THE STATESMAN'S YEAR-BOOK

1985–1986

Man hat behauptet, die Welt werde durch Zahlen regiert: das aber weiss ich, dass die Zahlen uns belehren, ob sie gut oder schlecht regiert werde.

GOETHE

Editors

Frederick Martin	1864–1883
Sir John Scott-Keltie	1883–1926
Mortimer Epstein	1911/27–1946
S. H. Steinberg	1946–1969
John Paxton	1963/69–

THE STATESMAN'S YEAR-BOOK

STATISTICAL AND HISTORICAL ANNUAL
OF THE STATES OF THE WORLD
FOR THE YEAR

1985–1986

EDITED BY

JOHN PAXTON

ST. MARTIN'S PRESS
NEW YORK

First published in 1864
122nd edition 1985

For information, write:
ST. MARTIN'S PRESS, INC.
175 Fifth Ave., New York, N.Y.10010

Typeset in Great Britain by
MB GRAPHIC (TYPESETTING) SERVICES
Dunstable, Bedfordshire

Printed in Great Britain by
RICHARD CLAY (THE CHAUCER PRESS), LTD
Bungay, Suffolk

Library of Congress Catalog Card No. 4–3776

ISBN 0–312–76099–X

This edition published in the United States of America in 1985

PREFACE

As a result of the excellent co-operation between the editor and his many correspondents every page of this, the 122nd edition of THE STATESMAN'S YEAR-BOOK, has received major or minor revisions. He is extremely grateful to all for that help and for the patience in answering his endless questions. Details of the voting, state by state, in the US Presidential elections are given, and the change of name of Upper Volta to Burkina Faso has been noted. A table on the production and trade in Computers and Telecommunications equipment in Western Europe is also included in this edition.

The third edition of THE STATESMAN'S YEAR-BOOK WORLD GAZETTEER is being fully revised and will be available in 1986.

J.P.

THE STATESMAN'S YEAR-BOOK OFFICE,
THE MACMILLAN PRESS LTD,
LITTLE ESSEX STREET,
LONDON, WC2R 3LF

WEIGHTS AND MEASURES

On 1 Jan. 1960 following an agreement between the standards laboratories of Great Britain, Canada, Australia, New Zealand, South Africa and the USA, an international yard and an international pound (avoirdupois) came into existence. 1 yard = 91·44 centimetres; 1 lb. = 453·59237 grammes.

The abbreviation 'm' signifies 'million(s)' and tonnes implies metric tons.

Length

Centimetre	0·394 inch
Metre	1·094 yards
Kilometre	0·621 mile

Liquid Measure

Litre	1·75 pints
Hectolitre	22 gallons

Surface Measure

Square metre	10·76 sq. feet
Hectare	2·47 acres
Square kilometre	0·386 sq. mile

Dry Measure

Litre	0·91 quart
Hectolitre	2·75 bushels

Weight—Avoirdupois

Gramme	15·42 grains
Kilogramme	2·205 pounds
Quintal (= 100 kg)	220·46 pounds
Tonne (= 1,000 kg)	0·984 long ton 1·102 short tons

Weight—Troy

Gramme	15·43 grains
Kilogramme	32·15 ounces 2·68 pounds

BRITISH WEIGHTS AND MEASURES

Length

1 foot	0·305 metre
1 yard	0·914 metre
1 mile (= 1,760 yds)	1·609 kilometres

Surface Measure

1 sq. foot	9·290 sq. decimetres
1 sq. yard	0·836 sq. metre
1 acre	0·405 hectare
1 sq. mile	2·590 sq. kilometres

Weight

1 ounce (= 437·2 grains)	28·350 grammes
1 lb. (= 7,000 grains)	453·6 grammes
1 cwt. (= 112 lb.)	50·802 kilogrammes
1 long ton (= 2,240 lb.)	1·016 tonnes
1 short ton (= 2,000 lb.)	0·907 tonne

Liquid Measure

1 pint	0·568 litre
1 gallon	4·546 litres
1 quarter	2·909 hectolitres

CONTENTS

Part I: International Organizations

Part II: Countries of the World A–Z

WHEAT

Countries	Area (1,000 hectares) Average 1974-76	1980	1981	1982	1983	Production (1,000 tonnes) Average 1974-76	1980	1981	1982	1983
Afghánistán	2,326	2,192	2,307	2,329	3,000	2,833	2,750	2,850	2,862	3,750*
Algeria	2,240	2,071	2,074*	1,850*	1,300	1,523	1,511	1,295	980*	810
Argentina	5,311	5,023	6,400	7,320	6,832	8,513	7,780	8,300	15,130	11,700
Australia [1]	8,606	11,283	11,885	11,546	12,690	11,721	10,856	16,360	8,879	21,780
Bulgaria [1,2]	911	968	1,032	1,059	1,128	3,180	3,847	4,443	4,913	3,600
Canada	9,888	11,098	12,427	12,554	13,697	17,990	19,292	24,802	26,790	26,914
Chile [1]	652	546	432	374	471	936	966	686	650	800
China [1]	27,683	29,231	28,279	27,914	28,801	45,522	55,213	59,643	68,422	81,392
Czechoslovakia [2]	1,240	1,189	1,083	1,068	1,100	4,690	5,386	4,325	4,606	5,820*
Egypt [1]	583	557	588	577	570	1,960	1,796	1,938	2,017*	1,996
France	4,099	4,582	4,753	4,849	4,828	16,715	23,683	22,857	25,342	24,781
Germany, Fed. Rep. of [2]	1,511	1,668	1,632	1,578	1,655	7,159	8,156	8,313	8,632	8,998
Greece	924	1,012	1,009	1,029	1,016	2,216	2,970	2,780	2,983	2,026
Hungary [1,3]	1,300	1,276	1,151	1,310	1,320	4,709	6,077	4,614	5,762	4,800
India	19,016	22,172	22,279	22,144	23,150	24,910	31,830	36,313	37,452	42,502
Iran	5,839	5,500	6,058*	6,060	6,046	5,438	5,700*	6,518*	6,500*	6,669
Iraq	1,513	1,500*	1,193	1,168	1,200	1,162	1,300	902	965	1,000
Italy	3,600	3,408	3,258	3,327	3,323	9,607	9,156	8,830	8,903	8,514
Japan [1]	87	191	224	228	229	232	583	587	742	747
Mexico	816	739	861	1,013	990	2,983	2,785	3,189	4,468	3,697
Morocco	1,843	1,715	1,647	1,686*	1,976	1,872	1,811	892	2,183	1,971
Pakistan [1]	6,012	6,912	6,982	7,223	7,398	7,998	10,805	11,474	11,304	12,414
Poland [1]	1,892	1,609	1,418	1,456	1,537	5,787	4,175	4,203	4,476	5,165
Romania [1]	2,378	2,244	2,111	2,155	2,150	5,530	6,427	5,310	6,460	5,000*
S. Africa, Republic of	1,718	1,620*	1,787*	1,974*	1,600*	1,876	1,470	2,340	2,420	1,770
Spain [2]	2,866	2,699	2,635	2,662	2,615	4,425	6,040	3,409	4,410	4,330
Turkey [2]	9,142	8,915	9,250	9,031	8,840	14,163	16,554	17,000	17,542	16,400
USSR [1]	60,376	61,475	59,232	57,278	50,856	82,340	98,182	80,000	87,000	82,000
UK	1,167	1,441	1,491	1,663	1,695	5,120	8,470	8,707	10,320	10,880
USA	27,760	28,727	32,784	31,963	24,885	54,955	64,619	76,169	76,538	66,010
Yugoslavia [2]	1,727	1,516	1,386	1,558	1,603	5,555	5,091	4,270	5,218	5,519
World total	227,349	236,873	240,195	239,530	230,034	383,370	446,107	453,821	486,423	498,182

* Unofficial figures. [1] Sown area. [2] Includes spelt. [3] Field crops and other crops.

RYE

Countries	Area (1,000 hectares) Average 1974–76	1980	1981	1982	1983	Production (1,000 tonnes) Average 1974–76	1980	1981	1982	1983
Argentina	338	210	162	174	156	303	155	149	148	142
Austria	120	109	101	100	83	391	383	320	348	348
Belgium	13	11	9	8*	34	47	42	35	32*	32
Bulgaria [1]	15	20	27	23	34	18	28	34	34	31
Canada	304	310	445	447	426	497	455	927	913	831
China	933	700	700	700	1,100	1,267	1,000	1,100	800	1,400
Czechoslovakia [2]	198	177	171	176	203	588	570	544	583	510
Denmark	56	56	50	53	77	181	199	208	235	321
Finland	59	53	41	16	47	131	124	64	35	116
France	115	130	117	110	106	312	408	342	322	307
German Demo. Rep.	610	678	656	653	702*	1,655	1,917	1,797	2,119	2,064*
Germany, Fed. Rep. of	665	547	484	407	445	2,262	2,098	1,729	1,639	1,599
Hungary [1, 3]	101	73	74	74	70	160	141	116	117	115
Netherlands	21	10	7	6	7	69	39	29	26	26
Poland [1]	2,955	3,039	3,002	3,273	3,448	7,024	6,566	6,731	7,792	8,781
Portugal	213	206	199	194	186	151	138	126	119	114
Romania [1]	36	35*	30*	35*	35	48	40*	35*	45*	45
Spain	233	217	220	212	212	236	284	212	169	247
Sweden	109	67	50	54	62	397	223	179	211	235
Turkey	565	443	410	313	309	683	525	530	430	430
USSR [1]	8,952	8,645	7,551	9,829	10,156	12,759	10,205	8,500	12,500	13,500
USA	301	273	286	292	374	409	419	478	532	715
Yugoslavia	84	55	54	53	51	108	79	75	84	83
World total	17,150	16,223	15,036	17,376	18,453	29,912	26,257	24,481	29,430	32,194

* Unofficial figures. [1] Sown area. [2] Includes mixture of wheat and rye. [3] Field crops and other crops.

BARLEY

Countries	Area (1,000 hectares) Average 1974–76	1980	1981	1982	1983	Production (1,000 tonnes) Average 1974–76	1980	1981	1982	1983
Australia [1]	2,159	2,452	2,685	2,454	3,232	2,846	2,682	3,450	1,798	4,910
Austria	320	374	362	340	339	1,177	1,514	1,220	1,437	1,442
Belgium	154	171	172	144*	159	625	865	824	800	745
Bulgaria [1]	525	426	382	352	323	1,705	1,375	1,406	1,436	1,046
Canada	4,532	4,634	5,476	5,189	4,461	9,604	11,394	13,724	14,074	10,616
China	1,740	1,239	1,201	1,141	1,201	3,001	2,700	3,100	2,500	3,400
Czechoslovakia	896	911	987	964	822	3,130	3,575	3,392	3,654	3,600
Denmark	1,453	1,577	1,541	1,489	1,353	5,308	6,044	6,044	6,357	4,450
Finland	471	533	570	540	550	1,253	1,534	1,080	1,599	1,764
France	2,753	2,581	2,579	2,391	2,143	9,303	11,423	10,231	10,044	8,865
German Demc. Rep.	889	969	964	982	891*	3,520	3,979	3,476	4,055	3,900*
Germany, Fed. Rep. of	1,719	2,002	2,044	2,021	2,035	6,835	8,826	8,687	9,460	8,900
Greece	398	331	312	311	312	943	950	768	853	572
Hungary [1, 2]	252	246	262	290	290	783	929	903	871	1,000
India	2,779	1,771	1,807	1,728	1,491	2,899	1,624	2,293	1,993	1,862
Iran	1,432	1,300	1,400	1,400	1,387	1,263	1,100	1,351*	1,400	1,413
Ireland	250	332	354	334	304	993	1,247	1,659	1,685	1,437
Italy	249	329	336	352	383	654	947	983	1,060	1,174
Japan [1]	79	122	122	123	124	221	385	383	390	380
Korea, South [1]	709	331	353	317	322	1,616	811	859	749	815
Morocco	2,026	2,150	2,228	2,047	2,151	2,279	2,210	1,039	2,334	1,228
Poland [1]	1,258	1,322	1,294	1,237	1,099	3,721	3,420	3,540	3,647	3,262
Romania [1]	418	809	917	943	800	1,033	2,466	2,571	3,052	2,000
Spain	3,176	3,575	3,508	3,615	3,634	5,868	8,705	4,757	5,269	6,571
Sweden	585	648	681	635	618	2,028	2,172	2,452	2,378	2,026
Syria	960	1,210	1,347	1,589	1,520	770	1,587	1,406	661	1,043
Turkey	2,599	2,800	2,965	3,137	2,750	4,243	5,300	5,900	6,400	5,600*
USSR [1]	32,629	31,583	31,781	29,706	31,831	53,185	43,450	39,000	41,000	54,000
UK	2,248	2,330	2,329	2,222	2,146	8,434	10,320	10,227	10,957	10,094
USA	3,370	2,944	3,706	3,688	4,008	7,699	7,859	10,436	11,374	11,300
World total	79,202	78,242	81,008	78,123	79,100	154,249	159,319	155,158	161,249	167,176

* Unofficial figures. [1] Sown area. [2] Field crops and other crops.

OATS

Countries	Area (1,000 hectares) Average 1974–76	1980	1981	1982	1983	Production (1,000 tonnes) Average 1974–76	1980	1981	1982	1983
Argentina	334	350	299	408*	397	430	433	339	637	538
Australia	960	1,093	1,388	1,213	1,995	1,029	1,128	1,617	851	2,360
Austria	96	92	92	91	83	293	316	304	325	292
Belgium	71	38	36	43*	34	262	136	172	200*	136
Canada	2,430	1,515	1,561	1,633	1,400	4,430	2,911	3,188	3,684	2,773
Chile	90	92	80	68	96	126	173	131	118	146*
China	533	400	400	450	450	700	500	600	500	800
Czechoslovakia [2]	201	121	147	161	154	553	421	431	488	410
Denmark	110	40	42	43	28	368	159	176	178	83
Finland	558	448	434	459	449	1,379	1,258	1,008	1,320	1,407
France	653	534	501	520	443	1,796	1,927	1,774	1,804	1,469
German Demo. Rep.	219	155	172	218*	163*	736	582	598	848*	500*
Germany, Fed.Rep.of	876	691	682	723	601	3,141	2,658	2,678	3,113	2,068
Ireland	45	26	23	23	22	151	90	89	101	103
Italy	237	226	222	219	209	469	450	418	359	307
Netherlands	31	18	21	24	14	142	94	115	136	61
Norway	103	112	118	133	116	309	428	463	495	413
Poland [1]	1,196	997	1,156	1,086	1,042	2,953	2,245	2,730	2,608	2,377
Spain	462	458	464	442	466	565	680	445	443	470
Sweden	450	452	474	477	404	1,409	1,567	1,816	1,663	1,268
Turkey	259	197	180	175	170	390	355	325	330*	330
USSR [1]	11,648	11,770	12,470	11,489	12,516	15,303	15,544	14,000	14,000	16,000
UK	241	148	144	129	108	838	600	619	576	465
USA	5,056	3,501	3,810	4,297	3,682	8,613	6,652	7,391	9,007	6,928
Yugoslavia	250	194	194	176	168	347	294	311	269	248
World Total	28,285	24,853	26,358	26,134	26,588	47,872	42,760	42,939	45,287	43,101

* Unofficial figures. [1] Sown area. [2] Includes spelt. [3] Field crops and other crops.

MAIZE

Countries	Area (1,000 hectares) Average 1974–76	1980	1981	1982	1983	Production (1,000 tonnes) Average 1974–76	1980	1981	1982	1983
Argentina	3,107	2,490	3,394	3,170	2,970	7,818	6,400	12,900	9,600	8,840
Austria	151	193	189	198	206	925	1,293	1,374	1,551	1,437
Brazil	10,882	11,451	11,502	12,601	10,750	16,786	20,372	21,117	21,865	18,756
Bulgaria	636	585	563	621	596	2,493	2,256	2,401	3,418	3,101
Canada	645	958	1,139	1,107	1,077	3,341	5,753	6,673	6,513	5,875
China	18,437	20,385	19,442	18,529	19,900	46,216	62,715	59,301	60,413	64,135
Egypt	767	800	808	813	756*	2,823	3,231	3,308	3,347	3,510*
France	1,755	1,757	1,571	1,617	1,606	7,511	9,358	8,956	10,381	10,143
Greece	129	172	161	163	169	484	1,279	1,337	1,448	1,622
Hungary	1,418	1,253	1,191	1,158	1,160	6,187	6,673	6,998	7,959	7,600
India	5,965	6,005	5,935	5,693	6,000	6,392	6,957	6,897	6,274	7,300
Indonesia	2,396	2,735	2,955	2,064	3,200	2,829	3,991	4,509	3,207	4,000*
Italy	892	942	998	1,011	976	5,230	6,377	7,197	6,847	6,900
Kenya	1,513	939	1,488*	1,236	1,720*	2,450	1,620	1,980	2,340	2,000*
Malawi	1,037	1,100	1,100*	1,200	1,200	1,127	1,165	1,245	1,415	1,500
Mexico	6,732	6,955	8,150	5,643	8,408	8,105	12,383	14,766	10,129	13,928
Nigeria	1,508	1,710	1,746	1,800	1,800*	1,258	1,550	1,580	1,750*	1,600*
Philippines	3,213	3,319	3,361	3,157	3,400	2,726	3,176	3,290	3,126	3,385
Portugal	379	377	365	367	365*	489	489	419	464	475*
Romania	3,215	3,288	3,327	3,055	3,000	9,421	11,153	11,892	12,620	10,500
S. Africa, Republic of	5,967	6,000	4,900	4,700	4,065	9,186	10,790	14,660	8,359	3,910
Spain	472	455	429	418	351	1,777	2,314	2,157	2,330	1,788
Tanzania	1,167	1,300	1,500	1,500	1,690	1,210	750	1,943	1,947	2,000
Thailand	1,180	1,335	1,465	1,306	1,668	2,679	2,998	3,449	3,002	3,552
Turkey	605	583	580	580	577	1,237	1,240	1,200	1,360	1,375
USSR [1]	3,303	2,977	3,545	4,161	5,189	9,857	9,454	8,000	12,000	14,000
USA	27,591	29,555	30,230	29,554	20,855	142,511	168,787	208,330	212,338	106,781
Yugoslavia	2,331	2,202	2,297	2,246	2,271	8,842	9,317	9,807	11,126	10,688
Zimbabwe	981	1,146	1,440	1,415	1,340	1,886	1,539	2,729	1,657	1,023
World total	123,354	128,014	130,863	126,150	122,997	333,721	395,949	452,030	451,080	344,103

* Unofficial figures. [1] For dry grain only.

RICE (Paddy)

Countries	Area (1,000 hectares) Average 1974–76	1980	1981	1982	1983	Production (1,000 tonnes) Average 1974–76	1980	1981	1982	1983
Bangladesh	10,001	10,309	10,460	10,586	10,600	17,900	20,821	20,444	21,322	21,700
Brazil	5,543	6,243	6,102	6,016	5,112	8,101	9,776	8,228	9,716	7,760
Burma	4,955	4,801	4,809	4,662	4,700	9,037	13,100	14,147	14,758	14,500
Cambodia	1,002	1,356*	1,350	1,680	1,755	1,312	1,470*	1,160*	1,400	1,700
China	36,568	34,517	33,928	33,682	33,980	128,435	142,993	147,042	164,493	172,184
Colombia	364	416	413	446	397	1,571	1,798	1,799	2,018	1,780
Egypt	446	408	402	431	423	2,322	2,384	2,236	2,441	2,440
India	38,625	40,152	40,708	37,794	41,000	65,351	80,312	79,883	69,948	90,000
Indonesia	8,458	9,005	9,382	9,022	9,100	22,705	29,652	32,774	34,104	34,300
Iran	452	300	320	330	312	1,436	1,212	1,500	1,400	1,400
Italy	181	176	169	178	181	988	968	893	964	1,060
Japan	2,756	2,377	2,278	2,257	2,273	16,116	12,189	12,824	12,838	12,958
Korea, North	638	800	800	810	820	3,783	4,960	4,900	5,000	5,200
Korea, South	1,212	1,233	1,224	1,188	1,228	6,636	5,311	7,149	7,308	7,608
Madagascar	1,069	1,178	1,186	1,139	1,219	2,009	2,109	2,012	1,967	2,147
Malaysia	741	718	675	720	700	2,029	2,070	2,177	1,832	2,000
Mexico	196	132	180	175	185	557	456	644	600	655
Nepál	1,252	1,270	1,280	1,230	1,290	2,481	2,464	2,560	1,833	2,744
Nigeria	234	550*	600*	650*	600*	476	1,090*	1,125*	1,376*	1,000
Pakistan	1,688	1,935	1,976	1,978	2,020	3,834	4,679	5,145	5,167	5,210
Philippines	3,555	3,637	3,433	3,240	3,300	6,092	7,836	8,108	7,731	8,150
Sri Lanka	677	824	842	746	926	1,336	2,137	2,229	2,156	2,200
Thailand	7,952	9,099	9,105	8,916	9,400	14,585	17,368	17,774	16,878	18,535
USSR	506	666	634	648	649	1,975	2,791	2,400	2,500	2,500
USA	1,056	1,340	1,535	1,320	878	5,390	6,629	8,289	6,967	4,523
Vietnam	5,134	5,544	5,615	5,750	5,900	11,213	11,679	12,570	14,500	14,500
World total	140,599	144,529	145,049	141,285	144,473	347,505	399,112	411,814	423,464	449,827

* Unofficial figures.

MILLET

Countries	Area (1,000 hectares) Average 1974–76	1980	1981	1982	1983	Production (1,000 tonnes) Average 1974–76	1980	1981	1982	1983
Argentina	211	182	187	132	160	241	188	238	154	179
Australia	30	19	27	35	34	28	14	27	39	30
Burkina Faso	857	800	900	909	900	364	330	443	441	300
Cameroon	433	450	500	513	515	389	400	351	423	360
Chad	959	1,150*	1,150	1,150	1,150	520	600	496*	450	450
China	5,271	3,874	3,892	4,041	155	6,522	5,448	5,768	6,583	625*
Egypt	205	172	173	161	4,102	786	635	653	596*	7,004
Ethiopia	261	233	227	225	230*	236	205	197	240	250*
Ghana	221	240*	157	160	150	140	66	119	90	80
India	18,338	18,158	18,180	16,692	17,500	9,042	9,337	10,136	8,986	10,500
Kenya	79	81	82	45	50	128	130	130	66	80
Korea, North	413	420	420	415	420	415	450	450	455	475
Korea, South	27	3	4	5	2	27	4	5	5	2
Mali	1,212	1,400	1,420	1,400	1,420	852	750	800	695	638
Nepal	124	120	120	120	118	140	122	122	121	113
Niger	2,150	3,072	3,038*	3,084*	3,139	828	1,364	1,314*	1,293	1,325
Nigeria	4,300	5,030*	5,030*	5,050*	4,070*	2,843	3,130*	3,180*	3,275*	2,300*
Pakistan	506	406	559	482	547	295	215	272	265	270
Senegal	1,004	1,115	1,177	991	800	658	540	736	585	352*
Sudan	1,092	1,300	1,100	999	1,100	372	450	573	339	314
Tanzania	200	220	220	220	220	129	160	150	150	150
Togo	142	170	170	170	170	110	128	107	120*	125*
Uganda	498	279	300	330	360	613	459	480	528	600
USSR	2,914	2,907	2,692	2,821	2,880	2,410	1,873	1,500	2,000	2,200
Zimbabwe [1]	360	380	279	266	280	173	180	138	98	100
World total	43,581	43,261	43,065	41,461	41,498	29,005	27,887	29,127	28,713	29,563

* Unofficial figures.

[1] Or farms and estates.

SORGHUM

Countries	Area (1,000 hectares) Average 1974–76	1980	1981	1982	1983	Production (1,000 tonnes) Average 1974–76	1980	1981	1982	1983
Argentina	2,115	1,279	2,135	2,510	2,520	5,391	2,960	7,603	8,060	8,250
Australia	518	519	658	649	698	1,029	922	1,204	1,311	986
Burkina Faso	1,131	850	1,084	1,048	1,000	666	559	659	609	600
China	4,550	2,696	2,614	2,786	2,803	8,584	6,785	6,662	9,478	10,014
Colombia	153	206	231	291	275*	366	431	532	568	579*
Ethiopia [1,2]	759	1,014	844	906	950	754	1,642	1,207	1,356	1,400
France	79	74	67	57	55	291	321	321	259	236
India	16,018	15,809	16,599	16,110	16,500	10,148	10,431	12,062	10,676	12,000
Mexico	1,284	1,579	1,767	1,275	1,896	3,778	4,812	6,296	4,717	6,367
Niger	649	768	982	1,136	1,114	253	368	322	357	362
Nigeria	5,793	6,000*	6,000*	6,025	5,925*	3,590	3,800*	3,700*	3,850*	2,660*
S. Africa, Republic of	317	450	400*	350	300	454	695	545	273	195
Sudan	2,415	3,000	3,901	3,583	3,500	1,798	2,200	3,350	1,919	1,819
Thailand	152	234	266	236	265*	210	237	274	236	327
Uganda	335	167	170	200	230	401	299	320	400	470
USA	5,892	5,068	5,551	5,766	4,006	17,678	14,712	22,333	21,372	12,270
Venezuela	48	265	229	220	163	76	403	347	377	280
Yemen Arab Republic	1,104	791	730	670	575*	835	692	635	580	248
World total	47,455	44,905	48,384	47,813	46,499	60,083	55,703	72,228	69,930	62,483

* Unofficial figures. [1] Includes teff. [2] Unspecified millet and sorghum.

CENTRIFUGAL RAW SUGAR
(in 1,000 tonnes)

Countries	*Average 1974–76*	*1978*	*1979*	*1980*	*1981*	*1982*	*1983*
Argentina	1,480	1,397	1,411	1,716	1,624	1,623*	1,635*
Australia [1]	3,000	2,902	2,963	3,329	3,435	3,500	3,075
Barbados [2]	104	101	114	132	94	89	83*
Brazil	6,867	7,767*	7,027*	8,547*	8,393*	9,314*	9,460*
Canada	141	123	106	107*	140*	122*	135*
China	2,700	3,213	3,587	3,650	4,191	4,649	5,041
Colombia	933	...	...	1,247	1,225*	1,318*	1,391*
Cuba	6,251	7,457	8,048	6,787	7,926	8,279	7,250*
Czechoslovakia	717	885*	910*	810*	747*	885	790*
Dominican Rep.	1,229	1,199	1,200	1,039*	1,108	1,255	1,281*
Egypt	595	635	668	662	677*	754	812*
France	3,049	4,065	4,332	4,253	5,576	4,800	3,875
Fiji [1]	280	347	473	396	470	487	270*
German Demo. Rep.	627	780*	679*	600*	747*	876*	730*
Germany, Fed. Rep. of	2,568	2,997	3,088	2,994	3,702	3,586	2,720*
Guyana	331	342	316	273	306	288	254*
India [3]	4,712	7,018	6,367	4,191	5,596	9,190	9,000
Indonesia [4]	1,037	1,105	1,307	1,250	1,247	1,629	1,650*
Italy	1,390	1,620	1,707	1,934	2,207	1,290	1,360*
Jamaica	367	292	283	232	205*	202	198*
Mauritius [4]	655	705	730	504	609	729	640
Mexico	2,761	3,072	3,078*	2,765*	2,586*	2,873*	2,900*
Pakistan [3]	631	936	663	624	925	1,414	1,225
Peru	965	856	716	552	493*	614	452*
Philippines	2,572	2,335	2,342	2,343	2,394	2,527	2,540
Poland	1,752	1,763*	1,762	1,186	1,872	2,011	2,141*
Puerto Rico	271	185*	174	158	137	102	91
S. Africa, Rep. of	1,909	2,082	2,079	1,611	2,218	2,304	1,473
Spain	984	1,143	750	972	1,111	1,242	1,318*
Sweden	294	327	350	327	374	389	304*
Thailand	1,272	...	...	1,098	1,641	2,930	2,268*
Trinidad	188	148*	144	114	94	79	77
Turkey	1,036	...	...	944*	1,521*	1,860*	1,740*
USSR	7,594	9,100*	7,700*	7,150*	6,200*	7,400	8,700*
UK	686	1,111	1,255	1,202	1,187	1,544	1,185
USA [5]	5,745	5,353	5,061	5,331	5,644	5,262	5,058
World total	79,496	90,258	88,984	84,047	92,778	102,422	97,173

[1] 94° net titre.
[2] Includes the sugar equivalent of fancy molasses.
[3] Includes sugar (raw value) refined from gur.
[4] Tel quel.
[5] Includes Hawaii.
* Unofficial figures.

WORLD ESTIMATED CRUDE OIL PRODUCTION [1]

(in 1,000 tonnes)

	1960	*1970*	*1983*	*1984*
North America				
USA	384,080	533,677	480,123	487,000
Canada	27,480	69,954	76,777	82,000
Caribbean Area				
Venezuela	148,690	193,209	95,345	95,000
Trinidad	6,075	7,225	8,523	8,000
Colombia	8,100	11,071	7,870	8,550
Other Latin America				
Mexico	14,125	21,877	147,295	150,000
Argentina	9,160	19,969	24,877	24,000
Brazil	390	8,009	16,915	24,000
Ecuador	2,680	191	12,080	12,800
Peru	450	3,450	8,476	9,000
Bolivia	990	1,128	1,027	950
Chile		1,620	1,840	1,800
Middle East				
Saudi Arabia	61,090	176,851	249,160	235,000
Iran	52,065	191,663	122,930	105,000
Iraq	47,480	76,600	46,760	58,500
Kuwait	81,860	137,397	53,380	58,000
Abu Dhabi	—	33,288	37,470	36,000
Qatar	8,210	17,257	12,985	18,800
Syria	—	4,350	9,360	9,000
Turkey	350	3,461	2,206	2,000
Bahrain	2,250	3,834	2,049	2,000
Sharjah	—	—	1,845	2,700
Africa				
Nigeria	880	53,420	61,050	68,000
Libya	—	159,201	53,260	52,500
Algeria	8,630	47,253	30,690	29,500
Gabon	850	5,460	7,685	8,000
Angola	70	5,066	8,303	9,500
Tunisia	—	4,151	5,578	5,400
Congo	—	—	4,241	4,500
Zaïre	—	—	1,214	1,200

[1] Excluding small scale production in Afghánistán, Bangladesh, Cuba, Guatemala, Israel, Mongolia, Morocco, New Zealand, Taiwan and Thailand.

WORLD ESTIMATED CRUDE OIL PRODUCTION
(contd.)

(in 1,000 tonnes)

	1960	*1970*	*1983*	*1984*
Western Europe				
UK	90	84	114,917	125,000
Norway	—	—	30,480	34,500
Germany, Fed. Rep. of	5,560	7,536	4,157	4,100
Austria	2,440	2,798	1,269	1,250
Spain	—	156	2,980	2,500
Netherlands	1,920	1,919	2,900	3,500
France	2,260	2,308	1,661	2,000
Italy	1,990	1,408	2,196	2,400
Denmark	—	—	2,153	2,335
Far East				
Indonesia	20,560	42,102	64,080	70,500
Australia	—	8,292	19,604	23,000
Brunei	4,690	6,916	8,750	8,000
India	440	6,809	25,100	28,000
Malaysia	—	—	18,500	21,000
Burma	530	750	1,355	1,400
Japan	510	750	423	430
Pakistan	360	486	560	900
USSR and Eastern Europe				
USSR	148,000	352,667	616,000	615,500
Romania	11,500	13,377	11,600	12,000
Yugoslavia	1,040	2,854	4,125	4,000
Albania	600	1,199	4,000	3,000
Hungary	1,215	1,937	2,005	2,000
Poland	195	424	250	250
German Dem. Rep.	—	60	60	60
Bulgaria	200	334	300	300
Czechoslovakia	140	203	95	95
China	5,000	20,000	105,972	110,000
World Total	1,090,080	2,336,153	2,754,364	2,817,002

WESTERN EUROPEAN COMPUTERS AND TELECOMMUNICATIONS EQUIPMENT

(1983 in US$1m.)

	Computers			*Telecommunications*		
Countries	*Production*	*Imports*	*Exports*	*Production*	*Imports*	*Exports*
Austria	111	345	94	201	50	17
Belgium	524	657	352	546	93	225
Denmark	93	373	88	67	51	39
Finland	78	275	50	165	61	79
France	3,096	2,680	1,856	3,085	92	474
Germany, Federal Republic of	4,050	3,389	2,966	2,905	115	692
Ireland	904	694	1,188	109	81	80
Italy	2,215	1,310	1,023	1,559	144	149
Netherlands	969	1,559	1,044	454	119	160
Norway	134	314	107	182	69	47
Portugal	–	53	52	–	16	14
Spain	286	417	176	531	37	41
Sweden	405	846	649	1,132	60	769
Switzerland	212	599	175	331	32	120
UK	2,597	3,817	2,497	2,209	302	235

TERRITORIAL SEA LIMITS (IN MILES)

State	*Territorial Sea*	*Jurisdiction over fisheries (measured from the baseline of the territorial sea)*
Albania	15 (1976)	—
Algeria	12 (1963)	—
Angola	20 (1975)	200 (1975)
Antigua and Barbuda	12 (1982)	200 (1982) [1]
Argentina	200 (1967)	—
Australia	3 (1878)	200 (1979)
Bahamas	3 (1878)	200 (1977)
Bahrain	3	—
Bangladesh	12 (1974)	200 (1974) [1]
Barbados	12 (1977)	200 (1978) [1]
Belgium	3	up to median line (1978)
Belize	3 (1878)	12 (1978)
Benin	200 (1976)	—
Brazil	200 (1970)	—
Bulgaria	12 (1951)	—
Burma	12 (1968)	200 (1977) [1]
Cambodia	12(1969)	200 (1979) [1]
Cameroon	50 (1974)	—
Canada	12 (1970)	200 (1977)
Cape Verde	12 (1978)	200 (1978) [1]
Chile	3	200 (1947–52) [1]
China	12 (1958)	—
Colombia	12 (1970)	200 (1978) [1]
Comoros	12 (1976)	200 (1976) [1]
Congo	200 (1977)	—
Costa Rica	12 (1972)	200 (1975) [1]
Cuba	12 (1977)	200 (1977) [1]
Cyprus	12 (1964)	—
Denmark (including Faroe Islands and Greenland)	3 (1966)	200 (1977)
Djibouti	12 (1971)	200 (1979) [1]
Dominica	12 (1981)	200 (1981) [1]
Dominican Republic	6 (1967)	200 (1977) [1]
Ecuador	200 (1966)	—
Egypt	12 (1958)	—
El Salvador	200 (1950)	—
Equatorial Guinea	12 (1970)	—
Ethiopia	12 (1953)	—
Fiji	12 (1976)	200 (1981) [1]
Finland	4 (1956)	12 (1975)
France	12 (1971)	200 (1977) [1] (except Mediterranean)
Gabon	100 (1972)	—
Gambia	12 (1969)	200 (1978)
German Democratic Republic	3	up to median line (1978)
Germany, Federal Republic of	In accordance with international law	200 (1977)
Ghana	200 (1977)	—
Greece	6 (1936)	—
Grenada	12 (1978)	200 (1978) [1]
Guatemala	12 (1934)	200 (1976) [1]
Guinea	12 (1980)	200 (1980) [1]
Guinea-Bissau	12 (1978)	200 (1978) [1]
Guyana	12 (1977)	200 (1977)
Haiti	12 (1972)	200 (1977) [1]
Honduras	12 (1965)	200 (1951) [1]

[1] Economic zone.

TERRITORIAL SEA LIMITS (IN MILES)—*contd.*

State	*Territorial Sea*	*Jurisdiction over fisheries (measured from the baseline of the territorial sea)*
Iceland	12 (1979)	200 (1979) [1]
India	12 (1967)	200 (1977) [1]
Indonesia	12 (1957) [2]	200 (1980) [1]
Iran	12 (1959)	[3]
Iraq	12 (1958)	—
Ireland	3 (1959)	200 (1977)
Israel	6 (1956)	—
Italy	12 (1974)	—
Ivory Coast	12 (1977)	200 (1977) [1]
Jamaica	12 (1971)	—
Japan	12 (1977)	200 (1977)
Jordan	3 (1943)	—
Kenya	12 (1969)	200 (1979) [1]
Kiribati	12 (1983)	200 (1983) [1]
Korea (North)	12	200 (1977) [1]
Korea (South)	12 (1978)	12
Kuwait	12 (1967)	—
Lebanon	—	6 (1921)
Liberia	200 (1976)	—
Libya	12 (1959)	—
Madagascar	50 (1973)	—
Malaysia	12 (1969)	200 (1980) [1]
Maldive, Republic of	3–55 [3]	(1976) [1, 4]
Malta	12 (1978)	25 (1978)
Mauritania	70 (1978)	200 (1978) [1]
Mauritius	12 (1970)	200 (1977) [1]
Mexico	12 (1969)	200 (1976) [1]
Monaco	12	—
Morocco	12 (1973) [5]	200 (1981) [1]
Mozambique	12 (1976)	200 (1976) [1]
Namibia	6 (1983)	12 (1963)
Nauru	12 (1971)	200 (1978) [1]
Netherlands	3	200 (1977)
New Zealand	12 (1977)	200 (1978) [1]
Nicaragua	200 (1979)	200 (1979) [1]
Nigeria	30 (1971)	200 (1978) [1]
Norway	4 (1812)	200 (1977) [1]
Oman	12 (1977)	200 (1981) [1]
Pakistan	12 (1966)	200 (1976) [1]
Panama	200 (1967)	—
Papua New Guinea	12 (1978)	200 (1978) (offshore waters)
Peru	200 (1947) [6]	200 (1947) [6]
Philippines	[7]	200 (1978) [1]

[1] Economic zone.

[2] The territorial sea of Indonesia is measured by straight lines surrounding the archipelago.

[3] Outer limits of the superjacent waters of the continental shelf. Median line in the Sea of Oman (1973).

[4] Territorial limits and economic zone defined by geographical co-ordinates.

[5] Limits with opposite or adjacent states to be fixed by agreement, failing which median line principle to apply.

[6] Sovereignty and jurisdiction over the sea, its soil and subsoil up to 200 miles (1947).

[7] The territorial sea of the Philippines is determined by straight base-lines joining appropriate points of the outermost islands forming the Philippine archipelago in accordance with Treaties of 1898, 1900 and 1930 (1961).

TERRITORIAL SEA LIMITS (IN MILES)—*contd.*

State	*Territorial Sea*	*Jurisdiction over fisheries (measured from the baseline of the territorial sea)*
Poland	12 (1977)	up to median line (1978)
Portugal	12 (1977)	200 (1977) [2]
Qatar	3	[1]
Romania	12 (1951)	—
St Christopher (St Kitts)—Nevis	3 (1878)	—
St Lucia	3 (1878)	—
St Vincent and the Grenadines	3 (1878)	—
São Tomé and Principe	12 (1978)	200 (1978) [2]
Saudi Arabia	12 (1958)	[1]
Senegal	150 (1976)	200 (1976)
Seychelles	12 (1977)	200 (1977) [2]
Sierra Leone	200 (1971)	—
Singapore	3 (1878)	—
Solomon Islands	12 (1978)	200 (1978)
Somalia	200 (1972)	—
South Africa, Republic of	12 (1977)	200 (1977)
Spain	12 (1977)	200 (1978) [2] (except Mediterranean)
Sri Lanka	12 (1971)	200 (1977) [2]
Sudan	12 (1960)	—
Suriname	12 (1978)	200 (1978) [2]
Sweden	4 (1779)	200 (1978)
Syria	35 (1981)	—
Tanzania	50 (1973)	—
Thailand	12 (1966)	200 (1982) [2]
Togo	30 (1977)	200 (1977) [2]
Tonga	[3]	—
Trinidad and Tobago	12 (1969)	—
Tunisia	12 (1973)	—
Turkey	6 (1964)	12 (1964)
Tuvalu	12 (1983)	200 (1983) [2]
USSR	12 (1909)	200 (1984) [2]
United Arab Emirates	3 [4]	[5]
UK	3 (1878)	200 (1977)
USA	3 (1793)	200 (1983) [2]
Uruguay	200 (1969)	—
Vanuatu	12 (1978–82)	200 (1978–82) [2]
Venezuela	12 (1956)	200 (1978) [2]
Vietnam	12 (1977)	200 (1977) [2]
Western Samoa	12 (1977)	200 (1981) [2]
Yemen, Peoples Dem. Rep. of	12 (1970)	200 (1978) [2]
Yemen, Republic of	12 (1967)	—
Yugoslavia	12 (1979)	—
Zaïre	12 (1974)	—

[1] Outer limits of the superjacent waters of the continental shelf (1974).
[2] Economic zone.
[3] Territorial limits defined by geographical co-ordinates (173–177° W. and 15–23° 30′ S.) (1887).
[4] Sharjah, 12 miles.
[5] Limits to be defined by agreement, failing which median line to apply (1980).

The table above, reproduced from a survey prepared by the FAO of the UN shows: *(a)* the territorial sea limit, and *(b)* jurisdiction over fisheries.

Books of Reference

Buzan, B., *Seabed Politics.* New York, 1976

Janis, M. W., *Sea Power and the Law of the Sea.* Lexington, 1977

Luard, E., *The Control of the Sea-Bed.* London, 1974

Moore, G., *Coastal State Requirements for Foreign Fishing. FAO Legislative Study No. 21.* Rev. 1. Rome, 1983

CHRONOLOGY

1984

April 3 Guinea. The Military Committee for National Recovery took office.

5 Guinea. Col. Lansana Conté took office as President and Col. Diarra Traore as Prime Minister.

India. Detention without trial was introduced in the Punjab, following the murder of a Rajya Sabha member.

6 Cocos (Keeling) Islands. A referendum decided by 231–30 votes in favour of integration with Australia.

11 Peru. Sandro Mariátegui became Prime Minister.

USSR. Konstantin Chernenko was elected President of the Presidium of the Supreme Soviet.

17 Antigua and Barbuda. A general election returned to office the ruling Labour Party, led by Vere Bird.

19 Tanzania. Ali Hassan Mwinyi was elected President of Zanzibar.

22 UK–Libya. Diplomatic relations were broken off, after a British policewoman was shot dead from a window of the Libyan Embassy in London.

24 Tanzania. Salim Ahmed Salim became Prime Minister.

26 Lebanon. Rashid Karami formed a new government.

29 Sudan. A state of emergency was declared and parts of the Constitution suspended.

May 6 Panama. Nicolás Ardito Barletta was elected President.

10 Nicaragua. The International Court of Justice forbade the USA to continue mining the approaches to Nicaraguan ports.

14 Philippines. A general election returned the ruling New Society Movement.

15 Yugoslavia. A new collective state presidency took office under Veselin Djuranovic.

16 El Salvador. José Napoleon Duarte was declared President-elect.

Guinea-Bissau. Gen. João Bernardo Vieira was elected Chairman of the Council of State.

20 Taiwan. Yu Kuo-hua became Prime Minister.

23 Sudan. The government was dissolved and replaced by a Presidential Council of Advisers.

Federal Republic of Germany. Richard von Weizsäcker was elected President.

27 Egypt. A general election returned the ruling National Democratic Party, led by Fuad Mohieddin.

June 6 Greenland. A general election returned the ruling Siumut Party, led by Jonathon Motzfeldt.

6–7 India. The army stormed the Golden Temple in Amritsar, Punjab, to evict armed Sikh militants.

12 Iran–Iraq. A moratorium began on bombing civilian targets; it was prompted by UN strictures on bombing vessels in the Persian Gulf.

CHRONOLOGY—*contd.*

1984

June 14 Netherlands. Parliament voted to deploy cruise missiles in 1988 unless the USSR had limited the number of SS-20s aimed at western Europe.

14–17 European Communities. Elections took place to the European Parliament.

16 Canada. John Turner was elected leader of the Liberal Party on the retirement of Pierre Trudeau.

17 Luxembourg. A general election returned parties of a coalition.

21 St Kitts-Nevis. A general election returned the ruling People's Action Party, led by Kennedy Simmonds.

25 NATO. Lord Carrington became Secretary-General.

European Communities. An agreement was reached (at Fontainebleau) on the European Community budget.

July 1 Guatemala. Members of a National Constituent Assembly were elected.

Liechtenstein. The franchise was extended to women.

3 Liberia. Parliament approved a new Constitution with an elected President.

4 Lebanon. The army resumed control of the 'Green Line' dividing Beirut.

5–15 Nigeria–UK. Respective High Commissioners were recalled after Alhaji Umaro Dikko, a former minister, was kidnapped in London.

11 Lebanon. A Shia Muslim group blew up the Libyan Peoples' Bureau in Beirut.

14 New Zealand. A general election returned the Labour Party, led by David Lange.

16 Egypt. Gen. Kamel Hassan Ali became Prime Minister.

17 France. Laurent Fabius became Prime Minister.

20 Luxembourg. A coalition government took office, led by Jacques Santer.

23 Israel. A general election returned Labour Alignment Party, led by Shimon Peres.

25–31 St Vincent and the Grenadines. A general election returned the New Democratic Party, led by James Mitchell.

28 USA. The Olympic Games began in Los Angeles, boycotted by the USSR and allied states.

30–31 Lebanon. The last US marines withdrew from Beirut.

Aug. 1 Zimbabwe. Curfew was lifted in Matabeleland.

4 Upper Volta. The country was re-named Burkina Faso.

8 Congo. Ange-Edouard Poungi became Prime Minister.

10 Colombia. Carlos Toledo Plata of the M-19 guerilla group, was shot dead.

12 Guyana. Hugh Desmond Hoyte became Prime Minister.

CHRONOLOGY—*contd.*

1984

Aug. 13 Libya–Morocco. A treaty establishing a 'union of states' was signed, to come into force on 1 Sept.

19 Burkina Faso (Upper Volta). The government was dissolved.

22–29 South Africa. Elections to new assemblies, the House of Representatives (Coloured) and the House of Delegates (Indian).

23–24 Colombia. The government signed a truce with the Communist Party, its armed branch (People's Liberation Army) and the Workers' Self-Defence Movement.

31 Burkina Faso (Upper Volta). A new government was installed.

Sept. 2–3 South Africa. A new Constitution came into force at midnight.

4 Canada. A general election returned the Progressive Conservative Party led by Brian Mulroney.

5 South Africa. P. W. Botha was elected President.

8 Botswana. A general election returned the ruling Botswana Democratic Party.

14 Morocco. A general election returned the *Union Constitutionelle* as the largest group (55 seats).

20 Lebanon. A lorry-bomb blew up part of the US Embassy in Beirut.

25 Chad. French troops began withdrawal.
Egypt–Jordan. Diplomatic relations were restored.

26 Hong Kong. China and Britain exchanged documents on the transfer of Hong Kong to China in 1997.

Oct. 1 Malta. The Roman Catholic Church closed its schools, in a dispute with the government about funds and control.

4 Ethiopia. A charities' press conference called European public attention to the famine.

10 UK. The National Union of Mineworkers was fined £200,000 for contempt of court in declaring the miners' strike (which they had called on 5 March) official.

12 UK. A bomb blew up part of the Grand Hotel, Brighton, during the Conservative Party conference.

13 Peru. Luis Percovich Roca became Prime Minister.

18 Argentina–Chile. A treaty on rights in the Beagle Channel was initialled.
Hong Kong. The Assembly approved the draft agreement between UK and China.

19 Poland. Father Jerzy Popieluszko was kidnapped by police. His body was found on 30 Oct.

31 India. Indira Gandhi was murdered by Sikh officers of her staff.

Nov. 4 Nicaragua. A general election returned the Sandinista Party, led by Daniel Ortega.

6 Poland. Gen. Jaruzelski, the Prime Minister, also took over the Interior Ministry.
USA. President Reagan was returned to office for a second term.

CHRONOLOGY—*contd.*

1984

Nov. 14 Belize. A general election returned the United Democratic Party, led by Manuel Esquivel.

16 USA. The space-shuttle *Discovery* made the first recovery of an off-course satellite.

16 New Caledonia. Elections were disrupted by the Kanak Liberation Front which demanded independence from France.

25 Uruguay. A general election returned the Colorado Party, led by J. Maria Sanguinetti.

26 New Caledonia. Karak separatists set up a provisional government under Jean-Marie Tjibaou. Europeans were evacuated on 30 Nov. following fresh violence.

USA–Iraq. Diplomatic relations were resumed (broken off in 1967).

Dec. 1 Australia. A general election returned the ruling Labour Party, led by Robert Hawke.

3 Grenada. A general election returned the New National Party, led by Herbert Blaize.

India. Leakage of methyl cyanate fumes from the Union Carbide factory at Bhopal killed about 2,500 people.

11 United Nations. Deadline for signatures to the Law of the Sea Treaty, 1982; 159 nations signed, but not the Federal Republic of Germany, the UK or the USA.

12 Mauritania. Lieut.-Col. Maaouya Ould Taya seized power in a *coup*.

19 Pakistan. A referendum decided that Gen. Zia-ul-Haq should continue as President after forthcoming elections.

China–UK. Agreement signed on transfer of Hong Kong to China in 1997.

20 USSR. Marshal Dmitry Ustinov, the Defence Minister, died.

22 Singapore. A general election returned the ruling People's Action Party, led by Lee Kuan Yew.

Malta. Dom Mintoff resigned, and was replaced as Prime Minister by Carmello Mifsud Bonnici.

24 India. Beginning of a general election, which returned the Congress (I) Party, led by Rajiv Gandhi.

27 USA–UK–Federal Germany. Launching of the first artificial comet (of barium) from a satellite.

31 UNESCO. The USA withdrew from membership.

1985

Jan. 1 Egypt. Pope Shenouda III, head of the Coptic church in Egypt, released from exile and returned to office.

Japan. Sanctions on North Korea (imposed in 1983) were lifted.

Comoros. Post of Prime Minister was abolished.

7 Cambodia. Vietnamese forces began the destruction of the Khmer People's National Liberation Front headquarters, at Ampil.

10 Nicaragua. Daniel Ortega was sworn in as President for a 6-year term.

CHRONOLOGY—*contd.*

1985

Jan. 12 New Caledonia. A state of emergency was proclaimed.

Greece–Albania. Frontier opened at Kakavia, where it had been closed since 1940.

14 Cambodia. Hun Sen was elected Prime Minister.

15 Brazil. Tancredo Neves was elected as first civilian president since 1964.

21 Canada. The *Parti Québécois* abandoned Quebec independence as its main goal.

Feb. 1 Greenland. Withdrew from the European Communities.

4–5 Gibraltar–Spain. Frontier was opened for vehicles, having been closed since 1969.

11 Uruguay. President General Gregorio Alvarez resigned. President-elect Julio Sanguinetti took office on 1 March.

13 South Korea. General election returned the ruling Democratic Justice Party.

16 Cambodia. Vietnamese forces took the headquarters of Khmer Rouge guerillas at Phum Thmei.

17 Lebanon. Israeli Army completed the first phase of a 3-phase withdrawal.

21 Argentina. Isabel Péron resigned as leader of the Péronist party.

22 Western Samoa. A general election returned the ruling Human Rights Protection Party.

25 Pakistan. A general election to the National Assembly returned: Pakistan People's Party, 47; Muslim League, 17; Jamaat Islami Party, 9; Provincial assemblies (elected 27 Feb.) would in turn elect a Senate.

March 2 Bangladesh. Elections due in April 1985 were abandoned and martial law reinstated.

5 UK. Coal strike ended without settlement.

10 USSR. President Konstantin U. Chernenko died and on 11 March, Mikhail S. Gorbachev became General Secretary of the Party.

30 Greece. Christos Sartzetakis took oath of office as President. President Caramanlis had resigned on 10 March.

April 6 Sudan. President Nemery was deposed in a military *coup* and the Constitution suspended.

11 Albania. Enver Hoxha, First Secretary of the Central Committee died, having ruled the country since 1944

ADDENDA

MALTA. *High Commissioner in London:* Francis F. A. Cassar.

BRAZIL. Cabinet appointed March 1985; the President-elect has been seriously ill since his election: *President of the Republic:* Tancredo Neves. *Vice-President:* José Sarney. *Foreign Affairs:* Olavo Setubal. *Planning:* João Sayad. *Finance:* Francisco Neves Dornelles. *Industry and Trade:* Roberto Gusmão. *Agriculture:* Pedro Simon. *Mines and Energy:* Aureliano Chavés. *Justice:* Fernando Lyra. *Health:* Carlos Santana. *Debureaucratization:* Paulo Lustosa. *Social Security:* Waldir Pires. *Transport:* Alfonso Camargo. *Education:* Marco Maciel. *Culture:* José Aparecido de Oliveira. *Interior:* Ronaldo Costa Couto. *Land:* Nelson Ribeiro. *Communications:* Antonio Carlos Magalhaes. *Labour:* Almir Pazzianotto Pinto Urban. *Housing and Services:* Flavio Peixoto da Silveira. *Administration:* Aluizio Alvés. *Science and Technology:* Renato Archer. *Army:* Gen. Leonidas Pires Goncalves. *Navy:* Adm. Henrique Saboya. *Air Force:* Brig. Otavio Moreira Lima. *Military Household:* Gen. Rubens Bayma Denys. *Civilian Household:* José Hugo Castelo Branco. *Secret Service:* Gen. Ivan de Sonza Mendes. *Armed Forces:* Adm. José Maria do Amaral Oliveira.

CHINA. Total population (1984) 1,036,040,000.

IRAQ. *UK Ambassador:* T. J. Clark.

VIETNAM. *UK Ambassador:* R. G. Talboys.

TAIWAN. *Economics Minister:* Lee Ta-hai.

BRUNEI. *Ambassador to UN:* Omar Bin Haji Servdin. *Ambassador to USA:* Pengiran Haji Iddriss. *US Ambassador to Brunei:* Barrington King.

VENEZUELA. Cabinet resigned in March 1985.

NEW ZEALAND. *Governor-General:* Most Rev. Paul Reeves, from Sept. 1985.

PAKISTAN. *Prime Minister:* Mohammad Khan Junejo.

GREECE. *President:* Christos Sartzetakis, from 30 March 1985.

JORDAN. *Prime Minister:* Zeid Refai.

SUDAN. President Jaafar Mohammed Nemery deposed in *coup* on 6 April 1985. Gen. Abdul-Rahman Swareddaheb became new military leader.

ALBANIA. *First Secretary of the Central Committee:* Enver Hoxha, died on 11 April 1985.

PART I

INTERNATIONAL ORGANIZATIONS

THE UNITED NATIONS

The United Nations is an association of states which have pledged themselves, through signing the Charter, to maintain international peace and security and to co-operate in establishing political, economic and social conditions under which this task can be securely achieved. Nothing contained in the Charter authorizes the organization to intervene in matters which are essentially within the domestic jurisdiction of any state.

The United Nations Charter originated from proposals agreed upon at discussions held at Dumbarton Oaks (Washington, D.C.) between the USSR, US and UK from 21 Aug. to 28 Sept., and between US, UK and China from 29 Sept. to 7 Oct. 1944. These proposals were laid before the United Nations Conference on International Organization, held at San Francisco from 25 April to 26 June 1945, and (after amendments had been made to the original proposals) the Charter of the United Nations was signed on 26 June 1945 by the delegates of 50 countries. Ratification of all the signatures had been received by 31 Dec. 1945. (For the complete text of the Charter *see* THE STATESMAN'S YEAR-BOOK, 1946, pp. xxi–xxxii.)

The United Nations formally came into existence on 24 Oct. 1945, with the deposit of the requisite number of ratifications of the Charter with the US Department of State. The official languages of the United Nations are Arabic, Chinese, English, French, Russian and Spanish.

The headquarters of the United Nations is in New York City, USA.

Flag: UN emblem in white centred on a light blue ground.

Membership. Membership is open to all peace-loving states whose admission will be effected by the General Assembly upon recommendation of the Security Council. The table on pp. 7–8 shows the member states of the United Nations.

The Principal Organs of the United Nations are: 1. The General Assembly. 2. The Security Council. 3. The Economic and Social Council. 4 The Trusteeship Council. 5. The International Court of Justice. 6. The Secretariat.

1. **The General Assembly** consists of all the members of the United Nations. Each member has only 1 vote. The General Assembly meets regularly once a year, commencing on the third Tuesday in Sept.; the session normally lasts until mid-December and is resumed for some weeks in the new year if this is required. Special sessions may be convoked by the Secretary-General if requested by the Security Council, by a majority of the members of the United Nations or by 1 member concurred with by the majority of the members. The Assembly also meets in emergency special session. The General Assembly elects its President for each session.

The first regular session was held in London from 10 Jan. to 14 Feb. and in New York from 23 Oct. to 16 Dec. 1946.

Special sessions have been held on Palestine (1947, 1948), Tunisia (1961), Financial Situation of UN (1963), South West Africa, Peace-Keeping, Postponement of Outer Space Conference (1967), Raw Materials and Development (1974), New International Economic Order (1975), Peace-keeping force in the Lebanon, Namibia, Disarmament (1978, 1982), Economic Issues (1980); Emergency Special sessions were held on Suez, Hungary (1956), Lebanon-Jordan-United Arab Republic dispute (1958), Congo (1960), Middle East (1967), Afghánistán, Palestine (1980) and Namibia (1981).

The work of the General Assembly is divided between 7 Main Committees, on which every member state is represented. These are: First committee (disarmament and related international security matters); special political committee; second committee (economic and financial matters); third committee (social, humanitarian and cultural matters); fourth committee (decolonisation matters); fifth committee (administrative and budgetary matters); sixth committee (legal matters).

In addition there is a General Committee charged with the task of co-ordinating the proceedings of the Assembly and its Committees; and a Credentials Committee which verifies the credentials of the delegates. The General Committee consists of 25 members, comprising the President of the General Assembly, its 17 Vice-Presidents and the Chairmen of the 7 Main Committees. The Credentials Committee consists of 9 members, elected at the beginning of each session of the General Assembly. The Assembly has 2 standing committees—an Advisory Committee on Administrative and Budgetary Questions, and a Committee on Contributions. The General Assembly establishes subsidiary and *ad hoc* bodies when necessary to deal with specific matters. These include: Special Committee on Peace-keeping Operations (33 members), Commission on Human Rights (32 members), Committee on the peaceful uses of outer space (28 members), Conciliation Commission for Palestine (3 members), Conference on Disarmament (42 members), International Law Commission (25 members), Scientific Committee on the effects of atomic radiation (15 members), Special Committee on the implementation of the declaration on the granting of independence to colonial countries and peoples (25 members), Special Committee on the policies of Apartheid of the Government of the Republic of South Africa (11 members), UN Commission on International Trade Law (29 members) and Committee on the Peaceful Uses of Sea-bed and Ocean Floor Beyond the Limits of National Jurisdiction (91 members).

The General Assembly may discuss any matters within the scope of the Charter, and, with the exception of any situation or dispute on the agenda of the Security Council, may make recommendations on any such questions or matters. For decisions on important questions a two-thirds majority is required, on other questions a simple majority of members present and voting. In addition, the Assembly at its fifth session, in 1950, decided that if the Security Council, because of lack of unanimity of the permanent members, fails to exercise its primary responsibility for the maintenance of international peace and security in any case where there appears to be a threat to the peace, breach of the peace or act of aggression, the General Assembly shall consider the matter immediately with a view to making appropriate recommendations to members for collective measures, including in the case of a breach of the peace or act of aggression the use of armed force when necessary, to maintain or restore international peace and security.

The General Assembly receives and considers reports from the other organs of the United Nations, including the Security Council. The Secretary-General makes an annual report to it on the work of the Organization.

2. **The Security Council** consists of 15 members, each of which has 1 vote. There are 5 permanent and 10 non-permanent members elected for a 2-year term by a two-thirds majority of the General Assembly.

Retiring members are not eligible for immediate re-election. Any other member of the United Nations will be invited to participate without vote in the discussion of questions specially affecting its interests.

The Security Council bears the primary responsibility for the maintenance of peace and security. It is also responsible for the functions of the UN in trust territories classed as 'strategic areas'. Decisions on procedural questions are made by an affirmative vote of 9 members. On all other matters the affirmative vote of 9 members must include the concurring votes of all permanent members (in practice, however, an abstention by a permanent member is not considered a veto), subject to the provision that when the Security Council is considering methods for the peaceful settlement of a dispute, parties to the dispute abstain from voting.

For the maintenance of international peace and security the Security Council can, in accordance with special agreements to be concluded, call on armed forces, assistance and facilities of the member states. It is assisted by a Military Staff Committee consisting of the Chiefs of Staff of the permanent members of the Security Council or their representatives.

The Presidency of the Security Council is held for 1 month in rotation by the member states in the English alphabetical order of their names.

The Security Council functions continuously. Its members are permanently represented at the seat of the organization, but it may meet at any place that will best facilitate its work.

The Council has 2 standing committees of Experts and on the Admission of New Members. In addition, from time to time, it establishes *ad hoc* committees and commissions such as the Truce Supervision Organization in Palestine.

Permanent Members: China, France, USSR, UK, USA.
Non-Permanent Members: Burkina Faso, Egypt, India, Peru, Ukraine (until 31 Dec. 1985); Australia, Denmark, Thailand, Trinidad and Tobago (until 31 Dec. 1986).

3. **The Economic and Social Council** is responsible under the General Assembly for carrying out the functions of the United Nations with regard to international economic, social, cultural, educational, health and related matters.

By Nov. 1977, 15 'specialized' inter-governmental agencies working in these fields had been brought into relationship with the United Nations. The Economic and Social Council may also make arrangements for consultation with international non-governmental organizations and, after consultation with the member concerned, with national organizations; by 1983 over 600 non-governmental organizations had been granted consultative status.

The Economic and Social Council consists of 54 Member States elected by a two-thirds majority of the General Assembly. Nine are elected each year for a 3-year term. Retiring members are eligible for immediate re-election. Each member has 1 vote. Decisions are made by a majority of the members present and voting.

The Council nominally holds 2 sessions a year, and special sessions may be held if required. The President is elected for 1 year and is eligible for immediate re-election.

The Economic and Social Council has the following commissions:

Regional Economic Commissions: ECE (Economic Commission for Europe. Geneva); ESCAP (Economic and Social Commission for Asia and the Pacific. Bangkok); ECLA (Economic Commission for Latin America. Santiago, Chile); ECA (Economic Commission for Africa. Addis Ababa). ECWA (Economic Commission for Western Asia. Baghdad). These Commissions have been established to enable the nations of the major regions of the world to co-operate on common problems and also to produce economic information.

Six functional commissions, including: (1) a Statistical Commission with sub-commission on Statistical Sampling. (2) Commission on Human Rights; with sub-commission on Prevention of Discrimination and Protection of Minorities; (3) Social Development Commission; (4) Commission on the Status of Women; (5) Commission on Narcotic Drugs; (6) Population Commission.

The Economic and Social Council has the following standing committees: The Economic Committee, Social Committee, Co-ordination Committee, Committee on Non-Governmental Organizations, Interim Committee on Programme of Conferences, Committee for Industrial Development, Advisory Committee on the Application of Science and Technology to Development, Committee on Housing, Building and Planning.

Other special bodies are the International Narcotics Control Board, the Interim Co-ordinating Committee for International Commodity Arrangements and the Administrative Committee on Co-ordination to ensure (1) the most effective implementation of the agreements entered into between the United Nations and the specialized agencies and (2) co-ordination of activities.

Membership: Bangladesh, Brazil, Colombia, France, Federal Republic of Germany, Guinea, Haiti, Iceland, India, Japan, Morocco, Nigeria, Romania, Senegal, Spain, Turkey, Venezuela, Zimbabwe (until 31 Dec. 1987). Argentina, Canada, China, Costa Rica, Finland, Indonesia, Papua New Guinea, Poland, Rwanda, Somalia, Sri Lanka, Sweden, Uganda, USSR, UK, Yugoslavia, Zaïre (until 31 Dec.

1986): Algeria, Botswana, Bulgaria, Congo, Djibouti, Ecuador, German Democratic Republic, Lebanon, Luxembourg, Malaysia, Mexico, Netherlands, New Zealand, Saudi Arabia, Sierra Leone, Suriname, Thailand, USA (until 31 Dec. 1985).

4. **The Trusteeship Council.** The Charter provides for an international trusteeship system to safeguard the interests of the inhabitants of territories which are not yet fully self-governing and which may be placed thereunder by individual trusteeship agreements. These are called trust territories.

All of the original 11 trust territories except one, the Pacific Islands (Micronesia), administered by the USA, have become independent or joined independent countries. The Trusteeship Council consists of the 1 member administering trust territories: USA; the permanent members of the Security Council that are not administering trust territories: China, France, USSR and UK. Decisions of the Council are made by a majority of the members present and voting, each member having 1 vote. The Council holds one regular session each year, and special sessions if required.

5. **The International Court of Justice** was created by an international treaty, the Statute of the Court, which forms an integral part of the United Nations Charter. All members of the United Nations are *ipso facto* parties to the Statute of the Court.

The Court is composed of independent judges, elected regardless of their nationality, who possess the qualifications required in their countries for appointment to the highest judicial offices, or are jurisconsuls of recognized competence in international law. There are 15 judges, no 2 of whom may be nationals of the same state. They are elected by the Security Council and the General Assembly of the United Nations sitting independently. Candidates are chosen from a list of persons nominated by the national groups in the Permanent Court of Arbitration established by the Hague Conventions of 1899 and 1907. In the case of members of the United Nations not represented in the Permanent Court of Arbitration, candidates are nominated by national groups appointed for the purpose by their governments. The judges are elected for a 9-year term and are eligible for immediate re-election. When engaged on business of the Court, they enjoy diplomatic privileges and immunities.

The Court elects its own President and Vice-Presidents for 3 years and remains permanently in session, except for judicial vacations. The full court of 15 judges normally sits, but a quorum of 9 judges is sufficient to constitute the Court. It may form chambers of 3 or more judges for dealing with a particular case or particular categories of cases, and forms annually a chamber of 5 judges to hear and determinc, at the request of the parties, cases by summary procedures. Taslim O. Elias (Nigeria) and José Sette-Camara (Brazil) are, respectively, President and Vice-President of the Court until 1985.

Competence and Jurisdiction. Only states may be parties in cases before the Court, which is open to the states parties to its Statute. The conditions under which the Court will be open to other states are laid down by the Security Council. The Court exercises its jurisdiction in all cases which the parties refer to it and in all matters provided for in the Charter, or in treaties and conventions in force. Disputes concerning the jurisdiction of the Court are settled by the Court's own decision.

The Court may apply in its decision: *(a)* international conventions; *(b)* international custom; *(c)* the general principles of law recognized by civilized nations; and *(d)* as subsidiary means for the determination of the rules of law, judicial decisions and the teachings of highly qualified publicists. If the parties agree, the Court may decide a case *ex aequo et bono.* The Court may also give an advisory opinion on any legal question to any organ of the United Nations or its agencies.

Procedure. The official languages of the Court are French and English. At the request of any party the Court will authorize the use of another language by this party. All questions are decided by a majority of the judges present. If the votes are equal, the President has a casting vote. The judgment is final and without appeal, but a revision may be applied for within 10 years from the date of the judgment on the ground of a new decisive factor. Unless otherwise decided by the Court, each party bears its own costs.

Judges. The judges of the Court, elected by the Security Council and the General Assembly, are as follows: (1) To serve until 5 Feb. 1988: Platon D. Morozov (USSR), Roberto Ago (Italy), Bedjaoui (Algeria), José Sette-Camara (Brazil), Stephen Schwebel (USA). (2) To serve until 5 Feb. 1991: Nagendra Singh (India), José Maria Ruda (Argentina), Sir Robert Jennings (UK), Guy Ladreit de Lacharrière (France), Kéba Mbaye (Senegal). (3) To serve until 5 Feb. 1994: Taslim Olawale Elias (Nigeria), Manfred Lachs (Poland), Jens Evensen (Norway), Shigeru Oda (Japan), Ni Zhengyu (China).

If there is no judge on the bench of the nationality of the parties to the dispute, each party has the right to choose a judge. Such judges shall take part in the decision on terms of complete equality with their colleagues.

The Court has its seat at The Hague, but may sit elsewhere whenever it considers this desirable. The expenses of the Court are borne by the UN.

Registrar: Santiago Torres Bernárdez (Spain).

6. **The Secretariat** is composed of the Secretary-General, who is the chief administrative officer of the organization, and an international staff appointed by him under regulations established by the General Assembly. However, the Secretary-General, the High Commissioner for Refugees and the Managing Director of the Fund are appointed by the General Assembly. The first Secretary-General was Trygve Lie (Norway), 1946–53; the second, Dag Hammarskjöld (Sweden), 1953–61; the third, U. Thant (Burma), 1961–71; the fourth, Kurt Waldheim (Austria), 1972–81.

The Secretary-General acts as chief administrative officer in all meetings of the General Assembly, the Security Council, the Economic and Social Council and the Trusteeship Council.

The financial year coincides with the calendar year; accountancy is in US$. Budget for 1984–85, $1,587,158,000.

Secretary-General: Javier Perez de Cuellar (Peru), appointed 1 Jan. 1982 for a 5-year term.

The Secretary-General is assisted by Under-Secretaries-General and Assistant Secretaries-General.

MEMBER STATES OF THE UN

(as in 1983 with percentage scale of contribution)

Afghánistán	0·01	1946
Albania	0·01	1955
Algeria	0·12	1962
Angola	0·01	1976
Antigua and Barbuda	0·01	1981
Argentina [1]	0·78	1945
Australia [1]	1·83	1945
Austria	0·71	1955
Bahamas	0·01	1973
Bahrain	0·01	1971
Bangladesh	0·04	1974
Barbados	0·01	1966
Belgium [1]	1·22	1945
Belize	...	1981
Benin	0·01	1960
Bhután	0·01	1971
Bolivia [1]	0·01	1945
Botswana	0·01	1966
Brazil [1]	1·27	1945
Brunei Darussalam	...	1984
Bulgaria	0·16	1955
Burkina Faso	0·01	1960
Burma	0·01	1948
Burundi	0·01	1962
Byelorussia [1]	0·39	1945
Cambodia	0·01	1955
Cameroon	0·01	1960
Canada [1]	3·28	1945
Cape Verde	0·01	1975
Central African Rep.	0·01	1960
Chad	0·01	1960
Chile [1]	0·07	1945
China [1]	1·62	1945
Colombia [1]	0·11	1945
Comoros	0·01	1975
Congo	0·01	1960
Costa Rica [1]	0·02	1945
Cuba [1]	0·11	1945
Cyprus	0·01	1960
Czechoslovakia [1]	0·83	1945
Denmark [1]	0·74	1945
Djibouti	0·01	1977
Dominica	0·01	1978
Dominican Republic [1]	0·03	1945
Ecuador [1]	0·02	1945
Egypt [1]	0·07	1945
El Salvador [1]	0·01	1945
Equatorial Guinea	0·01	1968

Ethiopia [1]	0·01	1945
Fiji	0·01	1970
Finland	0·48	1955
France [1]	6·26	1945
Gabon	0·02	1960
Gambia	0·01	1965
German Democratic Rep.	1·39	1973
Germany, Federal Rep. of	8·31	1973
Ghana	0·03	1957
Greece [1]	0·35	1945
Grenada	0·01	1974
Guatemala [1]	0·02	1945
Guinea	0·01	1958
Guinea-Bissau	0·01	1974
Guyana	0·01	1966
Haiti [1]	0·01	1945
Honduras [1]	0·01	1945
Hungary	0·33	1955
Iceland	0·03	1946
India [1]	0·60	1945
Indonesia	0·16	1950
Iran [1]	0·65	1945
Iraq [1]	0·12	1945
Ireland	0·16	1955
Israel	0·25	1949
Italy	3·45	1955
Ivory Coast	0·03	1960
Jamaica	0·02	1962
Japan	9·58	1956
Jordan	0·01	1955
Kenya	0·01	1963
Kuwait	0·20	1963
Laos People's Dem. Rep.	0·01	1955
Lebanon [1]	0·03	1945
Lesotho	0·01	1966
Liberia [1]	0·01	1945
Libyan Arab Jamahiriya	0·23	1955
Luxembourg [1]	0·05	1945
Madagascar	0·01	1960
Malawi	0·01	1964
Malaysia	0·09	1957
Maldives	0·01	1965
Mali	0·01	1960
Malta	0·01	1964
Mauritania	0·01	1961
Mauritius	0·01	1968
Mexico [1]	0·76	1945
Mongolia	0·01	1961
Morocco	0·05	1956
Mozambique	0·01	1975
Nepál	0·01	1955
Netherlands [1]	1·63	1945
New Zealand [1]	0·27	1945
Nicaragua [1]	0·01	1945
Niger	0·01	1960
Nigeria	0·16	1960
Norway [1]	0·50	1945

Oman	0·01	1971
Pakistan	0·07	1947
Panama [1]	0·02	1945
Papua New Guinea	0·01	1975
Paraguay [1]	0·01	1945
Peru [1]	0·06	1945
Philippines [1]	0·10	1945
Poland [1]	1·24	1945
Portugal	0·19	1955
Qatar	0·03	1971
Romania	0·21	1955
Rwanda	0·01	1962
St Christopher and Nevis	...	1983
St Lucia	0·01	1979
St Vincent and the Grenadines	0·01	1980
Samoa, Western	0·01	1976
São Tomé and Principe	0·01	1975
Saudi Arabia [1]	0·58	1945
Senegal	0·01	1960
Seychelles	0·01	1976
Sierra Leone	0·01	1961
Singapore	0·08	1965
Solomon Islands	0·01	1978
Somalia	0·01	1960
South Africa [1]	0·42	1945
Spain	1·70	1955
Sri Lanka	0·02	1955
Sudan	0·01	1956
Suriname	0·01	1975
Swaziland	0·01	1968
Sweden	1·31	1946
Syrian Arab Rep.[1]	0·03	1945
Tanzania	0·01	1961
Thailand	0·10	1946
Togo	0·01	1960
Trinidad and Tobago	0·03	1962
Tunisia	0·03	1956
Turkey [1]	0·30	1945
Uganda	0·01	1962
Ukrainian Soviet Socialist Rep.[1]	1·46	1945
USSR [1]	11·10	1945
United Arab Emirates	0·10	1971
UK [1]	4·46	1945
USA [1]	25·00	1945
Uruguay [1]	0·04	1945
Vanuatu	0·01	1981
Venezuela [1]	0·50	1945
Vietnam	0·03	1977
Yemen Arab Republic	0·01	1947
Yemen, P.D.R.	0·01	1967
Yugoslavia [1]	0·42	1945
Zaïre	0·02	1960
Zambia	0·02	1964
Zimbabwe	0·02	1980

[1] Original member.

Books of Reference

Yearbook of the United Nations. New York, 1947 ff. Annual

United Nations Chronicle. Quarterly

Monthly Bulletin of Statistics

General Assembly: Official-Records: Resolutions

Reports of the Secretary-General of the United Nations on the Work of the Organization. 1946 ff.

Documents of the United Nations Conference on International Organization, San Francisco, 1945. 16 vols.

Charter of the United Nations and Statute of the International Court of Justice. Text in English, French, Chinese, Russian and Spanish.
Repertory of Practice of UN's Organs. 5 vols. New York, 1955
Official Records of the Security Council, the Economic and Social Council, Trusteeship Council and the Disarmament Commission
Demographic Yearbook, 1948 ff. New York, 1969
Everyone's United Nations. New York. 9th ed., 1979
Statistical Yearbook. New York, 1947 ff.
United Nations Handbook 1984. New Zealand Ministry of Foreign Affairs, Wellington, 1984
Yearbook of International Statistics. New York, 1950 ff.
World Economic Survey. New York, 1947 ff.
Economic Survey of Asia and the Far East. New York, 1946 ff.
Economic Survey of Latin America. New York, 1948 ff.
Economic Survey of Europe. New York, 1948 ff.
Economic Survey of Africa. New York, 1960 ff.
Foote, W., *Dag Hammarskjöld—Servant of Peace.* London, 1962
Forsythe, D., *United Nations Peacemaking: The Conciliation Commission for Palestine.* Johns Hopkins Univ. Press, 1973
Hiscocks, R., *The Security Council: A Study in Adolescence.* New York, 1974
Lie, Trygve, *In the Cause of Peace.* London, 1954
Luard, E., *A History of the United Nations.* Vol. 1. London, 1982
Rikhye, I. J., Harbottle, M., Egge, B., *The Thin Blue Line.* London, 1974
Symonds, R., and Carder, M., *The United Nations and the Population Question.* London, 1973
Thant, U., *Towards World Peace.* New York, 1964
Urquhart, B., *Hammarskjöld.* London, 1973
Walters, F. P., *A History of the League of Nations.* 2 vols. London, 1952
Winton, H. N. M. (comp. and ed.), *Man and the Environment. A Bibliography of Selected Publications of the United Nations System 1946–1971.* New York, 1972
Witthauer, K., *Die Bevölkerung der Erde: Verteilung und Dynamik.* Gotha, 1958.—*Distribution and Dynamics Relating to World Population.* Gotha, 1969
Her Majesty's Stationery Office. *Sectional List 23* (currently revised) and *International Organizations Publications* contain a full list of publications on UN and Specialized Agencies, issued by HMSO.

United Nations Information Centre. 20 Buckingham Gate, London SW1E 6LB

UNITED NATIONS SYSTEM

The bulk of the work of the UN, measured in terms of money and personnel, is aimed at achieving the pledge made in Article 55 of the Charter to 'promote higher standards of living, full employment and conditions of economic and social progress and development'.

In addition to the 17 independent specialized agencies, there are some 14 major United Nations programmes and funds devoted to achieving economic and social progress in the developing countries.

Total contributions to the funds and programmes of the UN and specialized agencies for development activities amounted to $2,400m. (not including contributions to the World Bank group) in 1983. The highest total contributions went to the UN Development Programme (UNDP – $714m.) the UN Children's Fund (UNICEF – $297m.) and the UN Fund for Population Activities (UNFPA – $130m.). The World Food Programme, which provides food aid to support development projects and emergency relief operations, provided aid worth $900m. in 1983, making it the largest single source of development assistance in the UN system, apart from the World Bank.

The *United Nations Development Programme* (UNDP) is the world's largest agency for multilateral technical and pre-investment co-operation. It is the funding source for most of the technical assistance provided by the United Nations system, and UNDP is active in almost 150 countries and territories and in virtually every economic and social sector. UNDP assistance is provided only at the request of Governments and in response to their priority needs, integrated into over-all national and regional plans.

There are more than 5,000 UNDP-supported projects currently in operation at the national, regional, inter-regional and global levels, all aimed at helping developing countries make better use of their assets, improve living standards and expand productivity. The volume of such work was $1,200m. in 1983.

UNICEF, established in 1946 to deliver post-war relief to children, now concentrates its assistance on development activities aimed at improving the quality of life for children and mothers in developing countries. During 1983, UNICEF was working in over 110 countries with a child population of some 1,300m., concentrating on basic services for children and maternal health care, nutrition, water supply and sanitation and education. *The State of the World's Children Report: 1984*, published by UNICEF, has helped to spread acceptance by local and national leaders of a strategy for child health and nutrition which UNICEF estimates could save the lives of 7m. children. UNICEF has focused on popularising four primary health care techniques which are low in cost and produce results in a relatively short time. These include: oral rehydration therapy to fight the effects of diarrhoeal infections, which kill some 4m. children each year; expanded immunization against the 6 most common childhood diseases; child growth monitoring, and promotion of breast-feeding. The World Health Organization and UNICEF work closely together, providing training, equipment and the services of health care professionals. UNICEF is the world's largest supplier of vaccines and the 'cold chain' equipment needed to deliver them, as well as oral rehydration salts.

Executive Director: James P. Grant (USA).

The UN Fund for Population Activities (UNFPA) carries out programmes in over 130 countries and territories. The Fund's aims are to build up capacity to respond to needs in population and family planning; to promote awareness of population problems in both developed and developing countries and possible strategies to deal with them; to assist developing countries at their request in dealing with population problems. More than 25% of international population assistance to developing countries is channeled through UNFPA.

Executive Director: Rafael M. Salas (Philippines).

An International Conference on Population was convened by the United Nations in 1984 in Mexico City to review the World Population Plan of Action adopted by the 1974 population conference, and make recommendations for its future implementation.

Humanitarian relief to refugees and victims of natural and man-made disasters is also an important function of the UN system. Among the organizations involved in such relief activities are the Office of the UN Disaster Relief Co-ordinator (UNDRO), the Office of the UN High Commissioner for Refugees (UNHCR) and the UN Relief and Works Agency for Palestine Refugees in the Near East (UNRWA).

UNRWA was created by the General Assembly in 1949 as a temporary, non-political agency to provide relief to the nearly 750,000 people who became refugees as a result of the disturbances during and after the creation of the State of Israel in the former British Mandate territory of Palestine. 'Palestine refugees', as defined by UNRWA's mandate, are persons or descendants of persons whose normal residence was Palestine for at least 2 years prior to the 1948 conflict and who, as a result of the conflict, lost their homes and means of livelihood. UNRWA has also been called upon to assist persons displaced as a result of renewed hostilities in the Middle East in 1967. The situation of Palestine refugees in south Lebanon was of special concern to the Agency in 1984 which has carried out an emergency relief programme in that area for Palestine refugees affected in the aftermath of the Israeli invasion of Lebanon in 1982.

Over 2m. refugees are registered with the Agency which provides education, health care, supplementary feeding and relief services. Education and basic health care account for over 80% of the Agency's budget, which is financed by voluntary contributions from Governments. In 1984 its operating budget amounted to $230m., while cash contributions were expected to total only $170m.

Commissioner-General: Olof Rydbeck (Sweden).

The *Office of the United Nations High Commissioner for Refugees* (UNHCR) was established by the UN General Assembly with effect from 1 Jan. 1951, originally for three years. Since 1954, its mandate has been renewed for successive five-year periods.

The work of UNHCR is of a purely humanitarian and non-political character. The main functions of the Office are to provide international protection for refugees and to seek permanent solutions to their problems through voluntary repatriation, resettlement in other countries or integration into the country of present residence. UNHCR may also be called upon to provide emergency relief and ongoing material assistance where necessary.

UNHCR concerns itself with refugees who have been determined to come within its mandate under the Statute, and with persons in analogous circumstances whom it assists under the terms of the good offices resolutions adopted by the General Assembly.

The High Commissioner is elected by the General Assembly and follows policy directives given by the General Assembly or the Economic and Social Council.

International protection is the primary function of UNHCR. Its main objective is to promote and safeguard the rights and interests of refugees. In so doing UNHCR devotes special attention to promoting a generous policy of asylum on the part of Governments and seeks to improve the status of refugees in their country of residence. It also helps them to cease being refugees through the acquisition of the nationality of their country of residence when voluntary repatriation is not applicable. UNHCR pursues its objectives in the field of protection by encouraging the conclusion of intergovernmental legal instruments in favour of refugees, by supervising the implementation of their provisions and by encouraging Governments to adopt legislation and administrative procedures for the benefit of refugees.

The thirty-fifth session of the Executive Committee of the High Commissioner's Programme, held in Oct. 1984, noted with deep concern that an increasingly restrictive trend in the granting of asylum and refugee status by many Governments was eroding the rights of asylum-seekers in many parts of the world. It also expressed alarm at continued threats to the physical safety of refugees through military or armed attacks and piracy.

Throughout 1984 the numbers of refugees requiring material assistance from UNHCR remained relatively stable as there occurred no massive outflows of refugees of the kind so familiar in the late 1970's.

In Oct. 1984 the Executive Committee of the High Commissioner's Programme approved a revised financial target of US$352m. for UNHCR general programmes in 1984 and also approved the figure of US$368m. for projected requirements in 1985.

For its work on behalf of refugees around the world, UNHCR was awarded the Nobel Peace Prize in 1955 and again in 1981.

Headquarters: Palais des Nations, 1211, Geneva 10, Switzerland.
UK Office: 36 Westminster Palace Gardens, London, SW1P 1RR.

High Commissioner: Poul Hartling (Denmark).

UN funds and programmes participating in the 1984 pledging conference for development activities:
UN Development Programme; Special Measures Fund for the Least Developed Countries; UN Development Programme Energy Account; UN Capital Development Fund; UN Special Fund for Land-Locked Developing Countries; UN Revolving Fund for National Resources Exploration; Special Voluntary Fund for the UN Volunteers; UN Financing System for Science and Technology for Development; UN Trust Fund for Sudano-Sahelian Activities; UN Children's Fund; UN Fund for Population Activities; UN Industrial Development Fund; UN Trust Fund for African Development Activities; Voluntary Fund for the UN Decade for Women; UN Trust Fund for the International Research and Training Institute for the Advancement of Women; UN Centre for Human Settlements (Habitat): UN Habitat and Human Settlements Foundation; UN Trust Fund for the Transport and Communications Decade in Africa; Trust Fund for the UN Centre on Transnational Corporations; UN Institute for Training and Research; UN Fund for Drug

Abuse Control; UN Trust Fund for Social Defence; UN Development Programme Study Programme; Fund of the UN Environment Programme.

SPECIALIZED AGENCIES OF THE UN

INTERNATIONAL ATOMIC ENERGY AGENCY (IAEA)

Origin. The International Atomic Energy Agency came into existence on 29 July 1957. Its statute had been approved on 26 Oct. 1956, at an international conference held at UN Headquarters, New York. A relationship agreement links it with the United Nations. The IAEA had 112 member states in 1983.

Functions. (1) To accelerate and enlarge the contribution of atomic energy to peace, health and prosperity throughout the world, and (2) to ensure that assistance provided by it or at its request or under its supervision or control is not used in such a way as to further any military purpose. In addition, under the terms of the Non-Proliferation Treaty, to verify states' obligation to prevent diversion of nuclear energy from peaceful uses to nuclear weapons or other nuclear explosive devices.

The IAEA gives advice and technical assistance to developing countries on nuclear power development (provides a series of training courses on nuclear power project planning, construction and operation), on health and safety, on radioactive waste management, on legal aspects of the use of atomic energy, and on prospecting for and exploiting nuclear raw materials; in addition it promotes the use of radiation and isotopes in agriculture, industry, medicine and hydrology through expert services, training courses and fellowships, grants of equipment and supplies, research contracts, scientific meetings and publications. During this year, 1,348 scientists and technicians received training – primarily in nuclear engineering and nuclear safety (34%), agriculture (19%), medicine (11%) and industrial applications of isotopes and radiation techniques (10%). Thirty-five training courses were attended by 779 participants from developing countries. The IAEA has research laboratories in Austria and Monaco. At Trieste, the International Centre for Theoretical Physics was established in 1964 which is now operated jointly by UNESCO and IAEA.

In Dec. 1983, safeguards agreements were in force with 77 non-nuclear-weapon States pursuant to the NPT and/or the Tlatelolco Treaty. Other agreements were in force with a further 12 non-nuclear-weapon States. In addition, safeguards agreements were in force with three nuclear-weapon States for the Agency to apply safeguards to nuclear material in certain civil nuclear facilities. Negotiations are under way with a fourth nuclear-weapon State to conclude a similar agreement. The IAEA applied safeguards at 147 power reactors, 177 research reactors and critical assemblies, 7 conversion plants, 40 fuel fabrication plants, 6 reprocessing plants, 4 enrichment plants, 28 separate storage facilities, 46 other facilities and 425 other locations, in non-nuclear-weapon States. These figures include facilities safeguarded under the safeguards agreement with the European Atomic Energy Community and its non-nuclear-weapon States.

Organization. The Statute provides for an annual General Conference, a Board of Governors of 34 members and a Secretariat headed by a Director-General.

Headquarters: Vienna International Centre, PO Box 100, A-1400 Vienna, Austria.

Director-General: Hans Blix (Sweden).

INTERNATIONAL LABOUR ORGANISATION (ILO)

Origin. The ILO, established in 1919 as an autonomous part of the League of Nations, is an intergovernmental agency with a tripartite structure, in which representatives of governments, employers and workers participate. It seeks through international action to improve labour conditions, raise living standards and promote productive employment. In 1946 the ILO was recognized by the United Nations as a specialized agency. In 1969 it was awarded the Nobel Peace Prize. In 1984 it numbered 151 members.

Functions. One of the ILO's principal functions is the formulation of international standards in the form of International Labour Conventions and Recommendations. Member countries are required to submit Conventions to their competent national authorities with a view to ratification. If a country ratifies a Convention it agrees to bring its laws into line with its terms and to report periodically how these regulations are being applied. More than 5,100 ratifications of 159 Conventions had been deposited by mid-1984. Machinery is available to ascertain whether Conventions thus ratified are effectively applied.

Recommendations do not require ratification, but member states are obliged to consider them with a view to giving effect to their provisions by legislation or other action. By the end of 1984 the International Labour Conference had adopted 169 recommendations.

Organization. The ILO consists of the International Labour Conference, the Governing Body and the International Labour Office.

The Conference is the supreme deliberative organ of the ILO; it meets annually at Geneva. National delegations are composed of 2 government delegates, 1 employers' delegate and 1 workers' delegate.

The Governing Body, elected by the Conference, is the executive council. It is composed of 28 government members, 14 workers' members and 14 employers' members.

Ten governments hold permanent seats on the Governing Board because of their industrial importance, namely, Brazil, China, Federal Republic of Germany, France, India, Italy, Japan, USA, USSR and UK. The remaining 18 government seats were, at the end of 1984, held by Algeria, Angola, Argentina, Burkina Faso, Canada, Ethiopia, Finland, Ghana, Hungary, Indonesia, Iraq, Jamaica, Mongolia, Nicaragua, Pakistan, Ukraine, Venezuela, Zimbabwe.

The Office serves as secretariat, operational headquarters, research centre and publishing house.

The ILO budget for 1984–85 amounted to US$254·7m.

Activities. In addition to its research and advisory activities, the ILO extends technical co-operation to governments under its regular budget and under the UN Development Programme and Funds-in-Trust in the fields of employment promotion, human resources development (including vocational and management training), development of social institutions, small-scale industries, rural development, social security, industrial safety and hygiene, productivity, etc. Technical co-operation also includes expert missions and a fellowship programme. Some $94m. was spent on technical co-operation in 1983. Projects were in progress in some 115 countries and about 900 experts involved.

Major emphasis is being given to the ILO's World Employment Programme, launched in 1969 with the purpose of stimulating national and international efforts to increase the volume of productive employment, and so to counter the problem of rising unemployment in developing countries. Employment strategy missions were carried out under the Programme in Colombia, the Dominican Republic, Egypt, Iran, Kenya, Sri Lanka, Sudan and the Philippines. The work of these missions was complemented by an ILO programme of research designed to provide policy-makers with the information to promote employment. A World Employment Conference was held in June 1976.

The International Labour Conference (Geneva, June 1984) adopted a Recommendation on employment policy, and held first discussions on occupational health services and revision of Convention No. 63 (on statistics of wages and hours of work) with a view to the adoption of new instruments in these fields in 1985. The conference also evaluated the ILO's International Programme for the Improvement of Working Conditions and Environment.

In 1960 the ILO established in Geneva the International Institute for Labour Studies. The Institute specializes in advanced education and research on social and labour policy. It brings together for group study experienced persons from all parts of the world—government administrators, trade-union officials, industrial experts, management, university and other specialists.

A training institution was opened by the ILO in Turin, Italy, in 1965—the

International Centre for Advanced Technical and Vocational Training. The Centre provides opportunities for technical, vocational and management training for individuals who have advanced beyond the facilities available in their own countries. Courses are geared particularly to the needs of developing countries.

Headquarters: International Labour Office, CH-1211 Geneva 22, Switzerland.
Director-General: Francis Blanchard (France).
Chairman of the Governing Body: B. G. Deshmukh (India).
London Branch Office: 96/98 Marsham St., SW1.

The ILO has regional offices in Addis Ababa (for Africa), Bangkok (for Asia and the Pacific), Lima (for Latin America and the Caribbean) and Beirut (for Arab States).

Publications: Regular periodicals in English, French and Spanish include the *International Labour Review, Legislative Series, Bulletin of Labour Statistics, Year Book of Labour Statistics, Official Bulletin* and *Labour Education. Women at Work* and the *Social and Labour Bulletin* are issued in English and French.

Accident Prevention: A Workers' Education Manual; Collective Bargaining: A Response to the Recession in Industrialised Market Economy Countries; Economics: A Workers' Education Manual; Employment and Manpower Problems and Policy Issues in Arab Countries: Proposals for the Future; International Conflicts of Labour Law: A Survey of the Law Applicable to the International Employment Relation; Labour Co-operatives: Retrospect and Prospects; Microelectronics and Office Jobs; Occupational Safety and Health in the Iron and Steel Industry: An ILO Code of Practice; Rural Small-Scale Industries and Employment in Africa and Asia; Strategic Management of Development Programmes (All 1983).

FOOD AND AGRICULTURE ORGANIZATION OF THE UNITED NATIONS (FAO)

Origin. The UN Conference on Food and Agriculture in May 1943, at Hot Springs, Virginia, set up an Interim Commission in Washington in July 1943 to plan the Organization, which came into being on 16 Oct. 1945.

Aims and Activities. The aims of FAO are to raise levels of nutrition and standards of living; to improve the production and distribution of all food and agricultural products from farms, forests and fisheries; to improve the living conditions of rural populations; and, by these means, to eliminate hunger.

In carrying out these aims, FAO promotes investment in agriculture, better soil and water management, improved yields of crops and livestock, and the transfer of technology to, and the development of agricultural research in, developing countries. FAO promotes the conservation of natural resources and the rational use of fertilizers and pesticides. The Organization combats animal diseases, promotes the development of marine and inland fisheries, and encourages the rational use of forest resources. Technical assistance is provided in all these fields and others such as nutrition, agricultural engineering, agrarian reform, development communications, remote sensing for natural resources, and the prevention of food losses.

Special FAO programmes help countries prepare for, and provide relief in the event of, emergency food situations, in particular through the setting up of food reserves. Since the early 1980s, Africa has needed special emphasis. The Global Information and Early Warning System provides current information on the world food situation and identifies countries threatened by shortages to guide potential donors.

The Organization also has a major rôle in the collection, analysis and dissemination of information on natural resources and agricultural production.

FAO sponsors the World Food Programme (WFP) with the UN; WFP uses food commodities, cash and services contributed by member States of the UN to back programmes of social and economic development, as well as for relief in emergency situations.

Finance and Administration. The FAO Conference, composed of all member states, meets every other year to determine the policy and approve the budget and work programme of FAO. The Council, consisting of 49 member nations elected by the Conference, serves as FAO's governing body between Sessions of the Conference. At its 22nd Session in Nov. 1983, the Conference admitted four new member states, Antigua and Barbuda, Belize, St Kitts–Nevis–Anguilla, and Vanuatu, raising the total to 156. The Conference also approved a Regular Programme budget for the two years 1984–85 of $421m., an increase of 0·5% in real terms over the previous period. The Regular Programme, which is financed by contributions from member governments, covers the cost of the Organization's secretariat, its Technical Co-operation Programme and part of the cost of several Special Action Programmes.

FAO provides advice and assistance in the field through its Field Programmes, funded largely from external sources, such as the UN Development Programme (UNDP) and trust funds provided by governments. Funds available from UNDP have continued to fall – from $167m. in 1980 to around $117m. in 1984. The drop in funds from UNDP has been partially offset by increases in trust funds and in funds available through the Technical Co-operation Programme funded from FAO's own Regular Programme budget. Trust fund delivery in 1984 was expected to be about $135m. compared with $120m. the previous year. Delivery under the Technical Co-operation Programme in 1984 was expected to reach about $26m., compared with $23m. in 1983. Total Field Programme delivery in 1984 was expected to remain close to the 1982 figure of $278m., while falling significantly in real terms.

Headquarters: Viale delle Terme di Caracalla, Rome, Italy.
Director-General: Dr Edouard Saouma (Lebanon).

FAO publications include: FAO Books in Print 1980–81: The State of Food and Agriculture (annual), 1974 ff.; *The FAO World Food Report* (annual), 1983 ff.; *Animal Health Yearbook* (annual), 1957 ff.; *Production Yearbook* (annual), 1947 ff.; *Trade Yearbook* (annual), 1947 ff.; *FAO Commodity Review* (annual), 1961 ff.; *Yearbook of Forest Products Statistics* (annual), 1947 ff.; *Yearbook of Fishery Statistics* (in two volumes). *Ceres* (bi-monthly). *Food and Nutrition* (bi-annual), *FAO Fertilizer Yearbook, FAO Plant Protection Bulletin* (quarterly), *World Animal Review* (quarterly).

UNITED NATIONS EDUCATIONAL, SCIENTIFIC AND CULTURAL ORGANIZATION (UNESCO)

Origin. A Conference for the establishment of an Educational, Scientific and Cultural Organization of the United Nations was convened by the Government of the UK in association with the Government of France, and met in London, 1–16 Nov. 1945. UNESCO came into being on 4 Nov. 1946.

Functions. The purpose of UNESCO is to contribute to peace and security by promoting collaboration among the nations through education, science and culture in order to further universal respect for justice, for the rule of law and for the human rights and fundamental freedoms which are affirmed for the peoples of the world, without distinction of race, sex, language or religion, by the Charter of the United Nations.

Activities. The education programme has four main objectives: the extension of education; the improvement of education; and life-long education for living in a world community.

To train teachers specialized in the techniques of fundamental education UNESCO is helping to establish regional and national training centres. A centre for Latin America was opened in Mexico in 1951, one for the Arab States was set up in Egypt in 1953. UNESCO seeks to promote the progressive application of the right to free and compulsory education for all and to improve the quality of education everywhere.

In the natural sciences, UNESCO seeks to promote international scientific co-operation, such as the International Hydrological Programme which began in 1966. It encourages scientific research designed to improve the living conditions of mankind. Science co-operation offices have been set up in Montevideo, Cairo, New Delhi, Nairobi and Jakarta.

In the field of communication, UNESCO endeavours, by disseminating information, carrying out research and providing advice, to increase the scope and quality of press, film and radio services throughout the world.

Organization. The organs of UNESCO are a General Conference (composed of representatives from each member state), an Executive Board (consisting of 51 government representatives elected by the General Conference) and a Secretariat. UNESCO had 160 members in 1984.

National commissions act as liaison groups between UNESCO and the educational, scientific and cultural life of their own countries.

Budget for 1984–85: $374,410,000.

Headquarters: UNESCO House, 9 Place de Fontenoy, Paris (7eme).

Director-General: Amadou Mahtar M'Bow (Senegal).

Periodicals. Museum (quarterly, English and French); *International Social Science Journal* (quarterly, English and French); *Impact of Science on Society* (quarterly, English and French); *Unesco Courier* (monthly, English, French and Spanish); *Fundamental and Adult Education Bulletin* (quarterly, English, French and Spanish); *Copyright Bulletin* (twice-yearly, English and French); *Unesco News* (English, French and Spanish); *Unesco Bulletin for Libraries* (monthly, English, French and Spanish).

Hajnal, P. I., *Guide to UNESCO*. London and New York, 1983

WORLD HEALTH ORGANIZATION (WHO)

Origin. An International Conference, convened by the UN Economic and Social Council, to consider a single health organization resulted in the adoption on 22 July 1946 of the constitution of the World Health Organization. This constitution came into force on 7 April 1948.

Structure. The principal organs of WHO are the World Health Assembly, the Executive Board and the Secretariat. Each of the 164 member states and 1 Associate Member (1984) has the right to be represented at the Assembly, which meets annually usually in Geneva, Switzerland. The 30-member Executive Board is composed of technically qualified health experts designated by as many member states elected by the Assembly. The Secretariat consists of technical and administrative staff headed by a Director-General. Health activities in member countries are carried out through regional organizations which have been established in Africa (regional office, Brazzaville), South-East Asia (New Delhi), Europe (Copenhagen), Eastern Mediterranean (Alexandria) and Western Pacific (Manila). The Pan American Sanitary Bureau in Washington serves as the Regional Office of WHO for the Americas.

Functions. WHO's objective, as stated in the first article of the Constitution is 'the attainment by all peoples of the highest possible level of health'. As the directing and co-ordinating authority on international health it establishes and maintains collaboration with the UN, specialized agencies, government health administrations, professional and other groups concerned with health. The Constitution also directs WHO to assist governments to strengthen their health services, to stimulate and advance work to eradicate diseases, to promote maternal and child health, mental health, medical research and the prevention of accidents; to improve standards of teaching and training in the health professions, and of nutrition, housing, sanitation, working conditions and other aspects of environment health. The Organization also is empowered to propose conventions, agreements and regulations and make recommendations about international health matters; to revise the international nomenclature of diseases, causes of death and public health practices; to develop, establish and promote international standards concerning foods, biological, pharmaceutical and similar substances.

Methods of work. Co-operation in country projects is undertaken only on the request of the government concerned, through the 6 regional offices of the Organization. Worldwide technical services are made available by headquarters. Expert committees whose members are chosen from the 53 advisory panels of experts meet to advise the Director-General on a given subject. Scientific groups and consultative meetings are called for similar purposes. To further the education of health personnel of all categories, seminars, technical conferences and training courses are organized and advisors, consultants and lecturers are provided. WHO awards fellowships for study to nationals of member countries.

Activities. The main thrust of WHO's activities in recent years has been towards promoting national, regional and global strategies for the attainment of the main social target of the Member States for the next two decades: 'Health for All by the Year 2000', or the attainment by all citizens of the world of a level of health that will permit them to lead a socially and economically productive life.

Almost all countries indicated a high level of political commitment to this goal, and guiding principles for formulating corresponding strategies and plans of action were prepared.

The 37th World Health Assembly, meeting in May 1984 in Geneva, made an appeal to all industrialized countries to demonstrate absolute solidarity with the developing countries.

By far the most substantial debate was devoted to the global strategy of 'Health for All' and country reports on monitoring progress in its implementation.

The World Health Assembly urged all Member States to speed the reorientation and the modifications of health systems towards primary health care and to give the highest priority and assure full responsibility for the continuing monitoring and evaluation of their strategies.

The Organization's working budget for 1984–85 is $520·1m.

The role of universities. The potential of universities to make a great contribution to the strategies for Health for All was recognized and underlined by the Assembly following the Technical Discussions which brought together high-ranking academicians and health officials for two days of packed exchanges. In a resolution, the Assembly urged Member States to encourage universities and other higher learning institutions to include the social and technical concepts of Health for All in the education and training of all categories of students and post-graduates and to acquaint the general public with these concepts.

Essential Drugs. The Assembly urged Member States to intensify action to implement national drug policies and strategies with WHO support. It also called for the dissemination of unbiased and complete information on drugs and an exchange of information between Member States on drug use and marketing practices.

Prevention of blindness due to vitamin A deficiency. Some 10m. children are affected by vitamin A deficiency and xerophthalmia in Asia alone and more than 1m. become blind every year. The disease is also prevalent in Africa, the Western Pacific and limited areas of the Americas. Safe, effective and cheap techniques exist to control vitamin A deficiency. The Assembly therefore urged all Member States to give high priority to the prevention and control of vitamin A deficiency and xerophthalmia wherever these problems exist, through appropriate nutritional programmes, as a part of primary health care.

Emergency assistance to drought-stricken and famine-affected countries in Africa. With due consideration to the drought and famine in many African countries, and the fact that these countries are among the least developed in the world, the Assembly requested WHO to take appropriate steps to strengthen the mechanisms at present in function, in collaboration with the UN system, donor countries, governmental and non-governmental organizations, in order to improve the support of the international community to these countries.

Abuse of narcotics and psychotropic substances. The Assembly, recognizing the dramatic increase in drug addiction, all the more alarming in that the young are the chief victims of narcotics dependence, noted with satisfaction the development of the WHO programme on drug dependence, and requested the Organization to strengthen epidemiological surveillance systems.

Liberation struggle in southern Africa. Southern Africa front-line States, including Lesotho and Swaziland, still suffer from political and economic destabilization which hamper their development. The Assembly requested WHO to continue helping them to solve the acute health problems of the Namibian and South African refugees and to provide these States with health assistance, health personnel, pharmaceutical products and financial assistance to enable them to rehabilitate their damaged health infrastructure.

World Health Day. World Health Day, 7 April 1984, was devoted to the theme Children's Health – Tomorrow's Wealth. The theme chosen for World Health Day 1985 is Healthy Youth – Our Best Resource.

Headquarters: 1211 Geneva 27. *Regional Offices:* Alexandria, Brazzaville, Copenhagen, Manila, New Delhi, Washington.

Director-General: Dr Halfdan T. Mahler (Denmark).

Basic Documents. 34th ed., 1984 (Arabic, Chinese, English, French, Russian, Spanish)
Handbook of Resolutions and Decisions. Vol. I, 1973 and Vol. II, 1983 (Arabic, English, French, Russian, Spanish)
WHO Chronicle (bi-monthly from 1947; Arabic, Chinese, English, French, Russian and Spanish)
Bulletin of WHO (quarterly, 1947–51; 6 issues a year from 1978; English and French)
International Digest of Health Legislation (quarterly, from 1948; English)
World Health, the Magazine of WHO. 1957 ff. (10 issues a year; Arabic, English, French, German, Italian, Persian, Portuguese, Russian and Spanish)
WHO Technical Report Series, 1950 ff. (English, French, Russian, Spanish)
WHO Monograph Series, 1951 ff. (English, French, Russian, Spanish)
Public Health Papers, 1959 ff. (English, French, Russian, Spanish)
World Health Statistics Annual (from 1939; English, French and Russian)
World Health Statistics Quarterly (monthly, 1947–76 then quarterly; English and French)
Weekly Epidemiological Record (from 1926; English and French)
Publications of the WHO, 1947–57; a bibliography (1958).—*1958–62* (1965).—*1963–67* (1969).—*1968–72* (1974)
World Directories:
Dental Schools, 1963 (1967); *Medical Schools, 1979; Post-Basic and Post-Graduate Schools of Nursing* (1965); *Schools of Pharmacy, 1963* (1966); *Schools of Public Health, 1971* (1972); *Venereal Disease Treatment Centres at Ports* (1972); *Veterinary Schools, 1971* (1973). *Schools for Medical Assistants, 1973* (1976); *Auxiliary Sanitarians 1973* (1978); *Dental Auxiliaries 1973* (1977); *Medical Lab. Technicians and Assistants, 1973* (1977)
The International Pharmacopoeia. 3rd. ed., 1979 (English, French and Spanish)
Manual of the International Statistical Classification of Diseases, Injuries and Causes of Death. 9th rev. (1977; English, French, Russian, Spanish)
IARC Monographs on the Evaluation of Carcinogenic Risk of Chemicals to Humans. 1967 *ff.* (English)
International Histological Classification of Tumours. Books and slides, from 1967, No. 25, 1980 (English, French, Russian and Spanish)
Report on the World Health Situation. 1959 ff. (Arabic, Chinese, English, French, Russian, Spanish); Sixth report 1973–77 (1980)

INTERNATIONAL MONETARY FUND (IMF)

The International Monetary Fund was established on 27 Dec. 1945 as an independent international organization and began operations on 1 March 1947; its relationship with the UN is defined in an agreement of mutual co-operation which came into force on 15 Nov. 1947. The first amendment to the Fund's articles creating the special drawing right (SDR) took effect on 28 July 1969 and the second amendment took effect on 1 April 1978.

The capital resources of the Fund come from SDRs and currencies that the members pay under quotas calculated for them when they join the Fund. Members' quotas in the Fund at present amount to SDR 89,200m. and are closely related to (*i*) subscription to the Fund, (*ii*) their drawing rights on the Fund under both regular and special facilities, (*iii*) their voting power, and (*iv*) their share of any allocations of SDRs. Every Fund member is required to subscribe to the Fund an amount equal to its quota. An amount not exceeding 25% of the quota has to be paid in reserve assets, the balance in the member's own currency.

The Fund is authorized under its Articles of Agreement to supplement its resources by borrowing. In Jan. 1962, a 4-year agreement was concluded with 10 industrial members (Belgium, Canada, France, Federal Republic of Germany,

Italy, Japan, Netherlands, Sweden, UK, USA) who undertook to lend the Fund up to $6,000m. in their own currencies, if this should be needed to forestall or cope with an impairment of the international monetary system. Switzerland subsequently joined the group as an associate. These arrangements, known as the General Arrangements to Borrow (GAB), have been extended several times and the most recent 5-year renewal was to end in Oct. 1985. In early 1983 agreement was reached to increase the credit arrangements under the GAB to SDR 17,000m.; to permit use of GAB resources in transactions with Fund members that are not GAB participants; to authorize Swiss participation; and to permit borrowing arrangements with nonparticipating members to be associated with the GAB. Saudi Arabia and the Fund have entered into such an arrangement under which the Fund will be able to borrow up to SDR 1,500m. to assist in financing purchases by any member for the same purpose and under the same circumstances as in the GAB. The changes became effective by 26 Dec. 1983. The GAB have been used to finance drawings made by the UK in 1964, 1965, 1968, 1969, and 1977, by France in 1969 and 1970, and by USA in 1978. The Fund has also borrowed from member countries and official institutions for a supplementary financing facility and, more recently, from the Saudi Arabian Monetary Agency (SAMA).

Purposes: To promote international monetary co-operation, the expansion of international trade and exchange rate stability; to assist in the removal of exchange restrictions and the establishment of a multilateral system of payments; and to alleviate any serious disequilibrium in members' international balance of payments by making the financial resources of the Fund available to them, usually subject to conditions to ensure the revolving nature of Fund resources.

Activities. Each member of the Fund undertakes a broad obligation to collaborate with the Fund and other members to ensure the existence of orderly exchange arrangements and to promote a system of stable exchange rates. In addition, members are subject to certain obligations relating to domestic and external policies that can affect the balance of payments and the exchange rate. The Fund makes its resources available, under proper safeguards, to its members to meet short-term or medium-term payments difficulties. The first allocation of special drawing rights was made on 1 Jan. 1970 with five SDR allocations since then. SDRs in existence now total SDR 21,400m. To further enhance its balance of payments assistance to its members the Fund established a compensatory financing facility on 23 Feb. 1963, temporary oil facilities in 1974 and 1975, a trust fund in 1976, and an extended facility for medium term assistance to members with special balance of payments problems on 13 Sept. 1974 with additional financing now provided through a policy of enlarged access.

A Report on Reform of the International Monetary System was submitted to the Board of Governors at the 1972 annual meeting. During the meeting the Committee on Reform of the International Monetary System and Related Issues, generally known as the Committee of Twenty, held its first session, with the mandate to advise and report to the Board on all aspects of the international monetary system, including proposals for any amendments of the Articles of Agreement. The Committee of Twenty disbanded after submitting its final report in 1974. An Interim Committee of the Board of Governors on the International Monetary System and a Joint Ministerial Committee of the Boards of Governors of the World Bank and the Fund on the Transfer of Real Resources to Developing Countries (Development Committee) were established and held their initial meetings in Jan. 1975 and since then have met on a semi-annual basis.

Organization. The highest authority in the Fund is exercised by the Board of Governors on which each member government is represented. Normally the Governors meet once a year, although the Governors may take votes by mail or other means between annual meetings. The Board of Governors has delegated many of its powers to the executive directors in Washington, of whom there are 22, of which 6 are appointed by individual members and the other 16 elected by groups of countries. Each appointed director has voting power proportionate to the quota of the government he represents, while each elected director casts all the votes of the countries which elected him. The 6 appointed executive directors represent the US, UK, France, Federal Republic of Germany, Saudi Arabia and Japan.

The managing director is selected by the executive directors; he presides as chairman at their meetings, but may not vote except in case of a tie. His term is for 5 years, but may be extended or terminated at the discretion of the executive directors. He is responsible for the ordinary business of the Fund, under general control of the executive directors, and supervises a staff of about 1,500.

Headquarters: 700 19th St. NW, Washington, D.C., 20431. Offices in Paris and Geneva.

Managing Director: Jacques de Larosière (France).

Publications. Summary Proceedings of Annual Meetings of the Board of Governors.—Annual Report of the Executive Board.—Financial Statement (quarterly).—*International Financial Statistics* (monthly).—*IMF Survey* (bi-weekly).—*Balance of Payments Statistics.* Washington, monthly.—*IMF Staff Papers* (four times a year). Washington, from Feb. 1950.—*IMF Occasional Papers.—Annual Report on Exchange Arrangements and Exchange Restrictions.* Washington, 1950 ff.—*Finance and Development.* Washington, from June 1964 (quarterly).—*Direction of Trade.* Washington (monthly). *World Economic Outlook.* Washington (annual). *Government Finance Statistics Yearbook.*

de Vries, M. G., *The International Monetary Fund 1966–1971.* Washington D.C., 1976

INTERNATIONAL BANK FOR RECONSTRUCTION AND DEVELOPMENT (IBRD)

Conceived at the Bretton Woods Conference, July 1944, the 'World Bank' began operations in June 1946. Its purpose is to provide funds and technical assistance to facilitate economic development in its poorer member countries.

The Bank obtains its funds from the following sources: Capital subscribed by member countries; sales of its own securities; sales of parts of its loans; repayments; and net earnings. The subscribed capital of the Bank amounted to $56,011m. at 30 June 1984. On 4 Jan. 1980, the Board of Governors adopted a resolution that increased the authorized capital stock of the Bank by 331,500 shares. This represented an increase of approximately $40,000m. The resolution provides that the paid-in portion of the shares authorized to be subscribed under it will be 7·5%, compared with the 10% paid-in portion of existing capital stock. Borrowing in the market had reached more than $78,000m. by 30 June 1984, of which $45,029m. was outstanding, and sales of portions of Bank loans from portfolio had totalled $2,937m. The Bank is self-supporting. Its net earnings for year ending 30 June 1984 amounted to $600m.; in addition, the Bank had reserves of $3,450m.

By 30 June 1984 the Bank had made 2,429 loans totalling $101,565m. in 104 of its 148 member countries. Lending was for the following purposes: Agriculture and rural development, $21,021·6m.; Development Finance Companies, $9,925m.; education, $3,689m.; energy, $22,212·7m.; industry, $7,166·4m.; non-project, $3,689m.; population, health and nutrition, $381·3m.; small-scale enterprises, $217·4m.; telecommunications, $1,768·6m.; tourism, $364m.; transportation, $18,714m.; urban development, $2,697m.; water supply and sewerage, $4,798m., and technical assistance, $156m. In order to eliminate wasteful overlapping of development assistance and to ensure that the funds available are used to the best possible effect, the Bank has organized consortia or consultative groups of aid-giving nations for the following countries: Bangladesh, Colombia, Ghana, India, Kenya, Nepál, Pakistan, the Philippines, Somalia, Sri Lanka, Sudan, Uganda, Zaïre, Zambia and the Caribbean Group for Co-operation in Economic Development. The Bank furnishes a wide variety of technical assistance. It acts as executing agency for a number of pre-investment surveys financed by the UN Development Programme. Resident missions have been established in 29 developing member countries as well as 3 regional missions in East and West Africa and Thailand primarily to assist in the preparation of projects. The Bank helps member countries to identify and prepare projects for the development of agriculture, education and water supply by drawing on the expertise of the FAO, WHO, UNIDO and UNESCO through its co-operative agreements with these organizations. The Bank maintains a staff college, the Economic Development Institute in Washington, D.C., for senior officials of the member countries.

Headquarters: 1818 H St., NW, Washington, D.C., 20433, USA. *European office:* 66 avenue d'Iéna, 75116 Paris, France. *London office:* New Zealand House, Haymarket, SW1Y 4TE, England. *Tōkyō office:* Kokusai Building, 1-1, Marunouchi 3-chome, Chiyoda-ku, Tōkyō 100, Japan.

President: Alden W. (Tom) Clausen (USA).

Publications. Annual Reports. 1946 ff.—*Summary Proceedings of Annual Meetings.* 1947 ff.—*The World Bank Group.* 1971.—*The World Bank Atlas.* 1967 ff.—*Catalog of Publications,* 1982.—*World Development Report.* 1978 ff.

Payer, C., *The World Bank: A Critical Analysis.* London, 1982

INTERNATIONAL DEVELOPMENT ASSOCIATION (IDA)

A lending agency which came into existence on 24 Sept. 1960. Administered by the World Bank, IDA is open to all members of the Bank.

IDA concentrates its assistance on those countries with an annual *per capita* gross national product of less than $520 (1975 rate). Its resources consist mostly of subscriptions, general replenishments from its more industrialized and developed members, special contributions, and transfers from the net earnings of the Bank. IDA credits are made to Governments only. It had committed over $33,654m. for 1,389 development projects in 83 countries, by 30 June 1984.

INTERNATIONAL FINANCE CORPORATION (IFC)

The Corporation, an affiliate of the World Bank, was established in July 1956. Paid-in capital at 30 June 1984 was $544·2m., subscribed by 125 member countries. In addition, it has accumulated earnings of $230·1m. IFC supplements the activities of the World Bank by encouraging the growth of productive private enterprises in less developed member countries. Chiefly, IFC makes investments in the form of subscriptions to the share capital of privately owned companies, or long-term loans, or both. The Corporation will help finance new ventures, and it will also assist established enterprises to expand, improve or diversify their operations.

At 30 June 1984 IFC had approved investments amounting to $6,216m., in 84 countries. The total amount of loans and equity which IFC had sold or agreed to sell to other investors as of that date was $3,471m.

President: Alden W. (Tom) Clausen (USA).

Executive Vice-President: Hans A. Wuttke (Germany).

Publications. Annual Reports. 1956 ff.—*General Policies.* 1983

INTERNATIONAL CIVIL AVIATION ORGANIZATION (ICAO)

Origin. The Convention providing for the establishment of the International Civil Aviation Organization was drawn up by the International Civil Aviation Conference held in Chicago from 1 Nov. to 7 Dec. 1944. A Provisional International Civil Aviation Organization (PICAO) operated for 20 months until the formal establishment of ICAO on 4 April 1947.

The Convention on International Civil Aviation superseded the provisions of the Paris Convention of 1919, which established the International Commission for Air Navigation (ICAN), and the Pan American Convention on Air Navigation drawn up at Havana in 1928.

Functions. It assists international civil aviation by establishing technical standards for safety and efficiency of air navigation and promoting simpler procedures at borders; develops regional plans for ground facilities and services needed for international flying; disseminates air-transport statistics and prepares studies on aviation economics; fosters the development of air law conventions. As part of the UN Development Programme it provides technical assistance to States in developing civil aviation programmes.

Organization. The principal organs of ICAO are an Assembly, consisting of all members of the Organization, and a Council, which is composed of 33 states elected by the Assembly, for 3 years, and meets in virtually continuous session. In electing these states, the Assembly must give adequate representation to: (1) states of major importance in air transport; (2) states which make the largest contribution to the provision of facilities for the international civil air navigation; (3) those states not otherwise included whose election will ensure that all major geographical areas of the world are represented. The main subsidiary bodies are: the Air Navigation Commission, composed of 15 members appointed by the Council; Air Transport Committee, open to council members; and the Legal Committee, on which all members of ICAO may be represented. There are 152 members. Budget for 1984: US$35,195,000.

Headquarters: 1000 Sherbrooke St. West, Suite 400, Montreal, Quebec, Canada H3A 2R2.
President: Dr Assad Kotaite (Lebanon).
Secretary-General: Yves Lambert (France).

Annual Report of the Council. (English, French, Russian, Spanish)
ICAO Bulletin (Monthly)

UNIVERSAL POSTAL UNION (UPU)

Origin. The UPU was established on 1 July 1875, when the Universal Postal Convention adopted by the Postal Congress of Berne on 9 Oct. 1874 came into force. The UPU was known at first as the General Postal Union, its name being changed at the Congress of Paris in 1878. In 1980 there were 158 member countries.

Functions. The aim of the UPU is to assure the organization and perfection of the various postal services and to promote, in this field, the development of international collaboration. To this end, the members of UPU are united in a single postal territory for the reciprocal exchange of correspondence.

Organization. The UPU is composed of a Universal Postal Congress which usually meets every 5 years, a permanent Executive Council consisting of 40 members, a consultative Committee, which consists of 35 members elected on a geographical basis by each Congress, and an International Bureau, which functions as the permanent secretariat.

Since 1 July 1948 the Union has been governed by the revised Convention adopted by the twelfth Congress in Paris on 5 July 1947.

Budget for 1981: US$9·5m.

Headquarters: Weltpoststrasse 4, 3000, Berne 15, Switzerland.
Director-General: Mohamed Ibrahim Sobhi (Egypt).

Publications. Documents of the Lausanne Congress 1974. Bern, 1975.—*Universal Postal Convention: Paris, 5 July, 1948.* (Cmd. 7435).—*The Postal Union* (monthly, Arabic, Chinese, English, French, German, Spanish, Russian).—*The UPU: Its Foundation and Development.* Bern, 1959.

INTERNATIONAL TELECOMMUNICATION UNION (ITU)

Origin. The International Telegraph Union, founded in Paris in 1865, and the International Radiotelegraph Union, founded in Berlin in 1906, were merged by the Madrid Convention of 1932 to form the International Telecommunication Union. ITU came into being on 1 Jan. 1934. The ITU has been governed since 1 Jan. 1975 by the revised International Telecommunication Convention adopted on 23 Oct. 1973.

Functions. The ITU: (1) allocates radio frequencies and registers radio-frequency assignments; (2) seeks to establish the lowest rates possible, consistent with efficient service and taking into account the necessity for keeping the independent financial administration of telecommunication on a sound basis; (3) promotes the adoption of measures for ensuring the safety of life through telecommunication; and (4) makes studies and recommendations and collects and publishes information for the benefit of its members.

Organization. The ITU consists of the Plenipotentiary Conference, Administrative Conferences, the Administrative Council of 36 members, the General Secretariat, the International Frequency Registration Board, and 2 international consultative committees (radio, telephone and telegraph).

Budget for 1975: $62·32m.

Headquarters: Place des Nations, Geneva, Switzerland.
Secretary-General: Mohamed Mili (Tunisia).

Publications: International Convention on Telecommunications, Malaga-Torremolinos, 1973.—*Yearbook of Common Carrier Telecommunication Statistics (1964–73),* 1975.—*Telecommunication Journal* (monthly).—*Radio Regulations.* 1971.

WORLD METEOROLOGICAL ORGANIZATION (WMO)

Origin. A Conference of Directors of the International Meteorological Organization (set up in 1873), meeting in Washington in 1947, adopted a Convention creating the World Meteorological Organization. The WMO Convention became effective on 23 March 1950, and WMO was formally established on 19 March 1951, when the first session of its Congress was convened in Paris. An agreement to bring WMO into relationship with the United Nations was approved by this Congress and came into force on 21 Dec. 1951 with its approval by the General Assembly of the United Nations.

Functions. (1) To facilitate world-wide co-operation in the establishment of networks of stations for the making of meteorological observations as well as hydrological or other geophysical observations related to meteorology, and to promote the establishment and maintenance of meteorological centres charged with the provision of meteorological and related services; (2) to promote the establishment and maintenance of systems for the rapid exchange of meteorological and related information; (3) to promote standardization of meteorological and related observations and to ensure the uniform publication of observations and statistics; (4) to further the application of meteorology to aviation, shipping, water problems, agriculture and other human activities; (5) to promote activities in operational hydrology and to further close co-operation between meteorological and hydrological services; and (6) to encourage research and training in meteorology and, as appropriate, to assist in co-ordinating the international aspects of such research and training.

Organization. WMO is an inter-governmental organization of 152 member states and 5 member territories responsible for the operation of their own meteorological services. Constituent bodies of WMO are the World Meteorological Congress which meets every 4 years, the executive council composed of 36 members elected in their personal capacity and including the President and 3 Vice-Presidents of the Organization, 6 regional associations of members and 8 technical commissions established by the Congress. A permanent secretariat is maintained in Geneva.

Budget for 1984–87: $77,516,400.

Headquarters: Case postale 5, CH-1211, Geneva 20, Switzerland.
Secretary-General: G. O. P. Obasi (Nigeria).

Publications. WMO Bulletin. 1952 ff.—*Meteorological Services of the World.* 1982.—*Publications of the World Meteorological Organization, 1951–1983.*

INTERNATIONAL MARITIME ORGANIZATION (IMO)

Origin. The International Maritime Organization, until 1982 known as Inter-Governmental Maritime Consultative Organization (IMCO), was established as a specialized agency of the UN by a convention drawn up at the UN Maritime Conference held at Geneva in Feb./March 1948. The Convention became effective on 17 March 1958 when it had been ratified by 21 countries, including 7 with at least 1m. gross tons of shipping each. The International Maritime Organization started operations in Jan. 1959.

Functions. To facilitate co-operation among governments on technical matters affecting merchant shipping, especially concerning safety at sea; to prevent and control marine pollution caused by ships; to encourage abolition of discriminatory and restrictive practices affecting merchant shipping. The International Maritime Organization is responsible for convening international maritime conferences and for drafting international maritime conventions.

Organization. The International Maritime Organization had 126 members (and 1 associate member) in 1984. The Assembly, composed of all member states, normally meets every 2 years. The Council of 32 member states acts as governing body between Assembly sessions. The Maritime Safety Committee deals with all technical questions. It can establish specialized sub-committees to deal with specific problems and like the Marine Environment Protection Committee, Legal Committee, Facilitation Committee and Committee on Technical Co-operation is open to all International Maritime Organization members. The Secretariat is composed of international civil servants.

The International Maritime Organization is depositary authority for the International Convention for the Safety of Life at Sea, 1960, and the Regulations for Preventing Collisions at Sea, 1948 and 1960; the International Convention for the Prevention of Pollution of the Sea by Oil, 1954, as amended in 1962 and 1969; the Convention on Facilitation of International Maritime Traffic, 1965; the International Convention on Load Lines, 1966; the International Convention on Tonnage Measurement of Ships, 1969; the International Convention relating to Intervention on the High Seas in cases of Oil Pollution Casualties, 1969; the International Convention on Civil Liability for Oil Pollution Damage, 1969; Convention on International Compensation Fund for Oil Pollution Damage, 1971; Special Trade Passenger Ships Agreement, 1971; Convention on International Regulations for Preventing Collisions at Sea, 1972; the International Convention for Safe Containers, 1972; the International Convention on Prevention of Pollution from Ships, 1973; the International Convention for the Safety of Life at Sea, 1974; Athens Convention relating to the Carriage of Passengers and their Luggage by Sea, 1974; Convention on the International Maritime Satellite Organization, 1976; Convention on Limitation of Maritime Claims, 1976; Torremolinos International Convention for the Safety of Fishing Vessels, 1977; International Convention on Standards of Training, Certification and Watchkeeping for Seafarers, 1978; International Convention on Maritime Search and Rescue, 1979.

Headquarters: 4 Albert Embankment, London SE1 7SR.
Secretary-General: C. P. Srivastava (India).
Assistant General Secretary: T. A. Mensah (Ghana).
IMO News

GENERAL AGREEMENT ON TARIFFS AND TRADE (GATT)

Origin. The General Agreement on Tariffs and Trade was negotiated in 1947 and entered into force on 1 Jan. 1948. Its 23 original signatories were members of a Preparatory Committee appointed by the UN Economic and Social Council to draft the charter for a proposed International Trade Organization. Since this charter was never ratified, the General Agreement, intended as an interim arrangement, has instead remained as the only international instrument laying down trade rules accepted by countries responsible for most of the world's trade. In Nov. 1983 there were 90 contracting parties, with a further 31 countries participating under special arrangements.

Functions. GATT functions both as a multilateral treaty that lays down a common code of conduct in international trade and trade relations and as a forum for negotiation and consultation to overcome trade problems and reduce trade barriers. Key provisions of the Agreement guarantee most-favoured-nation treatment (exceptions being granted to customs unions and free trade areas, and for certain preferences in favour of developing countries); require that protection be given to domestic industry only through tariffs (apart from specified exceptions); provide for negotiations to reduce tariffs (which are then 'bound' against subsequent increase) and other trade distortions; and lay down principles (particularly in Part IV of the Agreement, added in 1965) to assist the trade of developing countries. The Agreement also provides for consultation on, and settlement of, disputes, for 'waivers' (the grant of authorization, when warranted, to derogate from specific GATT obligations) and for emergency action in defined circumstances.

Seven 'rounds' of multilateral trade negotiations, including the Kennedy Round of 1964–67, took place in GATT up to 1979. The latest in this series, the Tōkyō Round, although held in Geneva, was so called because it was launched at a Ministerial meeting in the Japanese capital in Sept. 1973.

Ninety-nine countries participated in the Tōkyō Round. In Nov. 1979, the negotiations were concluded with agreements covering: an improved legal framework for the conduct of world trade (which includes recognition of tariff and non-tariff treatment in favour of and among developing countries as a permanent legal feature of the world trading system); non-tariff measures (subsidies and countervailing duties; technical barriers to trade; government procurement; customs valuation; import licensing procedures; and a revision of the 1967 GATT anti-dumping code); bovine meat; dairy products; tropical products; and an agreement on free trade in civil aircraft. The agreements contain provisions for special and more favourable treatment for developing countries.

Participating countries also agreed to reduce tariffs on thousands of industrial and agricultural products, for the most part over a period of 7 years beginning on 1 Jan. 1980. As a result of these concessions, industrialized countries will reduce the average level of their import duties on manufactures by about 34%, a cut comparable to that achieved in the Kennedy Round.

The agreements providing an improved framework for the conduct of world trade took effect in Nov. 1979. The other agreements took effect on 1 Jan. 1980, except for those covering government procurement and customs valuation, which took effect on 1 Jan. 1981, and the concessions on tropical products which began as early as 1977. Committees were established to supervise implemention of each of the Tōkyō Round agreements. Negotiations continued on the one major unresolved Tōkyō Round issue of whether to revise GATT rules on emergency safeguard action against imports.

GATT's member governments met in Geneva 24–29 Nov. 1982. The purpose of the meeting was to 'examine the functioning of the multilateral trading system, and to reinforce the common efforts of the contracting parties to support and improve the system for the benefit of all nations'. They adopted by consensus a joint Ministerial declaration which included: (i) An agreement on the problems facing the world economy and international trade; (ii) reaffirmation of the member governments' commitment to the GATT rules and to the multilateral trading system; (iii) an undertaking to refrain from taking or maintaining any trade measures inconsistent with GATT; (iv) an undertaking to ensure the effective implementation of GATT rules and provisions concerning developing countries, thereby furthering the dynamic role of these countries in international trade; (v) an undertaking to bring agriculture more fully into the multilateral trading system; to this end a Committee on Trade in Agriculture was established to carry out a major two-year work programme in this area; (vi) an undertaking to bring into effect quickly a comprehensive understanding on safeguards to be based on the principles of the General Agreement.

The Ministerial declaration also included decisions to improve the GATT procedures for settling trade disputes between members, to study such issues as trade in certain natural resource products, and to exchange information through GATT on international trade in services.

To assist the trade of developing countries, GATT established in 1964 the International Trade Centre (since 1968 operated jointly with the UN Conference on Trade and Development) to provide information and training on export markets and marketing techniques. Other GATT action in favour of developing countries includes training courses on trade policy questions.

Budget for 1984: Sw. Frs. 51,805,000.

Headquarters: Centre William Rappard, 154 rue de Lausanne, 1211 Geneva 21, Switzerland.

Director-General: Arthur Dunkel (Switzerland).

Publications. Basic Instruments and Selected Documents. 4 vols. and 30 supplements 1952–82.—*International Trade* [i.e., annual review], 1952 ff. Annually from 1953.—*GATT, What It Is, What It Does* (1984).—*GATT Activities,* 1960 ff. Annually from 1972.—*GATT Focus.* Monthly from Feb. 1981.—*GATT Studies in International Trade.* 1971 ff. (irregular series).—*The Tokyo Round of Multilateral Trade Negotiations.* Report of the Director-General, 2 vols., 1979.—*Textile and Clothing in the World Economy,* 1984

Casadio, G. P., *Transatlantic Trade: USA–EEC Confrontation in the GATT Negotiations.* Farnborough, 1973

Dam, K. W., *The GATT: Law and International Economic Organization.* Chicago and London, 1970

Golt, S., *The GATT Negotiations, 1973–75: A Guide to the Issues.* London, 1974

Hudec, R. E., *The GATT Legal System and World Trade Diplomacy.* New York, 1975

Jackson, J. H., *World Trade and the Law of GATT: A Legal Analysis of the General Agreement on Tariffs and Trade.* New York, 1969

WORLD INTELLECTUAL PROPERTY ORGANIZATION (WIPO)

Origin. The Convention establishing WIPO was signed at Stockholm in 1967 by 51 countries, and entered into force in April 1970. In Dec. 1974 WIPO became a specialized agency of the UN.

Functions. To promote the protection of intellectual property throughout the world through co-operation among States and, where appropriate, in collaboration with any other international organization, and to ensure administrative co-operation among the Unions established by various treaties for the protection of intellectual property. The WIPO Convention provides expressly for the encouragement of the conclusion of international agreements designed to promote the protection of intellectual property, and for the provision of legal-technical assistance at the request of States.

Intellectual property means the legal rights which result from intellectual activity in the industrial, scientific, literary or artistic fields. The main examples are industrial property (patents and other rights in inventions, rights in trademarks and industrial designs etc.) and copyright and neighbouring rights (chiefly in literary, musical and artistic works, in films, records and broadcasts etc.) in all fields of human endeavour; scientific discoveries; industrial designs; trade-marks, service marks and commercial names and designations; protection against unfair competition and all other rights resulting from intellectual activity in the industrial, scientific, literary or artistic fields.

Membership in WIPO is open to any State which is a member of at least one of the Unions and to other States which are members of the organizations of the United Nations system, are party to the Statute of the International Court of Justice, or are invited to join by the General Assembly of WIPO. Membership of the Unions is open to any State. The total combined membership of WIPO and of the Unions on 31 Dec. 1983, was 124 states.

Organization. The bodies of WIPO are: The *General Assembly* consisting of all States members of WIPO which are members of any of the Unions. Among its other functions, the General Assembly appoints and gives instructions to the Director General, reviews and approves his reports and adopts the biennial budget of expenses common to the Unions. The *Conference,* consisting of all States members of WIPO whether or not they are members of any of the Unions. Among its other functions, the Conference adopts its biennial budget and establishes the biennial programme of legal-technical assistance. The *Co-ordination Committee,* consisting of the States members of WIPO which are members of the Executive Committees of the Paris or Berne Unions.

In addition, the Paris and Berne Unions have Assemblies and Executive Committees, with functions similar to those of the WIPO bodies in respect of the biennial and annual budgets and programmes of the Unions.

The *WIPO Permanent Committees for Development Co-operation Related to Industrial Property* and *Related to Copyright and Neighbouring Rights* plan and review activities in the said fields; the *WIPO Permanent Committee on Patent Information* is responsible for intergovernmental co-operation in patent search systems and in such matters as the classification, standardization and exchange of patent documents.

Headquarters: 34, chemin des Colombettes, 1211 Geneva 20, Switzerland.
Director-General: Arpad Bogsch (USA).

Principal publications. Industrial Property (monthly, in English and French).—*Copyright* (monthly, in English and French).—*Les Marques internationales* (monthly, in French).—*Brochures of Conventions and Agreements.—Collections of Laws and Treaties.—Model Laws for Developing Countries on Inventions, on Marks Trade Names and Acts of Unfair Competition on Designs on Copyright and on Neighbouring Rights* (in Arabic, English, French and Spanish).—*Licensing Guide for Developing Countries* (in Arabic, Chinese, English, French, Portuguese and Spanish).—*Glossaries – industrial property and copyright* (multilingual).—*Guide to the Berne Convention* (in Arabic, English, French, German, Hindi, Japanese, Portuguese, Russian, Spanish).—*Guide to the Rome and Phonograms Convention* (in English, French and Spanish).

INTERNATIONAL FUND FOR AGRICULTURAL DEVELOPMENT (IFAD)

The establishment of IFAD was one of the major actions proposed by the 1974 World Food Conference. The agreement for IFAD entered into force on 30 Nov. 1977 following attainment of initial pledges of $1,000m. and the agency began its operations the following month. IFAD's purpose is to mobilise additional funds for agricultural and rural development in developing countries through projects and programmes directly benefiting the poorest rural population. In line with the Fund's focus on the rural poor, its resources are being made available in highly concessional loans.

Organization. The Governing Council, consisting of the entire membership, directs the Fund's operations. The chief executive is the President, who is also the Chairman of the 18-member Executive Board.

President: Abdelmuhsin Al-Sudeary (Saudi Arabia).
Headquarters: 107 Via del Serafico, Rome, Italy.

THE COMMONWEALTH

The Commonwealth is a free association of sovereign independent states, numbering 49 at the beginning of 1984. There is no charter, treaty or constitution; the association is expressed in co-operation, consultation and mutual assistance for which the Commonwealth Secretariat is the central co-ordinating body.

The Commonwealth was first defined by the Imperial Conference of 1926 as a group of 'autonomous communities within the British Empire, equal in status, in no way subordinate one to another in any aspect of their domestic or foreign affairs, though united by a common allegiance to the Crown, and freely associated as members of the British Commonwealth of Nations'. The basis of the association changed from one owing allegiance to a common Crown, and the modern Commonwealth was born in 1949 when the member countries accepted India's intention of becoming a republic at the same time continuing 'her full membership of the Commonwealth of Nations and her acceptance of the King as the symbol of the free association of its independent member nations and as such the Head of the Commonwealth'. There are now (1985) 18 Queen's realms, 26 republics, and 5 indigenous monarchies in the Commonwealth. All acknowledge the Queen symbolically as Head of the Commonwealth.

The Queen's legal title rests on the statute of 12 and 13 Will. III, c. 3, by which the succession to the Crown of Great Britain and Ireland was settled on the Princess Sophia of Hanover and the 'heirs of her body being Protestants'. By proclamation of 17 July 1917 the royal family became known as the House and Family of Windsor. On 8 Feb. 1960 the Queen issued a declaration varying her confirmatory declaration of 9 April 1952 to the effect that while the Queen and her children should continue to be known as the House of Windsor, her descendants, other than descendants entitled to the style of Royal Highness and the title of Prince or Princess, and female descendants who marry and their descendants should bear the name of Mountbatten-Windsor. The Royal Style and Titles of Queen Elizabeth are: In *Antigua and Barbuda* 'Elizabeth the Second, by the Grace of God, Queen of Antigua and Barbuda and of Her other Realms and Territories, Head of the Commonwealth'. In *Australia*: 'Elizabeth the Second, by the Grace of God Queen of Australia and Her other Realms and Territories, Head of the Commonwealth'. In the *Bahamas*: 'Elizabeth the Second, by the Grace of God, Queen of the Commonwealth of the Bahamas and of Her other Realms and Territories, Head of the Commonwealth'. In *Barbados*: 'Elizabeth the Second, by the Grace of God, Queen of Barbados and of Her other Realms and Territories, Head of the Commonwealth'. In *Belize*: 'Elizabeth the Second, by the Grace of God, Queen of Belize and of Her Other Realms and Territories, Head of the Commonwealth'. In *Canada*: 'Elizabeth the Second, by the Grace of God of the United Kingdom, Canada and Her other Realms and Territories Queen, Head of the Commonwealth, Defender of the Faith'. In *Fiji*: 'Elizabeth the Second, by the Grace of God, Queen of Fiji and of Her other Realms and Territories, Head of the Commonwealth'. In *Grenada*: 'Elizabeth the Second, by the Grace of God, Queen of the United Kingdom of Great Britain and Northern Ireland and of Grenada and Her other Realms and Territories, Head of the Commonwealth'. In *Jamaica*: 'Elizabeth the Second, by the Grace of God of Jamaica and of Her other Realms and Territories Queen, Head of the Commonwealth'. In *Mauritius*: 'Elizabeth the Second, Queen of Mauritius and of Her other Realms and Territories, Head of the Commonwealth'. In *New Zealand*: 'Elizabeth the Second, by the Grace of God Queen of New Zealand and Her Other Realms and Territories, Head of the Commonwealth, Defender of the Faith'. In *Papua New Guinea*: 'Elizabeth the Second, Queen of Papua New Guinea and Her other Realms and Territories, Head of the Commonwealth'. In *Saint Christopher and Nevis*: 'Elizabeth the Second, by the Grace of God, Queen of Saint Christopher and Nevis and Her other Realms and Territories, Head of the Commonwealth'. In *Saint Lucia*: 'Elizabeth the Second, by the Grace of God, Queen of Saint Lucia and of Her other Realms and Territories, Head of Commonwealth'. In *Saint Vincent and the Grenadines*: 'Elizabeth the Second, by the Grace of God, Queen of Saint Vincent and the Grenadines and of Her other Realms and Territories, Head of the Commonwealth'. In *Solomon Islands*: 'Elizabeth the Second by the Grace of God Queen of Solomon Islands and of Her other Realms and Territories, Head of the Commonwealth'. In *Tuvalu*: 'Elizabeth the Second by the Grace of God Queen of Tuvalu and of Her other Realms and Territories, Head of the Commonwealth'. In the *United Kingdom*: 'Elizabeth the Second, by the Grace of God of the United Kingdom of Great Britain and Northern Ireland and of Her other Realms and Territories Queen, Head of the Commonwealth, Defender of the Faith'.

A number of territories, formerly under British jurisdiction or mandate did not join the Commonwealth: Egypt, Iraq, Transjordan, Burma, Palestine, Sudan, British Somaliland, South Cameroons, and Aden. Two countries, the Republic of South Africa in 1961 and Pakistan in 1972, have left the Commonwealth.

Maldives, Nauru, Tuvalu and Saint Vincent and the Grenadines are special members, with the right to participate in all functional Commonwealth meetings and activities but not to attend meetings of Commonwealth Heads of Government.

Member States. The following are the member countries, with their dates of independence, and, where appropriate, the date on which they became republics: *United Kingdom*; *Canada* 1 July 1867[1]; *Australia* 1 Jan. 1901[1]; *New Zealand* 26 Sept. 1907[1]; *India* 15 Aug. 1947 (Republic on 26 Jan. 1950); *Sri Lanka* 4 Feb. 1948 (Republic on 22 May 1972); *Ghana* 6 March 1957 (Republic on 1 July 1960);

Malaysia 31 Aug. 1957 as Federation of Malaya, 16 Sept. 1963 as Federation of Malaysia; *Cyprus* 16 Aug. 1960 (Republic on independence; joined Commonwealth on 13 March 1961); *Nigeria* 1 Oct. 1960 (Republic on 1 Oct. 1963); *Sierra Leone* 27 April 1961 (Republic on 19 April 1971); *Tanzania*–Tanganyika 9 Dec. 1961 (Republic on 9 Dec. 1962), Zanzibar 10 Dec. 1963 (Republic on 12 Jan. 1964), United Republic of Tanganyika and Zanzibar 26 April 1964; renamed United Republic of Tanzania 29 Oct. 1964; *Western Samoa* 1 Jan. 1962 (joined Commonwealth on 28 Aug. 1970); *Jamaica* 6 Aug. 1962; *Trinidad and Tobago* 31 Aug. 1962 (Republic on 1 Aug. 1976); *Uganda* 9 Oct. 1962 (Republic 8 Sept. 1967, second republic 25 Jan. 1971); *Kenya* 12 Dec. 1963 (Republic on 12 Dec. 1964); *Malawi* 6 July 1964 (Republic on 6 July 1966); *Malta* 21 Sept. 1964 (Republic on 13 Dec. 1974); *Zambia* 24 Oct. 1964 (Republic on independence); *The Gambia* 18 Feb. 1965 (Republic on 24 April 1970); *Maldives* 26 July 1965 (Republic on independence, joined Commonwealth on 9 July 1982); *Singapore* 16 Sept. 1963 as a state in the Federation of Malaysia, 9 Aug. 1965 as an independent state and republic not part of Malaysia; *Guyana* 26 May 1966 (Republic on 23 Feb. 1970); *Botswana* 30 Sept. 1966 (Republic on independence); *Lesotho* 4 Oct. 1966; *Barbados* 30 Nov. 1966; *Nauru* 31 Jan. 1968 (Republic on independence); *Mauritius* 12 March 1968; *Swaziland* 6 Sept. 1968; *Tonga* 4 June 1970; *Fiji* 10 Oct. 1970; *Bangladesh* seceded from Pakistan as Republic 16 Dec. 1971, recognized by United Kingdom 4 Feb. 1972 (joined Commonwealth on 18 April 1972); *Bahamas* 10 July 1973; *Grenada* 7 Feb. 1974; *Papua New Guinea* 16 Sept. 1975; *Seychelles* 29 June 1976 (Republic on independence); *Solomon Islands* 7 July 1978; *Tuvalu* 1 Oct. 1978; *Dominica* 3 Nov. 1978 (Republic on independence); *Saint Lucia* 22 Feb. 1979; *Kiribati* 12 July 1979 (Republic on independence); *Saint Vincent and the Grenadines* 27 Oct. 1979; *Zimbabwe* 18 April 1980 (Republic on independence); *Vanuatu* 30 July 1980 (Republic on independence); *Belize* 21 Sept. 1981; *Antigua* and *Barbuda* 1 Nov. 1981; *Saint Christopher and Nevis* 19 Sept. 1983; *Brunei*[2] 1 Jan 1984.

[1] These are the effective dates of independence, given legal effect by the Statute of Westminster 1931.

[2] Brunei was a sovereign state in treaty relationship with Britain, whereby Britain was responsible for the conduct of external affairs and had a consultative responsibility for defence. It had never been a dependent territory, and in 1971 had ceased to be a protected state. A Treaty of Friendship and Co-operation was signed on 7 Jan. 1979, becoming effective on 1 Jan. 1984 when Brunei assumed her full international responsibilities and Britain gave up her consultative commitment over defence matters.

Dependent Territories and Associated States. There are 15 British dependent territories, 7 Australian external territories, 2 New Zealand dependent territories and 2 New Zealand associated states. A dependent territory is a territory belonging by settlement, conquest or annexation to the British, Australian or New Zealand Crown.

United Kingdom dependent territories administered through the Foreign and Commonwealth Office comprise, in the Far East: Hong Kong; in the Indian Ocean: British Indian Ocean Territory; in the Mediterranean: Gibraltar; in the Atlantic Ocean: Bermuda, Falkland Islands, Falkland Islands Dependencies, British Antarctic Territory, St Helena, St Helena Dependencies (Ascension and Tristan da Cunha); in the Caribbean: Montserrat, British Virgin Islands, Cayman Islands, Turks and Caicos Islands, Anguilla; in the Western Pacific: Pitcairn Group of Islands. The Australian external territories are: Coral Sea Islands Territory, Cocos (Keeling) Islands, Christmas Island, Heard Island and McDonald Islands, Norfolk Island, Australian Antarctic Territory and the Territory of Ashmore and Cartier Islands. The New Zealand dependent territories are: Tokelau and Ross Dependency. The New Zealand associated states are: Cook Islands and Niue.

While constitutional responsibility to Parliament for the government of the British dependent territories rests with the Secretary of State for Foreign and Commonwealth Affairs, the administration of the territories is carried out by the Governments of the territories themselves.

British Government Department. With effect from 17 Oct. 1968, the Secretary of State for Foreign and Commonwealth Affairs is responsible for the conduct of relations with members of the Commonwealth as well as with foreign countries, and for the administration of British dependent territories.

Commonwealth Secretariat. The Commonwealth Secretariat is an international body at the service of all 49 member countries. It provides the central organization for joint consultation and co-operation in many fields. It was established in 1965 by Commonwealth Heads of Government and has observer status at the UN General Assembly.

The Secretariat disseminates information on matters of common concern, organizes and services meetings and conferences, co-ordinates many Commonwealth activities, and provides expert technical assistance for economic and social development through the multilateral Commonwealth Fund for Technical Co-operation. The Secretariat is organized in divisions and sections which correspond to its main areas of operation: International affairs, economic affairs, food production and rural development, youth, education, information, applied studies in government, science and technology, law and health. Within this structure the Secretariat organizes the biennial meetings of Commonwealth Heads of Government, annual meetings of Finance Ministers of member countries, and regular meetings of Ministers of Education, Law, Health, and others as appropriate.

To emphasize the multilateral nature of the association, meetings are held in different cities and regions within the Commonwealth. Heads of Government decided that the Secretariat should work from London as it has the widest range of communications of any Commonwealth city, as well as the largest assembly of diplomatic missions.

The Commonwealth Secretary-General, who has access to Heads of Government, is the head of the Secretariat which is staffed by officers from member countries and financed by contributions from member governments.

Headquarters: Marlborough House, Pall Mall, London, SW1Y 5HX.
Secretary-General: Shridath S. Ramphal (Guyana).

Books of Reference

Year-Book of the Commonwealth, HMSO, Annual
The Cambridge History of the British Empire. 8 vols. CUP, 1929 ff.
Bradley, K. (ed.), *The Living Commonwealth.* London, 1961
Burns, Sir Alan, *In Defence of Colonies.* London, 1957
Chadwick, J., *The Unofficial Commonwealth.* London, 1982
Dale, W., *The Modern Commonwealth.* London, 1983
Garner, J., *The Commonwealth Office, 1925–1968.* London, 1978
Hailey, Lord, *An African Survey.* Rev. ed. Oxford, 1957.—*Native Administration in the British African Territories.* 5 vols. HMSO, 1951 ff.
Hall, H. D., *Commonwealth: A History of the British Commonwealth.* London and New York, 1971
Holland, R. F., *Britain and the Commonwealth Alliance 1918–39.* London, 1981
Ingram, D. T., *The Commonwealth at Work.* London, 1969.—*The Imperfect Commonwealth.* London, 1977
Judd, D., and Slinn, P., *The Evolution of the Modern Commonwealth.* London, 1982
Keeton, G. W. (ed.), *The British Commonwealth: Its Laws and Constitutions.* 9 vols. London, 1951 ff.
McIntyre, W. D., *The Commonwealth of Nations: Origins and Impact 1869–1971.* Univ. of Minnesota Press and OUP, 1978
Mansbergh, N., *The Commonwealth Experience.* 2 vols. London, 1982
Maxwell, W. H. and L. F., *A Legal Bibliography of the British Commonwealth of Nations.* 2nd ed. London, 1956
Papadopoulos, A. N., *Multilateral Diplomacy within the Commonwealth: A Decade of Expansion.* The Hague, 1982
Smith, A., and Sanger, C., *Stitches in Time: The Commonwealth in World Politics.* New York, 1983
Smith, T. E., *Commonwealth Migration: Flows and Policies.* London, 1981
Wade, E. C. S., and Phillips, G. G., *Constitutional Law: An Outline of the Law and Practice of the Constitution, Including Central and Local Government and the Constitutional Relations of the British Commonwealth and Empire.* 8th ed. London, 1970

Wheare, K. C., *The Statute of Westminster and Dominion Status.* 5th ed. Oxford, 1953.—*Constitutional Structure of the Commonwealth.* Oxford, 1960

WORLD COUNCIL OF CHURCHES

The World Council of Churches was formally constituted on 23 Aug. 1948, at Amsterdam, by an assembly representing 147 churches from 44 countries. By 1984 the member churches numbered over 300, from more than 100 countries.

The basis of membership (1975) states: 'The World Council of Churches is a fellowship of Churches which confess the Lord Jesus Christ as God and Saviour according to the Scriptures and therefore seek to fulfil together their common calling to the glory of the one God, Father, Son and Holy Spirit.' Membership is open to Churches which express their agreement with this basis and satisfy such criteria as the Assembly or Central Committee may prescribe. Today 303 Churches of Protestant, Anglican, Orthodox, Old Catholic and Pentecostal confessions belong to this fellowship.

The World Council was founded by the coming together of several diverse Christian movements. These included the overseas mission groups gathered from 1921 in the International Missionary Council, the Faith and Order Movement founded by American Episcopal Bishop Charles Brent, and the Life and Work Movement led by Swedish Lutheran Archbishop Nathan Söderblom.

On 13 May 1938 at Utrecht a provisional committee was appointed to prepare for the formation of a World Council of Churches. It was under the chairmanship of William Temple, then Archbishop of York.

Assembly. The governing body of the World Council, consisting of delegates specially appointed by the member Churches. It meets every 6 or 7 years to frame policy and to consider some main theme. The Assembly has no legislative powers and depends for the implementation of its decisions upon the action of the member Churches. Assemblies have been held in Amsterdam (1948), Evanston (1954), New Delhi (1961), Uppsala (1968), and Nairobi (1975) and most recently in Vancouver, Canada in 1983 under the theme 'Jesus Christ – the Life of the World'. In between assemblies, a 150-member Central Committee meets annually to carry out the assembly mandate, with a smaller 22-member Executive Committee meeting twice a year.

Presidents. Hon. President: The Rev. Dr W. A. Visser't Hooft. *Presidium:* Dr Marga Bührig (Switzerland), Most Rev. W. P. K. Makhulu (Botswana), Dame R. Nita Barrow (Barbados), Bishop Johannes Hempel (German Democratic Republic), Dr Lois Wilson (Canada), Metropolitan Paulos Mar Gregorios (India), Patriarch Ignatios IV (Syria).

WCC programmes are organized from headquarters in Geneva, Switzerland, by a staff of 300 and a range of supervisory committees drawn from member churches. The 3 programme units are:

(i) Faith and Witness includes the Commission on Faith and Order, World Mission and Evangelism, Church and Society and the sub-unit on Dialogue with People of Living Faiths.

(ii) Justice and Service which includes Inter-Church Aid, Refugee and World Service (channelling over $35m. from member churches to areas of need); the Commission on the Churches' Participation in Development; the Commission of the Churches on International Affairs, the Programme to Combat Racism and the Christian Medical Commission.

(iii) Education and Renewal includes sections dealing with renewal and congregational life, women, youth, church related education, biblical studies, family ministry and the Programme on Theological Education.

A General Secretariat with a Communication Department, finance and central services co-ordinates the work of these 3 units.

Since 1975 the WCC has held several major world conferences on such diverse themes as 'Faith, Science and the Future', 'Your Kingdom Come', 'Family Power and Social Change', 'Strategies for Churches Combating Racism in the 1980's', 'The Community of Women and Men in the Church' and 'Giving an Account of the Hope that is in Us'.

Officers of the Central and Executive Committees: *Moderator:* Rev. Dr Heinz J. Held (Federal Republic of Germany). *Vice-moderators:* Dr Sylvia Ross Talbot (USA), Metropolitan Chrysostomos of Myra (Turkey). *General Secretary:* The Rev. Dr Emilio Castro.

Office: PO Box 66, 150 route de Ferney, 1211 Geneva 20, Switzerland.

The British Council of Churches, which is an associated national council of the World Council.

Books of Reference

Official Reports: The First [. . . *etc.*] *Assembly* (London, 1948, 1955, 1962, Geneva, 1968, 1975, 1983)
New Delhi to Uppsala 1961–68. Geneva, 1968
Uppsala to Nairobi 1968–75. Geneva, 1975
Nairobi to Vancouver. Geneva, 1983
Official Reports of the Faith and Order Conferences at Lausanne 1927, Edinburgh 1937, Lund 1952, Montreal 1963, Meeting of Faith and Order Commission, Louvain 1971, Accra 1974, Bangalore 1978
Official Reports of the Life and Work Conferences at Stockholm 1925 and Oxford 1937; World Conference on Church and Society 1966
Minutes of the Central Committee. Geneva, 1949 to date
Howell, L., *Acting in Faith: The World Council of Churches since 1975.* London, 1982
Hudson, D., *The World Council of Churches in International Affairs.* Leighton Buzzard, 1977
Paton, D. M., *Breaking Barriers—Nairobi 1975.* London, 1976
Potter, P., *Life in all its Fullness.* Geneva, 1981
van der Bent, A. J., *What in the World is the World Council of Churches?* Geneva, 1978.—*Handbook of Member Churches of the World Council of Churches*

INTERNATIONAL TRADE UNIONISM

There are three main international trade union confederations *(i)* the International Confederation of Free Trade Unions (ICFTU) which has in membership most of the national trade union confederations in the Western industrialized countries as well as democratic organizations in Asia, Africa, and Latin America; *(ii)* the World Federation of Trade Unions (WFTU) which draws its support mainly from Eastern Europe, but which also has affiliates in France and in several developing countries; and *(iii)* the World Confederation of Labour (WCL) which has affiliates in Western Europe, Latin America and a small number of African and Asian countries. In addition, national trade unions are frequently members of international trade union federations, set up to protect the interests of working people in particular industries or trades, which are associated with the international confederations. The International Trade Secretariats (ITS) are associated with the ICFTU; Trade Union Internationals (TUI) with the WFTU; and the International Trade Federations (ITF) with the WCL.

Coldrick, A. P., and Jones, P., *International Directory of the Trade Union Movement.* London, 1979

History. The international trade union structure in 1983 was shaped mainly by developments since 1945. In that year the WFTU was set up with world-wide membership. Attempts by trade unions in Eastern Europe to turn the WFTU into an organization voicing unquestioning support for the policies of the USSR led most of the affiliates in the Western European countries to break away from the WFTU and to form the ICFTU in 1949.

EUROPEAN TRADE UNION CONFEDERATION. In Feb. 1973 the European Trade Union Confederation was formed by trade unionists in 15 Western European countries to deal with questions of interest to European working people arising inside and outside the EEC. All the founding organizations were ICFTU affiliates but subsequently they accepted into membership European WCL affiliates, the Irish Congress of Trade Unions and the Italian Communist trade union centre (CGIL) and other national organizations. The ETUC Congress meets every 3 years and the Executive Committee 6 times a year. The membership is now about 43m. from 34 centres in 20 countries.

General Secretary: Mathias Hinterscheid.
Headquarters: Rue Montagne aux Herbes Potagères 37, 1000 Brussels.

INTERNATIONAL CONFEDERATION OF FREE TRADE UNIONS. The first congress of ICFTU was held in London in Dec. 1949. The constitution as amended provides for co-operation with the United Nations and the International Labour Organization and for regional organizations to promote free trade unionism, especially in less-developed countries.

Organization. The Congress meets every 4 years. It elects the Executive Board of 37 members nominated on an area basis for a 4-year period; the Board meets at least twice a year. Various committees cover policy *vis-à-vis* such problems as those connected with Atomic Energy and also the administration of the International Solidarity Fund. There are joint ICFTU–ITS committees for co-ordinating activities and also for women workers' problems.

Headquarters: 37–41, rue Montagne aux Herbes Potagères, Brussels 1000, Belgium.

General Secretary: John Vanderveken.

Regional organizations exist in America, offices in Mexico City and Caracas; Asia, offices in New Delhi and Singapore; and Africa.

Membership. The ICFTU has 134 affiliated organizations in 94 countries, which together represent about 85m. workers. The biggest groups were the American Federation of Labor and Congress of Industrial Organizations (13·6m.), the British Trades Union Congress (10·5m.), the Federal German Deutscher Gewerkschaftsbund (8m.), the Confederazione Italiana Sindacati Lavoratori (2·1m.), the Swedish Landsorganisationen (2·1m.), the Canadian Labour Congress (1·3m.), the Österreichischer Gewerkschaftsbund (1·7m.), the Belgian General Federation of Labour (925,000), the Indian National Trade Union Congress (3·6m.), Australian Council of Trade Unions (1·8m.), Japanese Confederation of Labour, Domei (1·4m.).

Publications (in 4 languages). *Free Labour World* (bi-monthly); *International Trade Union News* (fortnightly); *Economic and Social Bulletin* (bi-monthly).

THE WORLD FEDERATION OF TRADE UNIONS. The WFTU formally came into existence on 3 Oct. 1945, representing trade-union organizations in more than 50 countries of the world, both Communist and non-Communist, excluding Federal Republic of Germany and Japan, as well as a number of lesser and colonial territories. Representation from the USA was limited to the Congress of Industrial Organizations, as the American Federation of Labor declined to participate.

In Jan. 1949 the British, USA and Netherlands trade unions withdrew from WFTU, which had come under complete Communist control; and by June 1951 all non-Communist trade-unions, and the Yugoslavian Federation, had left WFTU.

Organization. The Congress meets every 4 years. In between, the General Council, of 134 members (including deputies), is the governing body, meeting (in theory) at least once a year. The Bureau controls the activities of WFTU between meetings of the General Council; it consists of the President, the General Secretary and members from different continents, the total number being decided at each Congress. The Bureau is elected by the General Council.

General Secretary: I. Zakaria (Sudan).

Membership. A total membership of 206m. from 90 national centres is claimed. The biggest groups are the Soviet All-Union Central Council of Trade Unions (107m.), the German Democratic Republic Free German Trade Union Federation (8m.), the Czechoslovak Central Council of Trade Unions (6m.), the Romanian General Confederation of Labour (6·4m.), the Hungarian Central Council of Trade Unions (4·5m.) and the French Confederation of Labour (CGT, 2m.).

Publications. World Trade Union Movement (monthly, in 9 languages); *Trade Union Press* (fortnightly, in 6 languages).

WORLD CONFEDERATION OF LABOUR. The first congress of the International Federation of Christian Trade Unions (IFCTU), as the WCL was then called, met in 1920; but a large proportion of its 3·4m. members were in Italy and Germany, where affiliated unions were suppressed by the Fascist and Nazi régimes, and in 1940 IFCTU went out of existence. It was reconstituted in 1945, and declined to merge with WFTU and, later, with ICFTU. The policy of IFCTU was based on the papal encyclicals *Rerum novarum* (1891) and *Quadragesimo anno* (1931), but in 1968, when the Federation became the WCL, it was broadened to include other concepts. The WCL now has Protestant, Buddhist and Moslem members as well as its mainly Roman Catholic members.

Organization. The WCL is organized on a federative basis which leaves wide discretion to its autonomous constituent unions. Its governing body is the Congress, which meets every 4 years. The Congress appoints (or re-appoints) the Secretary-General at each 4-yearly meeting. The General Council which meets at least once a year, is composed of the members of the Confederal Board (at least 22 members, elected by the Congress) and representatives of national confederations, international trade federations, and trade union organizations where there is no confederation affiliated to the WCL. The Confederal Board is responsible for the general leadership of the WCL, in accordance with the decisions and directives of the Council and Congress. Headquarters: 71 rue Joseph II, Brussels 1040, Belgium.

Secretary-General: Jan Kulakowski.

There are regional organizations in Latin America (office in Caracas), Africa (office in Banjul, Gambia) and Asia (office in Manila) There is also a liaison centre in Montreal.

Membership. A total membership of 14m. in about 90 countries is claimed. The biggest group is the Confederation of Christian Trade Unions of Belgium (1·1m.).

Publication. Labour Press and Information (11 each year, in 5 languages).

ORGANISATION FOR ECONOMIC CO-OPERATION AND DEVELOPMENT (OECD)

History and Membership. On 30 Sept. 1961 the Organisation for European Economic Co-operation (OEEC), after a history of 14 years (*see* THE STATESMAN'S YEAR-BOOK, 1961, p. 32), was replaced by the Organisation for Economic Co-operation and Development. The change of title marks the Organisation's altered status and functions: with the accession of Canada and USA as full members it ceased to be a purely European body; while at the same time it added development aid to the list of its other activities. The member countries are now Australia, Austria, Belgium, Canada, Denmark, Federal Republic of Germany, Finland, France, Greece, Iceland, Ireland, Italy, Japan, Luxembourg, the Netherlands, New Zealand, Norway, Portugal, Spain, Sweden, Switzerland, Turkey, UK and USA. Yugoslavia participates in the Organisation's activities with a special status. The Commission of the European Communities generally takes part in OECD's work.

Objectives. To promote economic and social welfare throughout the OECD area by assisting its member governments in the formulation of policies designed to this end and by co-ordinating these policies; and to stimulate and harmonize its members' efforts in favour of developing countries.

Organs. The supreme body of the Organisation is the Council composed of one representative for each member country. It meets either at Heads of Delegations level (about once a week) under the Chairmanship of the Secretary-General, or at Ministerial level (usually once a year) under the Chairmanship of a Minister elected annually. Decisions and Recommendations are adopted by mutual agreement of all members of the Council.

The Council is assisted by an Executive Committee composed of 14 members of the Council designated annually by the latter. The major part of the Organisation's work is, however, prepared and carried out in numerous specialized committees and working parties and sub-groups, of which there exist over 200. Thus, the Organisation comprises Committees for Economic Policy; Economic and Development Review; Development Assistance (DAC); Trade; Capital Movements and Invisible Transactions; Financial Markets; Fiscal Affairs; Restrictive Business Practices; Maritime Transport; International Investment and Multinational Enterprises; Tourism; Energy Policy; Industry; Steel; Scientific and Technological Policy; Information, Computer and Communications Policy; Education; Manpower and Social Affairs; Environment; Agriculture; Fisheries, etc. Moreover there exists a High-Level Group on Commodities and a Group on North-South Economic Issues.

Four autonomous or semi-autonomous bodies also belong to the Organisation: the International Energy Agency (IEA); the Nuclear Energy Agency (NEA); the Development Centre and the Centre for Educational Research and Innovation (CERI). Each one of these bodies has its own governing committee.

The Council, the committees and the other bodies are serviced by an international Secretariat headed by the Secretary-General of the Organisation.

All member countries have established permanent Delegations to OECD, each headed by an Ambassador.

Chairman of the Council (ministerial). Elected annually.
Chairman of the Council (official level): The Secretary-General.
Chairman of the Executive Committee: Hans Tabor (Denmark).
Secretary-General: Jean-Claude Paye (France).
Deputy Secretaries-General: Jacob M. Myerson (USA), Paul Lemerle (France).
Executive Director of the International Energy Agency: Ulf Lantzke (Federal Republic of Germany).
Headquarters: 2, rue André Pascal, 75775 Paris Cedex 16, France.

OECD publishes numerous reports and statistical papers. Regular features include:
Activities of OECD. Annual, from 1972
News from OECD. Monthly
Main Economic Indicators. Monthly, from 1965
The OECD Observer. Bi-monthly, from 1962
The OECD Economic Outlook. 1966 ff.
OEEC/OECD Economic Surveys of Member Countries. 1954 ff.
European Nuclear Energy Agency, Activity Report. 1959 ff.
The Flow of Financial Resources to Countries in Course of Economic Development. 1960 ff.
Development Assistance Efforts and Policies. 1962 ff.
Tourism Policy and International Tourism in OECD Member Countries. 1955 ff.
Energy Policies and Programmes of the IEA Member Countries. 1977 ff.

NORTH ATLANTIC TREATY ORGANIZATION (NATO)

Western perceptions of the political situation in Europe following World War II gave rise, in 1947, to 2 major US initiatives – the Truman Doctrine and the Marshall Plan. These policies were designed to increase the ability of Western

European countries to resist outside pressure and to assist them in bringing about their economic recovery. By 1948, on the initiative of the Foreign Secretary of the UK Ernest Bevin, 5 Western European nations had also entered into a treaty of mutual assistance in which they pledged themselves to come to each other's aid in the event of armed aggression against them (Brussels Treaty, 17 March 1948). The idea of a single mutual defence system involving North America as well as the European signatories of the Brussels Treaty was put forward by the Canadian Secretary of State for External Affairs in April 1948. It led, *via* the Vandenberg Resolution which enabled the US constitutionally to participate, to the creation of the Atlantic Alliance.

On 4 April 1949 the foreign ministers of Belgium, Canada, Denmark, France, Iceland, Italy, Luxembourg, the Netherlands, Norway, Portugal, the UK and the USA met in Washington and signed a treaty, the main clauses of which read as follows:

Article 1. The parties undertake, as set forth in the Charter of the United Nations, to settle any international disputes in which they may be involved by peaceful means in such a manner that international peace and security and justice are not endangered, and to refrain in their international relations from the threat or use of force in any manner inconsistent with the purposes of the United Nations.

Article 2. The parties will contribute toward the further development of peaceful and friendly international relations by strengthening their free institutions, by bringing about a better understanding of the principles upon which these institutions are founded, and by promoting conditions of stability and well-being. They will seek to eliminate conflict in their international economic policies and will encourage economic collaboration between any or all of them.

Article 3. In order more effectively to achieve the objectives of this treaty, the parties, separately and jointly by means of continuous and effective self-help and mutual aid, will maintain and develop their individual and collective capacity to resist armed attack.

Article 4. The parties will consult together whenever, in the opinion of any of them, the territorial integrity, political independence or security of any of the parties is threatened.

Article 5. The parties agree that an armed attack against one or more of them in Europe or North America shall be considered an attack against them all and consequently they agree that, if such an armed attack occurs, each of them, in exercise of the right of individual or collective self-defence recognized by article 51 of the Charter of the United Nations, will assist the party or parties so attacked by taking forthwith, individually and in concert with the other parties, such action as it deems necessary, including the use of armed force, to restore and maintain the security of the North Atlantic area. Any such armed attack and all measures taken as a result thereof shall immediately be reported to the Security Council. Such measures shall be terminated when the Security Council has taken the measures necessary to restore and maintain international peace and security.

Article 6. For the purpose of Article 5 an armed attack on one or more of the parties is deemed to include an armed attack *(i)* on the territory of any of the parties in Europe or North America, on the Algerian Departments of France, on the territory of Turkey or on the islands under the jurisdiction of any of the parties in the North Atlantic area north of the Tropic of Cancer; *(ii)* on the forces, vessels or aircraft of any of the parties, when in or over these territories or any other area in Europe in which occupation forces of any of the parties were stationed on the date when the treaty entered into force or the Mediterranean Sea or the North Atlantic area north of the Tropic of Cancer.

Article 8. Each party declares that none of the international engagements now in force between it and any other of the parties or any third state is in conflict with the provisions of this treaty, and undertakes not to enter into any international engagement in conflict with this treaty.

Article 10. The parties may, by unanimous agreement, invite any other European state in a position to further the principles of this treaty and to contribute to the security of the North Atlantic area to accede to this treaty. Any state so invited may become a party to the treaty by depositing its instrument of accession with the government of the United States of America. The government of the United States of America will inform each of the parties of the deposit of each such instrument of accession.

Article 12. After the treaty has been in force for 10 years, or at any time thereafter, the parties shall, if any of them so requests, consult together for the purpose of reviewing the treaty, having regard for the factors then affecting peace and security in the North Atlantic area, including the development of universal as well as regional arrangements under the Charter of the United Nations for the maintenance of international peace and security.

Article 13. After the treaty has been in force for 20 years, any party may cease to be a party one year after its notice of denunciation has been given to the government of the United States of America, which will inform the governments of the other parties of the deposit of each notice of denunciation.

The treaty came into force on 24 Aug. 1949. Greece and Turkey were admitted as parties to the treaty in 1952, the Federal Republic of Germany in 1955 and Spain in 1982.

NATO is an organization of sovereign states equal in status. Decisions taken are expressions of the collective will of member governments arrived at by common consent.

The North Atlantic Council is composed of representatives of the 16 member countries. At Ministerial Meetings of the Council, member nations are represented by Ministers of Foreign Affairs. These meetings are held twice a year. The Council also meets on occasion at the level of Heads of State and Government. In permanent session, at the level of Ambassadors, the Council meets at least once a week.

The Defence Planning Committee is composed of representatives of the member countries taking part in NATO's integrated military structure. Like the Council, it meets both in permanent session at the level of Ambassadors and twice a year at Ministerial level. At Ministerial Meetings member nations are represented by Defence Ministers.

The Council and Defence Planning Committee are chaired by the Secretary General of NATO at whatever level they meet. Opening sessions of Ministerial Meetings of the Council are presided over by the President, an honorary position held annually by the Foreign Minister of one of the member nations.

Nuclear matters are discussed by the Nuclear Planning Group in which 13 countries now participate. It meets regularly at the level of Permanent Representatives (Ambassadors) and twice a year at the level of Ministers of Defence.

The Permanent Representatives of member countries are supported by the National Delegations located at NATO Headquarters. The Delegations are composed of advisors and officials qualified to represent their countries on the various committees created by the Council. The Committees are supported by the International Staff responsible to the Secretary General.

Headquarters: 1110 Brussels, Belgium.
Secretary-General: Lord Carrington (UK).
Flag: Dark blue with a white compass rose of 4 points in the centre.

The *Military Committee* is responsible for making recommendations to the Council and the Defence Planning Committee on military matters and for supplying guidance to the Allied Commanders. Composed of the Chiefs-of-Staff of all member countries except France and Iceland (which has no military forces), the Committee is assisted by an International Military Staff. It meets at Chiefs-of-Staff level at least twice a year but remains in permanent session at the level of national military representatives. Liaison between the Military Committee and the French High Command is effected through the French Mission to the Military Committee. The permanent chairman of the Military Committee is elected by the Chiefs-of-Staff for a period of 2–3 years. The present chairman is Gen. Cornelis De Jager (Netherlands), appointed July 1983.

The area covered by the North Atlantic Treaty is divided among three commands: The Atlantic Ocean Command, the European Command and the Channel Command. Defence plans for the North American area are developed by the Canada–US Regional Planning Group.

The NATO commanders are responsible for the development of defence plans for their respective areas, for the determination of force requirements and for the deployment and exercise of the forces under their command.

The *Allied Command Europe* (ACE) covers the area extending from the North Cape to the Mediterranean and from the Atlantic to the eastern border of Turkey, excluding the UK and Portugal, the defence of which does not fall under any one major NATO Command. The European area, which is subdivided into a number of subordinate commands, is under the Supreme Allied Commander Europe

(SACEUR) whose Headquarters, near Mons in Belgium, are known as SHAPE (Supreme Headquarters Allied Powers Europe).

SACEUR has also under his orders the ACE Mobile Force, composed of both land and air force units from different member countries, which can be ready for action at very short notice in any threatened area. The present SACEUR is Gen. Bernard W. Rogers (USA).

Under the Supreme Allied Commander Atlantic (SACLANT) the *Atlantic Command* extends from the North Pole to the Tropic of Cancer and from the coastal waters of North America to those of Europe and Africa, but excludes the Channel and the British Isles. SACLANT, who would have the primary task in wartime of ensuring the security of the sea lanes in the whole Atlantic area, is an operational rather than an administrative commander. Under his direct command is the Standing Naval Force Atlantic (STANAVFORLANT) which is a permanent international squadron of ships drawn from NATO Navies which normally operate in the Atlantic.

The present SACLANT, whose Headquarters are in Norfolk (USA), is Admiral Wesley L. McDonald (US), appointed Sept. 1982.

The *Channel Command* covers the English Channel and the southern North Sea. Under the Allied Commander-in-Chief Channel (CINCHAN) its mission is to control and protect merchant shipping in the area, co-operating with SACEUR in the air defence of the Channel. The forces earmarked to the Command in emergency are predominantly naval but include maritime air forces. CINCHAN has also under his command the NATO Standing Naval Force Channel (STANAVFORCHAN) which is a permanent force comprizing mine countermeasure ships of different NATO countries. The present CINCHAN, with Headquarters at Northwood (UK), is Admiral Sir William Staveley (UK), appointed Oct. 1982.

The *Canada–US Regional Planning Group*, which covers the North American area, develops and recommends to the Military Committee plans for the defence of this area. It meets alternately in Washington and Ottawa.

Books of Reference

The NATO Handbook.—NATO: Facts and Figures.—The NATO Review (bi-monthly).—*NATO Pocket Guide.—NATO Folder.—NATO and the Warsaw Pact.—Economic and Scientific Publications.*

Henderson, N., *The Birth of NATO.* London, 1982
Hill-Norton, P., *No Soft Options: The Politico-Military Realities of NATO.* London, 1980
Kaplan, L. S., and Clawson, R. W., *NATO After Thirty Years.* Wilmington, 1981
Myers, K. A. (ed.), *NATO: The Next Twenty Years.* Boulder, 1980
Vigeveno, G., *The Bomb and European Security.* London, 1983
Yost, D. S., *NATO's Strategic Options: Arms Control and Defense.* Oxford and New York, 1981

WESTERN EUROPEAN UNION

On 17 March 1948 a 50-year treaty 'for collaboration in economic, social and cultural matters and for collective self-defence' was signed in Brussels by the Foreign Ministers of the UK, France, the Netherlands, Belgium and Luxembourg. (*See* THE STATESMAN'S YEAR-BOOK, 1954, pp. 32 f.)

On 20 Dec. 1950 the functions of the Western Union defence organization were transferred to the North Atlantic Treaty command, but it was decided that the reorganization of the military machinery should not affect the right of the Western Union Defence Ministers and the Chiefs of Staff to meet as they please to consider matters of mutual concern to the Brussels Treaty powers.

After the breakdown of the European Defence Community on 30 Aug. 1954 a conference was held in London from 28 Sept. to 3 Oct. 1954, attended by Belgium, Canada, France, the Federal Republic of Germany, Italy, Luxembourg, the Netherlands, the UK and the USA, at which it was decided to invite the Federal

Republic of Germany and Italy to accede to the Brussels Treaty, to end the occupation of Western Germany and to invite the latter to accede to the North Atlantic Treaty; the Federal Republic agreed that it would voluntarily limit its arms production, and provision was made for the setting up of an agency to control the armaments of the 7 Brussels Treaty powers; the UK undertook not to withdraw from the Continent her 4 divisions and the Tactical Air Force assigned to the Supreme Allied Commander against the wishes of a majority, *i.e.*, 4 of the Brussels Treaty powers, except in the event of an acute overseas emergency.

At a Conference of Ministers held in Paris from 20 to 23 Oct. 1954 these decisions were embodied in 4 Protocols modifying the Brussels Treaty which were signed in Paris on 23 Oct. 1954 and came into force on 6 May 1955.

The *Council of WEU* consists of the Foreign Ministers of the 7 powers or their representatives; it is so organized as to be able to exercise its functions continuously. An *Assembly,* composed of representatives of the Brussels Treaty powers to the Consultative Assembly of the Council of Europe, meets twice a year, usually in Paris. An *Agency for the Control of Armaments* and a *Standing Armaments Committee* have been set up in Paris. The social and cultural activities were transferred to the Council of Europe on 1 June 1960.

At a meeting of the Foreign, and Defence, Ministers of Western European Union held in Rome on 26–27 Oct. 1984, the Council adopted the 'Rome Declaration' and a document on the institutional reform of Western European Union. Member Governments support the reactivation of the Organization as a means of strengthening the European contribution to the North Atlantic Alliance and improving defence co-operation among the countries of Western Europe.

Headquarters: 9 Grosvenor Place, London, SW1X 7HL.
Secretary-General: Edouard F. T. Longerstaey.

COUNCIL OF EUROPE

In 1948 the 'Congress of Europe', bringing together at The Hague nearly 1,000 influential Europeans from 26 countries, called for the creation of a united Europe, including a European Assembly. This proposal, examined first by the Ministerial Council of the Brussels Treaty Organization, then by a conference of ambassadors, was at the origin of the Council of Europe, which is, with its 21 member States, the widest organization bringing together all European democracies. The Statute of the Council was signed at London on 5 May 1949 and came into force 2 months later. The founder members were Belgium, Denmark, France, Ireland, Italy, Luxembourg, the Netherlands, Norway, Sweden and the UK. Turkey and Greece joined in 1949, Iceland in 1950, the Federal Republic of Germany in 1951 (having been an associate since 1950), Austria in 1956, Cyprus in 1961, Switzerland in 1963, Malta in 1965, Portugal in 1976, Spain in 1977 and Liechtenstein in 1978.

Membership is limited to European States which 'accept the principles of the rule of law and of the enjoyment by all persons within [their] jurisdiction of human rights and fundamental freedoms'. The Statute provides for both withdrawal (Art. 7) and suspension (Arts. 8 and 9). Greece withdrew from the Council in Dec. 1969 and rejoined in Nov. 1974.

Structure. Under the Statute two organs were set up: an inter-governmental *Committee of* [*Foreign*] *Ministers* with powers of decision and of recommendation to governments, and an inter-parliamentary deliberative body, the *Parliamentary Assembly* (referred to in the Statute as the *Consultative Assembly*)—both of which are served by the Secretariat. In addition, a large number of committees of experts have been established, two of them, the Council for Cultural Co-operation and the Committee on Legal Co-operation, having a measure of autonomy; on municipal matters the Committee of Ministers receives recommendations from the Conference of Local and Regional Authorities of Europe.

The Committee of Ministers meets usually twice a year, their deputies 12 times a year.

The Parliamentary Assembly normally consists of 170 parliamentarians elected or appointed by their national parliaments (Austria 6, Belgium 7, Cyprus 3, Denmark 5, France 18, Federal Republic of Germany 18, Greece 7, Iceland 3, Ireland 4, Italy 18, Liechtenstein 2, Luxembourg 3, Malta 3, Netherlands 7, Norway 5, Portugal 7, Spain 12, Sweden 6, Switzerland 6, Turkey 12, UK 18); it meets 3 times a year for approximately a week. The work of the Assembly is prepared by parliamentary committees.

The *Joint Committee* acts as an organ of co-ordination and liaison between representatives of the Committee of Ministers and members of the Parliamentary Assembly and gives members an opportunity to exchange views on matters of important European interest.

The European Convention on Human Rights, signed in 1950, set up special machinery to guarantee internationally fundamental rights and freedoms. A *European Commission* investigates alleged violations of the Convention submitted to it either by States or, in most cases, by individuals. Its findings can then be examined by the *European Court of Human Rights* (set up in 1959), whose obligatory jurisdiction has been recognized by 19 States, or by the Committee of Ministers, empowered to take binding decisions by two-thirds majority vote.

In 1956 the Resettlement Fund for National Refugees and Over-Population was created, the Governor of the Fund is responsible to the governments collectively. With 19 member countries, the main purpose of the Fund is to give financial aid, particularly in the spheres of housing, vocational training, regional planning and regional development. Since its foundation, the total amount of loans thus granted comes to over US$2,244m. at 31 Dec. 1983.

In 1970 the Council set up a European Youth Centre at Strasbourg, where young people can discuss their own approach to international co-operation. More recently, a European Youth Foundation was created, and which provides money to subsidize activities by European Youth Organizations in their own countries.

Aims and Achievements. Art. 1 of the Statute states that the Council's aim is 'to achieve a greater unity between its members for the purpose of safeguarding and realising the ideals and principles which are their common heritage and facilitating their economic and social progress'; 'this aim shall be pursued . . . by discussion of questions of common concern and by agreements and common action'. The only limitation is provided by Art. 1 *(d)*, which excludes 'matters relating to national defence'.

Although without legislative powers, the Assembly acts as the power-house of the Council, initiating European action in key areas by making recommendations to the Committee of Ministers. As the widest parliamentary forum in Western Europe, the Assembly also acts as the conscience of the area by voicing its opinions on important current issues. These are embodied in resolutions. The Ministers' rôle is to translate the Assembly's recommendations into action, particularly as regards lowering the barriers between the European countries, harmonizing their legislation or introducing where possible common European laws, abolishing discrimination on grounds of nationality and undertaking certain tasks on a joint European basis.

In May 1976 the first plan of intergovernmental co-operation to be undertaken by the Council of Europe was adopted by the Committee of Ministers. The second one, adopted in Dec. 1980, will run until Dec. 1986, subject to a mid-term revision in 1983. The plan takes account of political developments and progress achieved, and covers 8 key areas: human rights, social and socio-economic questions, education and culture, youth, public health, environment and regional planning, local and regional government, and legal co-operation.

Some 120 Conventions and Agreements have been concluded covering such matters as social security, cultural affairs, conservation of European wild life and natural habitats, protection of achaeological heritage, extradition, medical treatment, equivalence of degrees and diplomas, the protection of television broadcasts, adoption of children and transportation of animals. Treaties in the legal field, were the adoption of the European Convention on the Suppression of Terrorism, the European Convention on the Legal Status of Migrant Workers and the Transfer of Sentenced Persons. In 1980 the Committee of Ministers adopted a European Convention for the protection of individuals with regard to the automatic processing of personal data. A Social Charter which came into force in 1965 sets out the social and economic rights which all member governments agree to guarantee to their citizens.

The official languages are English and French.

Chairman of the Committee of Ministers: (held in rotation).

President of the Parliamentary Assembly: Karl Ahrens (Federal Republic of Germany).

President of the European Court of Human Rights: Gérard J. Wiarda (Netherlands).

President of the European Commission of Human Rights: Carl Aage Nørgaard (Denmark).

Secretary-General: Marcelino Oreja Aguirre (Spain).

Headquarters: Palais de l'Europe, 67006, Strasbourg, Cedex, France.

Flag: Dark blue with a ring of 12 gold stars in the centre.

The Directorate of Press and Information, BP 431, R6-67006 Strasbourg-Cedex.
European Yearbook. The Hague, from 1955
Forum. Strasbourg, from 1978, 4 times a year
Yearbook on the Convention on Human Rights. Strasbourg, from 1958
Cook, C., and Paxton, J., *European Political Facts, 1918–84.* London, 1985

EUROPEAN COMMUNITIES

In May 1950 Belgium, France, the Federal Republic of Germany, Italy, Luxembourg and the Netherlands started negotiations with the aim of ensuring continual peace by a merging of their essential interests. The negotiations culminated in the signing in 1951 of the Treaty of Paris creating the European Coal and Steel Community (ECSC). After it was found impossible to create European Communities covering Defence and Foreign Affairs, two more communities with the aims of gradually integrating the economies of the 6 nations and of moving towards closer political unity, the European Economic Community (EEC) and the European Atomic Energy Community (EAEC or Euratom) were created in 1957 by the signing of the Treaties of Rome.

On 30 June 1970 membership negotiations began between the Six and the UK, Denmark, Ireland and Norway. On 22 Jan. 1972 those 4 countries signed a Treaty of Accession, although this was rejected by Norway in a referendum in Nov. 1972. On 1 Jan. 1973 the UK, Denmark and Ireland became full members. On 28 May 1979 the Greek Treaty of Accession was signed, and Greece joined the Community on 1 Jan. 1981. Negotiations for the accession of Spain and Portugal to the Communities culminated in 1984 in the signature of a treaty under which they will join on 1 Jan. 1986, although existing Community legislation will only apply after a transitionary period.

The institutional arrangements of the Communities provide an independent executive with powers of proposal (the Commission), various consultative bodies, and a decision-making body drawn from the Governments (the Council). Until 1967 the 3 Communities were completely distinct, although they shared some non-decision-making bodies: from that date the executives were merged in the European Commission, and the decision-taking bodies in the Council. The institutions and organs of the Communities are as follows:

The *Commission* consists of 14 members appointed by the member states to serve for 4 years; the President and Vice Presidents are appointed initially for 2 years, but are generally re-appointed for the rest of their term. The Commission acts independently of any country in the interests of the Community as a whole, with as its mandate the implementation and guardianship of the Treaties. In this it has the right of initiative (putting proposals to the Council for action); and execution (once the Council has decided); and can take the other institutions or individual countries before the Court of Justice (see below) should any of these renege upon its responsibilities.

President: Jacques Delors.
Address: 200 rue de la Loi, 1049, Brussels, Belgium.

The *Council of Ministers* consists of foreign ministers from the 10 national governments and represents the national as opposed to the Community interests. It is the body which takes decisions under the Treaties. Although legally most of its decisions should be made by majority, it has since 1966 sought unanimity wherever possible, using majority votes only rarely. Specialist Councils (*e.g.* the Agriculture Council) meet to discuss matters related to individual policies. Since 1974 the Heads of State and Government have met 3 times a year as the *European Council* to discuss Community, and also Foreign Policy, affairs. The Foreign Ministers also meet in Political Co-operation to discuss Foreign Policy matters. The Presidency of the Council is held for a 6-month term in the following order: Belgium, Denmark, Federal Republic of Germany, Greece, France, Ireland, Italy, Luxembourg, Netherlands, UK.

Address: 170 rue de la Loi, 1048, Brussels.

The *European Parliament* consists of 434 members, elected on 14 and 17 June 1984. France, the Federal Republic of Germany, Italy and the UK returned 81 members each, the Netherlands 25, Belgium and Greece 24, Denmark 16, Ireland 15 and Luxembourg 6. Party representation in the new Parliament was as follows: Socialists, 130; European People's Party (Christian Democratic Group), 110; European Democrats (formerly European Conservatives), 50; Communists and Allies, 41; Liberals, 31; European Democratic Alliance, 29; the "Rainbow" Group (a group of mixed tendencies) 20; the European Right, 16; Independents, 7. The Parliament has a right to be consulted on a wide range of legislative proposals, and forms one arm of the Communities' Budgetary Authority.

President: Pierre Pfimlin.
Address: Centre européen du Kirchberg, Luxembourg.

The *Economic and Social Committee* has an advisory role and consists of 156 representatives, employers, trade unions, consumers, etc. The *Consultative Committee*, of 84 members, performs a similar role for the ECSC.

President: Gert Muhr.
Address: 2, rue Ravenstein, 1000 Brussels.

The *European Court of Justice* is composed of 11 judges and 5 advocates-general, is responsible for the adjudication of disputes arising out of the application of the treaties, and its findings are enforceable in all member countries.

President: Lord Mackenzie Stuart.
Address: Palais de la Cour de Justice, Kirchberg, Luxembourg.

The *Court of Auditors* was established by a Treaty signed on 22 July 1975 which took effect on 1 June 1977. It consists of 10 members, and replaced the former *Audit Board*. It audits all income and current and past expenditure of the European Communities.

President: Marcel Mart.
Address: 29 Rue Aldringen, Luxembourg.

Annual Report of the Court of Auditors, from 1977

The *European Investment Bank* (EIB) was created by the EEC Treaty to which its statute is annexed. Its governing body is the Board of Governors consisting of ministers designated by member states. Its main task is to contribute to the balanced development of the common market in the interest of the Community by financing projects: developing less-developed regions; for modernizing or converting undertakings; or developing new activities, or those of common interest to several member states.

Address: 100, Boulevard Konrad Adenauer, Plateau du Kirchberg, Luxembourg.

Annual Report of the European Investment Bank

Community Law. Provisions of the Treaties and secondary legislation may be either directly applicable in Member States or only applicable after Member States have enacted their own implementing legislation. Secondary legislation consists of: regulations, which are of general application and binding in their entirety and directly applicable in all member states; directives which are binding upon each Member State as to the result to be achieved within a given time, but leave the national authority the choice of form and method of achieving this result; decisions, which are binding in their entirety on their addressees. In addition the Council and Commission can issue recommendations and opinions, which have no binding force.

The Community's Legislative Process starts with a proposal from the Commission (either at the suggestion of its services or in pursuit of its declared political aims) to the Council. The Council generally seeks the views of the European Parliament on the proposal, and the Parliament adopts a formal Opinion, after consideration of the matter by its specialist Committees. The Council may also (and in some cases is obliged to) consult the Economic and Social Committee, which similarly delivers an opinion. When these opinions have been received, the Council will decide. Most decisions are taken on a majority basis, but will take account of reserves expressed by individual member states. The text eventually approved may differ substantially from the original Commission proposal.

Community Finances. The general budget of the European Communities for 1984 was (in ECUm.):

Receipts		*Expenditure*	
Agricultural levies	2,950	Agriculture	17,288
Import duties	7,624	Social	1,628
VAT	14,566	Regional	1,455
Miscellaneous	221	Industry, energy, research	1,234
	25,361	Development aid	896
		Administration and miscellaneous	2,860
			25,361

The resources of the Community (the levies and duties mentioned above, and up to a 1% VAT charge) have been surrendered to it by Treaty. In the 1984 and 1985 budgets, the Community's own resources were not adequate to meet the budget, and the governments agreed to make extra payments to cover the deficit. Legislation was under way to increase the 1% VAT limit to 1·4%. The Budget is made by the Council and the Parliament acting jointly as the Budgetary Authority. The Parliament has control, within a certain margin, of non-obligatory expenditure (*i.e.*, expenditure where the amount to be spent is not set out in the legislation concerned), and can also reject the Budget totally (this has only been done once, for the 1980 Budget). Otherwise, the Council decides. ECSC operations are separately funded by a turnover levy (1984: 0·31%) on the coal and steel industries of the Community. The ECSC operating budget for 1983 was ECU332m.

THE EUROPEAN COAL AND STEEL COMMUNITY. The ECSC was the first of the 3 Communities, coming into existence on 10 Aug. 1952 following the signature of the Treaty of Paris on 18 April 1951. Its aim was to contribute towards economic expansion, growth of employment and a rising standard of living in Member States, through common action in the coal and steel sector, in a Community open to other nations. Since 1957 it has had the same membership as the other Communities.

The Common Market for Coal and Steel. This first aim of the ECSC was achieved for coal, iron ore and scrap in Feb. 1953, for steel in May 1953 and for special steels in Aug. 1954. The Common External Tariff on ECSC products is between 4-8%. Rules for fair competition within the Common Market, based on non-discrimination by nationality and the free movement of goods, have been established. The ECSC also gives readaptation and retraining grants to former workers in these industries, and makes capital grants for new industrial investment in former coal and steel areas.

The Commission has to approve take-overs and mergers of coal or steel undertakings, and has the power in the case of crisis (and with the approval of the Council) to set production quotas and minimum prices by product, with fines for non-observance. This power was first used in 1980.

THE EUROPEAN ECONOMIC COMMUNITY (EEC) or COMMON MARKET

Based on the Treaty of Rome of 25 March 1957 the EEC came into being on 1 Jan. 1958 with the same original members as the ECSC. The Treaty guarantees certain rights to the citizens of all Member States (*e.g.*, the outlawing of economic discrimination by nationality, and equal pay for equal work as between men and women) and sets out certain other areas where secondary legislation is to fill in the details. The most important policy areas are as follows:

Freedom of movement for persons, goods and capital. Under the Treaty individuals or companies from one Member State may establish themselves in another country (for the purposes of economic activity) or sell goods or services there on the same basis as nationals of that country. With a few exceptions, restrictions on the movement of capital have also been ended.

Customs Union and External Trade Relations. Goods or Services originating in one Member State have free circulation within the EEC, which implies common arrangements for trade with the rest of the world. Member States can no longer make bilateral trade agreements with third countries: this power has been ceded to the Community. The Customs Union was achieved in July 1968, with the abolition of internal customs tariffs (or equivalents) and quantitative restrictions, and the establishment of the Common External Tariff. Denmark, Ireland and the UK adopted these from July 1977; Greece is due to do so by Jan. 1986.

Following the 1973 accessions the Community made a series of agreements with the member states of EFTA to form an industrial free trade zone and to start the liberalization of agricultural trade. Association agreements which could lead to accession or customs union have been made with Cyprus, Malta and Turkey; and commercial, industrial, technical and financial aid agreements with Algeria, Egypt, Israel, Jordan, Lebanon, Morocco, Syria and Tunisia. In 1976 Canada signed a framework agreement for co-operation in industrial trade, science and natural resources.

In the *Development Aid* sector, the Community has an agreement (the Lomé Convention, originally signed in 1975 but renewed and enlarged in 1979 and 1984) with some 60 African, Caribbean and Pacific countries which removes customs duties without reciprocal arrangements for most of their imports to the Community, and under which ECU8,000m. of aid was granted between 1980–84. Negotiations for the renewal of the Convention were in progress in 1983. An economic and commercial agreement has also been signed with ASEAN.

The Common Agricultural Policy (CAP). The objectives set out in the Treaty are to increase agricultural productivity, to ensure a fair standard of living for the agricultural community, to stabilise markets, to assure supplies, and to ensure reasonable consumer prices. In Dec. 1960 the Council laid down the fundamental principles on which the CAP is based: a single market, which calls for common prices, stable currency parities and the harmonising of health and veterinary legislation; Community preference, which protects the single Community market from imports; common financing, through the European Agricultural Guidance and Guarantee Fund (EAGGF), which seeks to improve agriculture through its Guidance section, and to stabilise markets against world price fluctuations through market intervention, with levies and refunds on exports. At present common market organizations cover over 95% of EEC agricultural production. Greece is bringing its agricultural prices into line with the Community over a period of up to 7 years.

Following the disappearance of stable currency parities, artificial currency levels have been applied in the CAP. This factor, together with over-production due to high producer prices, means that the CAP consumes about two-thirds of the Communities' budget.

The European Monetary System (EMS), whose immediate objective is to create a zone of monetary stability in Europe by closer monetary co-operation, began operating in March 1979. All Member States (except Greece and the UK, 1984) limit fluctuations in the exchange rates of their currencies against a central rate denominated in ECU. The Greek drachma will join the EMS by 31 Dec. 1986.

Competition. The Competition (anti-trust) law of the Community is based on 2 principles: that businesses should not seek to nullify the creation of the common market by the erection of artificial national (or other) barriers to the free movement of goods; and against the abuse of dominant positions in any market. These two principles have led among other things to the outlawing of prohibitions on exports to other Member States, of price-fixing agreements and of refusal to supply; and to the refusal by the Commission to allow mergers or take-overs by dominant undertakings in specific cases. Increasingly heavy fines are imposed on offenders.

THE EUROPEAN ATOMIC ENERGY COMMUNITY (EURATOM)

Like the EEC, Euratom came into being on 1 Jan. 1958 following a Treaty signed in Rome on 25 March 1957, and it had the same Member States as the EEC. Its task is to promote common efforts between its members in the development of nuclear energy for peaceful purposes, and for this purpose it has monopoly powers of acquisition of fissile materials for civil purposes. It is in no way concerned with military uses of nuclear power; indeed, its members are forbidden under the Treaty to use nuclear materials obtained through Euratom for such purposes.

The execution of the Treaty now rests with the European Commission, which is advised by the Scientific and Technical Committee (28 members). Major decisions rest with the Council. Euratom has 1 substantial research institute of its own, at Ispra, in Italy; it does other work in co-operation with research institutes in the Member States, or in joint and international undertakings.

A common market for nuclear materials and equipment came into force, and external tariffs were suspended, in Jan. 1959. Although a recent Court of Justice decision has confirmed that Member States have ceded to Euratom the right to make supply contracts with outside suppliers (*e.g.* Australia, Canada or the USA), Euratom has generally been growing less effective in recent years, and most major new nuclear energy projects within the Member States have been undertaken outside its framework.

European Community Delegation to the US: 2111 M Street NW (Suite 707), Washington DC 20037.

Head of Delegation: Sir Roy Denman.

US Delegation to the European Community: 40 Boulevard du Régent, 1000 Brussels.

Head of Delegation. George S. Vest.

European Community Delegation to the United Nations: 1 Dag Hammarskjöld Plaza, 245 East 47th Street, New York NY 10017.

Head of Delegation: Michael Hardy.

Books of Reference

Official Journal of the European Communities.—General Report on the Activities of the European Communities (annual, from 1967).—*The Agricultural Situation in the Community 1983.—Thirteenth Report of Competition Policy.* 1983.—*Report on the Development of the Social Situation in the Community in 1983.—Basic Statistics of the Community* (annual).—*Bulletin of the European Community* (monthly).—*Register of Current Community Legal Instruments.* 1983

Europe (monthly), obtainable from the Information Office of the European Commission, 8 Storey's Gate, London, SW1P 3AT
Arbuthnott, H. and Edwards, G., (eds.), *A Common Man's Guide to the Common Market.* London, 1979
Coffey, P., *The External Economic Relations of the E.E.C.* London, 1976
Cook, C., and Francis, M., *The First European Elections.* London, 1979
Drew, J., *Doing Business with the European Community.* London, 1979
Fennell, R., *The Common Agricultural Policy of the European Community.* London, 1979
Fitzmaurice, J., *The European Parliament.* London, 1982
Goodhart, P., *Full-hearted Consent.* London, 1976
Hallstein, W., *Europe in the Making.* London, 1973
Korah, V., *An Introductory Guide to EEC Competition Law and Practice.* Oxford, 1979
Lodge, J., *The European Community: Bibliographical Excursions.* London, 1983
Mayre, R., *Postwar Europe.* London, 1983
Morris, B., *et al The European Community: A Practical Guide for Business and Government.* London, 1982
Palmer, D. M., *Sources of Information on the European Communities.* London, 1979
Parry, A., and Dinnage, J., *EEC Law.* London, 1982
Paxton, J., *The Developing Common Market.* London, 1976.—*A Dictionary of the European Communities.* 2nd ed. London, 1982
Shanks, M., *European Social Policy, Today and Tomorrow.* Oxford, 1977
Swann, D., *The Economies of the Common Market.* 4th ed. Harmondsworth, 1978
Twitchett, C. C., *Harmonisation in the EEC.* London, 1981
Wallace, W., and Herreman, I. (eds.), *A Community of Twelve?* Bruges, 1978
Walsh, A. E., and Paxton, J., *Competition Policy.* London, 1975

EUROPEAN FREE TRADE ASSOCIATION (EFTA)

The European Free Trade Association has 6 member countries: Austria, Iceland, Norway, Portugal, Sweden and Switzerland. A seventh country, Finland, is an associate member. The Stockholm Convention establishing the Association entered into force on 3 May 1960 and Finland became associated on 27 March 1961. Iceland joined EFTA on 1 March 1970 and was immediately granted duty-free entry for industrial goods exported to EFTA countries, while being given 10 years to abolish her own existing protective duties. Two founder members of EFTA, the UK and Denmark, left EFTA on 31 Dec. 1972 to join the EEC.

When the Association was created it had three objectives: to achieve free trade in industrial products between member countries, to assist in the creation of a single market embracing the countries of Western Europe, and to contribute to the expansion of world trade in general.

The first objective was achieved on 31 Dec. 1966, when virtually all inter-EFTA tariffs were removed. This was 3 years earlier than originally planned. Finland removed her remaining EFTA tariffs a year later on 31 Dec. 1967 and Iceland removed her tariffs on 31 Dec. 1979.

The fulfilment of the second aim was secured in 1972. On 22 Jan. 1972 the UK and Denmark signed the Treaty of Accession to the EEC whereby they became members of the enlarged Community from 1 Jan. 1973. On 22 July 1972, 5 other EFTA countries, Austria, Iceland, Portugal, Sweden and Switzerland signed Free Trade Agreements with the enlarged EEC. A similar agreement negotiated with Finland was signed on 5 Oct. 1973. Norway, whose intention of joining the EEC was reversed following a referendum, signed a similar agreement on 14 May 1973. Through these agreements virtually complete free trade in industrial goods was achieved in 16 Western European countries from July 1977. The free trade agreements apply also to Greece since its accession to the EEC on 1 Jan. 1981. A multilateral free trade agreement between the EFTA countries and Spain, a candidate for EEC membership, came into force on 1 May 1980 and the first tariff cuts were applied on 1 June 1980.

The third objective was to contribute to the expansion of world trade. In

1959 trade between the countries now in EFTA amounted to US$759m. and total exports from these countries were US$6,852m. In 1983 the respective figures were US$14,500m. and US$106,400m. More than half EFTA trade is with the EEC.

EFTA tariff treatment applies to those industrial products which are of EFTA origin, and these are traded freely between member countries. Each EFTA country remains free, however, to impose its own rates of duty on products entering from outside EFTA or the EEC.

Generally, agricultural products do not come under the provisions for free trade, but bilateral agreements have been negotiated to increase trade in these products.

The operation of the Convention is the responsibility of a Council assisted by a small secretariat. Each EFTA country holds the chairmanship of the Council for 6 months.

Secretary-General: Per Kleppe (Norway).
Headquarters: 9–11 rue de Varembé, 1211 Geneva 20, Switzerland.

Convention Establishing the European Free Trade Association
EFTA Bulletin (Four issues a year)
EFTA What it is, What it does
The European Free Trade Association

THE WARSAW PACT

On 14 May 1955 the USSR, Albania, Bulgaria, Czechoslovakia, the German Democratic Republic, Hungary, Poland and Romania signed, in Warsaw, a 20-year treaty of friendship and collaboration, after the USSR had (on 7 May) annulled the 20-year treaties of alliance with the UK (1942) and France (1944).

The main provisions of the treaty are as follows:

Article 4. In case of armed aggression in Europe against one or several States party to the pact by a State or group of States, each State member of the pact . . . will afford to the State or States which are the object of such aggression immediate assistance . . . with all means which appear necessary, including the use of armed force . . . These measures will cease as soon as the Security Council takes measures necessary for establishing and preserving international peace and security.

Article 5. The contracting Powers agree to set up a joint command of their armed forces to be allotted by agreement between the Powers, at the disposal of this command and used on the basis of jointly established principles. They will also take over agreed measures necessary to strengthen their defences.

Article 9. The present treaty is open to other States, irrespective of their social or Government regime, who declare their readiness to abide by the terms of the treaty in order to safeguard peace and security of the peoples.

Article 11. In the event of a system of collective security being set up in Europe and a pact to this effect being signed—to which each party to this treaty will direct its efforts—the present treaty will lapse from the day such a collective security treaty comes into force.

It is estimated (1981) that the armed forces of the Warsaw Pact countries total 4·82m., including 3·71m. Russians, compared with 4·99m. NATO forces.

Marshal Grechko was from July 1960 to April 1967 C.-in-C. of the united Armed Forces, with headquarters in Moscow. He was succeeded by Marshal I. I. Yakubovsky in 1967 and by Marshal V. G. Kulikov in Jan. 1977.

In 1962 Albania was no longer invited to the Warsaw Pact meetings without being formally expelled.

Two Soviet divisions are stationed in Poland, 20 divisions in German Democratic Republic, 4 divisions in Hungary and 5 in Czechoslovakia.

Clawson, R. W. and Kaplan, L. S. (eds.), *The Warsaw Pact: Political Purpose and Military Means.* Wilmington, 1982
Lewis, W. J., *The Warsaw Pact: Doctrine and Strategy.* Maidenhead, 1982

COUNCIL FOR MUTUAL ECONOMIC ASSISTANCE [1]

Membership. Founder members were USSR, Bulgaria, Czechoslovakia, Hungary, Poland and Romania. Later admissions were Albania (1949; ceased participation 1961), German Democratic Republic (1950), Mongolia (1962), Cuba (1972), Vietnam (1978). In 1964 Yugoslavia concluded an agreement with CMEA whereby Yugoslavia would participate in the work of some CMEA bodies (at present 21). Afghánistán, Angola, Ethiopia, Laos, Mexico, Mozambique, Nicaragua and the People's Democratic Republic of Yemen attend CMEA sessions as observers.

External relations. There are co-operation agreements with Finland, Iraq, Mexico and Nicaragua. Talks with the EEC at expert level on possible commercial co-operation were resumed in July 1980.

The Charter. The charter consists of a preamble and 18 articles. Extracts (in the language of the official English version) are as follows:

Article 1. Aims and Principles: 1 'The purpose of the Council is to promote, by uniting and co-ordinating the efforts of the member countries, the further extension and improvement of co-operation and the development of socialist economic integration, the planned development of their national economies, the acceleration of economic and technical progress in these countries, higher level of industrialization of the less industrialized countries, a continuous increase in labour productivity, a gradual approximation and equalization of economic development levels and a steady improvement in the wellbeing of the peoples. 2 The Council is based on the principles of the sovereign equality of all member countries.'

Article 2. Membership 'open to other countries which subscribe to the purposes and principles of the Council'.

Article 3. Functions and Powers to (a) 'organize all-round . . . co-operation of member countries in the most rational use of natural resources and acceleration of the development of their productive forces'; (b) 'foster the improvement of the international socialist division of labour by co-ordinating national economic development plans, and the specialization and co-operation of production in member countries'; (c) to assist in . . . carrying out joint measures for the development of industry and agriculture . . . transport . . . principal capital investments . . . [and] trade'.

Article 4. Recommendations and Decisions '. . . shall be adopted only with the consent of the interested member countries.'

The Structure. The supreme authority is the 'Session' of all members held (usually annually) in members' capitals in rotation under the chairmanship of the head of the delegation of the host country; all members must be present, and decisions must be unanimous. Delegations are usually led by prime ministers.

The *Executive Committee* is made up of 1 representative from each member state of deputy premier rank. It meets at least once every 3 months.

The administrative organ is the *Secretariat.*

Headquarters: Prospekt Kalinina, 56, Moscow, G-205.
Secretary: V. V. Sychev (appointed 1983).

There is a *Committee for Co-operation in the Field of Planning* and a *Committee for Scientific and Technical Co-operation* set up in 1971 and a *Committee for Material and Technical Supply* set up in 1974. There are *Permanent Commissions* on: Statistics, Foreign Trade, Currency and Finance, Electricity, Peaceful Uses of Atomic Energy, Geology, Coal Industry, Oil and Gas Industry, Chemical Industry, Iron and Steel Industry, Non-Ferrous Metals Industry, Engineering Industry, Radio Engineering and Electronics Industries, Light Industry, Food Industry, Agriculture, Construction, Transport, Posts and Telecommunications, Standardization, Civil Aviation, Public Health.

There are 7 *Standing Conferences:* for Legal Problems; of Ministers of Internal

---

[1] Abbreviations and Foreign Names. CMEA is the official abbreviation. Other unofficial abbreviations are COMECON and CEMA. The working language of the organization is Russian. The Russian form is *Sovet Ekonomicheskoi Vzaimopomoshchi* (SEV).

Trade; of Chiefs of Water Resources Authorities; of Chiefs of Patent Authorities; of Chiefs of Pricing Authorities; of Chiefs of Labour Authorities, and of Representatives of Freight and Shipping Organizations.

There are 3 semi-autonomous bodies within CMEA: The Institute of Standardization, The Bureau for the Co-ordination of Ship Freighting and The International Institute of Economic Problems of the World Socialist System.

In 1985 there were over 20 technical and economic agencies associated with CMEA.

Also associated with CMEA are:

The **International Bank for Economic Co-operation** was founded in 1963 with a capital of 300m. roubles and started operating on 1 Jan. 1964. It undertakes multilateral settlements in 'transferable roubles' (*i.e.*, used for intra-CMEA clearing accounts only) and advances credits to finance trading and other operations. The transferable rouble is a unit of account: gold content 0·987412 gramme.

The **International Investments Bank** was founded in 1970 and went into operation on 1 Jan. 1971 with a capital of 1,713m. roubles (70% transferable and 30% convertible or in gold).

Banking and Sources of Finance in Comecon. London, 1978
Charter of the Council for Mutual Economic Assistance. Moscow, 1980
Comecon Data 1983. London, 1984
Council for Mutual Economic Assistance: Thirty Years. Moscow, 1979
Comprehensive Programme for the Further Extension and Improvement of Co-operation and the Development of Socialist Economic Integration by the CMEA-member Countries. Moscow, 1971 (The official English-language version. This document also frequently referred to as the *Complex Programme,* etc.)
Ekonomicheskoe Sotrudnichestvo Stran-Chlenov SEV. Moscow, monthly
Multilateral Economic Co-operation of Socialist States: A Collection of Documents. Moscow, 1977
Statistical Year Book of CMEA Member Countries. Moscow, annual
Survey of CMEA Activities. Moscow, annual
Bautina, N. V., *CMEA Today: from Economic Co-operation to Economic Integration.* Moscow, 1975
Bystrický, R., *Le Droit de l'Intégration Économique Socialiste.* Geneva, 1979
Marrese, M., and Vanous, J., *Soviet Subsidization of Trade with Eastern Europe.* Berkeley, 1983
Saunders, C. T. (ed.), *Regional Integration in East and West.* London, 1983
Schiavone, G., *The Institutions of Comecon.* London, 1981
Szawlowski, R., *The System of the International Organizations of the Communist Countries.* Leyden, 1976
van Brabant, J. M. P., *Essays on Planning, Trade and Integration in Eastern Europe.* Rotterdam Univ. Press, 1974
Wilczynski, J., *Technology in Comecon.* London, 1974

COLOMBO PLAN

History: Founded in 1950 to promote the development of newly independent Asian member countries, the Colombo Plan has grown from its modest beginning as a group of seven Commonwealth nations into an international organization of 26 countries.

Originally the Plan was conceived for a period of six years. Its life has since been extended from time to time, generally at five-year intervals. The Consultative Committee, the Plan's highest deliberative body, at its meeting in Jakarta in 1980, gave the Plan an indefinite span of life; its need and relevance will henceforth be examined only if considered necessary.

The Plan is multilateral in approach but bilateral in operation: multilateral in that it takes cognizance of the problems of development of member countries in the Asia and Pacific region and endeavours to deal with them in a co-ordinated way; bilateral because negotiations for assistance are made direct between a donor and a recipient country.

Aims: The aims of the Colombo Plan are: *(a)* to promote interest in and support for the economic and social development in Asia and the Pacific; *(b)* to keep under review economic and social progress in the region and help accelerate development through co-operative effort; and *(c)* to facilitate development assistance to and within the region.

Member Countries: Afghánistán, Australia, Bangladesh, Bhutan, Burma, Cambodia, Canada, Fiji, India, Indonesia, Iran, Japan, Republic of Korea, Lao People's Democratic Republic, Malaysia, Maldives, Nepal, New Zealand, Pakistan, Papua New Guinea, Philippines, Singapore, Sri Lanka, Thailand, UK and USA.

Development Assistance: Colombo Plan aid covers all fields of socio-economic development and amounted to US$3,427·2m. in 1983. It takes two principal forms:

(i) *Capital Aid* including grants and loans for national projects mainly from the six developed member countries to the developing member countries of the Plan.
The total amount of capital aid provided by the leading donors under the plan in 1983 was as follows:

	US$1m.
Japan	1,569·6
USA	832·0
Australia	395·5
UK	374·3
Canada	267·5
New Zealand	11·3
Total	3,420·2

(ii) *Technical Co-operation: Assistance* is provided in the form of services of experts and volunteers, fellowships, and equipment for training and research. During 1983, 17,490 trainees and students received training, 7,457 experts and 1,425 volunteers were sent out, value of equipment supplied was $23·9m. Total disbursements on technical co-operation in 1983 amounted to $598·4m.

Structure: There are four organs which give focus to the Plan:

Consultative Committee: The Committee is the highest deliberative body of the Plan and consists of Ministers of member Governments who meet once in two years. The Ministerial meeting is preceded by a meeting of senior officials who are directly concerned with the operation of the Plan in various countries.

Colombo Plan Council: The Council is also a deliberative body which meets several times a year in Colombo, where most member countries have resident diplomatic missions, to review the economic and social development of the Asia-Pacific region and promote co-operation among member countries.

Colombo Plan Bureau: This is the only permanent organ of the Colombo Plan with headquarters in Colombo. Its functions include servicing the meetings of the Colombo Plan Council and the Consultative Committee, carrying out research, and dissemination of statistical and other information relating to activities under the Plan. Since 1973 the Bureau has been operating a Drug Advisory Programme to assist national and regional efforts to eliminate the causes and ameliorate the effects of drug abuse.

Colombo Plan Staff College: The Colombo Plan Staff College for Technician Education, located in Singapore, was opened in March 1975 to help member countries in developing their system of technician education. The College conducts training courses for senior technician educators and planners both at the College and in regional member countries.

Headquarters: Colombo Plan Bureau, 12 Melbourne Avenue, PO Box 596, Colombo 4, Sri Lanka.

The Colombo Plan (Cmd. 8080). HMSO, 1950; reprinted 1952.—*Annual Report.* HMSO 1952 to 1971 followed by Colombo Plan Bureaux, Sri Lanka, 1972–78, 1980, 1982 and 1984

Reports of the Council for Technical Co-operation. HMSO annually until 1966–67 followed by the Colombo Plan Bureau, Sri Lanka, 1967–68 to date

ASSOCIATION OF SOUTH EAST ASIAN NATIONS (ASEAN)

History and Membership. The Association of South East Asian Nations is a regional organization formed by the governments of Indonesia, Malaysia, the Philippines, Singapore and Thailand through the Bangkok Declaration which was signed by the Foreign Ministers of ASEAN countries on 8 Aug. 1967. Brunei joined in 1984.

Objectives. The main objectives are to accelerate economic growth, social progress and cultural development, to promote active collaboration and mutual assistance in matters of common interest, to ensure the stability of the South East Asian region and to maintain close co-operation with existing international and regional organizations with similar aims. Principal projects concern economic co-operation and development, with the intensification of intra-ASEAN trade and trade between the region and the rest of the world; joint research and technological programmes; co-operation in transportation and communications; promotion of tourism and South East Asian studies; including cultural, scientific, educational and administrative exchanges.

Organs. The highest authority in ASEAN are the Heads of Government of the Member Countries who meet as and when necessary to give directions to ASEAN. The highest policy-making body is the Meeting of Foreign Ministers, commonly known as the Annual Ministerial Meeting, which convenes in each of the ASEAN member countries on a rotational basis in alphabetical order. The Standing Committee, comprising the Foreign Minister of the country hosting the Ministerial Meeting in that particular year and the accredited ambassadors of the other member countries, carries out the work of the Association in between the Ministerial Meetings and handles the routine matters to ensure continuity and to make decisions based on the guidelines or policies set by the Ministerial Meetings and submit for the consideration of the Foreign Ministers all reports and recommendations of the various ASEAN committees. There are five economic committees under the ASEAN Economic Ministers and three non-economic committees that recommend and draw up programmes for ASEAN co-operation. These committees are responsible for the operation and implementation of ASEAN projects in their respective fields. Each ASEAN capital has an ASEAN National Secretariat. The central secretariat for ASEAN is located in Jakarta, Indonesia, and is headed by the Secretary General, a post that revolves among the member states in alphabetical order every 2 years. Bureau directors and other officers of the ASEAN Secretariat remain in office for 3 years.

Secretary-General: Phan Wannamethee (Thailand).

Books of Reference

Broinowski, A., *Understanding ASEAN.* London, 1982
Wawn, B., *The Economics of the ASEAN Countries.* London, 1982
Wong, J., *ASEAN Economics in Perspective.* London, 1979

ORGANIZATION OF AMERICAN STATES

On 14 April 1890 representatives of the American republics, meeting in Washington at the First International Conference of American States, established an 'International Union of American Republics' and, as its central office, a 'Commercial Bureau of American Republics', which later became the Pan American Union. This international organization's object was to foster mutual understanding and co-operation among the nations of the western hemisphere. Since that time, successive inter-American conferences have greatly broadened the scope of work of the organization.

This led to the adoption on 30 April 1948 by the Ninth International Conference of American States, at Bogotá, Colombia, of the Charter of the Organization of American States. This co-ordinated the work of all the former independent official entities in the inter-American system and defined their mutual relationships. The purposes of the OAS are to achieve an order of peace and justice, promote American solidarity, strengthen collaboration among the member states and defend their sovereignty, territorial integrity and independence. The OAS is a regional organization of the United Nations for the maintenance of peace and security.

Membership is on a basis of absolute equality. Each country has one vote in the Council of the Organization and its organs. The member countries were (1980): Antigua and Barbuda, Argentina, Bahamas, Barbados, Bolivia, Brazil, Chile, Colombia, Costa Rica, Cuba, Commonwealth of Dominica, Dominican Republic, Ecuador, El Salvador, Grenada, Guatemala, Haiti, Honduras, Jamaica, Mexico, Nicaragua, Panama, Paraguay, Peru, Saint Christopher (Kitts) and Nevis, Saint Lucia, Saint Vincent and the Grenadines, Suriname, Trinidad and Tobago, USA, Uruguay, Venezuela.

The OAS has been concerned increasingly in recent years with programmes to promote Latin American economic and social development. The OAS provides specialized training for thousands of Latin Americans each year in a wide variety of development-related fields. It also carries out several missions projects each year in response to requests from member governments.

On 27 Feb. 1967 the Third Special Inter-American Conference in Buenos Aires approved the Protocol of Amendment to the Charter of the OAS, which contained new standards for inter-American co-operation and a number of structural changes in the Organization.

On 14 April 1967 the Declaration of the Presidents of America, signed in Punta del Este, Uruguay, expressed the commitment of the American chiefs of state to promote Latin American economic integration; to join in efforts to increase substantially Latin American foreign-trade earnings; to modernize the living conditions of the rural population and raise agricultural productivity; and to expand programmes in education, science, technology and health.

On 22 Feb. 1968, in the Resolution of Maracay, the Inter-American Cultural Council launched new regional programmes for educational development and for scientific and technological development.

On 27 Feb. 1970, by ratification of more than the mandatory two-thirds of the OAS member states, the Protocol of Buenos Aires, modifying the 1948 Charter, entered into effect.

Under the amended Charter, the OAS accomplishes its purposes by means of:

(a) The *General Assembly*, which meets annually in various countries of the member states.

(b) The *Meeting of Consultation of Ministers of Foreign Affairs*, held to consider problems of an urgent nature and of common interest.

(c) Three councils of equal rank: the *Permanent Council*, which replaces the old OAS Council; the *Inter-American Economic and Social Council*; and the *Inter-American Council for Education, Science and Culture*. Functions are to direct and co-ordinate work in the areas of their competence and render the governments such specialized services as they may request. Each council is composed of 1 representative from each member state, appointed by his government.

(d) The *Inter-American Juridical Committee* which acts as an advisory body to the OAS on juridical matters and promotes the development and codification of international law. Eleven jurists, elected every 4 years by the General Assembly, represent all the American States.

(e) The *Inter-American Commission on Human Rights* which oversees the observance and protection of human rights. Seven members represent all the OAS member states.

(*f*) The *General Secretariat* is the central and permanent organ of the OAS.

(*g*) The *Specialized Conferences*, meeting to deal with special technical matters or to develop specific aspects of inter-American co-operation.

(*h*) The *Specialized Organizations*, inter-governmental organizations established by multilateral agreements to discharge specific functions in their respective fields of action, such as women's affairs, agriculture, child welfare, Indian affairs, geography and history, and health.

Secretary-General: João Clemente Baena Soares.

Assistant Secretary-General: Valerie McComie (Barbados).

The Secretary-General and the Assistant Secretary-General are elected by the General Assembly for 5-year terms. The General Assembly approves the annual budget for the Organization, which is financed by quotas contributed by the member governments.

General Secretariat: Washington, D.C., 20006, USA.
Flag: Light blue with the OAS seal in colour in the centre.

Books of Reference

Publications of the OAS General Secretariat include:

Charter of the Organization of American States. 1948.—*As Amended by the Protocol of Buenos Aires in 1967*
Americas. Illustrated bi-monthly, from 1949 (Spanish and English edition)
Organization of American States, a Handbook. Rev. ed. 1977
Organization of American States. Directory. Quarterly, from 1951
Report on the Tenth Inter-American Conference, Caracas 1954. 1955
Inter-American Review of Bibliography. Quarterly, from 1951
Annual Report of the Secretary-General
Status of Inter-American Treaties and Conventions. Annual
The Alliance for Progress: The Charter of Punta del Este. 1962
The Americas in the 1980s: An Agenda for the Decade Ahead. 1982

Publications on Latin America (*see also* the bibliographical notes appended to each country):

Revenue, Expenditure and Public Debts of the Latin American Republics. Division of Financial Information, US Department of Commerce. Annual
Boundaries of the Latin American Republics: An Annotated List of Documents, 1493–1943. Department of State, Office of the Geographer. Washington, 1944
Burgin, M. (ed.), *Handbook of Latin American Studies.* Gainesville, Fla., 1935 ff.
Hirschman, Albert O., *Latin American Issues:* [11] *Essays and Comments.* New York, 1961
Plaza, G., *The Organization of American States: Instrument for Hemispheric Development.* Washington, 1969.—*Latin America Today and Tomorrow.* Washington, 1971
Steward, J. H. (ed.), *Handbook of the South American Indian.* 7 vols. Washington, 1946–59
Thomas, A. V. W. and A. J., *The Organization of American States.* Southern Methodist Univ. Press, 1963

LATIN AMERICAN ECONOMIC GROUPINGS

The Economic Commission for Latin America, an organ of the United Nations, with headquarters in Santiago, Chile, has facilitated the co-operation of two groups of countries concerning production, tariffs and trade.

Latin American Free Trade Association was concluded in Montevideo on 18 Feb. 1961 by Argentina, Bolivia, Brazil, Chile, Mexico, Paraguay, Peru and Uruguay. Colombia (3 Oct. 1961), Ecuador (20 Oct. 1961) and Venezuela (1 Sept. 1966) have joined the ALALC/LAFTA Treaty. The permanent secretariat is at Montevideo. The 11 signatories held the 19th Extraordinary Conference at Acapulco, 16–27 June 1980. A Constitution was drawn up for a new Latin American Integration Association (LAIA) to take over after LAFTA expired on 31 Dec. 1980.

Central American Common Market (ODECA). On 13 Dec. 1960, at Managua, El

Salvador, Guatemala, Honduras and Nicaragua concluded a general treaty on Central American integration; a protocol on the equalization of import duties and charges; and an agreement establishing the Central American Bank for Economic Integration. Costa Rica acceded in 1962 and in Sept. 1963 ratified the charter of the Banco Centroamericano de Integración Económica (in Tegucigalpa), whose capital was thereupon increased to US$20m.

The San Salvador Charter, signed on 14 Dec. 1962, expanded these provisions, envisaging permanent political, economic, educational, defence, etc., councils. The permanent secretariat is at Guatemala City.

The Andean Group (Grupo Andino). On 26 May 1969 an agreement was signed by Bolivia, Chile, Colombia, Ecuador and Peru creating the Andean Group. Venezuela was initially actively involved but did not sign the agreement until 1973. The Group signed a further agreement on 31 Dec. 1970 on common regulations controlling foreign investments. Under the Cartagena Agreement of 1975 the development of an integrated petrochemical industry in each of the member countries was established.

Sistema Económico Latinoamericano (SELA) was created by 25 Latin American and Caribbean countries (Suriname joined in 1979) meeting at Panama, 17 Oct. 1975. The System provides member countries with permanent institutional machinery for joint consultation, co-ordination, co-operation and promotion in economic and social matters at both intraregional and extraregional level.

The River Plate Basin Development Group. A Treaty for the joint economic development of the River Plate Basin was signed by Argentina, Bolivia, Brazil, Paraguay and Uruguay in Brasilia in 1969. The aim was to jointly carry out development in the region and take steps to facilitate agreement on questions of navigation. An Inter-governmental Co-ordination Committee would meet annually and sub-committees on water resources and funding were established.

Chile was admitted as an observer in 1976.

The Amazon Pact. Representatives of Bolivia, Brazil, Colombia, Ecuador, Guyana, Peru, Suriname and Venezuela met in Belem on 23 Oct. 1980 to discuss joint policy for development in the region. It was agreed that Peru be responsible for reviewing development projects and the establishment of a fund for the improvement of communications in the region.

Urupabol. A tripartite commission for economic co-operation, trade and integration between Bolivia, Paraguay and Uruguay was constituted formally on 29 May 1981. This organization had existed informally since 1963 when the members started rotating a seat on the Inter-American Development Bank among themselves. By late 1981 both Paraguay and Uruguay had ratified membership of the new commission.

Britain and Latin America. Latin America Bureau, London (annual)
British Bulletin of Publications on Latin America, the Caribbean, Portugal and Spain. London, from June 1949 (half-yearly)
Hispanic and Luso–Brazilian Councils, Portuguese and Spanish Dictionaries. London, 1971
Instruments of Economic Integration in Latin America and the Caribbean. New York, 1975
Libre Comercio. Revista oficial de la Associación de Empresarios participantes de la ALALC. Montevideo, from June 1964 (monthly)
Committee on Latin America (COLA), *Latin American Serials.* 3 vols. London, 1969, 1973, 1977
Brooks, J. (ed.), *The South American Handbook.* Bath (Annual)
Loveman, B., and Davies, T. M., *The Politics of Antipolitics: The Military in Latin America.* Univ. of Nebraska Press, 1978
Morawetz, D., *The Andean Group: A Case Study in Economic Integration Among Developing Countries.* MIT Press, 1974
UN Economic Commission for Latin America. *The Latin America Economy.* Washington (annual)

CARIBBEAN COMMUNITY (CARICOM)

Establishment and Functions. The Treaty establishing the Caribbean Community, including the Caribbean Common Market, and the Agreement establishing the Common External Tariff for the Caribbean Common Market, was signed by the Prime Ministers of Barbados, Guyana, Jamaica and Trinidad and Tobago at Chaguaramas, Trinidad, on 4 July 1973, and entered into force on 1 Aug. 1973. Six less developed countries of CARIFTA signed the Treaty of Chaguaramas on 17 April 1974. They were Belize, Dominica, Grenada, Saint Lucia, St Vincent and Montserrat, and the Treaty came into effect for those countries on 1 May 1974. Antigua acceded to membership on 4 July 1974 and on 26 July the Associated State of St Kitts–Nevis–Anguilla signed the Treaty of Chaguaramas in Kingston, Jamaica, and became a member of the Caribbean Community, Bahamas became a member of the Community but not of the Common Market.

The Caribbean Community has 3 areas of activity: *(i)* economic co-operation through the Caribbean Common Market; *(ii)* co-ordination of foreign policy; *(iii)* functional co-operation in areas such as health, education and culture, youth and sports, science and technology, and tax administration.

The Caribbean Common Market provides for the establishment of a Common External Tariff, a common protective policy and the progressive co-ordination of external trade policies; the adoption of a scheme for the harmonization of fiscal incentives to industry; double taxation arrangements among member countries; the co-ordination of economic policies and development planning; and a special regime for the less developed countries of the community.

Membership: Antigua and Barbuda, Bahamas, Barbados, Belize, Dominica, Grenada, Guyana, Jamaica, Montserrat, St Kitts–Nevis, Saint Lucia, St Vincent and the Grenadines, and Trinidad and Tobago.

Structure: The *Heads of Government Conference* is the principal organ of the Community, and its primary responsibility is to determine the policy of the Community. It is the final authority of the Community and the Common Market, and for the conclusion of treaties and relationships between the Community and international organizations and States. It is responsible for financial arrangements for meeting the expenses of the Community.

The *Common Market Council* is the principal organ of the Common Market and consists of a Minister of Government designated by each member state. Decisions in both the Conference and the Council are in the main taken on the basis of unanimity.

The *Secretariat*, successor to the Commonwealth Caribbean Regional Secretariat, is the principal administrative organ of the Community and of the Common Market. The Secretary-General is appointed by the Conference on the recommendation of the Council for a term not exceeding 5 years and may be reappointed. The Secretary-General shall act in that capacity in all meetings of the Conference, the Council, and of the institutions of the Community.

Institutions of the Community, established by the Heads of Government Conference, are: Conference of Ministers responsible for Health; Standing Committees of Ministers responsible for Education, Industry, Labour, Foreign Affairs, Finance, Agriculture, Mines and Natural Resources, Industry, Science and Technology, and Transport, respectively.

Associate Institutions: Caribbean Development Bank; Caribbean Examinations Council, Caribbean Investment Corporation; Council of Legal Education; University of the West Indies; University of Guyana; Caribbean Meteorological Organization; West Indies Shipping Corporation.

Secretary-General: Roderick Rainford.
Deputy Secretary-General: Louis Wiltshire.

Headquarters: Bank of Guyana Building, PO Box 10827, Georgetown, Guyana.

The language of the Community is English.

Books of Reference

CARICOM Perspective. (Bi-monthly). *CARICOM Bibliography* (Bi-annual)

The Caribbean Community in the 1980's. Caribbean Community Secretariat, 1982

Axline, A. W., *Caribbean Integration: The Politics of Regionalism.* London and New York, 1979

Payne, A. J., *The Politics of the Caribbean Community 1961–79.* Manchester Univ. Press, 1980

THE LEAGUE OF ARAB STATES

Origin. The formation of the League of Arab States in 1945 was largely inspired by the Arab awakening of the 19th century. This movement sought to re-create and reintegrate the Arab community which, though for 400 years a part of the Ottoman Empire, had preserved its identity as a separate national group held together by memories of a common past, a common religion and a common language, as well as by the consciousness of being part of a common cultural heritage. The leaders of the Arab movement in the 19th century and of the Arab revolt against Turkey in the First World War sought to achieve these aims through secession from the Ottoman Empire into a united and independent Arab state comprising all the Arab countries in Asia. However the 1919 peace settlement divided the Arab world in Asia (with the exception of Saudi Arabia and the Yemen) into British and French spheres of influence and established in them a number of separate states and administrations (Syria, Lebanon, Iraq, Jordan and Palestine) under temporary mandatory control.

By 1943, however, 7 of these countries had substantially achieved their independence. An Arab conference therefore met in Alexandria in the autumn of 1944; it formulated the 'Alexandria Protocol', which delineated the outlines of the Arab League. It was found that neither a unitary state nor a federation could be achieved, but only a league of sovereign states. A covenant, establishing such a league, was signed in Cairo on 22 March 1945 by the representatives of Egypt, Iraq, Saudi Arabia, Syria, Lebanon, Jordan and Yemen. There were (1980) 21 members of the League: Algeria, Bahrain, Djibouti, Iraq, Jordan, Kuwait, Lebanon, Libya, Mauritania, Morocco, Oman, Palestine L.O., Qatar, Saudi Arabia, Somalia, Sudan, Syria, Tunisia, United Arab Emirates, P.D.R. of Yemen and Yemen Arab Republic.

Egypt's membership of the League was suspended, in accordance with a resolution passed at the Baghdad summit, in March 1979, at which time it was also agreed that the League secretariat should be moved from Cairo to Tunis. This action was taken in response to the signing of a bilateral peace treaty between Egypt and Israel.

Organization. The machinery of the League consists of a Council, a number of Special Committees and a Permanent Secretariat. On the Council each state has one vote. The Council may meet in any of the Arab capitals. Its functions include mediation in any dispute between any of the League states or a League state and a country outside the League. The Council has a Political Committee consisting of the Foreign Ministers of the Arab states.

The Permanent Secretariat of the League, under a Secretary-General (who enjoys, along with his senior colleagues, full diplomatic status), has its seat in Tunisia.

The League considers itself a regional organization within the framework of the United Nations at which its secretary-general is an observer.

Secretary-General: Chedli Klibi (Tunisia).

Flag: Dark green with the seal of the Arab League in white in the centre.

Arab Common Market. The Arab Common Market came into operation on 1 Jan.

1965. The agreement, reached on 13 Aug. 1964 and open to all the Arab League states, has been signed by Iraq, Jordan, Syria and Egypt. The agreement provides for the abolition of customs duties on agricultural products and natural resources within 5 years, by reducing tariffs at an annual rate of 20%. Customs duties on industrial products are to be reduced by 10% annually. The agreement also provides for the free movement of capital and labour between member countries, the establishment of common external tariffs, the co-ordination of economical development and the framing of a common foreign economic policy.

Books of Reference

Arab Maritime Data, 1979–80. London, 1979
Gomaa, A. M., *The Foundation of the League of Arab States.* London, 1977

ORGANIZATION OF THE PETROLEUM EXPORTING COUNTRIES

Aims. The Organization was founded in Baghdad, Iraq, in 1960 with the following founder members, Iran, Iraq, Kuwait, Saudi Arabia and Venezuela. The principal aims are unifying the petroleum policies of member countries and determining the best means for safeguarding their interests, individually and collectively; to devise ways and means of ensuring the stabilization of prices in international oil markets with a view to eliminating harmful and unnecessary fluctuations; and to secure a steady income for the producing countries, an efficient, economic and regular supply of petroleum to consuming nations, and a fair return on their capital to those investing in the petroleum industry.

Membership (1981). Algeria, Ecuador, Gabon, Indonesia, Iran, Iraq, Kuwait, Libya, Nigeria, Qatar, Saudi Arabia, United Arab Emirates and Venezuela. Membership is open to any other country having substantial net exports of crude petroleum, which has fundamentally similar interests to those of member countries.

OPEC Fund. The Fund was established in 1976 to provide financial aid to developing countries, other than OPEC members, on advantageous terms.

Acting Secretary-General: Dr Fadhil J. Al-Chalabi (Iraq).

Headquarters: Obere Donaustrasse 93, A–1020 Vienna, Austria.

Books of Reference

OPEC publications include: *Annual Statistical Bulletin. Annual Report. OPEC Bulletin* (monthly). *OPEC Review* (quarterly). *OPEC Papers* (bi-monthly).
Al-Chalabi, Dr F., *OPEC and the International Oil Industry: A Changing Structure.* OUP, 1980
Abolfathi, F., *The OPEC Market to 1985.* Lexington, 1977
El Mallakh, R., *OPEC: Twenty Years and Beyond.* London, 1982
Ghadar, F., *The Evolution of OPEC Strategy.* Lexington, 1977
Griffin, J., and Teece, D. J., *OPEC Behaviour and World Oil Prices.* London and Boston, 1982

ORGANIZATION OF AFRICAN UNITY

On 25 May 1963 the heads of state or government of 32 African countries, at a conference in Addis Ababa, signed a charter establishing an 'Organization of African Unity' *(Organisation de l'Unité Africaine)*

Its chief objects are the furtherance of African unity and solidarity; the co-ordination of the political, economic, cultural, health, scientific and defence policies and the elimination of colonialism in Africa.

The organs of the Organization are: (1) the assembly of the heads of state and government; (2) the council of foreign ministers; (3) the general secretariat; (4) a commission of mediation, conciliation and arbitration. Arabic, French and English are recognized as working languages.

Chairman: Mengistu Haile Mariam (Ethiopia).
Secretary-General a.i.: Dr Peter U. Onu (Nigeria).
Headquarters: Addis Ababa.
Flag: Horizontally green, white, green, with the white fimbriated yellow, and the seal of the OAU in the centre.

DANUBE COMMISSION

The Danube Commission was constituted in 1949 based on the Convention regarding the regime of navigation on the Danube, which was signed in Belgrade on 18 Aug. 1948. The Belgrade Convention reaffirmed that navigation on the Danube from Ulm to the Black Sea, with access to the sea through the Sulina arm and the Sulina Canal, is equally free and open to the nationals, merchant shipping and merchandise of all states as to harbour and navigation fees as well as conditions of merchant navigation.

The Danube Commission is composed of representatives from the countries on the Danube (1 for each of these countries), namely, Austria, Bulgaria, Hungary, Romania, Czechoslovakia, USSR and Yugoslavia. Since 1957, representatives of the Ministry of Transport from the Federal Republic of Germany have attended the meetings of the Commission as guests of the Secretariat.

The functions of the Danube Commission are to check that the provisions of the Convention are carried out, to establish a uniform buoying system on all the Danube's navigable waterways and to establish the basic regulations for navigation on the river. The Commission co-ordinates the regulations for river, customs and sanitation control as well as the hydrometeorological service and collects statistical data concerning navigation on the Danube.

The Danube Commission enjoys legal status. It has its own seal and flag. The members of the Commission and elected officers enjoy diplomatic immunity. The Commission's official buildings, archives and documents are inviolable. French and Russian are the official languages of the Commission.

Since 1954 the headquarters of the Commission have been in Budapest.

Flag: Blue, with a red strip fimbriated white along the bottom edge, and the initials of the Commission within a wreath in the canton—Latin letters on obverse Cyrillic on reverse.

Books of Reference

Danube Commission's publications include: *Summary Records and Documents Adopted by the Sessions of the Danube Commission. Rules of Procedure of the Danube Commission. Basic Regulations for Navigation on the Danube. Reports on the Maintenance of the Navigability of the Danube. Guidebook for Sailors. Hydrological Yearbooks. Statistical Yearbooks. Mileage Chart of the Danube. Ice Control on the Danube. Collection of Internal Laws Concerning Navigation on the Danube. Collection of International Agreements Relating to Navigation on the Danube. Radio-Codes for Navigation on the Danube.*

PART II

COUNTRIES OF THE WORLD

A—Z

AFGHÁNISTÁN

Capital: Kábul
Population: 17·15m. (1984)
GNP per capita: US$168 (1982)

De Afghanistan Democrateek Jamhuriat

HISTORY. A military *coup* on 17 July 1973 overthrew the monarchy of King Záhir Shàh. The *coup* was led by the King's cousin and brother-in-law Mohammad Daoud who declared a Republic. King Záhir abdicated on 24 Aug. 1973. President Daoud was killed in a military *coup* in April 1978 which led to the establishment of a pro-Soviet government of the People's Democratic Party of Afghánistán.

AREA AND POPULATION. Afghánistán is bounded north by the USSR, east and south by Pakistan and west by Iran.

The area is 251,773 sq. miles (652,090 sq. km). Population, according to the (1979) census, is 15,551,358, of which some 2·5m. are nomadic tribes. Estimate (1984) 17·15m. of whom 3m. are living in Pakistan and 1m. in Iran as refugees. The 1984 population estimate is doubted and 13m. is considered more accurate. Annual population growth rate (1981) 2·6%; infant mortality rate (1979) 182 per 1,000 live births.

Census (1979), Kábul 913,164; Kandahár, 178,409; Herát, 140,323; Mazár-i-Sharif, 103,372; Jalálábád, 53,915; Kunduz, 53,251; Baghlan, 39,228; Maimana, 38,251; Pul-i-Khomri, 31,101; Ghazni, 30,425; Charikar, 22,424; Shibarghan, 18,955; Gardez, 9,550; Faizabad, 9,098; Qala-i-nau, 5,340; Uiback, 4,938; Meterlam, 3,987; Cheghcherán, 2,974.

The main ethnic group are the Pathans. Other ethnic groups include the Tajiks, the Hazaras, the Turkomans and the Uzbeks.

CLIMATE. The climate is arid, with a big annual range of temperature and very little rain, apart from the period Jan. to April. Winters are very cold, with considerable snowfall, which may last the year round on mountain summits. Kabul. Jan. 27°F (–2·8°C), July 76°F (24·4°C). Annual rainfall 13″ (338 mm).

CONSTITUTION AND GOVERNMENT. The 1964 Constitution was abolished by Presidential decree in 1973 and on 14 Feb. 1977 a new Constitution was adopted by the *Loya-Jirgah* (Grand Assembly). The 1977 Constitution was abrogated in April 1978 by the new Head of State, Noor Mohammad Taraki. On 16 Sept. 1979 President Taraki was ousted in a *coup* and replaced by Hafizullah Amin. In Dec. 1979 Soviet troops invaded Afghánistán and Hafizullah Amin was deposed and replaced by Babrak Karmal. The pretext for the airlift of combat troops to Kábul was the Treaty of Friendship signed in Dec. 1978 between USSR and Afghánistán. In Oct. 1983 there were some 105,000 Soviet troops in Afghánistán.

President of the Revolutionary Council, Head of State: Babrak Karmal.

The Basic Law defines the People's Democratic Party of Afghánistán as the country's 'leading force'. It is governed by a 36-member Central Committee which elects a Political Bureau of 9 full and 2 alternate members to decide policy in association with the 9-member Presidium of the Revolutionary Council.

The Political Bureau of the PDPA comprised (1984): Babral Kamal *(General Secretary),* Sultan Ali Kishtmand *(President of the Council of Ministers),* Maj.-Gen. Mohammad Rafie *(Vice-President of the Council of Ministers),* Dr Saleh Mohammad Zearai *(Chairman of the National Fatherland Front),* Anahita Ratebzad, Ghulam Dastagir Panjsheri, Lieut.-Col. Mohammad Aslam Watanjar *(Minister of Communications),* Mohammad Najibullah.

National flag: Three equal horizontal stripes of red, black and green, with the national arms in the canton.

The official languages are Pushtu and Dari (Persian).

Local Government: There are 29 provinces each administered by an appointed governor.

DEFENCE. Conscription is for a period of 4 years, with reserve liability continuing for 3 years beginning 2 years from the end of the initial conscription period.

Army. The Army is organized in 3 armoured and 11 infantry divisions, 1 mechanized infantry brigade, 1 artillery brigade, 2 mountain infantry and 3 commando regiments. Equipment includes 50 T-34, 300 T-54/-55 and 100 T-62 battle tanks. Strength was (1985) about 40,000, but most units of the Army, effectively under Soviet control, are well below strength, largely as a result of desertions.

Air Force. The Air Force, which is Russian-equipped, has about 210 combat aircraft and 7,000 officers and men. Nominal strength comprises 1 squadron of Su-17 attack aircraft, 3 squadrons of MiG-21 interceptors (about 40 aircraft), 6 squadrons of MiG-17s and Su-7s (about 75 aircraft), 2 bomber squadrons each with about 10 twin-jet Il-28s, a helicopter attack force of at least 40 Mi-24s, a transport wing with 12 twin-turboprop An-26s, about 10 piston-engined An-2s, 15 Mi-8 and 10 Mi-4 helicopters and 1 or 2 turboprop Il-18s, and Yak-18, Aero L-39 and MiG-15UTI trainers. The main fighter station is Bagram, with facilities for the largest jet airliners and bombers. There is a bomber station at Shindand, a training station at Mazár-i-Sharif and an air academy at Sherpur. Large numbers of 'Guideline' and 'Goa' surface-to- air missiles are operational in Afghánistán. Strong Soviet forces in Afghánistán in 1983 included Su-25 attack aircraft, and large numbers of Mi-6, Mi-8 assault helicopters and Mi-24 helicopter gunships.

Police and Militia. In addition to the Army and Air Force there are a number of paramilitary units, including a 30,000-strong gendarmerie, secret police and 'Defence of the Revolution' forces.

INTERNATIONAL RELATIONS

Membership. Afghánistán is a member of UN and of the Colombo Plan.

ECONOMY

Planning. The 1979–84 5-year plan provides for expenditure of Afs. 105,000m. Industry and mining will receive 42% and agriculture 25%.

Budget. In 1983–84 the budget envisaged expenditure of Afs. 49,941m. and revenue of Afs. 34,120m.

Currency. The monetary system is on the silver standard. The unit is the *afgháni*, weighing 10 grammes of silver 0·900 fine, which is subdivided into 100 *puls*. Rates of exchange fluctuate round Afs. 100 = £1; Afs. 50 = US$1.

Banking. The Afghán State Bank *(Da Afghánistán Bank)* is the largest of the 3 main banks and also undertakes the functions of a central bank, holding the exclusive right of note issue. Total assets of the 3 main banks were: Da Afghánistán Bánk (1981), Afs. 22,839m.; Pashtany Tejaraty Bánk (1981), Afs. 6,997m.; Bánk-i-Milli (1981), Afs. 3,087m.

Weights and Measures. Weights and measures used in Kábul are: Weights: 1 *khurd* = 0·244 lb.; 1 *pao* = 0·974 lb.; 1 *charak* = 3·896 lb.; 1 *sere* = 16 lb.; 1 *kharwár* = 1,280 lb. or 16 maunds of 80 lb. each. Long measure: 1 yard or *gaz* = 40 in. The metric system is in increasingly common use. Square measures: 1 *jaríb* = 60 × 60 kábuli yd or ½ acre; 1 *kulbá* = 40 jaríbs (area in which 2½ kharwárs of seed can be sown); 1 jaríb yd = 29 in.

Local weights and measures are in use in the provinces.

ENERGY AND NATURAL RESOURCES

Electricity. Hydro-electric plants have been constructed at Sarobi, Nangarhár, Naghlu, Mahipár, Pul-i-Khumri and Kandahár; more hydro and thermal plants are projected. Production (1981) 1,035m. kwh.

Natural gas. Production (1984) 2,767m. cu. metres.

Minerals. Mineral resources are scattered and little developed. Coal is mined at Karkar in Pul-i-Khumri, Ishpushta near Doshi, north of Kábul and Dar-i-Suf south of Mazar (total production, 1983–84, 145,300 tonnes). Natural gas is found in northern Afghánistán around Shiberghan and Sar-i-Pol; over 2,000m. cu. metres, about 90% of production, is piped to the USSR annually. Rich, but as yet unexploited, deposits of iron ore exist in the Hajigak hills about 100 miles west of Kábul; beryllium has been found in the Kunar valley and barite in Bamian province. Other deposits include gold; silver (now unexploited, in the Panjshir valley); lapis lazuli (in the Panjshir valley and Badakhshán); asbestos; mica; sulphur (near Maimana); chrome (in the Logar valley and near Herát); and copper (in the north).

Agriculture. Although the greater part of Afghánistán is more or less mountainous and a good deal of the country is too dry and rocky for successful cultivation, there are many fertile plains and valleys, which, with the assistance of irrigation from small rivers or wells, yield very satisfactory crops of fruit, vegetables and cereals. It is estimated that there are 14m. hectares of cultivable land in the country, of which only 6% of the total land was being cultivated in 1982–83 (5·34m. hectares of this being irrigated land). Before 1979 Afghánistán was virtually self-supporting in foodstuffs (including wheat in 1973), apart from sugar. The USSR now provides wheat, sugar and other foodstuffs.

The castor-oil plant, madder and the asafœtida plant abound.

Fruit forms a staple food (with bread) of many people throughout the year, both in the fresh and preserved state, and in the latter condition is exported in great quantities. The fat-tailed sheep furnish the principal meat diet, and the grease of the tail is a substitute for butter. Wool and skins provide material for warm apparel and one of the more important articles of export. Persian lambskins (Karakuls) are one of the chief exports.

Cotton production, 1983–84, was estimated at 50,000 tonnes; wheat, 2·93m.; barley, 336,000; maize, 806,000; rice, 480,000.

Livestock (1984): Cattle, 3·8m.; horses, donkeys and mules, 1,755,000; sheep, 14·3m.; goats, 2·9m.; poultry, 26·7m.

INDUSTRY AND TRADE

Industry. At Kábul there are factories for the manufacture of cotton and woollen textiles, leather, boots, marble-ware, furniture, glass, bicycles, prefabricated houses and plastics. A large machine shop has been constructed and equipped by the USSR, with a capability of manufacturing motor spares. There is a wool factory and there are several cotton-ginning plants; a small cotton factory at Jabal-us-Seráj and a larger one at Pul-i-Khumri; a cotton-seed oil extraction plant at Lashkargah; a cotton textile factory at Gulbahar, and a cotton plant at Balkh.

An ordnance factory manufactures arms and ammunition, boots and clothing, etc. for the Army. There is a beet sugar plant at Baghlan (equipped with Soviet machinery) and a fruit-canning factory in Kandahár.

Industries include cement, coalmining, cotton textiles, small vehicle assembly plants, fruit canning, carpet making, leather tanning, footwear manufacture, sugar manufacture, preparation of hides and skins, and building. Most of these are relatively small and, with the exception of hides and skins, carpets and fruits, do not meet domestic requirements.

Commerce. Trade is supervised by the Government through the Ministries of Commerce and Finance and the Da Afghánistán Bank. The Association of Afghán Chambers of Commerce works in close liaison with the Ministry of Commerce. The Government monopoly controls the import of petrol and oil, sugar, cigarettes and tobacco, motor vehicles and consignment goods from bilateral trading countries. The principal surface routes for imports to Afghánistán are *via* the Soviet rail system and the border posts at Torghundi and Hairatan; and from Karachi *via* the border post at Torkham.

In the year ended 20 March 1984 Afghán imports totalled US$941m. and exports US$681m. Main export commodities were karakul skins (US$13·5m.), raw cotton (US$12·5m.), dried fruit and nuts (US$141m.), fresh fruit (US$53·3m.) and natural gas (US$302·4m.). Main items imported were petroleum products (US$164m.), textiles (US$122·5m.).

Total trade between Afghánistán and UK (in £1,000 sterling, British Department of Trade returns):

	1980	*1981*	*1982*	*1983*	*1984*
Imports to UK	20,174	22,822	20,855	19,837	20,776
Exports and re-exports from UK	6,818	7,725	9,344	10,310	11,892

Tourism. Owing to internal political instability there has been negligible tourism since 1979.

COMMUNICATIONS

Roads. There were in 1978 over 2,812 km of asphalted road and 15,940 km of other roads. The Americans asphalted the Kandahár–Chaman and Kábul–Torkham roads. The Russians constructed a road and tunnel through the Salang pass (over 11,000 ft) which was opened in Sept. 1964 and cut 120 miles off the old road from Kábul to the north; they continued this road to Kunduz and Sherkhan Bandar (Qizil Qala) on the Oxus. In addition, the Americans in 1966 completed the road between Kábul and Kandahár and the Russians constructed a concrete road between Kandahár and Herát. In 1968 the Americans completed an asphalt road from Herát to the Iranian frontier at Islam Qala. With Soviet assistance a metalled road from Pul-i-Khumri to Mazár-i-Sharif was completed in 1969 and Mazár-i-Sharif to Shiberghán in 1971. A Soviet-built road and rail bridge across the Oxus (Amu Darya) River was opened in May 1982. In 1978 there were 34,506 cars and 22,100 commercial vehicles.

Railways. There are no railways in the country, but the Oxus bridge opened in 1982, brought Soviet Railways' track into the country. A 200 km line of 1,520 mm gauge has been authorized from Termez to Pul-i-Khumri.

Aviation. On 29 June 1956 Afghánistán signed an agreement with the USA for the development of civil aviation, including the construction of the international airport at Kandahár, comprising a loan of $5m. and a grant of $9·56m. Kábul airport has been expanded with Russian assistance. New runways at Kábul and Kandahár airports have been completed. Provincial all-weather airports have been constructed at Herát, Qunduz, Jalálábád and Mazár-i-Sharif.

Ariana Afghan Airlines (a national airline) operates regular services to New Delhi, Prague, Tashkent and Moscow.

Bakhtar Afghan Airlines (the domestic national airline) began operations on 8 Feb. 1968 and regularly serves the main internal airfields.

Shipping. There are practically no navigable rivers in Afghánistán, and timber is the only article of commerce conveyed by water, floated down the Kunar and Kábul rivers from Chitral on rafts. A port has been built at Qizil Qala on the Oxus; barge traffic is increasing on the Oxus. Three river ports on the Amu Darya have been built at Sherkhan Bandar, Tashguzar and Hairatan, linked by road to Kábul.

Post and Broadcasting. Telephones, installed in most of the large towns, numbered 31,200 in 1978. There is telegraphic communication between all the larger towns and with other parts of the world. Kábul Radio broadcasts in Pushtu, Persian, Urdu, English, French, Russian and German. The first TV colour transmissions in Kábul began in mid-1978. An agreement was signed in 1981 under which the USSR undertook to assist with the development of communications. In 1978 there were 823,000 radio receivers and in 1982 12,000 television receivers

JUSTICE, RELIGION, EDUCATION AND WELFARE

Justice. A Supreme Court was established in June 1978. If no provision exists in the Constitution or in the general laws of the State, the courts follow the Hanafi jurisprudence of Islamic law.

Religion. The predominant religion is Islam, mostly of the Sunni sect, though there is a minority of about 1m. Shiah Moslems.

Education. There are elementary schools throughout the country, but secondary schools exist only in Kábul and provincial capitals. Both elementary and secondary education are free. In 1982 there were 1·1m. pupils (35,364 teachers) in primary education and 124,000 pupils (6,170 teachers) in secondary education. There are 3 teacher-training institutions in Kábul and 11 elsewhere; UNESCO is supporting an expansion programme. Technical, art, commercial and medical schools exist for higher education. Kábul University was founded in 1932 and has 9 faculties (medicine, science, agriculture, engineering, law and political science, letters, economics, theology, pharmacology). The University of Nangarhar in Jalálábád was founded in 1963. A Polytechnic in Kábul was completed in 1968. In 1982 there were 13,115 students in higher education, 4,427 in teacher-training schools and 1,230 in technical schools.

Health. In 1982 there were 1,215 doctors and 6,875 hospital beds. Two-thirds of the doctors and half the beds were in Kábul.

DIPLOMATIC REPRESENTATIVES

Of Afghánistán in Great Britain (31 Prince's Gate, London, SW7 1QQ)
Chargé d'Affaires: Mohammad Homayon Mokammil.

Of Great Britain in Afghánistán (Karte Parwan, Kábul)
Chargé d'Affaires. C. D. S. Drace-Francis.

Of Afghánistán in the USA (2341 Wyoming Ave., NW, Washington, D.C., 20008)
Chargé d'Affaires: Haider Refq.

Of the USA in Afghánistán (Wazir Akbar Khan Mina, Kábul)
Chargé d'Affaires: Edward Hurwitz.

Of Afghánistán to the United Nations
Ambassador: Mohammad Farid Zarif.

Books of Reference

Arnold, A., *Afghanistan: The Soviet Invasion in Perspective.* Oxford and Stanford, 1981.—*Afghanistan's Two-Party Communism.* Oxford and Santa Barbara, 1983
Bradsher, H. S., *Afghanistan and the Soviet Union.* Duke Univ. Press, 1983
Chaliand, G., *Rapport sur la résistance afghane.* Paris, 1981.—*Report from Afghanistan.* New York, 1982
Gilbertson, G. W., *Pakkhto Idiom Dictionary.* 2 vols. London, 1932
Gregorian, V., *The Emergence of Modern Afghanistan.* Stamford, 1970
Griffiths, J. C., *Afghanistan: Key to a Continent.* London, 1981
Hammond, T. T., *Red Star over Afghanistan.* Boulder and London, 1984
Hanifi, M. J., *Historical and Cultural Dictionary of Afghanistan.* Metuchen, 1976
Hyman, A., *Afghanistan under Soviet Domination 1964–81.* London, 1982
Male, B., *Revolutionary Afghanistan.* London, 1982
Misra, K. P., *Afghanistan in Crisis.* London, 1981
Newell, N. P. and Newell, R. S., *The Struggle for Afghanistan.* Cornell Univ. Press, 1981
Sykes, P. M., *A History of Afghanistan.* 2 vols. New York, 1975
Wilber, D. N. (ed.), *Afghanistan.* 2nd ed. New Haven, 1962.—(ed.), *Afghanistan. A Bibliography.* 2nd ed. New Haven, 1963

ALBANIA

Capital: Tirana
Population: 2·75m. (1982)
GNP per capita: US$840 (1979)

Republika Popullore Socialiste e Shqipërisë

HISTORY. After the death of Gjergi Kastrioti Skënderbeu (Skanderbeg), Albania's national hero, in 1468 Albania passed under Turkish suzerainty until 1912. Independence was proclaimed at Vlonë on 28 Nov. 1912, and the London conference of ambassadors decided upon its frontiers and nominated as its ruler Prince William of Wied, who arrived at Durrës on 7 March 1914, but on 3 Sept. 1914 left the country, which fell into a state of anarchy. By the secret Pact of London of 26 April 1915 provision was made for the partition of Albania; but this arrangement was repudiated on 3 June 1917, when the Italian C.-in-C. in Albania proclaimed at Gjirokastër the independence of Albania. In Jan. 1925 a republic was proclaimed and on 1 Sept. 1928 a monarchy. Ahmed Beg Zogu, President since 31 Jan. 1925, reigned as King Zog till April 1939, when, on the occupation of the country by the Italians, he fled to England. After the liberation he was deposed *in absentia* on 2 Jan. 1946. During the years 1939–44 the country was overrun by Italians and Germans. The official Albanian date of the liberation is 29 Nov. 1944.

On 10 Nov. 1945 the British, US and USSR Governments recognized the Provisional Government under Gen. Enver Hoxha, on the understanding that it would hold free elections. The elections of 2 Dec. 1945 resulted in a Communist-controlled assembly, which on 11 Jan. 1946 proclaimed Albania a republic.

In 1946 Great Britain and the USA broke off relations with Albania and vetoed its admission to the United Nations. Albania was finally admitted on 15 Dec. 1955.

Because of Albania's Stalinist and pro-Chinese attitudes diplomatic relations with USSR were broken off in 1961. In 1977 Albania terminated its special relationship with China. In Dec. 1981 the Prime Minister, Mehmet Shehu committed suicide. Later Hoxha alleged that Shehu had been a foreign agent. Massive purges of Shehu's associates in the leadership took place in 1982.

AREA AND POPULATION. The area of the country is 28,748 sq. km (11,101 sq. miles). By the peace treaty Italy restored the island of Sazan (Saseno) to Albania. At the census of Jan. 1979 the population was, 2,590,600 (34% urban; density, 90 per sq. km). Population in 1982, 2·75m. The capital is Tirana (1978 population (in 1,000), 198); other large towns are Shkodër (Shkodra, Scutari) (62·5), Durrës (Durrsi, Durazzo) (61), Vlorë (Vlona, Vlonë, Vlora, Valona) (58·4), Korçë (Korça, Koritza) (50·9), Elbasan (50·7). Other towns (1975): Berat (30), Fier (28), Gjirokastër (Argyrocastro) (22), Lushnjë (21), Kavajë, 1971 (18), Qytet Stalin (formerly Kuçovë) (14).

There is a Greek minority (1984 estimate, 400,000).

Vital statistics, 1980 (per 1,000): Births, 26·5; deaths, 6·4; marriages, 8·1; divorces, 0·8; natural increase, 20·1 per thousand. Population density, 93 per sq. km. Growth rate, 1945–79, 2·5%. Life expectancy in 1979 was 69 years.

The country is administratively divided into 26 districts (*rreth*, pl. *rrethët*) (*see* map in THE STATESMAN'S YEAR-BOOK, 1962. N.B. The district of Ersekë has been renamed Kolonjë). Districts are subdivided into *lokaliteteve*.

Districts	*Area (sq. km)*	*Population (in 1,000) (1973)*	*Districts*	*Area (sq. km)*	*Population (in 1,000) (1973)*
Berat	1,026	124·3	Gramsh	695	29·4
Dibrë	1,569	106·8	Gjirokastër	1,137	53·5
Durrës	859	182·4	Kolonjë	805	19·2
Elbasan	1,466	154·7	Korçë	2,181	175·4
Fier	1,191	171·5	Krujë	607	75·6

Districts	Area (sq. km)	Population (in 1,000) (1973)	Districts	Area (sq. km)	Population (in 1,000) (1973)
Kukës	1,564	71·4	Pukë	969	32·8
Lezhë	479	40·5	Sarandë	1,097	66·5
Librazhd	1,013	48·5	Skrapar	775	30·8
Lushnjë	712	94·1	Shkodër	2,528	178·5
Mat	1,028	53·5	Tepelenë	817	37·8
Mirditë	698	29·4	Tirana	1,222	272·0
Përmet	930	31·7	Tropojë	1,043	30·5
Pogradec	725	49·3	Vlorë	1,609	133·5

The districts are for the greater part named after their capitals; exceptions: Tropojë, chief town, Bajram Curri; Mat, Burrel; Mirditë, Rrëshen; Skrapar, Çorovodë.

The Albanian language is divided into two dialects—Gheg, north of the river Shkumbi, and Tosk in the south. Many places therefore have two forms of name: Vlonë (Gheg), Vlorë (Tosk), etc., and many are known also by an Italian name, *e.g.*, Valona. Since 1945 the official language has been based on Tosk.

CLIMATE. Mediterranean-type, with rainfall mainly in winter, but thunderstorms are frequent and severe in the great heat of the plains in summer. Winters in the highlands can be severe, with much snow. Tirana. Jan. 44°F (6·8°C), July 75°F (23·9°C). Annual rainfall 54″ (1,353 mm). Shkodër. Jan. 39°F (3·9°C), July 77°F (25°C). Annual rainfall 57″ (1,425 mm).

CONSTITUTION AND GOVERNMENT. The political structure derived from the Constitution of 14 March 1946 as amended in 1950, 1955, 1960 and 1963. In Dec. 1976 a new Constitution was adopted, by which Albania became a 'Socialist People's Republic'. The supreme legislative body is the single-chamber People's Assembly of 250 deputies, which meets twice a year, and delegates its day-to-day functions to a Presidium composed of a chairman, 3 deputy chairmen, a secretary and 10 members. Election to the People's Assembly is by universal suffrage (at 18) every 4 years.

In the elections of 14 Nov. 1982 a 100% turnout of the electorate of 1,627,968 was claimed to vote for the 250 candidates on the single list of the Democratic Front. (There were 8 spoiled papers and 1 vote against).

The Government consists of a prime minister (Chairman of the Council of Ministers), 2 deputy prime ministers, 15 ministers and the chairman of the State Planning Commission. Effective rule is exercised by the Albanian Labour (*i.e.*, Communist) Party, founded 8 Nov. 1941, whose governing body is the Politburo.

In 1981 the Party had 122,600 full members and candidates (in 1979 37·5% workers, 29% farmers, 27% women).

Titular Head of State: Chairman of the Presidium of the People's Assembly: Ramiz Alia, elected Nov. 1982. In March 1984 the chief Party and Government posts were filled as follows: Full members of the Politburo:

First Secretary of the Central Committee of the Party: Enver Hoxha. Adil Çarçani *(Prime Minister)*, Ramiz Alia, Hekuran Isai *(Minister of the Interior)*, Pali Miska, Manush Myftiu,[1] Rita Marko. Muho Asllani; Hajreddin Celiku *(Ministry of Industry)*; Simon Stefani; Ms. Lenka Çuko. Candidate members: Llambi Gegprifti; Qirjako Mihali *(Minister of Finance)*. Besnik Bekteshi [1], Foto Cami Prokop Murra *(Minister of Defence)*. Not in the Politburo: *Foreign Minister:* Reis Malile. *Minister of Foreign Trade:* Shane Korbeci. *Minister of Agriculture:* Ms. Themie Thomai. *Chairman, State Planning Commission:* Harilla Papajorgji.

[1] Deputy Prime Minister.

Local Government is carried out by People's Councils at village, *lokalitet*, town and district level. Councillors are elected for 3 years.

National flag: Red, with a black double-headed eagle and a red, gold-edged 5-pointed star above it. *Mercantile flag:* red, black, red (horizontal) with a red yellow-edged star in the centre.

National anthem: Rreth Flamurit te per bashkuar (The flag that united us in the struggle).

DEFENCE.

DEFENCE. Albania withdrew from the Warsaw Pact in 1968 in protest against the invasion of Czechoslovakia. The Constitution precludes the stationing of foreign troops in Albania. Conscription is for 2 years in the Army and 3 years in the Navy, Air Force and special forces.

Army. The Army consists of 1 tank brigade, 5 infantry brigades and 4 artillery regiments. Equipment includes 70 T-34, 15 T-54 and 15 T-59 main battle tanks. Strength is 30,000 (including 20,000 conscripts) and reserves number 150,000. There are also paramilitary internal security forces (5,000 men) and frontier guards (7,500).

Navy. The Navy consists of 3 submarines, 2 fleet minesweepers, 2 patrol vessels, 4 inshore minesweepers, 32 torpedo boats, 6 fast gunboats, 9 minesweeping boats, 1 degaussing ship, 4 oilers, 2 diving tenders, 2 torpedo recovery craft, 4 tugs and 12 small auxiliaries and service tenders. Navy personnel in 1985 exceeded 3,000 officers and ratings, including 300 coastal frontier guards. Service for ratings is 3 years. There are naval bases at Durrës and Vlorë.

Air Force. The Air Force, controlled by the Army, has about 8,000 officers and men, and in 1985 operates 80 combat aircraft received before relations with China were broken. The force included 20 Chinese-built F-7s and F-6s, some Il-28 twin-jet light bombers and 2 ground attack squadrons of F2s and F-2s. Transport and training types include 3 Il-14s, 10 An-2s, Mi-4 helicopters, Yak-18s and MiG-15UTIs.

INTERNATIONAL RELATIONS

Membership. Albania is a member of UN.

ECONOMY

Planning. For the first five 5-year plans *see* THE STATESMAN'S YEAR-BOOK, 1982–83. The sixth 5-year plan ran from 1976 to 1980. Annual average increases: national income, 5%; industrial production, 6·8%; agricultural production, 21·4%. The seventh 5-year plan covers 1981–85. Target increases: agricultural production, 32%, industrial, 34%. Emphasis is laid on industrial expansion, especially in the oil, mining and chemical industries. It is now stated that economic policy is founded on 'the revolutionary principle of self-reliance'.

Budget. Budget figures for 1983: Revenue, 8,800m. leks (8,200m. leks from enterprises and agricultural co-operatives); expenditure, 8,750m. leks (industry, 5,300m. leks; social, 2,300m. leks; defence, 910m. leks).

Currency. The monetary unit is the *lek* of 100 *qintars*. It replaced the gold franc *(franc ar)* in July 1947. In Aug. 1965 a new *lek* was introduced: 10 old *leks* = 1 new *lek*. There are 5, 10, 20 and 50 *qintar* coins and a 1 *lek* coin; notes are for 1, 3, 5, 10, 25, 50 and 100 *leks*. Exchange rates, Feb. 1985: US$1 = 9·33 *leks*; £1 = 9·82.

Banking. The Albanian State Bank was founded in 1925 with Italian aid. In 1970 savings deposits amounted to 572m. leks. In 1970 the Agricultural Bank was set up as a credit institution for agricultural co-operatives.

Weights and Measures. The metric system is in force.

ENERGY AND NATURAL RESOURCES

Electricity. Albania is rich in hydro-electric potential. Electric power production in 1973 was 1,603m. kwh., of which 1,127m. was hydro-electric. Total electrification was claimed in 1970.

Oil. The oil industry is being rapidly expanded. Output in 1973: Crude, 2,107,000 tonnes; refined, 1,596,000 tonnes. Refining capacity in 1970 was over 1 m. tonnes. Oil is produced chiefly at Qytet Stalin which a pipeline connects to the port of Vlorë. Natural gas is extracted.

Minerals. The mineral wealth of Albania is considerable but is only recently being developed. In 1971 there were 8 coal, 7 chromium (1977 output 9,000 tonnes) and 6 copper mines. Ferro-nickel ores are mined and output is increasing. In 1969 extensive coal deposits were discovered at Valias, near Tirana. There is no bituminous coal. Salt is extracted near Vlorë and bitumen mined at Selenicë. Production in tonnes (1973): Chrome ore, 611,000; copper ore, 435,000; ferro-nickel ore, 384,000; brown coal, 811,000; phosphate, 110,000; nitrogenous fertilizer, 106,000; bitumen (1964), 242,000; cement (1965), 133,600.

Agriculture. The country for the greater part is rugged, wild and mountainous, the exceptions being along the Adriatic littoral and the Korçë (Koritza) Basin, which are fertile. In 1973 a programme of land reclamation and anti-erosion measures was instituted. In 1970 arable land comprised 599,000 hectares and pasture 623,000 hectares. In 1980 366,000 hectares were irrigated.

Land is held by the State (largely forests and non-agricultural), state farms (50 in 1982 averaging 3,000 hectares of arable land) and co-operatives (500 in 1983 averaging 1,100 hectares). Co-operatives are divided into 'advanced' and 'ordinary'. There is a pension scheme for collective farmers. In 1982 there were 31 machine and tractor stations. Tractors in 1980 numbered 17,300 (in 15-h.p. units).

The yield of the main crops in 1981 was (in 1,000 tonnes): Wheat, 510; sugar-beet, 270; maize, 250; potatoes, 140; fruit, 132; grapes, 62; oats, 30; sorghum, 30; cotton, 26; barley, 25; sunflower seeds, 25; wine, 23; rice, 17; beans, 16; tobacco, 15.

Livestock, 1983: Cattle, 600,000; sheep, 1·2m.; goats, 700,000; pigs, 200,000; horses and mules, 65,000; poultry, 5m.

Forestry. 47% of the territory of Albania is forest land, of which 38% is oak forest, 26% elm and 18% pine and birch. Timber reserves reach 44·5m. cu. metres. In 1967 forests covered 1,242,100 hectares; 6,784 hectares were afforested, 10,000 hectares improved in 1967.

Fisheries. The catch in 1964 was 3,600 tonnes.

INDUSTRY AND TRADE

Industry. All industry is nationalized down to the smallest workshop. Output is small, and the principal industries are agricultural product processing, textiles, oil products and cement. Chemical and engineering industries are being built up. The metallurgical combine at Elbasan is being extended.

Labour. In 1973, 462,900 persons worked in the socialist sector of the national economy, of whom 34·7% were employed in industry. In 1976, 46% of wage-earners were women.

Minimum wages may not fall below one-third of maximum. A new labour code was introduced in 1980 normalizing an 8-hour day and 6-day week and 12 days yearly paid holiday. Retirement age is 60 for men and 55 for women.

Commerce. There are 1981–85 trade agreements with Bulgaria, Czechoslovakia, North Korea, Poland, Vietnam and Yugoslavia; and Albania also trades with Italy, France, Czechoslovakia and India. The establishment of joint companies with, and the acceptance of credits from, capitalist firms is forbidden by the constitution.

Exports which in 1983 were (estimate) US$500m. included crude oil, bitumen, chrome, nickel, copper, tobacco, fruit and vegetables.

Total trade between Albania and UK (British Department of Trade returns, in £1,000 sterling):

	1980	*1981*	*1982*	*1983*	*1984*
Imports to UK	107	110	45	60	1,097
Exports and re-exports from UK	1,478	2,445	4,453	240	4,481

COMMUNICATIONS

Roads. There were, in 1960, 3,100 km of roads suitable for motor traffic. The mountain districts of the north are still mostly inaccessible for wheeled vehicles, and communications are still by means of pack ponies or donkeys. Registered motor vehicles in 1960: Cars, 1,900; lorries and buses, 3,400. Road traffic carried 8·6m. passengers in 1970; goods carried, 34m. tonnes.

Railways. Total length, in 1983 was 253 km. They comprise the lines Durrës–Tirana, Durrës–Kavajë–Pegin–Elbasan, Vlorë–Memaliaj, Vlorë–Milot, Perrenjas–Pogradec, Durrës–Tirana-Shkodër. In 1974 a railway was opened from Elbasan to the iron mines at Pishkash. In 1981 the Laç–Shkodër section of the Tirana–Shkodër line opened. In April 1982 Albania and Yugoslavia signed an agreement for the construction of a line from Shkodër to Titograd and an extension of the main line from Fiër to Vlorë is also under construction. Goods carried in 1970 amounted to 2,324,000 tonnes; passengers (1971), 6·4m.

Aviation. There are regular scheduled flights from Tirana (Rinas Airport) to Belgrade, Bucharest, Budapest and East Berlin. Olympic Airways operate a weekly flight from Athens to Tirana.

Shipping. The ports are Shëngjin, Durrës, Vlorë and Sarandë. 567,000 tonnes of freight were carried in 1970. A ferry service from Trieste to Durrës opened in Nov. 1983.

Post and Broadcasting. Number of post and telegraph offices (1970), 292; telephones (1963), 10,150. There are 17 broadcasting stations, including Tirana and Korçë. Radio Tirana operates a foreign service in 18 languages. Radio receiving sets (1978), 200,000; television sets, 5,000. Regular television broadcasting began in 1971.

Cinemas and Theatres. In 1975 there were 410 cinemas (including mobile) and in 1973 27 theatres with an attendance of 1·6m. 14 full-length films were produced in 1980.

Newspapers. In 1978 there were 30 newspapers with an annual circulation of 57m. The Party paper is *Zëri i Popullit* (Voice of the People) (daily circulation, 105,000).

JUSTICE, RELIGION, EDUCATION AND WELFARE

Justice is administered by People's Courts. Minor crimes are tried by tribunals. Judges of the Supreme Court are elected by the People's Assembly for 4-year terms. The Office of the Procurator-General oversees the administration of justice. In 1983 an Investigator's Office was set up, separate from the Ministry of the Interior and answerable to the People's Assembly.

Religion. Albania is constitutionally an atheist state. In 1967 the Government closed all mosques and churches. For details of the situation before 1967 *see* THE STATESMAN'S YEAR-BOOK, 1969–70. The population had been mainly Moslem.

Education. Primary education is free and compulsory in 8-year schools from 7 to 15 years. Secondary education is available in 12-year (general), technical-professional or lower vocational schools. Periods of productive work and military service are intermingled with full-time education. There were, in 1979–80, 2,541 kindergartens with 83,697 pupils and 3,920 teachers and in 1973–74 1,470 primary schools with 569,600 pupils and 22,686 teachers; 39 secondary schools with 32,900 pupils; 116 technical–professional schools with 69,700 pupils (the last two categories had 3,990 teachers taken together); and (in 1969–70) 36 institutes of higher education with 36,525 students and 941 teachers, including a university in Tirana (founded 1957), a polytechnic, an agricultural college, a medical school, 5 teachers' training colleges and an institute of science. In 1969–70 there were 382 teachers and 12,783 full-time students at Tirana University. An Albanian Academy was founded in 1973.

Health. Medical services are free, though medicines are charged for. In 1978 there were 763 hospitals and 3,028 outpatient clinics. In 1982 there were 4,476 doctors and dentists, and 70 hospital beds per 1,000 inhabitants. In 1982 there were 730 maternity hospitals or hospital sections.

DIPLOMATIC REPRESENTATIVE

Of Albania to the United Nations
Ambassador: Justin Papajorgji.

Books of Reference

Vjetari Statistikor (Statistical Yearbook). Tirana, irregular, 1959–72
35 vjet Shqipëri socialiste (statistical handbook). Tirana, 1979
History of the Labour Party of Albania 1966–1980. Tirana, 1981
Portrait of Albania. Tirana, 1982
Bertolino, J., *Albanie: la Citadelle de Staline.* Paris, 1979
Duro, I., and Hysa, R., *Albanian-English Dictionary.* Tirana, 1981
Hetzer, A., and Roman, V. S. *Albania: A Bibliographic Research Survey.* Munich, 1983
Hoxha, E., *Réflexions sur la Chine.* Paris, 1979.—*Speeches, Conversations and Articles, 1969–1970.* Tirana, 1980.—*The Khrushchevites: Memoirs.* Tirana, 1980.—*The Anglo-American Threat to Albania.* Tirana, 1982
Logoreci, A., *The Albanians: Europe's Forgotten Survivors.* London, 1977
Marmullaku, R., *Albania and the Albanians.* London, 1975
Martin, N., *La Forteresse Albanaise: un Communisme National.* Paris, 1979
Pollo, S. and Arben, P., *The History of Albania.* London, 1981
Prifti, P. R., *Socialist Albania since 1944.* Cambridge, Mass., 1978
Russ, W., *Der Entwicklungsweg Albaniens.* Meisenheim-am-Glan, 1979
Schnytzer, A., *Stalinist Economic Strategy in Practice: The Case of Albania.* OUP, 1982
Tönnes, B., *Sonderfall Albanien: Enver Hoxhas 'Eigener Weg und die Historischen Ursprünge seiner Ideologie.* Munich, 1980

ALGERIA

Capital: Algiers
Population: 21·46m. (1984)
GNP per capita: US$2,140 (1981)

al-Jumhuriya al-Jazairiya ad-Dimuqratiya ash-Shabiya

HISTORY. On 1 Nov. 1954 the National Liberation Front (FLN) went over to open warfare against the French administration and armed forces. For details of history 1958–62 *see* p. 76 THE STATESMAN'S YEAR-BOOK, 1982–83. A cease-fire agreement was reached on 18 March 1962, and Gen. de Gaulle declared Algeria independent on 3 July 1962; the Republic was declared on 25 Sept. 1962.

The Government was overthrown by a junta of army officers which, on 19 June 1965, established a Revolutionary Council under Col. Houari Boumédienne.

AREA AND POPULATION. Algeria is bounded west by Morocco and Western Sahara, south-west by Mauritania and Mali, south-east by Niger, east by Libya and Tunisia, and north by the Mediterranean Sea. It has an area of 2,381,741 sq. km (919,595 sq. miles). Population (census 1977) 17,422,000; estimate (1984) 21,463,500.

The 31 departments were as follows in 1980; 17 additional departments were created in 1983:

Departments	*Area (sq. km)*	*Population (1980)*	*Departments*	*Area (sq. km)*	*Population (1980)*
Adrar	422,498	146,815	Médéa	8,704	511,070
al-Jazair (Algiers)	786	2,159,573	Mostaganem	7,024	791,688
Annaba (Bône)	3,489	544,519	M'Sila	19,825	477,614
Batna	14,882	633,723	Ouahran (Oran)	1,820	795,405
Béchar	306,000	156,107	Ouargla	559,234	226,728
Béjaia (Bougie)	3,444	590,979	Oum el Bouaghi	8,123	429,296
Biskra	109,728	585,403	Saida	106,177	469,348
al-Boulaida (Blida)	3,704	962,664	Sétif	10,350	1,061,161
Bouira	4,517	401,419	Sidi-Bel-Abbès	11,648	546,377
Qacentina (Constantine)	3,562	929,213	Skikda	4,748	520,359
Djelfa	22,905	722,927	Tamanrasset	556,000	60,702
al-Asnam (Orléansville)	8,677	384,694	Tébessa	16,575	403,278
Guelma	8,624	589,120	Tiaret	23,456	676,467
Jijel	3,704	529,651	Tizi-Ouzou	3,756	931,071
Laghouat	112,052	354,959	Tlemcen	9,284	618,856
Mascara	5,846	455,314			

The chief towns (estimates, 1974) are as follows: Algiers, 1,503,720; Oran, 485,139; Constantine, 350,183; Annaba, 313,174; Tizi-Ouzou, 223,702; Blida, 158,947; Sétif, 157,065; Sidi-Bel-Abbès, 151,148; Skikda, 127,968; Batna, 115,138; Tlemcen, 115,054; Al Asnam, 114,327; Bejaia, 103,996; Médéa, 102,336; Mostaganem, 101,780.

Arabic is spoken by 80·4% of the population and Berber by 18·7%.

CLIMATE. Coastal areas have a warm temperate climate, with most rain in winter, which is mild, while summers are hot and dry. Inland, conditions become more arid beyond the Atlas Mountains. Algiers. Jan. 54°F (12·2°C), July 76°F (24·4°C). Annual rainfall 30″ (762 mm). Biskra. Jan. 52°F (11·1°C), July 93°F (33·9°C). Annual rainfall 6″ (158 mm). Oran. Jan. 54°F (12·2°C), July 76°F (24·4°C). Annual rainfall 15″ (376 mm).

CONSTITUTION AND GOVERNMENT. A new Constitution was

approved by referendum in Nov. 1976. It provides for a single Party, the *Front de Libération Nationale*, working in parallel with state organs.

The President of the Republic is Head of State, Head of the Armed Forces, and Head of Government. He is nominated by the FLN Congress and elected by universal suffrage for 5-year terms (renewable).

Former Presidents of the Republic:

Ferhat Abbas, 25 Sept. 1962–15 Sept. 1963.
Ahmed Ben Bella, 15 Sept. 1963–19 June 1965 (deposed).
Col. Houari Boumediénne, 19 June 1965–27 Dec. 1978 (died).
Rabah Bitat (interim), 27 Dec. 1978–9 Feb. 1979.

President of the Republic, General Secretary of the FLN, Minister of Defence: Bendjedid Chadli (sworn in 9 Feb. 1979, re-elected on 12 Jan. 1984).

The President appoints a Prime Minister and other Ministers, and presides over meetings of the Council of Ministers.

The Council of Ministers, as in March 1984, consisted of:

Prime Minister: Abdelhamid Brahimi.

Foreign Affairs: Ahmed Taleb Ibrahimi. *Interior:* M'hamed Yala. *Finance:* Boualem Benhamouda. *Justice:* Boualem Baki. *Agriculture and Fisheries:* Abdellah Khalef. *Information:* Bachir Rouis. *Posts and Telecommunications:* Boualem Bessaieh. *Transport:* Salah Goudjil. *Energy, Chemical and Petrochemical Industries:* Belkacem Nabi. *Heavy Industry:* Salim Saadi. *Light Industry:* Zitouni Messaoudi. *Hydraulics, Environment and Forests:* Mohamed Rouighi. *Trade:* Abdelaziz Khelaf. *Education:* Mohamed Cherif Kherroubi. *Higher Education:* Rafik Abdelhak Brerhi. *Further Education and Labour:* Mohamed Nabi. *Youth and Sports:* Kamal Bouchama. *Public Health:* Djamal Eddine Houhou. *Social Security:* Z'hor Hounissi. *Veterans:* Djelloul Dakhti Nemiche. *Public Works:* Ahmed Benfreha. *Town Planning and Housing:* Abderrahmane Belayat. *Religious Affairs:* Abderrahmane Chibane. *Culture and Tourism:* Abdelmadjid Chibane.

Legislative power is held by the National People's Assembly, whose 261 members are elected for a 5-year term by universal suffrage from the single list of the FLN who nominate 3 candidates for each single-member seat.

National flag: Vertically green and white, a red crescent and star over all in centre.

The official language is Arabic, French being the principal foreign language.

DEFENCE. Conscription is for a period of 6 months at the age of 19.

Army. The Army had a strength of 110,000 in 1985, organized in 2 armoured, 5 mechanized and 6 motorized brigades; 28 infantry, 2 paratroop, 5 artillery, 11 air defence and 4 engineer battalions; and 12 companies of desert troops. Equipment includes 300 T-54/-55, 300 T-62 and 100 T-72 main battle tanks.

Navy. The Navy, largely supplied from the USSR, consists of 2 modern frigates, 4 new missile-armed corvettes, 2 fleet minesweepers, 6 patrol vessels, 18 fast missile boats, 4 torpedo boats, 2 fast gunboats, 2 logistic landing ships, 1 landing vessel, 1 diving tender, 2 training craft, 1 torpedo recovery vessel, 1 degaussing ship, 1 survey ship, 6 fishery protection craft and 18 coastguard cutters (16 Italian-built). Naval personnel in 1985 totalled 300 officers and cadets and 3,500 ratings.

There are naval bases at Algiers, Annaba and Mers el Kebir.

Air Force. Five MiG-15 jet-fighters were delivered in 1962 as the nucleus of an Algerian Air Force. Since then many more aircraft of Soviet design have followed, and the Air Force now has about 320 combat aircraft and 10,000 personnel. Training and technical assistance have been given by Egypt and the Soviet Union. There are 3 squadrons of MiG-21s, 3 squadrons of MiG-23 variable-geometry interceptors and fighter-bombers, 2 squadrons of MiG-17 fighter-bombers, 2 squadrons of Su-7 and Su-20 variable-geometry attack aircraft, 1 squadron of Il-28 twin-jet bombers, 2 squadrons with MiG-25 fighter and reconnaissance aircraft, more than

40 Mi-24 assault helicopters and gunships, 14 C-130H Hercules and 8 An-12 transports, an Il-18 and a variety of smaller transports, a wing of 4 Mi-6, 12 Mi-8, about 30 Mi-4, 5 Puma and 6 Hughes 269 helicopters, and training units equipped with CM.170 Magister armed jet counter-insurgency/trainers (20), 3 Beech Queen Air twin-engine/instrument trainers, MiG-15s and -15UTIs, and two-seat versions of operational types. Surface-to-air missile units have Soviet-built 'Guidelines', 'Goas', 'Gainfuls' and 'Gaskins'.

INTERNATIONAL RELATIONS

Membership. Algeria is a member of UN, OAU, the Arab League, OAPEC, OPEC and the Maghreb Organization.

ECONOMY

Planning. The third development plan (1980–84) gave priority to education, housing, water supply and agriculture.

Currency. The Algerian currency is the *dinar* (DA). There are in circulation banknotes of DA 5, 10, 50 and 100 and coins of 1, 2, 5, 20 and 50 centimes and DA 1, 5 and 10. In Feb. 1985, £1 = 5·54 DA; US$1 = 5·27 DA.

Budget. The budget (including extraordinary budget) was as follows in calendar years (in DA 1m.):

	1977	*1978*	*1979*	*1980*	*1981*
Revenue	33,479	36,782	46,429	59,344	68,305
Expenditure	25,472	29,946	33,514	43,214	67,788

Banking. The Banque Centrale d'Algérie is the government emission bank. Other banks operating in Algeria are Banque National d'Algérie, Crédit Populaire d'Algérie, Banque Extérieure d'Algérie, Caisse Algérienne de Développement, Banque Algérienne de Développement, Banque de l'Agriculture et du Développement.

Weights and Measures. The metric system is in use.

ENERGY AND NATURAL RESOURCES

Electricity. Production of energy in 1981 totalled 7·17m. kwh.

Oil. Two large oilfields went into production in 1957 around Edjélé and Hassi Messaoud and in 1959 at El Gassi. In 1960 about 200 wells were productive. Natural gas was discovered at Djebel Berga in 1954 and at Hassi-R'Mel in 1956. Oil pipelines from Edjélé to Skirra (Tunisia) and from Hassi Messaoud to Béjaia, and a gas pipeline from Hassi Messaoud *via* Hassi-R'Mel to Mostaganem–Oran–Algiers, have been completed. Oil production in 1982, 36·4m. tonnes. Production of natural gas in 1981 was 19,347m. cu. metres.

Minerals. Algeria possesses deposits of iron, zinc, lead, mercury, copper and antimony. Kaolin, marble and onyx, salt and coal are also found. Mineral output in 1980 (1,000 tonnes): Ferrous metals, 3,500; zinc, 7·6; copper, 0·8; lead, 2·7; phosphates, 1,025.

Agriculture. The greater part of Algeria is of limited value for agricultural purposes. In the northern portion the mountains are generally better adapted to grazing and forestry than agriculture, and a large portion of the native population is quite poor. In spite of the many excellent roads built by the Government, a considerable area of the mountainous region is without adequate means of communication and is accessible only with difficulty. There were an estimated 7·5m. hectares of agricultural land in 1978–79, of which 6·8m. hectares were arable; 200,000 hectares under vine and 31·7m. hectares pastures and brushlands.

The chief crops in 1982 were (in 1,000 tonnes): Wheat, 1,200; barley, 650; dates, 207; potatoes, 610; oranges, 250; mandarins and tangerines, 130; watermelons, 180; wine, 230; tomatoes, 140; olives, 120; onions, 120; oats, 80.

Livestock, 1983: 180,000 horses, 757,000 mules and asses, 1·4m. cattle, 13·75m. sheep, 2·78m. goats and 154,000 camels.

Forestry. The greater part of the state forests are mere brushwood, but there are very large areas covered with cork-oak trees, Aleppo pine, evergreen oak and cedar. The dwarf-palm is grown on the plains, alfa on the table-land. Timber is cut for firewood, also for industrial purposes, for railway sleepers, telegraph poles, etc., and for bark for tanning. Considerable portions of the forest area are also leased for tillage, or for pasturage for cattle and sheep.

Fisheries. There are extensive fisheries for sardines, anchovies, sprats, tunny fish, etc., and also shellfish. In 1977, 692 boats were employed in fishing. Fish taken in 1980 amounted to 33,615 tonnes, value DA 311m.

INDUSTRY AND TRADE

Industry. In 1981, 10·5m. tonnes of petroleum products were refined. Production of cement (1981) 4·45m. tonnes, crude steel (1980) 345,000 tonnes.

Labour. In 1980 the economically active population was estimated at 3,165,000 of whom 975,000 were in the agricultural sector, 374,000 in industry (plus 40,000 in the oil industry) and 461,000 in building and public works.

Trade Unions. The *Union Générale des Travailleurs Algériens* had in 1982 about 1m. members in 8 affiliated groups, while the *Union Nationale des Paysans Algériens* had 700,000.

Commerce. The foreign trade of Algeria was as follows (in DA 1m.):

	1978	*1979*	*1980*	*1981*
Imports	34,439	32,378	41,545	47,500
Exports	25,037	36,505	52,418	42,138

In 1980 imports came chiefly from France (23%), Federal Republic of Germany (14%), Italy (12%), USA (7%). Exports went mainly to USA (48%), Federal Republic of Germany (12%), France (13%).

Crude oil amounted to 78% and petroleum products 14%, of exports.

Total trade between Algeria and UK (British Department of Trade returns, in £1,000 sterling):

	1980	*1981*	*1982*	*1983*	*1984*
Imports to UK	114,054	159,470	176,304	157,645	274,155
Exports and re-exports from UK	142,552	172,964	199,234	233,425	272,438

Tourism. In 1981, 321,444 tourists visited Algeria.

COMMUNICATIONS

Roads. There were in 1984, 24,000 km of national highway. Motor vehicles in 1980 included 472,483 passenger cars and 283,966 commercial vehicles.

Railways. In 1983 there were 3,890 km of which 2,632 km is of standard gauge (298 km electrified) and 1,258 km of 1,055mm gauge railway open for traffic. In 1981 the railways carried 2,726m. tonne-km of freight and 2,156m. passenger-km.

Aviation. There are 5 international airports as well as another 65 airfields controlled by government and 135 owned by petroleum companies. Air Algeria serves the main Algerian cities, and an international network. Algeria is also served by Swissair, Royal Air Maroc and United Arab Airline. In 1980 the airports handled 2·84m. passengers and 22,479 tonnes of freight.

Shipping. In 1980, 63·2m. tonnes of goods were handled at Algerian ports.

A state shipping line, Compagnie Nationale Algérienne de Navigation, was formed in Jan. 1964.

Post and Broadcasting. There were, in 1980, 1,534 post offices; number of telephones (1982), 606,869, of which 186,312 were in Algiers and 48,428 in Oran. In 1982 *Radiodiffusion Télévision Algérienne* broadcast in Arabic, French and

Kabyle (Berber) from 16 radio stations to 3·24m. radio receivers and from 16 television stations to about 530,000 receivers.

Newspapers (1984). There were 4 daily newspapers, with a combined circulation of 480,000.

JUSTICE, RELIGION, EDUCATION AND WELFARE

Justice. There are appeal courts at Algiers, Constantine and Oran; and in the *arrondissements* are 17 courts of first instance. There are also commercial courts and justices of the peace with extensive powers. Criminal justice is organized as in France. The Supreme Court is at the same time Council of State and High Court of Appeal.

Religion. The overwhelming part of the population are Moslems. There are about 150,000 Christians, mainly Roman Catholic.

Education. In 1982 there were 9,263 state primary schools with 88,481 teachers and 4·6m. pupils; 1,128 secondary schools with 38,845 teachers and 1,029,884 pupils; and 71 technical and teacher-training colleges with 1,168 teachers and 12,903 students in technical education and 1,124 teachers and 13,315 students in teacher-training.

In 1981 there were 72,200 students in higher education including universities at Algiers (with 17,086 students), Oran (9,000), Constantine (8,340), Annaba (6,126), Sétif (5,800) and Boumedes. There are also Universities of Science and Technology at Algiers (11,500) and Oran (5,800) and university centres at Tlemcen, Tizi-Ouzou, Batna, Tiaret, Constantine, Mostaganem, Sidi-Bel-Abbès and Boulaida.

Health. There were in 1980, 182 general and specialized hospitals with together 45,160 beds; there were 6,081 doctors, 1,183 dentists, 778 pharmacists. There were also 1,422 dispensaries and consulting rooms, 747 health centres and 175 specializing centres for tuberculosis, venereal disease and trachoma.

DIPLOMATIC REPRESENTATIVES

Of Algeria in Great Britain (54 Holland Park, London, W11 3RS)
Ambassador: Ahmed Laïdi.

Of Great Britain in Algeria (Résidence Cassiopée, 7 Chemin des Glycines, Algiers)
Ambassador: A. G. Munro, CMG.

Of Algeria in the USA (2118 Kalorama Rd., NW, Washington, D.C., 20008)
Ambassador: Layachi Yaker.

Of the USA in Algeria (4 Chemin Cheikh Bachir Brahimi, Algiers)
Ambassador: Michael H. Newlin.

Of Algeria to the United Nations
Ambassador: Hocine Djoudi.

Books of Reference

Statistical Information: The Service de Statisque Générale (12, rue Bab-Azoun, Alger) publishes the annual *Statistique Générale de l'Algérie, Documents statistiques sur le commerce de l'Algérie* (from 1902). *Tableaux de l'économie algérienne* (1960).

Horne, A., *A Savage War of Peace: Algeria 1954–1962.* London, 1977
Ministère de l'Information et de la Culture, *La Révolution Algérienne: Réalités et Perspectives,* Algiers, 1972.—*Dix années de réalisations 19 juin 1965–19 juin 1975.* Algiers, 1976.—*Statistiques 1967–78.* Algiers, 1980
Lawless, R. I., *Algeria.* [Bibliography] Oxford and Santa Barbara, 1981
Ottaway, D., *Algeria: The Politics of a Socialist Revolution.* Berkeley, 1970
Quandt, W. B., *Revolution and Political Leadership: Algeria, 1954–68.* Cambridge, Mass., 1970

ANDORRA

Capital: Andorre-la-Vieille
Population: 41,627 (1984)

Principat d'Andorra

HISTORY AND CONSTITUTION. The political status of Andorra was regulated by the *Paréage* of 1278 which placed Andorra under the joint suzerainty of the Comte de Foix and of the Bishop of Urgel. The rights vested in the house of Foix passed by marriage to that of Bearn and, on the accession of Henri IV, to the French crown. The sovereignty is exercised jointly by the President of the French Republic and the Bishop of Urgel.

The co-princes are represented in Andorra by the *'Viguier français'* and the *'Viguier Episcopal'*. Each co-prince has set up a Permanent Delegation for Andorran affairs; the Prefect of the Eastern Pyrenees is the French Permanent Delegate.

The valleys pay every second year a due of 960 francs to France and 460 pesetas to the bishop.

A 'General Council of the Valleys' submits motions and proposals to the Permanent Delegations. Its 28 members are elected for 4 years; half of the council is renewed every 2 years.

The council nominates a First Syndic *(Syndic Procureur Général)* and a Second Syndic from outside its members.

In Jan. 1982 an Executive Council was appointed, following elections held in Dec. 1981, and legislative and executive powers were separated.

First Syndic: Francesc Cerqueda-Pascuet.

Head of Government and Finance: Josef Pintat Solans (from 21 May 1984).

Education and Culture: Roc Rossell Dolcet. *Tourism and Sports:* Joan Samarra Vila. *Public Works:* Pere Vila Font. *Agriculture, Commerce and Industry:* Francesc Forne Molne.

National flag: Three vertical strips of blue, yellow, red, with the arms of Andorra in the centre.

AREA AND POPULATION. The co-principality of Andorra is situated in the eastern Pyrenees on the French–Spanish border. The country consists of gorges, narrow valleys and defiles, surrounded by high mountain peaks varying between 1,880 and 3,000 metres. Its maximum length is 30 km and its width 20 km; it has an area of 465 sq. km (190 sq. miles) and a population of (1984) 41,627, scattered in 7 villages.

Catalan is the official and spoken language.

CLIMATE. Les Escaldes. Jan. 36°F (2·3°C), July 67°F (19·3°C). Annual rainfall 32" (808 mm).

ECONOMY

Budget. The 1979 budget balanced at 3,209m. pesetas.

Currency. French and Spanish currency are both in use.

Trade. Total trade between Andorra and UK (British Department of Trade returns, in £1,000 sterling):

	1982	*1983*	*1984*
Imports to UK	220	380	19
Exports and re-exports from UK	7,635	6,533	9,228

Tourism. Tourism is the main industry, and over 6m. people visited Andorra in 1982.

COMMUNICATIONS

Roads. A good road connects the Spanish and French frontiers by way of Sant Julià, Andorre-la-Vieille, les Escaldes, Encamp, Canillo and Soldeu: it crosses the Col d'Envalira (2,400 metres). Another road connects Andorre-la-Vieille with La Massana and Ordino. Motor vehicles (1983) 24,789.

Aviation. The nearest airports are at Seo de Urgel, Barcelona and Perpignan.

Post and Broadcasting. Number of telephones (1982) 17,719. Number of receivers (1977), radio, 7,000; TV, 3,000.

JUSTICE, RELIGION AND EDUCATION

Justice. Judicial power is exercised in civil matters in the first instance, according to the plaintiff's choice, by either the *Bayle Français* or the *Bayle Episcopal*, who are nominated by the respective co-princes. The judge of appeal is nominated alternately for 5 years by each co-prince; the third instance *(Tercera Sala)* is either the supreme court of Andorra at Perpignan or the supreme court of the Bishop at Urgel.

Criminal justice is administered by the *Corts* consisting of the 2 Viguiers, the judge of appeal, 2 *rahonadors* elected by the general council of the valleys, a general attorney and an attorney nominated for 5 years alternatively by each of the co-princes. The accused may be assisted by a barrister.

Religion. The prevailing religious denomination is Roman Catholic.

Education. In 1983–84 there were 1,798 pupils at infant schools, 3,452 at primary schools, 2,856 at secondary schools, 198 at technical schools and 46 at special schools.

Books of Reference

Brutails, *La Coutume d'Andorre.* Paris, 1904
Corts Peyret, J., *Geografia e Historia de Andorra.* Barcelona, 1945
Llobet, S., *El medio y la vida en Andorra.* Barcelona, 1947
Riberaygua-Argelich, B., *Les Valls d'Andorra.* Barcelona, 1946
Vidally Guitart, J. M., *Institutiones politicas y sociales de Andorra.* Madrid, 1949

ANGOLA

República Popular de Angola

Capital: Luanda
Population: 7·11m. (1983)
GNP per capita: US$470 (1980)

HISTORY. The first Europeans to arrive in Angola were the Portuguese in 1482, and the first settlers arrived there in 1491. Luanda was founded in 1575. Apart from a brief period of Dutch occupation from 1641 to 1648, Angola remained a Portuguese colony until 11 June 1951, when it became an Overseas Province of Portugal. On 11 Nov. 1975 Angola became fully independent as the People's Republic of Angola.

AREA AND POPULATION. Angola is bounded by Congo on the north, Zaïre on the north and north-east, Zambia on the east, South West Africa/Namibia on the south and the Atlantic ocean on the west. The area is 1,246,700 sq. km (481,351 sq. miles) including the 7,270 sq. km province of Cabinda, an enclave of territory separated by 30 km of Zaïre. The population at census, 1970, was 5,646,166, of whom 14% urban. Estimate (1983) 7,108,000, of whom 38% speak Umbundu, 27% Kimbundu, 13% Lunda and 11% Kikongo. Portuguese remains the official language. There were (1980) about 38,000 Cubans and 30,000 Europeans (mostly Portuguese) in Angola. Refugees living in Angola totalled 99,000 (1984) mainly Namibians.

The most important towns (with 1970 populations) are Luanda, the capital (480,613, 1982, 700,000), Huambo (61,885), Lobito (59,258), Benguela (40,996), Lubango (31,674) and Malange (31,559).

CLIMATE. The climate is tropical, with low rainfall in the west but increasing inland. Temperatures are constant over the year and most rain falls in March and April. Luanda. Jan. 78°F (25·6°C), July 69°F (20·6°C). Annual rainfall 13″ (323 mm). Lobito. Jan. 77°F (25°C), July 68°F (20°C). Annual rainfall 14″ (353 mm).

CONSTITUTION AND GOVERNMENT. Under the Constitution adopted at independence, the sole legal party is the *Movimento Popular de Libertação de Angola – Partido do Trabalho.* The supreme organ of state is the unicameral National People's Assembly, whose 203 members were first elected in Aug. 1980 for a 3-year term. There is an executive President, who appoints a Council of Ministers to assist him.

The Council of Ministers in Jan. 1985 was as follows:

President and Minister of Foreign Affairs: José Eduardo dos Santos.

Planning: Lopo Fortunato do Nascimento. *Defence:* Col. Pedro Maria Tonha (Pedale). *Justice:* Diogenes de Assis Boavida. *Education:* Augusto Lopes Teixeira (Tutu). *Health:* António Ferreira Neto. *Finance:* Augusto Teixeira de Matos. *Foreign Trade:* Ismael Gaspar Martins. *Internal Trade:* Adriano Perreira dos Santos Júnior. *Industry:* Henrique de Carvalho Santos (Onambwe). *Transport and Communications:* Manuel Bernardo de Sousa. *Labour and Social Security:* Horácio Perreira Brás da Silva. *Agriculture:* Evaristo Domingos Kimba. *State Security:* Col. Julião Mateus Paulo (Dino Matross). *Interior:* Manuel Alexandre Rodrigues (Kito). *Petroleum and Energy:* Pedro Castro Van-Dúnem (Loy). *Construction:* Jorge Henrique Varela de Melo Dias Flora. *Housing:* Lourenço Ferreira (Diandengue). *Provincial Co-ordination:* Evaristo Domingos Kimba. *Fisheries:* Emilio Guerra. There are 4 Secretaries of State.

Flag: Horizontally red over black, with a star and an arc of cogwheel crossed by a machete, all yellow over all in the centre.

Local government: Angola is divided into 18 provinces – (Cabinda, Zaïre, Uíge, Luanda, Cuanza Norte, Cuanza Sul, Malange, Lunda Norte, Lunda Sul, Benguela, Huambo, Bié, Moxico, Cuando-Cubango, Namibe, Huíla, Cunene and Bengo) each under a Provincial Commissioner, appointed by the President and an elected legislative of from 55 to 85 members.

DEFENCE. Conscription is for a period of 2 years.

Army. The Army has 2 motorized infantry, 17 infantry, and 4 air defence brigades; 10 tank and 6 artillery battalions; and 10 SAM batteries. Total strength (1985) 40,000. Equipment includes Soviet T-34, T-54, T-62 and PT-76 tanks.

Navy. Twenty Portuguese naval craft were transferred on independence in 1975 and 9 vessels were acquired from the Soviet Navy in 1977-79, when 8 merchant ships were taken over from local trade for naval use. There are 6 fast missile boats, 5 fast torpedo boats, 5 patrol craft, 9 coastal patrol boats, 18 landing craft, 1 survey ship and 8 auxiliary vessels. Naval personnel in 1985 totalled 1,500.

Air Force. The Angolan People's Air Force (FAPA) was formed in 1976. Combat equipment is mainly of Soviet origin, comprising about 20 MiG-21 and 20 MiG-17 fighters. FAPA also has 1 F.27 Maritime overwater reconnaissance aircraft, 1 Noratlas, 1 F.27 Friendship, 4 Nord 262, 15 An-26 and 3 C-47 transports, 8 Islander twin-engined light transports, 10 Do 27 and 2 Turbo-Porter liaison aircraft, 12 PC-7 Turbo Trainers, 24 L-39 jet trainers, 1 MiG-15UTI, and 27 Alouette III and 35 Mi-8 helicopters. 'Goa' surface-to-air missiles are deployed.

INTERNATIONAL RELATIONS

Membership. Angola is a member of UN and OAU.

ECONOMY

Budget. The 1981 budget balanced at 10,874m. kwanza.

Currency. The currency is the *kwanza* divided into 100 *lwei.* Coins are of 50 *lwei*, 1, 2, 5 and 10 *kwanza*; notes are of 20, 50, 100, 500 and 1,000 *kwanza.* In Feb. 1985, £1 = 32·73 *kwanza*; US$1 = 29·92 *kwanza.*

Banking. All banking was nationalized in 1975. The *Banco Nacional de Angola* is the central bank and bank of issue, while the *Banco Popular de Angola* handles all commercial activities throughout the country.

Weights and Measures. The metric system is in force.

ENERGY AND NATURAL RESOURCES

Electricity. Production (1981) totalled 1,500 m. kwh, mainly hydro-electricity. In Nov. 1984 an agreement was signed with Brazil and USSR to construct a hydro-electric plant on the river Kwanza, 250 miles south of Luanda.

Oil. Total production (1983) about 8m. tonnes.

Minerals. The country possesses valuable diamond deposits. Production of diamonds during 1983 totalled 1,034,000 carats (1978, 650,000). Production (1981) of salt, 38,900 tonnes. There has been no production of iron ore since 1975, but the mines at Kassinga were restarted in 1980 and a second project near Dondo started production in early 1981. Manganese and copper deposits exist.

Agriculture. The principal cash crops (with 1982 production, in 1,000 tonnes) were sugar-cane (410), coffee (35), bananas (280), palm oil (40), palm kernels (12), cotton (33); others include tobacco, citrus fruit and sisal. Food crops comprise cassava (1,950), maize (250), sweet potatoes (180) and beans (40).

Livestock (1983): 3·3m. cattle, 240,000 sheep, 950,000 goats, 450,000 pigs.

Fisheries. Total catch (1981) 174,100 tonnes.

Forestry. Mahogany and other hardwoods are exported, chiefly from the tropical rain forests of the north, especially Cabinda. Production (1981) 8·97m. cu. metres.

COMMERCE. Imports (1979, in 1m. kwanza), 28,093; exports, 39,531. The chief imports are textiles, transport equipment, foodstuffs, pig-iron and steel; chief exports are crude oil, coffee, diamonds, sisal, fish, maize, palm-oil. In 1981, crude petroleum represented 74% of exports, petroleum products, 10%, coffee 5% and diamonds 10%. In 1982 the USA provided 16% of imports, France 12%, Brazil 9% and the USSR 8%, while of exports 38% went to USA, 18% to the Bahamas.

Total trade between Angola and UK for calendar years (British Department of Trade returns, in £1,000 sterling):

	1981	*1982*	*1983*	*1984*
Imports to UK	6,388	7,368	45,732	158,636
Exports and re-exports from UK	39,507	25,781	22,847	35,581

COMMUNICATIONS

Roads. There were, in 1974, 72,323 km of roads, and in 1978, 143,100 cars and 42,600 commercial vehicles.

Railways. The length of railways open for traffic in 1984 was 2,952 km comprising 2,798 km of 1,067 mm gauge and 154 km of 600 mm gauge. The Benguela Railway runs from Lobito to the Zaïre border at Dilolo where it connects with the National Railways of Zaïre. Other lines link Luanda with Malange; Gunza with Gabela; and Moçâmedes with Menongue. In 1981 Angola's railways carried 7·6m. passengers and 725,000 tonnes of freight.

Aviation. Luanda has international air links to Lisbon, Rome, Paris, Moscow, Budapest, Brazzaville, Saõ Tomé, Lusaka, Maputo, Sal (Cape Verde Islands), Havana, Kinshasa, Libreville, Berlin, Tripoli, Lagos, Algiers, Niamey, Sofia, Malta, Rio de Janeiro and São Paulo.

Shipping. In 1975, 2·85m. tonnes were discharged and 16m. tonnes loaded in Angolan ports. In 1982 there were 56 merchant vessels (over 100 GRT) totalling 90,428 GRT.

Post and Broadcasting. Angola is connected by cable with east, west and south African telegraph systems. There were, in 1973, 1,808 km of telegraph lines, 77 telephone stations (with 29,796 instruments in 1978), 162 telegraph stations and 31 wireless stations.

Rádio Nacional de Angola is the largest of the 18 stations operating on medium- and short-waves. *Rádio Nacional* transmits 3 programmes as well as operating 2 regional stations. Number of radio receivers (1981)125,000 and television receivers 2,000.

Cinemas. There were, in 1972, 47 cinemas with seating capacity of 35,142.

Newspaper. The national daily newspaper is *Jornal de Angola*, with a circulation of 50,000 in 1984.

RELIGION, EDUCATION AND WELFARE

Religion. Article 7 of the Constitution of the People's Republic of Angola states that: 'The People's Republic of Angola is a secular state, where there is a complete separation of religious institutions from the state. All religions will be respected.

In 1979 46% of the population were Roman Catholic, 12% Protestant and 42% animist.

Education. In 1983 there were 2·4m. pupils in primary schools, 153,000 in secondary schools and 4,746 students in higher education. The *Universidade de Angola* (founded 1963) at Luanda with faculties at Huambo and Lubango, had 3,500 students in 1982.

Health. In 1972 there were 4 state, 14 regional and 70 rural hospitals and about 260 health centres and dispensaries, with a total of 18,011 hospital beds. In 1973 there were 383 doctors, 87 pharmacists, 284 midwives and 3,115 nursing personnel.

DIPLOMATIC REPRESENTATIVES

Of Angola in Great Britain
Ambassador: Elisio de Figueiredo (accredited 28 Nov. 1984).

Of Great Britain in Angola (Rua Diogo Cao, 4, Luanda)
Ambassador: M. I. Goulding, CMG.

Of Angola to the United Nations
Ambassador: Elísio de Figueiredo.

Books of Reference

Anuário Estatistico de Angola. Luanda, from 1897
Araújo, A. Correia de, *Aspectos do desenvolvimento económico e social de Angola.* Lisbon, 1964
Bender, G. J., *Angola under the Portuguese.* London, 1979
Davidson, B., *In the Eye of the Storm.* London, 1972
Dias, G. de Sousa, *Os portugueses em Angola.* Lisbon, 1959
Klinghoffer, A. J., *The Angolan War.* Boulder, 1980
Pélissier, R., *Les guerres grises.* Montamets, 1980.—*La Colonie du Minotaure.* Montamets, 1980.—*Le naufrage des coravelles.* Montamets, 1980
Wheeler, D. L., and Pélissier, R., *Angola.* London, 1971
Wolfers, M., and Bergerol., *Angola in the Frontline.* London, 1983
Zirka, A. K., *Angola Libre?* Paris, 1975

ANGUILLA

Capital: The Valley
Population: 7,000 (1984)

HISTORY. Anguilla was probably given its name by the Spaniards because of its eel-like shape. After British settlements in the 17th century, the territory was administered as part of the Leeward Islands. From 1825 it became more closely associated with St Kitts and ultimately incorporated in the colony of St Kitts-Nevis-Anguilla. Opposition to this association grew and finally in 1967 the island seceded unilaterally. Following direct intervention by the UK in 1969 Anguilla became *de facto* a separate dependency of Britain; and this was formalized on 19 Dec. 1980 under the Anguilla Act 1980. A new Constitution came into effect in April 1982.

AREA AND POPULATION. Anguilla is the most northerly of the Leeward Islands, some 70 miles (112 km) to the north-west of St Kitts and 5 miles (8 km) to the north of St Martin/St Maarten. The territory also comprises the island of Sombrero (on which there is an important lighthouse) and several other off-shore islets or cays. The total area of the territory is about 60 sq. miles (155 sq. km). Census population (1984) was 7,000. The capital is The Valley.

CONSTITUTION AND GOVERNMENT. The House of Assembly consists of a Speaker, 7 elected members, 2 nominated members and 2 official members.

Executive power is vested in the Governor who is appointed by HM The Queen. Apart from his special responsibilities (External Affairs, Defence, Internal Security, including the Police, and the Public Service) and his reserve powers in respect of legislation, the Governor discharges his executive powers on the advice of an Executive Council comprising a Chief Minister, 3 Ministers and 2 official members: Attorney-General and Permanent Secretary, Finance.

Governor: A. T. Baillie.
Chief Minister: Emile Gumbs.

ECONOMY

Budget. In 1984, the budget was: Expenditure EC$11·7m.; revenue EC$13·3m. Anguilla finances its recurrent budget but aid for capital projects comes from UK and other donors.

Currency. The currency is the Eastern Caribbean *dollar.*

NATURAL RESOURCES

Agriculture. Because of low rainfall agriculture potential is limited. Main crops are pigeon peas, corn and sweet potatoes. Livestock consists of sheep, goats, cattle and poultry.

Fisheries. Fishing is a thriving industry with exports to neighbouring islands.

INDUSTRY AND TRADE

Trade. Total trade between Anguilla and UK (British Department of Trade returns, in £1,000 sterling):

	1983 [1]	*1984*
Imports to UK	1,798	14
Exports and re-exports from UK	4,498	896

[1] Including St Christopher-Nevis.

Tourism. There are a few hotels of international standing and others are under construction. There are also several locally-owned hotels, guest houses and apartments.

COMMUNICATIONS

Roads. There are about 50 miles of tarred roads and 40 miles of secondary roads.

Aviation. There is a 3,600 ft surfaced runway at Wallblake Airport. Apart from regular air taxi and charter flights WINAIR (subsidiary of ALM) provides daily scheduled services between Juliana International Airport, St Maarten and Anguilla.

Shipping. The main seaports are Road Bay and Blowing Point, the latter serving passenger and cargo traffic to and from St Martin.

Post and Telecommunications. There is a modern internal telephone service with (1984) 1,200 exchange lines; and international telegraph, telex and telephone services, all operated by Cable & Wireless.

EDUCATION AND WELFARE

Education. There are 6 government primary schools and 1 secondary school. Tertiary education is provided at regional universities and similar institutions.

Health. There is a 24-bed cottage hospital, clinics and a modern dental clinic.

Book of Reference

Petty, C. L., *Anguilla: Where there's a Will, there's a Way.* Anguilla, 1984

ANTIGUA AND BARBUDA

Capital: St John's
Population: 79,000 (1984)
GNP per capita: US$ 1,550 (1981)

HISTORY. Antigua was discovered by Colombus in 1493 and named by him after a church in Seville (Spain). It was first colonized by English settlers in 1632; nearby Barbuda was colonized in 1661 from Antigua. Formed part of the Leeward Islands Federation from 1871 until 30 June 1956, when Antigua became a separate Crown Colony, which was part of the West Indies Federation from 3 Jan. 1958 until 31 May 1962. It became an Associated State of the UK on 27 Feb. 1967 and obtained independence on 1 Nov. 1981.

AREA AND POPULATION. Antigua and Barbuda comprises 3 islands of the Lesser Antilles situated in the Eastern Caribbean with a total land area of 442 sq. km (171 sq. miles); it consists of Antigua (280 sq. km), Barbuda, 40 km to the north (161 sq. km) and uninhabited Redonda, 40 km to the southwest (1 sq. km).

The population at the Census of 7 April 1970 was 65,525; the latest estimate (1984) is 79,000. The chief towns are St John's, the capital on Antigua (25,000 inhabitants in 1979) and Codrington, the only settlement on Barbuda.

CLIMATE. A tropical climate, but drier than most West Indies islands. The hot season is from May to Nov., when rainfall is greater. Mean annual rainfall is 40″ (1,000 mm).

CONSTITUTION AND GOVERNMENT. H.M. Queen Elizabeth, as Head of State, is represented by a Governor-General appointed by her on the advice of the Prime Minister. There is a bicameral legislature, comprising a 17-member Senate appointed by the Governor-General and a House of Representatives elected by universal suffrage for a 5-year term. The Governor-General appoints a Prime Minister and, on the latter's advice, other members of the Cabinet.

Governor-General: Sir Wilfred Ebenezer Jacobs, KCVO, OBE, QC.

Prime Minister. Right Hon. Vere C. Bird, Sen., PC.

At the general elections held on 17 April 1984, the ruling Antigua Labour Party won 16 seats and there was one independent.

Flag: Red, with a triangle based on the top edge, divided horizontally black, blue, white, with a rising sun in gold on the black portion.

ECONOMY

Budget. The budget for 1982–83 envisaged revenue at EC$99·3m.

Currency. The Eastern Caribbean $. In Feb. 1985, £1 = EC$2·87; US$1 = EC$2·70.

Banking. In government savings bank, 4,917 depositors on 31 Dec. 1971, $432,277 deposits. Barclays Bank International, Royal Bank of Canada, Canadian Imperial Bank of Commerce, the Virgin Islands National Bank, the Antilles International Trust Co. and the Bank of Nova Scotia have branches at St John's. The Antigua Co-operative Bank was opened in Jan. 1965.

AGRICULTURE. Sugar, cotton and fruits are the main crops. There were 40,000 lb. of cotton produced in 1981, 105,000 in 1980.

Livestock (1983): Cattle, 16,000; pigs, 7,000; sheep, 12,000; goats, 12,000.

INDUSTRY AND TRADE

Commerce. Imports in 1978 amounted to EC$111m. (of which 31% came from the USA and 28% from the UK) and exports to EC$34m. of which the major amount came from bunkering provided to ships.

Total trade between Antigua and Barbuda and UK (British Department of Trade returns, in £1,000 sterling):

	1982	*1983*	*1984*
Imports to UK	6,245	1,718	820
Exports and re-exports from UK	12,606	10,465	22,670

Tourism. There were 96,084 tourists (excluding cruise passengers) in 1981.

COMMUNICATIONS

Roads. There are 600 miles of roads (150 miles main road).

Shipping. The main harbour is the St John's deep water harbour. There are 2 tugs for the berthing of ships and all modern and efficient general cargo handling equipment. The harbour can also accommodate 3 large cruise ships simultaneously.

Post and Broadcasting. Telephone lines, 720 miles; 3,104 telephones.

RELIGION, EDUCATION AND WELFARE.

Religion. The vast majority of the population are Christian, preponderantly Anglican.

Education. In 1980–81 there were 10,660 pupils and 431 teachers in primary schools, and 4,526 pupils and 318 teachers in secondary schools.

Health. There is a general hospital (Holberton) with 215 beds, a mental hospital with 200 beds, a geriatric unit with 150 beds, 4 health centres and 16 dispensaries.

DIPLOMATIC REPRESENTATIVES

Of Antigua and Barbuda in Great Britain (15 Thayer St., London, W1)
High Commissioner: Ronald Sanders (accredited 29 Nov. 1984).

Of Great Britain in Antigua and Barbuda (38 St Mary's St., St John's)
High Commissioner: G. L. Bullard, CMG.

Of Antigua and Barbuda in the USA (2000 N. St., NW, Washington, D.C., 20036)
Ambassador: Edmund Hawkins Lake.

Of the USA in Antigua and Barbuda
Ambassador: Thomas H. Anderson, Jr. (resides in Bridgetown).

Of Antigua and Barbuda to the United Nations
Ambassador: Lloydstone Jacobs.

ARGENTINA

República Argentina

Capital: Buenos Aires
Population: 27·95m. (1980)
GNP per capita: US$2,560 (1981)

HISTORY. In 1515 Juan Díaz de Solis discovered the Río de La Plata. In 1534 Pedro de Mendoza was sent by the King of Spain to take charge of the 'Gobernación y Capitanía de las tierras del Rio de La Plata', and in Feb. 1536 he founded the city of the 'Puerto de Santa María del Buen Aire'. In 1810 the population rose against Spanish rule, and in 1816 Argentina proclaimed its independence. Civil wars and anarchy followed until, in 1853, stable government was established.

Military leaders supported by the Navy and Air Force staged a *coup d'état* on 27 June 1966, and the temporary Revolutionary Junta of the Commanders-in-Chief of the three Armed Services deposed Dr Illia and his Government elected in 1963. A former Commander-in-Chief of the Army, Lieut.-Gen. Onganía, was appointed President and the Junta dissolved. The previous Constitution remained in force in so far as it was consistent with the statutes and objectives of the Revolution. For details of earlier Constitutions *see* THE STATESMAN'S YEAR-BOOK, 1982–83.

AREA AND POPULATION. The Argentine Republic is bounded in the north by Bolivia, in the north-east by Paraguay, in the east by Brazil, Uruguay and the Atlantic Ocean and the west by Chile. The republic consists of 22 provinces, 1 federal district and the National Territories of Tierra del Fuego, the Antarctic and the South Atlantic Islands (census of 1980) as follows:

Provinces	*Area: sq. km. 1960*	*Population: census, 1980*	*Capital*	*Population census, 1980 (1,000)*
Litoral				
Federal Capital	200	2,922,829	Buenos Aires	2,908
Buenos Aires	307,804	10,865,408	La Plata	455
Corrientes	88,199	661,454	Corrientes	180
Entre Ríos	76,216	908,313	Paraná	160
Chaco	99,633	701,392	Resistencia	218
Santa Fé	133,007	2,465,546	Santa Fé	287
Formosa	72,066	295,887	Formosa	95
Misiones	29,801	588,977	Posadas	140
Norte				
Jujuy	53,219	410,008	San Salvador de Jujuy	124
Salta	154,775	662,870	Salta	260
Santiago del Estero	135,254	594,920	Santiago del Estero	148
Tucumán	22,524	972,655	San Miguel de Tucuman	497
Centro				
Córdoba	168,766	2,407,754	Córdoba	969
La Pampa	143,440	208,260	Santa Rosa	52
San Luis	76,748	214,416	San Luis	71
Andina				
Catamarca	99,818	207,717	Catamarca	88
La Rioja	92,331	164,217	La Rioja	67
Mendoza	150,839	1,196,228	Mendoza	597
San Juan	86,137	465,976	San Juan	118
Neuquén	94,078	243,850	Neuquén	90

Provinces	Area: sq. km. 1960	Population: census, 1980	Capital	Population census, 1980 (1,000)
Patagonia				
Chubut	224,686	263,116	Rawson	52
Rio Negro	203,013	383,354	Viedma	24
Santa Cruz	243,943	114,941	Rio Gallegos	43
Tierra del Fuego [2]	20,912	29,392	Ushuaia	11
Grand total	2,777,815 [1]	27,949,480		

[1] Total area claimed was 2,808,602 sq. km (1,084,120 sq. miles).

[2] The official census including the 'Antarctic Sector', and stated to comprise the 'Malvinas' (Falklands), South Orcadas (Orkneys), South Georgias, South Sandwich Islands and the 'sovereign territories of Argentina in the Antarctic': population 3,300.

Other large towns (1980 Census): Rosario (935,471), Mar del Plata (423,989), Bahia Blanca (233,126).

CLIMATE. The climate is warm temperate over the pampas, where rainfall occurs at all seasons, but diminishes towards the west. In the north and west, the climate is more arid, with high summer temperatures, while in the extreme south conditions are also dry, but much cooler. Buenos Aires. Jan. 74°F (23·3°C), July 50°F (10°C). Annual rainfall 37″ (950 mm). Bahia Blanca. Jan. 74°F (23·3°C), July 48°F (8·9°C). Annual rainfall 21″ (523 mm). Mendoza. Jan. 75°F (23·9°C), July 47°F (8·3°C). Annual rainfall 8″ (190 mm). Rosario. Jan. 76°F (24·4°C), July 51°F (10·6°C). Annual rainfall 35″ (869 mm). San Juan. Jan. 78°F (25·6°C), July 50°F (10°C). Annual rainfall 4″ (89 mm). San Miguel de Tucuman. Jan. 79°F (26·1°C), July 56°F (13·3°C). Annual rainfall 38″ (970 mm). Ushuaia. Jan. 50°F (10°C), July 34°F (1·1°C). Annual rainfall 19″ (475 mm).

CONSTITUTION AND GOVERNMENT. Presidential, congressional and municipal elections took place on 30 Oct. 1983 and a return to civilian rule took place on 10 Dec. 1983. With the return to constitutional rule the Constitution of 1853 (as amended up to 1898) is again in effect. The President and Vice-President are elected by a 600-member electoral college (directly elected by popular vote) for 6-year terms; both must be Roman Catholics of Argentine birth. The President is Commander-in-Chief of the Armed Services, and appoints to all civil and judicial offices.

The following is a list of Presidents from 1973 onwards:

Gen. Juan Domingo Perón. 12 Oct. 1973–1 July 1974.

Maria Estela (Isabel) Martinez Perón. 1 July 1974 (*a.i.* from 29 June 1974)–23 March 1976. (Deposed.)

Gen. Jorge Rafael Videla. 29 March 1976–29 March 1981.

Gen. Roberto Viola, 29 March–22 Dec. 1981.

Gen. Leopoldo Fortunato Galtieri, 22 Dec. 1981–17 June 1982.

Gen. Reynaldo Benito Antonio Bignone, 1 July 1982–10 Dec. 1983.

The National Congress consists of a Senate and a House of Deputies: The Senate comprises 46 members, 2 nominated by each provincial legislature and 2 from the Federal District for 9 years (one-third retiring every 3 years). The House of Deputies comprises 254 members directly elected by universal suffrage (at age 18).

In the General Elections held on 30 Oct. 1983, the Unión Cívica Radical won 129 seats in the House of Deputies, the Frente Justicialista de Liberación (Fréjuli) 111 seats and others 13 seats (1 vacancy); of the 600 seats in the electoral college, the UCR won 317, Fréjuli 259 and others 24 seats.

President of the Republic: Dr Raúl Alfonsín (sworn in 10 Dec. 1983).

Vice-President: Dr Víctor Martínez.

The Cabinet in Feb. 1985 was composed as follows:

Foreign Affairs: Dante Caputto. *Interior:* Dr Antonio Tróccili. *Treasury and Finance:* Juan Sourrouille. *Labour:* Hugo Barrionuevo. *Defence:* Raúl Borrás. *Education and Justice:* Dr Carlos Alconada Aramburú. *Public Health and Environment:* Aldo Neri. *Public Works:* Roque Carranza.

National flag: Three horizontal stripes of light blue, white and light blue, with the gold Sun of May in the centre.

National anthem: Oid, mortales, el grito sagrado Libertad (words by V. López y Planes, 1813; tune by J. Blas Parera).

Local Government. In Oct. 1983 the governors were elected by the people.

DEFENCE

Army. The Army is a National Militia, service in which is compulsory for all citizens from their 18th to their 45th year. Naturalized citizens are exempt for a period of 10 years. For the first 10 years the men belong to the 'active' Army, or first line. After completing 10 years in the first line the men pass to the National Guard, and serve in it for another 10 years, finishing their service with 5 years in the Territorial Guard; the latter is mobilized only in case of war. The period of continuous service, or training in the ranks with the permanent forces, is for 1 year for the Army or Air Force, and 14 months for the Navy. The reservists can be called out for training periodically.

The territory of the republic is divided into 5 military districts for administrative purposes. The Army is organized in 5 army corps; it consists of 2 armoured, 4 motorized infantry and 1 mechanized, 1 airborne, 3 mountain and 1 jungle brigades; 16 artillery, 1 aviation and 5 air defence battalions.

In 1985 the Army was 100,000 strong, of whom 80,000 were conscripts.

The trained reserve numbers about 250,000, of whom 200,000 belong to the National Guard and 50,000 to the Territorial Guard.

Navy. Principal ships of the Argentine Navy:[3]

Completed	*Name*	*Standard displacement Tons*	*Aircraft*	*Guns*	*Shaft horsepower*	*Speed Knots*
			Aircraft Carrier[1]			
1945	Veinticinco de Mayo[2]	15,892	18 fixed-wing, 4 helicopters	9 40mm	40,000	24·0

[1] The aircraft carrier *Independence*, ex-*Warrior*, purchased from the UK in 1958 was withdrawn from service in 1971.

[2] Ex-*Karel Doorman*, purchased from the Netherlands in 1968, ex-*Venerable*, purchased from UK in 1948.

[3] The cruiser *General Belgrano*, *ex-Phoenix*, purchased from the USA in 1951 was sunk by the British fleet submarine *Conqueror* in May 1982. Sister ship *Nueve de Julio* (ex-USS *Bloise*) was withdrawn from service in 1980. The cruiser *La Argentina* was stricken from the list in 1975.

There are 2 new German-built submarines, 2 modern German-built submarines, 4 new German-built destroyers, 2 new British-built destroyers (Type 42), 3 old *ex*-US destroyers, 2 new German-designed medium frigates, 3 new French-built small frigates, 2 old training frigates, 4 coastal minesweepers, 2 minehunters, 5 patrol vessels (armed ocean tugs), 2 fast patrol vessels, 2 torpedo boats, 6 patrol craft, 3 survey ships, 2 survey launches, 2 training ships, 5 transports, 3 oilers, 1 tank landing ship, 20 minor landing craft, 58 auxiliary amphibious craft, 2 polar ships, 20 ancillary vessels and service craft and 12 tugs.

The new construction programme includes 4 diesel powered patrol submarines (one building and three projected), and 4 fast frigates.

The diesel-powered submarine *Sante Fe,* ex-USS *Catfish,* was damaged and beached during the Falklands invasion in April 1982, and was later sunk in deep water.

The active personnel of the Navy in 1985 comprised 30,000 (2,000 officers and 28,000 ratings, including 12,000 conscripts). The Marine Corps numbered 6,000 including coast artillery.

The *Prefectura Naval Argentina* (PNA) for Coast Guard and rescue duties comprises five new 910-ton corvettes with helicopter and hangar, an ex-whaler of 1,000 tons, 8 patrol vessels, 40 coastal patrol craft and a training ship.

The Naval Aviation Service, formed on 17 Oct. 1919, has some 140 fixed-wing aircraft and helicopters with 2,000 personnel, in 6 wings. Aircraft include 14 Super Entendard fighters, 30 A-4Q Skyhawk attack bombers, 18 Aermacchi M.B. 326 and 7 M.B.339A light jet armed trainers, 3 P-2H Neptune and 6 S-2E ship-based Tracker anti-submarine aircraft, navalized Harvard trainers, and North American armed T-28s bought from France, and a dozen types of training, transport and general purpose aircraft, plus 3 types of helicopters. A variable mix of Super Entendards, Skyhawks, Trackers and Sea King and Alouette helicopters operated from the aircraft carrier.

Air Force. The Air Force, founded on 10 Aug. 1912 and autonomous since 4 Jan. 1945, is organized into Air Operations, Air Regions, Materiel and Personnel Commands. Air Operations Command, responsible for all operational flying, is made up of air brigades, each with 1 to 4 squadrons, usually operating from a single base. No. I Air Brigade is a military air transport service, with responsibility also for LADE (state airline) operations into areas of Argentina not served by civilian companies. Its equipment includes 8 C-130E/H Hercules and 10 F.27 Friendship/Troopship turboprop transports, 2 KC-130H Hercules tanker/transports, 5 twin-turbofan F.28 Fellowship freighters, 5 Twin Otters, 15 Guarani IIs, the Presidential Boeing 707-320B and 707-320C, 2 more 707s, 2 VIP Fellowships, and many older or smaller types. No. II Air Brigade has 5 Canberra twin-jet bombers and 2 Canberra trainers; a photographic squadron with Guarani IIs. No. III Air Brigade has 2 squadrons of IA 58 Pucara twin-turboprop COIN aircraft. No. IV Air Brigade comprises 2 ground attack squadrons equipped with about 15 A-4P Skyhawks and 15 Paris light jet combat and liaison aircraft. No. V Air Brigade comprises 2 squadrons with a total of about 30 A-4P Skyhawk strike aircraft. No. VI Air Brigade has 40 Dagger (Israeli-built Mirage III) fighters, equipping 2 squadrons. No. VII Air Brigade has 2 COIN, general-purpose, and search and rescue squadrons with 12 armed Hughes 500M, 5 Lama, 5 Sikorsky S-58T/S-61, 8 Bell 212 and 9 Bell UH-1 helicopters; and a COIN/training squadron of T-34 Mentors. No. VIII Air Brigade has 1 squadron with 14 Mirage IIIE fighter-bombers and 2 Mirage IIID trainers. Recent purchases, not listed above, include 22 Mirage III/5 fighters. There is a flying school at Córdoba, equipped with piston-engined T-34 Mentors and Paris jets. There are about 17,500 personnel and 180 combat aircraft.

INTERNATIONAL RELATIONS

Membership. Argentina is a member of UN, OAS and LAIA (formerly LAFTA).

ECONOMY

Budget. The financial year commences on 1 Nov. Budget receipts in 1980 33,459,261m. pesos and expenditure 37,248,461m. pesos.

Currency. The monetary system is on a gold-exchange standard, the unit for foreign transactions being, nominally, the *peso oro* (gold peso) and for domestic transactions, the *peso argentino* (paper peso), legal tender for all domestic debts.

The gold peso weighs 1·6129 grammes of gold 0·900 fine; it is divided into 100 *centavos*, but gold is not in circulation. Circulation consists chiefly of paper notes (issued since 1897) ranging from 1,000 down to 1 peso. The coins actually circulating, 1984, were steel-nickel, 1 peso, 50, 20 and 10 centavos. In Feb. 1985, US$1 = 253·3 new *pesos*; £1 = 268·5 new *pesos*. Inflation reached 776% in Feb. 1985.

Banking. A law promulgated 25 March 1946 nationalized the Central Bank (established in 1935), as an autonomous institution. Six decree-laws of Oct. 1957 have brought back a greater elasticity to the structure.

In 1984 there were 35 government banks, 141 private banks and 33 foreign banks. There are 6 Stock Exchanges.

The total foreign debt as 31 Dec. 1984 was US$48m.

Weights and Measures. Since 1 Jan. 1887 the use of the metric system has been compulsory.

ENERGY AND NATURAL RESOURCES

Electricity. Electric power production (1984) was 38,890 kwh.

Oil. Crude oil production (1983) 27,866,300 cu. metres from 873 oil wells. Investment of US$10,000m. is envisaged by 1985 in the oil industry with the aim of achieving self-sufficiency.

Gas. Natural gas production (1983) 13,500,000m. cu. metres.

Minerals. Argentina produced 600,000 tonnes of washed coal in 1983. Gold, silver and copper are worked in Catamarca, where there are also 2 tin-mines, and gold and copper in San Juan, La Rioja and the south-western territories. Iron ore (90,000 tonnes in 1983), tungsten, beryllium, mica, uranium (30 tonnes in 1983), lead (32,000 tonnes in 1983), barites, zinc (43,500 tonnes in 1972), tin (1·8m. tonnes in 1972), manganese and limestone are produced.

Agriculture. Argentina has an area of about 670,251,000 acres, of which about 41% is pasture land, 32% woodland and 11% (73·73m. acres) cultivated.

Livestock (1983): Cattle 53,670,000; sheep, 30m.; pigs, 3·8m.; horses, 3m. The Province of Buenos Aires has 38% of the cattle. Wool production, 1983, was 126,000 tonnes.

Crop statistics with area (in 1,000 hectares) and production (in 1,000 tonnes) are shown as follows:

	1976–77		*1977–78*[1]		*1978–79*[1]	
	Area	*Output*	*Area*	*Output*	*Area*	*Output*
Wheat	7,192	11,000	4,600	5,300	5,230	7,800
Linseed	722	617	950	810	900	630
Maize	2,980	8,300	3,100	9,700	3,300	9,000
Oats	1,471	530	1,480	570	1,545	676
Barley	962	650	890	353	761	554
Rye	2,300	330	2,140	170	1,722	210
Sunflower seed	1,460	900	2,200	1,600	1,745	1,270
Sugar-cane	360	16,000	356	13,600	350	14,100

[1]Provisional.

Argentina's meat exports are calculated in terms of actual weight; not 'carcase weight', as is the international practice. In 1983, 84·16m. tons of meat were exported.

Cotton, potatoes, vine, tobacco, citrus fruit, olives, rice, soya, and yerba maté (Paraguayan tea) are also cultivated. There are 36 cane-sugar mills and 1 beet-sugar factory; production, 1979, 14·12m. tonnes. Potato harvest, 1979, amounted to 1,694,000 tonnes. The area under tobacco, 1979, was 76,000 hectares; output 68,000 tonnes.

Sunflower seed, first grown by Russian immigrants in 1900, now furnishes the country's most popular edible oil. There are more than 10m. olive trees, of which 48% are in Mendoza. 672,000 tonnes of groundnuts were produced in 1979 (mainly in Córdoba). Argentina is the world's largest source of tannin.

Fisheries. Fish landings in 1983 amounted to 550,000 tonnes.

INDUSTRY AND TRADE

Industry. Production (1983 in tonnes) Paper, 873,000; steel, 2·95m.; sulphuric acid (1979), 279,066; cement (1979), 6·7m. Motor vehicles produced (1981) totalled, 172,350; television receivers, 262,000.

Commerce. Import values include charges for carriage, insurance and freight; export values are on a f.o.b. basis. Real values of foreign trade (in US$1m.), exclusive of coin and bullion:

	1978	*1979*	*1980*	*1981*	*1982*	*1983*
Imports	3,834	6,300	10,400	...	...	9,200
Exports	6,400	7,750	8,000	...	...	3,900

Total trade between Argentina and UK (British Department of Trade returns, in £1,000 sterling):

	1980	*1981*	*1982*	*1983*	*1984*
Imports to UK	114,286	136,892	58,728	194	65
Exports and re-exports from UK	172,830	161,192	37,349	4,472	5,232

Tourism. In 1983, 950,000 tourists visited Argentina.

COMMUNICATIONS

Roads. In 1978 there were 207,630 km of national and provincial highways. The 4 main roads constituting Argentina's portion of the Pan-American Highway were opened to traffic in 1942. In 1981 there were 3·19m. cars and 1·23m. commercial vehicles.

Railways. The system based on the 1949 amalgamation of 18 government, British and French-owned railways, comprises 6 railways with a total route-km in 1983 of 33,807 km (142 km electrified) on metre, 1,435 mm and 1,676 mm gauges. In 1981 railways carried 17·6m. tonnes of freight and 345m. passengers.

Aviation. There were (1980) 10 international airports. Commercial airlines flew a total of 94m. km in 1980, carrying 5·6m. passengers and 54,400 tonnes of freight.

Shipping. The merchant fleet, 31 Dec. 1976 (registered with Lloyd's), consisted of 1,869,662 GRT; traffic during 1971: vessels of 13·27m. GRT entered ports; 14m. tonnes of goods were unloaded and 10·6m. tonnes were loaded.

Post and Broadcasting. In 1949 the telephone service was nationalized; instruments numbered 3,041,475 in 1982. There were (1984) 122 radio stations and 4 television channels in Buenos Aires. In 1980 there were 7·5m. radio receivers and 5·6m. television receivers.

Cinemas (1972). Cinemas numbered 1,650, with seating capacity of 611,400.

Newspapers (1984). Daily newspapers numbered 297. Buenos Aires had (1984) 11 daily newspapers with a circulation of 2·5m.

JUSTICE, RELIGION, EDUCATION AND WELFARE

Justice. Justice is administered by federal and provincial courts. The former deal only with cases of a national character, or in which different provinces or inhabitants of different provinces are parties. The chief federal court is the Supreme Court, with 5 judges at Buenos Aires. Other federal courts are the appeal courts, at Buenos Aires, Bahía Blanca, La Plata, Córdoba, Mendoza, Tucumán and Resistencia. Each province has its own judicial system, with a Supreme Court (generally so designated) and several minor chambers. Trial by jury is established by the Constitution for criminal cases, but never practised, except occasionally in the provinces of Buenos Aires and Córdoba.

The death penalty was re-introduced in 1976 for the killing of government, military police and judicial officials, and for participation in terrorist activities.

The police force is centralized under the Federal Security Council.

Religion. The Roman Catholic religion is supported by the State and membership was 23·67m. in 1976.

There are several Protestant denominations with a total congregation (1983) of 500,000.

The Jewish congregation numbered 300,000 in 1983.

Education. In 1981 the primary schools had 218,294 teachers and 4,218,992 pupils; secondary schools had 191,096 teachers and 1,366,444 pupils.

There are National Universities at Buenos Aires (2), Córdoba (2), La Plata, Tucumán, Santa Fé (Litoral), Rosario, Corrientes (Nordeste,), Mendoza (Cuyo), Bahía Blanca (Sur), Catamarca, Tandil, Neuquén (Comahue), San Salvador de Jujuy, Salta, Santa Rosa (La Pampa), Mar del Plata, Comodoro Rivadavia (Patagonia), Río Cuarto, Entre Ríos, Resistencia, San Juan and Santiago del Estero. There are also private universities in Buenos Aires (6), Mendoza (3),

Córdoba, Comodoro Rivadavia, La Plata, Morón, Tucumán, Salta, Santa Fé and Santiago del Estero. In 1981 universities had 525,688 students and 54,039 lecturers.

Health. Free medical attention is obtainable from public hospitals. Many trade unions provide medical, dental and maternity services for their members and dependants. A Ministry of Social Welfare was set up in 1966. In 1971 there were 2,864 hospitals with 133,847 beds and in 1975 there were 48,693 doctors.

DIPLOMATIC REPRESENTATIVES

Diplomatic links with Argentina were broken by Great Britain in April 1982 following the invasion of the Falkland Islands.

Of Argentina in the USA (1600 New Hampshire Ave., NW, Washington, D.C., 20009)
Ambassador: Lucio Garcia del Solar.

Of the USA in Argentina (4300 Colombia, Palermo, Buenos Aires)
Ambassador: Frank V. Ortiz, Jr.

Of Argentina to the United Nations
Ambassador: Dr Carlos M. Muñiz.

Books of Reference

Boletin del comercio exterio Argentino y estadisticas económicas retrospectivas. Annual
Anuario de comercio exterior de la República Argentina. Annual
Economic Review, Banco de la Nación. Buenos Aires
Sintesis Estadistica Mensual. Dirección General de Estadistica. Buenos Aires, 1947 ff.
Boletin Internacional de Bibliografia Argentina. Ministry of Foreign Relations. Buenos Aires. Monthly
Geografia de la República Argentina. Ed. by the Sociedad Argentina de Estudios Geográficos. 7 vols. Buenos Aires. 1945–53
Bridges, E. L., *Uttermost Part of the Earth* [*Tierra del Fuego*]. New York, 1949
Ferns, H. S., *Britain and Argentina in the 19th Century.* OUP, 1960.—*The Argentine Republic 1516–1971.* Newton Abbot, 1973
Graham-Yooll, A., *The Forgotten Colony: A History of the English-Speaking Communities in Argentina.* London, 1981
Santillán, Diego A. de (ed.), *Gran Enciclopedia Argentina.* 9 vols. 1956–64
Snow, P. G., *Political Forces in Argentina.* Rev. ed. New York and London, 1979

AUSTRALIA

Capital: Canberra
Population: 15·45m. (1983)
GNP per capita: US$11,080 (1981)

HISTORY. On 1 Jan. 1901 New South Wales, Victoria, Queensland, South Australia, Western Australia and Tasmania were federated under the name of the 'Commonwealth of Australia', the designation of 'colonies' being at the same time changed into that of 'states'—except in the case of Northern Territory, which was transferred from South Australia to the Commonwealth as a 'territory' on 1 Jan. 1911.

In 1911 the Commonwealth acquired from the State of New South Wales the Canberra site for the Australian capital. Building operations were begun in 1923 and Parliament was opened at Canberra on 9 May 1927 by HRH the Duke of York (afterwards King George VI). A further area at Jervis Bay was acquired in 1915.

Territories under the administration of Australia in Jan. 1977, but not included in it, comprise Norfolk Island, the territory of Ashmore and Cartier Islands, and the Australian Antarctic Territory (24 Aug. 1936), comprising all the islands and territory other than Adélie Land, situated south of 60° S. lat. and between 160° and 45° E. long.

The British Government transferred sovereignty in the Heard Island and McDonald Islands to the Australian Government on 26 Dec. 1947. Cocos (Keeling) Islands on 23 Nov. 1955 and Christmas Island on 1 Oct. 1958 were also transferred to Australian jurisdiction.

AREA AND POPULATION. Area and resident population (estimate), 31 Dec. 1983:

States and Territories (capitals in brackets)	*Area (sq. km)*	*Males*	*Females*	*Total*	*Per 100 sq. km*
New South Wales (Sydney)	801,600	2,679,200	2,699,100	5,378,300	671
Victoria (Melbourne)	227,600	2,011,800	2,041,600	4,053,400	1,781
Queensland (Brisbane)	1,727,200	1,249,500	1,238,500	2,488,000	144
South Australia (Adelaide)	984,000	667,300	679,700	1,347,000	137
Western Australia (Perth)	2,525,500	693,800	679,900	1,373,700	54
Tasmania (Hobart)	67,800	215,900	218,700	434,700	641
Northern Territory (Darwin)	1,346,200	72,400	64,400	136,800	10
Aust. Cap. Terr. (Canberra)	2,400	120,000	120,000	240,100	10,004
Total	7,682,300	7,710,000	7,741,900	15,451,900	201

Resident population (estimate) in State capitals and other major cities, 30 June 1983 (preliminary):

Statistical division	*State*	*Persons*
Sydney	NSW	3,332,600
Melbourne	Vic.	2,864,600
Brisbane	Qld	1,138,400
Adelaide	SA	969,200
Perth	WA	969,100
Newcastle [1]	NSW	414,300
Canberra [1] [2]	ACT	255,900
Wollongong [1]	NSW	234,800
Hobart	Tas.	173,700
Gold Coast [1] [3]	Qld	192,000
Geelong [4]	Vic.	142,900
Darwin	NT	63,400

[1] Statistical District of 100,000 persons or more. [2] Includes Queanbeyan.
[3] Includes Tweed Heads. [4] Estimate at 30 June 1982.

The number of occupied dwellings in Australia (at 1981 census) was 4,691,425, distributed as follows: New South Wales, 1,669,596; Victoria, 1,243,453; Queensland, 703,964; South Australia, 433,841; Western Australia, 405,999;

Tasmania, 136,269; Northern Territory, 29,563; Australian Capital Territory, 68,740. There were also 469,742 unoccupied dwellings. Total completed new dwellings numbered 115,660 in 1982–3.

Vital statistics for 1982:

States and Territories	*Marriages*	*Divorces*	*Births*	*Deaths*	*Infant deaths*
New South Wales	41,955	14,378	83,489	42,352	823
Victoria	28,851	11,266	59,983	30,611	641
Queensland	18,928	6,770	40,540	18,149	432
South Australia	10,936	4,526	19,294	10,457	221
Western Australia	10,455	3,842	22,236	8,187	204
Tasmania	3,576	1,391	7,002	3,432	55
Northern Territory	818	369	2,880	573	57
Aust. Cap. Terr.	1,756	1,546	4,479	1,010	49
Total	11,275	44,088	239,903	114,771	2,482
Rate [1]	7·7	2·9	15·8	7·6	10·3 [2]

[1] Resident (estimate). [2] Per 1,000 live births registered.

Overseas arrivals during 1983 numbered 2,317,100 and departures 2,282,400. Of these 153,580 were long-term and permanent arrivals and 100,512 were long-term and permanent departures. Of these 78,390 came to Australia intending to settle. There were 25,870 Australian residents departing permanently.

Australian Bureau of Statistics, *Australian Demographic Statistics.* Quarterly. Canberra, June 1979 to date

National Population Inquiry, Population and Australia, A Demographic Analysis and Projection. Canberra, 1975

National Population Inquiry, Population and Australia: Recent Demographic Trends and their Implications. Canberra, 1978

CLIMATE. Over most of the continent, four seasons may be recognised. Spring is from Sept. to Nov., Summer from Dec. to Feb., Autumn from March to May and Winter from June to Aug., but because of its great size there are climates that range from tropical monsoon to cool temperate, with large areas of desert as well. In Northern Australia there are only two seasons, the wet one lasting from Nov. to March, but rainfall amounts diminish markedly from the coast to the interior. Central and southern Queensland are subtropical, north and central New South Wales are warm temperate, as are parts of Victoria, Western Australia and Tasmania, where most rain falls in winter. Canberra. Jan. 68°F (20°C), July 42°F (5·6°C). Annual rainfall 23″ (629 mm). Adelaide. Jan. 73°F (22·8°C), July 52°F (11·1°C). Annual rainfall 21″ (528 mm). Brisbane. Jan. 77°F (25°C), July 58°F (14·4°C). Annual rainfall 45″ (1,153 mm). Darwin. Jan. 83°F (28·3°C), July 77°F (25°C). Annual rainfall 59″ (1,536 mm). Hobart. Jan. 62°F (16·7°C), July 46°F (7·8°C). Annual rainfall 24″ (629 mm). Melbourne. Jan. 67°F (19·4°C), July 49°F (9·4°C). Annual rainfall 26″ (659 mm). Perth. Jan. 74°F (23·3°C), July 55°F (12·8°C). Annual rainfall 35″ (873 mm). Sydney. Jan. 71°F (21·7°C), July 53°F (11·7°C). Annual rainfall 47″ (1,215 mm).

CONSTITUTION AND GOVERNMENT. *Federal Government:* Under the Australian Constitution legislative power in Australia is vested in a Federal Parliament, consisting of the Queen, represented by a Governor-General, a Senate and a House of Representatives. Under the terms of the constitution there must be a session of parliament at least once a year.

The Senate comprises 64 Senators (10 for each State voting as one electorate and as from Aug. 1974, 2 Senators respectively for the Australian Capital Territory and the Northern Territory). Senators representing the States are chosen for 6 years. The terms of Senators representing the Territories expire at the close of the day next preceding the polling day for the general elections of the House of Representatives. In general, the Senate is renewed to the extent of one-half every 3 years, but in case of disagreement with the House of Representatives, it, together with the House of Representatives, may be dissolved, and an entirely new Senate elected. The House of Representatives consists, as nearly as practicable, of twice as many

Members as there are Senators, the numbers chosen in the several States being in proportion to population as shown by the latest statistics, but not less than 5 for any original State. The numerical size of the House after the election in 1980 was 125, including the Members for Northern Territory and the Australian Capital Territory. The Northern Territory has been represented by 1 Member in the House of Representatives since 1922, and the Australian Capital Territory by 1 Member since 1949 and 2 Members since May 1974. The Member for the Australian Capital Territory was given full voting rights as from the Parliament elected in Nov. 1966. The Member for the Northern Territory was given full voting rights in 1968. The House of Representatives continues for 3 years from the date of its first meeting, unless sooner dissolved. Every Senator or Member of the House of Representatives must be a British subject, be of full age, possess electoral qualifications and have resided for 3 years within Australia. The franchise for both Houses is the same and is based on universal (males and females aged 18 years) suffrage. Compulsory voting was introduced in 1925. If a Member of a State Parliament wishes to be a candidate in a federal election, he must first resign his State seat.

Executive power in Australia is vested in the Governor-General, who is advised by an Executive Council. This is presided over by the Governor-General, and its members hold office at his pleasure. All Ministers of State, who are members of the party or parties commanding a majority in the lower House, are members of the Executive Council under summons. A record of proceedings of meetings is kept by the Secretary to the Council. At Executive Council meetings the decisions of the Cabinet are (where necessary) given legal form, appointments made, resignations accepted, proclamations, regulations and the like made.

The policy of a ministry is, in practice, determined by the Ministers of State meeting without the Governor-General under the chairmanship of the Prime Minister. This group is known as the Cabinet. The Cabinet of the Liberal–National Country Party Coalition Government comprises the 14 senior Ministers. Other Ministers attend meetings of Cabinet only when required. Meetings of the full Ministry are held when necessary. There are 11 Standing Committees of the Cabinet comprising varying numbers of Cabinet and non-Cabinet Ministers. In Labour Governments all Ministers have been members of Cabinet. Cabinet meetings are private and deliberative and records of meetings are not made public. The Cabinet does not form part of the legal mechanisms of Government; the decisions it takes have, in themselves, no legal effect. The Cabinet substantially controls, in ordinary circumstances, not only the general legislative programme of Parliament but the whole course of Parliamentary proceedings. In effect, though not in form, the Cabinet, by reason of the fact that all Ministers are members of the Executive Council, is also the dominant element in the executive government of the country.

The legislative powers of the Federal Parliament embrace trade and commerce, shipping, etc.; taxation, finance, banking, currency, bills of exchange, bankruptcy, insurance; defence; external affairs, naturalization and aliens, quarantine, immigration and emigration; the people of any race for whom it is deemed necessary to make special laws; postal, telegraph and like services; census and statistics; weights and measures; astronomical and meteorological observations; copyrights; railways; conciliation and arbitration in disputes extending beyond the limits of any one State; social services; marriage, divorce etc.; service and execution of the civil and criminal process; recognition of the laws, Acts and records, and judicial proceedings of the States. The Senate may not originate or amend money bills; and disagreement with the House of Representatives may result in dissolution and, in the last resort, a joint sitting of the two Houses. No religion may be established by the Commonwealth. The Federal Parliament has limited and enumerated powers, the several State parliaments retaining the residuary power of government over their respective territories. If a State law is inconsistent with a Commonwealth law, the latter prevails.

The Constitution also provides for the admission or creation of new States. Proposed laws for the alteration of the Constitution must be submitted to the electors, and they can be enacted only if approved by a majority of the States and by a majority of all the electors voting.

The 34th Parliament was elected in Dec. 1984.

House of Representatives (following 1 Dec. 1984 elections): Australian Labor Party, 82 seats; Liberal Party, 45; National Party, 21.

Senate: See Addenda.

Governor-General: The Rt Hon. Sir Ninian Stephen, AK, GCMG, GCVO, KBE.

The following is a list of Governors-General of the Commonwealth:

Earl of Hopetoun	1901–02	HRH the Duke of Gloucester	1945–47
Lord Tennyson	1902–04	Sir William McKell	1947–53
Lord Northcote	1904–08	Viscount Slim	1953–60
Earl of Dudley	1908–11	Viscount Dunrossil	1960–61
Lord Denman	1911–14	Viscount De L'Isle	1961–65
Viscount Novar	1914–20	Lord Casey	1965–69
Lord Forster	1920–25	Sir Paul Hasluck	1969–74
Lord Stonehaven	1925–31	Sir John Kerr	1974–77
Sir Isaac Isaacs	1931–36	Sir Zelman Cowen	1977–82
Earl Gowrie	1936–45	Sir Ninian Stephen	1982–

National flag: The British Blue Ensign with a large star of 7 points beneath the Union Flag, and in the fly 5 stars of the Southern Cross, all in white.

The cabinet of the Labour administration in March 1985 was composed as follows:

Prime Minister: Robert Hawke.
Deputy Prime Minister and Attorney-General: Lionel Bowen.
Industry, Technology and Commerce: John Button.
Community Services: Don Grimes.
Employment and Industrial Relations: Ralph Willis.
Treasurer: Paul Keating.
Special Minister of State: Nick Young.
Finance: Peter Walsh.
Foreign Affairs: Bill Hayden.
Education: Susan Ryan.
Resources and Energy: Gareth Evans.
Trade: John Dawkins.
Primary Industry: John Kerin.
Housing and Construction: Stewart West.
Defence: Kim Beazley.
Immigration and Ethnic Affairs: Chris Hurford.
Social Security: Brian Howe.
Transport and Aviation: Peter Morris.
Sport, Recreation and Tourism: John Brown.
Health: Dr Neal Blewett.
Science: Barry Jones.
Territories: Gordon Scholes.
Communications: Michael Duffy.
Arts, Heritage and the Environment: Barry Cohen.
Aboriginal Affairs: Clyde Holding.
Veterans' Affairs: Arthur Gietzelt.
Local Government and Administrative Services: Tom Uren.

The Acts of the Parliament of the Commonwealth of Australia Passed from 1901 to 1973. 12 vols. Annual volumes, 1974 to date
The Australian Constitution Annotated. Attorney-General's Department, Canberra, 1980
Parliamentary Handbook of the Commonwealth of Australia. Canberra, 1915 to date
Commonwealth of Australia Directory [1921–1958 The Federal Guide; 1961–72 *Commonwealth Directory;* 1973–75 *Australian Government Directory*]. Prime Minister's Department. Canberra, 1924 to date
Crisp, L. F., *Australian National Government.* 3rd ed. Melbourne and London, 1975

Hughes, C. A., and Graham, B. D., *A Handbook of Australian Government and Politics.* Canberra, 1968
Odgers, J. R., *Australian Senate Practice.* 5th ed. Canberra, 1976
Paton, Sir George (ed.), *The Commonwealth of Australia: its Laws and Constitution.* London, 1952
Pettifer, J. A., *House of Representatives Practice.* Canberra, 1981
Sawer, G., *Australian Federal Politics and Law 1901–1929, 1929–1949.* 2 vols. Melbourne, 1974.—*Australian Government To-day.* 11th ed. Melbourne, 1973
Wynes, W. A., *Executive and Judicial Powers in Australia.* 5th ed. Sydney, 1976

State Government: In each of the 6 States (New South Wales, Victoria, Queensland, South Australia, Western Australia, Tasmania) there is a State government whose constitution, powers and laws continue, subject to changes embodied in the Australian Constitution and subsequent alterations and agreements, as they were before federation. The system of government is basically the same as that described above for the Commonwealth—*i.e.*, the Sovereign, her representative (in this case a Governor), an upper and lower house of Parliament (except in Queensland, where the upper house was abolished in 1922), a cabinet led by the Premier and an Executive Council. Among the more important functions of the State governments are those relating to education, health, hospitals and charities, law, order and public safety, business undertakings such as railways and tramways, and public utilities such as water supply and sewerage. In the domains of education, hospitals, justice, the police, penal establishments, and railway and tramway operation, State government activity predominates. Care of the public health and recreative activities are shared with local government authorities and the Federal Government, social services other than those referred to above are now primarily the concern of the Federal Government, and the operation of public utilities is shared with local and semi-government authorities.

Administration of Territories. Since 1911, responsibility for administration and development of the Australian Capital Territory has been vested in Federal Ministers and Departments. In 1930, the ACT Advisory Council was established, with both elected and appointed Members, to advise the Minister on administration of the Territory.

Late in 1974 the Government replaced the ACT Advisory Council with a Legislative Assembly of eighteen Members all of whom are elected and on 29 June 1979 the Legislative Assembly became the House of Assembly. While the Assembly has been accorded the forms of a legislature, it continues to perform an advisory function for the Minister for the Capital Territory.

On 1 July 1978 the Northern Territory of Australia became a self-governing Territory with expenditure responsibilities and revenue-raising powers broadly approximating those of a State, although the Territory is not a State under the Constitution.

Under self-government the Legislative Assembly and Ministers of the Northern Territory have responsibility in the areas of insurance, banking, taxation, provision of credit and assistance; Public Service of the Territory; maintenance of law and order and the administration of Justice etc.; civil liberties; markets and marketing; inquiries and administrative reviews; consumer affairs; sales and leases of goods and supply of services etc.; prices and rent control; industry and regulation of businesses and professions; tourism; printing and publishing; labour relations and industrial safety; mining and minerals; land and land use; transport; environment protection and conservation; fire prevention; water resources; energy planning, public utilities and public works; local government; housing, education, health, welfare etc.; censorship; Supreme Court, agreements between the Territory and the Commonwealth, State or States.

Local Government. The system of municipal government is broadly the same throughout Australia, although local government legislation is a State matter.

Each State is sub-divided into areas known variously as municipalities, cities, boroughs, towns, shires or district councils, totalling about 900. Within these areas the management of road, street and bridge construction, health, sanitary and garbage services, water supply and sewerage, and electric light and gas undertakings, hospitals, fire brigades, tramways and omnibus services and harbours is generally part of the functions of elected aldermen and councillors. The scope of their duties, however, differs considerably, for in all States the State Government, either directly or through semi-government authorities, also carries out some or all of these types of services.

In some instances, *e.g.*, in New South Wales, a number of local government authorities combine to conduct a public undertaking such as the supply of water or electricity.

DEFENCE. The Minister for Defence has responsibility under legislation for the control and administration of the Defence Force. The Chief of Defence Force Staff is vested with command of the Defence Force. He is the principal military adviser to the Minister. The Secretary, Department of Defence is the Permanent Head of the Department. He is the principal civilian adviser to the Minister and has statutory responsibility for financial administration of the Defence outlay. The Chief of Defence Force Staff and the Secretary are jointly responsible for the administration of the Defence Force except with respect to matters falling within the command of the Defence Force or any other matter specified by the Minister.

The Chief of Naval Staff, the Chief of the General Staff and the Chief of the Air Staff command the Navy, Army and Air Force respectively. They have delegated authority from the Chief of Defence Force Staff and the Secretary to administer matters relating to their particular Service.

The structure of Defence is characterized by 3 organizational types: *(i)* A Central Office comprising 5 groups of functional orientated Divisions: Strategic Policy and Force Development; Supply and Support; Manpower and Financial Services; Management and Infrastructure Services; and, Defence Science and Technology; *(ii)* the 3 Armed Services of the Defence Force, each having a Service Office element in addition to the command structure; and *(iii)* a small number of outrider organizations concerned with such specialist fields as intelligence and natural disasters.

Defence Support. Working within overall defence, industry and employment policies, the Department of Defence Support has as its goals the provision of optimum support for the nation's defence effort, the attainment of an appropriate technological and industrial infrastructure, and increased national self-reliance in defence support capacity.

Its specialist functions include defence purchasing and procurement, munitions and aircraft production, shipbuilding and other dockyard services and defence industry development.

In responding to the manifold needs of Australian defence, the Department: Undertakes the purchase of goods and services for defence purposes; provides technical expertise and other forms of assistance to encourage defence industry initiatives and the acquisition of modern industrial techniques and technologies; fosters participation by Australian industry in the procurement and support of defence equipment to the maximum practical extent; administers the Australian Offsets Program so as to stimulate technological advancement and broaden the capabilities of Australian industries of significance to this country's strategic and overall manufacturing needs; within overall defence policies develops proposals and provides advice in connection with the capacity, efficiency and capability of Australian industry particularly in so far as it is concerned with the design, export of defence materiel; manages the Government's munitions and aircraft factories, and dockyards; and consistent with the Government's defence and foreign affairs policies, markets defence and allied products and services to help maintain industrial capabilities of strategic significance.

These activities are carried out in pursuit of the Department's all encompassing goal of providing, within defence policy, optimum support for the nation's defence effort in peace and war.

The Department employs approximately 15,000 people (under the Public Service Act, the Supply and Development Act and the Naval Defence Act) who are located in establishments and offices in five states. This workforce includes some 2,100 professional and technical staff, 4,200 tradesmen and 1,500 apprentices.

Army. Overall organization and financial control of the Australian Army is vested in the Chief of General Staff. Under the Defence Force Re-organisation Act, which received the Royal Assent on 9 Sept. 1975, the Military Board, which was previously the controlling body of the Army, was abolished. The Act became effective on 1 Feb. 1976. A functional command structure, Headquarters Field Force Command, Headquarters Logistic Command, and Headquarters Training Command, with Headquarters in military districts, was introduced in 1973.

The strength of the Army was 32,212 as at 30 June 1984. There is emphasis in the field force organization on the combat element and high-priority logistic units to meet the requirements for limited war and tropical warfare with light air-portable formations. The Field Force is organized on the divisional structure, on the basis of 6 battalions organized in 3 brigades each with combat and logistic support.

The effective strength of the Army Reserve at 30 June 1984 was 30,058.

Staff and command training is carried out at the Command and Staff College, Queenscliff, Victoria, and the Land Warfare Centre, Canungra, Queensland.

In Jan. 1986 the Australian Defence Force Academy, Canberra, will accept its first officer cadets for the 3 Services. Cadets will study at the academy for degrees in arts, science and engineering. During semester breaks they will carry out military training with their particular Services.

At the end of 3 years at the academy, army officer cadets will undertake a year of military training at the Royal Military College, Duntroon. This will culminate with commissioning as a lieutenant.

In 1986 the Royal Military College will also take officer cadets for commissioning who previously would have attended the Officer Cadet School, Portsea, and the Women's Officer Cadet School, Sydney.

Navy. The overall control of the Royal Australian Navy is vested in the Chief of Naval Staff assisted by the Deputy Chief of Naval Staff with the Chief of Naval Personnel, the Chief of Naval Technical Services and the Chief of Naval Material. Under the Defence Re-organisation Act effective from 1 Feb. 1976 the Naval Board was abolished. The command, operation and administration of the Fleet is the responsibility of the Flag Officer Commanding HM Australian Fleet. The materiel support of the fleet is the responsibility of the Flag Officer Naval Support Command.

On 30 Sept. 1984 the RAN had 6 UK-built Oberon class submarines, *Onslow*, *Otway*, *Ovens* and *Oxley* (commissioned 1967–69) and *Orion* and *Otama* (commissioned in 1977–78); 3 US-built guided missile destroyers, *Brisbane*, *Hobart* and *Perth* (commissioned 1965–67; 4 US-built guided missile frigates, *Adelaide*, *Canberra*, *Sydney* and *Darwin* (commissioned 1981–84); 6 destroyer escorts; 4 oceanographic research and survey ships; 1 minehunter; 1 landing ship; 14 'Fremantle' and 2 'Attack' class patrol boats; plus 5 'Attack' class patrol boats (RANR); 6 landing craft; 1 fleet oiler; two training ships and 300 support craft. In addition an underway replenishment ship was being fitted out, the last planned 'Fremantle' class patrol boat was completing prior to commissioning in Dec. 1984, a prototype inshore minehunter was being built and the government announced plans to build 2 additional guided missile frigates at Williamstown, Victoria.

On 30 Sept. 1984, the Fleet Air Arm operated 39 Sea King, Wessex, Iroquois, Squirrel and Bell 206B helicopters and 2 HS748 fixed wing aircraft. Other fixed wing naval aviation ended on 30 June 1984.

The serving strength at 30 June 1984 totalled 16,692 personnel including 999 WRANS.

The main training establishments are HMAS *Cerberus* in Victoria; HMAS *Watson*, HMAS *Penguin* and HMAS *Nirimba* at Sydney; HMAS *Albatross* at Nowra, NSW, and HMAS *Creswell* (Royal Australian Naval College) at Jervis Bay, ACT. Reserve training is carried out in 7 major seaboard capital cities.

Navy estimates 1982–83, $A1,097,566,000; 1983–84, $A1,172,744,000.

Air Force. Command of the Royal Australian Air Force is vested in the Chief of the Air Staff (CAS) assisted by the Deputy Chief of the Air Staff, Chief of Air Force Operations and Plans, Chief of Air Force Materiel, Chief of Air Force Personnel, Chief of Air Force Technical Services, Director-General Supply—Air Force and Assistant Secretary Resources Planning.

The CAS administers and controls RAAF units through two commands: Operational Command and Support Command. Operational Command is responsible to the CAS for the command of operational units and the conduct of their operations within Australia and overseas. Support Command is responsible to the CAS for training of personnel, and the supply and maintenance of service equipment.

Flying establishment comprises 12 squadrons, of which 2 are equipped with 24 F-111 strike/reconnaissance aircraft. Of the others, 3 are equipped with missile-armed Mirage III-O Mach 2 fighters, 2 with Orion maritime reconnaissance aircraft. There are nine transport squadrons, 2 with Hercules turboprop transports, 1 with Caribou STOL transports, 1 with a mix of fixed-wing Caribou and Iroquois helicopters, 1 with Boeing Vertol CH-47C medium lift helicopters, 2 with Iroquois helicopters, and a special transport squadron equipped with BAC One-Eleven, Mystère 20 and HS 748 aircraft. There is also one squadron operating B707 aircraft. Training aircraft include piston-engined Airtrainers, built in New Zealand, Aermacchi MB 326H jets for pilot training, and HS 748 aircraft for navigator training.

Training for commissioned rank is carried out at the RAAF Academy and Officers' Training School, both located at Point Cook, Victoria. Other major training activities which lead to commissioned rank include basic aircrew training and technical and commercial cadet schemes. Basic ground training to tradesman level is conducted at RAAF technical training schools. Higher command and staff training is, in the main, carried out at the RAAF Staff College, Fairbairn, ACT.

The authorized service manpower ceiling for the Permanent Air Force is 22,677 for 1984–85. There is also an Australian Air Force Reserve.

Long, G. (ed.), *Australia in the War of 1939–45.* 22 vols. Canberra, 1952 ff.
O'Neil, R., and Horner, D. M., *Australian Defence Policy for the 1980s.* Univ. of Queensland Press, 1983

INTERNATIONAL RELATIONS

Membership. Australia is a member of the UN, the Commonwealth, OECD, Colombo Plan, the South Pacific Commission and the South Pacific Bureau for Economic Co-operation.

ECONOMY

Financial relations with the States. Since 1942 the Federal Government alone has levied taxes on incomes. In return for vacating this field of taxation, the State Governments are reimbursed by grants from the Federal Government out of revenue received. Payments to the States represent about one-third of Federal Government outlays, and in turn the payments State Governments receive from the Federal Government account for nearly half of their revenues.

The Financial Agreement of 1927 established the Australian Loan Council which consists of representatives of the Federal and six State Governments, and has the task of co-ordinating domestic and overseas borrowings by these governments including, *inter alia*, and setting of annual borrowing programmes. The Federal Government acts as a central borrowing agency in raising loans to finance the major part of those programmes. The Loan Council in 1984 agreed upon arrangements for the co-ordination of borrowings by semi-government and local authorities and government-owned companies.

Budget. In 1929, under a financial agreement between the Federal Government and States, approved by a referendum, the Federal Government took over all State debts existing on 30 June 1927 and agreed to pay $A15 17m. a year for 58 years towards the interest charges thereon, and to make substantial contributions towards a sinking fund on State debt. The Sinking Fund arrangements were revised under an amendment to the agreement in 1976.

Receipts, Financing Transactions and Outlays of the Federal Government for years ending 30 June (in $A1m.):

Receipts:	*1979–80*	*1980–81*	*1981–82*	*1982–83*[1]
Taxes on income	18,571	22,373	26,463	28,047
Employers payroll taxes	36	37	38	39
Taxes on property	72	45	36	71
Taxes on provision of goods and services excises	5,238	6,094	6,226	7,068
Taxes on international trade	1,630	1,916	2,158	2,105
Other	1,866	2,104	2,856	8,528
Total	*8,734*	*10,114*	*11,240*	*12,669*
Taxes on use of goods and performance of activities	47	52	83	101
Fees and fines	53	56	73	79
Total taxes, fees and fines	27,514	32,676	37,932	41,005
Net operating surpluses of trading enterprises	764	804	991	1,036
Property income				
Income from public financial enterprises	264	241	387	696
Other	1,631	1,910	2,150	2,338
Total	*1,895*	*2,151*	*2,537*	*3,034*
Other revenue	2	2	2	2
Total receipts	30,174	35,633	41,463	45,076
Financing transactions	3,054	2,162	1,879	6,097
Total funds available	33,228	37,794	43,341	51,172
Outlay:				
General public services	2,014	2,360	2,749	3,196
Defence	2,844	3,367	3,993	4,611
Public order and safety	199	218	255	322
Education:				
Primary and secondary education	848	990	1,194	1,431
Tertiary education	1,668	1,846	2,038	2,261
Total education	2,612	2,933	3,338	3,801
Health				
Hospital and other institutions	1,963	2,293	1,426	1,725
Other	1,199	1,348	1,482	1,698
Total health	3,162	3,641	2,908	3,423
Social Security and Welfare				
Sickness benefits	127	175	225	271
Benefits to Ex-Servicemen and their dependants	1,004	1,235	1,384	1,778
Invalid and other permanent disablement benefits	870	968	1,082	1,185
Old age benefits	3,529	3,963	4,538	4,915
Unemployment benefits	925	996	1,224	2,249
Family and child benefits	1,016	953	1,046	1,381
Family and child welfare	40	48	55	75
Aged and handicapped welfare	123	129	146	170
Other	1,170	1,455	1,823	2,079
Total social security, etc.	8,804	9,922	11,523	14,103
Housing and community amenities	363	350	352	725
Recreation and culture	315	401	476	528
Fuel and energy	94	–43	161	208
Agriculture, forestry, fishing and hunting	397	409	601	729
Mining, manufacturing and construction	368	445	487	509
Transport and communications	2,102	2,416	2,663	3,332
Other economic affairs	476	632	752	859
Other purposes	9,478	10,746	13,081	14,827
Total outlay	33,228	37,794	43,341	51,172

[1] Provisional.

The following table shows Government securities on issue on account of the Commonwealth Government and States, at 30 June 1984:

Currency in which repayable	*Australian Government*	*States*	*Total*
Australian Dollar ($A1,000)	23,016,365	16,833,415	39,849,779
Sterling (£1,000)	199,500	2,399	201,899
United States Dollar (US$1,000)	2,152,695	3,360	2,156,055
Swiss Francs (SW.F.1,000)	2,310,000	—	2,310,000
Netherlands Guilders (fl.1,000)	1,140,000	—	1,140,000
Deutsche Marks (DM 1,000)	2,650,936	—	2,650,936
European Units of Account (EUA1,000)	—	—	—
Japanese Yen (Yen 1m.)	324,233	—	324,233
Total ($A1,000 equivalents) [1]	30,092,550	16,841,077	46,933,627

[1] Converted at rate of exchange ruling at 30 June 1983.

Debt per head of population at 30 June 1984 was $A3,019, while the annual interest charge amounted to $A329 per head.

States: The following table presents a summary of the receipts and outlay of State and local authorities during 1981–82 (in $A1m.).

	NSW	*Vic.*	*Qld*	*SA*	*WA*	*Tas.*	*NT*	*All States*
Receipts and Financing Transactions								
Taxes, fees, fines, etc.	3,474	2,661	1,204	631	699	210	46	8,925
Income from public enterprises	127	402	249	113	62	94	–45	1,001
Grants from Commonwealth Government	4,037	3,089	2,208	1,331	1,426	551	540	13,181
Advances from Commonwealth Government (net)	282	198	102	76	71	52	80	862
All other	1,780	1,843	1,152	368	483	164	93	5,884
Total funds available	9,700	8,193	4,915	2,519	2,741	1,071	714	29,853
Outlay								
Final consumption expenditure	5,715	4,433	2,350	1,538	1,628	594	431	16,690
Interest paid	1,155	1,138	557	313	264	160	35	3,621
Gross fixed capital expenditure on new assets	3,343	2,557	1,890	606	800	285	182	9,663
All other	–513	65	118	62	49	32	66	–121
Total outlay	9,700	8,193	4,915	2,519	2,741	1,071	714	29,853

Australian National Accounts. Australian Bureau of Statistics. 1953–54 to date
Public Authority Finance: Commonwealth Government Finance, Australia. Australian Bureau of Statistics, 1962–63 to date
Public Authority Finance: State and Local Government Finance, Australia. Australian Bureau of Statistics, 1971–72 to date
Public Authority Finance: Government Financial Estimates. Australian Bureau of Statistics, 1975–76 to date
National Income and Expenditure. Australian Bureau of Statistics. Canberra, 1946 to date
Treasury Information Bulletin (and Supplements). Canberra Treasury Dept., 1956 to date (quarterly)
Hagger, A. J., *A Guide to Australian Economic and Social Statistics.* Sydney, 1983

Currency. On 14 Feb. 1966 Australia adopted a system of decimal currency. The currency unit, the *dollar* ($) is divided into 100 *cents*. The transition period ended on 31 July 1967. Decimal notes are issued in denominations of $2, 5, 10, 20, 50 and 100. Coins are issued in denominations of 1, 2, 5, 10, 20 and 50 cents and $1.

Australian notes, issued by the note-issue department of the Reserve Bank, are legal tender throughout Australia. The total value of notes in circulation on 30 June 1984 was $A7,205m., of which $A6,418m. was held by the public. In Feb. 1985, US$1 = 1·42 *dollars*; £1 = 1·52 *dollars*.

Banking. The banking system in Australia comprises:

(a) The Reserve Bank of Australia. This is the central bank which in addition to its central banking business (including the note-issue department) provides special financing facilities through the rural credits department for the processing, manufacture and marketing of primary produce.

(b) Four major trading banks: (i) The Commonwealth Bank of Australia; (ii) 3 private trading banks: The Australia and New Zealand Banking Group Ltd, Westpac Banking Corporation and the National Commercial Banking Corporation of Australia Ltd.

(c) Other trading banks: (i) 3 State Government banks—The State Bank of New South Wales, The State Bank of South Australia, and the Rural and Industries Bank of Western Australia; (ii) one joint stock bank—The Bank of Queensland Ltd, formerly The Brisbane Permanent Building and Banking Co. Ltd, which has specialized business in one district only; (iii) The Australian Bank Ltd; (iv) branches of 2 overseas banks—the Bank of New Zealand and the Banque Nationale de Paris, which are mainly concerned with financing trade, etc., between Australia and overseas countries.

(d) The Commonwealth Development Bank of Australia.

(e) The Australian Resources Development Bank Ltd opened on 29 March 1968. Its main objective is to assist Australian enterprises in the development of Australia's natural resources, through direct loans and equity investment or by re-financing loans made by trading banks. The bank is jointly owned by the 4 major Australian trading banks.

(f) The Primary Industry Bank of Australia Ltd commenced operations on 22 Sept. 1978. The equity capital of the bank consists of eight shares. Seven shares are held by the Australian Government and the major trading banks while the eighth share is held equally by the 4 State banks. The main objective of the bank is to facilitate the provision of loans to primary producers on longer terms than are otherwise generally available. The role of the bank is restricted to re-financing loans made by banks and other financial institutions.

(g) Savings Banks.

The Reserve Bank's functions and responsibilities derive from the Reserve Bank Act 1959 and the Banking Act 1959, which came into effect in 1960. They had their origins, however, in the development of the central banking role of the Commonwealth Bank, which was established in 1911 as a Government savings and trading bank.

Control of the Australian note issue was transferred from the Commonwealth Treasury to a Notes Board in 1920 and, in 1924, to the Bank. The Commonwealth Bank Act 1945 formally constituted the Bank as a central bank, and these powers were carried through into the 1959 Act establishing the Reserve Bank.

The Acts of 1959 provided for: (i) the separation of the central bank from the Commonwealth group of banking institutions and its reconstitution as the Reserve Bank of Australia; (ii) the establishment of an entirely separate Commonwealth Banking Corporation, with responsibilities for the non-central-banking elements that had developed from within the original Commonwealth Bank—namely the Commonwealth Trading Bank, the Commonwealth Savings Bank and the Commonwealth Development Bank, the latter being basically an amalgamation of the Mortgage Bank and Industrial Finance Department of the Commonwealth Bank.

At 30 June 1984 the capital of the Reserve Bank totalled $A49·4m. and reserve funds (including a special reserve for IMF special drawing rights) $A4,521m. The capital was distributed as follows: Central banking business, $A40m.; rural credits department, $A9m. Reserve funds held were: Central banking business, $A2,025m.; rural credits department, $A100m.; note issue department, $A2,396m. Profits for the year ended 30 June 1984 (including all departments) amounted to $A1,029m.

Particulars as at 30 June 1983 for the banks under the control of the Commonwealth Banking Corporation: Commonwealth Bank of Australia, capital, $A15m.;

reserve fund, $A200m.; profits for the year, $A46m. Commonwealth Development Bank, capital, $A62m.; reserve fund, $A179m.; profits for the year, $A23m. Commonwealth Savings Bank, reserve fund, $A404m.; profits for the year, $A68m.

At 30 June 1984 the 11 trading banks operating in Australia provided full banking facilities at 5,032 branches and 1,087 agencies all over Australia.

The weekly average of deposits in Australia with all trading banks (under *(b)* and *(c)* above) during June 1984 amounted to $A38,385m.; the average of advances owing to the banks was $A31,743m.; the average of total assets was $A62,627m.

At 30 June 1984, 11 savings banks were operating in Australia. These are the 4 major savings banks being wholly owned subsidiaries of the trading banks; the Bank of New Zealand Saving Bank Ltd; the Bank of Queensland Saving Bank Ltd; the State Bank of Victoria and the Savings Bank of South Australia; the Rural and Industries Bank of Western Australia, and 2 Trustee Savings Banks in Tasmania. At 30 June 1984 these savings banks provided savings facilities at 5,592 branches and 10,533 agencies throughout Australia. At end of June 1984 they held deposits in Australia amounting to $A34,328m.

The following table is a summary of banking business (in $A1m.) in the several States of the Commonwealth:

Particulars	*NSW*	*Vic.*	*Q'ld*	*SA*	*WA*	*Tas.*	*Australia (including A.C.T. and N.T.)*
All trading banks:[1]							
Fixed deposits	10,961	5,876	4,013	1,225	2,052	344	24,891
Current deposits	5,686	3,295	2,055	752	1,027	231	13,494
Advances	13,148	6,388	4,879	2,840	2,966	445	31,743
Savings bank deposits [2]	9,532	12,916	4,709	3,327	2,214	1,103	34,328

[1] Weekly averages for June 1984. [2] At June 1984.

Treasury Information Bulletin. Department of the Treasury. Canberra, 1956 to date (quarterly)

Reserve Bank of Australia. *Statistical Bulletin.* Sydney, 1937 to date (monthly)

Weights and Measures. Conversion to the metric system is in progress.

ENERGY AND NATURAL RESOURCES

Electricity. Total production 1983–84, 111,658m. kwh. (of which hydro, 12,793m.).

Minerals. The mineral output was valued ex-mine as follows (in $A1,000):

Mineral	*1981–82*	*1982–83*
Copper concentrate	231,952	264,144
Gold bullion [1]	200,408	...
Iron ore [2]	1,131,186	...
Lead concentrate	252,136	...
Tin concentrate	141,716	133,405
Zinc concentrate	...	220,546
Black coal	2,926,883	3,519,010
Brown coal [3]	137,138	150,788
Total (value of minerals and construction materials)	9,089,128	10,519,699

[1] Includes alluvial gold. [2] Includes iron ore for pellet production.
[3] Excludes value of brown coal used in making briquettes.

Gold production (metallic content) based on assay (kg), in 1978–79, 19,584; 1979–80, 18,273; 1980–81, 15,991; 1981–82, 22,328; 1982–83, 25,825.

Black coal (1,000 tonnes) mined in 1978–79, 81,197; 1979–80, 81,219; 1980–81, 96,074; 1981–82, 99,560; 1982–83, 107,768.

Agriculture. In 1983, of a total Australian area of 768m. hectares, 641·5m. hectares (83·5%) were Crown lands; private lands formed the remainder, of which 126·7m. hectares (16·5%) were alienated or in the process of alienation.

Area and production of the principal crops in 1983–84[2]:

Crops	Total area (1,000 hectares)	Total production (1,000 tonnes)
Wheat (grain)	12,909	22,064
Oats (grain)	1,743	2,270
Barley (grain)	3,163	4,617
Maize (grain)	63	...
Hay (cereal)	382	1,222
Potatoes (ordinary)	32	...
Sugar-cane (for crushing)	307	24,263
Vineyards	65	...
Wine made	...	...
Fruit	107	...

The following summary shows the production and gross value of the most important items or classes of production, classified by States:

1983–84 [2]	*NSW*	*Vic.*	*Q'ld*	*SA*	*WA*	*Tas.*	*Aust.*[1]
Area of crops (1,000 hectares)	6,534	2,643	3,065	3,075	6,492	95	21,910
Production of wheat (1,000 tonnes)	8,966	3,989	1,950	2,839	4,316	3	22,064
1983–84 [2]							
Total wool production (1,000m. tons)	248·8	140·2	65·4	108·7	142·7	21·8	728·1
1983–84 [2]							
Factory butter (1,000 kg)	2,832	93,884	5,371	1,733	1,269	6,191	111,280
All meat (tonnes, carcase weight)							
1981–82	538,006	622,455	644,050	194,673	201,490	65,320	2,307,284
1982–83	584,657	613,856	577,984	216,012	210,264	71,236	2,311,978
1983–84	486,769	428,571	623,620	171,939	177,418	56,628	1,987,720
Total Agriculture (value $A1m.) 1983–84[2]	4,503·3	3,196·0	3,098·9	1,796·8	1,953·5	356·8	14,997·0

[1] Includes Northern Territory and Australian Capital Territory. [2] Preliminary, subject to revision.

Livestock (in 1,000) at 31 March 1984 (preliminary):

	NSW	*Vic.*	*Q'ld*	*SA*	*WA*	*Tas.*	*N. Terr.*	*ACT*	*Australia*
Cattle	5,000	3,453	8,875	833	1,703	543	1,431	10	21,846
Sheep	51,000	24,425	12,942	16,088	29,467	4,594	1	108	138,625
Pigs	809	375	552	402	289	48	3	—	2,478

Forestry. At 31 March 1981 there were 741,000 hectares of coniferous plantations.

INDUSTRY AND TRADE

Industry. Statistics of the manufacturing industries in Australia in 1982–83: Number of establishments, 27,696; workers employed, 1,052,905; salaries and wages paid, $A17,403m.; value-added, $A31,059m. (excludes small single-establishment enterprises employing less than 4 persons).

Estimated gross value (in $A1,000) of the products of Australia:

Products	*1979–80*	*1980–81*	*1981–82*	*1982–83*	*1983–84* [1]
Crops	5,540·8	5,305·9	6,311·9	5,002·6	8,112·1
Livestock slaughtering and other disposals	3,658·8	3,474·3	3,295·6	3,489·6	3,391·3
Livestock products	2,564·3	2,804·8	3,100·6	3,210·2	3,493·3
Fishing	317·5	383·8	...	...	...
Mining and quarrying	7,143·7	8,158·2	9,089·1	10,519·7	...

[1] Preliminary, subject to revision.

Labour. The majority of wage and salary earners in Australia have their minimum wages and conditions of work prescribed in awards of industrial arbitration authorities established under federal and State legislation. However, in some

States, some conditions of work (*e.g.*, normal weekly hours of work, long-service leave, annual leave) are set down in State legislation. Practically all employees in Australia have a standard working week of 40 hours or less; paid annual leave of at least 4 weeks; and paid long-service leave (*i.e.*, leave granted to workers who remain with one employer over an extended period of time and in certain other areas) of at least 13 weeks after 15 years' continuous service. For most occupations equal pay for males and females has been granted.

In addition to the minimum rates of pay for a standard working week prescribed in awards of industrial arbitration authorities, many wage-earners are in receipt of over-award pay and payments for overtime. In Nov. 1983 it was estimated that the average weekly earnings of adult males (other than managerial, professional and higher supervisory staff) in full-time private and government employment was $A374 and average weekly hours 40.

Employees in all States are covered by workers' compensation legislation and by certain industrial award provisions relating to work injuries.

During 1983 industrial disputes involving stoppages of work of 10 man-days or more accounted for 1,641,400 working days lost. In these disputes 470,500 workers were involved.

The following table shows estimates (in 1,000) of the civilian population, by labour force status. The estimates are derived by the ABS from the population survey which is based on a sample of dwellings, carried out by personal interview, covering about two-thirds of 1% of the population of Australia. Prior to Feb. 1978, when monthly surveys were introduced, the surveys were conducted quarterly. The labour force estimates for Feb. 1978 and subsequent months are based on population estimates derived from the 1976 Population Census, adjusted for under-enumeration and were obtained using a new sample and revised questionnaire. Estimates for earlier periods have been revised to make them comparable with current surveys.

	May 1980	*May 1981*	*May 1982*	*May 1983*	*May 1984*
In the labour force	6,690·0	6,791·6	6,894·7	6,993·3	7,127·5
Employed	6,273·4	6,412·4	6,440·9	6,272·8	6,490·5
Unemployed	416·6	379·3	453·8	720·5	637·0
Not in the labour force	4,202·0	4,318·5	4,449·8	4,561·1	4,622·3
Civilian population aged 15 years and over	10,892·0	11,110·2	11,344·5	11,554·4	11,744·8

The following table shows population survey estimates (in 1,000) of employed persons in Australia classified by industry:

Industry [1]	*May 1981*	*May 1982*	*May 1983*	*May 1984*
Agriculture and services to agriculture	396·2	377·5	391·9	372·6
Forestry and logging, fishing and hunting	31·0	32·7	27·0	24·8
Mining	91·8	97·0	98·0	100·0
Manufacturing	1,266·8	1,249·1	1,148·9	1,148·0
Food, beverages and tobacco	175·3	183·5	190·8	181·4
Metal products	237·2	223·7	198·2	191·7
Other manufacturing	854·3	841·8	759·9	774·9
Electricity, gas and water	129·3	125·3	142·4	150·3
Construction	491·6	472·5	418·7	433·4
Wholesale trade	398·3	390·8	371·2	380·4
Retail trade	875·7	889·4	880·1	900·8
Transport and storage	346·1	368·4	355·7	367·2
Communication	123·7	142·1	133·5	136·8
Finance, property and business services	564·1	577·7	575·2	615·0
Public administration and defence	288·4	287·2	300·2	325·0
Community services	1,011·5	1,028·2	1,034·5	1,115·7
Recreation, personal and other services	397·9	403·0	395·3	420·7
Total employed	6,412·4	6,440·9	6,272·8	6,490·5

[1] Australian Standard Industrial Classification.

The following table shows the number of unemployed persons (from the population survey), job vacancies (from the ABS Job Vacancies survey) and the number of persons in receipt of unemployment benefit:

	May 1980	*May 1981*	*May 1982*	*May 1983*	*May 1984*
Persons unemployed	416,600	379,300	453,800	720,500	637,000
Job Vacancies	29,800	35,700	25,300	17,500	34,800 [2]
Unemployment benefit recipients [1]	311,200	314,500	390,700	635,000	584,500

[1] Data relates to the month of June [2] Not strictly comparable with earlier surveys.

Trade Unions. At the end of 1983 there were 319 trade unions reporting in Australia with an estimated membership of 2,985,200. About 55% of wage and salary earners were estimated to be members of unions. In 1983 there were 41 unions with fewer than 100 members and 9 unions with 80,000 or more members. Many of the larger trade unions are affiliated with central labour organizations, the oldest and by far the largest being the Australian Council of Trade Unions formed in 1927.

Labour Statistics. Australian Bureau of Statistics. Canberra, 1982
Isaac, J. E., and Ford, G. W., *Australian Industrial Relations.* Melbourne, 1971
O'Dea, R., *A Guide to Industrial Relations in Australia.* Sydney, 1967
Portus, J. H., *The Development of Australian Trade Union Law.* Melbourne, 1958
Rawson, D. W., *A Handbook of Australian Trade Unions and Employees' Associations.* Canberra, 1977
Walker, K. F., *Australian Industrial Relations Systems.* Cambridge, Mass., 1970

Commerce. Throughout Australia there are uniform customs duties, and trade between the States is free. For 1982–83 the gross revenue collected from customs duties amounted to $A2,065·9m. and from excise $A6,906·6m.

Value of the total imports and exports for years ending 30 June, in $A1,000:

		Exports (excluding ships' and aircraft stores)		
	Imports	*Australian produce*	*Re-exports*	*Total*
1981–82	23,004,930	18,816,343	758,863	19,575,206
1982–83	21,806,179	20,757,048	1,303,258	22,060,306
1983–84 [1]	24,062,896	23,550,377	1,254,866	24,805,243

[1] Preliminary, subject to revision.

The Australian customs tariff provides for preferences to goods produced in and shipped from certain specified countries such as UK, Canada, New Zealand and Ireland. Preferences occur as a result of reciprocal trade agreements between Australia and these countries.

Australia also has bilateral agreements with a number of other countries guaranteeing reciprocal treatment in matters of trade.

The Australia–New Zealand free-trade agreement came into force on 1 Jan. 1966 in certain scheduled goods.

In addition, Australia is a signatory to the multilateral General Agreement on Tariffs and Trade (GATT).

Principal commodities exported and imported from Australia (in $A1,000) in 1983–84 [1]:

	Exports	*Imports*
Live animals	246,846	36,575
Meat	1,394,511	14,099
Dairy products	366,226	67,915
Fish	394,403	260,547
Cereals	2,710,022	46,846
Fruit and vegetables	226,207	224,814
Sugar, etc., and honey	647,955	17,746
Coffee, tea, etc.	38,616	264,461
Food for animals	108,644	29,710
Miscellaneous food	22,045	52,612
Beverages	38,735	105,759
Tobacco	14,632	90,364
Hides, skins, etc.	268,841	3,228
Oil-seeds, nuts, kernels	15,154	23,006
Crude rubber	3,174	62,905
Wood, timber and cork	220,025	227,734
Pulp and waste paper	4,110	98,119
Textile fibres and their waste	2,057,104	103,641
Crude fertilizers and minerals	123,175	172,803
Metalliferous ores and metal scrap	4,109,712	16,366
Crude animal & vegetable materials, n.e.s.	53,904	54,325
Coal, coke & briquettes	3,320,801	4,186
Petroleum and products	1,401,160	2,198,601
Petroleum gases	502,061	1,326
Animal oils and fats	93,504	636
Fixed vegetable oils and fats	5,001	62,485
Animal and vegetable oils and fats	6,870	47,981
Organic chemicals	45,198	605,700
Inorganic chemicals	43,928	181,565
Dyeing, tanning and colouring materials	20,792	101,345
Medicinal and pharmaceutical products	118,529	221,239
Essential oils and perfumes, etc.	38,344	133,335
Fertilizers, manufactured	8,825	125,638
Explosives and pyrotechnic products	7,576	15,777
Plastic materials	127,652	485,504
Chemical materials and products, n.e.s.	89,979	280,971
Leather manufactures, n.e.s.	52,436	82,522
Rubber manufactures, n.e.s.	12,334	301,993
Wood and cork manufactures (except furniture)	6,843	118,020
Paper and paperboard	53,943	615,516
Textile yarn, fabrics, etc.	148,032	302,735
Non-metallic mineral manufactures, n.e.s.	152,899	423,367
Iron and steel	416,975	435,890
Non-ferrous metals	1,530,329	99,492
Manufactures of metal, n.e.s.	208,447	605,230

	Exports	*Imports*
Power generating machinery and equipment	186,455	586,528
Machinery specialized for particular industries	179,569	1,151,180
Metalworking machinery	30,580	145,740
General industrial machinery and equipment, n.e.s. and machine parts, n.e.s.	175,975	1,146,585
Office machines and automatic data processing equipment	118,107	1,141,066
Telecommunications and sound recording and reproducing apparatus and equipment	51,382	965,959
Electrical machinery, apparatus and appliances, n.e.s. and electrical parts thereof (including non-electrical counterparts n.e.s., of electrical household type equipment)	145,025	1,124,971
Road vehicles (including air cushion vehicles)	267,883	2,303,271
Other transport equipment	185,172	750,056
Sanitary, plumbing, heating and lighting fixtures and fittings, n.e.s.	8,531	44,989
Furniture and parts thereof	18,783	144,553
Travel goods, handbags and similar containers	2,273	107,261
Articles of apparel and clothing accessories	16,497	425,415
Footwear	5,201	160,335
Professional, scientific and controlling instruments and apparatus, n.e.s.	147,442	511,175
Photographic apparatus, equipment and supplies and optical goods, n.e.s.; watches and clocks	148,799	402,441
Miscellaneous manufactured articles, n.e.s.	163,128	1,323,466
Commodities and transactions of merchandise trade, not elsewhere classified [2]	711,189	691,943
Total merchandise trade	24,058,485	23,551,563
Commodities and transactions not included in merchandise trade	746,757	511,334
Total recorded trade	24,805,243	24,062,896

[1] Preliminary. [2] Industrial petroleum gases.

Total trade in ($A1,000) with the more important countries, according to origin (imports) and consignment (exports):

	1982–83		1983–84	
From or to	*Imports*	*Exports*	*Imports*	*Exports*
Belgium–Luxembourg	124,792	165,651	161,613	163,658
Canada	434,643	285,892	459,518	315,277
China–excl. Taiwan Province	278,891	643,792	311,623	608,435
Egypt, Arab Republic of	112	366,608	176	350,853
France	454,765	495,284	514,167	482,422
Germany, Fed. Republic of	6,273	548,615	8,581	720,509
Hong Kong	485,322	349,703	552,176	612,004
India	142,288	210,845	119,376	140,758
Indonesia	561,376	384,971	299,741	395,877
Iran	39,687	231,945	3,499	293,085
Italy	538,320	368,378	748,526	479,440
Japan	4,506,327	5,960,819	5,366,190	6,570,041
Kuwait	354,386	131,947	437,024	129,791
Malaysia	214,502	479,840	257,182	469,332
Netherlands	303,285	297,477	336,278	329,219
New Zealand	694,278	1,155,458	921,748	1,400,821
Pakistan	23,521	55,353	31,280	54,867
Papua New Guinea	69,042	508,220	76,679	494,387
Saudi Arabia	976,780	352,958	679,923	391,596
Singapore, Republic of	599,843	729,953	470,172	951,515
Sri Lanka	11,305	22,208	12,804	25,149
Sweden	277,859	34,136	342,686	37,511
Switzerland	197,395	31,034	229,166	57,900
USSR	12,314	506,952	12,094	581,756
UK	1,466,930	1,181,251	1,740,161	1,134,210
USA	4,766,424	2,241,119	5,188,392	2,704,744

Imports and exports for particular State ($A1,000):

	1982–83		1983–84	
States, etc.	*Imports*	*Exports*	*Imports*	*Exports*
New South Wales	8,610,870	5,433,293	10,027,948	5,771,969
Victoria	6,989,588	4,321,674	8,186,719	5,132,526
Queensland	1,994,645	4,463,889	2,086,980	5,442,927
South Australia	1,244,243	1,237,564	1,318,396	1,638,908
Western Australia	2,523,046	5,133,317	1,936,945	5,342,384
Tasmania	179,819	773,133	202,781	771,709
Northern Territory	239,856	565,153	279,941	590,735
Aust. Cap. Terr.	11,512	8,286	23,186	3,976
Total	21,806,015	22,060,306	24,062,896	24,805,243

In this table the value of goods sent from one state to another for transhipment abroad has been included in the State from which the goods were finally dispatched.

Overseas Trade. Australian Bureau of Statistics. Canberra, 1906 to date

Total trade between UK and Australia (British Department of Trade returns, in £1,000 sterling):

	1980	1981	1982	1983	1984
Imports to UK	484,112	395,387	493,196	552,642	612,087
Exports and re-exports from UK	815,652	863,636	1,043,615	940,279	1,186,521

Tourism. During 1983, 943,900 overseas visitors arrived in Australia intending to stay for less than 12 months, and international tourism receipts were $A1,187m.

Australian Bureau of Statistics, Canberra: *Rural Industries.* 1962–63 to date.—*Manufacturing Establishments: Details of Operations.* 1968–69 to date.—*Non-rural Primary Industries.* 1967–68 and 1968–69.—*Value of Production.* 1964–65 to 1968–69.—*Manufacturing Industry.* 1963–64 to 1967–68.—*Manufacturing Commodities.* 1963–64 and 1964–65.—*Building and Construction.* 1964–65 to date

Quarterly Review of Agricultural Economics. Bureau of Agricultural Economics. Canberra, 1948 to date

Developments in Australian Manufacturing Industry. Department of Trade. Melbourne, 1954–55 to date (annual)

The Australian Mineral Industry Review. Department of National Development—Bureau of Mineral Resources, Geology and Geophysics. Canberra, 1948 to date

Australian Economy. Department of the Treasury. Canberra, 1956 to date
Australasian Institute of Mining and Metallurgy. *Proceedings: New Series.* Melbourne, 1912 to date

COMMUNICATIONS

Roads. The length of roads in Australia for general traffic is about 817,000 km, of which approximately 238,000 is sealed, 211,000 of gravel, crushed stone or other improved surface, and 368,000 of cleared or formed surface only.

At 30 June 1983, 8,589,800 motor vehicles, including 6,469,600 cars and station wagons, 1,076,300 utilities and panel-vans, 642,000 truck type vehicles and buses and 402,000 motor cycles, were registered in Australia. New motor vehicle registration figures for 1983–84 include 461,018 cars and station wagons, 92,919 utilities and panel-vans, 49,777 truck type vehicles and buses and 46,684 motor cycles.

Railways. Government railways for the year ended 30 June 1983:

System	*Route-km open* [4]	*Revenue train-km run, 1,000*	*Passenger journeys, 1,000*	*Goods and livestock, carried, 1,000 tonnes*	*Gross earnings, $A1,000*	*Working expenses, $A1,000*
State:						
New South Wales	9,883	61,507	207,778	41,350	694,819	1,157,486
Victoria	5,815	30,166	84,323	8,570	247,945	625,848
Queensland	9,979	30,885	34,749	43,706	549,859	664,548
South Australia [3]	131	3,894	85,420	...	41,908	116,884
Western Australia	5,610	10,560	220 [5]	19,791	223,925	235,211
Australian National [1] [2]	7,647	10,795	357	10,676	193,854	300,410

[1] The Australian National Railways operates services of the former Commonwealth Railways, the non-metropolitan South Australian Railways and the Tasmanian Railways.
[2] Excludes Adelaide metropolitan rail passenger services and the Tasmanian Region.
[3] The South Australian State Transport Authority operates services in the Adelaide metropolitan area.
[4] Inter system traffic is included in the total for each system over which it passes.
[5] Excludes details of Western Australian suburban rail operations.

The State railway gauges are: New South Wales, 1,435 mm; Victoria, 1,600 mm (325 km 1,435 mm); Queensland, 1,067 mm (111 km 1,435 mm); South Australia, 1,600 mm for 2,533 km, 1,824 km 1,435 mm and the rest 1,067 mm; West Australia, 137 km, 1,435 mm and the rest 1,067 mm, and Tasmania, 1,067 mm. Of the Australian National Railways, the gauge of the Trans-Australian and Australian Capital Territory is 1,435 mm, and for the Central Australia 1,067 mm for 869 km and 1,435 mm for 350 km. Under various Commonwealth–State standardization agreements, all the State capitals are now linked by 1,435 mm gauge track. The Central Australia railway extends as far north as Alice Springs (now standard gauge on new alignment from Tarcoola to Alice Springs).

Aviation. All civil flying in Australia and its Territories is subject to legislative control by the Australian Government. In some cases intrastate air services are also subject to legislative control by the relevant State Government. The administration of the Air Navigation Act and Regulations and other Commonwealth aviation legislation is a function of the Commonwealth Department of Aviation under the Minister for Aviation.

All Australian-owned airlines, except Qantas Airways, operate regular internal air services. During 1982 hours flown numbered 259,388; the total distance flown was 134m. km; paying passengers carried numbered 11,005,796; weight of goods carried was 142,516 tonnes, and gross weight of mail was 17,005 tonnes.

During 1983 hours flown by Australian regular overseas services which are operated by or on behalf of Qantas numbered 81,684, km flown, 64m.; paying passengers, 2,073,438; freight, 81,340 tonnes; mail, 4,263 tonnes.

Expenditure by the Aviation Portfolio on air transport for the year 1983–84 was $A448·8m. Aviation related expenditure by other Australian Government Departments for the same period was $A71·6m.

At 30 June 1984 there were 441 licensed aerodromes and 71 governmental aerodromes in Australia.

Shipping. As at 30 June 1983 the Australian merchant marine (vessels of 150 tons gross and over) consisted of 74 coastal vessels of 1,146,505 tons gross and 30 overseas vessels of 924,037 tons gross.

Entrances and clearances of vessels (with cargo and in ballast) engaged in overseas trade:

	Entrances		*Clearances*	
	No.	*DWT*	*No.*	*DWT*
1981–82	10,483	328,628,782	10,331	328,066,585
1982–83	9,998	315,465,880	9,914	316,847,814

The following summary shows shipping activity by States, 1981–82:

Particulars	*NSW*	*Vic.*	*Q'ld*	*SA*	*WA*	*Tas.*	*N.T.*	*Unsp.*	*Aust.*
Overseas vessel arrivals									
Calls	2,398	1,705	2,014	743	2,481	438	219	...	9,998
DWT (1,000 tonnes)	68,954	34,720	61,707	14,977	117,625	10,993	6,489	...	315,466
Overseas cargo:									
Discharged: 1,000 gross weight tonnes	6,434	4,573	2,082	2,393	5,591	328	1,007	618	23,028
Discharged: 1,000 revenue tonnes	8,085	6,308	2,712	2,672	5,921	363	1,043	793	27,898
Overseas vessel departures									
Calls	2,426	1,637	1,986	739	2,477	421	224	4	9,914
DWT (1,000 tonnes)	70,826	33,931	61,398	14,721	118,587	10,724	6,613	115	316,848
Overseas cargo									
Loaded: 1,000 gross weight tonnes	31,861	5,330	34,234	2,734	84,940	4,776	4,024	1,671	169,572
Loaded: 1,000 revenue tonnes	32,050	5,738	34,313	2,787	85,012	4,816	4,030	1,771	170,517

Post and Broadcasting. Business, year ended 30 June 1983. Number of post offices, 4,843. Earnings: Postal, $A999·4m. Working expenses: $A990·6m.

At 30 June 1983, there were 5,591,667 telephone services, 70,191 data services, 39,388 telex services and 5,353 telephone exchanges.

Radio broadcasting stations are in operation in all State capitals and in other areas throughout Australia. The National Broadcasting and Television Service is provided by the Australian Broadcasting Corporation, which at 30 June 1983 operated 95 medium-wave, 25 frequency modulation and 6 high-frequency radio stations, and 10 high-frequency radio stations for overseas services. In addition, 130 medium-wave, and 7 frequency modulation, commercial broadcasting stations plus 38 public radio stations (both MW and FM) were operating.

Television services are provided in each State, the Northern Territory and the Australian Capital Territory by the ABC and by commercial television stations. There were 272 national stations (including translators) and 50 commercial television stations in 1983.

The Overseas Telecommunications Commission (OTC), established by the Overseas Telecommunications Act 1946, is responsible for the establishment, maintenance, operation and development of all public telecommunications' services between Australia and other countries, between Australia and its external territories and with ships at sea. In co-operation with Telecom and communications carriers in other countries, OTC provides ISD, other international telephone, telegram, facsimile, phototelegram, telex, leased circuit, audio broadcast and data transmission services to countries throughout the world by means of submarine cables, communications satellites and, in a decreasing number of cases, short wave radio. Television relay is provided to and from countries with access to satellite communications' facilities.

Cinemas (1971). There were 976 cinemas including 241 drive-in cinemas, with a total seating capacity of about 478,000.

Newspapers (1981). There was 1 national newspaper (average daily circulation 126,000) and 14 metropolitan daily newspapers in Australia with a combined daily circulation of 3·6m. Of these, 3 papers published in Melbourne accounted for 1·3m. and 4 published in Sydney for 1·2m.

Australian Transport. Sydney, Institute of Transport, 1937 to date (quarterly)

JUSTICE, RELIGION, EDUCATION AND WELFARE

Justice. The judicial power of the Commonwealth of Australia is vested in the High Court of Australia (the Federal Supreme Court), in the Federal courts created by the Federal Parliament (the Federal Court of Australia and the Family Court of Australia and in the State courts invested by Parliament with Federal jurisdiction.

High Court. The High Court consists of a Chief Justice and 6 other Justices, appointed by the Governor-General in Council. The Constitution confers on the High Court original jurisdiction, *inter alia*, in all matters arising under treaties or affecting consuls or other foreign representatives, matters between the States of the Commonwealth, matters to which the Commonwealth is a party and matters between residents of different States. Federal Parliament may make laws conferring original jurisdiction on the High Court, *inter alia*, in matters arising under the Constitution or under any laws made by the Parliament. It has in fact conferred jurisdiction on the High Court in matters arising under the Constitution and in matters arising under certain laws made by Parliament.

The High Court may hear and determine appeals from its own Justices exercising original jurisdiction, from any other Federal Court, from a Court exercising Federal jurisdiction and from the Supreme Courts of the States. It also has jurisdiction to hear and determine appeals from the Supreme Courts of the Territories. No appeal from the High Court to the Privy Council is permitted on questions as to the limits *inter se* of the constitutional powers of the States or the Commonwealth and the States except on the certificate of the High Court. No appeal to the Privy Council, whether special or otherwise, is permitted from a decision of Federal Courts (not being the High Court) or of the Supreme Court of a Territory. Appeal from the High Court to the Privy Council by special leave of the Privy Council is possible only in a matter in which the decision of the High Court was a decision that *(a)* was given on appeal from a decision of a Supreme Court of a State given otherwise than in the exercise of Federal jurisdiction and *(b)* did not involve the interpretation of the Constitution, a law made by the Federal Parliament or an instrument (including an ordinance, rule, regulation or by-law) made under a law made by the Parliament.

Other Federal Courts. Since 1924, 4 other Federal courts have been created to exercise special Federal jurisdiction, *i.e.* the Federal Court of Australia, the Family Court of Australia, the Australian Industrial Court and the Federal Court of Bankruptcy. The Federal Court of Australia was created by the Federal Court of Australia Act 1976 and commenced to exercise jurisdiction on 1 Feb. 1977. It exercises such original jurisdiction as is invested in it by laws made by the Federal Parliament including jurisdiction formerly exercised by the Australian Industrial Court and the Federal Court of Bankruptcy, and in some matters previously invested in either the High Court or State and Territory Supreme Courts. The Federal Court also acts as a court of appeal from State and Territory courts in relation to Federal matters. Appeal from the Federal Court to the High Court will be by way of special leave only. The State Supreme Courts have also been invested with Federal jurisdiction in bankruptcy.

State Courts. The general Federal jurisdiction of the State courts extends, subject to certain restrictions and exceptions, to all matters in which the High Court has jurisdiction or in which jurisdiction may be conferred upon it. In matters of non Federal jurisdiction a right of appeal is still possible, depending upon the nature of the matter involved, from the State courts direct to the Privy Council.

Industrial Tribunals. The major Federal industrial tribunal in Australia is the Australian Conciliation and Arbitration Commission, constituted by presidential members (with the status of judges) and commissioners. The Commission's functions include settling industrial disputes, making awards, determining the standard hours of work, wage fixation, etc. Questions of law, the judicial interpretation of awards, imposition of penalties, etc., in relation to industrial matters, are now dealt with by the Federal Court.

Australian Digest of Reported Decisions of the Australian Courts and of Australian Appeals to the Privy Council. 2nd ed. Sydney, Law Book Co. 1963—Supplements 1964 ff.
Baalman, J., *Outline of Law in Australia.* 4th ed. Sydney, 1979
Bates, N., *Introduction to Legal Studies.* 3rd ed. Melbourne, 1980
Benjafield, D. G., and Whitmore, H., *Principles of Australian Administrative Law.* 3rd ed. Sydney, 1966
Cowen, Z., *Federal Jurisdiction in Australia.* 2nd ed. Melbourne, 1978
Fleming, J. G., *The Law of Torts.* 5th ed. Sydney, 1977
Gunn, J. A. L., *Australian Income Tax Law and Practice.* 9th ed. by F. C. Bock and E. F. Mannix, Sydney, 1969, and *Butterworth's Taxation Service* to date
Howard, C., *Criminal Law.* 3rd ed. Sydney, 1975
Mills, C. P., and Sorrell, G. H., *Federal Industrial Law. (Nolan and Cohen.)* 5th ed. Sydney, 1975
O'Connell, D. P. (ed.), *International Law in Australia.* Sydney, 1966
Paterson, W. E., and Ednie, H. H., *Australian Company Law.* 2nd ed. Sydney, 1976, and *Butterworth's Company Service* to date
Sawer, G., *The Australian and the Law.* Melbourne, 1976
Twyford, J., *The Layman and the Law in Australia.* 2nd ed. Sydney, 1980
Wynes, A., *Legislative, Executive and Judicial Powers in Australia.* 5th ed. Sydney, 1976
Yorston, R. K., and Fortescue, E. E., *Australian Mercantile Law.* 14th ed. Sydney, 1971

Religion. Under the Constitution the Commonwealth cannot make any law to establish any religion, to impose any religious observance or to prohibit the free exercise of any religion, nor can it require a religious test as qualification for office or public trust under the Commonwealth. The figures in the table refer to those religions with the largest number of adherents at the census of 1981. The census question on religion was not obligatory, however.

Religion	*Persons*	*Religion*	*Persons*
Christian		Non-Christian	
Baptist	190,259	Hebrew	62,126
Brethren	21,489	Muslim	76,792
Catholic [1]	3,786,505	Other	23,577
Churches of Christ	89,424		
Church of England	3,810,469	Total Non-Christian	197,568
Congregational	23,017		
Jehovah's Witness	51,815	Indefinite	73,551
Orthodox	421,281	No religion	1,576,718
Lutheran	199,760	No reply	1,595,195
Methodist, inc. Wesley	490,767		
Presbyterian	637,818	Grand Total	14,576,330
Salvation Army	71,570		
Seventh-day Adventist	712,609		
Protestant (undefined)	220,679		
Other (including Christian undefined)	250,188		
Total Christian	11,133,298		

[1] Includes 'Catholic' and 'Roman Catholic'.

Education. The Governments of the Australian States and the Northern Territory have the major responsibility for education, including the administration and substantial funding of primary, secondary and technical and further education. In most States, a single Education Department is responsible for these three levels of education, but in New South Wales and South Australia there is a separate department responsible solely for technical and further education and in Victoria, a Technical and Further Education Board. Furthermore, in New South Wales an Education Commission advises the Minister on primary, secondary and post-secondary education.

The Australian Government is directly responsible for education services in the Australian Capital Territory, administered through an education authority, and for services to Norfolk Island, Christmas Island and the Cocos (Keeling) Islands. The

Australian Government provides supplementary finance to the States and is responsible for the total funding of universities and colleges of advanced education. It also has special responsibilities for student assistance, education programmes for Aboriginal people and children from non-English-speaking backgrounds, and for international relations in education.

The Australian Constitution empowers the Australian Government to make grants to the States and to place conditions upon such grants. This power has been used to provide financial assistance to the States specifically for educational purposes. There are two national Education Commissions which advise the Australian Government on the needs of educational institutions throughout Australia for the purpose of financial assistance. The Commonwealth Schools Commission, established in 1973, advises on the provision of financial assistance to the States for government and non-government schools. The Commonwealth Tertiary Education Commission, which was established in 1977 to replace three former commissions (the Universities Commission, the Commission on Advanced Education and the Technical and Further Education Commission), advises on the provision to the States of total funding for universities and colleges of advanced education and of supplementary financial assistance for their institutions of technical and further education.

In 1984 legislation was passed to reactivate the national Curriculum Development Centre (CDC) within the framework of the Commonwealth Schools Commission. The CDC's functions are to concentrate on co-ordination and dissemination and on sponsoring the development of materials through contract arrangements with other agencies.

School attendance is compulsory throughout Australia between the ages of 6 and 15 years (16 years in Tasmania), at either a government school or a recognized non-government educational institution. Many Australian children attend pre-schools for a year before entering school (usually in sessions of 2-3 hours, for 2-5 days per week). Government schools are usually co-educational and comprehensive. Non-government schools have been traditionally single-sex, particularly in secondary schools, but there is a developing trend towards co-education. Tuition is free at government schools, but fees are normally charged at non-government schools.

The following is a summary at July 1983 of primary and secondary school education:

	Schools		*Teachers* [1]		*Pupils* [2]	
States and Territories	*Government*	*Non-government*	*Government schools*	*Non-government schools*	*Government schools*	*Non-government schools*
New South Wales	2,237	831	45,800	13,965	778,410	251,506
Victoria	2,124	659	42,722	13,727	582,034	234,171
Queensland	1,260	363	21,586	5,654	373,097	107,991
South Australia	714	173	14,253	2,903	205,517	48,270
Western Australia	721	216	12,109	3,101	209,284	53,827
Tasmania	257	70	5,025	976	68,387	15,940
Northern Territory	137	16	1,663	269	24,490	4,720
Aust. Cap. Terr.	96	34	2,750	994	39,803	18,359
	7,546	2,362	145,908	41,589	2,281,022	734,784

[1] Full-time teachers plus the full-time equivalent of part-time teaching.
[2] Full-time pupils only.

Opportunities to pursue post-secondary education are available in universities, colleges of advanced education, technical and further education institutions and some more specialized post-school institutions. Tuition fees were abolished in 1974 and student allowances are provided for full-time students subject to a means test. Universities are autonomous institutions, as are the substantial majority of colleges of advanced education. While both offer degree courses, colleges also offer diploma and associate diploma courses and in general their courses have a more applied emphasis and are more vocationally oriented.

Universities and colleges of advanced education at 30 April 1983:

University and Advanced Education 1983:

	University			*Advanced Education* [1]		
States and Territories	*Students enrolled*	*Students completing courses*	*Staff* [2]	*Students enrolled*	*Students completing courses* [3]	*Staff* [2]
New South Wales	64,521	11,747	4,818	45,619	9,596	2,657
Victoria	44,303	9,342	3,525	59,206	11,053	3,527
Queensland	22,867	3,999	1,763	26,104	5,245	1,443
South Australia	13,242	2,387	1,143	17,158	3,578	1,023
Western Australia	12,977	2,381	1,051	21,377	3,805	1,105
Tasmania	5,229	993	415	2,852	291	191
Northern Territory	–	–	–	914	95	69
Australian Capital Territory	6,211	1,260	1,062	6,663	1,227	414
	169,350	32,109	13,778	179,893	34,890	10,429

[1] Advanced education courses are conducted mainly at colleges of advanced education.
[2] Full-time academic staff plus the full-time equivalent of part-time academic staff, rounded to whole numbers.
[3] Relates to students completing courses in the twelve months ended 31 Dec. 1982.

Technical and Further Education (TAFE) institutions offer a wide variety of courses of study which are classified into the following six streams: professional, para-professional, trades, other skilled, preparatory and adult or further education. The majority of TAFE courses are part-time, concurrent with employment, but there is also provision for full-time and external study. A network of over 900 government-run institutions facilitates access to these courses. Enrolments in 1982 numbered 1,027,052 of which 297,761 were classified as Stream 6, Adult Education (*i.e.* courses in home handicrafts, hobbies, self-expression and cultural appreciation). There were 959,934 internal enrolments, 55,665 external and 11,453 multimodal (*i.e.* a mixture of internal and external conditions) enrolments. 63,223 of the enrolled students undertook full-time courses (*i.e.* those involving 540 or more contact hours).

Teacher education usually takes place in colleges of advanced education, though a substantial number of secondary teachers and a few primary teachers receive their pre-service education in a university. Government school teachers are recruited by the State and Northern Territory departments of education, and in the Australian Capital Territory by the ACT Schools Authority and the Public Service Board. Non-government schools recruit their own teachers.

The Australian Government provides a number of schemes of assistance for students to facilitate access to education. The Secondary Allowances Scheme aims to help parents with a limited income to keep their children at school for the final 2 years of secondary education. The Assistance for Isolated Children Scheme provides special support to families whose children are isolated from schooling or are handicapped. The Adult Secondary Education Assistance Scheme provides assistance for mature-age students undertaking a full-time one-year matriculation level programme or a two-year programme if studies beyond the tenth year in the Australian secondary school system have not previously been undertaken. The Tertiary Education Assistance Scheme is a means-tested scheme to assist students enrolled for full-time study in approved courses at post-secondary institutions. Allowances are also available for post-graduate study and overseas study. Aboriginal students are eligible for assistance under the Aboriginal Secondary Grants Scheme and the Aboriginal Study Grants Scheme. The States also offer various schemes of assistance, principally at the primary and secondary levels.

There are a number of bodies at the national level which have an important co-ordinating, planning or funding rôle. These include: the Australian Education Council, comprising the Federal and State Ministers of Education, the Conference of Directors-General of Education and an advisory body, the National Aboriginal Education Committee.

Total expenditure on education in Australia in 1981–82 was estimated at $A8,684m.

Austin, A. G., *Australian Education 1788–1900*. Melbourne, 1961
Australian Education Directory. Canberra, 1983
Directory of Higher Education Courses 1982. Canberra, 1982
Education in Australia. Canberra, 1977
Jones, P. E., *Education in Australia*. Melbourne, 1974
Primary and Secondary Schooling in Australia. Canberra, 1977
Schools Commission, *Triennium 1982–84. Report for 1982*. Canberra, 1981
Tertiary Education Commission, *Report for 1982–84, Triennium Vol. 2: Recommendations for 1982*. Canberra, 1981

Social Security and Welfare. All Commonwealth Government social security pensions, benefits and allowances are financed from the Commonwealth Government's general revenue. In addition, assistance is provided for a wide range of welfare services. Total expenditure during 1983–84 was $A16,438·1m.

The following summarizes the rates and conditions of the major benefits provided at June 1984.

Age and invalid pensions—age pensions are payable to men 65 years of age or more and women 60 years of age or more who have lived in Australia for a specified period and, unless permanently blind, also satisfy an income test. Persons over 16 years of age who are permanently blind or permanently incapacitated for work to the extent of at least 85% may receive an invalid pension. There is no residence qualification for an invalid pension if the permanent incapacity or blindness occurred within Australia or during temporary absence from Australia. An income test must be satisfied for an invalid pension unless permanently blind. The maximum rates are $A89.40 a week in the case of the 'standard' rate pension, and in the case of the 'married' rate pension, $A149.10 a week ($A74.55 each). Additional amounts are paid to pensioners with dependent children. Supplementary assistance of up to $A10 a week for 'standard' rate pension and $A5 for each 'married' rate person may be paid to a pensioner paying rent or private lodging subject to an income test. Remote area allowance is payable to pensioners living in income tax zone A, except for those aged 70 or more receiving the special rate of age pension. Supplementary assistance, additional pension for children, mother's/guardian's allowance and remote area allowance are not taxable.

Wife's pension—payable to the wife of an age or invalid pensioner if she is not eligible for a pension in her own right. The maximum rate and the income test are identical to those for age and invalid pensioners.

Spouse carer's pension—payable to the husband of an age or invalid pensioner who is providing constant care and attention at home for his wife if he is not eligible for pension in his own right. The maximum rate and the income test are identical to those for age and invalid pensions.

Widow's pension—widows, divorcees, certain deserted wives, women who have been the dependant of a man for 3 years immediately prior to his death and women whose husbands have been convicted of an offence and have been imprisoned for not less than 6 months may, if they satisfy a residence requirement and an income test, receive a widow's pension. Such women may be paid a pension of up to $A89.40 a week. If they have any dependent children they also receive a mother's/guardian's allowance of $A8 a week plus an additional allowance of $A12 for each child. Persons who pay private rent may also receive supplementary assistance of up to $A10 a week subject to an income test. Pensions are subject to income tax, but not mother's allowances, additional pension for children, supplementary assistance, or remote area allowance.

Supporting parents benefit—sole parents who have custody, care and control of any dependent children may, if they satisfy a residence requirement and an income test, receive supporting parents benefit. It is payable at the same rate as the widow's pension and is subject to the same income test. Mother's/guardian's allowance, additional pension for each dependent child, supplementary assistance and remote area allowance are also payable

Sheltered employment allowance—is payable to disabled persons under age pension age engaged in approved sheltered employment who are qualified to receive invalid pension. The rates of payment and allowances and income test are the same as invalid pension.

Rehabilitation allowance—persons undertaking a rehabilitation programme with the Commonwealth Rehabilitation Service who are eligible for a social security pension or benefit are eligible to receive a non taxable rehabilitation allowance during treatment or training and for up to 6 months thereafter. The allowance is equivalent to the invalid pension and is subject to the same income test.

Family Allowance—is paid without income test to assist families with children under 16 years or dependent full-time students aged 16 years to under 25 years. It is not subject to income tax. Monthly rates payable are: first child, $A22.80; second child, $A32.55; third child, $A39; fourth child, $A39 and $A45.55 for each subsequent child. For each child or eligible student in an approved institution, the rate is $A39 per month.

Family income supplement—payable subject to an income test to families with one or more children eligible for family allowances so long as they are not in receipt of any Commonwealth pension, benefit or allowance which provides additional payment for dependent children. The maximum rate per child is $A12 a week and this is not taxable.

Handicapped child's allowance—payable to parents or guardians of severely physically or mentally handicapped children in the family home and needing constant care and attention. The allowance is $A85 per month and is free of an income test but is subject to a residence qualification similar to that for family allowance. It may also be paid, subject to an income test, in cases where the child is handicapped but not severely, and requires marginally less care and attention.

Double orphan's pension—the guardian of a child under 16 years of age or of a full-time student under 25, both of whose parents are dead, or one of whose parents is dead and the whereabouts of the other parent unknown, and for refugee children where both parents are outside Australia, may receive double orphan's pension of $A55.70 a month per child. The payment is not subject to an income test nor is it taxable.

Unemployment and sickness benefits—are paid, subject to an income test, to persons between the ages of 16 and age pension age who are unemployed, able and willing to work and making efforts to obtain work, or temporarily unable to work because of sickness or injury. The maximum weekly rates of benefit are for unemployment benefits $A45 (single, under 18 years), $A78.60 (single 18 and over without dependents), $A89.40 (single, 18 and over with dependents), $A149.10 (married); and for sickness benefits $A45 (single, under 18), $A89.40 (single, 18 and over), $A149.10 (married). To be granted benefit a person must have resided in Australia for at least 12 months preceding his claim or intend to remain in Australia permanently. For unemployment benefit purposes unemployment must not be due to industrial action by that person or by members of a union to which that person is a member.

Service Pension is a Social-Welfare type payment paid by the Department of Veterans' Affairs, similar to the age and invalid pensions provided by the Department of Social Security. Male Veterans who have reached the age of 60 years or are permanently unemployable, and who served in a theatre of war, are eligible for service pension subject to an income test. Female Veterans who served abroad or embarked for service abroad, and who have reached the age of 55 or are permanently unemployable, are also eligible. Wives of service pensioners are also eligible provided that they do not receive a pension from the Department of Social Security.

Disability pension is a compensatory payment in respect of incapacity attributable to war service. It is paid at a rate commensurate with the degree of incapacity suffered from service-related disabilities and is free of any income test. A separate allowance may be paid to dependents.

In addition to cash benefits, assistance is provided either directly or through State and Local government authorities and voluntary agencies, for a wide range of welfare services for people with special needs. Among the major areas involved were the provision of accommodation and home care for aged or disabled persons, the Commonwealth Rehabilitation Service and other welfare programmes for handicapped persons, assistance to homeless persons and the provision of children's services such as pre-schools, childcare and vacation care and assistance for Aboriginals and migrants.

Medicare. On 1 Feb. 1984 the Commonwealth Government introduced the new universal health scheme known as Medicare. The financing arrangements under the Medicare programme feature the following major elements: Automatic entitlement under a single public health fund to medical and optometrical benefits of 85% of the Medical Benefits Schedule fee, with a maximum patient payment for any service of $A10 where the Schedule fee is charged; access without direct charge to public hospital accommodation and to inpatient and outpatient treatment by doctors appointed by the hospital; the restoration of funds for community health to approximately the same real level as 1975; the reduction in charges for private treatment in shared wards of public hospitals to $A80 per day, and increases in the daily bed subsidy payable to private hospital to an average of $A30.

The Medicare programme is financed in part by a 1% levy on taxable incomes, with low income cut-off points. The tax rebate formerly paid for basic health insurance contributions ceased from 30 June 1983. In addition, the Commonwealth's annual contribution to the Health Benefits Reinsurance Trust Fund was reduced from $A100m. to $A20m. from 1 July 1983. Under the provisions of the National Health Act, the Commonwealth Government subsidises registered health insurance organizations by contributing to the Reinsurance Trust Fund for payments of benefits to patients with hospital treatment in excess of 35 days.

Eligibility for Medicare Benefits. Medicare benefits are available to all persons ordinarily resident in Australia with the exception of members of foreign diplomatic missions and their dependants.

Eligible persons include: All permanent Australian residents (including Repatriation beneficiaries and Defence Force Personnel); persons visiting Australia who obtain approval to stay for more than 6months – with eligibility to date from arrival in Australia; persons visiting Australia who originally obtain approval to stay less than 6 months, but are granted an extension which makes the total approved stay more than 6 months – with eligibility to date from when the extension was granted; foreign students who are undertaking courses in Australia for 6 months or less; persons visiting Australia who are residents of countries with whom Australia has a reciprocal health care agreement; Australian residents receiving medical services while travelling overseas.

Short-term visitors to Australia (i.e. for 6 months or less) are responsible for the full cost of their medical and hospital treatment. Such persons should therefore make some form of private insurance arrangements to cover such costs.

Medical Benefits. The Health Insurance Act provides for a Medical Benefits Schedule which lists medical services and the Schedule (standard) fee applicable in each State in respect of each medical service. The Schedule covers services attracting Medicare Benefits rendered by legally qualified medical practitioners, certain prescribed medical services rendered by approved dentists in the operating theatres of approved hospitals, and optometrical consultations by participating optometrists. Schedule fees are set and updated by an independent fees tribunal which is appointed by the Government. The fees so determined are to apply for Medicare benefits purposes. Medical services in Australia are generally delivered either by private medical practitioners on a fee-for-service basis, or by medical practitioners employed in hospitals.

Where a medical service is provided by a private medical practitioner on a fee-for-service basis, Medicare refunds 85% of the Medical Benefits Schedule fee cost or, the Schedule fee less $A10, whichever is the greater. It is not possible to insure with private, health insurance organizations to cover the 15% 'gap'. However, should an individual accumulate 'gap' payments in excess of $A150 in a year, Medicare will pay benefits at 100% of the Schedule fee for each service for the remainder of the year.

Under Medicare, medical practitioners are able to direct bill for any patient. In such cases, they receive the Medicare benefit as full payment. Previously, direct billing was limited to services rendered to eligible Pensioner Health Benefit and Health Care Cardholders, and their dependants.

Medicare medical benefits are administered by the Health Insurance Commission.

Hospital Care. From 1 Feb. 1984, through Medicare grants to the States, the cost of public hospital out-patient treatment, and inpatient accommodation in a shared ward with treatment by a doctor employed by a hospital, are covered. The scheme does not cover hospital charges raised for treatment as a private patient in a public hospital, where patients elect to be treated by their own doctor, nor does it cover private hospital charges. It is possible however for persons to take out insurance with private health funds to cover these situations.

Long Term Nursing Home Type Patients in Hospital. Patients who are accommodated in either private or public hospitals for extended periods and who are, in essence, nursing home type patients are required to make a non-insurable patient contribution in the same way that a patient in a nursing home does. For a long-term private patient in a public hospital, hospital charges and private health fund benefits are reduced to the level of the standard nursing home benefit. In a private hospital the fund benefits are reduced by the amount of the patient contribution.

Pharmaceutical Benefits. A comprehensive range of drugs and medicinal preparations is available. In general, a fee of $A4 is charged for each prescription.

Department of Territories, *Progress Towards Assimilation.* Canberra, 1958
Bilton, J., *The Royal Flying Doctor Service of Australia.* Sydney, 1961
Henderson, R., *People in Poverty.* Melbourne, 1970

DIPLOMATIC REPRESENTATIVES

Of Australia in Great Britain (Australia House, Strand, London, WC2B 4LA)
High Commissioner: Alfred R. Parsons.

Of Great Britain in Australia (Commonwealth Ave., Canberra)
High Commissioner: Sir John Leahy, KCMG.

Of Australia in the USA (1601 Massachusetts Ave., NW, Washington, D.C., 20036)
Ambassador: Sir Robert Cotton, KCMG.

Of the USA in Australia (Moonah Pl., Canberra)
Ambassador: Robert D. Nesen.

Of Australia to the United Nations
Ambassador: Richard A. Woolcott.

Books of Reference

Statistical Information: The Australian Bureau of Statistics (Cameron Offices, Belconnen, A.C.T., 2616) was established in 1906. All the activities of the Bureau are covered by the Census and Statistics Act, which confers authority to collect information and contains secrecy provisions to ensure that individual particulars obtained are not divulged. Under the provisions of the Statistics (Arrangements with States) Act which became law on 12 May 1956, the statistical services of all the States have been integrated with the Australian Bureau. An outline of the development of statistics in Australia is published in the *Official Year Book*, No. 51, 1965. *Australian Statistician:* Dr R. J. Cameron.

The principal publications of the Bureau are:

Official Year Book of Australia. 1907 to date
Pocket Year Book Australia. 1913 to date
Monthly Summary of Statistics Australia. Oct. 1937 to date
Digest of Current Economic Statistics Australia. Aug. 1959 to date
Catalogue of Publications, 1976 to date

Other Official Publications

Atlas of Australian Resources. Dept. of Resources and Energy, Division of National Mapping
Climatological Atlas of Australia. Bureau of Meteorology. Melbourne, 1940
Norfolk Island—Annual Report. Dept. of Territories and Local Government
Cocos (Keeling) Islands—Annual Report. Dept. of Territories and Local Government
Christmas Island—Annual Report. Dept. of Territories and Local Government
Australian Books: Select List of Works About or Published in Australia. National Library of Australia, Canberra, 1934 to date
Australian National Bibliography. Canberra, 1936 to date
Historical Records of Australia. 34 vols. National Library, Canberra, 1914–25
Australia Handbook. Dept. of Administrative Services. Australian Information Services
Annual Report. Dept. of Foreign Affairs, Canberra, 1932 to date
Australian Foreign Affairs Record. Dept. of Foreign Affairs, Canberra, 1936 to date
Australian Treaty List. Dept. of Foreign Affairs, Canberra, consolidated volume from Federation to 1970 with supplements to date
Coxon, H., *Australian Official Publications.* Oxford, 1981
Documents on Australian Foreign Policy 1937–49. Vols. I–VI. Dept. of Foreign Affairs, Canberra, 1975–83
Diplomatic List. Dept. of Foreign Affairs, Canberra. 1949 to date
Consular and Trade Representatives. Dept. of Foreign Affairs, Canberra. 1936 to date

Non-Official Publications

Australian Encyclopædia. 12 vols. Sydney, 1983
Australian Quarterly: A Quarterly Review of Australian Affairs. Sydney, 1929 to date
Ball, D., and Langtry, J. O., *Civil Defence and Australia's Security in a Nuclear Age.* Sydney, 1984
Chipman, E., *Australians in the Frozen South.* Melbourne, 1978
Ferguson, Sir John, *Bibliography of Australia, 1784–1900.* 7 vols. Sydney, 1941–69
Grant, B., *The Crisis of Loyalty: A Study of Australian Foreign Policy.* Rev. ed. Sydney, 1973
Hancock, Sir Keith, *Australia.* Brisbane, 1961
Hurst, J., *Hawke P. M.* Sydney, 1983
Inglis, K., *This is the ABC: The Australian Broadcasting Commission.* Melbourne, 1983
Kepars, I., *Australia.* [Bibliography] Oxford and Santa Barbara, 1984
Moore, D., and Hall, R., *Australia: Image of a Nation.* London, 1983
Serle, P., *Dictionary of Australian Biography.* 2 vols. Sydney, 1949
Who's Who in Australia. Melbourne, 1906 to date

National Library: The National Library, Canberra, A.C.T. *Director-General:* Harrison Bryan.

AUSTRALIAN TERRITORIES

AUSTRALIAN CAPITAL TERRITORY

HISTORY. The area, now the Australian Capital Territory, was first visited by white men in 1820 and settlement commenced in 1824. Until its selection as the seat of government it was a quiet pastoral and agricultural community.

AREA AND POPULATION. The area of the Australian Capital Territory is 2,432 sq. km (including Jervis Bay area). The population (estimate) at 30 June 1982 was 232,000. Previous census population:

	Males	*Females*	*Total*		*Males*	*Females*	*Total*
1911	992	722	1,714	1961	30,858	27,970	58,828
1921	1,567	1,005	2,572	1966	49,991	46,041	96,032
1933	4,805	4,142	8,947	1971	73,589	70,474	144,063
1947	9,092	7,813	16,905	1976	100,103	95,519	197,622
1954	16,229	14,086	30,315	1981	110,415	111,194	221,609

(Figures before 1961 exclude particulars of full-blood Aborigines.)

CONSTITUTION AND GOVERNMENT. The Constitution of Australia provided (Sec. 125) that the seat of government should be selected by parliament and that it should be within New South Wales but at least 161 km from Sydney. The present area was surrendered by New South Wales and accepted by the Australian Government from 1 Jan. 1911. In 1915 an additional 73 sq. km at Jervis Bay was transferred from New South Wales to the Commonwealth. In 1911 an international competition was held for the city plan. The plan chosen was that of W. Burley Griffin, of Chicago. Construction was delayed by the First World War, and it was not until 1927 that, with the transfer of parliament and certain departments, Canberra became in fact the seat of government. Most Australian Government departments now have their headquarters in Canberra.

The general administration of the Territory is in the hands of the Minister for the Capital Territory, but certain specific services are undertaken by other Federal Government Departments and Authorities. Since June 1979 the Minister has been advised on matters of local concern by the ACT House of Assembly consisting of 18 elected members. Prior to that date this function was performed by the ACT Legislative Assembly (from 1974), replacing the ACT Advisory Council which had been in existence since 1930 and consisted of both nominated and elected members.

The Australian Capital Territory Representation (House of Representatives) Act, 1973, provided for the representation of residents of the Territory by 2 elected members in the House of Representatives. The Senate (Representation of Territories) Act 1973 provided for the election of 2 Senators from the Territory. Elections took place in Nov. 1980.

FINANCE. The receipts and outlay of the Australian Capital Territory cover the transactions of the Australian Government in the Consolidated Revenue and other funds. They also include details of the ACT public corporations.

Receipts and outlay ($A1,000) for years ended 30 June:

	Receipts	*Capital*	*Current Outlay*	*Total*
1979	98,716	166,360	227,021	393,381
1980	102,297	139,947	260,248	400,195
1981	97,795	78,901	297,206	376,107
1982[1]	114,522	67,489	340,344	407,833

[1]Preliminary.

The chief sources of receipts in 1981–82 were taxes, fees and fines, $A67m.; and interest and rent, $A29m. Capital outlay comprised gross capital formation, $A58m., and net advances to other sectors, $A6m.

PRODUCTION. The Territory is predominantly pastoral. Livestock, 31 March 1984: 9,942 cattle, 10,232 sheep. A considerable amount of reafforestation (mostly pine) has been undertaken, the total area of commercial plantations at 30 June 1981 being 14,119 hectares. There is no secondary industry of any importance.

EDUCATION. In 1974 education in government schools became the direct responsibility of the Commonwealth Government. A Schools Authority was established to administer the Australian Capital Territory government school system. In July 1984 there were 95 government schools comprising 64 primary schools, 25 secondary schools and colleges and 6 special schools. Non-government schools numbered 35 in total of which there were 22 primary schools, 5 secondary schools and 8 schools with both primary and secondary enrolments. Students enrolled full-time in government schools in 1984 numbered 22,428 and 17,094 in primary and secondary school levels respectively. Enrolments at non-government schools comprised 10,311 primary school students and 8,758 secondary school students. Pre-school education is provided at 73 centres with a total enrolment of 4,670 (1984). The Canberra, Woden and Bruce Colleges of Technical and Further Education with a total enrolment of about 25,300 in 1983 provide trade, post-trade certificate, associate diploma, craft and leisure courses.

The Canberra School of Music, opened in 1965, had 736 students in 1983. The

Canberra School of Arts had 1,161 students in 1983. The Canberra College of Advanced Education commenced operation in 1970. Enrolments (1984) 5,129.

The Australian National University is situated in Canberra. Enrolments (1984) 6,194.

Books of Reference

A.C.T. Statistical Summary. Australian Bureau of Statistics. From 1960
Tomorrow's Canberra. National Capital Development Commission, 1970
Wigmore, L., *Canberra: A History of Australia's National Capital*. 2nd ed. Canberra, 1971

NORTHERN TERRITORY

HISTORY. The Northern Territory, after forming part of New South Wales, was annexed on 6 July 1863 to South Australia and in 1901 entered the Commonwealth as a corporate part of South Australia. The Commonwealth Constitution Act of 1900 made provision for the surrender to the Commonwealth of any territory by any state, and under this provision an agreement was entered into on 7 Dec. 1907 for the transfer of the Northern Territory to the Commonwealth, and it formally passed under the control of the Commonwealth Government on 1 Jan. 1911. For details of Constitutional development until 1978 *see* THE STATESMAN'S YEAR-BOOK 1980–81 pp. 123–24. The Commonwealth Government retained responsibility until Self-Government was granted on 1 July 1978.

AREA AND POPULATION. The Northern Territory is bounded by the 26th parallel of S. lat. and 129° and 138° E. long. Its total area is 1,346, 200 sq. km. The coastline is about 6,200 km in length, the principal port being Darwin. The greater part of the interior consists of a tableland rising gradually from the coast to a height of about 700 metres. On this tableland there are large areas of excellent pasturage. The southern part of the Territory is generally sandy and has a small rainfall, but water may be obtained by means of sub-artesian bores.

The capital and seat of Government, Darwin, is situated on the north coast. Darwin had a population of 60,923 in July 1982. The total population of the Territory is about 130,000. Other main centres include Katherine (3,883), 330 km south of Darwin; Alice Springs (19,610), in Central Australia; Tennant Creek (3,050), a rich mining centre 500 km north of Alice Springs; Nhulunbuy (3,864), a bauxite mining centre on the Gove Peninsula in eastern Arnhem Land; and Jabiru, a model town being built to serve the rich Uranium Province in eastern Arnhem Land with a planned population of 6,000. There also are a number of large self-contained Aboriginal communities.

Vital statistics for 1980: Births, 2,843; deaths, 603; marriages, 622; divorces, 289.

CONSTITUTION AND GOVERNMENT. The Northern Territory (Self-Government) Act 1978 established the Northern Territory as a body politic as from 1 July 1978, with Ministers having control over and responsibility for Territory finances and the administration of the functions of government as specified by the Federal Government by regulations made pursuant to the Act. Regulations have been made conferring executive authority for the bulk of administrative functions. Proposed laws passed by the Legislative Assembly in relation to a transferred function require the assent of the Administrator. Proposed laws in all other cases may be assented to by the Administrator or reserved by the Administrator for the Governor-General's pleasure. The Governor-General may disallow any law assented to by the Administrator within 6 months of the Administrator's assent.

The Northern Territory has federal representation, electing 1 member to the House of Representatives and 2 members to the Senate.

FINANCE. Budgets since the introduction of self-government in 1978 in $A1m.:

	1978–79	*1979–80*	*1980–81*	*1981–82*	*1982–83*
Revenue	349	530	656	744	850
Expenditure	348	529	656	746	852

The revenue available in 1980–81 comprised $A554m. in payments to the Northern Territory from the Commonwealth, as established by agreement at the time of self-government, together with $A102m. raised by the Northern Territory which included $A29m. through state-like taxes.

Expenditure during 1980–81 included $A92.1m. for education; $A72.8m. for lands and housing; $A79.5m. for health; $A49.5m. for community development and $A88m. on the capital works programme.

ENERGY AND NATURAL RESOURCES

Oil and Gas. Significant oil and gas reserves have been discovered in the Amadeus Basin. In 1981 the Territory's first petroleum leases were granted at Mereenie. There are estimated recoverable reserves of 28m. bbls of oil. Estimated gas reserves at Mereenie are 23,000m. cu. metres. A pipeline has been constructed from Palm Valley to carry natural gas 150 km to Alice Springs where it is providing fuel for the local power station. Proven reserves are 1,400m. cu. metres of gas.

Minerals. The Northern Territory's most important natural resources are minerals. In the calendar year 1982 the mining industry, by far the largest commercial industry in the Northern Territory, produced mineral products with a value of $A625m. Projects already committed will boost this amount to more than $A650m. by 1985.

At present there are five major mining organizations extracting bauxite, manganese, uranium, gold and copper; in addition, one firm is producing uranium oxide from stockpiled ore. There are also several smaller mining operations recovering tin, tantalum, gold, lead and silver. Significant amounts of rock, sand and gravel are also being produced for construction materials.

Gove Peninsula bauxite reserves are estimated at 250m. tonnes with an average alumina content of 50%. Over 4m. tonnes of bauxite were mined in 1982. Alumina is exported to Europe, the USA, Africa and Asia. More than half the bauxite goes to Japan.

One of the world's largest high-grade manganese mines is located on Groote Eylandt, which is Australia's largest known manganese deposit. In 1982 there were 1m. tonnes of manganese ore processed, much of which was shipped to Japan.

Copper, gold and bismuth are mined in the Tennant Creek area. Warrego Mine has a proven copper/gold ore resource of 4·8m. tonnes and Gecko Mine has a proven ore resource of 3·3m. tonnes. Nobles Nob has been producing gold since 1938 and currently mills 8,000 tonnes of ore per month. Gold bullion and concentrates with a total value of more than $A32m. were produced in the Territory in 1982.

The Alligator Rivers region is possibly the most prospective area in the world for high-grade uranium deposits. Four world-class deposits have been located to date. Of these, Ranger and Nabarlek are producing uranium oxide. The combined output from these two mines in 1981 was 2,622 tonnes, with a value of about $A175m.

Agriculture. Cattle and buffalo production, valued at $A78m. annually, constitutes the largest primary industry in the Northern Territory. The value of cattle and buffalo exports exceeded $A37m. in 1982.

There are 243 pastoral stations in the Northern Territory which produce cattle for Australian and overseas markets. They vary from small stations of 383 sq. km. to huge properties like Wave Hill Station which runs cattle over 12,380 sq. km.

In 1982, five export abattoirs in the Territory supplied 13,728 tonnes of beef, veal and fancy meats to more than 20 countries. The USA is the largest importer of Territory beef, followed by Japan, Taiwan, Saudi Arabia and Hong Kong. Total value of export beef is more than $A25m.

Live buffaloes and buffalo meat products are part of a growing export industry in the Northern Territory. Current value of these exports is more than $A6·5m. Processed buffalo meat for human consumption overseas is supplied by two export abattoirs in the Territory's Top End. In 1982 their combined exports of buffalo meat products was more than 2,800 tonnes.

General agriculture is conducted on a small scale in the Northern Territory. Small quantities of fruit, vegetables, eggs, dairy produce, poultry and pasture are produced. Properties in the Katherine and Douglas-Daly districts produce the Territory's four main crops – sorghum, maize, mung beans and peanuts.

Forestry. A forest development programme which commenced in 1970 has continued the multiple use management of Northern Territory forested areas; this included a softwood programme of 400 hectares per year, the introduction of additional suitable tree species in both arid and higher rainfall areas, conservation and management of native forests for production and recreational purposes, survey and assessment of resources, fire control activities and the creation of training opportunities for Aboriginals in forestry and allied saw-milling activities.

Local production of sawn timber, mainly Cypress pine, amounted to 870 cu. metres of pine in 1975–76. This was supplemented by 35,500 cu. metres of timber imported from interstate and overseas.

Local production of treated poles and rails amounted to 115 cu. metres. Only 280 hectares of plantation were established during the year because of complications arising from cyclone 'Tracy'.

During 1975–76 the Forestry Section of the Department of the Northern Territory redeveloped parks and open-space areas on behalf of the Darwin Reconstruction Commission.

Fisheries. The fishing industry is second only to beef cattle in Northern Territory primary industries. The total value (*ex*-vessel) of commercial fish products landed in the Northern Territory in 1981–82 was $A18·34m. Of this, prawns contributed $A15·25m. and barramundi $A1·9m. Threadfin salmon, spanish mackerel, mud crabs, reef fish and bay lobsters made up most of the remainder.

Prawns and barramundi provide an employment base for a large number of Territorians – not just in fishing, but in processing, distribution and ancillary services. Almost all products undergo some processing by land-based establishments before reaching the consumer. Some 95% of prawns landed in the Northern Territory are exported to Japan. The value of prawn exports in 1981–82 exceeded $A14·5m., mainly headless uncooked prawns. The bulk of barramundi and threadfin salmon is consigned in frozen packs to southern Australian markets.

INDUSTRY AND TRADE. In 1982–83 value added in the manufacturing industry, from 117 factories (with 4 or more persons employed) was $A91m. 2,434 persons were employed in these factories. In 1983, 75 trade unions had 20,600 members.

Tourism. In 1980–81, there were 363,000 tourists contributing about $A106m. to the economy.

National Parks and Reserves. About 43,000 sq. km have been set aside as wildlife sanctuaries under the Wildlife Conservation and Control Ordinance. They are controlled by the Chief Inspector of Wildlife who is an officer of the Department of the Northern Territory. 236,000 sq. km of Aboriginal reserves are also wild-life protected areas.

The Northern Territory Reserves Board administers some 37 national parks and reserves covering an area of over 249,926 hectares. The Board is responsible under the National Parks and Gardens Ordinance for the care, control and management of these reserves, and its functions include the preservation and protection of natural and historical features and the encouragement of public use and enjoyment of land set aside in such reserves.

COMMUNICATIONS

Roads. There are now 5,460 km of sealed road within the Northern Territory. They include three major interstate links: the Stuart Highway from Darwin to the South Australian border, the Barkly Highway, Tennant Creek to Mt. Isa, 444 km of which is in the Northern Territory, and the Victoria Highway, Katherine to the Western Australian border, a distance of 468 km. In addition to this there are 4,064 km of gravel roads, 4,834 km of formed roads and 6,670 km of unformed roads or tracks, totalling approximately 21,028 km of roads within the Northern Territory. In 1982–83 registrations of new motor vehicles included 3,260 cars, 2,517 utilities etc., 222 trucks, 52 buses and 425 motor cycles.

Railways. Alice Springs is linked to the Trans-continental network by a new standard (1,435 mm) gauge railway to Tarcoola (831 km), opened in 1980. This replaced the largely narrow gauge line to Port Augusta. The standard gauge railway is to be extended to Darwin by 1988, providing Australia with its first north-south rail link.

Aviation. Darwin is the first port of arrival in Australia for some aircraft from Europe and Asia. In 1982, 341,365 passengers were carried and 3,225 tonnes of freight. There are regular inland services connecting Darwin with all the State capitals and many inland towns.

Shipping. Regular freight shipping services connect Darwin with Western Australia, the eastern States and overseas. Passenger vessels also call at Darwin at irregular intervals.

The ports of Melville Bay (Gove) and Milner Bay (Groote Eylandt) are connected with Darwin, the eastern States and overseas by regular shipping freight services.

The inland and coastal communities around the coast are provided with regular freight barge services from Darwin. Some of these communities also receive a barge freight-transhipment service out of a Brisbane vessel which calls at Melville and Milner Bays, where the transhipment is effected.

EDUCATION AND WELFARE

Education. In June 1984 there were 139 government schools. Teachers totalled 1,788 and pupils 28,091. There were 18 private schools with 268 teachers and 5,078 pupils.

Health. In 1980 there were 6 hospitals with 756 beds. Community health services are provided from 9 urban Health Centres and 62 rural Health Centres including mobile units.

AUSTRALIAN EXTERNAL TERRITORIES

AUSTRALIAN ANTARCTIC TERRITORY. An Imperial Order in Council of 7 Feb. 1933 placed under Australian authority all the islands and territories other than Adélie Land situated south of 60° S. lat. and lying between 160° E. long. and 45° E. long. The Order came into force with a Proclamation issued by the Governor-General on 24 Aug. 1936 after the passage of the Australian Antarctic Territory Acceptance Act 1933. The boundaries of Adélie Land were definitively fixed by a French Decree of 1 April 1938 as the islands and territories south of 60° S. lat. lying between 136° E. long. and 142° E. long. The Australian Antarctic Territory Act 1954 declared that the laws in force in the Australian Capital Territory are, so far as they are applicable and are not inconsistent with any ordinance made under the Act, in force in the Australian Antarctic Territory.

In 1968 responsibility for the administration of this Act was transferred from the Minister for External Affairs to the Minister for Supply; in 1972 responsibility was transferred to the Minister for Science.

On 13 Feb. 1954 the Australian National Antarctic Research Expeditions (ANARE) established a station on Mac. Robertson Land at lat. 67° 37′ S. and long. 62° 52′ E. The station was named Mawson in honour of the late Sir Douglas Mawson. Meteorological and other scientific research is conducted at Mawson, which is the centre for coastal and inland survey expeditions.

A second Australian scientific research station was established on the coast of Princess Elizabeth Land on 13 Jan. 1957 at lat. 68° 34′ S. and long. 77° 58′ E. The station was named Davis in honour of Capt. John King Davis, Mawson's second-in-command on 2 expeditions. The station was temporarily closed down in Jan. 1965 and re-opened in Feb. 1969.

In Feb. 1959 the Australian Government accepted from the US Government custody of Wilkes Station, which was established by the US on 16 Jan. 1957 on the Budd Coast of Wilkes Land, at lat. 66° 15′ S. and long. 110° 32′ E. The station was named in honour of Lieut. Charles Wilkes, who commanded the 1838–40 US expedition to the area, and was closed in Feb. 1969. Operations were then transferred to the new station, Casey. Construction commenced on Casey station in Jan. 1965 and was continued, mainly during summer visits, until Feb. 1969, when it was opened. The station, specially designed to withstand blizzard winds and prevent inundation by snow, is situated 2·4 km south of Wilkes at lat. 66° 17′ S. and long. 110° 32′ E. The Antarctic Division has also operated a station, since March 1948, at Macquarie Island, about 1,370 km south-east of Hobart. Macquarie Island is a dependency of the State of Tasmania.

On 1 Dec. 1959 Australia signed the Antarctic Treaty with Argentina, Belgium, Chile, France, Japan, New Zealand, Norway, South Africa, the USSR, the UK and the USA. Poland, Czechoslovakia, German Democratic Republic, Netherlands, Romania, Brazil, Denmark, Bulgaria, Federal Republic of Germany, Italy, India, People's Republic of China, Spain, Papua New Guinea, Peru, Hungary and Uruguay have subsequently acceded to the Treaty. Poland became a full member of the Antarctic Treaty in 1977 and the Federal Republic of Germany in 1981 and India and Brazil in 1983. The Treaty reserves the Antarctic area south of 60° S. lat. for peaceful purposes, provides for international co-operation in scientific investigation and research, and preserves, for the duration of the Treaty, the *status quo* with regard to territorial sovereignty, rights and claims. The Treaty entered into force on 23 June 1961. Since then the Antarctic Treaty powers have held 12 consultative meetings. The 13th is scheduled to be held in Brussels, Belgium, in 1985.

COCOS (KEELING) ISLANDS. The Cocos (Keeling) Islands are 2 separate atolls comprising some 27 small coral islands with a total area of about 14·2 sq. km, and are situated in the Indian Ocean at 12° 05′ S. lat. and 96° 53′ E. long. They lie 2,768 km north-west of Perth and 3,685 km west of Darwin, while Colombo is 2,255 km to the north-west of the group.

The main islands in this Australian Territory are West Island (the largest, about 10 km from north to south) on which is an airport and an animal quarantine station, and most of the European community; Home Island, occupied by the Cocos Malay community; Direction, South and Horsburgh Islands, and North Keeling Island, 24 km to the north of the group.

Although the islands were discovered in 1609 by Capt. William Keeling of the East India Company, they remained uninhabited until 1826, when the first settlement was established on the main atoll by an Englishman, Alexander Hare, with a group of followers, predominantly of Malay origin. Hare left the islands in 1831, by which time a second settlement had been formed on the main atoll by John Clunies-Ross, a Scottish seaman and adventurer, who began commercial development of the islands' coconut palms.

In 1857 the islands were annexed to the Crown; in 1878 responsibility was transferred from the Colonial Office to the Government of Ceylon, and in 1886 to the Government of the Straits Settlement. By indenture in 1886 Queen Victoria granted all land in the islands to George Clunies-Ross and his heirs in perpetuity (with certain rights reserved to the Crown). In 1903 the islands were incorporated in the Settlement of Singapore and in 1942–46 temporarily placed under the Governor of Ceylon. In 1946 a Resident Administrator, responsible to the Governor of Singapore, was appointed.

On 23 Nov. 1955 the Cocos Islands were placed under the authority of the Australian Government as the Territory of Cocos (Keeling) Islands. An Administrator, appointed by the Governor-General, is the Government's representative in the

Territory and is responsible to the Minister for Territories and Local Government. The Cocos (Keeling) Islands Council, established as the elected body of the Cocos Malay community in July 1979, advises the Administrator on all issues affecting the Territory.

In 1978 the Australian Government purchased the Clunies-Ross family's entire interests in the islands, except for the family residence. A Cocos Malay co-operative has been established to take over the running of the Clunies-Ross copra plantation (160 tonnes of copra were exported in 1983–84) and to engage in other business with the Commonwealth in the Territory, including construction projects.

The population of the Territory at 30 June 1984 was 584, distributed between Home Island (376) and West Island (208).

The islands are low-lying, flat and thickly covered by coconut palms, and surround a lagoon in which ships drawing up to 7 metres may be anchored, but which is extremely difficult for navigation.

An equable and pleasant climate, affected for much of the year by the south-east trade winds. Temperatures range over the year from 68° F (20° C) to 88° F (31·1° C) and rainfall averages 80″ (2,000 mm) a year.

The Cocos (Keeling) Islands Act 1955 is the basis of the Territory's administrative, legislative and judicial systems. Under section 8 of this Act, those laws which were in force in the Territory immediately before the transfer continued in force there.

The *Singapore Ordinances Application Ordinance* 1979 repealed all those contained Ordinances and re-applied the provisions of 95 Ordinances of Singapore. These Ordinances can be amended, repealed or substituted by Ordinances made by the Governor-General.

Administrator: E. H. Hanfield.

CHRISTMAS ISLAND is in the Indian Ocean, lat. 10° 25′ 22″ S., long. 105° 39′ 59″ E. It lies 360 km S., 8° E. of Java Head, and 417 km N. 79° E. from Cocos Islands, 1,310 km from Singapore and 2,623 km from Fremantle. Area about 135 sq. km. The climate is pleasant and healthy with temperatures varying little over the year at 74–79° F (23–26° C). The wet season lasts from Nov. to April with an annual total of about 81″ (2,040 mm). The island was formally annexed by the UK on 6 June 1888, placed under the administration of the Governor of the Straits Settlements in 1889, and incorporated with the Settlement of Singapore in 1900. Sovereignty was transferred to the Australian Government on 1 Oct. 1958. The population (estimate, 1983), 3,000 (Europeans, 350; Chinese, 1,820; Malays, 750 and 90 others).

The legislative, judicial and administrative systems are regulated by the Christmas Island Act, 1958–73, which is administered by the Minister for Territories and Local Government with an Administrator, responsible for the local administration. The laws of Singapore which were in force before the transfer have been continued but can be amended, repealed or substituted by ordinances made by the Governor-General.

Extraction and export of rock phosphate dust is the island's only industry. In Dec. 1948 Australia and New Zealand bought the lease rights of the Christmas Island Phosphate Co. and set up the Christmas Island Phosphate Commission (CIPC), which conducted the mining operation until mid-1981. The Phosphate Mining Co. of Christmas Island Ltd (PMCI) acted as managing agents for the CIPC until the Commission was wound up and now mines in its own right. The export of phosphate rock during 1983–84 was 1,112,800 tonnes, which is shipped to Australia and New Zealand and other Asian nations.

There is direct radio communication with Australia and Singapore. Regular air charter flights commenced in 1974 to South-east Asia.

At 31 May 1983 there were 621 primary and secondary pupils at the Christmas Island Area School. There is a technical school which provides commercial, apprenticeship and adult education courses, with (1979) some 701 students.

Medical, dental and hospital services are provided free of charge by the Phosphate Mining Co. of Christmas Island Ltd.

Administrator: T. F. Paterson.

NORFOLK ISLAND. 29° 04′ S. lat. 167° 57′ E. long., area 3,455 hectares, population, approximately 1,800. The island was formerly part of the colony of New South Wales and then of Van Diemen's Land. It has been a distinct settlement since 1856, under the jurisdiction of the state of New South Wales; and finally by the passage of the Norfolk Island Act 1913, it was accepted as a Territory of the Australian Government. The Norfolk Island Act 1957 is the basis of the Territory's legislative, administrative and judicial systems. An Administrator, appointed by the Governor-General and responsible to the Minister for Territories and Local Government, is the senior government representative in the Territory.

The Norfolk Island Act 1979 equips Norfolk Island with responsible legislative and executive government to enable it to run its own affairs to the greatest practicable extent. Wide powers are exercised by the Norfolk Island Legislative Assembly and by an Executive Council, comprising the executive members of the Legislative Assembly who have ministerial-type responsibilities. The Act preserves the Commonwealth's responsibility for Norfolk Island as a Territory under its authority, with the Minister for Territories and Local Government being the responsible Minister, and indicates the Parliament's intention that consideration will be given to an extension of the powers of the Legislative Assembly and the political and administrative institutions of Norfolk Island within 5 years.

The Executive Council has executive authority over a prescribed range of matters.

The island's Supreme Court sits as required and a Court of Petty Sessions exercises both civil and criminal jurisdiction.

The Territory Administration is financed from local revenue which for 1982–83 totalled $A2,673,723. A further $A286,000 was provided by the Commonwealth during the year for the restoration and maintenance of historic structures.

Public revenue is derived mainly from the sale of postage stamps, customs duties, liquor sales and company registration and licence fees. Residents are not liable for income tax on earnings within the Territory, nor are death and personal stamp duties levied. In 1982–83 imports totalled $A15·1m. and exports $A3·1m.

An estimated 16,220 visitors travelled to Norfolk during 1982–83. Descendants of the *Bounty* mutineer families constitute the 'original' settlers and are known locally as 'Islanders', while later settlers, mostly from Australia, New Zealand and UK, are identified as 'mainlanders'. Over the years the Islanders have preserved their own lifestyle and customs, and their language remains a mixture of West Country English and Tahitian.

The Administration subsidises a public hospital and dispensary, and health services, together with free dental services for children, are provided by qualified government officers.

Norfolk Island's public school is staffed by the New South Wales Department of Education and follows the State's education system. A bursary scheme is available to provide students with secondary education on the mainland.

A radio telephone service between the island and Sydney is maintained by the Overseas Telecommunications Commission, and there is a local automatic telephone service. Number of telephones (1982) 987.

Administrator: Air Vice-Marshal R. E. Trebilco, DFC.

HEARD AND McDONALD ISLANDS. These islands, about 2,500 miles south-west of Fremantle, were transferred from UK to Australian control as from 26 Dec. 1947. Heard Island is about 43 km long and 21 km wide; Shag Island is about 8 km north of Heard. The total area is 412 sq. km (159 sq. miles). The McDonald Islands are 42 km to the west of Heard.

TERRITORY OF ASHMORE AND CARTIER ISLANDS. By Imperial Order in Council of 23 July 1931, Ashmore Islands (known as Middle,

East and West Islands) and Cartier Island, situated in the Indian Ocean, some 320 km off the north-west coast of Australia (area, 5 sq. km), were placed under the authority of the Commonwealth.

Under the Ashmore and Cartier Islands Acceptance Act, 1933, the islands were accepted by the Commonwealth under the name of the Territory of Ashmore and Cartier Islands, and the effective date was proclaimed by the Governor-General to be 10 May 1934. It was the intention that the Territory should be administered by the State of Western Australia, but owing to administrative difficulties the Territory was annexed to and deemed to form part of the Northern Territory of Australia (by amendment to the Act in 1938) with relevant laws of the Northern Territory, applying to the Territory of Ashmore and Cartier Islands. Responsibility for the administration of Ashmore and Cartier Islands rests with the Minister for Territories and Local Government.

On 16 Aug. 1983 a national nature reserve was declared over Ashmore Reef and the area so declared is now known as Ashmore Reef National Nature Reserve.

The islands are uninhabited but Indonesian fishing boats, which have traditionally plied the area, fish within the Territory and land to collect water in accordance with an agreement between the governments of Australia and Indonesia.

Periodic visits are made to the islands by ships of the Royal Australian Navy, and aircraft of the Royal Australian Air Force make aerial surveys of the islands and neighbouring waters.

TERRITORY OF CORAL SEA ISLANDS. The Coral Sea Islands became a Territory of the Commonwealth of Australia under the Coral Sea Islands Act 1969. It comprises scattered reefs and islands over a sea area of about 1m. sq. km. The Territory is uninhabited apart from a manned meteorological station on Willis Island.

Books of Reference

The Northern Territory: Annual Report. Dept. of Territories, Canberra, from 1911. Dept. of the Interior, Canberra, from 1966–67. Dept. of Northern Territory, from 1972

Australian Territories, Dept. of Territories, Canberra, 1960 to 1973. Dept. of Special Minister of State, Canberra, 1973–75. Department of Administrative Services, 1976

Northern Territory Statistical Summary. Australian Bureau of Statistics, Canberra, from 1960

Prospects of Agriculture in the Northern Territory. Dept. of Territories, Canberra, 1961

Holmes, J. M., *Australia's Open North.* Sydney, 1963

Lockwood, D. W., *Fair Dinkum.* London, 1960

NEW SOUTH WALES

HISTORY. New South Wales became a British possession in 1770; the first settlement was established at Port Jackson in 1788; a partially elective Council was established in 1843, and responsible government in 1856. New South Wales federated with the other Australian states to form the Commonwealth of Australia in 1901.

AREA AND POPULATION. New South Wales is situated between the 28th and 38th parallels of S. lat. and 141st and 154th meridians of E. long., and comprises 309,433 sq. miles (801,428 sq. km), inclusive of Lord Howe Island, 6 sq. miles (17 sq. km), but exclusive of the Australian Capital Territory (911 sq. miles, 2,359 sq. km) at Canberra and 28 sq. miles (73 sq. km), at Jervis Bay.

Lord Howe Island, 31° 33′ 4″ S., 159° 4′ 26″ E., which is part of New South Wales, is situated about 702 km north-east of Sydney; area, 1,656 hectares, of which only about 120 hectares are arable; resident population, estimate (30 June 1983), 300. The Island, which was discovered in 1788, is of volcanic origin. Mount Gower, the highest point, reaches a height of 866 metres.

The Lord Howe Island Board manages the affairs of the Island and supervises the Kentia palm-seed industry.

Census population of New South Wales (including full-blood Aboriginals from 1966):

	Males	Females	Persons	Population per sq. km	Average annual increase % since previous census
1901	710,264	645,091	1,355,355	2	1·86
1911	857,698	789,036	1,646,734	2	1·97
1921	1,071,501	1,028,870	2,100,371	3	2·46
1933	1,318,471	1,282,376	2,600,847	3	1·76
1947	1,492,211	1,492,627	2,984,838	4	0·99
1954	1,720,860	1,702,669	3,423,529	4	1·98
1961	1,972,909	1,944,104	3,917,013	5	1·94
1966	2,126,652	2,111,249	4,237,901	5	1·58
1971	2,307,210	2,293,970	4,601,180	6	1·66
1976	2,380,172	2,396,931	4,777,103	6	0·75
1981	2,548,984	2,577,233	5,126,217	6	1·42

At 30 June 1983 the resident population (estimate) of New South Wales was 5,360,400 (1982, 5,307,900). Sydney (Statistical Division), 3,334,950 (3,310,450); Newcastle (Statistical District), 414,700 (410,250); Wollongong (Statistical District), 235,000 (233,650). Population of principal country municipalities: Albury, 38,650 (38,100); Armidale, 19,500 (19,400); Bathurst, 24,250 (23,550); Broken Hill, 27,400 (27,700); Casino, 10,450 (10,400); Dubbo, 29,900 (29,350); Goulburn, 22,400 (22,250); Grafton, 17,300 (17,200); Hastings, 38,300 (37,000); Lake Macquarie, 159,000 (156,950); Lismore, 36,250 (35,500); Lithgow, Greater, 21,000 (20,850); Orange, 31,950 (31,750); Queanbeyan, 20,450 (20,150); Shellharbour, 45,200 (44,350); Shoalhaven, 54,350 (51,750); Tamworth, 33,100 (32,950); Taree, Greater, 33,950 (33,100); Wagga Wagga, 49,350 (48,950).

Vital statistics for calendar years:

	Live births	Marriages	Divorces	Deaths (excluding still-births)	Infantile mortality per 1,000 live births
1981	81,530	40,679	14,532	39,959	9·9
1982	83,489	41,955	14,378	42,352	9·9
1983	82,739	39,995	14,023	40,323	9·7

The annual rates per 1,000 of mean resident population (estimate) in 1983 were: Births, 15·4; deaths, 7·5; marriages, 7·5.

CONSTITUTION AND GOVERNMENT. Within the State there are three levels of government: the Commonwealth Government, with authority derived from a written constitution; the State Government with residual powers; the local government authorities with powers based upon a State Act of Parliament, operating within incorporated areas extending over almost 90% of the State.

The Constitution of New South Wales is drawn from several diverse sources; certain Imperial statutes such as the Colonial Laws Validity Act (1865) and the Commonwealth of Australia Constitution Act (1900); the Australian States Constitution Act (1907); the Letters Patent and the Instructions to the Governor; an element of inherited English law; amendments to the Commonwealth of Australia Constitution Act; the (State) Constitution Act and certain other State Statutes; numerous legal decisions; and a large amount of English and local convention.

The Parliament of New South Wales may legislate for the peace, welfare and good government of the State in all matters not specifically reserved to the Commonwealth Government.

The State Legislature consists of the Sovereign, represented by the Governor, and two Houses of Parliament, the Legislative Council (upper house) and the Legislative Assembly (lower house).

Australian citizens, and other British subjects who were enrolled at 25 Jan. 1984, men and women aged 18 years and over, are entitled to the franchise. Voting is compulsory.

The Legislative Council has 45 members elected by popular vote for a term of office equivalent to three terms of the Legislative Assembly, with 15 members retiring at the same time as the Legislative Assembly elections. In Oct. 1984, the Council consisted of the following parties: Labor, 24; Liberal, 11; National Party, 7; Australian Democrats, 1; Independents, 2.

The President of the Legislative Council has an annual salary (1984) of $A60,007; the Leader of the Opposition members, $A48,235; the Chairman of Committees, the Deputy Leader of the Government members (if not a Minister) and the Deputy Leader of the Opposition members (when a leader of a party), $A38,683 each; the Deputy Leader of the Opposition members (when not a leader of a party) and Government and Opposition Whips, $A35,539 each. The President is paid an annual expense allowance of $A8,752; the Leader of the Opposition members, $A5,200; the Chairman of Committees, the Deputy Leader of the Government members (if not a Minister) and the Deputy Leader of the Opposition members (when a leader of a party), $A4,810 each; the Deputy Leader of the Opposition members (when not a leader of a party) and Government and Opposition Whips, $A2,086 each. Other members who are not Ministers receive an annual salary of $A30,657. All members receive an annual electoral allowance of $A9,982. Special expenses allowances ($A4,664 or $A7,793) are paid to members who are not Ministers and reside in outlying electorates.

The Legislative Assembly has 99 members elected by popular vote for a maximum period of 4 years. The Legislative Assembly, elected on 24 March 1984, consisted in Oct. 1984 of the following parties: Labor, 58; Liberal, 22; National Party, 15; Independents, 4.

The Speaker of the Legislative Assembly and the Leader of the Opposition members receive a salary of (1984) $A64,873 each; the Chairman of Committees, Deputy Leader of the Opposition members and Leader of the National Party, $A48,235 each; Government and Opposition Whips, $A45,302 each. The Speaker and the Leader of the Opposition members also receive an expense allowance of $A9,462 each; the Chairman of Committees, Deputy Leader of the Opposition members and Leader of the National Party, $A5,200 each; Government and Opposition Whips, and Deputy Leader of the National Party, $A2,455 each. Members who are not Ministers receive an annual salary of $A39,558. All members receive an annual electoral allowance ranging from $A12,880 to $A23,075 according to the location of their constituencies. Special expenses allowances ($A5,182–$A7,793) are paid to members who represent outlying electorates.

Executive power is vested in the Governor, who is appointed by the Crown, and an Executive Council consisting of members of the Cabinet. Ministers receive the following annual salaries (1984): Premier, $A81,292; Deputy Premier, $A73,186; the Leader of the Government members in the Legislative Council, $A74,010; Deputy Leader of Government members in the Legislative Council, $A70,495; other Ministers, $A69,102. Ministers also receive an expense allowance (Premier, $A20,252; Deputy Premier, $A10,125; other Ministers, $A9,462 each). Ministers also receive an electoral allowance ranging from $A12,880 to $A23,075 to members of the Legislative Assembly, according to the location of their electorate; and $A9,982 to each member of the Legislative Council. A special expenses allowance of $A7,793 is paid to Ministers who represent or reside in outlying electorates.

Governor: Air Marshal Sir James Anthony Rowland, KBE, DFC, AFC (sworn in 20 Jan. 1981).

The Labor Party Cabinet, in Oct. 1984, was as follows:

Premier and Minister for the Arts: The Hon. N. K. Wran, QC, MP.

Deputy Premier and Minister for Health: The Hon. R. J. Mulock, MP. *Minister for Youth and Community Services and Minister for Housing:* The Hon. F. J. Walker, QC, MP. *Minister for Public Works and Ports and Minister for Roads:* The Hon. L. J. Brereton, MP. *Attorney-General:* The Hon. D. P. Landa, MP. *Minister for Industrial Relations:* The Hon. P. D. Hills, MP. *Minister for Police and Emergency Services:* The Hon. P. T. Anderson, MP. *Treasurer:* The Hon. K. G. Booth, MP. *Minister for Planning and Environment:* The Hon. T. W. Sheahan, MP. *Minister for Transport and Vice-President of the Executive Council:* The Hon. B. J.

Unsworth, MLC. *Minister for Agriculture and Fisheries:* The Hon. J. R. Hallam, MLC. *Minister for Education:* The Hon. R. M. Cavalier, MP. *Minister for Mineral Resources and Energy:* The Hon. P. F. Cox, MP. *Minister for Local Government:* The Hon. K. J. Stewart, MP. *Minister for Industry and Decentralisation and Minister for Small Business and Technology:* The Hon. E. L. Bedford, MP. *Minister for Sport and Recreation and Minister for Tourism:* The Hon. M. A. Cleary, MP. *Minister for Consumer Affairs and Minister for Aboriginal Affairs:* The Hon. George Paciullo, MP. *Minister for Natural Resources:* The Hon. Janice Crosio, MBE, MP. *Minister for Employment and Minister for Finance:* The Hon. R. J. Debus, MP. *Minister for Corrective Services:* The Hon. J. E. Akister, MP.

Agent-General in London: R. F. W. Watson, CMG (66 Strand, WC2N 5LZ).

Local Government. A system of local government extends over most of the State, including the whole of the Eastern and Central land divisions and almost three-quarters of the sparsely populated Western division. At 1 Jan. 1984 there were 62 municipalities, and 113 corporate bodies called shires. A number of the municipalities and shires have combined to form 43 county councils, which administer electricity or water supply undertakings or render other services of common benefit.

ECONOMY

Budget. State Consolidated Fund: statement of receipts and expenditure (in $A1m.) for financial years ending 30 June:

	1980–81	*1981–82*	*1982–83*	*1983–84*
Receipts: Recurrent	4,639	5,353	6,119	6,812
Capital	547	563	619	595
Total Receipts	5,186	5,916	6,737	7,407
Expenditure: Recurrent	4,669	5,422	6,301	6,955
Capital	564	553	477	486
Total Expenditure	5,233	5,976	6,777	7,441
Surplus/deficit	–46	–60	–40	–34

State Government receipts (in $A1m.) for 1983–84 included receipts from loan raisings, 317; Commonwealth general revenue assistance, 2,577; and state taxation, 2,969. Expenditure included capital works and services, 486; education, 2,135; health, 939; and public debt charges, 643.

Public Debt. In terms of the financial agreement between the Commonwealth and State Governments, the Commonwealth Government has assumed responsibility for debts of the Australian States, and contributes towards the interest thereon and sinking funds established for redemption of the debts. Loans for the States are raised by the Commonwealth Government in accordance with decisions of the Australian Loan Council.

The public debt of New South Wales at 30 June 1984 was $A5,567m. with less than 1% domiciled overseas. Interest liability for 1983–84 amounted to $A601m. Contributions to the sinking fund for New South Wales debt, $A78m., includes $A15m. contributed by the Commonwealth Government. The net cost of securities redeemed in the year was $A79m.

Banking. There were 8 trading banks operating in New South Wales at 30 June 1984, including the Commonwealth Trading Bank and State Bank (Government banks) and 1 New Zealand bank. The trading bank business is transacted chiefly by the Commonwealth Trading Bank, the State Bank and 3 private banks, all of which have their head offices in Australia. At 30 June 1984 the 8 banks operated 1,834 branches and 324 agencies in New South Wales.

The weekly average amount of deposits held in New South Wales by the 8 banks was $A16,646·7m. in June 1983, consisting of $A11,917·5m. bearing interest and $A4,729·2m. not bearing interest. Bank advances, overdrafts, bills discounted, etc., amounted to $A13,147·8m. A statement of other assets and liabilities of the banks in New South Wales is of little significance, as banking business is conducted on an Australia-wide basis.

Savings bank deposits at the end of June 1984 amounted to $A9,532·4m., representing $A1,772 per head of population.

ENERGY AND NATURAL RESOURCES

Minerals. New South Wales contains extensive mineral deposits. The most important minerals mined are: Coal (which accounts for 76% of the value of the State's mineral production); silver–lead–zinc (11%); construction materials (sand, gravel, stone, etc., 8%); and mineral sands (rutile, zircon, etc., 1%). At 30 June 1983, there were 577 mining establishments with an average employment of 28,665. During 1982–83, wages and salaries paid were $A808m., and value added was $A1,852m. Mine production of coal and metallic minerals (gross content) is shown below:

	1980–81	*1981–82*	*1982–83*	*1983–84*
Antimony (tonnes)	1,207	1,218	769	586
Cadmium (tonnes)	1,156	1,378	1,424	1,315
Coal (1,000 tonnes)	58,549	60,172	66,297	66,827
Cobalt (tonnes)	74	57	92	63
Copper (tonnes)	17,162	22,915	26,878	26,177
Gold (kg)	572	612	606	946
Lead (tonnes)	224,938	253,031	237,437	213,721
Silver (kg)	283,667	307,508	322,390	307,411
Sulphur (tonnes)	236,244	273,956	298,850	228,008
Tin (tonnes)	2,053	1,668	1,575	1,320
Titanium dioxide (tonnes)	111,021	80,454	47,612	41,662
Zinc (tonnes)	309,181	357,185	374,783	332,150
Zircon (tonnes)	113,009	88,479	55,588	59,181

The value of output in mining and quarrying in 1982–83 was $A2,504m.

Land settlement. The total area of land alienated or in process of alienation from the Crown on 30 June 1983 was 32,729,784 hectares; land resumed or reverted to the Crown was 2,866,746 hectares, with 29,863,038 hectares remaining alienated. 41,154,714 hectares (including 30,462,939 hectares of the Western Division) were held under lease from the Crown.

Agriculture. The area under cultivation in New South Wales during 3 years (ended 31 March) and the principal crops (in tonnes) produced were as follows:

	1981	*1982*	*1983*
Area of crops	5,376,115	5,993,393	5,307,063
Value (farm) of all crops	$A1,108m.	$A1,517m.	$A878m.

		1981		*1982*		*1983*	
Principal crops		*Hectares*	*Production*	*Hectares*	*Production*	*Hectares*	*Production*
Wheat	Grain	3,345,000	2,865,000	3,600,000	5,910,000	3,161,659	1,499,406
	Hay	33,081	67,830	22,239	62,796	29,340	43,692
Barley	Grain	455,481	413,325	539,967	766,362	386,555	189,398
	Hay	3,451	6,190	3,207	7,931	1,722	2,735
Oats	Grain	363,250	309,867	555,694	741,275	394,356	134,899
	Hay	42,716	90,151	58,419	171,180	35,452	45,636
Grain Sorghum		127,294	147,828	152,346	325,689	167,873	191,644
Potatoes		6,262	86,526	6,185	107,500	7,010	108,799
Lucerne (hay)		41,858	197,469	58,199	281,358	46,098	230,724
Rice		98,824	703,530	117,607	828,944	79,821	525,488
Cotton		53,743	173,428	63,508	248,665	69,615	205,501
Oilseeds		65,684	47,402	66,430	65,358	77,992	47,546

In 1982–83, 15,980 hectares of sugar-cane were cut for crushing, the production being 1,702,341 tonnes. The total area under grapes was 13,141 (including 677 not bearing) hectares; the production of table grapes was 5,411 tonnes; of wine, 102,804 tonnes; of dried vine fruits, 11,270 tonnes.

In 1982–83, 5,496 hectares of banana plantations; production from 5,011 hectares, 68,646 tonnes; there were 27,816 hectares of orchard fruit.

At 31 March 1983 the State had 48·1m. sheep and lambs, 5,018,021 cattle and 794,346 pigs. The production of wool in 1982–83 was 218·1m. kg (greasy). In the year ended 30 June 1984 production of butter was 2,832 tonnes; cheese, 14,140 tonnes, and bacon and ham, 21,083 tonnes.

Forestry. The estimated area of Crown and private lands is 16·3m. hectares. The total area of State forests amounts to 3·4m. hectares, and 252,000 hectares have been set apart as timber reserves.

In 1983–84, 3,244,000 cu. metres of timber (excluding firewood) were produced, including 1,168,000 cu. metres of forest hardwoood and 1,193,000 cu. metres of pulpwoods.

INDUSTRY AND TRADE

Industry. Approximately 20% of employed persons in New South Wales are employed in manufacturing industries.

A very wide range of manufacturing activities is undertaken in the Sydney area, and there are large iron and steel works and associated metal fabrication works in operation in proximity to the coalfields at Newcastle and Port Kembla.

The following table shows a summary of manufacturing industries' statistics for 1982–83:

Industry	*Establishments* [1] *No.*	*Employment* [2] *Males (No.)*	*Females (No.)*	*Wages and salaries* [3] *($A1m.)*	*Value added ($A1m.)*
Food, beverages and tobacco	1,014	38,631	16,277	956·0	1,905·6
Textiles	198	5,252	3,893	151·9	262·8
Clothing and footwear	769	4,347	15,419	237·2	372·4
Wood, wood products and furniture	1,428	20,005	3,892	327·6	585·6
Paper, paper products, printing and publishing	1,248	24,164	11,430	631·2	1,163·7
Chemical, petroleum and coal products	426	19,450	8,868	554·9	1,402·7
Non-metallic mineral products	569	12,926	1,748	289·8	523·3
Basic metal products	205	41,691	3,277	916·2	947·1
Fabricated metal products	1,727	30,906	7,046	610·9	1,006·1
Transport equipment	422	28,930	2,783	576·4	864·4
Other machinery and equipment	1,603	45,129	16,439	1,031·9	1,691·6
Miscellaneous manufacturing	862	14,514	7,591	354·5	607·2
Total manufacturing	10,471	285,945	98,663	6,638·4	11,332·4

[1] Operating at 30 June 1983. Excludes single-establishment manufacturing enterprises with less than 4 persons employed.

[2] Persons employed—average over whole year, including working proprietors.

[3] Excludes drawings of working proprietors.

Some of the principal articles manufactured in 1983–84 were:

Article	*Quantity*	*Article*	*Quantity*
Flour (1,000 tonnes)	528	Electric motors (1,000)	1,223
Woven fabric (1,000 sq. metres)	63,086	Clay bricks (1m.)	677
Raw steel (1,000 tonnes)	5,109	Electricity (1m. kwh.)	42,105

During 1983–84 the value of all building jobs commenced in New South Wales was $A3,902m. (of which jobs valued at $A981m. were being built for government ownership), jobs completed were valued at $A3,135m. ($A418m. for government ownership), and jobs under construction at the end of the period were valued at $A3,494m. ($A1,176m. for government ownership).

Labour. Two systems of industrial arbitration and conciliation for the adjustment of industrial relations between employers and employees are in operation—the State system which operates within the territorial limits of the State, and the Commonwealth system, which applies to industrial disputes extending beyond State borders.

The industrial tribunals are authorized to fix minimum rates of wages and other conditions of employment. Their awards may be enforced by law, as may be industrial agreements between employers and organizations of employees, when registered.

The principal State tribunal is the Industrial Commission of New South Wales. The Commission is empowered to exercise all the arbitration and conciliation powers conferred on subsidiary tribunals, and has in addition authority to determine any widely defined 'industrial matter', to adjudicate in case of illegal strikes and lockouts, etc., to investigate union ballots when irregularities are alleged and to hear appeals from subsidiary tribunals. Subsidiary tribunals are Conciliation Committees for various industries, each having an equal number representing employers and employees and a Conciliation Commissioner as chairman.

The chief industrial tribunals of the Commonwealth are the Industrial Division of the Federal Court of Australia, composed of judges, and the Australian Conciliation and Arbitration Commission, composed of presidential members, and commissioners.

Most State awards and agreements prescribe a basic wage. However, since 1974, the State Industrial Commission has also specified a minimum wage in line with Commonwealth awards. In Sept. 1984, the minimum wage payable in Sydney for a full week's work by an adult male or female was $A158.60 under both State and Commonwealth awards. For the June quarter 1984, average weekly earnings were $A422·60 for full-time adult males and $A320·10 for full-time adult females.

The standard working week is still regarded as 40 hours for employees under both Commonwealth and State awards. However, some awards prescribe less than 40 hours per week and, since early 1981, a campaign by trade unions has resulted in the extension of shorter working hours to more industries. Overtime is permitted under prescribed conditions.

Trade Unions. Registration of trade unions is effected under the New South Wales Trade Union Act, 1881, which follows substantially the Trade Union Acts of 1871 and 1876 of England. Registration confers a quasi-corporate existence with power to hold property, to sue and be sued, etc., and the various classes of employees covered by the union are required to be prescribed by the constitution of the union. For the purpose of bringing an industry under the review of the State industrial tribunals, or participating in proceedings relating to disputes before Commonwealth tribunals, employees and employers must be registered as industrial unions, under State or Commonwealth industrial legislation respectively. At 31 Dec. 1983, there were 186 trade unions with a total membership of 1,108,700. Approximately 59% (estimate) of wage and salary earners were members of trade unions.

Commerce. The external commerce of New South Wales, exclusive of interstate trade, is included in the statement of the commerce of Australia (*see* pp. 108–10). The overseas commerce of New South Wales is given in $A1,000 ending 30 June:

	Imports	*Exports*		*Imports*	*Exports*
1978–79	5,760,063	3,512,435	1981–82	9,235,864	4,194,663
1979–80	6,704,649	4,103,985	1982–83	8,610,543	4,956,145
1980–81	7,951,738	4,103,507	1983–84	10,027,948	5,231,459

The main exports from New South Wales of Australian produce in 1983–84 were coal (28·5%), cereals (11·4%), wool (8·9%), petroleum (5·8%), iron and steel (4·3%), meat (4·2%), metalliferous ores and metal scraps (3%). Principal imports were machinery and transport equipment (37·5%), chemicals (10%), petroleum and petroleum products (5·8%), textiles (4·9%), precision instruments and apparatus (2·6%), paper and paperboard (2·5%), metal manufactures (2·4%).

Principal destinations of all exports from New South Wales in 1983–84 were Japan (26·9%), EEC countries (12·6%), New Zealand (8·7%) ASEAN countries (7·9%), Republic of Korea (5·9%), USA (5·4%), China (4·9%). Major sources of supply were USA (23·9%), Japan (22·7%), EEC countries (21%), New Zealand (4·2%) and Saudi Arabia (2·2%).

COMMUNICATIONS

Roads. At 31 Dec. 1982 there were 195,127 km of roads and streets open for general traffic in New South Wales (excluding unincorporated and Lord Howe Island), comprising 73,247 km bitumen or concrete, 64,899 km gravel, crushed stone or other improved surface, 36,158 km earth formed and 20,805 km natural surface.

The principal bus services in Sydney and Newcastle are operated by the State Government.

The number of registered motor vehicles (excluding tractors and trailers) at 30 June 1984 was 2,873,206, including 1,806,734 cars, 356,353 station wagons, 166,273 utilities, 193,413 panel vans, 192,072 trucks, 25,646 buses and 132,715 motor cycles.

Railways. At 30 June 1984, 9,878 km of government railway were open. The revenue (including supplements) in 1982–83 was $A1,295·1m.; the expenditure from revenue, $A1,295·1m.; the number of passengers carried, 207·8m. Also open for traffic are 325 km of Victorian Government railways which extend over the border; 68 km of private railways (mainly in mining districts) and 53 km of Commonwealth Government-owned track.

Aviation. Sydney is the major airport in New South Wales and Australia's principal international air terminal. During the year ended 31 Dec. 1982 scheduled aircraft movements at Sydney totalled 93,665. Passengers totalled 5,685,185 on domestic services and 2,416,280 on international services. Freight handled on domestic and international services was 59,775 tonnes and 99,101 tonnes respectively.

Shipping. Arrivals of vessels engaged in overseas trade in the ports of New South Wales in 1982–83 numbered 2,396 and clearances numbered 2,426. The revenue tonnage of cargo discharged and loaded was 8·1m. and 32m. respectively. Sydney Harbour is the principal port of Australia. The number of overseas vessels which entered in 1982–83 was 1,350.

JUSTICE, RELIGION, EDUCATION AND WELFARE

Justice. Legal processes may be carried on in Lower or Magistrates' Courts, or in the Higher Courts presided over by judges. There is also an appellate jurisdiction. Persons charged with the more serious crimes must be tried before the Higher Courts.

Children's Courts have been established with the object of removing children as far as possible from the atmosphere of a public court. There are also a number of tribunals exercising special jurisdiction, *e.g.*, the Industrial Commission and the Workers' Compensation Commission.

In 1982 there were 3,973 distinct persons convicted at the Higher Criminal Courts. At 30 June 1983 there were 3,098 persons (including 135 females) held under sentence in prison.

Religion. There is no established church in New South Wales, and freedom of worship is accorded to all.

The following table shows the statistics of the religious denominations in New South Wales at the census in 1981, and of ministers of religion registered for the celebration of marriages in 1983:

Denomination	*Ministers*	*Adherents*	*Denomination*	*Ministers*	*Adherents*
Church of England	988	1,569,374	Other Christian	1,234	388,887
Roman Catholic	1,706	1,424,499	Muslim	10	25,176
Presbyterian	219	252,725	Hebrew	23	38,527
Uniting Church	578	179,271	Other Non-Christian	14	25,408
Orthodox	77	171,427	Others	...	954,564 [1]
Baptist	405	64,663			
Lutheran	45	31,696	Total	5,299	5,126,217

[1] Comprises 443,159 'no religion' and 511,405 'religion not stated' or 'inadequately described' (this is not a compulsory question in the census schedule).

Education. The State Government maintains a system of primary and secondary education, and attendance at school is compulsory from 6 to 15 years of age. In all government schools education is free. Non-government schools are subject to government inspection.

In July 1983 there were 2,237 government schools, comprising 1,679 primary and infant schools, 77 combined primary and secondary schools, 368 secondary schools and 113 special-purpose schools. In July 1983 the effective enrolment was 778,410 students, comprising 477,577 receiving primary instruction and 300,833 receiving secondary instruction. There were 45,800 teachers (including the full-time equivalent of part-time teachers) in 1983.

In July 1983 there were 831 non-government schools with 13,965 teachers (including the full-time equivalent of part-time teachers) and an effective enrolment of 251,506 students, including 604 Roman Catholic schools, having 10,600 teachers and 203,563 students, and 35 Anglican schools with 1,242 teachers and 18,066 students.

The University of Sydney, founded in 1850, had 18,404 students in 1983. There are 6 colleges providing residential facilities at the university. The University of New England at Armidale, previously affiliated with the University of Sydney, was incorporated in 1954, and in 1983 had 8,743 students.

The University of New South Wales was established in 1949. Enrolments in 1983 numbered 18,376. There are 8 colleges providing residential facilities at the university. The University of Newcastle, previously affiliated with the University of New South Wales, was granted autonomy from 1965, and in 1983 had 4,435 students. The University of Wollongong, also previously associated with the University of New South Wales, became autonomous in 1975, and in 1983 had 3,498 students. Macquarie University in Sydney, established in 1964, had 11,065 students in 1983.

Advanced education courses at Colleges of Advanced Education and other institutions provide tertiary training with a vocational emphasis. In 1983 there were 45,619 students (including 25,090 part-time students) enrolled in these courses.

Post-school technical and further education is provided at State technical colleges. Students enrolled in 1983 totalled 347,031 (including 25,593 external students).

State Government expenditure (including loan expenditure) on education in 1982–83 was $A2,030m.

Social Welfare. The Commonwealth Government makes provision for social benefits, such as age and invalid pensions, widows' pensions, supporting parents' benefits, family allowances, and unemployment, sickness and special benefits.

The number of age and invalid pensions (including wives' pensions) current in New South Wales on 30 June 1984 was: Age, 502,793 (males, 157,733; females, 345,060); invalid, 103,164 (males, 58,300; females, 44,864). Expenditure for the year ended 30 June 1984 was $A1,971m. for age pensions and $A420m. for invalid pensions.

Commonwealth Government widows' pensions current in New South Wales at 30 June 1984 numbered 58,731, the expenditure for 1983–84, $A307m. Supporting parents' benefits at 30 June 1984 numbered 57,581; expenditure in 1983–84 was $A345m.

Under the Family Allowance scheme, which commenced in 1976, payments to families and approved institutions for children under 16 years and full-time students under 25 years (1,464,927 such children or students) during 1983–84 amounted to $A538m.

Unemployment, sickness and special benefits commenced in 1945. During the year 1983–84 claims totalling $A1,350m. were paid in New South Wales. At 30 June 1984 unemployment benefit was being paid to an estimated 224,885 persons, and sickness and special benefits to 34,880 persons.

Direct State Government social welfare services are limited, for the most part, to the assistance of persons not eligible for Commonwealth Government benefit and the provision of certain forms of assistance not available from the Commonwealth Government. The State also subsidizes many approved services for needy persons. During 1982–83, expenditure on social security and welfare was $A323m.

Books of Reference

Statistical Information: The NSW Government Statistician's Office was established in 1886, and in 1957 was integrated with the Commonwealth Bureau of Census and Statistics (now called the Australian Bureau of Statistics). *Deputy Commonwealth Statistician:* T. J. Skinner. Its principal publications are:

New South Wales Year Book (1886/87–1900/01 under the title *Wealth and Progress of NSW*): latest issue, 1983
New South Wales Handbook of Local Statistics: latest issue, 1984
New South Wales Principal Subject Bulletins (previously published under the title *Statistical Register* (since 1858); latest issue of separate bulletins, 1981–82 and 1984
New South Wales Pocket Year Book. Published since 1913; latest issue, 1984
Monthly Summary of Statistics. Published since May 1931
New South Wales in Brief. 1984

New South Wales Dept. of Industrial Development and Decentralisation, *New South Wales Handbook for Industrialists.* 1984
State Planning Authority, *Sydney Region, 1970–2000 A.D.: Outline Plan.* Sydney, 1968
New South Wales Planning and Environment Commission, *Review: Sydney Region Outline Plan.* Sydney, 1980
New South Wales Government Information Service, *The Government of New South Wales: Directory of Administration and Services.* Sydney, 1982

State Library: The State Library of NSW, Macquarie St., Sydney. *State Librarian:* R. F. Doust, BA, M.Lib, FLAA.

QUEENSLAND

AREA AND POPULATION. Queensland comprises the whole north-eastern portion of the Australian continent, including the adjacent islands in the Pacific Ocean and in the Gulf of Carpentaria. Estimated area 1,727,000 sq. km.

The increase in the population as shown by the censuses since 1901 has been as follows:

	Census counts			*Intercensal increase*	
Year	*Males*	*Females*	*Total*	*Numerical*	*Rate per annum %*
1901	277,003	221,126	498,129	—	—
1911	329,506	276,307	605,813	107,684	1·98
1921	398,969	357,003	755,972	150,159	2·24
1933	497,217	450,317	947,534	191,562	1·86
1947	567,471	538,944	1,106,415	158,881	1·11
1954	676,252	642,007	1,318,259	211,844	2·53
1961	774,579	744,249	1,518,828	200,569	2·04
1966	849,390 [1]	824,934 [1]	1,674,324 [1]	144,857	1·84
1971	921,665 [1]	905,400 [1]	1,827,065 [1]	152,741 [1]	1·76 [1]
1976	1,024,611 [1]	1,012,586 [1]	2,037,197 [1]	210,132 [1]	2·20 [1]
1981	1,153,404 [1]	1,141,719 [1]	2,295,123 [1]	257,926 [1]	2·41 [1]

[1] Including Aboriginals.

Since the 1981 census, official population estimates are according to place of usual residence and are referred to as estimated resident population. Estimated resident populations at the census dates of 1971, 1976, and 1981 were 1,851,500; 2,092,400; and 2,345,200, respectively.

Statistics on birthplaces from the 1981 census are as follows: Australia, 1,932,810 (84·2%); UK and Ireland, 147,083 (6·4%); other countries, 183,067 (8%); at sea and not stated, 32,163 (1·4%).

Vital statistics (including Aboriginals) for calendar years:

	Total births	*Marriages*	*Divorces*	*Deaths*
1981	38,910	18,305	6,470	17,037
1982	40,606	18,928	6,770	18,011
1983	42,085	18,645	7,335	17,329

The annual rates per 1,000 population in 1983 were: Marriages, 7·5; births, 17; deaths, 7. The infant death rate was 9·9 per 1,000 births.

Brisbane, the capital, had on 30 June 1983 (estimate) a resident population of 1,138,370 (Statistical Division). The resident populations of the other major centres (Statistical Districts) at the same date were: Gold Coast, 166,050; Townsville, 99,560; Sunshine Coast, 77,020; Cairns, 62,700; Rockhampton, 56,440; Mackay, 48,140 and Bundaberg, 41,710. Other cities included Toowoomba, 74,450; Mount Isa, 25,350; Gladstone, 25,310; and Maryborough, 22,400.

CONSTITUTION AND GOVERNMENT. Queensland, formerly a portion of New South Wales, was formed into a separate colony in 1859, and responsible government was conferred. The power of making laws and imposing taxes is vested in a Parliament of one House—the Legislative Assembly, which comprises 82 members, returned from 4 electoral zones for 3 years, elected for single-member constituencies at compulsory ballot. Members are entitled to $A39,833 per annum, with individual electorate allowances for travelling, postage, etc., of from $A9,550 to $A24,630.

At the general election of 22 Oct. 1983 there were 1,458,206 persons registered as qualified to vote under the Elections Act 1983. This Act provides franchise for all males and females, 18 years of age and over, qualified by 6 months' residence in Australia and 3 months in the electoral district.

The Legislative Assembly, following the elections of 22 Oct. 1983, was composed of the following parties: National, 41; Liberal, 8; Australian Labor, 32; Independent, 1; total, 82. Subsequently, 2 Liberal Party members changed to the National Party of Australia.

Governor of Queensland: Cde Sir James Maxwell Ramsay, KCMG, KCVO,CBE, DSC (assumed office April 1977).

The Executive Council of Ministers, at 31 July 1984, consisted of the following members:

Premier and Treasurer: Sir Johannes Bjelke-Petersen, KCMG (National).

Deputy Premier and Assisting the Treasurer: William Angus Manson Gunn (National). *Local Government, Main Roads and Racing:* Russell James Hinze (National). *Works and Housing:* Claude Alfred Wharton (National). *Mines and Energy:* Ivan James Gibbs (National). *Industry, Small Business and Technology:* Michael John Ahern (National). *Transport:* Donald Frederick Lane (National). *Lands, Forestry and Police:* William Hamline Glasson (National). *Health:* Brian Douglas Austin (National). *Education:* Lionel William Powell (National). *Water Resources and Maritime Services:* John Philip Goleby (National). *Primary Industries:* Neil John Turner (National). *Employment and Industrial Affairs:* Vincent Patrick Lester (National). *Environment, Valuation and Administrative Services:* Martin James Tenni (National). *Justice and Attorney-General:* Neville John Harper (National). *Welfare Services, Youth and Ethnic Affairs:* Geoffrey Hugh Muntz (National). *Tourism, National Parks, Sport and the Arts:* Peter Richard McKechnie (National). *Northern Development and Aboriginal and Island Affairs:* Robert Carl Katter (National).

Each Minister has a salary of $A65,145, the Premier receives $A82,627, the Deputy Premier, $A70,934, and the Leader of the Opposition, $A56,288.

Agent-General in London: J. H. Andrews (392–3 Strand, WC2R 0LZ).

Local Government. Provision is made for local government by the subdivision of the State into cities, towns and shires. These are under the management of aldermen or councillors, who are elected by all persons 18 years and over. Local Authorities are charged with the control of all matters of a parochial nature, such as sewerage, cleansing and sanitary services, health services, domestic water supplies, and roads and bridges within their allotted areas. In addition to Government grants and subsidies, Local Authority revenue is derived from general rates, paid by landowners on the unimproved capital value of land, and by charging for some specific services.

For the year ended 30 June 1982, the receipts and expenditure (including loans) for the 134 Local Authorities were $A1,112·4m. and $A1,101·4m. respectively and their rateable values amounted to $A8,139·7m.

ECONOMY

Budget. Revenue and expenditure of the Consolidated Revenue Fund of Queensland during 5 years ending 30 June (in $A1,000):

	1979–80	*1980–81*	*1981–82*	*1982–83*	*1983–84*
Revenue	2,206,954	2,604,036	3,276,756	3,690,187	4,212,842
Expenditure	2,207,893	2,604,010	3,276,926	3,690,956	4,211,919

Total funds available to the Queensland Government in 1981–82 were $A3,505·8m., of which Taxation and Federal Government grants amounted to $A3,120·8m. Expenditure from these funds included: Education, $A1,097·6m.; economic services (roads, electricity, etc.), $A877m.; health, $A561·1m.

Revenue and expenditure of Commonwealth Government departments on account of Queensland are not included.

Debt. The gross public debt of the State at par rates of exchange amounted, on 30 June 1984, to $A2,291m. The debt was domiciled as follows (in $A1,000): Australia, 2,290,572; USA, 378. The annual interest charge on the public debt at 30 June 1984 was $A224·8m.

Banking. There were 7 trading banks operating in Queensland at 30 June 1984, including the Commonwealth Trading Bank of Australia, the 4 larger Australian trading banks, the Bank of Queensland Ltd, the Bank of New Zealand and the Banque Nationale de Paris. The Commonwealth Trading Bank had 159 branches and 62 agencies; the other banks had 674 branches and 142 agencies in the State. Queensland deposits of all trading banks, including the Commonwealth Trading Bank of Australia, amounted to $A6,067·8m.; and loans, advances and bills discounted in Queensland were $A4,878·8m. At 30 June 1984 savings bank business was conducted in Queensland by 6 banks, the Commonwealth Savings Bank with 168 branches and 1,192 agencies, and 5 other banks with 673 branches and 908 agencies. Depositors' balances amounted to $A4,709m. in 3·57m. accounts.

ENERGY AND NATURAL RESOURCES

Electricity. The State Electricity Commission, established in 1938 and under a single Commissioner since 1948, co-ordinates the electricity industry in Queensland.

Electricity generated by the principal stations in the year ended 30 June 1983 was 14,736m. kwh. Black coal was used to generate over 90% of the power; hydro-electric stations generated about 5% and the balance was generated by gas turbine and diesel power stations using light fuel oil. The Roma diesel power station also uses locally-produced natural gas.

Minerals. Principal minerals produced during 1982–83 were: Copper, 147,000 tonnes; coal, 35,812,000 tonnes; lead, 185,000 tonnes; zinc, 183,000 tonnes; silver, 501,274 kg; tin, 2,041 tonnes; gold, 766 kg; bauxite, 5,816,000 tonnes; mineral sands concentrates, 164,000 tonnes; nickel, 24,000 tonnes; uranium, 347 tonnes. Value of output, at the mine, was $A2,297m. The chief mines are Mount Isa (copper, silver, lead, zinc), Weipa (bauxite), Mount Morgan (gold), Moreton and Bowen Basin (coal), Greenvale (nickel) and Mary Kathleen (uranium).

Land Settlement. Of the total area of the State, 13·3m. hectares had been alienated at 31 Dec. 1981; in process of alienation, under deferred payment system, were 20·7m. hectares, leaving 138·8m. hectares, still the property of the Crown, or 80·4% of the total area. A large proportion of the area is leased for pastoral purposes (97·1m. hectares at 31 Dec. 1981).

In the western portion of the State water is comparatively easily found by sinking artesian bores. At 30 June 1982, 3,450 such bores had been drilled, of which 2,358 were flowing.

Agriculture. Livestock on farms and stations at 31 March 1983 numbered 9·35m. cattle, 12·23m. sheep and 551,000 pigs. The wool production (greasy) was, in 1982–83, 54m. kg, valued at $A137m. The total area under crops during 1982–83 was 2·65m. hectares.

Crop	Area (hectares) 1981–82	Area (hectares) 1982–83	Yield (tonnes) 1981–82	Yield (tonnes) 1982–83
Sugar-cane, crushed	301,658	302,503	23,587,934	23,114,767
Wheat	941,131	767,043	1,482,331	754,384
Maize	47,568	50,923	150,524	87,393
Sorghum	489,144	531,932	982,435	757,704
Barley	206,395	166,995	397,524	268,471
Oats	17,821	11,941	16,378	8,594
Potatoes	6,140	6,240	128,606	120,196
Pumpkins	4,031	4,351	27,673	37,840
Tomatoes	3,314	3,577	58,029	75,727
Peanuts	32,984	35,458	56,429	22,251
Tobacco	3,341	3,341	7,980	7,549
Apples [1]	3,404	3,399	35,957	28,790
Grapes [1]	1,441	1,430	4,212	5,706
Citrus [1]	1,981	1,942	43,723	36,910
Bananas [1]	2,531	2,558	57,146	61,362
Pineapples [1]	4,046	3,657	125,422	110,941
Green fodder [2]	321,082	379,643	...	...
Hay (all kinds)	38,912	38,218	220,664	198,067
Cotton (raw)	28,809	26,805	27,234	28,602

[1] Bearing area only. [2] Excluding lucerne and other pastures.

Forestry. A considerable area consists of natural forest, eucalyptus, pine and cabinet woods being the timbers mostly in evidence; a large quantity of ornamental woods is utilized by cabinet makers. The amount of timber processed, including plantation and imported, in 1982–83 was (in cu. metres): Conifers, 384,898; hardwoods, structural timbers and cabinet woods, 701,056.

INDUSTRY AND TRADE

Industry. The 1970s created a milestone in the State's industrial progress when the value added in production by the manufacturing sector exceeded the value of production in the agriculture, forestry, fishing and hunting sector. In 1982–83, there were 3,440 establishments, with four or more workers, employing 92,389 males and 22,257 females, and producing goods and services worth $A10,715m. The value added was $A3,445m. The manufacturing establishments contributing most to the overall production during 1982–83 were those predominantly engaged in the processing of food, beverages and tobacco.

The gross value of Queensland agricultural commodity production (in $A1,000) during 1982–83, amounted to 2,366,802, which included crops, 1,267,886; livestock disposals, 784,575; livestock products, 314,341.

Labour. Of the total population of 2·5m., 1,006,000 were in employment in Aug. 1984, 132,600 in manufacturing. Industrial wages and conditions are controlled partly by Federal and partly by State authorities. A State Industrial Commission is empowered to determine all industrial matters in relation to employers and employees, to fix minimum wage-rates and other conditions of employment. An Industrial Court hears appeals and decides points of industrial law. The Federal Court of Australia and the Conciliation and Arbitration Commission are superior within their jurisdictions. In Queensland most employees (67%) work under State awards; 25% under Federal awards.

Rates of wages for each occupation are prescribed by these courts. The minimum weighted average award rate of pay for adult male wage and salary earners was $A312·40 and for adult females $A285·80, at 30 June 1984, while for the June quarter 1984, average weekly earnings were $A403·70 for full-time adult males and $A322·30 for full-time adult females. (Average earnings include award, over-award and overtime payments.) A standard working week of either 38 or 40 hours is prescribed for most awards.

Trade Unions. Unions both of employees and employers must be registered with the State or Australian Commission. There were 71 employees' and 39 employers' unions registered with the State Commission at 31 Dec. 1983, the former comprising 386,787 and the latter 37,356 members.

Commerce. The overseas commerce of Queensland is included in the statement of the commerce of Australia (*see* pp. 108–10).

Total value of the direct overseas imports and exports of Queensland (in $A1,000) f.o.b. port of shipment for both imports and exports:

	1978–79	*1979–80*	*1980–81*	*1981–82*	*1982–83*	*1983–84*
Imports	1,027,709	1,321,062	1,882,815	2,179,752	1,994,608	2,086,980
Exports	3,285,778 [1]	4,261,697 [1]	4,501,290 [1]	4,414,452 [1]	4,470,870 [1]	5,399,667 [1]

[1] State of origin.

In 1983–84 interstate exports totalled $A2,039m. and imports $A4,759·6m. The chief exports overseas are minerals including alumina, coal, meat (preserved or frozen), sugar, wool, cereal grains, copper and lead, and manufactured goods. Principal overseas imports are machinery, motor vehicles, mineral fuels (including lubricants, etc.), chemicals and manufactured goods classified by material. Chief sources of imports in 1983–84 were Japan ($A686·1m.), USA ($A429·7m.), Italy ($A146m.); exports went chiefly to Japan ($A2,067m.), USA ($A637·4m.), UK ($A335·9m.), EEC, excluding UK ($A501·1m.).

COMMUNICATIONS

Roads. At 30 June 1982 there were 162,413 km of roads; of these, 141,211 km were formed roads, of which 48,996 km were surfaced with sealed pavement.

At 30 June 1983 motor vehicles registered in Queensland totalled 1,496,129, comprising 1,037,529 cars and station wagons, 197,895 utilities, 83,247 panel vans, 7,704 buses, 70,788 trucks and 98,966 motor cycles.

Railways. Practically all the railways are owned by the State Government. Total length of line at 30 June 1983 was 9,979 km. In 1982–83, 34·7m. passengers and 43·7m. tonnes of goods and livestock were carried.

Aviation. Queensland is well served with a network of air services, with overseas and interstate connexions. Subsidiary companies provide planes for taxi and charter work, and the Flying Doctor Service operates throughout western Queensland.

Shipping. In 1982–83, cargo discharged was 2·7m. revenue tonnes and cargo loaded was 34·3m. revenue tonnes.

Broadcasting. At 30 June 1983, 61 broadcasting and 43 television stations were in operation throughout Queensland.

JUSTICE, RELIGION, EDUCATION AND WELFARE

Justice. Justice is administered by a Supreme Court, District Courts, Magistrates' Courts and Children's Courts. The Supreme Court comprises a Chief Justice, a senior puisne judge, 16 puisne judges and 2 masters; the District Court, 22 district court judges. Stipendiary magistrates preside over the Lower Courts, except in the smaller centres, where justices of the peace officiate. A parole board may recommend prisoners for release.

The total number of persons convicted of serious offences by the superior courts in 1982–83 was 1,455; summary convictions and proven offences in lower courts numbered 120,655. There were, at 30 June 1983, 5 prisons, 2 prison farms conducted on the honour system and 1 prison for criminally-insane patients, with 1,728 male and 45 female prisoners. The total police force, was 4,869 at 30 June 1983.

Religion. There is no State Church. Membership, census 1981: Anglican, 601,537; Roman Catholic and Catholic (not further defined), 554,912; Uniting Church, 146,898; Presbyterian, 132,525; Methodist, 86,750; Lutheran, 50,401; Baptist, 34,323; other Christian, 166,611; Buddhist, 2,967; Muslim, 2,457; Hebrew, 2,021; all others (including not stated and no religion), 513,721.

Education. Education in Queensland ranges from pre-school level through to tertiary level. In addition, child care, kindergarten and adult education facilities are available. Education is compulsory between the ages of 6 and 15 years and is provided free in government schools. Expenditure on education by government authorities for 1981–82 was $A1,098m.

At July 1983, pre-school education and child care was provided at 1,149 centres with 3,460 staff and 61,917 children.

Primary and secondary education comprises 12 years of full-time formal schooling and is provided by both the government and non-government sectors. At July 1983, the State administered 1,047 primary, 78 primary/secondary, and 148 secondary schools with 250,955 primary students, 122,622 secondary students and 21,525 teachers. Special education, which is included in the above figures, was provided to 5,348 children at 62 special schools and 55 primary schools with special classes. Non-government enrolments at July 1983 were 58,264 primary students and 49,727 secondary students taught by 5,654 teachers at 225 primary, 60 primary/secondary and 78 secondary schools.

Post-secondary education in Queensland involves technical and further education, advanced education and university education. In 1982, students at TAFE institutions and colleges of advanced education numbered 64,168 and at rural training schools 524. In 1982, 664 students at TAFE institutions and 23,875 students at colleges of advanced education were enrolled in advanced education courses. At 30 April 1982 there were 22,528 university students.

Social Welfare. Public hospitals are maintained by State and Federal Government endowment, supplemented by fees from patients not in standard wards. Welfare institutions providing shelter and social care for the aged, the handicapped, and children, are maintained or assisted by the State. A maternal and child welfare service is provided throughout the State. Age, invalid, widows', disability and war service pensions, family allowances, and unemployment and sickness benefits are paid by the Federal Government. Age pensioners in the State at 30 June 1983 numbered 213,844; invalid pensioners, 32,390; disability pensioners, 134,536 (including dependants).

There were 21,424 widows' pensions current at 30 June 1983, and at the same date family allowances were being paid to 345,277 families in respect of 702,139 children under 16 years or students aged 16 or more but under 25. In addition, family allowances were paid to 2,222 children and students in institutions.

Housing. In 1983–84, 33,531 new dwelling units valued at $A1,409m. were approved for construction. This total comprised 25,956 houses and 7,575 individual other dwelling units contained in flats, semi-detached units, home units, villa units, town houses, etc. In 1982–83, 29,170 new dwelling units were completed and 10,020 were being built at 30 June 1983. The Queensland Housing Commission, financed by Federal and State Government loans, builds dwellings for sale and for rental. Building and co-operative housing societies are assisted by Federal and State Government loans.

Books of Reference

Statistical Information: The Statistical Office (345 Ann St., Brisbane) was set up in 1859. *Deputy Commonwealth Statistician:* D. N. Allen. *A Queensland Official Year Book* was issued in 1901, the annual *ABC of Queensland Statistics* from 1905 to 1936 with exception of 1918 and 1922. Present publications include: *Queensland Year Book.* Annual, from 1937 (omitting 1942, 1943, 1944).—*Queensland Pocket Year Book.* Annual from 1950.—*Monthly Summary of Queensland Statistics.* From Jan. 1961

Australian Sugar Year Book. Brisbane, from 1941
Johnston, W. R., *A Bibliography of Queensland History.* Brisbane, 1981
Endean, R., *Australia's Great Barrier Reef.* Brisbane, 1982
Queensland State Public Relations Bureau, *Queensland Resources Atlas,* Brisbane, 1980
Australian Department of Northern Development and Queensland Department of Commercial and Industrial Development, *Resources and Industry of the Mackay Region,* Canberra, 1974
School of Business Studies, Darling Downs Institute of Advanced Education, *Resources and Industry of Southern Inland Queensland,* Brisbane, 1975
Queensland Department of Commercial and Industrial Development, *Resources and Industry of Far North Queensland,* Brisbane, 1980

State Library: The State Library of Queensland, William St., Brisbane. *State Librarian:* S. L. Ryan.

SOUTH AUSTRALIA

AREA AND POPULATION. The total area of South Australia is 380,070 sq. miles (984,377 sq. km). The settled part is divided into counties and hundreds. There are 49 counties proclaimed, covering 23m. hectares, of which 19m. hectares are occupied. Outside this area there are extensive pastoral districts, covering 76m. hectares, 46m. of which are under pastoral leases.

Census population (exclusive of full-blood Aboriginals before 1966):

	Males	*Females*	*Total*		*Males*	*Females*	*Total*
1901	180,485	177,861	358,346	1961	490,225	479,115	969,340
1911	207,358	201,200	408,558	1966	550,196	544,788	1,094,984
1921	248,267	246,893	495,160	1971	586,051	587,656	1,173,707
1933	290,962	289,987	580,949	1976	620,162	624,594	1,244,756
1947	320,031	326,042	646,073	1981	635,696	649,337	1,285,033

The number of Aboriginals (as reported on Census schedules) in the State at the Census of 30 June 1981 was 9,476.

Vital statistics for calendar years:

	Live Births	*Marriages*	*Divorces*	*Deaths*
1981	19,351	10,252	4,132	9,706
1982	19,294	10,935	4,526	10,457
1983	19,865	10,550	4,431	9,882

The infant mortality rate in 1983 was 9·46 per 1,000 live births.

The Adelaide Statistical Division had 964,200 inhabitants at 30 June 1983 in 19 cities and 13 municipalities and other districts. Cities outside this area (with populations at the 1976 Census) are Whyalla (33,382), Mount Gambier (17,857), Port Augusta (13,082), Port Pirie (12,342) and Port Lincoln (9,807).

CONSTITUTION AND GOVERNMENT. South Australia was formed into a British province by letters patent of Feb. 1836, and a partially elective Legislative Council was established in 1851. The present Constitution bears date 24 Oct. 1856. It vests the legislative power in an elected Parliament, consisting of a Legislative Council and a House of Assembly. The former is composed of 22 members. Every 3 years half the members retire, and the resulting vacancies are filled at a general election on the basis of proportional representation with the State as one multi-member electorate. The qualifications of an elector are, to be an Australian citizen, or a British subject who on 25 Jan. 1984 was enrolled on a Commonwealth electoral roll and/or at some time between 26 Oct. 1983 and 25 Jan. 1984 inclusive was enrolled on an electoral roll for a South Australian Assembly district or a Commonwealth electoral roll in any State. The person must be of at least 18 years of age and to have lived continuously in Australia for at least 6 months, in South Australia for at least 3 months and in the sub-division for which he is enrolled for at least 1 month. War service may substitute for residential qualifications in some cases. By the Constitution Act Amendment Act, 1894, the franchise was extended to women, who voted for the first time at the general election of 25 April 1896. The qualifications for election as a member of both Houses are the same as for an elector. Certain persons are ineligible for election to either House.

The House of Assembly consists of 47 members elected for 3 years, representing single electorates. Election of members of both Houses takes place by preferential secret ballot. Voting is compulsory for those on the Electoral Roll.

The House of Assembly, elected on 6 Nov. 1982, consists of the following members: Liberal Party of Australia, 22; Australian Labor Party, 23; National Party of Australia, 1; Independent, 1. The Legislative Council consists of 11 Liberal Party of Australia, 9 Labor and 2 Australian Democrat members.

Each member of Parliament receives $A37,500 per annum with allowances of $A7,785–20,000 according to location of electorate, a free pass over government railways and superannuation rights. Electors enrolled (June 1982) numbered 858,295.

The executive power is vested in a Governor appointed by the Crown and an Executive Council, consisting of the Governor and the Ministers of the Crown. The

Governor has the power to dissolve the House of Assembly but not the Legislative Council unless that Chamber has twice consecutively with an election intervening defeated the same or substantially the same Bill passed in the House of Assembly by an absolute majority.

Governor: Lieut.-Gen. Sir Donald Dunstan, KBE, CB.

The South Australian Labor Ministry, in Sept. 1984 was as follows:

Premier, Treasurer, Minister of State and Development and Minister for the Arts: John Charles Bannon, MP.

Deputy Premier, Minister of Labour, Chief Secretary and Minister of Emergency Services: John David Wright, MP. *Attorney-General, Minister of Consumer Affairs and Minister of Corporate Affairs and Minister of Ethnic Affairs:* Christopher John Sumner, MLC. *Minister for Environment and Planning, Minister of Lands and Minister of Repatriation:* Donald Jack Hopgood, MP. *Minister of Transport and Minister of Marine:* Roy Kitto Abbott, MP. *Minister of Health:* John Robert Cornwall, MLC. *Minister of Education and Minister for Technology:* Lynn Maurice Ferguson Arnold, MP. *Minister of Tourism and Minister of Local Government:* Gavin Francis Keneally, MP. *Minister of Mines and Energy:* Ronald George Payne, MP. *Minister of Community Welfare and Minister of Aboriginal Affairs:* Gregory John Crafter, MP. *Minister of Water Resources and Minister of Recreation and Sport:* John William Slater, MP. *Minister of Housing and Construction and Minister of Public Works:* Terence Henry Hemmings, MP. *Minister of Agriculture, Minister of Fisheries, Minister of Forests and Minister of Correctional Services:* Frank Trevor Blevins, MLC.

Ministers are jointly and individually responsible to the legislature for all their official acts, as in the UK.

Agent-General in London: J. L. Rundle (50 Strand, WC2).

Local Government. The closely settled part of the State (mainly near the sea-coast and the River Murray) is incorporated into local government areas, and sub-divided into district councils (rural areas only), municipal corporations (mainly metropolitan, but including larger country towns) and cities (more densely populated areas with a qualification of 15,000 residents in the Adelaide metropolitan area, and 10,000 in the country). The main functions of councils are the construction and maintenance of roads and bridges, sport and recreational facilities and garbage collection and disposal.

The number and area of the sub-divisions, together with expenditure (in $A1,000) for the year ended 30 June 1983, were:

	No.	*Area (1,000 hectares)*	*Roads and bridges*	*Recreation and culture*	*All other*	*Total expenditure*
Adelaide statistical division	32	229·0	41,071	35,108	122,147	198,326
Other municipal corporations and district councils	96	15,138·6	35,213	11,048	61,122	107,383
Total	128	15,367·6	76,284	46,156	183,269	305,709

ECONOMY

Budget. Revenue and expenditure (in $A1,000) for years ended 30 June:

	1979	*1980*	*1981*	*1982*	*1983*	*1984*
Revenue	1,264,705	1,384,589	1,548,299	1,705,499	1,923,808	2,160,679
Expenditure	1,258,252	1,384,589	1,554,884	1,766,772	2,032,765	2,190,399

The public debt of the State amounted, on 30 June 1984, to $A2,010·3m.

Banking. There were 7 trading banks at 30 June 1984, including Commonwealth and State Government Banks. In June 1984 their average deposits were $A1,976·9m. and average loans and advances $A2,839·8m.

The 6 savings banks on 30 June 1984 had deposits amounting to $A3,327·1m. or $A2,470 per head of population.

NATURAL RESOURCES

Minerals. The value of minerals produced in 1981–82 was $A259·7m. The principal minerals produced are opals, natural gas, iron ore, copper, gypsum, salt, talc, clays, limestone, dolomite and sub-bituminous coal.

Agriculture. Of the total area of South Australia (984,377 sq. km), 164,242 sq. km were alienated, 527,046 sq. km were held under lease and 293,089 sq. km were unoccupied. Area used for agricultural purposes, at 31 March 1983, was 60,196 sq. km.

Soil Conservation. Under the direction of special officers in the Department of Agriculture, determined efforts are made to deal with the problems of erosion and soil conservation. Included in the programme are the planting of cereal rye, perennial rye and other grasses to check sand drifts; contour-furrowing and contour banking; contour planting with vines and fruit trees and several water-diversion schemes.

Irrigation. For the year ended 31 March 1981, 79,474 hectares were under irrigated culture, being used as follows: Vineyards, 20,253; orchards, 12,627; vegetables, 5,676, and other crops and pasture, 40,918. Most of these areas are along the river Murray.

Gross value of agricultural production (in $A1,000), 1982–83: Crops, 505,432; livestock slaughtering, 336,006; livestock products, 352,898. Total gross value, 1,194,336; local value (*i.e.* less marketing costs), 1,091,758.

	1981–82		*1982–83*	
Chief crops	*Hectares*	*Tonnes*	*Hectares*	*Tonnes*
Wheat	1,427,481	1,694,733	1,398,039	692,364
Barley	1,031,745	1,227,055	1,005,030	667,518
Oats	127,279	97,904	123,609	64,513
Hay	194,065	471,447	151,965	351,583
Vines	...	268,685,000 [1]	...	200,283,000 [1]

[1] Litres of wine.

Fruit culture is extensively carried on, and in 1982–83, 266,914 tonnes of fresh fruit were produced. Other products, in addition to all kinds of root crops and vegetables, are grass seeds and oil seeds. Livestock, March 1983: 828,282 cattle, 15,448,133 sheep and 405,146 pigs. In 1982–83, 103,007 tonnes of wool and 340m. litres of milk were produced.

INDUSTRY AND TRADE

Industry. The turnover for manufacturing industries for 1982–83 was $A6,708m.

Industry sub-division	*Establishments (No.)*	*Persons employed (No.)*	*Wages and salaries ($A1m.)*	*Turnover ($A1m.)*	*Value added ($A1m.)*
Food, beverages and tobacco	360	16,818	235	1,563	547
Textiles, clothing and footwear	124	6,742	84	326	142
Wood, wood products and furniture	297	7,014	93	398	149
Paper, paper products, printing and publishing	196	7,528	117	424	207
Chemical, petroleum and coal products	48	2,589	50	292	116
Non-metallic mineral products	129	3,159	54	303	136
Basic metal products	36	8,236	155	688	214
Fabricated metal products	327	7,166	103	451	176
Transport equipment	114	17,383	317	1,166	552
Other machinery and equipment	296	13,770	213	768	322
Miscellaneous manufacturing	172	5,501	81	329	146
Total	2,099	95,906	1,502	6,708	2,709

Practically all forms of secondary industry are to be found, the most important being, motor vehicle manufacture, saw-milling and the manufacture of household appliances, basic iron and steel, meat and meat products, and wine and brandy.

Labour. Two systems of industrial arbitration and conciliation for the adjustment of industrial relations between employers and employees are in operation—the State system, which operates when industrial disputes are confined to the territorial limits of the State, and the Federal system, which applies when disputes involve other parts of Australia as well as South Australia.

The industrial tribunals are authorized to fix minimum rates of wages and other conditions of employment, and their awards may be enforced by law. Industrial agreements between employers and organizations of employees, when registered, may be enforced in the same manner as awards. In April 1984 the minimum wage under State awards was $A158.20.

Commerce. The commerce of South Australia, exclusive of inter-state trade, is comprised in the statement of the commerce of Australia given under the heading of the Commonwealth, *see* pp. 108–10.

Overseas imports and exports in $A1,000 (year ending 30 June):

	1977–78	*1978–79*	*1979–80*	*1980–81*	*1981–82*	*1982–83*
Imports	628,568	865,554	882,457	1,072,449	1,337,301	1,244,243
Exports [1]	661,887	922,754	1,599,199	1,417,811	1,275,938	1,227,125

[1] From 1978–79 exports are recorded by 'State of Origin', whereas details prior to this are by 'State of Lodgment of Documents'.

Principal exports in 1982–83 were (in $A1,000): Wheat, 97,954 (543,844 tonnes); barley, 64,486 (371,433 tonnes); wool, 176,830 (59,283 tonnes); lead, 79,576 (159,578 tonnes); meat, 121,927 (73,142 tonnes); live sheep and lambs, 38,347 (1,604,000 head).

Principal imports in 1982–83 were (in $A1,000): Transport equipment, 144,514; petrol and products, 405,125; machinery, 287,005.

In 1982–83 the leading suppliers of imports were (in $A1m.): Saudi Arabia (347·7), Japan (290·6), USA (198·1), Federal Republic of Germany (60·4); main exports went to Japan (146·3), USA (97), USSR (95), UK (93·5), Saudi Arabia (83·7), New Zealand (75·5), Singapore (49·8).

Tourism. In June 1984 there were 285 hotels and motels with 7,662 rooms; 155 caravan parks had a total of 18,086 sites.

COMMUNICATIONS

Roads. At 30 June 1983, of the roads customarily used by the public, there were 2,568 km of national roads, 10,853 km of arterial roads and 88,979 km of local roads, totalling 102,400 km. Lengths of road classified by surface were as follows: Sealed, 21,767 km; unsealed, 80,633 km. Costs of construction and maintenance are shared by the State and Commonwealth governments and by the councils of the local areas. Motor vehicles registered at 30 June 1984 included 516,203 cars, 97,708 station wagons, 132,589 commercial vehicles and 37,655 cycles.

Railways. At June 1983, there were more than 5,900 km of railway, including the South Australian portion of the Transcontinental Railway from Port Pirie in South Australia to Kalgoorlie in Western Australia, which, in connexion with various State lines, completes a through rail connexion between Brisbane on the north-east coast and Fremantle on the west coast. The above figure includes the South Australian portion of the Australian National Railways from Tarcoola to the Northern Territory and private railways from Iron Knob to Whyalla and Coffin Bay to Port Lincoln and 152 km of railway which is operated by the State Transport Authority in the metropolitan area of Adelaide.

Aviation. For the year ended 30 June 1983 there were 1,635,663 passengers and 14,268 tonnes of freight handled at Adelaide, South Australia's principal airport. On 30 June 1983 there were 7 government and 25 licensed aerodromes.

Shipping. There are several good harbours, of which Port Adelaide is the principal one. In 1982–83, 753 vessels entered South Australia with 2,392,231 import tonnes of cargo and left with 3,000,249 export tonnes.

Post and Broadcasting. At 30 June 1983, there were 597 post offices. Telephone services connected totalled 532,107 on 30 June 1983. There were 26 radio and 32 television stations (including 9 translator and 11 satellite) at 1 Jan. 1984.

JUSTICE, RELIGION, EDUCATION AND WELFARE

Justice. There is a Supreme Court, which incorporates admiralty, civil, criminal, land and valuation, and testamentary jurisdiction; district criminal courts, which have jurisdiction in many indictable offences; local courts and courts of summary jurisdiction. Circuit courts are held at several places. In the year ended 30 June 1982, 1,541 cases were heard in higher courts and 185,784 cases in courts of summary jurisdiction. During the year ending 30 June 1983 there were 962 sequestrations and schemes under the Bankruptcy Act. There were 759 prisoners in custody on 1 July 1983, of whom 144 were on remand.

Religion. At the Census of 1981 the religious distribution of the population (as reported on Census schedules) was as follows: Anglican, 260,919; Roman Catholic and Catholic (so described), 255,332; Uniting Church, 108,857; Methodist, 85,935; Lutheran, 63,860; Baptist, 22,287; Presbyterian, 21,725; other Christians, 138,350; non-Christian, 7,128; indefinite, 6,529; no religion, 178,136; no reply, 135,970.

Education. Education is secular and is compulsory for children 6–15 years of age. Primary and secondary education at government schools is free. In 1983 there were 714 government schools, comprising 526 primary, 66 primary and secondary, 100 secondary schools and 22 special schools. There were 205,517 full-time students. The Department of Technical and Further Education is responsible for technical, adult and vocational education. In 1983 there were 26 colleges of technical and further education, among the facilities are an adult migrant education service, a centre for performing arts and schools of rural, maritime and external studies. Tertiary education, including teacher education, is provided by the 2 universities and 3 colleges of advanced education. There were 173 non-government schools and colleges, most of which are associated with religious denominations (48,270 students). In 1983 there were 509 day care and pre-school centres with a total enrolment of 33,847 pre-school children.

Social Welfare. Age, invalidity, war, etc., pensions are paid by the Commonwealth Government. The number of pensioners in South Australia at 30 June 1983 was: Disability and service, 70,450; age, 140,036; invalid, 30,238. There are schemes for family allowances, widows, supporting parents, unemployment and sickness and hospital and pharmaceutical benefits.

Books of Reference

Statistical Information: The State branch of the Australian Bureau of Statistics is in City Mutual Centre, 10–20 Pulteney St., Adelaide (GPO Box 2272). *Deputy Commonwealth Statistician:* G. C. Sims. Although the first printed statistical publication was the *Statistics of South Australia, 1854* with the title altered to *Statistical Register* in 1859, there is a written volume for each year back to 1838. These contain simple records of trade, demography, production, etc. and were prepared only for the use of the Colonial Office; one copy was retained in the State.

The publications of the State branch include the *South Australian Year Book*, the *Pocket Year Book of South Australia* and a *Monthly Summary of Statistics*, a quarterly bulletin of building activity, a quarterly bulletin of tourist accommodation and approximately 40 special bulletins issued each year as particulars of various sections of statistics become available.

South Australia: Development. Dept. of Industry and Commerce, Adelaide, 1977
Douglas, J., *South Australia from Space.* Adelaide, 1980
Finlayson, H. H., *The Red Centre: Man and Beast in the Heart of Australia.* 2nd ed. Sydney, 1952
Gibbs, R. M., *A History of South Australia.* Adelaide, 1969
Whitelock, D., *Adelaide, 1836–1976: A History of Difference.* Univ. of Queensland Press, 1977

State Library: The State Library of S.A., North Terrace, Adelaide. *State Librarian:* E. M. Miller, MA (Hons), Dip. NZLS, ANZLA, ALAA.

TASMANIA

HISTORY. Abel Janzoon Tasman discovered Van Diemen's Land (Tasmania) on 24 Nov. 1642. The island became a British settlement in 1803 as a dependency of New South Wales; in 1825 its connexion with New South Wales was terminated; in 1851 a partially elective Legislative Council was established, and in 1856 responsible government came into operation. On 1 Jan. 1901 Tasmania was federated with the other Australian states into the Commonwealth of Australia.

AREA AND POPULATION. Tasmania is an island separated from the mainland by the Bass Strait with an area (including islands) of 68,331 sq. km, or 6·83m. hectares, of which 6,441,000 hectares form the area of the main island. The population at 10 consecutive censuses was:

	Population	*Increase % per annum*		*Population*	*Increase % per annum*
1911	191,211	1·04	1961	350,340	1·82
1921	213,780	1·12	1966	371,436	1·18
1933	227,599	0·52	1971	398,100 [1]	0·99
1947	257,078	0·87	1976	412,300 [1]	0·70 [2]
1954	308,752	2·65	1981	427,200 [1]	0·72 [2]

[1] Resident population. [2] Not comparable with previous censuses.

The resident population (estimate) on 30 June 1981 consisted of 212,400 males and 214,900 females. At the census of 30 June 1981, 2·8% were born in the British Isles, 5·5% in other European countries and 88·7% in Australia. The last full-blooded Tasmanian Aboriginal died in 1876.

Vital statistics for calendar years:

	Marriages	*Divorces*	*Births*	*Deaths*	*Natural increase*
1981	3,515	1,139	7,188	3,320	3,868
1982	3,576	1,391	7,002	3,432	3,570
1983	3,644	1,359	7,028	3,311	3,718

The Hobart Statistical Division had 173,700 inhabitants at 30 June 1983; the state's largest cities and towns (with populations at the 1976 Census) are Hobart (50,381), Glenorchy (42,437), Clarence (42,201), Launceston (32,947) and Devonport (21,420).

CONSTITUTION AND GOVERNMENT. Parliament consists of the Governor, the Legislative Council and the House of Assembly. The Council has 19 members, elected by adults with 6 months' residence. Members sit for 6 years, 3 retiring annually and 4 every sixth year. There is no power to dissolve the Council. Vacancies are filled by by-elections. The House of Assembly has 35 members; the maximum term for the House of Assembly is 4 years. Members of both Houses are paid a basic salary of $A34,630 (Jan. 1984), plus an electorate allowance, according to the division represented. The annual allowance payable is calculated as a percentage of basic salary. The amounts vary from $A3,809 (11%) to $A12,120 (35%). Women received the right to vote in 1903. Proportional representation was adopted in 1907, the method now being the single transferable vote in 7-member constituencies. Casual vacancies in the House of Assembly are determined by a transfer of the preference of the vacating member's ballot papers to consenting candidates who were unsuccessful at the last general election.

A Minister must have a seat in one of the two Houses; all present Ministers are members of the House of Assembly.

In addition to the salary paid to Ministers as members of either House, the following allowances are payable: Premier, in conjunction with a ministerial office, $A43,287; Deputy Premier, in conjunction with a ministerial office, $A29,435; other Ministers, $A24,241. The Leader of the Opposition in the House of Assembly receives an allowance of $A24,241. The holders of some other offices receive allowances ranging from $A2,077 to $A11,542.

An election, precipitated by the House of Assembly wanting vote of confidence in the minority Labor Government, in May 1982 resulted in the Liberal Party forming a government in its own right. The composition of the new House of Assembly was Liberal, 19 seats, Labor, 14, Australian Democrats, 1 and 1 Independent.

The Legislative Council is predominantly independent without formal party allegiance; 2 members are Labor-endorsed.

Governor: Sir James Plimsoll, AC, CBE.

The Liberal Party Cabinet is composed as follows:

Premier, Treasurer, Minister for State Development, Energy and Forests: R. Gray.

Deputy Premier, Leader of the House, Attorney-General, Education, Industrial Relations, Tourism, Racing and Gaming: G. Pearsall. *Environment, Licensing, Construction and Administrative Services:* G. Davis. *Housing, Consumer Affairs and Small Business, Inland Fisheries:* B. Lyons. *Health, Community Welfare and the Elderly, Ethnic Affairs:* J. Cleary. *Primary Industry, Main Roads, Local Governments, Water Resources:* I. Braid. *Education, Lands and National Parks:* J. Beswick. *Mines, Transport, Road Safety, Sea Fisheries, Police and Emergency Services:* R. Groom.

Local Government. For the purposes of local government, the State is divided into 49 municipal areas comprising the cities of Hobart, Launceston, Glenorchy and Devonport and 45 municipalities. The cities and municipalities are managed by elected aldermen and councillors, respectively, with reference to local matters such as sanitation and health services, domestic water supplies and roads and bridges within each particular area. The chief source of revenue is rates (based on improved values) levied on owners of property.

Tasmanian Islands. Three inhabited Tasmanian islands (Bruny, King and Flinders) are organized as municipalities. Nearly 1,600 km south-east lies Macquarie Island, part of the State, and used only as an Australian research base and meteorological station.

ECONOMY

Budget. The revenue is derived chiefly from taxation (pay-roll, motor, lottery and land tax, business franchises and stamp duties), and from grants and reimbursements from the Federal Government. Customs, excise, sales and income tax are levied by the Federal Government, which makes grants to Tasmania for both revenue and capital purposes. Federal Government grants to Tasmania in 1983–84 totalled $A774m. These included General Purpose Revenue Funds, $A404m.; Specific Purpose Grants, $A308m.; Capital Grants, $A34m.; and Health Grants, $A27m.

Specific Purpose Grants are mainly used to provide essential services such as hospitals, housing, roads and educational services, while General Purpose Revenue Funds have been paid since 1942 to compensate the State for the loss of income tax to the federal government.

Consolidated Revenue Fund receipts and expenditure, in $A1,000, for financial years ending 30 June:

	1978–79	*1979–80*	*1980–81*	*1981–82*	*1982–83*	*1983–84*
Revenue	495,822	560,192	620,307	683,231	764,990	853,107
Expenditure	492,961	563,917	627,441	717,628	772,735	855,006

The public debt at current exchange rates amounted to $A1,155m. at 30 June 1984.

In 1983–84 State taxation revenue amounted to $A175m., of which pay-roll tax provided $A57·3m.; motor tax, $A17·5m.; stamp duties, $A39·3m.; business franchises, $A22·8m., and lottery tax, $A8·6m.

Banking. Trading bank activity in Tasmania is divided between 3 private banks and the Commonwealth Trading Bank. For the month of June 1984 liabilities represented by depositors' balances averaged $A575m. and assets represented by advances, $A445m. The 6 savings banks operating in Tasmania are the Commonwealth Savings Bank, 2 trustee savings banks and 3 private savings banks operated by trading banks. At 30 June 1984 total savings bank deposits were $A1,103m.

ENERGY AND NATURAL RESOURCES

Electricity. Tasmania has good supplies of hydro-electric power because of assured rainfall and high level water storages (natural and artificial). The Hydro-Electric Commission, Tasmania's sole commercial supplier of electricity, has been surveying water power resources of the State for many years and it is estimated that about 3m. kw. can be economically developed. By 31 Dec. 1982, 1,860,300 kw. of generating plant was in commission. In 1982 the peak loading was 1,266,100 kw. One project is currently in progress, the Pieman River Power Development, comprising 3 stations, scheduled for completion in 1986. The Gordon River Power Development Stage 2 (the Gordon-below-Franklin scheme) was halted by a High Court decision.

Minerals. The assayed content of principal metallic minerals contained in locally produced concentrates for 1981–82 was (in tonnes): Zinc, 84,214; iron, 1,387,310; copper, 23,033; lead, 30,820; tin, 7,197; gold, 2,000 kg; silver, 89,821 kg. Coal production, 395,347 tonnes.

Primary Industries. The estimated gross value of recorded production from agriculture in 1982–83 was (in $A1m.): Livestock products, 131·5; livestock slaughterings and other disposals, 100·7; crops, 107·5; total gross value, 338·5. Estimated gross value of fisheries was $A32·9m.

Agriculture. The area occupied by the 5,870 holdings in 1982–83 totalled 2,168,500 hectares, of which 1,001,500 were devoted to crops and sown pasture. The following table shows the area and production, in tonnes, of the principal crops:

	1980–81		*1981–82*		*1982–83*	
	Hectares	*Production*	*Hectares*	*Production*	*Hectares*	*Production*
Wheat	1,614	2,545	1,293	2,342	928	1,489
Barley	10,056	18,307	12,108	23,267	12,358	21,925
Oats	8,781	11,146	9,923	13,381	7,965	8,912
Green peas	7,097	26,547	7,973	30,946	8,022	31,159
Potatoes	4,335	155,965	4,438	160,797	4,749	173,147
Hay	64,088	249,348	63,854	242,593	51,329	165,906
Hops (bearing) (dry)	672	1,558	811	1,608	889	1,589

Livestock at 31 March 1983: Sheep, 4·5m.; cattle, 562,100; pigs, 50,600.

Wool produced during 1982–83 was 22m. kg, valued at $A59m. In 1983–84 butter production was 6,194 tonnes; cheese, 14,018 tonnes.

Forestry. Indigenous forests cover a considerable part of the State, and the sawmilling and woodchipping industries are very important. Production of sawn timber in 1983–84 was 281,600 cu. metres. 768,000 cu. metres of logs were used for milling in 1983–84 and a further 3·5m. cu. metres were used for chipping, grinding or flaking. Newsprint and paper are produced from native hardwoods, principally eucalypts.

INDUSTRY AND TRADE

Industry. The most important manufactures for export are refined metals, newsprint and other paper manufactures, pigments, woollen goods, fruit pulp, confectionery, butter, cheese, preserved and dried vegetables, sawn timber, and processed fish products. The electrolytic-zinc works at Risdon near Hobart treat large quantities of local and imported ore, and produce zinc, sulphuric acid, superphosphate, sulphate of ammonia, cadmium and other by-products. At George Town, large-scale plants produce refined aluminium and manganese alloys. During 1983–84, 3·5m. tonnes (green weight) of woodchips were produced. In

1982–83 the average employment in manufacturing establishments employing 4 or more persons was 24,085; wages and salaries (excluding proprietors' drawings), $A387·7m.; turnover, $A1,969m.; value added, $A695·1m.; and number operating at 30 June, 528.

Labour. The Commonwealth Industrial Court (judicial powers) and Commonwealth Conciliation and Arbitration Commission (arbitral powers) have jurisdiction over federal unions, *i.e.*, with interstate membership. Most Tasmanian employees are covered by federal awards.

State Industrial Boards, established for the various trades by resolution of Parliament or proclamation of the Governor, cover most of the remaining employees. Each Board consists of a Chairman appointed by the Governor with equal representation of employers and employees. The Boards have authority over minimum rates for wages or piecework, number of working hours for which the wage is payable, conditions of apprenticeship, annual leave and adjustment of wage and piecework rates. Industrial Boards follow to a large extent the wage rates fixed by the Conciliation and Arbitration Commission.

Commerce. Trade by sea and air in $A1m. for years ending 30 June:

	1978–79	*1979–80*	*1980–81*	*1981–82*	*1982–83*
Imports	836·8	1,168·8	1,207·1	1,258·5	1,339·1
Exports	1,180·2	1,451·5	1,540·2	1,574·6	1,728·9

In 1982–83 exports by sea and air totalled $A1,729m.; comprising $A956m. to other Australian states and $A773m. to overseas countries. The principal countries of destination (with values in $A1m.) for overseas exports were: Japan, 274; Malaysia, 104; USA, 89; Indonesia, 50; and China (excluding Taiwan), 36. Imports totalled $A1,339m.; comprising $A1,159m. from other Australian states and $A180m. from overseas countries. The principal countries of origin (with values in $A1m.) for overseas imports were: Japan, 24; USA, 24; Singapore, 20; New Zealand, 18; and Canada, 13.

The main commodities by value (with values in $A1m.) exported during 1982–83 were: Ores and concentrates (mainly iron, copper, lead, tin and tungsten), 245; refined zinc, 164; timber, 70; vegetables, 72; and greasy wool, 48. Other main exports, for which details are not available for separate publication were woodchips, newsprint, printing and writing papers, refined aluminium, ferro-alloys and chocolate confectionery. The main imports (with values in $A1m.) were: Petroleum products, 310; ores and concentrates, 110; new motor vehicles, 86; and machinery, clothing, cocoa beans and wood-pulp.

Tourism. In 1981 (estimate) 306,671 adult visitors spent at least one night in Tasmania.

COMMUNICATIONS

Roads. The total road length at 30 June 1983 was 22,209 km, consisting of a classified road system of 3,969 km maintained by the State Department of Main Roads, and the remainder maintained by local government authorities, the Forestry Commission and the Hydro-Electric Commission. Motor vehicles registered at 30 June 1984 comprised 195,000 cars and station wagons, 54,800 other vehicles and 6,100 motor cycles.

Railways. There is an 864-km network of 1,067-mm gauge lines linking Hobart and Launceston with coastal and country areas, formerly operated by Tasmanian Government Railways, but since 1 July 1975 worked by the Australian National Railways Commission. A private railway of 134 km, operated by the Emu Bay Railway Co. Ltd, connects Burnie with the mining settlements on the west coast.

Aviation. Regular daily passenger and freight air services connect the south, north and north-west of the State with the mainland of Australia. In 1982 there was a total of 30,514 scheduled aircraft movements at Tasmanian airports; a total of 987,424 passengers and 45,605 tonnes of freight, including mail, was carried.

Shipping. In 1982–83 overseas vessels made a total of 438 calls to Tasmanian ports discharging 362,716 revenue tonnes of cargo; departures numbered 421 with total cargo of 4,815,555 revenue tonnes.

For posts and telegraphs, *see* p. 112.

JUSTICE, RELIGION, EDUCATION AND WELFARE

Justice. The Supreme Court of Tasmania, with civil, criminal, ecclesiastical, admiralty and matrimonial jurisdiction, established by Royal Charter on 13 Oct. 1823, is a superior court of record, with both original and appellate jurisdiction, and consists of a Chief Justice and 6 puisne judges. There are also inferior civil courts with limited jurisdiction, licensing courts, mining courts, courts of petty sessions and coroners' courts.

During the year 1983, 18,853 matters were finalized in the lower courts, 1,407 in the Supreme Court and 3,994 in the children's courts. The total police force on 30 June 1984 was 1,009. There was 1 gaol, with 205 inmates at the end of June 1983.

Religion. There is no State Church. At the census of 1981 the following numbers of adherents of the principal religions were recorded:

Anglican Church	151,207	Other religions	32,213
Roman Catholic	78,143	No religion	36,222
Methodist	19,906	Not stated [1]	64,058
Uniting Church	17,668		
Presbyterian	11,575	Total [1]	418,957
Baptist	7,965		

[1] 'As counted' Census results.

Education. Education is controlled by the State and is free, secular and compulsory between the ages of 6 and 16. At 1 July 1983 government schools had a total enrolment of 68,387 pupils, including 27,942 at secondary level; private schools had a total enrolment of 15,940 pupils, including 7,364 at secondary level.

Technical and further education is conducted at technical and community colleges in the major centres throughout the state. In 1982 there were 17,931 students enrolled in the Division of Technical and Further Education, 14,912 students in the Division of Adult Education. Teaching staff was made up of 499 full-time and 2,238 part-time teachers.

Tertiary education is offered at the University of Tasmania in Hobart and the Tasmanian College of Advanced Education in Launceston. The University (established 1890) had (1983) 3,101 full-time and 2,128 part-time students, and 359 full-time teachers. There were 1,042 full-time and 1,492 part-time students at the College and a full-time teaching staff of 141.

Social Welfare. Old Age, Invalid, War Service and Widows' Pensions are paid by the Federal Government. The number of pensioners in Tasmania on 30 June 1983 was: Age, 40,838; invalid, 6,767; war (disability), 16,805; widows, 5,144. Benefit payments totalled $A229·2m. (including payments to wives).

Books of Reference

Statistical Information: The State Government Statistical Office (Commonwealth Government Centre, Hobart), established in 1877, became in 1924 the Tasmanian Office of the Australian Bureau of Statistics, but continues to serve State statistical needs as required.

Acting Deputy Commonwealth Statistician and Government Statistician of Tasmania: D. W. Rogers.

Main publications: *Annual Statistical Bulletins (e.g., Demography, Courts, Agricultural Industry, Finance, Manufacturing Establishments* etc.).—*Pocket Year Book of Tasmania.* Annual (from 1913).—*Tasmanian Year Book.* Annual (from 1967).—*Monthly Summary of Statistics* (from July 1945).

Department of Planning and Development, *Tasmanian Manufacturers Directory.* Hobart. Annual.
Angus, M., *The World of Olegas Truchanas.* Hobart, 1975
Green, F. C. (ed.), *A Century of Responsible Government.* Hobart, 1956
Townsley, W. A., *The Government of Tasmania.* Univ. of Queensland Press, 1976

State Library: The State Library of Tasmania, Hobart. *Librarian:* W. L. Brown, FLA, ALAA.

VICTORIA

AREA AND POPULATION. The State has an area of 227,600 sq. km, and a resident population (estimate) of 4,034,600 at 30 June 1983.

The resident population (estimate) of the Melbourne Statistical Division at 30 June 1983 was 2,864,600 or 71% of the population of the State. The resident population (estimate) of each statistical district in Victoria at 30 June 1982 was: Ballarat, 73,630; Bendigo, 60,980; Geelong, 142,890; Morwell, 17,230; Shepparton-Mooroopna, 36,760.

The census population (exclusive of full-blood aboriginals prior to 1961) was:

Date of census enumeration	*Population* *Males*	*Females*	*Total*	*On previous census* *Numerical increase*	*Increase* %
5 April 1891	598,222	541,866	1,140,088	278,522	32·33
31 March 1901	603,720	597,350	1,201,070	60,982	5·35
3 April 1911	655,591	659,960	1,315,551	114,481	9·53
4 April 1921	754,724	776,556	1,531,280	215,729	16·40
30 June 1933	903,244	917,017	1,820,261	288,981	18·87
30 June 1947	1,013,867	1,040,834	2,054,701	234,440	12·88
30 June 1954	1,231,099	1,221,242	2,452,341	397,640	19·35
30 June 1961	1,474,536	1,455,830	2,930,366	478,025	19·49
30 June 1966	1,614,240	1,605,977	3,220,217	289,851	9·89
30 June 1971	1,799,486	1,801,866	3,601,352	381,135	11·84
30 June 1976	1,900,488	1,909,938	3,810,426	209,074	5·81
30 June 1981	1,958,717	1,988,200	3,946,917	136,491	3·58

The population of urban Melbourne (capital city) on 30 June 1981 was 2,578,759. The population of urban Geelong was 125,279; urban Ballarat, 62,641; urban Bendigo, 52,741. Other urban centres: Shepparton-Mooroopna, 28,373; Warrnambool, 21,414; Moe-Yallourn, 18,159; Traralgon, 18,057; Morwell, 16,491; Wangaratta, 16,202; Mildura, 15,763; Sale, 12,968; Horsham, 12,034; Colac, 10,587; Hamilton, 9,751, Bairnsdale, 9,459; Portland, 9,353; Swan Hill, 8,398; Ararat, 8,336; Benalla, 8,151; Maryborough, 7,858; Warragul, 7,712; Castlemaine, 7,583.

Vital statistics for calendar years:

	Births	*Marriages*	*Divorces*	*Deaths*
1981	59,513	28,648	9,769	29,034
1982	59,983	28,851	11,266	30,611
1983	59,911	28,974	10,663	29,309

The annual rates per 1,000 of the mean resident population (estimate) in 1983 were: Marriages, 7·2; births, 14·8; deaths, 7·3; divorces, 2·6.

CONSTITUTION AND GOVERNMENT. Victoria, formerly a portion of New South Wales, was, in 1851, proclaimed a separate colony, with a partially elective Legislative Council. In 1855 responsible government was conferred, the legislative power being vested in a parliament of two Houses, the Legislative Council and the Legislative Assembly. At present the Council consists of 44 members who are elected for 6 years, one-half retiring every third year. The Assembly consists of 81 members, elected for 3 years from the date of its first meeting unless sooner dissolved by the Governor. As a result of the Constitution (Electoral Provinces and Districts) Act 1983, from the date of the next election the number of members in the Legislative Assembly will increase to 88. As a result of the Constitution (Duration of Parliament) Act 1984, the term of the Legislative Assembly will be a maximum of 4 years and the term of the Legislative Council will be two terms of the Legislative Assembly. Members and electors of both Houses must be aged 18 years and Australian citizens or those British subjects previously enrolled as electors, according to the Constitution (Qualification of Electors) Act 1982. Women are fully enfranchised. No property qualification is required, but judges, members of the Commonwealth Parliament and undischarged bankrupts may not be members of either House. Single voting (one elector one vote) and compulsory preferential voting apply to Council and Assembly elections. Enrolment for Council and Assembly electors is compulsory. The Council may not initiate or amend money bills, but may suggest amendments in such bills other than amendments which would increase any charge. Any Minister, with the consent of the House of which he is not a member, may sit and speak in that House to explain a bill relating to the department administered by him, but may not vote in that House. A bill shall not become law unless passed by both Houses, except that, in the event of a continued disagreement between the two Houses as to a bill passed by the Assembly, other than certain constitutional bills, the Governor having dissolved the Assembly may subsequently dissolve the Council, and if the disagreement still continues he may convene a joint sitting of the members of the Council and the Assembly; if at such joint sitting the bill in dispute is passed by an absolute majority of all members it shall become law.

Private members of both Houses receive salaries of $A41,302 per annum, additional allowances rising from $A12,163 to $A16,240, and a living-away-from-home allowance of $A57·15 for each day of attendance for each member (not being a responsible Minister or a metropolitan member).

Members holding the following offices receive the salaries and allowances specified: The President of the Council, $A72,278 salary and $A4,543 expense allowance; the Speaker of the Assembly, $A72,278 salary and $A4,543 expense allowance; the Chairman of Committees of the Council, $A54,518 salary and $A1,652 expense allowance; the Chairman of Committees of the Assembly, $A54,518 salary and $A1,652 expense allowance; the Leader of the Opposition in the Assembly, $A72,278 salary and $A7,434 expense allowance; the Deputy Leader of the Opposition in the Assembly, $A54,518 salary and $A2,478 expense allowance; the Leader of the Third Party, $A54,518 salary and $A2,478 expense allowance; a member of either House who is the Parliamentary Secretary of the Cabinet, $A54,518 salary and $A2,478 expense allowance; the Government Whip in the Assembly, $A48,736 salary; the Whip of any recognized Party which consists of at least 12 members of Parliament, of which Party no member is a responsible Minister, $A45,845 salary. All members have free passes over the Victorian Railways; country members are also entitled to certain allowances for air travel.

The Legislative Assembly, elected on 3 April 1982, and following several by-elections is composed as follows: Labor Party, 49; Liberal Party, 23; National Party, 9.

Governor: Rear-Adm. Sir Brian Stewart Murray, KCMG.

In the exercise of the executive power the Governor is advised by a Cabinet of responsible Ministers. Section 50 of the Constitution Act 1975 provides that the number of responsible Ministers shall not at any one time exceed 18, of whom not more than 6 may sit in the Legislative Council. No responsible Minister may hold office for more than 3 months unless he is or becomes a member of the Council or the Assembly.

Responsible Ministers receive the following amounts: The Premier, $A82,604 salary and $A17,346 expense allowance; the Deputy Premier, $A76,408 salary and $A8,673 expense allowance; 16 other responsible Ministers, $A72,278 salary and $A7,434 expense allowance. Each responsible Minister also receives an electorate allowance, an electorate office allowance, a residential allowance (where applicable) and, when travelling on business of the State, a travelling allowance. The President, Speaker, Chairman of Committees in the Assembly and in the Council, Parliamentary Secretary of the Cabinet, Leader and Deputy Leader of the Opposition in the Assembly, Leader of the Opposition in the Council and Leader in the Assembly of the Third Party, also receive a travelling allowance when travelling on official business. Members of Committees receive attendance fees and certain travelling expenses when on Committee duties.

The Labor Party Government (first appointed 8 April 1982) was as follows on 8 Sept. 1984:

Premier: John Cain, MP.

Deputy Premier, Minister of Education: R. C. Fordham, MP. *Planning and Environment and Public Works:* E. H. Walker, MLC. *Minerals and Energy and*

Water Supply: D. R. White, MLC. *Housing and Industry, Commerce and Technology:* I. R. Cathie, MP. *Transport and Industrial Affairs:* S. M. Crabb, MP. *Treasurer:* R. A. Jolly, MP. *Attorney-General:* J. H. Kennan, MLC. *Agriculture:* D. E. Kent, MLC. *Conservation, Forests and Lands:* R. A. Mackenzie, MLC. *Arts, Police and Emergency Services:* C. R. T. Mathews, MP. *Health:* T. W. Roper, MP. *Employment and Training:* J. L. Simmonds, MP. *Labour and Industry and Property and Services, Assistant Minister of Transport:* J. H. Simpson, MP. *Community Welfare Services:* P. T. Toner, MP. *Youth, Sport and Recreation:* N. B. Trezise, MP. *Local Government:* F. N. Wilkes, MP. *Consumer Affairs and Ethnic Affairs:* P. C. Spyker, MP. *Parliamentary Secretary of the Cabinet:* Dr K. A. Coghill, MP.

Agent-General in London: I. M. Haig (Victoria House, Melbourne Place, Strand, London, WC28 4LG).

Local Government. With the exception of Yallourn Works area (26·9 sq. km) and the unincorporated areas—French Island (154 sq. km), Lady Julia Percy Island (1·3 sq. km), the Bass Strait Islands and part of Gippsland Lakes (312·8 sq. km) and Tower Hill Lake Reserve (5 sq. km), the State is divided (at 30 June 1982) into 211 municipal districts, namely 65 cities, 6 towns, 7 boroughs and 133 shires. The constitution of cities, towns, boroughs and shires is based on statutory requirements concerning population, rate revenue and net annual value of rateable property.

ECONOMY

Budget. The receipts and payments (in $A1m.) of the Consolidated Fund in the years shown (ended 30 June) were:

	1980–81	*1981–82*	*1982–83*	*1983–84*
Receipts	4,482	5,466	7,203	7,781
Payments	4,502	5,473	7,209	7,752

The Consolidated Fund is divided into two sectors: the Current Account and the Works and Services (capital account).

Total receipts for 1982–83 of the Current Account sector were 6,183. Principal receipt items were: State taxation, 2,286; Commonwealth tax sharing, 1,743, other Commonwealth payments, 555 and railways operating income, 242.

The Works and Services sector contributed 1,019. Principal receipt items were: Commonwealth payments, 443; sale of railway assets, 162; loan raisings, 230 and the State Development Account (an investment account receiving deposits from various State Authorities), 130.

Of total Consolidated Fund payments during 1982–83 6,233 was paid through the Current Account sector. Principal payment items were: Debt charges, 518; education, 1,798; health, 955; railway operating expenditure, 572 and transport, 386.

The remaining 976 paid through the Works and Services sector was appropriated into the Works and Services Account, from which the Victorian Government makes its capital expenditure. The total receipts of the Works and Services Account was 1,042, which is the appropriation plus 65 in loan raisings by various boards and authorities. Payments from the account were 1,009. Principal payment items were: Road transport, 189; rail transport, 188; education, 170 and housing, 165.

The public debt of Victoria at 30 June 1983 was 4,045. Victoria had other liabilities due to the Commonwealth Government of 1,236 largely being advances for housing.

Banking. On 30 June 1984 there were 8·3m. operative accounts (excluding school bank accounts) in savings banks in Victoria. The total credit due to depositors amounted to $A12,916m., made up of State Savings Bank, $A5,941·9m.; Commonwealth Savings Bank, $A2,590·7m.; private savings banks, $A4,383·7m.

The weekly average of deposits and advances of trading banks operating in Victoria during June 1984 were as follows: Deposits, not bearing interest, $A2,685·2m.; deposits, bearing interest, $A6,485m.; total deposits, $A9,170·3m.; loans, advances, and bills discounted, $A6,387·7m. The weekly average of debits to customers' accounts (excluding debits to Federal and State Government accounts at City branches in State capitals) for the same period totalled $A19,075m.

ENERGY AND NATURAL RESOURCES

Electricity. All electricity in this State for public supply is generated by the largest electricity supply authority in Australia, the State Electricity Commission of Victoria. Through its network of 116,000 km of power lines the SEC supplies more than 1,362,000 customers. Another 277,600 customers take SEC power from 11 metropolitan councils which buy in bulk and distribute electricity through their own systems.

Electricity demand has almost doubled in 10 years and is now nearly 25,000 megawatt/hours a year. Generating capacity at 30 June 1983 was 6,344 megawatts compared with 3,863 in 1973.

About 75% of the power generated for the state system is supplied by base load generating stations, Yallourn, Morwell, Hazelwood and Yallourn W, located in the Latrobe Valley on one of the largest single brown coal deposits in the world 140 to 180 km east of Melbourne in Central Gippsland.

These plants and a new 2,000 megawatt brown coal station at Loy Yang, to come into operation after 1984, will provide the bulk of Victoria's power requirements until at least the turn of the century.

Oil and Natural Gas. Crude oil in commercially recoverable quantities was first discovered by the Esso/BHP partnership in 1967 in 2 large fields offshore in East Gippsland in Bass Strait between 65 and 80 km from land. These fields, Halibut and Kingfish, with 10 other fields since discovered—Marlin, Snapper, Barracouta, Mackerel, Tuna, Cobia, Flounder, Fortescue, Bream and Seahorse have been assessed as containing initial recoverable reserves of more than 2,930m. bbls of treated crude oil. Total production since 1969 from the producing fields has amounted to 1,568m. bbls, leaving a balance of recoverable reserves of 1,362m. bbls (31 Dec. 1982).

Gippsland crude now supplies approximately 72% of Australia's refinery requirements, and during 1982 a total of 122m. bbls were produced. Depletion of production from the 2 major fields, Kingfish and Halibut and the smaller Barracouta field, is now expected to occur in the late-1980s.

Natural gas was discovered offshore in East Gippsland in 1965. The initial recoverable reserves of treated gas are 220,400m. cu. metres. Reserves are sufficient for at least 30 years. Following an extensive development and distribution programme, natural gas was first connected to homes and industry in Victoria in April 1969. All gas consumers in Melbourne, Geelong, Ballarat, Bendigo, Shepparton, Euroa, Benalla, Wangaratta, Wodonga, Albury and a number of towns near Melbourne, in the Latrobe Valley and in East Gippsland, are now using natural gas. At 30 June 1983 a total of 941,623 consumers were being supplied with it. During the period 1 July 1982 to 30 June 1983 a total volume of 5,531m. cu. metres of gas was consumed in Victoria, including commercial sales and plant usage.

Natural gas and crude oil are conveyed from the producing fields to a large treatment plant at Longford in East Gippsland from where both hydrocarbons are distributed by a network of transmission lines to tank farms and city gate distribution points.

The crude oil is then distributed to refineries in Victoria by pipeline and to other States by seagoing tankers. Natural gas is distributed to residential and industrial consumers through a network of approximately 19,572 km of mains.

Liquefied petroleum gas is now being produced after extraction of the propane and butane fractions from the untreated oil and gas. For the year ended June 1982, approximately 1·8m. tonnes was exported by Esso and BHP, mainly to Japan.

Brown Coal. Major deposits of brown coal are located in the Central Gippsland region and comprise approximately 94% of the total resources in Victoria. The resource is estimated to be 108,000 megatonnes, of which about 35,000 megatonnes are economically winnable. It is young and soft with a water content of 60% to 70%. In the Latrobe Valley section of the region, the thick brown coal seams underlie an area from 10 to 30 km wide extending over approximately 70 kilometres from Yallourn in the west to the south of Sale in the east. It can be won continuously in large quantities and at low cost by specialized mechanical plant.

About 54% of the resources occur in areas where the overburden over the uppermost seam is less than 30·5 metres while 95% is in areas with less than 91·4 metres of overburden. The current primary use of these reserves is to fuel the major base load electricity generating stations located at Morwell and Yallourn.

Land Settlement. Of the total area of Victoria (22·76m. hectares), 14,063,683 hectares on 30 June 1982 were either alienated or in process of alienation. The remainder (8,696,317) constituted Crown land as follows: Perpetual leases, grazing and other leases and licences, 2,274,043; reservations including forest and timber reserves, water, catchment and drainage purposes, national parks, wildlife reserves, water frontages and other reserves, plus unoccupied and unreserved including areas set aside for roads, 6,422,274. Establishments with agricultural activity at 31 March 1982 numbered 48,608.

Minerals. The recorded production of certain metals and minerals raised in Victoria for the year 1981–82 was: Gold, 92,000 grammes, value $A881,000; coal, brown, 37·6m. tonnes, value $A137·1m.

Agriculture. The following table shows the area under the principal crops and the produce of each for 3 seasons (in 1,000 units):

	Total crop area	*Wheat*		*Oats*		*Barley*		*Potatoes*		*Hay*	
Season	*Hectares*	*Hectares*	*Tonnes*	*Hectares*	*Tonnes*	*Hectares*	*Tonnes*	*Hectares*	*Tonnes*	*Hectares*	*Tonnes*
1980–81	2,184	1,431	2,538	219	322	303	418	14	349	496	1,893
1981–82	2,184	1,322	2,467	245	306	315	459	14	354	556	1,982
1982–83	2,236	1,327	394	213	98	278	75	14	291	348	1,065

In 1982–83 there were 20,341 hectares of vines, yielding 64,900 tonnes of grapes for wine-making and 69,411 tonnes of grapes for drying or for table use. The area cut for green feed and silage covered 141,123 hectares, and orchards and vegetables, including potatoes and onions, occupied 46,337 hectares.

At March 1983 there were in the State 3·4m. head of cattle, 22,748,412 sheep and 386,901 pigs. In 1982–83, 680,769 tonnes of fresh meat was produced. The wool produced in the season 1982–83 amounted to 133m. kg, valued at $A324m. The quantity of butter produced in 1982–83 was 74·6m. kg.

The gross value of Victorian primary production in (rural and non-rural) 1982–83 was $A2,581m.

INDUSTRY AND TRADE

Industry. From the 1975–76 Census of Manufacturing Establishments onwards only a limited range of data—employment and wages and salaries—has been collected from single-establishment manufacturing enterprises with less than 4 persons employed. This procedure significantly reduces the statistical reporting obligations of small businesses. Data in respect of the larger manufacturers provides reliable information for the evaluation of trends in the manufacturing sector of the economy. From the 1977–78 census, the classification of census units to industry is based on the 1978 edition of the Australian Standard Industrial Classification. The following data relates to manufacturing establishments owned by multi-establishment enterprises, and single-establishment manufacturing enterprises with 4 or more persons employed.

The total number of manufacturing establishments in Victoria in 1982–83 (figures for 1981–82 in brackets) was 8,392 (8,916). Persons employed, including working proprietors, on the last pay day in June were males 247,629 (276,530) and females 102,050 (112,342). Salaries and wages paid were $A5,950m. ($A5,757m.), excluding drawings of working proprietors. The cost of purchases, transfers in, and selected expenses was $A17,060m. ($A17,031m.) and sales, transfers out and other operating revenue were $A27,747m. ($A27,208m.).

The preceding figures exclude gas and electricity producing and distributing establishments. In terms of persons employed the most important manufacturing activities were: Basic and fabricated metal products including transport equipment, other machinery and equipment, 145,900 (164,042); textiles, clothing and footwear, 58,598 (62,694); food, beverages and tobacco, 51,450 (53,139).

Trade Unions. There were 174 trade unions with a total membership of 788,200 operating in Victoria in Dec. 1983.

Commerce. The commerce of Victoria, exclusive of inter-state trade, is included in the statement of the commerce of Australia, *see* pp. 108–10.

The total value of the overseas imports and exports of Victoria, including bullion and specie but excluding inter-state trade, was as follows (in $A1,000):

	1977–78	*1978–79*	*1979–80*	*1980–81*	*1981–82*	*1982–83*[1]
Imports	3,855,619	4,694,481	5,506,400	5,929,278	7,167,713	6,987,715
Exports	2,505,768	2,702,452	3,782,993	3,993,482	3,981,601	4,023,680

[1] Preliminary.

The chief exports[1] in 1982–83 were: Cereals and cereal preparations, petroleum products and gases, vegetables and fruit, dairy products, meat, textile fibres and their wastes and road vehicles.

[1] From 1 July 1978 state export figures changed from 'State of Lodgement of documents with the Bureau of Customs' to 'State of Origin'.

COMMUNICATIONS

Roads. At 30 June 1982 there were 157,201 km of road open for general traffic consisting of 63,926 km of bituminous seal, etc., 47,905 km of waterbound macadam, gravel, etc., 23,503 km formed, but not paved, and 21,867 km not formed. The number of registered motor vehicles (other than tractors) at 30 June 1983 was 2,257,700.

Railways. All the railways are the property of the State and are under the management of a 9-member governing board, appointed by, and responsible to, the Victorian Government.

At 30 June 1983, 5,815 km of government railway were open. During the year 1982–83 the gross revenue amounted to $A248,129,365 and the total working expenses to $A680,409,404. 84,323,000 (estimate) passengers, 8,500,511 tonnes of freight and 69,117 tonnes of livestock were carried.

Aviation. During the year ended 31 Dec. 1983 there were 65,259 aircraft movements at Melbourne (Tullamarine) airport. Passengers totalled 4·4m. on domestic flights (international, 919,836). Freight handled, 69,645 tonnes, domestic flights (42,877 international).

JUSTICE, RELIGION, EDUCATION AND WELFARE

Justice. There is a Supreme Court with a Chief Justice and 20 puisne judges. There are magistrates' courts, county courts, a court of licensing, and a bankruptcy court.

Criminal matters proven for 1981 in the children's court were 18,117; magistrates' courts, 57,785; and higher (judges') courts, 3,330 (excluding driving and traffic offences).

There are 11 gaols in Victoria. At 30 June 1982 there were confined in these prisons, 1,809 persons.

Religion. There is no State Church in Victoria, and no State assistance has been given to religion since 1875. At the date of the 1981 census the following were the enumerated numbers of each of the principal religions: Catholic,[1] 524,612; Church of England, 371,873; Uniting, 97,611; Orthodox, 87,119; Presbyterian, 83,223;

Protestant (undefined), 46,403; Methodist, 43,030; other Christian, 34,361; Moslem, 15,666; Hebrew, 14,668; no religion, 258,249; no reply, 231,821.

[1] So described on individual census schedules.

Education. Education establishments in Victoria consist of 4 universities, established under special Acts and opened in 1855, 1961, 1967 and 1977; Colleges of Advanced Education; government schools (primary, primary-secondary, high and secondary technical, and further education colleges), and non-government schools.

The University of Melbourne, founded in 1853, had, in 1982, 16,060 students and 1,516 teaching and research staff.

Monash University, founded in 1958 in an eastern suburb of Melbourne, had, in 1982, 14,220 students and 1,169 teaching and research staff.

La Trobe University, founded in 1964 in a northern suburb of Melbourne, had 8,490 students and 585 teaching and research staff in 1982.

Deakin University (1974) near Melbourne had 5,380 students and 246 staff in 1982.

Primary education of children of the ages of 6 to 15 years inclusive is free, secular and compulsory. At 1 July 1983 there were 1,634 government primary schools and 75 special schools with 20,154 teachers and an enrolment of 333,089 pupils; 19 government primary-secondary schools had 563 teachers and an enrolment of 5,811 pupils. There were also 396 government secondary schools, including junior technical schools and high schools with 22,178 teachers and an enrolment of 243,134 pupils. In 1983 there were 181,482 students (excluding adult education programmes) enrolled in technical and further education schools and colleges.

Non-government Schools. There were at 1 July 1983, 659 non-government schools, excluding commercial colleges, with 15,244 teachers and 234,171 pupils enrolled. Of these schools, 492 were Roman Catholic.

Social Services. Victoria was the first State of Australia to make a statutory provision for the payment of Age Pensions. The Act providing for the payment of such pensions came into operation on 18 Jan. 1901, and continued until 1 July 1909, when the Australian Invalid and Old Age Pension Act came into force. The Social Services Consolidation Act, which came into operation on 1 July 1947, repealed the various legislative enactments relating to age (previously old-age) and invalid pensions, maternity allowances, child endowment, and unemployment, and sickness benefits and while following in general the Acts repealed, considerably liberalized many of their provisions: it has since been amended. On 30 June 1983 there were 380,350 aged and 77,257 invalid pensioners in Victoria, and the amount paid in pensions, including payments to wives of invalid pensioners, during 1982–83 was $A1,555·9m.

The number of disability pensions (members of the forces and their dependants) payable in Victoria on 30 June 1983 was 100,896, and the number of service pensions was 83,900. The amount paid in war and service pensions by the Federal Government during 1982–83 was $A420m.

Under the Australian Unemployment and Sickness Benefit Act 1944, there were 136,644 persons receiving benefits at June 1983 (excluding migrants in accommodation centres) and the amount paid in benefits totalled $A550·4m. in the year ended 30 June 1983.

The number of widows' pensions in force in Victoria at 30 June 1983 was 46,406, and the total amount paid in allowances during the year was $A209·6m.

The number of family allowances in force in Victoria at 30 June 1983 was 1,145,230 (including students). In addition (in 1983), endowment was being paid in respect of 2,527 children who were being maintained in approved institutions. The total amount paid in endowment in Victoria during the year ended 30 June 1983 was $A366m.

State Housing. The various State housing authorities were consolidated under the control of the Ministry of Housing early in 1973. The authorities include the Housing Commission, the Government Employee Housing Authority and the Co-operative Housing Registry.

The Housing Act 1983 abolished the Housing Commission and the Home Finance Trust, replacing these bodies by a Body Corporate under the name of the Director of Housing. All assets and rights, and liabilities and obligations, of the Housing Commission and the Home Finance Trust were, by the Housing Act 1983, vested in and became due by the Director. Part IVA – Government Finance – of the Co-Operative Housing Societies Act 1958 has been revoked, those provisions now being included in the Housing Act 1983. The Housing Advisory Council was abolished by the Housing Act 1983.

Including the construction and purchase of housing units 1938–84 of its antecedent authority, the Housing Commission, the Director of Housing has built and purchased 97,334 housing units, of which 50,785 have been sold. Approximately 36% of all construction since 1938 is located outside the Melbourne Metropolitan area.

Rental charges for the year ended 30 June 1984 were $A124,388,557, against which $A37,606,795 was allowed in rent rebates to tenants on low incomes, including pensioners.

Books of Reference

Statistical Information: Australian Bureau of Statistics (Commonwealth Banks Building, corner of Elizabeth and Flinders Streets, Melbourne, 3000). *Deputy Commonwealth Statistician:* Erle Bourke.

Victorian Year Book. (Annually since 1873)
Victorian Pocket Year Book. (Annually since 1956)
Victorian Statistical Register. (Annually from 1854 to 1916)
Monthly Summary of Statistics (from Jan. 1960)

Victoria: The First Century. Official History of Victoria. Melbourne, 1934
Victorian Municipal Directory. Melbourne, (From 1866). Melbourne, Arnall and Jackson
Grant, J., and Serle, G., *The Melbourne Scene 1803–1956.* Melbourne Univ. Press, 1956
Pratt, A., *The Centenary History of Victoria.* Melbourne, 1934

State Library: The State Library of Victoria, 328 Swanston St., Melbourne, 3000. *State Librarian:* W. Horton, BA, ALAA.

WESTERN AUSTRALIA

HISTORY. In 1791 Vancouver, in the *Discovery*, took formal possession of the country about King George Sound. In 1826 the Government of New South Wales sent 20 convicts and a detachment of soldiers to King George Sound and formed a settlement then called Frederickstown. In 1827 Captain (afterwards Sir) James Stirling surveyed the coast from King George Sound to the Swan River, and in May 1829 Captain (afterwards Sir) Charles Fremantle took possession of the territory. In June 1829 Captain Stirling, newly appointed Lieut.-Governor, founded the colony now known as the State of Western Australia. On 1 Jan. 1901 Western Australia became one of the 6 federated States within the Commonwealth of Australia.

AREA AND POPULATION. Western Australia lies between 113° 09′ and 129° E. long. and 13° 44′ and 35° 08′ S. lat.; its area is 2,525,500 sq. km.

The population at each census from 1933 was as follows [1]:

	Males	*Females*	*Total*		*Males*	*Females*	*Total*
1933	233,937	204,915	438,852	1966	432,569	415,531	848,100
1947	258,076	244,404	502,480	1971	534,100	509,000	1,043,100
1954	330,358	309,413	639,771	1976	596,800	573,100	1,169,800
1961	375,452	361,177	736,629	1981	656,400	642,700	1,299,100

[1] 1961 and earlier exclude full-blood Aboriginals; from 1966 figures refer to total population (*i.e.*, including Aboriginals).

Of the census population in 1981, 910,666 were born in Australia. Married persons numbered 585,465 (285,224 males and 283,241 females); widowers, 10,088; widows, 45,465; divorced, 16,180 males and 19,171 females; never married, 318,273 males and 267,761 females. The number of males under 21 was 240,210 and of females 228,155.

Perth, the capital, had an estimated resident population of 969,080 at June 1983. Of this, the area administered by the City of Perth had a population of 82,450 while the population in the area for which the City of Fremantle is responsible (which includes the chief port of the State) was 23,460.

Principal urban centres outside the metropolitan area, with population at 30 June 1983 (estimate): Bunbury, 23,630; Geraldton, 19,610; Kalgoorlie–Boulder, 21,800; Albany, 13,940; Northam, 7,030; Narrogin, 5,310.

Vital statistics for calendar years [1]:

	Births	*Ex-nuptial births*	*Marriages*	*Divorces*	*Deaths*
1981	21,877	3,300	10,111	3,481	7,993
1982	22,236	3,316	10,455	3,842	8,187
1983	23,046	3,642	10,519	3,822	8,359

[1] Including Aboriginals.

CONSTITUTION AND GOVERNMENT. In 1870 partially representative government was instituted, and in 1890 the administration was vested in the Governor, a Legislative Council and a Legislative Assembly. The Legislative Council was, in the first instance, nominated by the Governor, but it was provided that in the event of the population of the colony reaching 60,000, it should be elective. In 1893 this limit of population being reached, the Colonial Parliament amended the Constitution accordingly.

The Legislative Council consists of 34 members, 2 members representing each of the 17 electoral provinces. Each member is elected for a term of 6 years, one-half of the members retiring every 3 years.

There are 57 members of the Legislative Assembly, each member representing one of the 57 electoral districts of the State. Members are elected for the duration of the Parliament, normally 3 years. The qualifications applying to candidates and electors are identical for the Legislative Council and the Legislative Assembly. A candidate must have resided in Western Australia for a minimum of 12 months, be at least 18 years of age and free from legal incapacity, be an Australian citizen, and be enrolled, or qualified for enrolment, as an elector. A judge of the Supreme Court, the Sheriff of Western Australia, an undischarged bankrupt or a debtor against whose estate there is a subsisting order in bankruptcy may not be elected to Parliament. No person may hold office as a member of the Legislative Assembly and the Legislative Council at the same time. An elector must be at least 18 years of age, be an Australian citizen free from legal incapacity, must have resided in the Commonwealth of Australia for 6 and in Western Australia for 3 months continuously and in the electoral district for which he claims enrolment for a continuous period of 1 month immediately preceding the date of his claim. Enrolment is compulsory for all qualified persons except Aboriginal natives of Australia, who are entitled but not required to enrol. Voting at elections is on the preferential system and is compulsory for all enrolled persons.

Ordinary members of the legislature are paid a salary of $A37,622 a year, with an additional electorate allowance, ranging from $A10,410 to $A25,296 according to location of electorate. Members are entitled to free travel on Western Australian government railways and on the Metropolitan (Perth) Passenger Transport Trust omnibus and ferry services, and, by arrangement, once every year on government railways in other States. All members of Parliament contribute to superannuation benefits.

The Premier receives a salary, including an electorate allowance, of $A88,927, the Deputy Premier $A79,150, the Leader of the Government in the Legislative Council $A76,421, and all other Ministers $A71,145—86,031 according to location of electorate.

The Legislative Assembly, elected on 19 Feb. 1983, is composed as follows: Australian Labor Party, 32; Liberal Party, 19; National Country Party, 3; National

Party, 2; Independent, 1. The Legislative Council, one-half of which was elected on the same day, is composed of 19 Liberal Party, 13 Australian Labor Party, 1 National Country Party, 1 National Party.

Governor: Gordon Reid.

The Australian Labor Party Cabinet was, at 30 Sept. 1983:

Premier and Cabinet, Treasurer, Minister Co-ordinating Economic and Social Development, and Minister for Forests, Tourism and Women's Interests: Hon. Brian Thomas Burke, MLA.

Deputy Premier and Minister for Industrial Development, Technology and Defence Liaison: Hon. Malcolm John Bryce, BA, MLA. *Industrial Relations, Administrative Services and Leader of the Government in the Legislative Council:* Hon. Desmond Keith Dans, MLC. *Attorney-General, Budget Management, Prisons:* Hon. Joseph Max Berinson, LLB, MLC. *Water Resources, Parliamentary and Electoral Reform and Leader of the House:* Hon. Arthur Raymond Tonkin, BA, Dip Ed, MLA. *Police and Emergency Services, and Local Government:* Hon. Jeffrey Phillip Carr, BA, MLA. *Environment, Multi-Cultural and Ethnic Affairs, and the Arts:* Hon. Ronald Davies, MLA. *Agriculture, Fisheries and Wildlife and Minister Assisting the Minister for Forests:* Hon. Hywel David Evans, BA, MLA. *Education:* Hon. Robert John Pearce, BA, Dip Ed, MLA. *Health:* Hon. Barry James Hodge, MLA. *Works, and Lands and Surveys:* Hon. Kenneth Finlay McIver, MLA. *Minerals and Energy and Minister Assisting the Minister Co-ordinating Economic and Social Development:* Hon. David Charles Parker, BA, MLA. *Transport, and Regional Development and the North-West with special responsibility for 'Bunbury 2000':* Hon. Julian Fletcher Grill, LLB., MLA. *Housing, Youth and Community Services with special responsibility for Aboriginal Affairs, and Sport and Recreation:* Hon. Keith James Wilson, MLA. *Planning, Employment and Training and Consumer Affairs:* Hon. Peter M'Callum Dowding, LLB., MLC.

Agent-General in London: R. Douglas (Western Australia House, 115 Strand, WC2R 0AJ).

Local Government. The only unincorporated area in mainland Western Australia is King's Park, a public reserve of about 403 hectares in Perth. Including the lord-mayoralty of Perth there were 13 cities, 12 towns and 114 shires at 30 June 1984. The executive body in each of these districts is normally an elective council, presided over by a mayor (city and town) or a president (shire), but in certain circumstances it may be a commissioner appointed by the Governor. Their functions include road construction and repair, the provision of parks and recreation grounds, the administration of building controls and local services such as health. Finance is derived largely from rates levied on property owners as well as charges for services and government grants (mainly for road construction).

ECONOMY

Budget. The revenue and expenditure (in $A) of Western Australia in years ended 30 June, are given as follows:

	1981	*1982*	*1983*	*1984*[1]
Revenue	1,860,548,032	2,061,893,781	2,324,874,369	2,658,900,000
Expenditure	1,862,006,834	2,061,893,781	2,339,070,164	2,658,900,000

[1] Estimates.

Main items of revenue in 1982–83: Railways ($A210,225,502), taxation ($A475,314,902), lands, timber and mining ($A136,377,880), public utilities other than railways ($A56,484,547), from Federal funds ($A1,141,749,219). Western Australia had a net loan liability of $A1,547,497,840 on 30 June 1983, the charge for the year being $A171,628,379.

Banking. There are 8 trading banks in Western Australia including the Commonwealth Trading Bank and The Rural and Industries Bank of Western Australia. In the June quarter, 1984, the average of customers' balances was $A3,135·4m. and average advances $A2,955·9m.

At 30 June 1984, the 6 savings banks held deposits of $A2,214·4m., in 1,961,811 accounts.

ENERGY AND NATURAL RESOURCES

Minerals. The mining industry has been for many years of considerable significance in the Western Australian economy. Until the mid-1960s the major mineral produced was gold. However, in recent years gold has been displaced by iron ore in terms of value, and has at various times fallen behind nickel concentrates, bauxite, oil, mineral sands and salt.

The total ex-mine value of minerals from mining and quarrying in the State in 1982–83 was $A2,553·4m. Principal minerals produced in 1982–83 were: Iron ore, 75·3m. tonnes, value $A1,355·3m.; crude oil, 1·33m. cu. metres; gold bullion, 26·6m. grammes, value $A325·2m.; construction materials (excluding sand and gravel), value $A37·4m.; mineral sands, 1·27m. tonnes, value, $A79·2m.; black coal, 3·9m. tonnes, value $A95·5m.; salt, 4·15m. tonnes, value $A54·3m.; tin concentrates, 731 tonnes, value $A6·33m.; nickel concentrates, 483,283 tonnes; natural gas, 1,029·6m. cu. metres; diamonds, 2·75m. carats; copper concentrates, 55,127 tonnes and zinc concentrates, 71,522 tonnes.

Land Settlement. Up to 31 Dec. 1982, of the entire area of the State (252·55m. hectares) 17,281,000 hectares had been alienated; on that date 1·81m. hectares were in process of alienation; the area alienated and in process of alienation thus amounting to 19,092,000 hectares. There were in force leases comprising an area of 98,456,000 hectares, of which 95,739,000 hectares were pastoral, 374,000 hectares were timber, 193,000 hectares mining leases, 12,000 hectares miners' homestead leases and 2·09m. hectares for reserves, residential lots, special and perpetual leases.

Agriculture.

Crop	*1981–82* Area 1,000 hectares	*1981–82* Production 1,000 tonnes	*1982–83* Area 1,000 hectares	*1982–83* Production 1,000 tonnes
Wheat	4,593	4,803	4,865	5,534
Oats	432	442	461	534
Barley	580	576	603	717
Hay	255	711	250	749
Potatoes	2	67	2	69
Cauliflower	1	16	1	14

Crop	*1981–82* No. Trees Bearing (1,000)	*1981–82* Production Tonnes	*1982–83* No. Trees Bearing (1,000)	*1982–83* Production Tonnes
Apples	677	49,577	640	53,362
Pears	77	6,004	77	6,016
Oranges	184	7,676	178	7,834

Irrigation has been established by the Government along the south-western coastal plain and in the north of the State. Reservoirs with an aggregate capacity of 6,208m. cu. metres provided irrigation water for 30,000 hectares in 6 districts during 1982–83.

The livestock at 31 March 1983 consisted of 1,754,000 cattle, 30,164,000 sheep and 300,000 pigs.

The wool clip in 1982–83 was 145,526 tonnes; the overseas exports for 1982–83, greasy wool, 112,076 tonnes; degreased wool, 13,520 tonnes.

Forestry. The area of State forests and timber reserves (Forest Act 1918–76) at 30 June 1983 was 2,014,432 hectares; 1982–83 production of sawn timber was 265,340 cu. metres, principally Jarrah and Karri hardwoods.

Fisheries. The catch of fish, crustaceans and molluscs in Western Australia in 1982–83 totalled 36,967 tonnes for a gross value of $A126·2m. Of this, rock lobsters, with a total catch of 12,482 tonnes accounted for $A93·2m.

Value of Agricultural Commodities Produced. The estimated gross values of Western Australian agricultural commodities during 1982–83 were: Crops and pastures, $A1,368m.; livestock slaughterings and other disposals, $A354·95m.; livestock products, $A473·28m.

INDUSTRY AND TRADE

Industry. Perhaps the most significant change in Western Australia manufacturing came when the basis for an integrated industrial complex was established with the opening of a large oil refinery at Kwinana in 1954. Two of the plants in the Kwinana complex are directly concerned with metals processing. An alumina refinery commenced operations in 1964 and a nickel refinery commenced operations in 1970. Major mineral processing plants outside Kwinana also contribute to Western Australia's manufacturing industry. A plant at Australind, near Bunbury, which extracts titanium dioxide from ilmenite has been in operation since 1963. A nickel smelter commenced operations at Kalgoorlie in 1973 and another alumina refinery, at Pinjarra, began operating in 1972. In addition, two new alumina refineries are under construction, one at Wagerup and the other at Worsley.

Besides providing for heavy industry directly associated with minerals processing, the mining development of recent years, especially on the North West Shelf, has also given impetus to other manufacturing activity, particularly to industries associated with the provision of capital equipment and other manufactured goods for the major mining projects.

The following table shows manufacturing industry statistics for 1982–83 [1]:

Industry sub-division	*Number of establishments operating at 30 June*	*Persons employed* [2]	*Wages and salaries $A1,000*	*Turnover $A1,000*	*Value added $A1,000*
Food, beverages and tobacco	366	12,002	180,988	1,331,462	383,894
Textiles	29	688	9,251	36,756	11,872
Clothing and footwear	66	1,421	15,200	39,074	20,963
Wood, wood products and furniture	427	7,064	88,232	349,902	150,784
Paper, paper products, printing and publishing	209	6,858	102,765	316,634	155,874
Chemical, petroleum and coal products	81	3,150	65,977	441,007	154,276
Non-metallic mineral products	212	4,355	74,164	356,294	156,915
Basic metal products	39	5,655	131,709	1,340,917	408,120
Fabricated metal products	431	8,656	134,874	573,597	234,112
Transport equipment	156	4,838	75,059	196,582	103,809
Other machinery and equipment	316	7,807	124,788	449,153	197,705
Miscellaneous manufacturing	167	2,486	35,316	165,155	62,552
Total	2,499	64,980	1,038,325	5,596,534	2,040,876

[1] Excludes single establishment enterprises with less than 4 persons employed.
[2] Annual average. Includes working proprietors.

Labour. A Court of Arbitration was established in Western Australia in 1901 under the provisions of the 'Industrial Conciliation and Arbitration Act 1900'. The Court of Arbitration was replaced, with effect from 1 Feb. 1964, by the Western Australian Industrial Appeal Court and The Western Australian Industrial Commission, authorities constituted in terms of the *Industrial Arbitration Act 1912–1977*. These authorities continue to operate under the provisions of the *Industrial Arbitration Act 1979–81*.

The Western Australian Industrial Appeal Court consists of 3 Judges, one of whom is the Presiding Judge. The members are nominated by the Chief Justice of Western Australia. An appeal lies to the Court from decisions of the President of the Western Australian Industrial Commission, the Full Bench or the Commission in Court Session but only on the ground that the decision is erroneous in law or is in excess of jurisdiction.

The Western Australian Industrial Commission consists of a President, a Chief Industrial Commissioner, a Senior Commissioner, and 'such number of other Commissioners as may, from time to time, be necessary'. There were 5 'other

Commissioners' at 1 March 1984. A person shall not be appointed as President unless he is qualified to be a Judge, and on appointment he is entitled to the status of a Puisne Judge. The President or a Commissioner sitting or acting alone constitutes the Commission and may exercise the appropriate powers of the Commission.

The Commission can inquire into any industrial matter and make an award, order or declaration relating to such matter. 'Industrial matter' means any matter affecting or relating to the work, privileges, rights, or duties of employers or employees in any industry and includes any matter relating to the wages, salaries, allowances, or other remuneration of employees or the prices to be paid in respect of their employment; the hours of employment, sex, age, qualification or status of employees and the mode, terms and conditions of employment including conditions which are to take effect after the termination of employment. The Commission may also make inquiries where industrial action has occurred or is likely to occur.

The Commission in Court Session is constituted by not less than 3 Commissioners sitting or acting together, and may make General Orders, hear matters referred by the Commission, and hear appeals from decisions of Boards of Reference.

The Full Bench is constituted by not less than 3 members of the Commission, 1 of whom is the President, and may hear matters referred by the Commission on questions of law, and appeals from decisions of the Commission and Industrial Magistrates.

The following table shows details of the number of industrial awards, unions and members registered with The Western Australian Industrial Commission.

At 30 June	*1980*	*1981*	*1982*	*1983*	*1984*
Awards in force	494	459	483	488	491
Consent agreements in force [1]	... [2]	... [2]	... [2]	... [2]	... [2]
Unions of workers:					
Number	74	68	69	66	67
Membership	181,409	170,414	171,912	176,065	174,330
Unions of employers:					
Number	14	14	14	14	14
Membership	2,040	2,139	2,142	2,138	2,144

[1] Named as 'Industrial agreements' prior to 1980. [2] Included in 'Awards in force'.

Commerce. The external commerce of Western Australia, exclusive of interstate trade, is comprised in the statement of the commerce of Australia, *see* pp. 108–10.

The total value of imports and exports, including interstate trade, but excluding interstate value of horses, in 5 years (30 June) is, in $A1m., as follows:

	1978–79	*1979–80*	*1980–81*	*1981–82*	*1982–83*
Imports	3,205·6	3,787·5	4,504·5	5,676·2	3,160·8
Exports[1]	3,266·3	4,489·5	4,604·1	4,796·1	1,155·7

[1] Excluding ships' stores.

Selected overseas exports (in $A) for 1982–83 (excluding ships' stores): Iron ore and concentrates, 1,405,840,407; wheat, 845,854,994; wool, 392,665,286; petroleum and petroleum products, 259,729,955; gold bullion, 141,340,318; live sheep and lambs, 94,629,838; beef and veal, 88,686,614; rock lobster tails, 71,659,741; salt, 53,701,646; mutton and lamb, 43,132,646; barley, 28,234,084; prawns, 25,170,537; zirconium, 24,856,022; rutile, 23,374,434; ilmenite and leucoxene, 21,986,056; hides and skins (including fur skins), 19,331,593; whole rock lobsters, 16,515,248; fruit and nuts (fresh or dried), 12,714,899; animal oils and fats, 12,425,519; oats, 7,936,069; iron and steel, 29,519.

Selected overseas imports (in $A) for 1982–83: Petroleum and petroleum products, 959,616,019; machinery, 398,104,188; transport equipment, 269,799,450; iron and steel, 165,184,072; chemicals, 109,436,593; food, 40,391,122; crude fertilizer, 32,557,862; rubber manufactures, 27,065,306; paper and paperboard, 24,442,047.

The chief countries exporting to Western Australia in 1982–83 were (in $A): USA, 434,782,456; Japan, 369,368,817; Indonesia, 225,317,936; Singapore,

207,791,661; UAE, 194,659,440; Saudi Arabia, 141,922,351. Western Australian exports in 1982–83 (in $A) went chiefly to: Japan, 1,513,550,438; USA, 628,738,297; Egypt, 228,760,366; UK, 209,780,152; USSR, 199,601,757; China, People's Republic of, 176,066,386.

Tourism. In 1982, 493,900 (estimate) visitors contributed about $A270m. to the economy; interstate tourists, 4,904,000 (estimate) contributed $A648m. to the economy.

COMMUNICATIONS

Roads. At 30 June 1983 there were 118,193 km of prepared and formed roads in Western Australia, namely, 37,760 km of bituminous surface, 37,078 km other constructed surfaces and 43,355 km formed but not metalled or otherwise prepared. In addition, there are 21,218 km of roads unprepared except for clearing which are used for general traffic.

New motor vehicles registered in Western Australia during the year ended 30 June 1984 were 58,905.

Railways. At 30 June 1984 the State had 5,610 km of State government railway and 731 km of Federal line, the latter being the western portion of the Trans-Australian line (Kalgoorlie–Port Pirie), which links the State railway system to those of the other States of the Commonwealth. At 30 June 1982, mining companies operated 1,181 km of private railways for the transport of ore to ports on the north-west coast.

Aviation. An extensive system of regular air services operates in Western Australia for the transport of passengers, freight and mail. During the year ended 30 June 1982, Perth Airport handled a total of 18,555 aircraft movements, 28,760 tonnes of freight and 1,446,149 passengers on domestic and international services.

Shipping. In 1981–82, the number of overseas direct vessels through the major ports was: Port of Fremantle, 542 entered, 693 cleared; Dampier, 356 entered, 367 cleared; Port Hedland, 375 entered, 325 cleared; Port Walcott, 121 entered, 125 cleared. The gross weight (in tonnes) of overseas cargo through those ports was: Port of Fremantle, 4,706,197 discharged, 4,718,769 loaded; Dampier, 88,058 discharged, 30,523,912 loaded; Port Hedland, 257,256 discharged, 30,025,268 loaded; Port Walcott, 34,500 discharged, 14,803,147 loaded.

Post and Broadcasting. Postal, telephone and telegraph facilities are afforded at 453 offices. An additional 24 offices provide only telephone and telegraph facilities. Telephones connected totalled 690,417 at 30 June 1983.

There were 47 wireless broadcasting and 67 television stations, including translator stations, in operation at 30 June 1982.

JUSTICE, RELIGION, EDUCATION AND WELFARE

Justice. In Western Australia justice is administered by a Supreme Court, consisting of a Chief Justice, 7 puisne judges and 2 masters at 30 June 1984; a District Court comprising a chairman of judges and 9 district court judges and Magistrates' Courts exercising both civil and criminal jurisdiction. The lower courts are presided over by justices of the peace, except in the more important centres, where the court is constituted by a stipendiary magistrate. For juvenile offenders, a screening panel comprising a community welfare officer and a senior police officer may recommend a child be cautioned by a member of the Police Force or appear before a Children's Aid Panel or a Childrens Court. Childrens Aid Panels comprise a community welfare officer and a police or education departmental officer. Childrens Courts are presided over by magistrates.

Offences against law	*1978*	*1979*	*1980*	*1981*	*1982*
Charges	117,408	122,419	126,012	122,176	...
Lower Court convictions [1]	105,136	111,864	115,787	116,541	...
Higher Court convictions	1,204	1,584	...	1,759	1,857

[1] Includes convictions for traffic offences: 50,235 in 1978; 56,310 in 1979; 54,734 in 1980; 55,325 in 1981. In addition, small fines were imposed for minor traffic offences as follows: 1978, 307,396; 1979, 333,545; 1980, 332,754; 1981, 348,452; 1982, 379,444.

Persons in prison at 30 June 1984 numbered 1,464 males and 79 females.

Religion. There is no State Church, and freedom of worship is accorded to all. At the census, 30 June 1981, the principal denominations were: Church of England, 375,848; Roman Catholic and Catholic, 316,337; Methodist, 51,225; Presbyterian, 32,033; Baptist, 15,859; Church of Christ, 14,163; other Christian, 131,637; Hebrew, 3,156; all other, including not stated and no religion, 333,368.

Education. School attendance is compulsory from the age of 6 until the end of the year in which the child attains 15 years. Pre-school education is provided by a kindergarten system partly financed from government subsidy. In 1983 there were 680 government primary and secondary schools providing free education to 209,247 pupils and 216 non-government primary and secondary schools providing education, for which fees are charged, to 53,827 pupils.

Technical education is available at a number of technical colleges, schools and centres, which are staffed and controlled by the Education Department.

Tertiary Education at 30 April 1983:

	Teaching Staff[1]	*Students Enrolled*
University of Western Australia	669	9,808
Murdoch University	187	3,169
Western Australian Institute of Technology	702	12,262
Western Australian College of Advanced Education	426	8,958

[1] Comprises full-time teaching staff and part-time staff on the basis of equivalent full-time staff.

State Government expenditure from consolidated revenue on education, including financial assistance to the Universities, during the year ended 30 June 1983, amounted to $A610,116,645.

Social Welfare. At 30 June 1984 there were 47 general hospitals and 8 nursing homes maintained wholly by public funds and 43 general hospitals and 9 nursing homes partly assisted therefrom. In addition, there are numerous private hospitals.

The Health Department of Western Australia Psychiatric Services comprises 4 approved hospitals, 8 outpatient clinics for adults, 8 general rehabilitation units, 2 psychiatric extended care units and 1 rehabilitation hostel. Specifically for children are: 4 outpatient clinics and 2 residential units. The division for the intellectually handicapped comprises 51 units.

The Department for Community Welfare is responsible for the provision of welfare services throughout the State. In the country, there are 8 divisional offices, 28 district offices and 6 sub-offices. In the metropolitan area, there are 8 divisional offices and 3 sub-offices. Services to help families include emergency financial assistance, homemaker services, counselling and psychological service. Emergency financial relief was provided in more than 65,000 instances during the financial year ending June 1984.

There are specialist units working in the areas of child abuse, adoptions and youth activities.

A counselling service is provided through the Family Court; and a 24-hour emergency welfare service is available through the Crisis Care Unit.

Supervision of day care centres is carried out by the Dapartment.

The Department runs residential facilities for the temporary accommodation, care and training of children. These include 9 Community Support Hostels, 23 Hostels mainly for Aboriginal children, 12 Group Homes and 6 Hostels for children released from secure facilities.

There are 3 secure facilities for offenders.

Two centres, one residential and one non-residential, cater for children with behavioural and emotional problems at home and school.

Age, invalid, widows' and war and service pensions are paid by the Federal Government. The number of pensioners in Western Australia at 30 June 1983 was: Age, 105,784; invalid, 18,598; widows, 12,830; and disability, service, 64,357.

Housing. In 1982–83, 9,070 new houses and 4,020 new other dwellings were completed in Western Australia. Of these, the State Housing Commission provided 1,316 new dwelling units for sale and for rental.

The value of dwellings completed during this period was $A515·9m. Additions and alterations valued at $A10,000 or more to dwellings, were valued at $A47·4m.

Books of Reference

Statistical Information: The State Government Statistician's Office was established in 1897 and now functions as the Western Australian Office of the Australian Bureau of Statistics (1–3 St George's Tce, Perth). *Deputy Commonwealth Statistician and Government Statistician:* W. M. Bartlett. Its principal publications are: *Western Australian Year Book* (new series, from 1957). *Western Australian Pocket Year Book* (from 1919). *Monthly Summary of Statistics* (from 1958)

Battye, J. S., *Western Australia: A History from its Discovery to the Inauguration of the Commonwealth.* Oxford, 1924.—*The Cyclopedia of Western Australia.* Adelaide, Vol. 1 (1912), Vol. 2 (1913)
Crowley, F. K., and De Garis, B. K., *A Short History of Western Australia.* Melbourne, 1969
Kimberley, W. B., *History of Western Australia: A Narrative of Her Past.* Melbourne, 1978
Metropolitan Region Planning Authority, *The Corridor Plan for Perth.* Perth, 1970
Stannage, C. T. (ed.) *A New History of Western Australia.* Perth, 1980
Stephenson, G., and Hepburn, J. A., *Plan for the Metropolitan Region: Perth and Fremantle.* Perth, 1955

State Library: The State Library of Western Australia, Perth. *State Librarian:* R. C. Sharman, BA, FLAA.

AUSTRIA

Capital: Vienna
Population: 7·56m. (1981)
GNP per capita: US$10,210 (1981)

Republik Österreich

HISTORY. On 27 April 1945 a provisional government restored the Republic of Austria and was recognized by the Allied Control Council on 20 Oct. 1945.

AREA AND POPULATION. For the boundaries of Austria according to the Treaty of St Germain, signed in Sept. 1919, *see* THE STATESMAN'S YEAR-BOOK, 1920, pp. 674–75.

Federal States	*Area sq. km*	*Population (census 12 May 1981)*	*Percentage of population*	*Population per sq. km*
Vienna (Wien)	415	1,531,346	20·3	3,690
Lower Austria (Niederösterreich)	19,172	1,427,849	18·9	74
Burgenland	3,965	269,771	3·6	68
Upper Austria (Oberösterreich)	11,980	1,269,540	16·8	106
Salzburg	7,154	442,301	5·9	62
Styria (Steiermark)	16,387	1,186,525	15·7	72
Carinthia (Kärnten)	9,533	536,179	7·1	56
Tirol	12,647	586,663	7·8	46
Vorarlberg	2,601	305,164	4·0	117
Total	83,855 [1]	7,555,338	100·0	90

[1] 32,376 sq. miles.

Vital statistics for calendar years:

	Live births	*Still births*	*Deaths* [1]	*Marriages*	*Divorces*	*Emigration Austrians*	*Emigration Others*
1980	90,872	602	92,442	46,435	13,327	15	3,818
1981	93,942	511	92,693	47,768	13,369	9	6,909
1982	94,840	469	91,339	47,643	14,298	32	14,317
1983	90,118	481	93,041	56,171	14,692	24	5,441

[1] Excluding still births.

The population of the principal towns (excluding Vienna), according to the census of 12 May 1981 (area, 12 May 1981) was as follows:

Graz	243,166	Steyr	38,942	Feldkirch	23,745	Mödling	19,276
Linz	199,910	Dornbirn	38,641	Baden	23,140	Lustenau	17,401
Salzburg	139,426	Wiener Neustadt	35,006	Krems a.d.D.	23,056	Braunau am Inn	16,318
Innsbruck	117,287	Leoben	31,989	Klosterneuburg	22,975	Ternitz	16,120
Klagenfurt	87,321	Wolfsberg	28,097	Amstetten	21,989	Hallein	15,377
Villach	52,692	Kapfenberg	25,716	Traun	21,466	Bruck an der Mur	15,068
Wels	51,060	Bregenz	24,561	Leonding	19,389		
St Pölten	50,419						

CLIMATE. Climate ranges from cool temperate to mountain type according to situation. Winters are cold, with considerable snowfall, but summers are very warm. The wettest months are May to August.

Vienna, Jan. 28°F (−2°C), July 67°F (19·5°C). Annual rainfall 25·6″ (640 mm). Graz, Jan. 28°F (−2°C), July 67°F (19·5°C). Annual rainfall 34″ (849 mm). Innsbruck, Inn, 27°F (−2·7°C), July 66°F (18·8°C). Annual rainfall 34·7″ (868 mm). Salzburg, Jan. 28°F (−2·0°C), July 65°F (18·3°C). Annual rainfall 50·6″ (1,266 mm).

CONSTITUTION AND GOVERNMENT. Austria recovered its sovereignty and independence on 27 July 1955 by the coming into force of the Austrian State Treaty between the UK, the USA, the USSR and France on the one part and the Republic of Austria on the other part (signed on 15 May).

On 12 March 1938 Austria was forcibly absorbed in the German Reich until it was liberated by the American, British, French and Soviet armies in spring 1945. Already in the Moscow Declaration of Oct. 1943, UK, the USA and the USSR had resolved upon the re-establishment of a free and independent Austria.

On 27 April 1945 Dr Karl Renner set up a provisional government which restored the Republic of Austria in the spirit of the Constitution of 1920–29, and was recognized by the Four-Power Allied Control Council on 20 Oct. 1945. The last occupation forces left Austria in Oct. 1955.

President of the Republic: Dr Rudolf Kirchschläger, former Minister of Foreign Affairs, elected on 23 June 1974 and re-elected on 18 May 1980.

On 24 April 1983 the elections were held for the National Assembly, which returned 90 Socialists, 81 People's Party, 12 Freedom Party.

The Coalition government between the Socialist Party and the Freedom Party, which was formed in April 1983 was composed as follows in Feb. 1985:

Chancellor: Fred Sinowatz.

Vice-Chancellor and Trade, Commerce and Industry: Norbert Steger. *Finance:* Franz Vranitzky; Holger Bauer *(Minister of State). Social Welfare:* Alfred Dallinger. *Foreign Affairs:* Leopold Gratz. *Interior:* Karl Blecha. *Agriculture and Forestry:* Günther Haiden; Gerulf Murer *(Minister of State). Transport:* Ferdinand Lacina. *Justice:* Harald Ofner. *Trade, Commerce and Industry:* Erich Schmidt *(Minister of State). Defence:* Friedhelm Frischenschlager. *Construction and Technology:* (Vacant); Beatrix Eypeltauer *(Minister of State). Education and the Arts:* Herbert Moritz. *Family, Youth and Consumer Protection:* Gertrude Fröhlich-Sandner. *Science and Research:* Heinz Fischer. *Health and Environment:* Kurt Steyrer. Franz Löschnak *(Minister of State).* Johanna Dohnal *(Minister of State).*

The Federal Council *(Bundesrat)* which represents the federal provinces has 63 members and (1983) the Socialist Party had 31 members and the People's Party 32. The *Nationalrat* and *Bundesrat* together form the National Assembly.

National flag: Three horizontal stripes of red, white, red.

National anthem: Land der Berge, Land am Strome (words by Paula Preradovic; tune by W. A. Mozart).

The official language is German.

Local Government. The Republic of Austria comprises 9 Federal States (Vienna, Lower Austria, Upper Austria, Salzburg, Styria, Carinthia, Tirol, Vorarlberg, Burgenland). There is in every province an elected Provincial Assembly.

Every commune has a Council, which chooses one of its number to be head of the Commune (burgomaster) and a committee for the administration and execution of its resolutions.

DEFENCE. Conscription is for a 6-month period, with liability for 60 days reservist refresher training spread over 15 years.

Army. The Army consists of an alert force *(Bereitschaft truppe)*, mainly the 1st Armoured Division organized in 3 armoured infantry brigades; a mobile militia, comprising 8 motorized infantry brigades; and a stationary militia, comprising 26 regiments and security companies. The country is divided into 2 corps areas, I (Graz) and II (Salzburg). Strength was (1985) 45,300 (29,500 conscripts), and 158,000 reserves.

Army Aviation. *(Heeresfliegerkräfte):* The Army Air Division comprises 12 squadrons with about 4,500 personnel and 166 aircraft, organized in three Aviation Regiments each of which including air defence battalions. About 30 SAAB-105 Oe strike/trainer aircraft equip a surveillance wing of two squadrons with responsibility for defence of Austrian airspace and a fighter-bomber wing of two squadrons. Helicopters equip seven squadrons for transport/support, communications, observation, search and rescue duties. Types in service include Alouette III, armed Kiowa, JetRanger and Agusta-Bell 212. Fixed-wing transports comprise two Skyvans and 12 Turbo-Porters.

INTERNATIONAL RELATIONS

Membership. Austria is a member of UN and EFTA.

External debt. The external debt was (1982) 111·9m. schilling.

ECONOMY

Budget. The budget for calendar years provided revenue and expenditure (ordinary and extraordinary) as follows (in 1m. schilling):

	1978	*1979*	*1980*	*1981*	*1982*	*1983*[1]	*1984*[1]
Revenue	214,872	237,620	259,028	287,791	300,854	325,811	341,842
Expenditure	265,521	288,134	306,492	339,456	372,775	400,078	436,551

[1] Provisional.

Currency. The Austrian unit of currency is the *schilling* of 100 *groschen.* The rate of exchange in Feb. 1985, £1 = 25·58 *schilling,* US$1 = 23·56 *schilling.*

Banking. The National Bank of Austria, opened on 2 Jan. 1923, was taken over by the German Reichsbank on 17 March 1938. It was re-established on 3 July 1945. At 31 Aug. 1984 foreign exchange amounted to 71,237m. and note circulation to 87,857m. schilling.

Weights and Measures. The metric system of weights and measures is in use.

ENERGY AND NATURAL RESOURCES

Electricity. Electric energy produced (1m. kwh.): 1983, 42,625; 1982, 42,891.

Oil. The commercial production of petroleum began in the early 1930s. Production of crude oil (in tonnes): 1960, 2,448,391; 1971, 2,798,237; 1983, 1,268,573.

Minerals. The mineral production (in tonnes) was as follows:

	1982	*1983*		*1982*	*1983*
Lignite	3,297,488	3,041,260	Pig-iron	3,114,985	3,320,260
Iron ore	3,330,000	3,540,000	Raw steel	4,258,156	4,410,907
Lead and zinc ore[1]	841,027	883,134	Rolled steel	3,380,743	3,555,106
Raw magnesite[1]	1,031,404	1,005,768			

[1] Including recovery from slag.

Austria is one of the world's largest sources of high-grade graphite. Production, which averaged 20,000 tonnes yearly from 1929 to 1944, dropped to 246 in 1946, but rose to 102,237 in 1964, and fell again to 23,992 in 1970, 37,199 in 1980, 23,807 in 1981, 24,451 in 1982 and 40,418 in 1983.

Agriculture. In 1982 the total area sown amounted to 1,487,541 hectares.

The chief products (area in hectares, yield in tonnes) were as follows:

	1981		*1982*		*1983*	
	Area	*Yield*	*Area*	*Yield*	*Area*	*Yield*
Wheat	274,286	1,025,011	289,090	1,236,355	312,664	1,415,119
Rye	101,109	320,215	100,118	347,834	93,424	348,323
Barley	362,202	1,219,816	339,802	1,436,543	338,858	1,442,437
Oats	91,544	303,898	91,353	324,831	82,738	291,843
Potatoes	49,639	1,309,779	45,654	1,120,676	40,753	1,014,955

Production of raw sugar in 1949, 66,700; 1955, 219,300; 1960, 308,000; refined sugar: 1970, 298,000; 1980, 419,800, 1981, 446,900; 1982, 563,472 tonnes.

Livestock (1983): Cattle, 2,633,325; pigs, 3,880,662; sheep, 215,775; goats, 32,142; horses, 41,950; poultry, 15,614,206.

Forestry. Felled timber, in cu. metres: 1960, 10,015,925; 1970, 11,122,896; 1980, 12,732,507, 1983, 11,680,056.

INDUSTRY AND TRADE

Industry. On 26 July 1946 the Austrian parliament passed a government bill, nationalizing some 70 industrial concerns. As from 17 Sept. 1946 ownership of the 3 largest commercial banks, most oil-producing and refining companies and the principal firms in the following industries devolved upon the Austrian state: River navigation; coal extraction; non-ferrous mining and refining; iron-ore mining; pig-iron and steel production; manufacture of iron and steel products, including structural material, machinery, railroad equipment and repairs, and shipbuilding; electrical machinery and appliances. Six companies supplying electric power were nationalized in accordance with a law of 26 March 1947.

In 1983, 8,972 industrial establishments (including 2,242 sawmills) employed 573,948 persons, producing a gross output of 563m. schillings.

Commerce. Imports and exports are as follows (excluding coined gold):

	Imports			*Exports*		
	1981	*1982*	*1983*	*1981*	*1982*	*1983*
Quantity (1,000 tonnes)	35,848	34,248	32,906	15,317	15,299	16,505
Value (1m. sch.)	334,510	332,551	348,339	251,769	266,860	277,139

The total trade between Austria and UK (British Department of Trade returns, in £1,000 sterling):

	1980	*1981*	*1982*	*1983*	*1984*
Imports to UK	307,267	347,971	404,318	438,445	529,620
Exports and re-exports from UK	279,681	246,877	251,032	273,702	320,901

Tourism. Tourism is an important industry. In 1983, 21,700 hotels and boarding-houses had a total of 655,598 beds available; 19,913,775 foreigners visited Austria; of these 755,518 came from the UK and 687,116 from the USA.

COMMUNICATIONS

Roads. On 1 Jan. 1977 federal roads had a total length of 10,140 km, 743·2 km autobahn; provincial roads, 22,996 km. On 31 Dec. 1983 there were registered 3,650,446 motor vehicles, including 2,414,466 passenger cars, 197,125 lorries, 351,920 tractors and 233,335 trailers.

Railways. Austrian railways have been nationalized since before the First World War. Length of route (Dec. 1984), 5,759 km, of which 3,123 km were electrified. Twenty private railways have a total length of 562 km. Passengers in 1983 numbered 169m. and 50m. tonnes of freight.

Aviation. Austria has 6 airports in Vienna (Schwechat), Linz, Salzburg, Graz, Klagenfurt and Innsbruck. In 1983, 79,980 aircraft arrived and departed at Austrian airports on commercial air transport.

Shipping. Austria has no sea frontiers, but the Danube is an important waterway. Goods traffic (in tonnes): 6,587,190 in 1980; 6,108,263 in 1981; 5,531,373 in 1982; 5,661,753 in 1983. Ore and metal, coal and coke and iron ore comprise in bulk more than two-thirds of these cargoes. The Danube Steamship Co. (DDSG) is the main Austrian shipping company.

Post and Broadcasting. All postal, telegraph and telephone services are run by the State. In 1983 there were 2,522,401 telephones.

Österreicher Rundfunk transmits 3 regional and 10 local programmes, including one in English and one in French; there is also a 24 hours overseas service. All broadcasting is financed by licence payments and advertisements. There were 2·5m. registered listeners in Jan. 1983. Television was inaugurated in autumn 1955 and 2 programmes are transmitted, both in colour.

Cinemas (1982). There were 528 cinemas.

Newspapers (1983). There were 30 daily newspapers (6 of them in Vienna) with a combined circulation of 2·65m.

JUSTICE, RELIGION, EDUCATION AND WELFARE

Justice. The Supreme Court of Justice *(Oberster Gerichtshof)* in Vienna is the highest court in the land. Besides there are 4 higher provincial courts *(Oberlandesgerichte)*, 20 provincial and district courts *(Landes- und Kreisgerichte)* and 205 local courts *(Bezirksgerichte)*.

Religion. In 1981 there were 6,372,645 Roman Catholics (84·3%), 423,162 Protestants (5·6%), 118,866 others (1·6%), 452,039 without religious allegiance (6%) and 79,017 (1%) unknown. The Roman Catholic Church has 2 archbishoprics and 7 bishoprics.

Education (1983–84). There were in Austria 5,185 elementary and special schools with 66,152 teachers and 735,640 pupils. Of all kinds of secondary schools there were 1,563 with 559,879 pupils.

There were also 105 commercial academies with 35,573 students and 4,601 teachers. There were 215 schools of technical and industrial training (including schools of hotel management and catering) with 6,117 teachers and 58,315 pupils; 45 higher schools of women's professions (secondary level) with 12,662 pupils; 8 training colleges of social workers with 639 pupils. 138 trade schools had 24,274 pupils.

Austria has 12 universities and 6 colleges of arts maintained by the State: Universities at Vienna (2,751 teachers, 50,249 students), Graz (1,080 teachers, 19,390 students), Innsbruck (1,207 teachers, 16,847 students) and Salzburg (465 teachers, 8,773 students). There are also technical universities at Vienna (958 teachers, 11,546 students) and Graz (536 teachers, 6,498 students), a mining university at Leoben (170 teachers, 1,461 students), an agricultural university at Vienna (199 teachers, 3,993 students), a veterinary university at Vienna (167 teachers, 1,844 students), a commercial university at Vienna (222 teachers, 11,347 students), a university for social and economic sciences at Linz (326 teachers, 6,935 students) and a university for educational sciences at Klagenfurt (114 teachers, 2,004 students). There is an academy of fine arts at Vienna (147 teachers, 482 students), a college of applied arts at Vienna (188 teachers, 784 students), 3 colleges of music and dramatic art at Vienna (449 teachers, 2,120 students), 'Mozarteum', Salzburg (304 teachers, 1,119 students) and Graz (248 teachers, 983 students); the college for industrial design at Linz (113 teachers, 360 students).

Health. In 1983 there were 19,513 doctors, 323 hospitals and 83,141 hospital beds.

DIPLOMATIC REPRESENTATIVES

Of Austria in Great Britain (18 Belgrave Mews West, London, SW1X 8HU)
Ambassador: Dr Reginald Thomas (accredited 10 March 1982).

Of Great Britain in Austria (Reisnerstrasse 40, 1030 Vienna)
Ambassador: M. O'D. B. Alexander, CMG.

Of Austria in the USA (2343 Massachusetts Ave., NW, Washington, D.C., 20008)
Ambassador: Dr Thomas Klestil.

Of the USA in Austria (IX Boltzmangasse, 16, A-1091 Vienna)
Ambassador: Helene A. von Damm.

Of Austria to the United Nations
Ambassador: Dr Karl Fischer.

Books of Reference

Statistical Information: The Austrian Central Statistical Office was founded in 1863. *Address:* Neue Burg, Heldenplatz, A-1014 Vienna. *President:* Dr Josef Schmidl. Main publications:
Statistisches Handbuch für die Republik Österreich. New Series from 1950. Annually
Statistische Nachrichten. Monthly
Beiträge zur österreichischen Statistik (585 vols.)
Ergebnisse der Volkszählung vom 12 Mai 1981
Ergebnisse der Häuser- und Wohnungszählung vom 12 Mai 1981
HA-Taschenbuch 75. Annually from 1971
Statistiches Handbuch für die Republik Österreich. Annual.

Bobek, H. (ed.), *Atlas der Republik Österreich.* 3 vols. Vienna, 1961 ff
Österreich Lexikon. Wien-Munchen, 1966
Scheidl, L. G., and Lechleitner, H., *Österreich—Land, Volk, Wirtschaft.* Vienna, 1967
Sotriffer, K., *Greater Austria: 100 Years of Intellectual and Social Life from 1800 to the Present Time.* Vienna, 1982

National Library: Österreichische Nationalbibliothek, Vienna. *Librarian:* Dr Zessner-Spitzenberg.

THE COMMONWEALTH OF THE BAHAMAS

Capital: Nassau
Population: 228,000 (1984)
GNP per capita: US$3,620 (1981)

HISTORY. The Bahamas were discovered by Colombus in 1492 but the Spanish did not make a permanent settlement. British settlers arrived in the 17th century and it was occupied by Britain, except for a short period in the 18th century, until it gained independence.

AREA AND POPULATION. The Commonwealth of the Bahamas consists of 700 islands and more than 1,000 cays off the south-east coast of Florida. They are the surface protuberances of two oceanic banks, the Little Bahama Bank and the Great Bahama Bank. Land area, 5,353 sq. miles (13,864 sq. km).

Principal islands with census population in 1980: New Providence (135,437, containing capital, Nassau), Abaco (7,324), Andros (8,397), Cat Island (2,143), Eleuthera (10,600), Exuma (3,672), Grand Bahama (33,102), Inagua (939), Long Island (3,358). Total census population, with other islands and cays, 209,505. Estimate (1984) 228,000.

Vital statistics, 1977: Births, 4,871; deaths, 1,067 (excluding still-births); marriages, 1,297.

CLIMATE. Winters are mild and summers pleasantly warm. Most rain falls in May, June, Sept. and Oct., and thunderstorms are frequent in summer. Rainfall amounts vary over the islands from 30″ (750 mm) to 60″ (1,500 mm). Nassau. Jan. 71°F (21·7°C), July 81°F (27·2°C). Annual rainfall 47″ (1,179 mm).

CONSTITUTION AND GOVERNMENT. Internal self-government with cabinet responsibility was introduced 7 Jan. 1964.

Qualification for membership of the House of Assembly, under the 1973 Independence Constitution requires that a member shall be a citizen of the Bahamas of the age of 21 years or upwards, and shall have been ordinarily resident in the Bahamas for a period of not less than 1 year immediately before the date of his nomination for election. The Representation of the People's Act provides for adult suffrage. Women are eligible for election to the House of Assembly.

The Constitution of the Commonwealth of the Bahamas (1973) establishes the Bahamas as a free and democratic sovereign state. The constitution is the supreme law of the Bahamas and where any other law is inconsistent with it, the Constitution shall prevail and the other law shall, to the extent of the inconsistency be void.

The Constitution created the office of Governor-General, the holder of which is appointed by Her Majesty. There is a Senate of 16 members, 9 appointed by the Governor-General on the advice of the Prime Minister, 4 appointed by the Governor-General on the advice of the Leader of the Opposition and 3 appointed by the Governor-General on the advice of the Prime Minister after consultation with the Leader of the Opposition. The House of Assembly consists of 43 members. The life of a Parliament is 5 years, but it may be prorogued or dissolved at any time by the Governor-General on the advice of the Prime Minister.

At the elections of 11 June 1982 the Progressive Liberal Party obtained 32 seats and the Free National Movement 8 seats, others 3 seats.

Independence from Britain took place on 10 July 1973.

Governor-General: Sir Gerald Cash, GCMG, KCVO, OBE.

The Cabinet in Oct. 1984 was composed as follows:

Prime Minister, Minister of Economic Affairs: Rt. Hon. Sir Lynden O. Pindling.

External Affairs: Paul Adderley. *Tourism:* Clement Maynard. *Agriculture, Fisheries and Local Government:* Alfred T. Maycock. *Attorney-General and Local Government:* Philip M. Bethel. *Youth, Sports, Culture and Community Affairs:* Livingstone Coakley. *Works, National Insurance and Housing:* Darrell Rolle. *National Security:* A. Loftus Roker.

National flag: Three horizontal stripes of aquamarine, gold, aquamarine, with a black triangle on the hoist.

INTERNATIONAL RELATIONS

Membership. The Commonwealth of the Bahamas is a member of UN, the Commonwealth and an ACP state of EEC.

ECONOMY

Budget (in B$):

	1980	*1981*	*1982*
Revenue	255,257,167	295,923,300	305,100,000
Expenditure	287,408,577	336,339,638	369,700,000

The main sources of revenue were customs duties and receipts from fees, post office and public utilities.

Currency. A decimal system of currency was introduced in 1966. Bahamian $1.05 = £1 sterling (Feb. 1985). Notes: $0.50, 1, 3, 5, 10, 20, 50, 100; coins: 1, 5, 10, 15, 25, 50 cents, $1, 2, 5. Sterling currency has been withdrawn. American currency is generally accepted.

Bank of England and Canadian notes are not accepted, except at the banks from travellers from the UK.

Banking. The Central Bank of the Bahamas was established in June 1974 with assets (Dec. 1980) of B$154·95m. and capital and reserves of B$29·98m. Among these were the Royal Bank of Canada, the Bank of Nova Scotia, the Bank of Montreal, Chase Manhattan Bank, Barclays Bank International, the Canadian Imperial Bank of Commerce and Citibank. While the majority of banks are located in Nassau, there are branches on several of the other islands. The Bahamas Development Bank was established in 1974 and began operations in Jan. 1978; at Dec. 1980 it had total assets of B$7·45m. and paid-up capital of B$6m.

On 31 Dec. 1980 there were 314 institutions licensed to carry on banking and/or trust business under the Banks and Trust Companies Regulations Act. There were 17 designated institutions by the Exchange Control Department as authorized dealers and agents.

The post office savings bank, 31 Dec. 1980, had deposits of B$2·2m

Weights and Measures. The UK (Imperial) system is in force.

ENERGY AND NATURAL RESOURCES

Electricity. Electricity for lighting and power is available in New Providence, Grand Bahama and the Family Islands. Total units generated in New Providence/Paradise Island and Family Islands in 1979–80, 390m. kwh.

Agriculture. There were (1978) 4,246 agricultural holdings or parcels of farm land in the Bahamas, totalling 89,565 acres. About 40% of these holdings are cultivated with temporary and permanent crops. Livestock operations within the Bahamas are predominantly sheep and goat enterprises.

Several agricultural programmes exist to further stimulate agricultural production. Some of these programmes are subsidized by government and include land clearing and duty free importation of trucks and other farm implements. Farmers also have access to 2 credit programmes: a) The Agricultural Credit Guarantee Fund; b) The Stores on Credit Programme.

Total agricultural production including fisheries was valued at about B$30m. in 1980.

Livestock (1983): Cattle, 4,000; sheep, 38,000; goats, 18,000; pigs, 19,000; poultry, 1m.

Forestry. Production of cascarilla bark and pulp-wood in 1976 was B$1·8m., all of which was exported.

Fisheries. Crawfish exports were valued at B$12m. in 1982.

INDUSTRY AND TRADE

Industry. Tourism is the major industry. Several light industries have been established on Grand Bahama and New Providence in response to special encouragement legislation; these include garment manufacturing, ice, furniture, purified water, plastic containers, perfumes, industrial gases, jewellery and others. Larger industrial activities in the Bahamas include oil refining, oil transhipment, manufacture of alcoholic beverages, pharmaceuticals, aragonite mining, solar salt production and cement. Two industrial sites, one in New Providence and the other in Grand Bahama, have been developed as part of the industrialization programme.

Commerce. The principal exports in 1980 were hormones, rum, salt, crawfish, cement, aragonite and plywood.

The principal imports in 1977 were: Food, drink and tobacco, raw materials and articles mainly unmanufactured, articles wholly or mainly manufactured, animals not for food.

Imports and exports (excluding bullion and specie) for 6 calendar years in B$:

	Imports	*Exports*		*Imports*	*Exports*
1977	2,787,943	2,597,352	1980	5,506,577	4,836,366
1978	2,482,235	2,117,938	1981	4,203,000	3,515,000
1979	3,985,034	3,495,043	1982	3,051,000	2,444,000

The Bahamas became affiliated with CARIFTA (now CARICOM) in 1968.

Total trade between Bahamas and UK, in £1,000 sterling (British Department of Trade returns):

	1980	*1981*	*1982*	*1983*	*1984*
Imports to UK	59,123	30,915	18,273	24,013	38,478
Exports and re-exports from UK	77,366	171,347	26,364	17,815	220,356

Tourism. Tourism is the most important industry in the Bahamas. It accounts for approximately 58% of government revenue and 66% of employment. In 1982 there were 1,947,742 foreign arrivals in the Bahamas.

COMMUNICATIONS

Roads. There are 240 miles of paved roads in New Providence, and 426 miles in Grand Bahama. The other major islands have 400 miles of motorable roads. In 1978, 51,290 motor vehicles were registered. There are no railroads.

Aviation. Nassau international airport is located on the island of New Providence, about 10 miles from the city of Nassau. There is another international airport at Freeport. Scheduled flights—Air Canada: 3 times weekly from Toronto and once weekly from Montreal to Nassau; twice weekly from Toronto to Freeport and once weekly from Montreal to Freeport. Delta: twice daily from New York to Nassau; once daily from Boston and Newark. Eastern Airlines: 3 flights daily from New York, 3 times daily from Miami, once daily from Fort Lauderdale, twice weekly from Baltimore, Washington and Philadelphia, once daily from Boston and Newark, once daily from New York *via* Miami and Fort Lauderdale to Nassau; 3 times daily from Miami, once daily from Baltimore and Philadelphia to Freeport: Lufthansa: 3 times weekly from Frankfurt and Mexico and once weekly from Merida to Nassau. Air Jamaica: once daily from Chicago, Kingston and Montego Bay to Nassau. American Airlines: once daily from New York to Nassau and 4 times weekly from New York to Freeport. British Airways: 4 times weekly from London and Bermuda, twice weekly from Kingston and Panama and once weekly from Mexico City, all to Nassau; once weekly from London, Bermuda, Kingston and Panama to Freeport. There are numerous domestic schedules to the Family Islands and Florida. There are 53 airstrips on the various Family Islands and numerous water alighting areas. During 1977, 494,263 passengers landed at

Nassau and 38,840 aircraft arrivals. At Freeport in 1977, 407,772 passengers landed from 41,799 aircraft arrivals.

Shipping. In 1980, 678 cruise liners cleared Nassau carrying 499,527 passengers; 653 cargo vessels discharged 268,477 tons of cargo at Nassau. There are indirect cargo services with UK and Canada *via* the USA and passenger services with the USA only.

Telecommunications. New Providence and all the major islands have automatic telephone systems of the latest type in operation, together with an extensive system of underground cables. The total number of telephones in use at 1 Jan. 1982 was 75,071; 170 radio-telephone channels provide service *via* the USA to any part of the world. In 1971 direct dialling was introduced to the USA and in 1973 to Canada. All the important islands are connected with Nassau by means of radio-telegraphy, and in most cases radio-telephony is also available. Connexion through Nassau to the UK, the USA, Canada and Central America can be provided. Radio-teletype to Bermuda and Florida and ship-shore radio-telephone services are also available. Radio-teletype service is provided from Nassau to Freeport and West End in Grand Bahama. In 1976 a fully automated Telex exchange came into service. The Bahamas broadcasting station operates on 1,540, 1,240 and 810 kc.

Cinemas (1977). There are 16 cinemas and 3 drive-ins.

Newspapers (1985). There are 2 daily and 1 weekly newspapers in Nassau.

JUSTICE, EDUCATION AND WELFARE

Justice (1977). 9,655 cases (traffic, 3,550; criminal, 3,218; civil, 1,880; domestic, 1,007) were dealt with in the magistrates' court, and civil, 816; divorce, 256 in the Supreme Court. The strength of the police force (1973) was 932 officers and other ranks.

Education. Education is under the jurisdiction of the Ministry of Education and Culture. In 1980–81 there were 227 schools, and of these, 187 are fully maintained by Government and 40 are independent schools. Total school enrolment, 61,160. There are 38 government-owned schools in New Providence and 149 on the Family Islands. 24 independent schools are located on New Providence and 12 on the Family Islands. 181 students attended 4 special schools, 3 on New Providence and 1 on Grand Bahama; total staff, 38. Free education is available in ministry schools in New Providence and the Family Islands. Courses lead to the Bahamas Junior Certificate and the General Certificate of Education (GCE).

Independent schools provide education at primary, secondary and higher levels. Several schools of continuing education offer secretarial and academic courses. The Government-operated Princess Margaret Hospital offers a nursing course at two levels. The College of the Bahamas was established in 1974. It provides a 2- or 3-year programme leading to an associate degree in any of the 7 academic divisions. Several college degree programmes are offered in conjunction with the University of the West Indies and the University of Miami. The Hotel Training College offers a wide range of subjects up to middle management level in aspects of hotel work. Enrolment in this institution includes Bahamian as well as regional and international students.

Health. In 1980 there was a government general hospital in Nassau (460 beds) and 1 in Freeport (50). Grand Bahama has 4 clinics, 3 staffed by district medical officers and 1 by a nurse and the Family Islands have about 50 health centres. There are 2 private hospitals. Dental treatment is provided for smaller islands by a flying dentist service. There are 122 doctors, 387 nurses, 8 midwives and 5 dentists in the government service. There are many private doctors, dentists, nurses and midwives providing health care on a fee basis.

DIPLOMATIC REPRESENTATIVES

Of the Bahamas in Great Britain (39 Pall Mall, London, SW1Y 5JG)
High Commissioner: Richard C. Demerite (accredited 24 Oct. 1984).

Of Great Britain in the Bahamas (Bitco Bldg., East St., Nassau)
High Commissioner: Peter William Heap.

Of the Bahamas in the USA (600 New Hampshire Ave., NW, Washington, D.C., 20037)
Ambassador: Reginald L. Wood, CBE.

Of the USA in the Bahamas (Queen St., Nassau)
Ambassador: Lev E. Dobriansky.

Of the Bahamas to the United Nations
Ambassador: Dr Davidson L. Hepburn.

Books of Reference

Bahamas Handbook and Businessman's Annual (Annual)
Albury, P., *The Story of the Bahamas.* London, 1975.—*Paradise Island Story.* London, 1984
Barrett, P. J. H., *Grand Bahama.* London, 1982
Craton, M. A., *A History of the Bahamas.* London, 1962
Hughes, C. A., *Race and Politics in the Bahamas.* Univ. of Queensland Press, 1981
Hunte, G., *The Bahamas.* London, 1975

Library: Nassau Public Library.

BAHRAIN

Capital: Manama
Population: 384,221 (1983)
GNP per capita: US$8,960 (1981)

HISTORY. Treaties with Britain of 1882 and 1892 were replaced by a treaty of friendship which was signed on 15 Aug. 1971. Under the earlier treaties Britain had been responsible for Bahrain's defence and foreign relations. On the same day Bahrain declared its independence.

AREA AND POPULATION. The Bahrain islands form an archipelago in the Arabian Gulf, between the Qatar peninsula and the mainland of Saudi Arabia. The total area is about 255 sq. miles. Bahrain ('Two Seas'), largest island, is 30 miles long and 10 miles wide. Muharraq, to the north-east, 4 miles long and 1 mile wide, is connected with Bahrain by a causeway, nearly 1·5 miles long, carrying a motor road. Other islands are Sitra, to the east, 3 miles long and 1 mile wide; Umm An-Nassan, to the west, 3 miles by 2 miles; Jidda, also to the west, 1 mile by 0·5 mile, the Hawar group off Qatar and several islets, some uninhabited. From Sitra oil pipelines and a causeway carrying a road extend out to sea for 3 miles to a deep-water anchorage. The islands are low lying, the highest ground being a hill in the centre of Bahrain, 450 ft high.

The population in 1981 (census) was 350,798. Estimate (1983) 384,221. The majority of the people are Moslem Arabs.

Manama, the capital of the state and the commercial centre, is situated at the northern end of the largest island and extends for 1·5 miles along the shore. It has a population of 121,986 (1981 census). Electricity from the government power-station in Manama supplies light and power in Manama, Muharraq (61,853, 1981 census), Hidd (7,111), Rifa'a (28,150) and Isa Town (21,275) and the villages. Water is obtained from artesian wells and desalination plants, and there is a piped supply in Manama, Muharraq, Isa Town, Rifa'a and most villages.

CLIMATE. The climate is pleasantly warm between Nov. and March but from June to Sept. the conditions are very hot and humid. The period June to Nov. is virtually rainless. Bahrain. Jan. 66°F (19°C), July 97°F (36°C). Annual rainfall 5·2" (130 mm).

CONSTITUTION AND GOVERNMENT. A Constitution was ratified in June 1973 providing for a National Assembly of 30 members, popularly elected for a 4-year term, together with all members of the Cabinet (appointed by the Amir). Elections took place in Dec. 1973, but in Aug. 1975 the Amir dissolved the Assembly and has since ruled through the Cabinet alone.

Reigning Amir: The ruling family, the Al Khalifa, an Arab dynasty, who have been in power since 1782. The present Amir, HH Shaikh Isa bin Sulman Al Khalifa (born 1933) succeeded on 2 Nov. 1961. *Crown Prince and Minister of Defence:* Shaikh Hamed bin Isa Al Khalifa.

In Jan. 1985 the cabinet was composed as follows:

Prime Minister: Shaikh Khalifa bin Sulman Al-Khalifa.

Defence: Shaikh Hamed bin Isa Al-Khalifa. *Transport:* Ibrahim Mohammed Hassan Homaidan. *Housing:* Shaikh Khalid bin Abdulla Al-Khalifa. *Information:* Tariq Abdulrahman Almoayed. *Education:* Dr Ali Fakhro. *Health:* Jawad Salim Al-Arrayed. *Justice and Islamic Affairs:* Shaikh Abdullah bin Khalid Al-Khalifa. *Labour and Social Affairs:* Shaikh Khalifa bin Salman bin Mohammed Al-Khalifa. *Works, Power and Water:* Majid Jawad Al Jishi. *Interior:* Shaikh Mohammed bin Khalifa Al-Khalifa. *Foreign Affairs:* Shaikh Mohammed bin Mubarak Al-Khalifa. *Finance and National Economy:* Ebrahim Abdul-Karim. *Development and Industry:* Yusuf Ahmed Al-Shirawi. *Commerce and Agriculture:*

Habib Ahmed Qassim. *Acting Minister of State for Cabinet Affairs:* Yusuf Ahmed Al-Shirawi. *Minister of State for Legal Affairs:* Dr Hussain Al Baharna.

Flag: Red, with white serrated vertical strip on hoist.

DEFENCE

Army. The Army consists of 1 infantry battalion, 1 armoured car squadron, 1 artillery and 2 mortar batteries with a personnel strength of 2,300 (1985). Equipment included 8 Saladin armoured cars and 8 Ferret scout cars.

Navy. The Naval force consists of 2 fast missile craft and 2 fast gunboats; personnel (1985) 300. There is also a Coast Guard with 20 coastal patrol craft.

Air Wing. Formed in 1977. The only operational equipment (1984) was 3 MBB BO 105s. Police and security forces both also operate helicopters.

INTERNATIONAL RELATIONS

Membership. Bahrain is a member of UN, the Arab League, the Gulf Co-operation Council and OAPEC.

ECONOMY

Budget. The revenue of the State is derived from oil royalties and from customs duties, which are 10% *ad valorem* for luxury goods and 5% for essential goods. The exceptions are motor vehicles (20%); tobacco (30%); alcoholic beverages (100%); fresh fruit and vegetables (7%). Total revenues in 1982, BD 556·1m.; 1983, BD 484·8m.

On 2 Jan. 1958 Manama was declared a free transit port and the former 2% transit duty was abolished, but storage charges are levied.

Currency. The Bahrain *dinar* is divided into 1,000 *fils*. The Bahrain currency board issues notes of 10, 5, 1 and ½ *dinars*, and coins of 100, 50, 25 and 5 *fils*. £1 = BD 0·408 in Feb. 1985; US$1 = BD 0·377.

Banking. The Bahrain Monetary Agency has central banking powers. Other banking facilities are provided by the National Bank of Bahrain, the Bank of Bahrain and Kuwait and branches of the Chartered Bank, the British Bank of the Middle East, the Arab Bank, Habib Bank (Overseas), United Bank, Citibank, Banque du Caire, Chase Manhattan, Grindlays Bank, Bank Melli Iran, Algemene Bank, Bank Saderet Iran, Bank Paribas, National Bank of Abu Dhabi, Rafidain Bank, Bahrain Saudi Bank, Al-Ahli Commercial Bank. In Dec. 1983 there were 163 licensed banks and there were (1984) 75 licensed units of offshore banking facilities.

Weights and Measures. The metric system of weights and measures is officially in use.

ENERGY AND NATURAL RESOURCES

Electricity. Production (1980) 1,290m. kwh.

Oil. In 1931 oil was discovered. Operations were conducted by the Bahrain Petroleum Co., registered in Canada but owned by US interests, under a concession granted by the Shaikh. Production of crude oil in 1983 was 15·3m. bbls. A large oil refinery on Bahrain Island, besides treating crude oil produced locally, also processes oil from Saudi Arabia transported by pipeline.

In 1975 the Bahrain Government assumed a direct 60% interest in the Bahrain oilfield and related crude oil facilities of BAPCO. Bahrain's gas reserves are 100% government-owned.

Under the terms of the agreement signed between Bahrain and Saudi Arabia in 1958, Bahrain will receive 50% of the profits on any oil produced in the Abu Saafa area of sea between Bahrain and Saudi Arabia. Aramco, which is responsible for the development of this field, began production in 1966.

Gas. There is an abundant supply of natural gas with known reserves of 9,000,000m. cu. ft. Production, 1982, 130,507m. cu. ft.

INDUSTRY AND TRADE

Industry. Bahrain is being developed as a major manufacturing state, the first important enterprise being the Aluminium Bahrain Smelter, a company whose original shareholders included the Bahrain Government and British, Swedish, Federal German and US interests. In 1975, the government acquired a majority shareholding in the enterprise. The aluminium operation is the largest non-oil industry in the Gulf. Ancillary industries developed around aluminium smelting include the production of aluminium powder. Other projects at present under consideration include the further development of marine industries. The Arab Shipbuilding and Repair Yard (ASRY), commissioned in 1977, is now in service. The dry dock can handle up to 50 tankers (550,000 DWT each) annually. A US$207m. iron ore pelletizing plant was inaugurated in Dec. 1984 and a US$400m. petrochemical complex will go on-stream in 1985.

In addition to the traditional minor industries such as boat-building, weaving, pottery, etc., other modern industries have developed, which include the manufacture of building materials, furniture, soft drinks, drinking straws, paper bags, woollen garments, plastic and other consumer goods. There is also an important fishing industry and a fairly large farming community. The most important crops are dates and vegetables, and there is also poultry farming.

Livestock (1981): Cattle, 6,000; sheep, 7,000; goats, 15,000; poultry, 790,000.

The pearling industry for which Bahrain used to be famous has considerably declined. Only about 10 boats visit the pearl banks each year, as compared with the 600–1,000 that were employed 30 years ago.

Commerce. In 1983 imports totalled BD 1,226·4m.; exports and re-exports, non-oil, BD 200m. Total exports, BD 1,172·9m. Chief imports were manufactured goods, machinery and transport equipment, food and live animals, chemicals.

Import of arms and ammunition and telecommunication equipment is subject to special permission; the sale of alcoholic liquor is restricted and the import of cultured pearls is forbidden.

Total trade between Bahrain and UK (British Department of Trade returns, in £1,000 sterling):

	1980	*1981*	*1982*	*1983*	*1984*
Imports to UK	25,063	16,713	35,459	37,488	28,240
Exports and re-exports from UK	115,569	102,337	152,272	150,264	138,614

COMMUNICATIONS

Roads. In 1984 there were 94,700 registered vehicles.

Aviation. The airport, situated at Muharraq, can take the largest aircraft and is considered one of the most modern and efficient in the Middle East. British Airways, Gulf Air, Middle East Airlines, Pakistan International Airways, Qantas, Kuwait Airways, Air India International, Singapore Airlines, UTA, Saudi Arabian Airlines, KLM, Air Lanka, Cathay Pacific Airways, Iraqi Airways, Korean Airways, Philippine Airlines, Thai Airways International, Trans-Mediterranean Airways, Egyptair, Alia, Cyprus Airways, Ethiopia Airlines and Sudan Airways also operate to and from Bahrain. Bahrain International Airport is the Arabian Gulf's main air communication centre.

Shipping. Bahrain's traditional position as the entrepôt of the Southern Gulf has been supplemented by the development of Mina Sulman—the new modern harbour—as a free transit and industrial area. Local and international companies have developed industries in this area, which is also used as a storage centre for firms selling elsewhere in the Gulf. The facilities offered by Mina Sulman include engineering and ship repairing yards; the Basrec slipway is probably the largest between Rotterdam and Hong Kong.

Post and Broadcasting. There were, at Oct. 1984, 63,618 telephones. There is a state-operated radio and television station and in 1978 there were 93,500 radio and 80,000 television receivers.

Newspapers. In 1984 there were several Arabic and 2 English language newspapers (one weekly and one daily) published in Manama.

JUSTICE, RELIGION, EDUCATION AND WELFARE

Justice. Criminal law is codified, based on English jurisprudence.

Religion. In 1981 85% of the population were Moslem and 7·3% Christian.

Education. There were, in 1981–82, 125 state schools for boys and girls with 3,405 teachers and 71,177 pupils. Five boys' general and commercial schools had 2,177 pupils; 3 boys' industrial schools at secondary level, had 1,306 pupils. In addition there were 7 private schools. The Men's Teacher Training College (established 1966) and the Women's Teacher Training College (established 1967) give 2-year courses. In 1981–82, 2,619 Bahrainis were in higher education abroad. The Gulf Technical College opened in Bahrain in Sept. 1968 and Bahrain University in 1978. In 1981–82, 35 adult literacy centres were opened throughout Bahrain.

Health. There is a free medical service for all residents of Bahrain. In 1981–82, there were 45 government hospitals and health centres with 1,056 beds, an American mission hospital, an oil company hospital, a military hospital and an international hospital.

Social Security. In Oct. 1976, pensions, sickness and industrial injury benefits, unemployment, maternity and family allowances were established.

DIPLOMATIC REPRESENTATIVES

Of Bahrain in Great Britain (98 Gloucester Rd., London, SW7 4AU)
Ambassador: Salman Abdul Wahab Al Sabbagh (accredited 19 Dec. 1984).

Of Great Britain in Bahrain (21 Government Rd., P.O. Box 114, Manama)
Ambassador: F. S. E. Trew, CMG.

Of Bahrain in the USA (3502 International Dr., NW, Washington D.C., 20008)
Ambassador: Ghazi Mohammed Al-Gosaibi.

Of the USA in Bahrain (Shaikh Isa Road, P.O. Box 26431, Manama)
Ambassador: Donald Leidel.

Of Bahrain to the United Nations
Ambassador: Hussain Rashid Al-Sabbagh.

Books of Reference

Bahrain Business Directory. Manama (annual)
Statistical and General Information: Ministry of Information, PO Box 253, Manama
Statistical Abstract. Central Statistics Organisation (annual)

Belgrave, J. H. D., *Welcome to Bahrain.* 9th ed. Manama, 1975
Rumaihi, M. G., *Bahrain: Social and Political Change since the First World War.* New York and London, 1976
Unwin, P. T. H., *Bahrain.* [Bibliography]. London and Santa Barbara, 1984

BANGLADESH

People's Republic of Bangladesh

Capital: Dhaka
Population: 96m. (1983)
GNP per capita: US$140 (1981)

HISTORY. The state was formerly the Eastern Province of Pakistan. In Dec. 1970 Sheikh Mujibur Rahman's Awami League Party gained 167 seats out of 300 at the Pakistan general election and immediately made known their wish for greater independence for the then Eastern Province. Martial law was imposed following disturbances in Dhaka, and civil war developed in March 1971. The war ended in Dec. 1971 and Bangladesh was proclaimed an independent state.

AREA AND POPULATION. Bangladesh is bounded west and north-west by West Bengal (India), north by Assam and Meghalaya (India), east by Assam, Tripura (India) and Burma, south by the Bay of Bengal. The area is 55,598 sq. miles (143,999 sq. km). Bangladesh's population (1981 census), 87,120,000. An adjustment for underenumeration produced a revised census figure of 89,940,000. Population estimate, 1983, 96m. Growth rate (1983–84), 2·6%. Birth-rate 40·5 per 1,000, death-rate 15·5. The capital is Dhaka (population, 1981, 3,440,147) and its ports are Chittagong (1,391,877) and Khulna (646,359). Other large cities are Rajshahi (253,740) and Barisal (142,098). There are 21 districts:

	Area (sq. km)	*Population 1981*		*Area (sq. km)*	*Population 1981*
Dinajpur	6,566	3,198,000	Kushtia	3,440	2,292,000
Rangpur	9,593	6,510,000	Jessore	6,573	4,020,000
Bogra	3,888	2,728,000	Khulna	12,168	4,329,000
Rajshahi	9,456	5,270,000	Barisal	7,299	4,667,000
Pabna	4,732	3,424,000	Patuakhali	4,095	1,843,000
Rajshahi division	*34,238*	*21,132,000*	Khulna division	*33,575*	*17,151,000*
Tangail	3,403	2,444,000	Sylhet	12,718	5,656,000
Mymensingh	9,668	6,568,000	Comilla	6,599	6,881,000
Jamalpur	3,349	2,452,000	Noakhali	5,460	3,816,000
Dhaka	7,470	10,014,000	Chittagong	7,457	5,491,000
Faridpur	6,882	4,764,000	Chittagong Hill Tracts	8,679	580,000
Dhaka division	*30,772*	*26,242,000*	Bandarban	4,501	171,000
			Chittagong division	*45,414*	*22,595,000*

The official language is Bangla.

CLIMATE. A tropical monsoon climate with heat, extreme humidity and heavy rainfall in the monsoon season, from June to Sept. The short winter season is mild and dry. Rainfall varies between 50″ (1,250 mm) in the west to 100″ (2,500 mm) in the south-east and up to 200″ (5,000 mm) in the north-east. Dhaka. Jan. 66°F (19°C), July 84°F (28·9°C). Annual rainfall 81″ (2,025 mm). Chittagong. Jan. 66°F (19°C), July 81°F (27·2°C). Annual rainfall 108″ (2,831 mm).

GOVERNMENT AND CONSTITUTION. Bangladesh is a republic. The Constitution came into force on 16 Dec. 1972 and provided for a parliamentary democracy. On 25 Jan. 1975 Sheikh Mujibur Rahman took on the office of President, with an advisory Parliament. All political parties were abolished, and replaced by the new Bangladesh Krisha Sramik Awami League. On 15 Aug. 1975 Sheikh Mujibur Rahman and his family were killed; martial law was introduced on

20 Aug. and political parties were banned (including the new BKSAL) on 30 Aug. K. M.Ahmed was installed as President on 15 Aug. and replaced on 7 Nov. by former Chief Justice A. M. Sayem. Elections to parliament were promised for Feb. 1977 but postponed indefinitely in 1976. Political parties were made legal once again and requested to apply for registration in Aug. 1976.

On 29 Nov. 1976 Maj.-Gen. Ziaur Rahman became Chief Martial Law Administrator, with the Chiefs of Naval and Air Staff as his deputies. On 21 April 1977 President Sayem resigned and Maj.-Gen. Ziaur Rahman was sworn in as President. On 22 April 1977 the constitution of 1972 was amended to establish 'absolute trust and faith in Allah' as the first fundamental principle of state and to provide for a Supreme Judicial Council which would prescribe a code of conduct for judges and advise the President. Three political parties (JSD, Bangladesh Communist Party (pro-Soviet) and Democratic League) were dissolved in Oct. 1977. The President was confirmed in office by general election. Martial law ended in April 1979. President Ziaur Rahman was murdered by a group of army officers on 30 May 1981. Mr Justice Abdus Sattar was installed as Acting President and elected president in Nov. 1981.

A Presidential election was held on 15 Nov. 1981, resulting in a victory for Mr Justice Abdus Sattar.

On 23 March 1982 there was a bloodless military *coup*, by which Lieut.-Gen. Hossain Mohammad Ershad became chief martial law administrator. President Sattar was deposed. The Constitution was suspended and parliament ceased to function. Lieut.-Gen. Ershad, the commander of the army, said that a temporary military government was necessary to restore economic and social order and democratic civilian government would return as soon as possible. Assanuddin Chowdhury was sworn in as civilian president on 27 March. Lieut-Gen. Ershad assumed the presidency on 11 Dec. 1983.

Parliament has one chamber of 300 members directly elected every 5 years by citizens over 18. There are 30 seats reserved for women members elected by Parliament.

President and Chief Martial Law Administrator: Lieut.-Gen. Hossain Mohammad Ershad.

On 16 Jan. 1985 Lieut.-Gen. Ershad announced a relaxation of martial law, pending general elections which were to be held in April, however these were abandoned on 1 March 1985 and martial law was reimposed.

Lieut.-Gen. Ershad announced that a referendum would be held on 21 March 1985, to seek a vote of confidence on his continuance as President. The result was positive but disputed.

National flag: Bottle green with a red disc in the centre.

National anthem: Amar Sonar Bangla, ami tomay bhalobashi (My golden Bengal, I love you). Words by Rabindranath Tagore.

DEFENCE

Army. There are 5 infantry divisional headquarters, with 12 infantry brigades, and 2 armoured and 9 artillery regiments, and 7 engineer battalions. Strength (1985) 73,000, with an additional 80,000 paramilitary volunteers, including an armed police reserve and the Bangladesh Rifles. Equipment includes 30 Soviet T-54 and 20 Chinese Type-59 tanks.

Navy. Naval bases are at Chittagong (handed over by India on 14 Feb. 1972), Kaptai, Khulna and Dacca.

The fleet comprises 3 former British frigates (*Ali Hyder, ex*-HMS *Jaguar*, and *Abu Bakr*, *ex*-HMS *Lynx*, each 2,520 tons full load, transferred in July 1978 and March 1982, respectively, and *Umar Farooq, ex*-HMS *Llandaff*, 2,408 tons full load, transferred in Dec 1976); 1 new Chinese-built 390-ton fast attack craft, 2 *ex*-Yugoslav 200-ton patrol vessels, 8 *ex*-Chinese 155-ton fast gunboats, 2 *ex*-Indian 150-ton patrol craft, 1 British-built 140-ton patrol craft, 5 indigenously built

70-ton river gunboats, 1 support ship, 1 repair vessel and 1 training ship of 710 tons.

The manpower of the Navy in 1984 was 5,800, comprising 400 officers and 5,400 ratings.

Air Force. Deliveries, from the Soviet Union and China successively, have built up a current strength of about 30 J-6 (MiG-19) fighter-bombers; 1 An-24 and 3 An-26 turboprop transports; about 16 Mi-8, Bell 212 and Alouette III helicopters; 12 Chinese CJ-6 piston-engined primary trainers, 5 FT-2 (MiG-17) jet advanced trainers, 6 Magister armed jet trainers and some light aircraft. Personnel strength, 3,000.

INTERNATIONAL RELATIONS

Membership. Bangladesh is a member of the UN and all its related agencies, of the Colombo Plan and of the Islamic Conference.

External Debt. Estimated debt, Dec. 1981, US$4,000m. Most of this was in loans from the Western aid group through the World Bank.

Treaties. Bangladesh signed an economic and technical co-operation agreement with China on 4 Jan. 1977. The amended constitution of 1977 states that Bangladesh seeks fraternal relations with Moslem countries based on Islamic solidarity.

ECONOMY

Planning. The development budget for 1983–84 was allocated mainly to power (Tk.5,765m.); agriculture (Tk.4,758m.); water resources (Tk.4,696m.); industry (Tk.3,326m.); transport (Tk.2,859m.).

The second 5-year plan was launched in 1980, as part of a 20-year perspective plan; it aims at an annual growth rate of 7·2% (food-grain production, 7%, manufacturing 8·6%).

Budget. Details were as follows for the financial year 1983–84 (Tk.1m.):

Revenue receipts	*30,330*	*Expenditure*	*25,030*
Customs duties	10,000	Defence	4,271
Income and corporation tax	3,310	Education	3,652
Excise duties	6,000	Subsidies, grants and relief	2,632
Sales tax	3,450	Interest on domestic and foreign debt	2,743
Non-tax revenue	5,929		

Money supply (March 1984) stood at Tk.32,432m. and foreign exchange reserves at Tk.14,028m.

Currency. A new currency, the *Taka*, was floated in 1976 (Tk.27·85 = £1 and Tk.26·54 = US$1 in Feb. 1985).

Banking. The former private banking system, except for foreign banks, has been nationalized. Total bank deposits in March 1984 were Tk.60,592m.

Weights and Measures. Imperial measures are in use. Weight is in the *seer* (1 *seer* = 2 lb.); the *maund* (1 *maund* = 40 *seers*) and the ton. The metric system was to be introduced from July 1982.

ENERGY AND NATURAL RESOURCES

Electricity. Electric power is generated and distributed by the Bangladesh Power Development Board and the Rural Electrification Board. Production was not significant in 1983.

Water. On 5 Nov. 1977 India and Bangladesh signed an agreement on sharing the water of the river Ganges. The flow will be monitored daily at the Farakka barrage and two other points.

Oil. Supplies have been located in the Bay of Bengal. Drilling is in progress.

Gas. Natural gas from Titas is piped to Dhaka; drilling is in progress at other sites, and reserves are considered sufficient for 200 years. Production, 1981, 145m. cu. ft. per day.

Minerals. Coal has been found at Jamalpur (about 700m. tons). Other minerals include salt (750,000 tonnes in 1975), limestone, white clay, glass sand. The Rajshahi area has known reserves of deep-lying coal. In 1979 the Saudi fund for Development invested US$30m. for a limestone and cement project at Jaipurhat.

Agriculture. Agriculture contributes about 54% of GDP (Tk. 37,512m. in 1981–82) and employs about 80% of the economically active population; 64% of the total area is under cultivation; 80% of that is under rice and 9% under jute. Cultivable waste is about 1·5m. acres. About 2m. acres (1981–82) is irrigated. Rice is the most important food crop; production in 1983–84, 14·3m. tons. Other crops (1,000 tons): Sugar-cane, 6,986; wheat, 1,191; tobacco, 51,700; tea, 95m. lb.; potatoes, 11·5m. lb.

Livestock in 1983 (1,000): Poultry, 75,000; cattle, 36,000; goats, 12,000; sheep, 1m.; buffalo, 1·7m. Livestock products in 1981 (tonnes): beef and veal, 120,900; cow and buffalo milk, 705,000; goats' milk, 507,000; eggs, 1·4m.

Bangladesh produces about 70% of the world production of raw jute which is the principal foreign exchange earner. Production, 1983–84, 5·2m. tons.

Forestry. The total area under forests (1977) is 9,283 sq. miles, of which 5,105 sq. miles are Reserved Forests. The output of roundwood timber in 1980 (1,000 cu. metres): sawlogs, veneer logs and sleepers, 555; pulpwood, 63; fuel wood, 9,754.

Fisheries. Being bounded on the south by the Bay of Bengal and having numerous rivers, streams, khals and bils, the state is pre-eminently a fish-producing area and possesses great possibilities for the manufacture of various oils and fish products. Fish production, 1980–81, 640,000 tons, of which 517,000 was from inland water.

INDUSTRY AND TRADE

Industry. Out of the existing industries, the textile-mills, sugar factories, match factories, glass works, hosiery factories, a paper-mill, jute-mills, aluminium works and a cement factory, with a capacity of 2m. tons per annum, are the most prominent. New government policy in 1982 aimed to restore public-sector jute and textile mills to private ownership and encourage the private sector. Arms and ammunition, atomic energy, forestry, air transport, communications and electrical industries would remain in the public sector.

Refinery distillation capacity, 1·68m. tonnes. There is a steel mill at Chittagong with a capacity of 250,000 ingot-tons per annum. There is also a newsprint factory, 4 fertilizer factories, a shipyard, a dockyard and a liquified natural gas plant. Industry employs about 7% of the active population and provides 8·8% (1981–82) of the GNP. Industrial output grew by about 5% in 1982. Production, 1983–84: jute goods, 335,000 tons; cotton yarn, 87m. lb.; cotton cloth, 46m. yd.; cement, 320,000 tons; steel ingots, 137,000 tons; re-rolled steel products, 194,000 tons, refined sugar, 151,000 tons; newsprint, 3m. tons.

Labour. In 1974–75, 1,417 firms (employing more than 10 people) had 293,200 paid employees earning Tk.1,298·7m.; value added, Tk.3,781m.

Commerce. The main export commodities are jute goods, hide, skins, leather and tea. Bangladesh has resumed trade with Pakistan. In 1983–84 exports were valued at Tk.20,250m., of which Tk.9,000m. was from jute products; Tk.2,900m. from raw jute and mesta; Tk.2,110m. from leather hides and skins; Tk.1,760m. from tea. Principal imports (Tk.61,630m.) are food and live animals (Tk.12,410m.; machinery and transport equipment (Tk.12,280m.); manufactured goods (Tk.11,360m.); minerals, fuels and lubricants (Tk.8,860m.).

Total trade between Bangladesh and UK (British Department of Trade returns, in £1,000 sterling):

	1981	*1982*	*1983*	*1984*
Imports to UK	15,063	25,558	25,189	46,506
Exports and re-exports from UK	45,210	58,179	50,979	51,591

Tourism. In 1980 there were 64,162 visitors to Bangladesh. They spent TK.238m.

COMMUNICATIONS

Roads. The State is backward in the matter of road communications, but there are some 2,500 miles of paved and 2,000 miles of unpaved road. In 1979 there were 89,000m. motor vehicles.

Railways. In 1980 there were 2,883 km of railways, comprising 973 km of 1,676 mm gauge and 1,910 km of metre gauge. In 1982–83 the railways carried 3·2m. tonnes of freight and 102m. passengers.

Aviation. Bangladesh Biman (Bangladesh Airways) has domestic flights from Dhaka and international services to Calcutta, Kathmandu, Bombay, Dubai, Abu Dhabi, Jeddah, Bangkok, Singapore, London, Doha, Kuwait, Amsterdam, Rome, Karachi, Kuala Lumpur, Dahrain, Tripoli, Athens and Muscat.

Shipping. Navigable channels provide 5,000 miles of cheap water routes. There are 3 principal waterways, the Padma, Brahmaputra and Meghna. These are freely used by inland steam vessels, which serve areas where railways cannot be economically constructed. The Bangladesh Shipping Corporation owns 24 ships including a 93,000-ton oil tanker *(Banglar Noor)* and has the capacity to carry 20% of imports and 12% of exports. In 1982–83 ports handled 6m. tons of imports and 1·26m. tons of exports.

Post and Broadcasting. There were 122,190 telephones in 1982. Dhaka and Islamabad were linked by telephone in Oct. 1976 and a second telephone circuit was agreed on 11 April 1977. International communications are by satellite, Chittagong being linked to the Indian Ocean Intelsat IV satellite.

Newspapers. In Nov. 1981 there were 53 daily newspapers, 200 weeklies, 34 fortnightlies, 194 monthlies and 43 quarterly periodicals. Most papers are published in Dhaka. The Government has set up a paper *(Dainik Barta-at Rajshahi)* to stimulate a regional press. Most papers are privately owned. There is a Press Institute.

JUSTICE, RELIGION, EDUCATION AND WELFARE

Justice. The amended constitution in 1977 set up a Supreme Judicial Council to establish a code of conduct for Supreme Court and High Court judges, who may be removed from office by the President on the Council's recommendation.

Religion. Islam is the official religion, about 80% of the people being Muslim and the rest Hindus, Buddhists and Christians.

Education. In 1980 (estimate) under 24% of the population was literate. The compulsory primary education scheme has been replaced by model primary education. The Government has dissolved the District School Boards and taken over school administration.

In 1980 there were 43,634 primary schools, 8,946 secondary schools and about 600 intermediate and degree colleges. Primary schools had 8m. students, secondary schools about 2m. and technical colleges about 16,000. There were 6 universities including those at Dhaka, Rajshahi, Mymensingh and Chittagong (founded 1964); one university is for engineering and one for agriculture. Universities had about 28,000 students in 1977. There are 14 teacher training colleges, 47 primary training institutes, 16 polytechnics and 26 vocational institutes.

Health. In 1979 there were 405 hospitals, 1 mental and 5 tuberculosis and chest hospitals, 8 medical colleges and nursing training centres which train about 1,200 nurses annually. In 1979 the number of beds was 17,494.

DIPLOMATIC REPRESENTATIVES

Of Bangladesh in Great Britain (28 Queen's Gate, London, SW7)
High Commissioner: Fakhruddin Ahmed (accredited 11 June 1982)

Of Great Britain in Bangladesh (Abu Bakr Hse., Plot 7, Road 84, Gulshan Dhaka, 12)
High Commissioner: T. G. Streeton, CMG, MBE.

Of Bangladesh in the USA (2201 Wisconsin Ave., NW, Washington, D.C., 20007)
Ambassador: Humayun Rasheed Choudhury.

Of the USA in Bangladesh (Adamjee Court Bldg., Motijheel, Dhaka)
Ambassador: Howard B. Schaffer.

Of Bangladesh to the United Nations
Ambassador: Lieut.-Gen. Khwaja Wasiuddin.

Books of Reference

Bangladesh Planning Commission, *The First Five Year Plan—The Second Five Year Plan.*
Ministry of Finance. *Bangladesh Economic Survey.* 1979–80
Abdullah, T., and Zeidenstein, S., *Village Women of Bangladesh: Prospects for Change.* Oxford, 1981
Chen, L. C. (ed.), *Disaster in Bangladesh, Health Crisis in a Developing Nation.* OUP, 1973
Chowdhury, R., *The Genesis of Bangladesh.* London, 1972
Dutt, K., *Bangladesh Economy: An Analytical Study.* New Delhi, 1973
Franda, M., *Bangladesh: The First Decade.* New Delhi, 1982
Hartmann, B., and Boyce, J., *A Quiet Violence: View from a Bangladesh Village.* London, 1983
Kamal, K. A., *Sheikh Mujibur Rahman.* 2nd ed. Dhaka, 1970
Kashyap, S. C. (ed.), *Bangla Desh: Background and Perspectives.* New Delhi, 1971
Khan, A. R., *The Economy of Bangladesh.* London, 1972
de Lucia, R. J., and Jacoby, H. D., *Energy Planning for Developing Countries: A Study of Bangladesh.* John Hopkins Univ. Press, 1982
de Vylder, S., *Agriculture in Chains. Bangladesh: A Case Study in Contradictions and Constraints.* London, 1982
Rahman, M., *Bangladesh Today: An Indictment and a Lament.* London, 1978
Robinson, E. A. G., and Griffin, K. (ed.), *The Economic Development of Bangladesh.* London, 1974

BARBADOS

Capital: Bridgetown
Population: 251,800 (1983)
GNP per capita: US$3,661 (1982)

HISTORY. Barbados was occupied by the British in 1627 and during its colonial history never changed hands. Full internal self-government was attained in 1961. Barbados became an independent sovereign state within the Commonwealth on 30 Nov. 1966.

AREA AND POPULATION. Barbados lies to the east of the Windward Islands. Area 166 sq. miles (430 sq. km). In 1980 the census population was 248,983. Estimate (1983) 251,800. Bridgetown is the principal city: population, 7,466.

CLIMATE. An equable climate in winter, but the wet season, from June to Nov., is more humid. Rainfall varies from 50″ (1,250 mm) on the coast to 75″ (1,875 mm) in the higher interior. Bridgetown. Jan. 76°F (24·4°C), July 80°F (26·7°C). Annual rainfall 51″ (1,275 mm).

CONSTITUTION AND GOVERNMENT. The Legislature consists of the Governor-General, a Senate and a House of Assembly. The Senate comprises 21 members appointed by the Governor-General, 12 being appointed on the advice of the Prime Minister, 2 on the advice of the leader of the opposition and 7 in the Governor-General's discretion. The House of Assembly comprises 27 members elected every 5 years. In 1963 the voting age was reduced to 18.

The Privy Council is appointed by the Governor-General after consultation with the Prime Minister. It consists of 12 members and the Governor-General as chairman. It advises the Governor-General in the exercise of the royal prerogative of mercy and in the exercise of his disciplinary powers over members of the public and police services.

In the general election of June 1981 the Barbados Labour Party held 17 seats and the Democratic Labour Party 10 seats.

Governor-General: Sir Hugh Springer, GCMG, CBE.

The Cabinet, in March 1985, was composed as follows:

Prime Minister, Finance and Planning: H. Bernard St John.

Foreign Affairs and Attorney-General: Louis R. Tull. *Parliamentary Affairs:* Lionel S. Craig. *Education:* Miss Billie A. Miller. *Health:* O'Brien Trotman. *Information and Culture:* Nigel A. Barrow. *Transport and Works:* Victor L. Johnson. *Housing and Lands.* Lloyd B. Braithwaite. *Prime Minister's Office:* Clyde Griffith. *Labour and Social Security:* Delisle Bradshaw. *Agriculture, Food and Consumer Affairs:* Dr R. L. Johnny Cheltenham.

National flag: Three vertical strips of blue, gold, blue, with a black trident in the centre.

INTERNATIONAL RELATIONS

Membership. Barbados is a member of UN, OAS, CARICOM, the Commonwealth and an ACP state of EEC.

ECONOMY

Budget. The budget for 1983–84 envisaged expenditure of BD$638·2m.

Currency. The monetary unit is the *Barbados dollar* (BD$) divided into 100 *cents*. In Feb. 1985, £1 = BD$2.14; US$1 = 2.01.

Banking. Seven main commercial banks operate in Barbados including Barclays

Bank International, the Royal Bank of Canada, Canadian Imperial Bank of Commerce, the Bank of Nova Scotia, Chase Manhattan Bank, Caribbean Commercial Bank and Citibank, The Barbados National Bank.

Barbados is headquarters for the Caribbean Development Bank. The Barbados Development Bank opened on 15 April 1969 and Barbados became a member of the Inter-American Development Bank on 19 March 1969.

NATURAL RESOURCES

Electricity. Production (1982) 356·5m. kwh.

Oil. Crude oil production (1982) 258,500 bbls.

Gas. Output of gas (1982) 8·8m. cu. metres.

Agriculture. Of the total area of 106,240 acres, about 54,932 acres are arable land. The land is intensely cultivated, and sugar-cane occupies 64,000 acres, 34,720 were reaped in 1983. The agricultural sector accounted for 6·9% of GDP in 1983 (1946, 45%; 1967, 24%). In 1983, 8% of the total labour force were employed in agriculture. In 1983, 82,769 tonnes of sugar were produced. There are 6 sugar factories and 2 rum refineries in production.

Livestock (1983): Cattle, 19,000; sheep, 54,000; goats, 32,000; pigs, 66,000; poultry, 1m.

Fisheries. There are about 618 (1983) powered boats and many men and women are employed during the flying-fish season. Large numbers of these boats are laid up from July to Oct. The fish catch in 1983 was 6,522 tonnes.

INDUSTRY AND TRADE

Industry. Industrial establishments operating in Barbados in 1983 numbered approximately 300 and ranged from the manufacture of processed food to small specialized products such as garment manufacturing, furniture and household appliances, electrical components, plastic products and electronic parts.

Commerce. Total trade for calendar years in BD$1,000:

	1979	*1980*	*1981*	*1982*	*1983*
Domestic Imports [1]	852,446	1,070,724	1,165,910	1,106,589	1,257,961
Domestic Exports [1]	234,794	300,223	298,838	374,061	581,579

[1] Exclusive of bullion and specie.

In 1983 the principal imports (BD$1m.) were: Machinery and transport equipment, 465; manufactured goods, 318·8; lubricants, mineral fuels, etc., 153·7; food, 148·7; chemicals, 101·2; crude minerals, 26·4; animal and vegetable oils, 11·4. In 1983 the principal domestic exports (BD$1m.) were: Sugar, 38·7; clothing, 70·4; electrical parts, 262·3.

Total trade between Barbados and UK (British Department of Trade returns, in £1,000 sterling):

	1980	*1981*	*1982*	*1983*	*1984*
Imports from UK	7,630	9,390	14,887	11,899	22,509
Exports and re-exports to UK	29,860	35,409	26,886	31,938	30,654

Tourism. In 1983, 328,325 tourists visited Barbados spending BD$503·2m. The industry employs over 10,000 people.

COMMUNICATIONS

Roads. There are 1,020 miles of road open to traffic, of which 840 miles are all-weather roads. From June 1978 to May 1980 there were 24,177 private cars, 2,027 hired cars and taxis, 329 buses and 27,790 other vehicles including motorcycles and bicycles.

Aviation. There is an international airport at Seawell, Christ Church, Barbados, served by British Airways, BWIA, Leeward Islands Air Transport, PANAM, Air Canada, SAS, Caribbean Airways and Eastern Airlines, Cubana Airlines, Venezuelan Airlines.

Shipping. A deep-water harbour opened in 1961 at Bridgetown provides 8 berths for ships 500–600 ft in length, including one specially designed for bulk sugar loading. The number of merchant vessels entering in 1983 was 1,824 of 5,874,000 net tons.

Post and Telephone. There is a general post office in Bridgetown and 16 branches on the island. In June 1982 there were 78,000 telephones and stations in service.

Cinemas. There were (1984) 4 cinemas and 2 drive-in cinemas for 600 cars.

Newspapers. In 1984 there were 2 daily newspapers with a total circulation of 39,000.

JUSTICE, RELIGION, EDUCATION AND WELFARE

Justice. Justice is administered by the Supreme Court and by magistrates' courts. All have both civil and criminal jurisdiction. There is a Chief Justice and 3 puisne judges of the Supreme Court and 8 magistrates.

Religion. The majority (about 70%) of the population are Anglicans, the remainder mainly Methodists, Moravians and Roman Catholics.

Education. In 1982–83 children in 109 government primary schools numbered 32,061; in 21 secondary schools, 21,696; in 7 vocational centres, 595; in 15 private approved secondary schools, 4,289. There are 25 independent primary schools with 3,101 pupils and a number of independent schools for which no accurate figures are available. Education is free in all government-owned and maintained institutions from primary to university level.

In 1963 Erdiston College became one of the constituent Colleges of the University of the West Indies Institute of Education. The College of Arts and Sciences of the University of the West Indies in Barbados was opened in Sept. 1963 and Cave Hill campus in 1967. In 1979–80, 1,399 students attended the Cave Hill campus. The Barbados Community College for higher education at pre-university level was opened in 1969; in 1979–80, 1,800 students (full- and part-time) were enrolled. In 1980–81, 1,610 students (mainly part-time) attended the Samuel Jackman Prescod Polytechnic which was opened in Nov. 1969 to give training in, among other things, construction, electrical and engineering trades. Government expenditure on education during 1982–83 was estimated at BD$117m.

Health. In 1982 there were 2,151 hospital beds and 221 doctors.

DIPLOMATIC REPRESENTATIVES

Of Barbados in Great Britain (6 Upper Belgrave St., London, SW1X 8AZ)
High Commissioner: Dr H. McD. Forde (accredited 28 June 1984).

Of Great Britain in Barbados (147/9 Roebuck St., Bridgetown)
High Commissioner: G. L. Bullard, CMG.

Of Barbados in the USA (2144 Wyoming Ave., NW, Washington, D.C. 20008)
Ambassador: Randolph A. Fields.

Of the USA in Barbados (PO Box 302, Bridgetown)
Ambassador. Thomas H. Anderson, Jr.

Of Barbados to the United Nations
Ambassador: Harley S. L. Moseley.

Books of Reference

Statistical Information: The Barbados Statistical Service (NIS Bldg, Fairchild St, St Michael) produces selected monthly statistics and annual abstracts. *Director of Statistical Service:* Eric Straughn.

Chandler, M. J., *A Guide to Records in Barbados.* Univ. of the West Indies, 1965

Dann, G., *The Quality of Life in Barbados.* London, 1984.

Hoyos, F. A., *Barbados, Our Island Home.* London, 1970.—*Barbados: A History from the Amerindians to Independence.* London, 1978.—*Barbados: A Visitor's Guide.* London, 1983

Library: The Barbados Public Library, Bridgetown. *Acting Chief Librarian:* Edwin Igill.

BELGIUM

Capital: Brussels
Population: 9·86m. (1982)
GNP per capita: US$11,920 (1981)

Royaume de Belgique— Koninkrijk België

HISTORY. The kingdom of Belgium formed itself into an independent state in 1830, having from 1815 been part of the Netherlands. The secession was decreed on 4 Oct. 1830 by a provisional government, established in consequence of a revolution which broke out at Brussels, on 25 Aug. 1830. A National Congress elected Prince Leopold of Saxe-Coburg King of the Belgians on 4 June 1831; he ascended the throne 21 July 1831.

By the Treaty of London, 15 Nov. 1831, the neutrality of Belgium was guaranteed by Austria, Russia, Great Britain and Prussia. It was not until after the signing of the Treaty of London, 19 April 1839, which established peace between King Leopold I and the King of the Netherlands, that all the states of Europe recognized the kingdom of Belgium. In the Treaty of Versailles (28 June 1919) it is stated that as the treaties of 1839 'no longer conform to the requirements of the situation', these are abrogated and will be replaced by other treaties.

AREA AND POPULATION. Belgium is bounded north by the Netherlands, north-west by the North Sea, west and south by France, east by Federal Republic of Germany and Luxembourg. Belgium has an area of 30,519 sq. km (11,778 sq. miles). The Belgian exclave of Baarle-Hertog in the Netherlands has an area of 7 sq. km, and a population (1 Jan. 1984) of 1,089 males and 1,001 females.

By an agreement, 23 Sept. 1956, the frontier with Germany was slightly readjusted.

Census	*Population*	*Increase % per annum*	*Census*	*Population*	*Increase % per annum*
1900	6,693,548	1·03	1947	8,512,195	0·36
1910	7,423,784	1·09	1961	9,189,741	0·52
1920	7,465,782	0·06	1970	9,650,944	0·55
1930	8,092,004	0·84			

Provinces	*Provincial capitals*	*Area (hectares)*	*Estimated population (31 Dec.)* 1970[1]	1981	1982	1983
Antwerp (Anvers)	Antwerp	286,725	1,533,249	1,571,092	1,577,246	1,578,869
Brabant	Brussels	335,811	2,176,373	2,222,974	2,221,383	2,217,442
Flanders West	Bruges	313,439	1,054,429	1,081,913	1,084,350	1,086,574
Flanders East	Ghent	298,167	1,310,117	1,332,547	1,332,265	1,331,193
Hainaut	Mons	378,669	1,317,453	1,296,719	1,291,610	1,285,936
Liège	Liège	386,213	1,008,905	998,007	995,776	992,061
Limbourg	Hasselt	242,231	652,547	720,766	724,032	726,884
Luxembourg	Arlon	444,114	217,310	222,437	222,437	223,813
Namur	Namur	366,501	380,561	408,134	408,741	410,251
Total		3,051,871	9,650,944	9,854,589	9,858,017	9,853,023

[1] Census.

In 1984 there were 4,809,520 males and 5,043,503 females.

Foreigners numbered 890,873 on 1 Jan. 1984.

Vital statistics for calendar years:

	Births	*Deaths*	*Marriages*	*Divorces*	*Immigration*	*Emigration*
1979	123,658	112,156	65,476	13,499	54,854	59,552
1980	124,794	114,364	66,413	14,538	54,694	58,212
1981	124,827	113,308	65,076	15,704	49,298	60,191
1982	120,382	112,506	62,423	16,159	44,659	61,931
1983	117,395	114,814	59,467	17,232	43,657	61,339

	1981	1982	1983
Of the total births including still-born	*124,827*	*120,382*	*117,395*
Boys	64,295	61,930	60,440
Girls	60,532	58,452	56,955

The most important towns, with estimated population on 1 Jan. 1983:

Brussels and suburbs [1]	982,434	Tournai (Doornik)	67,291
Antwerp (Anvers) [2]	488,425	Hasselt	65,503
Ghent (Gand)	235,401	Seraing	62,832
Charleroi	213,041	Genk	61,532
Liège (Luik)	203,065	Mouscron (Moeskroen)	54,315
Brugge (Bruges)	118,146	Verviers	54,155
Namur (Namen)	101,861	Roeselare (Roulers)	51,712
Mons (Bergen)	91,216	Herstal	37,721
Leuven (Louvain)	84,908	Turnhout	37,438
Aalst (Alost)	77,767	Lokeren	33,851
Mechelen (Malines)	76,670	Vilvoorde (Vilvorde)	33,085
Kortrijk (Courtrai)	75,592	Lier (Lierre)	31,209
Oostende (Ostende)	69,039	Ronse (Renaix)	24,081
St Niklass (St Nicolas)	68,277		

[1] The suburbs comprise 18 distinct communes, viz., Anderlecht, Etterbeek, Forest Ixelles, Jette, Koekelberg, Molenbeek St Jean, St Gilles, St Josse-ten-Noode, Schaerbeek, Uccle, Woluwe-St Lambert, Auderghem, Watermael-Boitsfort, Woluwe-St Pierre, Berchem, Ste Agathe, Evere and Ganshoren.

[2] Including Berchem, Borgerhout, Deurne, Hoboken, Merksem and Wilrijk.

CLIMATE. Cool temperate climate, influenced by the sea, giving mild winters and cool summers. Brussels. Jan. 36°F (2·2°C), July 64°F (17·8°C). Annual rainfall 33″ (825 mm). Ostend. Jan. 38°F (3·3°C), July 62°F (16·7°C). Annual rainfall 31″ (775 mm).

KING. Baudouin, born 7 Sept. 1930, succeeded his father, Leopold III, on 17 July 1951, when he took the oath on the constitution before the two Chambers: married on 15 Dec. 1960 to Fabiola de Mora y Aragón, daughter of the Conde de Mora and Marqués de Casa Riera.

Brother and Sister of the King. (1) Josephine Charlotte, Princess of Belgium, born 11 Oct. 1927; married to Prince Jean of Luxembourg, 9 April 1953; (2) Albert, Prince of Liège, born 6 June 1934; married to Paola Ruffo di Calabria, 2 July 1959; *offspring:* Prince Philippe, born 15 April 1960; Princess Astrid, born 5 June 1962; married to Archduke Lorenz of Austria, 22 Sept. 1984; Prince Laurent, born 19 Oct. 1963. *Half-brother and half-sisters of the King.* Prince Alexandre, born 18 July 1942; Princess Marie Christine, born 6 Feb. 1951; Princess Maria-Esmeralda, born 30 Sept. 1956.

Aunt of the King. Princess Marie-José, born 4 Aug. 1906, married to Prince Umberto (King Umberto II of Italy in 1946) on 8 Jan. 1930.

BELGIAN SOVEREIGNS

Leopold I	1831–65	Leopold III	1934–44, 1950–51
Leopold II	1865–1909	Regency	1944–50
Albert	1909–34	Baudouin	1951–

CONSTITUTION AND GOVERNMENT. According to the constitution of 1831, Belgium is a constitutional, representative and hereditary monarchy. The legislative power is vested in the King, the Senate and the Chamber of Representatives. The royal succession is in direct male line in the order of primogeniture. By marriage without the King's consent, however, the right of succession is forfeited, but may be restored by the King with the consent of the two Chambers. No act of the King can have effect unless countersigned by one of his Ministers, who thus becomes responsible for it. The King convokes, prorogues and dissolves the Chambers. In default of male heirs, the King may nominate his successor with the consent of the Chambers. If the successor be under 18 years of age the two Chambers meet together for the purpose of nominating a regent during the minority.

National flag: Three vertical strips of black, yellow, red.

National anthem: Après des siècles d'esclavage (La Brabançonne; words by Jenneval, 1830; tune by F. van Campenhout, 1930).

French, Dutch and German are official languages.

Those sections of the Belgian Constitution which regulate the organization of the legislative power were revised in Oct. 1921. For both Senate and Chamber all elections are held on the principle of universal suffrage.

The Senate consists of members elected for 4 years, partly directly and partly indirectly. The number elected directly is equal to half the number of members of the Chamber of Representatives. The constituent body is similar to that which elects deputies to the Chamber; the minimum age of electors is 18 years, and the minimum length of residence required is 6 months. Women were given the suffrage at parliamentary elections on 24 March 1948. In the direct elections of members of both the Senate and Chamber of Representatives the principle of proportional representation was introduced by law of 29 Dec. 1899.

Senators are elected indirectly by the provincial councils, on the basis of 1 for 200,000 inhabitants. Every addition of 125,000 inhabitants gives the right to 1 senator more. Each provincial council elects at least 3 senators. There are at present 51 provincial senators. No one, during 2 years preceding the election, must have been a member of the council appointing him. Senators are elected by the Senate itself in the proportion of half the preceding category. The senators belonging to these two latter categories are also elected by the method of proportional representation. All senators must be at least 40 years of age. They receive 900,000 francs per annum. Sons of the King, or failing these, Belgian princes of the reigning branch of the royal family, are by right senators at the age of 18, but have no voice in the deliberations till the age of 25 years; this prerogative is hardly ever used.

The members of the Chamber of Representatives are elected by the electoral body. Their number, at present 212 (law of 3 April 1965), is proportional to the population, and cannot exceed one for every 40,000 inhabitants. They sit for 4 years. Deputies must be not less than 25 years of age, and resident in Belgium.

Each deputy has an annual allowance of 900,000 francs. Senators and deputies have also free railway passes.

The Senate and Chamber meet annually in October and must sit for at least 40 days; but the King has the power of convoking extraordinary sessions and of dissolving them either simultaneously or separately. In the latter case a new election must take place within 40 days and a meeting of the chambers within 2 months.

An adjournment cannot be made for a period exceeding 1 month without the consent of the Chambers.

After the revision of the Constitution by the laws of 24 Dec. 1970 and 28 July 1971 establishing three regions and two cultural councils, legislation on 'preparatory regionalization' was enacted in July 1974. Further revisions of the functions of the Cultural Councils took place on 8 and 9 Aug. 1980. The Cultural Councils became Community Councils with greater authority and the Regional Councils became competent on economic matters.

Parliament was dissolved on 6 Oct. 1981 and general elections were held on 8 Nov. 1981.

Parties in the Senate after the election: *Christelijke Volkspartij,* 22; *Parti social chrétien,* 8; *Socialistische Partij,* 13; *Parti Socialiste Belge,* 18; *Partij voor Vrijheid en Vooruitgang,* 14; *Parti Reformateur Libéral (PRL),* 11; *Other parties,* 20.

Parties in the Chamber of Representatives after the election: *Christelijke Volkspartij,* 43; *Parti social chrétien,* 18; *Parti Socialiste,* 35; *Socialistische Partij,* 26; *Partij voor Vrijheid en Vooruitgang,* 28; *Parti Reformateur Libéral,* 24; *Other parties,* 38.

A 4-party coalition government was formed in Dec. 1981 and in March 1985 was composed as follows:

Prime Minister: Dr Wilfried Martens (CVP).

Deputy Prime Ministers: Jean Gol, PRL (*Justice and Institutional Reform*);

Frans Grootjans, PVV (*Finance and Foreign Trade*); Charles-Ferdinand Nothomb, PSC (*Interior and Civil Service*). *Foreign Affairs:* Léo Tindemans (CVP). *Economic Affairs:* Mark Eyskens (CVP). *Public Works and Middle Classes:* Louis Olivier (PRL). *Posts and Telecommunications:* Herman de Croo (PVV). *Labour and Employment:* Michel Hansenne (PSC). *Education (Flemish):* Daniel Coens (CVP). *Budget, Scientific Policy and Research:* Philippe Maystadt (PSC). *Brussels Regional Affairs:* P. Hatry (PRL). *Defence:* Freddy Vreven (PVV). *Education (French-language):* A. Bertouille (PRL). *Social Affairs and Institutional Reform:* Jean-Luc Dehaene (CVP).

There are ten Secretaries of State.

Local Government. Belgium has 9 provinces and since the so-called 'Amalgamation Law' of 30 Dec. 1975, 589 communes (instead of 2,359). They have a large measure of autonomous government. According to the law of 9 June 1982, all Belgians over 18 years of age, who are recorded in the registers of population of the commune have the right to vote in the communal elections. Proportional representation is applied to the communal elections, and communal councils are to be renewed every 6 years. In each commune there is a college composed of the burgomaster as the president and a certain number of aldermen.

DEFENCE. Belgium is a full member of NATO since 1949 and of the Eurogroup since 1968. The need to extend European armaments co-operation led to the formation of the Independent European Program Group (IEPG) in 1976. Its members include Belgium.

According to the Military Law of 30 April 1962, the Belgian Army is recruited by annual calls to the colours and by voluntary enlistments.

Compulsory service lasts 8 or 10 months for private soldiers, 13 months for voluntary reserve officers and 15 for the paracommando regiment. Duration of military obligation is 8 years for most soldiers called for compulsory service.

Army. The Army comprises as major units 1 armoured and 3 mechanized brigades (2 of which are deployed as the Belgian divisions in the Belgian corps area in the Federal Republic of Germany) and 1 paracommando regiment. There are also 3 reconnaissance battalions. Total strength (1985) 65,102. *Gendarmerie,* 16,200.

Equipment includes nearly 330 LEOPARD Main Battle Tanks, 135 SCORPION Light Tanks, 150 SCIMITAR Armoured Fighting Vehicles, 1,150 Armoured Personnel Carriers and 80 JPK 90mm Self-Propelled Anti-Tank Guns; Artillery Battalions are equipped with 105mm, 155mm and 203mm Self-Propelled Howitzers, LANCE Surface-to-Surface Missiles, HAWK Surface-to-Air Missiles and GEPARD Armoured Vehicles with 35mm Anti-Aircraft Guns.

Other equipment in use: MILAN Anti-Tank Guided Weapon, STRIKER Armoured Fighting Vehicle with SWINGFIRE Anti-Tank Guided Weapon, Islander aircraft, Alouette II helicopters, Epervier Remotely Piloted Vehicle.

Navy. The naval forces include 4 frigates (Navy designed and built) completed in 1978, 7 ocean minehunters, 2 command and logistic support ships, 2 coastal minehunters, 5 coastal minesweepers, 14 inshore minesweepers, 2 research ships, 3 river patrol boats, 1 degaussing ship, 1 ammunition transport, 6 tugs and 2 service craft. Five tripartite minehunters are being built and five others (with a further 5 option) are projected. Naval personnel in 1985 totalled 4,590 officers and ratings.

The naval air arm comprises 3 Alouette III general utility helicopters.

Air Force. The Air Force has a strength of more than 20,000 personnel and more than 270 aircraft in 14 operational squadrons and support units. There are 5 flying wings. The all-weather fighter wing consists of 2 squadrons of F-16s. One fighter-bomber wing has 2 squadrons of F-16s; 2 others operate Mirage 5s, organized as 3 squadrons of Mirage 5Bs and Mirage 5BD two-seat trainers, and 1 squadron of Mirage 5BR photo-reconnaissance aircraft. The transport wing consists of 1 squadron equipped with 12 C-130H Hercules turboprop transports, and 1 squadron flying 2 Boeing 727s, 3 HS 748 twin-turboprop transports, 5 Swearingen Merlin III light turboprop transports and 2 light twin-jet Falcons. Other types in service include Sea King Mk 48 search and rescue helicopters, SIAI-Marchetti SF.260M and Alpha Jet training aircraft. Two surface-to-air missile wings, stationed in Germany, are equipped with Nike Hercules missiles. Aircraft on order include 44 more F-16s.

INTERNATIONAL RELATIONS

Membership. Belgium is a member of UN, EEC, Benelux Economic Union, Council of Europe, NATO, OECD and WEU.

ECONOMY

Budget. Revenue and expenditure for calendar years (in 1m. francs):

	1978	*1979*	*1980*	*1981*	*1982*	*1983*
Receipts						
Current	877,324	941,484	1,003,544	1,010,204	1,152,416	1,209,689
Capital	167,769	175,687	196,948	157,232	253,776	293,176
Total	1,045,093	1,171,171	1,200,492	1,167,436	1,406,192	1,502,865
Expenditure						
Current	1,012,521	1,092,766	1,186,367	1,384,078	1,516,884	1,610,580
Capital	113,351	119,212	146,697	185,481	172,036	214,278
Total	1,125,872	1,211,978	1,333,064	1,569,559	1,688,920	1,824,858

On 30 Dec. 1983 the Belgian public debt consisted of (in 1m. francs): Internal debt consolidated, 1,810,000; short and middle terms, 998,400; at sight, 83,700. External debt, 823,900.

Currency. The *franc*, containing 0·01826 gramme of fine gold, is the unit of currency.

No gold has been minted since 1882 (save only 5m. francs struck in 1914). New silver coins of 250 francs have been issued since 16 March 1976. Note circulation 31 Dec. 1983, 395,900m. francs.

The official rate of exchange in Feb. 1985 was US$1 = 68·64 francs; £1 = 73·25 francs.

Banking. The bank of issue in Belgium is the National Bank, instituted in 1850. It is the cashier of the State, and is authorized to carry on the usual banking operations. The note circulation on 31 Dec. 1983 amounted to 395,916m. francs. The articles of association of the National Bank of Belgium were modified on 13 Sept. 1948 so as to strengthen public control.

The savings banks are mainly operated by the *Caisse Générale d'Epargne et de Retraite* and by the private savings banks. *The Caisse Générale d'Epargne et de Retraite* (CGER), a state institution, consists of 2 parts: *the Caisse d'Epargne* which performs the whole range of banking activities and a further unit which embodies the funds engaged in social security and insurance activities; the CGER operates under the authority of the Minister of Finance. The *Commission bancaire* (bank commission) supervises the financial situation and the activities of the Caisse d'Epargne. It co-operates with the Belgian postal service, thus obviating any need of a postal-savings system. The savings deposits and savings bonds of the Caisse d'Epargne amounted to 573,200m. francs on 31 Dec. 1983. The private savings banks, whose liabilities expressed in savings accounts and bonds amounted to 775,900m. francs on 31 Dec. 1983, are controlled by the 'Commission bancaire'.

Weights and Measures. The metric system is in force.

ENERGY AND NATURAL RESOURCES

Electricity. The production of electricity (1m. kwh.) amounted to 51,015 in 1980; 48,179 in 1981; 47,936 in 1982; 49,912 in 1983.

Gas. Production of gas (in 1m. cu. metres): 675 in 1980; 690 in 1981; 594 in 1982; 623 in 1983.

Minerals. Output (in tonnes) for 5 calendar years:

	1979	*1980*	*1981*	*1982*	*1983*
Coal	6,124,503	6,324,034	6,136,446	6,538,874	6,097,428
Briquettes	152,492	81,597	53,981	49,836	45,265
Coke	6,450,359	6,047,504	6,003,730	5,216,692	5,105,675
Cast iron	10,775,843	9,844,629	9,786,077	7,831,469	8,033,206
Wrought steel	13,537,625	12,424,507	12,379,638	9,995,850	10,157,031
Finished steel	10,364,011	9,517,357	8,902,482	7,364,139	7,056,770

Agriculture. Of the total area of 3,051,871 hectares, there were, in 1983, 1,399,695 hectares under cultivation, of which 373,426 were under cereals, 24,654 vegetables, 122,883 industrial plants, 128,288 root crops, 686,452 pastures and meadows.

Chief crops	*Area in hectares*			*Produce in tonnes*		
	1981	*1982*	*1983*	*1981*	*1982*	*1983*
Wheat	166,092	170,426	187,260	875,426	1,010,009	1,003,346
Barley	152,403	131,176	138,676	751,885	745,109	670,198
Oats	26,418	33,716	20,980	108,842	153,408	79,724
Rye	8,349	7,101	6,399	31,978	29,752	24,510
Potatoes	34,272	32,626	34,473	1,195,291	1,310,043	977,492
Beet (sugar)	130,326	123,816	109,078	6,935,934	7,430,205	5,120,123
Beet (fodder)	16,201	17,249	15,012	1,547,953	1,934,621	1,304,706
Tobacco	481	477	485	1,604	1,701	1,638

In 1983 there were 29,154 horses, 3,086,028 cattle, 131,639 sheep, 7,524 goats and 5,314,150 pigs.

Forestry. In 1970 the forest area covered 19·7% of the land surface. In 1970, 2·85 cu. metres of timber were felled.

Fisheries. The total quantity of fish landed amounted to 37,207 tons valued at 2,131m. francs in 1982. The fishing fleet had a total tonnage of 21,847 gross tons at 31 Dec. 1982.

INDUSTRY AND TRADE

Industry. In 1983 there were 14 sugar factories, output 183,179 tonnes of raw sugar; 3 sugar refineries, output 227,375 tonnes; 10 distilleries, output 126,749 hectolitres of potable and industrial alcohol; 134 breweries, output 14,224,451 hectolitres of beer; margarine factories, output 158,605 tonnes.

Six trusts control the greater part of Belgian industry: the Société Générale (founded in 1822) owns about 40% of coal, 50% of steel, 65% of non-ferrous metals and 35% of electricity; Brufina-Confinindus operates in steel, coal, electricity and heavy engineering; the Groupe Solvay rules the chemical industry; the Groupe Copée has interests in steel and coal; Empain controls tramways and electrical equipment; the Banque Lambert owns petroleum firms and their accessories.

Commerce. By the convention concluded at Brussels on 25 July 1921 between Belgium and Luxembourg and ratified on 5 March 1922 an economic union was formed by the two countries, and the customs frontier between them was abolished on 1 May 1922. Dissolved in Aug. 1940, the union was re-established on 1 May 1945. On 14 March 1947, in execution of an agreement signed in London on 5 Sept. 1944, there was concluded a customs union between Belgium and Luxembourg, on the one hand, and the Netherlands, on the other. The union came into force on 1 Jan. 1948, and is now known as the Benelux Economic Union. A joint tariff has been adopted and import duties are no longer levied at the Netherlands frontier, but import licences may still be required. A full economic union of the three countries came into operation on 1 Nov. 1960.

Benelux information is supplied by the Secrétariat Général de l'Union Douaniére Néerlando-Belgo-Luxembourgeoise, Rue de la Régence, 39, 1000 Brussels. It publishes *Benelux. Bulletin Trimestriel de Statistique; Statistisch Kwartaalbericht* (1955 ff.).

Trade by selected countries (in 1,000 Belgian francs):

	Imports from			Exports to		
	1981	*1982*	*1983* [1]	*1981*	*1982*	*1983* [1]
France	315,952,138	367,217,886	395,996,562	395,582,544	464,092,390	482,909,573
USA	165,939,976	186,567,397	180,499,032	87,152,270	105,430,666	136,373,998
UK	171,442,793	185,727,003	243,337,219	177,660,091	230,640,748	261,121,114
Netherlands	394,397,768	471,529,721	510,568,987	305,357,063	339,968,747	377,366,469
German Dem. Rep.	6,053,009	6,204,025	6,578,304	3,156,944	2,340,007	5,470,610
Germany, Fed. Rep.	435,354,580	529,024,975	582,050,704	414,123,911	488,530,507	560,628,924
Argentina	4,727,455	6,578,622	10,693,533	2,877,342	2,537,641	2,771,822
Italy	77,632,033	95,099,121	103,453,065	104,735,092	120,582,881	123,770,478
Switzerland	80,538,132	61,360,255	78,800,831	64,787,862	76,936,334	75,404,891
Zaïre	35,989,008	26,492,300	20,131,155	7,304,624	8,833,248	8,888,939
Denmark	9,982,649	12,391,518	14,384,967	27,157,142	23,491,505	25,996,119
USSR	36,318,716	67,873,990	71,352,790	21,884,703	24,489,552	34,001,683
India	7,807,996	9,694,166	13,249,166	20,039,004	27,031,784	29,430,263
Rep. of S. Africa	14,535,344	17,687,165	15,879,683	11,159,909	10,400,260	11,309,297
Canada	19,822,425	18,627,442	15,727,568	8,982,712	9,146,689	11,353,771
Brazil	13,168,019	16,758,592	16,995,143	4,557,981	4,982,633	4,055,784
Australia	6,094,337	7,157,711	7,837,320	4,589,326	5,594,366	5,737,259

[1] Provisional.

Imports and exports for 6 calendar years (in 1,000 Belgian francs):

	Imports	*Exports*		*Imports*	*Exports*
1978	1,526,044,142	1,410,257,630	1981	2,309,761,017	2,062,315,689
1979	1,784,353,190	1,661,244,397	1982	2,653,362,108	2,393,152,616
1980	2,100,807,473	1,890,359,149	1983 [1]	2,817,019,308	2,650,761,959

[1] Provisional.

The total trade between Belgium and Luxembourg and UK was as follows (British Department of Trade returns, in £1,000 sterling):

	1980	*1981*	*1982*	*1983*	*1984*
Imports to UK	2,596,962	2,448,605	2,861,809	3,133,905	3,691,794
Exports and re-exports from UK	2,624,108	2,092,011	2,298,118	2,572,673	3,051,722

Principal Belgian-Luxembourg exports to UK in 1983 [1] (tonnes; francs): Textiles (128,698; 20,567m.); metals (534,473; 19,869m.); chemical and pharmaceutical products (536,421; 20,929m.); precious stones and manufactures thereof (362; 46,600m.).

Principal Belgian-Luxembourg imports from the UK in 1983[1] (tonnes; francs): Machinery and electrical apparatus (39,024; 19,047m.); vehicles, chiefly motor cars, and aircraft (102,808; 19,490m.); textiles (40,499; 7,444m.); precious stones (191; 66,681m.); base metals and manufactures thereof (270,320; 10,985m.).

[1] Provisional.

Tourism. In 1981 receipts totalled 27m. francs, comprising 20m. francs from Belgian tourists and 7m. francs from overseas visitors.

COMMUNICATIONS

Roads. The total length of the roads in Belgium on 31 Dec. 1982 was as follows: State roads (including 1,388 km of motorway), 13,297 km; provincial roads, 1,367 km; communal roads, 112,079 km. The majority of roads are metalled. Number of motor vehicles in Belgium, 1 Aug. 1983, 3,869,822, including 3,262,713 passenger cars, 17,866 buses, 261,126 lorries, 28,284 non-agricultural tractors, 136,868 agricultural tractors, 126,279 motor cycles and 36,686 special vehicles.

Railways. The main Belgian lines were a State enterprise from their inception in 1834. In 1926 the *Société Nationale des Chemins de Fer Belges (SNCB)* was formed to take over the railways. The State is sole holder of the ordinary shares of SNCB, which carry the majority vote at General Meetings. The length of railway operated on 31 Dec. 1983 was 3,842 km. Revenue (1983), 48,260m. francs; expenditure, 48,667m. francs. In 1983, 63·3m. tonnes of freight and 155·5m. passengers were carried.

Aviation. The national Belgian airline SABENA (*Société anonyme belge d'exploitation de la navigation aérienne*) was set up in 1923. Its capital is 750m. francs. In addition to its European network, SABENA operates different routes to North and South America, to North, Central and South Africa and to the Near, the Middle and the Far East. In 1983 its airfleet comprised 23 aircraft. In 1983 SABENA flew 48·6m. km, carrying 1,956,447 revenue passengers, 489·1m. ton-km of freight and 13·82m. ton-km of mail.

Shipping.[1] On 1 Jan. 1984 the Belgian merchant fleet was composed of 105 vessels of 2,183,585 tons. There were 52 shipping companies, of which the most important were the Compagnie Maritime Belge, with 17 ships, and the Belgian Fruit Lines, SA, with 5 ships.

[1] Belgian shipping returns are given in the official 'Moorsom tons', which may be converted into net tons by deducting 19·85% from the Moorsom total.

The navigation at the port of Antwerp in 1983 was as follows: Number of vessels entered, 16,152; tonnage, 109,596,000. Number of vessels cleared, 15,948; tonnage, 108,156,000.

The total length of navigable waterways (rivers and canals) was 1,559·5 km in 1984.

Post and Broadcasting. On 31 Dec. 1982 there were 1,862 post offices. The gross revenue of the post office in the year 1982 amounted to 22,573m. francs.

A régie of telegraphs and telephones for running the services on business lines was created in 1930. Telegraph offices for dispatching and receiving wires numbered 106; for dispatching only, 24. Receipts for 1982 were 4,983·23m. francs; expenditure, 4,548,865,000 francs.

In 1982 the telephone service comprised 690 exchanges, connecting 8,138 public telephone stations and 2,722,107 subscribers. Number of telephones, 1 Jan. 1982, 3,984,295. Receipts in 1982, 40,274,996m. francs; expenditure, 42,664,656m. francs.

Radio-Television belge de la Communauté française (RTBF) and *Belgische Radio en Televisie* (BRT) are public institutions broadcasting in French and Dutch respectively.

BRT has 5 radio programmes: BRT 1 is for service and information, documentary programmes, radio drama and light music; BRT 2 is for regional entertainments from each of the Flemish provinces. Both stations broadcast on medium-wave and on FM (stereo). BRT 3, on FM (stereo) is the cultural station; Studio Brussels (medium-wave and FM) gives local information and light music for 10 hours daily to Dutch-speaking residents; the World Broadcasting Station (short- and medium-wave) is for Belgians abroad and to publicise Flemish culture overseas.

RTBF has 5 radio programmes: RTBF 1 (medium-wave) for information; RTBF 2 (FM stereo) for entertainment and local information; RTBF 3 (FM stereo) for classical music; Radio 21 (FM stereo) a young people's popular music and news programme; *La Voix de l'Amitie* (short-wave) which broadcasts to Africa.

Each body has 2 television channels, one general and one mainly for sport, special events, cultural events, feature films; broadcasting is by PAL standards. Advertising is not allowed on radio or television, which are financed by the Flemish and French Community Councils. In 1984 the Flemish community had 2·76m. radio receivers and 1·7m. television sets of which 73·8% were colour sets; the French-speaking community had 1·8m. radio receivers and 1·3m. television sets of which 72% were colour sets; 73·8% of the Flemish and 89% of the French-speaking households were connected to a television cable-network. Number of receivers (1984), radio, 4,607,257; TV, 2,381,497.

Cinemas (1982). There were 470 cinemas, with a seating capacity of 146,132.

Newspapers (1984). There are 39 daily newspapers (some of them only regional or local editions of larger dailies), of which 23 are in French, 15 in Dutch and 1 in German.

JUSTICE, RELIGION, EDUCATION AND WELFARE

Justice. Judges are appointed for life. There is a court of cassation, 5 courts of appeal, and assize courts for political and criminal cases. There are 26 judicial districts, each with a court of first instance. In each of the 225 cantons is a justice and judge of the peace. There are, besides, various special tribunals. There is trial by jury in assize courts.

Religion. Of the inhabitants professing a religion the majority are Roman Catholic, but no inquiry as to the profession of faith is now made at the censuses. There are, however, statistics concerning the clergy, and according to these there were in 1983: Roman Catholic higher clergy, 130; inferior clergy, 6,956; Protestant pastors, 83; Anglican Church, 10 chaplains; Jews (rabbis and ministers), 27. The State does not interfere in any way with the internal affairs of any church. There is full religious liberty, and part of the income of the ministers of all denominations is paid by the State.

There are 8 Roman Catholic dioceses subdivided into 260 deaneries.

Estimated number of Protestants, 24,000; of Jews, 35,000.

The Protestant (Evangelical) Church is under a synod. There is also a Central Jewish Consistory, a Central Committee of the Anglican Church and a Free Protestant Church.

Education. On 8 Nov. 1962/2 Aug. 1963 a linguistic frontier was fixed between the Dutch-speaking, French-speaking and German-speaking parts of Belgium. In the north, Dutch is recognized as the official language, in the south, French, and along the eastern border, German. The city and *arrondissement* of Brussels are bilingual. The percentage of the population in the Flemish, French, German and bilingual regions was 57·4, 31·9, 0·7, 10·0 on 1 Jan. 1984. (*See* map in THE STATESMAN'S YEAR-BOOK, 1967–68.)

Higher Education (1982–83). Higher education is given in state universities: Ghent (12,939 students), Liège (9,447 students), Mons (1,395 students), the Polytechnic Faculty in Mons (489 students), the Antwerp State University Centre (2,055 students), the Gembloux Faculty of Agronomical Sciences (750 students), the Royal Military School in Brussels (728 students) and in the private universities: Catholic University of Louvain (39,407 students), the Free University of Brussels (18,417), University Institution Antwerp (1,498 students), St Ignatius Antwerp (3,175 students), Our Lady of Peace in Namur (3,064 students), Catholic University Faculty in Mons (724 students), St Louis in Brussels (366 students), St Aloysius in Brussels (691 students), the Limbourg University Centre (911 students) and the Protestant Faculty of Theology in Brussels (139 students). The total number of students in university colleges, faculties and institutes was 96,795.

There are 5 royal academies of fine arts and 5 royal conservatoires at Brussels, Liège, Ghent, Antwerp and Mons.

Secondary Education. 2,654 (1982–83) middle schools had a total of 150,765 pupils in the general classes and 215,189 in the technical classes in the traditional system and 482,102 pupils in the new system.

Elementary Education. There were 4,793 (1982–83) primary schools, with 812,092 pupils and 4,218 (1982–83) infant schools, with 389,732 pupils.

Normal Schools. Under the French and German linguistic systems there were 27 (1982–83) schools for training secondary teachers (3,595 students) in 1982–83; 43 (1982–83) for training elementary teachers (3,356 students) in 1980–81, 47 technical normal schools in 1982–83 with 3,452 students and 17 normal infant schools with 1,239 students in 1982–83.

Health. In 1982 there were 26,693 physicians (including 456 dentists), 4,670 other dentists and 10,177 pharmacists. Hospital beds numbered 92,686 on 1 Jan. 1982.

Social Security. Social security is based on the law of Dec. 1944. It applies to all workers subject to an employment contract, and is administered by the Central National Office of Social Security (ONSS), which collects from employers and employees all contributions referring to family allowances, health insurance, old age insurance, holidays and unemployment. These sums are distributed by the Central Office to the various institutions concerned with these benefits. Insurance against unemployment is organized through a common fund, which also undertakes to retrain the unemployed for another employment while providing for their families. Since 1944 further laws have increased allowances, made fresh provisions for housing (1945), injuries while working, professional illnesses, etc. (1948).

Apart from private charity, the poor are assisted by the communes through the agency of the *Centre Public d'Aide Sociale* in French-speaking parts of the country and *Openbaar Centrum voor Maatschappelijk Welzijn* in Dutch-speaking areas. Provisions of a national character have been made for looking after war orphans and men disabled in the war. Certain other establishments, either state or provincial, provide for the needs of the deaf-mutes and the blind, and of children who are placed under the control of the courts. Provision is also made for repressing begging and providing shelter for the homeless.

DIPLOMATIC REPRESENTATIVES

Of Belgium in Great Britain (103 Eaton Sq., London, SW1W 9AB)
Ambassador: Jean-Paul Van Bellinghen (accredited 24 Feb. 1984).

Of Great Britain in Belgium (Britannia Hse., rue Joseph II 28, 1040 Brussels)
Ambassador: Sir Edward Jackson, KCMG.

Of Belgium in the USA (3330 Garfield St., NW, Washington, D.C., 20008)
Ambassador: J. Raoul Schoumaker.

Of the USA in Belgium (Blvd. du Régent 27, 1000 Brussels)
Ambassador: Geoffrey Swaebe.

Of Belgium to the United Nations
Ambassador: Edmonde Dever.

Books of Reference

Statistical Information: The Institut National de Statistique (44 rue de Louvain, Brussels) was set up on 24 Jan. 1831, under the designation of Bureau de Statistique Générale; after several changes, it received its present name on 2 May 1946. *Director General:* E. Rosselle. *Main publications:*

Bulletin du Commerce Extérieur
Bulletin de Statistique. Monthly
Annuaire Statistique de la Belgique (from 1870).—*Annuaire statistique de poche* (from 1965)
Statistiques Agricoles. Monthly
Recensement général de la population au 31 déc. 1970. 13 vols.
Recensement de l'agriculture au 15 mai 1970. 3 vols.
Recensement de l'industrie et du commerce au 31 déc. 1970. 10 vols

Annuaire administratif et judiciaire de Belgique. Annual. Brussels
L'économie belge. Ministere des Affaires Economiques. Annual (from 1947)
Belgium, Investment Guide. Ministère des Affaires Economique, 1974
Guide des Ministères. Revue de l'Administration Belge. Brussels, Annual
Belgique: Un Panorama. Institut Belge d'Information et de documentation, Brussels, 1969
Molitor, A., *L'Administration de la Belgique.* Brussels, 1974.

BELIZE

Capital: Belmopan
Population: 157,700 (1983)
GNP per capita: US$1,080 (1981)

HISTORY. The early settlement of the territory was probably effected by British woodcutters about 1638; from that date to 1798, in spite of armed opposition from the Spaniards, settlers held their own and prospered. In 1780 the Home Government appointed a superintendent, and in 1862 the settlement was declared a colony, subordinate to Jamaica. It became an independent colony in 1884. Self-government was attained in 1964. Independence was achieved on 21 Sept. 1981.

AREA AND POPULATION. Belize is bounded north by Mexico, west by Guatemala and south and east by the Caribbean sea. Area, 22,963 sq. km. There are 6 districts:

	Sq. km	*Population census, 1980*		*Sq. km*	*Population census, 1980*
Corozal	1,860	22,902	Cayo	5,338	22,837
Belize	4,204	50,801	Stann Creek	2,176	14,181
Orange Walk	4,737	22,870	Toledo	4,649	11,762

Total population (census, 1980) 145,353. Estimate (1983) 157,700. In 1983 the birth rate per 1,000 was 38·6 and the death rate 4·2; infantile mortality 21·3 per 1,000 births; there were 954 marriages. English is the official language.

Main city, Belize City; population, census 1980, 39,771. Following the severe hurricane which struck the territory on 31 Oct. 1961 the capital Belmopan (population, 1980, 2,932) has been moved to a new site 50 miles inland; construction began in Jan. 1967 and it became the seat of government on 3 Aug. 1970. *See* map in the 1978–79 edition of The Statesman's Year-Book.

CONSTITUTION AND GOVERNMENT. Having achieved self-government in Jan. 1964 delays occurred in achieving independence because of the outstanding territorial claim by Guatemala. Attempts to reach agreement on the claim finally failed prior to independence being granted, but guarantees were given by Britain that a military force would remain. Talks were still in progress in 1984.

The Constitution, which came into force on 21 Sept. 1981, provided for a National Assembly, with a 5-year term, comprising a 28-member House of Representatives elected by universal adult suffrage, and a Senate consisting of 5 members appointed by the Governor-General on the advice of the Prime Minister and 3 other nominated members.

Governor-General: Dame Elmira Minita Gordon, DCMG.

Prime Minister and Minister of Finance and Defence: Manuel Amadeo Esqivel.

Flag: Blue with red band along the top and bottom edges. In the centre a white disc containing the coat of arms surrounded by a green garland.

CLIMATE. A tropical climate with high rainfall and small annual range of temperature. The driest months are Feb. and March. Belize. Jan. 74°F (23·3°C), July 81°F (27·2°C). Annual rainfall 76″ (1,890 mm).

DEFENCE. The Air Wing of the Belize Defence Force has two twin-engined BN-2B Defenders for maritime patrol and transport duties. RAF aircraft based temporarily in Belize include a detachment of Harrier V/STOL ground attack/reconnaissance aircraft. There is also a Maritime wing with 2 patrol boats used for anti-smuggling and coast guard duties.

ECONOMY

Budget. In 1983–84 revenue was $B75·8m. and expenditure $B84·8m.
Public debt, 31 March 1980, $B25,739,358; sinking fund, $B961,978.

Currency. There are notes of $B100, 20, 10, 5 and 1, and a subsidiary mixed metal coinage of 1-, 5-, 10-, 25- and 50-cent pieces. In Feb. 1985, £1 = $B2·12 and US$1 = $B2.

Banking. The Royal Bank of Canada took over the business of the local bank in 1912; it has 8 branches. There are 7 government savings banks.
Barclays Bank International have 7 branches, Bank of Nova Scotia have 5 branches and Atlantic Bank 3 branches.

NATURAL RESOURCES

Agriculture. The main agricultural export is sugar, followed by citrus fruit, chiefly grapefruit and oranges, whole, canned, juice and concentrates. Citrus production, 1983, 900,000 boxes. Sugar production in 1983 was 1,132,000 tonnes. Banana production began in 1973, and first shipments began in 1974; production, 1983, 531,000 boxes. [Ed. note: Box of grapefruit, 80 lb., oranges, 90 lb., bananas, 42 lb.]
Livestock (1983): Cattle, 51,000; sheep, 3,000; pigs, 17,000; poultry, 350,000.

Forestry. 2,964 sq. miles, 49% of the total land area, are under forests which include mahogany, cedar, Santa Maria, pine and rosewood, and many secondary hardwoods of known or probable market value, as well as woods suitable for pulp production. Exports of forest produce in 1982 amounted to $B3·8m.

Fisheries. Food and game fish are plentiful, and domestic consumption is heavy. The total exported in 1982 was valued at $B12·6m. Turtles—Hawksbill, Loggerhead and Green—are plentiful but as yet are not exported.

INDUSTRY AND TRADE

Industry. In 1983 production of the major commodities was: Sugar, 114,300 tons; molasses, 36,600 tons; cigarettes, 57·4m.; beer, 850,000 gallons; batteries, 5,000; wheat flour, 11m. lb.; rum, 4·9m. gallons; fertilizer, 3,080 tons; garments, 781,000.
The labour market alternates between full employment, often accompanied by local shortages in the citrus and sugar-cane harvesting (Jan.–July), and under-employment during the wet season (Aug.–Dec.), aggravated by the seasonal nature of the major industries.

Trade Unions. There are more than 25 accredited unions with an estimated membership of 30,000.

Commerce. In 1983 total imports amounted to $B223·6m. Total exports, $B115·5m. The principal domestic exports were timber, sugar, fish products, garments, bananas and citrus fruit.
Total trade between Belize and UK (British Department of Trade returns, in £1,000 sterling):

	1980	*1981*	*1982*	*1983*	*1984*
Imports to UK	13,168	15,050	13,326	11,565	15,911
Exports and re-exports from UK	11,824	9,995	10,455	8,726	11,501

COMMUNICATIONS

Roads. There are four major highways and all principal towns and villages are linked by road to Belmopan and Belize City. In 1983, there were 9,796 licensed vehicles.

Aviation. In 1983, 291,000 passengers arrived and departed on international flights.

Shipping (1981). Registered shipping, 55 sailing vessels, 1,348 net tons, and 323 motor vessels, 745,197 net tons.

Post. Number of telephones (1985), 8,800. The Belize Telecommunication

Authority has instituted a country-wide fully automatic telephone dialling facility. There are 6 post offices and 45 rural sub-post offices.

Cinemas (1985). There were 10 cinemas with seating capacity of 10,000.

Newspapers. There were 7 weekly newspapers and 2 monthly magazines in 1984.

JUSTICE, RELIGION, EDUCATION AND WELFARE

Justice. There are 3 magistrates' courts in Belize and 1 in each district town. The police force contained (1978) 30 officers and 470 n.c.o.s and constables.

Religion. In 1982 about 62% of the population was Roman Catholic and 28% Protestant, including Anglican, Methodist, Seventh Day Adventist, Mennonite, Nazarene, Jehovah's Witness, Pentecostal and Baptist. There was a small group of Bahai.

Education. In 1983, 199 primary schools had a total enrolment of 36,239 pupils; 22 secondary schools, 6,396 pupils; and 5 other technical schools with 526 students. In Sept. 1979 the Belize College of Arts, Science and Technology was opened for post-sixth form courses. The Teachers' College offers courses for primary school teachers. The 3-year course leads to a teachers' diploma granted by the University of the West Indies.

Health. In 1984 there was 1 general hospital and 6 district hospitals with 76 doctors and 576 hospital beds; one private hospital had 3 doctors and 15 beds.

DIPLOMATIC REPRESENTATIVES

Of Belize in Great Britain (15 Thayer St., London, W1)
High Commissioner: Rudolph Castillo, MBE (accredited 20 May 1983).

Of Great Britain in Belize (Belize Hse., Belmopan)
High Commissioner: John M. Crosby, MVO.

Of Belize in the USA (1575 I St., NW, Washington, D.C., 20005)
Ambassador: Henry Edney Conrad Cain.

Of the USA in Belize (Gabourel Lane, Belize City)
Ambassador: Malcolm R. Barnebey.

Of Belize to the United Nations
Ambassador: Robert Anthony Leslie.

Books of Reference

Abstract of Statistics 1981. Government Printer, Belize City, 1982
Bianchi, W. J., *Belize: The Controversy Between Guatemala and Great Britain.* New York, 1959
Dobson, D., *A History of Belize.* Belize, 1973
Grant, C. H., *The Making of Modern Belize.* CUP, 1976
Setzekorn, W. D., *Formerly British Honduras: A Profile of the New Nation of Belize.* Ohio Univ. Press, 1981
Woodward, R. L., Jr, *Belize.* [Bibliography] Oxford and Santa Barbara, 1980

BENIN

Capital: Porto Novo
Population: 3·83m. (1984)
GNP per capita: US$320 (1981)

République Populaire du Benin

HISTORY. The territory of the present State was occupied by France in 1892 and was constituted a division of French West Africa in 1904 under the name of Dahomey. It became an independent republic within the French Community on 4 Dec. 1958, and acquired full independence on 1 Aug. 1960.

In the sixth *coup* since independence, Maj. Mathieu (now Ahmed) Kerekou came to power on 26 Oct. 1972 and proclaimed a Marxist–Leninist state, whose name was altered from Dahomey to Benin on 1 Dec. 1975.

AREA AND POPULATION. Benin is bounded east by Nigeria, north by Niger and Burkina Faso, west by Togo and south by the Gulf of Guinea. The area is 112,622 sq. km, and the population, census 1979, 3,338,240. Estimate (1984) 3,832,000. In 1979, 48% of the inhabitants were male, 14·2% urban and 49% were under 15 years of age. The seat of government is Porto Novo (208,258 inhabitants in 1982); the chief port and business centre is Cotonou (487,020 in 1982); other important towns are Natitingou (50,800, 1979), Abomey (41,000), Kandi (31,000), Ouidah (30,000) and Parakou (23,000).

French is the official language, while 47% of the people speak Fon, 12% Adja, 10% Bariba, 9% Yoruba, 5% Somba and 5% Aizo.

CLIMATE. In coastal parts there is an equatorial climate, with a long rainy season from March to July and a short rainy season in Oct. and Nov. The dry season increases in length from the coast, with inland areas having rain only between May and Sept. Porto Novo. Jan. 82°F (27·8°C), July 78°F (25·6°C). Annual rainfall 52″ (1,300 mm). Cotonou. Jan. 81°F (27·2°C), July 77°F (25°C). Annual rainfall 53″ (1,325 mm).

CONSTITUTION AND GOVERNMENT. Under a *Loi fondamentale* adopted in Aug. 1977, the sole political party is the *Parti de la Revolution Populaire du Bénin;* its Congress held in Nov. 1979 elected a Central Committee of 45 members to direct Party policy and to appoint the 13-member Political Bureau.

There is a unicameral legislature, the National Revolutionary Assembly of 196 People's Commissioners elected on 10 June 1984 for 5 years from the sole list of the PRPB.

The Assembly elects the President, who appoints and leads a National Executive Council composed in March 1985 as follows:

President, Minister of National Defence: Brig.-Gen. Ahmed Kerekou (re-elected 31 July 1984).

President of National Executive Council, Minister of Defence: Brig.-Gen. Ahmed Mathieu Kerekou.

Ministers-Delegate to the Presidency: Maj. Edouard Zodehougan, Kifouli Salami. *Rural Development and Co-operative Action:* Maj. Adolphe Biaou. *Equipment and Transport:* Giriguissou Gado. *Finance and Economy:* Hospice Antonio. *Commerce, Crafts and Tourism:* Soule Dankoro. *Nursery and Primary Education:* Capt. Philippe Akpo. *Secondary and Higher Education:* Lieut.-Col. Michel Alladayé. *Culture, Youth and Sports:* Traoré Ali Moussa. *Labour and Social Affairs:* André Archade. *Public Health:* Vincent Guezodje. *Information and Communications:* Ali Houdou. *Foreign Affairs and Co-operation:* Frédéric Affo. *Justice:* Didier Dassi.

National flag: Green with a red star in the canton.

Local Government. The 6 provinces, Atakora, Borgou, Zou, Ouémé, Atlantique and Mono, each governed by an appointed Prefect and a Provincial Revolutionary Council, are divided into 84 districts.

DEFENCE. National service is for a period of 18 months.

Army. The Army consists of 3 infantry, 1 para-commando, 1 engineer and 1 service battalion, 1 armoured reconnaissance squadron and 1 artillery battery. Strength (1985) 3,000, with an additional 1,100-strong paramilitary gendarmerie.

Navy. A naval force was formed in 1979 with 4 fast gunboats and 2 fast torpedo boats transferred from the USSR, constituting a somewhat over-ambitious flotilla for such a short coastline. Personnel in 1985, 200.

Air Force. The Air Force has a strength of about 100 officers and men, 2 twin-turboprop An-26, 2 F.27, 2 C-47 and 3 An-2 transports, 1 Cessna Skymaster, 1 Aero Commander 500, 2 Broussard communications aircraft, up to 6 L-39 jet trainers, an Agusta-Bell 47G and an Alouette II helicopter. A twin-turbofan Corvette is operated by the Air Force on VIP missions for government agencies.

INTERNATIONAL RELATIONS

Membership. Benin is a member of UN, OAU and is an ACP country of EEC.

ECONOMY

Planning. A 10-year development plan (1980–90) envisages an expenditure of 958,800m. francs CFA.

Budget. The 1982 recurrent budget balanced at 46,863m. francs CFA and the investment budget at 96,730m. francs CFA.

Currency. The monetary unit is the *franc CFA (Communauté financière africaine)*, with a parity value of 50 *francs CFA* to 1 French *franc.* There are coins of 1, 2, 5, 10 and 25 *francs CFA*, and banknotes of 50, 100, 500, 1,000 and 5,000 *francs CFA*.

Banking. The *Banque Centrale des Etats de l'Afrique de l'Ouest* is the bank of issue and the central bank. The *Banque Commerciale du Bénin*, in Cotonou, conducts all government business.

ENERGY AND NATURAL RESOURCES

Electricity. The national electricity and water company, *Société Béninoise d'Electricité et d'Eau*, produced 5m. kwh in 1978 from generating plants at Cotonou, Porto-Novo and Parakou. Major development of hydro-electric resources along the Mono river are being conducted jointly with Togo.

Oil. The Semé oilfield, located 10 miles offshore, was discovered in 1968. Production is expected to commence in 1981–82 and should reach 150,000 bbls a day.

Agriculture. 90% of the population subsist by agriculture. The chief products, 1982 (in 1,000 tonnes) were: Cassava, 100; yams, 800; maize, 350; sorghum, 60; groundnuts, 65; beans, 50; rice,16; and sweet potatoes, 15, while cash crops were palm kernels, 75, and palm oil, 36. Cotton cultivation has been successfully introduced in the north; coffee cultivation has given good results in the south.

Livestock (1983 in 1,000): Cattle (880), sheep (1,080), goats (1,000), pigs (500), poultry (5m.), horses (6), asses (1).

Fisheries. Total catch in 1981 was 26,000 tonnes (80% from inland and lagoon waters).

Forestry. There are about 16,000 sq. km of classified forest, mainly in the north. Roundwood production in 1981 was 3·88m. cu. metres.

INDUSTRY AND TRADE

Industry. Industrial plants are few, limited mainly to palm-oil processing and brewing. Under the 1977–80 Plan, a sugar complex was built at Savé and a cement plant at Onigbolo. There are textile mills at Cotonou and Parakou.

Labour. In 1973 the small trade unions were amalgamated to form a single body, now named the *Union Nationale des Syndicats des Travaillers du Bénin.*

Commerce. Imports in 1978, 70,197m. francs CFA; exports, 6,140m. francs CFA of which cotton amounted to 36%, cocoa to 30% and palm oil 12% by value. In 1978, France provided 27% and the UK 13% of imports, while of exports the Netherlands took 28%, Japan 27% and France 24%.

Total trade between Benin and UK (British Department of Trade returns, in £1,000 sterling):

	1980	*1981*	*1982*	*1983*	*1984*
Imports to UK	2,856	896	1,227	2,887	2,101
Exports and re-exports from UK	13,119	18,611	14,941	10,577	6,829

Tourism. There were 23,033 foreign tourists in 1977.

COMMUNICATIONS

Roads. There were 7,200 km of roads in 1979. There were 9,592 motor cars and 6,927 goods vehicles in 1979.

Railways. There are 579 km of metre-gauge railway. One line connects Cotonou with Parakou (438 km) and is to be extended to Dosso (in Niger); the second runs from Cotonou *via* Porto-Novo to Pobé (107 km); and the third from Cotonou *via* Ouidah to Segboroué on the Togo frontier (34 km), continuing to Lomé. In 1981 1·9m. passengers and 419,000 tonnes of freight were carried.

Aviation. In 1981, 80,400 passengers used Cotonou airport. There are other airports at Abomey, Natitingou, Kandi and Parakou.

Shipping. In 1982, 1·08m. tonnes were unloaded and 53,800 tonnes loaded at the port of Cotonou. There were (1982) 12 vessels of 4,450 GRT registered in Benin.

Post and Broadcasting. There were, in 1975, 9,624 telephones. Telegraph lines connect Cotonou with Togo, Niger and Senegal. In 1983 there were 68,000 radios and 12,700 television receivers.

Cinemas. In 1976 there were 4 cinemas with a seating capacity of 4,400.

Newspapers. In 1984 there was 1 daily newspaper with a circulation of 10,000.

JUSTICE, RELIGION, EDUCATION AND WELFARE

Justice. The Supreme Court is at Cotonou. There are Magistrates Courts in Cotonou, Porto-Novo, Natitingou, Abomey, Kandi, Ouidah and Parakou, and a *tribunal de conciliation* in each district. Judges at provincial and district level are appointed by and responsible to the Executive Council.

Religion. 66% of the population follow animist beliefs, chiefly Voodoo, about 17% are Christian, mainly Roman Catholic, and 15% Moslem.

Education. There were, in 1983, 428,185 pupils in primary schools, 117,724 in secondary schools and 6,369 students in technical schools. The University of Benin (Cotonou) had 4,335 students in 1980.

Health. In 1978 there were 371 hospitals and dispensaries with 4,968 beds, and in 1979 there were 204 doctors, 13 dentists, 55 pharmacists and 1,294 midwives.

DIPLOMATIC REPRESENTATIVES

Of Benin in Great Britain
Ambassador: Souler Issoufou Idrissou (resides in Paris).

Of Great Britain in Benin
Ambassador: (Vacant).

Of Benin in the USA (2737 Cathedral Ave., NW, Washington, D.C., 20008)
Ambassador: Guy Landry Hazoume.

Of the USA in Benin (Rue Caporal Anani Bernard, Cotonou)
Ambassador: George E. Moose.

Book of Reference

Ronen, D., *Dahomey: Between Tradition and Modernity.* Cornell Univ. Press, 1975

BERMUDA

Capital: Hamilton
Population: 54,893 (1980)
GNP per capita: US$12,910 (1981)

HISTORY. The Spaniards visited the islands in 1515, but, according to a 17th-century French cartographer, they were discovered in 1503 by Juan Bermudez, after whom they were named. No settlement was made, and they were uninhabited until a party of colonists under Sir George Somers was wrecked there in 1609. A company was formed for the 'Plantation of the Somers' Islands', as they were called at first, and in 1684 the Crown took over the government.

AREA AND POPULATION. Bermuda consists of a group of some 150 small islands (about 20 inhabited), situated in the western Atlantic (32° 18′ N. lat., 64° 46′ W. long.); the nearest point of the mainland, about 570 miles distant, is Cape Hatteras, N.C., and 690 miles from New York.

The area is 20·59 sq. miles (53·3 sq. km), of which 2·3 sq. miles were leased in 1941 for 99 years to the US Government for naval and air bases. The civil population (*i.e.*, excluding British and American military, naval and air force personnel) in 1980 (Census) was 54,893.

Chief town, Hamilton; population, about 3,000.

In 1981 there were 783 live births, 579 marriages and 452 deaths; infantile mortality rate was 14 per 1,000 live births.

CLIMATE. A pleasantly warm and humid climate, with up to 60″ (1,500 mm) of rain, spread evenly throughout the year. Hamilton. Jan. 63°F (17·2°C), July 79°F (26·1°C). Annual rainfall 59″ (1,463 mm).

CONSTITUTION AND GOVERNMENT. Bermuda is a colony with representative government. Under the constitution of 8 June 1968 the Governor, appointed by the Crown, is normally bound to accept the advice of the Cabinet in matters other than external affairs, defence, internal security and the police, for which he retains special responsibility. The Cabinet is appointed from among members of the bicameral legislature, on the recommendation of the Premier. The Senate, of whom one or two members may serve on Cabinet, consists of 11 members. As a result of a Constitutional Conference held in Feb. 1979, it was decided that 5 Senators would be appointed by the Governor on the recommendation of the Premier, 3 by the Governor on the recommendation of the Opposition Leader and 3 by the Governor in his own discretion. The 40 members of the House of Assembly are elected 2 from each of 20 constituencies under full universal, adult suffrage. The general election on 18 May 1976 resulted in the return of 26 members of the United Bermuda Party and 14 members of the Progressive Labour Party. A by-election was held on 21 Sept. 1976 resulting in a total of 25 members of the United Bermuda Party and 15 members of the Progressive Labour Party. A general election was held on 6 Feb. 1983, which resulted in the United Bermuda Party being returned to power. The United Bermuda Party won 26 seats and the Progressive Labour Party, 14.

Governor: The Viscount Dunrossil, CMG.
Premier: John W. D. Swan.
Flag: The British Red Ensign with the badge of the Colony in the fly.

DEFENCE. The Bermuda Regiment had 630 men and women in 1983.

ECONOMY

Budget. Revenue and expenditure in $B for years ending 31 March:

	1979–80	*1980–81*	*1981–82* [1]	*1982–83*	*1983–84*
Revenue	105,207,166	125,232,000	131,966,000	155,129,150	165,498,190
Expenditure	101,224,172	122,936,000	129,821,000	154,858,550	165,466,440

[1] Estimate.

Expenditure in $B1,000 (excluding capital items) was earmarked as follows:

	1979–80	*1980–81*	*1981–82*	*1982–83*	*1983–84*
Education	19,189	24,717	21,928	25,919	24,068
Health and Social Services	18,189	21,353	28,478	30,386	41,855
Public Works	12,011	15,284	14,817	13,333	16,069
Police	8,006	9,244	10,623	12,427	13,933
Tourism	7,136	8,124	8,880	10,851	13,335
Marine and Air Services	4,539	8,028	8,312	3,794	4,678
Public Transportation	4,222	4,707	1,496	4,307	936
Agriculture and Fisheries	3,874	4,080	4,452	5,077	6,266
Post Office	2,939	3,429	3,404	4,169	5,022

Chief sources of revenue in 1983–84 were: Customs duties, $66·9m.; employment tax, $15·6m.; companies tax, $8,461,000; land tax, $8,355,000; hotel occupancy tax, $8·03m.; hospital levy, $15,540,000; vehicle licenses, $5,425,000; stamp duties, $4,750,000; passenger taxes, $5,250,000.

Public debt, as at 31 March 1981, was $4·3m.

Currency. Decimal currency based on a *Bermuda dollar* of 100 *cents* was introduced 6 Feb. 1970. In Feb. 1985 £1 = 1.05 Bermuda dollars and US$1 = 1 Bermuda dollar. The Bermuda Monetary Authority issues notes in denominations of $100, $50, $20, $10, $5 and $1, and coins in values of 50c, 25c, 10c, 5c and 1c.

Banking. There are 3 banks, the Bank of Bermuda, Ltd, the Bank of N. T. Butterfield and Son, Ltd, and the Bermuda Provident Bank, Ltd.

Weights and Measures. British, except that US instead of Imperial fluid measures are used.

AGRICULTURE. The chief products are fresh vegetables, bananas and citrus fruit. In 1983–84, 620 acres were under cultivation. In 1983 about 5% of the work force were engaged in agriculture, fishing and horticulture.

In 1983, total value of agricultural products was $B7,551,947.

Livestock (1983): Cattle, 1,000; pigs, 2,000; goats, 1,000; poultry (1982), 47,000.

TRADE UNIONS. Legislation providing for trade unions was enacted in Oct. 1946, and there are 9 trade unions with a total membership (1983) of 7,622.

COMMERCE. Imports and exports in $B:

	1980	*1981*	*1982*	*1983*
Imports	311,468,000	322,732,859	348,000,000	377,732,000
Exports	36,489,000	29,383,399	17,000,000	22,762,000

The visible adverse balance of trade is more than compensated for by invisible exports, including tourism and off-shore insurance business.

Imports in 1983 from USA, $212m.; UK, $31m.; Canada, $24m.; Japan, $18m.; West Indies, $5m.; Hong Kong, $6m.; France, $5m.; Federal Republic of Germany, $4m.; Netherlands, $2m.; Italy, $2m.

In 1980 the principal imports were food, drink and tobacco ($65m.), finished manufactures ($62m.), mineral fuels ($54m.), chemicals ($31m.); the principal local exports were beauty preparations ($443,000). The bulk of exports comprise sales of fuel to aircraft and ships, and re-exports of pharmaceuticals.

Total trade between Bermuda and UK, in £1,000 sterling (British Department of Trade returns):

	1980	*1981*	*1982*	*1983*	*1984*
Imports to UK	2,900	5,652	3,128	4,019	3,037
Exports and re-exports from UK	24,499	17,492	18,222	24,924	22,843

TOURISM. In 1983, 567,710 tourists visited Bermuda including those arriving by air and cruise ship. Tourism represents 41% of GDP.

COMMUNICATIONS

Roads. In 1948 the railway service was discontinued and a government-operated bus service introduced.

Between 1908 and Aug. 1946 the use of motor vehicles, with the exception of ambulances, fire engines and other essential services, was prohibited. With the passing of the Motor Car Act in 1946, the use of motor vehicles, subject to certain limitations on size and horse-power, became lawful. In 1981, out of 40,402 registered vehicles 14,442 were private cars.

Aviation. American Airlines, Pan American, Delta Airlines and Eastern Airlines maintain regular services between Bermuda and the USA. British Airways also have regular flights through Bermuda linking Bermuda with Baltimore and London. Air Canada Airlines call at Bermuda on their service between Toronto, Montreal and Halifax.

Shipping. In 1983, 496 commercial and pleasure vessels of 5,408,557 gross tons were registered in Hamilton. In 1981 the gross tonnage of 544 vessels entered and cleared was 4,494,572 tons.

Post and Broadcasting (1983). There are 15 post offices. The telephone company is privately owned and operated 40,000 telephones in 1983. Cables connect the islands with the USA, Halifax (N.S.) and Tortola, providing connexion with the world.

Radio and television broadcasting is commercial.

Newspapers (1984). There is 1 daily newspaper with a circulation of 14,000.

JUSTICE, EDUCATION AND WELFARE

Justice. There are 3 magistrates' courts, 2 Supreme Courts and a court of appeal. The police had a strength of 415 men and women in 1983.

Education. Education is compulsory between the ages of 5 and 16, and government assistance is given by the payment of grants, and, where necessary, of school fees. Free elementary education was introduced on 1 May 1949 and free secondary education in Sept. 1965. In 1981, there were 11 government nurseries, 6 special units for the handicapped, 18 government primary schools, 9 government secondary schools, the Bermuda College and 4 private, fee-paying schools. Total enrolment in 1984 was 10,962 pupils.

Health. In 1983 there were 108 doctors.

Books of Reference

Annual Report, 1971. HMSO, 1972
Bermuda Historical Quarterly. 1944 ff.
Dyer, H. T., *The Next 20 Years: A Report on the Development Plans for Bermuda.* Hamilton, 1963
Hayward, S. J., Holt-Gomez, V., and Sterrer, W., *Bermuda's Delicate Balance: People and the Environment.* Hamilton, 1981
Warwick, J. B., (ed.), *Who's Who in Bermuda 1980–81.* Hamilton, 1982
Wilkinson, H. C., *Bermuda from Sail to Steam.* OUP, 1973
Zuill, W. S., *The Story of Bermuda and Her People.* London, 1973

National Library: The Bermuda Library, Hamilton. *Head Librarian:* Mrs M. Skiffington.

BHUTÁN

Capital: Thimphu
Population: 1·25m. (1983)
GNP per capita: US$80 (1981)

Druk-yul

HISTORY. In 1774 the East India Company concluded a treaty with the ruler of Bhután. Under a treaty signed in Nov. 1865 the Bhután Government was granted an annual subsidy. By an amending treaty concluded in Jan. 1910 the British Government undertook to exercise no interference in the internal affairs of Bhután, and the Bhután Government agreed to be guided by the advice of the British Government in regard to its external relations.

The Government of India concluded a fresh treaty with Bhután on 8 Aug. 1949. Under this treaty the Government of Bhután continues to be guided by the Government of India in regard to its external relations, and the Government of India have undertaken not to interfere in the internal administration of Bhután. The subsidy paid to Bhután has been increased to Rs 500,000, and the Government of India agreed to retrocede to Bhután an area of about 32 sq. miles in the territory known as Dewangiri, which was annexed in 1865.

AREA AND POPULATION. Bhután is situated in the eastern Himalayas, bordered north by China and on all other sides by India. Extreme length from east to west 190 miles: extreme breadth 90 miles. Area about 18,000 sq. miles (46,600 sq. km); population estimated at approximately 1,247,000 (1983). Life expectancy (1977) was 46 years. The capital is at Thimphu (1952, 15,000 population). There are 17 districts.

CLIMATE. The climate is largely controlled by altitude. The mountainous north is cold, with perpetual snow on the summits, but the centre has a more moderate climate, though winters are cold, with rainfall under 40″ (1,000 mm). In the south, the climate is humid sub-tropical and rainfall approaches 200″ (5,000 mm).

KING. Jigme Singye Wangchuck, succeeded his father Jigme Dorji Wangchuck who died 21 July 1972.

GOVERNMENT. In 1907 the Tongsa Penlop (the governor of the province of Tongsa in eastern Bhután), Sir Ugyen Wangchuk, GCIE, KCSI, was elected as the first hereditary Maharaja of Bhután. The Bhutánese title is Druk Gyalpo, but his successor is now addressed as King of Bhután. From Oct. 1969 the absolute monarchy was changed to a form of 'democratic monarchy'. The National Assembly (*Tshogdu*) was reinstituted in 1953. It has approximately 150 members and meets twice a year. Two-thirds are representatives of the people and are elected for a 3-year term. All Bhutánese over 25 years may be candidates. Ten monastic representatives are elected by regional ecclesiastical bodies, while the remaining members are nominated by the King, and include members of the Council of Ministers and the Royal Advisory Council.

The official languages are Dzongkha, Nepali and English.

National flag: Diagonally yellow over orange, over all in the centre a white dragon.

Local government: There are 17 districts, each under a governor *(Dzongda)*.

DEFENCE

Army. There is an Army of about 4,000 men.

INTERNATIONAL RELATIONS

Membership. Bhután is a member of UN.

ECONOMY

Planning. The Government of Bhután has drawn up five 5-year development plans (1961–65, 1966–70, 1971–76, 1977–81, 1982–86), with the active co-operation and financial support of the Government of India. Educational facilities are being expanded and medical facilities are being provided. Forest and mineral wealth is to be exploited. About 1,900 km of new roads have been built.

Budget. The budget for 1982–83 envisaged expenditure of N635m. and revenue of N165m.

Currency. Paper currency has been introduced, known as the *Ngultrum*. Silver currency is known as *Tikchung*. Indian currency is also legal tender.

Banking. The Bank of Bhután was established in 1968. The headquarters are at Phuntsholing with 14 branches throughout the country.

ENERGY AND NATURAL RESOURCES

Electricity. In 1974 construction work began on the Chukha hydro-electric project at a cost of US$92m. and in 1979, 15 towns and 97 villages had electricity.

Minerals. Large deposits of limestone, marble, dolomite, graphite, lead, copper, slate, coal, talc, gypsum, beryl, mica, pyrites and tufa have been found.

Agriculture. The area under cultivation in 1978 was 5,534 sq. km. The chief products are rice, millet, wheat, barley, maize, cardomom, potatoes, oranges, apples, handloom cloth, timber and yaks. Extensive and valuable forests abound.

Livestock (1983): Horses, 16,000; asses, 18,000; cattle, 312,000; pigs, 74,000; sheep, 43,000; poultry (1982), 187,000.

INDUSTRY AND TRADE

Industry. In 1980 there were about 40 small-scale industrial units and also a cement plant, a fruit processing factory, a tea-chest ply veneer factory, a resin and turpentine factory and 3 distilleries.

Commerce. Trade with India is considerable but timber, cardomom and liquor are also exported to the Middle East, Singapore and Western Europe. Bhután imported from the UK in 1984 goods valued at £86,000.

Tourism. The country has been opened for tourism since 1974 and it is the largest source of foreign exchange. In 1979–80, 1,500 tourists visited Bhután.

COMMUNICATIONS

Roads. In 1978 there were about 1,775 km of roads. In 1979, there were 2,179 vehicles, of which 1,432 were private cars and 747 buses and trucks.

Post. A modern postal system was introduced in 1962. There are 53 general post offices and 28 branch post offices. In 1979 there were 1,086 km of telephone lines, 15 automatic exchanges and (1978) 1,355 telephones.

Newspapers. There is a government weekly newspaper published in 3 languages (English, Dzongkha and Nepali). Total circulation (1984) about 5,000.

JUSTICE, RELIGION, EDUCATION AND WELFARE

Justice. There is a Magistrate's Court in each district, under a *Thrimpon*, from which appeal is to the High Court in Paro.

Religion. The majority of the people are Mahayana Buddhists of the Drukpa subsect of the Karyud School which was first introduced from Tibet during the 12th century.

Education. In 1982 there were 22,288 pupils and 797 teachers in primary schools, 14,546 pupils and 520 teachers in secondary schools and 401 pupils and 49 teachers in technical schools. Many students receive training under the Colombo Plan in Australia, New Zealand, Japan, Singapore and UK.

Health. There were (1980) 12 general hospitals, 39 dispensaries, 43 basic health units, 4 indigenous dispensaries, 3 leprosy hospitals, 1 mobile hospital, 1 health school and 15 malaria eradication centres. In 1979 beds totalled 536 and there were 52 doctors.

DIPLOMATIC REPRESENTATIVE

Of Bhután to the United Nations
Ambassador: Dago Tshering.

The Government of Bhután is in diplomatic relations with Bangladesh and India at ambassadorial level. Honorary Consuls have also been appointed in Singapore and Hong Kong.

Books of Reference

Bhutan, Himalayan Kingdom. Bhután Government, Thimphu, 1979
Das, N., *The Dragon Country.* New Delhi, 1973
Labh, K., *India and Bhutan.* New Delhi, 1974
Mehra, G. N., *Bhutan: Land of the Peaceful Dragon.* New Delhi, 1974
Olschak, B. C., *Bhutan: Land of Hidden Treasures.* New Delhi, 1971
Rahul, R., *Royal Bhutan.* New Delhi, 1983
Ronaldshay, the Earl of, *Lands of the Thunderbolt.* 2nd ed. London, 1931
Rose, L. E., *The Politics of Bhutan.* Cornell Univ. Press, 1977
Rustomji, N., *Bhutan: The Dragon Kingdom in Crisis.* OUP, 1978

BOLIVIA

Capital: La Paz
Population: 6·25m. (1984)
GNP per capita: US$600 (1981)

República de Bolivia

HISTORY. Until 1884, when Bolivia was defeated by Chile, she had a strip bordering on the Pacific which contains extensive nitrate beds and at that time the port of Cobija (which no longer exists). She lost this area to Chile; but in Sept. 1953 Chile declared Arica a free port and, although it is no longer a free port for Bolivian imports, Bolivia still has certain privileges.

AREA AND POPULATION. Bolivia is a landlocked state with an area of some 424,165 sq. miles (1,098,581 sq. km).

The following table shows the area and population of the departments (the capitals of each are given in brackets):

Departments	*Area (sq. km)*	*Census 1976*	*Census 1982* [1]	*Per sq. km 1975*
La Paz (La Paz)	133,985	1,456,078	1,913,184	12·50
Cochabamba (Cochabamba)	55,631	720,952	908,674	15·57
Potosí (Potosí)	118,218	657,743	823,485	7·98
Santa Cruz (Santa Cruz)	370,621	710,724	942,986	1·36
Chuquisaca (Sucre)	51,524	358,516	435,406	9·69
Tarija (Tarija)	37,623	186,704	246,691	5·95
Oruro (Oruro)	53,588	310,409	385,121	6·93
Beni (Trinidad)	213,564	168,367	217,700	0·99
Pando (Cobija)	63,827	34,493	42,594	0·55
Total	1,098,581	4,687,718	5,915,841	4·85

[1] Preliminary.

Total population (estimate 1984) 6,252,250.

Population (estimate 1982) of the principal towns: La Paz, 881,404; Santa Cruz, 376,917; Cochabamba, 281,962; Oruro, 132,213; Potosí, 103,182; Sucre, 79,941; Tarija, 54,001.

The language of the educated classes is Spanish, that of the majority of Indians, Aymará (25·2%) or Quechua (34·4%).

CLIMATE. The very varied geography of Bolivia produces several different climates. The two most significant are the low-lying areas in the Amazon Basin, which are very warm and damp throughout the year, with heavy rainfall from Nov. to March, and the alti-plano, which is generally dry between May and Nov. with abundant sunshine, but the nights are cold in June and July, while the months from Dec. to March are the wettest. La Paz. Jan. 53°F (11·7°C), July 47°F (8·3°C). Annual rainfall 23″ (574 mm). Sucre. Jan. 55°F (13°C), July 49°F (9·4°C). Annual rainfall 27″ (675 mm).

CONSTITUTION AND GOVERNMENT. The Republic of Bolivia was proclaimed on 6 Aug. 1825; its first constitution was adopted on 19 Nov. 1826.

La Paz is the actual capital and seat of the Government, but Sucre is the legal capital and the seat of the judiciary.

The following is a list of presidents since 1966 and the date on which they took office:

Gen. René Barrientos Ortuño (Constitutional President killed in air accident), 6 Aug. 1966–27 April 1969.
Dr Luis Adolfo Siles Salinas (deposed), 27 April 1969–26 Sept. 1969.
Gen. Alfredo Ovando Candia, 26 Sept. 1969–6 Oct. 1970.
Gen. Juan José Torres, 7 Oct. 1970–21 Aug. 1971.
Gen. Hugo Banzer Suarez, 21 Aug. 1971–21 July 1978.
Gen. Juan Pereda Asbun, 21 July 1978–24 Nov. 1978.
Gen. David Padilla Arancibia, 24 Nov. 1978–8 Aug. 1979.
Dr Walter Guevara Arze (deposed), 8 Aug. 1979–1 Nov. 1979.
Dr Lydia Gueiler Tejada (deposed), 16 Nov. 1979–17 July 1980.
Maj.-Gen. Luis García Meza Tejada (resigned), 18 July 1980–4 Aug. 1981.
Military Junta, 4 Aug. 1981–4 Sept. 1981.
Gen. Celso Torrelio Villa, (resigned), 4 Sept. 1981–19 July 1982.
Brig.-Gen. Guido Vildoso Calderón, 21 July 1982–10 Oct. 1982.

Following elections in July 1979 which were inconclusive an interim President was chosen with the agreement of the three parties who had polled most votes. For details of political history 1970–78 *see* THE STATESMAN'S YEAR-BOOK, 1980–81 and for the period 1978–1980 *see* THE STATESMAN'S YEAR-BOOK, 1983–84.

The President and Vice-President are elected by universal suffrage for a four year term. The President appoints the members of his Cabinet from candidates nominated by the Senate. There is a bicameral legislature; the Senate comprises 27 members, 3 from each department, and the Chamber of Deputies 117 members, all elected for 4 years. The Congress elected on 29 June 1980 was dissolved following the *coup* on 17 July 1980, but reconvened on 6 Oct. 1982.

The Cabinet was composed as follows in Aug. 1984 but resigned in Jan. 1985.

President: Dr Siles Zuazo (sworn in 10 Oct. 1982).

Vice-President: Jaime Paz Zamora. *Foreign Affairs and Worship:* Dr Gustavo Fernández Saavedra. *Interior, Migration and Justice:* Vacant. *Defence:* Manuel Cárdenas Mallo. *Aeronautics:* Gen. Antonio Arnez Camacho. *Finance:* Gualberto Mercado. *Planning:* Ernesto Aranibar Quiroga. *Education and Culture:* Dr Alfonso Camacho Peña. *Transport and Communications:* Hernando Poppe Martínez. *Industry, Commerce and Tourism:* Freddy Justiniano. *Labour:* Dr Horst Grebe López. *Mining and Metallurgy:* Carlos Carvajal Nava. *Health:* Dr Javier Torrez Goitia. *Peasant Affairs and Agriculture:* Dr Julio Mendoza Huaynoca. *Energy and Hydrocarbons:* Dr Luis Saucedo Justiniano. *Housing:* Guillermo Capobianco Rivera. *Secretary-General to the Presidency:* Miguel Urioste Fernández. *Secretary-General of Integration:* Jorge Agreda Balderrama. *Secretary-General of Information:* Dr Mario Rueda Peña.

National flag: Three horizontal stripes of red, yellow, green, with the arms of Bolivia in the centre.

National anthem: Bolivianos, el hado propicio (words by I. de Sanjinés; tune by B. Vincenti).

Local Government: The republic is divided into 9 departments, established in Jan. 1826, with 98 provinces administered by sub-prefects, and 1,272 cantons administered by corregidores. The supreme authority in each department is vested in a prefect appointed by the President.

DEFENCE. Bolivia is divided into 8 military districts, with divisional headquarters in Viacha, Oruro, Villa Montes, Camiri, Roboré, Riberalta, Santa Cruz, Cochabamba; regional HQ are located at La Paz, Sucre, Tarija, Potosí, Trinidad and Cobija. There is selective conscription for 12 months at the age of 18 years.

Army. The Army consists of 13 infantry, 6 cavalry, 2 mechanized, 3 artillery, 2 ranger and 1 parachute regiments, and 2 armoured anti-tank and 6 engineer battalions. Equipment, 24 EE-9 Cascavel armoured cars. Strength (1985) 20,000.

Navy. A small Navy exists for river and lake patrol comprising 36 patrol craft operating in Lake Titicaca and the Bolivia-Paraguay 6,000-mile river systems, 1 transport (a gift from Venezuela for use to and from Bolivian free zones in Argentina and Uruguay) and 2 hospital ships (one a gift from USA).

Personnel in 1985 totalled 4,000 officers and men including marines. Most training of officers and petty officers is carried out in Argentina. The junior ratings are almost entirely converted soldiers.

Air Force. The Air Force, established in 1923, has 3 combat-capable squadrons, equipped with 6 F-86F jet fighters, 12 Canadian-built T-33 armed jet trainers, and 5 T-6G armed piston-engined trainers, for counter-insurgency operations. On order are 12 Mirage 50 fighters. A search and rescue helicopter squadron has 6 Brazilian-assembled Gaviãos (Lamas). Other types in service include Brazilian T-23 Uirapuru and American T-41 primary trainers, Italian SF.260M and Swiss turboprop-powered Pilatus PC-7 basic trainers, 16 PC-6 Turbo Porter utility aircraft, 1 Electra four-turboprop transport, 6 Fokker F.27 and 5 Israeli-built Arava twin-turboprop light transports, 3 Convair 580 twin-turboprop transports, 2 C-130H/L-100-30 Hercules, 8 C-47 and 2 Convair 440 piston-engined transports with which a military airline service is operated, about 30 Cessna single- and twin-engined light aircraft and helicopters. Personnel strength (1985) about 3,500.

INTERNATIONAL RELATIONS

Membership. Bolivia is a member of UN, OAS, LAIA (formerly LAFTA), the Andean Group and the Amazon Pact.

External Debt. The contracted external debt was US$3,641m., Dec. 1980.

ECONOMY

Budget. Revenue and expenditures in 1m. *pesos bolivianos* balanced as follows: In 1982 there was a projected budget deficit of $b.110,959m.

Currency. On 1 Jan. 1963 the *peso boliviano* ($b.) was introduced. Exchange rates were $b.45,000 = US$1 and $b.47,790 = £1 in Feb. 1985.

Banking. The Banco Central de Bolivia was established in 1911 as Banco de la Nacion Boliviana and re-organized in 1928. The Bank was nationalized in 1939. At 30 Dec. 1982 the Bank's gross gold and foreign exchange reserves amounted to US$214·1m.

Weights and Measures. The metric system of weights and measures is used by the administration and prescribed by law, but the old Spanish system is also employed.

ENERGY AND NATURAL RESOURCES

Electricity. Electric power production is expanding. Installed capacity was estimated at 428,595 kw. at the end of 1978. Estimated production from all sources (1978), 1,340,996 mwh.

Oil and Gas. There are petroleum and natural gas deposits in the Santa Cruz-Camiri areas. A pipeline for crude oil connects Caranda (Santa Cruz) with the Pacific coast at Arica (Chile) and a natural gas pipeline to Argentina was inaugurated in May 1972. All production, refining and internal distribution is now in the hands of *Yacimientos Petroliferos Fiscales Bolivianos* (the State Petroleum Organization). Total production of petroleum and condensates in 1981 was estimated at 8·1m. bbls. Production of natural gas in 1981 was estimated at 175,478m. cu. ft.

Minerals. Mining is the most important industry, accounting for about 69% of the foreign-exchange earnings. About half the mineral mined is tin. Tin mines are at altitudes of from 12,000 to 18,000 ft, where few except native Indians can stand the conditions; transport is costly. Bolivian tin is extracted by shaft-mining, frequently very deep; the ore yields only 0·7% or less of tin and is very refractory; tin is exported in concentrates called *barrilla,* through Pacific ports for refining. Smelting capacity was increased in 1980 and it is planned to smelt all the ores from the State Mining Co. but complex ores still have to be exported for smelting. Tin production in 1981 was 27,562 tonnes.

The state industry is being run by the *Corporación Minera de Bolivia* (COMIBOL) employing about 23,000 in mining and administrative capacities.

Alluvial gold deposits in the Alto Beni region are being exploited. Co-operative mines at Tipuani produced 770 kg in 1978.

Foreign firms are seeking exploration rights for uranium and a small uranium processing plant was opened in Oct. 1980 at Cotaje (Potosí province). Large deposits of salt are found near Lake Poopó and in the south of Bolivia.

Agriculture. The extensive and still largely undeveloped region east of the Andes comprises about three-quarters of the entire area of the country, and since the agrarian reform of 1952 sugar-cane, rice and cotton have been grown in this *Oriente* in increasing abundance, reaching self-sufficiency in all these products. Output in tonnes in 1980 was: Sugar-cane, 2·83m.; rice, 87,700; coffee, 19,600; maize, 327,700; potatoes, 720,000; wheat, 50,000; cotton (lint), 7,500; cocoa, 25,200.

The public lands of the State have an area of about 245,000 sq. miles, of which 104,000 sq. miles are reserved for special colonization.

A colony of Jewish refugees was established in 1940 at Buena Tierra, 60 miles east of La Paz and, more recently, Japanese and Okinawan settlements in the region of Santa Cruz. The Bolivian Development Corporation has a programme for relief of over-population on the barren altiplano and in 1964 resettled 1,217 families in tropical areas.

Livestock: In 1983 there were 4·2m. head of cattle, mostly in the Santa Cruz and Beni departments; some are exported to Peru; horses, 420,000; asses, 800,000; pigs, 1·7m.; sheep, 9·2m.; goats, 3·2m.; poultry, 10m.

Forestry. Tropical forests with woods ranging from the 'iron tree' to the light *palo de balsa* are beginning to be exploited. In 1962 the Forestry Service announced proved reserves of 46·3m. hectares, plus a similar amount available for immediate development.

INDUSTRY AND TRADE

Industry. There are few industrial establishments and the country relies on imports for the supply of many consumer goods. However a new investment law passed in 1971 provides incentives and protection for new investment, both foreign and domestic, and for reinvestment in various fields including manufacturing industry, mining, agriculture, construction and tourism.

Labour. The Ministry of Planning estimated economically active population in 1970 at 1·48m., of whom 1m. were employed in agriculture, 118,300 in industrial manufacture, 35,100 in construction, 74,000 in commerce and finance, 65,000 in central and local government, 47,800 in mining and 41,900 in transport. The ban on trade unions, imposed in 1974, was lifted in 1978 but re-imposed in 1980.

Commerce. The value of imports and exports in US$1,000 has been as follows:

	1977	*1978*	*1979*	*1980*	*1981*	*1982*
Imports	552,000	848,200	984,000	833,160	917,081	496,084
Exports	556,000	640,300	793,000	942,000	995,298	898,176

Tin ore remains the principal export. Total exports, 1982, of all minerals, in concentrates, ingots or solder, were valued at US$419·4m.

Bolivia having no seaport, imports and exports pass chiefly through the ports of Arica and Antofagasta in Chile, Mollendo-Matarani in Peru, through La Quiaca on the Bolivian-Argentine border and through river-ports on the rivers flowing into the Amazon. The chief imports are lard, flour, cooking oil, iron and steel products, mining machinery, pharmaceuticals, paper products and textiles.

Total trade between Bolivia and UK for 5 years (British Department of Trade returns in £1,000 sterling):

	1980	*1981*	*1982*	*1983*	*1984*
Imports to UK	33,179	36,800	20,899	14,834	20,052
Exports and re-exports from UK	8,684	12,676	4,943	4,711	17,170

COMMUNICATIONS

Roads. A highway, in poor condition, 497 km long, runs from Cochabamba to the lowland farming region of Santa Cruz. La Paz and Oruro are also connected by a metalled road. Of other main highways (unmetalled) there is one from La Paz through Guaqui into Peru, another from La Paz, *via* Oruro, Potosí, Tarija and Bermejo, into Argentina, with branches to Cochabamba, Sucre and Camiri, passable throughout the year except at the height of the rainy season, and others from Villazón to Villa Montes *via* Tarija, passable during the dry season. The total length of the road system is 37,708 km (1977). Motor vehicles in use in 1980, 134,790, including 65,540 cars, 69,250 heavy goods vehicles and buses and 1,133 agricultural tractors.

Railways. In 1964 Bolivian National Railways (ENFE) was formed by the amalgamation of the Bolivian Government Railways, Bolivian Railway Co. and the Bolivian section of the Antofagasta (Chile) & Bolivia Railway. The Guaqui-La Paz Railway, formerly operated by Peru, became part of ENFE in 1973. Access to the Pacific is by 3 routes: to Antofagasta and Arica in Chile, and to Mollendo in Peru *via* Guaqui, the Lake Titicaca train ferry to Puno (Peru), then rail to the coast. Construction began in 1978 of a 150-km line linking Puno with Desaguadero on the Bolivian border which would by-pass the train ferry, though gauge difference would still prevent through running to Peru. Current network totals 3,538 km of metre gauge, comprising unconnected Eastern (1,386 km) and Western (2,152 km) systems. In 1983 the railways carried 2·3m. passengers and 1·1m. tonnes of freight.

Aviation. The national airline is Lloyd Aéreo Boliviano. The airline runs regular services between La Paz and Lima, São Paulo, Buenos Aires, Miami, Caracas, Salta and Arica as well as many internal services. Eastern Airways runs regular flights between La Paz, Buenos Aires, Santiago and Asunción linking Bolivia to the USA. Lufthansa links Bolivia with Europe. Other airlines serving Bolivia are Aerolineas Argentinas, Cruzeiro, Aero Peru and Lan Chile.

Shipping. Traffic on Lake Titicaca between Guaqui and Puno is carried on by the steamers of the Peruvian Corporation. About 12,000 miles of rivers, in 4 main systems (Beni, Pilcomayo, Titicaca-Desaguadero, Mamoré), are open to navigation by light-draught vessels.

Post and Broadcasting. In Bolivia there were, in 1978, 458 post offices, of these, 205 provided telegraph and telephone services together with a further 245 offices for telegraph and telephone service only. There is telephone service in the cities of La Paz, Cochabamba, Oruro, Sucre, Potosí, Santa Cruz, Tarija, Camiri, Tupiza, Villazon, Riberalta and Trinidad with (1982), 144,300 telephones. There are about 119 broadcasting stations, of which 7 are state-owned. There is a commercial government television service.

Newspapers. There were (1984) 7 daily newspapers in La Paz, 2 in Oruro, and 1 in Cochabamba. Several other towns have regular newspapers devoted to local news, but most of them appear only a few times a week. An economic monthly journal *Revista Economica* and 4 daily newspapers are produced in Santa Cruz.

JUSTICE, RELIGION, EDUCATION AND WELFARE

Justice. Justice is administered by the Supreme Court, superior district courts (of 5 or 7 judges) and courts of local justice. The Supreme Court, with headquarters at Sucre, is divided into two sections, civil and criminal, of 5 justices each, with the Chief Justice presiding over both. Members of the Supreme Court are chosen on a two-thirds vote of Congress.

Religion. The Roman Catholic is the recognized religion of the state; the free exercise of other forms of worship is permitted. The Catholic Church is under a cardinal (in Sucre), an archbishop (in La Paz), 6 bishops (Cochabamba, Santa Cruz, Oruro, Potosí, Riberalta and Tarija) and vicars apostolic (titular bishops resident in Cueva, Trinidad, San Ignacio de Velasco, Riberalta and Rurrenabaque).

By a law of 11 Oct. 1911 all marriages must be celebrated by the civil authorities. Divorce is permitted by a law enacted on 15 April 1932.

Education. Primary instruction is free and obligatory between the ages of 6 and 14 years. Estimates for 1974 show that 989,858 children between 6 and 14 years attended school.

At Sucre, Oruro, Potosí, Cochabamba, Santa Cruz, Tarija, Trinidad and La Paz are universities; La Paz is the most important of them while the San Francisco Xavier University at Sucre is one of the oldest in America, founded in 1624.

Health. In 1972 there were 2,143 doctors.

DIPLOMATIC REPRESENTATIVES

Of Bolivia in Great Britain (106 Eaton Sq., London, SW1W 9AD)
Chargé d'Affaires: Carlos Quintanilla.

Of Great Britain in Bolivia (Avenida Arce 2732–2754, La Paz)
Ambassador: Alan White.

Of Bolivia in the USA (3014 Massachusetts Ave, NW, Washington, D.C., 20008)
Ambassador: Mariano Baptista Gumucio.

Of the USA in Bolivia (Banco Popular Del Peru Bldg, La Paz)
Ambassador: Edwin G. Corr.

Of Bolivia to the United Nations
Ambassador: Jorge Gumucio Granier.

Books of Reference

Anuario Geográfico y Estadístico de la República de Bolivia
Anuario del Comercia Exterior de Bolivia
Boletín Mensual de Información Estadística
Baptista Gumucio, M., *Cultural Policy in Bolivia.* UNESCO, 1978
Dunkerley, J., *Rebellion in the Veins: Political Struggle in Bolivia 1952–1982.* London, 1984
Fifer, J. V., *Bolivia: Land, Location and Politics Since 1825.* CUP, 1972
Guillermo, L., *A History of the Bolivian Labour Movement 1848–1971.* CUP, 1977
Klein, H., *Bolivia: The Evolution of a Multi-Ethnic Society.* OUP, 1982

BOTSWANA

Capital: Gaborone
Population: 941,027 (1981)
GNP per capita: US$1,010 (1981)

HISTORY. In 1885 the territory was declared to be within the British sphere; in 1889 it was included in the sphere of the British South Africa Company, but was never administered by the company; in 1890 a Resident Commissioner was appointed, and in 1895, on the annexation of the Crown Colony of British Bechuanaland to the Cape of Good Hope, the British Government was in favour of transferring the Protectorate to the BSA Company, but the three major chiefs of the Bakwena, the Bangwaketse and the Bamangwato went to England to protest against this proposal, and agreement was reached that their country should remain a British Protectorate if they ceded a strip of land on the eastern side of the country for railway construction. This railway was built in 1896–97.

On 30 Sept. 1966 the Bechuanaland Protectorate became an independent and sovereign member of the Commonwealth under the name of the Republic of Botswana.

AREA AND POPULATION. Botswana comprises the territory lying between the Molopo River on the south and the Zambezi on the north, and extending from the Transvaal Province and Zimbabwe on the east to South-West Africa on the west. Area about 222,000 sq. miles (582,000 sq. km); population, census of 1971, was 630,379 (census, 1981, 941,027).

The main business centres (with estimated population, 1984) are Gaborone (79,000), Francistown (36,000), Selebi-Pikwe (33,000), Kanye (22,000), Lobatse (22,000), Mochudi (20,000), Molepolole (19,000), Mahalapye (19,000), Maun (16,000).

The seat of government is at Gaborone.

The official language is English; the national language is Setswana.

CLIMATE. Most of the country is sub-tropical, but there are arid areas in the south and west. In winter, days are warm and nights cold, with occasional frosts. Summer heat is tempered by prevailing north-east winds. Rainfall comes mainly in summer, from Oct. to April, while the rest of the year is almost completely dry with very high sunshine amounts. Gaborone. Jan. 79°F (26·1°C), July 55°F (12·8°C). Annual rainfall 21″ (538 mm).

CONSTITUTION AND GOVERNMENT. The Constitution of the republic is based on the Constitution which came into effect in March 1965, with some minor alterations.

The executive rests with the President of the Republic who is responsible to the National Assembly.

The National Assembly consists of 36 members (32 elected by universal suffrage, 4 nominated by the President, the Attorney-General and the Speaker *ex-officio*). The general election, held in Sept. 1984, returned 29 members of the Botswana Democratic Party, 4 Botswana National Front and 1 Botswana People's Party.

The President is an *ex-officio* member of the Assembly. If the President is already a member of the National Assembly, a by-election will be held in the constituency of that member.

There is also a House of Chiefs to advise the Government. It consists of the Chiefs of the 8 tribes who were autonomous during the days of the British protectorate, and 4 members elected by and from among the sub-chiefs in 4 districts.

The first President of Botswana, who was re-elected 3 times, was Sir Seretse Khama, KBE, who died 13 July 1980.

President of the Republic: Dr Quett Ketumile Joni Masire (re-elected 1984).

In Sept. 1984 the Cabinet was as follows:

Vice President and Minister of Finance and Development Planning: P. S. Mmusi. *Public Service and Information:* D. K. Kwelagobe. *External Affairs:* D. K. Kwelagobe. *Health:* L. Makgekgenene. *Agriculture:* W. Meswele. *Local Government and Lands:* J. L. T. Mothibamele. *Works and Communications:* C. Blackbeard. *Commerce and Industry:* M. P. K. Nwako. *Mineral Resources and Water Affairs:* A. M. Mogwe. *Education:* K. P. Morake. *Home Affairs:* E. M. K. Kgabo. *Assistant for Finance and Development Planning:* P. H. K. Kedikilwe. *Assistants for Local Government and Lands:* M. R. Tshipinare, O. I. Chilume. *Assistant for Agriculture:* G. U. S. Matlhabaphiri. *Attorney-General:* Moleleki Mokama. *Speaker of the National Assembly:* J. G. Haskins.

National flag: Light blue with a horizontal black stripe, edged white, across the centre.

Local Government. Local government is carried out by 9 district councils and 4 town councils. Revenue is obtained mainly from local income tax, levied on all inhabitants in the area; from rates in the towns and from central government subventions in the districts.

DEFENCE

Army. A defence force has been created for border control and comprises 1 infantry battalion; group, strength, total armed forces (1985) 2,850.

Air Force. Equipment includes 5 Britten-Norman Defender armed light transports for border patrol, counter-insurgency and casualty evacuation duties, 6 Bulldog piston-engined basic trainers, 2 Skyvan turboprop passenger/cargo transports and 2 Cessna 152 light aircraft. Personnel total about 150.

INTERNATIONAL RELATIONS

Membership. Botswana is a member of UN, OAU, SADCC, the Commonwealth and is an ACP state of EEC.

ECONOMY

Planning. The National Development Plan 1979–85 envisages a total capital expenditure of P530m., GDP growth of 10·1% per annum, employment growth of 7% and a strong balance of payments.

Budget. Revenue and expenditure (in 1m. Pula) for financial years ending 31 March:

	1980–81	*1981–82*	*1982–83*
Revenues and grants	322	310	394
Expenditure and net lending	334	364	414

Currency. The currency was formerly the South African Rand but in Aug. 1976 a new currency, the *pula*, was introduced (P2·012 = £1 sterling and P1·867 = US$1 in Feb. 1985).

Banking. The Standard Bank Ltd and Barclays Bank International have branches in Francistown, Lobatse, Mahalapye, Maun and Gaborone and about 46 agencies throughout the country. A government-financed National Development Bank was founded in 1964. The Bank of Credit and Commerce (Botswana) Ltd opened in Nov. 1982.

NATURAL RESOURCES

Minerals. An important part of government revenue comes from the diamond mine at Orapa (production started in 1971, 021,914 carats; 1980 (estimate), P223,623,000) and the nickel–copper complex at Selebi-Pikwe (production started in 1974) with production (1980, estimate) valued at P83,258,000. An open-pit coalmine has been developed at Morupule, and produced (1978) 315,000 tonnes valued at P4·3m. A new diamond mine at Jwaneng produced 3m. carats in 1982.

Mineral resources in north-east Botswana are being investigated, including salt and soda ash on the Sua Pan of the Makgadikgadi Salt Pans, nickel–copper at Selkirk and Phoenix, copper south of Maun and close to Ghanzi, and coal at Mmamabula.

Agriculture. Cattle-rearing is the chief industry, but the country is more a pastoral than an agricultural one, crops depending entirely upon the rainfall. Increasing numbers of boreholes are being established where underground supply is adequate. However the rural economy is particularly vulnerable to drought and foot and mouth disease. The abattoir at Lobatse, opened in Oct. 1954, is of great importance to the country's economy. In 1983 the number of cattle was 3m.; goats, 670,000; sheep, 160,000; poultry, 1m.

LABOUR. In 1977, 68·8% of the labour force were engaged in agriculture, 12% was employed outside Botswana, mainly in the Republic of South Africa in the mining industry and 2·9% was engaged in domestic service. Total labour force was 384,000.

COMMERCE. In 1983 imports totalled P800m. and exports P700m.

Botswana is a member of the South African customs union with Lesotho, the Republic of South Africa and Swaziland.

Total trade between Botswana and UK (British Department of Trade returns, in £1,000 sterling):

	1980	*1981*	*1982*	*1983*	*1984*
Imports to UK	4,044	13,026	19,140	21,713	14,913
Exports and re-exports from UK	2,644	3,397	5,163	3,250	9,015

TOURISM. There were 82,193 tourists in 1983.

COMMUNICATIONS

Roads. On 31 Dec. 1982, 1,762 km of road were bitumen-surfaced, 1,626 km gravel and over 5,199 km earth. In 1979 there were 21,800 registered motor vehicles.

Railways. 714 km of the Cape Town to Zimbabwe railway line lie within Botswana. The railway is owned and operated by the National Railways of Zimbabwe but the Government of Botswana is preparing to take over the line of rail in Botswana and has formed the Botswana Railway Corporation.

In addition there are 2 Government-owned branch lines which serve the coal-mine at Morupule and the copper and nickel mining complex at Selebi Pikwe.

Aviation. The Seretse Khama International Airport at Gaborone opened in 1984. Regular international flights are flown by Air Botswana, Air Zimbabwe and SAA into Gaborone.

Post and Broadcasting. The telegraph, telephone and railway lines from Cape Town to Zimbabwe traverse Botswana. Wireless communication has been established between headquarters at Gaborone and various district offices and police stations. There are 39 post offices and 42 agencies. There were 10,833 telephones installed in 1978. A new earth station giving independent access to the international telecommunications system, was completed in 1980.

Newspapers. In 1984 there was 1 daily newspaper, circulation, 14,000.

JUSTICE, EDUCATION AND WELFARE

Justice. The Botswana Court of Appeal succeeded the Court of Appeal for Basutoland, Bechuanaland and Swaziland, which was established in 1954. It has jurisdiction in respect of criminal and civil appeals emanating from the High Court of Botswana. Further appeal lies in certain circumstances to the Judicial Committee of the Privy Council.

The High Court for Botswana succeeded the High Court for Bechuanaland, which was established in 1938. It has jurisdiction in all criminal and civil causes and proceedings. Subordinate courts and African courts are in each of the 12 administrative districts.

Police. The police force was 2,208 in 1980.

Education (1983). There were 512 primary, 41 secondary schools (of which 23 are Government or mission-aided), and 3 teacher training colleges. Primary education is controlled by district and town councils, the Ministry of Education being responsible for the training and deployment of teachers, curriculum, examinations and the inspectorate. In secondary education 18 schools are community based and controlled by boards of governors. Enrolment in primary schools was 202,444, and in secondary schools 215,000. There is a Polytechnic and an Auto Trades Training School. Throughout the country, Brigades provide lower level vocational training. The Department of Non-Formal Education offers secondary level correspondence courses and is the executing agency for the National Literacy Programme. The University of Botswana had 1,095 students, and there are about 190 students studying abroad.

In 1981, an estimated 66% of the total population were literate.

Welfare (1981). There were 13 general hospitals, 21 maternity centres, a mental home, 7 health centres, 104 clinics and 533 health posts. Total number of beds, 1,871 (1977). There were 113 registered medical practitioners, 8 dentists, and 1,157 nurses. The health facilities are the concern of central and local government, medical missions, mining companies and voluntary organizations. Government expenditure on medical services was P6·5m. for the year ended 31 March 1977.

DIPLOMATIC REPRESENTATIVES

Of Botswana in Great Britain (162 Buckingham Palace Rd., London, SW1)
High Commissioner. Samuel Akana Mpuchane (accredited 18 Feb. 1982).

Of Great Britain in Botswana (Private Bag 0023, Gaborone)
High Commissioner: W. Jones, CMG.

Of Botswana in the USA (4301 Connecticut Ave., NW, Washington, D.C., 20008)
Ambassador: Serara T. Ketlogetswe.

Of the USA in Botswana (PO Box 90, Gaborone)
Ambassador: Theodore C. Maino.

Of Botswana to the United Nations
Ambassador: Joseph Legwaila.

Books of Reference

General Information: The Director of Information and Broadcasting, PO Box 0060, Gaborone, Botswana publishes *Facts About Botswana*, the monthly *Kutlwano, The Botswana Daily News* and *Botswana Magazine*.
Statistical Bulletins. Quarterly. Central Statistical Office, Gaborone
Report on the Population Census, 1971. Government Printer, Gaborone, 1972
Campbell, A. C., *The Guide to Botswana.* Gaborone, 1980
Colclough, C. and McCarthy, S., *The Political Economy of Botswana.* OUP, 1980
Harvey, C., (ed.), *Papers on the Economy of Botswana.* London and Nairobi, 1981
Stevens, C., *Food Aid and the Developing World.* London, 1979

BRAZIL

Capital: Brasília
Population: 133m. (1984)
GNP per capita: US$2,220 (1981)

República Federativa do Brasil

HISTORY. Brazil was discovered on 22 April 1500 by the Portuguese Admiral Pedro Alvares Cabral, and thus became a Portuguese settlement; in 1815 the colony was declared 'a kingdom', and on 13 May 1822 Dom Pedro, eldest surviving son of King João VI of Portugal, was chosen 'Perpetual Defender' of Brazil by a National Congress. He proclaimed the independence of the country on 7 Sept. 1822, and was chosen 'Constitutional Emperor and Perpetual Defender' on 12 Oct. 1822. He resigned in 1831 and 9 years later, his 14-year-old son Pedro, became the second Emperor of Brazil.

AREA AND POPULATION. Brazil is bounded east by the Atlantic and on its north-west and southern borders by all the South American countries except Chile and Ecuador. Population as at 1 Sept. 1980 (census) and 1 July 1984 (estimate):

State and Capital	*Area (sq. km)*	*Census 1980*	*Estimate 1984*
North	3,581,180	5,880,268	7,074,000
Rondônia[1] (Porto Velho[2])	243,044	491,069	688,000
Acre (Rio Branco)	152,589	301,303	348,000
Amazonas[3] (Manaus)	1,564,445	1,430,089	1,674,000
Roraima (Boa Vista[2])	230,104	79,159	99,000
Pará (Bélem)[3]	1,250,722	3,403,391	4,058,000
Amapá (Macapá[2])	140,276	175,257	207,000
North-east	1,548,672	34,812,356	38,369,000
Maranhão (São Luis)	328,663	3,996,404	4,525,000
Piauí (Teresina)	250,934	2,139,021	2,378,000
Ceará (Fortaleza)[4]	150,630	5,288,253	5,785,000
Rio Grande do Norte (Natal)	53,015	1,898,172	2,085,000
Paraíba (João Pessoa)	56,372	2,770,176	2,971,000
Pernambuco (Recife)	98,281	6,141,993	6,662,000[10]
Alagoas (Maceió)	27,731	1,982,591	2,199,000
Fernando de Noronha[5]	26	1,279	...
Sergipe (Aracajú)	21,994	1,140,121	1,260,000
Bahia (Salvador)	561,026	9,454,346	10,504,000
South-east:	924,935	51,734,125	57,942,000
Minas Gerais (Belo Horizonte)	587,172	13,378,553	14,381,000
Espírito Santo[6] (Vitória)	45,597	2,023,340	2,239,000
Rio de Janeiro (Rio de Janeiro)[7]	44,268	11,291,520	12,502,000
São Paulo (São Paulo)	247,898	25,040,712	28,820,000
South	577,723	19,031,162	20,363,000
Paranå (Curitiba)	199,554	7,629,392	7,994,000
Santa Catarina (Florianópolis)	95,985	3,627,933	4,011,000
Rio Grande do Sul (Pórto Alegre)	282,184	7,773,837	8,358,000
Central West	1,879,455	7,544,795	8,832,000
Mato Grosso (Cuiabá)[8]	881,001	1,138,691	1,418,000
Mato Grosso do Sul (Campo Grande)[8]	350,548	1,369,567	1,562,000
Goiás (Goiânia)	642,092	3,859,602	4,347,000
Distrito Federal (Brasília)	5,814	1,176,935	1,505,000
Total	8,511,965[9]	119,002,706	132,580,000

For notes *see* p. 227.

Density of census population, 1980, was about 14 per sq. km.

The 1980 census showed 59,123,361 males and 59,879,345 females. The urban and suburban population comprised 44·7% in 1960, 55·9% in 1970 and 67·6% in 1980.

The language is Portuguese.

The new capital, Brasília, was inaugurated 21 April 1960. The federal district (5,814 sq. km) was detached from the west-central state of Goiás, about 1,000 km north-west of Rio de Janeiro. The *Distrito Federal* (DF) is the national capital; it is divided into 8 Administrative Regions by decree 488, 8 Feb. 1966. The 1st Region is Brasília.

Population of principal cities (1980 census):

São Paulo	7,032,547	Campinas	566,627
Rio de Janeiro	5,090,700	Santo André	549,556
Salvador	1,491,642	Nova Iguaçu	491,766
Belo Horizonte	1,441,567	Osasco	474,543
Recife	1,183,391	Guarulhos	426,693
DF	1,176,908	Brasília	410,999
Porto Alegre	1,114,867	Santos	410,933
Curitiba	842,818	Niterói	382,736
Belém	755,984	São Bernardo do Campo	381,097
Goiânia	702,858	Natal	376,446
Fortaleza	647,917	Maceió	375,771
Manaus	611,763		

CLIMATE. Because of its latitude, the climate is predominantly tropical, but factors such as altitude, prevailing winds and distance from the sea cause certain variations, though temperatures are not notably extreme. In tropical parts, winters are dry and summers wet, while in Amazonia conditions are constantly warm and humid. The N.E. sertao is hot and arid, with frequent droughts. In the south and east, spring and autumn are sunny and warm, summers are hot, but winters can be cold when polar air-masses impinge. Brasilia. Jan. 72°F (22·2°C), July 64°F (17·8°C). Annual rainfall 64″ (1,600 mm). Bahia. Jan. 80°F (26·7°C), July 74°F (23·3°C). Annual rainfall 76″ (1,900 mm). Belem. Jan. 79°F (26°C), July 79°F (26°C). Annual rainfall 97″ (2,438 mm). Manaus. Jan. 81°F (27·2°C), July 82°F (27·8°C). Annual rainfall 72″ (1,811 mm). Recife. Jan. 81°F (27·2°C), July 75°F (24°C). Annual rainfall 64″ (1,610 mm). Rio de Janeiro. Jan. 78°F (25·6°C), July 69°F (20·6°C). Annual rainfall 43″ (1,082 mm).

CONSTITUTION AND GOVERNMENT. On 15 Nov. 1889 Dom Pedro II (1825–91) was dethroned by a revolution, and Brazil declared a republic.

Presidents since the establishment of the republic:

Marshal Manuel Deodoro da Fonseca, 15 Nov. 1889–23 Nov. 1891 (resigned).
Marshal Floriano Peixoto (Acting), 23 Nov. 1891–15 Nov. 1894.
Dr Prudente José de Moraes Barros, 15 Nov. 1894–15 Nov. 1898.
Dr Manuel Ferraz de Campos Salles, 15 Nov. 1898–15 Nov. 1902.
Dr Francisco de Paula Rodrigues Alves, 15 Nov. 1902–15 Nov. 1906.
Dr Affonso Augusto Moreira Penna, 15 Nov. 1906–14 June 1909 (died).

---

[1] The name 'Território Federal do Guaporé' was changed to 'Território Federal de Rondônia' on 17 Feb. 1956 and became a state in 1981.

[2] Raised to the status of territorial capitals in 1943; previously, Pôrto Velho and Boa Vista belonged to the state of Amazonas and Macapá to the state of Pará.

[3] Including 2,680 sq. km in dispute with the state of Amazonas.

[4] Includes an area of 2,614 sq. km to be demarcated between states of Piauí and Ceará.

[5] Territory created in 1942, total area 26 sq. km. The archipelago comprises the main isle (of the same name) and about 20 islets.

[6] Including the islands of Trindade and Martim Vaz.

[7] According to Complementary Law no. 20 1 July 1974, the States of Rio de Janeiro and Guanabara were consolidated, since 15 March 1975, into a single political unit, the State of Rio de Janeiro with the City of Rio de Janeiro as its capital city.

[8] On 1 Jan. 1979, the former state of Mato Grosso was divided into Mato Grosso (capital, Cuiabá) and Mato Grosso do Sul (capital, Campo Grande).

[9] 3,286,000 sq. miles.

[10] Including Fernando de Noronha.

Dr Nilo Peçanha (Acting), 14 June 1909–15 Nov. 1910.
Marshal Hermes Rodrigues da Fonseca, 15 Nov. 1910–15 Nov. 1914.
Dr Wenceslau Braz Pereira Gomes, 15 Nov. 1914–15 Nov. 1918.
Dr Francisco de Paula Rodrigues Alves.[1]
Dr Delphim Moreira da Costa Ribeiro (Acting), 15 Nov. 1918–28 July 1919.
Dr Epitácio da Silva Pessoa, 28 July 1919–15 Nov. 1922.
Dr Arthur Bernardes, 15 Nov. 1922–15 Nov. 1926.
Dr Washington Luiz Pereira de Souza, 15 Nov. 1926–25 Oct. 1930 (deposed).
Dr Getúlio Dornelles Vargas, 26 Oct. 1930–29 Oct. 1945 (resigned).
Dr José Linhares (Provisional President), 30 Oct. 1945–31 Jan. 1946.
Gen. Eurico Gaspar Dutra, 31 Jan. 1946–31 Jan. 1951.
Dr Getúlio Dornelles Vargas, 31 Jan. 1951–died 24 Aug. 1954.
Dr João Café Filho, 24 Aug. 1954–8 Nov. 1955 (resigned).
Carlos Coimbra da Luz (Acting), 8 Nov. 1955–11 Nov. 1955 (deposed).
Nereu de Oliveira Ramos (Acting), 11 Nov. 1955–31 Jan. 1956.
Juscelino Kubitschek de Oliveira, 31 Jan. 1956–31 Jan. 1961.
Jânio da Silva Quadros, 31 Jan. 1961–25 Aug. 1961 (resigned).
João Belchior Marques Goulart, 7 Sept. 1961–31 March 1964 (deposed).
Marshal Humberto de A. Castelo Branco, 15 April 1964–15 March 1967.
Marshal Artur da Costa e Silva, 15 March 1967–31 Aug. 1969 (resigned).
Gen. Emilio Garrastazu Medici, 30 Oct. 1969–15 March 1974.
Gen. Ernesto Geisel, 15 March 1974–15 March 1979.
Gen. João Baptista de Oliveira Figueiredo, 15 March 1979–15 March 1985

[1] Died 10 Jan. 1919 before taking office.

On 24 Jan. 1967 both houses of Congress in joint session approved the new Constitution and press law which came into force on 15 March. An amendment to the Constitution, which came into force on 30 Oct. 1969, was issued on 17 Oct. The present Constitution provides for the indirect election of the President and Vice-President by an electoral college, comprising the members of Congress and delegates from the state legislatures; it grants powers to the President to issue decree-laws on matters connected with the economy and national security; it gives the President authority to intervene in any of the 23 states without consultation with Congress and the right to declare a state of siege and to rule by decree. President and Vice-President are elected for a 6-year term and are not immediately re-eligible.

Under the 1969 Constitution, Congress consists of a 69-member Senate and a 479-member Chamber of Deputies. The Senate is two-thirds directly elected (50% of these elected for 8 years in rotation) and one-third indirectly elected. The Chamber of Deputies is elected by universal franchise (with a literacy qualification) for 4 years.

The name of the country was changed from 'Estados Unidos do Brasil' to 'Brasil' and later to 'República Federativa do Brasil'.

Freedom of speech and press are not absolute: war propaganda, the teaching of 'subversive doctrines' and the dissemination of race or class prejudices are banned, as also are political parties opposed to democracy or to 'fundamental human rights' which include the right to own private property. The Supreme Electoral Court on 7 May 1947 declared the Communist Party illegal and on 20 Dec. 1979 the Political Parties Statute of 1965 was amended to allow for the formation of new political parties.

The Institutional Act No. 5 issued on 13 Dec. 1968 was incorporated into the new Constitution through an amendment on 17 Oct. 1969. It was repealed by the Constitutional Amendment Number 11 of 13 Oct. 1978. The Congress renewed its session on 22 Oct. 1969 and elections were held on 15 Nov. 1970, 1974, 1978 and 1982.

Voting is compulsory for men and women between the ages of 18 and 65 and optional for persons over 65. Enlisted men and illiterates (who numbered 339,849 at the 1980 census and, together with those 'without declaration' (22,436,851) comprise about 25% of the population 10 years old and older) may not vote. Elections were held 15 Nov. 1982.

President of the Republic: Tancred de Almeida Neves, assumed office 15 March 1985.

The cabinet was composed as follows in Sept. 1984:

Foreign Affairs: Ramiro Elysio Saraiva Guerreiro. *Planning:* Prof. Antônio Delfim Netto. *Finance:* Ernane Galvêas. *Justice:* Ibrahim Abi-Ackel. *Interior:* Mário David Andreazza. *Transport:* Cloraldino Soares Severo. *Communications:* Haraldo Corrêa de Mattos. *Agriculture:* Nestor Jost. *Labour:* Murilo Macedo. *Education and Culture:* Prof. Esther de Figueiredo Ferraz. *Health:* Dr Waldyr Mendes Arcoverde. *Industry and Commerce:* Murilo Bandaró. *Mines and Power:* César Cals de Oliveira Filho. *Welfare, Social Security:* Jarbas Gonçalves Passarinho. *Land Reform Affairs:* Gen. Danilo Venturini. *Army:* Gen. Walter Pires de Carvalho e Albuquerque. *Navy:* Adm. Alfredo Karam. *Air Force:* Brig. Délio Jardim de Mattos. *Head of President's Military Household:* Gen. Rubem Carlos Ludwig. *Head of President's Civilian Household:* João Leitão de Abreu. *Head of National Information Service* (SNI): Gen. Octávio Aguiar de Medeiros. *Head of General Staff* (EMFA): Air Lieut.-Brig. Waldyr Vasconcelos.

National flag: Green, with yellow lozenge on which is placed a blue sphere, containing 23 white stars and crossed with a band bearing the motto *Ordem e Progresso.*

National anthem: Ouviram do Ipiranga . . . (words by J. O. Duque Estrada; tune by F. M. da Silva).

Local Government. Brazil consists of 23 states, 3 federal territories (Roraima, Amapá, Fernando de Noronha) and 1 federal district. Each state has its distinct administrative, legislative and judicial authorities, its own constitution and laws, which must, however, agree with the constitutional principles of the Union. The states may unite or split or form new states. Taxes on interstate commerce, levied by individual states, are prohibited. The governors and members of the legislatures are elected, but magistrates are appointed and are not removable from office save by judicial sentence. Rio de Janeiro and Guanabara became one state in 1975.

DEFENCE. Under the constitution military service is compulsory for every Brazilian man from 21 years of age to 45. The terms of service are 9 years (from the 21st to the 30th years of age) in the Army 'first line' (1 in the ranks, the rest in the reserve) and 14 years (from the 30th to the 45th years of age) in the Army 'second line' (7 in the 'second line' and 7 in the reserve of the same). The men in the Territorial Army also have an annual training of 2 to 4 weeks.

Army. The Army is organized in 8 divisions, each with up to 6 armoured, 4 mechanized or motorized infantry brigades; in addition there are 5 light 'jungle' infantry battalions, 2 independent infantry and 1 independent parachute brigades; total strength (1985) 183,000.

Navy. The principal ship of the Brazilian Navy:

Completed	*Name*	*Standard displacement Tons*	*Aircraft*	*Guns*	*Shaft horsepower*	*Speed Knots*
			Aircraft Carrier			
1945	Minas Gerais [1]	15,890	16 fixed-wing, 4 helicopters	10 40mm AA	40,000	24·0

[1] Ex-*Vengeance*, purchased from Great Britain in 1956.

There are also 7 diesel-powered submarines (3 modern built in Britain and 4 old *ex*-US), 6 new destroyer leaders (or large frigates), the *Constituição, Defensora, Liberal* and *Niteroi*, built in Britain, and the *Independencia* and *Uniao*, built in Brazil, 10 old *ex*-US destroyers, 10 fleet tug type corvettes, 6 coastal minesweepers, 1 river monitor, 5 river patrol ships, 6 coastal gunboats, 1 submarine rescue ship, 2 tank landing ships, 4 transports, 18 local transports, 4 oilers, 1 repair ship, 6 training ships, 9 survey ships (2 carrying a helicopter), 6 survey launches, 35 minor landing craft, 12 tenders, 20 auxiliaries, 17 tugs and 3 floating docks.

Rather a static navy for such a large country which is apparently suffering from financial stringency. A considerable replacement programme is needed but this has been delayed.

The new construction plan was revised to replace old *ex*-US submarines and destroyers. A training ship (frigate) and a river support ship were projected.

Among the 50 new units planned are a carrier, submarines, guided missile leaders, frigates, minehunters and amphibious ships.

Naval bases are at Rio de Janeiro, Aratu (Bahia), Belém, Natal, Recife, Salvador, with a river base at Ladario.

The Fleet Air Arm was formed on 26 Jan. 1965. Aircraft for service on the carrier include 4 Sikorsky SH-3D helicopters and 8 S-2A/E Tracker anti-submarine aircraft from USA and 8 Seahawk A-4G from Australia. Nine Westland Wasp light helicopters were obtained from Britain, and operated on utility and search and rescue duties with 16 Bell Jet Ranger and 9 Esquilo (AS 350) helicopters. Nine Westland Lynx helicopters were provided for the destroyer leader/frigates of the 'Niteroi' class. Nine Jet Rangers were used for training.

The active personnel in 1985 totalled 50,300 (6,300 officers and 44,000 men), including 14,000 marines and auxiliary corps.

Air Force. The Air Force, formed in 1918, has been independent of the Army and Navy since 1941. It is organized in 6 zones, centred on Belém, Recife, Rio de Janeiro, São Paulo, Porto Alegre and Brasília. The 1a ALADA (air defence wing) has 12 Mirage IIIE fighters and 2 Mirage IIID trainers, integrated with Roland mobile short-range surface-to-air missile systems deployed by the Army, and a radar/communications/computer network. One fighter group has 2 squadrons of F-5E Tiger II supersonic fighter-bombers and two-seat F-5Bs; 2 others operate AT-26 (Aermacchi MB 326G) Xavante light jet attack/trainers, licence-built by Embraer in Brazil. Counter-insurgency squadrons are equipped with AT-26 Xavantes for reconnaissance and attack, and with Neiva Regente lightplanes, Universal armed piston-engined trainers, and UH-1D/H Iroquois and armed JetRanger helicopters for liaison and observation. There is an ASW group of S-2A/E Trackers for shore-based and carrier-based operations; a maritime patrol group (2 squadrons) with 12 EMB-111 (P-95) twin-turboprop aircraft developed from the Embraer Bandeirante transport; and 3 air-sea rescue units with RC-130E Hercules reconnaissance transports, SC-95B Bandeirantes, SA 330L Puma and SH-1D Iroquois helicopters. Equipment of transport units includes 1 group of C-130E/H Hercules transports and KC-130H Hercules tankers; 1 group made up of a squadron of HS 748 and C-95 Bandeirante turboprop transports and a second squadron of HS 748s with large freight doors; 1 troop-carrier group with DHC-5 Buffaloes; and 6 independent squadrons with Bandeirantes and Buffaloes. Light aircraft for liaison duties include 30 Embraer U-7s (licence-built Piper Senecas). The VIP transport group has 2 Boeing 737s, 8 HS 125 twin-jet light transports, some Bandeirantes, 6 Embraer Xingu (VU-9) twin-turboprop pressurized transports and 4 JetRanger helicopters. Training is performed primarily on locally-built Aerotec T-23 Uirapuru *ab initio* trainers, T-25 Universal and turboprop T-27 Tucano (EMB-312) basic trainers, and AT-26 Xavante armed jet basic trainers. Future equipment will include 79 AM-X jet attack aircraft, produced jointly by Embraer and Aeritalia/Aermacchi of Italy.

Personnel strength (1984) about 49,000, with more than 600 aircraft of all types.

INTERNATIONAL RELATIONS

Membership. Brazil is a member of UN, OAS and LAIA (formerly LAFTA).

ECONOMY

Budget. Receipts and expenditures for the federal government (excluding states, federal district and municipalities) for calendar years have been as follows in 1m. Cr$:

	1979	*1980*	*1981*	*1982*
Revenue	544,244	1,230,018	2,351,966	4,774,815
Expenditure	521,136	1,190,994	2,254,896	4,619,772

Chief items of revenue were in 1982 as follows (in Cr$1m.): Taxes, 3,900,940; government property, 69,366. Principal items of expenditure: Transport, 403,571;

education, 391,562; army, 221,772; aviation and navy, 311,580; welfare and security, 77,434; finance, 79,510.

The foreign debt (including states and municipalities) of Brazil on 31 Dec. 1983 amounted to US$81,319m. Internal federal debt, April 1984 was Cr$36,914,757m. Internal states and municipalities (main securities outstanding), April 1984, Cr$3,928,015m.

Currency. The *cruzeiro* (Cr$) is the monetary unit. The exchange rate was in Feb. 1985 US$1 = Cr$3,866; £1 = Cr$4,119.

Banking. The Bank of Brazil (founded in 1808 and reorganized in 1906, with an authorized capital of NCr$60m. from 1967) is not a central bank of issue but a closely controlled commercial bank; it had 2,400 branches in 1983 throughout the republic. On 31 Dec. 1983 deposits were Cr$3,875,789m.

On 31 Dec. 1964 the Banco Central da República do Brasil was founded.

The country's currency held by the public on 31 Dec. 1983 was Cr$1,841,889m. Since Sept. 1939 gold and dollar supply has risen from US$40m. to US$420m., of which the government's gold was US$288m. in May 1961. All banks had on 31 Dec. 1983 deposits of Cr$14,103,815m. and loans of Cr$63,743,124m.

Weights and Measures. The metric system has been in use in all official departments since 1862. It was made compulsory in 1872, but the ancient measures are still partly employed in remote districts. They are: *libra* = 1·012 lb. avoirdupois; *arroba* = 32·98 lb.; *quintal* = 129·54 lb.; *alqueire* (of Roi) = 1 Imperial bushel, or 40 litres; *oitava* = 55·34 grains.

ENERGY AND NATURAL RESOURCES

Electricity. Brazil's hydraulic potential capacity for electric power production was estimated at 106,570 mw. in 1980, one of the largest in the world, of which 34% belongs to the Amazon hydrographic basin. Installed electric power in 1982 was 39,019 mw.; gross production, 151,999 gwh.; consumption, 131,333 gwh.

Oil. There are 13 oil refineries, of which 11 are state owned. Crude oil output was 16,170,007 tonnes in 1983, of which 58% was from the continental shelf. Promising results have been obtained with the exploration of that area which in 1974 represented only 9% of all the national oil production.

The country imported substantial amounts of oil in 1983: 36,451,896 tonnes (value c.i.f US$8,498m.) representing 51% of total value of all Brazilian imports. Imports come mainly from Iraq and Saudi Arabia.

The government created the National Alcohol Program in 1975 with the aim of a gradual replacement of the consumption of petroleum by combustible alcohol specially produced from sugar-cane and cassava. About US$5,000m. will be invested by 1985. By May 1980, 281 sugar-cane alcohol distillery projects had been approved and their authorized capacity represents 61% of the national aim for 1985 (about 11m. cu. metres). An agreement between the automotive industry and the government was signed in Sept. 1979. In Dec. 1984 a major oil field was reported on the fringes of the existing Campos Basin oil field.

Minerals. Brazil is the only source of high-grade quartz crystal in commercial quantities; output, 1982, 67,527 tonnes raw, 53,426 tonnes processed; exports (1983) 9,629 tonnes. It is the first largest western producer of chrome ore (reserves of 7·3m. tonnes; output, 1982, 667,634 tonnes); other minerals are mica (571 tonnes in 1982); zirconium, 5,940; beryllium 14; graphite 359,991; titanium ore 2,859,559 tonnes, and magnesite 505,385 tonnes. Along the coasts of the states of Rio de Janeiro, Espírito Santo and Bahia are found monazite sands containing thorium; output, 1982, 1,967 tonnes; reserves are estimated at 25m. tonnes. Manganese ores of high content are important (reserves in the Amapá region alone are estimated at 8m. tonnes); output, 1982, 2,883,211 tonnes. Output of bauxite, 1982, 6,289,713 tonnes; salt, 2,887,803; tungsten ore, 532,222, unrough, 2,602; lead, 305,953; asbestos, 2,092,087; coal, 19,205,886. Deposits of coal exist in Rio

Grande do Sul, Santa Catarina, Paraná and Minas Gerais. Total reserves are estimated at 2,046·6m. tonnes.

Iron is found chiefly in Minas Gerais, notably the Cauê Peak at Itabira. The Government is now opening up what is believed to be one of the richest iron-ore deposits in the world, situated in Carajás, in the northern state of Pará, with estimated reserves of 18,000m. tonnes, representing the largest concentration of high-grade (66%) iron ore in the world. Total output of iron ore, 1982, mainly from the Cia. Vale do Rio Doce mine at Itabira, was 119,939,149 tonnes.

Production of tin ore (cassiterite, processed) was 15,250 tonnes in 1982. Output of barytes, 98,931 tonnes. Output of phosphate rock, 25m. tonnes.

Gold in large-scale mining was confined to a single mine in Minas Gerais; the production in 1982 (total), 18,765 kg. Large-scale gold deposits have been discovered at Serra Pelada in Pará; production, 1982, 15,824 kg processed and Minas Gerais, 4,563 kg. Silver output (processed), 1982, 23,625 kg. Diamond districts are Minas Gerais, Mato Grosso, Roraima, Bahia and São Paulo; output in 1982 was 212,039 carats (90,712 carats from Minas Gerais, 105,786 carats from Mato Grosso).

Agriculture. 32·41% of Brazil's population is rural. Production (in tonnes):

	1982	*1983*[1]		*1982*	*1983*[1]
Bananas (1,000 bunches)	454,766	440,468	Grapes	688,589	574,507
			Cocoa	363,519	380,182
Beans	2,906,259	1,586,993	Coffee	1,853,901	3,330,543
Cassava	24,009,355	21,568,757	Cotton, raw	1,935,091	1,599,235
Castor beans	192,428	171,650	Jute	14,222	12,919
Oranges	11,587,744	11,732,193	Maize	21,865,439	18,743,761
Potatoes	2,147,918	1,818,004	Soya	12,834,624	14,582,052
Rice	9,716,026	7,741,004	Sugar-cane	184,392,397	216,533,924
Sisal	249,236	180,859	Wheat	1,849,400	2,236,318

[1] Preliminary.

Land under coffee, 1983, 2·3m. hectares. The 4 states of São Paulo, Paraná, Espírito Santo and Minas Gerais are the principal districts for coffee-growing.

Land under cocoa, 544,331 hectares. Bahia furnished 90% of the output in 1982. Two crops a year are grown. Land under castor-bean, 271,366 hectares. Tobacco output was 421,532 tonnes in 1982. Brazil now ranks second only to the US in production of oranges.

Rubber is produced chiefly in the states of Acre, Amazonas and Pará. Output, 1983, 256,140 tonnes (natural and synthetic); peak reached in 1912 (when rubber realized US$3 a lb.) was 42,510 gross tons. Brazilian consumption of rubber in 1983, was 269,376 tonnes. Brazil is the chief source of carnaúba wax, used for electric insulation and gramophone records. Caroá fibre is grown as a substitute for Indian jute; production, 1982, 188 tonnes. Jute output, 1983, 12,919 tonnes. Plantations of tung trees established in 1930 (4m. trees in 1946) are beginning to yield tung oils in commercial quantities; output of tung, 1982, 7,116 tonnes.

Livestock (in 1,000): 1983, 93,000 cattle, 33,500 swine, 17,500 sheep, 8,500 goats, 5,200 horses, 1,480 asses and 1,690 mules. In 1982, 11·6m. cattle, 9m. swine, 901,000 sheep and lambs, 312,000 goats and 798m. poultry were slaughtered for meat.

Fisheries. The fishing industry had a 1982 catch of 833,933 tonnes.

INDUSTRY AND TRADE

Industry. The total number of persons engaged in industry (1980) was 5,004,522 and the value of production Cr$9,738,340m.

The National Iron and Steel Co. at Volta Redonda, State of Rio de Janeiro, furnishes a substantial part of Brazil's steel. Brazil's total output, 1983: Pig-iron, 12,944,772 tonnes; crude steel ingots castings, 14,659,281 tonnes.

Production of aluminium was started in Minas Gerais in 1945. Cement output, 1983, was 20,869,935 tonnes. A paper-mill, reported to be the largest pulp-and-paper mill in South America, is at Monte Alegre, Paraná. Brazil's output of paper, 1983, was 3,425,959 tonnes. Production of rubber tyres and tubes, 1983, 56m. units.

Commerce. Imports and exports for calendar years in Cr$1,000:

	1979	*1980*	*1981*	*1982*	*1983*
Imports	500,134,047	1,228,628,361	2,145,425,789	3,626,839,970	9,025,052,613
Exports	393,531,168	1,038,083,296	2,054,524,562	3,368,796,430	11,652,922,976

Principal imports in 1983 were (in US$1m.): Fuel and lubricants, 8,607; capital goods, 2,505; chemical products, 827; cereals, 905; steel and cast iron, 160; non-ferrous metals, 175.

Principal exports in 1983 were (in US$1m.): Coffee (green), 2,078; iron ore, 1,519; rolling stock and vehicles, 1,446; soybean bran, 1,792; machinery, 1,093.

Of exports (in US$1m.) in 1983, USA took 5,064; Japan, 1,431; Germany (Fed. Rep.), 1,130; Netherlands, 1,259; Italy, 980; France, 883; UK, 720; Argentina, 657; USSR, 670. Of 1983 imports, Saudi Arabia furnished 2,220; USA, 2,409; Iraq, 2,071; Venezuela, 663; Japan, 561; Germany (Fed. Rep.), 705; Mexico, 708; France, 456; Argentina, 358.

Total trade between Brazil and UK (according to British Department of Trade returns, in £1,000 sterling):

	1980	*1981*	*1982*	*1983*	*1984*
Imports to UK	269,340	389,898	443,956	560,277	637,702
Exports and re-exports from UK	218,159	174,361	158,837	157,758	238,717

Tourism. In 1982, 1,146,881 tourists visited Brazil, 223,911 were Argentinian, 210,870 Uruguayan, 118,210 US citizens, 84,422 Paraguayan, 44,684 German, 56,730 Chilean, 45,159 Italian, 21,762 British and 18,558 Japanese.

COMMUNICATIONS

Roads. There were (1982) 1,557,916 km of highways. In 1982 Brazil had 11,826,000 motor vehicles, including 8,754,881 passenger cars, 1,785,379 commercial vehicles, 128,141 buses and minibuses. 822,208 motor vehicles of all types were produced in 1983.

Railways. Public railways are operated by two administrations, the Federal Railways (RFFSA) formed in 1957 and São Paulo Railways (FEPASA) formed in 1971, which is confined to the state of São Paulo. RFFSA had a route-length of 23,087 km in 1982 and FEPASA 5,063 km. Principal gauges are metre and 1,600 mm. The share of the freight market declined to a low of 15% in 1967, but subsequent heavy government investment in reconstruction and new lines, coupled with a policy of forcing bulk commodities on to rail, had raised the share to over 20% in 1974. Continued investment in new wagons, electrification, gauge-conversion, and 'export corridor' routes to the ports will further improve this figure, and some new lines are planned up to the year 2000. Except in the urban areas of Rio de Janeiro and São Paulo, passenger traffic moving by rail is negligible. Traffic moved by RFFSA in 1983 amounted to 69·2m. tonnes of freight and 428·3m. passengers. FEPASA (1982) carried 21m. tonnes and 61m. passengers.

There are several important independent freight railways, including the Vitoria à Minas (773 km and 76m. tonnes of freight), the Corajas (890 km, opened in 1985) and the Amapa (194 km). The city of São Paulo has a rapid metropolitan transit railway, and a similar system opened in Rio de Janeiro city in 1979. Commuter railways are also being developed in Recife, Belo Horizonte, Porto Alegre (all opening in 1985), Fortaleza and Salvador.

Aviation. There were 32 companies (28 foreign) operating in 1983. The 4 largest Brazilian companies cover the whole territory and in 1983 they carried 13,542,660 passengers (11,809,242 in domestic traffic) and 2,327m. tonne-km of freight. Their commercial fleet consisted of 212 aircraft on 31 Dec. 1983. There were 204 taxi-plane companies on 31 Dec. 1983. The chief airline is Viação Aérea Rio Grande do Sul, (VARIG).

Shipping. Inland waterways, mostly rivers, are open to navigation over some

21,944 miles; number of vessels in 1982, 1,018. Rio de Janeiro and Santos are the 2 leading ports; there are 18 other large ports. Bolivia and Paraguay have been given free ports at Santos. During 1982, 36,409 vessels entered and cleared the Brazilian ports.

The Lloyd Brasileiro is owned and operated by the Government; its fleet comprised (1982), 36 vessels of 550,688 DWT. Brazilian shipping, 1982 (registered with Lloyds) amounted to 1,375 vessels of 9,384,668 DWT. Petrobrás, the government oil monopoly, took over the government tanker fleet of 26 vessels in 1958; total tanker fleet in 1982 was 166 vessels of 4,910,849 DWT (private and government-owned).

Post and Broadcasting. Of the telegraph system of the country, about half, including all interstate lines, is under control of the Government. There were 7,135 post and telegraph offices in 1982. There were 9,162,489 telephones in 1982 (São Paulo, 1,819,698; Rio de Janeiro, 1,155,586; Brasilia, 248,693). In 1981 there were 1,321 broadcasting and 119 television stations.

Cinemas (1980). Cinemas numbered 3,181 with a seating capacity of 1,891,385.

Newspapers (1981). There were 315 daily newspapers with a total yearly circulation of 1,205,481,000. Foreigners and corporations (except political parties) are not allowed to own or control newspapers or wireless stations. The press law of 1967 prohibits anonymous journalism and the publication of material defamatory to the armed forces and other public institutions.

JUSTICE, RELIGION, EDUCATION AND HEALTH

Justice. There is a Supreme Federal Court of Justice at Brasília. It has 11 judges; all are appointed by the President with the approval of the Senate. There are also federal courts in each state and the federal district and in the Territories, as well as 'electoral courts' to protect the elections, and labour tribunals. Justice is administered in the states in accordance with state law, by state courts, but in Brasília federal justice is administered. Judges are appointed for life. In Dec. 1977 the Senate approved laws for allowing marriages to be dissolved. Brazilian citizens can apply for one divorce only during their lifetime. In the case of a marriage partner becoming mentally ill, divorce proceedings cannot begin until 5 years after the illness has been proved. The death penalty was re-introduced in Sept. 1969.

Religion. The population is overwhelmingly Roman Catholic (89% at the census, 1980). In 1889 connexion between Church and State was abolished; it was restored by the 1934 constitution, but again abolished in 1946.

In 1980 (census) Catholics numbered 105,861,113; Protestants, 7,885,846, and Spiritualists, 1,538,230.

Education. Elementary education is compulsory. In 1980 (census) there were 69,703,993 persons 5 years of age or over who could read and write; this was 67·95% of that age group; 68·57% of the literates were men.

There were, in 1982, 192,976 first degree school units, with 22,297,583 pupils and 912,958 teachers; 8,454 second degree establishments (not school units), with 2,874,505 pupils and 203,676 teachers; 3,967 third degree units, with 1,203,468 pupils and 123,243 teachers.

There were, in 1982, 67 universities (including 20 private) and 811 faculties not belonging to universities (593 private), including the University of Rio de Janeiro (founded on 7 Sept. 1920), the University of Bahia (founded in 1946), the University of Recife (1946), the University of Paraná (1946), the Rural University (1948, State of Rio de Janeiro), the University of São Paulo (1934), the University of Minas Gerais (1927), the University of Rio Grande do Sul (1934), the University of Brasília (1960) and the University of Mato Grosso (1971). There are also 19 Catholic universities (all private) in Rio de Janeiro (1946), São Paulo (1946), Rio Grande do Sul (1948), Pernambuco (1951), Minas Gerais (1958), Bahia, Paraná, Brasília, Goiás, Mato Grosso and Piauí. Students in 1982 totalled 1,203,468.

Health. In 1981 there were 21,762 health establishments of which 6,342 were for inpatients; total number of beds, 522,769 (397,903 in private institutions).

DIPLOMATIC REPRESENTATIVES

Of Brazil in Great Britain (32 Green St., London, W1Y 3FD)
Ambassador: Mario Gibson Alves Barboza, GCMG (accredited 10 Dec. 1982).

Of Great Britain in Brazil (Setor de Embaixadas Sul, Quadra 801, Conjunto K, Brasília, D.F.)
Ambassador: J. B. Ure, CMG, MVO.

Of Brazil in the USA (3006 Massachusetts Ave., NW, Washington, D.C., 20008)
Ambassador: Sérgio Correa da Costa.

Of the USA in Brazil (Ave das Nocões, Lote 3, Brasília, D.F.)
Ambassador: Diego Asencio.

Of Brazil to the United Nations
Ambassador: George Alvares Maciel.

Books of Reference

Anuário do Transporte Aéreo. Ministério da Aeronáutica, DAC. Rio de Janeiro, 1983
Anuário Estatístico do Brasil. Vol. 44. Fundação Instituto Brasileiro de Geografia e Estatística, Rio de Janeiro, 1983
Anuário Mineral Brasileiro. Departamento Nacional da Produção Mineral. Brasília, 1983
Boletim do Banco Central do Brasil. Banco Central do Brasil. Brasília. Monthly
Autoridades Brasileiras. Empresa Brasileira de Notícias, 1984
A Profile of Brazil. Banco do Brazil, 1984
Anuario Sunumam, Superintendência Nacional da Marinha Mercante, 1982
Banco do Brasil, *Boletim Trimestral.* Brasília, D.F. From 1966
Burns, E. B., *A History of Brazil.* 2nd ed. Columbia Univ. Press, 1980
Campbell, G., *Brazil Struggles for Development.* London, 1973
Cowell, A., *The Tribe that Hides from Man.* London, 1973
Dickenson, J. P., *Brazil.* Harlow, 1982
Hanbury-Tenison, R., *A Question of Survival for the Indians of Brazil.* London, 1973
McDonough, P., *Power and Ideology in Brazil.* Princeton Univ. Press, 1981
Micallef, J., (ed.), *Brazil: Country with a Future.* London, 1982
Moraes, R. Borba de., *Bibliographia Brasiliana (1504–1900).* 2 vols. 1958
Selcher, W. E. (ed.), *Brazil in the International System: The Rise of a Middle Power.* Boulder, 1981
Trebat, T. J., *Brazil's State-Owned Enterprises.* CUP, 1983
Tyler, W. G., *The Brazilian Industrial Economy.* Aldershot, 1981
Young, J. M., *Brazil: Emerging World Power.* Malabar, 1982

National Library: Biblioteca Nacional Avenida Rio Branco 219–39, Rio de Janeiro, RJ.
Director: Maria Alice Barroso.

BRITISH ANTARCTIC TERRITORY

HISTORY. The British Antarctic Territory was established on 8 March 1962, as a consequence of the entry into force of the Antarctic Treaty, to separate those areas of the then Falkland Islands Dependencies which lay within the Treaty area from those which did not.

AREA AND POPULATION. The territory encompasses the lands and islands within the area south of 60°S latitude lying between 20°W and 80°W longitude (approximately due south of the Falkland Islands and the Dependencies). It covers an area of some 700,000 square miles, and its principal components are the South Orkney and South Shetland Islands, the Antarctic Peninsula (Palmer Land and Graham Land) and Coats Land.

British Antarctic Territory has no indigenous or permanently resident population. There is however an itinerant population of scientists and logistics staff of about 300, manning a number of research stations.

The territory is administered by a High Commissioner. Designated personnel of the scientific stations of the British Antarctic Survey are also appointed to exercise certain legal and administrative functions.

High Commissioner: Sir Rex Hunt, CMG (resides in Port Stanley).

Fox, R., *Antarctica and the South Atlantic.* London, 1985

BRITISH INDIAN OCEAN TERRITORY

HISTORY. This territory was established by an Order in Council on 8 Nov. 1965, consisting then of the Chagos Archipelago (formerly administered from Mauritius) and the islands of Aldabra, Desroches and Farquhar (all formerly administered from Seychelles). The latter islands being returned to the Seychelles when that country achieved independence on 29 June 1976, the territory now comprises the Chagos Archipelago, lying 1,180 miles (1,899 km) north-west of Mauritius.

AREA AND POPULATION. The group, with a total land area of 20 sq. miles (52 sq. km) comprises 5 coral atolls (Diego Garcia, Peros Banhos, Salomon, Eagle and Egmont) of which the largest and southern-most, Diego Garcia, covers 14 sq. miles (36 sq. km). The British Indian Ocean Territory was established to meet UK and US defence requirements in the Indian Ocean. In accordance with the terms of Exchanges of Notes between the UK and US governments in 1966 and 1976, a US Navy support facility has been established on Diego Garcia. There is no permanent population in the British Indian Ocean Territory.

Commissioner: P. C. F. Gregory-Hood (non-resident).
Administrator: D. H. Doble.

BRUNEI

Capital: Bandar Seri Begawan
Population: 214,440 (1983)
GNP per capita: US$17,380 (1981)

HISTORY. The Sultanate of Brunei was a powerful state in the early 16th century, with authority over the whole of the island of Borneo and some parts of the Sulu Islands and the Philippines. At the end of the 16th century its power had begun to decline and various cessions were made to Great Britain, the Rajah of Sarawak and the British North Borneo Company in the 19th century to combat piracy and anarchy. By the middle of the 19th century the State had been reduced to its present limits.

In 1847 the Sultan of Brunei entered into a treaty with Great Britain for the furtherance of commercial relations and the suppression of piracy, and in 1888, by a further treaty, the State was placed under the protection of Great Britain. Brunei was the only former British dependency inhabited by a Malay people that did not join the Federation of Malaysia in 1963.

AREA AND POPULATION. Brunei, on the northwest coast of Borneo, is bounded on all sides by Sarawak territory, which splits the State into two separate parts. Area, about 2,226 sq. miles (5,800 sq. km), with a coastline of about 100 miles. Population (1981 census) was 191,770. The 4 districts are Brunei/Muara (114,310), Belait (49,590), Tutong (21,640), Temburong (6,230). The capital is Bandar Seri Begawan, 9 miles from the mouth of Brunei River.

CLIMATE. The climate is tropical marine, hot and moist, but nights are cool. Humidity is high and rainfall heavy, varying from 100″ (2,500 mm) on the coast to 200″ (5,000 mm) inland. There is no dry season. Bandar Seri Begawan. Jan. 80°F (26·7°C), July 82°F (27·8°C). Annual rainfall 131″ (3,275 mm).

CONSTITUTION AND GOVERNMENT. On 29 Sept. 1959 the Sultan promulgated a Constitution. There is a Privy Council, an Executive and a Legislative Council. On 6 Jan. 1965 the constitution was amended to provide for general elections to the Legislative Council; at the same time the Executive Council was renamed Council of Ministers. The Legislative Council consists of 20 members and a Speaker appointed by the Sultan. The Council of Ministers is presided over by the Sultan and consists of 6 *ex-officio* members and 4 other members, all of whom except one are members of the Legislative Council. The Mentri Besar, who is one of the *ex-officio* members of the Legislative Council and the Council of Ministers, is responsible to the Sultan for the exercise of executive authority in the State. As a result of negotiations in June 1978, the Sultan and the British Government signed a new treaty on 7 Jan. 1979 under which Brunei became a fully sovereign and independent State on 31 Dec. 1983.

The official language is Malay, but English may be used for other purposes.

Sultan of Brunei: Duli Yang Maha Mulia Paduka Seri Baginda Sultan and Yang di-Pertuan Negeri Brunei Sir Muda Hassanal Bolkiah Mu'izzaddin Waddaulah ibni Duli Yang Teramat Mulia Paduka Seri Begawan Sultan Sir Muda Omar Ali Saifuddin Sa'adul Khairi Waddin, DK, PGGUB, DPKG, DPKT, PSPNB, PSNB, PSLJ, SPMB, PANB, GCMG, DMN, DK (Kelantan), DK (Johore), DK (Negeri Sembilan). The Sultan was crowned on 1 Aug. 1968.

General Adviser to HH The Sultan: The Most Hon., Pehin Orang Kaya Laila Setia Bakti Di-Raja Dato Laila Utama Awang Haji Isa bin Pehin Datu Perdana Mentri Dato Laila Utama Haji Ibrahim, DK, SPMB, DSNB, CVO, OBE, PHBS, PBLI, PJK.

Mentri Besar (Chief Minister, Acting): The Rt Hon. Pehin Orang Kaya Laila

Wijaya Dato Seri Setia Haji Abdul Aziz bin Begawan Pehin Udana Khatib Dato Seri Paduka Haji Umar, PSNB, DPMB, SLJ, PJK

Flag: Yellow, with 2 diagonal strips of white over black with the national arms in red placed over all in the centre.

DEFENCE

Army. The armed forces are known as the Royal Brunei Malay Regiment and contain the naval and air elements. Strength (1985) 3,950. Military units include 2 infantry battalions, 1 armoured reconnaissance squadron, 1 engineer squadron and 1 signals squadron. Equipment includes 16 Scorpion light tanks and 24 Sankey AT-104 armoured personnel carriers.

Navy. The Royal Brunei Malay Regiment Flotilla comprises 3 fast missile-armed attack craft of 200 tons (completed by Vosper, Singapore in 1978–79), 3 coastal patrol boats (built by Vosper-Thornycroft (Singapore)), 2 landing craft, 3 utility craft and 3 small patrol boats. Special Combat Division (formerly Special Boat Squadron) operates 24 fast assault boats. Personnel in 1985 numbered 450 (42 officers and 408 ratings) in the First Flotilla (for offshore work) and in the Special Combat Division and River Division.

Two coastal patrol craft built by Vosper, Singapore, were supplied in 1979 for the Marine Police.

Air Wing. The Air Wing of the Royal Brunei Malay Regiment was formed in 1965. Current equipment includes up to 6 MBB BO 105, 4 Bell 206B JetRanger and 11 Bell 212 helicopters, and 2 SF.260M piston-engined trainers.

Police. Establishment provides over 1,750 officers and men (1980). In addition, there is a small auxiliary force mostly employed on static guard duties.

ECONOMY

Planning. A fourth Five-Year National Development Plan was announced in 1980 to further improve the economic, social and cultural life of the people.

Budget. The budget for 1984 envisaged expenditure of B$2,600m. and revenue of B$6,500m.

Currency. The currency is the *Brunei dollar* with a par value of 0·290 299 gramme of gold.

INTERNATIONAL RELATIONS

Membership. Brunei is a member of ASEAN.

ENERGY AND NATURAL RESOURCES

Oil. The Seria oilfield, discovered in 1929, has passed its peak production. The high level of crude oil production is maintained through the increase of offshore oilfields production, which exceeds onshore oilfields production. Production was 65·3m. bbls in 1983. The crude oil is exported directly, and only a small amount is refined at Seria for domestic uses.

Gas. Natural gas is produced (828m. cu. feet per day, 1983) at one of the biggest liquefied natural gas plants in the world and is exported to Japan.

Agriculture. The chief agricultural products in 1981 were rice (10,000 tonnes) and bananas (3,000 tonnes).

Livestock in 1983: Cattle, 4,000; buffaloes, 15,000; pigs, 15,000; chickens, 1m.

Forestry. Most of the interior is under forest, containing large potential supplies of serviceable timber. Annual production averages 200,000 cu. metres.

INDUSTRY AND TRADE

Industry. Brunei depends primarily on its oil industry, which employs more than

7% of the entire working population. Crude oil accounts for 62% of the total value of the exports and re-exports. The second main export is liquefied natural gas, which contributes 31% and petroleum products 6%.

Other minor products are rubber, pepper, sawn timber, gravel and animal hides. Local industries include boat-building, cloth weaving and the manufacture of brass-and silverware.

Commerce. In 1983 imports totalled B$1,542m.; exports, B$7,171m.

Total trade between Brunei and UK (British Department of Trade returns, in £1,000 sterling):

	1980	*1981*	*1982*	*1983*	*1984*
Imports to UK	889	2,757	2,434	27,154	21,966
Exports and re-exports from UK	23,118	24,165	41,804	106,477	122,651

COMMUNICATIONS

Roads. The State has about 916 miles of road, of which 451 miles are bituminous surfaced. The main road connects Bandar Seri Begawan with Kuala Belait and Seria. The number of motor vehicles (1980) was 60,751.

Aviation. Royal Brunei Airlines (RBA) and Singapore Airlines provide daily services linking Brunei and Singapore. RBA also operates services to Bangkok, Manila, Kuala Lumpur, Kuching, Kota Kinabalu and Hong Kong. Cathay Pacific Airways also operates to Brunei and on to Western Australia from Hong Kong. British Airways provides a weekly service between Brunei and UK. Malaysian Airlines System has air connections from neighbouring regions.

Shipping. Regular shipping services operate from Singapore, Hong Kong, and from ports in Sarawak and Sabah to Bandar Seri Begawan. Private companies operate a passenger ferry service between Bandar Seri Begawan and Labuan, Sabah, 7 days a week.

Post and Broadcasting. There were 8 post offices (1980) and a telephone network (21,928 telephones in 1982) linking the main centres. Radio Brunei is operated by the Department of Radio and Television and operates on medium- and short-waves in Malay, Iban, Dusun, English and Chinese. Number of radio receivers, 38,000 and television sets, 32,000.

RELIGION AND EDUCATION

Religion. The official religion is Islam.

Education (1979). Free education in the Malay language is provided in government primary schools (29,934 pupils) and 4 government secondary Malay schools (1,218 pupils). Free education in English was provided in 30 government preparatory schools (8,546 pupils) and 7 government secondary schools (7,344 pupils) and one 6th form centre (819 pupils). The government also provided one Arabic preparatory school (203 pupils) and 2 Arabic secondary schools (251 pupils). Teacher-training was provided in 2 government teachers' colleges, in both Malay and English for 601 students. Eight non-government Mission schools provided education in English at kindergarten, primary and secondary level for a total of 6,745 pupils; 8 non-government Chinese schools provided education in Chinese at the same levels for a total of 5,813 pupils. One private kindergarten and primary school, administered by the Brunei Shell Petroleum Co., provided education in either English or Dutch for a total of 986 pupils, and there was also 1 private vocational school administered by the Brunei Shell Petroleum Co. (140 artisan-trainees). Two government vocational schools provided full training courses to 274 students in the engineering and building trades.

DIPLOMATIC REPRESENTATIVES

Of Brunei in Great Britain (49 Cromwell Rd, London, SW7 2ED)
High Commissioner: Pengiran Setia Raja Jaya (accredited 14 March 1984).

Of Great Britain in Brunei (Jalan Residency, Bandar Seri Begawan)
High Commissioner: R. F. Cornish.

BULGARIA

Capital: Sofia
Population: 8·93m. (1983)
GNP per capita: US$4,150 (1980)

Narodna Republika Bulgaria

HISTORY. The Bulgarian state was founded in 681, but fell under Turkish rule in 1396. By the Treaty of Berlin, which followed the Russo-Turkish war of 1878, the Principality of Bulgaria and the Autonomous Province of Eastern Rumelia, both under Turkish suzerainty, were constituted. In 1885 Rumelia was reunited with Bulgaria. On 5 Oct. 1908 Bulgaria declared her independence of Turkey. *Rulers:* Prince Alexander I of Battenberg, 1879–86; Prince (after 1908, Tsar) Ferdinand, 1887–1918 (abdicated); Tsar Boris III, 1918–43; Tsar Simeon II, lost his throne as a result of a referendum held on 8 Sept. 1946 (3,801,160 votes for a republic, 197,176 for the monarchy, 119,168 invalid).

In 1941 Bulgaria signed the Three Power Pact and the Anti-Comintern Pact. In 1944 Bulgaria asked the UK and the USA for an armistice. The USSR declared war on Bulgaria on 5 Sept. 1944. The Fatherland Front government (established 9 Sept.) asked the USSR for an armistice, which was signed on 28 Oct. 1944 by the USSR, the UK and the USA. The peace treaty was signed in Paris on 10 Feb. 1947.

AREA AND POPULATION. On 8 Sept. 1940 by the treaty of Craiova, Romania ceded to Bulgaria the Southern Dobrudja, fixing the new frontier on the 1912 line.

In April 1941 Bulgaria occupied the Yugoslav part of Macedonia, and the Greek districts of Western Thrace, Eastern Macedonia, Florina and Castoria. The peace treaty of 1947 restored the frontiers as on 1 Jan. 1941.

The area of Bulgaria is 110,911·5 sq. km (42,823 sq. miles) and is bounded in the north by Romania, east by the Black Sea, south by Turkey and Greece and west by Yugoslavia.

The country is divided into 28 provinces (*okrŭg,* plur. *okrŭzi).* Area and population in 1982:

Province	*Area (sq. km)*	*Pop. 1,000*	*Province*	*Area (sq. km)*	*Pop. 1,000*	*Province*	*Area (sq. km)*	*Pop. 1,000*
Blagoevgrad	6,490	340	Pleven	4,342	373	Sofia (City)	1,194	1,167
Burgas	7,608	438	Plovdiv	5,639	758	Stara Zagora	5,066	413
Gabrovo	2,035	179	Razgrad	2,669	194	Tolbukhin	4,704	253
Khaskovo	4,008	296	Ruse	2,570	298	Tŭrgovishte	2,732	172
Kŭrdzhali	4,035	289	Shumen	3,390	253	Varna	3,825	467
Kyustendil	3,041	198	Silistra	2,851	174	Veliko Tŭrnovo	4,686	344
Lovech	4,136	210	Sliven	3,614	236	Vidin	3,057	168
Mikhailovgrad	3,611	232	Smolyan	3,523	176	Vratsa	3,964	290
Pazardzhik	4,455	323	Sofia	7,166	307	Yambol	4,111	205
Pernik	2,391	175						

The population at the census of 2 Dec. 1975 was 8,727,771 (males, 4,357,820; urban, 5,061,087). Population on 1 Jan. 1983 was 8,929,332 (4·4m. males; 5·7m. urban). Population density 80·5 per sq. km.

Ethnic minorities are not identified. Some Turks have been repatriated, but 9% of the population may be Turkish. There were attempts forcibly to Bulgarianise these in preparation for the 1985 census. The remainder include Gipsies, Jews, Romanians and Armenians.

Population of principal towns (1982): Sofia, 1,082,315; Plovdiv, 367,195; Varna, 295,038; Ruse, 178,920; Burgas, 178,239; Stara Zagora, 141,722; Pleven, 135,899; Sliven, 100,637; Tolbukhin, 98,857; Shumen, 99,642; Pernik, 94,859; Khaskovo, 87,639; Yambol, 86,216; Gabrovo, 80,901; Pazardzhik, 77,830.

Vital statistics, 1982: Live births, 124,166; deaths, 100,293; marriages, 67,154; divorces, 13,282; crude birth rate, 14 per 1,000 population; crude death rate, 11·2; infant mortality, 18·2 per 1,000; growth rate, 2.7.

Expectation of life in 1980 was: men, 68·7 years, women 73·9.

CLIMATE. The southern parts have a Mediterranean climate, with winters mild and moist and summers hot and dry, but further north the conditions become more continental, with a larger range of temperature and greater amounts of rainfall in summer and early autumn. Sofia. Jan. 28°F(–2·2°C), July 69°F (20·6°C). Annual rainfall 25·4″ (635 mm).

CONSTITUTION AND GOVERNMENT. A People's Republic was proclaimed by the National Assembly on 15 Sept. 1946, and the existing 'Tŭrnovo' Constitution of 1879 was replaced by the 'Dimitrov' Constitution in 1947. This was in turn replaced by a new constitution on 18 May 1971. This provides for a single-chamber National Assembly *(Narodno Sŭbranie)*. The highest permanently operating organ of the state is the Council of State which consists of a chairman, 2 first vice-chairmen, 4 vice-chairmen, a secretary and 17 members; it is elected by the National Assembly from its members. Supreme power is vested in the National Assembly, which consists of 400 deputies elected from areas of equal population by direct, secret and universal suffrage (everybody at age of 18 being eligible to vote and hold office) for a term of 5 years; it is to meet at least three times every year. The National Assembly also elects the Council of State and the ministers who are responsible to it.

A general election was held on 27 Oct. 1946. The Fatherland Front, composed of the Workers (Communist), Agrarian, Socialist and Zveno Parties, and non-party independents, obtained 364 seats (277 of which went to the Communists) and the opposition 101. On 26 Aug. 1947 the oppositional Agrarian Union was dissolved; its leader, Nikola Petkov, was sentenced to death and hanged on 23 Sept. The Socialist Party was merged with the Workers' Party in Aug. 1948, and the Zveno Party dissolved itself.

The Fatherland Front became, in 1948, a unified mass organization with individual memberships. Inside the Fatherland Front, there remain two political parties, the Bulgarian Communist Party and the Bulgarian People's Agrarian Union. Petŭr Tanchev *(1st Vice-Chairman, Council of State)* is Secretary of the Agrarian Union and Pencho Kubadinski Chairman of the Fatherland Front's National Council.

In 1984 the membership of the Communist Party was 892,000; Young Communist League, (1976) 1·3m.; Agrarian Union, 120,000; Fatherland Front, 3,770,080.

At the elections of 7 June 1981, 99·96% of the electorate voted, and 99·93% of the votes were cast for the 400 candidates (87 women) of the Fatherland Front; there were no other candidates. The list comprised 271 Communists, 99 Agrarians and 30 independents. The President of the National Assembly is Stanko Todorov.

There is no constitutional single Head of State, but Todor Zhivkov *(Chairman of the Council of State, Secretary-General of the Communist Party)*, performs some of the functions of a Head of State.

The highest policy-making and executive body of the Bulgarian Communist Party is its Politburo. The Politburo is elected by and from the Central Committee.

The Politburo was in March 1985 composed as follows: FULL MEMBERS: Todor Zhivkov, Grisha Filipov *(Chairman, Council of Ministers, i.e. Prime Minister)*, Todor Bozhinov *(First Deputy Chairman, Council of Ministers, Minister of Energy and Raw Materials)*, Stanko Todorov, Pencho Kubadinski, Milko Balev, Chudomir Aleksandrov *(First Deputy Chairman, Council of Ministers)*, Gen. Dobri Dzhurov *(Defence Minister)*, Petŭr Mladenov *(Foreign Minister)*, Ognian Doinov *(Minister of Machine Building)*; Iordan Iotov. CANDIDATE MEMBERS: Petŭr Dyulgerov; Andrei Lukanov *(Deputy Chairman, Council of Ministers)*, Georgi Yordanov *(Deputy Chairman, Council of Ministers, Chairman, Committee for Culture)*. Grigor Stoichkov *(Deputy Chairman, Council of Ministers, Minister of Construction)*. Stanish Bonev *(Deputy Chairman, Council of Ministers, Chairman, State Planning Committee)*. Georgi Atanasov; Dimitŭr Stoianov *(Minister of Internal Affairs)*.

Ministers not in the Politburo include: Kiril Zarev *(Deputy Chairman, Council of Ministers)*, Georgi Karamanev, *(Deputy Chairman, Council of Ministers, Minister of Internal Trade)*, Khristo Khristov *(Foreign Trade)*, Belcho Belchev *(Finance)*, Svetla Daskalova *(Justice)*.

In May 1967 a second 20-year treaty of friendship, co-operation and mutual assistance with the Soviet Union was signed.

National flag: Three horizontal stripes of white, green, red, with the national emblem in the canton.

National anthem: An arrangement of Mila Rodino (Dear Fatherland), a popular patriotic song, was declared the national anthem in 1964.

Local Government. People's Councils for the 28 provinces, 29 urban areas and 299 other districts are elected for 30 months. In addition to their civic functions they also supervise the management of publicly owned enterprises. The Council's executive organs are Permanent Committees. 4,475 councillors were elected on 4 Dec. 1983.

DEFENCE. There is a compulsory service of 2 years in the Army and Air Force (3 years in the Navy).

Army. In 1985 the Army had a strength of 105,000, including 73,000 conscripts, and is organized in 8 motor rifle divisions and 5 tank brigades. Bulgaria is divided into 3 Military Districts, based on Sofia, Plovdiv and Sliven. Equipment includes 400 T-34, 1,400 T-54/-55 and 60 T-72 tanks. Paramilitary forces, including border guards, security police and People's Territorial Militia, number some 175,000.

Navy. The Navy consists of 2 *ex*-Soviet 'R' class submarines, 2 *ex*-Soviet 'Riga' class frigates, 3 *ex*-Soviet 'Poti' class corvettes, 5 *ex*-Soviet 'Osa' class missile boats, 6 *ex*-Soviet patrol vessels, 6 *ex*-Soviet torpedo boats, 2 fleet minesweepers, 6 coastal minesweepers, 4 inshore minesweepers, 18 minesweeping boats, 25 landing craft, 4 oilers, 3 survey ships, 2 salvage craft, 9 tugs, 2 training ships, 2 degaussing vessels, 2 diving tenders and 28 auxiliaries and service craft. Personnel in 1985 totalled 9,000 officers and ratings of whom 1,900 were afloat, 2,100 on coastal defence, 1,800 in training, 3,000 for shore support and 200 for naval aviation comprising 8 helicopters.

Air Force. The large tactical Air Force had (1984) about 250 Soviet-built combat aircraft and 30,000 personnel. There are 5 squadrons of MiG-21 interceptors; about 8 squadrons of fighter/ground attack MiG-23s and MiG-17s; 2 reconnaissance squadrons of MiG-17s; some Mi-24 helicopter gunships; a total of about 20 Tu-134, Il-14 and An-24/26 transport aircraft; a total of about 70 Mi-4, Mi-2, Ka-26, Mi-6, and Mi-8 helicopters; and L-29 Delfin, MiG-15UTI and MiG-21UTI trainers. Soviet-built 'Guideline', 'Goa' and 'Ganef' surface-to-air missiles have also been supplied to Bulgaria.

INTERNATIONAL RELATIONS

Membership. Bulgaria is a member of UN, Comecon and the Warsaw Pact.

External Debt. Agreements of 1955 and 1963 settled outstanding financial claims by the UK and USA respectively.

ECONOMY

Planning. State economic planning started in 1947. After 1964 there was a limited decentralization in planning, culminating in the economic reform of 1 Jan. 1969. A new economic mechanism was introduced on 1 Jan. 1982. This provides for direct linking of production to the market, a shift from extensive to intensive development, the establishment of profit as the sole criterion of success, the widening of enterprises' powers to make their own plans and the election of managerial staff (except the chief) by the workforce.

For the first seven 5-year plans *see* THE STATESMAN'S YEAR-BOOK for 1980–81 and 1981–82. The eighth 5-year plan (1981–85) envisages a rise in national income of 20%, in industrial production of 28% and in agriculture of 18%.

Budget. The revenue and expenditure of Bulgaria for calendar years were as follows (in 1m. leva):

	1972	*1973*	*1974*	*1975*	*1976*	*1977*	*1980*	*1981*	*1982*
Revenue	6,355	7,055	8,060	9,321	8,778	9,498	13,187	15,385	15,824
Expenditure	6,261	7,036	8,044	9,223	8,758	9,477	13,167	15,370	15,809

Of the 1984 revenue 92% came from the national economy. 1980 expenditure was: National economy, 5,777m. leva; social and education, 5,265m.; administration, 291m. Estimates (1985): Revenue, 18,097; expenditure, 18,087.

Currency. The unit of currency is the *lev* (pl. *leva*) divided into 100 *stotinki* (sing. *stotinka*). It has been linked to the Soviet rouble since May 1952. A new *lev*, equalling 10 old leva, was introduced on 1 Jan. 1962. The parity (clearing value) is 1 rouble = 1·30 *leva*. Official rate of exchange (March 1984) was £1 = 1·434 *leva*; US$1 = 0·999 *leva*. Rate of exchange for non-commercial transactions: £1 = 2·40 leva; US$1 = 1·65 *leva*.

Banking. The National Bank is the central bank and is responsible for issuing currency. It also plays an important part in the management of the economy: its chairman has ministerial rank. There is also a Foreign Trade Bank, a Mineral Bank and a State Savings Bank. In 1982, 9m. depositors had savings totalling 9,860m. leva. The State Savings Bank has advanced personal loans up to 500 leva at 3·5% interest to some 500,000 users. Interest on deposits is from 1% to 3%.

Weights and Measures. The metric system is in general use. On 1 April 1916 the Gregorian calendar came into force in Bulgaria.

ENERGY AND NATURAL RESOURCES

Energy. Bulgaria has little oil, gas or high-grade coal and energy policy is based on the exploitation of its low-grade coal and limited water resources.

Electricity. In 1982 there were 234 power stations with a potential of 9·5m. kw. (thermal, (146) 5·84m. kw.; hydroelectric, (87) 1·9m. kw.; nuclear, (1) 1·76m. kw.). Output, 1982, 40,455m. kwh.

Oil and Natural Gas. Oil is extracted in the Balchik district on the Black Sea, in an area 100 km north of Varna and at Dolni Dubnik near Pleven. Crude oil production was 129,000 tonnes in 1977. There are refineries at Burgas (annual capacity 5m. tonnes) and Dolni Dubnik (7m. tonnes). 190m. cu. metres of natural gas were produced in 1980.

Minerals. Ore production 1982: Manganese, 13,200 tonnes; iron, 474,000 tonnes. 33·6m. tonnes of coal including 406,000 tonnes of hard coal and 26·4m. tonnes of lignite were mined in 1982. 88 tonnes of salt were extracted in 1982.

Agriculture. In 1979 the National Agro-Industrial Union was formed, replacing the Ministry of Agriculture. It comprises state and collective organizations, and is responsible for agriculture, the food industry and agricultural machine building. In 1982 agricultural land covered 6,181,500 hectares, of which 4,654,700 hectares are cultivable.

Size of private plots (maximum, 1 hectare) is based on the number of members of a household. Total area of private plots in 1982 was 599,800 hectares. Collective and state farms have been incorporated into 'agricultural-industrial complexes'. There were 296 of these in 1982. There were 68 machine-tractor stations. 152,155 tractors (in 15-h.p. units) were in use and 19,097 combine harvesters.

In 1982, 26 irrigation systems and 161 dams irrigated 1,169,900 hectares.

Yield in 1982 (in 1,000 tonnes): Wheat, 4,913; rye, 34; maize, 3,418; barley, 1,436; oats, 50; rice, 75; sunflower seed, 511; unginned cotton, 20; tobacco, 145; tomatoes, 853; potatoes, 469; grapes, 1,246. Bulgaria produces 80% of the world supply of attar of roses; annual production, 1,200 kg.

Other products (in 1,000 tonnes) in 1982: Meat, 1,179; wool, 35; sugar, 399; 2,489m. eggs were produced and 2,350m. litres of milk.

Livestock (1983): 118,559 horses, 1,782,649 cattle, including 694,066 milch cows, 10,761,395 sheep, 3,809,800 pigs, 42,853,108 poultry and 565,522 bee-hives.

Forestry. The forest area, 1982, was 3,859,000 hectares (34% coniferous, 26% oak). Oak forests are in a poor condition due to indiscriminate felling in the past. 39,006 hectares were afforested in 1982. 7·6m. cu. metres of timber were cut in 1982.

Fisheries. The catch of sea fish was 89,500 tonnes in 1979.

INDUSTRY AND TRADE

Industry. All industry was nationalized in 1947.

Industrial production	*1977*	*1978*	*1979*	*1980*	*1981*	*1982*
Crude steel (1,000 tonnes)	2,589	2,470	2,482	2,565	2,484	2,584
Pig-iron (1,000 tonnes)	1,664	1,538	1,501	1,583	1,512	1,558
Cement (1,000 tonnes)	4,665	5,149	5,401	5,359	5,433	5,614
Sulphuric acid (1,000 tonnes)	860	974	998	852	920	916

In 1982 there were also produced (in 1,000 tonnes): Coke, 1,274; rolled steel, 3,253; artificial fertilizers, 2,976; calcinated soda, 1,459; cotton fabrics, 367m. metres; woollens, 37m. metres.

Labour. There is 42½-hour 5-day working week. The average wage (excluding peasantry) was 207 leva per month in 1983. Population of working age (males 16–60; females 16–55), 1982, 5·06m. (2·7m. males). The labour force (excluding peasantry) in 1982 was 4,100,259 (2,624,829 female), of whom 1,401,997 worked in industry, 349,029 in building and 954,488 in agriculture and forestry.

Commerce. Foreign trade is controlled by the Ministry of Foreign Trade. Bulgarian trade has developed as follows (in 1m. leva):

	1977	*1978*	*1979*	*1980*	*1981*	*1982*
Imports	6,061	6,801	7,363	8,283	9,860	10,976
Exports	6,022	6,650	7,667	8,902	9,958	10,880

Structure of imports and exports in 1982: Producers' goods, 86%, 75%; consumer goods, 14%, 25%; industrial products, 99%, 91%; agricultural products, 11%, 24%.

Main exports are food products, tobacco, non-ferrous metals, cast iron, leather articles, textiles and (to Communist countries) machinery; main imports are machinery, oil, natural gas, steel, cellulose and timber.

74% of Bulgaria's trade is with the Communist countries (54% with USSR). Agreements with USSR envisage the co-ordination of the Soviet and Bulgarian 5-year plans in the spirit of 'socialist internationalism'. In 1979 a 10-year plan of economic specialization and co-operation was signed with the USSR. Libya is Bulgaria's biggest non-Communist export market, Federal Republic of Germany her major non-Communist supplier.

Indebtedness to the West was some US$1,800m. in 1983.

Total trade between Bulgaria and UK (British Department of Trade returns, in £1,000 sterling):

	1980	*1981*	*1982*	*1983*	*1984*
Imports to UK	14,425	13,353	21,009	12,355	17,345
Exports and re-exports from UK	35,242	33,838	46,104	44,577	55,917

In 1979 there were 40 joint Western-Bulgarian industrial ventures in operation. Western share participation may exceed 50%.

COMMUNICATIONS

Roads. In 1982 there were 32,597 km of roads, including 164 km of motorways and 2,914 km of main roads. 880m. tonnes of freight and 790m. passengers were carried.

Railways. In 1983 Bulgaria had 4,341 km of standard gauge railway, including

1,650 km electrified. 97m. passengers and 83·9m. tons of freight were carried in 1982.

Aviation. BALKAN (Bulgarian Airlines) operates internal flights from Sofia (airport: Vrazhdebna) to Burgas, Khaskovo, Pleven, Plovdiv, Ruse, Silistra, Stara Zagora, Tŭrgovishte, Veliko Tŭrnovo, Varna, Vidin and Yambol and international flights to Algiers, Amsterdam, Athens, Baghdad, Bratislava, Belgrade, Benghazi, Berlin, Brussels, Bucharest, Budapest, Cairo, Casablanca, Copenhagen, Damascus, Dresden, Frankfurt, Istanbul, London, Madrid, Moscow, Nicosia, Paris, Prague, Rome, Stockholm, Syktyvkar, Tunis, Vienna, Warsaw and Zurich. There are also flights from Burgas to Leningrad and Kiev, and from Varna to Leningrad, Kuwait, Athens and Stockholm. In 1982 BALKAN carried 2·3m. passengers and 28,218 tonnes of freight.

Shipping. Ports, shipping and shipbuilding are controlled by the Bulgarian United Shipping and Shipbuilding Corporation. The mercantile marine in 1982 possessed 194 ocean-going vessels and tankers with a total loading capacity of 1·6m. DWT. Burgas is a fishing and oil-port open to tankers of 20,000 tons. Varna is the other important port. In Nov. 1978 a rail ferry, with an initial capacity of 4·5m. tonnes of freight a year, was opened between Varna and Ilitchovsk (USSR). In 1982, 710,000 passengers and 26m. tonnes of cargo were carried.

Post and Broadcasting. In 1982 there were 2,916 post offices, 1,513,397 telephones, 57 broadcasting stations and 27 television stations. Radio Sofia, the government broadcasting station, transmits 2 programmes on medium- and short-waves. There is also a special tourist service, broadcast *via* the Varna II transmitter on 1,124 kHz. Advertisements are broadcast for half an hour a day. Bulgaria participates in the East European TV link 'Intervision'. Colour programmes by SECAM system. Radio receiving sets licensed in 1982, 2,085,376; television, 1,682,697.

Cinemas and Theatres (1982). There were 36 theatres, 18 puppet theatres, 8 opera houses, 1 operetta house and 3,302 cinemas. 532 films were made (33 full-length).

Newspapers and Books. In 1982 there were 14 dailies with a circulation of 2·1m. The Party newspaper is *Rabotnicheskoto Delo* ('The Workers' Cause') with a circulation of 820,000 in 1984. 5,070 book titles were published in 1982.

JUSTICE, RELIGION, EDUCATION AND WELFARE

Justice. A law of Nov. 1982 provides for the election (and recall) of all judges by the National Assembly. The lower courts include lay assessors as well as professional judges. There are a Supreme Court, 28 provincial courts (including Sofia), 105 regional courts and 'Comrades' Courts' for minor offences.

The maximum term of imprisonment is now 20 years except for 'exceptionally dangerous crimes' which carry the death penalty.

The Prosecutor General, elected by the National Assembly for 5 years and subordinate to it alone, exercises supreme control over the correct observance of the law by all government bodies, officials and citizens. He appoints and discharges all Prosecutors of every grade. The powers of this office were extended and redefined by a law of 1980 to put a greater emphasis on crime prevention and the rights of citizens.

Religion. 'The traditional church of the Bulgarian people' (as it is officially described), is that of the Eastern Orthodox Church. It was disestablished under the 1947 Constitution. In 1953 the Bulgarian Patriarchate was revived. The present Patriarch is Metropolitan Maksim of Lovech (enthroned 1971). The seat of the Patriarch is at Sofia. There are 11 dioceses, each under a Metropolitan, 10 bishops, 2,600 parishes, 1,700 priests, 400 monks and nuns, 3,700 churches and chapels, one seminary and one theological college.

The Constitution provides for freedom of conscience and belief but forbids propaganda against the Government. The State provides 17% of Church funds.

Churches may not maintain schools or colleges, except theological seminaries, or organize youth movements.

In 1976 there were some 50,000 Roman Catholics in 3 bishoprics with 40 priests and 30 churches. In 1984 there were 5 Protestant groups: Pentecostals (10,000 members, 120 churches, 40 pastors); Baptists (1,000 members, 20 churches); Methodists; Congretationalists; Adventists. There were estimated to be about 700,000 practising Moslems in 1984.

Education. Education is free, and compulsory for children between the ages of 7 and 16. The gradual introduction of unified secondary polytechnical schools offering compulsory education for all children from the ages of 7 to 17 was begun in 1973–74. Complete literacy is claimed. Schools are classified according to which years of schooling they offer: Elementary (1–4), primary (1–8), preparatory (5–8), secondary (9–11), complete secondary (1–11).

Educational statistics for 1982–83: 5,733 kindergartens (403,518 children, 29,257 teachers); 777 elementary schools; 2,267 primary schools; 54 preparatory schools; 94 secondary schools; 349 complete secondary schools. Numbers of teachers and pupils: School years 1 to 4, 24,975 and 430,433; 5 to 8, 35,261 and 623,432; 9 to 11, 8,459 and 116,569. There were also 3 vocational-technical schools (71 teachers, 1,667 students), 232 technical colleges (9,133 teachers, 93,226 students), 23 post-secondary institutions (973 teachers, 9,899 students) and 29 institutes of higher education (13,254 teachers, 83,633 students). There are 3 universities: the Kliment Ohrid University in Sofia (founded 1888) had 1,195 teachers and 12,616 students (in 1977–78); the Kirill i Metodii University in Veliko Tŭrnovo (founded 1971) had 250 teachers and 3,670 students and the Paisi Hilendarski University in Plovdiv (founded 1972) had 274 teachers and 3,500 students in 1980–81.

The Academy of Sciences was founded in 1869.

Social Welfare. Retirement and disablement pensions and temporary sick pay are calculated as a percentage of previous wages (respectively 55–80%, 35–100%, 69–90%) and according to the nature of the employment.

Monthly family allowances for children under 16: 15 leva for 1 child, 25 leva for 2 children and 45 leva for 3 children.

In 1982, 2·12m. persons received pensions totalling 1,974m. leva.

All medical services are free. In 1982 there were 186 hospitals (including 16 mental hospitals and addiction treatment centres) with 74,656 beds. There were 23,081 doctors and 5,201 dentists.

DIPLOMATIC REPRESENTATIVES

Of Bulgaria in Great Britain (186 Queen's Gate, London, SW7 5HL)
Ambassador: Kiril Shterev (accredited 26 Nov. 1980).

Of Great Britain in Bulgaria (Blvd. Marshal Tolbukhin 65–67, Sofia)
Ambassador: J. M. O. Snodgrass, CMG.

Of Bulgaria in the USA (1621 22nd St., NW, Washington, D.C., 20008)
Ambassador: Stoyan I. Zhulev.

Of the USA in Bulgaria (1 Stamboliiski Blvd., Sofia)
Ambassador: Robert L. Barry.

Of Bulgaria to the United Nations
Ambassador: Boris Tsvetkov.

Books of Reference

Kratka Bŭlgarska Entsiklopediia (Short Bulgarian Encyclopaedia), 5 vols. Sofia, 1963–69
Statisticheski Godishnik (Statistical Yearbook). Sofia from 1956
Constitution of the People's Republic of Bulgaria. Sofia, 1971
Information Bulgaria. Oxford, 1985
Modern Bulgaria: History, Politics, Economy, Culture. Sofia, 1981
Atanasova, T., *et al., Bulgarian-English Dictionary.* Sofia, 1975

Dobrin, B., *Bulgarian Economic Development Since World War II.* New York, 1973
Feiwel, G. R., *Growth and Reforms in Centrally Planned Economies: the Lessons of the Bulgarian Experience.* New York, 1977
Markov, M., *System of Social Administration in Bulgaria.* Sofia, 1969
Oren, N., *Communism Administered: Agrarianism and Communism in Bulgaria.* Baltimore, 1973
Pundeff, M. V., *Bulgaria: A Bibliographic Guide.* Library of Congress, 1965
Spasov, B., *La Bulgarie.* Paris, 1973
Todorov, N., and others, *Bulgaria: Historic and Geographical Outline.* Sofia, 1965
Zhivkov, T., *Modern Bulgaria: Problems and Tasks in Building an Advanced Socialist Society.* New York, 1974

BURKINA FASO

Capital: Ouagadougou
Population: 6·70m. (1983)
GNP per capita: US$240 (1981)

République de Burkina Faso

HISTORY. A separate colony of Upper Volta was in 1919 carved out of the colony of Upper Senegal and Niger, which had been established in 1904. In 1932 it was abolished and most of its territory transferred to Ivory Coast, with small parts added to French Sudan and Niger, but it was re-constituted with its former borders on 4 Sept. 1947. Upper Volta became an autonomous republic within the French Community on 11 Dec. 1958 and reached full independence on 5 Aug. 1960.

On 3 Jan. 1966 the government of Maurice Yameogo was overthrown by a military *coup* led by Lieut-Col. Sangoulé Lamizana, who assumed the Presidency. Constitutional rule was resumed on 21 June 1970 but suspended from 8 Feb. 1974 until May 1978. In a further *coup* on 25 Nov. 1980, President Lamizana was overthrown and a military regime assumed power. Further *coups* took place on 7 Nov. 1982 and 4 Aug. 1983. The name of the country was changed to Burkina Faso on 4 Aug. 1984.

AREA AND POPULATION. Burkina Faso is bounded north and west by Mali, east by Niger, south by Benin, Togo, Ghana and the Ivory Coast. The republic covers an area of 274,122 sq. km; population (census, 1975) 5,638,203. Estimate (1984) 6,695,000. The largest cities (1982) are: Ouagadougou, the capital (286,453 inhabitants), Bobo-Dioulasso (165,171), Koudougou (44,089), Ouahigouya (38,374), Kaya (18,402), Banfora (12,358). The principal ethnic groups are the Mossi (48%), Fulani (10%), Lobi-Dagari (7%), Mandé (7%), Bobo (7%), Sénoufo (6%), Gourounsi (5%), Bissa (5%), Gourmantché (5%).

CLIMATE. A tropical climate with a wet season from May to Nov. and a dry season from Dec. to April. Rainfall decreases from south to north. Ouagadougou. Jan. 76°F (24·4°C), July 83°F (28·3°C). Annual rainfall 36″ (894 mm).

CONSTITUTION AND GOVERNMENT. Following the *coup* of 25 Nov. 1980, the 1977 Constitution was suspended and the 57-member National Assembly dissolved. Supreme political power is now vested in a new 12-member People's Salvation Council (CSP), ruling through an appointed Cabinet composed in Sept. 1984 of:

President of CNR, Head of State and Government: Capt. Thomas Sankara.

National Defence and War Veterans' Affairs: Maj. Jean-Baptiste Lingani. *Minister of State to the Presidency, Justice:* Capt. Blaise Compaoré. *Foreign Affairs and Co-operation:* Laitar Basile Guissou. *Territorial Administration and Security:* Ernest Ouedraogo. *Information and Culture:* Wattamou Lamien. *Economic Promotion:* Capt. Henri Zongo. *Financial Resources:* Justin Damou Barro. *Budget:* Adele Ouegraogo. *Planning and People's Development:* Youssouf Ouegraogo. *Commerce and People's Supply:* Alain Koeffe. *Agriculture and Animal Husbandry:* Seydou Traoré. *Water Resources:* Michel Tapsoba. *Equipment:* Leonard Compaoré. *Transport and Communications:* Omar Diawara. *Labour, Social Security and Civil Service:* Fidèle Toe. *Environment and Tourism:* Raymond Poda. *Family Welfare and National Solidarity:* Josephine Ouedraogo. *Public Health:* Maj. Abdul Salam Kaboré. *Sport and Leisure:* Rita Sawadogo. *National Education:* Philippe Somé. *Higher Education and Scientific Research:* Issa Tiendrebéogo. *Secretary-General to the Cabinet:* Rayatigoungou Kaboré Zongo.

National flag: Horizontally red over green with a yellow star over all in the centre.

Local government: The country is divided into 25 provinces.

DEFENCE

Army. The Army consists of 3 infantry regiments, 1 reconnaissance squadron and support units. Equipment includes 25 armoured cars. Strength (1985), 3,700 with a further 900 men in paramilitary forces.

Air Force. Creation of a small air arm to support the land forces began, with French assistance, in 1964. Equipment now comprises 2 HS.748 twin-turboprop freighters, 2 C-47s, 2 twin-turboprop Frégates, an Aero Commander 500, 2 Broussard and 4 Reims/Cessna Super Skymasters for transport and liaison duties, and 3 Dauphin and Aloutte III helicopters. Personnel total about 75.

INTERNATIONAL RELATIONS

Membership. Burkina Faso is a member of UN, OAU and is an ACP state of the EEC.

ECONOMY

Planning. The Third Development Plan 1977–81 aimed at an 8·4% average annual real growth in GDP.

Budget. Government revenue and expenditure balanced in 1983 at 57,949m. francs CFA.

Currency. The unit of currency is the *franc* CFA with a parity rate of 50 *francs* CFA to 1 French *franc*. In Feb. 1985, £1 = 558 *francs*; US$1 = 512 *francs*.

Banking. The *Banque Centrale des Etats de l'Afrique de l'Ouest* is the bank of issue. The main commercial bank is the *Banque Internationale des Voltas*. In Dec. 1982 the savings banks had deposits of 25,957,000 *francs* CFA.

ENERGY AND NATURAL RESOURCES

Electricity. Production of electricity (1982) was 123m. kwh.

Minerals. There are deposits of manganese near Tambao in the north, but exploitation is limited by existing transport facilities. Magnetite, bauxite, zinc, lead, nickel and phosphates have been found in the same area.

Agriculture. Production (1981–82, in tonnes): Sorghum, 657,986; millet, 442,771; maize, 125,204; groundnuts, 77,667; rice (paddy, 1980), 28,657; cotton, 59,474; sesame, 8,017. Rice and groundnuts are of increasing importance.

Livestock (1983): 2·9m. cattle, 2m. sheep, 2·5m. goats, 70,000 horses, 200,000 donkeys.

INDUSTRY AND TRADE

Industry. In 1981 gross manufacturing (including energy) was 40,189,000 francs CFA, of which textiles (3,461,000 francs CFA) and metal products (2·28m. francs CFA). In 1972 there were 91 industrial units.

Labour. In 1982 the labour force was 3,503,610 of whom (1979) 2,941,000 were engaged in agriculture, forestry and fishing. There were (1981) 4 trade unions.

Commerce. In 1982 imports totalled 113,708m. francs CFA and exports 18,109m. francs CFA. In 1982 the major exports were cotton (41·9%), almonds (16%) and livestock (14·1%). In 1982 France provided 26·7%, the Ivory Coast 12·4% and USA 6·6% of imports, while the Ivory Coast took 21%, France 14·5%, Federal Republic of Germany 7·4% and UK 6·6% of exports.

Total trade between Burkina Faso and UK (British Department of Trade returns, in £1,000 sterling):

	1981	*1982*	*1983*	*1984*
Imports to UK	2,864	1,289	1,514	3,695
Exports and re-exports from UK	5,311	2,166	3,048	2,065

Tourism. There were 50,049 tourists in 1982.

COMMUNICATIONS

Roads. The road system comprises 13,134 km, of which 4,396 km are national, 1,744 km departmental, 2,364 km regional and 1,940 km unclassified roads. In 1982 there were 33,769 vehicles, comprising 16,463 private cars, 419 buses, 14,852 commercial vehicles, 411 special vehicles and 1,123 tractors.

Railway. Ouagadougou is the terminus of the Abidjan-Niger railway, of which 517 km lie in Burkina Faso. A 355-km extension to the manganese deposits at Tambao is planned with the first 107-km section to Kaya under construction.

Aviation. Ouagadougou and Bobo-Dioulasso are regularly served by UTA and Air Afrique and in 1982 dealt with 120,684 passengers and 6,778 tonnes of freight. Air Volta operates all internal flights to 47 domestic airports.

Post and Broadcasting. There were, in 1982, some 42 post offices and (1978) 3,564 telephones. There are radio stations at Ouagadougou and Bobo-Dioulasso and (1981) 90,000 receivers. The state television service, Voltavision, broadcasts 3 days a week in Ouagadougou; there were (1981) 5,500 receivers.

Newspapers. 3 daily newspapers were published in Ouagadougou in 1984.

JUSTICE, RELIGION, EDUCATION AND WELFARE

Justice. There are courts of first instance at Ouagadougou, Bobo-Dioulasso, Ouahigouya and Fada N'Gourma. The Supreme Court, High Court of Justice and Court of Appeal are all in Ouagadougou.

Religion. The majority of the population (53%) follow animist religions; 36% are Moslem and 11% Christian (mainly Roman Catholic).

Education. There were at 1 Jan. 1983, 251,169 pupils in 1,176 primary schools. In 1981–82 there were 25,283 in secondary schools, and 5,122 in technical schools and (1980) 495 students in teacher-training establishments. The Université d'Ouagadougou had 2,887 students in 1982–83.

Health (1980). There were 5 hospitals, 178 dispensaries with maternity units and 60 maternity units alone, 50 health centres, 131 dispensaries and 99 special dispensaries with a total of 4,587 beds. There were 119 doctors, 14 surgeons, 52 pharmacists, 163 health assistants, 229 midwives and 1,345 nursing personnel.

A 10-year health programme started in 1979, providing for 7,000 village health centres, 515 district health centres, regional and sub-regional medical centres, 10 departmental hospitals, 2 national hospitals and a university centre of health sciences in Ouagadougou.

DIPLOMATIC REPRESENTATIVES

Of Burkina Faso in Great Britain
Ambassador: Amadé Ouedraogo (accredited 11 July 1984).

Of Great Britain in Burkina Faso
Ambassador: J. M. Willson (resides in Abidjan).

Of Burkina Faso in the USA (2340 Massachusetts Ave., NW, Washington, D.C., 20005)
Ambassador: Doulaye Corentin Ki.

Of the USA in Burkina Faso (PO Box 35, Ouagadougou)
Ambassador: Julius W. Walker, Jr.

Of Burkina Faso to the United Nations
Ambassador: Léandre Bassole.

BURMA

Capital: Rangoon
Population: 35·31m. (1983)
GNP per capita: US$190 (1981)

Pyidaungsu Socialist Thammada Myanma Naingngandaw

HISTORY. The Union of Burma came formally into existence on 4 Jan. 1948 and became the Socialist Republic of the Union of Burma in 1974. In 1948 Sir Hubert Rance, the last British Governor, handed over authority to Sao Shwe Thaike, the first President of the Burmese Republic, and Parliament ratified the treaty with Great Britain providing for the independence of Burma as a country not within His Britannic Majesty's dominions and not entitled to His Britannic Majesty's protection. This treaty was signed in London on 17 Oct. 1947 and enacted by the British Parliament on 10 Dec. 1947.

For the history of Burma's connexion with Great Britain *see* THE STATESMAN'S YEAR-BOOK, 1950, p. 836.

AREA AND POPULATION. Burma is bounded east by China, Laos and Thailand, west by the Indian ocean, Bangladesh and India. The total area of the Union is 261,789 sq. miles (678,000 sq. km). Some small rectifications of the border with China were agreed upon in 1960 and with Pakistan in 1964. The population in 1983 (census) was 35,313,905. Birth rate (1977 estimate), 29·1; death rate, 10·4 per 1,000 population; infant deaths, 56·3 per 1,000 live births. The leading towns are: Rangoon, the capital (1983), 2,458,712; other towns (1973), Mandalay, 417,266; Bassein, 355,588; Henzada, 283,658; Pegu, 254,761, Myingyan, 220,129; Moulmein, 202,967; Prome, 148,123; Akyab, 143,215; Tavoy, 101,536.

The population of the States and Divisions at the 1983 census (provisional): Kachin State, 903,982; Kayah State, 168,355; Karen State, 1,057,505; Chin State, 368,985; Sagaing Division, 3,855,991; Tenasserim Division, 917,628; Pegu Division, 3,800,240; Magwe Division, 3,241,103; Mandalay Division, 4,580,923; Mon State, 1,682,041; Rakhine State, 2,045,891; Rangoon Division, 3,973,782; Shan State, 3,718,706; Irrawaddy Division, 4,991,057.

The Burmese belong to the Tibeto-Chinese (or Tibeto-Burman) family.

CLIMATE. The climate is equatorial in coastal areas, changing to tropical monsoon over most of the interior, but humid temperate in the extreme north, where there is a more significant range of temperature and a dry season lasting from Nov. to April. In coastal parts, the dry season is shorter. Very heavy rains occur in the monsoon months May to Sept. Rangoon. Jan. 77°F (25°C), July 80°F (26·7°C). Annual rainfall 104″ (2,616 mm). Akyab. Jan. 70°F (21·1°C), July 81°F (27·2°C). Annual rainfall 206″ (5,154 mm). Mandalay. Jan. 68°F (20°C), July 85°F (29·4°C). Annual rainfall 33″ (828 mm).

CONSTITUTION. A new Constitution was approved by referendum in Dec. 1973. On 2 March 1974 military rule ended and Burma became a one party socialist republic. Elections to the People's Assembly took place in Jan. and Feb. 1974. U Ne Win became President under the new Constitution and in Jan. 1978 his term of office was extended for 4 years. For earlier Constitutions *see* THE STATEMAN'S YEAR-BOOK, 1981–82, p. 252.

In Nov. 1981, U San Yu was elected Head of State by the People's Assembly.

The State Council has 27 members with U San Yu as Chairman and U Aye Ko as secretary.

In Jan. 1984 the Council of Ministers consisted of:

Prime Minister: U Maung Maung Kha.

Deputy Prime Minister, Planning and Finance: U Tun Tin. *Deputy Prime Minister, Defence:* Gen. Thura Kyaw Htin. *Agriculture and Forests:* U Ye Goung. *Co-operatives:* U Sein Tun. *Transport and Communications:* Thura U Saw Pru. *Foreign Affairs:* U Chit Hlaing. *Industry:* U Tint Swe, U Maung Cho. *Construction:* U Hla Tun. *Mines:* U Than Tin. *Trade:* U Khin Maung Ghi. *Education:* U Kyaw Nyein. *Information and Culture:* U Aung Kyaw Myint. *Home and Religious Affairs:* Maj.-Gen. Min Gaung. *Labour and Social Welfare:* U Ohn Kyaw. *Health:* U Tun Wai. *Livestock and Fisheries:* U Sein Tun.

National flag: Red with a blue canton bearing 2 ears of rice within a cog-wheel and a ring of 14 stars, all in white.

Language: The official language is Burmese; the use of English is permitted.

Local government: Burma is divided into 7 states and 7 administrative divisions; these are sub-divided into townships and thence into villages and wards.

DEFENCE

Army. The strength of the Army (1985) was 163,000. The Army is organized into 9 regional commands comprising 3 light infantry divisions, 16 brigades, and 2 armoured, 85 independent infantry and 4 artillery battalions and 1 anti-aircraft battery. Equipment includes 24 Comet tanks, 40 Humber armoured cars and 45 Ferret scout cars. In addition, there are 2 paramilitary units: People's Police Force (38,000) and People's Militia (35,000).

Navy. The fleet includes 2 old escort patrol vessels (*ex*-USA PCE and MSF types), 2 small indigenously built corvettes, 3 new patrol craft, 20 gunboats, 20 river gunboats, 40 small river patrol craft, 1 support ship, 2 survey vessels, 12 fishery protection cutters (3 offshore, 3 coastal, 6 inshore), 10 auxiliaries and 12 landing craft. Personnel in 1985: 10,000 including 800 marines.

Air Force. The Air Force is intended primarily for internal security duties. Its combat force comprises about 5 T-33A jet fighter/trainers supplied under MAP, supplemented by 9 SIAI-Marchetti SF.260W light piston-engined attack/trainers. Other training aircraft include 10 piston-engined SF.260Ms, 16 turboprop Pilatus PC-7s and 10 jet-powered T-37Cs. Transport and second-line units are equipped with 4 FH-227, Turbo-Porter and 10 Cessna 180 aircraft, 4 Japanese-built Bell 47 (H-13) and Vertol KV-107-II, Bell UH-1, and Alouette III helicopters. Personnel about 7,000.

INTERNATIONAL RELATIONS

Membership. Burma is a member of the UN and Colombo Plan.

ECONOMY

Planning. The economy has been controlled since 1972 through a series of 4-year plans. The fourth 4-year plan began in 1983.

Budget. The budget estimates (in K.1m.) for fiscal year 1 April 1981–31 March 1982 was revenue K.38,750m. and expenditure K.48,493m.

The largest items, in 1980–81, of revenue were commodities and service tax (K.2,360·1m.) and customs (K.590m.); of expenditure, processing and manufacturing (K.8,769m.); trade (K.5,222·3m.); transport and communication (1,736·2m.).

Currency. The currency unit is now the *kyat* divided into 100 *pyas*. There are notes of *kyat* 25, 20, 10, 5 and 1, and coins of *kyat* 1; *pyas* 100, 50, 25, 10, 5 and 1.

In Feb. 1985, £1 = K.9·86 and US$1 = K.8·89.

Banking. Banks include the Union of Burma Bank, the Myanma Economic Bank, the Myanma Foreign Trade Bank and the Myanma Agricultural Bank and the corporation is the Myanma Insurance Corporation.

ENERGY AND NATURAL RESOURCES

Electricity. In 1979 the total installed capacity of power plants was 642,230 kw., of which 168,500 was hydro-electricity and 158,850 gas turbine; there were 264 towns and 709 villages with electricity. Production (1981-82) 1,405m. kwh.

Oil. Production (1981–82) of crude oil was 1·7m. tonnes; natural gas 665,000 cu. metres.

Minerals. Production in 1977–78 (provisional): Silver, 410,000 oz.; zinc, 6,000 tons; copper matte, 90 tons; refined lead, 5,198 tons; nickel speiss, 75 tons; antimony, 1,455 tons; tin, 866 tons; tungsten, 568 tons; tin tungsten-scheelite, 500 tons; coal (1981), 30,000 tons; gypsum, 28,000 tons; limestone, 1m. tons.

Agriculture. Production (1981) in 1,000 tonnes: Paddy, 13,923; sugar-cane, 2,569; groundnuts, 558; jute, 32; cotton, 107.

Livestock (1983): Cattle, 9·4m.; buffaloes, 2·1m.; pigs, 2·9m.

In 1979–80 the area irrigated by government-controlled irrigation works was 2,417,769 acres.

Forestry. The area of reserved forests in 1977–78 was 23,477,000 acres; other forests, 55,986,000 acres. Teak extracted in 1979–80 (provisional), 400,250 cu. tons; hardwood, 1,049,000 cu. tons. All the teak and about 50% of the hardwood is from the state sector. Other forest produce (1977–78) included 13m. tons of firewood and 680,000 bamboo canes. 2,780 elephants are at work on extraction.

Fisheries. In 1979 sea fishing produced 413,000 tonnes and freshwater fisheries 153,000 tonnes. The contribution of state-owned fishing vessels (32 trawlers and 43 other craft) is about 3%.

INDUSTRY AND TRADE

Industry. Production (1981) in 1,000 tonnes: Cement, 372; salt, 242; fertilizers, 132; sugar, 42; paper, 23; cotton, 15.

Trade Unions. Labour disputes are dealt with by the government labour sub-committees.

Commerce. All foreign trade is handled by the government trading organizations.

Imports and exports (US$1m.) for the calendar years.

	1980	*1981*	*1982*
Imports	785·6	860·2	881·9
Exports	427·7	530·9	421·5

Total trade between Burma and UK (British Department of Trade returns, in £1,000 sterling):

	1980	*1981*	*1982*	*1983*	*1984*
Imports to UK	5,379	3,613	5,342	4,726	6,420
Exports and re-exports from UK	20,494	28,036	44,242	21,927	16,488

Tourism. There were 28,230 tourists in 1981.

COMMUNICATIONS

Roads. There were 13,948 miles of road in 1977–78, of which 2,452 miles were union highway.

Railways. The Burma Railways were nationalized in 1948 and the present Burma Railways Corporation took over in 1972. In 1980 there were 3,137 km of route on metre gauge. In 1977–78 the railway carried 2·29m. tons of freight and 64·2m. passengers.

Aviation. Burma Airways Corporation, formerly Union of Burma Airways, started its internal service in Sept. 1948 and its external service in Nov. 1950. International services were in 1963 maintained between Rangoon and Bangkok and Calcutta. The routes were extended to Hong Kong in 1969 and to Dacca and Káthmándu in 1970. There were, in 1971, 43 civil aerodromes and landing grounds.

Shipping. Burma has 60 miles of navigable canals. The Irrawaddy is navigable up to Myitkyina, 900 miles from the sea, and its tributary, the Chindwin, is navigable for 390 miles. The Irrawaddy delta has nearly 2,000 miles of navigable water. The Salween, the Attaran and the G'yne provide about 250 miles of navigable waters around Moulmein. The Inland Water Transport Board runs services from Bhamo to Myitkyina.

Post and Broadcasting. There were 1,101 post offices in 1977. Number of telephones was 32,616 in 1978, of which 22,456 are in Rangoon. There is one television broadcasting station in Rangoon.

Cinemas. In 1971 there were about 418 cinemas.

Newspapers. In 1983 there were 7 daily newspapers with a readership of over 800,000.

JUSTICE, RELIGION, EDUCATION AND WELFARE

Justice. Since March 1974 the highest judicial authority has been the Council of People's Justices, appointed by the People's Assembly from its own members, which serves as the Supreme Court and Central Criminal Court. At lower levels courts are appointed by the local People's Councils from among their own membership.

Religion. The Revolutionary Government, having repealed the amendment of 1961 which made Buddhism the state religion, recognizes 'the right of everyone freely to profess and practise his religion'.

Education. The medium of instruction in all schools is Burmese; English is taught as a compulsory second language from kindergarten level.

Education is free in the primary, junior secondary and vocational schools; fees are charged in senior secondary schools and universities.

In 1977–78 there were 586 state high schools with 189,146 pupils, 1,262 state middle schools with 825,195 pupils and 21,999 state primary schools with 3,841,687 pupils; the total teaching staff was 111,339, of which 80,343 were in primary schools.

Beside the Arts and Science University, there are independent degree-giving institutes of engineering, education, medicine, agriculture, economics and commerce, and veterinary sciences. The University of Mandalay has been similarly decentralized. A foreign-languages institute in Rangoon has about 800 students learning English, French, German, Russian, Japanese, Chinese and Italian.

There are intermediate colleges at Taunggyi, Magwe, Akyab and Myitkyina, and degree colleges at Moulmein and Bassein, and several technical and agricultural institutes at higher and middle level. 4,656 school teachers were being trained in 15 training colleges in 1977–78. Technical high schools had 2,488 students; agricultural schools, 1,077; other vocational colleges, 1,438, and university colleges, 63,292.

A correspondence course for universities and colleges was introduced in 1975–76.

Health. In 1977 there were 5,787 doctors and 512 hospitals with 22,755 beds. There were 1,459 health centres.

DIPLOMATIC REPRESENTATIVES

Of Burma in Great Britain (19A Charles St., London, W1X 8ER)
Ambassador: U Myo Aung (accredited 16 Dec. 1981).

Of Great Britain in Burma (80 Strand Rd., Rangoon)
Ambassador: N. M. Fenn, CMG.

Of Burma in the USA (2300 S St., NW, Washington, D.C., 20008)
Ambassador: U Maung Maung Gyi.

Of the USA in Burma (581 Merchant St., Rangoon)
Ambassador: Daniel A. O'Donohue.

Of Burma to the United Nations
Ambassador: Saw Hlaing.

Books of Reference

Burma: Treaty between the Government of the United Kingdom and the Provisional Government of Burma. (Treaty Series No. 16, 1948.) HMSO, 1948
Cornyn, W. S., and Musgrave, J. K., *Burmese Glossary.* New York, 1958
Lehman, F. K., *The Structure of Chin Society.* Univ. of Illinois Press, 1963
Silverstein, J., *Burma: Military Rule and the Politics of Stagnation.* Cornell Univ. Press, 1978.
—*Burmese Politics: The Dilemma of National Unity.* Rutgers Univ. Press, 1980
Steinberg, D. I., *Burma.* Boulder, 1982
Stewart, J. A., and Dunn, C. W., *Burmese–English Dictionary.* London, 1940 ff.

BURUNDI

Capital: Bujumbura
Population: 4·92m. (1983)
GNP per capita: US$230 (1981)

HISTORY. Tradition recounts the establishment of a Tutsi kingdom under successive Mwamis as early as the 16th century. German military occupation in 1890 incorporated the territory into German East Africa. From 1919 Burundi formed part of Ruanda-Urundi administered by the Belgians, first as a League of Nations mandate and then as a United Nations trust territory. Elections supervised by the United Nations in Sept. 1961 resulted in a large majority for the Unité et Progrès National party (UPRONA). Internal self-government was granted on 1 Jan. 1962, followed by independence on 1 July 1962. An agreement, signed with Rwanda under United Nations auspices at Addis Ababa in April 1962, provided for a monetary and customs union. This union and all organizations operated jointly by the two governments were dissolved by 30 Sept. 1964.

On 8 July 1966 Prince Charles Ndizeye deposed his father Mwami Mwambutsa IV, suspended the constitution and made Capt. Michel Micombero Prime Minister. On 1 Sept. Prince Charles was enthroned as Mwami Ntare V. On 28 Nov., while the Mwami was attending a Head of States Conference in Kinshasa (Congo), Micombero declared Burundi a republic with himself as president.

On 31 March 1972 Prince Charles returned to Burundi from Uganda and was placed under house arrest. On 29 April 1972 President Micombero dissolved the Council of Ministers and took full power; that night heavy fighting broke out between rebels from both Burundi and neighbouring countries, and the ruling Tutsi, apparently with the intention of destroying the Tutsi hegemony. Prince Charles was killed during the fighting and it was estimated that up to 120,000 were killed. On 14 July 1972 President Micombero reinstated a Government with a Prime Minister. On 1 Nov. 1976 President Micombero was deposed by the Army. A Supreme Revolutionary Council of the Armed Forces was established which appointed Col. Jean-Baptiste Bagaza president.

AREA AND POPULATION. Burundi is bounded north by Rwanda, east and south by Tanzania and west by Zaïre, and has an area of 27,834 sq. km (10,759 sq. miles). It lies astride the main Nile–Congo dividing crest (6,000–7,000 ft) bounded on the west by the narrow plain of the Ruzizi River and Lake Tanganyika (2,534 ft). The interior is a broken plateau at an average height of about 5,000 ft, sloping eastwards down to Tanzania and the valley of the Maragarazi River. The southernmost tributary of the Nile system, the Luvironza, rises in the south of the country.

The population at the census in 1979 was 4,111,310. There are three ethnic groups—Hutu (Bantu, forming the great majority): Tutsi (Nilotic, less than 15%); Twa (pygmoids, less than 1%). There are some 3,500 Europeans and 1,500 Asians. In 1974 some 49,000 Tutsi refugees from Rwanda were living in Burundi.

Bujumbura, the capital, had (1979 census) 141,040 inhabitants. Kitega (15,943 inhabitants) was formerly the royal residence.

CLIMATE. An equatorial climate, modified by altitude. The eastern plateau is generally cool, the easternmost savanna several degrees hotter. The wet seasons are from March to May and Sept. to Dec. Bujumbura. Jan. 73°F (22·8°C), July 73°F (22·8°C). Annual rainfall 33″ (825 mm).

CONSTITUTION AND GOVERNMENT. A new Constitution was promulgated on 21 Nov. 1981 and provides for a one-party state. The 65-member National Assembly elected in Oct. 1982 comprised 52 members elected by universal suffrage from a list of 104 candidates nominated by UPRONA *(Parti de l'Unité et du Progrès National du Burundi)*, together with 13 members appointed by the President. President Bagaza became Party Chairman and Head of the Central Committee for a 5-year term in Jan. 1980 and was re-elected for a second 5-year term in Sept. 1984. He won 99·63% of the 1·7m. votes cast.

President of the Republic: Col. Jean-Baptiste Bagaza.
Foreign Affairs: Laurent Nzeyimana.
Finance: Edouard Kadigiri.

Flag: White diagonal cross dividing triangles of red and green, in the centre a white disc bearing 3 red green-bordered 6-pointed stars.

Local Government: The administrative divisions are: 15 provinces, each under a military governor, and 114 communes.

DEFENCE. The national armed forces total (1985), 5,200 (there are also about 1,500 in paramilitary units) and include a small naval flotilla and air force flight of 3 SF 260, 2 Cessna 150 and 2 Do 27 liaison aircraft and 4 Alouette III helicopters. The Army comprises 2 infantry battalions, 1 parachute battalion, 1 commando battalion and 1 armoured-car company.

INTERNATIONAL RELATIONS

Membership. Burundi is a member of UN and OAU and is an ACP state of EEC.

ECONOMY

Planning. The 1982–87 Plan aims at greater diversification of agriculture.

Budget. The 1984 budget envisaged receipts of 15,171m. Burundi francs and expenditure at 17,348m. Burundi francs.

Currency. The currency is administered by the Bank of the Republic of Burundi. The rate was 138·85 *Burundi francs* = £1 and 128·3 *Burundi francs* = US$1 in Feb. 1985.

Weights and Measures. The metric system operates.

ENERGY AND NATURAL RESOURCES

Electricity. Electricity generation capacity was (1980) 44·7m. kwh.

Minerals. Mineral ores such as bastnasite and cassenite were formerly mined but output is now insignificant. Deposits of nickel (280m. tonnes) remain to be exploited.

Agriculture. The main economic activity and the main source of employment of the country is subsistence agriculture, which accounts for well over half of the gross national product. Beans, kassava, maize, sweet potatoes, groundnuts, peas, sorghum and bananas are grown according to the climate and the region.

The main cash crop is coffee, of which about 95% is arabica. It accounts for 90% of exports and taxes and levies on coffee constitute a major source of revenue. A coffee board (OCIBU) manages the grading and export of the crop. Production (1982) 24,000 tonnes. The main food crops (production 1982, in 1,000 tonnes) are cassava (1,200), yams (930), bananas (960), beans (181), maize (140), sorghum (98), groundnuts (42) and peas (37). Among cash crops are cotton (3) and tea (2).

Cattle play an important traditional role, and there were about 560,000 head in 1983. The quality is poor, but efforts are being made to improve it. There were (1983) some 760,000 goats, 310,000 sheep and 36,000 pigs.

Fisheries. There is a small commercial fishing industry on Lake Tanganyika which produced 7,941 tonnes in 1973 and which dropped to 4,118 tonnes in 1981.

INDUSTRY AND TRADE

Industry. Industrial development is rudimentary. In Bujumbura there are plants for the processing of coffee and by-products of cotton, a brewery, cement works, a textile factory, a soap factory, a shoe factory and small metal workshops.

Commerce. The total value of exports 1982 was 7,883m. Burundi francs, and of imports, 19,159m. Burundi francs. Main exports in 1981 were coffee, (5,352m. Burundi francs); cotton, (188m.); tea, (181m.). Main imports, petrol products, food, vehicles and textiles.

Total trade between Burundi and the UK (British Department of Trade returns, in £1,000 sterling):

	1980	*1981*	*1982*	*1983*	*1984*
Imports to UK	1,881	6,329	8,737	3,485	1,924
Exports and re-exports from UK	583	1,479	1,522	3,155	1,710

Tourism. Tourism is developing and there were 13,000 visitors Jan.–June 1976.

COMMUNICATIONS

Roads. There is a road network of 6,400 km connecting with Rwanda, Congo and Tanzania but in 1982 only 310 km were macadamized. In 1978 there were 5,307 cars and 2,951 commercial vehicles.

Aviation. In 1980, 38,441 passengers arrived or departed through Bujumbura International airport, and there are local airports at Gitega, Nyanza-Lac, Kiofi and Nyakagunda.

Shipping. There are lake services from Bujumbura to Kigoma (Tanzania) and Kalémié (Zaïre). The main route for exports and imports is *via* Kigoma, and thence by rail to Dar es Salaam.

Post and Broadcasting. Number of telephones (1982), 5,601. Radio receivers (1982) 180,000.

Newspapers. There was (1984) one daily newspaper *(Le Renouveau)* with a circulation of 20,000.

JUSTICE, RELIGION, EDUCATION AND WELFARE

Justice. There is a Supreme Court, an appeal court and a *tribunal de première instance* at Bujumbura and provincial tribunals in each arrondissement.

Religion. About 78% of the population is Roman Catholic; there is a Roman Catholic archbishop and 3 bishops. The Anglican Missions under a bishop fall within the archdiocese of Uganda.

Education. In 1981 the number of children in primary school was 206,408 and 18,544 pupils were receiving secondary education. The university of Bujumbura had (1981) 1,793 students.

The local language is Kirundi, a Bantu language. French is also an official language. Kiswahili is spoken in the commercial centres.

Health. In 1979 there were about 130 doctors and 21 hospitals.

DIPLOMATIC REPRESENTATIVES

Of Burundi in Great Britain
Ambassador: Cyprien Mbonimpa (resides in Brussels).

Of Great Britain in Burundi
Ambassador: N. P. Bayne, CMG (resides in Kinshasa).

Of Burundi in the USA (2233 Wisconsin Ave., NW, Washington, D.C., 20007)
Ambassador: Simon Sabimbona.

Of the USA in Burundi (Chaussée Prince Louis Rwagasore, Bujumbura)
Ambassador: James R. Bullington.

Of Burundi to the United Nations
Ambassador: Melchior Bwakira.

Books of Reference

Lemarchand, R., *Rwanda and Burundi.* London, 1970
Melady, T. P., *Burundi: The Tragic Years.* Maryknoll, New York, 1974
Mpozapara, G., *La République du Burundi.* Paris, 1971
Weinstein, W., *Historical Dictionary of Burundi.* Metuchen, 1976

CAMBODIA

Democratic Kampuchea

Capital: Phnom Penh
Population: 6·7m. (1981)
GNP per capita: No accurate estimate available (1981)

Since April 1975 the situation in Cambodia has been such that it has been impossible to obtain reliable statistical and other information.

HISTORY. The recorded history of Cambodia starts at the beginning of the Christian era with the Kingdom of Fou-Nan, whose territories at one time included parts of Thailand, Malaya, Cochin-China and Laos. The religious, cultural and administrative inspirations of this state came from India. The Kingdom was absorbed at the end of the 6th century by the Khmers, under whose monarchs was built, between the 9th and 13th centuries, the splendid complex of shrines and temples at Angkor. Attacked on either side by the Vietnamese and the Thai from the 15th century on, Cambodia was saved from annihilation by the establishment of a French protectorate in 1863. Thailand eventually recognized the protectorate and renounced all claims to suzerainty in exchange for Cambodia's north-western provinces of Battambang and Siem Reap, which were, however, returned under a Franco-Thai convention of 1907, confirmed in the Franco-Thai treaty of 1937. In 1904 the province of Stung Treng, formerly administered as part of Laos, was attached to Cambodia. For history to 1969 *see* THE STATESMAN'S YEAR-BOOK, 1973–74, p. 1112.

Following a period of increasing economic difficulties and growing indirect involvement in the Vietnamese war Prince Sihanouk was deposed in March 1970 and on 9 Oct. 1970 the Kingdom of Cambodia became the Khmer Republic. From 1970 hostilities extended throughout most of the country involving North and South Vietnamese and US forces as well as Republican and anti-Republican Khmer troops. During 1973 direct American and North Vietnamese participation in the fighting came to an end, leaving a civil war situation which continued during 1974 with large-scale fighting between forces of the Khmer Republic supported by American arms and economic aid and the forces of the United National Cambodian Front including 'Khmer Rouge' communists supported by North Vietnam and China.

After unsuccessful attempts to capture Phnom Penh in 1973 and 1974, the Khmer Rouge ended the 5-year war in April 1975, when the remnants of the republican forces surrendered the city.

From April 1975 the Khmer Rouge instituted a harsh and highly regimented régime. They cut the country off from normal contact with the world and expelled all foreigners. All cities and towns were forcibly evacuated and the population were set to work in the fields.

The régime had difficulties with the Vietnamese from 1975 and this escalated into full-scale fighting in 1977–78. On 7 Jan. 1979, Phnom Penh was captured by the Vietnamese, and the Prime Minister, Pol Pot, fled. In March 1982 Pol Pot still commanded 30,000 guerrillas fighting the Vietnamese in Kampuchea.

In June 1982 the Khmer Rouge (who claim to have abandoned their Communist ideology and to have disbanded their Communist Party) entered into a coalition with Son Sann's Kampuchean People's National Liberation Front and Prince Sihanouk's group. This government is recognized by the UN.

President of the Coalition Government: Prince Norodom Sihanouk. *Deputy President:* Khieu Samphan. *Prime Minister:* Son Sann.

AREA AND POPULATION. Cambodia is bounded north by Laos and Thailand, in the west by Thailand, east by Vietnam and south by the Gulf of

Thailand. It has an area of about 181,000 sq. km (71,000 sq. miles), divided into 17 provinces: Kompong Thom (population, 322,000), Kompong Cham (820,000), Battambang (551,860), Kampot (337,879), Siem Reap (313,000), Kompong Chhang (273,000), Kompong Speu (307,000), Takeo (467,000), Kratié (136,000), Stung Treng (136,000), Svay Rieng (287,000), Prey Veng (492,000), Pursat (180,000), Kandal (population, excluding Phnom Penh, 706,000), Ratanakiri (49,400), Mondolkiri (14,300), Koh Kong (38,700).

The total population of 6,682,000 (1981) included Chinese and Chams. In the uplands and in the north-east live various groups of hillmen, known as Khmer-Loeu.

The chief towns are Phnom Penh, the capital located at the junction of the Mekong and Tonle Sap rivers, and Battambang. Populations of major towns have fluctuated greatly since 1970 by flows of refugees from rural areas and from one town to another. Phnom Penh formerly had a population of at least 2·5m. but a 1983 estimate puts it at 500,000. Khmer is the official language.

CLIMATE. A tropical climate, with high temperatures all the year. Phnom Penh. Jan. 78°F (25·6°C), July 84°F (28·9°C). Annual rainfall 52″ (1,308 mm).

CONSTITUTION AND GOVERNMENT. Following the ousting of the Khmer Rouge régime, the Vietnamese-backed Kampuchean National United Front for National Salvation (KNUFNS) on 8 Jan. 1979 proclaimed a People's Republic and established a People's Revolutionary Council to administer the country. A 117-member National Assembly was elected on 1 May 1981 for a 5-year term; in June 1981 it ratified a new Constitution under which it appointed a 7-member Council of State and a 16-member Council of Ministers, replacing the Revolutionary Council.

President of the Council of State: Heng Samrin.
Prime Minister: Hun Sen.

National flag: Red with a five-towered silhouette of the temple of Angkor Wat in the centre in yellow.

DEFENCE. Since the end of the war in April 1975 there has been no accurate data on defence and the three sections below should be treated with severe reserve. There is conscription into the armed forces.

Army. Strength (1985) 30,000 including 4 infantry divisions and some 50 supporting units. Equipment reported includes T-54/-55 and PT-76 tanks. There are also paramilitary police and militia units.

Navy. The Marine Royale Khmer was established on 1 March 1954 and became Marine Nationale Khmer on 9 Oct. 1970. It recently included 15 coastal patrol craft, 25 river patrol boats, 3 surveying craft, 1 tug, 2 floating docks and a dozen small craft, converted junks, etc. Less than a third of this force is operational and the residual navy has little fighting value. Two patrol vessels and 2 support (landing) gunboats escaped from Khmer Rouge, and 2 torpedo boats were believed to have sunk. Units since stricken include 7 amphibious vessels, 8 coastal patrol craft and 60 river patrol boats and service craft.

Naval active personnel provided for in 1985 did not exceed 4,000. In addition there was a battalion of marines numbering some 4,000.

Air Force. In 1974 the Air Force had a strength of about 7,000 officers and men, including 120 pilots, with about 200 aircraft, none of them jets. It was not known (1985) how many aircraft remain serviceable.

ECONOMY

Currency. In 1978 money was officially abolished and no wages or salaries were paid, but in 1980 the use of money was restored.

Banking. In 1964 all bank functions were taken over by government banks. In 1972 legislation permitted the re-opening of foreign banks but by the end of Dec. 1973 only a few representational offices had opened. In 1979 there was no longer anything that could be called a normal banking system.

NATURAL RESOURCES

Minerals. A phosphate factory, jointly controlled by the State and private interests, was set up in 1966 near a deposit of an estimated 350,000 tons. Another deposit of about the same size is earmarked for exploitation. High-grade iron-ore deposits (possibly as much as 2·5m. tons) exist in Northern Khmer, but are not exploited commercially because of transportation difficulties. Some small-scale gold panning (6,687 troy oz. in 1963) and gem (mainly zircon) mining is carried out at Pailin where there is potential for considerable expansion.

Agriculture. The overwhelming majority of the population is normally engaged in agriculture, fishing and forestry. Of the country's total area of 44m. acres, about 20m. are cultivable and over 20m. are forest land. In 1980, 1·5m. hectares were cultivated. Before the spread of war the high productivity provided for a low, but well-fed standard of living for the peasant farmers, the majority of whom owned the land they worked. A relatively small proportion of the food production entered the cash economy. The war and unwise pricing policies have led to a disastrous reduction in production to a stage in which the country had become a net importer of rice.

A crop of about 900,000 tonnes of paddy were produced in 1982, 200,000 tonnes short of domestic requirements. Rubber production in 1982 amounted to 12,000 tonnes. Other products are maize, and, in usual order of value, livestock, timber, pepper, haricot beans, soybeans and fish.

Livestock (1983) FAO estimate: Cattle, 1·1m.; buffaloes, 468,000; sheep, 1,000; pigs, 717,000; horses, 10,000; poultry, 6m.

Forestry. Much of Cambodia's surface is covered by potentially valuable forests, 3·8m. hectares of which are reserved by the Government to be awarded to concessionaires, and are not at present worked to an appreciable extent. The remainder is available for exploitation by the local residents, and as a result some areas are over-exploited and conservation is not practised. There are substantial reserves of pitch pine.

Fisheries. Cambodia has the greatest freshwater fish resources in South-East Asia but production in 1970 (30,000 tons) was about a third of that for 1966.

INDUSTRY AND TRADE

Industry. Some development of industry had taken place before the spread of open warfare in 1970. Industry established and in operation in Jan. 1970 included a motor-vehicle assembly plant, 3 cigarette manufacturing concerns, a modern factory, several metal fabricating concerns, a distillery, a saw-mill, textile, fish canning, plywood, paper, cement, sugar sack, tyre, pottery and glassware factories and a cotton-ginnery. In the private sector there are about 3,200 manufacturing enterprises, producing a wide range of goods; most of them are small family concerns. An oil refinery at Kompong Som came into production in 1969 but was put out of action by an attack in early 1971. Since April 1975 a programme for repairing factories has been started and some 70 are back in production.

Commerce. Principal imports by order of value (1972) were petroleum products, metals and machinery (including vehicles), general foodstuffs and chemicals.

The only recorded export in 1972 was 7,328 tonnes of rubber. Much of the country's trade is with Hong Kong and Singapore.

Total trade between Cambodia and UK (British Department of Trade returns, in £1,000 sterling):

	1980	*1981*	*1982*	*1983*	*1984*
Imports to UK	73	91	92	184	72
Exports and re-exports from UK	825	645	479	826	635

COMMUNICATIONS

Roads. There were, in 1970, 2,574 km of asphalt roads (including the 'Khmer-American Friendship Highway' from outside Phnom Penh to close to Kompong Som, built under the US aid programme and opened in July 1959), 359 km of macadamized roads, and about 1,213 km of improved dirt roads. Since 1970 many road bridges have been destroyed and long stretches of highway closed to traffic or open only to escorted convoys.

Railways. A line of 385 km (metre gauge) links Phnom Penh to Poipet (Thai frontier). In 1969 traffic amounted to 170m. passenger-km and 76m. ton-km. Work was completed during 1969 on a line Phnom Penh-Kompong Som *via* Takeo and Kampot. Total length, 649 km but by 1973 only a short stretch between Battambang and the Thai border remained in operation, the remainder having been closed by military action. Passenger and freight trains were running over about 80% of the network in 1980.

Aviation. The Pochentong airport is 10 km from Phnom Penh. Air Kampuchea has 2 small aircraft.

Shipping. The port of Phnom Penh can be reached by the Mekong (through Vietnam) by ships of between 3,000 and 4,000 tons. In 1970, 97 ocean-going vessels imported 51,300 tons of cargo at Phnom Penh and exported 86,400 tons.

A new ocean port has been built under the French aid programme at Kompong Som (formerly Sihanoukville) on the Gulf of Siam and is being increasingly used by long-distance shipping.

Post. There were 58 post offices functioning in 1968 but in 1979 it was doubtful if any offices operate. There are telephone exchanges in all the main towns; number of telephones in 1968, 6,325. There is an International Telex network in Phnom Penh and direct telephone and telegraphic links with Singapore.

RELIGION. The majority of the population practised Theravada Buddhism before 1975. The Constitution of 1976 ended Buddhism as the State religion. There are small Roman Catholic and Moslem minorities.

EDUCATION (1970–71). There were 1,490 primary schools (337,290 pupils) compared with 5,699 and 989,464 in 1969–70, 95 secondary schools (81,611 pupils) and 12,453 students in higher education. These figures show the disruption caused by the spread of war in 1970 which led to the concentration of all university education in Phnom Penh and closed many schools in rural areas and provincial towns. In 1980 there were 1·3m. pupils in all types of school.

DIPLOMATIC REPRESENTATIVES

UK and USA Embassies have been closed as have Cambodian Embassies in London and Washington.

Of Cambodia to the United Nations
Ambassador: Thiounn Prasith.

Books of Reference

Barron, J., and Paul, A., *Murder of a Gentle Land.* New York, 1977.—*Peace with Horror.* London, 1977
Debré, F., *La Révolution de la Forêt.* Paris, 1976
Etcheson, C., *The Rise and Demise of Democratic Kampuchea.* London, 1984
Kiljunen, K., (ed.) *Kampuchea: Decade of the Genocide.* London, 1984
McDonald, M., *Angkor.* London, 1958
Ponchaud, F., *Cambodia, Year Zero.* London, 1978
Vickery, M., *Cambodia: 1975–1982.* London, 1984

CAMEROON

République du Cameroun

Capital: Yaoundé
Population: 9·06m. (1983)
GNP per capita: US$880 (1981)

HISTORY. The former German colony of Kamerun was occupied by French and British troops in 1916. The greater portion of the territory (422,673 sq. km) was in 1919 placed under French administration, excluding the territory ceded to Germany in 1911, which reverted to French Equatorial Africa. The portion under French trusteeship was granted full internal autonomy on 1 Jan. 1959 and complete independence was proclaimed on 1 Jan. 1960.

The portion assigned to British trusteeship consisted of 2 parts where separate plebiscites were held in Feb. 1961. The northern part decided in favour of joining Nigeria, while the southern part decided to join the Cameroon Republic. This was implemented on 1 Oct. 1961 with the formation of a Federal Republic of Cameroon. As a result of a national referendum, Cameroon became a unitary republic on 2 June 1972. Amadou Babatoura Ahidjo, President since independence, resigned on 6 Nov. 1982.

AREA AND POPULATION. Cameroon is bounded west by the Gulf of Guinea, north-west by Nigeria and east by Chad, with Lake Chad at its northern tip, and the Central African Republic, and south by Congo, Gabon and Equatorial Guinea. The total area is 465,054 sq. km (179,558 sq. miles). Population (1976 census) 7,663,246 (28·5% urban). Estimate (1983) 9·06m.

The areas, populations and chief towns of the 7 provinces at the 1976 census (now 10 provinces) were:

Province	*Sq. km*	*Census 1976*	*Chief town*	*Census 1976*
Centre-Sud	116,036	1,491,945	Yaoundé (capital)	313,706
Est	109,011	366,235	Bertoua	18,450
Littoral	20,239	935,166	Douala	458,426
Nord	163,513	2,233,257	Garoua	69,285
Nord-Ouest	17,810	980,531	Bamenda	67,184
Ouest	13,872	1,035,597	Bafoussam	62,239
Sud-Ouest	24,471	620,515	Buea	13,000

Other large towns (1976 census): Nkongsamba (71,298), Maroua (67,187), Foumban (59,701), Kumba (44,175) and Limbe (formerly Victoria) (31,222).

The population is composed of Sudanic-speaking people in the north (Sao, Fulani and Kanuri) and Bantu-speaking groups, mainly Fang, Bamileke and Duala, in the rest of the country. The official languages are French and English.

CLIMATE. An equatorial climate, with high temperatures and plentiful rain, especially from March to June and Sept. to Nov. Further inland, rain occurs at all seasons. Yaoundé. Jan. 76°F (24·4°C), July 73°F (22·8°C). Annual rainfall 62″ (1,555 mm). Douala. Jan. 79°F (26·1°C), July 75°F (23·9°C). Annual rainfall 160″ (4,026 mm).

CONSTITUTION AND GOVERNMENT. The 1972 Constitution, amended 1975 and 1984, provides for a President as head of state and commander of the armed forces, who is elected for a 5-year term, and a Council of Ministers whose members must not be members of parliament.

The National Assembly, elected by universal adult suffrage for 5 years, consists of 120 representatives. Elections took place in May 1983. Since 1966 the sole legal party is the *Union National Camerounaise*.

The Economic and Social Council consists of 85 members appointed for 5 years by the President of the Republic to represent various social and economic interests; its chairman, appointed by decree, is assisted by a board appointed for 1 year.

President: Paul Biya (assumed office 6 Nov. 1982).

Foreign Affairs: Felix Tonye Mbog.

National flag: Three vertical strips of green, red, yellow, with a gold star in the centre.

National anthem: O Cameroun, berceau de nos ancêtres.

Local Government: The provinces are each administered by a governor appointed by the President. They are sub-divided into *départements* (each under a *préfet*) and then into *arrondissements* (each under a *sous-préfet*). In Aug. 1983, 3 additional provinces were created by the division of Centre-Sud and Nord provinces into 2 and 3 new provinces respectively.

DEFENCE. Compulsory military service was introduced in 1975.

Army. The Army consists of 1 armoured car, 1 para-commando, 1 engineer and 4 infantry battalions and 11 artillery batteries. Equipment includes M-8 armoured and Ferret scout cars. Total strength (1985) 6,600, there are an additional 5,000 paramilitary troops.

Navy. The Navy operates 2 fast attack craft, 2 patrol vessels (1 new French-built), 3 small patrol craft, 6 coastal patrol launches, 12 inshore cutters and 32 auxiliaries. Personnel in 1985 numbered 360.

Air Force. The Air Force has 3 C-130H Hercules turboprop transports, 4 Buffalo and 1 Caribou STOL transports, 3 C-47s for transport and communications duties, 7 Broussard liaison aircraft, 4 Magister armed jet basic trainers, 6 Alpha Jet close support/trainers, and 2 Alouette II helicopters. Some of 4 Gazelle light helicopters are armed with anti-tank missiles. A small VIP transport fleet, maintained in civil markings, comprises 1 Boeing 727 jet aircraft, 1 Alouette III helicopter, 1 Gulfstream II and a twin-engined Puma helicopter. Radar-equipped Dornier 128-6 twin-turboprop aircraft were delivered in 1982 for offshore oilfield patrol. Personnel total about 350.

INTERNATIONAL RELATIONS

Membership. Cameroon is a member of UN, OAU and is an ACP state of EEC.

ECONOMY

Planning. The Fourth 5-year Development Plan, 1976–81 envisaged expenditure of 725,232m. francs CFA.

Budget. The budget for 1982–83 balanced at 410,000m. francs CFA.

Currency. The unit of currency is the *franc CFA*, with a parity rate of 50 *francs CFA* to 1 French *franc*.

Banking. The Banque des Etats de l'Afrique Centrale is the sole bank of issue. The main banks are Banque Internationale pour l'Afrique Occidentale, Société Camerounaise de Banque, Société Générale de Banques au Cameroun, Banque International pour le Commerce et l'Industrie du Cameroun and Cameroon Bank. Most of the banks operate in all the large cities and towns throughout the Republic.

ENERGY AND NATURAL RESOURCES

Electricity. There are 3 hydro-electric power stations at Edéa on the Sanaga river with a capacity of 180,000 kw, and another on the Wouri river near Douala. Total production (1981) 1,660m. kwh.

Oil. Production (estimate, 1981) mainly from Kole oilfield was 6m. tonnes.

Minerals. There are considerable deposits of bauxite and kyanite around

Ngaoundéré. Further deposits of bauxite and cassiterite remain to be exploited in the Adamawa plateau.

Agriculture. At the 1976 Census, 80% of the working population were engaged in agriculture. The main food crops (with 1982 production in 1,000 tonnes): Cassava, 1,020; millet, 408; maize, 526; plantains, 1,030; yams, 140; groundnuts, 120; bananas, 100. Cash crops include palm oil, 81; palm kernals, 47; cocoa, 120; coffee, 105; rubber, 17; cotton, 34; raw sugar (1981), 36.

Livestock (1983): 3m. cattle, 2·19m. sheep, 2·4m. goats, 1·2m. pigs.

Fisheries. In 1979 the total catch was 69,400 tonnes.

Forestry. Over a third of Cameroon consists of forests, ranging from tropical rain forests in the south (producing hardwoods such as mahogany, ebony and sapele) to semi-deciduous forests in the centre and wooded savannah in the north. Production in 1982 amounted to 10·3m. cu. metres.

INDUSTRY AND TRADE

Industry. There is a major aluminium smelting complex at Edéa; aluminium production in 1980 amounted to 43,000 tonnes. Production of cement totalled 227,000 tonnes in 1980. There are also factories producing shoes, soap, oil and food products, cigarettes.

Commerce. Imports and exports in 1m. francs CFA were as follows:

	1979	*1980*	*1981*	*1982*
Imports	271,160	337,602	386,089	392,600
Exports	243,699	290,614	299,716	326,900

In 1981, 19% (by value) of exports went to France, 15% to the Netherlands and 38% to the USA, while France provided 41% of imports; the main exports (1980) were coffee (23%), cocoa (21%), crude oil (31%) and timber (11%).

Total trade between Cameroon and UK (British Department of Trade returns, in £1,000 sterling):

	1980	*1981*	*1982*	*1983*	*1984*
Imports to UK	9,798	24,022	9,108	52,481	132,539
Exports and re-exports from UK	17,470	24,014	22,462	26,445	23,254

Tourism. There were an estimated 126,337 foreign visitors in 1979. There are 13 National Parks and reserves, with a total area of nearly 20,000 sq. km.

COMMUNICATIONS

Roads. There were (1977) 2,155 km of tarred roads, 9,284 km earth roads and 15,482 km of secondary roads. In 1978 there were 134,900 vehicles in use.

Railways. Cameroon Railways (1,168 km in 1983) link Douala with Nkongsamba and Ngaoundére, with branches M'Banga–Kumba and Makak–M'Balmayo.

Aviation. Douala is the main international airport; other airports are at Yaoundé and Garoua. In 1976, 342,000 passengers and 20,000 tonnes of freight passed through the airports.

Shipping. The merchant-marine consisted (1980) of 44 vessels (over 100 GRT) of 62,080 GRT. The major port of Douala handled (1978) 2·03m. tonnes of imports and 811,000 tonnes of exports. Timber is exported mainly through the south-west ports of Kribi (145,850 tonnes out of 162,496 tonnes of exports in 1975) and Campo (50,000 tonnes). In 1975 ports of Bota and Tiko (at Nimbe) handled 26,305 tonnes and Garoua on the river Benue 21,041 tonnes (comprising 6,022 tonnes fertilizer imports and 15,019 tonnes cotton exports).

Post and Broadcasting. There were (1975) 150 post offices supplemented by a mobile postal service; telephone lines, 2,677 km; main telephones (1978), 14,321; radio stations, 36 with (1983) 774,000 receivers.

Cinemas. There were (1977) 45 cinemas with a capacity of 25,000 seats.

Newspapers. There was (1984) 1 daily newspaper with a circulation of 20,000.

JUSTICE, RELIGION, EDUCATION AND WELFARE

Justice. The Supreme Court sits at Yaoundé, as does the High Court of Justice (consisting of 9 titular judges and 6 surrogates all appointed by the National Assembly). There are magistrates' courts situated in the provinces.

Religion. In 1980, 21% of the population is Roman Catholic, 22% Moslem, 18% Protestant, while 39% follow traditional (animist) religions.

Education (1979–80). There were 1,302,974 pupils and 25,289 teachers in 4,721 primary schools, 153,618 pupils and 5,602 teachers in 317 secondary schools, 51,561 students and 2,596 teachers in 157 vocational schools and 1,926 students and 176 teachers in teacher-training colleges. The University of Yaoundé (established 1962) had 11,901 students and 439 teaching staff at 10 higher education establishments, including the *Université National* with its main campus at Yaoundé (established 1962) and new university centres at Douala, Buea, Dschang and Ngaoundére.

Health. In 1976 there were 85 hospitals with 16,734 beds, and 347 dispensaries and health centres. In 1977 there were 477 doctors, 19 dentists, 93 pharmacists, 1,805 midwives and 3,533 nursing personnel.

DIPLOMATIC REPRESENTATIVES

Of Cameroon in Great Britain (84 Holland Pk., London, W11 3SB)
Ambassador: Ferdinard Leopold Oyono (accredited 13 Feb. 1985).

Of Great Britain in Cameroon (Ave. Winston Churchill, BP 547, Yaoundé)
Ambassador: Michael Glaze.

Of Cameroon in the USA (2349 Massachusetts Ave., NW, Washington, D.C., 20008)
Ambassador: Vincent Paul-Thomas Pondi.

Of the USA in Cameroon (Rue Nachtigal, BP 817, Yaoundé)
Ambassador: Myles R. Frechette.

Of Cameroon to the United Nations
Ambassador: Paul Bamela Engo.

Books of Reference

Statistical Information: The Service de la Statistique Générale, at Douala, set up in 1945, publishes a monthly bulletin (from Nov. 1950)

Le Vine, V. T., *The Cameroon Federal Republic.* Cornell Univ. Press, 1971
Ndongko, W. A., *Planning for Economic Development in a Federal State: The Case of Cameroon, 1960–71.* New York, 1975
Rubin, N., *Cameroon.* New York, 1972

CANADA

Capital: Ottawa
Population: 25·1m. (1984)
GNP per capita: US$11,400 (1981)

HISTORY. The territories which now constitute Canada came under British power at various times by settlement, conquest or cession. Nova Scotia was occupied in 1628 by settlement at Port Royal, was ceded back to France in 1632 and was finally ceded by France in 1713, by the Treaty of Utrecht; the Hudson's Bay Company's charter, conferring rights over all the territory draining into Hudson Bay, was granted in 1670; Canada, with all its dependencies, including New Brunswick and Prince Edward Island, was formally ceded to Great Britain by France in 1763; Vancouver Island was acknowledged to be British by the Oregon Boundary Treaty of 1846, and British Columbia was established as a separate colony in 1858. As originally constituted, Canada was composed of Upper and Lower Canada (now Ontario and Quebec), Nova Scotia and New Brunswick. They were united under an Act of the Imperial Parliament, 'The British North America Act, 1867', which came into operation on 1 July 1867 by royal proclamation. The Act provided that the constitution of Canada should be 'similar in principle to that of the United Kingdom'; that the executive authority shall be vested in the Sovereign, and carried on in his name by a Governor-General and Privy Council; and that the legislative power shall be exercised by a Parliament of two Houses, called the 'Senate' and the 'House of Commons'.

On 30 June 1931 the British House of Commons approved the enactment of the Statute of Westminster freeing the Provinces as well as the Dominion from the operation of the Colonial Laws Validity Act, and thus removing what legal limitations existed as regards Canada's legislative autonomy. A joint address of the Senate and the House of Commons was sent to the Governor-General for transmission to London on 10 July 1931. The statute received the royal assent on 12 Dec. 1931.

Provision was made in the British North America Act for the admission of British Columbia, Prince Edward Island, Newfoundland, Rupert's Land and Northwest Territory into the Union. In 1869 Rupert's Land, or the Northwest Territories, was purchased from the Hudson's Bay Company. On 15 July 1870, Rupert's Land and the Northwest Territory were annexed to Canada and named the Northwest Territories, Canada having agreed to pay the Hudson's Bay Company in cash and land for its relinquishing of claims to the territory. By the same action the Province of Manitoba was created from a small portion of this territory and they were admitted into the Confederation on 15 July 1870. On 20 July 1871 the province of British Columbia was admitted, and Prince Edward Island on 1 July 1873. The provinces of Alberta and Saskatchewan were formed from the provisional districts of Alberta, Athabaska, Assiniboia and Saskatchewan and originally parts of the Northwest Territories and admitted on 1 Sept. 1905. Newfoundland formally joined Canada as its tenth province on 31 March 1949.

In Feb. 1931 Norway formally recognized the Canadian title to the Sverdrup group of Arctic islands. Canada thus holds sovereignty in the whole Arctic sector north of the Canadian mainland.

In Nov. 1981 the Canadian government agreed on the provisions of an amended constitution, to the end that it should replace the British North America Act and that its future amendment should be the prerogative of Canada. These proposals were adopted by the Parliament of Canada and were enacted by the UK Parliament as the Canada Act of 1982.

The enactment of the Canada Act was the final act of the UK Parliament in Canadian constitutional development. The Act gave to Canada the power to amend the Constitution according to procedures determined by the Constitutional Act 1982, which was proclaimed in force by the Queen on 17 April 1982. The Constitution Act 1982 added to the Canadian Constitution a charter of Rights and Freedoms, and provisions which recognize the nation's multi-cultural heritage, affirm the existing rights of native peoples, confirm the principle of equalization of benefits among the provinces, and strengthen provincial ownership of natural resources.

AREA AND POPULATION. Population of the area now included in Canada:

1851	2,436,297	1901	5,371,315	1951	14,009,429
1861	3,229,633	1911	7,206,643	1961	18,238,247
1871	3,689,257	1921	8,787,949	1971	21,568,311
1881	4,324,810	1931	10,376,786 [1]	1981	24,343,181
1891	4,833,239	1941	11,506,655 [1]		

[1] From 1951 figures include Newfoundland.

Population (estimated), 1 June 1984, was 25,127,900.

Areas of the provinces, etc. (in sq. km) and population at recent censuses:

Province	*Land area*	*Fresh water area*	*Total land and fresh water area*	*Population, 1971*	*Population, 1976*	*Population, 1981*
Newfoundland	371,690	34,030	405,720	522,104	557,725	567,681
Prince Edward Island	5,600	—	5,660	111,641	118,229	122,506
Nova Scotia	52,840	2,650	55,490	788,960	828,571	847,442
New Brunswick	72,090	1,350	73,440	634,557	677,250	696,403
Quebec	1,356,790	183,890	1,540,680	6,027,764	6,234,445	6,438,403
Ontario	891,190	177,390	1,068,580	7,703,106	8,264,465	8,625,107
Manitoba	548,360	101,590	649,950	988,247	1,021,506	1,026,241
Saskatchewan	570,700	81,630	652,330	926,242	921,323	968,313
Alberta	644,390	16,800	661,190	1,627,874	1,838,037	2,237,724
British Columbia	929,730	18,070	947,800	2,184,621	2,466,608	2,744,467
Yukon	478,970	4,480	483,450	18,388	21,836	22,135
Northwest Territories	3,293,020	133,300	3,426,320	34,807	42,609	45,471
Total	9,215,430	755,180	9,970,610	21,568,311	22,992,604	24,343,181

Of the total population in 1981, 20,216,340 were Canadian born, 3,867,160 foreign born, 312,015 of the latter being USA born and 2,586,080 European born.

The population (1981) born outside Canada in the provinces was in the following ratio (%): Newfoundland, 1·7; Prince Edward Island, 3·7; Nova Scotia, 4·9; New Brunswick, 3·9; Quebec, 8·2; Ontario, 23·5; Manitoba, 14·2; Saskatchewan, 8·6; Alberta, 16·3; British Columbia, 23; Yukon, 12·5; Northwest Territories, 6·1.

In 1981, figures for the population, according to origin, were [1]:

Single origins	22,244,885	Polish	254,485
Austrian	40,630	Portuguese	188,105
Belgian and Luxembourg	43,000	Romanian	22,485
British	9,674,245	Russian	48,435
Czech and Slovak	67,695	Scandinavian	282,795
Chinese	289,245	Spanish	53,540
Dutch	408,240	Swiss	29,805
Finnish	52,315	Ukrainian	529,615
French	6,439,100	Other single origins:	1,204,685
German	1,142,365		
Greek	154,365	*Multiple origins:*	1,838,615
Magyar (Hungarian)	116,390	British and French	430,255
Italian	747,970	British and Other	859,800
Japanese	40,995	French and Other	124,940
Native Peoples	413,380	Others	423,620

[1] The 1981 Census was the first to accept more than one ethnic origin for an individual. Therefore, this table includes counts of single and multiple origins.

The native Indian registered population numbered 367,810 in 1981 and the Eskimo population was 25,390 in 1981.

Populations of Census Metropolitan Areas (CMA) and Cities (proper), 1981 census:

	CMA	*City proper*		*CMA*	*City proper*
Toronto	2,998,947	559,217	Winnipeg	584,842	564,473
Montreal	2,828,349	980,354	Quebec	576,075	166,474
Vancouver	1,268,183	414,281	Hamilton	542,095	306,434
Ottawa-Hull	717,978	295,163	St Catharines-Niagara	304,353	—
Edmonton	657,057	532,246	St Catharines	—	124,018
Calgary	592,743	592,743			

	CMA	*City proper*		*CMA*	*City proper*
Niagara Falls	—	70,960	Saskatoon	154,210	154,210
Kitchener	287,801	139,734	Sudbury	149,923	91,829
London	283,668	254,280	Chicoutimi-Jonquiere	135,172	—
Halifax	277,727	114,594	Chicoutimi	—	60,064
Windsor	246,110	192,083	Jonquiere	—	60,354
Victoria	233,481	64,379	Thunder Bay	121,379	112,486
Regina	164,313	162,613	Saint John	114,048	80,521
St John's	154,820	83,770	Trois Rivieres	111,453	50,466
Oshawa	154,217	117,519			

The total 'urban' population of Canada in 1981 was 18,435,927, against 17,366,970 in 1976.

While the registration of births, marriages and deaths is under provincial control, the statistics are compiled on a uniform system by Statistics Canada.

The following table gives the results for the year 1983, estimate:

Province	*Living births Number*	*Marriages Number*	*Deaths Number*
Newfoundland	9,630	3,250	3,140
Prince Edward Island	1,960	940	1,000
Nova Scotia	12,090	6,270	6,930
New Brunswick	10,590	4,660	5,280
Quebec	90,140	38,750	44,430
Ontario	125,490	69,590	66,440
Manitoba	16,500	8,060	8,480
Saskatchewan	16,300	7,480	7,410
Alberta	45,400	18,910	12,130
British Columbia	43,040	21,060	20,160
Yukon Territory	530	240	120
N.W. Territories	1,250	280	240
	372,920	179,490	175,760

Immigrant arrivals by country of last permanent residence:

Country	*1982*	*1983*
UK	16,445	5,737
France	2,393	1,651
Germany	4,425	2,518
Netherlands	1,827	672
Greece	885	601
Italy	1,506	826
Portugal	1,388	820
Other Europe	17,281	11,487
Asia	41,617	36,906
Australasia	938	478
USA	9,360	7,381
West Indies	8,674	7,216
All other	14,408	12,864
Total	121,147	89,157

CLIMATE. The climate ranges from polar conditions in the north to cool temperate in the south, but with considerable differences between east coast, west coast and the interior, affecting temperatures, rainfall amounts and seasonal distribution. Winters are very severe over much of the country, but summers can be very hot inland. *See* individual provinces for climatic details.

CONSTITUTION AND GOVERNMENT. The members of the Senate are appointed until age 75 by summons of the Governor-General under the Great Seal of Canada. Members appointed before 2 June 1965 may remain in office for life. The Senate consists of 104 senators, namely, 24 from Ontario, 24 from Quebec, 10 from Nova Scotia, 10 from New Brunswick, 4 from Prince Edward Island, 6 from Manitoba, 6 from British Columbia, 6 from Alberta, 6 from Saskatchewan, 6 from Newfoundland, 1 from the Yukon Territory and 1 from the Northwest Territories.

Each senator must be at least 30 years of age, a born or naturalized subject of the Queen and must reside in the province for which he is appointed and his total net worth must be at least $4,000. The House of Commons is elected by the people, for 5 years, unless sooner dissolved. Women have the vote and are eligible. From 1867 to the election of 1945 representation was based on Quebec having 65 seats and the other provinces the same proportion of 65 which their population had to the population of Quebec. In the General Election of 1949 readjustments were based on the population of all the provinces taken as a whole. Generally speaking, this format for representation has prevailed in all subsequent elections with readjustments made after each decennial census. However, on 31 Dec. 1974, the law was changed so that it has reverted somewhat to the type of system that had prevailed initially. That is to say, Quebec is to be assigned a fixed number of seats in the House of Commons and the representation of the other provinces calculated by a quotient which reflects this fact.

The thirty-second Parliament, elected in Sept. 1984, comprises 282 members and the provincial and territorial representation are: Ontario, 95; Quebec, 75; Nova Scotia, 11; New Brunswick, 10; Manitoba, 14; British Columbia, 28; Prince Edward Island, 4; Saskatchewan 14; Alberta, 21; Newfoundland, 7; Yukon Territory, 1; Northwest Territories, 2.

State of parties in the Senate (Sept. 1984): Liberals, 73; Progressive Conservative, 23; Independent, 3; Independent Liberal, 1; Vacant, 4; total 104.

State of the parties in the House of Commons (Sept. 1984): Progressive Conservatives, 211; Liberals, 40; New Democratic Party, 30; Independent, 1; total, 282. Elections took place on 4 Sept. 1984.

The following is a list of Governors-General of Canada:

Viscount Monck	1867–1868	Viscount Willingdon	1926–1931
Lord Lisgar	1868–1872	Earl of Bessborough	1931–1935
Earl of Dufferin	1872–1878	Lord Tweedsmuir	1935–1940
Marquess of Lorne	1878–1883	Earl of Athlone	1940–1946
Marquess of Lansdowne	1883–1888	Field-Marshal Viscount Alexander of Tunis	1946–1952
Lord Stanley of Preston	1888–1893	Vincent Massey	1952–1959
Earl of Aberdeen	1893–1898	Georges Philias Vanier	1959–1967
Earl of Minto	1898–1904	Roland Michener	1967–1974
Earl Grey	1904–1911	Jules Léger	1974–1979
HRH the Duke of Connaught	1911–1916	Edward Schreyer	1979–1984
Duke of Devonshire	1916–1921		
Viscount Byng of Vimy	1921–1926		

Governor-General: Jeanne Sauve.

National flag: Vertically red, white, red with the white of double width and bearing a stylized red maple leaf.

The office and appointment of the Governor-General are regulated by letters patent, signed by the King on 8 Sept. 1947, which came into force on 1 Oct. 1947. In 1977 the Queen approved the transfer to the Governor-General functions discharged by the Sovereign. He is assisted in his functions, under the provisions of the Act of 1867, by a Privy Council composed of Cabinet Ministers.

The following is the list of the Conservative Cabinet in March 1985, in order of precedence, which in Canada attaches generally rather to the person than to the office:

Prime Minister: Brian Mulroney.
Veterans Affairs: George Hees.
Government Leader in Senate: Senator Duff Roblin.
External Affairs: Joe Clark.
Employment and Immigration: Flora MacDonald.
Deputy Prime Minister and Defence, President of Privy Council: Erik Nielsen.
Justice, Attorney-General: John Crosbie.
Public Works: Roch LaSalle.
Transport: Donald Mazankowski.
Solicitor General: Elmer MacKay.
Health and Welfare: Jake Epp.

Fisheries and Oceans: John Fraser.
Regional Industrial Expansion: Sinclair Stevens.
Agriculture: John Wise.
Government Leader in House: Ramon Hnatyshyn.
Indian Affairs and Northern Development: David Crombie.
Treasury Board: Robert René de Cotret.
National Revenue: Perrin Beatty.
Finance: Michael Wilson.
Multiculturalism: Jack Murta.
Supply and Services: Harvie Andre.
Fitness and Amateur Sport: Otto Jelinek.
Science and Technology: Thomas Siddon.
Wheat Board: Charles Mayer.
Labor: William McKnight.
Secretary of State: Walter McLean.
Tourism: Thomas McMillan.
Energy, Mines and Resources: Pat Carney.
Small Businesses: André Bissonnette.
Environment: Suzanne Blais-Grenier.
Minister of State for Transport: Benoit Bouchard.
Youth: Andrée Champagne.
Consumer and Corporate Affairs: Michel Côté.
International Trade: James Kelleher.
Mines: Robert Layton.
Communications: Marcel Masse.
Minister of State for Finance: Barbara McDougall.
Forestry: Gerald Merrithew.
External Relations: Monique Vézina.

The salary of a member of the House of Commons is $52,800 with a tax-free allowance of $17,600. The salary of a senator is $52,800 with a tax-free allowance of $8,600. The salary and allowances of the Prime Minister total $132,700. The salary of the Speaker of the House of Commons is $93,200; the salary of the Speaker of the Senate is $78,400; the salary of the Opposition Leader is $93,200 and that of the National Democratic Party Leader, $77,100; all these also have tax-free allowances of from $12,600–$21,600.

Future increases are to be pegged at 1% less than increases in the consumer price index or industrial composite index, whichever is lower.

An Act to provide retiring allowances, on a contributory basis, to members of the House of Commons was given the Royal Assent on 4 July 1952. This Act was amended in July 1963; a member can now opt for a reduced retiring allowance in favour of an additional allowance for the widow; and provision has been made for retiring allowance for former Prime Ministers and their widows.

The Canadian Parliamentary Guide. Annual. Ottawa

Report of the Royal Commission on Dominion–Provincial Relations, Canada 1867–1939. 3 vols. Ottawa, 1940

Byers, R. B. (ed.), *Canada Challenged: The Viability of the Confederation.* Toronto, 1979

Information Canada, *Organization of the Government of Canada.* Loose-leaf service. Ottawa, 1970

Kennedy, W. F. M., *Statutes, Treaties and Documents of the Canadian Constitution, 1713–1929.* Toronto, 1930

Kernaghan, N. (ed.), *Bureaucracy in Canadian Government. Selected Readings.* Toronto, 1969

Morton, W. L., *The Kingdom of Canada; A General History From Earliest Times.* Toronto, 1969

Olmsted, R. A., *Decisions of the Judicial Committee of the Privy Council Relating to the British North America Act, 1867, and the Canadian Constitution, 1867–1954.* Ottawa, Queens' Printer, 1954

Russell, P. H. (ed.), *Leading Constitutional Decisions; Cases on the British North America Act.* Toronto, 1968

DEFENCE. The Department of National Defence was created by the National Defence Act, 1922, which established one civil Department of Government in place of the previous Departments of Militia and Defence, Naval Service and the Air Board. The Department now operates under authority of RSC 1970, c.N1-4. The Minister of National Defence has the control and management of the Canadian Forces and all matters relating to national defence establishments and works for the defence of Canada. He is the Minister responsible for presenting before the Cabinet, matters of major defence policy for which Cabinet direction is required. He is also responsible for the Canada Emergency Measures Organization which was renamed 'Emergency Planning Canada' in 1976.

In Dec. 1976, the Minister of National Defence was named as minister responsible for all aspects of air Search and Rescue in the areas of Canadian SAR responsibility, and for the overall co-ordination of marine search and rescue including provision of air resources for marine SAR within Canadian territorial waters and in designated oceanic areas off the Pacific and Atlantic Coasts in accordance with agreements made with the United States Coast Guard. A group from Transport Canada, the Department of National Defence and the Department of Fisheries and Oceans was set up at the same time, as a co-ordinating body.

Command Structure. The Canadian forces are organized on a functional basis to reflect the major commitments assigned by the Government. All forces devoted to a primary mission are grouped under a single commander who is assigned sufficient resources to discharge his responsibilities. Specifically, the Canadian forces consist of National Defence Headquarters and the following major commands reporting to the Chief of the Defence Staff:

1. *Mobile Command* provides units trained and equipped to support the United Nations or other peacekeeping operations; provides ground forces for the protection of Canadian territory; maintains combat formations in Canada for support of overseas commitments. It is comprised of 3 airportable combat groups in Canada; the United Nations force in Cyprus; the Canadian Airborne Regiment, and 1 combat training centre. The Militia and Air Reserve components are also controlled by Mobile Command. Strength (1984), 17,900.

2. *Maritime Command.* All maritime forces are under the Commander, Maritime Command, with headquarters in Halifax, Nova Scotia. In addition, he also exercises operational control of aircraft assigned to him by the commander Maritime Air Group for Maritime operations. The Commander Maritime Forces (Pacific), who is the Deputy Commander, has his headquarters in Esquimalt, British Columbia. Maritime Command is to defend Canada against attack from the sea; provide anti-submarine defence in support of NATO; provide sea transport in support of Mobile Command. Composition of the maritime forces includes 3 submarines, 4 destroyers, 19 smaller destroyer-escorts (of which 3 are in reserve), 3 supply ships, 1 maintenance ship, 6 patrol craft, 7 small support ships, 6 training vessels (*ex*-coastal minesweepers), 3 research ships and 30 auxiliaries and service craft. There are 16 naval reserve personnel units in major Canadian cities which form an essential component of Maritime Command.

Active naval personnel strength in Maritime Command ships and shore establishments in 1984 was 19,017.

3. *Air Command.* Air Command's main task is to provide operationally-ready regular and reserve air forces to meet Canada's national, continental and international commitments, with regional commitments in the Prairie Region (Saskatchewan, Alberta, Manitoba and north west Ontario). The Command's headquarters are at Winnipeg, and it is organized in 6 operational groups:

Fighter group (headquarters at North Bay, Ontario) maintains the sovereignty of Canada's air space, supports Mobile Command and Maritime Command training, and provides combat aircrew to meet Canada's North American Aerospace Defence (NORAD) and NATO commitments. It has command of all fighter aircraft resources in Canada. This includes two CF-5, two CF-101, and one CF-18 operational squadrons, as well as CF-5 and CF-18 training squadrons. As the

CF-18 aircraft are brought in, the CF-5 and CF-101 operational squadrons will be phased out. Fighter Group also has command of two trans-continental radar lines, a space sensor unit and an electronic warfare squadron.

The Air Transport Group (headquarters at Trenton, Ontario) provides airlift resources for Canadian Forces. It also undertakes national and international tasks as directed by the government. The group provides search and rescue service for downed aircraft and marine search and rescue operations. The heavy transport resources consist of 26 C-130 Hercules aircraft and five Boeing 707 aircraft. At Winnipeg, there are four of the Hercules equipped for navigation training. A squadron at Ottawa provides medium-range passenger transport with Cosmopolitan Falcon and Challenger aircraft. Two Dash 7 aircraft in Lahr, Germany, provide passenger transport in Europe.

Transport and Rescue squadrons located at Comox, B.C., Edmonton, Trenton and Summerside, P.E.I., are equipped with a combination of Fixed Wing Aircraft and Helicopters. Either Buffalo or Twin Otter aircraft together with Twin Huey, Voyageur or Labrador helicopters are utilized. Squadrons at Edmonton operate Twin Otters and Hercules. Three helicopters are now based at Gander, Nfld., as 103 Rescue Unit, to enable a quicker response to emergency situations in Newfoundland, Labrador and surrounding waters.

Search and rescue activities are co-ordinated from four centres located at Victoria, Edmonton, Trenton and Halifax. Rescue co-ordination centres are manned by Canadian Forces personnel with Canadian Coast Guard officers attached as advisors on liaison duties in all centres except Edmonton.

In addition to the dedicated aircraft specially equipped and manned for search and rescue duties, other aircraft at various locations across Canada are also tasked and in some instances kept on standby to augment the SAR capability

Air Movements Units are located at Ottawa, Trenton, Edmonton and Lahr, Federal Republic of Germany, with detachments at Comox, B.C., Vancouver, Winnipeg, Greenwood, N.S., and Shearwater, N.S. The units provide passenger and cargo-processing services in support of the group's operations.

Maritime Air Group, with headquarters at Halifax, N.S., is responsible for management of all air resources engaged in maritime patrol, maritime surveillance and anti-submarine warfare.

The Commander of Maritime Air Group is responsible to the Commander Air Command but provides aircraft and crews to the Commander Maritime Command for the conduct of maritime surveillance patrols and anti-submarine operations. A close working relationship between Maritime Command and Maritime Air Group enables them to utilize a common operations centre.

The group conducts surveillance flights over Canada's coastal waters and the Arctic archipelago. It also provides anti-submarine air forces as part of Canada's contribution to NATO.

Mobile Command has operational control over Air Command's 10 Tactical Air Group whose headquarters are co-located at St. Hubert, Que. The group operates all rotary wing air resources engaged in the close support of land forces. This involves helicopter fire-support, reconnaissance and tactical transport over the battle area.

14 Training Group, located in Winnipeg, was formed in 1981 and is responsible to the Commander of Air Command for aircrew selection, aircrew training to wings standard, junior leadership and survival training, and meteorological training. This group develops training policy for Air Command and is responsible for monitoring and evaluating all Air Command training.

On 1 April 1976, a new formation was added to the Air Command family; the Air Reserve Group. Commanded by a reserve officer of Brigadier General rank, the Air Reserve has its headquarters at Winnipeg. The Group was formed in recognition of the growing importance of the air reserves which, in the recent past, have seen developments in their numbers and in the types of aircraft flown.

The Air Reserves comprises two wings from each with two squadrons located in Montreal and Toronto and three other squadrons located in Winnipeg, Edmonton and Summerside, P.E.I. In addition, Air Reserve Augmentation flights at nine different bases in Canada have been formed to provide a cadre of trained personnel available for war establishment augmentation and for base expansion. Other Air Reserve Augmentation flights are being planned.

4. *Canadian Forces Training System.* The Canadian Forces Training System headquarters is located at CFB Trenton, Ont. Its functions include the planning and conduct of all recruit, trades, specialist and other officer classification training common to more than one command. The Commander of Canadian Forces Training System also assumes regional commitments in the Central Region (the province of Ontario).

5. *Canadian Forces Communications Command (CFCC)* manages, operates and maintains strategic communications for the Canadian Forces and, in the event of emergencies, for the federal and provincial governments. The Command also provides points for interconnecting strategic and tactical networks and CFCC manages, operates and maintains the major DND automatic data processing centres.

6. *The Reserves* are composed of the Naval Reserve, the Militia and the Air Reserve.

Projected National Defence expenditures for 1983–84 were $7,937m. at 31 Oct. 1983. Strength of the Regular Forces in 1984 was about 84,500.

7. *Canadian Forces Europe.* The Canadian Forces allocated to support NATO in Europe are part of Canadian Forces Europe. The land element is No. 4 Canadian Mechanized Brigade Group operationally responsible to the Central Army Group. The air element, No. 1 Canadian Air Group, consisting of 3 CF-104 Starfighter squadrons, is operationally assigned to No. 4 Allied Tactical Air Force. These elements are located in the Baden-Baden area of Federal Republic of Germany and are supported administratively by CFB Europe at Lahr.

8. *Functional Regional Organization.* Functional Commanders have been assigned a regional as well as a functional responsibility for such actions as representation to provincial governments, aid of the Civil Power, emergency and survival operations, and administration of cadets, as well as regional support services for all units in the region.

Canada has been divided into six regions, five of which have been assigned to functional Commanders as follows: Atlantic (Newfoundland, Nova Scotia, Prince Edward Island, New Brunswick) – Maritime Command; Eastern (Quebec) – Mobile Command; Ontario, except N.W. Ontario – Canadian Forces Training System; Prairie (Manitoba, Saskatchewan, Alberta and N.W. Ontario) – Air Command; and Pacific (British Columbia) – Maritime Forces Pacific. One region, comprising the Yukon Territory and Northwest Territories, has been assigned to Commander Northern Region with Headquarters in Yellowknife, NWT.

9. *Northern Region.* Northern Region headquarters is located in Yellowknife, NWT. They act as a DND agency for contact and assistance to the territorial governments and federal government departments in the north. They also provide support to military activities by serving as liaison between elements of the operational commands and the various settlements in which they exercise.

Police Forces. The police forces of Canada are organized in three groups: (1) the federal force, which is the Royal Canadian Mounted Police; (2) provincial police forces—the Provinces of Ontario and Quebec have their own provincial police forces, but all other provinces engage the services of the Royal Canadian Mounted Police to perform parallel functions within their borders, and (3) municipal police forces—each urban centre of reasonable size maintains its own police force or engages the services of the provincial police, under contract, to attend to police matters.

In addition, the Canadian National Railways, the Canadian Pacific Railway Company and the National Harbours Board have their own police forces.

Royal Canadian Mounted Police. The Royal Canadian Mounted Police is a civil force maintained by the federal government. It was established in 1873, as the

North-West Mounted Police for service in what was then the North-West Territories and, in recognition of its services, was granted the use of the prefix 'Royal' by King Edward VII in 1904. Its sphere of operations was expanded in 1918 to include all of Canada west of Thunder Bay. In 1920 the force absorbed the Dominion Police, and its headquarters was transferred from Regina to Ottawa, and its title was changed to Royal Canadian Mounted Police. The force is responsible to the Solicitor-General of Canada and is controlled and managed by a Commissioner who holds the rank and status of a Deputy Minister. The Commissioner is empowered under the Royal Canadian Mounted Police Act to appoint members to be peace officers in all provinces and territories of Canada.

The responsibilities of the Royal Canadian Mounted Police are national in scope. The administration of justice within the provinces, including the enforcement of the Criminal Code of Canada, is part of the power and duty delegated to the provincial governments.

All provinces except Ontario and Quebec have entered into contracts with the Royal Canadian Mounted Police to enforce criminal and provincial laws under the direction of the respective Attorneys-General. In addition, in these 8 provinces the Force is under agreement to provide police services to 187 municipalities, thereby assuming the enforcement responsibility of municipal as well as criminal and provincial laws within these communities. The Royal Canadian Mounted Police is also responsible for all police work in the Yukon and Northwest territories enforcing federal law and territorial ordinances. The 16 Operational Divisions, alphabetically designated, make up the strength of the Force across Canada; they comprise 48 sub-divisions which include 712 detachments. Headquarters Division, as well as the Office of the Commissioner, is located in Ottawa. The Force maintains liaison officers in 31 countries and represents Canada in the International Criminal Police Organization which has its headquarters in Paris.

Thorough training is emphasized for members of the Force. Recruits receive 6 months of basic training at the Royal Canadian Mounted Police Academy in Regina. This is followed by a further 6 months of supervised on-the-job training. The RCMP also operates the Canadian Police College at which its members and selected representatives of other Canadian and foreign police forces may study the latest advances in the fields of crime prevention and detection.

Many of these advances have been incorporated into the operation of the Force. A teletype system links the widespread divisional headquarters with the administrative centre at Ottawa and a network of fixed and mobile radio units operates within the provinces. The focal point of the criminal investigation work of the Force is the Directorate of Laboratories and Identification; its services, together with those of divisional and sub-divisional units, and of 8 Crime Detection Laboratories, are available to police forces throughout Canada. The Canadian Police Information Centre at RCMP Headquarters, a duplexed computer system, is staffed and operated by the Force. Law Enforcement agencies throughout Canada have access *via* a series of remote terminals to information on stolen vehicles, licences and wanted persons.

In Oct. 1982, the Force had a total strength of 21,642 including regular members, special constables, civilian members and Public Service employees. It maintained 6,071 motor vehicles, 76 police service dogs and 144 horses.

The Force has 13 divisions actively engaged in law enforcement, 1 Headquarters Division and 2 training divisions. In addition it maintains Marine Services and Air Services with headquarters at Ottawa. The Air Directorate has stations throughout Canada and maintains 36 aircraft.

Eayrs, J., *In Defence of Canada: Growing up Allied.* Univ. of Toronto Press, 1980

Feasby, W. R. (ed.), *Official History of the Canadian Medical Services, 1939–45.* 2 vols. Dept. of National Defence. Ottawa, 1953–56

Swettenham, J., *Canada and the First World War.* Toronto, 1970

INTERNATIONAL RELATIONS

Membership. Canada is a member of UN, the Commonwealth, OECD, NATO and Colombo Plan.

ECONOMY

Budget. Budgetary revenue and expenditure of the Government of Canada for years ended 31 March (in Canadian $1m.):

	1980–81	*1981–82*	*1982–83*	*1983–84*[1]	*1984–85*[1]
Revenue	45,200	54,068	55,123	58,626	67,326
Expenditure	59,350	67,674	79,776	90,076	96,926

[1] Estimate.

Budgetary revenue, main items, 1984–85 (estimates in Canadian $1m.):

Income tax, personal	32,810	Non-resident tax	1,050
Income tax, corporation	9,806	Oil export charge	125
Sales	7,315	Natural gas tax	...
Customs duties	3,600	Non-tax revenue	6,050

Details of budget estimates[1], 1984–85 (in Canadian $1m.):

Energy	4,016	External affairs	2,721
Economic development	11,251	Defence	8,782
Social affairs	39,707	Parliament	192
Justice and legal affairs	2,037	Services to government	4,274
Public debt charges	20,350		

[1] The Department of Finance now manages expenditure under a new system of broad categories (listed above) called 'envelopes'.

On 31 March 1984 the net debt (estimate) was $151,876m.

Canadian Tax Foundation. *The National Finances: An Analysis of the Revenues and Expenditures of the Government of Canada.* Toronto. Annual

Currency. The denominations of money in the currency of Canada are dollars and cents. The cent is one-hundredth part of a dollar. Subsidiary coins of the denominations of 1, 5, 10, 25 and 50 cents and $1 are in use. The monetary standard is gold of 900 millesimal fineness (23·22 grains of pure gold equal to 1 gold dollar). The Currency Act provides for gold coins in the denominations of $5, $10 and $20, which are legal tender. The British and US gold coins are also legal tender, at the par rate of exchange. The legal equivalent of the British sovereign is $4.86⅔.

The Bank of Canada has the sole right to issue paper money for circulation in Canada. Restrictions introduced by the 1944 revisions of the Bank Act cancelled the right of chartered banks to issue or re-issue notes after 1 Jan. 1945; and in Jan. 1950 the chartered banks' liability for such of their notes as then remained outstanding was transferred to the Bank of Canada in return for payment of a like sum to the Bank of Canada. On 31 May 1970 the Canadian dollar which was stabilized at 92·50 US cents was allowed to fluctuate. The value of the US$ in Canadian funds was $1·39 and £1 sterling = Canadian $1·48 in Feb. 1985.

The Bank of Canada issues notes, which are legal tender, in denominations of $1, $2, $5, $10, $20, $50, $100, $500 and $1,000. Under the terms of the Bank of Canada Act, the bank is required to sell gold in bars of 400 oz. to any person tendering legal tender. This obligation is at the present time suspended by Order-in-Council. The exportation of gold from Canada is prohibited except by licence issued by the Minister of Finance to the Bank of Canada or a chartered bank.

The Ottawa Mint was established in 1908 as a branch of the Royal Mint, in pursuance of the Ottawa Mint Act, 1901. In Dec. 1931 control of the Mint was passed over to the Canadian Government, and since that time has operated as the Royal Canadian Mint. The Mint issues silver, nickel, bronze and steel coins for circulation in Canada. In 1967, in celebration of Canada's Centennial of Confederation, a $20 gold piece was minted, the first gold coin struck since 1919. In 1935, on the occasion of His Majesty's Silver Jubilee, the Royal Canadian Mint issued the first Canadian silver dollars. Commemorative dollars were also issued in 1939 on the occasion of the visit of King George VI and Queen Elizabeth to Canada; in 1949, when Newfoundland became the tenth Province of Canada; in 1958, the one-hundredth anniversary of the establishment of the Colony of British Columbia; in 1964, the centennial of the Charlottetown and Quebec Conferences which paved the way to confederation. The silver dollar bearing the design of the canoe manned by an Indian and a Voyageur has been issued in the years 1935–38, 1945–48, 1950–57, 1959–63, 1965, 1966 and 1972. For centennial year the Canada goose replaced the usual canoe design on the silver dollar. Because of a world-wide shortage of silver, the Government, in Aug. 1967, authorized the Mint to change the metal content of the 25-cent and 10-cent coins. Commencing in Sept. 1968, the 10-cent, 50-cent and $1 coins were minted in pure nickel. Gold refining is one of the principal activities of the Mint. In 1983 the refinery treated over 3·8m. troy oz. of gold-containing materials and returned over 3m. troy oz. of fine gold to its clients. Of this total, 1,924,590 troy oz. of rough bullion were received from Canadian gold mines for treatment, containing 1,559,306 troy oz. of fine gold and 243,509 troy oz. of fine silver. Coin issued: Gold, $59,010,600; silver, $667,784; other metals, $56,309,560.

Banking. Commercial banks in Canada are known as chartered banks and are incorporated under the terms of the Bank Act, which imposes strict conditions as to capital, notes in circulation, returns to the Dominion Government, types of lending operations and other matters. In Oct. 1983 there were 71 chartered banks (13 domestic banks and 58 foreign bank subsidiaries) incorporated under the provisions of the Bank Act; the 13 had 7,300 branches serving 2,000 communities in all provinces in Canada and nearly 300 branches in other countries. There was also one bank incorporated under the Quebec Savings Bank Act. The foreign bank subsidiaries operate 200 offices in Canada including 58 head offices. The Bank Act is subject to revision by Parliament every 10 years. Bank charters expire every 10 years and are renewed at each decennial revision of the Bank Act. The chartered banks make detailed monthly and yearly returns to the Minister of Finance and are subject to periodic inspection by the Inspector-General of Banks, an official appointed by the Government.

There were 14 domestic banks at 31 July 1984 with assets of gold coin and bullion, $527m., Bank of Canada deposits and notes, $5,603m., deposits with banks, $249,884m.; cheques and other items in transit, $1,223m.; loans, $249,884m. (including mortgage loans, $37,248m.); total assets, $362,998m.

The Bank of Canada Act, passed on 3 July 1934, provided for the establishment of a central bank for the Dominion. This bank commenced operations on 11 March 1935 with a paid-up capital of $5m. By reason of certain changes introduced into the composition of stockholders of the bank (for which *see* THE STATESMAN'S YEAR-BOOK, 1944 pp. 322–23), the Minister of Finance on behalf of Canada is the sole registered owner of the capital stock of the bank. The revised Bank Act, which came into force on 1 May 1967, requires the chartered banks, beginning Feb. 1968, to maintain a statutory cash ratio of 12% on demand deposits and 4% on other deposits, in the form of reserves with and notes on the Bank of Canada. A secondary reserve of 7% in treasury bills, government bonds, etc., is also required. All gold held in Canada by the chartered banks was transferred to the Bank of Canada along with the gold held by the Government as reserve against Dominion notes outstanding at the time of the commencement of operations of the Bank of Canada. The liability of the Dominion notes outstanding at the commencement of business of the Bank of Canada was assumed by the bank.

In the year ending 31 March 1984, the Federal Business Development Bank authorized 2,157 loans for a total of $321m.

Weights and Measures. The legal weights and measures are in transition from the Imperial to the International system of units. The Metric Commission, established in June 1971, co-ordinates Canada's conversion to the metric system.

ENERGY AND NATURAL RESOURCES

Electricity. The net generation of electricity in 1983 was 395,464,438 mwh., of which utilities accounted for 357,422,816 mwh. Of the total, 263,363,135 mwh. was from hydro-electricity, 82,755,312 mwh. from conventional steam plants and 46,220,094 mwh. from nuclear plants. Demand (1983) was 359,811,922 mwh.

Oil and Natural Gas. With the discovery of large oilfields in Alberta and development of the Alberta oil sands, the production of petroleum became a major Canadian industry. The Interprovincial Pipeline, Canada's longest oil pipeline, moves crude oil from Edmonton, Alberta, to Montreal, Quebec. The pipeline serves Canadian refineries from Edmonton to Montreal and since the middle of 1982, Canadian crude has been delivered from Montreal to Atlantic provinces and many in the USA. Another pipeline, Trans-Mountain, extends from Edmonton to Vancouver. Nine refineries, 5 in Canada and 4 in Washington State, are served by the pipeline. At the end of 1983 Canada's oil pipeline system had 36,357 km of line in operation. Net oil deliveries in 1981 were 145,616,106 cu. metres. The Trans-Canada natural gas pipeline is the longest in the world (10,626 km). It brings natural gas from the Alberta–Saskatchewan border across the prairies, through northern Ontario to Toronto, then eastward to Montreal. Natural gas pipeline mileage totalled 162,000 km in 1983. Total gas received from fields and processing plants in 1983, 65,132·3m. cu. metres; total gas supplied to gas utilities, 49,663·1m. cu. metres.

Minerals. Alberta, Ontario, British Columbia, Saskatchewan and Quebec are the chief mining provinces. Total value of minerals produced in 1983 (preliminary) was $35,976,477,000. Principal minerals produced in 1983 (preliminary) were as follows:

	Quantity (1,000)	*Value ($1,000)*
Metallics		
Copper (kg)	624,998	1,307,307
Nickel (kg)	121,836	766,351
Zinc (kg)	970,803	1,116,423
Iron ore (tonnes)	32,382	1,143,380
Gold (grammes)	70,746	1,186,411
Lead (kg)	258,904	152,883
Silver (kg)	1,106	500,441
Molybdenum (kg)	10,523	103,651
Others	...	961,095
Total metallics	...	7,237,942
Non-metallics		
Asbestos (tonnes)	829	402,280
Potash (K_2O) (tonnes)	6,203	620,912
Salt (tonnes)	8,950	174,261
Sulphur, elemental (tonnes)	6,327	428,119
Gypsum (tonnes)	7,481	56,790
Others	...	220,166
Total non-metallics	...	1,902,528
Fuels		
Crude petroleum (cu. metres)	76,874	14,470,793
Natural gas (1,000 cu. metres)	69,266	6,623,158
Natural gas by-products (cu. metres)	17,408	2,568,635
Coal (tonnes)	44,250	1,300,000
Total fuels	...	24,962,586
Structural materials		
Cement (tonnes)	7,828	650,833
Sand and gravel (tonnes)	199,293	514,609
Stone (tonnes)	62,359	269,394
Clay products (bricks, tiles, etc.)	...	127,357
Lime (tonnes)	2,126	139,638
Total structural materials	...	...

Value (in Canadian $1,000) of mineral production by provinces:

Provinces	1982	1983[1]
Newfoundland	646,762	690,366
Pr. Ed. Island	1,774	1,500
Nova Scotia	281,211	248,501
New Brunswick	497,556	513,673
Quebec	2,065,011	1,916,634
Ontario	3,148,013	3,566,696
Manitoba	529,706	637,629
Saskatchewan	2,312,503	2,736,136
Alberta	20,913,347	22,218,213
British Columbia	2,768,954	2,826,730
Yukon Territory	169,120	59,362
N.W. Territories	503,065	561,037
Total	33,837,022	35,976,477

[1] Preliminary.

Agriculture. Though the manufacturing industries now predominate, agriculture is still very important to the Canadian economy. It contributes about 2·9% of the net value of production and in 1982 accounted for about 12·1% of the value of commodities exported.

According to the census of 1981 the total land area is 2,278·6m. acres of which 162·8m. acres are agricultural land.

Grain growing, dairy farming, fruit farming, ranching and fur farming are all carried on successfully. Total farm receipts (1983) $18,725m.

The following table shows the estimated value of selected agricultural production for 1983, in Canadian $1,000:

Wheat	4,239,866	Tobacco	287,033
Oats and barley	974,218	Cattle and calves	3,430,321
Rapeseed	726,364	Hogs	1,711,865
Potatoes	293,672	Sheep and lambs	27,754
Other vegetables	436,757	Dairy products	2,757,856
Fruit	268,003	Poultry and eggs	1,253,515

Number of occupied farms (census of 1982) was 316,770; average farm size, 540 acres.

Field Crops. The estimated acreage and yield of the principal field crops, by provinces, 1984 were:

	Wheat		*Tame hay*		*Oats*	
Provinces	*1,000 acres*	*1,000 bu.*	*1,000 acres*	*1,000 bu.*	*1,000 acres*	*1,000 bu.*
Prince Edward Island	8	392	125	281	30	1,830
Nova Scotia	6	312	177	425	19	1,154
New Brunswick	12	492	172	361	37	1,961
Quebec	91	4,777	2,470	5,699	408	24,316
Ontario	536	29,820	2,570	7,880	300	18,000
Manitoba	4,450	129,100	1,300	2,300	570	28,000
Saskatchewan	20,050	407,000	1,800	2,300	850	30,000
Alberta	7,250	171,800	3,900	6,800	1,250	66,000
British Columbia	160	5,400	740	1,480	60	3,500
Total, Canada	32,563	749,093	13,254	27,526	3,524	174,761

	Barley		*Rye*		*Corn for Grain*	
Provinces	*1,000 acres*	*1,000 bu.*	*1,000 acres*	*1,000 bu.*	*1,000 acres*	*1,000 bu.*
Prince Edward Island	53	2,862	—	—	—	—
Nova Scotia	12	652	4	224	6	433
New Brunswick	17	816	—	—	—	—
Quebec	334	19,979	9	197	544	53,147
Ontario	465	28,100	86	3,180	2,200	211,000
Manitoba	1,800	85,000	220	7,710	180	12,000
Saskatchewan	3,200	110,000	370	8,650	—	—
Alberta	5,100	205,000	210	5,550	16	1,200
British Columbia	105	8,000	10	330	—	—
Total, Canada	11,176	460,409	909	25,841	2,946	277,780

Provinces	Canola-Rapeseed-Colza 1,000 acres	1,000 bu.	Mixed grains 1,000 acres	1,000 bu.	Soybeans 1,000 acres	1,000 bu.
Prince Edward Island	—	—	82	5,002	—	—
Nova Scotia	—	—	5	342	—	—
New Brunswick	—	—	2	125	—	—
Quebec	—	—	131	8,084	—	—
Ontario	28	950	670	43,100	1,030	34,700
Manitoba	1,200	23,000	125	5,600	—	—
Saskatchewan	2,950	55,000	80	2,400	—	—
Alberta	2,900	54,000	140	5,900	—	—
British Columbia	285	4,900	15	640	—	—
Total, Canada	7,363	137,850	1,251	71,193	1,030	34,700

Livestock. In parts of Saskatchewan and Alberta stockraising is still carried on as a primary industry, but the livestock industry of the country at large is mainly a subsidiary of mixed farming. The following table shows the numbers of livestock (in 1,000) by provinces in July 1984:

Provinces	Milch cows	Other cattle	Sheep and lambs	Swine
Newfoundland	3·0	4·2	5·6	19·5
Prince Edward Island	23·3	77·7	8·4	122·0
Nova Scotia	35·2	106·8	44·8	158·0
New Brunswick	28·4	80·6	11·0	133·0
Quebec	675·0	895·0	125·0	3,405·0
Ontario	540·0	2,031·0	242·0	3,490·0
Manitoba	78·0	957·0	37·0	1,028·0
Saskatchewan	85·0	2,149·0	66·0	625·0
Alberta	157·0	3,623·0	190·0	1,400·0
British Columbia	88·0	672·0	61·0	275·0
Total	1,712·9	10,596·3	790·8	10,655·5

Net production[1] of farm eggs in 1982, 493·5m. doz. ($471·5m.); 1983, 504·8m. doz. ($493·0m.).

[1] Includes exports.

Wool production (in tonnes), 1979, 1,066; 1980, 1,173; 1981, 1,407; 1982, 1,417; 1983, 1,380.

Dairying. The dairy products industry has shown a marked tendency towards centralization; the number of establishments decreased between 1961 and 1982 from 1,710 to 402 (76·5%), whereas the number of employees has decreased only 23%. Production, 1983: Creamery butter, 103,579 tonnes; cheddar cheese, 99,446 tonnes; concentrated whole milk products, 168,853 kl; skim milk powder, 123,408 tonnes.

Fruit Farming. The value of fruit production (excluding apples) in 1983 was (estimated in $1,000): Ontario, 72,735; British Columbia, 57,062 ; Quebec, 17,549; Nova Scotia, 11,379; New Brunswick, 5,618; Prince Edward Island, 1,756. Total apple production in Canada in 1983 was 484,853 tonnes.

Tobacco. Commercial production of tobacco is confined to Ontario and Quebec. Farm cash receipts in 1983 totalled $280m.

Forestry. As of 1982, the total area of land covered by forests is estimated at about 4,364,000 sq. km, of which 2,641,000 sq. km are classed as productive forest land.

Lumber production (in cu. metres) in 1982 was 37,452,090.

Lumber shipments from sawmills and planing mills in 1982 was 37,078,694 cu. metres valued at $3,103·7m. Pulp production was 18·5m. tonnes in 1982 and 20·6m. tonnes in 1981. In 1982 mill shipments of paper amounted to 12·1m. tonnes valued at $6,739,712,000.

Fur Trade. In 1982–83 (year ended 30 June), 4,303,704 pelts valued at $91,130,048, were taken. In wild-life pelt production beaver led in total value, followed by muskrat, fox, lynx and raccoon. The most important animal raised on fur farms is mink, with 99% of the total production. The value of mink pelts from fur farms in 1983 was $43,357,145. There were, in 1983, 696 fur farms reporting fox and 618 mink.

Fisheries. During 1983, landings in Canadian commercial fisheries reached 1,340,824 tonnes. The landed value was $874·2m. and the estimated market value was $2,109·9m. The landed value of principal fish in 1983 was (in $1,000): Salmon, 108,797; cod, 188,529; lobster, 141,883; herring, 67,604; scallops, 70,755; freshwater fish, 50,800; halibut, 21,101. Exports of fisheries' products, 1983, were valued at $1,571·5m.

Canadian Mines Handbook. Annual. Toronto, from 1931
Canadian Fisheries, Highlights 1983. Dept. of Fisheries and Oceans, 1984

INDUSTRY AND TRADE

Industry. Industry groups ranked by value of shipments, survey of 1982:

Industry	*Production workers*	*Wages ($1,000)*	*Cost of materials ($1,000)*	*Value of shipments ($1,000)*
Food and beverages	153,499	2,891,993	22,220,366	33,016,551
Tobacco products	5,562	128,487	827,505	1,493,756
Rubber and plastics	42,222	760,074	2,265,008	4,433,639
Leather industries	19,614	248,662	549,584	1,105,960
Textile industries	45,869	711,416	2,416,680	4,507,573
Knitting mills	15,798	195,029	491,615	947,795
Clothing industries	79,051	935,061	1,902,606	3,962,352
Wood industries	80,800	1,654,550	4,097,919	7,173,003
Furniture and fixtures	39,024	567,186	1,183,540	2,494,082
Paper and allied industries	91,824	2,286,024	7,371,202	14,783,955
Printing, publishing and allied industries	62,066	1,252,157	2,530,515	6,779,341
Primary metal industries	82,186	2,157,186	6,724,186	12,402,450
Metal fabricating industries	107,014	2,189,796	5,940,207	11,765,669
Machinery industries	59,717	1,281,729	3,831,438	7,662,220
Transport equipment	120,289	2,804,979	15,299,844	22,656,564
Electrical products industries	75,536	1,430,758	3,905,482	8,714,421
Non-metallic mineral products	33,997	751,915	1,725,280	4,385,269
Petroleum and coal products	8,275	266,022	19,352,020	21,709,154
Chemical and chemical prods.	45,485	1,059,958	7,571,228	14,095,400
Miscellaneous manufacturing	44,596	688,611	1,913,924	3,930,165
All industries	1,212,424	24,261,593	112,120,148	188,019,319

Labour. In Sept. 1984 the industrial distribution of the employed was estimated as follows (in 1,000): Service, 3,502; manufacturing, 1,966; trade, 867; transport, communication and other utilities, 1,959; construction, 580; public administration, 765; finance, insurance and real estate, 650; agriculture, 466; non-agriculture, 10,596; other primary industries, 301; total employed, 11,045; unemployed, 1,472.

Union returns filed for 1982 in compliance with the Corporations and Returns Act (1962), show 183 labour organizations reporting on 13,598 local union branches in Canada. Union membership in 1982 was 3·05m. 33·3% of the wage and salary workers in major industry groups were members of reporting labour organizations, with about 61·4% of the organized workers members of unions affiliated with the Canada Labour Congress. Over 1·42m. of the union members were in international unions, which have branches both in Canada and the USA and in most cases belong to central labour organizations in both countries.

It is generally established by legislation, both federal and provincial, that a trade union to which the majority of employees in a unit suitable for collective bargaining belong, is given certain rights and duties. An employer is required to meet and negotiate with such a trade union to determine wage-rates and other working conditions of his employees. The employer, the trade union and the employees affected are bound by the resulting agreement. If an impasse is reached in negotiation conciliation services provided by the appropriate government board are available. Generally, work stoppages may not take place until an established conciliation procedure has been carried out and are prohibited while an agreement is in effect. Almost 28% of the workers affected by collective agreements are in the manufacturing industry.

Freedom of association is a civil right in Canada, and under common law workers are at liberty to join unions and participate in their activities. This right has also been guaranteed by statutes which make it an offence to interfere with freedom of association.

Certain specific minimum standards in regard to working conditions are set by law, for the most part by provincial labour legislation. Minimum wages, maximum hours of work or an overtime rate of pay after a specified number of hours, minimum weekly rest periods and annual vacations with pay are established for the majority of workers.

Dept. of Labour, *Working Conditions in Canadian Industry.* Annual. Ottawa

Commerce. In the past the custom tariff of Canada has been protective, with a preferential tariff in favour of the UK, the Dominions, a number of Crown Colonies, and the Irish and South African Republics. At the Imperial Economic Conference of 1932, held in Ottawa, the UK developed further the policy of preferential tariffs to the Dominions, and on the part of the latter there was a general lowering of the existing tariffs against certain lines of UK manufacturers. Canada is one of the signatories of the General Agreement on Tariffs and Trade (GATT) and of the Kennedy Round agreements.

Imports for home consumption and domestic exports (in Canadian $1,000) for calendar years (merchandise only):

	Imports	*Exports*		*Imports*	*Exports*
1960	5,842,695	5,255,575	1982	67,855,703	81,824,824
1970	13,951,903	16,820,098	1983[1]	75,586,566	88,506,249
1980	69,273,844	74,445,976			

[1] Estimate

Exports (domestic) by countries in 1983 (in Canadian $1,000):

Australia	437,996	Sierra Leone	891
Bahamas	28,659	Singapore	126,735
Bahrain	4,697	South Africa, Republic of	165,770
Bangladesh	114,622	Sri Lanka	52,911
Barbados	38,660	Tanzania	17,023
Belize	1,978	Trinidad and Tobago	150,838
Bermuda	29,162	Uganda	3,090
Britain (UK)	2,448,796	Zambia	2,902
British Oceania	230		
Cyprus	11,797	Afghánistán	61
Falkland Islands	20	Albania	26
Fiji	2,596	Algeria	448,531
Gambia	84	Angola	3,445
Ghana	22,627	Argentina	67,184
Gibraltar	128	Austria	49,991
Guyana	3,919	Belgium and Luxembourg	700,126
Hong Kong	221,176	Benin	688
India	261,683	Bolivia	3,782
Ireland	89,150	Brazil	596,246
Jamaica	64,366	Burma	1,536
Kenya	12,319	Cameroon Republic	18,387
Leeward and Windward Islands	31,793	Chile	69,963
Malawi	1,054	China	1,607,242
Malaysia	114,003	Colombia	204,641
Malta	1,913	Costa Rica	21,846
Mauritius and Dependencies	363	Cuba	360,592
New Zealand	122,362	Czechoslovakia	15,026
Nigeria	50,252	Denmark	66,608
Pakistan	65,441	Dominican Republic	45,070
Qatar	9,951	Ecuador	45,123

Exports *(continued)*

Egypt (UAR)	136,226	Netherlands Antilles	10,052
El Salvador	18,574	Nicaragua	15,930
Ethiopia	27,619	Norway	230,490
Finland	86,952	Panama	29,544
France	626,034	Paraguay	1,203
French Africa	12,435	Peru	82,014
French Guiana	22	Philippines	76,828
French Oceania	1,367	Poland	43,747
French West Indies	2,034	Portugal	60,694
Gabon	925	Portuguese Africa	314
German Democratic Rep.	202,195	Puerto Rico	121,654
Germany, Fed. Rep. of	1,155,674	Romania	16,398
Greece	48,677	Saudi Arabia	364,772
Greenland	3,468	Senegal	19,259
Guatemala	15,266	Somalia	823
Guinea	1,262	Spain	137,079
Haiti, Republic of	15,034	Spanish Africa	220
Honduras	11,482	St Pierre and Miquelon	23,763
Hungary	14,838	Sudan	15,476
Iceland	5,450	Suriname	3,494
Indonesia	209,890	Sweden	146,727
Iran	206,177	Switzerland	197,805
Iraq	116,276	Syria	79,009
Israel	124,827	Taiwan	342,180
Italy	549,357	Thailand	146,486
Ivory Coast	3,056	Togo	4,943
Japan	4,728,174	Tunisia	47,195
Jordan	12,809	Turkey	102,094
Korea, North	1,244	USSR	1,761,789
Korea, South	556,088	United Arab Emirates	31,001
Kuwait	64,652	USA	64,527,697
Lebanon	14,236	US Oceania	1,678
Liberia	4,253	US Virgin Islands	24,640
Libya	78,466	Uruguay	6,617
Madagascar	1,748	Venezuela	231,779
Mauritania	3,891	Vietnam (South)	1,203
Mexico	375,260	Yemen (South)	1,794
Morocco	59,385	Yugoslavia	48,878
Mozambique	10,516	Zaïre	11,589
Netherlands	958,139	Zimbabwe	4,554

Imports (for consumption) by countries in 1983 (in Canadian $1,000):

Australia	357,487	Malta	2,263
Bahamas	50,583	Mauritius and Dependencies	6,240
Bahrain	523	New Zealand	156,571
Bangladesh	10,465	Nigeria	192,692
Barbados	8,759	Pakistan	18,526
Belize	8,133	Qatar	67
Bermuda	18,828	Sierra Leone	80
Britain (UK)	1,809,806	Singapore	168,444
British Oceania	4	South Africa, Republic of	194,143
Cyprus	353	Sri Lanka	21,669
Falkland Islands	3	Tanzania	2,117
Fiji	6,031	Trinidad and Tobago	9,030
Gambia	36	Uganda	333
Ghana	3,174	Zambia	29
Gibraltar	—		
Guyana	19,214	Afghánistán	209
Hong Kong	820,316	Albania	9
India	101,118	Algeria	150,103
Ireland	107,266	Angola	6
Jamaica	109,697	Argentina	52,917
Kenya	11,417	Austria	108,103
Leeward and Windward Islands	1,455	Belgium and Luxembourg	296,024
Malawi	6,361	Benin	14
Malaysia	115,581	Bolivia	16,557

Imports *(continued)*

Brazil	499,958	Madagascar	725
Burma	292	Mauritania	2
Cameroon Republic	1,290	Mexico	1,079,233
Chile	134,158	Morocco	15,818
China	245,767	Mozambique	301
Colombia	94,249	Netherlands	349,382
Costa Rica	62,506	Netherlands Antilles	11,932
Cuba	56,287	Nicaragua	32,120
Czechoslovakia	54,443	Norway	313,517
Denmark	136,925	Panama	46,551
Dominican Republic	19,432	Paraguay	3,689
Ecuador	62,035	Peru	119,627
Egypt (UAR)	98,733	Philippines	88,290
El Salvador	35,026	Poland	39,512
Ethiopia	2,048	Portugal	58,337
Finland	75,763	Portuguese Africa	15
France	840,977	Puerto Rico	146,669
French Africa	593	Romania	50,131
French Guiana	—	Saudi Arabia	94,044
French Oceania	501	Senegal	1,285
French West Indies	79	Somalia	366
Gabon	2,951	Spain	181,945
German Democratic Rep.	10,117	Spanish Africa	—
Germany, Fed. Rep. of	1,576,555	St Pierre and Miquelon	520
Greece	44,119	Sudan	692
Greenland	2,388	Suriname	7,376
Guatemala	20,823	Sweden	415,843
Guinea	19,297	Switzerland	408,161
Haiti, Republic of	10,753	Syria	50,201
Honduras	35,962	Taiwan	925,451
Hungary	27,984	Thailand	60,554
Iceland	3,234	Togo	2
Indonesia	40,043	Tunisia	1,549
Iran	526,750	Turkey	12,809
Iraq	897	USSR	33,252
Israel	55,872	United Arab Emirates	2,432
Italy	798,389	USA	54,103,299
Ivory Coast	10,450	US Oceania	243
Japan	4,409,441	US Virgin Islands	1,172
Jordan	199	Uruguay	32,767
Korea, North	79	Venezuela	1,004,453
Korea, South	791,405	Vietnam, South	178
Kuwait	18,283	Yemen	65
Lebanon	769	Yugoslavia	29,007
Liberia	92	Zaïre	17,011
Libya	126	Zimbabwe	6,470

Categories of imports in 1983, estimate (in Canadian $1,000):

Live animals	132,165	Fabricated materials, inedible	14,005,689
Food, feed, beverages and tobacco	4,870,314	End products, inedible	48,397,209
Crude materials, inedible	7,201,111	Special transactions	980,078

Categories of exports (Canadian produce) in 1983, estimate (in Canadian $1,000):

Live animals	339,761	Fabricated materials, inedible	30,011,051
Food, feed, beverages and tobacco	10,073,910	End products, inedible	33,472,277
Crude materials, inedible	14,392,802	Special transactions	216,449

Total trade of Canada with UK (British Department of Trade returns, in £1,000 sterling):

	1980	*1981*	*1982*	*1983*	*1984*
Imports to UK	1,412,156	1,508,756	1,439,619	1,522,187	1,617,476
Exports and re-exports from UK	758,367	844,978	851,703	968,269	1,183,231

Tourism. The number of visitors to Canada in 1983 was 34,255,508 (1982, 34,406,501). In 1983, 32,479,769 came from USA (1982, 32,431,840).

COMMUNICATIONS

Roads. The total highway mileage in Canada in March 1981 was 928,258 km. Of this total, federal highways 10,823 km, provincial highways 256,092 km and municipal highways 661,343 km. Expenditure (1981–82) on roads, bridges, ferries, etc., from federal and provincial/territorial governments $4,139m. Federal expenditure was chiefly devoted towards the upkeep of national-park roadways and nationally owned bridges and ferries, although for the 'Mackenzie Highway' from Grimshaw, Alberta, to Hay River, Northwest Territories, the federal government paid about 68% of the total cost. In general, however, highways are provincially controlled and maintained, and the responsibility of assisting municipalities and townships falls directly on the provinces.

The Alaska Highway is part of the Canadian highway system. For the Trans-Canada Highway *see* map in THE STATESMAN'S YEAR-BOOK, 1962.

Registered motor vehicles totalled 14,560,903 in 1983 (preliminary); they included 10,731,520 passenger cars and taxis, 3,362,972 trucks and buses and 466,411 motor cycles.

Urban Transit. In 1982 urban transit systems (urban and suburban passenger transportation, electrical railway, trolly coach, bus or subway) carried 1,331,649,961 fare passengers 710,436,750 km for an operating revenue of $1,465,327,081. In 1982, intercity and rural bus operations carried 29,772,000 fare passengers 195,104,087 km, earning revenues of $323,512,665.

Railways. The total length of track operated during 1982 in Canada was 98,927 km. Mainline track, 38,030 km; branch line, 34,647 km; industrial and siding track, 26,250 km.

Canada has 2 great trans-continental systems: the Canadian National Railway system (CN), a government-owned body which operates 52,507 km (1982) of track, and the Canadian Pacific Railway, a joint-stock corporation operating 34,771 km (1982). From 1 April 1978, a government funded organization known as Via Rail took over passenger services formerly operated by CP and CN.

Selected statistics of Canadian railways for 1982: Passenger revenue $195·8m.; freight revenue, $4,514·5m.; total railway operating revenues, $6,301·3m.; total operating expenses, $6,185·2m.

Aviation. Civil aviation in Canada is under the jurisdiction of the federal government. The technical and administrative aspects are supervised by the Administrator of Air Transportation, while the economic functions are assigned to the Canadian Transportation Commission.

In 1982 Canadian airports handled 45,035,953 passengers, 138,184,000 kg of mail and 473,657,000 kg of cargo. Operating revenue (1982) was $4,664·7m.; operating expenditure, $4,679·2m.

Shipping. The registered shipping on 31 Dec. 1983, including vessels for inland navigation, totalled 35,622 with a gross tonnage of 5,360,433. A total of 50,539 vessels (international shipping) visited Canadian ports in 1983, loading and unloading 178m. tonnes of cargo.

The major canals in Canada are those of the St Lawrence–Great Lakes waterway with their 7 locks, providing navigation for vessels of 25·75-ft draught from Montreal to Lake Ontario; the Welland Canal by-passing the Niagara River between Lake Ontario and Lake Erie with its 8 locks; and the Sault Ste Marie Canal and lock between Lake Huron and Lake Superior. These 16 locks overcome a drop of 582 ft from the head of the lakes to Montreal. The St Lawrence Seaway was opened to navigation on 1 April 1959 (*see* map in THE STATESMAN'S YEAR-BOOK, 1957). In 1983, traffic on the Montreal–Lake Ontario Section of the Seaway numbered 3,870 vessels carrying 45·1m. cargo tonnes; on the Welland Canal Section, 4,707 vessels with 50·1m. gross tonnes. Value of fixed assets was $602,095,285 and investments, $42,529,388 at 31 March 1984.

Coast Guard. The Canadian Coast Guard (formed in 1962) is responsible to the Minister of Transport. In 1984 it comprised 7 heavy icebreakers; a heavy icebreaker/cable repair vessel; 7 medium icebreakers; 3 light icebreakers; 25 aid tenders; 3 special shallow draft vessels; 60 search and rescue vessels (all types and sizes); 4 hovercraft and 34 helicopters.

Post. In May 1984 there were 8,376 postal facilities in operation and 6,400m. pieces of mail were processed. Gross revenue (estimate 1982–83) was $2,200m.; gross expenditure, $2,600m.

There were 919,143 miles (1,479,216 km) of telegraph wire in Canada in 1979 (including external cable landed in Canada). There were 16·2m. telephones in July 1984.

Broadcasting. There were 991 originating stations operating in Canada at 31 March 1984, of which 109 were Canadian Broadcasting Corporation stations, 116 were CBC affiliates and 489 were privately owned and operated. Included were 410 AM radio stations, 312 FM radio stations and 211 television stations. Radio and television licence fees were abolished in 1953.

Wireless 'beam' stations are operated at Montreal for direct communications with Great Britain and Australia, and a station at Louisburg, N.S., provides a long-distance service to ships.

Cinemas (1982). There were 983 cinemas with a seating capacity of 619,511 and 270 drive-in theatres with a capacity of 136,241 cars.

Newspapers (1983). There were 118 daily newspapers, of which 106 were in English, 10 in French and 2 others.

JUSTICE, RELIGION, EDUCATION AND WELFARE

Justice. There is a Supreme Court in Ottawa, having general appellate jurisdiction in civil and criminal cases throughout Canada. There is an Exchequer Court, which is also a Court of Admiralty. There is a Superior Court in each province and county courts, with limited jurisdiction, in most of the provinces, all the judges in these courts being appointed by the Governor-General. Police, magistrates and justices of the peace are appointed by the provincial governments.

For the year ended 31 Dec. 1983, 2,143,256 Criminal Code Offences were reported and 402,851 persons were charged.

Canadian Legal and Directory. Toronto. Annual

Religion. Membership of the leading denominations in 1981:

Province	*Roman Catholic*	*United Church of Canada*	*Anglican Church of Canada*	*Presbyterian*	*Lutheran*
Newfoundland	204,430	104,835	153,530	2,700	460
Prince Edward Island	56,415	29,645	6,850	12,620	210
Nova Scotia	310,140	169,605	131,130	38,285	12,315
New Brunswick	371,100	87,460	66,260	12,070	1,810
Quebec	5,609,685	126,275	132,115	34,625	17,655
Ontario	2,986,175	1,655,550	1,164,315	517,020	254,175
Manitoba	269,070	240,395	108,220	23,910	58,830
Saskatchewan	279,840	263,375	77,725	16,065	88,785
Alberta	573,495	525,480	202,265	63,890	144,675
British Columbia	526,355	548,360	374,055	89,810	122,395
Yukon	5,470	3,310	4,665	615	915
Northwest Territories	18,215	3,725	15,295	505	665
Total, Canada	11,210,385	3,758,015	2,436,375	812,110	702,905

Other denominations: Baptist, 696,850; Greek Orthodox, 314,870; Jewish, 296,425; Ukrainian (Greek) Catholic, 190,585; Pentecostal, 338,790; Mennonite, 189,370; other, 3,136,815.

Education. Under the Constitution the various provincial legislatures have power over education. These powers are subject to certain qualifications respecting the rights of denominational and minority language schools. Newfoundland and Quebec legislations provide for Roman Catholic and Protestant school boards. School Acts in Ontario, Saskatchewan and Alberta provide tax support for both public and separate schools. School board revenues derive from local taxation on real property and government grants from general provincial revenue.

Except in Quebec the number of private elementary and secondary schools is small; their enrolments in 1983–84 were less than 5% of the total elementary-secondary enrolment. Indian and Northern Affairs Canada finances schools for Indian and Inuit children; the enrolment in 1983–84 was 38,937.

In 1982–83, 426,400 full-time regular students (graduates and under-graduates) were enrolled in universities. In 1982 some 28,800 took first degrees in social sciences, commerce, economics, law, political science and geography; 16,200 in education; 8,700 in humanities; 7,200 in engineering and applied sciences; 5,000 in agriculture; 6,100 in health subjects; 4,900 in mathematics and physical sciences and 2,800 in fine and applied arts. Unclassified, 7,700.

The following statistics give information, for 1983–84, about all elementary and secondary schools, public, federal, private and blind and deaf:

Province	*Schools*	*Teachers*	*Pupils*
Newfoundland	629	8,236	148,052
Prince Edward Island	73	1,319	25,575
Nova Scotia	595	10,611	180,587
New Brunswick	471	7,596	147,847
Quebec	2,788	71,560	1,165,378
Ontario	5,539	94,721	1,864,514
Manitoba	836	12,324	219,401
Saskatchewan	1,057	11,252	211,118
Alberta	1,656	24,640	464,358
British Columbia	1,891	27,860	529,920
Yukon	26	250	4,548
Northwest Territories	72	660	12,901
National Defence (overseas)	10	230	3,003
Total	15,643	271,259	4,977,202

Health. Canada achieves national health insurance through a series of interlocking provincial plans which qualify the provinces for federal financial support if they meet the minimum criteria of the federal legislation with respect to comprehensiveness of coverage with regard to services, universality of coverage with regard to people, accessibility to services uninhibited by user charges, portability of benefits and non-profit administration by a public agency. There are also related, unconditional, federal contributions made by yielding points to provinces. The federal contributions to the provinces cover about 50% of the provincial costs for the insured services of the national health program. (In the health field the federal government also furnishes the provinces with *per capita* cash contributions towards the cost of extended health care services; *e.g.*, nursing home care, certain home care services; these are unconditional except that the provinces must provide appropriate information.

The Canadian approach to the development of national health programmes has been to progressively provide major segments of personal health care on a publicly financed basis to virtually the whole population, and this is achieved with the co-operation of the provinces, which exercise the primary constitutional prerogative in health matters.

The insurance programmes are designed to ensure that all residents of Canada have reasonable access to needed medical and hospital care on a prepaid basis. The insured services of the Hospital Insurance Programme, which commenced in 1958, include in-patient care (including necessary drugs, diagnostic tests, etc.); out-patient services, although optional under the national programmes, are insured in all provinces. Complementing the protection of the Hospital Insurance Programme was the Medical Care Programme, inaugurated in 1968, which covered all medically required services rendered by medical practitioners no matter where the services are rendered, and certain surgical–dental procedures undertaken by dental surgeons in hospital. All 10 provinces and the 2 northern territories participated in both programmes, which provided a health insurance coverage for over 99% of the population (or over 24m. people). From April 1, 1984 the original federal health insurance legislation was consolidated under the Canada Health Act. The Act retains and further clarifies the five programme conditions that the provinces must satisfy in order to qualify for full federal funding.

The approach taken by Canada is one of state-sponsored health insurance. Accordingly, the advent of insurance programmes produced little change in the ownership of hospitals, almost all of which are owned by non-government non-profit corporations, or in the rights and privileges of private medical practice. Patients are free to choose their own general practitioners and/or specialists without losing their insured benefits (there is a minor exception in Quebec involving the non-emergency services of a few physicians). Except for 0·5% of the population whose care is provided for under other legislation (such as serving members of the Canadian Armed Forces), all residents are eligible, regardless of whether they are in the work force. Benefits are available without upper limit so long as they are medically necessary, provided any registration obligations are met. Benefits are also portable during any temporary absence from Canada anywhere in the world—subject to any limitation a province may impose upon treatment electively sought outside the particular province without prior approval. Provinces may prescribe limits on benefits payable for out-of-province care.

In addition to the benefits qualifying for federal contributions, provinces are free to provide additional benefits at their own discretion. Most provinces provide such benefits, which cover a variety of services (*e.g.*, optometric care, children's dental programme, drug benefits) depending upon the province. Most provinces fund their portion of health insurance costs out of general provincial revenues. Three provinces and one territory levy premiums which meet part of the provincial costs, 2 provinces impose a levy on employers, and 1 province utilizes part of its sales tax revenues for this purpose. Four provinces have nominal co-charges for short-term hospital care. Several provinces have charges for long-term hospital care geared, approximately, to the room and board portion of the OAS–GIS payment mentioned under Social Welfare.

Social Welfare. The social security network provides financial benefits to individuals and their families through a variety of programmes administered by federal, provincial and municipal governments. Federally, the Department of National Health and Welfare is responsible for research into the areas of health and social issues, provision of grants and contributions for various social services, improvement and construction of health facilities and the administration of several of Canada's income security programmes. These programmes are: The Family Allowances programme, introduced in 1945 and amended in 1973; the Old Age Security programme, introduced in 1952 and to which were added the Guaranteed Income Supplement in 1966 and the Spouse's Allowance in 1975, and the Pension Plan which came into being in 1966. Also implemented in 1966 was the Assistance Plan, which provides for federal-provincial cost-sharing of social assistance payments and social service programs provided by provincial and, in some cases, municipal governments.

The 1973 Family Allowances Act provides for the payment of a monthly Family Allowance ($29.95 in 1984) in respect of a dependent child under the age of 18 who is a resident of Canada, who is wholly or substantially maintained by a parent or guardian. At least one parent must be a Canadian citizen, or admitted to Canada as a permanent resident under the Immigration Act, or admitted to Canada for a period of not less than 1 year, if during that time his or her income is subject to Canadian Income Tax. Benefits are also paid under prescribed circumstances to Canadian citizens living abroad. A Special Allowance ($44.68 monthly in 1984) is paid on behalf of a child under the age of 18 who is maintained by a welfare agency, a government department or an institution. In some cases, payment is made directly to a foster parent. The Special Allowance was paid on behalf of 36,259 children across Canada in March 1984.

Family Allowances are considered as income for income-tax purposes for the parent who claims an exemption for the child; Special Allowances are not taxable.

During the month of March 1984, over 3·6m. Canadian families (including 6·6m. eligible children) received Family Allowances; the total bill for FA and Special Allowances in the 1983–84 fiscal year was (estimate) $2,328m.

Family Allowance benefits are increased each year in Jan. in accordance with the Consumer Price Index; for 1983 and 1984, however, indexation for regular benefits, (Special Allowances are excluded from this provision), has been limited to 6% and 5% respectively, in accordance with a federal policy on fiscal restraints announced in late 1982. The Family Allowances Act specifies that a provincial government may request the federal government to vary the allowance rates payable within the province subject to the fulfilment of stipulated conditions. Only the provinces of Alberta and Quebec have exercised this option.

The Old Age Security (OAS) pension is payable to persons 65 years of age and over who satisfy the residence requirements stipulated in the Old Age Security Act. The amount payable, whether full or partial, is also governed by stipulated conditions, as is the payment of an OAS pension to a recipient who absents himself from Canada. OAS pensioners with little or no income apart from OAS may, upon application, receive a full or partial supplement known as the Guaranteed Income Supplement (GIS). Entitlement is normally based on the pensioner's income in the preceding year, calculated in accordance with the Income Tax Act. The spouse of an OAS pensioner, aged 60 to 64, meeting the same residence requirements as those stipulated for OAS, may be eligible for a full or partial Spouse's Allowance (SA). SA is payable, on application, the annual combined income of the couple being subject to an income test which does not include the OAS pension or the Guaranteed Income Supplement. In 1979, the SPA program was expanded to include a spouse, who is eligible for SPA in the month the pensioner spouse dies, until the age of 65 or until remarriage. This provision is called the Extended Spouse's Allowance.

The OAS pension is taxable; GIS and SA are not taxable. However, they must be included in computing the net income of a dependant for income-tax purposes. OAS, GIS and SA are subject to an increase every Jan., April, July and Oct. to reflect increases in the Consumer Price Index.

In Oct. 1984, the basic OAS pension was $272.17 monthly; the maximum Guaranteed Income Supplement was $298.47 monthly for a single pensioner or a married pensioner whose spouse was not receiving a pension or a Spouse's Allowance, and $210.67 monthly for each spouse of a married couple where both are pensioners. The maximum Spouse's Allowance for the same quarter was $482.84 monthly (equal to the basic pension plus the maximum GIS married rate) and $508.06 for the spouse of a deceased pensioner.

The Canada Pension Plan (CPP) is designed to provide workers with a basic level of income protection in the event of retirement, disability or death. Benefits are determined by the contributor's earnings and contributions made to the Plan, and are adjusted annually to reflect cost of living increases. Contribution is compulsory for most employed and self-employed Canadians 18 to 65 years of age. The Canada Pension Plan does not operate in Quebec, which has exercised its constitutional prerogative to establish a similar plan, the Quebec Pension Plan (QPP), to operate in lieu of CPP; there is reciprocity between the two to ensure coverage for all adult Canadians in the labour force.

CPP/QPP contributions are deductible for income tax purposes, while benefits are taxable. Benefits are adjusted annually to fully reflect increases in the Consumer Price Index.

Both CPP and QPP are funded by equal contributions of 1·8% of pensionable earnings from the employer and 1·8% from the employee (self-employed persons contribute the full 3·6%), in addition to the interest on the investment of excess funds. In 1983, the range of yearly pensionable earnings was from $2,000 to $20,500; a person who earned and contributed at less than the maximum level receives monthly benefits at rates lower than the maximum allowable under CPP/QPP.

For CPP, an advisory committee representing employers, employees, self-employed persons and the public regularly reviews the operation of the plan, the state of investments and the adequacy of coverage and benefits, and reports to the Minister of National Health and Welfare. CPP authorizes reciprocal agreements with other countries to achieve portability of pensions. Such agreements have been made with Italy, France and Portugal, and agreements with the US, Greece and Jamaica have been signed, but are not yet (1983) in force. In general, parallel provisions apply under QPP. In March 1984, over 1·6m. Canadians received Canada Pension Plan benefits; an additional 518,000 persons received Quebec Pension Plan benefits. Total expenditures during 1983–84 were just over $3,657m. for CPP and $1,281m. for QPP.

Under the Canada Assistance Plan, the federal government pays 50% of the cost, to the provinces, of assistance to persons in need; welfare services provided to persons who are in need or likely to become in need if they do not receive such services (welfare services means services having as their object the lessening, removal or prevention of the causes and effects of poverty, child neglect or dependence on public assistance); and work activity projects which are designed to improve the employability of persons who have unusual difficulty in finding or retaining jobs or in undertaking job training.

'Need' is defined by each province and is determined by the 'budget deficit' method, that is, the difference between an applicant's requirements and his income and resources. The rates of assistance payable are also determined by provincial authorities and are non-taxable. Provinces generally adjust social assistance rates once a year in accordance with certain economic indicators.

In addition to persons in need as defined in the Plan, federal contributions may be made towards agency costs of providing welfare services to persons who are likely to become in need, if such services are not provided. The amount of federal subsidy is dependent on the proportion of eligible persons as determined by the use of an income test or a pre-determined income level for different sized families.

In March 1983, close to 1·8m. Canadians (representing 985,000 households) were in receipt of direct financial assistance from provincial programmes shareable under the Canada Assistance Plan. Total payments to the provinces under the Plan (including General Assistance, Homes for Special Care, Child Welfare, Health Care, Welfare Services and Work Activity) for the 1982–83 financial year were over $3,190m.; this amount includes the estimated value of income tax points transferred to the province of Quebec by the Department of Finance under the Interim Arrangements Act.

Unemployment Insurance covers about 95% of workers. To be insurable, workers must be employed by the same employer for at least 15 hours a week or make at least $85.00 a week (1984). Neither the self-employed nor workers over 65 may insure their earnings. Benefit rate is 60% of average weekly insurable earnings. Maximum weekly benefit (1984) $255.

Workers' compensation coverage is compulsory for employees in specified trades and industries. Maximum compensation is 75% of gross earnings except in Quebec, Alberta and New Brunswick where it is 90% of net earnings.

The New Horizons Program, established in 1972 and administered by the Department of National Health and Welfare, is designed to encourage the self-determination and community involvement of retired Canadians. From inception late in 1972 until July 1983, close to $119m. had been approved for over 19,000 projects.

DIPLOMATIC REPRESENTATIVES

Of Canada in Great Britain (Macdonald House., Grosvenor Sq., London, W1X 0AB)
High Commissioner: Roy McMurtry.

Of Great Britain in Canada (80 Elgin St., Ottawa, K1P 5K7)
High Commissioner: Sir Derek Day, KCMG.

Of Canada in the USA (1746 Massachusetts Ave., NW, Washington, D.C., 20036)
Ambassador: Allan E. Gotlieb.

Of the USA in Canada (100 Wellington St., Ottawa)
Ambassador: Paul H. Robinson, Jr.

Of Canada to the United Nations
Ambassador: Stephen Lewis.

Books of Reference

Statistical Information: Statistics Canada, Ottawa, has been the official central statistical organization for Canada since 1918. The Bureau, which reports to Parliament through the Minister of Industry, Trade and Commerce, serves as the statistical agency for federal government departments; co-ordinates the statistics of the provincial governments along national lines; and channels all Canadian statistical data to internal organizations. *Statistician Chief of Canada:* Dr Martin B. Wilk.

Publications of Statistics Canada are classified as periodical (issued more frequently than once a year), annual, biennial and occasional publications. The occasional publications frequently supplement the annual reports and usually contain historical information. A complete list is contained in the 1978–79 edition of the Statistics Canada catalogue and supplements, available on request. Official publications include:

The Canada Year Book. Annual, from 1905
Canada, Official Handbook. Annual, from 1930
Canadian Statistical Review. Monthly, with weekly supplements, from 1948
Eleventh Decennial Census of Canada, 1971. Ottawa, 1972
Atlas and Gazetteer of Canada. Dept. of Energy, Mines and Resources. Ottawa, 1969
Cambridge History of the British Empire. Vol. VI. Canada and Newfoundland. Cambridge, 1930
Canadian Almanac and Directory. Toronto. Annual
Canadian Annual Review. Annual, from 1960
Canadian Dictionary: French–English. Toronto, 1970
Canadiana; A List of Publications of Canadian Interest. National Library, Ottawa. Monthly, with annual cumulation. 1951 ff.
Cook, R., *French-Canadian Nationalism; An Anthology.* Toronto, 1970.—*The Maple Leaf Forever; Essays on Nationalism and Politics in Canada.* Toronto, 1971
Creighton, Donald G., *Canada's First Century.* Toronto, 1970.—*Towards the Discovery of Canada.* Toronto, 1974
Dewitt, D. B., and Kirton, J. J., *Canada as a Principal Power: A Study in Foreign Policy.* Toronto, 1983
Dictionnaire Bélisle de la langue française au Canada, dictionnaire oxford. 1970
Dictionnaire canadien; français–anglais–français. Toronto, 1962
Encyclopedia Canadiana. 10 vols. Rev. ed. Ottawa, 1967
Granatstein, J. L., *Twentieth Century Canada.* Toronto, 1983
Hardy, W. G., *From Sea to Sea; Canada, 1850–1920: The Road to Nationhood.* Toronto, 1960
Hockin, T. A., *Government in Canada.* London, 1976
Kerr, D. G. G., *Historical Atlas of Canada.* Toronto, 1960
Leacy, F. H., (ed.) *Historical Statistics of Canada.* Government Printer, Ottawa, 1983
Lower, A. R. M., *Colony to Nation: A History of Canada.* 4th ed. Toronto, 1964
McCann, L. D., (ed.) *Heartland and Hinterland: A Geography of Canada.* Scarborough, Ontario, 1982
Mallory, J. R., *The Structure of Canadian Government.* Toronto, 1971
Moir, J., and Saunders, R., *Northern Destiny: A History of Canada.* Toronto, 1970
Nurgitz, N., and Segal, H., *No Small Measure: The Progressive Conservatives and the Constitution.* Ottawa, 1983
Smith, D. L., (ed.) *History of Canada: An Annotated Bibliography.* Oxford and Santa Barbara, 1983

National Library: The National Library of Canada, Ottawa, Ontario. *Librarian:* J. Guy Sylvestre.

CANADIAN PROVINCES

The 10 provinces have each a separate parliament and administration, with a Lieut.-Governor, appointed by the Governor-General in Council at the head of the executive. They have full powers to regulate their own local affairs and dispose of their revenues, provided only they do not interfere with the action and policy of the central administration. Among the subjects assigned exclusively to the provincial legislatures are: the amendment of the provincial constitution, except as regards the office of the Lieut.-Governor; property and civil rights; direct taxation for revenue purposes; borrowing; management and sale of Crown lands; provincial hospitals, reformatories, etc.; shop, saloon, tavern, auctioneer and other licences for local or provincial purposes; local works and undertakings, except lines of ships, railways, canals, telegraphs, etc., extending beyond the province or connecting with other provinces, and excepting also such works as the Dominion Parliament declares are for the general good; marriages, administration of justice within the province; education.

Local Government. Under the terms of the British North America Act the provinces are given full powers over local government. All local government institutions are, therefore, supervised by the provinces, and are incorporated and function under provincial acts.

The acts under which municipalities operate vary from province to province. A municipal corporation is usually administered by an elected council headed by a mayor or reeve, whose powers to administer affairs and to raise funds by taxation and other methods are set forth in provincial laws, as is the scope of its obligations to, and on behalf of, the citizens. Similarly, the types of municipal corporations, their official designations and the requirements for their incorporation vary between provinces. The following table sets out the classifications as at 1 Jan. 1977.

Type and size of group	*Nfld.*	*PEI*	*NS*	*NB*	*Que.*	*Ont.*	*Man.*
Type:							
Regional municipalities	—	—	—	—	75	39	—
Metropolitan and regional municipalities [1]	—	—	—	—	3	12	—
Counties and regional districts	—	—	—	—	72	27	—
Unitary municipalities	129	36	65	112	1,500	784	185
Cities	2	1	3	6	64	45[2]	5
Towns	127[3]	8	38	21	195	144	35
Villages	—	27	—	85	242	120	40
Rural municipalities[4]	—	—	24	—	999	475	105
Quasi-municipalities[5]	171	—	—	—	—	13	17
Total	300	36	65	112	1,575	836	202
Population size group (1976 census):							
Unitary municipalities—							
Over 100,000	—	—	1	—	4	17	1
50,000 to 99,999	1	—	2	2	14	14	—
10,000 to 49,999	5	1	17	5	72	76	3
Under 10,000	123	35	45	105	1,410	677	181
Total	129	36	65	112	1,500	784	185

Type and size of group	*Sask.*	*Alta.*	*BC*	*YT*	*NWT*	*Canada*
Type:						
Regional municipalities	—	—	28	—	—	142
Metropolitan and regional municipalities[1]	—	—	—	—	—	15
Counties and regional districts	—	—	28	—	—	127
Unitary municipalities	783	327	140	3	7	4,071
Cities	11	10	33	2	1	183
Towns	135	102	10	1	4	820
Villages	344	167	59	—	2	1,086
Rural municipalities[4]	293	48	38	—	—	1,982
Quasi-municipalities[5]	7	22	—	4	10	244
Total	790	349	168	7	17	4,457

[1] Includes urban communities in Quebec; and Metropolitan Toronto, regional municipalities and the district municipality in Ontario.

[2] Includes the 5 boroughs of Metropolitan Toronto. [3] Includes 11 rural districts.

[4] Includes municipalities in Nova Scotia; parishes, townships, united townships and municipalities in Quebec; townships in Ontario; rural municipalities in Manitoba and Saskatchewan; municipal districts and counties in Alberta; and districts in British Columbia.

[5] Includes local government communities, local improvement districts and the metropolitan area in Newfoundland; improvement districts in Ontario and Alberta; local government districts in Manitoba; local improvement districts in Saskatchewan and the Yukon Territory; and hamlets in the Northwest Territories.

Type and size of group	*Sask.*	*Alta.*	*BC*	*YT*	*NWT*	*Canada*
Population size group (1976 census):						
Unitary municipalities—						
Over 100,000	2	2	3	—	—	30
50,000 to 99,999	—	—	9	—	—	42
10,000 to 49,999	6	14	26	1	—	227
Under 10,000	775	311	102	2	7	3,772
Total	783	327	140	3	7	4,071

ALBERTA

HISTORY. The southern half of the province of Alberta was part of Rupert's land which was granted by royal charter in 1670 to the Hudson's Bay Company. The intervention by the North West Company in the fur trade after 1783 led to the establishment of trading posts. In 1869 Rupert's land was transferred from the Hudson's Bay Company (which had absorbed its rival in 1821) to the new Dominion, and in the following year this land was combined with the former Crown land of the North Western Territories to form the Northwest Territories.

In 1882 'Alberta' first appeared as a provisional 'district', consisting of the southern half of the present province. In 1905 the Athabasca district to the north was added when provincial status was granted to Alberta.

Four parties have held office: the Liberals 1905–21; the United Farmers 1921–35; Social Credit 1935–71, and Progressive Conservative since Sept. 1971.

AREA AND POPULATION. The area of the province is 661,188 sq. km; 644,392 sq. km being land area and 16,796 sq. km water area. The population (estimate 1 Oct. 1984) was 2,356,800; the urban population (1982), centres of 1,000 or over, was 1,727,545 and the rural 510,179. Population of the principal cities (30 June 1984): Calgary, 619,814; Edmonton, 560,085; Lethbridge, 58,586; Red Deer, 51,070; Medicine Hat, 41,493; St Albert, 35,529; Fort McMurray, 35,352; Grande Prairie, 24,411; Camrose, 12,571; Leduc, 12,471, Wetaskiwin, 10,022; Lloydminster (Alberta portion), 9,226; Drumheller, 6,671.

Vital statistics, *see* p. 269.

Religion, *see* p. 286.

CLIMATE. A cold continental climate, modified at times by the warm Chinook wind. Rainfall amounts are greatest between May and Sept. Edmonton. Jan. 5°F (–15°C), July 61°F (16·1°C). Annual rainfall 18" (439 mm).

CONSTITUTION AND GOVERNMENT. The constitution of Alberta is contained in the British North America Act of 1867, and amending Acts; also in the Alberta Act of 1905, passed by the Parliament of the Dominion of Canada, which created the province out of the then Northwest Territories. All the provisions of the British North America Act, except those with respect to school lands and the public domain, were made to apply to Alberta as they apply to the older provinces of Canada. On 1 Oct. 1930 the natural resources were transferred from the Dominion to provincial government control. The province is represented by 6 members in the Senate and 21 in the House of Commons of Canada.

The executive is vested nominally in the Lieut.-Governor, who is appointed by the federal government, but actually in the Executive Council or the Cabinet of the legislature. Legislative power is vested in the Assembly in the name of the Queen.

Members of the Legislative Assembly are elected by the universal vote of adults over the age of 18 years.

There are 79 members in the legislature (elected 2 Nov. 1982): 75 Progressive Conservative, 2 New Democratic Party, 2 Independent.

Lieut.-Governor: His Hon. Frank Lynch-Staunton (sworn in 4 Oct. 1979).
Flag: Blue with the shield of the province in the centre.

The members of the Ministry (all Progressive Conservative) are as follows:

Premier, President of Executive Council: Hon. Peter Lougheed.

Provincial Treasurer: Hon. L. D. Hyndman. *Attorney-General and Government House Leader:* Hon. N. Crawford. *Hospitals and Medical Care:* Hon. D. J. Russell. *Transportation:* Hon. M. E. Moore. *Municipal Affairs:* Hon. J. G. J. Koziak. *Federal and Intergovernmental Affairs, Deputy Government House Leader:* Hon. J. D. Horsman. *Economic Development:* Hon. H. Planche. *Advanced Education:* Hon. D. Johnston. *Education:* Hon. D. King. *Labour:* Hon. L. G. Young. *Public Works, Supply and Services:* Hon. T. W. Chambers. *Tourism and Small Business:* Hon. J. A. Adair. *Energy:* Hon. J. B. Zaozirny. *Agriculture:* Hon. E. L. Fjordbotten. *Utilities and Telecommunications:* Hon. R. J. Bogle. *Social Services and Community Health:* Hon. Dr P. N. Webber. *Housing:* Hon. L. R. Shaben. *International Trade:* Hon. H. A. Schmid. *Consumer and Corporate Affairs:* Hon. C. E. Osterman. *Environment:* Hon. F. D. Bradley. *Solicitor-General:* Hon. G. L. Harle. *Culture:* Hon. M. J. LeMessurier. *Recreation and Parks:* Hon. P. Trynchy. *Minister responsible for Native Affairs:* Hon. M. G. Pahl. *Manpower:* Hon. E. D. Isley. *Associate Minister of Public Lands and Wildlife:* Hon. D. Sparrow. *Minister responsible for Workers' Health, Safety and Compensation:* Hon. B. W. Diachuk. *Minister responsible for Personnel Administration:* Hon. G. P. Stevens. *Minister without Portfolio:* Hon. W. E. Payne.

Local Government. The local government units are City, Town, New Town, Village, Summer Village, County, Municipal District and Improvement District.

There are 12 cities in Alberta, namely: Calgary, Camrose, Drumheller, Edmonton, Fort McMurray, Grande Prairie, Lethbridge, Lloydminster, Medicine Hat, Red Deer, St Albert and Wetaskiwin. These cities operate under the Municipal Government Act. The governing body consists of a mayor and a council of from 6 to 20 members. A city can be incorporated by order of the Lieut.-Governor-in-Council. A population of 10,000 is required.

There are no limits of area specified in the statutes for any of the different local government units. The population requirement for a Town as specified in the Municipal Government Act is 1,000 people, and the area at incorporation is that of the original village.

A Village must contain 75 separate and occupied dwellings. The Municipal Government Act requires each dwelling to have been occupied continuously for a period of at least 6 months. A Summer Village must contain 50 separate dwellings.

A rural county area is an area incorporated through an order of the Lieut.-Governor-in-Council under the provisions of the County Act. One board of councillors deal with both municipal and school affairs.

A rural Municipal District is an area which has been incorporated under the Municipal Government Act. In Municipal Districts separate boards control municipal and school affairs.

Areas not incorporated as counties or Municipal Districts are termed Improvement Districts or Special Areas. Sparsely populated, such districts are administered and taxed by the Department of Municipal Affairs of the provincial government. There are no requirements as to the minimum number of residents of a County or Municipal District.

FINANCE. The budgetary revenue and expenditure (in Canadian $) for years ending 31 March were as follows:

	1980–81	*1981–82*	*1982–83*	*1983–84* [1]	*1984–85* [1]
Revenue	6,578,000,000 [2]	7,084,710,000 [2]	7,085,000,000 [2]	8,840,000,000 [2]	9,386,000,000
Expenditure	5,561,000,000	7,043,707,000	9,133,575,000	9,813,262,000	9,644,000,000

[1] Estimates. [2] Excludes funds allocated to Alberta Heritage Savings Trust Fund.

Personal income *per capita* (1982), $14,137.

ENERGY AND NATURAL RESOURCES

Oil. In 1983, 64,464,000 cu. metres of crude oil and condensate were produced with gross sales value of $12,282,894,000. Alberta produced 84·9% of Canada's crude petroleum output in 1983. Production of natural gas by-product was 17,097,000 cu. metres, valued at $2,523,359,000.

The 4 major deposits of oil sands are found in areas totalling 106,600 sq. km in northern and eastern Alberta. There are 4 major deposits of oil sands, the Athabasca, Cold Lake, Peace River and Buffalo Head Hills deposits; total area, 105,320 sq. km. A limited part of the deposits along the Athabasca River can be exploited through open-pit mining. The rest of the Athabasca, and all the deposits in the other areas, are deeper reserves which must be developed through in situ techniques. These reserves reach depths of 760 metres.

One recovery plant, situated 25 miles north of Fort McMurray, began production in 1967. The deposit being produced is sufficiently close to the surface to permit strip mining. A second plant, to produce 20,000 cu. metres per day of synthetic crude oil, began production in 1978.

Gas. Natural gas is found in abundance in numerous localities. In 1983, 61,632,000 cu. metres valued at $6,227,597,000 were produced.

Minerals. In 1983 the ultimate remaining recoverable coal resources of Alberta were estimated at 18,400m. tonnes.

Value of total mineral production increased from $20,913,347,000 in 1982 to $22,218,213,000 in 1983.

Agriculture. Total area of farms (1981) 47,218,170 acres; improved land, 30,951,142; under crops, 20,858,765; improved pasture, 3,907,830; summer fallow, 5,449,831; other improved land, 734,716; unimproved land, 16,267,083; woodland, 1,217,420; other unimproved land, 15,049,663.

For particulars of agricultural production and livestock, *see under* CANADA, pp. 279–80. Farm cash receipts in 1983 totalled $3,704,859,000, of which crops contributed $2,018,447,000; livestock and products, $1,659·04m., and other sources, $126,572,000.

Forestry. Total woodland (1981) 1·2m acres. Alberta has an estimated net merchantable volume of 1,700m. cu. metres of timber comprised of 700m. cu. metres of hardwood and 1,000m. cu. metres of softwood. In 1983–84, 6,173,328 cu. metres of lumber and plywood were produced.

Fisheries. The lakes of the province contain whitefish, pike and tullibee. Commercial catches are marketed through the Freshwater Fish Marketing Corporation which was inaugurated in May 1969 as the result of an agreement between the federal government and the provinces for the buying and exporting of freshwater fish. Marketed value of commercially caught fish 1983–84 was $2,735,091. This value includes fish not marketed through the corporation.

INDUSTRY. The leading manufacturing industries are food and beverages, petroleum refining, metal fabricating, wood industries, primary metal, chemical and chemical products and non-metallic mineral products industries. There were in 1981 approximately 2,452 manufacturing establishments, in which were employed about 86,356 persons, who earned in salaries and wages $1,853,709,000.

Manufacturing shipments had a total value of $12,762·53m. in 1983. Chief among these shipments were: Food and beverages, $3,642,538,000; petroleum and coal products, $3,550,007,000; chemicals and chemical products, $1,497,611,000; metal fabricating, $633,637,000; primary metals, $529,803,000; non-metallic mineral products, $504,617,000; printing and publishing, $456,806,000; wood, $413,396,000; paper, $362,837,000; machinery, $359,525,000; electrical products, $157,748,000; textiles, $110,798,000.

Total retail sales (1983) $11,304m.

Tourism is of increasing importance and in 1983 contributed $1,990·3m. to the economy.

COMMUNICATIONS

Roads. In 1983 there were 151,470 km of roads and highways, including 102,681 km gravelled and 15,237 km paved.

At 31 March 1984 there were 2,055,262 motor vehicles registered, including 1,277,502 passenger cars, 438,799 trucks, 247,629 trailers, 8,023 buses and 59,456 motor cycles.

Railways. In 1984 the length of main railway lines was 10,178·2 km. In 1984 there was a rail rapid transit network in Edmonton (10·3 km) and Calgary (22·2 km).

Post and Telecommunications. Alberta's modern telephone system is owned and operated by the provincial government, except in the city of Edmonton (owned and operated by Edmonton) and some rural lines. There were 1,057,530 telephones in service in April 1984.

JUSTICE AND EDUCATION

Justice. The Supreme Judicial authority of the province is the Court of Appeal. Judges of the Court of Appeal and Court of Queen's Bench are appointed by the Dominion Government and hold office until retirement at the age of 75. There are courts of lesser jurisdiction in both civil and criminal matters. The Court of Queen's Bench has full jurisdiction over civil proceedings. A Provincial Court which has jurisdiction in civil matters up to $1,000 is presided over by provincially appointed judges. Juvenile Courts have power to try boys and girls 16 and under for offences against the Juvenile Delinquents Act.

The jurisdiction of all criminal courts in Alberta is enacted in the provisions of the Criminal Code. The system of procedure in civil and criminal cases conforms as nearly as possible to the English system.

Education. Schools of all grades are included under the term of public school (including those in the separate school system which are publicly supported). The same board of trustees controls the schools from kindergarten to university entrance. In 1982–83 there were 423,690 pupils enrolled in elementary, junior high schools and high schools. The University of Alberta (in Edmonton), organized in 1907, had, in 1983–84, 22,908 full-time students. The University of Calgary, formerly part of the University of Alberta and autonomous from April 1966, had in 1983–84, 14,557 full-time students. The University of Lethbridge, organized in 1966, had in 1983–84, 2,442 full-time students. The Athabasca University had in 1983–84, 9,496 full-time students. The full-time enrolment at Alberta's 10 public colleges totalled 14,513 students in 1983–84.

Books of Reference

Statistical Information: The Alberta Bureau of Statistics (Dept. of Treasury, Edmonton), which was established in 1939, collects, compiles and distributes information relative to Alberta. Among its publications are: *Alberta Statistical Review* (Annual).—*Alberta Statistical Review* (Quarterly).—*Alberta Economic Accounts* (Annual).—*Alberta Pay and Benefits* (Annual).—*Retail and Service Trade Statistics, Alberta* (Annual).—*Alberta Facts* (Annual).—*Principal Manufacturing Statistics, Alberta* (Annual).—*Population Projections, Alberta* (Occasional).—*Quarterly Population Growth, Alberta* (Quarterly).—*Place-to-Place Price Comparisons for Selected Alberta Communities* (Annual).
Dept. of Economic Development, *Alberta Profile.* Edmonton, (Annual)

Barr, J. J., *The Dynasty: The Rise and Fall of Social Credit in Alberta.* Toronto, 1974
MacGregor, J. G., *A History of Alberta.* 2nd ed. Edmonton, 1981
Richards, J., *Prairie Capitalism: Power and Influence in the New West.* Toronto, 1979
Wiebe, Rudy., *Alberta, a Celebration.* Edmonton, 1979

BRITISH COLUMBIA

HISTORY. Vancouver Island was organized as a colony in 1849; the mainland as far as the watershed of the Rocky Mountains was organized as a colony following a gold rush on the Fraser River in 1858. The two were united as the colony of British Columbia in 1866; this became a Canadian Province in 1871.

AREA AND POPULATION. British Columbia has an area of 948,596 sq. km. The capital is Victoria. The province is bordered westerly by the Pacific ocean and Alaska Panhandle, northerly by the Yukon and Northwest Territories, easterly by the Province of Alberta and southerly by the USA along the 49th parallel. A chain of islands, the largest of which are Vancouver Island and the Queen Charlotte Islands, affords protection to the mainland coast.

The June 1981 census population was 2,744,467; estimate, 1984, 2,870,700.

The principal cities and their populations (1983) are as follows: Greater Vancouver, 1,310,600; Greater Victoria, 240,400; Prince George, 68,628; Kamloops, 64,434; Kelowna, 60,827; Nanaimo, 49,347; Penticton, 24,142; Vernon, 20,508; Port Alberni, 19,555; Prince Rupert, 16,786; Cranbrook, 16,513; Fort St. John, 14,174.

Vital statistics, *see* p. 269.

Religion, *see* p. 286.

CLIMATE. The climate is cool temperate, but mountain influences affect temperatures and rainfall very considerably. Driest months occur in summer. Vancouver. Jan. 36°F (2·2°C), July 64°F (17·8°C). Annual rainfall 58" (1,458 mm).

CONSTITUTION AND GOVERNMENT. British Columbia (then known as New Caledonia) originally formed part of the Hudson's Bay Company's concession. In 1849 Vancouver Island and in 1858 British Columbia were constituted Crown Colonies; in 1866 the two colonies amalgamated. The British North America Act of 1867 provided for eventual admission into Canadian Confederation, and on 20 July 1871 British Columbia became the sixth province of the Dominion.

British Columbia has a unicameral legislature of 57 elected members. Government policy is determined by the Executive Council responsible to the Legislature. The Lieut.-Governor is appointed by the Governor-General of Canada, usually for a term of 5 years, and is the head of the executive government of the province.

Lieut.-Governor: The Hon. Robert Gordon Rogers.

Flag: A banner of the arms, *i.e.*, blue and white wavy stripes charged with a setting sun in gold, across the top of a Union Flag with a gold coronet in the centre.

The Legislative Assembly is elected for a maximum term of 5 years. Every male or female Canadian citizen 18 years and over, having resided a minimum of 6 months in the province, duly registered, is entitled to vote. Representation of the parties at 5 May 1983: Social Credit Party, 35; New Democratic Party, 22; total, 57.

The province is represented in the Federal Parliament by 28 members in the House of Commons, and 6 Senators.

The Executive Council was composed as follows, Sept. 1984:

Premier: William Richards Bennett.

Agriculture and Food. Harvey W. Schroeder. *Attorney-General:* Brian R. D. Smith. *Consumer and Corporate Affairs:* James J. Hewitt. *Education:* John H. Heinrich. *Energy, Mines and Petroleum Resources:* Stephen Rogers. *Environment, Lands, Parks and Housing:* A. J. Brummet. *Finance:* Hugh A. Curtis. *Forests:* Thomas M. Waterland. *Health:* James Nielsen. *Industry and Small Business Development:* Donald M. Phillips. *Intergovernmental Relations:* Garde B. Gardom. *Labour:* Robert H. McClelland. *Municipal Affairs:* William S. Ritchie. *Provincial Secretary:* James R. Chabot. *Tourism:* Claude Richmond. *Transportation and Highways:* Alexander V. Fraser. *Universities, Science and Communications:* Patrick L. McGeer.

Agent-General in London: Alexander H. Harte, QC (British Columbia House, 1 Regent St., London, SW1Y 4NS).

Local Government. Vancouver City was incorporated by statute and operates under the provisions of the Vancouver Charter of 1953 and amendments. This is the only incorporated area in British Columbia not operating under the provisions of the Municipal Act. Under this Act municipalities are divided into the following classes: *(a)* a village with a population between 500 and 2,500, governed by a council consisting of a mayor and 4 aldermen; *(b)* a town with a population between 2,500 and 5,000, governed by a council consisting of a mayor and 4 aldermen; *(c)* a city where the population exceeds 5,000 governed by a council consisting of a mayor and 6 or 8 aldermen depending on population; *(d)* a district where the area exceeds 810 hectares and the average density is less than 5 persons per hectare, governed by a council consisting of a mayor and 6 or 8 aldermen depending on population.

There are two other forms of local government: the regional district covering a number of areas both incorporated and unincorporated, governed by a board of directors; and the improvement district governed by a board of 3 trustees.

Revenue for municipal services is derived mainly from real-property taxation, although additional revenue is derived from licence fees, business taxes, fines, public utility projects and grants-in-aid from the provincial government.

ECONOMY

Budget. Current provincial revenue and expenditure, including all capital expenditures, in Canadian $1m. for fiscal years ending 31 March:

	1980–81	*1981–82*	*1982–83*	*1983–84*
Revenue	5,802·7	6,903·4	6,529·1	7,262·6
Expenditure	6,059·5	7,087·5	7,513·3	8,339·9

The main sources of current revenue are the income taxes, contributions from the federal government, and privileges, licences and natural resources taxes and royalties.

The main items of expenditure in 1983–84 (preliminary) are as follows: Health and social services, $3,889m.; education, $1,728·7m.; transport and communication, $800m.; natural resources and industry, $446·3m.; protection of persons and property, $369·1m.

Banking. Cheques cashed (in $1m.): 1979, 286,902; 1980, 382,836; 1981, 519,386; 1982, 488,102; 1983, 523,629.

ENERGY AND NATURAL RESOURCES

Electricity. Generation in 1983 totalled 47,279m. kwh. of which a net 4,975m. kwh. were exported. Consumption within the province was 44,749m. kwh.

Minerals. Copper, coal, natural gas, crude oil, molybdenum and silver are the most important minerals produced. The 1983 total of mineral production was estimated at $2,859·6m. Total value of mineral fuels produced in 1983 was estimated at: Coal, $560·7m.; oil and gas, $896·8m.

Agriculture. Only 2·4m. hectares or 3% of the total land area is arable or potentially arable. Farm cash receipts, in 1983, were $901·6m.

Forestry. About 55% of British Columbia's land is forest land, with 47·8m. hectares bearing commercial forest. Over 94% of the forest area is owned or administered by the provincial government. The total cut from forests in 1983 was 71·4m. cu. metres.

Fisheries. In 1983 the wholesale market value of fish products was estimated at $441m.

INDUSTRY AND TRADE

Industry. The selling value of factory shipments from all manufacturing industries reached an estimated $16,812m. in 1983.

Commerce. Exports through British Columbia customs ports during 1983 totalled $15,691m. in value, while imports amounted to $6,450m. About 40% of exports through British Columbia customs ports are products from other provinces, primarily grains, potash and fuels from the Prairie Provinces. USA is the largest market for products exported through British Columbia customs ports ($6,248·6m. in 1983) followed by Japan ($3,902·7m.).

Exports were valued at $9,925m. in 1983. The leading exports were: Lumber, $2,631·8m.; pulp, $1,427·2m.; coal, $821·87m.; newsprint, $577·5m.; natural gas, $446·1m.; copper ore and ingots, $370·8m.; fisheries products, $361·1m.; aluminium ingots, $306·8m.

COMMUNICATIONS

Roads. At 31 March 1984 there were 43,668 km of provincial roads and rights of way in the province, of which 18,242 km were paved.

Railways. The province is served by two transcontinental railways, the Canadian Pacific Railway and the Canadian National Railway. British Columbia is also served by the publicly owned British Columbia Railway, the Railway Freight Service of the B.C. Hydro and Power Authority, the Northern Alberta Railways Company and the Burlington Northern Inc. The combined route-mileage of mainline track operated by the CPR, CNR and BCR totals 7,344 km. The system also includes CPR and CNR railcar barge connections to Vancouver Island, between Prince Rupert and Alaska, and interchanges with American railways at southern border points.

Aviation. International airports are located at Vancouver and Victoria. Daily interprovincial and intraprovincial flights serve all main population centres. Small public and private airstrips are located throughout the province.

Shipping. The major ports are Vancouver, New Westminster, Victoria, Nanaimo and Prince Rupert. The volume of domestic and international cargo handled during 1983 was 47m. tonnes and 55m. tonnes respectively.

The British Columbia Ferries connect Vancouver Island with the mainland and also provide service to other coastal points. Service by other ferry systems is also provided between Vancouver Island and the USA. The Alaska State Ferries connect Prince Rupert with centres in Alaska.

Post and Broadcasting. The British Columbia Telephone Company have 1·3m. telephones in service. In March 1983 there were 63 AM radio, 18 FM radio and 12 television stations originating in British Columbia. In addition there were 539 rebroadcasting stations in the province.

EDUCATION AND WELFARE

Education. Education, free up to Grade XII levels, is financed jointly from municipal and provincial government revenues. Attendance is compulsory from the age of 6 to 15. There were 497,312 pupils enrolled in public schools from kindergarten to Grade XII in Sept. 1983.

The universities had a full-time enrolment of 37,500 for 1983–84 (preliminary). They include University of British Columbia, Vancouver; University of Victoria, Victoria and Simon Fraser University, Burnaby. The regional colleges are Camosun College, Victoria; Capilano College, North Vancouver; Cariboo College, Kamloops; College of New Caledonia, Prince George; Douglas College, New Westminster; East Kootenay Community College, Cranbrook; Fraser Valley College, Chilliwack/Abbotsford; Kwantlen College, Surrey; Malaspina College, Nanaimo; North Island College, Comox; Northern Lights College, Dawson Creek/Fort St John; Northwest Community College, Terrace/Prince Rupert; Okanagan College, Kelowna with branches at Salmon Arm and Vernon, Selkirk College, Castlegar; Vancouver Community College, Vancouver.

There are also the British Columbia Institute of Technology, Burnaby; Emily Carr College of Art and Design, Vancouver; Justice Institute of British Columbia, Vancouver; Open Learning Institute, Richmond; Pacific Marine Training Institute, North Vancouver; Pacific Vocational Institute, Burnaby/Maple Ridge/

Richmond. A televised distance education and special programmes through KNOW, the Knowledge Network of the West is provided.

Health. The Government operates a hospital insurance scheme giving universal coverage after a qualifying period of 3 months' residence in the province. The province has come under a national medicare scheme which is partially subsidized by the provincial government and partially by the federal government.

Books of Reference

Statistical Information: Central Statistics Bureau (Ministry of Industry and Small Business Development, Hon. Don Phillips—Minister, Parliament Buildings, Victoria, B.C.V8V 1 × 4), collects, compiles and distributes information relative to the Province.

Publications include *B.C. Economic Bulletin* (bi-monthly); *B.C. Industry Review* (annual); *Manufacturers' Directory; External Trade Report* (Annual); *B.C. Manual of Facts and Statistics* Annual).

Ministry of Finance, *British Columbia Financial and Economic Review.* Victoria, B.C. (Annual)

Fifteenth British Columbia Natural Resources Conference, *Inventory of the Natural Resources of British Columbia,* 1964

MANITOBA

HISTORY. The Hudson's Bay Company formed a colony on the Red River in 1812. This being part of territory annexed to Canada in 1870. The Metis colonists (part-Indian, mostly French-speaking, Catholic) objected to the arrangements for the purchase of the Company territory by Canada and the province of Manitoba was created to accommodate them. It was extended northwards and westwards in 1881 and to Hudson Bay in 1912.

AREA AND POPULATION. The area of the province is 250,946 sq. miles (649,046 sq. km), of which 211,721 sq. miles are land and 39,225 sq. miles water. From north to south it is 793 km and the widest point is 493 km.

The population (June 1984) was 1,056,500. Population of the principal cities (June 1983): Winnipeg (capital), 600,700; Brandon, 36,242; Thompson, 14,288; Portage la Prairie, 13,086; Selkirk, 10,037; Flin Flon, 7,894.

Vital statistics, *see* p. 269.

Religion, *see* p. 286.

CLIMATE. The climate is cold continental, with very severe winters but pleasantly warm summers. Rainfall amounts are greatest in the months May to Sept. Winnipeg. Jan. -3°F (-19·4°C), July 67°F (19·4°C). Annual rainfall 21″ (539 mm).

CONSTITUTION AND GOVERNMENT. Manitoba was known as the Red River Settlement before its entry into the Dominion in 1870. The provincial government is administered by a Lieut.-Governor and a legislative assembly of 57 members elected for 5 years. Women were enfranchised in 1916. The Electoral Division Act, 1955, created 57 single-member constituencies and abolished the transferable vote. The Electoral Divisions Act, 1979, created 27 rural electoral divisions, and 30 urban electoral divisions. The province is represented by 6 members in the Senate and 14 in the House of Commons of Canada.

Lieut.-Governor: Pearl McGonigal (sworn in 23 Oct. 1981).
Flag: The British Red Ensign with the shield of the province in the fly.

State of parties in the Legislative Assembly (sworn in 30 Nov. 1981): New Democratic Party, 32; Progressive Conservative, 23; Independent, 2.

The members of the New Democratic Party Ministry are as follows (Sept. 1982):

Premier, President of the Council, Minister of Federal-Provincial Relations: Howard Russell Pawley.

Health, Sport, Minister charged with the administration of The Boxing and

Wrestling Commission Act, The Fitness and Amateur Sport Act, The Manitoba Lotteries Foundation Act: Laurent Louis Desjardins. *Business Development and Tourism, Minister responsible for the administration of the Manitoba Telephone Act:* Samuel Uskiw. *Employment Services and Economic Security:* Leonard Salusbury Evans. *Agriculture:* Billie Uruski. *Government Services:* A. R. Adam. *Co-operative Development:* Jay Marine Cowan. *Energy and Mines, Minister responsible for the administration of the Manitoba Hydro Act:* Wilson D. Parasiuk. *Finance, Crown Investments, Minister responsible for The Civil Service Act, The Civil Service Superannuation Act, The Civil Service Special Supplementary Severance Benefit Act, The Public Servants Insurance Act, The Manitoba Development Corporation Act (with respect to A. E. McKenzie Co. Ltd):* Victor Schroeder. *Education:* Maureen Lucille Hemphill. *Culture, Heritage and Recreation, Industry, Trade and Technology, Minister responsible for and charged with the administration of The Manitoba Data Services Act, The Manitoba Development Corporation Act (except with respect to A. E. McKenzie Co. Ltd):* Eugene Michael Kostyra. *Attorney-General, Consumer and Corporate Affairs, Keeper of the Great Seal, Minister responsible for the administration of The Liquor Control Act:* Roland Penner. *Community Services:* Muriel Ann Smith. *Natural Resources:* Alvin Henry Mackling. *Labour, Urban Affairs, Minister responsible for the Status of Women:* Mary Elizabeth Dolin. *Northern Affairs, Minister responsible for and charged with the administration of The Communities Economic Development Fund Act, The Manitoba Natural Resources Development Act (with respect to Channel Area Loggers Ltd or to Moose Lake Loggers Ltd) and Manitoba Forestry Resources Ltd:* Jerry Thomas Storie. *Highways and Transportation:* John S. Plohman. *Housing, Minister charged with the administration of The Manitoba Public Insurance Corporation Act:* John Bucklaschuk. *Municipal Affairs:* Andrue Anstett. *Environment and Workplace Safety and Health:* Gerard Lecuyer.

Local Government. Rural Manitoba is organized into rural municipalities which vary widely in size. Some have only 4 townships (a township is 36 sq. miles), while the largest has 22 townships. The province has 105 rural municipalities, as well as 35 incorporated towns, 40 incorporated villages and 5 incorporated cities.

On 1 Jan. 1972, the cities and towns comprising the metropolitan area of Winnipeg were amalgamated to form the City of Winnipeg. A mayor and council are elected to a central government, but councillors also sit on 'community committees' which represent the areas or wards they serve. These committees are advised by non-elected residents of the area on provision of municipal services within the community committee jurisdiction. Taxing powers and overall budgeting rest with the central council. The mayor is elected at the same time as the councillors in a city-wide vote. Revisions to the City of Winnipeg Act came into effect with the municipal elections held in Oct. 1977.

Since Jan. 1945, 17 Local Government Districts have been formed in the less densely populated areas of the province. They are administered by a provincially appointed person, who acts on the advice of locally elected councils.

In the extreme north, many communities have locally elected councils, while others are administered directly by the Department of Northern Affairs. This department provides most of the funding in all these northern settlements.

FINANCE. Provincial revenue and expenditure (current account) for fiscal years ending 31 March (in Canadian $):

	1980–81	*1981–82*	*1982–83* [1]	*1983–84* [1]	*1984–85* [2]
Revenue	1,968,405,039	2,180,821,120	2,408,961,000	2,799,688,000	2,968,950,900
Expenditure	2,057,913,309	2,431,863,998	2,843,608,000	3,226,403,000	3,457,626,900

[1] Preliminary unaudited. [2] Budgetted

ENERGY AND NATURAL RESOURCES

Electricity. The total generating capacity of Manitoba's power stations is 4·1m. kw. The Manitoba Hydro system, owned by the province, provides most of this power, while the city-owned Winnipeg Hydro provides about 190,000 kw. The systems have about 423,542 customers and consumption was 14·4m. kwh. in 1983.

Oil. Crude oil production in 1983 was valued at $153m. for the 730,000 cu. metres produced.

Minerals. Total value of minerals in 1983 was about $659·4m. Principal minerals mined are nickel, zinc, copper, and small quantities of gold and silver. Manitoba has the world's largest deposits of caesium ore.

Agriculture. Rich farmland is the main primary resource, although the area of Manitoba in farms is only about 14% of the total land area. In 1983 the total value of agricultural production in Manitoba was $1,899·7m., with $1,305·2m. from crops, $594·5m. from livestock and from the sale of other products including furs, hides and honey.

Forestry. About 40% of the land area is wooded, of which 139,000 sq. km is productive forest land. Total sales of wood-using industries (1982, estimate) $441m.

Fur Trade. Value of fur production to the trapper was $3·5m. in 1983–84.

Fisheries. From 22,000 sq. miles of rivers and lakes fisheries production was about $21m. in 1981–82. Whitefish, sauger, pickerel, pike, trout and perch are the principal varieties of fish caught.

INDUSTRY AND TRADE

Industry. Manufacturing, the largest industry in the province, encompasses almost every major industrial activity in Canada. Estimated shipments in 1983 totalled $4,819·3m. Manufacturing employed about 59,000 persons. Due to the agricultural base of the province, the food and beverage group of industries is by far the largest, valued at $1,563·4m. in 1982, accounting for about 32·4% of the total value. The next largest segments are machinery, $354·3m. (7·4%), transportation equipment, $339·7m. (7%) and clothing and textiles, $329·7m. (6·8%).

Trade. Products grown and manufactured in Manitoba find ready markets in other areas of Canada, in the USA, particularly the upper midwest region, and in other countries. Export shipments to foreign countries from Manitoba in 1983 were valued at about $1,364·9m., with $1,093·4m. (80·1%) going to the US. Of total exports about 29% are raw materials and about 71% are processed and manufactured products.

Tourism. In 1982, Canadian, US and overseas tourists numbered 2·4m. contributing $592m. to the economy.

COMMUNICATIONS

Roads. Highways and provincial roads totalled 18,877 km in 1983.

Railways. At 31 Dec. 1981 the province had 6,430 km of track, not including industrial track, yards and sidings.

Aviation. A total of 102 licensed commercial air carriers operate from bases in Manitoba, as well as 8 regularly scheduled major national and international airlines.

Post. All of the province's 765,902 (1983) telephones are dial-operated.

EDUCATION. Education is controlled through locally elected school divisions. There are about 200,000 children enrolled in the province's elementary and secondary schools. Manitoba has 3 universities with an enrolment of about 45,000 during the 1983–84 year; the University of Manitoba, founded in 1877, in Winnipeg, the University of Winnipeg, and Brandon University. Expenditure (estimate) on education in the 1984–85 fiscal year was $654m.

Three community colleges, in Brandon, The Pas and Winnipeg, offer 2-year diploma courses in a number of fields, as well as specialized training in many trades. They also give a large number and variety of shorter courses, both at their campuses and in many communities throughout the province.

Books of Reference

General Information: Inquiries may be addressed to the Information Services Branch, Room 29, Legislative Building, Winnipeg, R3C OV8.

The Department of Agriculture publishes: *Year Book of Manitoba Agriculture*
Information Services Branch publishes: *Manitoba Facts*
Manitoba Statistical Review. Manitoba Bureau of Statistics, Quarterly
Tenth Census of Canada: Manitoba. Statistics Canada, 1971

NEW BRUNSWICK

HISTORY. Touched by Jacques Cartier in 1534, New Brunswick was first explored by Samuel de Champlain in 1604. It was ceded by the French in the Treaty of Utrecht in 1713 and became a permanent British possession in 1763. It was separated from Nova Scotia and became a province in June 1784, as a result of the great influx of United Empire Loyalists. Responsible government came into being in 1848, and consisted of an executive council, a legislative council (later abolished) and a House of Assembly.

AREA AND POPULATION. The area of the province is 28,354 sq. miles (73,000 sq. km), of which 27,633 sq. miles (71,569 sq. km) are land area. The population (census 1976) was 677,250. Of the total population (1971) about 58% are of British origin, 37% French and the remainder are principally of Netherlands, German and Scandinavian descent, and in 1980 there were about 5,300 Indians. Census population of urban centres: Saint John, 85,956; Moncton, 55,934; Fredericton (capital), 45,248; Bathurst, 16,301; Edmundston, 12,710; Campbellton, 9,282.

Vital statistics, *see* p. 269.

Religion, *see* p. 286.

CLIMATE. A cool temperate climate, with rain at all seasons but temperatures modified by the influence of the Gulf Stream. Saint John. Jan. 19°F (–7·2°C), July 65°F (18·3°C). Annual rainfall 51″ (1,278 mm).

CONSTITUTION AND GOVERNMENT. The government is vested in a Lieut.-Governor and a Legislative Assembly of 58 members each of whom is individually elected to represent the voters in one constituency or riding. A simultaneous translation system is used in the Assembly. Any Canadian subject of full age and 6 months' residence is entitled to vote. As a result of the provincial election held on 23 Oct. 1978 and subsequent by-elections, the Assembly is composed of 30 Progressive Conservatives and 28 Liberals. The province has 10 members in the Canadian Senate and 10 members in the federal House of Commons.

Lieut.-Governor: George F. S. Stanley (appointed 23 Dec. 1981).

Flag: A banner of the Arms, *i.e.*, yellow charged with a black heraldic ship on wavy lines of blue and white; across the top a red band with a gold lion.

The members of the Progressive Conservative Ministry are as follows (Dec. 1982):

Premier and President of the Executive Council: Richard Hatfield.

Attorney-General and Justice: Fernand Dube, QC. *Finance and Minister Responsible for New Brunswick Housing Corporation:* John B. M. Baxter, QC. *Chairman of the Treasury Board:* Harold N. Fanjoy. *Supply and Services:* Edwin G. Allen. *Transportation:* Wilfred G. Bishop. *Natural Resources and Minister Responsible for Energy Policy:* Gerald Merrithew. *Agriculture and Rural Development:* Malcolm N. MacLeod. *Health:* Charles G. Gallagher. *Social Services:* Nancy E. Clark Teed. *Labour and Manpower:* Joseph W. Mombourquette. *Education:*

Mabel M. DeWare. *Municipal Affairs:* Yvon R. Poitras. *Commerce and Development:* Paul W. Dawson. *Fisheries:* Jean Gauvin. *Environment:* C. W. (Bill) Harmer. *Tourism:* Omer Leger. *Youth and Recreation:* Leslie I. Hull. *Cultural and Historical Resources:* Jean-Pierre Ouellet.

Local Government. Under the reforms introduced in 1967 the province has assumed complete administrative and financial responsibility for education, health, welfare and administration of justice. Local government is now restricted to provision of services of a strictly local nature. Under the new municipal structure, units include existing and new cities, towns and villages. Counties have disappeared as municipal units. Areas with limited populations have become local service districts. The former local improvement districts have become towns, villages or local service districts depending on their size.

FINANCE. The ordinary budget (in Canadian $) is shown as follows (financial years ended 31 March):

	1981	*1982*	*1983*	*1984*
Gross revenue	1,534,987,829	1,772,232,788	1,945,154,091	2,213,420,941
Gross expenditure	1,505,252,819	1,795,554,444	2,147,955,484	2,344,948,500

Funded debt and capital loans outstanding (exclusive of Treasury Bills) as of 31 March 1984 was $2,428m. Sinking funds held by the province at 31 March 1984, $630m. The ordinary budget excludes capital spending.

ENERGY AND NATURAL RESOURCES

Electricity. Hydro-electric, thermal and nuclear generating stations of the New Brunswick Electric Power Commission had an installed capacity of 3,136,576 kw. at 31 March 1984, consisting of 14 generating stations. The Mactaquac hydro-electric development near Fredericton, has a nominal capacity of 600,000 kw. The largest thermal generating station, Coleson Cove, near Saint John, has over 1m. kw. of installed capacity. Atlantic Canada's first nuclear generating station, a 630,000 kw. CANDU plant built on a promontory jutting out in the Bay of Fundy, near Saint John, went into commercial operation in Jan. 1983. New Brunswick is electrically inter-connected with utilities in neighbouring provinces of Quebec, Nova Scotia and Prince Edward Island, as well as the New England States. Electricity export sales accounted for over 40% of revenue in 1983–84; energy purchases, mainly from the large Hydro Quebec system, supplied about 23% of in-province energy requirements.

Minerals. A considerable variety of metals, industrial minerals, fuels and structural materials occur in the province. These include zinc, lead, copper, cadmium, bismuth, nickel, gold, silver, cobalt, tungsten, tin, molybdenum, antimony, potash, salt, glauberite, limestone, dolomite, gypsum, oil, gas, coal, uranium, oil shales, sand, gravel, clay, peat, diatomite and marl. Not all have been explored sufficiently. 52% of the value of minerals produced in 1983, which totalled $513m., was attributed to zinc produced from 2 mines in the Bathurst–Newcastle area. In Canada, New Brunswick ranks second in zinc production, second in lead, third in silver and fifth in copper. Exploration continues in this area. The antimony mine at Lake George, near Fredericton, is scheduled to resume production during 1985. The tungsten-molybdenum mine at Mount Pleasant continues operation. The Potash Company of America has commenced production of potash and salt near Sussex, while Denison-Potacan expects to commence production in 1985. A third company is now in the exploration stage and will make a decision shortly concerning production. Limestone and gypsum are quarried at Havelock and Hillsborough and small quantities of oil and natural gas continue to be produced from the Stoney Creek field south of Moncton. Coal is mined at Grand Lake and exploration is underway for other deposits of this important energy resource.

Agriculture. The total area under crops is estimated at 130,526 hectares, exclusive of improved pasture land (41,479 hectares). Farms numbered 4,063 and averaged 107·8 hectares each (census 1981). Potatoes account for 30% of total farm cash income. Mixed farming is common throughout the province. Dairy farming is centred around the larger urban areas, and is located mainly along the Saint John River Valley and in the south-eastern sections of the province. For particulars of agricultural production and livestock, *see under* CANADA, pp. 279–80. Farm cash receipts in 1983 were approximately $195·1m.

Forestry. New Brunswick contains some 62,000 sq. km of productive forest lands. The gross value of forest production is over $1m. and it accounts for almost one-quarter of all goods produced in the province. The pulp and paper and allied industry group is the largest component of the industry contributing about 70% of the value of output. Timber-using plants employ about 16,000 men for all aspects of the forest industry, including harvesting, processing and transportation. Practically all forest products are exported from the province's numerous ports and harbours near which many of the mills are located or sent by road or rail to the USA.

Fisheries. Commercial fishing is one of the most important primary industries of the province. Nearly 50 commercial species of fish and shellfish are landed, of which scallop, shrimp, crab, herring and cod are the most valuable. Landings in 1983 (109,111 tonnes) amounted to $79·7m. In 1983 there were 125 fish processing plants employing more than 11,000 people in peak periods. The total market value of fish products in 1982 was approximately $288·9m. Estimate (1983) $320m. Exports (1983) $210·9m.

INDUSTRY. In 1984 there were 1,357 manufacturing and processing establishments, employing about 37,950 persons. New Brunswick's location, with deep-water harbours open throughout the year and container facilities at Saint John, makes it ideal for exporting. Industries include food and beverages, paper and allied industries, timber products. About 20% of the industrial labour force work in Saint John.

TOURISM. Tourism is a major industry. During 1983, more than 4m. tourists spent approximately $375m.

COMMUNICATIONS

Roads. There are about 2,133 km of arterial highways and 2,321 km of collector roads, over 99% of which are hard-surfaced. 12,910 km of local roads provide access to most areas in the province. The main highway system, including 617 km of the Trans-Canada Highway, links the province with the principal roads in Quebec and Nova Scotia, as well as the Interstate Highway System in the eastern seaboard states of the USA. Passenger vehicles, 31 March 1984, numbered 259,102; commercial vehicles, 113,640; motor cycles, 11,640.

Railways. New Brunswick is served by main lines of both Canadian Pacific and Canadian National railways.

Post and Broadcasting. In 1980 the New Brunswick Telephone Co. Ltd had 389,466 telephones in service. The province is served by 16 radio stations. Twelve are privately owned and 4 owned by the Canadian Broadcasting Corporation. Three stations broadcast in the French language, 1 is bilingual and the CBC International Service broadcasts in several languages from its station at Sackville. The province is served by 3 television stations, 1 of which broadcasts in French.

Newspapers. New Brunswick had (1983) 5 daily newspapers, and 23 weekly newspapers, 7 in French or bilingual.

EDUCATION. Public education is free and non-sectarian. There are 4 universities. The University of New Brunswick at Fredericton (founded 13 Dec. 1785 by the Loyalists, elevated to university status in 1823, reorganized as the University of New Brunswick in 1859) had 6,556 full-time students at the Fredericton campus and 914 full-time students at the Saint John campus (1983–84); Mount Allison University at Sackville had 1,625 full-time students; the Université de Moncton at Moncton, 3,203 full-time students; St Thomas University at Fredericton, 1,197 full-time students. During the period 1 July 1983 to 30 June 1984, there were 11,505 students enrolled full-time at 10 Community College campuses and at various campus training centres.

There were, in Sept. 1983, 145,524 students and 7,598 full-time (equivalent) teachers in the province's 445 schools. There are 41 school boards.

Books of Reference

Industrial Information: Dept. of Commerce and Development, Fredericton. *Economic Information:* Dept. of Finance, Economics and Statistics Branch. Fredericton. *General Information:* NB Information Service, Fredericton.

New Brunswick and Its People. Fredericton, 1962

Department of Commerce and Development, *Annual Report.* Fredericton, 1973.—*New Brunswick in Profile.* Fredericton

NEWFOUNDLAND AND LABRADOR

HISTORY. Archaeological finds at L'Anse-au-Meadow in northern Newfoundland suggest that the Vikings had established a colony there at about A.D. 1000. Newfoundland was discovered by John Cabot 24 June 1497, and was soon frequented in the summer months by the Portuguese, Spanish and French for its fisheries. It was formally occupied in Aug. 1583 by Sir Humphrey Gilbert on behalf of the English Crown, but various attempts to colonize the island remained unsuccessful. Although British sovereignty was recognized in 1713 by the Treaty of Utrecht, disputes over fishing rights with the French were not finally settled till 1904. By the Anglo-French Convention of 1904, France renounced her exclusive fishing rights along part of the coast, granted under the Treaty of Utrecht, but retained sovereignty of the offshore islands of St Pierre and Miquelon.

AREA AND POPULATION. Area, 143,489 sq. miles (371,635 sq. km). In March 1927 the Privy Council decided the boundary between Canada and Newfoundland in Labrador. This area, now part of the Province of Newfoundland and Labrador, is 102,486 sq. miles. The coastline is extremely irregular. Bays, fiords and inlets are numerous and there are many good harbours with deep water close to shore. The coast is rugged with bold rocky cliffs from 200 to 400 ft high; in the Bay of Islands some of the islands rise 500 ft, with the adjacent shore 1,000 ft above tide level. The interior is a plateau of moderate elevation and the chief relief features trend north-east and south-west. Long Range, the most notable of these, begins at Cape Ray and extends north-east for 200 miles, the highest peak reaching 2,673 ft. Approximately one-third of the area is covered by water. Grand Lake, the largest body of water, has an area of about 200 sq. miles. The principal rivers flow towards the north-east. On the borders of the lakes and water-courses good land is generally found, particularly in the valleys of the Terra Nova River, the Gander River, the Exploits River and the Humber River, which are also heavily timbered.

Census population, 1981, was 567,681.

The capital of Newfoundland is the City of St John's (154,820, metropolitan area). The only other city is Corner Brook (24,339); important towns are Labrador City (11,538), Gander (10,404), Stephenville (8,876), Grand Falls (8,765), Happy Valley–Goose Bay (7,103), Marystown (6,299), Channel-Port aux Basques (5,988), Windsor (5,747), Carbonear (5,335), Bonavista (4,460), Wabana (4,254), Wabush (3,155).

Vital statistics, *see* p. 269.

Religion, *see* p. 286.

CLIMATE. The cool temperate climate is marked by heavy precipitation, distributed evenly over the year, a cool and cheerless summer and frequent fogs in winter. St. John's. Jan. 23°F (–5°C), July 59°F (15°C). Annual rainfall 54″ (1,367 mm).

CONSTITUTION AND GOVERNMENT. Until 1832 Newfoundland was ruled by the Governor under instructions of the Colonial Office. In that year a Legislature was brought into existence, but the Governor and his Executive Council were not responsible to it. Under the constitution of 1855, which lasted until its suspension in 1934, the government was administered by the Governor appointed by the Crown with an Executive Council responsible to the House of Assembly of 27 elected members and a Legislative Council of 24 members nominated for life by the Governor in Council. Women were enfranchised in 1925. At the Imperial Conference of 1917 Newfoundland was constituted as a Dominion.

In 1933 the financial situation had become so critical that the Government of Newfoundland asked the Government of the UK to appoint a Royal Commission to investigate conditions. On the strength of their recommendations, the parliamentary form of government was suspended and Government by Commission was inaugurated on 16 Feb. 1934.

A National Convention, elected in 1946, made, in 1948, recommendations to H.M. Government in Great Britain as to the possible forms of future government to be submitted to the people at a national referendum. Two referenda were held. In the first referendum (June 1948) the three forms of government submitted to the people were: commission of government for 5 years, confederation with Canada and responsible government as it existed in 1933. No one form of government received a clear majority of the votes polled, and commission of government, receiving the fewest votes, was eliminated. In the second referendum (July 1948) confederation with Canada received 78,408 and responsible government 71,464 votes.

In the Canadian Senate on 18 Feb. 1949 Royal assent was given to the terms of union of Newfoundland and Labrador with Canada, and on 23 March 1949, in the House of Lords, London, Royal assent was given to an amendment to the British North America Act made necessary by the inclusion of Newfoundland and Labrador as the tenth Province of Canada.

Under the terms of union of Newfoundland and Labrador with Canada, which was signed at Ottawa on 11 Dec. 1948, the constitution of the Legislature of Newfoundland and Labrador as it existed immediately prior to 16 Feb. 1934 shall, subject to the terms of the British North America Acts, 1867 to 1946, continue as the constitution of the Legislature of the Province of Newfoundland and Labrador until altered under the authority of the said Acts.

The franchise was in 1965 extended to all male and female residents who have attained the age of 19 years and are otherwise qualified as electors.

The House of Assembly (Amendment) Act, 1979, established 52 electoral districts and 52 members of the Legislature.

In Sept. 1984 there were 43 Progressive-Conservatives, 8 Liberals and 1 seat vacant.

The province is represented by 6 members in the Senate and by 7 members in the House of Commons of Canada.

Lieut.-Governor: Hon. Dr W. A. Paddon (assumed office 10 July 1981).

Flag: White, in the hoist 4 solid blue triangles; in the fly 2 red triangles voided white, and between them a yellow tongue bordered in red.

The Progressive-Conservative Executive Council was, at 2 Oct. 1984, composed as follows:

Premier: Brian Peckford.

President of the Council and Petroleum Directorate: W. Marshall. *Finance:* J. Collins. *Justice:* G. Ottenheimer. *Development:* N. Windsor. *Municipal Affairs:* N. Doyle. *Health:* H. Twomey. *Fisheries (Acting):* J. Goudie. *Forest Resources and Lands:* L. Simms. *Rural Agricultural and Northern Development:* J. Goudie. *Labour:* J. Dinn. *Transportation, Mines and Energy:* R. Dawe. *Consumer Affairs and Communications:* H. Newhook. *Social Services:* T. Hickey. *Culture, Recreation and Youth:* T. Rideout. *Environment:* H. Andrews. *Public Works and Services:* H. Young. *Education:* L. Verge. *Career Development:* C. Power. *Without Portfolio:* W. House.

Agent-General in London: H. Watson Jamer (60 Trafalgar Sq., WC2).

FINANCE. Budget [1] in Canadian $1,000 for fiscal years ended 31 March:

	1979–80	*1980–81*	*1981–82*	*1982–83*	*1983–84* [2]	*1984–85* [3]
Gross revenue	1,215,697	1,359,209	1,511,019	1,652,046	1,785,728	1,922,957
Gross expenditure	1,174,091	1,310,018	1,504,752	1,689,339	1,850,430	1,955,212

[1] Current amount only. [2] Revised estimates. [3] Estimates.

Public debenture debt as at 31 March 1984 (preliminary) was $2,717·9m.; sinking fund, $577·9m.

ENERGY AND NATURAL RESOURCES

Electricity. The electrical energy requirements of the province are met mainly by hydro-electric power, with petroleum fuels being utilized to provide the balance. The total amount of energy generated in the province in 1983 (preliminary) was 39,993,569 mwh., of which approximately 98% was derived from hydro-electric facilities. The greater part of the energy produced in 1983 (preliminary) came from Churchill Falls, of which 31,233,755 mwh. was sold to Hydro-Quebec under the terms of a long-term contract. Energy consumed in the province during 1983 (preliminary) totalled 8,759,814 mwh., with approximately 8,155,690 mwh., or 93%, coming from hydro-electric facilities.

At 31 Dec. 1982 total electrical generating capacity in the province was 6,962,527 kw., with hydro-electric plants accounting for 6,210,256 kw., or 89%. A 75 mw hydro project started in 1978 at Hind's Lake in central Newfoundland and was completed in 1981. It is estimated that potential additional hydro-electric generating capacity of up to 4·5m. kw. can be developed at various sites in the Labrador part of the province.

Oil. In 1981 the province consumed refined petroleum at the rate of 39,000 bbls a day with 30% of this being refined in the province. The refining capacity of the province is 114,000 bbls per day, this refinery was closed in June 1983.

Since 1965, 92 wells have been drilled on the Continental Margin of the Province. In 1983 it is estimated that offshore exploration expenditures would be between $450m. and $500m.

In Oct. 1974, two natural gas finds off the coast of Labrador were announced. Tests of these two wells resulted in rates of flow of 13–20m. cu. ft per day respectively, with some condensate and no water present. Additional natural gas finds with flows of 9·8m. cu. ft per day and 32m. cu. ft per day, with significant condensates and no water present, were announced in 1976 and 1978 respectively.

In 1979, a discovery of oil was made on the Hibernia geological structure located 164 nautical miles east of Cape Spear. The discovery well, Hibernia P–15, tested medium gravity, sweet crude from several intervals with a reported total producing capability in excess of 20,000 bbls of oil per day.

Minerals. The mineral resources are vast but only partially documented. Large deposits of iron ore, with an ore reserve of over 5,000m. tons at Labrador City, Wabush City and in the Knob Lake area are supplying approximately half of Canada's production. Other large deposits of iron ore are known to exist in the Julienne Lake area.

There are a variety of other minerals being produced in the province in more limited amounts.

Uranium deposits in the Kaipokak Bay area near Makkovik in Labrador are presently being studied by Brinex. The Central Mineral Belt, which extends from the Smallwood Reservoir to the Atlantic coast near Makkovik, holds uranium, copper, beryllium and molybdenite potential.

Production in 1983 (preliminary): Iron ore, 18,123,000 tonnes ($601,078,000); copper, 184 tonnes ($384,000); zinc, 36,649 tonnes ($42,146,000); asbestos, 32,000 tonnes ($16·85m.); lead, 1,521 tonnes ($898,000); silver, 2,000 kg ($846,000); gold, 10,000 grammes ($162,000); gypsum, 500,000 tonnes ($3m.); pyrophyllite, soapstone and talc (. . .); cement (. . .); clay products (. . .); sand and gravel, 2,900,000 tonnes ($9,320,000); stone, 280,000 tonnes ($1·3m.); quartz (. . .).

Agriculture. The estimated value of agricultural products sold, including livestock, 1983, was $33·7m.

Forestry. The forestry economy in the province is mainly dependent on the operation of 3 newsprint mills. In 1982 the value of newsprint exported from these 3 mills totalled $260·7m. Lumber mills, saw-log operations produced 33m. f.b.m. in 1982–83.

Fisheries. The principal fish landings are cod, flounder, redfish, Queen crabs (in shell), lobster, salmon and herring. In 1982 a yearly average of some 9,100 persons were employed by the fish-processing industry and there were 27,379 licensed full-, part-time and casual fishermen engaged in harvesting operations. Approximately 218 processing operations were licensed in 1983. The production of fresh and frozen fish products was $504·5m. in 1982.

The total catch in 1983 was 455,839 tonnes valued at $165,739,085, which comprised: Cod, 295,046 tonnes ($100,309,758); flounder, 51,662 ($14,006,878); herring, 9,401 tonnes ($1,986,682); redfish, 17,458 ($3,362,557); lobster, 2,403 ($11,934,927); salmon, 1,029 ($3,553,980); capelin, 29,836 ($5,605,703); crab, 11,120 ($10,413,092); shrimp, 4,083 ($4,782,240).

The seal fishery in 1983 had 1 large licensed and 85 small licensed vessels with 371 men who landed 19,368 pelts. The number of pelts landed by landsmen totalled 23,244.

INDUSTRY. The total value of manufacturing shipments in 1983 was $1,142m. This consists largely of first-stage processing of primary resource products with two of the largest components being paper and fish products.

TRADE UNIONS. There were (1982) 408 unions representing 73,929 members of international and national unions and government employee associations.

COMMUNICATIONS

Roads. In 1983 there were 8,729 km, of which 5,510 were paved.

Railways. In 1981 there were 1,457·8 km of railway, of which the Canadian National Railways operated 1,130·6 (3 ft 6 in.), the Quebec North Shore and Labrador Railway 324·8 (4 ft 8½ in.) and there were 2·4 km of private line. Car and passenger ferries operate from Port aux Basques and Argentia to North Sydney, Nova Scotia. On the island of Newfoundland, the Canadian National Railways operates a trans-island bus and rail freight service in addition to a coastal service for both passengers and freight. In the months that the Labrador coast is ice-free, usually from June to Nov., the Canadian National Railways operates a scheduled coastal steamer service every week.

Aviation. The province is linked to the rest of Canada by regular air services provided by Air Canada, Eastern Provincial Airways, Quebecair and a number of smaller air carriers.

Shipping. In 1983 there were 1,608 ships registered in Newfoundland.

Post. There were 481 post offices open in 1984, and 2 telegraph offices in the Newfoundland and Labrador postal district. Telephone connexions in the province numbered 268,237 in 1982.

EDUCATION. The number of schools in 1983–84 was 627. The enrolment was 147,603; teachers numbered 8,219. The Memorial University, offering courses in arts, science, engineering, education, nursing and medicine, had approximately 12,442 full- and part-time students. Total expenditure for education by the Government in 1983–84 was $595m.

Books of Reference

Blackburn, R. H. (ed.), *Encyclopaedia of Canada: Newfoundland Supplement.* Toronto, 1949
Bruet, E., *Le Labrador et le Nouveau-Québec.* Paris, 1949

Horwood, H., *Newfoundland.* Toronto, 1969
Loture, R. de, *Histoire de la grande pêche de Terre-Neuve.* Paris, 1949
Mercer, G. A., *The Province of Newfoundland and Labrador: Geographical Aspects.* Ottawa, 1970
Perlin, A. B., *The Story of Newfoundland, 1497–1959.* St John's, 1959
Tanner, V., *Outlines of Geography. Life and Customs of Newfoundland–Labrador.* 2 vols. Helsinki, 1944, and Toronto, 1947
Taylor, T. G., *Newfoundland: A Study of Settlement.* Toronto, 1946

NOVA SCOTIA

HISTORY. The first permanent settlement was made by the French early in the 17th century, and the province was called Acadia until finally ceded to the British by the Treaty of Utrecht in 1713.

AREA AND POPULATION. The area of the province is 21,425 sq. miles (55,000 sq. km), of which 20,401 sq. miles are land area, 1,024 sq. miles water area. The population (census 1981) was 847,442; estimate (1984) 869,900.

Population of the principal cities and towns (census 1981): Halifax, 114,594; Dartmouth 62,277; Sydney, 29,444; Glace Bay, 21,466; Truro, 12,552; New Glasgow, 10,464; Amherst, 9,684; Sydney Mines, 8,501; North Sydney, 7,820; Yarmouth, 7,475.

Vital statistics, *see* p. 269.
Religion, *see* p. 286.

CLIMATE. A cool temperate climate, with rainfall occurring evenly over the year. The Gulf Stream moderates the temperatures in winter so that ports remain ice-free. Halifax. Jan. 23°F (–5°C), July 64°F (17·8°C). Annual rainfall 56″ (1,412 mm).

CONSTITUTION AND GOVERNMENT. Under the British North America Act of 1867 the legislature of Nova Scotia may exclusively make laws in relation to local matters, including direct taxation within the province, education and the administration of justice. The legislature of Nova Scotia consists of a Lieut.-Governor, appointed and paid by the federal government, and holding office for 5 years, and a House of Assembly of 52 members, chosen by popular vote not more than every 5 years. The province is represented in the Canadian Senate by 10 members, and in the House of Commons by 11.

The franchise and eligibility to the legislature are granted to every person, male or female, if of age (19 years), a British subject or Canadian citizen, and a resident in the province for 1 year and 2 months before the date of the writ of election in the county or electoral district of which the polling district forms part, and if not by law otherwise disqualified. State of parties in Oct. 1984: 35 Progressive Conservatives, 15 Liberals, 1 New Democrat, 1 independent.

Lieut.-Governor: Alan R. Abraham.

Flag: A banner of the Arms, *i.e.*, white with a blue diagonal cross, bearing in the centre the royal shield of Scotland.

The members of the Progressive Conservative Ministry are as follows:

Premier, President of the Executive Council, Chairman of the Policy Board, Minister of Intergovernmental Affairs: John M. Buchanan, QC.

Finance: Greg Kerr. *Development and Minister in Charge of Administration of the Research Foundation Corporation Act:* Roland J. Thornhill. *Attorney-General, Provincial Secretary and Minister in Charge of Administration of the Regulations Act:* Ronald Giffen. *Education and Minister in Charge of Administration of the Advisory Council on Status of Women Act:* Terence Donahoe. *Lands and Forests:* Kenneth Streatch. *Health, Minister in Charge of Administration of the Drug Dependency Act and Registrar-General:* Gerald Sheehy. *Mines and Energy and Minister in Charge of the Nova Scotia Energy Council:* Joel Matheson. *Agriculture and Marketing:* Roger S. Bacon. *Fisheries:* John Leefe. *Tourism:* Fisher Hudson. *Municipal Affairs:* Thomas McInnis. *Labour and Manpower:* David Nantes. *Chairman of the Management Board, Minister in Charge of Administration of the Civil Service Act and Minister in Charge of Administration of the Liquor Control Act:* Ronald Russell. *Transportation:* John MacIsaac. *Social Services:* Edmund Morris. *Government Services, Minister in Charge of Administration of Communication and Information Act:* Gerald Lawrence. *Environment:* George Moody. *Minister in Charge of Administration of the Nova Scotia Emergency Measures Act and Regulations (EMO) and Chairman of Resource Development Sector Committee Board:* Milne Pickings. *Culture, Recreation and Fitness, Minister in Charge of the Nova Scotia Heritage Property Act and Minister Responsible for Lotteries:* William MacLean. *Consumer Affairs, Minister in Charge of Administration of Human Rights Act, Minister in Charge of Administration of the Residential Tenancies Act and Chairman of Social Development Sector Committee Board:* Laird Stirling. *Minister Without Portfolio:* George Henley.

Agent-General in London: Donald M. Smith (14 Pall Mall, SW1Y 5LU).

Local Government. The main divisions of the province for governmental purposes are the 3 cities, the 39 towns and the 24 rural municipalities, each governed by a council and a mayor or warden. The cities have independent charters, and the various towns take their powers from and are limited by The Towns Act, and the various municipalities take their powers from and are limited by The Municipal Act as revised in 1967. The majority of municipalities comprise 1 county, but 6 counties are divided into 2 municipalities each. In no case do the boundaries of any municipality overlap county lines. The 18 counties as such have no administrative functions.

Any city (of which there are 3) or incorporated town (of which there are 39) that lies within the boundaries of a municipality is excluded from any jurisdiction by the municipal council and has its own government.

FINANCE. Revenue is derived from provincial sources, payments from the federal government under the Federal-Provincial Fiscal Arrangements and Established Programs Financing Act. Recoveries consist generally of amounts received under various federal cost-shared programmes. Main sources of provincial revenues include income and sales taxes.

Revenue, expenditure and debt (in Canadian $1m.) for fiscal years ending 31 March:

	1980	*1981*	*1982*	*1983*	*1984*[1]
Budgetary Transactions					
Current Expenditure	1,524·3	1,769·6	2,117·7	2,387·8	2,558·8
Current Revenues and Recoveries	1,565·2	1,750·1	1,937·4	2,119·1	2,323·9
Operating Deficit (Surplus)	(40·9)	19·5	180·3	268·7	234·9
Sinking fund Instalments and Serial Retirements	30·9	32·2	34·3	45·1	51 3
Net Capital Expenditures	122·7	160·9	249·6	186·4	203·7
Net Budgetary Transactions	112·7	212·6	464·2	500·2	489·9
Non-Budgetary Transactions					
Capital Expenditures	2·5	10·2	3·2	3·0	10·3
Net Increase (Decrease) in Advances and Investments	86·4	108·5	75·6	29·1	(9·3)
Net Other Transactions	23·8	21·9	25·1	19·7	7·7
Non-Budgetary Transactions	112·7	140·6	103·9	51·8	8·7
	225·4	353·2	568·1	552·0	498·6

[1] Estimate.

NATURAL RESOURCES

Minerals. Principal minerals in 1983 were: Coal, 3m. tonnes, valued at $146·7m.; gypsum, 5·4m. tonnes, valued at $38·4m.; salt, 725,000 tonnes, valued at $31·7m.; sand and gravel, 6·2m. tonnes, valued at $15·3m. Total value of mineral production in 1983 was about $248·5m.

Agriculture. Dairying, poultry and egg production, livestock and fruit growing are the most important branches. Farm cash receipts for 1983 were estimated at $239·3m., with an additional $6·2m. going to persons on farms as income in kind.

Cash receipts from sale of dairy products was $67·8m., with total milk production of 170,541,000 litres.

The production of poultry meat in 1983 was 16,494 tonnes, of which 13,503 tonnes were chickens, 1,180 tonnes were fowls and 1,811 tonnes were turkeys. Egg production was 19·3m. dozen.

The main 1983 fruit crops were apples, 53,342 tonnes; blueberries, 8,846 tonnes; and strawberries, 2,439 tonnes.

Forestry. The estimated forest area of Nova Scotia is 15,555 sq. miles (40,298 sq. km), of which about 25% is owned by the province. The principal trees are spruce, balsam fir, hemlock, pine, larch, birch, oak, maple, poplar and ash. 2,192,316 cu. metres of round forest products were produced in 1983.

Fisheries. The fisheries of the province in 1983 had a landed value of $276·5m. of sea fish including scallop fishery, $60·3m., and lobster fishery, $68·2m. In 1982 there were about 6,693 employees in the fish processing industry; the value of shipment of goods was $431·5m.

INDUSTRY. The number of manufacturing establishments was 781 in 1982; the number of employees was 34,646; wages and salaries, $671·5m.; value of shipments was $3,728m. The value of shipments in 1983, was $3,962·4m., and the leading industries were petroleum and coal products, food and beverages, paper and allied industries and transportation equipment.

TRADE UNIONS. Total union membership during 1984 was 103,694 belonging to 103 unions comprised of 618 individual branches. The largest percentage of the total union membership was in the service sector followed by public administration and defence sector. An estimated 48,916 members in 366 branches were affiliated with the Canadian Labour Congress.

COMMUNICATIONS

Roads. In March 1984 there were 25,716 km of highways; 2,623 km of paved arterial highways; 4,683 km of collector highways (of which 4,419 km are paved); 18,441 km of local highways (of which 4,556 km are paved).

Railways. The province is covered with a network of railways, 1,470·3 km in extent.

Aviation. There is a direct air service to major Canadian and USA cities, London, Amsterdam and Bermuda.

Shipping. Ferry services connect Nova Scotia with Newfoundland, Prince Edward Island, New Brunswick and Maine. Direct service by container vessels is provided from the Port of Halifax to ports in Europe, Asia and the Caribbean.

JUSTICE AND EDUCATION

Justice. There is a Supreme Court which is a Court of common law and equity possessing original and appellate jurisdiction in civil and in criminal cases. The Supreme Court consists of an appeal division of 7 judges and a trial division of 9 judges. There are also county courts, family courts, probate courts, magistrates' courts, municipal and justices' courts. Bodies, sometimes referred to as courts, are established for the revision of assessment rolls, voters' lists and like purposes.

Young offenders under 16 years are now tried by Youth Courts. The Courts were established in April 1984. In 1985, the Youth Courts have the jurisdiction to adjudicate charges against 16- and 17- year-old offenders.

For the year ending 31 Dec. 1983 there were 4,855 admissions to provincial jails, of these, 3,523 were sentenced. There were 3,123 admissions to probationary supervision.

Education. Public education in Nova Scotia is free, compulsory and undenominational through elementary and high school. Attendance is compulsory to the age of 16. In addition to 582 public schools there are the Atlantic Provinces Resource Centres for the Hearing Handicapped and for the Visually Impaired; the Nova Scotia School for Boys and the Nova Scotia School for Girls for delinquent children; and the Nova Scotia Youth Training Centre for mentally handicapped children. The province has 14 universities and colleges of which the largest is Dalhousie University in Halifax. The Nova Scotia Agricultural College and the Nova Scotia Teachers' College are located at Truro. The Technical University of Nova Scotia at Halifax grants degrees in engineering and architecture.

The Vocational and Technical Training Section of the Nova Scotia Department of Education administers 2 institutes of technology and a nautical institute. It also provides in-school training for the Department of Labour Apprenticeship programme.

The Department of Education offers financial support and organizational assistance to local school boards for provision of weekend and evening courses in academic and avocational subjects, and citizenship for new Canadians. It also provides local authorities with specialist support services to assist them in providing community workshops and it operates a correspondence study service for children and adults.

Occupational courses at the high school level are provided by 14 regional vocational schools under the jurisdiction (except in 3 school areas) of the Department of Education.

Total estimated expenditure on education for the year 1982–83 was $503.8m., of which 81% was borne by the provincial government. In 1983–84, classrooms operated in 582 school houses, with 11,183 teachers and 177,240 pupils, of whom 91,113 were in elementary school grades and junior auxiliary classes, 83,351 in junior and senior high school grades and vocational education, and 2,776 in special education.

Books of Reference

Atlantic Provinces Economic Council. *The Atlantic Vision, 1990.* Halifax, 1979

Public Archives of Nova Scotia. *Place Names and Places of Nova Scotia.* Halifax, 1967

Beck, Murray, *The Government of Nova Scotia.* Toronto, 1957.—*Joseph Howe. The Voice of Nova Scotia.* 1964.—*The Evolution of Municipal Government in Nova Scotia, 1749–1973.* 1973

Elliott, S. B., *Nova Scotia Book of Days: A Calendar of the Province's History.* Halifax, 1979

Fergusson, C. B., *Nova Scotia in Encyclopedia Canadiana,* Vol. VII. Toronto, 1968

McCreath, P., and Leefe, J., *History of Early Nova Scotia.* Halifax, 1982

Raddall, T. H., *Halifax, Warden of the North.* Toronto, 1972

Vaison, R., *Nova Scotia Past and Present: A Bibliography and Guide.* Halifax, 1976

ONTARIO

HISTORY. The French explorer Samuel de Champlain explored the Ottawa River from 1613. The area was governed by the French, first under a joint stock company and then as a royal province, from 1627 and was ceded to Great Britain in 1763. A constitutional act of 1791 created there the province of Upper Canada, largely to accommodate loyalists of English descent who had immigrated after the United States war of independence. Upper Canada entered the Confederation as Ontario in 1867.

AREA AND POPULATION. The total area is about 412,600 sq. miles (1,068,630 sq. km), of which some 344,100 sq. miles (891,220 sq. km) are land area and some 68,500 sq. miles (177,420 sq. km) are fresh water.

The province extends 1,000 miles from east to west and 1,050 miles from north to south.

Ontario is bounded on the north by the waters of Hudson and James Bay, on the east by Quebec, on the west by Manitoba, and on the south by the states of New York, Pennsylvania, Ohio, Michigan, Wisconsin and Minnesota.

The population of the province (census, 1 June 1981) was 8,625,107. Population of the principal cities (1982): Hamilton, 308,102 (city), 542,095 (census metropolitan area); Kitchener, 141,438 (city), 287,801 (census metropolitan area); London, 266,319 (city); Ottawa (federal capital), 303,144 (city), 562,782 (census metropolitan area); Sudbury, 91,388 (city), 159,779 (regional municipality); Toronto (provincial capital), 614,763 (city), 2,998,947 (census metropolitan area); Windsor, 192,546 (city).

Vital statistics, *see* p. 269.

Religion, *see* p. 286.

CLIMATE. A temperate continental climate, but conditions are quite severe in winter, though proximity to the Great Lakes has a moderating influence on temperatures. Ottawa. Jan. 12°F (−11·1°C), July 69°F (20·6°C). Annual rainfall 35″ (871 mm). Toronto. Jan. 23°F (−5°C), July 69°F (20·6°C). Annual rainfall 33″ (815 mm).

CONSTITUTION AND GOVERNMENT. The provincial government is administered by a Lieut.-Governor, a cabinet and one chamber elected by a general franchise for a period of 5 years. Women have the vote and can be elected to the chamber. The minimum voting age is 18 years.

In Oct. 1981 the provincial legislature was composed as follows: Progressive Conservatives, 70; Liberals, 34; New Democrats, 21; total 125.

Lieut.-Governor: Hon. John B. Aird, QC, BA, LLD (appointed 15 Sept. 1980).

Flag: The British Red Ensign with the shield of Ontario in the fly.

The members of the Executive Council in Feb. 1985 were as follows (all Progressive Conservatives):

Premier and President of the Council: F. S. Miller.

Deputy Premier and Attorney-General: R. Welch, QC. *Treasurer and Minister of Economics:* L. Grossman, QC. *Municipal Affairs and Housing and Women's Issues:* D. R. Timbrell. *Northern Affairs:* L. Bernier. *Tourism and Recreation and Chairman of Cabinet:* C. Bennett. *Chairman of Management Board of Cabinet:* B. M. Stephenson. *Education and Colleges and Universities:* K. C. Norton, QC. *Transportation and Communications:* G. McCague. *Provincial Secretary for Justice:* R. Baetz. *Community and Social Services:* R. G. Elgie. *Consumer and Commercial Relations:* G. Walker, QC. *Revenue:* B. Gregory. *Health:* A. W. Pope, QC. *Correctional Services:* N. G. Leluk. *Energy:* G. L. Ashe. *Labour:* R. H. Ramsay. *Industry and Trade:* A. S. Brandt. *Citizenship and Culture:* S. Fish. *Agriculture and Food:* P. Andrewes. *Provincial Secretary for Social Development:* G. H. Dean. *Provincial Secretary for Resources Development:* E. Eves. *Natural Resources:* M. Harris. *Environment:* M. Kells. *Government Services:* R. Runciman. *Solicitor General:* J. Williams. *Ministers Without Portfolio:* J. W. Snow, P. Gillies, A. McLean, R. Mitchell, R. Piché, A. Robinson, D. Rotenburg.

Local Government. Local government in Ontario is divided into two branches, one covering municipal institutions and the other education.

The present municipal system dates from The Municipal Corporations Act enacted by The Province of Canada in 1849. It has been considerably modified in recent years with the creation of the Municipality of Metropolitan Toronto in 1954 and the launching of the Government of Ontario's local government restructuring programme in 1968. Generally, there are two levels of municipal government in Ontario. The upper level consists of 27 counties plus 12 restructured regional municipalities. The local level comprises more than 800 cities, towns and townships. Cities in the traditional county system function independently of the county in which they lie, as do 5 towns which have been separated for municipal purposes. There are no separated municipal units in regional governments.

Ontario's local municipalities are governed by councils elected by popular vote. A city council usually consists of a mayor, aldermen and, sometimes, an executive committee known as a board of control.

Councils of towns, villages and townships usually consist of a mayor, reeve, deputy reeve, councillors and, in the case of the newer regional municipalities, one or more regional councillors who represent the area municipalities on the regional council.

County and regional government councils are federated assemblies.

A county council consists of the reeves and deputy reeves of the towns, villages and townships. The head of the county council is the warden, who is elected by the council from among its own members.

A regional council consists of the heads of council of the local municipalities, as well as a varying number of regional councillors, who are elected on the basis of representation, either directly or indirectly. The head of the regional council is the chairman who is elected by council but who, unlike a county warden, need not have been a council member.

No municipality in Ontario may incur long-term debts without the sanction of the tribunal created by the Provincial Legislature and known as the Ontario Municipal Board. Debenture obligations incurred by municipalities for utility undertakings (water-works and electric light and power systems) are discharged ordinarily out of revenues derived from the sale of utility services and do not fall upon the ratepayers.

Municipal councils have no jurisdiction for education beyond the collection of taxes for school purposes. Responsibility for providing, operating and maintaining school facilities, and for the supply of teachers, rests with local education authorities known as boards of education or school boards. These boards are now generally organized on a county or regional basis. Apart from some of the larger cities, local municipal school boards no longer exist.

Municipal institutions come under the jurisdiction of the Provincial Ministry of Intergovernmental Affairs. One of the principal functions of the Ministry is to advise and assist municipalities on such matters as accounting, reporting, auditing, budgeting and planning. Educational support and guidance at the provincial level is the responsibility of the Ministry of Education, which deals with the training of teachers and the formulation of curriculum. (At the university and community college level, education support services are provided by the Ministry of Colleges and Universities.)

There are considerable areas in the northernmost parts of Ontario where as yet there is little or no settlement of population. In such areas no municipal organization exists, and control for all purposes over such areas remains in the hands of the Provincial Government.

FINANCE. The gross revenue and expenditure and the net cash requirements (in Canadian $1,000) for years ending 31 March were as follows:

	1980–81	*1981–82*	*1982–83*	*1983–84*	*1984–85*
Gross revenue	16,470	18,886	20,395	22,647	24,773
Gross expenditure	17,273	20,389	22,943	24,936	26,801
Net cash requirement	803	1,503	2,548	2,289	2,028

Gross revenue and expenditure figures include all non-budgetary transactions, *i.e.*, the lending and investment activity of the Government to Crown corporations, agencies and municipalities as well as the repayment of these loans or recovery of investments. Transactions on behalf of Ontario Hydro are excluded.

ENERGY AND NATURAL RESOURCES

Electricity (1982). Ontario Hydro recorded for the calendar year an installed generating capacity of 25·5m. kw. and a net energy output generated and purchased of 118,550m. kwh.

Minerals (1983, preliminary). The total value of shipments (in $1m.) in the mineral products industry were: Nickel, 595; copper, 412; iron ore, 181; gold, 363. The total value of mineral production was $3,533m. in 1983. The mining industry employed about 50,000 people in 1982.

Agriculture. In 1982, 3·5m. hectares were under field crops with total farm receipts of $5,000m.

Forestry. According to the most recent inventory (1984) the total area of productive forest is 34·7m. hectares, comprising: Softwoods, 22·9m.; hardwoods, 11,837,000. The growing stock equals 4,431m. cu. metres. The estimated value of shipments by the forest products industry (including logging) was (1983) $7,145·3m.

INDUSTRY AND TRADE

Industry (1982). Ontario is Canada's most highly industrialized province. About 73% of value added in commodity-producing industries is accounted for by manufacturing. Construction is next with 13%.

In 1982, the labour force was 4·57m. Total labour income was $89,236·5m. The Gross Provincial Product (GPP) was $147,210m.

The leading manufacturing industries are motor vehicles and parts, iron and steel, meat and meat preparations, dairy products, paper and paperboard, chemical products, petroleum and coal products, machinery and equipment, metal stamping and pressing and communications equipment.

Trade. In 1982 Ontario exported 43% ($36,603·4m.) of Canada's total foreign trade.

COMMUNICATIONS

Roads. There were, in 1983, 151,880·2 km of roads. Motor licences numbered (1982) approximately 5·3m., of which 3·8m. were passenger cars, 1,031,320 trucks and tractors, 23,827 buses, 65,754 trailers, 119,642 motor cycles and 169,385 snow vehicles.

Railways. The provincially-owned Ontario Northland Railway has about 550 miles of track and the Algoma Central Railway 325 miles. The Canadian National and Canadian Pacific Railways operate a total of about 9,500 miles in Ontario. There is a metro and tramway network in Toronto.

Post (1983). Telephone service is provided by 31 independent systems (278,619 telephones) and Bell Canada (9·3m. telephones).

EDUCATION. There is a complete provincial system of elementary and secondary schools as well as private schools. In 1983 publicly financed elementary and secondary schools had a total enrolment of 1,777,829 pupils.

In 1965 Ontario established Colleges of Applied Arts and Technology (CAATS). There are now 22 of these publicly owned colleges with full-time enrolment (1983) of 97,484 in academic courses.

The University of Toronto, founded in 1827 (full-time enrolment, 1983, 35,749), and 14 other major universities (total full-time enrolment, 1983, 183,094), all receive provincial grants. The net general expenditure of the provincial ministries of education and colleges and universities for the fiscal year ending 31 March 1983 was $5,044m.

Books of Reference

Statistical Information: Annual publications of the Ontario Ministry of Treasury and Economics include: *Ontario Statistics; Ontario Budget; Public Accounts; Financial Report.*

PRINCE EDWARD ISLAND

HISTORY. The earliest discovery of the island is not satisfactorily known, but the first recorded visit was by Jacques Cartier in 1534, who named it Isle St-Jean; it was first settled by the French, but was taken from them in 1758. It was annexed to Nova Scotia in 1763, and constituted a separate colony in 1769. Prince Edward Island entered the Confederation on 1 July 1873.

AREA AND POPULATION. The province, which is the smallest in Canada, lies in the Gulf of St Lawrence, and is separated from the mainland of New Brunswick and Nova Scotia by Northumberland Strait. The area of the island is 2,184 sq. miles (5,656 sq. km). Total population (census, 1981), 124,200. Population of the principal cities: Charlottetown (capital), 15,282; Summerside, 7,828.

Vital statistics, *see* p. 269.

Religion, *see* p. 286.

CLIMATE. The cool temperate climate is affected in winter by the freezing of the St. Lawrence, which reduces winter temperatures. Charlottetown. Jan. 19°F (–7·2°C), July 67°F (19·4°C). Annual rainfall 43″ (1,077 mm).

CONSTITUTION AND GOVERNMENT. The provincial government is administered by a Lieut.-Governor-in-Council (Cabinet) and a Legislative Assembly of 32 members who are elected for up to 5 years. In Feb. 1985, parties in the Legislative Assembly were: Progressive Conservatives, 20; Liberals, 12.

Lieut.-Governor: Joseph Aubin Doiron (sworn in 14 Jan. 1980).

Flag: A banner of the arms, *i.e.*, a white field bearing 3 small trees and a larger tree on a compartment, all green, and at the top a red band with a golden lion; on 3 sides a border of red and white rectangles.

Premier and President of Executive Council: James M. Lee.

Finance and Tourism: Lloyd G. MacPhail. *Justice and Attorney-General and Community and Cultural Affairs:* George R. McMahon, QC. *Agriculture:* Prowse G. Chappell. *Energy and Forestry:* Frederick L. Driscoll. *Health and Social Services:* Albert Fogarty. *Fisheries and Labour:* R. B. (Roddy) Pratt. *Education:* Leone Bagnall. *Industry:* Wilbur MacDonald. *Transportation and Public Works:* Gordon Lank.

Local Government. The Village Service Act, 1954, provides for the incorporation of villages. The city of Charlottetown and the town of Summerside have been incorporated under Special Acts. The Town Act, 1951, provides for the incorporation of all towns. The Community Improvement Act, 1968, provides for the establishment of Community Improvement Committees in the unincorporated areas of the province.

FINANCE. Revenue and expenditure (in Canadian $) for 6 financial years ending 31 March:

	1979–80	*1980–81*	*1981–82*	*1982–83*	*1983–84*	*1984–85*
Revenue	273,375,400	307,566,300	352,556,900	380,883,900	394,641,400	432,222,600
Expenditure	273,074,300	306,789,900	351,486,200	386,878,700	415,444,500	440,300,700

ENERGY AND NATURAL RESOURCES

Electricity. Electric power is supplied to 98% of the population. The province's net generated and purchased consumption of electricity increased during 1982 from 510m. kwh to 531m. kwh. In 1983, peak demand for electricity was 103 mw. In 1977 the province completed the laying of an undersea power cable which links the island with New Brunswick and the Maritime Power Grid. In 1980, 30 miles of additional 138 kv transmission line was added to the PEI system. In 1983, about 98% of power requirements were supplied through this system.

Agriculture. Total area of farms occupied approximately 699,367 acres in 1981 out of the total land area of 1,399,040 acres. Farm cash receipts in 1983 were $176m. with cash receipts from potatoes accounting for 37% of the total. Cash receipts from dairy products, cattle and hogs followed in importance. The land in natural forest covered 161,697 acres in 1981 and total value of forest products sold in 1980 was $363,221. For particulars of agricultural production and livestock, *see under* CANADA, pp. 279–80.

Fisheries. The fishery of the province in 1983 had a landed value of $44·2m. Lobsters accounted for 65·7% of the total. Value of groundfish landings accounted for 11%; pelagic and estuarial, 8%; shellfish, other than lobster, 12%; Irish moss, 3·2%.

INDUSTRY AND TRADE

Industry. Value of manufacturing shipments for all industries in 1981 was $312·9m.

Commerce. Average personal income rose from $8,943 in 1982 to $10,056 in 1983. The average weekly wage rose from $278.53 in 1982 to $295.45 in 1983. The labour force averaged 55,000 in 1983, while employment averaged 48,000.

In 1982, provincial GDP for manufacturing was $62·9m.; construction, $47·4m.

In 1983, total value of retail trade was $471,714,000.

Tourism. The value of the tourist industry was estimated at $50·1m. in 1983 with 220,590 (estimate) tourist parties.

COMMUNICATIONS

Roads. The province has a total of 5,278 km of road, including 3,687 km of paved highway.

Railways. Rail service is provided over 274 miles of track within the province and connects with the national railways system *via* the New Brunswick–Prince Edward Island ferry service.

Aviation. Air service for passengers, mail and cargo is scheduled to provide 8 flights daily in each direction between the province and various points in eastern Canada. A daily bus service operates between various centres in the province as well as to Nova Scotia during the summer months.

Shipping. A ferry service provides rail and highway communication with New Brunswick by means of 4 large ferries, 2 of which are powerful ice-breakers. Another ferry service employing 2 ferries plus an additional 2 for summertime operates between the province and Nova Scotia throughout the season of open navigation. A third ferry service employing 1 ferry operates between the province and Magdalen Islands, Quebec, during the open navigation season.

Post. In 1983 there were approximately 74,594 telephones.

EDUCATION (1982–83). Under the regional school boards there are 72 public schools, 1,382 teaching positions, 25,120 students. There is one undergraduate university (1,676 full-time students), and a college of applied arts and technology (928 full-time post-secondary students), both in Charlottetown. Total expenditure in education in the year ending 31 March 1984 is forecast to be $101,854,500.

Books of Reference

Clark, A. H., *Three Centuries and the Island.* Toronto, 1959
Hocking, A., *Prince Edward Island.* Toronto, 1978
MacKinnon, F., *The Government of Prince Edward Island.* Toronto, 1951

QUEBEC—QUÉBEC

HISTORY. Quebec was formerly known as New France or Canada from 1534 to 1763; as the province of Quebec from 1763 to 1790; as Lower Canada from 1791 to 1846; as Canada East from 1846 to 1867, and when, by the union of the four original provinces, the Confederation of the Dominion of Canada was formed, it again became known as the province of Quebec (Québec).

The Quebec Act, passed by the British Parliament in 1774, guaranteed to the people of the newly conquered French territory in North America security in their religion and language, their customs and tenures, under their own civil laws.

In the referendum held 20 May 1980, 59·5% voted against and 40·5% for 'separatism'.

AREA AND POPULATION. The area of Quebec (as amended by the Labrador Boundary Award) is 1,667,926 sq. km (594,860 sq. miles), of which 1,315,134 sq. km is land area and 352,792 sq. km water. Of this extent, 911,106 sq. km represent the Territory of Ungava, annexed in 1912 under the Quebec Boundaries Extension Act. The population (estimated 1 June 1983) was 6,514,900.

Principal cities (1983): Quebec (capital), 163,800; Montreal, 1,005,000; Laval, 273,000; Sherbrooke, 73,000; Verdun, 60,100; Hull, 55,100; Trois-Rivières, 50,000.

Vital statistics, *see* p. 269.
Religion, *see* p. 286.

CLIMATE. Cool temperate in the south, but conditions are more extreme towards the north. Winters are severe and snowfall considerable, but summer temperatures are quite warm. Rain occurs at all seasons. Quebec. Jan. 10°F (–12·2°C), July 66°F (18·9°C). Annual rainfall 40″ (1,008 mm). Montreal. Jan. 11°F (–11·7°C), July 67°F (19·4°C). Annual rainfall 41″ (1,025 mm).

CONSTITUTION AND GOVERNMENT. There is a Legislative Assembly consisting of 122 members, elected in 122 electoral districts for 4 years. There were, June 1984, 71 *Parti Québecois*, 48 Liberals, 2 Independent, 1 vacant seat.

Lieut.-Governor: The Hon. Gilles Lamontagne.

Flag: The Fleurdelysé flag, blue with a white cross, and in each quarter a white fleur-de-lis.

The members of the Executive Council as on 10 March 1985, are as follows:

Prime Minister: René Lévesque.

Justice and Minister of Intergovernmental Affairs: Pierre Marc Johnson. *Communications:* Jean-François Bertrand. *Administrative Reform:* Michel Clair. *Industry, Commerce and Tourism:* Rodrigue Biron. *Recreation and Sport:* Guy Chevrette. *Transport:* Jacques Léonard. *Energy and Resources:* Yves L. Duhaime. *Work:* Raynald Fréchette. *Agriculture, Fisheries and Food:* Jean Garon. *Planning and Regional Development:* François Gendron. *Cultural Communities and Immigration:* Gérald Godin. *Social Affairs:* Camille Laurin. *External Trade and International Relations:* Bernard Landry. *Education:* Yves Bérubé. *Public Relations:* Denis Lazure. *Municipal Affairs, Public Works and Functions:* Alain Marcoux. *Revenue:* Robert Dean. *Women's Affairs:* Denise Leblanc-Bantey. *Environment:* Adrien Ouellette. *Science and Technology:* Gilbert Paquette. *Finance:* Jacques Parizeau. *Cultural Affairs:* Clément Richard. *Consumer Protection and Housing:* Guy Tardif.

General-delegate in London: Patrick Hindman (59 Pall Mall, London SW1Y 5JH).

General-delegate in New York: Rita Dion Marsolais (17 West 50th St., Rockefeller Center, New York 10020).

General-delegate in Paris: Louise Beaudoin (66 Pergolèse, Paris 75116).

ECONOMY

Budget. Ordinary revenue and expenditure (in Canadian $1,000) for fiscal years ending 31 March:

	1978–79	*1979–80*	*1980–81*	*1981–82*	*1982–83*
Revenue	11,928,343	13,306,680	14,718,305	17,471,594	19,210,266
Expenditure	13,402,830	15,123,200	17,596,659	20,359,807	22,259,296

The total net debt at 31 March 1983 was $14,225,644,000.

ENERGY AND NATURAL RESOURCES

Electricity. Water power is one of the most important natural resources of the province of Quebec. Its turbine installation represents about 40% of the aggregate of Canada. At the end of 1982 the installed generating capacity was 27,745 mw. Production, 1983, was 110,566 gwh.

Minerals (1983). The estimated value of the mineral production (metal mines only) was $1,091,142,000. Chief minerals: Iron ore, $346,197,000; copper, $123,386,000; gold, $441,459,000; zinc, $77,837,000.

The second major iron-ore development in northern Quebec is, like the one at Knob Lake which gave birth to Schefferville, based on the Quebec–Labrador Trough which extends from Lac Jeannine to the northern tip of Ungava peninsula. The port of Sept-Iles and the railway connecting it with Schefferville allow easy shipment to the furnaces and steel mills of Canada, the USA and Europe. The setting-up of a steel industry is being explored.

Non-metallic minerals produced include: Asbestos ($315,696,000; about 87% of Canadian production), titane-dioxide ($108,300,000), industrial lime, dolomite and brucite, quartz and pyrite. Among the building materials produced were: Stone, $111,358,000; cement, $124,108,000; sand and gravel, $77,599,000; lime, $21,673,000.

Agriculture. In 1983 the total area (estimate) of the principal field crops was 2,124,800 hectares. The yield of the principal crops was (in 1,000 tonnes):

Crops	*Yield*	*Crops*	*Yield*
Tame hay	4,000	Fodder corn	2,500
Oats for grain	335	Maize for grain	975
Potatoes	295	Barley	335
Mixed grains	130	Buckwheat	12

The farm cash receipts from farming operations in 1983 amounted to $2,844,371,000. The principal items being: Livestock and products, $2,200,933,000; crops, $412,872,000; dairy supplements payments, $127,502,000, forest and maple products, $48,105,000.

Forestry. Forests cover an area of 764,279 sq. km. About 556,044 sq. km are classified as productive forests, of which 652,956 sq. km are provincial crown land and 108,992 sq. km are privately owned. Quebec leads the Canadian provinces in pulpwood production, having nearly half of the Canadian estimated total.

In 1982 production of lumber was softwood and hardwood, 6,516,857 cu. metres; woodpulp, 6,282,713 tonnes; paper and paperboard, 5,480,898 tonnes.

Fisheries. The principal fish are cod, herring, red fish, lobster and salmon. Total catch of sea fish, 1983, 68,784 tonnes, valued at $54,705,846.

INDUSTRY AND TRADE

Industry. In 1982 there were 10,753 industrial establishments in the province; employees, 482,337; salaries and wages, $9,915,886,480; cost of materials, $32,543,904,029; value of shipments, $54,293,104,947. Among the leading industries are petroleum refining, pulp and paper mills, smelting and refining, dairy products, slaughtering and meat processing, motor vehicle manufacturing, women's clothing, saw-mills and planing mills, iron and steel mills, commercial printing.

Commerce. In 1983 the value of Canadian exports through Quebec custom ports was $18,274,864,000; value of imports, $13,840,684,000.

COMMUNICATIONS

Roads. In 1983 there were 59,749 km of roads and (1983) 3,823,820 registered motor vehicles.

Railways. There were (1982) 8,322 km of railway. There is a metro system in Montreal.

Aviation. In 1983 Quebec had 2 international airports, Dorval (Montreal) with landing runway of 8·4 km and Mirabel (Montreal) with 7·3 km.

Post and Broadcasting. Telephones numbered 4,077,038 in 1983 and there were 25 television and 119 radio stations in 1982.

Newspapers (1983). There were 10 French- and 2 English-language daily newspapers.

EDUCATION. The province has 7 universities: 3 English-language universities, McGill (Montreal) founded in 1821, Bishop (Lennoxville) founded in 1845 and the Concordia University (Montreal) granted a charter in 1975; 4 French-language universities: Laval (Quebec) founded in 1852, Montreal University, opened in 1876 as a branch of Laval and became independent in 1920, Sherbrooke University founded in 1954 and University of Quebec founded in 1968.

In 1983–84 there were 96,900 full-time university students and 96,800 part-time students.

In 1982–83, in pre-kindergartens, there were 7,501 pupils; in kindergartens, 91,655; primary schools, 550,073; in secondary schools, 515,347; in colleges (post-secondary, non-university), 149,956; and in classes for children with special needs, 93,953. The school boards had a total of 66,030 teachers.

Expenditure of the Department of Education for 1982–83, $6,108,932,000 net. This included $959,104,000 for universities, $3,712,393,000 for public primary and secondary schools, $173,916,000 for private primary and secondary schools and $803,624,000 for colleges.

Books of Reference

Statistical Information: The Quebec Bureau of Statistics was established in 1912. The Bureau, which reports to the Executive council since Sept. 1981, collects, compiles and distributes statistical information relative to Quebec. *Director:* Nicole Gendreau.

A statistical information list is available on request. Among the most important publications are: *Annuaire du Québec* (Quebec Yearbook), *Statistiques* (quarterly), *Comptes économiques du Québec* (annual), *Perspectives démographiques* (annual), *Situation démographique* (annual), *Exportations internationales du Québec* (annual), *Statistiques du travail et de la main-d'oeuvre* (annual), *Investissements privés et publics* (annual), *Eléments de prévisions économiques* (quarterly), *Statistiques manufacturières* (annual).

Atlas du Québec: L'Agriculture. Ministère de l'Industrie et du Commerce, Quebec, 1966
Baudoin, L., *Le Droit civil de la province de Québec.* Montreal, 1953
Blanchard, R., *Le Canada-français.* Paris, 1959
Hamelin, J., *Histoire du Québec.* St-Hyacinthe, 1978
Jacobs, J., *The Question of Separatism: Quebec and the Struggle for Sovereignty.* London, 1981
McWhinney, E., *Quebec and the Constitution.* Univ. of Toronto Press, 1979
Ouellet, F., *Histoire de la Chambre de Commerce de Québec, 1809–1959.* Québec, 1959
Raynauld, A., *Croissance et structure économiques de la province de Québec.* Québec, 1961
Trofimenkoff, S. M., *Action Française.* Univ. of Toronto Press, 1975
Wade, F. M., *The French Canadians, 1760–1967.* Toronto, 1968.—*Canadian Dualism: Studies of French–English Relations.* Quebec–Toronto, 1960

SASKATCHEWAN

HISTORY. Saskatchewan derives its name from its major river system, which the Cree Indians called 'Kis-is-ska-tche-wan', meaning 'swift flowing'. It officially became a province when it joined the Confederation on 1 Sept. 1905.

In 1670 King Charles II granted to Prince Rupert and his friends a charter covering exclusive trading rights in 'all the land drained by streams finding their outlet in the Hudson Bay'. This included what is now Saskatchewan. The trading company was first known as The Governor and Company of Adventurers of England; later as the Hudson's Bay Company. In 1869 the Northwest Territories was formed, and this included Saskatchewan. In 1882 the District of Saskatchewan was formed. By

1885 the North-West Mounted Police had been inaugurated, with headquarters in Regina (now the capital), and the Canadian Pacific Railway's transcontinental line had been completed, bringing a stream of immigrants to southern Saskatchewan. The Hudson's Bay Company surrendered its claim to territory in return for cash and land around the existing trading posts. Legislative government was introduced.

AREA AND POPULATION. Saskatchewan is bounded on the west by Alberta, on the east by Manitoba, to the north by the Northwest Territories; to the south it is bordered by the US states of Montana and North Dakota. The area of the province is 251,700 sq. miles (570,113 sq. km), of which 220,182 sq. miles is land area and 31,518 sq. miles is water. The population, 1981 census, was 968,313 (1984, estimate, 1,007,700). Population of principal cities, 1981 census (1984 estimate): Regina (capital), 162,984 (172,340); Saskatoon, 154,210 (170,748); Moose Jaw, 33,941 (35,118); Prince Albert, 31,380 (32,957); Yorkton, 15,339 (15,895); Swift Current, 14,747 (15,772); North Battleford, 14,030 (14,702); Estevan, 9,174 (10,056); Weyburn, 9,523 (10,038); Lloydminster, 6,034 (6,312); Melfort, 6,010 (6,458); Melville, 5,092 (5,320).

Vital statistics, *see* p. 269.
Religion, *see* p. 286.

CLIMATE. A cold continental climate, with severe winters and warm summers. Rainfall amounts are greatest from May to Aug. Regina. Jan. 0°F (−17·8°C), July 65°F (18·3°C). Annual rainfall 15″ (373 mm).

CONSTITUTION AND GOVERNMENT. The provincial government is vested in a Lieut.-Governor, an Executive Council and a Legislative Assembly, elected for 5 years. Women were given the franchise in 1916 and are also eligible for election to the legislature. State of parties in July 1984: Progressive Conservative, 55; New Democratic Party, 8; Liberal, 1.

Lieut.-Governor: F. W. Johnson.
Flag: Green over gold, with the shield of the province in the canton, and a green and red prairie lily in the fly.

The Progressive Conservative Ministry in March 1985 was composed as follows:

Premier: Grant Devine.
Deputy Premier, Economic Development and Trade, Provincial Secretary, Saskatchewan Power Corporation: Eric Berntson. *Finance and Leader of the House:* Bob Andrew. *Energy and Mines, Potash Corporation of Saskatchewan:* Paul Schoenals. *Agriculture:* Lorne Hepworth. *Justice and Attorney-General, Saskatchewan Telecommunications:* Gary Lane. *Urban Affairs:* Tim Embury. *Parks and Renewable Resources:* Colin Maxwell. *Culture and Recreation:* Rick Folk. *Education:* Patricia Smith. *Social Services:* Gordon Dirks. *Labour:* Lorne McLaren. *Tourism and Small Business:* Jack Klein. *Science and Technology, Telephones, Advanced Education and Manpower:* Gordon Currie. *Health:* Graham Taylor. *Environment:* Neal Hardy. *Highways:* Jim Garner. *Revenue and Financial Services:* Paul Rousseau. *Consumer and Commercial Affairs:* Joan Duncan. *Supply and Services, Deputy Leader of the House:* George McLeod. *Co-operation and Co-operative Development:* Jack Sandberg. *Rural Development:* Louis Domotor. *Ministers without Portfolio:* Sid Dutchak *(Indian and Native Affairs, Saskatchewan Housing Corporation)*, Gerald Muirhead *(Saskatchewan Crop Insurance)*.

Agent-General in London: R. A. Larter, 21 Pall Mall, SW1Y 5LP.

Local Government. The organization of a city requires a minimum population of 5,000 persons; that of a town, 500; that of a village, 100 people. No requirements as to population exist for the rural municipality and the local improvement district.

Cities, towns, villages and rural municipalities are governed by elected councils, which consist of a mayor and 6–20 aldermen in a city; a mayor and 6 councillors in a town; a mayor and 2 other members in a village; a reeve and a councillor for each division in a rural municipality (usually 6). Local improvement districts are administered by the Department of Municipal Affairs.

FINANCE. Budget and net assets (years ending 31 March) in Canadian $1,000[2]:

	1980–81[1 2]	*1982–83*[2]	*1983–84*	*1984–85*[1]
Budgetary revenue	2,019,345	2,523,803	2,699,216	2,912,701
Budgetary expenditure	2,018,303	2,821,554	3,041,095	3,211,304

[1] Estimate.
[2] Excludes Consolidated Fund, Community Capital Fund, Saskatchewan Heritage Fund, Energy and Resource Development Fund and The Marketing Development Fund.

ENERGY AND NATURAL RESOURCES. Agriculture used to dominate the history and economics of Saskatchewan, but the 'prairie province' is now a rapidly developing mining and manufacturing area. It is a major supplier of oil; has the world's largest deposits of potash; and net value of non-agricultural production account for (1983 estimate) 61% of the provincial economy.

Electricity. The Saskatchewan Power Corporation generated 10,668m. kwh. in 1983.

Minerals. The 1983 mineral production was valued at $2,651,400,000, including (in $1,000): Petroleum 1,612,399; natural gas, 60,415; coal, 91,600; gold, 2,573; silver, 2,222; copper, 13,676; zinc, 6,782; potash, 620,912; salt, 20,821; uranium, 119,600; sodium sulphate, 39,427.

Agriculture. Saskatchewan produces normally about two-thirds of Canada's wheat. Wheat production in 1982 (in 1,000 tonnes), was 15,622 from 20·7m. acres; oats, 648 from 1·1m. acres; barley, 2,613 from 3m. acres; rye, 203 (1979) from 360,000 acres; rapeseed, 1,089,000 from 1·4m. acres; flax, 259 (1979) from 800,000 acres. Livestock (1 July 1983): Cattle and calves, 2,275,000; swine, 545,000; sheep and lambs, 68,000. Poultry in 1982: Chickens, 4,793,000; turkeys 459,000. Cash income from the sale of farm products in 1983 was $3,060m. At the June 1981 census there were 67,318 commercial farms in the province, each being a holding having agricultural sales of $2,500 or more.

The South Saskatchewan River irrigation project, whose main feature is the Gardiner Dam, was completed in 1967. It will ultimately provide for an area of 200,000 acres of irrigated cultivation in Central Saskatchewan. In 1981, 38,023 acres were developed. Total irrigated land, 138,164 acres.

Forestry. Half of Saskatchewan's area is forested, but only 115,000 sq. km are of commercial value at present. Forest products valued at $171m. were produced in 1983. The province's first pulp-mill, at Prince Albert, went into production in 1968; its daily capacity is 1,000 tons of high-grade kraft pulp.

Fur Production. In 1983–84 wild fur production was estimated at $4,029,591. Ranch-raised fur production amounted to $132,236.

Fisheries. The lakeside value of the 1983–84 commercial fish catch of 2,817,948 kg was $2,224,136.

INDUSTRY. In 1982 Saskatchewan had 749 manufacturing establishments, employing 20,115 persons. The net value of gross domestic production was $2,500m. in 1982. Manufacturing accounted for $2,500m., construction for $2·5m. in 1980.

TOURISM. An estimated 1·5m. out of province tourists spent $150m. in 1982.

COMMUNICATIONS

Roads. In 1983 there were 23,190 km of provincial highways, 180,647 km of municipal roads (including prairie trails). Motor vehicles registered totalled (1983) 694,372. Bus services are provided by 2 major lines.

Railways. There were (1983) approximately 11,857 km of main railway track in operation.

Aviation. Saskatchewan had 2 major airports, 176 airports and landing strips in 1983.

Post and Broadcasting. There were (1984) 720 post offices (excluding sub-post offices), 85 TV and re-broadcasting stations and 52 AM and FM radio stations. 695,964 telephones were connected to the Saskatchewan Telecommunications system.

EDUCATION. The University of Saskatchewan was established at Saskatoon on 3 April 1907. In 1984–85 it had 13,195 (day-time) degree students, 1,214 (part-time) and 1,000 full-time teaching staff; and 5,149 (full-time) and 3,353 (part-time) students and 350 full-time faculty members at the University of Regina which was established 1 July 1974.

The Saskatchewan public education system in 1984–85 consisted of 122 school units and districts serving 143,468 elementary pupils, 58,011 high-school students and 3,292 students enrolled in special classes. In addition, 3 provincial technical and vocational schools provided training for approximately 24,108 technical students. There are also 22 Roman Catholic separate school districts and 2 separate high-school districts. In addition there are 16 community colleges with an enrolment of approximately 100,000 registrations per year.

Books of Reference

Tourist and industrial publications, descriptive of the Government's programme, are obtainable from the Department of Industry and Commerce; other government publications from Government Information Services (Legislative Building, Regina).
Saskatchewan Economic Review. Executive Council, Regina. Annual
Morton, A. S., *Saskatchewan, the Making of a University.* Toronto, 1959
Richards, J. S., and Fung, K. I. (eds.), *Atlas of Saskatchewan.* Univ. of Saskatchewan, 1969

THE NORTHWEST TERRITORIES

HISTORY. The Territory was developed by the Hudson's Bay Company and the North West Company (of Montreal) from the 17th century. The Canadian Government bought out the Hudson's Bay Company in 1869 and the Territory was annexed to Canada in 1870. The Arctic Islands lying north of the Canadian mainland were annexed to Canada in 1880 by Queen Victoria.

AREA AND POPULATION. The total area of the Territories is 1,304,903 sq. miles (3,379,700 sq. km), divided into 5 districts, namely, Inuvik, Fort Smith, Keewatin, Baffin and Kitikmeot. The population in Dec. 1982 was 48,346, about 58% of whom were Indians or Inuit (Eskimo). Main centres (Dec. 1982): Inuvik (3,511), Fort Smith (2,302), Hay River (3,057), Frobisher Bay (2,525), Fort Simpson (984). When the transfer of governmental responsibility from Ottawa to the Territorial capital at Yellowknife took place in 1967, the population of Yellowknife increased by the influx of civil servants from 3,741 in 1966 to 10,394 in 1982.

CLIMATE. Conditions range from cold continental to polar, with long hard winters and short cool summers. Precipitation is low. Yellowknife. Jan. –15°F (–26°C), July 61°F (16·1°C). Annual rainfall 10″ (256 mm).

CONSTITUTION AND GOVERNMENT. The Northwest Territories comprises all that portion of Canada lying north of the 60th parallel of N. lat. except those portions within the Yukon Territory and the Provinces of Quebec and Newfoundland: it also includes the islands in Hudson Bay, James Bay and Ungava Bay except those within the Provinces of Manitoba, Ontario and Quebec.

The Northwest Territories is governed by a Commissioner and a Legislative Assembly. The Assembly is composed of 24 members elected for a 4-year term of office. The seat of government was transferred from Ottawa to Yellowknife when it was named territorial capital on 18 Jan. 1967.

Commissioner: J. H. Parker.

Flag: Vertically, blue, white, blue, with the white of double width and bearing the shield of the Territory.

Legislative powers are exercised by the Executive Council on such matters as taxation within the Territories in order to raise revenue, maintenance of justice, licences, solemnization of marriages, education, public health, property, civil rights and generally all matters of a local nature.

The Territorial Government has now assumed responsibility for the administration of the entire Northwest Territories. In a Territories-wide plebiscite in April 1982, a majority of residents favoured dividing the Northwest Territories into two jurisdictions. The Legislative Assembly has asked the Federal Government to agree to division and to establish a Commission to determine a boundary.

ENERGY AND NATURAL RESOURCES

Oil and Gas. As of March 1983, 1,531 permits for oil and gas exploration were held for 40·86m. hectares, of which 107 leases were on the mainland, 1,142 were on the arctic islands and 282 on the marine coast.

Crude oil, discovered in 1920, is produced and refined at Norman Wells on the Mackenzie River. In 1982, oil production was 173,294 cu. metres.

Minerals. Mineral production for the year 1983, from 11 producing mines, was valued at $516,671,000, of which zinc accounted for $282,509,000; gold, $158,559,000; lead, $38,335,000; tungsten, $3,281,000; silver, $33,145,000; arsenic trioxide, $595,000; copper, $236,000 and cadmium, $11,000.

Yellowknife continues to be the centre of goldmining activity and Canada's Cominco Ltd has completed construction of a lead-zinc mine, the Polaris Project, on Little Cornwallis Island in the central high arctic.

Trapping and Game. Fur produced during the 1982–83 season was valued at $2,574,120·54, primarily in muskrat, fox, lynx and marten. A herd of some 6,500 buffalo is protected in Wood Buffalo National Park. Barren ground caribou are increasing, due to more effective management techniques.

Forestry. The principal trees are white and black spruce, jack-pine, balsam, poplar and birch. In 1983, 27,163 cu. metres of lumber, 5,649 cu. metres of round timber and 16,268 cu. metres of fuelwood were cut.

Fisheries. Commercial fishing, principally on Great Slave Lake, in 1981–82 produced fish valued at $1·3m., principally trout, char and whitefish.

CO-OPERATIVES. There are 36 active co-operatives in the Northwest Territories. They are active in handicrafts, furs, fisheries, retail stores, print shops, provision of housing, contracting for services, etc. Total sales in 1980–81 were more than $20m.

COMMUNICATIONS

Roads. The Mackenzie Route connects Grimshaw, Alberta, with Hay River, Pine Point, Fort Smith, Fort Providence, Rae-Edzo and Yellowknife. The Mackenzie Highway extension to Fort Simpson and a road between Pine Point and Fort Resolution have both been opened.

Clearing began in 1972 for extending the Mackenzie Highway north of Fort Simpson to the arctic coast. Highway service to Inuvik in the Mackenzie Delta was opened in spring 1980, extending north from Dawson, Yukon as the Dempster Highway. The Liard Highway connecting the communities of the Liard River valley to British Columbia opened in 1984.

Railways. The Great Slave Lake Railway runs from Pine Point and Hay River, on the south shore of Great Slave Lake, 435 miles south to Grimshaw, Alberta, where it connects with the CN Rail's main system.

Aviation (1979). Fourteen licensed and 1 unlicensed airports are operated by the federal Ministry of Transport and there are 17 licensed and 18 unlicensed airports operated by the Government of the Northwest Territories. Two licensed and 10 unlicensed airports are operated by private owners. Regular mail, passenger and express services are maintained throughout the Territories. A seaplane base is operated by the Ministry of Transport and there are 17 private seaplane bases. Scheduled services join major points with centres in southern Canada.

Shipping. A direct inland-water transportation route for about 1,700 miles is provided by the Mackenzie River and its tributaries, the Athabasca and Slave rivers. Subsidiary routes on Lake Athabasca, Great Slave Lake and Great Bear River and Lake total more than 800 miles.

Post and Broadcasting (1982). There were 54 post offices. The CBC northern service operated radio stations at Yellowknife, Inuvik, Frobisher Bay and Rankin Inlet. Virtually all communities of 150 or over were receiving television in 1982 *via* satellite. Telephone service is provided by common carriers to nearly all communities in the Northwest Territories. Those few communities without service have high frequency or very high frequency radios for emergency use.

EDUCATION AND WELFARE

Education. In 1982–83 the Government of the Northwest Territories operated 71 schools with 731 teachers. In addition, one public school district operated at Yellowknife, one Roman Catholic separate school district at Yellowknife, and one school society operated a school at Rae-Edzo. The total enrolment was 12,760 in 1983, of whom about 65% were Inuit (Eskimos) and Indians. Three large and 4 small residences accommodate 400 students. Free correspondence courses are available to any pupil in a settlement where appropriate instruction is not available. There is a full range of courses available in the school system: academic, industrial arts, home economics, commercial, technical and occupational training. The continuing and special education programme provides courses and financial assistance to residents who have left the school system or are taking post high school training.

Health. In 1980 there were 7 hospitals in the Territories, 4 operated by the territorial government (Yellowknife, Hay River, Frobisher Bay and Fort Smith) and 3 operated by the federal government. Thirty-nine nursing stations, 6 health stations and 8 health centres were in operation.

Welfare. Welfare services are provided by professional social workers. Facilities included (1978) 5 children's receiving homes, 2 homes for the aged and 1 transient centre.

Books of Reference

Annual Report of the Department of Indian Affairs and Northern Development, 1974–75
Annual Report of the Government of the Northwest Territories, 1980
Boyle, E., and Sprudz, A., *Arctic Cooperatives, Canada 1965–68*
Dawson, C. A., *The New North-West.* Toronto, 1947
MacKay, D., *The Honorable Company.* Toronto, 1949

YUKON TERRITORY

HISTORY. Formerly part of the North-West Territory, Yukon was joined to the Dominion as a separate territory in 1898.

AREA AND POPULATION. The Yukon Territory is situated in the extreme north-western section of Canada and comprises 531,844 sq. km. The census population in 1981 was 23,153; 1983 (estimate), 23,216. Principal centres are Whitehorse (capital), 15,771; Faro, 1,700; Watson Lake, 1,325; Dawson City, 1,244; Mayo-Elsa, 659.

Vital statistics, *see* p. 269.
Religion, *see* p. 286.

CLIMATE. A cold climate, with considerable annual range of temperature and moderate rainfall. Whitehorse. Jan. 5°F (–15°C), July 56°F (13·3°C). Annual rainfall 10″ (250 mm). Dawson City. Jan. –22°F (–30°C), July 57°F (13·9°C). Annual rainfall 13″ (320 mm).

CONSTITUTION AND GOVERNMENT. The Yukon Territory was constituted a separate territory in June 1898. It is governed by a 5-member Executive Council (Cabinet) appointed from among the 16-member elected Legislative Assembly. The members are elected for a 4-year term. The seat of government is at Whitehorse. A federally appointed Commissioner has the final signing authority for all legislation passed by the Assembly.

Commissioner: Doug Bell.

Flag: Vertically green, white, blue, in the proportions 2 : 3 : 2, charged in the centre with the arms of the Territory.

The legislative authority of the Assembly includes direct taxation, education, property and civil rights, territorial civil service, municipalities and generally all matters of local or private nature. All other major administration including Crown lands, income tax, natural resources and particularly that which requires the spending of large sums of money, is federally controlled.

ECONOMY

Planning. There are very few major development projects at present or in the foreseeable future as the future of the mining industry, the backbone of the economy, is highly uncertain. One mine, Whitehorse Copper, has closed permanently; another, United Keno Hill, is only working at 50% capacity. The largest, Cyprus Anvil, is still not back in production; the mine is expected to re-open in 1985. In 1981 the opening of 5 new mines in eastern Yukon, the extension of railways from southern Canada and Alaska and a proposed aluminium smelter were under consideration but by 1983 many of these plans were shelved, because of the recession.

Finance. The territorial revenue and expenditure (in Canadian $1,000) for fiscal years ended 31 March was:

	1979–80	*1980–81*	*1981–82*	*1982–83*
Revenue	88,442	122,252	145,021	173,559
Expenditure	103,839	125,442	142,047	161,682

ENERGY AND NATURAL RESOURCES

Minerals. Mining remains the main industry. Lead, zinc, silver and gold are the chief minerals. Production figures for year ending 31 Dec. 1983 (provisional) in tonnes were: Lead, 391; zinc (1981), 86,486 kg; silver, 18; gold, 3. The value of mining production sales in 1983 was approximately $58·8m.

Forestry. The forests are part of the great Boreal forest region of Canada which stretches from the east coast of Canada into Alaska and north well above the Arctic Circle. Vast areas are covered by coniferous stands in the southern portion of Yukon with white spruce and lodgepole pine forming pure stands on wet sites and in northern aspects. Deciduous species form pure stands or occur mixed with conifers throughout forest areas.

The forestry industry remained very depressed in 1983. The major operator, Cattermole Timber, operated on only a very small scale.

Game and Furs. The country abounds with big game, such as moose, goat, caribou, mountain sheep and bear (grizzly and black). In 1979–80, 52,800 pelts were taken for a market value of $917,048. Lynx was the most valuable fur and made up 45% of the total harvest bringing in $416,458 in revenues.

TOURISM. In 1983, 394,000 tourists visited Yukon and spent $77m.

COMMUNICATIONS

Roads. The Alaska Highway and its side roads connect Yukon's main communities with Alaska and the provinces and with adjacent mining centres. Interior roads connect the mining communities of Elsa (silver–lead), Faro (lead–zinc–silver). Tungsten (tungsten) and mineral exploration properties (lead–zinc and tungsten) north of Ross River. The Dempster Highway north of Dawson City connects with Inuvik, on the Arctic coast; this highway, the first public road to be built to the Arctic ocean, was opened in Aug. 1979. The Carcross–Skagway road was opened in May 1979, providing a new access to the Pacific ocean. There are 4,230 km of roads in the Territory, of which about 380 km are paved. The rest are all-weather gravel.

Railways. The 176-km White Pass and Yukon Railway connected Whitehorse with year-round ocean shipping at Skagway, Alaska, but was suspended in 1982.

Aviation. Commercial airlines provide regular services between Whitehorse, Watson Lake, Edmonton and Vancouver. Regularly scheduled air services extend from Whitehorse to interior communities of Faro, Mayo, Dawson City, Old Crow, Ross River, Watson Lake, MacMillan Pass, Juneau with connecting service to Anchorage, Seattle, Fairbanks and other points in Alaska. There are several commercial bush plane operations for charter service.

Shipping. Some goods are shipped into the Territory by air or *via* the Alaska Highway, but most are containerized in Vancouver and brought up the coast by ship to Skagway, Alaska. The containers are then taken by train from Skagway to Whitehorse, and then hauled by truck to the outlying communities. Many of these trucks then return to Whitehorse hauling ore to be shipped out. Some goods are transported within the Territory by air. Although navigable, the rivers are no longer used for shipping.

Post and Broadcasting. There are 2 radio stations in Whitehorse and 13 low-power relay radio transmitters operated by CBC. There are also 12 cable-TV channels in Whitehorse, TV channels in Whitehorse and private cable operations in Faro (provided by Canadian Satellite), Dawson City and Watson Lake. Live CBC national television is provided by the Anik satellite to virtually every community in the Territory. All telephone and telecommunications in the Territory are provided by NorthwesTel, a subsidiary of Canadian National Telecommunications. Almost all pole lines have been replaced with microwave transmission.

Newspapers. In 1984 there were 2 newspapers, each 3 days a week, in Whitehorse. Faro has a two-monthly newspaper.

EDUCATION AND WELFARE

Education In Sept. 1982, the Territory had 26 schools with 4,849 pupils. In addition to the courses given in the Yukon Vocational and Technical Centre, the Yukon offers a limited number of post-secondary courses through the University of Alberta, University of Victoria and Red Deer College. A Yukon Teacher Education Programme started in 1977 to train local residents to obtain Bachelor of Education degrees in Education and a Teaching Certificate. The course is conducted by the University of British Columbia. The Government provides financial assistance to students requiring further education elsewhere.

Health. The health care system provides all residents with the care demanded by illness or accident. The federal government operates 1 general hospital at Whitehorse, 3 cottage hospitals, 2 nursing stations, with a total of 150 beds, 11 health centres and 4 health stations. The territorial government also operates a medical evacuation programme to send patients to Edmonton or Vancouver for specialized treatment not available in the Territory.

Books of Reference

Annual Report of the Commissioner.
Yukon Territorial Government, *Statistical Review.*
Berton, P., *Klondike.* Toronto, 1963
McCourt, E., *The Yukon and Northwest Territories.* Toronto, 1969

CAPE VERDE

Capital: Praia
Population: 296,093 (1980)
GNP per capita: US$340 (1981)

República de Cabo Verde

HISTORY. The Cape Verde Islands were discovered in 1460 by Diogo Gomes, the first settlers arriving in 1462. In 1587 its administration was unified under a Portuguese governor. The colony became an Overseas Province in 1951.

On 30 Dec. 1974 Portugal transferred power to a transitional government headed by the Portuguese High Commissioner. Full independence was granted on 5 July 1975.

AREA AND POPULATION. Cape Verde is situated in the Atlantic Ocean 620 km WNW of Senegal and consists of 10 islands and 5 islets. Praia is the capital. The islands are divided into 2 groups, named Barlavento (windward) and Sotavento (leeward). The total area is 4,033 sq. km (1,557 sq. miles). The population (census, 1980) was 296,093.

The areas and populations (1980, census) of the islands are:

	Sq. km	*Population*		*Sq. km*	*Population*
Santo Antão	779	43,198	Maio	269	4,103
Sao Vicente [1]	227	41,792	São Tiago	991	145,923
São Nicolau	388	13,575	Fogo	476	31,115
Sal	216	6,006	Brava	67	6,984
Boa Vista	620	3,397			
			Sotavento	1,803	188,125
Barlovento	2,230	107,968			
			Total	4,033	296,093

[1] Includes Santa Luzia which is uninhabited.

The main towns are Mindelo on São Vicente (28,797, 1970 census) and Praia on São Tiago, the capital (37,500, 1980 census).

Crioulo serves as the common language of the islands, although the official language is Portuguese.

CLIMATE. The climate is arid, with a cool dry season from Dec. to June and warm dry conditions for the rest of the year. Rainfall is sparse, rarely exceeding 5″ (127 mm) in the northern islands or 12″ (304 mm) in the southern ones. There are periodic severe droughts. Praia. Jan. 72°F (22·2°C), July 77°F (25°C). Annual rainfall 10″ (250 mm).

CONSTITUTION AND GOVERNMENT. The Constitution adopted on 12 Feb. 1981 removed all reference to possible future union with Guinea-Bissau, and the *Partido Africano da Independencia de Cabo Verde*, founded 20 Jan. 1981, became the sole legal party. The legislature consists of a unicameral People's National Assembly of 56 members elected for 5 years by universal suffrage; it elects the President, who appoints and leads a Council of Ministers. Elections were held on 7 Dec. 1980.

President: Aristides Maria Pereira (assumed office 5 July 1975; re-elected 1980).

In April 1984 the Council of Ministers comprised:

Prime Minister: Maj. Pedro Verona Rodrigues Pires.

Foreign Affairs: Col. Silvino Manuel da Luz. *Defence:* Col. Honorio Chantre. *Interior:* Col. Julio de Carvalho. *Economy and Finance:* Cmdt Osvaldo Lopez da Silva. *Education and Culture:* José Araújo. *Transport and Telecommunications.* Herculano Vieira. *Health and Social Affairs:* Dr Ireneu Gomes. *Justice:* Dr David Hopffer Cordeiro Almada. *Rural Development:* Cmdt João Pereira Silva. *Housing and Public Works:* Tito Livio Santos de Oliveira Ramos. *Secretaries of State:* Jose Brito *(Planning and Co-operation)*, Virgilio Fernandes *(Trade, Tourism and*

Crafts), Dr Arnaldo Vasconcellos Franca *(Finance)*, Miguel Lima *(Fishing)*, Adao Rocha *(Industry and Energy)*, Dr Corsino Antonio Fortes *(Social Communications)*.

National flag: Horizontally yellow over green, with a vertical red strip in the hoist charged slightly above the centre with a black star surrounded by a wreath of maize, and beneath this a yellow clam shell.

Local government: The 2 *distritos* (Barlovento and Sotavento) are sub-divided into 14 *conçelhos* – Ribeira Grande, Paúl, Porto Novo (these 3 covering Santo Antão island), São Vicente (including Santa Luzia), São Nicolau, Sal, Boa Vista, Maio, Praia, Santa Catarina, Tarrafal, Santa Cruz (these 4 covering Sao Tiago island), Fogo and Brava.

DEFENCE

Army. The Popular Revolutionary Armed Forces had a strength of 1,100 in 1985. There is also a paramilitary People's Militia.

Navy. There are 3 fast gunboats and 2 fast attack craft (*ex*-torpedo boats), all 5 *ex*-Soviet. A small *ex*-Portuguese hydrographic vessel is also reportedly in service (1985). Personnel (1985) 75.

Air Force. An embryo air force has been formed with two An-26 twin-turboprop transports and about 25 personnel.

INTERNATIONAL RELATIONS

Membership. Cape Verde is a member of UN, OAU and an ACP state of EEC.

ECONOMY

Budget. In 1981, the budget included revenue of 944m. escudos Caboverdianos and expenditure, 1,082m.

Currency. *Escudo Caboverdianos.* In Feb. 1985, 90·80 *Escudo* = £1 and 89·27 *Escudo* = US$1.

Banking. The Banco de Cabo Verde is the bank of issue and commercial bank, with branches at Praia, Mindelo and Espargos (Sal).

ENERGY AND NATURAL RESOURCES

Electricity. Production in 1972 amounted to 6·8m. kwh; capacity, 6,032 kw.

Minerals. Salt is obtained on the islands of Sal, Boa Vista and Maio. Volcanic rock (pozzolana) is mined for export.

Agriculture. Mostly confined to irrigated inland valleys, the chief crops (production, 1981, in tonnes) are: Sugar-cane, 15,000; bananas, 9,000; cassava, 6,000, sweet potatoes, 5,000; maize, 3,000 and coffee. Bananas and coffee are mainly for export.

Livestock (1983): 75,000 goats, 13,000 cattle, 22,000 pigs and 6,000 asses.

Fisheries. About 8,000 tonnes of tuna and 200 tonnes of lobsters are caught annually.

COMMERCE. Imports in 1981 totalled 3,451·6m. escudos Caboverdianos, of which 40% came from Portugal; exports in 1981 totalled 147m. escudos Caboverdianos, of which 62% went to Portugal, 10% to Angola. In 1978 32% by value of exports were fish, 17% salt and 10% bananas.

Total trade of Cape Verde with UK (British Department of Trade returns, in £1,000 sterling):

	1980	*1981*	*1982*	*1983*	*1984*
Imports to UK	207	22	49	122	211
Exports and re-exports from UK	1,047	1,260	2,068	1,245	1,162

COMMUNICATIONS

Roads. There were 2,250 km of roads (560 km paved) in 1981 and there were 4,000 private cars and 1,343 commercial vehicles.

Aviation. Amilcar Cabral International Airport, on Sal, is a major refuelling point on flights to Africa and South America, with 21,200 passengers disembarking and 23,106 embarking in 1982.

Shipping. The main ports are Mindelo and Praia. In 1982 the ports handled 371,812 tonnes of imports and 146,822 tonnes of exports. In 1981, the merchant marine comprised 20 vessels of 10,793 GRT.

Broadcasting. The private broadcasting stations are operating on shortwaves. There were (1982) 42,000 radio receivers and (1981) 1,739 telephones.

Cinemas. In 1972 there were 6 cinemas with 2,800 seats.

JUSTICE, RELIGION, EDUCATION AND WELFARE

Justice. There is a network of People's Tribunals, with a Supreme Court in Praia.

Religion. In 1980, over 96% of the population were Roman Catholic.

Education. In 1980 there were 50,778 pupils and 1,436 teachers at 436 primary schools, 6,500 pupils and 207 teachers at 15 preparatory schools, 2,216 pupils and 141 teachers at 3 secondary schools, and 679 students and 40 teachers at a technical school. In 1978 there were 198 students and 32 teachers in a teacher-training college and about 500 students were at foreign universities.

Health. In 1977 there were 23 hospitals and dispensaries with 640 beds; there were also 43 doctors, 2 dentists, 6 pharmacists and 148 nursing personnel.

DIPLOMATIC REPRESENTATIVES

Of Great Britain in Cape Verde
Ambassador: P. L. O'Keeffe, CMG, CVO (resides in Dakar).

Of Cape Verde in the USA (3415 Massachusetts Ave., NW, Washington, D.C., 20007)
Ambassador: José Luis Fernandes Lopes.

Of the USA in Cape Verde (Rua Hoji Ya Yenna 81, Praia)
Ambassador: John M. Yates.

Of Cape Verde to the United Nations
Ambassador: Dr Corentino Virgílio Santos.

Books of Reference

Annuario Estatistico de Cabo Verde. Praia. Annual
Andrade, E., *The Cape Verde Islands: From Slavery to Modern Times.* Dakar, 1973
Carreira, A., *The People of the Cape Verde Islands.* London, 1982
Lobban, R., *The Cape Verde Islands.* New York, 1974

CAYMAN ISLANDS

Capital: George Town
Population: 18,750 (1983)

HISTORY. The islands were discovered by Columbus on 10 May 1503 and were ceded (with Jamaica) to Britain in 1670. Grand Cayman was settled in 1734 and the other islands in 1833. They became a separate Crown Colony on 4 July 1959, administered by the same governor as Jamaica until the latter's independence on 6 Aug. 1962 when they received their own Administrator.

AREA AND POPULATION. Cayman Islands consist of Grand Cayman, Little Cayman and Cayman Brac. Situated in the Caribbean Sea, about 200 miles NW of Jamaica. Area, 100 sq. miles (260 sq. km). Census population of 1979, 16,677. Grand Cayman (population 15,000), 22 miles long, 4–8 miles broad; capital: George Town (population 7,617). Little Cayman, 10 miles long, 1 mile broad. Cayman Brac, 12 miles long and 1¼ miles wide. Total population of the lesser islands, 1,677. Vital statistics (1983): Births, 387; marriages, 204; deaths, 105.

CLIMATE. The climate is tropical maritime, with a cool season from Nov. to March and temperatures some 10°F warmer for the remaining months. Rainfall averages 56″ (1,400 mm) a year at George Town. Hurricanes may be experienced between July and Nov.

CONSTITUTION AND GOVERNMENT. A new Constitution came into force in Aug. 1972. The Legislative Assembly consists of the Governor, not less than 2 nor more than 3 official members, and 12 elected members.

The Executive Council consists of 3 official members appointed from among the official members of the Legislative Assembly, and 4 elected members elected by the elected members of the Assembly with the Governor as Chairman.

Governor: G. Peter Lloyd, CMG, CVO.

Flag: British Blue Ensign with the arms of the Colony on a white disc in the fly.

ECONOMY

Budget. Revenue 1983, CI$49·89m.; expenditure, CI$36·8m. Public debt (31 Dec. 1983), CI$9·5m.; total reserves, CI$11m.

Banking. Thirty-three commercial banks and trust companies hold category 'A' licences, which permit the holders to offer services to the public. Barclays Bank International has offices at George Town and Cayman Brac.

INDUSTRY AND TRADE

Industry. Finance and tourism are the main industries.

Commerce. Exports (estimate), 1982 (f.o.b.), totalled CI$2m. and included primary turtle products. Imports, estimate (c.i.f.), CI$110m.; principally foodstuffs, manufactured items, textiles, building materials, automobiles and petroleum products.

Total trade between Cayman Islands and UK (British Department of Trade returns, in £1,000 sterling):

	1982	*1983*	*1984*
Imports to UK	613	610	12,911
Exports and re-exports from UK	6,717	4,046	4,905

Tourism. Tourism is now the chief industry of the islands and in recent years 19 hotels have been completed. There were 307,978 visitors in 1983.

COMMUNICATIONS

Roads. There were (1982) about 110 miles of road and over 8,600 motor vehicles.

Aviation. Cayman Airways provides regular services between Grand Cayman and Miami, Houston and Jamaica. Republic Airways provide a daily service between Miami and Grand Cayman. CAL provides a regular inter-island service. Air Jamaica also provides services between Grand Cayman and Jamaica.

Shipping. Motor vessels ply regularly between the Cayman Islands, Jamaica, Costa Rica and Florida. Shipping registered at George Town, 615 vessels (23 Aug. 1984).

Post and Broadcasting. There were 5,985 telephones in 1983 and there are 2 broadcasting stations in the islands.

Newspapers. The *Caymanian Compass* is published 5 days a week, *The Cayman Islands Sun, The Cayman Pilot* and the *Caymanian Herald* are published twice weekly.

JUSTICE, RELIGION, EDUCATION AND WELFARE

Justice. There is a Grand Court, sitting 6 times a year at George Town under a Chief Justice. 2 Summary Courts (one civil and one criminal) sit at other times.

Religion. There are Anglican, Roman Catholic, Presbyterian and other Christian communities represented in the islands.

Education. In 1983 there were 9 government primary schools with 1,097 pupils, 6 private elementary schools with 868 pupils and 4 private secondary schools with 212 pupils. Post-primary education at the government high schools and the government middle school and private schools was attended by 2,090 pupils. There was also a private institution for further education and a government school for special educational needs.

Health. In 1983 there was a fully-equipped general hospital in George Town with 12 doctors, a dental clinic, 4 district clinics and a hospital in Cayman Brac.

Books of Reference

Annual Report, 1983. Cayman Islands Government, 1984
Statistical Abstract of the Cayman Islands, 1983. Cayman Islands Government Statistics Unit, 1984

CENTRAL AFRICAN REPUBLIC

Capital: Bangui
Population: 2·52m. (1983)
GNP per capita: US$320 (1981)

République centrafricaine

HISTORY. Central African Republic became independent on 13 Aug. 1960, after having been one of the 4 territories of French Equatorial Africa (under the name of Ubangi Shari) and from 1 Dec. 1958 a member state of the French Community. In Jan. 1959 the 4 republics formed an 'economic, technical and customs union'. A new Constitution was adopted by a special congress of the *Mouvement pour l'évolution sociale de l'Afrique noire* on 4 Dec. 1976. It provided for the country to be a parliamentary democracy and to be known as the Central African Empire. President Bokassa became Emperor Bokassa I. The Emperor was overthrown in a *coup* on 20–21 Sept. 1979 and the empire was abolished. On 15 March 1981 David Dacko was again elected President but was deposed on 1 Sept. 1981 by General André Kolingba.

AREA AND POPULATION. The Central African Republic is bounded north by Chad, east by Sudan, south by Zaïre and Congo, and west by Cameroon. The area covers 622,436 sq. km (240,324 sq. miles); its population in 1975 census, 2,054,610 and estimate in 1983 was 2·52m. The capital is Bangui (387,100 inhabitants in 1981): other towns, Berberati (95,000) and Bouar (51,000).

The principal ethno-linguistic groups are the Banda (27·4% of the population), Baya (24·4%), Mandja (21·2%), Ubangi (12·2%), Sara (7%), Mbum (6%) and Fertit (2·4%). The national language is Sango, used as a *lingua franca* throughout the country; French is the official language.

CLIMATE. A tropical climate with little variation in temperature. The wet months are May, June, Oct. and Nov. Bangui. Jan. 80°F (26·5°C), July 77°F (25°C). Annual rainfall 61″ (1,525 mm). Ndele. Jan. 83°F (28·3°C), July 77°F (25°C). Annual rainfall 57″ (1,417 mm).

CONSTITUTION AND GOVERNMENT. Following the bloodless *coup* of 1 Sept. 1981, all legislative and executive power was held by a 23-member Military Committee for National Recovery (CMRN), ruling through an appointed Council of Ministers. The constitution and political parties were suspended.

The Council of Ministers in Jan. 1984 was composed as follows:

Chairman of CMRN, Head of State and Government, Minister of Defence and Veterans' Affairs: Gen. André Kolingba (assumed office 1 Sept. 1981).

Ministers of State: Lieut.-Col. Jean-Louis Gervil Yambala *(Economy and Finance)*, Col. Alphonse Gombadi *(Rural Development)*.

Foreign Affairs and International Co-operation: Second-Lieut. Clément Michel N'Gai Voueto. *Interior:* Lieut.-Col. Christophe Grelombe. *Public Works and Urban Affairs:* Maj.-Gen. Abel Nado. *Public Health and Social Affairs:* Maj-Gen. Xavier Sylvestre Yangongo. *Education:* Maj. Gabriel Ngaindiro. *Justice:* Maj. Gaspard Kalene. *Civil Service, Labour and Social Security:* Maj. Stanislas Pollagba. *Posts and Telecommunications:* Capt. Samuel Ngaiouma. *Trade and Industry:* Capt. Luc Nganafei. *Transport and Civil Aviation:* Capt. Raymond Ndougou. *Secretaries of State:* Col. Francois Diallo *(Defence, War Veterans, Energy and Water Resources)*, Lieut. Michel Salle *(General Secretariat)*.

National flag: Four horizontal stripes of blue, white, green, yellow; over all in the centre a vertical red strip, and in the canton a yellow star.

Local Government: Central African Republic is divided into 14 prefectures, 2 'economic prefectures' and the autonomous commune of Bangui (the capital).

DEFENCE. Selective national service for a 2-year period is in force.

Army. The Army consisted (1984) of about 2,000 men, comprising an infantry battalion, with supporting engineer, signals and transport companies. Equipment includes 4 T-55 tanks, 22 BRDM-2 reconnaissance vehicles and 10 Ferret scout cars. There is also a 1,500-strong paramilitary force.

Navy. The naval force has 9 river patrol craft and (1985) 85 personnel.

Air Force. The Air Force has 12 Argentine-built 1A 58 Pucara attack aircraft, 2 Rallye Guerrier armed light aircraft, 1 twin-jet Caravelle, 1 DC-4 and 4 C-47 transports, 2 Reims-Cessna 337, 10 Aermacchi AL.60 and 6 Broussard liaison aircraft, 1 Alouette and 4 H-34 helicopters. It also maintains and operates the Corvette twin-jet VIP aircraft. Personnel strength (1984) about 300.

INTERNATIONAL RELATIONS

Membership. Central African Republic is a member of UN, OAU and an ACP state of EEC.

ECONOMY

Planning. The third 5-year development plan (1976–80) provided for expenditure of 23,623m. francs CFA.

Budget. The budget for 1982 provided for expenditure of 38,203m. francs CFA, and for revenue of 29,995m. francs CFA. The deficit is met by aid, mainly from France.

Currency. The unit of currency is the *franc CFA* with a parity of 50 *francs CFA* to 1 French *franc*.

Banking. The *Banque des Etats de l'Afrique Centrale* is the bank of issue.

ENERGY AND NATURAL RESOURCES

Electricity. Production in 1981 totalled 65m. kwh (94% hydro-electric).

Minerals. 250,000 carats of gem diamonds were mined in 1980.

Agriculture. Over 90% of the working population is occupied in subsistence agriculture. The main crops (production 1982, in 1,000 tonnes) are cassava, 1,040; groundnuts, 128; bananas, 84; plantains, 63; millet, 51; maize, 40; cotton, 13; coffee, 18; rice, 15.

Livestock (1983): Cattle, 1·5m.; goats, 960,000; sheep, 80,000; pigs, 140,000.

Forestry. The extensive hardwood forests, particularly in the south-west, provide mahogany, obeche and limba for export. Production (1979) 2·9m. cu. metres.

INDUSTRY AND TRADE

Industry. The small industrial sector includes factories producing cotton fabrics (2·6m. metres in 1978) and radios.

Commerce. Imports and exports in 1m. francs CFA:

	1979	*1980*	*1981*
Imports	14,816	17,009	40,100
Exports	16,937	24,384	31,900

In 1980, France took 52% of exports and provided 61% of imports. Of all exports, coffee comprised 27% (by value), diamonds 25%, timber 29% and cotton 7%.

Total trade of Central African Republic with UK (British Department of Trade returns, in £1,000 sterling):

	1980	*1981*	*1982*	*1983*	*1984*
Imports to UK	1,466	702	878	902	357
Exports and re-exports from UK	738	373	576	535	722

Tourism. There were about 4,000 visitors in 1974.

COMMUNICATIONS

Roads. In 1984 there were 21,000 km of roads and (1974) there were 9,100 passenger cars and 3,900 commercial vehicles in use.

Railways. There are no railways, but a proposal exists (1979) for an 800 km line (1,435 mm gauge) from Bangui through Cameroon and Congo to connect with the Trans-Gabon railway at Belinga.

Aviation. There is an international airport at Mpoko, near Bangui, and Air Centrafrique operates extensive internal services to several airstrips.

Post and Broadcasting. There were (1979) 400 television and 80,000 radio receivers and (1984) 5,000 telephones.

Cinemas. In 1971 there were 8 cinemas.

Newspapers. In 1984 there was one daily newspaper.

JUSTICE, RELIGION, EDUCATION AND WELFARE

Justice. The Criminal Court and Supreme Court are situated in Bangui. There are 7 civil courts throughout the country.

Religion. About 57% of the population follow animist beliefs, 20% are Roman Catholic, 15% Protestant and 8% Moslem.

Education. The University of Bangui was founded in 1970 and had 1,489 students in 1980. In 1978 there were 241,201 pupils at primary schools and 46,084 at secondary schools; technical schools held 2,523 students, while (1976) 615 were at the 2 teacher-training establishments.

Health. In 1977 there were 61 hospitals and dispensaries with 2,983 beds and 106 doctors, 3 dentists, 16 pharmacists, 142 midwives and 1,200 nursing personnel.

DIPLOMATIC REPRESENTATIVES

Of Central African Republic in Great Britain
Ambassador: (Vacant).

Of Great Britain in Central African Republic
Ambassador: Michael Glaze (resides in Yaoundé).

Of Central African Republic in the USA (1618 22nd St., NW, Washington, D.C. 20008)
Ambassador: Christian Lingama-Toleque.

Of the USA in Central African Republic (Ave. President Dacko, Bangui)
Ambassador: Edmund T. DeJarnette.

Of Central African Republic to the United Nations
Ambassador: Michel Gbezera-Bria.

CHAD

République du Tchad

Capital: N'djaména
Population: 5·12m. (1984)
GNP per capita: US$110 (1981)

HISTORY. France proclaimed a protectorate over Chad on 5 Sept. 1900, and in July 1908 the territory was incorporated into French Equatorial Africa. It became a separate colony March 1920, and in 1946 one of the four constituent territories of French Equatorial Africa. On 1 Jan. 1959 Chad became an autonomous republic within the French Community and achieved full independence on 11 Aug. 1960, although the northern prefecture of Borkou-Ennedi-Tibesti remained under French military administration until 1965.

Conflicts between the central government of President François (later Ngarta) Tombalbaye and secessionist groups, particularly in the Moslem north and centre of Chad, began in 1965 and continued despite attempts at reconciliation. President Tombalbaye was assassinated on 13 April 1975 following an Army *coup d'etat*. A Supreme Military Council of 9 members, under the Presidency of Gen. Felix Malloum, ruled until 29 Aug. 1978, when the Council was dissolved and Malloum formed a new government of 'national unity'. After further fighting an accord was finally signed in Lagos on 21 Aug. between representatives of 11 warring factions. A 22-member Transitional Government of National Unity (GUNT) was formed on 10 Nov. under the Presidency of Goukouni Oueddei. The reconciliation agreement broke down on 25 April 1980, and civil war continued until June 1982 when the *Forces Armées du Nord* (FAN) led by Hissène Habré gained control of the country.

AREA AND POPULATION. Chad is bounded west by Cameroon, Nigeria and Niger, north by Libya, east by Sudan and south by Central African Republic. Area, 1,284,000 sq. km; its population in 1984 was estimated at 5,122,000 (census 1975, 4,029,917). The capital is N'djaména, formerly Fort Lamy with 303,000 inhabitants in 1979, other large towns being Moundou (66,000), Sarh (65,000) and Abéché (54,000).

Préfecture	*sq. km*	*Population 1979*	*Capital*
Borkou-Ennedi-Tibesti	600,350	88,000	Faya-Largeau
Biltine	46,850	175,000	Biltine
Ouaddaï	76,240	347,000	Abéché
Batha	88,800	354,000	Ati
Kanem	114,520	200,000	Mao
Lac	22,320	139,000	Bol
Chari-Baguirmi	82,910	676,000	N'djaména
Guéra	58,950	207,000	Mongo
Salamat	63,000	107,000	Am Timan
Moyen-Chari	45,180	524,000	Sarh
Logone Oriental	28,035	307,000	Doba
Logone Occidental	8,695	295,000	Moundou
Tandjilé	18,045	302,000	Laï
Mayo-Kabbi	30,105	684,000	Bongor

More than 100 different languages and dialects are spoken. The largest ethnic group is the Sara of southern Chad. Arabic serves as a common language throughout the semi-tropical (Sahelian) centre and the Saharan north.

CLIMATE. A tropical climate, with adequate rainfall in the south, though Nov. to April are virtually rainless months. Further north, desert conditions prevail. N'djaména. Jan. 75°F (23·9°C), July 82°F (27·8°C). Annual rainfall 30" (744 mm).

CONSTITUTION AND GOVERNMENT. Hissène Habré was sworn in as President on 21 Oct. 1982 and a 31-member government was appointed.

In June 1983 the Libyan-backed forces of former President Goukouni Oueddei re-occupied Borkou-Ennedi-Tibesti, and in early 1985 the country remained partitioned between the two sides.

The official language is French.

National flag: Three vertical strips of blue, yellow, red.

Local Government: The 14 *préfectures* are divided into 53 *sous-préfectures.*

DEFENCE

Army. A new national army, the Forces Armées Nationales Tchadiennes (FANT) was formed in Dec. 1982. In 1985 the strength was 4,000 and there was a paramilitary force of 6,000.

Air Force. The Air Force has at least 1 Noratlas, 1 VIP Caravelle, 1 C-54 and 9 C-47 transports, 4 Reims-Cessna F337 light aircraft, 2 Turbo-Porters, 2 Broussard communications aircraft and about 14 Puma and Alouette III helicopters. Personnel (1985) about 200.

INTERNATIONAL RELATIONS

Membership. Chad is a member of UN, OAU and is an ACP state of EEC.

ECONOMY

Budget. The budget for 1983 balanced at 37,750m. francs CFA of which defence was 7,000m.

Currency. The unit of currency is the *franc CFA* with a parity value of 50 *francs CFA* to 1 French *franc.*

Banking. The *Banque des Etats de l'Afrique Centrale* is the bank of issue, and the principal commercial banks are the *Banque de Développement du Tchad* and the *Banque Tchadienne de Crédit et de Dépôts.*

ENERGY AND NATURAL RESOURCES

Electricity. Production (1980) amounted to 64m. kwh.

Oil. The oilfield in Kanem préfecture has been linked by pipeline to a new refinery at Laï (in Tandjilé).

Minerals. Salt (about 4,000 tonnes per annum) is mined around Lake Chad, and deposits of uranium, gold and bauxite are to be exploited.

Agriculture. In 1981, 82·7% of the 1,738,000 work force were occupied in agriculture, forestry and fishing. Cotton growing (in the south) and animal husbandry (in the central zone) are the most important industries. Production (1982, in 1,000 tonnes) was: Millet, 580; unginned cotton (1981), 195; groundnuts, 118; cassava, 190; rice (1981), 47.

Livestock (1983): Cattle, 3·6m.; sheep, 2·3m.; goats, 2·1m.; chickens, 3m.

Fisheries. Fish production from Lake Chad and the Chari and Logone rivers, was estimated at 115,000 tonnes in 1981.

TRADE (in 1m. francs CFA):

	1974	*1975*	*1976*	*1977*
Imports	20,859	28,325	27,593	11,255
Exports	9,053	10,103	14,861	6,862

Total trade with UK (British Department of Trade returns, in £1,000 sterling):

	1980	*1981*	*1982*	*1983*	*1984*
Imports to UK	279	12	3	8	626
Exports and re-exports from UK	361	375	1,082	2,244	3,521

COMMUNICATIONS

Roads. In 1976 there were 30,725 km of roads, of which only 240 km are surfaced. In 1977 there were 7,636 private cars and 9,668 commercial vehicles.

Aviation. There is an international airport at N'djaména, from which UTA and Air Afrique run 4 flights per week to Paris; there are also flights to Douala, Bangui and Kinshasa. Air Tchad operates internal services to 12 secondary airports.

Post and Broadcasting. In 1978 there were 3,850 telephones and (1981), 70,000 radios in use.

Cinemas. In 1977 there were 13 cinemas with 12,400 seats.

JUSTICE, RELIGION, EDUCATION AND WELFARE

Justice. There are criminal courts and magistrates courts in N'djaména, Moundou, Sarh and Abéché, with a Court of Appeal situated in N'djaména.

Religion. The northern and central parts of the country are predominantly Moslem (52% of the total population) and the southern part is mainly animist (43%) or Christian (5%).

Education. In 1977 there were 229,191 pupils in primary schools, 18,382 in secondary schools, 649 in technical schools and 549 students in teacher-training establishments. The University of Chad (founded 1971) at N'djaména had (1980) 800 students and 62 teaching staff.

Health. There were 33 hospitals with 3,353 beds in 1977 and in 1978 90 doctors, 4 dentists, 9 pharmacists, 98 midwives and 993 nursing personnel.

DIPLOMATIC REPRESENTATIVES

Of Chad in Great Britain
Ambassador: (Vacant).

Of Great Britain in Chad
Ambassador: M. F. Daly (resides in London).

Of Chad in the USA (2002 R. St., NW, Washington, D.C., 20009)
Ambassador: Mahamat Ali Adoum.

Of the USA in Chad (Ave., Felix Ebouc, N'djaména)
Ambassador: J. Peter Moffat.

Of Chad to the United Nations
Ambassador: Ramadane Barma.

Books of Reference

Aperçu sur le Tchad. Publication of the President. 2nd ed. N'djaména, 1973
L'essentiel sur le Tchad. Publication of the President. 2nd ed. N'djaména, 1972
Thompson, V., and Adloff, R., *Conflict in Chad.* London and Berkeley, 1981
Westebbe, R., *Chad: Development Potential and Constraints.* Washington, D.C., 1974

CHILE

República de Chile

Capital: Santiago
Population: 11·7 (1983)
GNP per capita: US$1,965 (1983)

HISTORY. The Republic of Chile threw off allegiance to the crown of Spain, constituting a national government on 18 Sept. 1810, finally freeing itself from Spanish rule in 1818.

AREA AND POPULATION. Chile is bounded north by Peru, east by Bolivia and Argentina, and south and west by the Pacific ocean.

Many islands to the west and south belong to Chile, including Easter Island (Isla de Pascua; 63·9 sq. miles), discovered in 1722. The coastline is about 2,650 miles in length; the average width of the country, 120 miles. Area, 756,626 sq. km or 292,135 sq. miles.

In 1940 Chile declared, and in each subsequent year has reaffirmed, its ownership of the sector of the Antarctic lying between 53° and 90° W. long.; and asserted that the British claim to the sector between the meridians 20° and 90° W. long. overlapped the Chilean by 27°. Five Chilean bases were established in Antarctica in 1947, 1948, 1951 and 1962. A law promulgated 21 July 1955 put the Intendente of the Province of Magallanes in charge of the 'Chilean Antarctic Territory'.

Three thinly-settled southern provinces of Magallanes, Chiloé and Aysén and the northern provinces of Arica and Iquique are known as 'free zones', which implies that all commodities imported into those areas from abroad are not subject to all national import duties.

The total population at the census in 1970 was 8,884,768. Census (1982) 11,275,440. Estimate (1983) 11,682,260.

The areas of the 13 regions and their populations (census, 1982) were as follows:

Region	*Sq. km*	*Census 1982*	*Capital*	*Estimate 1983*
Taracapá	58,073	273,427	Iquique	112,872
Antofagasta	125,306	341,203	Antofagasta	169,824
Atacama	78,268	183,071	Copiapó	39,942 [3]
Coquimbo	39,647	419,178	La Serena	61,889 [3]
Aconcagua	16,109	1,204,693	Valparaiso	266,726
Metropolitan	13,808	4,294,938	Santiago	4,132,293
Liberador	18,193	584,989	Rancagua	142,473
Maule	30,518	723,224	Talca	137,981
Bíobío	36,823	1,516,552	Concepción	209,925
Araucanía	31,760	692,924	Temuco	165,301
Los Lagos	67,090	843,430	Puerto Monti	62,748 [1]
Aisén	108,998	65,478	Coihaique	...
Magallanes	132,033	132,333	Punta Arenas	67,600 [2]

[1] 1970. [2] 1975. [3] 1980.

Vital statistics (1981): Revised birth rate 23·4 per 1,000 population; death rate, 6·2; marriage rate, 8; infantile mortality rate, 27 per 1,000 live births. Life expectancy: men, 63·7 years, women, 70·4.

The majority of the population is mixed or *mestizo*, due to the free intermarriage between the early Spaniards and women of indigenous tribes; language and culture remain of European origin. In urban areas the majority is white, because of European immigration during the nineteenth century. The indigenous inhabitants are of 3 branches: The *Fuegians*, mostly nomadic, living in or near Tierra del Fuego; the *Araucanians* in the valleys or on the western slopes of the Andes; the *Changos*, who inhabit the northern coast region and work as labourers and fishermen.

Other large towns (estimate, 1983) are: Viña del Mar (298,663), Talcahuano (212,865), Chillán (123,571), Arica (123,211), Valdivia (115,681) and Osorno (71,000 in 1975).

CLIMATE. With its enormous range of latitude and the influence of the Andean Cordillera, the climate of Chile is very complex, ranging from extreme aridity in the north, through a Mediterranean climate in Central Chile, where winters are wet and summers dry, to a cool temperate zone in the south, with rain at all seasons. In the extreme south, conditions are very wet and stormy. Santiago. Jan. 67°F (19·5°C), July 46°F (8°C). Annual rainfall 15″ (375 mm). Antofagasta. Jan. 69°F (20·6°C), July 57°F (14°C). Annual rainfall 0·5″ (12·7 mm). Valparaiso. Jan. 64°F (17·8°C), July 53°F (11·7°C). Annual rainfall 20″ (505 mm).

CONSTITUTION AND GOVERNMENT. The Marxist coalition government of President Salvador Allende Gossens was ousted on 11 Sept. 1973 by the 3 Armed Services and the *Carabineros* (para-military police). These forces formed a government headed by a Junta of the 4 Commanders-in-Chief. Gen. Augusto Pinochet Ugarte, Commander-in-Chief of the Army, took over the presidency. President Allende was killed on the day of the *coup*.

Marxist parties were outlawed and all political activities banned. The new Government assumed wide-ranging powers but the 'state of siege' ended in March 1978. A new Constitution was approved by 67·5% of the voters on 11 Sept. 1980 and came into force on 11 March 1981. It provided for a return to democracy after a minimum period of 8 years. Gen. Pinochet would remain in office during this period after which the Junta would nominate a single candidate for President.

On 7 Nov. 1984 Gen. Pinochet declared a national state of siege: he assumed power to control movement, communication, political activity and the media.

For details of the 1925 Constitution and earlier political history *see* THE STATESMAN'S YEAR-BOOK 1975–76, p. 808.

The capital is Santiago, founded on 12 Feb. 1541.

National flag: Two horizontal bands, white, red, with a white star on blue square in top sixth next to staff.

National anthem: Dulce patria, recibe los votos (words by E. Lillo, 1847; tune by Ramón Carnicer, 1828).

The following is a list of the presidents since 1942:

Juan Antonio Rios, 1 April 1942–27 June 1946 (died).
Alfredo Duhalde (Acting), 27 June–3 Aug. 1946 (resigned).
Vice-Admiral Vicente Merino Bielech (Acting), 3 Aug.–3 Nov. 1946.
Gabriel González Videla, 3 Nov. 1946–3 Nov. 1952.
Carlos Ibáñez del Campo, 3 Nov. 1952–3 Nov. 1958.
Jorge Alessandri Rodriguez, 3 Nov. 1958–3 Nov. 1964.
Eduardo Frei Montalva, 3 Nov. 1964–3 Nov. 1970.
Salvador Allende Gossens, 3 Nov. 1970–11 Sept. 1973 (deposed).

President of the Republic: Gen. Augusto Pinochet Ugarte.

Local Government. For the purposes of local government the Military Junta in pursuance of its policy of administrative decentralization, has divided the republic into 13 regions (12 and Greater Santiago). Each Region is presided over by a *Gobernador,* while the provinces (40) included in it are in charge of an *Intendente* who represents the central government. The provinces are divided into municipalities under an *alcalde* (mayor). All these officials are appointed by the President.

DEFENCE. Military service is for a period of 2 years at the age of 19 (Army and Navy only). Ex-conscripts are liable to 12 years' service in the active reserve and 13 in the second reserve.

Army. The Army is organized in 2 armoured, 8 cavalry and 24 infantry regiments; 10 artillery and 7 engineer battalions; and 1 helicopter-borne ranger unit. Equipment includes 150 M-4A3 and 21 AMX-30 tanks, 75 light tanks and 200 armoured cars. Strength (1985) 53,000 (30,000 conscripts) and 240,000 reserves.

Navy. The principal ships[1] of the Chilean Navy are as follows:

The British guided missile armed destroyer *Norfolk,* 5,440 tons standard, completed in 1970, was purchased in 1982 and re-named *Prat* on transfer; and her sister-ship *Antrim* of the same age was purchased in 1984 and re-named *Cochrane*.

There are 2 new West German-built small diesel-electric submarines, 2 modern diesel powered patrol submarines (British 'Oberon' class), 6 destroyers (2 British built and 2 old *ex*-US), 2 frigates (modern British 'Leander' class, *Condell* and *Lynch*), 2 fast missile craft, 4 torpedo boats, 6 patrol vessels, 12 coastal patrol craft, 1 submarine support vessel, 2 amphibious transports, 3 landing ships, 2 landing craft, 1 survey ship, 5 transports, 2 training ships, 1 antarctic patrol ship, 2 harbour patrol boats, 3 oilers, 4 floating docks and 2 tugs.

Naval personnel in 1985 totalled 22,260 (2,050 officers, 18,170 ratings, 2,040 marines).

[1] Of the three cruisers, *Prat* (ex-*Nashville*) and *O'Higgins* (ex-*Brooklyn*), both 10,000 tons standard, completed in 1938 and purchased from USA in 1951, were discarded in 1981 and 1983 respectively; and *Latorre* (ex-*Göta Lejou*) 8,200 tons, completed in 1947, acquired from Sweden in 1971, was stricken from the list in 1984. See full particulars and notes in the 1984–85 and earlier editions.

Air Force. Approximate strength (1985) is 11,000 personnel, with 110 first-line and 150 second-line aircraft, divided among 12 groups, each comprising 1 squadron, within 4 combat and support wings. Groups 1 and 12 have twin-jet A-37Bs, from a total of 34 acquired for light strike/reconnaissance duties. Group 3 is equipped for general duties with about 12 UH-1H Iroquois and Puma helicopters. Group 4 has 14 Mirage 50 fighters. Group 5 has 14 Twin Otters for light transport and survey duties. Group 6 operates 3 civil-registered Learjet 35 and King Air 100 aircraft on photo survey duties. Group 7 received 15 F-5E Tiger II fighter-bombers and 3 F-5F trainers. Groups 8 and 9 are also fighter-bomber units, with a total of 30 Hunter F.71s, *ex*-RAF FGA.9s, and T.72s. Group 10 is a transport wing, with 2 C-130H Hercules and 5 DC-6Bs. Group 11 has 9 twin-turboprop Beech 99A instrument/navigation trainers. Three *ex*-RAF Canberra PR.9s have been acquired for reconnaissance duties. Training aircraft include piston-engined Piper Dakota and T-35 Pillan basic trainers and T-37 jets have been replaced. The A-37Bs are being replaced by up to 60 Spanish-built CASA C-101BB Aviojets.

INTERNATIONAL RELATIONS

Membership. Chile is a member of the UN, OAS and LAIA (formerly LAFTA).

ECONOMY

Budget. In 1983 revenue was US$3,025·7m. and expenditure, US$3,485·3m.

Currency. In Jan. 1960 a system came into force based on the *escudo* (equivalent of 1,000 *pesos*), the *centésimo* (10 *pesos*) and the *milésimo (1 peso)*. On 29 Sept. 1975 the currency reverted to *pesos* with a value of 1,000 escudos to the new peso.

In Feb. 1985 there were 140·60 *pesos* = £1 and 143 *pesos* = US$1.

Banking. Notes in circulation and deposits in currency were 300,877m. pesos at 31 Dec. 1983; total deposits in the commercial banks stood at 197,796m. pesos (1983).

Commercial banks, since Feb. 1983, must maintain cash reserves of 60% of all sight deposits and 20% of time deposits over 30 days.

Inflation has fluctuated as follows: 31·2% (1980), 9·5% (1981), 20·7% (1982) and 23·1% (1983).

Weights and Measures. The metric system has been legally established in Chile since 1865, but the old Spanish weights and measures are still in use to some extent.

ENERGY AND NATURAL RESOURCES

Electricity. In 1983 production of electricity was 12,658·4m. kwh.

Oil. Petroleum was discovered in 1945 in the southern area of Magallanes; output, 2,284,000 cu. metres of crude oil and 4,803,000 cu. metres of natural gas in 1983.

Minerals. The wealth of the country consists chiefly in its minerals, especially in the northern provinces of Atacama and Tarapacá.

Copper is the most important source of foreign exchange (about 48% of exports) and government revenues (over 30%). The copper industry's output in 1983 was 1,257,200 tonnes. Exports during 1983 were valued at US$1,871m.

Nitrate of soda is found in the Atacama deserts. Exports were US$84m. in 1983. Production was 622,513 tonnes in 1983. Iodine is a by-product: 1983 production totalled 2,793 tonnes. The use of solar evaporation as a means of reducing costs has developed the production of potassium salts as an additional by-product.

Iron ore, of which high-grade deposits estimated at over 1,000m. tons exist in the provinces of Atacama and Coquimbo, has overtaken nitrate as Chile's second mineral. Production in 1983 was 5,973,674 tonnes, of which 3,071,900 were in pellet form.

Coal reserves exceed 2,000m. tons, partially low in thermal unit. Net 1983 production was 1,095,230 tonnes.

In 1983 other minerals include molybdenum (15,264 tonnes, pure), zinc (5,993 tonnes), manganese (26,050 tonnes), lead (1,679 tonnes).

Agriculture. Agriculture and forestry contribute one-twelfth of the national product, although one-third of the population take part in it. Total area of land being exploited (census of 1968) was 52·4m. hectares; 14·9% for agriculture, 26·7% for pasture, 28·8% for forest; 29·6% is desert or unproductive.

Some principal crops were as follows:

Crop	Area sown, 1,000 hectares 1983–84	Production, 1,000 quintals 1983–84	Crop	Area sown, 1,000 hectares 1983–84	Production, 1,000 quintals 1983–84
Wheat	471	5,860	Potatoes	81	6,836
Oats	96	1,463	Beans	85	844
Barley	33	732	Lentils	24	138
Maize	138	5,116	Peas	10	57
Rice	40	1,156	Sugar-beet	48	16,428

There were in 1955 over 300 large farms, each with more than 12,250 acres, while 500,000 peasants live on less than 4 acres per family. The military government has opted in most cases to increase the number of settlements with access to individual property. The process was completed in early 1979 with some 24,000 property titles issued, a large proportion of which were in co-operative schemes.

Production of animal products in 1983 was (in 1,000 tonnes): Cattle, 208·1; sheep, 13·3; pork, 59·2; poultry, 79. Eggs, 1,184m.; milk, 900m. litres.

Livestock (1983): Cattle, 3,865,000; horses, 440,000; asses, 28,000; sheep, 6,434,000; goats, 600,000; pigs, 1·26m.; poultry, 21m.

Forestry. According to the Forestry Institute, by late 1982, there were 825,000 hectares of artificial forests from Maule to Magallanes, the most important species being the pine (*pinus radiata*) which covers 640,000 hectares. Eucalyptus and poplar cover some 72,000 hectares. Native species of importance amounted to 9m. hectares in 1978.

Production during 1983 amounted to about 173m. in. of sawn timber. Exports of forestry products in 1983 were valued at US$116m.

Fisheries. Chile's catch of fish and shellfish in 1982 was 3·8m. tonnes; shellfish, 269,000 tonnes. Exports of seafood in 1982 were US$352m., of which fishmeal accounted for US$307m.

INDUSTRY AND TRADE

Industry. A nationally owned steel plant operates from Huachipato, near Concepción. Output, 1983, 593,000 tonnes of steel ingots. Cellulose and wood-pulp are two industries which are rapidly developing; in 1983, 637,800 tonnes of cellulose were produced. Cement (1·25m. tonnes) and fishmeal (520,700 tonnes) are also important.

Labour. In Feb. 1984 the 'economically active' numbered 3·1m. Professional and 'white-collar' workers numbered 1,336,000; agriculture employed 487,600; manufacturing, 396,000; mining, 58,300; construction, 399,200, and transport, 191,200.

Trade unions began in the middle 1880s.

Commerce. Imports and exports in US$1m.:

	1978	*1979*	*1980*	*1981*	*1982*	*1983*
Imports	2,917	4,200	5,821	7,368	3,580	2,969
Exports	2,480	3,800	4,818	4,000	3,798	3,835

In 1983 imports (in US$1m.) from USA, were valued at 764; Venezuela, 225; Brazil, 190; Japan, 161; Federal Republic of Germany, 185; Argentina, 201; Spain, 64; France, 83; UK, 61; Italy, 51.

In 1983 the principal imports were (in US$1m.): Fuels, 572; chemicals, 434; industrial equipment, 257; transport equipment, 73; spares, 174, and live animals and foodstuffs, 120. The principal exports in 1982 were (in US$1m.): Copper, 1,836; paper and pulp, 208; iron ore, 112; timber, 116; nitrate, 84.

Total trade between Chile and UK for 5 years (British Department of Trade returns, in £1,000 sterling):

	1980	*1981*	*1982*	*1983*	*1984*
Imports to UK	126,273	87,939	111,206	107,644	108,420
Exports and re-exports from UK	55,741	62,227	56,897	43,520	74,997

Tourism. There were 295,406 foreign visitors in 1983.

COMMUNICATIONS

Roads. In 1981 there were in Chile 78,025 km of highways. There were in 1982 (estimate), 850,000 automobiles, 185,000 goods vehicles and 22,500 buses.

Railways. The total length of state railway lines was (1981) 6,302 km, including 907 km electrified, of broad- and metre-gauge. In 1980 the railways carried 14·7m. tonnes and 9·4m. passengers. Further electrification is in progress between Concepción and Puerto Montt (600 km). An underground railway in Santiago was opened in Sept. 1975.

Aviation. There are 7 international airports, 16 domestic airports and about 300 landing grounds. Chile is served by 19 commercial air companies (2 Chilean). In 1980, 325,800 passengers were carried into and out of Chile on international services; 265,400 passengers were carried on internal routes.

Shipping. The mercantile marine had, in 1982, 60 ships of over 100 tons (825,076 DWT) but most of the fleet operates under flags of convenience. Valparaíso is the chief port. The free ports of Magallanes, Chiloé and Aysén serve the southern provinces. Chilean ports handled 45·6m. tons in 1982. There are 2,185 km of navigable rivers.

Post and Broadcasting. There are 1,486 post offices and agencies. The length of telegraph lines in 1971 was 12,870 km. In 1982 there were 595,108 (Santiago, 364,527) telephones in use.

A chain of wireless stations along the coast for shore-to-ship transmission is operated by the Navy. At the end of 1982 there were 267 commercial broadcasting stations. Three television stations are operated by the Universities and there is a national television station using NTSC 525 line colour standards. On 9 Aug. 1968 the satellite station at Longovilo, 50 miles south-west of Santiago, was inaugurated to cover transmissions (including colour) from the USA and Europe. In 1977 there were 2m. radio receivers and (1976) 710,000 television receivers.

Cinemas (1982). Cinemas numbered 170; 50 of them are in Santiago.

Newspapers (1981). There were 59 daily newspapers and 96 magazines.

JUSTICE, RELIGION, EDUCATION AND WELFARE

Justice. There are a High Court of Justice in the capital, 12 courts of appeal distributed over the republic, tribunals of first instance in the departmental capitals and second-class judges in the sub-delegations. The police force had (1975) about 27,000 officers and men; it is organized and regulated by the Ministry of Defence.

Religion. The Roman Catholic religion was disestablished in 1925; it remains, however, a national Church in a state wherein 89·5% of the population are Catholics. There are 1 cardinal-archbishop, 5 archbishops, 22 bishops and 2 vicars apostolic. Latest estimates show 6·7m. Roman Catholics, 880,500 Protestants and 25,000 Jews.

Education. Education is in 3 stages: Basic (6–14 years), Middle (15–18) and University (19–23). Enrolment (1981): 2,139,319 pupils in the basic schools, 392,940 pupils in the middle schools and 161,809 pupils in technical schools; teachers in 1980 numbered 66,354 in basic, 24,387 in middle and 4,176 in technical schools.

University education is provided in the state university (founded in 1842), the Catholic University at Santiago (1888), the University of Concepción (1919), the Catholic University at Valparaíso (1928), the Universidad Técnica Federico Santa María at Valparaíso (1930), the Universidad Técnica del Estado (1952), Universidad Austral, Valdivia (1954) and Universidad del Norte, Antofagasta (1957) with a total student population of 118,978 in 1981.

Health. In 1982 there were 205 hospitals, 296 health centres and 888 emergency posts. State-owned hospitals had 33,879 beds; private hospitals, 4,088. Total expenditure (1982), US$1,000m.

DIPLOMATIC REPRESENTATIVES

Of Chile in Great Britain (12 Devonshire St., London, W1N 2FS)
Ambassador: Francisco Orrego.

Of Great Britain in Chile (La Concepción 177, Casilla 72-D, Santiago)
Ambassador: J. K. Hickman, CMG.

Of Chile in the USA (1732 Massachusetts Ave., NW, Washington, D.C., 20036)
Ambassador: Hernán Felipe Errázuriz.

Of the USA in Chile (Agustinas 1343, Santiago)
Ambassador: James D. Theberge.

Of Chile to the United Nations
Ambassador: Pedro Daza.

Books of Reference

Statistical Information: The Instituto Nacional de Estadística (Santiago), was founded 17 Sept. 1847. *Director General:* Alvaro Vial Donoso. Principal publications: *Anuario Estadística* and the bi-monthly *Estadística Chilena.*

Other sources are: *Geografía Económica,* by the Corporación de Fomento de la Production, and *Boletín Mensual,* by the Banco Central de Chile.

Allende, S., *Chile's Road to Socialism.* Harmondsworth, 1973
De Vylder, S., *Allende's Chile.* CUP, 1976
Empresa Periodística, *Diccionario biográfico de Chile.* 8th ed. Santiago, 1952
Horne, A., *Small Earthquake in Chile. A Visit to Allende's South America.* London, 1972
Lasaga, M., *The Copper Industry in the Chilean Economy. An Econometric Analysis.* Aldershot, 1981
MacEoin, G., *No Peaceful Way: Chile's Struggle for Dignity.* New York, 1974
Petras, J., and Merino, H. Z., *Peasants in Revolt: A Chilean Case Study.* Univ. of Texas Press, 1972
Pinochet de la Barra, O., *La Antartida Chilena.* Santiago de Chile, 1948
Porteous, J. D., *The Modernization of Easter Island.* Victoria, B.C., 1981

PEOPLE'S REPUBLIC OF CHINA

Capital: Peking (Beijing)
Population: 1,015m. (1983)
GNP per capita: US$300 (1981)

Zhonghua Renmin Gonghe Guo

HISTORY. In the course of 1949 the Communists obtained full control of the mainland of China, and in 1950 also over most islands off the coast, including Hainan.

On 1 Oct. 1949 Mao Zedong (Tse-tung) proclaimed the establishment of the People's Republic of China.

AREA AND POPULATION. China is bounded north by the USSR and Mongolia, east by Korea, the Yellow Sea and the East China Sea, with Hong Kong and Macao as enclaves on the south-east coast; south by Vietnam, Laos, Burma, India, Bhután and Nepál; west by India, Pakistan, Afghánistán and the USSR. China is composed of 22 provinces (this figure includes Taiwan), 5 autonomous regions originally entirely or largely inhabited by national minorities (owing to the immigration of Han Chinese the original nationality is sometimes outnumbered, *e.g.,* by 10 to 1 in Inner Mongolia), namely Inner Mongolia, Xinjiang–Uygur, Guangxi–Zhuang, Ningxia–Hui, Tibet and 3 centrally controlled municipalities (Peking, Shanghai, Tianjin).

The capital is Peking (Beijing).

See map in THE STATESMAN'S YEAR-BOOK, 1968–69.

The total area is estimated at 9,597,000 sq. km (3,704,400 sq. miles).

A census took place in July 1982 when the population was 1,008,175,288 (including 4,238,210 servicemen); China claims a total population of 1,031,882,511 by adding to this 18,270,749 in Taiwan, 5,378,627 in Hong Kong (Xianggang) and Macao (Aomen) and 57,847 in Quemoy (Jinmen) and Matsu (Mazu). Han Chinese numbered 936·7m. There are 55 ethnic minorities; the 3 largest were Zhuang (1·3m.), Hui (0·7m.) and Uighur (0·6m.).

Population in 1983: 1015·4m. (523·1m. male; 211·5m. urban). Vital statistics, 1982: birth rate, 2·1%; death rate, 0·7%; growth rate, 1·5%. Population density, 108 per sq. km.

Estimates of persons of Chinese race outside China, Taiwan and Hong Kong in 1980 varied from 15m. to 20m. China permits the emigration of a limited number of persons to Hong Kong annually. There were 70,456 in 1979.

A number of widely divergent varieties of Chinese are spoken. The official 'Modern Standard Chinese' is based on the dialect of North China, and the Government is promoting its use generally. The ideographic writing system is uniform throughout the country, and has undergone systematic simplification. In 1958 a phonetic alphabet (*Pinyin*) was devised to transcribe the characters, and on 1 Jan. 1979 this was officially adopted for use in all texts in the Roman alphabet (*see also* Post and Broadcasting, p. 355). The decision of press agencies to use the *Pinyin* transcription led to the supersession of the system previously widely used in English-speaking countries (Wade). Starting with THE STATESMAN'S YEAR-BOOK, 1979–80 new names were introduced in *Pinyin*. In this edition with a few exceptions *Pinyin* forms are used for all names. *Pinyin* forms are not used in Taiwan.

From 1949 to 1955 the country was divided into 6 large administrative regions. This system was terminated in 1955, but in 1961 was revived in the form of 6 regional Party Bureaux. These ceased to function during the Cultural Revolution. The table below shows the Provinces, Autonomous Regions and Government-controlled Municipalities grouped regionally. The cities shown in brackets are the seats of the former regional Party Bureaux.

	Area (in 1,000 sq. km)	*Census 1982 (in 1m.)*	*Capital*
North-Eastern Region (Shenyang)			
Heilongjiang	463·6	32,665,546	Harbin
Jilin	187·0	22,502,207	Changchun
Liaoning	151·0	35,721,693	Shenyang
Northern Region (Peking)			
Hebei	202·7	53,005,875	Shijiazhuang
Inner Mongolia (Aut. Region) [1]	450·0	19,274,279	Hohhot
Peking (Beijing) [2]	17·8	9,230,687	—
Shanxi	157·1	25,291,389	Taiyuan
Tianjin [2]	4·0	7,764,141	
Eastern Region (Shanghai)			
Shandong	153·3	74,419,054	Jinan
Jiangxi	164·8	33,184,827	Nanchang
Jiangsu	102·2	60,521,114	Nanking (Nanjing)
Shanghai [2]	5·8	11,859,748	—
Anhui	139·9	49,665,724	Hefei
Zhejiang	101·8	38,884,603	Hangzhou
Fujian	123·1	25,931,106	Fuzhou
Taiwan	36·0	18,270,749	Taibei
Central-Southern Region (Wuhan)			
Henan	167·0	74,422,739	Zhengzhou
Hubei	187·5	47,804,150	Wuhan
Hunan	210·5	54,008,851	Changsha
Guangdong	231·4	59,299,220	Canton (Guangzhou)
Guangxi–Zhuang (Aut. Region)	220·4	36,420,960	Nanning
South-Western Region (Chongqing)			
Sichuan	569·0	99,713,310	Chengdu
Guizhou	174·0	28,552,997	Guiyang
Yunnan	436·2	32,553,817	Kunming
Tibet (Aut. Region)	1,221·6	1,892,392 [3]	Lhasa
North-Western Region (Xian)			
Shaanxi	195·8	28,904,423	Xian
Gansu [1]	530·0	19,569,261	Lanzhou
Ningxia–Hui (Aut. Region) [1]	170·0	3,895,578	Yinchuan
Qinghai	721·0	3,895,706	Xining
Xinjiang–Uygur (Aut. Region)	1,646·8	13,081,681	Urumqi

[1] Boundaries restored to approximately the pre-1970 position in 1979.
[2] Centrally controlled municipality. [3] Estimate, 1980.

Population of largest towns in 1982: Shanghai, 6·27m.; Peking, 5·55m.; Tianjin, 5·13m.; Shenyang, 4·02m.; Wuhan, 3·23m.; Guangzhou (Canton), 3·12m.; Chongqing, 2·65m.; Harbin, 2·55m.

Manchuria, a term not used by the Chinese, is roughly identical with the 3 provinces of the N.E. Region.

Tibet. For events before the revolt of 1959 *see* THE STATESMAN'S YEAR-BOOK, 1964–65, under TIBET. After the revolt was suppressed the Preparatory Committee for the Autonomous Region of Tibet (set up 1955) took over the functions of local government, led by its Vice-Chairman, the Banqen Lama, in the absence of its Chairman, the Dalai Lama, who had fled to India in 1959. In Dec. 1964 both the Dalai and Banqen Lamas were removed from their posts and on 9 Sept. 1965 Tibet became an Autonomous Region. 301 delegates were elected to the first People's Congress, of whom 226 were Tibetans and in 1968 a Revolutionary Committee was established to administer the Region. This gave way to a People's Government in Aug. 1979. The Banqen Lama was re-elected to the Standing Committee of the Chinese People's Political Consultative Conference in March 1978—he became one of its Vice-Chairmen in July 1979—and has made several appeals to the Dalai Lama to return to China. In 1982 the population was reported to be 1,892,393, of which 1·7m. is Tibetan, 4·25m. Tibetans live outside Tibet, in China, and in India and Nepál. Chinese efforts to modernize Tibet include irrigation, road-building and the establishment of light industry: more than 260 small and medium-sized factories and mines have been set up producing electric power, coal, building materials, lumber, textiles, chemicals and animal products.

In 1979, 1·6m. were engaged in agriculture, including 0·5m. nomadic herdsmen. Agricultural communes were first introduced in 1965; by 1975 99% of villages had formed them. By 1984, however, a large measure of autonomy for the peasantry had been re-introduced: compulsory deliveries and some taxes were abolished and private ownership of livestock and 30-year disposition of land were granted. There were 23m. cattle in 1984. In 1975 Tibet became self-sufficient in grain for the first time. There are now 21,000 km of highways, and air routes link Lhasa with Chengdu and Xian.

It was officially admitted in Peking in 1980 that the administration of Tibet had been badly conducted hitherto. The borders were opened for trade with neighbouring countries.

Efforts are being made to revive Tibetan culture as part of China's new liberal policy towards minorities. 45 Buddhist monasteries closed in the Cultural Revolution were open in 1984. There were 1,300 monks. In 1984 a Buddhist seminary in Lhasa opened with 200 students. Circulation of the Tibetan-language *Xizang Daily* now totals 38,000. In 1983 there were 2,542 primary schools, 55 secondary schools, 13 technical schools and 3 higher education institutes. In 1984 only 56% of children were at school. A university is said to be opening in 1985. There were more than 7,000 medical workers, some 5,000 rural doctors and 962 hospitals, with a total of 4,500 beds.

The Dalai Lama, *My Land and My People* (ed. D. Howarth). London, 1962
Dawa Norbu, *Red Star Over Tibet*. London, 1974
Harrer, H., *Return to Tibet*. London, 1984
Jäschke, H. A., *A Tibetan–English Dictionary*. London, 1934
Mele, F., *Tibet*. Paris, 1975
Richardson, H. E., *Tibet and its History*. OUP, 1962
Shakabpa, T. W. D., *Tibet: A Political History*. Yale Univ. Press, 1967
Thubten, J. N., and Turnbull, C., *Tibet: Its History, Religion and People*. Harmondsworth, 1972

CLIMATE. Most of China has a temperate climate but, with such a large country, extending far inland and embracing a wide range of latitude as well as containing large areas at high altitude, many parts experience extremes of climate, especially in winter. Most rain falls during the summer, from May to Sept., though amounts decrease inland. Peking (Beijing). Jan. 24°F (–4·4°C), July 79°F (26°C). Annual rainfall 24·9″ (623 mm). Chongqing. Jan. 45°F (7·2°C), July 84°F (28·9°C). Annual rainfall 43·7″ (1,092 mm). Shanghai. Jan. 39°F (3·9°C), July 82°F (27·8°C). Annual rainfall 45·4″ (1,135 mm). Tianjin. Jan. 24°F (–4·4°C), July 81°F (27·2°C). Annual rainfall 21·5″ (533·4 mm).

CONSTITUTION AND GOVERNMENT. On 21 Sept. 1949 the 'Chinese People's Political Consultative Conference' met in Peking, convened by the Chinese Communist Party. The Conference adopted a 'Common Programme' of 60 articles and the 'Organic Law of the Central People's Government' (31 articles). Both became the basis of the Constitution adopted on 20 Sept. 1954 by the 1st National People's Congress, the supreme legislative body. The Consultative Conference continued to exist after 1954 as an advisory body. Both bodies stopped functioning in the Cultural Revolution. The People's Congress was revived in 1975 and the Consultative Conference in 1978, when Deng Xiaoping was elected as its head. In 1979 it had 1,734 members.

In Jan. 1975 the 4th National People's Congress approved a constitution, under which China was defined as a 'socialist state of the dictatorship of the proletariat'. The 1975 Constitution was a simpler document than its predecessor emphasizing the role of politics in society, especially the thought of Mao, but giving fewer organizational details. In March 1978 the 5th National People's Congress adopted a new constitution of 60 articles which revived several of the provisions of the 1954 constitution dropped in the 1975 document and eliminated much of the latter's innovatory radicalism. More administrative detail was given.

A new Constitution was adopted in 1982. It defines 'socialist modernisation' as

China's basic task. Its most striking change is the restoration of the post of State President (*i.e.* Head of State).

The National People's Congress is the highest organ of state power. It can amend the Constitution, elects and has power to remove from office the highest State dignitaries, decides on the national economic plan, etc. The Congress elects a *Standing Committee* (which supervises the State Council) and the State President, currently Li Xiannian.

The Constitution provides that the Congress be elected for a 5-year term and should meet once a year. It is composed of deputies elected on a constituency basis by direct secret ballot. Any voter, and certain organizations, may nominate candidates. Nominations may exceed seats by 50–100%. 2,978 deputies were elected to the 6th Congress in June 1983.

Government structure was streamlined in 1983, the number of Ministries, Commissions and other agencies of the State Council being reduced from 98 to 52. In 1985 there were 33 Ministries and 7 Commissions under the State Council. The number of Vice-Premiers was reduced from 13 to 4. Many of the former Vice-Premiers have taken the newly-created post of State Councillor, of which there are 10. Some of these are also Ministers, *i.e.* Wu Xueqian *(Foreign Affairs),* Chen Muhua *(Foreign Trade and Economic Relations),* Zhang Aiping *(Defence),* Wang Bingqian *(Finance).* Song Ping heads the Economic Commission and Fang Yi the Scientific and Technological Committee. The Premier is Zhao Ziyang. *Vice-Premiers:* Li Peng, Tian Jiyun, Yao Yilin, Wan Li.

Since 1970 when China began to emerge from the isolation of the Cultural Revolution, her diplomatic relations have expanded considerably. On 25 Oct. 1971 the UN voted for the People's Republic to take over the China seat from the Nationalists by 76 votes to 35 with 17 abstentions. US President Nixon visited China in Feb. 1972 and in 1973 'liaison offices' were opened in the capitals of the two countries. On 1 Jan. 1979 the US recognized the Peking government as the sole legal government of China and diplomatic relations were established. In Jan.–Feb. 1979 Deng Xiaoping paid an official visit to USA. On 12 Aug. 1978 China and Japan signed a 10-year treaty of peace and friendship (ratified 22 Oct. 1978). China has announced that it will not renew its treaty of friendship with the USSR which expired in 1980.

State emblem: 5 stars above Peking's Gate of Heavenly Peace, surrounded by a border of ears of grain entwined with drapings, which form a knot in the centre of a cogwheel at the base; the colours are red and gold.

National flag: Red with a large star and 4 smaller stars all in yellow in the canton.

National anthem: 'March of the Volunteers' composed 1935 by Tien Han. (Replacing the 1978 version).

De facto power is in the hands of the Communist Party of China, which had 39·6m. members in 1982. A 3-year campaign to expel Maoists began in 1985. There are 8 other parties, all members of the Chinese People's Political Consultative Conference. In mid-1966 the Party Chairman, Mao Tse-tung, launched the 'Great Proletarian Cultural Revolution' to eradicate 'revisionism' and numerous Party and State officials were dismissed. The Cultural Revolution can be taken to have terminated by April 1969 when the long-delayed 9th Party Congress was convened, although it was not officially declared to have been brought to a 'victorious conclusion' until Aug. 1977. The 9th Congress adopted a new Party Constitution which proclaimed the leading rôle of the Party in the State and designated Lin Biao as Chairman Mao's successor. A factional dispute developed, however, centred on Lin Biao (killed in an air crash in Mongolia in Sept. 1971) and in Aug. 1973 the 10th Party Congress adopted amendments to the Party Constitution, removing references to Lin Biao and the succession to Chairman Mao, and electing a new Central Committee which appointed a new Politburo and Standing Committee. In Jan. 1975 the Central Committee appointed as a vice-chairman of the Politburo Deng Xiaoping, former Party Secretary-General dismissed during the Cultural Revolution. In April 1976 a 'radical' faction in the Politburo engineered a second dismissal of Deng from all his posts, and Hua Guofeng was appointed First Party Vice-Chairman as well as Premier. On the death of Mao Tse-tung on 9 Sept. 1976 Hua became Party Chairman. In Oct. 1976 the 'radical' faction (now identified and branded as the 'Gang of Four': Mao's widow, Jiang Qing, Zhang Chunqiao, Wang Hongwen and Yao Wenyuan) were placed under arrest. At the 11th Party Congress in Aug. 1977 a new Party Constitution was adopted, and a new Central Committee was elected. Changes in the leadership saw the elimination of the 'radical' faction and a second reinstatement of Deng to his Party and government posts. In Feb. 1980 Liu Shaoqi, former head of state denounced by Mao as a traitor, was posthumously reinstated, and 4 Politburo members of Maoist persuasion were dismissed. Hua Guofeng was replaced as Premier by Zhao Ziyang in Sept. 1980. The 'Gang of Four', along with Chen Boda (a former secretary of Mao), were brought to trial only on 20 Nov. 1980. At the same time the trial opened of five generals accused of complicity with Lin Biao in an attempt to seize power. All 10 accused were found guilty on 25 Jan. 1981. Suspended death sentences were passed on Jiang Qing and Zhang Chunqiao. Hua Guofeng was removed from the Party Chairmanship in June 1981 and replaced by Hu Yaobang. At the 12th Party Congress (Sept. 1982), the posts of Chairman and Vice-Chairman of the CPC were abolished, and greater stress laid on the position of General Secretary of the Central Committee. The members of the Standing Committee of the Politburo elected at the 12th Party Congress are Hu Yaobang *(General Secretary)*, Ye Jianying, Deng Xiaoping *(Chairman of the Military Commission of the Central Committee)*, Zhao Ziyang, Li Xiannian and Chen Yun *(Chairman of the Central Commission for Discipline Inspection)*. Other members of the Politburo are: Wan Li, Xi Zhongxun, Wang Zhen, Wei Guoqing, Ulanhu, Fang Yi, Deng Yingchao, Li Desheng, Yang Shangkun, Yang Dezhi, Yu Qiuli, Song Renqiong, Zhang Tingfa, Hu Qiaomu, Nie Rongzhen, Ni Zhifu, Xu Xiangqian, Peng Zhen. A new central Party body—the Central Advisory Commission, chaired by Deng Xiaoping—was elected by the Congress.

Local Government. There are 4 administrative levels: (1) Provinces, Autonomous Regions and the municipalities directly administered by the Government; (2) prefectures and autonomous prefectures (*zhou*); (3) counties, autonomous counties and municipalities; (4) towns. A policy began in 1982 of replacing rural communes by townships as the basic unit of rural local government. Local government after 1968 was in the hands of Revolutionary Committees. From 1 Jan. 1980 these were replaced by elected People's Congresses and People's Governments. These exist at provincial, county and township levels and in national minority autonomous prefectures, but not in ordinary prefectures which are just agencies of the provincial government. Up to county level Congresses are elected directly.

DEFENCE. China is divided into 11 military regions. The military commander also commands the air, naval and civilian militia forces assigned to each region.

Conscription is compulsory but for organizational reasons selective: only some 10% of potential recruits are called up. Service is 3 years with the Army and 4 years with the Air Force and Navy.

Marks of rank were abolished in 1965 but restored in 1984.

Army. The Army (PLA: 'People's Liberation Army') is divided into main and local forces. Main forces, administered by the military regions in which they are stationed but commanded by the Ministry of Defence, are available for operation anywhere and are better equipped. Local forces concentrate on the defence of their own regions. The Army consists of 191 divisions including 31 artillery, 13 armoured, 118 infantry, 3 airborne and 73 local divisions. Land-based missile forces consisted of (1985 estimate): 4 intercontinental, 60 intermediate range and 50 medium range ballistic missiles. Total strength in 1985 was 3·16m.

The security forces, including the armed police, number some 300,000.

The People's Militia consists of the Armed Militia of up to 6m. strength, the Ordinary Militia of several million, unarmed but with some basic military training, which includes the Urban Militia.

Navy. The steady new construction programme of all classes of warships in modernized yards, many with advanced nuclear and/or missile capability, has been maintained. Chinese naval strength is an important factor in the present and future balance of power in the eastern hemisphere.

Strength (1985) comprised 2 nuclear powered and ballistic missile armed submarines, 1 diesel-powered submarine with ballistic missile tubes, 6 nuclear propelled fleet submarines, 113 patrol submarines, 20 destroyers, 26 frigates, 14 patrol escorts, 220 missile boats, 21 large patrol boats, 40 fast patrol craft, 350 fast gunboats, 260 fast torpedo boats, 24 ocean minesweepers, 80 mine warfare craft, 110 river patrol craft, 35 coastal patrol craft, 40 survey and research ships, 36 supply ships, 16 support ships, 32 oilers, 9 boom defence vessels, 2 repair ships, 44 landing ships, 530 landing craft, 7 salvage ships, 2 icebreakers, 43 tugs, 375 coast and river defence craft and 525 vessels of the Maritime Militia.

Active personnel in 1985 exceeded 300,000 officers and men, including 30,000 in the naval air force and over 28,000 marines.

Main naval bases: Qingdao (North Sea Fleet); Shanghai (East Sea Fleet); Tsamkong (Zhanjiang) (South Sea Fleet).

The largely land-based naval air force of 720 aircraft, primarily for defensive and anti-submarine service, includes MiG-17, MiG-19 and MiG-15 fighters, some 130 Il-28 torpedo bombers, Madge flying boats, Hound Mi4 and Super Frelon helicopters and communications and transport aircraft.

Air Force. In 1984 the Air Force was estimated at 5,300 front-line aircraft, organized in over 100 regiments of jet-fighters and about 12 regiments of tactical bombers, plus reconnaissance, transport and helicopter units. Each regiment is made up of 3 or 4 squadrons (each 12 aircraft), and 3 regiments form a division.

Equipment is predominantly Russian in design and includes about 500 J-7 (MiG-21), 2,000 F-6 (MiG-19) and 500 F-5 (MiG-17) interceptors and fighter-bombers, with about 400 H-5 (Il-28) jet-bombers, about 120 H-6 Chinese-built copies of the Soviet Tu-16 twin-jet strategic bomber, and a few piston-engined Tu-4 (Soviet copy of Boeing B-29) strategic bombers, plus 350 Q-5 twin-jet fighter-bombers (known in the west as 'Fantan'), evolved from the MiG-19. Under development is a new fighter designated J-8 (known in the west as 'Finback'). Transport aircraft include about 300 Y-5 (An-2), Y-8 (An-12), An-24/26, 100 Li-2, 30 Il-14 and a few three-turbofan Trident fixed wing types, plus 300 Z-5 (Mi-4) and Mi-8 helicopters. The MiG fighters and Antonov transports have been manufactured in China, initially under licence, and other types have been assembled there, including several hundred JJ-5 (2-seat MiG-17) trainers.

Total strength (1983) about 490,000, including 220,000 in air defence organization.

At least 26 nuclear tests have been made since 1964 and a nuclear force capable of reaching large parts of the USSR and Asia is operational. Land-based missile forces thought to be deployed consist of 4 intercontinental, 60 intermediate-range (approximately 3–5,000 km) and 50 medium-range (1,100 km) ballistic missiles. Missile forces are controlled by the Second Artillery, the missile arm of the PLA.

INTERNATIONAL RELATIONS

Membership. The People's Republic of China is a member of UN.

ECONOMY

Planning. For planning history 1953–73 *see* THE STATESMAN'S YEAR-BOOK, 1973–74, p. 817.

The long-term aim of the present leadership is to transform China by the year 2000 into a modern developed economic power by the implementation of 'the 4 modernizations', *i.e.*, of agriculture, industry, defence and science and technology. In 1978, as a first step to the realization of the '4 modernizations', a 10-year plan (1976–85) was introduced. However this proved in practice to be over-ambitious; many of the planned targets were too high and the scale of capital construction was too great. The pursuit of the plan caused serious imbalances in the economy. Since

1979 a policy of 'readjusting, restructuring, consolidating and improving' the economy has been followed.

Agriculture and light industry receives higher priority in investment compared to heavy industry. The total value of industrial and agricultural output was 33% higher in 1982 than in 1978. A fundamental economic reform was introduced in 1985, to be fully implemented by 1990. Enterprises are to be taxed by the state to the extent of 80% of profits, and are free to dispose of the rest. The economic plan will apply only to 70 basic products. Wages will vary according to work performed, and prices will gradually increase to a 'realistic' level. The next 5-year plan will run from 1986 to 1990.

Budget. 1982 revenue was 112,397m. yuan; expenditure, 115,331m. yuan.

Revenue, 1982 (in million yuan): enterprises, 39,069; taxation, 67,951. Expenditure: capital construction, 30,270; social, 19,000; defence, 17,780; administration, 8,000. Income tax was introduced in 1980. Registration of British claims for loss of assets of £61m. in 1949 was requested by the Foreign Compensation Commission in Jan. 1981. A credit of 450m. SDF was granted by IMF in March 1981.

China's reserves at 31 Dec. 1983 were US$14,342m. of foreign exchange and 12·8m. troy oz. of gold.

Currency. The currency is called Renminbi (RMB, *i.e.,* People's Currency). The unit of currency is the *yuan* which is divided into 10 *jiao*, the *jiao,* into 10 *fen*. The official rate of exchange is £1 = 3·21 *yuan*; US$1 = 2·53 *yuan*; Hong Kong $1 = 0·32 *yuan*; 1 rouble = 2·222 *yuan* (non-commercial, 1 rouble = 1·29 *yuan*).

Notes are issued for 1, 2 and 5 *jiao* and 1, 2, 5 and 10 *yuan* and coins for 1, 2 and 5 *fen*.

Banking. A re-organization of the banking system in 1983 resulted in the People's Bank of China assuming the role of a Central Bank. Its former commercial role was taken over by a new specialized bank, The Industrial and Commercial Bank. The Bank of China will continue to be responsible for foreign banking operations.

Savings bank deposits were 65,740m. yuan in 1982.

Weights and Measures. The metric system is in general use alongside traditional units of measurement, for which *see* THE STATESMAN'S YEAR-BOOK, 1975–76, p. 826 and 1954, pp. 877–88.

ENERGY AND NATURAL RESOURCES

Electricity. Sources of energy in 1982: coal 73·8%; oil, 18·76%; hydroelectric power, 4·87%; gas, 2·57%. Hydroelectric potential is 676m. kw. Generating is not centralized; local units range between 30 and 60 mw of output. Output in 1983: 351,400m. kwh.

Oil. China has made rapid progress in oil extraction and refining. There are probably about 100 oilfields, of which the largest are at Daqing, Shengli, Dagang and Karamai. Offshore resources in Bohai Bay are also being exploited and exploration is taking place in the South China and Yellow Seas. Oil reserves may be as much as 10,000m. tonnes. Crude oil production was 106·07m. tonnes in 1983.

Gas. Natural gas is available from fields near Canton and Shanghai and in Sichuan province. Production was 12,210m. cu. metres in 1983, but is only used locally.

Minerals. *Coal.* Most provinces contain coal, and there are 70 major production centres, of which the largest are in Hebei, Shanxi, Shandong, Jilin and Anhui. Coal reserves are estimated at 740,000m. tonnes. Coal production was 715m. tonnes in 1983.

Iron. Iron ore deposits are estimated at 447,000m. tonnes and are abundant in the anthracite field of Shanxi, in Hebei and in Shandong and are found in conjunction with coal and worked in Manchuria. Estimated output of iron ore in 1981, 70m. tonnes. The biggest steel bases are at Anshan (in Manchuria) with a capacity of 6m. tons, Wuhan (capacity 3·5m. tonnes), Baotou and Maanshan (both 2·5m. tonnes) and Baoshan near Shanghai.

Tin. Tin ore is plentiful in Yunnan, where the tin-mining industry has long existed. Tin production was 15,000 tonnes in 1981.

Tungsten. China is the world's principal producer of wolfram (tungsten ore), producing 14,000 tonnes in 1981. Mining of wolfram is carried on in Hunan, Guangdong and Yunnan.

Production of other minerals in 1978 (in tonnes): Phosphate rock, 4·5m.; aluminium, 225,000; copper, 200,000; lead, 120,000; zinc, 125,000; antimony, 9,000; manganese, 2m.; (1973) sulphur, 130,000; (1967) bauxite, 350,000; (1973) salt, 18,000; (1969) asbestos, 160,000. Other minerals produced: barite, bismuth, gold, graphite, gypsum, mercury, molybdenum, silver.

Agriculture. China remains essentially an agricultural country. 224m. hectares are under cultivation. Intensive agriculture and horticulture have been practised for millennia. Present-day policy aims to avert the traditional threats from floods and droughts by soil conservancy, afforestation, irrigation and drainage projects, and to increase the 'high stable yields' areas by introducing fertilizers, pesticides and improved crops. Crop priorities: food grains; raw materials for industry (especially cotton); crops for export (especially oil seeds). Among livestock, priority is given to pig production.

Since 1958 modifications have been made in the commune system, including size reductions. There were 54,352 in 1982.

Since 1978 more flexible methods of management have been adopted comprising 'responsibility systems', whereby individual households or other small units are contracted to supply to the commune or government purchasing agency a quantity of crops to be produced from an allotted area of commune land. Any surplus is at the disposal of the household, to be consumed or marketed. In 1984 peasants were granted contracts to commune land with inheritance rights, and were permitted to hire up to 7 labourers. Production has improved.

In 1981 there were estimated to be 145m. hectares of arable land and 792,000 large and medium-sized tractors.

Agricultural production, 1982 (in 1m. tonnes); rice, 161; wheat, 68; maize, 60; soybeans, 9; tubers, 26; tea, 0·4; cotton, 4·6; oilseed crops, 10·5; sugar-cane, 37. The gross value of agricultural output in 1982 was 312,100m. yuan.

Livestock, 1982: Horses and cattle, 68·4m.; sheep and goats, 182m.; pigs, 306m. Pork and mutton production in 1982 was 13·51m. tonnes.

Forestry. In 1982 there were 2·6m. hectares of timber forest. The chief forested areas are in Heilongjiang, Sichuan and Yunnan. Timber output in 1982 was 50·4m. cu. metres.

Fisheries. Sea-water catch in 1982: 3·6m. tonnes; fresh-water 1·6m. tonnes. Fresh-water production (estimate) 1m. tonnes annually.

INDUSTRY AND TRADE

Industry. 'Cottage' industry is very old in the economy and persists into the 20th century. Modern industrial development began with the manufacture of cotton textiles, and the establishment of silk filatures, steel plants, flour-mills and match factories. In 1982 there were 388,600 industrial enterprises, of which 301,900 were collectives and 86,100 state-owned. Only 1,584 were classified as 'large'. Expanding sectors of manufacture are: steel, chemicals, cement, agricultural implements, plastics and lorries.

1983 production (in tonnes): Chemical fertilizer, 13·79m.; chemical fibres, 541,000; pig-iron. 37·3m.; cement, 108m.; cotton cloth, 14,880m. metres; motor vehicles, 240,000; tractors, 37,000; bicycles, 27·58m.; (1982) steel, 37m.; rolled steel, 29m.; coke, 33m.; paper, 5·9m., sugar, 3·4m.; drugs 42,200; cotton yarn, 3·4m. and 5·9m. TV sets.

The gross value of industrial output in 1983 was 608,800m. yuan.

Labour. Total workforce, 1983: 447m., including 112·8m. industrial workers, 1·47m. urban artizans and 332·8m. rural workers. Average annual non-agricultural wage in 1983: 826 yuan. There is a 6-day 48-hour working week.

Commerce. Foreign trade is being decentralized. Trade authorities are being established in the main cities, to date Beijing (Peking), Shanghai and Tianjin, and in selected provinces, to date Guangdong and Fujian. The quasi-governmental China International Trust and Investment Corporation also handles foreign trade. Special Economic Zones have been set up in the provinces of Guangdong and Fujian, in which concessions are made to foreign businessmen to encourage their investment. In 1984 14 coastal cities and Hainan Island were opened for technological imports. A law of July 1979 permits the establishment of joint ventures with foreign firms. There is no maximum limit on the foreign share of the holdings; the minimum limit is 25%. Foreign indebtedness was US$3,020m. in 1983.

Imports include grain, raw materials and semi-manufactured products for agriculture (primarily chemical fertilizers), light industry and textiles, advanced equipment, particularly whole plants and consumer goods. Exports include heavy industrial goods including petroleum, chemicals, minerals, machinery and equipment, light industrial goods and agricultural products.

Trade in 1983: Imports, US$21,500m.; exports, US$22,400m.

90% of China's trade is with non-Communist countries. Japan is China's biggest trading partner. Other major trading partners are USA, Hong Kong, Federal Republic of Germany and Canada. Customs duties on imports and exports between Taiwan and the mainland were abolished in April 1980.

Total trade between China and UK (British Department of Trade returns, in £1,000 sterling):

	1980	*1981*	*1982*	*1983*	*1984*
Imports to UK	153,433	184,069	193,231	231,417	278,474
Exports and re-exports from UK	169,500	120,048	103,051	159,722	317,256

In April 1978 a most-favoured-nation agreement was signed with EEC, and in 1980 the EEC extended preferential tariffs to China.

On 15 Nov. 1978 a science and technology agreement was signed by UK and China and on 4 March 1979 an agreement on economic co-operation. In July 1979 the USA and China signed a 3-year trade agreement which accords China most-favoured-nation status from 1980.

China gained representation in the IMF in Apr. 1980, and in the IBRD in May 1980 and became an observer at GATT in Nov. 1984.

Tourism. 764,500 foreigners, 42,700 overseas Chinese and 7·1m. citizens of Hong Kong, Taiwan and Macao visited China in 1982.

COMMUNICATIONS

Roads. The total road length was 915,000 km in 1983. Highways are well graded but mostly unmetalled. 90% of townships can be reached by road.

In 1983, 790m. tonnes of freight and 3,390m. passengers were transported by road.

Railways. Chinese railway history begins in 1876, when the Wusong–Shanghai line was opened. In 1983 there were some 51,604 km of railway including 2,334 km electrified.

The principal railways are:

(1) The great north–south trunk lines: (*a*) Peking–Canton Railway (over 2,300 km), *via* Zhengzhou–Wuhan–Zhuzhou–Hengyang. (*b*) Tianjin–Shanghai Railway (1,500 km), *via* Pukow and Nanjing (double-tracked in July 1976). (*c*) Baoji–Chongqing Railway, *via* Chengdu (1,174 km). Chongqing with the east–west route from Hengyang to the Vietnam border, and to Kunming, connecting there with the Yunnan Railway to the Vietnam border. Two further lines connect Baoji.

(2) Great east–west trunk lines: (*a*) Longhai Railway; Lianyungkang–Xuzhou–Zhengzhou (on the Peking–Canton line) –Xian–Baoji–Tianshui–Lanzhou (1,500 km). The Baoji–Lanzhou section was upgraded in 1978. (*b*) Lanzhou–Xinjiang Railway: Lanzhou–Yumen–Hami–Turfan–Urumqi (1,800 km); (c) Shanghai–

Youyiguan (Vietnam border) *via* Hangzhou, Nanchang, Hengyang (on the Peking–Canton line), Guilin, Liuzhou and Nanning. (*d*) Peking–Lanzhou *via* Xining (from which a branch connects with the lines through Mongolia to the Trans-Siberian Railway), Dadong (from which a branch serves the province of Shanxi), Baotou and Yinchuan (Ningxia). (*e*) Zhuzhou–Guiyang (632 km). A new east–west line was opened in 1978 between Xiangfan and Chongqing.

Branches link coastal areas (*e.g.*, Fujian province) and the smaller inland centres with the main parts of the system. Surveys have been made for a new 500-km railway, linking the trunk line with the oilfield of Karamai in Xinjiang.

(3) The Manchurian system: (*a*) Chinese Eastern (Changchun) Railway (2,370 km), from Manzhouli on the Soviet border through northern Inner Mongolia and Manchuria *via* Qiqihar, Harbin and Mudanjiang to the Soviet border near Vladivostok. (*b*) South Manchuria Railway (705 km, 1,120 km with branches), Changchun–Shenyang–Luda. (*c*) Peking–Shenyang Railway, with branches in Manchuria (854 km, 1,350 km with branches).

Branches give connexions with outlying parts of Manchuria and Inner Mongolia as well as international links with Korean railways. Chinese railways are all constructed to the standard gauge except for some 600 mm gauge in Yunnan. Trunk routes are being converted from single to double track. The route between Baoji and Chengdu (676 km) was electrified in 1975 and that between Yangpingguan (on the Baoji–Chengdu route) and Ankang in 1977.

Capacity is being expanded under the 1976–85 development plan: 6 new lines are to be built by 1985. Lines are planned to link Tibet with the Chinese network (opened as far as Golmud in 1979) and to bridge gaps in the system such as Liuzhou–Canton, Kantang–Taiyuan and southern Xinjiang.

In 1983 the railways carried 1,160m. tons of freight and 1,094m. passengers.

Aviation. Since 1985 the Civil Aviation Administration of China has become the administrative body for 5 new airlines: Air China (based on Beijing), Eastern Airways (Shanghai); Southern Airways (Canton); South-Western Airways (Chengdu) and the Capital Helicopter Company. There are services to Pyongyang, Hanoi, Rangoon, Karachi, Tōkyō, Moscow, Teheran, Addis Ababa, Bucharest, Belgrade, Zurich, Paris, Frankfurt, Manila, New York, San Francisco, London, Sydney and Hong Kong. Route lengths in 1982: international, 9·99m. km; domestic, 13·28m. km. British Airways have a direct flight London-Beijing. Japan Airlines have a route from Tōkyō to Beijing (*via* Osaka and Shanghai), Air France Paris to Beijing (*via* Athens and Karachi), Pakistan Airlines Karachi to Beijing, Aeroflot Moscow to Beijing, Ethiopian Airlines Addis Ababa to Shanghai, Tarom Bucharest to Beijing, Swissair Geneva to Beijing and Shanghai, Iran Air Paris to Peking and PANAM Beijing *via* Tōkyō.

In 1982 CAAC carried 4·45m. passengers and 102,000 tonnes of freight.

Air services agreements have been signed with 42 countries.

Shipping. In 1980 the ocean-going merchant fleet consisted of 431 vessels with a total DWT of 7·92m.

The major ports are at Tianjin, Shanghai, Qingdao, Luda and Canton. New ports are under construction at Changchiang, Huangpu, Qinhuangdao, Yantai and Lienyunkang. Ports cannot accommodate vessels over 100,000 GRT and most harbours have a draught limitation of 35 ft. In 1982 46m. tonnes of freight were carried.

Inland waterways totalled 108,600 km in 1982. 397m. tonnes of freight were carried.

Pipeline. A pipeline links the Daqing oilfield to the port of Luda and to refineries in Peking. There is a pipeline from Lanzhou to Lhasa. There were 10,400 km of pipeline in 1982 which carried a load of 108·6m. tonnes.

Post and Broadcasting. There were 49,700 post offices in 1982. The use of *Pinyin* transcription of place names has been requested for mail to addresses in China (*e.g.*, 'Beijing' *not* 'Peking'; 'Tianjin' *not* 'Tientsin'; 'Guangzhou' *not* 'Canton', etc.).

In 1983 there were 122 radio and 52 television stations and in 1981 9·02m. TV receivers. Most are communally owned.

Cinemas. Cinemas numbered 162,000 in 1983.

Newspapers and books. In 1983 there were 277 newspapers with a circulation of 15,150m. and 3,100 periodicals. The Party newspaper is *Renmin Ribao* (People's Daily). In 1979 it had a daily circulation of 7m. 31,784 book titles were produced in 5·8m. copies in 1982.

JUSTICE, RELIGION, EDUCATION AND WELFARE

Justice. Six new codes of law (including criminal and electoral) came into force in 1980, to regularize the legal unorthodoxy of previous years. There is no provision for *habeas corpus*. An anti-crime campaign was launched in Aug. 1983. The death penalty has been extended from treason and murder to include rape, embezzlement, smuggling, drug-dealing, bribery and robbery with violence. Courts will no longer be subject to the intervention of other state bodies, and their decisions will be reversible only by higher courts. 'People's courts' are divided into some 30 higher, 200 intermediate and 2,000 basic-level courts, and headed by the Supreme People's Court. The latter tries cases, hears appeals and supervises the people's courts.

People's courts are composed of a president, vice-presidents, judges and 'people's assessors' who are the equivalent of jurors. 'People's conciliation committees' are charged with settling minor disputes.

There are also special military courts.

Procuratorial powers and functions are exercised by the Supreme People's Procuracy and local procuracies.

Religion. Confucianism, Buddhism and Taoism have long been practised. Confucianism has no ecclesiastical organization and appears rather as a philosophy of ethics and government. Taoism—of Chinese origin—copied Buddhist ceremonial soon after the arrival of Buddhism two millennia ago. Buddhism in return adopted many Taoist beliefs and practices. It is no longer possible to estimate the number of adherents to these faiths. A more tolerant attitude towards religion had emerged by 1979, and the Government's Bureau of Religious Affairs was reactivated.

Ceremonies of reverence to ancestors have been observed by the whole population regardless of philosophical or religious beliefs.

Moslems are found in every province of China, being most numerous in the Ningxia–Hui Autonomous Region, Yunnan, Shaanxi, Gansu, Hebei, Honan, Shandong, Sichuan, Xinjiang and Shanxi. They totalled 10m. in 1980.

Roman Catholicism has had a footing in China for more than 3 centuries. In 1985 there were about 3m. Catholics who are members of the Patriotic Catholic Association, which declared its independence of Rome in 1958. In 1979 there were about 1,000 priests. In 1977 there were 78 bishops and 4 apostolic administrators, not all of whom were permitted to undertake religious activity. This figure included 46 'democratically elected' bishops not recognized by the Vatican. A bishop of Peking was consecrated in 1979 without the consent of the Vatican and 2 auxiliary bishops of Shanghai in 1984.

Protestants are members of the All-China Conference of Protestant Churches.

Education. After the radical experimentalism of the Cultural Revolution 1977 marked the beginning of a return to a more conventional educational system, and by 1978 3 out of every 4 children were attending school. University entry now normally follows from secondary schooling and is dependent upon entrance examinations in which political reliability tests are accompanied by tests in academic subjects. Obligatory manual labour has been reduced to 1 month per year. In 1978 a system of 'key' schools for the best-performing pupils was set up, and it was announced that new universities and colleges would be established. It was also announced that several thousand students would be sent to Western universities. In 1982 there were 715 universities and institutes of higher education, with some 1·15m. students. In 1982 there were some 140m. pupils in 880,000 primary schools, and 47m. pupils in 108,000 secondary schools.

The Academy of Sciences had in 1964 some 20 provincial branches and an Academy of Social Sciences was established in 1977.

Among the universities are the following: People's University of China, Peking (founded 1912 by Dr Sun Yat-sen; reorganized 1950; about 3,000 students); Peking University, Peking (1898, enlarged 1945; about 10,000 students); Xiamen University, Fujian (1921 and 1937); Fudan University, Shanghai (1905); Inner Mongolia University, Hohhot; Lanzhou University, Lanzhou (Gansu Prov.); Nankai University, Tianjin (1919); Nanjing University, Nanjing (1888 and 1928); Jilin University, Changchun (Jilin Prov.); North-West University, Xian (Shanxi Prov.); Shandong University, Qingdao (1926); Sun Yat-sen University, Canton (founded 1924 by Dr Sun Yat-sen); Sichuan University, Chengdu (1931); Qinghua University, Peking, Wuhan University, Wuhan (Hubei Prov.; 1905 and 1928); Yunnan University, Kunming. In 1958 a university of science and technology was set up by the Academy of Sciences.

Chen, T. H., *Chinese Education since 1949.* Oxford, 1981.

Health. Medical treatment is free only for certain groups of employees, but where costs are incurred they are partly borne by the patient's employing organization. In 1982 there were 1,002,000 Western-style doctors and 303,000 doctors of Chinese medicine. In rural areas there were also 1·5m. 'bare-foot doctors', who receive 3 months' training and remain in the community treating simple ailments and implementing public health directives.

In 1982 there were 66,149 hospitals with 2·05m. beds (59·4% in rural areas).

DIPLOMATIC REPRESENTATIVES

Of China in Great Britain (31 Portland Place, London, W1N 3AG)
Ambassador: Chen Zhaoyuan.

Of Great Britain in China (Guang Hua Lu 11, Jian Guo Men Wai, Peking)
Ambassador: Sir Richard Evans, KCMG.

Of China in the USA (2300 Connecticut Ave., NW, Washington, D.C., 20008)
Ambassador: Zhang Wenjin.

Of the USA in China (Guang Hua Lu 17, Peking)
Ambassador: Arthur W. Hummel, Jr.

Of China to the United Nations
Ambassador: Ling Qing.

Books of Reference

Beijing Review. Peking, weekly
China Directory [in Pinyin and Chinese]. Tōkyō, annual
The China Investment Guide, 1984–85. London, 1984
The China Quarterly. London, from 1960
China Reconstructs. Peking, monthly
China's Foreign Trade. Bimonthly. Peking, from 1966
Bartke, W., *Who's Who in the People's Republic of China.* New York, 1981
Bennett, G. (ed.), *China's Finance and Trade: a Policy Reader.* London, 1978
Boardman, R., *Britain and the People's Republic of China, 1949–1974.* London, 1976
Bonavia, D., *The Chinese.* New York, 1980.—*The Chinese: A Portrait.* London, 1981
Boorman, H. L., and Howard, R. C., (eds.) *Biographical Dictionary of Republican China.* 5 vols. Columbia Univ. Press, 1967 ff.
Brady, J. P., *Justice and Politics in People's China: Legal Order or Continuing Revolution?* London, 1982
Brugger, B. (ed.), *China since the Gang of Four.* London, 1980
The Cambridge History of China. 14 vols. CUP, 1978 ff.
Cheng, C., *China's Economic Development.* Boulder, 1982
Cheng, P., *China.* [Bibliography] Oxford and Santa Barbara, 1983
Chu, G. C. and Hsu, F. L., (eds.) *China's New Social Fabric.* London, 1983
Croll, E., *The Family Rice Bowl: Food and the Domestic Economy in China.* London, 1983
Duncanson, D., *Changing Qualities of Chinese Life.* London, 1982
Fairbank, J. K., *The United States and China.* 4th ed. Cambridge, Mass., 1979

Fung, K. K. (ed.), *Current Economic Problems in China.* Boulder, 1982
Garside, R., *Coming Alive: China after Mao.* New York, 1980
Gray, J., and White, G., *China's New Development Strategy.* London, 1982
Harding, H. (ed.), *China's Foreign Relations in the 1980's.* Yale UP, 1984
Hinton, H. C. (ed.), *The People's Republic of China: A Handbook.* Boulder, 1979.—*The People's Republic of China 1949–1979.* 5 vols. Wilmington, 1980
Ho, A.-K., *Developing the Economy of the People's Republic of China.* NY, 1982
Hook, B. (ed.), *The Cambridge Encyclopaedia of China.* CUP, 1982
Houn, F. W., *A Short History of Chinese Communism.* 2nd ed. Englewood Cliffs, N.J., 1973
Hsieh, C. M., *Atlas of China.* New York, 1973
Hsu, I. C., *China without Mao: the Search for a New Order.* OUP, 1983
Hsu, R. C., *Ford for One Billion.* Boulder, 1982
Hsüeh, C.-T. (ed.), *Dimensions of China's Foreign Relations.* New York, 1977
Jingrong, W. (ed.), *The Pinyin-Chinese Dictionary.* Beijing and San Francisco, 1979
Kallgren, J. (ed.), *The People's Republic of China after 30 years.* Berkeley, 1979
Kaplan, F. M. (ed.), *Encyclopedia of China Today.* 3rd ed. London, 1982
Kim, S. S., *China, the United Nations and World Order.* Princeton, 1979
Klein, D. W., and Clark, A. B., *Biographic Dictionary of Chinese Communism, 1921–1965.* Harvard U.P., 1971
Lardy, N. R., *Economic Growth and Distribution in China.* CUP, 1978; *Agriculture in China's Modern Economic Development.* CUP, 1983
Mao Tse-tung, Selected works. 5 vols. Peking, 1965–77
Mathews, R. H., *Chinese-English Dictionary.* Cambridge, Mass., 1943–47
Maxwell, N., and McFarlane, B. (eds.), *China's Changed Road to Development.* Oxford, 1984
Meyer, C., *China Observed.* London, 1981
Moody, P. R., *Chinese Politics after Mao.* NY, 1983
Moser, M. J. (ed.), *Foreign Trade Investment and the Law in the People's Republic of China.* OUP, 1984
Nee, V., and Mozingo, D. (eds.), *State and Society in Contemporary China.* Cornell UP, 1983
O'Leary, G., *The Shaping of Chinese Foreign Policy.* London, 1980
Pannell, C. W., and Laurence, J. C., *China: the Geography of Development and Modernization.* London, 1983
Rodzinski, W., *A History of China.* Oxford, 1981–84
Schaller, M., *The United States and China in the Twentieth Century.* OUP, 1979
Scott, G. L., *Chinese Treaties: The Post-revolutionary Restoration of International Law and Order.* New York, 1975
The Times Atlas of China. London, 1974
Thornton, R. C., *China: A Political History, 1917–1980.* Boulder, 1982
Tung, R. L., *Chinese Industrial Society after Mao.* Lexington, Mass., 1982
Walker, K. R., *Food Grain Procurement and Consumption in China.* CUP, 1984
Wei, L., and Chao, A. (eds.), *China's Economic Reforms.* Philadelphia UP, 1982
Wickert, E., *The Middle Kingdom: Inside China Today.* London, 1983
Wilson, D., *Chou: The Story of Zhou En lei, 1898–1976.* London, 1984
Yahuda, M. B., *Towards the End of Isolationism: China's Foreign Policy after Mao.* London, 1983

TAIWAN

'Republic of China'

Capital: Taipei
Population: 18·8m. (1984)
GNP per capita: US$2,682 (1983)

HISTORY. The island of Taiwan (Formosa) was ceded to Japan by China by the Treaty of Shimonoseki on 8 May 1895. After the Second World War the island was surrendered to Gen. Chiang Kai-shek in Sept. 1945 and was placed under Chinese administration on 25 Oct. 1945. USA broke off diplomatic relations with Taiwan on 1 Jan. 1979 on establishing diplomatic relations with the Peking Government. Relations between the USA and Taiwan are maintained through the American Institute on Taiwan and the Taiwan Co-ordination Council for North American Affairs, set up in 1979 and accorded diplomatic status in Oct. 1980.

AREA AND POPULATION. Taiwan lies between the East and South China

Seas about 100 miles from the coast of Fujian province. The total area of Taiwan Island and the Penghu Archipelago is 13,968 sq. miles (36,174 sq. km). Population (1984), 18·8m., of whom some 2m. are mainland Chinese who came with the Nationalist Government. There are also some 300,000 aboriginals. Population density: 520·4 per sq. km.

In 1983, birth rate was 2·1%; death rate, 0·49%; rate of growth, 1·67% per annum.

Taiwan is divided into two special municipalities (Taipei, the capital, population 2·4m. in 1983 and Kaohsiung, population 1·26m. in 1983), 5 municipalities (Taichung, the seat of the Provincial Government, Keelung, Tainan, Chiayi and Hsinchu) and 16 counties (*hsien*): Changhua, Chiayi, Hsinchu, Hualien, Ilan, Kaohsiung, Miaoli, Nantou, Penghu, Pingtung, Taichung, Tainan, Taipei, Taitung, Taoyuan, Yunlin.

CLIMATE. A tropical climate with hot, humid conditions and heavy rainfall in the summer months but cooler from Nov. to March when rainfall amounts are not so great. Typhoons may be experienced. Taipei. Jan. 63°F (17·2°C), July 82°F (27·8°C). Annual rainfall 72″ (1,803 mm).

CONSTITUTION AND GOVERNMENT. Taiwan is controlled by the remnants of the Nationalist Government. On 1 March 1950, Chiang Kai-shek resumed the presidency of the 'Republic of China'. He died 5 April 1975 and was succeeded by Dr Yen Chia-kan who was replaced in the presidential elections of 21 March 1978 by Chiang Kai-shek's eldest son Chiang Ching-kuo (nominated for a second 6-year term in 1984). There are 3 political parties: the ruling Kuomintang (2m. members in 1982), which has a youth movement (China Youth Corps) of over 1m. members, the Young China Party and the China Democratic Socialist Party.

The National Assembly was elected in 1947. In Jan. 1984 it had 1,080 delegates. The National Assembly operates through 5 councils (Executive, Legislative, Judicial, Examination, and Control *Yuan*). The highest administrative organ is the Executive Yuan, headed by the premier, which includes a number of ministers. The highest legislative body is the Legislative Yuan, elected in 1948, which in June 1984 numbered 368 members. The National Assembly, Legislative Yuan and Control Yuan are elected bodies. Their terms of office have been extended indefinitely. As the number of original delegates dwindled, regulations introduced in 1966 and 1972 provided for the election of additional members to the National Assembly and Legislative Yuan, and elections were held in 1969, 1972, 1975, 1980 and 1984, the latter resulting in the election of 62 Kuomintang candidates and 9 independents to the Legislative Yuan. Opposition parties were forbidden to campaign. There is also a Provincial Assembly of which the current Seventh Assembly with 77 members was elected on 14 Nov. 1981.

A political campaign calling on the Kuomintang to abandon its claim to represent all China and hold representative elections resulted in the sentencing of the prime movers at a court-martial in March 1980.

State emblem: A 12-pointed white sun in a blue sky.
National flag: Red with a blue first quarter bearing the state emblem in white.
National anthem: 'San Min Chu I', words by Dr Sun Yat-sen; tune by Cheng Mao-yun.

Prime Minister: Yu Kuo hua.
Vice-Premier: Lin Yang-kang. *Foreign Minister:* Chu Fu sung. *Minister of National Defence:* Adm. Soong Chang-chih. *Minister of the Interior:* Wu Po-hsiung. *Minister of Finance:* Loh Jen-kang. *Minister of Education:* Li Huan. *Minister of Justice:* Shih Chi-yang. *Minister of Economic Affairs:* Hsi Li-teh. *Minister of Communications:* Lien Chan. *Governor of Taiwan Province:* Lee Teng-hui.

DEFENCE

Army. The Army, which embodies the remnants of the forces which escaped to Taiwan with Chiang Kai-shek at the end of the civil war in 1949, numbered about 330,000 in 1985. It was reorganized, re-equipped and trained by the USA and in 1985 consisted of 12 heavy and 6 light infantry divisions, 6 armoured infantry and 3 airborne brigades, 4 tank groups, 20 field artillery and 5 SAU battalions. There is a conscription system for 2 years and reserve liability. US supplies of military equipment were resumed in 1980 after a moratorium in 1979. US forces were withdrawn by 1 May 1979.

Navy. Most of the 236 vessels in naval service are former US Navy ships now well over 30 years old and overdue for replacement. There are 2 diesel powered patrol submarines, 26 destroyers, 10 frigates, 1 new corvette, 3 escort vessels, 35 fast missile craft, 9 defence boats, 14 coastal minesweepers, 1 coastal minelayer, 9 minesweeping boats, 28 coastal patrol craft, 2 dock landing ships, 1 amphibious flagship, 26 landing ships, 22 utility landing craft, 2 repair ships, 4 surveying ships, 12 support ships, 2 transports, 7 oilers, 1 supply ship, 17 tugs, 5 floating docks and 25 service craft. There are also 260 LCMs and 150 minor landing craft. Customs have 18 coastguard cutters.

Active personnel in 1985 exceeded 7,100 naval officers and 28,000 ratings; 3,000 marine officers and 26,000 men.

The Navy has 12 anti-submarine torpedo helicopters and operational control of 2 squadrons of Air Force anti-submarine warfare Tracker aircraft; and the Marine Corps operates a number of observation aircraft and helicopters.

Air Force. The Nationalist Air Force is equipped mainly with aircraft of US design, including F-5E fighters built in Taiwan. It has 13 squadrons of F-104G Starfighter, F-5A/B/E/F and F-100 Super Sabre fighter-bombers, 1 interceptor squadron of F-104S Starfighters, and 1 tactical reconnaissance squadron of RF-104G Starfighters. The 6 transport squadrons are equipped with a VIP Boeing 720, 4 Boeing 727s, 5 C-54s, 20 C-47s, about 40 C-119Gs and 10 C-123 Providers. There is a naval co-operation squadron with S-2A/E Trackers and an ASW squadron with Hughes 500 MD helicopters. Search and rescue units operate Albatross amphibians and Iroquois helicopters, and there are other helicopter and large training elements, some equipped with AT-3 twin-jet trainers designed and built in Taiwan. Total strength in 1983: 77,000 personnel and 485 combat aircraft.

INTERNATIONAL RELATIONS. By a treaty of 1 Dec. 1954 the USA was pledged to protect Taiwan, but this treaty lapsed 1 year after the USA established diplomatic relations with the People's Republic of China on 1 Jan. 1979. In April 1979 the US Congress approved a law to maintain commercial, cultural and other relations between USA and Taiwan.

The People's Republic took over the China seat in the UN from the Nationalists on 25 Oct. 1971.

ECONOMY

Planning. Government policy is to 'develop industry through agriculture and expand agriculture through industry'. There have been a series of development plans. The seventh (1976–81) discontinued the promotion of labour-intensive in favour of capital- and technology-intensive industry and envisaged a GNP annual growth rate of 8·5%. A 4-year plan (1982–85) envisages a GNP annual growth rate of 8%.

Budget. There are 2 budgets, the national together with a special defence budget (partly secret) and the provincial (*i.e.,* for Taiwan proper). For the fiscal year 1984 (July 1983–June 1984) tax revenue was NT$521,841m.; expenditure, NT$520,672m.

Currency. The unit of currency is the New Taiwan dollar, divided into 100 cents, which is linked to the US$. There are coins of NT$ 1, 5 and 10 and notes of NT$ 10, 50, 100, 500 and 1,000. There are no cent coins or notes. Exchange rates (Feb. 1985): £1 = NT$41·58; US$1 = NT$39·28.

Banking. The Central Bank of China (reactivated in 1961) regulates the money market, manages foreign exchange and issues currency. The former Bank of China, a foreign exchange bank with branches in New York, Chicago, Tōkyō, Osaka, Panama, Bangkok, Colon Free Zone and Los Angeles, was reorganized in 1972 as a private bank for export financing and renamed the International Commercial Bank of China (paid-in capital NT$3·300m. in 1983).

The Bank of Taiwan is the largest commercial bank and the fiscal agent of the Government. In addition, there are 15 domestic commercial banks and 31 local branches of foreign banks.

Other banking institutions include the China Development Corporation.

ENERGY AND NATURAL RESOURCES

Electricity. Output of electricity in 1983 was 45,517m. kwh.; total generating capacity was 12·4m. kw. 3 nuclear power-stations (capacities 1m., 1m. and 0·6m. kw.) came into use in 1977, 1981 and 1984, and a fourth is envisaged.

Minerals. There are reserves of coal (185m. tonnes), gold (2·1m. tonnes), copper (4·8m. tonnes), sulphur (2·4m. tonnes), oil (1·4m. kl.) and natural gas (21,630 cu. metres). In 1976 an offshore gas-field south-west of Taiwan was discovered with an annual capacity of 500m. cu. metres. In 1983, coal production was 2·2m. tonnes; petroleum, 134,644 kl.; natural gas, 1,237·1m. cu. metres.

Agriculture. The cultivated area was 894,326 hectares in 1983, of which 500,901 hectares were paddy fields. Production in 1,000 tonnes, in 1983: Rice, 2,485 (2,482 in 1982); tea, 24; bananas, 196; pineapples, 115; sugar-cane, 7,070; sweet potatoes, 560; wheat, 1·6; soybeans, 9; peanuts, 62·5.

Livestock (1983): Cattle, 129,852; pigs, 5,888,198; goats, 196,987.

Forestry. Forest area, 1983: 1,865,141 hectares; forest reserves, 326,421,000 cu. metres; timber production, 694,773 cu. metres.

Fisheries. The fleet comprised 4,393 vessels over 20 GRT in 1983; the catch was 930,582 tonnes in 1983.

INDUSTRY AND TRADE

Industry. Output (in tonnes) in 1982 (and 1983): Crude steel, 1·7m. (1·7m.); pig-iron, 148,110 (166,546); aluminium, 10,120 ( ); shipbuilding, 925,323 (861,201); sugar, 662,944 (658,380); cement, 13·4m. (14·8m.); compound fertilizers, 246,626 (274,854); paper, 485,919 (467,297); cotton fabrics, 661m. metres (822m.).

In 1983, 20,801m. litres of crude oil were refined; the main refinery at Kaohsiung has an annual capacity of 17,675m. litres.

Labour. In 1983 the labour force was 7m., of whom 1·3m. worked in agriculture, forestry and fisheries, 2·9m. in industry (including 2·3m. in manufacturing and 0·5m. in building), 1·2m. in commerce, 0·4m. in transport and communications, and 1·2m. in other services. 197,000 were registered unemployed.

Commerce. Foreign trade affairs are handled by the China External Trade Development Council (founded 1970), which operates branches in 22 countries under the name of Far East Trade Service. Principal exports: textiles, electrical machinery, foodstuffs, agricultural products, machinery, plastic products. Principal imports: minerals, oil, agricultural products, metal products, machinery. Total trade, in US$1m.:

	1976	*1977*	*1978*	*1979*	*1980*	*1981*	*1982*	*1983*
Imports	7,599	8,511	11,027	14,774	19,733	21,200	18,888	20,287
Exports	8,166	9,361	12,678	16,103	19,811	22,611	22,204	25,123

The USA, Japan and Saudi Arabia are Taiwan's major trade partners followed by Hong Kong, Kuwait and the Federal Republic of Germany.

Total trade between Taiwan and UK (British Department of Trade returns, in £1,000 sterling):

	1980	*1981*	*1982*	*1983*	*1984*
Imports to UK	253,915	321,082	335,537	458,307	585,246
Exports and re-exports from UK	92,386	120,038	125,183	128,467	150,648

COMMUNICATIONS

Roads. In 1983 there were 19,833·4 km of roads (16,513 km surfaced). 6,674,135 motor vehicles were registered in 1983 including 687,860 passenger cars, 20,458 buses, 324,560 trucks and 5,594,609 motor cycles. 2,055m. passengers and 180m. tons of freight were transported (excluding urban buses).

Railways. Total route length in 1983 was 2,812 km (1,067 mm to 762 mm gauge), of which a large proportion is owned by the Taiwan Sugar Corporation and other concerns. The state network consists of 1,100·7 km. Electrification of the west trunk line of the state network from Keelung and Kaohsiung was completed in 1979. Freight traffic in 1983 amounted to 30·8m. tons and passenger traffic to 130·4m.

Aviation. There are 2 international airports: Chiang Kai-shek at Taoyuan near Taipei, and Kaohsiung which operates daily flights to Hong Kong. There are 6 domestic airlines, including China Airlines (CAL), which also operates international services to Bangkok, Kuala Lumpur, Manila, Seoul, Singapore, Amsterdam, Saudi Arabia, Japan and USA.

Shipping. The merchant marine in 1983 comprised 200 vessels over 200 GRT, totalling 2,915,009 GRT; it included 22 passenger ships and 198 freighters. Ocean-going freight-traffic was 38·7m. tonnes.

The 4 international ports, Kaohsiung, Keelung, Hualien and T'aichung, are being extensively redeveloped. The first two are container centres. The lesser port of Suao is also being built up.

Post and Broadcasting. In 1983 there were 12,224 postal establishments. Number of telephones in 1983, 4,854,861. In 1978 there were 8m. radio receivers and 3m. TV receivers. There are 3 TV networks.

Cinemas (1983). Cinemas numbered 665.

Newspapers (1983). There were 31 daily papers and 2,543 periodicals.

RELIGION, EDUCATION AND WELFARE

Religion. The predominant faith is Confucianism, and there were 5,000 temples in 1976. There were 1·52m. Taoists in 1983 with 6,174 temples and 18,432 priests, and 0·8m. Buddhists with 1,157 temples and 3,471 priests. There are some 600,000 Christians, of whom there were 291,598 Catholics and 305,200 Protestants in 1983.

Education. Since 1968 there has been free compulsory education for 9 years (6–15). In that year the curriculum was modernized to give more emphasis to science while retaining the traditional basis of Confucian ethics. There were, in 1983–84, 2,464 primary schools with 70,648 teachers and 2,242,641 pupils; 1,047 secondary schools with 74,873 teachers and 1,682,364 students; 105 schools of higher learning, including 28 universities and colleges, with 19,166 full-time teachers and 395,153 students.

Health. In 1982 there were 112,687 registered medical personnel, including 21,526 doctors, 4,716 dentists and 4,690 'herb doctors', and 11,615 health and medical care facilities, including 1,083 public health and medical care facilities and 10,532 private hospitals and clinics.

Books of Reference

Statistical Yearbook of the Republic of China. Taipei, annual
Republic of China: A Reference Book. Taipei, 1983
Taiwan Statistical Data Book. Taipei, annual
Annual Review of Government Administration, Republic of China. Taipei, annual
Chiu, H., (ed.) *China and the Taiwan Issue.* New York, 1979
Clough, R. N., *Island China.* Cambridge, Mass., 1978
Fei, J. C. H., *et al; Growth with Equity: the Taiwan Case.* OUP, 1981
Ho, S. P. S., *Economic Development of Taiwan, 1860–1970.* Yale Univ. Press, 1978
Hsiung, J. C., (ed.) *Contemporary Republic of China.* New York, 1981
Simon, D. F. S., *Taiwan, Technology Transfer, and Transnationalism.* Boulder, 1983
Tierney, J., (ed.) *About Face: The China Decision and its Consequences.* New Rochelle, 1979

COLOMBIA

República de Colombia

Capital: Bogotá
Population: 28·2m. (1984)
GNP per capita: US$1,380 (1981)

HISTORY. The Vice-royalty of New Granada gained its independence of Spain in 1819, and was officially constituted 17 Dec. 1819, together with the present territories of Panama, Venezuela and Ecuador, as the state of 'Greater Colombia', which continued for about 12 years. It then split up into Venezuela, Ecuador and the republic of New Granada in 1830. The constitution of 22 May 1858 changed New Granada into a confederation of 8 states, under the name of Confederación Granadina. Under the constitution of 8 May 1863 the country was renamed 'Estados Unidos de Colombia', which were 9 in number. The revolution of 1885 led the National Council of Bogotá, composed of 2 delegates from each state, to promulgate the constitution of 5 Aug. 1886, forming the Republic of Colombia, which abolished the sovereignty of the states, converting them into departments, with governors appointed by the President of the Republic, though they retained some of their old rights, such as the management of their own finances.

AREA AND POPULATION. Colombia is bounded north by the Caribbean sea, north-west by Panama, west by the Pacific ocean, south-west by Ecuador and Peru, north-east by Venezuela and south-east by Brazil. The estimated area is 1,138,914 sq. km (456,535 sq. miles). It has a coastline of about 2,900 km, of which 1,600 km are on the Caribbean sea and 1,300 km on the Pacific ocean. Population estimate (1984) 28,240,000. Bogotá, the capital, (1981) 4,486,000.

Départmentos	*Area (sq. km)*	*Population 1983*	*Capital*	*Population 1980*
Antioquia	63,612	4,081,700	Medellín	1,812,000
Atlantico	3,388	1,379,100	Barranquilla	900,000
Bolívar	25,978	1,076,800	Cartagena	368,000
Boyacá	23,189	1,100,400	Tunja (M.E.)	66,000
Caldas	7,888	870,600	Manizales	302,000
Caquetá	88,965	88,920 [1]	Florencia	55,000
Cauca	29,398	821,700	Popayán	93,000
César (El)	22,905	542,600	Valledupar	180,000
Chocó	46,530	253,500	Quibdó	34,000
Córdoba	25,020	861,900	Montería	117,000
Cundinamarca	22,623	1,288,000	Bogotá	4,000,000
Huila	19,890	272,900	Neiva	135,000
Guajira (La)	20,848	510,200	Riohacha	36,000
Magdalena	23,188	610,100	Santa Marta	120,000
Meta	85,635	384,800	Villavicencio	116,000
Nariño	33,268	947,000	Pasto	182,000
Norte de Santander	21,658	878,300	Cúcuta	272,000
Quindío	1,845	352,700	Armenia	192,000
Risaralda	4,140	630,800	Pereira	309,000
Santander	30,537	1,367,600	Bucaramanga	459,000
Sucre	10,917	398,400	Sincelejo	89,000
Tolima	23,562	1,128,900	Ibagué	238,000
Valle del Cauca	22,140	2,848,600	Cali	1,232,000

[1] 1973.

Intendencias	*Area (sq. km)*	*Population 1978*	*Capital*
Arauca	23,818	27,497 [1]	Arauca
Casanare	44,640	[2]	El Yopal
Putumayo	24,885	29,137 [1]	Mocoa
San Andrés y Providencia	44	22,719 [1]	San Andrés

[1] 1973. [2] Included in figure for Boyacá.

Comisarías	*Area (sq. km)*	*Population 1978*	*Capital*
Amazonas	109,665	12,962 [1]	Leticia
Guainía	72,238	3,602 [1]	Puerto Inírida
Guaviare	42,327	—	—
Vaupés	65,268	13,403 [1]	Mitú
Vichada	100,242	12,330 [1]	Puerto Carreño

[1] 1973.

The bulk of the population lives at altitudes of from 4,000 to 9,000 ft above sea-level. It is divided broadly into: 68% mestizo, 20% white, 7% Indio and 5% Negro.

The language spoken is Spanish.

CLIMATE. The climate includes equatorial and tropical conditions, according to situation and altitude. In tropical areas, the wettest months are March to May and Oct. to Nov. Bogotá. Jan. 58°F (14·4°C), July 57°F (13·9°C). Annual rainfall 42″ (1,052 mm). Baranquilla. Jan. 80°F (26·7°C), July 82°F (27·8°C). Annual rainfall 32″ (799 mm). Cali. Jan. 75°F (23·9°C), July 75°F (23·9°C). Annual rainfall 37″ (915 mm). Medellin. Jan. 71°F (21·7°C), July 72°F (22·2°C). Annual rainfall 64″ (1,606 mm).

CONSTITUTION AND GOVERNMENT. The legislative power rests with a Congress of 2 houses, the Senate, of 112 members, and the House of Representatives, of 199 members, both elected for 4 years. Congress meets annually at Bogotá on 20 July. Women were given the vote, which is now open to citizens of either sex, over 18 years of age, on 25 Aug. 1954.

The President is elected by direct vote of the people for a term of 4 years, and is not eligible for re-election until 4 years afterwards. Congress elects, for a term of 2 years, one substitute to occupy the presidency in the event of a vacancy during a presidential term. There are 13 Ministries. The Governors of Departments and the Mayor of Bogotá are nominated by the national government.

A National Economic Council, functioning since May 1935, went through several transformations, becoming in 1954 a Directorate of Planning.

National Flag: Three horizontal stripes of yellow, blue, red with the yellow of double width.

National anthem: Oh! Gloria inmarcesible (words by R. Núñez; tune by O. Síndici).

The following is a list of presidents since 1953:

Gen. Gustavo Rojas Pinilla, 13 June 1953–10 May 1957.
Military Junta, Maj.-Gen. Gabriel París and 4 others, 10 May 1957–7 Aug. 1958.
Dr Alberto Lleras Camargo (Lib.), 7 Aug. 1958–7 Aug. 1962.
Dr Guillermo León Valencia (Cons.), 7 Aug. 1962–7 Aug. 1966.
Dr Carlos Lleras Restrepo (Lib.), 7 Aug. 1966–7 Aug. 1970.
Dr Misael Pastrana Borrero (Cons.), 7 Aug 1970–7 Aug. 1974.
Dr Alfonso López Michelsen (Cons./Lib.), 7 Aug. 1974–7 Aug. 1978.
Dr Julio Cesar Turbay Ayala (Lib.), 7 Aug. 1978–7 Aug. 1982.

President: Dr Belisario Betancur Cuartas. He was elected on 30 May 1982 and took office on 7 Aug. 1982.

The Cabinet was composed as follows in Nov. 1984:

Foreign Affairs: Dr Augusto Ramírez Ocampo. *Interior:* Alfonso Gomez Gomez. *Defence:* Gen. Gustavo Matamoros d'Acosta. *Finance:* Roberto Jungito. *Agriculture:* Gustavo Castro Guerrero. *Economic Development:* Rodrigo Marin Bernal. *Justice:* Enrique Parejo Gonzalez. *Labour and Social Security:* Guillermo Alberto Gonzalez Mosquera. *Public Health:* Jaime Arias Ramirez. *Mines and Energy:* Dr Carlos Martinez Simahan. *Education:* Rodrigo Escobar Navia. *Communications:* Dr Bernardo Ramirez. *Public Works and Transportation:* Hernan Beltz Peralta. *Industry and Commerce:* Oscar Bonifaz. *Aviation:* Gen. Antonio Arnez.

Local government: The country is divided into 23 *départmentos*, 4 *intendencias*,

5 *comisarías* and a Special District. The governor of each is appointed by the President, but each has also a directly-elected legislature. The *départmentos* are subdivided into municipalities, each with a mayor appointed by the departmental governor.

DEFENCE. Men become liable for 2 years' military service at age 18, although the system is applied selectively. *Ex*-conscripts remain in the reserve, divided into 3 classes, until age 45.

Army. The Army consists of 10 infantry and 1 training brigades, artillery, cavalry, engineer and motorized troops and the usual services. The peace effective is 57,000 men (conscripts, 28,500); reserves 70,000. Number of national police, about 50,000.

Navy. Colombia has 2 Federal German-built 1,200-ton diesel-electric powered patrol submarines completed in 1975, 2 Italian-built midget submarines; 2 destroyers completed in Sweden in 1958; 4 new German-built missile-armed frigates; 4 old patrol vessels (*ex*-US fleet tugs); 4 fast patrol gunboats; 4 river gunboats; 4 surveying vessels; 9 coastguard patrol vessels; 10 patrol motor launches; 1 oiler; 4 small transports, 1 training ship, 5 service craft, and 12 tugs. Personnel in 1985 exceeded 700 officers and 6,500 men. The Navy has also a brigade of marines with 2,500 officers and men.

Air Force. Formed in 1922, the Air Force has been independent of the Army and Navy since 1943, when its reorganization began with US assistance. In 1983 it had about 300 aircraft, including a squadron of Mirage 5-COA fighter-bombers, 5-COR reconnaissance aircraft and 5-COD two-seat operational trainers; a squadron of A-37B jets for counter-insurgency duties, a transport group equipped with 3 C-130, 17 C-47s, 3 C-54s and a small number of Arava, Beaver and Turbo-Porter light transports; a presidential F-28 Fellowship jet transport; 1 Boeing 707, UH-1B/H utility helicopters; and a reconnaissance unit with Hughes OH-6A, 300C and TH-55 helicopters. Eleven more C-47s, 1 C-54 and 2 HS.748 transports are flown by the Air Force operated airline SATENA. Thirty Cessna T-41D primary trainer/light transports were delivered in 1968 and were followed by 10 T 37C jet advanced trainers to supplement piston-engined T-34s and T-33A armed jet trainers. Total strength (1985) 5,000 personnel.

INTERNATIONAL RELATIONS

Membership. Colombia is a member of the UN, OAS, the Andean Group and LAIA (formerly LAFTA).

ECONOMY

Budget. Ordinary revenue and expenditure in 1981 balanced at 196,500 pesos.

Currency. Coins include 50 *centavos* (90% steel and 10% nickel) and 1, 2, 5, 10 and 20 pesos. There are also notes representing 10, 20, 50, 100, 200, 500, 1,000 and 2,000 *gold pesos*. Exchange rate Feb. 1985, 122·86 *pesos* = £1 sterling; 118·34 *pesos* = US$1.

Banking. On 23 July 1923 the Banco de la República was inaugurated as a semi-official central bank, with the exclusive privilege of issuing bank-notes in Colombia; its charter, in 1951, was extended to 1973. Its note issues must be covered by a reserve in gold of foreign exchange of 25% of their value.

There are 25 domestic commercial banks of importance and 5 foreign banks (English, Canadian, American, French and Franco-Italian). External public debt was US$6,000m. in 1982.

Weights and Measures. The metric system was introduced in 1857, but in ordinary commerce Spanish weights and measures are generally used; according to new definitions by the Ministry of Development, *e.g.*, *botella* (750 grammes), *galón* (5 *botellas*), *vara* (70 cm), *arroba* (25-lb., of 500 grammes; 4 *arrobas* = 1 quintal).

ENERGY AND NATURAL RESOURCES

Electricity. Capacity of electric power (1983) is 5·54m. kw. Electric power produced in 1983, 22,825,000 kwh. There is increasing utilization of natural gas.

Oil. Production in 1983 was 54·2m. bbls (of 42 gallons).

Minerals. Colombia is rich in minerals; gold is found chiefly in Antioquia and moderately in Cauca, Caldas, Tolima, Nariño and Chocó; output in 1983, 430,978 troy oz.

Other minerals are silver (78,689 troy oz. in 1983), copper, lead, mercury, manganese, emeralds and platinum; production of platinum, 1983, 10,301 troy oz. The chief emerald mines are those of Muzo and Chivor.

The Government holds the monopoly, which is leased to the Banco de la República, for extracting salts from the outstanding Zipaquirá mines (several hundred feet in depth and several hundred square miles in area) and for evaporating many sea salt pans; salt production in 1983 was 229,967 tons of land salt from the Zipaquirá mines and 291,378 tons of sea salt from Manaure and Galerazamba on the Caribe coast. Colombia's coal reserves were estimated at 16,500m. tonnes in 1983; production (1983) 5·58m. tonnes.

Agriculture. Very little of the country is under cultivaton, but much of the soil is fertile and is coming into use as roads improve. The range of climate and crops is extraordinary; the agricultural colleges have different courses for 'cold-climate farming' and 'warm-climate farming'. Some 6m. acres are described as arable, 96m. pasture and 148m. forest.

Coffee covers an area (1983) of 1m. hectares; production, 816,000 tons. Crops are grown by smallholders, and are picked all the year round. Production (1983, in 1,000 tons): Potatoes, 2,188; rice, 1,780·3; bananas, 1,173; maize, 863·8; sorghum, 595·2.

The rubber tree grows wild, and its cultivation has begun; output is a few hundred tons. Fibres are being exploited, notably the 'fique' fibre, which furnishes all the country's requirements for sacks and cordage; output about 12,000 tons. Tolú balsam is cultivated, and copaiba trees are tapped but are not cultivated. Tanning is an important industry.

Livestock (1983): 26,022,000 cattle, 2,279,000 pigs, 2,734,000 sheep, 33m. poultry (1982).

Fishery. In Sept. 1963 a *Sección de Caza y Pesca* was set up in the Ministry of Agriculture. It extended territorial waters to 200 nautical miles.

INDUSTRY AND TRADE

Industry. Production (1983): Iron, 436,068 tonnes; cement, 4,720,792 tonnes; motor cars, 21,614; industrial vehicles, 6,719.

Commerce. For the 'Charter of Quito' trading agreement in 1948 between Colombia, Ecuador, Panama and Venezuela, *see* THE STATESMAN'S YEAR-BOOK, 1956, p. 882. Colombia's entry into the Latin American Free Trade Area (ALALC) was ratified on 29 Sept. 1961. A fresh impulse to this effort was given by the Bases for an Immediate Action Programme under the 'Charter of Bogotá' signed by Colombia, Chile, Equador, Peru and Venezuela on 16 Aug. 1966.

Imports (c.i.f. values) and exports (f.o.b. values) (excluding export tax) for calendar years (in US$1m.):

	1980	*1981*	*1982*	*1983*
Imports	4,662	5,199	5,478	4,968
Exports	3,945	2,956	3,095	3,081

Important articles of export in 1983 (in US$1m.) were coffee (1,494), bananas (166), flowers (122·8), sugar (68·7), clothing and textiles (62·4). The chief imports are machinery, vehicles, tractors, metals and manufactures, rubber, chemical products, wheat, fertilizers and wool.

Imports in 1983 (in US$1,000) from USA were valued at 1,744,952; Venezuela, 426,404; Japan, 396,073; Federal Republic of Germany, 229,200; Brazil, 146,999. Exports (in US$1,000) went to USA, 783,344; Federal Republic of Germany, 568,623; Netherlands, 147,680; Venezuela, 116,244; Italy, 67,717.

Total trade between Colombia and UK (British Department of Trade returns, in £1,000 sterling).

	1980	*1981*	*1982*	*1983*	*1984*
Imports to UK	34,289	32,951	34,502	56,458	80,387
Exports and re-exports from UK	41,920	45,145	50,328	51,023	43,485

Tourism. Foreign visitors totalled 1·1m. in 1982.

COMMUNICATIONS

Roads. Owing to the mountainous character of the country, the construction of arterial roads and railways is costly and difficult. Total length of highways, about 75,000 km in 1983. Of the 2,300-mile Simón Bolívar highway, which runs from Caracas in Venezuela to Guayaquil in Ecuador, the Colombian portion is complete. Buena Ventura and Cali are linked by a highway (Carreterra al Mar). Motor vehicles numbered 927,520, of which 430,531 were passenger cars and 99,110 lorries in 1977.

Railways. There are 5 divisions of the State Railway with a total length of 3,403 km in 1983 and a gauge of 914 mm. The Pacific Railway connects Bogotá with the port of Buenaventura. The Atlantic line from Bogotá to Sta. Marta was opened in July 1961. Three connecting links are planned to improve the operating efficiency of the network. Total railway traffic, 1983, was 1·3m. passengers and 1·3m. tonnes of freight.

Aviation. In civil aviation Colombia ranks perhaps second, after Brazil, among South American countries. There are 670 landing grounds of all kinds. In 1982 the national airports moved 6,386,000 passengers and 92,177 tonnes of cargo.

Shipping. Vessels entering Colombian ports in 1982 unloaded 7·1m. tonnes of imports and loaded 5·4m. tonnes of exports. The Colombian merchant fleet in 1966 owned 23 vessels of 187,906 net tons, and leased 20 of 164,360 net tons; in 1965 it carried 1·9m. tonnes.

The Magdelena River is subject to drought, and navigation is always impeded during the dry season, but it is an important artery of passenger and goods traffic. The river is navigable for 900 miles; steamers ascend to La Dorada, 592 miles from Barranquilla.

Post and Broadcasting. The length of telephone lines in service is 705,832 km (Bogotá only); instruments in use, 1 Jan. 1982, 1,747,689, of which 642,000 were in Bogotá. The cable company is government owned. Television was established in 1954 and in 1978 there were 1·75m. sets in use. In 1983 there were 485 radio stations.

Cinemas (1978). There were 715 cinemas.

Newspapers (1984). There were 31 daily newspapers, with daily circulation totalling 1·5m.

JUSTICE, RELIGION, EDUCATION AND WELFARE

Justice. The Supreme Court, at Bogotá, of 20 members, is divided into 3 chambers—civil cassation (6), criminal cassation (8), labour cassation (6). Each of the 61 judicial districts has a superior court with various sub-dependent tribunals of lower juridical grade. Communism was outlawed by government decree on 5 March 1956.

Religion. The religion is Roman Catholic, with the Cardinal Archbishop of Bogotá as Primate of Colombia and 7 other archbishops in Cartagena, Manizales, Medellín, Pamplona, Popayán, Cali and Tunja, 26 bishops, 1,546 parishes and 4,020 priests. Other forms of religion are permitted so long as their exercise is 'not contrary to Christian morals or to the law'.

Education. Primary education is free but not compulsory, and facilities are limited. Schools are both state and privately controlled. In 1983 there were 4,396 pre-primary schools with 221,262 pupils, 33,101 primary schools with 3,749,859 pupils. In 5,495 secondary schools there were 1,816,599 pupils and in 216 higher education establishments there were 365,772 students.

The National University in Bogotá was founded in 1867 and there are 97 other universities with 171,002 students and 17,963 lecturers.

Health. In 1979 there were 729 hospitals and clinics. There were also 1,499 health centres.

DIPLOMATIC REPRESENTATIVES

Of Colombia in Great Britain (3 Hans Crescent, London, SW1X 0LR)
Ambassador: Dr Bernardo Ramirez (accredited 20 Feb. 1985).

Of Great Britain in Colombia (Calle 38, No. 13–35, Bogotá)
Ambassador: J. A. Robson, CMG.

Of Colombia in the USA (2118 Leroy Pl., NW, Washington, D.C., 20008)
Ambassador: Alvaro Gomez.

Of the USA in Colombia (Calle 37, 8-40, Bogotá)
Ambassador: Lewis A. Tambs.

Of Colombia to the United Nations
Ambassador: Dr Carlos Alban-Holguin.

Books of Reference

Anuario General de Estadística de Colombia. Bogotá. Annual
Anuario de Comercio Exterior de Colombia. Annual
Anuario Estadístico Bogotá D. E. Annual
Boletín Mensual de Estadística. Monthly
Economía y Estadística. Occasional
Informe Financiero del Contralor General. Annual
Informe del Gerente de la Caja de Crédito Agrario, Industrial y Minero. Annual
Memorias (13) de los Ministros al Congreso Nacional. Annual
McGreevey, W. P., *An Economic History of Colombia, 1845–1930.* CUP, 1970
Morairetz, D., *Why the Emperor's New Clothes are not made in Colombia.* OUP, 1982

COMOROS

Capital: Moroni
Population: 385,000 (1983)
GNP per capita: US$320 (1981)

Republique fédérale islamique des Comores

HISTORY. The 3 islands forming the present state became French protectorates at the end of the 19th century, and were proclaimed colonies on 25 July 1912. With neighbouring Mayotte they were administratively attached to Madagascar from 1914 until 1947, when the 4 islands became a French Overseas Territory, achieving internal self-government in Dec. 1961.

In referenda held on each island on 22 Dec. 1974, the 3 western islands voted overwhelmingly for independence, while Mayotte voted to remain French. The Comoran Chamber of Deputies unilaterally declared the islands' independence on 6 July 1975, but Mayotte remained a French dependency.

The first government of Ahmed Abdallah was overthrown on 3 Aug. 1975 by a *coup* led by Ali Soilih (who assumed the Presidency on 2 Jan. 1976), but Ahmed Abdallah regained the Presidency after a second *coup* ousted Ali Soilih in May 1978.

AREA AND POPULATION. The Comoros consists of 3 islands in the Indian ocean between the African mainland and Madagascar. The majority of the population throughout the islands speak Kiswahili, but a small proportion speak French or Arabic. Population (estimate, 1983) 385,000.

	Area sq. km	*Population census 1966*	*Population census 1980*	*Chief town*
Njazidja (Grande Comore)	1,148	126,205	189,000	Moroni
Mwali (Mohéli)	290	10,300	19,000	Fomboni
Nzwami (Anjouan)	424	80,082	148,000	Mutsamudu
	1,862	216,587	356,000	

Population of the capital, Moroni (1978) 16,000; Fomboni, 4,500; Mutsamudu, 10,000.

The indigenous population are a mixture of Malagasy, African, Malay and Arab peoples; the vast majority speak Comoran, an Arabised dialect of Swahili, but a small proportion speak French or Arabic.

CLIMATE. There is a tropical climate, affected by Indian monsoon winds from the north, which gives a wet season from Nov. to April. Moroni. Jan. 81°F (27·2°C), July 75°F (23·9°C). Annual rainfall, 113″ (2,825 mm).

CONSTITUTION AND GOVERNMENT. Under the new Constitution approved by referendum on 1 Oct. 1978 (amended 1983), the Comoros are a Federal Islamic Republic. Mayotte has the right to join when it so chooses.

The President is Head of State, directly elected for a 6-year term (renewable once). He appoints a Prime Minister and up to 9 other Ministers to form the Council of Government, on which each island's Governor has a non-voting seat. There is a 39-member unicameral Federal Assembly, directly elected for 5 years. Each of the 3 islands is administered by a Governor (nominated by the President), up to 4 Commissioners whom he appoints to assist him, and a Legislative Council directly elected for 5 years.

President: Ahmed Abdallah Abderemane (elected Oct. 1978 and re-elected Oct. 1984).

The Council of Government, as re-organized March 1984, comprised:

Prime Minister: Ali Mroudjae.

Foreign Affairs, Co-operation and External Trade: Saïd Madi Kafe. *Home Affairs:* Omar Tamou. *Equipment, Environment and Town Planning:* Saïd Mohamed Saïd Turqui. *Justice:* Mohamed Moumine. *Agriculture, Industry and Handicraft:* Mohamed Chaher Ben Saïd Massoundé. *Economy and Finance:* Ali Nassor. *Public Health and Population:* Abdou Moustakin. *National Education:* Ahmed Ali Mohamed. *Secretaries of State:* Antoy Abdou *(Transport and Tourism),* Yahaya Djamadar *(Civil Service),* Abdillah Mbae *(Posts and Telecommunications).*

National flag: Green with a crescent and 4 stars all in white in the centre, tilted towards the lower fly.

DEFENCE

Army. The army had a strength of about 700 in 1983.

Navy. An *ex*-British landing craft built in 1945 was transferred from France in 1976 and another vessel, with ramps, was purchased in 1981. Two small patrol boats were supplied by Japan in 1982.

Air Arm. Equipment, acquired since 1977–78, comprises 3 SIAI-Marchetti SF.260W Warrior armed trainers built in Italy and a Cessna 402B communications aircraft.

INTERNATIONAL RELATIONS

Membership. Comoros is a member of UN and an ACP state of EEC.

ECONOMY

Budget. In 1982, current revenue amounted to 1,898m. francs CFA and current expenditure to 3,208m. francs CFA; the separate capital budget totalled 667m. francs CFA revenue against 854m. francs CFA expenditure.

Currency. The unit of currency is the *franc CFA,* with a parity value of 50 *francs CFA* to 1 French *franc.*

Banking. The Institut d'émission des Comores was established as the new bank of issue in 1975. The chief commercial banks are the Banque des Comores, established in 1974 by the separation of the former Comoran section of the Banque de Madagascar et des Comores and the Banque de Développement des Comores.

Weights and Measures. The metric system is in force.

NATURAL RESOURCES

Agriculture. The chief product was formerly sugar-cane, but now vanilla, copra, cacao, sisal, coffee, cloves and essential oils (citronella, ylang, lemon-grass) are the most important products. Production (1981 in tonnes): Cassava, 88,000; coconuts, 53,000; bananas, 32,000; sweet potatoes, 16,000 and rice, 14,000.

Livestock (1983): Cattle, 83,000; sheep, 9,000; goats, 90,000; asses, 4,000.

Forestry. Njazídja has a fine forest and produces timber for building.

Fisheries. In 1980 the catch was (estimate) 4,000 tonnes.

COMMERCE. Imports in 1980 amounted to 6,147m. francs CFA, exports to 2,712m. francs CFA. In 1977 France provided 41% of imports and (in 1978) took 71% of exports. The main exports (1978) were vanilla (735m. francs CFA), essential oils (640m.), cloves (460m.) and copra (205m.).

Trade between Comoros and UK (British Department of Trade returns, in £1,000 sterling):

	1980	*1981*	*1982*	*1983*	*1984*
Imports to UK	40	188	108	278	236
Exports and re-exports from UK	155	212	258	597	316

Tourism. There are about 2,000 visitors each year.

COMMUNICATIONS

Roads. In 1983 there were 750 km of classified roads, of which 262 km were tarmac. There were 3,600 registered vehicles.

Aviation. There is an international airport at Hahaya (on Njazídja). Air Comores have twice-weekly flights to Antanarivo, Dar es Salaam and Mombasa. Air France and Air Madagascar also have twice-weekly flights to Antanarivo. Air Comores has daily internal flights between Moroni and Nzwami, and 5 per week between Moroni and Mwali.

Shipping. In 1973, 279 vessels entered Comoran ports (excluding internal traffic) to discharge 54,391 tonnes and load 8,700 tonnes.

Post and Broadcasting. There were 1,035 telephones in 1977. *Comores-Inter* broadcasts in French and Comorian on short-wave and FM for approximately 8 hours a day. Number of radios (1982): 37,750.

Cinemas. In 1973 there were 2 cinemas with a seating capacity of 800.

JUSTICE, RELIGION, EDUCATION AND WELFARE

Justice. The Supreme Court comprises 7 members, 2 each appointed by the President and the Federal Assembly, and 1 by each island's Legislative Council.

Religion. Islam is the official religion, adhered to by the vast majority of the population.

Education. In 1981 there were 59,709 pupils and 1,292 teachers in primary schools; secondary schools had 13,528 pupils and 432 teachers, technical schools held 151 students with 9 teachers, and a teacher-training college had 119 students and 8 teachers.

Health. In 1978 there were 20 doctors, 1 dentist, 2 pharmacists, 35 midwives and 124 nursing personnel.

DIPLOMATIC REPRESENTATIVE

Of the Comoros in the USA
Ambassador: Ali Mlahaili (resides in Moroni).

CONGO

Capital: Brazzaville
Population: 1·74m. (1984)
GNP per capita: US$1,110 (1981)

République Populaire du Congo

HISTORY. First occupied by France in 1882, the Congo became (as 'Middle Congo') a territory of French Equatorial Africa from 1910–58, when it became a member state of the French Community. It became an independent Republic on 15 Aug. 1960.

The first President, Fulbert Youlou, was deposed on 15 Aug. 1963 by a *coup* led by Alphonse Massemba-Débat, who became President on 19 Dec. Following a second *coup* in Aug. 1968, the Army took power under the leadership of Major Marien Ngouabi, whose colleague, Major Alfred Raoul, was appointed President from 3 Sept. until 1 Jan. 1969, when Ngouabi himself became President.

The country's present name was established on 3 Jan. 1970, when a Marxist-Leninist state was introduced. Ngouabi was assassinated on 18 March 1977, and succeeded by Col. Joachim Yhombi-Opango, who in turn was replaced on 5 Feb. 1979 by Col. Denis Sassou-Nguesso.

AREA AND POPULATION. The Congo is bounded by Cameroon and the Central African Republic in the north, Zaïre to the east and south, the Cabinda province of Angola and the Atlantic to the south-west and Gabon to the west, and covers 342,000 sq. km; census population (1974), 1,300,120. Estimate (1984) 1·74m. The main towns (population in 1980) are Brazzaville, the capital (422,402) and Pointe-Noire, the main port and oil centre (185,105); other large towns are N'Kayi (formerly Jacob) (32,520) and Loubomo (30,830).

In 1974, 45% spoke Kongo dialects, 15% Téké, 15% Sanga, 12% Ubangi; there are also about 12,000 pygmies and 12,000 Europeans (mainly French). French is the official language.

CLIMATE. An equatorial climate, with moderate rainfall and a small range of temperature. There is a long dry season from May to Oct. in the S.W. plateaux, but the Congo Basin in the N.E. is more humid, with rainfall approaching 100″ (2,500 mm). Brazzaville. Jan. 78°F (25·6°C), July 73°F (22·8°C). Annual rainfall 59″ (1,473 mm).

CONSTITUTION AND GOVERNMENT. In July 1979 a new Constitution was approved by referendum. Executive power was vested in the President, elected for a 5-year term by the National Congress of the *Parti congolais du travail* (the sole legal party since 1969). The President is assisted by a Council of Ministers, appointed and led by him. The PCT Congress elects a Central Committee of 75 members and a Political Bureau of 13 to administer it; it nominates all candidates for the 153-member People's National Assembly and for the regional, district and local councils, all of which were last elected on 11 Aug. 1984. The PCT accepted a constitutional amendment which increases the power of the presidency and reduces the role of the Prime Minister to that of a co-ordinator rather than Head of Government.

President, Defence and Security: Col. Denis Sassou-Nguesso.
Prime Minister: Ange-Edouard Poungui.
Foreign Affairs: Antoine Ndinga Oba.

National flag: Red, in the canton the national emblem of a crossed hoe and mattock, a green wreath and a gold star.

Local Government: The republic is divided into the capital district of Brazzaville and 9 regions (each under an appointed Commissioner and an elected Council), which are sub-divided into 46 districts.

DEFENCE

Army. The Army consists of 6 battalions, 1 armoured, 1 artillery, 2 infantry, 1 engineering, and 1 paracommando. Equipment includes 35 T-54/-55 and T-59 tanks. Total personnel (1985) 8,000.

Navy. The flotilla includes 3 new Spanish-built fast attack craft, 1 *ex*-Soviet torpedo boat, 2 *ex*-Chinese gunboats, 4 *ex*-Chinese river patrol craft, 2 guard vessels, 4 small patrol cutters, 2 French-built new tugs and 12 small river patrol boats. Personnel in 1985 totalled 250 officers and men.

Air Force. The Air Force had (1985) about 500 personnel, 15 MiG-17 jet fighters, 2 twin-turbofan F28 Fellowship and 1 Corvette for VIP transport, 1 Frégate and 5 Antonov An-24/26 turboprop transports, 5 C-47 and 5 Il-14 piston-engined transports, 3 Broussard communications aircraft, 6 L-39 jet trainers and 2 Alouette II and 1 Alouette III light helicopters.

INTERNATIONAL RELATIONS

Membership. Congo is a member of UN, OAU and is an ACP state of EEC.

ECONOMY

Planning. The National Plan runs 1982–86.

Budget. The ordinary budget in 1983 balanced at 388,000m. francs CFA. Oil revenues finance 53% of the operational budget.

Currency. The unit of currency is the *franc CFA* with a parity value of 50 *francs CFA* to 1 French franc.

Banking. The *Banque des États de l'Afrique Centrale* is the bank of issue. There are 4 commercial banks situated in Brazzaville, including the *Banque Commerciale Congolaise* and the *Union Congolaise de Banques.*

ENERGY AND NATURAL RESOURCES

Electricity. Production in 1981 was 165m. kwh from a hydro-electric plant at Djoué near Brazzaville and from about 6 thermal plants.

Oil. Oil reserves are estimated at 500–1,000m. tonnes. Output in 1982 was almost 5m. tonnes from the 26 offshore oil platforms operated by Elf Congo and Agip Congo. A refinery at Pointe-Noire came on stream in Dec. 1982.

Minerals. Lead, copper, zinc and gold (16 kg in 1978) are the main minerals.

Agriculture. Production (1982, in 1,000 tonnes): Cassava, 530; sugar-cane, 225; pineapples, 107; bananas, 32; plantains, 34; yams, 26; groundnuts, 14; palm-oil, 9; coffee, 5; cocoa, 4.

Livestock (1983): Cattle, 68,000; pigs, 25,000; sheep, 60,000; goats, 160,000; poultry, 1m.

Forestry. Equatorial forests cover 20m. hectares (60% of the total land area) from which (in 1980) 800,000 cu. metres of timber were produced, mainly okoumé from the south and sapele from the north. Hardwoods (mainly mahogany) are also exported.

Fisheries. In 1977 the catch amounted to 16,400 tonnes.

INDUSTRY AND TRADE

Industry. There is a growing manufacturing sector, located mainly in the 4 major towns, producing processed foods, textiles, cement (34,000 tonnes in 1980), metal industries and chemicals; in 1970 it employed 21·5% of the labour force.

Trade Unions. In 1964 the existing unions merged into one national body, the *Confédération Syndicale Congolaise.*

Commerce. Imports in 1982 totalled 265,250m. francs CFA (mainly machinery) and exports 321,030m. (of which petroleum 97%). In 1980 50% of imports were from France; 31% of exports were to Italy and 24% to France.

Total trade between the Congo and UK (British Department of Trade returns, in £1,000 sterling):

	1980	*1981*	*1982*	*1983*	*1984*
Imports to UK	3,416	3,670	2,393	4,335	1,958
Exports and re-exports from UK	2,943	4,434	9,766	9,560	6,207

COMMUNICATIONS

Roads. There were (1980) 8,246 km of all-weather roads. In 1980 there were 20,000 cars and 14,000 commercial vehicles.

Railways. A railway (517 km, 1,067 mm gauge) and a telegraph line connect Brazzaville with Pointe-Noire and a 200 km branch railway links Mont-Belo with Mbinda on the Gabon border.

Aviation. The principal airports are at Maya Maya (near Brazzaville) and Pointe-Noire. In addition there are 22 airfields served by the local airline, Lina-Congo.

Shipping. Pointe-Noire handled (1979) 2·4m. tonnes of goods including manganese from Gabon. There were (1979) 16 vessels of 6,942 GNT registered.

Post and Broadcasting. Telephones (1982) numbered 8,899. In 1980 there were 92,000 radios and 3,500 TV sets in use.

Cinemas. In 1973 there were 7 cinemas with a seating capacity of 5,100.

JUSTICE, RELIGION, EDUCATION AND WELFARE

Justice. The Supreme Court, Court of Appeal and a criminal court are situated in Brazzaville, with a network of *tribunaux de grande instance* and *tribunaux d'instance* in the regions.

Religion. In 1977, 50% of the population were Christian (40·5% Roman Catholic and 9·5% Protestant), 47% followed animist beliefs and 3% were Moslem.

Education. In 1981 there were 390,676 pupils and 7,186 teachers in 1,310 primary schools, 168,718 pupils and 3,649 teachers in 122 secondary schools, 16,933 students with 1,239 teachers in 36 technical schools and 1,934 students with 229 teachers in teacher-training establishments. The Université Marien-Ngouabi (founded 1972) in Brazzaville had 6,848 students and 681 teaching staff in 1980.

Health. There were (1978) 274 doctors, 2 dentists, 28 pharmacists, 413 midwives, 1,915 nursing personnel and 473 hospitals and dispensaries with 6,876 beds.

DIPLOMATIC REPRESENTATIVES

Of the Congo in Great Britain
Ambassador: (Vacant).

Of Great Britain in the Congo
Ambassador: N. P. Bayne, CMG.

Of the USA in the Congo (PO Box 1015, Brazzaville)
Ambassador: Kenneth L. Brown.

Of Congo to the USA and United Nations
Ambassador: Nicolas Mondjo.

COSTA RICA

República de Costa Rica

Capital: San José
Population: 2·4m. (1984)
GNP per capita: US$1,430 (1981)

HISTORY. The republic of Costa Rica (the 'Rich Coast') has been independent since 1821, although it formed, from 1824 to 1838, part of the Confederation of Central America.

AREA AND POPULATION. Costa Rica is bounded north by Nicaragua, east by the Caribbean, southeast by Panama, and south and west by the Pacific. The area is estimated at 51,100 sq. km (19,344 sq. miles). The population at the census of 14 May 1973 was 1,871,780.

The area and census (provisional) of population for 1 Jan. 1984 (2,450,226) was as follows:

Province	*Population*	*Area (sq. km)*	*Capital*	*Population*
San José	893,254	4,959·63	San José	245,370
Alajuela	430,634	9,753·23	Alajuela	33,929
Cartago	269,860	3,124·67	Cartago	23,884
Heredia	195,389	2,656·27	Heredia	20,867
Guanacaste	193,024	10,140·71	Liberia	14,093
Puntarenas	291,008	11,276·97	Puntarenas	47,851
Limón	187,057	9,188·52	Limón	43,158

Vital statistics for calendar years:

	Marriages	*Births*	*Deaths*
1981	16,654	72,260	8,990
1982	18,444	73,089	9,136
1983	18,507	72,953	9,432

The population of European descent, many of them of pure Spanish blood, dwell mostly around the capital of the republic, San José, and in the principal towns of the provinces. Limón, on the Caribbean coast, and Puntarenas, on the Pacific coast, are the chief commercial ports. The United Fruit Co., who in 1941 abandoned their banana plantations on the Atlantic coast in favour of large new plantations on the Pacific coast, have constructed ports at Quepos and Golfito. The Standard Fruit Co. and others have cleared land since 1958 in the Atlantic coast area and now have 2,325 acres producing some 4·2m. stems a year. There are some 15,000 West Indians, mostly in Limón province. The indigenous Indian population is dwindling and is now estimated at 1,200.

Spanish is the language of the country.

CLIMATE. The climate is tropical, with a small range of temperature and abundant rains. The dry season is from Dec. to April. San José. Jan. 66°F (18·9°C), July 69°F (20·6°C). Annual rainfall 72" (1,793 mm).

CONSTITUTION AND GOVERNMENT. The Constitution, promulgated on 7 Dec. 1871, has been modified very frequently, last in 1949. The Constitution forbids the establishment or maintenance of an army. The legislative power is normally vested in a single chamber called the Legislative Assembly, which since 1962 consists of 57 deputies, 1 for every 25,214 inhabitants, elected for 4 years. The President is elected for 4 years; the candidate receiving the largest vote, provided it is over 40% of the total, is declared elected, but a second ballot is required if no candidate gets 40% of the total. Suffrage is universal, there being no exemption for reasons of economic status, race or sex. The vote is direct by secret ballot for all nationals of 18 years or over. Elections are normally held on the first Sunday in

February. Voting for President, Deputies and Municipal Councillors is secret and compulsory for all men under 70 years of age. Independent non-party candidates are barred from the ballot.

Elections for the Legislative Assembly took place on 7 Feb. 1982; and Partido de Liberacíon won 33 and Partido Unidad 18 of the 57 seats.

The Cabinet was composed as follows in Jan. 1985:

President: Luis Alberto Monge, elected 7 Feb. 1982.

Foreign Affairs and Religion: Carlos José Gutiérrez Gutiérrez. *Interior:* Enrique Obregón Valverde. *Justice:* Hugo Alfonso Muñoz. *Public Security:* Benjamín Piza Carranza. *Finance:* Porfirio Morera Batres. *Education:* Eugenio Rodríguez Vega. *Agriculture and Livestock:* Carlos Manuel Rojas López. *Public Works and Transport:* Hernán Azofaifa Víquez. *Industry, Energy and Mines:* Calixto Chávez Zamora. *Economy and Commerce:* Odalier Villalobos. *Planning:* Juan Manuel Villasusa. *Labour and Social Security:* Guillermo Sandóval Aguilar. *Health:* Dr Juan Jaramillo Antillón. *Culture, Youth and Sport:* Hernán González Gutiérrez. *Presidency:* Danilo Jiménez Veiga. *Exports and Investments:* Jorge Manuel Dengo Obregón. *Counsellor for Foreign Dept:* Federico Vargas Peralta.

The powers of the President are limited by the constitution, which leaves him the power to appoint and remove at will members of his cabinet. All other public appointments are made jointly in the names of the President and of the minister in charge of the department concerned.

National flag: Five unequal stripes of blue, white, red, white, blue, with the national arms on a white disc near the hoist.

National anthem: Noble patria, tu hermosa bandera (words by J. M. Zeledón, 1903; tune by M. M. Gutiérrez, 1851).

DEFENCE

Army. The Army was abolished in 1948, and replaced by a Civil Guard reputed to be 7,000 strong. There has never been compulsory military service or training.

Navy. The flotilla includes 1 fast patrol craft and 1 armed tug on the Atlantic coast and 5 small coastguard cutters and 3 smaller patrol boats on the Pacific coast. Personnel (1985) 90 officers and men.

Air Wing. The Civil Guard operates a small air wing equipped with 3 Otter STOL utility transports, plus a few lightplanes and helicopters.

INTERNATIONAL RELATIONS

Membership. Costa Rica is a member of UN and OAS.

ECONOMY

Budget. The budget for 1980 balanced at 8,029m. colones. The income-tax law of 10 March 1972 raised the maximum rate to 50% for personal incomes of 350,000 colones and over, and to 40% for corporate incomes of 1m. colones and over.

External government debt on 31 Dec. 1982 was US$3,500m.

Currency. The unit of currency is the *colone* (₡). The official rate in Feb. 1985 was ₡48·20 = US$1; 51·90 = £1. The official rate is used for all imports on an essential list and by the Government and autonomous institutions and a free rate is used for all other transactions.

The currency is chiefly notes. The Banco Central issue notes for 5, 10, 20, 50, 100, 500 and 1,000 colones. Silver coins of 1 colone, 50 centimos and 25 centimos were in 1935 replaced by coins (2 and 1 colones and 50 and 25 centimos) made up of 3 parts copper and 1 part nickel, and given the same value as the subsidiary silver currency. There are copper coins (and chromium stainless steel coins) of 10 and 5 centimos.

Banking. By a law passed on 28 Jan. 1950 a Central Bank was established for the organization and direction of the national monetary system and of dealings in foreign exchange, the promotion of facilities for credit and the supervision of all banking operations in the country. The bank has a board of 7 directors appointed by the Government, including *ex officio* the Minister of Finance and the Planning Office Director.

The National Insurance Institute *(Instituto Nacional de Seguros)* is a Government organization, created in 1924, which has a monopoly of new insurance business.

Weights and Measures. The metric system is legally established; but in the country districts the following old Spanish weights and measures are found: *libra* = 1·014 lb. avoirdupois; *arroba* = 25·35 lb. avoirdupois; *quintal* = 101·40 lb. avoirdupois, and *fanega* = 11 Imperial bushels.

ENERGY AND NATURAL RESOURCES

Electricity. Electricity, derived from water power in the highlands, is increasingly used as motive power. Output, 1980, was 1,902m. mwh.

Minerals. Gold output is about 3,000 troy oz. per year. Salt production from sea water is about 10,000 tonnes annually. Haematite ore was discovered on the Nicoya Peninsula late in 1960 and sulphur near San Carlos in 1966. The United Nations have offered US$1m. towards a 3-year mining survey.

Agriculture. Agriculture is the principal industry. The cultivated area is about 1m. acres; grass lands cover 1·8m. acres; forests and woodlands, 9,855,000 acres. There are thousands of square miles of public lands that have never been cleared on which can be found quantities of rosewood, cedar, mahogany and other cabinet woods. The principal agricultural products are coffee, bananas, sugar and cattle. Coffee normally accounts for about half the country's foreign-exchange earnings. Cocoa, maize, sugar, tobacco, rice and potatoes are commonly cultivated. The distillation of spirits is a government monopoly.

Coffee production in 1981 was 112,089 tonnes. Sugar production (1981) 2,521,020 tonnes.

Dairy-farming and cattle-raising are substantial pursuits. In 1983 cattle numbered 2·28m. and pigs 236,000.

Costa Rica is the seat of the Inter-American Institute of Agricultural Sciences, with headquarters at Turrialba.

INDUSTRY AND TRADE

Industry. The main manufactured goods are foodstuffs, textiles, fertilizers, pharmaceuticals, furniture, cement, tyres, canning, clothing, plastic goods, plywood and electrical equipment.

Industrial production was valued at 25·1m. colones in 1980, compared with 1·499m. in 1972.

Labour. As Costa Rica is still essentially an agricultural country, the organization of labour has made progress only in the larger centres of population, and even there it is not a strong movement. There are two main trade unions, *Rerum Novarum* (anti-Communist) and *Confederación General de Trabajadores Costarricenses* (Communist).

Commerce. The value of imports into and exports from Costa Rica in 5 years was as follows in US$:

	1979	*1980*	*1981*	*1982*	*1983*
Imports	1,396,812,332	1,523,797,000	1,208,529,000	867,000,000	987,826,445
Exports	934,391,357	1,001,742,230	1,030,203,040	870,800,000	559,951,375

The value (in US$1m.) of the principal imports in 1983 were: Machinery, including transport equipment, 163·5; manufactures (1982), 227·9; chemicals, 200·5; fuel and mineral oils, 189; foodstuffs, 72·5.

Chief exports (in US$1m.) in 1982 were: Manufactured goods and other products, 126·4; coffee, 236·9 (mostly to Federal Republic of Germany and USA); bananas, 234·5 (to USA); sugar, 13·2; cocoa, 2·4.

Total trade between Costa Rica and UK (British Department of Trade returns in £1,000 sterling):

	1980	*1981*	*1982*	*1983*	*1984*
Imports to UK	5,424	6,433	15,068	22,299	21,248
Exports and re-exports from UK	8,302	4,791	5,455	11,041	9,138

Tourism. There was a total of 371,582 visitors in 1982.

COMMUNICATIONS

Roads. In 1981 there were about 28,525 km of all-weather motor roads open. On the Costa Rica section of the Inter-American Highway it is possible to motor to Panama during the dry season. The Pan-American Highway into Nicaragua is metalled for most of the way and there is now a good highway open almost to Puntarenas. Motor vehicles, 1980, numbered 195,105.

Railways. The nationalized railway system *(Ferrocarriles de Costa Rica)*, totalling 700 km (260 km electrified) of 1,067 mm gauge, connect San José with Limón, the Atlantic port, and San José with Puntarenas, the Pacific port. Total railway traffic in 1982 was 1·2m. tonnes of freight and 1·4m. passengers.

Aviation. Passenger movement in and out of Costa Rica is almost entirely by air *via* the local company, LACSA, PANAM and TACA. LACSA links San José by daily services with all the more important towns. The international airport at Juan Santamaría was opened in June 1955.

Shipping. In 1981, 1,221 ships entered and cleared the ports of the republic (Puerto Limón, Puntarenas and Golfito); combined cargo, 1,395 tonnes.

Post and Broadcasting. There were 255,898 telephones in 1982.

The commercial wireless telegraph stations are operated by *Cia Radiográfica Internacional de Costa Rica.* The stations are located at Cartago, Limón, Puntarenas, Quepos and Golfito. The Government has 19 wireless telegraph stations in its local network. The principal or central station at San José also maintains international radio-telegraph circuits to Nicaragua, Honduras, San Salvador and Mexico. The Government has 202 telegraph offices and 88 official telephone stations. The official list of broadcasting stations shows 28 long-wave stations and 7 short-wave stations. Television was inaugurated in May 1960; there were 6 stations and (estimate) 277,694 receivers in 1980.

Cinemas (1979). Cinemas numbered 106, with seating capacity of 105,000.

Newspapers (1984). There were 4 daily newspapers all published in San José.

JUSTICE, RELIGION, EDUCATION AND WELFARE

Justice. Justice is administered by the Supreme Court, 5 appeal courts divided into 5 chambers; the Court of Cassation, the Higher and Lower Criminal Courts, and the Higher and Lower Civil Courts. There are also subordinate courts in the separate provinces and local justices throughout the republic. Capital punishment may not be inflicted.

Religion. Roman Catholicism is the religion of the State, which contributes to its maintenance but controls the Church Patronage and insists on lay instruction in history, economics and similar subjects; there is entire religious liberty under the constitution, but religious appeals are forbidden in current political discussions. The Archbishop of Costa Rica has 4 bishops at Alajuela, Limón, San Isidro el General and Tilarán.

Protestants number about 40,000.

Education. Costa Rica has a very low illiteracy rate. Elementary instruction is compulsory and free; secondary education (since 1949) is also free. Elementary schools are provided and maintained by local school councils, while the national government pays the teachers, besides making subventions in aid of local funds. In 1982 there were 3,509 public primary schools with 11,615 teachers and administrative staff and 377,274 enrolled pupils; there were 242 public and private secondary schools with 165,649 pupils. The University of Costa Rica, founded in San José in 1843, has 2,337 professors in 13 faculties and 38,629 students. A medical school was opened in 1961. The budget for 1971 provides ₡250m. for public education. Since 1944 English has been taught in all secondary schools.

Social Welfare. The labour code of 1943 provides considerable protection for the workers, while a system of social insurance against sickness covering 756,347 workers in 1968, old age and death covering 68,949 is gradually being extended throughout the country.

DIPLOMATIC REPRESENTATIVES

Of Costa Rica in Great Britain (225 Cromwell Rd., London SW5)
Ambassador: Jorge Borbón Zeller (accredited 20 July 1982).

Of Great Britain in Costa Rica (Edificio Centro Colon, Apartado 815, San José)
Ambassador and Consul-General: Peter Wayre Summerscale.

Of Costa Rica in the USA (2112 S St., NW, Washington D.C., 20008)
Ambassador: Claudio A. Volio.

Of the USA in Costa Rica (Avenida 3, Calle 1, San José)
Ambassador: Curtin Winsor, Jr.

Of Costa Rica to the United Nations
Ambassador: Dr Fernando Zumbado Jimenez.

Books of Reference

Statistical Information: Official statistics are issued by the Director General de Estadística (Ministerio de Industria y Comercio, San José) as they become available. The compilation of statistics was started in 1861.

Ameringer, C. D., *Democracy in Costa Rica*. New York, 1982
Biesanz, R., *(et al), The Costa Ricans.* Hemel Hempstead, 1982
Fernandez Guardia, L., *Historia de Costa Rica.* 2nd ed., 2 vols. San José, 1941
Seligson, M. A., *Peasants of Costa Rica and the Development of Agrarian Capitalism.* Univ. of Wisconsin Press, 1980
Trejos, Juan, *Geografía ilustrada de Costa Rica.* San José, 1948

CUBA

Capital: Havana
Population: 10m. (1984)
GNP per capita: US$2,696 (1981)

República de Cuba

HISTORY. Cuba, except for the brief British occupancy in 1762–63, remained a Spanish possession from its discovery by Columbus in 1492 until 10 Dec. 1898, when the sovereignty was relinquished under the terms of the Treaty of Paris, which ended the struggle of the Cubans against Spanish rule. Cuba thus became an independent republic, but the United States stipulated under the 'Platt Amendment' (abrogated by Roosevelt in 1934) that Cuba must enter into no treaty relations with a foreign power, which might endanger its independence. A convention which assembled on 5 Nov. 1900 adopted the first constitution of the republic on 21 Feb. 1901.

The revolutionary movement against the Batista dictatorship, led by Dr Fidel Castro, started on 26 July 1953 (now a national holiday). It achieved power on 1 Jan. 1959 when Batista fled the country.

An invasion force of émigrés and adventurers landed in Cuba on 17 April 1961; the main body was defeated at the Bay of Pigs (Mantanzas province) and mopped up by 20 April.

The US Navy blockaded Cuba from 22 Oct. to 22 Nov. 1962.

AREA AND POPULATION. The island of Cuba forms the largest and most westerly of the Greater Antilles group and lies 135 miles south of the tip of Florida, USA. It has an area of 44,206 sq. miles (114,524 sq. km); the Isle of Youth (formerly Isle of Pines) has 1,180 sq. miles, and other islands about 1,350 sq. miles. Estimated population in 1984 was 10m.

The area, population and density of population of the 14 provinces and the special Municipality of the Isle of Youth were as follows (1982 estimate):

	Area sq. km	*Population*		*Area sq. km*	*Population*
Pinar del Rió	10,860	649,653	Camagüey	14,134	680,549
La Habana	5,671	594,866	Las Tunas	6,373	444,136
Ciudad de La Habana	740	1,951,373	Holguín	9,105	922,129
Matanzas	11,669	565,648	Granma	8,452	746,771
Cienfuegos	4,149	332,234	Santiago de Cuba	6,343	919,158
Villa Clara	8,069	772,721	Guantánamo	6,366	469,421
Sancti Spíritus	6,737	404,110			
Ciego de Avila	6,485	328,426	Isla de la Juventud	2,199	60,794

CLIMATE. Situated in the sub-tropical zone, Cuba has a generally rainy climate, affected by the Gulf Stream and the N.E. Trades, though winters are comparatively dry after the heaviest rains in Sept. and Oct. Hurricanes are liable to occur between June and Nov. Havana. Jan. 72°F (22·2°C), July 82°F (27·8°C). Annual rainfall 48″ (1,224 mm).

CONSTITUTION AND GOVERNMENT. The previous Constitution was suspended in Jan. 1959. The first socialist Constitution came into force on 24 Feb. 1976.

Since the last representative in Cuba of the King of Spain, Gen. Don Adolfo Jiménez Castellanos, handed over the island on 1 Jan. 1899 the following have been at the head of the administration:

US Military Governors	*Took office*	*President of the Republic*	*Took office*
Maj.-Gen. John R. Brooke	1 Jan. 1899	Tomas Estrada Palma	20 May 1902
Maj.-Gen. Leonard Wood	23 Dec. 1899		

	Took office
US Provisional Governors	
William Howard Taft	29 Sept. 1906
Charles Edward Magoon	13 Oct. 1906
Presidents of the Republic	
Gen. José Miguel Gómez	28 Jan. 1909
Gen. Mario García Menocal	20 May 1913
Dr Alfredo Zayas y Alfonso	20 May 1921
Gen. Gerardo Machado y Morales	20 May 1925
Dr Carlos Manuel de Céspedes	12 Aug. 1933
Dr Ramón Grau San Martín	10 Sept. 1933
Col. Carlos Mendieta	Jan. 1934
Dr José A. Barnet	12 Dec. 1935
Dr Miguel Mariano Gómez y Arias	20 May 1936
Dr Federico Laredo Bru	24 Dec. 1936
Gen. Fulgencio Batista y Zaldívar	10 Oct. 1940
Dr Ramón Grau San Martín	10 Oct. 1944
Dr Carlos Prío Socarrás	10 Oct. 1948
Gen. Fulgencio Batista y Zaldívar	10 March 1952
Dr Manuel Urratia Lleo	2 Jan. 1959
Osvaldo Dorticos Torrado	17 July 1959

President: Dr Fidel Castro Ruz became President of the Council of State on 3 Dec. 1976. He is also President of the Council of Ministers, First Secretary of the Cuban Communist Party and C.-in-C. of the Revolutionary Armed Forces. From Jan. 1980 he took overall charge of Defence, Interior, Health and Culture.

Dr Castro on 2 Dec. 1961 proclaimed 'a Marxist–Leninist programme adapted to the precise objective conditions existing in our country'. The provisional *Organizaciones Revolucionarias Integradas* (ORI) were established as an intermediate stage towards a single (communist) party, and gave way to the *Partido Unido de la Revolución Socialista* (PURS). This brought together the *Partido Socialista Popular, Movimiento de 26 Julio* and (Students') *Directorio Revolucionario.* The PURS in turn became (3 Oct. 1965) the *Partido Comunista de Cuba.* The Communist Party had been outlawed by Batista in 1954, but legally reinstated after the revolution.

National flag: 3 blue, 2 white stripes (horizontal); a white 5-pointed star in a red triangle at the hoist.

National anthem: Al combate corred bayameses (words and tune by P. Figueredo, 1868).

Local Government. The country is divided into 14 provinces the special Municipality (the Isle of Youth) and 169 municipalities. Local Government is the responsibility of the organizations of Peoples' Power. Elections were held in 1976, 1979, 1981 and 1984 for delegates to the Provincial and Municipal Assemblies and in 1976 and 1981 to the National Assembly.

DEFENCE. On 13 Nov. 1963 conscription was introduced for all men between the ages of 16 and 45, later raised to 50 (3 years), women of the 17–35 age groups may volunteer (for 2 years).

Army. The strength was 200,000 officers and men (75,000 conscripts) in 1984. Reserves are estimated at 200,000.

The Army is organized in 15 infantry brigades, 3 armoured brigades and 8 independent battalions. Equipment includes 350 T-34, 250 T-54/-55, 60 T-62 and a few T-72 tanks. Para-military forces total 15,000 and the new Territorial Militia, 1·2m. including reservists, all armed.

Navy. The Navy consists of 4 *ex*-Soviet diesel-powered submarines (of which 1 is in static reserve), 2 *ex*-Soviet guided missile-armed frigates, 36 missile boats, 9 hydrofoil attack craft, 13 patrol vessels, 18 torpedo boats, 22 fast gunboats, 2 minehunters, 12 inshore minesweepers, 12 motor launches, 14 coastguard vessels, 13 survey vessels, 3 landing ships, 7 landing craft and 10 service craft. The large majority of over 160 craft are former units of the Soviet Navy. Personnel in 1985 exceeded 6,000 officers and ratings. One of the 3 old *ex*-US patrol frigates still exists as a harbour hulk. The USA is still in possession of the Guantanámo naval base, but the Cuban Government refuses to accept the nominal rent of US$5,000 per annum.

Air Force. The Air Force has been extensively re-equipped with aircraft supplied by USSR and in 1984 had a strength of some 16,000 officers and men and 280 combat aircraft. About 16 interceptor and 4 ground-attack squadrons fly MiG-23, MiG-21 and MiG-17 jet fighters. There is a squadron of An-26 twin-turboprop transports, some An-24 twin-turboprop transports, piston-engined Il-14s, and about 100 Mi-24 gunship, Mi-8 (some armed) and Mi-4 helicopters, Zlin 326 piston-engined trainers and MiG-15UTI, MiG-21U and MiG-23U jet trainers. Many An-2M biplanes are operated by the Air Force, mainly on agricultural and liaison duties. Soviet-built surface-to-air ('Guideline', 'Goa' and 'Gainful') and coastal defence ('Samlet') missiles are in service.

INTERNATIONAL RELATIONS

Membership. Cuba is a member of the UN, SELA and COMECON.

ECONOMY

Planning. The Cuban economy is now centrally planned. Since July 1972 Cuba has been a member of the Council for Mutual Economic Assistance (COMECON) and, since Jan. 1974, of the two COMECON international banks.

Budget. Revenue in 1984 was 11,471·3m. pesos and expenditure, 11,249·6m. pesos.

Currency. The *peso* is not a freely exchangeable currency but an official exchange rate is announced monthly reflecting any changes in the strength of the US$. In Feb. 1985, the sterling-peso rate was £1 = 0·966 *pesos*. The old gold *pesos* and all US currency are no longer legal tender. US currency is accepted in tourist/hotel shops, but is not normally legal tender.

Copper-nickel coins of 1 *peso* and 40, 20, 5 and 1 *cent* are issued. Notes are for 100, 50, 20, 10, 5, 3 and 1 *peso*.

Banking. On 23 Dec. 1948 the president signed the law creating a central bank (with capital of US$10m.) and which began operating 27 April 1950.

On 14 Oct. 1960 all banks were nationalized, except the Royal Bank of Canada and the Bank of Nova Scotia, which were bought out later. All banking is now carried out by the National Bank of Cuba through its 250 agencies. In 1964, 1·6m. small savings accounts totalled US$738m.

All insurance business was nationalized in Jan. 1964. A National Savings Bank was established in 1983.

Weights and Measures. The metric system of weights and measures is legally compulsory, but the American and old Spanish systems are much used. The sugar industry uses the Spanish long ton (1·03 tonnes) and short ton (0·92 tonne). Cuba sugar sack = 329·59 lb. or 149·49 kg. Land is measured in *caballerías* (of 13·4 hectares or 33 acres).

ENERGY AND NATURAL RESOURCES

Electricity. Installed capacity 1982 was 2,418 mw. Production in 1983 was 11,553·4m. kwh.

Minerals. Iron ore abounds, with deposits estimated at 3,500m. tons, of which 90% were held as reserves by American steel interests but are now controlled by the Cuban Mining Institute; output (tonnes), wrought iron (1980), 1,180; steel (1983), 363,700.

Output of copper (1982) was 1,465 tonnes; refractory chrome (1982), 27,300 tonnes. Other minerals are nickel and cobalt (1983, 39,300 tonnes), silica and barytes. Gold and silver are also worked. Cuba has a small output of petroleum (1983: 7·4m. tonnes). Salt output from the solar evaporation of sea water was 92,900 tonnes in 1983.

Agriculture. In May 1959 all land over 30 *caballerías* was nationalized and has since been turned into state farms. In Oct. 1963 private holdings were reduced to a maximum of 5 *caballerías* (approximately 67 hectares). By 1960, 764 co-operative farms had been formed, and by late 1966 almost 65% of farm land was state-owned; the balance being in private hands.

In Sept. 1982 there were 1,402 co-operatives comprising 47,357 *caballerías* of land. The total cultivated land included state-owned, 3,398,200 hectares, and in the private sector, 475,400 hectares.

The most important product is sugar, of which Cuba is the world's second largest producer; with its by-products it furnishes nearly 80% by value of the national exports. The 1983–84 crop was estimated at 8·2m. tonnes. There are 152 mills, including 40 of the largest, which were taken over from US interests, and which represent 39% of total capacity. Tobacco, coffee, cotton, maize, rice and potatoes are grown.

Production of other important crops in 1982 was (in tonnes): Tobacco, 45,700; rice (1983), 517,600; maize, 21,561; coffee, 28,684.

Tobacco is grown mainly in the Vuelta–Abajo district, near Pinar del Río. Coffee is grown chiefly in the province of Oriente.

Output of henequén fibre in 1964 was 233,919 tons. A fast-growing fibre, *kenaf*, originally from India, soft in texture, is replacing jute for sacking (production, 1982, 15,773 tonnes); the tobacco industry uses *majagua*, another local fibre, while a third fibre, *yarey*, from palms is also used. 206,700 tonnes of potatoes were produced in 1983. A nitrate plant has been built at Nuevitas and a large British-built urea plant at Cienfuegos. The principal fruits exported are pineapples, citrus fruit, tomatoes and pimentos. A rice cultivation plan began in 1967 in the south of Havana province. Cultivation is highly mechanized and the area so far sown produces two crops a year.

In 1983 citrus fruit production was 615,000 tonnes.

In 1962, 2,105 *caballerías* were allocated to cotton; cotton produced, 1982, was 3,000 tons against 13,000 tons in 1962.

In 1983 the livestock included 867,200 pigs; 812,000 horses; 375,300 sheep and goats; 5·1m. head of cattle.

Forestry. Cuba has extensive forest lands. These forests contain valuable cabinet woods, such as mahogany and cedar, besides dye-woods, fibres, gums, resins and oils. Cedar is used locally for cigar-boxes, and mahogany is exported. During the re-forestation campaign of 1959–60, 34,000 eucalyptus saplings were planted over 1,120 *caballerías*. Cedars, mahogany, *majagua*, teca, etc., are also being raised and planted out. In 1983 saplings planted included: Eucalyptus, 12·9m.; pine, 36·9m.; majagua, 5·5m.; mahogany, 2 1m.; cedar, 2·1m.; casuarina, 15·5m.

Fisheries. Fishing is the third most important export industry, after sugar and nickel. Catch (1981) 150,000 tonnes.

INDUSTRY AND TRADE

Industry. Production in 1983 was: Textiles, 170·7m. sq. metres; cement, 3·2m. tonnes; wheat flour, 428,700 tonnes; fuel oil (1982), 3,298,100 tonnes; diesel oil (1982), 1,126,600 tonnes; 353,200 tyres; 266,300 inner tubes; leather shoes, 13·1m. pairs; paint (1982), 68,988 hectolitres; soft drinks, 2,051,200 hectolitres; 359m. cigars; 16,801,900m. cigarettes; fertilizers, 1,081,700 tonnes.

Trade Unions. All workers have a right to join a trade union. The Workers' Central Union of Cuba, to which 23 unions are affiliated, had 2m. members in 1978.

Commerce. Imports and exports (including bullion and specie) for calendar years (in 1m. pesos):

	1980	*1981*	*1982*	*1983*
Imports	4,059	5,081	5,537	6,224
Exports	3,967	4,259	4,939	5,537

Cuba's principal exports are sugar, minerals, tobacco and fish, which in 1974 were planned to furnish 86%, 6·4%, 2·7% and 2·3% respectively by value. The main imports from non-Communist countries are chemicals and engineering and electrical machinery and transport equipment.

Sugar accounts for approximately 80% of the exports. In 1983 over 1,600,000 tons were sold in free world markets, the balance going mainly to Eastern Europe under long-term guaranteed price contracts. Tobacco, fish and nickel are the other major exports. Most trade is with Eastern Europe, particularly with the USSR which supplies approximately 70% of total Cuban imports.

Total trade between Cuba and UK (British Department of Trade returns, in £1,000 sterling):

	1980	*1981*	*1982*	*1983*	*1984*
Imports to UK	26,208	16,829	17,688	14,010	13,020
Exports and re-exports from UK	35,272	27,656	64,835	45,737	64,377

Tourism. In 1982 there were 200,000 visitors (280,000 in 1957).

COMMUNICATIONS

Roads. In 1982 there were 11,746 km of paved highways open to traffic, traversing the island for 760 miles from Pinar del Río to Santiago. In 1983 there were 49,841 hire cars (including coaches and buses).

Railways. There were (1982) 5,158 km of public railway (mainly 1,435 mm gauge) of which 147 km is electrified. In 1982 it carried 23m. passengers and 16·6m. tonnes of freight. In addition, the large sugar estates have 9,441 km of lines on 1,435, 914 and 760 mm gauges.

Aviation. The state airline CUBANA operates all internal services, and from Havana to Mexico City, Madrid, Berlin, Montreal, Prague, and also to Lima, Panama, Kingston, Bridgetown, Port of Spain, Georgetown. The other regular foreign services are Mexican, Spanish, Soviet, Czech, East German and Canadian. In Dec. 1977 the first charter flights since 1960 started operating between USA and Cuba.

Shipping. The coastline is over 3,500 miles long and has many fine harbours. The merchant marine, in 1983, consisted of 107 sea-going vessels of 1,083,800 DWT.

Post and Broadcasting. There are 3,545 miles of public and 8,902 miles of private telegraph wires. Cuba has 103 broadcasting stations and 2 television stations. Radio receiving sets, 1974, numbered 909,000; television sets, 300,000. The national telephone system (1984) had 430,000 instruments.

Cinemas. In 1983 there were 520 (35mm) and 843 (16mm) cinemas.

Newspapers. In 1983 there were 29 newspapers of which 16 were daily newspapers.

JUSTICE, RELIGION, EDUCATION AND WELFARE

Justice. There is a Supreme Court in Havana and 7 regional courts of appeal. The provinces are divided into judicial districts, with courts for civil and criminal actions, with municipal courts for minor offences. The civil code guarantees aliens the same property and personal rights as are enjoyed by nationals.

The 1959 Agrarian Reform Law and the Urban Reform Law passed on 14 Oct. 1960 have placed certain restrictions on both. Revolutionary Summary Tribunals have wide powers.

Religion. There is no state Church, though Roman Catholics predominate. There is a bishop of the American Episcopal Church in Havana; there are congregations of Methodists in Havana and in the provinces. Protestants numbered 265,000 in 1962; they have been organized as the Cuban Council of Evangelical Churches.

Education. Education is compulsory (between the ages of 6 and 14) and free, and now available everywhere. In 1964 illiteracy was officially declared to have been completely eliminated.

In 1982–83 the universities had 173,403 students and 12,222 teaching staff. There were 1,363,078 pupils and 71,251 teachers at primary schools; 118,072 at pre-primary, 774,400 pupils at intermediate schools; 173,403 students at higher schools; 392,945 students at adult primary and intermediate schools; and 56,721 students at other schools.

The Camilo Cienfuegos school city in the Sierra Maestra was designed for 12,000 boys and 8,000 girls by 1970 (1965: 4,000, total). In 1974 the V. I. Lenin vocational school opened as a forerunner of 6 such schools.

Health. There were (1982) 17,026 posts for doctors and (1983) 268 hospitals. The 1984 health and education budget was 2,405m. pesos.

Free medical services are provided by the state polyclinics, though some doctors still have private practices. All serious tropical diseases are effectively kept under control, and virtually all children under the age of 15 have been vaccinated against poliomyelitis.

DIPLOMATIC REPRESENTATIVES

Of Cuba in Great Britain (167 High Holborn, London, WC1)
Ambassador: Hermes Herrera (accredited 16 Feb. 1982).

Of Great Britain in Cuba (Edificio Bolivar, Carcel 101–103, Havana)
Ambassador: Patrick Robin Fearn, CMG.

Of Cuba to the United Nations
Ambassador: Oscar Oramas Oliva.

The USA broke off diplomatic relations with Cuba on 3 Jan. 1961 but in 1977 Interest Sections were opened, officially attached to the Swiss Embassy in Havana and to the Czech Embassy in Washington respectively.

Books of Reference

Anuario Estadístico de a República de Cuba. Havana, 1914, 1953, 1957, 1972, 1973, 1979
Boletín Oficial, Ministerio de Comercio. Monthly
Estadística General: Commercio Exterior. Quarterly and Annual.—*Movimiento de Población.* Monthly and Annual. Havana
Anuario azucarero de Cuba. Havana, from 1937
Brundenius, C., *Revolutionary Cuba: The Challenge of Economic Growth with Equity.* Oxford, 1984
Canet, G., and Raisz, E., *Atlas de Cuba.* Cambridge, Mass., 1949
Carpentier, A., *Reasons of State.* London, 1976
Caute, D., *¿Cuba, Yes?* London, 1974
Domínguez, J. I., *Cuba: Order and Revolution.* Harvard Univ. Press, 1978
Guerra y Sánchez, R., and others, *Historia de la Nación Cubana.* 10 vols. Havana, 1952
MacEwan, A., *Revolution and Economic Development in Cuba.* London, 1981
Mesa-Lago, C., *The Economy of Socialist Cuba: A Two-Decade Appraisal.* Univ. of New Mexico Press, 1981
Meyer, K. E., and Szulc, T., *The Cuban Invasion.* New York, 1962
Miller, W., *The Lost Plantation.* London, 1961
Montaner, C. A., *Informe secreto sobre la revolución cubana.* Madrid, 1975
Nelson, L., *Cuba: The Measure of the Revolution.* Univ. of Minnesota Press, 1972
O'Connor, J., *The Origins of Socialism in Cuba.* London, Cornell Univ. Press, 1970
Ritter, A. R. M., *The Economic Development of Revolutionary Cuba: Strategy and Performance.* New York, 1974
Thomas, H., *Cuba: Or the Pursuit of Freedom.* London, 1971
Vives, J., *Les Maîtres de Cuba.* Paris, 1981

CYPRUS

Capital: Nicosia
Population: 655,100 (1983)
GNP per capita: US$3,193 (1982)

Kypriaki Dimokratia—
Kıbrıs Cumhuriyeti

HISTORY. About the middle of the 2nd millennium B.C. Greek colonies were established in Cyprus and later it formed part of the Persian, Roman and Byzantine empires. In 1193 it became a Frankish kingdom, in 1489 a Venetian dependency and in 1571 was conquered by the Turks. They retained possession of it until its cession to England for administrative purposes under a convention concluded with the Sultan at Constantinople, 4 June 1878. On 5 Nov. 1914 the island was annexed by Great Britain and on 1 May 1925 given the status of a Crown Colony.

For the history of Cyprus from 1931 to 1974 *see* THE STATESMAN'S YEAR-BOOK, 1958, pp. 237–38, 1959, p. 236, and 1983–84, p. 385.

On 15 July 1974 a *coup* was staged in Cyprus by the men of the Greek ruling junta, for the overthrow of President Makarios. The President left the island and the *coup* was short-lived. On 23 July power was handed over to the President of the House of Representatives, Glafcos Clerides, in accordance with the Constitution. He acted as President until the return of President Makarios on Dec. 7.

Turkey invaded the island on 20 July, eventually landing 40,000 troops supported with heavy armament and tanks. In two military operations 20–30 July and 14–16 Aug. the Turkish troops managed to occupy 40% of the northern part of Cyprus. As a result 200,000 Greek Cypriots fled to live as refugees in the south. The Cyprus crisis was raised in the UN and the General Assembly unanimously adopted resolutions calling for the withdrawal of all foreign troops from Cyprus and the return of refugees to their homes, but without result.

On 13 Feb. 1975 at a special meeting of the executive council and legislative assembly of the Autonomous Turkish Cypriot Administration a Turkish Cypriot Federated State was proclaimed. Rauf Denktash was appointed President and he declared that the state would not seek international recognition. The proclamation was denounced by President Makarios and the Greek Prime Minister but welcomed by the Turkish Prime Minister. In 1984 the UN Secretary-General initiated talks on a possible federal state but these failed in Jan. 1985.

AREA AND POPULATION. The island lies in the eastern Mediterranean, about 50 miles off the south coast of Turkey and (at the nearest points) 65 miles off the coast of Syria. Area 3,572 sq. miles (9,251 sq. km); about 150 miles is greatest length from east to west, and about 60 miles is greatest breadth from north to south. Populations by religions:

Religion	*1946*	*1960*	*1980*	*1982*	*1983*
Greek Orthodox	361,199	441,656	507,500	520,900	528,700
Turkish Moslem	80,548	104,942	118,000	121,100	122,900
Others	8,367	26,968	3,500	3,500	3,500
Total	450,114	573,566	629,000	645,500	655,100

Population estimate (1983) 655,100, of which 81% are Greek Cypriot (Armenian, Maronite and Latin minorities included) and 19% Turkish Cypriot. Principal towns with populations (1982 estimate): Nicosia (the capital), 161,100 (Greek Cypriots); Limassol, 107,200; Famagusta, 39,500; Larnaca, 48,400.

As a result of the Turkish invasion and the occupation of part of Cyprus, 200,000 Greek Cypriots were displaced and forced to find refuge in the south of the island. The urban centres of Famagusta, Kyrenia and Morphou were completely evacuated.

Vital statistics. The birth rate per 1,000 population in 1983 was 22·3; death rate, 8·5; infantile mortality per 1,000 live births, 17.

CLIMATE. The climate is Mediterranean, with very hot, dry summers and variable winters. Maximum temperatures may reach 112°F (44·5°C) in July and Aug., but minimum figures may fall to 22°F (–5·5°C) in the mountains in winter when snow is experienced. Rainfall is generally between 10 and 27″ (250 and 675 mm) and occurs mainly in the winter months, but it may reach 48″ (1,200 mm) in the Troodos mountains. Nicosia. Jan. 50°F (10·0°C), July 83°F (28·3°C). Annual rainfall 15″ (371 mm).

CONSTITUTION AND GOVERNMENT. The legislative power is exercised by the House of Representatives of 50 members, of whom 35 were elected by the Greek community and 15 by the Turkish community. As from Dec. 1963 the Turkish members have ceased to attend.

On 13 Dec. 1959 Archbishop Makarios was elected President of the Republic, having received 144,501 votes (against 71,753 cast for the candidate sponsored by the Left). Dr Fazil Kuchuk was elected Vice-President unopposed; he resigned on 4 Jan. 1964. On 13 Feb. 1975, Rauf Denktash the Turkish-Cypriot leader announced the formation of a Turkish-Cypriot state within a federal republic and on 15 Nov. 1983 a unilateral declaration of independence, as the Turkish Republic of Northern Cyprus, was announced.

When President Makarios died in Aug. 1977 Spyros Kyprianou became acting President and was proclaimed President on 31 Aug. 1977 and was elected for a 5-year term on 26 Jan. 1978 and re-elected 13 Feb. 1983.

Flag: White with a copper-coloured outline of the island with 2 green olive-branches beneath.

The elections held on 25 May 1981 returned 8 Democratic Party, 12 Akel Party (Communists), 3 EDEK (Socialist Party), 12 Democratic Rally. The Turks have not participated in the proceedings of the House since Dec. 1963.

The Council of Ministers in Jan. 1985 was as follows:

Foreign Affairs: George Iacovou. *Interior:* Roes Nicolaides. *Finance:* Demetrios Liveras. *Minister to the President:* Dinos Michaelides. *Commerce and Industry:* Michalakis Michaelides. *Education:* Andreas Christofides. *Communications and Works:* Christos Mavrellis. *Agriculture and Natural Resources:* Andreas Papasolomontos. *Labour and Social Insurance:* Andreas Moushoutas. *Health:* Dr Christos Pelekanos. *Justice:* Phivos Clerides. *Deputy Minister of the Interior:* Elias Eliades. *Defence:* Stelios Katsellis.

DEFENCE

Army. Total strength (1985) 10,000 organized in 1 armoured, 2 reconnaissance/mechanized infantry and 20 infantry battalions, with artillery and support units. The National Guard has a twin-engined Maritime Islander light transport. There is also a para-military force of 3,000 armed police.

The Turkish-Cypriot Security Force: about 25,000 men and some T-34 tanks.

INTERNATIONAL RELATIONS

Membership. Cyprus is a member of UN, the Commonwealth, the Council of Europe and the Non-Aligned Movement.

ECONOMY

Planning. A fourth emergency action plan (1982–86) envisages expenditure of £C398m. for development projects.

Budget. Revenue and expenditure for calendar years (in £C1m.):

	1980	*1981*	*1982*	*1983*
Current domestic revenue	161·1	191·2	232·7	275·4
Current expenditure	163·2	216·5	249·7	301·0
Investment expenditure	34·3	36·1	33·8	41·8

Main sources of ordinary revenue in 1983 (in £C1m.) were: Import duties, 63; excise duties, 42·5; income tax, 51·6; rents, royalties and interest, 18·6; sales of goods and services, 14·5; other duties and taxes, 22·6; social security contributions, 48·5.

Main divisions of ordinary expenditure in 1983 (in £C1m.): Wages and salaries, 123·2; pensions and gratuities, 9·5; commodity subsidies, 30·1; expenditures on goods and services, 39·9; public debt charges, 55·2; social insurance benefits, 45·8.

Development expenditure for 1983 (in £C1m.) included 10·9 for water development, 5·2 for agriculture, forests and fisheries, 2·9 for rural development, 11 for roads, 4·8 for airports and 0·7 for tourism. (An independent Ports Authority with its own funds was set up in 1977.)

The outstanding public debt as at 31 Dec. 1983 was £C292·9m., excluding sinking fund reserves, and accumulated sinking funds totalled £C15·7m. Outstanding loans as at 31 Dec. 1983 totalled £C57·2m.; including £C7·9m. to the Electricity Authority of Cyprus and £C3m. to the Cyprus Telecommunications Authority.

Currency. From Oct. 1983 the *Cyprus £* has been divided into 100 *cents*. Notes of the following denominations are in circulation: £10, £5, £1, 50 *cents*. Coins in circulation: Cupro-zinc-nickel: 20, 10, 5, 2, 1 *cent* and ½ *cent* in aluminium. Rate of exchange, Feb. 1985: £1 = £C0·733; US$1 = £C0·909.

Banking. There is a Central and Issuing Bank exercising monetary functions, and the Cyprus Development Corporation created by the Government as a major source of loan funds for industrial development. Commercial banks carrying on business in Cyprus are: Bank of Cyprus Ltd, Turkish Bank Ltd, Cyprus Popular Bank Ltd, Barclays Bank International, National Bank of Greece, Hellenic Bank Ltd, Cyprus Turkish Co-operative Central Bank Ltd, Mortgage Bank of Cyprus Ltd, Turkiye Ish Bankasi, The Housing and Finance Corporation, The Arab Bank Ltd, The Co-operative Central Bank and Lombard Banking (Cyprus) Ltd.

Turkiye Ish Bankasi are operating in the Turkish occupied area of the republic and consequently no control or supervision is exercised by the Central Bank of Cyprus.

The Central Bank of Cyprus, established in 1963, is responsible for the issue of currency, the regulation of money supply and credit, administration of the exchange control law and the foreign-exchange reserves of the republic. The Bank also acts as a banker of the banks operating in Cyprus and of the Government.

At the end of Dec. 1983 total deposits in banks were £C689m. The country's foreign exchange reserves at the end of Dec. 1982 were £C289m.

Weights and Measures. Cyprus weights and measures follow the standard weights and measures of Great Britain. The metric system may also be lawfully used. In internal trade the following special Cyprus weights and measures are in use: 1 *pic* = ⅔ yd; 1 *oke* = 2·8 lb.; 1 *kilé* = 8 Imperial gallons. The Cyprus *donum* is approximately ⅓ acre.

ENERGY AND NATURAL RESOURCES

Water resources. In 1983 £C13·1m. was spent on water dams, water supplies, hydrological research and geophysical surveys. Existing dams had (1984) a capacity of 150m. cu. metres as against 6m. cu. metres before independence.

Minerals. The principal minerals exported during 1983 were (in tonnes): Asbestos, 13,416; iron pyrites, 10,857; chromium ores and concentrates, 10,896; cement copper, 1,086. Mining products provided about 2·5% of all exports in 1983. Total value of minerals exported in 1983 was £C4·4m.

Agriculture. Chief agricultural products in 1983 (1,000 tonnes): Grapes, 210; potatoes, 188; milk, 93·1; cereals (wheat and barley), 71·3; citrus fruit, 125; meat, 42·9; carobs, 13·2; fresh fruit, 25·5; olives, 3; other vegetables, 96; eggs, 8·2m. dozen.

Of the island's 2·3m. acres, approximately 1m. are cultivated. 21·1% (1983) of the economically active population are engaged in agriculture.

Livestock in 1983 (in 1,000): Cattle, 34·2; sheep, 325; goats, 230; pigs, 243·4; poultry, 2·4.

Forestry. By Dec. 1982, the reforesting of burnt areas in the Paphos Forest was completed and an area of 7,492 ha (56,000 donums) was reforested. Reforestation work in other bare areas of state forests was carried out in an area of 5,729 ha (42,828 donums). Total forest area, 1,740 sq. km.

In 1983 the chief forest products were timber, valued at £C600,000; firewood, £C200,000; figures relate to the area of Cyprus not occupied by Turkey.

Fisheries. Catch (1983) 2,042 tonnes valued at £C3·4m.

INDUSTRY AND TRADE

Industry. Cyprus has no heavy industry, but a wide variety of light manufacturing industries. The establishment of a Development Bank in 1963 has given further impetus to industrial activity. Manufacturing industry in 1983 contributed about £C178·9m. to the GDP and gave employment to 44,100 of the economically active population.

The highest increases in output in 1983 were production of chemicals, clothing, petroleum, leather and fur products. Industrial exports rose to £C133·3m. in 1983 and accounted for 74·1% of total domestic exports.

Trade Unions and Associations. Registration of trade unions and employers' associations is compulsory and freedom of association is constitutionally and statutorily guaranteed.

Commerce. The commerce and the shipping, exclusive of coasting trade, for calendar years were (in £C1,000):

	1979	*1980*	*1981*	*1982*	*1983*
Imports [1]	357,603	424,292	489,536	577,551	641,962
Exports [2]	161,871	188,036	234,773	263,809	260,525

[1] Excluding Naafi imports of about £C1·5m. in 1982.
[2] Including re-exports and ships' stores of about £C59m. in 1982.

Chief civil imports, 1983 (in £C1,000):

Petroleum and petroleum products	115,593	Feeding stuff for animals	11,667
Textile yarn and fabrics made up	51,336	Tobacco and manufactures	13,810
Iron and steel	21,797	Meat and meat preparations	7,339
Cereals and cereal preparations	35,407	Animal and vegetable oils, fats and waxes	6,929
Machinery and Transport equipment	145,417	Non-metallic mineral manufactures	15,449
Paper, paperboard and pulp and articles thereof	18,292	Medicinal and pharmaceutical products	9,266
Artificial resins and plastics	13,520	Manufactures of metal, n.e.s.	17,960
		Dairy products and eggs	6,070

Chief domestic exports, 1983 (in £C1,000):

Grapes	3,476	Cigarettes	5,956
Grapefruit	4,596	Paper products	5,290
Lemons	4,563	Cement	10,234
Oranges	4,257	Clothing	38,382
Potatoes	12,372	Footwear	15,770
Wine	9,219		

In 1983 the EEC countries supplied 49·6% of the imports; Arab countries, 11·2%; others, 39·2%. Of the exports (1983), 49·6% went to Arab countries; 36·2% to EEC countries, 9% to Eastern Europe and 5·2% to other countries.

Total trade between Cyprus and UK (British Department of Trade returns, in £1,000 sterling):

	1980	*1981*	*1982*	*1983*	*1984*
Imports to UK	128,386	80,580	89,908	87,436	94,381
Exports and re-exports from UK	153,754	115,597	111,882	127,837	146,773

Tourism. Foreign tourists (1983), 620,726 and 94,771 excursionists.

COMMUNICATIONS

Roads. In 1983 the total length of roads was 11,227 km, of which 5,385 km were paved and 5,842 km were earth or gravel roads. The main roads which are maintained by the Ministry of Communications and Works (Public Works Department) totalled 2,841 km, of which 2,760 km were paved. The total of urban streets was 1,718 km, of which 1,205 were paved. Village roads and streets totalled 6,976 km, of which 1,345 km were paved, the rest being of earth or gravel surface. There were also 2,433 km of unpaved forest roads. On 31 Dec. 1983, there were 239,525 motor vehicles including 1,854 buses and 42,876 goods vehicles.

The area controlled by the Government of the Republic and that occupied by Turkey are now served by separate transport systems, and there are no services linking the two areas.

Aviation. Nicosia airport has been closed since Aug. 1974. During 1983, 1,651,770 persons travelled and 31,040 tonnes of commercial air-freight was handled through Larnaca airport. Paphos International airport started operations in 1983.

Shipping. In 1983, 4,831 ships of 10,634,062 net tons entered Cyprus ports. Ships under Cyprus registry (Sept. 1983) numbered 1,300 of 4·4m. tons. Famagusta has been closed to international traffic since Oct. 1974.

Post and Broadcasting. In 1983 there were 53 post offices and 583 postal agencies. There are 17 post offices and 368 postal agencies in the Turkish occupied area. Telephones (1983) 158,000. Wireless licences issued (1981) were 247,000, including television licences.

Cyprus Broadcasting Corporation broadcasts mainly in Greek, but also in Turkish, English, and Armenian on medium-waves. The corporation also broadcasts one TV programme. There are also 2 foreign broadcasting stations.

Cinemas (1982). In the Greek part of Cyprus there were 56 cinemas.

Newspapers (1983). There are 9 Greek, 4 Turkish and 1 English daily newspapers and 10 Greek, 6 Turkish and 1 English weeklies.

JUSTICE, RELIGION, EDUCATION AND WELFARE

Justice. The administration of justice is exercised by separate and independent judiciary. Under the 1960 Constitution and other legislation in force there are the Supreme Court of the Republic, Assize Courts, District Courts, Ecclesiastical Courts and Turkish Family Courts.

The Supreme Court is composed of 5-7 judges one of whom is the President of the Court. There is an Assize Court and a District Court for each district. The Assize Courts have unlimited criminal jurisdiction and may order the payment of compensation up to £C800. The District Courts exercise original civil and criminal jurisdiction, the extent of which varies with the composition of the Bench.

There is a Supreme Council of Judicature, consisting of the Attorney-General of the Republic, the President and Judges of the Supreme Court, entrusted with the appointment, promotion, transfers, termination of appointment and disciplinary control over all judicial officers, other than the Judges of the Supreme Court.

Religion. *See* Area and Population, p. 386.

Education. Until 31 March 1965 each community in Cyprus managed its own schooling through its respective Communal Chamber. Intercommunal education had been placed under the Minister of the Interior, assisted by a Board of Education for Intercommunal Schools, of which the Minister was the Chairman. In 1965 the Greek Communal Chamber was dissolved and a Ministry of Education was established to take its place. Intercommunal education has been placed under this Ministry.

Greek-Cypriot Education. Elementary education is compulsory and is provided free in 6 grades to children between 5½ and 12 years of age. In some towns and large villages there are separate junior schools consisting of the first three grades. Apart from schools for the deaf and blind and the Lambousa School for juvenile offenders, there are also 7 schools for handicapped children. In 1983–84 the Ministry ran 183 kindergartens for children from low-income families; there were 150 privately run pre-primary schools. There were 413 primary schools with 46,653 pupils and 2,221 teachers in 1983–84.

Secondary education is free for the first 4 years and is fee-paying for the rest, although senior pupils can be wholly or partially exempt from payment. The secondary school is 6 years, 3 years at the gymnasium followed by 3 years at the lykeion. There were 3 types of lykeia: classical, science, economic. There are 5- to 6-year technical schools. In 1983–84 there were 101 secondary schools with 3,137 teachers and 49,274 pupils.

Post-secondary education is provided at the Pedagogical Academy, which organizes 3-year courses for the training of pre-primary and primary school teachers, and at the Higher Technical Institute, which provides 3-year courses for technicians in civil, electrical and mechanical engineering. There is also a 2-year Forestry College (administered by the Ministry of Agriculture), a Hotel and Catering Institute and a 3-year Nurses' School and 1-year School for Health Inspectors (Ministry of Health). Adult education is conducted through youth centres in rural areas, foreign language institutes in the towns and private institutions offering courses in business administration and secretarial work.

In 1983–84, 9,967 students were studying in universities abroad, mainly in Greece and the UK.

Turkish-Cypriot Education. The Office of Education of the Turkish Community of Cyprus caters for some 18% of the island's population and (1976) administered 10 kindergartens, 167 elementary schools (16,014 pupils), 18 secondary schools (7,190 pupils), 6 technical schools (735 pupils) and 1 teacher-training college (13 students). There were 43 evening institutes for adult education.

Greek is the language of 82% of the population and Turkish of 18%. English is widely spoken. English and French are compulsory subjects in secondary schools. Illiteracy is largely confined to older people.

Social Security. The administration of the social-security services in Cyprus is in the hands of the Ministry of Labour and Social Insurance, with the Ministry of Health providing medical services through public clinics and hospitals on a means test, except medical treatment for employment accidents, which is given free to all insured employees and financed by the Social Insurance Scheme.

DIPLOMATIC REPRESENTATIVES

Of Cyprus in Great Britain (93 Park St., London, W1Y 4ET)
High Commissioner: Tasos Panayides.

Of Great Britain in Cyprus (Alexander Pallis St., Nicosia)
High Commissioner: W. J. A. Wilberforce, CMG.

Of Cyprus in the USA (2211 R. St., NW, Washington, D.C., 20008)
Ambassador: Andrew J. Jacovides.

Of the USA in Cyprus (Therissos St., Nicosia)
Ambassador: Raymond C. Ewing.

Of Cyprus to the United Nations
Ambassador: Constantine Moushoutas.

Books of Reference

Statistical Information. Statistics and Research Department, Nicosia.
Alastos, D., *Cyprus in History.* London, 1955.—*Cyprus Guerilla.* London, 1960
Attalides, M., *Cyprus Nationalism and International Politics.* Edinburgh, 1979
Ditsios, D. E., *Cyprus: The Vulnerable Republic.* Thessaloniki, 1975
Christodoulou, D., *The Evolution of the Rural Land use Pattern in Cyprus.* Bude, 1960
Crawshaw, N., *The Cyprus Revolt: An Account of the Struggle for Union with Greece.* London, 1978

Denktash, R., *The Cyprus Triangle*. London, 1982
Emilianides, A., *Histoire de Chypre*. Paris, 1962.—*The Zurich and London Agreements and the Cyprus Republic*. Athens, 1962
Georghallides, G. S., *A Political and Administrative History of Cyprus 1918–1926*. Nicosia, 1979
Halil, K., *The Rape of Cyprus*. London, 1982
Hill, Sir George F., *A History of Cyprus*. 4 vols. Cambridge, 1940–52
Hitchins, C., *Cyprus*. London, 1984
Hunt, D., *Footprints in Cyprus*. London, 1982
Kitromilides, P. M., and Evriviades, M. L., *Cyprus*, [Bibliography]. Oxford and Santa Barbara, 1982
Kosut, H., *Cyprus 1946–68*. New York, 1970
Kyle, K., *Cyprus*. London, 1984
Loizos, P., *The Heart Grows Bitter: A Chronicle of Cypriot War Refugees*. CUP, 1982
Mayes, S., *Makarios*. London, 1981
Oberling, P., *The Road to Bellapais: The Turkish Cypriot Exodus to Northern Cyprus*. Boulder, 1982
Polyviou, P. G., *Cyprus: The Tragedy and the Challenge*. London, 1975.—*Cyprus in Search of a Constitution*. Nicosia, 1976.—*Cyprus: Conflict and Negotiation, 1960–1980*. London, 1980
St John-Jones, L. W., *The Population of Cyprus*. London, 1983

CZECHOSLOVAKIA

Capital: Prague
Population: 15·4m. (1982)
GNP per capita: US$5,820 (1980)

Československá Socialistická Republika

HISTORY. The Czechoslovak State came into existence on 28 Oct. 1918, when the Czech *Národní Výbor* (National Committee) took over the government of the Czech lands upon the dissolution of Austria–Hungary. Two days later the Slovak National Council manifested its desire to unite politically with the Czechs. On 14 Nov. 1918 the first Czechoslovak National Assembly declared the Czechoslovak State to be a republic with T. G. Masaryk as President (1918–35).

The Treaty of St Germain-en-Laye (1919) recognized the Czechoslovak Republic, consisting of the Czech lands (Bohemia, Moravia, part of Silesia) and Slovakia. To these lands were added as a trust the autonomous province of Subcarpathian Ruthenia.

This territory was broken up for the benefit of Germany, Poland and Hungary by the Munich agreement (29 Sept. 1938) between UK, France, Germany and Italy.

In March 1939 the German-sponsored Slovak government proclaimed Slovakia independent, and Germany incorporated the Czech lands into the Reich as the 'Protectorate of Bohemia and Moravia'. A government-in-exile, headed by Dr Beneš, was set up in London in July 1940.

Liberation by the Soviet Army and US Forces was completed by May 1945.

Territories taken by Germans, Poles and Hungarians were restored to Czechoslovak sovereignty. Subcarpathian Ruthenia was transferred to the USSR.

Elections were held in May 1946, at which the Communist Party obtained about 38% of the votes.

A coalition government under a Communist Prime Minister, Klement Gottwald, remained in power until 20 Feb. 1948, when 12 of the non-Communist ministers resigned in protest against infiltration of Communists into the police.

In Feb. a predominantly Communist government was formed by Gottwald. In May elections resulted in an 89% majority for the government and President Beneš resigned.

In the first months of 1968 mounting pressure for liberalization culminated in the overthrow of the Stalinist President and Party Secretary, Antonín Novotný, and his associates. Under a new leadership the Communist Party introduced in April 1968 an 'Action Programme' of far-reaching political and economic reforms.

Soviet pressure to abandon this programme was exerted between May and Aug. 1968, and finally, Warsaw Pact forces occupied Czechoslovakia on 21 Aug. The enforced Moscow agreement of 26 Aug. bound the Czechoslovak government to a policy of 'normalization' (*i.e.*, abandonment of most reforms) and to the stationing of Soviet forces on Czechoslovak soil. This situation was confirmed by the Czechoslovak–Soviet 'Status of Forces Agreement' of 16 Oct. In 1969–1970 Soviet pressure led to extensive changes in the Party and Government. In Oct. 1969 Czechoslovakia repudiated its condemnation of the Warsaw Pact invasion.

A Czechoslovak–Soviet 20-year Treaty of Friendship, Co-operation and Mutual Assistance was signed in May 1970. Since 1977 a dissident civil rights movement 'Charter 77' has been active despite official efforts to supress it.

On 11 Dec. 1973 the German Federal Republic and Czechoslovakia signed a treaty normalizing relations and annulling the Munich agreement of 1938. This was ratified by both countries' parliaments in July 1974.

AREA AND POPULATION. At the census of 11 Nov. 1980 the population was 15,283,095 (4,991,168 in Slovakia; 7·9m. females). Population in 1983,

15,395,970 (Slovakia, 5,073,861; females 7,899,119). There are 12 administrative regions *(Kraj)*, one of which is the capital, Prague (Praha) and one the capital of Slovakia, Bratislava.

Region	*Chief city*	*Area in sq. km*	*Population 1983*
Czech			
Prague	—	495	1,185,693
Středočeský	Prague (Praha)	11,003	1,147,837
Jihočeský	České Budějovice	11,345	692,803
Západočeský	Plzeň (Pilsen)	10,876	878,882
Severočeský	Ústí nad Labem	7,810	1,172,357
Východočeský	Hradec Králové	11,240	1,248,274
Jihomoravský	Brno	15,028	2,048,569
Severomoravský	Ostrava	11,067	1,942,676
Slovak			
Bratislava	—	368	394,644
Západoslovenský	Bratislava	14,491	1,696,986
Středoslovenský	Banská Bystrica	17,985	1,543,189
Východoslovenský	Košice	16,188	1,422,354

The area of Czechoslovakia is 127,896 sq. km (Slovakia, 49,032 sq. km). Population density in 1982: 120 per sq. km. Growth rate in 1982, 3·5 per 1,000. Expectation of life in 1982 was 67 (males); 74 (females).

Ethnic minorities have equal political and cultural rights. In 1982 there were (in 1,000): Czechs, 9,800; Slovaks, 4,727; Hungarians, 582; Poles, 69; Germans, 60; Ukrainians, 47; Russians, 7. There were 303,000 gipsies in 1983.

Official languages are Czech and Slovak.

The population of the principal towns in 1983 was as follows (in 1,000):

Prague (Praha)	1,185	Hradec Králové	97	Karviná	78
Bratislava	394	Pardubice	93	Prešov	76
Brno	379	České Budějovice	92	Kladno	72
Ostrava	323	Havířov	91	Banská Bystrica	71
Košice	213	Ústí nad Labem	90	Trnava	66
Plzeň	173	Žilina	87	Frýdek-Místek	61
Olomouc	103	Gottwaldov	84	Most	61
Liberec	99	Nitra	80	Opava	61

Vital statistics for calendar years:

	Live births	*Marriages*	*Divorces*	*Deaths*
1980	248,901	117,921	33,863	186,116
1981	237,728	116,805	34,595	180,039
1982	233,284	117,208	34,371	179,983

Infant mortality in 1982 (per 1,000 live births), 11·7.

CLIMATE. A humid continental climate, with warm summers and cold winters. Precipitation is generally greater in summer, with thunderstorms. Autumn, with dry, clear weather and spring, which is damp, are each of short duration. Prague. Jan. 29·5°F (–1·5°C), July 67°F (19·4°C). Annual rainfall 19·3″ (483mm). Brno. Jan. 31°F (–0·6°C), July 67°F (19·4°C). Annual rainfall 21″ (525mm).

CONSTITUTION AND GOVERNMENT. For details of previous constitutions, *see* THE STATESMAN'S YEAR-BOOK, 1968–69, pp. 927–28.

Since 1 Jan. 1969 Czechoslovakia has been a federal socialist republic consisting of two nations of equal rights: the Czech Socialist Republic (the Czech lands, previously Bohemia, Moravia and part of Silesia), and the Slovak Socialist Republic (Slovakia). Each Republic is governed by a National Council (the Czech with 200 deputies, the Slovak with 150), which delegates to an overall Federal Assembly responsibility for constitutional and foreign affairs, defence and important economic decisions. The Federal Assembly consists of the Chamber of Nations, which has 75 Czech and 75 Slovak delegates elected by their respective National Councils, and the Chamber of the People, which has 200 deputies elected by national suffrage.

The previous constitution (1960) remains in force as amended by Constitutional Acts 143 and 144 of 1968. Since 1971 deputies are elected for a 5-year term so as to coincide with Communist Party congresses. Minimum age of voters is 18, of deputies, 21 years. At the elections of 5–6 June 1981 a single list of National Front candidates was presented. Turnout was 10,736,312 from an electorate of 10,789,574 (99·5%). 99·96% of the votes were cast for the official candidates.

President of the Republic: Gustáv Husák (born 1913), *President of the Federal Assembly:* Alois Indra.

The *de facto* primary source of power is the Communist Party of Czechoslovakia, of which the Communist Party of Slovakia (*First Secretary:* Jozef Lenárt) is a constituent part. Communists head the National Front, which incorporates the remaining political parties (Czechoslovak Socialist Party, Czechoslovak People's Party, Slovak Reconstruction Party, Slovak Freedom Party) and the trade unions and youth organizations. The Communist Party had 1,584,011 members and 123,000 candidate members on 1 Oct. 1982. In March 1985 the Presidium consisted of Gustáv Husák *(General Secretary)*; Vasil Bil'ak; Peter Colotka *(Deputy Prime Minister)*; Karel Hoffmann *(Chairman, Central Council of Trade Unions)*; Alois Indra; Miloš Jakeš; Antonín Kapek; Josef Kempný; Josef Korčák *(Deputy Prime Minister)*; Jozef Lenárt; Lubomír Štrougal *(Prime Minister)*. Candidate members: Jan Fojtík, Josef Hamán, Miloslav Hruškovič.

In March 1985 members of the government not mentioned above included: *(Deputy Prime Ministers)* Ladislav Gerle; Karol Laco; Matej Lúčan; Jaromír Obzina; Svatopluk Potáč *(Chairman, State Planning Commission)*; Rudolf Rohlíček; (other ministers) Bohumil Urban *(Foreign Trade)*; Milan Vaclavik *(Defence)*; František Ondřich *(Chairman, Czechoslovak Control Commission)*; Bohuslav Chňoupek *(Foreign)*; Leopold Lér *(Finance)*; Miloslav Boda *(Labour and Social Welfare)*; Vratislav Vajnar *(Interior)*; Vlastimir Ehrenberger *(Fuel and Power)*.

The Czech Prime Minister is Josef Korčák; the Slovak, Peter Colotka.

Local government is carried on by National Committees consisting of deputies elected for 5 year terms. There are 10 regional Committees, 2 City Committees with the same status for Prague and Bratislava, 108 district Committees and 7,979 town and community Committees. Elections were held in 1981.

National flag: White and red (horizontal), with a blue triangle of full depth at the hoist, point to the fly.

National anthem: Kde domov můj (words by J. K. Tyl, tune by F. J. Škroup, 1834); combined with, Nad Tatru sa blyska (words by J. Matuška, 1844).

DEFENCE. Defence is the responsibility of the Defence Council set up in Feb. 1969 and headed by the First Secretary of the Party.

The Warsaw Pact invasion of Aug. 1968 brought an estimated 500,000 occupation troops into the country. By early 1970 this number had been reduced to 80,000 Soviet troops, the presence of which is legalized by the Czech–Soviet 'Status of Forces' Agreement of Oct. 1968.

In Feb. 1969 the government announced an increase in defence capacity, and Czechoslovakia resumed participation in Warsaw Pact meetings.

Military service is for 2 years in the Army and 3 years in the Air Force.

Army. The Army had a strength (1985) of 148,000 (100,000 conscripts). It consists of 5 armoured, 5 motor rifle and 1 artillery divisions, 1 airborne brigade, 6 engineer battalions and 5 regiments of Civil Defence Troops. Equipment includes 3,500 T-54/-55/-72 tanks. There are also 2 paramilitary forces: Border Troops (11,000) and People's Militia (120,000).

Air Force. The Air Force is organized as a tactical force, under overall army command, and has a strength of some 56,000 personnel and 475 combat aircraft. Six interceptor regiments (each 3 squadrons of 14 aircraft) are equipped with MiG-23 and MiG-21 jets, and there are 4 regiments of Su-7, Su-20, MiG-23 and MiG-21 ground attack aircraft, as well as Mi-24 gunship helicopters. MiG-21s and adapted L-39 Albatros jet trainers are used for tactical reconnaissance. Transport units have a total of 70 Let L-410, An-24/26, Il-14, Tu-134, and Tu-154 aircraft and about 100 Mil Mi-2 (armed), Mi-4 and Mi-8 helicopters. Training units are equipped with 2-seat MiG-23s and MiG-21s and Czech-built aircraft, including L-39 Albatros jet advanced trainers. Surface-to-air ('Guideline', 'Goa', 'Ganef', 'Gainful' and 'Gaskin') missile units are operational.

INTERNATIONAL RELATIONS

Membership. Czechoslovakia is a member of UN, COMECON and the Warsaw Pact.

ECONOMY

Planning. For the first five 5-year plans *see* THE STATESMAN'S YEAR-BOOK, 1978–79, p. 385. Economic reforms of the period 1965–68 were abandoned after the Soviet intervention of 1968, and the economy reverted to the traditional communist centrally planned type. In 1980 some rationalizations in the planning system, which have become known as the 'Set of measures', were applied. Food prices were raised in Jan. 1982.

The sixth 5-year plan for 1976–80 saw an increase of 3% in national income, 3·2% in industrial, and 6% in agricultural, production. Targets were not met. The 7th 5-year plan is running from 1981 to 1985. National income is to rise by 2·8%, industrial production by 2·7%, agricultural by 2·6%.

Budget. Budgets for calendar years (in Kčs. 1m.):

	1976	*1977*	*1978*	*1979*	*1980*	*1981*	*1982*
Revenue	292,165	280,786	286,267	294,638	306,262	311,568	314,203
Expenditure	290,071	278,301	283,912	292,403	304,182	310,928	314,046

Main items of the 1982 budget were (in Kčs. 1,000m.): Revenue: from the economy, 222; direct taxes, 43. Expenditure: national economy, 78; health and social services, 85; defence, 25; administration, 4. The 1984 budget was estimated to balance at 324,300.

Currency. The monetary unit in the Czechoslovak Republic is the *koruna* (Kčs.) or crown of 100 *haler*. Notes in circulation: Kčs. 10, 20, 50, 100, 500. Coin: 5, 10, 20, 50 *halers*, and Kčs. 1, 2, 5. The *koruna* is based on a gold content of 0·123426 gramme of pure gold and pegged on the rouble at Kčs. 1·80 = R.1. The International Monetary Fund did not approve this change of the par value, and Czechoslovak membership was terminated in 1954, and ceased to be a member of the International Bank. Official rates of exchange (1984): £1 = Kčs. 15·50; US$1 = Kčs. 5·89; 1 Soviet rouble = Kčs. 10. Tourist rate: £1 = Kčs. 16·36.

The return of 18·4 tonnes of gold seized by Nazi Germany and held in London and New York since the nationalization of Western assets in 1948 was agreed in Jan. 1982 by the Czech, British and US governments in exchange for compensation of the asset-holders.

Banking. For previous banking history *see* THE STATESMAN'S YEAR-BOOK, 1971–72, pp. 858–59. The central bank and bank of issue is the State Bank (Statní Banka), which controls foreign exchange reserves, and is a savings bank and a commercial credit bank to enterprises, except foreign trade enterprises. These are financed by the Commercial Bank (Obchodní Banka) which carries out all foreign trade transactions. The Trade Bank (Živnostenská Banka) provides banking services for private foreign clients, and maintains branches abroad. There is also an Investment Bank (Investiční Banka), one of whose functions is to manage foreign securities. 'Foreign exchange points' (*e.g.*, hotels) have partial foreign exchange authorization. There were 17·8 savings accounts totalling 3,200m. Kčs in 1982.

Weights and Measures. The metric system is in force.

ENERGY AND NATURAL RESOURCES

Energy. There is an oil pipeline from the USSR with branches to Bratislava and Zaluzi and a natural gas pipeline which supplies the German Federal and Democratic Republics, Austria and Italy as well as Czechoslovakia. A second is under construction. Production of electricity in 1982: 74,749m. kwh. In 1984 there were 3 nuclear power stations.

Minerals. Czechoslovakia is not rich in minerals. There are hard and soft coal reserves (chief coalfields: Most, Chomutov, Kladno, Ostrava and Sokolov). There is also uranium, glass sand and salt, and small quantities of iron ore, graphite, copper and lead. Production in 1982 (in tonnes): Coal, 27,059,000; lignite and brown coal, 95,504,000.

Agriculture. In 1982 there were 6·9m. hectares of agricultural land (4·8m. hectares arable, 0·8m. meadow, 0·8m. pasture), of which 4·3m. were held by collective farms, 2·1m. by state farms and 93,000 as private plots (maximum size 1 hectare).

In 1982 there were 1,701 collective farms with 986,325 members and 220 state farms with 160,706 employees. Crop production in 1982 (in 1,000 tonnes): Sugar-beet, 8,210; wheat, 4,606; potatoes, 3,608; barley, 3,654; maize, 941; rye, 583.

Livestock. In 1983 the number of livestock was: Cattle, 5·1m. (including 1·9m. milch cows); horses, 44,000; pigs, 7·1m.; sheep, 990,000; poultry, 49·2m. In 1982 production of meat was 1,580,000 tonnes (live weight); milk, 5,753m. litres; 5,030m. eggs. In 1982 there were 132,286 tractors.

Forestry. Czechoslovakia is a richly wooded country, and the timber industry is important. Forest area in 1982 was 4,581,833 hectares (50% spruce, 16% beech and pine, 7% oak). The area reafforested in 1982 was 80,154 hectares. The timber yield was 18·96m. cu. metres in 1982.

INDUSTRY AND TRADE

Industry. Industrialization is well developed and antedates the Communist régime. All industry is nationalized.

Output in 1982 (in 1,000 tonnes): Pig-iron, 9,525; crude steel, 14,992; coke, 10,566; rolled-steel products, 10,654; cement, 10,325; paper, 928; sulphuric acid, 1,252; nitrogenous fertilizers, 566; phosphate fertilizers, 335; plastics, 956; synthetic fibres, 180; sugar, 894; beer, 24·9m. hectolitres; cars, 173,517 (no.).

Textile production (in 1m. metres) in 1982: Cotton, 583; linen, 103; woollen, 61; shoes, 128m. pairs (57·6m. leather).

Labour. There were 8,697,786 persons of employable age in 1982 (*i.e.*, males, 15–59; females 15–54). 7·43m. persons (excluding collective farmers) were employed in 1982 (3·38m. women): 5·6m. in production (industry, 2·8m.; agriculture, 0·9m.; building, 0·6m.; commerce, 0·7m.); and 1·8m. in services.

A 5-day 42-hour week with 4 weeks annual holiday is standard. Average monthly wage in 1983: Kčs. 2,790. In 1983 the trade union movement had 7m. members.

Commerce. Total trade (in Kčs. 1m.) for calendar years:

	1977	*1978*	*1979*	*1980*	*1981*	*1982*
Imports	63,213	68,074	75,760	81,540	86,276	94,177
Exports	58,246	63,609	70,156	80,163	87,689	95,314

In 1982, trade with Communist countries amounted to 142,809m. Kčs. (79,951m. Kčs. with the USSR, 17,583m. Kčs. with the German Democratic Republic, 11,881m. Kčs. with Poland). The UK is Czechoslovakia's fourth biggest non-Communist trade partner after the Federal German Republic, Austria and Switzerland.

Major exports in 1982 (percentage of total). Machinery, 50·6; industrial consumer goods, 16; raw materials and fuel, 25·3. Imports: Machinery, 31·2; raw materials and fuel, 50·5. Oil imports in 1980, 19·3m. tonnes, 98% from USSR (96% in 1982).

There are 11 foreign trade agencies (independent legal entities with their own capital run by state-appointed managers). Western firms are permitted to set up their own offices on Czechoslovak soil. Enterprises must obtain agreement from the Ministry of Foreign Trade before trading with foreign firms. Foreign indebtedness was US$3,000m. in 1982; US$3,600m. (1981).

In 1972 an Anglo-Czech Agreement on Co-operation was signed. Under this an

Anglo-Czech Joint Commission was established to further the development of trade and industrial and scientific co-operation.

UK-Czechoslovak trade has been conducted since 1 Jan. 1975 on the basis of autonomous EEC measures.

Total trade between Czechoslovakia and UK for calendar years (British Department of Trade returns, in £1,000 sterling):

	1980	*1981*	*1982*	*1983*	*1984*
Imports to UK	87,812	70,503	82,007	101,302	117,188
Exports and re-exports from UK	81,026	70,686	70,105	69,456	78,075

Tourism. In 1982, 7,732,052 tourists visited Czechoslovakia (576,723 from the West) and 4,849,668 Czechoslovak tourists made visits abroad (200,657 to the West).

COMMUNICATIONS

Roads. In 1982 there were 73,881 km of motorways and first-class roads and 2,441,472 passenger cars. In 1982 state road transport carried 2,196m. passengers and 368m. tonnes of freight.

Railways. In 1983 the length of railway track was 13,142 km. Of this, 3,171 km were electrified. Traction, 1982: electric 62·9%; diesel, 37·1%. In 1982, 412m. passengers and 289m. tonnes of freight were carried.

Aviation. Air transport is run by ČSA (Czechoslovak Airlines). The main airports are: Prague (Ruzyně), Brno (Cernovice), Bratislava (Vajnory), Olomouc (Holice), Košice (Barca). In 1982, 1·1m. passengers and 21,400 tonnes of freight were flown. There are 6 internal and 53 international flights from Prague. British Airways operates air traffic London–Prague, Air France Paris–Prague–Bucharest.

Shipping. In 1983 Czechoslovak Maritime Shipping *(Československá námorní plavba)* (founded 1959) had 14 freighters totalling 264,167 DWT, based on Szczecin. In 1982, 1,787m. tonnes of cargo were carried. Freight transport within Czechoslovakia totalled 11·39m. tonnes. There are fleets on the Danube and Elbe.

Czechoslovak Danube Shipping *(Československá plavba dunajská)* operate 5 ships in the Mediterranean from the port of Bratislava.

Post and Broadcasting. Number of telephones in service in 1982 was 3,306,155. *Československý Rozhlas*, the governmental broadcasting station, broadcasts on 2 networks; 1 from Prague with 3 programmes in Czech and Slovak and 1 from Bratislava with 2 programmes in Slovak and additional broadcasts in Hungarian and Ukrainian. *Československá Televise* broadcast 2 television programmes nation-wide, including colour broadcasts. In 1982, 4·1m. people held wireless and 4·3m. TV licences.

Cinemas and Theatres (1982). There were 2,891 cinemas and 81 theatres. 44 full-length films were made in 1982.

Newspapers and Books (1982). There were 30 daily newspapers, including 12 in Slovak and 1,070 other periodicals. The party daily *Rudé Právo* ('Red Justice') has a circulation of about 1m. 7,164 book titles were published in 1982 in 97m. copies.

JUSTICE, RELIGION, EDUCATION AND WELFARE

Justice. The criminal and criminal procedure codes date from 1 Jan. 1962, as amended in April 1973.

Police powers were strengthened in July 1974.

There is a Federal Supreme Court and federal military courts, with judges elected by the Federal Assembly. Both republics have Supreme Courts and a network of regional and district courts whose professional judges are elected by the republican National Councils. Lay judges are elected by regional or district local authorities. Local authorities and social organizations may participate in the decision-making of the courts.

Religion. Churches are controlled by the Federal Secretariat for Church Affairs and the Ministries of Culture. In 1984 there were 18 different faiths with 4,860 clergy and 8,200 churches. The largest single church is the Roman Catholic (10m. members, 5,000 churches, 1983): its main support is in Slovakia. Cardinal František Tomášek was installed as archbishop of Prague in 1978. The archbishoprics of Trnava and of Olomouc are vacant. In 1983 there were 5 bishops (the remaining 8 dioceses are directed by Government-appointed capitulary vicars) and 1 archbishop and 5 bishops working among émigrés. There were 6 seminaries in 1984.

In 1981 there were 600,000 Hussites in 5 dioceses, 270,000 Czech Brethren with 272 parishes, 450,000 Slovak Lutherans with 326 parishes, 46,700 Silesian Lutherans and 180,000 Reformed Christians with 310 parishes. In 1981 there were 15,000 Jews (mainly in Prague, where there is a synagogue). The Uniate Church was suppressed in 1950. Official estimate of believers among the population over 15 based on opinion surveys of 1980: 36% (30% in the Czech lands, 51% in Slovakia).

Education. In 1982–83 there were 11,397 kindergartens for children from 3 to 6 years of age, with 49,437 teachers and 714,921 pupils. Education is free and compulsory for 10 years. Children of 6 to 14 yrs attend primary school for 8 years. Selection then takes place for secondary schools (4 years), vocational secondary schools (4 years) or apprentice centres (2–4 years). University entrance is from secondary schools. The respective proportions of entrants are approximately 20%:20%:60%. In 1982–83 there were 6,516 primary schools with 1,956,634 pupils and 90,702 teachers.

336 secondary schools with 9,014 teachers and 150,638 pupils and 573 secondary vocational schools with 310,856 students and 17,161 teachers. In higher education in 1982–83, there were 154,421 full-time students, and 21,146 teachers. There are 36 institutions of higher education, with 110 faculties. These include 5 universities—the Charles University in Prague (founded 1348); the Purkyně (formerly Masaryk) University in Brno (1919); the Comenius University in Bratislava (1919); the Palacký University in Olomouc (1573); the Šafárik University in Košice (1959); and 12 technical universities or institutes.

Welfare. Medical care is free. In 1982 Kčs. 27,807m. were spent on health insurance benefits. There were, in 1982, 227 hospitals with a total of 120,907 beds, and 52,493 doctors and dentists. Family allowances (Kčs. per month): 1 child, 130; 2 children, 610; 3, 1,150. Old age pensions averaging 67% of salary are paid at the age of 60 (men), 53–57 (women).

DIPLOMATIC REPRESENTATIVES

Of Czechoslovakia in Great Britain (25 Kensington Palace Gdns., London, W8 4QY)
Ambassador: Dr Miroslav Houštecky (accredited 8 Dec. 1983)

Of Great Britain in Czechoslovakia (Thunovská 14, Prague 1)
Ambassador: Stephen Barrett.

Of Czechoslovakia in the USA (3900 Linnean Ave., NW, Washington, D.C., 20008)
Ambassador: Dr Stanislav Suja.

Of the USA in Czechoslovakia (Tržiste 15–12548 Praha, Prague)
Ambassador: William H. Luers.

Of Czechoslovakia to the United Nations
Ambassador: Jaroslav César.

Books of Reference

The Constitution of the Czechoslovak Socialist Republic [English ed.]. Prague, 1960
Statistická ročenka ČSSR [Statistical Yearbook]. Prague, annual since 1958
Czechoslovak Foreign Trade. Prague, monthly
Bradley, J. F. N. *Politics in Czechoslovakia, 1945–1971.* Lanham, 1981

Czechoslovak Chamber of Commerce and Industry. *Facts on Czechoslovak Foreign Trade.* Prague, annual since 1967.—*Your Trade Partners in Czechoslovakia.* Prague, 1979
Demek, J., and others, *Geography of Czechoslovakia.* Prague, 1971
Eidlin, F. H. *The Logic of 'Normalization': The Soviet Intervention in Czechoslovakia of 21 August 1968 and the Czechoslovak Response.* Columbia Univ. Press, 1980
Hermann, A. H., *A History of the Czechs.* London, 1975
Hejzlar, Z., and Kusin, V. V., *Czechoslovakia, 1968–1969.* New York, 1975
Jičinský, J., and Skála, J. *The Czechoslovak Federation,* Prague, 1969
Kalvoda, J., *Czechoslovakia's Role in Soviet Strategy.* Washington, 1981
Kolafová, V., and Slaba, D. *Czech-English and English-Czech dictionary.* Prague, 1979
Korbel, J., *Twentieth-Century Czechoslovakia: The Meanings of its History.* Columbia Univ. Press, 1977
Krejčí, *Social Change and Stratification in Postwar Czechoslovakia.* London, 1972
Krystufek, Z., *The Soviet Régime in Czechoslovakia.* Columbia Univ. Press, 1981
Kusin, V. V., *From Dubček to Charter 77.* Edinburgh, 1978
Littell, R. (ed.), *The Czech Black Book; prepared by the Institute of History of the Czechoslovak Academy of Sciences.* London, 1969
Mamatey, V. S., and Luža, R. (eds.), *A History of the Czechoslovak Republic 1918–1948.* Princeton Univ. Press, 1973
Mlynař, Z., *Night Frost in Prague: the End of Humane Socialism.* New York, 1980
Procházka, J., *English–Czech and Czech–English Dictionary.* 16th ed. London, 1959
Şejna, J. *We Will Bury You.* London, 1982
Šik, O., *Czechoslovakia: The Bureaucratic Economy.* New York, 1972
Sperling. W., *Tschechoslowakei: Beiträge zur Landeskunde Ostmitteleurapas.* Stuttgart, 1981
Suda, Z. L., *Zealots and Rebels: A History of the Communist Party in Czechoslovakia.* Stanford, 1980
Teplý, J., *Economie Nationale de la Tchécoslovaquie Contemporaine.* Paris, 1977
Wallace, W. V., *Czechoslovakia.* London, 1977

DENMARK

Capital: Copenhagen
Population: 5·11m. (1984)
GNP per capita: US$13,120 (1981)

Kongeriget Danmark

HISTORY. First organized as a unified state in the 10th century, Denmark acquired approximately its present boundaries in 1815, having ceded Norway to Sweden and its north German territory to Prussia. Denmark became a constitutional monarchy in 1849.

AREA AND POPULATION. According to the census held on 9 Nov. 1970 the area of Denmark proper was 43,075 sq. km (16,631 sq. miles) and the population 4,937,579. Population, Jan. 1984: 5,112,130.

Administrative divisions		*Area (sq. km) 1984*	*Population 1970*	*Population 1984*	*Population 1984 per sq. km*
København (Copenhagen)	(city)	88	622,773	482,937	5,480
Frederiksberg	(borough)	9	101,874	88,114	10,047
Københavns	(county)	522	615,343	616,210	1,180
Frederiksborg	,,	1,347	259,442	332,852	247
Roskilde	,,	891	153,199	207,059	232
Vestsjællands	,,	2,984	259,057	277,839	93
Storstrøms	,,	3,398	252,363	257,585	76
Bornholms	,,	588	47,239	47,243	80
Fyns	,,	3,486	432,699	453,921	130
Sønderjyllands	,,	3,930	238,062	249,762	64
Ribe	,,	3,131	197,843	215,217	69
Vejle	,,	2,997	306,263	326,725	109
Ringkøbing	,,	4,853	241,327	264,071	54
Aarhus	,,	4,561	533,190	579,839	127
Viborg	,,	4,122	220,734	230,618	56
Nordjyllands	,,	6,173	456,171	482,108	78
Total		43,080	4,937,579	5,112,130	119

The population is almost entirely Scandinavian; in July 1976, of the inhabitants of Denmark proper, 97·2% were born in Denmark, including Faroe Islands and Greenland.

On 1 Jan. 1984 the population of the capital, Copenhagen (comprising Copenhagen, Frederiksberg and Gentofte municipalities), was 638,163 (including suburbs, 1,365,760); Aarhus, 250,404; Odense, 170,961; Aalborg, 154,840; Esbjerg, 80,534; Randers, 61,410; Kolding, 56,519; Helsingør, 56,161; Herning, 55,923; Horsens, 54,717.

Vital statistics for calendar years:

	Living births	*Still births*	*Marriages*	*Divorces*	*Deaths*	*Emigration*	*Immigration*
1979	59,464	309	27,842	13,044	54,654	27,731	33,183
1980	57,293	253	26,448	13,593	55,939	29,913	30,311
1981	53,089	281	25,411	14,425	56,359	29,719	27,874
1982	52,658	269	24,330	14,621	55,368	28,328	28,223
1983	50,822	265	27,096	14,763	57,156	25,999	27,718

Illegitimate births: 1980, 33·2%; 1981, 35·8%; 1982, 38·3%; 1983, 40·6%.

CLIMATE. The climate is much modified by marine influences, and the effect of the Gulf Stream, to give winters that are cold and cloudy but warm and sunny summers. In general, the east is drier than the west, though few places have more than 27″ (675 mm) of rain a year. Long periods of calm weather are exceptional and windy conditions are common. Copenhagen. Jan. 33°F (0·5°C), July 63°F

(17°C). Annual rainfall 22·8″ (571 mm). Esbjerg. Jan. 33°F (0·5°C), July 59°F (15°C). Annual rainfall 32″ (800 mm).

REIGNING QUEEN. Margrethe II, born 16 April 1940; married 10 June 1967 to Prince Henrik, born Count de Monpezat; *offspring:* Crown Prince Frederik, born 26 May 1968; Prince Joachim, born 7 June 1969. She succeeded to the throne on the death of her father, King Frederik IX, on 14 Jan. 1972.

Mother of the Queen: Queen Ingrid, born Princess of Sweden, 28 March 1910.
Sisters of the Queen: Princess Benedikte, born 29 April 1944 (married 3 Feb. 1968 to Prince Richard of Sayn-Wittgenstein-Berleburg); Princess Anne-Marie, born 30 Aug. 1946 (married 18 Sept. 1964 to King Constantine of Greece).

The crown of Denmark was elective from the earliest times. In 1448 after the death of the last male descendant of Swein Estridsen the Danish Diet elected to the throne Christian I, Count of Oldenburg, in whose family the royal dignity remained for more than 4 centuries, although the crown was not rendered hereditary by right till 1660. The direct male line of the house of Oldenburg became extinct with King Frederik VII on 15 Nov. 1863. In view of the death of the king, without direct heirs, the Great Powers signed a treaty at London on 8 May 1852, by the terms of which the succession to the crown of Denmark was made over to Prince Christian of Schleswig-Holstein-Sonderburg-Glücksburg, and to the direct male descendants of his union with the Princess Louise of Hesse-Cassel, niece of King Christian VIII of Denmark. In accordance with this treaty, a law concerning the succession to the Danish crown was adopted by the Diet, and obtained the royal sanction 31 July 1853. Linked to the constitution of 5 June 1953, a new law of succession, dated 27 March 1953, has come into force, which restricts the right of succession to the descendants of King Christian X and Queen Alexandrine, and admits the sovereign's daughters to the line of succession, ranking after the sovereign's sons.

Subjoined is a list of the kings of Denmark, with the dates of their accession, from the time of election of Christian I of Oldenburg:

House of Oldenburg

Christian I	1448	Christian IV	1588	Frederik V	1746
Hans	1481	Frederik III	1648	Christian VII	1766
Christian II	1513	Christian V	1670	Frederik VI	1808
Frederik I	1523	Frederik IV	1699	Christian VIII	1839
Christian III	1534	Christian VI	1730	Frederik VII	1848
Frederik II	1559				

House of Schleswig-Holstein-Sonderburg-Glücksburg

Christian IX	1863	Christian X	1912	Margrethe II	1972
Frederik VIII	1906	Frederik IX	1947		

CONSTITUTION AND GOVERNMENT. The present constitution of Denmark is founded upon the 'Grundlov' (charter) of 5 June 1953.

The legislative power lies with the Queen and the *Folketing* (Diet) jointly. The executive power is vested in the Queen, who exercises her authority through the ministers. The judicial power is with the courts. The Queen must be a member of the Evangelical-Lutheran Church, the official Church of the State. The Queen cannot assume major international obligations without the consent of the *Folketing*. The *Folketing* consists of one chamber. All men and women of Danish nationality of more than 18 years of age and permanently resident in Denmark possess the franchise and are eligible for election to the *Folketing*, which is at present composed of 179 members; 135 members are elected by the method of proportional representation in 17 constituencies. In order to attain an equal representation of the different parties, 40 *tillægsmandater* (additional seats) are divided among such parties which have not obtained sufficient returns at the constituency elections. Two members are elected for the Faroe Islands and 2 for Greenland. The term of the legislature is 4 years, but a general election may be called at any time.

The *Folketing* must meet every year on the first Tuesday in October. Besides its legislative functions, it appoints every 6 years judges who, together with the ordinary members of the Supreme Court *(Højesteret)*, form the *Rigsret*, a tribunal which can alone try parliamentary impeachments. The ministers have free access to the House, but can vote only if they are members.

Folketing, elected 10 Jan. 1984: 56 Social Democrats, 10 Radical Liberals, 42 Conservatives, 21 Socialist People's Party, 8 Centre Democrats, 5 Christian People's Party, 22 Liberals, 5 Left Socialists, 6 Progress Party, 2 Faroe Islands and 2 Greenland representatives.

The executive (called the State Council *(Statsraadet)* when acting with the Queen presiding) is a minority non-Socialist coalition government, consisting of the Conservatives, the Liberals, the Centre Democrats and the Christian People's Party; it was in March 1984 as follows:

Prime Minister: Poul Schlüter.

Foreign Affairs: Uffe Ellemann-Jensen. *Finance:* Palle Simonsen. *Economy:* Anders Andersen. *Industry:* Ib Stetter. *Greenland:* Tom Høyem. *Social Affairs:* Elsebeth Kock-Petersen. *Agriculture:* Niels Anker Kofoed. *Fisheries:* Henning Grove. *Education:* Bertel Haarder. *Culture:* Mimi Stilling Jakobsen. *Defence:* Hans Engell. *Labour:* Grethe Fenger Møller. *Housing:* Niels Bollman. *Inland Revenue:* Isi Foighel. *Energy:* Knud Enggaard. *Interior:* Britta Schall Holberg. *Justice:* Erik Ninn-Hansen. *Environment and Nordic Affairs:* Christian Christensen. *Public Works:* Arne Melchior. *Ecclesiastical Affairs:* Mette Madsen.

The ministers are individually and collectively responsible for their acts, and if impeached and found guilty, cannot be pardoned without the consent of the *Folketing*.

In 1948 a separate legislature *(Lagting)* and executive *(Landsstyre)* were established for the Faroe Islands, to deal with specified local matters and in 1979 a separate legislature *(Landsting)* and executive *(Landsstyre)* were established for Greenland, also to deal with specified local matters.

National flag: Red with white Scandinavian cross (Dannebrog).

National anthems: Kong Kristian stod ved højen Mast (words by J. Ewald, 1778, tune by J. E. Hartmann, 1780) and Der er et yndigt land.

Local Government. For administrative purposes Denmark is divided into 275 municipalities *(kommuner)*; each of them has a district council of between 5 and 25 members, headed by an elected mayor. The city of Copenhagen forms a district by itself and is governed by a city council of 55 members, elected every 4 years, and an executive *(magistraten)*, consisting of the chief burgomaster *(overborgmesteren)* and 6 burgomasters, appointed by the city council for 4 years. There are 14 counties *(amtskommuner)*, each of which is administered by a county council *(amstråd)* of between 13 and 31 members, headed by an elected mayor. All councils are elected directly by universal suffrage and proportional representation for 4-year terms. A third council, the Metropolitan Council, with a constitution similar to the counties was established 1 April 1974. The Metropolitan Council is responsible for overall development within Metropolitan Copenhagen.

The counties and Copenhagen are superintended by a ministry of interior affairs. The municipalities are superintended by 14 local supervision committees, headed by a state county prefect *(statsamtmand)* who is a civil servant appointed by the Queen.

DEFENCE. The Danish military defence is organized in accordance with the Defence Act of May 1982 and the overall organization of the Danish Armed Forces comprises the Defence Command, the Army, the Navy, the Air Force and inter-service authorities and institutions. To this should be added the Home Guard, which is an indispensable part of Danish military defence. The Home Guard is based on the Home Guard Act of May 1982.

In accordance with the Defence Act the Chief of Defence has full command of the three services: the Army, the Navy and the Air Force. The Chief of Defence, and the Defence Staff constitute the Defence Command. The Inspector Generals of the Army, the Navy and the Air Force are members of the Defence Staff.

The Minister of Defence is assisted by a Defence Council consisting of the Chief of Defence, the Chief of Defence Staff, the Chief of Danish Operational Forces, the Inspector Generals of the Army, the Navy and the Air Force and the Chief of the Home Guard.

The Constitution of 1849 declared it the duty of every fit man to contribute to the national defence, and this provision is still in force. According to the Personnel Act of May 1982, the military personnel comprises officers, n.c.o.s and privates. Private personnel are provided by enlistment and by recruiting of volunteers. Selection of conscripts takes place at the age of 18–19 years, and the conscripts are normally called up for 9 months service ½–1½ years later. Afterwards conscripts may be recalled for refresher training or musters. From 1986 the initial training period for conscripts in combat and engineer units will be 12 months.

Army. The peace-time Army strength is about 20,500. The Army comprises field army formations and the local defence forces. The field army formations are organized in a covering force and in reserve units (comprising 6 regimental formations and some independent battalions). The covering force numbers about 16,000 men and comprises a standing force (regulars and conscripts with more than six months' service), and a supplementary force consisting of men newly released from service. The standing force number about 10,000 men organized in standing brigade units, headquarters units and support units. The brigade units are organized in 5 mechanized infantry brigades. The field army is equipped with 200 medium battle tanks and about 650 armoured personnel carriers as well as artillery including 72 self-propelled howitzers. The local defence units consist of about 14,000 men organized in 9 infantry battalions and some artillery battalions. The men of the latest annual service groups form the troops of the line, while those of the previous years form the local defence, the reserve and the reserve for the Home Guard. The mobilization units of the field army and the local defence force will total about 55,000 men.

Navy. The Navy comprises the fleet and coast-defence which includes several permanent fortifications. The fleet includes 4 submarines, 2 frigates, 3 small frigates, 5 ocean escorts (for fishery protection and surveying duties), 10 fast missile craft, 6 fast torpedo boats, 4 ocean minelayers, 3 coastal minelayers, 6 coastal minesweepers, 2 torpedo recovery vessels, 22 patrol vessels, 8 coastal patrol launches, 2 oilers, 20 auxiliary vessels and the royal yacht. The Naval Air Arm comprises 8 helicopters (one is carried in each of the ocean escorts).

Total strength of the Navy is 8,400 officers and men (1,300 officers, 3,200 regular ratings, 1,300 national service, 2,600 civilians). Reserves total 10,000 (the mobilization force is 4,000 men).

The Naval Home Guard has 37 vessels and 5,300 officers and men.

Air Force. The operational units of the Air Force comprise 8 surface-to-air missile squadrons and 6 flying squadrons.

The air defence force consists of the 8 Hawk surface-to-air missile squadrons and 4 all-weather air-defence squadrons with a total unit establishment of 32 F-16s. All squadrons have an air-defence and a fighter-bomber rôle.

The fighter bomber force comprises 1 squadron with a unit establishment of 16 F 35 Drakens, and 1 reconnaissance squadron with a unit establishment of 16 RF 35 Drakens.

In addition the Air Force has a number of supplementary units, including 1 transport squadron (C-130 Hercules and Gulfstream III), 1 helicopter rescue squadron (S-61As), and a control and warning system.

Total strength of the Air Force is about 7,000, and the mobilization force about 10,000 men.

Home Guard. The overall Home Guard organization comprises the Home Guard Command, the Army Home Guard, the Naval Home Guard and the Air Force Home Guard.

The personnel of the Home Guard is recruited on a voluntary basis. The personnel establishment of the Home Guard is at present about 77,500 persons (60,000 in the Army Home Guard, 5,300 in the Navy Home Guard and 12,200 in the Air Force Home Guard).

INTERNATIONAL RELATIONS

Membership. Denmark is a member of UN, NATO, OECD and EEC.

ECONOMY

Budget. The budget *(Finanslovforslag)* must be laid before the Parliament *(Folketing)* not later than 4 months before the beginning of a new fiscal year.

The following shows the actual revenue and expenditure as shown in central government accounts for the calendar years 1980, 1981 and 1982, the approved budget figures for 1983 and the budget for 1984 (in 1,000 kroner):

	1980	*1981*	*1982*	*1983*	*1984*
Revenue	106,707,623	111,997,031	120,561,873	115,810,266	128,328,368
Expenditure	124,602,838	145,863,972	169,981,027	184,267,276	187,653,064

Receipts and expenditures of special government funds and expenditures on public works are included.

The 1982 budget envisages revenue of 62,327m. kroner from income and property taxes and 78,193m. from consumer taxes.

The central government debt on 31 Dec. 1981 amounted to 190,271m. kroner.

Currency. The monetary unit is the *krone* of 100 *øre*. In 1931 Denmark went off the gold standard, as established in 1873.

Small change: 10-kroner and 5-kroner pieces of copper-nickel, 1-krone pieces of copper-nickel; 25-øre and 10-øre pieces of copper-nickel, and 5-øre pieces of copper–steel–copper clad. In Feb. 1985, £1 = 13·07 *kroner*; US$1 = 12·25 *kroner*.

Banking. On 31 Dec. 1982 the accounts of the National Bank balanced at 122,726m. kroner. The assets included 4,759m. kroner in gold bullion. The liabilities included 14,601m. kroner note issue, 14,484m. kroner general capital fund and reserve fund. On 31 Dec. 1981 there were 157 savings banks, with 6·4m. accounts and deposits of 53,922m. kroner. Their advances amounted to 42,673m. kroner.

On 31 Dec. 1982 there were 73 other banks for commercial, agricultural and industrial purposes; their deposits amounted to 141,684m. kroner; advances were 103,557m. kroner.

Weights and Measures. The use of the metric system of weights and measures has been obligatory in Denmark since 1 April 1912.

ENERGY AND NATURAL RESOURCES

Electricity. Owing to the concentration of power production, the number of generating power stations has declined from 371 in 1949–50 to 23 in 1980, while the net power production (in 1m. kwh.) has risen from 1,689 in 1949–50 to 20,366 in 1982.

Agriculture. Land ownership is widely distributed. In June 1983 (census) there were 98,680 holdings with at least 5 hectares of agricultural area (or at least a production equivalent to that from 5 hectares of barley). About 10,000 holdings were below the census threshold. There were 20,762 small holdings (with less than 10 hectares), 64,835 medium sized holdings (10–50 hectares) and 13,083 holdings with more than 50 hectares.

The number of agricultural workers declined from 120,442 in July 1961 to 27,309 in June 1983.

In June 1983 the cultivated area was utilized as follows (in 1,000 hectares): Grain, 1,698; peas and beans, 22; root crops, 234; other crops, 239; green fodder and grass, 640; fallow, 17; total cultivated area, 2,846.

	Area (1,000 hectares)			Production (in 1,000 tonnes)		
Chief crops	*1981*	*1982*	*1983*	*1981*	*1982*	*1983*
Wheat	150	181	242	835	1,207	1,548
Rye	50	55	77	208	235	315
Barley	1,541	1,485	1,347	6,044	6,357	4,423
Oats	42	43	29	176	178	86
Mixed grain	4	4	3	14	16	8
Potatoes	36	35	31	1,053	1,229	853
Other root crops	209	208	203	10,277	11,958	8,705

Livestock, 1983: Horses, 33,000; cattle, 2,852,000; pigs, 9,253,000; poultry, 14,766,000.

Production (in 1,000 tonnes) in 1983: Milk, 5,427; butter, 131; cheese, 251; beef, 257; pork and bacon, 1,102; eggs, 81.

In June 1982 farm tractors numbered 183,135 and harvester-threshers, 37,578.

Fisheries. The total value of the fish caught was (in 1m. kroner): 1950, 156; 1955, 252; 1960, 376; 1965, 650; 1970, 854; 1975, 1,442; 1979, 2,888. The fishing fleet in 1977 consisted of 7,340 motor boats, 182 sailing boats and 2,761 rowing boats.

INDUSTRY AND TRADE

Industry. The following table sets forth the gross factor income (in 1m. kroner) by industrial origin in 3 calendar years:

	1981		*1982*		*1983*	
	Current Prices	*1975 Prices*	*Current Prices*	*1975 Prices*	*Current Prices*	*1975 Prices*
Agriculture, fur-farming, forestry, etc.	18,879	11,961	23,960	13,426	22,196	11,875
Fishing	2,015	1,003	2,277	1,436	2,312	1,282
Total	20,894	12,964	26,238	14,862	24,508	13,158
Mining and quarrying	1,081	173	2,991	562	3,580	648
Manufacturing	69,197	44,786	77,273	44,555	86,876	46,397
Electricity, gas and water	5,295	3,260	8,090	3,836	8,754	4,089
Construction	22,326	13,417	24,922	12,986	27,820	13,636
Total	97,900	61,636	113,276	61,938	127,031	64,770
Wholesale and retail trade	45,281	32,616	49,986	33,603	54,882	34,794
Restaurants and hotels	4,138	2,251	4,954	2,436	5,359	2,406
Transport and storage	24,879	15,828	25,687	15,560	28,771	15,499
Communication	4,834	4,080	5,648	4,136	7,020	4,108
Financing and insurance	9,282	5,821	11,034	6,199	12,623	6,540
Dwellings	32,210	16,864	36,346	16,557	40,722	16,674
Business services	14,917	9,090	17,976	9,680	21,971	10,815
Market services of education, health	4,984	3,508	5,459	3,561	6,082	3,735
Recreational and cultural services	3,568	2,293	4,259	2,435	4,722	2,504
Household services, incl. auto repair	9,751	5,740	11,103	5,780	12,180	5,855
Total	153,844	98,090	172,454	99,949	194,333	102,929
Other producers, excl. government	2,459	1,319	2,896	1,376	3,216	1,426
Producers of government services	83,253	51,480	97,464	54,110	105,570	55,149
Total	85,712	52,799	100,360	55,487	108,786	56,575

	1981 Current Prices	1981 1975 Prices	1982 Current Prices	1982 1975 Prices	1983 Current Prices	1983 1975 Prices
Imputed bank service charges	-11,048	-6,457	-11,445	-6,051	-13,067	-6,303
Gross domestic product at factor cost	347,302	219,031	400,882	226,184	441,591	231,128
Plus indirect taxes	75,096	26,467	82,062	27,666	91,720	28,945
Less subsidies	12,742		15,019		17,285	
Gross domestic product at market prices	409,656	245,498	467,925	253,850	516,026	260,073

According to the registration of business units for VAT settlement there were in 1982 a total of 33,000 manufacturing enterprises. In the following table 'number of wage-earners' refers to 6,400 establishments with 6 employees or more, while 'gross-output' and 'value-added' cover 2,800 kind-of-activity units of enterprises with 20 employees or more.

Branch of industry	*Number of wage-earners (1,000)*	*Gross output in factor values (1m. kroner)*	*Value added in factor values (1m. kroner)*
Mining and quarrying	0·8	406	282
Food products	47·8	68,371	15,844
Beverages	8·0	5,910	3,506
Tobacco	1·8	1,369	686
Textiles	10·8	5,768	2,632
Wearing apparel	8·7	2,720	1,343
Leather and products	0·9	394	188
Footwear	2·3	972	388
Wood products	6·6	3,116	1,381
Furniture and fixtures	9·1	3,590	1,869
Paper and products	6·2	5,031	2,113
Printing, publishing	14·1	8,153	5,394
Industrial chemicals	11·3	16,621	8,340
Other chemical products, petroleum refineries, petroleum coal products and rubber	2·4	10,947	1,325
Plastic products	5·4	2,991	1,506
Pottery, china, glass and products	4·3	1,509	986
Non-metal products	8·4	5,329	3,000
Iron, steel and non-ferrous metals	4·6	3,355	1,366
Metal products	21·4	11,095	5,516
Machinery	35·0	18,432	10,058
Electrical machinery	14·7	8,765	4,880
Transport equipment	22·5	12,325	5,385
Controlling equipment	5·0	3,155	2,059
Other industries	4·0	2,387	1,459
Total manufacturing	256·1	202,305	81,224

Labour. In 1983, 7% of the working population lived on agriculture, forestry and fishery, 24% on industries and handicrafts, 7% on construction, 14% on commerce, etc., 8% on transport and communication, and 40% on administration, professional services, etc.

Commerce. The following table shows the value, in 1,000 kroner, of special trade imports and exports (including trade with the Faroe Islands and Greenland) for calendar years:

	1978	*1979*	*1980*	*1981*	*1982*	*1983*[1]
Imports	81,405,158	96,838,868	109,388,313	124,169,649	138,864,990	148,524,576
Exports	65,307,647	77,361,446	95,670,845	113,796,938	128,172,776	146,301,192

[1] Preliminary.

Imports and exports (in 1,000 kroner) for calendar years:

Leading commodities	1982 Imports	1982 Exports	1983[1] Imports	1983[1] Exports
Live animals, meat, etc.	170,369	18,476,235	218,120	18,504,363
Dairy products, eggs	504,553	7,097,159	460,823	7,240,201
Fish and fish preparations	2,442,124	6,391,598	2,777,016	7,093,359
Cereals and cereal preparations	1,139,665	2,471,571	1,438,954	2,849,523
Sugar and sugar preparations	640,809	1,163,699	709,174	1,293,189
Coffee, tea, cocoa, etc.	2,006,656	426,678	2,085,633	404,486
Feeding stuff for animals	4,213,246	1,395,495	4,711,955	1,608,164
Wood, lumber and cork	1,465,098	661,780	2,019,890	661,282
Textiles, fibres, yarns, fabrics, etc.	4,972,484	2,996,838	5,613,647	3,354,121
Fuels, lubricants, etc.	29,602,278	2,811,333	27,736,949	6,410,539
Pharmaceutical products	1,647,507	3,388,219	1,848,839	4,009,761
Fertilizers, etc.	1,630,462	859,772	2,159,048	963,805
Metals, manufactures of metals	13,549,350	6,014,864	14,012,412	7,316,784
Machinery, electrical, equipment, etc.	21,088,558	24,483,167	23,860,565	26,342,779
Transport equipment	8,398,408	5,753,862	9,535,341	8,321,948

[1] Preliminary.

Distribution of Danish foreign trade (in 1,000 kroner) according to countries of origin and destination, for calendar years:

Countries	Imports 1981	Imports 1982	Imports 1983[1]	Exports 1981	Exports 1982	Exports 1983[1]
Belgium	4,442,668	3,750,825	4,314,524	1,968,438	2,326,964	2,614,909
Finland	4,603,002	5,796,852	6,052,580	2,353,222	2,791,009	2,939,203
France	5,039,250	5,741,221	6,695,408	5,473,225	7,016,666	8,063,987
Germany (Fed. Rep.)	23,053,477	28,693,963	29,705,317	19,016,954	22,380,850	25,185,295
Norway	5,339,757	5,207,150	6,132,454	7,082,878	8,294,524	9,376,648
Sweden	14,957,255	16,376,313	19,598,925	13,084,262	13,909,987	15,381,089
Switzerland	2,037,630	2,485,574	2,757,672	2,648,222	2,722,724	2,954,757
UK	14,832,377	15,209,732	15,790,050	15,453,691	18,046,456	19,768,673
USA	10,545,243	9,380,502	8,376,990	6,046,825	7,489,738	10,676,995
Allied forces in Fed. Rep. Germany	—	—	—	146,734	170,873	194,003

[1] Preliminary.

Total trade between Denmark (without the Faroe Islands) and UK (British Department of Trade returns, in £1,000 sterling):

	1980	1981	1982	1983	1984
Imports to UK	1,103,590	1,179,065	1,335,640	1,512,620	1,660,447
Exports and re-exports from UK	1,032,525	2,812,957	1,096,642	1,159,184	1,197,381

Tourism. In 1983, foreigners visiting Denmark spent some 11,952m. kroner. In 1983 foreigners spent 4·50m. nights in hotels and 4·67m. nights at camping sites.

Industrial Statistics. Danmarks Statistik. Copenhagen (annually)
Quarterly Statistics for the Industry: Commodity Statistics. Danmarks Statistik, Copenhagen
Statistics on Agriculture, Horticulture and Forestry. Danmarks Statistik. Copenhagen (annually)
Agricultural Statistics 1900–1965. Vol. I: *Agricultural Area and Harvest and Utilization of Fertilizers.*—Vol. II: *Livestock and Livestock Products, and Consumption of Feeding Stuffs.* Danmarks Statistik. Copenhagen, 1968–69
External Trade of Denmark. Danmarks Statistik, Copenhagen
Danish Industry in Facts and Figures. Federation of Danish Industries. Copenhagen (annually)
Energy Supply of Denmark, 1900–58 and *1948–65.* Danmarks Statistik. Copenhagen, 1959, 1967. Annual Supplements 1966–75 have been published in Statistical News
Report on Fisheries. Ministry of Fisheries, Copenhagen (annually)
Nash, E. F., and Attwood, E. A., *The Agricultural Policies of Britain and Denmark.* London, 1961

COMMUNICATIONS

Roads. Denmark proper had (1 Jan. 1984), 518 km of motorways, 4,123 km of other state roads, 6,948 km of provincial roads and 58,238 km of commercial roads. Motor vehicles registered at 31 Dec. 1983 comprised 1,379,800 passenger cars, 235,621 lorries, 10,539 taxicabs (including 3,992 for private hire), 7,762 buses and 38,637 cycles.

Railways. In 1983 there were 2,448 km of State railways (142 km electrified), which carried 4,391m. passenger-km and 1,627m. tonne-km. There were also 483 km of private railways in 1982.

Aviation. On 1 Oct. 1950 the 3 Scandinavian airlines, Det Danske Luftfartsselskab, ABA and DNL, combined in Scandinavian Airlines System. In 1983 SAS flew 121·2m. km and carried 9,367,606 passengers.

SAS inaugurated its transpolar routes Copenhagen–Los Angeles on 15 Nov. 1954 and Copenhagen–Tōkyō on 25 Feb. 1957, and its trans-Asian express route Copenhagen–Bangkok–Singapore *via* Tashkent on 4 Nov. 1967.

Shipping. On 31 Dec. 1983 the Danish merchant fleet consisted of 2,856 vessels (above 20 GRT) of 5,075,168 GRT.

In 1983, 35,646 vessels of 53m. GRT entered the Danish ports, unloading 39m. tonnes and loading 16m. tonnes of cargo; traffic by passenger ships and ferries is not included.

Post and Broadcasting. There were, in 1982, 1,307 post offices. On 31 Dec. 1983 the length of telephone circuits of private companies was 12,158,582 km. On 31 Dec. 1983 there were 3,717,174 telephone instruments (including those in the Faroe Islands and Greenland). Postal revenues, 1982, 5,724m. kroner; expenditure, 6,096m. kroner.

Danmarks Radio is the government broadcasting station and is financed by licence fees. Television is broadcast by *Danmarks Radio* with colour programmes by PAL system. Number of receivers: Radio, 1·95m.; television, 2·13m., including 1·59m. colour sets.

Cinemas. In 1983 there were 463 cinema rooms with a seating capacity of 97,545.

Newspapers. In 1982 there were 47 daily newspapers with a combined circulation of 1·81m. on weekdays; 9 of them (873,000) appeared in Copenhagen.

JUSTICE, RELIGION, EDUCATION AND WELFARE

Justice. The lowest courts of justice are organized in 84 tribunals *(byretter)*, where cases are dealt with by a single judge. The tribunals at Copenhagen have 33 judges, Aarhus 12, Odense 9, Aalborg 8, and the other tribunals have 1 to 4. Cases of greater consequence are dealt with by the superior courts *(Landsretterne)*; these courts are also courts of appeal for the above-named cases. Of superior courts there are two: *Østre Landsret* in Copenhagen with 46 judges, *Vestre Landret* in Viborg with 23 judges. From these an appeal lies to the Supreme Court *(Højesteret)* in Copenhagen, composed of 16 judges. Judges under 65 years of age can be removed only by judicial sentence.

In 1980, 11,402 men and 995 women were convicted of violations of the penal code, fines not included. In 1983, the daily average population in penal institutions, local prisons, etc, was 3,131 men and 125 women, of whom 796 men and 47 women were on remand.

Religion. At the Reformation in 1536 the Danish Church ceased to exist as a legally independent unit, a part of the Roman Catholic Church, and became instead a Lutheran Church under the direction of the State. Since that time the State has, in one form or another, continued to exercise supreme authority in the affairs of the Church, and has regulated these by the passing of laws, by royal decree, or other appropriate means. The great majority of Danish citizens (about 90%) belongs to the National Church. Administratively, Denmark is divided into 10 dioceses each with a Bishop who, within the framework of the law, is the supreme diocesan authority in ecclesiastical affairs. The Bishop together with the Chief Administrative Officer of the county make up the diocesan governing body, responsible for all matters of ecclesiastical local finance and general administration. Bishops are appointed by the Crown after an election at which the clergy and parish council members of the diocese have had the opportunity of voting for the candidates nominated. Each diocese is divided into a number of deaneries (about 107 in the whole country) each with its Dean and Deanery Committee, who have certain financial powers. Local government at parish level (there are about 2,200 parishes in all) is in the hands of Parish Councils, who are elected for a 4-year period of office.

Since the Constitution of 1849 complete religious toleration is extended to every sect, and no civil disabilities attach to Dissenters.

Kjær, J. C., *History of the Church of Denmark*. Blair, Nebr., 1945
Roesen, August, *Religion in Denmark*. Copenhagen, 1963

Education. Education has been compulsory since 1814. The *folkeskole* (public primary and lower secondary school) comprises a pre-school class *(børnehaveklassen)*, a 9-year basic school corresponding to the period of compulsory education and 1-year voluntary tenth form. Compulsory education may be fulfilled either through attending the *folkeskole* or private schools or through home-instruction, the only requirement being that the instruction given should be comparable to that offered in the *folkeskole. Folkeskolen* are mainly municipal and no fees are paid. In the year 1982–83, 2,278 primary and lower secondary schools had 757,936 pupils and employed 65,563 teachers. Approximately 14% of the total number of schools were private schools and they were attended by 8% of the total number of pupils. The 9-year basic school is in practice not streamed. However, a certain differentiation may take place in the eighth and ninth forms.

After the completion of the eighth and ninth forms the pupils may sit for the leaving examination of the *folkeskole (folkeskolens afgangsprøve)*. After the completion of the tenth form the pupils may sit for either the leaving examination of the *folkeskole (folkeskolens afgangsprøve)* or the advanced leaving examination of the *folkeskole (folkeskolens udvidede afgangsprøve)*.

Under certain conditions the pupils may continue their education either in a 3-year gymnasium ending with *studentereksamen* or in the 2-year higher preparatory school ending with the *højere forberedelseseksamen*. There were (1982–83) 144 of these upper secondary schools with 76,348 pupils and 7,764 teachers.

Youth and leisure-time education: 294 schools (continuation schools, youth residential schools, home economics schools, folk high schools, youth high schools and agricultural schools) with 21,307 pupils.

Vocational education and training consists of Basic Vocational Training in trade and commerce with (1982–83) 23,732 students, and 15,606 received training in technical education. There were 2,818 apprentices commencing training in the field of trade and commerce, and 10,998 trainees in the technical branches. Finally, 10,609 students were admitted to the diploma courses for trade and commerce, and 7,819 students were admitted to the technical diploma courses. In 1982–83, vocational education and training totalled 71,582 students.

There were 30 teacher-training colleges with 9,542 students and 34 colleges for training of teachers for kindergartens and leisure-time activities with 6,481 students.

Degree-courses in engineering: The Technical University of Denmark had 3,866 students. The Engineering Academy had 1,580 students and 8 engineering colleges with 4,419 students.

Universities: The University of Copenhagen (founded 1479) 24,691 students. The University of Aarhus (founded in 1928) 12,272 students. The University of Odense (founded in 1964) 5,015 students. Roskilde University Centre (founded in 1972) 2,326 students. Aalborg University Centre (founded in 1974) 2,668 students.

Other types of post-secondary education: The Royal Veterinary and Agricultural College had 2,216 students. The two dental colleges had 1,198 students. The Danish School of Pharmacy had 745 students. The 11 colleges of economics and business administration had 16,289 students. The 2 schools of architecture had 1,962 students. Five academies of music had 825 students. The Danish School of Librarianship had 873 students. The Royal Danish School of Educational Studies had 2,219 students. The Danish State Institute of Physical Education had 222 students. The 4 schools of social work had 884 students. The Danish School of

Journalism had 675 students. Six colleges of physiotherapy had 1,082 students. One School of Midwifery Education had 151 students.

Andresén, A., *The Danish Folk High School To-day.* Copenhagen, 1981
Struve, K., *Schools and Education in Denmark.* Copenhagen, 1981
Thomsen, O. B., *Some Aspects of Education in Denmark.* Toronto, 1976
Thorsen, L., *Public Libraries in Denmark.* English and French eds., Copenhagen, 1972
Trane, E., *Education and Culture in Denmark.* Copenhagen, 1958

Social Security. The main body of Danish social welfare legislation is consolidated in 7 acts concerning (1) public health security, (2) sick-day benefits, (3) social pensions (for disablement, early retirement and old age), (4) employment injuries insurance, (5) employment services and unemployment insurance, (6) social assistance including assistance to handicapped, rehabilitation, child and juvenile guidance, day-care institutions, care of the aged and sick, and (7) family allowances.

Public health security, covering the entire population, provides free medical care, substantial subsidies for certain essential medicines together with some dental care and a funeral allowance. Hospitals are primarily municipal and the hospital treatment is normally free. Wage-earners are granted daily sickness allowances, others can have limited daily sickness allowances. Daily cash benefits are granted in the case of temporary incapacity for work because of illness, injury or childbirth to all persons who earn an income derived from personal work. The benefit is paid at the rate of 90% of the average weekly earnings. There was a maximum rate of 2,008 kroner a week (Oct. 1984).

Social pensions cover the entire population. Entitlement to old-age pensions at the full rates is subject to the condition that the beneficiary has been ordinarily resident in Denmark for a number of years (40). For a shorter period of residence, the benefits are reduced proportionally. The basic amount of the old-age pension in Oct. 1984 was 65,376 kroner to married couples and 35,580 to single persons. Various supplementary allowances, depending on age and income, may be payable with the basic amount. Persons aged 55–66 may, depending on health and income, apply for an early-retirement pension. Persons over 67 years of age are entitled to the basic amount. The pensions to a married couple are calculated and paid to the husband and the wife separately. Invalidity pension is payable, having regard to the degree of disability, at a rate of up to 81,348 kroner to a single person. Invalidity and early-retirement pensions may be subject to income regulation.

Employment injuries insurance provides for disablement or survivors' pensions and funeral allowances. The scheme covers practically all employees.

Employment services are provided by regional public employment agencies. The insurance against unemployment provides daily allowances. The unemployment insurance funds had in Oct. 1983 a membership of 1,826,046, of which 1,596,625 were full-time insured and 229,421 part-time.

The *Social Assistance Act* applies to the field of social legislation which rules the individually granted benefits in contrast to the other fields of social legislation which apply to fixed benefits.

Total social expenditure, including hospital and health services, statutory pensions, etc, amounted in the financial year 1982 to 138,077m. kroner.

Bibliography of Foreign Language Literature on Industrial Relations and Social Services in Denmark. Ministries of Labour and Social Affairs, Copenhagen, 1975
Social Conditions in Denmark. Vols 1–8. Ministries of Labour and Social Affairs, Copenhagen
Marcussen, E., *Social Welfare in Denmark.* 4th ed. Copenhagen, 1980

THE FAROE ISLANDS
Færøerne

HISTORY. A Norwegian province 1380–1709, the islands secured the restoration of their Parliament in 1852 and since 1948 they have been a self-governing region of the Kingdom of Denmark.

AREA AND POPULATION. Area, 1,399 sq. km (540 sq. miles); population (31 Dec. 1983), 44,805. Capital, Thorshavn. Population (31 Dec. 1983) 14,473.

GOVERNMENT. The parliament *(Lagting)*, elected on 8 Nov. 1980, consists of 32 members: 8 Samband Party, 7 Social Democrats, 6 Folkeflok, 2 Progressive Party, 3 Home Rule Party, 6 Republicans.

Flag: White with a red blue-edged Scandinavian cross.

From 1 Jan. 1972 the Faroe Islands were no longer members of EFTA.

COMMERCE. The main industries are fisheries and crafts. Exports, mainly fresh, frozen, filleted and salted fish, amounted to 1,379m. kroner in 1983; imports to 2,199m. kroner.

Total trade with UK (British Department of Trade returns, in £1,000 sterling):

	1980	*1981*	*1982*	*1983*	*1984*
Imports to UK	10,559	12,530	8,925	15,932	17,649
Exports and re-exports from UK	2,434	2,568	2,397	2,332	5,140

BROADCASTING. *Utvarp Føroya* is the broadcasting station and the number of receivers 16,000.

EDUCATION. In 1983–84 there were 5,610 primary and 3,098 secondary school pupils with 503 teachers.

Books of Reference

Årbog for Færøerne. 1983
Faroes in Figures. Thorshavn, annual, from 1956
Rutherford, G. K., (ed.) *The Physical Environment of the Færoe Islands.* The Hague, 1982
West, J. F., *Faroe.* London, 1973

GREENLAND
Grønland/Kalaallit Nunaat

HISTORY. A Danish possession since 1380, Greenland became on 5 June 1953 an integral part of the Danish kingdom. Following a referendum in Jan. 1979, home rule was introduced from 1 May 1979, and full internal self-government was attained in Jan. 1981 after a transitional period.

AREA AND POPULATION. Area 2,175,600 sq. km (840,000 sq. miles), made up of 1,833,900 sq. km of ice cap and 341,700 sq. km of ice-free land. The population, 1 Jan. 1984, numbered 52,347; West Greenland, 47,033; East Greenland, 3,286; North Greenland (Thule), 787, and 1,241 not belonging to any specific municipality. Of the total, 9,217 were born outside Greenland. Capital, Godthaab (Nuuk) (1984), 9,997.

CONSTITUTION. Greenland has the same rights as other counties in Denmark with a democratically elected council *(landsråd)*. A referendum held in Jan. 1979 approved of home rule from 1 May 1979. At the elections held on 12 April 1983 for the new 26-member Parliament, *Landsting*, the *Siumut* gained 12 seats, the *Atassut*, 12 seats and the *Inuit Ataqatigiit*, the remaining 2 seats. The Premier, Jonathan Motzfeldt, formed a 6-member administration, *Landsstyre*.

INDUSTRY. Until the beginning of this century, the hunting of land and sea mammals, especially seals, was the main occupation of the population; now fishing is most important. Fish-processing industries, construction and trade are also important occupations.

Coal production ceased in 1972. A deposit of the valuable mineral cryolite has been mined at Ivigtut. The mine is now worked out, but exports from stock will continue for some years. In 1973 the Danish company Greenex A/S began producing lead and zinc concentrate near Umanak. Annual production of lead and zinc concentrates is about 34,000 tonnes and 153,000 tonnes respectively. In 1975, 6 groups of oil companies were granted 13 oil concessions off the west coast. These concessions were terminated by 31 Dec. 1978.

Public authorities are investigating uranium and coal deposits in Greenland as well as possibilities of hydro-electric power and there are other private prospectors for various minerals.

COMMERCE. Imports (c.i.f. Greenland) (in 1,000 kroner): 1978, 980,292; 1979, 1,447,904; 1980, 1,847,877; 1981 2,096,192; 1982 2,318,622; 1983 (provisional), 2,421,025. Exports (f.o.b. Greenland) (in 1,000 kroner): 1978, 559,274; 1979, 866,926; 1980, 1,199,301; 1981, 1,324,808; 1982, 1,431,987; 1983 (provisional), 1,644,662. Trade is mainly with Denmark.

Total trade with UK (British Department of Trade returns, in £1,000 sterling):

	1980	*1981*	*1982*	*1983*	*1984*
Imports to UK	282	270	1,095	3,114	3,983
Exports and re-exports from UK	5,930	2,502	288	140	99

COMMUNICATIONS

Roads. There were (1970) 150 km of roads, of which 60 km were paved.

Aviation. There is an international airport at Søndre Srømfjord, and about 12 local airports with scheduled services.

Broadcasting. *Grønlands Radio* broadcasts in Greenlandic and Danish. The short wave transmitters are located at Godthaab. Several towns have local television stations.

JUSTICE, RELIGION, EDUCATION AND WELFARE

Justice. The High Court *(Landsret)* in Godthaab comprises one professional judge and 2 lay magistrates, while there are 18 district courts under lay assessors.

Religion. About 88% of the population are Evangelical Lutherans.

Education. There were (1983–84) 10,269 pupils in primary comprehensive schools, of whom 7,556 were in the course of compulsory education (9 years). On 1 Jan. 1983, 1,609 students were enrolled in vocational training.

Health. The medical service is free to all inhabitants. There is a central hospital in Godthaab and 16 smaller district hospitals. In 1982 there were 57 doctors and 616 hospital beds.

Books of Reference

Greenland. R. Danish Ministry of Greenland. Copenhagen. Annual from 1968

Indkomst- og erhvervsforholdene i Grønland ved Hjemmestyrets indførelse (Income and Business Conditions in Greenland at the Introduction of Home Rule), Statistiske Undersøgelser nr. 40, Danmarks Statistik 1984

Meddelelser om Grønland. Ed. Kommissionen for videnskabelige undersøgelser i Grønland. Copenhagen, 1899 ff. Since 1979 issued in 3 separate series: 'Bioscience', 'Geoscience' and 'Man and Society'

Statistiske Efterretninger (Statistical News), from 1983 special series: *Færøerne og Grønland* (Faroe Islands and Greenland)

Gad, F., *A History of Greenland.* Vol. 1. London, 1970.—Vol. 2. London, 1973

Hertling, K. (ed.) *Greenland Past and Present.* Copenhagen, 1970

DIPLOMATIC REPRESENTATIVES

Of Denmark in Great Britain (55 Sloane St., London, SW1X 9SR)
Ambassador: Tyge Dahlgaard (accredited 28 Feb. 1981).

Of Great Britain in Denmark (36–40 Kastelsvej, DK-2100, Copenhagen)
Ambassador: James Mellon, CMG.

Of Denmark in the USA (3200 Whitehaven St., NW, Washington, D.C., 20008)
Ambassador: Eigil Jørgensen.

Of the USA in Denmark (Dag Hammarskjolds Alle 24, Copenhagen)
Ambassador: Terence A. Todman.

Of Denmark to the United Nations
Ambassador: Ole Bierring.

Books of Reference

Statistical Information: Danmarks Statistik (Sejrøgade 11, 2100 Copenhagen Ø.) was founded in 1849 and reorganized in 1966 as an independent institution; it is administratively placed under the Minister of Economic Affairs. *Chief:* N. V. Skak-Nielsen. Its main publications are: *Statistisk Årbog* (Statistical Yearbook). From 1896; *Statistiske Efterretninger* (Statistical News). From 1909; *Statistiske Meddelelser* (Statistical Reports). From 1852; *Handelsstatistiske Meddelelser* (Reports on Foreign Trade). From 1910; *Statistiske Tabelværker* (Statistical Tables). From 1850; *Statistiske Undersøgelser* (Statistical Inquiries).

Ministry of Foreign Affairs, *Danish Foreign Office Journal. Commercial and General Review.—Denmark.* 1961.—*Economic Survey of Denmark* (annual).—*Facts About Denmark.* 1959.—Hæstrup, J., *From Occupied to Ally: the Danish Resistance Movement.* 1963
Atlas over Danmark. R. Danish Geog. Society. Copenhagen, 1963
Bibliografi over Danmarks Offentlige Publikationer. Institut for International Udveksling, Copenhagen. Annual
Dania polyglotta. Annual Bibliography of Books ... in Foreign Languages Printed in Denmark. State Library, Copenhagen. Annual
Kongelig Dansk Hof og Statskalender. Copenhagen. Annual
Brynildsen, F., *A Dictionary of the English and Dano-Norwegian Languages.* 2 vols. Copenhagen, 1902–07
Danstrup, J., *History of Denmark.* 2nd ed. Copenhagen, 1949
Krabbe, L., *Histoire de Danemark.* Copenhagen and Paris, 1950
Nielsen, B. K., *Engelsk–Dansk Ordbog.* Copenhagen, 1964
Trap, J. P., *Kongeriget Danmark.* 5th ed. 11 vols. Copenhagen, 1953 ff.
Vinterberg, H., and Bodelsen, C. A., *Dansk-Engelsk Ordbog.* Copenhagen, 1966

National Library: Det Kongelige Bibliotek, Copenhagen. *Librarian:* P. Birkelund.

DJIBOUTI

Jumhouriyya Djibouti

Capital: Djibouti
Population: 340,000 (1983)
GNP per capita: US$480 (1981)

HISTORY. At a referendum held on 19 March 1967, 60% of the electorate voted for continued association with France rather than independence and the new statute for the territory came into being on 5 July 1967. In Jan. 1976, following discussions between Ali Aref and President Giscard d'Estaing, it was announced that the French Government affirmed that the Territory of the Afars and the Issas was destined for independence but no date was fixed. Legislative elections were held on 8 May and independence as the Republic of Djibouti was achieved on 27 June 1977.

AREA AND POPULATION. Djibouti is bounded north-east by the Gulf of Aden, south-east by Somalia and all other sides by Ethiopia.

Djibouti has an area of 23,000 sq. km (8,880 sq. miles). The population was estimated in 1983 at 340,000, of whom 48% were Somali, 38% Afar, 9% European and 5% Arab. There were (1982) about 40,000 refugees from Ethiopia. Djibouti, the seat of government, had (1981) 150,000 inhabitants; other towns are Tadjoura, Obock, Dikhil and Ali-Sabieh. There are 5 administrative districts.

CLIMATE. Conditions are hot throughout the year, with very little rain. Djibouti. Jan. 78°F (25·6°C), July 96°F (35·6°C). Annual rainfall 5" (130 mm).

CONSTITUTION AND GOVERNMENT. Under an organic law approved by the Constituent Assembly on 10 Feb. 1981, the President is directly elected for a 6-year term (renewable once) and the Constituent Assembly became a 65-member Chamber of Deputies, with a 5-year term. In Oct. 1981, the Assembly declared Djibouti a one-Party state, the ruling Party being the *Rassemblement Populaire pour le Progrès*. Elections for the Chamber of Deputies were held 21 May 1982, when 26 Somali, 23 Afar and 16 Arab members were elected.

President: Hassan Gouled Aptidon (elected 1977 and re-elected 1981).
Prime Minister and Ports: Barkat Gourad Hamadou.
Foreign Affairs: Moumin Báhdon Farah.

National flag: Horizontally blue over green, with a white triangle based on the hoist charged with a red star.

DEFENCE

Army. The Army comprises 1 infantry regiment, 1 armoured squadron, 1 support battalion, 1 border commando battalion and 1 parachute company. Equipment includes 22 armoured cars. The strength of the Army (of which the Navy and Air Force form part) was (1985) about 2,700 men. There is also a paramilitary force of some 2,000 men.

Navy. The nucleus of a naval force was acquired in 1977 with the commissioning of a coastal patrol craft and in 1984, 3 minor landing craft.

Air Force. As the nucleus of an air force, the French *Armée de l'Air* transferred to the Djibouti Government 1 Noratlas piston engined tactical transport aircraft.

INTERNATIONAL RELATIONS

Membership. Djibouti is a member of UN, OAU, the Arab League and an ACP State of the EEC.

ECONOMY

Budget. The ordinary budget for 1983 envisaged an expenditure of 22,269m. Djibouti francs.

Currency. The currency is the *Djibouti franc*. In Feb. 1985, £1 = 183 *Djibouti francs*; US$1 = 198·16 *Djibouti francs*.

Banking. The Banque Nationale de Djibouti is the bank of issue. There are 6 commercial banks.

NATURAL RESOURCES

Minerals. Minerals supposed to exist are gypsum, mica, amethyst and sulphur.

Agriculture. Mainly market gardening at the oasis of Ambouli and near urban areas. Livestock (1983): 43,000 cattle, 380,000 sheep, 540,000 goats, 7,000 donkeys, 52,000 camels.

Fisheries. The catch in 1980 was 2,000 tonnes.

INDUSTRY AND TRADE

Industry. Industry provides employment for 1,500 and the main industry is a bottling plant opened in 1981.

Commerce. The main economic activity is the operation of the port. The chief imports are cotton goods, sugar, cement, flour, fuel oil and vehicles; the chief exports are hides, cattle and coffee (transit from Ethiopia). Trade in 1m. Djibouti francs:

	1979	*1980*	*1981*
Imports	28,436	33,782	36,654
Exports	14,147	19,171	20,348

In 1979 France provided 47% of imports and took 87% of exports.

Total trade between Djibouti and UK (British Department of Trade returns, in £1,000 sterling):

	1980	*1981*	*1982*	*1983*	*1984*
Imports to UK	303	227	53	184	59
Exports and re-exports from UK	6,682	6,555	6,521	7,712	8,896

COMMUNICATIONS

Roads. There were (1982) 2,795 km of roads, of which 300 km were hard-surfaced. In 1977 there were 11,800 passenger cars and 3,300 lorries.

Railway. For the line Djibouti–Addis Ababa *see* p. 450. In 1983 the railway carried 249,000 tonnes of freight and 1·4m. passengers.

Aviation. Air Djibouti provides services to Addis Ababa, Nairobi, Jidda and the Gulf. Other airlines serving Djibouti international airport (Ambouli) are Ethiopian Airlines, Air France, Air Tanzania and Yemen Airways Corporation. In 1981 there were 2,983 inward flights.

Shipping. In 1981 there entered at Djibouti 1,753 vessels, unloading 307,800 tonnes and loading 151,900 tonnes of merchandise. In 1981 the merchant marine comprised 8 vessels of 3,185 GRT. Djibouti became a free port in 1981.

Post and Broadcasting. Number of telephones (1980), 4,348. *Radiodiffusion-Télévision de Djibouti* broadcasts on medium- and short-waves in French, Somali, Afar and Arabic. There is a television transmitter in Djibouti, broadcasting for 19 hours a week. Number of receivers (1982): radio, 17,200; TV, 10,550.

Cinemas. In 1975 there were 4 cinemas with a seating capacity of 5,800.

JUSTICE, RELIGION, EDUCATION AND WELFARE

Justice. There is a Court of First Instance and a Court of Appeal in the capital. The judicial system is based on Islamic law.

Religion. The vast majority of the population is Moslem, with about 12,000 Roman Catholics.

Education. In 1984 there were 21,847 pupils and 503 teachers at primary schools, 6,331 pupils and 280 teachers at secondary and technical schools.

Health. There were (1975) 11 hospitals and dispensaries with 1,028 beds; 52 physicians.

DIPLOMATIC REPRESENTATIVES

Of Djibouti in Great Britain
Ambassador: Ahmed Ibrahim Abdi (resides in Paris).

Of Great Britain in Djibouti
Ambassador: (Vacant).

Of the USA in Djibouti (Villa Plateau du Serpent Blvd., Djibouti)
Ambassador: Alvin P. Adams, Jr.

Of Djibouti to the United Nations and in the USA
Ambassador: Saleh Hadji Farah Dirir.

Books of Reference

Poinsot, J.-P., *Djibouti et la Côte française des Somalis.* Paris, 1965
Thompson, V., and Adloff, R., *Djibouti and the Horn of Africa.* Stanford Univ. Press, 1967

COMMONWEALTH OF DOMINICA

Capital: Roseau
Population: 74,859 (1981)
GNP per capita: US$761 (1982)

HISTORY. Dominica was discovered by Columbus. It was a British possession from 1805, a member of the Federation of the West Indies 1958–62, an Associated State of the UK, 1967–78 and became an independent republic as the Commonwealth of Dominica on 3 Nov. 1978.

AREA AND POPULATION. Dominica is an island in the Windward group of the West Indies situated between Martinique and Guadeloupe. It has an area of 751 sq. km (290 sq. miles) and a population at the 1981 Census of 74,859. The chief town, Roseau, had about 20,000 inhabitants in 1981.

The population is mainly of Negro and mixed origins, with small white and Asian minorities. There is a Carib settlement of about 500, almost entirely of mixed blood.

CLIMATE. A tropical climate, with pleasant conditions between Dec. and March, but there is a rainy season from June to Oct., when hurricanes may occur. Rainfall is heavy, with coastal areas having 70″ (1,750 mm) but the mountains may have up to 250″ (6,250 mm). Roseau. Jan. 76°F (24·2°C), July 81°F (27·2°C). Annual rainfall 78″ (1,956 mm).

CONSTITUTION AND GOVERNMENT. The House of Assembly has 21 elected and 9 nominated members. The Speaker is elected from among the members of the House or from outside. The Cabinet is presided over by the Prime Minister and consists of 6 other Ministers including the Attorney-General. Elections were held in July 1980. The Dominica Freedom Party won 17 seats, Dominica Democratic Labour Party, 2 seats and Independents 2 seats.

President: Aurelius Marie, MBE.
The Cabinet in Feb. 1985 was composed as follows:

Prime Minister and Minister of Finance, Foreign Affairs, Trade, Tourism, Development and Industry: Mary Eugenia Charles.

Attorney-General and Minister of Legal Affairs: Ronan David. *Home Affairs, Women's Affairs, Industrial Relations and Housing:* Brian G. K. Alleyne. *Agriculture, Lands, Co-operatives and Fisheries:* Heskeith Alexander. *Communications and Works:* Alleyne Carbon. *Education, Health, Youth Affairs, Sports and Culture:* Charles Maynard. *Minister without portfolio in the Prime Minister's Office with special responsibility for Trade and Industry, Tourism and Information:* Charles Savarin.

National flag: Green with a cross over all of yellow, black, and white pieces, and in the centre a red disc charged with a Sisserou parrot in natural colours within a ring of 10 green yellow-bordered stars.

INTERNATIONAL RELATIONS

Membership. The Commonwealth of Dominica is a member of UN, OAS, CARICOM, the Commonwealth and is an ACP state of EEC.

ECONOMY

Budget. In 1982–83 there was a deficit of EC$11·9m.

Currency. The French *franc,* the £ sterling and the East Caribbean *dollar* are legal tender. In March 1984, EC$2·70 = US$1 and EC$3·98 = £1.

Banking. Savings bank (Dec. 1982), 2,862 depositors, with $593,659 deposits. There are branches of Barclays Bank International, Royal Bank of Canada and

Dominica Cooperative Bank in Roseau, and a branch of Barclays at Portsmouth. The National Commercial and Development Bank was opened in 1977 and Banque Française Commerciale opened in 1979.

NATURAL RESOURCES

Agriculture. Hurricanes in 1979 and 1980 devastated large agricultural areas and damaged infrastructure. Production (1982): Bananas, 34,354 tonnes; coconuts, 11,455,000 nuts; beef, 457,428 lb; pork, 588,993 lb.

Livestock (1983): Cattle, 4,000; pigs, 9,000; sheep, 4,000; goats, 6,000; poultry, (1982) 115,000.

INDUSTRY AND TRADE

Industry. The main industries are agriculture and tourism.

Commerce (1982). Imports, EC$128,190,856; exports, EC$61,516,134. Chief products: Bananas, soap, fruit juices, essential oils, coconuts, vegetables, fruit and fruit preparations, and alcoholic drinks.

Total trade between Dominica and UK (British Department of Trade returns, in £1,000 sterling):

	1981	*1982*	*1983*	*1984*
Imports to UK	14,462	11,376	12,251	14,961
Exports and re-exports from UK	7,924	7,423	7,653	8,359

Tourism. Tourists (1982) totalled 10,419.

COMMUNICATIONS

Roads. In 1976 there were 467 miles of road and 282 miles of track. Vehicles totalled (Sept. 1983) 5,717.

Post and Broadcasting. Telephone lines, 136 route miles; number of telephones, 3,193 (Sept. 1983). Radio receivers (1982) 13,405.

Cinemas. In 1982 there were 2 cinemas with a seating capacity of 1,000.

JUSTICE, RELIGION, EDUCATION AND WELFARE

Justice. There are 4 magistrates' courts. In 1981, 4,891 cases were filed and 4,388 were disposed of. There is also a supreme court which dealt with 38 criminal and 319 civil cases in 1981. The police force consists of 10 officers and 431 other ranks.

Religion. 80% of the population is Roman Catholic.

Education. In 1982 there were 18,780 primary and 6,195 secondary school pupils and 3 colleges of higher education.

Health. In Sept. 1983 there were 3 hospitals with 237 beds, 26 doctors, 7 dentists, 10 pharmacists and 153 nursing personnel.

DIPLOMATIC REPRESENTATIVES

Of Dominica in Great Britain (10 Kensington Ct., London, W8)
High Commissioner: Arden Shillingford, MBE (accredited 13 Dec. 1978).

Of Great Britain in Dominica
High Commissioner: G. L. Bullard, CMG (resides in Bridgetown).

Of Dominica to the USA and the United Nations
Ambassador: Franklin A. M. Baron.

Book of Reference

Commonwealth of Dominica. HMSO, 1979

Library: Public Library, Roseau. *Librarian:* Miss C. Henry.

DOMINICAN REPUBLIC

Capital: Santo Domingo
Population: 6·3m. (1982)
GNP per capita: US$1,260 (1981)

República Dominicana

HISTORY. On 5 Dec. 1492 Columbus discovered the island of Santo Domingo, which he called La Española; for a time it was called Hispaniola. The city of Santo Domingo, founded by his brother, Bartholomew, in 1496, is the oldest city in the Americas. The western third of the island—now the Republic of Haiti—was later occupied and colonized by the French, to whom the Spanish colony of Santo Domingo was also ceded in 1795. In 1808 the Dominican population, under the command of Gen. Juan Sánchez Ramirez, routed an important French military force commanded by Gen. Ferrand, at the famous battle of Palo Hincado. This battle was the beginning of the end for French rule in Santo Domingo and culminated in the successful siege of the capital. Eventually, with the aid of a British naval squadron, the French were forced to capitulate and the colony returned again to Spanish rule, from which it declared its independence in 1821. It was invaded and held by the Haitians from 1822 to 1844, when they were expelled, and the Dominican Republic was founded and a constitution adopted. Independence day 27 Feb. 1844. Great Britain, in 1850, was the first country to recognize the Dominican Republic. The country was occupied by American Marines from 1916 until 1924. In 1936 the name of the capital city was changed from Santo Domingo to Ciudad Trujillo; and back again in 1961.

AREA AND POPULATION. The Dominican Republic occupies the eastern portion (about two-thirds) of the island of Hispaniola, Quisqueya or Santo Domingo, the western division forming the Republic of Haiti. It consists of the National District (containing the capital, Santo Domingo; population, census 1970, 817,067), and 26 provinces.

Area is 48,442 sq. km (18,700 sq. miles) with 870 miles of coastline, 193 miles of frontier line with Haiti (marked out in 1936).

The populations of the 26 provinces at the 1970 census were:

La Altagracia	88,231	Puerto Plata	186,112
Azua	90,590	La Romana	58,341
Bahoruco	66,398	Salcedo	89,204
Barahona	111,162	Samaná	53,420
Dajabón	51,069	Sánchez Ramírez	106,289
Duarte	200,478	San Cristóbal	324,673
Espaillat	140,508	San Juan	190,624
La Estrelleta	53,598	San Pedro de Macorís	105,463
Independencia	32,632	Santiago	385,625
María Trinidad Sánchez	97,109	Santiago Rodríguez	49,376
Montecristi	69,056	El Seibo	135,156
Pedernales	12,382	Valverde	76,825
Peravia	128,144	La Vega	293,573

Census (1981) 5,647,977. Estimate (1983) 5,982,000.

Population of the principal municipalities (Census 1981): National District (including Santo Domingo) 1,313,172; Santiago de los Caballeros, 278,638; La Romana, 91,571; San Pedro de Macoris, 78,562; San Francisco de Macoris, 64,906; La Vega, 52,432; San Juan de la Managuana, 49,764; Barahona, 49,334; Puerto Plata, 45,348.

The population is partly of Spanish descent, but is mainly composed of a mixed race of European and African blood.

CLIMATE. A tropical maritime climate with most rain falling in the summer months. The rainy season extends from May to Nov. and amounts are greatest in the north and east. Hurricanes may occur from June to Nov. Santo Domingo. Jan. 75°F (23·9°C), July 81°F (27·2°C). Annual rainfall 56″ (1,400 mm).

CONSTITUTION AND GOVERNMENT. A new Constitution was promulgated on 28 Nov. 1966.

The President is elected for 4 years, by direct vote. In case of death, resignation or disability, he is succeeded by the Vice-president. There are 12 secretaries of state, a judicial adviser with secretary-of-state rank and 2 ministers without portfolio in charge of departments. Citizens are entitled to vote at the age of 18, or less when married.

Recent Presidents have been: Dr Joaquín Balaguer, 4 Aug. 1960–62; Lic. Rafael Bonnelly, 18 Jan. 1962; Professor Juan Bosch, 27 Feb.–25 Sept. 1963 (deposed); Dr Héctor Gracía Godoy, 3 Sept. 1965–1 July 1966; Joaquín Balaguer, 1 July 1966–15 Aug. 1978; Antonio Guzan, 26 May 1978–4 July 1982.

President: Salvador Jorge Blanco (assumed office 14 Aug. 1982).

The country's first free elections for nearly 40 years were held in Dec. 1962 when Juan Bosch was elected President with a clear majority, after which a new Constitution was approved on 29 April 1963. Bosch was overthrown by a military *coup d'état* in Sept. 1963 and the declared aim of the Constitutionalist side in the Civil War of April–Sept. 1965 was the restoration of Bosch as President and a return to the 1963 Constitution.

On 29 April 1965 USA landed a force of 44,000 Marine and Army, later assisted by Organization of American States contributions. The capital remained divided between these forces and various rival factions of nationals. A provisional government was eventually installed on 3 Sept. 1965.

Until elections on 1 June 1966 there was government by decree.

National flag: Blue, red; quartered by a white cross.

National anthem: Quisqueyanos valientes, alzemos (words by E. Prud'homme; tune by J. Reyes, 1883).

DEFENCE. The armed forces are under the command of the President of the Republic, acting through the Secretary of State for the Armed Forces.

Army. The Army has a strength (1985) of about 14,000. It is organized in 3 infantry brigades, 1 artillery regiment and support battalions, and has some light tanks and armoured cars.

Navy. The Navy, largely comprising former US vessels, consists of 1 very old frigate (built 1944) acting as the staff flagship (former training ship, *ex*-presidential yacht), 2 escort (*ex*-fleet) minesweepers, 3 patrol vessels (*ex*-netlayers), 1 medium landing ship, 2 landing craft, 5 coastguard vessels, 8 patrol cutters, 4 small training craft, 2 oilers, 3 survey craft and 10 tugs. Personnel in 1985 totalled 4,050 officers and men.

Air Force. The Air Force, with HQ at San Isidoro, has 1 squadron of 10 F-51D Mustang piston-engined fighters, supported by 11 T-34B Mentors; 1 squadron with a total of about 16 Bell 205A-1, UH-1, UH-12E, OH-6A, H-19 and Alouette II/III helicopters; 1 transport squadron with 5 C-47s and some smaller communications aircraft; a Presidential Dauphin 2 helicopter, and an assortment of trainers. Personnel strength was (1985) 4,000.

INTERNATIONAL RELATIONS

Membership. The Dominican Republic is a member of UN and OAS.

ECONOMY

Budget. The 1982 budget balanced at RD$1,029·2m.

Currency. In Oct. 1947 the *peso oro*, equal to the US$, was formally made the unit of currency. In March 1985, £1 = RD$1·069; US$1 = RD$1.

There are silver coins for 50, 25 and 10 centavos, a copper-nickel 5-centavo piece and a copper 1-centavo piece.

Banking. There are 4 foreign banks—the Royal Bank of Canada with 12 branches, the Bank of Nova Scotia with 11 branches, the Citibank with 6 branches, the Chase Manhattan Bank with 7 branches and the Bank of America with 4 branches. An agricultural and mortgage bank, with paid-up capital of RD$500,000, was established in 1945; in 1950 its capital was increased to RD$5m. In 1947 the Central Bank of the Dominican Republic was established. A Banco Popular Dominicano, with an authorized capital of RD$5m., opened in Jan. 1964.

Weights and Measures. The metric system was nominally adopted on 1 Aug. 1913, but English and Spanish units have remained in common use in ordinary commercial transactions; on 17 Sept. 1954 a more drastic law requiring the decimal metric system was passed.

ENERGY AND NATURAL RESOURCES

Electricity. Hurricane 'David' (Aug. 1979) damaged 3 of the hydro-electric plants which produce 30% of electricity supply. 2,225·4m. kwh. of electricity was generated in 1982.

Minerals. Bauxite output in 1982 was 152,250 tonnes. Silver and platinum have been found, and near Neiba there are several hills of rock salt (production 1977, 48,592 tonnes). Ferronickel production (1982) 13,817 tonnes. The Rosario Dominicana goldmines were nationalized in Oct. 1979. Exports of Doré, a gold and silver alloy, (1982) RD$163·6m.

Agriculture. Agriculture is the chief source of wealth, sugar cultivation being the principal industry. Of the total area, 27,411 hectares are cultivable.

Livestock in 1983: 1,951,000 cattle, 143,000 pigs, 56,000 sheep.

The largest sugar estates are in the south-eastern part of the republic. Sugar production, 1982, was 10·92m. tonnes.

Coffee is exported mainly to USA. Output, 1982, 126,984 tonnes. Production of rice for home consumption and export is fostered; output, 1982, 446,913 tonnes. Cocoa is the second principal crop and covers 2m. *tareas* (340,000 acres); output in 1982, 34,921 tonnes. There are useful crops of yucca (1977: 162,287 tonnes) and beans (1982: 58,075 tonnes) for local consumption. Scientific growing of bananas (1977: 290,837 tonnes) and of leaf tobacco (1982: 33,184 tonnes) is progressing.

Fisheries. The total catch (1981) was 14,500 tonnes.

INDUSTRY AND TRADE

Industry. In 1975, 1,286 industrial establishments employed 130,000 men and women, who earned RD$157·57m. Important manufactures are sugar (114,000 tonnes in 1981), cotton and rayon textiles (17m. metres in 1979), cement (960,000 tonnes in 1981).

Commerce. Total imports and exports in RD$1m. (equal to US$1m.):

	1977	*1978*	*1979*	*1980*	*1981*	*1982*
Imports	847·8	860·9	1,080·4	1,498·4	1,450·2	1,255·8
Exports	780·4	675·3	868·6	961·9	1,188·0	767·7

The principal exports in 1980 were (in RD$1m.): Sugar and by-products, 242·9; coffee, 48·5; ferronickel, 92·7; Doré, 184.

Total trade between the Dominican Republic and UK (British Department of Trade returns, in £1,000 sterling):

	1980	*1981*	*1982*	*1983*	*1984*
Imports to UK	4,788	7,013	5,752	6,662	5,620
Exports and re-exports from UK	11,514	10,860	10,161	11,594	12,535

Tourism. 175,000 tourists visited the Dominican Republic in 1982.

COMMUNICATIONS

Roads. Three main trunk highways, with branches, extend from Santo Domingo eastward to Higuey (106 miles), northward to Santiago and Montecristi and Dajabón (204 miles) and westward to San Juan (128 miles) and Elías Piña on the Haitian border (161 miles). At Elías Piña the road joins the Haitian road to Port-au-Prince. Total highway system in 1977 was 5,224 km first-, 1,538 km second- and 2,505 km third-class roads; there were 647 bridges. Road transport is the chief means of travel. There were 82,001 cars, 40,626 commercial vehicles and 34,967 motor cycles in 1977.

Railways. Some 142 km of the Dominican Government Railway remains in use between La Vega and the port of Sánchez. Twelve lines, including the Central Romana Railway, exist to serve the sugar industry, totalling 1,600 km.

Aviation. The country is reached from the American continent and the Caribbean islands by 8 international airlines. Two local aviation companies provide interior services and connect Santo Domingo with San Juan in Puerto Rico, Curaçao, Aruba and Miami.

Shipping. Santo Domingo is the leading port; Puerto Plata ranks next. In 1971, vessels of 9,833,000 tons entered the ports to discharge 3,009,000 tonnes of cargo, and vessels of 5,276,000 tons cleared the ports having loaded 1,986,000 tonnes.

Post and Broadcasting. Number of telephone instruments (1982), 175,054, of which 138,169 in Santo Domingo. The telephone system is mainly operated by an American company. The telegraph has a total length of about 500 km, privately owned; they have been leased to All-America Cables, Inc., which also controls submarine cables connecting, in the north, Puerto Plata with Puerto Rico and New York, and in the south, Santo Domingo with Puerto Rico, Cuba and Curaçao.

There were (1980) 105 broadcasting stations in Santo Domingo and other towns; this includes the 2 government stations. There are 4 television stations.

Cinemas (1978). Cinemas numbered 72, with seating capacity of about 40,000.

Newspapers (1984). There were 7 daily newspapers with a circulation of 155,000.

JUSTICE, RELIGION, EDUCATION AND WELFARE

Justice. The judicial power resides in the Supreme Court of Justice, the courts of appeal, the courts of first instance, the communal courts and other tribunals created by special laws, such as the land courts. The Supreme Court consists of a president and 8 judges chosen by the Senate, and the procurator-general, appointed by the executive; it supervises the lower courts. Each province forms a judicial district, as does the *Distrito Nacional*, and each has its own procurator fiscal and court of first instance; these districts are subdivided, in all, into 72 municipalities and 18 municipal districts, each with one or more local justices. The death penalty was abolished in 1924.

Religion. The religion of the state is Roman Catholic; other forms of religion are permitted.

Education. Primary instruction (5,956 schools) is free and obligatory for children between 7 and 14 years of age; there are also secondary, normal, vocational and special schools, all of which are either wholly maintained by the State or state-aided; in 1981, primary schools had 22,672 teachers and 1·1m. pupils, 1,963 intermediate and secondary schools had 11,716 teachers and 331,471 pupils.

The University of Santo Domingo (founded 1538) had (1975) 27,675 students; 5 other universities had 14,573 students.

Health. In 1978, 18 towns had complete waterworks. There were, in 1975, 1,310 doctors, 121 hospitals, health centres and polyclinics with 8,389 beds.

DIPLOMATIC REPRESENTATIVES

Of the Dominican Republic in Great Britain (4 Braemar Mansions, London, SW7 4AG)
Ambassador: (Vacant).

Of Great Britain in the Dominican Republic (Ave. Independencia 506, Santo Domingo)
Ambassador: Roy G. Marlow.

Of the Dominican Republic in the USA (1715 22nd St., NW, Washington, D.C., 20008)
Ambassador: Carlos Despradel.

Of the USA in the Dominican Republic (Calle Cesar Nicolas Penson, Santo Domingo)
Ambassador: Robert Anderson.

Of the Dominican Republic to the United Nations
Ambassador: Dr E. Knipping-Victoria.

Books of Reference

Anuario estadístico de la República Dominicana, 1944–45. Ciudad Trujillo. 1949. This has been succeeded by separate annual reports covering foreign trade, vital statistics, banking, insurance, housing and communications.

Dirección General de Estadística. *21 años de estadísticas dominicanas 1936–1956.* Ciudad Trujillo, 1957.—*Republica Dominicana en Cifras 1978.* Ciudad Trujillo, 1979

Official Guide to the Dominican Republic, 79–80. Tourist Information Center, Santo Domingo, 1980

Atkins, G. P., *Arms and Politics in the Dominican Republic.* London, 1981

Bell, I., *The Dominican Republic.* London, 1980

Diederich, B., *Trujillo: The Death of the Goat.* London, 1978

Wiarda, H. J., and Kryzanek, M. J., *The Dominican Republic: A Caribbean Crucible.* Boulder, 1982

ECUADOR

República del Ecuador

Capital: Quito
Population: 8·42m. (1984)
GNP per capita: US$1,180 (1981)

HISTORY. The Spaniards under Francisco Pizarro founded a colony after their victory at Cajamarca (16 Nov. 1532). Their rule was first challenged by the rising of 10 Aug. 1809. Marshal Sucre defeated the Spaniards at Pichincha in 1821, and in 1822 Bolívar persuaded the new republic to join the federation of Gran Colombia. The Presidency of Quito became the Republic of Ecuador by amicable secession 13 May 1830.

AREA AND POPULATION. Ecuador is bounded on the north by Colombia, on the east and south by Peru, on the west by the Pacific ocean. The frontier with Peru has long been a source of dispute between the two countries. The latest delimitation of it was in the treaty of Rio, 29 Jan. 1942, when, after being invaded by Peru, Ecuador lost over half her Amazonian territories. Ecuador unilaterally denounced this treaty in Sept. 1961. *See* map in THE STATESMAN'S YEAR-BOOK, 1942. Fighting between Peru and Ecuador began again in Jan. 1981 over this border issue but a ceasefire was agreed in early Feb.

No definite figure of the area of the country can yet be given, as a portion of the frontier has not been delimited. One estimate of the area of Ecuador is 270,670 sq. km, excluding the litigation zone between Peru and Ecuador, which is 190,807 sq. km.

Ecuador has 3 distinct zones: the *Sierra* or uplands of the Andes, consisting of high mountain ridges with valleys, with 2·57m. of the population and high-priced farming land; the *Costa*, the coastal plain between the Andes and the Pacific, with 2·02m., whose permanent plantations furnish bananas, cacao, coffee, sugar-cane and many other crops; the *Oriente*, the upper Amazon basin on the east, consisting of tropical jungles threaded by large rivers.

The population is predominantly of Amerindians, with small proportions of people of European or African descent.

The official language is Spanish. The Amerindians of the highlands speak mainly the Quechua language; in the Oriental Region various tribes have languages of their own.

Census population in 1982, 8,072,702. Estimate (1984) 8·42m.

The population 28 Nov. 1982 was distributed by provinces (capitals in brackets):

Provinces	*Area (sq. km)*	*Population Census 1982* [1]
Azuay (Cuenca)	7,799	440,571
Bolívar (Guaranda)	3,216	148,161
Cañar (Azogues)	2,677	180,285
Carchi (Tulcán)	3,582	128,113
Chimborazo (Riobamba)	6,161	329,922
Cotopaxi (Latacunga)	4,614	279,622
El Oro (Machala)	7,451	335,630
Esmeraldas (Esmeraldas)	15,866	247,870
Guayas (Guayaquil)	21,259	2,116,819
Imbabura (Ibarra)	4,903	244,421
Lojá (Loja)	28,900	358,558
Los Ríos (Babahoyo)	5,937	451,064
Manabí (Portoviejo)	18,963	874,803
Pichincha (Quito)	16,438	1,369,059
Tungurahua (Ambato)	3,204	328,070

[1] Provisional.

Provinces	Area (sq. km)	Population Census 1982[1]
Napo (Tena)	296,390	113,042
Pastaza (Puyo)		32,536
Morona-Santiago (Macas)		67,094
Zamora-Chinchipe (Zamora)		44,841
Colon (Galápagos)	7,844	6,201
Total	455,454	8,053,280

[1] Provisional.

There are 115 cantons, 212 urban parishes and 715 rural parishes. The chief cities (population census, 1982) are the capital, Quito (1,110,248), Guayaquil (1,300,868), Cuenca (272,397), Ambato (221,392), Portoviejo (167,070), Riobamba (149,757), Esmeraldas (141,030), Machala (117,243).

Vital statistics for calendar years: Births, (1964) 219,137, (1965) 226,436, (1966) 220,930; deaths, (1964) 58,989, (1965) 60,202, (1966) 59,618.

CLIMATE. The climate varies from equatorial, through warm temperate to mountain conditions, according to altitude. This affects temperatures and rainfall. In coastal areas, the dry season is from May to Dec., but only from June to Sept. in mountainous parts, where temperatures may be 20°F colder than on the coast. Quito Jan. 59°F (15°C), July 58°F (14·4°C). Annual rainfall 44″ (1,115 mm). Guayaquil. Jan. 79°F (26·1°C), July 75°F (23·9°C). Annual rainfall 39″ (986 mm).

CONSTITUTION AND GOVERNMENT. On 22 June 1970 President José Maria Velasco Ibarra assumed dictatorial powers, following months of strife between student and security forces. For details of governments 1963–70, *see* THE STATESMAN'S YEAR-BOOK, 1974–75, pp. 875–76. On 15 Feb. 1972 President Velasco Ibarra was deposed. A National Military Government under Gen. Guillermo Rodriguez Lara was formed and the 1945 Constitution reintroduced. President Rodriguez Lara resigned in Jan. 1976 and a military Junta assumed power until the 1979 elections. A new Constitution came into force on 10 Aug. 1979. Elections take place in May 1984.

National flag: Three horizontal stripes of yellow, blue, red, with the yellow of double width, and in the centre over all the national arms.

National anthem: Salve, oh patria! (words by J. L. Mera; tune by A. Neumann, 1866).

The following is a list of the presidents and provisional executives since 1940:

Carlos Alberto Arroyo del Rio, elected 12 Jan. 1940; resigned 30 May 1944.
Dr José María Velasco Ibarra, elected by Constituent Assembly, Aug. 1944; re-elected 11 Aug. 1946, but deposed 24 Aug. 1947.
Col. Carlos Mancheno, seized power 24 Aug. 1947; deposed 3 Sept. 1947.
Mariano Suárez Veintimilla (Vice-President), 3–15 Sept. 1947.
Carlos Julio Arosemena Tola (provisional), 15 Sept. 1947–31 Aug. 1948.
Galo Plaza Lasso, 1 Sept. 1948–31 Aug. 1952.
Dr José María Velasco Ibarra, 1 Sept. 1952–31 Aug. 1956.
Dr Camilo Ponce Enríquez, 1 Sept. 1956–31 Aug. 1960.
Dr José María Velasco Ibarra, 1 Sept. 1960–8 Nov. 1961 (withdrew).
Dr Carlos Julio Arosemena Monroy, 8 Nov. 1961–11 July 1963 (deposed).
Military Junta, 11 July 1963–31 March 1966.
Clemente Yerovi Indaburu, 31 March–16 Nov. 1966 (interim).
Dr Otto Arosemena Gómez, 17 Nov. 1966–1 Sept. 1968.
Dr José María Velasco Ibarra, 1 Sept. 1968–15 Feb. 1972 (deposed).
Gen. Guillermo Rodriguez Lara, 16 Feb. 1972–11 Jan. 1976 (resigned).
Adm. Alfredo Poveda Burbano, 11 Jan. 1976–10 Aug. 1979.
Jaime Roldós Aguilera, 10 Aug. 1979–24 May 1981.
Osvaldo Hurtado Larrea, 24 May 1981–10 Aug. 1984.

President: León Febres Cordero (sworn in on 10 Aug. 1984).

The Cabinet in Jan. 1984 was as follows:

Vice-President and President of the National Development Council: Léon Roldós Aguilera. *Administration:* Vladimiro Alvarez. *Foreign Affairs:* Dr Luis Valencia. *Social Welfare:* Alfredo Mancero. *Public Finance:* Pedro Pinto. *Education and Culture:* Dr Ernesto Albán. *Health:* Dr Luis Sarrazín. *Natural Resources and Energy:* Gustavo Galindo. *Labour:* Dr Jamil Mahauat. *Industry, Trade and Integration:* José Bermeo. *Public Works:* Edwin Ripalda. *Agriculture:* Fausto Jordán. *National Defence:* Jorge Arciniegas. *Secretary-General of Administration:* Andrés Crespo. *Secretary of Administration:* Ramiro Rivera. *President of the Central Bank:* Abelardo Pachano B.

Local Government. The country is divided politically into 20 provinces; 4 of them comprise the 'Región Oriental' and one the Archipelago of Galápagos, officially called 'Colón', situated in the Pacific ocean about 600 miles to the west of Ecuador and comprising 15 islands. The provinces are administered by governors, appointed by the Government; their sub-divisions, or cantons, by political chiefs and elected cantonal councillors; and the parishes by political lieutenants. The Galápagos Archipelago is administered by the Ministry of National Defence.

DEFENCE. Military service is selective, with a 2-year period of conscription. The country is divided into 4 military zones, with headquarters at Quito, Guayaquil, Cuenca and Pastaza.

Army. The Army consists of 9 infantry, 2 armoured and 1 parachute brigade. Strength (1985) 27,500, with about 50,000 reservists. Equipment includes 45 American M-3 and 150 French AMX-13 light tanks.

Navy. The Navy consists of 2 Federal Republic of Germany-built diesel-electric powered patrol submarines; 1 old *ex*-US destroyer (completed in 1946), 1 old frigate (*ex*-US destroyer escort transport, built in 1943), 6 Italian-built new corvettes, 6 fast missile boats, 7 coastal patrol craft, 1 landing ship, 2 medium landing ships, 1 supply ship, 3 survey vessels, 16 coastguard service craft, 1 repair vessel, 2 training ships, 1 floating dock and 6 tugs. Naval personnel in 1985 totalled 3,800 officers and men. There are 16 Coast Guard cutters.

Air Force. The Air Force, formed with Italian assistance in 1920, was reorganized and re-equipped with US aircraft after Ecuador signed the Rio Pact of Mutual Defence in 1947 but latest equipment acquired from Europe and Brazil. Current strength of about 4,800 personnel and 52 combat aircraft includes a strike squadron equipped with 10 single-seat and 2 two-seat Jaguars; an interceptor squadron of 15 single-seat and 2 two-seat Mirage F.1s; a bomber squadron with 3 Canberra B.6s; 2 counter-insurgency units equipped with 11 Cessna A-37B and 12 Strikemaster light jet attack and training aircraft, 1 squadron with 1 piston-engined DC-6 and 2 C-130, 2 Buffalo and 4 HS 748 turboprop transports; Alouette III, SA 330 Puma and SA 315B Lama helicopters; and Cessna 150, T-33, T-34C-1 and T-41A/D trainers; 14 EMB-326 Xavante light jet attack/trainers were acquired from Brazil in 1982. Many other transports are operated by the military airline TAME.

INTERNATIONAL RELATIONS

Membership. Ecuador is a member of UN, OAS and LAIA (formerly LAFTA).

ECONOMY

Budget. Estimated revenue in 1983 was 71,000m. sucres and expenditure, 81,200m. sucres.

Net international reserves, 31 Dec. 1983, were US$600m.

Currency. The monetary unit is the *sucre*, divided into 100 *centavos*. In circulation are a pure nickel 1-sucre and copper-nickel and copper-zinc 50-, 20-, 10- and 5-centavo pieces. The currency consists mainly of the notes of the Central Bank in denominations of 5, 10, 20, 50, 100, 500 and 1,000 sucres. In March 1985, US$1 = 95·75; £1 = 129·20.

Banking. The Central Bank of Ecuador, at Quito, with a capital of 20m. sucres, is modelled after the Federal Reserve Banks of US: through branches opened in 12 towns it now deals in mortgage bonds. All commercial banks must be affiliated to the Central Bank. The Bank of London and Montreal, Ltd, had branches in Quito and Guayaquil.

Weights and Measures. By a law of 6 Dec. 1856 the metric system was made the legal standard but the Spanish measures are in general use. The quintal is equivalent to 101·4 lb.

The meridian of Quito has been adopted as the official time.

ENERGY AND NATURAL RESOURCES

Electricity. In 1982, total capacity of hydraulic and thermal plants was 990,000 kw. Estimated output was 2,000m. kwh.

Oil. Production of crude petroleum in 1982 was 77·1m. bbls; 1983, 86m. New drilling along the coast has had some success, but Ecuador has to import some crude oil. Proven oil reserves (1981, estimate) 1,100m. bbls.

Gas. In 1982, natural gas production was 400,257·9m. cu. ft.

Minerals. Production (1980): Silver, 24,000 troy oz; gold, 3,344 troy oz; copper, 723,000 kg; zinc, 330,000 kg.

The country has some copper, iron and lead. There are coal deposits in the Biblián area, but their exploitation has so far proved uneconomic.

Agriculture. Ecuador is divided into two agricultural zones: the coast and lower river valleys, where tropical farming is carried on in an average temperature of from 18° to 25° C.; and the Andean highlands with a temperate climate, adapted to grazing, dairying and the production of cereals, potatoes, pyrethrum and vegetables suitable to temperate climes. Some wheat has to be imported.

124,000 acres of rich virgin land in the Santo Domingo de los Colorados area has been set aside for settlement of smallholders.

Excepting the two agricultural zones and a few arid spots on the Pacific coast, Ecuador is a vast forest. Roughly estimated, 10,000 sq. miles on the Pacific slope extending from the sea to an altitude of 5,000 ft on the Andes, and the Amazon Basin below the same level containing 80,000 sq. miles, nearly all virgin forest, are rich in valuable timber, but much of it is still not commercially accessible.

The staple export products are bananas, cacao and coffee. Main crops, in 1,000 tonnes, in 1982: Rice, 384; potatoes, 416; maize, 324; coffee, 84; barley, 35; cocoa, 97; bananas, 2,752.

Livestock (1982): Cattle, 3m.; sheep, 2·35m.; pigs, 3·6m.; horses, 303,000; poultry, 42m.

Forestry. In 1981, 4·5m. cu. metres of timber were cut. Exports approximately US$10m. per annum.

Fisheries. Fisheries and fish product exports were valued at US$91,823,000 in 1980 (31,717 tonnes).

INDUSTRY AND TRADE

Industry. Production in 1978: Sugar, 178,000 tonnes; beer, 1,560,000 hectolitres; cement 1·06m. tonnes.

Commerce. Imports and exports for calendar years, in US$1m.:

	1979	*1980*	*1981*	*1982*	*1983*
Imports (c.i.f.)	1,986	2,250	2,246	1,988	1,300
Exports (f.o.b.)	2,173	2,506	2,541	2,140	2,199

Of the total exports (1982); petroleum, US$1,184,218m.; bananas, US$213,297m.; cocoa, US$63,064m.; coffee, US$138,758m.

USA furnished 35% of imports in 1970 and took 43% of thc exports.

Total trade between Ecuador and UK (British Department of Trade returns, in £1,000 sterling):

	1980	*1981*	*1982*	*1983*	*1984*
Imports to UK	8,844	5,050	9,288	11,022	12,951
Exports and re-exports from UK	30,930	34,149	60,792	35,008	34,323

Tourism. There were 239,000 visitors in 1981, mainly from South American countries, spending US$131m.

COMMUNICATIONS

Roads. In 1981, there were 32,185 km of roads of all types in this mountainous country, but most are narrow and subject to landslides. A trunk highway through the coastal plain is under construction which will link Machala in the extreme south-west with Esmeraldas in the north-west and with Quito and the northern section of the Pan-American Highway. In 1981, there were 232,600 cars and 23,900 commercial vehicles.

Railways. A 1,067 mm gauge line runs from São Lorenzo through Quito to Guayaquil and Cuenca, total 971 km.

Aviation. There are 2 international airports. The following international lines operate: Air France, Avianca, Eastern, British Caledonian, Ecuatoriana de Aviación, KLM, Lufthansa, Iberia, LAN Chile, and Aerovías Peruanas. They connect Quito with Panama, Bogotá (Colombia), Guayaquil, New York and Europe. All the leading towns are connected by an almost daily service, but landing fields are small.

Shipping. Ecuador has 7 seaports, of which Guayaquil is the chief. The merchant navy comprises 39,964 tons of seagoing and 21,232 tons of river craft. In 1970 ships totalling 8·88m. GRT entered Ecuadorean ports, unloading 1·52m. tons, and loading 1·77m. tons.

There is river communication, improved by dredging, throughout the principal agricultural districts on the low ground to the west of the Cordillera by the rivers Guayas, Daule and Vinces (navigable for 200 miles by river steamers in the rainy season).

Post and Broadcasting. Quito is connected by telegraph with Colombia and Peru, and by cable with the rest of the world. The main towns in the country are connected by radio-telephone. There are over 300 radio stations.

In 1982 there were 290,200 telephones in use, 109,600 in Quito and 109,200 in Guayaquil; most were operated by the Government; 99% were automatic. Television was inaugurated in 1960 in Guayaquil, in 1961 in Quito and in 1967 in Cuenca. In 1980 there were 1·8m. radio receivers and 1·3m. television receivers.

Cinemas. (1974). Cinemas numbered about 185 with total seating capacity of 114,600.

Newspapers (1984). There were 22 daily newspapers with an aggregate daily circulation of 526,000; 7 papers in Quito and Guayaquil have the bulk of the circulation.

JUSTICE, RELIGION, EDUCATION AND WELFARE

Justice. The Supreme Court in Quito is the highest tribunal and consists of 5 justices and the Minister Fiscal. Of the 15 superior courts, 4 are composed of 6 judges and 11 of 3 judges each. There are numerous lower courts. The popular jury was abolished in 1928, and criminal cases are heard before a 'special jury' consisting of 1 judge and 3 members of the Ecuadorean bar, appointed annually by the superior courts. Capital punishment and all forms of torture are prohibited under the constitution, as are imprisonment for debt and contracts involving personal servitude or slavery. Substantial amendments expediting judicial procedure were introduced in 1936, and salaries for all judicial officials replaced remuneration by fees.

Religion. The state recognizes no religion and grants freedom of worship to all. Civil registration of births, deaths and marriages is obligatory. Divorce is permitted. Illegitimate children have the same rights as legitimate ones with respect to education and inheritance.

Education. Primary education is free and in principle obligatory. Private schools, both primary and secondary, are under some state supervision. There were (1979–80), primary schools with 1·4m. pupils; secondary schools with 535,000 pupils and universities with 230,637 students.

Social Welfare. From 1 May 1964 social benefits are extended to professional men, artisans and domestic workers; and to agricultural workers from 1 May 1965. The Ministry of Social Welfare and Labour was in 1967 divided into the Ministries of Social Welfare and of Public Health. In 1970 there were 199 hospitals with 14,024 beds.

DIPLOMATIC REPRESENTATIVES

Of Ecuador in Great Britain (3 Hans Crescent, London, SW1X 0LS)
Ambassador: Dr Mauricio Gándara.

Of Great Britain in Ecuador (Calle Gonzalez Suarez 111, Quito)
Ambassador: A. C. Buxton, CMG.

Of Ecuador in the USA (2535 15th St., NW, Washington, D.C., 20009)
Ambassador: Rafael Garcia-Velasco.

Of the USA in Ecuador (120 Avenida Patria, Quito)
Ambassador: Samuel F. Hart.

Of Ecuador to the United Nations
Ambassador: Dr Miguel A. Albornoz.

Books of Reference

Anuario de Legislación Ecuatoriana. Quito. Annual
Boletín del Banco Central. Quito
Boletín General de Estadistica. Tri-monthly
Boletín Mensual del Ministerio de Obras Públicas. Monthly
Informes Ministeriales. Quito. Annual
Bibliografia Nacional, 1756–1941. Quito, 1942
Invest in Ecuador. Banco Central del Ecuador, Quito, 1980
Buitrón, A., and Collier, Jr, J., *The Awakening Valley: Study of the Otavalo Indians.* New York, 1950
Cueva, A., *The Process of Political Domination in Ecuador.* London, 1982
Martz, J. D., *Ecuador: Conflicting Political Culture and the Quest for Progress.* Boston, 1972
Middleton, A., *Class, Power and the Distribution of Credit in Ecuador.* Glasgow, 1981

EGYPT

Jumhuriyat Misr al-Arabiya

Capital: Cairo
Population: 46m. (1984)
GNP per capita: US$650 (1981)

HISTORY. Part of the Ottoman Empire from 1517 until Dec. 1914 when it became a British protectorate, Egypt became an independent monarchy on 28 Feb. 1922. Following a revolution on 23 July 1952, a Republic was proclaimed on 18 June 1953. Egypt merged with Syria on 22 Feb. 1958 to form the United Arab Republic, retaining that name when Syria broke away from the union on 28 Sept. 1961, finally re-adopting the name of Egypt on 2 Sept. 1971.

AREA AND POPULATION. Egypt is bounded east by Israel, the Gulf of Aqaba and the Red Sea, south by Sudan, west by Libya and north by the Mediterranean. The total area is 1,002,000 sq. km (386,900 sq. miles), but the cultivated and settled area, that is, the Nile valley, delta and oases, covers only about 35,580 sq. km.

The area, population (1976 Census) and capitals of the governerates are:

Governorate	*Sq. km*	*1976 census*	*Capital*
Sinai	60,714	10,104	Al-Arish
Suez	17,840	194,001	Suez
Ismailia	1,442	351,889	Ismailia
Port Said	72	262,620	Port Said
Sharqîya	4,180	2,621,208	Zagazig
Daqahlîya	3,471	2,732,756	Mansûra
Damietta	589	557,115	Damietta
Kafr el-Sheikh	3,437	1,403,468	Kafr el-Sheikh
Alexandria	2,679	2,318,655	Alexandria
Behera	4,589	2,517,292	Damanhur
Gharbîya	1,942	2,294,303	Tanta
Menûfiya	1,612	1,710,982	Shibin el-Kom
Qalyûbîya	971	1,674,006	Benha
Cairo	214	5,084,463	Cairo
Gîza	1,010	2,419,247	Gîza
Faiyûm	1,827	1,140,245	Faiyûm
Beni Suef	1,322	1,108,615	Beni-Suef
Minya	2,262	2,055,739	Minya
Asyût	1,530	1,695,378	Asyût
Sohag	1,547	1,924,960	Sohag
Qena	1,851	1,705,594	Qena
Aswân	679	619,932	Aswân
al-Bahr al-Ahmar	203,685	56,191	Al-Ghurdaqah
al-Wadi al Jadid	376,505	84,645	Al-Kharijah
Mersa Matruh	298,735	112,772	Matruh
Total		36,656,180	

The principal towns, with their census 1976 populations, are:

Cairo	5,074,016	Mansûra	257,866	Minya	146,423
Alexandria	2,317,705	Asyût	213,983	Ismailia	145,978
Gîza	1,246,713	Zagazig	202,637	Aswân	144,377
Shubra el-Khema	393,700	Suez	193,965	Beni-Suef	118,148
Mahalla el-Kubra	292,853	Damanhûr	188,927	Shibin el-Kom	102,840
Tanta	284,636	Faiyûm	167,081	Sohag	101,758
Port Said	262,760	Kafr el-Dwar	160,554		

Population (1984) 46m. and of Greater Cairo (1979) 8.54m. The 1976 census total excluded an estimated 1,572,000 nationals living abroad.

CLIMATE. The climate is mainly dry, but there are winter rains along the

Mediterranean coast. Elsewhere, rainfall is very low and erratic in its distribution. Winter temperatures are everywhere comfortable, but summer temperatures are very high, especially in the south. Cairo. Jan. 56°F (13·3°C), July 83°F (28·3°C). Annual rainfall 1·2″ (28 mm). Alexandria. Jan. 58°F (14·4°C), July 79°F (26·1°C). Annual rainfall 7″ (178 mm). Aswan. Jan. 62°F (16·7°C), July 92°F (33·3°C). Annual rainfall trace. Giza. Jan. 55°F (12·8°C), July 78°F (25·6°C). Annual rainfall 16″ (389 mm). Ismailia. Jan. 56°F (13·3°C), July 84°F (28·9°C). Annual rainfall 1·5″ (37 mm). Luxor. Jan. 59°F (15°C), July 86°F (30°C). Annual rainfall trace. Port Said. Jan. 58°F (14·4°C), July 78°F (27·2°C). Annual rainfall 3″ (76 mm).

CONSTITUTION AND GOVERNMENT. The Constitution was approved by referendum on 11 Sept. 1971. It defines Egypt as 'an Arab Republic with a democratic, socialist system' and the Eyptian people as 'part of the Arab nation' with Islam as the state religion and Arabic as the official language.

The President of the Republic is nominated by the People's Assembly and confirmed by plebiscite for a 6-year term. He is the supreme commander of the armed forces and presides over the defence council.

Presidents since the establishment of the Republic have been:

Gen. Mohamed Neguib, 18 June 1953–14 Nov. 1954 (deposed).
Col. Gamal Abdel Nasser, 14 Nov. 1954–28 Sept. 1970 (died).
Col. Mumammad Anwar Sadat, 28 Sept. 1970–6 Oct. 1981 (assassinated).
Lieut.-Gen. Muhammad Hosni Mubarak, 7 Oct. 1981–.

The People's Assembly is a unicameral legislature consisting of 458 members directly elected for a 5-year term; the President of the Republic may appoint up to 10 additional members. At the general elections held in May 1984, the National Democratic Party gained 390 seats and the New *Wafd* Party 58.

The President may appoint one or more Vice-Presidents, and appoints a Prime Minister and a Council of Ministers, whom he may remove as he wishes.

President of the Republic: Hosni Mubarak.

The Council of Ministers in Jan. 1985 was composed as follows:

Prime Minister: Gen. Kamel Hassan Ali.

Deputy Prime Minister and Minister of Education and Scientific Research: Dr Mustapha Kamal Hilmi. *Deputy Prime Minister and Minister of Defence and War Production:* Mohammed Abdel-Karim Abu Ghazalah. *Foreign Affairs:* Dr Ahmed Esmat Abdel Meguid. *Finance:* Dr Mohammed Salaheddin Hamid. *Social Insurance and Social Affairs:* Dr Amal Abd ar-Rahim Osman. *Reconstruction, New Societies and Land Reclamation:* Hasaballah Mohammed al-Kafrawi. *Manpower and Training:* Saad Mohammed Ahmad. *Justice:* Mamdouh Atteya. *Transport, Communications and Maritime Transport:* Soleiman Metwali Soleiman. *Electricity and Energy:* Mohammed Mahir Osman Abazah. *Culture:* Mohammed Abdel Hamid Radwan. *Information:* Sawfat Sharif. *Health:* Dr Mohammed Sabri Zaki. *Planning and International Co-operation:* Dr Kamal Ahmed Ganzouri. *Local Government:* Gen. Hassan Soliman Abu Basha. *Agriculture and Food Sufficiency:* Dr Yusuf Amin Wali. *Tourism and Civil Aviation:* Dr Waguih Shindy. *Economy and Foreign Trade:* Dr Mustapha Kamal as-Said. *People's Assembly and Shura Affairs:* Tewfik Abu Ismail. *Supply and Internal Trade:* Mohammed Nagi-Shatlah. *Interior:* Ahmad Rushdi. *Irrigation:* Isam Radi Abdul Hamid Radi. *Industry:* Mohammed Mahmud Faraj Abdul Wahab. *Petroleum and Mineral Resources:* Abdul Hadi Mohammed Qandil. *Cabinet Affairs and Administrative Development:* Dr Atif Mohammed Mohammed Ubayd. *Education:* Dr Abdessalam Abdul Kadir Abdul Ghaffer. *Housing and Utilities:* Abdul Fattah Sidqi. *Waqfs (Religious Trusts):* Dr Mohammed al-Ahmadi Abu an-Nur. There are 3 Ministers of State.

National flag: Three horizontal stripes of red, white, black, with the national emblem in the centre in gold.

Local Government. There are 26 governorates: 16 provinces, 5 cities and 4 frontier districts.

DEFENCE. Conscription is for 3 years, between the ages of 20 and 35.

Army. The Army comprises 3 armoured, 5 mechanized infantry, and 4 infantry divisions; 2 Republican Guard, 2 independent armoured, 9 independent infantry, 2 airmobile, 1 parachute, 12 artillery, 2 heavy mortar, and 6 anti-tank guided weapon brigades; 7 commando groups; and 2 surface-to-surface missile regiments. Strength (1985) 315,000 (180,000 conscripts) and about 300,000 reservists. Equipment includes 800 T-54/-55, 600 T-62 and 350 AM-60 tanks. There are also paramilitary forces of about 139,000.

Navy. There are 14 elderly diesel-driven *ex*-Soviet and *ex*-Chinese submarines (most nearing the end of their hull lives and of which little more than half can be operational – 4 having been used for spares and several under refit), 5 old destroyers, 2 new Spanish-built frigates, 3 very old frigates, 24 missile boats, 33 torpedo boats, 2 fast attack craft, 6 new patrol gunboats, 12 submarine chasers, 10 fleet minesweepers, 2 inshore minesweepers, 3 medium landing ships, 14 landing craft, 10 minor landing craft, 2 survey vessels, 10 service craft, 2 tenders, 3 hovercraft, 1 large training ship (*ex*-Royal Yacht), 7 auxiliaries and 4 tugs. There are 65 Coast Guard cutters.

Naval bases are at Alexandria, Port Said, Mersa Matru, Port Tewfik, Hurghada and Safaqa. The Naval Academy is at Abu Qir.

Naval personnel in 1985 exceeded 20,000 officers and men, including the Coastguard, but not reserves of about 15,000.

Air Force. Until 1979, the Air Force was equipped largely with aircraft of USSR design, but subsequent re-equipment involves aircraft bought in the West, as well as some supplied by China. Strength (1985) is about 30,000 personnel and 500 combat aircraft, of which the interceptors are operated by an independent Air Defence Command, in conjunction with many 'Guideline', 'Goa', 'Gainful', Hawk and Crotale missile batteries. There are about 16 Tu-16 twin-jet strategic bombers, some equipped to carry 'Kelt' air-to-surface missiles. The strike force includes 10 Il-28 twin-jet bombers, and about 50 Su-7B and 20 Su-20 supersonic fighter-bombers. Other interceptor/ground attack fighter divisions are equipped with 64 F-16 Fighting Falcons, 75 Mirage 5s, 35 F-4E Phantoms, 50 F-6s (Chinese built MiG-19s), and more than 120 MiG-21s, with 34 F-7s (Chinese-built MiG-21s) being delivered for assembly in Egypt (some for Iraq). Transport units have 21 C-130H Hercules turboprop heavy freighters, 10 twin-turboprop Buffaloes and up to 175 Gazelle, Mi-4, Mi-6, Mi-8, Sea King/Commando and Agusta-built CH-47C helicopters; some Commando helicopters and 2 EC-130H Hercules are equipped for electronic warfare duties. Training units are equipped with Gomhouria piston-engined trainers, Czech-built L-29 Delfin jet trainers, single-seat and two-seat versions of the MiG-15, MiG-17s, two-seat FT-6s, Mirage IIIs, MiG-21Us and Su-7Us, and Gazelle helicopters. Delivery has begun of 45 Alpha Jets, of which 15 are equipped for close air support duties, to replace MiG-17s, MiG-15s and L-29s. On order for mid-80s delivery are 2 (of a planned force of 4) E-2C Hawkeye AWACS aircraft. Main aircrew training centre is the EAF Academy at Bilbeis.

INTERNATIONAL RELATIONS

Membership. Egypt is a member of UN, OAU, the Arab League and OAPEC.

ECONOMY

Planning. A 5-year development plan runs 1982/83–1986/87 and provides for investments totalling £E35,000m.

Budget. Ordinary revenue and expenditure for fiscal years ending 30 June, in £E1m.:

	1980–81	*1981–82*
Revenue	5,970	7,890
Expenditure	5,700	7,150

Currency. By decree of 18 Oct. 1916 (20 Zi-El-Higga 1934), the monetary unit of Egypt is the gold Egyptian pound of 100 *piastres* of 1,000 *millièmes.* Coins in circulation are 20, 10, 5, 2 piastres (silver); 2, 1 piastre, 5 millièmes, 1 millième (bronze). Gold coins are no longer in circulation. Silver coin is legal tender only up to £E1, and bronze coins up to 10 piastres. The Treasury issues 5- and 10-piastre currency notes. Bank-notes are issued by the National Bank in denominations of 5, 10, 25 and 50 piastres, £E1, 5, 10, 20, and 100.

In March 1985, £1 sterling = £E1·23; US$ = £E1·83.

Banking. On 18 Aug. 1960 a Central Bank of Egypt was established by decree. It manages the note issue, the Government's banking operations and the control of commercial banks. At the same date the National Bank founded in 1898 ceased to be the central bank and became a purely commercial bank. In 1981, 79 foreign and private banks were authorized to deal.

Weights and Measures. In 1951 the metric system was made official with the exception of the feddân and its subdivisions.

Capacity. Kadah = 1/96th ardeb = 3·36 pints. *Rob* = 4 kadahs = 1·815 gallons. *Keila* = 8 kadahs = 3·63 gallons. *Ardeb* = 96 kadahs = 43·555 gallons, or 5·44439 bu., or 198 cu. decimetres.

Weights. Rotl = 144 dirhems = 0·9905 lb. *Oke* = 400 dirhems = 2·75137 lb. *Qantâr* or 100 rotls or 36 okes = 99·0493 lb. 1 *Qantâr* of unginned cotton = 315 lb. 1 *Qantâr* of ginned cotton = 99·05 lb. The approximate weight of the ardeb is as follows: Wheat, 150 kg; beans, 155 kg; barley, 120 kg; maize, 140 kg; cotton seed, 121 kg.

Surface. Feddân, the unit of measure for land = 4,200·8 sq. metres = 7,468·148 sq. pics = 1·03805 acres. 1 sq. pic = 6·0547 sq. ft = 0·5625 sq. metre.

ENERGY AND NATURAL RESOURCES

Electricity. Electricity generated in 1980 was 18,500m. kwh.

Oil. The first commercial discovery of oil in the Middle East outside Iran was made in Egypt in 1909, but production long remained low and often insufficient to meet Egypt's domestic requirements. In 1979 production was rising again and with the newly-regained Sinai oilfields was 25·5m. tonnes. Policy is controlled by the Egyptian General Petroleum Corporation (EGPC) a wholly state-owned corporation answerable to the Minister of Petroleum. EGPC is whole or part-owner of the various production and refining companies and controls supplies to the domestic marketing companies.

In 1983, 36m. tonnes of crude petroleum.

Minerals. Production (1973 in tonnes): Phosphate rock (1980), 658,000; iron ore, 656,000; marine salt, 454,000.

Agriculture. Rain seldom falls in Upper Egypt, and only at irregular intervals in Cairo, where the average for the year is no more than 1·2 in. At Alexandria the average is 8 in.

The cultivated area of Egypt proper was estimated in 1981 at 6·3m. feddâns (1 feddân = 1·038 acres) and of this (1971), 4,869,000 feddâns were under winter crops, 5,012,000 under summer crops and 613,000 under Nile crops.

Irrigation occupies a predominant place in the economic development of the country. The Aswân reservoir can now hold up to 5,500m. cu. metres of water, and the Gebel Aulia reservoir, completed in 1937, holds 2,000m. cu. metres. Barrages have been erected at Nag' Hammâdi, Asyût and Zifta, and at the bifurcation of the Nile below Cairo. Esna, Nag' Hammâdi barrage, completed in 1930, ensures full basin supplies even in low flood to Girga province, and will facilitate perennial irrigation when basin lands are converted. Asyût barrage, having been remodelled, will meet the greater demands of the area it now commands. The Esna barrage now secures basin irrigation to lands in Qena province. New barrages (Mohamed Ali barrages) have been completed at the bifurcation of the Nile below Cairo to replace the existing structures which, built in 1861, are now unable to meet the conditions following the increase in summer supplies, the reclamation of large areas of waste lands and the earlier watering of food crops.

On 8 Nov. 1959 the United Arab Republic and Sudan concluded agreements on the sharing of the Nile waters (after construction of the Aswân High Dam), and trade, payments and Customs dues. The agreement provides that from the time the High Dam started to store water (15 May 1964) Sudan will be entitled to 18,500m. cu. metres of the total annual flow and Egypt to 55,500m.

In 1982 the area (1,000 hectares) and production (1,000 tonnes) were: Wheat, 577(2,017); barley, 45(122); beans (dry), 7(13); lentils, 5(6); onions, 21(657); maize, 817(2,709); millet, 174(633); sugar-cane, 108(8,700).

The rice crop was 2·3m. tonnes in 1977.

Livestock (1983): 1,826,000 cattle, 2,393,000 buffaloes, 1,394,000 sheep, 1,498,000 goats, 80,000 camels and 15,000 pigs.

Fisheries. The catch of the Egyptian sea, Nile and lake fisheries in 1981 amounted to 138,500 tonnes.

INDUSTRY AND TRADE

Industry. In 1979 there were 1·5m. Egyptians employed in manufacturing. Production in 1981–82 included 690,000 tonnes of crude steel, 4m. tonnes of nitrogenous fertilizers and 4m. tonnes of cement.

Trade Unions. Trade unions were first recognized in 1942. In 1952 the acts concerning trade unions, individual contracts, and conciliation and arbitration were recast. Employment exchanges and unemployment statistics were introduced in 1953. Social insurance was enacted in 1955.

Commerce. Imports and exports for 5 years (in £E1,000):

	1978	*1979*	*1980*	*1981*	*1982*
Imports	2,632,180	2,686,200	3,092,600	5,588,500	5,776,800
Exports	679,754	1,287,800	2,132,800	2,263,000	2,184,100

In 1979, raw cotton and cotton products represented 34% of total exports, crude oil 31% and petroleum products 11%; 27% of exports went to Italy, 8% to the USSR and 8% to the Netherlands; 18% of imports came from the USA, 11% from Federal Republic of Germany.

Total trade between Egypt and UK (British Department of Trade returns, in £1,000 sterling):

	1980	*1981*	*1982*	*1983*	*1984*
Imports to UK	336,595	414,599	412,802	79,826	164,946
Exports and re-exports from UK	346,688	325,141	338,645	370,489	427,688

Tourism. In 1983 there were 1·5m. tourists spending US$600m.

COMMUNICATIONS

Roads. In 1980, the total length of roads was 21,637 km, of which 16,182 km were paved. Motor vehicles, in 1981, 580,000 private cars, 165,000 commercial vehicles (including buses).

Railways. In 1982 there were 4,321 km of state railways (1,435 mm gauge) which carried 486m. passengers and 7·5m. tonnes of freight.

Aviation. There is an international airport at Cairo. The national airline Egyptair operates scheduled flights connecting Cairo with Athens, Rome, Frankfurt, Zürich, London, Khartoum, Tōkyō, Bombay, Aden, Jeddah, Doha, Dharan, Kuwait, Beirut, Baghdad, Tripoli, Benghazi, Algiers, Entebbe, Nairobi, Dar-es-Salaam, Kano, Lagos, Accra, Abidjan, Damascus, Amman, Manilla, Paris, Munich, Copenhagen, Nicosia, Karachi, Aleppo, Bahrain, Abu Dhabi, Dubai, Sharjah, Sanaa and Vienna. In addition, Egyptair operates scheduled flights on a widespread domestic network connecting Cairo with Port Said, Mersa Matruh, Asyût, Luxor, Aswân. In 1982, 62,000 tonnes of cargo were carried.

Shipping. The Egyptian merchant navy in 1980 consisted of 75 steamers of 387,460 tons.

In 1977, 3,050 ships of 11,432,000 tons entered the port of Alexandria and 876 ships of 4,583,000 tons entered Port Said.

Suez Canal. The Suez Canal was opened for navigation on 17 Nov. 1869. By the convention of Constantinople of 29 Oct. 1888 the canal is open to vessels of all nations and is free from blockade, except in time of war, but the UAR Government did not allow Israeli ships to use the canal until May 1979, when the embargo was lifted. It is 173 km long (excluding 11 km of approach channels to the harbours), connecting the Mediterranean with the Red Sea. Its minimum width is 197 ft at a depth of 33 ft, and its depth permits the passage of vessels up to 38 ft draught.

In 1976 a 2-stage development project was started. The first stage which was completed in 1980 allowing vessels, of up to 150,000 tons, fully loaded, and up to 370,000 tons in ballast to pass through the canal and give a draught of 53 ft.

During the war with Israel in June 1967 the Canal was blocked. The canal was cleared and re-opened to shipping on 5 June 1975. This is part of a programme to develop and rebuild the whole area of Suez to make it one of the largest tax-free industrial zones. Canal toll fees reached £621·8m. in 1981, and in 1980 21,603 vessels (281·3m. tons) went through the canal.

On 1 Jan. 1981 charges were increased by 30%. The first tunnel below the canal, located 10 miles north of Suez City, was completed on 30 April 1980.

Marlow, J., *The Making of the Suez Canal.* London, 1964

Post and Broadcasting. There were, in 1980–81, 1,821 postal agencies, 1,812 mobile offices (1978), 1,747 government and 2,956 private post offices. Number of telephones in 1982, 521,625. Number of wireless licences in 1982, 12m. and 6m. TV licences.

The internal telecommunications system is owned and operated by the Telecommunications Organization. Government landlines connect with those of the Gaza sector and the Sudan.

Cinemas (1971). There were 152 cinemas with a seating capacity of 140,900.

Newspapers. In 1984 there were 11 dailies published in Cairo and 6 in Alexandria.

JUSTICE, RELIGION, EDUCATION AND WELFARE

Justice. The National Courts in 1981 were as follows: Court of Cassation with a bench of 5 judges which constitutes the highest court of appeal in both criminal and civil cases; Courts of Appeal with 3 judges situated in Cairo and 4 other cities; Assize Courts with 3 judges which deal with all cases of serious crime; Central Tribunals with 3 judges which deal with ordinary civil and commercial cases; Summary Tribunals presided over by a single judge which hear civil disputes in matters up to the value of £E3,250, and criminal offences punishable by a fine or imprisonment of up to 3 years.

Religion. In 1947 the population (excluding Nomads) consisted of 17,397,946 Moslems (91·46%); 1,186,353 Orthodox Copts; 86,918 Protestant Copts; 72,764 Roman Catholic Copts; 89,062 other Orthodox; 50,200 other Roman Catholics; 16,338 other Protestants; 1,547 Jews, other and unknown.

There are in Egypt large numbers of native Christians connected with the various Oriental Churches; of these, the largest and most influential are the Copts, who adopted Christianity in the 1st century. Their head is the Coptic Patriarch. There are 25 metropolitans and bishops in Egypt; 4 metropolitans for Ethiopia, Jerusalem, Khartoum and Omdurman, and 12 bishops in Ethiopia. Priests must be married before ordination, but celibacy is imposed on monks and high dignitaries. The Copts use the Diocletian (or Martyrs') calendar, which begins in A.D. 284.

Education. Education was made compulsory for all children between the ages of 6 and 12 in 1933; primary education (6 years) was made free in 1944, secondary and technical education in 1950. Compulsory education is provided in primary schools (6 years).

In 1981–82 there were 4·48m. primary school pupils and (1978–79) 127,021 teachers; 1·56m. secondary school pupils and (1978–79) 67,567 teachers; and 568,000 technical school pupils with (1978–79) 29,353 teachers. Teacher-training colleges had 40,595 students and 3,373 teaching staff in 1978–79.

There are 18 universities in Egypt. Cairo University, founded in 1908 as a private institution and taken over by the Government in 1925; Alexandria University, founded by the Government in 1942; the Ein Shams University, founded by the Government in Cairo in 1950 and universities at Asyût Al-Azhar, Tanta, Mansûra, Zagazig, Helwan, Suez Canal, Minya and Menoufia. Education is free at universities depending entirely on grades achieved. The number of students at universities was 476,537 in 1977–78.

Health. In 1983–84 there were about 73,300 doctors and 85,350 hospital beds.

DIPLOMATIC REPRESENTATIVES

Of Egypt in Great Britain (26 South St., London, W1Y 8EL)
Ambassador: Yousef Sharara (accredited 29 Nov. 1984).

Of Great Britain in Egypt (Ahmed Ragheb St., Garden City, Cairo)
Ambassador: Sir Alan Urwick, KCMG.

Of Egypt in the USA (2310 Decatur Pl., NW, Washington, D.C., 20008)
Ambassador: Dr Ashraf A. Ghorbal.

Of the USA in Egypt (5 Sharia Latin America, Cairo)
Ambassador: Nicholas Veliotes.

Of Egypt to the United Nations
Ambassador: Ahmed Tawfik Khalil.

Books of Reference

Statistical Information: The Department of Statistics and Census (15, Sharia Mansour, Cairo) was formed in 1905. *Chief:* Under Secretary of State for Statistical Affairs, Dr Hasan M. Husein. Previously, various government departments had their own statistical sections. Estimates of population were made in 1800, 1821 and 1846; the first census took place in 1873. Among the publications of the Department are the following: *Annuaire Statistique* (Arabic and French). *Annual Return of Shipping* (Arabic and English). *Monthly Summary and Annual Statement of Foreign Trade* (Arabic and English). *Monthly Bulletin of Agriculture and Economic Statistics* (Arabic and English). *Vital Statistics* (Arabic and English). *Statistical Pocket Year-Book* (Arabic and English).

The Egyptian Almanac. Annual
Le Mondain Egyptien (Who's Who). Cairo. Annual
Cooper, M. N., *The Transformation of Egypt.* London, 1982
Dawisha, A. I., *Egypt in the Arab World.* London, 1976
Elias, E. A., *Modern Dictionary English–Arabic.* 5th ed. Cairo, 1946
Hansen, B., and Radwan, S., *Employment Opportunities and Equity in Egypt.* Geneva, 1982
Heikal, M., *Autumn of Fury: Assassination of Sadat.* London, 1983
Hirst, D., and Beeson, I., *Sadat.* London, 1981
Hopwood, D., *Egypt: Politics and Society 1945–1981.* London, 1982
Springberg, R., *Family, Power and Politics in Egypt.* Univ. of Pennsylvania Press, 1982
Vatikiotis, P. J., *The History of Egypt: From Muhammad Ali to Sadat.* 2nd ed. London, 1980
Waterbury, J., *The Egypt of Nasser and Sadat.* Princeton Univ. Press, 1983

EL SALVADOR

Capital: San Salvador
Population: 5·3m. (1984)
GNP per capita: US$650 (1981)

República de El Salvador

HISTORY. In 1839 the Central American Federation, which had comprised the states of Guatemala, El Salvador, Honduras, Nicaragua and Costa Rica, was dissolved, and El Salvador declared itself formally an independent republic in 1841.

AREA AND POPULATION. El Salvador is the smallest and most densely populated (248 inhabitants per sq. km) of the Central American states. Its area (including 247 sq. km of inland lakes) is estimated at 21,393 sq. km (8,236 sq. miles) with population (census 1981) of 4,672,900. Estimate (1984) 5·3m.

A Treaty was signed in Peru on 30 Oct. 1980 settling the border dispute between El Salvador and Honduras which caused 4 days of fighting in July 1979.

The republic is divided into 14 departments, each under an appointed governor. Their areas (in sq. km) and populations at census 1971 were:

Department	*Area*	*Population*	*Department*	*Area*	*Population*
San Salvador	892	681,656	La Paz	1,155	194,196
Santa Ana	1,829	375,186	Chalatenango	2,507	186,003
San Miguel	2,532	337,325	Ahuachapán	1,281	183,682
Usulután	1,780	304,369	Marazán	1,364	170,706
La Libertad	1,650	293,076	San Vicente	1,175	160,534
Sonsonate	1,133	239,688	Cuscatlán	766	158,458
La Unión	1,738	230,103	Cabañas	1,075	139,312

Important towns (with population 1983) were: San Salvador (the capital), 884,093; Santa Ana, 208,322; San Miguel, 161,156; Mejicanos (1978), 73,626; Delgado (1978), 55,912; Nueva San Salvador (1978), 45,384; Sonsonate (1978), 41,389.

There has been considerable emigration into nearby states. There are no tribal Indians. The language of the country is Spanish.

CLIMATE. Despite its proximity to the equator, the climate is warm rather than hot and nights are cool inland. Light rains occur in the dry season from Nov. to April while the rest of the year has heavy rains, especially on the coastal plain. San Salvador. Jan. 71°F (21·7°C), July 75°F (23·9°C). Annual rainfall 71″ (1,775 mm). San Miguel. Jan. 77°F (25°C), July 83°F (28·3°C). Annual rainfall 68″ (1,700 mm).

CONSTITUTION AND GOVERNMENT. A new Constitution was enacted in Dec. 1983. The Executive Power is vested in a President elected for a non-renewable term of 5 years, with Ministers and Under-Secretaries appointed by him. The Legislative power is an Assembly of 52 members elected by universal suffrage and proportional representation for a term of 3 years. The judicial power is vested in a Supreme Court, of a President and 9 magistrates elected by the Legislative Assembly for renewable terms of 3 years; and subordinate courts. For governments, 1961–79 *see* STATESMAN'S YEAR-BOOK 1982–83, p. 436.

Elections were held in March 1984.

President: José Napoleon Duarte (elected May 1984).

In June 1984 the Cabinet was composed as follows:

Presidency: Julio Adolfo Rey Prendes. *Foreign Affairs:* Dr Jorge Eduardo Tenorio. *Planning and Co-ordination of Economic and Social Development:* Dr Fidel Chávez Mena. *Interior and Vice-President:* Rodolfo Castillo Claramount. *Justice:* Dr Manuel Francisco Cardona H. *Finance:* Ricardo J. López. *Foreign*

Trade: Manuel Morales Erlich. *Economics:* Dr Ricardo González Camacho. *Education:* Professor Alberto Buendía Flores. *Defence and Public Safety:* Carlos Eugenio Vides Casanova. *Labour and Social Security:* Dr Julio Alfredo Samayoa. *Public Health and Social Welfare:* Dr Benjamín Valdez H. *Agriculture and Livestock:* Carlos Aquilino Duarte Funes. *Works:* Ramón Ernesto Rodríguez.

During 1982–84, there was continuing fighting between government forces and guerrillas and it was estimated that 17,153 people were killed in 1983 as a result of the violence.

National flag: Blue, white, blue (horizontal): the white stripe charged with the arms of the republic.

National anthem: Saludemos la patria orgullosos (words by J. J. Cañas; tune by J. Aberle).

DEFENCE. There is selective national service for 2 years.

Army. The Army comprises 4 infantry brigades, 1 mechanized cavalry regiment, 1 artillery brigade, 1 engineer, 1 anti-aircraft, 1 parachute and 1 special forces battalion. Equipment includes 12 AMX-13 light tanks and 18 AML-90 armoured cars. Strength was (1985) 39,000. There are also National Guard, National Police and Treasury Police, paramilitary units, numbering (1985) about 10,000 and a territorial civil defence force of up to 70,000.

Navy. The Navy includes 4 patrol boats, 1 new French-built tug, 2 cutters and 25 service launches. Personnel in 1985 totalled 130 officers and men.

Air Force. The Air Force underwent a major re-equipment programme in 1974–75, with most aircraft coming from Israel and US aid for transport units, but lost 18 aircraft in a guerrilla attack in Jan. 1982. Combat squadron now has 6 A-37 and 4 Ouragan jet fighter-bombers, supported by 6 Israeli-built Magister jets and 15 piston-engined Rallyes for light attack duties, and 4 Cessna O-2s for reconnaissance. Transports include 3 C-47s and 4 Israeli-built light twin-engined Aravas, plus 3 Lamas, 3 Alouette III and 30 UH-1H helicopters. Training types include about 15 piston-engined T-41Cs, T-6s and T-34s. Strength totalled about 2,500 personnel in 1985.

INTERNATIONAL RELATIONS

Membership. El Salvador is a member of UN and OAS.

ECONOMY

Budget. Revenue and expenditure for fiscal years ending 31 Dec., in 1,000 cólones:

	1979	*1980*	*1981*	*1982*	*1983*	*1984*
Revenue	1,541,017	1,376,337	1,740,424	1,730,899	1,723,333	2,298,442
Expenditure	1,303,707	1,606,335	1,757,600	1,864,699	1,847,065	2,298,442

External debt amounted to US$1,650m. in 1983.

Currency. The monetary unit is the *colón* (₡) of 100 *centavos*. The *colón* (₡) is issued in denominations of 1, 2, 5, 10, 25 and 100 *colónes*; 25 and 50 *centavos* (silver); 1, 2, 5 and 10 *centavos* (copper–nickel and copper–zinc); 1 centavo (nickel). In March 1985, £1 = ₡2·68; US$1 = ₡2·50.

Banking. There are 10 native commercial banks, including the Banco Salvadoreño (paid-up capital, 6m. colónes). The Bank of London and South America, the Citibank Bank of America and the Bank of Santander and Panama S. A. are the only foreign institutions. The Central Reserve Bank of El Salvador, constructed in 1934 out of the Banco Agricola Comercial, was nationalized on 20 April 1961.

Weights and Measures. On 1 Jan. 1886 the metric system was made obligatory. But other units are still commonly in use, of which the principal are as follows: *Libra* = 1·014 lb. av.; *quintal* = 101·4 lb. av.; *arroba* = 25·35 lb. av.; *fanega* = 1·5745 bushels.

ENERGY AND NATURAL RESOURCES

Electricity. A 200 ft high dam begun in 1950, and completed in 1954 was the construction across the (unnavigable) Lempa River, 35 miles north-east of San Salvador, with an annual capacity of 344m. kwh. The San Lorenzo dam, completed in 1983, has an annual capacity of 722m. kwh. Production in 1981, 1,512m. kwh.; consumption, 1,322m. kwh.

Oil. Production of petroleum derivatives during 1971 totalled ₡422,476,000.

Minerals. The mineral output of the republic is now negligible, but the Ministry of Public Works has recently started to investigate 2 new silver mines in the department of Morazán.

Agriculture. El Salvador is predominantly agricultural; 32·5% of its total area is used for crops and 30·2% for pasture. Area devoted to coffee (1982–83) was about 516,615 acres, entirely owned by nationals. In 1981, 35·5% of the working population was engaged in farming.

Production (1982–83, in 1m. quintales, 46 kg each): Coffee, 3·5 (1981 value ₡1,155·07m.); cotton, 2·8 (1981 value, ₡190,884,000); grain (including maize, beans, rice, sorghum), 14 (1981 value of maize, ₡186,612,000); sugar, 3·3. A little rubber is exported.

Livestock (1983): 954,000 cattle, 450,000 pigs, 4,000 sheep, 14,000 goats.

Forestry. In the national forests are found dye woods and such woods as mahogany, cedar and walnut. Balsam trees also abound: El Salvador is the world's principal source of this medicinal gum. Production, 1981, ₡36,148,000.

Fisheries. In 1982, fish products were valued at ₡56m.

INDUSTRY AND TRADE

Industry. Total production was valued at ₡3,390,991m. in 1982, which included (in 1,000 colones): Food, ₡1,274,877; textiles, ₡202,589; chemicals, ₡205,017; footwear and clothing, ₡208,274.

Commerce. The imports (including parcels post) and exports have been as follows in calendar years in 1,000 colónes:

	1977	*1978*	*1979*	*1980*	*1981*	*1982*
Imports	2,356,100	2,559,900	2,529,900	2,404,269	2,461,458	2,250,000
Exports	2,431,900	1,577,400	2,579,300	2,683,953	1,991,940	1,845,600

Of total exports (1982), coffee furnished about 32·2% by weight and 57·6% by value. The coffee is of the 'mild' variety; it is sold in bags of 60 kg, but trade statistics use a bag of 69 kg.

In 1982 US took 640·65m. colónes of exports and furnished 603,737,000 colónes of the imports. The chief imports in 1982 were manufactured goods (25·7%), chemical and pharmaceutical products (21%), non-edible crude materials, mainly crude oil (19·8%), electric machinery, tools and appliances and transport equipment (12·9%). The other Central American Republics, the Federal Republic of Germany, Japan, Canada, France, the Netherlands and the UK are also important trading partners.

Total trade between El Salvador and UK for 5 years (British Department of Trade returns, in £1,000 sterling):

	1980	*1981*	*1982*	*1983*	*1984*
Imports to UK	2,889	1,962	2,017	425	2,551
Exports and re-exports from UK	4,603	3,652	5,244	7,653	7,589

Tourism. There were 69,111 visitors in 1981.

COMMUNICATIONS

Roads. In 1981 there were 9,336·1 km of national roads in the republic, including 1,662 km of main paved roads; 3,276 km main asphalted roads; other roads, 4,397·9 km. Motor vehicles registered, 1979, 137,000.

Railways. All railways (602 km) came under the control of National Railways of El Salvador *(Fenadesal)* in 1975. Lines run from Acajutla to San Salvador; Cutuco to San Salvador; between San Salvador and Santa Ana, San Miguel and Sonsonate; there is also a link to the Guatemalan system. Total railway traffic in 1983 was 364,530 tonnes of freight and 246,814 passengers.

Aviation. The airport at Ilopango, 8 km from San Salvador, now a military airport, and the new international airport at Cuscatlán, 40 km from San Salvador, opened in 1979. In 1980, 265,000 passengers were carried.

Shipping. The principal ports are La Unión, La Libertad and Acajutla, all on the Pacific. Passengers (and some freight) use the Guatemalan port of Puerto Barrios on the Atlantic, reaching El Salvador by rail or road.

Post and Broadcasting. The telephone and telegraph systems are government-owned; the radio-telephone systems are partly private, partly government-owned. Telephone instruments, 1982, 86,316. There were (1983) over 50 radio stations. Radio El Salvador is state-owned. There were (1983) 3 commercial television channels and 2 educational channels sponsored by the Ministry of Education.

Cinemas (1976). Cinemas numbered 65.

Newspapers (1984). There are 5 daily newspapers in San Salvador and 1 in Santa Ana.

JUSTICE, RELIGION, EDUCATION AND WELFARE

Justice. Justice is administered by the Supreme Court of Justice, courts of first and second instance, besides minor tribunals. Magistrates of the Supreme Court and courts of second instance are elected by the Legislative Assembly for a renewable 3-year term.

An anti-Communist law, effective 29 Sept. 1962, has made the propagation of totalitarian or Communist doctrines an offence punishable by imprisonment; supplementary offences, contrary to democratic principles, are punished by prison terms of from 3 to 7 years.

Religion. The dominant religion is Roman Catholicism. Under the 1962 Constitution churches are exempted from the property tax; the Catholic Church is recognized as a legal person, and other churches are entitled to secure similar recognition. There is an archbishop in San Salvador and bishops at Santa Ana, San Miguel, San Vicente, Santiago de María and Usulután.

Education. Education is free and obligatory. In 1929 the State took over control of all schools, public and private, but the provision that the teaching in government schools must be wholly secular was removed in 1945.

In 1983 there were 57,739 pupils in nursery schools, 885,893 in secondary schools, 59,843 students at universities and polytechnics and 42,700 students receiving adult education.

Social Welfare. The Social Security Institute now administers the sickness, old age and death insurance, covering industrial workers and employees earning up to ₡700 a month. Employees in other private institutions with salaries over this amount are included but are excluded from the medical and hospital benefits.

DIPLOMATIC REPRESENTATIVES

Of El Salvador in Great Britain (62 Welbeck St., London, W1)
Chargé d'Affaires: Roberto Tomás Rivas Gardiner.

Of Great Britain in El Salvador
Ambassador and Consul-General: B. O. White (resides in Tegucigalpa).

Of El Salvador in the USA (2308 California St., NW, Washington, DC., 20008)
Chargé d'Affaires: Roberto Jimenez-Ortiz.

Of the USA in El Salvador (25 Ave. Norte, Colonia Dueñas, San Salvador)
Ambassador: Thomas R. Pickering.

Of El Salvador to the United Nations
Ambassador: Dr Mauricio Rosales-Rivera.

Books of Reference

Statistical Information: The Dirección General de Estadistica y Censos (Villa Fermina, Calle Arce, San Salvador) dates from 1937. *Director General:* Lieut.-Col. José Castro Meléndez. Its publications include *Anuario Estadistico.* Annual from 1911.—*Boletin Estadístico.* Quarterly.—*El Salvador en Gráficas.* Annual.—*Atlas Censal de El Salvador.* 1955 only.—Revista Mensual, Banco Central de Reserva de El Salvador.

Angel Gallardo, M., *Cuatro Constituciones Federales de Centro América y Las Constituciones Politicas de El Salvador.* San Salvador, 1945
Armstrong, R., and Shenk, J., *El Salvador: The Face of Revolution.* London, 1982
Baloyra, E. A., *El Salvador in Transition.* Univ. of North Carolina Press, 1982
Bevan, J., *El Salvador. Education and Repression.* London, 1981
Browning, D., *El Salvador: Landscape and Society.* OUP, 1971
Devire, F. J., *El Salvador: Embassy under Attack.* New York, 1981
Didion, J., *Salvador.* London, 1983
Erdozain, P., *Archbishop Romero: Martyr of El Salvador.* Guildford, 1981
Montgomery, T.S., *Revolution in El Salvador: Origins and Evolution.* Boulder, 1982
North, L., *Bitter Grounds: Roots of Revolt in El Salvador.* London, 1981
Schmidt, S. W., *El Salvador: America's Next Vietnam.* Salisbury (N.C.), 1983

EQUATORIAL GUINEA

Capital: Malabo
Population: 398,000 (1984)
GNP per capita: US$180 (1981)

República de Guinea Ecuatorial

HISTORY. The Republic of Equatorial Guinea became independent on 12 Oct. 1968 after having been a Spanish colony (Territorios Españoles del Golfo de Guinea) until 1959. From 1959 to 1963 the territory was made into two Spanish provinces with a status comparable to the metropolitan provinces. From 1964 to 1968 this Equatorial Region became an autonomous entity still retaining the status of two Spanish provinces, but with a certain amount of internal self-government. Serious political disturbances in Rio Muni occurred in March–April 1969. This led to the partial withdrawal of the Spanish community. Agreements for co-operation in education and economic development were signed with Spain in 1971, 1972 and 1979. From 1968–79 the republic depended heavily on the Soviet bloc including Cuba and the People's Republic of China, Spanish economic, technical and social co-operation has become essential since 1979.

AREA AND POPULATION. The total area is 28,051 sq. km (10,831 sq. miles). Total population, 245,989 (1960 census); 1984 estimate, 398,000.

The 6 provinces consist of 2 on the islands of Bioko and Pagalu, and 4 on the mainland, with these separate areas having the following areas (in sq.km) and populations:

	Sq. km	*Census 1960*	*Estimate 1984*	*Chief town*
Bioko	2,034 [1]	62,612 [1]	105,000	Malabo
Rio Muni	26,017 [2]	183,377	293,000	Bata

[1] Including 1,415 on the island of Pagalu (17 sq. km).
[2] Including the adjacent islets of Corisco, Elobey Grande and Elobey Chico (17 sq. km).

The majority of the Rio Munian population is Fang (Pámues in Spanish). Along the coast and in the islets are the Combes, the Bengas, the Bujebas, etc.

In Bioko the aborigines are called Bubis. These are now a minority (perhaps 15,000). Other ethnic groups are the Fernandinos (descendants of English-speaking Creoles), the Fangs, coast people from Rio Muni and formerly naturalized migrant workers from Nigeria, Cameroon and São Tomé. A fluctuating mass of plantation workers were about twice as numerous as the Equatorial Guineans. Pagalu is peopled by descendants of slaves brought by the Portuguese; they still speak a Portuguese patois. Pidgin English was the lingua franca in Bioko in spite of the official Spanish. Because of political and economic difficulties about 110,000 citizens are reported to live in neighbouring countries and Spain.

CLIMATE. The climate is equatorial, with alternate wet and dry seasons. In Rio Muni, the wet season lasts from Dec. to Feb.

CONSTITUTION AND GOVERNMENT. A 10-member cabinet was established and the country was placed under military rule and in Aug. 1982, under a new Constitution, the President's mandate was extended for 7 years. A 41-member National Assembly was elected on 28 Aug. 1983.

President: Lieut.-Col. Teodoro Obiang Nguema Mbasogo.

National flag: Three horizontal stripes of green, white, red; a blue triangle based on the hoist; in the centre the national arms.

DEFENCE. Under President Macías the *Guardia Nacional* consisted mainly of Fang soldiers with Cuban and Chinese military advisers. Total strength about 1,500. Since the 1979 *coup*, Moroccan troops and Spanish military and police personnel have replaced Soviet bloc advisers.

INTERNATIONAL RELATIONS

Membership. Equatorial Guinea is a member of UN, OAU and is an ACP state of EEC.

ECONOMY

Budget. The 1982 budget envisaged income at 2,980m. Bikuele and expenditure at 4,038m. Bikuele.

Currency. In July 1973 the Guinean *peseta* was redesignated the *Ekuele* (plural, *Bikuele*). In Dec. 1984 the currency joined the franc zone.

Banking. The Banco Central de Guinea Ecuatorial in Malabo was established in 1969 with Spanish technical and financial assistance.

NATURAL RESOURCES

Agriculture. The chief products are cocoa (71,000 hectares in 1979), coffee (17,000 hectares) and wood; in 1982 production was about 8,000 tonnes of cocoa, most of it high-grade exported to Spain and the US. Coffee, of mediocre quality, is chiefly a Fang product. Production (1982) 7,000 tonnes; palm oil, 5,000; palm kernels, 3,000; bananas, 16,000. Food crops include cassava, 55,000; sweet potatoes, 34,000.

Livestock (1983): Cattle, 4,000; sheep, 34,000; goats, 7,000.

Forestry. Wood was almost entirely exported from Rio Muni to Spain and the Federal Republic of Germany. Production: 1981, 465,000 cu. metres. Plantations in the hinterland have been abandoned by their Spanish owners and except for cocoa, commercial agriculture is under serious difficulties.

INDUSTRY AND TRADE

Industry. Bioko has very few industries. Electricity production in 1980: 15·54m. kwh. Rio Muni has no industry except lumbering. Post-independence political conditions have not been conducive to private investment. Since 1979 the lumber industry has resumed activity but there was (1981) a shortage of labour.

Commerce. In 1981 imports amounted to 7,982m. Bikuele (of which 80% came from Spain) and exports to 2,502m. Bikuele (of which Spain took 87%). Cocoa amounted to 71% of all exports and timber to 24%.

Total trade between Equatorial Guinea and UK (British Department of Trade returns, in £1,000 sterling):

	1981	*1982*	*1983*	*1984*
Imports to UK	19	156	13	559
Exports and re-exports from UK	142	633	10	553

COMMUNICATIONS

Roads. Bioko had a good tarmac road network, but Rio Muni had few surfaced roads; the main artery is Mbini–Bata–Micomeseng–Ebebiyin. Road reconstruction is envisaged.

Aviation. An international airfield exists in Malabo (28,029 passengers in 1967). Bata has more modest facilities (15,031 passengers in 1967). The line Madrid–Malabo–Bata is subsidized by Spain. Links with Douala (from Malabo) and Libreville (Gabon) exist.

Shipping. Malabo is the main port. The other ports are Luba, formerly San Carlos (bananas, cocoa) in Bioko and Bata, Kogo and Mbini (wood) in Rio Muni. A new harbour in Bata has been completed. In 1981 47,731 tonnes were unloaded and 50,843 loaded.

Post and Broadcasting. Estimated number of telephones (1969), 1,451. In 1977 there were 80,000 radio and 1,000 TV receivers.

JUSTICE, RELIGION, EDUCATION AND WELFARE

Justice. The Constitution guarantees an independent judiciary. The Supreme Tribunal is the highest court of appeal and is located at Malabo.

Religion. The population of Equatorial Guinea is nominally Roman Catholic with influential Protestant groups in Malabo and Rio Muni. By order of the President most churches were closed in 1975 and in June 1978 the Roman Catholic Church was banned. Since 1979, religious services have been restored.

Education. There were in 1981 about 40,110 pupils and 647 teachers in primary schools and 3,013 pupils and 288 teachers in secondary schools.

Health. In 1967 there were 16 hospitals and dispensaries with 1,637 beds. In 1975 there were only 5 doctors, 2 midwives and 248 nursing personnel.

DIPLOMATIC REPRESENTATIVES

Of Equatorial Guinea in Great Britain
Ambassador: Jesús Ele Abeme.

Of Great Britain in Equatorial Guinea
Ambassador: Michael Glaze (resides at Yaoundé).

Of the USA in Equatorial Guinea (Calle de 65 Ministros, Malabo)
Ambassador: Alan M. Hardy.

Of Equatorial Guinea to the USA and the United Nations
Ambassador: Florencio Maye Ela.

Books of Reference

Atlas Historico y Geográfico de Africa Espanola. Madrid, 1955
Plan de Desarrollo Económico de la Guinea Ecuatorial. Presidencia del Gobierno. Madrid, 1963
Resumén estadistico del Africa española, 1965–66. Madrid, 1967
Berman, S., *Spanish Guinea: An Annotated Bibliography.* Microfilm Service, Catholic University. Washington, D.C. 1961
Liniger-Goumaz, M., *La Guinée équatoriale un pays méconnu.* Paris, 1980
Pélissier, R., *Les Territoires espagnols d'Afrique.* Paris, 1963.—*Los territorios españoles de Africa.* Madrid, 1964.—*Etudes Hispano-Guinéennes.* Orgeval, 1969

ETHIOPIA

Hebretesebawit Ityopia

Capital: Addis Ababa
Population: 40m. (1984)
GNP per capita: US$140 (1981)

HISTORY. The ancient empire of Ethiopia has its legendary origin in the meeting of King Solomon and the Queen of Sheba. Historically, the empire developed in the centuries before and after the birth of Christ, at Aksum in the north, as a result of Semetic immigration from South Arabia. The immigrants imposed their language and culture on a basic Hamitic stock. Ethiopia's subsequent history is one of sporadic expansion southwards and eastwards, checked from the 16th to early 19th centuries by devastating wars with Moslems and Gallas. Modern Ethiopia dates from the reign of the Emperor Theodore (1855–68).

Menelik II (1889–1913) defeated the Italians in 1896 and thereby safeguarded the empire's independence in the scramble for Africa. By successful campaigns in neighbouring kingdoms within Ethiopia (Jimma, Kaffa, Harar, etc.) he united the country under his rule and created the empire as it is today.

In 1936 Ethiopia was conquered by the Italians, who were in turn defeated by the Allied forces in 1941 when the Emperor returned.

The former Italian colony of Eritrea, from 1941 under British military administration, was in accordance with a resolution of the General Assembly of the UN, dated 2 Dec. 1950, handed over to Ethiopia on 15 Sept. 1952. Eritrea thereby became an autonomous unit within the federation of Ethiopia and Eritrea.

This federation became a unitary state on 14 Nov. 1962 when Eritrea was fully integrated with Ethiopia.

A provisional military government assumed power on 12 Sept. 1974 and deposed the Emperor. On 24 Nov. 1974 the Provisional Military Government announced that on 23 Nov. it had executed 60 former military and civilian leaders including Gen. Aman Andom who was Chairman of the Provisional Military Administrative Council.

On 3 Feb. 1977 it was announced that Brig.-Gen. Teferi Bante, the Chairman of PMAC and 6 other members of the ruling military council were executed.

In mid-1977 Somalia invaded Ethiopia and took control of the Ogaden region. After an offensive mounted with strong USSR and Cuban support the area was recaptured and in March Somalia withdrew all troops from the area. Control was re-established by Ethiopia later in 1978 and nationalist guerrillas were pushed back but sporadic fighting continues (1985) in the Ogaden and along the border.

AREA AND POPULATION. Ethiopia is bounded north-east by the Red Sea, east by Djibouti and Somalia, south by Kenya and west by Sudan. It has a total area of 1,221,900 sq. km (471,800 sq. miles) and total population (1983) 33,008,000. The first census was carried out in 1984 and the population is expected to exceed 40m.

The dominant race of Ethiopia, the Amhara, inhabit the central Ethiopian highlands. To the north of them are the Tigréans, akin to the Amhara and belonging to the same Christian church, but speaking a different, though related, language. Both these races are of mixed Hamitic and Semitic origin, and further mixed by intermarriage with Oromo (Galla) and other races. The Oromos, some of whom are Christian, some Moslem and some pagan, comprise about 40% of the entire population, and are a pastoral and agricultural people of Hamitic origin. Somalis, another Hamitic race, inhabit the south-east of Ethiopia, in particular the Ogaden desert region. These like the closely related Afar people, are Moslem. The Afar stretch northwards from Wollo region into Eritrea.

Region	Area (sq. km)	Population July 1980	Chief town	Population July 1980
Addis Ababa	218	1,277,159	—	—
Arussi	23,500	1,149,400	Assela	34,874
Bale	124,600	879,200	Goba	6,116 [1]
Eritrea	117,600	2,426,200	Asmara	424,532
Gemu Gofa	39,500	1,003,400	Arba Minch	8,914 [1]
Gojjam	61,600	2,037,900	Debre Markos	40,686
Gondar (Begemdir)	74,200	2,053,400	Gondar	76,932
Hararge	259,700	3,125,200	Harar	62,921
Illubabor	47,400	810,800	Mattu	8,115 [1]
Kefa	54,600	1,615,400	Jimma	63,837
Shoa	85,200	5,085,000	—	—
Sidamo	117,300	2,808,300	Awassa	23,038 [1]
Tigre	65,900	2,162,100	Mekele	46,846
Wollega	71,200	2,019,200	Lekemti	21,694 [1]
Wollo	79,400	2,612,600	Dessie	75,616

[1] Jan. 1978.

Other large towns (population, Jan. 1980): Dire Dawa, in Hararge, 82,024; Nazret, in Shoa, 69,865; Bahr Dar, 52,188; Debre Zeit, 49,570.

Local Government. The country is divided into 15 administrative regions, each under a Chief Administrator, and under the administrative control of the Minister of the Interior. The regions are divided into 103 *awraja* (sub-regions), and thence into 505 *woredo* (districts).

CLIMATE. The wide range of latitude produces many climatic variations between the high, temperate plateaus and the hot, humid lowlands. The main rainy season lasts from June to Aug., with light rains from Feb. to April, but the country is very vulnerable to drought. Addis Ababa. Jan. 59°F (15°C), July 59°F (15°C). Annual rainfall 50″ (1,237 mm). Harar. Jan. 65°F (18·3°C), July 64°F (17·8°C). Annual rainfall 35″ (897 mm). Massawa. Jan. 78°F (25·6°C), July 94°F (34·4°C). Annual rainfall 8″ (193 mm)

CONSTITUTION AND GOVERNMENT. Pending the promulgation of a new constitution, Ethiopia is controlled by a Provisional Military Administration Council (the *Derg*) to whom the Council of Ministers is responsible. A Commission for Organizing the Party of the Working Peoples of Ethiopia (COPWE) was established in early 1980 and charged with the task of preparing the formation of a civilian party which will ultimately take over from the PMAC. The second congress of COPWE was held in Jan. 1983 and elected a 91 member central committee and a 7-member executive committee, both chaired by Mengistu. The Workers Party of Ethiopia (WPE) was founded in 1984. An 11-member Politbureau was elected which includes all 7 members of the former COPWE executive committee. The central committee was increased to 136 members, including most former COPWE central committee members. The WPE is the leading organ of the state but the transition to civilian government still awaits the promulgation of the new Constitution. Mengistu leads the new party.

Chairman of the PMAC, Head of State, Chairman of the Council of Ministers: Lieut.-Col. Mengistu Haile Mariam.

Vice-Chairman of the Council of Ministers: and *Secretary-General of the PMAC:* Capt. Fikre Selassie Wogderesse.

Foreign Affairs: Lieut.-Col. Goshu Wolde.

National flag: Three horizontal stripes of green, yellow and red.

National anthem. Ityopya, Ityopia Kidemi (tune by Daniel Yohannes, 1975).

DEFENCE. Ethiopia's military rulers have moved away from US military assistance since they came to power and now rely on USSR for most of their military aid. Large amounts of USSR military equipment have been sent to help her in her conflict with Somalia over the Ogaden desert region.

Selective conscription was introduced in 1983 for a period of 30 months is in force. Some 1,400 Soviet, 3,000 Cuban and 250 East German military advisers and technicians are reported to be serving with the armed forces.

Army. The Army, comprises 23 infantry divisions with some 20 tank battalions, 4 para-commando brigades, 30 artillery battalions and 30 air defence battalions. Equipment includes 700 T-54/-55, 150 T-34 and 40 M-47 tanks. Strength (1985) 300,000 including a People's Militia.

Navy. The Navy, with headquarters at Addis Ababa, consists of 1 *ex*-Soviet light frigate, 4 *ex*-Soviet fast missile boats, 2 *ex*-Soviet fast torpedo boats, 1 training ship (1,768 tons; *ex*-US seaplane tender), 1 *ex*-Netherlands coastal minesweeper, 4 patrol craft (*ex*-US coastguard motor gunboats), 4 patrol boats, 1 *ex*-Yugoslav submarine chaser, 3 *ex*-Soviet coastal cutters, 4 harbour defence craft, 2 medium landing ships, 2 landing craft and 4 minor landing craft. The Naval Base and College is at Massawa.

Personnel in 1985, totalled 1,500 officers and men. It is presumed that Soviet advisers remain embarked in the 6 attack craft recently acquired until Ethiopian naval officers and ratings have sufficient experience to operate independently the missiles and torpedoes.

Air Force. The Air Force, trained originally by Swedish and American personnel, but now operating aircraft of Soviet origin, has its headquarters at Debre Zeit, near Addis Ababa. It includes a training school and a central workshop. Of 6 ground-attack fighter squadrons, 4 have MiG-21s, the others MiG-23s and MiG-17s respectively. There is a squadron of Mi-24 helicopter gunships, and a transport squadron equipped with An-12s, and An-26s. Training aircraft include two-seat MiG-21s and L-39 jet basic trainers. More than 40 Mi-8 helicopters are in service. Personnel, 3,500 officers and men.

INTERNATIONAL RELATIONS

Membership. Ethiopia is a member of UN, OAU and is an ACP state of EEC.

ECONOMY

Planning. A 10-year development plan (1984–94) places emphasis on socialist development and a growth rate of 6%.

Budget. Revenue and expenditure estimates for financial years (ended 7 July) were as follows (in EB1m.):

	1975–76	*1976–77*	*1977–78*	*1978–79*	*1979–80*
Revenue	1,331	1,466	1,601	2,119	2,365
Expenditure	1,331	1,466	1,601	2,119	2,365

Of the estimated revenue in 1979–80, EB1,327m. is expected to come from taxes and EB417m. from external assistance. Of the 1979–80 expenditure, EB1,655m. is on current account and EB710m. for capital expenditure.

Currency. The Ethiopian *birr*, divided into 100 cents, is the unit of currency; it is based on 5·52 grains of fine gold. It consists of notes of EB1, 2, 10, 50 and 100 denominations, and bronze 1-, 5-, 10-, 25- and 50-cent coins. *Birr* 2·21 = £1 sterling; *Birr* 2·02 = US$1 (in March 1985).

Banking. The State Bank was renamed the National Bank of Ethiopia in Oct. 1963, when its commercial activities were transferred to the newly established Commercial Bank of Ethiopia. At the same time another new bank, the Investment Bank of Ethiopia, was set up with a capital of EB10m., of which the Government held the majority of shares. In Sept. 1965 it became the Ethiopian Investment Corporation, which is a substantial shareholder in a number of industrial and other ventures.

The Investment Corporation has now been merged with the Development Bank of Ethiopia and the two are now known as the Agricultural and Industrial Development Bank, SC.

Two Italian banks have subsidiaries in Asmara, and one has a subsidiary in Addis Ababa. The Addis Ababa Bank Share Co. is connected with National & Grindlays Bank Ltd.

On 1 Jan. 1975 the Government nationalized all banks, mortgage and insurance companies.

Weights and Measures. The metric system of weights and measures is officially in use. Traditional weights and measures vary considerably in the various provinces: the principal ones are: *Frasilla* = approximately 37½ lb.; *gasha*, the principal unit of land measure, which is normally about 100 acres but can vary between 80 and 300 acres, depending on the quality of the land.

ENERGY AND NATURAL RESOURCES

Electricity. Production in 1979 totalled 544m. kwh.

Oil. A Russian built state-owned oil refinery at Assab came on stream in 1967 with a capacity of 600,000 tonnes of crude per annum.

Gas. A natural gas-strike was made offshore near Massawa in Dec. 1969, but it was not exploited. Traces of gas and oil have been found in south-east Ethiopia.

Minerals. Ethiopia has little proved mineral wealth. Salt is produced mainly in Eritrea, while a placer goldmine is worked by the Government of Adola in the south. Gold production, in 1980, was 373 kg. Small quantities of other minerals are produced including platinum.

Agriculture. Coffee is by far the most important source of rural income accounting for 70% of foreign earnings in 1982. Harari coffee (long berry Mocha) is cultivated in the east.

Teff (*Eragrastis abyssinica*) is the principal food grain, followed by barley, wheat, maize and durra. Pulses and oilseeds are imported for local consumption and export. Cane sugar is an important crop.

Production (1982 in 1,000 tons): Maize, 1,000; sorghum, 1,300; barley, 1,150; pulses, 1,002.

Livestock (1983): 26·3m. cattle, 23·4m. sheep, 17·24m. goats; smaller numbers of donkeys, horses, mules and camels. Hides and skins and butter (ghee) are important for home consumption and export. Sheep, cattle and chickens are the main providers of meat. In 1983 85% of the population were engaged in agriculture, producing 40% of GDP. The continuing drought has had a devastating effect on production.

INDUSTRY AND TRADE

Industry. The most important products of the small but growing industries are cotton yarn (9,600 tons in 1978) and fabrics, cement (100,000 tons), sugar, salt, cigarettes, canned foodstuffs, beer, building materials, footwear, pharmaceuticals, tyres and paint. Most industry is centred around Addis Ababa and Asmara. Industry around Asmara has been severely hit by actions of Eritrean guerrillas.

Commerce. Coffee is by far the most important export, followed by pulses, oilseeds, hides and skins. Imports are textiles, foodstuffs, vehicles, machinery, manufactured goods and petroleum products.

Imports and exports (in US$1m.) for 4 years.

	1978	*1979*	*1980*	*1981*
Imports	440·1	521·3	649·6	629·8
Exports	308·3	429·1	419·3	374·1

Total trade between Ethiopia and UK (British Department of Trade returns, in £1,000 sterling):

	1980	*1981*	*1982*	*1983*	*1984*
Imports to UK	10,281	0,079	10,877	12,071	13,733
Exports and re-exports from UK	20,962	19,569	27,584	34,092	63,434

Tourism. There were 55,000 tourists in 1982.

COMMUNICATIONS

Roads. There were (1984) 30,000 km of roads. Addis Ababa is linked with Nairobi by a highway.

Motor vehicles (1984): Cars, 41,300; lorries and trucks, 8,800; buses, 3,041.

Railways. The former Franco-Ethiopian Railway Co. (782 km, metre-gauge) became the Ethiopian-Djibouti Railway Corp. in 1982, when the remaining France-owned shares were bought out. In 1983 the railway carried 249,000 tonnes of freight and 1·4m. passengers.

Aviation. Ethiopian Air Lines, formed in 1946, carried 242,924 passengers in 1980 and 8,613 tonnes of freight.

Shipping. A state shipping line was established in 1964. The ports unloaded 1·7m. tonnes in 1980 and loaded 518,000.

Post and Broadcasting. The postal system serves 301 offices, mainly by air-mail. All the main centres are connected with Addis Ababa by telephone or radio telegraph. International telephone services are available at certain hours to most countries in Europe, North America and India. Number of telephones (1982), 100,783.

The Ethiopian Broadcasting Service makes sound broadcasts on the medium and short waves in English, Amharic and in the vernacular languages spoken within the country. There were about 45,000 television sets and 2m. radio receivers in 1982.

Cinemas (1974). There were 31 cinemas, with seating capacity of about 25,600.

Newspapers. There were (1984) 3 government-controlled daily newspapers with a combined circulation of about 47,000.

JUSTICE, RELIGION, EDUCATION AND WELFARE

Justice. The legal system is said to be based on the Justinian Code. A new penal code came into force in 1958 and Special Penal Law in 1974. Codes of criminal procedure, civil, commercial and maritime codes have since been promulgated.

The extra-territorial rights formerly enjoyed by foreigners have been abolished, but any person accused in an Ethiopian court has the right to have his case transferred to the High Court, provided he asks for this before any evidence has been taken in the court of first instance.

Provincial and district courts have been established, and High Court judges visit the provincial courts on circuit. The Supreme Court at Addis Ababa is presided over by the Chief Justice.

Religion. About 45% of the population are Moslem and 40% Christian, mainly belonging to the Ethiopian Orthodox Church.

Education. In the academic year 1980–81 there were more than 2·13m. pupils in primary schools. In secondary schools there were 400,000 students. Higher education is co-ordinated under the National University, chartered in 1961; in 1979–80, there were 14,562 students. The University College, the Engineering, Building and Theological Colleges are in Addis Ababa, the Agricultural College in Harar and the Public Health College in Gondar.

The government claims to have reduced illiteracy from 95% to 54% since 1974.

Health. In 1977 there was one doctor for every 75,000 people and in 1981 it was found that Ethiopia has the shortest life expectancy in the world, at 40 years.

DIPLOMATIC REPRESENTATIVES

Of Ethiopia in Great Britain (17 Prince's Gate, London, SW7 1PZ)
Ambassador: Ato Ayalew Wolde-Giorgis.

Of Great Britain in Ethiopia (Fikre Mariam Abatechan St., Addis Ababa)
Ambassador: B. L. Barder.

Of Ethiopia in the USA (2134 Kalorama Rd., NW, Washington D.C., 20008)
Chargé d'Affaires: Tamene Eshete.

Of the USA in Ethiopia (Entoto St., Addis Ababa)
Chargé d'Affaires: David A. Korn.

Of Ethiopia to the United Nations
Ambassador: Berhanu Dinka.

Books of Reference

Gilkes, P., *The Dying Lion: Feudalism and Modernisation in Ethiopia.* London, 1975
Halliday, F. and Molyneaux, M., *The Ethiopian Revolution.* London, 1981
Hancock, G., *Ethiopia: The Challenge of Hunger.* London, 1985
Hess, R. L., *Ethiopia: The Modernization of Autocracy.* Cornell Univ. Press, 1970
Holmberg, J., *Grain Marketing and Land Reform in Ethiopia.* Uppsala, 1977
Mosley, L., *Haile Selassie.* London, 1964
Pool, D., *Eritrea: Africa's Longest War.* London, 1982
Scholler, H. and Brictzke, P., *Ethiopia: Revolution, Law and Politics.* New York, 1976
Thompson, B., *Ethiopia: The Country That Cut Off Its Head.* London, 1975
Ullendorff, E., *The Ethiopians.* New York, 1973
Wolde-Mariam, M., *An Atlas of Ethiopia.* Rev. ed. Addis Ababa, 1970

FALKLAND ISLANDS AND DEPENDENCIES

Capital: Stanley
Population: 1,813 (1980)

HISTORY. France established a settlement in 1764 and Britain a second settlement in 1765. In 1770 Spain bought out the French and drove off the British. In 1806 Spanish rule was overthrown in Argentina, and the Argentinians claimed to succeed Spain in the French and British settlements in 1820. The British objected and reclaimed their settlement in 1832 as a Crown Colony.

On 2 April 1982 Argentine forces invaded the Falkland Islands and the Governor was expelled. At a meeting of the UN Security Council, held on 3 April, the voting was 10 to 1 in favour of the resolution calling for Argentina to withdraw. Britain regained possession on 14–15 June after the Argentinians surrendered.

AREA AND POPULATION. The Crown Colony is situated in the South Atlantic Ocean about 480 miles north-east of Cape Horn. The numerous islands cover 4,700 sq. miles. The main East Falkland Island, 2,610 sq. miles; the West Falkland, 2,090 sq. miles, including the adjacent small islands. The Dependency of South Georgia lies 800 miles south-east of the Falklands, has an area of 1,450 sq. miles; the South Sandwich group, 470 miles south-east of South Georgia, has an area of 130 sq. miles.

The population of the Falkland Islands at census 1980 was 1,813. The only town is Stanley, in East Falkland, with a population of just over 1,000. A large garrison of British servicemen was stationed near Stanley in 1985. The population of South Georgia varies with the season, but the resident population in 1980 was 22 (males). The South Sandwich are uninhabited.

South Georgia, once a base for whaling and sealing operations, is now occupied by members of the British Antarctic Survey at the base at King Edward Point.

The population of the Falkland Islands is nearly all of British descent, with about 80% born in the islands.

CLIMATE. A harsh climate, much affected by strong winds, particularly in spring. Stanley. Jan. 49°F (9·4°C), July 35°F (1·7°C). Annual rainfall 27″ (681 mm).

CONSTITUTION AND GOVERNMENT. The present Constitution came into force on 21 Nov. 1977. On 18 June 1982, a Falkland Islands and Dependencies (Interim Administration) Order was introduced which made provision for the interim administration by the establishment of a Civil Commissioner and a Military Commissioner. Under the Order the Military Commissioner has responsibility for the defence and internal security (with the exception of the police). The Civil Commissioner is required to consult the Military Commissioner on any matter which falls within the responsibility of the Military Commissioner and accept any advice on such matters tendered by the Military Commissioner. The Order suspended the office of Governor and Commander-in-Chief and vested the functions of that office in the Civil Commissioner who is assisted by an Executive Council consisting of the Chief Executive and Financial Secretary, both *ex-officio*; 2 members elected by the Legislature and 2 appointed members; and a Legislative Council composed of the Chief Executive and Financial Secretary, both *ex-officio*; 3 elected members representing Stanley, 1 elected member from the East Falkland and 1 from the West Falkland and 1 representing the Camp as a whole.

Governor: Sir Rex Hunt, CMG.
Chief Executive: D. G. P. Taylor.
Government Secretary: B. E. Pauncefort, OBE.
Flag: British Blue Ensign with arms of Colony on a white disc in the fly.

DEFENCE. Since 1982 the Islands have been defended by a garrison of several thousand servicemen. The garrison is commanded by a Military Commissioner who is responsible for all military matters in the Islands. He liaises with the Civil Commissioner on civilian and political matters, and advises him on matters of internal security. Apart from their strictly defence role, the military are taking an active part in the rehabilitation and reconstruction of the Islands.

ECONOMY

Budget. Revenue and expenditure (in £ sterling) for fiscal years ending 30 June:

	1977–78	*1978–79*	*1979–80*	*1980–81*	*1981–82*	*1982–83*
Revenue	1,803,151	1,820,561	2,427,934	2,298,325	2,533,425	3,653,895
Expenditure	1,382,744	1,792,780	2,057,928	2,775,697	2,648,432	3,118,763

Currency. The Falkland £ is at parity with the £ sterling.

Banking. On 1 Dec. 1983 the government savings bank was dissolved, and all savings bank deposits were transferred to the Standard Chartered Bank, which has a branch in Stanley, and provides a full range of banking facilities.

SHEEP FARMING. The whole acreage of the Colony is divided into large sheep runs. Wool is the principal product, but hides are exported. In 1983 there were 669,144 sheep, 7,648 cattle and 2,324 horses in the islands.

DEVELOPMENT. The economy is mainly dependent on the production of wool for export. The Falkland Islands Development Corporation commenced operations during July 1984 with the aim of encouraging the economic development of the Falkland Islands. The first projects assisted by the Development Corporation include inshore and offshore fisheries surveys to establish potential catch size and value, the introduction of agricultural improvement schemes to encourage investment in the land, and the establishment of a wool spinning and knitting factory to process a portion of the islands main product.

TRADE. Total imports, 1981, amounted to £3,193,437 and exports to £2,304,446.

Total trade between the Falkland Islands and UK (British Department of Trade returns, in $1,000 sterling).

	1982	*1983*	*1984*
Imports to UK	2,568	4,022	5,202
Exports and re-exports from UK	4,150	7,259	9,516

COMMUNICATIONS

Roads. There are 20 km of made-up roads in and around Stanley. Roadworks presently under construction will add another 53 km to this figure. Between Stanley and Bluff Cove there is a 23 km all-weather road. Other settlements outside of Stanley are linked by tracks, which are passable, with high axle clearing four-wheel drive vehicles in all but the worst weather.

Aviation. Air communication is currently *via* Ascension Island by means of Hercules aircraft manned by the RAF. There are no external civil air links. A new airfield which is expected to be operational by mid-1985 and completed in 1986, is sited at Mount Pleasant. Internal air links are provided by the government operated air service, which carries passengers, mail and medical patients between the settlements and Stanley on non-scheduled flights.

Shipping. A charter vessel calls 4 or 5 times a year to/from the UK. Communication with the Colony, the Dependencies and the British Antarctic Territory is kept up by the Royal research ships *John Biscoe* and *Bransfield* and by the ice-patrol vessel HMS *Endurance*.

Post and Broadcasting. Number of telephones (1984) 500. There is a government-operated broadcasting station at Stanley.

EDUCATION AND WELFARE

Education. Education is compulsory between the ages of 5 and 15 years. In 1984 there were 339 children receiving education in the Colony. Almost 75% attended schools in Stanley, the others were taught in settlement schools or by itinerant teachers. 5 children were being educated abroad.

Health. The Government Medical Department is responsible for preventative and curative medical services in the territory. A board of health deals with public health problems as they arise. The Senior Medical Officer, who sits on the board is responsible for advising the Falkland Islands Government on health policy. The Military Environmental Health Officer also sits on the board.

Since the destruction by fire in April 1984 of the hospital in Stanley, separate temporary civilian and military hospitals have been established. Medical services for the Islands are run from the civilian hospital, including a general practitioner service to Stanley and a routine and emergency flying doctor service for outlying farm settlements.

WILD LIFE. The Falkland Islands and South Georgia are noted for their outstanding wild life, including penguin and seal. Four Nature Reserves have been declared and 18 Wild Animal and Bird Sanctuaries gazetted. The brown trout introduced between 1947 and 1952 can now be found in nearly all the rivers.

Books of Reference

Falkland Islands: The Facts. HMSO, London, 1982
Falkland Islands Journal. Stanley, from 1967
Falkland Islands Review [Franks Report] Cmnd. 8787. HMSO, London, 1983
Falklands/Malvinas, Whose Crisis? Latin American Bureau, London, 1982
Calvert, P., *The Falklands Crisis: The Rights and the Wrongs.* London, 1982
Hanrahan, B., and Fox, R., *'I counted them all out and I counted them all back'.* London, 1982
Hastings, M., and Jenkins, S., *The Battle for the Falklands.* London, 1983
Headland, R. K., *The Island of Georgia.* CUP, 1985
Hoffmann, F. L., and Hoffmann, O. M., *Sovereignty in Dispute.* London, 1984
Phipps, C., *What Future for the Falklands?* London, 1977
Shackleton, E., *Falkland Islands Economic Study 1982.* HMSO, London, 1982

FIJI

Capital: Suva
Population: 663,485 (1982)
GNP per capita: US$2,000 (1981)

HISTORY. The Fiji Islands were discovered by Tasman in 1643 and visited by Capt. Cook in 1774, but first recorded in detail by Capt. Bligh after the mutiny of the *Bounty* (1789). In the 19th century the search for sandalwood, in which enormous profits were made, brought many ships. Deserters and shipwrecked men stayed on; firearms salvaged from wrecks were used in native wars, new diseases swept the islands, and rum and muskets became regular articles of trade. Tribal wars became bloody and general until Fiji was ceded to Britain on 10 Oct. 1874, after a previous offer of cession had been refused. British administrators produced order out of chaos, and since then there has been steady political, social and economic progress. Fiji gained independent status on 10 Oct. 1970.

AREA AND POPULATION. Fiji comprises about 332 islands and islets (about 110 inhabited) lying between 15° and 22° S. lat. and 174° E. and 177° W. long. The largest is Viti Levu, area 10,429 sq. km (4,027 sq. miles), next is Vanua Levu, area 5,556 sq. km (2,145 sq. miles). The island of Rotuma (47 sq. km, 18 sq. miles), about 12° 30′ S. lat., 178° E. long., was added to the colony in 1881. Total area, 7,078 sq. miles (18,333 sq. km).

A population census is taken every 10 years. Total population (census, Dec. 1977), 601,485; 1983 (estimate) 671,712. The mid 1983 total population consisted of the following: 300,945 (44·8%) Fijians; 336,028 (50%) Indians; 11,276 (1·7%) Part Europeans; 3,753 (0·6%) Europeans; 8,311 (1·2%) Rotumans; 4,596 (0·7%) Chinese; 6,624 (0·9%) other Pacific Islanders; 179 others.

Suva, the capital, is on the south coast of Viti Levu; population (1982), 71,255. Suva was proclaimed a city on 2 Oct. 1953. Lautoka had 26,000 in 1982.

Vital statistics, 1982: Crude birth rate per 1,000 population, Fijian, 28·5, Indian, 33; crude death rate per 1,000 population, Fijian, 5·4, Indian, 6·2.

CLIMATE. A tropical climate, but oceanic influences prevent undue extremes of heat or humidity. The S.E. Trades blow from May to Nov., during which time nights are cool and rainfall amounts least. Suva. Jan. 80°F (26·7°C), July 73°F (22·8°C). Annual rainfall 117″ (2,974 mm).

CONSTITUTION AND GOVERNMENT. Fiji became an independent nation within the Commonwealth on 10 Oct. 1970. This had been agreed at a constitutional conference held in London in April 1970. There is a Lower House, the House of Representatives, which consists of 52 elected members and an Upper House, the Senate, of 22 members (8 nominations by the Council of Chiefs, 7 by the Prime Minister, 6 by the Leader of the Opposition and 1 by the Rotuma Council). Elections are held every five years.

At elections held in July 1982 for the 52 seats in the House of Representatives the Alliance Party won 28 seats, the National Federation Party won 22 seats and the Western United Front won 2 seats. In Jan. 1982, the National Federation Party entered into a formal agreement with the Western United Front to form a coalition.

Local Government. The Fijian Administration, established in 1876, had jurisdiction over all Fijians.

Fiji is divided into 13 provinces, each with its own council. Elections to these councils in 90 constituencies were conducted for the first time in 1967 on a full adult franchise amongst Fijians.

The councils have wide powers to make by-laws and draw up their own budget subject to confirmation by the Fijian Affairs Board. Each council has its own treasury and levies rates to raise its revenue. These provincial rates vary from $F6 to $F9 per annum for every male adult, but those maintaining 5 or more children pay lower rates until their children become taxpayers. A start has been made, however, to change over to a system of land rating based upon the unimproved value of Fijian-owned land. This is considered to be more equitable and related to ability to pay.

These newly elected councils held their inaugural and 1968 budget meetings towards the end of 1967, when the chairman for each of these 13 councils was also elected from among its members. Members were elected for 2 years and new elections were held in 1969.

At the apex of the Fijian Administration is the Great Council of Chiefs presided over by the Minister for Fijian Affairs. The Council of Chiefs consists of 22 Fijian members elected to the House of Representatives, 30 representatives, elected by the Provincial Councils and 15 representatives nominated by the Minister for Fijian Affairs.

The Council of Chiefs advises the Government generally on Fijian affairs.

Governor-General: Ratu Sir Penaia Ganilau, GCMG, KCVO, KBE, DSO.

Prime Minister, Minister for Fijian Affairs and Information: Ratu Sir Kamisese Mara, GCMG, KBE.

Deputy Prime Minister and Minister for Economic Planning and Development: Ratu David Toganivalu. *Foreign Affairs, Tourism and Civil Aviation:* Jonati Mavoa, CMG. *Employment and Industrial Relations:* Mohammed Ramzan, MBE. *Housing and Urban Affairs:* Edward J. Beddoes. *Communications, Transport and Works:* Semesa K. Sikivou, CBE. *Home Affairs:* Militoni V. Leweniqila. *Attorney-General and Justice:* Qoriniasi Bale. *Finance:* Mosese Qionibaravi, CMG. *Education:* Dr Ahmed Ali. *Health and Social Welfare:* Dr Apenisa Kurisaqila. *Lands, Energy and Mineral Resources:* J. B. Naisara. *Primary Industries:* Charles Walker.

There are 3 Ministers of State.

Flag: Light blue with the Union Flag in the canton and the shield of Fiji in the fly.

DEFENCE. The Fiji Military Forces Ordinance, 1949, provides for the maintenance of a small regular force, with territorial units and trained reserves. This force, comprising 3 infantry battalions, numbers (1985), 2,500.

Navy. A naval squadron was authorized in 1974 to perform fishery protection, surveillance, hydrographic surveying and coastguard duties. Present strength is 3 coastal minesweepers (*ex*-US MSC), 1 utility vessel and 2 survey craft. Naval personnel (trained in Australia) in 1985 numbered 170 officers and ratings. The naval base is HMFS *Viti* in Suva.

INTERNATIONAL RELATIONS

Membership. Fiji is a member of the UN, the Commonwealth, the Colombo Plan and is an ACP state of the EEC.

ECONOMY

Budget. The financial year corresponds with the calendar year. All figures are in $1m. Fijian.

	1979	*1980*	*1981*	*1982*	*1983*[1]
Revenue	198·7	232·6	259·4	258·3	296·4
Expenditure	189·0	223·1	239·6	273·2	304·1

[1] Preliminary.

Currency. The National Bank of Fiji had, in 1983, deposits amounting to $F58·2m. due to 242,441 accounts. The headquarters are at Suva, and there are 48 agencies, 8 branches and 3 sub-branches throughout Fiji. Fiji changed to decimal currency on 13 Jan. 1969, with the major unit being $F1. In March 1985, £1 = $F1·28; US$ = $F1·20.

Banking. The Westpac Banking Corporation has 8 branches and 18 agencies; the Bank of New Zealand has 8 branches, and 15 agencies; the Australia and

New Zealand Bank has 3 branches and 3 agencies and the Bank of Baroda has 8 branches and 5 agencies in Fiji. Barclays International has 3 branches in Suva and 1 agency.

NATURAL RESOURCES

Agriculture. Some 600,000 acres of land are in agricultural use. Sugar-cane is the principal cash crop (production, 1983, 2,202,000 tonnes), accounting for more than two-thirds of Fiji's export earnings; one quarter of the population depend on it directly for their livelihood. Copra, Fiji's second major cash crop (output, 1983, 24,000 tonnes), provides coconut oil and other products for export and employs nearly as many workers as the sugar industry. Ginger is the third major export crop replacing bananas which has declined through disease and hurricane. Other agricultural products include rice, cocoa, maize, tobacco and a variety of fruits and vegetables. There is a small, but fast developing, livestock industry.

Livestock (1983): Cattle, 157,000; horses, 40,000; goats, 55,000; pigs, 28,000; poultry, 1m.

Forestry. Fiji supplies the bulk of its own timber requirements. A comprehensive pine scheme has been implemented with the aim of planting 186,000 acres by 1988.

Fisheries. Catch (1982) 26,000 tonnes.

INDUSTRY AND TRADE

Industry. Major industries include 4 large sugar-mills, the goldmines (1,250 kg in 1983) and 3 mills which process copra into coconut oil and coconut meal. There is a great variety of light industries.

Trade Unions. In 1982 there were 45 trade unions operating with about 45,000 members.

Commerce. Exports in 1983, $F244,902,000 (including re-exports). Imports, $F493,206,000. Chief exports: Sugar, gold, molasses and canned fish.

Total trade between Fiji and UK (British Department of Trade returns, in £1,000 sterling):

	1979	*1980*	*1981*	*1982*	*1983*	*1984*
Imports to UK	43,694	36,739	31,144	39,826	46,943	70,209
Exports and re-exports from UK	14,154	12,786	11,401	9,088	12,184	11,281

Tourism. In 1983, there were 192,000 visitors contributing $F136m. to the economy.

COMMUNICATIONS

Roads. Total road mileage is 2,019, of which 218 are sealed (paved), 1,663 are gravelled and 138 are unimproved. In 1983, there were 57,018 vehicles including 24,013 private cars, 18,049 goods vehicles, 1,188 buses, 4,028 tractors and (1980) 2,599 motor cycles.

Railway. Fiji Sugar Cane Corporation runs 600 mm gauge railways at four of its mills on Viti Levu and Vanua Levu, totalling 595 km.

Aviation. Fiji provides an essential staging point for long-haul trunk-route aircraft operating between North America, Australia and New Zealand. Under the South Pacific Air Transport Council, which comprises the UK, Australia, New Zealand and Fiji, the international airport at Nadi has been developed and administered. Thirteen other airports are in use for domestic services.

Shipping. In 1981, 234 vessels of 19,479 net tons were registered. Suva has 4 slipways of 100, 200, 500 and 1,500 tons, and there are 3 shipbuilding and repair firms.

Post. There are 42 post offices and 158 postal agencies. Overseas telephone and telegram services are available through the Commonwealth cable to most countries except those in the South Pacific, which are served by direct radio circuits. The automatic telex network operates through New Zealand into the international telex system. There are ship-to-shore radio facilities. There were 49,542 telephones in 1983.

Cinemas. In 1979 there were 48 cinemas with a seating capacity of 28,100.

JUSTICE, RELIGION AND EDUCATION

Justice. An independent Judiciary is guaranteed under the Constitution of Fiji. The Constitution allows for a Supreme Court of Fiji which has unlimited original jurisdiction to hear and determine any civil or criminal proceedings under any law.

The Supreme Court also has jurisdiction to hear and determine constitutional and electoral questions including the membership of members of the House of Representatives and the Senate.

The Chief Justice of Fiji is appointed by the Governor-General acting after consultation with the Prime Minister and the Leader of the Opposition.

Parliament prescribes the number of puisne judges. They are appointed by the Governor-General acting after consultation with the Judicial and Legal Services Commission.

The Constitution provides that a person cannot be qualified to be appointed as a judge of the Supreme Court unless he holds, or has held, high judicial office in some part of the Commonwealth or in any country outside the Commonwealth that may be prescribed by Parliament, or unless he has qualified to practise in the Supreme Court for not less than three years.

The Fiji Court of Appeal of which the Chief Justice is *ex officio* President is formed by four specially appointed Justices of Appeal. The Justices of Appeal are appointed by the Governor-General acting after consultation with the Judicial and Legal Services Commission. Generally any person convicted of any offence has a right of appeal from the Supreme Court to the Fiji Court of Appeal. The final appellant court is the Privy Council. Most matters coming before the Superior Courts originate in Magistrates' Courts.

Police. The Royal Fiji Police Force had (1983) a total strength of 1,410.

Religion. The 1976 census showed: Christians, 299,960; Hindus, 234,520; Moslems, 45,247; Confucians, 731.

Education (1983). School attendance is not compulsory in Fiji. There were 837 schools scattered over 56 islands, staffed by 7,254 teachers, of whom about 88·4% (1982) were trained. There were also 140 pre-schools. The primary and secondary schools had 164,659 pupils. The technical and vocational schools had 2,344 students and the teachers' colleges 285. There were 4 teacher-training colleges, 1 medical and 2 agricultural schools.

The University of the South Pacific opened in Feb. 1968 at Laucala Bay in Suva. It had about 1,500 full-time and 1,500 part-time students in 1983. The University has 3 schools, social and economic development, natural resources and education.

Total government expenditure on education in 1980 was over $F55·5m.

Health. In 1982 there were 27 hospitals with 1,720 beds, 325 doctors, 54 dentists and 1,342 nurses.

DIPLOMATIC REPRESENTATIVES

Of Fiji in Great Britain (34 Hyde Park Gate, London, SW7 5DN)
High Commissioner: Ratu Josua Brown Toganivalu, CBE (accredited 19 May 1981).

Of Great Britain in Fiji (Civic Centre, Stinson Parade, Suva)
High Commissioner: R. A. R. Barltrop, CVO.

Of Fiji in the USA (1140 19th St., NW, Washington, D.C., 20036)
Ambassador: Ratu Jone Filipe Radrodro.

Of the USA in Fiji (31 Loftus St., Suva)
Ambassador: Carl Dilery.

Of Fiji to the United Nations
Ambassador: Ratu Jone Radrodro.

Books of Reference

Statistical Information: A Bureau of Statistics was set up in 1950 (Government Buildings, Suva).
Trade Report. Annual (from 1887 [covering 1883–86]). Bureau of Statistics, Suva.
Journal of the Fiji Legislative Council. Annual (from 1914 [under different title from 1885]). Suva
Fiji Today. Suva, Annual
Fiji Facts and Figures. Suva, 1983
Report of Commission of Inquiry Into Natural Resources and Population Trends in Fiji. Suva, Government Press, 1960
Capell, A., *New Fijian Dictionary.* 2nd ed. Glasgow, 1957
Hoare, M., *The Winds of Change: Norfolk Island 1950–82.* Suva, 1983
Nayacakalou, R. R., *Leadership in Fiji.* OUP, 1976
Roth, G. K., *The Fijian Way of Life.* 2nd ed. OUP, 1973

FINLAND

Capital: Helsinki
Population: 4·87m. (1983)
GNP per capita: US$8,727 (1983)

Suomen Tasavalta—Republiken Finland

HISTORY. Since the Middle Ages Finland was a part of the realm of Sweden. In the 18th century parts of south-eastern Finland were conquered by Russia, and the rest of the country was ceded to Russia by the peace treaty of Hamina in 1809. Finland became an autonomous grand-duchy which retained its previous laws and institutions under its Grand Duke, the Emperor of Russia. After the Russian revolution Finland declared itself independent on 6 Dec. 1917. The Civil War began in Jan. 1918 between the 'whites' and 'reds', the latter being supported by Russian bolshevik troops. The defeat of the red guards in May 1918 consequently meant freeing the country from Russian troops. A peace treaty with Soviet Russia was signed in 1920.

On 30 Nov. 1939 Soviet troops invaded Finland, after Finland had rejected territorial concessions demanded by the USSR. These, however, had to be made in the peace treaty of 12 March 1940, amounting to 32,806 sq. km and including the Carelian Isthmus, Viipuri and the shores of Lake Ladoga.

When the German attack on the USSR was launched in June 1941 Finland again became involved in the war against the USSR. On 19 Sept. 1944 an armistice was signed in Moscow. Finland agreed to cede to Russia the Petsamo area in addition to cessions made in 1940 (total 42,934 sq. km) and to lease to Russia for 50 years the Porkkala headland to be used as a military base. Further, Finland undertook to pay 300m. gold dollars in reparations within 6 years (later extended to 8 years). The peace treaty was signed in Paris on 10 Feb. 1947. The payment of reparations was completed on 19 Sept. 1952. The military base of Porkkala was returned to Finland on 26 Jan. 1956.

AREA AND POPULATION. The area and the population of Finland on 31 Dec. 1983 (Swedish names in brackets):

Province	*Area (sq. km)*[1]	*Population*[2]	*Population per sq. km*[2]
Uusimaa (Nyland)	9,898	1,162,871	117·5
Turku-Pori (Åbo-Björneborg)	22,169	709,897	32·0
Ahvenanmaa (Åland)	1,527	23,435	15·4
Häme (Tavastehus)	17,010	672,096	39·5
Kymi (Kymmene)	10,783	342,432	31·8
Mikkeli (St Michel)	16,343	209,062	13·8
Pohjois-Karjala (Norra Karelen)	17,782	177,625	10·0
Kuopio	16,511	254,799	15·4
Keski-Suomi (Mellersta Finland)	16,230	246,242	15·2
Vaasa (Vasa)	26,447	442,073	16·7
Oulu (Uleåborg)	56,866	429,450	7·6
Lappi (Lappland)	93,057	199,876	8·2
Total	304,623	4,869,858	16·0

[1] Excluding inland water area which totals 33,522 sq. km. [2] Resident population.

The growth of the population, which was 421,500 in 1750, has been:

End of year	*Urban*	*Rural*	*Total*	*Percentage urban*
1800	46,600	786,100	832,700	5·6
1900	333,300	2,322,600	2,655,900	12·5
1950	1,302,400	2,727,400	4,029,800	32·3
1960	1,707,000	2,739,200	4,446,200	38·4
1970	2,340,308	2,258,028	4,598,336	50·9
1980	2,865,063	1,922,715	4,787,778	59·8
1983	2,910,467	1,959,391	4,869,858	59·8

The population on 31 Dec. 1983 by language primarily spoken: Finnish, 4,557,191; Swedish, 299,916; other languages, 11,347; Lappish, 1,404.

The principal towns with resident census population, 31 Dec. 1983, are (Swedish names in brackets):

Helsinki (Helsingfors)—capital	484,471	Kajaani	35,703
(metropolitan area)	932,376	Imatra	35,606
Tampere (Tammerfors)	167,344	Kokkola (Gamlakarleby)	34,337
(metropolitan area)	249,606	Rovaniemi	31,910
Turku (Åbo)	163,002	Kouvola	31,365
(metropolitan area)	256,687	Rauma (Raumo)	30,770
Espoo (Esbo)	149,057	Mikkeli (St Michel)	29,243
Vantaa (Vanda)	139,202	Savonlinna (Nyslott)	28,563
Oulu (Uleåborg)	96,243	Kemi	26,600
Lahti	94,466	Seinäjoki	25,827
Pori (Björneborg)	78,935	Kerava	25,380
Kuopio	76,792	Järvenpää	25,169
Jyväskylä	64,600	Varkaus	24,716
Kotka	59,973	Riihimäki	24,196
Vaasa (Vasa)	54,297	Nokia	23,978
Lappeenranta (Villmanstrand)	53,967	Iisalmi	23,225
Joensuu	45,920	Valkeakoski	22,594
Hämeenlinna (Tavastehus)	42,387	Kuusankoski	22,317
Hyvinkää (Hyvinge)	38,264		

Vital statistics in calendar years:

	Living births	*Of which illegitimate*	*Still-born*	*Marriages*	*Deaths (exclusive of still-born)*	*Emigration*
1979	63,428	7,603	269	29,277	43,737	16,661
1980	63,064	8,247	266	29,388	44,398	14,824
1981	63,469	8,431	260	30,100	44,404	10,042
1982	66,106	9,007	263	30,454	43,408	7,403
1983	67,023	...	...	29,498	45,444	7,120

In 1983 the rate per 1,000 was: Births, 13·8; marriages, 6·1; deaths, 9·4, and infantile deaths (1982, per 1,000 live births), 6.

Population and Housing Census 1980. 19 vols. Helsinki, 1981–83
Population. Annual. Helsinki

CLIMATE. The climate is severe in winter, which lasts about 6 months, but mean temperatures in south and south-west are less harsh, 21°F (–6°C). In the north, mean temperatures may fall to 8·5°F (–13°C). Snow covers the ground for three months in the south and for over six months in the far north. Summers are short but quite warm, with occasional very hot days. Precipitation is light throughout the country, with one third falling as snow, the remainder mainly as convectional rain in summer and autumn. Helsinki (Helsingfors). Jan. 21°F (–6°C), July 62°F (16·5°C). Annual rainfall 24·7″ (618 mm).

CONSTITUTION AND GOVERNMENT. Finland is a republic according to the Constitution of 17 July 1919.

Parliament consists of one chamber of 200 members chosen by direct and proportional election in which all Finnish citizens (men or women) who are 18 years have the vote (since 1972). The country is divided into 15 electoral districts with a representation proportional to their population. Every citizen over the age of 20 is eligible for Parliament, which is elected for 4 years, but can be dissolved sooner by the President.

The President is elected for 6 years by a college of 301 electors, elected by the votes of the citizens in the same way as the members of Parliament.

President of Finland: Dr Mauno Koivisto (elected 27 Jan. 1982).

State of Parties for Parliament elected on 20–21 March 1983: Conservative 44; Swedish Party, 11 (including 1 for Coalition of Åland); Centre, 38; Rural, 17; Social Democratic Party, 57, Communists, 27, Christian League, 3, Constitutional Party, 1. In addition there were 2 representatives of the Greens.

The Council of State (Cabinet), appointed by the President in May 1983 was composed as follows:

Prime Minister: Kalevi Sorsa.

Agriculture and Forestry: Toivo Yläjärvi. *Deputy Prime Minister and Foreign Affairs:* Paavo Väyrynen. *Justice:* Christoffer Taxell. *Environment:* Matti Ahde. *Interior:* Kaisa Raatikainen. *Defence:* Veikko Pihlajamäki. *Finance:* Ahti Pekkala. *Finance (Deputy):* Pekka Vennamo. *Education:* Kaarina Suonio. *Education (Deputy):* Gustav Björkstrand. *Communication:* Matti Luttinen. *Trade and Industry:* Seppo Lindblom. *Social Affairs and Health:* Eeva Kuuskoski-Vikatmaa. *Social Affairs and Health (Deputy):* Matti Puhakka. *Labour:* Urpo Leppänen. *Foreign Trade:* Jermu Laine.

National flag: White with a blue Scandinavian cross.

National anthem: Maamme; Swedish: Vårt land (words by J. L. Runeberg, 1843; tune by F. Pacius, 1848).

Finnish and Swedish are the official languages of Finland.

Local Government. For administrative purposes Finland is divided into 12 provinces (*lääni*, Sw.: *län*). The administration of each province is entrusted to a governor (*maaherra*, Sw.: *landshövding*) appointed by the President. He directs the activities of the provincial office (*lääninhallitus*, Sw.: *länsstyrelse*) and of local sheriffs (*nimismies*, Sw.: *länsman*). In 1984 the number of sheriff districts was 224.

The unit of local government is the commune. Main fields of communal activities are local planning, roads and harbours, sanitary services, education, health services and social aid. The communes raise taxes independent from state taxation. Two different kinds of communes are distinguished: Urban communes (*kaupunki*, Sw.: *stad*) and rural communes. In 1984 there were altogether 461 communes of which 84 were urban and 377 rural. In all communes communal councils are elected for terms of 4 years; all inhabitants (men and women) of the commune who have reached their 18th year are entitled to vote and eligible. The executive power is in each commune vested in a board which consists of members elected by the council and one or a few chief officials of the commune. Several communes often form an association for the administration of some common institution, *e.g.*, a hospital or a vocational school.

The autonomous county *(landskap)* of Åland has a county council *(landsting)* of one chamber, elected according to rule corresponding to those for parliamentary elections. In addition to its provincial governor it has a county board with executive power in matters within the field of the autonomy of the county.

Constitution Act and Parliament Act of Finland. Helsinki, 1978
The Finnish Parliament. Porvoo, 1969

DEFENCE. The period of military training is 240 to 330 days and refresher training 40 to 100 days. Total strength of trained and equipped reserves is about 700,000.

Army. The country is divided into 7 military regions. The Army consists of 1 armoured brigade, 7 infantry brigades, 7 independent infantry battalions, 3 field-artillery regiments, 2 independent field-artillery battalions, 2 coastal artillery regiments, 3 independent coastal artillery battalions, 1 anti-aircraft regiment, 1 surface-to-air missile battalion, 4 independent anti-aircraft battalions, 2 engineering battalions, 1 signals regiment and 1 signals battalion, making a total strength in 1985, of about 30,900.

Navy. The Fleet comprises 2 corvettes, 2 minelayers (including a modified *ex*-Soviet frigate), 1 coastal minelayer, 6 missile craft, 1 missile experimental craft, 10 fast patrol boats, 6 inshore minesweepers, 5 patrol boats capable of minelaying, 6 support ships, 1 headquarters ship, 10 transport craft, 14 landing craft, 3 tugs, 1 supply ship, 1 cable ship and 9 icebreakers. There is a naval academy. Personnel in 1985 totalled 2,500 (200 officers and 2,300 ratings).

The Frontier Guard comprises 4 large patrol vessels, 10 coastal defence craft and 36 coastal patrol boats.

Air Force. The Air Force has 2 fighter squadrons, 1 transport squadron, 1 training squadron, a military school of aviation, a technical school, a signal school and a depot. The fighter squadrons have MiG-21bis and Saab J35 Draken aircraft (1 additional J35 squadron to be formed). Other equipment includes 30 Valmet

Vinka piston-engined primary trainers of Finnish design, 50 Hawk trainers, MiG-21U and Saab J35C jet advanced trainers, C-47 and Fokker F.27 transport aircraft, Cessna 402 liaison aircraft, Learjet 35A target tugs, Piper Chieftain utility transports, and Mi-8 and Hughes 500 helicopters. Personnel total 3,000 officers and men.

INTERNATIONAL RELATIONS

Membership. Finland is a member of UN, the Nordic Council, OECD and an associate member of EFTA.

Treaties. A Treaty of friendship, co-operation and mutual assistance between Finland and the USSR was concluded in Moscow on 6 April 1948 for 10 years, extended on 19 Sept. 1955 to cover a period of 20 years, extended on 19 July 1970 for a further period of 20 years and extended again on 6 June 1983 for a further period of 20 years.

Treaty of Peace with Finland (10 Feb. 1947). Cmd. 7484

ECONOMY

Budget. Actual revenue and expenditure for the calendar years 1978–83, the ordinary budget for 1984 and the proposed budget for 1985 in 1m. marks:

	1978	*1979*	*1980*	*1981*	*1982*	*1983*	*1984*	*1985*
Revenue	40,393	43,319	48,916	58,795	63,043	76,354	84,548	92,928
Expenditure	38,938	45,036	50,812	57,797	68,008	77,190	84,547	92,927

Of the total revenue, 1983, 23% derived from sales tax, 25% from income and property tax, 14% from excise duties, 11% from other taxes and similar revenue, 14% from loans and 13% from miscellaneous sources. Of the total expenditure, 1983, 17% went to education and culture, 16% to social security, 9% to transport, 10% to agriculture and forestry, 9% to general administration, public order and safety, 9% to health, 5% to communities and housing policy, 6% to defence, 3% to promotion of industry and 16% to other expenditures.

At the end of Dec. 1983 the foreign loans totalled 21,723m. marks. The internal loans amounted to 16,401m. marks, of which, 16,383m. were consolidated debt. The cash deficit was 1,088m. marks. The total public debt was 38,124m. marks.

Currency. The unit of currency, starting 1 Jan. 1963, is the new *mark* of 100 *pennis*, equalling 100 old *marks*. The gold standard was suspended on 12 Oct. 1931. Aluminium bronze coins are 50, 20 and 10 *pennis*; copper coins, 5 and 1 *pennis*; aluminium coins, 5 and 1 *pennis*; silver, 1 *mark* pieces. Exchange rate in March 1985: 7·48 marks = £1; 7·10 marks = US$1.

Banking. The Bank of Finland (founded in 1811) is owned by the State and under the guarantee and supervision of Parliament. It is the only bank of issue, and the limit of its right to issue notes is fixed equal to the value of its assets of gold and foreign holdings plus 500m. marks. Notes of 500, 100, 50, 10, 5 and 1 marks are in circulation, and their total value at the end of 1981 was 6,029m. marks.

At the end of 1983 the deposits in banking institutions totalled 108,888m. marks and the loans granted by them 116,990m. marks. The most important groups of banking institutions were:

	Number of institutions	*Number of offices*	*Deposits (1m. marks)*	*Loans (1m. marks)*
Commercial banks	7	1,389	37,528	44,012
Savings banks	270	1,407	31,756	29,367
Postipankki	1	40 [1]	13,378	12,680
Co-operative banks	371	1,275	26,226	27,288

[1] In addition: 3,283 post offices.

Bank of Finland Monthly Bulletin. Helsinki, from 1926
Unitas. Quarterly Review, issued by Union Bank of Finland. Helsinki, from 1929
Economic Review (issued quarterly by Kansallis Osake Pankki). Helsinki, from 1948

Weights and Measures. The metric system of weights and measures was introduced in 1887 and is officially and universally employed.

Economic Survey of Finland. Annual

ENERGY AND NATURAL RESOURCES

Electricity. Electricity production was (in 1m. kwh.) 8,605 in 1960; 22,562 in

1970; 38,710 in 1980; 39,354 in 1982 and 40,120 in 1983, of which 33% was hydro-electric.

Minerals. The most important mines are Outokumpu (copper, discovered in 1910) and Otanmäki (iron, discovered in 1953). In 1982 the metal content (in tonnes) of the output of copper concentrates was 38,145, of zinc concentrates 54,665, of nickel concentrates 6,335, of iron concentrates and pellets 562,000 and of lead concentrates 1,882.

Agriculture. The cultivated area covers only 9% of the land and of the economically active population 9·2% were employed in agriculture and forestry in 1980. The arable area was divided in 1982 into 212,630 farms, and the distribution of this area by the size of the farms was: Less than 5 hectares cultivated, 64,040 farms; 5–20 hectares, 117,935 farms; 20–50 hectares, 27,500 farms; 50–100 hectares, 2,768 farms; over 100 hectares, 387 farms.

The principal crops (area in 1,000 hectares, yield in tonnes) were in 1983:

Crop	*Area*	*Yield*	*Crop*	*Area*	*Yield*
Rye	47	116,100	Oats	449	1,406,000
Barley	550	1,764,400	Potatoes	45	804,000
Wheat	159	549,500	Hay	490	2,057,400

The total area under cultivation in 1983 was 2,466,600 hectares. Production of dairy butter in 1983 was 84,000 tonnes, and of cheese, 72,000 tonnes.

Livestock (1984): Horses, 19,200; cattle, 1,657,500; pigs, 1,957,600; poultry, 7,957,600; reindeer, 347,000.

Forestry. The total forest land amounts to 30–31m. hectares. The productive forest land covers 19·73m. hectares. The growing stock was valued at 1,520m. cu. metres in 1971–76 and the annual growth at 57·4m. cu. metres.

In 1982 there were exported: Round timber, 766,685 cu. metres; sawn wood, 4,936,220 cu. metres; plywood and veneers, 691,927 cu. metres.

Monthly Review of Agriculture. Board of Agriculture
Agriculture 1982: Annual Statistics of Agriculture. Helsinki

INDUSTRY AND TRADE

Industry. The following data cover establishments with a total personnel of 5 or more in 1983 [1]:

Industry	*Establishments*	*Personnel* [2]	*Value of production: Gross (1m. marks)*	*Value of production: Value added (1m. marks)*
Mining and quarrying	114	7,728	1,855	1,079
Metal ore mining	13	4,344	842	474
Other mining	101	3,384	1,013	605
Manufacturing	7,557	523,570	180,265	63,924
Manufacture of food, beverages and tobacco	1,100	60,373	33,589	8,189
Textile, wearing apparel and leather industries	955	63,539	10,145	4,999
Manufacture of textiles	304	20,824	3,914	1,839
Manufacture of wearing apparel, except footwear	459	31,905	4,391	2,319
Manufacture of wood and wood products, incl. furniture	1,175	53,805	12,161	4,408
Manufacture of paper and paper prod., printing, publishing	967	84,409	38,147	13,000
Manufacture of paper and paper products	191	46,991	28,832	7,708
Printing, publishing, etc.	776	37,418	9,315	5,292
Manufacture of chemicals and chemical, petroleum, coal, rubber and plastic products	472	39,883	27,639	7,215
Manufacture of industrial chemicals	158	14,122	8,094	2,154
Manufacture of other chemical products	115	10,409	3,301	1,724
Petroleum refineries	2	2,696	13,048	1,803
Manufacture of non-metallic mineral products	434	21,276	5,700	2,931
Basic metal industries	89	19,134	11,993	2,443
Iron and steel basic industries	59	13,987	8,335	1,996
Non-ferrous metal basic industries	30	5,147	3,658	447

[1] Preliminary. [2] Working proprietors, salaried employees and wage earners.

Industry	*Establish-ments*	*Person-nel* [1]	*Value of production* *Gross (1m. marks)*	*Value added (1m. marks)*
Manufacture of fabricated metal products, machinery, etc.	2,242	176,124	40,024	20,237
Manufacture of fabricated metal products, excl. machinery	831	33,942	7,743	4,002
Manufacture of machinery, except electrical	792	65,745	14,672	7,651
Manufacture of electrical machinery, apparatus, etc.	228	30,095	6,338	3,466
Manufacture of transport equipment	308	41,684	10,317	4,469
Other manufacturing industries	123	5,027	866	502
Electricity, gas and water	523	28,031	23,351	8,388
All industry	8,194	559,329	205,471	73,391

[1] Working proprietors, salaried employees and wage earners.

GDP (at market prices) *per capita* (1983) 56,658 marks.

Industrial Statistics of Finland. Annual

Commerce. Imports and exports for calendar years, in 1m. marks:

	1979	*1980*	*1981*	*1982*	*1983*
Imports	44,222	58,250	61,269	64,751	71,528
Exports	43,430	52,795	60,308	63,026	69,692

The trade with some principal import and export countries was (in 1,000 marks):

Country	*Imports* *1982*	*1983*	*Exports* *1982*	*1983*
Australia	145,343	207,149	527,617	614,602
Austria	806,389	836,780	422,100	518,329
Belgium–Luxembourg	1,148,099	1,254,935	869,615	1,085,190
Brazil	468,401	503,595	178,879	186,868
Canada	573,188	531,826	440,951	412,463
China	147,686	196,038	193,110	255,487
Colombia	327,534	313,454	79,638	99,919
Czechoslovakia	338,757	307,203	268,887	274,248
Denmark	1,501,357	1,728,022	2,282,487	2,580,832
France	2,023,280	2,336,073	2,486,551	2,847,854
German Dem. Rep.	387,220	440,929	337,314	374,047
Germany (Fed. Rep.)	8,585,831	9,464,208	5,699,772	6,668,796
Greece	48,995	118,608	341,983	374,053
Hungary	276,920	255,544	363,290	215,398
Iran	323,397	719,440	476,113	443,087
Iraq	1,150	455	728,401	422,381
Ireland	205,296	240,802	402,787	374,349
Israel	164,932	187,293	203,844	246,820
Italy	1,707,913	2,140,662	1,134,317	1,300,198
Japan	2,723,217	3,903,263	677,793	789,315
Netherlands	1,714,545	1,903,228	1,928,125	2,771,250
Norway	1,456,549	1,884,965	3,084,494	2,376,799
Poland	938,492	904,641	86,328	115,067
Portugal	365,211	433,934	143,250	143,877
Saudi Arabia	1,362,691	772,702	538,842	566,978
Spain	453,791	529,959	530,082	523,789
Sweden	7,869,684	7,995,607	7,547,167	8,635,151
Switzerland	1,059,441	1,208,265	838,689	947,274
USSR	14,909,962	18,388,772	16,805,316	18,243,551
UK	4,641,997	4,765,931	6,827,279	7,199,712
USA	3,947,018	4,042,955	2,007,538	2,860,340

Principal imports 1983 (in 1m. marks): Machinery, apparatus and appliances, 20,877; mineral fuels, lubricants, etc., 19,246; chemicals, 6,703; food and live animals, 3,725; road vehicles, 4,547; crude materials, inedible, except fuels, 4,403; textile yarn, fabrics, etc., 2,627; iron and steel, 2,035.

Principal exports in 1983 (in 1m. marks): Paper and paper-board, 15,672;

machinery and transport equipment, 17,168; wood shaped or simply worked, 3,919; wood pulp, 3,260; ships, 6,261; clothing, 2,799; veneers, plywood, etc., and other wood manufactures, 1,536; food and live animals, 2,385; road vehicles, 1,215.

Total trade between Finland and UK (British Department of Trade returns, in £1,000 sterling):

	1980	*1981*	*1982*	*1983*	*1984*
Imports to UK	793,218	844,379	849,933	995,017	1,248,561
Exports and re-exports from UK	525,488	524,973	513,558	539,721	684,477

Foreign Trade. Annual

Tourism. In 1983 tourism contributed 2,845m. marks to the economy.

COMMUNICATIONS

Roads. In Jan. 1983 there were 75,448 km of public roads, of which 37,817 km were paved. At the end of 1983 there were 1,410,438 registered cars, 53,056 lorries, 114,775 vans and 9,102 buses.

Railways. On 31 Dec. 1983 the total length of the line operated was 6,090 km (1,257 km electrified), of which all except 21 km was owned by the State. The gauge was 1,524 mm. In 1983 the number of passengers carried was 42m. and the amount of goods carried was 29·1m. tonnes. The total revenue in 1983 was 2,497m. marks and the total expenditure 3,381m. marks.

Aviation. The scheduled traffic of Finnish airlines covered 37m. km in 1983. The number of passengers was 2,797,318 and the number of passenger-km 2,629·8m. The air transport of freight and mail amounted to 77m. tonne-km.

Shipping. The total registered mercantile marine on 31 Dec. 1983 was 484 vessels of 2·36m. gross tons. In 1983 the total number of vessels arriving in Finland from abroad was 15,695 and the goods discharged amounted to 30·9m. tonnes. The goods loaded for export from Finland ports amounted to 1·78m. tonnes.

The lakes, rivers and canals are navigable for about 6,100 km. Timber floating is important, and there are about 9,200 km of floatable inland waterways. In 1983 bundle floating was about 5·4m. tonnes and free floating 1·7m. tonnes.

On 27 Aug. 1963 the USSR leased to Finland the Russian part of the canal connecting Lake Saimaa with the Gulf of Finland. After extensive rebuilding the canal was opened for traffic in 1968. The Saimaa Canal and deepwater channels on Lake Saimaa (755 km) can be used by vessels with dimensions not larger than as follows: length 82 metres, width 11·8 metres, draught 4·2 metres and height of mast 24·5 metres.

Post and Broadcasting. In 1983 there were 3,632 post offices and 581 telegraph offices. The total length of telegraph wires was 577,201 km and that of domestic trunk and net group telephone wires 6·1m. km. The number of telephones was (1983), 2,777,073. All post and telegraph systems are administered by the State jointly with a large part of the telephone services. The total revenues from postal services were 2,496m. marks and from (wire and radio) telegraph services 2,518m. marks.

On 31 Dec. 1983 the number of television licences, 1,737,810, of which licences for colour television, 1,204,411. *Oy Yleisradio AB* broadcasts 2 programmes in Finnish and 1 in Swedish on long-, medium- and short-waves, and on FM. Two TV programmes (1 commercial) are broadcast.

Cinemas. In Dec. 1983 there were 368 cinemas with a seating capacity of 85,000.

Newspapers. In 1983 the number of newspapers published more often than once a week was 154, of which 142 in Finnish and 12 in Swedish.

JUSTICE, RELIGION, EDUCATION AND WELFARE

Justice. The lowest courts of justice are the municipal courts in towns and district courts in the country. Municipal courts are held by the burgomaster and at least 2 members of court, district court by judge and 5 jurors, the judge alone deciding, unless the jurors unanimously differ from him, when their decision prevails. From these courts an appeal lies to the courts of appeal *(Hovioikeus)* in Turku, Vaasa, Kuopio, Kouvola and Helsinki. The Supreme Court *(Korkein oikeus)* sits in Helsinki. Appeals from the decisions of administrative authorities are in the final instance decided by the Supreme Administration Court *(Korkein hallinto-oikeus)*, also in Helsinki. Judges can be removed only by judicial sentence.

Two functionaries, the *Oikeuskansleri* or Chancellor of Justice, and the *Oikeusasiamies*, or Solicitor-General, exercise control over the administration of justice. The former acts also as counsel and public prosecutor for the Government; while the latter, who is appointed by the Parliament, exerts a general control over all courts of law and public administration.

At the end of 1983 the prison population numbered 4,495 men and 161 women; the number of convictions in 1983 was 349,657, of which 323,495 were for minor offences with maximum penalty of fines and 26,137 with penalty of imprisonment. 11,516 of the prison sentences were unconditional.

Religion. Liberty of conscience is guaranteed to members of all religions. National churches are the Lutheran National Church and the Greek Orthodox Church of Finland. The Lutheran Church is divided into 8 bishoprics (Turku being the archiepiscopal see), 78 provostships and 594 parishes. The Greek Orthodox Church is divided into 3 bishoprics (Kuopio being the archiepiscopal see) and 25 parishes, in addition to which there are a monastery and a convent.

Percentage of the total population at the end of 1982: Lutherans, 90; Greek Orthodox, 1·1; others, 0·8; not members of any religion, 8·1.

Education (1982–83). *Primary and Secondary Education:*

	Number of institutions	*Teachers*	*Students*
First-level Education	*4,238*	*24,752*	*365,965*
(Lower sections of the comprehensive schools, grades I–VI)			
Second-level Education	*1,613*	*37,098*	*432,761*
General education	1,078	22,279	325,763
(Upper sections of the comprehensive schools, grades VII–IX, and senior secondary schools)			
Vocational education	*535*	*14,819*	*106,998*

Higher Education. Education at the third level (including universities and third level education at vocational institutes) was provided for 127,657 students. Education at universities was provided at 21 institutions with 6,618 teachers and 87,488 students.

University Education. Universities and similar types of institutions and the number of teachers and students are:

	Founded	*Teachers*	*Students Total*	*Students Women*
Universities				
Helsinki	1640	1,687	24,147	13,593
Turku (Swedish)	1919	289	3,512	2,184
Turku (Finnish)	1922	758	8,738	5,111
Jyväskylä	1958	470	6,161	3,920
Oulu	1958	728	7,251	3,341
Tampere	1966	499	8,902	5,519
Joensuu	1969	269	3,433	2,288
Kuopio	1972	216	1,773	1,092
Lapland	1979	57	621	289
Vaasa	1968	74	1,434	741
Polytechnic, Lappeenranta	1969	97	1,252	181
Polytechnic, Helsinki	1849	547	8,074	1,333
Polytechnic, Tampere	1972	193	2,840	285
College of Veterinary Medicine, Helsinki	1946	50	257	188
Schools for Economics				
Helsinki (Finnish)	1911	150	3,514	1,498
Helsinki (Swedish)	1927	86	1,609	672
Turku (Finnish)	1950	61	1,361	611
Swedish school of social work and local administration	1964 [1]	20	340	245

[1] Previously Swedish Civic College since 1943.

	Founded	Teachers	Students Total	Students Women
Universities of Art				
Sibelius Academy	1939	177	783	384
University of Industrial Arts	1949	137	875	511
Theatre Academy	1979	53	111	48
Teachers' training colleges [2]				

[2] Included in data for the universities above.

General adult education (at civic institutes, folk high schools and study centres) had 866,307 students.

General Education. Central Statistical Office, Helsinki (annual), *Higher Education.* Central Statistical Office, Helsinki (annual), *Vocational Education.* Helsinki (annual)

Health. In 1982 there were 10,057 physicians, 4,234 dentists and 75,026 hospital beds.

Social Security. The Social Insurance Institution administers general systems of old age pensions (to all persons over 65 years of age and disabled younger persons) and of health insurance. An additional system of compulsory old age pensions paid for by the employers is in force and works through the Central Pension Security Institute. Systems for child welfare, care of vagrants, alcoholics and drug addicts and other public aid are administered by the communes and supervised by the National Social Board and the Ministry of Social Affairs and Health.

The total cost of social security amounted to 58,090·1m. marks in 1982. Out of this 16,495·9m. (28·4%) was spent for health, 1,098·2m. (1·9%) for industrial accidents, 3,613·8m. (6·2%) for unemployment, 22,399·9m. (38·6%) old age and disability, 9,637·7m. (16·4%) for family allowances and child welfare, 339·1m. (0·6%) for general welfare purposes, 1,579·9m. (2·7%) for war-disabled, etc., 1,005m. (1·7%) as tax reductions for children. Out of the total expenditure 30% was financed by the State, 15% by local authorities, 44% by employers, 7% by the beneficiaries and 4% by users.

Labour Protection in Finland. Helsinki, 1980
Social Welfare in Finland. Helsinki, 1980
Social Security in the Nordic Countries 1981. Statistical Reports of the Nordic Countries, vol. 44. Helsinki, 1984
Arajarvi, E., *Social Expenditure in 1981 and Preliminary Data for 1982.* Official Statistics of Finland, Helsinki, 1983
Ellala, Esa, Suominen Risto, and Kotiranta, Maija-Liisa, *The Development of Social Security in Finland from 1950 to 1977.* Official statistics of Finland, special social studies XXXII : 56. Helsinki, 1978

DIPLOMATIC REPRESENTATIVES

Of Finland in Great Britain (38 Chesham Place, London, SW1X 8HW)
Ambassador: Ilkka Olavi Pastinen, KCMG (accredited 24 Feb. 1983).

Of Great Britain in Finland (16–20 Uudenmaankatu, Helsinki 12)
Ambassador: Alan Brooke Turner, CMG.

Of Finland in the USA (3216 New Mexico Ave., NW, Washington, D.C., 20016)
Ambassador: Richard Müller.

Of the USA in Finland (Itäinen Puistotie 14A, Helsinki 14)
Ambassador: Keith F. Nyborg.

Of Finland to the United Nations
Ambassador: Dr Keijo Korhonen.

Books of Reference

Statistical Information: The Central Statistical Office (Tilastokeskus, Swedish: Statistikcentralen; address: PO Box 504, SF-00101 Helsinki 10) was founded in 1865 to replace earlier official statistical services dating from 1749 (in united Sweden–Finland). Statistics on foreign trade, agriculture, forestry, navigation, health and social welfare are produced by other state authorities. Its publications include: *Statistical Yearbook of Finland* (from 1879) and *Bulletin of Statistics* (monthly, from 1924). A bibliography of all official statistics of Finland was published in Finnish, Swedish and English in *Statistical publications 1856–1979.* Helsinki, 1980.

Constitution Act and Parliament Act of Finland. Helsinki, 1978
Suomen valtiokalenteri (*State Calendar of Finland;* a Swedish version *Finlands statskalender* is published separately). Helsinki. Annual
Facts About Finland. Helsinki. Annual (Union Bank of Finland)
Facts about Finland. Helsinki, 1984
Finland in Figures. Helsinki, Annual
Finland in Maps. Helsinki, 1979
Finnish Press Laws. Helsinki, 1984
Making and Applying Law in Finland. Ministry of Justice, 1983
Statistical Yearbook of Finland. Helsinki, Annual
Yearbook of Finnish Foreign Policy. Helsinki, Annual
The Finnish Banking System. Helsinki, 1983
Finnish Industry. Helsinki, 1984
Finnish Local Government. Helsinki, 1982
Health Services in Finland. Helsinki, 1980
Hurme-Malin-Syväoja, *Finnish-English General Dictionary.* Helsinki, 1984
Hurme-Pesonen, *English–Finnish General Dictionary.* Helsinki, 1982
Jutikkala, E., and Pirinen, K., *A History of Finland.* 3rd ed. New York, 1979
Kekkonen, U., *President's View.* London, 1982
Kirby, D. G., *Finland in the Twentieth Century.* 2nd ed. London, 1984
Klinge, M., *A Brief History of Finland.* Helsinki, 1984
Layton, R., *Sibelius: The Master Musician.* London, 1978
Nousiainen, J., *The Finnish Political System.* Harvard Univ. Press, 1971
Paasivirta, J., *Finland and Europe. The Period of Autonomy and the International Crises 1808–1914.* London, 1981
Puntila, L. A., *The Political History of Finland, 1809–1966.* Helsinki, 1974
University of Turku, *Political Parties in Finland.* Turku, 1984

FRANCE

Capital: Paris
Population: 54·54m. (1984)
GNP per capita: US$12,190 (1981)

République Française

HISTORY. The republic proclaimed on the fall of the Bourbon monarchy in 1792 lasted until the First Empire, under Napoleon I, was established in 1804. The Bourbon monarchy was restored in 1814 and (with an interval during 1815) lasted until the abdication of Louis Philippe in 1848. The Second Republic was established on 12 March 1848, the Second Empire (under Louis Napoleon) on 2 Dec. 1852. The Third Republic was established on 4 Sept. 1870 following the capture and imprisonment of Louis Napoleon in the Franco-Prussian war, and lasted until the German occupation of 1940. The Fourth Republic was established on 24 Dec. 1946 and lasted until 4 Oct. 1958.

AREA AND POPULATION. France is bounded north by the English Channel *(La Manche)*, north-east by Belgium and Luxembourg, east by Federal Republic of Germany, Switzerland and Italy, south by the Mediterranean (with Monaco as a coastal enclave), south-west by Spain and Andorra, and west by the Atlantic Ocean The total area is 543,965 sq. km (210,033 sq. miles).

The population (present in actual boundaries) at successive censuses has been:

1801	27,349,003	1881	37,672,048	Mar. 1946	40,506,639
1821	30,461,875	1891	38,342,948	May 1954	42,777,174
1841	34,230,178	1901	38,961,945	Mar. 1962	46,519,997
1861	37,386,313	1911	39,604,992	Mar. 1968	49,778,540
1866	38,067,064	1921	39,209,518	Feb. 1975	52,655,802
1872	36,102,921	1931	41,834,923	Mar. 1982	54,334,871

The 1975 total included 3,442,415 foreigners, of whom 758,925 were Portuguese, 710,690 Algerian, 497,480 Spanish and 462,940 Italian.

The latest population estimate (at 30 June 1984) is 54,539,000.

Vital statistics for calendar years:

	Marriages	*Divorces*	*Live births*	*Stillborn*	*Deaths*
1976	374,003	59,200	720,395	7,522	557,114
1977	368,000	72,000	745,830	8,600	535,900
1978	354,628	73,200	737,062	7,852	546,916
1979	340,405	86,900	757,354	7,570	541,805
1980	334,377	...	800,376	7,900	547,107
1981	314,600	...	805,680	7,735	555,360

Live birth rate in 1980 was 15 per 1,000 inhabitants; death rate, 10·3; marriage rate, 5·8; divorce rate, 1·6; infant mortality, 9·6 per 1,000 live births. Life expectation at birth; men, 70·2; women, 78·5. Population growth rate, 4·5 per 1,000.

The areas, populations and chief towns of the 22 Metropolitan regions were as follows:

Regions	*Area (sq. km)*	*Census April 1975*	*Census March 1982*	*Chief town*
Alsace	8,280	1,517,330	1,566,048	Strasbourg
Aquitaine	41,308	2,550,340	2,656,544	Bordeaux
Auvergne	26,013	1,330,479	1,332,678	Clermont-Ferrand
Basse-Normandie	17,589	1,306,152	1,350,979	Caen
Bourgogne (Burgundy)	31,582	1,570,943	1,596,054	Dijon
Bretagne (Brittany)	27,208	2,595,431	2,707,886	Rennes
Centre	39,151	2,152,500	2,264,164	Orléans
Champagne-Ardenne	25,606	1,336,832	1,345,935	Reims
Corse (Corsica)	8,680	289,842	240,178	Ajaccio
Franche-Comté	16,202	1,060,317	1,084,049	Besançon
Haute-Normandie	12,317	1,595,695	1,655,362	Rouen

Regions	Area (sq. km)	Census April 1975	Census March 1982	Chief town
Île-de-France	12,012	9,878,524	10,073,059	Paris
Languedoc-Roussillon	27,376	1,789,474	1,926,514	Montpellier
Limousin	16,942	738,726	737,153	Limoges
Lorraine	23,547	2,330,821	2,319,905	Nancy
Midi-Pyrénées	45,348	2,268,245	2,325,319	Toulouse
Nord-Pas-de-Calais	12,414	3,913,773	3,932,939	Lille
Pays de la Loire	32,082	2,767,163	2,930,398	Nantes
Picardie	19,399	1,678,644	1,740,321	Amiens
Poitou-Charentes	25,810	1,528,118	1,568,230	Poitiers
Provence-Côte d'Azur	31,400	3,675,730	3,965,209	Marseille
Rhône-Alpes	43,698	4,780,723	5,015,947	Lyon

Populations of the principal conurbations and towns at Census 1975:

	Conurbation	Town		Conurbation	Town
Paris	8,549,898 [1]	2,317,227	Limoges	167,664	147,406
Lyon	1,170,660	462,841	Avignon	162,562	93,024
Marseille	1,070,912	914,356	Mantes-la-Jolie	154,988	42,564
Lille	935,882 [2]	177,218	Amiens	152,997	135,992
Bordeaux	612,456	226,281	Béthune	145,155	28,279
Toulouse	509,939	383,176	Thionville	141,881	44,191
Nantes	453,500	263,689	Briey	133,853	10,048
Nice	437,566	346,620	Montbéliard	132,343	31,591
Grenoble	389,088	169,740	Nîmes	131,638	133,942
Rouen	388,711	118,332	Pau	126,859	85,860
Toulon	378,430	185,050	Troyes	126,611	75,500
Strasbourg	365,323	257,303	Besançon	126,349	126,187
Valenciennes	350,599	43,202	Bayonne	121,474	44,706
St-Étienne	334,846	221,775	Saint-Nazaire	119,418	69,769
Lens	328,741	40,281	Perpignan	117,689	107,971
Nancy	280,569	111,493	Bruay-en-Artois	116,340	25,951
Le Havre	264,422	219,583	Trappes	112,353	22,905
Cannes	258,479	71,080	Aix-en-Provence	110,659	114,014
Clermont-Ferrand	253,244	161,203	Lorient	105,797	71,923
Tours	245,631	145,441	Valence	104,330	70,307
Rennes	229,310	205,733	Annecy	103,543	54,954
Mulhouse	218,743	119,326	La Rochelle	100,649	77,494
Montpellier	211,430	195,603	Boulogne-sur-Mer	100,581	49,284
Douai	210,508	47,570	Angoulême	100,528	50,500
Orléans	209,234	109,956	Calais	100,327	79,369
Dijon	208,432	156,787	Poitiers	98,554	85,466
Reims	197,021	183,610	Forbach	97,970	25,385
Le Mans	192,057	155,245	Maubeuge	97,494	35,474
Brest	190,812	172,176	Béziers	88,619	85,677
Angers	188,695	142,966	Chambéry	88,081	56,788
Dunkerque	186,314	83,759	Bourges	86,041	80,379
Caen	181,390	122,794	Roanne	83,561	56,498
Metz	181,191	117,199	Colmar	83,435	67,410

[1] Including towns of Boulogne-Billancourt (103,948) and Argenteuil (103,141).
[2] Including towns of Roubaix (109,797) and Tourcoing (102,543).

Recensement de la population de 1982. Paris, Institut National de la Statistique et des Etudes Economiques, 1983
Scargill, I., *Urban France.* London, 1983

CLIMATE. The north west has a moderate maritime climate, with small temperature range and abundant rainfall, but inland, rainfall becomes more seasonal, with a summer maximum, and the annual range of temperature increases. Southern France has a Mediterranean climate, with mild moist winters and hot dry summers. Eastern France has a continental climate and a rainfall maximum in summer, with thunderstorms prevalent.

Paris. Jan. 37°F (3°C), July 64°F (18°C). Annual rainfall 22·9″ (573 mm). Bordeaux. Jan. 41°F (5°C), July 68°F (20°C). Annual rainfall 31·4″ (786 mm). Lyon. Jan. 37°F (3°C), July 68°F (20°C). Annual rainfall 31·8″ (794 mm).

CONSTITUTION AND GOVERNMENT. The Constitution of the Fifth Republic, superseding that of 1946, came into force on 4 Oct. 1958. It consists of a preamble, dealing with the Rights of Man, and 92 articles.

France is a Republic, indivisible, secular, democratic and social; all citizens are equal before the law (Art. 2). National sovereignty resides with the people, who exercise it through their representatives and by referenda (Art. 3). Political parties carry out their activities freely, but must respect the principles of national sovereignty and democracy (Art. 4).

The President of the Republic sees that the Constitution is respected; he ensures the regular functioning of the public authorities, as well as the continuity of the state. He is the protector of national independence and territorial integrity (Art. 5). He is elected for 7 years by direct universal suffrage (Art. 6). He appoints a Prime Minister and, on the latter's advice, appoints and dismisses the other members of the Government (Art. 8). He presides over the Council of Ministers (Art. 9). He can dissolve the National Assembly, after consultation with the Prime Minister and the Presidents of the two Houses (Art. 12). He appoints to the civil and military offices of the state (Art. 13). In times of crisis, he may take such emergency powers as the circumstances demand; the National Assembly cannot be dissolved during such a period (Art. 16).

Previous Presidents of the Fifth Republic:

General Charles André Joseph de Gaulle, 8 Jan. 1959–28 April 1969 (resigned); Alain Poher (interim), 28 April 1969–20 June 1969; Georges Jean Raymond Pompidou, 20 June 1969–2 April 1974 (died); Alain Poher (interim), 2 April 1974–27 May 1974; Valéry Giscard d'Estaing, 27 May 1974–21 May 1981.

President of the Republic: François Mitterrand (elected 10 May 1981; took office 21 May 1981).

The government determines and conducts the policy of the nation (Art. 20). The Prime Minister directs the operation of the Government, is responsible for national defence and ensures the execution of laws (Art. 21). Members of the Government must not be members of Parliament (Art. 23).

The Council of Ministers was composed as follows in March 1985:

Prime Minister: Laurent Fabius (Soc.)
Finance and Budget: Pierre Bérégovoy (Soc.)
Social Affairs and National Solidarity, Government Spokesman: Georgina Dufoix (Soc.)
Interior and Decentralization: Pierre Joxe (Soc.)
Planning and Regional Development: Gaston Defferre (Soc.)
Justice: Robert Badinter (Soc.)
Foreign Affairs: Roland Dumas (Soc.)
Defence: Charles Hernu (Soc.)
Agriculture: Michel Rocard (Soc.)
Research and Technology: Hubert Curien (Soc.)
Education: Jean-Pierre Chevènement (Soc.)
Industrial Redeployment and Foreign Trade: Edith Cresson (Soc.)
Town Planning, Housing and Transport: Paul Quilés (Soc.)
Commerce, Craft Trades and Tourism: Michel Crépeau (MRG)
Environment: Huguette Bouchardeau (PSU)
Labour, Employment and Vocational Training: Michel Delebarre (Soc.)
Ministers-Delegate: Jack Lang *(Culture),* Yvette Roudy *(Women's Rights),* Alain Calmat *(Youth and Sports),* André Labarrère *(Parliamentary Relations),* Christian Nucci *(Overseas Co-operation and Development),* Louis Mexandeau *(Posts and Telecommunications).*

The Government also includes 20 Secretaries of State.

Parliament consists of the National Assembly and the Senate; the National Assembly is elected by direct suffrage and the Senate by indirect suffrage (Art. 24). It convenes as of right in two ordinary sessions per year, the first on 2 Oct. for 80 days and the second on 2 April for not more than 90 days (Art. 28).

The National Assembly comprises 491 Deputies, elected for a 5-year term from single-member constituencies – 474 in Metropolitan France, 11 in Overseas Departments, 1 for Mayotte (a 'special collectivity'), and 5 in Overseas Territories. The latest General Elections, held in June 1981, resulted in a new composition of 269 *Parti Socialiste*, 44 *Parti Communiste Français*, 14 *Mouvement des Radicaux de Gauche* and 6 others supporting the Government, together with 88 *Rassemblement Pour la République* (Gaullists), 63 *Union de la Démocratie Française* (Giscardians and Centrist Union), and 7 others forming the opposition. On 17 Sept. 1984 the PCF withdrew support and joined the opposition.

The Senate comprises 318 Senators elected for 9-year terms (one-third every 3 years) by an electoral college in each Department or Overseas Territory, made up of all members of the Departmental Council or Territorial Assembly together with all members of Municipal Councils within that area; 298 Senators represent Metropolitan France, 8 Overseas Departments, 1 Mayotte, 3 Overseas Territories and 8 Frenchmen residing outside France. Following the partial elections in Sept. 1983, the Senate was composed of 70 *Groupe Socialiste*, 72 *Union Centriste*, 49 *Union des Républicans et des Indépendants* (Giscardians), 58 RPR (Gaullists), 27 *Gauche Démocratique*, 24 *Groupe Communiste*, 12 MRG, 5 *non-inscrits* (unaffiliated) and 1 seat vacant.

The Constitutional Council is composed of 9 members whose term of office is 9 years (non-renewable), one-third every 3 years; 3 are appointed by the President of the Republic, 3 by the President of the National Assembly, and 3 by the President of the Senate; in addition, former Presidents of the Republic are, by right, life members of the Constitutional Council (Art. 56). It oversees the fairness of the elections of the President (Art. 58) and Parliament (Art. 59) and of referenda (Art. 60), and acts as a guardian of the Constitution (Art. 61).

The Economic and Social Council advises on Government and Private Members' Bills (Art. 69). It comprises representatives of employers', workers' and farmers' organizations in each Department and Overseas Territory.

National flag: The Tricolour of three vertical stripes of blue, white, red.

National anthem: La Marseillaise (words and music by C. Rouget de Lisle, 1792).

Local Government: France is divided into 22 regions for national development work, for planning and for budgetary policy. Under far-reaching legislation on decentralisation promulgated in March 1982, state appointed Regional Prefects were abolished and their executive powers transferred to the Presidents of the Regional Councils, which are to be directly elected.

There are 96 *départements* within the 22 regions each governed by a directly-elected *Conseil Général*. From 1982 their Presidents' powers are greatly extended to take over local administration and expenditure from the former Departmental prefects, now called 'Commissioners of the Republic' with responsibility for public order. The *arrondissement* (324 in 1975) and the *canton* (3,509 in 1975), have little administrative significance.

The unit of local government is the *commune*, the size and population of which vary very much. There were, in 1975, in the 96 metropolitan departments, 36,394 communes. Most of them (31,593) had less than 1,500 inhabitants, and 16,550 had less than 300, while 229 communes had more than 30,000 inhabitants. The local affairs of the commune are under a Municipal Council, composed of from 9 to 36 members, elected by universal suffrage for 6 years by French citizens of 21 years or over after 6 months' residence. Each Municipal Council elects a mayor, who is both the representative of the commune and the agent of the central government.

In Paris the *Conseil de Paris* is composed of 109 members elected from the 20 *arrondissements*. It combines the functions of departmental *Conseil Général* and Municipal Council.

d'Estaing, V. G., *French Democracy.* New York, 1977
Suleiman, E. N., *Politics, Power, and Bureaucracy in France.* Princeton Univ. Press, 1974
Wright, V., *The Government and Politics of France.* London, 1978

DEFENCE. The President of the Republic exercises command over the Armed

Forces. He is assisted by the research organization of the High Council of Defence (*Conseil Supérieur de la Défense Nationale*) and two Committees (*Comité de Défense* and *Comité de Défense restreint*) which formulate directives. The Prime Minister is responsible for the national defence; he exercises his military responsibilities through the General Secretariat of National Defence (SGDN). Under the Prime Minister's authority, the *Comité d'Action Scientifique de Défense* co-ordinates research.

On 5 July 1969 the Army Ministry was replaced by the Ministry of State for National Defence which is responsible for the Army, Air Force and Navy. In addition to the powers of the Army Ministry, the Ministry of State prepares general directives for negotiations relating to defence. It is assisted by the Departmental Assistant for Weapons, the Secretary-General for Administration, the Chief of Staff of the Armed Forces and the Chiefs of Staff of the 3 Armed Forces—Army, Navy and Air.

In 1962 the Armed Forces were reorganized in 3 groups: (1) nuclear strategic force; (2) operational forces; (3) home defence forces. Total strength (1984) 471,350.

French forces are not formally committed to NATO.

Army. The Army consists of regular officers and n.c.o.s, long-term n.c.o.s and soldiers, and conscripts serving 12 months.

The peace-time units comprise infantry, armoured troops and cavalry, artillery, engineering, signals, transport, matériel, naval infantry and artillery. In addition, there are the Foreign Legion, mountain and airborne troops and other specialized units.

In 1984 the effective strength of the Army was 305,000 all ranks (excluding *Gendarmerie).*

Higher military instruction is provided in 3 stages: the staff school (*École d'État-major*) for officers of formation staffs; the *École Supérieure de Guerre* for officers earmarked for the higher command; the *Institut des Hautes Études de Défense Nationale* where high-ranking officers and civilians study together the problems of national defence.

Light Army Aircraft. Formed in 1952, the *Aviation Légère de l'Armée de Terre* (ALAT) is a well-equipped force, with 75 light aeroplanes and more than 560 helicopters for observation, reconnaissance, combat area transport, liaison and supply duties. Effective strength, 1984, 6,600.

The *Gendarmerie* is an integral part of the Armed Forces but also co-operates with the civil administration in maintaining public order. Effective strength, 1984, 85,312.

Navy. The Navy is under the supreme direction of the Minister of Defence, being administered by the Chief and Deputy Chiefs of Naval Staff.

All naval aircraft and coastal defences are under the control of the Navy, and have been reorganized in 3 coast 'naval frontier' districts (with headquarters in Cherbourg, Brest and Toulon), in relation to the aircraft attached to the fleet.

The French Navy is manned partly by conscription but mainly by voluntary enlistment. In 1985 the active personnel was 67,720 officers and men, including the Naval Air Arm.

The following is a summary of the strength of the fleet at the end of the years shown:

	1976	*1977*	*1978*	*1979*	*1980*	*1981*	*1982*	*1983*	*1984*
Aircraft carriers	3[1]	3[1]	3[1]	3[1]	3[1]	3[1]	3[1]	3[1]	3[1]
Submarines	24[2]	26[2]	27[2]	29[3]	28[3]	27[3]	28[3]	24[4]	26[4]
Cruisers	1	1	1	1	1	1	1	1	1
Destroyers	20	21	22	20	19	20	20	18	18
Frigates	27	29	27	24	22	22	25	26	26

[1] Including 1 helicopter-carrier.
[2] Including 4 nuclear-powered ballistic missile submarines.
[3] Including 5 nuclear-powered ballistic missile submarines.
[4] Including 6 nuclear-powered ballistic missile submarines.

The principal ships of the French Navy are as follows:

Completed	Name	Standard displacement Tons	Aircraft	Principal armament	Shaft horsepower	Speed Knots
			Aircraft Carriers			
1963	Foch	27,300	30 fixed wing,	8 3·9 in.	126,000	32·0
1961	Clemenceau	(normal)	4 helicopters			
			Helicopter Carrier			
1964	Jeanne d'Arc[1]	10,000	8 helicopters	6 'Exocet' (singles) 4 3·9 in.	40,000	26·5
			Cruiser			
1959	Colbert	8,500	—	4 'Exocet' (singles) 1 twin 'Masurca' 2 3·9 in. AA	86,000	32·0

[1] Cruiser type forward, flat-topped midships to aft.

Capital (Strategic) Submarines

Class	No.	Displacement (submerged) tons	Missile Tubes (vertical)	Nuclear Reactors	Shaft horsepower	Speed Knots
'611'	6	8,940	16 M 20	1	16,000	25 dived 20 surface

In order of completion: *Le Redoutable* (1971), *Le Terrible* (1973), *Le Foudroyant* (1974), *L'Indomptable* (1976), *Le Tonnant* (1980), **L'Inflexible* (1985)

*The latter, with M4 missiles, is of intermediate type between her predecessors and a new class. One more is reportedly planned and two or three more of an improved class envisaged.

All the named vessels above are also armed with four 21-inch torpedo tubes.

There are also 2 nuclear-powered fleet submarines of 2,670 tons (submerged), 1 large experimental missile submarine, 17 diesel-powered submarines, 18 destroyers, 26 frigates, 5 fast missile craft, 4 fast attack craft, 5 offshore patrol vessels, 10 large minehunters (*ex*-ocean minesweepers), 8 coastal minehunters, 14 coastal minesweepers (4 used as patrol vessels and 4 as diving ships), 8 inshore minesweepers (used as diving and utility tenders), 7 surveying vessels, 2 dock landing ships, 9 tank landing ships, 18 landing craft, 36 minor landing craft, 7 maintenance, repair and depot ships, 6 oilers, 11 boom defence vessels, 8 support ships, 18 transports, 16 training vessels, 42 auxiliary ships and 105 tugs.

One more nuclear-powered ballistic missile submarine, 3 nuclear-powered fleet (torpedo-armed) submarines, 4 guided missile destroyers and 8 *avisos* (escorts) are under construction. One nuclear-powered aircraft carrier, *Charles de Gaulle*, 36,000 tons, 40 aircraft, for keel-laying in 1986 and commissioning in 1995; 4 more nuclear-powered fleet, torpedo-armed (hunter-killer) submarines, 3 frigates and 7 mine-hunters are projected.

The naval air arm, known usually as *Aéronavale*, includes 2 squadrons of nationally designed Super Etendard transonic fighter-bombers, 1 squadron of Super Etendard reconnaissance fighters, 2 squadrons of US-built Crusader all-weather fighters, 3 squadrons of Alizé turboprop anti-submarine aircraft, 5 maritime reconnaissance squadrons with Atlantic and Neptune aircraft and 3 anti-submarine and assault squadrons with Super Frelon, Lynx and HSS-1 helicopters. Strength is 410 aircraft comprising 310 fixed-wing and 100 helicopters.

Air Force. Formed as the *Service Aéronautique* in April 1910, the *Armeé de l'Air* is organized in 7 major commands. Its bases and installations were regrouped and modernized in 1967. The *Commandement des Forces Aériennes Stratégiques* (CFAS) commands the nuclear deterrent force. The *Commandement de la Force*

Aérienne Tactique (FATAC) directs the tactical air forces, commands the air force reserve and is responsible for support of the ground forces. Under FATAC the 1st *Commandement Aérien Tactique* (1° CATAC) controls tactical air units based in eastern France; the 2nd *Commandement Aérien Tactique* (2° CATAC) controls the reserve forces and the air component of the *Force d'Intervention*. The *Commandement du Transport Aérien Militaire* (COTAM) is responsible for air transport operations and for the training and transport of airborne forces. The *Commandement Air des Forces de Défense Aérienne* (CAFDA) controls air defence forces. The *Commandement des Écoles de l'Armée de l'Air* (CEAA) is responsible for training the personnel for all branches of the Air Force. The *Commandement des Transmissions* has responsibility for communications and electronic warfare. Finally, the *Commandement du Génie de l'Air,* made up mainly of Army personnel, undertakes airbase construction and maintenance under Air Force control.

The home-based French Air Force is divided territorially among 4 metropolitan air regions (Metz, Villacoublay, Bordeaux, Aix-en-Provence); overseas, small air units are integrated into the local joint-service commands. There are about 40 combat squadrons plus about 30 transport, helicopter and support squadrons, and the Air Force uses a total of 66 bases.

The strategic, tactical and air defence forces are equipped entirely with jet aircraft. The CFAS has 96 first-line Mirage IV supersonic nuclear bombers, and 10 reserves, deployed in 2 wings (each 3 squadrons) supported by 11 C-135F refuelling tanker transports. The 1° CATAC deploys 7 wings (20 squadrons), with about 180 Mirage III-E and 5F ground-attack fighters, and 135 Jaguar strike aircraft, plus 2 OCUs equipped with Mirage III-Bs and Jaguars. Five of these squadrons can deliver AN 52 nuclear weapons. The 3 reconnaissance squadrons were re-equipped with Mirage F1-CRs. The air defence forces have 4 wings, with 8 squadrons of Mirage F1 multi-mission fighters and 1 squadron of Mirage III-Cs (to be replaced by Mirage 2000s). The COTAM is organized into 4 wings, equipped with 45 Transall C.160 turboprop transports, 50 Nord 250ls, 4 DC-8s and 92 helicopters. Training aircraft include CAP-10 piston-engined primary trainers, Epsilon piston-engined and Magister jet basic trainers, Alpha Jet and Mirage III-B advanced trainers, and two-seat Jaguars; 25 EMB-121 Xingus bought from Brazil and dual-purpose training/liaison aircraft.

Total officers and other ranks (1983) 100,225; 495 combat aircraft.

INTERNATIONAL RELATIONS

Membership. France is a member of UN, the Council of Europe, NATO and EEC.

ECONOMY

Planning. For the history of planning in France from 1947 to 1980, *see* THE STATESMAN'S YEAR-BOOK, 1982–83, p. 474. The eighth plan, covering the 1981–85 period, was set aside after the change of government in May 1981 and replaced by an interim plan for 1982–83, followed by a new ninth plan for 1984–88.

Budget. Receipts and expenditure (in 1m. francs) for calendar years:

Receipts	*1983*	*%*	*1984*	*%*
Direct taxation				
Income tax	200,592	21·4	219,907	21·9
Corporation tax	90,800	9·7	89,290	8·9
Wealth and other taxes	65,092	6·9	71,342	7·1
Indirect taxation				
Value-added tax	385,685	41·2	415,800	41·4
Petrol tax	58,010	6·2	67,396	6·7
Stamp duty and other taxes	90,869	9·7	86,302	8·6
Non-fiscal receipts	45,770	4·9	54,002	5·4
Gross total	936,818		1,004,039	
Net budget receipts (gross total taxes minus various deductions)	772,234		817,198	

Expenditure	*1982*	%	*1983*	%
Public authorities and general administration	83,724	10·3	92,980	10·3
Education and culture	188,655	23·1	208,757	23·1
Social affairs, health, employment	176,517	21·6	199,911	22·1
Agriculture and countryside	21,946	2·7	22,886	2·5
Housing and town planning	41,904	5·1	48,211	5·4
Transport and communications	36,342	4·5	41,592	4·6
Industry and services	43,408	5·3	46,313	5·1
External affairs	21,921	2·7	25,639	2·9
Defence	131,452	16·1	141,505	15·7
Miscellaneous expenditure	70,408	8·6	75,317	8·3
Total expenditure	816,277		903,111	

The accounts of revenue and expenditure are examined by a special administrative tribunal (*Cour des Comptes*), instituted in 1807.

Currency. The unit of currency is the *franc.* Coins are issued for 5, 10, 20 and 50 centimes, 1, 2, 5 and 10 francs; and bank-notes for 10, 50, 100 and 500 francs. In March 1985, £1 sterling = 11·03 *francs*; US$1 = 10·48 *francs*.

Banking. The *Banque de France*, founded in 1800, and placed under the authority of a state-appointed Governor in 1806, has the monopoly (since 1848) of issuing bank-notes throughout France. Note circulation at 31 Dec. 1981 was 151,900m. francs.

On 2 Dec. 1945 a law was passed to nationalize the *Banque de France* and the principal deposit banks. It also established a new body, the National Credit Council, formed to regulate banking activity and consulted in all political decisions on monetary policy. This new body comprises 45 members nominated by the Government; its president is the Minister for the Economy, its vice-president is the Governor of the *Banque de France* which as a Central Bank puts monetary policy into effect and supervises its application. On 11 Feb. 1982, a law was passed to nationalize the remaining deposit banks, the principal ones being: (*i*) those nationalized in 1945: Crédit Lyonnais (founded 1863), Banque Nationale de Paris (founded by amalgamation 1966) and the Société Générale (founded 1864), and (*ii*) among those nationalized in 1982: Crédit Industriel et Commercial, Crédit Commercial de France, the Banque de Paris et des Pays-Bas and the Crédit du Nord. Total deposits and short- and medium-term held bills by the banks at 31 Dec. 1981 was 1,302,800m. francs. The rest of the banking system comprises the popular banks, the Crédit agricole, the Crédit mutuel, the Banque française du commerce exterieur and the various financial establishments.

The state savings organization (*Caisse nationale d'epargne*) is administered by the post office on a giro system. On 31 Dec. 1981 the private savings banks (*Caisses d'epargne et de prévoyance*), numbering about 500 had 434,000m. francs in deposits; the state savings banks had 206,300m. francs in deposits. Deposited funds are centralized by a non-banking body, the *Caisse de Dépôts et Consignations*, which finances a large number of local authorities and state aided housing projects, and carries an important portfolio of transferable securities.

Weights and Measures. The metric system is in general use.

ENERGY AND NATURAL RESOURCES

Electricity. Production of electrical power (in 1m. kwh.): 1980, 243,282; 1981, 260,759; 1982, 262,813. In 1978, 37% was hydro electric and 9% nuclear.

Oil. In 1982 1·64m. tonnes of crude oil were produced. The greater part came from the Parentis oilfield in the Landes. France has an important oil-refining industry, utilizing imported crude oil. Total yearly capacity at the end of 1979 was about 166·84m. tonnes. The principal plants are situated in Basse Seine (capacity in tonnes, 1979), 56·1m.; Mediterranean, 45·5m.; Atlantic, 15·9m.; Nord, 14·8m.; Alsace, 13·9m.; Paris region, 11·6m.; Lyonnais, 9m.

There has been considerable development of the production of natural gas and sulphur in the region of Lacq in the foothills of the Pyrenees. Production of natural gas was 7,757m. cu. metres in 1979, 7,529 in 1980, 7,080 in 1981.

Minerals. Principal minerals and metals produced, in 1,000 tonnes:

	1976	*1977*	*1978*	*1979*
Coal	21,879	21,293	19,690	18,612
Lignite	3,189	3,080	2,732	2,454
Iron ore	45,181	36,630	33,454	31,627
Bauxite	2,330	2,059	1,978	1,969
Potash salts	1,738	1,719	1,928	2,075
Pig-iron	19,024	18,257	18,497	19,415
Crude Steel	23,221	22,094	22,841	23,360
Aluminium	385	400	391	395

Agriculture. Of the total area of France (54·9m. hectares) 17·3m. were under cultivation, 12·9m. were pasture, 1·2m. were under vines, 14·3m. were forests and 8·3m. were uncultivated land in 1980.

The following table shows the area under the leading crops and the production for 4 years:

	Area (1,000 hectares)				*Produce (1,000 tonnes)*			
Crop	*1977*	*1978*	*1979*	*1980*	*1977*	*1978*	*1979*	*1980*
Wheat	4,126	4,167	4,063	4,580	17,546	21,057	19,411	23,668
Rye	129	138	116	128	389	432	353	405
Barley	2,909	2,814	2,816	2,648	10,319	11,414	11,238	11,758
Oats	625	611	539	534	1,938	2,194	1,865	1,927
Potatoes	279	269	252	227	8,190	7,459	6,698	6,722
Sugar-beet	585	556	547	541	24,500	24,488	26,444	26,206
Maize	1,639	1,802	2,003	1,754	8,316	9,473	10,293	9,254

Other crops in 1980 (figures for 1979 in brackets) include (in 1,000 tonnes): Rice, 27 (29); tobacco, 48 (53); flax, 293 (307).

France is the world's second largest producer of wine (after Italy); production in 1978 amounted to 5,882,000 tonnes.

The annual production of wine (in 1,000 hectolitres) appears as follows:

	Vineyards (1,000 hectares)	*Wine produced*
1938	1,513	60,332
1948	1,433	47,437
1958	1,315	47,735
1968	1,228	66,460
1977	1,180	53,137
1978	1,141	58,599
1979	1,219	80,319
1980	1,174	71,546

The production of fruits (other than for cider making) for 4 years was (in 1,000 tonnes) as follows:

	1977	*1978*	*1979*	*1980*
Apples	1,243	1,867	1,716	1,810
Pears	273	366	418	422
Plums	73	165	158	136
Peaches	319	406	386	397
Apricots	72	81	59	71
Cherries	53	99	112	106
Nuts	18	37	30	30
Grapes	211	234	213	192
Strawberries	77	68	82	85

In 1983 the numbers of farm animals (in 1,000) were (figures for 1982 in brackets): Horses, 312 (315); cattle, 23,656 (23,493); sheep, 12,103 (13,090); goats, 1,243 (1,242); pigs, 11,709 (11,421); poultry, 213,000 (215,000).

Forestry. The total area of forested land (1982) was 137,651 sq. km. Timber sold (1982), 28,342m. cu. metres valued at 7,581m. francs.

Fisheries. (1982). There were 75,060 fishermen, and 10,780 sailing-boats, steamers and motor-boats. Catch (in 1,000 tonnes): Fish, total, 640; crustaceans, 29; shell fish, 191.

INDUSTRY AND TRADE

Industry. Industrial production (in 1,000 tonnes) for 3 years was as follows:

	1980	*1981*	*1982*
Sulphuric acid	4,952	4,412	4,143
Caustic acid	1,333	1,314	1,448
Sulphur	1,839	1,700	1,839
Polystyrene	254	262	445

	1980	1981	1982
Polyvinyl	725	710	789
Polyethylene	1,074	883	912
Wool	64	54	49
Cotton	172	158	161
Linen	2·3	2	1·8
Silk	51	46	48
Man-made fibres, yarns	68	55	46
Jute	8	7	5
Cheese	1,067	1,098	1,125
Chocolate	116	118	115
Biscuits	368	379	380
Sugar	3,921	5,130	4,436
Fish preparations	85	87	92
Jams and jellies	116	120	125
Cement	29,104	28,229	26,141

Engineering production (in 1,000 units) for 3 years:

	1980	1981	1982
Motor vehicles	3,378	3,019	3,148
Television sets	1,928	1,960	2,155
Radio sets	2,141	2,266	2,733
Tyres	50,601	43,196	41,478

See map in THE STATESMAN'S YEAR-BOOK, 1968–69, Industrial Redeployment.

Employment (1975). Out of an economically active population of 21,061,215 persons, there are 2·01m. engaged in agriculture; 1,841,083 in building and public works; 6,327,818 in other manufacturing industries; 829,289 in transport; 3,632,478 in business, banking and insurance; 3,543,881 in services; 2,522,544 in commerce. In 1981, there were 23,044,900 employed (40·9% female), of whom 1,427,000 were foreign workers; in April 1982, there were 1,928,200 unemployed.

Trade Unions. The main confederations recognized as nationally representative are: the CGT (Confédération Générale du Travail), founded in 1895; the CGT-FO (Confédération Générale du Travail–Force Ouvrière) which broke away from the CGT in 1948 as a protest against Communist influence therein; the CFTC (Confédération Française des Travailleurs Chrétiens), which was founded in 1919 and divided in 1964, with a breakaway group retaining the old name and the main body continuing under the new name of CFDT (Confédération Française Démocratique du Travail); and the CGC (Confédération Générale des Cadres) formed in 1944 which only represents managerial and supervisory staff.

Membership is estimated because unions are not required to publish figures; but at elections held on 8 Dec. 1982 for labour tribunals, the CGT was supported by 2·8m. members, the CGT–FO by 1·4m., the CFDT by 1·8m., the CFTC by 650,000 and the CGC by 740,000. Except for the CGC unions operate within the framework of industries and not of trades.

Commerce. Imports (c.i.f.) and exports (f.o.b.) in 1m. francs for 5 calendar years were (including gold):

	1979	1980	1981	1982	1983
Imports	457,100	569,900	653,100	757,595	799,993
Exports	414,700	470,400	548,700	632,198	695,028

The chief imports for home use and exports of home goods are to and from the following countries, in 1m. francs (including gold):

	Imports (c.i.f)		Exports (f.o.b.)	
Countries	1982	1983[1]	1982	1983[1]
Algeria	25,815	23,447	13,991	18,591
Belgium-Luxembourg	58,488	64,268	52,329	59,360
Germany (Fed. Rep.)	127,573	135,500	89,559	108,076
Italy	72,782	79,394	68,383	74,132
Netherlands	41,988	47,688	27,950	33,005
Saudi Arabia	48,204	26,603	12,886	13,752
Spain (excluding Canary Is.)	23,106	27,084	18,823	22,103

[1] Provisional.

Countries	Imports (c.i.f.) 1982	Imports (c.i.f.) 1983[1]	Exports (f.o.b.) 1982	Exports (f.o.b.) 1983[1]
Sweden	11,171	12,029	6,950	9,023
Switzerland (and Liechtenstein)	15,244	16,068	24,162	29,045
USSR	18,668	21,425	10,169	17,003
UK	45,975	56,718	43,883	52,692
USA	59,738	61,687	34,327	43,835

[1] Provisional.

Total trade between France and UK (British Department of Trade returns, in £1,000 sterling):

	1980	1981	1982	1983	1984
Imports to UK	3,899,174	3,978,646	4,269,103	5,043,118	5,885,715
Exports and re-exports from UK	3,651,470	3,625,923	4,486,458	5,651,521	7,082,389

Tourism. In 1983 foreign visitors contributed about 55,052m. francs to the French economy.

COMMUNICATIONS

Roads. At the end of 1978 the French road system consisted of 4,248 km of motorway, 29,068 km of national roads, 345,990 km of departmental roads and 424,950 km of local roads. Total, 804,256 km. In 1982, there were 20·3m. passenger cars and 2·70m. commercial vehicles in use.

Railways. As from 1 Jan. 1938 all the independent railway companies were merged with the existing state railway system in a Société Nationale des Chemins de Fer Français, which became a public industrial and commercial establishment in 1983.

In 1982, the State railway totalled 34,599 km (10,600 km electrified) of 1,435 mm gauge, and carried 184m. tonnes of freight and 713m. passengers. A new railway for high-speed trains was completed in 1983 between Paris and Lyon.

The Paris transport network consisted in 1982 of 466 km of underground railway (métro) and regional express railways and 2,115 km of bus routes. In 1982 it carried 1,376m. passengers on the métro and 724m. by bus.

Aviation. Air France, UTA and Air Inter, the national airlines, had (31 Dec. 1979) a fleet of 166 aircraft, servicing Europe, North America, Central and South America, West and East Africa, Madagascar, the Near, Middle and Far East. There are local networks in the West Indies and Central America.

In 1982 Air France, UTA and Air Inter flew 2,298m. tonne-km (excluding mail) and 37,846m. passenger-km.

Shipping. French merchant ships of more than 100 tons, on 1 Oct. 1981, numbered 399 vessels of 10·58m. GRT.

Shipping (excluding fishing vessels) in foreign trade in 1979: Entered, 85,026 vessels and disembarked 259·2m. tonnes of imports and loaded 71·6m. tonnes of exports. Total cargo traffic 330·8m. tonnes.

In 1981 there were 8,623 km of navigable rivers, waterways and canals (of which 1,617 km accessible to vessels over 3,000 tons), with a total traffic of 83·6m. tonnes.

Post and Broadcasting. In 1977 the receipts on account of posts, telegraphs and telephones amounted to 56,275m. francs.

On 31 Dec. 1982 the telephone system (government-owned) had 26,940,296 subscribers; the Paris region (including the Paris and Seine-et-Marne, Yvelines, Essonne, Hauts-de-Seine, Seine-Saint-Denis, Val-de-Marne and Val-d'Oise departments) accounted for 4,153,586 in 1978.

Radio and television broadcasting was reorganized under the Act of 7 Aug. 1974 which replaced the Office de Radiodiffusion Télévision Française with 4 broadcasting companies, a production company and an audio-visual institute. Organization, development, operation and the maintenance of networks and installations became the responsibility of the Public Broadcasting Establishment. Radio programmes are broadcast from 298 transmitters (including 260 VHF) by 3 stations:

France Inter, France Musique and *France Culture*. Television programmes are broadcast from 325 transmitters and 4,661 relay stations on 3 channels. There were about 19m. sets in use in 1981 (of which 8·9m. in colour).

Cinemas (1981). There were 4,532 cinemas with a seating capacity (1979) of 1,472,400; attendances totalled 187·6m.

Newspapers (1980). There were 71 daily papers published in the provinces with a circulation of 7·5m. copies, and 13 published in Paris with a national circulation of 3·8m. Among Paris dailies *France-Soir* sells 550,000; *Le Monde* 550,000; *Le Parisien Libéré* 438,000; *Le Figaro* 407,000, and *L'Aurore* 220,000. Among provincial dailies *Ouest-France* (Rennes) sells 783,000; *Le Progrés* (Lyon) 447,000; *La Voix du Nord* (Lille) 372,000; *Sud-Ouest* (Bordeaux) 430,000; *La Dauphine Libérée* (Grenoble) 401,000 and *Le Provençal* (Marseilles) 345,000.

JUSTICE, RELIGION, EDUCATION AND WELFARE

Justice. Since 1958, 474 *tribunaux d'instance* (11 in overseas departments), under a single judge each and with increased material and territorial jurisdiction, have replaced the former *juges de paix* (1 in each canton); and 181 *tribunaux de grande instance* (6 in overseas departments) have taken the place of the 357 *tribunaux de première instance* (1 in each *arrondissement*).

The *tribunaux de grande instance* usually have a collegiate composition, however a law dated 10 July 1970 has allowed them to administer justice under a single judge in some civil cases.

All petty offences (*contraventions*) are disposed of in the Police Courts (*Tribunaux de Police*) presided over by a Judge on duty in the *tribunal d'instance*. The Correctional Courts pronounce upon all graver offences (*délits*), including cases involving imprisonment up to 5 years. They have no jury, and consist of 3 judges who administer both criminal and civil justice. An Act of 29 Dec. 1972 established that there is only 1 judge; in some cases, the correctional courts may consist of a single judge each. In all cases of a *délit* or a *crime* the preliminary inquiry is made in secrecy by an examining magistrate (*juge d'instruction*), who either dismisses the case or sends it for trial before a court where a public prosecutor (*Procureur*) endeavours to prove the charge.

The Conciliation Boards (*Conseils des Prud'hommes*) composed of an equal number of employers and employees deal with labour disputes. Commercial litigation goes to the Commercial Courts (*Tribunaux de Commerce*) composed of tradesmen and manufacturers elected for 2 years. The judges hold office for 2 years and they can be re-elected; 3 years for the President.

When the decisions of any of these Tribunals are susceptible of appeal, the case goes to one of the 35 Courts of Appeal (*Cours d'Appel*), (including 3 in overseas departments and 2 in overseas territories), composed each of a president and a variable number of members.

The Courts of Assizes (*Cours d'Assises*), composed each of a president, assisted by 2 other magistrates who are members of the Courts of Appeal, and by a jury of 9 people, sit in every *département*, when called upon to try very important criminal cases. The decisions of the Courts of Appeal and the Courts of Assizes are final; however, the Court of Cassation (*Cour de Cassation*) has discretion to verify if the law has been correctly interpreted and if the rules of procedure have been followed exactly. The Court of Cassation may annul any judgment, and the cases have to be tried again by a Court of Appeal or a Court of Assizes.

The State Security Court, established in 1963, was abolished by law on 4 Aug. 1981. Capital punishment was abolished in the same month.

On 24 Jan. 1973 the first Ombudsman (*médiateur*) was appointed for a 6-year period.

The French penal institutions consist of: (1) *maisons d'arrêt* and *de correction*, where persons awaiting trial as well as those condemned to short periods of imprisonment are kept; (2) central prisons (*maisons centrales*) for those sentenced to long imprisonment; (3) special establishments, namely (*a*) schools for young adults, (*b*) hostels for old and disabled offenders, (*c*) hospitals for the sick and psychopaths, (*d*) institutions for recidivists. Special attention is being paid to classified treatment and the rehabilitation and vocational re-education of prisoners including work in open-air and semi-free establishments. There are 2 penal institutions for women.

Juvenile delinquents go before special judges and courts; they are sent to public or private institutions of supervision and re-education.

The population at 1 June 1984 of all penal establishments was 40,870 men and women.

Religion. No religion is officially recognized by the State. Under the law promulgated on 9 Dec. 1905, which separated Church and State, the adherents of all creeds are authorized to form associations for public worship (*associations culturelles*). The law of 2 Jan. 1907 provided that, failing *associations culturelles*, the buildings for public worship, together with their furniture, would continue at the disposition of the ministers of religion and the worshippers for the exercise of their religion; but in each case there was required an administrative act drawn up by the *préfet* as regards buildings belonging to the State or the departments and by the *maire* as regards buildings belonging to the communes.

There are 18 archbishops and 92 bishops of the Roman Catholic Church, with (1974) 43,557 clergy of various grades and 45·3m. church members. The Protestants of the Augsburg confession are, in their religious affairs, governed by a General Consistory, while the Reformed Church is under a Council of Administration, the seat of which is in Paris. In 1975 communicant Protestants numbered 750,000. There were (1978) about 2m. Moslems.

Education. The primary, secondary and higher state schools constitute the 'Université de France'. The Supreme Council of 84 members has deliberative, administrative and judiciary functions, and as a consultative committee advises respecting the working of the school system, the inspectors-general are in direct communication with the Minister. For local education administration France is divided into 25 academic areas, each of which has an Academic Council whose members include a certain number elected by the professors or teachers. The Academic Council deals with all grades of education. Each is under a Rector, and each is provided with academy inspectors, 1 for each department.

By decree of 6 Jan. 1959 the whole system of public instruction was reorganized and the structure of the Ministry of National Education has consequently been modified. A further Education Act was passed on 11 July 1975. Compulsory education is now provided for children of 6–16. The educational stages are as follows:

1. Non-compulsory pre-school instruction for children aged 2–5, to be given in infant schools or infant classes attached to primary schools.

2. Compulsory elementary instruction for children aged 6–11, to be given in primary schools and certain classes of the *lycées*. It consists of 3 courses: preparatory (1 year), elementary (2 years), intermediary (2 years). Physically or mentally handicapped children are cared for in special institutions or special classes of primary schools.

3. Lower secondary education (*Enseignement du premier cycle du Second Degré*) for pupils aged 11–15, consists of 4 years of study in the *lycées* (grammar schools), *Collèges d'Enseignement Secondaire* or *Collèges d'Enseignement Général*.

4. Upper secondary education (*Enseignement du second cycle du Second Degré*) for pupils aged 15–18:

Long, général or *professionel* provided by the *lycées* and leading to the *baccalauréat* or to the *baccalauréat de technicien* after 3 years.

Court, professional courses of 3, 2 and 1 year are taught in the *lycées d'enseignement professionel*, or the specialized sections of the *lycées*, CES or CEG.

The following table shows the various types of schools in 1981 and the numbers of enrolled pupils:

Description	*State*	*Private*	*Total*
Pre-primary	2,070,060	313,386	2,383,446
Primary	3,940,782	668,660	4,609,442
Secondary:			
First and second cycle	3,983,623	1,030,043	5,013,666
Specialized	233,296	8,728	242,024
Total	10,227,761	2,020,817	12,248,578

The state schools in 1978 had 64,676 nursery, 172,969 primary, 18,908 special school, 143,572 secondary and 44,624 secondary technical school and 65,797 grammar school (*lycée*) teachers.

Higher Instruction is supplied by the State in the universities and in special schools, and by private individuals in the free faculties and schools. The law of 12 July 1875 provided for higher education free of charge. This law was modified by that of 18 March 1880, which granted the state faculties the exclusive right to confer degrees. A decree of 28 Dec. 1885 created a general council of the faculties, and the creation of universities, each consisting of several faculties, was accomplished in 1897, in virtue of the law of 10 July 1896.

The law of 12 Nov. 1968 laying down future guidelines for higher education redefined the activities and working of universities. Bringing several disciplines together, 780 units for teaching and research (UER–Unités d'Enseignement et de Récherche) were formed which decided their own teaching activities, research programmes and procedures for checking the level of knowledge gained. They and the other parts of each university must respect the rules designed to maintain the national standard of qualifications.

The UERs form the basic units of the 69 Universities, and 3 National Polytechnic Institutes, which have university status. They are grouped geographically into 25 *académies* with student populations in 1978–79 as follows:

Academie	*1978–79*	*Academie*	*1978–79*	*Academie*	*1978–79*
Aix-Marseille	47,292	Lille	39,375	Paris	224,655
Amiens	10,661	Limoges	7,668	Poitiers	13,026
Besançon	11,149	Lyon	50,720	Reims	12,528
Bordeaux	42,985	Montpellier	36,604	Rennes	33,262
Caen	12,490	Nancy-Metz	28,223	Rouen	12,775
Clermont	15,191	Nantes	26,219	Strasbourg	27,495
Créteil	24,599	Nice	19,030	Toulouse	45,211
Dijon	13,297	Orléans-Tours	18,746	Versailles	44,901
Grenoble	31,896				
				Total	849,998

The following table shows the number of students by faculties, for 5 years:

Students of	*1974–75*	*1975–76*	*1976–77*	*1977–78*	*1978–79*
Law and economics	178,215	183,566	182,533	184,361	183,592
Medicine and dentistry	146,912	154,660	159,874	160,900	160,917
Science	117,389	121,028	122,205	125,945	129,441
Letters	233,954	251,421	252,134	253,364	260,090
Pharmacy	31,599	33,510	33,474	34,821	36,014
Technology	41,949	43,526	44,243	47,398	50,237
Multi discipline courses	4,843	18,527	21,818	25,329	29,707
Total	754,861	806,238	816,281	838,118	849,998

There are also Catholic university facilities in Paris, Angers, Lille, Lyon and Toulouse with (1981–82) 34,118 students.

Outside the university system, higher education (academic, professional and technical) is provided by over 400 schools and institutes, including the various Grand Écoles with 96,726 students in 1981.

In 1978–79 there were also 99,000 students in preparatory classes leading to the Grande Écoles, the Sections de Techniciens Supérieurs and other bodies; there were also 21,000 students in Écoles normales d'instituteurs (teacher-training).

Health. On 1 Jan. 1981 there were 108,054 physicians, 37,820 pharmacists, 31,872 dentists, 249,450 nursing personnel and 8,479 midwives practising. On 1

Jan. 1982 there were 934 public hospitals (446,901 beds) excluding mental hospitals and 2,420 private hospitals (180,769 beds) including private mental homes.

Social Welfare. An order of 4 Oct. 1945 laid down the framework of a comprehensive plan of Social Security and created a single organization which superseded the various laws relating to social insurance, workmen's compensation, health insurance, family allowances, etc. All previous matters relating to Social Security are dealt with in the Social Security Code, 1956; this has been revised several times, and finally by orders laid down on 21 Aug. 1967, which were ratified on 31 July 1968. The Social Security general scheme covers all wage-earning workers in industry and commerce that are not covered by a special scheme of their own.

Contributions. All wage-earning workers or those of equivalent status are insured regardless of the amount or the nature of the salary or earnings. The funds for the general scheme are raised mainly from professional contributions, these being fixed within the limits of a ceiling (assessed at 68,760 francs per annum on 1 Jan. 1981) and calculated as a percentage of the salaries. The calculation of contributions payable for family allowances, old age and industrial injuries relates only to this amount; on the other hand, the amount payable for sickness, maternity expenses, disability and death is calculated partly within the limit of the 'ceiling' and partly on the whole salary. These contributions are the responsibility of both employer and employee, except in the case of family allowances or industrial injuries, where they are the sole responsibility of the employer.

Contributions and benefits paid in 1982 (in 1m. francs) were:

	Contributions	*Benefits*
Health service	260,300	254,900
Old age pensions	123,900	125,000
Family benefits	103,000	114,900

Self-employed Workers. From 17 Jan. 1948 allowances and old-age pensions were paid to self-employed workers by independent insurance funds set up within their own profession, trade or business. Schemes of compulsory insurance for sickness were instituted in 1961 for farmers and in 1966, with modifications in 1970, for other non-wage-earning workers.

Social Insurance. The orders laid down in Aug. 1967 ensure that the whole population can benefit from the Social Security Scheme; at present all elderly persons who have been engaged in the professions, as well as the surviving spouse, are entitled to claim an old-age benefit; 98% of the population, both working and retired, are covered by a compulsory scheme of insurance for sickness, the remaining 2% who are not covered by a compulsory insurance scheme have been able to participate in a voluntary scheme since 1967; the whole population benefit from the legislation regarding family allowances.

Sickness Insurance refunds the costs of treatment required by the insured and the needs of dependants. A decree of 12 Oct. 1976 laid down conditions on which students of 20 or over at public or private educational institutions, who do not benefit from a social security scheme in their own right, are guaranteed insurance benefits for sickness or maternity, holding their parents entitlement until the end of the academic year in which they attain their 21st birthday, provided they have proof that their studies have been interrupted by illness. The general principles relating to medical care consist of: a free choice by the patient of his doctor, his pharmaceutical chemist, his place of treatment, etc.; the medical practitioner is granted freedom of prescription. Reimbursement is not as a rule made in full; the insured person usually pays between 10% and 30% of the legal rate except in cases of exemption. The insured who is recognized as medically unfit for work receives daily allowances equal to half of the wage which has been used to calculate the contributions, or to two-thirds of this if the person has 3 or more children. These allowances may be paid for 3 years, plus 1 additional year if the insured undergoes re-adaptation treatment or takes up fresh vocational training.

Maternity Insurance covers the costs of medical treatment relating to the pregnancy, confinement and lying-in period; the beneficiaries being the insured person or the spouse. The daily allowances are equal to 90% of the salary on which contributions were calculated.

Insurance for Invalids is divided into 3 categories: (1) those who are capable of working; (2) those who cannot work; (3) those who, in addition, are in need of the help of another person. According to the category, the pension rate varies from 30 to 50% of the average salary for the last 10 years, with additional allowance for home help for the third category.

Old-age Pensions for workers were introduced in 1910 and are now fixed by the Social Security Code of 28 Jan. 1972. Since 1983 people who have paid insurance for at least 37½ years (150 quarters) receive at 60 a pension equal to 60% of basic salary. People who have paid insurance for less than 37½ years but no less than 15 years can expect a pension equal to as many 1/150ths of the full pension as their quarterly payments justify. In the event of death of the insured person, the husband or wife of the deceased person receives half the pension received by the latter. Compulsory supplementary schemes ensure benefits equal to 70% of previous earnings.

Family Allowances. The system comprises: (*a*) Family allowances proper, equivalent to 25·5% of the basic monthly salary (1,246 francs) for 2 dependent children, 46% for the third child, 41% for the fourth child, and 39% for the fifth and each subsequent child; a supplement equivalent to 9% of the basic monthly salary for the second and each subsequent dependent child more than 10 years old and 16% for each dependent child over 15 years. (*b*) Family supplement (519 francs) for persons with at least 3 children or one child aged less than 3 years. (*c*) Antenatal grants. (*d*) Maternity grant equal to 260% of basic salary; increase for multiple births or adoptions, 198%; increase for birth or adoption of third or subsequent child, 457%. (*e*) Allowance for specialized education of handicapped children. (*f*) Allowance for orphans. (*g*) Single parent allowance. (*h*) Allowance for opening of school term. (*i*) Allowance for accommodation, under certain circumstances. (*j*) Minimum family income for those with at least 3 children. Allowances (*b*), (*g*), (*h*) and (*j*) only apply to those whose annual income falls below a specified level.

Workmen's Compensation. The law passed by the National Assembly on 30 Oct. 1946 forms part of the Social Security Code and is administered by the Social Security Organization. Employers are invited to take preventive measures. The application of these measures is supervised by consulting engineers (assessors) of the local funds dealing with sickness insurance, who may compel employers who do not respect these measures to make additional contributions; they may, in like manner, grant rebates to employers who have in operation suitable preventive measures. The injured person receives free treatment, the insurance fund reimburses the practitioners, hospitals and suppliers chosen freely by the injured. In cases of temporary disablement the daily payments are equal to half the total daily wage received by the injured. In case of permanent disablement the injured person receives a pension, the amount of which varies according to the degree of disablement and the salary received during the past 12 months.

A law promulgated on 11 Oct. 1946 has created a medical labour service of doctors who hold a diploma of 'industrial health specialists'. These doctors are entrusted with the control of hygiene and health matters in all industrial undertakings or groups of undertakings. In addition, it is the duty of this medical service to examine wage-earners when they are engaged, to carry out periodical medical examinations and to ensure the application of the existing rules relating to safety in work.

Unemployment Benefits vary according to circumstances (full or partial unemployment) which are means-tested. Since 1926 unemployment benefits have been paid from public funds. Full unemployment benefit amounts to 13·50 francs per day for the head of the family and 5·40 francs for the spouse or a dependent person. After 3 months the payment is reduced to 12·40 francs.

A collective agreement signed on 31 Dec. 1958 between the national council of employers and certain trade unions has established a system of special allowances for totally unemployed workers in industry and trade. The costs are shared by employers (2·76% of wages) and employees (0·84%) and the benefits vary according to circumstances. The system is now governed by the law of 16 Jan. 1979. A similar agreement of 21 Feb. 1968 extends the system to partial unemployment.

Social Security in France. I.N.S.E.E., 1970
Questions de Sécurité Sociale. Paris, 1970

DIPLOMATIC REPRESENTATIVES

Of France in Great Britain (58 Knightsbridge, London, SW1X 7JT)
Ambassador: Jacques Viot (accredited 8 Feb. 1985).

Of Great Britain in France (35 rue du Faubourg St Honoré, Paris)
Ambassador: Sir John Fretwell, KCMG.

Of France in the USA (2535 Belmont Rd., NW, Washington, D.C., 20008)
Ambassador: Bernard Vernier-Palliez.

Of the USA in France (2 Ave. Gabriel, Paris)
Ambassador: Evan G. Galbraith.

Of France to the United Nations
Ambassador: Luc de la Barre de Nanteuil.

Books of Reference

Statistical Information: The Institut national de la Statistique et des Études économiques (18, Boulevard Adolphe Pinard, 75014 Paris) is the central office of statistics. It was established by a law of 27 April 1946, which amalgamated the Service National des Statistiques (created in 1941 by merging the Direction de la Statistique générale de la France and the Service de la Démographie) with the Institut de Conjoncture (set up in 1938) and some statistical services of the Ministry of National Economy. The Institut comprises the following departments: Metropolitan statistics, Overseas statistics, Market research and economic studies, Documentation, Research statistics and economics, Informatics, Foreign Economic Studies.

The main publications of the Institut include:

Annuaire statistique de la France (from 1878)
Annuaire statistique des Territoires d'Outre-Mer (from 1959)
Bulletin mensuel de statistique (monthly)
Documentation économique (bi-monthly)
Données statistiques africaines et Malgaches (quarterly)
Economie et Statistique (monthly)
Tableaux de l'Economie Française (biennially, from 1956)
Tendances de la Conjoncture (monthly)

Caron, F., *An Economic History of Modern France.* London, 1979
Chambers, F. J., *France.* [Bibliography] London and Santa Barbara, 1984
Coffey, P., *The Social Economy of France.* London, 1973
Crozier, M., *A Strategy for Change: The Future of French Society.* MIT Press, 1982
Dyer, C., *Population and Society in Twentieth Century France.* London, 1978
Hoffman, S., *Decline or Renewal? France Since the 1930's.* New York, 1973
Peyrefitte, A., *The Trouble with France.* New York, 1981
Tuppen, J. N., *France.* Folkestone, 1981

OVERSEAS DEPARTMENTS

GUADELOUPE

HISTORY. Discovered by Columbus in Nov. 1493, the two main islands were then known as *Karukera* (Isle of Beautiful Waters) to the Carib inhabitants, who resisted Spanish attempts to colonize. A French colony was established on 28 June 1635, and apart from short periods of occupancy by British forces, Guadeloupe has since remained a French possession. On 19 March 1946 the status of Guadeloupe was changed to that of an Overseas Department; in 1973 it additionally became an administrative region.

AREA AND POPULATION. Guadeloupe consists of a group of islands in the Lesser Antilles. The two main islands, Basse-Terre to the west and Grande-Terre to the east, are separated by a narrow channel, called Rivière Salée. Adjacent to these are the islands of Marie Galante *(Ceyre* to the Caribs) to the south-east, La Désirade to the east, and the Îles des Saintes to the south. The islands of St Martin and St Barthélemy lie 250 km to the north-west.

	Area in sq. km	*Census 1974*	*Census 1982*	*Chief town*
St Martin[1]	54	6,191	8,072	Marigot
St Barthélemy	21	2,491	3,059	Gustavia
Basse-Terre	848	135,746	141,313	Basse-Terre
Grande-Terre	585	159,424	157,696	Pointe-à-Pitre
Îles des Saintes	14	3,084	2,901	Terre-de-Bas
La Désirade	22	1,682	1,602	Grande Anse
Marie-Galante	158	15,912	13,757	Grand-Bourg
	1,702	324,530	328,400	

[1]Northern part only; the southern third belongs to the Netherlands.

Population (estimate, 1984) 329,400. The vast majority are black or mulatto, but the populations of St Barthélemy and Les Saintes are still mainly descended from 17th-century Breton and Norman settlers. French is the official language, but a Creole dialect is also widely used.

The seat of government is Basse-Terre (13,656 inhabitants in 1974) at the south-west end of that island but the largest towns are Pointe-à-Pitre (25,310 inhabitants), the economic centre with a large commercial harbour, and its suburb Abymes (53,165).

Vital statistics (1982): Births, 6,657; deaths, 2,115.

CONSTITUTION AND GOVERNMENT. Guadeloupe is administered by an elected *Conseil Général* of 36 members (assisted by an Economic and Social Committee of 40 members) and an elected Regional Council of 41 members. It is represented in the National Assembly by 3 deputies, in the Senate by 2 senators and on the Economic and Social Council by 2 councillors. There are 3 *arrondissements*, sub-divided into 34 communes, each administered by an elected municipal council. The French government is represented by an appointed Commissioner.

Commissioner: Robert Miguet.
President of the Conseil Général: Lucette Michaux-Chevry.

ECONOMY

Budget. The budget for 1982 balanced at 1,196,207,767 francs.

Banking. The Banque des Antilles Françaises (founded 1853), with a capital of 32,583,000 francs and reserve funds amounting to 1·44m. francs, advances loans chiefly for agricultural purposes; it has 6 branches in the department. The Banque Populaire de la Guadeloupe has a capital of 5m. francs and 6 branches in the department. The Banque Nationale de Paris has 12 branches in the department, the Crédit Agricole 25, the Banque Française Commerciale 7, and the Société Generale de Banque aux Antilles and the Chase Manhattan Bank 1 each. The Caisse Centrale de Coopération économique is the official banking institution of the department, enjoying the privilege of issuing bank-notes.

ENERGY AND NATURAL RESOURCES

Electricity. Production in 1982 totalled 394,972,000 kwh.

Agriculture. Chief products (1982) are bananas (165,000 tonnes), sugar (868,357 tonnes), rum (92,172 hectolitres of pure alcohol), vegetables (46,586 tonnes), fruit (3,115 tonnes), flowers (no.) 8,505,000.

Livestock (1983): Cattle, 90,000; goats, 36,000; sheep, 3,000; pigs, 51,000.

Forestry. In 1982, 421 cu. metres of wood were produced.

Fisheries. The catch in 1982 was 8,362 tonnes; crustacea (120 tonnes), shell fish (300 tonnes), turtles (20 tonnes).

COMMERCE. Trade for 1982 (in 1m. francs) was imports 4,117 and exports 548·4. In 1982, 62·5% of imports were from France, while 67·8% of exports went to France and 18% to Martinique; bananas formed 50·69% of the exports and sugar 17·47%. St Martin and St Barthélemy are free ports.

There are Chambers of Commerce and Industry at Basse-Terre and Pointe-à-Pitre. There is a British consular agent at Pointe-à-Pitre.

Tourism. In 1982 there were 337,500 tourists.

COMMUNICATIONS

Roads. In 1982 there were 2,059 km of roads of which 330 km were national roads. There were 87,785 passenger cars and 33,350 commercial vehicles in 1981.

Aviation. Air France and 7 other airlines call at Guadeloupe. In 1982 there were 48,480 arrivals and departures of aircraft and 1,177,489 passengers at Raizet (Pointe-à-Pitre) airport making it the sixth most frequented French airport.

Shipping. Guadeloupe is in direct communication with France by means of 12 steam navigation companies. In 1982, 1,159 vessels arrived to disembark 31,078 passengers and 1,074,660 tonnes of freight and to embark 30,646 passengers and 426,535 tonnes of freight.

Post and Broadcasting. In 1982 there were 47 post offices and 47,247 telephones. ORTF broadcasts for 17 hours a day in French and television broadcasts for 6 hours a day. There were (1977) 13,979 radio and (1981) 32,886 TV receivers.

Newspapers. There was (1984) 1 daily newspaper *(France-Antilles)* with a circulation of 25,000.

JUSTICE, RELIGION, EDUCATION AND WELFARE

Justice. There are 4 *tribunaux d'instance* and 2 *tribunaux de grande instance* at Basse-Terre and Pointe-à-Pitre; there is also a court of appeal and a court of assizes at Basse-Terre.

Religion. The majority of the population are Roman Catholic.

Education. In 1982 there were 61,511 pupils at pre-primary schools and primary schools and 45,876 at secondary schools. The *University Antilles-Guyane* had 4,637 students in 1982–83, of which Guadeloupe itself had 1,719.

Health. The medical services in 1983 included 12 public hospitals (2,974 beds), 15 private clinics (1,261 beds) and 42 dispensaries. There were 418 physicians, 80 dentists, 127 pharmacists, 76 midwives and 1,196 nursing personnel.

Books of Reference

Information: Office du Tourisme du départemente, Point-à-Pitre. *Director:* Eric W. Rotin.
Lasserre, G., *La Guadeloupe, étude géographique.* 2 vols. Bordeaux, 1961

GUIANA

Guyane Française

HISTORY. A French settlement on the island of Cayenne was established in 1604 and the territory between the Maroni and Oyapock rivers finally became a French possession in 1817. Convicts settlements were established from 1852, that on off-shore Devil's Island being most notorious; all were closed by 1945. On 19 March 1946 the status of Guiana was changed to that of an Overseas Department.

AREA AND POPULATION. French Guiana is situated on the north-east coast of South America, and has an area of about 83,533 sq. km (32,252 sq. miles) and a population at the 1982 Census of 73,022 (Estimate, 1984, 79,000), of whom 4,500 are tribal Indians. Cayenne, the chief town, has a population of (1982) 38,135. These figures are exclusive of the floating population of miners, officials and troops.

Vital statistics (1981): Live births, 2,081; deaths, 417.

CONSTITUTION AND GOVERNMENT. French Guiana is administered by an elected *Conseil Général* of 16 members and an elected Regional Council of 31 members. It is represented in the National Assembly by 1 deputy and in the Senate by 1 senator. The French government is represented by an appointed Commissioner. There are 2 *arrondissements* (Cayenne and Saint-Laurent-du-Maroni) sub-divided into 20 communes.

Commissioner: Claude Silberzahn.
President of the Conseil Général: Emmanuel Bellony.
President of the Conseil Regional: Georges Othily.

ECONOMY

Budget. The budget for 1982 balanced at 578m. francs, excluding duplicated items and national expenditure.

Banking. The Bank of Guiana has a capital of 10m. francs and reserve fund of 2·39m. francs. Loans totalled 206m. francs in 1981. Other banks include Bank National of Paris-Guyane and Banc Française Commerciale.

ENERGY AND NATURAL RESOURCES

Electricity. Production in 1981 totalled 97m. kwh.

Agriculture. The country has immense forests (about 80,000 sq. km) rich in many kinds of timber. Only 10,436 hectares are under cultivation. The crops (1981, in tonnes) consist of rice (983, 1983), maize (280), manioc (7,650), bananas (680) and sugar-cane (7,900, 1983) as well as a large variety of other fruits, vegetables and spices (3,000 tonnes, 1983).

Livestock (1983): 12,000 cattle, 10,000 swine and (1982) 100,000 poultry.

Fisheries. The fishing fleet for shrimps comprises 59 US, 22 Japanese and 11 French boats. The catch in 1982 totalled 4,503 tonnes, of which shrimps comprised 3,000 tonnes, exports 2,750 tonnes. Production of *Macrobrachium Rosenbergii* (an edible river shrimp) is now established.

COMMERCE. Trade in 1,000 tonnes and 1m. francs:

	1980		*1981*		*1982*	
	Quantity	*Value*	*Quantity*	*Value*	*Quantity*	*Value*
Imports	859·7	1,087	222·6	1,355	261·1	1,643
Exports	54·0	108	32·7	192	30·3	212

In 1981, 15% of imports came from Trinidad and Tobago, 53% from France and 10% from the USA, while 54% of exports went to the USA, 17% to Japan and 15% to France. In 1981, shrimps formed 73% of exports and timber, 11%.

Total trade between Guiana and UK (British Department of Trade returns, in £1,000 sterling):

	1980	*1981*	*1982*	*1983*	*1984*
Imports to UK	117	844	1,956	853	795
Exports and re-exports from UK	1,264	7,117	6,840	897	3,106

COMMUNICATIONS

Roads. Three chief and some secondary roads connect the capital with most of the coastal area by motor-car services. There are (1981) 321 km of national and 269 km of departmental roads. Connexions with the interior are made by waterways which, despite rapids, are navigable by local craft.

Aviation. Air France calls at Cayenne (Rochambeau Airport) 4 times a week, Air Suriname Airways and Cruseiro do Sul once a week; Air Guyane services interior connexions. In 1981, about 150,000 passengers and 3,600 tonnes of freight passed through the airport.

Shipping. The chief ports are: Cayenne, St-Laurent-du-Maroni and Kourou. Dégrad des Cannes, the port of Cayenne is visited regularly by ships of the Compagnie Général Maritime, the Compagnie Maritime des Chargeurs Réunis and Marseille Fret. In 1981, 594 arrivals and departures of vessels were registered in French Guiana (113,219 tonnes of petroleum products arrived and 165,140 tonnes of other freight arrived and departed).

Post and Broadcasting. An automatic telephone system connects Cayenne with 10 other communes as well as with Europe and most parts of North and South America. Number of telephones (1983), 13,755. There are wireless stations at Cayenne, Oyapoc, Régina, St-Laurent-du-Maroni and numerous other locations.

RFO-Guyane (Guiana Radio) broadcasts for 116 hours each week on medium- and short-waves and FM in French. Television is broadcast for 43 hours each week on 7 transmitters. In 1980 there were 35,000 radio and 9,063 TV receivers.

Newspapers. There was (1984) 1 daily newspaper *(Presse de la Guyane)* with a circulation of 16,000, a bi-weekly paper *(France-Guyane)* with a circulation of 3,500 and a weekly *(Debout Guyane)*.

JUSTICE, RELIGION, EDUCATION AND WELFARE

Justice. At Cayenne there is a *tribunal d'instance* and a *tribunal de grande instance*, from which appeal is to the regional *cour d'appel* in Martinique.

Religion. The majority of the population is Roman Catholic.

Education. Primary education has been free since 1889 in lay schools for the two sexes in the communes and many villages. In 1981 public primary schools had 580 teachers and 11,953 pupils, the *lycées* and *collèges d'enseignement secondaire*, 510 teachers and 7,277 pupils. Private schools had 119 teachers and 2,528 pupils. The *Institut Henri Visioz* forms part of the *Université des Antilles-Guyane,* with 236 students.

Health. There were (1981) 80 physicians, 14 dentists, 18 pharmacists, 16 midwives and 309 nursing personnel. In 1980 there were 5 hospitals with 907 beds and 3 private clinics.

Books of Reference

Abonnec, A., Hurrault, J., Saban, R., *Bibliographie de la Guyane Française.* 2 vols. Paris, 1957
Henry, *Guyane Française, son histoire 1604–1946*. Cayenne
Hurrault, J., *Guide du voyageur en Guyane*. Paris, 1949
Masse, D., *La Guyane Française: Histoire, Géographie, Possibilités*. Abbeville, 1978

MARTINIQUE

HISTORY. Discovered by Columbus in 1493, the island was known to its inhabitants as *Madinina*, from which its present name was corrupted. A French colony was established in 1635 and, apart from brief periods of British occupation, has since remained under French control. On 19 March 1946 its status was altered to that of an Overseas Department.

AREA AND POPULATION. The island, situated in the Lesser Antilles between Dominica and St Lucia, occupies an area of 1,079 sq. km (417 sq. miles). The total population, 1982 Census was 328,566 (estimate, 1984, 329,500), of whom 99,844 lived in Fort-de-France, the capital and chief commercial town, which has a landlocked harbour nearly 40 sq. km in extent.

French is the official language, but the majority of the population use a Creole dialect.

Vital statistics (1983): Live births 5,641; deaths 2,207.

CONSTITUTION AND GOVERNMENT. The island is administered by an elected *Conseil Général* of 36 members and an elected Regional Council of 41 members. The French government is represented by an appointed Commissioner. There are 3 *arrondissements*, sub-divided into 34 communes, each administered by an elected municipal council. Martinique is represented in the National Assembly by 3 deputies, in the Senate by 2 senators and on the Economic and Social Council by 2 councillors.

Commissioner: Jean Chevance.

President of the Conseil Général: Émile Maurice.

ECONOMY

Budget. The budget, 1983, balanced at 1,249m. francs.

Banking. The Institut d'Émission des Départements d'Outre-mer is the official bank of the department. The Caisse Centrale de Coopération économique is used by the Government in assisting the economic development of the department.

The Banque des Antilles Françaises (with a capital of 10·8m. francs), the Crédit Martiniquais (11·4m. francs), branches of the Banque Nationale de Paris (22·6m. francs), Crédit Agricole, The Chase Manhattan Bank, Société Générale de Banque and Banque Française Commerciale are operating at Fort-de-France.

ENERGY AND NATURAL RESOURCES

Electricity. Production in 1983 totalled 375m. kwh.

Agriculture. Bananas, sugar and rum are the chief products, followed by pineapples, food and vegetables. In 1983 there were 4,546 hectares under sugarcane, 6,960 hectares under bananas and 650 hectares under pineapples. Production (1983): Sugar, 3,949 tonnes; industrial rum, 22,313 hectolitres; agricultural rum, 64,945 hectolitres; cane for sugar, 82,986 tonnes; cane for rum, 116,360 tonnes.

Livestock (1983): 40,260 cattle, 32,993 (1982) sheep, 23,560 pigs, 13,666 (1982) goats and 840 horses.

COMMERCE. Trade in 1m. francs:

	1980	*1981*	*1982*	*1983*
Imports	3,523	4,142	4,943	5,578
Exports	554	977	1,016	867

In 1981 the main items of import were foodstuffs; main items of export were petroleum products (43%), bananas (22%) and rum (6%); 58% of imports came from France and 32% of exports went to France and 50% to Guadeloupe.

Total trade of the French West Indian Islands with UK (British Department of Trade returns, in £1,000 sterling):

	1980	*1981*	*1982*	*1983*	*1984*
Imports to UK	578	295	34	35	229
Exports and re-exports from UK	2,588	2,268	2,400	3,029	2,980

The Chamber of Commerce and Industry administers the port, airport and industrial zones.

Tourism. In 1983 there were 144,580 tourists.

COMMUNICATIONS

Roads. In 1983 there were 7 km of motorway, 260 km of national roads, 618 km of district roads and 980 km of local roads. In 1982 there were 8,734 passenger cars and 1,915 commercial vehicles registered.

Aviation. In 1983, 924,302 passengers arrived and departed by air.

Shipping. The island is visited regularly by French and American steamers. In 1982, 1,650 vessels called at Martinique.

Post and Broadcasting. There were, in 1983, 46 post offices and, 43,127 telephones. Radio-telephone service to Europe is available. In 1983 there were 41,500 radio and 39,570 TV receivers.

Newspapers. In 1984 there was 1 daily newspaper with a circulation of 30,000.

JUSTICE, RELIGION, EDUCATION AND WELFARE

Justice. Justice is administered by 2 *tribunaux d'instance*, a *tribunal de grande instance*, a regional court of appeal, a commercial court, a court of assizes and an administrative court.

Religion. The majority of the population is Roman Catholic.

Education. Education is compulsory between the ages of 6 and 16 years. In 1982–83, there were 57,132 pupils in primary schools, and 45,603 pupils in secondary and technical schools. The *Institut Henri Visioz*, which forms part of the *Centre Universitaire Antilles-Guyane*, had (1980) 1,475 students.

Health. There were (1982) 18 hospitals with 3,973 beds and in 1980 there were 364 physicians, 138 pharmacists, 120 midwives and 101 dentists.

Books of Reference

Annuaire statistique I.N.S.E.E. 1977–80. Martinique, 1982
La Martinique en quelques chiffres. Martinique, 1982
Guide Economique des D.O.M.-T.O.M., Paris, 1982

MAYOTTE

HISTORY. Mayotte was a French colony from 1843 until 1914, when it was attached, with the other Comoro islands, to the government-general of Madagascar. The Comoro group was granted administrative autonomy within the French Republic and became an Overseas Territory.

When the other 3 islands voted to become independent (as the Comoro state) in 1974, Mayotte voted against this and remained a French dependency. In 1976, it became (following a further referendum) a *collectivité territoriale,* being an intermediate status between Overseas Territory and Overseas Department.

AREA AND POPULATION. Mayotte, east of the Comoro Islands, has an area of 374 sq. km (144 sq. miles) and a 1978 Census population of 47,246 (1984, estimate, 56,000). The main towns are Mamoundzou (7,800) and the capital, Dzaoudzi (4,147 inhabitants) situated on a tiny offshore islet. The main languages are Mahorian (a Swahili dialect) and French.

GOVERNMENT. The island is administered by an appointed Commissioner and an elected *Conseil Général* of 17 members. Mayotte is represented by 1 deputy in the National Assembly and by 1 member in the Senate.

Commissioner: Christian Pellerin.
President of the Conseil Général: Younoussa Bamana.

ECONOMY

Budget. The budget for 1982 balanced at 144·3m. French francs.

Currency. Since Feb. 1976 the currency has been the (metropolitan) *French franc.*

NATURAL RESOURCES

Agriculture. The main products are vanilla, ylang-ylang, coffee and copra.

Fisheries. A lobster and shrimp industry has recently been created. Annual catch is about 2,000 tonnes.

COMMERCE. In 1982, exports totalled 5·1m. francs (81% to France) and imports 121·7m. francs (57% from France). Ylang-ylang formed 67% of exports and vanilla, 9%. Total trade between Mayotte and UK (1984): Imports to UK, £67,000 and exports and re-exports from UK, £343,000.

COMMUNICATIONS

Roads. In 1982 there were 96 km of main roads (72 km bitumenized) and 120 km of local roads, with about 1,300 motor vehicles.

Aviation. In 1981, 7,458 passengers and 739 tonnes of freight arrived by air and 9,100 passengers (314 tonnes) departed.

JUSTICE, RELIGION AND EDUCATION

Justice. There is a *tribunal d'instance* and a *tribunal supérieur d'appel.*

Religion. The population is 99% Moslem, with a small Christian (mainly Roman Catholic) minority.

Education. In 1982 there were 11,338 pupils and 317 teachers in primary schools and 794 pupils and 40 teachers in secondary and technical schools.

RÉUNION

HISTORY. Réunion (formerly Île Bourbon) became a French possession in 1638 and remained so until 19 March 1946, when its status was altered to that of an Overseas Department; in 1972 it additionally became an administrative region.

AREA AND POPULATION. The island of Réunion, about 640 km east of Madagascar, has an area of 2,512 sq. km (968·5 sq. miles) and population of 515,814 (March 1982 census), estimate (1984) 545,300. The capital is Saint-Denis (1982 census) 109,072.

Vital statistics (1983): Live births, 12,461; deaths, 3,280.

The small islands of Juan de Nova, Europa, Bassas da India, Îles Glorieuses and Tromelin, with a combined area of about 60 sq. km, are all uninhabited and lie at various points in the Indian Ocean adjacent to Madagascar. They remained integral parts of the French Republic after Madagascar's independence in 1960, and are now administered by Réunion. Both Mauritius and the Seychelles have laid claim to Tromelin (which had been transferred by the UK from the Seychelles to France in 1954), and Madagascar to all 5 islands.

CLIMATE. A sub-tropical maritime climate, free from extremes of weather, though the island lies in the cyclone belt of the Indian Ocean. Conditions are generally humid and there is no well-defined dry season. Saint-Denis. Jan. 80°F (26·7°C), July 70°F (21·1°C). Annual rainfall 56″ (1,400 mm).

GOVERNMENT. The island is administered by an elected *Conseil Général* of 36 members and an elected Regional Council of 45 members. Réunion is represented in the National Assembly by 3 deputies, in the Senate by 3 senators, and in the Economic and Social Council by 1 councillor. There are 4 *arrondissements* sub-divided into 24 communes each administered by an elected municipal council. The French government is represented by an appointed Commissioner.

Commissioner: Michel Blangy.
President of the Conseil Général: Auguste Legros.

ECONOMY

Budget. The budget for 1983 balanced at 7,314m. French francs.

Banking. The Institut d'émission des Départements d'Outre-mer has the right to issue bank-notes. Banks operating in Réunion are the Banque de la Réunion (Crédit Lyonnais), the Banque Nationale de Paris Internationale, the Caisse Régionale de Crédit Agricole Mutuel de la Réunion, the Banque Française Commerciale (BFC) and the Banque Populaire Fédérale de Développement.

NATURAL RESOURCES

Agriculture (1983). The chief produce is sugar (223,700 tonnes), rum (84,100 hectolitres), maize (10,690 tonnes), potatoes (3,602 tonnes), onions (1,379 tonnes), vanilla, essences and tobacco. The forests occupy about 100,500 hectares.

Livestock (1983): 19,660 cattle, 71,680 pigs, 2,900 sheep, 42,900 goats and 2,827,000 poultry.

Fisheries. In 1983 the catch was 2,777 tonnes.

INDUSTRY AND TRADE

Industry (1983). Total number of workers (in 418 firms employing 10 or more) 18,846. The sugar industry employed 2,846.

Commerce. Trade in 1m. French francs:

	1978	*1979*	*1980*	*1981*	*1982*	*1983*
Imports	2,659	3,230	3,749	4,282	5,304	6,490
Exports	519	594	554	573	668	875

The chief export is sugar, forming (1983) 79·7% by value. In 1983 (by value) 61·9% of imports were from, and 53·1% of exports to, France.

Total trade between Réunion and UK (British Department of Trade returns, in £1,000 sterling):

	1980	*1981*	*1982*	*1983*	*1984*
Imports to UK	60	290	74	73	407
Exports and re-exports from UK	3,022	3,117	2,889	3,684	3,327

COMMUNICATIONS

Roads. There were, in 1983, 2,710 km of roads. There were 108,725 passenger cars and 50,000 other vehicles in 1982.

Aviation. Air France maintains an air service 6 times a week. In 1983, 202,472 passengers and 5,655 tonnes of freight arrived and 200,628 passengers and 2,460 tonnes of freight departed at Saint-Denis-Gillot airport.

Shipping. Four shipping lines serve the island. In 1983, 259 vessels visited the island to discharge 1,104,583 tonnes of freight and 1,814 passengers, and load 340,997 tonnes of freight and 1,814 passengers at Pointe-des-Galets.

Post and Broadcasting. There are telephone and telegraph connexions with Mauritius, Madagascar and metropolitan France. There are 38 post offices and a central telephone office; number of telephones (1984), 74,000.

France Régions 3 broadcast in French on medium- and short-waves for more than 18 hours a day. There are 2 television channels broadcasting for 70 hours a week. In 1984 there were 114,500 radio and 107,500 TV receivers.

Cinemas. In 1972 there were 25 cinemas with a seating capacity of 10,200.

Newspapers. There were (1983) 3 daily newspapers with a combined circulation of 68,000.

JUSTICE, RELIGION, EDUCATION AND WELFARE

Justice. There are 3 *tribunaux d'instance,* 2 *tribunaux de grande instance,* 1 *Cour d'Appel,* 1 *tribunal administratif* and 2 *conseils de prud'homme.*

Religion. The vast majority of the population is Roman Catholic.

Education. Secondary education is provided in (1983–84) 6 *lycées*, 50 *collèges*, and 9 *lycées d'enseignement technique* with 66,653 pupils altogether and in 13 private secondary schools with 3,407 pupils. Primary education is given in 336 public schools with 4,018 teachers and 106,437 pupils; and in 28 private schools, with 306 teachers, and 8,827 pupils. The *Université Française de l'Océan Indien* (founded 1971) had 2,928 students in 1983.

Health. In 1983 there were 21 hospitals with 4,183 beds; in 1983 there were 608 physicians, 181 dentists, 174 pharmacists, about 90 midwives and 1,620 nursing personnel.

Books of Reference

Bulletin de l'Académie de la Réunion. Biennial
Bulletin de la Chambre d'Agriculture de la Réunion
Panorama de l'Economie de la Reunion. 1983
Statistiques et Indicateurs Economiques. 1983

ST PIERRE AND MIQUELON

HISTORY. The tiny remaining fragment of the once extensive French possessions in North America, the archipelago was settled from France in the 17th century and finally became a French territory from 1816 until July 1976, when its status was altered to that of an Overseas Department.

AREA AND POPULATION. The department consists of 8 small islands off the south coast of Newfoundland, with a total area of 242 sq. km, comprising the Saint-Pierre group (26 sq. km) and the Miquelon-Langlade group (216 sq. km). The population (census, 1982) was 6,041 of whom 5,415 were on Saint-Pierre and 626 on Miquelon. The chief town is St Pierre.

Vital statistics (1982): Births, 127; marriages, 33; deaths, 44.

GOVERNMENT. The department is administered by an appointed Commissioner and an elected *Conseil Général* of 14 members, directly elected for a 6-year term; it is represented in the National Assembly by 1 deputy, in the Senate by 1 senator and in the Economic and Social Council by 1 councillor.

Commissioner: Gérard Lefebvre.
President of the Conseil Général: Marc Plantegenest.

BUDGET. The ordinary budget for 1982 balanced at 51·4m. francs.

INDUSTRY AND TRADE

Industry. The islands, being mostly barren rock, are unsuited for agriculture. The chief industry is fishing.

Commerce. Trade in 1,000 tonnes and 1,000 francs:

	1980		*1981*		*1982*	
	Quantity	*Value*	*Quantity*	*Value*	*Quantity*	*Value*
Imports	47·7	177,203	58·6	220,910	58·6	275,390
Exports	4·3	24,213	4·9	38,658	3·6	41,045

In 1981, 66% of imports came from Canada and 28% from France, while 58% of exports were to USA, 17% to France and 11% to UK.

The main exports are fish (88%), shellfish (6%) and fishmeal (5%).

Total trade between St Pierre and Miquelon and UK (British Department of Trade returns in £1,000 sterling):

	1980	*1981*	*1982*	*1983*	*1984*
Imports to UK	3	1,352	254	578	743
Exports and re-exports from UK	884	481	363	250	523

Tourism. There were (1982) 11,293 visitors.

COMMUNICATIONS

Roads. In 1982 there were 108 km of roads, of which 43 km were paved. In 1981 there were about 1,637 passenger cars and 531 commercial vehicles.

Aviation. Air Saint-Pierre connects the department with Halifax and Sydney (Nova Scotia), and there are occasional flights to and from St John's (Newfoundland), Gander and New York.

Shipping. St Pierre is in regular motor-vessel communication with North Sydney, Fortune (Newfoundland) and Halifax. In 1980, about 47,600 tonnes of freight were unloaded and 4,250 tonnes loaded. 1,033 ships (615,176 gross tonnage) entered the harbour in 1981.

Post and Broadcasting. There were 2,907 telephones in 1982. *France Régions 3* broadcasts in French on medium-waves. St Pierre is connected by radio-telecommunication with most countries of the world. Radio licences totalled 4,300 and TV 1,950 in 1980.

Cinemas. There were (1983) 2 cinemas with a seating capacity of 760.

JUSTICE, RELIGION, EDUCATION AND WELFARE

Justice. There is a *tribunal de premier instance* and a *tribunal supérieur d'appel* at St Pierre.

Religion. The population is chiefly Roman Catholic.

Education. Primary instruction is free. There were, in 1982–83, 7 nursery and primary schools with 1,023 pupils and 3 secondary schools (including 1 technical school) with 693 pupils.

Health. There was (1983) 1 hospital on St Pierre with 100 beds; 11 doctors and 2 dentists.

Books of Reference

De Curton, E., *Saint-Pierre et Miquelon.* Paris, 1944
De La Rüe, E. A., *Saint-Pierre et Miquelon.* Paris, 1963
Ribault, J. Y., *Histoire de Saint-Pierre et Miquelon: Des Origines à 1814.* St Pierre, 1962

OVERSEAS TERRITORIES

SOUTHERN AND ANTARCTIC TERRITORIES

Terres Australes et Antarctiques Françaises

The Territory of the TAAF was created on 6 Aug. 1955. It comprises the Kerguelen and Crozet archipelagoes, the islands of Saint Paul and Amsterdam (formerly Nouvelle Amsterdam), all in the southern Indian ocean, and Terre Adélie.

The Administrator is assisted by a 7-member consultative council which meets twice yearly in Paris; its members are nominated by the Government for 5 years. The 12 members of the Scientific Council are appointed by the Senior Administrator after approval by the Minister in charge of scientific research. A 15-member Consultative Committee on the Environment, created in Nov. 1982, meets at least once a year to discuss all problems relating to the preservation of the environment. The administration has its seat in Paris.

Administrateur supérieur: Vice-Adm. Claude Piéri.

There are 4 postal agencies; the TAAF has its own postage stamps.

The scientific stations of the TAAF which took an important part in the International Geophysical Year, 1956–58, have been made permanent; the staff of the French bases (168 in 1983) is renewed annually and forms the only population.

Kerguelen islands, situated 48–50° S. lat., 68–70° E. long., consists of 1 large and 85 smaller islands and over 200 islets and rocks with a total area of 7,215 sq. km (2,786 sq. miles), of which Grande Terre occupies 6,675 sq. km (2,577 sq. miles). It was discovered in 1772 by Yves de Kerguelen, but was effectively occupied by France only in 1949. Port-aux-Français has several scientific research stations (76 members). Reindeer, trout and sheep have been acclimatized.

Crozet islands, situated 46° S. lat., 50–52° E. long., consists of 5 larger and 15 tiny islands, with a total area of 505 sq. km (195 sq. miles); the western group includes Apostles, Pigs and Penguins islands; the eastern group, Possession and Eastern islands. The archipelago was discovered in 1772 by Marion Dufresne, whose mate, Crozet, annexed it for Louis XV. A meteorological and scientific station (33 members) at Base Alfred-Faure on Possession Island was built in 1964.

Amsterdam Island and **Saint-Paul Island,** situated 38–39° S. lat., 77° E. long. Amsterdam, with an area of 54 sq. km (21 sq. miles) was discovered in 1522 by Magellan's companions; Saint-Paul, lying about 100 km to the south, with an area of 7 sq. km (2·7 sq. miles), was probably discovered in 1559 by Portuguese sailors. Both were first visited in 1633 by the Dutch explorer, Van Diemen, and were annexed by France in 1843. They are both extinct volcanoes. The only inhabitants are at Base Martin de Vivies, established in 1949 on Amsterdam Island, with several scientific research stations, hospital, communication and other facilities (33 members). Crayfish are caught commercially on Amsterdam.

Terre Adélie comprises that section of the Antarctic continent between 136° and 142° E. long., south of 60° S. lat. The ice-covered plateau has an area of about 432,000 sq. km (166,800 sq. miles), and was discovered in 1840 by Dumont d'Urville. A research station (26 members) is situated at Base Dumont d'Urville, which is maintained by the French Polar Expeditions.

Books of Reference

T.A.A.F. Revue trimestrielle. Paris, 1957 ff.
Expéditions Polaires Françaises. Études et Rapports. Paris, 1948–59

NEW CALEDONIA

Nouvelle Calédonie

HISTORY. New Caledonia was annexed by France in 1853 and, together with most of its former dependencies, became an Overseas Territory in 1958.

AREA AND POPULATION. The territory comprises the island of New Caledonia and various outlying islands, all situated in the south-west Pacific with a total land area of 19,103 sq. km (7,375 sq. miles). In 1983 the population (census) was 145,368, including 53,974 Europeans (majority French), 61,870 Melanesians, 7,700 Vietnamese and Indonesians, 5,570 Polynesians, 12,174 Wallisians, 4,080 others; 1984 (estimate) 147,200. The capital, Noumea had (1983) 60,112 inhabitants.

Vital statistics (1983): Live births, 3,516; deaths, 787.

The main islands are:

1. The island of New Caledonia with an area of 16,627 sq. km, has a total length of about 400 km, and an average breadth of 50 km, and a population (census, 1983) of 127,885.
2. The Loyalty Islands, 100 km (60 miles) east of New Caledonia, consisting of 3

large islands, Maré, Lifou and Uvéa, and many small islands with a total area of about 2,353 sq. km and a population (census, 1983) of 15,510, nearly all Melanesians except on Uvéa, which is partly Polynesian. The chief culture in the islands is that of coconuts: the chief export, copra.
3. The Isle of Pines, 50 km (30 miles) to the south-east of Nouméa, with an area of 153 sq. km and a population of 1,287 (census 1983), is a tourist and fishing centre.
4. The Bélep Archipelago, about 50 km north-west of New Caledonia, with an area of 70 sq. km and a population of 686 (census 1983).

The remaining islands are all very small and none have permanent inhabitants, although many were formerly exploited for their guano deposits. The largest are the Chesterfield Islands, a group of 11 well-wooded coral islets with a combined area of 10 sq. km, about 550 km west of the Bélep Archipelago. The Huon Islands, a group of 4 barren coral islets with a combined area of just 65 hectares, are 225 km north of the Bélep Archipelago. Walpole, a limestone coral island of 1 sq. km, lies 150 km east of the Isle of Pines; Matthew Island (20 hectares) and Hunter Island (2 sq. km), respectively 250 km and 330 km east of Walpole, are spasmodically active volcanic islands also claimed by Vanuatu.

CONSTITUTION AND GOVERNMENT. From Jan. 1976 State affairs are administrated by the High Commissioner and Territorial affairs by a Council of Government of 7 elected members (until 1976 the Council was advisory). A Territorial Assembly of 42 elected members decides the more important territorial affairs including local revenue.

New Caledonia is represented in the National Assembly by 2 deputies, in the Senate by 1 senator and in the Economic and Social Council by 1 councillor.

At territorial elections held 18 Nov. 1984, the *Rassemblement Pour la Calédonie dans la République* (Gaullists) gained 34 seats, the Kanak Socialist Independence Party 6 seats and others 2 seats.

The Territory is divided into 6 counties (of which the Loyalty Islands form one), and sub-divided into 32 communes which are administered by locally elected councils and mayors.

President of the Territorial Assembly: Dick Ukeiwé.
High Commissioner: Edgard Pisani.
President of the Territorial Assembly: Jean Leques.

ECONOMY

Budget. The budget for 1983 balanced at 28,939m. francs CFP. Revenues included special grants by France totalling 7,440m. francs CFP.

Currency. The unit of currency is the *franc* CFP, with a parity of CFP *francs* 18·18 to the French *franc*.

Banking. There are branches of the Banque de Indosuez, the Banque Nationale de Paris, the Banque de Paris et des Pays-Bas, and the Société Générale, and the Banque de la Nouvelle-Calédonie (Crédit Lyonnais).

ENERGY AND NATURAL RESOURCES

Electricity. In 1983, production totalled 737m. kwh.

Minerals. The mineral resources are very great; nickel, chrome and iron abound; silver, gold, cobalt, lead, manganese, iron and copper have been mined at different times. The nickel deposits are of special value, being without arsenic. Production of nickel ore in 1982, 2·2m. tonnes. About 467,000 hectares of mining land are owned, and 97,000 hectares have been granted for exploitation. In 1983 the furnaces produced 4,578 tonnes of matte nickel and 21,717 tonnes of ferro-nickel.

Agriculture. Of the total area only about 6% is cultivable; about 416,000 hectares are pasture land; about 6,000 hectares are commercially cultivated and about 250,000 hectares contain forest; forest produce, 1976, 19,849 cu. metres. There are 4 forms of landownership: native reserves belonging to the local tribes, private estates, public land belonging to the New Caledonian territory and public land belonging to the metropolitan government. The chief agricultural products are beef, pork, poultry, coffee, maize, fruit and vegetables.

Livestock (1983): Cattle, 100,000; pigs, 20,000; goats, 8,000; poultry.

Fisheries. The catch in 1982 totalled 2,299 tonnes.

INDUSTRY AND TRADE

Industry. Local industries include chlorine and oxygen plants, cement, soft drinks, barbed wire, nails, pleasure and fishing boats, clothing, pasta, household cleaners and confectionery.

Commerce. Imports and exports in 1m. francs CFP for 5 years:

	1979	*1980*	*1981*	*1982*	*1983*
Imports	27,791	35,041	40,434	43,735	42,201
Exports	28,549	29,652	33,435	27,707	22,035

In 1981, 32·5% of the imports came from, and 67% of the exports went to France.

Chief imports in 1983 were (in 1m. francs CFP): Food, 10,452; fuels and minerals, 5,160; machines and electrical equipment, 3,986. Chief exports: Nickel metal, 13,871; nickel ore, 3,082. Iron alloys (mainly ferro-nickel) formed 50% of exports, nickel 26% and nickel ore 19%.

COMMUNICATIONS

Roads. There were, in 1980, 5,496 km of roads, excluding 470 km on minor islands.

Aviation. New Caledonia is connected by air routes with France (by UTA), Australia (UTA and Qantas), New Zealand (UTA and Air New Zealand), Fiji (by UTA Cal International and Air Pacific), Vanuatu, Wallis archipelago and Tahiti (by UTA), and Nauru (by Air Nauru). In 1983, 125,317 passengers arrived and 127,157 departed *via* La Tontouta airport, near Nouméa.

Shipping. In 1983, 350 vessels entered Nouméa unloading 694,600 tonnes of goods and loading 1,273,800 tonnes. A new harbour for deep-water alongside discharge was completed in 1974.

Post and Broadcasting. There were 32 post offices and telex, telephone, radio and television services. There were (1982) 30,058 telephones. *Radio Nouméa* belongs to *Société Nationale des Programmes* and broadcasts in French on medium- and short-waves. *Télé Nouméa* broadcasts 1 television programme 48 hours a week. Number of receivers (1978): radio, 65,000; TV, 28,000.

Cinemas. In 1983 there were 9 cinemas.

Newspapers. In 1984 there was 1 daily newspaper with a circulation of 16,000 and 16 other periodicals.

JUSTICE, RELIGION, EDUCATION AND WELFARE

Justice. There is a *Tribunal de Grande Instance* and a *Cour d'Appel* in Nouméa.

Religion. Over 60% of the population are Roman Catholic and 30% Protestant.

Education. In 1983, there were 34,055 pupils and 1,672 teachers in primary schools, 11,943 pupils and 981 teachers in secondary schools, 4,934 students and 308 teachers in technical and vocational schools and 580 students and 52 teaching staff in higher education.

Health. In 1982 there were 200 physicians, 53 dentists, 47 pharmacists, 15 midwives and 561 nursing personnel. In 1983, 6 hospitals and 27 dispenseries had a total of 1,224 beds.

Books of Reference

Journal Officiel de la Nouvelle Calédonie et Dépendances
Annuaire Statistique de la Nouvelle Calédonie et Dépendances
Tableaux de l'Economie Calidonierre, 1983–1985

FRENCH POLYNESIA

Polynésie Française

HISTORY. French protectorates since 1843, these islands were annexed to France 1880–82 to form 'French Settlements in Oceania', which opted in Nov. 1958 for the status of an Overseas Territory within the French Community.

AREA AND POPULATION. The total land area of these 5 archipelagoes, scattered over a wide area in the Eastern Pacific is 3,941 sq. km (1,522 sq. miles). The population, Census, 1983, was 166,753; estimate (1984) 172,000. The islands are administratively divided into 5 *circonscriptions:*

1. The **Windward Islands** (Îles du Vent) (123,069 inhabitants in 1983) comprise Tahiti with an area of 1,042 sq. km and (1977) 95,604 inhabitants; Moorea with an area of 132 sq. km and 5,788 inhabitants; and the smaller Mehetia, Tetiaoro and Tubuai Manu. The capital is Papeete (62,735 inhabitants including suburbs).

2. The **Leeward Islands** (Îles sous le Vent) (19,060 (1983) inhabitants), comprise the volcanic islands of Huahine (3,140), Raiatéa (6,376), Tahaa (3,513), Bora-Bora (2,572), and Maupiti (710) together with 4 small atolls, the group having a total area of 507 sq. km. The chief town is Uturoa (2,517 inhabitants) on Raiatéa.

The Windward and Leeward Islands together are called the Society Archipelago (Archipel de la Société). Tahitian, a Polynesian language, is spoken throughout the archipelago and used as a *lingua franca* in the rest of the territory.

3. The **Tuamotu Archipelago**, consisting of two parallel ranges of 78 atolls lying between 135° and 143° W. long. and 14° and 23° S. lat., east of the Society Archipelago, have a total area of 774 sq. km; its major islands are Rangiroa, Hao and Turéia. The *circonscription* (total 11,793 inhabitants) also includes the **Gambier Islands** further east (of which Mangareva is the principal), with an area of 36 sq. km and a population of 556 (1977); the chief centre is Rikitea.

4. The **Austral or Tubuai Islands**, lying south of the Society Archipelago, comprise a 1,300 km chain of volcanic islands and reefs. They include Rimatara, Rurutu, Tubuai, Raivaevae and, 500 km to the south, Rapa-Iti, with a combined area of 174 sq. km and 6,283 inhabitants; the chief centre is Mataura on Tubuai.

5. The **Marquesas Islands**, lying north of the Tuamotu Archipelago, with a total area of 1,274 sq. km and 6,548 inhabitants, comprise Nuku-Hiva, Ua Pu, Ua Huka, Hiva-Oa, Tahuata, Fatu-Hiva and 4 smaller (uninhabited) islands; the chief centre is Taiohae on Nukuhiva.

CONSTITUTION AND GOVERNMENT. Under the 1984 Constitution, the Territory is administered by a Council of Ministers, whose President is elected by the Territorial Assembly from among its own members; he appoints a Vice-President and 9 other ministers. There is an advisory Economic and Social Committee. French Polynesia is represented in the National Assembly by 2 deputies, in the Senate by 1 senator, and in the Economic and Social Council by 1 councillor. The French government is represented by a High Commissioner.

The Territorial Assembly comprises 30 members elected every 5 years by universal suffrage.

At the elections held in May 1982, the *Tahoeraa Huiratira* (Gaullists) won 13 seats, the *Pupu Here Ai'a* (moderate autonomists) 6 seats and others 11 seats.

High Commissioner: Alain Ohrel.
President of the Government: Gaston Flosse.

ECONOMY

Budget. The ordinary budget for 1982 balanced at 28,100m. francs CFP.

Currency. The unit of currency is the *franc* CFP, with a parity of CFP *francs* 18·18 to the French *franc*.

Banking. There are 4 commercial banks, the Bank Indosuez, the Bank of Tahiti, the Banque de Polynésie and Paribas.

ENERGY AND NATURAL RESOURCES

Electricity. Production in 1981 (Tahiti only) amounted to 151·7m. kwh.

Agriculture. An important product is copra (coconut trees covering the coastal plains of the mountainous islands and the greater part of the low-lying islands), production (1982) 19,181 tonnes. Tropical fruits, such as bananas, pineapples, oranges, etc., are grown only for local consumption.

Livestock (1983): Cattle, 9,000; horses, 2,000; pigs, 30,000; sheep, 2,000; goats, 3,000; poultry (1982), 600,000.

Fisheries. The catch in 1979 amounted to 4,217 tonnes of fish.

COMMERCE. Trade in 1m. francs CFP:

	1980	*1981*	*1982*
Imports	42,030	54,843	62,307
Exports	2,340	2,861	3,349

Total trade between the French possessions in the Pacific and UK (British Department of Trade returns, in £1,000 sterling):

	1980	*1981*	*1982*	*1983*	*1984*
Imports to UK	32	8	2	93	2
Exports and re-exports from UK	2,154	1,421	1,962	2,601	3,276

Chief imports (by value) include metalwork, textiles, petrol, sugar and flour. Chief exports are coconut oil, cultured pearls, vanilla and citrus fruits. In 1982, France provided 45% of imports and USA, 21% while 68% of exports went to France.

Tourism is very important, earning almost half as much as the visible exports. There were 114,000 tourists in 1982.

COMMUNICATIONS

Roads. In 1981 there were 741 km of roads.

Aviation. Seven international airlines connect Tahiti with Paris, Los Angeles and many Pacific locations. There is also a regular air service between Faaa airport (on Tahiti), Moorea and the Leeward Isles with occasional connexions to the other groups. In 1981, 351,489 passengers arrived and 338,006 departed *via* Faaa airport and (1976) 210,300 *via* Moorea airport.

Shipping. Several shipping companies connect France, San Francisco, New Zealand, Japan, Australia, South East Asia and most Pacific locations with Papeete.

Post and Broadcasting. Number of telephones (1982), 24,818. *Radio Tahiti* belongs to *Office de Radiodiffusion-Télévision Française* and broadcasts in French, Tahitian and English on medium- and short-waves and also broadcasts 1 television programme *via* 5 transmitters. Number of receivers (1980): radio, 80,000; TV, 25,000.

Cinemas. In 1975 there were 6 cinemas with a seating capacity of 3,200.

Newspapers. In 1984 there were 2 daily newspapers with a combined circulation of 12,000.

JUSTICE, RELIGION, EDUCATION AND WELFARE

Justice. There is a *tribunal de grande instance* and a *cour d'appel* at Papeete.

Religion. In 1975 it was estimated that 50% of the inhabitants were Protestants, 34% Roman Catholic and 6% Mormon.

Education. Education at primary level was reorganized in 1974 and secondary education in 1975. There were, in 1979-80, 38,964 pupils and 1,687 teachers in primary schools, 9,613 pupils and 610 teachers in secondary schools, 2,757 pupils and 214 teachers in technical schools, and 225 students and 20 lecturers at teacher-training colleges.

Health. There were (1979) 125 physicians, 46 dentists, 19 pharmacists, 15 midwives and 408 nursing personnel. There was a main hospital at Mamao (on Tahiti), 6 secondary hospitals, 41 dispensaries and medical centres and 45 first aid posts with (1978) 890 hospital beds.

DEPENDENCY. The uninhabited Clipperton Island, 1,000 km off the west coast of Mexico, is administered by the High Commissioner for French Polynesia but does not form part of the Territory; it is an atoll with an area of 5 sq. km.

Books of Reference

Journal Officiel des Etablissements Françaises de l'Océanie, and *Supplement Containing Statistics of Commerce and Navigation*. Papeete
Andrews, E., *Comparative Dictionary of the Tahitian Language*. Chicago, 1944
Bounds, J. H., *Tahiti*. Bend, Oregon, 1978
Luke, Sir Harry, *The Islands of the South Pacific*. London, 1961
O'Reilly, P., and Reitman, E., *Bibliographie de Tahiti et de la Polynésie française*. Paris, 1967
O'Reilly, P., and Teissier, R., *Tahitiens. Répertoire bio-bibliographique de la Polynésie française*. Paris, 1963

WALLIS AND FUTUNA

HISTORY. French dependencies since 1842, the inhabitants of these islands voted on 22 Dec. 1959 by an overwhelming majority in favour of exchanging their status to that of an Overseas Territory, which took effect from 29 July 1961.

AREA AND POPULATION. The Territory comprises two groups of islands (total area 274 sq. km) in the central Pacific, The Îles de Hoorn lie 240 km north-east of Fiji and consist of 2 main islands–Futuna (64 sq. km) and uninhabited Alofi (51 sq. km). The Wallis Archipelago lies another 160 km further north-east, and comprises one main island – Uvea (159 sq. km), with a surrounding coral reef. The capital is Mata-Utu on Uvea.

The resident population (census March 1982) was 11,943 (estimate, 1984, 13,000), comprising 7,843 on Uvea and 4,100 on Futuna. About 11,000 Wallisians and Futunians live abroad, mainly in New Caledonia and Vanuatu. Wallisian and Futunian are distinct Polynesian languages.

CONSTITUTION AND GOVERNMENT. The Senior Administrator carries out the duties of Head of the Territory, assisted by an elected 20-member Territorial Assembly. The territory is represented by 1 deputy in the National Assembly, by 1 senator in the Senate, and by 1 member on the Economic and Social Council. There are 3 districts: Singave and Alo (both on Futuna) and Wallis.

Administrateur supérieur: Robert Thil.
President of the Territorial Assembly: Falakito Gata.

ECONOMY

Budget. The 1982 budget provided for expenditure of 303·8m. francs CFP.

Currency. The unit of currency is the *franc* CFP, with a parity of CFP *francs* 18·18 to the French *franc*.

AGRICULTURE. The chief products are copra, yams, taro roots and bananas.

Livestock: Cattle, 100 (1976); pigs, 22,000 (1983); horses, 400 (1978); goats, 7,000 (1983).

COMMERCE. Imports (1981) amounted to 667m. francs CFP. There are few exports.

COMMUNICATIONS

Roads. In 1977 there were 100 km of roads on Uvea.

Aviation. In 1980 there were 581 aircraft arrivals and departures at Hihifo airport, on Uvea. There is a weekly flight *via* Vila (Vanuatu) to Noumea (New Caledonia) and three flights each week to Futuna (Point Vele air strip).

Shipping. A regular service links wharves at Mata-Utu and at Singave (Futuna) with Nouméa (New Caledonia).

Post and Broadcasting. In 1979 a radio station was established on Uvea. In 1982 there were 151 telephones.

RELIGION, EDUCATION AND WELFARE

Religion. The majority of the population is Roman Catholic.

Education. In 1983, there were 3,962 pupils in 13 primary and lower secondary schools.

Health. In 1974 there were 3 physicians and 26 nursing personnel (including 10 midwives). There were (1972) 5 small hospitals and dispensaries with 108 beds.

GABON

République Gabonaise

Capital: Libreville
Population: 1·37m. (1984)
GNP per capita: US$3,810 (1981)

HISTORY. First colonized by France in the mid-19th century, Gabon was annexed to French Congo in 1888 and became a separate colony in 1910 as one of the 4 territories of French Equatorial Africa. It became an autonomous republic within the French Community in 1958 and achieved independence on 17 Aug. 1960. The first President, Leon M'ba, died on 30 Nov. 1967 and was succeeded on 2 Dec. by his Vice-President, Albert-Bernard (now Omar) Bongo.

AREA AND POPULATION. Gabon is bounded west by the Atlantic ocean, north by Equatorial Guinea and Cameroon and east and south by Congo. The area covers 267,667 sq. km; its population at the 1970 census was 950,007; estimate (1984) is 1,367,000. The capital is Libreville (350,000 inhabitants, 1983), other large towns (1975) being Port-Gentil (77,611) and Lambaréné (22,682).

Vital statistics (1975): Birth rate, 3·22%; death rate, 2·22%.

Provincial areas, populations (estimate 1976, in 1,000) and capitals are as follows:

Province	*sq. km*	*1976*	*Capital*	*Province*	*sq. km*	*1976*	*Capital*
Estuaire	20,740	311	Libreville	Nyanga	21,285	89	Tchibanga
Woleu-Ntem	38,465	162	Oyem	Ngounié	37,750	123	Mouila
Ogooué-Ivindo	46,075	57	Makokou	Ogooué-Lolo	25,380	51	Koulamoutou
Moyen-Ogooué	18,535	51	Lambaréné	Haut-Ogooué	36,547	188	Franceville
Ogooué-Maritime	22,890	172	Port-Gentil				

The largest ethnic groups are the Fang (30%) in the north, Eshira (25%) in the south-west, and the Adouma (17%) in the south-east. French is the official language.

CLIMATE. The climate is equatorial, with high temperatures and considerable rainfall. Mid-May to mid-Sept. is the long dry season, followed by a short rainy season, then a dry season again from mid-Dec. to mid-Feb., and finally a long rainy season once more. Libreville. Jan. 80°F (26·7°C), July 75°F (23·9°C). Annual rainfall 99″ (2,510 mm).

CONSTITUTION AND GOVERNMENT. The 1967 Constitution (as subsequently revised) provides for an Executive President directly elected for a 7-year term, who appoints a Council of Ministers to assist him. The unicameral National Assembly consists of 84 members, directly elected for a 5-year term (latest elections, Feb. 1980) and a further 9 members nominated by the President.

The sole legal political party is the *Parti democratique gabonais* founded in 1968.

President: Omar Bongo (re-elected on 25 Feb. 1973 and 30 Dec. 1979).
Prime Minister: Léon Mébiame.
Foreign Minister: Martin Bongo.
Flag: Three horizontal stripes of green, yellow, blue.
Local government: The 9 provinces, each administered by a governor appointed by the President, are divided into 37 *départements*, each under a prefect.

DEFENCE

Army. The Army consists of 1 all-arms Presidential Guard battalion group with support units, totalling (1985), 3,900 men.

Navy. The small naval flotilla in 1985 comprised 4 fast attack craft, 1 patrol craft and 3 landing craft with a base at Port-Gentil. Personnel, 170 officers and men. The Coastguard has 9 small patrol craft and 1 service tender.

Air Force. The Air Force has 5 single-seat and 2 two-seat Mirage 5 ground-attack aircraft, and 1 EMB-111 maritime patrol aircraft. Transport duties are performed primarily by 3 Hercules and 4 EMB-110 Bandeirante turboprop aircraft, supported by 3 C-47s and 3 Nord 262s. Single Gulfstream III, Mystère 20, YS-11 and DC-8 aircraft are used for VIP duties; a Cessna Skymaster for liaison. Four T-34C-1 armed turboprop aircraft are operated for *La Présidentiale Garde.* Also in service are 5 Puma and 5 Alouette III helicopters. Personnel (1985) 500.

INTERNATIONAL RELATIONS

Membership. Gabon is a member of UN, OAU and OPEC; it is an ACP state of the EEC.

ECONOMY.

Planning. The 1982–84 Interin Development Plan proposed public expenditure of 362,512m. francs CFA, of which 188,202m. were to develop the transport infrastructure.

Budget. The provisional budget for 1983 balanced at 562,000m. francs CFA.

Currency. The unit of currency is the franc CFA, divided into 100 centimes, with a parity value of 50 francs CFA to 1 French franc.

Banking. The *Banque des États de l'Afrique Centrale* is the bank of issue. There are 6 commercial banks situated in Gabon. The *Banque Gabonaise de Développement* and the *Union Gabonaise de Banque* are Gabonese controlled.

ENERGY AND NATURAL RESOURCES

Electricity. The semi-public *Société d'energie et d'eau du Gabon* produced 734m. kwh. in 1983, mainly from thermal plants but increasingly from hydro-electric schemes at Kinguélé (near Libreville), Tchimbélé and Poubara (near Franceville).

Oil. Extraction from offshore fields totalled 7·9m. tonnes in 1983. Gabon operates 2 refineries, at Port-Gentil and at nearby Pointe Clairette.

Gas. Natural gas production (1983) was 82m. cu. metres.

Minerals. Production (1983) of manganese ore (from deposits around Moanda in the south-east) amounted to 1·92m. tonnes. Uranium is mined nearby (1,358 tonnes in 1983). An estimated 850m. tonnes of iron ore deposits, discovered 1971 at Mékambo (near Bélinga in the north-east) await completion of the branch railway line to be exploited. Gold (50 kg in 1978), zinc and phosphates also occur.

Agriculture. Agriculture, forestry and fisheries occupy 85% of the working population. The major crops (production, 1981, in 1,000 tonnes) are: Sugar-cane, 14; cassava, 100; plantains, 63; maize, 10; bananas, 8; palm products, 547; cocoa (1983, 167,000); coffee (1983, 616) and rice.

Livestock (1983): 7,000 cattle, 80,000 sheep, 60,000 goats, 145,000 pigs.

Forestry. Gabon's equatorial forests covering 78% of the land area produced 1·1m. cu. metres of *okoumé* and hardwoods in 1983. Hardwoods (mahogany, ebony and walnut) are also exported.

Fisheries. The total catch (1980) amounted to 26,400 tonnes in the Atlantic and 400 tonnes in inland waters.

TRADE. In 1981 imports totalled 226,800m. francs CFA and exports (1980) 477,760m. francs CFA. France and USA are Gabon's principal trading partners. In 1978 petroleum made up 72% of exports; metals, 18% and timber, 6%.

Total trade between Gabon and the UK (British Department of Trade returns, in £1,000 sterling):

	1980	1981	1982	1983	1984
Imports to UK	10,657	36,726	27,634	66,135	70,775
Exports and re-exports from UK	9,155	12,099	14,179	18,798	20,548

COMMUNICATIONS

Roads. There were (1982) 7,393 km of roads and there were 36,240 (10,200 goods) vehicles.

Railways. A 1,435-mm gauge (Transgabonais) railway runs from Owendo *via* N'Djole to Booué and Lastourville, and is being extended to Moanda and Franceville with a projected branch from Booué to Bélinga.

Aviation. There are 3 international airports at Port-Gentil, Franceville, and Libreville; internal services link these to 65 domestic airfields.

Shipping. Owendo (near Libreville), Mayumba and Port-Gentil are the main ports. In 1980, 10·1m. tonnes were loaded and 617,000 tonnes unloaded at the ports. In 1978 there were 15 merchant vessels of 98,645 gross tons.

Post and Broadcasting. Telephones (1982), 11,133. In 1982 there were 10,000 television and 98,000 radio licences.

Cinemas. In 1974 there were 6 cinemas with a seating capacity of 4,100.

Newspapers. There were (1984) 2 newspapers published in Libreville; *Gabon-Matin* (daily) has a circulation of 18,000 and *L'Union* (weekly) 15,000.

JUSTICE, RELIGION, EDUCATION AND WELFARE

Justice. There are *tribunaux de grande instance* at Libreville, Port-Gentil, Lambaréné, Mouila, Oyem, Franceville and Koulamoutou, from which cases move progressively to a central Criminal Court, Court of Appeal and Supreme Court, all 3 located in Libreville.

Civil police number about 900.

Religion. It is estimated that 50% of the population is Christian (mainly Roman Catholic), the majority of the balance following animist beliefs. There are about 2,000 Moslems.

Education. Education is compulsory between 6–16 years. In 1981 there were 155,081 pupils with 3,281 teachers in primary schools; 22,005 pupils with 1,088 teachers in secondary schools; 3,465 students with 266 teachers in 9 technical schools; and 2,119 students with 120 teaching staff at 13 teacher-training schools.

The Université Omar Bongo, founded in 1970 in Libreville, had (1978) 1,284 students; about 750 Gabonese students study abroad.

Health (1977). There were 207 doctors, 20 dentists, 28 pharmacists (1971), 99 midwives and 823 nursing personnel. In 1981 there were 16 hospitals and 87 medical centres, with a total of 4,815 beds, as well as 258 local dispensaries.

DIPLOMATIC REPRESENTATIVES

Of Gabon in Great Britain (48 Kensington Ct., London, W8)
Ambassador: Léon N'Dong.

Of Great Britain in Gabon (Bâtiment Sogame, Blvd de l'Indépendance, Libreville)
Ambassador: R. H. T. Bates.

Of Gabon in the USA (2034 20th St., NW, Washington, D.C., 20009)
Ambassador: Mocktar Abdoulaye-Mbingt.

Of the USA in Gabon (Blvd de la Mer, Libreville)
Ambassador: Francis McNamara.

Of Gabon to the United Nations
Ambassador: Jean-Félix Oyoue.

Books of Reference

Bory, P., *The New Gabon*. Monaco, 1978
Remy, M., *Gabon Today*. Paris, 1977

THE GAMBIA

Capital: Banjul
Population: 695,886 (1983)
GNP per capita: US$344 (1983)

HISTORY. The Gambia was discovered by the early Portuguese navigators, but they made no settlement. During the 17th century various companies of merchants obtained trading charters and established a settlement on the river, which, from 1807, was controlled from Sierra Leone; in 1843 it was made an independent Crown Colony; in 1866 it formed part of the West African Settlements, but in Dec. 1888 it again became a separate Crown Colony. The boundaries were delimited only after 1890. The Gambia achieved full internal self-government on 4 Oct. 1963 and became an independent member of the Commonwealth on 18 Feb. 1965. The Gambia became a republic within the Commonwealth on 24 April 1970. The Gambia, with Senegal formed the Confederation of Senegambia on 1 Feb. 1982.

AREA AND POPULATION. The Gambia is bounded west by the Atlantic ocean and on all other sides by Senegal. Area of Banjul (formerly Bathurst) and environs, 87·8 sq. km. In the provinces (area, 10,601·5 sq. km) the settled population (1971) was 275,469, not including temporary immigrants. Total population (census, April 1983), 695,886. The largest tribe is the Mandingo (1973) (186,241), followed by the Fulas (79,994), Woloffs (69,291), Jolas (41,988) and Sarahulis (38,478). The capital is Banjul, 1983 census (44,536), and the surrounding urban area, Kombo St Mary (102,858).

CONSTITUTION AND GOVERNMENT. Parliament consists of the House of Representatives which consists of a Speaker, Deputy Speaker and 35 elected members; in addition, 4 Chiefs are elected by the Chiefs in Assembly; 5 nominated members are without votes and the Attorney-General is appointed and has a vote. *See* Senegal for details about Senegambia.

A general election was held on 4–5 May 1982. State of parties (Jan. 1984): The People's Progressive Party 29, the National Convention Party 3, and Independents 3 seats.

The Government was in Sept. 1984 composed as follows:

President: Sir Dawda Kairaba Jawara.

Vice-President (Information and Tourism): Bakary B. Darbo. *External Affairs:* Alhaji Lamine Kiti Jabang. *Finance and Trade:* Sherif Sisay. *Agriculture (Finance and Trade):* Saikou Sabally. *Education, Youth, Sport and Culture:* Alhaji Abdoulie K. N'Jie. *Health, Labour and Social Welfare:* Momodou Cherno Jallow. *Works and Communications:* Lamine Bora M'Boge. *Economic Planning and Industrial Development:* Dr Momodou S. K. Manneh. *Justice and Attorney-General:* Hassan Jallow. *Water Resources and Environment:* Omar A. Jallow. *Information and Tourism:* Landing Jallow Sonko. *Interior:* A. E. W. F. Badji. *Local Government and Lands:* Amulai Janneh.

National flag: Three horizontal stripes of red, blue, green, with the blue edged in white.

Local Administration. The Gambia is divided into 35 districts, each traditionally under a Chief, assisted by Village Heads and advisers. These districts are grouped into 6 Area Councils containing a majority of elected members, with the Chiefs of the district as *ex-officio* members. The city of Banjul is administered by a City Council.

CLIMATE. The climate is characterized by two very different seasons. The dry season lasts from Nov. to May, when precipitation is very light and humidity moderate. Days are warm but nights quite cool. The SW monsoon is likely to set in with spectacular storms and produces considerable rainfall from July to Oct., with increased humidity. Banjul. Jan. 73°F (22·8°C), July 80°F (26·7°C). Annual rainfall 52″ (1,295 mm).

INTERNATIONAL RELATIONS

Membership. The Gambia is a member of UN, OAU, the Commonwealth, the Non-Aligned Conference and is an ACP state of EEC.

ECONOMY

Budget. Revenue and expenditure for years ending 30 June are (in dalasi):

	1979–80	*1980–81*	*1981–82*	*1982–83*
Revenue	88,045,000	85,001,700	134,286,323	104,947,970
Expenditure	81,190,000	96,792,176	137,268,189	144,220,280

Currency. The currency is the *dalasi* and is divided into 100 *butut.* 5 *dalasi* = £1 sterling; 4·74 *dalasi* = US$1 (March 1985).

Banking. There are 4 banks in the Gambia, the Standard Bank of Gambia Ltd, Central Bank of the Gambia, Commercial and Development Bank and la Banque Internationale pour le Commerce et l'Industrie (BICI). On 30 Nov. 1978 the government savings bank had about 36,000 depositors holding approximately 992,496 dalasi.

NATURAL RESOURCES

Minerals. Heavy minerals, including ilmenite, zircon and rutile, have been discovered (1m. tons up to 31 Dec. 1980) in Sanyang, Batakunku and Kartong areas.

Agriculture. Almost all commercial activity centres upon the marketing of groundnuts, which is the only export crop of financial significance; in 1982–83, 128,000 tonnes were produced. Cotton is also exported on a limited scale. Rice is of increasing importance for local consumption.

Livestock (1983): 300,000 cattle, 194,000 goats, 185,000 sheep, 12,000 pigs and (1982) 300,000 poultry.

Fisheries. Total catch (1975) 10,800 tonnes, of which 800 tonnes were from inland waters.

LABOUR. There are 4 large and 10 small trade unions.

TRADE. Chief items of imports are textiles and clothing, vehicles and machinery, metal goods and petroleum products.

Imports and exports, in 1,000 dalasi:

	1978–79	*1979–80*	*1980–81*	*1981–82*	*1982–83*
Imports	221,014	500,000	275,800	220,600	218,900
Exports	94,913	417,000	...	82,900	86,000

Chief items of exports are groundnuts, palm kernels, dried and smoked fish, hides and skins and groundnut oil.

Total trade between the Gambia and UK (British Department of Trade returns, in £1,000 sterling):

	1980	*1981*	*1982*	*1983*	*1984*
Imports to UK	2,417	2,335	2,031	3,781	3,407
Exports and re-exports from UK	17,792	11,889	10,087	13,251	10,233

TOURISM. In 1982–83, 24,800 tourists visited the Gambia.

COMMUNICATIONS

Roads. There are 2,990 km of motorable roads, of which 1,718 km rank as all-weather roads including 306 km of bituminous surface and 531 km of laterite gravel. Number of licensed motor vehicles (1981): 7,400 private cars, 800 buses and coaches, 750 goods vehicles, and 800 motorcycles.

Aviation. The Gambia is served by Air Guinea, Air Mali, British Caledonian Airways, Ghana Airways and Nigeria Airways. Air movements at Yundum Airport in 1975 numbered 2,756, including scheduled services.

Shipping. The chief port, Banjul, handled 303 ships of 686,300 DWT in 1975–76. A new 400 ft berth will take one large vessel of up to 36 ft draught. Internal communication is maintained by steamers and launches.

The Gambia River Development Organization was founded in 1978 as a joint project with Senegal to develop the river and its basin. Guinea and Guinea-Bissau were also members in 1984.

Post and Broadcasting. There are several post offices and agencies; postal facilities are also afforded to all river towns by means of a travelling post office on the government river mail-steamers. Banjul is connected with St Vincent (Cape Verde islands) and with Sierra Leone by cable. Banjul is in wireless communication with London and the main centres up river. A trans-Gambia telephone system provides direct communications with Dakar and Ziguinchor. Telephones numbered 3,476 in Jan. 1980. A telex service was introduced in 1968.

Radio Gambia, a government station, broadcasts for about 12 hours a day; Radio Syd, a commercial station, broadcasts for 15 hours. Number of radio receivers (1983, estimate), 66,000.

Cinemas. In 1979 there were 10 cinemas.

Newspapers. There is an official newspaper and several news-sheets.

JUSTICE, RELIGION, EDUCATION AND WELFARE

Justice. Justice is administered by a Supreme Court consisting of a chief justice and puisne judges. It has unlimited jurisdiction but there is a Court of Appeal. Two magistrates' courts and divisional courts are supplemented by a system of travelling magistrates. There are also Moslem courts, group tribunals dealing with cases concerned with customs and traditions, and one juvenile court.

Religion. About 70% of the population is Moslem. Banjul is the seat of an Anglican and a Roman Catholic bishop. There are some Methodist missions. Some sections of the population retain their original animist beliefs.

Education (1979–80). There were 133 primary schools (1,371 teachers, 37,644 pupils), 17 secondary technical schools (260 teachers, 5,274 pupils), 7 senior secondary schools (179 teachers, 3,040 pupils) and 1 post-secondary school; total number of teachers, 1,810. Gambia College, which is to replace Yundum College as a teacher-training and vocational centre, opened for agricultural and health students in 1979.

Health. In 1980 there were 43 government doctors, 23 private doctors and about 635 hospital beds.

DIPLOMATIC REPRESENTATIVES

Of the Gambia in Great Britain (57 Kensington Ct., London, W8 5DG)
High Commissioner. Samuel J. O. Sarr, MBE.

Of Great Britain in the Gambia (48 Atlantic Rd., Fajara, Banjul)
High Commissioner: John D. Garner, MVO.

Of the Gambia in the USA (1785 Massachusetts Ave., NW, Washington, D.C., 20036)
Ambassador: Dr Lamin A. Mbye.

Of the USA in the Gambia (Pipeline Road, Kombo St. Mary, Banjul)
Ambassador: Robert T. Hennemeyer.

Books of Reference

The Gambia since Independence 1965–1980. Banjul, 1980
Tomkinson, M., *The Gambia: A Holiday Guide.* London, 1983

GERMANY

POST-WAR HISTORY. Since the unconditional surrender of the German armed forces on 8 May 1945 there has been no central authority whose writ runs in the whole of Germany. Consequently no peace treaty has been signed with a government representing the whole of Germany, and the country is virtually partitioned between the Federal Republic of Germany and the German Democratic Republic.

By the Berlin Declaration of 5 June 1945 the governments of the USA, the UK, the USSR and France assumed supreme authority over Germany. Each of the 4 signatories was given a zone of occupation, in which the supreme power was to be exercised by the C.-in-C. in that zone (*see* map in THE STATESMAN'S YEAR-BOOK, 1947). Jointly these 4 Cs.-in-C. constituted the Allied Control Council in Berlin, which was to be competent in all 'matters affecting Germany as a whole'. The territory of Greater Berlin, divided into 4 sectors, was to be governed as an entity by the 4 occupying powers.

At the Potsdam Conference (17 July–2 Aug. 1945) the northern part of the Province of East Prussia, including its capital Königsberg (renamed Kaliningrad), was transferred to the Soviet Union, pending final ratification by a peace treaty; and it was agreed that, pending the final peace settlement, Poland should administer those parts of Germany lying east of a line running from the Baltic Sea immediately west of Swinemünde along the river Oder to its confluence with the Western Neisse and thence along the Western Neisse to the Czechoslovak frontier.

The agreements between the war-time allies concerning the occupation zones (12 Sept. 1944) and control of Germany (1 May 1945) were repudiated by the USSR on 27 Nov. 1958.

A Treaty was signed in East Berlin between the German Democratic Republic and the Federal Republic of Germany on 21 Dec. 1972 agreeing the basis of relations between the two countries.

GERMAN DEMOCRATIC REPUBLIC

Capital: Berlin (East)
Population: 16·7m. (1983)
GNP per capita: US$7,180 (1980)

Deutsche Demokratische Republik

HISTORY. For the immediate post-war history *see* p. 510.

AREA AND POPULATION. Area and population, 30 June 1983 (in 1,000):

Districts	*Area in sq. km*	*Population Male*	*Population Female*	*Population Total*	*Per sq. km*
Berlin (East)	403	552·5	633·1	1,185·5	2,924
Cottbus	8,262	423·0	460·8	883·9	107
Dresden	6,738	836·5	959·9	1,796·3	267
Erfurt	7,349	586·3	652·3	1,238·6	169
Frankfurt	7,186	341·3	367·7	709·0	99
Gera	4,004	350·5	392·6	743·1	186
Halle	8,771	854·2	955·8	1,810·0	206
Karl-Marx-Stadt	6,009	882·4	1,020·5	1,903·0	317
Leipzig	4,966	646·0	746·6	1,392·6	280
Magdeburg	11,526	594·7	664·3	1,259·0	109
Neubrandenburg	10,948	300·5	320·5	621·0	57
Potsdam	12,568	533·8	588·1	1,121·9	89
Rostock	7,074	431·2	464·7	895·9	127
Schwerin	8,672	282·8	309·1	592·0	68
Suhl	3,856	261·1	288·6	549·7	143
German Democratic Republic	*108,333*	*7,876·9*	*8,824·5*	*16,701·5*	*154*

An agreement proclaiming the Oder–Neisse line the permanent frontier between Germany and Poland was concluded between the German Democratic Republic and Poland on 6 July 1950. A protocol on the delimitation of the frontier was signed on 27 Jan. 1951.

Resident population of the principal towns as at 30 June 1982:

Berlin (East), capital	1,185,533	Rostock	241,146	Schwerin	124,975
Leipzig	558,994	Halle	236,139	Zwickau	120,486
Dresden	522,532	Erfurt	214,231	Cottbus	120,723
Karl-Marx-Stadt	318,917	Potsdam	135,922	Jena	106,555
Magdeburg	289,075	Gera	129,891	Dessau	103,738

Vital statistics:

	Live births	*Marriages*	*Divorces*	*Deaths*
1980	245,132	134,195	44,794	238,254
1981	237,543	128,174	48,567	232,244
1982	240,102	124,890	49,874	227,975
1983	233,756	125,429	49,624	222,702

Crude birth rate per 1,000 population was 13·9 in 1978; 14 in 1979; 14·6 in 1980; 14·2 in 1981; 14·4 in 1982; 13·3 in 1983; marriage rate, 8·4 in 1978; 8·2 in 1979; 8 in 1980; 7·7 in 1981; 7·5 in 1982; 7·5 in 1983; death rate, 13·9 in 1978; 13·9 in 1979, 14·2 in 1980; 13·9 in 1981; 13·7 in 1982; 13·3 in 1983; infantile mortality per 1,000 live births, 7 in 1978 and 1979; 6·7 in 1980; 6·9 in 1981; 5·9 in 1982; 5·6 in 1983.

CLIMATE. The continental-type climate makes winters crisp and clear, but with cold easterly winds bringing very low temperatures and appreciable snowfall. Summers are hot, but with much convectional rainfall. Berlin. Jan. 31°F (–0·5°C), July 66°F (19°C). Annual rainfall 22·5″ (563 mm). Dresden. Jan. 30°F (–1°C), July 65°F (18·5°C). Annual rainfall 27·2″ (680 mm). Leipzig. Jan. 31°F (–0·6°C), July 65°F (18·5°C). Annual rainfall 24″ (605 mm).

CONSTITUTION AND GOVERNMENT. Upon the establishment of the Federal Republic of Germany, the People's Council of the Soviet-occupied zone, appointed in 1948, was converted into a provisional People's Chamber.

On 7 Oct. 1949 the provisional People's Chamber enacted a constitution of the 'German Democratic Republic'.

In July 1952 the 5 Länder of Mecklenburg, Saxony-Anhalt, Brandenburg, Saxony and Thuringia were replaced by 14 districts *(Bezirke)*.

A new 'socialist constitution' was approved by a referendum on 6 April 1968 (revised in 1974), when 94·54% of the electorate voted for the constitution; it came into force on 8 April 1968. The People's Chamber, of 500 deputies, is 'the supreme organ of state power'; it elects the Council of State, the Council of Ministers, the National Defence Council and the judges of the Supreme Court. Latest elections to the People's Chamber were in June 1981: the National Front candidates won 99·86% of the vote. The State Presidency was abolished after the death of Wilhelm Pieck in 1960.

Council of State. This consists of a chairman, 6 deputy chairmen, 18 members and a secretary. The Council is authorized to issue decisions and to interpret existing laws. The Chairman of the Council of State represents the GDR in international law. *Chairman:* Erich Honecker.

In March 1985 the Council of Ministers was composed as follows:

Chairman (i.e. Premier): Willi Stoph.

First Deputy Chairmen: Alfred Neumann, Werner Krolikowski.

Deputy Chairmen: Günther Kleiber, Wolfgang Rauchfuss, Gerhard Schürer *(Chairman, State Planning Commission)*, Dr Gerhard Weiss, Dr Herbert Weiz, Manfred Flegel, Hans-Joachin Heusinger *(Minister of Justice)*, Dr Hans Reichelt *(Minister for the Environment)*, Rudolph Schulze.

The Presidium of the Council of Ministers consists of the above-mentioned, and Ernst Höfner *(Minister of Finance)*, Walter Halbritter *(Director, Office of Prices)*, and Horst Sölle *(Foreign Trade Minister)*. There are 39 other members, including Heinz Hoffman *(Defence)*, Oskar Fischer *(Foreign Affairs)*, and Friedrich Dickel *(Interior)*.

De facto political power is exercised by the Politburo of the Socialist Unity (*i.e.* Communist) Party (SED), which in March 1985 consisted of: Erich Honecker *(Secretary-General)*; Hermann Axen; Horst Dohlus; Werner Felfe; Kurt Hager; Joachim Herrmann; Heinz Hoffmann; Egon Krenz; Werner Krolikowski; Erich Mielke; Günter Mittag; Erich Mueckenberger; Konrad Naumann; Alfred Neumann; Horst Sindermann; Willi Stoph; Harry Tisch; Paul Verner. There were also 7 candidate members.

National flag: Black, red, golden (horizontal); in the centre, on both sides, the coat of arms showing a hammer and compass with a wreath of grain entwined with a black, red and golden ribbon.

National hymn: Auferstanden aus Ruinen (tune by Hanns Eisler).

East Berlin ('Democratic Berlin') is the capital of the German Democratic Republic. *Mayor:* Erhard Krack.

DEFENCE. On 18 Jan. 1956 the People's Chamber established a 'national people's army' and a defence ministry. A 12-member defence council, under the chairmanship of E. Honecker, General Secretary of the Central Committee, was set up on 10 Feb. 1960.

The 'law for the defence of the GDR', of 20 Sept. 1960, makes military service (in case of emergency) and civil defence compulsory for all citizens.

Conscription for men between 18 and 25 years was introduced on 24 Jan. 1962 (18 months' service in the army, 2 years in the navy and air force).

Twenty Soviet divisions of about 258,000 men with about 1,000 heavy tanks and 6,000 armoured vehicles are stationed in the German Democratic Republic, chiefly along the Polish border.

Army. The Army, set up on 1 March 1956, is organized in 2 army corps, including 2 armoured divisions and 4 motorized infantry divisions. Operationally these divisions are subordinate to the Soviet formations of the Warsaw Pact forces. They are armed with about 3,100 tanks (mostly Soviet T-54, T-55 and T-72), 216 self-propelled guns and ground-to-air 'Guideline' missiles. The Border Police was incorporated in the Army in Sept. 1961. Total army strength was (1985) 120,000 (71,500 conscripts) with a reserve of 580,000 men.

Police. The Police force *(Volkspolizei)* numbered 25,000 security and 46,500 border troops. There are also 450,000 militiamen organized in combat groups. The militia receive military instruction from the People's Police.

Navy. The 'People's Navy' *(Volksmarine)* includes 2 frigates, 13 corvettes, 15 missile boats, 50 torpedo boats, 6 patrol vessels, 46 coastal minesweepers, 3 intelligence ships, 16 coastguard boats, 12 tank landing ships, 10 oilers, 2 training ships, 4 supply ships, 5 survey vessels, 9 small survey craft, 13 buoy tenders, 3 diving vessels, 1 cable layer, 2 torpedo recovery craft, 2 icebreakers, 30 auxiliary ships and service craft and 13 tugs. Personnel in 1985 totalled 14,600 officers and men, including the GBK Coastal Frontier Guards *(Grenz Brigade Küste)*.

Air Force. The *ex*-'air-police', set up in Nov. 1950, had in 1985 a strength of about 37,000 officers and men and 375 combat aircraft. Two air defence divisions consist respectively of 2 and 4 regiments (each with 3 squadrons of 12 aircraft), plus a fighter training division, equipped with MiG-21 and a small number of MiG-23 supersonic day and all-weather interceptors. There is 1 squadron of MiG-21 reconnaissance fighters. Four ground attack squadrons have begun replacing MiG-17s with MiG-27s, and Mi-24 gunship helicopters have been delivered to the German Democratic Republic. Other units include a regiment of Mi-2, Mi-4 and Mi-8 helicopters, a regiment of An-2, Let L.410, Il-14, An-26 and Tu-134 transports and a Flight Training Division with Yak-18, Trener, L-29 Delfin, L-39 Albatros, MiG-15UTI and MiG-21U training aircraft. 'Guideline' and 'Goa' surface-to-air missile units are operational.

INTERNATIONAL RELATIONS

Membership. The German Democratic Republic is a member of UN and Comecon.

ECONOMY

Budget. The budget of the German Democratic Republic was as follows (in M 1m.) for calendar years:

	1978	*1979*	*1980*	*1981*	*1982*	*1983*
Revenue	132,612	140,633	160,652	167,466	182,836	192,410
Expenditure	132,103	140,223	160,283	167,159	182,071	191,689

Of the 1982 expenditures, 54,875m. was earmarked for health and social services, education and *Kultur*.

Currency. The circulating Reichsmark notes were in June 1948 exchanged for 'Deutsche Mark' (East), renamed 'Mark of the German Bank of Issue' (MDN) from 1 Aug. 1964 and further renamed 'the Mark of the GDR' (M) from 1967. The circulation of notes and coins at 31 Dec. 1980 was M 12,250m. In March 1985, £1 = 3·60 M; US$1 = 3·43 M.

Banking. The most important banking institutions of the GDR are the Staatsbank der DDR Berlin, which is the bank of issue, and the Industrie- und Handelsbank der DDR. Savings, as at 31 Dec. 1983, totalled M 113,193m.

Weights and Measures. The metric system is in force.

ENERGY AND NATURAL RESOURCES

Electricity. Generation of electric power (in 1m. kwh.): 1950, 19,466; 1960, 40,305; 1970, 67,650; 1977, 91,996; 1978, 95,963; 1979, 96,845; 1980, 98,808; 1981, 100,720; 1982, 102,906; 1983, 104,928.

Minerals. In the production of lignite, the German Democratic Republic takes first place in world output. Rare metals, such as uranium, cobalt, bismuth, arsenic and antimony, are being exploited in the western Erzgebirge and eastern Thuringia.

The principal minerals are as follows (in 1,000 tonnes):

	1980	*1981*	*1982*	*1983*
Coal	258	267	...	...
Lignite	258,097	266,734	276,038	277,968
Potash	3,422	3,460	3,434	3,431

Agriculture. In 1983 the arable land was 4·74m. hectares; meadows and pastures, 1,250,271 hectares. In 1983 there were 3,938 collective farms with 5·36m. hectares of land cultivated independently and 70,726 hectares co-operatively, and 477 state farms of 436,421 hectares.

The yield of the main crops in 1983 was as follows (in 1,000 tonnes): Potatoes, 7,063; sugar-beet, 5,711; barley, 3,882; wheat, 3,550; rye, 2,092; oats, 498.

Livestock (in 1,000) in 1983: Cattle, 5,768 (including 2,096 milch cows); pigs, 13,058; sheep, 2,359; goats, 24; horses, 88; poultry, 53,018.

Forestry. In 1983 there were 2,963,138 hectares of forest. Timber production was 10,432,800 cu. metres. The industry employed 45,877 people in 1982.

Fisheries. Total catch (1983) 266,015 tonnes. Inland catch was 22,310 tonnes, of which 12,041 tonnes was carp.

INDUSTRY AND TRADE

Industry. Industry produced about 69% of the national income in 1982; the nationally owned and co-operative undertakings were responsible for 96·5% of the net product. The percentage of privately owned enterprises was 32·8 in 1950 and 2·9 in 1982.

There were, at 31 Dec. 1982, 4,029 industrial establishments with 3,190,361 employees.

Production of iron and steel (in 1,000 tonnes):

	1977	*1978*	*1979*	*1980*	*1981*	*1982*	*1983*
Crude steel	6,850	6,976	7,023	7,308	7,467	7,168	7,219
Rolled steel	4,802	5,002	5,100	5,128	5,061	4,959	5,084

Leading chemical products in 1983 were (in 1,000 tonnes): Sulphuric acid, 926; nitrogen fertilizers, 968; calcined soda, 887; caustic soda, 687; other industrial products: cement, 11,782; passenger cars (no.), 188,300; television receivers (no.), 667,100; shoes, 82m. pairs; plastics and synthetic resins, 1,045.

Commerce. Total trade was as follows (in 1m. Valuta-Mark):

	Total Imports	*Total Exports*
1970	20,357	19,240
1980	62,970	57,131
1981	67,000	65,927
1982	69,878	75,231
1983	76,197	84,227

In 1983 machinery made up 48% of exports and fuels and metal ores 40% of imports. Largest trading partners: USSR, Czechoslovakia, Federal Germany.

Total trade between the German Democratic Republic and UK (British Department of Trade returns, in £1,000 sterling):

	1980	*1981*	*1982*	*1983*	*1984*
Imports to UK	88,127	93,507	133,921	157,625	190,130
Exports and re-exports from UK	94,124	82,975	63,665	60,997	92,270

COMMUNICATIONS

Roads. There were, in 1983, 47,380 km of classified roads. 3,463m. passengers and

141·7m. tonnes of goods were carried by public transport in 1983. There were 3,019,875 cars, 223,186 lorries, 1,306,788 motorcycles and 53,178 buses.

Railways. There were, in 1983, 13,933 km of standard gauge line, of which 2,096 km were electrified. 620m. passengers and 325·6m. tonnes of freight were carried in 1983.

Aviation. Interflug operates services between Berlin and Prague, Warsaw, Budapest, Bucharest, Moscow, Sofia, Belgrade, Tirana, Cairo, Baghdad, Beirut and other capitals. Passengers carried (1983), 1,358,700; freight, 29,000 tonnes.

Shipping. In 1983 the merchant fleet had 174 vessels of 1,223,865 GRT. 11·9m. tonnes of freight were carried. Navigable inland waterways had a total length of 2,319 km. 7m. passengers and 17·47m. tonnes of freight were carried.

Pipeline. 1,301 km in 1983. Materials transported in 1983: 37·2m. tonnes.

Post and Broadcasting. In 1983 there were 11,971 post offices and agencies and 3,441,484 telephone subscribers. *Staatliches Kommittee für Rundfunk*, the governmental broadcasting station, broadcasts 4 programmes on long-, medium- and short-waves, and on FM. The foreign service is broadcast in 11 languages on medium-and short-waves, using the name Radio Berlin International. The transmitters are located at Königswusterhausen, Leipzig and Nauen. Radio Volga transmits on long-waves from Burg and broadcasts in Russian for the Soviet Armed Forces in Germany. More than 80% of the programmes are relays from Radio Moscow. Radio Moscow is using relay transmitters on medium-waves at Leipzig for programmes in German. *Deutsche Freiheitssender 904* and *Deutsche Soldatensender* are clandestine stations claiming to be operating from the Federal Republic although they are located not far from Burg. *Fernsehen der DDR* broadcasts 2 TV programmes in colour, using SECAM-system. Number of wireless licences (1983), 6·49m.; TV licences, 5·93m.

Cinemas and Theatres (1983). There were 824 cinemas with a seating capacity of 255,132, and 195 theatres with a capacity of 56,853.

Newspapers. There were 519 newspapers and periodicals in 1983.

RELIGION, EDUCATION AND WELFARE

Religion. According to the census of 1950, 80·5% of the population were Protestants and 11% were Roman Catholics.

Education. There are 2 types of schools: *(a)* the General polytechnical secondary schools, with 10 grades (the former elementary and middle schools), numbering (1983) 5,183 with 1,973,902 pupils; *(b)* the Extended polytechnical secondary schools, with the 11th and 12th grades, numbering (1983) 214 with 44,985 pupils. There were 171,914 teachers in 1983.

In addition there were (1983), 969 vocational schools *(Berufsschulen)* with 16,777 teachers and 411,166 pupils and 240 technical schools with 167,864 pupils. There were also 54 universities and other higher education institutes with 108,120 full-time students, including 57,281 women.

Health. In 1983, 541 hospitals had 170,996 beds. There were 581 polyclinics. There were 36,181 doctors and 10,903 dentists.

DIPLOMATIC REPRESENTATIVES

Of the German Democratic Republic in Great Britain (34 Belgrave Sq., London, SW1X 8QB)

Ambassador: Dr Gerhard Lindner (accredited 27 July 1984).

Of Great Britain in the German Democratic Republic (108 Berlin, Unter den Linden 32/34)

Ambassador: T. J. Everard, CMG.

Of the German Democratic Republic in the USA (1717 Massachusetts Ave., NW, Washington, D.C., 20036)
Ambassador: Dr Gerhard Herder.

Of the USA in the German Democratic Republic (108 Berlin, Neustädtische Kirchstrasse 4-5)
Ambassador: Rozanne L. Ridgway.

Of the German Democratic Republic to the United Nations
Ambassador: Harry Ott.

Books of Reference

Statistical Information: The central statistical agency is the Staatliche Zentralverwaltung für Statistik (Hans-Beimler-Str. 70–72, 102, Berlin).
Statistisches Jahrbuch der Deutschen Demokratischen Republik, annual (from 1956).—*Statistisches Taschenbuch der DDR* (annual, from 1959; also Arabic, English, French, Russian, Spanish editions).—*Statistische Praxis* (from 1946).
The Constitution of the German Democratic Republic. 3rd ed. Berlin, 1974
Deutsche Demokratische Republik, Handbuch. Leipzig, 1979
Handbook of the Economy of the German Democratic Republic. Farnborough, 1979

Biermann, W., *Demokratiserung in der DDR?* Cologne, 1978
Childs, D., *East Germany.* London, 1969.—*The GDR: Moscow's German Ally.* London, 1983
Heitzer, H., *GDR: An Historical Outline.* Dresden, 1981
Honecker, E., *Reden und Aufsätze.* Berlin, 1975–; *The German Democratic Republic, Pillar of Peace and Socialism.* New York, 1979
Krisch, H., *German Politics under Soviet Occupation.* New York and London, 1974
Legters, L. H., *The German Democratic Republic: A Developed Socialist Society.* Boulder, 1978
McCauley, M., *The German Democratic Republic since 1945.* London, 1984

National Library: Deutsche Bücherei, Leipzig C.1. *Director:* Helmut Rötzsch.—Deutsche Staatsbibliothek, Berlin. *Director:* Professor H. Kunze.

FEDERAL REPUBLIC OF GERMANY

Capital: Bonn
Population: 61·4m. (1983)
GNP per capita: US$13,450 (1981)

Bundesrepublik Deutschland

HISTORY. The Federal Republic of Germany became a sovereign independent country on 5 May 1955 and is a member of EEC, the Council of Europe, Western European Union, NATO, the European Coal and Steel Community, Euratom, the European Monetary Agreement and the Agencies of the UN.

In June 1948 USA, UK and France agreed on a central government for the 3 western zones. An Occupation Statute, which came into force on 30 Sept. 1949, reduced the responsibilities of the occupation authorities. Formally, the Federal Republic of Germany came into existence on 21 Sept. 1949. The Petersberg Agreement of 22 Nov. 1949 freed the Federal Republic of numerous restrictions of the Occupation Statute. In 1951 USA, UK and France as well as other states terminated the state of war with Germany; the Soviet Union followed on 25 Jan. 1955. On 5 May 1955 the High Commissioners of USA, UK and France signed a proclamation revoking the Occupation Statute. On the same day, the Paris and London treaties, signed in Oct. 1954, came into force and established the sovereignty of the Federal Republic of Germany.

AREA AND POPULATION. In April 1949 some minor frontier rectifications were carried out in favour of the Netherlands (68 sq. km), Belgium (18 sq. km), Luxembourg (6 sq. km) and France (7 sq. km), subject to a final peace settlement. Belgium (1956) and the Netherlands (1963) returned most of this territory to Germany.

Area and estimated population as at 30 June 1983:

Länder	*Area in sq. km*	*Population Male*	*Female*	*Total*	*Per sq. km*
Schleswig-Holstein	15,720	1,262,900	1,354,200	2,617,100	166
Hamburg	755	756,500	861,300	1,617,800	2,144
Lower Saxony	47,426	3,480,200	3,770,700	7,250,900	153
Bremen	404	321,100	361,300	682,400	1,688
North Rhine-Westphalia	34,067	8,070,900	8,830,600	16,901,500	496
Hessen	21,114	2,683,300	2,900,800	5,584,100	264
Rhineland-Palatinate	19,846	1,736,200	1,896,400	3,632,600	183
Baden-Württemberg	35,752	4,455,400	4,800,800	9,256,100	259
Bavaria	70,551	5,248,300	5,715,900	10,964,200	155
Saarland	2,571	499,900	553,800	1,053,700	410
Berlin (West)	480	848,800	1,011,600	1,860,500	3,875
Federal Republic	*248,687*[1]	*29,363,400*	*32,057,300*	*61,420,700*	*247*

[1] 96,018 sq. miles.

Vital statistics for calendar years:

	Marriages	*Live births*	*Of these illegitimate*	*Deaths*
1981	359,658	624,557	49,363	722,192
1982	361,966	621,173	52,750	715,857
1983	369,628	594,177	52,442	718,337

Crude birth rate in 1983 was 9·7 per 1,000 population; marriage rate, 6; death rate, 11·7; infantile mortality 10·2.

In 1983 there were 489,200 emigrants and 372,000 immigrants. Migrants from Eastern Germany to the Federal Republic, including West Berlin, totalled about 2,022,000 between 1955 and 1961. The East German Government tried to stop the outflow by erecting a concrete wall which later became a heavily fortified barrier along the border in Berlin on 13 Aug. 1961; despite the Berlin wall, the figures registered for persons moving from Eastern Germany and East Berlin into the Federal Republic were 20,700 in 1970, 15,400 in 1979 and 15,544 in 1982; most of them are older people with permission to emigrate. Migrants from the Federal Republic to Eastern Germany totalled about 279,000 between 1955 and 1961, 2,500 in 1969, 1,300 in 1979 and 1,528 in 1982.

The resident population of the principal towns was estimated as follows on 30 June 1983:

Town	*Land*	*Population*	*Town*	*Land*	*Population*
Berlin (West)	Berlin (West)	1,860,500	Freiburg im Breisgau	Baden-Württ.	178,400
Hamburg	Hamburg	1,617,800	Herne	N. Rhine-Westph.	177,700
München	Bavaria	1,284,300	Mülheim a.d. Ruhr	N. Rhine-Westph.	177,200
Köln	N. Rhine-Westph.	953,300	Hamm	N. Rhine-Westph.	170,000
Essen	N. Rhine-Westph.	635,200	Solingen	N. Rhine-Westph.	161,100
Frankfurt am Main	Hessen	614,700	Leverkusen	N. Rhine-Westph.	157,400
Dortmund	N. Rhine-Westph.	595,200	Ludwigshafen am Rhein	Rhinel.-Pal.	157,400
Düsseldorf	N. Rhine-Westph.	579,800	Osnabrück	Lower Saxony	156,100
Stuttgart	Baden-Württ.	571,100	Neuss	N. Rhine-Westph.	146,800
Bremen	Bremen	545,100	Oldenburg	Lower Saxony	138,800
Duisburg	N. Rhine-Westph.	541,800	Darmstadt	Hessen	137,800
Hanover	Lower Saxony	524,300	Bremerhaven	Bremen	137,300
Nürnberg	Bavaria	476,400	Heidelberg	Baden-Württ.	133,600
Bochum	N. Rhine-Westph.	391,300	Göttingen	Lower Saxony	132,700
Wuppertal	N. Rhine-Westph.	386,000	Regensburg	Bavaria	132,000
Bielefeld	N. Rhine-Westph.	307,900	Würzburg	Bavaria	129,500
Mannheim	Baden-Württ.	299,700	Remscheid	N. Rhine-Westph.	125,500
Gelsenkirchen	N. Rhine-Westph.	295,400	Wolfsburg	Lower Saxony	124,000
Bonn	N. Rhine-Westph.	292,900	Recklinghausen	N. Rhine-Westph.	119,100
Münster (Westf.)	N. Rhine-Westph.	273,500	Bottrop	N. Rhine-Westph.	113,400
Wiesbaden	Hessen	272,600	Koblenz	Rhinel.-Pal.	112,200
Karlsruhe	Baden-Württ.	270,300	Salzgitter	Lower Saxony	111,100
Mönchengladbach	N. Rhine-Westph.	258,200	Heilbronn	Baden-Württ.	111,000
Braunschweig	Lower Saxony	257,100	Paderborn	N. Rhine-Westph.	110,300
Kiel	Schleswig-Holstein	248,400	Siegen	N. Rhine-Westph.	109,800
Augsburg	Bavaria	246,700	Offenbach am Main	Hessen	108,600
Aachen	N. Rhine-Westph.	243,700	Pforzheim	Baden-Württ.	105,200
Oberhausen	N. Rhine-Westph.	226,200	Witten	N. Rhine-Westph.	104,200
Krefeld	N. Rhine-Westph.	222,100	Erlangen	Bavaria	102,400
Lübeck	Schleswig-Holstein	216,100	Hildesheim	Lower Saxony	101,900
Hagen	N. Rhine-Westph.	212,500	Bergisch Gladbach	N. Rhine-Westph.	100,900
Kassel	Hessen	190,400			
Saarbrücken	Saarland	190,100			
Mainz	Rhinel.-Pal.	186,400			

CLIMATE. Oceanic influences are only found in the north-west where winters are quite mild but stormy. Elsewhere a continental climate is general. To the east and south, winter temperatures are lower, with bright frosty weather and considerable snowfall. Summer temperatures are fairly uniform throughout. Rainfall is well distributed over the year, varying from 20″ (500 mm) on low ground to 80″ (2,000 mm) in Alpine parts.

CONSTITUTION. The Constituent Assembly (known as the 'Parliamentary Council') met in Bonn on 1 Sept. 1948, and worked out a Basic Law which was approved by a two-thirds majority of the parliaments of the participating Länder and came into force on 23 May 1949.

The Basic Law *(Grundgesetz)* consists of a preamble and 146 articles. The first section deals with the basic rights which are legally binding for legislation, administration and jurisdiction.

The Federal Republic of Germany is a democratic and social federal state. For the time being the Basic Law applies to the Länder Baden-Württemberg, Bavaria, Bremen, Greater Berlin (temporarily suspended), Hamburg, Hessen, Lower Saxony, North Rhine-Westphalia, Rhineland-Palatinate, Saarland and Schleswig-Holstein. The Basic Law decrees that the general rules of international law form part of the federal law. The constitutions of the Länder must conform to the principles of a republican, democratic and social state based on the rule of law. Executive power is vested in the Länder, unless the Basic Law prescribes or permits otherwise. Federal law supersedes Land law.

The organs of the Federal Republic are:

The Federal Diet *(Bundestag)*, elected in universal, direct, free, equal and secret elections, for a term of 4 years.

The Federal Council *(Bundesrat)*, consisting of members of the governments of the Länder. Each Land has at least 3 votes. Länder with more than 2m. inhabitants have 4, Länder with more than 6m. inhabitants have 5 votes.

The Federal President *(Bundespräsident)* is elected by the Federal Assembly for a term of 5 years and represents the Federal Republic in international relations. Re-election is admissible only once. The Federal Assembly (which meets only for the election of the Federal President) consists of the members of the Federal Diet and an equal number of members elected by the popular representative bodies of the Länder according to a particular system of semi-proportional representation.

The Federal Government consists of the Federal Chancellor, elected by the Federal Diet on the proposal of the Federal President, and the Federal Ministers, who are appointed and dismissed by the Federal President upon the proposal of the Federal Chancellor.

The Federal Republic has exclusive legislation on: (1) foreign affairs (2) federal citizenship; (3) freedom of movement, passports, immigration and emigration, and extradition; (4) currency, money and coinage, weights and measures, and regulation of time and calendar; (5) customs, commercial and navigation agreements, traffic in goods and payments with foreign countries, including customs and frontier protection; (6) federal railways and air traffic; (7) post and telecommunications; (8) the legal status of persons in the employment of the Federation and of public law corporations under direct supervision of the Federal Government; (9) trade marks, copyright and publishing rights; (10) co-operation of the Federal Republic and the Länder in the criminal police and in matters concerning the protection of the constitution, the establishment of a Federal Office of Criminal Police, as well as the combating of international crime; (11) federal statistics.

For concurrent legislation in which the Länder have legislative rights if and as far as the Federal Republic does not exercise its legislative powers, *see* THE STATESMAN'S YEAR-BOOK, 1956, p. 1038.

Federal laws are passed by the Federal Diet and after their adoption submitted to the Federal Council, which has a limited veto. The Basic Law may be amended only upon the approval of two-thirds of the members of the Federal Diet and two-thirds of the votes of the Federal Council.

The foreign service, federal finance, railways, postal services, waterways and shipping are under direct federal administration.

In the field of finance the Federal Republic has exclusive legislation on customs and financial monopolies and concurrent legislation on: (1) excise taxes and taxes on transactions, in particular, taxes on real-estate acquisition, incremented value and on fire protection; (2) taxes on income, property, inheritance and donations; (3) real estate, industrial and trade taxes, with the exception of the determining of the tax rates.

The Federal Republic can, by federal law, claim part of the income and corporation taxes to cover its expenditures not covered by other revenues. Financial jurisdiction is uniformly regulated by federal legislation.

National flag: Three horizontal stripes of black, red, gold.

National anthem: Einigkeit und Recht und Freiheit (words by H. Hoffmann, 1841; tune by J. Haydn, 1797).

GOVERNMENT. The *Federal Diet*, elected in March 1983 was composed of 498 members. In addition, there are 22 members for Berlin who, however, have no vote.

State of the parties: Social Democrats (SPD), 193 (1980: 218); Christian Democrats (CDU), 191 (174); Free Democrats (FDP), 34 (53); Christian Socialists (CSU), 53 (52); The Greens 27 (–).

Bonn on the Rhine is the capital of the Federal Republic.

Federal President: Dr Richard von Weizsäcker (sworn in 1 July 1984).

The Cabinet, a coalition of Christian Democrats, Christian Socialists and Free Democrats, in March 1984, was as follows:

Chancellor: Dr Helmut Kohl (CDU).
Deputy Chancellor, Minister of Foreign Affairs: Hans-Dietrich Genscher (FDP).
Interior: Dr Friedrich Zimmermann (CSU).
Justice: Hans A. Engelhard (FDP).
Finance: Dr Gerhard Stoltenberg (CDU).
Economics: Dr Otto Count Lambsdorff (FDP).
Food, Agriculture and Forestry: Ignaz Kiechle (CSU).
Intra-German Relations: Heinrich Windelen (CDU).
Labour and Social Affairs: Dr Norbert Blüm (CDU).
Defence: Dr Manfred Wörner (CDU).
Youth, Family Affairs and Health: Dr Heiner Geissler (CDU).
Transport: Dr Werner Dollinger (CSU).
Posts and Telecommunications: Dr Christian Schwarz-Schilling (CDU).
Regional Planning, Building and Urban Development: Dr Oscar Schneider (CSU).
Research and Technology: Dr Heinz Riesenhuber (CDU).
Education and Science: Dr Dorothee Wilms (CDU).
Economic Co-operation: Dr Jürgen Warnke (CSU).

DEFENCE. The Paris Treaties, which entered into force in May 1955, stipulated a contribution of the Federal Republic to western defence within the framework of NATO and the Western European Union. The Federal Armed Forces *(Bundeswehr)* had a total strength (1985) of 495,000 all ranks (236,000 conscripts) and a further 750,000 reserves.

Army. The Army is divided into the Field Army, containing the units assigned to NATO in event of war, and the Territorial Army. The Field Army is organized in 3 corps, comprising 17 armoured, 15 armoured infantry, 1 mountain and 3 airborne brigades. Equipment includes 1,232 M-48, 2,437 Leopard I and 800 Leopard II tanks. The Territorial Army is organized into 5 Military Districts, under 3 Territorial Commands. Its main task is to defend rear areas and remains under national control even in wartime. Total strength was (1985) 335,500 (conscripts 181,000; Territorial Army 44,000).

Navy. The Federal Navy comprises 24 diesel-powered coastal submarines, 7 destroyers, 8 frigates, 6 corvettes, 40 fast missile boats (Exocet armed), a light cruiser type training ship, 10 frigate-type support ships, 18 coastal minesweepers and minehunters, 21 fast minesweepers, 20 inshore minesweepers, 22 utility landing craft, 28 smaller landing craft, 12 supply and support ships, 2 fleet replenishment ships, 8 oilers, 8 coast patrol boats, 12 torpedo recovery vessels, 9 coastguard cutters, 2 repair ships, 24 tugs and 45 auxiliaries and service craft.

The projected construction programme includes 12 submarines, 2 more guided missile frigates and 10 minehunters.

The Naval Air Arm operates 160 fixed-wing aircraft, comprising 50 Tornados, 70 Starfighters, 20 Atlantics and 20 Dorniers; and 34 helicopters (22 Sea Kings and 12 Lynx).

Navy personnel in 1985 totalled 5,600 officers and 32,900 men, including 6,700 in the Naval Air Arm.

Air Force. Since Oct. 1970, the *Luftwaffe* has comprised the following commands: German Air Force Tactical Command, German Air Force Support Command (including two German Air Force Regional Support Commands—North and South) and General Air Force Office. Its strength in 1984 was approximately 105,900 officers and other ranks and about 500 first-line combat aircraft. Combat units, including 12 heavy fighter-bomber squadrons, 7 light ground attack/reconnaissance squadrons, 4 reconnaissance squadrons, 8 surface-to-surface missile squadrons, and an air defence force of 4 interceptor squadrons, 24 batteries of *Nike-Hercules* and 36 batteries of *Improved Hawk* surface-to-air missiles, are assigned to NATO. There are 4 F-4F Phantom interceptor squadrons, 3 Tornado attack squadrons, 5 F-104G fighter-bomber squadrons (re-equipping with Tornados), 4 attack squadrons of F-4Fs, 4 RF-4E Phantom reconnaissance squadrons, and 7 light attack/reconnaissance squadrons of Alpha Jets. Four transport squadrons (each 15 aircraft) with turboprop Transall C-160 aircraft and 1 wing of 5 helicopter squadrons with UH-1D Iroquois add to the air mobility of the *Bundeswehr*. There are also VIP, support and light transport aircraft, and Piaggio P.149D initial training aircraft. Guided weapons in service include 8 squadrons of *Pershing* surface-to-surface missiles and 6 battalions of *Nike-Hercules* and 9 battalions of *Improved Hawk* surface-to-air missiles.

Pilots undergo basic and advanced training in USA.

INTERNATIONAL RELATIONS

Membership. The Federal Republic of Germany is a member of UN, OECD, EEC, NATO and the Council of Europe.

ECONOMY

Budget. Since 1 Jan. 1979 tax revenues have been distributed as follows: Federal Government. Income tax, 42·5%; capital yield and corporation tax, 50%; turnover tax, 67·5%; trade tax, 15%; capital gains, insurance and accounts taxes, 100%; excise duties (other than on beer), 100%. Länder. Income tax, 42·5%; capital yield and corporation tax, 50%; turnover tax, 32·5%; trade tax, 15%; other taxes, 100%. Local authorities. Income tax, 15%; trade tax, 70%; local taxes, 100%.

Budgets for 1982 and 1983 (in DM1m.):

	All public authorities		*Federal portion*	
Revenue	*1982*	*1983*	*1982*	*1983*
		Current		
Taxes	366,643	383,378	184,574	191,865
Economic activities	34,941	36,545	15,294	16,010
Interest	2,821	2,813	1,259	1,131
Current allocations and subsidies	182,118	182,438	2,052	3,252
Other receipts	46,756	49,074	4,045	3,764
minus equalising payments	83,268	82,809	...	...
	458,951	480,220	206,198	214,396
		Capital		
Sale of assets	6,294	6,563	413	226
Allocations for investment	51,854	51,658	32	32
Repayment of loans	7,762	7,758	1,805	1,757
Public sector borrowing	2,229	2,158	...	...
minus equalising payments	23,825	23,731	...	...
	477,339	498,797	208,431	216,394

Expenditure	*All public authorities* 1982	1983	*Federal portion* 1982	1983
		Current		
Staff	176,142	181,117	34,398	35,139
Materials	85,697	88,553	34,807	36,672
Interest	45,042	51,423	22,107	26,618
Allocations and subsidies	562,552	548,294	315,535	300,374
minus equalising payments	83,268	82,805	...	...
	451,391	461,370	210,975	213,016
		Capital		
Construction	40,297	37,263	5,515	5,682
Acquisition of property	10,780	10,606	1,440	1,436
Allocations and subsidies	95,292	101,856	40,645	39,099
Loans	15,728	17,377	6,507	6,921
Acquisition of shares	3,818	3,484	1,351	1,729
Repayments in the public sector	1,327	1,316	...	...
minus equalising payments	23,825	23,731	...	...
	547,162	553,613	246,110	248,334

Major areas of expenditure in 1984 (and 1983) in DM1m.: Social, 75·9 (76·1); defence, 47·8 (46·7); transport, 24·6 (24·8); agriculture, 6·1 (5·9).

Currency. 100 *pfennig* (pf.)=1 *deutsche Mark* (DM). There are 1, 2, 5, 10, 50 pf., 1, 2, 5 and 10 DM coins and 5, 10, 20, 50, 100, 500 and 1,000 DM notes. Money in circulation in 1983, DM 99,294m. In March 1985, £1=3·60 DM; US$1=3·43.

Banking. On 14 Feb. 1948 the Bank deutscher Länder was established in Frankfurt as the central bank.

The Länder and Berlin central banks were merged from 1 Aug. 1957 when it became Deutsche Bundesbank. Its assets were DM 197,148m. in 1983.

Weights and Measures. The metric system is in force.

ENERGY AND NATURAL RESOURCES

Electricity. In 1982, 366,876m. kwh. were produced.

Oil. In 1983, 33·17m. tonnes of petroleum and 11·67m. tonnes of diesel oil were produced.

Minerals. The great bulk of the minerals in Germany is produced in North Rhine-Westphalia (for coal, iron and metal smelting-works), Central Germany (for brown coal), Lower Saxony (Salzgitter for iron ore; the Harz for metal ore). The chief oil-fields are in Lower Saxony (Emsland).

The quantities of the principal minerals raised in the Federal Republic were as follows (in 1,000 tonnes):

Minerals	*1978*	*1979*	*1980*	*1981*	*1982*	*1983*
Coal	83,936	86,319	87,146	88,460	89,014	82,202
Lignite	123,559	130,579	129,833	130,619	127,307	124,281
Iron ore	1,608	1,655	1,945	1,572	1,304	976
Potash	25,260	27,674	29,317	28,192	22,536	27,200
Crude oil	5,059	4,774	4,631	4,459	4,256	4,116

Production of iron and steel (in 1,000 tonnes):

	1978	*1979*	*1980*	*1981*	*1982*	*1983*
Pig-iron	30,148	35,167	33,873	31,876	27,621	26,598
Steel ingots and castings	41,253	46,040	43,838	41,610	35,880	35,729
Rolled products finished	31,102	33,616	...	...	...	26,063

Agriculture. In 1983 agricultural holdings with a farm area of 1 hectare or more cultivated 11·98m. hectares, including arable, 7·22m.; pasture, 4·58m.

In 1983 the number of agricultural holdings classified by area farmed was:

	Total	*1–5 hectares*	*5–20 hectares*	*20–100 hectares*	*Over 100 hectares*
Schleswig-Holstein	31,525	6,236	5,993	18,119	1,177
Hamburg	1,365	836	307	209	13
Lower Saxony	116,728	31,646	33,962	49,353	1,767
Bremen	466	153	114	196	3
North Rhine-Westphalia	94,696	29,092	34,254	30,773	577
Hessen	58,665	22,521	23,021	12,906	217
Rhineland-Palatinate	57,514	23,528	21,960	11,899	127
Baden-Württemberg	128,917	52,536	52,847	23,198	336
Bavaria	249,582	64,496	129,299	55,173	614
Saarland	4,212	1,789	1,281	1,113	29
Berlin (West)	143	84	35	24	—
Federal Republic	*743,813*	*232,917*	*303,073*	*202,963*	*4,860*

Area (in 1,000 hectares) and yield (in 1,000 tonnes) of the main crops in the Federal Republic, were as follows:

	Area				*Yield*			
	1979	*1980*	*1981*	*1982*	*1979*	*1980*	*1981*	*1982*
Wheat	1,627	1,668	1,631	1,578	8,061	8,156	8,313	8,632
Rye	564	546	484	407	2,114	2,098	1,729	1,639
Barley	1,989	2,001	2,044	2,021	8,184	8,826	8,687	9,460
Oats	728	691	682	723	2,994	2,658	2,678	3,113
Potatoes	276	258	246	238	8,716	6,694	7,585	7,049
Sugar-beet	393	395	444	418	18,340	19,122	24,380	22,732

Wine must production (in 1m. hectolitres): 7·4 in 1960; 9·9 in 1970; 9·2 in 1975; 8·7 in 1976; 10·4 in 1977; 7·3 in 1978; 8·2 in 1979; 4·6 in 1980; 7·2 in 1981; 15·4 in 1982; 13 in 1983.

Livestock on 3 Dec. 1983 was as follows: Cattle, 15,002,600 (including 5,516,500 milch cows); horses, 257,300; sheep, 981,200; pigs, 22,178,400; goats, 36,000 (1981); poultry (1982), 79,697,800.

Forestry. Forestry is of great importance, conducted under the guidance of the State on scientific lines. In recent years enormous depredation has occurred through pollution with acid rain. Forest area in 1983 was 5·27m. hectares, of which 2·22m. were owned by the State. In 1982 29m. cu. metres of timber were cut.

Fisheries. In 1983 the yield of sea and coastal fishing in the Federal Republic was 273,617 tonnes live weight, valued at DM 323,708,000.

At the end of 1982 the number of vessels of the fishing fleet was 29 trawlers (62,575 gross tons), 2 luggers and 625 cutters.

INDUSTRY AND TRADE

Industry. In 1982, 55,564 establishments (with 20 and more employees; production industries including handicrafts) in the Federal Republic employed 8,539,000 persons; of these 991,000 were employed in machine construction; 262,000 in the textile industry; 954,000 in electrical engineering; 238,000 in mining; 579,000 in chemical industry (average of 12 months).

The production of important industrial products in the Federal Republic was as follows:

Products	*1979*	*1980*	*1981*	*1982*	*1983*
Aluminium (1,000 tonnes)	742	731	729	723	743
Potassium fertilizers, K_2O (1,000 tonnes)	2,616	2,737	2,592	2,057	2,419
Sulphuric acid, SO_3 (1,000 tonnes) [1]	4,136	3,900	3,945	3,601	3,543
Soda, Na_2CO_3 (1,000 tonnes) [1]	1,401	1,411	1,189	1,105	1,218
Cement (1,000 tonnes) [1]	35,659	34,551	31,498	30,079	30,466
Rayon:					
Staple fibre (1,000 tonnes)	76	73	149	136	142
Continuous rayon filament (1,000 tonnes) [1]	62	70			
Cotton yarn (1,000 tonnes) [1]	161	170	148	168	181
Woollen yarn (1,000 tonnes) [1]	56	60	52	47	46
Passenger cars (1,000) [2]	3,943	3,530	3,590	3,771	3,875
Bicycles (1,000)	3,099	3,643	3,441	3,089	3,334

[1] Including the quantities processed in the same factories. [2] Including dual-purpose vehicles.

Labour. 25·19m. persons were employed in 1983, including 9·56m. women and 1·71m. foreign workers (Turks, 0·54m.; Yugoslavs, 0·31m.; Italians, 0·24m.; Greeks, 0·11m.). Unemployment was 2·26m. Major categories: manufacturing industries, 10·57m.; services, 8·64m.; commerce and transport, 4·61m.; self-employed, 2·36m.; agriculture, 1·38m.

Trade Unions. The majority of trade unions belong to the *Deutscher Gewerkschaftsbund* (DGB, German Trade Union Federation), which had (women in brackets) 7·75m. (1·64m.) members in 1983, including 5·21m. (0·82m.) workers, 1·71m. (0·69m.) white-collar workers and 0·82m. (0·13m.) civil servants in 1984. Of these 2·54m. (0·36m.) worked in the metal industries, 1·17m. (0·34m.) in public services, 0·52m. in building and 0·37m. in mining. DGB unions are organized in industrial branches such that only one union operates within each enterprise. Outside the DGB lie several smaller unions: The *Deutscher Beamtenbund* (DBB) or civil servants union with 0·8m. (0·2m.) members, the *Deutsche Angestellten-Gewerkschaft* (DAG) or union of salaried staff with 0·5m. (0·23m.) members and the *Deutscher Handels-und Industrieangestellten-Verband* (DHIV) or commercial and industrial salaried staffs association with 0·06m. (0·02m.) members.

Commerce. Distribution of imports and exports by country (in DM 1m.):

Country	*Imports*			*Exports*		
	1981	*1982*	*1983*	*1981*	*1982*	*1983*
Argentina	1,125·8	1,399·5	1,386·8	2,360·6	1,495·7	3,056·2
Australia	1,405·6	1,487·9	1,377·1	2,703·9	3,193·5	2,762·7
Austria	10,279·3	11,115·1	12,603·7	20,009·7	20,620·4	22,123·3
Belgium–Luxembourg	24,674·8	25,480·2	28,092·6	28,907·0	31,081·6	31,849·4
Brazil	3,449·4	4,191·7	4,310·1	2,277·1	2,162·6	1,555·3
Canada	3,278·3	3,360·9	3,316·8	2,740·6	2,528·1	3,103·8
Denmark	5,926·9	6,547·1	6,983·2	7,525·8	8,451·6	8,582·8
Finland	3,363·8	3,201·2	3,626·1	3,697·1	4,220·1	4,185·7
France	40,123·8	42,878·0	44,566·8	51,909·9	60,128·7	55,563·8
Greece	2,946·5	2,747·7	2,751·0	4,653·0	4,686·2	4,612·7
India	1,278·6	1,267·9	1,254·9	2,249·4	2,102·1	2,117·2
Iran	1,527·0	1,738·5	1,571·1	3,639·5	3,402·9	7,720·5
Italy	27,562·0	28,710·0	31,570·2	31,306·5	32,374·8	32,088·0
Japan	12,910·0	12,646·6	14,819·1	4,758·7	5,165·8	5,602·8
Libya	7,417·1	7,232·0	6,316·5	3,379·9	2,835·0	2,141·7
Netherlands	44,322·9	45,946·3	48,143·0	33,884·0	36,144·1	37,857·3
Norway	9,418·1	9,901·4	10,808·5	4,950·3	5,536·6	5,027·4
Rep. of South Africa	3,184·0	3,075·5	2,741·8	6,160·5	6,128·9	4,982·0
Spain	4,662·4	5,036·6	5,793·7	6,283·9	7,462·8	7,587·1
Sweden	7,681·5	7,496·2	8,427·6	10,426·7	11,350·0	11,271·1
Switzerland	12,615·2	12,927·6	13,971·4	20,727·8	21,691·2	22,376·0
USSR	9,224·8	11,357·7	11,788·4	7,621·4	9,395·0	11,244·8
UK	27,502·2	27,001·9	27,137·7	26,162·9	31,316·7	35,400·9
USA	28,387·5	28,212·6	27,711·7	25,975·9	28,120·1	32,847·0

Principal imports in 1983 (in DM1m.) were finished manufactures (208,433) and semi-finished manufactures (73,144); exports, finished manufactures (364,198) and semi-finished manufactures (34,328).

Total trade between the Federal Republic of Germany and UK (British Department of Trade returns, in £1,000 sterling):

	1980	*1981*	*1982*	*1983*	*1984*
Imports to UK	5,700,861	5,941,130	7,414,073	9,667,444	11,090,227
Exports and re-exports from UK	5,113,032	5,515,965	5,414,733	6,063,989	7,458,042

Tourism. In 1982–83, 9·69m. arrivals and 1·3m. overnight stays by foreign visitors were registered.

COMMUNICATIONS

Roads. On 1 Jan. 1983 the total length of classified roads in the Federal Republic was 172,973 km, including 7,919 km autobahn, 32,239 km federal highways,

65,780 km first-class and 67,035 km second-class country roads. Motor vehicles licensed in the Federal Republic on 1 July 1983 numbered 29,122,300 (including 24,580,500 passenger cars, 1,277,500 trucks, 71,300 buses and 1,680,400 tractors.

Road casualties in 1983 totalled 489,148 injured and 11,715 killed.

Railways. Length of Federal Railway in 1983 was 28,016 km (1,435 mm gauge) of which 11,202 km was electrified. In 1983 it carried 60,732m. tonne-km and 51,139m. passenger-km. There are also some 3,000 km of privately-owned and other minor railways.

Aviation. The Deutsche Lufthansa AG (set up on 6 Jan. 1953, as AG für Luftverkehrsbedarf and renamed on 6 Aug. 1954), with headquarters at Cologne, has capital of DM 900m. The Federal Republic owns 74·3%, Land North Rhine-Westphalia 2·2%, the Federal Railways, 0·9%, Federal Post 1·8%, Kreditanstalt für Wiederaufbau 3% and private industry 17·8%.

Lufthansa operate internal, European, African, North and South Atlantic, Near and Far East routes. In 1983 the Lufthansa carried 36·2m. passengers, and 629,000 tonnes of cargo.

Shipping. On 31 Dec. 1982 the mercantile marine comprised 1,971 ocean-going vessels of 7,060,000 BRT.

The inland-waterways fleet on 31 Dec. 1982 included 2,467 motor freight vessels of 2·1m. tonnes and 461 tankers of 560,000 tonnes. The length of the navigable rivers and canals in use was 4,429 km.

Sea-going ships (foreign trade only) in 1982 loaded 42·7m. tonnes clearing and unloaded 88·4m. tonnes entering in the ports of the Federal Republic. Inland waterways carried 222m. tonnes in 1982.

Post and Broadcasting. In 1982 there were 18,280 post offices. Number of telephones (1982) 30,122,023.

The post office savings banks had, in 1982, 19,695,000 depositors with DM 30,205m. to their credit.

In 1982 postal revenues amounted to DM 45,080m. and the expenditure to DM 43,408m.

Arbeitsgemeinschaft der öffentlich-rechtlichen Rundfunkanstalten der Bundesrepublik Deutschland (ARD) is an organization for co-operation between the German broadcasting stations. ARD also broadcast a common TV programme under the name *Deutsches Fernsehen* throughout the Federal Republic. In addition regional programmes are broadcast. Number of wireless licences, (1983) 24·3m.; of television licences, 22·1m.

Cinemas and Theatres. In 1981 there were 3,144 cinemas and 15 drive-in cinemas. In 1983 there were 258 theatres with a seating capacity of 144,779.

Newspapers. In 1981, 6,486 newspapers and periodicals were published.

JUSTICE, RELIGION, EDUCATION AND WELFARE

Justice. Justice is administered by the federal courts and by the courts of the Länder. In criminal procedures, civil cases and procedures of non contentious jurisdiction the courts on the Land level are the local courts *(Amtsgerichte)*, the regional courts *(Landgerichte)* and the courts of appeal *(Oberlandesgerichte)*. On the federal level decisions regarding these matters are taken by the Federal Court *(Bundesgerichtshof)* at Karlsruhe. In labour law disputes the courts of the first and second instance are the labour courts and the Land labour courts and in the third instance, the Federal Labour Court *(Bundesarbeitsgericht)* at Kassel. Disputes about public law in matters of social security, unemployment insurance, maintenance of war victims and similar cases are dealt with in the first and second instances by the social courts and the Land social courts and in the third instance by the Federal Social Court *(Bundessozialgericht)* at Kassel. In most tax matters the finance courts of the Länder are competent and in the second instance, the Federal Finance Court *(Bundesfinanzhof)* at Munich. Other controversies of public law in non-constitutional matters are decided in the first and second instance by the administrative and the higher administrative courts *(Observerwaltungsgerichte)* of the Länder, and in the third instance by the Federal Administrative Court *(Bundesverwaltungsgericht)* at Berlin.

For the inquiry into maritime accidents the admiralty courts *(Seeämter)* are competent on the Land level and in the second instance the Federal Admiralty Court *(Bundesoberseeamt)* at Hamburg.

The constitutional courts of the Länder decide on constitutional questions. The Federal Constitutional Court *(Bundesverfassungsgericht)* as the supreme German court decides such questions as loss of basic rights, unconstitutional character of political parties, validity of laws, charges against judges and complaints regarding violations of basic rights by the public force.

The death sentence is abolished.

Religion. Census (1970) 49% of the population were Protestants, 44·6% Roman Catholics and 0·1% Jews.

The Evangelical (Protestant) Church consists of 18 member-churches in the Federal Republic and West Berlin (7 Lutheran Churches, 8 United-Lutheran-Reformed, 2 Reformed Churches and 1 Confederation of United member Churches: 'Church of the Union'). Its organs are the Synod, the Church Conference and the Council under the chairmanship of Bishop Dr Eduard Lohse (Hanover). The Protestants numbered about 26·5m. in 1978. There are also some 12 Evangelical Free Churches.

There are 5 Catholic archbishops and 17 bishoprics. Chairman of the German Bishops' Conference is Cardinal Höffner, Archbishop of Cologne. A concordat between Germany and the Holy See was signed on 20 July and ratified on 10 Sept. 1933.

The 'Old Catholics', who are in full communion with the Anglican Churches, numbered about 30,000 in 1977; they have a bishop at Bonn.

Evangelische Kirche in Deutschland. Hanover, 1979
Taschenbuch der evangelischen Kirche in Deutschland. Frankfurt, 1980
Kirchliches Handbuch. Amtliches statistisches Jahrbuch der Katholischen Kirche Deutschlands
Pastoral der Kirche fremden—Eroffnungsreferat der Deutschen Bischofskonferenz 1979 in Fulda—von Kardinal Joseph Höffner. Bonn, 1979
Alt-Katholisches Jahrbuch. Bonn, 1978
Katholiken und ihre Kirche, Protestanten und ihre Kirche. Munich, 1977

Education. Schools providing general education are primary and post-primary schools *(Grund- und Hauptschulen)*, special schools *(Sonderschulen)*, secondary modern schools *(Realschulen)*, grammar schools *(Gymnasien)* and comprehensive schools. Primary schools: Attendance is compulsory for all children having completed their 6th year of age. Compulsory education extends 9 years. After the first 4 (or 6) years at primary school children may attend post-primary schools, secondary modern schools, grammar schools and other schools of general secondary education. The secondary modern school comprises 6, the grammar school 9 years. The final Grammar School Certificate (Abitur-Higher School Certificate) entitles the holder to enter any institution of higher education. There are also special schools for retarded, physically or mentally handicapped and socially maladjusted children.

In 1982 there were in the Federal Republic 18,468 primary and post-primary schools with 4,500,991 pupils; 2,820 special schools with 319,254 pupils, 2,639 secondary modern schools with 1,278,092 pupils; 2,489 grammar schools with 2,050,466 pupils; 285 comprehensive schools (primary and secondary stage) with 226,303 pupils.

Vocational education is provided in part-time, full-time and advanced vocational schools (*Berufs-*, *Berufsaufbau-*, *Berufsfach-* and *Fachschulen*, including *Fachschulen für Technik* and *Schulen des Gesundheitswesens*). Running parallel to the occupation, part-time vocational schools offer 6 to 12 hours per week of additional compulsory schooling. All young people who are apprentices, in some other employment or even unemployed have to attend them in general up to the age of 18 years or until the completion of the practical vocational training. Full-time vocational schools comprise courses of at least one year. They prepare for commercial and domestic occupations as well as specialized occupations in the field of handicrafts. Advanced full-time vocational schools are attended by pupils having completed their 18th year of age; courses vary from 6 months to 3 or more years.

In 1982 there were 7,281 full- and part-time vocational schools with 75,683 teachers and 2,493,477 pupils (1,093,463 female); 2,970 advanced vocational schools with 9,065 teachers and 207,148 pupils (133,255 female).

Higher Education. Universities and equivalent institutions; teacher-training colleges and equivalent institutions which train teachers for primary schools, special schools, intermediate schools and schools providing vocational education; colleges of music, fine arts and the college for physical education in Cologne.

Higher technical colleges offer highly qualified full-time vocational instruction. There were, in the winter term 1979–80, 111 higher technical colleges with 180,651 students (50,609 female).

During the winter term 1979–80 there were 228 academic institutions of higher education with 981,808 students (353,432 female; 56,601 foreigners); they comprise 64 universities with 728,334 students (258,422 female); 6 Roman Catholic theological colleges and 4 Protestant theological colleges with together 2,182 students (591 female).

In the winter term 1979–80 there were 17 teacher-training colleges and equivalent institutions with 53,665 students (36,133 female); 15 colleges of music, 10 colleges of fine arts and the college of film and television with together 16,976 students (7,677 female).

Health. In 1982 there were 146,221 doctors (including 64,305 in private practice and 68,757 in hospitals) and 33,679 dentists. There were 3,130 hospitals (including 917 private) with 683,624 beds.

Social Welfare. *Social Health Insurance* (introduced in 1883). Wage-earners and apprentices, salaried employees with an income below a certain limit and social-insurance pensioners are compulsorily insured. Voluntary insurance is also possible.

Benefits: Medical treatment, medicines, hospital and nursing care, maternity benefits, death benefits for the insured and their families, sickness payments and out-patients' allowances.

35·8m. persons were insured in 1982 (20·8m. compulsorily) and 10·4m. persons (including 6·4m. women) were drawing pensions. Number of cases of incapacity for work totalled 21·8m., and 368·1m. working days were lost. Total disbursements DM 97,224m.

Accident Insurance (introduced in 1884). Insured are all persons in employment or service, apprentices and the greater part of the self-employed and the unpaid family workers.

Benefits in the case of industrial injuries and occupational diseases: Medical treatment and nursing care, sickness payments, pensions and other payments in cash and in kind, surviving dependants' pensions.

Number of insured in 1982, 28·5m.; number of current pensions, 1m.; total expenditure, DM 12,524m.

Workers' and Employees' Old-Age Insurance Scheme (introduced in 1889). All wage-earners and salaried employees, the members of certain liberal professions and—subject to certain conditions—self-employed craftsmen are compulsorily insured. The insured may voluntarily continue to insure when no longer liable to do so or increase the insurance.

Benefits: Measures designed to maintain, improve and restore the earning capacity; pensions paid to persons incapable for work, old age and surviving dependants' pensions.

Number of insured in 1983, 30·3m. (14·2m. women); number of current pensions, 11m.; pensions to widows and widowers, 3·8m.; pensions to orphans, 0·5m. Total disbursements in 1982, DM 170,469m.

There are also special retirement and unemployment pension schemes for miners and farmers.

Assistance for War Victims (war-disabled and dependants).

Benefits: Medical treatment and nursing care, aid to war victims, disablement pensions, basic and equalization pensions paid to widows and orphans, parents' pensions, allowances for nursing care, compensation for occupational detriment, funeral allowances, lump-sum indemnification and indemnification paid upon marriage.

Persons (including those with permanent residence abroad) qualifying for pensions in 1983, 1·8m., of which disabled persons, 0·8m.; widows and widowers, 0·9m.; orphans, 0·02m.; parents, 0·05m. Total disbursements, DM 1,767m.

Public relief and compensation payments are payable to members of German minorities in East European countries expelled after the Second World War and persons who suffered damage because of the war or in connexion with the currency reform.

Benefits: Basic compensation, war-damage pensions, compensation for household equipment, accommodation assistance, currency-conversion compensation, compensation for holders of 'old savings', training grants, loans and other promotive measures.

DM 110·6m. were paid in 1983 to 201,351 recipients.

Family Allowances. The monthly allowance is for the first child DM 50, for the second, DM 100 and for the third and any further child, DM 200.

Accommodation Allowances averaging DM 109 a month were paid in 1982 to 1·6m. persons whose monthly income averaged DM 1,323.

Public Welfare. Benefits were instituted in 1962. In 1982 DM 16·3m. were distributed to 1·6m. recipients.

Public Youth Welfare. For supervision of foster children, official guardianship, assistance with adoptions and affiliations, social assistance in juvenile courts, educational assistance and correctional education under a court order. Total expenditure in 1982, DM 5,753m.

Übersicht über die soziale Sicherung. Bundesministerium für Arbeit und Sozialordnung. 9th ed. Bonn, 1977
Tietz, G., *Zahlenwerk zur Sozialversicherung in der Bundesrepublik Deutschland* (and supplements). Berlin, 1963
Arbeits- und Sozialstatistik. Bundesminister für Arbeit und Sozialordnung, Bonn (from 1950)
Fachserie 13 Sozialleistungen. Statistisches Bundesamt (from 1951)
Fachserie 12 Gesundheitswesen. Statistisches Bundesamt (from 1946)

DIPLOMATIC REPRESENTATIVES

Of the Federal Republic of Germany in Great Britain (21–23 Belgrave Sq., London, SW1X 8PZ)
Ambassador: Baron Rüdiger von Wechmar (accredited 7 Feb. 1984).

Of Great Britain in the Federal Republic of Germany (Friedrich-Ebert-Allee 77, 5300, Bonn)
Ambassador: Sir Julian Bullard, KCMG.

Of the Federal Republic of Germany in the USA (4645 Reservoir Rd, NW, Washington, D.C., 20007)
Ambassador: Guenther van Well.

Of the USA in the Federal Republic of Germany (Delchmannsaue, 5300, Bonn)
Ambassador: Robert Burt.

Of the Federal Republic of Germany to the United Nations
Ambassador: Dr Hans Werner Lautenschlager.

Books of Reference

Statistical Information: The central statistical agency is the Statistisches Bundesamt, 62

Wiesbaden, Gustav Stresemann Ring 11. *President:* Franz Kroppenstedt. Its publications include:

Statistisches Jahrbuch für die Bundesrepublik Deutschland; Wirtschaft und Statistik (monthly, from 1949); *Das Arbeitsgebiet der Bundesstatistik* (latest issue 1981; also in English: *Survey of German Federal Statistics*).

Berghahn, V. R., *Modern Germany: Society, Economy and Politics in the Twentieth Century.* CUP, 1982
Childs, D., *Germany since 1918.* 2nd ed. New York, 1980
Craig, G. A., *Germany, 1866–1945.* OUP, 1981
Gatzke, H. W., *Germany and the United States: a 'Special Relationship'?* Harvard Univ. Press, 1980
Grosser, A., *Germany in our Time: A Political History of the Postwar Years.* New York, 1971
Hardach, K., *The Political Economy of Germany in the Twentieth Century.* California Univ. Press, 1980
Kohl, W. L., and Basevi, G., *West Germany: A European and Global Power.* London, 1982
Mann, A., *Comeback: Germany 1945–1952.* London, 1980
Pachter, H., *Modern Germany: A Social, Cultural and Political History.* Boulder, 1978
Pasley, M., (ed.). *Germany: a Companion to German Studies*
Pounds, N. J. G., *The Economic Pattern of Modern Germany.* 2nd ed. London, 1966
Roberts, G. K., *West German Politics.* London, 1972
Ryder, A. J., *Twentieth-Century Germany: From Bismarck to Brandt.* London, 1973
Trene, W., *Germany Since 1884.* Bad Godesberg, 1969
Who's Who in Germany. Munich, 1980
Wild, T., (ed). *Urban and Rural Change in West Germany.* London, 1983

National Library: Deutsche Bibliothek, Zeppelinallee 4–8; Frankfurt (Main). *Director:* Professor Dr Kurt Köster.

THE LÄNDER

BADEN-WÜRTTEMBERG

AREA AND POPULATION. Baden-Württemberg comprises 35,751 sq. km, with a population (at 31 March 1984) of 9,241,932 (4,446,758 males, 4,795,174 females).

The Land is administratively divided into 4 areas, 9 urban and 35 rural districts, and numbers 1,111 communes. The capital is Stuttgart.

Vital statistics for calendar years:

	Live births	*Marriages*	*Divorces*	*Deaths*
1981	100,673	52,521	14,006	93,979
1982	100,268	53,768	14,736	93,197
1983	95,447	54,785	15,434	95,750

CONSTITUTION. The Land Baden-Württemberg is a merger of the 3 Länder, Baden, Württemberg-Baden and Württemberg-Hohenzollern, which were formed in 1945. The merger was approved by a plebiscite held on 9 Dec. 1951, when 70% of the population voted in its favour.

The Diet, elected on 25 March 1984, consists of 68 Christian Democrats, 41 Social Democrats, 8 Free Democrats, 9 Ecologists.

The Government is formed by Christian Democrats, with Lothar Späth (CDU) as Prime Minister.

AGRICULTURE. Area and yield of the most important crops:

	Area (in 1,000 hectares)			*Yield (in 1,000 tonnes)*		
	1981	*1982*	*1983*	*1981*	*1982*	*1983*
Rye	17·9	14·0	14·1	65·4	54·8	53·5
Wheat	224·3	215·9	223·1	1,114·0	1,071·1	1,046·0
Barley	193·8	202·2	198·8	802·7	901·3	821·4
Oats	93·7	93·2	87·0	385·2	370·1	337·1
Potatoes	23·0	20·4	19·0	693·4	584·7	422·6
Sugar-beet	24·4	22·6	22·3	1,298·8	1,233·8	940·1

Livestock (3 Dec. 1982): Cattle, 1,832,799 (including 683,422 milch cows); horses, 48,985; pigs, 2,210,520; sheep, 199,374; poultry, 6,054,972.

INDUSTRY. In May 1984 9,498 establishments (with 20 and more employees) employed 1,350,677 persons; of these, 238,306 were employed in machine construction (excluding office machines, data processing equipment and facilities); 77,544 in textile industry; 221,685 in electrical engineering; 205,605 in car building.

LABOUR. The economically active persons totalled 4,280,100 at the 1%-sample survey of the microcensus of April 1982. Of the total 361,400 were self-employed, 125,100 unpaid family workers, 3,773,600 employees; 270,000 were engaged in agriculture and forestry; 2,143,700 in power supply, mining, manufacturing and building, 614,400 in commerce and transport, 1,312,000 in other industries and services.

ROADS. On 1 Jan. 1984 there were 27,835 km of 'classified' roads, including 926 km of autobahn, 4,872 km of federal roads, 12,729 km of first-class and 9,308 km of second-class highways. Motor vehicles, at 1 Jan. 1984, numbered 4,587,085, including, 3,886,437 passenger cars, 8,569 buses, 191,003 lorries, 301,543 tractors and 156,469 motor cycles.

JUSTICE. There are a constitutional court *(Staatsgerichtshof)*, 2 courts of appeal, 17 regional courts, 108 local courts, a Land labour court, 9 labour courts, a Land social court, 8 social courts, a finance court, a higher administrative court *(Verwaltungsgerichtshof)*, 4 administrative courts.

RELIGION. On 1 Jan. 1983, 44% of the population were Protestants and 47·1% Roman Catholics.

EDUCATION. In 1983–84 there were 2,558 primary schools with 32,966 teachers and 605,069 pupils; 538 special schools with 7,834 teachers and 50,232 pupils; 436 intermediate schools with 12,459 teachers and 230,909 pupils; 412 high schools with 19,830 teachers and 307,103 pupils; 25 *Freie Waldorf* schools with 934 teachers and 13,108 pupils; 15 *Integrierte Gesamtschulen* (comprehensive schools) including stage of orientation, with 863 teachers and 11,873 pupils; 170 *Berufliche Gymnasien* (technical secondary schools) with 33,241 pupils; 398 part-time vocational schools with 277,916 pupils; 1,104 full-time vocational schools with 92,926 pupils; 207 advanced vocational schools with 10,659 pupils; 227 schools for public health occupations with 14,719 students; there were also 64 (full- and part-time) institutions for the training of technicians with 5,024 participants and 36 *Fachhochschulen* (colleges of engineering and others) with 41,794 students; in all vocational schools there were 15,199 teachers.

In the winter term 1983–84 there were 9 universities (Freiburg, 21,541 students; Heidelberg, 25,453; Konstanz, 5,354; Tübingen, 21,862; Karlsruhe, 15,466; Stuttgart, 16,308; Hohenheim, 4,731; Mannheim, 8,886; Ulm, 4,042); 10 teacher-training colleges with 11,629 students; 5 colleges of music and 2 colleges of fine arts, comprising together 3,691 students.

Statistical Information: Statistisches Landesamt Baden-Württemberg (P.O.B. 898, D7000 Stuttgart 1) (*President:* Prof. Max Wingen), publishes: Monatsschrift *'Baden-Wurttemberg in Wort und Zahl'; Jahrbücher für Statistik und Landeskunde von Baden-Württemberg; Statistik von Baden-Württemberg* (series); *Statistischer und prognostischer Jahres-bericht* (latest issue 1983–84); *Statistisches Taschenbuch* (latest issue 1982–83).

State Library: Württembergische Landesbibliothek, Konrad-Adenauer-Str. 8, 7000 Stuttgart 1. *Director:* Dr Hans-Peter Geh.

BAVARIA
Bayern

AREA AND POPULATION. Bavaria has an area of 70,553 sq. km. The capital is Munich. There are 7 areas, 96 urban and rural districts and 2,052 communes. The population (31 March 1984) numbered 10,969,106 (5,252,190 males, 5,716,916 females).

Vital statistics for calendar years:

	Live births	*Marriages*	*Divorces*	*Deaths*
1981	117,063	65,409	15,456	123,736
1982	116,576	65,764	16,538	123,033
1983	112,644	65,941	18,420	125,362

CONSTITUTION. The Constituent Assembly, elected on 30 June 1946, passed a constitution on the lines of the democratic constitution of 1919, but with greater emphasis on state rights; this was agreed upon by the Christian Social Union and the Social Democrats.

The elections for the Diet, held on 10 Oct. 1982, had the following results: 133 Christian Social Union, 71 Social Democrats. The cabinet of the Christian Social Union is headed by Minister President Dr Franz Josef Strauss (CSU).

AGRICULTURE. Area and yield of the most important products:

	Area (1,000 hectares)			*Yield (1,000 tonnes)*		
	1981	*1982*	*1983*	*1981*	*1982*	*1983*
Wheat	489·6	443·5	494·9	2,047·5	2,142·1	2,627·9
Rye	69·2	56·2	62·0	239·3	189·9	227·3
Barley	510·6	558·3	540·6	2,073·2	2,395·6	2,262·6
Oats	148·5	150·6	131·6	540·8	589·3	497·8
Potatoes	99·0	94·4	87·0	2,951·1	2,747·8	2,244·3
Sugar-beet	92·5	84·7	79·3	5,580·2	4,911·4	3,794·7

Livestock (3 Dec. 1983): 5,107,300 cattle (including 2,047,900 milch cows); 56,100 horses; 303,600 sheep; 4,172,300 pigs; 14,140,400 poultry.

INDUSTRY. In 1984, 9,561 establishments (with 20 and more employees) employed 1,266,292 persons; of these, 217,346 were employed in electrical engineering; 172,798 in mechanical engineering; 126,224 in clothing industry.

LABOUR. The economically active persons totalled 5,117,400 at the 0·4% sample survey of the microcensus of June 1983. Of the total, 552,400 were self-employed, 339,200 unpaid family workers, 4,225,800 employees; 2,225,600 in power supply, mining, manufacturing and building; 795,600 in commerce and transport; 1,571,000 in other industries and services.

ROADS. There were, on 1 Jan. 1983, 40,157·5 km of 'classified' roads, including 1,736·3 km of autobahn, 7,158 km of federal roads, 13,752·3 km of first-class and 17,510·8 km of second-class highways. Number of motor vehicles, at 1 July 1984, was 5,690,924, including 4,549,955 passenger cars, 225,849 lorries, 12,628 buses, 557,645 tractors, 289,877 motor cycles.

JUSTICE. There are a constitutional court *(Verfassungsgerichtshof)*, a supreme Land court *(Oberstes Landesgericht)*, 3 courts of appeal, 21 regional courts, 72 local courts, 2 Land labour courts, 11 labour courts, a Land social court, 7 social courts, 2 finance courts, a higher administrative court *(Verwaltungsgerichtshof)*, 6 administrative courts.

RELIGION. At the census of 27 May 1970 there were 69·9% Roman Catholics and 25·7% Protestants.

EDUCATION. In 1983–84 there were 2,821 primary schools with 43,971 teachers and 798,785 pupils; 396 special schools with 4,944 teachers and 41,291 pupils; 336 intermediate schools with 8,835 teachers and 167,799 pupils; 397 high schools with 19,313 teachers and 311,785 pupils; 242 part-time vocational schools with 7,200 teachers and 374,477 pupils, including 58 special part-time vocational schools with 395 teachers and 6,598 pupils; 553 full-time vocational schools with 3,558 teachers and 64,447 pupils including 220 schools for public health occupations with 694 teachers and 15,375 pupils; 278 advanced full-time vocational schools with 1,917 teachers and 25,371 pupils; 82 vocational high schools *(Berufsoberschulen, Fachoberschulen)* with 1,759 teachers and 31,503 pupils.

In the winter term 1983–84 there were 10 universities with 142,774 students (Augsburg, 6,289; Bamberg, 4,006; Bayreuth, 3,937; Eichstätt, 2,018; Erlangen–Nürnberg, 22,722; München, 51,106; Passau, 3,173; Regensburg, 12,014; Würzburg, 16,803; the Technical University of München, 20,706); 2 *Gesamthochschulen* with 3,109 students, the college of philosophy, München, 336 and a philosophical-theological college in Benediktbeuern with 99 students. There were also 2 colleges of music, 2 colleges of fine arts and 1 college of television and film, with together 2,254 students; 13 vocational colleges *(Fachhochschulen)* with 47,625 students including one for the civil service *(Bayerische Beamtenfachhochschule)* with 5,016 students.

Statistical Information: Bayerisches Landesamt für Statistik und Datenverarbeitung, 51 Neuhauser Str. 8000 Munich, was founded in 1833. *President:* Dr Hans Helmut Schiedermaier. It publishes: *Statistisches Jahrbuch für Bayern.* 1894 ff.—*Bayern in Zahlen.* Monthly (from Jan. 1947).—*Zeitschrift des Bayerischen Statistischen Landesamts.* July 1869–1943; 1948 ff.—*Beiträge zur Statistik Bayerns.* 1850 ff.—*Statistische Berichte.* 1951 ff.—*Schaubilderhefte.* 1951 ff.—*Kreisdaten.* 1972 ff.—*Gemeindedaten.* 1973 ff.

Nawiasky, H., and Luesser, C., *Die Verfassung des Freistaates Bayern vom 2. Dez. 1946.* Munich, 1948; supplement, by H. Nawiasky and H. Lechner, Munich, 1953

State Library: Bayerische Staatsbibliothek, Munich 22. *Director:* Dr Franz G. Kaltwasser.

BERLIN

GOVERNMENT. Greater Berlin was under quadripartite Allied government (Kommandatura) until 1 July 1948, when the Soviet element withdrew. On 30 Nov. 1948, a separate Municipal Government was set up in the Soviet Sector (*see* p. 510).

AREA. The total area of Berlin is 883 sq. km, of which Western Berlin covers 480 sq. km and the Soviet Sector 403 sq. km. The *British Sector* includes the administrative districts of Tiergarten, Charlottenburg, Wilmersdorf and Spandau; the *American Sector* those of Kreuzberg, Neukölln, Tempelhof, Schöneberg, Zehlendorf and Steglitz; the *French Sector* covers the administrative districts of Wedding and Reinickendorf, and the *Soviet Sector*, those of Mitte, Friedrichshain, Prenzlauer Berg, Pankow, Weissensee, Lichtenberg, Treptow and Köpenick. The British, American and French sectors form an administrative unit, called Berlin (West).

On 13 Aug. 1961 the East German Government completely severed all communications between West and East Berlin.

BERLIN (WEST)

POPULATION. Population, 31 Dec. 1983, 1,854,502 (847,480 males, 1,007,022 females). According to the census of 27 May 1970, 70·2% were Protestants and 12·5% Roman Catholics.

Vital statistics for calendar years:

	Live births	*Marriages*	*Divorces*	*Deaths*
1981	18,955	12,658	6,500	34,485
1982	18,662	11,503	6,709	34,528
1983	17,819	12,762	5,950	33,145

CONSTITUTION AND GOVERNMENT. According to the constitution of 1 Sept. 1950, Berlin is simultaneously a Land of the Federal Republic (though not yet formally incorporated) and a city. It is governed by a House of Representatives (at least 200 members); the executive power is vested in a Senate, consisting of the Governing Mayor, the Mayor and not more than 16 senators.

In the municipal elections, held on 10 May 1981, the Christian Democrats obtained 65 seats; the Social Democrats, 51; the Alternative List, 9; the Free Democrats, 7.

Governing Mayor: Eberhard Diepgen (Christian Democrat).

ECONOMY

Currency. The legal tender of Berlin (West) is the German Mark (DM).

Banking. On 20 March 1949 when the DM (West) became the only legal tender of the Western Sectors, the Zentralbank of Berlin was established. Its functions were similar to those of the Zentralbanks of the Länder of the Federal Republic. The Berlin Central Bank was merged with the Bank deutscher Länder as from 1 Aug. 1957, when the latter became the Deutsche Bundesbank. The legal tender for the Western Sectors of Berlin is being issued by the Deutsche Bundesbank (formerly Bank deutscher Länder).

AGRICULTURE. Agricultural area (May 1983), 1,415 hectares, including 957 hectares arable land and 170 hectares gardens, orchards, nurseries.

Livestock (3 Dec. 1982): Cattle, 661; pigs, 3,679; horses, 3,090; sheep, 1,025.

INDUSTRY. In 1983 (monthly averages), 1,079 establishments (with 20 or more employees) employed 159,616 persons; of these, 54,675 were employed in electrical engineering, 16,443 in machine construction, 11,039 in the manufacture of chemicals (in 1982), 3,800 in steel construction and 3,246 in textiles.

LABOUR. The economically active persons totalled 802,700 at the 1%-sample survey of the microcensus of April 1982. Of the total, 66,700 were self-employed including unpaid family workers, 736,000 employees; 9,300 were engaged in agriculture and forestry; 286,400 in power supply, manufacturing and building; 124,400 in commerce and transport; 382,900 in other industries and services.

ROADS. There were, on 1 Jan. 1983, 137 km of 'classified' roads, including 42 km of autobahn and 94 km of federal roads. On 1 July 1983, 685,510 motor vehicles were registered, including 545,658 passenger cars, 38,037 lorries, 83,036 motor cycles, and 2,373 buses.

JUSTICE. There are a court of appeal *(Oberlandesgericht)*, a regional court, 7 local courts, a Land Labour court, a labour court, a Land social court, a social court, a higher administrative court, an administrative court and a finance court.

EDUCATION. In 1983 (preliminary figures) there were 452 schools providing general education (excluding special schools) with 15,051 teachers and 205,545 pupils; 63 special schools with 1,253 teachers and 8,120 pupils. There were a further 198 vocational schools with 2,675 teachers and 63,408 pupils.

In the winter term 1983–84 there was 1 university (50,358 students); 1 technical university (26,215); 1 theological (evangelical) college (501); 1 college of fine arts with 3,850 students; 1 vocational college (for economics) (1,186); 2 colleges for social work (1,437); 1 technical college (3,844), 1 college of the Federal postal administration (524) and 1 college for public administration (2,162).

Statistical Information: The Statistisches Landesamt Berlin was founded in 1862 (Fehrbelliner Platz 1, 1000 Berlin 31). *Director:* Günther Appel. It publishes: *Statistisches Jahrbuch* (from 1867): *Berliner Statistik* (monthly, from 1947).—*100 Jahre Berliner Statistik* (1962).

Childs, D. and Johnson, J., *West Berlin: Politics and Society.* London, 1981

Hillenbrand, M. J., *The Future of Berlin*. Monclair, 1981

State Library: Amerika-Gedenkbibliothek-Berliner Zentralbibliothek-, Blücherplatz 1, D1000 Berlin 61. *Director*: Dr Peter K. Liebenow.

BREMEN
Freie Hansestadt Bremen

AREA AND POPULATION. The area of the Land, consisting of the towns and ports of Bremen and Bremerhaven, is 404 sq. km. Population, 31 Dec. 1983, 676,933 (318,213 males, 358,720 females).

Vital statistics for calendar years:

	Live births	*Marriages*	*Divorces*	*Deaths*
1981	5,966	3,854	1,835	9,246
1982	5,892	3,726	1,951	8,824
1983	5,700	3,933	2,059	8,692

CONSTITUTION. Political power is vested in the House of Burgesses *(Bürgerschaft)* which appoints the executive, called the Senate.

The elections of 25 Sept. 1983 had the following result: 58 Social Democratic Party, 37 Christian Democrats, 5 Die Grünen. The Senate is only formed by Social Democrats; its president is Hans Koschnick (Social Democrat).

AGRICULTURE. Agricultural area comprised (1983), 10,510 hectares: yield of grain crops (1983), 6,658 tonnes; potatoes, 211 tonnes.

Livestock (3 Dec. 1982): 16,807 cattle (including 4,802 milch cows); 4,939 pigs; 357 sheep; 1,153 horses; 17,820 poultry.

INDUSTRY. In 1983, 372 establishments (20 and more employees) employed 78,940 persons; of these, 12,871 were employed in shipbuilding (except naval engineering); 6,812 in machine construction; 9,535 in electrical engineering; 2,894 in coffee and tea processing.

LABOUR. The economically active persons totalled 282,400 at the 1%-sample survey of the microcensus of April 1982. Of the total, 19,300 were self-employed, 261,000 employees; 93,100 in power supply, mining, manufacturing and building, 79,800 in commerce and transport, 106,800 in other industries and services.

ROADS. On 1 Jan. 1976 there were 139 km of 'classified' roads, including 45 km of autobahn, 82 km of federal roads, 7 km of first-class and 5 km of second-class highways. Registered motor vehicles on 1 July 1983 numbered 270,217, including 241,038 passenger cars, 14,488 trucks, 2,234 tractors, 656 buses and 8,913 motor cycles.

SHIPPING. Vessels entered in 1983, 9,576 of 44,110,376 net tons; cleared, 9,494 of 44,097,241 net tons. Sea traffic, 1983, incoming 15,184,250 tonnes; outgoing, 11,427,441 tonnes.

JUSTICE. There are a constitutional court *(Staatsgerichtshof)*, a court of appeal, a regional court, 3 local courts, a Land labour court, 2 labour courts, a Land social court, a social court, a finance court, a higher administrative court, an administrative court.

RELIGION. On 27 May 1970 (census) there were 82·4% Protestants and 10·2% Roman Catholics.

EDUCATION. In 1983 there were 331 new system schools with 5,911 teachers and 84,556 pupils; 28 special schools with 611 teachers and 3,715 pupils; 23 part-time vocational schools with 28,312 pupils; 36 full-time vocational schools with 6,896 pupils; 8 advanced vocational schools (including institutions for the training of technicians) with 1,059 pupils; 11 schools for public health occupations with 1,047 pupils.

In the winter term 1983–84 about 8,179 students were enrolled at the university. In addition to the university there were 4 other colleges in 1983–84 with about 5,478 students.

Statistical Information: Statistisches Landesamt Bremen (An der Weide 14–16 (P.B. 101309), D2800 Bremen 1), founded in 1850. *Director:* Ltd Reg. Dir. Volker Hannemann. Its current publications include: *Statistische Mitteilungen Freie Hansestadt Bremen* (from 1948).—*Monatliche Zwischenberichte* (1949–53); *Statistische Monatsberichte* (from 1954).—*Statistische Berichte* (from 1956).—*Statistisches Handbuch für das Land Freie Hansestadt Bremen (1950–60,* 1961; *1960–64,* 1967; *1965–69,* 1971; *1970–74,* 1975; *1975–80,* 1982).—*Bremen im statistischen Zeitvergleich 1950–1976.* 1977.—*Bremen in Zahlen.* 1983.

Beutin, L., *Bremen und Amerika.* Bremen, 1953

University Library: Universitats Str., D2800 Bremen 33. *Director:* Dr Koch.

HAMBURG
Freie und Hansestadt Hamburg

AREA AND POPULATION. In 1938 the territory of the town was reorganized by the amalgamation of the city and its 18 rural districts with 3 urban and 27 rural districts ceded by Prussia. Total area, 754·7 sq. km (1982), including the islands Neuwerk and Scharhörn (7 sq. km). Population (31 Dec. 1983), 1,609,531 (753,749 males, 855,782 females).

Vital statistics for calendar years:

	Live births	*Marriages*	*Divorces*	*Deaths*
1981	13,494	9,042	5,037	23,746
1982	13,262	8,991	4,762	23,761
1983	12,819	9,198	4,970	22,537

CONSTITUTION. The constitution of 6 June 1952 vests the supreme power in the House of Burgesses *(Bürgerschaft)* of 120 members. The executive is in the hands of the Senate, whose members are elected by the Bürgerschaft.

The elections of 19 Dec. 1982 had the following results: Social Democrats, 64; Christian Democrats, 48, Green Alternatives, 8. The First Burgomaster is Dr Klaus von Dohnanyi (Social Democrat).

The territory has been divided into 7 administrative districts.

AGRICULTURE. The agricultural area comprised 15,600 hectares in 1983. Yield, in tonnes, of cereals, 21,000; potatoes, 1,100.

Livestock (3 Dec. 1982): Cattle, 13,288 (including 3,404 milch cows); pigs, 9,651; horses, 2,877; sheep, 2,323; poultry, 66,543.

FISHERIES. In 1983 the yield of sea and coastal fishing was 14,180 tonnes valued at DM 20m.

INDUSTRY. In June 1983, 895 establishments (with 20 and more employees) employed 150,961 persons; of these, 19,575 were employed in electrical engineering; 17,343 in machine construction; 12,978 in shipbuilding (except naval engineering); 14,309 in chemical industry.

LABOUR. The economically active persons totalled 721,600 at the 0·4%-sample survey of the microcensus of June 1983. Of the total, 57,200 were self-employed, 4,000 unpaid family workers, 660,400 employees; 4,800 were engaged in agriculture and forestry, 202,600 in power supply, mining, manufacturing and building, 196,600 in commerce and transport, 318,200 in other industries and services.

ROADS. On 1 Jan. 1981 there were 3,628 km of roads, including 60 km of autobahn, 157 km of federal roads. Number of motor vehicles (1 July 1983), 644,157, including 572,859 passenger cars, 35,098 lorries, 1,734 buses, 4,686 tractors, 22,042 motor cycles and 7,738 other motor vehicles.

SHIPPING. Hamburg is the largest port in the Federal Republic.

Vessels		*1938*	*1958*	*1978*	*1982*	*1983*
Entered:	Number	18,149	19,033	16,636	15,619	14,159
	Tonnage	20,567,311	27,454,640	61,785,643	65,345,047	57,263,715
Cleared:	Number	19,316	20,363	17,414	16,116	14,482
	Tonnage	20,547,148	27,579,914	62,028,141	65,281,211	57,392,802

JUSTICE. There is a constitutional court *(Verfassungsgericht)*, a court of appeal *(Oberlandesgericht)*, a regional court *(Landgericht)*, 6 local courts *(Amtsgerichte)*, a Land labour court, a labour court, a Land social court, a social court, a finance court, a higher administrative court, an administrative court.

RELIGION. On 27 May 1970 (census) Evangelical Church and Free Churches 73·6%, Roman Catholic Church 8·1%.

EDUCATION. In 1983 there were 393 schools of general education (not including *Internationale Schule*) with 8,190 teachers and 179,649 pupils; 60 special schools with 914 teachers and 7,986 pupils; 45 part-time vocational schools with 52,284 pupils; 23 schools with 2,664 pupils in their vocational preparatory year; 23 schools with 1,824 pupils in manual instruction classes; 52 full-time vocational schools with 11,361 pupils; 9 economic secondary schools with 2,752 pupils; 28 advanced vocational schools with 3,855 pupils; 38 schools for public health occupations with 2,728 pupils; 11 vocational introducing schools with 344 pupils and 21 technical superior schools with 2,726 pupils; all these vocational and technical schools have a total number of 2,932 teachers.

In the winter term 1983–84 there was 1 university with 39,367 students; 1 technical university with 119 students; 1 college of music and 1 college of fine arts with together 2,024 students; 1 high school of the *Bundeswehr* with 1,857 students; 1 professional high school *(Fachhochschule)* with 11,120 students; 1 high school for economics and politics with 1,622 students; 1 high school of public administration with 999 students, as well as 1 private professional high school with 156 students.

Statistical Information: The Statistisches Landesamt der Freien und Hansestadt Hamburg (Steckelhörn 12, D2000 Hamburg 11) publishes: *Hamburg in Zahlen, Statistische Berichte, Statistisches Taschenbuch, Statistik des Hamburgischen Staates.*

Klessmann, E., *Geschichte der Stadt Hamburg.* Hamburg, 1981
Meyer-Marwitz, B., *Das Hamburg Buch.* Hamburg, 1981
Ohlig, J., *Porträt einer Weltstadt.* Hamburg, 1974
Studt, B., and Olsen, H., *Hamburg—eine kurzgefaßte Geschichte der Stadt.* Hamburg, 1964

State Library: Staats- und Universitätsbibliothek, Carl von Ossietzky, Von-Melle-Park 3, D2000 Hamburg 13. *Director:* Prof. Dr Horst Gronemeyer.

HESSEN

AREA AND POPULATION. The state of Hessen comprehends the areas of the former Prussian provinces Kurhessen and Nassau (excluding the exclaves belonging to Hessen and the rural counties of Westerwaldkreis and Rhine-Lahn) and of the former Volksstaat Hessen, the provinces Starkenburg (including the parts of Rheinhessen east of the river Rhine) and Oberhessen. Hessen has an area of 21,114 sq. km. Its capital is Wiesbaden. Since 1 Jan. 1981 there have been 3 areas with 5 urban and 21 rural districts and 421 communes. Population, 31 Dec. 1983, was 5,564,964 (2,673,045 males, 2,891,919 females).

Vital statistics for calendar years:

	Live births	*Marriages*	*Divorces*	*Deaths*
1981	54,132	30,306	9,388	64,570
1982	54,015	30,596	10,546	63,603
1983	50,860	32,286	10,252	63,945

CONSTITUTION. The constitution was put into force by popular referendum on 1 Dec. 1946. The Diet, elected on 25 Sept. 1983, consists of 51 Social Democrats, 44 Christian Democrats, 8 Free Democrats, 7 *Die Grünen*.

The Social Democrat cabinet is headed by Minister President Holger Börner (SPD).

AGRICULTURE. Area and yield of the most important crops:

	Area (in 1,000 hectares)			*Yield (in 1,000 tonnes)*		
	1981	*1982*	*1983*	*1981*	*1982*	*1983*
Wheat	142·0	135·2	142·0	664·0	773·2	749·3
Rye	35·2	31·4	32·4	131·4	124·0	118·9
Barley	139·0	143·0	140·8	565·6	728·4	651·2
Oats	73·6	75·2	67·7	280·7	308·3	217·8
Potatoes	12·6	12·1	11·1	308·1	325·4	225·7
Sugar-beet	24·2	22·4	21·3	1,216·0	1,118·5	876·3

Livestock, 3 Dec. 1983: Cattle, 871,200 (including 295,900 milch cows); horses (1982), 32,200; pigs, 1·32m.; sheep (1982), 115,200; poultry (1982), 4,223,800.

INDUSTRY. In June 1984, 3,657 establishments (with 20 and more employees) employed 597,864 persons; of these, 93,087 were employed in chemical industry; 76,898 in electrical engineering; 85,804 in car building; 71,879 in machine construction; 29,575 in food industry.

LABOUR. The economically active persons totalled 2·44m. at the 0·4%-labour force sample survey of June 1983. Of the total, 208,800 were self-employed, 74,800 unpaid family workers, 2,158,400 employees; 101,200 were engaged in agriculture and forestry, 967,600 in power supply, mining, manufacturing and building, 465,600 in commerce and transport, 907,600 in other services.

ROADS. On 1 Jan. 1984 there were 16,634 km of 'classified' roads, including 916 km of autobahn, 3,586 km of federal highways, 7,130 km of first-class highways and 5,001 km of second-class highways. Motor vehicles licensed on 1 July 1984 totalled 2,795,389, including 2,419,180 passenger cars, 5,655 buses, 114,894 trucks, 138,121 tractors and 92,415 motor cycles.

JUSTICE. There are a constitutional court *(Staatsgerichtshof)*, a court of appeal, 9 regional courts, 58 local courts, a Land labour court, 12 labour courts, a Land social court, 7 social courts, a finance court, a higher administrative court *(Verwaltungsgerichtshof)*, 4 administrative courts.

RELIGION. On 27 May 1970 (census) there were 60·5% Protestants and 32·8% Roman Catholics.

EDUCATION. In 1983 there were 1,258 primary schools with 14,181 teachers and 280,762 pupils; 240 special schools with 2,766 teachers and 22,513 pupils; 157 intermediate schools with 2,843 teachers and 58,622 pupils; 154 high schools with 8,931 teachers and 143,282 pupils; 185 *Gesamtschulen* (comprehensive schools) with 11,100 teachers and 188,166 pupils, 114 part-time vocational schools with 4,183 teachers and 170,632 pupils; 253 full-time vocational schools with 2,416 teachers and 39,048 pupils; 56 advanced vocational schools with 349 teachers and 5,087 pupils; 174 schools for public health occupations with 9,693 pupils; there were a further 37 full- and part-time institutions for the training of technicians with 3,121 participants.

In the winter term 1983–84 there were 3 universities (Frankfurt/Main, 28,208 students; Giessen, 16,487; Marburg, 15,196); 1 technical university in Darmstadt (13,917); 1 *Gesamthochschule* (8,735); 15 *Fachhochschulen* (29,250); 2 Roman

Catholic theological colleges and 1 Protestant theological college with together 479 students; 1 college of music and 2 colleges of fine arts with together 1,144 students.

Statistical Information: The Hessisches Statistisches Landesamt (Rheinstr. 35–37, D6200 Wiesbaden). *President:* Götz Steppuhn. Main publications: *Statistisches Handbuch für das Land Hessen* (1978–79).—*Statistisches Taschenbuch für das Land Hessen* (1982–83).—*Staat und Wirtschaft in Hessen* (monthly).—*Beiträge zur Statistik Hessens.—Statistische Berichte.* —*Hessische Gemeindestatistik 1960–61* (5 vols., 1963 ff.).—*Hessische Gemeindestatistik 1970* (5 vols., 1972 ff.).—*Hessische Gemeindestatistik* (annual, 1980 ff.).

State Library: Hessische Landesbibliothek, Rheinstr. 55–57, D6200 Wiesbaden. *Director:* Dr Helmut Schwitzgebel.

LOWER SAXONY
Niedersachsen

AREA AND POPULATION. Lower Saxony (excluding the town of Bremerhaven, and the districts on the right bank of the Elbe in the Soviet Zone) comprises 47,447 sq. km, and is divided into 4 administrative districts, 38 rural districts, 9 towns and 1,019 communes; capital, Hanover.

Estimated population, on 31 Dec. 1983, was 7,248,536 (3,479,399 males, 3,769,137 females).

Vital statistics for calendar years:

	Live births	*Marriages*	*Divorces*	*Deaths*
1981	72,022	40,282	11,383	86,364
1982	71,407	40,938	12,779	85,867
1983	68,490	41,284	13,231	85,375

GOVERNMENT. The Land Niedersachsen was formed on 1 Nov. 1946 by merging the former Prussian province of Hanover and the *Länder* Brunswick, Oldenburg and Schaumburg-Lippe. The Diet, elected on 21 March 1982, consists of 87 Christian Democrats, 63 Social Democrats; Free Democrats, 10 and *Die Grünen,* 11.

The cabinet of the Christian Democratic Union is headed by Minister President Dr Ernst Albrecht (CDU).

AGRICULTURE. Area and yield of the most important crops:

	Area (in 1,000 hectares)			*Yield (in 1,000 tonnes)*		
	1980	*1981*	*1982*	*1980*	*1981*	*1982*
Wheat	293	279	301	1,475	1,449	1,694
Rye	217	198	164	841	675	668
Barley	498	513	464	2,226	2,203	2,077
Oats	175	163	185	691	634	871
Potatoes	72	72	72	2,210	2,436	2,239
Sugar-beet	148	169	160	6,334	7,509	7,712

Livestock, 3 Dec. 1983: Cattle, 3,314,978 (including 1,192,676 milch cows); horses, 75,549; pigs, 7,242,251; sheep, 163,121; poultry, 33,871,020.

FISHERIES. In 1983 the yield of sea and coastal fishing was 101,360 tonnes valued at DM 120m.

INDUSTRY. In Sept. 1983, 4,535 establishments (with 20 and more employees) employed 649,149 persons; of these 60,470 were employed in machine construction; 139,216 in car building; 59,624 in electrical engineering.

LABOUR. The economically active persons totalled 3,022,600 at the 0·4%-sample survey of the microcensus of April 1983. Of the total 262,400 were self-employed, 149,000 unpaid family workers, 2,611,200 employees; 226,800 were engaged in agriculture and forestry, 1,180,200 in power supply, mining, manufacturing and building, 559,400 in commerce and transport, 1,056,200 in other industries and services.

ROADS. At 1 Jan. 1983 there were 27,918 km of 'classified' roads, including 1,045 km of autobahn, 5,134 km of federal roads, 8,710 km of first-class and 13,029 km of second-class highways.

Number of motor vehicles, 1 Jan. 1984, was 3,367,484 including 2,848,896 passenger cars, 145,672 lorries, 8,829 buses, 242,960 tractors, 129,867 motor cycles.

JUSTICE. There are a constitutional court *(Staatsgerichtshof)*, 3 courts of appeal, 11 regional courts, 79 local courts, a Land labour court, 15 labour courts, a Land social court, 8 social courts, a finance court, a higher administrative court (together with Schleswig-Holstein), 3 administrative courts.

RELIGION. On 27 May 1970 (census) there were 74·6% Protestants and 19·6% Roman Catholics.

EDUCATION. In 1980 there were 2,307 primary schools with 28,092 teachers and 502,497 pupils; 293 special schools with 4,743 teachers and 43,450 pupils; 320 stages of orientation with 179,811 pupils; 270 intermediate schools with 7,157 teachers and 165,699 pupils; 241 grammar schools with 12,623 teachers and 207,542 pupils; 9 evening high schools with 138 teachers and 1,514 pupils; 20 integrated comprehensive schools with 1,684 teachers and 24,492 pupils; 17 co-operative comprehensive schools with 1,490 teachers and 26,186 pupils; 142 part-time vocational schools with 211,447 pupils; 114 year of basic vocational training with 21,071 pupils; 538 full-time vocational schools with 38,008 pupils; 89 *Fachgymnasien* with 8,696 pupils; 126 *Fachoberschulen* with 7,557 pupils (full-time vocational schools leading up to vocational colleges); 56 vocational extension schools with 1,544 pupils, 151 advanced full-time vocational schools (including schools for technicians) with 9,662 pupils; 219 public health schools with 11,527 pupils.

In the winter term 1982–83 there were 4 universities (Göttingen, 27,706 students; Hanover, 22,698; Oldenburg, 7,305; Osnabrück, 5,899); 2 technical universities (Braunschweig, 12,733; Clausthal, 3,241); the medical college of Hanover (3,460), the veterinary college in Hanover (1,726) and the colleges of Hildesheim (1,679) and Lüneburg (1,282).

Statistical Information: The Niedersächsisches Landesverwaltungsamt—Statistik' (Geibelstr. 65, D3000 Hanover 1) fulfils the function of the 'Statistisches Landesamt für Niedersachsen'. *Head of Division:* Abteilungsdirektor Dr Günter Koop. Main publications are: *Statistisches Jahrbuch Niedersachsen* (from 1950).—*Statistische Monatshefte Niedersachsen* (from 1947).—*Statistik Niedersachsen.*

State Library: Niedersächsische Staats- und Universitätsbibliothek, Prinzenstr. 1, 3400, Göttingen. *Director:* Helmut Vogt; Niedersächsische Landesbibliothek, Waterloostr. 8, D3000 Hannover 1. *Director:* Dr Wilhelm Totok.

NORTH RHINE-WESTPHALIA
Nordrhein-Westfalen

AREA AND POPULATION. The Land comprises 34,062 sq. km. It is divided into 5 areas, 23 urban and 31 rural districts. Capital Düsseldorf. Population, 31 Dec. 1983, 16,836,519 (8,035,185 males, 8,801,334 females).

Vital statistics for calendar years:

	Live births	*Marriages*	*Divorces*	*Deaths*
1981	169,704	101,603	32,709	196,773
1982	169,191	102,049	35,381	195,044
1983	161,589	105,022	36,198	194,905

GOVERNMENT. The Land Nordrhein-Westfalen is governed by Social Democrats; Minister President, Johannes Rau (SPD). The Diet, elected on 11 May 1980, consists of 106 Social Democrats and 95 Christian Democrats.

AGRICULTURE. Area and yield of the most important crops:

	Area (in 1,000 hectares)			*Yield (in 1,000 tonnes)*		
	1981	*1982*	*1983*	*1981*	*1982*	*1983*
Wheat	214·1	215·9	234·6	1,164·4	1,293·0	1,353·7
Rye	72·1	56·4	59·5	272·7	241·5	224·0
Barley	382·5	343·8	362·1	1,682·8	1,731·7	1,746·4
Oats	104·4	121·2	89·8	422·4	555·2	318·7
Potatoes	20·4	19·8	18·4	681·0	644·7	535·9
Sugar-beet	89·0	85·5	80·3	4,927·6	4,649·4	3,338·7

Livestock, 3 Dec. 1983: Cattle, 2,051,151 (including 665,558 milch cows); pigs, 5,977,610; sheep, 165,711; horses, 79,680; poultry, 12,397,408.

INDUSTRY. In June 1983, 10,999 establishments (with 20 and more employees) employed 1,971,337 persons; of these, 175,158 were employed in mining; 274,739 in machine construction; 167,951 in iron and steel production; 193,004 in chemical industry; 171,039 in electrical engineering; 61,683 in textile industry.

Output and/or production in 1,000 tonnes, 1983: Hard coal, 71,654; lignite, 117,391; pig-iron, 16,992; raw steel ingots, 21,372; rolled steel, 14,350; castings (iron, steel and malleable castings), 1,308; cement, 11,326; fireproof products, 1,191; sulphuric acid (including production of cokeries), 1,921; staple fibres and rayon, 298; metalworking machines, 101; equipment for smelting works and rolling mills, 129; machines for mining industry, 228; cranes and hoisting machinery, 58; installation implements, 978,000 (pieces); cables and electric lines, 205; springs of all kinds, 185; chains of all kinds, 80; locks and fittings, 321; spun yarns, 179; electric power, 170,567m. kwh. Of the total population, 11·7% were engaged in industry.

LABOUR. The economically active persons totalled 6,772,600 at the labour force sample survey of European Communities of June 1983. Of the total, 513,600 were self-employed, 133,800 unpaid family workers, 6,075,200 employees; 200,000 were engaged in agriculture and forestry, 3,040,400 in power supply, mining, manufacturing and building, 1·21m. in commerce and transport, 2,269,400 in other industries and services.

ROADS. There were (1 Jan. 1984) 29,635 km of 'classified' roads, including 1,908 km of autobahn, 5,520 km of federal roads, 12,283 km of first-class and 9,924 km of second-class highways. Number of motor vehicles, 1 July 1984, 7,727,854, including 6,253,579 passenger cars, 544,840 lorries, 321,942 motor lorries/trucks, 16,898 buses, 206,083 tractors and 320,069 motor cycles.

JUSTICE. There are a constitutional court *(Verfassungsgerichtshof)*, 3 courts of appeal, 19 regional courts, 130 local courts, 3 Land labour courts, 30 labour courts, a Land social court, 8 social courts, 3 finance courts, a higher administrative court, 7 administrative courts.

RELIGION. On 27 May 1970 (census) there were 41·9% Protestants and 52·5% Roman Catholics.

EDUCATION. In 1983 there were 4,714 primary schools with 69,256 teachers and 1,203,520 pupils; 742 special schools with 12,377 teachers and 96,137 pupils; 555 intermediate schools with 16,583 teachers and 325,640 pupils; 75 *Gesamtschulen* (comprehensive schools) with 5,001 teachers and 63,731 pupils; 641 high schools with 39,399 teachers and 604,875 pupils; in 1983 there were 293 part-time vocational schools with 449,463 pupils; vocational preparatory year 248 with 31,498 pupils; 326 full-time vocational schools with 114,213 pupils; 91 *Berufsaufbauschulen* with 2,596 pupils; 234 full-time vocational schools leading up to vocational colleges with 27,594 pupils; 146 advanced full-time vocational schools with 14,624 pupils; 555 schools for public health occupations with 9,343 teachers and 30,892 pupils; 21 schools within the scope of a pilot system of courses with 47,574 pupils and 1,743 teachers.

In the winter term 1983–84 there were 8 universities (Bielefeld, 13,136 students; Bochum, 28,693; Bonn, 38,594; Dortmund, 17,474; Düsseldorf, 13,998; Cologne, 42,574; Münster, 43,502; Witten, 27); the Technical University of Aachen (34,800); 4 Roman Catholic and 2 Protestant theological colleges with together 1,110 students. There were also 3 colleges of music, 1 college of fine arts and the college for physical education in Cologne with together 10,132 students; 19 *Fachhochschulen* (vocational colleges) with 80,555 students, and 6 *Gesamthochschulen* with together 70,961 students.

Statistical Information: The Landesamt für Datenverarbeitung und Statistik Nordrhein-Westfalen (Mauerstr. 51, D4000 Düsseldorf 1) was founded in 1946, by amalgamating the provincial statistical offices of Rhineland and Westphalia. *President:* A. Benker. The Landesamt publishes: *Statistisches Jahrbuch Nordrhein-Westfalen.* From 1949. More than 550 other publications yearly.

Müller-Wille, W., *Westfalen.* Münster, 1981.

Land Library: Universitätsbibliothek, Universitätsstr. 1, D4000 Düsseldorf. *Director:* Dr G. Gattermann.

RHINELAND-PALATINATE
Rheinland-Pfalz

AREA AND POPULATION. Rhineland-Pfalz comprises 19,845 sq. km. Capital Mainz. Population (at 31 Dec. 1983), 3,633,488 (1,737,107 males, 1,896,381 females).

Vital statistics for calendar years:

	Live births	*Marriages*	*Divorces*	*Deaths*
1981	37,402	22,710	6,172	44,269
1982	37,132	23,002	6,965	43,567
1983	35,422	23,317	6,747	44,459

CONSTITUTION. The constitution of the Land Rheinland-Pfalz was approved by the Consultative Assembly on 25 April 1947 and by referendum on 18 May 1947, when 579,002 voted for and 514,338 against its acceptance.

The elections of 6 March 1983 returned 57 Christian Democrats, 43 Social Democrats.

The cabinet is headed by Bernhard Vogel (Christian Democrat).

AGRICULTURE. Area and yield of the most important products:

	Area (1,000 hectares)			*Yield (1,000 tonnes)*		
	1981	*1982*	*1983*	*1981*	*1982*	*1983*
Wheat	119·1	112·7	113·4	554·8	574·9	527·4
Rye	31·5	27·2	28·0	119·5	103·8	98·8
Barley	137·1	140·5	137·0	531·7	622·1	489·8
Oats	50·8	51·4	45·0	203·3	193·0	129·2
Potatoes	13·2	13·4	12·9	345·6	349·3	264·9
Sugar-beet	24·1	22·5	22·0	1,374·9	1,209·6	970·2
Wine (1,000 hectolitres)	57·9	58·0	58·9	5,305·3	10,560·7	8,932·0
Tobacco	1·1	1·0	1·0	...	...	...

Livestock (2 Dec. 1983): Cattle, 638,200 (including 230,300 milch cows); horses, 19,500; sheep, 92,300; pigs, 677,000; poultry, 3,325,100.

INDUSTRY. In Sept. 1983, 2,728 establishments (with 20 and more employees) employed 364,939 persons; of these 69,870 were employed in chemical industry; 21,120 in production of leather goods and footwear; 46,779 in machine construction; 15,746 in processing stones and earthenware.

LABOUR. The economically active persons totalled 1,585,700 at the census of June 1983. Of the total, 140,800 were self-employed, 68,000 unpaid family workers, 1,350,400 employees; 96,000 were engaged in agriculture and forestry, 646,000 in power supply, mining, manufacturing and building, 266,600 in commerce and transport, 550,600 in other industries and services.

ROADS. There were (1 Jan. 1984) 18,535 km of 'classified' roads, including 727 km of autobahn, 3,216 km of federal roads, 6,949 km of first-class and 7,643 km of second-class highways. Number of motor vehicles, 1 July 1984, was 1,917,987, including 1,581,556 passenger cars, 78,643 lorries, 4,903 buses, 145,792 tractors and 91,644 motor cycles.

JUSTICE. There are a constitutional court *(Verfassungsgerichtshof)*, 2 courts of appeal, 8 regional courts, 47 local courts, a Land labour court, 5 labour courts, a Land social court, 4 social courts, a finance court, a higher administrative court, 4 administrative courts.

RELIGION. On 27 May 1970 (census) there were 40·7% Protestants and 55·7% Roman Catholics.

EDUCATION. In 1983 there were 1,193 primary schools with 15,333 teachers and 253,414 pupils; 156 special schools with 2,703 teachers and 15,023 pupils; 106 intermediate schools with 3,191 teachers and 62,215 pupils; 137 high schools with 6,896 teachers and 115,964 pupils; 99 vocational schools with 122,863 pupils; 127 advanced vocational schools and institutions for the training of technicians (full-and part-time) with 7,082 pupils; 117 schools for public health occupations with 355 teachers and 7,344 pupils.

In the winter term 1983–84 there were the University of Mainz (25,613 students), the University of Kaiserslautern (5,777 students), the University of Trier (6,362 students), the *Hochschule für Verwaltungswissenschaften* in Speyer (403 students), the Roman Catholic Theological College in Trier (398 students) and the Roman Catholic College in Vallendar (56 students). There were also the Teacher-Training College of the Land Rheinland-Pfalz *(Erziehungswissenschaftliche Hochschule)* with 2,697 students, the *Fachhochschule des Landes Rheinland-Pfalz* (college of engineering) with 12,354 students and 4 *Verwaltungsfachhochschulen* with 2,736 students; also 2 private colleges for social-pedagogy (850 students).

Statistical Information: The Statistisches Landesamt Rheinland-Pfalz (Mainzer Str., 15–16, D5427 Bad Ems) was established in 1948. *President:* Dr Weis. Its publications include: *Statistisches Jahrbuch für Rheinland-Pfalz* (from 1948); *Statistische Monatshefte Rheinland-Pfalz* (from 1958); *Statistik von Rheinland-Pfalz* (from 1949) 309 vols. to date; *Rheinland-Pfalz im Spiegel der Statistik* (1968); *Die kreisfreien Städte und Landkreise in Rheinland-Pfalz* (1977); *Rheinland-Pfalz heute* (from 1973); *Benutzerhandbuch des Landesinformationssystems* (1976); *Rheinland-Pfalz heute und morgen* (Mainz, 1981); *Raumordnungsbericht 1981 der Landesregierung Rheinland-Pfalz* (Mainz, 1981). *Landesentwicklungsprogramm 1980* (Mainz, 1980).

Klöpper, R., and Korber, J., *Rheinland-Pfalz in seiner Gliederung nach zentralörtlichen Bereichen.* Remagen, 1957

Süsterhenn, A., and Schäfer, H., *Verfassung von Rheinland-Pfalz: Kommentar.* Koblenz, 1950

SAARLAND

HISTORY. In 1919 the Saar territory was placed under the control of the League of Nations. Following a plebiscite, the territory reverted to Germany in 1935. In 1945 the territory became part of the French Zone of occupation, and was in 1947 accorded an international status inside an economic union with France. In pursuance of the German–French agreement signed in Luxembourg on 27 Oct. 1956 the territory returned to Germany on 1 Jan. 1957. Its re-integration with Germany was completed by 5 July 1959.

AREA AND POPULATION. Saarland has an area of 2,570 sq. km. Estimated population, 31 Dec. 1983, 1,052,794 (499,557 males, 553,237 females). The capital is Saarbrücken.

Vital statistics for calendar years:

	Live births	*Marriages*	*Divorces*	*Deaths*
1980	10,511	7,587	1,628	13,061
1981	10,496	7,400	2,012	13,097
1982	10,287	7,213	2,459	12,832

CONSTITUTION. Saarland now ranks as a *Land* of the Federal German Republic and is represented in the Federal Diet by 8 members. The constitution passed on 15 Dec. 1947 is being revised.

The Saar Diet, elected on 27 April 1980, is composed as follows: 24 Social Democrats, 23 Christian Democrats,4 Free Democrats.

Saarland is governed by Christian Democrats and Free Democrats in spite of deadlock in Parliament. Minister President: Werner Zeyer (Christian Democrat).

AGRICULTURE AND FORESTRY. The cultivated area occupies 123,500 hectares or slightly more than half the total area; the forest area comprises nearly 32% of the total.

Area and yield of the most important crops:

	Area (1,000 hectares)			*Yield (1,000 tonnes)*		
	1981	*1982*	*1983*	*1981*	*1982*	*1983*
Wheat	7·3	6·7	6·9	28·6	29·1	27·3
Rye	6·4	5·1	5·4	21·6	17·7	19·3
Barley	11·7	12·7	11·1	44·3	52·9	35·0
Oats	7·1	7·4	6·0	28·1	26·7	16·9
Potatoes	0·7	0·6	0·6	15·0	13·9	7·7
Sugar-beet	...	...	...	...	1·0	0·2

Livestock, Dec. 1983: Cattle, 71,609 (including 25,411 milch cows); pigs, 44,183; sheep, 10,471; horses, 3,817; poultry, 349,210.

INDUSTRY. In June 1983, 587 establishments (with 20 and more employees) employed 143,247 persons; of these 25,605 were engaged in coalmining, 24,304 in iron and steel production, 11,774 in machine construction, 8,968 in steel construction. In 1983 the coalmines produced 10m. tonnes of coal. Four iron foundries had 9 blast furnaces working and produced 3·4m. tonnes of pig-iron and 3·8m. tonnes of crude steel.

LABOUR. The economically active persons totalled 407,100 at the 1%-sample survey of the microcensus of April 1982. Of the total, 26,300 were self-employed, 5,600 unpaid family workers, 375,200 employees; 6,500 were engaged in agriculture and forestry, 199,500 in power supply, mining, manufacturing and building, 72,500 in commerce and transport, 128,600 in other industries and services.

ROADS. At 1 Jan. 1981 there were 2,139 km of 'classified' roads, including 163 km of autobahn, 443 km of federal roads, 765 km of first-class and 767 km of second-class highways. Number of motor vehicles, 31 Dec. 1983, 501,002, including 440,772 passenger cars, 19,721 lorries, 1,499 buses, 12,391 tractors and 21,098 motor cycles.

JUSTICE. There are a constitutional court (*Verfassungsgerichtshof*), a court of appeal, a regional court, 11 local courts, a Land labour court, 3 labour courts, a Land social court, a social court, a finance court, a higher administrative court, an administrative court.

RELIGION. On 27 May 1970 (census) 73·8% of the population were Roman Catholics and 24·1% were Protestants.

EDUCATION. In 1983–84 there were 333 primary schools with 3,990 teachers and 67,655 pupils; 53 special schools with 663 teachers and 4,229 pupils; 38 intermediate schools with 1,133 teachers and 16,816 pupils; 37 high schools with 2,008 teachers and 28,903 pupils; 2 *Gesamtschule* (comprehensive high schools) with 137 teachers and 2,076 pupils; 2 *Freie Waldorfschulen* with 43 teachers and 574 pupils; 41 part-time vocational schools with 33,174 pupils; year of commercial basic training: 87 institutions with 237 classes and 5,042 pupils; 22 advanced full-time vocational schools and schools for technicians with 2,375 pupils; 57 full-time vocational schools with 6,783 students; 19 vocational extension schools with 1,277 pupils; 25 *Fachoberschulen* (full-time vocational schools leading up to vocational colleges) with 3,291 students; 39 schools for public health occupations with 2,239 pupils; 2 evening high schools and 1 *Saarland-Kolleg* with together 401 pupils. The number of pupils visiting the vocational schools amounts to 55,757. They are instructed by 1,751 teachers.

In the summer term 1983 there was the University of the Saarland with 14,623 students; 1 conservatory with 257 students; 1 vocational college (economics, engineering and design) with 1,906 students; 1 vocational college for social affairs with 152 students; 1 vocational college for public administration with 196 students.

Statistical Information: The Statistisches Amt des Saarlandes (Hardenbergstrasse 3, D6600 Saarbrücken 1) was established on 1 April 1938. As from 1 June 1935, it was an independent agency; its predecessor, 1920–35, was the Statistical Office of the Government Commission of the Saar. *Chief:* Direktor Alois Spross. The most important publications are: *Statistisches Handbuch für das Saarland,* from 1950.—*Statistisches Taschenbuch für das Saarland,* from 1959.—*Saarländische Bevölkerungsund Wirtschaftszahlen.* Quarterly, from 1949. —*Saarland in Zahlen* (special issues).—*Einzelschriften zur Statistik des Saarlandes,* from 1950—*Statistische Nachrichten,* from 1981.

Fischer, P., *Die Saar zwischen Deutschland und Frankreich.* Frankfurt, 1959
Osang, R.M., *Saarland ABC.* Saarbrücken, 1975
Schmidt, R. H., *Saarpolitik 1945–57.* 3 vols. Berlin, 1959–62

SCHLESWIG-HOLSTEIN

AREA AND POPULATION. The area of Schleswig-Holstein is 15,721 sq. km; it is divided into 4 urban and 11 rural districts and 1,131 communes. The capital is Kiel. The population (estimate, 31 Dec. 1983) numbered 2,616,598 (1,262,847 males, 1,353,751 females).

Vital statistics for calendar years:

	Live births	*Marriages*	*Divorces*	*Deaths*
1981	24,650	13,873	5,030	31,927
1982	24,481	14,416	5,676	31,601
1983	23,470	14,840	5,568	31,017

GOVERNMENT. The elections of 13 March 1983 gave the Christian Democrats 39, the Social Democratic Party 34 and the South Schleswig Association 1 seat. Minister President, Dr Uwe Barschel (Christian Democrat).

AGRICULTURE. Area and yield of the most important crops:

	Area (1,000 hectares)			*Yield (1,000 tonnes)*		
	1981	*1982*	*1983*	*1981*	*1982*	*1983*
Wheat	154·4	144·8	148·5	918·6	1,040·4	982·6
Rye	52·7	51·5	52·6	198·3	233·0	207·9
Barley	153·7	154·5	149·2	773·3	939·8	803·3
Oats	39·4	38·4	26·7	179·4	193·9	88·4
Potatoes	4·8	5·0	4·4	152·8	142·5	93·5
Sugar-beet	21·0	19·4	17·5	888·7	686·2	589·0

Livestock, 2 Dec. 1983: 32,241 horses, 1,615,957 cattle (including 573,649 milch cows), 1,732,550 pigs, 142,578 sheep, 3,810,443 poultry.

FISHERIES. In 1982 the yield of small-scale deep-sea and inshore fisheries was 47,000 tonnes valued at DM57·9m.

INDUSTRY. In 1983 (average), 1,610 establishments (with 20 and more employees) employed 165,909 persons; of these, 14,160 were employed in shipbuilding (except naval engineering); 30,379 in machine construction; 23,023 in food and kindred industry; 15,790 in electrical engineering.

LABOUR. The economically active persons totalled 1·12m. at the 1%-sample survey of the microcensus of April 1982. Of the total, 105,000 were self-employed, 31,000 unpaid family workers, 987,000 employees; 69,000 were engaged in agriculture and forestry, 368,000 in power supply, mining, manufacturing and building, 227,000 in commerce and transport, 459,000 in other industries and services.

ROADS. There were (1 Jan. 1984) 9,742·5 km of 'classified' roads, including 381·5 km of autobahn, 1,940 km of federal roads, 3,525 km of first-class and 3,896 km of second-class highways. Number of motor vehicles, 1 Jan. 1984, was 1,200,149, including 1,024,552 passenger cars, 53,780 lorries, 2,809 buses, 73,054 tractors, 33,472 motor cycles.

SHIPPING. The Kiel Canal, 98·7 km (51 miles) long, is on Schleswig-Holstein territory. In 1938, 53,530 vessels of 22·6m. net tons passed through it; in 1981, 52,641 vessels of 53·3m. net tons; in 1982, 49,100 vessels of 52·7m. net tons; in 1983, 49,320 vessels of 50·9m. net tons.

JUSTICE. There are a court of appeal, 4 regional courts, 30 local courts, a Land labour court, 6 labour courts, a Land social court, 4 social courts, a finance court, an administrative court.

RELIGION. On 27 May 1970 (census) there were 86·5% Protestants and 6% Roman Catholics.

EDUCATION. In 1983–84 there were 695 primary schools with 6,239 teachers and 166,956 pupils; 168 special schools with 1,596 teachers and 16,473 pupils; 178 intermediate schools with 3,212 teachers and 75,613 pupils; 96 high schools with 4,480 teachers and 81,059 pupils; 6 *Integrierte Gesamtschulen* (comprehensive schools) with 228 teachers and 4,049 pupils; 41 part-time vocational schools with 1,558 teachers and 92,011 pupils; 139 full-time vocational schools with 447 teachers and 12,145 pupils; 57 advanced vocational schools with 293 teachers and 5,406 pupils; 55 schools for public health occupations with 3,717 pupils; 48 vocational grammar schools with 385 teachers and 6,611 pupils; 5 *Fachhochschulen* (vocational colleges) with 8,211 pupils in the summer term 1984.

In the summer term 1984 the University of Kiel had 16,325 students, 2 teacher-training colleges had 2,753 students, 1 music college had 339 students and 1 *Medizinische Hochschule* in Lübeck had 814 students.

Statistical Information: Statistisches Landesamt Schleswig-Holstein (Fröbel Str. 15–17, D2300 Kiel 1). *Director:* Dr Mohr. Publications: *Statistisches Taschenbuch Schleswig-Holstein,* since 1954.—*Statistisches Jahrbuch Schleswig-Holstein,* since 1951.—*Statistische Monatshefte Schleswig-Holstein,* since 1949.—*Statistische Berichte,* since 1947.—*Beiträge zur historischen Statistik Schleswig-Holstein,* since 1967.—*Lange Reihen,* since 1977.

Baxter, R. R., *The Law of International Waterways.* Harvard Univ. Press, 1964
Brandt, O., *Grundriss der Geschichte Schleswig-Holsteins.* 5th ed. Kiel, 1957
Handbuch für Schleswig-Holstein. 22nd ed. Kiel, 1984

State Library: Schleswig-Holsteinische Landesbibliothek, Kiel, Schloss. *Director:* Prof. Dr Klaus Friedland.

GHANA

Capital: Accra
Population: 12·21m. (1984)
GNP per capita: US$400 (1981)

HISTORY. The State of Ghana came into existence on 6 March 1957 when the former Colony of the Gold Coast and the Trusteeship Territory of Togoland attained Dominion status. The name of the country recalls a powerful monarchy which from the 4th to the 13th century A.D. ruled the region of the middle Niger.

The Ghana Independence Act received the royal assent on 7 Feb. 1957. The General Assembly of the United Nations in Dec. 1956 approved the termination of British administration in Togoland and the union of Togoland with the Gold Coast on the latter's attainment of independence.

The country was declared a Republic within the Commonwealth on 1 July 1960 with Dr Kwame Nkrumah as the first President. On 24 Feb. 1966 the Nkrumah regime was overthrown in a military *coup* and ruled by the National Liberation Council until 1 Oct. 1969 when the military regime handed over power to a civilian regime under a new constitution. Dr K. A. Busia was the Prime Minister of the Second Republic. On 13 Jan. 1972 the armed forces and police took over power again from the civilian regime in a *coup*.

In Oct. 1975 the National Redemption Council was subordinated to a Supreme Military Council (SMC). In 1979 the SMC was toppled in a *coup* led by Flight-Lieut. J. Rawlings. The new government permitted elections already scheduled and these resulted in a victory for Dr Hilla Limann and his People's National Party. However on 31 Dec. 1982 by another *coup* led by Flight-Lieut. Rawlings dismissed the government and Parliament, suspended the Constitution and established a Provisional National Defence Council to exercise all government powers.

AREA AND POPULATION. Ghana is bounded west by Ivory Coast, north by Burkina Faso, east by Togo and south by the Gulf of Guinea. The area of Ghana is 92,010 sq. miles (238,305 sq. km); census population 1984, 12,205,574.

The capital is Accra (population, 1970, 636,067).

Ghana is divided into 9 regions:

Regions	*Area (sq. km)*	*Population census 1970*	*Capital*	*Population census 1970*
Eastern	19,833	1,262,882	Koforidua	69,804
Western	24,214	770,089	Sekondi-Takoradi	254,543
Central	9,469	890,135	Cape Coast	71,594
Ashanti	25,123	1,505,049	Kumasi	351,629
Brong-Ahafo	39,709	766,509	Sunyani	61,772
Northern	70,338	728,572	Tamale	120,000
Volta	20,651	947,012	Ho	46,348
Upper	16,877	862,723	Bolgatanga	18,896
Greater Accra	2,023	903,445	Accra	636,067

Other chief towns (population, census, 1970); Asamankese, 101,144; Tema, 60,767; Nsawam, 57,350; Tarkwa, 50,570; Oda, 40,740; Obuasi, 40,001; Winneba, 36,104; Keta, 27,461; Swedru (Agona), 23,843.

Estimated birth rate, between 47 and 52 per 1,000; death rate, about 23 per 1,000.

In the south and centre of Ghana, the people are of the Kwa ethno-linguistic group, mainly Akan (Ashante, Fante, etc.), Ewe (in the Volta region) and Ga, while the 20% living in the north belong to Gur peoples (Dagbane, Gurma and Grusi).

CLIMATE. The climate ranges from the equatorial type on the coast to savannah in the interior and is typified by the existence of well-marked dry and wet seasons.

Temperatures are relatively high throughout the year. The amount, duration and seasonal distribution of rain is very marked, from the south, with over 80″ (2,000 mm) to the north, with under 50″ (1,250 mm). In the extreme north, the wet season is from March to Aug., but further south it lasts until Oct. Near Kumasi, two wet seasons occur, in May and June and again in Oct. and this is repeated, with greater amounts, along the coast of Ghana. Accra. Jan. 80°F (26·7°C), July 77°F (25°C). Annual rainfall 29″ (724 mm). Kumasi. Jan. 77°F (25°C), July 76°F (24·4°C). Annual rainfall 58″ (1,402 mm). Sekondi-Takoradi. Jan. 79°F (25°C), July 76°F (24·4°C). Annual rainfall 47″ (1,181 mm). Tamale. Jan. 82°F (27·8°C), July 78°F (25·6°C). Annual rainfall 41″ (1,026 mm).

CONSTITUTION AND GOVERNMENT. Since the *coup* of 31 Dec. 1982, supreme power is held by the Provisional National Defence Council, which in Sept. 1984 consisted of: Flight-Lieut. Jerry John Rawlings (Chairman), Warrant Officer Joseph Adjei Buadi, Aanaa Enin, Edo Tawiah, J. S. Annan and Suzanna Alhassan. Ministerial responsibilities are exercised by Secretaries appointed by the PNDC, comprising in Sept. 1984:

Co-ordinating Secretariat (i.a. Prime Minister): P. V. Obeng.

Foreign Affairs: Dr Obed Asamoah. *Finance and Economic Planning:* Dr Kwesi Botwe. *Interior:* Koffi Gwyn. *Agriculture:* John A. Ndebugre. *Culture and Tourism:* Dr Ben Abdallah. *Education:* Dr V. C. Dadson. *Fuel and Power:* Appiah Korang. *Health:* E. J. Tandoh. *Industry, Science and Technology:* Dr Charles Boadu. *Information:* Joyce Aryee. *Justice:* G. E. K. Aikins. *Lands and Natural Resources:* G. A. Renner. *Local Government:* Kwame Dwemo Kessie. *Roads and Highways:* Yaw Donkor. *Rural Development and Co-operatives:* Kwaku Ankomah. *Trade:* Ato Ahwoi. *Transport and Communications:* Mahamad Idrisu. *Labour and Social Welfare:* Ato Austin. *Works and Housing:* Hassan Abubakr. *Youth and Sports:* Maj. Amarke Amarteifo.

National flag: Red, gold, green (horizontal); a black star in the centre.

National anthem: Hail the name of Ghana.

Local government: The 9 Regions, each under a Regional Secretary appointed by the PNDC, are divided into 62 districts and thence into local council areas, each level being administered by Provisional Defence Committees.

DEFENCE. The Ministry of Defence is responsible for the armed services, the military academy and the border guards. The Military Academy provides a 2-year course for army officers, a 1-year course for later entrants in the flying-training school and a preliminary 6-month course for navy cadets.

Army. The Ghana Army consists of 6 infantry battalions, 1 reconnaissance battalion, 1 field engineer battalion, 1 mortar battalion, 5 with armoured cars,: and ancillary units. Total strength, (1985) 10,000. There are also 3 battalions of people's militia and a border guard of 5,000.

Navy. The Ghana Navy was formed in 1959. It comprises 2 British-built 500-ton corvettes, 4 fast attack craft, 2 patrol craft, 2 old seaward defence boats, 4 coastal patrol boats and 2 service craft. Naval personnel in 1985 numbered 840 officers and ratings.

Air Force. The Ghana Air Force was formed in 1959, when an Air Force Training School was established at Accra. Its first combat unit has 6 Italian-built Aermacchi M.B.326K light ground attack jets ordered in 1976. It has, for training, transport, search and rescue, and air survey operations, 5 Fokker Friendship twin-turboprop transports, and a twin-turbofan Fokker Fellowship for Presidential use, all built in the Netherlands; 6 Shorts Skyvan twin-turboprop STOL transports, some Islanders, and 11 Bulldog primary trainers, all built in the UK; 2 Bell 212 helicopters built in the US; 2 French-built Alouette III helicopters, 8 Italian-built SF.260TP turboprop trainers, and 6 Aermacchi M.B.326F armed jet trainers. There are air bases at Takoradi and Tamale. Personnel strength (1983) about 1,400.

INTERNATIONAL RELATIONS

Membership. Ghana is a member of UN, the Commonwealth, OAU, ECOWAS and is an ACP state of EEC.

ECONOMY

Planning. In Jan. 1983 a 4-year economic reconstruction and development programme was announced and aims at increasing state involvement in economic activity.

Budget. In 1984–85 budget provided for revenue of ₵22,600m. and expenditure of ₵28,500m.

Currency. The monetary unit is the *cedi* (₵), divided into 100 *pesewas* (P). Notes are issued of 1, 2, 5, 10 and 50 ₵; copper coins of ½ and 1 P, and cupro-nickel coins of 2½, 5, 10 and 20 P. In March 1985, £1 = ₵64·18; US$1 = ₵50.

Banking. The Bank of Ghana was established in Feb. 1957 as the central bank of the country. The Ghana Commercial Bank, also established in Feb. 1957, is the former Bank of the Gold Coast. It is a purely commercial institution and has 120 branches in the country, 1 in London and 1 in Lomé (Togo). Barclays Bank (Ghana) Ltd has 54 branches and agencies and the Standard Bank (Ghana) Ltd has 27 branches.

The Ghana National Investment Bank, opened in June 1963, is a finance-cum-development agency. The former post office savings bank has been transformed into the Ghana Savings Bank. The Bank for Housing and Construction opened in 1973.

ENERGY AND NATURAL RESOURCES

Electricity. Production (1981) 5,053m. kwh, mainly from the Volta Dam at Akosombo, opened in 1966, which has a capacity of 912 mw.

Oil. The Government announced in Jan. 1978 that oil had been found in commercial quantities with known reserves (1980) 7m. bbls and in Oct. 1983 formed the Ghanaian National Petroleum Corporation with exploration rights in all areas not covered by existing agreements.

Minerals. In 1982 gold production was 10,300 kg; diamonds, 684,000 carats; manganese, 160,000 tons; bauxite, 64,000 tons.

Agriculture. Cocoa is by far the most important crop and covers about 2m. acres. Production (1982) 190,000 tons. There has been considerable increase in cocoa yields as a result of the Capsid control and the introduction of improved varieties. A Cocoa Affairs Ministry has been established to formulate policy and provide technical supervision for developing cocoa, coffee, shea-nuts, copra and bananas. Coffee, improved types of oil-palm and coconut are being planted on an increased scale and production from these crops is increasing. Progress has been made in the planting of Clonal rubber in south-west Ghana. In the south-east coastal belt irrigation works have been constructed and black-clay farming is being successfully undertaken in the Accra plains.

Of the main foodstuffs in south and central Ghana, maize, rice, cassava, plantain, groundnuts, yam and cocoyam predominate. Tobacco is proving an attractive and very important cash crop in food-crop producing areas.

In northern Ghana the chief food crops are groundnuts, rice, maize, guinea corn, millet and yams, with tobacco and cotton as important cash crops.

Agricultural cash crops, *e.g.*, pepper, ginger, pineapple, avocado and citrus, etc., are being extensively cultivated for export. Active steps have also been taken to provide within the next few years industrial raw materials, *e.g.*, kenaf, cotton, tobacco, palm-oil, mango, pineapple, sugar-cane, etc., to feed the local factories. The trend is towards diversification of agriculture.

Production of main food crops (1982) was: Cassava, 1·9m. tons; plantain, 950,000 tons; coconut, 160,000; maize, 420,000; plantains, 950,000; millet, 90,000; sugar-cane, 220,000; sorghum, 150,000; rice, 90,000; tomatoes, 160,000.

Livestock, 1983: Cattle, 800,000; sheep, 2m.; goats, 2m.; horses, 4,000; pigs, 375,000; poultry, 13m.

Forestry. Area of closed forest is 82,576 sq. km, (16,852·2 sq. km are reserved).

Fisheries. Catch (1982) 224,100 tonnes (40,000 from inland waters).

INDUSTRY AND TRADE

Industry. The aluminium smelter at Tema is the centre of industrial development, mainly concentrated on Accra/Tema, Kumasi and Takoradi/Sekondi. Production (1981) 173,300 tonnes.

Commerce. In 1982 exports were ₵ 2,402m.; imports, ₵ 1,939m. Principal exports: cocoa, timber and gold; imports were raw materials, capital equipment, petroleum and food.

Total trade between Ghana and UK (British Department of Trade returns, in £1,000 sterling):

	1980	*1981*	*1982*	*1983*	*1984*
Imports to UK	104,545	61,167	74,438	58,192	61,561
Exports and re-exports from UK	88,511	87,849	66,709	82,234	82,897

Tourism. In 1981 there were 42,400 tourists.

COMMUNICATIONS

Roads. The total mileage of roads maintained by the Public Works Department in 1980 was 33,000.

The number of vehicles in use (1977) was 121,700, of which private cars, 49,300.

Railways. Total length of railways open in 1983 was 953 km of 1,067 mm gauge. In 1983 railways carried 357,040 tonnes and 3·6m. passengers.

Aviation. There is an international airport at Kotoka (Accra) and domestic airports at Takoradi, Kumasi, Tamale and Sunyani. Total aircraft freight in 1980 was 32m. ton-km.

Shipping. The chief ports are Takoradi and Tema. In 1978, 2m. tons of cargo were imported and 1·6m. tons were exported by 1,082 ships.

Post and Broadcasting. There were 431 telephone exchanges and 742 call offices with (1982) 70,653 telephones in use. There are internal wireless stations at Accra, Kumasi, Bawku, Lawra, Kete-Krachi, Tamale, Yendi, Kpandu, Tumu and Sekondi-Takoradi. In 1982 there were 1·88m. radio and 60,000 television receivers.

Cinemas. In 1977 there were 8 cinemas with a seating capacity of 13,200.

Newspapers. There were (1984) 4 daily and 15 weekly newspapers.

JUSTICE, RELIGION, EDUCATION AND WELFARE

Justice. In June 1983 the legal system was being re-organized. The Courts were constituted as follows:

Supreme Court. The Supreme Court consists of the Chief Justice who is also the President and not less than 6 other Justices of the Supreme Court. The Supreme Court is the final court of appeal in Ghana. The final interpretation of the provisions of the constitution has been entrusted to the Supreme Court.

Court of Appeal. The Court of Appeal consists of the Chief Justice together with not less than 5 other Justices of the Appeal court and such other Justices of Superior Courts as the Chief Justice may nominate. The Court of Appeal is duly constituted by 3 Justices. The Court of Appeal is bound by its own previous decisions and all courts inferior to the Court of Appeal are bound to follow the decisions of the Court of Appeal on questions of law. Divisions of the Appeal Court may be created, subject to the discretion of the Chief Justice.

High Court of Justice. The Court has jurisdiction in civil and criminal matters as well as those relating to industrial and labour disputes including administrative complaints. The High Court of Justice has supervisory jurisdiction over all inferior Courts and any adjudicating authority and in exercise of its supervisory jurisdiction has power to issue such directions, orders or writs including writs or orders in the nature of habeas corpus, certiorari, mandamus, prohibition and quo warrantto. The High Court of Justice has no jurisdiction in cases of treason. The High Court consists of the Chief Justice and not less than twelve other judges and such other Justices of the Superior Court as the Chief Justice may appoint.

Religion. Christians represent 52% of the population (Protestant, 37%; Roman Catholic, 15%), Moslem, 13%, animist, 30%.

Education. In 1985 there were kindergartens for the age-groups 4–6 years. Primary schools are free and attendance is compulsory. In 1978–79 there were 11,422 primary schools with 1,784,834 pupils. In 1979 there were 300 secondary schools with 626,168 pupils. At the beginning of the 1979 academic year there were 41 training colleges with 12,350 students. In 1979–80 there were 8,286 students at the 3 universities (University of Ghana, the University of Science and Technology and the University of the Cape Coast). University education is free.

Health. Medical facilities include 50 government hospitals, 116 health centres and posts, 4 university hospitals, 3 mental hospitals, 4 leprosaria, 7 military hospitals, 1 prison hospital, 40 mission hospitals and 16 private hospitals. In addition, there are 30 nurses and midwives training schools.

There were 1,224 doctors, 7,608 nurses and 4,168 midwives at work in 1976.

DIPLOMATIC REPRESENTATIVES

Of Ghana in Great Britain (13 Belgrave Sq., London, SW1X 8PR)
High Commissioner: Kenneth Kweku Sinaman Dadzie (accredited 13 Oct. 1982).

Of Great Britain in Ghana (Barclays Bank Bldg., High St., Accra)
High Commissioner: K. F. X. Burns, CMG.

Of Ghana in the USA (2460 16th St., NW, Washington, D.C., 20009)
Ambassador: Eric K. Otoo.

Of the USA in Ghana (Ring Rd., East, Accra)
Ambassador: Robert E. Fritts.

Of Ghana to the United Nations
Ambassador: James Victor Gbeho.

Books of Reference

Digest of Statistics. Accra. Quarterly (from May 1953)
Ghana. Official Handbook. Annual
The Volta River Project. 3 vols. HMSO, 1956
Davidson, B., *Black Star.* London, 1973
James, C. L. R., *Nkrumah and the Ghana Revolution.* London, 1977
Jones, T., *Ghana's First Republic 1960–1966.* London, 1975
Killick, T., *Development Economics in Action: A Study of Economic Policies in Ghana.* London, 1978

GIBRALTAR

Population: 29,073 (1983)
GNP per capita: US$4,690 (1981)

HISTORY. The Rock of Gibraltar was settled by Moors in 711; they named it after their chief Jebel Tariq, 'the Mountain of Tarik'. In 1462 it was taken by the Spaniards, from Granada. It was captured by Admiral Sir George Rooke on 24 July 1704, and ceded to Great Britain by the Treaty of Utrecht, 1713. The cession was confirmed by the treaties of Paris (1763) and Versailles (1783).

On 10 Sept. 1967, in pursuance of a United Nations resolution on the decolonization of Gibraltar, a referendum was held in Gibraltar in order to ascertain whether the people of Gibraltar believed that their interests lay in retaining their link with Britain or in passing under Spanish sovereignty. Out of a total electorate of 12,762, 12,138 voted to retain the British connexion, while 44 voted for Spain.

On 15 Dec. 1982 the border between Gibraltar and Spain was re-opened for Spaniards and Gibraltarian pedestrians who are residents of Gibraltar. The border was closed by Spain in June 1969. Following an agreement signed in Brussels in Nov. 1984 the border was fully opened on 5 Feb. 1985.

AREA AND POPULATION. Area, 2½ sq. miles (6·5 sq. km). Total population, including port and harbour (census, 1981), 28,719. Estimate (31 Dec. 1983) 29,073 (of which 20,021 were British Gibraltarian). The population is mostly of Genoese, Portuguese and Maltese as well as Spanish descent.

Vital statistics (1983): Births, 510; marriages, 432; deaths, 252.

CLIMATE. The climate is warm temperate, with westerly winds in winter bringing rain. Summers are pleasantly warm and rainfall is low. Frost or snow is very rare. Jan. 55°F (12·8°C), July 75°F (23·9°C). Annual rainfall 29" (772 mm).

CONSTITUTION AND GOVERNMENT. Following a Constitutional Conference held in July 1968, a new Constitution was introduced in 1969. The Legislative and City Councils were merged to produce an enlarged legislature known as the Gibraltar House of Assembly. Executive authority is exercised by the Governor, who is also Commander-in-Chief. The Governor, while retaining certain reserved powers, is normally required to act in accordance with the advice of the Gibraltar Council, which consists of 4 *ex-officio* members (the Deputy Governor, the Deputy Fortress Commander, the Attorney-General and the Financial and Development Secretary) together with 5 elected members of the House of Assembly appointed by the Governor after consultation with the Chief Minister. Matters of primarily domestic concern are devolved to elected Ministers, with Britain responsible for other matters, including external affairs, defence and internal security. There is a Council of Ministers presided over by the Chief Minister.

The House of Assembly consists of a Speaker appointed by the Governor, 15 elected and 2 *ex-officio* members (the Attorney-General and the Financial and Development Secretary).

A Mayor of Gibraltar is elected from among the members of the Assembly by the elected members of the Assembly.

Governor and C.-in-C.: Admiral Sir David Williams, GCB.

Chief Minister: Sir Joshua Hassan, CBE, MVO, QC.

Flag: White with a red strip along the bottom, a red triple-towered castle with a gold key depending from the gateway.

DEFENCE. The Gibraltar Regiment is a part-time infantry battalion with a small regular cadre. There is also a resident battalion from the British Army.

ECONOMY

Budget. Revenue and expenditure (in £ sterling):

	1981–82	*1982–83*	*1983–84*	*1984–85*
Revenue	44,265,500	47,789,100	59,770,420	60,184,807
Expenditure	42,594,000	51,980,283	60,354,175	62,854,244

Currency. The legal currency consists of Gibraltar government notes in denominations of £20, £10, £5 and £1 and UK silver and copper-cupro-nickel coins. The amount of local currency notes in circulation at 31 March 1984 was £8,309,910.

Banking. There are 5 banks, including a branch of Barclays Bank International. In addition there are 3 offshore banks. Government savings banks had 643 depositors and £708,690 savings at 31 March 1984.

INDUSTRY AND TRADE

Industry. There are a number of relatively small industrial concerns engaged in the bottling of beer and mineral waters, etc., mainly for consumption. There is a small but important commercial ship-repair yard.

Employment. The total insured labour force at 31 Dec. 1983, was 12,163. The labour supply from the local population is insufficient to meet the demand and since the withdrawal of the Spanish frontier workers in June 1969, a substantial part of the labour has had to come from other places. A quota system is in existence which takes into account the demand from the various industries and seasonal variations and the issue of employment permits is based on this. Approximately 60% of the local labour force is employed by the UK departments or the Gibraltar government.

Trade Unions. A considerable proportion of the workers are organized in one or other of the 12 registered employees' trade unions, of which the Transport and General Workers Union has the largest membership; 7 of these are local branches of parent associations in the UK.

Commerce. Imports and exports (in £ sterling):

	1980	*1981*	*1982*	*1983*
Imports	63,141,753	65,826,282	68,393,000	61,600,000
Exports	4,182,217 [1]	5,701,416 [1]	23,800,000	24,500,000

[1] Exclusive of petroleum and petroleum products.

Britain and the Commonwealth provide the bulk of the imports, but fresh vegetables, fruit and fish come mainly from Morocco, Portugal and the Netherlands. Exports of local produce are negligible. Gibraltar depends largely on tourism, the entrepôt trade and the provision of supplies to visiting ships.

Total trade between Gibraltar and UK (British Department of Trade returns, in £1,000 sterling):

	1982	*1983*	*1984*
Imports to UK	4,229	4,266	5,333
Exports and re-exports from UK	29,712	26,495	31,978

Tourism. The number of tourists in 1983 was 782,630. On 15 Dec. 1982 the land frontier with Spain was re-opened for pedestrians only on a restricted basis.

COMMUNICATIONS

Roads. There are 31 miles of roads including 4·25 miles of pedestrian way.

Aviation. There are 5 weekly flights between London and Gibraltar (3 operated by Gibraltar Airways and 2 by British Airways) during the winter; these are increased to daily flights during the summer.

Shipping. Gibraltar is a naval and air base of strategic importance. There is a deep Admiralty harbour of 440 acres. A total of 2,226 merchant ships, 21,545,985 GRT, entered the port during 1983, including 1,254 deep-sea ships of 20,963,577 GRT. An additional 5,573 calls were made by yachts, 106,523 GRT.

Post and Broadcasting. An automatic telephone system exists in the town; number of telephones (1982), 9,870. There is also world-wide communication *via* the cable and/or wireless circuits of Cable & Wireless Ltd and international direct dialling facilities. Air-mails arrive by British Airways daily. A direct air-mail service between Gibraltar and Tangier is run by Gibraltar Airways, Ltd. Surface mails arrive direct and through France, Spain and Tangier. Radio Gibraltar broadcasts for 17 hours daily, in English and Spanish, and there are about 40 hours of television per week. Number of receivers (31 Dec. 1983), TV (including radio), 6,816.

Cinemas. In 1983 there were 3 cinemas with a seating capacity of 2,400.

Newspapers. There were (1985) 1 daily and 5 weeklies.

JUSTICE, RELIGION, EDUCATION AND WELFARE

Justice. The judicial system is based on the English system. There is a Court of Appeal, a Supreme Court, presided over by the Chief Justice, a court of first instance and a magistrates' court.

Religion. Religion of civil population mostly Roman Catholic; 1 Anglican and 1 Roman Catholic cathedral and 2 Anglican and 6 Roman Catholic churches; 1 Presbyterian and 1 Methodist church and 4 synagogues; annual subsidy to each communion, £500.

Education. Free compulsory education is provided for children between ages 5 and 15 years. Scholarships are made available for universities, teacher-training and other higher education in Britain. The comprehensive system was introduced in Sept. 1972. There were (1983) 7 first, 4 middle, 1 primary school and 2 comprehensive schools. All first and middle schools are mixed but the comprehensives are single-sex. In addition, there are 2 Services primary schools and 1 private primary school. A new purpose-built Special School for Handicapped Children was opened in 1977. Technical education is available at the Gibraltar and Dockyard Technical College managed by the UK Ministry of Defence for which Government pays 50% of all recurrent costs and scholarships are made available in Britain for university, teacher-training and other forms of higher education. In Sept. 1983, there were 1,354 pupils at government first schools, 1,318 at government middle schools, 200 at private and 777 at services schools; 17 at the special school; 841 at the boys' comprehensive school and 908 at the girls' comprehensive. In addition there were 68 full-time and 204 part-time students in the Technical College. Total full-time pupils in all educational institutions, 5,483. In 1982–83, government expenditure on education was £4,082,670.

Health. In 1983 there were 3 hospitals with 262 beds and 22 doctors. Total expenditure on medical and health services during year ended 31 March 1983 was £4,939,395.

Books of Reference

Annual Report on Gibraltar, 1972. London, 1974
Gibraltar Year Book. Gibraltar, (Annual)
Dennis, P., *Gibraltar.* Newton Abbot, 1977
Ellicott, D., *Our Gibraltar.* Gibraltar, 1975
Garcia, S., *Gibraltar: An Analysis of How the Economy was Affected by the Spanish Restrictions 1963–72* (unpublished). Garrison Library, 1974
Green, M. M., *A Gibraltar Bibliography.* London, 1980.—*Supplement.* London, 1982
Hills, G., *Rock of Contention: A History of Gibraltar.* London, 1974
Howes, H. W., *The Story of Gibraltar.* London, 1946

GREECE

Elliniki Dimokratia

Capital: Athens
Population: 9·74m. (1981)
GNP per capita: US$3,540 (1983)

HISTORY. Greece gained her independence from Turkey in 1821–29, and by the Protocol of London, of 3 Feb. 1830, was declared a kingdom, under the guarantee of Great Britain, France and Russia. For details of the subsequent history to 1947 *see* THE STATESMAN'S YEAR-BOOK, 1957, pp. 1069–70 and for details of the monarchy *see* THE STATESMAN'S YEAR-BOOK, 1973–74, p. 1000.

AREA AND POPULATION. Greece is bounded north by Albania, Yugoslavia and Bulgaria, east by Turkey and the Aegean Sea, south by the Mediterranean and west by the Ionian Sea. The total area is 131,957 sq. km (50,949 sq. miles), of which the islands account for 25,042 sq. km (9,669 sq. miles).

The population was 9,740,417 according to the census of 5 April 1981.

Athens is the capital; population of Greater Athens, in 1981, 3,027,331.

The following table shows the prefectures *(Nomoi)* and their population:

Nomoi	*Area in sq. km*	*Population 1981*	*Capital*	*Population 1981*
Greater Athens [1]	*433*	*3,027,331*	Athens	885,737
			(Piraeus)	196,389
Central Greece and Euboea [2]	*24,475*	*1,099,841*		
Aetolia and Acarnania	5,447	219,764	Missolonghi	10,164
Attica [2]	2,496	342,093	Athens	885,737
Boeotia	3,211	117,175	Levadeia	16,864
Euboea	3,908	188,410	Chalcis	44,867
Evrytania	2,045	26,182	Karpenissi	5,100
Phthiotis	4,368	161,995	Lamia	41,667
Phokis	2,121	44,222	Amphissa	7,156
Peloponnessos	*21,439*	*1,012,528*		
Argolis	2,214	93,020	Nauplion	10,609
Arcadia	4,419	107,932	Tripolis	21,311
Akhaïa	3,209	275,193	Patras	141,529
Elia	2,681	160,305	Pyrgos	21,958
Korinthia	2,289	123,042	Korinthos	22,658
Lakonia	3,636	93,218	Sparte	11,911
Messenia	2,991	159,818	Calamata	41,911
Ionian Islands	*2,307*	*182,651*		
Zakynthos	406	30,014	Zante	9,764
Kerkyra	641	99,477	Kerkyra	33,561
Kefallenia	935	31,297	Argostolion	6,788
Lefkas	325	21,863	Levkas	6,415
Epirus	*9,203*	*324,541*		
Arta	1,612	80,044	Arta	18,283
Thesprotia	1,515	41,278	Hegoumenitsa	5,879
Yannina	4,990	147,304	Yannina	44,829
Preveza	1,086	55,915	Preveza	12,662
Thessaly	*13,904*	*695,654*		
Karditsa	2,576	124,930	Karditsa	27,291
Larissa	5,354	254,295	Larisa	102,048
Magnessia	2,636	182,222	Volos	71,378
Trikkala	3,338	134,207	Trikkala	40,857

[1] Comprising parts of Attica and Piraeus prefectures.
[2] Excluding figures for the parts of Attica and Piraeus prefectures within Greater Athens.

Nomoi	*Area in sq. km*	*Population 1981*	*Capital*	*Population 1981*
Macedonia	*34,203*	*2,121,953*		
Grevena	2,338	36,421	Grevena	7,433
Drama	3,468	94,772	Drama	36,109
Imathia	1,699	133,750	Verria	37,087
Thessaloniki	3,560	871,580	Thessaloniki	406,413
Kavalla	2,109	135,218	Kavala	56,375
Kastoria	1,685	53,169	Kastoria	17,133
Kilkis	2,597	81,562	Kilkis	11,148
Kozani	3,562	147,051	Kozani	30,994
Pella	2,506	132,386	Edessa	16,054
Pieria	1,548	106,859	Katerini	38,016
Serres	3,987	196,247	Serres	45,213
Florina	1,863	52,430	Florina	12,562
Khalkidiki	2,945	79,036	Polyghyros	4,075
Aghion Oros Mount Athos	336	1,472	Karyai (locality)	235
Thrace	*8,578*	*345,220*		
Evros	4,242	148,486	Alexandroupolis	34,535
Xanthi	1,793	88,777	Xanthi	31,541
Rodopi	2,543	107,957	Komotini	34,051
Aegean Islands	*9,071*	*428,533*		
Cyclades	2,572	88,458	Hermoupolis	13,876
Lesvos	2,154	104,620	Mitylini	24,115
Samos	778	40,519	Samos	5,575
Khios	904	49,865	Khios	24,070
Dodecanese	2,663	145,071	Rhodes	40,392
Crete	*8,331*	*502,165*		
Iraklion	2,641	243,622	Heraklion	101,634
Lassithi	1,818	70,053	Aghios Nikolaos	8,130
Rethymnon	1,496	62,634	Rethymnon	17,736
Canea	2,376	125,856	Canea	47,338

In 1981 cities (*i.e.*, communes of more than 10,000 inhabitants, including Greater Athens) had 5,659,528 inhabitants (58·1%), towns (*i.e.*, communes with between 2,000 and 9,999 inhabitants), 1,125,547 (11·6%), villages and rural communities (under 2,000 inhabitants), 2,955,342 (30·3%).

Mount Athos, the easternmost of the three prongs of the peninsula of Chalcidice, is a self-governing community composed of 20 monasteries. (*See* THE STATESMAN'S YEAR-BOOK, 1945, p. 983.) For centuries the peninsula has been administered by a Council of 4 members and an Assembly of 20 members, 1 deputy from each monastery. The Greek Government on 10 Sept. 1926 recognized this autonomous form of government; Articles 109–112 of the Constitution of 1927 gave legal sanction to the Charter of Mount Athos, drawn up by representatives of the 20 monasteries on 20 May 1924. Article 103 of the 1952 Constitution and Article 105 of the 1975 Constitution confirmed the special status of Mount Athos.

Vital statistics (1983): 132,608 live births; 1,174 still births; 2,050 illegitimate live births; 71,143 marriages; 90,580 deaths; 16,510 emigrants (Jan.–Sept. 1977); 12,572 immigrants (Jan.–Sept. 1977).

CLIMATE. Coastal regions and the islands have typical Mediterranean conditions, with mild, rainy winters and hot, dry, sunny summers. Rainfall comes almost entirely in the winter months, though amounts vary widely according to position and relief. Continental conditions affect the northern mountainous areas, with severe winters, deep snow cover and heavy precipitation, but summers are hot. Athens. Jan. 48°F (8·6°C), July 82·5°F (28·2°C). Annual rainfall 16·6" (414·3 mm).

CONSTITUTION AND GOVERNMENT. A *coup d'état* took place on 21 April 1967, 'to avert the danger of a communist threat against the nation'. A Military Government was formed, which suspended the 1952 Constitution. Following the unsuccessful counter-*coup* in 1967, King Constantine went abroad. Voting took place on 29 July 1973 in the referendum to change Greece from a

Monarchy to a Republic and to elect a President. 77·2% of the valid votes were cast for a republican régime.

On 25 Nov. 1973, in a bloodless *coup*, President Papadopoulos was overthrown and Lieut.-Gen. Phaedon Ghizikis was sworn in. The military dictatorship collapsed on 23 July 1974 and the 1952 Constitution was reintroduced in a modified form. A new Constitution was introduced in June 1975. Parliamentary elections took place on 12 Nov. 1974.

A further referendum on the Monarchy took place on 8 Dec. 1974 and 69·2% of the valid votes were cast for an 'uncrowned democracy'.

Elections were again held on 18 Oct. 1981. The results were New Democracy, 115; Pan-Hellenic Socialist Movement, 172; Communists, 12.

President: Konstantinos Karamanlis (elected President in May 1980).

The Cabinet in Sept. 1984:

Prime Minister and Minister of Defence: Andreas Papandreou.

Agriculture: Constantine Simitis. *Commerce:* Nikolaos Akritidis. *Communications:* Giannis Papadonikolakis. *Culture and Sciences:* Melina Mercouri. *Education and Religion:* Apostolos Kaklamanis. *Energy and National Resources:* Eleftherios Verivakis. *Finance and National Economy:* Gerassimos Arsenis. *Foreign Affairs:* Ioannis Haralambopoulos. *Health and Welfare and Social Security:* George Gennimatas. *Interior:* Agamemnon Koutsogiorgas. *Justice:* George Alex Mangakis. *Labour:* Evangelos Yannopoulos. *Merchant Marine:* George Katsifaras. *Northern Greece:* Vassilis Intzes. *Physical Planning, Housing and Environment:* Evangelos Kouloumbis. *Minister to the Presidency:* Apostolos Lazaris. *Minister to the Prime Minister:* Apostolos Tsohatzopoulos. *Public Order:* Ioannis Skoularikis. *Research and Technology:* George Lianis. *Public Works:* George Perrakis.

National flag: Nine horizontal stripes of blue and white, with a canton of blue with a white cross.

National anthem: Hymn to Freedom, Imnos eis tin Eleftherian (words by Dionysios Solomos, 1824; tune by N. Mantzaros, 1828).

DEFENCE. In Aug. 1950 the Ministries of War, Marine and Military Aviation were fused into a single Ministry of National Defence. The General Staff of National Defence is directly responsible to the Minister on general defence questions, besides the special staffs for Army, Navy and Air Force. Military service in the Armed Forces is compulsory and universal. Liability begins in the 21st year and lasts up to the 50th. The normal terms of service are Army 22 months, Navy 26 months, Air Force 24 months, followed by 19 years in the First Reserve and 10 years in the Second Reserve.

Army. The Army is organized into 3 Military Regions, comprising 1 armoured, 1 mechanized, 1 para-commando and 11 infantry divisions; 3 armoured brigades; 13 field artillery, 7 anti-aircraft, 2 surface-to-surface missile, 2 surface-to-air missile, and 2 army aviation battalions; and 4 independent aviation companies. Equipment includes 350 M-47, 1,125 M-48, 200 AMX-30 and 106 Leopard I main battle tanks. Strength (1985) 135,000 (99,500 conscripts), with a further 350,000 reserves. There is also a paramiltary gendarmerie of 25,000 men.

Navy. The Hellenic Navy includes 2 modern Netherlands-built leader-size guided missile frigates, 10 submarines (8 modern German (Fed. Rep.)-built small and 2 old *ex*-US large), 14 old *ex*-US destroyers, 1 *ex*-German support frigate, 1 new armed training ship carrying a helicopter, 4 old *ex*-US frigates (small DE type), 2 coastal minelayers, 14 fast missile boats, 10 fast torpedo boats, 15 coastal minesweepers, 11 coastal patrol boats, 1 dock landing ship, 8 tank landing ships, 5 medium landing ships, 10 landing craft, 68 minor landing craft, 1 ammunition ship, 6 oilers, 2 transports, 1 depot ship, 2 surveying craft, 2 light-house tenders, 6 water carriers, 1 netlayer and 14 fleet tugs.

Personnel in 1985 totalled 2,500 officers and 17,000 ratings (200 women).

Air Force. The Hellenic Air Force had a strength (1985) of about 24,500 officers and men and 275 combat aircraft, consisting of 4 squadrons of F-4E Phantom air-superiority fighters, 2 squadrons of F-104G Starfighters, 2 squadrons of Mirage F.1 fighters, 3 squadrons of A-7H Corsair II attack aircraft, 2 squadrons of F-5 fighters, 1 squadron of RF-4E and RF-5A reconnaissance fighters and 1 squadron of HU-16B Albatross ASW amphibians. There are also transport squadrons equipped with C-130H Hercules (12), Noratlas, NAMC YS-11 and C-47 aircraft, 7 Canadair CL-215 twin-engined amphibians, 36 T-2E Buckeye training/attack aircraft, other training and helicopter units, and anti-aircraft units equipped with Nike-Hercules and Hawk surface-to-air missiles.

The HAF is organized into Tactical, Training and Air Materiel Commands.

INTERNATIONAL RELATIONS

Membership. Greece is a member of UN, EEC, the Council of Europe and the military and political wings of NATO.

ECONOMY

Budget. The estimated revenue and expenditure for calendar years were as follows (in 1m. drachmai):

	1980	*1981*	*1982*	*1983*
Revenue	423,117	733,079	728,734	1,001,387
Expenditure	423,115	733,077	794,295	1,055,218

Currency. On 11 Nov. 1944 the Greek currency was stabilized at 1 new *drachma* equalling 50,000m. old *drachmai*. Further readjustments took place in 1946, 1949 and 1953. A 'new issue' of notes and coins was put into circulation on 1 May 1954, 1 new drachma equalling 1,000 old drachmai (72 drachmai = £1; 30 drachmai = US$1). The 'new issue' comprises notes of 50, 100, 500 and 1,000 drachmai and metal coins of 1, 2, 5, 10 and 20 drachmai and 10, 20 and 50 *lepta*. Rate of exchange, March 1985, £1 = 151·51 drachmai; US$1 = 143·73.

Banking. The Bank of Greece *(Trapeza Tis Ellados)* is the bank of issue.

The National Investment Bank for industrial development was set up in Dec. 1963; of its capital of 180m. drachmai, the National Bank provided 60%.

Other important banks are the Ionian and Popular Bank of Greece, the Commercial Bank of Greece, the National Mortgage Bank, the Hellenic Industrial Development Bank, the Investment Bank, the Commercial Credit Bank and the General Bank of Greece.

Weights and Measures. The metric system was made obligatory in 1959; the use of other systems is prohibited. The Gregorian calendar was adopted in Feb. 1923.

ENERGY AND NATURAL RESOURCES

Electricity. Total installed capacity of the Public Power Corporation was 5,410m. mw as at 31 Dec. 1980. Total net production in 1981 was 21,657m. kwh.

Minerals. Greece produces a variety of ores and minerals, including iron-pyrites (115,976 tonnes in 1982), bauxite (2·84m. tonnes, 1982), nickel (523,405 tonnes, 1982), magnesite (967,106 tonnes, 1982), dead burnt magnesite (285,572 tonnes, 1982), mixed sulphur ores (752,000 tonnes, 1976), barytes, chromite, marble (white and coloured) and various other earths, chiefly from the Laurium district, Thessaly, Euboea and the Aegean islands. There is little coal, and lignite of indifferent quality (27·19m. tonnes, 1982). Oil was struck in 1963 by British Petroleum at Kleisoura in west central Greece. Salt production (1970) 68,471 tonnes.

Agriculture. Of the total area only 33% is cultivable, but it supports about 45% of the whole population. The total area under cultivation in 1971 was 3,586,232 hectares, forest area (1965) was 2,512,418 hectares (443,713 of which were privately owned). The average holding was 3·42 hectares in 1975.

Yield (1,000 tonnes) of the chief crops (1982):

Wheat	2,983	Table grapes	267
Tobacco	130	Wine	470
Cotton	290	Citrus fruit	863
Sugar-beet	2,426	Other fruit	911
Currants and raisins	132	Milk	1,700
Olive oil	321	Meat and poultry	524

About 496,260 hectares of olives are under cultivation.

Rice is cultivated in Macedonia, the Peloponnese, Epirus and Central Greece. Successful experiments have been made in growing rice on alkaline land previously regarded as unfit for cultivation. The main kinds of cheese produced are sliced cheese in brine (commercially known as Fetta) and hard cheese, such as Kefalotyri.

Livestock (1983): 850,000 cattle, 1,000 buffaloes, 1·4m. pigs, 8·4m. sheep, 4·63m. goats, 97,000 horses, 105,000 mules, 220,000 asses, 36m. poultry.

Fisheries. In 1981, 10,762 fishermen were active and landed 90,869 tonnes of fish. 37,182 kg of sponges were produced in 1981.

INDUSTRY AND TRADE

Industry. The main products are canned vegetables and fruit, fruit juice, beer, wine, alcoholic beverages, cigarettes, textiles, yarn, leather, shoes, synthetic timber, paper, plastics, rubber products, chemical acids, pigments, pharmaceutical products, cosmetics, soap, disinfectants, fertilizers, glassware, porcelain sanitary items, wire and power coils and household instruments.

Production, 1976 (1,000 tonnes): Textile yarns, 137; cement, 8,714; fertilizers, 1,554; ammonia, 287; iron (concrete-reinforcing bars), 589; iron-nickel, 16; alumina, 450; aluminium, 133; electrical domestic goods (1,000 pieces), 325.

Labour. Of the economically active population in 1971, 1·92m. were engaged in agriculture. 677,451 in industry and 1,000,684 in other employment.

Pepelasis, A. A., and Yotopoulos, P. A., *Surplus Labor in Greek Agriculture, 1953–60.* Athens, 1962

Trade Unions. The status of trade unions in Greece is regulated by the Associations Act 1914. Trade-union liberties are guaranteed under the Constitution, and a law of June 1982 altered the unions' right to strike.

The national body of trade unions in Greece is the Greek General Confederation of Labour.

Commerce. Foreign trade (in US$1m.) for 4 calendar years was:

	1979	*1980*	*1981*	*1982*
Imports	10,110	10,903	11,468	10,079
Exports	3,932	4,094	4,772	4,139

Total trade between Greece and UK (British Department of Trade returns, in £1,000 sterling):

	1980	*1981*	*1982*	*1983*	*1984*
Imports to UK	142,456	167,655	151,688	164,917	279,367
Exports and re-exports from UK	224,619	254,154	255,281	280,204	354,332

Tourism. Tourists visiting Greece in 1984 numbered 5,523,192. They spent the equivalent of US$1,310m.

COMMUNICATIONS

Roads. There were, in 1982, 37,365 km of roads, of which 8,689 were national and 28,676 provincial roads.

Number of motor vehicles in Dec. 1983: 1,658,193, of which 1,073,411 were passenger cars, 519,194 goods vehicles, 19,121 buses.

Railways. In 1983 the State network, Hellenic Railways (CH), totalled 2,479 km comprising 1,565 km of 1,435 mm gauge, 872 km of 1,000 mm gauge, and 22 km of 750 mm gauge, and carried 670m. tonne-km and 1,629m. passenger-km.

Aviation. Olympic Airways connects Athens with all important cities of the country, Europe, the Middle East and USA. Thirty-four foreign companies connect Athens with the principal cities of the world.

The principal airport is at Athens. In 1983, 95,923 aircraft arrived, carrying 8·4m. passengers.

Shipping. In Dec. 1983 the merchant navy comprised 3,863 vessels of 36,806,000 GRT. Greek-owned ships under foreign flags totalled more than 7,283,000 GRT.

There is a canal (opened 9 Nov. 1893) across the Isthmus of Corinth (about 4 miles).

Post and Broadcasting. In 1983 there were 2,691 telephone exchanges, handling 4,700m. calls. There were (1983) 3,331,143 telephones.

Elliniki Radiophonia Tileorasis (ERT), the Hellenic National Radio and Television Institute, is the government broadcasting station. ERT broadcasts 2 TV programmes. Number of receivers: radio, 5m.; television, 1·4m.

Cinemas (1981). There were 1,150 cinemas.

Newspapers (1984). There were 35 daily newspapers published in Athens.

JUSTICE, RELIGION, EDUCATION AND WELFARE

Justice. Under the 1975 Constitution judges are appointed for life by the President of the Republic, after consultation with the judicial council. Judges enjoy personal and functional independence. There are three divisions of the courts: administrative, civil and criminal and they must not give decisions which are contrary to the Constitution. Final jurisdiction lies with a Special Supreme Tribunal.

Some laws, passed before the 1975 Constitution came into force, and which are not contrary to it, remain in force.

Religion. The Christian Eastern Orthodox faith is the established religion to which 98% of the population belong.

The Greek Orthodox Church is under an archbishop and 67 metropolitans, 1 archbishop and 7 metropolitans in Crete, and 4 metropolitans in the Dodecanese. The Roman Catholics have 3 archbishops (in Naxos and Corfu and, not recognized by the State, in Athens) and 1 bishop (for Syra and Santorin). The Exarchs of the Greek Catholics and the Armenians are not recognized by the State.

Complete religious freedom is recognized by the Constitution of 1968, but proselytizing from, and interference with, the Greek Orthodox Church is forbidden.

Education. Public education is provided in nursery, primary and secondary schools, starting at 6 years of age and since 1963 free at all levels.

In 1981–82 there were 4,743 nursery schools with 6,901 staff and 151,626 pupils; 9,400 public day primary schools with 37,947 staff and 891,488 pupils. There were 2,291 secondary schools with 33,613 staff and 669,812 pupils.

In 1981–82 there were 13 universities with 87,476 students and 7,489 lecturers.

Illiteracy in the age groups of 10 years and over was 18% in 1961 (8% among men). 1972 estimate 12%.

The Greek language consists of 2 branches, *katharevousa*, a conscious revival of classical Greek and *demotiki*. Demotiki is the official language both spoken and written.

Health (1983). There were 626 hospitals and sanatoria with a total of 57,496 beds. There were 27,607 doctors and 8,286 dentists.

DIPLOMATIC REPRESENTATIVES

Of Greece in Great Britain (1A Holland Park, London, W11 3TP)
Ambassador: Nikolaos Kyriazides.

Of Great Britain in Greece (1 Ploutarchou St., Athens 139)
Ambassador: Sir Peregrine Rhodes, KCMG.

Of Greece in the USA (2221 Massachusetts Ave., NW, Washington, D.C., 20008)
Ambassador: George D. Papoulias.

Of the USA in Greece (91 Vasilissis Sophias Blvd., Athens)
Ambassador: Monteagle Stearns.

Of Greece to the United Nations
Ambassador: Mihalis Dountas.

Books of Reference

Clogg, R. and M. J., *Greece.* [Bibliography] Oxford and Santa Barbara, 1980
Holden, D., *Greece Without Columns: The Making of the Modern Greeks.* London, 1972
Katris, J. A., *Eyewitness in Greece: The Colonels Come to Power.* St Louis, 1971
Kayser, B., *Géographie humaine de la Grèce.* Paris, Presses Universitaires, 1964
Kolodny, E. Y., *La Population des Îles de la Grèce.* Aix-en-Provence, 1973
Kousoulas, D. G., *Revolution and Defeat: The Story of the Greek Communist Party.* OUP, 1965
Kykkotis, I., *English–Modern Greek and Modern Greek–English Dictionary.* 3rd ed. London, 1957
Mouzelis, N. P., *Modern Greece.* London, 1978
Munkman, C. A., *American Aid to Greece.* New York, 1958
Phillipson, A., *Die griechischen Landschaften: eine Landeskunde.* 4 vols. Frankfurt, 1951–59
Pring, J. T., *The Oxford Dictionary of Modern Greek, Greek-English, English-Greek.* OUP, 1965–82
Tsoukalis, L., *Greece and the European Community.* Farnborough, 1979
Woodhouse, C. M., *The Struggle for Greece, 1941–1949.* London, 1976.—*Karamanlis: The Restorer of Greek Democracy.* OUP, 1982
Xydis, S. G., *Greece and the Great Powers, 1944–47.* Thessaloniki, 1963
Young, K., *The Greek Passion.* London, 1967

GRENADA

Capital: St George's
Population: 115,000 (1981)
GNP per capita: US$850 (1981)

HISTORY. Grenada became an independent nation within the Commonwealth on 7 Feb. 1974. Grenada was formerly an Associated State under the West Indies Act, 1967. The 1973 Constitution was suspended in 1979 following a revolution.

AREA AND POPULATION. Grenada is the most southerly island of the Windward Islands with an area of 133 sq. miles (344 sq. km); population, census 1970, 92,775; estimated population 1981, 115,000. The borough of St George's, the capital, had population (1978) 30,813. The largest of the Grenadines attached to Grenada is Carriacou, area 32 sq. km; population 1970, 5,950 (including Petit Martinique).

Vital statistics (1978): Births, 2,521; deaths, 765; infant deaths, 73; marriages, 360.

CLIMATE. The tropical climate is very agreeable in the dry season, from Jan. to May, when days are warm and nights quite cool, but in the wet season there is very little difference between day and night temperatures. On the coast, annual rainfall is about 60″ (1,500 mm) but it is as high as 150–200″ (3,750–5,000 mm) in the mountains.

CONSTITUTION AND GOVERNMENT. On 19 Oct. 1983 the army took control after a power struggle led to the killing of Maurice Bishop the Prime Minister. At the request of a group of Caribbean countries, Grenada was invaded by US-led forces on 24–28 Oct. On 1 Nov. a State of Emergency was imposed which ended on 15 Nov. when an interim government was installed. Elections were held for the 15-seat House of Representatives on 3 Dec. 1984 The New National Party won 14 seats and the Grenada United Labour Party, 1.

Governor-General: Sir Paul Scoon, GCMG.

Prime Minister, Finance, Security and Home Affairs: Herbert Blaize.

National flag: Divided into 4 triangles of yellow, top and bottom, and green, hoist and fly; in the centre a red disc bearing a gold star; along the top and bottom edged red stripes each bearing 3 gold stars; on the green triangle near the hoist a pod of nutmeg.

DEFENCE

Army. A People's Revolutionary Army was created in 1979. Personnel about 6,500 organized into 3 infantry battalions and an artillery battery.

INTERNATIONAL RELATIONS

Membership. Grenada is a member of the UN, OAS, Caricom, the Commonwealth and is an ACP state of EEC.

ECONOMY

Budget. The 1981 estimates balanced at EC$169m. Public debt at 31 Dec. 1970 was EC$15,168,705.

Currency. The currency is the *Eastern Caribbean dollar.* In March 1985, £1 = EC$2·88; US$ = EC$2·70.

Banking. In 1981 there were 5 commercial banks in Grenada: The National Commercial Bank, Barclays Bank International, Royal Bank of Canada, Bank of Nova Scotia and the Grenada Co-operative Bank. The Grenada Agricultural Bank was established in 1965 to encourage agricultural development. In 1981, bank deposits were EC$164·7m.

AGRICULTURE (1981). The principal crops (production in lb.) are: Cocoa (6,409,227), nutmegs (6,767,199), bananas (25,609,408), and mace (506,950); coconuts, corn and pigeon peas, citrus, sugar-cane, root-crops and vegetables are also grown, in addition to small scattered cultivations of cotton, cloves, cinnamon, pimento, coffee and fruit trees The fish catch was about 3m. lb.

Livestock (1983): Cattle, 6,000; sheep, 16,000; goats, 13,000; pigs, 11,000; poultry (1982), 260,000.

COMMERCE (1981). Total value of imports, EC$146,709,830; exports, EC$50,275,362. The main exports are cocoa, nutmegs and bananas.

Of exports in 1981, UK took 35·6%; Netherlands, 15·8%; Trinidad, 15·6%; Federal Republic of Germany, 9%; Canada, 2·8%; USA, 2·5%. Of 1981 imports, Trinidad furnished 19·2%; USA, 18·6%; UK, 16·6%; Canada, 5·5%; Netherlands, 1·6%; Federal Republic of Germany, 1·3%.

Total trade between Grenada and UK (British Department of Trade returns, in £1,000 sterling):

	1980	*1981*	*1982*	*1983*	*1984*
Imports to UK	5,225	4,890	4,704	5,387	5,703
Exports and re-exports to UK	3,371	3,839	3,687	7,293	8,319

TOURISM. In 1981, there were 102,668 visitors; 131 cruise ships and 1,376 yachts visited the island.

COMMUNICATIONS

Roads. The scheduled road mileage is 577, of which 377 have an oiled surface and 210 are graded as third- and fourth-class roads. Vehicles registered (1979) 6,676.

Aviation. A new international airport was inaugurated in Oct. 1984 at Point Salines. Pearls Airport has daily connexions to London, New York and South America *via* nearby islands. There is a small airstrip on Carriacou.

Shipping. Total shipping for 1978 was 927 motor and steamships and 166 sailing and auxiliary vessels, with a total net tonnage of 2,210,532 and 7,479 respectively.

Post and Broadcasting. The telephone system is owned and operated by the Grenada Telephone Co. Ltd. The Government of Grenada is a shareholder. The system is completely automatic, and in 1981 served 5,648 subscribers. Cable & Wireless (W.I.) Ltd operates a VHF radio system (telephone and telegraph) to Trinidad and Barbados, from where connexion is made to all other parts of the world. There were (1978) 63,500 radios.

JUSTICE, RELIGION AND EDUCATION

Justice. The Grenada Supreme Court, situated in St George's, comprises a High Court of Justice, a Court of Magisterial Appeal (which hears appeals from the lower Magistrates' Courts exercising summary jurisdiction) and an Itinerant Court of Appeal (to hear appeals from the High Court).

Religion. The majority of the population are Roman Catholic; the Anglican and Methodist churches are also well represented.

Education. There are 20 primary schools, 4 junior schools and 16 secondary schools, as well as 46 schools taking the full age range. There is a Technical Centre in each district and a Technical Institute in St George's, where there is also a Teacher Training College and a branch of the University of the West Indies. There were 28,745 primary and 4,773 secondary school pupils in 1973.

DIPLOMATIC REPRESENTATIVES

Of Grenada in Great Britain (1 Collingham Gdns., London, SW5)
High Commissioner: O. M. Gibbs, CMG (accredited 15 March 1984).

Of Great Britain in Grenada
High Commissioner: G. L. Bullard, CMG (resides at Bridgetown).

Of Grenada in the USA (1701 New Hampshire Ave., NW, Washington, DC., 20009)
Ambassador: (Vacant).

Of the USA in Grenada
Ambassador: (Vacant).

Of Grenada to the United Nations
Ambassador: (Vacant).

Books of Reference

Hodge, M. and Searle, C. (eds), *Is Freedom We Making.* Govt. Information Service, 1981
O'Shaughnessy, H., *Grenada: Revolution, Invasion and Aftermath.* London, 1984
Page, A., Sutton, P., and Thorndike, T., *Grenada and Invasion.* London, 1984
Searle, C., *Grenada: The Struggle against Destabilization.* London, 1983
Searle, C. and Rojas, D. (eds), *To Construct from Morning.* Grenada, 1982
Wheaton, P. and Sunshine, C. (eds), *Grenada: The Peaceful Revolution.* Washington, 1982

GUATEMALA

República de Guatemala

Capital: Guatemala City
Population: 6·58m. (1984)
GNP per capita: US$1,140 (1981)

HISTORY. From 1524 to 1821 Guatemala was a Spanish captaincy-general, comprising the whole of Central America. It became independent in 1821 and formed part of the Confederation of Central America from 1823 to 1839, when Rafael Carrera dissolved the Confederation.

AREA AND POPULATION. Guatemala is bounded on the north and west by Mexico, south by the Pacific ocean and east by El Salvador, Honduras and Belize, and the area is 108,889 sq. km (42,042 sq. miles). In March 1936 Guatemala, El Salvador and Honduras agreed to accept the peak of Mount Montecristo as the common boundary point.

The census population was 6,043,559 in 1981. Estimate (1984) 6,577,000. About 45% are pure Indians, of 21 different groups descended from the Maya; most of the remainder are mixed Indian and Spanish and these supply the ruling classes. Density of population, 1984, 60 per sq. km.

Vital statistics, 1980: Births, 303,643; deaths, 51,769.

Guatemala is administratively divided into 22 departments, each with a governor appointed by the President. Population, 1982:

Departments	*Area (sq. km)*	*Population*	*Departments*	*Area (sq. km)*	*Population*
Alta Verapaz	8,686	383,178	Petén	35,854	102,803
Baja Verapaz	3,124	152,374	Quezaltenango	1,951	447,428
Chimaltenango	1,979	267,182	Quiché	8,378	430,003
Chiquimula	2,376	215,409	Retalhuleu	1,858	206,543
El Progreso	1,922	101,203	Sacatepéquez	465	137,815
Escuintla	4,384	496,522	San Marcos	3,791	552,094
Guatemala	2,126	1,785,665	Santa Rosa	2,955	249,930
Huehuetenango	7,403	524,829	Sololá	1,061	173,401
Izabal	9,038	290,203	Suchitepéquez	2,510	304,826
Jalapa	2,063	162,907	Totonicapán	1,061	236,033
Jutiapa	3,219	329,185	Zacapa	2,690	149,267

The capital is Guatemala City with about 1·3m. inhabitants (1983). Other towns are Quezaltenango (65,733), Puerto Barrios (38,956), Mazatenango (38,319), Antigua (26,631), Zacapa (35,769) and Cobán (43,538). An earthquake in central Guatemala in Feb. 1976 killed 24,103 people and destroyed 200,000 dwellings.

CLIMATE. A tropical climate, with little variation in temperature and a well marked wet season from May to Oct. Guatemala City. Jan. 63°F (17·2°C), July 69°F (20·6°C). Annual rainfall 53″ (1,316 mm).

CONSTITUTION AND GOVERNMENT. On 23 March 1982 a junta, consisting of Brig.-Gen. Efrain Ríos Montt, Gen. Horacio Maldonado and Col. Francisco Gordillo, took power in a bloodless *coup*. Gen. Ríos Montt later became President. The Constitution and political activity were suspended, Congress abolished and government was to be by decree. A further *coup* on 8 Aug. 1983 removed Brig.-Gen. Montt from the presidency. Brig.-Gen. Oscar Humberto Mejía Victores became Chief of State. Elections to a National Constituent Assembly were held on 1 July 1984 and a return to civilian rule was promised in 1985.

National flag: Three vertical strips of blue, white, blue, with the national arms in the centre.

National anthem: ¡Guatemala! feliz (words by J. J. Palma; tune by R. Alvarez).

DEFENCE. There is conscription into the armed forces for 24–30 months.

Army. The Army numbers 38,000, organized in 17 infantry, 1 armoured, 2 parachute and 1 engineer battalions, 4 field artillery groups, 1 anti-aircraft artillery group and 4 reconnaissance squadrons. Equipment includes light tanks and armoured cars.

Navy. A Naval force was formed in 1959. It comprises 12 small patrol craft, 1 landing craft, 2 small troop carriers, 6 motor launches, 2 utility cutters, 30 river patrol craft and 1 tug. Since 1973 the base at Santo Tomas has had a 230-ton marine elevator (synchrolift), greatly improving naval repair facilities. Personnel in 1985 numbered 1,000 comprising 125 officers and 875 men (including marines).

Air Force. There is a small Air Force with 10 A-37B light attack aircraft, 1 DC-6, 10 C-47, 2T-33s and 8 Israeli-built Arava transports, 12 Pilatus PC-7 turboprop trainers, and a number of light aircraft and helicopters, including a few armed UH-1 Iroquois. Total strength is about 550 personnel and 70 aircraft.

INTERNATIONAL RELATIONS

Membership. Guatemala is a member of UN, OAS and Cacom.

External Debt. In 1983 the external debt was Q.503·9m.

ECONOMY

Planning. The 1979–82 National Economic Development Plan involved government investment of Q.1,937·5m.

Budget. The estimates of ordinary revenue and expenditure balanced as follows, in quetzales (1 quetzal = US$1): 1982, 1,481m.; 1983, 1,314m.

Currency. The gold *quetzal* was established 7 May 1925 equal to 60 old Guatemala paper pesos, with a gold content equal to that of the US$. Coins of 25, 10, 5 and 1 *centavos* were issued by the Banco de Guatemala on 16 Sept. 1965; they are of a lower content value than the previous ones. There are also paper notes of 100, 50, 20, 10, 5, 1 and ½ *quetzales* (50 *centavos*). In March 1985, £1 = Q.1·07; US$1 = Q.1.

Banking. By an Act effective 4 Feb. 1946 the Central Bank of Guatemala (founded in 1926 as a mixed central and commercial bank) was superseded by a new institution, the Banco de Guatemala, to operate solely as a central bank. Savings and term deposits at commercial banks were Q.1,428·5m. at the end of 1983. Total currency circulation (backed by a gold reserve fixed by law at a minimum of 40%) on 31 Dec. 1983 was Q.1,159·5m.; total net international reserves amounted to Q.–25·5m. on 31 Dec. 1983. In July 1965 the country's quota with the IMF was increased from US$15m. to 25m.

There are 17 banks, including the Banco de Guatemala, Banco Nacional de Desarollo, set up in 1971 to promote agricultural development, its counterpart for small industries (Banco de los Trabajadores) set up in Jan. 1966 with initial capital of US$1·3m., a branch of Lloyds Bank International Ltd and a branch of the Bank of America.

Weights and Measures. The metric system has been officially adopted, but is little used in local commerce.

Libra of 16 oz.	= 1·014 lb.	*League*	= 3 miles
Arroba of 25 libras	= 25·35 lb.	*Vara*	= 32 in.
Quintal of 4 arrobas	= 101·40 lb.	*Manzana*	= 100 varas sq.
Tonelada of 20 quintals	= 18·10 cwt	*Caballeria* of 64 manzanas	= 110 acres
Fanega	= 1½ Imp. bushels		

ENERGY AND NATURAL RESOURCES

Electricity. 1,045m. kwh. of electricity were generated in 1976. A large-scale hydro-electric development is now underway and others are planned.

Oil. Guatemala began exporting crude oil in 1980; exports, 1983, were valued at Q.60m. Production is from wells in Alta Verapaz department from where the oil is piped to Santo Tomas de Castilla. Further exploration is proceeding in the Petén.

Minerals. Mineral production includes zinc and lead concentrates, some antimony and tungsten, a small amount of cadmium and silver; some copper is also being mined. Exports (1983) Q.2m. In 1965 a subsidiary of International Nickel Company of Canada was granted a 40-year concession to extract and process nickel ore in northern Guatemala. Production and exports started in 1977 but production had ceased temporarily in 1982.

Agriculture. The Cordilleras divide Guatemala into two unequal drainage areas, of which the Atlantic is much the greater. The Pacific slope, though comparatively narrow, is exceptionally well watered and fertile between the altitudes of 1,000 and 5,000 ft, and is the most densely settled part of the republic. The Atlantic slope is sparsely populated, and has little of commercial importance beyond the chicle and timber-cutting of the Petén, coffee cultivation of Cobán region and banana-raising of the Motagua Valley and Lake Izabal district. Soil erosion is serious and a single week of heavy rains suffices to cause flooding of fields and much crop destruction.

The principal crop is coffee; there are about 12,000 coffee plantations with 138m. coffee trees on about 338,000 acres, but 80% of the crop comes from 1,500 large coffee farms employing 426,000 workers. Coffee exports in 1983 were valued at Q.350·6m. mainly to USA and Federal Republic of Germany.

Bananas are still an important export crop, but exports have at times been seriously reduced, partly by labour troubles and by hurricanes. Exports 1980 were worth Q.40m.

Cotton exports in 1983 were valued at Q.46m. Other important exports (1983) were sugar, Q.126·7m.; beef, Q.14·9m. Guatemala is, after Mexico, the largest producer of chicle gum (used for chewing-gum manufacture in USA). Rubber development schemes are under way, assisted by US funds. Guatemala is one of the largest sources of essential oils (citronella and lemon grass); exports in 1983 were valued at Q.1·9m. Cardamom, exported mainly to the Arab countries, was valued at Q.31·4m. in 1983.

Livestock (1983): Cattle, 2·3m.; pigs, 870,000; sheep, 550,000; horses, 100,000; poultry, 15m.

Forestry. The forest area has an extent of 17,784,000 acres. The department of Petén is rich in mahogany and other woods. Production (1980) 11·23m. cu. metres.

Fisheries. Exports were about Q.8·9m. in 1983.

INDUSTRY AND TRADE

Industry. The principal industries are food and beverages, tobacco, chemicals, hides and skins, textiles, garments and non-metallic minerals. New industries include electrical goods, plastic sheet and metal furniture.

Trade Unions. Trade unions are small. In 1954 the trade unions were ordered to reorganize and there are now two main federations.

Commerce. Values in Q.1,000 (1 quetzal = US$1) were:

	1979	*1980*	*1981*	*1982*	*1983*
Imports (c.i.f.)	1,503,900	1,615,000	1,773,600	1,387,000	1,135,000
Exports (f.o.b.)	1,241,400	1,522,000	1,281,200	1,120,000	1,150,000

Total trade between Guatemala and UK for 6 years (British Department of Trade returns, in £1,000 sterling):

	1980	*1981*	*1982*	*1983*	*1984*
Imports to UK	23,657	8,197	13,476	9,764	9,565
Exports and re-exports from UK	13,835	11,280	8,127	7,440	10,660

Tourism. There were 235,166 foreign visitors in 1983.

COMMUNICATIONS

Roads. In 1985 there were 18,000 km of roads, of which 2,850 are paved. There is a trunk highway from coast to coast *via* Guatemala City. There are 2 trunk highways from the Mexican to the Salvadorean frontier: the Pacific Highway serving the fertile coastal plain and the Pan-American Highway running through the highlands and Guatemala City. Motor vehicles number about 200,000.

Railways. The principal railway system is the government-owned (since 1968) *Ferrocarriles de Guatemala.* All railways are of 914 mm gauge. Total length of all lines is 820 km. Passengers carried, 1976, numbered 386,000, and freight carried (1983), 617,700 short tons. The bridge across the Suchiate River between Mexico and Guatemala in 1942 linked the railways of North and Central America, though differences in gauge make it necessary to change trains at Ayutla.

Aviation. The government-owned airline, Aviateca, furnishes both domestic and international services; 6 other airlines handle international traffic.

Shipping. The chief ports on the Atlantic coast are Puerto Barrios and Santo Tomás de Castilla: on the Pacific coast, San José and Champerico. Total tonnage handled was, 1983, 6·17m. tons.

Post and Broadcasting. The Government own and operate the telegraph and telephone services; there were (1982) 97,670 telephone instruments. There are some 70 broadcasting stations. Radio receiving sets in use, 1976, numbered about 1m. There are 4 commercial TV stations, 1 government station and about 192,000 TV receivers.

Cinemas (1983). Cinemas numbered approximately 100.

Newspapers (1984). There are 8 daily newspapers.

JUSTICE, RELIGION, EDUCATION AND WELFARE

Justice. Justice is administered in a Supreme Court, 6 appeal courts and 28 courts of first instance. Supreme Court and appeal court judges are elected by Congress. Judges of first instance are appointed by the Supreme Court.

All holders of public office have to show on entering office, and again on leaving, a full account of their private property and income.

Religion. Roman Catholicism is the prevailing faith; but all other creeds have complete liberty of worship. Guatemala has an archbishopric.

Education. In 1980 there were 7,708 primary schools with 24,242 teachers and an attendance of 826,613 pupils; these figures include private schools. There are 753 secondary and other schools having 9,613 teachers and an attendance of 171,903 pupils; the autonomous University of San Carlos de Borromeo, founded in 1678, was reopened in 1910 with 7 faculties and schools and there are 4 new universities. Students at state university (1977) approximately 25,925. All education is in theory free, but owing to a grave shortage of state schools private schools flourish. The 1964 census showed that 63% of those 10 years of age and older were illiterate.

Social Welfare. A comprehensive system of social security was outlined in a law of 30 Oct. 1946. Medical personnel include about 1,250 doctors and 275 dentists for the whole republic. There are about 60 public hospitals and about 100 dispensaries.

DIPLOMATIC REPRESENTATIVES

Of Guatemala in the USA (2220 R St., NW, Washington, D.C., 20008)
Ambassador: Federico Fahsen.

Of the USA in Guatemala (7–01 Avenida de la Reforma, Zone 10, Guatemala City)
Ambassador: Alberto M. Piedra.

Of Guatemala to the United Nations
Ambassador: Arturo Fajardo Maldonado.

Guatemala broke off diplomatic relations with UK on 31 July 1963 and consular relations were broken on 7 Sept. 1981 but there is a British Interests Section of the Embassy of Switzerland. *First Secretary:* David T. Handley.

Books of Reference

The official gazette is called *Diario de Centro America.*

Banco de Guatemala, *Memoria annual, Estudio económico* and *Boletin Estadistico*
Bloomfield, L. M., *The British Honduras–Guatemala Dispute.* Toronto, 1953
Franklin, W. B., *Guatemala.* [Bibliography] Oxford and Santa Barbara, 1981
Glassman, P., *Guatemala Guide.* Dallas, 1977
Humphreys, R. A., *The Diplomatic History of British Honduras 1638–1901.* London, 1961
Immerman, R. H., *The CIA in Guatemala: The Foreign Policy of Intervention.* Univ. of Texas Press, 1982
Mendoza, J. L., *Britain and Her Treaties on Belize.* Guatemala, 1946
Morton, F., *Xeláhuh.* London, 1959
Plant, R., *Guatemala: Unnatural Disaster.* London, 1978
Schlesinger, S., and Kinzer, S., *Bitter Front: The Untold Story of the American Coup in Guatemala.* London and New York, 1982

National Library: Biblioteca Nacional, 5a Avenida y 8a Calle, Zona 1, Guatemala City.

GUINEA

Capital: Conakry
Population: 5·41m. (1983)
GNP per capita: US$300 (1981)

République populaire et révolutionnaire de Guinée

HISTORY. Guinea was proclaimed a French protectorate in 1888 and a colony in 1893. It became a constituent territory of French West Africa in 1904. The independent republic of Guinea was proclaimed on 2 Oct. 1958, after the territory of French Guinea had decided at the referendum of 28 Sept. to leave the French Community. Following the death of the first President, Ahmed Sekou Touré, on 27 March 1984 the armed forces staged a *coup* and dissolved the National Assembly.

AREA AND POPULATION. Guinea, a coastal state of West Africa, is bounded north-west by Guinea-Bissau and Senegal, north-east by Mali, south-east by the Ivory Coast, south by Liberia and Sierra Leone, and west by the Atlantic Ocean.

The area is 245,857 sq. km (94,926 sq. miles), and the population, census, 1972, was 5,143,284, including an estimated 1·5m. living abroad (estimate, 1983, 5,412,000.). The capital, Conakry, had 763,000 inhabitants in 1980; other large towns (1972) were Kankan (85,310), Kindia, (79,861), Labé (79,670), and N'Zérékoré (about 23,000).

The ethnic composition is Fulani (40·3%, predominant in Moyenne-Guinée), Malinké (or Mandingo, 25·8%, prominent in Haute-Guinée), Susu (11%, prominent in Guinée-Maritime), Kissi (6·5%) and Kpelle (4·8%) in Guinée Forestière, and Dialonka, Loma and others (11·6%).

CLIMATE. A tropical climate, with high rainfall near the coast and constant heat, but conditions are a little cooler on the plateau. The wet season on the coast lasts from May to Nov., but only to Oct. inland. Conakry. Jan. 80°F (26·7°C), July 77°F (25°C). Annual rainfall 172″ (4,293 mm).

CONSTITUTION AND GOVERNMENT. Following the coup of 3 April 1984, supreme power rests with a 25-member *Comité Militaire de Redressement National*, ruling through a Council of Ministers composed as follows in Dec. 1984:

President: Col. Lansana Conté (assumed office 5 April 1984).
Prime Minister: Col. Diarra Traoré.

Foreign Affairs: Capt. Fanciné Touré. *International Co-operation:* Capt. Fode Mono Camara. *Defence:* Capt. Lanciné Keita. *Interior and Security:* Herve Vincent. *Economic Affairs:* Richard Haba. *Finance:* Kémoko Keita. *State Control:* Maj. Sory Doumbiya. *Planning and Statistics:* Capt. Bahourou Condé. *Internal Trade:* Capt. Abou Camara. *Foreign Trade:* Capt. Mohamed Oumar Kebeh. *Public Works:* Capt. Youssouf Diallo. *Transport:* Maj. Abdoulrahmane Kaba. *Town Planning, Housing and Estates:* Capt. Kerfala Camara. *Mining and Geology:* Capt. Jean Traoré. *Industry:* Capt. Mohamed Laminé Sakho. *Energy:* Maj. Abraham Kabassan Keita. *Small and Medium-Scale Enterprises:* Capt. Mamadou Pathé Barry. *Agriculture:* Maj. Alhousség Fofana. *Fisheries and Livestock:* Capt. Alfa Oumar Diallo. *Higher Education:* Maj. Sidi Mohamed Keita. *Secondary Education:* Abou Camara. *Technical Education and Vocational Training:* Zaïnoul Sanoussi Abidiné. *Justice:* Maj. Lama Kolipé. *Posts and Telecommunication:* Capt. Ahmadou Kouyaté. *Labour and Public Services:* Capt. Mamadou Baldet. *Public Health:* Dr Mamadou Bah Kaba. *Social Affairs:* Dr Mariama Dielo Barry. *Islamic Affairs:* al-Hadj Thierno Ibrahima Bah al-Labé. *Information:* Capt. Mohamed Traoré. *Youth:* Capt. Mamady Bayo. *Secretaries of State:* Lieut. Mamadou Thiana Diallo *(Water Resources and Forestry)*, Sgt.-Maj. Joseph Gbago Zoumanigui *(Energy)*. *Governor of Banks and Insurance:* Capt. Kabiné Kaba. *Secretary-General of the Government:* Capt. Sekou Traoré. *Secretary-General to the Presidency:* Capt. Ahmadou Mangata.

Local Government: The administrative division comprises 33 regions, grouped into 4 'supra-regions' which correspond to the 4 major geographical and ethnic areas: Guinée-Maritime (Lower Guinea, headquarters at Kindia); Moyenne-Guinée (Fouta Djallon, head-quarters at Labé); Haute-Guinée (Upper Guinea, headquarters at Kankan) and Guinée-Forestière (Forest-Guinea, headquarters at N'Zérékoré).

National flag: Three vertical strips of red, gold, green.

Besides French, there are 8 official languages taught in schools: Fulani, Malinké, Susu, Kissi, Kpelle, Loma, Basari and Koniagi.

DEFENCE

Army. The Army of 8,500 men (1985), which comprises 1 armoured, 5 infantry, 1 commando and 1 engineer, 1 artillery and 1 special force battalions. Equipment includes 45 T-34 and 20 PT-76 tanks. There are also 3 paramilitary forces: People's Militia (7,000), Gendarmerie (1,000) and Republican Guard (1,000).

Navy. The Navy comprises an ocean minesweeper, 6 fast gunboats, 12 fast attack craft, 16 coastal patrol craft, and 4 small landing craft. There are bases at Conakry and Kakanda. Personnel in 1985 exceeded 600 officers and men.

Air Force. The Air Force, formed with Soviet assistance, is reported to be equipped with 6 MiG-17 jet-fighters and 2 MiG-15UTI trainers, 2 Il-18 turboprop transports, 4 An-14 and 4 Il-14 piston-engined transports and a Yak-40 jet aircraft for VIP duties, all Russian built, plus a few helicopters, piston-engined Yak-18 and L-29 jet trainers. Personnel about 800.

INTERNATIONAL RELATIONS

Membership. Guinea is a member of UN, OAU and is an ACP state of EEC.

ECONOMY

Planning. The Fourth Development Plan, 1981–85 envisaged expenditure of 38,000m. sylis.

Budget. The budget for 1979 balanced at 11,250m. sylis.

Currency. The monetary unit is the *syli*, divided into 100 *cauris*, introduced in 1972. The issue consists of notes of 100, 50, 25 and 10 *sylis*, and coins of 50 *cauris*, 5, 2 and 1 *sylis*. In March 1985, £1 = 27·56 *sylis*; US$1 = 26 *sylis*.

Banking. In 1980 the Central Bank was replaced by a National Currency Institute, through which a governor with ministerial rank controls all banking and insurance, state monopolies since Jan. 1962.

ENERGY AND NATURAL RESOURCES

Electricity. Production of electrical energy was 498m. kwh. in 1981. The development of 2 new dams (1981) on the Konkouré river will expand capacity, primarily for the aluminium industry.

Minerals. Bauxite is mined at Fria, Boké and elsewhere in Guinée-Maritime; output 12,833,000 tonnes in 1981. Reserves (estimate,1982) 8,000m. tonnes. Production of iron ore from the Nimba and Simandou mountains commenced in 1981, following exhaustion of the Kaloum peninsula deposits. Diamond mining was suspended in 1978 but resumed in 1981; output 37,000 carats.

Agriculture. There are experimental fruit gardens at Camayenne near Conakry, Kindia and Dalaba, 2 stations for rice selection (Kankan, Koba) and an experimental quinine station at Seredou. Coffee is grown in forest districts. Fouta Djallon contains cattle in abundance.

The chief crops (production, 1982, in 1,000 tonnes) are: Cassava, 620; rice, 400; plantains, 230; sugar-cane, 220; bananas, 110; groundnuts, 85; sweet potatoes, 75; maize, 87; palm-oil, 45; palm kernels, 35; pineapples, 18; coffee, 15; coconuts, 15.

Livestock (1983): Cattle, 1·9m.; sheep, 450,000; goats, 440,000; pigs, 44,000.

Forestry: There were 5,756 sq. km of classified forests in 1977. Round-wood production amounted to 3·62m. cu. metres in 1981.

Fisheries: Catch (1980) 18,500 tonnes, 90% in coastal waters.

COMMERCE. In 1979 imports totalled 5,637m. sylis; exports, 6,925m. sylis. Alumina forms about 30% and bauxite 58% of the exports.

Total trade between Guinea and the UK (British Department of Trade returns, in £1,000 sterling):

	1980	*1981*	*1982*	*1983*	*1984*
Imports to UK	10,777	844	1,956	668	1,171
Exports and re-exports from UK	26,596	7,117	6,840	7,190	6,469

COMMUNICATIONS

Roads. There are 28,400 km of roads and tracks, of which 520 km are bitumenized. In 1978 there were 9,948 cars and 9,992 commercial vehicles.

Railways. A railway connects Conakry with Kankan (662 km) and may be extended to Bamako in Mali. A line 134 km long linking bauxite deposits at Sangaredi with Port Kamsar was opened in 1973 and a third line links Conakry and Fria (144 km).

Aviation. There are airports at Conakry and Kankan; in 1978, 71,000 passengers disembarked and embarked.

Shipping. There are ports at Conakry (facilities expanded 1976–80) and for bauxite exports at Kamsar (opened 1973). There were (1983) 18 vessels of 6,944 GRT registered in Guinea.

Post and Broadcasting. The territory is connected by cable with France and Pernambuco; also with Freetown, Monrovia and other places. There is a wireless station at Conakry affording communication with all territories of West Africa. Telephones, 1972, numbered about 7,488. There were 123,000 radio receivers and 7,000 television receivers in 1983.

JUSTICE, RELIGION, EDUCATION AND WELFARE

Justice. There are *tribunaux du premier degré* at Conakry and Kankan, and a *juge de paix* at N'Zérékoré. The High Court, Court of Appeal and Superior Tribunal of Cassation are at Conakry.

Religion. In 1980, about 69% of the population was Moslem, 1% Christian and 30% followed tribal religions.

Education. In 1980–81, 257,547 pupils and 7,165 teachers in primary schools, 89,900 pupils and 3,520 teachers in secondary schools, 2,776 in technical schools and 8,437 in teacher-training colleges and (1979) 20,739 in higher education.

Health. In 1976 there were 314 hospitals and dispensaries with 7,650 beds; there were also 277 doctors, 21 dentists, 159 pharmacists, 394 midwives and 1,533 nursing personnel.

DIPLOMATIC REPRESENTATIVES

Of Guinea in Great Britain
Ambassador: (Vacant).

Of Great Britain in Guinea
Ambassador: P. L. O'Keeffe, CMG, CVO (resides in Dakar).

Of Guinea in the USA (2112 Leroy Pl., NW, Washington, D.C., 20008)
Ambassador: Thierno Habib Diallo.

Of the USA in Guinea (2nd Blvd. and 9th Ave., Conakry)
Ambassador: James D. Rosenthal.

Of Guinea to the United Nations
Ambassador: Alpha Ibrahima Diallo.

Books of Reference

Bulletin Statistique et Economique de la Guinée. Monthly. Conakry
Adamolekun, L., *Sékou Touré's Guinea.* London, 1976
Camara, S. S., *La Guinée sans la France.* Paris, 1976
Rivière, C., *Guinea: The Mobilization of a People.* Cornell Univ. Press, 1977
Taylor, F. W., *A Fulani-English Dictionary.* Oxford, 1932

GUINEA-BISSAU

Capital: Bissau
Population: 844,000 (1984)
GNP per capita: US$190 (1981)

HISTORY. Guinea-Bissau, formerly Portuguese Guinea, on the coast of Guinea, was discovered in 1446 by Nuno Tristão. It became a separate colony in 1879. It is bounded by the limits fixed by the convention of 12 May 1886 with France. In 1951 Guinea-Bissau became an overseas province of Portugal. The struggle against colonial rule began in 1963. Independence was declared on 24 Sept. 1973. In 1974 Portugal formally recognized the independence of Guinea-Bissau.

AREA AND POPULATION. Guinea-Bissau is bounded by Senegal in the north, the Atlantic ocean in the west and by Guinea in the east and south. It includes the adjacent archipelago of Bijagoz, with the island of Bolama. The capital and chief port is Bissau, population (census 1979), 109,486. Other ports are Bolama and Cacheu. Area is 36,125 sq. km (13,948 sq. miles); population (census, 1979), 767,739 (estimate, 1984) 844,000.

The regional populations at the 1979 Census were as follows:

Bissau City	109,214	Bolama-Bijagós	25,473	Gabú	104,227
Bafatá	116,032	Buba	35,532	Oio	135,114
Biombo	56,463	Cacheu	130,227	Tombali	55,099

The main ethnic groups were (1979) the Balante (27%), Fulani (23%), Malinké (12%), Mandjako (11%) and Pepel (10%). Portuguese remains the official language, but Crioulo is spoken throughout the country.

CLIMATE. The tropical climate has a wet season from June to Nov., when rains are abundant, but the hot, dry Harmattan wind blows from Dec. to May. Bissau. Jan. 76°F (24·4°C), July 80°F (26·7°C). Annual rainfall 78″ (1,950 mm).

CONSTITUTION AND GOVERNMENT. A new Constitution was promulgated on 16 May 1984. The Revolutionary Council, established following the 1980 *coup*, remains in being as the supreme political institution, but in April 1984 a new National People's Assembly was elected comprising 150 Representatives elected by and from the directly-elected regional councils. The sole political movement is the *Partido Africano da Independencia da Guiné e Cabo Verde* (PAIGC). The President is Head of State and Government, leading a Council of Ministers which in Dec. 1984 was composed as follows:

President, Minister of Defence and the Interior: Maj. João Bernardo Vieira.

First Vice-President, Minister of State for Justice and Local Authorities: Col. Paulo Alexandre Nunes Correia. *Second Vice-President, Minister of State for the Armed Forces:* Col. Iafai Camara. *Foreign Affairs:* Julio Semedo. *Presidency, Economic Affairs:* Dr Vasco Cabral. *Rural Development and Fisheries:* Carlos Correia. *Education, Culture and Sports:* Dr Fidelis Cabral d'Almada. *Social Affairs:* Maj. Manuel dos Santos. *National Security and Public Order:* Maj. José Pereira. *Natural Resources and Industry:* Filinto de Barros. *Finance:* Dr Vítor Freire Monteiro. *Health:* Adelino Nunes Correia. *Trade and Tourism:* Mario Cabral. *Economic Planning and International Co-operation:* Bartolomeu Simões Pereira: *Information and Telecommunications:* Musa Djassi. *Governor of Central Bank:* Pedro Godinho Gomes.

National flag: Horizontally yellow over green with red vertical strip in the hoist bearing a black star.

Local government. The administrative division is in 8 regions (each under an elected regional council), in turn subdivided into 37 sectors; and the city of Bissau, treated as a separate region.

DEFENCE

Army. The Army consisted in 1985 of 4 infantry battalions, 1 engineer unit and 1 tank squadron. Equipment includes 10 T-34 tanks. Personnel, 6,000 men.

Navy. The naval flotilla includes 6 fast attack craft, 11 coastal patrol craft, 4 utility landing craft, 2 river craft, 4 minor landing craft and 1 survey ship. Based at Bissau. Personnel in 1985 exceeded 250 officers and men.

Air Force. Formation of a small Air Force began in 1978 with the delivery of a French-built Cessna FTB-337 twin-engined counter-insurgency and general-purpose light transport. It has been followed by about 12 Czechoslovak-built L-39 jet trainers, an Mi-8 and 2 Alouette III helicopters, an An-26 twin-turboprop transport and 2 Dornier Do 27 utility aircraft.

INTERNATIONAL RELATIONS

Membership. Guinea-Bissau is a member of UN, OAU and is an ACP state of EEC.

ECONOMY

Budget. The revenue in 1981 was 1,137m. pesos; the expenditure, 1,944m. pesos.

Currency. The monetary unit is the *peso* divided into 100 *centavos*. In March 1985, £1 = 93·84 *pesos*; US$1 = 88·53 *pesos*.

Banking. The Banco Nacional da Guiné-Bissau, founded 1976, is the bank of issue and also the commercial bank. There are also state-owned savings institutions.

ENERGY AND NATURAL RESOURCES

Electricity. Production (1977) 24m. kwh.

Minerals. Mining is very little developed although bauxite (200m. tonnes) has been located in the Boé area. Exploration for oil is taking place but no finds have been reported.

Agriculture. Chief crops (production, 1981, in 1,000 tonnes) are: Groundnuts, 30; sugar-cane, 25; plantains, 25; coconuts, 25; rice, 23; rubber, 23; palm kernels, 10; millet, 6; palm-oil, 5; sorghum, 5; maize, 4; timber, hides, seeds and wax.

Livestock (1983): Cattle, 225,000; sheep, 65,000; goats, 145,000; pigs, 130,000; poultry (1982), 420,000.

Fishing. Total catch (1978) 2,000 tonnes. Fishing is the most important export industry.

Forestry. Production (1981) 526,000 cu. metres.

COMMERCE. Imports in 1980, 1,860m. pesos; exports, 382m. of which 27% went to Portugal and 25% to Spain. In 1980, fish formed 33% of exports, groundnuts, 24% and coconuts, 17%.

Total trade between Guinea-Bissau and UK (British Department of Trade returns, in £1,000 sterling):

	1981	*1982*	*1983*	*1984*
Imports to UK	–	–	94	–
Exports and re-exports from UK	595	431	477	499

COMMUNICATIONS

Roads. There were (1979) 3,570 km of roads.

Aviation. There is an international airport at Bissalanca (for Bissau).

Shipping. In 1974, 169 vessels entered the ports unloading 134,000 tonnes.

Post. In 1973 there were 2,723 telephones and (1983) 11,000 radio receivers.

Cinemas. There were 7 cinemas (1972) with a seating capacity of 3,000.

Newspapers (1984). There was one daily newspaper, with a circulation of 3,000.

JUSTICE, RELIGION, EDUCATION AND WELFARE

Justice. Following the 1980 *coup*, the judicial system has been subject to the authority of the Council of the Revolution.

Religion. In 1980 about 38% of the population were Moslem and about 10% Christian (mainly Roman Catholic).

Education. There were, in 1981, 75,143 pupils in primary schools with 3,351 teachers; 4,068 pupils in secondary schools with 387 teachers, 569 students in technical schools with 54 teachers and 557 students in teacher-training establishments with 62 teachers.

Health. In 1978 there were 10 hospitals with 910 beds and 88 doctors, 2 dentists, 2 pharmacists, 70 midwives and 292 nursing personnel.

DIPLOMATIC REPRESENTATIVES

Of Great Britain in Guinea-Bissau
Ambassador: P. L. O'Keeffe, CMG, CVO (resides in Dakar).

Of Guinea-Bissau in the USA
Ambassador: Inacio Semedo, Jr.

Of the USA in Guinea-Bissau (Ave. Domingos Ramos, Bissau)
Ambassador: Wesley W. Egan, Jr.

Of Guinea-Bissau to the United Nations
Ambassador: Dr Inacio Semedo, Jr.

Books of Reference

Relatório e Mapas do Movimento Comercial e Maritimo da Guiné. Bolama, Annual
Cabral, A., *Revolution in Guinea.* London, 1969.—*Return to the Source.* New York, 1973
Davidson, B., *Growing from the Grass Roots.* London, 1974
Gjerstad, O., and Sarrazin, C., *Sowing the First Harvest: National Reconstruction in Guinea-Bissau.* Oakland, 1978
Rudebeck, L., *Guinea-Bissau: A Study of Political Mobilization.* Uppsala, 1974

GUYANA

Capital: Georgetown
Population: 965,000 (1984)
GNP per capita: US$720 (1981)

HISTORY. The territory, including the counties of Demerara, Essequibo and Berbice, named from the 3 rivers, was first partially settled by the Dutch West Indian Company about 1620. The Dutch retained their hold until 1796, when it was captured by the English. It was finally ceded to Great Britain in 1814 and named British Guiana. On 26 May 1966 British Guiana became an independent member of the Commonwealth under the name of Guyana and the world's first Co-operative Republic on 23 Feb. 1970.

AREA AND POPULATION. Guyana is situated on the north-east coast of South America on the Atlantic ocean, with Suriname on the east, Venezuela on the west and Brazil on the south and west. Area, 83,000 sq. miles (214,969 sq. km). Estimated population (1983), 900,000. Births (1972), 25,065; deaths (1974), 3,418. In 1976, the population comprised 362,700 Indians, 218,400 Africans, 2,100 Europeans, 3,400 Chinese, 800 others. The Greater Georgetown area had in 1983 an estimated population of 188,000.

Venezuela demanded the return of the Essequibo region in 1963. It was finally agreed in March 1983 that the UN Secretary-General should mediate. There was also an unresolved claim (1984) by Suriname for the return of an area between the New river and the Courantyne river.

CLIMATE. A tropical climate, with rainy seasons from April to July and Nov. to Jan. Humidity is high all the year but temperatures are moderated by sea-breezes. Rainfall increases from 90″ (2,280 mm) on the coast to 140″ (3,560 mm) in the forest zone. Georgetown. Jan. 79°F (26·1°C), July 81°F (27·2°C). Annual rainfall 87″ (2,175 mm).

CONSTITUTION AND GOVERNMENT. A new Constitution was promulgated in Oct. 1980. The National Assembly consists of 65 elected members. Elections are held under the single-list system of proportional representation, with the whole of the country forming one electoral area and each voter casting his vote for a party list of candidates. The legislature is elected for 5 years unless earlier dissolved.

The elections held on 15 Dec. 1980 gave the People's National Congress 41 seats, the People's Progressive Party 10 seats, the Liberator Party 2 seats. The PNC with an overall majority formed a 25-member cabinet.

The Cabinet was in Nov. 1984 composed as follows:

President: L. F. S. Burnham.

Prime Minister and First Vice-President: H. Desmond Hoyle.

Vice-President and Social Infrastructure: H. Green. *Vice-President, Party and State Matters:* B. Ramsaroop. *Vice-President and Attorney-General:* Dr M. Shahabuddeen. *Education, Social Development and Culture:* R. Chandisingh. *National Mobilisation:* R. H. O. Corbin. *Foreign Affairs:* R. E. Jackson. *Home Affairs:* J. R. Thomas. *Energy and Mines:* H. Rashid. *Finance and Economic Planning:* C. B. Greenidge. *Information and Public Service:* Y. V. Harewood-Benn. *Manpower and Co-operatives:* K. W. E. Denny. *Office of the Prime Minister:* U. E. Johnson. *Agriculture:* Sallahuddin. *Youth and Sport:* R. C. Fredericks. *Transport:* S. Prashad. *Health and Public Welfare:* Dr R. A. VanWest Charles.

There are 2 Ministers of State.

National flag: Green with a yellow triangle based on the hoist, edged in white, charged with a red triangle edged in black.

DEFENCE

Army. The Guyana Army has a strength of 7,000 (which includes all armed services), including a women's army corps. It comprises 3 infantry battalions and 1 artillery battery.

Air Force. The Air Command is equipped with light aircraft and helicopters, including 2 Skyvan and 1 Super King Air 200 twin-turboprop transports, 6 Islander twin-engined STOL transports, a Cessna U206F utility lightplane, and 4 Bell 206/212 light helicopters.

INTERNATIONAL RELATIONS

Membership. Guyana is a member of UN, the Commonwealth, Caricom and is an ACP state of EEC.

ECONOMY

Budget. Revenue and expenditure for calendar years (in G$1,000):

	1976 [1]	*1977*	*1978*	*1979*	*1980*	*1981*
Revenue	500,942	442,475	539,591	693,921	803,460	1,009,936
Expenditure	746,329	567,322	632,749	868,664	1,049,836	1,176,678

[1] Revised estimates.

Currency. The Bank of Guyana, established in 1965, issued Guyana dollar notes of $1, 5, 10 and 20 and coins of 1-, 5-, 10-, 25- and 50-cent pieces. In March 1985: £1 = 4·55 G$; US$1 = 4·12 G$.

Banking. Barclays Bank International and the Royal Bank of Canada maintain branches in Berbice, Demerara and Essequibo while the Bank of Baroda (India) has branches in Demerara and Berbice. The Chase Manhattan Bank (USA) and the Bank of Nova Scotia each have a branch in Georgetown. The Guyana National Co-operative Bank opened in Feb. 1970 with headquarters in Georgetown and 12 branches throughout the country. In 1973 the Guyana Agricultural and Industrial Development Bank (Gaibank) and the Guyana Co-operative Mortgage Finance Bank were established.

NATURAL RESOURCES

Minerals. Placer gold mining commenced in 1884, and was followed by diamond mining in 1887. From 1884 to 1973 the output of gold was 431,413 bullion oz. (11,000 oz. in 1980). From 1901 to 1973 the production of diamonds was 4,008,211 metric carats (10,200 in 1980). There are large deposits of bauxite; 2,717,000 tons, 2,111,000 tons of alumina and 318,000 tonnes of alumina hydrate were produced in 1980. Full-scale production of manganese began in 1960 and other minerals include uranium, oil, copper and molybdenum.

Agriculture. Production, 1982: Sugar-cane, 292,000 tonnes; rice, 182,000 tonnes. Other important products are coconuts, ground provisions and citrus fruit. Other tropical fruits and vegetables are grown mostly in scattered plantings; they include mangoes, papaws, avocado pears, melons, bananas and gooseberries. Other important crops are tomatoes, cabbages, black-eye peas, peanuts, carrots, onions, turmeric, ginger, pineapples, red kidney beans, soybeans, eschallot and tobacco. Large areas of unimproved land in the coastal region, which vary in width up to about 30 miles from the sea, are still available for agricultural and cattle-grazing projects.

Livestock estimate (1983): Cattle, 310,000; pigs, 142,000; sheep, 117,000; goats, 75,000; poultry, 14m.

Forestry. Guyana can be divided roughly into 3 regions: (1) A low coastal region varying in width up to about 30 miles and constituting the agricultural area; (2) an intermediate area about 100 miles wide, of slightly higher undulating land containing the chief mineral and forest resources of the country; and (3) a hinterland of several mountain ranges and extensive savannahs. 19,844,170 hectares of the land area is forested out of 21,497,000 hectares.

COMMERCE. Imports and exports (in G$) for calendar years:

	1978	*1979*	*1980*	*1981*	*1982*
Imports	711,056,000	811,000,000	1,009,664,425	1,236,488,611	840,442,362
Exports	739,589,440	732,900,000	992,608,557	974,327,562	775,544,161

Chief imports (1981): Wheat flour, 555,000 kg, $999,000; unmilled wheat, 42,569,000 kg, $30,311,000; milk, 4,748,000 gallons, $31,617,000; textile fabrics, 18,195,000 sq. metres, $25,221,000.

Chief domestic exports (1981): Sugar, 267,000 tonnes, $327·81m.; rice, 78,000 tonnes, $110m.; bauxite, dried, 1,011,000 tonnes, $78,123,000; bauxite, calcined, 496,000 tonnes, $259,464,000; alumina and alumina hydrate, 152,000 tonnes, $91,915,000; rum, 3,204,000 proof gallons, $24,046,000; timber, 36,000 cu. metres, $15,582,000; molasses, 85,344,000 kg, $12,902,000; shrimps, 477 kg, $7,849,000.

Imports (exclusive of transhipments), 1981, from CARICOM Territories, 35%; from USA, 25%; from UK, 16%; from Canada, 4%; exports (exclusive of transhipments) to UK, 26%; to CARICOM Territories, 17%; to Canada, 5%.

Total trade between Guyana and UK (British Department of Trade returns, in £1,000 sterling):

	1980	*1981*	*1982*	*1983*	*1984*
Imports to UK	47,143	50,841	50,495	42,810	57,884
Exports and re-exports from UK	30,191	28,969	13,145	13,585	14,845

COMMUNICATIONS

Roads. Roads and vehicular trails in the national, provincial and urban systems amount to 8,870 km. Motor vehicles, as of 31 Dec. 1976, totalled 64,272, including 26,599 passenger cars (1980, 28,400), 6,979 lorries and vans, 9,072 tractors and trailers, and 19,109 motor cycles. The main road on the Atlantic Coast, some 290 km (180 miles) long extends from Charity on the Pomeroon River to Crabwood Creek on the Corentyne, there are two unbridged gaps made by the Berbice and Essequibo Rivers, and the banks of the Demerara River are linked by a 1,853 metre (6,074 ft) floating bridge.

Railways. There is a government-owned railway in the North West District, while the Guyana Mining Enterprise operates a standard gauge railway of 133 km from Linden on the Demerara River to Ituni and Coomacka.

Aviation. Guyana Airways Corporation operates scheduled services within the state and also to Trinidad, Barbados, Paramaribo, New York, Miami and Brazil. In 1982, Guyana Airways Corporation carried 108,402 passengers and 1·6m. kg of freight on its international service and 46,373 passengers and 1·5m. kg freight locally. Other services in operation: British Airways 4 times weekly to the Caribbean, Europe and North America: PANAM 3 times weekly to North, Central and South America: Air France, to and from Guadeloupe, Paramaribo and Cayenne 4 times a week; British West Indian Airways, Ltd, to and from Trinidad 3 times a week, providing direct connexion with New York and London; Cubana Airlines once weekly; Suriname Airways. The International Airport at Timehri serves Arrow Air Airlines, BWIA, Cubana Airways, and Suriname Airways.

Shipping. In 1975, 1,273 vessels of 2,823,912 NRT entered and 1,225 of 2,266,220 NRT cleared the port of Georgetown. There are 217 nautical miles of river navigation. There are ferry services across the mouths of the Demerara, Berbice and Essequibo rivers, the last providing a link between the islands of Leguan and Wakenaam and the mainland at Adventure, and a number of coastal and river-boat services carrying both passengers and cargo. A number of launch services are operated in the more remote areas by private concerns.

Georgetown harbour, about ½ mile wide and 2½ miles long, has a minimum depth of 24 ft. New Amsterdam harbour is situated at the mouth of the Berbice

River; there are wharves for coastal vessels only. Bauxite is loaded on ocean-going freighters at Mackenzie, 67 miles up the Demerara River, and at Everton on the Berbice River, about 10 miles from the mouth of the waterway. The Essequibo River has several timber-loading berths ranging from 20 to 40 ft. Springlands on the Corentyne River is the point of entry and departure of passengers travelling by launch services to and from Suriname. In 1984 the merchant marine comprised 84 vessels of 20,248 GRT.

Post and Broadcasting. The inland public telegraph and radio communication services are operated and maintained by the Telecommunication Corporation, established on 1 March 1967. On 31 Dec. 1976 there were 57 post offices and 94 agencies (including travelling post offices and agencies).

The telephone exchanges had at the end of 1979 a total of 17,464 direct exchange lines with (1982), 28,468 telephone instruments. The number of route miles in the coastal and inland areas was 2,982 km. 39 land-line stations were maintained at post offices in the coastal area, and 8 telegraph stations in the interior provide communication with the coastal area through a central telegraph office in Georgetown.

The Guyana Broadcasting Corporation, which came into operation on 1 July 1980, has 2 channels.

Cinemas (1981). There are 52 cinemas.

Newspapers (1984). There is 1 daily newspaper with a circulation of 60,000 and 4 weekly papers with a combined circulation of about 100,000.

JUSTICE, EDUCATION AND WELFARE

Justice. The law, both civil and criminal, is based on the common and statute law of England, save that the principles of the Roman–Dutch law have been retained in respect of the registration, conveyance and mortgaging of land.

The Supreme Court of Judicature consists of a Court of Appeal and a High Court.

Education. In Sept. 1976 the Government assumed total responsibility for education from nursery school to university. Private education was abolished. In Sept. 1983, the total number of schools was 879: Nursery, 368; primary, 423; secondary and community high, 30; general secondary, 58.

There are now 5 technical and vocational schools and 2 schools for the teaching of home economics and domestic crafts. Training in co-operatives is provided by the Kuru-Kuru Co-operative College and agriculture by the Guyana School of Agriculture and the Burnham Agricultural Institute. Art training is provided by the Burrowes School of Art. The training of primary and secondary school teachers is undertaken by 3 institutions. Higher education is also provided by the University of Guyana which was established in 1963 with faculties of natural science, social science, art, technology and education as well as first year students in law. There were 2,004 students in July 1983. The total number of pupils in all schools was 233,723 in 1983.

Health. In 1981 there were 29 hospitals, 149 health centres and stations, 4 dispensaries and 11 medical outposts. There were (1982) 270 doctors and 24 dentists.

DIPLOMATIC REPRESENTATIVES

Of Guyana in Great Britain (3 Palace Court, London, W2 4LP)
High Commissioner: Cedric L. Joseph (accredited 17 Feb. 1982).

Of Great Britain in Guyana (44 Main St., Georgetown)
High Commissioner: John Massingham.

Of Guyana in the USA (2490 Tracy Place, NW, Washington, D.C., 20008)
Ambassador: Dr Cedric Hilburn Grant.

Of the USA in Guyana (31 Main St., Georgetown)
Ambassador: (Vacant).

Of Guyana to the United Nations
Ambassador: Noel G. Sinclair.

Books of Reference

Braveboy-Wagner, J. A., *The Venezuela-Guyana Border Dispute: Britain's Colonial Legacy in Latin America.* London, 1984
Daly, P. H., *From Revolution to Republic.* Georgetown, 1970
Daly, Vere T., *A Short History of the Guyanese People.* Rev. ed. London, 1975
Hope, K. R., *Development Policy in Guyana: Planning, Finance and Administration.* London, 1979
Spinner, T. J., *A Political and Social History of Guyana, 1945–83.* Epping, 1985

HAITI

République d'Haiti

Capital: Port-au-Prince
Population: 5·2m. (1984)
GNP per capita: US$300 (1981)

HISTORY. Haiti occupies the western third of the large island of Hispaniola which was discovered by Christopher Columbus in 1492. The Spanish colony was ceded to France in 1697 and became her most prosperous colony. After the extirpation of the Indians by the Spaniards (by 1533) large numbers of African slaves were imported whose descendants now populate the country. The slaves obtained their liberation following the French Revolution, but subsequently Napoleon sent his brother-in-law, Gen. Leclerc, to restore French authority and re-impose slavery. Toussaint Louverture, the leader of the slaves who had been appointed a French general and governor, was kidnapped and sent to France, where he died in gaol. However, the reckless courage of the Negro troops and the ravages of yellow fever forced the French to evacuate the island and surrender to the blockading British squadron.

The country declared its independence on 1 Jan. 1804, and its successful leader, Gen. Jean-Jacques Dessalines, proclaimed himself Emperor of the newly-named Haiti. After the assassination of Dessalines (1806) a separate régime was set up in the north under Henri Christophe, a Negro general who in 1811 had himself proclaimed King Henry. In the south and west a republic was constituted, with the mulatto Alexander Pétion as its first President. Pétion died in 1818 and was succeeded by Jean-Pierre Boyer, under whom the country became re-united after Henry had committed suicide in 1820. From 1822 to 1844 Haiti and the eastern part of the island (later the Dominican Republic) were united. After one more monarchical interlude, under the Emperor Faustin (1847–59), Haiti has been a republic. From 1915 to 1934 Haiti was under United States occupation.

Following a military *coup* in 1950, and subsequent uprisings, Dr François Duvalier was elected President on 22 Oct. 1957 and subsequently became President for Life in 1964. He died on 21 April 1971 and was succeeded as president for life by his son, Jean-Claude Duvalier.

AREA AND POPULATION. The area is 27,750 sq. km (10,700 sq. miles), of which about three-quarters is mountainous. The population at the census in 1982 was 5,032,000. Estimate (1984) 5,198,000.

The areas and populations of the 5 *départements* are as follows:

Département	*Sq km*	*1977*	*Chief town*	*1975*
Nord-Ouest	2,750	247,326	Port-de Paix	21,733
Nord	4,100	747,360	Cap Haïtien	54,691
Artibonite	6,800	748,357	Gonaïves	36,736
Ouest	7,900	1,983,826	Port-au-Prince	458,675
Sud	6,200	1,041,232	Les Cayes	27,222
Totals	27,750	4,768,101		

The Île de la Gonave, some 40 miles long, lies in the gulf of the same name. Among other islands is La Tortue, off the north peninsula. The majority of the population are Negroes, with an important minority of mulattoes and only about 5,000 white residents, almost all foreign.

Haiti is the only French speaking republic in the Americas. The standard French of government, parliament and the press is spoken by the small literate minority, but the great majority of the people habitually speak the dialect known as Créole.

CLIMATE. A tropical maritime climate with a small range of temperature. The wet season extends from May to Sept. Port-au-Prince. Jan. 77°F (25°C), July 84°F (28·9°C). Annual rainfall 53″ (1,321 mm).

CONSTITUTION AND GOVERNMENT. The 1983 Constitution, provides for an Executive President who is elected for life and may nominate his successor. He nominates a Cabinet to assist him and, in cases of national emergency, may dismiss both the Cabinet and the National Assembly and govern by decree.

The unicameral National Assembly comprises 59 deputies elected for 6-year terms (renewable) by universal suffrage at age 18. Of the deputies elected on 12 Feb. 1984, all but one belonged to the Parti de l'Unité Nationale of President Duvalier. From 11 May 1984, all other political activity was banned.

The Cabinet in Oct. 1984 was composed as follows:

President: Jean-Claude Duvalier.

Ministers of State: Dr Roger Lafontant *(Interior and Defence),* Théodore Achille *(Labour and Social Affairs),* Jean-Marie Chanoine *(Presidency, Information and Public Relations),* Franz Merceron *(National Economy, Finance and Industry),* Fritz Benjamin *(Public Works, Transport and Communications).*

Foreign Affairs and Worship: Jean-Robert Estimé. *Agriculture, Natural Resources and Rural Development:* Luckner Saint-Dic. *Public Health and Population:* Ary Bordes. *Commerce:* Odonel Fenestor. *Justice:* Casimir Rodriguez. *Planning:* Yves Blanchard. *Mines and Energy Resources:* Claude Mompoint. *Education:* Franck Saint-Victor. *Youth and Sports:* Arnold Blain. *Trade:* Stanley Théard.

National flag: Vertically black and red, with a small white panel in the centre bearing the national arms.

National anthem: 'La Dessalinienne': Pour le pays, pour les ancêtres (words by J. Lhérisson; tune by N. Geffrard, 1903).

DEFENCE. The Haitian Defence Force (*Forces Armées d'Haiti*) totalling about 7,500 men, is divided into Army, Navy, and Air Force. The President is Commander-in-Chief and appoints the officers.

Army. Total strength, about 7,000, organized into 9 Military Departments and the 'Leopards'. Three of the Departments are in Port-au-Prince and consist of the Presidential Guard (4 Companies); the Dessalines Barracks (7 Companies including the Dessalines Battalion and Headquarters troops); and the Port-au-Prince Police (6 Companies in blue uniforms). The other 6 Military Departments are located outside Port-au-Prince; their troops (21 Companies) operate as District Police. The Fire Brigade and the Prison Guard Company are also part of the Armed Forces. Only the Presidential Guard, the Dessalines Battalion and the Leopards (2 companies of 'Commandos' or Special Forces) with a third company of about 200 recruits, now in training, have any potential for tactical military operations. They are armed mainly with light infantry weapons but have a few elderly pieces of light artillery, 9 light tanks and 6 V-150 commando vehicles.

Navy. The Navy/coastguard of 40 officers and 260 men has 1 *ex*-US armed tug, and 14 coastal patrol boats. The base is at Port-au-Prince.

Air Force. Personnel strength is about 200, with about 28 aircraft of some 12 varieties. They include 8 Summit/Cessna O2-337 Sentry twin piston-engined counter-insurgency aircraft, 3 DC-3s, 5 light transports, 5 training/liaison aircraft, and 7 Hughes and Sikorsky helicopters.

Militia. There is in addition a volunteer civilian force, the *Volontaires de la Sécurité Nationale*, total strength is now estimated at about 14,900, about half of whom have access to antiquated rifles. This force, formerly of some importance as Dr François Duvalier's 'private army' of tough, devoted followers (sometimes called Tontons Macoute or Bogeymen) is much less prominent since his death, having been reduced in strength and reorganized under Defence Force Headquarters on lines roughly parallel to the regional Military Departments.

INTERNATIONAL RELATIONS

Membership. Haiti is a member of UN and OAS.

ECONOMY

Budget. Revenue (fiscal year ending 30 Sept.) in US$1m. (5 gourdes = US$1), 1979–80, 775m.; expenditure, 1,270m.

Currency. The unit of currency is the *gourde* and its value fixed at 5 *gourdes* = US$1. In March 1985, £1 = 5·34 *gourdes.* There are copper–nickel coins for 50, 20, 10 and 5 *centimes* and copper–zinc–nickel coins of 10 and 5 centimes.

Banking. The Banque Nationale de la République d'Haiti, owned by the State, was established 21 Oct. 1910 with a capital of US$5m., and has a monopoly of the note issue. US dollars may be included in the minimum required reserves. The Royal Bank of Canada, the Citibank, the Bank of Nova Scotia, the Bank of Boston, the Banque de l'Union Haitienne (mainly local capital with participation from American, Canadian and Dominican Republic Banks), Banque Nationale de Paris and First National Bank of Chicago all have branches in Port-au-Prince.

Weights and Measures. The metric system is officially accepted.

ENERGY AND NATURAL RESOURCES

Electricity. Production (1980) 315m. kwh.

Minerals. A US company is engaged in mining bauxite (466,000 tonnes in 1980). Copper exists but is at present uneconomic to exploit. Haiti may possess undeveloped mineral resources of oil, gold, silver, antimony, sulphur, coal and lignite, nickel, gypsum and porphyry.

Agriculture. Only one-third of the country is arable and most people own the tiny plots they farm; the resulting pressure of population is the main cause of rural poverty. Number of farms is estimated at over 500,000.

The occupations of Haiti are nine-tenths agricultural, carried on in 7 large plains, from 200,000 to 25,000 acres, and in 15 smaller plains down to 2,000 acres. Irrigation is used in some areas. Haiti's most important product is coffee of good quality, classified as 'mild', and grown by peasants. Production in 1981 totalled about 33,000 tonnes. Second most important crop is sugar. Sisal is grown extensively. Much of the fibre is exported as or for cordage. New types of cotton are being tried with success. New varieties of rice should significantly boost future production, especially in the Artibonite Valley. Output of main crops in 1981 (in 1,000 tonnes) was: Sugar, 3,000; mangoes, 330; plantains; 300; sweet potatoes, 270; cassava, 255; bananas, 210; maize, 180; sorghum, 110; rice, 90; sisal, 10; cotton, 5; cocoa, 3.

Rum and other spirits are distilled. Essential oils from vetiver, neroli and amyris are important. Cattle and horse breeding are encouraged.

Livestock (1983); Cattle, 1·3m.; sheep, 92,000; pigs, 800,000; goats, 1·1m.; horses, 425,000; poultry, 5m.

Fisheries. Production (1980) 4,000 tonnes.

INDUSTRY AND TRADE

Industry. Light manufacturing industries assembling or finishing goods for re-export constitute the fastest growing sector. There are 2 textile mills producing cheap denim with a total of 550 looms and 14,000 spindles. Soap factories produce laundry soap, toilet soap and detergent. A cement factory located near the capital produced 243,000 tonnes in 1980. A steel plant making rods, beams and angles was opened in 1974. There are also a pharmaceutical plant, a tannery, a plastics plant, 2 paint works, 2 shoe factories, a large factory producing enamel cookingware, 2 pasta-making factories, a tomato cannery and a flour-mill, all located in or near Port-au-Prince.

Labour. Trade unions were recognized in Feb. 1946. Strong government influence is exercised over the insignificant portion of the labour force that is unionized and organized labour has virtually no strength in Haiti.

Commerce. In 1982 exports were US$150m. and imports, US$330m.

The leading imports are foodstuffs, textiles, machinery, mineral oils, raw materials for transformation industries and vehicles.

Total trade between Haiti and UK (British Department of Trade returns, in £1,000 sterling):

	1980	*1981*	*1982*	*1983*	*1984*
Imports to UK	915	1,439	2,615	1,646	1,402
Exports and re-exports from UK	2,818	2,541	3,704	4,171	3,736

Tourism. In 1978, 112,000 tourists visited Haiti.

COMMUNICATIONS

Roads. Total length of roads is some 4,000 km, little of which is practicable in ordinary motors in the rainy season. There were (1980) about 35,000 vehicles in Haiti.

Railways. The only railway is owned by the Haitian American Sugar Company.

Aviation. An airport capable of handling jets was opened at Port-au-Prince in 1965. US and French carriers provide daily direct services to New York, Miami, Jamaica, Puerto Rico and the French Antilles. There are also services to the Dominican Republic and the Netherlands Antilles. A Haitian company provides a cargo service to the US and Puerto Rico. Air services connecting Port-au-Prince with other Haitian towns are operated by Haiti Air Inter.

Shipping. US, French, Federal Republic of Germany, Dutch, British, Canadian and Japanese lines connect Haiti with the US, Latin America (except Cuba), Canada, Jamaica, Europe and the Far East.

Post and Broadcasting. Most principal towns are connected by the government telegraph system, telephones and wireless.

The telephone company, of which the Haitian Government is now the majority stockholder, is in process of being modernized. Telephone subscribers totalled 22,000 in 1980.

In 1982 there were 105,000 radio and 65,000 television receivers.

Cinemas (1980). There were 15 cinemas in Port-au-Prince.

Newspapers (1984). There were 6 daily newspapers in Port-au-Prince, also a monthly in English and 1 weekly newspaper in Cap Haitien.

JUSTICE, RELIGION, EDUCATION AND WELFARE

Justice. Judges, both of the lower courts and the court of appeal, are appointed by the President. The legal system is basically French. The divorce law has recently been amended to permit parties to obtain 'quick and painless' divorces at a moderate cost, in the hope of attracting the US trade, now that the Mexican 'divorce mills' have closed down. This has developed a useful flow of dollar revenue.

Police. The Police number about 750 in Port-au-Prince and are part of the armed forces.

Religion. Since the Concordat of 1860, the official religion is Roman Catholicism, under an archbishop with 5 suffragan bishops. There are still quite a number of foreigners, French and French Canadians mainly, among the clergy but the first Haitian archbishop took office in 1966. The Episcopal Church now has its first Haitian bishop who was consecrated in 1971. Other Christian churches number perhaps 10% of the population. The folk religion is Voodoo.

Education. Education is divided into primary (first 6 years), secondary (the next 7 years) and finally superior or university. The school system is modelled on that of France. The law calls for free and compulsory elementary education in the French language.

For the 1973–74 academic year, urban primary schools numbered 360 (221 lay and 139 religious) attended by 127,330 pupils with 3,532 teachers. There were, for the same period, at the secondary level, 21 public secondary *lycées* with 15,760 students (4,163 of them girls), 563 teachers (39 of them women). In the private secondary sector, 129 schools were reported with 35,414 students (16,398 girls), 1,172 teachers (107 women). Professional education is divided into 3 categories: (*a*) 41 pre-vocational schools; (*b*) 18 vocational schools which prepare trained workers, and (*c*) 5 vocational schools preparing technicians. There are also 10 licensed private commercial schools. The total number of students was 13,000, 2,000 of whom were in the private sector.

Higher education is offered at the University of Haiti.

Health. There were, in 1972, 332 doctors and 104 dentists in practice, 44 hospitals, and 196 health centres and rural clinics. The hospitals had 3,329 beds, of which 776 were in private and charitable establishments.

DIPLOMATIC REPRESENTATIVES

Of Haiti in Great Britain (33 Abbots Hse., St Mary Abbots Terr., London, W14)
Ambassador: Théo Duval (accredited 6 Dec. 1984).

Of Great Britain in Haiti
Ambassador: H. M. S. Reid, CMG (resides in Kingston).

Of Haiti in the USA (2311 Massachusetts Ave., NW, Washington, D.C., 20008)
Ambassador: Fritz N. Cineas.

Of the USA in Haiti (Harry Truman Blvd., Port-au-Prince)
Ambassador: Clayton E. McManaway, Jr.

Of Haiti to the United Nations
Ambassador: Serge Elie Charles.

Books of Reference

The official gazette is *Le Moniteur*.

Revue Agricole d'Haïti. From 1946. Quarterly
Bellegarde, D., *Histoire du Peuple Haïtien.* Port-au-Prince, 1953
Chambers, F. J., *Haiti.* [Bibliography] Oxford and Santa Barbara, 1983
Laguerre, M. S., *The Complete Haitiana.* [Bibliography] London and New York, 1982
Lundahl, M., *The Haitian Economy: Man, Land and Markets.* London, 1983
Nicholls, D., *From Dessalines to Duvalier: Race, Colour and National Independence in Haiti.* CUP, 1979

National Library: Bibliothèque Nationale, Rue du Centre, Port-au-Prince.

HONDURAS

República de Honduras

Capital: Tegucigalpa
Population: 4·24m. (1984)
GNP per capita: US$661 (1982)

HISTORY. On 5 Nov. 1838 Honduras declared itself an independent sovereign state, free from the Federation of Central America, of which it had formed a part.

AREA AND POPULATION. Honduras is bounded north by the Caribbean, east and south-east by Nicaragua, west by Guatemala, south-west by El Salvador and south by the Pacific ocean. Area is 112,088 sq. km (43,277 sq. miles), with a population, census (1974) of 2,656,948. Estimate (1983) 4,092,175.

The chief cities (populations, 1982) were Tegucigalpa, the capital (533,626), San Pedro Sula (397,937), El Progreso (105,372), Choluteca (88,988), Danli (77,005) and the Atlantic coast ports of La Ceiba (68,911), Puerto Cortés (62,250) and Tela (61,188); other towns include Olanchito (53,568), Juticalpa (49,817) and Comayagua (28,121 in 1971).

The areas and populations of the 18 departments and federal district were as follows:

Department	*Sq. km*	*1983*	*Department*	*Sq. km*	*1983*
Atlántida	4,251	242,235	Intibucá	3,072	111,412
Choluteca	4,211	289,637	Islas de la Bahía	261	18,744
Colón	8,875	128,370	La Paz	2,331	86,627
Comayagua	5,196	211,465	Lempira	4,290	174,916
Copán	3,203	217,258	Ocotepeque	1,680	64,151
Cortés	3,954	624,090	Olancho	24,350	228,122
El Paraíso	7,218	206,601	Santa Bárbara	5,115	286,854
Federal District	1,648	532,519	Valle	1,565	125,640
Francisco Morazán	6,298	203,753	Yoro	7,939	304,310
Gracias a Dios	16,630	35,471			

Aboriginal tribes number over 35,000, principally Miskito, Payas and Xicaques Indians and Sambos (the latter a mixture of Miskito and Negro), each speaking a different dialect. The Spanish-speaking inhabitants are chiefly *mestizos*, Indians with an admixture of Spanish blood. Gracias a Dios is still largely unexplored and is inhabited by pure native races who speak little or no Spanish.

In 1980 the birth rate was 49·3 per 1,000; death rate, 12·4 per 1,000 and infant mortality rate, 11·8 per 1,000 live births.

CLIMATE. The climate is tropical, with a small annual range of temperature but with high rainfall. Upland areas have two wet seasons, from May to July and in Sept. and Oct. The Caribbean Coast has most rain in Dec. and Jan. and temperatures are generally higher than inland. Tegucigalpa. Jan. 66°F (19°C), July 74°F (23·3°C). Annual rainfall 64″ (1,621 mm).

CONSTITUTION AND GOVERNMENT. Following Presidential and Congressional elections held on 29 Nov. 1981, a new Constitution was promulgated on 20 Jan. 1982. The President is directly elected for a 4-year term.

President: Dr Roberto Suazo Córdova (sworn in 27 Jan. 1982).

Cabinet of ministers to assist him, which was composed as follows in Aug. 1984:

Foreign Affairs: Edgardo Paz Barniça. *Interior and Justice:* Abogado Oscar Mejía Arellano. *Defence:* Col. Amilcar Castillo Suazo. *Education:* (Vacant). *Finance:* Manuel Fontecha. *Economy:* Miguel Orellana Maldonado. *Economic Planning:* Edgardo Sevilla Idiáquez. *Presidency:* Ubudore Arriaga. *Labour and Social Security:* Amado Nuñez. *Health:* Dr Rubén García Martínez. *Culture and*

Tourism: Victor Cáceres Lara. *Communications, Public Works and Transport:* Carlos Handal. *Natural Resources:* Miguel Angel Bonilla. *Director of National Agrarian Institute:* Ubudoro Arriaga Iraheto.

The legislature is a 82-member Congress of Deputies, composed following the elections of 29 Nov. 1981 of 44 deputies of the *Partido Liberal,* 34 of the *Partido Nacional,* 3 of the *Partido de Innovación y Unidad,* and 1 of the *Partido Demócrata Cristiano.*

National flag: Three horizontal stripes of blue, white, blue, with 5 blue stars in the centre.

National anthem: Tu bandera es un lampo de cielo (words by A. C. Coello; tune by C. Hartling).

Local government: Honduras comprises a Federal District (containing the cities of Tegucigalpa and Comayaguela) and 18 departments (each administered by an appointed Governor), sub-divided into 282 municipalities (each under an elected Council).

DEFENCE. Conscription into the Armed Forces is for approximately 12 months. Although there is no actual reserves programme, those men who have served on active duty for 1 year or more, are eligible for recall.

Army. The Army consists of 1 infantry brigade, 1 Presidential Guard and 3 infantry, 3 artillery, 1 engineer and 1 special forces battalions and 1 armoured car regiment. Equipment includes 16 Scorpion light tanks. Strength (1985) 15,500 (12,000 conscripts). There is also a paramilitary Public Security Force of 4,500 men.

Air Force. Equipment includes 12 (probably unserviceable) J52-engined Super Mystère fighters acquired from Israel, 5 A-37B jet light attack aircraft, 4 Spanish-built CASA C 101BB armed jet trainers, 3 RT-33A reconnaissance aircraft, some Summit/Cessna O2-337 Sentry twin piston-engined COIN aircraft, 3 Israeli-built Arava and 1 Westwind transports, some helicopters, and T 28 and T-41A trainers. Total strength is about 1,200 personnel, of whom many are civilian maintenance staff.

INTERNATIONAL RELATIONS

Membership. Honduras is a member of UN and OAS.

ECONOMY

Budget. In 1983 revenue (in 1m. lempiras) was 2,580 (1982, 2,304); expenditure, 2,580 (1982, 2,304).

Sources of income (1983) included (in 1m. lempiras): Income tax, 190; production (and domestic transactions) taxes, 251; import taxes, 202; export taxes, 78.

Total external debt (1983) was (in 1m. lempiras), 2,525 and net reserves of foreign currency, 35.

Currency. The unit of the monetary system is the *lempira* also known as a *peso,* comprising 100 *centavos.* Notes are issued by the Banco Central de Honduras which has the sole right to issue, in denominations of 100, 50, 20, 10, 5, 2 and 1 *lempiras.* Coins in circulation are 50 and 20 *centavos* in silver, 10 and 5 *centavos* in cupro-nickel and 2 and 1 *centavos* in copper.

Rate of exchange, March 1985: £1 = 2·15 *lempiras;* US$1 = 2 *lempiras.*

Banking. The central bank of issue is the Banco Central de Honduras. The Banco Atlántida has branches in Tegucigalpa, San Pedro Sula, Comayaguela, Puerto Cortés, La Ceiba, Tela, El Progreso, Choluteca and other towns. The Banco de Honduras which operates in many parts of the country is controlled by the Citibank. The Bank of America has branches in Tegucigalpa and San Pedro Sula. The Bank of London and Montreal has branches in Tegucigalpa, San Pedro Sula, Comayaguela and La Ceiba. The Central American Bank for Economic Integration has its head office in Tegucigalpa.

Weights and Measures. The metric system has been legal since 1 April 1897, but English pounds and yards and the old Spanish system are still in use: 1 *vara* = 32 in.; 1 *manzana* (10,000 sq. *varas*) = 700 sq. metres; 1 *arroba* = 25 lb.; 1 *quintal* = 100 lb.; 1 *tonelada* = 2,000 lb.

NATURAL RESOURCES

Minerals. Mineral resources include gold, silver, lead, copper, zinc and iron ore, which are exported. There are probably reserves of other minerals which have not yet been exploited. The Rosario Resources Company, which owned and operated the famous Rosario mines near Tegucigalpa from 1882 to 1954, developed and now operates a mine at El Mochito (Department of Santa Barbara) while the Compañia Minera Los Angeles SA has a mine currently extracting lead, zinc and silver at Valle de Angeles (Department of Francisco Morazán).

Agriculture. Although Honduras is essentially an agricultural country, less than a quarter of the total land area is cultivated and by far the larger portion of this is on the Caribbean and Pacific coastal plains. Agriculture employs 58·9% of the working population and provides 80% of the exports. The main agricultural crops are: Bananas, coffee, sugar and tobacco. Exports of meat amounted to 62·6m. lempiras in 1983.

Livestock (1983): Cattle, 2,418,000; sheep, 5,000; pigs, 409,000; goats, 22,000; horses, 152,000; poultry, 5m.

Forestry. Forests cover nearly 45% of the total land area. Honduras has an abundance of hard- and soft-woods. Large stands of mahogany and other hardwoods—granadino, guayacán, walnut and rosewood—grow in the north-eastern part of the country, in the interior valleys, and near the southern coast. Stands of pine occur almost everywhere in the interior, but are severely damaged by bark beetle and fires. In 1983, total wood exports amounted to 79·3m. lempiras. The Olancho Forest Development Programme involving the construction of saw- and pulp-mills is in progress.

Fisheries. Commercial fishing in territorial waters is restricted to Honduran nationals and Honduran companies in which the controlling share of the capital is owned by a Honduran national. Shrimps and lobsters are important catches; exports (1983) 68·3m. lempiras.

INDUSTRY AND TRADE

Industry. Small-scale local industries include beer and mineral waters, cement, flour, vegetable lard, coconut oil, sweets, cigarettes, cigars, textiles and clothing, panama hats, plastics, nails, matches, plywood, furniture, paper bags, soap, candles, fruit juices and household chemicals. An important hydro-electric scheme has been built at Rio Lindo to serve the Central and North Coast regions. The El Cajon hydro-electric project is now under construction and will come on stream in 1985 (290 mw). A small integrated steel-mill may be erected in Agalteca (Department of Francisco Morazán). The manufacturing industry employed 7·5% of the working population in 1983.

Labour. The organization of trade unions was begun in 1954 with the assistance of ORIT (Inter-American Regional Organization) sponsored by the USA trade unions. In 1972 there were 166 trade unions, of which only 119 were active, with about 67,956 members. A 'Charter of Labour' was granted in Feb. 1955 and an advanced Labour Code and Social Security Bill passed into law in May 1959. A Ministry of 'Labour, Social Assistance and the Middle Class' was created in 1955; the last four words of its title were expunged in 1957.

Commerce. Imports in 1983 were valued at 1,511·7m. lempiras and exports at 1,360·6m. lempiras.

Imports (1983) in 1m. lempiras: Fuel and lubricants, 341·6; chemical products, 314·8; transport machinery and equipment, 257·4; food products, 139·2.

Exports (1983) in 1m. lempiras: Bananas, 415·3; coffee, 302·4; timber, 79·3; refrigerated meats, 62·6; sugar, 55·7; cotton, 9·4.

Trade with main countries in 1m. lempiras (1982) was: USA, 1,224·5; Trinidad and Tobago, 244·3; Japan, 163·8; Federal Republic of Germany, 163·3; Guatemala, 144·3; Belgium, 90·6; Netherlands, 60·6; Spain, 53·5.

Total trade between Honduras and UK (British Department of Trade returns, in £1,000 sterling):

	1980	*1981*	*1982*	*1983*	*1984*
Imports to UK	3,687	4,065	4,695	7,082	12,360
Exports and re-exports from UK	11,835	8,617	4,659	9,539	7,382

Tourism. There were 157,715 tourists in 1983.

COMMUNICATIONS

Roads. Honduras is connected with Guatemala, El Salvador and Nicaragua by the Pan-American Highway. Out of a total of 18,280 km of road (1983), 1,828 were paved and 9,379 are useable throughout the year. There are good asphalted highways between Puerto Cortés in the north and Choluteca in the south passing through San Pedro Sula and Tegucigalpa with branches to Guatemala and El Salvador. In 1981 there were 95,997 motor vehicles.

Railways. Only 4 railways exist; they are confined to the north coastal region and are used mainly for transportation of bananas. Tegucigalpa, the capital, is not served by any railway, and there are no international railway connexions. The total railways operating in 1983 were 1,004 km of 1,067 mm and 914 mm gauge.

Aviation. Over a large part of the country the aeroplane is the normal means of transport for both passengers and freight. There are international airports at Tegucigalpa, San Pedro Sula, La Ceiba and over 30 smaller airstrips in various parts of the country.

Shipping. Sailings to the Atlantic coast port of Puerto Cortés from Europe are frequent, mainly operated by the Harrison Line, Cia Generale Transatlantique, the Royal Netherlands Steamships Co., Hapag Lloyd and vessels owned or chartered by the Tela Railroad Co., a subsidiary of United Brands, and the Standard Fruit Co.

Post and Broadcasting. The Government in April 1972 operated 18,845 km of telephone lines and 12,526 km of telegraph lines. Number of telephones in use, 1983, 35,365; telephone exchanges, 56; number of telegraph offices, 262; combined telephone and telegraph offices, 184; radio stations, 187; commercial television channels, 4. There were (1979) about 27,000 receivers in use. Transmission in colour commenced mid-1973.

Cinemas (1982). Cinemas numbered about 60 with seating capacity of some 60,000.

Newspapers (1984). The 4 most important daily papers are *El Heraldo* and *La Tribuna* in Tegucigalpa, *La Prensa* and *El Tiempo* in San Pedro Sula. Several others exist but their circulation is low and their influence is very limited.

JUSTICE, RELIGION, EDUCATION AND WELFARE

Justice. The judicial power resides in the Supreme Court, with 7 judges elected by the National Constituent Assembly in 1980 for 6 years; it appoints the judges of the courts of appeal, labour tribunals and the district attorneys who, in turn, name the justices of the peace.

Religion. Roman Catholicism is the prevailing religion, but the constitution guarantees freedom to all creeds, and the State does not contribute to the support of any.

Education. Instruction is free, compulsory (from 7 to 15 years of age) and secular. In 1983 the 6,422 primary schools had 704,612 children (19,300 teachers); the 354 secondary, normal and technical schools had 129,606 pupils (5,916 teachers); the teachers' college had 2,604 students in 1981 (168 teachers). In 1982, the three universities had a total of 29,261 students and 1,825 teachers; one teachers' training college with 5,841 students.

The illiteracy rate was 40% of those 10 years of age and older in 1983.

Health. In 1981 there were about 1,370 doctors. In 1983 there were 44 hospitals (25 private) with 5,506 beds, and 571 health centres.

DIPLOMATIC REPRESENTATIVES

Of Honduras in Great Britain (47 Manchester St., London, W1M 5PB)
Ambassador: Max Velasquez Diaz (accredited 7 June 1984).

Of Great Britain in Honduras (Edificio Palmira, Ave. República de Chile, Tegucigalpa)
Ambassador: B. O. White.

Of Honduras in the USA (4301 Connecticut Ave., NW, Washington, D.C., 20008)
Ambassador: Juan Agurcia Ewing.

Of the USA in Honduras (Ave. La Paz, Tegucigalpa)
Ambassador: J. D. Negroponte.

Of Honduras to the United Nations
Ambassador: Dr Roberto Herrera Cácares.

Books of Reference

The *Anuario Estadístico* (latest issue, *Comercio Exterior de Honduras*, 1980) is published by the Dirección de Estadísticas y Censos, Tegucigalpa. *Director:* Elizabeth Zavala de Turcios.

Monthly Bulletin.—Honduras en Cifras. Banco Central de Honduras, 1980
Checchi, V. (and others), *Honduras, a Problem in Economic Development.* New York, 1959
Morris, J. A., *Honduras: Caudillo Politics and Military Rulers.* Boulder, 1984
Rubio Melhado, A., *Geografía General de la Republica de Honduras.* Tegucigalpa, 1953
Stokes, W. S., *Honduras: An Area Study in Government.* Madison, Wisc., 1950

HONG KONG

Population: 5·36m. (1984)
GDP per capita: US$5,738 (1981)

HISTORY. Hong Kong Island and the southern tip of the Kowloon peninsula were ceded by China to Britain after the first and second Anglo-Chinese Wars respectively by the Treaty of Nanking 1842 and the Convention of Peking 1860. Northern Kowloon was leased to Britain for 99 years by China in 1898. Since then, Hong Kong has been under British administration, except from Dec. 1941 to Aug. 1945 during the Japanese occupation. Talks began in Sept. 1982 between Britain and China over the future of Hong Kong after the lease expiry in 1997. On 19 Dec. 1984, the two countries signed an agreement whereby China would recover sovereignty over Hong Kong (including Hong Kong Island, Kowloon and the New Territories) from 1 July 1997 and establish it as a Special Administrative Region where the existing social and economic systems, and the present life-style, would remain unchanged for another 50 years.

AREA AND POPULATION. Hong Kong island is 32 km east of the mouth of the Pearl River and 130 km south-east of Canton. The area of the island is 78·12 sq. km. It is separated from the mainland by a fine natural harbour. On the opposite side is the peninsula of Kowloon (10·48 sq. km), which, with Stonecutters Island (0·75 sq. km), was added to the Territory by the Convention of Peking, 1860. By a further convention, signed at Peking on 9 June 1898, about 950 sq. km, consisting of all the immediately adjacent mainland and numerous islands in the vicinity, were leased to Great Britain by China for 99 years. This area is known as the New Territories. Total area of the territory is 1,066·53 sq. km (including recent reclamations), a large part of it being steep and unproductive hillside. Some 40% of the territory is conserved as country parks. Shortage of land suitable for development for housing and industry, is a serious problem. Since 1945, the Government has reclaimed about 1,897 hectares from the sea, principally from the seafronts of Hong Kong and Kowloon, facing the harbour. In the New Territories, the new town of Tsuen Wan, incorporating Tsuen Wan, Kwai Chung and Tsing Yi, already houses 688,000 of its planned ultimate population of 918,000. The construction of 5 further new towns at Sha Tin, Tuen Mun, Tai Po, Fanling and Yuen Long is now well underway, with designed population capacities of 833,000, 547,000, 220,000, 195,000 and 140,000 respectively. Planning has started for a new town at Junk Bay to house 380,000 people.

The population was 5,109,812 at 1981 census. Estimate (mid-1984) 5,364,000. During the war years the population of Hong Kong fluctuated sharply. In Sept. 1945, at the end of the Japanese occupation, it was about 600,000. In mid-1950 it was estimated at 2·24m. Since 1971 the average annual growth rate has been 2·2%. Of the present population about 32·5% are under 20 years of age. About 57% of the population was born in Hong Kong.

CLIMATE. The climate is warm sub-tropical being much affected by monsoons, the winter being cool and dry and the summer hot and humid, May to Sept. being the wettest months. Jan. 60°F (15·6°C), July 83°F (28·3°C). Annual rainfall 85″ (2,162 mm).

CONSTITUTION AND GOVERNMENT. The administration is in the hands of a Governor, aided by an Executive Council, composed of the Chief Secretary, the Commander, British Forces, the Financial Secretary, the Attorney-General (who are members *ex officio*) and such other members, both official and unofficial, as may be appointed by the Queen upon the Governor's nomination. In Sept. 1984 there were, in addition to the 4 *ex-officio* members, 2 nominated officials and 10 appointed unofficial members. There is also a Legislative Council, presided over by the Governor. In 1984 it consisted of 3 *ex-officio* members, namely the Chief Secretary, the Financial Secretary, the Attorney-General, and 30 appointed unofficial members and 13 nominated official members. Chinese and English are the official languages. District boards with elected members were set up in 1982 in the 18 administrative districts of Hong Kong. They have mainly an advisory role to perform and have a substantial influence over district affairs.

Governor and C.-in-C.: Sir Edward Youde, GCMG, MBE.
Commander British Forces: Maj.-Gen. Derek Boorman, CB.
Chief Secretary: David Akers-Jones, CMG.
Flag: British Blue Ensign with the arms of the Territory on a white disc in the fly.

DEFENCE. The Hong Kong garrison, under the Commander British Forces, comprises units of all three services. Its principal rôle is to assist the Hong Kong Government in maintaining security and stability.

Army. The Army constitutes the bulk of the garrison. It comprises a UK battalion, based at Stanley Fort, and 4 Gurkha infantry battalions, one based at Lyemun, the other 3 in the New Territories; supporting units include the Queen's Gurkha Engineers, the Queen's Gurkha Signals, the Gurkha Transport Regiment, and 660 Squadron Army Air Corps.

Navy. The Naval Base is at HMS *Tamar*. The Hong Kong Squadron comprising five patrol craft, converted Ton-class old wooden minesweepers were replaced in 1984 and 1985 by five new larger, faster and better-armed patrol vessels of the 'Peacock' class specially designed for the purpose (HMS *Peacock* and HMS *Plover* were the first, joined by *Starling*, *Swallow* and *Swift*) all built by Hall Russell, Aberdeen, Scotland.

Air Force. The Royal Air Force is based at Shek Kong. No. 28 (Army Cooperation) Squadron operates 8 Wessex helicopters. In addition to its operational rôle in support of the army and navy, the RAF carries out search and rescue and medical evacuation tasks. It is also responsible for air traffic control services at Shek Kong, and provides a territory-wide air traffic advisory service.

Auxiliary Forces. The local auxiliary defence units, consisting of the Royal Hong Kong Regiment and the Royal Hong Kong Auxiliary Air Force, are administered by the Hong Kong Government, but, if called out, would come under the command of the Commander British Forces. The Royal Hong Kong Regiment (The Volunteers) has a strength of about 950. It is fully mobile and its rôle is to operate in support of regular army battalions stationed in Hong Kong. The Royal Hong Kong Auxiliary Air Force is intended mainly for internal security and air-sea rescue duties. It has a strength of about 131, operating a fleet of seven aircraft – a twin-engined Britten-Norman Islander, a twin-engined Cessna 404 Titan Courier, two Scottish Aviation Bulldog Trainers and three Aérospatiale Dauphin 365C1 helicopters.

ECONOMY

Budget. The public revenue and expenditure for financial years ending 31 March were as follows (in HK$):

	1980–81	*1981–82*	*1982–83*	*1983–84* [1]
Revenue	30,290,300,000	34,312,900,000	31,097,600,000	32,269,700,000
Expenditure	23,593,500,000	27,778,200,000	34,597,800,000	35,474,900,000

[1] Estimate.

The revenue is derived chiefly from rates, licences, duties on liquor, tobacco, hydrocarbon oils and methyl alcohol, a tax on earnings and profits, land sales and various duties.

Currency. The unit of currency is the Hong Kong *dollar*. Banknotes (of denominations of $10 upwards) are issued by the Hongkong and Shanghai Banking Corporation, and the Chartered Bank. Their combined note and coin issue was, at 31 July 1984, HK$13,376m. Subsidiary currency consisting of HK$5, HK$2, HK$1, 50-cent, 20-cent, 10-cent, 5-cent copper-nickel-alloy coins and 1-cent notes is issued by the Hong Kong Government and at 31 July 1984 totalled HK$1,354m.

Since Oct. 1983 the HK$ has been linked to the US$1 at a fixed exchange rate of US$1 = HK$7·80.

Since 1975, the Hong Kong Government has issued annually a limited quantity of HK$1,000 gold coins. The first in the series was issued to commemorate the Queen's visit to Hong Kong in 1975. Gold coins have since been minted to mark the Chinese Lunar Years of the Dragon, the Snake, the Horse, the Goat, the Monkey, the Cockerel, the Dog, the Pig and the Rat.

Banking. There are 140 licensed banks and 105 of them are foreign-incorporated. Deposits at 30 June 1984 totalled HK$266,484m.

Weights and Measures. Metric, British Imperial, Chinese and US units are all in current use in Hong Kong. However Government Departments have now effectively adopted metric units; all new legislation uses metric terminology and existing legislation is being progressively metricated. Metrication is also proceeding in the private sector.

The statutory equivalent for the *chek* is 14 5/8 inches. The variation of the size of the *chek* with usage still persists in Hong Kong but the *chek* and derived units are now used much less than in the past.

AGRICULTURE. In 1983, 153,000 tonnes of vegetables were produced. Livestock (1983): Cattle, 860; pigs, 392,290; poultry, 32m.

WATER. The provision of sufficient reservoir capacity to store the summer rainfall in order to meet supply requirements has always been a serious problem. Over the years no less than 17 impounding reservoirs have been constructed with a total capacity of 586m. cu. metres. The major among these are the Plover Cove Reservoir (230m. cu. metres) finally completed in 1973 and the High Island Reservoir (280m. cu. metres) completed in 1978, both involving the conversion of sea water inlets into fresh water lakes.

There are no sites remaining in Hong Kong suitable for development as storage reservoirs. Consequently the purchase of water from China has been of increasing importance and the future needs of Hong Kong will be met to a large extent from this source. During the financial year 1984–85 water purchased from China will be in the order of 290m. cu. metres which represents about 45% of Hong Kong's demand. The agreement with China allows for annual increases up to a total figure of 620m. cu. metres per annum by 1994–95 which will represent around 60% of Hong Kong's demand at that time.

These resources can be further supplemented when necessary by up to 181,000 cu. metres of fresh water a day from a desalting plant completed in 1976 and now considered as a reserve resource.

INDUSTRY AND TRADE

Industry. An economic policy based on free enterprise and free trade; an industrious work force; an efficient and aggressive commercial infrastructure; modern and efficient sea-port (including container shipping terminals) and airport facilities: its geographical position relative to markets in North America and its traditional trading links with Britain have all contributed to Hong Kong's success as a modern industrial complex.

In March 1984, there were 46,862 factories employing 869,296 people out of a total population of approximately 5·3m. The type of factory involved ranges from the small cottage type to large highly complex modern establishments. Given the scarcity of land it is most common for light industry to operate in multi-storey buildings specially designed for this purpose. The main industry is textiles and clothing, which employed 41% of the total industrial workforce and accounted for 40% of total domestic exports in 1983. Other major light manufacturing industries include electronic products, clocks and watches, toys, plastic products, metalware, footwear, cameras and travel goods. Heavy industry includes ship-building, ship-repairing, aircraft engineering and the manufacture of machinery. Agriculture, fishing and some mining are the main primary industries.

Commerce. Hong Kong's industries are mainly export oriented. The total value of domestic exports in 1983 was HK$104,405m. The major markets were USA (42%), UK (8·2%), Federal Republic of Germany (7·7%), China (6%), Japan (3·7%) and Canada (3·6%). There is also a sizeable and flourishing entrepôt trade which accounted for another HK$56,294m. in 1983.

The total value of imports in 1983 was HK$175,442m., mainly from China (24·4%), Japan (23%), USA (10·9%), Taiwan (7·1%), Singapore (6%) and UK (4·2%).

The chief import items were manufactured goods (28·2%), machinery and transport equipment (22·5%), foodstuffs (10·8%), chemicals (7·4%), mineral fuel, lubricants and related materials (6·6%).

Imports from the Commonwealth countries (HK$25,358m. in 1983) amounted to 14·4% of total imports, and exports to the Commonwealth countries (HK$20,173m.) accounted for 19·3% of Hong Kong's domestic exports.

Duties are levied only on tobacco, hydrocarbon oils, methyl alcohol and alcoholic liquors, whether imported into or manufactured in Hong Kong for local consumption.

All imports (apart from foodstuffs, which are subject to a flat charge of HK50 cents for every $1,000 worth of goods shipped) and exports are subject to a varying *ad valorem* charge.

The adverse balance on visible trade is offset by a favourable balance from exchange, shipping and insurance transactions, an inflow of capital, ship-repairing, a flourishing tourist industry, etc.

Hong Kong has a free exchange market. Foreign merchants may remit profits or repatriate capital. Import and export controls are kept to the minimum, consistent with strategic requirements.

Total trade between Hong Kong and UK (British Department of Trade returns, in £1,000 sterling) is given as follows:

	1980	*1981*	*1982*	*1983*	*1984*
Imports to UK	850,340	898,634	872,545	1,178,343	1,266,965
Exports and re-exports from UK	559,420	618,525	732,489	726,711	897,419

Tourism. 2,775,014 tourists spent HK$11,375·68m. in Hong Kong during 1983.

COMMUNICATIONS

Roads. In 1983 there were 1,238 km of roads, distributed as follows: Hong Kong Island, 360; Kowloon and New Kowloon, 345, and New Territories, 533. A cross-harbour tunnel, 1·8 km in length, opened to traffic in Aug. 1972, now links Hong Kong Island with the Kowloon peninsula. The 1·4 km twin-tube Lion Rock Tunnel, which links Kowloon with Sha Tin New Town and other areas of the north-eastern New Territories, became fully operational in Oct. 1978. The 1·8 km twin-tube Aberdeen Tunnel, which connects Aberdeen and Wanchai, became operational in March 1983.

Railways. There is an electric tramway with a total track length of 30·4 km, and a cable tramway connecting the Peak district with the lower levels in Victoria. The Kowloon-Canton Railway runs for 34 km from the terminus at Hung Hom in Kowloon to the border point at Lo Wu. On 4 April 1979 a direct 'through' passenger train to Guangzhou (Canton) was re-introduced after a lapse of nearly 30 years. A second express train came into operation on 11 Feb. 1980 and a third train was introduced in July 1984. The trains are invariably full and cater mainly for the business and tourist communities as well as Hong Kong residents visiting friends and relatives in China. There are also other passenger services to Lo Wu to allow for connexions to be made for onward trains at the Shenzhen border point (Chinese section). Mail and freight are conveyed across the border without transhipment.

The railway completed its five-year, HK$3,500m. modernization and electrification project in July 1983. All existing stations were rebuilt and three new stations were constructed for Tai Wai, Fo Tan (due to be opened in Jan. 1985) and Kowloon Tong. The Kowloon Tong Station is designed as an interchange with the underground Mass Transit Railway.

The status of the Kowloon-Canton Railway changed from a government department to a public corporation on 1 Jan. 1983. The decision was taken in view of the major development of the KCR into a much expanded and more sophisticated railway.

An underground Mass Transit Railway system, comprising 25 stations, is now in operation. The system consists of two lines, one linking the Central District of Hong Kong Island with Tsuen Wan in the west of Kowloon, and the other linking Kwun Tong in East Kowloon with Waterloo in Nathan Road. Cross platform interchange facilities are provided at Prince Edward and Argyle stations for passengers travelling between the two lines. The system is about 26 km in length.

Work began at the end of 1981 on the Island Line, which will serve the northern foreshore of Hong Kong Island. Scheduled to be fully operational in mid-1986, the new line will run for 12·5 km and add 12 new stations to the system.

Aviation. Hong Kong International Airport is situated on the north shore of Kowloon Bay. It is regularly used by 30 airlines and many charter airlines which provide frequent services throughout the Far East to Europe, North America, Africa, the Middle East, Australia and New Zealand. British Airways operates 10 passenger and cargo services per week, to UK, Africa and many Asian countries. Cathay Pacific Airways, the Hong Kong-based airline, operates 413 passenger and cargo services to the UK, Europe, the Far and Middle East, Australasia and Canada weekly. During 1980, British Caledonian Airways also commenced scheduled services on the Hong Kong to London route. About 1,000 scheduled services are operated weekly to and from Hong Kong by various airlines. In 1983, 54,281 aircraft arrived and departed on international flights, carrying 8·8m. passengers and 368,000 tonnes of freight.

Shipping. The port of Hong Kong, which ranks among the top three container ports in the world, handled 1·83m. twenty-foot equivalent units in 1983. The Kwai Chung Container Port has six berths with more than 2,300 metres of quay backed by about 88 hectares of cargo handling area. In 1983, some 11,400 ocean-going vessels called at Hong Kong and loaded and discharged more than 37m. tonnes of cargo. This included 32m. tonnes of general goods, 34% of which was containerized cargo.

Telecommunications, Post and Broadcasting. There were 94 post offices in 1983, postal revenue totalled HK$656·8m.; expenditure, HK$457·3m.; 490m. letters and parcels were handled. Telephone services are provided by the Hong Kong Telephone Co. Ltd. It operates through a network of 65 fully automatic main exchanges and served (1984) over 2m. subscribers. Cable and Wireless (Hong Kong) Ltd, which is owned jointly by Cable and Wireless PLC and the Hong Kong Government, provides the international telecommunication services as well as local telegram and telex services. These include public telegram, telex, telephone, television programmes transmission and reception, leased circuits, facsimile, switched data, ship-shore and air-ground communications. International facilities are provided through submarine cables, microwave, tropospheric scatter and satellite radio systems.

There is a government broadcasting station, Radio Television Hong Kong, with daily transmissions in English and Chinese. A commercial station, the Commercial Broadcasting Co. Ltd, transmits daily in English and Cantonese. Two radio stations operate 8 channels with 4 providing 24-hour service.

Television Broadcasts Ltd and Asia Television Ltd transmit commercial television in English and Chinese on 4 channels, in colour.

Cinemas. In Sept. 1984 there were 96 cinemas with a seating capacity of over 108,649. Attendance 61m. during 1983.

Newspapers. In Sept. 1984 there were 68 daily or weekly newspapers, registered and in circulation, including 13 English-language papers; the remainder are almost all in Chinese.

JUSTICE, EDUCATION AND WELFARE

Justice. There is a Supreme Court which comprises the Court of Appeal and the High Court. While the Court of Appeal hears appeals on all matters, civil and criminal from the lower courts, the High Court has unlimited jurisdiction in both civil and criminal matters including bankruptcy, company winding-up, adoptions, probate and lunacy matters. The District Court has civil jurisdiction to hear monetary claims up to HK$60,000 or, where the claims are for recovery of land, the annual rent or rateable value does not exceed HK$45,000. In its criminal jurisdiction, it may try more serious offences except murder, manslaughter and rape; the maximum term of imprisonment it can impose is seven years. The Magistrates' Court exercises criminal jurisdiction over a wide range of indictable and summary offences. Its powers of punishment are generally restricted to a maximum of two years' imprisonment, or a fine of HK$10,000, though cumulative sentences of imprisonment up to three years may be imposed. The Coroner's Court inquires into the identity of a deceased person and the cause of death. The Juvenile Court has jurisdiction to hear charges against young people aged under 16 for any offence other than homicide. Children under the age of seven are not deemed to have reached the age of criminal responsibility. The Lands Tribunal determines on statutory claims for compensation over land and certain landlord and tenant matters. The Labour Tribunal provides inexpensive and speedy settlements to individual monetary claims arising from disputes between employers and employees. The Small Claims Tribunal deals with monetary claims involving amounts not exceeding HK$5,000.

Police. At the end of 1983, the establishment of the Royal Hong Kong Police Force was 24,211. In addition, there were 5,432 auxiliary officers. During the year, 86,000 crimes were reported. The overall detection rate was 42·9% and a total of 34,773 people were arrested and prosecuted.

The Marine Police is responsible for patrolling some 1,836 sq. km of territorial waters and involved in the control of some 7,250 small local craft with a maritime population of about 50,000. At the end of 1983, it consisted of a disciplined staff of 2,676 and a fleet of 104 vessels.

Education. The majority of schools have to be registered with the Education Department under the Education Ordinance. They are required to comply with regulations as to staff, building, fire and health requirements. From Sept. 1971, free and compulsory primary education was introduced in government and the majority of government-aided schools. Free junior secondary education of 3 years' duration was introduced in 1978 and it was made compulsory in Sept. 1979.

In March 1984 there were 217,507 pupils in kindergartens (all private), another 546,388 in primary schools and 448,591 in secondary schools.

There are 5 technical institutes with a total full-time and part-time enrolment of 39,142, 1 technical teachers' college and 3 colleges of education with a total enrolment of 4,632.

The University of Hong Kong had 5,423 undergraduates in 1984 and the Chinese University of Hong Kong, inaugurated in Oct. 1963, had 5,001 undergraduates. The Hong Kong Polytechnic, 1983, had a total of 25,600 students. In Oct. 1984, the City Polytechnic was opened with a full- and part-time enrolment of 1,228.

Health. In June 1984 there were 3,875 doctors and about 22,453 hospital beds.

Social Security. The Government co-ordinates and implements expanding programmes in social welfare, which include social security, family services, child care, services for the elderly, youth and community work, probation and corrections and rehabilitation. More than 138 voluntary welfare agencies are subsidised by public funds.

The Government gives non-contributory cash assistance to needy families, unemployed able-bodied adults, the severely disabled and the elderly. Caseload in July 1984 totalled 303,595. Victims of natural disasters, crimes of violence and traffic accidents are financially assisted.

Books of Reference

Statistical Information: The Census and Statistics Department is responsible for the preparation and collation of Government statistics. These statistics are published mainly in the *Hong Kong Monthly Digest of Statistics* which is also available in a collected annual edition. The Department also publishes monthly trade statistics, economic indicators, annual review of overseas trade, etc. Statistical information is also published in the annual reports of Government departments. *Hong Kong 1984*, and other government publications are available from the Hong Kong Government Publications Centre, GPO Building, Connaught Place, Hong Kong, and the Hong Kong Government Office in London, 6 Grafton Street, London, W1X 3LB.

The Hong Kong Trade Development Council, Connaught Centre, Connaught Place, Hong Kong, issues a monthly *Hong Kong Enterprise* and other publications.

Hong Kong 1984. Hong Kong Government Press, 1984
Beazer, W. F., *The Commercial Future of Hong Kong.* New York, 1978
Bonavia, D., *Hong Kong 1997.* London, 1984
Endacott, G. B., *A History of Hong Kong.* 2nd ed. OUP, 1973.–*Government and People in Hong Kong, 1841–1962. A Constitutional History.* OUP, 1965
Hopkins, K., *Hong Kong: The Industrial Colony.* OUP, 1971
Rabushka, A., *The Changing Face of Hong Kong: New Departures in Public Policy.* Washington, 1973
Tregear, E. R., *Land Use in Hong Kong.* Hong Kong Univ. Press, 1958.—*Hong Kong Gazetteer.* Hong Kong Univ. Press, 1958.—*The Development of Hong Kong as Told in Maps.* Hong Kong Univ. Press, 1959
Youngson, A. J., *Hong Kong: Economic Growth and Policy.* OUP, 1982

HUNGARY

Magyar Népköztársaság

Capital: Budapest
Population: 10·68m. (1984)
GNP per capita: US$2,100 (1981)

HISTORY. Hungary first became an independent kingdom in 1001. For events in Hungary since 1918 *see* THE STATESMAN'S YEAR-BOOK, 1945, pp. 1006–7, and 1957, p. 1096.

On 23 Oct. 1956 an anti-Stalinist revolution broke out, and the newly formed coalition government of Imre Nagy on 1 Nov. withdrew from the Warsaw Pact and asked the UN for protection. János Kádár, formed a counter-government on 3 Nov. and asked the USSR for support.

Russian troops suppressed the revolution and abducted Nagy and his Ministers, who were later secretly executed.

On 7 Sept. 1967 the Soviet-Hungarian treaty of friendship was renewed for 20 years.

In 1978 the crown of St Stephen, the symbol of Hungarian nationhood, which had been in US hands since 1945, was returned to Hungary.

AREA AND POPULATION. Hungary is bounded north by Czechoslovakia, north-east by the USSR, east by Romania, south by Yugoslavia and west by Austria. The peace treaty of 10 Feb. 1947 restored the frontiers as of 1 Jan. 1938. The area of Hungary is 93,032 sq. km (35,911 sq. miles).

The official language is Hungarian (Magyar), which is a member of the Finno-Ugrian group.

At the census of 1 Jan. 1980 the population was 10,709,550 (5,195,300 males). Population in 1984: 10,679,000 (males, 5,164,000). Ethnic composition, 1984: Hungarians, 96·6%; Germans, 1·6%; Slovaks, 1·1%; Romanians, 0·2%; others, 0·5%. There were 0·38m. Gypsies in 1985.

54% of the population is urban (19% in Budapest). Population density, 114·8 per sq. km. Birth rate, 1983, 11·9 per 1,000. The population is decreasing, by 5·3 per 1,000 in 1983; expectation of life (1982): males, 66; females, 74. There is a world-wide Hungarian diaspora, and Hungarian minorities in Romania, Yugoslavia and Czechoslovakia.

Vital statistics, 1983: Births, 128,425; marriages, 75,978; divorces, 29,000; deaths, 148,776; abortions, 77,000 (approx.); infant mortality, 19 per 1,000 live births.

Area (in sq. km) and population (in 1,000) of counties, county boroughs and county towns:

Counties (1984)	*Area*	*Population*	*Chief town (1984)*	*Population*
Baranya	4,487	434	Pécs	175
Bács-Kiskun	8,363	564	Kecskemét	102
Békés	5,632	429	Békéscsaba	69
Borsod-Abaúj-Zemplén	7,248	801	Miskolc	212
Csongrád	4,263	453	Hódmezovásárhely	54
Fejér	4,374	423	Székesfehérvár	109
Győr-Sopron	4,012	430	Győr	128
Hajdú-Bihar	6,212	552	Debrecen	205
Heves	3,637	346	Eger	64
Komárom	2,250	323	Tatabánya	77
Nógrád	2,544	237	Salgótarján	50
Pest	6,394	983	Budapest	2,064
Somogy	6,035	357	Kaposvár	74
Szabolcs-Szatmár	5,938	586	Nyíregyháza	114
Szolnok	5,608	441	Szolnok	78
Tolna	3,702	268	Szekszárd	38
Vas	3,337	283	Szombathely	86
Veszprém	4,689	389	Veszprém	60
Zala	3,786	316	Zalaegerszeg	60

County boroughs (1984)	*Area*	*Population*	*County boroughs (1984)*	*Area*	*Population*
Budapest (capital)	525	2,064	Szeged	145	176
Miskolc	224	212	Pécs	113	175
Debrecen	446	205	Győr	175	128

CLIMATE. A humid continental climate, with warm summers and cold winters. Precipitation is generally greater in summer, with thunderstorms. Dry, clear weather is likely in autumn, but spring is damp and both seasons are of short duration. Budapest. Jan. 32°F (0°C), July 71°F (21·5°C). Annual rainfall 25″ (625 mm). Pécs. Jan. 30°F (–0·7°C), July 71°F (21·5°C). Annual rainfall 26·4″ (661 mm).

CONSTITUTION AND GOVERNMENT. On 1 Feb. 1946 the National Assembly proclaimed a republic.

The present People's Republic was established by a constitution adopted on 18 Aug. 1949. Supreme power is vested in Parliament. Parliament elects a Presidential Council, which exercises the functions of Parliament between sessions. It can dissolve government bodies and annul legislation. The 1949 Constitution was amended in 1972. The distinction between 'working people' and 'citizens' disappears. Citizens are stated to have both indirect (through elected representatives) and direct (through local and enterprise councils) democratic rights. State and co-operative property are recognized as co-existing with equal status. Personal property is 'recognized and protected' up to the limit set by law (this includes for private artisans and, since 1 Jan. 1982, for various classes of small companies and 'economic working groups', places of business and machinery).

Ethnic minorities have equal rights and education in their own tongue.

National flag: Three horizontal stripes of red, white, green.

National anthem: God bless the Hungarians–Isten áldd meg a magyart (words by Ferenc Kölcsey, tune by Ferenc Erkel).

Chairman of the Presidential Council (Head of State): Pál Losonczi, appointed on 14 April 1967. *Deputy Chairmen:* Sándor Gáspár and Rezső Trautmann.

In 1949 the Hungarian Working People's Party (Communists), the Smallholders' Party, the National Peasant Party, the Trade Union Federation, the Association of Working Peasants, the Democratic Women's Association and the Federation of Working Youth were merged in the Hungarian People's Independence Front. In 1954 a new comprehensive organization was formed, the People's Patriotic Front. The Communist Youth Association (KISZ) had 875,000 members in 1985.

The Communist Party was reorganized after the 1956 revolution and changed its name to 'Hungarian Socialist Workers' Party'. It had 852,000 members in 1983 (32% women; 46% manual workers and peasants in 1980). Supreme *de facto* power is in the hands of the Party's Politburo, composed in March 1985 of: János Kádár, *First Secretary of the Central Committee*; György Aczél *(Secretary of the Central Committee)*; Valéria Benke; Sándor Gáspár; Ferenc Havasi; Mihály Korom; György Lázár; Pál Losonczi; László Maróthy; Lajos Méhes; Károly Németh; Miklos Ovári; István Sárlos.

Prominent members of the Government in March 1985 were:

Prime Minister: György Lázár.

Deputy Prime Ministers: Judith Csehak, Gen. Lajos Czinege, Lajos Faluvégi *(Chairman, State Planning Committee)*, József Marjai, László Maróthy, István Sárlos. *Finance:* Dr István Hetényi. *Foreign Affairs:* Péter Várkonyi. *Speaker, National Assembly:* Antal Apró. *Interior:* Dr István Horváth. *Culture:* Dr Béla Köpeczi. *Defence:* Gen. István Olah. *Foreign Trade:* Péter Veress. *Justice:* Imre Markója.

Parliament consists of 352 deputies (106 women) elected for a 5-year term by all citizens over 18 years.

The right to select candidates is vested solely in pre-election nomination meetings open to all voters. More than one candidate is permitted to stand in each constituency. Such 'alternative' candidates must receive 30% of the votes at nomination meetings. All candidates must support the Patriotic People's Front (PPF).

To be elected candidates must gain at least 50% of the votes cast. A law of 1983 made multiple candidatures compulsory in the elections of 1985. Candidates coming second with more than 25% of the votes become deputy members. 10% of deputies are elected on a national list voted upon by all citizens.

Elections were held on 8 June 1980. Electorate, 7,661,361; votes cast, 7,577,401; votes for PPF candidates, 7,462,953; against, 54,070. Alternative candidates stood in 15 constituencies.

Local Government. Hungary is divided into the capital, Budapest, 19 counties *(megyék)* and 5 county boroughs (large towns with county status), which are subdivided into towns and boroughs. All of these are administered by a hierarchy of local councils which in turn elect Executive Committees to carry on day-to-day administration. Members of county councils are elected by the lower councils. Elections are held every 5 years. Local elections were held in 1985. At the June 1980 elections 59,270 councillors were elected (18,240 women). County districts were abolished in 1983.

DEFENCE. The 1947 Treaty authorized Hungary to have an army up to a strength of 65,000 personnel, and an air force of 90 aircraft, of which not more than 70 may be combat types with a personnel strength of 5,000.

By a law of 1976 the Presidential Council may establish a National Defence Council which in times of war would exercise supreme control over defence.

Men between the ages of 18 and 23 are liable for 18 months' conscription in the Army, 24 months in the Air Force. Compulsory military service age-limits are 18 to 55 (18 to 45 women).

The security police (BKH) is controlled by the Ministry of the Interior.

The Workers' Militia is a para-military organization armed with automatic weapons. Strength (1985), 60,000.

Four Soviet divisions are stationed in Hungary.

Army. Hungary is divided into 4 army districts: Budapest, Debrecen, Kiskunfélegyháza, Pécs. The strength of the Army was (1985) 84,000 (including 50,000 conscripts). It is organized in 1 tank division, 5 motor rifle divisions, 1 artillery and 1 surface-to-surface missile brigade, 1 anti-aircraft regiment, 3 surface-to-air missile regiments and 1 airborne battalion. Equipment includes 1,200 T-54/-55, 30 T-72 and 100 PT-76 tanks.

Navy. The maritime wing of the Army in 1985 deployed 500 officers and men operating 45 vessels, comprising 10 patrol craft of 100 tons, 5 utility landing craft and 30 other craft including river mine-warfare vessels, troop transports of up to 1,000 tons, river monitors, icebreakers and tugs, constituting the River Guard, and Army amphibious logistic and bridging vessels are active along the Danube.

Air Force. The Air Force is an integral part of the Army, with a strength (1985) of about 21,000 officers and men and 200 combat aircraft. The interceptor division has 2 regiments of MiG-23 and MiG-21 fighters. Other combat aircraft include about 20 Mi-24 helicopter gunships. Transport units are equipped with An-2, An-24, An-26 and Il-14 aircraft. Other types in service include Ka-26, Mi-2 and Mi-8 helicopters and L-29 Delfin and MiG-15UTI trainers. 'Guideline' and 'Goa' surface-to-air missiles are also operational.

INTERNATIONAL RELATIONS

Membership. Hungary is a member of UN, the Warsaw Pact and Comecon and, since 1982, IMF and IBRD.

External Debt. Hungary settled its debt to the UK in 1967. By an agreement of 6 March 1973 Hungary is to meet US claims of US$189m. arising from war damage and nationalization in 20 yearly instalments. Hungarian indebtedness to the West was US$8,300m. in 1983. A US$400m. loan was made by IBRD in 1983.

ECONOMY

Planning. For details of past plans *see* THE STATESMAN'S YEAR-BOOK, 1975–76. A 'New Economic Mechanism' (NEM) came into effect on 1 Jan. 1968. It restricted central direction to overall policies, replaced direct by financial control and gave local managers more initiative. Reforms aimed ultimately at adapting the economy to world prices by reducing costs, bringing salaries into line with productivity, re-deploying labour, cutting import subsidies and encouraging exports were set in train in 1980. Since 1976, enterprises have been required to repay state investment credits in full, usually over 10 years, and to cover unscheduled increases in costs. Regulations introduced in 1982 allow the creation of various types of small private enterprises. Targets for the sixth 5-year plan (1976–80) were not met. The seventh 5-year plan (1981–85) was one of consolidation and envisaged rises of only 6% in real incomes and 15% in the national income. There were large price increases in 1983 and 1985. Inflation was over 7% in 1984.

Budget. The budget for calendar years was as follows (in 1,000 forints):

	1976	*1977*	*1978*	*1979*	*1980*	*1981*	*1982*
Revenue	320,384	361,272	382,900	411,600	423,500	472,600	485,800
Expenditure	322,874	364,808	386,400	415,200	428,000	482,400	498,000

1982 revenue included (in 1,000m. forints): 256·2 from enterprises, 15·2 from collective farms, 11·4 from personal taxation and 71·8 turnover tax. Expenditure included: subsidies to enterprises, 82·4; investment, 53·3; welfare, 25·4; social security 98·5; culture, 47·6.

Currency. A decree of 26 July 1946 instituted a new monetary unit, the *forint* sub-divided into 100 *fillér*. The rate of exchange (March 1985) 56·39 forints to the £1 sterling, 52·73 forints = US$1. A uniform exchange rate was established in Oct. 1981 as a final step before the introduction of external, central-bank convertibility for foreign trade. Since 1983 the forint has been devalued several times by a total of 20%.

Banking. Banking activities are controlled by the National Bank, including the National Savings Bank, which handles local government, as well as personal, accounts. (Deposits in 1983: 197,100m. forints.) The National Bank finances investment to individual enterprises and is the main authority over foreign-exchange transactions. Since 1983 a number of small specialized financial institutions have been set up to function alongside the National Bank. There is also a Foreign Trade Bank for Hungarian enterprises trading abroad. The State Development Bank (formerly Investment Bank) finances large-scale investment projects and oversees national investment trends.

The National Credit Institute of Co-operatives handles all credit transactions for farmers, artisans and co-operatives. The Hungarian International Trade Bank opened in London in 1973. In 1980 the Central European International Bank was set up in Budapest with 7 Western banks holding 66% of the shares.

Weights and Measures. The metric system of weights and measures is in use. For land measure a cadastral yoke (1 acre = 0·7033 cadastral yoke) is used.

ENERGY AND NATURAL RESOURCES

Electricity. Capacity of all power stations in 1983 was 6,050 mw. There is an 880-mw nuclear power station at Paks. A 750 kv power line links Albertirsa with the Soviet grid at Vinnitsa. 25,808m. kwh were produced in 1983, and 10,815m. kwh imported.

Oil. Oil and natural gas have been found in the Szeged basin and in Zala county. Production in 1983: oil, 2m. tonnes; gas, 6,497m. cu. m. There are pipelines for crude oil ('Friendship' I and II from USSR, section of the Adria oil pipeline from Rijeka to Czechoslovakia) and natural gas totalling 4,752 km in 1982. Imports in 1983 (in 1,000 tonnes): Oil, 8,864; gas, 4,071.

Minerals. Production in 1983 (in 1,000 tonnes): coal, 2,827; lignite, 7,980; brown coal, 14,406; bauxite, 2,917; iron ore, 441.

Agriculture. Agricultural land was collectivised in 1950. A law of 1968 permits collectives to own land, and guarantees individuals' rights to private plots. Collectives meet in a National Council of Agricultural Co-operatives.

In 1983 the agricultural area was (in 1,000 hectares) 6,571, of which 4,681 were arable, 1,279 meadows and pastures, and 272 orchards and vineyards.

In 1984 there were 1,285 collective farms with 5·7m. hectares of land (including 319,700 hectares of household plots) and 129 state farms with 925,900 hectares of land. The irrigated area was 175,000 hectares; 55,000 tractors were in use.

Production statistics (in 1,000 tonnes):

Crops	*1981*	*1982*	*1983*	*Crops*	*1981*	*1982*	*1983*
Wheat	4,602	5,747	5,961	Maize	6,813	7,730	6,215
Rye	115	116	136	Potatoes	1,112	975	791
Barley	899	865	1,007	Sugar-beet	4,719	5,363	3,765
Oats	159	123	118	Sunflower seed	624	577	581

Livestock in 1984 was (in 1,000 head) as follows: Cattle, 1,907; pigs, 9,843; poultry, 41,245; sheep, 2,975; horses, 111,000.

Livestock products (1983): Eggs, 4,481m.; milk, 2,689m. litres; wool, 13,030 tonnes; animals for slaughter, 2,335,000 tonnes.

The north shore of Lake Balaton and the Tokaj area are important wine-producing districts. Wine production in 1983 was 609m. litres.

Forestry. The area under forest in 1983 was 1·63m. hectares. 21,000 hectares were afforested and 8m. cu. metres of timber were cut.

Fisheries. There are fisheries in the rivers Danube and Tisza and Lake Balaton, and in 1984 there were 26,000 hectares of commercial fishponds. Catch in 1983: 43,857 tonnes.

INDUSTRY AND TRADE

Industry. Production (in 1,000 tonnes):

	1979	*1980*	*1981*	*1982*	*1983*
Pig-iron	2,369	2,214	2,193	2,183	2,047
Crude steel	3,907	3,763	3,643	3,703	3,617
Rolled steel	3,240	3,046	2,816	2,856	2,820
Aluminium	72	73	74	74	74
Alumina	793	811	792	745	836
Cement	4,857	4,660	4,635	4,369	4,243
Artificial fertilizers	1,043	1,045	647	726	761
Synthetic materials (PVC, etc.)	294	328	314	326	344
Sulphuric acid	588	590	573	569	606
Sugar	497	468	490	459	476
Cotton cloth (1m. sq. metres)	349	335	320	310	307
Woollen (1m. sq. metres)	41	43	45	41	37
Silk and rayon (1m. sq. metres)	57	56	59	57	55
Leather footwear (1m. pairs)	45	43	44	44	43,501

Labour. In 1983 there were 4,970,100 wage-earners (2,243,500 female) in the following categories: working-class, 56·1%; white-collar, 26·1%; co-operative peasantry, 14·1%; self-employed tradesmen, 3·7%. 4,779,000 worked in the socialist sector. Percentage distributions of the workforce: industry, 31·7; agriculture, 21·8; social and cultural services, 10·7; trade, 10; transport and communications, 7·9; building, 7·5. In 1981 to simplify administration the Ministry of Labour was abolished and replaced by a National Office for Wages and Labour. A 40-hour 5-day week was introduced in 1984. Average monthly wages of employed persons in 1984: 5,240 forints. Minimum wage in 1984: 2,000 forints. Retirement age: Men, 60; women, 55. Leave entitlement, 15-24 days in 1985.

Trade Unions. Trade union membership was 4·9m. in 1984.

Commerce. Hungary is heavily dependent on foreign trade, which even under the 'New Economic Mechanism' remains basically under state control. Trade for calendar years (in 1m. forints):

	1977	*1978*	*1979*	*1980*	*1981*	*1982*	*1983*
Imports	267,300	300,900	308,900	299,900	314,300	324,800	365,000
Exports	238,600	240,700	282,100	281,000	299,400	324,500	374,100

In 1983 Hungary's trade with communist countries (in 1,000m. forints): imports,

191·9; exports, 203·2. In 1983 USSR was Hungary's major trading partner (28·6% of imports, 31·6% of exports), ahead of West Germany (10·2%, 7·4%) and East Germany (6·7%, 5·9%). Major exports to communist countries: Machinery, industrial consumer goods, raw materials; elsewhere, raw materials and industrial consumer goods.

All exports and imports require licensing by the Ministry of Foreign Trade, and may be handled by 29 specialized foreign-trade agencies. Enterprises may handle their own foreign trade relations, set up companies abroad and participate in foreign companies. Hard currency is available through the National Bank. Tax-free zones for foreign companies exporting their own products were established in 1983. The Marketexpo branch of the Hungarian National Market Research Institute will conduct research for foreign firms. The agency Interag acts for Western firms in Hungary. Main imports from the West are machinery, fuel and consumer goods.

Joint ventures with Western firms holding up to 49% of the capital are permitted, and foreign companies may set up offices in Hungary. In Nov. 1978 the US and Hungary signed a most-favoured-nation trade agreement. In May 1982 Hungary was granted membership of the IMF.

Total trade between Hungary and UK (British Department of Trade returns, in £1,000 sterling):

	1980	*1981*	*1982*	*1983*	*1984*
Imports to UK	43,327	40,684	44,051	53,834	75,905
Exports and re-exports from UK	68,977	84,181	77,446	91,845	100,502

Tourism. In 1983, 10·46m. foreigners visited Hungary (2·94m. from the West), of whom 6·76m. were tourists (1·54m. from the West); and 4·75m. Hungarians travelled abroad (0·55m. to the West) of whom 3·93m. (0·48m.) were tourists.

COMMUNICATIONS

Roads. In 1983 there were 29,684 km of roads, including motorways, 78 km; highways, 152 km and other first class main roads, 1,934 km. In 1983 passenger cars numbered 1,258,498 (1,223,481 private). 235m. tonnes of freight and 673m. passengers were transported by road in 1983 (excluding intra-urban passengers).

Railways. Route length of public lines in 1983, 7,759 km, of which 1,604 km are electrified. 124m. tonnes of freight and 237m. passengers were carried.

Aviation. Hungarian Air Lines (Malév) operate from Ferihegy airport, 16 km from Budapest. 1983 arrivals, 797,800; departures, 801,700. Malév has 22 aircraft and flies 40 routes (including one to UK), and in 1983 carried 1m. passengers. British Airways, PANAM, Air France, SABENA, Swissair, OS, Lufthansa and KLM have services to Budapest.

Shipping. Permanently navigable waterways have a length of 1,688 km; 4·1m. tonnes of cargo were carried in 1983 and 3·9m. passengers.

Post and Broadcasting. Number of post offices (1983), 2,537; number of telephones, 1,383,200 (1983). Radio licences were abolished in 1980; television licences, (1983) 2,864,000. *Magyar Rádio és Televízió* broadcasts 3 programmes on medium-waves and FM and also regional programmes, including transmissions in German, Romanian and Serbo-Croat. Two TV programmes are broadcast, averaging 91 hours a week in 1983. Colour broadcasts are only transmitted in Budapest, using the SECAM system.

Cinemas and Theatres (1983). There were 3,700 cinemas; attendance 69m. 31 full-length feature films were made. There were 40 theatres; attendance 6·1m.

Newspapers and Books. In 1982 there were 29 dailies and 980 other periodicals. The Party daily is *Népszabadság* ('People's Freedom') (average daily circulation, 727,000). 7,600 book titles were published in 1983 in 99·4m. copies.

JUSTICE, RELIGION, EDUCATION AND WELFARE

Justice. The administration of justice is the responsibility of the Procurator General, who is elected by Parliament for a term of 6 years. Civil and criminal cases fall under the jurisdiction of the district courts, county courts and the Supreme

Court in Budapest. Criminal proceedings are dealt with by district courts through 3-member councils and by county court and the Supreme Court in 5-member councils. A new Civil Code was adopted in 1978 and a new Criminal Code in 1979.

District Courts act only as courts of first instance; county courts as either courts of first instance or of appeal. The Supreme Court acts normally as an appeal court, but may act as a court of first instance in cases submitted to it by the Public Prosecutor. All courts, when acting as courts of first instance, consist of 1 professional judge and 2 lay assessors, and, as courts of appeal, of 3 professional judges. Local government Executive Committees may try petty offences.

District or county judges and assessors are elected by the district or county councils, all members of the Supreme Court by Parliament.

There are also military courts of the first instance. Military cases of the second instance go before the Supreme Court.

Judges are elected by the Presidential Council. 60,282 sentences were imposed on adults in 1983, including 27,295 of imprisonment (of which 12,329 were suspended). Juvenile convictions: 5,865.

Religion. There are 20 authorized religious denominations which share proportionally an annual state subsidy of 70m. forints. 8·5m. of the population professed a religious faith in 1976; the number of active church members was put between 1m. and 1·5m.

Senior church appointments require the consent of the Presidential Council. Lower ones are ratified by the State Office for Church Affairs. Certain appointments become valid if the Office makes no comment within 15 days, and for the most minor church appointments neither state consent nor prior notification is required. Ecclesiastics are required to take an oath of allegiance to the state.

In 1976 there were 5·25m. Roman Catholics with 11 dioceses, 4,000 priests and 4,400 churches, and 500,000 uniates. In 1979 there were 3 seminaries and 1 uniate seminery, a theological academy, and 8 secondary schools. The Primate of Hungary is the Archbishop of Esztergom, Laszló Lekai, appointed Feb. 1976. There are also 2 archbishops, 8 bishops and an apostolic administrator. There is one Uniate bishopric.

In 1976 there were 2m. Calvinists with 4 dioceses, 1,300 ministers and 1,567 churches. There were 2 theological colleges (20% of students female) with 16 teachers, and 1 secondary school. There were 500,000 Lutherans with 16 dioceses, 374 ministers and 673 churches. There is a theological college with 6 teachers. The 10 denominations in the Association of Free Churches had 37,000 members, 230 ministers and 675 churches. There are 4 Orthodox denominations with 40,000 members in 1979. The Unitarian Church has 10,000 members, 11 ministers and 6 churches. In 1979 there were 80,000–100,000 Jews (825,000 in 1939) with 130 synagogues, 26 rabbis, a rabbinical college with 6 teachers and a secondary school.

Education. Education is free and compulsory from 6 to 14. Primary schooling ends at 14; thereafter education may be continued at secondary, secondary technical or secondary vocational schools, which offer diplomas entitling students to apply for higher education, or at vocational training schools which offer tradesmen's diplomas. Students at the latter may also take the secondary school diploma examinations after 2 years of evening or correspondence study.

In 1983–84 there were 4,842 kindergartens with 32,715 teachers and 455,205 pupils; 3,546 primary schools with 83,469 teachers and 1,269,900 pupils; 545 secondary schools with 16,889 teachers and 225,300 pupils; and 269 vocational training schools with 174,800 students and 11,090 teachers. There are 4 universities proper (Budapest, Pécs, Szeged, Debrecen), and 14 specialized universities (6 technical, 4 medical, 3 arts, 1 economics). At these and at 40 other institutions of higher education there were, in 1983–84, 62,900 students and 14,452 teachers.

Libraries and Museums. In 1983 there were 4,842 public and 5,430 trade union libraries. Major national libraries (1983): National Széchenyi, 6m. volumes; Budapest University, 3·3m.; Academy of Sciences, 1·7m.; National Technical Library and Documentation Centre, 1·3m. In 1983 there were 557 museums with 18·59m. visitors.

Health. In 1983 there were 33,035 doctors and dentists and 99,098 hospital beds.

Social Security. Medical treatment is free. Patients bear 15% of the cost of medicines. Sickness benefit is 75% of wages, old age pensions (at 60 for men, 55 for women) 60–70%. In 1983, 111m. forints were paid out in social insurance benefits. In 1983 family allowances were paid to 1,334,000 families. Rates (in forints): 1 child, 670; 2, 1,340; 3, 2,190; 4, 2,920.

DIPLOMATIC REPRESENTATIVES

Of Hungary in Great Britain (35 Eaton Place, London, SW1X 8BY)
Ambassador: Dr Mátyás Domokos (accredited 22 Nov. 1984).

Of Great Britain in Hungary (Harmincad Utca 6, Budapest V)
Ambassador: P. W. Unwin, CMG.

Of Hungary in the USA (3910 Shoemaker St., NW, Washington, D.C., 20008)
Ambassador: Dr Vencel Hazi.

Of the USA in Hungary (Szabadság Tér 12, Budapest V)
Ambassador: Nicolas Salgó.

Of Hungary to the United Nations
Ambassador: Pál Rácz.

Books of Reference

Report of the Hungarian Statistical Office on the Economic Development and Plan Fulfilment. Budapest, annual from 1973
Statisztikai Évkönyv. Budapest, annual; since 1871, abridged English version, *Statistical Year Book*
Statistical Year-Book. (in English and Russian). Budapest, annual from 1982
Statistical Pocket Book of Hungary (in English). Budapest, annual from 1959
Hungarian Digest. Budapest, 6 a year from 1980
The Hungarian Economy: a Quarterly Economic and Business Review. Budapest, since 1972
Hungary 66 (*67* etc.). Budapest, annual from 1966
Marketing in Hungary. Budapest, quarterly
Quarterly Review of the National Bank of Hungary. From 1983
Information Hungary. Budapest, 1980
The Constitution of the Hungarian People's Republic. Budapest, 1972
Bako, E., *Guide to Hungarian Studies.* 2 vols. Stanford Univ. Press, 1973
Berend, I. T., and Ranki, G., *Hungary: A Century of Economic Development.* New York and Newton Abbot, 1974; *Underdevelopment and Economic Growth: Studies in Hungarian Social and Economic History.* Budapest, 1979
Cave, M., *Alternative Approaches to Economic Planning.* London, 1981
Donath, F., *Reform and Revolution: Transformation of Hungary's Agriculture, 1945–1970.* Budapest, 1980
Enyedi, G., *Hungary: An Economic Geography.* Boulder, 1976
Fekete, J., *Back to the Realities: Reflections of a Hungarian Banker.* Budapest, 1982
Gadó, O., *The Economic Mechanism of Hungary.* Leiden and Budapest, 1976
Halász, Z., *Hungary: A Guide with a Difference.* 2nd ed. Budapest, 1979
Hare, P. G., and others (eds.), *Hungary: a Decade of Economic Reform.* London, 1981
Hegedüs, A., *The Structure of Socialist Society.* London, 1977
Ignotus, P., *Hungary.* London, 1972
Kabdebo, T., *Hungary.* [Bibliography] Oxford and Santa Barbara, 1980
Kádár, J., *For a Socialist Hungary.* Budapest, 1974
Kornai, J., *Economics of Shortage.* Oxford, 1980
Kourig, B., *Communism in Hungary.* Stanford, 1979
Kozma, F., *Economic Integration and Economic Strategy.* The Hague, 1982
Macartney, C. A., *Hungary: A Short History.* London, 1962
Németh, G. (ed.), *Hungary: A Comprehensive Guide.* Budapest, 1980
Országh, L., *Hungarian-English Dictionary.* Budapest, 1977.—*English-Hungarian Dictionary.* Budapest, 1970
Pamlényi, E. (ed.), *A History of Hungary.* Budapest, 1975
Pécsi, M. and Sárfalvi, B., *Physical and Economic Geography of Hungary.* 2nd ed. Budapest, 1979
Toma, P. A., and Volgyes, I., *Politics in Hungary.* San Francisco, 1977
Vardy, S. B., and Vardy, A. H., (eds.) *Society in Change.* Boulder, 1983

ICELAND

Capital: Reykjavík
Population: 238,175 (1983)
GNP per capita: US$12,860 (1981)

Lýðveldið Ísland

HISTORY. The first settlers came to Iceland in 874. Between 930 and 1264 Iceland was an independent republic, but by the 'Old Treaty' of 1263 the country recognized the rule of the King of Norway. In 1381 Iceland, together with Norway, came under the rule of the Danish kings, but when Norway was separated from Denmark in 1814, Iceland remained under the rule of Denmark. Since 1 Dec. 1918 it has been acknowledged as a sovereign state. It was united with Denmark only through the common sovereign until it was proclaimed an independent republic on 17 June 1944.

AREA AND POPULATION. Iceland is a large island in the North Atlantic, close to the Arctic Circle, and comprises an area of about 103,000 sq. km (39,758 sq. miles), with its extreme northern point (the Rifstangi) lying in 66° 32′ N. lat., and its most southerly point (Dyrhólaey, Portland) in 63° 24′ N. lat., not including the islands north and south of the land; if these are included, the country extends from 67° 10′ N. (the Kolbeinsey) to 63° 19′ N. (Geirfuglasker, one of the Westman Islands). It stretches from 13° 30′ (the Gerpir) to 24° 32′ W. long. (Látrabjarg). The skerry *Hvalbakur* (The Whaleback) lies 13° 16′ W. long.

The 25 constituencies of the country are now grouped in 7 districts.

District	*Inhabited land (sq. km)*	*Mountain pasture (sq. km)*	*Waste-land (sq. km)*	*Total area (sq. km)*	*Population (1 Dec. 1983)*
Reykjanes area	1,266	716	—	1,982	142,564
West	5,011	3,415	275	8,711	15,115
Western Peninsula	4,130	3,698	1,652	9,470	10,426
Northland West	4,867	5,278	2,948	13,093	10,710
Northland East	9,890	6,727	5,751	22,368	26,190
East }	16,921	17,929	12,555	21,991	13,093
South }				25,214	20,077
Iceland	42,085	37,553	23,181	102,819	238,175

In 1983, 26,855 were domiciled in rural districts and 211,320 in towns and villages (of over 200 inhabitants.) The population is almost entirely Icelandic.

In 1983 foreigners numbered 3,561; of these 1,010 were Danish, 691 US, 339 British, 291 Norwegian and 236 German (Fed. Rep.) nationals.

The capital, Reykjavík, had on 1 Dec. 1983, a population of 87,309; other towns were Akranes, 5,349; Akureyrí, 13,745; Bolungarvík, 1,275; Dalvík, 1,374; Eskifjörður, 1,084; Garðabaer, 5,764; Grindavík, 2,021; Hafnarfjörður, 12,683; Húsavík, 2,514; Ísafjörður, 3,400; Keflavík, 6,886; Kópavogur, 14,433; Neskaupstaður, 1,684; Njarðvík, 2,208; Ólafsfjörður, 1,207; Sauðárkrókur, 2,324; Selfoss, 3,602; Seltjarnarnes, 3,598; Seyðisfjörður, 993; Siglufjörður, 1,915; Vestmannaeyjar, 4,743.

Vital statistics for calendar years:

	Living births	*Still-born*	*Marriages*	*Divorces*	*Deaths*	*Infant deaths*
1981	4,345	21	1,357	463	1,655	26
1982	4,337	17	1,303	421	1,583	31
1983	4,371	14	1,396	495	1,653	27

CLIMATE. The climate is cool temperate oceanic and rather changeable, but mild for its latitude because of the Gulf Stream and prevailing S.W. winds. Precipitation is high in upland areas, mainly in the form of snow. Reykjavik. Jan. 34°F (1°C), July 52°F (11°C). Annual rainfall 34″ (860 mm).

CONSTITUTION AND GOVERNMENT. On 24 May 1944 the people of Iceland decided in a referendum to sever all ties with the Danish Crown. The voters were asked whether they were in favour of the abrogation of the Union Act, and whether they approved of the bill for a republican constitution: 70,725 voters were for severance of all political ties with Denmark and only 370 against it; 69,048 were in favour of the republican constitution, 1,042 against it and 2,505 votes were invalid. On 17 June 1944 the republic was formally proclaimed, and as the republic's first president the Alþingi elected Sveinn Björnsson for a 1-year term (re-elected 1945 and 1949; died 25 Jan. 1952). The President is now elected for a 4-year term.

President of the Republic of Iceland: Vigdís Finnbogadóttir (elected 29 June 1980, with 43,611 out of 129,049 valid votes, inaugurated 1 Aug. 1980); re-elected unopposed in 1984.

National flag: Blue with a red white-bordered Scandinavian cross.

National anthem: Ó Guð vors lands (words by M. Jochumsson, 1874; tune by S. Sveinbjørnsson).

The official language is Icelandic (*íslenzka*).

The *Alþingi* (Parliament) is divided into two Houses, the Upper House and the Lower House. The former is composed of one-third of the members elected by the whole Alþingi in common sitting. The remaining two-thirds of the members form the Lower House. The members of the Alþingi receive payment for their services.

The budget bills must be laid before the two Houses in joint session, but all other bills can be introduced in either of the Houses. If the Houses do not agree, they assemble in a common sitting and the final decision is given by a majority of two-thirds of the voters, with the exception of budget bills, where a simple majority is sufficient. The ministers have free access to both Houses, but can vote only in the House of which they are members.

The electoral law enacted in 1959 provides for an Alþingi of 60 members. Of these, 49 are elected in 8 constituencies by proportional representation; the remaining 11 are apportioned to the parties according to their total vote.

At the elections held on 23 April 1983 the following parties were returned: Independence Party, 23; Progressives, 14; People's Alliance, 10; Social Democrats, 6; Social Democratic Alliance, 4; Women's Alliance, 3.

The executive power is exercised under the President by the Cabinet. The coalition Cabinet, as constituted in May 1983, was as follows:

Prime Minister: Steingrímur Hermannsson (Progress).

Foreign Affairs: Geir Hallgrímsson (Ind.). *Finance:* Albert Guðmundsson (Ind.). *Social Affairs:* Alexander Stefánsson (Progress). *Fisheries:* Halldór Ásgrímsson (Progress). *Agriculture, Justice and Church:* Jón Helgason (Progress). *Health and Social Security, Communications:* Matthías Bjarnason (Ind.). *Commerce:* Matthías A. Mathiesen (Ind.). *Education:* Ragnhildur Helgadóttir (Ind.). *Energy and Industry:* Sverrir Hermannsson (Ind.).

The ministers take responsibility for their acts. They can be impeached by the Alþingi, and in that case their cause will be decided by the *Landsdómur*, a special tribunal for parliamentary impeachments.

Local Administration. Iceland is divided into 224 communes, of which 23 have the status of towns, while the 201 remaining communes make up 23 counties *(sýslur)*. The commune and county councils are elected by universal suffrage (men and women 20 years of age and over), in town and other urban communes by proportional representation, but in rural communes by simple majority. The county councils consist of one representative for each of the constituent communes, their purpose being the superintendence of local government within the county. Town councils and county councils come under the supervision of the Ministry of Social Affairs. For national government there are 27 divisions, consisting of towns and counties, single or combined, with the exception of Keflavik Airport. In the capital the different branches of national government are independent (courts, police, customs), while in other national government divisions they are the charge of one official, who, in the case of counties, presides over the county council as well.

DEFENCE. Iceland possesses neither an army nor a navy. Under the North Atlantic Treaty, US forces are stationed in Iceland as the Iceland Defence Force. Three armed fishery protection vessels are maintained by the Coastguard, with 1 patrol aircraft and 2 helicopters. Coastguard Service personnel in 1983 totalled about 130 officers and men.

INTERNATIONAL RELATIONS

Membership. Iceland is a member of UN, EFTA, OECD, the Council of Europe, NATO and the Nordic Council.

ECONOMY

Budget. Current revenue and expenditure for calendar years (in 1,000 new kr.):

	1979	*1980*	*1981*	*1982*	*1983*	*1984*
Revenue	2,089,508	3,461,773	5,514,780	7,967,266	13,007,315	17,894,777
Expenditure	2,022,864	3,432,401	5,457,475	7,909,270	12,972,958	18,283,464

Main items of the Treasury accounts for 1983 (in 1,000 new kr.):

Revenue		*Expenditure*	
Direct taxes	2,614,289	Presidency	8,899
Indirect taxes	12,867,661	Alþingi	99,817
Profit from government enterprises	82,097	Cabinet	24,730
		Justice and ecclesiastical affairs	972,718
		Culture and education	2,659,074
		Social affairs	623,123
		Commerce	1,159,698
		Foreign affairs	242,965
		Fisheries and agriculture	889,527
		Finance	640,138
		Communications	1,627,671

The public debt of Iceland was on 31 Dec. 1983, 10,797m. new kr., of which the foreign debt amounted to 3,903m. new kr. and the internal debt to 6,894m. new kr.

Currency. The Icelandic monetary units are the *króna*, pl. *krónur* and the *eyrir*, pl. *aurar*. There are 100 *aurar* to the *króna*. On 1 Jan. 1981 a currency reform took place and 100 old krónur equal 1 new króna. In March 1985, US\$1 = kr. 42·92; £1 = kr. 45·82. Note and coin circulation, 31 Dec. 1982, was 825m. new kr.

Banking. By Act of 29 March 1961 the Central Bank of Iceland was established, which took over the central bank function up to that date exercised by the *Landsbanki Íslands* (The National Bank of Iceland, owned entirely by the State). Other banks are: *Búnaðarbanki Íslands* (the Agricultural Bank of Iceland), a state bank, founded in 1930; *Útvegsbanki Íslands* (the Fisheries Bank of Iceland), founded in 1930 as a joint-stock bank, which in 1957 became a state bank; *Ísðnaðarbanki Íslands* (Industrial Bank of Iceland Ltd), a joint-stock bank, established 1953, part of the shares being owned by the Government; *Verzlunarbanki Íslands* (Iceland Bank of Commerce Ltd), established in 1961; *Samvinnubanki Íslands* (The Icelandic Co-operative Bank), established in 1963; *Alþýðubankinn* (The People's Bank Ltd) established 1971. On 31 Dec. 1983 the accounts of the Central Bank balanced at 15,514m. new kr.

At the end of 1983 there were 40 savings banks with deposits amounting to 2,974m. new kr.

Weights and Measures. The metric system of weights and measures is obligatory.

ENERGY AND NATURAL RESOURCES

Electricity. The installed capacity of public power plants at the end of 1983 totalled 907,900 kw., of which 752,000 kw. comprised hydro-electric plants. Total energy production in public-owned plants in 1983 amounted to 3,766m. kwh.; in privately-owned plants, 15m. kwh.

Agriculture. Of the total area of Iceland, about six-sevenths is unproductive, but only about 0·5% is under cultivation, which is confined to hay, potatoes and turnips. In 1983 the total hay crop was 3,249,000 cu. metres; the crop of potatoes, 3,600 tonnes, and of turnips 366 tonnes. At the end of 1983 the livestock was as follows: Horses, 52,060; cattle, 68,540 (including 33,189 milch cows); sheep, 711,936; pigs, 2,203; poultry, 294,425.

Fisheries. Fishing vessels in Dec. 1983 numbered 836 with a gross tonnage of 111,772. Total catch in 1982, 766,000 tonnes; 1983, 835,000 tonnes.

The Icelandic Government announced that the fishery limits off Iceland were extended from 12 to 50 nautical miles from Sept. 1972. An interim agreement for 2 years signed by the UK and Iceland in Nov. 1973 expired in Nov. 1975.

On 15 July 1975 the Icelandic Government issued a decree that from 15 Oct. 1975 the fishery limits of Iceland were extended from 50 to 200 nautical miles. The Icelandic Government maintain that this extension is necessary to protect the fish stocks in Icelandic waters because the fishing industry is of vital importance to the national economy.

COMMERCE. Total value of imports and exports in 1,000 new kr.:

	1979	*1980*	*1981*	*1982*	*1983*
Imports	2,913,072	4,801,616	7,484,684	11,647,000	20,605,978
Exports	2,784,515	4,459,529	6,536,214	8,479,000	18,632,993

Leading exports (in 1,000 kg and 1,000 new kr.):

	1982		*1983*	
	Quantity	*Value*	*Quantity*	*Value*
Fish and whale products	365,219,200	6,354,366	332,480,400	12,667,465
Agricultural products	6,051,000	107,088	6,290,900	206,892

Leading imports (in 1,000 tonnes and 1,000 new kr.):

	1982		*1983*	
	Quantity	*Value*	*Quantity*	*Value*
Ships (number)	15	302,026	8	540,868
Fuel oil	399,824·5	1,208,479	378,164·0	2,246,755
Cereals	15,365,·5	79,291	13,242·1	140,580
Animal feed	65,113·7	175,550	72,722·6	375,277
Gasoline	94,222·7	346,257	93,732·3	664,803
Motor vehicles (number)	10,565	616,149	5,982	707,689
Fishing nets and other gear	1,843·1	128,483	1,368·6	191,629

Value of trade with principal countries for 3 years (in 1,000 new kr.):

	1981		*1982*		*1983*	
	Imports (c.i.f.)	*Exports (f.o.b.)*	*Imports (c.i.f.)*	*Exports (f.o.b.)*	*Imports (c.i.f.)*	*Exports (f.o.b.)*
Austria	45,612	4,486	81,093	6,099	124,547	26,450
Belgium	200,980	82,664	305,040	117,630	508,860	403,097
Brazil	66,218	6,905	70,100	12,821	90,548	47,169
Canada	83,724	44,028	66,677	44,581	82,117	70,010
Czechoslovakia	39,698	49,379	44,249	21,854	69,302	46,214
Denmark	777,025	111,851	1,133,722	148,238	2,002,029	288,975
Faroe Islands	33,103	55,919	1,280	65,988	1,337	114,137
Finland	168,599	92,481	289,005	130,242	508,157	193,369
France	169,693	124,716	304,956	243,790	470,430	682,076
German Dem. Rep.	20,660	1,118	41,471	2,570	67,775	5,126
Germany, Fed. Rep. of	858,270	420,803	1,422,183	600,492	2,426,220	1,812,324
Greece	989	73,317	1,265	115,127	4,417	188,803
Hungary	5,617	6,596	8,020	4,961	11,632	13,606
India	12,430	—	20,145	1	26,665	—
Ireland	12,865	12,338	25,447	10,788	42,743	6,057
Israel	8,285	832	8,890	4,868	15,709	16,274
Italy	174,253	209,161	289,555	321,938	499,429	587,596
Japan	336,011	108,870	545,186	273,719	807,752	521,783
Netherlands	555,424	75,638	852,213	80,103	1,310,917	282,373
Nigeria	188	858,368	226	325,335	302	888,441
Norway	734,028	78,697	871,681	62,935	1,642,559	131,801

	1981		1982		1983	
	Imports (c.i.f.)	*Exports (f.o.b.)*	*Imports (c.i.f.)*	*Exports (f.o.b.)*	*Imports (c.i.f.)*	*Exports (f.o.b.)*
Poland	27,510	56,463	39,192	41,390	49,365	36,543
Portugal	135,171	702,137	268,449	999,498	490,611	1,142,564
Spain	76,038	243,620	120,130	345,865	193,250	610,292
Sweden	623,416	110,218	963,472	118,377	1,717,205	218,809
Switzerland	85,002	165,371	106,463	300,017	220,340	1,056,507
USSR	600,045	403,040	1,063,158	639,827	2,133,474	1,384,598
UK	573,204	933,349	1,015,647	1,118,684	1,810,767	2,207,225
USA	581,709	1,361,079	982,751	2,188,650	1,622,300	5,266,130

Total trade between Iceland and UK (British Department of Trade returns, in £1,000 sterling):

	1980	*1981*	*1982*	*1983*	*1984*
Imports to UK	82,042	75,729	72,721	66,505	86,104
Exports and re-exports from UK	47,223	50,558	102,714	65,176	64,242

TOURISM. There were 77,592 visitors to Iceland in 1983.

COMMUNICATIONS

Roads. There are no railways in Iceland. Iceland possesses between 11,000–12,000 km of high roads and country roads. Motor vehicles registered at the end of 1983 numbered 108,254, of which 97,307 were passenger cars and 10,947 trucks; there were also 804 motor cycles. On 26 May 1968 Iceland changed from left-hand to right-hand traffic.

Aviation. One large and some small companies maintain regular services between Reykjavík and various places in Iceland (the large one 1983: 202,501 passengers; 881 tonnes of mail; 2,250 tonnes of freight). The large company maintains regular services between Iceland and the UK, the Scandinavian countries, some other European countries and USA. In 1983 the company carried in scheduled foreign flights 360,147 passengers, 1,478 tonnes of mail and 5,763 tonnes of freight.

Shipping. The mercantile marine of Iceland consisted in Dec. 1983 of 4 steam vessels (1,953 gross tons) and 936 motor vessels (190,359 gross tons).

Post and Broadcasting. At the end of 1983 the number of post offices was 150 and telephone and telegraph offices 115; number of telephones, 124,951. The government station, *Rikisútvarpid,* broadcasts 1 programme on long and medium-waves and on FM. *Rikisútvarpid-Sjónvarp* uses 130 transmitters and broadcasts 1 TV programme. Number of licenced receivers: radio, about 70,000; television, about 66,000.

Cinemas (1980). There were 29 cinemas with a seating capacity of about 12,000.

Newspapers (1984). There are 5 daily newspapers, all in Reykjavík, with a combined circulation of about 125,000.

JUSTICE, RELIGION, EDUCATION AND WELFARE

Justice. The lower courts of justice are those of the provincial magistrates (*sýslumenn*) and town judges (*bæjarfógetar*). From these there is an appeal to the Supreme Court (*hæstiréttur*) in Reykjavík, which has 8 judges.

Religion. The national church, and the only one endowed by the State, is Evangelical Lutheran. But there is complete religious liberty, and no civil disabilities are attached to those not of the national religion. The affairs of the national church are under the superintendence of a bishop. In 1982, 4,444 persons (1·9%) were Dissenters and 2,946 persons (1·2%) did not belong to any religious community.

Education. Compulsory education for children began in 1907, and a university was founded in Reykjavík in 1911. There is in Reykjavík a teachers' training college and a technical high school; various specialized institutions of learning and a number of second-level schools are scattered throughout the country. There are many part-time schools of cultural activities, including music.

Compulsory education comprises 8 classes, 7-14 years of age. After completion of a facultative 9th class, attended by 93%-95% of the relevant age group, there is access to further schooling free of charge. Some 65% of the age groups 15-19 years old attend schools. Around 15%-20% of each age group go into handicraft apprenticeship. About 30% pass matriculation examination, generally at the age of 20. Approximately one third-level student out of every four goes abroad for studies, two-thirds of them to Scandinavia, the rest mainly to English- and German-speaking countries.

Immatriculation in Iceland in autumn 1983: Preceding the first level, 3,989. First-level (1st-6th class) 25,280. Second-level first stage (7th-9th class) 11,732. Second-level second stage general programmes (4-year courses) 7,048. Second-level second stage vocational programmes (3 or 4 year courses) 8,023. Third-level first stage non-university 562. Third-level first and second stage university and equivalent 4,650.

Social Welfare. The main body of the Icelandic social welfare legislation is consolidated in six main acts:

(i) The social security legislation (a) health insurance, including sickness benefits; *(b)* social security pensions, mainly consisting of old age pension, disablement pension and widows' pension, and also children's pension; *(c)* employment injuries insurance.

(ii) The unemployment insurance legislation, where daily allowances are paid to those who have met certain conditions.

(iii) The subsistence legislation. This is controlled by municipal government, and social assistance is granted under special circumstances, when payments from other sources are not sufficient.

(iv) The tax legislation. In 1975 family allowances were abolished and children's support included in the tax legislation, according to which a certain amount is subtracted from levied taxes for each child in a family.

(v) The rehabilitation legislation.

(vi) Child and juvenile guidance.

Health insurance covers the entire population. Citizenship is not demanded and there is no waiting period. Most hospitals are both municipally and state run, a few solely state run and all offer free medical help. Medical treatment out of hospitals is partly paid by the patient, the same applies to medicines, except medicines of life-long necessary use, which are paid in full by the health insurance. Dental care is free for the age groups 6-15, but is paid 75% for those five years or younger and the age group 16 but 50% for old age and disabled pensioners. Sickness benefits are paid to those who lose income because of periodical illness. The daily amount is fixed and paid from the 11th day of illness. On 1 Nov. 1984 it was 173 new kr. a day.

Entitlement to old age and disablement pensions at the full rates is subject to the condition that the beneficiary has been resident in Iceland for 40 years at the age period of 16–67. For shorter period of residence, the benefits are reduced proportionally. Entitled to old age pension are all those who are 67 years old, and have been residents in Iceland for 3 years of the age period of 16–67. Entitled to disablement pension are those who have lost 75% of their working capacity and have been residents in Iceland for 3 years before application or have had full working capacity at the time when they became residents. Old age and disablement pension are of equally high amount, in the year 1984 the total sum was 41,969 new kr. for an individual. Married pensioners are paid 90% of two individuals' pensions. In addition to the basic amount, supplementary allowances are paid according to social circumstances and income possibilities. Widows' pensions are the same amount as old age and disablement pension, provided the applicant is over 60 when she becomes widowed. Women at the age 50–60 get reduced pension. Women under 50 are not entitled to widows' pensions.

The employment injuries insurance covers medical care, daily allowances, disablement pension and survivors' pension and is applicable to practically all employees.

All benefits within the above-mentioned laws shall go up in step with general wages within 6 months from their increase.

Social assistance is primarily municipal and granted in cases outside the social security legislation. Domestic assistance to old people and disabled is granted within this legislation, besides other services.

Child and juvenile guidance is performed by chosen committees according to special laws, such as home guidance and family assistance. In cases of parents' disablement the committees take over the guidance of the children involved.

DIPLOMATIC REPRESENTATIVES

Of Iceland in Great Britain (1 Eaton Terrace, London, SW1W 8EY)
Ambassador: Einar Benediktsson (accredited 11 Nov. 1982).

Of Great Britain in Iceland (Laufásvegur 49, 101 Reykjavík)
Ambassador and Consul-General: Richard Thomas.

Of Iceland in the USA (2022 Connecticut Ave., NW, Washington, D.C., 20008)
Ambassador: Hans G. Andersen.

Of the USA in Iceland (Laufasvegur 21, 101 Reykjavík)
Ambassador: Marshall Brement.

Of Iceland to the United Nations
Ambassador: Hörður Helgason.

Books of Reference

Statistical Information: The Icelandic Statistical Office, Hagstofa Íslands (Reykjavík) was founded in 1914. *Director:* Klemens Tryggvason. Its main publications are:

Hagskýrslur Íslands. Statistics of Iceland (from 1912)
Hagtíðindi (Statistical Journal) (from 1916)
Statistical Bulletin. Issued quarterly by the Statistical Bureau of Iceland and the Central Bank of Iceland (from 1931 to 1962, monthly). Ceased publication May 1980
Economic Statistics. Central Bank of Iceland (quarterly from 1980)
Icelandic Currency Reform January 1st 1981. Central Bank of Iceland, 1980
Heilbrigðisskýrslur. Public Health in Iceland (latest issue for 1977; published 1980)
Cleasby, R., *An Icelandic-English Dictionary.* 2nd ed. Oxford, 1957
Foss, H. (ed.), *Directory of Iceland.* Annual. Reykjavík, 1907–40, 1948 ff.
Hermannsson, Halldór, *Islandica.* An annual relating to Iceland and the Fiske Icelandic Collection in Cornell University Library. Ithaca (from 1908)
Hood, J. C. F., *Icelandic Church Saga.* London, 1946
Horton, J. J., *Iceland.* [Bibliography] Oxford and Santa Barbara, 1983
Leaf, H., *Iceland Yesterday and Today.* London, 1949
Magnússon, S. A., *Northern Sphinx: Iceland and the Icelanders from the Settlement to the Present.* London, 1977
Nordal, J., and Kristinsson, V. (eds), *Iceland 874–1974.* Central Board of Iceland, Reykjavík, 1975
Þórðarson, Matthias, *The Althing, Iceland's Thousand-Year-Old Parliament, 930–1930.* Reykjavík, 1930
Þorsteinsson, Þorsteinn, *Iceland, 1946: A Handbook Published on the 60th Anniversary of the National Bank of Iceland.* 4th ed. Reykjavík, 1946
Zoëga, G. T., *Íslensk-ensk (and Ensk-íslensk) orðabók.* 3rd ed. 2 vols. Reykjavík, 1932–51

National Library: Landsbókasafnið, Reykjavík, *Librarian:* Dr Finnbogi Guðomundsson.

INDIA

Capital: New Delhi
Population: 684m. (1981)
GDP per capita: US$260 (1981)

Bharat

HISTORY. The Indus civilization was fully developed by *c.* 2500 B.C., and collapsed *c.* 1750 B.C. An Aryan civilization spread from the west as far as the Ganges valley by 500 B.C.; separate kingdoms were established and many of these were united under the Mauryan dynasty established by Chandragupta in *c.* 320 B.C. The Mauryan Empire was succeeded by numerous small kingdoms. The Gupta dynasty (A.D. 320–600) was followed by the first Arabic invasions of the north-west. Moslem, Hindu and Buddhist states developed together with frequent conflict until the establishment of the Mogul dynasty in 1526. The first settlements by the East India Company were made after 1600 and the company established a formal system of government for Bengal in 1700. During the decline of the Moguls frequent wars between the Company, the French and the native princes led to the Company's being brought under British Government control in 1784; the first Governor-General of India was appointed in 1786. The powers of the Company were abolished by the India Act, 1858, and its functions and forces transferred to the British Crown. Representative government was introduced in 1909, and the first parliament in 1919. The separate dominions of India and Pakistan became independent within the Commonwealth in 1947 and India became a republic in 1950.

EVENTS. More than 2,000 people were killed by a leakage of methyl isocyanate gas from a pesticide plant in Bhopal, Madhya Pradesh, in Dec. 1984.

AREA AND POPULATION. India is bounded north-west by Pakistan, north by China, Tibet, Nepál and Bhután, east by Burma, south-east, south and south west by the Indian ocean. The far eastern states and territories are almost separated from the rest by Bangladesh as it extends northwards from the Bay of Bengal. The area of the Indian Union (excluding the Pakistan and China occupied parts of Jammu and Kashmir) is 3,166,829 sq. km. Its population according to the 1981 census (preliminary figures) was 683,810,051 (excluding the occupied area of Jammu and Kashmir); this represents an increase of 24·8% since 1971. Sex ratio was 940 females per 1,000 males (929 in 1971); density of population, 221 per sq. km. About 23·7% of the population was urban in 1981 (in Maharashtra, 35%; in Himachal Pradesh, 7·7%).

Many births and deaths go unregistered. Data from certain areas of better registration and field studies suggest that the average annual birth rate for the decade 1971–80 was about 36 per 1,000 population, the death rate 14·8 per 1,000. In 1980 (estimate) the age-group 0–14 years represented 39·7% of the population and only 5·5% were over 60. In 1981 expectation of life for men was 52 years, for women 50.

Marriages and divorces are not registered. The minimum age for a civil marriage is 18 for women and 21 for men; for a sacramental marriage, 14 for girls and 18 for youths.

The main details of the census of 1 March 1971 and of 1 March 1981 are:

Name of State	*Land area in sq km (1981)*	*Population 1971*	*Population 1981*
States			
Andhra Pradesh	276,814	43,502,708	53,403,619
Assam	78,523	14,625,152	19,902,826
Bihar	173,876	56,353,369	[illegible]
Gujarat	195,984	26,697,475	33,960,905
Haryana	44,222	10,036,808	12,850,902
Himachal Pradesh	55,673	3,460,434	4,237,569
Jammu and Kashmir[1]	101,283	4,617,000	5,981,600

[1] Excludes the Pakistan-occupied area.

Name of State	Land area in sq. km (1981)	Population 1971	Population 1981
Karnataka	191,773	29,299,014	37,043,451
Kerala	38,864	21,347,375	25,403,217
Madhya Pradesh	442,841	41,654,119	52,131,717
Maharashtra	307,762	50,412,235	62,693,898
Manipur	22,356	1,072,753	1,433,691
Meghalaya	22,489	1,011,699	1,327,824
Nagaland	16,527	516,449	773,281
Orissa	155,782	21,944,615	26,272,054
Punjab	50,362	13,551,060	16,669,755
Rajasthan	342,214	25,765,806	34,102,912
Sikkim	7,299	...	315,682
Tamil Nadu	130,069	41,199,168	48,297,456
Tripura	10,477	1,556,342	2,060,189
Uttar Pradesh	294,413	88,341,144	110,858,019
West Bengal	87,853	44,312,011	54,485,560
Union Territories			
Andaman and Nicobar Islands	8,293	115,133	188,254
Arunachal Pradesh	83,578	467,511	628,050
Chandigarh	114	257,251	450,061
Dadra and Nagar Haveli	491	74,170	103,677
Delhi	1,485	4,065,698	6,196,414
Goa, Daman and Diu	3,813	857,771	1,082,117
Lakshadweep	32	31,810	40,237
Mizoram	21,087	332,390	487,774
Pondicherry	480	471,707	604,136
Grand total	3,166,829	547,949,809	683,810,051

Greatest density occurs in Delhi (4,178 per sq. km), Chandigarh (3,948), Lakshadweep (1,257) and Pondicherry (1,228). The lowest occurs in Arunachal Pradesh (7).

There were (1981) 353,347,249 males and 330,462,802 females.

In 1981, 502m. were rural (*c.* 76%) and 156m. were urban.

Cities and Urban Agglomerations (with states in brackets) having more than 250,000 population at the 1981 census were (1,000):

Agra (U.P.)	770
Ahmedabad (Guj.)	2,515
Ajmer (Raj.)	374
Aligarh (U.P.)	320
Allahabad (U.P.)	642
Amravati (Mah.)	261
Amritsar (Pun.)	589
Asansol (W.B.)	365
Aurangabad (Mah.)	316
Bangalore (Kar.)	2,914
Bareilly (U.P.)	438
Belgaum (Kar.)	300
Bhavnagar (Guj.)	308
Bhopal (M.P.)	672
Bikaner (Raj.)	280
Bokaro Steel City (Bih.)	261
Bombay (Mah.)	8,227
Calcutta (W.B.)	9,166
Calicut (Ker.)	546
Chandigarh (Ch.)	421
Cochin (Ker.)	686
Coimbatore (T.N.)	917
Cuttack (Ori.)	326
Dehra Dun (U.P.)	294
Delhi	5,714
Dhanbad (Bih.)	677
Durgapur (W.B.)	306
Durg-Bhilainagar (M.P.)	490
Erode (T.N.)	275
Faridabad agglomeration	327
Ghaziabad (U.P.)	292
Gorakhpur (U.P.)	306
Guntur (A.P.)	367
Gwalior (M.P.)	560
Hubli-Dharwar (Kar.)	526
Hyderabad (A.P.)	2,528
Indore (M.P.)	827
Jabalpur (M.P.)	758
Jaipur (Raj.)	1,005
Jalandhar (Pun.)	406
Jamnagar (Guj.)	317
Jamshedpur (Bih.)	670
Jhansi (U.P.)	281
Jodhpur (Raj.)	494
Kanpur (U.P.)	1,688
Kolhapur (Mah.)	351
Kotah (Raj.)	347
Lucknow (U.P.)	1,007
Ludhiana (Pun.)	606
Madras (T.N.)	4,277
Madurai (T.N.)	904
Mangalore (Kar.)	306
Meerut (U.P.)	538
Moradabad (U.P.)	348
Mysore (Kar.)	476
Nagpur (Mah.)	1,298
Nasik (Mah.)	429
Patna (Bih.)	916
Pondicherry	251
Pune (Mah.)	1,685
Raipur (M.P.)	339
Rajahmundry (A.P.)	268
Rajkot (Guj.)	444
Ranchi (Bih.)	501
Rourkela (Ori.)	321
Saharanpur (U.P.)	294
Salem (T.N.)	515
Sangli (Mah.)	269
Sholapur (Mah.)	514
Srinagar (J. & K.)	520[1]
Surat (Guj.)	913
Thana (Mah.)	389
Tiruchirapalli (T.N.)	608
Tirunelveli (T.N.)	324
Trivandrum (Ker.)	520
Tuticorin (T.N.)	251
Ujjain (M.P.)	282
Ulhasnagar (Mah.)	648
Vadodara (Guj.)	744
Varanasi (U.P.)	794
Vijayawada (A.P.)	545
Visakhapatnam (A.P.)	594
Warangal (A.P.)	336

[1] Estimate.

Report of the Officials of the Government of India and the People's Republic of China on the Boundary Question. New Delhi, Ministry of External Affairs, 1961
Census of India: Reports and Papers, Decennial Series. (Government of India.)
Annual Report on the Working of Indian Migration. Government of India, from 1956
Report of the Commissioner for Scheduled Castes and Scheduled Tribes. Government of India. Annual
Public Health. Report of the Public Health Commission with the Government of India. Annual
Agarwala, S. N., *India's Population Problems.* New York, 1973

CLIMATE. India has a variety of climatic sub-divisions. In general, there are four seasons. The cool one lasts from Dec. to March, the hot season is in April and May, the rainy season is June to Sept., followed by a further dry season till Nov. Rainfall, however, varies considerably, from 4″ (100 mm) in the N.W. desert to over 400″ (10,000 mm) in parts of Assam.

Range of temperature and rainfall: New Delhi. Jan. 57°F (13·9°C), July 88°F (31·1°C). Annual rainfall 26″ (640 mm). Bombay. Jan. 75°F (23·9°C), July 81°F (27·2°C). Annual rainfall 72″ (1,809 mm). Calcutta. Jan. 67°F (19·4°C), July 84°F (28·9°C). Annual rainfall 64″ (1,600 mm). Cherrapunji. Jan. 53°F (11·7°C), July 68°F (20°C). Annual rainfall 432″ (10,798 mm). Cochin. Jan. 80°F (26·7°C), July 79°F (26·1°C). Annual rainfall 117″ (2,929 mm). Darjeeling. Jan. 41°F (5°C), July 62°F (16·7°C). Annual rainfall 121″ (3,035 mm). Hyderabad. Jan. 72°F (22·2°C), July 80°F (26·7°C). Annual rainfall 30″ (752 mm). Madras. Jan. 76°F (24·4°C), July 87°F (30·6°C). Annual rainfall 51″ (1,270 mm). Patna. Jan. 63°F (17·2°C), July 90°F (32·2°C). Annual rainfall 46″ (1,150 mm).

CONSTITUTION AND GOVERNMENT. On 26 Jan. 1950 India became a sovereign democratic republic. India's relations with the British Commonwealth of Nations were defined at the London conference of Prime Ministers on 27 April 1949.

Unanimous agreement was reached to the effect that the Republic of India remains a full member of the Commonwealth and accepts the Queen as 'the symbol of the free association of its independent member nations and, as such, the head of the Commonwealth'. This agreement was ratified by the Constituent Assembly of India on 17 May 1949.

The constitution was passed by the Constituent Assembly on 26 Nov. 1949 and came into force on 26 Jan. 1950. It has since been amended 44 times.

India is a Union of States and comprises 22 States and 9 Union territories. Each State is administered by a Governor appointed by the President for a term of 5 years while each Union territory is administered by the President through an administrator appointed by him.

The capital is New Delhi.

Presidency. The head of the Union is the President in whom all executive power is vested, to be exercised on the advice of ministers responsible to Parliament. He is elected by an electoral college consisting of all the elected members of Parliament and of the various state legislative assemblies. He holds office for 5 years and is eligible for re-election. He must be an Indian citizen at least 35 years old and eligible for election to the Lower House. He can be removed from office by impeachment for violation of the constitution.

There is also a Vice-President who is *ex officio* chairman of the Upper House of Parliament.

Central Legislature. The Parliament for the Union consists of the President, the Council of States *(Rajya Sabha)* and the House of the People *(Lok Sabha)*. The Council of States, or the Upper House, consists of not more than 250 members; in 1980 there were 232 elected members and 12 members nominated by the President. The election to this house is indirect; the representatives of each State are elected by the elected members of the Legislative Assembly of that State. The Council of States is a permanent body not liable to dissolution, but one-third of the members retire every second year. The House of the People, or the Lower House, consists of 544 members, 525 directly elected on the basis of adult suffrage from territorial constituencies in the States, and 17 members to represent the Union territories, chosen in such manner as the Parliament may by law provide; in March 1982 there were 542 elected members and 2 members nominated by the President. The House of the People unless sooner dissolved continues for a period of 5 years from the date appointed for its first meeting; in emergency, Parliament can extend the term by 1 year.

State Legislatures. For every State there is a legislature which consists of the Governor, and *(a)* 2 Houses, a Legislative Assembly and a Legislative Council, in the States of Andhra Pradesh, Jammu and Kashmir, Karnataka, Madhya Pradesh, Maharashtra, Tamil Nadu and Uttar Pradesh, and *(b)* 1 House, a Legislative Assembly, in the other States. Every Legislative Assembly, unless sooner dissolved, continues for 5 years from the date appointed for its first meeting. In emergency the term can be extended by 1 year. Every State Legislative Council is a permanent body and is not subject to dissolution, but one-third of the members retire every year. Parliament can, however, abolish an existing Legislative Council or create a new one, if the proposal is supported by a resolution of the Legislative Assembly concerned.

Legislative Councils have one-third of the total membership of the Assemblies but not less than 40 members, of whom one-third are elected by local authorities, one-third by members of the Assembly, one-twelfth by state university graduates and one-twelfth by teachers of secondary school upwards; the rest are named by the Governor. Legislative Assemblies have between 60 and 500 directly elected members.

Legislation. The various subjects of legislation are enumerated in three lists in the seventh schedule to the constitution. List I, the Union List, consists of 97 subjects (including defence, foreign affairs, communications, currency and coinage, banking and customs) with respect to which the Union Parliament has exclusive power to make laws. The State legislature has exclusive power to make laws with respect to the 66 subjects in list II, the State List; these include police and public order, agriculture and irrigation, education, public health and local government. The powers to make laws with respect to the 47 subjects (including economic and social planning, legal questions and labour and price control) in list III, the Concurrent List, are held by both Union and State governments, though the former prevails. But Parliament may legislate with respect to any subject in the State List in circumstances when the subject assumes national importance or during emergencies.

Other provisions deal with the administrative relations between the Union and the States, interstate trade and commerce, distribution of revenues between the States and the Union, official language, etc.

Fundamental Rights. Two chapters of the constitution deal with fundamental rights and 'Directive Principles of State Policy'. 'Untouchability' is abolished, and its practice in any form is punishable. The fundamental rights can be enforced through the ordinary courts of law and through the Supreme Court of the Union. The directive principles cannot be enforced through the courts of law; they are nevertheless fundamental in the governance of the country.

Citizenship. Under the Constitution, every person who was on the 26 Jan. 1950, domiciled in India and *(a)* was born in India or *(b)* either of whose parents was born in India or *(c)* who has been ordinarily resident in the territory of India for not less than 5 years immediately preceding that date became a citizen of India. Special provision is made for migrants from Pakistan and for Indians resident abroad. Under the Citizenship Act, 1955, which supplemented the provisions of the Constitution, Indian citizenship is acquired by birth, by descent, by registration and by naturalization. The Act also provides for loss of citizenship by renunciation, termination and deprivation. The right to vote is granted to every person who is a citizen of India and who is not less than 21 years of age on a fixed date and is not otherwise disqualified.

Parliament. Parliament and the state legislatures are organized according to the following schedule (figures show distribution of seats in March 1982):

	Parliament: House of the People (Lok Sabha)	Parliament: Council of States (Rajya Sabha)	State Legislatures: Legislative Assemblies (Vidhan Sabhas)	State Legislatures: Legislative Councils (Vidhan Parishads)
States:				
Andhra Pradesh	42	18	294	90
Assam	14	7	126	–
Bihar	54	22	324	–
Gujarat	26	11	182	–
Haryana	10	5	90	–
Himachal Pradesh	4	3	68	–
Karnataka	28	12	224	63
Kerala	20	9	140	–
Madhya Pradesh	40	16	320	90
Maharashtra	48	19	288	78
Manipur	2	1	60	–
Meghalaya	2	1	60	–
Nagaland	1	1	60	–
Orissa	21	10	147	–
Punjab	13	7	117	–
Rajasthan	25	10	200	–
Sikkim	1	1	32	–
Tamil Nadu	39	18	234	63
Tripura	2	1	60	–
Uttar Pradesh	85	34	425	108
West Bengal	42	16	294	–
Jammu and Kashmir	6	4	76[2]	36[4]
Union Territories:				
Andaman and Nicobar Islands	1	–	–	–
Arunachal Pradesh	2	1[3]	30	–
Chandigarh	1	–	–	–
Dadra and Nagar Haveli	1	–	–	–
Delhi	7	3	61	–
Goa, Daman and Diu	2	–	30	–
Lakshadweep	1	–	–	–
Mizoram	1	1	30	–
Pondicherry	1	1	30	–
Nominated by the President under Article 80 (1) (a) of the Constitution	–	12	–	–
Total	544[1]	244	4,034	528

[1] Includes 2 nominated members to represent Anglo-Indians.
[2] Excludes 25 seats for Pakistan-occupied areas of the State which are in abeyance.
[3] Nominated by the President.
[4] Excludes seats for the Pakistan-occupied areas.

The number of seats allotted to scheduled castes and scheduled tribes in the House of the People is 77 and 42 respectively. Out of the 3,864 seats allotted to the Legislative Assemblies, 521 are reserved for scheduled castes and 329 for scheduled tribes.

Following the general election of Dec. 1984 (the 14 Assam and 13 Punjab seats were not contested) the composition of the House of the People was: Indira Congress 402; Telugu Desam, 30; Communist Party (Marxist) 22; All India Anna DMK, 12; Janata, 10; Communist Party, 6; Congress (S), 1; National Conference (F), 3; Dalit Mazdoor Kisan Party, 3; Independents and others, 20; nominated, 2; vacant, 30.

The Council of States was composed as follows: Indira Congress 154; CPI (Marxist) 13; All-India Anna DMK 11; Janata, 9; Bharatiya Janata, 8; Lok Dal, 5; CPI, 5; Telugu Desam, 5; DMK, 3; National Conference (F), 3; Congress (S), 2; Akali Dal, 2; Forward Bloc, 2; Others, 7; Independent 4; Nominated 6; Vacant 5.

National flag: Three horizontal stripes of saffron (orange), white and green, with the wheel of Asoka in the centre in blue.

National anthem: Jana-gana-mana (words by Rabindranath Tagore).

Indian Independence Act, 1947. (Ch. 30.) London, 1947
The Constitution of India (Modified up to 15 April 1967). Delhi, 1967
Appadorai, A., *Indian Political Thinking in the Twentieth Century: From Naoroji to Nehru.* OUP, 1971.—*Documents on Political Thought in Modern India.* OUP, 1974
Austin, G., *The Indian Constitution.* OUP, 1972
Gandhi, I., *The Speeches and Reminiscences of Indira Gandhi.* London, 1975
Mansergh, N., ed. *The Transfer of Power 1942–47.* 5 vols. HMSO, 1970–75
Menon, V. P., *Transfer of Power in India.* Bombay, 1957
Pylee, M. V., *Constitutional Government in India.* 2nd ed. Bombay, 1965
Rao, K. V., *Parliamentary Democracy of India.* 2nd ed. Calcutta, 1965
Seervali, H. M., *Constitutional Law of India.* Bombay, 1967

Language. The Constitution provides that the official language of the Union shall be Hindi in the Devanagari script. It was originally provided that English should continue to be used for all official purposes until 1965. But the Official Languages Act 1963 provides that, after the expiry of this period of 15 years from the coming into force of the Constitution, English might continue to be used, in addition to Hindi, for all official purposes of the Union for which it was being used immediately before that day, and for the transaction of business in Parliament. According to the Official Languages (Use for official purposes of the Union) Rules 1976, an employee may record in Hindi or in English without being required to furnish a translation thereof in the other language and no employee possessing a working knowledge of Hindi may ask for an English translation of any document in Hindi except in the case of legal or technical documents.

The following 15 languages are included in the Eighth Schedule to the Constitution: Assamese, Bengali, Gujarati, Hindi, Kannada, Kashmiri, Malayalam, Marathi, Oriya, Punjabi, Sanskrit, Sindhi, Tamil, Telugu, Urdu.

There are numerous mother tongues grouped under each language. Hindi, Bengali, Telugu and Marathi languages (including mother tongues grouped under each) are spoken by 162·6m., 44.8m., 44·8m. and 42·3m. of the population respectively.

Ferozsons English–Urdu, Urdu–English Dictionary. 2 vols. 4th ed. Lahore, 1961
Fallon, S. W., *A New English–Hindustani Dictionary.* Lahore, 1941
Grierson, Sir G. A., *Linguistic Survey of India.* 11 vols. (in 19 parts). Delhi, 1903-28
Mitra, S. C., *Student's Bengali–English Dictionary.* 2nd ed. Calcutta, 1923
Scholberg, H. C., *Concise Grammar of the Hindi Language.* 3rd ed. London, 1955
University of Madras, *Tamil Lexicon.* 7 vols. Madras, 1924-39
Vyas, V. G., and Patel, S. G., *Standard English–Gujarati Dictionary.* 2 vols. Bombay, 1923

Government. *President of the Republic:* Zail Singh (sworn in July 1982).
Vice-President: R. Venkataraman (took office 31 Aug. 1984).

There is a Council of Ministers to aid and advise the President of the Republic in the exercise of his functions; this comprises Ministers who are members of the Cabinet and Ministers of State who are not. A Minister who for any period of 6 consecutive months is not a member of either House of Parliament ceases to be a Minister at the expiration of that period. The Prime Minister is appointed by the President; other Ministers are appointed by the President on the Prime Minister's advice.

The salary of each Minister is Rs 27,000 per annum, and that of each Deputy Minister is Rs 21,000 per annum. Each Minister is entitled to the free use of a furnished residence and a chauffeur-driven car throughout his term of office. A Cabinet Minister has a sumptuary allowance of Rs 500 per month, other Ministers (but not Deputy Ministers) of up to Rs 500. At the administrative head of each Ministry is a Secretary of the Government.

Following was the composition of the Cabinet in Jan. 1985:

Prime Minister: Rajiv Gandhi.
Portfolios held by the Prime Minister:
Planning, Environment and Forest, Science and Technology, Atomic Energy, Culture, Electronics, Ocean Development, Personnel and Administrative Reforms, Space, Tourism and Civil Aviation, Youth Affairs, Sports and other subjects not allocated to the Cabinet.

Ministers or Ministers of State:
Foreign Affairs: R. Bhandari.
Works and Housing: Abdul Ghafoor.
Law and Justice: Ashoke Sen.
Irrigation and Power: B. Shankaranand.
Railways: Bansi Lal.
Agriculture and Rural Development: Buta Singh.
Parliamentary Affairs: H. K. L. Bhagat.
Education: K. C. Pant.
Health and Family Welfare: Mohsina Kidwai.
Defence: P. V. Narasimha Rao.
Food and Civil Supplies: Rao Birendra Singh.
Home: S. B. Chavan.
Steel, Mines and Coal: Vasant Sathe.
Chemicals and Fertilizers, Industry and Company Affairs: Veerendra Patil.
Finance, Commerce and Supply: Vishwanath Pratap Singh.
Women and Social Welfare: M. Chandrasekhar.

There were also 6 Ministers of State with independent charges and 19 Ministers of State.

Local Government. There were in 1980, 40 municipal corporations, 1,274 municipalities, 815 town area and notified area committees and 62 cantonment boards. The municipal bodies have the care of the roads, water supply, drainage, sanitation, medical relief, vaccination and education. Their main sources of revenue are taxes on the annual rental value of land and buildings, octroi and terminal, vehicle and other taxes. The municipal councils enact their own bye-laws and frame their budgets, which in the case of municipal bodies other than corporations generally require the sanction of the State government. All municipal councils are elected on the principle of adult franchise.

For rural areas there is a 3-tier system of *panchayati raj* at village, block and district level, although the 3-tier structure may undergo some changes in State legislation to suit local conditions. All *panchayati raj* bodies are organically linked, and representation is given to special interests. Elected directly by and from among villagers, the *panchayats* are responsible for agricultural production, rural industries, medical relief, maternity and child welfare, common grazing grounds, village roads, tanks and wells, and maintenance of sanitation. In some places they also look after primary education, maintenance of village records and collection of land revenue. They have their own powers of taxation. There are some judicial *panchayats* or village courts.

Panchayati raj now cover all the States with the exception of Nagaland and Meghalaya, although Nagaland has area, range and tribal councils. They exist in all the Union Territories except Mizoram and Lakshadweep. In Pondicherry they have been created by declaring existing Municipal Communes to be Commune Panchayat Councils; this is a transition arrangement. In Arunachal Pradesh and Chandigarh the 3-tier system of *panchayati raj* has been introduced. With most of the country covered by *panchayati raj*, the emphasis now is on consolidation and clarifying their role in rural development.

The powers and responsibilities of *panchayati raj* institutions are derived from State Legislatures, and from the executive orders of State governments.

NAGARLOK (Municipal Affairs Quarterly). Quarterly. Institute of Public Administration. Delhi
Proceedings of the 13th Meeting of the Central Council of Local Self Government. Delhi, 1970
Report of the Committee on Budgetary Reforms in Municipal Administration. Delhi, 1974
State Machinery for Municipal Supervision. Institute of Public Administration. Delhi, 1970
Statistical Abstract of India. Annual. Delhi.

DEFENCE. The Supreme Command of the Armed Forces vests in the President of the Indian Republic. Policy is decided at different levels by a number of committees, including the Political Affairs Committee presided over by the Prime

Minister and the Defence Minister's Committee. Administrative and operational control rests in the respective Service Headquarters, under the control of the Ministry of Defence.

The Ministry of Defence is the central agency for formulating defence policy and for co-ordinating the work of the three services. Among the organizations directly administered by the Ministry are the Research and Development Organization, the Production Organization, the National Defence College, the National Cadet Corps and the Directorate-General of Armed Forces Medical Services.

The Research and Development Organization (headed by the Scientific Adviser to the Minister) has under it about 30 research establishments. The Production Organization controls 8 public-sector undertakings and 28 ordnance and 2 departmental factories.

The National Defence College, New Delhi, was established in 1960 on the pattern of the Imperial Defence College (UK): the 1-year course is for officers of the rank of brigadier or equivalent and for senior civil servants. The Defence Services Staff College, Wellington, trains officers of the three Services for higher command for staff appointments. There is an Armed Forces Medical College at Pune.

The National Defence Academy, Khadakvasla, gives a 3-year basic training course to officer cadets of the three Services prior to advanced training at the respective Service establishments.

Army. The Army Headquarters functioning directly under the Chief of the Army Staff is divided into the following main branches: General Staff Branch; Adjutant General's Branch; Quartermaster-General's Branch; Master-General of Ordnance Branch; Engineer-in-Chief's Branch; Military Secretary's Branch.

The Army is organized into 4 commands–eastern, central, western and southern–each divided into areas, which in turn are subdivided into sub-areas.

Recruitment of permanent commissioned officers is through the Indian Military Academy, Dehra Dun. It conducts courses for ex-National Defence Academy, National Cadet Corps and direct-entry cadets, and for serving personnel and technical graduates.

The Territorial Army came into being in Sept. 1949, its role being to: (1) relieve the regular Army of static duties and, if required, support civil power; (2) provide anti-aircraft units, and (3) if and when called upon, provide units for the regular Army. The Territorial Army is composed of practically all arms of the Services.

The authorized strength of the Army is 944,000, that of the Territorial Army, 40,000. There are 2 armoured, 17 infantry and 10 mountain divisions, 5 independent armoured brigades, 1 independent infantry, 14 independent artillery brigades, 1 commando and 2 parachute brigades.

Navy. Since 26 Jan. 1950 the former Royal Indian Navy, which traced its history in an unbroken line from the foundation in 1613 of the East India Company's Marine, has been known as 'Indian Navy', and the ships referred to as 'INS' instead of 'HMIS'. There are 2 commands: Eastern and Southern; and 2 fleets: Eastern and Western.

Principal ships of the Indian Navy:

Completed	*Name*	*Standard displacement Tons*	*Armour Belts in.*	*Armour Turrets in.*	*Principal armament*	*Shaft horse-power*	*Speed Knots*
		Aircraft Carrier					
1961	Vikrant (*ex*-Hercules)	16,000	–	–	7 40 mm. AA (22 aircraft)	40,000	24·5
		Cruisers [1]					
1940	Mysore (*ex*-Nigeria)	8,700	3-4½	2	9 6-in.; 8 4-in.	72,500	31·5

[1] The cruiser *Delhi* (ex-*Achilles*) completed in 1933, was scrapped in 1979.

The fleet also includes 8 *ex*-Soviet submarines, 3 new Soviet-built guided missile armed destroyers, 2 new 'stretched', or improved 'Leander' type missile frigates and 6 broad-beamed 'Leander' class general purpose frigates (all eight built in India), 2 anti-submarine frigates and 3 anti-aircraft frigates (all five built in Great Britain), 1 old *ex*-British frigate, 12 Soviet-built escorts, 3 *ex*-Soviet corvettes, 16 fast attack craft (most of them missile armed), 6 *ex*-Soviet ocean minesweepers, 4 *ex*-British coastal minesweepers, 10 inshore minesweepers, 4 patrol craft, 7 landing ships, 4 landing craft, 7 survey ships, 1 repair ship, 1 submarine parent ship, 1 submarine rescue ship, 7 oilers, 20 service craft and 7 tugs.

New construction includes 2 Federal German-built patrol submarines, 2 indigenously built similar submarines, 4 Soviet built larger submarines, 3 more Soviet destroyers, 4 more frigates and 4 corvettes. India plans to acquire an aircraft carrier to replace *Vikrant*, see above.

The major training establishments of the Navy include INS *Venduruthy* at Cochin (Basic and Divisional, Gunnery, Torpedo and Anti-Submarine, Navigation and Direction, Communication), INS *Vaisura* at Jamnagar (Electrical), INS *Shivaji* at Lonavla (Engineering), INS *Hansa* at Goa (Aviation), INS *Hamla* at Bombay (Supply and Secretariat) and INS *Satyavahana* (Submarine) and INS *Circars* (Boys') at Vishakhapatnam.

The Fleet Requirement Unit of the Naval Aviation Station, INAS *Garuda*, is at Cochin. Over 110 aircraft include Sea Harriers for HMS *Vikrant*, Sea Hawk fighters, Alize anti-submarine aircraft and Sea King anti-submarine helicopters acquired for the aircraft carrier.

Naval personnel in 1985 comprised 47,000 officers and ratings, including the Naval Air Arm.

The Coast Guard was constituted as an independent para-military service by 1978 Act of Parliament. It comprised the frigates *Kirpan* and *Kuthar* and five patrol craft all transferred from the Indian Navy and 2 larger patrol vessels custom-built. It has recently been augmented by new specifically built ships and aircraft, including three 1,040-ton offshore patrol vessels with aircraft and hangar, three inshore protection craft, 5 *ex*-Soviet cutters, 8 South Korean-built launches and 4 Japanese-built vedettes. There are 5 aircraft. The Coast Guard is administered by a Director-General (Vice-Admiral) and a Deputy Director-General (Commodore). It functions under the Defence Ministry but is funded by the Revenue Department.

Air Force. The Indian Air Force Act was passed in 1932, and the first flight was formed in 1933.

The Air Headquarters, under the Chief of Air Staff, consists of 4 main branches, viz., Air Staff, Administration, Policy and Plans, and Maintenance. Units of the IAF are organized into 4 operational commands–Western at Delhi, Central at Allahabad, Eastern at Shillong and South-Western at Jodhpur. Training Command HQ is at Bangalore, Maintenance Command at Nagpur. Nominal strength in 1983 was more than 100,000 personnel and 1,400 aircraft of all types, in 45 squadrons of fixed-wing aircraft, 14 helicopter squadrons and about 30 squadrons of 'Guideline' and 'Goa' surface-to-air missiles, and close-range missiles such as 'Gainful' and Tigercat.

Air defence units include 2 squadrons of MiG-23 variable-geometry interceptors, and 19 squadrons of MiG-21s. Initial delivery of MiG-21s from the Soviet Union was followed by large-scale licence production in India. There are 2 squadrons of Sukhoi Su-7s, 1 of Indian-designed Maruts, 3 of Ajeet (Gust Mk 2) fighters, 3 of Canberras, 2 of Jaguars, 2 of Hunter F56s, 3 of MiG-23 supersonic fighter-bombers and one of MiG-25 reconnaissance aircraft plus a MiG-25U two seat trainer. Canberra and Hunter squadrons are being re-equipped with at least 76 Jaguars, assembled in India, to create a force of 5 Jaguar squadrons. Some of those flying MiG-21s and SU-7s will re-equip with MiG-27s licence-built in India; also on order are 40 Mirage 2000s from France.

The large transport force includes An-12s, jet-boosted C-119Gs, C-47s, HS 748s, Caribou, 2 Boeing 737s, and smaller aircraft and helicopters for VIP and other duties. Replacement of the C-119Gs and Caribou with An-32s is under way. C-47s, Otters and Devons will be replaced with Dornier 228s. Helicopter units have Mi-8s (6 squadrons), Chetaks (Aero spatiale Alouette IIIs) and licence-built Cheetahs (Aerospatiale Lamas); main training types are the Hindustan HT-2 and Kiran, Polish built TS-11 Iskra, Hunter T.66 (to be replaced with 2-seat Ajeets), MiG-21UT1, MiG-23U and Su-7U. Replacement of the HT-2s with HPT-32s is expected to begin in 1985-86.

Primary flying training is provided at the Elementary Flying School, Bidar, and advanced flying training at the Air Force Academy, Dundigal, Hyderabad. There is a Navigation and Signals School at Begumpet. The IAF Technical College, Jalahalli, imparts technical training, while the IAF Administrative College, Coimbatore, trains officers of the ground duty branch. There are also land-air warfare, flying instructors' and medical schools.

INTERNATIONAL RELATIONS

Membership. India is a member of the UN, the Commonwealth and the Colombo Plan.

External Debt. At the end of Dec. 1982 India's external public debt was Rs 205,330m.

Treaties. India pursues a general policy of non-alignment; the exception is a Treaty of Peace, Friendship and Cooperation with the USSR, 1971; the parties agreed to mutual support short of force in the event of either being attacked by a third party.

ECONOMY

Planning. The sixth plan (1980–85) envisages total investment of Rs 1,587,100m., of which Rs 975,000m. is for the public sector. The amount of this financed from abroad would be Rs 90,630m. The aim is an annual 5·2% growth rate and the prime objective is to alleviate rural poverty. Intended investment in energy, Rs 265,350m.; in social services, Rs 140,350m.; transport and industry both get Rs 124,110m.

Ministry of Agriculture. *Serving the Small Farmer: Policy Choices in Indian Agricultural Development.* 1975

Dutt, A. K. (ed.), *India: Resources, Potentialities and Planning.* Rev. ed. Dubuque, India, 1973

Singh, T., *India's Development Experience.* London, 1975

Budget. Revenue and expenditure (on revenue account) of the central government[1] for years ending 31 March, in crores of rupees:

	1982–83	*1983–84*[2]	*1984–85*[3]
Revenue	18,091	20,965	23,744
Expenditure	19,345	23,339	26,342

[1] Excluding states' share of excise duties and other taxes.
[2] Revised. [3] Budget estimates.

Important items of revenue and expenditure on the revenue account of the central government for 1984–85 (estimates), in Rs 1m.:

Revenue		*Expenditure*	
Net tax revenue	175,267	General Services	143,825
Non-tax revenue	64,897	Defence	60,756
		Grants in aid to States, etc.	51,886

Total capital account receipts (1984–85), Rs 167,570m.; capital account disbursements, Rs 161,940m. Total (revenue and capital) receipts, Rs 405,010m.; disbursements, Rs 425,360m.

Under the Constitution (Part XII and 7th Schedule), the power to raise funds has been divided between the central government and the states. Generally, the sources of revenue are mutually exclusive. Certain taxes are levied by the Union for the sake of uniformity and distributed to the states. The Finance Commission (Art. 280 of the Constitution) advises the President on the distribution of the taxes which are distributable between the centre and the states, and on the principles on which grants should be made out of Union revenues to the states. The main sources of central revenue are: customs duties; those excise duties levied by the central government; corporation, income and wealth taxes; estate and succession duties on non-agricultural assets and property, and revenues from the railways and posts and telegraphs. The main heads of revenue in the states are: taxes and duties levied by the state governments (including land revenues and agricultural income tax); civil administration and civil works; state undertakings; taxes shared with the centre; and grants received from the centre.

Currency. A decimal system of coinage was introduced in 1957. The Indian *rupee* is divided into 100 *paise* (until 1964 officially described as *naye paise*), the decimal coins being 1, 2, 3, 5, 10, 20, 25 and 50 *paise*.

The rupee is valued in relation to a package of main currencies. The £ is the currency of intervention. In March 1985 Rs 14.05 = £1; Rs 13.15 = US$1.

The paper currency consists of: (1) Reserve Bank notes in denominations of Rs 2, 5, 10, 20, 50 and 100; and (2) Government of India currency notes of denominations of Re 1 deemed to be included in the expression 'rupee coin' for the purposes of the Reserve Bank of India Act, 1934.

According to the Reserve Bank of India, the total money supply with the public on the last Friday of June 1982 was Rs 26,423 crores.

100,000 rupees are called 1 lakh; 100 lakhs are called 1 crore.

Banking. The Reserve Bank, the central bank for India, was established in 1934 and started functioning on 1 April 1935 as a shareholder's bank; it became a nationalized institution on 1 Jan. 1949. It has the sole right of issuing currency-notes. The Bank acts as adviser to the Government on financial problems and is the banker for central and state governments, commercial banks and some other financial institutions. The Bank manages the rupee public debt of central and state governments. It is the custodian of the country's exchange reserve and supervises repatriation of export proceeds and payments for imports. The Bank gives short-term loans to state governments and scheduled banks and short and medium-term loans to state co-operative banks and industrial finance institutions. The Bank has extensive powers of regulation of the banking system, directly under the Banking Regulation Act, 1949, and indirectly by the use of variations in Bank rate, variation in reserve ratios, selective credit controls and open market operations. Bank rate was raised to 10% in July 1981.

Except refinance for food credit and export credit, the Reserve Bank's refinance facility to commercial banks has been placed on a discretionary basis. The net profit of the Reserve Bank of India for the year ended June 1982, after making the usual or necessary provisions, amounted to Rs 210 crores.

The commercial banking system consisted of 201 scheduled banks (*i.e.*, banks which are included in the 2nd schedule to the Reserve Bank Act) and 4 non-scheduled banks on 30 June 1982; scheduled banks included 121 Regional Rural Banks. Total deposits in commercial banks, June 1982, stood at Rs 45,831 crores. The business of non-scheduled banks forms less than 0.1% of commercial bank business. Of the 201 scheduled banks, 18 are foreign banks which specialize in financing foreign trade but also compete for domestic business. The largest scheduled bank is the State Bank of India, constituted by nationalizing the Imperial Bank of India in 1955. The State Bank acts as the agent of the Reserve Bank and the subsidiaries of the State Bank act as the agents of the State Bank for transacting government business as well as undertaking commercial functions. Fourteen banks with aggregate deposits of not less than Rs 50 crores were nationalized on 19 July 1969. Six banks were nationalized in April 1980. The 28 public sector banks (which comprise the State Bank of India and its seven associate banks and 20 nationalised banks) account for over 90% of deposits and bank credit of all scheduled commercial banks.

Reserve Bank of India: Report on Currency and Finance.—Report on the Trend and Progress of Banking in India.—Report of the Central Board of Directors. Annual. Bombay

Weights and Measures. Uniform standards of weights and measures, based on the metric system, were established for the first time by the Standards of Weights and Measures Act, 1956, which provided for a transition period of 10 years. So far the system has been fully adopted in trade transactions but there are a few fields such as engineering, survey and land records and the building and construction industry where it has not; efforts are being made to complete the change as early as possible.

In order to align this legislation with the latest international trends an expert committee (Weights and Measures (Law Revision) Committee) was set up by the central government to suggest a revised Bill which was passed by Parliament in April 1976. The new Standards of Weights and Measures Act, 1976, has recognized the International System of Units and other units recommended by the General Conference on Weights and Measures and is in line with the recommendations of the International Organisation of Legal Metrology (OIML). The new Act also covers the system of numeration, the approval of models of weights and measures, regulation and control of inter-state trade in relation to weights and measures. The Act also protects consumers through proper indication of weight, quantity, identity, source, date and price on packaged goods. A draft Standards of Weights and Measures (Enforcement) Bill has also been prepared by the committee for adoption either by Parliament or State legislatures, as enforcement is now in the 'concurrent' list of legislation.

The provisions of the 1976 Act came into force in Sept. 1977, as did the accompanying Standards of Weights and Measures (Packaged Commodities) Rules, 1977.

While the Standards of Weights and Measures are laid down in the Central Act, enforcement of weights and measures laws is entrusted to the state governments; the central Directorate of Weights and Measures is responsible for co-ordinating activities so as to ensure national uniformity.

An Indian Institute of Legal Metrology trains officials of the Weights and Measures departments of India and different developing countries. The Institute is being modernized with technical assistance from the Federal Republic of Germany.

There are 2 Regional Reference Standards laboratories at Ahmedabad and Bhubaneswar which (besides calibrating secondary standards of physical measurements) also provide testing facilities in metrological and industrial measurements. These laboratories are equipped with Standards next in line to the National Standards of physical measurements which are maintained at the National Physical Laboratory in New Delhi.

For weights previously in legal use under the Standards of Weight Act, 1956, *see* THE STATESMAN'S YEAR-BOOK, 1961, p. 171.

Calendar. The dates of the Saka era (named after the north Indian dynasty of the first century A.D.) are being used alongside Gregorian dates in issues of the *Gazette of India*, news broadcasts by All-India Radio and government-issued calendars, from 22 March 1957, a date which corresponds with the first day of the year 1879 in the Saka era.

ENERGY AND NATURAL RESOURCES

Electricity. In March 1983 about 55% of all villages had electricity. Total installed capacity (1981, provisional) was 33m. kw. Production of electricity in 1981–82 was 122,000m. kwh., of which 72,400m. kwh. came from thermal and nuclear stations and 49,600m. kwh from hydro-electric stations.

Oil and Gas. The Oil and Natural Gas Commission, Oil India Ltd and the Assam Oil Co. are the only producers of crude oil. Total production, 1983, about 26m. tonnes; consumption, about 35m. tonnes. The main fields are in Assam and offshore in the Gulf of Cambay (the Bombay High field). Natural gas production, 1981–82, 1,655m. cu. metres.

Water. The net area of 57m. hectares (1982) under irrigation exceeds that of any other country except China, and equals about 38% of the total area under cultivation. Irrigation projects have formed an important part of all three Five-Year Plans. The possibilities of diverting rivers into canals being nearly exhausted, the emphasis is now on damming the monsoon surplus flow and diverting that. Usable surface and groundwater resources were assessed (1972) at 870,000m. cu. metres. Utilization (1974) 337,000m. cu. metres. Irrigation plant in operation in 1976 could make use of 67m. hectare-metres of surface water and 26·5m. hectare-metres of ground water. Ultimate potential of irrigation is assessed at 107m. hectares, total cultivated land being 142m. hectares. In 1977 India and Bangladesh reached an agreement to share the water of the Ganges at the Farakka barrage: India needs this supply to supplement the Hooghly River in flushing silt from Calcutta port. A further agreement (1982) also includes the waters of the Brahmaputra.

Minerals. Bihar, West Bengal and Madhya Pradesh produce 42%, 25% and 19% of all coal, respectively. The coal industry was nationalized in 1973; planned state investment during sixth five-year plan (1980-85), Rs 2,573 crores. Production, 1981–82, 125m. tonnes; reserves (including lignite) are estimated at 114,000m. tonnes. (Coal in seams at least 1·2 metres thick and down to a depth of 600 metres, 86,428m. tonnes; lignite, 2,100m. tonnes). Sixth-plan investment in the Neyveli Lignite Corporation, Rs 647 crores. Production of other minerals, 1982 (in 1,000 tonnes): Iron ore, 40,824; bauxite, 1,860; chromite 336; copper ore, 2,016; manganese ore, 1,452; gold, 2,204 kg. Other important minerals are lead, zinc, limestone, apatite and phosphorite, dolomite, magnesite and silver. Value of mineral production, 1982 (provisional), Rs 53,912m. of which mineral fuels produced Rs 48,140m., metallic minerals Rs 2,671m. and non-metallic Rs 3,102m.

Agriculture. The chief industry of India has always been agriculture. About 70% of the people are dependent on the land for their living. In 1981-82 it provided 35·4% of GDP; growth rate, 1981–82, 5·5%.

Agricultural commodities account for about 26% by value of Indian exports, while agricultural commodities, machinery and fertilizers account for about 20% of imports. Tea accounted for about 19% of agricultural exports in 1982–83; exports have since been limited.

An increase in food production of at least 2% per annum is necessary to keep pace with the rising population. Foodgrain production, 78·4m. tons in 1962–63, was 151·54m. tonnes in 1983–84.

The Indian Council of Agricultural Research works through 37 institutes and research centres, and 70 national research projects. It supports the establishment of at least 1 agricultural university in each of the states.

The farming year runs from July to June through three crop seasons: kharif (monsoon); rabi (winter) and summer.

Agricultural production, 1981-82 (in 1,000 tonnes): rice, 53,593; wheat, 37,833; total foodgrains, 133,061; coffee, of which the main cash varieties are Arabica and Robusta (main growing areas Karnataka, Kerala and Tamil Nadu), 150; sugarcane 183,647; cotton, 7·8m. bales (of 170 kg), jute is grown in West Bengal (half total yield), Bihar and Assam, total yield, 6·8m. bales; oilseeds, 12,073; maize, 6,761; pulses, 11,351; milk, 33,000.

The tea industry is important, with production concentrated in Assam, West Bengal, Tamil Nadu, Kerala and Karnataka. Total crop in 1983–84, about 585,000 tonnes from 370,000 hectares.

Livestock (1983). Cattle, 182m.; sheep, 41·7m.; pigs, 8·6m.; horses, 900,000; asses, 1m.; goats, 78m.; buffaloes, 63m.

Fertilizer consumption in 1983–84 was 7·2m. tonnes.

Land Tenure. There are three main traditional systems of land tenure: *ryotwari* tenure, where the individual holders, usually peasant proprietors, are responsible for the payment of land revenues; *zamindari* tenure, where one or more persons own large estates and are responsible for payment (in this system there may be a number of intermediary holders); and *mahalwari* tenure, where village communities jointly hold an estate and are jointly and severally responsible for payment.

Agrarian reform, initiated in the first Five-Year Plan, being undertaken by the state governments includes: (1) The abolition of intermediaries under *zamindari* tenure. (2) Tenancy legislation designed to scale down rents to ¼–⅕ of the value of the produce, to give permanent rights to tenants (subject to the landlord's right to resume a minimum holding for his personal cultivation), and to enable tenants to acquire ownership of their holdings (subject to the landlord's right of resumption for personal cultivation) on payment of compensation over a number of years. (3) Fixing of ceilings on existing holdings and on future acquisition; the holding of a family is between 4·05 and 7·28 hectares if it has assured irrigation to produce two crops a year; 10·93 hectares for land with irrigation facilities for only one crop a year; and 21·85 hectares for all other categories of land. Tea, coffee, cocoa and cardamom plantations have been exempted. (4) The consolidation of holdings in community project areas and the prevention of fragmentation of holdings by reform of inheritance laws. (5) Promotion of farming by co-operative village management (*see* p. 627).

The average size of holding for the whole of India is 2·63 hectares. Andhra Pradesh, 2·87; Assam, 1·46; Bihar, 1·53; Gujarat, 4·49; Jammu and Kashmir, 1·43; Karnataka, 4·11; Kerala, 0·75; Madhya Pradesh, 3·99; Maharashtra, 4·65; Orissa, 1·98; Punjab, 3·85; Rajasthan, 5·5; Tamil Nadu, 1·49; Uttar Pradesh, 1·78; West Bengal, 1·56.

Of the total 71m. rural households possessing operational holdings, 34% hold on the average less than 0·20 hectare of land each.

Opium. By international agreement the poppy is cultivated under licence, and all raw opium is sold to the central government. Opium, other than for wholly medical use, is available only to registered addicts.

Fisheries. Total catch (1981–82) was 2·4m. tonnes, of which Kerala, Tamil Nadu, and Maharashtra produced about half. Of the total catch, 1,441,000 tonnes were marine fish. There were 102 commercial deep-sea fishing boats, including trawlers, operating in 1982–83 and about 20,000 small craft. Fishermen's co-operatives had 552,000 members in 1981; their total sales were worth Rs 177m.

Forestry. The lands under the control of the state forest departments are classified as 'reserved forests' (forests intended to be permanently maintained for the supply of timber, etc., or for the protection of water supply, etc.), 'protected forests' and 'unclassed' forest land.

In 1982–83 the total forest area was 75m. hectares. Main types are teak and sal. Production, 1983, 39m. tonnes. About 16% of the area is inaccessible, of which about 45% is potentially productive. Forest revenue, 1981–82 (provisional), Rs 5,239·3m. There are about 3,000 sawmills. In 1981–82 1·3m. saplings were planted; this is considered insufficient to meet future demands for fuel and industrial wood. Fuel wood consumption, 1983, 133m. tonnes. Some states have encouraged planting small areas around villages.

INDUSTRY AND TRADE

Industries. Railways, air transport, armaments and atomic energy are government monopolies. In a number of industries (including the manufacture of iron and steel and mineral oils, shipbuilding and the mining of coal, iron and manganese ores, gypsum, gold and diamonds) new units are set up only by the state. In a further group of industries (road transport, manufacture of chemicals such as drugs, dyestuffs, plastics and fertilizers) the state established new undertakings, but private enterprise may develop either on its own or with state backing, which may take the form of loans or purchase of equity capital. Nationalized industries employed 4m. in 1981. Under the Industries (Development and Regulation) Act, 1951, as amended, industrial undertakings are required to be licensed; 162 industries are within the scope of the Act. The Government are authorized to examine the working of any undertaking, to issue directions to it and to take over its control if this be deemed necessary. A Central Advisory Council has been set up consisting of representatives of industry, labour, consumers and primary producers. There are Development Councils for individual industries and (1981) 4 national development banks.

Foreign investment is encouraged by a tax holiday on income up to 6% of capital employed for 5 years. There are special depreciation allowances, and customs and excise concessions for export industries.

Oil refinery installed capacity, 1983, was 37·8m. tonnes; production of refined oils (1982–83), 33·2m. tonnes. The Indian Oil Corporation was established in 1964 and had (1984) most of the market.

Industry, particularly steel, has suffered from a shortage of power and coal. There is expansion in petrochemicals, based on the oil and associated gas of the Bombay High field, and gas from Bassein field. Small industries (initial outlay on capital equipment of less than Rs 2m.) are important; they employ about 7m. and produced (1980) goods worth Rs 209,000m. The industrial growth rate, 1982–83 was 4%.

Industrial production, 1981–82 (in 1,000 tonnes): Pig-iron and ferro-alloys, 9,832 (1982); steel ingots, 10,940; finished steel, 7,270; aluminium, 207; motor cycles (nos.), 315,900; commercial vehicles (nos.), 91,000; petroleum products, 28,200; sulphuric acid, 2,137; cement, 20,900; board and paper, 1,237; nitrogen fertilizer, 3,144; phosphate fertilizer, 949; jute goods, 1,337; cotton yarn, 989; cotton cloth, 7,983m. metres; man-made fibre and yarn, 242·7; diesel engines, 172,000 engines; electric motors, 4·4m. h.p.; refractories, 875 (estimate); sugar, 8,434.

Labour. At the 1981 census there were 222·5m. workers, of whom 92·5m. were cultivators, 55·5m. agricultural labourers; in 1983 there were 6·3m. in manufacturing, 9·1m. in social, community and personal services, 1·2m. in construction and 2·9m. in transport, communications and storage. There were in 1983 over 30,000 unions. The bond labour system was abolished in 1975. Man-days lost by industrial disputes, 1983, 21·55m., of which 2·54m. were in the central sector. An ordnance of July 1981 gave the government power to ban strikes in essential services; the ordnance was to remain in force for six months and would then be renewable.

Dasgupta, A. K., *A Theory of Wage Policy*. OUP, 1976

Companies. The total number of companies limited by shares at work in India, 31 March 1983, was 82,903; aggregate paid-up capital was Rs 19,909 crores. There were 11,780 public limited companies with an aggregate paid-up capital of Rs 5,339·1 crores, and 71,123 private limited companies (Rs 14,569·8 crores). There were also 252 companies with unlimited liability.

During 1982–83, 10,764 new limited companies were registered in the Indian Union under the Companies Act 1956 with a total authorized capital of Rs 1,386·2 crores; 1,278 were public limited companies (Rs 527·5 crores) and 9,486 were private limited companies (Rs 855·7 crores). There were 33 private companies with unlimited liability also registered in 1982–83, authorized capital Rs 0·49 crores. Of the new non-government limited companies, 126 had an authorized capital of Rs 1 crore and above, and 182 of between Rs 50 lakhs and Rs 1 crore. During 1982–83, 97 companies with an aggregate paid-up capital of Rs 11·47 crores went into liquidation and 162 companies (Rs 36 lakhs) were struck off the register.

On 31 March 1983 there were 943 government companies at work with a total paid-up capital of Rs 14,722·5 crores; 409 were public limited companies and 534 were private limited companies.

On 31 March 1983, 320 companies incorporated elsewhere were reported to have a place of business in India; 128 were of UK and 67 of USA origin.

Department of Company Affairs, Govt. of India. *Annual Report on the Working and Administration of the Companies Act, 1956*. New Delhi, 1983

Co-operative Movement. In 1983 there were 290,000 co-operative societies with a total membership of about 115m. There were 3,632 Primary Co-operative Marketing Societies, 29 State Co-operative Marketing Federations and the National Agricultural Co-operative Marketing Federation of India. There were also 8 State Co-operative Commodity Marketing Federations, and 8 State Tribal Co-operative Development Corporations/Federations.

There were, on 31 March 1983, 27 State Co-operative Banks, 337 Central Co-operative Banks, 94,019 Primary Agricultural Societies, 19 State Land Development Banks, and 1,731 Primary Land Development Banks/branches which provide long-term investment credit.

Total agricultural credit disbursed by Co-operatives in 1982–83 was Rs 2,588 crores including Rs 1,957 crores in short-term credit, Rs 223 crores in medium-term credit and Rs 408 crores in long-term credit. Total credit disbursed in 1983–84 (estimate), Rs 3,000 crores.

Value of agricultural produce marketed by Co-operatives in 1982–83 was about

Rs 2,300 crores. They procured 2·1m. tons of wheat, 0·28m. tons of paddy, 43·5m. tons of sugarcane, 2·4m. bales of cotton and 0·25m. bales of jute.

In June 1983 there were 2,004 processing units; in 1982–83, 157 sugar factories produced 4·5m. tons; 66 spinning mills (capacity 600,000 spindles) produced 110m. kg. of yarn; there were 307 oil mills and similar units; total storage capacity was 6·4m. tons, and an extra 139 cold stores had been installed (capacity 290,000 tons) by Feb. 1984.

In 1982–83 there were 64,645 retail depots distributing Rs 1,270 crores' worth of fertilizers.

Indian Labour Guide. Monthly. Delhi
Co-operative Movement in India, Statistical Statements Relating to. Annual. Reserve Bank of India, Bombay

Commerce. The external trade of India (excluding land-borne trade with Tibet and Bhután) was as follows (in 1,000 rupees):

	Imports	*Exports and Re-exports*
1977–78	6,020,42,65	5,407,93,26
1978–79	6,811,29,75	5,726,14,82
1979–80	9,142,87,66	6,418,49,30
1980–81	12,549,15,00	6,710,70,00
1981–82	13,607,56,00	7,805,90,00
1982–83	14,359,99,00	8,834,21,00

The distribution of commerce by countries and areas was as follows in the year ended 31 March 1983 (in 100,000 rupees):

Countries	*Exports to*	*Imports from*
Afghánistán	1,307	1,187
Argentina	215	772
Australia	10,235	27,872
Bangladesh	3,720	964
Bahrain	3,213	14,137
Belgium	21,102	61,762
Brazil	232	17,683
Burma	362	1,747
Canada	5,571	25,100
Czechoslovakia	5,319	5,270
Denmark	3,442	1,874
Egypt	8,405	380
Federal Rep. of Germany	34,315	80,129
France	14,831	41,378
German Dem. Republic	7,449	5,932
Hong Kong	19,168	4,773
Hungary	985	3,893
Iran	7,404	78,265
Iraq	5,735	88,407
Italy	14,185	24,123
Japan	79,463	106,998
Kenya	1,872	627
Korea, Republic of	5,593	22,490
Kuwait	12,901	28,243
Malaysia	5,513	20,840
Nepál	8,389	5,200
Netherlands	11,575	25,487
New Zealand	1,977	2,497
Nigeria	5,966	40
Poland	7,153	5,481
Rumania	8,683	6,080
Saudi Arabia	22,729	149,624
Singapore	19,419	36,193
Sri Lanka	9,733	1,225
Sudan	3,133	179
Sweden	3,245	8,015
Spain	3,587	9,699
Switzerland	9,563	11,118
Thailand	3,059	1,970
United Arab Emirates	21,921	36,512
USSR	155,830	151,340
UK	45,716	88,558
USA	95,025	137,066
Yugoslavia	1,670	2,678

The value (in 100,000 rupees) of the leading articles of merchandise was as follows in the year ended 31 March 1983:

Exports	*Value*
Meat and meat preparations	8,057
Fish, crustaceans, molluscs and preparations thereof	34,945
Rice	19,950
Vegetables and fruits	29,277
Coffee and coffee substitutes	18,420
Tea and mate	36,753
Spices	8,893
Oilcake	14,935
Tobacco unmanufactured and tobacco refuse	20,854

Exports	*Value*
Raw cotton	10,116
Iron ore	37,379
Crude vegetable materials	8,102
Cotton fabrics	26,552
Cotton madeup articles	9,701
Readymade garments	52,750
Jute manufactures including twist and yarn	20,276
Leather and leather manufactures (except footwear)	34,588
Pearls, precious and semi-precious stones	82,491
Works of art	10,961
Handmade carpets	16,857
Metal manufactures except iron and steel	20,156
Machinery including transport equipments	58,460
Mineral fuel, lubricants and related products	13,403
Chemicals and allied products	30,820
Iron and steel	5,575
Jewellery	6,912
Sugar and sugar preparations	6,235
Imports	
Wheat	29,227
Milk and cream	5,987
Crude rubber including synthetic and reclaimed	5,408
Synthetic and regenerated fibre	12,473
Fertilisers, crude	5,551
Sulphur and unroasted iron pyrites	6,933
Metalliferous ores and metal scrap	15,222
Petroleum, Petroleum products and related materials	560,496
Edible oil	22,627
Organic chemicals	23,814
Inorganic chemicals	14,889
Medical and pharmaceutical products	8,058
Fertilisers, manufactured	14,564
Artificial resins, plastic materials etc	12,571
Chemical materials and products	7,323
Paper, paper board and manufactures thereof	14,747
Textile yarn, fabrics and madeup articles	11,239
Pearls, precious and semi-precious stones	67,743
Non-metallic mineral manufactures exclg. pearls	14,139
Iron and steel	114,596
Non-ferrous metal	27,906
Manufactures of metal	13,647
Machinery other than electric	138,311
Electrical machinery	24,819
Transport equipment	60,049
Professional, scientific, controlling instruments, photographic, optical goods, watches and clocks	18,984

Total trade between India and UK (British Department of Trade returns, in £1,000 sterling):

	1980	*1981*	*1982*	*1983*	*1984*
Imports to UK	315,858	294,323	379,169	366,928	571,470
Exports and re-exports from UK	529,007	638,867	805,321	804,779	780,997

Annual Statement of the Foreign Trade of India. 2 vols. Calcutta
Monthly Statistics of the Foreign Trade of India. Calcutta
Review of the Trade of India. Annual. Delhi
India–Handbook of Commercial Information. 3 vols. Calcutta
Guide to Official Statistics of Trade, Shipping, Customs and Excise Revenue of India. Rev. ed. Calcutta

Tourism. There were 1·3m. visitors in 1983 bringing Rs 8,250m. in foreign exchange.

COMMUNICATIONS

Roads. In 1983–84 there were 1,675,000 km of roads, of which 794,000 km were surfaced. Roads are divided into 5 main administrative classes, namely, national highways, state highways, major district roads, other district roads and village roads. The national highways (31,398 km in 1984) connect capitals of states, major ports and foreign highways. The national highway system is linked with the ESCAP (Economic and Social Commission for Asia and the Pacific) international highway system. The state highways are the main trunk roads of the states, while the major district roads connect subsidiary areas of production and markets with distribution centres, and form the main link between headquarters and neighbouring districts.

There were (31 March 1983) 6,297,131 motor vehicles in India, comprising 1,197,159 private cars and jeeps, 3·4m. motor cycles and scooters, 127,072 taxis, 173,814 buses and 633,643 goods vehicles.

Railways. The Indian railway system is government-owned and (under the control of the Railway Board) is divided into 9 zones; route-km at 31 March 1983:

Zone	*Headquarters*	*Route-km*
Central	Bombay	6,371 km (657 km electrified)
Eastern	Calcutta	4,238 km (1,218 km)
Northern	Delhi	10,688 km (572 km)
North Eastern	Gorakhpur	5,163 km
North East Frontier	Gauhati	3,844 km
Southern	Madras	6,700 km (391 km)
South Central	Secunderabad	7,023 km (388 km)
South Eastern	Calcutta	7,041 km (1,421 km)
Western	Bombay	10,292 km (496 km)

Principal gauges are 1,676 mm. and metre, with networks also of 762 and 610 mm. gauge.

Passengers carried in 1981 were approximately 3,612m.; freight, 196m. tonnes. Revenue-earning-goods traffic, 1983–84, 230m. tonnes.

Indian Railways pay to the central government a fixed dividend of 4·5% on capital-at-charge.

Financial years	*Gross traffic receipts (Rs crores)*	*Working expenses (Rs crores)*	*Net revenues (Rs crores)*	*Net surplus or deficit (Rs crores)*
1979–80	2,337·84	2,142·38	227·29	–66·24
1980–81[1]	2,707·22	2,468·61	272·09	–52·34
1981–82[2]	3,276·75	2,913·14	399·80	+49·89

[1] Revised estimate. [2] Budget.

Aviation. The air transport industry in India was nationalized in 1953 with the formation of two Air Corporations: Air India for operating long-distance international air services, and Indian Airlines for operating air services within India and to adjacent countries. A third airline, Vayudoot, was formed in 1981 as an internal feeder airline. Air India has 10 Boeing 747s and 5 707s, and 3 Airbus A-300B4s; it operates from Bombay, Delhi, Madras, Trivandrum and Amritsar to Africa (Addis Ababa, Nairobi, Accra, Lagos, Seychelles, Mauritius, Dar es Salaam, Lusaka and Harare); to Europe (London, Birmingham, Paris, Amsterdam, Frankfurt, Geneva, Zurich, Brussels, Moscow and Rome); to western Asia (Doha, Abu Dhabi, Dharan, Cairo, Dubai, Bahrain, Kuwait, Aden, Muscat, Jeddah, Ras al Khaymah, Sharjah, Baghdad and Sanna); to east Asia (Dakha, Bangkok, Hong Kong, Tōkyō, Osaka, Kuala Lumpur, Singapore, Perth and Sydney); to North America (New York and Montreal).

Indian Airlines has a fleet of 54 aircraft consisting of Airbus A-300B2, Boeing 737, F-27 and HS-748 aircraft (Sept. 1984). During 1983–84 they carried 7·7m. passengers; net profit Rs 45·85 crores. Flights cover over 74,000 unduplicated route km. Vayudoot serves remote areas of India; it has a network of 19 stations.

The Civil Aviation Department maintains and operates 86 civil aerodromes and 24 terminals at military aerodromes. The management of the 4 international airports at Bombay (Santa Cruz), Calcutta (Dum Dum), Delhi (Palam) and Madras is vested in the International Airports Authority of India.

Shipping. In Dec. 1983, 405 ships totalling 6,045,000 GRT were on the Indian

Register; of these, 72 ships of 337,264 GRT were engaged in coastal trade, and 333 ships of 5,754,649 GRT in overseas trade. Traffic of major ports, 1983–84, was as follows:

Port	Ships entered	Imports (1m. tonnes)	Exports (1m. tonnes)
Calcutta	1,264	2·87	1·02
Bombay	3,881	10·74	13·99
Madras	1,064	7·83	5·01
Cochin	768	4·21	0·92
Mormugao	448	0·94	11·90
Vishakhapatnam	495	4·29	5·59
Kandla	555	13·27	0·89
Paradip	92	0·32	1·05
New Mangalore	255	–	–
Tuticorin	342	2·97	0·58
Haldia	410	3·99	2·39

The shipyard at Vishakhapatnam is capable of building vessels of a maximum of 21,500 DWT. Present capacity is about 64,500 DWT per year. The Cochin Shipyard can build Panamax type bulk carriers of 85,000 DWT each. On full development the capacity of the shipyard will be 2 such ships a year. Garden Reach Shipbuilders and Engineers are building bulk carriers of 26,000 DWT, ferry ships (6,000 DWT), hydrographic research ships, tugs and fast patrol craft. There are about 5,200 km of major rivers navigable by motorised craft, of which 1,700 km are used. Canals, 4,300 km, of which 485 km are navigable by motorised craft (331 km are used).

Post and Broadcasting. On 31 March 1980 there were 137,000 post offices and 28,300 telegraph offices (including (1979) 2,570 licensed offices, 23,867 combined offices and 346 DTOs). Of the post offices, 117,260 were rural and 13,728 urban in 1979.

The telephone system is in the hands of the Indian Posts and Telegraphs Department. In 1982 there were 2,981,609 telephones. There were (1979) 117 telex exchanges and 16,449 subscribers.

There were (1978) 82 radio stations and 2 auxiliary centres; on 31 Dec. 1976, 17,359,710 receiver licences were in force and programmes were sent out from 155 transmitters. A communications satellite ('APPLE') went into operation in July 1981. 'Home Service' broadcasts reach 87·75% of the population. The television service was started at Delhi, 15 Sept. 1959. There were (1974) 275,424 television receiver licences. There were 7 television centres and a relay station at Pune. Entertainment films occupy 29·3% of broadcasting time, news and current affairs, 21·3%.

Cinemas. In 1976 there were 9,017 cinemas, including about 2,660 touring cinemas: about 500 feature films were produced.

Newspapers. In Jan. 1981 the total number of newspapers and periodicals was 18,140; about 30% were published in Delhi, Bombay, Calcutta and Madras. There were 1,173 daily and 5,280 weekly papers. Circulation of dailies, 13·2m., of weeklies, 12·9m. Hindi papers have the highest number and circulation, followed by English. Circulation of dailies per 1,000 of the literate population in other languages was highest in Gujarati, followed by Malayalam, Marathi and Urdu.

Annual Report of the Register of Newspapers for India. New Delhi

JUSTICE, RELIGION, EDUCATION AND WELFARE

Justice. All courts form a single hierarchy, with the Supreme Court at the head, which constitutes the highest court of appeal. Immediately below it are the high courts and subordinate courts in each state. Every court in this chain, subject to the usual pecuniary and local limits, administers the whole law of the country, whether made by Parliament or by the state legislatures.

The states of Andhra Pradesh, Assam (in common with Nagaland, Meghalaya, Manipur and Tripura and the Union territories of Arunachal Pradesh and Mizoram), Bihar, Gujarat, Himachal Pradesh, Jammu and Kashmir, Karnataka,

Kerala, Madhya Pradesh, Maharashtra, Orissa, Punjab (in common with the state of Haryana and the Union Territory of Chandigarh), Rajasthan, Tamil Nadu, Uttar Pradesh, West Bengal and Sikkim have each a High Court. The jurisdiction of Bombay High Court extends to the Territory of Goa. There is a separate High Court for Delhi. For the Andaman and Nicobar Islands the Calcutta High Court, for Pondicherry the High Court of Madras, and for Lakshadweep the High Court of Kerala are the highest judicial authorities; in Dadrá and Nagar Haveli the High Court of Bombay is the relevant high court. The Allahabad High Court has a Bench at Lucknow, the Bombay High Court has a Bench at Nagpur, the Madhya Pradesh High Court has Benches at Gwalior and Indore, the Patna High Court has a Bench at Ranchi and the Rajasthan High Court has a Bench at Jaipur. Judges and Division Courts of the Gauhati High Court also sit in Meghalaya, Manipur, Nagaland and Tripura. Below the High Court each state is divided into a number of districts under the jurisdiction of district judges who preside over civil courts and courts of sessions. There are a number of judicial authorities subordinate to the district civil courts. On the criminal side magistrates of various classes act under the overall supervision of the High Court.

The Code of Criminal Procedure, 1898, has been replaced by the Code of Criminal Procedure, 1973 (2 of 1974), which came into force with effect from 1 April 1974. The new Code provides for complete separation of the Judiciary from the Executive throughout India.

Police. The states control their own police force through the state Home Ministers. The Home Minister of the central government co-ordinates the work of the states and controls the Central Detective Training School, the Central Forensic Laboratory, the Central Fingerprint Laboratory as well as the National Police Academy at Mount Abu (Rajasthan) where the Indian Police Service is trained. This service is recruited by competitive examination of university graduates and provides all senior officers for the state police forces. The Central Bureau of Investigation functions under the control of the Cabinet Secretariat.

The cities of Pune, Ahmedabad, Nagpur, Bangalore, Calcutta, Madras, Bombay and Hyderabad have separate police commissionerates.

Sarkar, P. C., *Civil Laws of India and Pakistan.* 2 vols. Calcutta, 1953.—*Criminal Laws of India and Pakistan.* 2nd ed. 2 vols. Calcutta, 1956
Setalvad, M. C., *The Common Law of India.* London, 1960
Sharma, S. R., *Supreme Court in the Indian Constitution.* Delhi, 1959

Religion. The principal religions in 1971 (census) were: Hindus, 453·2m. (82·7%); Moslems, 61·4m. (11·21%); Christians, 14·2m. (2·6%); Sikhs, 10·3m. (1·89%); Buddhists, 3·8m. (0·7%); Jains, 2·6m. (0·47%).

In 1971 the Christian population consisted of 8·2m. Roman Catholics, 2·69m. Anglicans of the Church of South India, 1·37m. Anglicans of the Church of North India and about 2m. nonconformists.

Sundkler, B., *Church of South India.* London, 1954

Education. Literacy. According to the 1981 census the literacy percentage in the country (excluding age-group, 0-4) was 36 (34·45 in 1971): 46·74% among males, 24·88% among females. Of the states and territories, Chandigarh and Kerala have the highest rates.

Educational Organization. With some exceptions, education is the concurrent responsibility of state and Union governments. In the union territories it is the responsibility of the central government. The Union Government is directly responsible for the central universities and all institutions declared by parliament to be of national importance; the promotion of Hindi as the federal language; co-ordinating and maintaining standards in higher education, research, science and technology. Professional education rests with the Ministry or Department concerned, e.g., medical education, the Ministry or Department of Health. The Union Minister of Education is in overall charge of the separate Departments of Education and Culture, assisted by a Minister of State. There are several autonomous organizations attached to the Department of Education. The Central Advisory

Board of Education meets to recommend directions for educational policy. The University Grants Commission is a statutory body and is responsible for the funding of the central universities and some institutions deemed to be universities, besides providing developmental assistance to the state universities as well. The Commission also influences the policies and the course curricula of the universities. The National Council of Educational Research and Training provides advisory and consultancy services in respect of school education, and also produces standard school textbooks which can be used all over the country. The Union Ministry of Education is also concerned with non-formal education, youth activities, promotion of regional languages, sports, the institution of scholarships, the award of foreign scholarships, liaison with Unesco and its organizations and promoting book production.

School Education. The school system in India can be divided into four stages: primary, middle, secondary and senior secondary.

Primary education is imparted either at independent primary (or junior basic) schools or primary classes attached to middle or secondary schools. The period of instruction in this stage varies from 4 to 5 years and the medium of instruction is in most cases the mother tongue of the child or the regional language. Free primary education is available for all children. Legislation for compulsory education has been passed by 16 state governments and 3 Union Territories but it is not practicable to enforce compulsion when the reasons for non-attendance are socio-economic.

The period for the middle stage varies from 2 to 3 years.

Under the new system, general education has been recommended up to Class X, with compulsory study of languages, sciences, mathematics and social sciences, health, physical education, fine arts and socially useful productive work.

After that there are diversified courses both academic and vocational.

Most states and territories have adopted this system.

There are, in addition, schools for professional subjects such as agriculture, commerce, fine arts, forestry, medicine, veterinary science, physical education, social service, teachers' training, technical, industrial and crafts subjects. There are also special schools for the physically and mentally handicapped and reformatory pupils. There are schools of oriental studies and adult education centres.

Higher Education. Higher education is given in arts, science or professional colleges, universities and all-India educational or research institutions. In Aug. 1982 there were 118 universities, 10 institutions of national importance and 13 institutions deemed as universities. Of the 118 universities, 7 are central: Aligarh Muslim University; Banaras Hindu University; University of Delhi; University of Hyderabad; Jawaharlal Nehru University; North Eastern Hill University; Visva Bharati. The rest are state universities. Total enrolment at universities, 1981–82, 2·95m., of which 2·59m. were undergraduates. Women students, 817,000.

Grants are paid through the University Grants Commission to the central universities and institutions deemed to be universities for their maintenance and development and to state universities for their development projects only; their maintenance is the concern of state governments. During 1981–82 the University Grants Commission sanctioned grants of Rs 93·14 crores.

Technical Education. The number of institutions awarding degrees in engineering and technology in 1979–80 was 149 (in 1947: 38), and those awarding diplomas in engineering and technology numbered 306 (in 1947: 53); the former admitted about 28,000, the latter about 47,500 students; enrolment in some has been less than capacity, following a period of unemployment in engineering. There were also 7 rural institutes and 30 Girls' Polytechnics with about 455 and 4,090 students respectively. For training high-level engineers and technologists 5 Institutes of Technology, the Indian Institute of Science, Bangalore, and 89 other institutions conduct postgraduate and research courses.

Adult Education. In spite of the improvement in the literacy rate, the number of adult illiterates over 14 was over 423m. in 1981. Adult education is, therefore, being accorded a high priority; it forms part of the Minimum Needs Programme under the sixth Five-Year Plan (1980–85), in which it is proposed to cover all illiterate persons in the age-group 15–35 by 1990. A National Board of Adult Education has been established for this purpose; effort is concentrated on backward areas, women, scheduled castes, scheduled tribes and migrant labourers. The Rural Functional Literacy Project and the programme for urban workers still operate. The Directorate of Adult Education, established in 1971, is the national resource centre responsible for producing teaching/learning materials, training and orientation, monitoring and evaluating the programme.

There were about 108,000 adult education centres in March 1982.

Educational statistics for the year 1980–81:

Type of recognized institution	*No. of institutions*	*No. of students on rolls*	*No. of teachers*
Primary/junior basic schools	485,538	51,330,138	1,345,376
Middle/senior basic schools	116,447	27,493,826	830,649
High/higher secondary schools	51,594	24,633,848	901,329
Training schools and colleges	1,397	173,838[1]	–
Arts, Science and Commerce colleges	2,425	2,177,769[2]	–

[1] Enrolment by stages of teachers' training courses at school and college level.
[2] Enrolment by stages of all post-graduate and graduate courses.

Primary pupils represent 83·1% of the age-group 6–11; middle school pupils, 40% of 11s-14s.

Expenditure (on recognized institutions) during the Sixth Plan (1980–85) is estimated at Rs 1,986 crores.

Health. Health programmes are primarily the responsibility of the state governments. The Union Government has sponsored and supported major schemes for disease prevention and control which are implemented nationally. These include the prevention and control of malaria, filaria, tuberculosis, leprosy, venereal diseases, smallpox, trachoma and cancer. There are also Union Government schemes in connexion with water supply and sanitation, and with nutrition. The Nutrition Advisory Committee of the Indian Council of Medical Research sponsors schemes for research and advises the Government. The National Nutrition Advisory Committee is to formulate a national nutrition policy and recommend measures for improving national standards.

Medical relief and service is primarily the responsibility of the states. Medical education is also a state responsibility, but there is a co-ordinating Central Health Educational Bureau. Family planning is centrally sponsored and locally implemented. The goal is to reduce the birth-rate by means of education in family planning methods.

The central government budget for 1984–85 provided Rs 469·7 crores for family welfare (including family planning) and Rs 343 crores for health; Rs 124·4 crores was for prevention and control of disease.

Social Security. Annual plan expenditure (estimate) 1977-78, Rs 1,286·65 lakhs: services for children in need of care, Rs 210 lakhs; assistance to voluntary organizations, Rs 375 lakhs; integrated child development services, Rs 107 lakhs; hostels for working women, Rs 161·5 lakhs; education for employment and vocational training for adult women, Rs 80 lakhs; national institute for the handicapped, Rs 65 lakhs; functional literacy, Rs 57·5 lakhs.

DIPLOMATIC REPRESENTATIVES

Of India in Great Britain (India House, Aldwych, London, WC2 4NA)
Acting High Commissioner: R. C. Arora.

Of Great Britain in India (Chanakyapuri, New Delhi 21, 1100-21)
High Commissioner: Sir Robert Wade-Gery, KCMG, KCVO.

Of India in the USA (2107 Massachusetts Ave., NW, Washington, D.C., 20008)
Ambassador: K. Shankar Bajpai.

Of the USA in India (Shanti Path, Chanakyapuri, New Delhi 21)
Ambassador: Harry G. Barnes, Jr.

Of India to the United Nations
Ambassador: Natarajan Krishnan.

Books of Reference

Special works relating to States are shown under their separate headings.

India: A Reference Annual. Delhi Govt. Printer. Annual
Cambridge History of India. 6 vols. CUP, 1922-47. Supp., 1953
The Times of India Directory and Yearbook. Bombay and London. Annual
Cassen, R. H., *India: Population, Economy and Society.* London, 1978
Chatterjee, S. P., *Indian Climatology.* Calcutta, 1956.(ed.), *National Atlas of India* (*Preliminary* (Hindi) *edition*). Calcutta, 1957
Fishlock, T., *India File: Inside the Subcontinent.* London, 1983
von Fürer-Haimendorf, C., *Tribes of India: the Struggle for Survival.* Univ. of California Press, 1983
Kesavan, B. S., and Kulkarni, V. Y. (eds), *The National Bibliography of Indian Literature, 1901–53,* New Delhi, 1963 ff.
Gupta, G. K. and Kharbas, D. S., *India.* [Bibliography] Oxford and Santa Barbara, 1984
Hall, A., *The Emergence of Modern India.* Columbia Univ. Press, 1981
Hart, D., *Nuclear Power in India: a Comparative Analysis.* London, 1983
Majumdar, R. C., Raychandhuri, H. C., and Datta, K., *An Advanced History of India.* 2nd ed. London, 1950
Mitra, H. N., *The Indian Annual Register.* Calcutta, from 1953
Nanda, B. R. (ed.), *Socialism in India.* Delhi, Bombay, Bangalore, Kanpur, London, 1972
Pachauri, R. K., *Energy and Economic Development in India.* New York, 1977
Philips, C. H. (ed.), *The Evolution of India and Pakistan: Select Documents.* OUP, 1962 ff.—*Politics and Society in India.* London, 1963
Poplai, S. L. (ed.), *India, 1947–50* (select documents). 2 vols. Bombay and London, 1959
Ray, R. K., *Industrialisation of India.* OUP, 1983
Smith, V. E., *Oxford History of India.* 3rd ed. OUP, 1958
Spear, P., *India: A Modern History.* 2nd ed. Univ. of Michigan Press, 1972
Sutton, S. C., *Guide to the India Office Library (founded in 1801).* HMSO, 1952
Thomas, R., *India's Emergence as an Industrial Power.* Royal Institute of International Affairs, London, 1982
Yazdani, G. (ed.), *Early History of the Deccan.* 2 vols. London, 1960

STATES AND TERRITORIES

The Republic of India is composed of the following 22 States and 9 centrally administered Union Territories:

States	*Capital*	*States*	*Capital*
Andhra Pradesh	Hyderabad	Manipur	Imphal
Assam	Dispur	Meghalaya	Shillong
Bihar	Patna	Nagaland	Kohima
Gujarat	Ahmedabad	Orissa	Bhubaneswar
Haryana	Chandigarh	Punjab	Chandigarh
Himachal Pradesh	Simla	Rajasthan	Jaipur
Jammu and Kashmir	Srinagar	Sikkim	Gangtok
Karnataka	Bangalore	Tamil Nadu	Madras
Kerala	Trivandrum	Tripura	Agartala
Madhya Pradesh	Bhopal	Uttar Pradesh	Lucknow
Maharashtra	Bombay	West Bengal	Calcutta

Union Territories

Andaman and Nicobar Islands; Arunachal Pradesh; Chandigarh; Dadra and Nagar Haveli; Delhi; Goa, Daman and Diu; Lakshadweep; Mizoram; Pondicherry.

States Reorganization. The Constitution, which came into force on 26 Jan. 1950, provided for 9 Part A States (Assam, Bihar, Bombay, Madhya Pradesh, Madras, Orissa, Punjab, Uttar Pradesh and West Bengal) which corresponded to the previous governors' provinces; 8 Part B States (Hyderabad, Jammu and Kashmir, Madhya Bharat, Mysore, Patalia-East Punjab (PEPSU), Rajasthan, Saurashtra and Travancore-Cochin) which corresponded to Indian states or unions of states; 10

Part C States (Ajmer, Bhopal, Bilaspur, Coorg, Delhi, Himachal Pradesh, Kutch, Manipur, Tripura and Vindhya Pradesh) which corresponded to the chief commissioners' provinces; and Part D Territories and other areas (*e.g.*, Andaman and Nicobar Islands). Part A States (under governors) and Part B States (under rajpramukhs) had provincial autonomy with a ministry and elected assembly. Part C States (under chief commissioners) were the direct responsibility of the Union Government, although Kutch, Manipur and Tripura had legislatures with limited powers. Andhra was formed as a Part A State on its separation from Madras in 1953. Bilaspur was merged with Himachal Pradesh in 1954.

The States Reorganization Act, 1956, abolished the distinction between Parts A, B and C States and established two categories for the units of the Indian Union to be called States and Territories. The following were the main territorial changes: the Telugu districts of Hyderabad were merged with Andhra; Mysore absorbed the whole Kannada-speaking area (including Coorg, the greater part of 4 districts of Bombay, 3 districts of Hyderabad and 1 district of Madras); Bhopal, Vindhya Pradesh and Madhya Bharat were merged with Madhya Pradesh, which ceded 8 Marathi-speaking districts to Bombay; the new state of Kerala, comprising the majority of Malayalam-speaking peoples, was formed from Travancore-Cochin with a small area from Madras; Patalia-East Punjab was included in Punjab; Kutch and Saurashtra in Bombay; and Ajmer in Rajasthan; Hyderabad ceased to exist.

On 1 May 1960 Bombay State was divided into two parts: 17 districts (including Saurashtra and Kutch) in the north and west became the new state of Gujarat; the remainder was renamed the state of Maharashtra.

In Aug. 1961 the former Portuguese territories of Dadra and Nagar Haveli became a Union territory. The Portuguese territory of Goa and the smaller territories of Daman and Diu, occupied by India in Dec. 1961, were constituted a Union territory in March 1962. In Aug. 1962 the former French territories of Pondicherry, Karikal, Mahé and Yanaon were formally transferred to India and became a Union territory. In Sept. 1962 the Naga Hills Tuensang Area was constituted a separate state under the name of Nagaland. On 1 Nov. 1966, under the Punjab Reorganization Act 1966, a new state of Haryana and a new Union Territory of Chandigarh were created from parts of Punjab (India); for details, *see* pp. 643 and 676. On 26 Jan. 1971 Himachal Pradesh became a state. In 1972 the North East Frontier Agency and Mizo hill district were made Union territories (as Arunachal Pradesh and Mizoram) and Manipur, Meghalaya and Tripura full states. Sikkim became a state in 1975.

Report of the States Reorganization Commission. Government of India. Delhi, 1956

ANDHRA PRADESH

HISTORY. Andhra was constituted a separate state on 1 Oct. 1953, on its partition from Madras, and consisted of the undisputed Telugu-speaking area of that state. To this region was added, on 1 Nov. 1956, the Telangana area of the former Hyderabad State, comprising the districts of Hyderabad, Medak, Nizamabad, Karimnaga, Warangal, Khammam, Nalgonda and Mahbubnaga, parts of the Adilabad district and some taluks of the Raichur, Gulbarga and Bidar districts, and some revenue circles of the Nanded district. On 1 April 1960, 221·4 sq. miles in the Chingleput and Salem districts of Madras were transferred to Andhra Pradesh in exchange for 410 sq. miles from Chittoor district. The district of Prakasam was formed on 2 Feb. 1970. Hyderabad was split into 2 districts on 15 Aug. 1978. A new district, Vizianagaram, was formed in 1979.

AREA AND POPULATION. Andhra Pradesh is in south India and is bounded south by Tamil Nadu, west by Karnataka, north and northwest by Maharashtra, northeast by Madhya Pradesh and Orissa, east by the Bay of Bengal. The state has an area of 275,068 sq. km and a population (1981 census) of 53·5m. Density, 195 per sq. km. Growth rate 1971–81, 23·19%. The principal language is

Telugu. Cities with over 250,000 population (1981 census), see p. 614. Other large cities (1981): Nellore (236,879); Kakinada (226,600); Kurnool (206,700); Nizamabad (183,135); Eluru (168,074); Machilipatnam (138,525); Anantapur (119,536); Tenali (119,200); Tirupati (115,200); Vizianagaram (115,200); Adoni (108,900); Proddatur (107,100); Cuddapah (103,006); Bheemavaram (101,940).

CONSTITUTION AND GOVERNMENT. Andhra Pradesh has a bicameral legislature. There are 295 seats in the Legislative Assembly and 90 in the Legislative Council. At the election of March 1985, the Telegu Dasam party continued in office.

For administrative purposes there are 23 districts in the state. The capital is Hyderabad.

Governor: Ram Lal.
Chief Minister: N. T. Rama Rao.

BUDGET. The budget (estimate) for 1983–84 showed total receipts on revenue account of Rs 2,145·04 crores, and expenditure of Rs 2,105·29 crores.

ENERGY AND NATURAL RESOURCES

Gas. Natural gas was found at Reyzole in 1983.

Electricity. There are hydro-electric plants at Machkund, Upper Sileru, Nizam Sagar, Nellore and Kothagudam. Installed capacity, 1982, 2,298 mw., power generated 8,874m. kwh. In 1983 there were 20,159 electrified towns and villages and 532,000 electric pump sets.

Water. The irrigation potential of the state in 1982 was 10,300,000 hectares; actual area under irrigation, 3,693,000 hectares. A joint project with Tamil Nadu, agreed in 1983, will irrigate about 230,000 hectares.

Minerals (1981). Production of principal minerals (in 1,000 tonnes): Coal, 9,800; limestone, 3,142; barytes, 340·7; iron ore (1980), 390. The state also has bauxite, asbestos, steatite, mica and chromite.

Agriculture. There were (1981–82) about 13·04m. hectares of cropped land, of which 35·9% is irrigated. Yield per hectare, in kg: Sugar cane, 9,142; rice, 2,102; ground-nuts, 990; tobacco, 1,053; jowar, 602; cotton, 239; castor, 208.

Livestock (1979 census): Cattle, 12·03m.; buffaloes, 7·16m.; goats, 4·4m.; sheep, 7·07m.

Forests. In 1982 it was estimated that forests occupy 23·3% of the total area of the state or 64,154 sq. km; main forest products are teak, eucalyptus, cashew, casuarina, softwoods and bamboo.

Fisheries. Production 1981–82, 118,300 tonnes of marine fish and 124,170 tonnes of inland water fish. The state has a coastline of 974 km.

INDUSTRY. The main industries are textile manufacture, sugar-milling machine tools, pharmaceuticals, cement, chemicals, glass, fertilizers, electronic equipment, heavy electrical machinery, aircraft parts and paper-making. There is an oil refinery at Vishakhapatnam, where India's only major shipbuilding yards are situated. In 1983 a steel plant was under construction at Vishakhapatnam and a railway repair shop at Tirupathi.

Cottage industry includes the manufacture of carpets, wooden and lacquer toys, brocades, bidriware, filigree and lace-work. The wooden toys of Nirmal and Kondapalli are particularly well known. Sericulture is developing rapidly. District Industries Centres have been set up to promote small-scale industry.

Tourism is growing; the main centres are Hyderabad, Nagarjunasagar, Warungal, Araku Valley, Horsley Hills and Tirupathi.

COMMUNICATIONS

Roads. In 1981–82 there were 2,437 km of national highways, 8,387 km of state highways, 18,072 km of major district roads, 74,930 km of other roads. Number of vehicles, 1981–82: 170,040 motor cycles and scooters, 41,224 cars and jeeps, 36,605 goods vehicles and 10,156 buses.

Railways. In 1981–82 there were approximately 4,813 route-km of railway, of which 3,079 km were broad gauge.

Aviation. There are airports at Hyderabad, Tirupathi, Vijayawada and Vishakapatnam, with regular scheduled services to Bombay, Delhi, Calcutta, Bangalore and Madras.

Shipping. The chief port is Vishakhapatnam. There are minor ports at Kakinada, Machilipatnam, Bheemunipatnam, Narsapur, Krishnapatnam, Vadarevu and Calingapatnam.

JUSTICE, RELIGION AND EDUCATION

Justice. The high court of Judicature at Hyderabad has a Chief Justice and 19 puisne judges.

Religion. At the 1971 census Hindus numbered 38,119,279; Moslems, 3,520,166; Christians, 1,823,436; Jains 16,103; Sikhs, 12,591; Buddhists, 10,035.

Education. In 1981, 29·94% of the population were literate (39·13% of men and 20·52% of women). There were, in 1980–81 40,408 primary schools (5,368,000 students); 4,577 upper primary (882,000); 3,706 secondary (811,000). Education is free for children up to 14.

There were in 1981–82 387 degree colleges, 468 junior colleges, 53 oriental colleges and 10 universities: Osmania University, Hyderabad; Andhra University, Waltair; Sri Venkateswara University, Tirupathi; Kakatiya University, Warangal; Nagarjuna University, Guntur; Sri Jawaharlal Nehru Technological University, Hyderabad; Central University, Hyderabad; A.P. Agricultural University, Hyderabad; Sri Krishnadevaraya University, Anantapur; Smt. Padmarathi Mahila Vishwaridyalayam (University for Women), Tirupathi. An Open University was inaugurated at Nagarjunasagar in 1982.

ASSAM

HISTORY. Assam first became a British Protectorate at the close of the first Burmese War in 1826. In 1832 Cachar was annexed; in 1835 the Jaintia Hills were included in the East India Company's dominions, and in 1839 Assam was annexed to Bengal. In 1874 Assam was detached from Bengal and made a separate chief commissionership. On the partition of Bengal in 1905, it was united to the Eastern Districts of Bengal under a Lieut.-Governor. From 1912 the chief commissionership of Assam was revived, and in 1921 a governorship was created. On the partition of India almost the whole of the predominantly Moslem district of Sylhet was merged with East Bengal (Pakistan). Dewangiri in North Kamrup was ceded to Bhután in 1951. The Naga Hill district, administered by the Union Government since 1957, became part of Nagaland in 1962. The autonomous state of Meghalaya within Assam, comprising the districts of Garo Hills and Khasi and Jaintia Hills, came into existence on 2 April 1970, and achieved full independent statehood in Jan. 1972, when it was also decided to form a Union Territory, Mizoram, from the Mizo Hills district.

EVENTS. The issue of immigration from Bangladesh has continued to inspire violent incidents and unrest. The central government proposes to build a frontier fence to prevent unauthorized entry from Bangladesh.

AREA AND POPULATION. Assam is in eastern India, almost separated from central India by Bangladesh. It is bounded west by West Bengal, north by Bhután and the Territory of Arunachal Pradesh, east by Nagaland, Manipur and

Burma, south by Meghalaya, Bangladesh and Tripura. The area of the state is now approximately 78,523 sq km. Its population (1981 census) 19·9m. Density, 254 per sq. km. Growth rate since 1971, 36·09%. Principal towns with population (1971) are; Gauhati, 122,981; Dibrugarh, 80,344; Tinsukia, 55,392; Nowgong, 52,892; Silchar, 52,612. The principal language is Assamese.

CONSTITUTION AND GOVERNMENT. Assam has a unicameral legislature of 126 members. In Feb. 1983 elections were held despite unrest and an outbreak of communal violence against Bangladeshi immigrants. A congress (I) government was returned. The capital is Gauhati.

Governor: B. N. Singh.
Chief Minister: H. Saikia.

BUDGET. The budget estimates for 1984–85 showed revenue account receipts of Rs 656·51 crores and expenditure of Rs 752·22 crores.

ENERGY AND NATURAL RESOURCES

Electricity. In 1978 there was an installed capacity of 141·5 mw and 2,260 villages (out of 21,995) with electricity. A further 583 mw capacity is to be installed by 1984. New power stations are under construction at Bongaigaon and Lakwa.

Oil. Assam contains important oilfields and produces about 50% of India's crude oil. There is also natural gas.

Water. In 1978, 88,300 hectares were irrigated and 228 projects were in hand. Intended Sixth Plan outlay, Rs 300 crores.

Minerals. Coal production (1973), 436,000 tonnes. The state also has limestone, refractory clay, dolomite, and corundum.

Agriculture. There are 756 tea plantations, and growing tea is the principal industry. Production in 1976, 276m. kg, over 50% of Indian tea. Over 72% of the cultivated area is under food crops, of which the most important is rice. Total foodgrains, 1976–77, 21·47m. tonnes. Main cash crops: jute, tea, cotton, oilseeds, sugar-cane, fruit and potatoes. Wheat has been introduced recently and yielded 71,045 tonnes in 1976–77. Cattle are important; milk production, 1976–77, 343m. litres.

Forestry. There are 1·62m. hectares of reserved forests under the administration of the Forest Department and 1,229,000 hectares of unclassed forests, altogether about 30% of the total area of the state. Revenue from forests, 1978–79, Rs 821 lakhs.

INDUSTRY. Sericulture and hand-loom weaving, both silk and cotton, are important home industries together with the manufacture of brass, cane and bamboo articles. Hand-loom weaving of silk is stimulated by state and central development schemes; outlay, Rs 18,34·5 lakhs. There is a silk-spinning mill and 2 cotton-mills. The main heavy industry is petro-chemicals; there are 3 oil refineries. Other industries include manufacturing paper, fertilizers, sugar, jute and plywood products, rice and oil milling.

COMMUNICATIONS

Roads. In 1972 there were 17,839 km of road maintained by the Public Works Department in Assam, including national highway. There were 63,616 motor vehicles in the state in 1976.

Railways. The open length of railways in 1974 was 2,193·65 km, of which 105·22 km are broad gauge.

Aviation. Daily scheduled flights connect the principal towns with the rest of India. There are airports at Gauhati, Tezpur, Jorhat, Dimapur, Silchar and Dibrugarh.

Shipping. Water transport is important in Lower Assam; the main waterway is the Brahmaputra River.

JUSTICE, RELIGION AND EDUCATION

Justice. The seat of the High Court is Gauhati. It has a Chief Justice and 6 puisne judges.

Religion. At the 1971 census Hindus numbered 10,604,618; Moslems, 3,592,124; Christians, 381,010; Buddhists, 22,565; Jains, 12,914; Sikhs, 11,920.

Education. The 1971 census showed 28·74% of the population to be literate.

In 1976 there were 26,000 primary schools; 2,504 middle schools; 1,657 high schools; 70 higher secondary schools; in 1977 there were 25,768 schools altogether, 126 general colleges and institutions for professional education, 507 vocational and technical schools, 31 teacher-training colleges and 3 universities.

Goswami, P. C., *Economic Development of Assam.* London, 1963
Reid, Sir Robert, *History of the Frontier Areas Bordering on Assam.* Shillong, 1942

BIHAR

The state contains the ethnic areas of North Bihar, Santhalpargana and Chota Nagpur. In 1956 certain areas of Purnea and Manbhum districts were transferred to West Bengal.

AREA AND POPULATION. Bihar is in north India and is bounded north by Nepál, east by West Bengal, south by Orissa, south-west by Madhya Pradesh and west by Uttar Pradesh. The area of Bihar is 173,876 sq. km and its population (1981 census, revised), 69,914,734, a density of 402 per sq. km. Growth rate since 1971, 23·9%. Population of principal towns, *see* p. 614. Other large towns (1981): Muzaffarpur, 189,765; Darbhanga, 175,879; Biharsharif, 151,305; Munghyr, 129,187; Arrah, 124,614; Katihar, 121,693; Dhanbad, 119,807; Chapra, 111,407; Purnea, 109,649; Bermo, 101,502.

The official language is Hindi and the second language Urdu.

CONSTITUTION AND GOVERNMENT. Bihar has a unicameral legislature. The Legislative Assembly consists of 325 elected members. After the elections in March 1985 a Congress government was returned. For the purposes of administration the state is divided into 10 divisions covering 38 districts. The capital is Patna.

Governor: P. Venkatasubbiah.
Chief Minister: B. Dbuey.

BUDGET. The budget estimates for 1981–82 show total receipts of Rs 15,221·3m and expenditure of Rs 14,443·5m. Per capita income (1983) Rs 870.

ENERGY AND NATURAL RESOURCES

Electricity. Installed capacity (1983) 939·68 mw. Power generated (1983–84), 2,219m. kw. In Feb. 1984 there were 29,702 villages with electricity. Hydro-electric projects in hand in 1984 will add about 50mw. capacity.

Minerals. Bihar is very rich in minerals, with about 40% of national production. There are huge deposits of copper, capatite and kyanite and sizeable deposits of coal, mica and china clay. Bihar is a principal producer of iron ore. Other important minerals: manganese, limestone, graphite, chromite, asbestos, barytes, dolomite, feldspar, columbite, pyrites, saltpetre, glass sands, slate, lead, silver, building stones and radio-active minerals.

Agriculture. About 26% of the cultivable area is irrigated. Cultivable land, 11·5m.

hectares, of a total area of 17·4m. hectares. Total cropped area, 1984, 8·5m. hectares. Main food crops are rice, wheat, maize, rabi and pulses. Main cash crops are jute, sugar-cane, oilseeds, tobacco and potato.

Forests in 1984 covered 30,896 hectares. There are 12 protected forests.

INDUSTRY. Main plants are the Tata Iron and Steel Co., the Tata Engineering and Locomotive Co., the steel plant at Bokaro, oil refinery at Barauni, Heavy Engineering Corporation and Foundry Forge project at Ranchi, and aluminium plant at Muri. Other important industries are machine tools, fertilizers, electrical engineering, sugar-milling, paper-milling, silk-spinning, manufacturing explosives and cement. There is a copper smelter at Ghatsila and a zinc plant at Tundo. Industrial disputes lost 1·18m. man-days in 1979.

TOURISM. The main tourist centres are Bodh Gaya, Patna, Nalanda, Jamshedpur, Sasaram, Betla, Hazaribagh and Vaishali.

COMMUNICATIONS

Roads. In 1972 the state had 116,575 km of highway (including 88,040 km of unmetalled roads). Passenger transport has been nationalized in 7 districts. There were 181,694 motor vehicles in 1980–81.

Railways. The North Eastern and Eastern railways traverse the state.

Aviation. There are airports at Patna and Ranchi with regular scheduled services to Calcutta and Delhi.

Shipping. The length of waterways open for navigation is 900 miles.

JUSTICE, RELIGION, EDUCATION AND WELFARE

Justice. There is a High Court (constituted in 1916) at Patna, and a bench at Ranchi, with a Chief Justice, 32 puisne judges and 4 additional judges.

Police. The police force is under a Director General of Police; in 1983 there were 957 police stations (and 56 for railway police).

Religion. At the 1961 census Hindus numbered 39,347,050; Moslems, 5,785,631; Christians, 502,195; Sikhs, 44,413; Jains, 17,598; Buddhists, 2,885.

Education. At the census of 1981 the number of literates was 18·16m. (26%: males 37·78%; females, 13·58%). There were, 1971, 2,581 high and higher secondary schools with 601,000 pupils, 8,025 middle schools with 965,000 pupils, 46,582 primary schools with 5,009,000 pupils. Primary schools had 144,559 teachers, higher secondary and high schools 25,740. Education is free for children aged 6-11.

There were 7 universities in academic year 1972–73; Patna University (founded 1917) with 12,577 full-time students (1970); Bihar University, Muzaffarpur (1952) with 4 constituent colleges, 35 affiliated colleges and 41,640 students (1970); Bhagalpur University (1960) with 40,746 students (1970); Ranchi University (1960) with 36,892 students (1968–69); Darbhanga Sanskrit University (1961); Magadha University, Gaya (1962) and Mithila University (1972), Darbhanga.

Health. In 1983 there were 259 hospitals with 19,583 beds, and 861 dispensaries with 4,166 beds.

Das, A. N., *Agrarian Movements in India. Studies in 20th Century Bihar.* London, 1982

GUJARAT

HISTORY. On 1 May 1960, as a result of the Bombay Reorganization Act, 1960, the state of Gujarat was formed from the north and west (predominantly Gujarati-speaking) portion of Bombay State, the remainder being renamed the state of Maharashtra. Gujarat consists of the following districts of the former state of

Bombay: Banas Kantha, Mehsana, Sabar Kantha, Ahmedabad, Kaira, Panch Mahals, Vadodara, Bharuch, Surat, Dangs, Amreli, Surendranagar, Rajkot, Jamnagar, Junagadh, Bhavnagar, Kutch, Gandhinagar and Bulsar.

EVENTS. Floods in Saurashtra region in June 1983 caused over 600 deaths and extensive damage; monsoon rains caused Fodana dam to burst.

AREA AND POPULATION. Gujarat is in western India and is bounded north by Pakistan and Rajasthan, east by Madhya Pradesh, south-east by Maharashtra, south and west by the Indian ocean and Arabian sea. The area of the state is 195,984 sq. km and the population at the 1981 census was 33,960,905; a density of 173 per sq. km. Growth rate 1971–81, 27·2%. The chief cities, *see* p. 614. Gujarati and Hindi in the Devanagari script are the official languages.

CONSTITUTION AND GOVERNMENT. Gujarat has a unicameral legislature, the Legislative Assembly, which has 182 elected members. After the elections in March 1985 a Congress government was returned.

The capital is Gandhinagar. There are 19 districts.

Governor: B. K. Nehru.
Chief Minister: M. Solanki.

BUDGET. The budget estimates for 1983–84 showed a surplus on revenue account of Rs 176·64 crores and an overall deficit of Rs 29·07 crores.

ENERGY AND NATURAL RESOURCES

Electricity. In 1983 the total generating capacity was 2,770 mw of electricity, serving 14,150 towns and villages and 264,392 wells and tube-wells. A thermal power station of 1,260 mw eventual capacity was commissioned at Vanakbori in 1981.

Oil and Gas. There were crude oil and gas reserves in 23 fields in 1982–83. Production: Crude oil, 3·2m. tonnes; gas, 658·5m. cu. metres.

Minerals. Chief minerals produced in 1982 (in tonnes) included chalk (90,897), lime stone (2·8m.), agate stone (1,317), calcite (323), quartz (51,775), bauxite (492,241), china clay (49,320), other clays (11,131), dolomite (260,042), crude fluorite (115,586), silica-glass sand (156,333) and lignite (510,230). Enormous reserves of coal were found under the Kalol and Mehsana oil and gas fields in May 1980. The deposit, mixed with crude petroleum, is estimated at 100,000m. tonnes, extending over 500 km.

Agriculture. Cropped area, 1979–80, was 10·6m. hectares. Area and production of principal crops, 1979–80 (in 1,000 hectares and 1,000 tonnes): Rice, 550,516; groundnuts, 2,108, 1,856; cotton, 1,717, 1,797,000 bales of 170 kg. Estimates, 1982–83: Rice, 476, 489; groundnuts, 2,057, 133; cotton, 1,496, 1,558,000 bales.

Livestock (1982): Buffaloes, 4·43m.; other cattle, 6·93m.; sheep, 2·33m.; goats, 3·26m.; horses and ponies, 24,000.

Fisheries. There were (1982) about 81,000 active fishermen and 187 fishing co-operatives. There were (1983) 11,014 fishing vessels (4,016 motor vessels). The catch for 1982–83 (estimate) was 212,419 tonnes.

INDUSTRY. Gujarat is one of the 4 most industrialized states. In 1981 there were over 10,000 registered factories including over 2,000 textile factories. There were about 77 industrial estates. There were also about 35,000 small units. Principal industries are textiles, general and electrical engineering, petrochemicals, machine tools, heavy chemicals, pharmaceuticals, dyes, sugar, soda ash and cement. Large fertilizer plants have been set up and there is an oil refinery at Koyali near Vadodara, with a developing petro-chemical complex.

State production of soda-ash is about 85% of national output, and of salt, about 60%. The capacity of state cement plants (1983) was 3·5m. tonnes a year.

COMMUNICATIONS

Roads. In 1983 there were 52,621 km of roads. Gujarat State Transport Corporation operated 11,932 routes.

Railways. In 1982 the state had 3,057 km metre gauge railway, 1,099 km narrow gauge and 1,422 km broad gauge.

Aviation. Ahmedabad is the main airport. There are 5 services daily between Ahmedabad and Bombay, Jaipur and Delhi. There are 8 other airports: Baroda, Bhavnagar, Bhuj, Jamnagar, Kandla, Keshod, Porbandar and Rajkot.

Shipping. The largest port is Kandla. There are 45 other ports, including Okha, Bedi, Bhavnagar, Verawal, Sikka and Porbandar.

Post. There were (March 1983) 8,522 post offices, 1,647 telegraph offices. Ahmedabad has direct dialling telephone connexion (or night S.T.D.) with 26 cities and telex connexions with 19 cities.

JUSTICE, RELIGION, EDUCATION AND WELFARE

Justice. The High Court of Judicature at Ahmedabad has a Chief Justice and 10 puisne judges.

Religion. At the 1971 census Hindus numbered 23,835,471; Moslems, 2,249,055; Jains, 451,578; Christians, 109,341; Sikhs, 18,233; Buddhists, 5,469.

Education. In 1981 the number of literates was 14·85m. (43·7%). Primary and secondary education are free. In 1982–83 there were 26,908 primary schools; nearly all villages with more than 200 people have one within 1·5 km. In 1980–81 there were 2,186 secondary schools and 967 higher secondary schools with 1,027,000 pupils.

There are 6 universities in the state. Gujarat University, Ahmedabad, founded in 1949, is teaching and affiliating; it has 149 affiliated colleges. The Maharaja Sayajirao University of Vadodara (1949) is residential and teaching. The Sardar Patel University, Vallabh-Vidyanagar, (1955) has 16 constituent and affiliated colleges. The 2 newer universities (1967) are Saurashtra University at Rajkot with 54 affiliated colleges, and South Gujarat at Surat with 37. Bhavnagar University (1978) is residential and teaching with 7 affiliated colleges. In 1980–81 the total number of students was 180,303. Gujarat Vidyapith at Ahmedabad is deemed a university under the University Grants Commission Act. There were also 1 agricultural and 1 Ayurvedic university.

There are 9 technical institutions for degree courses (student capacity 2,226) and 27 for full-time diploma courses (4,491).

Health. In 1983 there were 251 primary health centres and 13,000 hospital beds. The annual intake at 5 medical colleges was 675.

Rushbrook Williams, L. F., *The Black Hills: Kutch in History and Legend.* London, 1958
Desai, I. F., *Untouchability in Rural Gujarat.* Bombay, 1977

HARYANA

HISTORY. The state of Haryana, created on 1 Nov. 1966 under the Punjab Reorganization Act, 1966, was formed from the Hindi-speaking parts of the state of Punjab (India). It comprises the districts of Hissar, Mohindergarh, Gurgaon, Rohtak and Karnal; parts of Sangrur and Ambala districts; and part of Kharar tehsil.

AREA AND POPULATION. Haryana is in north India and is bounded north by Himachal Pradesh, east by Uttar Pradesh, south and west by Rajasthan and north-west by Punjab. Delhi forms an enclave on its eastern boundary. The state has an area of 44,222 sq. km and a population (1981) of 12,850,902; density, 291 per sq. km. Growth rate, 1971–81, 28·04%. The principal language is Hindi.

CONSTITUTION AND GOVERNMENT. The state has a unicameral legislature with 90 members. After the elections of May 1982 when 89 seats were contested, Congress (I) held 36 seats; Lok Dal, 31; independents, 12 and others, 10. The state shares with Punjab (India) a High Court, a university and certain public services. The capital (shared with Punjab) is Chandigarh (*see* p. 676). There are 12 districts.

Governor: G. D. Tapase.
Chief Minister: Bhajan Lal.

BUDGET. Budget estimates for 1981–82 show income of Rs 872 crores and expenditure of Rs 921 crores.

ENERGY AND NATURAL RESOURCES

Electricity. Approximately 1,000 mw are supplied to Haryana, mainly from the Bhakra Nangar system. In 1976 installed capacity was 612 mw and all the 3,302 villages had electric power.

Minerals. Minerals include iron ore, limestone, china clay and marble. Value of production, 1976, Rs 8·6m.

Agriculture. Haryana has sandy soil and erratic rainfall, but the state shares the benefit of the Sutlej-Beas scheme. Agriculture employs over 82% of the working population; in 1981 there were about 900,000 holdings (average 3·7 hectares), and the gross irrigated area was 1·97m. hectares. Area under high-yielding varieties of foodgrains, 2·2m. hectares. During 1980–81 foodgrain production was 6·2m. tonnes; sugar (gur), oilseeds, and cotton, are important.

Forests cover 3·3% of the state.

INDUSTRY. Haryana has a large market for consumer goods in neighbouring Delhi. In 1981 there were 233 large and medium scale industries employing 100,000 and producing goods worth Rs 8,000m. There were 25,000 small units. The main industries are cotton textiles (11 mills in 1976), agricultural machinery, woollen textiles, scientific instruments, glass, cement, paper and sugar milling.

COMMUNICATIONS

Roads. There were (1984) about 19,415 km of metalled roads, linking all villages. Road transport was nationalized by 1971.

Railways. The state is crossed by lines from Delhi to Agra, Ajmer, Ferozepur and Chandigarh. The main stations are at Ambala and Kurukshetra.

Aviation. There is no airport within the state but Delhi is on its eastern boundary.

JUSTICE AND EDUCATION

Justice. Haryana shares the High Court of Punjab and Haryana at Chandigarh which had (1968) a Chief Justice and 16 puisne judges.

Education. In 1981 the number of literates was 4·6m. In 1969-70 there were 5,967 schools and colleges with 1,250,590 attending. This includes 4,362 primary schools, 776 high and higher secondary schools, 777 middle schools and 47 colleges.

HIMACHAL PRADESH

HISTORY. The territory came into being on 15 April 1948 and comprised 30 former Hill States. The state of Bilaspur was merged with Himachal Pradesh in

1954. The 6 original districts were: Mahasu, Sirmur, Mandi, Chamba, Bilaspur and Kinnaur. On 1 Nov. 1966, under the Punjab Reorganization Act, 1966, certain parts of the state of Punjab (India) were transferred to Himachal Pradesh. These comprise the districts of Simla, Kulu, Kangra, and Lahaul and Spiti; and parts of Hoshiarpur and Ambala districts, with an estimated population (1967) of 1·5m.

AREA AND POPULATION. Himachal Pradesh is in north India and is bounded north by Kashmir, east by Tibet, south-east by Uttar Pradesh, south by Haryana, south-west and west by Punjab. The area of the state is 55,673 sq. km and it had a population at the 1981 census of 4,280,818. Density, 77 per sq. km. Growth rate, 1971–81, 23·71%. Principal language is Pahari.

CONSTITUTION AND GOVERNMENT. Full statehood was attained, as the 18th state of the Union, on 25 Jan. 1971.

On 1 Sept. 1972 districts were reorganized and 2 new districts created, Hamirpur and Una, making a total of 12. The capital is Simla.

There is a unicameral legislature. After the elections in March 1985 a Congress government was returned.

Governor: H. Sema.
Chief Minister: V. Bhadra Singh.

BUDGET. Budget estimates for 1980–81 showed revenue receipts of Rs 193 crores and expenditure on revenue account of Rs 161 crores. The capital account showed a deficit of Rs 73·57 crores.

ENERGY AND NATURAL RESOURCES

Electricity. In 1983–84, 13,360 villages had electricity. Power generation is the first priority of the seventh 5-year plan.

In 1984 the state signed an agreement with neighbouring states to generate 3,000 mw of hydro-electricity.

Water. An artificial confluence of the Sutlej and Beas rivers has been made, directing their united flow into Govind Sagar Lake.

Minerals. The state has rock salt, slate, gypsum, limestone, barytes, dolomite and pyrites.

Agriculture. Farming employs 76% of the people. Irrigated area is 24% of the area sown. Main crops are seed potatoes, wheat, maize, rice and fruits such as apples, peaches, apricots, nuts, pomegranates.

Production of foodgrains (1983) 1·06m. tonnes.

Livestock (1977 census): Buffaloes, 384,497; other cattle, 2,106,220; goats, 1,035,337.

Forestry. Himachal Pradesh forests cover 38·3% of the state and supply the largest quantities of coniferous timber in northern India. They are the main source of revenue of Pradesh. The forests also ensure the safety of the catchment areas of the Jumna, Sutlej, Beas, Ravi and Chenab rivers.

INDUSTRY. The main sources of employment are the forests and their related industries; there are factories making turpentine and rosin, fertilizers, cement and TV sets. There is a foundry and a brewery. Other industries include salt production and handicrafts, including weaving.

COMMUNICATIONS

Roads. The national highway from Chandigarh runs through Simla; other main highways from Simla serve Kulu, Manali, Kangra, Chemba and Pathankot. The rest are minor roads. Pathankot is also on national highways from Punjab to Kashmir.

Railways. There is a line from Chandigarh to Simla, and the Jammu-Delhi line runs through Pathankot.

Aviation. The state has no airport, but Chandigarh is on its southern boundary. In 1984 an airport was under construction at Jubbarhath, near Simla.

JUSTICE. The state has its own High Court at Simla.

EDUCATION. The number of literates in 1984 was 1·8m.

JAMMU AND KASHMIR

HISTORY. The state of Jammu and Kashmir, which had earlier been under Hindu rulers and Moslem sultans, became part of the Mogul Empire under Akbar from 1586. After a period of Afghan rule from 1756, it was annexed to the Sikh kingdom of the Punjab in 1819. In 1820 Ranjit Singh made over the territory of Jammu to Gulab Singh. After the decisive battle of Sobraon in 1846 Kashmir also was made over to Gulab Singh under the Treaty of Amritsar. British supremacy was recognized until the Indian Independence Act, 1947, when all states decided on accession to India or Pakistan. Kashmir asked for standstill agreements with both. Pakistan agreed, but India desired further discussion with the Government of Jammu and Kashmir State. In the meantime the state became subject to armed attack from the territory of Pakistan and the Maharajah acceded to India on 26 Oct. 1947, by signing the Instrument of Accession. India approached the UN in Jan. 1948; India-Pakistan conflict ended by ceasefire in Jan. 1949. Further conflict in 1965 was followed by the Tashkent Declaration on Jan. 1966. Following further hostilities between India and Pakistan a ceasefire came into effect on 17 Dec. 1971, followed by the Simla Agreement in July 1972, whereby a new line of control was delineated bilaterally through negotiations between India and Pakistan and came into force on 17 Dec. 1972.

AREA AND POPULATION. The state is in the extreme north and is bounded north by China, east by Tibet, south by Himachal Pradesh and Punjab and west by Pakistan. The area is 222,236 sq. km, of which about 78,932 sq. km is occupied by Pakistan and 42,735 sq. km by China; the population of the territory on the Indian side of the line, 1981 census, was 5,981,600. Growth rate, 1971–81, 29·57%. For the population of Srinagar, *see* p. 614. The official language is Urdu; other commonly spoken languages are Kashmiri, Dogri, Balti, Ladakhi and Punjabi.

CONSTITUTION AND GOVERNMENT. The Maharajah's son, Yuvraj Karan Singh, took over as Regent in 1950 and, on the ending of hereditary rule (17 Oct. 1952), was sworn in as Sadar-i-Riyasat. On his father's death (26 April 1961) Yuvraj Karan Singh was recognized as Maharajah by the Indian Government; he decided not to use the title while he was elected head of state.

The permanent Constitution of the state came into force in part on 17 Nov. 1956 and fully on 26 Jan. 1957. There is a bicameral legislature; the Legislative Council has 36 members and the Legislative Assembly has 76. The state of the parties in the Legislative Assembly in autumn 1983 was: Congress (I) 26; National Conference, 47; Panthers Party, 1; Peoples' Conference, 1; Independent, 1. Since the 1967 elections the 6 representatives of Jammu and Kashmir in the central House of the People are directly elected; there are 4 representatives in the Council of States. The Council of Ministers consists of 7 Ministers and 4 Junior Ministers.

Kashmir Province has 8 districts and Jammu Province has 6 districts. Srinagar is the summer and Jammu the winter capital.

Governor: Jag Mohan.
Chief Minister: G. Muhammed Shah.

BUDGET. Budget estimates for 1980–81 show revenue of Rs 576·62 crores, and expenditure of Rs 578·37 crores.

Total planning expenditure for 1980–81 was Rs 147·48 crores., of which agriculture and allied sectors received Rs 26·38 crores; power Rs 21·25 crores; water supply Rs 16·50 crores and irrigation and flood control Rs 16·00 crores.

ENERGY AND NATURAL RESOURCES

Electricity. Installed capacity (1980) 208·78 mw.; 4,631 villages had electricity.

Minerals. Value of production, 1976, Rs 5·46m. Minerals include coal, bauxite and gypsum.

Agriculture. About 80% of the population are supported by agriculture. Rice, wheat and maize are the major cereals. The total area under food crops (1978-79) was estimated at 1,847,000 acres. Total foodgrains produced, 1980, 1·4m. quintals. Fruit is important; exports (1980–81 estimate), 360,000 tonnes.

The Agrarian Reforms Act came into force in July 1978; the Debtors Relief Act and the Restriction of Mortgage Properties Act also alleviate rural distress. The redistribution of land to cultivators is continuing.

Livestock (1977 census): Cattle, 2,138,000; buffaloes, 501,000; goats, 1,216,000; horses, 629,000, and poultry, 2,039,000.

Forestry. Forests cover about 21,080 sq. km., forming an important source of revenue, besides providing employment to a large section of the population. About 7,480 sq. km of forests yield valuable timber; state income in 1978–79 was Rs 231·1m.

INDUSTRY. The largest industrial complex is the Bari Brahmara estate in Jammu which covers 320 acres and accommodates diverse manufacturing, as does the Khanmuh estate. The Sopore industrial area in Kashmir Division is intended for industries based on horticulture. There are 6,386 small units (1980) with production valued at Rs 661·3m., employing 34,000. The main traditional handicraft industries are silk spinning and carpet-weaving.

COMMUNICATIONS

Roads. Kashmir is linked with the rest of India by the motorable Jammu Pathankot road. The Jawahar Tunnel, through the Banihal mountain, connects Srinagar and Jammu, and maintains road communication with the Kashmir Valley during the winter months. In 1981 there were 7,866 km of roads; work on the Batote–Kishtwar road was in progress, up-grading to National Highway standard.

There were 33,361 motor vehicles in 1979–80.

Railways. Kashmir was linked with the Indian railway system on 3 Dec. 1972 when the line between Jammu and Pathankot was opened.

Aviation. Major airports, with daily service from Delhi, are at Srinagar and Jammu. Srinagar airport is being developed as an international airport.

Post. There were 1,290 post offices in 1980, 82 telephone exchanges and approximately 12,120 private telephones.

JUSTICE, RELIGION, EDUCATION AND WELFARE

Justice. The High Court, at Srinagar and Jammu, has a Chief Justice and 4 puisne judges.

Religion. The majority of the population, except in Jammu, are Moslems. At the 1971 census Moslems numbered 3,040,129, Hindus, 1,404,292; Sikhs, 105,873; Buddhists, 57,956; Christians, 7,182; Jains, 1,150.

Education. The proportion of literates was 18·59% in 1980. Education is free. There are (1981) 9,715 schools and about 953,000 children attend. Jammu and Srinagar Universities (founded 1948) have 37 teaching departments and 42 affiliated colleges. There are 2 medical colleges, an engineering college, 1 agricultural college, 2 polytechnics, 12 professional colleges, 8 oriental colleges and an Ayurvedic college.

Health. In 1979–80 there were 43 hospitals, 279 primary health units, 279 sub-centres, about 530 clinics and dispensaries, and 50 other units. There were 800 doctors. Expenditure on health was Rs 27·15 in 1980–81. There is a National Institute of Medical Sciences under construction.

Bamzai, P. N. K., *A History of Kashmir.* Delhi, 1962
Gupta, S., Kashmir: *A Study in IndiaPakistan Relations.* London, 1967

KARNATAKA

HISTORY. The state of Karnataka, constituted as Mysore under the States Reorganization Act, 1956, brought together the Kannada-speaking people distributed in 5 states, and consisted of the territories of the old states of Mysore and Coorg, the Bijapur, Kanara and Dharwar districts and the Belgaum district (except one taluk) in former Bombay, the major portions of the Gulbarga, Raichur and Bidar districts in former Hyderabad, and South Kanara district (apart from the Kasaragod taluk) and the Kollegal taluk of the Coimbatore district in Madras. The state was renamed Karnataka in 1973.

AREA AND POPULATION. The state is in south India and is bounded north by Maharashtra, east by Andhra Pradesh, south by Tamil Nadu and Kerala, west by the Indian ocean and north-east by Goa. The area of the state is 191,791 sq. km, and its population (1981 census), 37,135,714, an increase of 26·43% since 1971. Density, 193 per sq. km. Kannada is the language of administration and is spoken by about 66% of the people. Other languages include Telugu (8·2%), Urdu (9%), Marathi (4·5%), Tamil (3·6%), Tulu and Konkani. Principal cities, *see* p. 614.

CONSTITUTION AND GOVERNMENT. Karnataka has a bicameral legislature. The Legislative Council has 63 members. The Legislative Assembly consists of 223 elected members and 1 nominated member. After elections in March 1985 the Janata party formed a government.

The state has 19 districts (of which Coorg is one) in 4 divisions: Bangalore, Mysore, Belgaum and Gulbarga. The capital is Bangalore.

Governor: A. N. Banerjee.
Chief Minister: Ramakrishna Hegde.

BUDGET. Budget estimates for 1981–82 showed a deficit of Rs 461·1m.

ENERGY AND NATURAL RESOURCES

Electricity. In 1980 the state's installed capacity was 1,334·8 mw., to be revised (by the Kalinadi project) to 2,000 mw.

Water. About 1·3m. hectares were irrigated in 1984.

Minerals. Karnataka has India's only sources of gold and silver. The estimated reserves of high grade iron ore are 5,000m. tonnes. These reserves are found mainly in the Chitradurga belt. The National Mineral Development Corporation of India has indicated total reserves of nearly 1,000m. tonnes of magnesite and iron ore (with an iron content ranging from 25 to 40) which have been found in Kudremukh Ganga-Mula region in Chickmagalur District. The estimated reserves of manganese are over 100m. tonnes.

Limestone is found in many regions; deposits (1984) are about 2,104m. tonnes.

Karnataka is the largest producer of chromite. It is one of the only two states of India producing magnesite. The other minerals of industrial importance are corundum and garnet.

Agriculture. Agriculture forms the main occupation of more than three-quarters of the population. Physically, Karnataka divides itself into four regions–the coastal region, the southern and northern 'maidan' or plain country, comprising roughly the districts of Bangalore, Tumkur, Chitaldrug, Kolar, Bellary, Mandya and Mysore, and the 'malnad' or hill country, comprising the districts of Chickmagalur, Hassan and Shimoga. Rainfall is heavy in the 'malnad' tracts, and in this area there is dense forest. The greater part of the 'maidan' country is cultivated. Coorg district is essentially agricultural.

The main food crops are rice and jowar, and ragi which is also about 30% of the national crop. Sugar, groundnut, castor-seed, safflower, mulberry silk and cotton are important cash crops. The state grows about 70% of the national coffee crop.

Production, 1980 (1,000 tonnes): Cotton, 219·3; sugar-cane, 109·2; tobacco, 158·2; chillies, 131·3; ground nuts, 119·9; caster seed, 134·7; sesamum, 252·9.

Livestock (1977): Buffaloes, 3,215,873; other cattle, 10,018,714; sheep, 662,420; goats, 726,016.

Forestry. Total forest in the state (1979) is 18% of the land area, producing sandal wood, bamboo and other timbers, and ivory.

INDUSTRY. The Visvesvaraya Iron and Steel Works is situated at Bhadravati, while at Bangalore are national undertakings for the manufacture of aircraft, machine tools, light engineering and electronics goods. Other industries include textiles, vehicle manufacture, cement, chemicals, sugar, paper, porcelain and soap. In addition, much of the world's sandalwood is processed, the oil being one of the most valuable productions of the state. Sericulture is a more important cottage industry giving employment, directly or indirectly, to about 2·4m. persons; production is about 3,000 tonnes, over two-thirds of national production.

COMMUNICATIONS

Roads. In 1982–83 the state had 102,151 km of roads.

Railways. In 1982–83 there were 2,936 km of railway (including 154 km of narrow gauge) in the state.

Aviation. There are airports at Bangalore, Mangalore and Belgaum, with regular scheduled services to Bombay, Calcutta, Delhi and Madras.

Shipping. Mangalore is a deep-water port for the export of mineral ores. Karwar is being developed as an intermediate port.

JUSTICE, RELIGION AND EDUCATION

Justice. The seat of the High Court is at Bangalore. It has a Chief Justice and 11 puisne judges.

Religion. At the 1971 census Hindus numbered 25,332,388; Moslems, 3,113,298; Christians, 613,026; Jains, 218,862; Buddhists, 114,139; Sikhs, 6,830.

Education. The number of literates, according to the 1981 census, was 14·2m. In 1977 the state had 33,137 primary schools, 2,326 high schools, 314 schools for professional and technical education and 30 polytechnic and engineering schools. Education is free up to pre-university level.

The University of Mysore (founded in 1916) at Mysore has 7 university colleges at Mysore and 134 affiliated colleges. Karnatak University (1950) at Dharwar has 4 constituent colleges and 95 affiliated colleges. Bangalore University (1964) has 46 constituent colleges, the University of Agricultural Sciences, Hebbal, Bangalore, (1964) has 3 constituent colleges. There are two other universities: Gulbarga and Mangalore.

The Indian Institute of Science. Bangalore, is unaffiliated; it conducts diploma courses in engineering, metallurgy and technology. There are 415 other colleges, including medical, law and commercial.

Learmouth, A. T. A., and Bhat, L. T., *Mysore State.* 2 vols. London, 1961–62

KERALA

HISTORY. The state of Kerala, created under the States Reorganization Act, 1956, consists of the previous state of Travancore-Cochin, except for 4 taluks of the Trivandrum district and a part of the Shencottah taluk of Quilon district. It took over the Malabar district (apart from the Laccadive and Minicoy Islands) and the Kasaragod taluk of South Kanara (apart from the Amindivi Islands) from Madras State.

AREA AND POPULATION. Kerala is in south India and is bounded north by Karnataka, east and south-east by Tamil Nadu, south-west and west by the Indian ocean. The state has an area of 38,863 sq. km. The 1981 census showed a population of 25,453,680; density of population was 655 per sq. km (highest of any state). Growth rate, 1971–81, 19%. Population of principal cities, *see* p. 614.

Languages spoken in the state are Malayalam, Tamil and Kannada.

The physical features of the land fall into three well-marked divisions: (1) the hilly tracts undulating from the Western Ghats in the east and marked by long spurs, extensive ravines and dense forests; (2) the cultivated plains intersected by numerous rivers and streams; and (3) the coastal belt with dense coconut plantations and rice fields.

CONSTITUTION AND GOVERNMENT. The state has a unicameral legislature of 140 members including the Speaker. After the elections of May 1982 the Indian National (I) Congress Party and allies held 77 seats, the Left Front (CPI, CPI (M) and allies), 63.

The state has 14 districts. The capital is Trivandrum.

Governor: P. Ramachandran.
Chief Minister: K. Karunakaran.

BUDGET. Revised budget estimates for 1983–84 showed total revenue receipts of Rs 958·54 crores, expenditure Rs 1,030·57 crores. Annual Plan expenditure, Rs 355 crores.

ENERGY AND NATURAL RESOURCES

Electricity. Installed capacity (1983), 1,011·5 mw.; energy generated in 1982–83 was 4,487·7m. kw. Stage I of the Idukki hydro-electric plant has a capacity of 390 mw, the Sabarigiri scheme 300mw.

Minerals. Next to Bihar, Kerala possesses the widest variety of economic mineral resources among the Indian States. The beach sands of Kerala contain monazite, ilmenite, rutile, zircon, sillimanite, etc. There are extensive whiteclay deposits; other minerals of commercial importance include mica, graphite, limestone, quartz sand and lignite. Iron ore has been found at Kozhikode (Calicut). Value of mineral production, 1982–83, Rs 3·22m.

Agriculture. The state suffered three successive monsoon failures up to 1983, with severe effects on crops. The chief agricultural products are rice, tapioca, coconut, arecanut, cashewnut, oilseeds, pepper, sugar-cane, rubber, tea, coffee and cardamom. About 98% of Indian black pepper and about 95% of Indian rubber is produced in Kerala. Area and production of principal crops, 1982–83 (in 1,000 hectares and 1,000 tonnes): Rice, 778·5, 1,306; black pepper, 107·9, 26·8; arecanut, 58, 8,463 (million nuts); bananas and other plantains, 49·3, 293·8; cashewnuts, 139·5, 81·2; coconuts, 658·5, 2,444 (million nuts); tea, 36·1, 48·7; coffee, 57·9, 21·7; rubber, 256·2, 152·6; tapioca, 245·6, 3,486·6; cardamom, 54·5, 1·9.

Livestock (1972, provisional); Buffaloes, 469,515; other cattle, 2,855,856; sheep, 10,390; goats, 1,450,587. In 1981–82 production was: milk, 982,000 tonnes; meat, 17,500; feeds, 3,093. Egg production, 1982–83, 3,366,000.

Forestry. About 24% of the area is comprised of forests, including teak, sandal wood, ebony and blackwood and varieties of softwood. Net forest revenue, 1981–82, Rs 51·9 crores, from timber, bamboos, reeds and ivory.

Fisheries. Fishing is a flourishing industry; the catch in 1982 was about 351,000 tonnes. Fish exports, 1982–83, 32,525 tonnes valued at Rs 141·5 crores.

INDUSTRIES. Most of the major industrial concerns are either owned or sponsored by the Government. Among the privately owned factories are the numerous cashew and coir factories. Other important factory industries are rubber, tea, tiles, oil, textiles, ceramics, fertilizers and chemicals, zinc-smelting, sugar, cement, rayon, glass, matches, pencils, monazite, ilmenite, titanium oxide, rare earths, aluminium, electrical goods, paper, shark-liver oil, etc.

The number of factories registered under the Factories Act 1948 on 31 Dec. 1982 was 9,099, with daily average employment of 303,588.

Among the cottage industries, coir-spinning and handloom-weaving are the most important, forming the means of livelihood of a large section of the people. Other industries are the village oil industry, ivory carving, furniture-making, bell metal, brass and copper ware, leather goods, screw-pines, mat-making, rattan work, bee-keeping, pottery, etc. These have been organized on a co-operative basis.

COMMUNICATIONS

Roads. In 1983 there were 99,185 km of roads in the state; national highways, 839 km. There were 246,923 motor vehicles in 1982–83.

Railways. There is a coastal line from Mangalore (Karnataka) which serves Cannanore, Mahe, Kozhikode (Calicut), Ernakulam (for Cochin), Quilon and Trivandrum, and connects them with main towns in Tamil Nadu. In 1982–83 there were 806 km broad gauge and 113 km metre gauge lines.

Aviation. There are airports at Cochin and Trivandrum with regular scheduled services to Bombay and Madras; international flights leave Trivandrum for Sri Lanka.

Shipping. Port Cochin, administered by the central government, is one of India's major ports; in 1983 it became the out-port for the Inland Container Depot at Coimbatore (Tamil Nadu). There are 13 other ports and harbours.

JUSTICE, RELIGION AND EDUCATION

Justice. The High Court at Ernakulam has a Chief Justice and 11 puisne judges and 4 additional judges.

Religion. The majority are Hindus; other important faiths are Christianity and Islam. There are also some Jains.

Education. Kerala is the most literate Indian State with 17m. literates at the 1981 census (70%). Education is free up to the age of 14.

In 1982–83 there was a total school enrolment of 5·64m. students. There were 6,817 lower primary schools 2,763 upper primary schools and 2,154 high schools.

Kerala University (established 1937) at Trivandrum, is affiliating and teaching; in 1982–83 it had 99 affiliated arts and science colleges. The University of Cochin is federal, and for post-graduate studies only. The University of Calicut (established 1968) is teaching and affiliating and has 69 affiliated colleges. Kerala Agricultural University (established 1971) has 3 constituent colleges. Gandhiji University at Kottayam was established in 1983.

MADHYA PRADESH

HISTORY. Under the provisions of the States Reorganization Act, 1956, the State of Madhya Pradesh was formed on 1 Nov. 1956. It consists of the 17 Hindi districts of the previous state of that name, the former state of Madhya Bharat (except the Sunel enclave of Mandsaur district), the former state of Bhopal and Vindhya Pradesh and the Sironj subdivision of Kotah district, which was an enclave of Rajasthan in Madhya Pradesh.

For information on the former states, *see* THE STATESMAN'S YEAR-BOOK, 1958, pp. 180–84.

EVENTS. More than 2,000 were killed by a leakage of toxic gas from a pesticide plant near Bhopal in Dec. 1984. the plant (Union Carbide) was closed.

AREA AND POPULATION. The state is in central India and is bounded north by Rajasthan and Uttar Pradesh, east by Bihar and Orissa, south by Andhra Pradesh and Maharashtra, west by Gujarat. Madhya Pradesh is the largest Indian state in size, with an area of 442,841 sq. km. In respect of population it ranks sixth. Population (1981 census), 52,138,467, an increase of 25·15% since 1971. Density, 118 per sq. km.

Cities with over 250,000 population, *see* p. 614. Other large cities (1981): Sagar, 207,401; Bilaspur, 186,885; Ratlam, 156,490; Burhanpur, 141,142; Mudwari-Katni, 125,096; Khandwa, 114,463; Rewa, 100,519.

The number of persons speaking each of the more prevalent languages (1971 census) were: Hindi, 32,873,079; Urdu, 988,275; Marathi, 1,385,952; Gujarati, 155,723.

CONSTITUTION AND GOVERNMENT. Madhya Pradesh is one of the 9 states for which the Constitution provides a bicameral legislature, but the Vidhan Parishad or Upper House (to consist of 90 members) has yet to be formed. The Vidhan Sabha or Lower House has 320 elected members. Following the election of March 1985, a Congress government was returned, with 250 out of 350 seats.

For administrative purposes the state has been split into 11 divisions with a Commissioner at the head of each; the headquarters of these are located at Bhopal, Bilaspur, Gwalior (2), Hoshangabad, Indore, Jabalpur, Raipur, Rewa, Sagar and Ujjain. There are 45 districts.

The seat of government is at Bhopal.

Governor: Prof. K. M. Chandy.
Chief Minister: (Vacant).

BUDGET. Budget estimates for 1982–83 showed total revenue of Rs 14,26,51·83 lakhs, and expenditure of Rs 12,68,30 lakhs. Receipts included: Contributions and adjustments between central and state governments, Rs 4,84,55·97 lakhs; taxes on income, Rs 81,92 lakhs; state excise, Rs 68,63·70 lakhs; stamps and registration, Rs 26,45 lakhs; forests, Rs 1,95,00 lakhs; sales tax, Rs 2,40,96 lakhs; vehicles taxes, Rs 26,11 lakhs; debt services, Rs 77,49·27 lakhs; civil administration, Rs 22,39·68 lakhs; land revenue, Rs 12,98·00 lakhs. Expenditure included: Education, Rs 2,11,24·16 lakhs; public works and improvements, Rs 55,26·89 lakhs; irrigation, embankment, etc., Rs 40,24·01 lakhs; medical, and public health, Rs 1,34,46·65 lakhs; police, Rs 83,32·72 lakhs; agriculture, Rs 40,94·18 lakhs; general administration, Rs 20,13·25 lakhs; debt services, Rs 1,19,05·35 lakhs; community projects and local development, Rs 65,80·76 lakhs; industries, Rs 16,41·25 lakhs; forests, Rs 1,05,66·69 lakhs; social security and welfare, Rs 71,88·49 lakhs.

ENERGY AND NATURAL RESOURCES

Electricity. Madhya Pradesh is rich in low-grade coal suitable for power generation, and also has immense potential hydro-electric energy. The present installed capacity is 1,630·5 mw; of this 193 mw from hydro-electric power stations. The thermal power stations are at Korba in Bilaspur district, Amarkantak in Shahdol district and Satpura in Betul district; new stations are being built. The only hydro-electric power station is at Gandhi Sagar lake in Mandsaur district; this, with a maximum water surface of 165 sq. miles, is the biggest man-made lake in Asia.

Water. Major irrigation projects include the Chambal Valley scheme (started in 1952 with Rajasthan), the Tawa project in Hoshangabad district, the Barna and Hasdeo schemes, the Mahanadi canal system and schemes in the Narmada valley at Bargi and Narmadasagar. Total irrigation potential in 1983, 10m. hectares, of which 3m. had been achieved.

Minerals. The state has extensive mineral deposits including coal (35% of national deposits), iron ore (30%) and manganese (50%), bauxite (44%), ochre, sillimanite, limestone, dolomite, rock phosphate, copper, lead, tin, fluorite, barytes, china clay and fireclay, corundum, gold, diamonds, pyrophyllite and diaspore, lepidolite, asbestos, vermiculite, mica, glass sand, quartz, felspars, bentonite and building stone.

In 1980 the output of major minerals was (in tonnes): Coal, 25·1m.; limestone, 6·53m.; dolomite, 770,000; diamonds, 14,432 carats; bauxite, 470,000; iron ore, 9·7m.; manganese ore, 270,000. Value of production, 1980, Rs 3,626m.

Agriculture. Agriculture is the mainstay of the state's economy and 80% of the people are rural. Over 42% of the land area is cultivable, of which 13% is irrigated. The Malwa region abounds in rich black cotton soil, the low-lying areas of Gwalior, Bundelkhand and Baghelkhand and the Chhatisgarh plains have a lighter sandy soil, while the Narmada valley is formed of deep rich alluvial deposits. Production of principal crops, 1980–81 (in tonnes): Foodgrains, 12·4m.; sugar-cane (gur), 107,000; oilseeds, 608,000, and cotton, 268,000 bales (of 170 kg).

Livestock (1977 census): Buffaloes, 5,852,549; other cattle, 34,256,725; sheep, 968,595; goats, 6,573,467; horses and ponies, 121,908.

Forestry. In 1982 155,411 sq. km, or about 35% of the state's area was covered by forests. The forests are chiefly of sal, saja, bija, bamboo and teak. They are the chief source in India of best-quality teak; they also provide firewood for about 60% of domestic fuel needs, and form valuable watershed protection.

INDUSTRY. The major industries are the steel plant at Bhilai, Bharat Heavy Electricals at Bhopal, the aluminium plant at Korba, the security paper mills at Hoshangabad, the Bank Note Press at Dewas, the newsprint mill at Nepanagar and alkaloid factory at Neemuch, cement factories, vehicle factory, ordnance factory, and gun carriage factory. There are also 23 textile mills, 7 of them nationalized.

The Bhilai steel plant near Durg is one of the 6 major steel mills. A power station at Korba (Bilaspur) with a capacity of 420 mw serves Bhilai, the aluminium plant and the Korba coalfield.

The heavy electricals factory was set up by the Government of India at Bhopal during the second plan period. This is India's first heavy electrical equipment factory and also one of the largest of its type in Asia. It makes a variety of highly complicated equipment required for generation, transmission, distribution and utilization of electric power.

Other industries include cement, sugar, straw board, paper, vegetable oil, refractories, potteries, textile machinery, steel casting and rerolling, industrial gases, synthetic fibres, drugs, biscuit manufacturing, engineering, tools, rayon and art silk. The number of heavy and medium industries in the state is 193, with 181 ancillary industries; the number of small-scale industries in production is 77,360. Thirty-nine out of 45 districts in the state are categorized as industrially backward districts.

The main industrial development agencies are Madhya Pradesh Financial Corporation, Madhya Pradesh Audyogik Vikas Nigam Ltd, Madhya Pradesh State Industries Corporation, Madhya Pradesh Laghu Udyog Nigam, Madhya Pradesh State Textile Corporation, Madhya Pradesh Handicrafts Board, Khadi and Village Industries Board and Madhya Pradesh State Mining Corporation.

The state is known for its traditional village and home crafts such as handloom weaving, best developed at Chanderi and Maheshwar, toys, pottery, lacework, woodwork, zari work, leather work and metal utensils. The ancillary industries of dyeing, calico printing and bleaching are centred in areas of textile production.

COMMUNICATIONS

Roads. Total length of roads in 1982 was 65,889 km, of which 50,934 km were surfaced. In 1977–78 there were 225,278 motor vehicles.

Railways. Bhopal, Bilaspur, Katni, Khandwar and Ratlam are important junctions for the central and northern networks.

Aviation. There are airports at Bhopal, Indore, Jabalpur, Khajuraho and Raipur with regular scheduled services to Bombay, Calcutta and Delhi.

JUSTICE, RELIGION AND EDUCATION

Justice. The High Court of Judicature at Jabalpur has a Chief Justice and 21 puisne judges.

Religion. At the 1971 census Hindus numbered 39,024,162; Moslems, 1,815,685; Christians, 286,072; Buddhists, 81,823; Sikhs, 98,973.

Education. The 1981 census showed 14·5m. people to be literate. Education is free for children aged up to 14.

In 1975–76 there were 355 higher educational institutions. Primary schools (1974–75) had 3·5m. pupils and higher secondary schools, 620,897 pupils.

There are 10 universities in Madhya Pradesh: the University of Sagar (established 1946), at Sagar, had 53 affiliated colleges and 26,516 students in 1975; Jabalpur University (1957) had 30 affiliated colleges and 12,962 students; Vikram University (1957), at Ujjain, had 46 affiliated colleges and 38,011 students; Indira Kala Sangeet Vishwavidyalaya (1956), at Khairagarh, had 9 affiliated colleges and 1,164 students on roll (this university teaches music and fine arts); Indore University (1964) had 21 affiliated colleges and 22,915 students; Jivagi University (1963), at Gwalior, had 43 affiliated colleges and 31,462 students; Jawaharlal Nehru Krishi University (1964), at Jabalpur, had 9 affiliated colleges and 2,274 students in 1964; Ravishankar University (1964), at Raipur, had 63 affiliated colleges and 41,607 students. In 1975–76 there were 256 degree-granting colleges, 19 teacher-training colleges, and 71 professional colleges including polytechnics.

MAHARASHTRA

HISTORY. Under the States Reorganization Act, 1956, Bombay State was formed by merging the states of Kutch and Saurashtra and the Marathi-speaking areas of Hyderabad (commonly known as Marathwada) and Madhya Pradesh (also called Vidarbha) in the old state of Bombay, after the transfer from that state of the Kannada-speaking areas of the Belgaum, Bijapur, Kanara and Dharwar districts which were added to the state of Mysore, and the Abu Road taluka of Banaskantha district, which went to the state of Rajasthan.

By the Bombay Reorganization Act, 1960, which came into force 1 May 1960, 17 districts (predominantly Gujarati-speaking) in the north and west of Bombay State became the new state of Gujarat, and the remainder was renamed Maharashtra.

The state of Maharashtra consists of the following districts of the former Bombay State: Ahmednagar, Akola, Amravati, Aurangabad, Bhandara, Bhir, Buldana, Chanda, Dhulia (West Khandesh), Greater Bombay, Jalgaon (East Khandesh), Kolaba, Kolhapur, Nagpur, Nanded, Nasik, Osmanabad, Parbhani, Pune, Ratnagiri, Sangli, Satara, Sholapur, Thana, Wardha, Yeotmal; certain portions of Thana and Dhulia districts have become part of Gujarat.

AREA AND POPULATION. Maharashtra is in central India and is bounded north and east by Madhya Pradesh, south by Andhra Pradesh, Karnataka and Goa, west by the Indian ocean and north-west by Daman and Gujarat. The state has an area of 307,762 sq. km. The population at the 1981 census was 62,693,898 (an increase of 24·36% since 1971), of whom about 30m. were Marathi-speaking.

Density, 204 per sq. km. The area of Greater Bombay was 603 sq. km. and its population 8,227,000. For other principal cities, *see* p. 614.

CONSTITUTION AND GOVERNMENT. Maharashtra has a bicameral legislature. The Legislative Council has 78 members. The Legislative Assembly has 287 elected members and 1 member nominated by the Governor to represent the Anglo-Indian community. Following the election of March 1985 Congress (I) held 161 seats; Congress (U), 56; JMM, 20; CPI, 16; others, 35.

The Council of Ministers consists of the Chief Minister, 13 other Ministers, 12 Ministers of State and 5 Deputy Ministers.

The capital is Bombay.

Governor: H. Latif.
Chief Minister: Vasant Patil.

BUDGET. Budget estimates, 1980–81, show revenue receipts of Rs 1,921·97 crores, revenue account expenditure Rs 1,857·39 crores. Capital account receipts, Rs 799·03 crores; expenditure, Rs 873·33 crores. The estimates for 1981–82 showed a deficit of Rs 291m.

ENERGY AND NATURAL RESOURCES

Electricity. Installed capacity, 1984, 4,358 mw. (2,351 mw. thermal, 1,897 mw. hydro-electricity and 210 mw. nuclear).

Minerals. Value of production, 1976, Rs 26·7m. The state has coal, chromite, limestone, iron ore, manganese, bauxite.

Agriculture. About 10% of the cropped area is irrigated. In 1984–85 there was severe drought in 21 of the state's 30 districts. The 1984 monsoon-season harvest failed, and the winter-season harvest was poor.

In normal seasons the main food crops are rice, wheat, jowar, bajri and pulses. Main cash crops: cotton, sugar-cane, groundnuts.

Livestock (1972 census): Buffaloes, 3,300,746; other cattle, 14,705,147; sheep, 2,128,036; goats, 5,910,554; horses and ponies, 58,287; poultry, 12,216,567.

Forestry. Forests occupy 17·4% of the state.

INDUSTRY. Industry is concentrated mainly in Bombay, Pune and Thana. The main groups are chemicals and products, textiles, electrical and non-electrical machinery, petroleum and products, and food products. The state industrial development corporation had invested Rs 840m. in 57 industrial estates by 1980.

COMMUNICATIONS

Roads. On 31 March 1975 there were 89,007 km of roads, of which 41,484 km were surfaced. There were 432,901 motor vehicles in 1976. Passenger and freight transport has been nationalized.

Railways. The total length of railway is about 5,162 km. The main junctions and termini are Bombay, Manmad, Akola, Nagpur, Pune and Sholapur.

Aviation. The main airport is Bombay, which has national and international flights. Nagpur airport is on the route from Bombay to Calcutta and there are also airports at Pune and Aurangabad.

Shipping. Maharashtra has a coastline of 720 km. Bombay is the major port, and there are 42 minor ports.

JUSTICE, RELIGION AND EDUCATION

Justice. The High Court has a Chief Justice and 27 judges. There are 8 additional judges. The seat of the High Court is Bombay, but it has a bench at Nagpur.

Religion. At the 1961 census Hindus numbered 32,530,901; Moslems, 3,034,332; Buddhists, 2,789,501; Christians, 560,594; Jains, 485,672; Sikhs, 57,617.

Education. The number of literates, according to the 1981 census, was 29·6m.

The total number of recognized institutions in 1975 was 56,656, with 10,528,258 students. Higher and secondary schools numbered 6,579 with 2,986,636 pupils; primary schools, 48,018, with 7,367,045 pupils; pre-primary schools, 827 with 62,781.

Bombay University, founded in 1857, is mainly an affiliating university. It has 99 constituent colleges and 21 post-graduate departments in Bombay with a total (1975–76) of 137,922 students. Colleges in Goa can affiliate to Bombay University. Nagpur University (1923) is both teaching and affiliating. In addition to the 26 post-graduate departments there were (1975–76) 140 affiliated colleges and constituent colleges with 87,153 students. Pune University, founded in 1948, is teaching and affiliating; in 1975–76 it had 103 affiliated colleges and constituent colleges, 26 post-graduate departments and a total of 88,232 students. The SNDT Women's University had, in 1975–76, 16 constituent colleges and affiliated colleges with a total of 9,911 students. Marathwada University, Aurangabad, was founded in 1958 as a teaching and affiliating body to control colleges in the Marathwada or Marathi-speaking area, previously under Osmania University; in 1975–76 there were 82 affiliated and constituent colleges and 6 post-graduate departments and 71,419 students. Shiwaji University, Kolhapur, was established in 1963 to control affiliated colleges previously under Pune University. In 1975–76 it had 84 affiliated and constituent colleges and 14 post-graduate departments and 65,526 students. There are 4 agricultural universities with 16 affiliated colleges and 6,114 students in 1975–76. There were altogether 682 institutions for higher education in 1975–76, with 474,067 students.

Statistical Information: The Director of Publicity, Sachivalaya, Bombay.
Annual Statistical Abstract (from 1951)
Tindall, G., *City of Gold*, London, 1982

MANIPUR

HISTORY. Formerly a state under the political control of the Government of India, Manipur, on 15 Aug. 1947, entered into interim arrangements with the Indian Union and the political agency was abolished. The administration was taken over by the Government of India on 15 Oct. 1949 under a merger agreement, and it is centrally administered by the Government of India through a Chief Commissioner. In 1950–51 an Advisory form of Government was introduced. In 1957 this was replaced by a Territorial Council of 30 elected and 2 nominated members. Later in 1963 a Legislative Assembly of 30 elected and 3 nominated members was established under the Government of Union Territories Act 1963. Because of the unstable party position in the Assembly, it had to be dissolved on 16 Oct. 1969 and President's Rule introduced. The status of the administrator was raised from Chief Commissioner to Lieut.-Governor with effect from 19 Dec. 1969. On the 21 Jan. 1972 Manipur became a state and the status of the administrator was changed from Lieut.-Governor to Governor.

AREA AND POPULATION. The state is in north-east India and is bounded north by Nagaland, east by Burma, south by Burma and Mizoram, and west by Assam. Manipur has an area of 22,356 sq. km and a population (1981) of 1,433,691. Density, 64 per sq. km. Growth rate, 1971–81, 33·65%. The valley, which is about 1,813 sq. km, is 2,600 ft above sea-level. The hills rise in places to nearly 10,000 ft, but are mostly about 5,000–6,000 ft. The average annual rainfall is 65 in. The hill areas are inhabited by various hill tribes who constitute about one-third of the total population of the state. There are about 40 tribes and sub-tribes falling into two main groups of Nagas and Kukis. Manipuri and English are the official languages. A large number of dialects are spoken, while Hindi is gradually becoming prevalent.

CONSTITUTION AND GOVERNMENT. With the attainment of statehood, Manipur has a Legislative Assembly of 60 members, of which 19 are from reserved tribal constituencies. There are 6 districts. Capital, Imphal (population, 1981, 155,639). Presidential rule was imposed in Feb. 1981.

Governor: Gen. K. V. Krishna Rao.

BUDGET. Revised estimates for 1977–78 show revenue of Rs 4,247·82 lakhs and expenditure on revenue account of Rs 4,774·24 lakhs.

ENERGY AND NATURAL RESOURCES

Electricity. Installed capacity (1983) is 22 mw. from diesel generators. This has been augmented since 1981 by the North Eastern Regional Grid. In 1983 there were 488 villages with electricity.

Water. The main power, irrigation and flood-control schemes are the Loktak Lift Irrigation scheme (irrigation potential, 40,000 hectares of which (1983) 19,000 have been achieved); the Singda scheme (potential 4,000 hectares, and improved water supply for Imphal); the Thoubal scheme (potential 34,000 hectares, 7·5 mw. of electricity and 10 MGD of water supply), and four other large projects.

Agriculture. Rice is the principal crop; with wheat, maize and pulses. Total foodgrains, 1982–83, 358,000 tonnes.

Agricultural work force, about 348,000. Only 210,000 hectares are cultivable, of which 186,000 are under paddy. Fruit and vegetables are important in the valley, including pineapple, oranges, bananas, mangoes, pears, peaches and plums. Soil erosion, produced by shifting cultivation, is being halted by terracing.

Forests. Forests occupy about 15,154 sq km. The main products are teak, jurjan, pine; there are also large areas of bamboo and cane, especially in the Jiri and Barak river drainage areas, yielding about 300,000 tonnes annually. Total revenue from forests, 1981–82, Rs 3·9m.

Fisheries. Landings in 1981–82, 3,450 tonnes.

INDUSTRY. Handloom weaving is a popular industry. Larger-scale industries include sugar, cement, starch and glucose. Sericulture produces about 45 tonnes of raw silk annually. Estimated non-agricultural work force, 240,000.

COMMUNICATIONS. A national highway from Kazirangar (Assam) runs through Imphal to the Burmese frontier. There are no railways, but the highway runs through Dimapur which has a rail head, 215 km. from Imphal. There is an airport at Imphal with regular scheduled services to Gauhati and Calcutta.

EDUCATION AND HEALTH

Education. The 1981 census gave the number of literates as 600,000. In 1982–83 there were 2,821 primary schools, 459 middle schools, 301 high and higher schools and 23 colleges, as well as Manipur University.

Health. In 1977–78 there were 33 hospitals (including primary health centres) and 125 dispensaries (including primary health centres).

MEGHALAYA

HISTORY. The state was created under the Assam Reorganization (Meghalaya) Act 1969 and inaugurated on 2 April 1970. Its status was that of a state within the State of Assam until 21 Jan. 1972 when it became a fully independent state of the Union. It consists of the former Garo Hills district and United Khasi and Jaintia Hills district of Assam.

AREA AND POPULATION. Meghalaya is bounded north and east by Assam, south and west by Bangladesh. In 1981 (census figure) the area was 22,489 sq. km and the population 1,327,824. Density 59 per sq. km. Growth rate, 1971–81, 31·25%. The people are mainly of the Khasi, Jaintia and Garo tribes.

CONSTITUTION AND GOVERNMENT. Meghalaya has a unicameral legislature. The Legislative Assembly has 60 seats. Party position in summer 1984: Meghalaya Democratic Front, 37 (including 31 Congress I); opposition, 13.

There are 2 districts. The capital is Shillong.

Governor: B. N. Singh.
Chief Minister: W. A. Sangma.

BUDGET. Budget estimates for 1981–82 showed a deficit of Rs 6·6m. Annual Plan expenditure, 1984–85, Rs 65 crores.

ENERGY AND NATURAL RESOURCES

Electricity. Total installed capacity (1977) was 65·2 mw. 388 villages had electricity.

Minerals. The United Khasi and Jaintia Hills district produces coal, sillimanite (95% of India's total output), limestone, white clay and corundum. The state also has deposits of coal (estimated reserves 1,200m. tonnes), limestone (2,100m.), fire clay (100,000) and sandstone which are virtually untapped because of transport difficulties. Value of production, 1976, Rs 3·26m.

Agriculture. About 80% of the people depend on agriculture, and 27% of the cultivable area is irrigated. Principal crops are potatoes, fresh fruit and cotton. Production 1978 (in 1,000 tonnes): Foodgrains, 130; potatoes, 71; tapioca, 5; jute, 50,000 bales (of 180 kg). Annual production (in 1,000 tonnes, estimated) of pineapples, 70; oranges, 80; bananas, 35.

Forest products are the state's chief resources.

INDUSTRY. Apart from agriculture the main source of employment is the extraction and processing of minerals; there are also important timber processing mills.

COMMUNICATIONS. A national highway from Gauhati (Assam) runs through Dispur and Shillong. The state has no railways. There is no airport but Gauhati airport is on the northern boundary.

JUSTICE. There is a High Court at Shillong which is common to Assam, Meghalaya, Nagaland, Manipur, Tripura and the Union Territories of Mizoram and Arunachal Pradesh.

NAGALAND

HISTORY. The territory was constituted by the Union Government in Sept. 1962. It comprises the former Naga Hills district of Assam and the former Tuensang Frontier division of the North-East Frontier Agency; these had been made a Centrally Administered Area in 1957, administered by the President through the Governor of Assam. In Jan. 1961 the area was renamed and given the status of a state of the Indian Union, which was officially inaugurated on 1 Dec. 1963.

For some years a section of the Naga leaders sought independence. Military operations from 1960 and the prospect of self-government within the Indian Union led to a general reconciliation, but rebel activity continued. A 2-month amnesty in mid 1963 had little effect. A 'ceasefire' in Sept. 1964 was followed by talks between a Government of India delegation and rebel leaders. The peace period was extended and the 'Revolutionary Government of Nagaland' (a breakaway group from the Naga Federal Government) was dissolved in 1973. Further talks with the Naga underground movement resulted in the Shillong Peace Agreement of Nov. 1975.

AREA AND POPULATION. The state is in the extreme north-east and is bounded west and north by Assam, east by Burma and south by Manipur. Nagaland has an area of 16,527 sq. km and a population (1981) census of 773,281. Density 47 per sq. km. Growth rate, 1971–81, 49·73%. Towns include Kohima, Mokokchung, Tuensang and Dimapur. The chief tribes in numerical order are: Angami, Ao, Sema, Konyak, Chakhesang, Lotha, Phom, Khiamngan, Chang, Yimchunger, Zeliang-Kuki, Rengma and Sangtam.

CONSTITUTION AND GOVERNMENT. An Interim Body (Legislative Assembly) of 42 members elected by the Naga people and an Executive Council (Council of Ministers) of 5 members were formed in 1961, and continued until the State Assembly was elected in Jan. 1964. The initial strength of this Assembly was 46, with 8 cabinet ministers. Since 1974 there have been 60 members. The Governor has extraordinary powers, which include special responsibility for law and order. On 17 Nov. 1982 a Congress (I) government took office.

There are 10 cabinet ministers and 10 ministers of state.

The state has 7 districts (Kohima, Mon, Zunheboto, Wokha, Phek, Mokokchung and Tuensang). The capital is Kohima.

Governor: Gen. K. V. Krishna Rao.
Chief Minister: S. C. Jamir.

BUDGET. The budget (estimate) for 1984–85 is Rs 187·18 crores. Plan outlay, Rs 56 crores; non-plan, Rs 131·18 crores.

ENERGY AND NATURAL RESOURCES

Electricity. Installed capacity (1984) 5·12 mw; 580 towns and villages (out of 814) had electricity in 1984.

Agriculture. More than 80% of the people derive their livelihood from agriculture. The Angamis, in Kohima district, practise a fixed agriculture in the shape of terraced slopes, and wet paddy cultivation in the lowlands. In the other two districts a traditional form of shifting cultivation (*jhumming*) still predominates, but some farmers have begun tea and coffee plantations and horticulture. About 66,120 hectares were under terrace cultivation and 44,810 under *jhumming* in 1982. Production of rice (1981) was 135,000 tonnes.

Forests covered 288,252 hectares in 1981.

INDUSTRY. There is a forest products factory at Tijit; a paper-mill (100 tonnes daily capacity) at Tuli, a distillery unit and a sugar-mill (1,200 tonnes daily capacity) at Dimapur. There are also over 1,000 small units.

COMMUNICATIONS. There is a national highway from Kaziranga (Assam) to Kohima and on to Manipur. There are state highways connecting Kohima with the district headquarters. There were 16,972 motor vehicles in 1983. Dimapur has a rail-head and a daily air service to Calcutta.

RELIGION AND EDUCATION

Religion. Christianity is the main religion; there are also Hindus, Moslems, and followers of indigenous faiths.

Education. The 1981 census records 300,000 literates, or 41·9%: 49·16% of men and 33·72% of women. In 1981 there were 3 government and 10 private colleges, 59 government and 50 private high schools, 173 government and 147 private middle schools and 1,224 primary schools, 1 polytechnic, 1 agricultural college, 2 law colleges. The North Eastern Hill University opened in 1978.

Aram, M., *Peace in Nagaland,* New Delhi, 1974

ORISSA

HISTORY. Orissa, ceded to the Mahrattas by Alivardi Khan in 1751, was conquered by the British in 1803. In 1803 a board of 2 commissioners was appointed to administer the province, but in 1805 it was designated the district of Cuttack and was placed in charge of a collector, judge and magistrate. In 1829 it was split up into 3 regulation districts of Cuttack, Balasore and Puri, and the non-regulation tributary states which were administered by their own chiefs under the ægis of the British Government. Angul, one of these tributary states, was annexed in 1847, and with the Khondmals, ceded in 1835 by the tributary chief of the Boudh state, constituted a separate non-regulation district. Sambalpur was transferred from the Central Provinces to Orissa in 1905. These districts formed an outlying tract of the Bengal Presidency till 1912, when they were transferred to Bihar, constituting one of its divisions under a commissioner. Orissa was constituted a separate province on 1 April 1936, some portions of the Central Provinces and Madras being transferred to the old Orissa division.

The rulers of 25 Orissa states surrendered all jurisdiction and authority to the Government of India on 1 Jan. 1948, on which date the Provincial Government took over the administration. The administration of 2 states, viz., Saraikella and Kharswan, was transferred to the Government of Bihar in May 1948. By an agreement with the Dominion Government, Mayurbhanj State was finally merged with the province on 1 Jan. 1949. By the States Merger (Governors' Provinces) Order, 1949, the states were completely merged with the state of Orissa on 19 Aug. 1949.

EVENTS. Serious flooding in Aug. 1982 caused the deaths of about 1,000 people.

AREA AND POPULATION. Orissa is in eastern India and is bounded north by Bihar, north-east by West Bengal, east by the Bay of Bengal, south by Andhra Pradesh and west by Madhya Pradesh. The area of the state is 155,707 sq. km, and its population (1981 census), 26,370,271, density 169 per sq. km. Growth rate, 1971–81, 20·17%. The second-largest city next to Cuttack (327,412) is Rourkela (322,610). The principal language is Oriya, which will be the official language from 1 April 1985.

CONSTITUTION AND GOVERNMENT. The Legislative Assembly has 147 members. After the election in March 1985 a Congress government was returned.

The state consists of 13 districts.

The capital is Bhubaneswar (18 miles south of Cuttack).

Governor: B. N. Pandey.
Chief Minister: J. B. Patnaik.

BUDGET. Budget estimates, 1980–81 showed total revenue of Rs 1,257·3 crores and expenditure of Rs 1,235·6 crores (capital and revenue accounts).

ENERGY AND NATURAL RESOURCES

Electricity. The Hirakud Dam Project on the river Mahanadi (started 1949) irrigates 628,000 acres and has a scheduled capacity of 270,000 kw. The dam (the largest earth dam in the world) was completed in 1957. Hydro-electric power totalling 85,000 kw. is now serving a large part of the state. The installed capacity of the Machkund hydro-electric project (financed jointly with Andhra Pradesh) is 114,750 kw. Total installed capacity, 1979, 923 mw.; there were 20,953 electrified villages in 1981.

Minerals. Orissa is India's leading producer of chromite (95% of national output), dolomite (50%), manganese ore (25%), graphite (80%), iron ore (16%), fire-clay (34%), limestone (20%), and quartz-quartzite (18%). Production in 1980 (1,000 tonnes): iron ore, 7,019; manganese ore, 568; chromite, 261; coal, 3,042; limestone, 2,591; dolomite, 761; fire-clay, 100; china clay, 31; graphite, 32; quartz and quartzite, 53; lead ore, 40. About 56,000 workers are employed in the mines. Value of mineral production annually is about Rs 900m.

Agriculture. The cultivation of rice is the principal occupation of nearly 80% of the population. Production amounted to 4·44m. tonnes in 1978–79; only a very small amount of other cereals is grown. Production of foodgrains (1978–79) totalled 5·7m. tonnes from 6·7m. hectares. Jute (439,000 tonnes), wheat (110,000 tonnes), oilseeds (426,950 tonnes) and sugar-cane (281,000 tonnes) are also grown. Turmeric is cultivated in the uplands of the districts of Ganjam, Phulbani and Koraput, and is exported.

Livestock (1977 census): Buffaloes, 1,358,451; other cattle, 12·1m.; sheep, 1·5m.; goats, 3·4m.; horses and ponies, 3,675.

Forests. Forests occupy about 43% of the area of the state, the most important species being sal, teak, kendu, sandal, sisu, bija, kuruma, kongada and bamboo.

Fisheries. There were, in 1981, 484 fishery co-operative societies.

INDUSTRY. Fifty-five large industries have been set up (1978–79), mostly based on minerals, including the steel plant of Hindustan Steel Ltd at Rourkela, a pig-iron plant at Barbil, a ferrochrome plant, 2 ferromanganese plants at Joda and Rayagada, 1 ferrosilicon plant at Theruvelli and an aluminium smelter plant at Hirakud, 4 refractory plants and 2 cement plants. There are 3 large paper mills at Rayagada, Chowdwar and Brajrajnagar, two fertilizer plants, a caustic soda plant, a salt manufacturing unit and an industrial explosives plant. An aluminium-alumina plant at Damanjodi was begun in 1981.

Other industries of importance are sugar, glass, aluminium, heavy machine tools, a re-rolling mill and textile mills.

There are cottage and small-scale industries in the state, e.g., handloom weaving and the manufacture of baskets, wooden articles, hats and nets; silver filigree work and hand-woven fabrics are specially well known.

TOURISM. Tourist traffic is concentrated mainly on the 'Golden Triangle', Konark, Puri and Bhubaneswar, and its temples. Tourists also visit Gopalpur, the Similipal Forest and Chilka Lake.

COMMUNICATIONS

Roads. On 31 March 1980 length of roads was: State highway, 2,821 km; national highway, 1,631 km; major district roads, 4,974 km; other district roads, 2,748 km; village roads, about 5,796 km. There were 94,156 motor vehicles in 1979. A 144-km expressway, part national highway, connects the Daitari mining area with Paradip Port.

Railways. The total length of railway in 1979 was 1,948 km, of which 1,310 km was single line.

Aviation. There is an airport at Bhubaneswar with regular scheduled services to New Delhi, Calcutta, Vizag and Hyderabad.

Shipping. Paradip was declared a 'major' port in 1966 and has been developed to handle 1m. tons of traffic. Other minor ports at Chandbali and Gopalpur.

JUSTICE, RELIGION AND EDUCATION

Justice. The High Court of Judicature at Cuttack has a Chief Justice and 6 puisne judges.

Religion. There were in 1971: Hindus (including scheduled castes and scheduled tribes), 21,121,056; Christians, 378,888; Moslems, 326,507; Sikhs, 10,204; Buddhists, 8,462; Jains, 6,521.

Education. The percentage of literates in the population is 34·12% (males, 46·9%, females, 21·11%).

In 1981–82 there were 32,797 primary, 7,413 middle English and 2,466 high schools.

Utkal University was established in 1943 at Cuttack and moved to Bhubaneswar in 1962; it is both teaching and affiliating. It has 2 university colleges (law) and 113 affiliated colleges. Berhampur University has 20 affiliated colleges and Orissa University of Agriculture and Technology 4 constituent colleges. Sambalpur University has 42 affiliated colleges. Sri Jagannath Sanskrit Viswavidyalaya University was established in 1981 for oriental studies.

PUNJAB (INDIA)

HISTORY. The Punjab was constituted an autonomous province of India in 1937. In 1947, the province was partitioned between India and Pakistan into East and West Punjab respectively, under the Indian Independence Act, 1947, the boundaries being determined under the Radcliffe Award. The name of East Punjab was changed to Punjab (India) under the Constitution of India. On 1 Nov. 1956 the erstwhile states of Punjab and Patiala and East Punjab States Union (PEPSU) were integrated to form the state of Punjab. On 1 Nov. 1966, under the Punjab Reorganization Act, 1966, the state was reconstituted as a Punjabi-speaking state comprising the districts of Gurdaspur (excluding Dalhousie), Amritsar, Kapurthala, Jullundur, Ferozepore, Bhatinda, Patiala and Ludhiana; parts of Sangrur, Hoshiarpur and Ambala districts; and part of Kharar tehsil. The remaining area comprising an area of 18,000 sq. miles and an estimated (1967) population of 8·5m. was shared between the new state of Haryana and the Union Territory of Himachal Pradesh. The existing capital of Chandigarh was made the joint capital of Punjab and Haryana.

EVENTS. The Akali Dal party has continued its campaign for Sikh autonomy; violent incidents precipitated the imposition of President's rule. Armed separatists were driven out of their headquarters in the Golden Temple at Amritsar by government troops, on 6 June 1984. In retaliation for this, two Sikhs murdered the Prime Minister, Indira Gandhi, on 31 Oct. 1984.

AREA AND POPULATION. The Punjab is in north India and is bounded at its northernmost point by Kashmir, north-east by Himachal Pradesh, south-east by Haryana, south by Rajasthan, west and north-west by Pakistan. The area of the state is 50,376 sq. km, with census (1981) population of 16,669,755. Density 331 per sq. km. Growth rate, 1971–81, 23·01%. The largest cities, *see* p. 614. The official language is Punjabi.

CONSTITUTION AND GOVERNMENT. Punjab (India) has a unicameral legislature of 117 members. The Legislative Council was abolished in Jan. 1970. The Legislative Assembly was composed as follows after the election of May 1980: Congress (I), 64; Akali Dal, 36; others, 17. President's rule was imposed in Oct. 1983, and later extended.

There are 12 districts. The capital is Chandigarh (*see* p. 676). There are 104 municipalities, 118 community development blocks and 9,331 elected village *panchayats*.

Governor: A. Singh.

BUDGET. Budget estimates, 1984–85, showed a surplus of Rs 135·52 crores on revenue account and a deficit of Rs 240·61 crores on capital account.

ENERGY AND NATURAL RESOURCES

Electricity. Installed capacity, 1979, was 1,541 mw; all villages had electricity.

Agriculture. About 75% of the population depends on agriculture. Agricultural prosperity is mainly due to irrigation. The irrigated area rose from 2·21m. hectares in 1950-51 to 5·5m. hectares in 1978–79: total production of foodgrains rose from 1·99m. tonnes to 11·9m. tonnes in 1980–81. Production in 1,000 tonnes (area in 1,000 hectares) in 1980–81: Wheat, 7,677 (2,812); maize, 605 (378); rice, 3,223 (1,178); oil-seeds, 167 (220); sugar-cane (gur), 397 (72); cotton, 605,000 bales (of 180 kg) from 1,178 hectares.

Livestock (1972 census): Buffaloes, 3,839,200; other cattle, 3·41m.; sheep and goats, 1,205,400; horses and ponies, 54,700; poultry, 3m.

Forestry. In 1981 there were 260,235 hectares of forest land, of which 130,008 hectares belonged to the Forest Department.

INDUSTRY. In Jan. 1981 the number of registered factories in the Punjab (India) was 7,397; 7,053 operational factories employed about 210,735 people. The chief manufactures are textiles (especially woollen hosiery), sewing machines, sports goods, sugar, starch, fertilizers, bicycles, scientific instruments, electrical goods, machine tools and pine oil. In 1981 there were 61,667 important small manufacturing units.

COMMUNICATIONS

Roads. The total length of metalled roads on 31 March 1980 was 33,288 km. State transport services cover 671,000 route km daily with a fleet of 2,776 buses carrying a daily average of 1m passengers. Coverage by private operators is estimated as 40%. In 1978 there were 276,748 motor vehicles.

Railways. The Punjab possesses an extensive system of railway communications, served by the Northern Railway. Total length, (1980) 3,511·4 km.

Aviation. There is an airport at Amritsar, and Chandigarh airport is on the north-eastern boundary; both have regular scheduled services to Delhi.

JUSTICE, RELIGION, EDUCATION AND WELFARE

Justice. The Punjab and Haryana High Court exercises jurisdiction over the states of Punjab and Haryana and the territory of Chandigarh. It is located in Chandigarh. It consists (1981) of a Chief Justice and 19 puisne judges.

Religion. At the 1971 census Hindus numbered 5,037,235; Sikhs, 8,159,172; Moslems, 114,447; Christians, 162,202; Jains, 21,383; Buddhists, 1,374.

Education. Compulsory education was introduced in April 1961; at the same time free education was introduced up to 8th class for boys and 9th class for girls as well as fee concessions. The aim is education for all children of 6-11.

In 1980 there were 17,784 primary schools, 1,432 middle schools and 2,313 higher secondary schools.

Punjab University was established in 1947 at Chandigarh as an examining, teaching and affiliating body. It is shared with Haryana and Himachal Pradesh. In 1962 Punjabi University was established at Patiala and an agricultural university at Ludhiana. Guru Nanak University has been established at Amritsar to mark the 500th anniversary celebrations for Guru Nanak Dev, first Guru of the Sikhs. Altogether there are 202 affiliated colleges, 160 for arts and science, 18 for teacher training, 8 medical, 2 dental, 2 engineering and 12 for other studies.

Health. Punjab claims the longest life expectancy (57·9 years for women, 58·5 for men) and lowest death rate (8·9 per 1,000). There were (1980) 254 hospitals, 467 Ayurvedic and Unani hospitals and dispensaries, 129 primary health centres and 1,485 dispensaries.

Singh, Khushwant, *A History of the Sikhs.* 2 vols. Princeton and OUP, 1964–67

RAJASTHAN

HISTORY. As a result of the Implementation of the States Reorganization Act, 1956, the erstwhile state of Ajmer, Abu Taluka of Bombay State and the Sunel

Tappa enclave of the former state of Madhya Bharat were transferred to the state of Rajasthan on 1 Nov. 1956, whereas the Sironj subdivision of Rajasthan was transferred to the state of Madhya Pradesh.

AREA AND POPULATION. Rajasthan is in north-west India and is bounded north by Punjab, north-east by Haryana and Uttar Pradesh, east by Madhya Pradesh, south by Gujarat and west by Pakistan. The area of the state is 342,239 sq. km and its population (census 1981, revised), 34,261,862, density 100 per sq. km. Growth rate, 1971–81, 32·36%. The chief cities, *see* p. 614.

CONSTITUTION AND GOVERNMENT. There is a unicameral legislature, the Legislative Assembly, having 200 members. After the election in March 1985 a Congress government was returned.

The capital is Jaipur. There are 27 districts.

Governor: Air Chief-Marshal O. P. Mehra.
Chief Minister: H. D. Joshi.

BUDGET. Revised estimates for 1983–84 show total revenue receipts of Rs 1,148·82 crores, and expenditure of Rs 1,111·61 crores. Receipts included: share in Central taxes, Rs 242·01 crores; state excise, Rs 59·42 crores, sales tax, Rs 248 crores; vehicles taxes, Rs 53 crores; non-tax revenue, Rs 476·77 crores. Expenditure included: Education, Rs 262·46 crores; water and power, Rs 121·25 crores; medical and public health, Rs 88·85 crores; agriculture, Rs 150·93 crores. Gross Plan expenditure, Rs 450·68 crores (of which Rs 200·98 crores were for irrigation and power).

ENERGY AND NATURAL RESOURCES

Electricity. Installed capacity in March. 1984, 1,713 mw.; 18,900 villages and 255,000 wells had electric power.

Water. In 1984 the Bhakra Canal irrigated 300,000 hectares, the Chambal Canal, 200,000 and the Rajasthan Canal, 450,000. The Rajasthan is the main canal system, of which (1984) 189 km. of main canal and 2,950 km of distributors had been built. Cost, at 1 March 1984, Rs 419 crores.

Minerals. The state is rich in minerals. In 1983, 959,000m. tonnes of gypsum and 585,300 tonnes of rock phosphate were produced. Other minerals include silver, asbestos, felspar, copper, limestone and salt. Total value of mineral production in 1983 was about Rs 180 crores. Lead-zinc reserves have been found near Rampura-Agucha, estimated at 61m. tonnes.

Agriculture. The state has suffered drought for 5 years. The cultivable area is (1984) about 26·6m. hectares, of which 3·9m. is irrigated. Production of principal crops (in 1,000 tonnes), 1983–84: pulses, 2,272; sugar-cane (gur), 1,715; total oilseeds, 954; cotton, 596,000 bales (of 180 kg). Total foodgrains, 8,540.

Livestock (1983): Buffaloes, 6,034,743; other cattle, 13,466,474; sheep, 15,389,100; goats, 15,397,993; horses and ponies, 45,381; camels, 7,528,287.

INDUSTRY. In 1984 there were 7,377 registered factories and 10,000 small industrial units. There were 148 industrial estates. Total capital investment (1983), Rs 13,000m., of which small units, Rs 3,250m. Chief manufactures are textiles, cement, glass, sugar, sodium, oxygen and acetylene units, pesticides, insecticides, dyes, caustic soda, calcium, carbide, nylon tyre cords and refined copper.

COMMUNICATIONS

Roads. In 1984 there were 48,422 km of roads including 12,091 km of unsurfaced roads in Rajasthan; there were 2,521 km of national highway. Motor vehicles numbered 429,012 in 1983.

Railways. Jodhpur, Marwar, Udaipur, Ajmer, Jaipur, Khota, Bikaner and Sawai Madhopur are important junctions of the north-western network.

Aviation. There are airports at Jaipur, Jodhpur, Khota and Udaipur with regular scheduled services by Indian Airlines.

JUSTICE, RELIGION, EDUCATION AND WELFARE

Justice. The seat of the High Court is at Jodhpur. There is a Chief Justice and 11 puisne judges. There is also a bench of 5 judges at Jaipur.

Religion. At the 1971 census Hindus numbered 23,093,895; Moslems, 1,778,275; Jains, 513,548; Sikhs, 341,182; Christians, 30,202.

Education. The proportion of literates to the total population was 24·39% at the 1981 census.

In 1984 there were 24,360 primary schools, 6,511 middle schools, 1,796 secondary and 723 higher secondary schools. Elementary education is free but not compulsory.

In 1983–84 there were 159 colleges. Enrolment at these was 168,345. Rajasthan University, established at Jaipur in 1947, is teaching and affiliating; Jodhpur University and Udaipur University were founded in 1962. There are also 4 agricultural colleges, 1 veterinary and animal science college, 6 engineering colleges, 3 Ayurvedic colleges and 10 polytechnics.

Health. In 1983–84 there were 1,285 hospitals and dispensaries, 248 primary health centres, 59 Unani, 63 homoepathic and 2 naturopathy hospitals. There were 111 maternity centres, and 2,795 Ayurvedic hospitals and dispensaries. There were 5 medical colleges and a nursing college.

SIKKIM

HISTORY. Sikkim became the twenty-second state of the Indian Union in May 1975. It is inhabited chiefly by the Lepchas, who are a tribe indigenous to Sikkim with their own dress and language, the Bhutias, who originally came from Tibet, and the Nepalis, who entered from Nepál in large numbers in the late 19th and early 20th century. The main languages spoken are Bhutia, Lepcha and Nepali. Being a small country Sikkim had frequently been involved in struggles over her territory, and as a result her boundaries have been very much reduced over the centuries. In particular the Darjeeling district was acquired from Sikkim by the British East India Company in 1839. The Namgyal dynasty had been ruling Sikkim since the 14th century; the first consecrated ruler was Phuntsog Namgya I who was consecrated in 1642 and given the title of 'Chogyal', meaning 'King ruling in accordance with religious laws', derived from Cho–religion and Gyalpo–king. The last Chogyal was deposed in 1975 and died in America in 1982.

Sikkim is a land of wide variation in altitude, climate and vegetation, and is known for the great number and variety of birds, butterflies, wild flowers and orchids to be found in the different regions. It is a fertile land and to the Sikkimese is known as Denjong, The Valley of Rice.

AREA AND POPULATION. Sikkim is in the Eastern Himalayas and is bounded north by Tibet, east by Tibet and Bhután, south by West Bengal and west by Nepál. Area, 7,298 sq. km. Census population (1981), 314,999, of whom 36,768 lived in the capital, Gangtok. Density 43 per sq km. Growth rate, 1971–81, 50·01%.

CONSTITUTION AND GOVERNMENT. Sikkim was joined to the British Empire by a treaty in 1886 until 1947, but that relationship ceased when Britain withdrew from India in 1947. Thereafter there was a standstill agreement between India and Sikkim until a treaty was signed on 5 Dec. 1950 between India and Sikkim by which Sikkim became a protectorate of India and India undertook to be responsible for Sikkim's defence, external relations and strategic communications. The Chogyal had governed Sikkim with the help of the Sikkim Council, consisting of 18 elected members and 6 members nominated by the Chogyal. Sikkim parties represented were: National Party, Sikkim National Congress and, later, Sikkim Janta Congress.

Political reforms were demanded by the National Congress and the Janta Congress in March-April 1973 and Indian police took over control of law and order at the request of the Chogyal. On 13 April it was announced that the Chogyal had agreed to meet most of the political demands. Elections were held in April 1974 to a popularly-elected assembly. By the Government of Sikkim Act, June 1974, the Chogyal became a constitutional monarch with power of assent to the Assembly's legislation. By the Constitution (Thirty-Sixth Amendment) Act 1974 Sikkim became a state associated with the Indian Union. The office of Chogyal was abolished in April 1975. By the Constitution (Thirty-Eighth Amendment) Act 1975 Sikkim became the twenty-second state of the Indian Union. The Assembly has 32 members with a cabinet of 10 ministers including the Chief Minister. After the election of March 1985 a Sangram Parishad government was returned.

Governor: K. P. Rao.
Chief Minister: N. Bahadur Bhandari.

The official language of the Government is English. Lepcha, Bhutia, Nepali and Limboo have also been declared official languages.

Sikkim is divided into 4 districts for administration purposes, Gangtok, Mangan, Namchi and Gyalshing being the headquarters for the Eastern, Northern, Southern and Western districts respectively. Each district is administered by a District Collector. Within this framework are the Panchayats or Village Councils.

ECONOMY

Planning. The sixth Five-Year Plan covered 1980–85.

Budget. The annual budget for 1984–85 is Rs 35·08 crores.

ENERGY AND NATURAL RESOURCES

Electricity. There are 4 operational hydro-electric power stations; the Lagyap project is also being implemented by the Government of India as aid to meet the growing demand for electrical power for new industries. The first of its two 6 mv generators was commissioned 1 Sept. 1979.

Agriculture. The economy is mainly agricultural; main food crops are rice, maize, millet, wheat and barley; cash crops are cardamom (a spice), mandarin oranges, apples, potatoes, and buckwheat. Foodgrain production, 1983, 84,000 tonnes. A tea plantation has recently been started. Forests occupy about 1,000 sq. km. of the land area (excluding hill pastures) and the potential for a timber and wood-pulp industry is being explored. Some medicinal herbs are exported.

INDUSTRY AND TRADE

Industry. There is a state Industrial Development Investment Corporation and an Industrial Training Institute offering 7 trades. There are two cigarette factories (at Gangtok and Rangpo), two distilleries and a tannery at Rangpo and a fruit preserving factory at Singtam. Copper, zinc and lead are mined by the Sikkim Mining Corporation. A recent survey by the Geological Survey of India and the Indian Bureau of Mines has confirmed further deposits of copper, zinc, silver and gold in Dikchu, North Sikkim. There is a jewel-bearing factory for the production of industrial jewels. A watch factory has been set up in collaboration with Hindustan Machine Tools (India). A number of small manufacturing units for leather, wire nails, storage cells batteries, candles, safety matches and carpets, are already producing in the private sector. Local crafts include carpet weaving, making handmade paper, wood carving and silverwork. To encourage trading in indigenous products, particularly agricultural produce, the State Trading Corporation of Sikkim has been established.

Tourism. There is great potential for the tourist industry; a 78-bed lodge at Gangtok and a 50-bed tourist lodge in West Sikkim have been opened. Tourism has been stimulated by the opening of new roads from Pemayangtse to Yuksam in West Sikkim and from Yuksam to the Dzongri Glacier.

COMMUNICATIONS

Roads. There are 1,201 km. of metalled roads, all on mountainous terrain, and 18 major bridges under the Public Works Department. Public transport and road haulage is nationalized.

Railways. The nearest railhead is at Siliguri (115 km from Gangtok).

Aviation. The nearest airport is at Bagdogra (128 km from Gangtok).

Post and Broadcasting. There are 1,118 telephones (1983) and 32 wireless stations. A radio broadcasting station, Akashvani Gangtok, was built in 1982, and a permanent station was under construction in 1983.

RELIGION, EDUCATION AND WELFARE

Religion. The state religion is Mahayana Buddhism, but a large proportion of the population is Hindu. There are some Christians, Moslems and members of other religions.

Education. At the 1981 census there were 100,000 literates. Sikkim has (1983) 100 pre-primary schools, 438 primary schools, 99 junior high schools and high schools, and 11 higher secondary schools. Education is free up to class XII; text books are free up to class V. There are 500 adult education centres. There is also a training institute for primary teachers, a law college and a degree college. Estimated spending on education, 1980–81, Rs 29·78m.

Health. There are (1983) 4 district hospitals at Singtam, Gyalshing, Namchi and Mangan, and one central referral hospital at Gangtok, besides 16 primary health centres, 62 sub-centres and 8 dispensaries, a maternity ward, chest clinic and 2 blocks for tuberculosis patients. There is a blood bank at Gangtok. There are 81 doctors. Medical and hospital treatment is free; there is a health centre for every 20,000 of the population. Small-pox and Kala-azar have been completely eliminated and many schemes for the provision of safe drinking water to villages and bazaars have been implemented.

Coelho, V. H., *Sikkim and Bhutan.* New Delhi, 1970
Mele, F., *Sikkim.* Paris, 1974

TAMIL NADU

HISTORY. The first trading establishment made by the British in the Madras State was at Peddapali (now Nizampatnam) in 1611 and then at Masulipatnam. In 1639 the English were permitted to make a settlement at the place which is now Madras, and Fort St George was founded. By 1801 the whole of the country from the Northern Circars to Cape Comorin (with the exception of certain French and Danish settlements) had been brought under British rule.

Under the provisions of the States Reorganization Act, 1956, the Malabar district (excluding the islands of Laccadive and Minicoy) and the Kasaragod district taluk of South Kanara were transferred to the new state of Kerala; the South Kanara district (excluding Kasaragod taluk and the Amindivi Islands) and the Kollegal taluk of the Coimbatore district were transferred to the new state of Mysore; and the Laccadive, Amindivi and Minicoy Islands were constituted a separate Territory. Four taluks of the Trivandrum district and the Shencottah taluk of Quilon district were transferred from Travancore-Cochin to the new Madras State. On 1 April 1960, 405 sq. miles from the Chittoor district of Andhra Pradesh were transferred to Madras in exchange for 326 sq. miles from the Chingleput and Salem districts. In Aug. 1968 the state was renamed Tamil Nadu.

AREA AND POPULATION. Tamil Nadu is in south India and is bounded north by Karnataka and Andhra Pradesh, east and south by the Indian ocean and west by Kerala. Area, 130,357 sq. km. Population (1981 census), 48,297,456, density of 371 per sq. km. Growth rate, 1971–81, 17·23%. Tamil is the principal language and has been adopted as the state language with effect from 14 Jan. 1958. The principal towns, *see* p. 614.

CONSTITUTION AND GOVERNMENT. The Governor is aided by a Council of 16 ministers. There is a bicameral legislature; the Legislative Council has 63 members and the Legislative Assembly has 234 members. The Legislative Assembly was composed as follows after the election of May 1980: All-India Anna DMK, 129; DMK, 38; Congress (I), 30; CPM, 11; CPI, 10; others, 16.

There are 18 districts. The capital is Madras.

Governor: S. L. Khurana.
Chief Minister: M. G. Ramachandran.

BUDGET. Budget estimates for 1981-82, revenue receipts, Rs 1,128·3 crores, revenue account expenditure, Rs 1,137·8 crores. Capital outlay, Rs 434·4 crores; capital account receipts, Rs 289·9.

ENERGY AND NATURAL RESOURCES

Electricity. Installed capacity 1983 amounted to 3,344 mw of which 1,344 mw was hydro-electricity and 1,170 mw thermal. 99·8% of villages were supplied with electricity. The Kalpakkam nuclear power plant became operational in 1983; initial capacity, 230 mw.

Water. A joint project with Andhra Pradesh was agreed in 1983, to supply Madras with water from the Krishna river, also providing irrigation, *en route,* for Andhra Pradesh.

Minerals. Value of mineral exports, 1983, Rs 1·5 crores. The state has magnesite, salt, coal, chromite, bauxite, limestone, manganese, mica, quartz, gypsum and feldspar.

Agriculture. Agriculture engages 29% of the population. The land is a fertile plain watered by rivers flowing east from the Western Ghats, particularly the Cauvery and the Tambaraparani. Temperature ranges between 18°C. and 43°C., rainfall between 25 in. and 75 in. Of the total land area (13·01m. hectares), 7,698,000 hectares were cultivable and 3m. hectares were irrigated in 1977. The staple food crops grown are paddy, maize, jawar, bajra, pulses and millets. Important commercial crops are sugar-cane, oilseeds, cashewnuts, cotton, tobacco, coffee, tea, rubber and pepper. Production 1983–84, in 1,000 tons, (and area, 1,000 hectares): rice 5,000 (2,282); millet 1,900 (1,652); sugar cane 2,500 (132); pulses 115 (333); cotton 3m. bales (169); oilseeds 752 (825).

Livestock (1966 census): Buffaloes, 2,753,049; other cattle, 11,009,368; sheep, 6,641,843; goats, 3,796,736; swine, 874,880; horses, ponies, mules, camels, etc., 185,336; poultry, 10,898,862.

Forestry. Forest area, 1983, 2,201,000 hectares, of which 1,812,000 were reserved forest. Forests cover about 17% of land area. Main products are teak, soft wood, wattle, sandalwood, pulp wood, cashew and cinchona bark.

Fisheries. Landings, 1976, 510,000 tonnes.

INDUSTRY AND TRADE

Industry. The contribution of the industrial sector to the state income was Rs 373 crores in 1972-73. The number of registered factories was 6,713 in 1973. The consumption of power in the industrial sector was 49·5% of total state consumption in 1974. The biggest central sector project is Salem steel plant. Man-days lost in industrial disputes, 1979, 8·38m.

Cotton textiles is one of the major industries. There are nearly 180 cotton textile mills and most of the spinning mills supplying yarn to the decentralized handloom industry. Other important industries are tanning, manufacture of textile machinery, power-driven pumps, bicycles, electrical machinery, tractors, rubber tyres and tubes, bricks and tiles and silk. Tamil Nadu is the second largest producer of cement, while its sugar industry has been expanding rapidly.

Public sector undertakings include the Neyveli lignite complex, integral coach factory, high-pressure boiler plant, photographic film factory, surgical instruments factory, teleprinter factory, oil refinery, continuous casting plant and defence vehicles manufacture. Main exports: tanned hides and skins, leather and cotton goods, tea, coffee, spices, engineering goods, motor-car ancillaries.

Tourism. In 1982, 229,000 foreign tourists visited the state.

COMMUNICATIONS

Roads. On 1 April 1982 the state had approximately 35,746 km of national and state highways, major and other district roads. In 1983 there were 100,037 registered motor vehicles and 326,977 others not covered by permits.

Railways. In 1970 there were 6,038 km of railway. Madras and Madurai are the main centres.

Aviation. There are airports at Madras, Tiruchirapalli and Madurai, with regular scheduled services to Bombay, Calcutta and Delhi. Madras is the main centre of airline routes in South India.

Shipping. Madras and Tuticorin are the chief ports. Important minor ports are Cuddalore and Nagapattinam. There are 9 intermediate ports. The Inland Container Depot at Coimbatore has a capacity of 50,000 tonnes of export traffic; it is linked to Cochin (Kerala).

JUSTICE, RELIGION AND EDUCATION

Justice. There is a High Court at Madras with a Chief Justice and 18 judges. *Police.* Strength of armed police battalions, 1973, 4,420; strength of the armed reserve (1972) in the state and in Madras, 356,461.

Religion. At the 1971 census Hindus numbered 36,674,150 (89·2%), Christians, 5·75%; Moslems, 5·11%.

Education. At the 1981 census 22·1m. people were literate.

Education is free up to pre-university level. In 1973-74 there were 2,823 high schools with a total enrolment of 1,627,030 students. The number of primary schools was 26,726, and their enrolment, 3,759,140, 5,773 upper primary schools had 2,113,981 pupils. Allotment of expenditure for education for 1974-75, Rs 1,08·52 crores.

There are 3 universities. Madras University (founded in 1857) is affiliating and teaching. It had (1968) 119 colleges for arts and sciences with 106,571 students. Annamalai University, Annamalainagar (founded 1928) is residential; Madurai University (founded 1966) is an affiliating and teaching university.

Statistical Information: The Department of Statistics (Fort St George, Madras) was established in 1948 and reorganized in 1953. *Director:* D. S. Rajabushanam, MA. Main publications: *Annual Statistical Abstract; Decennial Statistical Atlas; Season and Crop Report; Quinquennial Wages Census; Quarterly Abstract of Statistics.*

TRIPURA

HISTORY. A Hindu state of great antiquity having been ruled by the Maharajahs for 1,300 years before its accession to the Indian Union on 15 Oct. 1949. With the reorganization of states on 1 Sept. 1956 Tripura became a Union Territory. The Territory was made a State on 21 Jan. 1972.

EVENTS. Tribal insurgents have caused violent disturbances, largely because of large-scale immigration from Bangladesh.

AREA AND POPULATION. Tripura is bounded on the north, west and south by Bangladesh, and on the east by Mizoram. The major portion of the state is hilly and mainly jungle. It has an area of 10,477 sq. km and a population of 2,060,189 (1981 census); Density, 196 per sq. km. Growth rate, 1971-81, 32·37%.

The predominant language is Bengali.

GOVERNMENT. There is a Legislative Assembly of 60 members. The election of Jan. 1983 was won by the Communist Party of India (Marxist). The territory has 1 district, divided into 10 administrative sub-divisions, namely, Sadar, Khowai, Kailasahar, Dharmanagar, Sonamura, Udaipur, Belonia, Kamalpur, Sabroom and Amarpur.

The capital is Agartala.

Governor: Gen. K. V. Krishna Rao.
Chief Minister: N. Chakravarty.

BUDGET. Budget estimates 1980-81 show revenue receipts of Rs 107·1 crores, and expenditure on revenue account of Rs 108·8 crores. Annual plan expenditure, Rs 35 crores.

ENERGY AND NATURAL RESOURCES

Electricity. Installed capacity (1980), 14·72 mw; there were (1976) 245 electrified villages.

Agriculture. About 23% of the land area is cultivable. The tribes practise shifting cultivation, but this is being slowly replaced by modern methods. The main crops are rice, wheat, jute, mesta, potatoes, oilseeds and sugar-cane. Foodgrain production (1979-80), 310,000 tonnes. There are 56 registered tea gardens producing 4,500,000 kg. per year, and employing about 10,000. In 1983, 5,000 hectares were under new rubber plantations.

Forestry. Forests cover about 65% of the land area. They have been much depleted by clearance for shifting cultivation and, recently, for refugee settlements of Bangladeshis. About 8% of the forest area still consists of dense natural forest; losses elsewhere are being replaced by plantation. Commercial rubber plantation has also been encouraged and covers over 65,000 hectares.

INDUSTRY. There is a jute mill, a steel re-rolling mill and a flour mill at Agartala; a second flour mill at Dharmanagar. Small scale industries produce diverse manufacture. The main village industries are hand-loom weaving, sericulture and cane-work. The Tripura Handloom and Handicrafts Development Corporation marketed goods worth Rs 6m. in 1979-80.

COMMUNICATIONS

Roads. Total length of motorable roads (1974) 3,692 km, of which 1,123 km were surfaced. Vehicles registered, 31 March 1980, 7,889.

Railways. There is a railway between Dharmanagar and Kalkalighat (Assam).

Aviation. There is 1 airport and 3 airstrips. The airport (Agartala) has regular scheduled services to Calcutta.

EDUCATION AND WELFARE

Education. In autumn 1978 there were 1,885 primary schools (209,836 pupils); 436 middle schools (51,418); 144 high schools (21,238), and 52 higher grade schools (6,202). There were 6 colleges of general education (7,772). 9 colleges of professional and technical education (1,346) and 859 social education centres.

Health. There were (1980) 12 hospitals, with 1,357 beds, 128 dispensaries, 297 doctors and 459 nurses. There were 26 primary health centres and about 35 other medical units.

UTTAR PRADESH

HISTORY. In 1833 the then Bengal Presidency was divided into two parts, one of which became the Presidency of Agra. In 1836 the Agra area was styled the North-West Province and placed under a Lieut.-Governor. The two provinces of Agra and Oudh were placed, in 1877, under one administrator, styled Lieut.-Governor of the North-West Province and Chief Commissioner of Oudh. In 1902 the name was changed to 'United Provinces of Agra and Oudh', under a Lieut.-Governor, and the Lieut.-Governorship was altered to a Governorship in 1921. In 1935 the name was shortened to 'United Provinces'. On Independence, the states of Rampur, Banaras and Tehri-Garwhal were merged with United Provinces. In 1950 the name of the United Provinces was changed to Uttar Pradesh.

AREA AND POPULATION. Uttar Pradesh is in north India and is bounded north by Himachal Pradesh, Tibet and Nepál, east by Bihar, south by Madhya Pradesh and west by Rajasthan, Haryana and Delhi. The area of the state is 294,413 sq. km. Population (1981 census), 110,862,013, a density of 377 per sq. km. Growth rate, 1971–81, 25·52%. Cities with more than 250,000 population, *see* p. 614. The official language is Hindi.

CONSTITUTION AND GOVERNMENT. Uttar Pradesh has had an autonomous system of government since 1937. There is a bicameral legislature. The Legislative Council has 108 members; the Legislative Assembly has 426, of which 423 are elected. After the elections in March 1985 a Congress government was returned.

There are 12 administrative divisions, each under a Commissioner, and 57 districts.

The capital is Lucknow.

Governor: M. Usman Arif

Chief Minister: N. D. Tiwari.

BUDGET. Budget estimates 1984–85 show revenue and capital receipts of Rs 4,356·28 crores; revenue and capital account expenditure, Rs 4,629 crores.

ENERGY AND NATURAL RESOURCES

Electricity. The State Electricity Board had, 31 March 1983, an installed capacity of 3,852 mw. There were (March 1984) 57,733 villages with electricity.

Minerals. The state has magnesite, fire-clay, coal, copper, dolomite, limestone, soapstone, gypsum, bauxite, diaspore, ochre, phosphorite, pyrophyllite, silica sand and steatite among others.

Agriculture. Agriculture occupies 78% of the work force. About 9m. hectares are irrigated. The state is India's largest producer of foodgrains; production (1982–83), 26·5m. tonnes; sugar-cane 81·4m.; oilseeds, 1·22m. The state is one of India's main producers of sugar. There were (1981) 1,199 veterinary centres for cattle.

Forests cover (1982) about 5·3m. sq. km.

INDUSTRY. Sugar production is important; other industries include edible oils, textiles, distilleries, brewing, leather working, agricultural engineering, paper and chemicals. There is an aluminium smelter at Renukoot. An oil refinery at Mathura has capacity of 6m. tonnes per annum. Large public-sector enterprises have been set up in electrical engineering, pharmaceuticals, locomotive building, general engineering, electronics and aeronautics. Village and small-scale industries are important; there were 90,237 small units in 1983. About one-third of cloth output is from hand-looms. Total working population (1981) 30·8m., of whom 6·8m. were non-agricultural.

COMMUNICATIONS

Roads. There were, 31 March 1983, 273,011 km of motorable roads, of which 66,034 km were metalled. (This excludes forest roads.) In 1983 there were 674,049 motor vehicles of which 391,307 were motorcycles.

Railways. Lucknow is the main junction of the northern network; other important junctions are Agra, Kanpur, Allahabad and Varanasi.

Aviation. There are airports at Lucknow, Kanpur, Varanasi, Allahabad, Agra, Jhansi, Lalitpur and Gorakhpur.

JUSTICE, RELIGION AND EDUCATION

Justice. The High Court of Judicature at Allahabad (with a bench at Lucknow) has a Chief Justice and 52 puisne judges including additional judges. There are 56 sessions divisions in the state.

Religion. At the 1971 census Hindus numbered 73,997,597; Moslems, 13,676,533; Sikhs, 369,672; Christians, 131,810; Jains, 124,728; Buddhists, 39,639.

Education. At the 1981 census 30·1m. people were literate. In 1983–84 there were 72,519 junior basic schools, 13,984 senior basic schools and 5,650 higher secondary schools.

Uttar Pradesh has 19 universities: Allahabad University (founded 1887); Agra University (1927); the Banaras Hindu University, Varanasi (1916); Lucknow University (1921); Aligarh Muslim University (1920); Roorkee University (1948), formerly Thomason College of Civil Engineering (established in 1847); Gorakhpur University (1957); Varanasaya Sanskrit Vishwavidyalaya, Varanasi (1958); Kashi Vidyapith, Varanasi (1963). Kanpur University and Meerut University were founded in 1966. Govind Ballabh Pant University, Pantnagar (1969); Garhwal University, Srinagar, (1973). Two universities of agriculture were founded in 1974–75 and Avadh, Kumaon, Rohilkhand and Jhansi Universities in 1975.

There are also two institutions with university status: Gurukul Kangri and Dayal Bagh Educational Institute. There are 9 medical colleges.

HEALTH. On 31 Dec. 1982 there were 3,363 allopathic and 3,344 ayurvedic and unani hospitals. There were 6,083 allopathic doctors and 3,332 allopathic nurses in state service. There were TB hospitals and clinics with 3,437 beds.

WEST BENGAL

HISTORY. For the history of Bengal under British rule, from 1633 to 1947, *see* THE STATESMAN'S YEAR-BOOK, 1952, p. 183.

Under the terms of the Indian Independence Act, 1947, the Province of Bengal ceased to exist. The Moslem majority districts of East Bengal, consisting of the Chittagong and Dacca Divisions and portions of the Presidency and Rajshahi Divisions, became what was then East Pakistan (now Bangladesh).

AREA AND POPULATION. West Bengal is in north-east India and is bounded north by Sikkim and Bhután, east by Assam and Bangladesh, south by the Bay of Bengal and Orissa, west by Bihar and north-west by Nepál. The total area of West Bengal is 87,853 sq. km. At the 1981 census its population was 54,580,647, an increase of 23·17% since 1971, the density of population 621 per sq. km. Population of chief cities, *see* p. 614. The principal language is Bengali.

CONSTITUTION AND GOVERNMENT. The state of West Bengal came into existence as a result of the Indian Independence Act, 1947. The territory of Cooch-Behar State was merged with West Bengal on 1 Jan. 1950, and the former French possession of Chandernagore became part of the state on 2 Oct. 1954. Under the States Reorganization Act, 1956, certain portions of Bihar State (an area of 3,157 sq. miles with a population of 1,446,385) were transferred to West Bengal.

The Legislative Assembly has 295 seats. Distribution March 1984: Communist Party of India (Marxist), 170; Forward Bloc, 27; Revolutionary Socialist Party, 19; Communist Party of India, 7; Revolutionary Communist Party of India, 2; Forward Bloc (Marxist), 2; Democratic Socialist Party, 2; Socialist Party, 3. Total "Left Front", 236. Opposition: Indian National Congress, 55; others, 2; vacant, 2.

The capital is Calcutta.

For administrative purposes there are 3 divisions (Jalpaiguri, Burdwan and Presidency), under which there are 16 districts, including Calcutta. The Calcutta Metropolitan Development Authority has been set up to co-ordinate development in the metropolitan area (1,250 sq. km). For the purposes of local self-government there are 15 *zilla parishads* (district boards), 339 *panchayat samities* (regional boards), and 3,305 *gram* (village) *panchayats*. There are 99 municipalities, 2 Corporations, 3 Town Committees and 10 Notified Areas. The Calcutta Corporation was reconstituted in 1969 with a mayor and deputy mayor, a commissioner, aldermen and standing committees.

Governor: U. S. Dikshit.
Chief Minister: J. Basu.

BUDGET. Budget estimates for 1984–85 showed a deficit of Rs 544m.

ENERGY AND NATURAL RESOURCES

Electricity. Installed capacity, 1983–84, 2,553 mw; 19,964 villages had electricity.

Water. The major irrigation and power scheme at present under construction is (1984) the Teesta barrage. Major irrigation schemes are the Mayurakshi, Kansabati and Damodar Valley. During 1981–82 government canals irrigated 1m. hectares. At March 1983 there were 5,701 tubewells and 3,108 riverlift irrigation schemes.

Minerals. Value of production, 1981, Rs 3,131·9m. The state has coal (the Raniganj field is one of the 3 biggest in India) including coking coal. Coal production (1982) 198m. tonnes.

Agriculture. About 4·8m. hectares are rice-paddy, one-third of it irrigated. Total foodgrain production, 1982–83, 5·8m. tonnes; oilseeds (provisional), 170,700 tonnes; jute and other fibres, 3·8m. bales (180 kg.); wheat, 605,500 tonnes. The state produces 55% of the national output of jute.

Livestock (1976 census): 11,968,000 cattle, 758,000 buffaloes; 1981 census, 758,000 sheep and goats, and 15,052,000 poultry.

Forests cover 13·4% of the state.

Fisheries. Landings, 1983–84, about 385,000 tonnes. During 1980–86 Rs 280m. was to be invested in fishery schemes.

INDUSTRY. The total number of registered factories, 1982, was 6,954; average daily employment in public sector industries, 1·6m. The coalmining industry had 116 units with average daily employment of 129,000.

There is a large automobile factory at Uttarpara, and there are aluminium rolling-mills at Belur and Asansol. At Durgapur a major steel plant was completed in 1962. Durgapur has other industries under the state sector—a thermal power plant, coke oven plant, fertilizer factory, alloy steel plant and ophthalmic glass plant. There are a locomotive factory and cable factory at Chittaranjan and Rupnarayanpur. A refinery and fertilizer factory are operating at Haldia.

Small industries are important; 12,265 units were registered in 1981–82, (91,605 jobs); 12,265 units (provisional) in 1982–83 (97,952).

COMMUNICATIONS

Roads. In 1980 the length of national highway was 1,471 km, of state highway 3,147 km and of other motorable roads 138,666 km. In 1982 the state had 321,291 motor vehicles.

Railways. The length of railways within the state (1981–82) is 6,085 km. The main centres are Howrah, Sealdah, Kharagpur, Asansol and New Jalpaiguri. The first section of the Calcutta Metro opened in Nov. 1984.

Aviation. The main airport is Calcutta which has national and international flights. The second airport is at Bagdogra in the extreme north, which has regular scheduled services to Calcutta.

Shipping. Calcutta is the chief port: a barrage is being built at Farakka to control the flow of the Ganges and to provide a rail and road link between North and South Bengal. A second port is being developed at Haldia, halfway between the present port and the sea, which is intended mainly for bulk cargoes. West Bengal possesses 779 km of navigable canals.

JUSTICE, RELIGION AND EDUCATION

Justice. The High Court of Judicature at Calcutta has a Chief Justice and 38 puisne judges. The Andaman and Nicobar Islands *(see below)* come under its jurisdiction.

Police. In 1983 the police force numbered 52,772, under a director-general and an inspector-general. Calcutta has a separate force under a commissioner directly responsible to the Government; its strength was 20,777 in 1982.

Religion. At the 1971 census Hindus numbered 34,611,864; Moslems, 9,064,338; Christians, 251,752; Buddhists, 121,504; Sikhs, 35,084; Jains, 32,203.

Education. At the 1981 census 22·2m. people were literate. In 1983–84 there were 50,090 primary schools, with about 7·6m. pupils and 3,247 junior and 10,190 secondary schools with about 3·5m. pupils. Primary education is free.

The University of Calcutta (founded 1857) is affiliating and teaching; in 1976–77 it had 234,661 students. Visva Bharati, Santiniketan, was originally established in 1951 and is residential and teaching; it had 2,911 students in 1977–78. The University of Jadavpur, Calcutta (1955), had 4,222 students in 1977–78. Burdwan University was established 15 June 1960 with 31 affiliated colleges previously under the supervision of the University of Calcutta; in 1977–78 there were 48,550 students. Kalyani University was established in 1960 (1,839 students in 1977). The University of North Bengal (1962) had 17,728 students in 1977–78. Rabindra Bharati University had 2,783 students in 1977–78. Bidhan Chandra Krishi Viswavidyalaya (1974) had 1,047 students in 1977–78.

UNION TERRITORIES

ANDAMAN AND NICOBAR ISLANDS. The Andaman and Nicobar Islands are administered by the President of the Republic of India acting through a Lieut.-Governor. There is a Pradesh Council, 5 members of which are selected by the Chief Commissioner as advisory counsellors. The seat of administration is at Port Blair, which is connected with Calcutta (1,255 km away) and Madras (1,190 km) by steamer service which calls about every 10 days; there is a bi-weekly air service from Calcutta and a weekly service from Madras. Roads in the islands, 691 km black-topped and 26 km others. There are 2 districts.

The population (1981 census) was 188,254; density 23 per sq. km.; growth rate 1971–81, 63·5%. Port Blair (1981), 49,634.

The climate is tropical, with little variation in temperature. Heavy rain (125″ annually) is mainly brought by the south-west monsoon. Humidity is high.

Revised estimates for 1983–84 show total revenue receipts of Rs 8,00·95 lakhs, and total expenditure on revenue account of Rs 48,73·39 lakhs, and total capital expenditure of Rs 29,28·22 lakhs. Estimates for 1984–85 show revenue, Rs 8,12·45 lakhs, expenditure Rs 53,81·85 lakhs, and capital expenditure Rs 31,44·56 lakhs.

Lieut.-Governor: M. L. Kampani.

The **Andaman Islands** lie in the Bay of Bengal, 193 km from Cape Negrais in Burma, 1,255 from Calcutta and 1,190 from Madras. Five large islands grouped together are called the Great Andamans, and to the south is the island of Little Andaman. There are some 204 islets, the two principal groups being the Ritchie Archipelago and the Labyrinth Islands. The total area is about 6,340 sq. km. The Great Andaman group is about 467 km long and, at the widest, 51 km broad.

The original inhabitants live in the forests by hunting and fishing; they are of a small Negrito type and their civilization is about that of the Stone Age. Their exact numbers are not known, as they avoid all contact with civilization. The total population of the Andaman Islands (including about 430 aboriginals) was 157,821 in 1981. Main aboriginal tribes, Andamanese, Onges, Jarawas and Sentinelese. Under a central government scheme started in 1953, some 4,000 displaced families, mostly from East Pakistan, had been settled in the islands by May 1967.

Japanese forces occupied the Andaman Islands on 23 March 1942. Civil administration of the islands was resumed on 8 Oct. 1945.

From 1857 to March 1942 the islands were used by the Government of India as a penal settlement for life and long-term convicts, but the penal settlement was abolished on re-occupation in Oct. 1945.

The Great Andaman group, densely wooded, contains many valuable trees, both hardwood and softwood. The best known of the hardwoods is the *padauk* or Andaman redwood; *gurjan* is in great demand for the manufacture of plywood. Large quantities of softwood are supplied to match factories. Annually the Forest Department export about 25,000 tons of timber to the mainland. Coconut, coffee and rubber are cultivated. The islands are slowly being made self-sufficient in paddy and rice, and now grow approximately half their annual requirements. Livestock (1982): 27,400 cattle, 9,720 buffaloes, 17,600 goats and 21,220 pigs. Fishing is important. There is a sawmill at Blair and a coconut-oil mill at Dunbar Point.

The islands possess a number of harbours and safe anchorages, notably Port Blair in the south, Port Cornwallis in the north and Elphinstone and Mayabandar in the middle.

The **Nicobar Islands** are situated to the south of the Andamans, 121 km from Little Andaman. The British were in possession 1869–1947. There are 19 islands, 7 uninhabited; total area, 1,953 sq. km. The islands are usually divided into 3 subgroups (southern, central and northern), the chief islands in each being respectively, Great Nicobar, Camotra with Nancowrie and Car Nicobar. There is a fine land-locked harbour between the islands of Camotra and Nancowrie, known as Nancowrie Harbour.

The population numbered, in 1981, 30,433, including about 22,200 of Nicobarese and Shompen tribes. The coconut and arecanut are the main items of trade, and coconuts are a major item in the people's diet.

The Nicobar Islands were occupied by the Japanese in July 1942; and Car Nicobar was developed as a big supply base. The Allies reoccupied the islands on 9 Oct. 1945.

ARUNACHAL PRADESH. On 21 Jan. 1972 the former North East Frontier Agency of Assam was created a Union Territory. The territory includes the Kameng, Tirap, Subansiri, Siang and Lohit frontier divisions and has an area of 81,426 sq. km and a population (1981 census) of 628,050, density, 7 per sq. km; growth rate, 1971–81, 34·34%.

There is a Legislative Assembly of 30 members and a Council of Ministers. The election of 1978 was won by the Janata party.

There are 5 districts. The centre of administration is at Itanagar.

Chief Commissioner: S. M. Krishnatry.
Chief Minister: Prem Khandu Thungon.

About 60% of the land area is forest. Agriculture employs 18·5% of the people. In 1970 there were 200,000 acres under cultivation, 32,600 acres of it irrigated. Crops include rice (13,000 tonnes, 1976), rubber, coffee, coconut, arecanut, fruits and spices. There were about 100 co-operatives. The budget estimates for 1980–81 provided Rs 81·7 crores, of which Rs 1·16 crores was allotted to agriculture.

CHANDIGARH. On 1 Nov. 1966 the city of Chandigarh and the area surrounding it was constituted a Union Territory. Population (1981), 450,061; density, 3,948 per sq. km.; growth rate, 1971–81, 74·9%. Area, 114 sq. km. It serves as the joint capital of both Punjab (India) and the state of Haryana, and is the seat of a High Court and of a university serving both states. The city will ultimately be the capital of just the Punjab; joint status is to last while a new capital is built for Haryana.

There is some cultivated land (foodgrain production, 1977, 8,000 tonnes) and some forest (27·5% of the territory).

Evenson, N., *Chandigarh.* Berkeley, Cal., 1966

DADRA AND NAGAR HAVELI. Formely Portuguese, the territories of Dadra and Nagar Haveli were occupied in July 1954 by nationalists, and a pro-India administration was formed; this body made a request for incorporation into the Union, 1 June 1961. By the 10th amendment to the constitution the territories became a centrally administered Union Territory with effect from 11 Aug. 1961, forming an enclave at the southernmost point of the border between Gujarat and Maharashtra. Area 491 sq. km.; population (1981), 103,676 (males 52,515, females 51,161); density 211 per sq. km; growth rate, 1971–81, 39·78%. There is an Administrator appointed by the Government of India. The day-to-day business is done by various departments, co-ordinated by the Administrator's secretary and headed by a Collector. Headquarters are at Silvassa. The territory is tribal and organised in 72 villages. Languages used are Bhilli, Gujarat, Bhilodi (83%), Marathi and Hindi.

Administrator: K. T. Satarawala
Collector: H. Haukhum

Electricity. Electricity is supplied by Gujarat, and 62 villages had been electrified by 1983.

Water. A joint project with the governments of Gujarat, Goa, Daman and Diu has been set up; a reservoir at Damanganga is being built with irrigation potential of 8,280 hectares.

Agriculture. Farming is the chief occupation, and about 21,400 hectares were under crops in 1982–83. Much of the land is terraced and there is a 75% subsidy for soil conservation. The major food crops are rice and ragi; wheat, small millets and pulses are also grown. There is little irrigation (915 hectares). There are veterinary centres, an agricultural research centre and breeding centres to improve strains of cattle and poultry. During 1982–83 the Administration distributed 256 tonnes of high yielding paddy seed, and high yielding wheat seed, and 302 tonnes of fertilizer.

Forests. About 20,200 hectares or 41·2% of the total area is forest, mainly of teak, sadad and khair. Timber production provides the largest simple contribution to the territory's revenue.

Industry. Industrial estates have been set up at Piparia, Masat and Khadoli. There are 133 small units, and 3 medium scale, employing about 3,000. Concessions are available for small industries, and the whole Territory is aided as a backward area.

Communications. There are (1978) 167 km of motorable road. The railway line from Bombay to Ahmedabad runs through Silvassa. The nearest airport is Bombay.

Justice. The territory is under the jurisdiction of the Bombay (Maharashtra) High Court. There is a District and Sessions Court and one junior Division Civil Court at Silvassa.

Education. Literacy was 14·86% of the population at the 1971 census. In 1982–83 there were 70 adult education centres (2,225 students); there were 141 government primary schools, 12 government-aided mission schools and one unaided; there were 2 higher secondary schools and 5 high schools. Total primary enrolment was 16,962; high-school and higher secondary, 1,893.

Health. The territory has 1 cottage hospital, 3 primary health centres and 7 dispensaries; there is also a mobile dispensary.

DELHI. Delhi became a Union Territory on 1 Nov. 1956.

Area and Population. The territory forms an enclave inside the eastern frontier of Haryana in north India. Delhi has an area of 1,485 sq. km. At the 1981 census its population was 6,220,406 (density per sq. km, 4,189). Growth rate, 1971–81, 53%. In the rural area of Delhi there are 214 inhabited and 17 deserted villages and 27 census towns. They are distributed in 5 community development blocks.

Government. The Lieut-Governor is the Administrator, assisted by 4 Executive Councillors (1 Chief Executive Councillor and 3 Executive Councillors) appointed by the President of India on the recommendation of the Union Home Ministry. There is a Metropolitan Council of 61 members including 5 nominated by the President of India. The Territory is covered by 3 local bodies: Delhi Municipal Corporation, New Delhi Municipal Committee and Delhi Cantonment Board.

Lieut.-Governor: M. M. K. Wali.

Budget. Revised estimates 1984–85 show total revenue of Rs 5,113m. and expenditure of Rs 18,018m. Plan expenditure: Rs 2,890m.; power, Rs 435m.; transport and communication, Rs 403·6m.; water and sewerage, Rs 410·4m.; general education, Rs 390m.; urban development, Rs 324m.; medical services, Rs 252·5m.

Agriculture. The contribution to the economy is not significant. About 98,930 hectares are cultivated. Animal husbandry is increasing and mixed farms are common. Chief crops in 1982–83, (production in 1,000 tonnes) were: Wheat, 130; jowar and bajra, 15; gram, 0·6; sugar-cane (gur), 0·13; fruit, vegetables and flowers.

Industry. The modern city of Delhi and New Delhi is not only the largest commercial centre in northern India but is also an important industrial centre. Since 1947 a large number of industrial concerns have been established; these include factories for the manufacture of razor blades, sports goods, radios and television and parts, bicycles and parts, plastic and PVC goods including footwear, textiles, chemicals, fertilizers, medicines, hosiery, leather goods, soft drinks, hand and machine tools. There is also metal forging, casting, galvanising and electro-plating, printing and warehousing. The number of industrial units functioning was about 54,000 in 1982–83; average number of workers employed was 507,000. Production was worth Rs 2,352 crores and investment was about Rs 1,035 crores.

Some traditional handicrafts, for which Delhi was formerly famous, still flourish; among them are ivory carving, miniature painting, gold and silver jewellery and papier mâché work. The handwoven textiles of Delhi were particularly fine; this craft is being successfully revived.

Delhi publishes 13 major daily newspapers, including the *Times of India, Hindustan Times, Indian Express, Statesman, Nav Bharat Times* and *Hindustan.*

Roads. Five national highways pass through the city. There were (1983) 724,495 registered motor vehicles in Delhi including 8,258 taxis. The Transport Corporation had 5,115 buses in 1983–84.

Railways. Delhi is an important rail junction with three main stations: Delhi, New Delhi, Hazart Nizamuddin. There is an electric ring railway for commuters.

Aviation. Palam airport operates internal and international flights.

Religion. At the 1971 census Hindus numbered 3,407,835; Sikhs, 291,123; Moslems, 263,019; Jains, 50,513; Christians, 43,720; Buddhists, 8,720.

Education. The proportion of literates to the total population was 61·54% at the 1981 census (68·4% of males and 53·07% of females).

The total number of educational institutions in 1982–83 was 4,658, with an enrolment of 1,532,502 students.

The University of Delhi was founded in 1922; it had 65 constituent colleges and institutions in 1983–84, with a total of 105,522 students. There are also Jawaharlal Nehru university and Jamia Millia Islamia; the Indian Institute of Technology at Haus Khaz; the Indian Agricultural Research Institute at Pusa; the All India Institute of Medical Science at Ansari Nagar and the Indian Institute of Public Administration.

GOA, DAMAN AND DIU. The coast was captured for Portugal by Alfonso de Albuquerque in 1510 and the inland area was added in the 18th century. Daman (Damão) on the Gujarat coast, 100 miles (160 km) north of Bombay, was seized by the Portuguese in 1531 and ceded to them (1539) by the Shar of Gujarat. The island of Diu, captured in 1534, lies off the south-east coast of Kathiawar (Gujarat); there is a small coastal area. In Dec. 1961 the territories were occupied by India and incorporated into the Indian Union.

Area and Population. Goa, bounded on the north by Maharashtra and on the east and south by Karnataka, has a coastline of 105 km. The area of the territory is 3,813 sq. km, that of Goa itself being about 3,701 sq. km. Daman, 72 sq. km; Diu, 40 sq. km. Population (1981) 1,082,117. Density, 285 per sq. km. Growth rate, 1971–81, 26·15%. Estimated population, 1983, 1,146,000. Panaji is the largest town, population (urban agglomeration, 1981) 76,839. The languages spoken are Gujarati, Marathi, Konkani, Portuguese and English.

Government. The Indian Parliament passed legislation in March 1962 by which Goa, Daman and Diu became a Union Territory with retrospective effect from 20 Dec. 1961. Goa is represented by 2 elected members in the Indian House of the People. For judicial purposes there is a Panaji bench of the High Court of Bombay. The capital is Panaji. There are 195 village *panchayats*.

There is a Legislative Assembly of 30 members.

Lieut.-Governor: Gopal Singh.
Chief Minister: P. R. Rane.

Budget. Annual Plan expenditure, 1984–85, Rs 655m.

Electricity. Units sold, 251·9m. kwh. in 1982–83. Seventeen towns and 393 villages were supplied with electric power by March 1984. Power is generated in neighbouring states.

Minerals. Resources include manganese ore and iron ore, both of which are exported. There are also reserves of bauxite, limestone and clay.

Agriculture. Agriculture is the main occupation; important crops are rice, ragi, pulses, groundnuts, fruit and coconuts. The net area sown is 133,575 hectares. Area irrigated, 13,000 hectares. Area under paddy (1983–84), 37,145 hectares of high-yielding strain (producing 186,120 tonnes). Area under pulses, 11,668; ragi, 7,840. Government poultry and dairy farming schemes yielded 180m. eggs and 30,000 litres of milk in 1983–84.

Fisheries. The fishing industry is important; fish is the territory's staple food. In 1983 the catch of seafish was 29,915 tonnes (value Rs 1,303·02 lakhs). The whole territory has a coastline of about 140 km. There are about 3,996 active fishing vessels.

Industry. In 1983 there were 36 large and medium industrial projects and 2,943 small units registered. There were 9 government industrial estates. Small units were mainly occupied in making nylon fishing-nets, ready made clothing, pesticides, pharmaceuticals and footwear.

Employment. In 1980 there were 86 unions with 42,300 members.

Roads. In 1983 there were 5,721 km of motorable road (national highway, 223 km). In 1983 there were 49,714 registered vehicles.

Railways. There is a metre gauge line from the Pune–Bangalore line into Goa. There are no railways on Diu or in Daman.

Aviation. There are regular services to Bombay and Bangalore from Dabolim (Goa).

Shipping. The main port is Marmagoa, which handled 11·38m. tonnes of cargo, mainly iron ore, in 1983–84. There is a daily steamer service between Panaji and Bombay.

Post and Telegraphs. There are (1983) 253 post offices and 40 telephone exchanges providing links to 60 countries. There are 3 telex exchanges.

Justice. The territory comes under the High Court of Bombay.

Religion. About 62% of the population is Hindu, 36% Christian, 2% Muslim and other communities.

Education. The 1981 census recorded 57% literacy. Education is free up to grade VIII. In 1983–84 primary schools numbered 1,265 with 141,195 pupils, middle schools 430 with 79,313 pupils and secondary schools 281 with 54,088 pupils. There were 22 higher secondary schools, with 9,802 pupils, and 18 arts, commercial and science colleges with 7,570 students.

Health. There were (1983) 102 hospitals (3,580 beds) including 3 tuberculosis hospitals; also mobile and specialist clinics. There were also 188 health centres and about 1,287 doctors. There is 1 medical college and 1 dental college.

Richards, J. M., *Goa.* London, 1982
Soeiro de Brito, R., *Goa e as Praças do Norte.* Lisbon, 1966

LAKSHADWEEP. The territory consists of a group of 27 islands (10 inhabited), about 300 km off the west coat of Kerala. It was constituted a Union Territory in 1956 as the Laccadive, Minicoy and Amindivi Islands, and renamed in Nov. 1973. The total area of the islands is 32 sq. km. The northern portion is called the Amindivis. The remaining islands are called the Laccadives (including Minicoy Island). Androth is the largest island, 4·8 sq. km, and is nearest to Kerala. An Advisory Committee associated with the Union Home Minister and an Advisory Council to the Administrator assist in the administration of the islands; these are constituted annually. Population (1981 census), 40,237, nearly all Moslems. Density, 1,257 per sq. km.; growth rate, 1971–81, 26·49%. The language is Malayalam, but the language in Minicoy is Mahl. There were, in 1984, 9 high schools and 9 nursery schools, 17 junior basic schools, 4 senior basic schools and 2 junior colleges. There are 2 hospitals and 7 primary health centres. The staple products are coconut-husk fibre (coir), coconuts and fish. There is a tourist resort at Bangarem, an uninhabited island with an extensive lagoon. Headquarters of administration, Kavaratti Island.

Administrator: O. Saigal.

MIZORAM. On 21 Jan. 1972 the former Mizo Hills District of Assam was created a Union Territory. The area is approximately 21,090 sq. km and the population (1981 census), 487,774, of whom about 55% are literate and 90% are Christian. Density, 23 per sq. km.; growth rate, 1971–81, 46·75%.

There is a Council of Ministers responsible to a Legislative Assembly with 30 seats. The present ministry (Congress I) took office in May 1984. The nationalist Mizo National Front was banned in 1982. The main town is Aizawl, which is connected by a main road (not a national highway) to Silchar, Assam; Silchar is also the nearest airport. There are no railways.

The budget for 1980–81 estimated receipts of Rs 52·28 crores on revenue account and Rs 24·50 crores on capital account. Outlay for the sixth Five-Year Plan is Rs 24·50 crores.

Agriculture employs 46% of the people and 17% of cultivated land is irrigated; there are some terraced holdings, elsewhere shifting cultivation is practised in forest clearings. Industry is based on the forests. Total installed power capacity, 1975, 3·4 mw supplying 61 villages.

Lieut.-Governor: K. A. A. Raja.
Chief Minister: M. Lalthanwala.

PONDICHERRY. Formerly the chief French settlement in India, Pondicherry was founded by the French in 1674, taken by the Dutch in 1693 and restored to the French in 1699. The English took it in 1761, restored it in 1765, re-took it in 1778, restored it a second time in 1785, retook it a third time in 1793 and finally restored it to the French in 1814. Administration was transferred to India on 1 Nov. 1954. A Treaty of Cession (together with Karikal, Mahé and Yanam) was signed on 28 May 1956; instruments of ratification were signed on 16 Aug. 1962 from which date (by the 14th amendment to the Indian Constitution) Pondicherry, comprising the 4 territories, became a Union Territory.

Area and Population. The territory forms an enclave on the Coromandel Coast of Tamil Nadu, with Karikal forming a separate enclave further south. The total area of Pondicherry is 492 sq. km, divided into 4 Districts: Pondicherry, Karikal, Mahe and Yanam. Population (1981 census), 604,471; density, 1,229 per sq. km.; growth rate, 1971–81, 28·15%. Pondicherry Municipality had (1981) 162,639 inhabitants. The principal languages spoken are French, English, Tamil, Telegu and Malayalam.

Government. By the Government of Union Territories Act 1963 Pondicherry is governed by a Lieut.-Governor, appointed by the President, and a Council of Ministers responsible to a Legislative Assembly. The election in March 1985 returned a Congress and Anna-DMK coalition.

Lieut.-Governor: K. Prabhakara Rao.

Planning. Outlay for 1983–84 was Rs 205m. Of this, Rs 32·3m. was for agriculture, Rs 93·6m. for social and community services, Rs 28·4m. for irrigation, flood control and power development, Rs 20·4m. for transport and communications and Rs 14·9m. for industry.

Budget. Budget estimates for 1982–83 show revenue receipts of Rs 399·3m.

Electricity. Power is bought from neighbouring states. All main villages have electricity and there is a programme under the Sixth Plan to bring power to hut-dwellers. Consumption, 1982–83, 183·96m. units: 51·5% in industry, 28% in agriculture. Peak demand, 46·69 mw.

Agriculture. Nearly 45% of the population is engaged in agriculture and allied pursuits; 89% of the cultivated area is irrigated. The main food crop is rice. Estimated foodgrain production, 120,000 tonnes from 39,915 hectares in 1981–82, of which 99,000 tonnes was paddy; cash crops include groundnuts (11,700 tonnes), cotton (9,350 bales of 180 kg) and sugar-cane (200,000 tonnes).

Industry. There are 12 large and medium-scale industries manufacturing consumer goods such as textiles, sugar, cotton yarn, paper, spirits and beer, and employing 14,143 people in 1983. There were 11,766 people employed in 1,738 small industrial units engaged in varied manufacturing.

Railways. Pondicherry is on a branch from the main Madurai–Madras line.

Aviation. The nearest airport is Madras.

Education. There were, in July 1983, 97 pre-primary schools (4,399 pupils and 124 teachers), 324 primary schools (42,195 and 1,357), 103 middle schools (44,137 and 1,388), 61 high schools (33,658 and 1,253) and 18 higher secondary schools (16,783 and 582). There were 9 general education colleges, a medical college, a law college, a technical higher secondary school and a polytechnic; these had a total of 6,077 students; there were also professional and vocational colleges.

Health. In 1983 there were 10 hospitals and 40 health centres, one doctor to each 1,100 population, and one hospital bed to each 250.

INDONESIA

Capital: Jakarta
Population: 158m. (1983)
GNP per capita: US$520 (1982)

Republik Indonesia

HISTORY. In the 16th century Portuguese traders in quest of spices settled in some of the islands, but were ejected by the British, who in turn were ousted by the Dutch (1595). From 1602 the Netherlands East India Company conquered the Netherlands East Indies, and ruled them until the dissolution of the company in 1798. Thereafter the Netherlands Government ruled the colony from 1816 to 1941, when it was occupied by the Japanese until 1945. An independent republic was proclaimed by Dr Sukarno and Dr Hatta on 17 Aug. 1945.

Complete and unconditional sovereignty was transferred to the Republic of the United States of Indonesia on 27 Dec. 1949, except for the western part of New Guinea, the status of which was to be determined through negotiations between Indonesia and the Netherlands within one year after the transfer of sovereignty. A union was created to regulate the relationship between the two countries. A settlement of the New Guinea (Irian Jaya) question was, however, delayed until 15 Aug. 1962, when, through the good offices of the United Nations, an agreement was concluded for the transfer of the territory to Indonesia on 1 May 1963. In Feb. 1956 Indonesia abrogated the union and in Aug. 1956 repudiated Indonesia's debt to the Netherlands.

During 1950 the federal system which had sprung up in 1946–48 (*see* THE STATESMAN'S YEAR-BOOK, 1950, p. 1233) was abolished, and Indonesia was again made a unitary state. The provisional constitution was passed by the Provisional House of Representatives on 14 and came into force on 17 Aug. 1950. On 5 July 1959 by Presidential decree, the Constitution of 1945 was reinstated and the Constituent Assembly dissolved. For history 1960–66 *see* THE STATESMAN'S YEAR-BOOK, 1982–83, p. 678.

On 11–12 March 1966 the military commanders under the leadership of Lieut. Gen. Suharto took over the executive power while leaving President Sukarno as the head of State. The Communist Party was at once outlawed and the National Front was dissolved in Oct. 1966. On 22 Feb. 1967 Sukarno handed over all his powers to Gen. Suharto.

AREA AND POPULATION. Indonesia, covering a total land area of 741,101 sq. miles (1,919,400 sq. km), consists of some 13,700 islands extending about 3,200 miles east to west through three time-zones (East, Central and West Standard time) of 1 hour's difference. Among the largest islands are Sumatra, Java and Madura, Bali, Kalimantan (Indonesian Borneo), Sulawesi (Celebes) and Irian Jaya (the western part of New Guinea). In addition there are two large groups of islands: Maluku (the Moluccas) and Nusa Tenggara (the Lesser Sundas).

The total population in 1980 (census) was 147,490,298, distributed as follows:

Province	*Sq. km*	*Census 1980*	*Chief town*	*Census 1980*
Aceh (D.I.)	59,904	2,611,271	Banda Aceh	...
Sumatera Utara	71,104	8,360,894	Medan	1,378,955
Sumatera Barat	49,333	3,406,816	Padang	480,922
Riau	124,084	2,168,535	Pakanbaru	186,262
Jambi	62,150	1,445,994	Telanaipura	230,373
Sumatera Selatan	104,363	4,629,801	Palembang	787,187
Bengkulu	20,760	768,064	Bengkulu	...
Lampung	33,866	4,624,785	Tanjungkarang	284,275
Sumatra	524,097	28,016,160		

Province	*Sq. km*	*Census 1980*	*Chief town*	*Census 1980*
Jakarta Raya (D.C.I.)	592	6,503,449	Jakarta	6,503,449
Jawa Barat	49,144	27,453,525	Bandung	1,462,637
Jawa Tengah	34,353	25,372,889	Semarang	1,026,671
Yogyakarta (D.I.)	3,090	2,750,813	Yogyakarta	398,727
Jawa Timur	46,865	29,188,852	Surabaya	2,027,913
Jawa and Madura	134,044	91,269,528		
Kalimantan Barat	157,066	2,486,068	Pontianak	304,778
Kalimantan Tengah	156,552	954,353	Palangkaraya	...
Kalimantan Selatan	33,966	2,064,649	Banjarmasin	381,286
Kalimantan Timur	202,619	1,218,016	Samarinda	264,718
Kalimantan	550,203	6,723,086		
Sulawesi Utara	24,200	2,115,384	Menado	217,159
Sulawesi Tengah	88,655	1,289,635	Palu	...
Sulawesi Selatan	83,799	6,062,212	Ujung Padang	709,038
Sulawesi Tenggara	32,454	942,302	Kendari	...
Sulawesi	229,108	10,409,533		
Bali	5,623	2,469,930	Denpasar	...
Nusu Tenggara Barat	21,740	2,724,664	Mataram	...
Nusu Tenggara Timur	48,889	2,737,166	Kupang	...
Loro Sae [1]	14,925	555,350	Dili	...
Maluku	83,675	1,411,006	Amboina	208,898
Irian Jaya	421,981	1,173,875	Jajapura	...
Palau–Palau Lain	596,833	11,071,991		
Totals	2,034,255	147,490,298		

[1] Formerly Portuguese East Timor.

Other major cities (census 1980): Malang, 511,780; Surakarta, 469,888; Bogor, 247,409; Cirebon, 223,776; Kediri, 221,830 and Madiun, 150,502 (all on Java); Balik papan on Kalimantan, 280,875. Estimate (1983) 158m.

The principal ethnic groups are the Aceh, Bataks and Minangkabaus in Sumatra, the Javanese and Sundanese in Java, the Madurese in Madura, the Balinese in Bali, the Sasaks in Lombok, the Menadonese, Minahas, Torajas and Buginese in Sulawesi, the Dayaks in Kalimantan, Irianese in Irian Jaya, the Ambonese in the Moluccas and Timorese in Timor Timur.

Bahasa Indonesia is the official language of the Republic.

CLIMATE. Conditions vary greatly over this spread of islands, but generally the climate is tropical monsoon, with a dry season from June to Sept. and a wet one from Oct. to April. Temperatures are high all the year and rainfall varies according to situation on lee or windward shores. Jakarta. Jan. 78°F (25·6°C), July 78°F (25·6°C). Annual rainfall 71″ (1,775 mm). Padang. Jan. 79°F (26·7°C), July 79°F (26·7°C). Annual rainfall 177″ (4,427 mm). Surabaya. Jan. 79°F (27·2°C), July 78°F (25·6°C). Annual rainfall 51″ (1,285 mm).

CONSTITUTION AND GOVERNMENT. Indonesia is a sovereign, independent republic.

The People's Consultative Assembly is the supreme power. It has 920 members and it sits at least once every 5 years. The House of People's Representatives has 460 members, 360 of them elected and 100 nominated by the President upon recommendation and sits for a 5-year term.

General elections to the 360 elected seats in the House of Representatives were held on 4 May 1982 and 244 seats were won by the Golkar Party

President, Prime Minister and Minister of Defence: Gen. Suharto, elected by the People's Consultative Assembly in 1968 and re-elected in 1973, 1978 and 1983.

Vice-President: Gen. Umar Wirahadikusumah. *Minister Coordinator for Political Affairs and Security:* Surono. *Minister Coordinator for the Economy, Finance, Industry and Development Supervision:* Dr Ali Wardhana. *Minister Coordinator for Public Welfare:* H. Alamsjah Ratu Perwiranegara. *State Minister and Secretary of State:* Sudharmono. *State Minister for National Development Planning and Chairman of the National Development Planning Agency:* Dr J. B. Sumarlin. *State Minister for Research and Technology and Chairman of the Agency for Research and Applied Technology:* Prof. B. J. Habibie. *State Minister for Population Affairs and the Environment:* Dr Emil Salim. *State Minister for Housing:* Dr Cosmas Batubara. *State Minister for Youth Affairs and Sports:* Dr Abdul Gafur. *State Minister for Administrative Reform and Vice Chairman of the National Development Planning Agency:* Dr Saleh Afiff. *State Minister for Women's Affairs:* L. Soetanto. *Minister of Home Affairs:* Soepardjo Roestam. *Foreign Affairs:* Dr Mochtar Kusumaatmadja. *Defence and Security:* Gen. S. Poniman. *Justice:* Ismail Saleh. *Information:* H. Harmoko. *Finance:* Dr Radius Prawiro. *Trade:* Dr Rachmat Saleh. *Cooperatives:* Bustanil Arifin. *Agriculture:* Achmad Affandi. *Forestry:* Soedjarwo. *Industries:* Hartarto. *Mines and Energy:* Dr Subroto. *Public Works:* Suyono Sosrodarsono. *Communications:* Roesmin Nurjadin. *Tourism, Post and Telecommunications:* Achmad Tahir. *Manpower:* Sudomo. *Transmigration:* Martono. *Education and Culture:* Dr Nugroho Notosusanto. *Health:* Dr Suwardjono Surjaningrat. *Religious Affairs:* H. Munawir Sjadzali. *Social Affairs:* Nani Soedarsono. *Commander-in-Chief of the Armed Forces:* Gen. L. B. Murdani.

There are 5 junior ministers.

National flag: Horizontally red over white.

National anthem: Indonesia Raya (tune by Wage Rudolf Supratman, 1928).

DEFENCE. The Indonesian Armed Forces were formally set up on 5 Oct. 1945. On 11 Oct. 1967 the Army, Navy, Air Force and Police were integrated under the Department of Defence and Security. Their commanders no longer hold cabinet rank. There is selective military service.

Army. There are 4 infantry divisions, 1 armoured cavalry brigade, 2 independent infantry brigades, 2 airborne infantry brigades, 1 artillery regiment, 1 engineer and 2 air defence regiments, 15 artillery battalions. Equipment includes 93 AMX-13 and 41 PT-76 light tanks. Total strength in 1985 was 210,000.

Navy. The fleet comprises 2 diesel powered patrol submarines, 10 small frigates, 4 fast missile boats, 2 fast torpedo boats, 14 patrol vessels, 2 fleet minesweepers, 8 small patrol craft, 15 landing ships, 2 landing craft, 3 training ships, 4 surveying vessels, 2 command and submarine support ships, 1 destroyer depot ship, 1 repair ship, 1 cable ship, 4 oilers, 10 auxiliaries, 60 minor landing craft, 20 service craft and 10 tugs. Of the 104 ships acquired from the USSR very few now remain. The naval air arm has 73 aircraft, including 23 helicopters. There are 71 customs patrol cutters, 6 maritime security agency boats, 35 Army vessels, 6 Air Force boats and 30 armed marine police craft.

Naval personnel in 1985 numbered 35,000 officers and men, including 5,000 of the Marine Commando Corps and 1,000 in the Naval Air Arm.

Air Force. Operational combat units comprise two squadrons of A-4E Skyhawk attack aircraft, and single squadrons of F-5E Tiger II fighters and OV-10F Bronco twin-turboprop counter-insurgency aircraft. There are 3 transport squadrons, equipped with turboprop C-130 Hercules, Nurtanio/CASA NC-212 Aviocar and F27 Friendship aircraft, and piston-engined C-47s, plus 3 specially equipped Boeing 737 dual-purpose maritime surveillance/transports; and an assortment of other aircraft in transport, helicopter and training units including 16 Hawk attack/trainers, 25 T-34C-1 armed turboprop trainers, and 20 Swiss-built AS 202 Bravo piston-engined primary trainers. On order are 32 CN-235 twin-turboprop transports and a large number of MBB NBO 105, Super Puma and Bell 412 helicopters, all from Nurtanio of Indonesia. Personnel (1984) approximately 25,000.

INTERNATIONAL RELATIONS

Membership. Indonesia is a member of UN and ASEAN.

ECONOMY

Planning. The fourth Five-Year Development Plan (1984–89) gives priority to increasing production and services in agriculture, manufacturing, mining, communications and transportation, and tourist industries.

Budget. The ordinary budget, excluding the development budget, was as follows in 1983–84 (in Rp. 1m.): Gross revenue, 16,565,000m.; gross expenditure, 16,565,000m.

Currency. The monetary unit is the *rupiah* (abbreviated Rp.), divided into 100 *sen.* There are banknotes of 1, 2½, 5, 10, 25, 50 and 100 rupiahs and aluminium coins of 1, 5, 10, 25 and cupro-nickel coins of 50 sen.

In March 1985 there were 1,168 rupiahs=£1 sterling; 1,097 rupiahs=US$1.

Banking. The Bank Indonesia, formerly the Java Bank, established in 1828, was made the central bank of Indonesia on 1 July 1953. It had an original capital of Rp. 25m.; a reserve fund of Rp. 18m. and a special reserve of Rp. 84m.

There are 86 commercial banks, 29 development banks and several other financial institutions. Commercial banking is dominated by 5 state-owned banks: Bank Rakyat Indonesia provides services to smallholder agriculture and rural development; Bank Bumi Daya, estate agriculture and forestry; Bank Negara Indonesia 1946, industry; Bank Dagang Negara, mining; and Bank Ekspor-Imurpor Indonesia, production of exports.

There are 70 private national commercial banks owned and operated by Indonesians and 10 of these are licensed to deal in foreign exchange. The 11 foreign banks (of which one is a joint-venture) include the Chartered Bank, the Hongkong and Shanghai Banking Corporation, the Bank of America, the Citibank, the Bank of Tōkyō, Chase Manhattan and the American Express International Banking Corporation.

Weights and Measures. The metric system of weights and measures was officially introduced in Feb. 1923, and came into full operation on 1 Jan. 1938.

The following are the old weights and measures: *Pikol* = 136·16 lb. avoirdupois; *Katti* = 1·36 lb. avoirdupois; *Bau* = 1·7536 acres; *Square Pal* = 227 hectares = 561·16 acres; *Jengkal* = 4 yd; *Pal* (Java) = 1,506 metres; *Pal* (Sumatra) = 1,852 metres.

ENERGY AND NATURAL RESOURCES

Electricity. All gas and electricity undertakings were nationalized by presidential decree of 3 Oct. 1953, retroactive from 23 Dec. 1952. Three large-scale hydro-electric plants are operating on the Jatiluhur and Brantas rivers in Java and on the Asahan River in Sumatra. Electricity capacity, 1984, 4,631m. mw.

Oil. Indonesia is the principal producer of petroleum in the Far East, production coming from Sumatra, Kalimantan (Indonesian Borneo) and Java, where Anglo-Dutch and US interests operate. Indonesia is the tenth largest OPEC producer. The 1983 (preliminary) output of crude oil was 387m. bbls.

Gas. Pertamina, the state oil company, started to pump natural gas to Jakarta in 1979.

Minerals. The high cost of extraction means that little of the large mineral resources outside Java is exploited; however, there is copper mining in Irian Jaya, nickel mining and processing on Sulawesi, aluminium smelting in northern Sumatra. Coal production (1982) 480,985 tons. Output (in 1,000 tons, 1982) of bauxite was 700·25; iron sand, 136·52; copper, 223·70; silver, 3,051·74 kg; gold, 222·37 kg; nickel 1,640·92. In 1982 tin production was 26,218 tons.

Agriculture. Rice production (1983), 23·5m. tonnes. In 1982 production was (in

1,000 tons): Copra, 1,736; sugar, 1,862; rubber, 861; palm oil, 873; tea, 92; cloves, 32.

Livestock (1983): Cattle, 6,734,000; buffaloes, 2,513,000; horses, 658,000; sheep, 4,231,000; goats, 7,891,000; pigs, 3,587,000.

Forestry. The forest area is 113m. hectares. Production (1981): All timber, 27·38m. cu. metres.

Fisheries. In 1983 the catch of sea fisheries was 2m. tonnes.

INDUSTRY AND TRADE

Industry. There are shipyards at Jakarta Raya, Surabaya, Semarang and Amboina. There are many textile factories (total production in 1982–83, 1,708·9m. metres), large paper factories (296,900 tons, 1982–83), match factories, automobile and bicycle assembly works, large construction works, tyre factories, glass factories, a caustic soda and other chemical factories. Production (1982–83): Cement, 7,650,000 tons; fertilizers, 2,153,000 tons; glass, 43,571,720 tons; 7·4m. cycle tyres; 6,806,000 cu. metres of oxygen; 305,000 cu. metres of acetylene.

For details of nationalization *see* THE STATESMAN'S YEAR-BOOK, 1981–82, p. 677.

Trade Unions. The largest group of trade unions in Indonesia is the Serekat Organasasi Karyawan Seluruh Indonesia (SOKSI), the Central Council of All Indonesia Trade Unions, with a membership of 2·6m., to which 28 national unions and 832 local unions are affiliated. The second largest is the Kongres Buruh Seluruh Indonesia (KBSI), the All Indonesia Trades Union Congress, with a membership of nearly 400,000. To the KBSI 25 national unions and 54 local unions are affiliated. There are also the HISSBI (Federation of Indonesian Trade Unions) with a membership of 180,203, and the KBKI (Indonesian Democratic Labour Organization), with a membership of 94,477. In addition, there are also trade-union centres which are closely connected with the Islamic Parties.

Commerce. Imports and exports (including oil) in US$1m. for year April–March:

	1979	*1980*	*1981*	*1982*
Imports	7,202·3	10,834·4	13,272·0	16,858·9
Exports	15,590·1	21,908·9	22,260·3	22,293·3

The main export items (in US$1m.) in 1982 were: Oil and gas, 18,365·7; coffee, 341·7; rubber, 602·1; palm-oil and kernels, 97·2; tin ore, 378·8; tea, 89·5; tobacco, 38·0; copper, 117·6; forestry products, 965·8; fishery products, 229·5.

The main import items are non-crude oil, rice, consumer goods, fertilizer, chemicals, weaving yarn, iron and steel, industrial and business machinery.

Total trade between Indonesia and UK (British Department of Trade returns, in £1,000 sterling):

	1980	*1981*	*1982*	*1983*	*1984*
Imports to UK	56,971	73,756	91,704	169,454	181,490
Exports and re-exports from UK	112,170	139,236	212,066	193,642	186,736

Tourism. In 1983 about 644,000 tourists visited Indonesia mainly from USA, Australia, Japan, Netherlands, Germany, France, UK and Singapore.

COMMUNICATIONS

Roads. Most cities on Java, Sumatra, Sulawesi and Bali are connected by highways or secondary roads. The Trans-Sumatra trunk road connecting Aceh (north) and Lampung (south) and the Trans-Sulawesi highway were nearing completion in 1984. The feeder-road between West Sumatra and Riau provinces was completed with the building of the bridge over the Kampai River at Pekanbaru in 1971. Motor vehicles, at 31 Dec. 1979, totalled 577,345 passenger cars, 383,648 vans and trucks, 69,545 buses and about 2,266,183 motor cycles.

Railways. In 1982 the State Railways totalled 6,877 km, comprising 4,922 km of 1,067 mm gauge on Java, and 1,458 km of 1,067 mm gauge and 497 km of 750 mm gauge on Sumatra. In 1982–83, railways carried 6,105m. passenger-km and 917m. tonne-km.

Aviation. Indonesia has 14 major airports: 4 on Java, 3 on Sumatra, 2 on Sulawesi and one each on Bali, Kalimantan, Timor, Maluku and Irian Jaya. Construction of a new international airport, 18 miles west of Jakarta at Cengkareng, began in 1981. This will replace Jakarta's present international airport. The Government and KLM in 1949 set up 'Garuda Indonesian Airways' as a mixed enterprise on a 50–50 capital basis under KLM management. The agreement was to last until 1960. In 1954, however, the Government bought up the shares held by KLM for 15m. guilders and nationalized GIA; and in Jan. 1958, the Government unilaterally terminated the contracts with the technical assistants provided by KLM. GIA maintains a direct service between Jakarta and Manila, Bangkok, Hong Kong, Tōkyō and Amsterdam.

Shipping. There are 16 ports for oceangoing ships, the largest of which is Tanjung Priok, which serves the Jakarta area and has a container terminal. The national shipping company Pelajaran Nasional Indonesia (PELNI) maintains interinsular communications. The Jakarta Lloyd maintains regular services between Jakarta, Amsterdam, Hamburg and London.

Post and Broadcasting. In 1979 the postal and telegraph services of Indonesia included 2,796 post offices. There were 660 telegraph offices which handled 3·9m. domestic and 488,000 international cables. Post offices handled 176m. letters and Rp. 250,000m. in money orders, Giro and postal cheques. Deposits with post office savings accounts, Rp. 31,210m. Number of telephones (1982), 600,643.

Radio Republik Indonesia, under the Department of Information, operates 26 stations. In 1982 there were 1·8m. television and 20m. radio receivers.

Newspapers (1980). There were about 120 daily newspaper publishers with estimated daily circulation of 1·7m. There were 270 publishers of weekly papers and magazines with a circulation of 3·5m.

JUSTICE, RELIGION, EDUCATION AND WELFARE

Justice. There are courts of first instance, high courts of appeal in every provincial capital and a Supreme Court of Justice for the whole of Indonesia in Jakarta. Administrative matters on judicial organization are under the direction of the Department of Justice.

In civil law the population is divided into three main groups: Indonesians, Europeans and foreign Orientals, to whom different law systems are applicable. When, however, people from different groups are involved, a system of so-called 'inter-gentile' law is applied.

The present criminal law, which has been in force since 1918, is codified and is based on European penal law. This law is equally applicable to all groups of the population. For private and commercial law, however, there are various systems applicable for the various groups of the population. For the Indonesians, a system of private and agrarian law is applicable; this is called Adat Law, and is mainly uncodified. For the other groups the prevailing private and commercial law system is codified in the Private Law Act (1847) and the Commercial Law Act (1847). These Acts have their origins in the French *Code Civile* and *Code du Commerce* through the similar Dutch codifications. These Acts are entirely applicable to Indonesian citizens and to Europeans, whereas to foreign Orientals they are applicable with some exceptions, mainly in the fields of family law and inheritance. Penal law was in the process of being codified in 1981.

Religion. Religious liberty is granted to all denominations. The majority of the Indonesians are Moslems. There are nearly 6m. Christians; their main strength is in Central and East Java, North Sulawesi, East Nusa Tenggara, the Moluccas and Irian Jaya. There are also about 1m. Buddhists, probably for the greater part Chinese. Hinduism has 6m. members, of whom 2·5m. are on Bali.

In 1978–79 there were 423,570 Islamic houses of worship, 24,215 Christian (7,052 of them Catholic), 4,365 Hindu and 1,762 Buddhist.

Education. Pupils and teachers in 1982 (1,000):

	Pupils	*Teachers*
Primary	23,900	713
Secondary	5,532	328
Technological	300	27

English is the first foreign language taught in schools. Literacy rate was 72% in 1984.

There are 51 universities (23 are private).

Health. In 1981–82 there were 1,224 hospitals, 17,000 health centres and 15,400 doctors.

DIPLOMATIC REPRESENTATIVES

Of Indonesia in Great Britain (38 Grosvenor Sq., London W1X 9AD)
Ambassador: Sjahabuddin Arifin (accredited on 12 Nov. 1981).

Of Great Britain in Indonesia (Jalan, M.H. Thamrin, 75, Jakarta)
Ambassador: Alan E. Donald, CMG.

Of Indonesia in the USA (2020 Massachusetts Ave., NW, Washington, D.C., 20036)
Ambassador: A. Hasnan Habib.

Of the USA in Indonesia (Medan Merdeka Selatan 5, Jakarta)
Ambassador: John H. Holdridge.

Of Indonesia to the United Nations
Ambassador: Ali Alatas.

Books of Reference

Economic Update 1984. National Development Information Office, Jakarta, 1984
Indonesia 1984. Department of Information, Jakarta, 1984
Bee, O. J., *The Petroleum Resources of Indonesia.* OUP, 1982
Bemmelen, R. W. van, *Geology of Indonesia.* 2 vols. The Hague, 1949
Echols, J. M., and Shadily, H., *An Indonesian–English Dictionary.* 3rd ed. Cornell Univ. Press, 1975
Leifer, M., *Indonesia's Foreign Policy.* London, 1983
McDonald, H., *Suharto's Indonesia.* Univ. Press of Hawaii, 1981
Neill, W. T., *Twentieth-Century Indonesia.* Columbia Univ. Press, 1973
Papenek, G., *The Indonesian Economy.* Eastbourne, 1980
Polomka, P., *Indonesia Since Sukarno.* London, 1971
Taylor, A. M., *Indonesian Independence and the United Nations.* Cornell Univ. Press, 1960

IRAN

Jomhori-e-Islami-e-Irân

Capital: Tehrán
Population: 43·83m. (1984)
GNP per capita: US$2,160 (1977)

HISTORY. Persia was ruled by the Shahs as an absolute monarchy until 30 Dec. 1906 when the first Constitution was granted. Reza Khan took control after a *coup d'état* on 31 Oct. 1925 deposed the last Shah of the Qajar Dynasty, and became Reza Shah Pahlavi on 12 Dec. 1925. The country's name was changed to Iran on 21 March 1935. Reza Shah abdicated on 16 Sept. 1941 (and died 25 July 1944) in favour of his son, Mohammad Reza Pahlavi (born 26 Oct. 1919).

Following widespread civil unrest, the Shah left Iran with his family on 17 Jan. 1979 (and died in Egypt 27 July 1980). The Ayatollah Ruhollah Khomeini, spiritual leader of the Shi'a Moslem community, returned from 15 years exile on 1 Feb. 1979 and appointed a provisional government on 5 Feb. The Shah's government resigned and Parliament dissolved itself on 11 Feb. Following a referendum in March, an Islamic Republic was proclaimed on 1 Apr. 1979. In 1980 Iraq invaded Iran and the war was continuing in early 1984.

In Sept. 1980 war began with Iraq with destruction of some Iranian towns and damage to the oil installations at Abadán. The war was still in progress in early 1985.

AREA AND POPULATION. Iran is bounded north by the USSR and the Caspian Sea, east by Afghánistán and Pakistan, south by the Gulf of Oman and the Persian Gulf, and west by Iraq and Turkey. It has an area of about 1,648,000 sq. km (636,000 sq. miles), but a vast portion is desert, and the average density is only (1982) 25 inhabitants to the sq. km.

The population at recent censuses was as follows: (1956) 18,944,821; (1966) 25,781,090; (1976) 33,708,744. Estimate (1984) 43·83m.

The populations (census 1976) and capitals of the provinces *(ostán)* were:

Azarbáiján Bákhtari	1,407,970	Rezáyeh	Hamadán	1,093,079	Hamadán
Azarbáiján Khavari	3,204,761	Tabriz	Ilam	242,812	Abdanan
Bakhtiári va Chahár Mahál	398,807	Shahr Kord	Kermán	1,085,097	Kermán
Balúchestán va Sistán	662,677	Záhedán	Kermánsháhán	1,025,257	Kermánsháh
Boyer ahmadi va Kohkiluyeh	242,207	Yasoof	Khorásán	3,250,085	Mashhad
Bushehr	347,703	Bushehr	Khuzestán	2,187,198	Ahváz
Esfáhán	1,971,745	Esfáhán	Kordestán	783,740	Sánándáj
Fárs	2,020,942	Shiráz	Lorestan	932,297	Khorramábád
Gilán	1,579,317	Rasht	Markazi	6,954,729	Tehrán
			Mázándárán	2,386,956	Sári
			Semnán	487,531	Semnán
			Yazd	358,082	Yazd
			Zanjan	577,286	Zanjan

The principal cities at census 1976 were:

Tehrán	4,496,159	Qom	246,831	Karaj	138,774
Esfáhán	671,825	Rasht	187,203	Qazvin	138,527
Mashhad	670,180	Rezáyeh	163,991	Yazd	135,978
Tabriz	598,576	Hamadán	155,846	Arak	114,507
Shiráz	416,408	Ardabil	147,404	Desful	110,287
Ahváz	329,006	Khorramshahr	146,709	Khorramábád	104,928
Abadán	296,081	Kermán	140,309	Borujerd	100,103

The national language is Farsi or Persian, spoken by 45% of the population. 23% spoke related languages, including Kurdish and Luri in the west and Baluchi in the south-east, while 26% spoke Turkic languages, primarily the Azarbáijáni-speaking peoples of the north-west and the Turkomen of Khorásan in the north-east.

CLIMATE. Mainly a desert climate, but with more temperate conditions on the shores of the Caspian Sea. Seasonal range of temperature is considerable. Abadán. Jan. 54°F (12·2°C), July 97°F (36·1°C). Annual rainfall 8" (204 mm). Tehrán. Jan. 36°F (2·2°C), July 85°F (29·4°C). Annual rainfall 10" (246 mm).

CONSTITUTION AND GOVERNMENT. The Constitution of the Islamic Republic was approved by a national referendum in Dec. 1979. It gives supreme authority to a religious leader (*wali faqih*), which position will be held by Ayatollah Khomeini for the rest of his natural life, and thereafter be elected by the Moslem clergy.

The President of the Republic is popularly-elected for a 4-year term and is head of the executive; he appoints a Prime Minister and other Ministers, subject to approval by the *Majlis*.

Presidents since the establishment of the Islamic Republic:

Abolhassan Bani-Sadr, 4 Feb. 1980–22 June 1981 (deposed)

Mohammad Ali Raja'i, 24 July 1981–30 Aug. 1981 (assassinated).

The Cabinet was composed as follows in Aug. 1984.

President: Hojatolislam Sayed Ali Khamenei (from 12 Oct. 1981).

Prime Minister: Mir Hussein Moussavi.

Foreign Affairs: Dr Ali Akbar Vellayati. *Interior:* Hojatolislam Ali Akbar Nateq Nouri. *Defence:* (Vacant). *Labour and Social Affairs:* Abdul Ghasem Sar Hadizadeh. *Education and Training:* Ali Akbar Parvaresh. *Islamic Guidance:* (Vacant). *Commerce:* Hassen Abedi Jafari. *Health:* Dr Ali Reza Marandi. *Posts and Telecommunications:* Morteza Nabavi. *Justice:* Dr Hassan Ebrahim Habibi. *Roads and Transport:* Hadinezhad Hoseyniyan. *Industry:* Sayyed Mostafa Hashemi. *Higher Education and Culture:* Dr Iraj Fazel. *Mines and Metals:* Hussain Nili Ahmad Abadi. *Agriculture:* Abbas Ali Zali. *Housing and Urban Development:* Sarajuddin Karerumi. *Energy:* Dr Hassan Ghafuri-Fard. *Oil:* Sayyed Mohammed Gharazi. *Heavy Industry:* Behzad Nabavi. *Economic Affairs and Finance:* Dr Hussein Namazi. *Ministers of State:* Dr Mohammad Taqi Banki *(Planning and Budget)*, Gholamreza Agazadeh *(Executive Affairs)*.

Legislative power is held by a 270-member Islamic Consultative Assembly *(Majlis)*, directly elected for a 4-year term on 17 May 1984; but all legislation is subject to approval by a 12-member Council of Guardians who ensure it is in accordance with the Islamic code and with the Constitution. Six members of this constitutional Council are appointed by the *wali faqih* and six by the judiciary.

National flag: Three horizontal stripes of green, white and red; on the borders of the green and red stripes the legend *Allah Akbar* in white Kufi script repeated 22 times in all; in the centre of the white stripe the national emblem in red.

Local Government. The country is divided into 21 provinces *(ostán)* and 2 governor-generalships; these are sub-divided into 172 *shahrestán* (counties), each under a *farmándár* (governor) and thence into 499 *bakhsh* (districts), each under a *bakhshdár*. The districts are sub-divided into *dehistán* (groups of villages) each under a *dehdár*, each village having its elected *kadkhodá* (headman).

DEFENCE. Two years' military service is compulsory.

Army. The Army consisted (1985) of 250,000 men (100,000 conscripts), with some 400,000 reservists. It is organized in 3 armoured, 7 infantry and 1 airborne divisions, and auxiliary units. Equipment includes 190 T-54/-55/ 62, 100 T-72, 300 Chieftain, 300 M-47/ 48 and 150 M-60A1 main battle tanks. There is also a 250,000-strong Revolutionary Guard Corps.

Navy. The fleet, declining since the revolution, before the war comprised 3 very old destroyers, 4 frigates, 4 old corvettes, 3 old coastal minesweepers, 2 inshore minesweepers, 7 patrol boats, 14 hovercraft, 2 landing ships, 1 landing craft, 2 supply ships, 1 repair ship, 2 oilers, 4 survey vessels, 1 water carrier and 3 tugs. There were also 30 coastguard cutters and 2 customs craft.

The construction of 12 fast missile craft in France was to have been completed by mid-1979, but later boats did not receive their missiles and the last 3 boats were embargoed in France. They eventually sailed on 2 Aug. 1981 but one was seized by a Royalist group off Cadiz and after she surrendered to the French all three were sent to Iran in a merchant ship to obviate further trouble.

The naval air arm comprised 14 assorted aircraft and 20 helicopters.

Naval personnel nominally totalled 20,000 officers and ratings including cadets, apprentices and marines, but considerably fewer than 10,000 were active in 1985.

With war following revolution and withdrawal of UK and US maintenance teams the fleet lacks spares and the navy has run down, several ships being laid up. The situation was worsened by cessation of foreign help in training semi-illiterate conscripts and with poor morale following general instability and casualties the above ships do not represent an efficient maritime force.

Claims of sinkings during the Iran-Iraq war have not been officially confirmed. Figures for ship and personnel strengths should be interpreted with caution.

Air Force. In Aug. 1955 the Air Force became a separate and independent arm, and had a strength of about 23 first-line squadrons (each 15 aircraft, plus reserves), with 100,000 personnel before the 1979 revolution. Strength (1985) was estimated at 20,000 personnel and 50 serviceable combat aircraft. The latter include some MiG-19/Chinese-built F-6 fighter-bombers, supplied via North Korea, and surviving US fighters that might total 40 F-5E Tiger II and 4 F-4D/E Phantom II fighter-bombers, plus a few RF-4E reconnaissance-fighters. Transport aircraft include F27s and Boeing 707s and 747s, some equipped as flight refuelling tankers. The status of the large fleet of CH-47C Chinook, Bell Model 214 and other helicopters is not known; but two P-3F Orion maritime patrol aircraft remain operational. Training aircraft include Bonanza basic trainers and 6 turboprop PC-7 Turbo-Trainers.

INTERNATIONAL RELATIONS

Membership. Iran is a member of UN, OPEC and the Colombo Plan.

ECONOMY

Planning. The sixth 5-year development plan, 1978–83 was abandoned following the revolution.

Budget. Budget estimate for year commencing 21 March 1981: Revenue 2,025,000m. *rials*; expenditure 3,300,000m. *rials*.

Currency. The Iranian unit of currency is the *rial* sub-divided into 100 *dinars*.

Notes in circulation are of denominations of 5–10,000 *rials*. Coins in circulation are bronze–aluminium and copper, 50 *dinar*; silver alloy, 1, 2, 5, 10 and 20 *rials*. In March 1985, US$1 = 97·21 *rials*; £1 = 102 *rials*.

Banking. The *Bank Markazi Iran* was established in 1960 as the note-issuing authority and government bank of Iran. All other banks were nationalized in June 1979, and re-organized into 8 new state banking corporations.

All insurance companies were nationalized in June 1979.

Weights and Measures. By a law passed on 8 Jan. 1933, the official weights and measures are those of the metric system.

The Iranian year is a solar year running from 21 March to 20 March; the Hejira year 1362 corresponds to the Christian year 21 March 1984–20 March 1985.

ENERGY AND NATURAL RESOURCES

Electricity. Electric energy installed capacity, 1980, was 5·3m. kw., and 17,150m. kwh. was generated.

Oil. For a history of Iran's oil industry 1951–79, *see* STATESMAN'S YEAR-BOOK, 1982–83.

The petroleum industry was seriously disrupted by the 1979 revolution, and many facilities, including the vast refinery at Abadan, the new refinery at Bandar Khomeini and the tanker terminal at Kharg Island, have been destroyed or put out of action during the Gulf war with Iraq. All operating companies were nationalised in 1979 and operations are now run by the National Petrochemical Company.

Total production of petroleum, 73·7m. tonnes, 1980 (113·2m. tonnes, 1979).

Gas. Natural gas production (1979) was 44,300m. cu. metres.

Minerals. Iran has substantial mineral deposits relatively underdeveloped. Production figures for 1977 (in 1,000 tonnes): Iron ore, 670; coal, 900; zinc, 62; lead, 40; manganese, 15; chromite, 80; salt (1973), 500.

Agriculture. Reliable statistics of production are not available. It is estimated, however, that out of 164·8m. hectares of land area only 16,857,000 are crop land (including 10,300 hectares fallow), 27·8m. hectares are forests and ranges and 32·7m. hectares are potentially cultivable waste.

Crop returns for 1982 (in 1,000 tonnes): Wheat, 6,500; barley, 1,200; rice, 1,400; sugar-beet, 2,100; sugar-cane, 1,300; tobacco, 24.

Wool comes principally from Khorásán, Kermánsháh, Mázandarán and Azerbáiján. Production, 1972, 20,000 tonnes.

Rice is grown largely on the Caspian shores.

Tobacco is grown along the shores of the Caspian. It is purchased by the Tobacco Monopoly and manufactured in the government factory at Tehrán.

Opium, until 1955, was an important export commodity in Iran. On 7 Oct. 1955 an Act was approved by Parliament to prohibit the cultivation and usage of opium.

Livestock (1983): 34·5m. sheep, 13·8m. goats, 8·6m. cattle, 350,000 horses, 27,000 camels, 30,000 pigs, 220,000 buffaloes, and 1·8m. donkeys.

Fisheries. The Caspian Fisheries Co. (Shilát) is a government monopoly. Exports of caviar (1975) were valued at US$72m.

INDUSTRY AND TRADE

Industry. Iran's chief natural products are oil, wool, cotton, silk, fruit, nuts, cereals, vegetables, gum, timber, oil seeds, copper and other metalliferous ores, coal, cattle, sheep and goats. Its principal manufactured or processed products are textiles, carpets, skins, casings, vegetable oil, soap, metal products, plastic products, furniture, beet sugar, tea, tobacco and cigarettes, wine, vodka, soft drinks, caviar, footwear, petroleum products, glass products, tiles, bricks, cement, leather and leather goods, dairy products and manufactured foodstuffs, and printed matter.

Apart from the oil industry, the industries employing most workers are textiles, sugar refining, flour-milling, fruit processing, tea, furniture, printing, leather, matches, glass, building materials and light metal goods. The most popular carpets are manufactured in the environs of Tabriz, Kermán, Arák, Káshán, Esfahán, Shiráz and Hamadán. Esfahán is the traditional textile manufacturing centre, but in recent years important textile mills, particularly cotton, have been built in other towns, including Tehrán. A number of automobile assembly plants have been set up in recent years employing several thousand workers. A steel-mill, a machine-tool factory, a tractor plant and a huge petrochemical complex are also going into production.

Commerce. Imports totalled 863,300m. rials and exports 963,500m. rials in 1980. Crude oil amounted to 73% of exports and refined products to 21%; 27% of exports went to Japan and 12% to Federal Republic of Germany while these two countries each provided 14% of imports.

Total trade between Iran and UK (British Department of Trade returns, in £1,000 sterling):

	1980	*1981*	*1982*	*1983*	*1984*
Imports to UK	107,176	154,385	225,971	100,545	368,572
Exports and re-exports from UK	393,335	402,753	333,715	629,980	703,097

COMMUNICATIONS

Roads. In 1980 there were 24,806 km of first-class roads and 20,484 km of second-class (graded, all weather) roads, and 11,825 km of third class (earth) roads.

In 1974 passenger cars and taxis numbered 119,851; commercial vehicles, 13,193; buses, 2,611, and motor cycles, 19,785.

Railways. The State Railways total 4,567 km, comprising 4,473 km of 1,435 mm gauge of which 145 km electrified and 94 km of 1,676 mm gauge. In 1981–82 the railways ran 4,734m. passenger-km and 5,566m. tonne-km. Construction started in 1983 of a link from Kermán to Zahedán to connect with the network in Pakistan.

Aviation. The principal airlines which link Tehrán with Europe and the Middle East are Air France, British Airways, Ariana, Alitalia, Swissair, LIA, KLM, PIA, SAS, Qantas, SABENA, Lufthansa, Aeroflot and Middle East Air Lines. British Airways, Qantas, Lufthansa, PANAM and Air France also connect Tehrán with the Far East. Aryana (Afghánistán) Airline connects Tehrán with Lebanon, Syria and Afghánistán. British Airways, KLM and SAS operate services to Tehrán and Iran National Airlines Corporation, registered on 29 March 1962, has monopoly rights on all internal flights and also operates in the Persian Gulf; in 1965 it inaugurated European services. The Iranian Government owns 51% of its shares.

Shipping. In 1979, 80·22m. tonnes of goods were loaded at Iranian ports and 15m. tonnes were unloaded.

Navigation on the Lake of Rezáyeh, from Sharaf-Khaneh to Kolmankháneh, is served by some 5 tugs and 9 barges for the transport of goods and passengers. The service runs twice a week. On the river Karun likewise, from Khorramshahr to Ahwáz, an irregular service for cargo only both ways is run by the Iran Transport Co. and the Karun Navigation Co., and some local firms run daily trips by motor boat, for passengers and merchandise. By changing into lighter-draught boats at Ahwáz both can be taken up to Shallili near Shushtar.

Post and Broadcasting. Postal, telegraph and telephone services are administered by the Iranian Ministry of Posts, Telegraphs and Telephones.

There is wireless-telegraph communication between Tehrán and Tabriz, Meshed, Kermánshah, Kermán, Khorramshahr, Bushehr, Yezd, Shiráz and Lingeh and a wireless-telephone link between Tehrán and Tabriz. Tehrán is also in wireless communication with Europe and is linked by wireless telephone with Baghdad, London, Berne and New York. In 1982 the number of telephones was 1,041,939, of which some 423,861 were in Tehrán. Wireless sets numbered 10m. in 1980, and television sets 2·1m.

Cinemas (1975). There were 430 cinemas with 299,191 seats.

Newspapers. There were in 1982, 17 daily papers in Tehrán and other cities. Their circulation is relatively small, *Ettela'át* and *Kayhán* leading with about 220,000 and 350,000 respectively. Two English-language and a French-language daily ceased publication in March 1979.

JUSTICE, RELIGION, EDUCATION AND WELFARE

Justice. A new legal system based on Islamic law was introduced by the new constitution in 1979. The President of the Supreme Court and the public Prosecutor-General are appointed by the *wali faqih* (Ayatollah Khomeini). The Supreme Court has 16 branches and 109 offences carry the death penalty.

Religion. The official religion is the Shia branch of Islam, known as the *Ithna-Ashariyya,* which recognizes 12 Imáms or spiritual successors of the Prophet Mohammad. Of the total population, 96% are *Shiá,* 3% are *Sunni* and 1% non-Moslem (mainly Armenian Christians).

The Gregorian National Armenians form 3 dioceses. There are also a few thousand Roman Catholic Armenians, who have a bishop of their own rite at Esfahán, the bishop of the Latin rite residing at Rezayeh (Urmia). There is an Anglican bishop residing at Esfahán.

Education. The great majority of primary and secondary schools are state schools. Grants are made to private schools. Elementary education in state schools and university education are free; small fees are charged for state-run secondary schools. Text-books are issued free of charge to pupils in the first 4 grades of elementary schools.

In 1978–79 there were 4,403,106 pupils in primary schools and 2,370,341 in secondary schools; there were 256,303 students in technical schools and 57,832 in teacher-training establishments. There were 17 universities and almost 200 other institutes of higher education, with 175,675 students in 1978–79. The Free Islamic University was established after the revolution and in 1983 the International University of Islamic Studies was being organized.

A literary movement was established in 1981 and by 1985, 3m. citizens have participated.

Health. The Ministry of Health controls the health of the country through the Department of Public Health, which has achieved some remarkable results in the fight against malaria; large areas along the Caspian and the Persian Gulf and in Azerbáiján are now free from malaria. Opium addiction has been greatly reduced, and the cultivation of the poppy has been practically eradicated. Programmes to combat tuberculosis, smallpox, trachoma, venereal diseases, etc., have been introduced.

In 1981 about 62,056 hospital beds (33% of them in Tehrán) were available in 579 hospitals. Medical personnel included 10,054 physicians and surgeons and 1,462 dentists.

Social Security. A system of social security benefits covering accident, sickness, retirement, death, marriage, maternity and childbirth and free medical attention and hospitalization for insured contributors and their families is embodied in the Workers' Social Insurance Law, 1960. This law provides for the insurance under the scheme of all workers in receipt of wages or salaries, but is at present being applied to some 683,496 workers employed mainly in industrial and mining establishments employing 10 or more workers. It also provides for the compulsory payment by employers of family allowances to workers with 2 or more children.

DIPLOMATIC REPRESENTATIVES

Of Iran in Great Britain (27 Prince's Gate, London, SW7 1PX)
Chargé d'Affaires: Seyed Jalal Sadatian.

Of Great Britain in Iran (Ave. Ferdowsi, Tehrán)
Head of Interests Section: M. K. O. Simpson-Orlebar, CMG (at Swedish Embassy).

Of Iran in the USA (3005 Massachusetts Ave., NW, Washington, D.C., 20008)
Ambassador: (Vacant).

Of the USA in Iran (260 Takhte Jamshid Ave., Tehrán)
Ambassador: (Vacant).

Of Iran to the United Nations
Ambassador: Dr Said Rajaie-Khorassani.

Books of Reference

Statistical Information: The principal statistical agencies of the Government are. (1) Department of Census, Civil Registration, and Statistics (Ministry of the Interior). *Director-General:* Sayyed Mehdi Hesabi, Publications on demographical statistics, in Persian. (2) Publicity and Information Department of the Seven-year Plan Organization. *Director:* Dr Mohammed Ali Rashti; Publications on industry, labour, agriculture, in English and Persian. (3) Statistical and Economic Research Department of the Bank Melli Iran; Publishes *Monthly Bulletin*, in English and Persian. (4) Customs Department (Ministry of Finance), publishes monthly and annual reports, in French and Persian. (5) and (6) Ministry of Labour and Ministry of Industry and Mines, publish statistical year-books.

Adli, Abolfazl, *Aussenhandel und Aussenwirtschaftspolitik des Iran*. Berlin, 1960
Arberry, A. J. (ed.), *The Cambridge History of Iran*. 8 vols. CUP, 1968ff.
Benard, C., and Zalmay, K., '*The Government of God' Iran's Islamic Republic*. Columbia Univ. Press, 1984
Forbis, W. H., *Fall of the Peacock Throne*. New York, 1979

Haim, S., *Shorter Persian–English Dictionary*. Tehran, 1958
Heikal, M., *Iran: The Untold Story*. New York, 1982
Hiro, D., *Iran under the Ayatollahs*. London, 1985
Katouzian, H., *The Political Economy of Iran*. London, 1981
Keddie, N., *Roots of Revolution*. Yale Univ. Press, 1981
Lambton, A. K. S., *Landlord and Peasant in Persia*. OUP, 1953.—*Persian Vocabulary*. CUP, 1954
Looney, R. E., *The Economic Development of Iran: A Recent Survey with Projections to 1981*. New York, 1973
Nashat, G., *Women and Revolution in Iran*. Boulder, 1983
Rubin, B., *Paved with Good Intentions: The American Experience in Iran*. OUP, 1981
Steinglass, F. J., *A Comprehensive Persian–English Dictionary*. 2nd ed. London, 1930
Stempel, J. D., *Inside the Iranian Revolution*. Indiana Univ. Press, 1981
Sullivan, W. H., *Mission to Iran*. New York, 1981
Zabih, S., *Iran's Revolutionary Upheaval: An Interpretive Essay*. San Francisco, 1979.—*The Mosadegh Era: Roots of the Iranian Revolution*. Chicago, 1982.—*Iran since the Revolution*. London, 1982
Zakhoder, B. N. (ed.), *Sovremennyi Iran*. Moscow, 1957

IRAQ

Capital: Baghdad
Population: 14m. (1982)
GNP per capita: US$3,020 (1980)

al Jumhouriya al 'Iraqia

HISTORY. Part of the Ottoman Empire from the 16th century, Iraq was captured by British forces in 1916 and became in 1921 a Kingdom under a League of Nations mandate, administered by Britain. It became independent on 3 Oct. 1932 under the Hashemite Dynasty, which was overthrown on 14 July 1958 by a military *coup* which established a Republic, controlled by a military-led Council of Sovereignty under Gen. Qassim. The republican régime terminated the adherence of Iraq to the Arab Federation (*see* THE STATESMAN'S YEAR-BOOK, 1958, p. 806). In 1963 Qassim was overthrown and Gen. Abdul Salam Aref became President, to be succeeded in 1966 by his brother Abdul Rahman Aref. In 1968 a successful *coup* was mounted by the Ba'th Party, which brought Gen. Ahmed Al Bakr to the Presidency. His Vice-President, from 1969, Saddam Hussein, became President in a peaceful transfer of power in 1979.

An attempt at succession by the Kurdish minority in the north-east of Iraq flared up in 1962, and fighting continued until the acceptance of a peace plan in June 1966. The Revolutionary Command Council formed after the 17 July 1968 *coup* announced in March 1970 a complete and constitutional settlement of the Kurdish issue. This was not, however, fully accepted by the Kurdish opposition leader.

In Sept. 1980 Iraq invaded Iran in a dispute over territorial rights in the Shatt-al Arab waterway. Fighting was continuing in early 1985.

AREA AND POPULATION. Iraq is bounded north by Turkey, east by Iran, south-east by the Gulf, south by Kuwait and Saudi Arabia, and west by Jordan and Syria. The country has an area of 434,924 sq. km (167,925 sq. miles) and its population census (1977) was 12,029,700 and (estimate) 1982, 14m.

The areas, populations (1976 estimate) and capitals of the governorates were:

Governorate	*sq. km*	*1976*	*Capital*	*1970*
Al-Anbar	89,540	405,000	Ar-Ramadi	79,488
Al-Basrah	19,702	897,000	Al-Basrah	333,684
Al-Muthanna	49,206	184,000	As-Samawah	33,473 [2]
Al-Qadisayah	8,569	395,000	Ad-Diwaniyah	60,553 [2]
An-Najaf	26,834	354,000	An-Najaf	179,160
As-Sulaymaniyah [1]	16,482	656,000	As-Sulaymaniyah	98,063
Babil (Babylon)	5,503	565,000	Al-Hillah	128,811
Baghdad	5,023	3,036,000	Baghdad	2,183,760
Dahuk [1]	6,374	217,000	Dahuk	19,736
Dhi Qar	13,668	617,000	As-Nasiriyah	62,368
Diyala	19,047	663,000	Ba'qubah	39,186
Irbil [1]	14,428	492,000	Irbil	107,355
Karbala	52,856	243,000	Karbala	107,496
Maysan	16,774	419,000	Al-Amarah	80,078
Ninawa (Nineveh)	41,320	1,158,000	Mosul	293,079
Salah ad-Din	21,326	356,000	Samarra	62,008
Ta'min	9,426	439,000	Kirkuk	207,852
Wasit	17,922	386,000	Al Kut	58,647

[1] Forming Kurdish Autonomous Region [2] Census 1965

The national language is Arabic, spoken by 81% of the population. There is a major minority group of Kurdish-speakers in the north-east (15·5%) and smaller groups speaking Turkic, Aramaic and Iranian languages.

CLIMATE. The climate is mainly arid, with small and unreliable rainfall and a large annual range of temperature. Summers are very hot and winters cold. Al-Basrah. Jan. 55°F (12·8°C), July 92°F (33·3°C). Annual rainfall 7″ (175 mm).

Baghdad. Jan. 50°F (10°C), July 95°F (35°C). Annual rainfall 6″ (140 mm). Mosul. Jan. 44°F (6·7°C), July 90°F (32·2°C). Annual rainfall 15″ (384 mm).

CONSTITUTION AND GOVERNMENT. The Provisional Constitution was published on 22 Sept. 1968 and promulgated on 16 July 1970. The highest state authority remains the 9-member Revolutionary Command Council (RCC) but some legislative power has now been given to the 250-member National Assembly, elected 20 June 1980 for a 4-year term.

The only legal political grouping is the National Progressive Front (founded July 1973) comprising the Arab Socialist Renaissance (Ba'th) Party and various Kurdish parties; the Iraqi Communist Party left the Front in March 1979.

The President and Vice-President are elected by the RCC; the President appoints and leads a Council of Ministers responsible for administration.

President: Saddam Hussein at-Takriti (assumed office 17 July 1979).
Vice-President: Taha Moheddin Marouf.

The RCC was composed as follows in Jan. 1985:

Saddam Hussein at-Takriti *(Chairman)*, Taha Moheddin Marouf, Izzat Ibrahim *(Vice-Chairman)*, Na'im Hamid Haddad *(Secretary-General of the National Progressive Front)*, Taha Yasin Ramadan *(First Deputy Prime Minister)*, Gen. Adnan Khairallah *(Deputy Prime Minister, Defence)*, Tariq Aziz Isa *(Deputy Prime Minister, Foreign Affairs)*, Sa'doun Shakir Mahmud *(Interior)*, Hasan Ali Nasar al-Amiri *(Trade)*.

Besides those named above, the Council of Ministers comprises 7 Ministers of State, 19 other Ministers and 7 Presidential advisors with ministerial status.

National flag: Three horizontal stripes of red, white, black, with 3 green stars on the white stripe.

Local Government. Iraq is divided into 18 governorates *(liwa)*, each administered by an appointed Governor; three of the governorates form a (Kurdish) Autonomous Region, with an elected 57-member Kurdish Legislative Council. Each governorate is divided into *qadhas* (under Qaimaqams) and *nahiyahs* (under Mudirs).

DEFENCE. Military training is compulsory for all men when they reach the age of 18. This consists of 2 years' service with the colours and 18 years on the reserve. However, a man may volunteer for service in the army or change his conscript service into voluntary service. In such circumstances voluntary service is for 2 years, and he may extend it by periods of 2 years until he reaches the age of 45. The 2-year compulsory service can be extended in a national emergency as in the present war with Iran. Many technicians and technically qualified officers serve up to 4 or 5 years.

Army. The Army is organized into 6 armoured, 5 mechanized, and 5 infantry divisions; 2 Republican Guard armoured, 3 special forces, 9 Reserve and 15 People's Army brigades. Equipment includes Soviet T-54/-55/-62/-72 and Chinese Type-69 main battle tanks. Strength (1985) 600,000, with an additional 75,000 reserves and the paramilitary People's Army of 650,000.

Navy. The Navy comprises 1 new frigate/training ship, 4 new Italian-built missile corvettes, 12 *ex*-Soviet missile boats, 12 *ex*-Soviet torpedo boats, 4 *ex*-Soviet but Polish-built medium landing ships, 3 Danish-built landing craft, 3 *ex*-Soviet submarine chasers, 2 fleet minesweepers, 3 inshore minesweepers, 1 training ship, 16 gunboats, 8 coastal patrol craft, 10 harbour patrol boats, 3 mine warfare boats, 1 presidential yacht, 1 harbour authority craft (former presidential yacht), 5 diving craft and 10 service tenders.

In 1985 naval personnel totalled over 3,000 officers and ratings, to be increased on the acquisition of 4 frigates and 2 more missile corvettes being built in Italy with a replenishment tanker, if this 1981 contract is fulfilled.

Air Force. Except for a few Hunter jet fighter-bombers bought from Britain and 89 Mirage F.1E/B fighters, 5 Exocet missile-armed Super Etendard attack aircraft, about 40 Alouette III, 10 Super Frelon, 40 Puma and 59 Gazelle helicopters acquired from France, the combat and transport squadrons are equipped primarily with aircraft of Soviet design, including 10 Tu-22 supersonic medium bombers, 30 Su-7 and 50 Su-20 fighter-bombers, 40 MiG-23 interceptors and fighter-bombers, and 50 Chinese-built F-7 and MiG-21 interceptors, 40 Chinese-built F-6 (MiG-19) fighters, 40 Mi-24 gunship helicopters, 50 Mi-8 helicopters, and four-turbofan Il-76, turboprop An-12 and An-24/26 transports. A few Il-14s and smaller types are used in a transport/communications role. Hunter, L-29 Delfin and L-39 Albatros aircraft are employed for training, with Swiss-built Bravo piston-engined primary trainers and Pilatus PC-7 turboprop basic trainers, Soviet MiG-15UTI trainers and other types in the Air Force College and operational conversion unit. Total strength is about 45,000 personnel and 400 combat aircraft. Soviet 'Guideline', 'Goa', 'Gainful', 'Gaskin' and Roland surface-to-air missiles are operational.

INTERNATIONAL RELATIONS

Membership. Iraq is a member of UN, Arab League and the Non-Aligned Movement.

ECONOMY

Planning. A new plan for 1981–85 was introduced but has been affected, to some extent, by the hostilities with Iran.

Budget. Revenue and expenditure (in 1,000 Iraqi dinars) for 1981 balanced at I.D. 19,250m.

Oil revenues account for nearly 50%, customs and excise for about 26% of the total revenue.

Currency. The monetary unit is the *Iraqi dinar* (I.D.) = 1,000 *fils* = 10 *riyals* = 20 *dirhams*. Silver alloy coins for 100 and 50 fils (*dirham*) and 25 fils are in circulation, and other coins for 10, 5 and 1 fils. Notes are for ¼, ½ and 1 dinar, and for 5 and 10 dinars. In March 1985, £1 = 0·34 *dinar*; US$1 = 0·311 *dinar*.

Banking. All banks were nationalized on 14 July 1964. The Central Bank of Iraq is the sole bank of issue. In 1941 the Rafidain Bank, financed by the Iraqi Government, was instituted to carry out normal banking transactions with head office in Baghdad and branches in the chief towns and abroad, including London. In addition, there are 4 government banks which are authorized to issue loans to companies and individuals: the Industrial Bank, the Agricultural Bank, the Estate Bank, and the Mortgage Bank.

Weights and Measures. The metric system is in general use.

ENERGY AND NATURAL RESOURCES

Electricity. Production in 1978 amounted to 6,950m. Kwh.

Oil. Following the nationalization of the Iraqi oil industry in June 1972, the Iraqi National Oil Company (INOC) is responsible for the exploration, production, transport and marketing of Iraqi crude oil and oil products.

The total crude petroleum production was (1980) 130·2m. tonnes and of natural gas (1980) 1,760m. cu. ft. Oil exports are essential for the economy but oil terminals in the Gulf were destroyed in 1980 and the trans-Syria pipeline closed in 1982. Iraq is now wholly reliant on the 625 mile pipeline from Kirkuk to the Mediterranean *via* Turkey.

Water. The soil of the country is rich, but there are vast areas which can be cultivated only if irrigated by canals or pumps. The Irrigation Ministry operates several canal systems, new dams have been completed and other irrigation works are under construction.

Agriculture. The chief winter crops (1980) are wheat, 1·3m. tonnes and barley, 575,000 tonnes. The chief summer crop is rice, 220,000 tonnes. The date crop is important (395,000 tonnes), the country furnishing about 80% of the world's trade in dates (exports, 1975, I.D.11,493,000); the chief producing area is the totally irrigated riverain belt of the Shatt-el-Arab. Wool is also an important export (1975: I.D.1,013,000). In 1975, I.D.20,000 of cotton were exported.

Livestock (1983): Cattle, 3m.; buffaloes, 240,000; sheep, 12m.; goats, 3·8m.; horses, 65,000; camels, 250,000; chickens, 20m.

INDUSTRY AND TRADE

Industry. Constructional establishments employed the largest number of workers. Other large employers were the brick industry, water and electricity services, date packing, the textile industry, cigarette factories, oil refining and the cement industry. Iraq is still relatively under-developed industrially but work has begun on 13 new industrial plants which are being established with Soviet equipment and technical assistance.

Commerce. Imports and exports for 4 calendar years were (in 1m. Iraqi dinars):

	1977	*1978*	*1979*	*1980*
Imports	1,151	1,244	2,225	4,440
Exports	2,854	3,251	6,350	7,782

In 1980, crude oil formed 99% of all exports, of which 18% went to France, 15% to Brazil and 14% to Japan. 18% of imports came from Japan, 15% from Federal Republic of Germany and 9% from France.

Total trade between Iraq and UK for 5 years (British Department of Trade returns, in £1,000 sterling):

	1980	*1981*	*1982*	*1983*	*1984*
Imports to UK	532,483	72,644	79,764	30,334	69,047
Exports and re-exports from UK	321,883	623,889	875,179	400,259	343,120

Tourism. About 700,000 tourists visited Iraq in 1978.

COMMUNICATIONS

Roads. About 9,291 km of roads and tracks had been developed for vehicular traffic. The main surfaced roads are: (1) the road north from Baghdad *via* Kirkuk, Arbil and Nineveh to a point near the Turkish frontier at Zakho, with branches from Kirkuk to the northern province of Sulaimaniya, from Arbil to the Iranian frontier, and from Nineveh to Sinjar; (2) about 350 miles of the main road west from Baghdad to the Jordan frontier; (3) the road east of Baghdad, which connects the road system of Iran near Khanaqin; and (4) the road south from Baghdad to Hilla and the holy city of Kerbela.

Vehicles registered in 1982 totalled 230,000 passenger cars and 145,000 commercial vehicles.

Railways. The Iraqi Republic Railways were originally largely metre gauge but now comprise a 1,435 mm gauge main line from Um Qasr through Basra to Baghdad, Mosul and Tel-Kotchek on the Syrian frontier, and the remaining metre gauge route from Baghdad to Khanaqin, Kirkuk and Erbil. A 1,435 mm gauge line was opened in 1983 from Baghdad to Husaiba (404 km) on the Syrian frontier, which will form part of a through route to the Mediterranean port of Latakia, together with a branch to Akashat. A branch of 155 km has opened to serve phosphates deposits at Akashat. In 1981 the railways carried 5m. tonnes of freight and 3·8m. passengers.

Aviation. Baghdad airport is served by British Airways, Lufthansa, Alitalia, SAS, Swissair, KLM, Middle East Air Lines, PIA, Iraqi Airways, Air Liban, United Arab Airlines and Aeroflot. In 1977 there were 728,266 passengers using Iraqi airports and 10,000 tons of cargo handled.

Shipping. The merchant fleet in 1980 comprised 142 vessels (over 100 gross tons) with a total tonnage of 1,465,949. The ports of Basra and Um Qasr have been closed since Sept. 1980.

Post and Broadcasting. Wireless telegraph services exist with UK, USA, UAR,

Lebanon and Saudi Arabia, and wireless telephone services with UK, USA, Italy, UAR and USSR. Telephones, 1978, 319,591. In 1983 there were 2·1m. radio and 530,000 television receivers.

Cinemas (1979). There were 87 cinemas.

Newspapers (1983). In Baghdad there are 4 main daily newspapers (one of which is in English with a circulation of 200,000).

JUSTICE, RELIGION, EDUCATION AND WELFARE

Justice. The courts are established throughout the country as follows: For civil matters: the court of cassation in Baghdad; 6 courts of appeal at Baghdad (2), Basra, Babylon, Mosul and Kirkuk; 18 courts of first instance with unlimited powers and 150 courts of first instance with limited powers, all being courts of single judges. In addition, 6 peace courts have peace court jurisdiction only. Tribal law was abolished in Aug. 1958.

For *Shara'* (religious) matters: the Shara' courts at all places where there are civil courts, constituted in some places of specially appointed Qadhis (religious judges) and in other places of the judges of the civil courts. For criminal matters: the court of cassation; 6 sessions courts (2 being presided over by the judge of the local court of first instance and 4 being identical with the courts of appeal). Magistrates' courts at all places where there are civil courts, constituted of civil judges exercising magisterial powers of the first and second class. There are also a number of third-class magistrates courts, powers for this purpose being granted to municipal councils and a number of administrative officials. Some administrative officials are granted the powers of a peace judge to deal with cases of debts due from cultivators.

Religion. In 1965 there were 7,711,712 Moslems, 232,406 Christians (1979), 2,500 Jews, 69,653 Yazidis and 14,262 Sabians.

Education. Primary and secondary education is free and primary education became compulsory in Sept. 1976. Primary school age is 6–12. Secondary education is for 6 years, of which the first 3 are termed intermediate. The medium of instruction is Arabic; Kurdish is used in primary schools in northern districts.

There were, in 1976–77, 8,156 primary schools with 1,947,182 pupils, and 1,320 secondary schools with 555,184 pupils. Eighty-two vocational schools had 28,365 students and 43 teacher-training colleges had 21,186 students.

There are 6 universities with (1977) 71,536 students and 15 other higher educational establishments with 9,962 students.

Health. In 1974 there were 4,734 doctors (including dentists); 162 hospitals with 21,582 beds.

DIPLOMATIC REPRESENTATIVES

Of Iraq in Great Britain (21–22 Queen's Gate, London, SW7 5JG)
Ambassador: Dr Wahbi Abdul-Razzaq Al Qaraghuli (accredited 19 Nov. 1982).

Of Great Britain in Iraq (Sharia Salah Ud-Din, Karkh, Baghdad)
Ambassador: S. John Moberly, KBE, CMG.

Of Iraq to the United Nations
Ambassador: Dr Riyadh Mahmoud Al Qaisi.

Iraq broke off diplomatic relations with USA on 7 June 1967.

Books of Reference

Statistical Information: The Central Statistical Organization, Ministry of Planning, Baghdad (*President:* Dr Salah Al-Shaikhly) publishes an annual *Statistical Abstract* (latest issue 1973). Foreign Trade statistics are published annually by the Ministry of Planning.

Abdulrahman, A. J., *Iraq.* Oxford and Santa Barbara, 1984
Arfa, H., *The Kurds.* OUP, 1966
Ghareeb, E., *The Kurdish Question in Iraq.* Syracuse Univ. Press, 1981
Khadduri, M., *Independent Iraq.* OUP, 1960.—*Republican Iraq.* OUP, 1970.—*Socialist Iraq: A Study of Iraqi Politics since 1968.* OUP, 1978
Postgate, E., *Iraq. International Relations and National Development.* London, 1983

IRELAND

Capital: Dublin
Population: 3·44m. (1981)
GNP per capita: US$4,855 (1981)

Éire

HISTORY. In April 1916 an insurrection against British rule took place and a republic was proclaimed. The armed struggle was renewed in 1919 and continued until 1921. The independence of Ireland was reaffirmed in Jan. 1919 by the National Parliament (*Dáil Éireann*), elected in Dec. 1918.

In 1920 an Act was passed by the British Parliament, under which separate Parliaments were set up for 'Southern Ireland' (26 counties) and 'Northern Ireland' (6 counties). The Unionists of the 6 counties accepted this scheme, and a Northern Parliament was duly elected on 24 May 1921. The rest of Ireland, however, ignored the Act.

On 6 Dec. 1921 a treaty was signed between Great Britain and Ireland by which Ireland accepted dominion status subject to the right of Northern Ireland to opt out. This right was exercised, and the border between *Saorstát Éireann* (26 counties) and Northern Ireland (6 counties) was fixed in Dec. 1925 as the outcome of an agreement between Great Britain, the Irish Free State and Northern Ireland. The agreement was ratified by the three parliaments.

Subsequently the constitutional links between *Saorstát Éireann* and the UK were gradually removed by the *Dáil.* The remaining formal association with the British Commonwealth by virtue of the External Relations Act, 1936, was severed when the Republic of Ireland Act, 1948, came into operation on 18 April 1949.

AREA AND POPULATION. The Republic of Ireland lies in the Atlantic ocean, separated from Great Britain by the Irish Sea to the east, and bounded north-east by Northern Ireland.

Counties and county boroughs	*Area in hectares* [1]	*Population, 1981* Males	Females	Total
Province of Leinster				
Carlow	89,635	20,195	19,625	39,820
Dublin County Borough	11,499	248,016	277,866	525,882
Dublin [2]	78,937	209,533	213,253	422,786
Dun Laoghaire Borough	1,720	24,793	29,703	54,496
Kildare	169,425	53,967	50,155	104,122
Kilkenny	206,167	36,395	34,411	70,806
Laoighis	171,954	26,774	24,397	51,171
Longford	104,387	16,234	14,906	31,140
Louth	82,334	44,125	44,389	88,514
Meath	233,587	48,957	46,462	95,419
Offaly	199,774	30,290	28,022	58,312
Westmeath	176,290	31,388	30,135	61,523
Wexford	235,143	50,336	48,745	99,081
Wicklow	202,483	43,663	43,786	87,449
Total of Leinster	1,963,335	884,666	905,855	1,790,521
Province of Munster				
Clare	318,784	45,366	42,201	87,567
Cork County Borough	3,731	66,177	70,167	136,344
Cork	742,257	136,211	129,910	266,121
Kerry	470,142	63,492	59,278	122,770
Limerick County Borough	1,904	29,723	31,013	60,736
Limerick	266,676	51,872	49,053	100,925
Tipperary, N. R.	199,622	30,247	28,737	58,984
Tipperary, S. R.	225,836	39,256	37,021	76,277

[1] Exclusive of certain rivers, lakes and tideways.
[2] Excludes Dun Laoghaire borough.

Counties and county boroughs	*Area in hectares*[1]	*Males*	*Population, 1981* *Females*	*Total*
Province of Munster—contd.				
Waterford County Borough	3,809	18,751	19,722	38,473
Waterford	179,977	25,762	24,356	50,118
Total of Munster	2,412,738	506,857	491,458	998,315
Province of Connacht				
Galway	593,966	88,330	83,688	172,018
Leitrim	152,476	14,699	12,910	27,609
Mayo	539,846	58,987	55,779	114,766
Roscommon	246,276	28,653	25,890	54,543
Sligo	179,608	28,183	27,291	55,474
Total of Connacht	1,712,172	218,852	205,558	424,410
Province of Ulster (part of)				
Cavan	189,060	28,338	25,517	53,855
Donegal	483,058	63,962	61,150	125,112
Monaghan	129,093	26,679	24,513	51,192
Total of Ulster (part of)	801,211	118,979	111,180	230,159
Total	6,889,456	1,729,354	1,714,051	3,443,405

[1] Exclusive of certain rivers, lakes and tideways.

Principal towns (1981 census): Greater Dublin including Dún Laoghaire, 915,115; Cork, 149,792; Limerick, 75,520; Galway, 41,861; Waterford, 39,636.

Vital statistics for 6 calendar years:

	Births	*Marriages*	*Deaths*		*Births*	*Marriages*	*Deaths*
1977	68,892	20,016	33,632	1980	74,064	21,792	33,472
1978	70,299	21,184	33,794	1981	72,158	20,612	32,929
1979	72,539	20,806	33,771	1982	70,933	20,441	32,876

CLIMATE. Influenced by the Gulf Stream, there is an equable climate with mild south-west winds, making temperatures almost uniform over the whole country. The coldest months are Jan. and Feb. (39–45°F, 4–7°C) and the warmest July and Aug. (57–61°F, 14–16°C). May and June are the sunniest months, averaging 5·5 to 6·5 hours each day, but over 7 hours in the extreme S.E. Rainfall is lowest along the eastern coastal strip. The central parts vary between 30–44″ (750–1,125 mm), and up to 60″ (1,500 mm) may be experienced in low-lying areas in the west. Dublin. Jan. 41°F (5°C), July 59°F (15°C). Annual rainfall 30″ (750 mm). Cork. Jan. 43°F (6·1°C), July 60°F (15·6°C). Annual rainfall 41″ (1,025 mm).

CONSTITUTION AND GOVERNMENT. Ireland is a sovereign independent, democratic republic. Its parliament exercises jurisdiction in 26 of the 32 counties of Ireland.

The first Constitution of the Irish Free State came into operation on 6 Dec. 1922. Certain provisions which were regarded as contrary to the national sentiments were gradually removed by successive amendments, with the result that at the end of 1936 the text differed considerably from the original document. On 14 June 1937 a new Constitution was approved by Parliament (*Dáil Éireann*) and enacted by a plebiscite on 1 July 1937. This Constitution came into operation on 29 Dec. 1937. Under it the name Ireland (Éire) was restored.

The Constitution provides that, pending the reintegration of the national territory, the laws enacted by the Parliament established by the constitution shall have the same area and extent of application as those of the Irish Free State.

The *Oireachtas* or National Parliament consists of the President and two Houses, viz., a House of Representatives, called *Dáil Éireann*, and a Senate, called *Seanad Éireann*, consisting of 60 members. The *Dáil*, consisting of 166 members, is elected by adult suffrage. Of the 60 members of the Senate, 11 are nominated by the *Taoiseach* (Prime Minister), 6 are elected by the universities and the remaining

43 are elected from 5 panels of candidates established on a vocational basis, representing the following public services and interests: (1) national language and culture, literature, art, education and such professional interests as may be defined by law for the purpose of this panel; (2) agricultural and allied interests, and fisheries; (3) labour, whether organized or unorganized; (4) industry and commerce, including banking, finance, accountancy, engineering and architecture; (5) public administration and social services, including voluntary social activities. The electing body is a college of about 1,032 members, comprising members of the *Dáil*, Senate, county boroughs and county councils.

A maximum period of 90 days is afforded to the Senate for the consideration or amendment of Bills sent to that House by the *Dáil*, but the Senate has no power to veto legislative proposals.

No amendment of the Constitution can be effected except with the approval of the people given at a referendum.

Agreement on the establishment of a Council of Ireland was reached at a meeting held at Sunningdale on 6–9 Dec. 1973. Members of the Irish and UK governments attended together with the Northern Ireland Executive-designate.

Irish is the first official language; English is recognized as a second official language. For further details of the Constitution *see* THE STATESMAN'S YEAR-BOOK, 1952, pp. 1123–34.

President: Pádraig Óhlrighile (Patrick Hillery), installed on 3 Dec. 1976 and re-elected for a second 7-year term in 1983.

Former Presidents: Dr Douglas Hyde (1938–45); Seán T. O. Ceallaigh (1945–59; 2 terms); Éamon de Valéra (1959–73; 2 terms); Erskine Childers (1973–74; died in office); Cearbhall Ó Dálaigh (1974–76; resigned).

A general election was held on 24 Nov. 1982: Fianna Fáil, 75 (Feb. 1982 election, 81); Fine Gael, 70 (66); Labour Party, 16 (15); Workers' Party, 2 (3); Independents, 3 (4).

There are no formal party divisions in the Senate.

The National Coalition Government consisted of the following members in Feb. 1983 (Fine Gael and Labour Parties):

Taoiseach (Prime Minister): Dr Garret Fitzgerald.

Tanaiste (Deputy Prime Minister) and Minister for Energy: Dick Spring. *Finance:* Alan Dukes. *Agriculture:* Austin Deasy. *Industry, Trade, Commerce and Tourism:* John Bruton. *Foreign Affairs:* Peter Barry. *Education:* Gemma Hussey. *Justice:* Michael Noonan. *Communications:* Jim Mitchell. *Gaeltacht, Fisheries and Forestry:* Paddy O'Toole. *Health and Social Welfare:* Barry Desmond. *Labour:* Ruaici Quinn. *Environment:* Liam Kavanagh. *Defence:* Paddy Cooney. *Public Service:* John Boland.

There were 15 Ministers of State.

National flag: Three vertical strips of green, white, orange.

National anthem: The Soldier's Song (words by P. Kearney; music by P. Heaney).

Local Government. The elected local authorities comprise 27 county councils, 4 county borough corporations, 7 borough corporations, 49 urban district councils and 25 Boards of Town Commissions. All the members of these authorities are elected under a system of proportional representation, normally every 5 years. All residents of an area who have reached the age of 18 are entitled to vote in the local election for their area. Women are eligible for election as members of local authorities in the same manner and on the same conditions as men. Elected members are not paid, but provision is made for the payment of travelling expenses and subsistence allowances.

The range of services for which local authorities are responsible is broken down into 8 main programme groups as follows: Housing and Building; Road Transportation and Safety; Water Supply and Sewerage; Development Incentives and Controls; Environmental Protection; Recreation and Amenity; Agriculture, Education, Health and Welfare and Miscellaneous Services. Because of the small size of their administrative areas the functions carried out by town commissioners and some of the smaller urban district councils have tended to become increasingly limited, and the more important tasks of local government have tended to become the responsibility of the county councils.

The local authorities have a system of government which combines an elected council and a whole-time manager. The elected members have specific functions reserved to them which include the striking of rates (local tax), the borrowing of money, the adoption of development plans, the making, amending or revoking of bye-laws and the nomination of persons to other bodies. The managers, who are paid officers of their authorities, are responsible for the performance of all functions which are not reserved to the elected members, including the employment of staff, making of contracts, management of local authority property, collection of rates and rents and the day-to-day administration of local authority affairs. The manager for a county council is manager also for every borough corporation, urban district council and board of town commissioners whose functional area is wholly within the county. A central body called the Local Appointments Commission is charged with the duty of selecting suitable persons to be appointed by local authorities to chief executive offices, professional offices and other prescribed offices. Where a prescribed office becomes vacant, the local authority must request the Commissioners to recommend to them a suitable person. The Commissioners normally select persons for appointment by the machinery of selection boards.

The revenue expenditure of local authorities is financed by a local tax, called rates, on the occupation of immovable property, grants and subsidies from the central government and payments for certain services which they provide.

Since 1978 full rates relief has applied to houses, the domestic element of mixed property, *i.e.* property embodying a domestic as well as a non-domestic use, secondary schools, community halls and farm buildings not previously de-rated. A grant not exceeding the aggregate of these allowances is made to the local authorities by central government. Since 1983 such relief also applies in relation to all land.

DEFENCE. Under the direction of the President, and subject to the provisions of the Defence Act, 1954, the military command of the Defence Forces is exercisable by the Government through the Minister for Defence. To aid and counsel the Minister for Defence on all matters in relation to the business of the Department of Defence on which he may consult it, there is a Council of Defence consisting of the Minister for State at the Department of Defence, the Secretary of the Department of Defence, the Chief of Staff, the Adjutant-General and the Quartermaster-General. Establishments provide at present for a Permanent Defence Force of approximately 18,000 all ranks including the Air Corps and the Naval Service. The Reserve Defence Force caters for 23,000 all ranks. Recruitment is on a voluntary basis. Minimum term of enlistment is 3 years in the Permanent Defence Force and 6 years in the Reserve.

The Defence Estimates for the year ending 31 Dec. 1984 provide for an expenditure of £229,715,000.

Since May 1978 an Irish contingent has formed part of the United Nations force in Lebanon. The contingent now comprises 740 men (all ranks). 21 Irish officers are at present serving with the UN Truce Supervision Organization and the UN Disengagement Observer Force in the Middle East. There is a small detachment with the UN force in Cyprus.

Army. The Army has 4 brigades three of which have two infantry battalions and the fourth one, a field artillery regiment and a squadron/coy size unit from each Corps. There is in addition a special Infantry force consisting of two battalions. The establishment strength of the Army is 15,517 all ranks.

Navy. The Naval Service comprises 1 new frigate-size patrol vessel (with helicopter), 4 offshore patrol vessels built in Cork between 1972 and 1980, two coastal minesweepers purchased from Great Britain in 1971 for fishery protection purposes, one supply and training ship and 8 other craft. The Naval Base is at Haulbowline Island in Cork Harbour. The establishment strength of the Naval Service is 1,277 officers and men but in 1985 personnel were fewer.

Air Force. The Air Corps has an establishment of 800 all ranks, and 37 aircraft. There are 6 Fouga – Magister armed jet trainers, SF 260W armed piston-engined trainers, 8 Alouette III and 2 Gazelle helicopters, 3 twin-turbo prop Super Beech King 200 for coastal fishery patrol and a BAe 125/700 twin turbofan aircraft.

INTERNATIONAL RELATIONS

Membership. Ireland is a member of UN, OECD, the Council of Europe and EEC.

ECONOMY

Budget. Current revenue and expenditure (in IR£1m.):

Current revenue	*1983*	*1984*
Customs duties	78·1	92·6
Excise duties	1,182·0	1,241·6
Estate, etc, duties	1·6	1·0
Residential Property Tax	1·0	1·1
Capital taxes	24·0	28·0
Stamp duties	103·9	112·2
Income tax	1,664·2	1,966·5
Income levy	40·1	78·1
Corporation tax	215·0	209·7
Value-added tax	1,192·6	1,361·6
Agricultural levies (EEC)	11·4	17·4
Motor vehicle duties	93·7	110·8
Youth employment levy	73·8	83·3
Post Office	416·5	–
Total (including other items)	5,711·0	5,952·2
Current expenditure		
Debt service	1,456	1,710
Industry and Labour	184	195
Agriculture	360	408
Fisheries, Forestry, Tourism	63	65
Health	973	1,000
Education	804	894
Social Welfare	1,909	2,167
Less: Receipts, e.g. social security	(–)1,095	(–)1,226
Total (including other items)	6,309	7,060

Capital expenditure amounted to £1,862m. in 1983, and £1,936m. in 1984.

On 31 Dec. 1980 the liabilities totalled £7,896m. The assets were: Electricity scheme, £42·6m.: local loans fund, £1,313·2m.; national transport organization, £33·3m.; industrial credit, £59·8m.; turf development, £29·6m.; reconstruction finance, £33m.; shares in companies established under state auspices, £240·7m.; exchequer balance, £613,000; other assets, £150·2m.; total, £1,903m.

Currency. The unit of currency is the Irish *pound* or *an punt Eirennach*. From 10 Sept. 1928 when the first Irish legal-tender notes were issued, the Irish currency was linked to Sterling on a one-for-one basis. This relationship was discontinued on 30 March 1979 when, following Ireland's adherence to the European Monetary System, market forces pushed sterling exchange rates beyond the upper intervention limit established for the Irish pound against the Belgian franc.

The Central Bank has the sole right of issuing legal tender notes; token coinage is issued by the Minister for Finance through the Bank. In March 1985, £1 = IR£1·16; US$ = IR£0·98.

The volume of legal-tender notes outstanding in Sept. 1984 was £901·91m. Total notes and coins outstanding amounted to £949·22m.

Banking. The Central Bank, which was established as from 1 Feb. 1943, in accordance with the Central Bank Act, 1942, replaced the Currency Commission, which was set up under the Currency Act, 1927, and had been responsible *inter alia* for the regulation of the note issue. In addition to the powers and functions of the

Currency Commission the Central Bank has the power of receiving deposits from banks and public authorities, of rediscounting Exchequer bills and bills of exchange, of making advances to banks against such bills or against Government securities, of fixing and publishing rates of interest for rediscounting bills, or buying and selling certain Government securities and securities of any international bank or financial institution formed wholly or mainly by governments. The Bank also collects and publishes information relating to monetary and credit matters. The Central Bank Act, 1971, gives further powers to the Central Bank in the regulation of banking including licensing of banks, the supervision of their operations and control of liquidity and reserve ratios. The capital of the Bank is £40,000, of which £24,000 has been paid up and is held by the Minister for Finance.

The Board of Directors of the Central Bank consists of a Governor, appointed by the President on the advice of the Government, and 8 directors, all appointed by the Minister for Finance, 6 direct and 2 from among directors of the Associated Banks (the term applied to the 4 shareholding banks associated with the former Currency Commission).

There are 4 commercial banks associated with the Central Bank: The Bank of Ireland, Allied Irish Banks Ltd, the Ulster Bank and the Northern Bank.

At 16 Feb. 1983 the Associated Banks had liabilities, within the State, of £6,089·5m. including current and deposit accounts amounting to £4,967·5m.; assets, within the State, amounted to £6,338m., of which the main components were liquid assets of £735·2m. and lending of £5,147·6m. At the same date liabilities, outside the State, stood at £5,569·9m. and assets at £5,320·9m., giving a net external liability of £249m. Total liabilities and assets balanced at £11,659·4m. The commercial banking system also includes 40 licensed banks not 'associated' with the Central Bank. At 16 Feb. 1983 these non-associated banks had total liabilities and assets, within the State and elsewhere, balancing at £6,410·6m.

The post office savings bank has approximately 2·7m. (including 1·2m. dormant) accounts and the amount due at 31 Aug. 1983 was IR£322m. The trustee savings banks had deposits of IR£285m. at 31 Aug. 1983.

Weights and Measures. The Imperial system is in use but conversion to metric is in progress.

ENERGY AND NATURAL RESOURCES

Electricity. The generating and supplying of electricity and the construction and maintenance of the nationwide electricity distribution system is the function of the Electricity Supply Board, a State-sponsored body established in 1927. The total generating capacity is 3,260 mw. In the year ending 31 March 1984 the total sales of electricity amounted to 8,904m. units supplied to 1,145,818 consumers. Electricity generated by fuel source (1983–84): Oil, 20%; natural gas, 54%; peat, 18%; hydro, 7%.

Oil. About 551,000 sq. km of the continental shelf has been made an exploration area; at its furthest point the limit of jurisdiction is 520 nautical miles from the coast. An exploration well drilled by Gulf Oil on block 49/9 in 1983 flowed oil on test from three different levels at an aggregate 9,901 bbls per day. A fourth level flowed gas at 2·1m. cu. ft per day. Further appraisal work must be carried out on the block to determine the commerciality or otherwise of this discovery. Since 1970, 83 exploratory offshore oil wells have been drilled.

Gas. There has been one commercial discovery of natural gas, off the south-west coast at Kinsale Head. The total reserves of the field are 1·35m. cu. ft. Gas Transmission is controlled by the Irish Gas Board (BGE), who sell the gas into electricity generation, fertilizer production, and distribution systems for domestic and industrial use.

Peat. The country has very little indigenous coal, but possesses large reserves of peat, the development of which is handled by Bord na Mona (Peat Board). To date, the Board has acquired over 200,000 hectares of bog and has established 23 locations around the country. In the year ending 31 March, 1984, production totalled

5·3m. tonnes, of which 3m. tonnes went to generate electricity and 0·8m. tonnes for the domestic market. In addition moss peat production for the year was 1·3m. cu. metres.

Minerals. Lead and zinc concentrates are important. Metal content of production, 1983: zinc, 185,900 tonnes; lead, 33,600 tonnes. Barytes and gypsum are also important, and there is some dolomite, limestone, aggregates, coal, green and black marble. About 30 companies are prospecting.

Agriculture. General distribution of surface (in hectares) in 1980: Crops and pasture, 4,695,751; other land, including grazed mountain, 2,193,646; total, 6,889,195.

Estimated area (hectares) under certain crops calculated from sample returns:

	Area [1]			
Crops	*1981*	*1982*	*1983*	*1984*
Wheat	48,100	57,000	59,300	78,100
Oats	22,500	22,600	22,000	24,500
Barley	354,200	334,200	304,300	293,600
Potatoes	35,000	36,900	32,300	34,600
Sugar-beet	34,900	34,300	36,100	...

[1] Provisional.

Gross agricultural output (excluding value changes in livestock) for the year 1983 was valued at £2,447·91m.

Livestock (1984): Cattle, 6·76m.; sheep, 3·75m.; pigs, 1·03m.; horses (1980), 68,500; poultry (1983), 8·39m.

Forestry. The total area of state forests at 31 Dec. 1982 was 386,622·3 hectares.

Fisheries. The number of vessels engaged in fishing in 1983 were 1,449 boats propelled by outboard engines, sails and oars and 1,571 other fishing boats; men 8,572. The quantities and values of fish landed during 1982 were: Demersal fish, 35,000 tonnes, value £13,908,000; pelagic fish, 144,000 tonnes, value £17,992,000; shellfish, 16,000 tonnes, value £11,909,000. Total quantity: 195,000 tonnes; total value, £43,809,000.

INDUSTRY AND TRADE

Industry. The census of industrial production for 1980 gives the following details of the values (in £1,000) of gross and net output for the principal manufacturing industries. The figures for net output are those of gross output minus cost of materials, including fuel, light and power, repairs to plant and machinery and amounts paid to others in connexion with products made.

	Gross output	*Net output*
Slaughtering, preparing and preserving meat	908·3	125·6
Dairy products	876·3	133·8
Bread, biscuit and flour confectionery	160·3	68·0
Sugar, cocoa, chocolate and sugar confectionery	237·4	70·2
Grain milling, animal and poultry foods	388·5	69·9
Brewing and malting	162·7	101·4
Tobacco products	75·4	40·2
Paper and paper products	138·0	50·7
Printing and publishing	197·1	128·7
Production and preliminary processing of metals	70·4	22·6
Manufacture of metal articles	352·3	162·9
Manufacture of non-metallic mineral products	469·2	222·2
Chemicals, including fertilizers and manmade fibres	720·0	375·4
Mechanical engineering	190·7	87·0
Manufacture of office machinery and data-processing machinery	329·8	143·6
Electrical engineering	324·2	151·1
Manufacture of motor vehicles, parts and accessories	181·5	37·9
Manufacture of other means of transport	87·0	49·1
Textiles (including knitting industry)	352·9	123·8
Footwear and clothing	214·2	100·1
Timber and wooden furniture	171·4	73·1
Processing rubber and plastics	202·7	80·5
Gas, water and electricity	548·1	263·7
All other industries [1]	1,163·3	528·9
Total (all industries)	8,521·7	3,210·4

[1] Including mining, fuel production, instrument engineering, various food and drink industries, etc.

Labour. The total labour force at mid-April 1983 was about 1,309,000, of which about 155,000 persons were out of work.

The number of trade unions holding negotiation licences in Sept. 1983 was 79, of which 63 were workers' trade unions and the remainder employers' trade unions. The total membership of these unions is estimated at 500,796, of whom 10,480 were in the employers' trade unions. Approximately 314,767 were organized in 6 general unions catering for both white-collar and manual workers.

Commerce. Value of imports and exports of merchandise for calendar years (in £):

	1979	*1980*	*1981*	*1982*	*1983*
Imports	4,827,922,798	5,420,704,523	6,578,406,480	6,816,154,975	7,355,394,884
Exports	3,477,738,139	4,082,496,312	4,777,570,799	5,691,441,609	6,935,861,156

The values of the chief imports and total exports are shown in the following table (in £):

	Imports		*Exports*	
	1982	*1983*	*1982*	*1983*
Live animals and food	753,379,640	845,170,876	1,535,173,452	1,743,398,194
Raw materials	186,541,592	221,175,720	229,614,384	284,412,079
Mineral fuels and lubricants	1,009,561,613	993,018,886	36,016,177	79,498,517
Chemicals	737,216,396	838,557,214	805,419,687	963,616,035
Manufactured goods	1,153,504,966	1,172,459,092	640,347,955	725,544,593
Machinery and transport equipment	1,872,485,385	2,119,812,778	1,394,387,526	1,814,131,254
Manufactured articles [1]	832,825,516	892,517,759	645,992,983	831,738,151

[1] Not elsewhere specified.

Distribution of trade, by principal countries of origin in the case of imports and destination in the case of exports (in £):

	Imports		*Total exports*	
Country	*1982*	*1983*	*1982*	*1983*
Belgium and Luxembourg	148,103,626	155,656,579	254,440,348	274,678,619
Canada	83,169,537	91,703,372	69,270,047	80,578,188
Denmark	55,573,710	73,997,262	38,614,495	55,379,543
Finland	57,575,067	60,530,583	29,960,406	31,066,120
France	316,055,734	343,071,698	494,997,715	572,137,020
Germany, Fed. Rep. of	523,627,428	585,485,028	531,594,324	685,909,006
Hong Kong	30,334,489	43,398,587	8,466,986	11,206,146
India	16,120,398	14,933,931	6,922,027	6,828,558
Iran	162,824	70,626	4,342,971	42,647,419
Iraq	186,189	325,667	58,960,538	16,673,287
Israel	18,254,429	16,507,905	6,498,439	11,976,836
Italy	179,621,326	176,312,834	166,266,356	208,312,962
Japan	200,568,021	244,121,611	72,408,144	155,747,758
Kuwait	124,301	16,934	11,663,977	8,908,577
Malaysia	17,133,919	19,200,343	5,930,000	8,046,545
Netherlands	258,368,837	271,075,258	295,991,014	405,373,873
New Zealand	9,404,985	8,472,402	7,458,413	7,422,223
Norway	22,391,249	24,448,939	32,313,219	43,470,853
Poland	33,347,263	48,063,551	1,936,137	3,880,871
Portugal	22,157,736	26,447,035	17,213,484	21,513,683
Saudi Arabia	54,495,655	6,834,683	48,533,865	55,627,216
South Africa, Rep. of, and Namibia	13,419,227	12,925,579	23,774,488	31,940,590
Spain	68,393,756	85,304,012	69,769,021	79,157,566
Sweden	105,341,034	112,171,827	79,962,608	106,701,284
Switzerland	72,335,487	72,100,104	55,207,676	75,974,032
USSR	37,811,091	39,817,622	29,993,248	48,205,054
UK	3,273,070,994	3,336,051,240	2,207,979,609	2,559,703,109
USA	877,615,460	1,080,660,814	406,738,422	560,605,059

An Anglo-Irish free-trade agreement to remove progressively all duties between July 1966 and July 1975 was signed in London on 14 Dec. 1965.

Total trade between Ireland and UK (British Department of Trade returns, in £1,000 sterling):

	1980	*1981*	*1982*	*1983*	*1984*
Imports to UK	1,784,329	1,787,065	2,000,033	2,290,067	2,635,039
Exports and re-exports from UK	2,660,024	2,812,957	2,890,497	3,055,275	3,393,499

Tourism. Estimated number of visits by foreigners (including cross-border movement) in 1983 was 9,797,000; they spent £524·3m.

COMMUNICATIONS

Roads. At 31 Dec. 1983 there were 92,294 km of public roads, consisting of 5,365 km of national roads, 10,616 km of main (trunk and link) roads other than national roads, 73,975 km of county roads and 2,338 km of county borough and urban roads; of the total length 87,679 km (95%) was paved. Five miles of motorway were opened in 1983.

Number of licensed motor vehicles at 30 Sept. 1983: Private cars, 718,555; public-service vehicles, 6,909; goods vehicles, 69,978; agricultural tractors, 64,854; motor cycles, 25,208; other vehicles, 11,777.

The total number of km run by road motor passenger vehicles of the omnibus type during 1983 was 95,802,000. Passengers carried numbered 221,731,000 and the gross receipts from passengers were £88,240,000.

Railways. The total length of railway open for traffic at 31 Dec. 1984 was 1,994 km (30 km electrified), all 1,600 mm gauge. Córas Iompair Éireann, the national transport undertaking, operates all rail services in the State.

Railway statistics for years ending 31 Dec.	*1981*	*1982*
Passengers (no.)	15,374,000	12,813,000
Miles run by coaching trains	5,300,000	5,025,000
Merchandise and mineral traffic conveyed (tons)	3,664,000	3,680,000
Miles run by freight trains	3,281,000	2,843,000
Receipts (£)	45,445,595	49,943,000
Expenditure (£)	105,663,970	121,607,000

Aviation. During the year ended 31 March 1984 Aer Lingus-Irish International Airlines carried 1,933,569 passengers, 37,183 short tons of cargo and 1,217 short tons of mail on its European services and 279,394 passengers, 18,498 short tons of cargo and 1,389 short tons of mail on its trans-Atlantic services.

Shipping. The Irish merchant fleet, of vessels of 100 gross tonnes or over, consisted of 65 vessels totalling 197,462 GRT at 31 Dec. 1983. Total cargo traffic passing through the country's ports amounted to 17·2m. tonnes in 1983.

Inland Waterways. The principal inland waterways open to navigation are the Shannon Navigation (130 miles) and the Grand Canal and Barrow Navigation (156 miles). Merchandise traffic is not now transported on them and navigation is confined to pleasure craft operated either privately or commercially.

Post and Broadcasting (31 Dec. 1982). Number of post offices, 2,096; telegraph offices, 1,340; telephones, 580,000; public telephones, 3,939; telephone exchanges, 1,097.

Radio and television broadcasting is operated by Radio Telefis Éireann, a statutory public body appointed by the Minister for Posts and Telegraphs under the Broadcasting Authority Acts. On 31 Dec. 1982 there were 695,500 holders of current television licences.

Cinemas. There are 160 cinemas and 169 (estimate) screens.

Newspapers (1983). There are 7 daily newspapers (all in English) with a combined circulation of 711,319; 5 of them are published in Dublin (circulation, 609,858).

JUSTICE, RELIGION, EDUCATION AND WELFARE

Justice. The Constitution provides that justice shall be administered in public in Courts established by law by Judges appointed by the President on the advice of the Government. The jurisdiction and organization of the Courts are dealt with in the Courts (Establishment and Constitution) Act, 1961, the Courts (Supplemental Provisions) Acts, 1961–81. These Courts consist of Courts of First Instance and a Court of Final Appeal, called the Supreme Court. The Courts of First Instance are the High Court with full original jurisdiction and the Circuit and the District Courts with local and limited jurisdiction. A judge may not be removed from office except for stated misbehaviour or incapacity and then only on resolutions passed by both Houses of the *Oireachtas*. Judges of the Supreme, High and Circuit Courts are appointed from among practising barristers. Judges of the District Court (called District Justices) may be appointed from among practising barristers or practising solicitors.

The Supreme Court, which consists of the Chief Justice (who is *ex officio* an additional judge of the High Court) and 5 ordinary judges, has appellate jurisdiction from all decisions of the High Court. The President may, after consultation with the Council of State, refer a Bill, which has been passed by both Houses of the *Oireachtas* (other than a money bill and certain other bills), to the Supreme Court for a decision on the question as to whether such Bill or any provision thereof is repugnant to the Constitution.

The High Court, which consists of a President (who is *ex officio* an additional Judge of the Supreme Court) and 14 ordinary judges, has full original jurisdiction in and power to determine all matters and questions, whether of law or fact, civil or criminal. In all cases in which questions arise concerning the validity of any law having regard to the provisions of the Constitution, the High Court alone exercises original jurisdiction. The High Court on Circuit acts as an appeal court from the Circuit Court.

The Court of Criminal Appeal consists of the Chief Justice or an ordinary Judge of the Supreme Court, together with either 2 ordinary judges of the High Court or the President and one ordinary judge of the High Court. It deals with appeals by persons convicted on indictment where the appellant obtains a certificate from the trial judge that the case is a fit one for appeal, or, in case such certificate is refused, where the court itself, on appeal from such refusal, grants leave to appeal. The decision of the Court of Criminal Appeal is final, unless that court or the Director of Public Prosecutions certifies that the decision involves a point of law of exceptional public importance, in which case an appeal is taken to the Supreme Court.

The High Court exercising criminal jurisdiction is known as the Central Criminal Court. It consists of a judge or judges of the High Court, nominated by the President of the High Court. The Court sits in Dublin and tries criminal cases which are outside the jurisdiction of the Circuit Court or which may be sent forward to it for trial from the Circuit Court on the application of the Director of Public Prosecution.

The country is divided into a number of circuits for the purposes of the Circuit Court. The President of the Circuit Court is *ex officio* an additional judge of the High Court. The jurisdiction of the court in civil proceedings is limited to £15,000 in contract and tort, £15,000 in actions founded on hire-purchase and credit-sale agreements, £5,000 in equity and £5,000 in probate and administration, save by consent of the parties, in which event the jurisdiction is unlimited. In criminal matters it has jurisdiction in all cases except murder, treason, piracy and allied offences. The Circuit Court acts as an appeal court from the District Court.

The District Court has summary jurisdiction in a large number of criminal cases where the offence is not of a serious nature. In civil matters the Court has jurisdiction in contract and tort (except slander, libel, seduction, slander of title and false imprisonment) where the claim does not exceed £2,500; in proceedings founded on hire-purchase and credit-sale agreements, the jurisdiction is £2,500.

All criminal cases, except those of a minor nature, are tried by a judge and a jury of 12. Juries are also used in many civil cases in the High Court. In a criminal case the jury must be unanimous in reaching a verdict, but in a civil case the agreement of 9 members is sufficient.

Religion. According to the census of population taken in 1981 the principal religious professions were as follows:

	Leinster	*Munster*	*Connacht*	*Ulster (part of)*	*Total*
Roman Catholics	1,645,038	949,708	406,656	202,172	3,203,574
Church of Ireland	58,330	18,065	5,976	12,959	95,339
Presbyterians	4,342	540	342	9,028	14,252
Methodists	3,343	1,293	330	847	5,813
Other religious denominations	9,087	2,567	746	480	12,880
Not stated or no religion	70,372	26,142	10,360	4,673	111,547

Education. *Elementary.* Elementary education is free and was given in about 3,398 national schools (including 112 special schools) in 1981. The average daily enrolment of pupils in 1984 was 571,003; the number of teachers of all classes about 20,720, including remedial teachers and teachers of special classes. Average daily pupil attendance is about 91%. There are 6 Colleges of Education for the training of primary school teachers, all co-educational. The estimated state expenditure on elementary education for 1984 is £350,847,000, excluding the cost of administration.

Special provision is made for handicapped and deprived children in special schools which are recognized on the same basis as primary schools, in special classes attached to ordinary schools and in certain voluntary centres where educational services appropriate to the needs of the children are provided. Categories of handicapped children catered for include visually handicapped, hearing impaired, physically handicapped, mentally handicapped, emotionally disturbed, travelling children and other socially disadvantaged children. Provision is also being made on an increasing scale for children with dual or multiple handicaps. In each case a programme suited to the needs of the particular kind of handicap is provided. The number of children in each class in such schools is very much smaller than in ordinary classes in a primary school and because of the size of the catchment areas involved an extensive system of school transport has been developed. Many handicapped children who have spent some years in a special school or class are integrated into normal schools for part of their school career, if necessary with special additional facilities such as nursing services, special equipment, etc. For others who cannot progress within the ordinary school system the special schools or classes provide both the primary and secondary level of education. In addition to the services being provided on a full-time basis many children are being catered for by the provision of part-time teaching facilities in hospitals, child guidance clinics, rehabilitation workshops, special 'Saturday-morning' centres and home teaching schemes.

Special schools (1982–83) were numbered 112 with 8,383 pupils. There were 189 special classes attached to ordinary schools with 2,377 pupils. 737 remedial teachers were employed for backward pupils in ordinary schools. 35 peripatetic teachers were employed for children with hearing or visual impairments.

Secondary. Voluntary secondary schools are under private control and are conducted in most cases by religious orders; all schools receive grants from the State and are open to inspection by the Department of Education. The number of recognized secondary schools during the school year 1983–84 was 511, and the number of pupils in attendance was 209,197. Total estimated state expenditure for 1984 is £214,354,500.

Grants for the provision of a wide range of audio visual teaching aids are available to secondary schools. The schools television service, *Telefis Scoile*, provides programmes in Irish, English, history, geography, mathematics and science subjects for senior and junior pupils. The vast majority of secondary schools now have at least one television receiving set which was purchased with the aid of a state grant.

Vocational Education Committee schools provide courses of general and technical education. The number of vocational schools during the school year 1983–84 was 248, full-time students, 71,968. These schools are controlled by the local Vocational Education Committees, and are maintained partly from the rates and partly by state grants. The estimated state expenditure for 1984 was £113m., and the estimated expenditure from the local rates, £2,437,000.

Comprehensive Schools which are financed by the State combine academic and technical subjects in one broad curriculum so that each pupil may be offered a range of educational options structured to his needs, abilities and interests. Pupils are prepared for the State examinations and for entrance to universities and institutes of further education. The number of comprehensive schools during the school year 1983–84 was 15 with 8,705 students.

Community Schools continue to be established through the amalgamation of existing voluntary secondary and Vocational Education Committee schools where this is found feasible and desirable and in new areas where a single larger school is considered preferable to 2 smaller schools under separate managements. These schools cater for all aspects of second-level education and provide adult education facilities in the areas in which they are situated. They also make facilities available to voluntary organizations and to the adult community generally. The number of community schools during the school year 1983–84 was 42 with 26,029 students. The estimated State expenditure on running costs for 1984 is £35,751,000 for community and comprehensive schools.

Regional Technical Colleges and Colleges of Technology. Apprentice, technician and professional courses are provided in the colleges of technology of the City of Dublin Vocational Education Committee, the Limerick College of Technology and 9 regional technical colleges at Athlone, Carlow, Cork, Dundalk, Galway, Letterkenny, Sligo, Tralee and Waterford. Students (full-time) 1983–84, 16,284.

University Education is provided by the National University of Ireland, founded in Dublin in 1908, and by the University of Dublin (Trinity College), founded in 1592. The National University comprises 3 constituent colleges–University College, Dublin, University College, Cork, and University College, Galway. St Patrick's College, Maynooth, Co. Kildare, is a national seminary for Catholic priests and a pontifical university with the power to confer degrees up to doctoral level in philosophy, theology and canon law. It also admits lay students (men and women) to the courses in arts, celtic studies, science and education which it provides as a recognized college of the National University. Besides the University medical schools, the Royal College of Surgeons in Ireland, provides medical qualifications which are internationally recognized. There are six Colleges of Education for the training of primary school teachers. For degree awarding purposes, three of these colleges are associated with Trinity College, two with University College, Dublin and one with University College, Cork. Third-level courses with a technological bias, leading to degree, diploma and certificate qualifications are also provided by the National Institutes for Higher Education, Limerick and Dublin. The Thomond College of Education, Limerick, is a specialist teacher-training institution concerned with the training of post-primary teachers in the areas of physical education, rural and general science, metalwork and engineering science, woodwork and building science and commercial and secretarial subjects.

The National Council for Educational Awards, established on a statutory basis in 1979, is the validating and awarding authority for degree, diploma and certificate courses in the third-level non-university sector.

Agricultural. An Chomhairle Óiliuna Talmhaíochta (ACOT) is the agency responsible for providing agricultural advisory and training services. Full-time instruction in agriculture is provided for all sections of the farming community. There are 4 agricultural colleges for young people, administered by ACOT, and 7 private ACOT- aided agricultural colleges, at each of which a 1-year course in agriculture is given. Second-year courses in farm machinery and dairying are provided at a number of the colleges. Advanced courses in pig and poultry husbandry and management are also provided. Scholarships tenable at these colleges, all of which are residential, are awarded by ACOT which also provides a comprehensive agricultural advisory service and conducts winter classes in agriculture and horticulture at local centres. A more comprehensive course is provided in winter farm schools, which are intended, in general, for persons of not less than 17 years of age who are engaged in farming. A comprehensive 3-year training programme leading to a 'Certificate in Farming' involving both formal instruction and a period of supervised on-farm work experience, was introduced by ACOT in 1982.

Horticultural. A 2-year course in commercial horticulture is provided at 3 residential colleges. There is also a 2-year course in amenity horticulture at the National Botanic Gardens in Dublin.

A scheme of farm apprenticeship and a trainee farmer scheme are operated by the Farm Apprenticeship Board, which represents various agricultural interests. The scheme provides for practical training on well-managed commercial farms.

Higher Education in Agriculture, Horticulture, Dairy Science and Veterinary Science. Higher education in general agriculture and horticulture is provided by University College, Dublin, and in dairy science by University College, Cork. Training in veterinary medicine and surgery is provided at the Veterinary College, Ballsbridge, Dublin.

Health Services. Persons in the lower income group (those who are unable to afford general practitioner services for themselves and their dependants) are entitled to a free comprehensive health service (family doctor, hospital and specialist services, maternity and infant-welfare services, dental, ophthalmic and aural services). Persons and dependants in the middle-income groups (less than £12,500 per annum income) are entitled to in-patient and out-patient hospital services including specialist services, free maternity care and help towards the cost of drugs and medicines. Such persons must pay a contribution of 1% of income, subject to a maximum of £120 per year, towards the cost of these services. All persons, irrespective of income, qualify for the benefit of assistance towards the cost of prescriptions, which limits the total outlay of a family to £28 per month. Hospital treatment for tuberculosis and certain other infectious diseases as well as for children suffering from certain long-term diseases and disabilities is provided free of charge to all classes of the community. Persons suffering from diabetes and other specified long-term conditions are eligible for a free supply of drugs and other necessary medicines, etc.

Pupils of national (elementary) schools are provided with a free school health-examination service and are also eligible for free dental, ophthalmic and aural services for defects discovered at school health examinations.

A free child-welfare clinic service for children under 6 years of age is available in many urban areas. A disabled persons maintenance allowance is payable in cases of need to chronically disabled persons over 16 who are not living in institutions. The disabled are also entitled to free travel and in certain circumstances to a free electricity allowance, a free television licence, free telephone rental and fuel vouchers. There is a mobility allowance of £300 per year for those unable to walk. The mother of a severely handicapped child maintained at home may qualify for a constant care allowance. There are also schemes which provide for the education of the blind, and for the training and placement in suitable employment of the blind and the disabled. Welfare services include day care services for children, families in stress and the old. Home helps, meals-on-wheels, home nursing etc, are provided where neccessary. All these services are provided by regional health boards under the direction and control of the Minister for Health.

Social Security. Social-welfare services concerned primarily with income maintenance are under the general control of the Minister for Social Welfare. The services administered by the Department of Social Welfare are divided into Insurance and Assistance schemes.

Insurance Services. All employees irrespective of their level of earnings are compulsorily insured from age 16 to 66 years and are liable for pay-related social insurance contributions. The majority of employees pay a contribution of 8·5% of their earnings prescribed up to a ceiling of £12,000 while a contribution of 7·5% of their earnings continues to be deducted up to a ceiling of £13,000. Their employers pay a further 12·1% up to a prescribed ceiling of £13,000. (The insured population is approximately 1·2m.) Subject to appropriate statutory conditions (but without regard to the recipients' means) the following flat-rate insurance benefits are available: Disability benefit, invalidity pension, unemployment benefit, maternity benefit, widow's pension, deserted wife's benefit, orphan's allowance, treatment benefit, retirement pension payable at 65, old-age pension payable at 66 and a death grant. Pay-related benefit is payable with disability benefit, unemployment benefit, maternity allowance and injury benefit to persons whose employment is insurable at certain class rates of pay-related social insurance contribution. The cost of the flat-rate and pay-related benefits is met by pay-related social insurance contributions from employers and employees and by a state grant.

The insurance services also provide for payment of benefits in respect of injury, disablement or death, as well as medical care resulting from an occupational accident or disease. These benefits are available to employees, irrespective of age, and are paid from an Occupational Injuries Fund which is financed by employers' contributions and income from investments.

Assistance Services. Children's allowances are payable without a means test in respect of each child under 16 years of age and children between 16 and 18 who are at school or incapacitated for a prolonged period. The following Assistance services are subject to a means test: Non-contributory widows' and orphans' pensions to the survivors of persons whose lack of insurance (or inadequate insurance record) precludes payment of contributory pensions; deserted wife's allowance to women who have been deserted by their husbands and for whom the deserted wife's benefit is similarly precluded; allowances for unmarried mothers, prisoners' wives and single women between the ages of 58 and 66 years; old age pensions payable at age 66 to persons not entitled to insurance pensions; blind pensions (under the same general conditions as apply to old age pensions) payable at age 18; unemployment assistance payable during unemployment to persons not entitled to receive unemployment benefit; supplementary welfare allowance, payable when a person has no other resources or when such resources are insufficient to meet his needs.

DIPLOMATIC REPRESENTATIVES

Of Ireland in Great Britain (17 Grosvenor Place, London, SW1X 7HR)
Ambassador: Noel Dorr (accredited 19 Oct. 1983).

Of Great Britain in Ireland (33 Merrion Rd., Dublin, 4)
Ambassador: A. C. Goodison, CMG, CVO.

Of Ireland in the USA (2234 Massachusetts Ave., NW, Washington, D.C., 20008)
Ambassador: Tadhg F. O' Sullivan.

Of the USA in Ireland (42 Elgin Rd., Ballsbridge, Dublin)
Ambassador: Robert F. Kane.

Of Ireland to the United Nations
Ambassador: Robert McDonagh.

Books of Reference

Statistical Information: The Central Statistics Office (Earlsfort Terrace, Dublin, 2) was established in June 1949, and is attached to the Department of the Taoiseach. *Director.* T. P. Linehan, B.E., B.Sc.

The Central Statistics Office took over the work carried out since 1922 by the Statistics Branch, Department of Industry and Commerce, which in turn had continued the statistical work carried out by the Department of Agriculture and Technical Instruction (since 1900) and by the Irish Department of the Ministry of Labour, London (since 1919). Vital statistics from 1864, annual agricultural statistics prior to 1900 and decennial census of population were compiled by the Registrar-General for Ireland. The population censuses were carried out in 1926, 1936 and 1946 by the Statistics Branch of the Department of Industry and Commerce and are now the responsibility of the Central Statistics Office, which has also, as from July 1950, taken over from the Registrar-General the compilation of Vital Statistics. The Statistics Act 1926 confers wide powers for the collection, compilation and publication of statistics. Other Acts under which statistics are collected are Workmen's Compensation Act, Merchant Shipping Act, Customs Consolidation Act and Road Transport Act.

Principal publications of the Central Statistics Office are *National Income and Expenditure* (annually), *Statistical Abstract* (annually), *Census of Population Reports, Census of Industrial Production Reports, Trade and Shipping Statistics* (annually and monthly), *Trend of Employment and Unemployment* (annually), *Reports on Vital Statistics* (annually), *Irish Statistical Bulletin* (quarterly).

Aspects of Ireland (Series). Dublin Department of Foreign Affairs.
Atlas of Ireland. Royal Irish Academy, Dublin, 1979
Facts About Ireland. Dublin Department of Foreign Affairs, 5th ed. 1981
The Gill History of Ireland. 11 vols. Dublin
Bartholomew, P. C., *The Irish Judiciary.* Dublin, Institute of Public Administration, 1974
Brown, T., *Ireland: A Social and Cultural History, 1922–1979.* London, 1981
Chubb, B., *The Constitution and Constitutional Change in Ireland.* Dublin, 1978
Delaney, V. T. H., *The Administration of Justice in Ireland.* 4th ed. Dublin, Institute of Public Administration, 1975

Eager, A. R., *A Guide to Irish Bibliographical Material.* 2nd ed. London, 1980
Encyclopaedia of Ireland. Dublin, 1968
Freeman, T. W., *Ireland: A General and Regional Geography.* 4th ed. London, 1972
Harbison, P., *Guide to the National Monuments of Ireland.* Dublin, 1975
Hickey, D. J. and Doherty, J. E., *A Dictionary of Irish History since 1800.* Dublin, 1980
Johnston, T. J., and others, *A History of the Church of Ireland.* Dublin, 1953
Keatinge, P., *Formulation of Irish Foreign Policy.* Dublin, 1973.—*A Place Among the Nations: Issues of Irish Foreign Policy.* Dublin, 1978
Kee, R., *The Green Flag.* London, 1972
Kelly, J. M., *Fundamental Rights in the Irish Law and Constitution.* 2nd ed. Dublin, 1967
Lehane, B., *The Companion Guide to Ireland.* London, 1973
Lyons, F. S. L., *Ireland Since the Famine.* London, 1971
McDunphy, Michael, *The President of Ireland: His Powers, Functions and Duties.* Dublin, 1945
Nevill, W. E., *Geology and Ireland.* Dublin, 1963
Thom's Directory of Ireland. 2 vols. (Dublin, Street Directory, Commercial). Dublin, 1979–80
Tobin, F., *Ireland in the 1960s.* Dublin, 1984

ISRAEL

Capital: Jerusalem
Population: 4·15m. (1984)
GNP per capita: US$5,160 (1981)

Medinat Israel—State of Israel

HISTORY. In 1967, following some years of uneasy peace, local clashes on the Israeli-Syrian border were followed by Egyptian mass concentration of forces on the borders of Israel. The UN emergency force was expelled and a blockade of shipping to and from Israel was imposed by Egypt in the Red Sea. Israel struck out at Egypt on land and in the air on 5–9 June 1967. Jordan joined in the conflict which spread to the Syrian borders. By 11 June the Israelis had occupied the Gaza Strip and the Sinai peninsula as far as the Suez Canal in Egypt, West Jordan as far as the Jordan valley and the heights east of the Sea of Galilee, including Quneitra in Syria.

A further war broke out on 6 Oct. 1973 when an Egyptian offensive was launched across the Suez Canal and Syrian forces struck on the Golan Heights. Following UN Security Council resolutions a ceasefire finally came into being on 24 Oct. In Dec. agreement was reached by Egypt and Israel on disengagement and a disengagement agreement was signed with Syria on 31 May 1974. A further disengagement agreement was signed between Israel and Egypt in Sept. 1975.

Developments in 1977 included President Sadat of Egypt's visit to Israel and peace inititative and in March 1978 Israeli troops entered southern Lebanon but later withdrew after the arrival of a UN peace-keeping force.

In Sept. 1978 President Carter convened the Camp David conference at which Egypt and Israel agreed on frameworks for peace in the Middle East with treaties to be negotiated between Israel and her neighbours. Negotiations began in USA between Egypt and Israel in Oct. 1978 and a peace treaty was signed in Washington 26 March 1979.

Under the Israel-Egypt peace treaty signed in Washington on 26 March 1979, Israel withdrew from the Sinai Desert in two phases, part was achieved on 26 Jan. 1980 and the final withdrawal by 26 April 1982.

AREA AND POPULATION. The area of Israel, within the boundaries defined by the 1949 armistice agreements with Egypt, Jordan, the Lebanon and Syria, is 20,770 sq. km (8,017 sq. miles), with a population (May 1972 census) of 3·2m. (estimated, Jan. 1984, 4·15m.). Population of areas under Israeli administration as a result of the 6-day war was: Judaea and Samaria (West Bank), 767,300, Gaza Strip, 493,700, and the Golan Heights, 19,700.

Crude birth rate per 1,000 population of Jewish population (1983), 22·4; non-Jewish, 34·7; crude death rate, Jewish, 7·4; non-Jewish, 4·1; infant mortality rate per 1,000 live births, Jewish, 11·7; non-Jewish, 22.

Israel is administratively divided into 6 districts:

District	*Area (sq. km)*	*Population* [1]	*Chief town*
Northern	4,946	656,000	Nazareth
Haifa	854	575,300	Haifa
Central	1,242	830,000	Ramla
Tel Aviv	170	1,000,200	Tel Aviv
Jerusalem [2]	627	472,900	Jerusalem
Southern	14,107	478,800	Beersheba

[1] 1983. [2] Includes East Jerusalem, annexed from Jordan after 1967 War.

On 23 Jan. 1950 the Knesset proclaimed Jerusalem the capital of the State and on 14 Dec. 1981 extended Israeli law into the Golan Heights. Population of the main towns (4 June 1983): Tel-Aviv/Jaffa, 327,300; Jerusalem, 428,700; Haifa, 225,800; Ramat Gan, 117,100; Bat-Yam, 128,700; Holon, 133,500; Petach Tikva, 123,900; Beersheba, 110,800.

The official languages are Hebrew and Arabic.

Immigration. The following table shows the numbers of Jewish immigrants entering Palestine (Israel), including persons entering as travellers who subsequently registered as immigrants. For a year-by-year breakdown, *see* THE STATESMAN'S YEAR-BOOK, 1951, p. 1167.

1919–32	129,349	1940–47	101,173	1969–79	384,066
1933–39	235,170	1948–68	1,290,610	1980–83	63,656

During the period 1948–68, 45·5% of the immigrants came from Europe and America and 54·5% from Asia and Africa; during the period 1969–79, 79·5% came from Europe and America and 20·5% from Asia and Africa.

The Jewish Agency, which, in accordance with Article IV of the Palestine Mandate, played a leading role in laying the political, economic and social foundations on which the State of Israel was established, continues to be instrumental in organizing immigration.

CLIMATE. From April to Oct., the summers are long and hot, and almost rainless. From Nov. to March, the weather is generally mild, though colder in hilly areas, and this is the wet season. Jerusalem. Jan. 48°F (9°C), July 73°F (23°C). Annual rainfall 21″ (528 mm). Tel Aviv. Jan. 57°F (14°C), July 81°F (27°C). Annual rainfall 22″ (550 mm).

CONSTITUTION AND GOVERNMENT. Israel is an independent sovereign republic, established by proclamation on 14 May 1948. For the history of the British Mandate, *see* THE STATESMAN'S YEAR-BOOK, 1920–49, under PALESTINE.

In 1950 the Knesset (*Parliament*), which in 1949 had passed the Transition Law dealing in general terms with the powers of the Knesset, President and Cabinet, resolved to enact from time to time fundamental laws, which eventually, taken together, would form the Constitution. The first of these fundamental laws, dealing with the Knesset, Israel Lands and the President, were passed in 1958, 1960 and 1964 respectively and with the Government in 1968.

National flag: White with 2 horizontal blue stripes, the blue Shield of David in the centre.

National anthem: Hatikvah (The Hope). Words by N. N. Imber (1878); adopted as the Jewish National Anthem by the first Zionist Congress (1897).

The Knesset, a one-chamber Parliament, consists of 120 members. It is elected for a 4-year term by secret ballot and universal direct suffrage. The system of election is by proportional representation. After the July 1984 elections the Knesset was composed as follows: Alignment, 44; Likud, 41; National Religious Party, 5; Tehiya, 5; Hadash, 4; Shas, 4; Shinui, 3; Civil Rights, 3; Yahad, 3; PLP, 2; Agudat Israel, 2; Morasha, 2; Tami, 1; Kach, 1; Ometz, 1. It was agreed that for the first 25 months of the parliamentary term Shimon Peres should be Prime Minister and Itzhak Shamir, Deputy Prime Minister and after that the roles would be reversed. The President is elected by the Knesset by secret ballot by a simple majority; his term of office is 5 years. He may be re-elected once.

Former Presidents of the State: Chaim Weizmann (1949–52); Izhak Ben-Zvi (1952–63); Zalman Shazar (1963–68); Ephraim Katzir (1968–78); Yitzhak Navon (1978–83).

President: Chaim Herzog, elected 22 March 1983 by 61 votes to 56 against with 3 abstentions.

The Cabinet in Sept. 1984 was composed as follows:

Prime Minister and Minister of Interior and Religious Affairs: Shimon Peres (Labour).

Deputy Prime Minister and Minister of Foreign Affairs: Itzhak Shamir (Herut).

Vice-Premier and Minister of Education: Itzhak Navon (Labour). *Vice-Premier and Minister of Housing and Construction:* David Levi (Herut). *Trade and Industry:* Ariel Sharon (Herut). *Police:* Haim Bar-Lev (Labour). *Health:* Mordechai Gur (Labour). *Minister in the Prime Minister's Office:* Ezer Weizmann (Yahad). *Economics and Planning:* Gad Yaakobi (Labour). *Finance:* Itzhak Moda'i (Liberal). *Agriculture:* Arye Nehamkin (Labour). *Justice:* Moshe Nissim (Liberal). *Science and Development:* Gideon Patt (Liberal). *Integration of Immigrants:* Yaacov Tsur (Labour). *Transport:* Haim Corfu (Herut). *Labour and Social Affairs:* Moshe Katzav (Herut). *Defence:* Itzhak Rabin (Labour). *Communications:* Amnon Rubinstein (Shinui). *Energy and Infrastructure:* Moshe Shahal (Labour). *Tourism:* Avraham Sharir (Liberal). *Without Portfolio:* Moshe Arens (Herut), Dr Josef Burg (NRP), Yigael Hurwitz (Ometz), Itzhak Peretz (Shas), Josef Shapira (Morasha).

Local Government. Local authorities are of three kinds, namely, municipal corporations, local councils and regional councils. Their status, powers and duties are prescribed by statute. Regional councils are local authorities set up in agricultural areas and include all the agricultural settlements in the area under their jurisdiction. All local authorities exercise their authority mainly by means of bye-laws approved by the Minister of the Interior. Their revenue is derived from rates and a surcharge on income tax. Local authorities are elected for a 4-year term of office concurrently with general elections.

There are 36 municipalities (2 Arab), 115 local councils (46 Arab and 6 Druze) and 49 regional councils (1 Arab) comprising 700 villages.

DEFENCE. The Defence Service Law, provides a compulsory 39-month conscription for men between the ages of 18 and 26 and a 30-month conscription for men in the age-group of 27–29 years. Unmarried women aged 18–26 serve 24 months. After their term of military service, men are on the reserves until the age of 55 years. Until they are 40, men usually report for 31 days training annually and from then until they are 55, for 14 days. Commissioned and n.c.o.s usually serve 7 extra days a year.

The Israel Defence Force is a unified force, in which army, navy and air force are subordinate to a single chief-of-staff. The Minister of Defence is *de facto* commander-in-chief but from Oct. 1973 the cabinet formed a defence committee with authority to make decisions on military operations.

Army. The Army is organized in 11 armoured divisions, 33 armoured brigades, 10 mechanized infantry brigades, 12 territorial/border infantry brigades and 15 artillery brigades. Equipment includes some 3,600 main battle tanks and 4,000 other armoured fighting vehicles. Strength (1985) 104,000 (conscripts 88,000), rising to 600,000 on mobilization.

Navy. The Navy includes 3 diesel-electric patrol submarines (built in Britain), 27 missile vessels (6 of 500 tons with helicopter and hangar, 8 of 415 tons, 12 of 220 tons and 1 of 47 tons, the smallest missile craft yet built), 2 missile-armed hydrofoils of 105 tons, 45 coastal patrol craft, 2 transports, 3 medium landing ships, 6 landing craft, 1 'firefish', 1 support ship, 1 training ship, 4 coastguard cutters, and 3 minor landing craft.

New construction includes 2 missile armed corvettes of 850 tons, and 10 improved guided-missile hydrofoils of 105 tons, all being built in Israel.

The former Nautical School in Haifa has been reorganized as a Naval Officers' School in Acre. The repair base at Eilat has a syncrolift. Naval personnel in 1985 totalled 800 officers and 5,800 men, of whom 3,500 are conscripts, including a Naval Commando. There are also 1,000 naval reservists available on mobilization.

Air Force. The Air Force has a personnel strength of about 30,000, with about 580 first-line aircraft, all jets, of Israeli, US and French manufacture. There are 2 squadrons with about 50 F-15s, 4 squadrons with about 100 Israeli-built Kfirs, and 3 squadrons with the first 95 of a planned 145 F-16s in an interceptor role; 5 squadrons with 130 F-4E Phantoms, 2 squadrons with 65 Kfirs, and 4 squadrons with A-4E/H/N Skyhawks in the fighter-bomber/attack role; and 12 RF-4E reconnaissance fighters; supported by 4 E-2C Hawkeye airborne early warning and control aircraft and a few OV-1 Mohawk and RU-21 elint aircraft. There are transport squadrons of turboprop C-130/KC-130 Hercules, C-47, Arava, Islander, and Boeing 707 (some equipped for tanker or ECM duties) aircraft, helicopter squadrons of CH-53, Super Frelon, AH-1G/S HueyCobra, Hughes 500MD/TOW Defender, JetRanger, Agusta-Bell 205 and 212 aircraft, and training units with locally-built Magister jet trainers, which can be used also in a light ground attack role. Missiles in service include surface-to-air Hawks and surface-to-surface Lances.

INTERNATIONAL RELATIONS

Membership. Israel is a member of UN.

ECONOMY

Budget. The budget year runs from 1 April to 31 March (in shekel 1 m.):

	1980–81	*1981–82*
Revenue	101,423	228,506
Revenue for development budget	20,156	44,804
Business enterprises	11,323	22,506
Expenditure	101,423	228,506

In 1981–82 the main items of expenditure (in shekel 1 m.) were: Defence, 63,816; education and culture, 15,202; health, 3,722; labour and social welfare, 8,070.

Currency. The unit of currency is the *shekel* and was introduced in Feb. 1980. Currency in circulation on 31 Dec. 1978 was I£6,860m. (bank-notes and coins). In March 1985, £1 = 824 *shekel*; US$ = 783 *shekel.*

Banking. The Bank of Israel was established by law in 1954 as Israel's central bank. Its Governor is appointed by the President on the recommendation of the Cabinet for a 5-year term. He acts as economic adviser to the Government and has ministerial status.

There are 21 commercial banks headed by Bank Leumi Le Israel, Bank Hapoalim and Israel Discount Bank.

Weights and Measures. The metric system is in general use. The (metrical) *dunam* = 1,000 sq. metres (about 0·25 acre).

Jewish Year. The Jewish year 5745 corresponds to 27 Sept. 1984–15 Sept. 1985; 5746 to 16 Sept. 1985–3 Oct. 1986; 5747 to 4 Oct. 1986–23 Sept. 1987.

ENERGY AND NATURAL RESOURCES

Electricity. Electric-power consumption amounted during 1983 to 12,555m. kwh.

Oil and Gas. Oil was first discovered in Sept. 1955 at Heletz in the Negev. Crude oil production in 1983 was 13m. litres and natural gas 66m. cu. metres.

Minerals. The most valuable natural resources of the country are the potash, bromine and other salt deposits of the Dead Sea, which are exploited by the Dead Sea Works, Ltd. Geological research and exploration of the natural resources in the Negev are undertaken by the Israel Mining Corporation. Potash production in 1983 was 1,518,000 tons.

Agriculture. In the coastal plain (Sharon, Emek Hefer and the Shephelah) mixed farming, poultry raising, citriculture and vineyards are the main agricultural activities. The Emek (the Valley of Jezreel) is the main agricultural centre of Israel. Mixed farming is to be found throughout the valleys; the sub-tropical Beisan and Jordan plainlands are also centres of banana plantations and fish breeding. In Galilee mixed farming, olive and tobacco plantations prevail. The Hills of Ephraim are a vineyard centre; many parts of the hill country are under afforestation. In the northern Negev farming has been aided by the Yarkon–Negev water pipeline. This has become part of the overall project of the 'National Water Carrier', which is to take water from the Sea of Galilee (Lake Kinnereth) to the south. The plan includes a number of regional projects such as the Lake Kinnereth –Negev pipeline which came into operation in 1964; it has an annual capacity of 320m. cu. metres.

The area under cultivation (in 1,000 dunams) in 1982–83 was 4,370, of which 2,200 were under irrigation. Of the total cultivated area 2,500 dunams were under field crops, 340 under vegetables, potatoes, pumpkins and melons, 930 under citrus and orchards, 37 under fish ponds and 190 under miscellaneous crops, including auxiliary farms, nurseries, flowers, etc.

Industrial crops, such as cotton and sugar-beet, have successfully been introduced. In 1982–83 the area under cotton totalled 570,800 dunams.

Livestock (1983) included 330,000 cattle, 240,000 sheep, 115,000 goats, 95,000 pigs, 4,000 horses, 26m. chickens.

Characteristic types of rural settlement are, among others, the following: (1) The *Kibbutz* and *Kvutza* (communal collective settlement), where all property and earnings are collectively owned and work is collectively organized. (2) The *Moshav Ovdim* (workers' co-operative smallholders' settlement) which is founded on the principles of mutual aid and equality of opportunity between the members, all farms being equal in size; hired labour is prohibited. (3) The *Moshav Shitufi* (co-operative settlement), which is based on collective ownership and economy as in the *Kibbutz,* but with each family having its own house and being responsible for its own domestic services. (4) The *Moshav* (smallholders' settlement), which resembles the *moshav ovdim* but lacks the latter's rigid ideological basis; hired labour, for instance, is permitted. (5) The *Moshava* (village), in which land and property are privately owned and every resident is responsible for his own well-being.

INDUSTRY AND TRADE

Industry. A wide range of products is manufactured, processed or finished in the country, including chemicals, metal products, textiles, tyres, diamonds, paper, plastics, leather goods, glass and ceramics, building materials, precision instruments, tobacco, foodstuffs, electrical and electronic equipment.

Labour. The General Federation of Labour (Histadrut) founded in 1920, had, in 1973, 1,259,200 members (including 89,000 Arab and Druze members); including workers' families, this membership represents 56·1% of the population covering 85% of all wage-earners. Several trades unions of lesser importance also exist.

Commerce. External trade, in US$1,000, for calendar years:

	1977	*1978*	*1979*	*1980*	*1982*	*1983*
Imports	4,844	5,843	7,511	8,024	7,960	8,370
Exports	3,082	3,921	4,546	5,540	5,017	4,894

The main exportable commodities are citrus fruit and by-products, fruit-juices, wines and liquor, sweets, polished diamonds, chemicals, tyres, textiles, metal products, machinery, electronic and transportation equipment, flowers. The main exports were, in 1983 (US$1m.): Diamonds, 1,207·7; chemical and oil products, 582; food, beverages and tobacco, 312·9; citrus fruit, 166·5.

Total trade between Israel and UK (British Department of Trade returns, in £1,000 sterling):

	1980	*1981*	*1982*	*1983*	*1984*
Imports to UK	236,599	256,000	275,139	314,148	392,757
Exports and re-exports from UK	231,658	212,000	224,362	354,860	393,025

Tourism. In 1983 there were about 1·16m. tourists.

COMMUNICATIONS

Roads. There were 12,482 km of paved roads in 1983. Registered motor vehicles in 1983 totalled 729,567, including 7,870 buses, 110,786 trucks and 571,515 private cars.

Railways. Internal communications (1982) are provided by 336 km of standard gauge line. Construction is in progress (1982) of 215 km of new line linking Eilat on the Gulf of Aqaba with Sedom and the existing rail network by means of the 34 km line opened between Oron and Nahal Zin in Nov. 1977. In 1983, 2·8m. passengers and 5·8m. tonnes of freight were carried.

Aviation. Air communications are centred in the airport of Ben Gurion, near Tel-Aviv. In 1983, 9,757 planes landed at Israeli airports on international flights; 1,558,000 passengers arrived, 1,549,000 departed. In 1983, 64,455 tons of freight were loaded and 61,253 tons unloaded. The Israeli airline El Al maintains regular flights to London, Paris, Rome, Amsterdam, Brussels, Athens, Vienna, New York, Zurich, Munich, Nicosia, Istanbul, Johannesburg, Nairobi, Frankfurt and Copenhagen. In 1980–81 El Al carried 1·25m. passengers.

Shipping. Israel has 3 commercial ports, Haifa, Ashdod and Eilat. In 1983, 3,274 ships anchored in Israeli ports; 15·3m. tons. of freight were handled. The merchant fleet consisted in 1983 of 94 vessels, totalling 1,849,000 GRT.

Post and Broadcasting. The Ministry of Posts controls the postal, telegraph and telephone service. In 1983 there were 601 post offices and postal agencies, 49 mobile post offices and 1·4m. telephones.

The broadcasting station in Jerusalem, *Kol Israel*, is controlled by the Broadcasting Authority, established in 1965. Wireless licences in 1974 numbered approximately 460,000 and television licences 385,000.

Cinemas (1979). There were 214 cinemas with a seating capacity of approximately 152,300.

Newspapers (1984). There were 36 daily newspapers, including 17 in Hebrew.

JUSTICE, RELIGION, EDUCATION AND WELFARE

Justice. *Law.* Under the Law and Administration Ordinance, 5708/1948, the first law passed by the Provisional Council of State, the law of Israel is the law which was obtaining in Palestine on 14 May 1948 in so far as it is not in conflict with that Ordinance or any other law passed by the Israel legislature and with such modifications as result from the establishment of the State and its authorities.

Capital punishment was abolished in 1954, except for support given to the Nazis and for high treason.

The law of Palestine was derived from three main sources, namely, Ottoman law, English law (Common Law and Equity) and the law enacted by the Palestine legislature, which to a great extent was modelled on English law. The Ottoman law in its turn was derived from three main sources, namely, Moslem law which had survived in the Ottoman Empire, French law adapted by the Ottomans and the personal law of the non-Moslem communities.

Civil Courts. Municipal courts, established in certain municipal areas, have criminal jurisdiction over offences against municipal regulations and bye-laws and certain specified offences committed within a municipal area.

Magistrates courts, established in each district and sub-district, have limited jurisdiction in both civil and criminal matters.

District courts, sitting at Jerusalem, Tel-Aviv and Haifa, have jurisdiction, as courts of first instance, in all civil matters not within the jurisdiction of magistrates courts, and in all criminal matters, and as appellate courts from magistrates courts and municipal courts.

The Supreme Court has jurisdiction as a court of first instance (sitting as a High Court of Justice dealing mainly with administrative matters) and as an appellate court from the district courts (sitting as a Court of Civil or of Criminal Appeal).

In addition, there are various tribunals for special classes of cases, such as the Rents Tribunals and the Tribunals for the Prevention of Profiteering and Speculation. Settlement Officers deal with disputes with regard to the ownership or possession of land in settlement areas constituted under the Land (Settlement of Title) Ordinance.

Religious Courts. The rabbinical courts of the Jewish community have exclusive jurisdiction in matters of marriage and divorce, alimony and confirmation of wills of members of their community other than foreigners, concurrent jurisdiction with the civil courts in such matters of members of their community who are foreigners if they consent to the jurisdiction, and concurrent jurisdiction with the civil courts in all other matters of personal status of all members of their community, whether foreigners or not, with the consent of all parties to the action, save that such courts may not grant a decree of dissolution of marriage to a foreign subject.

The courts of the several recognized Christian communities have a similar jurisdiction over members of their respective communities.

The Moslem religious courts have exclusive jurisdiction in all matters of personal status over Moslems who are not foreigners, and over Moslems who are foreigners, if under the law of their nationality they are subject in such matters to the jurisdiction of Moslem religious courts.

Where any action of personal status involves persons of different religious communities, the President of the Supreme Court will decide which court shall have jurisdiction, and whenever a question arises as to whether or not a case is one of personal status within the exclusive jurisdiction of a religious court, the matter must be referred to a special tribunal composed of 2 judges of the Supreme Court and the president of the highest court of the religious community concerned in Israel.

Religion. Religious affairs are under the supervision of a special Ministry, with departments for the Christian and Moslem communities. The religious affairs of each community remain under the full control of the ecclesiastical authorities concerned: in the case of the Jews, the Sephardi and Ashkenazi Chief Rabbis, in the case of the Christians, the heads of the various communities, and in the case of the Moslems, the Qadis. The Druze were officially recognized in 1957 as an autonomous religious community.

In 1984 there were: Moslems, 548,600; Christians, 96,200; Druze and others, 67,700.

The Jewish Sabbath and Holy Days are observed as days of rest in the public services. Full provision is, however, made for the free exercise of other faiths, and for the observance by their adherents of their respective days of rest and Holy Days.

Education. Laws passed by the Knesset in 1949 and 1978 provide for free and compulsory education from 5 to 16 years of age. There is free education until 18 years of age.

The State Education Law of 12 Aug. 1953 established a unified state-controlled elementary school system with a provision for special religious schools. The standard curriculum for all elementary schools is issued by the Ministry with a possibility of adding supplementary subjects comprising not more than 25% of the total syllabus. Many schools in towns are private, a number are maintained by municipalities and some are administered by teachers' co-operatives or trustees.

Statistics relating to schools under government supervision, 1983–84:

Type of School	*Schools*	*Teachers*	*Pupils*
Hebrew Education			
Primary schools	1,292	36,113	468,609
Schools for handicapped children	209	2,959	11,632
Schools of intermediate division	263	11,792	95,476
Secondary schools	499		166,097
Vocational schools	305	20,643	79,713
Agricultural schools	26		4,698
Arab Education			
Primary schools	315	6,423	135,649
Schools for handicapped children	13	112	962
Schools of intermediate division	51	1,299	19,207
Secondary schools	75		29,462
Vocational schools	36	1,774	4,031
Agricultural schools	2		584

There are also a number of private schools maintained by religious foundations—Jewish, Christian and Moslem—and also by private societies.

The Hebrew University of Jerusalem, founded in 1925, comprises faculties of the humanities, social sciences, law, science, medicine and agriculture. In 1978–79 it had a teaching staff of 2,184 and 14,000 students.

The Technion in Haifa had, in 1978–79, 21 faculties and departments with 1,500 teachers and 7,800 students. The Weizmann Institute of Science in Rehovoth is engaged in research in chemistry, mathematics, physics and biology; founded in 1949, it had a staff of 400 and 486 students in 1978–79.

In 1978–79 the Tel Aviv University had 16 faculties, some 2,388 teachers and 19,000 students. The religious Bar-Ilan University at Ramat Gan, opened in 1965 had, in 1978–79, 5 faculties (Jewish studies, humanities, natural sciences, social sciences, philology), 900 teachers and 7,600 students. The Haifa University had, in 1978–79, 29 faculties with 568 teachers and 7,522 students. The Ben Gurion University had, in 1978–79, 28 departments with 628 teachers and 4,300 students.

Social Welfare. In 1983 Israel had 150 hospitals with 26,402 beds. The 'Malben' organization cares for the aged. The Women's International Zionist Organization has a number of children's homes, crèches and kindergartens as well as vocational schools and training institutions for nurses. In addition, there are several other voluntary bodies providing specific services to the community.

The National Insurance Law, which took effect in April 1954, provides for old-age pensions, survivors' insurance, work-injury insurance, maternity insurance, family allowances and unemployment benefits.

DIPLOMATIC REPRESENTATIVES

Of Israel in Great Britain (2 Palace Green, London, W8 4QB)
Ambassador: Yehuda Avner (accredited 3 Aug. 1983).

Of Great Britain in Israel (192 Rehov Hayarkon, Tel Aviv 63405)
Ambassador: C. W. Squire, CMG, MVO.

Of Israel in the USA (3514 International Drive, NW, Washington, D.C., 20008)
Ambassador: Meir Rosenne.

Of the USA in Israel (71 Hayarkon St., Tel Aviv)
Ambassador: Samuel W. Lewis.

Of Israel to the United Nations
Ambassador: Benjamin Netanyahu.

Books of Reference

Statistical Information: There is a Central Bureau of Statistics and Economic Research at the Prime Minister's Office, Jerusalem. It publishes monthly bulletins of economic statistics, social statistics, foreign trade statistics and an English summary.
Government Yearbook. Government Printer, Jerusalem. 1951 ff. (latest issue, 1971/72)
Facts about Israel. Government Printer, Jerusalem, 1979
Statistical Abstract of Israel. Government Printer, Jerusalem (from 1949/50)
Israel Yearbook. Tel-Aviv, 1948–49 ff.
Statistical Bulletin of Israel. 1949 ff.
Reshumoth (Official Gazette)
Middle East Record, ed. Y. Oron. London, 1960 ff.
Laws of the State of Israel. Authorized translation. Government Printer, Jerusalem, 1958 ff.
Alkalay, R., *The Complete English–Hebrew Dictionary.* 4 vols. Tel-Aviv, 1959–61
Atlas of Israel. Amsterdam, Jerusalem and London, 1970
Ben-Gurion, D., *Ben-Gurion Looks Back.* London, 1965.—*The Jews in Their Land.* London, 1966.—*Israel: A Personal History.* New York, 1971
Churchill, R. S. and W. S., *The Six-Day War.* London, 1967
Dayan, M., *Breakthrough.* New York, 1981
Efrat, E. and Orni, E., *Geography of Israel.* Jerusalem, 1976
Frankel, W., *Israel Observed.* London, 1980
Gilbert, M., *The Arab-Israeli Conflict: Its History in Maps.* 3rd ed. London, 1981
Goldman, N., *The Jewish Paradox.* New York, 1978
Harris, W., *Taking Root: Israeli Settlement in the West Bank, The Golan and Gaza Sinai 1967–1980.* Chichester, 1981
Hyamson, A. M., *Palestine under Mandate, 1920–48.* London, 1951

Jiryis, S., *The Arabs in Israel.* New York, 1976
Kieval, G. R., *Party Politics in Israel and the Occupied Territories.* Westport, 1983
Laquer, W. (ed.), *The Israel–Arab Reader.* London, 1970.—*A History of Zionism.* New York, 1972
Likhovski, E. S., *Israel's Parliament: The Law of the Knesset.* Oxford, 1971
Lucas, N., *A Modern History of Israel.* London and New York, 1975
Luttwak, E., and Horowitz, D., *The Israeli Army.* London, 1975
Peretz, D., *The Government and Politics of Israel.* Folkestone, 1979
Peri, Y., *Between Battles and Ballots: Israeli Military in Politics.* CUP, 1983
Pryce-Jones, D., *The Face of Defeat: Palestinian Refugees and Guerrillas.* New York, 1973
Sachar, H., *A History of Israel.* London and New York, 1976
Schick, A. P., (ed.) *Research Contributions to the Physical Geography of Israel.* Jerusalem, 1982
Segal, R., *Whose Jerusalem? The Conflicts of Israel.* London, 1973
Shimshoni, D., *Israeli Democracy: The Middle of the Journey.* New York, 1982
Who's Who in Israel. Tel-Aviv, 1978
Wolffsohn, M., *Politik in Israel.* Opladen, 1983

National Library: The Jewish National and University Library, Jerusalem.

ITALY

Repubblica Italiana

Capital: Rome
Population: 56·9m. (1983)
GNP per capita: US$6,960 (1981)

HISTORY. On 10 June 1946 Italy became a republic on the announcement by the Court of Cassation that a majority of the voters at the referendum held on 2 June had voted for a republic. The final figures, announced on 18 June, showed: For a republic, 12,718,641 (54·3% of the valid votes cast, which numbered 23,437,143); for the retention of the monarchy, 10,718,502 (45·7%); invalid and contested, 1,509,735. Total 24,946,878, or 89·1% of the registered electors, who numbered 28,005,449. For the results of the polling in the 13 leading cities, *see* THE STATESMAN'S YEAR-BOOK, 1951, p. 1175. Voting was compulsory, open to both men and women 21 years of age or older, including members of the Civil Service and the Armed Forces; former active Fascists and a few other categories were excluded.

On 18 June the then Provisional Government without specifically proclaiming the republic, issued an 'Order of the Day' decreeing that all court verdicts should in future be handed down 'in the name of the Italian people', that the *Gazzetta Ufficiale del Regno d'Italia* should be re-named *Gazzetta Ufficiale della Repubblica Italiana,* that all references to the monarchy should be deleted from legal and government statements and that the shield of the House of Savoy should be removed from the Italian flag.

Thus ended the reign of the House of Savoy, whose kings had ruled over Piedmont for 9 centuries and as Kings of Italy since 18 Feb. 1861. (For fuller account of the House of Savoy, *see* THE STATESMAN'S YEAR-BOOK, 1946, p. 1021.) The Crown Prince Umberto, son of King Victor Emmanuel III, became Lieut.-Gen. (*i.e.*, Regent) of the kingdom on 5 June 1944. Following the abdication and retirement to Egypt of his father on 9 May 1946, Umberto was declared King Umberto II; his reign lasted to 13 June, when he left the country. King Victor Emmanuel III died in Alexandria on 28 Dec. 1947.

AREA AND POPULATION. The population (present in actual boundaries) at successive censuses were as follows:

31 Dec. 1881	29,277,927	21 April 1936	42,302,680
10 Feb. 1901	33,370,138	4 Nov. 1951	47,158,738
10 June 1911	35,694,582	15 Oct. 1961	49,903,878
1 Dec. 1921	37,403,956	24 Oct. 1971	53,744,737
21 April 1931	40,582,043	25 Oct. 1981	56,243,935

The following table gives area and population of the Regions (census 1981 and estimate, 1983):

Regions	*Area in sq. km (1981)*	*Resident pop. census, 1981*	*Resident pop. estimate, 1983*	*Density per sq. km (1981)*
Piemonte	25,399	4,479,031	4,431,064	175
Valle d'Aosta	3,262	112,353	113,418	35
Lombardia	23,856	8,891,652	8,891,318	373
Trentino-Alto Adige	13,613	873,413	875,780	64
Bolzano-Bozen	*7,400*	*430,568*	*432,231*	*58*
Trento	*6,213*	*442,845*	*443,549*	*71*
Veneto	18,364	4,345,047	4,361,527	235
Friuli-Venezia Giulia	7,846	1,233,984	1,228,280	157
Liguria	5,416	1,807,893	1,789,225	332
Emilia Romagna	22,123	3,957,513	3,952,304	178
Toscana	22,992	3,581,051	3,581,291	155
Umbria	8,456	807,552	813,507	95
Marche	9,694	1,412,404	1,420,829	145
Lazio	17,203	5,001,684	5,056,119	289

Regions	Area in sq. km (1981)	Resident pop. census, 1981	Resident pop. estimate, 1983	Density per sq. km (1981)
Abruzzi	10,794	1,217,791	1,236,060	113
Molise	4,438	328,371	331,670	73
Campania	13,595	5,463,134	5,563,230	398
Puglia	19,347	3,871,617	3,946,871	199
Basilicata	9,992	610,186	614,522	60
Calabria	15,080	2,061,182	2,098,137	135
Sicilia	25,708	4,906,878	5,006,684	189
Sardegna	24,090	1,594,175	1,617,265	66
Total	301,268	56,556,911	56,929,101	187

Vital statistics for calendar years:

	Marriages	Living births: Legitimate	Living births: Illegitimate	Living births: Total	Still-born	Deaths excl. of still-born
1977	347,928	715,414	25,689	741,103	7,219	545,694
1978	331,416	681,350	27,693	709,043	6,564	540,671
1979	323,930	643,835	26,386	670,221	5,748	534,563
1980	322,968	612,945	27,456	640,401	5,139	554,510
1981[1]	313,736	595,195	26,610	621,805	4,950	542,204
1982[1]	310,938	589,342	28,165	617,507	4,739	531,632
1983[1]	300,855	571,628	28,590	600,218	4,361	561,214

[1] Provisional.

Emigrants to non-European countries, by sea and air: 1978, 23,589; 1979, 21,302; 1980, 20,360; 1981, 20,628; 1982, 22,324. Since 1960 nearly nine-tenths of these emigrants have gone to Canada, USA and Australia.

Communes of more than 100,000 inhabitants, with population resident at the census of 25 Oct. 1981 and (estimate) on 31 Dec. 1983:

	1981	1983		1981	1983
Roma (Rome)	2,840,259	2,830,650	Ferrara	149,453	147,328
Milano (Milan)	1,604,773	1,561,438	Perugia	142,348	144,064
Napoli (Naples)	1,212,387	1,208,545	Ravenna	138,034	136,786
Torino (Turin)	1,117,154	1,069,013	Pescara	131,330	131,974
Genova (Genoa)	762,895	746,785	Reggio nell'E.	130,376	131,075
Palermo	701,782	712,342	Rimini	127,813	129,506
Bologna	459,080	447,971	Monza	123,145	122,476
Firenze (Florence)	448,331	440,910	Bergamo	122,142	121,033
Catania	380,328	380,370	Sassari	119,596	119,781
Bari	371,022	369,576	Siracusa (Syracuse)	117,615	118,690
Venezia (Venice)	346,146	340,873	La Spezia	115,392	112,606
Verona	265,932	261,947	Vicenza	114,598	112,771
Messina	260,233	263,924	Terni	111,564	111,347
Trieste	252,369	246,305	Forlì	110,806	110,943
Taranto	244,101	243,120	Piacenza	109,039	107,617
Padova (Padua)	234,678	230,744	Cosenza	106,801	106,373
Cagliari	233,848	225,009	Ancona	106,498	105,657
Brescia	206,661	204,278	Bolzano	105,180	103,009
Modena	180,312	178,985	Pisa	104,509	103,894
Parma	179,019	177,062	Torre del Greco	103,605	104,654
Livorno (Leghorn)	175,741	176,298	Novara	102,086	102,279
Reggio di C.	173,486	175,646	Udine	102,021	101,179
Prato	160,220	161,705	Catanzaro	100,832	101,622
Salerno	157,385	156,921	Alessandria	100,523	–
Foggia	156,467	157,371			

CLIMATE. The climate varies considerably with latitude. In the south, it is warm temperate, with little rain in the summer months, but the north is cool temperate with rainfall more evenly distributed over the year.

Florence, Jan. 42°F (5·6°C), July 76°F (25°C). Annual rainfall 36" (901 mm). Milan, Jan. 35°F (2°C), July 75°F (24°C). Annual rainfall 32" (802 mm). Naples, Jan. 48°F (8·9°C), July 77°F (25·6°C). Annual rainfall 34" (850 mm). Palermo, Jan. 52°F (11·1°C), July 79°F (26·1°C). Annual rainfall 28" (702 mm). Rome, Jan. 44·5°F (7°C), July 77°F (25°C). Annual rainfall 26" (657 mm). Venice, Jan. 38°F (3·3°C), July 75°F (23·9°C). Annual rainfall 29" (725 mm).

CONSTITUTION AND GOVERNMENT. The new Constitution was

passed by the constituent assembly by 453 votes to 62 on 22 Dec. 1947; it came into force on 1 Jan. 1948. The Constitution consists of 139 articles and 18 transitional clauses. Its main dispositions are as follows:

Italy is described as 'a democratic republic founded on work'. Parliament consists of the Chamber of Deputies and the Senate. The Chamber is elected for 5 years by universal and direct suffrage and it consists of 630 deputies. The Senate is elected for 5 years on a regional basis; each Region having at least 7 senators, consisting of 315 elected senators; the Valle d'Aosta is represented by 1 senator only. The President of the Republic can nominate 5 senators for life from eminent men in the social, scientific, artistic and literary spheres. On the expiry of his term of office, the President of the Republic becomes a senator by right and for life, unless he declines.

The President of the Republic is elected in a joint session of Chamber and Senate, to which are added 3 delegates from each Regional Council (1 from the Valle d'Aosta). A two-thirds majority is required for the election, but after a third indecisive scrutiny the absolute majority of votes is sufficient. The President must be 50 years or over; his term lasts for 7 years. The President of the Senate acts as his deputy.

The President can dissolve the chambers of parliament, except during the last 6 months of his term of office.

The Cabinet can be forced to resign only on a motivated motion of censure; the defeat of a government bill does not involve the resignation of the Government.

A Constitutional Court, consisting of 15 judges who are appointed, 5 each, by the President of the Republic, Parliament (in joint session) and the highest law and administrative courts, has rights similar to those of the Supreme Court of the USA. It can decide on the constitutionality of laws and decrees, define the powers of the State and Regions, judge conflicts between the State and Regions and between the Regions, and try the President of the Republic and the Ministers. The court was set up in Dec. 1955.

The reorganization of the Fascist Party is forbidden. Direct male descendants of King Victor Emmanuel are excluded from all public offices, have no right to vote or to be elected, and are banned from Italian territory; their estates are forfeit to the State. Titles of nobility are no longer recognized, but those existing before 28 Oct. 1922 are retained as part of the name.

National flag: Three vertical strips of green, white, red.

National anthem: Fratelli d'Italia (words by G. Mameli; tune by M. Novaro, 1847).

The peace treaty was signed in Paris on 10 Feb. 1947, and ratified on 15 Sept. 1947. Italy ceded to France 4 frontier districts on the Little St Bernard Pass, the Mont-Cenis Plateau, the Mont-Thabor and Chaberton areas, and the upper valleys of the Tinée, Vésubie and Roya (*see* map in THE STATESMAN'S YEAR-BOOK, 1948); to Yugoslavia, nearly the whole of the provinces of Venezia Giulia, the commune of Zara and the island of Pelagosa; to Greece, the Dodecanese; to Albania, the island of Saseno; to China the Italian concession at Tientsin. Italy also gave up her former colonies.

Under the peace treaty Italy was to pay reparations to the following states: Greece, US$105m.; Yugoslavia, US$125m.; USSR, US$100m.; Ethiopia, US$25m.; Albania, US$5m. By 30 Nov. 1967 the whole debt had been paid.

Head of State: On 8 July 1978 Chamber and Senate in joint session elected by an absolute majority (832 votes out of 1,008 votes cast) Alessandro Pertini (Socialist; born 1896), President of the Republic.

Former Presidents of the Republic: Luigi Einaudi (1948–55); Giovanni Gronchi (1955–62); Antonio Segni (1962–64); Giuseppe Saragat (1964–71); Giovanni Leone (1971–78).

General elections for the Senate and Chamber of Deputies took place on 26 June 1983.

Senate. Christian Democrats, 120; Communists, 107; Socialists, 38; Italian Social Movement, 18; Social Democrats, 8; Republicans, 10; Liberals, 6; other groups, 8. Total: 315.

Chamber. Christian Democrats, 225; Communists, 198; Socialists, 73; Italian

Social Movement, 42; Republicans, 29; Social Democrats, 23; Liberals, 16; Radical Party, 11; other groups, 13. Total: 630.

The coalition government was composed as follows in Aug. 1984.

Prime Minister: Benedetto Craxi (PSI).
Vice Prime Minister: Arnaldo Forlani (DC).
Foreign Affairs: Giulio Andreotti (DC).
Interior: Oscar Scalfaro (DC).
Justice: Fermo Martinazzoli (DC).
Budget: Pier Luigi Romita (PSDI).
Finance: Bruno Visentini (PRI).
Treasury: Giovanni Goria (DC).
Defence: Giovanni Spadolini (PRI).
Education: Franca Falcucci (DC).
Public Works: Franco Nicolazzi (PSDI).
Agriculture: Filippo Pandolfi (DC).
Transport: Claudio Signorile (PSI).
Post: Antonio Gava (DC).
Industry: Renato Altissimo (PLI).
Labour: Gianni De Michelis (PSI).
Foreign Trade: Nicola Capria (PSI).
Merchant Navy: Gianuario Carta (DC).
State Industry: Clelio Darida (DC).
Health: Costante Degan (DC).
Tourism: Lelio Lagorio (PSI).
Culture: Antonino Gullotti (DC).
EEC Affairs: Francesco Forte (PSI).
Public Administration: Remo Gaspari (DC).
Scientific Research: Luigi Granelli (DC).
Southern Affairs: Salverino De Vito (DC).
Regional Affairs: Carlo Vizzini (PSDI).
Relations with Parliament: Oscar Mammi (PRI).
Civil Protection: Giuseppe Zamberletti (DC).
Ecology: Alfredo Biondi (PLI).

Allum, P. A., *Italy. Republic Without Government.* New York, 1974
Cross, E. (ed.), *La Constitution Italienne de 1948.* Paris, 1950
Ruini, M., and others, *La Nuova Costituzione Italiana.* Rome, 1947

Regional Administration. Italy is administratively divided into regions (*regioni*), provinces (*province*) and municipalities (*comuni*).

Art. 116 of the 1948 constitution provided for the establishment of 5 autonomous regions with special statute (*regioni autonome con statuto speciale*) and 15 autonomous regions with ordinary statute (*regioni autonome con statuto normale*). The regions have their own parliaments (*consiglio regionale*) and governments (*giunta regionale e presidente*) with certain legislative and administrative functions adapted to the circumstances of each region.

A government commissioner co-ordinates regional and national activities. The results of the last regional elections were as follows:

Regions	*Election date*	*Christian Democrats*	*Communists*	*Socialists*	*Social Movement*	*Social Democrats*	*Republicans*	*Liberals*	*Others*	*Total*
Piemonte	8 June 1980	20	20	9	2	3	2	3	1	60
Valle d'Aosta [1]	26 June 1983	7	6	3	1	1	1	1	15[2]	35
Lombardia	8 June 1980	34	23	11	3	3	2	2	2	80
Trentino-Alto Adige [1]	20 Nov. 1983	19	6	4	3	1	3	1	33[3]	70
Veneto	8 June 1980	32	13	7	2	2	1	1	2	60
Friuli-Venezia Giulia [1]	26 June 1983	23	14	7	3	3	3	1	8[4]	62
Liguria	8 June 1980	13	15	5	2	2	1	2	–	40
Emilia-Romagna	8 June 1980	13	26	4	1	2	2	1	1	50
Toscana	8 June 1980	15	25	5	1	1	1	1	1	50
Umbria	8 June 1980	9	14	4	1	1	1	–	–	30
Marche	8 June 1980	16	15	4	1	1	1	1	1	40

Regions	Election date	Christian Democrats	Communists	Socialists	Social Movement	Social Democrats	Republicans	Liberals	Others	Total
Lazio	8 June 1980	22	19	6	6	3	2	1	1	60
Abruzzi	8 June 1980	20	12	4	2	1	1	–	–	40
Molise	8 June 1980	17	5	3	1	2	1	1	–	30
Campania	8 June 1980	25	15	7	7	3	1	1	1	60
Puglia	8 June 1980	22	13	6	4	2	1	1	1	50
Basilicata	8 June 1980	14	8	4	2	2	–	–	–	30
Calabria	8 June 1980	18	10	7	2	2	1	–	–	40
Sicilia [1]	21 June 1981	38	16	13	6	2	5	3	7	90
Sardegna [1]	24 June 1984	27	24	8	3	4	3[5]	–	12[6]	81

[1] Autonomous regions with special statute.
[2] Including 4 Democrates Populaires – Union Valdôtaine Progressiste, 9 Union Valdôtaine.
[3] Including 25 Südtiroler Volkspartie.
[4] Including 1 Slovenian Union, 2 Movimento Friuli, 4 Lista per Trieste.
[5] Republican-Liberal.
[6] Sardinian Action Party.

DEFENCE. Most of the restrictions imposed upon Italy in Part IV of the peace treaty signed on 10 Feb. 1947 were repudiated by the signatories on 21 Dec. 1951, only the USSR objecting.

Head of the armed forces is the Defence Chief of Staff. In 1947 the ministries of war, navy and air were merged into the ministry of defence. The technical and scientific council for defence directs all research activities.

National service lasts 12 months in the Army and Air Force, and 18 months in the Navy.

Army. The Army is divided into the expeditionary force and the national defence force. It is composed of 1 armoured division, 3 mechanized divisions, 2 independent mechanized and 4 independent motorized brigades, 5 Alpine brigades, 1 airborne brigade, 2 amphibious battalions and 1 missile brigade. Equipment includes 550 M-47, 300 M-60A1 and 920 Leopard I main battle tanks. The Army air corps operates light aircraft and helicopters. Strength (1985) 260,000 (189,000 conscripts), with 545,000 reserves. There is also the paramilitary Carabinieri of 90,000 men.

Navy. Particulars of the principal surface ships in the Italian Navy:

Completed	Name	Standard displacement Tons	Aircraft	Principal armament	Torpedo tubes	Shaft horsepower	Speed Knots
			Light Aircraft Carrier				
1985	Giuseppe Garibaldi	10,100	16 Sea King helicopters	4 Teseo launchers for Otomat; 2 Albatross systems with Aspide missiles	6 A/S	80,000	30
			Cruisers				
1969	Vittorio Veneto	7,500	9 helicopters	8 3-in.; twin 'Terrier';	6	73,000	32
1964 1964	Andrea Doria [1] Caio Duilio [1]	6,000	4 helicopters	8 3-in.; twin 'Terrier';	6	60,000	31

[1] Rated as guided-missile escort cruisers.

There are also 10 diesel-powered submarines, 4 guided-missile destroyers, 15 frigates, 8 corvettes, 4 ocean minesweepers, 12 minehunters, 12 coastal minesweepers, 5 inshore minesweepers, 7 hydrofoil missile boats, 2 fast torpedo-boats, 2 fast gunboats, 2 landing ships, 3 surveying vessels, 2 salvage ships, 1 transport, 1 support ship, 5 training ships, 2 replenishment oilers, 14 water carriers, 1 netlayer,

7 repair craft, 18 auxiliaries, 5 coastal transports (landing craft), 7 motor transports (minor landing craft), and 42 tugs.

One frigate, 4 corvettes and 2 minehunters are under construction. Two submarines, 8 corvettes, 4 minehunters and 2 landing ships are projected.

The coastline of the peninsula is divided into zones, with headquarters at Spezia, Naples, Taranto and Ancona; all are under the jurisdiction of flag officers with the status of C.-in-C. The admirals commanding on the coasts of Sardinia and Sicily do not rank as C.-in-C.

Other localities of strategic importance under naval administration are Brindisi, where there is an admiral commanding, and Genoa, Leghorn, Augusta and Venice, each of which is under a senior naval officer.

The personnel of the Navy in 1985 numbered 42,200 officers and ratings, including the naval air arm and the marine battalion.

Air Force. Control is exercised through 2 regional HQ near Taranto and Milan. Units assigned to NATO comprise the 1st air brigade of Nike-Hercules surface-to-air missiles, 6 fighter-bomber, 3 light attack, 6 interceptor and 2 tactical reconnaissance squadrons, with supporting transport, search and rescue, and training units. Three of the fighter-bomber squadrons have Tornados, others have F-104S Starfighters and Aeritalia G91Ys. The light attack squadrons operate G91Rs. F-104S Starfighters have been standardized throughout the interceptor squadrons. The reconnaissance force operates RF-104G Starfighters. A total of 187 AM-X jet aircraft, built jointly by Aeritalia, Aermacchi and Embraer of Brazil, will replace G91R, G91Y and F-104G/S aircraft in eight squadrons in 1986–90.

One transport squadron has turboprop C-130H Hercules aircraft; 2 others have turboprop Aeritalia G222s. There is a VIP and personnel transport squadron, equipped with DC-9, PD-808 and P.166M aircraft. Electronic warfare duties are performed by specially equipped G222s, PD-808s and MB 339s. Two land-based anti-submarine squadrons operate Breguet Atlantics. ASW helicopters, including Italian-built SH-3D Sea Kings, operate from ships of the Italian Navy. Search and rescue are performed by 12 Agusta-Sikorsky HH-3F helicopters and smaller types. There are also strong support and training elements; some MB 339 jet trainers have armament provisions for secondary close air support and anti-helicopter roles.

Air Force strength in mid-1983 was about 70,600 officers and men, about 300 combat aircraft, 500 fixed-wing second-line aircraft and over 100 helicopters.

INTERNATIONAL RELATIONS

Membership. Italy is a member of UN, NATO and EEC.

ECONOMY

Budget. Total revenue and expenditure for fiscal years, in 1m. lire:

	Revenue	*Expenditure*		*Revenue*	*Expenditure*
1976	37,882,716	50,036,796	1980	88,303,000	128,994,000
1977	43,666,361	59,548,331	1981	105,343,000	149,246,000
1978	51,696,512	78,844,114	1982	150,842,000	206,444,000
1979	62,431,447	92,127,557	1983	177,148,000	250,230,000

In the revenue for 1983 turnover and other business taxes accounted for 46,132,000m. lire, customs duties and indirect taxes for 14,290,000m. lire.

The public debt at 31 Dec. 1983 totalled 367,699,500m. lire, including consolidated debt of 42,100m. lire and the floating debt 204,492,200m. lire.

Currency. The standard coin is the *lira*. From 30 March 1960 the gold standard was formally established as equal to 0·00142187 gramme of gold per lira.

State metal coins are of 5, 10, 20, 50, 100, 200, and 500 lire. There are also in circulation State notes of 500 and bank-notes of 1,000, 2,000, 5,000, 10,000, 20,000, 50,000 and 100,000 lire; they are neither convertible into gold as foreign moneys nor exportable abroad, nor importable from abroad into Italy (except for certain specified small amounts).

Circulation of money at 31 March 1984: State coins and notes, 949,200m. lire; bank-notes, 35,428,400m. lire.

In Sept. 1985 the rate of exchange was 2,235 lire per US$1 and 2,136 lire per £1 sterling.

Banking. According to the law of 6 May 1926 there is only one bank of issue, the Banca d'Italia. Its gold reserve amounted to 43,399,000m. lire in Dec. 1983; the foreign credit reserves of the Exchange Bureau (*Ufficio Italiano Cambi*) amounted to 22,903,000m. lire at the same date.

Since 1936, all credit institutions have been under the control of a State organ, named 'Inspectorate of Credit'; the Bank of Italy has been converted into a 'public institution', whose capital is held exclusively by corporate bodies of a public nature. Other credit institutions, totalling 1,092, are classified as: (1) 6 chartered banks (Banco di Napoli, Banco di Sicilia, Banca Nazionale del Lavoro, Monte dei Paschi di Siena, Istituto di S. Paolo di Torino, Banca di Sardegna); (2) 3 banks of national interest (Banca Commerciale Italiana in Milan, Credito Italiano in Genoa and Banco di Roma); (3) banks and credit concerns in general, including 157 joint-stock banks and 148 co-operative banks; (4) 87 savings banks and Monti di pegno (institutions granting loans against personal chattels as security); (5) 686 *Casse rurali e agrarie* (agricultural banks, established as co-operative institutions with unlimited liability of associates); (6) 5 Istituti di Categoria.

At 31 Dec. 1983 there were 295 credit institutes handling 95% of all deposits and current accounts, with capital and reserves of 29,626,913m. lire.

On 31 Dec. 1983 the post office savings banks had deposits and current accounts of 54,951,000m. lire; credit institutions, 373,295,000m. lire.

Insurance. By a decree of 29 April 1923 life-assurance business is carried on only by the National Insurance Institute and by other institutions, national and foreign, authorized by the Government. At 31 Dec. 1982 the insurances vested in the *Istituto Nazionale delle Assicurazioni* amounted to 7,823,842m. lire, including the decuple of life annuities.

Weights and Measures. The metric system is in general use.

ENERGY AND NATURAL RESOURCES

Electricity. Italy has greatly developed her water-power resources. In 1983 the total power generated was 182,880m. kwh., of which 44,216m. kwh. were generated by hydro-electric plants.

Oil. Production in 1983 amounted to 2,197,582 tonnes, of which 732,206 came from Sicily.

Minerals. The Italian mining industry is most developed in Sicily (Caltanissetta), in Tuscany (Arezzo, Florence and Grosseto), in Sardinia (Cagliari, Sassari and Iglesias), in Lombardy (particularly near Bergamo and Brescia) and in Piedmont.

Italy's fuel and mineral resources are wholly inadequate. Only sulphur and mercury outputs yield a substantial surplus for exports. In 1983 outputs, in tonnes, of raw steel were 21,810,787; rolled iron, 18,862,738; cast-iron ingots, 10,312,716; solid fuels (1981), 1,957,958.

Production of metals and minerals (in tonnes) was as follows:

	1978	*1979*	*1980*	*1981*	*1982*	*1983*
Iron pyrites	786,666	804,469	858,992	680,988	666,964	646,209
Iron ore	352,611	218,762	434,374	345,604	195,034	67,700
Manganese	9,741	9,782	9,165	8,756	8,727	7,205
Zinc	120,492	100,825	116,191	83,476	76,878	81,050
Crude sulphur	523,355	108,309	100,852	96,172	88,848	40,858
Bauxite	24,410	26,095	23,260	19,000	23,810	13,118
Mercury	5	–	–	20,017	17,163	–
Lead	31,110	27,237	40,477	37,191	49,197	45,580
Aluminium	270,770	266,814	265,803	243,959	232,893	144,167

Agriculture. The area of Italy in 1983 comprised 301,277 sq. km, of which 264,212 sq. km was agricultural and forest land and 37,065 sq. km was unproductive; the former was mainly distributed as follows (in 1,000 hectares): Forage and pasture, 8,696; woods, 6,393; cereals, 5,127; vines, 1,134; olive trees, 1,254; garden produce, 556; leguminous plants, 308. This does not include vines and olives grown among other crops.

At the second general census of agriculture (25 Oct. 1970) agricultural holdings numbered 3,620,799 and covered 25,091,267 hectares. 3,142,608 owners (86·8%) farmed directly 14,706,204 hectares (58·6%); 278,157 owners (7·7%) worked with hired labour on 8,523,107 hectares (34%); 130,648 share-croppers (3·6%) tilled 1,271,485 hectares (5·1%); the remaining 69,408 holdings (1·9%) of 590,471 hectares (2·3%) were operated in other ways.

According to the labour force survey in July 1978 persons engaged in agriculture numbered 3·17m. (2·02m. males and 1·15m. females).

In 1982, 1,139,050 farm tractors were being used.

The production of the principal crops (in 1,000 metric quintals) in 1983: Sugar beet, 102,441; wheat, 85,850; maize, 67,226; tomatoes, 59,729; potatoes, 26,130; oranges, 23,786; rice, 10,306; barley, 11,830; lemons, 8,890; oats, 3,109; olive oil, 6,200; tangerines, 4,795; other citrus fruit, 600; rye, 285.

Production of wine, 1983, 82,200,000 hectolitres; of tobacco, 141,000 tonnes.

In 1983 consumption of chemical fertilizers in Italy was as follows (in 1,000 tons): Perphosphate, 652·9; nitrate of ammonia, 737·3; sulphate of ammonium, 340·5; potash salts, 147·5; nitrate of calcium $^{15}/_{16}$, 56·9; deposed slags, 48.

Livestock estimated in 1983: Cattle, 9,221,000; pigs, 9,187,000; sheep and goats, 10,316,000; horses, 253,000; donkeys, 101,000; mules, 59,000.

Fisheries. The Italian fishing fleet comprised in 1982, 23,385 motor boats (323,512 gross tons) and 11,694 sailing vessels (14,612 gross tons). The catch in 1983 was 414,704 tonnes.

INDUSTRY AND TRADE

Industry. The main branches of industry are: (% of industrial value added at factor cost in 1982) Textiles, clothing, leather and footwear (17·7%), food, beverages and tobacco (10·4%), energy products (7·9%), agricultural and industrial machines (7·7%), metal products except machines and means of transport (7%), mineral and non-metallic mineral products (7%), timber and wooden furniture (6·6%), electric plants and equipment (6·3%), chemicals and pharmaceuticals (6·2%), means of transport (6·1%).

Production, 1983. Steel, 21,664,381; motor vehicles, 1,575,224; cement, 39,216,609 tonnes; artificial and synthetic fibres (including staple fibre and waste), 568,284 tonnes; ethylene, 1,014,839 tonnes; polyethylene resins, 690,849 tonnes.

Labour. As at April 1982, 20·1m. persons were employed, 1·9m. unemployed (figures from a new series of statistics on the labour force, 1977, which is not comparable with previous series).

Trade Unions. Membership of the 4 main groups: Confederazione Generale Italiana del Lavoro (Communist-dominated), 4,485,930 (1977); Confederazione Italiana Sindacati Lavoratori (Catholic), 3,059,800 (1980); Unione Italiana del Lavoro, 1,151,370 (1977); Confederazione Italiana Sindacati Nazionali Lavoratori, 1,015,988 (1961).

Commerce. The territory covered by foreign trade statistics includes Italy, the Republic of San Marino, but excludes the municipalities of Livigno and Campione.

The following table shows the value of Italy's foreign trade (in 1m. lire):

	1978	*1979*	*1980*	*1981*	*1982*	*1983*
Imports	47,867,899	64,397,204	83,304,303	103,674,405	116,215,679	122,001,933
Exports	47,505,301	59,926,272	66,719,410	86,039,719	99,230,877	110,537,204

The following table shows trade by countries in 1m. lire:

Countries	*Imports into Italy from* 1981	1982	1983	*Exports from Italy to* 1981	1982	1983
Argentina	476,796	515,888	597,447	491,201	298,284	396,143
Australia	580,140	616,191	648,654	575,103	689,448	983,147
Austria	1,878,070	1,953,207	2,147,344	1,914,230	2,141,152	2,601,268
Belgium-Luxembourg	3,205,365	3,747,101	4,127,557	2,370,425	2,872,654	3,176,743
France	12,938,148	14,531,270	15,362,342	11,686,202	15,103,288	16,253,746
Germany, Fed. Rep. of	16,190,684	18,657,976	19,371,821	13,351,362	15,490,512	18,331,355
Japan	1,435,861	1,477,210	1,688,409	762,691	1,068,557	1,201,810
Netherlands	4,287,907	5,023,524	5,941,564	2,615,611	3,048,588	3,308,070
Switzerland	3,300,745	3,984,053	4,734,343	3,454,960	3,960,965	4,578,457
USSR	3,536,935	4,791,094	5,456,788	1,467,690	2,042,829	2,850,334
UK	4,011,549	4,601,251	4,749,509	4,998,901	6,219,338	7,019,308
USA	7,032,025	7,863,746	7,245,994	5,841,374	6,999,295	8,526,145
Yugoslavia	840,963	1,138,215	1,538,595	1,235,970	1,333,240	1,517,341

In 1982 the main imports were maize, wood, greasy wool, metal scrap, pit-coal, petroleum, raw oils, meat, paper, rolled iron and steel, copper and alloys, mechanical and electric equipment, motor vehicles. The main exports were fruit and vegetables, fabrics, footwear and other clothing articles, rolled iron and steel, machinery, motor vehicles, plastic materials and petroleum by-products.

Italy's balance of trade (in 1,000m. lire) has been estimated as follows:

	Goods and services *Export*	*Import*	*Balance*	*Income from investments and work, balance*	*Net balance*
1977	49,412	47,277	+2,135	–142	+1,993
1978	58,866	53,465	+5,401	+184	+5,585
1979	74,377	71,123	+3,254	+922	+4,176
1980	83,710	93,967	–10,257	+927	–9,330
1981	105,630	113,721	–8,091	–1,995	–10,086
1982	123,439	128,787	–5,348	–3,228	–8,576
1983	138,943	136,303	+2,640	–3,622	–982

Remittances from Italians abroad (in US$1m. until 1969 and then 1,000m. lire): 1950, 72; 1960, 214; 1970, 289; 1975, 338; 1976, 385; 1977, 626; 1978, 785; 1979, 956; 1980, 1,059; 1981, 1,325; 1982, 1,607; 1983, 1,727.

Total trade between Italy and UK (British Department of Trade returns, in £1,000 sterling):

	1980	*1981*	*1982*	*1983*	*1984*
Imports to UK	2,311,071	2,330,349	2,745,094	3,188,219	3,814,163
Exports and re-exports from UK	1,899,181	1,742,514	2,022,711	2,292,788	2,902,666

Tourism. In 1983, 46·6m. foreigners visited Italy; they included 10·4m. German, 10·2m. Swiss, 7·9m. French, 4·6m. Austrian, 1·1m. Yugoslav, 1·9m. British, 1·7m. Dutch and 1·7m. US citizens. They spent about 13,721,000m. lire.

COMMUNICATIONS

Roads. Italy's roads totalled (31 Dec. 1983) 297,698 km, of which 45,461 km were state roads, 104,670 km provincial roads, 141,666 km communal roads. Motor vehicles, Dec. 1982: Cars, 19·6m.; buses, 66,688; lorries, 1,575,018; motor cycles, light vans, etc., 4,793,979.

The Mont Blanc tunnel road (11·6 km) from Entreves to Les Pelerins (France) was opened on 16 July 1965.

Railways. Railway history in Italy begins in 1839, with a line between Naples and Portici (8 km). Length of railways (31 Dec. 1983), 19,782 km, including 16,148 km of state railways, of which 7,386 had not yet been electrified. The first section of a new high-speed direct railway linking Rome and Florence opened in Feb. 1977. In 1983 the state railways carried 380m. passengers and 49m. tonnes of goods. The Rome Underground opened in Feb. 1980.

Aviation. The Italian airline Alitalia (with a capital of 280,800m. lire, of which 99·1% is owned by the State) operates flights to every part of the world. Airports include 25 international, 36 national and 75 club airports. Domestic and international traffic in 1983 registered 14,866,398 passengers arrived and 14,861,167 departed, while freight and mail (excluding luggage) amounted to 155,380 tonnes unloaded and 224,288 tonnes loaded.

Shipping. The mercantile marine at 31 Dec. 1983 consisted of 2,115 vessels of 9,619,814 gross tons, not including pleasure boats (yachts, etc.), sailing and motor vessels. There were 1,391 motor vessels of 100 gross tons and over.

In 1983, 238,792,391 tonnes of cargo were unloaded, and 85,296,567 tonnes of cargo were loaded in Italian ports.

In 1972 navigable waterways had a length of 2,237 km (849 km of which were canals).

Post and Broadcasting. On 31 Dec. 1982 there were 14,107 post offices and 13,503 telegraph offices. The maritime radio-telegraph service had 20 coast stations. On 1 Jan. 1982 the telephone service had 20,452,749 apparatus. *Radiotelevisione Italiana* broadcasts 3 programmes and additional regional programmes, including transmissions in English, French, German and Slovenian on medium- and short-waves and on FM. It also broadcasts 2 TV programmes. Radio licences numbered 532,800; television and radio licences, 13,400,609.

Cinemas. There were 7,475 cinemas in 1980.

Newspapers. There were (1984) 74 daily newspapers with a combined circulation of 6·71m. copies; of the papers 15 are published in Rome and 8 in Milan. One daily each is published in German and Slovene, and 2 in English.

JUSTICE, RELIGION, EDUCATION AND WELFARE

Justice. Italy has 1 court of cassation, in Rome, and is divided for the administration of justice into 23 appeal court districts (and 3 detached sections), subdivided into 159 tribunal *circondari* (districts), and these again into *mandamenti* each with its own magistracy (*Pretura*), 899 in all. There are also 90 first degree assize courts and 26 assize courts of appeal. For civil business, besides the magistracy above mentioned, *Conciliatori* have jurisdiction in petty plaints (those to a maximum amount of 1m. lire).

On 31 Dec. 1983 there were 25,016 male and 1,448 female prisoners in establishments for preventive custody, 10,819 males and 409 females in penal establishments and 1,255 males and 98 females in establishments for the execution of safety measures.

Religion. The treaty between the Holy See and Italy, of 11 Feb. 1929, confirmed by article 7 of the Constitution of the republic, lays down that the Catholic Apostolic Roman Religion is the only religion of the State. Other creeds are permitted, provided they do not profess principles, or follow rites, contrary to public order or moral behaviour.

The appointment of archbishops and of bishops is made by the Holy See; but the Holy See submits to the Italian Government the name of the person to be appointed in order to obtain an assurance that the latter will not raise objections of a political nature.

Catholic religious teaching is given in elementary and intermediate schools. Marriages celebrated before a Catholic priest are automatically transferred to the civil register. Marriages celebrated by clergy of other denominations must be made valid before a registrar. In 1972 there were 279 dioceses with 28,154 parishes and 43,714 priests. There were 187,153 members (154,796 women) of about 20,000 religious houses.

In 1962 there were about 100,000 Protestants and about 50,000 Jews.

Annuario Cattolico d'Italia, a cura del CNEC. 14th ed. 1969–70, Rome, 1970
Annuario di Pastorale. Rome, 1970
Burgalassi, S., *La Sociologia della Religione in Italia dalle originial 1967.* Rome, 1967

Education. Education is compulsory from 6 to 14 years of age. An optional pre-school education is given to the children between 3 and 5 years in the preparatory schools (kindergarten schools). Illiteracy of males over 6 years was 4% in 1971, of females 6·3%.

Compulsory education can be classified as primary education (5-year course) and junior secondary education (3-year course).

Senior secondary education is subdivided in classical (*ginnasio* and classical *liceo*), scientific (scientific *liceo*), language lyceum, professional institutes and technical education: agricultural, industrial, commercial, technical, nautical institutes, institutes for surveyors, institutes for girls (5-year course) and teacher-training institutes (4-year course).

University education is given in Universities and in University Higher Institutes (4, 5, 6 years, according to degree course).

Statistics for the academic year 1983–84:

Elementary schools	*No.*	*Pupils*
Kindergarten	29,183	1,680,236
Public elementary schools	26,370	3,753,055
Private elementary schools Private elementary recognized schools (*parificate*)	2,416	315,269

Government secondary schools		*Total students*
Junior secondary schools	10,057	2,821,580
Classical lyceum	754	206,180
Lyceum for science	972	344,131
Language lyceum	306	48,478
Teachers' schools	209	30,686
Teachers' institutes	689	193,261
Professional institutes	1,666	493,711
Technical institutes, of which:		
Industrial institutes	625	284,953
Commercial institutes	1,149	551,724
Surveyors' institutes	503	153,233
Agricultural institutes Nautical institutes Technical institutes for tourism Managerial institutes Girls technical schools	387	137,038
Artistic studies	248	64,644

Universities and higher institutes	*Date of foundation*	*Students 1983–84*	*Teachers 1982–83*
Ancona	1965	6,792	311
Arezzo	1971	1,129	94
Bari	1924	50,489	1,754
Bergamo	1970	2,818	110
Bologna	1200	58,720	2,900
Brescia	1970	5,670	103
Cagliari	1626	17,081	1,095
Camerino (Macerata)	1727	2,754	233
Cassino (Frosinone)	1968	2,338	42
Catania	1434	32,936	1,496
Catanzaro	1983	3,608	–
Chieti	1965	4,904	109
Cosenza	1972	5,571	495
Feltre (Belluno)	1969	424	24
Ferrara	1391	5,454	463
Firenze	1924	43,412	2,210
Genova	1243	31,040	1,896
L'Aquila	1956	6,037	553
Lecce	1959	6,892	314
Macerata	1290	4,477	190
Messina	1549	24,263	1,180
Milano	1924	116,586	4,015
Modena	1678	8,204	649
Napoli	1224	112,953	3,993
Padova	1222	41,212	2,139
Palermo	1805	42,912	2,232
Parma	1502	14,781	973
Pavia	1390	17,765	1,433
Perugia	1276	18,563	1,097
Pescara	1965	8,450	150
Piacenza	1924	621	68
Pisa	1338	28,336	1,786
Potenza	1983	900	–
Reggio di C.	1968	9,070	132
Roma	1303	155,365	6,358
Salerno	1944	21,279	557
Sassari	1677	8,424	504
Siena	1300	10,140	765
Teramo	1965	4,307	80
Torino	1404	57,260	2,357
Trento	1965	2,615	204
Trieste	1924	13,276	949
Udine	1969	3,089	255
Urbino	1564	12,182	428
Venezia	1868	21,619	758
Verona	1969	7,554	365
Viterbo	1980	961	25

Health. In 1981 there were 190,196 doctors and 529,221 hospital beds.

Social Security. Social expenditure is made up of transfers which the central public departments, local departments and social security departments, make to families.

Payment is principally for pensions, family allowances and health services. Expenditure on subsidies, public assistance to various classes of people and people injured by political events or national disasters are also included.

DIPLOMATIC REPRESENTATIVES

Of Italy in Great Britain (14 Three Kings Yard, London, W1Y 2EH)
Ambassador: Andrea Cagiati, GCVO (accredited 20 Feb. 1980).

Of Great Britain in Italy (Via XX Settembre 80A, 00187, Rome)
Ambassador: The Lord Bridges, KCMG.

Of Italy in the USA (1601 Fuller St., NW, Washington, D.C., 20009)
Ambassador: Rinaldo Petrignani.

Of the USA in Italy (Via Veneto 119/A, Rome)
Ambassador: Maxwell M. Rabb.

Of Italy to the United Nations
Ambassador: Maurizio Bucci.

Books of Reference

Statistical Information: The Istituto Centrale di Statistica (16 Via Cesare Balbo 00100 Rome) was set up by law of 9 July 1926 as the central institute in charge of census and all statistical information. *President:* Prof. Guido Mario Rey. *Director-General:* Dr Luigi Pinto. Its publications include:

Annuario statistico italiano. 1984
Compendio statistico italiano. 1984
Bollettino mensile di statistica. Monthly, from 1950
Annuario di statistiche industriali. 1982
Annuario di statistiche demografiche. 1982
Annuario di statistica agraria. 1982
Annuario statistico della navigazione marittima. 1983
Annuario statistico del commercio interno e del turismo. 1982
Statistica annuale del commercio con l'estero. 1982
Statistica mensile del commercio con l'estero. Monthly
Annuario di statistiche del lavoro. 1983
Censimento generale dell'agricoltura. 1982
Censimento generale della popolazione, 1981. Vol. I, II and III
Censimento generale dell'industria e del commercio. 1981
Sintesi Statistica di un Ventennio di Vita Economica Italiana, 1951–71
Cinquanta anni di attivita, 1926–1976. 1978

Italy. Documents and Notes. Servizi delle Informazioni, Rome. 1952 ff.
Italian Books and Periodicals. Bimonthly from 1958
Banco di Roma, *Review of the Economic Condition in Italy* (in English). Bimonthly, 1947 ff.
Credito Italiano, *The Italian Economic Situation.* Bimonthly. Milan, from June 1961 (in Italian), from June 1962 (in English)
Compendio Economico Italiano. Rome, Unione Italiana delle Camere di Commercio. Annually from 1954
Allum, P. A., *Italy: Republic Without Government.* London, 1973
Carone, G., *Il Turismo nell'economia internazionale.* Milan, 1959
Clough, S. B., *The Economic History of Modern Italy.* Columbia Univ. Press, 1964
Di Vittorio, G. (ed.), *I sindacati in Italia.* Bari, 1955
Grindrod, M., *The Rebuilding of Italy, 1945–55.* R. Inst. of Int. Affairs, 1955
Large, P. and Tarrow, S. (eds.), *Italy in Transition – Conflict and Consensus.* London, 1980
Nichols, P., *Italia, Italia.* London, 1974
Wiskemann, E., *Italy Since 1945.* London, 1971
Woolfe, S. J. (ed.), *The Rebirth of Italy, 1943–50.* New York, 1972

National Library: Biblioteca Nazionale Centrale Vittorio Emanuele II Viale Castro Pretorio, Rome. *Director:* Dr L. M. Crisari.

IVORY COAST

République de la Côte d'Ivoire

Capital: Abidjan
Population: 8·5m. (1984)
GNP per capita: US$1,200 (1981)

HISTORY. France obtained rights on the coast in 1842, but did not actively and continuously occupy the territory till 1882. On 10 Jan. 1889 Ivory Coast was declared a French protectorate, and it became a colony on 10 March 1893; in 1904 it became a territory of French West Africa. On 1 Jan. 1933 most of the territory of Upper Volta was added to the Ivory Coast, but on 1 Jan. 1948 this area was returned to the re-constituted Upper Volta, now Burkina Faso. The Ivory Coast became an autonomous republic within the French Community on 4 Dec. 1958 and achieved full independence on 7 Aug. 1960.

AREA AND POPULATION. Ivory Coast is bounded west by Liberia and Guinea, north by Mali and Burkina Faso, east by Ghana, and south by the Gulf of Guinea. It has an area of 322,463 sq. km and a population at the 1975 census of 6,702,866 (of whom 31·8% were urban). Estimate (1984) 8·5m.

The areas and populations of the 26 departments at the 1975 census were:

Department	*Sq. km*	*Population*	*Department*	*Sq. km*	*Population*
Abengourou	6,713	175,891	Danané	4,650	169,589
Abidjan	14,819	1,388,321	Dimbokro	13,822	478,054
Aboisso	6,135	146,876	Divo	9,869	275,171
Adzopé	5,151	159,502	Ferkéssédougou	19,292	90,901
Agboville	3,900	140,250	Gagnoa	6,873	256,006
Biankouma	2,897	74,408	Guiglo	14,232	135,252
Bondoukou	16,465	293,838	Katiola	8,469	75,909
Bouaflé	8,362	265,875	Korhogo	12,164	276,846
Bouaké	23,405	805,359	Man-Danané	7,004	277,648
Bouna	21,470	77,232	Odienné	21,336	124,196
Boundiali	10,273	132,160	Sassandra	26,263	195,620
Dabakala	8,694	55,356	Séguéla	22,861	157,644
Daloa	13,918	367,414	Touba	8,767	77,696

The principal cities (populations, census 1975) are the capital, Abidjan (685,828; estimate 1982, 1·85m.), Bouaké (173,248, 640,000), Daloa (59,500), Man-Danané (48,521, 450,000), Korhogo (45,146, 280,000) and Gagnoa (42,000). The new capital will be at Yamoussoukro (70,000 in 1983).

The population includes 60 ethnic groups, the main ones being, the Akan, the Krou and the Senoufo.

CLIMATE. A tropical climate, affected by distance from the sea. In coastal areas, there are wet seasons from May to July and in Oct. and Nov., but in central areas the periods are March to May and July to Nov. In the north, there is one wet season from June to Oct. Abidjan. Jan. 81°F (27·2°C), July 75°F (23·9°C). Annual rainfall 84" (2,100 mm). Bouaké. Jan. 81°F (27·2°C), July 77°F (25°C). Annual rainfall 48" (1,200 mm).

CONSTITUTION AND GOVERNMENT. The 1960 Constitution was amended in 1971, 1975 and 1980. Under it, the sole legal Party is the *Parti Démocratique de la Côte d'Ivoire.* There is a 147-member National Assembly elected by universal suffrage (latest elections, Nov. 1980) for a 5-year term. The President is also directly elected for a 5-year term (renewable).

The Government was in Sept. 1984 composed as follows:

President: Félix Houphouët-Boigny. (Re-elected for a fifth 5-year term in 1980).

Ministers of State: Auguste Denise, Mathieu Ekra, Camille Alliali, Maurice Seri Gnoleba, Emile Kei Boguinard. *Health and Population:* Alphonse Djedje Mady. *Cultural Affairs:* Bernard B. Dadie. *Information:* Amadou Thiam. *Commerce:* Nicolas Kouandi Angba. *Labour and 'Ivorization' of Personnel:* Albert Vanie Bi Tra. *Navy:* Lamine Fadiga. *Public Works:* Jean-Jacques Bechio. *Tourism:* Duon Sadia. *Social Affairs:* Yaya Ouattara. *Youth, Popular Education and Sport:* Laurent Dona Fologo. *Mines:* Paul Gui Dibo. *Internal Security:* Oumar N'daw. *Justice:* Lazeni N. P. Coulibaly. *Defence and Civic Service:* Konan Banny. *Interior:* Konan Koffi Léon. *Foreign Affairs:* Simeon Ake. *Economy and Finance:* Abdoulaye Kone. *Agriculture, Water and Forests:* Denis Bra Kanon. *Education and Scientific Research:* Balla Keita. *Posts and Telecommunications, Construction and Town Planning:* Ange Barry Battesti. *Industry:* Bernard K. Ehui. *Rural Development:* Gilles Laubouet. *Relations with the National Assembly:* Emile Brou.

National flag: Three vertical strips of orange, white, green.

Local government: Since the 1975 census, 8 further *départements* have been created (Bongouanou, Issia, Lakota, Mankono, Oumé, Soubré, Tengréla and Zuénoula) bringing the total to 34 *départements*, sub-divided into 163 sub-prefectures.

DEFENCE

Army. The Army consisted of 3 infantry battalions and support units in 1985. Equipment includes 5 AMX-13 light tanks and 7 ERC-90 armoured cars. Total strength, 4,500.

Navy. Offshore, riverine and coastal patrol squadrons include 2 fast missile craft, 2 patrol vessels, 3 river defence craft, 1 training vessel, 1 light transport, 10 fast assault boats, 6 small protection launches and 2 minor landing craft. Personnel in 1985 totalled 70 officers and 630 ratings.

Air Force. The Air Force, formed in 1962, has 6 Alpha Jet advanced trainers, with combat potential, 2 turbofan F-28 Fellowship and 1 turbofan Gulfstream II and 1 Gulfstream III transports, 2 Reims-Cessna 150s, 6 Beech F-33Cs and 2 Reims-Cessna 337s for liaison and training, and 3 SA330 Puma, 4 Dauphin 2 and 3 Alouette II/III helicopters. Other transport aircraft are leased to the national airline. Personnel total 570.

INTERNATIONAL RELATIONS

Membership. Ivory Coast is a member of UN, OAU and is an ACP state of EEC.

ECONOMY

Planning. The 1975–80 Five Year Plan provided 1·4m. francs CFA for investment, aiming to raise GDP by 25%, and was followed by a new Plan for 1980–85.

Budget. The budget for 1982 balanced at 712,200m. francs CFA.

Currency. The currency is the *franc CFA* with a parity rate of 50 *francs CFA* to 1 French *franc*. In March 1985, £ sterling = 551·25 francs CFA; US$1 = 523·75 francs CFA.

Banking. The *Banque Centrale des Etats de l'Afrique de l'Ouest* is the bank of issue. Numerous foreign and domestic banks have offices in Abidjan, and *Société Ivoirienne de Banque*, *Banque Internationale pour le Commerce et l'Industrie de la Côte d'Ivoire* and *Banque Internationale pour l'Afrique Occidentale* maintain wide branch networks throughout the country.

ENERGY AND NATURAL RESOURCES

Electricity. Production in 1981 amounted to 1,903m. kwh mostly from new hydroelectric projects at Kassou and Taabo on the Bandama river, Buyo on the Sassandra river, and from 2 older dams on the Bia river.

Oil. Petroleum has been produced (offshore) since Oct. 1977. Production (1979) 1·57m. tonnes.

Minerals. Annual diamond extraction had dwindled to 25,000 carats by 1979, and manganese mining ceased. Exploitation of iron ore deposits at Bangolo in the west await completion of hydro-electric projects.

Agriculture. The main export crops (production 1981 in 1,000 tonnes) are coffee (250), cocoa (390), bananas (150), pineapples (350), palm oil (177), palm kernels (38), cotton (60) and rubber (25); food crops include yams (2,000), cassava (800), plantains (830), rice (500), maize (300), millet (49) and groundnuts (60). Sugar-cane (800,000 tonnes in 1979) is grown on new plantations in the north at Ferkessedougou and elsewhere.

Several factories produce palm-oil, fruit preserves and fruit juice.

Livestock, 1983: 780,000 cattle, 1·38m. sheep, 1·38m. goats, 400,000 pigs, 1,000 horses and 1,000 donkeys.

Fisheries. The catch in 1981 amounted to 80,000 tonnes.

Forestry. Production in 1981 was 12·03m. cu. metres.

INDUSTRY AND TRADE

Industry. Industrialization has developed rapidly since independance, particularly food processing, textiles and sawmills.

Commerce. Trade for calendar years in 1m. francs CFA:

	1978	*1979*	*1980*	*1981*	*1982*
Imports	522,515	528,850	631,900	653,320	718,590
Exports	524,380	534,847	663,900	689,300	747,450

In 1981 exports of coffee furnished 18% of exports, cocoa 34%, timber 14% and petroleum products, 8%. 19% went to France, 13% to the Netherlands, 11% to the USA, 8% to Italy and 7% to Federal Republic of Germany. Of the imports, France supplied 31%, Venezuela 8%, the USA 5% and Japan 5%.

Total trade between the Ivory Coast and UK (British Department of Trade returns, in £1,000 sterling):

	1980	*1981*	*1982*	*1983*	*1984*
Imports to UK	53,563	63,055	56,097	79,255	93,875
Exports and re-exports from UK	27,916	30,128	28,238	25,591	25,347

Tourism. In 1980 there were 137,750 foreign tourists.

COMMUNICATIONS

Roads. In 1982 roads totalled 45,200 km and there were 236,400 vehicles.

Railways. From Abidjan a metre-gauge railway runs to Léraba and thence through Burkina-Faso to Ouagadougou (1,140 km). An extension to Tambao is proposed and a new network for the export of iron ore from the port of San Pedro is under study. In 1982 the railways carried 910m. passenger-km and 622m. tonne-km of freight.

Aviation. The main airport is at Abidjan-Port-Buet. In 1981 it handled 870,000 passengers and 33,000 tonnes of freight and mail. Air Ivoire provides domestic services to 25 regional airports and landing strips.

Shipping. The main ports are Abidjan and San Pedro. In 1981 Abidjan port handled 5·8m. tonnes and San Pedro 1·5m. tonnes.

Post and Broadcasting. There were 78,370 telephones in 1980 and (1978), 939 telex machines. In 1980 there were 300,000 television and 900,000 radio receivers.

Cinemas. There were 60 cinemas in 1977 with a seating capacity of 41,000.

Newspapers. In 1982 there were 3 daily newspapers (*Fraternité-Matin* circulation, 80,000).

JUSTICE, RELIGION, EDUCATION AND WELFARE

Justice. There are 28 courts of first instance, 3 assize courts and a court of appeal.

Religion. Of the total population, 23·5% are Moslems, 12·5% Christians and 65% animists.

Education. There were, in 1979, 954,656 pupils and 21,640 teachers in 2,697 primary schools, 172,280 pupils and 4,026 teachers in secondary schools and (1979) 22,437 in technical schools. The *Université Nationale de Côte d'Ivoire,* at Abidjan (founded 1964), had 12,765 students in 1980.

Health. In 1978 there were 9,962 hospital beds, 429 doctors, 36 dentists, 615 midwives, 3,052 nurses and 76 pharmacists.

DIPLOMATIC REPRESENTATIVES

Of the Ivory Coast in Great Britain (2 Upper Belgrave St., London, SW1X 8BJ)
Ambassador: Seydou Diarra (accredited 9 Dec. 1983).

Of Great Britain in the Ivory Coast (Immeuble 'Les Harmonies', Blvd. Corde, Abidjan)
Ambassador: John M. Willson.

Of the Ivory Coast in the USA (2424 Massachusetts Ave., NW, Washington, D.C., 20008)
Ambassador: Rene Amany.

Of the USA in the Ivory Coast (5 Rue Jesse Owens, Abidjan)
Ambassador: Robert H. Miller.

Of the Ivory Coast to the United Nations
Ambassador: Amara Essy.

Books of Reference

Statistical Information: Service de la Statistique, Abidjan. It publishes *Bulletin Statistique Mensuel and Inventoire Économique de la Côte d'Ivoire.*

La Côte d'Ivoire en Chiffre. Abidjan, 1979

Panorama de la Côte d'Ivoire, 1978, ed. Direction de l'Information, Abidjan

Holas, B., *Industries et cultures en Côte d'Ivoire.* Abidjan, 1979

Zartman, I. W., and Delgado, C., *The Political Economy of Ivory Coast.* New York, 1984

Zolberg, A. R., *One-Party Government in the Ivory Coast.* Rev. ed. Princeton Univ. Press, 1974

JAMAICA

Capital: Kingston
Population: 2·31m. (1983)
GNP per capita: US$1,180 (1981)

HISTORY. Jamaica was discovered by Columbus in 1494, and was occupied by the Spaniards between 1509 and 1655, when the island was captured by the English; their possession was confirmed by the Treaty of Madrid, 1670. Self-government was introduced in 1944 and gradually extended until Jamaica achieved complete independence within the Commonwealth on 6 Aug. 1962.

AREA AND POPULATION. The area of Jamaica is 4,411 sq. miles (11,425 sq. km). The population at the census of 7 April 1970 was 1,861,300, distributed on the basis of the 14 parishes of the island as follows: Kingston and St Andrew, 550,100 (estimate 1977, 643,800); St Thomas, 71,400 (78,800); Portland, 68,500 (74,300); St Mary, 100,000 (108,900); St Ann, 121,300 (134,300); Trelawny, 61,300 (67,600); St James, 103,700 (122,800); Hanover, 59,000 (64,200); Westmoreland, 113,200 (121,600); St Elizabeth, 126,000 (139,000); Manchester, 123,500 (142,600); St Catherine, 186,000 (217,900); Clarendon, 176,600 (193,900).

Estimated population, in 1983, was 2·31m.

Vital statistics (1983): Births, 61,400 (26·8 per 1,000 population); deaths, 12,600 (5·5); migration loss, 4,300.

CLIMATE. A tropical climate but with considerable variation. High temperatures on the coast are usually mitigated by sea breezes, while upland areas enjoy cooler and less humid conditions. Rainfall is plentiful over most of Jamaica, being heaviest in May and from Aug. to Nov. The island lies in the hurricane zone. Kingston. Jan. 76°F (24·4°C), July 81°F (27·2°C). Annual rainfall 32″ (800 mm).

CONSTITUTION AND GOVERNMENT. A new Constitution was enacted with independence in Aug. 1962. The Crown is represented by a Governor-General appointed by the Crown on the advice of the Prime Minister. The Governor-General is assisted by a Privy Council.

The Legislature comprises two chambers, an elected House and a nominated Senate. The executive is chosen from both chambers.

The Executive comprises the Prime Minister, who is the leader of the majority party, and Ministers appointed by the Prime Minister. Together they form the Cabinet, which is the highest executive power. An Attorney-General is a member of the House and is legal adviser to the Cabinet.

The Senate consists of 20 senators appointed by the Governor-General, 12 on the advice of the Prime Minister, 8 on the advice of the Leader of the Opposition. The House of Representatives (60 members, Dec. 1976) is elected by universal adult suffrage for a 5-year period. Electors and elected must be Jamaican or Commonwealth citizens resident in Jamaica for at least 12 months before registration. The powers and procedure of Parliament correspond to those of the British Parliament.

The Privy Council consists of 6 members appointed by the Governor-General in consultation with the Prime Minister.

Governor-General: Florizel Augustus Glasspole.

National flag: A yellow diagonal cross dividing triangles of green, top and bottom, and black, hoist and fly.

The elections to House of Representatives, held on 30 Oct. 1980, returned 51 members of the Jamaica Labour Party and 9 members of the People's National Party.

The Cabinet in March 1985 was comprised as follows:

Prime Minister and Minister of Finance, Planning and Information: Edward Seaga.

Deputy Prime Minister and Minister of Foreign Affairs and Foreign Trade: Hugh Shearer. *Construction with responsibility for Electoral Matters:* Bruce Golding. *Agriculture:* Dr Percival Broderick. *Public Service:* Errol Anderson. *Social Security:* Neville Gallimore. *Labour and Leader of Government Business in the House of Representatives:* J. A. G. Smith. *Education:* Dr Mavis Gilmour. *Industry and Commerce:* Douglas Vaz. *Health:* Dr Kenneth Baugh. *Local Government:* Neville Lewis. *Youth and Community Development:* Edmund Bartlett. *Mining, Energy and Tourism:* Hugh Hart. *National Security and Justice:* Winston Spaulding. *Public Utilities and Transport:* Pearnel Charles. *Without Portfolio:* Oswald Harding.

DEFENCE

Army. The Jamaica Defence Force consists of a Regular and a Reserve Force. The Regular Force is comprised of the 1st battalion, Jamaica Regiment and Support Services which include the Air Wing and Coast Guard. The Reserve Force consists of the 3rd battalion, Jamaica Regiment. Total strength (all services, 1985), 3,500.

Air Force. The Air Wing of the Jamaica Defence Force was formed in July 1963 and has since been expanded and trained successively by the British Army Air Corps and Canadian air force personnel. Equipment for army liaison, search and rescue, police co-operation, survey and transport duties includes 2 Defender armed STOL transports; 1 Beech King Air, 1 Cessna 210 and 1 Cessna 337 light transports; 4 JetRanger and 3 Bell 212 light helicopters.

INTERNATIONAL RELATIONS

Membership. Jamaica is a member of UN, the Commonwealth, OAS, CARICOM and is an ACP state of EEC.

ECONOMY

Budget. Revenue and expenditure for fiscal years ending 31 March (in J$1m.):

	1980–81	*1981–82*	*1982–83*	*1983–84*
Revenue	1,233	1,555	1,750	1,718
Expenditure	1,547	1,655	2,707	3,396

The chief heads of recurrent revenue are customs and excise duties, income tax, motor vehicle licences and post office receipts. Capital revenue is derived mainly from royalties. The chief items of recurrent expenditure are public debt, education, health and grants to local government.

Official foreign debt at 31 Dec. 1983, J$5,410·3m.

Currency. The currency, is the *dollar*, divided into 100 cents. Currency circulation in Dec. 1980 was J$302·1m., comprising notes of J$283·6m. and J$18·5m. coin. In March 1985, £1 = J$5·65; US$1 = J$5·17.

Banking. On 1 May 1961 the Bank of Jamaica opened as Jamaica's Central Bank. It has the sole right to issue notes and coins in Jamaica, acts as Banker to the Government and to the commercial banks, and administers the island's external reserves and exchange control. Foreign exchange reserves (31 Dec. 1983), US$75m.

There are 8 commercial banks with about 170 branches and agencies in operation, with main offices in Kingston. Six of these banks are subsidiaries of major British and North American banks, of which 4 are incorporated locally. The Workers' Savings and Loan Bank is owned by the Government, Trade Unions and the private sector. The National Commercial Bank (Jamaica) Ltd, formally Barclays Bank Jamaica Ltd, is 100% government-owned. The other 6 banks which operate are: The Bank of Nova Scotia (Jamaica) Ltd, City Bank of North America, Royal Bank (Jamaica) Ltd, Bank of Commerce, Jamaica Citizens Bank Ltd and First National Bank of Chicago (Jamaica) Ltd.

Total deposits in commercial banks, 31 Dec. 1983, J$3,254·8m., of which J$1,410·7m. were time deposits and J$1,223·8m. were savings.

ENERGY AND NATURAL RESOURCES

Electricity. The Jamaica Public Service Co. is the public supplier of electricity. The bauxite companies, sugar estates and the Caribbean Cement Co. generate their own electricity. Total public installed capacity, 31 Dec. 1983, 448·2 mw., of which 336 mw. is in steam units. Total generation, 1983, 1,458 mwh., of which 1,295·7 mwh. was from steam.

Minerals. Bauxite, ceramic clays, marble, silica and gypsum are commercially valuable. Jamaica has become the world's third largest producer of bauxite and alumina. The bauxite deposits are worked by a Canadian and 4 American companies. In 1983, 7,683,000 tonnes of bauxite ore was mined, gypsum, 108,000; marle, 3·3m.; sand and gravel, 3·65m.; industrial lime, 121,300.

Agriculture (1983). Production: Sugar-cane, 2,286,000 tons; sugar (commercial), 193,000 tons; rum, 3,974,000 proof gallons; molasses, 92,500 tons; bananas, 23,500 tons; citrus fruit, 685,000 boxes; cocoa, 2,738,000 tons; spices, 2,666,000 tons; copra, 2,373 short tons; domestic food crops, 428,000 short tons.

Livestock (1983): Cattle, 315,000; goats, 410,000; pigs, 270,000; poultry, 5m.

INDUSTRY AND TRADE

Industry. Three bauxite-mining companies also process bauxite into alumina; production, 1983, 1·9m. tonnes. From processing only a few agricultural products—sugar, rum, condensed milk, oils and fats, cigars and cigarettes—the island is now producing clothing, footwear, textiles, paints, building materials (including cement), agricultural machinery and toilet articles. There is an oil refinery in Kingston. In 1983 manufacturing contributed J$1,273·8m. to the total GDP at current prices.

Labour. Average total labour force (1983), 999,800, of whom 735,700 were employed. Government and services employed 358,500; agriculture, forestry, fishing and mining, 255,200; manufacture 94,400; construction and installation, 35,000.

Commerce. Value of imports and domestic exports for calendar years (in J$1m.):

	1979	*1980*	*1981*	*1982*	*1983*
Imports	1,002·0	1,173·0	2,623·4	2,460·3	2,841·0
Domestic exports	814·7	959·3	1,735·1	1,367·0	1,392·0

Principal imports in 1983: Minerals, fuels and lubricants, 31·4%; machinery and transport equipment, 16·9%; food, 15·4%; manufactured goods, 15%.

Principal exports, 1983: Alumina and bauxite, 62·6%; food, including sugar, 16·9%.

Total trade between Jamaica and UK (British Department of Trade returns, in £1,000 sterling):

	1980	*1981*	*1982*	*1983*	*1984*
Imports to UK	95,578	114,219	92,760	95,036	77,895
Exports and re-exports from UK	33,122	42,650	56,025	116,188	48,088

Tourism. In 1983, 782,940 tourists arrived in Jamaica, spending about US$399·2m.; direct employment, 11,437.

COMMUNICATIONS

Roads (1978). The island has 2,944 miles of main roads, and over 7,264 miles of parochial and subsidiary roads. Main roads in the corporate area of Kingston and St Andrew are constructed and maintained by that corporation, those elsewhere by the Public Works Department of the Ministry of Public Utilities. Parochial or subsidiary roads are constructed and maintained by parish councils. In 1983 there were 65,534 licensed vehicles.

Railways. There are 294 km of railway open of 1,435 mm gauge, operated by the Jamaica Railway Corporation, which also operates 31 km (Alcoa Mineral Railway) on behalf of one of the bauxite companies. In 1983 the railway carried 94 tonne-km and 573,251 passengers.

Aviation. Scheduled commercial international airlines operate through the Norman Manley and Sangster international airports at Palisadoes and Montego Bay. In 1983 Norman Manley airport had 36,970 aircraft movements, handled 954,183 passengers and 16,443 tonnes of freight. Sangster had 33,508 movements, with 1·3m. passengers and 2,165 tonnes of freight. Trans-Jamaica Airlines Ltd operates internal flights; in 1983 it carried 42,100 passengers. Air Jamaica, originally set up in conjunction with BOAC and BWIA in 1966, became a new company, Air Jamaica (1968) Ltd, and is affiliated to Air Canada. In 1969 it began operations as Jamaica's national airline. In 1983 Air Jamaica carried 725,000 passengers and operated at a net loss of J$33m.

Shipping. In 1983 there were 2,053 visits to all ports; 9·4m. tons of cargo were handled. Kingston had 1,315 visits and handled 1·9m. tons. The outports had 738 visits and handled 7·5m. tons, of which 5·7m. was loaded and 1·7m. landed.

Post and Broadcasting. In the financial year 1980 there were 318 post offices and 471 postal agencies.

The Jamaica Telephone Co. operates the telephone system. In Jan. 1982 there were 124,258 telephones in use. All telephone exchanges are automatic. Jamaica is linked to USA by a submarine telephone cable. Jamaica International Telecommunications Ltd (JAMINTEL) established in 1971, provides a wide range of international telecommunications services for Jamaica. There are 1 commercial and 1 publicly owned broadcasting stations; the latter also operates a television service.

Cinemas. In 1981 there were 25 cinemas and 3 drive-in cinemas.

JUSTICE, RELIGION, EDUCATION AND WELFARE

Justice. The Judicature comprises a Supreme Court, a court of appeal, a revenue court, resident magistrates' courts, petty sessional courts, coroners' courts, a traffic court and a family court which was instituted in 1975. The Chief Justice is head of the judiciary. All prosecutions are initiated by the Director of Public Prosecutions.

Police. The Constabulary Force in 1980 stood at approximately 6,000 officers, sub-officers and constables (men and women). There are, in addition, district constables and special constables.

Religion. Freedom of worship is guaranteed under the Constitution. The main Christian denominations are Anglican, Baptist, Roman Catholic, Methodist, Church of God, United Church of Jamaica, and Grand Cayman (Presbyterian–Congregational) Moravian, Seventh-day Adventists, Pentecostal, Salvation Army, Quaker, and Disciples of Christ. Pocomania is a mixture of Christianity and African survivals. Non-Christians include Hindus, Jews, Moslems and Bahai followers. There is also a growing number of Rastafarians who believe in the deity of the late Emperor, Hailé Selassié of Ethiopia.

Education. In Sept. 1973 education became free for all government grant-aided schools (the majority of all schools) and for all Jamaicans entering the University of the West Indies, the College of Arts, Science and Technology and the Jamaica School of Agriculture. In 1983–84 there were 1,635 pre-primary schools and departments (124,010 pupils); 289 primary schools (181,022 pupils); 495 all-age schools (234,825 pupils).

There were 140 secondary and vocational schools (164,599). Teacher-training colleges had 4,052 students; community colleges had 1,932; the College of Arts, Science and Technology had 3,568, the College of Agriculture, 119 and the University of the West Indies, 4,055.

Health. In 1983 the public health service had 5,433 staff in medicine, nursing and pharmacology; 331 in dentistry; 417 public health inspectors; 79 in nutrition. There were 371 primary health centres, 6,062 public hospital beds and 284 private beds.

DIPLOMATIC REPRESENTATIVES

Of Jamaica in Great Britain (50 St James's St., London, SW1A 1JS)
High Commissioner: H. S. Walker.

Of Great Britain in Jamaica (Trafalgar Rd., Kingston 10)
High Commissioner: H. M. S. Reid, CMG.

Of Jamaica in the USA (1850 K. St., NW, Washington, D.C., 20006)
Ambassador: Keith Johnson.

Of the USA in Jamaica (2 Oxford Rd., Kingston)
Ambassador: William Hewitt.

Of Jamaica to the United Nations
Ambassador: Lloyd M. H. Barnett.

Books of Reference

Statistical Information: The Department of Statistics (93 Hanover St., Kingston) was set up in 1945—the nucleus being the Census Office, which undertook the operations of the 1943 Census of Jamaica and its Dependencies. *Director:* Mrs C. P. McFarlane. Publications of the Bureau include the *Bulletin of Statistics on External Trade* and the *Annual Abstract of Statistics.*

Economic and Social Survey, Jamaica. Planning Institute of Jamaica, Kingston (Annual)
Social and Economic Studies. Institute of Social and Economic Research, Univ. of the West Indies. Quarterly
Beckford, G. and Witter, M., *Small Garden ... Bitter Weed. The Political Struggle and Change in Jamaica.* 2nd ed. London, 1982
Black, C. V., *History of Jamaica.* London, 1965
Cassidy, F. G., and Le Page, R. B., *Dictionary of Jamaican English.* CUP, 1966
Delattre, R., *A Guide to Jamaica Reference Material.* Kingston, 1965
Floyd, B., *Jamaica: An Island Microcosm.* London, 1979
Ingram, K. E., *Jamaica.* [Bibliography] Oxford and Santa Barbara, 1984
Jefferson, O., *The Post-War Economic Development of Jamaica.* Kingston, 1972
Kuper, A., *Changing Jamaica.* London and Boston, 1976
Lacey, T., *Violence and Politics in Jamaica, 1960–70.* Manchester Univ. Press, 1977
Manley, M., *A Voice at the Work Place.* London, 1975.—*Jamaica: Struggle in the Periphery.* London, 1983
Post, K., *Strike the Iron, A Colony at War: Jamaica 1939–1945.* 2 vols. Atlantic Highlands, N.J., 1981
Sherlock, P., *Keeping Company with Jamaica.* London, 1985
Stone, C., *Class, Race and Political Behaviour in Urban Jamaica.* Kingston, 1973. —*Democracy and Clientalism in Jamaica.* London and New Brunswick, N.J., 1981
Bibliography of Jamaica, 1900–1963. Jamaica Library Service, 1963

Libraries: Institute of Jamaica, Kingston. Jamaica Library Service, Kingston.

JAPAN

Capital: Tōkyō
Population: 120·02m. (1984)
GNP per capita: US$9,706 (1983)

Nippon (*or* Nihon)

HISTORY. The house of Yamato, from about 500 B.C. the rulers of one of several kingdoms, in about A.D. 200 united the nation; the present imperial family are their direct descendants. From 1186 until 1867 successive families of Shoguns exercised the temporal power. In 1867 the Emperor Meiji recovered the imperial power after the abdication on 14 Oct. 1867 of the fifteenth and last Tokugawa Shogun Keiki (in different pronunciation: Yoshinobu). In 1871 the feudal system (Hōken Seido) was abolished; this was the beginning of the rapid westernization.

At San Francisco on 8 Sept. 1951 a Treaty of Peace was signed by Japan and representatives of 48 countries. For details *see* THE STATESMAN'S YEAR-BOOK, 1953, p. 1169. On 26 Oct. 1951 the Japanese Diet ratified the Treaty by 307 votes to 47 votes with 112 abstentions. On the same day the Diet ratified a Security Treaty with the US by 289 votes to 71 votes with 106 abstentions. The treaty provided for the stationing of American troops in Japan until she was able to undertake her own defence. The peace treaty came into force on 28 April 1952, when Japan regained her sovereignty. In 1960 Japan signed the Japan–US Mutual Security Treaty, valid for 10 years, which was renewed in 1970. In June 1971 the Okinawa Reversion Agreement providing for the return from the US to Japan of Okinawa on 15 May 1972 was signed.

AREA AND POPULATION. Japan consists of 4 major islands, Honshu, Hokkaido, Kyushu and Shikoku and many small islands with an area of 377,765 sq. km. Census (1980) 117,060,396. Estimate, 1 Oct. 1983, 119,483,000 (males 58,790,000, females 60,693,000). Foreigners registered 31 Dec. 1983 were 817,129, of whom 674,581 were Koreans, 63,164 Chinese, 26,434 Americans, 7,516 Philippines, 6,087 British, 3,472 Vietnamese, 3,037 West Germans, 2,368 Indians, 2,233 Thais, 2,148 French, 1,963 Canadians, 1,962 stateless persons.

Japanese overseas, Oct. 1983, 471,873; of these 132,306 lived in USA, 130,433 in Brazil, 16,567 in UK, 16,041 in Argentina, 14,953 in Canada, 14,708 in the Federal Republic of Germany, 10,287 in Singapore, 9,391 in France, 8,436 in Hong Kong, 7,735 in Peru.

The leading cities, with population, 31 March 1983 (in 1,000), are:

Akita	286	Kitakyushu	1,055	Otaru	180
Amagasaki	507	Kōbe	1,370	Sagamihara	458
Aomori	290	Kōchi	304	Sakai	807
Asahikawa	359	Koriyama	290	Sapporo	1,451
Chiba	757	Kumamoto	520	Sasebo	252
Fujisawa	314	Kurashiki	410	Sendai	657
Fukuoka	1,082	Kure	233	Shimonoseki	262
Fukushima	265	Kyoto	1,461	Shizuoka	461
Fukuyama	355	Machida	301	Suita	332
Funabashi	489	Maebashi	271	Takamatsu	320
Gifu	408	Matsudo	412	Takatsuki	341
Hachioji	399	Matsuyama	412	Tokushima	250
Hakodate	320	Miyazaki	266	Tōkyō	8,151
Hamamatsu	501	Nagano	327	Toyama	307
Higashiosaka	499	Nagasaki	446	Toyohashi	312
Himeji	447	Nagoya	2,058	Toyonaka	396
Hirakata	369	Naha	302	Toyota	289
Hiroshima	898	Nara	311	Urawa	365
Ichinomiya	253	Neyagawa	254	Utsunomiya	390
Ichikawa	376	Niigata	457	Wakayama	403
Iwaki	352	Nishinomiya	401	Yao	267
Kagoshima	512	Oita	368	Yokkaichi	258
Kanazawa	412	Okayama	550	Yokohama	2,868
Kawaguchi	392	Omiya	362	Yokosuka	427
Kawasaki	1,039	Osaka	2,535		

Vital statistics (in 1,000) for calendar years:

	1974	1975	1976	1977	1978	1979	1980	1981	1982
Births	2,030	1,901	1,833	1,755	1,709	1,643	1,616	1,546	1,515
Deaths	710	702	703	690	696	690	722	725	712

Crude birth rate of Japanese nationals in present area, 1982, was 12·8 per 1,000 population (1947: 34·3); crude death rate, 6; crude marriage rate, 6·6; infant mortality rate per 1,000 live births, 6·6.

CLIMATE. The islands of Japan lie in the temperate zone, north-east of the main monsoon region of S.E. Asia. The climate is temperate with warm, humid summers and relatively mild winters except in the island of Hokkaido and northern parts of Honshu facing the Japan Sea. There is a month's rainy season in June-July, but the best seasons are spring and autumn, though Sept. may bring typhoons. There is a summer rainfall maximum. Tōkyō. Jan. 40·5°F (4·7°C), July 77·4°F (25·2°C). Annual rainfall 63″ (1,460 mm). Hiroshima. Jan. 39·7°F (4·3°C), July 78°F (25·6°C). Annual rainfall 61″ (1,603 mm). Nagasaki. Jan. 43·5°F (6·4°C), July 79·7°F (26·5°C). Annual rainfall 77″ (2,002 mm). Osaka. Jan. 42·1°F (5·6°C), July 80·6°F (27°C). Annual rainfall 53″ (1,400 mm). Sapporo. Jan. 23·2°F (–4·9°C), July 68·4°F (20·2°C). Annual rainfall 47″ (1,158 mm).

EMPEROR. The Emperor bears the title of Nihon-koku Tennō ('Emperor of Japan'). **Hirohito,** born in Tōkyō, 29 April 1901; succeeded his father, Yoshihito, 25 Dec. 1926; married 26 Jan. 1924, to Princess Nagako, born 6 March 1903. Living sons: (1) Prince Akihito (Tsugunomiya), born 23 Dec. 1933; formally installed as Crown Prince on 10 Nov. 1952; married to Michiko Shoda (born 20 Oct. 1934), 10 April 1959. *Offspring:* Prince Naruhito (Hironomiya), born 23 Feb. 1960; Prince Fumihito (Ayanomiya), born 30 Nov. 1965; Princess Sayako (Norinomiya), born 18 April 1969. (2) Prince Masahito (Hitachinomiya), born 28 Nov. 1935; married to Hanako Tsugaru, 30 Sept. 1964.

By the Imperial House Law of 11 Feb. 1889, revised on 16 Jan. 1947, the succession to the throne was fixed upon the male descendants.

CONSTITUTION AND GOVERNMENT. Japan's Government is based upon the Constitution of 1947 which superseded the Meiji Constitution of 1889. In it the Japanese people pledge themselves to uphold the ideas of democracy and peace. The Emperor is the symbol of the States and of the unity of the people. Sovereign power rests with the people. The Emperor has no powers related to government. Japan renounces war as a sovereign right and the threat or the use of force as a means of settling disputes with other nations. Fundamental human rights are guaranteed.

National flag: White, with a red disc.

National anthem: Kimi ga yo wa (words 9th century, tune by Hiromori Hayashi, 1881).

Legislative power rests with the Diet, which consists of the House of Representatives (of 511 members), elected by men and women over 20 years of age for a 4-year term, and the House of Councillors of 252 members (100 elected by party list system with proportional representation according to the d'Hondt method and 152 from prefectural districts), one-half of its members being elected every 3 years. The Lower House controls the budget and approves treaties with foreign powers.

The former House of Peers is replaced by the House of Councillors, whose members, like those of the House of Representatives, are elected as representatives of all the people. The House of Representatives has pre-eminence over the House of Councillors.

On 21 Nov. 1984 the House of Representatives consisted of 264 Liberal-Democrats-New Liberal Club National Union, 111 Socialists, 59 Komeito, 38 Democratic Socialists, 27 Japan Communist Party, 3 Social Democratic Federation and 6 Independents.

The Cabinet, as constituted in Nov. 1984, was as follows:

Prime Minister: Yasuhiro Nakasone.
Justice: Hitoshi Shimasaki.
Foreign Affairs: Shintaro Abe.
Finance: Noboru Takeshita.
Education: Hikaru Matsunaga.
Health and Welfare: Hiroyuki Masuoka.
Agriculture, Forestry and Fishery: Moriyoshi Sato.
Trade and Industry: Keijiro Murata.
Transport: Tokuo Yamashita.
Postal Service: Megumu Sato.
Labour: Toshio Yamaguchi.
Construction: Yoshiaki Kibe.
Home Affairs: Toru Furuya.

Local Government. The country is divided into 47 prefectures (*Todōfuken*), including Tōkyō-to (the capital), Ōsaka-fu and Kyōto-fu, Hokkai-dō, and 43 *Ken*. Each *Todōfuken* has its governor (*Chiji*) elected by the voters in the area. The prefectural government of Tōkyō-to is also responsible for the urban part (formerly Tōkyō-shi) of the prefecture. Each prefecture, city, town and village has a representative assembly elected by the same franchise as in parliamentary elections.

New legislation, which came into effect on 1 July 1954, has given the central government complete control of the police throughout the country.

DEFENCE

Army. The 'Ground Self-Defence Force' had in 1984 an authorized strength of 180,000 uniformed personnel, plus a reserve of 43,000 men. The Army is organized in 12 infantry divisions, 1 armoured division, 1 airborne brigade, 2 air defence brigades, 1 artillery, 5 engineer, 1 signal, 2 composite and 1 helicopter brigades in addition to 4 anti-aircraft artillery groups. Equipment includes 1,040 tanks.

The Northern Army, stationed in Hokkaido, consists of 4 divisions (1 of which is armoured), an artillery brigade, an anti-aircraft artillery brigade, a tank group and an engineering brigade. The Western Army, stationed in Kyushu, consists of 2 divisions and 1 composite brigade. The North-Eastern Army (2 divisions), the Eastern Army (2 divisions) and 1 airborne brigade, the Middle Army (3 divisions and 1 composite brigade). The infantry division establishment is approximately 9,000 with 4 infantry regiments or 9,000 (lower establishment) with 4 infantry regiments. Each infantry division has an artillery unit, an anti-tank unit, a tank battalion and an engineering battalion in addition to administrative units.

Navy. The 'Maritime Self-Defence Force' comprises 48 destroyers including 2 large destroyers of 5,200 tons each and 2 destroyers of 4,700 tons each, 14 submarines, 40 mine warfare vessels, 19 patrol vessels, 8 landing ships, 37 auxiliary ships including 1 ice breaker and 3 training vessels, and 320 support ships.

The Fleet Air Arm, numbering 6 air wings, includes 90 patrol aircraft and 16 flying boats for anti-submarine patrol, 76 trainers and 103 helicopters plus transports, rescue planes and others.

Personnel in 1985 numbered 46,000 officers and ratings including the Naval Air Arm. There are also 4,300 in civil maritime defence.

Air Force. An 'Air Self-Defence Force' was inaugurated on 1 July 1954. In 1984 its equipment included 2 interceptor squadrons of F-15J/DJ Eagles (total of 100 aircraft to be acquired by 1987); 3 squadrons of F-104J Starfighters, and 6 of F-4EJ Phantoms; 3 squadrons of Mitsubishi F-1 close-support fighters; 1 squadron of RF-4E reconnaissance fighters; the first 6 of 8 E-2C Hawkeye AWACS aircraft; ECM flight with 2 YS-11Es; 3 squadrons of turbofan Kawasaki C-1 and turboprop C-130H Hercules and NAMC YS-11 transports. About 35 helicopters, mostly KV-107s (to be replaced with CH-47 Chinooks), and MU-2 twin-turboprop aircraft perform search, rescue and general duties. Training units use piston-engined Fuji T-3 basic trainers, Fuji T-1 jet intermediate trainers, T-33 jet trainers and supersonic Mitsubishi T-2 jet advanced trainers. The T-1s and T-33s will be replaced with Kawasaki T-4s in the late '80s. Six surface-to-air missile groups (19 squadrons) are in service. Total strength (1985) about 350 combat aircraft and 46,000 officers and men.

INTERNATIONAL RELATIONS

Membership. Japan is a member of UN, the Colombo Plan and OECD.

ECONOMY

Planning. The 1981–85 Plan envisages an onward growth rate of 5·5%. The real growth rate for 1985 is envisaged at 4·6% and the nominal 6·1%.

Budget. Ordinary revenue and expenditure for fiscal year ending 31 March 1985 balanced at 50,627,000m. yen.

Of the proposed revenue in 1984, 34,596,000m. was to come from taxes and stamps, 12,680,000m. from public bonds. Main items of expenditure: Social security, 9,321,000m.; public works, 6,520,000m.; local government, 9,069,000m.; education, 4,867,000m.; defence, 2,935,000m.

The outstanding national debt incurred by public bonds was estimated in March 1983 to be 97,862,580m. yen, including 11,290m. yen of Japan's foreign currency bonds.

The estimated 1984 budgets of the prefectures and other local authorities forecast a total revenue of 48,289,000m. yen, to be made up partly by local taxes and partly by government grants and local loans.

Currency. Coins of 1, 5, 10, 50, 100 and 500 *yen* are in circulation as well as notes of the Bank of Japan, of 100, 500, 1,000, 5,000 and 10,000 *yen*. Bank-notes for 100 *yen* are still in circulation in country districts but are gradually being replaced by coins. In March 1985, £1 = 277 *yen*; US$1 = 261·77 *yen*.

In Dec. 1983 the currency in circulation consisted of 22,466,000m. yen Bank of Japan notes and 1,307,000m. yen subsidiary coins.

Banking. The modern banking system dates from 1872. The Nippon Ginko (Bank of Japan) was founded in 1882. The Bank of Japan has undertaken to finance the Government and the banks; its function is similar to that of a Central Bank in other countries. The Bank undertakes the actual management of Treasury funds and foreign exchange control.

Gold bullion and cash holdings of the Bank of Japan at 31 Dec. 1983 stood at 263,000m. yen.

The Yokohama Specie Bank (specializing in foreign exchange) became the Bank of Tōkyō in Aug. 1954. Total assets of all banks at 31 Dec. 1983 was 299,508,000m. yen.

The post office savings bank is modelled upon the British; deposits amounted to 82,505,650m. yen in Nov. 1983.

Many foreign banks operate branches in Japan including: Bank of Indo-China, Hongkong & Shanghai Banking Corporation, Chartered Bank of India, Australia and China, Bank of India, Mercantile Bank of India, Bank of Korea, Bank of China, Algemene Bank Nederland NV, National Handelsbank NV, Bank of America, National City Bank of New York, Chase Manhattan Bank, Bangkok Bank and American Express Co.

Weights and Measures. The metric system was made obligatory by a law passed in March 1921, and the period of grace for its compulsory use ended on 1 April 1966.

ENERGY AND NATURAL RESOURCES

Electricity. In 1982 generating facilities were capable of an output of 154,645,000 kw.; electricity produced was 581,133m. kwh.

Oil and Gas. Output of crude petroleum, 1982, was 467,000 kl, almost entirely from oilfields on the island of Honshu, but 214,685,000 kl crude oil had to be imported. Output of natural gas, 1982, 2,047m. cu. metres.

Minerals. Ore production in tonnes, 1982, of chromite, 11,129; coal, 17,606,000;

iron, 361,813; zinc, 251,356,000; molybdenum (1980), 100; manganese, 78,045; copper, 50,658; lead, 45,873; tungsten, 1,825; silver, 306,167 kg.; gold, 3,239 kg.

Agriculture. Agricultural workers in 1983 were 6,462,000, including 794,000 subsidiary and seasonal workers; 9% of the labour force as opposed to 24·7% in 1962. The arable land area in 1983 was 5,411,000 hectares (5,796,000 in 1970). Division of ordinary fields to non-agricultural use accounted largely for this decrease. Rice cultivation accounted for 2,257,000 hectares in 1982. The area planted with industrial crops such as rapeseed, tobacco, tea, rush, etc., was 258,000 hectares in 1982.

In 1983 there were 4,405,000 power cultivators and tractors in use together with 3·67m. power sprayers and power dusters and 2,025,000 rice power planters.

Output of rice was 12m. tonnes in 1979, 9·6m. in 1980, 10,259,000 in 1981 and 10·27m. in 1982.

Production in 1982 (in 1,000 tonnes) of barley was 390; wheat, 742; soybeans, 226. Sweet potatoes, which in the past mitigated the effects of rice famines, have, in view of rice over-production, decreased from 4,955,000 tons in 1965 to 1,384,000 tons in 1982. Domestic sugar-beet and sugar-cane production accounted for only 28·8% of requirement in 1982. In 1982, 2,169,000 tonnes were imported, 26% of this being imported from Australia, 22·8% from South Africa, 17·1% from Thailand, 14% from Cuba, 12·5% from Philippines, 6% from Formosa.

Fruit production, 1982 (in 1,000 tonnes): Mandarins, 2,864; apples, 923·5; pears, 492; grapes, 338·3; peaches, 227·5; and persimmons, 333·7.

Livestock (1983): 4,590,000 cattle (including about 2·1m. milch cows), 24,000 horses, 10·27m. pigs, 21,000 sheep, 57,000 goats, 307m. chickens. Milk (1981), 6·75m. tonnes.

Forestry. Forests and grasslands cover about 25m. hectares (nearly 70% of the whole land area), with an estimated timber stand of 2,484m. cu. metres in 1981. In 1981, 39,498,000 cu. metres were felled.

Fisheries. Before the War, Japanese catch represented one-half to two-thirds of the world's total fishing, in 1981 it was 14·3%. The catch in 1982 was 11·38m. tonnes, excluding whaling. Japan now ranks first in whaling.

INDUSTRY AND TRADE

Industry. Japan's industrial equipment, 1981, numbered 743,300 plants of all sizes, employing 11,218,000 production workers.

Since 1920 there has been a shift from light to heavy industries. The production of electrical appliances and electronic machinery has made great strides: television sets (1982: 13,898,000), radio sets (1982: 15,000,000), cameras (1982: 13,850,000), computing machines and automation equipment are produced in increasing quantities. The chemical industry ranks third in production value after machinery and metals (1981). Production, 1982, included (in tonnes): Sulphuric acid, 6,531,000; caustic soda, 2,709,000; ammonium sulphate, 1·69m.; calcium superphosphate, 532,000.

Output (1982), in 1,000 tonnes, of pig iron was 77,658; crude steel, 99,548; ordinary rolled steel, 76,295.

In 1982 paper production was 10·35m. tonnes; paperboard, 7·09m. tonnes.

Japan's textile industry before the War had 13m. cotton-yarn spindles. After the War she resumed with 2·78m. spindles; in 1964, 8·42m. spindles were operating. Output of cotton yarn, 1982, 170,000 tonnes, and of cotton cloth, 2,030m. sq. metres.

In wool, Japan aims at wool exports sufficient to pay for the imports of raw wool. Output, 1982, 120,000 tonnes of woollen yarns and 295m. sq. metres of woollen fabrics.

Output, 1982, of rayon woven fabrics, 740m. sq. metres; synthetic woven fabrics, 3,024m. sq. metres; silk fabrics, 129m. sq. metres.

Shipbuilding has been decreasing and in 1982, 7·97m. gross tons were launched, of which 3,024,000 GRT were tankers.

Labour. Total labour force, Oct. 1982, was 56·38m., of which 5·02m. were in agriculture and forestry, 460,000 in fishing, 100,000 in mining, 5·4m. in construction, 13·8m. in manufacturing, 15·02m. in commerce and finance, 3·83m. in transport and other public utilities, 10·65m. in services (including the professions) and 1·95m. in government work.

In 1982 there were 12,526,000 workers organized in 74,091 unions. The largest federation is the 'General Council of Japanese Trade Unions' (Sōhyō) with 4·55m. members. The 'Japanese Confederation of Labour' (Dōmei Kaigi) had 2,187,000 members. The 'Federation of Independent Unions' (Chūritsu Rōren) founded in 1956 had 1,429,000 members.

In Nov. 1982, 1·36m. (2·3%) were unemployed. In 1983, 507,000 working days were lost in industrial stoppages.

Commerce. Trade (in US$1m.)

	1977	*1978*	*1979*	*1980*	*1981*	*1982*	*1983*
Imports	70,808	79,343	110,672	140,528	152,030	138,831	126,393
Exports	80,494	97,543	103,031	129,807	143,289	131,931	146,927

Distribution of trade by countries (customs clearance basis) (US$1m.):

	Exports		*Imports*	
	1982	*1983*	*1982*	*1983*
Africa	4,167	2,904	1,610	1,348
Australia	4,581	4,280	6,961	6,642
Canada	2,861	3,625	4,441	4,430
China	3,511	4,912	5,352	5,087
Fed. Rep. of Germany	5,018	5,877	2,355	2,414
Hong Kong	4,718	5,289	622	670
Latin America	9,086	6,379	6,268	6,451
Philippines	1,803	1,744	1,576	1,306
South-east Asia	31,873	34,498	29,985	27,925
Thailand	1,907	2,506	1,041	1,019
USSR	3,899	2,821	1,682	1,456
UK	4,813	4,983	1,874	1,940
USA	36,330	42,829	24,179	24,647

Principal items in 1983, with value in 1m. yen were:

Imports, c.i.f.		*Exports, f.o.b.*	
Mineral fuels	13,986,000	Machinery and transport equipment	23,653,000
Foodstuffs	3,539,000	Metals and metal products	4,365,000
Metal ores and scrap	1,547,000	Textile products	1,572,000
Machinery and transport equipment	1,644,000	Chemicals	1,659,000

Total trade between Japan and UK (British Department of Trade returns, in £1,000 sterling):

	1980	*1981*	*1982*	*1983*	*1984*
Imports to UK	1,712,108	2,236,170	2,657,977	3,355,450	3,768,019
Exports and re-exports from UK	597,147	620,273	681,483	797,848	925,311

Tourism. In 1982, 1,708,306 foreigners visited Japan, 352,208 of whom came from USA, 151,545 from UK. Japanese travelling abroad totalled 4,086,138 in 1982.

COMMUNICATIONS

Roads. The total length of roads (including urban and other local roads) was 1,123,030 km at 1 April 1982; the 'national' roads extended 46,275 km, of which 44,063 km were paved. Motor vehicles, at 31 Dec. 1983, numbered 42,053,000, including 26,385,000 passenger cars and 15,437,000 commercial vehicles.

Railways. The first railway was completed in 1872, between Tōkyō and Yokohama (29 km). Total length of railways, in March 1982, was 27,029 km, of which the national railways had 21,419 km (8,435 km electrified) and private railways, 5,610 km (4,923 km electrified). In 1982 the national railways carried 6,742m. passengers (private, 11,527m.) and 98m. tons of freight (private, 38m.).

Aviation. The principal airlines are Japan Airlines and All Nippon Airways. Japan Airlines, founded in 1953, operate international services from Tōkyō to the USA,

Europe, the Middle East and Southeast Asia, including flights to London over the North Pole and to Moscow by way of Siberia. In 1982 Japanese companies carried 40,461,300 passengers in domestic services and 5,624,000 passengers in international services.

Shipping. On 30 June 1983 the merchant fleet consisted of 8,666 vessels of 100 gross tons and over; total tonnage 39m. gross tons; there were 707 ships for passenger transport (1,131,000 gross tons), 2,679 cargo ships (2,460,000 gross tons) and 1,564 oil tankers (15,430,000 gross tons).

Coastguard. The 'Maritime Safety Agency' (Coastguard) consists of 11 regional MS headquarters, 65 MS offices, 52 MS bases, 14 air bases, 7 District Communications Centres, 1 Traffic Advisory Service Centre, 4 hydrographic observatories and 136 navigation aids offices (with 4,927 navigation aids facilities) and controls 43 large patrol vessels, 47 medium patrol vessels, 19 small patrol vessels, 231 patrol craft, 22 hydrographic service vessels, 5 firefighting vessels, 10 firefighting boats, 63 guard and rescue boats and 80 navigation aids service supply vessels. Personnel in 1984 numbered 12,061 officers and men.

The Coastguard aviation service includes 23 fixed-wing aircraft and 35 helicopters.

Post and Broadcasting. The telephone services, operated by a public corporation, at 31 March 1983 had 61,208,000 instruments.

On 31 March 1983, 98·8% of all households owned colour television sets.

Cinemas (1982). Cinemas numbered 2,267 with an annual attendance of 155m. (1960: 1,014m.).

Newspapers (1982). Daily newspapers numbered 125 with aggregate circulation of 68,142,000, including 4 major English-language newspapers.

JUSTICE, RELIGION, EDUCATION AND WELFARE

Justice. The Supreme Court is composed of the Chief Justice and 14 other judges. The Chief Justice is appointed by the Emperor, the other judges by the Cabinet Every 10 years a justice must submit himself to the electorate. All justices and judges of the lower courts serve until they are 70 years of age.

Below the Supreme Court are 8 regional higher courts, district courts (*Chihosaibansho*) in each prefecture (4 in Hokkaidō) and the local courts.

The Supreme Court is authorized to declare unconstitutional any act of the Legislature or the Executive which violates the Constitution.

Religion. There has normally been religious freedom, but Shintō (literally, The Way of the Gods) was given the status of *quasi*-state-religion in the 1930s; in 1945 the Allied Supreme Command ordered the Government to discontinue state support of Shintō. State subsidies have ceased for all religions, and all religious teachings are forbidden in public schools.

In Dec. 1982 Shintoism claimed 103,046,565 adherents, Buddhism 86,642,598; these figures obviously overlap. Christians numbered 1,511,845, of whom 1,124,538 are Protestants and 387,307 Catholics.

Education. Education is compulsory and free between the ages of 6 and 15. Almost all national and municipal institutions are co-educational. On 1 May 1983 there were 15,093 kindergartens with 99,810 teachers and 2,192,853 pupils; 23,988 elementary schools with 474,018 teachers and 11,739,456 pupils; 10,840 junior high schools with 273,739 teachers and 5,706,811 pupils, 5,142 senior high schools with 252,649 teachers and 4,715,162 pupils; 532 junior colleges with 17,202 teachers and 379,427 pupils.

There were also 782 special schools for handicapped children (37,330 teachers, 94,372 pupils).

Japan has 7 main state universities, formerly known as the Imperial Universities: Tōkyō University (1877); Kyōto University (1897); Tōhoku University, Sendai (1907); Kyūshū University, Fukuoka (1910); Hokkaidō University, Sapporo

(1918); Osaka University (1931), and Nagoya University (1939). In addition, there are various other state and municipal as well as private universities of high standing, such as Keio (founded in 1859), Waseda, Rikkyō, Hōsei, Maiji universities, and several women's universities, among which Tōkyō and Ochanomizu are most notable. There are 458 colleges and universities with (1 May 1983) 1,834,495 students and 109,135 teachers.

Social Welfare. Hospitals at the end of 1982 numbered 9,403 with 1,401,999 beds. Physicians at the end of 1982 numbered 167,952; dentists, 58,362.

There are in force various types of social security schemes, such as health insurance, unemployment insurance and old-age pensions. The total population come under one or more of these schemes.

In 1982 17,488,592 persons and 9,244,655 households received some form of regular public assistance, the total of which came to 1,329,923·11m. yen.

DIPLOMATIC REPRESENTATIVES

Of Japan in Great Britain (43-46 Grosvenor St., London, W1X 0BA)
Ambassador: Toshio Yamazaki (accredited 20 Feb. 1985).

Of Great Britain in Japan (1 Ichiban-cho, Chiyoda-ku, Tōkyō 102)
Ambassador: Sir Sydney Giffard, KCMG.

Of Japan in the USA (2520 Massachusetts Ave., NW, Washington, D.C., 20008)
Ambassador: Yoshio Ōkawara.

Of the USA in Japan (10–1, Akasaka 1-chome, Minato-Ku, Tōkyō)
Ambassador: Michael J. Mansfield.

Of Japan to the United Nations
Ambassadors: Mizuo Kuroda and Tomohiko Kobayashi.

Books of Reference

Statistics Bureau of the Prime Minister's Office: *Statistical Year-Book* (from 1949).—*Statistical Abstract* (from 1950)).—*Statistical Handbook of Japan 1977.—Monthly Bulletin* (from April 1950)
Economic Planning Agency: *Economic Survey* (annual), *Economic Statistics* (monthly), *Economic Indicators* (monthly)
Ministry of International Trade: *Foreign Trade of Japan* (annual)
Kodansha Encyclopedia of Japan. 9 vols. Tōkyō, 1983
Japan Times Year Book. (I. Year Book of Japan. II. Who's Who in Japan. III. Business Directory of Japan.) Tōkyō, first issue 1933
Treaty of Peace with Japan. (Cmd. 8392). HMSO, 1951; (Cmd. 8601). HMSO, 1952
Allen, G. C., *Short Economic History of Modern Japan.* London, 1946.—*The Japanese Economy.* London, 1981
Baerwald, H. H., *Japan's Parliament.* CUP, 1974
Burks, A. W., *Japan: Profile of an Industrial Power.* Boulder, 1981
Kahn, H., and Pepper, T., *The Japanese Challenge.* New York, 1979
Kenkyusha's *New Japanese–English [and English–Japanese] Dictionary.* 2 vols. New ed. Cambridge, Mass., and Berkeley, Cal., 1960
Langdon, F. C., *Japan's Foreign Policy.* Univ. of British Columbia Press, 1973
McNelly, T., *Politics and Government in Japan.* 2nd ed. London, 1972
Miyazaki, S., *The Japanese Dictionary Explained in English.* Tōkyō, 1950
Morishima, U. *Why has Japan 'Succeeded'?* CUP, 1984
Murata, K., *An Industrial Geography of Japan.* London, 1980
Nippon: A Chartered Survey of Japan. Tsuneta Yano Memorial Society. Tōkyō, annual
Prindl, A., *Japanese Finance: Guide to Banking in Japan.* Chichester, 1981
Sansom, G. B., *The Western World and Japan.* New York, 1950.—*A History of Japan.* 3 vols. London, 1958–64
Simonis, H. and U. E. (ed.), *Japan: Economic and Social Studies in Development.* Wiesbaden, 1974
Tanaka, K., *Building a New Japan: A Plan for Remodelling the Japanese Archipelago.* Tōkyō, 1973
Tsoukalis, L., (ed.), *Japan and Western Europe.* London, 1982
Vogel, E. F., *Japan as Number One.* Harvard Univ. Press, 1979
Yabuki, K. (ed.), *Japan Bibliographic Annual.* 2 vols. Tōkyō, annual

THE HASHEMITE KINGDOM OF JORDAN

Capital: Amman
Population: 2·25m. (1982) E. Bank
1·25m. (1982) W. Bank
GNP per capita: US$1,620 (1981)

Al Mamlaka al Urduniya al Hashemiyah

HISTORY. By a Treaty, signed in London on 22 March 1946, Britain recognized Transjordan as a sovereign independent state. A new Anglo-Transjordan treaty was signed in Amman on 15 March 1948. The treaty was to remain in force for 20 years, but by mutual consent was terminated on 13 March 1957.

The Arab Federation between the Kingdoms of Iraq and Jordan, which was concluded on 14 Feb. 1958, lapsed after the revolution in Iraq of 14 July 1958, and was officially terminated by royal decree on 1 Aug. 1958.

On 25 May 1946 the Amir Abdullah assumed the title of King, and when the treaty was ratified on 17 June 1946 the name of the territory was changed to that of 'The Hashemite Kingdom of Jordan'. The legislature consists of a lower house of 60 members elected by universal suffrage (30 from East Jordan and 30 from West Jordan), and a senate of 30 members nominated by the King.

AREA AND POPULATION. The part of Palestine remaining to the Arabs under the armistice with Israel 3 April 1949, with the exception of the Gaza strip, was in Dec. 1949 placed under Jordan rule and formally incorporated in Jordan on 24 April 1950. For the frontier lines *see* map in THE STATESMAN'S YEAR-BOOK, 1951. On 10 Aug. 1965 a treaty with Saudi Arabia provided for an exchange of about 6,000–7,000 sq. km in order to facilitate the development of the port of Aqaba.

Total East Bank area, 91,000 sq. km. West Bank enclaves 5,000 sq. km: census population (18 Nov. 1961), 1,706,226; estimate, 1982, 3·5m. (2·25m. in East Bank, 1·25m. in West Bank).

The country is divided into 8 districts (*muhafaza*), viz., Amman, Irbid, Balqa, Karak, Ma'an, Jerusalem, Hebron and Nablus. The last 3 named districts are known collectively as the West Bank, which, since the hostilities of June 1967, has been occupied by Israel.

The largest towns, with estimated population, 1980: Amman, the capital, 1,232,600; Zarka, 269,780 (1977); Irbid, 140,000.

In 1979 registered births numbered 91,622; deaths, 6,547; marriages, 15,491; divorces, 3,295.

CLIMATE. Predominantly a Mediterranean climate, with hot dry summers and cool wet winters, but in hilly parts summers are cooler and winters colder. Those areas below sea-level are very hot in summer and warm in winter. Eastern parts have a desert climate. Amman. Jan. 46°F (7·5°C), July 77°F (24·9°C). Annual rainfall 12″ (290 mm). Aqaba. Jan. 61°F (16°C), July 89°F (31·5°C). Annual rainfall 1·5″ (35 mm).

KING. The Kingdom is a constitutional monarchy headed by HM King **Hussein**, GCVO, eldest son of King Talal, who, being incapacitated by mental illness, was deposed by Parliament on 11 Aug. 1952 and died 8 July 1972. The King was born 14 Nov. 1935, and married Princess Dina Abdul Hamid on 19 April 1955 (divorced 1957), Toni Avril Gardiner (Muna al Hussein) on 25 May 1961 (divorced 1972), Alia Toukan on 26 Dec. 1972 (died in air crash 1977) and Elizabeth Halaby on 15 June 1978. *Offspring:* Princess Alia, born 13 Feb. 1956; Prince Abdulla, born 30 Jan. 1962; Prince Faisal, born 11 Oct. 1963; Princesses Zein and Aisha, born 23 April 1968; Princess Haya, born 3 May 1974; Prince Ali, born 23 Dec. 1975; Prince Hamzah, born 1 April 1980; Prince Hashem, born 10 June 1981; Princess Iman, born 4 April 1983. *Crown Prince* (appointed 1 April 1965): Prince Hassan, younger brother of the King.

CONSTITUTION AND GOVERNMENT. The Constitution passed on 7 Nov. 1951 provides that the Cabinet is responsible to Parliament.

On 5 Feb. 1976 both Houses of Parliament approved amendments to the Constitution by which the King was empowered to postpone calling elections until further notice. The lower house was dissolved. This step was taken because no elections could be held in the West Bank which has been under Israeli occupation since June 1967.

Parliament was reconvened on 9 Jan. 1984. By-elections were held in March 1984 and 6 members were nominated for the West Bank bringing Parliament to 60 members. Women voted for the first time in 1984.

The Cabinet, in Jan. 1984, was composed as follows:

Prime Minister and Defence: Ahmed Obaidat.

Deputy Prime Minister and Interior: Sulaiman Arar. *Minister of State for the Prime Ministry and Minister of Justice:* Ahmed Abdelkareem Al Tarawneh. *Foreign Affairs:* Taher Al Masri. *Communication:* Dr Mahammad Adoub Al Zaben. *Supplies:* Ibrahim Ayoub. *Education:* Hekmat Al Saket. *Industry and Trade and Tourism:* Dr Jawad Alanani. *Transport:* Taher Hekmat. *Finance:* Dr Hanna Owdeh. *Information:* Lyla Sharaf. *Municipal and Rural Affairs:* Hamadallah Al Nabulsi. *Awqaf and Religious Affairs:* Ebed Khala Dawoudeyeh. *Agriculture:* Mohammed Basheer. *Labour:* Dr Tayseer Abdel Jaber. *Occupied Territories Affairs:* Shawkat Mahmoud. *Health:* Dr Kamal Alajlouni. *Public Works:* Raef Najm. *Culture, Youth and Antiquities:* Dr Abdellah Awaydat. *Social Development:* Abdelsalam Kenaan.

National flag: Three horizontal stripes of black, white, green, with a red triangle based on the hoist, bearing a white 7-pointed star.

The official language of the country is Arabic.

DEFENCE

Army. The Army is organized in 6 armoured, 1 special forces and 4 mechanized brigades, 1 independent Royal Guards brigade and 16 artillery battalions. Total strength (1985) 68,000 men.

Navy. The Coastal Guard or Jordan Sea Force has 14 patrol launches and 1 support craft based at Aqaba. Personnel (1985) totalled 300 officers and ratings.

Air Force. The Air Force has 2 interceptor and 3 ground attack squadrons equipped respectively with Mirage F1 and F-5E Tiger II fighters, and 2-seat F-5Fs, plus an OCU equipped with F-5A fighters and 2-seat F-5Bs. There are 5 C-130B/H Hercules and 2 CASA Aviocar turboprop transports, S-76, Alouette III and Hughes 500D helicopters, piston-engined Bulldog and AS 202 Bravo basic trainers and T-37B jet trainers. Aircraft on order include 24 AH-1S HueyCobra anti-tank helicopters for 1985 delivery. Hawk surface-to-air missiles equip 14 batteries. Strength (1985) about 7,000 officers and men.

INTERNATIONAL RELATIONS

Membership. Jordan is a member of the UN and the Arab League.

ECONOMY

Planning. A 5-year plan (1981–85) aims at achieving a growth rate of 10·4% per annum.

Budget. The budget estimates for the year 1981 provide for revenue of JD.656,900,000 and expenditure of JD.654,100,000.

Currency. The Jordan *dinar,* divided into 1,000 *fils.* The following bank-notes and coins are in circulation: 10, 5 dinars, 1 dinar, 500 fils (notes), 250, 100, 50, 25, 20 fils (cupronickel), 10, 5, 1 fils (bronze). In March 1985, £1 = JD.0·408; US$ = JD.0·453.

Banking. The Central Bank of Jordan started operations on 1 Oct. 1964, taking over the sterling assets and the commitments of the Jordan Currency Board.

NATURAL RESOURCES

Oil. Oil was discovered in 1982 at Azraq, 70 km east of Amman but was (1985) totally dependent on imports costing US$577m. in 1983.

Minerals. Phosphates production in 1981 was 4,243,000 tons. Potash is found in the Dead Sea. Reserves, over 800m. tonnes. A potash plant is being built on the southeast shore to extract compounds by solar evaporation. Cement production (1982), 964,000 tons.

Agriculture. The country east of the Hejaz Railway line is largely desert; north-western Jordan is potentially of agricultural value and an integrated Jordan Valley project began in 1973; 21,000 hectares had been irrigated by 1980. The main crops are tomatoes and other vegetables, fruit, wheat.

Production in 1981 included (in tonnes): Tomatoes, 204,500; citrus fruit, 53,800; wheat, 90,000.

Livestock (1983): 1m. sheep; 500,000 goats; 40,000 cattle; 15,000 camels.

INDUSTRY AND TRADE

Industry. The most important activity is processing potash and other minerals. There is a large chemical fertilizer plant at Aqaba, an oil refinery at Zarka and a cement plant at Fuhers. Production (1981): Iron, 134,000 tons; textiles, 1·3m. yards; cigarettes, 4,711m.

Commerce. Imports in 1983 were valued at US$3,088m. and exports and re-exports at US$448m. Total remittances from Jordanians working abroad reached US$1,150m. in 1983.

Total trade between Jordan and UK (British Department of Trade returns, in £1,000 sterling):

	1980	*1981*	*1982*	*1983*	*1984*
Imports to UK	8,157	10,300	17,487	28,680	18,114
Exports and re-exports from UK	100,318	203,651	295,274	262,503	192,508

Tourism. In 1981, 2·22m. foreigners visited Jordan.

COMMUNICATIONS

Roads. Asphalt roads connect Amman with all the chief towns in the country. Unmetalled roads have been constructed, making motor traffic possible from Amman to most other areas. The road from Amman to Ma'an and Aqaba (394 km) has branches to Karak, Tafileh, Shobak and Wadi Musa (Petra). The town of Jerash is joined by a good road to Amman. The normal asphalted route from Amman to Deraa (in Syria) and thence to Damascus is through Jerash. The oasis of Azraq may be reached by motor car from Mafraq, Zarka or Amman. Total length of public highways, 4,095 km. Motor vehicles in 1980 included 73,078 private passenger cars, 11,207 taxis, 1,415 buses, 29,517 goods vehicles, 4,888 motor cycles.

Railways. The 1,050 mm gauge Hejaz Jordan and Aqaba Railway runs from the Syrian border at Nassib to Ma'an and Naqb Ishtar and Aqaba Port (total, 618 km). In 1981 the railways carried 57,753 passengers and 10,000 tons of freight.

Aviation. The Queen Alia International airport, at Zizya, 30 km south of Amman was inaugurated in 1983. There are other international airports at Amman and Aqaba.

Shipping (1980). The port of Aqaba handled 6,598,591 tons of cargo.

Post. In 1982 there were 791 post offices and 60,533 telephones in 1980.

Cinemas (1975). Cinemas numbered 40 with a total attendance of 4,341,900.

Newspapers (1984). There were 4 daily (including 1 in English) and 5 weekly papers.

RELIGION, EDUCATION AND WELFARE

Religion. About 80% of the population are Sunni Moslems.

Education (1980, East Bank only). There were 189 pre-primary schools with 639 teachers and 17,160 pupils; 1,095 primary schools with 13,898 teachers and 448,411 pupils; 341 secondary schools had 3,648 teachers and 80,173 pupils and 16 teacher-training institutes had 362 teachers and 8,621 students. The University of Jordan, inaugurated on 15 Dec. 1962 had in 1980-81, 10,767 students and 431 teachers. The Yarmouk University (Irbid) was inaugurated in 1976 with (1980-81) 5,677 students and 225 teachers.

Health (1980). There were 1,715 physicians, 351 dentists and 35 hospitals with 2,743 beds.

DIPLOMATIC REPRESENTATIVES

Of Jordan in Great Britain (6 Upper Phillimore Gdns., London, W8 7HB)
Ambassador: Hani Tabbara, GCVO (accredited 23 March 1984).

Of Great Britain in Jordan (Third Circle, Jebel Amman)
Ambassador: A. J. Coles, CMG.

Of Jordan in the USA (3504 International Dr., NW, Washington, D.C., 20008)
Ambassador: Ibrahim Izziddin.

Of the USA in Jordan (Jebel Amman, Amman)
Ambassador: Richard N. Viets.

Of Jordan to the United Nations
Ambassador: Abdullah Salah.

Books of Reference

The Department of Statistics, Ministry of National Economy, publishes a *Statistical Yearbook* (in Arabic and English), latest issue 1968, and a *Statistical Guide,* latest issue 1965.—*External Trade Statistics*, 1968.—*National Accounts and Input-Output Analysis, 1959–65,* 1967

The Constitution of the Hashemite Kingdom of Jordan. Amman, 1952

Glubb, J. B., *The Story of the Arab Legion.* London, 1948.—*A Soldier with the Arabs.* London, 1957

Gubser, P., *Jordan.* Boulder, 1982

Haas, J., *Husseins Königreich: Jordaniens Stellung in Nahen Osten.* Munich, 1975

Morris, J., *The Hashemite Kings.* London, 1959

Seton, C. R. W., *Legislation of Transjordan, 1918-30.* London, 1931. [Continued by the Government of Jordan as an annual publication: *Jordan Legislation.* Amman, 1932 ff.]

Toni, Y. T., and Mousa, S., *Jordan: Land and People.* Amman, 1973

KENYA

Capital: Nairobi
Population: 19·5m. (1985)
GNP per capita: US$420 (1981)

Jamhuri ya Kenya

HISTORY. Until Kenya became independent on 12 Dec. 1963, it consisted of the colony and the protectorate. The protectorate comprised the mainland dominions of the Sultan of Zanzibar, viz., a coastal strip of territory 10 miles wide, to the northern branch of the Tana River; also Mau, Kipini and the Island of Lamu, and all adjacent islands between the rivers Umba and Tana. The Sultan on 8 Oct. 1963 ceded the coastal strip to Kenya with effect from 12 Dec. 1963.

The colony and protectorate, formerly known as the East African Protectorate were, on 1 April 1905, transferred from the Foreign Office to the Colonial Office and in Nov. 1906 the protectorate was placed under the control of a governor and C.-in-C. and (except the Sultan of Zanzibar's dominions) was annexed to the Crown as from 23 July 1920 under the name of the Colony of Kenya, thus becoming a Crown Colony.

The territories on the coast became the Kenya Protectorate.

A Treaty was signed (15 July 1924) with Italy under which Great Britain ceded to Italy the Juba River and a strip from 50 to 100 miles wide on the British side of the river. Cession took place on 29 June 1925. The northern boundary is defined by an agreement with Ethiopia in 1947.

AREA AND POPULATION. Kenya is bounded by Ethiopia in the north, Uganda in the west, Tanzania in the south and the Somali Republic and the Indian ocean in the east. The total area is 224,960 sq. miles (582,600 sq. km), of which 219,790 sq. miles is land area. In the 1979 census, the population was 15,327,000, of which 15,100,000 were Africans, 78,600 Asians, 39,900 Europeans, 39,140 Arabs. Estimate (1985) 19·5m.

On the coast the Arabs and Swahili predominate, farther inland the races speaking Bantu languages, and non-Bantu tribes, such as the Luo, the Nandi and Kipsigis, the Masai, the Somali and the Gallas. There are more than forty tribes.

Population of the provinces (1979): Rift Valley, 3·24m.; Eastern, 2,719,000; Nyanza, 2,643,000; Central, 2,345,000; Coast, 1,342,000; Western, 1,832,000; Nairobi district, 835,000; North-Eastern, 373,000.

Nairobi, the capital, was given a Royal charter on 30 March 1950; the 1979 census showed a population of 827,775. Estimate (1985) 1·2m.

Population of the largest towns: Mombasa, 341,000; Kisumu, 153,000; Nakuru, 93,000; Machakos, 84,000; Meru, 70,000; Eldoret, 51,000; Thika, 41,000. A new town is being developed (in 1981) at Bura, which will be the centre of a production area using irrigated water from the Tana river.

CLIMATE. The climate is tropical, with wet and dry seasons, but considerable differences in altitude make for varied conditions between the hot, coastal lowlands and the plateau, where temperatures are very much cooler. Heaviest rains occur in April and May, but in some parts there is a second wet season in Nov. and Dec. Nairobi. Jan. 65°F (18·3°C), July 60°F (15·6°C). Annual rainfall 39″ (958 mm). Mombasa. Jan. 81°F (27·2°C), July 76°F (24·4°C). Annual rainfall 47″ (1,201 mm).

CONSTITUTION AND GOVERNMENT. A Constitution conferring internal self government was brought into force on 1 June 1963, and full independence was achieved on 12 Dec. 1963. On 12 Dec. 1964 Kenya became a republic.

President of the Republic: Daniel Arap Moi (elected 1979, re-elected 1983).
Vice-President and Home Affairs: Mwai Kibaki.

Foreign Affairs: Elijah Mwagale.

The House of Representatives and the Senate were in Dec. 1966 amalgamated into one National Assembly consisting of 158 elected Members, 12 nominated members, together with the Speaker and the Attorney-General.

On 10 Nov. 1964 Kenya became a one-party state of the Kenya African National Union (KANU) when the voluntary dissolution of the Kenya African Democratic Union (KADU) was declared. Later a second party, the Kenya People's Union (KPU) was formed but on 30 Oct. 1969 was proscribed.

At general elections held in Sept. 1983 there were over 740 candidates for 153 seats. The turnout was low, ranging from 27% to 40%.

National flag: Three horizontal stripes of black, red, green, with the red edged in white; bearing in the centre an African shield in black and white with 2 crossed spears behind.

Administration. The country is divided into the Nairobi Area and 7 provinces. There are 40 districts. The provinces are: Coast, Central, Eastern, Rift Valley, Western, Nyanza and North Eastern.

Kiswahili became the official language in 1974 but English is in general use.

DEFENCE

Army. The Army consists of 2 armoured, 1 armoured reconnaissance, 6 infantry, 2 artillery, 1 parachute, 1 independent air cavalry and 2 engineer battalions. Equipment includes 76 Vickers Mk 3 main battle tanks. 32 Hughes Defender helicopters, of which 15 are armed with TOW missiles. Total strength (1985) 13,000, and there is also a paramilitary police force of 1,800.

Navy. The Navy in 1985 consists of 7 British built patrol craft and 1 tug. Personnel totalled 350 officers and ratings. The base is at Mombasa which has a dry dock with a capacity of 18,000 tons. There are also 2 British-built marine police cutters.

Air Force. An air force, formed 1 June 1964, was built up with RAF assistance and is under Army command. Equipment includes 13 F-5E/F-5F supersonic combat aircraft/trainers, 12 Hawk and 5 BAC 167 Strikemaster light jet attack/trainers, 6 twin-turboprop Buffaloes and 5 twin-engined Caribou for transport, air ambulance, anti-locust spraying and security duties, 6 Skyservant and 1 VIP Navajo Chieftain light twin, 14 Bulldog piston-engined primary trainers and Puma, Gazelle and Bell 47 helicopters. Personnel about 2,300 in 1983.

INTERNATIONAL RELATIONS

Membership. Kenya is a member of UN, the Commonwealth, OAU and is an ACP state of EEC.

ECONOMY

Planning. The 1984–88 development plan aims at an average annual growth rate of 6·3%.

Budget. Ordinary revenue and expenditure for 1982–83: Revenue, KSh.16,017m.; expenditure, KSh.22,605m.

Currency. The monetary unit is the Kenya *Shilling* divided into 100 *cents*; 20 shillings = K£1. In March 1985, £1 = 17·66 *Shilling*; US$1 = 15·57 *Shilling.*

Banking. Banks operating in Kenya: the National & Grindlays Bank International, Ltd; the Standard Bank, Ltd; Barclays Bank International; Algemene Bank Nederland NV; Bank of India, Ltd; Bank of Baroda, Ltd; Habib Bank (Overseas), Ltd; Commercial Bank of Africa, Ltd; Citibank; The Co-operative Bank of Kenya, Ltd; National Bank of Kenya, Ltd; The Kenya Commercial Bank; The Central Bank of Kenya.

ENERGY AND NATURAL RESOURCES

Electricity. Hydropower supplies 20% of energy needs from 4 power stations on the Tana river.

Minerals. Mineral production in 1981 was: Soda ash, 159,385 tonnes; gold, 114 grammes; salt, 27,766 tonnes. Other minerals comprised barytes, magnesite, felspar, sapphires, fluorspar ore, garnets, sand and raw soda.

Agriculture. As agriculture is possible from sea-level to altitudes of over 9,000 ft, tropical, sub-tropical and temperate crops can be grown and mixed farming can be advocated. Four-fifths of the country is range-land which produces mainly livestock products and wild game which constitutes the major attraction of the country's tourist industry.

The main areas of crop production are the Central, Rift Valley, Western and Nyanza Provinces and parts of Eastern and Coastal Provinces. Coffee, tea, sisal, pyrethrum, maize and wheat are crops of major importance in the Highlands, while coconuts, cashew nuts, cotton, sugar, sisal and maize are the principal crops grown at the lower altitudes. Principal crops with production for sale (in 1,000 tonnes, 1982): Wheat, 220; maize, 495; rice paddy 44; pyrethrum extract, 0·2; sugar-cane, 4,042; clean coffee, 94·6; sisal, 52; tea, 93.

Livestock (1983): Cattle, 11·5m.; sheep, 6·5m.; goats, 8m.; pigs, 100,000; poultry, 19m.

Forestry. The total area of gazetted forest reserves in Kenya amounts to 16,800 sq. km, of which the greater part is situated between 6,000 and 11,000 ft above sea-level, mostly on Mount Kenya, the Aberdares, Mount Elgon, Tinderet, Londiani, Mau watershed, Elgeyo and Charangani ranges. These forests may be divided into coniferous, broad-leaved or hardwood and bamboo forests. The upper parts of these forests are mainly bamboo, which occurs mostly between altitudes of 8,000 and 10,000 ft and occupies some 10% of the high-altitude forests. Production (1981): Softwood, 350,000 cu. metres; hardwood, 475,000.

INDUSTRY AND TRADE

Industry. Processing of agricultural products is one of the major industries, followed by beer brewing, cement, chemicals, footwear and textiles. Heavy industries include manufacture of tyres and assembly of trucks and pick-ups. Production, 1981 (in tonnes): Maize meal, 329,000; wheat flour, 282,000; cement, 1·32m.; cigarettes (no.), 5m.

Commerce. Total domestic exports (1983) K£613·6m.; imports K£945·2m.

Chief imports (1980): Mineral fuels, K£325m.; machinery and transport equipment, K£274m. Chief exports (1980): Petroleum products, K£163m.; unroasted coffee, K£108m.; tea, K£58m.

Total trade between Kenya and UK (British Department of Trade returns, in £1,000 sterling):

	1980	*1981*	*1982*	*1983*	*1984*
Imports to UK	105,443	95,238	104,312	128,464	203,243
Exports and re-exports from UK	259,103	173,663	153,858	111,249	176,061

Tourism. In 1983, about 360,300 overseas visitors travelled to Kenya spending KSh.1,800m.

COMMUNICATIONS

Roads. In 1981 there were 6,540 km of bitumen surfaced roads and 47,037 km of gravel-surfaced roads.

Railways. On 11 Feb. 1977 the independent Kenya Railways Corporation was formed following break-up of the East African Railways administration. The network totals 2,654 km of metre-gauge and extensive upgrading and re-equipment was in progress in 1984. In 1983, the railways carried 2·2m. passengers and 3·9m. tonnes of freight.

Aviation. Total number of passengers handled at the 3 main airports (1981) was 1,975,000. Jomo Kenyatta Airport, Nairobi, handles nearly 30 international airlines as well as Kenya Airways.

Shipping. A national shipping service is planned (1984) to be based in Mombasa, the Kenyan main port at Kilindini on the Indian Ocean. The port handles cargo freight both for Kenya as well as for the neighbouring East African states. The Port Authority also runs a modern harbour college.

Post and Broadcasting. The Voice of Kenya operates 2 national services (Swahili–English) from Nairobi and regional services in Kisumu, Nairobi and Mombasa. The television service provides programmes mainly in English and Swahili. A new television station opened in Mombasa in 1970. Telephones (1982) 216,674.

Cinemas (1971). Cinemas numbered 32, with seating capacity of 18,800.

JUSTICE, RELIGION, EDUCATION AND WELFARE

Justice. The courts of justice comprise the High Court, established in 1921, with full jurisdiction both civil and criminal over all persons and all matters in Kenya, including Admiralty jurisdiction arising on the high seas and elsewhere, and Subordinate Courts. The High Court has its headquarters at Nairobi and consists of the Chief Justice and 24 puisne judges; it sits continuously at Nairobi, Mombasa, Nakuru and Kisumu; civil and criminal sessions are held regularly at Eldoret, Nyeri, Meru, Kitale, Kisii and Kericho.

The Subordinate Courts are presided over by Senior Resident, Resident or District Magistrates and are established in the main centres of all districts. They sit throughout the year. There are also Moslem Subordinate Courts established in areas where the local population is predominantly Moslem; they are presided over by Kadhis and exercise limited jurisdiction in matters governed by Moslem law.

Religion. The indigenous African background is largely influenced by belief in God in Judaic forms, but Christianity is making an important contribution to the life of the whole territory, not only through the educational and medical services of Christian missions, but by the growth of churches under African leadership, and by its impact on the thought and policy of the country. The Roman Catholic Church (about 4m. adherents) has been developed mainly by Irish, British, Dutch and Italian missionary bodies and is now organized in 12 dioceses under the archbishop of Nairobi.

The Protestant Churches (about 2·5m. adherents) were started mainly by British and American mission societies; most of them are now linked together by the National Christian Council of Kenya. The Church of the Province of Kenya, formerly the Anglican Church Province of East Africa, was inaugurated on 3 Aug. 1970; at the same time the first Archbishop of Kenya was enthroned. The East African Yearly Meeting of Friends (Religious Society of Friends) has 90,000 adherents.

The Arabs on the coast are Moslems, and Islam has spread among some of the African coastal tribes and the cities. The Asians are Hindus and Moslems, with the exception of the Goans, who are Roman Catholics.

Education. *Primary* (1982). 11,500 primary schools with 4·2m. pupils and 71,000 teachers.

Secondary (1982). There were 2,131 secondary schools with a total enrolment of 465,000 and 8,611 teachers.

Technical (1982). 17 technical colleges with 9,200 pupils and 343 teachers.

Teacher training (1982). 14,000 students were training as teachers in 20 colleges with 900 lecturers.

Higher Education. The University of Nairobi was inaugurated on 10 Dec. 1970 and provides courses in arts, science, education, agriculture, medicine, art, architecture, engineering, veterinary, law and domestic science. In 1982 there were 8,772 students and 900 lecturers. Moi University opened in 1985 with 90 students.

Health. In 1981 beds in hospitals (including mission hospitals) totalled 28,108. 1,328 health centres, including sub-centres and dispensaries, were in operation. Free medical service for all children and adult out-patients was launched in 1965.

DIPLOMATIC REPRESENTATIVES

Of Kenya in Great Britain (45 Portland Pl., London, W1N 4AS)
High Commissioner: Benjamin K. Kipkulei (accredited 22 March 1984).

Of Great Britain in Kenya (Bruce Hse., Standard St., Nairobi)
High Commissioner: Sir Leonard Allinson, KCVO, CMG.

Of Kenya in the USA (2249 R. St., NW, Washington, D.C., 20008)
Ambassador: Wafula Wabuge.

Of the USA in Kenya (Moi/Haile Selassie Ave., Nairobi)
Ambassador: Gerald E. Thomas.

Of Kenya to the United Nations
Ambassador: Raphael Muli Kiilu.

Books of Reference

Kenya Development Plan, 1984–88. Nairobi, 1984
Kenya Economic Survey, 1983. Nairobi, 1984
Statistical Abstract. Government Printer, Nairobi, 1982
Standard English–Swahili Dictionary. Ed. Inter-territorial Language Committee of East Africa. 2 vols. London, 1939
Who's Who in Kenya 1982–1983. London, 1983
Arnold, G., *Kenyatta and the Politics of Kenya.* London, 1974.—*Modern Kenya.* London, 1982
Bienen, H., *Kenya: The Politics of Participation and Control.* Princeton Univ. Press, 1974
Bolton, K., *Harambee Country: A Guide to Kenya.* London, 1970
Collison, R. L., *Kenya.* [Bibliography] London and Santa Barbara, 1982
Harbeson, J. W., *Nation-Building in Kenya: The Role of Land Reform.* Northwestern Univ. Press, 1973
Hazlewood, A., *The Economy of Kenya: The Kenyatta Era.* OUP, 1980
Huxley, E., and Perham, M., *Race and Politics in Kenya.* Rev. ed. London, 1956
Langdon, S. W., *Multinational Corporations in the Political Economy of Kenya.* London, 1981
Mutalik-Desai, P., *Economic and Political Development in Kenya.* Bombay, 1979
Tomkinson, M., *Kenya: A Holiday Guide.* 5th ed. London and Hammamet, 1981

KIRIBATI

Capital: Tarawa
Population: 60,302 (1982)
GNP per capita: US$420 (1981)

HISTORY. The Gilbert and Ellice Islands were proclaimed a protectorate in 1892 and annexed (at the request of the native governments) as the Gilbert and Ellice Islands Colony on 10 Nov. 1915 (effective on 12 Jan. 1916). On 1 Oct. 1975 the former Ellice Islands severed its constitutional links with the Gilbert Islands and took a new name Tuvalu.

Internal self-government was obtained on 1 Nov. 1976 and independence achieved on 12 July 1979 as the Republic of Kiribati.

AREA AND POPULATION. Kiribati consists of 3 groups of coral atolls and one isolated volcanic island, spread over a large expanse of the Central Pacific with a total land area of 717·1 sq. km (276·9 sq. miles). It comprises Banaba or Ocean Island (5 sq. km), the 16 Gilbert Islands (295 sq. km), the 8 Phœnix Islands (55 sq. km), and 8 of the 11 Line Islands (329 sq.km), the other 3 Line Islands (Jarvis, Palmyra and Kingman Reef) being uninhabited dependencies of the US. Population, 1978 census, 56,213; 1982 estimate, 60,302 (Tarawa, 20,050). Banaba, all 16 Gilbert Islands, and 3 atolls in the Line Islands (Teraina, Tabuaeran and Kiritimati—formerly Washington, Fanning and Christmas Islands respectively) are inhabited; their populations in 1980 were as follows:

Banaba (Ocean Is.)	300	Kuria	803	Arorae	1,527
Makin	1,419	Aranuki	850	Teraina	416
Butaritari	3,149	Nonouti	2,284	Tabuaeran	434
Marakei	2,335	Tabiteuea	4,157	Kiritimati	1,265
Abaiang	3,447	Beru	2,212	Aboard ships	255
Tarawa	22,148	Nikunau	1,829	In Nauru and Overseas	2,299
Maiana	1,688	Onotoa	2,034		
Abemama	411	Tamana	1,349		
				Total	58,518

The remaining 13 atolls have no permanent population; the 8 Phœnix Islands comprise Birnie, Rawaki (formerly Phœnix), Enderbury, Kanton (or Abariringa), Manra (formerly Sydney), Orona (formerly Hull), McKean and Nikumaroro (formerly Gardner), while the others are Malden and Starbuck in the Central Line Islands and Caroline, Flint and Vostok in the Southern Line Islands. The population is almost entirely Micronesian.

CLIMATE. The Line Islands, Phœnix Islands and Banaba have a maritime equatorial climate, but the islands further north and south are tropical. Annual and daily ranges of temperature are small and mean annual rainfall ranges from 50″ (1,250 mm) near the equator to 120″ (3,000 mm) in the north. Tarawa. Jan. 83°F (28·3°C), July 82°F (27·8°C). Annual rainfall 79″ (1,977 mm).

CONSTITUTION AND GOVERNMENT. Under the independence Constitution the republic has a unicameral legislature, comprising 36 members elected from 20 constituencies for a 4-year term. The *Beretitenti* (President) is both Head of State and of Government.

In May 1983 the government was composed as follows:

President and Foreign Affairs: Ieremia Tabai, GCMG.

Vice-President, Home Affairs and Decentralization: Teatao Teannaki. *Trade, Industry and Labour:* Teewe Arobati. *Finance:* Boanareke Boanareke. *Health and Family Planning:* Baitika Toum. *Natural Resource Development:* Babera Kirata, OBE. *Education:* Baitika Toum. *Communications:* Taomati Iuta, OBE. *Minister for the Line and Phœnix Group of Islands:* Uera Rabaua. *Works and Energy:* Tiwau Awira. *Attorney-General:* Michael Takabwebwe.

Flag: Red, with blue and white wavy lines in base, and in the centre a gold rising sun and a flying frigate bird.

INTERNATIONAL RELATIONS

Membership. Kiribati is a member of the Commonwealth and is an ACP state of the EEC.

ECONOMY

Budget. Revenue for the calendar year 1982 amounted to $A15,871,000; principal items: customs duties, $A3,587,000; direct taxation, $A1m. Expenditure in 1982 amounted to $A16,956,000.

Currency. The currency in use is the Australian *dollar.*

NATURAL RESOURCES

Minerals. Phosphate production was discontinued in 1979.

Agriculture. The land is basically coral reefs upon which coral sand has built up, and then been enriched by humus from rotting vegetation and flotsam which has drifted ashore. The principal tree is the coconut, which grows prolifically on all the islands except some of the Phœnix Islands. Other food-bearing trees are the pandanus palm and the breadfruit. As the amount of soil is negligible, the only vegetable which grows in any quantity is a coarse calladium (alocasia) with the local name 'babai', which is cultivated most laboriously in deep pits. Pigs and fowls are kept throughout the Colony, and there is an abundance of fish.

Copra production is mainly in the hands of the individual landowner, who collects the coconut products from the trees on his own land. Production (1982) 8,081 tonnes.

Livestock (1983): Pigs, 10,000; poultry (1982), 163,000.

TRADE. The principal imports are rice, flour, cotton piece-goods, tobacco and manufactured articles such as bicycles. The value of imports for 1981 amounted to $A20m.; exports, $A3·6m. Exports are almost exclusively copra.

Total trade between Kiribati and UK (British Department of Trade returns, in £1,000 sterling):

	1982	*1983*	*1984*
Imports to UK	79	42	20
Exports and re-exports from UK	321	371	401

COMMUNICATIONS

Roads. There are 640 km of roads.

Shipping. The main ports are at Banaba and at Betio (Tarawa). In 1980, 71 vessels were handled at Betio.

Aviation. Air Tungaru is the national carrier. It operates services from Tarawa to the other 15 outer Islands in the Gilbertese Group, services varying between one and four flights each week. It also operates a weekly service to Christmas Island, in the Line Islands, which continues to Honolulu. A weekly service operates externally to Apia, Funafuti, Majuro, Nandi and Pago Pago. There are five flights per week to Nauru, while Air Nauru also has five flights from Nauru to Tarawa. There are air fields at Maiana and Christmas Island from which local services link to Tarawa.

Post and Broadcasting. There were 821 telephones in 1982. Radio Tarawa transmits daily in English and I-Kiribati. A telephone line to Australia was installed in 1981. There were (1983 estimate) 10,000 radio receivers.

Cinemas. In 1974 there were 5 cinemas with a seating capacity of 2,000.

Newspapers. There was (1980) 1 weekly newspaper and 1 monthly.

JUSTICE, RELIGION, EDUCATION AND WELFARE

Justice. In 1978 Kiribati had a police force of 188 under the command of a Commissioner of Police. The Commissioner of Police is also responsible for prisons, immigration, fire service (both domestic and airport) and firearms licensing.

Religion. The majority of the population belong to the Roman Catholic or Protestant (Congregational) church; there are small numbers of Seventh-day Adventist and Baha'i.

Education (1979). The Government maintains a co-educational boarding school, the King George V and Elaine Bernacchi School at Tarawa, with (1977) 211 boys and 178 girls, 87 primary schools, with a total of 13,092 pupils, 1 government secondary school with 385 pupils, and 4 community high schools with 562 pupils attending the first year of a new rurally oriented 3-year post-primary course. The Government also maintains a teachers' training college with 100 students and a marine training school with 180 full-time students. The Tarawa Technical Institute at Betio offers a variety of part-time and evening technical and commercial courses to about 500 students each year in addition to providing full-time courses for 34 students. The Marine Training School, also at Betio, offers training for 150 merchant seamen every year. There are in addition 4 Mission secondary schools with a total enrolment of 213 boys and 230 girls.

In 1978, 120 islanders were in overseas countries for secondary and further education or training.

Welfare. Government maintains free medical and other services. There are few towns, and the people are almost without exception landed proprietors, thus eliminating child vagrancy and housing problems to a large extent, except in the Tarawa urban area. Destitution is almost unknown. There were 19 doctors in 1979.

DIPLOMATIC REPRESENTATIVES

Of Kiribati to Great Britain and to the USA
High Commissioner: Atenroi Ba'teke, OBE (resides in Tarawa).

Of Great Britain in Kiribati (Tarawa)
High Commissioner: Charles Thompson.

Books of Reference

Kiribati, Aspects of History. Univ. of South Pacific, 1979
Bailey, E., *The Christmas Island Story.* London, 1977
Cowell, R., *Structure of Gilbertese.* Suva, 1950
Grimble, Sir Arthur, *A Pattern of Islands.* London, 1953.—*Return to the Islands.* London, 1957
Maude, H. E., *Of Islands and Men.* London, 1968.—*Evolution of the Gilbertese Boti.* Suva, 1977
Sabatier, E., *Astride the Equator.* Melbourne, 1978
Whincup, T., *Nareau's Nation.* London, 1979

KOREA

Han Kook

Capital: Seoul
Population: 39·95m. (1983)
GNP per capita: US$1,700 (1981)

HISTORY. Korea was united in a single kingdom under the Silla dynasty from 668. China, which claimed a vague suzerainty over Korea, recognized Korea's independence in 1895. Korea concluded trade agreements with the USA (1882), Great Britain, Germany (1883). After the Russo-Japanese war of 1904–5 Korea was virtually a Japanese protectorate until it was formally annexed by Japan on 29 Aug. 1910 thus ending the rule of the Yi dynasty which had begun in 1392.

Following the collapse of Japan in 1945, American and Russian forces entered Korea to enforce the surrender of the Japanese troops there, dividing the country for mutual military convenience into two portions separated by the 38th parallel of latitude. Negotiations between the Americans and Russians regarding the future of Korea broke down in May 1946.

On 25 June 1950 the North Korean forces crossed the 38th parallel and invaded South Korea. The same day, the Security Council of the United Nations asked all member states to render assistance to the Republic of Korea. When the UN forces had reached the Manchurian border Chinese troops entered the war on the side of the North Koreans on 26 Nov. 1950 and penetrated deep into the south. By the beginning of April 1951, however, the UN forces had regained the 38th parallel. On 23 June 1951 Y. A. Malik, President of the Security Council, suggested a cease-fire, and on 10 July representatives of Gen. Ridgway met representatives of the North Koreans and of the Chinese Volunteer Army. An agreement was signed on 27 July 1953.

For the contributions of member-nations of the United Nations to the war, *see* THE STATESMAN'S YEAR-BOOK, 1954, p. 1195, and 1956, p. 1180.

On 16 Aug. 1953 the USA and Korea signed a mutual defence pact and on 28 Nov. 1956 a treaty of friendship, commerce and navigation.

On 4 July 1972 it was announced in Seoul and Pyongyang (North Korea) that talks had taken place aimed at 'the peaceful unification of the fatherland as early as possible'. In Nov. 1984 agreement was reached to form a joint economic committee.

A North Korean–UN agreement of 6 Sept. 1976 established a joint security area 850 metres in diameter, divided into 2 equal parts to ensure the separation of the two sides.

AREA AND POPULATION. South Korea is bounded north by the demilitarized zone (separating it from North Korea), east by the Sea of Japan, south by the Korea Strait (separating it from Japan) and west by the Yellow Sea. After a transfer of some frontier districts by the United Nations command on 12 Aug. 1954, the area of South Korea is now 98,992 sq. km (38,221 sq. miles). The population (census, 1 Oct. 1983) was 39,950,743 (male, 20,161,398).

The areas (in sq. km) and 1983 census populations of the provinces are as follows:

Province	*sq. km*	*1983*	*Province*	*sq. km*	*1983*
Seoul	627	9,204,344	South Chungchong	8,807	3,038,329
Pusan	433	3,395,171	North Cholla	8,052	2,302,509
Taegu	455	1,958,812	South Cholla	12,189	3,817,763
Inchon	201	1,220,311	North Kyongsang	19,427	3,128,876
Kyonggi	10,875	4,358,199	South Kyongsang	11,850	3,518,401
Kangwon	16,894	1,824,324	Cheju	1,825	477,861
North Chungchong	7,430	1,424,915			

The chief cities (populations in 1980) are:

Seoul	8,366,756	Kwangchu	727,627	Seongnam	376,447
Pusan	3,160,276	Taejon	651,642	Chonchu	366,997
Taegu	1,607,458	Ulsan	418,415	Suweon	310,757
Inchon	1,084,730	Masan	386,773		

CLIMATE. The extreme south has a humid warm temperate climate while the rest of the country experiences continental temperate conditions. Rainfall is concentrated in the period April to Sept. and ranges from 40″ (1,020 mm) to 60″ (1,520 mm). Pusan. Jan. 36°F (2·2°C), July 76°F (24·4°C). Annual rainfall 56″ (1,407 mm). Seoul. Jan. 23°F (–5°C), July 77°F (25°C). Annual rainfall 50″ (1,250 mm).

CONSTITUTION AND GOVERNMENT. A new constitution was approved by national referendum on 22 Oct. 1980 and came into force on 27 Oct. It provides for a President with reduced executive powers, to be indirectly elected for a single 7-year term (by an electoral college of 5,271 directly-elected members), a State Council of ministers whom he appoints and leads, and a National Assembly (276 members) directly elected for 4 years (184 from 2-member constituencies and 92 by proportional representation).

The National Assembly elected on 25 March 1981 comprised 151 members of the Democratic Justice Party, 81 Democratic Korea Party, 25 Korean National Party, 8 from other parties and 11 independents.

President of the Republic: Gen. Chun Doo-Hwan (took office 2 Sept. 1980, re-elected 25 Feb. 1981).

The Cabinet at March 1985 was composed as follows:

Prime Minister: Lho Shin Yong.

Deputy Premier and Economic Planning: Shin Byong Hyun. *Foreign Affairs:* Lee Won Kyung. *Interior:* Chung Suk Mo. *Finance:* Kim Mahn Je. *Justice:* Kim Suk Hwi. *Defence:* Yoon Sung Min. *Education:* Sohn Jae Souk. *Agriculture and Fisheries:* Hwang In Sung. *Trade and Industry:* Kum Jin Ho. *Energy and Resources:* Choi Dong Kyu. *Construction:* Kim Sung Bae. *Health and Welfare:* Rhee Hai Won. *Transport:* Sohn Ik. *Communications:* Lee Ja Hon. *Culture and Information:* Lee Won Hong. *Government Administration:* Park Sae Jik. *Science and Technology:* Kim Sung Jin. *National Unification:* Lee Se Ki. *Labour:* Cho Chul Kwon. *State Affairs (Responsibility for Political Affairs):* Chung Jae Chull. *Sport:* Lee Young Ho.

National flag: White charged in the centre with the *yang-um* in red and blue and with 4 black *pal-kwar* trigrams.

Local government: South Korea is divided into 9 provinces (Do) and 4 cities with provincial status (Seoul, Pusan, Taegu and Inchon); the provinces are sub-divided into 138 districts (Gun) and 46 cities (Si).

DEFENCE. Military service is compulsory for 30 months in the Army and Marines and 3 years in the Navy and Air Force.

Army. The Army is organized in 20 infantry divisions, 2 mechanized infantry divisions, 11 independent special forces brigades, 2 anti-aircraft artillery brigades, 2 surface-to-air missile brigades, 1 army aviation brigade and 2 surface-to-surface battalions. Equipment includes 1,200 M-47/-48 main battle tanks. Strength (1985) 540,000, with a Regular Army Reserve of 1·4m. and a Homeland Reserve Defence Force of 3·3m.

Navy. The Fleet comprises 1 indigenously built modern frigate, 11 aged (1943–46) *ex*-US destroyers, 7 equally old *ex*-US frigates (1 of destroyer-escort type and 6 former fast transports, *ex*-destroyer escorts), 9 fast missile patrol craft, 7 new corvettes, 33 fast attack craft, 3 *ex*-US submarine chasers, 12 fast gunboats, 30 coastal patrol boats, 8 coastal minesweepers, 1 minesweeping boat, 8 landing ships, 9 medium landing craft, 20 utility landing craft, 1 repair ship, 6 surveying vessels, 2 salvage ships, 4 supply ships, 6 oilers, 13 auxiliary ships, 35 service craft, and 2 tugs. Nearly all South Korea's naval vessels are *ex*-US ships.

It was reported that the first submarine built in South Korea entered service in 1983. Probably the first of a class of four or five, she displaces only 175 tons.

The South Korean Coastguard operates 30 vessels including rescue craft and tugs.

Personnel in 1985 totalled 29,000 in the Navy; plus 20,000 in the Marine Corps.

Air Force. With a 1984 strength of about 32,600 men, the Air Force is undergoing rapid expansion with US assistance. Its combat aircraft include about 55 F-4D/E Phantoms, 78 F-5A/B tactical fighters, more than 200 F-5E/F tactical fighters (being delivered from local production), 8 RF-5A reconnaissance fighters, 10 O-2A forward air control aircraft and 10 Hughes 500-D Defender ASW helicopters. There are also 6 C-130H turboprop transports, 10 C-123 piston-engined transports, 2 VIP HS 748s; UH-1D and Bell 212 helicopters, and T-41, T-28, T-33 and T-37C trainers. Aircraft on order include 36 F-16 Fighting Falcons for delivery from 1986.

ECONOMY

Planning. The fifth 5-year social and economic plan (1982–86) aims at an annual growth rate of 7–8%.

Budget. The 1984 budget balanced at 10,386,300m. won.

Currency. Notes are issued by the Bank of Korea in denominations of 10,000, 5,000 and 500 *won* and coin in denominations of 500, 100, 50, 10, 5 and 1 *won*. The exchange rate is determined daily by the Bank of Korea. In March 1985, 843·80 *won*=US$1; 910·28 *won*=£1 sterling.

Banking. State-run banks include the Bank of Korea, the Korean Development Bank, the Medium & Small Industry Bank, the Citizen's National Bank, the Korea Exchange Bank, the National Agricultural Co-operatives Federation, the Federation of Fisheries Co-operatives serving as banking and credit institutions for farmers and fishermen, the Korea Housing Bank, the Export and Import Bank of Korea.

There are 5 commercial banks: the Bank of Seoul & Trust Co. Ltd, the Cho Heung Bank Ltd, the Commercial Bank of Korea, the Korea First Bank, the Hanil Bank, Ltd, the Taegu Bank Ltd. The Bank of Korea is the central bank and the only note-issuing bank, the authorized purchaser of domestically produced gold.

In addition, there are non-bank financial institutions consisting of 19 insurance companies, the Land Bank of Korea, the Credit Guarantee Fund, 10 short-term financial companies, 211 mutual credit companies, and the Merchant Banking Corporation.

ENERGY AND NATURAL RESOURCES

Electricity. Electricity generated (1983) was 48,850m. kwh.

Minerals. In 1979, 1,779 mining companies employed 79,229 people. Mineral deposits are mostly small, with the exception of tungsten; the Sangdong mine is one of the world's largest deposits of tungsten. Korea's output, 1984, included (in 1,000 tonnes): Anthracite coal (1983), 18,945; iron ore, 591; tungsten concentrate (1983), 4,132 short tons; kaolin, 223 (1983); copper ore, 8·4 (1983); lead ore, 21; gold refined (1982), 1,505 kg; silver refined (1983), 48,992 kg.

Agriculture. The arable land in South Korea comprises 24·4m. acres, of which over 5·5m. acres are cultivated.

The chief crops are rice (1983: 5·4m. tonnes), barley, wheat, beans, grain of all kinds and tobacco.

Output of tobacco manufactures, a government monopoly, was 94,524 tonnes in 1983.

Raising of livestock has recently become a flourishing industry. In 1983 cattle numbered 1·94m.; pigs, 3·6m.; poultry, 49m.

Fisheries. Fishery exports (1982) US$947m. In 1982, 895 Korean deep-sea fishing vessels were engaged based on 46 overseas fishing bases, 345 in the Atlantic, 143 in the Indian and 361 in the Pacific oceans. In 1982, there was a total of 86,515 boats (808,570 gross tons) and the fish catch (inland and marine) was 2,644,000 tonnes.

INDUSTRY AND TRADE

Industry. Manufacturing industry, which (1983) employed 3·3m. persons, was concentrated primarily in the production of light consumer goods for domestic consumption and export. This is now shifting towards heavy and petro-chemical industries rapidly.

Output of principal products in 1983 (in tonnes): Cotton yarn, 271,338; Portland cement, 21·2m.; urea fertilizers, 737,000.

Trade Unions. Membership of trade unions at 31 Dec. 1977 was 954,682.

Commerce. In 1983 the total exports were equal to US$24,445m., while imports (including 'aid goods') were US$26,192m. USA provided 5·3% and Japan 17·6% of imports; USA received 32·8% of exports, Japan 1·3%.

Total trade between Korea and UK (British Department of Trade returns, in £1,000 sterling):

	1981	*1982*	*1983*	*1984*
Imports to UK	325,650	321,691	440,354	443,819
Exports and re-exports from UK	158,811	167,752	168,942	219,406

Tourism. In 1982 there were 1,145,044 tourists. They spent the equivalent of US$502,318,000.

COMMUNICATIONS

Roads. In 1983 there were 53,936 km of roads. Motor vehicles totalled 785,316 including 304,158 trucks, 87,282 buses, 380,993 passenger cars.

Railways. In Dec. 1983, 3,121 km of railways existed, including 411 km electrified.

Shipping. In Dec. 1983, there were 24 first-grade ports and 22 second-grade ports, and 7·4m. gross tons in various vessels. Of the total tonnage, national-flag ocean-going vessels accounted for 6·01m. tons, charted vessels for 1·01m. tons and coastal passenger-cargo vessels for some 356,000 tons. Passenger ships accounted for 44,000 tons.

Aviation. In Dec. 1983, 32 countries maintained aviation agreement with Korea. The Ministry of Transportation also opened Seoul-Singapore and Seoul-Baghdad routes in 1983.

In 1982, Korean Air Lines carried 1,844,000 passengers in domestic and 3,501,000 in international services, and transported 263,400 tons of cargo, mostly on international routes.

Post. Post offices total 2,182 (1983); telephones (all government-owned) were 5,357,499 in 1983.

Cinemas. In 1983 there were 452 with a seating capacity of 400,000.

Newspapers (1982). There were 25 daily papers, including 6 national dailies and 2 in English appearing in Seoul.

RELIGION, EDUCATION AND WELFARE

Religion. Basically the religions of Korea have been Animism, Buddhism (introduced A.D. 372) and Confucianism, which was the official faith from 1392 to 1910. Catholic converts from China introduced Christianity in the 18th century, but the ban on Roman Catholics was not lifted until 1882. Christian population in 1983 was 9,348,322.

Education. In 1983 Korea had 5,257,164 pupils enrolled in 6,500 elementary schools, 2,672,307 pupils in 2,254 middle schools and 2,013,046 pupils in 1,494 high schools (including 639 vocational schools).

For higher education, 1,063,406 students who attended 424 universities, colleges and junior colleges. There are 190 graduate schools granting master's degrees in 2 years and doctor's degrees in 4 years, where 60,282 students attended in 1983. An Open University was inaugurated in March 1982.

The Korean language belongs to the Ural–Altaic group, is polysyllabic, agglutinative and highly developed syntactically. The modern Korean alphabet of 10 vowels and 14 consonants forms a script known as Hangul.

Health. In Dec. 1982 there were 28,365 physicians (including herb doctors), 4,266 dentists, 4,222 midwives (1980), 101,445 nurses (including assistant nurses, 1980), 4,712 technicians (1980) and 27,000 pharmacists. There were 11,181 hospitals and clinics in 1980.

DIPLOMATIC REPRESENTATIVES

Of Korea in Great Britain (4 Palace Gate, London, W8 5NF)
Ambassador: Young Choo Kim (accredited 14 Feb. 1985).

Of Great Britain in Korea (4 Chung-Dong, Chung-Ku, Seoul)
Ambassador and Consul-General: J. N. T. Spreckley, CMG.

Of Korea in the USA (2370 Massachusetts Ave., NW, Washington, D.C., 20008)
Ambassador: Yu Pyong-huon.

Of the USA in Korea (Sejong-Ro, Seoul)
Ambassador: Richard L. Walker.

Books of Reference

A Handbook of Korea. 4th ed. Seoul, 1982
Economic Planning Board. *Guide to Investment in Korea.* Seoul, 1980
Korea Annual 1983. 20th ed. Seoul, 1983
Korea Statistical Year Book. Seoul, 1981
Guide to Geographical Names in Korea (Chosen). United States Board of Geographical Names. Washington, 1945
Major Economic Indicators, 1979–80. Seoul, 1980
Monthly Statistics of Korea. Seoul, 1980
Lew, H. J., *New Life Korean–English, English–Korean Dictionary.* 2 vols. Seoul, 1947–50
Martin, S. F. (ed.), *A Korean–English Dictionary.* Yale Univ. Press, 1968
Srivastava, M. P., *The Korean Conflict: Search for Unification.* New Delhi, 1982
Wright, E. R., *Korean Politics in Transition.* Univ. of Washington Press, 1976

NORTH KOREA

Capital: Pyongyang
Population: 18·49m. (1983)
GNP per capita: US$736 (1982)

Chosun Minchu-chui Inmin Konghwa-guk

HISTORY. In northern Korea the Russians, arriving on 8 Aug. 1945, one month ahead of the Americans, established a Communist-led 'Provisional Government'. The newly created Korean Communist Party merged in 1946 with the New National Party into the Korean Workers' Party. In July 1946 the KWP, with the remaining pro-Communist groups and non-party people, formed the United Democratic Patriotic Front. On 25 Aug. 1948 the Communists organized elections for a Supreme People's Assembly, both in Soviet-occupied North Korea (212 deputies) and in US-occupied South Korea (360 deputies, of whom a certain number went to the North and took their seats). A People's Democratic Republic was proclaimed on 9 Sept. 1948. In 1973 North Korea was admitted to WHO, and granted observer status at the UN. Talks between North and South Korea on reunification began in 1980, but were broken off by the North. In 1981 North Korea announced a new reunification plan, but plans put forward by South Korea were rejected. In Sept. 1984 North Korea sent supplies estimated at a value of US$12m. to aid flood victims in the South, and agreed to proposals of a meeting on 15 Nov. which was subsequently cancelled.

AREA AND POPULATION. North Korea is bounded north by China, east by the sea of Japan, west by the Yellow Sea and south by South Korea, from which it is separated by a demilitarized zone of 1,262 sq km. Its area is 122,098 sq. km. Population estimate in 1983, 18·49m. Rate of population increase, 2·2% per annum. Death rate, 1979: 4·4 per mille. Marriage is discouraged before the age of 32 for men and 29 for women. Expectation of life in 1984 was 74 years. The capital is Pyongyang, with 1·28m. inhabitants in 1981. Other large towns (with 1972 population): Hamhung (420,000); Chongjin (265,000); Kimchaek (formerly Songjin) (265,000).

The country is divided into 13 administrative units: 4 cities (Pyongyang, Chongjin, Hamhung and Kaesong) and 9 provinces (capitals in brackets): South Pyongan (Nampo), North Pyongan (Sinuiji), Jagang (Kanggye), South Hwanghai (Haeju), North Hwanghai (Sariwon), North Kangwon (Wonsan), South Hamgyong (Hamheung), North Hamgyong (Chongjin), Yanggang (Hyesan).

CLIMATE. There is a warm temperate climate, though winters can be very cold in the north. Rainfall is concentrated in the summer months. Pyongyang. Jan. 18°F (–7·8°C), July 75°F (23·9°C). Annual rainfall 37" (916 mm).

CONSTITUTION AND GOVERNMENT. The political structure is based upon the Constitution of 27 Dec. 1972. The Constitution provides for a Supreme People's Assembly elected every 4 years by universal suffrage. Citizens of 17 years and over can vote and be elected. Elections were held in 1948, 1957, 1962, 1972, 1977 and 1 March 1982. At the latter it was claimed that 100% of the electorate voted for the candidates presented. There are 615 deputies. The government consists of the Administration Council directed by the Central People's Committee (*Secretary,* Kim I Hun).

In practice the country is ruled by the Korean Workers' (*i.e.*, Communist) Party which elects a Central Committee which in turn appoints a Politburo, the first 3 members of which constitute its Standing Committee. In March 1985 this was composed of: Marshal Kim Il Sung, *(General Secretary of the Party, President of the Republic, Chairman of the Central People's Committee, Supreme Commander of the Armed Forces)*; Kim Jong Il (Kim Il Sung's son and designated successor)

(Vice-President of the Republic); O Jin U *(Defence Minister)*; Li Jong Ok *(Vice-President of the Republic)*; Pak Sung Chul *(Vice-President of the Republic);* Rim Chun Chu *(Vice-President of the Republic);* So Chol; Kim Yong Nam *(Deputy Prime Minister, Foreign Minister)*; Chon Mun Sop; Kim Hwan *(Deputy Prime Minister)*; Yon Hyong Muk; O Guk Ryol; Kang Song San *(Prime Minister)*; Paek Hak Rim; Choe Yong Rim; So Yun Sok, Ho Dam *(Deputy Prime Minister).*

Ministers not full members of the Politburo include Kye Ung Tae *(Deputy Prime Minister)*; Yun Gi Jong *(Finance)*; Choe Jong Gun *(Trade)*; Chong Song Nam *(Foreign Economic Affairs)*; Hong Song Ryong *(Deputy Prime Minister, Chairman, State Planning Commission)*; Lee Jin Su *(Public Security)*; Kong Jin Tae, Choe Gwang, Chong Jun Gi, Kim Chang Ju, Kim Bok Sin, Cho Se Ung *(Deputy Prime Ministers).*

In 1981 the Party had some 2m. members.

There are also the puppet religious Chongu and Korean Social Democratic Parties and various organizations combined in a Fatherland Front.

National flag: Blue, red and blue horizontal stripes separated by narrow white bands. The red stripe bears a white circle within which is a red 5-pointed star.

National anthem: 'A chi mun bin na ra i gang san' (Shine bright, o dawn, on this land so fair'). Words by Pak Se Yong; music by Kim Won Gyun.

Local government is administered by People's Assemblies at city (or province), county (or district) and *ri* (town, workers' or rural commune) level. The latest elections were on 6 March 1983. There are 24,562 local deputies.

DEFENCE. Military service is compulsory at the age of 17 for periods of 5 years in the Army and Navy and 3–4 years in the Air Force. In 1982 defence spending was 23·8% of GNP.

Army. The Army is organized in 2 armoured, 3 motorized infantry and 34 infantry divisions; 5 armoured, 4 infantry and 26 special forces brigades; 2 independent tank, 5 independent infantry and 5 river-crossing regiments; 250 artillery, 82 multiple-rocket-launcher and 5 surface-to-surface missile battalions. Equipment includes 2,500 T 34/-55/-62 and 175 Type-59 main battle tanks. Strength (1985) 760,500, with 260,000 reserves. There is also a paramilitary militia of some 1·8m. men and a ranger commando force of 100,000.

Navy. The Navy comprises 20 diesel-powered patrol submarines (16 *ex*-Chinese and indigenously-built and 4 *ex*-Soviet), 2 small frigates, 38 fast missile boats, 140 fast torpedo boats, 160 fast gunboats, 50 patrol vessels, 30 coastal patrol craft, 20 light gunboats, 4 medium landing ships, 10 utility landing craft, 20 mechanised landing craft, 100 small assault landing craft, 30 trawlers and auxiliaries, 2 *ex*-Soviet ocean tugs and 100 service craft. Up to 5 small submarines are reported as built locally with a dozen X-craft in commission. Personnel in 1985 totalled 31,000 officers and men, plus 40,000 reservists.

Air Force. The Air Force has a total of about 930 aircraft and 51,000 personnel. Equipment is believed to include about 180 supersonic MiG-21 interceptors, more than 100 F-6s (Chinese-built MiG-19s), 250 MiG-17s for ground attack and reconnaissance, 50 Su-7 fighter-bombers, 60 Il-28 twin-jet light bombers, and a variety of transport and training aircraft and helicopters.

ECONOMY

Planning. For previous plans *see* THE STATESMAN'S YEAR-BOOK, 1983–84. A 7-year plan for 1978–84 gave priority to the fuel and mining industries, foreign trade development and transport, and achieved an annual industrial growth rate of 12·8%.

Budget (in 1m. won) for calendar years:

	1979	*1980*	*1981*	*1982*	*1983*	*1984*
Revenue	17,478	19,139	20,479	22,680	24,384	26,237
Expenditure	16,972	18,837	20,479	22,204	24,018	26,237

In 1984, 3,831m. won were spent on defence (3,602m. in 1983). 1984 expenditure (in 1m. won): economy, 16,640; social welfare, 5,262; administration, 547. Personal taxation was abolished in 1974.

Currency. The monetary unit is the *won*, divided into 100 *jun*. In March 1985, US$1 = 0·94 *won*; £1 = 1·57 *won*.

Weights and Measures. While the metric system is in force traditional measures are in frequent use. The *jungbo* = 1 hectare; the *ri* = 3,927 metres.

ENERGY AND NATURAL RESOURCES

Oil. An oil pipeline from China came on stream in 1976. Crude oil refining capacity was 80,000 barrels a year in 1981.

Electricity. There are thermal power stations at Pyongyang, Unggi and Chongchongang. There are hydro-electric plants at Kanggye, Unbong and Sodusu, and another is under construction at Taedonggang. Output in 1981, was 22,150m. kwh. Installed capacity was 5·1m. kw in 1981. Hydroelectric potential exceeds 8m. kw.

Minerals. North Korea is rich in minerals. Estimated reserves in tonnes: Iron ore, 3,300m.; copper, 2·15m.; lead, 6m.; zinc, 12m.; coal, 11,990m.; uranium, 26m.; manganese, 6,500m. Oilwells went into production in 1957. Refining capacity in 1984: 4m. tonnes a year. 33·45m. tonnes of coal were mined in 1982. 16m. tonnes of iron ore were extracted in 1984.

Agriculture. In 1982 there were 2·1m. hectares of arable land, including 635,000 hectares of paddy fields. In 1982, 38% of the population made a living from agriculture.

Collectivization took place between 1954 and 1958, when there were 13,309 'co-operatives' averaging 130 *jungbo*. In 1958 these were merged into 3,843 larger units *(ri)*, averaging 500 *jungbo*. 90% of the cultivated land is farmed by co-operatives, of which there were 3,700 in 1970. There is no private property in land; land belongs either to the State or to co-operatives, and it is intended gradually to transform the latter into the former. Livestock farming is mainly carried on by large state farms. There were 200 state farms in 1970.

There were 37,600 km of irrigation canals in 1976. The 6-year plan (1971–76) extended irrigation so as to make possible 2 rice harvests a year. In 1982 there were 133,000 tractors (15 h.p. units). The technical revolution in agriculture (nearly 95% of ploughing, etc., is mechanized) considerably increased the yield of grain (sown on 2·3m. *jungbo* of land); this was 9·5m. tonnes in 1982 (mainly rice). 268,000 tonnes of potatoes were produced in 1981.

Livestock, 1983: 1m. cattle, 2·5m. pigs, 18m. poultry.

Forestry. Between 1961 and 1970, 800,000 hectares were afforested, 500,000 hectares of oil-bearing trees are scheduled for planting.

Fishery. Catch in 1982: 1·5m. tonnes. There is a fishing fleet of 28,000 vessels including 19,000 motor vessels.

Labour. The economically-active population was 9m. in 1982. Industrial workers make up some 40% of the work force. Average monthly wage, 1984: 90 *won*.

INDUSTRY AND TRADE

Industry. Industries were intensively developed by the Japanese, notably cotton spinning, hydro-electric power, cotton, silk and rayon weaving, and chemical fertilizers. Production (in tonnes) in 1982: Pig-iron, 4m.; crude steel, 4m.; rolled steel, 3·2m.; lead, 30,000; zinc, 140,000; copper, 48,000; ship-building, 400,000; chemical fertilizers, 620,000; chemicals, 20,000; synthetic resins, 90,000; cement, 8,700; textiles, 120m. metres; woven goods, 600m. metres; shoes, 40m. pairs; motor-cars, 15,000; TV sets, 150,000; refrigerators, 10,000. There is a steel complex at Kangson with an annual productive capacity of 4m. tonnes.

Commerce. North Korea trades with some 60 countries. Largest trade partners are

USSR, China and Japan; in Jan. 1985 the latter lifted sanctions imposed after the assassination of members of the South Korean Government in Rangoon in Oct. 1983. Exports in 1981: US$1,260m.; imports, US$1,610m. 51·5% of trade was with Communist countries (85% in 1971). In 1981 manufactured goods formed 59% of exports. In 1982 North Korea's indebtedness was estimated at US$3,500m. (US$2,300m. to the West). An agreement regulating the repayment of North Korea's debt to Japan over 10 years was signed in 1979. The chief exports are metal ores and products, the chief imports machinery and petroleum products.

Joint ventures with foreign firms have been permitted since 1984.

Exports to the USSR in 1980 (and 1981) were worth 284·2m. (250·3m.) roubles; imports from the USSR, 287·9m. (278·9m.) roubles.

Total trade between North Korea and UK (British Department of Trade returns, in £1,000 sterling):

	1980	*1981*	*1982*	*1983*	*1984*
Imports to UK	391	701	235	362	456
Exports and re-exports from UK	981	727	3,857	2,527	2,935

COMMUNICATIONS

Roads. There were 20,800 km of road in 1981, including 240 km of motorways. There were 180,000 motor cars in 1982.

Railways. The two trunk-lines Pyongyang–Sinuiji and Pyongyang–Myongchon are both electrified, and the Pyongyang–Sariwon trunk is in course of electrification. The 'Wonra' line runs from Wonsan to Rajin and is electrified from Myongchon to Rajin and beyond to Tumangang. The Namdokchon–Toknam line was opened in 1983. Lines are under construction from Pukchong to Toksong, from Palwon to Kujang and Kanggye *via* Hyesan to Musan. The Hyesan–Samsok section of the latter opened to traffic in 1971. In 1981 there were 4,380 km of track, of which 2,706 km were electrified. In 1980, 87% of trains were hauled by electricity and 30·6m. tonnes were transported in 1969. A weekly service from Pyongyang to Beijing opened in 1983.

Aviation. Flights are made once or twice a week from Pyongyang to Moscow, Khabarovsk and Beijing by 17 propeller-driven aircraft operated by the Air Force. There are domestic flights from Pyongyang to Hamhung and Chongjin.

Shipping. The leading ports are Chongjin and Hungnam (near Hamhung). Nampo, the port of Pyongyang, has been dredged and expanded. Pyongyang is connected to Nampo by railway and river. In 1983 the ocean-going merchant fleet numbered 56 vessels totalling 651,180 tonnes.

The biggest navigable river is the Yalu, 698 km up to the Hyesan district.

Post and Broadcasting. In 1982 there were some 200,000 television receivers. The Pyongyang central broadcasting station was rebuilt about 1955. There were some 10,000 telephones in 1983.

Newspapers. The party newspaper is *Nodong* (or *Rodong*) *Sinmun* (Workers' Daily News). Circulation about 600,000.

JUSTICE, RELIGION, EDUCATION AND WELFARE

Justice. The judiciary consists of the Supreme Court, whose judges are elected by the Assembly for 3 years; provincial courts; and city or county people's courts. The procurator-general, appointed by the Assembly, has supervisory powers over the judiciary and the administration; the Supreme Court controls the judicial administration.

Religion. According to the 1972 Constitution 'The people shall enjoy the freedom of religion as well as the freedom of anti-religious propaganda'. There are 3 religious organizations: The Buddhist League, the Chondoist Society and the Christians' League.

Education. In 1975–76 the 10-year system of free compulsory universal technical education was extended to 11 years (1 pre-school year, 4 years primary education starting at the age of 6, followed by 6 years secondary).

In 1970–71, 9,260 schools of all grades were attended by 3·2m. pupils, including 214,000 students in institutes of higher education, two-thirds of whom were studying technical and engineering subjects. There were some 100,000 teachers. In 1975–76 there were 5–6m. children in the 11-year system and nearly 1m. students in higher education. In 1980 there were 170 institutes of higher education, including 3 universities—Kim Il Sung University (founded 1946), Kim Chaek Technical University, Pyongyang Medical School—and an Academy of Sciences (founded 1952).

In 1977–78 Kim Il Sung University had some 17,000 students.

Health. Medical treatment is free. In 1982 there were 1,531 general hospitals, 979 specialised hospitals and 5,414 clinics. There were 24 doctors and 130 hospital beds per 10,000 population.

DIPLOMATIC REPRESENTATIVE

Of North Korea to the United Nations
Ambassador: Li In-Ho (accredited 10 Jan. 1984).

Books of Reference

An, T. S., *North Korea in Transition.* Westport, 1983;–*North Korea: a Political Handbook.* Washington, 1983
Baik Bong, *Kim Il Sung: Biography.* 3 vols. New York, 1969–70
Brun, E., and Hersh, J., *Socialist Korea: A Case Study in the Strategy of Economic Development.* New York, 1976
Chung, C.-S., (ed.), *North Korean Communism: A Comparative Analysis.* Seoul, 1980
Kim Han Gil, *Modern History of Korea.* Pyongyang, 1979
Kim Il Sung, *Works.* Pyongyang, 1980–83
Kim, Y. S., (ed.), *The Economy of the Korean Democratic People's Republic, 1945–1977.* Kiel, 1979
Lee, C.-S., *The Korean Workers' Party: A Short History.* Stanford, 1978
McCormack, G., and Selden, M. (eds.), *Korea North and South: The Deepening Crisis.* New York, 1978
Park, J. K., and Kim, J.-G., *The Politics of North Korea.* Boulder, 1979
Scalapino, R. A., and Lee, C.-S., *Communism in Korea. Part I: The Movement. Part II: The Society.* Univ. of Calif. Press, 1972
Suh, D.-S., *Korean Communism, 1945–1980: A Reference Guide to the Political System.* Honolulu, 1981
Yang, S. C., *Korea and Two Regimes: Kim Il Sung and Park Chung Hee.* Cambridge, Mass., 1981

KUWAIT

Dowlat al Kuwait

Capital: Kuwait
Population: 1·91m. (1985)
GNP per capita: US$20,900 (1981)

HISTORY. The ruling dynasty was founded by Shaikh Sabah al-Owel, who ruled from 1756 to 1772. In 1899 the then ruler Shaikh Mubarak concluded a treaty with Great Britain wherein, in return for the assurance of British protection, he undertook not to alienate any of his territory without the agreement of Her Majesty's Government. In 1914 the British Government recognized Kuwait as an independent government under British protection. On 19 June 1961 an agreement reaffirmed the independence and sovereignty of Kuwait and recognized the Government of Kuwait's responsibility for the conduct of internal and external affairs; the agreement of 1899 was terminated and Her Majesty's Government expressed their readiness to assist the Government of Kuwait should they request such assistance.

AREA AND POPULATION. Kuwait is bounded east by the Gulf, north and west by Iraq and south by Saudi Arabia, with an area of about 7,000 sq. miles (17,818 sq. km); the total population at the census of 1981 was 1,466,431, of which about 59% were non-Kuwaitis; 1985 (estimate), 1,910,856.

The country is divided into 3 governorates, Kuwait (the capital, 60,525 population (census, 1980) and its suburbs Hawalli (152,402) and as-Salmiyah (145,991).

The Neutral Zone (3,560 sq. miles, 5,700 sq. km), jointly owned and administered by Kuwait and Saudi Arabia from 1922 to 1966, was partitioned between the two countries in May 1966, but the exploitation of the oil and other natural resources will continue to be shared.

CLIMATE. Kuwait has a dry, desert climate which is cool in winter but very hot and humid in summer. Rainfall is extremely light. Kuwait. Jan. 56°F (13·5°C), July 99°F (36·6°C). Annual rainfall 5″ (125 mm).

RULER. HH Shaikh Jabir al-Ahmad al-Jabir al-Sabah the 13th Amir of Kuwait, succeeded on 31 Dec. 1977.

CONSTITUTION AND GOVERNMENT. Elections for a National Assembly of 50 members were held on 27 Jan. 1975 but in Aug. 1976 the Amir dissolved the Assembly and at the same time parts of the Constitution were suspended. Elections were held in Feb. 1985 for the National Assembly.

The official language is Arabic; English is used as the second language.

The Cabinet in Nov. 1983 was composed as follows:

Prime Minister: Shaikh Saad al-Abdullah al-Salem al-Sabah.

Deputy Prime Minister, Foreign Affairs and Information: Shaikh Sabah al-Ahmad al-Jaber al-Sabah. *Interior:* Shaikh Nawwaf al-Ahmad al-Jaber al-Sabah. *Defence:* Shaikh Salem al-Sabah al-Salem al-Sabah. *Oil, Finance and Planning.* Shaikh Ali al-Khalifah al-Sabah. *Public Health:* Abdel Rahman Abdullah al-Awadi. *Social Affairs, Labour and Housing:* Hamad Isa al-Rajib. *Public Works:* Abdullah al-Rushid. *Electricity and Water:* Khalaf Ahmad al-Khalaf. *Justice, Legal Affairs and Administrative Affairs:* Shaikh Salman al-Duaij al-Sabah. *Education:* Yacoub Yousef al-Ghunaim. *Commerce and Industry:* Jassem al-Marzouk. *Communications:* Isa al-Mazidi. *Awqaf and Islamic Affairs:* Ahmad Saad al-Jasser. *Minister of State (Cabinet Affairs):* Abdel-Aziz Hussain. *Amiri Diwan Affairs:* Shaikh Khaled A. al-Sabah.

Flag: Three horizontal stripes of green, white, red, with a black trapezium based on the hoist.

DEFENCE. Military service is compulsory for 18 months.

Army. Kuwait maintains a small, well-equipped and mobile army of 1 armoured and 2 mechanized infantry brigades and 1 surface-to-surface missile battalion. Equipment includes 70 Vickers Mk I, 10 Centurion and 160 Chieftain main battle tanks. Strength (1985) about 10,000 men.

Navy. The several new flotillas comprise 6 fast missile craft, 2 larger fast gunboats (all eight West German-built); 40 coastal patrol craft built by Vosper/Thornycroft; 7 US-built very fast cutters; 10 general purpose launches; 6 Vosper Singapore-built landing craft and 4 tugs.

Six hovercraft are reportedly to be ordered, and probably fast attack craft, patrol vessels and minecountermeasures vessels.

A Japanese firm was awarded the contract for the construction of a base to accommodate the planned expansion of the coastguard force.

In 1985 personnel exceeded 1,100 officers and men.

Air Force. From a small initial combat force the Air Force has grown rapidly. It has 1 squadron with 16 Mirage F1-C fighters and 2 Mirage F1-B 2-seat trainers; and 2 squadrons with 28 A-4KU/TA-4KU Skyhawk attack aircraft; 24 more Mirage F1s have been ordered. Other equipment includes 2 DC-9 jet transports, 1 L-100-20 and 4 L-100-30 Hercules turboprop transports, 9 BAC 167 Strikemaster armed jet trainers (to be replaced with 12 Hawks), 10 Puma, 6 Exocet missile-armed Super Puma and 23 missile-armed Gazelle helicopters. Hawk surface-to-air missiles are in service. Personnel strength (1985) about 1,900.

INTERNATIONAL RELATIONS

Membership. Kuwait is a member of UN, the Arab League, OPEC and OAPEC.

ECONOMY

Budget. The financial year runs 1 April–31 March. In 1983–84 revenue, KD 3,037m.; expenditure, KD 3,605m.

Currency. The Kuwait *dinar* of 1,000 *fils* replaced the Indian external rupee on 1 April 1961. In March 1985, £1 sterling = KD 0·329; US$1 = KD 0·307. Coins in circulation are, 1, 5, 10, 20, 50 and 100 fils and notes of KD, 10, 5, 1, ½ and ¼.

Banking. In addition to the Central Bank, ten banks operate in Kuwait: the Bank of Kuwait and Middle East, the Kuwait National Bank, the Commercial Bank of Kuwait Ltd, the Gulf Bank of Kuwait, the Alahli Bank, The Burgan Bank, Savings and Credit Bank, the Industrial Bank of Kuwait, Real Estate Bank of Kuwait, the Bank of Kuwait and Bahrain.

Weights and Measures. The metric system was adopted in 1962.

ENERGY AND NATURAL RESOURCES

Electricity. 11,699m. kw. were produced in 1982.

Oil. Kuwait oil comes mainly from the Burgan oilfields, the residential and administrative centre for oil operations being at Ahmadi. Oil reserves in Kuwait and its share of the Neutral Zone was estimated at 77,000m. bbls in 1975. The Kuwait Petroleum Gas and Energy Co. (KPGEC) formed in 1974 as a result of the Government's take-over of 60% of oil production, is controlling all oil exploration and the processing and marketing of oil and gas. Production of crude oil (in 1,000 bbls); 1982, 300,211; 1983, 331,200.

Gas. Production (1983) 170,200m. cu. ft.

Agriculture. Major crops (production, 1981, in tonnes) are melons (5,000), tomatoes (12,000), onions (3,000), dates (1,000), radishes, clover.

Livestock (1983): Cattle, 18,000; sheep, 550,000; goats, 300,000; poultry, 8m.

Fisheries. Shrimp fishing is becoming one of the important non-oil industries.

INDUSTRY AND TRADE

Industry. Industries, apart from oil, include boat building, fishing, food production, petrochemicals, gases and construction. The manufacture or import of alcoholic drinks is prohibited.

Labour. Of the working population 75% are foreigners.

Commerce. The port of Kuwait formerly served mainly as an entrepôt for goods for the interior, for the export of skins and wool, and for pearl fishing. Entrepôt trade continues but, with the development of the oil industry, is declining in importance. Pearl fishing is now on a small scale. Dhows and launches of traditional construction are still built.

In 1982 total imports were KD1,945m.; exports, KD4,531m. Oil accounted for more than 80% of exports.

Total trade between Kuwait and UK (British Department of Trade returns, in £1,000 sterling):

	1980	*1981*	*1982*	*1983*	*1984*
Imports to UK [1]	655,024	477,262	104,793	67,281	141,606
Exports and re-exports from UK	258,696	281,203	333,247	333,273	301,520

[1] Including oil.

COMMUNICATIONS

Roads. In 1982 there were 3,100 km and the number of private cars 435,000; lorries and vans, 146,000.

Aviation. Kuwait Airways flew over 9,000 flights in 1980, carrying 1·76m. passengers and 25,000 tonnes of freight. British Airways, Kuwait Airways, Iraqi Airways, Iranian Airways, United Arab Airlines, Middle East Airlines, Saudi Arabian Airways, Lebanese International Airways, Air Liban, Air India, Lufthansa, Japanese Airlines, TWA, PIA, Aden Air Lines, Air France, Alitalia, SAS, Swiss Air, SABENA, KLM and Gulf Aviation operate scheduled air services.

Shipping. The Kuwaiti merchant fleet in 1982 comprised 217 vessels (of over 100 tonnes) with a total gross tonnage of 2,014,379. The oil terminal is at Mina al-Ahmadi, while the main ports for other traffic are at Shuwaikh and at Shuaiba.

Post and Broadcasting. There were (1982), 231,643 telephones and there is a broadcasting and a television station.

Cinemas. In 1976 there were 10 cinemas with a seating capacity of 13,000.

Newspapers. In 1984 there were 5 daily newspapers in Arabic and 2 in English, with a combined circulation of about 418,000.

RELIGION, EDUCATION AND WELFARE

Religion. In 1980 about 78% of the population were Sunni Moslems, 14% Shia Moslems, 6% Christians and 2% others.

Education. In 1982 there were 334,942 pupils at 481 government schools. In 1980–81 there were 4,143 students at teacher-training institutes (608 teachers) and teacher-training colleges had 1,584 students (289 teachers). A technical college was opened in 1954 and in 1970 had 931 students (212 teachers). The University of Kuwait had 14,000 students in 1984.

Health. Medical services are free to all residents. There were (1982) 15 hospitals with over 5,563 beds in the State and 232 clinics and health centres. The Ministry of Health employs 2,348 physicians and 708 dentists.

DIPLOMATIC REPRESENTATIVES

Of Kuwait in Great Britain (45 Queen's Gate, London, SW7)
Ambassador: Ghazi Mohammed Amin Al-Rayes (accredited 12 Feb. 1981).

Of Great Britain in Kuwait (Arabian Gulf St., Kuwait)
Ambassador: M. R. Melhuish, CMG.

Of Kuwait in the USA (2940 Tilden St., NW, Washington, D.C., 20008)
Ambassador: Shaikh Saud Nasir Al-Sabah.

Of the USA in Kuwait (PO Box 77, Safat, Kuwait)
Ambassador: Anthony Quainton.

Of Kuwait to the United Nations
Ambassador: Mohammad A. Abulhasan.

Books of Reference

Arabian Year Book. Kuwait, 1978
Annual Statistical Abstract of Kuwait. Kuwait
The Oil of Kuwait: Facts and Figures. 3rd ed. Kuwait Government Press, 1970
Khouja, M. W., and Sadler, P. G., *The Economy of Kuwait.* London, 1979
Sabah, Y. S. F., *The Oil Economy of Kuwait.* London, 1980

LAOS

Capital: Vientiane
Population: 3·52m. (1979)
GNP per capita: US$80 (1981)

HISTORY. The Lao People's Democratic Republic was founded on 2 Dec. 1975. Until that date Laos was a Kingdom, once called Lanxang (the land of a million elephants).

In 1893 Laos became a French protectorate and in 1907 acquired its present frontiers. In 1941 French authority was suppressed by the Japanese. When the Japanese withdrew in 1945 an independence movement known as Lao Issara (Free Laos) set up a government under Prince Phetsarath, the Viceroy of Luang Prabang. This government collapsed with the return of the French in 1946 and the leaders of the movement fled to Thailand.

Under a new Constitution of 1947 Laos became a constitutional monarchy under the Luang Prabang dynasty, and in 1949 became an independent sovereign state within the French Union. Most of the Lao Issara leaders returned to Laos but a few remained in dissidence under Prince Souphanouvong, who allied himself with the Vietminh and subsequently formed the 'Pathet Lao' (Lao State) rebel movement.

The war in Laos from 1953 to 1973 between the Royal Lao Government (supported by American bombing and Thai mercenaries) and the Patriotic Front *Pathet Lao* (supported by large numbers of North Vietnamese troops) ended in 1973 when an agreement and a protocol were signed. A provisional coalition government was formed by the two sides in 1974. However, after the communist victories in neighbouring Vietnam and Cambodia in April 1975, the *Pathet Lao* took over the running of the whole country, although maintaining the façade of a coalition. On 29 Nov. 1975 HM King Savang Vatthana signed a letter of abdication and the People's Congress proclaimed a People's Democratic Republic of Laos. For the history of *Pathet Lao* and the military intervention of the Vietminh, *see* THE STATESMAN'S YEAR-BOOK, 1971–72, pp. 1126–28 and 1975–76 ed., pp. 1115–16.

AREA AND POPULATION. Laos is a landlocked country of about 91,400 sq. miles (236,800 sq. km) bordered on the north by China, the east by Vietnam, the south by the People's Republic of Democratic Kampuchea (Cambodia) and the west by Thailand and Burma. Apart from the Mekong River plains along the border of Thailand, the country is mountainous, particularly in the north, and in places densely forested. The climate is of a tropical monsoon type with a wet season from May to Oct. and a dry one from Nov. to April. Most of northern Laos receives about 40–80 in. of rainfall annually, while parts of the Bolovens Plateau in southern Laos have over 150 in.

Estimates place the population at about 3·5m. but the first complete census will be undertaken, with UN assistance, in March 1985. The most heavily populated areas are the Mekong River plains by the Thailand border. Otherwise, the population is sparse and scattered, particularly in the northern provinces, and the eastern part of the country has been depopulated by war. The majority of the population is officially divided into 4 groups: about 56% Lao-Lum (Valley-Lao), 34% Lao-Theung (Lao of the mountain sides); and 9% Lao-Soung (Lao of the mountain tops), who comprise the Meo and Yaoe. Other minorities include Vietnamese, Chinese, Europeans, Indians and Pakistanis.

The Lao-Lum and Lao-Tai belong to the Lao branch of the Tai peoples, who migrated into South-East Asia at the time of the Mongol invasion of South China. The valley Lao are Buddhists, following the Hinayana (Theravada) form. The majority of the Lao-Theungma diverse group consisting of many tribes but mostly belonging to the Mon-Khmer group—are animists.

The Meo and Yaoe live in northern Laos. Far greater numbers live in both North

Vietnam and China, having migrated over the last century. Their religions have strong Confucian and animistic features but some are Christians.

There are 16 provinces. Compared with other parts of Asia, Laos has few towns. The administrative capital and largest town is Vientiane, with a population of estimate (1984) 120,000. Other important towns are Luang Prabang, 44,244; Pakse, 44,860, in the extreme south, and Savannakhet, 50,690.

Language: Lao is the official language of the country. The liturgical language of Theravada Buddhism is Pali.

CLIMATE. A tropical monsoon climate, with high temperatures throughout the year and very heavy rains from May to Oct. Vientiane. Jan. 70°F (21·1°C), July 81°F (27·2°C). Annual rainfall 69" (1,715 mm).

CONSTITUTION AND GOVERNMENT. On 1–2 Dec. 1975 a national congress of 264 people's representatives met and declared Laos a People's Democratic Republic. A People's Supreme Council was appointed to draw up a new Constitution.

President: Prince Souphanouvong.

Prime Minister, Secretary General of the Central Committee of the Lao People's Revolutionary Party: Kaysone Phomvihane.

There are 4 deputy prime ministers.

National flag: Three horizontal stripes of red, blue, red, with blue of double width with in the centre a large white disc.

National anthem: Peng Sat Lao (Hymn of the Lao People).

Provincial Administration: All provincial administration is in the hands of the Lao People's Revolutionary Party. Orders come from the Central Committee through a series of 'People's Revolutionary Committees' at the province, town and village level.

DEFENCE. Military service is compulsory for 18 months.

Army. The Army is organized in 4 infantry and 1 artillery divisions; 7 independent infantry regiments and 65 independent infantry companies; and 5 artillery and 9 anti-aircraft battalions. Equipment includes 30 T-34, T-54, T-55 main battle tanks. Strength (1985) about 50,000.

Navy. In 1985 there were nominally 4 squadrons comprising 42 small river patrol craft of 6 different types, of which 14 were in commission and 28 in reserve. Some 70 river patrol boats were reportedly transferred from Vietnam. Naval personnel totalled 550 officers and ratings.

Air Force. Since 1975, the Air Force has received aircraft from the USSR, including 30 MiG-21 fighters, 6 An-24 and 3 An-26 turboprop transports and 10 Mi-8 helicopters. They may be supplemented by a few of the C-47 and C-123 transports, supplied by the USA to the former régime. Personnel strength, about 2,000.

INTERNATIONAL RELATIONS

Membership. Laos is a member of UN.

Aid. Foreign aid in 1983 (estimate), was US$50m.

ECONOMY

Planning. Following the completion of the original 3-year Development Plan 1978–80, a 5-year plan (1981–85), which is basically a list of investment projects, was drawn up by the government with Soviet assistance.

Budget. Total revenue 1983, K.3,496m.; total expenditure, K.6,695m.

Currency. The currency is the *kip*. 1 *kip* = 100 *att*. Coinage, 1, 2 and 5 *att*; banknotes, 1, 5, 10, 20 and 50 *kip*. The official rate of exchange was

(March 1985) K.35 = US$1; £1 = K37·38, but in June 1983 a new 'non-commercial' rate of K.108 = US$1 was established.

ENERGY AND NATURAL RESOURCES

Electricity. Only a few towns in Laos have an electricity service. A power plant with a capacity of 8,000 kw. is installed at Vientiane, but there are only small thermo-electric plants in other towns. The Nam Ngum Dam situated about 45 miles north of Vientiane was inaugurated in Dec. 1971 with an initial installed capacity of 30,000 kw. and a planned ultimate capacity of 150,000 kw. The generators of Phase II of the scheme were brought into operation in 1978, giving an installed capacity of 110,000 kw. The installation of a fifth generator (Phase III) was due for completion in 1984. Transmission lines to Vientiane and to Thailand have been constructed. Other sources of electric power are the dams on the Sedone River about 20 miles north of Pakse and on the Nam Dong about 5 miles south of Luang Prabang, with installed capacities of 2,400 and 1,200 kw. respectively. Production (1979) 840m. kwh.

Minerals. Various minerals are found, but only tin is mined to any significant extent at present, and only at 2 mines (Tin exports (1980) US$500,000). There are extremely rich deposits of high-quality iron in Xieng Khouang province and potash near Vientiane.

Agriculture. The chief products are rice (production in 1980, 1m. tonnes; 1978, estimate, 420,000 tonnes), maize (production 27,200 tonnes), tobacco (4,200 tonnes), cotton (2,100 tonnes), citrus fruits, sticklack, benjohn tea and in the Boloven plateau coffee (2,070 tonnes), potatoes, cardamom and cinchara. Opium is produced but its manufacture is controlled by the state.

Livestock (1983): Cattle, 490,000; buffaloes, 910,000; horses, 37,000; pigs, 1·3m.; goats, 58,000; poultry, 6m.

Forestry. The forests, which cover over 50% of the country, produce valuable woods such as teak. Their potential is being exploited with Swedish and Soviet aid.

INDUSTRY AND TRADE

Industry. Industry is limited to beer, cigarettes, matches, soft drinks, plastic bags, saw-mills, rice-mills, weaving, pottery, distilleries, ice, plywood, bricks, etc. but most factories have been working at limited capacity in recent years. Plans for increased production are limited by lack of funds and skilled machine operators.

Commerce. In 1981 imports (estimate) amounted to US$121m. and exports to US$48m. The main imports were food and beverages, petroleum products and agricultural and other machinery. The chief supplying countries were Thailand and Japan. The main exports were timber, coffee and electricity.

Total trade between Laos and UK (British Department of Trade returns, in £1,000 sterling):

	1980	*1981*	*1982*	*1983*	*1984*
Imports to UK	32	65	355	56	238
Exports and re-exports from UK	720	542	880	626	721

COMMUNICATIONS

Roads. In 1981 the national road network, consisted of 1,300 km paved, 5,300 km gravel and 3,600 km earth roads.

Railways. There is no railway in Laos, but the Thai railway system extends to Nongkhai, on the Thai bank of the Mekong, which is connected by ferry with Thadeua about 12 miles east of Vientiane.

Aviation. Lao Aviation provides scheduled domestic air services linking major towns in Laos and international services to Bangkok, Phnom Penh and Hanoi. Thai Airways, Aeroflot and Air Vietnam provide flights from Bangkok, Hanoi, Rangoon, Ho Chi Min City and Moscow.

Shipping. The river Mekong and its tributaries are an important means of transport, but rapids, waterfalls and narrow channels often impede navigation and make trans-shipments neccessary.

Telecommunications. There is a radio network in Laos as well as a limited TV service with the main station at Vientiane. A ground station constructed near Vientiane under the Soviet aid programme enables USSR television programmes to be received in the capital. It also provides a telephone service to Hanoi and Eastern Europe.

In 1974 there were 5,506 telephones in Laos.

RELIGION, EDUCATION AND WELFARE

Religion. The majority of the population is Buddhist (Hinayana).

Education. In 1978–79 school year there were 5,900 elementary schools (451,000 pupils); 260 secondary schools (60,400 pupils); 86 senior high schools (7,800 pupils); 72 nursery schools (3,400 pupils); 24 teacher training schools (8,300 students) and 7 technical schools (2,000 students).

Literacy has improved from 40% in 1975, 65% in 1978 to 85% in 1981 according to official reports.

There is 1 teachers' training college, 1 college of education, 1 school of medicine, 1 agricultural college and an advanced school of Pali.

Health. In 1982 there were about 40 qualified doctors and 8,729 hospital beds.

DIPLOMATIC REPRESENTATIVES

Of Laos in Great Britain (5 Palace Green, London, W8 4QA)
Chargé d'Affaires: Ouan Phommachack.

Of Great Britain in Laos (Rue Pandit J. Nehru, Vientiane)
Ambassador: W. B. J. Dobbs.

Of Laos in USA (2222 S St., NW, Washington, D.C., 20008)
Chargé d'Affaires: Bounkeut Sangsomsak.

Of USA in Laos (Rue Bartholonie, Vientiane)
Chargé d'Affaires: Theresa Tull.

Of Laos to the United Nations
Ambassador: Dr Kithong Vongsay.

Books of Reference

La Constitution du Laos. Notes et Etudes. 1957

International Conference on the Settlement of the Laotian Question. Geneva, 12th May 1961–23rd July 1962 (Cmnd. 1828). HMSO, 1962

Declaration and Protocol on the Neutrality of Laos. Geneva, 23rd July 1962 (Cmnd. 2025). HMSO, 1963

White Book on the Violations of the Geneva Accords of 1962 by the Government of North Vietnam. Ministry of Foreign Affairs, Vientiane, 1968

Halpern, Joel M., *Economy and Society of Laos: Brief Survey.* Yale Univ. Press, 1964.—*Government, Politics and Social Structure in Laos.* Yale Univ. Press, 1964

Stuart-Cox, M., *Contemporary Laos.* Univ. of Queensland Press, 1983

Zasloff, J. J., *The Pathet Lao: Leadership and Organization.* Lexington, Toronto and London, 1973

LEBANON

Capital: Beirut
Population: 3·5m. (1984)
GNP per capita: No reliable figures available.

al-Jumhouriya al-Lubnaniya

HISTORY. After 20 years' French mandatory regime, Lebanon was proclaimed independent at Beirut on 26 Nov. 1941. On 27 Dec. 1943 an agreement was signed between representatives of the French National Committee of Liberation and of Lebanon, by which most of the powers and capacities exercised hitherto by France were transferred as from 1 Jan. 1944 to the Lebanese Government. The evacuation of foreign troops was completed in Dec. 1946.

In early May 1958 the opposition to President Chamoun, consisting principally (though not entirely) of Moslem pro-Nasserist elements, rose in insurrection; and for 5 months the Moslem quarters of Beirut, Tripoli, Sidon and the northern Bekaa were in insurgent hands. On 15 July the US Government acceded to President Chamoun's request and landed a considerable force of army and marines who re-established the authority of the Government.

Israeli attacks on Lebanon resulted from the presence and activities of armed Palestinian resistance units. Internal problems, which had long been latent in Lebanese society, were exacerbated by the politically active Palestinian population and by the deeply divisive question of the Palestine problem itself. An attempt to regulate the activities of Palestinian fighters through the secret Cairo agreement of 1969 was frustrated both by the inability of the Government to enforce its provisions and by an influx of battle-hardened fighters expelled from Jordan in Sept. 1970. A further attempt to control the guerrillas in 1973 also failed. From March 1975, Lebanon was beset by civil disorder causing considerable loss of life and economic life was brought to a virtual standstill.

By Nov. 1976 it was estimated that 40,000 people had been killed and up to 100,000 injured. By the end of the year, however, large scale fighting had been brought to an end by the intervention of the Syrian-dominated Arab Deterrent Force which ensured sufficient security to permit Lebanon to establish quasi-normal conditions under President Sarkis. Large areas of the country, however, remained outside Governmental control, including West Beirut which was the scene of frequent conflict between opposing militia groups. The South, where the Arab Deterrent Force could not deploy, remained unsettled and subject to frequent Israeli attacks. In March 1978 there was an Israeli invasion following a Palestinian attack inside Israel. Israeli troops eventually withdrew in June, but instead of handing over all their positions to UN Peacekeeping Forces they installed Israeli-controlled Lebanese militia forces in border areas. Severe disruption continued in the South. In June 1982, following on the attempted assassination of the Israeli ambassador in London, Israeli forces once again invaded, this time in massive strength, and swept through the country, eventually laying siege to and devastatingly bombing Beirut. In Sept. Palestinian forces, together with the PLO leadership, evacuated Beirut. On 23 Aug. 1982 Bachir Gemayel was elected President of Lebanon. On 14 Sept. he was assassinated. His brother, Amin Gemayel, was elected in his place on 21 Sept. Since then there has been a state of 'no peace, no war' with intermittent clashes between the various *de facto* forces on the ground. Israeli forces started a complete withdrawal on 16 Feb. 1985.

AREA AND POPULATION. Lebanon is a mountainous country about 135 miles long and varying between 20 and 35 miles wide, bounded on the north and east by Syria, on the west by the Mediterranean and on the south by Israel. Between the two parellel mountain ranges of Lebanon and Anti-Lebanon lies the fertile Bekaa Valley. About one-half of the country lies at an altitude of over 3,000 ft.

The area of Lebanon is estimated at 10,452 sq. km (4,036 sq. miles) and the population at 3·5m. (1984, estimate). The principal towns, with estimated population (1980), are: Beirut (the capital), 702,000; Tripoli 175,000; Zahlé, 46,800; Saida (Sidon), 24,740; Tyre, 14,000.

The official language is Arabic. French and, increasingly, English are widely spoken in official and commercial circles.

CLIMATE. A Mediterranean climate with short, warm winters and long, hot and rainless summers, with high humidity in coastal areas. Rainfall is largely confined to the winter months and can be torrential, with snow on high ground. Beirut. Jan. 55°F (13°C), July 81°F (27°C). Annual rainfall 35·7" (893 mm).

CONSTITUTION AND GOVERNMENT. Lebanon is an independent republic. The first Constitution was established under the French Mandate on 23 May 1926. It has since been amended in 1927, 1929, 1943 (twice) and 1947. It is a written constitution based on the classical separation of powers, with a President, a single chamber elected by universal adult suffrage, and an independent judiciary. The Executive consists of the President and a Prime Minister and Cabinet appointed by him. The system is, however, adapted to the peculiar communal balance on which Lebanese political life depends. This is done by the electoral law which allocates deputies according to the confessional distribution of the population, and by a series of constitutional conventions whereby, *e.g.,* the President is always a Maronite Christian, the Prime Minister a Sunni Moslem and the Speaker of the Chamber a Shia Moslem. There is no highly developed party system other than on religious confessional lines. The Constitution was amended on 11 April 1976 to allow a new President to be elected up to 6 months before the end of the incumbent's term.

Former Presidents of the Republic:

Bishara al-Khuri, 1 Jan. 1944–23 Sept. 1952
Camille Chamoun, 23 Sept. 1952–23 Sept. 1958
Gen. Fouad Chehab, 23 Sept. 1958–23 Sept. 1964
Charles Hélou, 23 Sept. 1964–17 June 1970
Suleiman Frangié, 17 June 1970–13 Sept. 1976
Elias Sarkis, 13 Sept. 1976–23 Sept. 1982
Bachir Gemayel, 23 Aug. 1982–14 Sept. 1982 (assassinated)

President of the Republic: Amin Gemayel (elected on 21 Sept. 1982 and took office on 23 Sept.).

On 5 Feb. 1984 the government resigned and the following day Moslem militiamen took over West Beirut from the Lebanese army. Fighting between the various factions became intense. On 5 March, President Gemayel issued a statement that the unratified military withdrawal agreement of 17 May 1982 with Israel was null and void. Later in March the re-convened Conference of National Reconciliation met in Lausanne. On 1 May 1984, a new government was formed and aims to achieve constitutional and power-sharing reforms on the basis of a wide measure of consensus.

The Cabinet was composed as follows in Dec. 1984:

Prime Minister, Foreign Affairs: Rashid Karanie.

Labour and Education: Dr Selim Hoss. *Public Works, Transport and Tourism:* Walid Jumblatt. *Posts and Communications, Health and Social Affairs:* Pierre Gemayel. *Finance, Housing and Co-operatives:* Camille Chamoun. *Justice, Hydroelectricity, Minister of State for Reconstruction and for Southern Lebanon:* Nabi Berri. *Defence, Agriculture:* Adel Osseirane. *Information:* Joseph Skaff. *Interior:* Abdullah al-Rassi. *Economy, Trade and Industry:* Victor Kassir.

National flag: Three horizontal stripes of red, white, red, with the white of double width and bearing in the centre a green cedar of Lebanon.

National anthem: Kulluna lil watan lil 'ula lil' alam (words by Rashid Nachleh, tune by Mitri El-Murr).

DEFENCE. Compulsory military service was made law in 1975, but enjoys limited application.

Army. The strength of the Army was about 19,000 in 1985 but it is in a state of flux and most of its units are well below strength. Its equipment includes M-48 and AMX-13 tanks and Saladin armoured cars. In addition, there are numerous private militias under arms in Lebanon, divided between the Maronite-Christian factions, notably the Phalange of some 10,000 men, and the Muslim-Leftist groups, such as the Druze Free Lebanese Militia led by Walid Jumblat.

Navy. The small flotilla consisted in 1985 of 4 French-built patrol boats (2 similar craft to be acquired) and 8 coastal patrol craft (2 British-built). Personnel totalled 400 officers and men.

Air Force. The Air Force had (1985) about 800 men and 50 aircraft. In addition to 6 Hunter jet fighter-bombers, it has (in storage) 9 Mirage III supersonic fighters and 1 Mirage 2-seat trainer. Other aircraft include 1 Dove light transport, 11 Alouette II and III and 2 Agusta-Bell 212 helicopters, and 10 Fouga Magister jet and piston-engined Bulldog trainers.

INTERNATIONAL RELATIONS

Membership. Lebanon is a member of UN and the Arab League.

ECONOMY

Planning. Since the civil war a Development and Reconstruction Council has been responsible for co-ordinating all efforts.

Budget. The budget for 1985 provides for a total expenditure of £Leb.10,000m.

Currency. The Lebanese *pound*, divided into 100 *piastres*, is issued by the Banque du Liban, which commenced operations on 1 April 1964. There is a fluctuating official rate of exchange, fixed monthly (March 1985: £Leb.17·89 = £1 sterling; £Leb.18·75 = US$1), this in practice is used only for the calculation of *ad-valorem* customs duties on Lebanese imports and for import statistics. For other purposes the free market is used.

Banking. Beirut was an important international financial centre, and there were about 80 banks registered with the central bank in 1979, including 2 British banks, the British Bank of the Middle East and the Chartered Bank. As a result of the civil war in 1975–76, Beirut lost much of its status as an international and regional banking centre; in general only local offices for banks remain.

Weights and Measures. The use of the metric system is legal and obligatory throughout the whole of the country. In outlying districts the former weights and measures may still be in use. They are: 1 *okiya* = 0·47 lb.; 6 *okiyas* = 1 *oke* = 2·82 lb.; 2 *okes* = 1 *rottol* = 5·64 lb.; 200 *okes* = 1 *kantar*.

ENERGY AND NATURAL RESOURCES

Oil. There are 2 oil refineries in Lebanon, one at Tripoli, which refines oil brought by ship from Iraq, and the other at Sidon, which refines oil brought from Saudi Arabia by a pipeline owned by the Trans-Arabian Pipeline Co. These refineries were not fully active in 1984 and the country depends on imports.

Minerals. Iron ore exists but is difficult to work. Other minerals known to exist are iron pyrites, copper, bituminous shales, asphalt, phosphates, ceramic clays and glass sand; but the available information is of doubtful value.

Agriculture. Lebanon is essentially an agricultural country, although owing to its physical character only about 38% of the total area of the country is at present cultivated.

The estimated yield (in 1,000 tonnes) of the main crops in 1982 was as follows: Citrus fruits, 315; apples, 130; grapes, 161; potatoes, 126; sugar-beet, 61; wheat, 23; bananas, 15; olives, 75. No reliable estimates available for 1984.

Livestock (estimated, 1983): Goats, 440,000; sheep, 140,000; cattle, 50,000; pigs, 19,000; horses, 2,000; donkeys, 10,000; mules, 4,000.

Forestry. The forests of the past have been denuded by exploitation.

INDUSTRY AND TRADE

Industry. Industry suffered badly during the civil war. The manufacturing industry was small but had doubled in size in the 10 years before the war. As a result of the war some industrial concerns have closed but others are working at reduced capacity.

Commerce. Foreign as well as local wholesale and retail trade is the principal source of income in Lebanon and provides about 31% of the total. Because of the protectionist policies followed in some neighbouring countries, this sector has been declining, the sectors to gain being those of banking, real estate, government and services.

In 1978 imports were estimated at £Leb.5,220m.; exports were valued at £Leb.1,639m. Imports came mainly from USA, Federal Republic of Germany, France, Italy and UK. Exports went mainly to Saudi Arabia, Kuwait, Syria, Libya and Iraq. Reliable trade figures have not been published in recent years.

Total trade between Lebanon and UK (British Department of Trade returns, in £1,000 sterling):

	1980	*1981*	*1982*	*1983*	*1984*
Imports to UK	9,076	7,470	24,237	11,521	6,859
Exports and re-exports from UK	70,692	61,945	67,640	81,435	76,223

Customs duties are usually imposed on an *ad-valorem* basis: the receipts are the Lebanese Government's main source of income; actual yield in 1978, £Leb.509m. The considerable adverse balance of trade is offset by invisible receipts, including foreign capital investment in Lebanese real estate, remittances from émigrés and receipts from tourism and international arbitrage operations.

Tourism. Receipts from tourism were £Leb.573m. in 1973; since 1975 they have been negligible, this sector having suffered badly as a result of the war.

COMMUNICATIONS

Roads. The main roads in Lebanon are not good by international standards. The surface is normally of asphalt and they are well maintained in normal times. Roads between Beirut and the provinces were (1984) controlled by various militia.

In 1985 there were about 300,000 cars and taxis.

Railways. There are 3 railway lines in Lebanon, all operated by the *Office des Chemins de Fer de l'Etat Libanais* (CFL): (1) Nakoura–Beirut–Tripoli (standard gauge); the Nakoura–Sidon section has been idle since the establishment of Israel: (2) a narrow-gauge line running from Beirut to Riyak in the Bekaa Valley (now closed) and thence to Damascus, Syria; (3) a standard-gauge line from Tripoli to Homs and Aleppo in Syria, providing access to Ankara and Istanbul. From Homs a branch of the CFL line extends south and re-enters Lebanon, terminating at Riyak. Total length 417 km. These lines were idle in 1984–85 because of insecurity and large sections needed repairs.

Aviation. Beirut International Airport is used by some international airlines. There are 2 national airlines, Middle East Airlines/Air Liban and Trans-Mediterranean Airways. Over the past few years, Beirut airport was closed several times.

Shipping. Beirut is the largest port, followed by Tripoli, Jounieh and Sidon. Illegal ports have mushroomed on the coast, very much reducing the legal ports' activity. No reliable figures about tonnage were available in 1984.

Post and Broadcasting. There is an automatic telephone system in Beirut which is being extended to other parts of the country. There are no telegraph, postal or telephone communications with Israel. Number of telephones (1978), 231,000.

The state radio transmits in Arabic, French, English and Armenian. Teté-Liban, which is 50% government-owned was the only television station in operation in 1984. There were 325,000 sets in 1975.

Cinemas (1973). There were 161 cinemas with a seating capacity of about 77,400.

Newspapers (1985). There were about 30 daily newspapers in Arabic, 2 in French, 1 in English and 4 in Armenian.

RELIGION, EDUCATION AND WELFARE

Religion. Probably less than half the population are Christians, some of whom have been indigenous since the earliest time of Christianity. The Christians include the Maronites, Greek Orthodox, Armenians, Greek and Roman Catholics, Armenian Catholics and the Protestants. Moslems include the Sunnis, the Shiites and the Druzes. No reliable figures on the numbers of these communities are available. Most Jews left the country after the 1975 disturbances.

Education. Government schools in 1984 comprise primary and secondary schools. There were also private primary and secondary schools. There are also 5 teachers' training colleges and 5 universities, namely the Lebanese (State) University, the American University of Beirut, the French University of St Joseph (founded in 1875), the Arab University, a branch of Alexandria University and Beirut University College. The French Government runs the École Supérieure de Lettres and the Centre d'Études Mathématiques. The Maronite monks run the University of the Holy Spirit at Kaslik.

The Lebanese Academy of Fine Arts includes schools of architecture, art, music, political and social science.

Health. There are several government-run hospitals, and many private ones.

DIPLOMATIC REPRESENTATIVES

Of Lebanon in Great Britain (21 Kensington Palace Gdns., London, W8 4QM)
Ambassador: Gen. Ahmad al-Hajj (accredited 25 May 1983).

Of Great Britain in Lebanon (Shamma Bldg., Ras Beirut)
Ambassador: H. D. A. C. Miers, CMG.

Of Lebanon in the USA (2560 28th St., NW, Washington, D.C., 20008)
Ambassador: Dr Abdallah Bouhabib.

Of the USA in Lebanon
Ambassador. Reginald Bartholomew.

Of Lebanon to the United Nations
Ambassador: Rashid Fakhouri.

Books of Reference

Statistical Information: Import and export figures are produced by the Conseil Supérieur des Douanes. The Service de Statistique Générale (M. A. G. Ayad, *Chef du Service*) publishes a quarterly bulletin (in French and Arabic) covering a wide range of subjects, including foreign trade, production statistics and estimates of the national income.

Cowan, J. M., *Dictionary of Modern Arabic.* Wiesbaden, 1961
Deeb, M., *The Lebanese Civil War.* New York, 1980
Gilmour, D., *Lebanon: The Fractured Country.* Oxford and New York, 1983
Gordon, D. C., *The Republic of Lebanon: Nation in Jeopardy.* London, 1983
Khairallah, S., *Lebanon.* [Bibliography] Oxford and Santa Barbara, 1979
Rabanovich, I., *The War for Lebanon, 1970–1983.* Cornell Univ. Press, 1984
Randal, J., *The Tragedy of Lebanon.* London, 1982
Salem, E. A., *Modernization Without Revolution: Lebanon's Experience.* Indiana Univ. Press, 1973
Salibi, K. S., *Modern History of Lebanon.* London, 1965.—*Crossroads to Civil War: Lebanon 1958–76.* New York, 1976

National Library: Dar el Kutub, Parliament Sq., Beirut.

LESOTHO

Capital: Maseru
Population: 1·47m. (1984)
GNP per capita: US$540 (1981)

HISTORY. Basutoland first received the protection of Britain in 1868 at the request of Moshoeshoe I, the first paramount chief. In 1871 the territory was annexed to the Cape Colony, but in 1884 it was restored to the direct control of the British Government through the High Commissioner for South Africa.

On 4 Oct. 1966 Basutoland became an independent and sovereign member of the Commonwealth under the name of the Kingdom of Lesotho.

AREA AND POPULATION. Lesotho, an enclave within the Republic of South Africa is bounded on the west by the Orange Free State, on the north by the Orange Free State and Natal, on the east by Natal, and on the south by Transkei. The altitude varies from 1,500 to 3,482 metres. The area is 11,720 sq. miles (30,355 sq. km). Lesotho is a purely African territory, and the few European residents are government officials, traders, missionaries and artisans.

The census taken on 12 April 1976 showed a total population of 1,216,815 persons. Estimate (1984) 1·47m.

The capital is Maseru (population, 1976, 45,000).

The official languages are Sesotho and English.

CLIMATE. A healthy and pleasant climate, with variable rainfall, but averaging 29″ (725 mm) a year over most of the country. The rain falls mainly in the summer months of Oct. to April, while the winters are dry and may produce heavy frosts in lowland areas and frequent snow in the highlands. Temperatures in the lowlands range from a maximum of 90°F (32·2°C) in summer to a minimum of 20°F (–6·7°C) in winter.

CONSTITUTION AND GOVERNMENT. Lesotho is a constitutional monarchy with HM the King as ceremonial Head of State.

Parliament consists of the National Assembly (60 members elected by adult suffrage) and a Senate (22 principal chiefs and 11 members nominated by the King). The elections of 27 Jan. 1970 were declared invalid on 31 Jan. Parliamentary rule, with a National Assembly of nominated members, was reintroduced in April 1973. Elections are planned for 1985.

A new Constitution will add up to 20 nominated members to the 60 elected members of the National Assembly, and will limit the Senate to 22 principal chiefs.

Ruler: Constantine Bereng Seeiso Motlotlehi Moshoeshoe II, Paramount Chief of the Sotho people since 1940, became King at independence on 4 Oct. 1966.

Prime Minister: Chief Leabua Jonathan. *Minister of the Interior:* Chief Sekhonyana 'Maseribane.

The College of Chiefs settles the recognition and succession of Chiefs and adjudicates cases of inefficiency, criminality and absenteeism among them.

National flag: Blue with a white Basuto hat; in the hoist 2 vertical strips of green and red.

Local Government. The country is divided into 10 districts as follows: Maseru, Qacha's Nek, Mokhotlong, Leribe, Butha–Buthe, Teyateyaneng, Mafeteng, Mohale's Hoek, Quthing, Thaba–Tseka. Each district is subdivided into wards, most of which are presided over by hereditary chiefs allied to the Moshoeshoe family.

DEFENCE

Police Mobile Unit. Formed in 1978, to facilitate deployment of men and equipment to less accessible regions, this small air wing has 2 Skyvan twin-turboprop transports, 1 Do 27 and 1 Do 28 liaison aircraft, and a total of 5 Bell 412, BO 105 and Bell 47 helicopters. The Skyvans are available also as ambulance aircraft.

INTERNATIONAL RELATIONS

Membership. Lesotho is a member of UN, OAU, the Commonwealth and is an ACP state of the EEC.

ECONOMY

Planning. A third 5-year plan (1981–84), to exploit natural resources and promote investment was published in 1983.

Budget. Expenditure (1982–83) M269m.; revenue, M216m.

The major items of expenditure in 1983–84 were education (M25·8m.), agriculture (M10·1m.) and health (M8·4m.). The revenue situation was greatly improved by the re-negotiation of the Republic of South Africa's customs agreement in 1970.

Currency. The currency is the *Loti* (plural *Maloti*) divided into 100 *Lisente* which is at par with the South African *Rand.* In March 1985, £1 = 2·22 *Maloti*; US$1 = 2·06 *Maloti.*

Banking. The Standard Bank of South Africa and Barclays Bank International have branches at Maseru, Mohale's Hoek and Leribe. The Lesotho Bank has branches throughout the country.

ENERGY AND NATURAL RESOURCES

Electricity. A feasibility study was announced (1982) to be undertaken by the Republic of South Africa and Lesotho to divert river waters from Lesotho to South Africa and to provide hydro-electricity for Lesotho.

Agriculture. The chief crops were (1983 production in 1,000 tonnes): wheat, 15; maize, 79; sorghum, (31); barley, oats, beans, peas and other vegetables are also grown. The land is held in trust for the nation by the King and may not be alienated.

Soil conservation and the improvement of crops and pasture are matters of vital importance. A total area of 1,006,817 acres has been protected against soil erosion by means of terracing, training banks, tree planting and grass strips. Efforts are being made to secure the general introduction of rotational grazing in the mountain area.

Livestock (1983): Cattle, 600,000; horses, 105,000; donkeys, 100,000; pigs, 65,000; sheep, 1·4m.; goats, 1m.; mules, 1,000; poultry, 1m.

INDUSTRY AND TRADE

Industry. Industrial development is progressing under the National Development Corporation. Diamond production (1981) 52,000 carats.

Commerce. Lesotho, Botswana and Swaziland are members of the South African customs union, by agreement dated 29 June 1910.

Total values of imports and exports into and from Lesotho (in Mm.):

	1979	*1980*	*1981*	*1982*
Imports	312	372	453	541
Exports	38	45	43	38

Principal imports were food, livestock, drink and tobacco, machinery and transport equipment, mineral fuels and lubricants; principal exports were wool and mohair and diamonds.

The majority of international trade is with the Republic of South Africa.

Total trade between Lesotho and UK (British Department of Trade returns, in £1,000 sterling):

	1980	*1981*	*1982*	*1983*	*1984*
Imports to UK	340	489	682	216	78
Exports and re-exports from UK	394	1,483	1,260	2,080	633

Tourism. In 1980 there were 150,000 visitors.

COMMUNICATIONS

Roads. There were (1983) 311 km of tarred roads and 1,500 km of gravel-surfaced roads. In addition to the main roads there were (1983) 931 km of food aid tracks leading to trading stations and missions. Communications into the mountainous interior are by means of bridlepaths suitable only for riding and pack animals, but a mountain road of 80 miles has been constructed, and some parts are accessible by air transport, which is being used increasingly. In 1977 there were 11,509 motor vehicles.

Railways. A railway built by the South African Railways, 1 mile long, connects Maseru with the Bloemfontein–Natal line at Marseilles.

Aviation. There is a scheduled passenger service between Maseru and Jan Smuts Airport, Johannesburg, operated jointly by Lesotho National Airways and SAA. There are also 30 airstrips for light aircraft.

Post and Broadcasting. There were 5,409 telephones in 1983. Radio Lesotho transmits daily in English and Sesotho. Radio receivers (1983), 37,786.

Cinemas. In 1971 there were 2 cinemas with a seating capacity of 800.

JUSTICE, RELIGION, EDUCATION AND WELFARE

Justice. An appeal court for Lesotho was established at Maseru on 4 Oct. 1966.

The police force on 31 Dec. 1982 had an establishment of 348 officers and subordinate officers and 1,530 other ranks.

Religion. About 70% of the population are Christians, 40% being Roman Catholics.

Education. Education is largely in the hands of the 3 main missions (Paris Evangelical, Roman Catholic and English Church), under the direction of the Ministry of Education. In 1982 the total enrolment in 1,103 primary schools was 277,945; in 108 secondary schools, 27,799; in the National Teacher-Training College enrolment was 1,136. University education is provided at the National University of Lesotho established in 1975 at Roma; enrolment in 1982–83, 1,139.

Health. The government medical staff of the territory consists of 1 Permanent Secretary for Health, 1 Director of Health Services, 1 medical superintendent, 8 district medical officers and a total of 102 doctors including 20 specialists.

There are 11 government hospitals staffed by 308 matrons, sisters and nurses. There is accommodation for 2,175 patients in government hospitals. The 360-bed Queen Elizabeth II hospital in Maseru was completed in 1957. There are 9 mission hospitals subsidized by the Government with 153 staff and 729 beds. 116 health centres (319 beds) and mountain dispensaries provide outpatient medical facilities and maternity services to people living in remote areas. The leper settlement 5 miles out of Maseru had 67 patients in 1983.

Typhus and plague occur.

DIPLOMATIC REPRESENTATIVES

Of Lesotho in Great Britain (10 Collingham Rd., London, SW5)
High Commissioner: Odilon Tlali Sefako (accredited 25 Oct. 1983).

Of Great Britain in Lesotho
High Commissioner: P. E. Rosling, MVO.

Of Lesotho in the USA (1601 Connecticut Ave., NW, Washington, D.C., 20009)
Ambassador: 'M'alineo N. Tau.

Of the USA in Lesotho (P.O. Box MS 333, Maseru, 100)
Ambassador: S. L. Abbott.

Of Lesotho to the United Nations
Ambassador: Thabo Makeka.

Books of Reference

Statistical Information: Bureau of Statistics, PO Box 455, Maseru, Lesotho.
Ashton, H., *The Basuto.* 2nd ed. OUP, 1967
Hailey, Lord, *The Republic of South Africa and the High Commission Territories.* OUP, 1963
Murray, C., *Families Divided: The Impact of Migrant Labour in Lesotho.* OUP, 1981
Spence, J. E., *Lesotho.* OUP, 1968
Stevens, C., *Food, Aid and the Developing World.* London, 1979

LIBERIA

Capital: Monrovia
Population: 1·9m. (1984)
GNP per capita: US$520 (1981)

HISTORY. The Republic of Liberia had its origin in the efforts of several American philanthropic societies to establish freed American slaves in a colony on the West African coast. In 1822 a settlement was formed near the spot where Monrovia now stands. On 26 July 1847 the State was constituted as the Free and Independent Republic of Liberia. The new State was first recognized by Great Britain and France, and ultimately by other powers.

AREA AND POPULATION. Liberia has about 350 miles of coastline, extending from Sierra Leone, on the west, to the Ivory Coast, on the east, and it stretches inland to a distance, in some places, of about 250 miles.

The total area is about 43,000 sq. miles (112,600 sq. km). A census taken in 1978 gave the total population as 1,715,973 (872,105 males). Estimate (1984) 1·9m. The indigenous natives belong in the main to 4 principal stocks: Mendetan, West Atlantic, Mande-fu, and Kru. These are in turn subdivided into 16 major tribes, namely: Bassa, Belle, Gbandi, Mende, Gio, Dey, Mano, Gola, Kpelle, Kissi, Krahn, Kru, Loma, Mandingo, Vai and Grebo.

Monrovia, the capital, had (1984) a population of 425,000. It is one of the 4 ports of entry along the 350 miles of coast, the others being Buchanan (Grand Bassa), River Cess, Greenville (Sinoe), Harper (Maryland). Other towns are Kolba City, Voinjama, Tubmanburg, Bensonville, Zorzor, Kakata, Suakoko, Gbarnga, Ganta, Sanniquellie, Saclape, Tappita, Robertsport, Bendja, Yekepa and Zwedru.

The country is divided into 11 counties and 4 territories and the district of Monrovia.

CLIMATE. An equatorial climate, with constant high temperatures and plentiful rainfall, though Jan. to May is drier than the rest of the year. Monrovia. Jan. 79°F (26·1°C), July 76°F (24·4°C). Annual rainfall 206″ (5,138 mm).

CONSTITUTION AND GOVERNMENT. The Constitution of the Republic is modelled on that of the US. The executive power is vested in a President and the legislative power in a legislature of 2 Houses, the Senate (27 members) and the House of Representatives (71 members). The President is elected for 6 years in the first instance, the House of Representatives for 4 and the Senate for 6 years. A Legislative Act was approved on 22 July 1974, setting up a National Commission to give consideration to possible changes in the Constitution in preparation for a return to civilian rule in 1985.

On 12 April 1980, President Tolbert was assassinated; his government was overthrown and the Constitution suspended. President Tolbert's party, the True Whig Party, was formed in 1860 and had been in power since 1870. Recent economic decline and pressure for change had undermined the Government. In March 1980, the newly formed People's Progressive Party was banned and its leaders arrested. The *coup* was led by Master-Sergeant Doe who was later installed as Head of State and Commander-in-Chief of the army.

Executive power is vested in the Head of State and a Cabinet of 17 which is supervised by a People's Redemption Council. A draft Constitution was published in 1983 and approved in a referendum held in July 1984, and a return to civilian rule is envisaged for 1985.

Head of State and Commander-in-Chief: Samuel Kanyon Doe.
Foreign Minister: T. Ernest Eastman.
The official language is English.

National flag: Six red and 5 white horizontal stripes alternating. In the upper corner, nearest the staff, is a square of blue covering a depth of 5 stripes. In the centre of this blue field is a 5-pointed white star.

National anthem: All hail, Liberia, hail! (words by President Warner; tune by O. Lucas, 1860).

DEFENCE

Army. The establishment organized on a militia basis numbers 4,900 (1985), divided into 5 infantry battalions with support units. There is in addition an enlisted frontier force, the Liberian National Guard, of 93 officers and 2,200 men. Equipment includes 12 M-3A1 scout cars.

Navy. The small naval service or coastguard comprises 3 small patrol boats, 3 coastguard cutters and 1 aircraft. Personnel in 1985 totalled 445 officers and men.

Air Force. The nucleus of an Air Force has been formed, as the Air Reconnaissance Unit, to support the Liberian Army. Equipment includes 2 C-47 transports, an Israeli-built Arava twin-turboprop light transport and a small number of Cessna 172, 185, 207 and 337G light aircraft. HAL Chetak (licence-built Alouette III) helicopters are expected to follow from India. Personnel about 250.

INTERNATIONAL RELATIONS

Membership. Liberia is a member of UN, OAU, ECOWAS and is an ACP state of EEC.

ECONOMY

Planning. The 1981–85 Development Plan has planned expenditure of US$615m. of which US$203m. is devoted to the development of agriculture.

Budget. Revenue and expenditure was as follows (in US$1,000):

	1981–82	*1982–83*	*1983–84*
Revenue	279,300	390,100	357,000
Expenditure	385,800	420,100	387,000

Currency. The legal currency of Liberia is the *dollar* which is equivalent to US$1 which itself has been in circulation since 3 Nov. 1942, but there is a Liberian coinage in silver and copper. Official accounts are kept in dollars and cents. The Liberian coins are as follows: Silver,$5, $1, 50-, 25-, 10- and 5-cent pieces; alloy, 2-and 1-cent pieces. The Government has not yet issued paper money. In March 1985, £1 = 1·07 Liberian $; US$1 = 1 Liberian $.

Banking. The First National City Bank (Liberia) was founded in 1935. An Italian bank, Tradevco, started business in 1955. The International Trust Co. of Liberia opened a commercial banking department at the end of 1960. A branch of the Chase Manhattan Bank opened in 1961. The Liberian Bank for Development and Investment (LBDI) was founded in 1964 and began operations in 1965. The National Bank of Liberia opened on 22 July 1974, to act as a central bank. The National Housing and Savings Bank opened on 20 Jan. 1972. The Liberian Finance & Trust Corporation was incorporated Oct. 1976 and began operations in May 1977. The Liberian Agricultural and Co-operative Development Bank started operations in 1978. The Bank of Credit & Commerce International opened in Sept. 1978.

Weights and Measures. Weights and measures are the same as in UK and USA.

NATURAL RESOURCES

Minerals. The National Iron Ore Co. near the Mano River, the Liberian Swedish Mineral Co. in the Nimba Mountains and the Bong Mining Co. (DELIMCO) at Bong Mountain Range are exploiting their iron-ore concession areas. Iron ore production was valued at US$241·1m. tonnes in 1982. Total employment in iron ore mining was 8,815 in 1981. Gold is found on a small scale and diamond production (1982) 337,732 carats valued at US$20·8m.

Agriculture. The soil is productive, but due to excessive rainfall (from 160 to 180 in. per year), there are large swamp areas. Rice, cassava, coffee, citrus and sugar-cane are cultivated. The Government is negotiating the financing of large-scale investment in rice production aimed at making the country self-sufficient in rice production. Coffee, cocoa and palm-kernels are produced mainly by the traditional agricultural sector. In 1981, the total volume of coffee and cocoa exports alone were 18·3m. lb. (US$19·4m.), and 14·8m. lb. (US$13·8m.), respectively.

The Liberia Produce Marketing Corporation (LPMC) operates an oil-mill in Monrovia, processing most of the palm-kernels. There were 2 large commercial oil-palm plantations in the country. The Liberia Industrial Co-operative (LBINC) has 6,000 acres of oil-palm (of which 5,000 acres are in production) in Grand Bassa County,and West Africa Agricultural Co. (WAAC) has 4,020 acres in production in Grand Cape Mount County.

Livestock (1983): Cattle, 42,000; pigs, 115,000; sheep, 232,000; poultry, 3m.

Forestry. The Firestone Plantation Co. have large rubber plantations, employing over 40,000 men. Their concession comprises about 1m. acres and expires in the year 2025. About 100,000 acres have been planted. Independent producers have a further 65,000 acres planted. In 1976 the total area under rubber cultivation was 294,400 acres, of which 195,800 acres were under actual production.

Other rubber producing companies include Goodrich Rubber Plantation, Allen L. Grant, L. A. C. and Salala Rubber Co. Together, the foreign concessions produced 131·6m. lb. in 1981 while independent Liberian farmers produced 148·7m. lb. in 1981.

The production of logs in 1981 was 451m. cu. metres; 1980, 745m.

INDUSTRY AND TRADE

Industry. There are a number of small factories (brick and tile, soap, nails, mattresses, shoes, plastics, paint, oxygen, acetylene, tyre retreading, a brewery, soft drinks, cement, matches, candy and biscuits).

Commerce. Foreign trade for 6 calendar years was as follows (in US$1m.):

	1977	*1978*	*1979*	*1980*	*1981*	*1982*
Imports	463·5	486	537	533·8	477·4	353·9
Exports	447·4	481	505	600·4	529·2	...

The principal exports in 1981 were: Iron ore, and concentrates, US$325·4m.; rubber, US$86·7m.; logs and lumber, US$36·8m. The principal imports in 1981 were machinery and transport equipment (US$118·9m.) and manufactured goods (US$61·3m.). Main suppliers in 1981 were: Asia and European countries (US$200m.), USA (US$142·1m.), other countries (US$136·3m.).

Total trade between Liberia and UK (British Department of Trade returns, in £1,000 sterling):

	1980	*1981*	*1982*	*1983*	*1984*
Imports to UK	8,671	6,014	8,213	7,181	6,975
Exports and re-exports from UK	46,412	24,262	14,069	13,877	30,980

The figures for exports from the UK include the value of shipping transferred to the Liberian flag; the genuine exports are considerably lower.

Tourism. The National Bureau of Culture and Tourism was created in July 1981.

COMMUNICATIONS

Roads. In 1981, there were 4,794 miles of public roads (1,165 primary, 366 paved, 799 all-weather, 3,629 secondary and feeder) and 1,474 miles of private roads (93 paved, 1,381 laterite and earth). The principal highway connects Monrovia with the road system of Guinea, with branches leading into the Eastern and Western areas of Liberia. The latter branch reaches the Sierra Leone border and joins the Sierra Leone road system. A bridge over the St Paul River carries road and rail traffic to the iron-ore mines at Bomi Hills.

Railway. A railway (for freight only) was built in 1951, connecting Monrovia with the Bomi Hills iron-ore mines about 69 km distant; this has been extended to the

National Iron Ore Co. area by 79 km. A line from Nimba to Lower Buchanan (267 km) was completed in 1963 and another line from Bong to Monrovia (78 km) was completed in 1965.

Aviation. The airport for Liberia is Roberts Airport (30 miles from Monrovia). The James Spriggs Payne Airfield, 5 miles from Monrovia, can be used by light aircraft and mini jumbo jets. Air services are maintained by PANAM, Ghana Airways, Nigeria Airways, UTA, Middle East Airlines, Air Mali, Air Afrique, SAS, KLM, Swissair, British Caledonian, Air Guinée, SABENA, Iberia Airlines, Romanian Airlines and Air Liberia.

Shipping. In 1981, 2,277 vessels entered Monrovia.

The Liberian merchant navy, in 1976, consisted of 2,666 ships of 76,412,842 GRT. The Liberian Government requires only a modest registration fee and an almost nominal annual charge and maintains no control over the operation of ships flying the Liberian flag.

Post and Broadcasting. There is cable communication (French) with Europe and America *via* Dakar, and a wireless station is maintained by the Government at Monrovia. There is a telephone service (7,079 telephones, 1980), in Monrovia, which is gradually being extended over the whole country. An earth station constructed by Itacable in 1976 is equipped for 24 telephone type channels and its traffic can be increased to 60 telephone type channels. With the aid of the satellite, automatic telephone and telegraph services to and from many countries are transmitted on a 24-hour basis.

There are wireless stations at Monrovia, Bassa, Harper, Kolahun, Cape Mount and Sinoe. There were (1982) 320,000 radio and 21,000 television receivers.

JUSTICE, RELIGION, EDUCATION AND WELFARE

Justice. Justice is administered by a Supreme Court of 5 judges, circuit courts and lower courts. A new Liberian code of laws has been published (5 vols. to 1956).

Religion. The main denominations represented in Liberia are Methodist, Baptist, Episcopalian, African Methodist, Pentecostal, Seventh-day Adventist, Lutheran and Roman Catholic, working through missionaries and mission schools. There are about 670,000 Moslems.

Education. Schools are classified as: (1) Public schools, maintained and run by the Government; (2) Mission schools, supported by foreign Missions and subsidized by the Government, and operated by qualified Missionaries and Liberian teachers; (3) Private schools, maintained by endowments and sometimes subsidized by the Government.

In 1984 there were estimated to be 1,830 schools with 8,344 teachers and 443,688 pupils.

Health. There were 236 doctors in 1981 and about 3,000 hospital beds.

DIPLOMATIC REPRESENTATIVES

Of Liberia in Great Britain (21 Prince's Gate, London, SW7 1QB)
Chargé d'Affaires: James H. Stevens.

Of Great Britain in Liberia (Mamba Point, Monrovia)
Ambassador and Consul-General: D. G. Reid, CMG.

Of Liberia in the USA (5201 16th St., NW, Washington, D.C., 20011)
Ambassador: Dr G. Toe Washington.

Of the USA in Liberia (United Nations Drive, Monrovia)
Ambassador: William L. Swing.

Of Liberia to the United Nations
Ambassador: Dr Abeodu B. Jones.

Books of Reference

Economic Survey of Liberia, 1981. Ministry of Planning and Economic Affairs
Dunn, D. E., *The Foreign Policy of Liberia during the Tubman Era, 1944–71.* London, 1979
Fraenkel, M., *Tribe and Class in Monrovia.* OUP, 1964
Wilson, C. M., *Liberia: Black Africa in Microcosm.* New York, 1971

LIBYA

Capital: Tripoli
Population: 3·5m. (1982)
GNP per capita: US$8,450 (1981)

Al-Jamahiriyah Al-Arabiya Al-Libya Al-Shabiya Al-Ishtirakiya

HISTORY. Tripoli fell under Turkish domination in the 16th century, and though in 1711 the Arab population secured some measure of independence, the country was in 1835 proclaimed a Turkish vilayet. In Sept. 1911 Italy occupied Tripoli and on 19 Oct. 1912, by the Treaty of Ouchy, Turkey recognized the sovereignty of Italy in Tripoli.

After the expulsion of the Germans and Italians in 1942 and 1943, Tripolitania and Cyrenaica were placed under British, and the Fezzan under French, military administration. Britain recognized the Amir Mohammed Idris Al-Senussi as Amir of Cyrenaica in June 1949.

Libya became an independent, sovereign, federal kingdom under the Amir of Cyrenaica, Mohammed Idris Al-Senussi, as King of the United Kingdom of Libya, on 24 Dec. 1951, when the British Residents in Tripolitania and Cyrenaica and the French Resident in the Fezzan transferred their remaining powers to the federal government of Libya, in pursuance of decisions passed by the United Nations in 1949 and 1950.

On 1 Sept. 1969 King Idris was deposed by a group of army officers. Twelve of the group of officers formed the Revolutionary Command Council chaired by Col. Muammar Qadhafi and proclaimed a republic.

AREA AND POPULATION. The area is estimated at 1,759,540 sq. km (679,358 sq. miles). The population, according to the census of 1973, was 2,249,237. Estimate (1982) 3·5m.

The country is divided administratively in 25 municipalities with the following main population centres: Tripoli, 980,000; Benghazi, 650,000; Misurata, 285,000; Zavia, 247,000; Sebha (the main town in the southern province) 113,000.

CLIMATE. The coastal region has a warm temperate climate, with mild wet winters and hot dry summers, though most of the country suffers from aridity. Tripoli. Jan. 52°F (11·1°C), July 81°F (27·2°C). Annual rainfall 16" (400 mm). Benghazi. Jan. 56°F (13·3°C), July 77°F (25°C). Annual rainfall 11" (267 mm).

CONSTITUTION AND GOVERNMENT. Under the new 1977 Constitution, Libya is now divided into 25 municipalities and 126 'Basic People's Congresses', which form the primary level of government. The General People's Congress, created in Jan. 1976 as the national legislature, comprises 3 delegates from each of the 186 Basic People's Congresses. The General People's Committee, which replaced the Council of Ministers, is assisted by the 5-member General People's Secretariat, which replaced the Revolutionary Command Council. It was ruled by the Revolutionary Command Council (RCC) under the leadership of Col. Muammar Qadhafi.

In March 1977 a new form of direct democracy, the 'Jamahiriya' (state of the masses) was promulgated and the official name of the country was changed to Socialist Peoples Libyan Arab Jamahiriya. At local level authority is now vested in 186 Basic and 25 Municipal People's Congresses which appoint Popular Committees to execute policy. Officials of these Congresses and Committees form at national level the General People's Congress, a body of some 1,000 delegates which normally meets for about a week twice a year. This is the highest policy-making body in the country. The General People's Congress appoints its own General Secretariat and the General People's Committee, whose members head the 20 government departments which execute policy at national level. The Secretary of the General People's Committee has functions similar to those of a Prime Minister.

Following the re-organization of March 1979 Col. Qadhafi retained his position as leader of the Revolution. But neither he nor his former RCC colleagues have any formal posts in the new administration.

Arabic is the official language. Tripoli is the capital.

Secretary-General of the General Secretariat of the General People's Congress: Muhamed Az-Zaruq Rajab.

National flag: Plain green.

DEFENCE. Libyans are liable for 18 months' service at the age of 18. Enrolment in the reserves, numbering about 40,000, continues until aged 49.

Army. The Army is organized into 20 tank battalions, 30 mechanized infantry, 1 National Guard, 10 artillery, 2 anti-aircraft and 2 surface-to-surface missile battalions. Equipment includes 2,600 T-54/-55/-62 and 300 T-72 main battle tanks. Strength (1985) 58,000. The paramilitary Pan-African Legion numbers about 10,000.

Navy. The fleet comprises 6 *ex*-Soviet diesel-driven submarines, 1 missile-armed frigate, 7 missile-armed corvettes, 1 gun corvette, 6 ocean minesweepers, 25 fast missile craft, 14 fast gunboats, 8 patrol boats, 1 medium (dock type) logistic support ship, 2 landing ships, 3 medium landing ships, 20 landing craft, 1 maintenance repair craft, 1 diving ship, 1 salvage ship, 1 transport and 7 tugs. Under construction or projection are 1 missile-armed corvette and 30 landing craft.

Libya has procured naval equipment and weapons from both the East (particularly the USSR) and the West; and the increasing and up-to-date fleet constitutes a force of crucial importance in the Mediterranean.

Personnel in 1985 exceeded 4,000 officers and ratings, including coastguard. A large proportion of naval personnel have been trained in the Soviet Union since 1975.

Air Force. The creation of an Air Force began in 1959. In 1974, delivery was completed of a total of 110 Mirage 5 combat aircraft and trainers, of which about 50 remain. They have been followed by 20 Tu-22 supersonic reconnaissance bombers, 50 MiG-25 interceptors and reconnaissance aircraft, 100 Su-22 ground attack fighters, 94 MiG-21s, and about 140 MiG-23 variable-geometry fighters and fighter-bombers from the USSR. Other equipment includes 40 Mirage F1 fighters from France, 6 Mirage F1-B two-seat trainers, 20 Mi-24 gunship helicopters, Mi-14 anti-submarine helicopters, 9 C-130H Hercules and 20 Aeritalia G222T transports, 8 Super Frelon and 20 Agusta-built CH-47C Chinook heavy-lift helicopters, and a total of 16 Bell 212, Bell 47, Alouette III and Mi-8 helicopters. Training is performed on piston-engined SF.260Ms (some of which are armed for light attack duties) from Italy; L-39 Albatros, Galeb and Magister jet aircraft; and twin-engined Xingus built in Brazil. Personnel total about 8,500, with many of the combat aircraft operated by foreign aircrew. Aircraft on order include more Mirage F1 fighters from France and MiG-23s from the USSR.

INTERNATIONAL RELATIONS

Membership. Libya is a member of UN, OAU and the Arab League.

ECONOMY

Planning. Declining oil revenues (50% down on 1980 levels) has meant postponing of most projects envisaged in the 5-year development plan (1981–85).

Budget. A development budget of LD2,370m. was announced for 1983 but is likely to be under-spent by 50%.

Currency. The currency is the Libyan *dinar* which is divided into 1,000 *millemes*. Rate of exchange, March 1985: LD0·32 = £1; LD0·30 = US$1.

Banking. A National Bank of Libya was established in 1955; it was renamed the Central Bank of Libya in 1972. All foreign banks were nationalized by Dec. 1970. In 1972 the Libyan Government set up the Libyan Arab Foreign Bank whose function is overseas investment and to participate in multinational banking corporations. The National Agricultural Bank, which has been set up to give loans and subsidies to farmers to develop their land and to assist them in marketing their crops, has offices in Tripoli, Benghazi, Sebha and other agricultural centres. The National Industrial and Real Estate Bank has been divided to form a Real Estate Bank to provide loans for house-buyers and the Development Bank to finance industrial projects.

Weights and Measures. Although the metric system has been officially adopted and is obligatory for all contracts, the following weights and measures are still used: *oke* = 1·282 kg; *kantar* = 51·28 kg; *draa* = 46 cm; *handaza* = 68 cm.

ENERGY AND NATURAL RESOURCES

Electricity. Electricity output capacity in 1980 was 1,950 mw and under the development plan was scheduled to rise to 3,878 mw by 1985.

Oil. Production (1981) 420m. bbls. Reserves (1981) 21,000m. bbls. The Libyan National Oil Corporation (NOC) was established in March 1970 to be the state's organization for the exploitation of Libya's oil resources. NOC does not participate in the production of oil but has a majority share in all the operating companies with the exception of two small producers Aquitaine-Libya and Wintershall Libya.

The largest producers are Oasis (59·2% NOC, Marathon and Conoco, 16·3% and Amerada Hess 8·2%) and AGOCO (100% NOC) who together produce more than 50% of total production. The other significant producers are Occidental Libya (51% NOC, 49% Occidental US) AGIP N.A.M.E. (50% NOC, 50% AGIP Italy) SIRTE Oil Co. (formerly ESSO Libya until EXXON withdrew in Oct. 1981) and Mobil Oil Libya Ltd. (82·8% NOC, 17·2% Veba-Gelsenberg) who continue to use the Mobil name despite the fact that Mobil Inc. followed EXXON's example and withdrew in July 1982.

Gas. Reserves (1982) 670,000m. cu. metres. Production (1982) 29,000m. cu. metres. In 1983 a gas pipeline was under construction which will take gas from Brega, along the coast to Misurata.

Minerals. There were (1984) 5 cement factories with a capacity of 4·75m. tonnes per annum. Two new plants were under construction in 1984 with a capacity of 2·5m. tonnes. Gypsum output (1975) 15,000 tonnes. Iron ore deposits have been found in the south.

Agriculture. Tripolitania has 3 zones from the coast inland—the Mediterranean, the sub-desert and the desert. The first, which covers an area of about 17,231 sq. miles, is the only one properly suited for agriculture, and may be further subdivided into: (1) the oases along the coast, the richest in North Africa, in which thrive the date palm, the olive, the orange, the peanut and the potato; (2) the steppe district, suitable for cereals (barley and wheat) and pasture; it has olive, almond, vine, orange and mulberry trees and ricinus plants; (3) the dunes, which are being gradually afforested with acacia, robinia, poplar and pine; (4) the Jebel (the mountain district, Tarhuna, Garian, Nalut-Yefren), in which thrive the olive, the fig, the vine and other fruit trees, and which on the east slopes down to the sea with the fertile hills of Msellata. Of some 25m. acres of productive land in Tripolitania, nearly 20m. are used for grazing and about 1m. for static farming. The sub-desert zone produces the alfa plant. The desert zone and the Fezzan contain some fertile oases, such as those of Ghadames, Ghat, Socna, Sebha, Brak.

Cyrenaica has about 10m. acres of potentially productive land, most of which, however, is suitable only for grazing. Certain areas, chief of which is the plateau known as the Barce Plain (about 1,000 ft above sea-level), are suitable for dry farming; in addition, grapes, olives and dates are grown. With improved irrigation, production, particularly of vegetables, could be increased, but stock raising and dry farming will remain of primary importance. About 143,000 acres are used for settled farming; about 272,000 acres are covered by natural forests. The Agricultural Development Authority plans to reclaim 6,000 hectares each year for agriculture.

In the Fezzan there are about 6,700 acres of irrigated gardens and about 297,000 acres are planted with date palms.

Production (1980, in tonnes): Wheat, 141,000; barley, 71,000; milk, 85,000; meat, 119,000. Olive trees number about 3·4m. and productive date-palm trees about 3m.

Livestock (1983): 4·8m. sheep, 1·5m. goats, 200,000 cattle, 7m. poultry.

INDUSTRY AND TRADE

Industry. Among the traditional industries of Tripolitania and Cyrenaica are sponge fishing, tunny fishing, tobacco growing and processing, dyeing and weaving of local wool and imported cotton yarn, and olive oil. Tripolitania also produces bricks, salt, leather and esparto grass for paper-making. Home industries of both territories include the making of matting, carpets, leather articles and fabrics embroidered with gold and silver. The Government has embarked on an ambitious programme of industrial development aimed at the local manufacture of building materials (steel and aluminium pipes and fittings, electric cables, cement, bricks, glass, etc.), foodstuffs (dairy products, flour, tinned fruits and vegetables, dates, fish processing and canning, etc.), textiles and footwear (ready-made clothing, woollen and cotton cloth, blankets, leather footwear, etc.) and development of mineral deposits (iron ore, phosphates, mineral salts). Small scale private sector industrialization is encouraged by government loans and subsidies.

On 21 Sept. 1969 a decree laid down that all business concerns should be 100% Libyan-owned, but oil companies and banks were excluded.

Commerce. Total imports in 1982 were valued at US$13,000 (f.o.b.) and exports of US$13,948 (f.o.b.), mostly crude oil.

Total trade between Libya and UK (British Department of Trade returns, in £1,000 sterling):

	1980	*1981*	*1982*	*1983*	*1984*
Imports to UK	46,528	74,810	342,476	224,050	155,276
Exports and re-exports from UK	288,358	520,416	260,937	274,169	246,467

COMMUNICATIONS

Roads. Good motor roads connect Tripoli through Zuara with Tunis, and through Homs and Misurata with Benghazi and thence with Tobruk and Alexandria, although the border with Egypt has been closed for some years. Other roads go south and south-west from Tripoli to Tiagura, Garian, Yefren, Nalut and Ghadames. A road connects Sebha in the south with the main coastal road. An ambitious road building programme is being implemented and a road will eventually link Libya with Chad and Niger through Sebha. A further main road is being built to link Kufra, a major agricultural centre in the south-eastern part of Libya with the coastal road.

Surface communication between Benghazi and Tripoli is by frequent bus service, and there are also bus services between Benghazi and Alexandria, and between Tripoli, Tunis and Algiers.

Railways. There were in 1982 no railways, but a major railway project has been planned to run along the coast from the Tunisian to the Egyptian border.

Aviation. Benghazi and Tripoli are both served by international airlines, linking them with each other and Athens, Rome, Malta, Tunis, Frankfurt, Paris, Amsterdam, Algiers, Lagos and London. British Caledonian has 5 flights weekly between Tripoli and London.

A national airline, the Libyan Arab Airlines (LAA), was inaugurated on 30 Sept. 1965. Apart from internal flights LAA operate to Athens, London, Rome, Beirut, Paris, Malta, Algiers, Moscow, Cotonou and Tunis.

Post and Broadcasting. Tripoli is connected by telegraph cable with Malta and by microwave link with Bengardane (Tunis). There are overseas wireless-telegraph stations at Benghazi and Tripoli, and radio-telephone services connect Libya with most countries of western Europe. In 1971 some 41,495 telephones were in use and in 1982 there were 150,000 radio sets and 160,000 television receivers.

Newspapers. There was (1984) one daily in Tripoli with a circulation of about 40,000.

JUSTICE, RELIGION, EDUCATION AND WELFARE

Justice. The Civil, Commercial and Criminal codes are based mainly on the Egyptian model. Matters of personal status of family or succession matters affecting Moslems are dealt with in special courts according to the Moslem law. All other matters, civil, commercial and criminal, are tried in the ordinary courts, which have jurisdiction over everyone.

There are civil and penal courts in Tripoli and Benghazi, with subsidiary courts at Misurata and Derna; courts of assize in Tripoli and Benghazi, and courts of appeal in Tripoli and Benghazi.

Religion. Islam is declared the State religion, but the right of others to practise their religions is provided for.

Education. There were (1980–81) 675,000 pupils in primary schools, 223,000 in preparatory schools and 40,000 in secondary schools. There are 2 universities of Al Fatah (in Tripoli) and Garyounes (in Benghazi).

Social Welfare. In 1980 there were 14,472 hospital beds and 4,300 physicians and dentists.

DIPLOMATIC REPRESENTATIVES

UK broke off diplomatic relations with Libya on 22 April 1984. Saudi Arabia looks after Libyan interests in UK and Italy looks after UK's interests in Libya.

USA suspended all embassy activities in Tripoli on 2 May 1980.

Of Libya to the United Nations
Ambassador: Dr Ali A. Treiki.

Books of Reference

Allen, J. A., *Libya: The Experience of Oil.* London and Boulder, 1981.—*Libya since Independence.* London, 1982
Ansell, M. O., and al-Arif, I. M., *The Libyan Revolution.* London, 1972
Bianco, M., *Gadafi: Voice from the Desert.* London, 1975
Cooley, J. K., *Libyan Sandstorm: The Complete Account of Qaddafi's Revolution.* London and New York, 1983
Fergiani, M. B., *The Libyan Jamahiriya.* London, 1984
Waddhams, F. C., *The Libyan Oil Industry.* London, 1980
Wright, J., *Libya: A Modern History.* London, 1982

LIECHTENSTEIN

Capital: Vaduz
Population: 26,512 (1983)
GNP per capita: US$16,440 (1980)

HISTORY. The Principality of Liechtenstein, situated between the Austrian province of Vorarlberg and the Swiss cantons of St Gallen and Graubünden, is a sovereign state whose history dates back to 3 May 1342, when Count Hartmann III became ruler of the county of Vaduz. Additions were later made to the count's domains, and by 1434 the territory reached its present boundaries. It consists of the two former counties of Schellenberg and Vaduz (until 1806 immediate fiefs of the Roman Empire). The former in 1699 and the latter in 1712 came into the possession of the house of Liechtenstein and, by diploma of 23 Jan. 1719, granted by the Emperor Charles VI, the two counties were constituted as the Principality of Liechtenstein.

AREA AND POPULATION. Liechtenstein is bounded on the east by Austria and the west by Switzerland. Area, 160 sq. km (61·8 sq. miles); population, of Alemannic race (census 1980), 25,215; estimate, 1983, 26,512. In 1983 there were 350 births and 156 deaths. Population of Vaduz (census 1980), 4,606; estimate, 1983, 4,896.

REIGNING PRINCE. Francis Joseph II, born 16 Aug. 1906; succeeded his great uncle, 26 July 1938; married on 7 March 1943 to Countess Gina von Wilczek; there are 4 sons, Princes Hans Adam (*heir apparent*, born 14 Feb. 1945; married on 30 July 1967 to Countess Marie Aglaë Kinsky), Philipp Erasmus (married on 11 Sept. 1971 to Isabelle de l'Arbre de Malander), Nikolaus Ferdinand (married on 20 March 1982 to Princess Margaretha of Luxembourg) and Franz Josef Wenzel, and one daughter, Princess Nora Elisabeth. The monarchy is hereditary in the male line.

National flag: Horizontally blue over red, with a gold coronet in the first quarter.

National anthem: Oben am jungen Rhein (words by H. H. Jauch, 1850; tune, 'God save the Queen').

CONSTITUTION AND GOVERNMENT. Liechtenstein is a constitutional monarchy ruled by the hereditary princes of the House of Liechtenstein. The present constitution of 5 Oct. 1921 provides for a unicameral parliament (Diet) of 15 members elected for 4 years. Election is by universal adult suffrage and is on the basis of proportional representation. The prince can call and dismiss the parliament. On parliamentary recommendation, he appoints the prime minister and the 4 councillors for a 4-year term. Any group of 900 persons or any 3 communes may propose legislation (initiative). Bills passed by the parliament may be submitted to popular referendum. A law is valid when it receives a majority approval by the parliament and the prince's signed concurrence. The capital and seat of government is Vaduz and there are 10 more communes all connected by modern roads. The 11 communes are fully independent administrative bodies within the laws of the principality. They levy additional taxes to the state taxes. Since Feb. 1921 Liechtenstein has had the Swiss currency, and since 29 March 1923 has been united with Switzerland in a customs union. Switzerland has also since 1919 represented the Principality diplomatically.

At the elections for the Diet, on 7 Feb. 1982, the Fatherland Union obtained 8 seats, the opposition Progressive Citizens' Party, 7 seats.

Head of Government: Hans Brunhart.

INTERNATIONAL RELATIONS

Membership. Liechtenstein is a member of EFTA, the Council of Europe and the International Court of Justice.

ECONOMY

Budget. Budget estimates for 1984: Revenue, 272,692,000 Swiss francs; expenditure, 269,254,000 Swiss francs. There is no public debt.

Currency. The Swiss *franc*.

Banking. There were (1984) 3 banks: Liechtensteinische Landesbank, Bank in Liechtenstein Ltd, Verwaltungs-und Privatbank Ltd.

Weights and Measures. The metric system is in force.

ENERGY AND NATURAL RESOURCES

Electricity. Electricity produced in 1983 was 52·28m. kwh.

Agriculture. The rearing of cattle, for which the fine alpine pastures are well suited, is highly developed. In March 1984 there were 6,260 cattle (including 2,758 milch cows), 165 horses, 2,265 sheep, 123 goats, 3,575 pigs. Total production of dairy produce, 1983, 10,558,022 kg.

INDUSTRY AND TRADE

Industry. The country has a great variety of light industries (textiles, ceramics, steel screws, precision instruments, canned food, pharmaceutical products, heating appliances, etc.).

Since 1945 Liechtenstein has changed from a predominantly agricultural country to a highly industrialized country. The farming population has gone down from 70% in 1930 to only 3% in 1983. The rapid change-over has led to the immigration of foreign workers (Austrians, Germans, Italians, Spaniards). Industrial undertakings in 1983 employed 5,978 workers earning 259m. Swiss francs.

Commerce. Exports of home produce in 1983 amounted to 919m. Swiss francs. 30·7% went to EFTA countries, of which Switzerland took 210·8m. (22·9%) and 37·9% went to EEC countries.

Total trade with UK is included with Switzerland from 1968.

Tourism. In 1983, 79,426 foreign visitors stayed in Liechtenstein.

COMMUNICATIONS

Roads. There are 250 km of roads. Postal buses are the chief means of public transportation within the country and to Austria and Switzerland.

Railways. The 18·5 km of main railway passing through the country is operated by Austrian Federal Railways.

Post and Broadcasting. In 1983 there were 11,480 telephones, 426 telex, 8,234 wireless sets and 7,743 television sets. The post and telegraphs are administered by Switzerland.

Cinemas. There were 3 cinemas in 1983.

Newspapers. In 1983 there were 2 daily newspapers with a total circulation of 14,700.

JUSTICE, RELIGION, EDUCATION AND WELFARE

Justice. The principality has its own civil and penal codes. The lowest court is the county court, *Landgericht*, presided over by one judge, which decides minor civil cases and summary criminal offences. The criminal court, *Kriminalgericht*, with a bench of 5 judges is for major crimes. Another court of mixed jurisdiction is the court of assizes (with 3 judges) for misdemeanours. The superior court, *Obergericht*, and Supreme Court, *Oberster Gerichtshof*, are courts of appeal for civil and criminal cases (both with benches of 5 judges). An administrative court of appeal from government actions and the State Court determines the constitutionality of laws.

Police. The principality has no army. Police force, 42; auxiliary police, 20 (1984).

Religion. In 1983, 85·5% of the population was Roman Catholic and 8·6% was Protestant.

Education (1984). In 14 primary, 3 upper, 4 secondary, 1 grammar and 3 (for backward children) schools there were 3,700 pupils and 330 teachers. There is also an evening technical school, a music school and a children's pedagogic-welfare day school.

Health. In 1984 there was 1 hospital, but Liechtenstein has an agreement with the Swiss cantons of St Gallen and Graubünden that her citizens may use certain hospitals.

DIPLOMATIC REPRESENTATIVES

British Consul-General: G. N. Smith (resident in Zürich).
USA Consul-General: Dr Alfred P. Brainard (resident in Zürich).

Books of Reference

Statistical Information: Amt für Volkswirtschaft, Vaduz.

Rechenschaftsbericht der Fürstlichen Regierung. Vaduz. Annual, from 1922
Jahrbuch des Historischen Vereins. Vaduz. Annual since 1901
Kranz, W., *The Principality of Liechtenstein.* Press and Information Office. 5th ed. Vaduz, 1981
The Economy of the Principality of Liechtenstein. Press and Information Office, Vaduz, 1984
Batliner, E. H., *Das Geld- und Kreditwesen des Fürstentums Liechtenstein in Vergangenheit und Gegenwart.* 1959
Green, B., *Valley of Peace.* Vaduz, 1967
Larke, T. A. T., *Index and Thesaurus of Liechtenstein.* 2nd ed. Berkeley, 1984
Malin, G., *Kunstführer Fürstentum Liechtenstein.* Berne, 1977
Raton, P., *Liechtenstein: History and Institutions of the Principality.* Vaduz, 1970
Seger, O., *A Survey of Liechtenstein History.* 2nd English ed. Vaduz, 1970
Steger, G., *Fürst und Landtag nach Liechtensteinischem Recht.* Vaduz, 1950

LUXEMBOURG

Capital: Luxembourg
Population: 365,800 (1984)
GNP per capita: US$15,910 (1981)

Grand-Duché de Luxembourg

HISTORY. The country formed part of the Holy Roman Empire until it was conquered by the French in 1795. In 1815 the Grand Duchy of Luxembourg was formed under the house of Orange-Nassau, also sovereigns of the Netherlands. In 1839 the Walloon-speaking area was joined to Belgium. In 1890 the personal union with the Netherlands ended with the accession of a member of another branch of the house of Nassau, Grand Duke Adolphe of Nassau-Weilburg.

AREA AND POPULATION. Luxembourg has an area of 2,586 sq. km (998 sq. miles) and is bounded on the west by Belgium, south by France, east by the Federal Republic of Germany. The population (1984) was 365,800. The capital, Luxembourg, had 79,000 inhabitants; Esch-Alzette, the centre of the mining district, 25,142; Differdange, 8,588; Dudelange, 14,074, and Petange, 6,416. In 1983 the foreign population was about 96,700.

Vital statistics (1983): 4,185 births, 4,129 deaths, 1,982 marriages.

CLIMATE. Cold, raw winters with snow covering the ground for up to a month are features of the upland areas. The remainder resembles Belgium in its climate, with rain evenly distributed throughout the year. Jan. 31°F (0·5°C), July 63°F (17·5°C). Annual rainfall 29·6″ (740 mm).

REIGNING GRAND DUKE. Jean, born 5 Jan. 1921, son of Grand Duchess Charlotte and the late Prince Felix of Bourbon-Parma; succeeded 12 Nov. 1964 on the abdication of his mother; married to Princess Joséphine-Charlotte of Belgium, 9 April 1953. *Offspring:* Princess Marie Astrid, born 17 Feb. 1954, married Christian of Habsbourg-Lorraine 6 Feb. 1982; Prince Henri, *heir apparent*, born 16 April 1955, married Maria Teresa Mestre 14 Feb. 1981; (*Offspring:* Prince Guillaume Jean Joseph Marie, born 11 Nov. 1981, Prince Felix Marie Guillaume, born 3 June 1984). Prince Jean and Princess Margaretha (married Prince Nikolaus of Liechtenstein 20 March 1982), born 15 May 1957; Prince Guillaume, born 1 May 1963.

The civil list is fixed at 300,000 gold francs per annum, to be reconsidered at the beginning of each reign.

On 28 Sept. 1919 a referendum was taken in Luxembourg to decide on the political and economic future of the country. The voting resulted as follows: For the reigning Grand Duchess, 66,811; for the continuance of the Nassau-Braganza dynasty under another Grand Duchess, 1,286; for another dynasty, 889; for a republic, 16,885; for an economic union with France, 60,133; for an economic union with Belgium, 22,242. But France refused in favour of Belgium, and on 22 Dec. 1921 the Chamber of the Grand Duchy passed a Bill for the economic union between Belgium and Luxembourg. The agreement, which is for 60 years, provides for the disappearance of the customs barrier between the two countries and the use of Belgian, in addition to Luxembourg, currency as legal tender in the Grand Duchy. It came into force on 1 May 1922.

The Grand Duchy was under German occupation from 10 May 1940 to 10 Sept. 1944. The Grand Duchess Charlotte and the Government carried on an independent administration in London. Civil government was restored in Oct. 1944.

National flag: Three horizontal stripes of red, white and light blue.

National anthem: Ons Hemecht (words by M. Lentz, 1859; tune by J. A. Zinnen).

CONSTITUTION AND GOVERNMENT. The Grand Duchy of Luxembourg is a constitutional monarchy, the hereditary sovereignty being in the Nassau family. The constitution of 17 Oct. 1868 was revised in 1919, 1948, 1956 and 1972. The revision of 1948 has abolished the 'perpetually neutral' status of the country and introduced the concepts of right to work, social security, health services, freedom of trade and industry, and recognition of trade unions. The revision of 1956 provides for the devolution of executive, legislative and judicial powers to international institutions.

The national language is Luxemburgish; French, German and English are widely used.

The country forms 4 electoral districts. An elector must be a citizen (male or female) of Luxembourg and have completed 18 years of age; to be eligible for election the citizen must have completed 21 years of age.

The Chamber of Deputies consists of 25 Christian Social, 21 Socialists, 14 Democrats, and 2 Communists, and 2 Green alternatives (Ecologists) deputies (elections of 17 June 1984). Members are elected for 5 years; they receive a salary and a travelling allowance.

The head of the state takes part in the legislative power, exercises the executive power and has a certain part in the judicial power. The constitution leaves to the sovereign the right to organize the Government, which consists of a Minister of State, who is President of the Government, and of at least 3 Ministers.

The Cabinet was, in Aug. 1984, composed as follows:

President of the Government, Minister of State, Minister for Finance: Jacques Santer.

Vice-President of the Government, Foreign Affairs, Foreign Trade and Co-operation, Economy and Middle Classes, Exchequer: Jacques F. Poos. *Health and Social Security:* Benny Berg. *Justice, Cultural Affairs, Environment:* Robert Krieps. *National Education and Youth, Tourism:* Fernand Boden. *Interior, Family Affairs, Social Solidarity:* Jean Spautz. *Labour, Finance and Budget:* Jean-Claude Juncker. *Transport, Public Works, Energy:* Marcel Schlechter. *Agriculture and Viticulture, Armed Forces, Civil Service, Physical Education and Sports:* Marc Fischbach. *Secretary of State for Economy:* Johny Lahure. *Secretary of State for Agriculture and Viticulture:* René Steichen. *Secretary of State for Foreign Affairs, Foreign Trade and Co-operation, Middle Classes:* Robert Goebbels.

Besides the Cabinet there is a Council of State. It deliberates on proposed laws and Bills, and on amendments; it also gives administrative decisions and expresses its opinion regarding any other question referred to it by the Grand Duke or the Government. The Council of State is composed of 21 members chosen for life by the sovereign, who also chooses a president from among them each year.

DEFENCE. A law passed by Parliament on 29 June 1967 abolished compulsory service and instituted a battalion-size army of volunteers enlisted for 3 years. Strength (1985) 720. The defence estimates for 1985 amounted to 1,715m. francs. Luxembourg is an original member of NATO and the battalion is committed to NATO ACE mobile force.

INTERNATIONAL RELATIONS

Membership. Luxembourg is a member of the UN, Benelux, the EEC, OECD, the Council of Europe, NATO and WEU.

ECONOMY

Budget. Revenue and expenditure (including extraordinary) for years ending 30 April (in 1m. francs):

	1980	*1981*	*1982*[1]	*1983*[1]	*1984*[2]	*1985*[2]
Revenue	48,244·0	53,411·2	59,897·5	71,921·4	68,464·3	73,764·9
Expenditure	48,918·4	54,968·9	59,927·2	74,030·1	67,656·4	70,440·6

[1] Provisional. [2] Budget.

Consolidated debt at 31 Dec. 1983 amounted to 37,076·6m. francs (long-term) and 3,554·5m. francs (short-term).

Currency. On 14 Oct. 1944 the Luxembourg *franc* was fixed at par value with the Belgian franc. Notes of the Belgian National Bank are legal tender in Luxembourg.

Banking. On 31 Dec. 1983 there were 303,285 depositors in the State Savings Bank with a total of 35,211m. francs to their credit. There are 114 banks established in Luxembourg which has become an international financial centre.

Weights and Measures. The metric system is in force.

ENERGY AND NATURAL RESOURCES

Electricity. Power production was 801m. kwh. in 1983.

Minerals. The mining and metallurgical industries are the most important. In 1983 production (in tonnes) of pig-iron, 2,316,300; of steel, 3,293,760.

Agriculture. Agriculture is carried on by about 7,500 of the population; 127,422 hectares were under cultivation in 1983. The principal crops are potatoes, barley, beet, oats and wheat.

Livestock (1983): 1,363 horses, 224,645 cattle, 71,957 pigs, 3,540 sheep.

INDUSTRY AND TRADE

Commerce. By treaty of 5 Sept. 1944, signed in London, and the treaty of 14 March 1947, signed in The Hague, the Grand Duchy, together with Belgium and the Netherlands, became a party to the Benelux Customs Union, which came into force on 1 Jan. 1948. For further particulars *see* p. 199.

Total trade between Luxembourg and UK included with Belgium from 1974.

Tourism. In 1983 there were 406,000 tourists.

COMMUNICATIONS

Roads. In 1983 the network had a total of 5,157 km. Motor vehicles registered in Luxembourg on 1 Jan. 1984 included 145,850 passenger cars, 9,110 trucks, 700 buses, 17,610 tractors and special vehicles.

Railways. In 1983 there were 270 km of railway (standard gauge) of which 162 km electrified.

Aviation. Findel is the airport for Luxembourg.

Post and Broadcasting. In 1982 the telephone system had more than 5,200 km of telegraph and telephone line, 142,100 telephones (1983), 104 post offices and 393 telegraph offices. *Compagnie Luxembourgeoise de Télédiffusion* broadcasts 1 programme in Luxembourgian on FM. Powerful transmitters on long-, medium- and short-waves are used for commercial and religious programmes in French, Dutch, German, English and Italian. Ten TV programmes are broadcast. Colour transmission by SECAM system.

Cinemas (1983). There were 11 cinemas.

Newspapers (1984). There were 5 daily newspapers with an aggregate circulation of 140,000.

RELIGION, EDUCATION AND WELFARE

Religion. The population is Catholic, save (31 Dec. 1970) 3,900 Protestants, 700 Jews, 2,100 belonging to other denominations and 3,700 without religion (or having given no indication on this subject). The Protestant Church is organized on an interdenominational basis.

Education (1983–84). Education is compulsory for all children between the ages of 6 and 15. The nursery schools had 7,827 pupils; primary schools had 25,806[1] pupils; technical secondary schools, 16,212[1] pupils; secondary schools, 9,009[1] pupils; the Superior Institute of Technology, 298 pupils; pedagogic education, 150 pupils; university studies, 350 pupils.

[1] Provisional.

Health. In 1982 there were 580 doctors and 4,816 hospital beds.

DIPLOMATIC REPRESENTATIVES

Of Luxembourg in Great Britain (27 Wilton Crescent, London, SWIX 8SD)
Ambassador: Roger Hastert, CMG.

Of Great Britain in Luxembourg (28 Boulevard Royal, Luxembourg)
Ambassador and Consul-General: Richard Oliver Miles, CMG.

Of Luxembourg in the USA (2200 Massachusetts Ave., NW, Washington, D.C., 20008)
Ambassador: Paul Peters.

Of the USA in Luxembourg (22 Blvd. Emmanuel Servais, Luxembourg)
Ambassador: John E. Dolibois.

Of Luxembourg to the United Nations
Ambassador: André Philippe.

Books of Reference

Statistical Information: The Service Central de la Statistique et des Études Économiques was founded in 1900 and reorganized in 1962 (19–21 boulevard Royal, C.P. 304 Luxembourg-City). *Director:* Georges Als. Main publications: *Bulletin du Statec.—Annuaire statistique.—Cahiers économiques.*

Bulletin de Documentation. Government Information Service. From 1945 (monthly)
The Institutions of the Grand Duchy of Luxembourg. Press and Information Service, Luxembourg, 1982
Als, G., *Le Luxembourg, situation politique, économique et sociale.* Luxembourg, 1982
Calmes, C., *Au Fil de l'Histoire.* Luxembourg, 1977
Heiderscheid, A., *Aspects de Sociologie Religieuse du Diocèse de Luxembourg.* 2 vols. Luxembourg, 1961
Hury, C. and Christophory, J., *Luxembourg.* [Bibliography] Oxford and Santa Barbara, 1981
Majerus, P., *Le Luxembourg independant.* Luxembourg, 1948.—*L'État Luxembourgeois.* Luxembourg, 1983
Newcomer, J., *The Grand Duchy of Luxembourg: The Evolution of Nationhood, 963 A.D. to 1983.* Washington, 1983
Trausch, G., *Le Luxembourg à l'Époque Contemporaine.* Luxembourg, 1975

Archives of the State: Luxembourg-City. *Director:* Paul Spang.
National Library: Luxembourg-City, 14a Boulevard Royal. *Director:* Jules Christophory.

MADAGASCAR

Capital: Antananarivo
Population: 9·74m. (1984)
GNP per capita: US$330 (1981)

Repoblika Demokratika n'i Madagaskar

HISTORY. Madagascar was discovered by the Portuguese, Diego Diaz, in 1500. The island was unified under the Imérina monarchy between 1797 and 1861, but French claims to a protectorate led to hostilities culminating in the establishment of a protectorate on 30 Sept. 1895. The monarchy was abolished and Madagascar became a French Colony on 6 Aug. 1896.

Madagascar became an Overseas Territory in 1946, and on 14 Oct. 1958, following a referendum, was proclaimed the autonomous Malagasy Republic within the French Community, achieving full independence on 26 June 1960.

The government of Philibert Tsiranana, President from independence, resigned on 18 May 1972 and executive powers were given to Maj.-Gen. Gabriel Ramanantsoa, who replaced Tsiranana as President on 11 Oct. 1972. On 5 Feb. 1975, Col. Richard Ratsimandrava became Head of State, but was assassinated 6 days later. A National Military Directorate under Brig.-Gen. Gilles Andriamahazo was established on 12 Feb. On 15 June it handed over power to a Supreme Revolutionary Council (SRC) under Didier Ratsiraka.

AREA AND POPULATION. Madagascar is situated off the south-east coast of Africa, from which it is separated by the Mozambique channel, the least distance between island and continent being 250 miles; its length is 980 miles; greatest breadth, 360 miles.

The area is 587,041 sq. km (226,658 sq. miles). In 1975 (census) the population was 7,603,790. Estimate (1984) 9,735,000.

Province	*Area in sq. km*	*Population 1978*	*Chief town*	*Population 1978*
Antseranana	42,725	620,228	Antseranana	48,000
Mahajanga	152,165	857,610	Mahajanga	57,500
Toamasina	72,212	1,254,639	Toamasina	59,100
Antananarivo	57,775	2,322,019	Antananarivo	400,000
Fianarantsoa	100,326	1,908,465	Fianarantsoa	55,500
Toliary	162,283	1,084,083	Toliary	34,000

Vital statistics, 1975: Births, 338,850; deaths, 100,450.

The indigenous population are of Malayo-Polynesian stock, divided into 18 linguistic groups of which the principal are Merina (30%) of the central plateau, the Betsimisaraka (15%) of the east coast, and the Betsileo (14%) of the southern plateau. Foreign communities include Europeans, mainly French (40,000), Indians (16,000), Chinese (9,000), Comorians and Arabs.

CLIMATE. A tropical climate, but the mountains cause big variations in rainfall, which is very heavy in the east and very light in the west. Antananarivo. Jan. 70°F (21·1°C), July 59°F (15°C). Annual rainfall 54″ (1,350 mm). Toamasina. Jan. 80°F (26·7°C), July 70°F (21·1°C). Annual rainfall 128″ (3,256 mm).

CONSTITUTION AND GOVERNMENT. The new Constitution of the Democratic Republic of Madagascar was approved by referendum on 21 Dec. 1975 and came into force on 30 Dec. It provides for a bicameral Parliament, comprising a Senate of 50 members and a National People's Assembly of 137 members elected by universal suffrage for a 5-year term from the single list of the *Front National pour la Défense de la Révolution Malgache;* following the general elections held on 28 Aug. 1983, this comprised 117 members of the *Avant-garde de* *la Révolution Malgache,* 9 of the *Parti du Congrès de l'Indépendence* and 11 others. Executive power is vested in the President, elected for 7 years, who appoints a Council of Ministers to assist him, with the guidance of the 20-member Supreme Revolutionary Council.

President: Didier Ratsiraka (re-elected 7 Nov. 1982).

The Council of Ministers in Oct. 1983 was composed as follows:

Prime Minister: Lieut.-Col. Désiré Rakotoarijaona.

Foreign Affairs: Jean Bemanjara. *Defence:* Capt de Vaisseau Guy Sibon. *Interior:* Ampy Portos. *Civil Service and Labour:* Georges Ruphin. *Finance:* Pascal Rakotomavo. *Health:* Jean-Jacques Séraphin. *Commerce:* Georges Solofoson. *Industry, Energy and Mines:* René Andrianarivo Tantely. *Animal Production, Water Resources and Forestry:* Joseph Randrianasolo. *Agricultural Production and Agrarian Reform:* Yves Léone Ramélison. *Posts and Telecommunications:* Rakotovao Andriantiana. *Secondary and Basic Education:* Charles Zany. *Higher Education:* Ignace Rakoto. *Scientific Research:* Antoine Zafera. *Information and Ideological Guidance:* Bruno Rakotomavo. *Revolutionary Art and Culture:* Gisêle Rabesahala. *Transport, Supply and Tourism:* Joseph Bedo. *Public Works:* Lieut.-Col. Victor Ramahatra. *Population, Social Welfare, Youth and Sport:* Dr Rémi Tiandraza. *Justice:* Gilbert Sambson. *Special Economic Advisor:* Mirina Andriamanerasoa.

National flag: Horizontally red over green, in the hoist a vertical white strip.

National anthem: Ry tanindrazanay malala ô!

Malagasy, which is a language of Malayo-Polynesian origin, is the official language. French and English are understood and taught in Malagasy schools.

Local Government: The six provinces are sub-divided into 18 prefectures, which in turn are divided in 92 sub-prefectures and finally into 11,000 *fokontany* (the traditional communal divisions). Each level is governed by an elected council.

DEFENCE

Army. The Army is organized in 2 battalion groups, and 1 engineer, 1 signals, 1 service and 7 construction regiments. Equipment includes PT-76 light tanks and M-8 armoured cars. Strength (1985) 20,000.

Navy. The small maritime guard in 1985 had a strength of 600 (including a company of marines), equipped with 1 large patrol craft, 5 patrol boats, 1 landing ship, 7 small landing craft and a large trawler training ship.

Air Force. Created in 1961, the Malagasy Air Force received its first combat equipment in 1978, with the arrival of 8 MiG-21 and 4 MiG-17 fighters, plus flying and ground staff instructors, from North Korea. Other equipment includes An-12 and 4 An-26 turboprop transports, 6 L-39 jet trainers, 1 Britten-Norman Defender armed transport, 5 C-47s, 1 HS. 748 and 2 Yak-40s for VIP use, 1 Aztec, 3 Cessna Skymasters, 4 Cessna 172Ms and 6 helicopters, comprising 2 Mi-8s, 1 Bell 47, 1 Alouette II and 2 Alouette IIIs. Personnel about 500.

INTERNATIONAL RELATIONS

Membership. Madagascar is a member of UN, OAU and is an ACP state of EEC.

ECONOMY

Budget. The general budget 1982, envisaged expenditure of 274,530m. FMG.

Currency. The Malagasy *franc* is divided into 100 *centimes*. In March 1985, £1 = 744·60 FMG; US$1 = 719·84 FMG.

Banking. A Central Bank was formed in July 1973, replacing the former *Institut d'Emission Malgache* as the central bank of issue. All commercial banking and insurance was nationalised in June 1975. Industrial development is financed through the *Bankin'ny Indostria,* and other commercial banking undertaken by the *Bankin'ny Tantsaha Mpamokatra* and the *Banky Fampandrosoana ny Varotra.*

Weights and Measures. The metric system is in use.

ENERGY AND NATURAL RESOURCES

Electricity. Production (1983) 360,186,000 kwh.

Oil. The oil refinery at Toamasina has a capacity of 12,000 bbls a day.

Minerals. Mining production (in tonnes) in 1983 included: Graphite, 13,496; chromite, 42,920; zircon, 2,000; beryl, (industrial), 120,514; gold, 2·6 kg; garnet, (industrial), 2,065.

Agriculture. In 1978, 83% of the working population was employed in agriculture. The principal agricultural products in 1982 were (in 1,000 tonnes): Rice, 2,000; cassava, 1,807; mangoes, 175; bananas, 280; potatoes, 271; sugar-cane, 1,525; maize, 127; sweet potatoes, 422; coffee, 80; oranges, 88; pineapples, 58; groundnuts, 38; sisal, 20; cotton, 31; tobacco, 5.

Cattle breeding and agriculture are the chief occupations. There were, in 1983, 10,322,000 cattle, 1·3m. pigs, 630,000 sheep, 1·75m. goats and 18m. poultry.

Forestry. The forests contain many valuable woods, while gum, resins and plants for tanning, dyeing and medicinal purposes abound.

Fisheries. The fish catch in 1980 was 54,000 tonnes.

INDUSTRY AND TRADE

Industry. Industry, hitherto confined mainly to the processing of agricultural products, is now extending to cover other fields.

Commerce. Trade in 1m. FMG:

	1979	*1980*	*1981*	*1982*
Imports (c.i.f)	135,319	126,775	147,977	148,601
Exports (f.o.b)	83,826	84,781	85,742	108,347

The chief exports in 1980 were coffee (53%) and cloves (8%); France took 20% of exports, the USA 20% and Japan 10%, while France provided 41% of imports, Federal Republic of Germany 10% and Japan 5%.

Total trade between Madagascar and UK (British Department of Trade returns, in £1,000 sterling):

	1981	*1982*	*1983*	*1984*
Imports to UK	2,937	3,355	3,731	1,529
Exports and re-exports from UK	5,322	3,548	4,907	6,936

COMMUNICATIONS

Roads. In 1979 there were 27,556 km of roads of which 4,526 km bitumenized, with 57,000 passenger cars and 50,000 commercial vehicles (including buses).

Railways. In 1983 there were 883 km of railways, all metre gauge. In 1983, 2·5m. passengers and 622,220m. tonnes of cargo were transported.

Aviation. Air France and Air Madagascar connect Antananarivo with Paris, Alitalia connects with Rome. Several weekly services operated by Air Madagascar connect the capital with the ports and the chief inland towns. The main airfields are at Ivato, Toamasina, Toliary and Mahajanga. In 1979, 326,275 passengers arrived and 8,684 tonnes of cargo arrived and departed on international flights.

Shipping. In 1981 there were 232,000 tons loaded and 705,000 tons unloaded at Toamasina, the main port, and 86,000 tons loaded and 282,000 tons unloaded at Mahajanga and other minor ports. In 1980, registered merchant marine was 56 vessels (of more than 100 GRT) with a total of 91,211 GRT.

Post and Broadcasting. There were in 1971, 547 post offices and agencies and 55 wireless telegraph stations. The telegraph line has a length of 17,400 km. There were 66,000 km of telephone line and, in 1978, 28,686 telephone subscribers. In Dec. 1979, there were 1·15m. radio receivers and (1980) 9,000 television receivers.

Cinemas. There were, in 1974, 31 cinemas with a seating capacity of 12,500.

JUSTICE, RELIGION, EDUCATION AND WELFARE

Justice. The Supreme Court and the Court of Appeal are in Antananarivo. In each provincial capital there is a Court of First Instance (for civil and commercial cases) and a *juge de paix* (for criminal cases).

Religion. 50% of the population follow animist religions; 25% are Roman Catholic, 20% Protestant (mainly belonging to the Fiangonan'i Jesosy Kristy eto Madagaskar) and 5% Moslem.

Education. Education is compulsory from 6 to 14 years of age in the primary schools. In 1978 there were 1,311,000 pupils and 23,937 teachers in public primary schools, while in 1976 there were 114,468 pupils in secondary schools and about 7,000 in technical schools. The University of Madagascar has a main campus at Antananarivo and 5 university centres in the other provincial capitals, with 33,449 students in 1982. There are also 4 agricultural schools at Nanisana, Ambatondrazaka, Marovoay and Ivoloina.

Health. In 1978 there were 749 hospitals and dispensaries with 16,401 beds; there were also 811 doctors, 88 dentists, 86 pharmacists, 1,227 midwives and 2,309 nursing personnel.

DIPLOMATIC REPRESENTATIVES

Of Madagascar in Great Britain
Ambassador: Jean Ernest Bezaza (resides in Paris).

Of Great Britain in Madagascar (Immeuble Ny Havana, Cite de 67 Ha, Antananarivo)
Ambassador: D. Malcolm McBain, MVO.

Of Madagascar in the USA (2374 Massachusetts Ave., NW, Washington, D.C., 20008)
Ambassador: Leon M. Rajaobelina.

Of USA in Madagascar (14 rue Rainitovo, Antsahavola, Antananarivo)
Ambassador: Robert B. Keating.

Of Madagascar to the United Nations
Ambassador: Blaise Rabetafika.

Books of Reference

Statistical Information: The Service de Statistique Générale in Antananarivo published the *Bulletin mensuel de Madagascar* (from 1971); continuation of the trimestrial *Bulletin de statistique générale* (1949–71), the *Revue de Madagascar,* the *Madagascar à travers ses provinces* (latest issue, 1953), the *Annuaire Statistique de Madagascar* (vol. 1, 1938–51, published 1953, the *Situation Economique au Janvier 1968, Population de Madagascar au 1er Jan. 1971,* and the *Statistiques du Commerce Extérieur de Madagascar).*
Bulletin de l'Académie Malgache (from 1902)
Brown, M., *Madagascar Rediscovered.* London, 1978
Deschamps, H., *Histoire de Madagascar.* Paris, 4th ed. 1972
Heseltine, N., *Madagascar.* London and New York, 1971

MALAWI

Capital: Lilongwe
Population: 6·1m. (1981)
GNP per capita: US$200 (1981)

HISTORY. Malawi was formerly the Nyasaland (until 1907 British Central Africa) Protectorate, constituted on 15 May 1891.

Nyasaland became a self-governing country on 1 Feb. 1963, and on 6 July 1964 an independent member of the Commonwealth under the name of Malawi. It became a republic on 6 July 1966.

AREA AND POPULATION. Malawi lies along the southern and western shores of Lake Malawi (the third largest lake in Africa), and is otherwise bounded north by Tanzania, south by Mozambique and west by Zambia. Land area (excluding inland water of Lakes Palombe, Chilwa and Chiuta) 36,325 sq. miles, divided into 3 regions and 24 districts, each administered by a District Commissioner.

Lake Malawi waters belonging to Malawi are 9,250 sq. miles and the whole Lake Malawi (including the waters under Mozambique by an agreement made between the two countries in 1950) is 11,650 sq. miles.

Census 1977, 5,547,460 (males, 2,673,589). Estimate (1981), 6·1m. Over 90% of the population live in rural areas.

Population of main towns (census 1977) was as follows: Blantyre, 219,011; Lilongwe, 98,718; Zomba, 24,234; Mzuzu, 16,108.

Population of the regions, 1966 (and census 1977): Northern, 497,491 (648,853); Central, 1,474,952 (2,143,716); Southern, 2,067,140 (2,754,891).

CLIMATE. The tropical climate is marked by a dry season from May to Oct. and a wet season for the remaining months. Rainfall amounts are variable, within the range of 29–100″ (725–2,500 mm), and maximum temperatures average 75–89°F (24–32°C), and minimum temperatures 58–67°F (14·4–19·4°C). Lilongwe. Jan. 73°F (22·8°C), July 60°F (15·6°C). Annual rainfall 36″ (900 mm). Blantyre. Jan. 75°F (23·9°C), July 63°F (17·2°C). Annual rainfall 45″ (1,125 mm). Zomba. Jan. 73°F (22·8°C), July 63°F (17·2°C). Annual rainfall 54″ (1,344 mm).

CONSTITUTION AND GOVERNMENT. The President of the republic is also head of Government and of the Malawi Congress Party. Malawi is a one-party state. Parliament is composed of 101 elected members elected for up to 5 years, and any number of nominated members. Elections were held in June 1983.

Life President, External Affairs, Agriculture, Justice, Works and Supplies: Ngwazi Dr H. Kamuzu Banda. (Took office 6 July 1966 and became Life President on 6 July 1971).

The Cabinet in Jan. 1985 was composed as follows:

Finance: Edward Chitsulo Isaac Bwanali. *Trade, Industry and Tourism:* Stephen Chimwemwe Hara. *Education and Culture:* Louis J. Chimango. *Local Government:* B. L. Kapichila Banda. *Labour:* E. C. Katola Phiri. *Health:* Dalton S. Katopola. *Youth:* Stanford Demba. *Transport and Communications:* Wadson B. Deleza. *Community Services:* George Afwawaka Kandawire. *Forestry and Natural Resources:* Poulton Mtenje. *At Large:* Sydney B. Somanje. *Without Portfolio, Administrative Secretary of Malawi Congress Party:* Robson Watayachanga Chirwa.

National flag: Three equal horizontal stripes of black, red, green, with a red rising sun on the centre of the black stripe.

DEFENCE. All services form part of the Army and have a strength (1985) 4,650.

Army. The army is organized into 3 infantry battalions and 1 support battalion. Equipment includes scout cars.

Navy. There are 3 small lake patrol boats and 1 gunboat. Uniformed personnel in 1985 totalled 30.

Air wing. To support the infantry battalion, the Air Wing has 4 C-47 Transport aircraft, 1 Defender armed light transport, 12 Do 28D Skyservant light transports, 6 Do 27 training aircraft, and 6 Puma and 1 Alouette III helicopters. An HS 125 jet is used for VIP transport.

INTERNATIONAL RELATIONS

Membership. Malawi is a member of UN, the Commonwealth, OAU, and is an ACP state of EEC.

ECONOMY

Planning. The Government of Malawi operates a 3-year 'rolling' public-sector investment programme, revised annually to take into account changing needs and the expected level of resources available. The greatest part of the development programme is annually financed from external aid, and priority in the use of resources has always been given to providing the counterpart contributions to funds received from external sources. The balance of these local resources is used for financing projects commanding high national priority for which no external funds can be secured.

Budget. Revenue Account receipts and expenditure (in K.1,000) for years ending 31 March:

	1980–81	*1981–82*	*1982–83*	*1983–84*
Revenue	282,962	344,484	340,723	458,140
Expenditure	199,793	257,282	259,507	449,747

Currency. The currency is the *kwacha* (dawn), which is subdivided into 100 *tambala* (cockerels). From 9 June 1975 the kwacha has been pegged to Special Drawing Rights. In March 1985: £1 sterling = K.1·75, US$1 = K.1·64.

Banking. In July 1964 the Reserve Bank of Malawi was set up with a capital of K.1m. to be responsible for the issue of currency and the holding of external reserves and to issue treasury bills and local registered stock on behalf of the Government. Since then, the Reserve Bank has fully assumed the responsibilities of a Central Bank.

The National Bank of Malawi has a total of 14 branches in major urban areas and 25 static and 41 mobile agencies in rural areas. The Commercial Bank of Malawi Ltd opened in 1970 and has branches at Limbe, Lilongwe, Mzuzu and Zomba and an agency in Dedza and headquarters at Blantyre. It has 4 permanent and 65 mobile agencies.

In 1972 The Investment Development Bank of Malawi was established in Blantyre. Its resources are derived from domestic and foreign official sources and its objective is to provide medium and long-term credits to private entities considered of importance to the economy.

The post office savings bank had (1985) 257 offices conducting savings business throughout the country, and the New Building Society has agencies in Limbe, Mzuzu, Zomba and Blantyre with its head office in Lilongwe.

In 1972 the Investment and Development Bank (Inde Bank) was established in Blantyre. Its resources are derived from domestic and foreign official sources and provides medium and long-term credits to private entities considered important to the economy.

Weights and Measures. The metric system became fully operational in 1982.

ENERGY AND NATURAL RESOURCES

Electricity. The Electricity Supply Commission of Malawi is the sole supplier of electrical power and energy and the demand and supply of electricity and power on the inter-connected system was met from the hydro-electric generator sets installed at Tedzani Falls and Nkula Falls stations which together have a total capacity of

124 mw as at 1984. The inter-connected system extends from the Shire River hydro stations and covers most areas of the Southern and Central Regions, and part of the Northern Region. Transmission is at 132 and 66 kw. The present installed capacity will meet the forecast demand up to 1986 when a further 20 mw set will be commissioned at Nkula Falls Station.

Thermal plant of 23·8 mw capacity is available on the inter-connected system and there are stations at Blantyre, Lilongwe, Mtunthama, Kasungu, and Mzuzu. The capacity of the isolated station at Karonga was increased to 480 kw with the installation of 120 kw diesel generator set.

Minerals. The main product in 1976 was marble (149,254 tonnes) for the manufacture of cement.

Agriculture. Malawi is predominantly an agricultural country. Up to 1982 816,000 of the rural population had been reached by self-help piped water projects. In 1983 agriculture contributed about 43% to the GDP, and agricultural produce accounted for 90% of total exports. Of the total area of 23·3m. acres, 13·1m. could be cultivated and, in 1969, 3·36m. were being cultivated, of which 2·64m. were under maize. Maize is the main subsistence crop and is grown by over 95% of all smallholders. Tea cultivation is of growing importance; in 1982, 38m. kg were produced. Almost all the surplus crops produced by smallholders are sold to the Agricultural Development and Marketing Corporation. In 1982 the corporation purchased crops valued at K.41·2m., including maize (K.27·3m.), cotton, tobacco, groundnuts and rice.

Livestock in 1983: Cattle, 900,000; sheep, 87,000; goats, 750,000; pigs, 210,000.

Forestry. In 1981 10,419 cu. metres of sawn timber were removed.

Fisheries. Landings in 1981 were 51,400 tonnes.

INDUSTRY AND TRADE

Industry. Index of manufacturing output (1970 = 100): manufacturing for domestic consumption 177·7 (229·5 in 1980); of this consumer goods were at 191·9 (252·5) and intermediate goods mainly for building and construction were at 128·6 (150·4). Manufacturing for export, 172·3 (201·6).

Labour:

	1978		
	Private	*Government*	*Total*
Agriculture, forestry, fishing	147,962	21,371	169,333
Mining and quarrying	564	–	564
Manufacturing	34,862	1,093	35,955
Electricity and water	2,459	463	2,922
Building and construction	27,418	4,052	31,470
Trade, hotels, restaurants	26,829	382	27,211
Transport storage, communications	13,809	3,808	17,617
Financial services	6,194	623	6,817
Community, social, personal services	10,794	36,601	47,395
Total	270,891	68,393	339,284

Commerce. The main items of export in 1982 were (in K.1m.): Tobacco, 145·78; tea, 45·25; sugar, 23·15; groundnuts, 8·7. Imports (in K.1m.) included capital equipment, 38·3; means of transport, 29·3; consumer goods, 41·7; building materials, 19·3.

Trade statistics for calendar years are (in K.1m.):

	1979	*1980*	*1981*	*1982*
Imports	324·8	356·2	321·9	322·1
Exports	181·7	238·2	257·5	269·0

Total trade between Malawi and UK (British Department of Trade returns, in £1,000 sterling):

	1981	*1982*	*1983*	*1984*
Imports to UK	34,744	42,478	42,060	65,327
Exports and re-exports from UK	21,503	20,893	18,183	22,995

Tourism. There were 37,252 visitors to Malawi in 1983.

COMMUNICATIONS

Roads. In 1982 there were 2,745 km of main road, of which 1,685 were bitumen-surfaced and 138 gravel; 2,740 km of secondary roads, of which 227 were surfaced, 111 km of gravel and 2,402 km of earth roads. In 1983 there were 14,000 cars, 13,500 commercial vehicles and 268 buses and coaches.

Railways. Malawi Railways (789 km–1,067 mm gauge) operates a main line from Salima to the Mozambique border near Nsanje, from which running powers over the Trans-Zambesia Railway allow access to the port of Beira; a branch opened in 1970 runs eastwards from a point 16 km south of Balaka to the Mozambique border to give a direct route to the deep-water port of Nacala. The 26-km section from Nsanje to the border is operated by the Central Africa Railway Co. Ltd. An extension of 111 km from Salima to the new state capital of Lilongwe was opened in Feb. 1979, and a further extension to Mchinji on the Zambian border (120 km) was completed in 1981. In 1981, 1·2m. tonnes hauled, 77·9m. passenger-km run.

Aviation. In 1983 the Kamuzu International Airport at Lilongwe was inaugurated. It handled (1984) 56,580 passengers and 893 tonnes. In 1982 Chileka Airport handled 184,700 passengers and 5,598 tonnes of freight.

Shipping. In 1982 lake ships carried 1·48m. passengers.

Post and Broadcasting. Number of telephones (1982) 16,445. The Malawi Broadcasting Corporation broadcasts in English and Chichewa. There were 1m. radio sets in 1983.

Newspapers (1984). *The Daily Times* (English, Monday to Friday); 14,000 copies daily. *Malawi News* (English and Chichewa, Saturdays); 21,000 copies weekly. *The Odini* (English and Chichewa, 7,000 fortnightly).

JUSTICE, RELIGION, EDUCATION AND WELFARE

Justice. Justice is administered in the High Court, the magistrates' courts and traditional courts. There are 23 magistrates' courts, 176 traditional courts and 23 local appeal courts.

Appeals from traditional courts are dealt with in the traditional appeal courts and in the national traditional appeal court. Appeals from magistrates' courts lie to the High Court, and appeals from the High Court to Malawi's Supreme Court of Appeal.

Religion. In 1983 the Roman Catholic Church claimed 1·2m. members; Church of Central Africa Presbyterian, 366,377; Diocese of Southern Malawi and Lake Malawi (part of the Province of Central Africa (the Anglican Communion), 70,606; Seventh Day Adventist Church (1984), 59,319. Zambezi Evangelical Church (formerly Nyasa mission), 26,000; Assembly of God, 10,000; Seventh Day Baptist (Central Africa Conference), 5,198; Church of Christ, 50,000+; African Evangelical Church, 6,000. Moslems are estimated to number about 500,000.

Education (1981–82). The Ministry of Education and Culture controls all aspects of education.

The number of pupils in the 2,250 primary schools was 882,903; in the 62 secondary schools, 19,329. There were 11,425 teachers in primary schools and 739 in secondary schools. The primary school course is of 8 years duration, followed by a 4-year secondary course. English is taught from the 1st year and becomes the general medium of instruction from the 4th year.

Teacher-training is undertaken in 5 residential colleges, 2 of which are directly controlled by the Ministry; the others receive grants in aid as assisted institutions. Courses last 3 years. Enrolment 8,303. Technical and trade courses are offered in commerce, building, woodwork and mechanical engineering, as well as home craft for girls; 1,904 trainees undertook courses at government and voluntary schools in 1966.

The University of Malawi was inaugurated on 6 Oct. 1965. In 1981–82 there were 1,718 students taking degree and diploma courses.

Health. In 1984 there were two central hospitals, one general hospital, one mental hospital, 43 hospitals of which 21 are government district hospitals. There are 6,596 hospital beds of which 1,448 are for maternity.

DIPLOMATIC REPRESENTATIVES

Of Malawi in Great Britain (33 Grosvenor St., London, W1X 0DE)
High Commissioner: C. M. Mkona.

Of Great Britain in Malawi (Lingadzi Hse., Lilongwe, 3)
High Commissioner: A. H. Brind, CMG.

Of Malawi in the USA (1400 20th St., NW, Washington, D.C., 20036)
Ambassador: Nelson T. Mizere.

Of the USA in Malawi (PO Box 30016, Lilongwe)
Ambassador: W. Adams.

Of Malawi to the United Nations
Ambassador: N. T. Mizere.

Books of Reference

General Information: The Chief Information Officer, PO Box 494, Blantyre.
Roeder, R. B. *Malawi.* [Bibliography] Oxford and Santa Barbara, 1981
McMaster, C., *Malawi: Foreign Policy and Development.* London, 1974
Williams, T. D., *Malawi: The Politics of Despair.* Cornell Univ. Press, 1979

MALAYSIA

Capital: Kuala Lumpur
Population: 15·07m. (1984)
GNP per capita: US$1,840 (1981)

HISTORY. On 16 Sept. 1963 Malaysia came into being, consisting of the Federation of Malaya, the State of Singapore and the colonies of North Borneo (renamed Sabah) and Sarawak. The agreement between the UK and the 4 territories was signed on 9 July (Cmnd. 2094); by it, the UK relinquished sovereignty over Singapore, North Borneo and Sarawak from independence day and extended the 1957 defence agreement with Malaya to apply to Malaysia. Malaysia became automatically a member of the Commonwealth of Nations. *See* map in THE STATESMAN'S YEAR-BOOK, 1964–65.

On 9 Aug. 1965, by a mutual agreement dated 7 Aug. 1965 between Malaysia and Singapore, Singapore seceded from Malaysia to become an independent Sovereign nation.

POPULATION. 1980 census gave 11,800,000 in Peninsular Malaysia, 1,034,000 in Sabah, and 1,323,000 in Sarawak. Estimate (1984) 15·07m.

CLIMATE. Malaysia is affected by the monsoon climate. The N.E. monsoon prevails from Oct. to Feb., bringing rain to the east coast of the peninsula. The S.W. monsoon lasts from mid-May to Sept. and affects the opposite coastline the most. Temperatures are uniform throughout the year. Kuala Lumpur. Jan. 81°F (27·2°C), July 81°F (27·2°C). Annual rainfall 97·6″ (2,441 mm). Penang. Jan. 82°F (27·8°C), July 82°F (27·8°C). Annual rainfall 109·4″ (2,736 mm).

CONSTITUTION AND GOVERNMENT. The Constitution of Malaysia is based on the Constitution of the former Federation of Malaya, but includes safeguards for the special interests of Sabah and Sarawak. It was amended in 1983.

The federal capital is Kuala Lumpur, established on 1 Feb. 1974 with an area of approximately 94 sq. miles. The official language is Bahasa Malaysia.

The Constitution provides for one of the 9 Rulers of the Malay States to be elected from among themselves to be the *Yang di-Pertuan Agong* (Supreme Head of the Federation). He holds office for a period of 5 years. The Rulers also elect from among themselves a Deputy Supreme Head of State, also for a period of 5 years.

Supreme Head of State (Yang di-Pertuan Agong): HM Sultan Mahmood Iskandar ibni Al-Marhum Sultan Ismail DK, SPMJ, SPDK, DK (Brunei) SSIJ, PIS, BSI, elected as 8th *Yang di-Pertuan Agong* from 26 April 1984.

Raja of Perlis: HRH Tuanku Syed Putra ibni Al-Marhum Syed Hassan Jamalullail, DK, DKM, DMN, SMN, SPMP, SPDK, acceded 12 March 1949.

Sultan of Kedah: HRH Tuanku Haji Abdul Halim Mu'adzam Shah ibni Al-Marhum Sultan Badlishah, DK, DKH, DKM, DMN, DUK, SPMK, SSDK, acceded 20 Feb. 1959.

Regent of Johore: HRH Tengku Ibrahim Ismail ibni Sultan Mahmood Iskandar Al-Haj, DK, SPMJ, appointed from 15 Nov. 1984.

Sultan of Selangor: HRH Sultan Salahuddin Abdul Aziz Shah ibni Al-Marhum Sultan Hisamuddin 'Alam Shah Al-Haj, DK, DMN, SPMS, SPDK, acceded 3 Sept. 1960.

Raja of Perak: HRH Raja Tun Azlan Shah, DK, DMN, PMN, SPCM, SPMP, acceded 3 Feb. 1984.

Yang di-Pertuan Besar of Negeri Sembilan: HRH Tuanku Ja'afar ibni Al-Marhum Tuanku Abdul Rahman, DMN, DK, acceded 8 April 1968.

Sultan of Kelantan: HRH Sultan Ismail Petra ibni Al-Marhum Sultan Yahya Petra, DK, SPMK, SJMK, SPSM, appointed 29 March 1979.

Sultan of Trengganu: HRH Sultan Mahmud Al Marhum ibni Al-Marhum Tuanku Al-Sultan Ismail Nasiruddin Shah, DK, SPMT, SPCM, appointed 2 Sept. 1979.

Sultan of Pahang: Sultan Haji Ahmad Shah Al-Musta'in Billah Ibni Al-Marhum Sultan Abu Bakar Ri'Ayatuddin Al-Mu'Adzam Shah, DKM, DKP, DK, SSAP, SPCM, SPMJ.

Yang di-Pertua Negeri Pulau Pinang: HE Tun Dr Awang bin Hassan, DUPN, SPMJ, appointed 1 May 1981.

Governor of Malacca: HE Tun Haji Syed Zahiruddin bin Syed Hassan, SMN, PSM, DUNM, SPMP, JMN, PJK, appointed 23 May 1975; re-appointed 23 May 1979.

Yang di-Pertua Negeri Sarawak: HE Tan Sri Dr Haji Abdul Rahman bin Ya'kub, DP, PMN, SPMJ, SIMP, SPMK, SSDK, SPMP, SPMS, SPDK, appointed 2 April 1981.

Yang di-Pertua Sabah: HE Datuk Mohamad Adnan Roberts, SMN, SPDK, SPMP, DUPN, DP, appointed 26 June 1978.

Parliament consists of the *Yang di-Pertuan Agong* and two *Majlis* (Houses of Parliament) known as the *Dewan Negara* (Senate) of 68 members and *Dewan Rakyat* (House of Representatives) of 154 members. There are 149 members from the states in Malaysia and 5 from the Federal Territory. Appointment to the Senate is for 3 years. The maximum life of the House of Representatives is 5 years, subject to its dissolution at any time by the *Yang di-Pertuan Agong* on the advice of his Ministers.

National flag: Fourteen horizontal stripes of red and white, with a blue quarter bearing a crescent and a star of 14 points, all in gold.

The elections to the House of Representatives held on 22 April 1982, returned the following members: National Front, 139; Democratic Action Party, 9; PAS, 5; Independent, 8.

The Cabinet was in July 1984 composed as follows:

Prime Minister and Minister of Defence: Datuk Seri Dr Mahathir Mohamad, SSDK, SSAP, SPMS, SPMJ, DP(Sk), DUPN, SPNS, SPDK, SPCM, SSMT, DUMN.

Deputy Prime Minister and Home Affairs: Datuk Musa Hitam. *Housing and Local Government:* Datuk Dr Neo Yee Pan. *Foreign Affairs:* Tengku Datuk Ahmad Rithaudeen bin Tengku Ismail. *Trade and Industry:* Tengku Tan Sri Razaleigh Hamzah. *Finance:* Encik Daim Zainuddin. *Transport:* Tan Sri Datuk Seri Chong Hon Nyan. *Justice:* Datuk Dr James Ongkili. *Primary Industries:* Datuk Seri Paul Leong Kee Seong. *Energy, Telecommunications and Posts:* Datuk Leo Moggie Anak Irok. *Works:* Datuk S. Samy Vellu. *Public Enterprises:* Datin Paduka Rafidah Aziz. *Culture, Youth and Sports:* Datuk Dr Sulaiman bin Haji Daud. *National and Rural Development:* Datuk Sanusi bin Junid. *Education:* Datuk Abdullah bin Haji Ahmad Badawi. *Information:* Datuk Rais Yatim. *Labour:* Datuk Mak Hon Kam. *Land and Regional Development:* Datuk Seri Mohd Adib bin Haji Mohd Adam. *Science, Technology and Environment:* Datuk Amar Stephen Yong. *Health:* Datuk Chin Hon Ngian. *Federal Territory:* Datuk Shahrir bin Abdul Semad. *Agriculture:* Encik Anwar Ibrahim. *Welfare Services:* Datuk Abu Hassan Omar.

DEFENCE. The Malaysian Armed Forces are made up of the Malaysian Army, the Royal Malaysian Navy and the Royal Malaysian Air Force. Each Service has its own component of reserves.

The Malaysian Constitution provides for the *Yang di-Pertuan Agong* (Supreme Head of State) to be the Supreme Commander of the Armed Forces who exercises his powers and authority in accordance with the advice of the Cabinet. Under the general authority of the Yang di-Pertuan Agong and the Cabinet, there is the Armed Forces Council which is responsible for the command, discipline and administration of all other matters relating to the Armed Forces, other than those relating to its operational use.

The Armed Forces Council is chaired by the Minister of Defence and its membership consists of the chief of the Defence Forces, the 3 Service Chiefs and 2 other senior military officers, the Secretary-General of the Ministry of Defence, a representative of State Rulers and an appointed member.

The chief of the Armed Forces Staff is the professional head of the Armed Forces and the senior military member in the Armed Forces Council. He is the principal adviser to the Minister of Defence on the military aspects of all defence matters. The chief of the Armed Forces Staff's committee, established under the authority of the Armed Forces Council, is the highest level at which joint planning and co-ordination with the Armed Forces are carried out. The Committee is chaired by the chief of the Armed Forces Staff and its membership consists of the chief of the Army, Navy and Air Force, the chief of Personnel Staff, the chief of logistic Staff and the chief of Staff of the Ministry of Defence.

Army. The Army is organized into 4 divisions, comprising 12 infantry brigades made up of 36 infantry battalions; 3 cavalry, 4 field artillery, 1 armoured personnel carrier, 1 special service, 5 engineer and 5 signals regiments and 2 anti-aircraft batteries. Equipment includes 25 Scorpion light tanks. Strength (1985) about 100,500, with as reserves the Malaysian Territorial Army (45,000), the Local Defence Corps (15,000) and the regular reservists who have completed their full-time service.

Navy. The Royal Malaysian Navy is commanded by the Chief of the Navy from the integrated Ministry of Defence in Kuala Lumpur. The main naval bases are KD Malaya situated on Singapore Island, KD Sri Labuan on Labuan Island and KD Pelandok in Lumut, Perak. These establishments are responsible for the operation and administration of the ships, and KD Pelandok for the training of personnel.

The ships include 2 British (Yarrow)-built frigates (including the former HMS *Mermaid*), 2 logistic support ships, 8 fast missile craft, 6 fast gunboats, 22 patrol craft, 2 landing ships, 1 diving tender, 1 survey vessel and 6 tugs. The peace-time tasks include fishery protection and anti-piracy patrols. There are also 48 armed patrol launches, 46 operated by the Royal Malaysian Police and 2 by the Government of Sabah (North Borneo) which also operates 3 patrol boats, 1 landing craft and a yacht.

New construction includes 2 corvettes or light frigates, 4 minehunters, 2 off-shore patrol vessels and 12 marine police patrol boats.

Naval personnel in 1984 totalled 11,000 officers and ratings, including 1,000 reservists and 800 volunteer reserve.

Air Force. Formed on 1 June 1958, the Royal Malaysian Air Force is equipped primarily to provide air defence and air support for the Army, Navy and Police. Its secondary rôle is to render assistance to Government departments and civilian organizations, especially during periods of national disasters. There were in early 1984 11 squadrons, of which 6 operated transport aircraft and helicopters. Up to 45 *ex*-US Navy A-4L/C Skyhawks are being refurbished progressively as the primary attack force. Other equipment includes 14 F-5E Tiger II jet fighter-bombers, 2 RF-5E reconnaissance-fighters, and 4 F-5F trainers, 2 F.28 Fellowship VIP transports, 16 Caribou twin-engined STOL transports, 35 Sikorsky S-61A-4 Nuri heavy troop and cargo transport helicopters, 20 Alouette III, 3 Agusta-Bell 212, 9 Bell 47 and 5 Bell 206B JetRanger helicopters, 12 Cessna 402Bs for twin-engine training and liaison, 44 PC-7 Turbo-Trainers and 2 H.S. 125 Merpati twin-jet executive transports. Personnel (1984) totalled about 12,000.

Volunteer Forces. The Army Volunteer Force (Territorial Army) consists of first-line infantry, signals, engineer and logistics units able to take the field with the active army, and a second-line organization to provide local defence. There is also a small Naval Volunteer Reserve with Headquarters in Penang and Kuala

Lumpur. The Royal Malaysian Air Force Volunteer Reserve has both air and ground elements.

INTERNATIONAL RELATIONS

Membership. Malaysia is a member of UN, the Commonwealth, Non-Aligned countries, the Colombo Plan, Organization of Islamic Conference and ASEAN.

ECONOMY

Planning. The fourth 5-year plan, 1981–85 envisages an expenditure of M$42,830m. and aims at national unity through the two-pronged objectives of eradicating poverty irrespective of race and of restructuring society to eliminate the identification of race with economic functions.

Budget. Revenue and expenditure for calendar years, in M$1m.:

	1979	*1980*	*1981*	*1982*[1]	*1983*[2]
Revenue	10,505	13,926	15,806	16,434	17,266
Operating expenditure[3]	10,040	13,617	15,686	16,185	17,079
Development expenditure	4,282	7,463	11,358	10,434	11,270

[1] Latest Estimate. [2] Budget Estimate.
[3] Including contribution to sinking fund from 1975.

Currency. Bank Negara Malaysia (Central Bank of Malaysia) assumed sole currency issuing authority in Malaysia on 12 June 1967. The unit of currency issued by Bank Negara Malaysia is the Malaysian *ringgit* ($) which is divided into 100 *sen.* Currency notes are of denominations of $1, 5, 10, 20, 50, 100, 500 and $1,000. Coins are of denominations of 1 *sen*, 5, 10, 20, 50 *sen* and $1, $5 and $100. The circulation of currency on 31 Dec. 1981 was M$5,493m.

Rate of exchange, March 1985: 2·60 *ringgit* = US$1; 2·79 *ringgit* = £1.

Banking. Thirty-eight banks were operating in Dec. 1983; of these 22 were domestic banks with a total of 664 banking offices. Five were banks incorporated in Singapore with 63 banking offices and the remaining 12 banks were foreign incorporated with 85 banking offices. Total deposits amounted to M$40,429·8m. on 31 Dec. 1983 and loans and advances amounted to (1981) M$25,521·4m.

The National Savings Bank (formerly known as the post office savings bank) held M$973·8m. due to 3,600,948 depositors at 31 Dec. 1978.

TRADE. Total trade of Malaysia with UK (British Department of Trade returns, in £1,000 sterling):

	1981	*1982*	*1983*	*1984*
Imports to UK	188,327	185,239	222,673	320,325
Exports and re-exports from UK	196,213	210,805	248,239	283,269

COMMUNICATIONS

Post. The Postal Services in Malaysia are under the Ministry of Energy, Telecommunications and Post and are headed by the Director-General of Post, Malaysia.

Cinemas. In 1974 there were 500 cinemas with a seating capacity of 345,400.

JUSTICE. By virtue of Art. 121(1) of the Federal Constitution judicial power in the Federation is vested on 2 High Courts of co-ordinate jurisdiction and status namely the High Court of Malaya and the High Court of Borneo, and the inferior courts. The Federal Court with its principal registry in Kuala Lumpur is the Supreme Court in the country.

The Lord President as the supreme head of the Judiciary, the 2 Chief Justices of the High Courts and 6 other Judges form the constitution of the Federal Court. Apart from having exclusive jurisdiction to determine appeals from the High Court the Federal Court is also conferred with such original and consultative jurisdiction as is laid out in Articles 128 and 130 of the Constitution.

A panel of 3 Judges or such greater uneven number as may be determined by the Lord President preside in every proceeding in the Federal Court.

The right of appeal to the Yang di-Pertuan Agong (who in turn refers the appeal to the Judicial Committee of the British Privy Council) from a decision of the Federal Court in respect of criminal and constitutional matters was abolished on 1 July 1978.

DIPLOMATIC REPRESENTATIVES

Of Malaysia in Great Britain (45 Belgrave Sq., London, SW1X 8QT)
High Commissioner: M. H. Kassim (accredited 16 March 1983).

Of Great Britain in Malaysia (Wisma Damansara, Jalan Semantan, Kuala Lumpur)
High Commissioner: D. H. Gillmore, CMG.

Of Malaysia in the USA (2401 Massachusetts Ave., NW, Washington, D.C., 20008)
Ambassador: Dato' Lew Sip Hon.

Of the USA in Malaysia (A.I.A. Bldg., Jalan Tun Razak, Kuala Lumpur)
Ambassador: Thomas P. Shoesmith.

Of Malaysia to the United Nations
Ambassador: Zain Azraai.

Books of Reference

Statistical Information: The Department of Statistics, Malaysia, Kuala Lumpur, was set up in 1963, taking over from the Department of Statistics, States of Malaya. *Chief Statistician:* Khoo Teik Huat. Main publications: *Peninsular Malaysia Monthly* and *Annual Statistics of External Trade; Malaysia External Trade* (quarterly); *Peninsular Malaysia Statistical Bulletin* (monthly); *Rubber Statistics* (monthly); *Rubber Statistics Handbook* (annual); *Oil Palm Statistics* (monthly); *Oil Palm, Coconut and Tea Statistics* (annual); *Survey of Manufacturing Industries, 1974; National Accounts Statistics, 1973–1977; Malaysia Industrial Classification, 1972; Monthly Industrial Statistics, Malaysia; Census of Selected Service Trades, 1973.*

Anand, S., *Inequality and Poverty in Malaysia.* OUP, 1983
Gullick, J., *Malaysia: Economic Expansion and National Unity.* Boulder and London, 1982
Huk Tee, L., and Sook Jean, W., *Malaysia.* [Bibliography] Oxford and Santa Barbara, 1983
Meerman, J., *Public Expenditure in Malaysia.* OUP, 1980
Snodgrass, D. R., *Inequality and Economic Development in Malaysia.* OUP, 1982

PENINSULAR MALAYSIA

AREA AND POPULATION. The total area of Peninsular Malaysia is about 50,806 sq. miles (131,587 sq. km). The federal capital is Kuala Lumpur (244 sq. km).

State	*Area (sq. miles)*	*Population (1980 Census)*	*Capital*	*Population (1980 Census)*
Johore	7,330	1,601,504	Johore Bharu	249,880
Kedah	3,639	1,102,200	Alor Star	71,682
Kelantan	5,765	877,575	Kota Bharu	170,559
Malacca	637	453,153	Malacca	88,073
Negeri Sembilan	2,565	563,955	Seremban	136,252
Pahang	13,886	770,644	Kuantan	136,625
Penang	399	911,586	Georgetown	250,578
Perak	8,110	1,762,288	Ipoh	300,727
Perlis	307	147,726	Kangar	12,956
Selangor	3,074	1,467,441	Shah Alam	24,138
Trengganu	5,002	542,280	Kuala Trengganu	186,608
Federal Territory	94	937,875	Kuala Lumpur	937,875
Peninsular Malaysia	50,806	11,138,227		

Population by races (1981 estimate): 11,428,000. Malays, 6,168,000; Chinese, 3,995,000; Indians, 1,183,000; others, 82,000. In 1974 Kuala Lumpur became a

Federal District. Shah Alam became capital of Selangor. Vital statistics (1979): Births, 336,848; deaths, 64,345.

CONSTITUTION AND GOVERNMENT. The States of the Federation of Malaya, now known as Peninsular Malaysia, comprises the 11 States of Johore, Pahang, Negeri Sembilan, Selangor, Perak, Kedah, Perlis, Kelantan, Trengganu, Penang and Malacca. On 31 Aug. 1957 the Federation became the 11th sovereign member-state of the Commonwealth of Nations.

For earlier history of the States and Settlements *see* THE STATESMAN'S YEAR-BOOK, 1957, p. 241.

The Constitution is based on the agreements reached at the London conference of Jan.-Feb. 1956, between HM Government in the UK, the Rulers of the Malay states and the Alliance Party (which at the first federal elections on 27 July 1955 obtained 51 of the 52 elected members), and subsequently worked out by the Constitutional Commission appointed after that conference.

ECONOMY

Budget. See p. 819.

Weights and Measures. The standard measures are the imperial yard, pound and gallon. The Weights and Measures Act of 1972 provides for a 10-year transition to the metric system, and was completed by 31 Dec. 1981.

ENERGY AND NATURAL RESOURCES

Electricity. In 1983, 10,616m. kwh. were generated; commerce and industry are the main consumers.

Oil. Production (1983) 18,286,900 tonnes of crude oil.

Minerals. Production (in tonnes): Tin-in-concentrates: 1983, 41,400; 1982, 52,300. Iron ore: 1983, 113,700; 1982, 340,300. Bauxite: 1983, 501,800; 1982, 589,000. Copper: 1983, 123,400; 1982, 128,800. Gold: 1980, 4,621 troy oz.; 1979, 5,273.

Agriculture. Total area under agricultural crops, 1978, 8m. acres. This included 251,830 acres of second season rice crops. Rice: Production in 1983, 1,818,100 tonnes from 654,900 hectares. Rubber: Production in 1983, 1·53m. tonnes; Oil-palms: Production in 1983 (estimate), 3m. tonnes of palm oil; 67,300 tonnes of cocoa; 72,000 tonnes of coconut oil.

Tea: Production in 1980, 3,202,000 kg.

Livestock: (1983) Cattle, 600,000; buffaloes, 300,000; sheep, 66,000; pigs, 2·1m.; goats, 350,000.

Forestry (1982). Reserved forests, 4·9m. hectares. Production of logs (1983, estimate), 11·2m.cu. metres; sawn timber, 1983, 8m. cu. metres; plywood, 88,168,000 sq. metres (5mm thickness). Exports of veneer, 31·9m. sq. metres (5mm thickness).

Fisheries. Landings in 1983 (estimate), 730,300 tons; 1982, 676,500 tons. Number of vessels in 1979, 21,439 powered, 5,955 non-powered.

INDUSTRY AND TRADE

Trade Unions. There were, on 31 Dec. 1981, 292 registered trade unions with 549,000 members in Peninsular Malaysia.

Commerce. In 1983 exports totalled M$32,922m. and imports M$30,724m.

Chief imports (1983, provisional); Machinery and transport equipment, M$13,453m.; manufactured goods, M$4,948m.; food, M$2,969m.

Chief exports (1982): Rubber, 704,000 tonnes (M$1,373m.); crude petroleum (M$3,702m.); sawn timber, 8,649,000 cu. metres (M$1,554m.); other exports (1981) palm oil, 2·35m. tonnes (M$2,710m.); palm oil, crude, 2,822,000 tonnes (M$1,177m.); saw logs, 15,816,000 cu. metres (M$2,473m.); bauxite (1980), 718,300 tonnes (M$20·8m.).

In 1982 imports came chiefly from Japan (M$3,023m.), USA (M$2,299m.), Australia (M$699m.), Thailand (M$686m.), UK (M$464m.), Saudi Arabia (M$454m.), China (M$238m.), Singapore (M$211m.). Exports went mainly to Singapore (M$2,663m.), Japan (M$2,332m.), Netherlands (M$439m.), USA (M$406m.), Thailand (M$318m.), Korea (M$293m.), Taiwan (M$213m.), UK (M$134m.), India (M$131m.).

Tourism. In 1978, 3,017,864 foreigners visited Peninsular Malaysia.

COMMUNICATIONS

Roads. In 1982 the Public Works Department maintained 29,934 km of public roads, of which 15,983·44 km was of bituminous metalled surface, 81·44 km waterbound metalled surface, 1,799 km hard surface bitumen sealed, 2,931·99 km hard surface waterbound and 1,038·67 km earth surface.

In 1980, 374,939 motor vehicles were registered, including 124,428 private cars, 854 buses, 23,436 lorries and vans, 210,682 motor cycles.

Railways. The Malayan Railway main line runs from Singapore to Butterworth opposite Penang Island. From Bukit Mertajam 8 miles south of Butterworth a branch line connects Peninsular Malaysia with the State Railways of Thailand at the frontier station of Padang Besar. Other branch lines connect the main line with Port of Klang, Teluk Anson, Port Dickson and Ampang. The east-coast line, branching off the main line at Gemas, runs for over 300 miles to Tumpat, Kelantan's northernmost coastal town; a 13-mile branch line linking Pasir Mas with Sungei Golok makes a second connexion with Thailand.

In 1982 there were 1,639 km (metre gauge) which carried 7·4m. passengers and 3·4m. tonnes of freight.

Aviation (1980). There are 9 airports used by scheduled air services and international air services are operated into Kuala Lumpur and Penang airports. The national carrier, Malaysian Airlines System (MAS), began operation on 1 Oct. 1972 to provide both domestic and international services. The Malaysian Airlines System (MAS) operate international services to Amsterdam, Bandar Seri Begawan, Bangkok, Dubai, Frankfurt, Haadyai, Hong Kong, Jakarta, Jeddah, Kuwait, London, Madras, Manila, Medan, Melbourne, Paris, Perth, Seoul, Singapore, Sydney, Taipei and Tōkyō. The number of domestic points served by the airline is 37. Charter services are provided within Peninsular Malaysia by Malaysia Air Charter Co., Pan Malaysia Air Charter, Wira Kris, Genting Helicopter Service and Kris Udara Malaysia. The following airlines operate scheduled services through Kuala Lumpur besides MAS: Air Lanka, Cargoluse Airways, Bangladesh Beiman, Iraqi Airways, Philippine Airlines, PIA, Aeroflot Soviet Airlines, Air India, British Airways, Cathay Pacific Airways, Czechoslovakia Airlines, Garuda Indonesian Airways, Japan Airlines, KLM, PANAM, SAS, SABENA, Singapore Airlines, Thai International Airways and Trans Mediterranean Airways. The airlines operating scheduled services through Penang besides MAS are Garuda Indonesian Airways, Cathay Pacific Airways, Thai Airways Co. and Thai Airways International.

Civil aviation statistics for airports in Peninsular Malaysia (1980): Aircraft movements, 90,530; terminal passengers, 3,940,078; freight, 37,511 tonnes; mail, 3,473 tonnes.

Shipping. The major ports of Peninsular Malaysia are Penang, Malacca, Port Klang, Pasir Gudang, Port Dickson and Kuantan. The volume of shipping (vessels of over 75 NRT only) handled at these ports, exclusive of coasting trade, was as follows (in 1,000 NRT):

		Arrivals		*Departures*	
Ports		*Number*	*Tonnage*	*Number*	*Tonnage*
Penang	1979	1,711	7,236	1,720	7,244
	1980	1,805	7,627	1,796	7,610
Port Klang	1979	2,794	16,463	2,799	16,434
	1980	2,785	15,891	2,796	15,996
Total (all ports)	1979	5,399	34,103	5,408	34,090
	1980	5,611	34,132	5,558	34,072

The total cargo handled in all ports during 1979 was 25·37m. tonnes; 1980, 27·25m. tonnes.

Post and Broadcasting. As at 31 Dec. 1979, 445 post offices, 1,381 postal agencies, 177 mobile post offices and 1 riverine postal office were operating in Malaysia, and the cash turnover for the year amounted to M$4,688,113,241.

There were 825,289 telephones on 1 Jan. 1982. In 1979, 208,731 wireless licences and 911,749 television licences were issued.

JUSTICE, RELIGION, EDUCATION AND WELFARE

Justice. Unlike the Federal Court and the High Court which were established under the Constitution, the subordinate courts in Peninsular Malaysia comprising the sessions court, the Magistrate's court and the Penghulu's court were established under a Federal Law (the subordinate Courts Act, 1948 (Revised 1972)).

All offences other than those punishable with death are tried before a Sessions Court President who is empowered to pass any sentence allowed by law other than the sentence of death. In civil matters, the sessions court has jurisdiction to hear all actions and suits where the amount in dispute does not exceed M$25,000.

A First Class Magistrate's criminal jurisdiction is limited to offences for which the maximum term provided by law does not exceed 10 years' imprisonment and to certain specified offences where the term of imprisonment provided for may be extended to 14 years' imprisonment or which are punishable with fine only.

Juvenile courts established under the Juvenile Courts Act, 1947 for juvenile offenders below the age of 18 are presided over by a First Class Magistrate assisted by 2 advisers.

There are 30 penal institutions, including Borstal establishments and an open prison camp. The average prison population (1979) was 9,254.

Religion. More than half the population are Muslims, and Islam is the official religion. In 1970 there were 4,673,670 Muslims, 765,250 Hindus, 220,897 Christians and 2,495,739 Buddhists.

Education. In 1981 there were 4,357 state assisted primary schools with 2,003,803 pupils and 4,357 teachers and in 1980, 208 private primary schools with 5,130 pupils and 224 teachers.

In 1981 there were 2,855 secondary schools with 1,160,967 pupils and 46,960 teachers.

There were (1980): 10 special schools with 1,312 pupils and 104 teachers; 401 classes for further education with 10,281 students and 997 teachers; 25 teacher training colleges with over 12,000 students.

In the academic year 1980–81 there were 10 institutions of higher learning:

	1981–82	
	Staff	*Students*
Ungku Omar Polytechnic, Ipoh	112	2,449
Kuantan Polytechnic, Kuantan	49	575
MARA Institute of Technology, Shah Alam	665	11,108
Tunku Ab. Rahman College, Kuala Lumpur	156	6,285
University of Malaya, Kuala Lumpur	1,085	9,310
University of Kebangsaan, Bangi	864	7,514
University of Science, Penang	417	4,387
University of Agriculture, Serdang	502	4,136
University of Technology, Kuala Lumpur	431	4,862

The International Islamic University opened in 1983.

Health. In 1981 Government maintained 65 general, district hospitals with 29,712 beds, 2 institutions with 2,688 beds for the treatment of Hensens' disease, 2 mental institutions with 6,577 beds and 1 institution (293 beds) for tuberculosis treatment. For the care of the rural population there were 3,131 medical and health facilities comprising 65 main health centres, 254 health sub-centres, 1,375 midwives' clinics, 414 static, 284 travelling dispensaries, 739 dental clinics, 41 maternal and child health clinics. The Government also maintains an Institute for Medical Research with 2 branch laboratories at Ipoh and Penang.

Books of Reference

Morris, M. W., *Local Government in Peninsular Malaysia.* London, 1980
Wilkinson, R. J., *Malay-English Dictionary.* 2 vols. New ed. London, 1956
Winstedt, Sir R., *Malaya and Its History.* 3rd ed. London, 1953.—*An English–Malay Dictionary.* 3rd ed. Singapore, 1949.—*The Malays: A Cultural History.* London, 1959

SABAH

HISTORY. The territory now named Sabah, but until Sept. 1963 known as North Borneo, was in 1877-78 ceded by the Sultans of Brunei and Sulu and various other rulers to a British syndicate, which in 1881 was chartered as the British North Borneo (Chartered) Company. The Company's sovereign rights and assets were transferred to the Crown with effect from 15 July 1946. On that date, the island of Labuan (ceded to Britain in 1846 by the Sultan of Brunei) became part of the new Colony of North Borneo. On 16 Sept. 1963 North Borneo joined the new Federation of Malaysia and became the State of Sabah.

AREA AND POPULATION. Area, about 28,460 sq. miles (73,711 sq. km), with a coastline of 973 miles (1,577 km). The interior is mountainous, Mount Kinabalu being 13,455 ft (4,175 metres) high. Population, 1980 census 1,012,608, (1983 estimate, 1,116,000), of whom, 838,141 were Pribumis, 163,996 Chinese, 5,613 Indians, 3,296 others. The native population comprises Kadazans (largest and mainly agricultural), Bajaus and Bruneis (agriculture and fishing), Muruts (hill tribes), Suluks (mainly seafaring) and several smaller tribes.

The island of Labuan became Federal territory on 16 April 1984, 35 sq. miles (75 sq. km) in area, lying 6 miles (9·66 km) off the north-west coast of Borneo is a free port. It has a fine port, Victoria Harbour.

The principal towns are situated on or near the coast. They include Kota Kinabalu, the capital (formerly Jesselton), 1980 census population (preliminary), 108,725, Tawau (113,708), Sandakan (113,496), Keningau in the hinterland (41,204), and Kudat (38,397).

CLIMATE. The climate is tropical monsoon, but on the whole is equable, with temperatures around 80°F (26·5°C) throughout the year. Annual rainfall varies, according to locality, from 10″ (250 mm) to 148″ (3,700 mm). The north-east monsoon lasts from Dec. to April and chiefly affects the east coast, while the south-west monsoon from May to Aug. gives the west coast its wet season.

CONSTITUTION AND GOVERNMENT. The Constitution of the State of Sabah provides for a Head of State, called the *Yang Dipertua Negeri Sabah.* Executive authority is vested in the State Cabinet headed by the Chief Minister.

Head of State: Tun Datuk Mohamed Adam Robert, SMN, SPDK, SPMP, SPMK, DUPN, DP.

Flag: Horizontally blue over white with a red triangle based on the hoist.

The Cabinet was composed as follows in Nov. 1984:

Chief Minister: Datuk Harris Mohd. Salleh.

Deputy Chief Minister and Minister of Infrastructure Development: Tan Sri Haji Mohd. Suffian Koroh. *Financial Planning and Development:* Datuk Haji Mohd. Noor Mansoor. *Social Services:* Toh Puan Datuk Hajjah Rahimah Stephens. *Agriculture and Fisheries Development:* Datuk Lim Guan Sing. *Town and Country Development:* Datuk Ayub Aman. *Culture, Youth and Sports:* Datuk Conrad Mojuntin. *Resources Development:* Stephen Wong Soon Yu. *Industrial Development:* Datuk Clarence Mansul.

The Legislative Assembly consists of the Speaker, 48 elected members and not more than 6 nominated members.

The official language was English for a period of 10 years from Sept. 1963 but in

Aug. 1973 Bahasa Malaysia was introduced and in 1974 was declared the official language. English is widely used especially for business.

ECONOMY

Budget. Budgets for calendar years, in M$:

Ordinary Budget	*1977*	*1978*	*1979*	*1980*	*1981*
Revenue	716,291,841	777,282,219	1,439,748,354	1,538,251,203	1,206,110,099
Expenditure	556,660,409	637,510,015	926,035,864	1,383,481,653	1,738,218,335
Development Budget					
Revenue	184,895,412	198,347,347	201,937,626	331,753,502	898,051,408
Expenditure	165,749,561	186,816,759	264,620,018	396,634,910	798,727,173

Banking. There are branches of The Chartered Bank at Kota Kinabalu, Sandakan, Tawau, Labuan, Kudat, Tenom and Lahad Datu. The Hongkong and Shanghai Bank has branches at Kota Kinabalu, Sandakan, Labuan, Beaufort, Papar and Tawau. The Hock Hua Bank (S) has branches at Kota Kinabalu, Sandakan and Tawau. The Chung Khiaw Bank has branches at Kota Kinabalu, Tuaran and Sandakan. Malayan Banking Ltd has branches at Kota Kinabalu, Tawau, Semporna and Sandakan. United Overseas Bank and the Overseas Chinese Banking Corporation have each a branch at Kota Kinabalu. Bank Bumiputra Malaysia has branches at Kota Kinabalu. Lahad Datu, Sandakan and Keningau. Overseas Union Bank and the Development and Commercial Bank have each a branch at Sandakan. The Sabah Bank Berhad and Sabah Development Bank were established in Kota Kinabalu in 1979.

The National Savings Bank has taken over the functions of the post office savings bank as from 1 Dec. 1974 and had (1983) M$29·4m. due to 139,212 depositors. It also provides additional services to depositors including the granting of loans for housing.

COMMERCE. The main imports are machinery, tobacco, provisions, petroleum products, metals, rice, textiles and apparel, vehicles, sugar, building material. Statistics for calendar years, in M$:

	1979	*1980*	*1981*	*1982*	*1983*
Imports	2,035,061,720	3,060,819,153	3,644,281,463	3,217,971,724	3,802,333,624
Exports	4,132,247,959	4,455,982,812	4,357,069,182	5,726,240,301	5,432,972,223

The main imports and exports were (in M$1m.):

Imports	*1960*	*1970*	*1980*	*1981*	*1982*	*1983*
Rice	8·4	15·4	47·9	86·7	75·0	88·2
Provisions	22·3	45·7	218·8	261·7	261·8	309·4
Textiles and apparel	9·2	20·5	87·9	109·0	99·8	124·2
Tobacco, cigars and cigarettes	12·8	32·9	92·2	96·0	79·2	112·9
Sugar	3·5	6·7	34·0	38·6	32·3	44·9
Vehicles	8·1	47·6	389·1	394·9	279·2	384·6
Machinery	30·0	109·0	138·3	168·4	160·2	218·2
Petroleum products	16·1	28·6	332·9	437·9	332·3	244·8
Metals	12·1	36·8	296·8	407·5	416·4	469·4
Building materials	2·8	13·0	89·7	128·7	120·4	145·0
Exports						
Rubber	49·5	36·5	82·3	56·2	36·5	45·1
Timber	90·7	396·8	1,855·1	1,777·6	2,319·1	2,037·2
Hemp	5·2	0·3	–	–	–	–
Fish, fresh, dried and salted	0·9	8·0	31·3	40·7	41·7	68·6
Copra (including re-exports)	40·2	6·8	33·3	22·5	17·0	15·5
Cocoa beans	15·8	4·4	67·6	83·1	104·6	119·1
Veneer sheets	0·5	2·5	10·4	18·1	19·0	32·8
Palm oil	–	18·1	159·6	159·6	182·7	192·9
Copper concentrates	–	–	177·3	167·3	152·3	162·6
Crude petroleum	–	–	1,779·7	1,567·0	2,238·0	2,141·1

Tourism. In 1983 some 68,329 tourists visited Sabah.

COMMUNICATIONS

Roads (1983). There were 6,471 km of roads, of which 1,997 km were bitumen surfaced, 4,300 km gravel surfaced and 190 km of earth road. Work is in progress on a network of roads, notably the Kota Kinabalu-Sandakan and Sandakan-Lahad Datu road links.

Railways. A metre-gauge railway, 140 km, runs from Kota Kinabalu on Gaya Bay to Tenom in the interior. It carried 315,000 passengers in 1983.

Aviation. External communications are provided from the international airport at Kota Kinabalu by Cathay Pacific Airways Ltd to Hong Kong; Malaysian Airways to Hong Kong, Manila, Brunei, Kuching, Singapore and Kuala Lumpur; Brunei Airways to Brunei and Kuching and Philippine Airlines to Manila.

The total air traffic handled at Sabah airports during 1983 was 2,181,833 passengers, 16,983,717 kg freight and 3,211,263 kg mail.

Shipping (1983). Merchant shipping totalling 16,065,853 NRT used the ports, handling 16,236,743 tonnes of cargo.

Post. As at 31 Dec. 1976 there were 32 post offices, 13 mobile post offices and 84 postal agencies. There were 65,101 telephones on 31 Dec. 1983. As at 31 Dec. 1983, there were 62,540 wireless and 78,363 television licences issued.

JUSTICE, EDUCATION AND WELFARE

Justice. Pursuant to the Subordinate Courts Ordinance (Cap. 20) (1951) Courts of a Magistrate of the First Class, Second Class and Third Class were established to adjudicate upon the administration of civil and criminal law. The civil jurisdiction of a First Class Magistrate is limited to cases where the amount in dispute does not exceed M$1,000. but provision is made for the Chief Justice to enlarge that jurisdiction to M$3,000. This has been established so as to confer this jurisdiction on all stipendiary magistrates. A Second Class Magistrate can only try suits where the amount involved does not exceed M$500 and a Third Class Magistrate where it does not exceed M$100.

The criminal jurisdiction of these Magistrates' Courts is limited to offences of a less serious nature although stipendiary magistrates have enhanced jurisdiction. There are no Juvenile Courts.

There are also Native Courts with jurisdiction to try cases arising from breach of native law and custom (including Moslem Law and custom) where all parties are natives or one of the party is a native (if the matter is a religious, matrimonial or sexual one). Appeals from Native Courts lie to a District Judge or a Native Court of Appeal presided over by a Judge.

In 1982, 3,996 convictions were obtained in 999 cases taken to court.

Education. In 1983, there were 169,481 primary and 75,619 secondary pupils. There are 837 primary schools (657 government, 169 grant-aided and 11 private), and 106 general secondary schools (55 government, 37 grant-aided and 14 private) throughout the State. There are 3 teacher-training colleges, with (1983) 958 students.

The Government also runs 5 vocational schools in Kota Kinabalu and Sandakan offering carpentry, motor mechanics, electrical installation, fitting/turning, radio and television and heavy plant fitting.

The Department of Education also runs further education classes in most towns and districts. The main medium of instruction in primary schools is Bahasa Malaysia although there are some Chinese medium primary schools. Secondary education is principally English but this is progressively being replaced by Bahasa Malaysia.

Health. The principal diseases are malaria, pulmonary tuberculosis and intestinal infestations. Specific control programmes for malaria and tuberculosis have drastically reduced the incidence of these two diseases.

As at 31 Dec. 1983 there were 16 hospitals (2,950 beds). Seventy-six fixed dispensaries in outlying districts providing in-patient and out-patient care are staffed by hospital assistants under the supervision of district medical officers. There are mental hospitals at Sandakan and Kota Kinabalu. There are 17 district health centres and 45 travelling clinics throughout the State providing maternal and child health care.

Book of Reference

Statistical Information: Director, Federal Department of Information, Kota Kinabalu.

Tregonning, K. G., *North Borneo.* HMSO, 1960

SARAWAK

HISTORY. The Government of part of the present territory was obtained on 24 Sept. 1841 by Sir James Brooke from the Sultan of Brunei. Various accessions were made between 1861 and 1905. In 1888 Sarawak was placed under British protection. On 16 Dec. 1941 Sarawak was occupied by the Japanese. After the liberation the Rajah took over his administration from the British military authorities on 15 April 1946. The Council Negri, on 17 May 1946, authorized the Act of Cession to the British Crown by 19 to 16 votes, and the Rajah ceded Sarawak to the British Crown on 1 July 1946.

On 16 Sept. 1963 Sarawak joined the Federation of Malaysia.

AREA AND POPULATION. The area is about 48,250 sq. miles (124,449 sq. km), with a coastline of 450 miles and many navigable rivers.

The population at 1980 census was 1,294,753 (1978 estimate, 1,173,906, including 386,260 Dayaks; 182,700 Malays; 103,194 other natives; 294,020 Chinese; 9,735 others). The annual rate of increase is 2·4% (estimate). Working population (1980), 710,000.

The chief towns are the capital, Kuching, about 21 miles inland, on the Sarawak River (1900 population: 120,000), Sibu, 80 miles up the Rejang River, which is navigable by large steamers (1980 population: 86,000), and Miri, the headquarters of the Sarawak Shell Ltd (1980 population: 66,000).

CONSTITUTION AND GOVERNMENT. On 24 Sept. 1941 the Rajah began to rule through a constitution. Since 1855 two bodies, known as Majlis Mesyuarat Kerajaan Negeri (Supreme Council) and the Dewan Undangan Negeri (State Legislature), had been in existence. By the constitution of 1941 they were given, by the Rajah, powers roughly corresponding to those of a colonial executive council and legislative council respectively. Sarawak has retained a considerable measure of local autonomy in state affairs. The State or Legislature consists of 48 elected members and sits for 5 years unless sooner dissolved.

A ministerial system of government was introduced in 1963. The Chief Minister presides over the Supreme Council, which contains no more than 8 other Council Negri members, all of whom are Ministers.

Elections to the State Legislature on 29 Dec. 1983 returned 3 Independents and 45 members of the Sarawak Barisan Nasional comprising the Party Pesaka Bumiputra Bersatu, the Sarawak United Peoples' Party, Sarawak National Party and Party Bansa Dayak Sarawak.

Sarawak has 24 seats in the Malaysia House of Representatives (154 members) and 5 seats in the Senate (58 members).

Sarawak has 7 divisions each under a Resident.

Head of State: Tun Datuk Patinggi Tan Sri Haji Abdul Rahman Ya'kub, DPSS, SMN, SSMT, DP, SPMJ, SPMK, SIMP, SPMS, SSDK, SPMP, SPDK, PNBS.

Chief Minister: Datuk Patinggi Haji Abdul Taib Mahmud, DP, SPMJ, PGDK.

Deputy Chief Ministers: Tan Sri Datuk Amar Sim Kheng Hong, PSM, DA, PGDK (*Finance and Development*), Datuk Daniel Tajem anak Miri, PNBS (*Agriculture and Community Development*), Datuk Alfred Jabu anak Numpang, PNBS, KMN (*Housing*). *Communications and Works:* Datuk Dr Wong Soon Kai, PNBS.

Local Government: Datuk Edward Jeli Bhayong, PNBS. *Forestry:* Datuk Haji Noor Tahir, PNBS, AMN. *Special Functions:* Hafsah Harun, JMN.

State Secretary: Datuk Amar Abang Haji Yusuf Puteh, DA, PNBS, PGDK, JSM. *State Attorney-General:* Datuk Jemuri Serjan, PNBS, JBS. *State Financial Secretary:* Datuk Haji Bujang mohd Nor, PNBS, JBS, JSM.

The official languages are Malay and English. The continuing use of English as official language in Sarawak will be reviewed in 1985.

Flag: Horizontally red over white with a blue triangle on the hoist.

ECONOMY

Budget. In 1982 State revenue was M$536·3m.; expenditure, M$543·8m. The revenue is mainly derived from royalties on oil and timber.

The fourth Malaysian 5-year development plan (1981-85) provides for Sarawak an expenditure of M$3,567m.; of this sum over 90% is to be spent on roads and bridges, land development, port development, education, electricity and water supply and agriculture.

Currency. The Malaysian *dollar* is on a par of £0·334 or US$0·426.

Banking. The National savings bank had 86,157 depositors at the beginning of 1981; the amount to their credit was M$38·8m. There is a branch of Bank Negara Malaysia in Kuching, and branches of the Chartered Bank, the Hongkong & Shanghai Bank, Bank Bumiputra Malaysia, the Overseas Chinese Banking Corporation, the Malayan Bank and 9 other banks.

PRODUCTION. The State produces rubber (exports, 1982, 15,919 net tons, M$24·2m.; 1981, 28,158 net tons, M$57·6m.), timber logs (exports, 1982, 9·2m. tons, M$1,261m.; 1981, 6·9m. tons, M$812m.), sawn timber (exports, 1982, 183,759m. tons, M$100m.; 1981, 162,963m. tons, M$84·8m.), palm oil (exports, 1982, 31,919 tons, M$23·8m.; 1981, 18,660 tons, M$21·9m.), pepper (exports, 1982, 25,010 tons, M$65·7m.; 1981, 28,606 tons, M$81·3m.), and other jungle produce. There are also gold (1981, 2,108 grammes), antimony ore (1981, 318 tons) and silica sand (1981, 141,048 tons).

INDUSTRY AND TRADE

Commerce. Export of crude oil in 1982 was 4·41m. tons (M$2,725m.), about 60% of total exports. The bulk of crude production was exported to Japan, USA, Philippines and Thailand.

Total import value, 1982, M$3,313m.; 1981, M$3,001m. Export, 1982, M$4,967m.; 1981, M$4,514m.

Tourism. Tourism is expanding and new hotels were under construction in 1985.

COMMUNICATIONS

Roads. There are no railways. In 1982 there were 3,296 miles of roads, consisting of 830 miles of bitumen surfaced, 2,389 miles of gravel or stone surfaced and 75 miles of earth roads.

Aviation. There are daily Malaysian Airline System (MAS) B737 and Airbus flights between Kuching and Kuala Lumpur *via* Singapore, and also scheduled flights between Kuching, Brunei and Hong Kong. Major towns in Sarawak are linked up by internal air routes.

Shipping. In 1981 Sarawak ports loaded 12,164,000 tons (1980: 10·58m. tons) and discharged 1·38m. tons (1980: 900,000 tons). New Kuching wharf, operational since Dec. 1974, can accommodate vessels up to 15,000 tons.

Post and Broadcasting. There are 52 post offices, 18 mobile offices and 200 postal agencies. A telephone system with 57 exchanges (64,310 telephones) covers the country. There is communication by wireless with Singapore and other Commonwealth countries. The government radio and television service had, at the end of 1981, 33,202 registered receivers.

Newspapers (1982). There are 1 Malay, 2 English and 7 Chinese daily; 1 English weekly; 1 Malay and 1 Iban (Sea Dayak) monthly newspapers as well as a weekly news review in Malay and Iban published by Government.

JUSTICE, RELIGION, EDUCATION AND WELFARE

Justice (1980). In Sarawak subordinate courts were established pursuant to the Subordinate Courts Ordinance (Cap. 42) (1952). The limits of civil and criminal jurisdiction of a First Class, Second Class and Third Class Magistrate are the same as in Sabah. As in Sabah, here too there is provision for the Chief Justice to enhance the jurisdiction of a First Class Magistrate in civil and criminal matters, the reason being that there are no Sessions Courts in both Sabah and Sarawak.

Native Courts were set up under the Native Courts Ordinance (Cap. 43) (1955) with the same limited jurisdiction as Native Courts in Sabah. In addition these courts have jurisdiction to try civil cases where the amount in dispute does not exceed M$50. Appeals from Native Courts lie to a Resident's Native Court and, subject to some limitations, to the Native Court of Appeal which is presided over by a High Court Judge. There are no Juvenile Courts. There are 5 prisons. There were 1,866 admissions, of whom 1,028 were sentenced to penal imprisonment and 723 committed on remand or awaiting trial, and 75 paid fines. Daily average prison population was 409.

Police. There is a Royal Malaysia Police, Sarawak Component, with a total establishment of about 8,000 regular officers and men.

Religion. There are Church of England, Roman Catholic, American Methodist, Seventh-day Adventist and Borneo Evangelical missions. There is a large Moslem population and many Buddhists. Islam is the national religion.

Education (1982). All schools (government, missions, private) numbered about 1,500 with 313,900 pupils, of whom about 100,276 were in secondary classes. There are 3 teacher-training centres and an agricultural university campus conducting pre-university courses.

Health. At the end of 1982 there were 16 government hospitals (2,908 beds), 140 static and 94 travelling dispensaries, 121 public dental and school dental clinics and 158 maternal and child health centres. There were 181 registered doctors.

Books of Reference

Population and Housing Census of Malaysia, 1980. Dept. of Statistics, Kuala Lumpur
Sarawak Annual of Statistics. Dept. of Statistics, Kuching, 1981
Sarawak Annual External Trade Statistics. Dept. of Statistics, Kuching, 1982
1983 Sarawak Budget. Information Dept., Sarawak
Milne, R. S., and Ratnam, K. J., *Malaysia, New States in a New Nation: Political Development of Sarawak and Sabah in Malaysia.* London, 1974
Runciman, S., *The White Rajahs.* CUP, 1960
Scott, N. C., *Sea Dyak Dictionary.* Govt. Printing Office, Kuching, 1956

National Library: The Sarawak Central Library, Kuching.

MALDIVES

Capital: Malé
Population: 168,000 (1983)
GNP per capita: US$308 (1980)

Divehi Jumhuriya

HISTORY. The islands were under British protection from 1887 to mid–1965. They now enjoy complete independence under the agreement signed in Colombo on 26 July 1965. Maldives became a republic on 11 Nov. 1968.

AREA AND POPULATION. The Republic of Maldives, 400 miles to the south-west of Sri Lanka, consists of some 2,000 low-lying coral islands (only 220 inhabited), grouped into 12 clearly defined clusters of atolls but divided into 19 districts for administrative purposes. Area 115 sq. miles (298 sq. km). Population (census 1978), 143,046. Estimate (1983) 168,000. Capital Malé (40,000 inhabitants).

CONSTITUTION AND GOVERNMENT. The President is elected every 5 years by universal adult suffrage. He is assisted by the Ministers' *Majlis*, a cabinet of ministers of his own choice whom he may dismiss at will. There is also a Citizens' *Majlis* (House of Representatives) which consists of 54 members, 8 nominated by the President, 8 elected from Malé and 2 elected from each of the 19 atolls. The life of the Citizens' *Majlis* is 5 years. There are no political parties.

President and Prime Minister: Maumoon Abdul Gayoom.

External Affairs: Fathulla Jameel. *Justice:* Ibrahim Fareed Didi. *Home Affairs:* Umar Zahir. *Provincial Affairs:* Abdulla Hameed. *Education:* Mohamed Zahir Hussain. *Health:* Adulla Jameel Hussain. *Fisheries:* Abdul Sattar. *Agriculture:* Vacant. *Transport:* Ahmed Mujuthaba.

The official language is Divehi, which is akin to Elu or old Sinhalese.

National flag: Red with a green panel bearing a white crescent.

INTERNATIONAL RELATIONS.

Membership. The Republic of the Maldives is a member of UN and a special member of the Commonwealth.

ECONOMY

Budget. There is no direct taxation.

Currency. The *rufiyaa* (Maldivian rupee) is divided into 100 *laaris*; there are notes of 1, 2, 5, 10, 50 and 100 rufiyaa.

NATURAL RESOURCES

Agriculture. The islands are covered with coconut palms and yield millet and fruit as well as coconut produce.

Production in 1981 included (in 1,000 tonnes): Coconuts, 9; copra, 2.

Fisheries. The Maldivian economy is based on the fishing industry.

INDUSTRY AND TRADE

Commerce. Bonito ('Maldive fish') is the main export commodity and Japan the main buyer. Exports (1981) US$27·9m.: imports, US$38·8m.

Total trade between the Republic of Maldives and UK (British Department of Trade returns, in £1,000 sterling):

	1980	*1981*	*1982*	*1983*	*1984*
Imports to UK	294	254	57	44	529
Exports and re-exports from UK	1,121	2,403	615	840	747

Tourism. Tourism, introduced in 1972, is expanding and there were 74,000 visitors in 1983.

COMMUNICATIONS

Aviation. The Maldives' national airline, Maldives International Airline, was established in 1977, and is a joint venture between the Maldives' government and Indian Airlines. It replaced an earlier airline, Air Maldives which was wound up in 1977. The airline operates one Boeing 737, leased from Indian Airlines, from Hulule airport on Malé atoll. Hulule airport is being extended. The Maldives' government hopes to reactivate the former RAF staging post on Gan in order to attract additional tourist traffic.

Shipping. The merchant fleet consists of about 50 vessels of 200,000 GRT.

Post and Broadcasting. There were (1982) 1,540 telephones. An external telephone service links Tortola with Bermuda and the rest of the world, and cable communications also exist to all parts of the world. Radio ZBVI transmits 10,000 watts and has stand-by transmitting facilities of 1,000 watts. Cable and Wireless operate a commercial cable television service to provide subscribers with good quality reception of approximately 7 television channels plus a number of FM stereo broadcasting stations.

JUSTICE, RELIGION EDUCATION AND WELFARE

Justice. Justice is based on the Islamic Shari'ah.

Religion. The State religion is Moslem of the Sunni sect.

Education. In 1978 there were 8,749 pupils in primary and 3,652 in secondary schools.

Health. In 1977 there was a 40-bed hospital in Malé, and 9 doctors, 1 dentist, 177 midwives and 34 nursing personnel.

DIPLOMATIC REPRESENTATIVES

Of Great Britain in the Republic of Maldives
High Commissioner: J. A. B. Stewart, CMG, OBE (resides in Colombo)

Of the Republic of Maldives to the United Nations
Ambassador: M. Musthafa Hussain.

Books of Reference

Bell, H. C. P., *History, Archaeology and Epigraphy of the Maldive Islands.* Ceylon Govt. Press, Colombo, 1940
Bernini, F. and Corbin, G., *Maldive.* Turin, 1973

MALI

Capital: Bamako
Population: 7·72m. (1984)
GNP per capita: US$190 (1981)

République du Mali

HISTORY. Annexed by France between 1881 and 1895, the region became the territory of French Sudan as a part of French West Africa. It became an autonomous state within the French Community on 24 Nov. 1958, and on 4 April 1959 joined with Sénégal to form the Federation of Mali. The Federation achieved independence on 20 June 1960, but Sénégal seceded on 22 Aug. and Mali proclaimed itself an independent republic on 22 Sept. The National Assembly was dissolved on 17 Jan. 1968 by President Modibo Keita, whose government was then overthrown by an Army *coup* on 19 Nov. 1968; power was assumed by a Military Committee for National Liberation led by Lieut. (now General) Moussa Traoré, who became President on 19 Sept. 1969.

AREA AND POPULATION. Mali is a landlocked state, consisting of the Middle and Upper Niger basin in the south, the Upper Sénégal basin in the south-west, and the Sahara in the north. It is bounded west by Sénégal, north-west by Mauritania, north-east by Algeria, east by Niger and south by Burkina Faso, the Ivory Coast and Guinea. The republic covers an area of 1,240,142 sq. km (478,832 sq. miles) and had a population of 6,398,914 at the 1976 Census; the latest estimate (1984) is 7,722,000. The chief cities (with populations in 1976) are Bamako, the capital (404,022), Ségou (64,890), Mopti (53,885), Sikasso (47,030), Kayes (44,736), Gao (30,714), Tombouctou (20,483) and Koulikoro (16,876).

The population of the regions (census 1976): Kayes, 871,871; Koulikoro, 916,148; Capital district, 404,022; Sikasso, 1,044,664; Ségou, 1,111,810; Mopti, 1,104,708; Tombouctou, 487,278; Gao, 367,819.

The various indigenous languages belong chiefly to the Mande group; of these the principal are Bambara (spoken by 60% of the population), Soninké, Malinké and Dogon; non-Mande languages include Fulani, Songhai, Senufo and Minianka. The official language is French.

CLIMATE. A tropical climate, with adequate rain in the south and west, but conditions become increasingly arid towards the north and east. Bamako. Jan. 76°F (24·4°C), July 80°F (26·7°C). Annual rainfall 45″ (1,120 mm). Kayes. Jan. 76°F (24·4°C), July 93°F (33·9°C). Annual rainfall 29″ (725 mm). Tombouctou. Jan. 71°F (21·7°C), July 90°F (32·2°C). Annual rainfall 9″ (231 mm).

CONSTITUTION AND GOVERNMENT. A new constitution was announced on 26 April 1974 and approved by a national referendum on 2 June; it was amended by the National Assembly on 2 Sept. 1981. The sole legal party is the *Union démocratique du peuple malien* (UDPM), formally constituted on 30 March 1979 and governed by a 19-member Central Executive Bureau responsible to a 137-member National Council who nominate all candidates for election.

The President is directly elected and his term of office is now 6 years; Gen. Moussa Traoré was elected unopposed on 19 June 1979. The 82-member National Assembly is also directly elected (latest elections, 13 June 1982); its term of office is now 3 years.

The Council of Ministers in June 1984 comprised:

President, Head of Government, Defence and Security: Gen. Moussa Traoré.

Ministers of State: Brig.-Gen. Amadou Baba Diarra *(Equipment),* Oumar Coulibaly *(Economy and Plan).*

Foreign Affairs and Co-operation: Alioune Blondin N'guéye. *Planning:* Ahmed

Mohamed Ag Hamani. *Agriculture:* Nfagnanama Kone. *Education:* Lieut.-Col. Sékou Ly. *Labour and Civil Service:* Modibo Keita. *Rural Development:* Mady Diallo. *Justice:* Lieut.-Col. Issa Ongoiba. *Public Works and Transport:* Mamadou Haidara. *Health and Social Affairs:* Dr Ngolo Traoré. *Finance and Commerce:* Ydrissa Keita. *State Enterprises:* Bandiougou Bidia Doucoure. *Interior:* Lieut.-Col. Abdourahmane Maiga. *Information and Telecommunications:* Gakou Nee Fatou Niang. *Sports, Arts and Culture:* N'tji Idrissa Mariko.

National flag: Three vertical stripes of green, yellow, red.

Local Government: Mali is divided into the Capital District of Bamako and 7 regions, sub-divided into 46 *cercles* and then into 279 *arrondissements.*

DEFENCE. There is a selective system of 2 years' military service.

Army. The Army consists of 3 infantry battalions, 1 tank battalion, 1 artillery battalion and support units. Equipment includes 21 T-34 tanks. Strength (1985) 4,600. There is also a paramilitary force of 5,000 men.

Air Force. The Air Force has 5 MiG-17 jet fighters, 1 MiG-15UTI jet trainer, some Yak-18 piston-engined trainers, 2 An-24, 1 An-26 and 3 An-2 transports, and 3 Mi-8 and Mi-4 helicopters from USSR. A twin-turbofan Corvette is used for VIP transport. Personnel total about 300.

INTERNATIONAL RELATIONS

Membership. Mali is a member of UN, OAU and is an ACP state of EEC.

ECONOMY

Planning. The 1981–85 Four Year Plan provides for expenditure of MF 795,200m.

Budget. The budget for 1982 balanced at MF 88,800m.

Currency. Mali introduced its own currency, the *Mali franc,* in July 1962 but reverted to the franc CFA on 1 June 1984, with a parity value of 50 francs CFA to 1 French franc.

Banking. The *Banque Centrale du Mali* (founded in 1968) is the bank of issue. There are 4 domestic and 2 French-owned banks.

ENERGY AND NATURAL RESOURCES

Electricity. Production (1981) totalled 91m. kwh. Hydro-electric dams have been built at Selingué (near Bamako) on the Upper Niger and at Manantali (near Kayes) on the Sénégal river.

Minerals. Mineral resources are limited, but marble (at Bafoulabé) and limestone (at Diamou) are being extracted in the Upper Sénégal valley; iron ore deposits in this area await development. Salt is mined at Taoudenni in the far north (3,000 tonnes a year) and phosphates at Bouren (10,000 tonnes).

Agriculture. Production in 1982 included (in 1,000 tonnes): Millet, 950; sugar-cane, 225; groundnuts, 178; rice, 145; maize, 81; cottonseed, 60; cotton lint, 36; cassava, 65; sweet potatoes, 30.

Livestock, 1983: Cattle, 5·4m.; horses, 140,000; asses, 425,000; sheep, 6·45m.; goats, 7·5m.; camels, 240,000; chickens, 14m.

Important irrigation schemes have been carried out in the Ségou and Mopti districts on the Niger River, of which the Sansanding Barrage and the Sahel Canal are the most important; 50,000 hectares of cotton and rice lands are being irrigated.

Fisheries. About 100,000 tonnes of fish per annum are caught in the rivers.

TRADE. Imports in 1982 totalled MF 218,400m., exports, 95,800m. Chief imports are foodstuffs, automobiles, petrol, building material, sugar, salt and beer.

France and Ivory Coast are the main trading partners. Cotton formed 39% of exports in 1981.

Total trade between Mali and UK (British Department of Trade returns, in £1,000 sterling):

	1980	*1981*	*1982*	*1983*	*1984*
Imports to UK	11,318	4,534	3,385	3,833	5,646
Exports and re-exports from UK	7,878	2,761	4,403	15,856	5,471

Tourism. There were 19,853 foreign tourists in 1977.

COMMUNICATIONS

Roads. There were (1980) 13,360 km of roads, of which 6,869 km are usable in all seasons; they include 2,606 km of metalled road Dakar–Niger (of which 1,693 km are in Mali). There were 19,500 road vehicles in 1974.

Railways. Mali has a railway from Kayes to Koulikoro by way of Bamako, a continuation of the Dakar–Kayes line in Sénégal. Total length 642 km and in 1983 the railways ran 156m. passenger-km and 132m. tonne-km.

Aviation. Air services connect the republic with Paris, Dakar and Abidjan. There are international airports at Bamako and Mopti, and Air Mali operates domestic services to 10 other airports.

Shipping. For about 7 months in the year small steamboats perform the service from Koulikoro to Tombouctou and Gao, and from Bamako to Kouroussa.

Post and Broadcasting. There were, in 1982, 8,485 telephones and in 1983, 100,000 radio receivers.

JUSTICE, RELIGION, EDUCATION AND WELFARE

Justice. The Supreme Court was established at Bamako in 1969 with both judicial and administrative powers. The Court of Appeal is also at Bamako, at the apex of a system of regional tribunals and local *juges de paix.*

Religion. In 1979, 65% of the population were Sunni Moslems, 30% animists and 5% Christians.

Education. In 1979 there were 293,227 pupils and 6,877 teachers in primary schools, 70,625 pupils and 3,004 teachers in secondary schools, (1977) 2,609 in technical schools, (1979) 2,511 in teacher-training colleges and 5,281 students in higher educational establishments. A further 30,000 students were at 1,321 adult literacy centres.

Health. In 1980 there were 12 hospitals, 327 health centres and 445 dispensaries, with a total of 3,200 beds; there were 319 doctors, 18 surgeons, 14 dentists (1978), 24 pharmacists (1978), 250 midwives and 1,312 nursing personnel.

DIPLOMATIC REPRESENTATIVES

Of Mali in Great Britain
Ambassador: Yaya Diarra (resides in Brussels).

Of Great Britain in Mali
Ambassador: P. L. O'Keeffe, CMG, CVO (resides in Dakar).

Of Mali in the USA (2130 R. St., NW, Washington, D.C., 20008)
Ambassador: Lassana Keita.

Of the USA in Mali (Rue Testard and Rue Mohamed V, Bamako)
Ambassador: Parker W. Borg.

Of Mali to the United Nations
Ambassador: Seydou Niare.

Books of Reference

Hopkins, N. S., *Popular Government in an African Town.* Univ. of Chicago Press, 1972
Jones, W., *Planning and Economic Policy: Socialist Mali and Her Neighbors.* New York, 1974

MALTA

Capital: Valletta
Population: 329,189 (1983)
GNP per capita: US$3,600 (1981)

Repubblika Ta' Malta

HISTORY. Malta was held in turn by Phoenicians, Carthaginians and Romans, and was conquered by Arabs in 870. From 1090 it was joined to Sicily until 1530, when it was handed over to the Knights of St John, who ruled until dispersed by Napoleon in 1798. The Maltese rose in rebellion against the French and the island was subsequently blockaded by the British aided by the Maltese from 1798 to 1800. The Maltese people freely requested the protection of the British Crown in 1802 on condition that their rights and privileges be preserved. The islands were finally annexed to the British Crown by the Treaty of Paris in 1814.

On 15 April 1942, in recognition of the steadfastness and fortitude of the people of Malta during the Second World War, King George VI awarded the George Cross to the island.

AREA AND POPULATION. The area of Malta is 246 sq. km (94·9 sq. miles); Gozo, 67 sq. km (25·9 sq. miles); Comino, 3 sq. km (1·1 sq. miles); total area, 316 sq. km (121·9 sq. miles). Population, census 27 Nov. 1967, 314,216; estimate (31 Dec. 1983) 329,189. Malta, 305,545; Gozo and Comino, 23,644. Chief town and port, Valletta, population 14,040 (1983).

Vital statistics, 1983, estimate: Births, 5,651; deaths, 3,137; marriages, 2,780; emigrants, 641; returned emigrants, 1,052.

CLIMATE. The climate is Mediterranean, with hot, dry and sunny conditions in summer and very little rain from May to Aug. Rainfall is not excessive and falls mainly between Oct. and March. Average daily sunshine in winter is 6 hours and in summer over 10 hours. Valletta. Jan. 55°F (12·8°C), July 78°F (25·6°C). Annual rainfall 23" (578 mm).

CONSTITUTION AND GOVERNMENT. Malta became independent on 21 Sept. 1964 and became a republic within the Commonwealth on 13 Dec. 1974. For earlier constitutional and government history *see* THE STATESMAN'S YEAR-BOOK, 1980–81, p. 837.

In 1971 Malta began to follow a policy of strict non-alignment and closed the NATO base. In March 1972 agreement was reached on the phasing out of the British Military base which was closed down completely on 31 March 1979.

Malta is a democratic republic and the Constitution, which has been amended 7 times, the last in 1977, provides for a Parliament consisting of a President of the Republic, a House of Representatives of elected members and a Cabinet consisting of the Prime Minister and such number of Ministers as may be appointed. The Constitution which is founded on work, makes provision for the protection of fundamental rights and freedom of the individual, and ensures that all persons in Malta shall have full freedom of conscience and religious worship.

Maltese and English, and such other language as may be prescribed by Parliament, are the official languages.

Elections were held on 12 Dec. 1981. State of parties in Feb. 1983: Malta Labour Party, 34; Nationalist Party, 31.

President: Agatha Barbara.

The Cabinet (Malta Labour Party) was as at Jan. 1985:

Prime Minister and Minister of the Interior and of Education: Dr Karmenu Mifsud Bonnici. *Senior Deputy Prime Minister and Minister of Justice and Parliamentary Affairs:* Dr Joseph Cassar. *Deputy Prime Minister and Minister of Finance and Customs:* Wistin Abela. *Works and Housing:* Lorry Sant. *Labour and Social Services:* Freddie Micallef. *Health:* Dr Vincent Moran. *Parastatal and People's Investments:* Dr Philip Muscat. *Tourism:* Joseph Grima. *Industry:* Karmenu Vella. *Foreign Affairs:* Dr Alex Sceberras Trigona. *Economic Planning and Trade:* Lino Spiteri. *Agriculture and Fisheries:* Joseph Debono Grech.

National flag: Vertically white and red, with a representation of the George Cross medal in the canton.

DEFENCE. The Maltese armed forces include 800 personnel, organized into 1 infantry battalion, and supported by a Helicopter Flight equipped with 4 Bell 47G-2 and 1 JetRanger light helicopters received in 1972–73, and 1 Agusta-Bell 204 received subsequently. Duties of the Flight include patrol, search and rescue. There is also a para-military force of 1,100.

A coastal patrol force of small craft was formed in 1973. It is manned by the Maltese Regiment and primarily employed as a coastguard. In 1985 it comprised 15 patrol craft and customs launches manned by 150 officers and men.

All UK forces were withdrawn in March 1979.

INTERNATIONAL RELATIONS

Membership. Malta is a member of UN, the Commonwealth and the Council of Europe.

ECONOMY

Planning. The Development Plan (1981–85) aims at continued economic growth as a means towards improving living standards and towards enhancing the quality of life of the community. Given the lack of national resources and the small size of the home market, the development strategy is based on export-led growth in the production of goods and services and, in particular, in manufacturing industry as the mainstay of the economy; ship repair and shipbuilding; food production and the service sector including tourism and transhipment. This should enable the further diversification of the productive base of the economy and generate new employment opportunities.

Budget. Revenue and expenditure (in Lm):

	1979[1]	*1980*[2]	*1981*[2]	*1982*[2]	*1983*[2]
Revenue	98,708,773	170,152,444	204,661,944	210,724,438	224,522,930
Expenditure	105,603,164	161,490,920	192,435,435	216,494,068	220,908,608

[1] Nine months. April–Dec. [2] Calendar year.

The most important sources of revenue are customs duties, income tax, National Insurance contributions, receipts from the Central Bank of Malta and until 1979, rent from defence facilities.

Currency. The Maltese currency is (Lm) *Lira Maltija* (Maltese Lira). Central Bank of Malta notes of Lm1, Lm5 and Lm10 denominations are in circulation. Malta coins are issued in the following denominations: 50, 25, 10, 5, 2 and 1 cents; 5, 3 and 2 *mils*. Total notes in circulation on 31 Dec. 1983 was Lm279·8m.; coins, Lm5·3m. In March 1985, £1 sterling = Lm0·548; US$1 = Lm1·95.

Banking. The Central Bank of Malta was founded in 1968. Commercial banking facilities are provided by Bank of Valletta Ltd, Lombard Bank (Malta) Ltd and Mid-Med Bank Ltd. The other domestic banking institutions are the Investment Finance Bank (long-term industrial loans), the Apostleship of Prayer Savings Bank Ltd, Lohombus Corporation Ltd (house mortgage) and Melita Bank International Ltd (offshore bank).

ENERGY AND NATURAL RESOURCES

Electricity. All towns and villages in Malta and Gozo are provided with electric current. Up to Sept. 1978 the islands obtained their electricity power supplies from 2 interconnected power stations located at Marsa (Malta) having a total installed capacity of 115 mw. The bigger power station with a generating capacity of 85 mw is also equipped with distillation plant capable of also producing fresh water for public consumption at the rate of 4m. gallons per day. An expansion programme is currently under way for the erection of two 30 mw turbo-generating sets and boiler plant which will increase the installed capacity to 175 mw.

In Oct. 1978 another power station, which was formerly used to supply foreign military installations on the Island, was handed over to the Government of Malta and has been integrated in the national electricity supply system. The station has a generating capacity of 12 mw.

The gross electricity generated in 1983–84 was 715·7m. kwh.

Agriculture. In 1983 agriculture contributed Lm18·1m. to the Gross Domestic Product as against Lm16·1m. in 1982. (The 1983 figure represents a share of 4·3% in the GDP.) In 1983 there was a slight decrease in the cultivable area, which totalled 11,491 hectares as against 11,639 hectares in 1982. In 1983 agriculture employed 4,373 full-time farmers, 341 full-time wage earners and 10,903 part-time farmers against, 4,332, 346 and 11,026 respectively in 1982.

In 1983 the value of Malta's main agricultural exports reached Lm1·27m. The 1983 exports consisted mainly of: Potatoes, Lm423,692; seeds, cut-flowers and plants, Lm569,975; wine, Lm167,808; onions, Lm2,326; hides and skins, Lm89,757; capers, Lm20,209.

Livestock (1983): Cattle, 12,794; pigs, 53,366; sheep, 4,719; goats 4,569; poultry, 1m.

Fisheries. In 1983 the fishing industry occupied 1,052 power propelled and 93 other fishing boats, engaging 269 full-time and 676 part-time fishermen. The catch in 1983 was 993 tonnes valued at Lm837,548 at first sale.

INDUSTRY AND TRADE

Industry. Investors in industry in Malta are offered the following advantages: political stability, excellent industrial relations, a strategic geographic location, a special association agreement with the EEC, a fully developed and highly functional infrastructure, free repatriation of profits and capital, easily trainable and highly adaptable labour force, financing facilities at favourable rates of interest, ready-built factories at attractive rents. About 260 aided firms are in operation in various industrial sectors, of which the majority are foreign-owned or have foreign interests. The Malta Development Corporation is the Government agency responsible for promoting and implementing new industrial projects, including joint ventures. The Corporation may also participate by way of equity capital, in certain projects jointly with Maltese or foreign industrialists.

Labour. The total work force in Dec. 1983 was 121,560; males, 91,851; females, 29,709, distributed as follows: Agriculture and fisheries, 5,478; manufacturing, 29,444; building, construction and quarrying, 6,992; services, 36,155; electricity, gas and drydocks, 5,947; government, 24,384; armed forces, 763; Dejma and auxiliary workers, 1,476. The number of registered unemployed under Part I of the Employment Register was 10,283, and under Part II, 638.

There were 14 trade unions registered as at 30 June 1984, with a total membership of 46,134 and 20 employers' associations with a total membership of 7,326.

Commerce. Imports and exports including bullion and specie (in Lm1,000):

	1977	*1978*	*1979*	*1980*	*1981*	*1982*	*1983*
Imports	217,681	221,505	271,960	323,737	332,269	325,073	316,633
Exports	121,791	131,949	152,169	166,722	173,725	169,036	156,748

In 1983 the principal items of imports were: Semi-manufactures, Lm92·8m.; machinery and transport, Lm77·5m.; food, Lm41·7m.; fuels, Lm38·2m.; manufactures, Lm22·9m.; chemicals, Lm22m.; others, Lm21·5m. Of domestic exports: Manufactures, Lm92·9m.; machinery and transport, Lm20·7m.; semi-manufactures, Lm13·3m., beverages and tobacco, Lm5·3m.; food, Lm3·9m.; others, Lm3·5m.

In 1983, Lm84·8m. of the imports came from Italy, Lm53·4m. from UK,

Lm50·6m. from Federal Republic of Germany, Lm35·9m. from USA, Lm12·8m. from Asia, Lm9·8m. from the EFTA, Lm3·5m. from Africa, Lm2·1m. from Oceania, Lm20·9m. from other European countries; of domestic exports, Lm48·3m. to Federal Republic of Germany, Lm24·6m. to UK, Lm14·9m. to Italy, Lm9·8m. to Africa, Lm7m. to Asia, Lm4·4m. to USA, Lm3·7m. to EFTA and Lm8·7m. to other European countries.

Total trade between Malta and UK (British Department of Trade returns, in £1,000 sterling):

	1980	*1981*	*1982*	*1983*	*1984*
Imports to UK	46,609	40,713	42,792	40,852	45,076
Exports and re-exports from UK	87,527	78,286	71,823	71,895	89,468

Tourism. In 1983, 490,812 tourists visited Malta, 312,302 from UK, 34,578 from Italy, 18,382 from Scandinavia, 26,422 from Federal Republic of Germany, 15,014 from Libya, 18,239 from France and 6,217 from USA. In 1983, gross tourist expenditure was Lm67·8m. (estimate).

COMMUNICATIONS

Roads. Every town and village is served by motor omnibuses. There are ferry services running between Malta and Gozo; cars can be transported on the ferries. Motor vehicles registered at 31 Dec. 1983 totalled 105,252, of which 73,448 were private cars, 2,772 hire cars, 16,037 commercial vehicles, 138 buses, 12,019 motor cycles and 838 other motor vehicles.

Aviation. In 1983 the principal airlines, Air Malta, Alitalia, British Airways, Libyan Arab Airlines, Yugoslav Air Transport, Austrian Airlines, Balkan Airlines and Tunisavia, operated scheduled services between Malta and UK, Austria, Belgium, Bulgaria, Egypt, Federal Republic of Germany, France, Italy, Libya, Netherlands, Nigeria, Switzerland, Tunisia and Yugoslavia. In 1983 there were 12,948 civil aircraft movements at Luqa Airport. 1,083,230 passengers, 4,869 tonnes of freight and 517 tonnes of mail were handled.

Shipping. The number of ships registered in Malta on 31 Dec. 1983 was 455; 972,660 GRT. Ships entering harbour during 1983, 2,928.

Post and Telecommunications. Telegraph and telephone services are administered by Telemalta Corporation with exchanges at Malta and Gozo. On 31 Dec. 1983 there were 110,191 telephones. A world-wide cable and telex service is also operated.

Cinemas (1983). There were 26 cinemas with a seating capacity of 18,561.

Newspapers. There were (1983) 1 English, 3 Maltese daily newspapers and 5 weekly papers.

JUSTICE, RELIGION, EDUCATION AND WELFARE

Justice. The number of persons convicted of crimes in 1983 was 2,391; those convicted for contraventions against various laws and regulations numbered 9,673. Eighty-eight were committed to prison and 10,181 were awarded fines.

Police. On 31 Dec. 1983 police numbered 41 officers and 1,213 other ranks, including 22 women police.

Religion. The majority of the population belong to the Roman Catholic Church.

Education. Education in Malta is compulsory between the ages of 6 and 16 and free in government schools. In 1983 there were 162 kindergarten groups, with nearly 3,489 children in 62 centres throughout Malta and Gozo. The primary level enrols children between 5 and 11 years in a 6-year course. There were 24,825 children (12,952 boys and 11,873 girls) in 80 government schools. Four new Junior Lyceums (2 on Malta and 2 on Gozo) were opened in Sept. 1981 with a total of 3,660 students (1,473 boys, 2,187 girls). There were 31 other government secondary schools with a total of 11,796 (5,145 boys, 6,651 girls). Secondary schools run 5-year courses leading to GCE 'O' level. Two-year courses leading to GCE 'A' level on a worker/pupil system which alternates work with study periods are provided for in the New Lyceum, *i.e.*, upper secondary schools (1,326 students). Enrolment in craft and technician courses in 3 technical institutes amounted to 1,117, while 4,079 (3,041 boys and 1,038 girls) were enrolled in the 12 trade schools for boys and 6 trade schools for girls. Other students are enrolled in specialized vocational schools. Trade schools offer 2- to 4-year courses in specialized trades and are open to students who finish their third year of secondary education. The number of children in special education amounted to 906.

There were 80 private schools with a population of 4,215 at the nursery level, 9,540 at the primary level and 6,854 at the secondary level.

About 4,500 students attended evening courses in academic, commercial, technical and practical subjects established in 82 centres. Other schools run on a mainly part-time basis by the Education Department for adult students are the School of Art, the School of Music and the School of Art and Design.

The University of Malta consists of 6 faculties: Law, Medicine and Surgery, Engineering and Architecture, Dental Surgery, Education and Management Studies (1,223 students in 1983–84). Degrees in Law, Mechanical Engineering, Electrical Engineering, Architecture and Civil Engineering, Accountancy, Business Management, Public Administration, Education, Medicine and Surgery, Pharmacy and Dental Surgery are conferred by the University.

Welfare. The National Insurance Act, 1956, provides cash benefits for marriage, maternity, sickness, unemployment, widowhood, orphanhood, invalidity, old age, children's allowances and industrial injury. An agreement, signed on 26 Oct. 1956, established reciprocity in matters of social insurance between Malta and the UK.

The total number of persons in receipt of benefits on 31 Dec. 1983 was 82,965, viz., 884 in receipt of sickness benefit, 818 unemployment benefit, 49 injury benefit, 218 disablement benefit, 87 death benefit, 20,154 retirement pensions, 7,910 widows' pensions, 12 widows' special allowance, 21 guardian's allowance, 5,087 invalidity pensions, 47,355 children's allowances and 370 maternity benefit.

The National Assistance Act, 1956, provides for the payment of social assistance and medical assistance, while the Old Age Pensions Act of 1948 provides for the payment of non-contributory pensions to persons over 60 years of age, to blind persons over the age of 14 years and to handicapped persons over the age of 16 years.

The number of households in receipt of social assistance and of medical assistance on 31 Dec. 1983 was 5,388 and 5,978 respectively, and the number of pensioners in receipt of a non-contributory pension under the Old Age Pensions Act, 1948, was 7,357.

DIPLOMATIC REPRESENTATIVES

Of Malta in Great Britain (16 Kensington Sq., London, W8 5HH)
Deputy High Commissioner: Francis Cassar.

Of Great Britain in Malta (7 St Anne St., Floriana)
High Commissioner: S. F. St. C. Duncan.

Of Malta in the USA (2017 Connecticut Ave., NW, Washington, D.C., 20008)
Chargé d'Affaires: Lawrence Farrugia.

Of the USA in Malta (Development Hse., St Anne St., Floriana)
Ambassador: James Malone Rentschler.

Of Malta to the United Nations
Ambassador: Victor J. Gauci.

Books of Reference

Statistical Information: The Central Office of Statistics (Auberge d'Italie, Valletta) was set up in 1947. It publishes *Statistical Abstracts of the Maltese Islands*, a quarterly digest of statistics, quarterly and annual trade returns, annual vital statistics and annual publications on shipping and aviation, education, agriculture and industry and National Accounts and Balance of Payments.

Government publications: Information Division (Kastilja, Malta), set up in 1955, publishes *The Malta Government Gazette* (twice weekly), *Il-Gzejjer* (monthly), *Malta Review* (bi-monthly), *Malta Handbook, Economic Survey, Malta: Guidelines for Progress, Development Plan for Malta 1981–85* and *Supplement Paper Currency in Malta, Heritage of an Island, Reports on the Working of Government Departments.* Malta, 1982.

Annual Reports. Central Bank of Malta
Trade Directory. Chamber of Commerce (annual)
The Year Book. Sliema (annual)
Malta Independence Constitution (Cmnd 2406). HMSO, 1964
Constitution of the Republic of Malta. Information Division, 1975
Malta Manufacturers and Exporters. Department of Industry, 1981
Economic Survey 1983. Malta, 1983
Bannerman, D. A., and Vella-Graffiero, J. A., *Birds of the Maltese Archipelago.* Valetta, 1976
Blouet, Brian, *The Story of Malta.* London, Rev. ed. 1981
Busuttil, E. D., *Kalepin Dizzjunarju Malti-Ingliz.* Valletta, 1971.—*Kalepin Dizzjunarju Ingliz-Malti.* 1976
Cassar, P., *Medical History of Malta.* London, 1966
Cremona, J. J., *The Malta Constitution of 1835 and its Historical Background.* Malta, 1959.—*The Constitutional Developments of Malta under British Rule.* Malta Univ. Press, 1963.—*Human Rights Documentation in Malta.* Malta Univ. Press, 1966
Gerada, E. and Zuber, C., *Malta: An Island Republic.* Paris, 1979
Haslam, S. M., Sell, P. D., and Wolseley, P. A., *A Flora of the Maltese Islands.* Malta Univ. Press, 1977
Luke, Sir Harry, *Malta.* 2nd ed. London, 1962
Price, G. A., *Malta and the Maltese: A Study in 19th-century Migration.* Melbourne, 1954
Smith, Harrison, *Britain in Malta.* 2 vols. Malta, 1954

MAURITANIA

Capital: Nouakchott
Population: 1·83m. (1984)
GNP per capita: US$460 (1981)

République Islamique de Mauritanie

HISTORY. Mauritania became a French protectorate in 1903 and a colony in 1920. It became an autonomous republic within the French Community on 28 Nov. 1958 and achieved full independence on 28 Nov. 1960. Under its first President, Moktar Ould Daddah, Mauritania became a one-party state in 1964, but following his deposition by a military *coup* on 10 July 1978, the ruling *Parti du peuple mauritanien* was dissolved.

Following the Spanish withdrawal from Western Sahara on 28 Feb. 1976, Mauritania occupied the southern part (88,667 sq. km) of this territory and incorporated it under the name of Tiris el Gharbia; on 8 Aug. seven additional members of the National Assembly were nominated to represent this territory. However in Aug. 1979 Mauritania renounced sovereignty and withdrew from Tiris el Gharbia.

Following the *coup* of 10 July 1978, power was placed in the hands of a Military Committee for National Recovery (CMRN); the constitution was suspended and the 70-member National Assembly dissolved. Col. Mustafa Ould Salek, Head of the CMRN, assumed the Presidency on 20 March 1979, and on 6 April the CMRN was renamed the Military Committee for National Salvation (CMSN). On 3 June Col. Salek was replaced as President by Lieut.-Col. Mohamed Mahmoud Ould Ahmed Louly, who was in turn replaced on 4 Jan. 1980 by his Prime Minister, Lieut.-Col. Mohamed Khouna Ould Haydalla.

AREA AND POPULATION. Mauritania is bounded west by the Atlantic ocean, north by Western Sahara, north-east by Algeria, east and south-east by Mali, and south by Sénégal. The total area is 1,030,700 sq. km (398,000 sq. miles), and the population at the Census of 1976 was 1,419,939 including 12,897 in Tiris el Gharbia; latest estimate (1984) 1,834,500. The main towns (with 1976 populations) are the capital Nouakchott (134,986), Nouâdhibou (21,961), Kaédi (20,848), Zouérate (17,474), Rosso (16,466) and Atâr (16,326).

In 1976, 22% of the population were urban and 36% were nomadic. 68% of the inhabitants are Moorish, speaking the Hassaniyah dialect of Arabic, while the other 32% consist of Negro peoples, speaking mainly Tukulor (20%), Sarakole (10%), and Wolof, all inhabiting the Sénégal valley in the extreme south.

The official languages are French and Arabic.

CLIMATE. A tropical climate, but conditions are generally arid, even near the coast, where the only appreciable rains come in July to Sept. Nouakchott. Jan. 71°F (21·7°C), July 82°F (27·8°C). Annual rainfall 6″ (158 mm).

CONSTITUTION AND GOVERNMENT. A draft Constitution was published on 19 Dec. 1980, but not promulgated. Pending a return to constitutional rule, the 24-member CMSN wields all executive and legislative powers, working through an appointed Council of Ministers composed as follows in Oct. 1984:

President, Prime Minister, Minister of Defence: Lieut.-Col. Mohamed Khouna Ould Haydalla (assumed office 4 Jan. 1980). *See* Addenda.

Foreign Affairs and Co-operation: Maj. Ahmed Ould Minnih. *Interior:* Lieut-Col. Yall Abdoulaye. *Justice and Islamic Affairs:* Lieut.-Col. Cheikh Ould Boyda. *Planning and Territorial Management:* Ahmed Ould Zein. *Economy and Finance:* Sidi Ould Ahmed Deya. *Fisheries and Maritime Economy:* Capt. Mohamed Lemine Ould N'Diayane. *Mines and Energy:* Dr Diabira Maroufa. *Industry:*

Lieut.-Col. Ann Amadou Baraly. *Rural Development:* Dr Louleid Ould Weddad. *Equipment and Transport:* Maj. Gabriel Cimper. *Education:* Hassiny Ould Didi. *Higher Education, Cadre Training and Civil Service:* Maj. Athie Hamath. *Health and Employment:* Maj. Mohamed Mahmoud Ould Deh. *Culture, Youth and Sports:* Mahmoud Ba. *Telecommunications and Information:* Dr Mohamed Salem Ould Zein. *Secretary-General of the Government:* Mohamed Ould Amar. *Minister-Counsellor to the Presidency:* Col. Ahmed Mahmoud Ould el-Hussein.

National flag: Green, with a crescent beneath a star in yellow in the centre.

Local Government: Mauritania is divided into the District of Nouakchott and 12 regions—Hodh ech Chargui, Hodh el Gharbi, Assaba, Gorgol, Brakna, Trarza, Adrar, Dakhlet Nouâdhibou, Tagent, Guidimaka, Tiris Zemmour and Inchiri. The regions are sub-divided into 44 *départements*.

DEFENCE

Army. The Army consists of 1 infantry and 1 artillery battalion, 3 armoured car squadrons and support units; total strength, 8,500 in 1985.

Navy. The Navy consists of 4 patrol vessels and 4 small patrol craft. Personnel (1985) 320.

Air Force. The Air Force has 6 Britten-Norman Defender armed light transports, 2 Maritime Surveillance Cheyennes for coastal patrol, 1 Buffalo and 2 Skyvan transports and 2 Islander aircraft, and 4 Reims-Cessna 337 Milirole twin-engined counter-insurgency, forward air control and training aircraft. Personnel (1984) 200.

INTERNATIONAL RELATIONS

Membership. Mauritania is a member of UN, OAU, the Arab League and is an ACP state of EEC.

ECONOMY

Planning. The 1981–85 development plan stresses the development of agriculture and light industry.

Budget. The ordinary budget for 1984 balanced at 13,800m. ouguiyas.

Currency. The monetary unit is *ouguiya* which is divided into 5 *khoums*. Banknotes of 1,000, 200 and 100 *ouguiya* and coins of 20, 10, 5 and 1 *ouguiya* and 1 *khoum* are in circulation. In March 1985, £1 = 71·73 *ouguiya*; US$1 = 67·16 *ouguiya*.

Banking. *The Banque Centrale de Mauritanie* (created 1973) is the bank of issue, and there are 5 commercial banks situated in Nouakchott.

ENERGY AND NATURAL RESOURCES

Electricity. Production (1979) 100m. kwh.

Minerals. Iron ore deposits of (estimate) 200m. tonnes are found at Zouérate. Production (1981) 8·9m. tonnes. Copper mining, suspended in 1978, resumed in 1983.

Agriculture. Agriculture is mainly confined to the south, in the Sénégal river valley. Production (tonnes) (1981) of millet, 67,000; dates, 14,000; potatoes, 4,000; maize, 6,000; sweet potatoes, 2,000; rice, 6,000; groundnuts, 4,000.

In 1983 there were 750,000 camels, 1·5m. cattle, 143,000 asses, 15,000 horses, 5m. sheep, 3m. goats.

Fisheries. About 300,000 tonnes of fish are caught in Mauritanian coastal waters each year, but only 34,200 tonnes (1978) are landed in the country (mainly at Nouâdhibou).

Forestry. There are 151,340 sq. km of forests, chiefly in the southern regions, where wild acacias yield the main product, gum arabic.

TRADE. In 1982 imports totalled 14,213m. ouguiya, and exports, 12,050 ouguiya of which, iron ore comprised 60% of exports and salted and dried fish 40%; 26% of all exports went to Italy, 21% to France, and 20% to Japan, while France provided 29% of imports and Spain 9%.

Total trade between Mauritania and UK (British Department of Trade returns, in £1,000 sterling):

	1980	*1981*	*1982*	*1983*	*1984*
Imports to UK	9,438	9,679	5,462	6,044	10,343
Exports and re-exports from UK	5,647	3,517	1,943	1,719	2,656

Tourism. In 1975 there were 20,700 tourists.

COMMUNICATIONS

Roads. There were 8,900 km of roads in 1983. In 1980 there were 8,300 passenger cars and 3,300 commercial vehicles.

Railways. A 652-km railway links Zouérate with the port of Point-Central, 10 km south of Nouâdhibou, and is used primarily for iron ore exports.

Aviation. There are international airports at Nouakchott, Nouâdhibou and Néma.

Shipping. The major ports are at Point-Central (for mineral exports), Nouakchott and Nouâdhibou.

Post and Broadcasting. There were, in 1977, over 2,000 telephones and 82,000 radio receivers.

Cinemas. In 1977 there were 12 cinemas with a seating capacity of 8,800.

JUSTICE, RELIGION, EDUCATION AND WELFARE

Justice. There are *tribunaux de première instance* at Nouakchott, Atar, Kaédi, Aïoun el Atrouss and Kiffa. The Appeal Court and Supreme Court are situated in Nouakchott. Islamic jurisprudence was adopted in Feb. 1980.

Religion. Over 99% of Mauritanians are Moslem, mainly of the Qadiriyah sect.

Education. In 1981 there were 90,530 pupils in primary schools, 20,248 in secondary schools, 1,004 in technical schools and 850 in teacher-training establishments.

Health. In 1976 there were 9 hospitals with 567 beds, there were 71 doctors, 4 dentists, 5 pharmacists, 20 midwives and 560 nursing personnel.

DIPLOMATIC REPRESENTATIVES

Of Mauritania in Great Britain
Ambassador: Ely Ould Allaf (accredited 15 Dec. 1983).

Of Great Britain in Mauritania
Ambassador: P. L. O'Keeffe, CMG, CVO. (resides in Dakar).

Of Mauritania in the USA (2129 Leroy Pl., NW, Washington, D.C., 20008)
Ambassador: Abdellah Ould Daddah.

Of the USA in Mauritania (PO Box 222, Nouakchott)
Ambassador: Edward L. Peck.

Of Mauritania to the United Nations
Ambassador: Mohamed Mahjoub Ould Boye.

Books of Reference

Stewart, C. C., and Stewart, E. K., *Islam and Social Order in Mauritania.* New York, 1970
Westebbe, R. M., *The Economy of Mauritania.* New York, 1971

MAURITIUS

Capital: Port Louis
Population: 969,191 (1983)
GNP per capita: US$1,270 (1981)

HISTORY. Mauritius was known to Arab navigators probably not later than the 10th century. It was probably visited by Malays in the 15th century, and was discovered by the Portuguese between 1507 and 1512, but the Dutch were the first settlers (1598). In 1710 they abandoned the island, which was occupied by the French under the name of Ile de France (1715). The British occupied the island in 1810, and it was formally ceded to Great Britain by the Treaty of Paris, 1814. Mauritius attained independence on 12 March 1968.

AREA AND POPULATION. Mauritius has an area of about 720 sq. miles (1,865 sq. km). According to the census of 30 June 1972, the population of the island was 826,199 (413,580 males, 412,619 females); that of the dependencies was 25,135 (30 June 1972). Estimated population of the island at the end of 1983 was 969,191, and the population of Port Louis, the capital with its suburbs, numbered 149,900. Port Louis was granted city status on 25 Aug. 1966. Other towns: Beau Bassin-Rose Hill, 88,890; Curepipe, 58,611; Quatre Bornes, 57,487; Vascoas-Phoenix, 56,756.

Rodrigues (formerly a dependency but now a part of Mauritius) is about 350 miles east of Mauritius, 9½ miles long, 4½ miles broad. Area, 40 sq. miles (103·6 sq. km). Population (31 Dec. 1983, estimate), 35,594. Imports, 1983, Rs 96·3m. Exports, 1983, Rs 9·7m. There are 5 government, 5 aided primary, 1 private and 1 state secondary school.

Vital statistics, June 1983: Births, 19,948 (20·5 per 1,000); marriages, 10,067; deaths, 6,322 (6·6 per 1,000).

The official language is English.

Outer Islands. Agalega and St Brandon Group. St Brandon is 250 miles from Mauritius. Area, 71 sq. km. Total population of the islands, census 1972, 366; estimated population on 31 Dec. 1983, 350. In 1965 the Chagos Archipelago was transferred to the British Indian Ocean Territory.

CLIMATE. The sub-tropical climate produces quite a difference between summer and winter, though conditions are generally humid. Most rain falls in the summer so that the pleasantest months are Sept. to Nov. Rainfall amounts vary between 40″ (1,000 mm) on the coast to 200″ (5,000 mm) on the central plateau, though the west coast only has 35″ (875 mm). Mauritius lies in the cyclone belt, whose season runs from Nov. to April, but is seldom affected by intense storms. Port Louis. Jan. 73°F (22·8°C), July 81°F (27·2°C). Annual rainfall 40″ (1,000 mm).

CONSTITUTION AND GOVERNMENT. Mauritius became an independent state and a monarchial member of the British Commonwealth on 12 March 1968 after 7 months of internal self-government. The Governor-General is the local representative of HM the Queen, who remains the Head of the State.

The Cabinet is presided over by the Prime Minister. Each of the other 18 members of the Cabinet is responsible for the administration of specified departments or subjects and is bound by the rule of collective responsibility. 10 Parliamentary Secretaries may also be appointed by the Governor-General on the advice of the Prime Minister.

The Legislative Assembly consists of a Speaker, elected from its own members, and 62 elected members (3 each for the 20 constituencies of Mauritius and 2 for Rodrigues) and 8 additional seats in order to ensure a fair and adequate representation of each community within the Assembly. General Elections are held every 5 years on the basis of universal adult suffrage.

The Constitution also provides for the Public Service Commission and the

Judicial and Legal Service Commission, which have both assumed executive powers for appointments to the Public Service. An Ombudsman assumed office on 2 March 1970. Adequate provision is also made for the protection of fundamental rights and freedoms of the individual.

Elections were held in Aug. 1983.

Governor-General: The Rt Hon. Sir Seewoosagur Ramgoolam, GCMG.

The Cabinet was composed as follows in Oct. 1984:

Prime Minister, Defence and Internal Security, Information, Reform Institutions and External Communications: Aneerood Jugnauth.

Deputy Prime Minister, Attorney-General and Minister of Justice: Gaetan Duval. *Finance:* Seetanah Lutchmeenaraidoo. *Economic Planning and Development:* Beergoonath Ghurburrun. *Trade and Shipping:* Abdool Kader Ahmed Bhayat. *Employment and Social Security, National Solidarity:* Diwakur Bundhun. *External Affairs, Tourism and Emigration:* Anil Kumarsingh Gayan. *Agriculture, Fisheries and Natural Resources:* Nunkeswarsingh Deerpalsingh. *Works:* Rohit Niemo Beedassy. *Education, Arts and Culture:* Armoogum Parsuraman. *Housing, Lands and the Environment:* Dwarkanath Gungah. *Energy and Internal Communications:* Mahyendrah Utchanah. *Health:* Rajkeswur Purryag. *Industry:* Ramsamy Chedumbarum Pillay. *Labour and Industrial Relations:* Joseph Herve Duval. *Women's Rights and Family Welfare:* Mrs Sheilabai Bappoo. *Youth and Sports:* Michael James Kevin Glover. *Rodrigues and the Outer Islands:* France Felicite. *Local Government and Co-operatives:* Karl Offman.

National flag: Horizontally 4 stripes of red, blue, yellow and green.

DEFENCE. The Mauritius Police, which is responsible for defence, is equipped with arms; its strength at 30 June 1982 was 4,082 officers and men.

INTERNATIONAL RELATIONS

Membership. Mauritius is a member of UN, the Commonwealth, OAU and is an ACP state of EEC.

ECONOMY

Budget. Revenue and expenditure (in Rs) for years ending 30 June:

	1978–79	*1979–80*	*1980–81*	*1981–82*	*1982–83*
Revenue	1,486,394,583	1,863,872,536	2,163,055,708	2,398,000,000	2,928,644,798
Expenditure	1,769,964,582	2,016,144,439	2,525,190,433	3,075,000,000	3,709,755,222

Principal sources of revenue, 1982–83 (estimate): Direct taxes, Rs 510·9m.; indirect taxes, Rs 1,919·3m.; receipts from public utilities, Rs 135m.; receipts from public services Rs 102·5m.; interest and reimbursement, Rs 102·5m. Capital expenditure, June 1983, was Rs 1,009·4. Capital revenue, Rs 842·1m. On 30 June 1983 the public debt of Mauritius was Rs 6,096,744,688 after deducting the value of accumulated sinking funds.

Currency. The unit of currency is the Mauritius *Rupee*, divided into 100 *cents*.

The currency consists of: (i) Bank of Mauritius notes of Rs 50, 25, 10 and 5; (ii) Cupro-nickel coins of 1 rupee, ½ rupee, ¼ rupee and 10 cents; (iii) Bronze coins of 5 cents, 2 cents and 1 cent. In March 1985, £1 = 17·68 *rupees*; US$1 = 16·84.

Banking. The Bank of Mauritius was established in 1966, with an authorized capital of Rs 10m., to exercise the function of a central bank. There are 12 commercial banks, the Mauritius Commercial Bank Ltd (established 1838), Barclays Bank International, the Bank of Baroda Ltd, The Hong Kong and Shanghai Banking Corporation, the Mauritius Co-operative Central Bank Ltd, Banque Nationale de Paris (Intercontinentale), the Habib Bank (Overseas) Ltd, Citibank, the State Commercial Bank, the Bank of Credit and Commerce International SA, Indian Ocean International Bank Ltd and Habib Bank (Zurich). Other financial institutions include the Mauritius Housing Corporation, the Development Bank of Mauritius and the post office savings bank.

On 31 Dec. 1983 the post office savings bank held deposits amounting to Rs 129·6m., belonging to 207,524 depositors.

NATURAL RESOURCES

Agriculture (1983). The area planted with sugar-cane was 209,010 acres. There were 21 factories in operation and the amount of sugar produced was: Raw sugar (1983), 558,000 tonnes; white sugar, 52,975 tonnes; molasses, 161,780 tonnes.

The main secondary crops are tea (9,241 acres, yielding 6,142 tonnes of tea), tobacco (1,759 acres, yielding 800 tonnes of tobacco), potatoes (15,000 tonnes) and onions (1,684 tonnes).

Livestock (1983): Cattle, 25,485; goats, 72,696; poultry, 1·7m.

Forestry. The total forest area is estimated at 21,005 hectares including some 11,578 hectares of plantations; if scrub and grazing are included the total area is approximately 56,197 hectares.

In 1983 sales of forest produce from Crown land totalled 29,876 cu. metres, round wood.

INDUSTRY AND TRADE

Industry. Manufactures include: Knitwear, clothing, diamond cutting, watch straps, fertilizers.

Labour. There were on 31 Dec. 1983, 360 registered trade unions with a total membership of 81,502 (on roll).

Commerce. Total trade (in Rs) for calendar years:

	1979	*1980*	*1981*	*1982*	*1983*
Imports [1]	3,634,400,000	4,721,400,000	4,976,800,000	5,048,200,000	5,155,900,000
Exports [2]	2,432,700,000	3,341,300,000	2,999,200,000	3,988,700,000	4,311,300,000

[1] Excluding bullion and specie.
[2] Including value of sugar quota certificates.

In 1983, Rs 611·5m. of the imports came from France, Rs 449·2m. from South Africa, Rs 449·4m. from UK and Rs 242·3m. from Australia; Rs 2,182·1m. of the exports went to UK, Rs 1,009·9m. to France, Rs 166·8m. to Federal Republic of Germany and Rs 366·2m. to USA.

Sugar exports in 1983, 569,501 tonnes (Rs 2,597·8m.).

Total trade between Mauritius and UK (British Department of Trade returns, in £1,000 sterling):

	1980	*1981*	*1982*	*1983*	*1984*
Imports to UK	145,227	97,435	119,450	128,437	160,042
Exports and re-exports from UK	24,688	21,612	20,857	22,499	24,358

Tourism. In 1983, 123,820 tourists visited Mauritius.

COMMUNICATIONS

Roads. There are 25·5 miles of motorway, 523 miles of main roads, 361 miles of urban roads and 216 miles of rural roads. All the main urban and rural roads have a bitumen surface. At 31 Dec. 1983 there were 26,024 cars, including 2,954 for public hire, 1,418 buses, 8,523 motor cycles and 18,653 auto cycles. Commercial vehicles comprised 13,548 lorries and vans.

Aviation. Mauritius is linked by air with Europe, Africa, Asia and Australia by the following airlines: Air France, Air India, Air Malawi, Air Mauritius, British Airways, Lufthansa, South African Airways and Zambia Airways. In addition to passenger services a weekly cargo flight is operated by Air France on the Mauritius–Paris route.

Air Mauritius operates a Boeing 707 service to London *via* Nairobi and Rome and to Bombay *via* the Seychelles, and Twin Otter services to Réunion and Rodrigues. The company has commercial arrangements with Air France, Lufthansa, Alitalia, Zambia Airways and Air Malawi for the operation of services to Paris, Frankfurt, Rome, Lusaka and Blantyre.

Shipping. In 1983 898 vessels entered Port Louis; total tonnage of cargo, about 1·8m. tonnes.

Post and Broadcasting. In Dec. 1983 there were 31 telephone exchanges and 48,462 individual telephone installations in Mauritius and Rodrigues. Communication with other parts of the world is established *via* satellite.

Television was introduced in Feb. 1965. At 31 Dec. 1983 there were 95,063 television sets and 125,625 radio sets.

Cinemas (1984). There were 46 cinemas, with a seating capacity of about 46,000.

Newspapers. There were (1984) 5 French daily papers (with occasional articles in English) and 2 Chinese daily papers with a combined circulation of about 66,000.

RELIGION, EDUCATION AND WELFARE

Religion. At the 1972 census there were 245,570 Roman Catholics, 7,050 Protestants (Church of England and Church of Scotland). The Hindus numbered 421,707 and the Moslems. 136,997. State aid is granted to the churches and Rs 7m. is budgeted for 1984–85.

Education. Primary education is free but not compulsory, though under the Education Ordinance of 1957 compulsion may be introduced as circumstances permit. In 1983 there were 219 government and 49 state-aided primary schools, 2 Hindu and 47 Roman Catholic. Enrolment at government schools was 105,467 and at state-aided primary schools 26,466. There were 8 special schools (blind, deaf, educationally sub-normal and industrial).

For secondary education there were in 1983, 5 government boys' schools (one of which has technical and commercial streams), 16 junior secondary schools (including one in Rodrigues) and 3 government girls' schools and 103 private secondary schools (including Mahatma Gandhi Institute) with 75,963 pupils.

There is also a teachers' training college, known as the Mauritius College of Education, and 8 private vocational and technical training centres, 650 on roll including students following part-time courses.

Health. In 1983 there were 690 doctors, including 120 specialists, and 2,841 hospital beds.

DIPLOMATIC REPRESENTATIVES

Of Mauritius in Great Britain (32–33 Elvaston Pl., London, SW7)
High Commissioner: D. Gian Nath (accredited 13 Dec. 1983).

Of Great Britain in Mauritius (Cerné Hse., Chausée, Port Louis)
High Commissioner: James Nicholas Allan, CBE.

Of Mauritius in the USA (4301 Connecticut Ave., NW, Washington, D.C., 20008)
Ambassador: Chitmansing Jesseramsing.

Of the USA in Mauritius (Rogers Bldg., John Kennedy St., Port Louis)
Ambassador: George Roberts Andrews.

Of Mauritius to the United Nations
Ambassador: Rameschand Seereekissoon.

Books of Reference

Statistical Information: The Central Statistical Information Office (Rose Hill, Mauritius) was founded in July 1945. Its main publication is the *Bi-annual Digest of Statistics.*

Brouard, N. R., *A History of Woods and Forests in Mauritius.* Government Printer, 1964
Buckory, S., *Our Constitution.* Port Louis, 1971.—*An Outline of Local Government.* Port Louis, 1970
Chelin, A., *Une île et son passé (1507–1947).* Mauritius Printing, 1973
Ministry of Information and Broadcasting, *Fruits of Political and Social Democracy.—Mauritius Facts and Figures 1980*
Napal, D., *Les constitutions de l'Ile Maurice.* Port Louis, 1962
Simmons, A. S., *Modern Mauritius: The Politics of Decolonization.* Indiana Univ. Press, 1982
Société de l'Histoire de l'Ile Maurice. *Dictionnaire de biographie mauricienne.* Port Louis, 1967
Toussaint A., *History of Mauritius.* London, 1978

Library: The Mauritius Institute Public Library, Port Louis.

MEXICO

Capital: Mexico City
Population: 76·79m. (1984)
GNP per capita: US$2,250 (1981)

Estados Unidos Mexicanos

HISTORY. Mexico's history falls into four epochs: the era of the Indian empires (before 1521), the Spanish colonial phase (1521–1810), the period of national formation (1810–1910), which includes the war of independence (1810–21) and the long presidency of Porfirio Díaz (1876–80, 1884–1911), and the present period which began with the social revolution of 1910–21 and is regarded by Mexicans as the period of social and national consolidation.

AREA AND POPULATION. Mexico is at the southern extremity of North America and is bounded in the north by USA, west and south-west by the Pacific, south by Guatemala and Belize and east by the Gulf of Mexico. It comprises 1,958,201 sq. km (756,198 sq. miles), including uninhabited islands (5,073 sq. km) offshore.

The population at recent censuses has been as follows:

1900	13,607,272	1960	34,923,129	1980	66,846,833
1930	16,552,722	1970	48,225,238		

The areas (in sq. km), populations and capitals of the states are:

States	*Sq. km*	*Census 1980*	*Capital*
Aguascalientes	5,471	519,439	Aguascalientes
Baja California	69,921	1,177,886	Mexicali
Baja California Sur	73,475	215,139	La Paz
Campeche	50,812	420,553	Campeche
Chiapas	74,211	2,084,717	Tuxtla Gutiérrez
Chihuahua	244,938	2,005,477	Chihuahua
Coahuila	149,982	1,557,265	Saltillo
Colima	5,191	346,293	Colima
Distrito Federal	1,479	8,831,079	México City
Durango	123,181	1,182,320	Victoria de Durango
Guanajuato	30,491	3,006,110	Guanajuato
Guerrero	64,281	2,109,513	Chilpancingo
Hidalgo	20,813	1,547,493	Pachuca de Soto
Jalisco	80,836	4,371,998	Guadalajara
México	21,355	7,564,335	Toluca de Lerdo
Michoacán de Ocampo	59,928	2,868,824	Morelia
Morelos	4,950	947,089	Cuernavaca
Nayarit	26,979	726,120	Tepic
Nuevo León	64,924	2,513,044	Monterrey
Oaxaca	93,952	2,369,076	Oaxaca de Juárez
Puebla	33,902	3,347,685	Puebla de Zaragoza
Querétaro	11,449	739,605	Querétaro
Quintana Roo	50,212	225,985	Chetumal
San Luis Potosí	63,068	1,673,893	San Luis Potosí
Sinaloa	58,328	1,849,879	Culiacán Rosales
Sonora	182,052	1,513,731	Hermosillo
Tabasco	25,267	1,062,961	Villahermosa
Tamaulipas	79,384	1,924,484	Ciudad Victoria
Tlaxcala	4,016	556,597	Tlaxcala
Veracruz	71,699	5,387,680	Jalapa Enríquez
Yucatán	38,402	1,063,733	Mérida
Zacatecas	73,252	1,136,830	Zacatecas

At the 1980 census 33,039,307 were males, 33,807,526 females. Urban population was 66·3% and rural population was 33·7%. Estimate (1984) 76,791,819. The official language is Spanish, the mother tongue of over 92% of the population, but there are 5 indigenous language groups (Náhuatl, Maya, Zapotec, Otomi and Mixtec) from which are derived a total of 59 dialects spoken by 5,181,038 inhabitants (1980 census). In 1980, about 16% of the population were of European ethnic origin, 55% mestizo and 29% Amerindian.

The populations (1980 Census) of the largest cities were:

México [1]	12,932,116	Morelia	353,055	Tepic	177,007
Guadalajara [2]	2,244,715	Hermosillo	340,779	Ensenada	175,425
Monterrey [2]	1,916,472	Saltillo	321,758	Poza Rica de Hidalgo	166,799
Netzahualcóyotl	1,341,230	Victoria de Durango	321,148	Tuxtla Gutiérrez	166,476
Puebla de Zaragoza	835,759	Veracruz Llave	305,456	Salamanca	160,040
Léon de los Aldamas	655,809	Querétaro	293,586	Oaxaca de Juárez	157,284
Ciudad Juárez	567,365	Tampico	267,957	Ciudad Victoria	153,206
Culiacán Rosales	560,011	Villa Hermosa	250,903	Campeche	151,805
Mexicali	510,554	Mazatlán	249,988	Uruapan	146,998
Tijuana	461,257	Irapuato	246,308	Minatitlán	145,268
Mérida	424,529	Matamoros	238,840	Pachuca de Soto	135,248
Acapulco de Juárez	409,335	Cuernavaca	232,355	Ciudad Madero	132,444
Chihuahua	406,830	Celaya	219,010	Cordoba	126,179
San Luis Potosí	406,630	Jalapa Enríquez	212,769	Monclova	119,609
Torreón	363,886	Reynosa	211,412	Orizaba	114,848
Aguascalientes	359,454	Nuevo Laredo	203,286		
Toluca de Lerdo	357,071	Coatzacoalcos	186,129		

[1] Metropolitan Area (including Netzahualcóyotl). [2] Metropolitan Area.

Vital statistics for calendar years:

	Marriages	*Births*	*Deaths*
1978	463,157	2,346,862	418,381
1979	488,270	2,448,774	428,217
1980	483,151	2,428,499	434,465

Crude birth rate in 1980 was 36·3 per 1,000 population; crude death rate, 6·5; marriage rate 7·2.

CLIMATE. Latitude and relief produce a variety of climates. Arid and semi-arid conditions are found in the north, with extreme temperatures, whereas in the south there is a humid tropical climate, with temperatures varying with altitude. Conditions on the shores of the Gulf of Mexico are very warm and humid. In general, the rainy season lasts from May to Nov. Mexico City. Jan. 55°F (12·6°C), July 61°F (16·1°C). Annual rainfall 30″ (747 mm). Guadalajara. Jan. 59°F (15·2°C), July 69°F (20·5°C). Annual rainfall 36″ (902 mm). La Paz. Jan. 64°F (17·8°C), July 85°F (29·4°C). Annual rainfall 6″ (145 mm). Mazatlan Jan. 66°F (18·9°C), July 82°F (27·8°C). Annual rainfall 33″ (828 mm). Merida. Jan. 72°F (22·2°C), July 83°F (28·3°C). Annual rainfall 38″ (957 mm). Monterey. Jan. 58°F (14·4°C), July 81°F (27·2°C). Annual rainfall 23″ (588 mm). Puebla de Zaragoza. Jan. 54°F (12·2°C), July 63°F (17·2°C). Annual rainfall 34″ (850 mm).

CONSTITUTION AND GOVERNMENT. A new Constitution was promulgated on 5 Feb. 1917 and has been amended from time to time. Mexico is a representative, democratic and federal republic, comprising 31 states and a federal district, each state being free and sovereign in all internal affairs, but united in a federation established according to the principals of the Fundamental Law. Citizenship, including the right of suffrage, is vested in all nationals of 18 years of age and older who have 'an honourable means of livelihood'.

There is complete separation of legislative, executive and judicial powers (Art. 49). Legislative power is vested in a General Congress of 2 chambers, a Chamber of Deputies and a Senate (Art. 50). The Chamber of Deputies consists of 400 members directly elected for 3 years, 300 of them from single-member constituencies and 100 chosen under a system of proportional representation (Arts. 51–55). At the general elections held on 4 July 1982, 299 of the single-member seats were won by the *Partido Revolucionario Institucional* (PRI) and 1 by the *Partido de Acción Nacional* (PAN); of the extra 100 seats, 50 were won by PAN, 17 by the *Partido*

Socialista Unificado de México, 10 by the *Partido Popular Socialista,* 11 by the *Partido Socialista de los Trabajadores* and 12 by the *Partido Demócrata Mexicano.* The Senate comprises 64 members, 2 from each state and 2 from the federal district, directly elected for 6 years (Arts.56–58). At the elections of 4 July 1982, the PRI won all 64 seats. Members of both chambers are not immediately re-eligible for election (Art.59). Congress sits from 1 Sept. to 31 Dec. each year; during the recess there is a permanent committee of 15 deputies and 14 senators appointed by the respective chambers.

The President is the supreme executive authority. He appoints the members of the Council of Ministers and the senior military and civilian officers of the state. He is directly elected for a single 6-year term.

The names of the presidents from 1934 are as follows:

Gen. Lázaro Cárdenas, 1 Dec. 1934–30 Nov. 1940.
Gen. Manuel Avila Cámacho, 1 Dec. 1940–30 Nov. 1946.
Miguel Alemán Valdés, 1 Dec. 1946–30 Nov. 1952.
Adolfo Ruiz Cortinez, 1 Dec 1952–30 Nov. 1958.
Adolfo López Mateos, 1 Dec. 1958–30 Nov. 1964.
Gustavo Díaz Ordaz, 1 Dec. 1964–30 Nov. 1970.
Luis Echeverría Alvarez, 1 Dec. 1970–30 Nov. 1976.
José López Portillo y Pacheco, 1 Dec. 1976–30 Nov. 1982.

President: Miguel de la Madrid Hurtado (born in 1934), formerly Minister of Planning, elected 4 July 1982. He assumed office on 1 Dec. 1982.

In Nov. 1984 the Council of Ministers was composed as follows:

Agrarian Reform: Luis Martínez Villicaña. *Agriculture and Water Resources:* Eduárdo Pesqueira Olea. *Commerce and Industrial Development:* Héctor Hernández Cervantes. *Communication and Transport:* Rodolfo Félix Valdés. *Finance and Public Credit:* Jesús Silva Herzog Flores. *Foreign Relations:* Bernardo Sepúlveda Amor. *Interior:* Manuel Bartlett Díaz. *Health and Assistance:* Dr Guillermo Soberón Acevedo. *Urban Development and Energy:* Marcelo Javelly Girard. *Labour and Social Welfare:* Arsenio Farell Cubillas. *National Defence:* Gen. Juan José Arévalo Gardoqui. *Navy:* Adm. Miguel Angel Gómez Ortega. *Energy, Mines and State Industries:* Francisco Labastida Ochoa. *Planning and Budget:* Carlos Salinas de Gortari. *Public Education:* Jesús Reyes Heroles. *Tourism:* Antonio Enríquez Savignac. *Fisheries:* Pedro Ojeda Paullada. *Comptroller-General:* Francisco Rojas Gutierréz. *Attorney-General:* Sergio García Ramírez. *Governor of the Federal District:* Ramón Aguirre Velázquez. *Attorney-General of the Federal District:* Sra. Victoria Adato de Ibarra. *Head of Petróleos Mexicanos (PEMEX):* Mario Ramón Beteta. *Governor of the Bank of Mexico:* Miguel Mancera Aguayo.

National flag: Three vertical strips of green, white, red, with the national arms in the centre.

National anthem: Mexicanos, al grito de guerra (words by F. González Bocanegra; tune by Jaime Nunó, 1854).

Local Government. Mexico is divided into 31 states and a Federal District. The latter is co-extensive with Mexico City and is administered by a Governor appointed by the President. Each state has its own constitution, with the right to legislate and to levy taxes (but not inter-state customs duties); its Governor is directly elected for 6 years and its unicameral legislature for 3 years; judicial officers are appointed by the state governments.

DEFENCE. Supreme command is vested in the President, exercised through the Ministries of Defence (for Army and Air Force) and Marine.

Army. Enlistment into the regular army is voluntary, but there is conscription into a part-time militia, which numbers some 250,000. The regular army consists of 1 mechanized brigade group, 2 infantry brigade groups, 1 parachute brigade, 1 reconnaissance regiment, 1 armoured regiment, a garrison for each of the country's 35 military zones, and support units. Equipment includes 40 M-3A1 and 20 M-5A1 light tanks and some 140 armoured cars. Strength of the regular army (1985) 95,000.

Navy. The fleet comprises 3 very old *ex*-US destroyers, 5 very old *ex*-US frigates (including 4 former destroyer escort transports), 6 modern light frigate or corvette-type with small helicopter and hangar and 1 frigate-size listed as patrol ships, 1 ancient frigate-size armed transport and 6 old *ex*-US armed tugs used as patrol ships, 18 old *ex*-US fleet minesweepers, 16 old *ex*-US escort minesweepers, 21 fishery protection cutters of 130 tons built in Britain in 1974–76 and 10 similar-design patrol craft built in Mexico in 1978–80, 18 patrol boats, 7 survey ships, 1 transport, 3 armed landing ships (2 used for rescue and 1 (with helicopter landing deck) for light forces repair), 2 oilers, 1 training ship, 21 auxiliary vessels and 8 tugs. There are 5 naval zones on the Gulf and 11 on the Pacific coast and 6 naval air bases holding 54 aircraft. Naval personnel in 1985 totalled 23,650 officers and men including naval air force and 3,800 marines.

Air Force. The Air Force has a strength of about 5,500 officers and men, and has nine operational groups, each with one or two squadrons. No. 1 Group comprises No. 208 Squadron with 10 IAI Aravas for transport, search and rescue and counter-insurgency duties; and No. 209 Squadron with Bell 205A, 206B Jet-Ranger, 212, Alouette III and Puma helicopters. No. 2 Group has two Squadrons (Nos. 206 and 207) of Swiss-built Pilatus PC-7 Turbo-Trainers for light attack duty. No. 3 Group (203 and 204 Squadrons) also operates PC-7s; No. 4 Group (201 and 205 Squadrons) is in process of conversion to PC-7s. No. 5 Group consists of No. 101 communications Squadron and a photo-reconnaissance unit, both equipped with Aero Commander 500S piston-engined light twins. Nos. 301 and 302 Squadrons, in No. 6 Group, operate a total of 5 C-54, 2 C-118A and 1 DC-7 piston-engined transports. The main combat Group, No. 7, comprises No. 401 Squadron with 12 F-5E Tiger II and F-5F 2-seat fighters; and No. 202 Squadron with AT-33A jet trainer/fighter-bombers. No. 8 Group has 7 C-47s in a VIP transport squadron. No. 9 Group operates the Air Force's remaining 12 or more C-47s in Nos. 311 and 312 transport Squadrons. There is a Presidential Squadron with 9 Boeing 727s, 1 737-247, 1 HS.125, 1 JetStar, 1 Islander and 1 Bell 212. The Military Academy continues to fly 14 veteran Stearman PT-17 biplanes. Other training aircraft include 20 Mudry CAP 10Bs, 20 Beech Musketeers, 20 Bonanzas, and PC-7 Turbo-Trainers.

INTERNATIONAL RELATIONS

Membership. Mexico is a member of UN, OAS and ALIDE (formerly LAFTA).

External Debt. The public sector external debt (Dec. 1983) was US$62,556m. and private sector US$14,000m.

ECONOMY

Budget. The 1984 budget provides for expenditure of 12,023,282m. pesos.

Currency. The monetary unit is the *peso* divided into 100 *centavos*. There are coins of 20 and 50 *centavos* and 1, 5, 10, 50 and 100 *pesos*; and banknotes of 100, 500, 1,000, 2,000, 5,000 and 10,000 *pesos*.

Rate of exchange, March 1985: 203 pesos = US$1; 216 pesos = £1.

Banking. The Bank of Mexico, established 1 Sept. 1925, is the central bank of issue; it is modelled on the Federal Reserve system, with large powers to 'manage' the currency. On 1 Sept. 1982 the private banking sector was nationalized.

Weights and Measures. The metric system was introduced in 1896, and its sole use is enjoined by law of 14 Dec. 1928.

ENERGY AND NATURAL RESOURCES

Electricity. In 1983 the 498 generating plants had installed capacity of 19m. kw. Production, 1983, 79,951m. kwh.

Oil. The chief Mexican oilfields had proven reserves of oil and gas, in 1983, of 72,500m. bbls. In 1982 the oil industry generated 6·3% of the GDP and supplied about 85% of the energy consumed in the country. Since the nationalization of the industry in 1938, Petróleos Mexicanos, a government-owned enterprise, has exclusive rights to the exploitation, refining and sale of oil and its by-products. Initially centred on the northeast coasts of the Gulf of Mexico, the industry developed with the discovery of rich fields in the south and southeast, particularly in Veracruz, Tabasco and Chiapas. Offshore wells and those from the southeast now provide the main yields. Exploration has been primarily in recent years in deep waters on the continental shelf in the Gulf coast area, as well as in the northern and southern zones inland. Crude petroleum output was 150m. tonnes in 1984.

Gas. Natural gas production came to 41,880m. cu. metres in 1983.

Minerals. Uranium deposits were discovered in the states of Chihuahua, Durango, Sonora and Queretaro in 1959, rich deposits have been located in Nuevo León. Total reserves (proven 1982) 15,000 tonnes of uranium 308; potential reserves, 150,000 tonnes.

Silver output (in tonnes) was 1,911 in 1983; gold 6,930 kg.

Mexico has large coal resources, calculated at 5,448m. tonnes, including 1,675m. tonnes (65% cokeable) including high-grade coking coal in Coahuila.

Output, 1983 (in 1,000 tonnes): Lead, 167·4; copper, 206·1; zinc, 257·4; fluorite, 557; pig iron, 5,306; sulphur, 1,602; manganese, 133.

Agriculture. About 80% of Mexico's territory is unsuitable for agriculture. Irrigation is needed, 50% of the land having less than 500 mm of rain a year. In 1981 Mexico had 21·9m. hectares of arable land, 74·4m. hectares of meadows and pastures, 48·1m. hectares of forests, 1·6m. hectares of permanent crops and 40·6m. hectares of other land. In 1980, the government launched the *Sistema Alimentario Mexicano* to raise food production and rationalize land tenure, with the aim of achieving self-sufficiency in basic crops. Grains occupy most of the cultivated land, with about 43% given to maize, 10% to sorghum and 5% to wheat. In 1982 there were 146,083 tractors. It is estimated that Mexico should be self-supporting with at least 17m. hectares of land under irrigation and 20·3m. hectares under cultivation.

Livestock (1983): Cattle, 37·5m.; sheep, 6·3m.; pigs, 19·4m.; horses, 6m.; goats, 9·8m.; mules, 3·1m.; donkeys, 3·1m.; poultry, 204m.

Mexico's basic food crop is maize, and a rapid expansion of this crop is one of the chief aims of Mexican agricultural policy, balanced by the demand for 'cash crops' for export, such as cotton, sugar, garbanzos (chick peas), bananas, winter vegetables and coffee.

Production of crops for 1983 was as follows (in 1,000 tonnes):

Crop	*1983*	*Crop*	*1983*	*Crop*	*1983*
Maize	13,191	Sugar-cane	33,860	Oranges	1,758
Sorghum	4,827	Tomatoes	1,093 [1]	Bananas	1,382
Wheat	3,463	Potatoes	868 [1]	Lemons	601
Barley	557	Dry beans	1,296	Pineapples	635
Rice	1,416	Soybeans	687	Apples	312
Cottonseed	340	Coconuts	113 [1]	Grapes	478
Cotton lint	182	Coffee	313	Mangoes	750

[1] 1981.

Sugar-cane is linked closely with the export markets, although not to the same degree as coffee, in view of the fact that despite the large crop, the national consumption of sugar, at approximately 35 kg a year per person, is one of the highest in the world. Exports have however remained more or less stable: 1972 exports represented 25% of total output.

Forestry. Forests extended over 48m. hectares in 1981, containing pine, spruce, cedar, mahogany, logwood and rosewood. There are 14 forest reserves (nearly 800,000 hectares) and 47 national park forests of 750,000 hectares. In 1983 total roundwood production amounted to 8·75m. cu. metres.

Fisheries. Catch (1983, in tonnes): sardines, 303,290; anchoveta, 84,662; shrimp and prawns, 67,555; oysters, 27,810; tunny, 17,541; shark, 17,436; sea perch (*mojarras*), 63,989; sea bass, 10,723. Total catch in 1983 was 972,627 tonnes.

INDUSTRY AND TRADE

Industry. In 1983, the primary sector (agriculture etc.) provided 7·9% of GDP, the mining, oil and petrochemical industry 11·2%, manufacturing and construction 27·4% and the service sector (commerce, transport and communications, power supply and other services) 54·6%.

Labour. In 1980, the economically active population was 22,066,084, of whom 5·7m. were engaged in the primary sector and 2·6m. in manufacturing. Approximately 5m. people belong to trade unions, of whom 85% are affiliated to the *Congreso del Trabajo*.

Commerce. Trade for calendar years in US$1m.:

	1980	*1981*	*1982*	*1983*
Imports	19,801	25,061	15,057	8,200
Exports	15,134	19,420	21,230	21,012

Of total imports in 1983, 60% came from USA, 4·5% from Federal Republic of Germany and 4·5% from France. Leading imports were maize, sorghum, transport equipment, machine tools, parts and spares.

Of total exports in 1983, 58% went to USA, 7·6% to Spain, 7·1% to Japan and 4·3% to UK. The main exports (1983) were crude oil, coffee and vehicles.

Total trade between Mexico and UK (British Department of Trade returns, in £1,000 sterling):

	1980	*1981*	*1982*	*1983*	*1984*
Imports to UK	111,636	108,749	106,067	160,978	175,487
Exports and re-exports from UK	188,133	209,596	162,946	95,674	150,126

Tourism. Tourism is the largest single source of dollar income. In 1983, there were 4,749,000 tourists; gross revenue, including border visitors, amounted to US$1,625m.

COMMUNICATIONS

Roads. Total length, (1982) 214,073 km, of which 1,178 km were motorways. Motor vehicles registered in 1982 comprised 5,221,200 passenger cars, and 1,891,400 commercial vehicles.

Railways. In 1937 the main railway lines were nationalized. The principal group is the *Ferrocarriles Nacionales de México*, with 25,474 km of track. Three lines (215 km) remain privately owned. In 1982, FNM carried 70m. tonnes of freight and 22m. passengers. In Mexico City an urban railway system opened in 1969 had 78 km of track and 5 lines in 1982.

Aviation. Mexico has an excellent air service. There are 32 international and 40 national airports. Each of the larger states has a local airline which links them with main airports, which, in turn, furnish services to US, Central and South America and Europe. In 1983, 34 companies maintained international services, of which 2 were Mexican. Domestic flights are handled by 77 companies. In 1983 commercial aircraft carried 20m. national and international passengers and some 127,000 tonnes of mail and freight.

Shipping. Mexico has 49 ocean ports, of which, on the Gulf coast, the most important include Tampico, Veracruz, Coatzacoalcos, Progreso and Yucalpetén. On the Pacific are Ensenada, La Paz, Santa Rosalía, Guaymas, Mazatlán, Manzanillo, Acapulco and Salina Cruz.

Merchant shipping loaded 73·6m. tonnes and unloaded 12·8m. tonnes in 1982. Passengers (1982), embarked and disembarked 2·8m. In 1982, the merchant marine comprised 545 vessels (of over 100 GRT) with a total tonnage of 1,251,630 GRT.

Post and Broadcasting. In 1980 the telegraph and telephone system had 7,140 offices and 184,641 km of telegraph lines and 30·56m. km of telephone line. *Teléfonos de México*, a state-controlled company, controls about 98% of all the telephone service. Telephones in use, Jan. 1983, 6,395,000.

In 1983 there were 1,014 commercial radio stations and 47 cultural government radio stations while (1982) 10,338,024 homes had receiving sets. In 1982 commercial television stations numbered 191 and cultural stations 8; there were 4,589,170 homes with receiving sets.

Cinemas (1982). Cinemas numbered 1,789 with annual attendance of 278m.

Newspapers (1982). There were 362 dailies and 36 weeklies, with an aggregate circulation of 9·5m. In Mexico City the main dailies are, *Excelsoir, El Sol de México, Uno más Uno, La Pressa, El Heraldo de México, Novedades, El Universal* and *Esto,* with a combined circulation (1984) 1·8m.

JUSTICE, RELIGION, EDUCATION AND WELFARE

Justice. Magistrates of the Supreme Court are appointed for 6 years by the President and confirmed by the Senate; they can be removed only on impeachment. The courts include the Supreme Court with 21 magistrates, 12 collegiate circuit courts with 3 judges each and 9 unitary circuit courts with 1 judge each, and 68 district courts with 1 judge each.

The penal code of 1 Jan. 1930 abolished the death penalty, except for the armed forces, and set up a commission of alienists and other specialists, in place of courts, to deal with criminal cases (for federal offences); each state also appoints its own local magistrates.

The Mexican Constitution provides a guarantee of individual rights by means of a judicial procedure known as *amparo*, which gives any injured person whose constitutional rights have, in his opinion, been infringed, right to immediate access to the courts and full remedy, combining the swiftness of the Anglo-Saxon writ of *habeas corpus* and the breadth of remedy available through the injunction.

Religion. The prevailing religion is the Roman Catholic (92·6% of the population in 1980); with (1983) 3 cardinals, 12 archbishops and 87 bishops, but by the constitution of 1857, the Church was separated from the State, and the constitution of 1917 provided strict regulation of this and all other religions. No ecclesiastical body may acquire landed property, and since 1917 the property of the Church has been held to belong to the State. In the 1920s the Government suppressed the political influence of the priesthood and temporarily (1929–31) closed the churches. An understanding between State and Church was, however, reached, and all churches eschewing public affairs flourish freely. At the 1980 census there were also 3·3% Protestants, and 4·1% members of other religions.

Education. Primary and secondary education is free and compulsory, and secular. Clergy are forbidden to establish primary schools. All private schools must conform to government standards. In the Federal District education is controlled by the national government; elsewhere by the state authorities.

In 1981–82 there were:

	Establishments	*Teachers*	*Students*
Nursery	17,937	43,531	1,411,316
Primary	76,652	400,417	14,981,028
Secondary	15,753	222,785	3,987,964
Preparatory/Vocational	2,163	66,027	1,140,610
Teacher-training	512	13,127	203,557
Higher education	941	74,944	1,009,123

The most important university is the Universidad Nacional Autónoma de México (UNAM) in México City which, with its associated institutions, had, in 1982, 136,534 students (excluding post-graduates). UNAM was founded in 1551, re-organized in 1910, and granted full autonomy in 1920. Other universities of particular importance in México City are the Instituto Politécnico Nacional, specializing in technology and applied science, with 52,694 students, and the Universidad Autónoma Metropolitana with 27,452 students, opened in 1973.

Outside México City the principal universities are the Universidad de Guadalajara (in Guadalajara) with 65,799 students; the Universidad Veracruzana (in Jalapa) with 57,755 students; the Universidad Autónoma de Nueva León (in Monterrey) with 48,124 students; the Universidad Autónoma de Puebla (in Puebla) with 39,505 students; the Universidad Autónoma de Sinaloa (in Culiacán) with 33,366 students; and the Universidad Michoacana (in Morelia) with 23,935 students.

Health. In 1980 Mexico had 66,373 physicians; there were 6,315 state and private hospitals and clinics with 82,717 beds.

Social Welfare. The social welfare system administered mainly by the Mexican Social Security Institute covered 27m. on 31 Dec. 1983.

DIPLOMATIC REPRESENTATIVES

Of Mexico in Great Britain (8 Halkin St., London, SW1X 7DW)
Ambassador: Francisco Cuevas-Cancino (accredited 11 Feb. 1983).

Of Great Britain in Mexico (Lerma 71, Col. Cuauhtémoc, México City 06500, D.F.)
Ambassador: C. M. James, CMG.

Of Mexico in the USA (2829 16th St., NW, Washington, D.C., 20009)
Ambassador: Jorge Espinosa de los Reyes.

Of the USA in Mexico (Paseo de la Reforma 305, México City 5, D.F.)
Ambassador: John A. Gavin.

Of Mexico to the United Nations
Ambassador: Porfirio Muñoz Ledo.

Books of Reference

Anuario Estadístico de los Estados Unidos Mexicanos. Annual
Revista de Estadística (Monthly); *Revista de Economia* (Monthly)
Alba, V., *A Concise History of Mexico.* London, 1973
Banco de México S.A., Annual report
Banco Nacional de Comercio Exterior. *Comercio Exterior,* monthly.—*Mexico.* Annual (in Spanish or English)
Bazant, J., *A Concise History of Mexico.* CUP, 1977
Carrada-Bravo, F., *Oil, Money, and the Mexican Economy.* Boulder, 1982
Davies, N., *The Aztecs.* London, 1973
Dominguez, J. I., (ed.) *Mexico's Political Economy: Challenges at Home and Abroad.* London, 1982
Johnson, K. F., *Mexican Democracy: A Critical View.* Rev. ed. New York, 1978
Kaufman, S., (ed.) *The Politics of Mexican Oil.* Univ. of Pittsburgh Press, 1981
Millor, M. R., *Mexico's Oil.* Boulder, 1982
Robbins, N., *Mexico.* [Bibliography] Oxford and Santa Barbara, 1984
Velasco, S. J-A., *Impacts of Mexican Oil Policy on Economic and Political Developments.* Aldershot, 1983
Wyman, D. L., (ed) *Mexico's Economic Crisis: Challenges and Opportunities.* San Diego, 1983

MONACO

Capital: Monaco
Population: 27,063 (1982)

HISTORY. Monaco is a small Principality on the Mediterranean, surrounded by the French Department of Alpes Maritimes except on the side towards the sea. From 1297 it belonged to the house of Grimaldi. In 1731 it passed into the female line, Louise Hippolyte, daughter of Antoine I, heiress of Monaco, marrying Jacques de Goyon Matignon, Count of Torigni, who took the name and arms of Grimaldi. The Principality was placed under the protection of the Kingdom of Sardinia by the Treaty of Vienna, 1815, and under that of France in 1861. Prince Albert I (reigned 1889–1922) acquired fame as an oceanographer; and his son Louis II (1922–49) was instrumental in establishing the International Hydrographic Bureau.

AREA AND POPULATION. The area is 195 hectares or 481 acres. The Principality is divided into 4 districts: Monaco-Ville, la Condamine, Monte-Carlo and Fontvieille. Population (1982), 27,063. The official language is French.

CLIMATE. A Mediterranean climate, with mild moist winters and hot dry summers. Monaco. Jan. 50°F (10°C), July 74°F (23·3°C). Annual rainfall 30″ (758 mm).

REIGNING PRINCE. Rainier III, born 31 May 1923, son of Princess Charlotte, Duchess of Valentinois, daughter of Prince Louis II, 1898–1977 (married 19 March 1920 to Prince Pierre, Comte de Polignac, who had taken the name Grimaldi, from whom she was divorced 18 Feb. 1933). Prince Rainier succeeded his grandfather Louis II, who died on 9 May 1949. He married on 19 April 1956 Miss Grace Kelly, a citizen of the USA (died 14 Sept. 1982). *Issue:* Princess Caroline Louise Marguerite, born 23 Jan. 1957; married Philippe Junot on 28 June 1978, divorced, 9 Oct. 1980, married Stefano Casiraghi on 29 Dec. 1983, offspring: Prince Andrea, born 8 June 1984; Prince Albert Alexandre Louis Pierre, born 14 March 1958 *(heir apparent)*; Princess Stephanie Marie Elisabeth, born 1 Feb. 1965.

CONSTITUTION AND GOVERNMENT. Prince Rainier III on 28 Jan. 1959 suspended the Constitution of 5 Jan. 1911, thereby dissolving the National Council and the Communal Council. On 28 March 1962 the National Council (18 members elected every 5 years, last elections 1983) and the Communal Council (16 members elected every 4 years, last elections 1983) were re-established as elected bodies.

On 17 Dec. 1962 a new constitution was promulgated. It maintains the hereditary monarchy, though Prince Rainier renounces the principle of divine right. The supreme tribunal becomes the custodian of fundamental liberties, and guarantees are given for the right of association, trade union freedom and the right to strike. It provides for votes for women and the abolition of the death penalty.

The constitution can be modified only with the approval of the elected National Council. Women were given the vote in 1945.

Monegasque relations with France were based on a convention of neighbourhood and administrative assistance of 1951. This was terminated by France on 11 Oct. 1962, but has been replaced by several new conventions signed on 18 May 1963.

National flag: Horizontally red over white.

ECONOMY

Planning. A 55-acre site has been reclaimed from the sea at Fontvieille. This land has been earmarked for office and residential development. The present industrial zone is to be reorganized and developed with a view to attracting new light industry to the Principality.

Budget. The budget (in 1,000 francs) was as follows:

	1978	*1979*	*1980*	*1981*	*1982*
Revenue	671,035	784,319	987,158	1,258,654	1,429,968
Expenditure	518,129	551,632	629,449	814,333	1,171,757

Currency. The monetary unit is the French *franc* divided into 100 *centimes.*

Weights and Measures. The metric system is in use.

INDUSTRY AND TRADE

Tourism. There were 216,110 tourists in 1982.

Trade Unions. Membership of trade unions is estimated at 2,500 out of a work force of 21,588 (1984).

Commerce. International trade is included with France.

COMMUNICATIONS

Roads. There were 47·8 km of roads in 1984.

Railways. The 1·6m. km of main line passing through the country is operated by the French National Railways (SNCF).

Aviation. The nearest airport is at Nice, France and a heliport at Fontvieille.

Shipping. The harbour has an area of 47 acres, depth at the entrance 90 ft, and alongside the quay 24 ft at least.

Post and Broadcasting. Telephone subscribers numbered about 17,700 in 1984 and telex subscribers, 597. Monaco issues its own postage stamps.

Radio Monte Carlo broadcasts 2 commercial programmes in French (long- and medium-waves). Radio Monte Carlo owns 55% of Radio Monte Carlo Relay Station on Cyprus. The foreign service is dedicated exclusively to religious broadcasts and is maintained by free-will contributions. It operates in 36 languages under the name 'Trans World Radio' and has relay facilities on Bonaire, West Indies, and is planning to build relay facilities in the southern parts of Africa. *Télé Monte-Carlo* broadcasts TV programmes in French, Italian and English.

Cinemas. In 1981 there were 3 cinemas (one open air) with seating capacity of 800.

JUSTICE, RELIGION, EDUCATION AND WELFARE

Justice. There is a Court of First Instance as well as a Juge de Paix's Court.

Police. There is an independent police force *(Surîté Publique)* which comprised (1985) 350 policemen and inspectors.

Religion. There has been since 1887 a Roman Catholic bishop elevated since 1982 to an archbishop, directly dependent on the Holy See.

Education. In 1984 there were 5,200 pupils with over 487 teachers.

Health. In 1985 there were 515 hospital beds and 63 physicians.

DIPLOMATIC REPRESENTATIVES

British Consul-General (resident in Marseille). D. A. S. Gladstone.
British Honorary Consul (resident in Nice): Lieut.-Col. R. W. Challoner, OBE.
Consul-General for Monaco in London: I. S. Ivanovic.

Books of Reference

Journal de Monaco. Bulletin Officiel. 1858 ff.
Handley-Taylor, G., *Bibliography of Monaco.* London, 1968
La Gorce, P. M. de, *Monaco.* Lausanne, 1969

MONGOLIAN PEOPLE'S REPUBLIC

Capital: Ulan Bator
Population: 1·82m. (1984)
GNP per capita: US$940 (1978)

Bügd Nayramdakh Mongol Ard Uls

HISTORY. Outer Mongolia was a Chinese province from 1691 to 1911, an autonomous state under Russian protection from 1912 to 1919 and again a Chinese province from 1919 to 1921. On 13 March 1921 a Provisional People's Government was established which declared the independence of Mongolia and on 5 Nov. 1921 signed a treaty with Soviet Russia annulling all previous unequal treaties and establishing friendly relations. On 26 Nov. 1924 the Government proclaimed the country the Mongolian People's Republic.

On 5 Jan. 1946 China recognized the independence of Outer Mongolia after a plebiscite in Mongolia (20 Oct. 1945) had resulted in an overwhelming vote for independence. A Sino-Soviet treaty of 14 Feb. 1950 guaranteed this independence.

AREA AND POPULATION. Mongolia is bounded north by the USSR, east and south and west by China. Area, 1,565,000 sq. km (604,250 sq. miles); population (1984) 1,820,000 (in 1977 719,000 urban; 51% male). Density, 1·12 per sq. km. Birth rate (1981), 37·9 per 1,000; death rate, 10·4 per 1,000. Rate of increase, 1982, 3%. The population is predominantly made up of Mongolian peoples (75% Khalkha). There is a Turkic Kazakh minority (5·2% of the population) and 8 Mongol minorities. The official language is Mongol. Expectation of life in 1983 was 65 years. 50% of the population is under 16.

The republic is administratively divided into 3 cities (Ulan Bator, the capital, population 400,000 (1978), Darkhan, 52,000 (1981) and Erdenet 35,000 (1978)), and 18 provinces *(aimag)*. Local government is administered by People's Deputies' Khurals. The provinces are sub-divided into districts *(somon)*.

CLIMATE. A very extreme climate, with six months of mean temperatures below freezing, but much higher temperatures occur for a month or two in summer. Rainfall is very low and limited to the months mid-May to mid-Sept. Ulan Bator. Jan. –14°F (–25·6°C), July 61°F (16·1°C). Annual rainfall 8″ (208 mm).

CONSTITUTION AND GOVERNMENT. According to the fourth Constitution (1960) legislative power is vested in the *Great People's Khural* of deputies elected for 5 years by universal suffrage of voters over 18 years of age on a basis of 1 deputy per 2,500 inhabitants. It elects from its number 9 members of the Presidium, which carries on current state affairs.

The last general election took place on 21 June 1981; 99·99% of an electorate of 792,896 were said to have voted for the 370 deputies (344 Party members; 100 industrial workers; 90 women).

The Chairman of the Presidium of the Khural is Dr Jambyn Batmunkh. *De facto* power is in the hands of the only political party, the Mongolian People's Revolutionary (*i.e.*, Communist) Party, which had 76,240 members and candidates in 1981 (workers 33%; peasants, 18%; women, 27%). The youth organization had over 180,000 members in 1982. The *General Secretary of the Party* is Dr

Batmunkh. The other members of the Politburo of the Party are: D. Sodnom, *Prime Minister:* D. Maydar, *First Deputy Prime Minister and Chairman, State Committee for Science and Technology;* T. Ragchaa, *First Deputy Prime Minister;* D. Molomjamts. D. Gombojav, B.-O. Altangerel, Ts. Namsraí, B. Dejid. *Candidate members:* N. Jagvaral, S. Luvsangombo. Ministers not in the Politburo include: *Minister of Defence:* Col.-Gen. J. Yondon; *Minister of Public Security:* O. Choijilsuren; *Foreign Minister:* Mangalyn Dügesüren; *Minister of Foreign Trade:* Yë Ochir. *Minister of Agriculture:* S. Sodnomdorj.

National flag: Red–sky-blue–red (vertical), with a golden 5-pointed star and under it the golden *soyombo* emblem on the red stripe nearest to the flagpole.

The last local elections to the 380 *khurals* took place in June 1984. Turn-out was announced to be 99·99% of the electorate. There are some 15,000 councillors. White-collar, 50%; collective farmers, 30%; industrial workers, 20%; Communist Party members, 60%; women, 33%; under-30, 20%, first term of office, 50%.

DEFENCE. Military service is 3 years.

Army. The Army comprises 2 infantry divisions and 1 infantry brigade. Equipment includes T-54/-55/-62 main battle tanks. Strength (1985) 33,000, with reserves of 40,000. There is a paramilitary Ministry of Public Security force of about 15,000 men. A civil defence force was set up in 1970. There were (1985) some 25,000 Soviet service personnel.

Air Force. The Air Force has about 100 pilots and more than 60 aircraft, including 12 MiG-21 fighters; a total of about 40 An-2, An-24 and An-26 transports used mainly on civil air services; 3 Wilga utility aircraft; 10 Mi-4 and 3 Mi-8 helicopters; and Yakovlev trainers.

INTERNATIONAL RELATIONS

Membership. Mongolia is a member of UN and Comecon.

Aid. Mongolia receives economic aid from the USSR and other communist countries. There is also a UN development aid programme running at US$2m. per annum.

Treaties. Relations with the USSR were based on treaties of friendship and mutual aid (27 Feb. 1946), trade (17 Dec. 1957), economic and technical assistance (9 Sept. 1960), now replaced by a 20-year treaty of friendship, co-operation and mutual assistance (15 Jan. 1966).

Sino-Mongolian relations have deteriorated since the estrangement between China and USSR.

On 28 Oct. 1961 Mongolia was admitted to the United Nations.

ECONOMY

Planning. Mongolia has had for centuries a traditional nomadic pastoral economy, which the Government aims to transform into an 'agricultural–industrial economy'. For earlier plans *see* THE STATESMAN'S YEAR-BOOK, 1976–77, p. 1156. The 5 year plan (1976–80) increased national income by 30·9%, industrial production by 50% and agricultural production by 6·3% (Targets were 42%, 63% and 30%). The seventh 5-year plan is running from 1981 to 1985. Industrial output is scheduled to rise by 58%, agricultural by 25%. There is also a long-term plan to 1990 which emphasizes energy production, mining, metallurgy, chemicals, food processing and building.

Budget (in 1m. tugriks):

	1973	*1974*	*1975*	*1976*	*1977*	*1978*	*1980*
Revenue	2,678	2,718	2,696	2,988	3,312	3,660	4,070
Expenditure	2,530	2,670	2,686	2,973	3,300	3,630	4,058

In the 1971–75 planning period 7,010m. tugriks were invested in the national economy. During the 1976–80 plan period overall investment was doubled.

Currency. 100 *möngö* = 1 *tugrik*. Official exchange rates: £1 = 5·10 *tugriks*; 1 rouble = 4·44 *tugriks*; US$1 = 3·36 *tugriks*.

Weights and Measures. The metric system is in use.

ENERGY AND NATURAL RESOURCES

Electricity. There are 6 thermal electric power stations. Production of electricity, 1980, 1,400m. kwh.

Minerals. There are large deposits of copper, nickel, zinc, molybdenum, phosphorites, tin, wolfram and fluorspar; annual production of the latter is 300,000 tonnes, entirely exported to the USSR. The ore-dressing plant at Erdenet was completed in 1981. Coal reserves are 17,000m. tonnes. Coal accounted for 74·6% of energy production in 1980. There are major coalmines near Ulan Bator and Darkhan. Coal (mainly lignite) production in 1981 was 4·1m. tonnes.

Agriculture. The economy remains predominantly agricultural (70% of agricultural production derives from cattle-raising). In 1981 there were 2,028,000 horses, 2,396,000 cattle, 14,955,000 sheep, 570,000 camels and 4,802,000 goats. Pastures occupy 84% of the total area, forests 10·5%. In 1983 there were 719,000 hectares of arable land. In 1981 there were 255 collective farms, 30 inter-farm associations and 57 state farms. All cultivated land and 75% of livestock belong to collective or state farms. Farms cover vast areas. In 1978 collective farms averaged 64,000 head of cattle and state farms about 36,000.

The sown area 1978 was some 680,000 hectares, 500,000 hectares of which were sown to grain. The 1980 crop was 207,000 tonnes of wheat; 1,700 tonnes of rye; 31,800 tonnes of barley. Production of hay fodder was 10·4m tonnes in 1977. 6·5m. litres of fermented mare's milk were produced in 1984. In 1981 there were 7,500 tractors (15 h.p. units) and 2,000 combine harvesters.

Forestry. Forests, chiefly larch, cedar, fir and birch, occupy 156,700 sq. km. Production, 1976: 1,067,000 cu. metres of timber.

INDUSTRY AND TRADE

Industry. Industry though still small in scale and local in character, is being vigorously developed and now accounts for a greater share of GNP than agriculture. The food industry accounts for 20% of industrial production. The main industrial centre is Ulan Bator; others Erdenet and Baga-Nuur, and another is under construction at Khutul. Production figures (1980): textiles, 1·4m. cu metres; leather, 1·4m. tonnes; cement, 178,000 tonnes; leather footwear, 2·1m. pairs; meat, 56,700 tonnes; animal fat, 3,800 tonnes; beer 98,000 hectolitres.

Employment. The labour force was 370,000 in 1980, including 130,000 shepherds. Average wage was 500 tugriks per month in 1981. Trade union membership was 400,000 in 1982.

There is a serious labour shortage necessitating the employment of military personnel, and workers from the USSR and Eastern Europe.

Commerce. Foreign trade is a state monopoly. Trade figures for 1976 (in 1m. tugriks): exports, 775; imports, 1,007, Mongolia has been a member of Comecon since 1962. The main exports are live cattle and horses, wool and hair, meat, grain, hides, furs, ores, and butter. 96% of foreign trade is with communist countries (80% with USSR). There is a chronic trade deficit. Just over 25% of imports are consumer goods and the remainder are machinery and industrial raw materials. In 1976 trade with China was 28m. tugriks. Trade with Japan, previously valued at US$1m. per annum, increased slightly after the establishment of diplomatic relations in 1972.

Total trade between Mongolia and UK (British Department of Trade returns, in £1,000 sterling):

	1982	*1983*	*1984*
Imports to UK	3,861	1,350	4,561
Exports and re-exports from UK	64	242	100

COMMUNICATIONS

Roads. There are surfaced roads in and around Ulan Bator, from Ulan Bator to Darkhan and at points on the frontier with USSR. Truck services run throughout the country where there are no surfaced roads. 120m. passengers were carried in 1981. 70·2% of all freight was carried by lorry in 1983.

Railways. The Trans-Mongolian Railway (1,423 km in 1983) connects Ulan Bator with the Soviet Union and China. The Moscow–Ulan Bator–Peking express runs each way once a week. There are spur lines to Erdenet and to the coalmines at Nalaykha and Sharin Gol. A separate line connects Choybalsan in the east with Borzya on the Trans-Siberian railway. 1·1m. passengers and 8·1m. tonnes of freight were carried in 1976.

Aviation. Mongolair operates internal services and a flight to Irkutsk which links with the Moscow service. 7,000 tons of freight were carried in 1976 and 370,000 passengers. Soviet airlines (Aeroflot) and Mongolair jointly operate a daily service to Moscow.

Shipping. There is a steamer service on the Selenge River and a tug and barge service on Hobsgol Lake. 3,000 tonnes of freight were carried in 1976.

Post and Broadcasting. There were, in 1976, 382 post offices and 218 telephone exchanges. Number of telephones (1977), 37,792.

There are wireless stations at Ulan Bator, Gobi Altai and Olgiy. In 1978 there were 128,000 radio and 3,800 television receivers. Television services began in 1967. A Mongolian television station opened in 1970. Mongolia is a member of the international TV organisation Intervision.

Cinemas. In 1976 there were 23 cinemas, 439 mobile cinemas and, in 1981, 10 theatres.

Newspapers and books. In 1984, 12 newspapers and 32 journals were published. The Party daily paper *Ünen* ('Truth') had a circulation of 112,000 in 1978. 400 book titles were published in 1982 in 70m. copies

JUSTICE, RELIGION, EDUCATION AND WELFARE

Justice. The Procurator-General is appointed, and the Supreme Court elected, by the *Khural* for 4 years. There are also courts at province, town and district level. Lay assessors sit with professional judges.

Religion. Tibetan Buddhist Lamaism was the prevalent form of religion. The Church was suppressed in the 1930s, and only one functioning monastery exists today, at Ulan Bator.

Education. In 1983 there were 620 nurseries with 52,000 children. Schooling begins at the age of 8. There are 8- and 10-year schools. In 1983-84 there were 579 'general' schools with 394,000 pupils, 25 specialised secondary schools and 37 vocational technical schools with 22,000 pupils. There is a state university (founded 1942) at Ulan Bator (40 professors, 240 lecturers and 10,000 students in 1982), and 6 other institutes of higher learning (teacher training, medicine, agriculture, economics, etc.) with 14,000 students in 1982 under the supervision of an Academy of Sciences (founded 1953) which has 15 institutes and 190 research workers. In 1977 there were 23,550 students in institutes of higher learning, and some 6,000 students a year are sent to study abroad, principally in the USSR. In 1982–83 there were 885 'general' schools with 385,000 pupils and 37 technical schools with 21,100 pupils.

In 1946 the Mongolian alphabet was replaced by a modern Cyrillic alphabet.

Health. In 1983 there were 22 doctors and 107 hospital beds per 10,000 inhabitants.

DIPLOMATIC REPRESENTATIVES

Of Mongolia in Great Britain (7 Kensington Ct., London, W8 5DL)
Ambassador: Jambalyn Banzar (accredited 20 Dec. 1984).

Of Great Britain in Mongolia (30 Enkh Taivny Gudamzh, Ulan Bator)
Ambassador: A. G. R. Butler.

Of Mongolia to the United Nations
Ambassador: Gendengiin Nyamdoo.

Books of Reference

The Central Statistical Office: *Economic Statistics of the MPR for 40 Years.* 1961.—*40 Years of the MPR Revolution.* 1961.—*National Economy MPR 1973.* 1974

Bawden, C. R., *The Modern History of Mongolia.* London, 1968
Boberg, F., *Mongolian–English, English–Mongolian Dictionary.* 3 vols. Stockholm, 1954–55
Haltod, M. (ed.), *Mongolian–English Dictionary.* Berkeley, Cal., 1961
Jagchid, S., and Hyer, P. *Mongolia's Culture and Society.* Folkestone, 1979
Lattimore, O., *Nationalism and Revolution in Mongolia.* Leiden, 1955.—*Nomads and Commissars.* OUP, 1963
Lörinc, L., *Histoire de la Mongolie des Origines à nos Jours.* Budapest, 1984
News from Mongolia. Ulan Bator, fortnightly, Jan. 1980
Petrov. V. P., *Mongolia: A Profile.* London, 1971
Rupen, R. A., *How Mongolia is Really Ruled: A Political History of the Mongolian People's Republic, 1900–1978.* Stanford, 1979
Sanders, A. J. K., *The People's Republic of Mongolia: A General Reference Guide.* OUP, 1968
Shirendev, B., and Sanjdorj, M. (eds.), *History of the Mongolian People's Republic.* Vol. 3 (vols. 1 and 2 not translated). Harvard Univ. Press, 1976
Socialist Mongolia. Ulan Bator, 1981

MONTSERRAT

Capital: Plymouth
Population: 12,074 (1980)
GNP per capita: US$2,200 (1983)

HISTORY. Montserrat was discovered by Columbus in 1493 and colonized by Britain in 1832 who brought in Irish settlers.

AREA AND POPULATION. Montserrat is situated in the Caribbean Sea 25 miles south-west of Antigua. The area is 39·5 sq. miles (106 sq. km). Population, 1980, 12,074. Chief town, Plymouth, 3,200 inhabitants.

CLIMATE. A tropical climate but with no well-defined rainy season, though July to Dec. shows slightly more rainfall, with the average for the year being about 60″ (1,500 mm). Dec. to March is the cooler season while June to Nov. is the hotter season, when hurricanes may occur. Plymouth. Jan. 76°F (24·4°C), July 81°F (27·2°C). Annual rainfall 65″ (1,628 mm).

CONSTITUTION AND GOVERNMENT. Montserrat is a crown colony. The Executive Council is composed of 4 elected Ministers (the Chief Minister and 3 other Ministers) and 2 civil service officials (Attorney-General and Financial Secretary). The Legislative Council consists of 7 elected and 2 civil service officials (the Attorney-General and Financial Secretary) and 2 nominated members. The Executive Council is presided over by the Governor and the Legislative Council by the Speaker.

Governor: A. C. Watson.
Chief Minister: Dr J. A. Osborne.
Flag: The British Blue Ensign with the shield of Montserrat in the fly.

FINANCE. In 1982 the budget expenditure was at EC$35m. of which EC$12m. was capital expenditure. In 1981 the territorial budget ceased to be grant-aided by the British Government.

AGRICULTURE. Agriculture has been in decline for several years, but is likely to recover with the progress of the Integrated Sea Island Cotton Project and revised land tenure and settlement arrangements associated with the government's acquisition of a number of estates.

Livestock (1983); Cattle, 4,000; pigs, 400; sheep, 4,500; goats, 4,500; poultry, 60,000.

INDUSTRY AND TRADE

Industry. Considerable light industry was attracted to the territory from abroad during 1979–81 and there is 83,000 sq. ft of modern factory space available.

Commerce. Imports in 1983 totalled EC$54m. (US$20m.); domestic exports, EC$4m. Chief imports were manufactured goods, food and beverages, machinery and transport equipment and fuel. Chief exports in 1983 were hot peppers, live plants, cattle and manufactured articles.

Total trade between Montserrat and UK (British Department of Trade returns, in £1,000 sterling):

	1981	*1982*	*1983*	*1984*
Imports to UK	397	193	164	115
Exports and re-exports from UK	935	1,786	2,159	1,999

Tourism. In 1983, 18,800 tourists arrived in Montserrat.

COMMUNICATIONS

Aviation. At the modernized Blackburne airport 3,598 aircraft landed in 1983, disembarking 20,634 passengers and 278 tons of cargo.

Shipping. In 1982, 311 vessels arrived, landing 34,698 and loading 789 tons of cargo.

Post. Number of telephones (1983), 2,600; telex, 17.

JUSTICE, RELIGION, EDUCATION AND WELFARE

Justice. There are 2 magistrates' courts, at Plymouth and Cudjoe Head. Strength of the police force (1983), 3 gazetted officers, 3 inspectors and 101 other ranks.

Religion. In 1981 there were 1,329 Roman Catholics, 4,332 Anglicans, 3,249 Methodists, 804 Seventh Day Adventists, 1,091 Pentecostals and 254 members of the Church of God. There is also a Christian Council of Churches.

Education. There are 9 government elementary, 1 government secondary, 2 grant-aided denominational elementary schools, 2 government junior secondary schools, 2 preparatory private schools for children between the ages of 5 and 12 and 11 nursery schools. In 1983, 1,723 children were enrolled in the primary schools, with 66 teachers; 871 in the secondary schools, with 60 teachers. There was 1 technical college with 66 students and 9 teachers.

Health. In 1983 there were 6 doctors and 67 hospital beds.

Books of Reference

Overseas Trade 1983. Montserrat Government
Preliminary National Account Statistics, 1975–1982. 1982
Vital Statistics Report. Montserrat Government, 1982
Statistical Digest 1984. Montserrat Government
Fergus, H.A., *Montserrat: Emerald Isle of the Caribbean.* London, 1983

Library: Public Library, Plymouth. *Librarian:* Miss J. Grell.

MOROCCO

al-Mamlaka al-Maghrebia

Capital: Rabat
Population: 21·16m. (1984)
GNP per capita: US$860 (1981)

HISTORY. From 1912 to 1956 Morocco was divided into a French protectorate (established by the treaty of Fez concluded between France and the Sultan on 30 March 1912), a Spanish protectorate (established by the Franco-Spanish convention of 27 Nov. 1912) and the international zone of Tangier (set up by France, Spain and Great Britain on 18 Dec. 1923).

On 2 March 1956 France and the Sultan terminated the treaty of Fez; on 7 April 1956 Spain relinquished her protectorate, and on 29 Oct. 1956 France, Spain, Great Britain, Italy, USA, Belgium, the Netherlands, Sweden and Portugal abolished the international status of the Tangier Zone. The northern strip of Spanish Sahara was ceded by Spain on 10 April 1958, and on 30 June 1969 the former Spanish province of Ifni was returned to Morocco.

A tripartite agreement was announced on 14 Nov. 1975 providing for the transfer of power from Spanish Sahara (Western Sahara) to the Moroccan and Mauritanean governments on 28 Feb. 1976. Spanish troops left El Aaiún on 20 Dec. 1975. On 14 April 1976 a Convention was signed by Mauritania and Morocco in which the 2 countries agreed to partition the former Spanish territory, but on 14 Aug. 1979 Mauritania renounced its claim to its share of the territory (Tiris El-Gharbiya) which was added by Morocco to its area.

AREA AND POPULATION. Morocco is bounded by Algeria to the east and south-east, Western Sahara to the south-west, the Atlantic ocean to the north-west and the Mediterranean to the north. Excluding the Western Saharan territory claimed and occupied since 1976 by Morocco, the total area is 458,730 sq. km and its total population at the Sept. 1982 census was 20,255,687; the latest estimate (1984) is 21·16m.

The areas (in sq. km) and populations (census 1982) of the provinces are:

Province	*Sq. km*	*1982*
Agadir	5,910	579,741
Taroudant	16,460	558,501
Al-Hoceima	3,550	311,298
Azilal	10,050	387,115
Beni Mellal	7,075	668,703
Ben Slimane	2,760	174,464
Boulemane	14,395	131,470
Casablanca-Anfa [1]		923,630
Aïn Chok-Hay Hassani [1]		298,376
Ben Msik-Sidi Othmane [1]	1,615	639,558
Hay Mohamed-Aïn Sebâa [1]		421,272
Mohamedia-Znata [1]		153,828
Chechaouèn	4,350	309,024
El Jadida	6,000	763,351
El Kelâa-Srarhna	10,070	577,595
Er Rachidia	59,585	421,207
Es Saouira	6,335	393,683
Fez	5,400	805,464
Figuig	55,990	101,359
Guelmim	28,750	128,676
Kénitra	4,745	715,967
Sidi Kacem	4,060	514,127
Khémisset	8,305	405,836
Khénifra	12,320	363,716
Khouribga	4,250	437,002
Marrakesh	14,755	1,200,695
Meknès	3,995	626,868
Ifrane	3,310	100,255

Province	*Sq km*	*1982*
Nador	6,130	593,255
Ouarzazate	41,550	533,892
Oujda	20,700	780,762
Rabat-Salé [1]	1,275	1,020,001
Safi	7,285	706,618
Settat	9,750	692,359
Tangier	1,195	436,227
Tan-Tan	17,295	47,040
Taounate	5,585	535,972
Tata	25,925	99,950
Taza	15,020	613,485
Tétouan	6,025	704,205
Tiznit	6,960	313,140
Morocco	458,730	20,255,687
Boujdour (Bojador)	100,120	8,481
Es Semara (Smara)	61,760	20,480
Laâyoune (Al Aaiún)	39,360	113,411
Oued Ed Dahab	50,880	21,496
Sahara	232,120	163,868

[1] Urban prefectures

The population of the largest municipalities (census) June 1971: Casablanca, 1,506,373; Rabat (capital), 367,620; Marrakesh, 332,741; Fez, 325,327; Meknès, 248,369; Tangier, 187,894; Oujda, 175,532; Salè, 155,557; Kenitra, 139,206; Tétouan, 139,105; Safi, 129,113; Khouribga, 73,667; Mohammedia, 70,392; Agadir, 61,192; El Jadida, 55,501.

The official language is Arabic, spoken by 75% of the population; the remainder speak Berber. French and Spanish are considered subsidiary languages.

CLIMATE. The climate ranges from semi-arid in the south to warm temperate Mediterranean conditions in the north, but cooler temperatures occur in the mountains. Rabat. Jan. 55°F (12·9°C), July 72°F (22·2°C). Annual rainfall 23″ (564 mm). Agadir. Jan. 57°F (13·9°C), July 72°F (22·2°C). Annual rainfall 9″ (224 mm). Casablanca. Jan. 54°F (12·2°C), July 72°F (22·2°C). Annual rainfall 16″ (404 mm). Marrakesh. Jan. 52°F (11·1°C), July 84°F (28·9°C). Annual rainfall 10″ (239 mm). Tangier. Jan. 53°F (11·7°C), July 72°F (22·2°C). Annual rainfall 36″ (897 mm).

REIGNING KING. Hassan II, born on 9 July 1929, succeeded on 3 March 1961, on the death of his father Mohammed V, who reigned 1927–61. The royal style was changed from 'His Sherifian Majesty the Sultan' to 'His Majesty the King' on 18 Aug. 1957. *Heir apparent:* Crown Prince Sidi Mohammed, born 21 Aug. 1963.

The King holds supreme civil and religious authority; the latter in his capacity of Emir-el-Muminin or Commander of the Faithful. He resides usually at Rabat, but occasionally in one of the other traditional capitals, Fez (founded in 808), Marrakesh (founded in 1062), or at Skhirat.

CONSTITUTION AND GOVERNMENT. A new Constitution was approved by referendum in March 1972 and amendments were approved by referendum in May 1980. The Kingdom of Morocco is a constitutional monarchy with a legislature of a single chamber composed of 306 deputies. Deputies for 102 seats are elected by indirect vote through an electoral college representing the town councils, the regional assemblies, the chambers of commerce, industry and agriculture, and the trade unions. Deputies for the remaining 204 seats are by general election. The King, as sovereign head of State, appoints the Prime Minister and other Ministers, has the right to dissolve Parliament and approves legislation.

In the General Elections held on 14 Sept. 1984, the new *Union constitutionelle* (founded Jan. 1983) won 83 seats, the *Rassemblement nationale des indépendants* 38 seats, the *Union socialiste des forces populaires* 61 seats, the *Mouvement populaire* 47 seats, and *Istiqlal* (Independence) 41 seats.

National flag: Red, with a green pentacle star in the centre.

Cabinet in Jan. 1985:

Prime Minister: Mohamed Karim Lamrani.

Justice: Moulay Mustapha Belarbi Alaoui. *Interior:* Driss Basri. *Foreign Affairs:* Abdelouahed Belakziz. *Information:* Abdellatif Filali. *Planning:* Abdelhaq Tazi. *National Education:* Azzeddine Laraki. *Economic Affairs:* Taib Bencheikh. *Finance:* Abdellatif Jouahri. *Trade, Industry and Tourism:* Azzeddine Guessous. *Handicrafts and Social Affairs:* Abbas el Fassi. *Transport:* Mansouri Ben Ali. *Energy and Mining:* Moussa Saadi. *Health:* Rahhali Rahal. *Maritime Fishing and Merchant Navy:* Bensalem Smili. *Secretary-General of the Government:* Abbas Kaissi. *Cultural Affairs:* Said Bel Bachir. *Housing, Urban Affairs and Protection of the Environment:* Mfadel Lahlou. *Equipment, Executive and Professional Training:* Mohamed Kabbaj. *Minister at the Prime Minister's Office:* Abdelkrim Ghallab. *Posts and Telecommunications:* Mohand Laensar. *Agriculture and Land Reform:* Otman Demnati. *Relations with Parliament:* Ahmed Belhadj. *Youth and Sports:* Abdellatif Semlali. *Minister in charge of Co-operation:* Abdelouahed Radi. *Labour:* Moulay Zine Zahidi. *Waqfs and Islamic Affairs:* Abdelkbar Alaoui Medaghri. There are 8 Ministers of State, 4 Secretaries and 1 Under Secretary of State.

Local Government: The country is administratively divided into 39 provinces and 6 urban prefectures.

DEFENCE. Military service is compulsory for 18 months.

Army. The Army comprises 4 mechanized infantry, 1 light security, 1 parachute and 1 anti-aircraft brigades; 10 mechanized infantry regiments; 9 artillery groups; 7 armoured, 1 Royal Guard, 5 camel corps, 2 desert cavalry, 1 mountain, 3 commando and 4 engineer battalions; and 4 armoured car squadrons. Equipment includes 120 M-48 and 15 T-54 main battle tanks, 80 light tanks and 1,000 armoured cars. Strength (1985) 125,000 men. There are also 30,000 paramilitary troops.

Navy. Navy includes 1 new missile-armed light frigate, 4 new missile armed large patrol vessels or small corvettes, 2 modern fast attack (corvette size) gunboats, 1 coastal minesweeper, 1 patrol vessel, 1 gunboat, 1 seaward patrol craft, 9 coastal patrol boats, 4 landing craft acquired from France, 2 logistic support vessels and 1 yacht training vessel. The construction of 5 corvettes of new design is under discussion. Personnel in 1985 totalled 1,800 officers and ratings including 500 marines. There were also 12 small customs cutters and a coastguard picket.

Air Force. The Air Force was formed in Nov. 1956. Equipment in current use is mainly of US and West European origin. It includes 45 Mirage F1s, a total of 26 F-5A/B/E/F fighter-bombers and RF-5A reconnaissance-fighters, 4 OV-10 Bronco counter-insurgency aircraft, a Falcon 20 for electronic warfare, and 24 Hughes 500MD Scout Defender armed helicopters, 24 Alpha Jet advanced trainers, 22 Magister armed jet basic trainers, 12 T-34C-1 turboprop armed basic trainers, 10 Swiss-built Bravo primary trainers, 2 Mudry CAP 10B aerobatic trainers, 4 Broussard liaison aircraft, 75 Agusta-Bell 205 and 212, Puma and JetRanger helicopters, 10 Do 28D Skyservants for coastal patrol, 9 CH-47C heavy-lift helicopters, 12 C-130H turboprop transport aircraft, 3 KC-130H tanker/transports, a Falcon 50 VIP transport and 5 turboprop King Air light transports. The T-34C-1s are intended to be replaced in the mid-80s by locally designed Gepal Mk IV 550 turboprop trainers. Personnel strength (1984) about 10,000.

INTERNATIONAL RELATIONS

Membership. Morocco is a member of UN, OAU, the Non-Aligned Movement, the Islamic Conference and the Arab League.

ECONOMY

Planning. A 5-year plan (1973–77) envisaged a total investment of 11,751,874m. DH. A new 3-year plan (1978–80) was approved in Dec. 1978. The 5-year plan (1981–85) was approved in June 1981.

Budget. The budget for 1982 envisaged revenue of 39,900m. DH and expenditure of 46,800m. DH.

Currency. In Oct. 1959, a national currency was introduced. Its unit is the *dirham* (abbreviated DH), equalling 100 *centimes*. Notes: 5, 10, 50, 100 DH; coins: 0·02, 0·05, 0·10, 0·20, 0·50, 1 DH. The exchange rate in March 1985 was £1 sterling = 10·50 DH; US$1 = 9·95 DH.

Banking. The bank of issue is the Banque du Maroc in Rabat. Other important institutions are the Banque Marocaine du Commerce Extérieur (Casablanca), the Banque Nationale pour le Développement Economique (Rabat), Crédit Populaire and the Crédit Immobilier et Hotelier (Casablanca). There are 23 other banks in Casablanca, 3 in Tangier and 1 each in Tétouan, Fez, Kenitra, Meknès, Oujda and Rabat.

Weights and Measures. The metric system of weights and measures is the sole legal system.

ENERGY AND NATURAL RESOURCES

Electricity. Electric power-plants produced 5,077·4m. kwh. in 1982.

Oil. Crude oil production, 48,000 tonnes 1980.

Minerals. The principal mineral exploited is phosphate, the output of which (under a state monopoly) was 17·09m. tonnes in 1982. Other important minerals (in 1,000 tonnes) are: Iron ore (223·8), lead (148·5), cobalt (6), zinc (22·4), manganese (94·1), silver (27). Production of minerals (1978) 2,829,284m. dirhams.

Agriculture. Agriculture is by far the most important industry, on which 70% of the population exists. The principal crops are cereals, especially wheat and barley; beans, chickpeas, fenugreek and other legumens; canary seed; cumin and coriander; linseed; olives; almonds and other fruits, especially citrus. The almost universal wild palmetto is put to various uses, including the manufacture of *crin végétal*. The trees include cork, cedar, arar, argon, oak and various conifers. Wine production, 1975, 830,000 hectolitres. Tizra wood is exported for tanning purposes. Stock-raising is an important industry.

Production in 1982: Barley, 19·1m.; wheat, 18·2m.; maize, 315,000; sugar-cane, 630,000; citrus fruit, 1m.

Livestock (in 1,000 heads), 1983: Camels, 240; horses, 315; cattle, 3,000; pigs, 11; sheep, 15,000; goats, 6,270; poultry, 25m.

Fishing. The chief fishing centres are Agadir, Safi, Essaouira and Casablanca. There are over 5,000 fishing vessels and about 100 freezing and processing plants. The industry employs 50,000 workers. Total catch in 1982 was 413,999 tonnes.

COMMERCE. Imports and exports were (in 1m. DH):

	1978	*1979*	*1980*	*1981*	*1982*
Imports	12,361	14,327	16,792	22,455	25,990
Exports	6,262	7,622	9,645	12,002	12,439

Main imports, 1982, consumer goods and industrial products. Main exports, (1982 in 1m. DH), phosphates (3,445), fruit and vegetables (1,086), phosphoric acid (1,586) and clothing (549).

Main trading partners (1982): Exports, France (24%), Federal Republic of Germany (8%), Spain (6·7%), Italy (6·7). Imports, France (24·1%), Saudi Arabia (13·5%) Spain (7·1%), USA (6%).

A royal proclamation of 30 Aug. 1959 abrogated the former economic status of Tangier and integrated the zone in the Kingdom. However, Tangier was declared a free port from 1 Jan. 1962; and commercial transactions within the free zone were further liberalized by decree of 8 Nov. 1965.

Total trade between Morocco and UK (British Department of Trade returns, in £1,000 sterling):

	1980	*1981*	*1982*	*1983*	*1984*
Imports to UK	62,582	67,697	60,219	75,602	79,738
Exports and re-exports from UK	69,223	55,939	95,487	99,727	79,850

TOURISM. In 1982, 1·9m. foreign visitors came to Morocco.

COMMUNICATIONS

Roads. In 1983 there were 57,592 km of classified roads, of which (1978) 27,671 km were surfaced. At the end of 1981 there were in use 207,370 lorries, 445,000 private cars and 18,424 motor cycles.

Railways. In 1982 there were 1,779 km of railways, of which 709 km were electrified. The principal standard-gauge lines are from Casablanca eastward to the Algerian border, forming part of the continuous rail line to Tunis; Casablanca to Marrakesh with 2 important branches, one eastward to Oued Zem tapping the Khouribga phosphate mines, the other westward to the port of Safi. Another branch serves the manganese mines at Bou Arfa. Two new double-track electrified lines are to serve a new deep-water port at Jorf Lasfar, and a 650 km south-east extension from Marrakesh to Laayoun in the south Sahara is planned.

In 1982 the railways ran 1,374m. passenger-km and 3,851m. tonne-km of goods.

Aviation. There are 19 airfields, of which Casablanca–Arfa and Casablanca–Nouaceur are the most important. Total international air services in 1982 comprised 2,395,856 passengers arrived and departed and 32,445 tonnes of freight including mail.

Shipping. In 1982, 18,974 vessels entered and cleared the ports of Morocco. In 1980 the merchant marine consisted of 145 vessels (of over 100 gross tons) with a total tonnage of 359,552 GRT.

Post and Broadcasting. Communication with Europe is maintained by cables between Casablanca and Brest, Tangier–Casablanca–Le Havre, Tangier–Gibraltar, Tangier–Cádiz, Larache–Cádiz *via* Algeciras.

Telephone subscribers totalled 241,000 in 1982.

Broadcasting is done in Arabic, Berber, French, Spanish and English from Rabat and Tangier; television in Arabic and French began in 1962. In 1977 there were 1·6m. radio and 597,000 television receivers.

Cinemas. There were about 235 cinemas in 1971.

JUSTICE, RELIGION, EDUCATION AND WELFARE

Justice. A uniform legal system is being organized, based mainly on French and Islamic law codes and French legal procedure. The judiciary consists of a Supreme Court, courts of appeal, regional tribunals and magistrates' courts.

Religion. Islam is the established state religion. 98% are Sunni Moslems of the Malekite school and 2% are Christians, mainly Roman Catholic.

Education. In 1959 a standardization of the various school systems (French, Spanish, Israeli, Moslem, etc.) was begun. Education has been made compulsory from the age of 7 to 13.

In 1982–83 there were 2,377,568 pupils and 65,521 teachers in state primary schools; 902,234 pupils and 42,728 teachers in secondary schools; 10,020 (1981) students in technical schools and 16,148 (1981) students in teacher-training establishments.

The language of instruction in primary and secondary schools is Arabic. Some scientific courses were (1985) still taught in French.

There are six universities, Mohamed V at Rabat, Hassan II at Casablanca, Mohamed Ben Abdallah at Fez, Quaraouyine at Fez, Oujda and Marrakesh with a total enrolment of 82,944 students and 4,007 teaching staff in 1982–83.

Health. In 1982 there were 1,308 doctors and (1979) 24,453 hospital beds.

DIPLOMATIC REPRESENTATIVES

Of Morocco in Great Britain (49 Queen's Gate Gdns., London, SW7 5NE)
Ambassador: Mohamed Medhi Benabdeljalil (accredited 11 Feb. 1982).

Of Great Britain in Morocco (17 Blvd de la Tour Hassan, Rabat)
Ambassador: R. A. C. Byatt.

Of Morocco in the USA (1601 21st St., NW, Washington, D.C., 20009)
Ambassador: Maati Jorio.

Of the USA in Morocco (2 Ave. de Marrakech, Rabat)
Ambassador: Joseph V. Reed, Jr.

Of Morocco to the United Nations
Ambassador: Ali Ben Jelloun.

Books of Reference

Statistical Information: The Service Central des Statistiques (BP 178, Rabat) was established in 1942. Its publications include: *Annuaire de Statistique Générale.—La Conjoncture Économique Marocaine* (monthly; with annual synthesis). *Bulletin économique et social du Maroc* (trimestral)

Bulletin Officiel (in Arabic and French). Rabat. Weekly
Findlay, A. M. and A. M., and Lawless, R. I., *Morocco.* [Bibliography] Oxford and Santa Barbara, 1984
Kinross, Lord, and Hales-Gary, D., *Morocco.* London, 1971
Rivière, P. L., *Précis de Législation marocaine.* New ed. in collaboration with G. Catteriz. 2 vols. Caen, 1942–46

National Library: Bibliothèque Générale et Archives, Rabat.

MOZAMBIQUE

República Popular de Moçambique

Capital: Maputo
Population: 13·14m. (1983)
GNP per capita: US$270 (1980)

HISTORY. Trading settlements were established by Arab merchants at Sofala (Beira), Quelimane, Angoche and Mozambique Island in the fifteenth century. Mozambique Island was visited by Vasco da Gamba's fleet on 2 March 1498, and Sofala was occupied by Portuguese in 1506. At first ruled as part of Portuguese India, a separate administration was created in 1752, and on 11 June 1951 Mozambique became an Overseas Province of Portugal. Following a decade of guerrilla activity, Portugal and the nationalists jointly established a transitional government on 20 Sept. 1974. Independence was achieved on 25 June 1975. In March 1984 the Republic of South Africa and Mozambique signed a non-agression pact.

AREA AND POPULATION. Mozambique is bounded east by the Indian ocean, south by South Africa, south-west by Swaziland, west by South Africa and Zimbabwe and north by Zambia, Malawi and Tanzania. It has an area of 799,380 sq. km (308,642 sq. miles) and a population, according to the census of 1980, of 12·13m. Estimate (1983) 13·14m. of whom (1982) 850,000 lived in the capital, Maputo. The areas, populations and capitals of the 10 provinces are:

Province	*Sq. km*	*Census 1970*	*Capital*
Cabo Delgado	78,374	546,113	Pemba
Niassa	120,135	285,329	Lichinga
Nampula	78,265	1,716,486	Nampula
Zambézia	102,880	1,747,888	Quelimane
Tete	100,714	488,668	Tete
Manica Sofala	129,854	1,079,718	Chimoio Beira
Inhambane	68,470	748,575	Inhambane
Gaza	82,534	756,654	Xaixai
Maputo	16,783	799,502	Maputo

At the 1970 census, Maputo had 354,684 inhabitants; other large towns are Nampula (126,126) and Beira (113,770). The main ethnolinguistic groups are the Makua/Lomwe (37% of the population), mainly in Nampula and Zambézia provinces in the north, the Shona (10%) in Manica and Sofala, and the Thonga (23%) in the south. Portuguese remains the official language, but Swahili serves as a lingua franca, particularly north of the Zambézi.

CLIMATE. A humid tropical climate, with a dry season from June to Sept. In general, temperatures and rainfall decrease from north to south. Maputo. Jan. 78°F (25·6°C), July 65°F (18·3°C). Annual rainfall 30″ (760 mm). Beira. Jan. 82°F (27·8°C), July 69°F (20·6°C). Annual rainfall 60″ (1,522 mm).

CONSTITUTION AND GOVERNMENT. Under the Constitution adopted at independence on 25 June 1975, the directing power of the state is vested in the *Frente de Libertação de Moçambique* (FRELIMO), the liberation movement, which in Feb. 1977 was reconstituted as sole political Party. The legislative organ is the People's Assembly of 210 members, elected in Dec. 1977.

The Council of Ministers in Dec. 1983 consisted of:

President, and Commander-in-Chief of the Armed Forces, with overall responsibility for the Ministry of Defence: Samora Moises Machel.

Foreign Affairs: Joaquim Alberto Chissano. *Defence:* Lieut.-Gen. Alberto Joaquim Chipande. *Interior:* Armando Emílio Guebuza. *Security:* Mariano de Araújo Matsinhe. *Deputy Minister of Defence and Chief of Staff of the Armed*

Forces: Sebastião Marcos Mabote. *Minister in the Presidency for Economic Affairs:* Jacinto Soares Veloso. *Planning:* Mário da Graça Machungo. *Justice:* Dr José Oscar Monteiro. *Finance:* Dr Rui Baltazar dos Santos Alves. *Education and Culture:* Graça Simbine Machel. *Information:* José Luís Cabaço. *Public Works:* Júlio Zamith Carrilho. *Foreign Trade:* Joaquim Ribeiro de Carvalho. *Agriculture:* João dos Santos Ferreira. *Mineral Resources:* José Carlos Lobo. *Industry and Energy:* António José Lima Rodigues Branco. *Health:* Pascual Manuel Mucumbi. *Ports, Railways and Shipping:* Luis Maria Alcântara Santos. *Posts and Telecommunications:* Rui Jorge Gomes de Lousã. *Domestic Trade:* Manuel Jorge Aranda da Silva. *Governor of the Bank of Mozambique:* Prakash Ratilal.

There are 8 Deputy Ministers and 9 Secretaries of State.

National flag: Horizontally green, black, yellow with the black fimbriated in white; a red triangle based on the hoist, charged with a yellow star surmounted by an open white book and a crossed rifle and hoe in black.

DEFENCE. Selective conscription for 2 years is in force.

Army. The Army consists of 1 tank brigade and 7 infantry brigades. Equipment includes T-34/-54/-55 main battle tanks. Strength (1985) 11,000. There are also 4,000 Border Guards and various militias.

Navy. The small flotilla comprises 6 former Portuguese coastal patrol boats, 6 *ex*-Soviet gunboats, 4 *ex*-Netherlands patrol craft, 1 *ex*-Portuguese survey ship (former British fleet minesweeper), 1 *ex*-Portuguese landing craft (used as a transport) and 2 *ex*-Portuguese minor landing craft. Naval personnel in 1985 totalled 700 officers and men.

Air Force. The Air Force is reported to have about 20 MiG-17 and 30 MiG-21 fighters, probably flown by Cuban pilots, An-26 turboprop transports, a Tu-134A for VIP use. Mi-8 helicopters, about 28 L-39 jet trainers, Zlin 326 primary trainers and a few *ex*-Portuguese Air Force transport/liaison aircraft.

INTERNATIONAL RELATIONS

Membership. Mozambique is a member of UN, OAU and SADCC.

ECONOMY

Budget. In 1982 the revenue was 18,500m. meticais; expenditure, 21,370m. meticais.

Currency. In June 1980 the currency became the *metical* (pl. *meticais*) divided into 100 *centavos.* The *metical* was established at par with the former *escudo*. In March 1985, £1 = 47·98 *meticais*; US$1 = 44·87 *meticais.*

Banking. Most banks had been nationalized by 1979. The *Banco de Moçambique* (bank of issue) and the *Banco Popular de Desenvolvimento* (state investment bank) each have a capital of 1,000m. meticais.

Weights and Measures. The metric system is in force.

ENERGY AND NATURAL RESOURCES

Electricity. Production (1980) 14,000m. kwh. Capacity (1977) 1,213 mw. The hydro-electric dam at Cabora Bassa on the Zambezi is the largest producer in Africa.

Minerals. Coal mining is the main mineral being exploited. Output reached 160,000 tonnes in 1981 but has since fallen. Coal reserves (estimate) 400m. tonnes. Small quantities of bauxite, gold, titanium, fluorite and colombo-tantalite are produced. Iron ore deposits and natural gas are known to exist.

Agriculture. Production in tonnes (1981): Cereals, 495,000; tea, 18,000; maize, 270,000; bananas, 65,000; sisal, 12,000; rice, 162,000; groundnuts, 80,000; copra, 70,000.

Livestock 1983: 1·44m. cattle, 350,000 goats, 112,000 sheep, 135,000 pigs, 20,000 asses.

Forestry. Production (1981) 13·57m. cu. metres.

Fisheries. In 1981 the catch was 30,000 tonnes.

INDUSTRY AND TRADE

Industry. Although the country is overwhelmingly rural, there is some substantial industry in and around Maputo (steel, engineering, textiles, processing, docks and railways).

Commerce. Imports in 1981 totalled 25,800m. meticais and exports 13,100m. meticais. 15·3% of imports came from the Republic of South Africa and 12·7% from the Federal Republic of Germany. Exports (1976 in tonnes): Coal, 204,843 while 27% of exports went to USA and 16% to Portugal. In 1977 cashew nuts formed 30%, textiles, 9% and tea, 8% of all exports.

Total trade between Mozambique and UK (British Department of Trade returns, in £1,000 sterling):

	1980	*1981*	*1982*	*1983*	*1984*
Imports to UK	11,416	5,716	10,611	9,176	8,549
Exports and re-exports from UK	11,345	21,763	14,473	28,618	15,671

COMMUNICATIONS

Roads. There were, in 1982, 26,000 km of roads, of which 4,600 km were tarred. Motor vehicles, in 1980, included 99,400 passenger cars and 24,700 lorries and buses. The Government is devoting effort to constructing a new North/South road link, and to improving provincial rural feeder road systems.

Railways. The Mozambique State Railways consist of 5 independent networks known as the Maputo, Mozambique, Sofala (Beira), Inhambane and Gaza, and Quelimane systems. The Maputo system has links with the Republic of South Africa, Swaziland and Zimbabwe railways; the Sofala system links with Zimbabwe at Machipanda and by way of the Trans–Zambesia Railway with Malawi at Dona Ana; and the Mozambique system links with Malawi at Entre Lagos. The Inhambane and Quelimane systems have no international connections. Total route-km (1980), 3,696 km (1,067 mm gauge), and 147 km (762 mm gauge). Trans–Zambesia Railway, 318 km (1,067 mm gauge). In 1981, 12m. passengers and 5,166m. tonne-km of goods were carried. Rail links with Zimbabwe reopened in 1979.

Aviation. There are international airports at Maputo, Beira and Nampula with regular services to European and Southern African destination by several foreign airlines and by *Linhas Aéreas de Moçambique*, who also serve 13 domestic airports.

Shipping. The total tonnage handled by Mozambique ports (1981) was 9·12m. The principal ports are Maputo, Beira, Naçala and Quelimane.

Post and Broadcasting. Maputo is connected by telegraph with the Transvaal system. Quelimane has telegraphic communication with Chiromo. Number of telephones (1982), 56,305.

Radio Moçambique broadcasts 5 programmes in Portuguese, English, Afrikaans, Ronga and Shangane as well as 4 regional programmes in 8 languages. Number of receivers (1984): radio, 450,000; (1979) TV, 1,500.

Cinemas. There were, in 1971, 31 cinemas with a seating capacity of 20,195.

Newspapers. There were (1984) 2 daily newspapers in Mozambique: *Noticias,* published in Maputo, and *Diario de Mozambique.* There are also 2 weekly magazines.

JUSTICE, RELIGION, EDUCATION AND WELFARE

Justice. A system of People's Courts exists at all levels.

Religion. About 60% of the population follow traditional animist religions, while some 18% are Christian (mainly Roman Catholic) and 16% Moslem.

Education. In 1981 there were 1,376,865 pupils in primary schools and 135,956 in secondary schools. The *Universidade Eduardo Mondlane* had 836 students in 1980. About 500,000 attend adult literacy classes.

Health. There were (1980) 321 hospitals and medical centres and 13,180 hospital beds; there were 823 doctors, 96 dentists, 8 pharmacists, 457 midwives and 2,156 nursing personnel.

DIPLOMATIC REPRESENTATIVES

Of Great Britain in Mozambique (Ave. Vladimir I Lenine, 310, Maputo)
Ambassador: E. V. Vines, CMG, OBE.

Of Mozambique in the USA (1990 M St., NW, Washington, D.C., 20037)
Ambassador: Valeriano Ferrao.

Of USA in Mozambique (35 Rua Da Mesquita, Maputo)
Ambassador: Peter Jon de Vos.

Of Mozambique to the United Nations
Ambassador: Manuel dos Santos.

Books of Reference

Henriksen, T. H., *Mozambique: A History.* London and Cape Town, 1978
Houser, G., and Shore, H., *Mozambique: Dream the Size of Freedom.* New York, 1975
Isaacman, A., *A Luta Continua: Building a New Society in Mozambique.* New York, 1978.
—*Mozambique: From Colonization to Revolution, 1900–1982.* Aldershot and Boulder, 1984
Mondlane, E., *The Struggle for Mozambique.* London, 1983
Munslow, B., *Mozambique: The Revolution and its Origins.* London and New York, 1983

NAURU *Population:* 8,421 (1982)

HISTORY. The island was discovered by Capt. Fearn in 1798, annexed by Germany in Oct. 1888, and surrendered to the Australian forces in 1914. It was administered under a mandate, effective from 17 Dec. 1920, conferred on the British Empire and approved by the League of Nations until 1 Nov. 1947, when the United Nations General Assembly approved a trusteeship agreement with the governments of Australia, New Zealand and UK as joint administering authority. Independence was gained in 1968.

AREA AND POPULATION. The island is situated 0° 32′ S. lat. and 166° 56′ E. long. Area, 5,263 acres (2,130 hectares). It is an oval-shaped upheaval coral island of approximately 12 miles in circumference, surrounded by a reef which is exposed at low tide. There is no deep water harbour but offshore moorings, reputedly the deepest in the world, are capable of holding medium-sized vessels, including 30,000 tonne capacity bulk carriers. On the seaward side the reef dips abruptly into the deep waters of the Pacific at an angle of 45°. On the landward side of the reef there is a sandy beach interspersed with coral pinnacles. From the sandy beach the ground rises gradually, forming a fertile section ranging in width from 150 to 300 yd and completely encircling the island. There is an extensive plateau bearing phosphate of a high grade, the mining rights of which were vested in the British Phosphate Commissioners until 1 July 1970, subject to the rights of the Nauruan landowners. In July 1970 the Nauru Phosphate Corporation assumed control and management of the enterprise. It is chiefly on the fertile section of land between the sandy beach and the plateau that the Nauruans have established themselves. With the exception of a small fringe round a shallow lagoon, about 1 mile inland, the plateau, which contains the phosphate deposits, has few foodbearing trees and is not settled by the Nauruans.

At the census held on 22 Jan. 1977 the population totalled 7,254, of whom 4,174 were Nauruans. Estimate (1983) 8,421.

Vital statistics, 1982: Births, 286 (224 Nauruan); deaths, 77 (42 Nauruan).

CLIMATE. A tropical climate, tempered by sea breezes, but with a high and irregular rainfall, averaging 82″ (2,060 mm). Jan. 81°F (27·2°C), July 82°F (27·8°C). Annual rainfall 75″ (1,862 mm).

CONSTITUTION AND GOVERNMENT. A Legislative Council was established by the Nauru Act, passed by the Australian Parliament in Dec. 1965 and was inaugurated on 31 Jan. 1966. The trusteeship agreement terminated on 31 Jan. 1968, on which day Nauru became an independent republic but having special relationship with the Commonwealth. An 18-member Parliament is elected on a 3-yearly basis.

President and Minister for Foreign Affairs: Hammer DeRoburt, OBE.

National flag: Blue with a narrow horizontal gold stripe across the centre, beneath this near the hoist a white star of 12 points.

FINANCE. Revenue and expenditure (in $A) for financial year ending 30 June 1983 (estimate): revenue, 97,279,300; expenditure, 111,284,800 (health, 1,602,200; education, 2,004,200).

The interests in the phosphate deposits were purchased in 1919 from the Pacific Phosphate Company by the governments of the UK, the Commonwealth of Australia and New Zealand at a cost of £Stg3·5m., and a Board of Commissioners representing the 3 governments was appointed to manage and control the working of the deposits. In May 1967, in Canberra, the British Phosphate Corporation agreed to hand over the phosphate industry to Nauru and on 15 June 1967 agreement was reached that the Nauruans could buy the assets of the B.P.C. for approximately $A20m. over 3 years. It is estimated that the deposits will be exhausted by 1993.

COMMERCE. The export trade consists almost entirely of phosphate shipped to Australia, New Zealand and Japan. The imports consist almost entirely of food supplies, building construction materials and machinery for the phosphate industry.

Total trade between Nauru and UK (British Department of Trade returns, in £1,000 sterling):

	1980	*1981*	*1982*	*1983*	*1984*
Imports to UK	70	83	32	1,421	916
Exports from UK	821	326	1,843	1,715	1,332

COMMUNICATIONS

Aviation. There is an airfield on the island capable of accepting medium size jet aircraft. Air Nauru, a wholly owned government subsidiary, operates services with Boeing 727 and 737 aircraft to Melbourne, Sydney, Apia, Honiara, Guam, Tarawa, Majuro, Kagoshima, Okinawa, Noumea, Port Vila, Suva, Nadi, Ponape, Manila, Taipei, Truk, Saipan, Korer (Pelan), Honolulu, Singapore, Auckland, Pago Pago and Niue.

Shipping. The Nauru Local Government Council, through its agency the Nauru Pacific Shipping Line, owns 6 ships and 2 fishing boats. These ships ply between Australia, Pacific Islands, west coast of USA, New Zealand, Japan, Singapore etc. Other shipping coming to the island consists of those under charter to the phosphate industry.

Telecommunications. An earth satellite station became operational in 1976, offering 24 hour telephone, telegram and telex services world-wide. Number of telephones (1978) 1,500. Direct daily high frequency service is maintained with Tarawa and both long- and short-wave transmissions with merchant shipping. A separate tele-radio service exists between Nauru and Ocean Island.

Cinemas. In 1978 there were 7 cinemas with seating capacity of 1,500.

JUSTICE, RELIGION AND EDUCATION

Justice. The highest Court is the Supreme Court of Nauru. It is the Superior Court of record and has the jurisdiction to deal with constitutional matters in addition to its other jurisdiction. There is also a District Court which is presided over by the Resident Magistrate who is also the Chairman of the Family Court and the Registrar of Supreme Court. The laws applicable in Nauru are its own Acts of Parliament and a large number of British statutes and the common law have been adopted for Nauru.

Religion. The population is mainly Roman Catholic or Protestant

Education. Attendance at school is compulsory for all children between the ages of 6 and 16. In June 1983 there were 8 infant and primary schools and 2 secondary schools. There were 44 teachers and 2,164 pupils in infant, primary and secondary schools. In addition, there is a trade school with 4 instructors and an enrolment of 74 trainees. Scholarships are available for Nauruan children to receive secondary and higher education and vocational training in Australia and New Zealand. In June 1983, 77 Nauruans were receiving secondary education abroad in Australia and New Zealand and 10 were enrolled in university and vocational training courses in Australia, New Zealand and Fiji.

DIPLOMATIC REPRESENTATIVES

Of Great Britain in Nauru
High Commisioner: R. A. R. Barltrop, CVO (resides in Suva).

Of Nauru in the USA
Ambassador: T. W. Star (resides in Melbourne).

Books of Reference

Text of Trusteeship Agreement. (Cmd. 7290; Treaty Series No. 89, 1947)
Packett, C. N., *Guide to the Republic of Nauru.* Bradford, 1970
Pittman, G. A., *Nauru, the Phosphate Island.* London, 1959
Viviani, N., *Phosphate and Political Progress.* Canberra, 1970

NEPÁL

Sri Nepala Sarkar

Capital: Káthmándu
Population: 16·10m. (1982)
GNP per capita: US$150 (1981)

HISTORY. From 1846 to 1951 Nepál was virtually ruled by the Ráná family, a member of which always held the office of prime minister, the succession being determined by special rules. The last Ráná prime minister (and, until 18 Feb. 1951, Supreme C.-in-C.) was HH Máháraja Mohan Shumsher Jung Bahádur Ráná, who resigned in Nov. 1951.

AREA AND POPULATION. Nepál, situated between 26° 20′ and 30° 10′ N. lat. and between 80° 15′ and 88° 15′ E. long., is bounded on the north by Tibet, on the east by Sikkim and West Bengal, on the south and west by Bihar and Uttar Pradesh. On 5 Oct. 1961 a treaty was signed in Peking, according to which the Chinese–Nepalese boundary line 'runs generally south-eastwards along the mountain ridge, passing through Cho Oyu mountain, Pumoli mountain, Mount Chomo Lungma (the Chinese name for Everest) and Lhotse Too Makalu mountain'. Nepál gained about 300 sq. miles of territory. Area 56,136 sq. miles (145,391 sq. km); population (estimate, 1982), 16·10m.; (census, 1981) 15,020,451 of whom 52·5% were Nepali-speaking and 18·5% Bihari-speaking.

Capital, Káthmándu, 75 miles from the Indian frontier; population about 195,260. Other towns (1971) include Pátan (also called Lalitpur), 48,577; Moráng (Biratnagar), 44,938; Bhádgáon (Bhaktapur), 40,112.

The aboriginal stock is Mongolian with a considerable admixture of Hindu blood from India. They were originally divided into numerous hill clans and petty principalities, one of which, Gorkha or Gurkha, became predominant in 1559 and has since given its name to men from all parts of Nepál. The 15 feudal chieftainships were integrated into the kingdom on 10 April 1961.

The country is administratively divided into 14 zones and 75 development districts.

CLIMATE. The rainfall is high, with maximum amounts from May to Sept., but conditions are very dry from Nov. to Jan. The range of temperature is moderate. Káthmándu. Jan. 50°F (10°C), July 76°F (24·4°C). Annual rainfall 57″ (1,428 mm).

RULING KING. The sovereign is HM Mahárájádhirája **Birendra Bir Bikram Sháh Dev**, who succeeded his father Mahendra Bir Bikram Sháh Dev on 31 Jan. 1972.

CONSTITUTION AND GOVERNMENT. On 18 Feb. 1951 the King proclaimed a constitutional monarchy, and on 16 Dec. 1962 a new Constitution of the 'Constitutional Monarchical Hindu State'. The village and town *panchayat*, recognized as the basic units of democracy, elect the district *panchayat*, these elect the zonal *panchayat*, and these finally the 112 members of the national *panchayat*. The Constitution was amended in 1975. In addition, 28 representatives of professional organizations and royal nominees not exceeding 15% of the elected members, will be included in the national *panchayat*. The executive power is vested in the King, who appoints a council of ministers from the national *panchayat*. A state council will advise the King and proclaim the successor or, if the heir is a minor, a regency council. Art. 81 empowers the King to declare a state of emergency and to suspend the Constitution.

The Cabinet appointed in July 1983 was as follows:

Prime Minister: Lokendra Bahadur Chand.

Parliament and Local Development: Jog Mehar Shrestha. *Home Affairs:* Padma Sunder Lawati. *Water Resources and Supply:* Pashupati Shumsher Rana. *Agricul-*

ture and Land Reform: Hem Bahadur Malla. *Commerce, Industry and Health:* Narayan Dutta Bhatta. *Law and Justice:* Bakhan Singh Gurung. *Foreign Affairs:* Padma Bahadur Khatri. *Public Works and Transport:* Damber Narayan Yadau. *Finance and Communications:* Prakash Chandra Lohani.

There were also 4 Ministers of State and 7 Assistant Ministers.

National flag: Two triangular parts of red, with a blue border all round, bearing symbols of the moon and the sun in white.

National anthem: 'May glory crown our illustrious sovereign' (1952).

DEFENCE

Army. The Army consists of 6 infantry brigades, and single artillery, engineer, signals, parachute and transport battalions, and 1 air squadron. Equipment includes AMX-13 light tanks. Strength (1985) about 25,000, and there is also a 15,000-strong paramilitary police force.

Air Force. Independent of the army since 1979, the Air Force has 1 Skyvan transport aircraft, 1 Puma helicopter, 3 Chetak trainers, and 2 Alouette III helicopters. An H.S. 748 turboprop transport and a Puma helicopter are operated by the Royal Flight.

INTERNATIONAL RELATIONS

Membership. Nepál is a member of UN and the Colombo Plan.

ECONOMY

Planning. The sixth (1980–85) plan envisages expenditure of NRs 33,940m. Priority will be given to transport, communications, power, agriculture, irrigation, training of technicians and schools.

Budget. The general budget for the fiscal year 1983–84 envisages total expenditure of NRs 2,439m. Revenues are estimated at NRs 4,306m.

Currency. The Nepalese *rupee* is 171 grains in weight, as compared with the Indian rupee, which weighs 180 grains. The rate of exchange is 135 Nepalese rupees for 100 Indian rupees. 100 Nepalese *pice* = 1 Nepalese rupee. Coins of all denominations are minted. The Rástra Bank also issues notes of 1, 5, 10, 100 and 1,000 rupees. In March 1985, US$1 = 19 *rupees*; £1 = 20·29 *rupees*.

ENERGY AND NATURAL RESOURCES

Electricity. Production (1981) 232 kwh. A hydro-electric power scheme costing US$120m. was inaugurated in Dec. 1982.

Agriculture. Nepál has valuable forests in the southern part of the country. In the northern part, on the slopes of the Himálayas, there grow large quantities of medicinal herbs which find a world-wide market. Of the total area, nearly one-third (11·2m. acres) is under forest; 5·4m. acres is covered by perpetual snow; 9·6m. acres is under paddy, 2·9m. maize and millet, 800,000 wheat. Production (1982 in 1,000 tonnes): Rice, 2,560; maize, 752; wheat, 526; sugar-cane, 590; potatoes, 320; millet, 122.

Livestock (1983); Cattle, 6·98m., including about 470,000 cows; 4·46m. buffaloes; sheep, 2·48m.; goats, 2·65m.; pigs, 365,000; poultry, 24m.

INDUSTRY AND TRADE

Industry. Industries, such as jute- and sugar-mills, match, leather, cigarette, and shoe factories, and chemical works have been established, including two industrial estates at Pátan and Baluju. Production (1982 in 1,000 tonnes): Jute goods, 15·7; sugar, 21·1; cement, 30; iron goods, 7·4.

Commerce. The principal articles of export are food grains, jute, timber, oilseeds, ghee (clarified butter), potatoes, medicinal herbs, hides and skins, cattle. The chief imports are textiles, cigarettes, salt, petrol and kerosene, sugar, machinery, medicines, boots and shoes, paper, cement, iron and steel, tea.

Imports and exports in NRs 1,000:

	1979	*1980*	*1981*	*1982*
Imports	3,509,600	3,911,700	4,332,400	4,930,000
Exports	1,136,900	964,200	1,797,500	1,492,000

Total trade between Nepál and UK (British Department of Trade returns, in £1,000 sterling):

	1980	*1981*	*1982*	*1983*	*1984*
Imports to UK	2,253	2,324	3,844	6,115	5,564
Exports and re-exports from UK	2,956	2,980	4,650	5,011	6,453

Tourism. There were 175,448 tourists in 1983.

COMMUNICATIONS

Roads. With the co-operation of India and the USA 900 miles of motorable roads are being constructed, including the East-West Highway through southern Nepál. A road from the Tibetan border to Káthmándu was recently completed with Chinese aid.

There are about 1,300 miles motorable roads. A ropeway for the carriage of goods covers the 14 miles from Dhursing above Bhimphedi into the Káthmándu valley.

A road connects Káthmándu with Birgung.

Railways. Railways (762 mm gauge) connect Jayanagar on the North Eastern Indian Railway with Janakpur and thence with Bijulpura (54 km).

Aviation. The Royal Nepál Airline Corporation has linked Káthmándu, the capital, with 11 districts of Nepál; and 23 more airfields are under construction. The Royal Nepalese Airline Corporation has services between Káthmándu and Calcutta, Patna, New Delhi, Bangkok, Rangoon and Dacca, employing Boeing 727 jet aircraft.

Post and Broadcasting. Káthmándu is connected by telephone with Birganj and Raxaul (North Eastern Indian Railway) on the southern frontier with Bihar; and with the eastern part of the Terai foothills; an extension to the western districts is being completed. Number of telephones (1978) 9,425, of which 5,431 were in Káthmándu. Under an agreement with India and the USA, a network of 91 wireless stations exists in Nepál, with further stations in Calcutta and New Delhi. Radio Nepál at Káthmándu broadcasts in Nepáli and English. Wireless telecommunication was inaugurated on 1 Oct. 1964.

All post, telephone and telegraph services have been taken over from India. The Indian, originally English, post office, established 1816, closed on 13 April 1965.

JUSTICE, RELIGION, EDUCATION AND WELFARE

Justice. The Supreme Court Act, established a uniform judicial system, culminating in a supreme court of a Chief Justice and no more than 6 judges. Special courts to deal with minor offences may be established at the discretion of the Government.

Religion. Sánáton of Pauranic, *i.e.*, traditional or ancient Hinduism, and Buddhism are the religions of the bulk of the people. Christian missions are admitted, but conversion is forbidden.

The royal family is Hindu.

Education. In 1982 there were 1,475,000 primary school pupils, 370,000 secondary school pupils and the Tribhuvan University (founded 1960).

About 20% of the population are literate. The national language is Nepáli.

Health. There were about 420 doctors and 2,586 hospital beds in 1979.

DIPLOMATIC REPRESENTATIVES

Of Nepál in Great Britain (12a Kensington Palace Gdns., London, W8 4QU)
Ambassador: Ishwari Raj Pandey (accredited 4 Aug. 1983).

Of Great Britain in Nepál (Láincháur, Káthmándu)
Ambassador: A. G. Hurrell, CMG.

Of Nepál in the USA (2131 Leroy Pl., NW, Washington, D.C., 20008)
Ambassador: Bhekh Bahadur Thapa.

Of the USA in Nepál (Pani Pokhari, Káthmándu)
Ambassador: Carleton S. Coon.

Of Nepál to the United Nations
*Ambassador:*Uddhav Deo Bhatt.

Books of Reference

Statistical Information: A Department of Statistics was set up in Káthmándu in 1950.

Baral, L. S., *Political Development in Nepal.* London,1980
Bezruchka, S., *A Guide to Trekking in Nepal.* Leicester, 1981
Turner, R. L., *Nepali Dictionary.* 1980.
Wadhwa, D. N., *Nepal.* [Bibliography] Oxford and Santa Barbara, 1983

THE NETHERLANDS

Koninkrijk der Nederlanden

Capital: Amsterdam
Seat of Government: The Hague
Population: 14·31m. (1982)
GNP per capita: US$11,790 (1981)

HISTORY. William of Orange (1533–84), as the German count of Nassau, inherited vast possessions in the Netherlands and the Princedom of Orange in France. He was the initiator of the struggle for independence from Spain (1568–1648); in the Republic of the United Netherlands he and his successors became the 'first servants of the Republic' with the title of 'Stadhouder' (governor). In 1689 William III acceded to the throne of England, becoming joint sovereign with Mary II, his wife. William III died in 1702 without issue, and after a stadhouderless period a member of the Frisian branch of Orange–Nassau was nominated hereditary stadhouder in 1747; but his successor, Willem V, had to take refuge in England, in 1795, at the invasion of the French Army. In Nov. 1813 the United Provinces were freed from French domination.

The Congress of Vienna joined the Belgian provinces, the 'Austrian Netherlands' before the French Revolution, to the Northern Netherlands. The son of the former stadhouder Willem V was proclaimed King of the Netherlands at The Hague on 16 March 1815 as Willem I. The union was dissolved by the Belgian revolution of 1830, and the treaty of London, 19 April 1839, constituted Belgium an independent kingdom.

Netherlands Sovereigns

Willem I	1815–1840 (died 1843)	Wilhelmina	1890–1948 (died 1962)
Willem II	1840–1849	Juliana	1948–1980
Willem III	1849–1890	Beatrix	1980–

AREA AND POPULATION. The Netherlands is bounded north and west by the North Sea, south by Belgium and east by the Federal Republic of Germany. Growth of census population:

1829	2,613,298	1909	5,858,175	1960	11,461,964
1849	3,056,879	1920	6,865,314	1971	13,060,115
1869	3,579,529	1930	7,935,565		
1889	4,511,415	1947	9,625,499		

Area, density and estimated population on 1 Jan. 1974 and 1984:

Province	*Land area (in sq. km) 1984*	*Population 1974*	*Population 1984*	*Density per sq. km 1984*
Groningen	2,335·24	532,649	561,532	240
Friesland	3,335·72	547,223	597,236	179
Drenthe	2,653·56	393,739	427,336	161
Overijssel	3,811·24	966,806	1,042,077	273
Gelderland	5,005·61	1,601,045	1,735,780	347
Utrecht	1,331·54	849,266	929,401	698
Noord-Holland	2,667·86	2,282,686	2,307,447	865
Zuid-Holland	2,907·34	3,018,525	3,139,189	1,080
Zeeland	1,785·36	322,891	355,514	199
Noord-Brabant	4,956·80	1,910,347	2,103,003	424
Limburg	2,169·76	1,038,253	1,083,561	499
Almere [1]	148·40	...	33,037	223
Dronten [1]	332·56	14,297	22,224	67
Lelystad [1]	270·60	...	55,141	204

[1] Almere, Dronten and Lelystad are municipalities (ex-Zuidelijke Ijsselmeerpolders) and have not been incorporated into any province.

Province	Land area (in sq. km) 1984	Population 1974	Population 1984	Density per sq. km 1984
Zeewolde [1]	222·70	...	821	4
Zuideijke Ijsselmeerpolders [1]	—	10,638	—	—
Central Population Register [2]	—	2,655	1,290	—
Total	33,935·52[3]	13,491,020	14,394,589	424

[1] Zeewolde is a municipality (ex-Zuideijke Ijsselmeerpolders) and has not been incorporated into any province. The Zuidelijke Ijsselmeerpolders (drained in 1957) are part of the former Zuiderzee, now called Ijsselmeer; they have not been incorporated into any province.

[2] The Central Population Register includes persons who are residents of the Netherlands but who have no fixed residence in any particular municipality (living in caravans and houseboats, population on inland vessels, etc.).

[3] Including 1·25 sq. km not municipally classified.

Of the total population on 1 Jan. 1982, 7,081,566 were males, 7,204,263 females.

The total area of the Netherlands is 41,548 sq. km (16,042 sq. miles), of which 33,930 sq. km (13,100 sq. miles) is land area.

On 14 June 1918 a law was passed concerning the reclamation of the Zuiderzee. The work was begun in 1920; the following sections have been completed: 1. The Noordholland–Wieringen Barrage (2·5 km), 1924; 2. The Wieringermeer Polder (210 sq. km), 1930 (inundated by the Germans in 1945, but drained again in the same year); 3. The Wieringen–Friesland Barrage (30 km), 1932; 4. The Noordoost Polder (501 sq. km), 1942; 5. Oost Flevoland (604 sq. km), 1957; 6. Zuidelijk Flevoland (499 sq. km), 1967.

The polder Markerwaard (400 sq. km) is being reclaimed. A portion of what used to be the Zuiderzee behind the barrage will remain a fresh-water lake: Ijsselmeer (1,400 sq. km). The 'Delta-project', scheduled to be completed in the 1980s, comprises the building of (semi) enclosure dams in the estuaries between the islands in the south-western part of the country, excluding the sea-entrances to the ports of Rotterdam and Antwerp; it will also create fresh-water reservoirs. *See* map in THE STATESMAN'S YEAR-BOOK, 1959.

Vital statistics for calendar years.

	Live births Total	Live births Illegitimate	Still births	Marriages	Divorces	Deaths	Net migration
1981	178,569	8,609	1,122	85,574	28,509	115,515	+16,988
1982	172,071	10,080	1,010	83,516	30,877	117,264	+3,233
1983	170,246	11,857	1,002	78,451	32,589	117,761	+5,978

Population of principal municipalities on 1 Jan. 1984:

Aalsmeer	20,379	Bussum	33,401	Geldermalsen	20,907
Achtkarspelen	27,030	Capelle a/d Ijssel	53,444	Geldrop	26,568
Alkmaar	83,892	Casticum	22,726	Geleen	34,828
Almelo	62,941	Delft	86,733	Gendringen	20,131
Almere	33,037	Delfzijl	24,953	Gilze en Rijen	21,170
Alphen a/d Rijn	54,560	Deurne	28,492	Goes	31,155
Amersfoort	86,896	Deventer	64,823	Gorinchem	27,538
Amstelveen	68,518	Doetinchem	39,755	Gouda	60,026
Amsterdam	676,439	Dongen	20,543	's-Gravenhage	445,213
Apeldoorn	144,108	Dongeradeel	24,969	Groningen	167,866
Arnhem	128,431	Dordrecht	107,475	Haarksbergen	21,959
Assen	46,745	Dronten	22,224	Haarlem	152,511
Baarn	24,693	Edam-Volendam	24,019	Haarlemmermeer	83,428
Barneveld	38,464	Ede (Gld.)	86,816	Hardenberg	31,799
Bergen op Zoom	45,568	Eindhoven	192,854	Harderwijk	32,505
Beverwijk	34,947	Emmen	91,010	Heemskerk	31,782
de Bilt	31,834	Enschede	144,938	Heemstede	25,730
Boxtel	24,475	Epe	33,465	Heerenveen	37,407
Breda	118,662	Ermelo	24,473	Heerhugowaard	34,383
Brummen	20,295	Etten-Leur	30,659	Heerlen	93,283
Brunssum	29,595	Franekeradeel	21,130	Heiloo	20,908

Den Helder	63,826	Nijkerk	24,266	Tilburg	154,094
Hellendoorn	33,508	Nijmegen	147,102	Uden	33,557
Hellevoetsluis	30,291	Oldebroek	20,192	Uithoorn	21,796
Helmond	60,582	Oldenzaal	28,827	Utrecht	230,414
Hengelo (O.)	76,855	Oosterhout	45,927	Valkenswaard	28,539
's-Hertogenbosch	89,059	Ooststellingwerf	24,533	Veendam	28,532
Hilversum	88,417	Opsterland	26,240	Veenendaal	43,228
Hoogeveen	45,031	Oss	50,086	Veghel	25,246
Hoogezand-Sappemeer	34,980	Papendrecht	25,787	Veldhoven	35,519
		Poortugaal	22,110	Velsen	58,287
Hoorn	50,473	Purmerend	45,829	Venlo	62,935
Huizen	35,741	Raalte	25,481	Venray	33,808
Kampen	31,944	Renkum	33,738	Vlaardingen	76,466
Katwijk	38,659	Rheden	47,934	Vlissingen	46,150
Kerkrade	53,231	Ridderkerk	47,124	Voorburg	41,945
Krimpen a/d Ijssel	28,238	Roermond	38,209	Voorschoten	21,665
Landgraaf	39,918	Roosendaal	56,519	Voorst	23,149
Leeuwarden	85,435	Rosmalen	24,121	Vught	23,205
Leiden	104,261	Rotterdam	555,349	Waalwijk	28,808
Leiderdorp	21,352	Rucphen	20,133	Waddinxveen	21,769
Leidschendam	30,597	Rijssen	22,538	Wageningen	32,083
Lelystad	55,141	Rijswijk (Z.-H.)	49,790	Wassenaar	26,950
Leusden	24,174	Scharsterland	22,699	Weert	39,402
Lisse	20,135	Schiedam	69,849	Weststellingwerf	24,493
Loon op Zand	20,063	Schijndel	20,510	Wierden	21,531
Losser	21,771	Sittard	43,889	Winschoten	20,660
Maarssen	32,768	Sliedrecht	22,746	Winterswijk	27,782
Maassluis	33,107	Smallingerland	50,724	Wisch	20,042
Maastricht	113,277	Sneek	29,473	Woerden	25,629
Meerssen	20,319	Soest	40,355	Wÿchen	29,772
Meppel	22,752	Spijkenisse	54,381	Zaanstad	128,413
Middelburg	38,854	Stadskanaal	34,095	Zeist	60,478
Naaldwijk	26,145	Steenwijk	21,084	Zevenaar	26,383
Nieuwegein	53,601	Stein	26,513	Zoetermeer	77,632
Noordoostpolder	37,884	Terneuzen	35,339	Zutphen	31,683
Noordwijk	24,270	Tiel	29,849	Zwolle	87,340
Nunspeet	23,134	Tietjerksteradeel	29,564	Zwijndrecht	39,862

Urban agglomerations as at 1 Jan. 1984: Rotterdam, 1,025,466; Amsterdam, 994,062; The Hague, 672,127; Utrecht, 501,357; Eindhoven, 374,109; Arnhem, 291,399; Enschede-Hengelo, 266,095; Heerlen-Kerkrade, 248,200; Tilburg, 233,992; Nijmegen, 221,684; Haarlem, 217,191; Groningen, 206,611; Dordrecht-Zwijndrecht, 199,156; 's-Hertogenbosch, 177,410; Geleen-Sittard, 186,946; Leiden, 176,360; Maastricht, 157,329; Breda, 153,517; Zaanstreek, 140,354; Velsen-Beverwijk, 125,016; Hilversum, 105,570.

CLIMATE. A cool temperate maritime climate, marked by mild winters and cool summers, but with occasional continental influences. Coastal temperatures vary from 37°F (3°C) in winter to 61°F (16°C) in summer, but inland the winters are slightly colder and the summers slightly warmer. Rainfall is least in the months Feb. to May, but inland there is a well-defined summer maximum in July and Aug.

The Hague. Jan. 37°F (2·7°C), July 61°F (16·3°C). Annual rainfall 32·8″ (820 mm). Amsterdam. Jan. 36°F (2·3°C), July 62°F (16·5°C). Annual rainfall 34″ (850 mm). Rotterdam. Jan. 36·5°F (2·6°C), July 62°F (16·6°C). Annual rainfall 32″ (800 mm).

REIGNING QUEEN. Beatrix Wilhelmina Armgard, born 31 Jan. 1938 daughter of Queen Juliana and Prince Bernhard; married to Claus von Amsberg on 10 March 1966; succeeded to the crown on 1 May 1980, on the abdication of her mother. *Offspring:* Prince Willem-Alexander, born 27 April 1967; Prince Johan Friso, born 25 Sept. 1968; Prince Constantijn, born 11 Oct. 1969.

Mother of the Queen: Queen Juliana Louise Emma Marie Wilhelmina, born 30 April 1909, daughter of Queen Wilhelmina (born 31 Aug. 1880, died 28 Nov. 1962) and Prince Henry of Mecklenburg-Schwerin (born 19 April 1876, died 3

July 1934); married to Prince Bernhard Leopold Frederick Everhard Julius Coert Karel Godfried Pieter of Lippe-Biesterfeld (born 29 June 1911) on 7 Jan. 1937. Abdicated in favour of her daughter, the Reigning Queen, on 30 April 1980.

Sisters of the Queen: Princess Irene Emma Elisabeth, born 5 Aug. 1939, married to Prince Charles Hugues de Bourbon-Parma on 29 April 1964, divorced 1981 (*sons:* Prince Carlos Javier Bernardo, born 27 Jan. 1970; Prince Jaime Bernardo, born 13 Oct. 1972; *daughters:* Princess Margarita Maria Beatriz, born 13 Oct. 1972; Princess Maria Carolina Christina, born 23 June 1974); Princess Margriet Francisca, born in Ottawa, 19 Jan. 1943, married to Pieter van Vollenhoven on 10 Jan. 1967 (*sons:* Prince Maurits, born 17 April 1968; Prince Bernhard, born 25 Dec. 1969; Prince Pieter-Christiaan, born 22 March 1972; Prince Floris, born 10 April 1975); Princess Maria Christina, born 18 Feb. 1947, married to Jorge Guillermo on 28 June 1975 (*sons:* Bernardo, born 17 June 1977; Nicolas Daniel Mauricio, born 6 July 1979; *daughter:* Juliana, born 8 Oct. 1981).

CONSTITUTION AND GOVERNMENT. According to the Constitution of the Kingdom of the Netherlands, the Kingdom consists of the Netherlands and the Netherlands Antilles. Their relations are regulated by the 'Statute' for the Kingdom, which came into force on 29 Dec. 1954. Each part enjoys full autonomy; they are united, on a footing of equality, for mutual assistance and the protection of their common interests.

The first Constitution of the Netherlands after its restoration as a Sovereign State was promulgated in 1814. It was revised in 1815 (after the addition of the Belgian provinces, and the assumption by the Sovereign of the title of King), 1840 (after the secession of the Belgian provinces), 1848, 1884, 1887, 1917, 1922, 1938, 1946, 1948, 1953, 1956, 1963, 1972 and 1983.

The Netherlands is a constitutional and hereditary monarchy. The royal succession is in the direct male or female line in the order of primogeniture. The Sovereign comes of age on reaching his 18th year. During his minority the royal power is vested in a Regent—designated by law—and in some cases in the Council of State.

The central executive power of the State rests with the Crown, while the central legislative power is vested in the Crown and Parliament (the *Staten-Generaal*), consisting of 2 Chambers. After the 1956 revision of the Constitution the Upper or First Chamber is composed of 75 members, elected by the members of the Provincial States, and the Second Chamber consists of 150 deputies, who are elected directly from all Netherlands nationals who are aged 18 or over on polling day. Members of the States-General must be Netherlanders or recognized as Netherlands subjects and 21 years of age or over, they may be men or women. They receive an allowance.

First Chamber (as constituted in 1983): Labour Party, 17; Christian Democratic Appeal, 26; People's Party for Freedom and Democracy, 17; Democrats '66, 6; Party of Political Radicals, 1; Communist Party, 2; Pacifist Socialist Party, 2; Calvinist Party, 2; Reformed Political Federation, 1; Calvinist Political Union, 1.

Second Chamber (elected on 8 Sept. 1982): Labour Party, 47; Christian Democratic Appeal, 45; People's Party for Freedom and Democracy, 36; Democrats '66, 6; Communist Party, 3; Party of Political Radicals, 2; Pacifist Socialist Party, 3; Calvinist Party, 3; Reformed Political Federation, 2; Calvinist Political Union, 1; Evangelical People's Party, 1; Conservative Nationalist Party, 1.

The revised Constitution of 1917 has introduced an electoral system based on universal suffrage and proportional representation. Under its provisions, members of the Second Chamber are directly elected by citizens of both sexes who are Netherlands subjects not under 18 years (since 1972).

The members of the First Chamber and of the Second Chamber are elected for 4 years, and retire in a body. The Sovereign has the power to dissolve both Chambers of Parliament, or one of them, subject to the condition that new elections take place within 40 days, and the new House or Houses be convoked within 3 months.

Both the Government and the Second Chamber may propose Bills; the First Chamber can only approve or reject them without inserting amendments. The meetings of both Chambers are public, though each of them may by a majority vote decide on a secret session. It is a fixed custom, that Ministers and Secretaries of State, on their own initiative or upon invitation of the Parliament, attend the sessions to defend their policy, their budget, their proposals of Bills, etc., when these are in discussion. A Minister or Secretary of State, however, cannot be a member of Parliament at the same time.

The Constitution can be revised only by a Bill declaring that there is reason for introducing such revision and containing the proposed alterations. The passing of this Bill is followed by a dissolution of both Chambers and a second confirmation by the new States-General by two-thirds of the votes. Unless it is expressly stated, all laws concern only the realm in Europe, and not the oversea part of the kingdom, the Netherlands Antilles.

Every act of the Sovereign has to be covered by a responsible Minister.

The Ministry, a coalition of Christian Democrats and Liberals, was composed as follows in Nov. 1982:

Prime Minister: Ruud Lubbers (CDA).

Deputy Prime Minister and Economic Affairs: Gijs van Aardenne (VVD). *Foreign Affairs:* Hans van den Broek (CDA). *Finance:* Herman Ruding (CDA). *Defence:* Jacob de Ruiter (CDA). *Development Aid Co-operation:* Eegje Schoo (VVD). *Social Affairs and Employment:* Jan de Koning (CDA). *Home Affairs:* Koos Rietkerk (VVD). *Justice:* Frits Korthals Altes (VVD). *Agriculture and Fisheries:* Gerrit Braks (CDA). *Welfare, Public Health and Culture:* Elco Brinkman (CDA). *Education and Science:* Wim Deetman (CDA). *Transport and Public Works:* Neelie Smit-Kroes (VVD). *Housing, Physical Planning and Environment:* Pieter Winsemius (VVD).

There are also 16 state secretaries.

The Council of State *(Raad van State)*, appointed by the Crown, is composed of a vice-president and not more than 28 members. The Queen is president, but the day-to-day running of the council is in the hands of the vice-president. The Council can be consulted on all legislative matters. Decisions of the Crown in administrative disputes are prepared by a special section of the Council.

The Hague is the seat of the Court, Government and Parliament; Amsterdam is the capital.

National flag: Three horizontal stripes of red, white, blue.

National anthem: Wilhelmus van Nassoue (words by Philip Marnix van St Aldegonde, *c.* 1570).

Local Government. The kingdom is divided in 11 provinces and about 750 municipalities. The creation of a new province in the Zuiderzee area is in preparation. Each province has its own representative body, the Provincial States. The members must be 21 years of age or over; they are elected for 4 years, directly from the Netherlands inhabitants of the province who are 18 years of age or over. The electoral register is the same as for the Second Chamber. The members retire in a body and are subject to re-election. The number of members varies according to the population of the province, from 83 for Zuid-Holland to 43 for Zeeland. The Provincial States are entitled to issue ordinances concerning the welfare of the province, and to raise taxes pursuant to legal provisions. The provincial budgets and the provincial ordinances and resolutions relating to provincial property, loans, taxes, etc., must be approved by the Crown. The members of the Provincial States elect the First Chamber of the States-General. They meet twice a year, as a rule in public. A permanent commission composed of 6 of their members, called the 'Deputy States', is charged with the executive power and, if required, with the enforcement of the law in the province. Deputy as well as Provincial States are presided over by a Commissioner of the Queen, appointed by the Crown, who in the former assembly has a deciding vote, but attends the latter in only a deliberative capacity. He is the chief magistrate in the province. The Commissioner and the members of the Deputy States receive an allowance.

Each municipality forms a Corporation with its own interests and rights, subject to the general law, and is governed by a Municipal Council, directly elected from the Netherlands inhabitants of the municipality who are 18 years of age or over, for 4 years. All Netherlands inhabitants aged 21 or over are eligible, the number of members varying from 7 to 45, according to the population. The Municipal Council has the right to issue bye-laws concerning the communal welfare. The Council may levy taxes pursuant to legal provisions; these ordinances must be approved by the Crown. All bye-laws may be vetoed by the Crown. The Municipal Budget and resolutions to alienate municipal property require the approbation of the Deputy States of the province. The Council meets in public as often as may be necessary, and is presided over by a Burgomaster, appointed by the Crown. The day-to-day administration is carried out by the Burgomaster and 2–7 Aldermen *(wethouders)*, elected by and from the Council; this body is also charged with the enforcement of the law. The Burgomaster may suspend the execution of a resolution of the council for 30 days, but is bound to notify the Deputy States of the province. In maintaining public order, the Burgomaster acts as the chief of police. The Burgomaster and Aldermen receive allowances.

DEFENCE. The Netherlands are bordered on the south by Belgium, on the east by the Federal Republic of Germany. On both sides the country is quite level and has no natural defences, except the barriers of some large rivers, running east to west and south to north. The country has an excellent roadnet and a vast railway system, enabling rapid movement. The west part of the country is densely populated.

Army. Service is partly voluntary and partly compulsory; the voluntary enlistments bear a small proportion to the compulsory. The total peacetime strength amounts to 72,000, including Military Police. The number of regulars is 24,000. The Army also employs 13,000 civilians. The legal period of active service for national servicemen is 22–24 months; the actual service period is 14 months for other ranks and 16 months for reserve-officers and n.c.o.s. The balance may be spent at will as 'short leave'. After their period of actual service or short leave, conscript personnel are granted long leave. However, they will be liable to being called up for refresher training or in case of mobilization until they have reached the age of 35 (n.c.o.s 40, reserve officers 45).

The 1st Netherlands Army Corps is assigned to NATO. It consists of 10 brigades and Corps troops. The active part of the Corps comprises 2 armoured brigades and 4 armoured infantry brigades, grouped in two divisions and 40% of the Corps troops. Part of this force is stationed in the Federal Republic of Germany. The peacetime strength of the active brigades is 80% of the war-authorized strength.

The mobilizable part of the Corps comprises 1 armoured brigade, 2 armoured infantry brigades, 1 infantry brigade and the remaining Corps troops.

The mechanized brigades comprise tank battalions (Centurion and Leopard 1), armoured infantry battalions (YP-408 and YPR-765), medium artillery battalions (155 mm self-propelled), armoured engineer units, armoured reconnaissance units and armoured anti armour units. The Corps troops comprise headquarters units, combat-support units, including Engineer and Corps artillery (203 mm, 155 mm and Lance) and service-support units. Helicopter squadrons are also available.

The National Territorial Command forces consist of territorial brigades, security forces, some logistical units and staffs. The major part of these units is mobilizable. Some units in the Netherlands are earmarked for assignment to the United Nations as peace keeping forces. Since Dec. 1983 an infantry company, composed of regulars and conscripts, has been involved in the UN peace-keeping operations in Lebanon. For civil defence purposes there are a number of mobilizable fire-fighting, rescue and medical battalions. The army is responsible for the training of these units which in time of war are placed under the command of the National Commander of the Civil Defence.

Navy. The Royal Netherlands Navy has its main base in the Netherlands at Den Helder and minor bases at Flushing and Curaçao (Netherlands Antilles). The Ministry of Defence is located in The Hague.

The fleet comprises 6 diesel-electric patrol submarines, 18 frigates, 2 fast combat support ships, 1 mine countermeasures support ship (*ex*-ocean minesweeper), 11 coastal minehunters, 10 coastal minesweepers, 3 diving vessels, 1 torpedo maintenance vessel (*ex*-ocean minesweeper), 5 patrol vessels, 3 hydrographic survey ships, 10 minor landing craft, 2 training ships, 12 tugs and 30 small auxiliary ships.

Two diesel-electric patrol submarines, 2 large frigates, 4 medium frigates, 8 coastal minehunters and 12 minor landing craft are under construction. The future construction programme includes two more diesel-electric patrol submarines.

In 1985 personnel totalled 16,800 officers and other ranks, including the Naval Air Service, 410 female, and the Royal Netherlands Marine Corps.

The naval air service (1,700 personnel) maintains 13 Orion P3C, 5 Breguet Atlantics (SP-13A), 23 Westland Lynx SH14B/C embarked and 5 Lynx UH 14A for SAR, utility and transport.

Naval estimates (in 1m. guilders): 1981, 2,218; 1982, 2,352; 1983, 2,446; 1984, 2,418.

Air Force. The Royal Netherlands Air Force was established 1 July 1913. Its current strength is approximately 19,000 personnel and it has a first-line combat force of 9 squadrons of aircraft and 3 groups of surface-to-air missiles. All squadrons are operated by Tactical Air Command. Aircraft operated are F-16 (4 squadrons for air defence and ground attack, 1 for tactical reconnaissance), and NF-5A/B fighter-bombers (4 squadrons, to re-equip with F-16s in 1985–91). Also under control of Tactical Air Command is 1 squadron of the USAF, flying F-15C/D Eagles in the air defence role. 3 squadrons of Alouette III and Bölkow Bö 105C helicopters are under control of the Royal Netherlands Army, but flown and maintained by the RNethAF for use in the communications and observation roles. Also operated is 1 squadron of F.27 Friendship/Troopship transport aircraft, and another (based in Curaçao) with 2 F.27 maritime patrol aircraft.

Training of RNethAF pilots is undertaken in the USA. The surface-to-air missile force consists of 1 group of Nike Hercules (high altitude) and 2 groups of Hawk (low and medium altitude). The Nike will be replaced by Patriot missiles from 1987.

INTERNATIONAL RELATIONS

Membership. The Netherlands is a member of UN, EEC, OECD, the Council of Europe and NATO.

ECONOMY

Budget. The revenue and expenditure of the central government (ordinary and extraordinary) were, in 1m. guilders, for calendar years:

	1978 [2]	*1979* [2]	*1980* [2]	*1981* [2]	*1982* [3]	*1983* [4]	*1984* [6]
Revenue [1]	92,262	98,810	107,165	110,866	113,923	114,227	119,514
Expenditure [5]	101,067	110,776	121,081	130,455	141,715	145,752	154,926

[1] Without the revenue of loans. [2] Accounts. [3] Preliminary accounts.
[4] Revised budget figures. [5] Without redemption of loans. [6] Budget figures.

The revenue and expenditure of the Agriculture Equalization Fund, the Fund for Central Government roads, the Property Acquisition Fund (established in 1971), the Fund for the Development of a fast Breeder Reactor (established in 1972 but discontinued in 1978) and of the Investment Account Fund (established in 1978) have been incorporated in the general budget.

The national debt, in 1m. guilders, was on 31 Dec.:

	1979	*1980*	*1981*	*1982*	*1983*
Internal funded debt	64,086	78,090	96,830	122,777	153,262
,, floating ,,	20,314	21,433	21,629	21,878	21,535
Total	84,400	99,523	118,459	144,655	174,797

Currency. The monetary unit is the *gulden* (guilder, florin) of 100 *cents*. In March 1985 the rate of exchange was US\$1 = 3·88 guilders; £1 = 4·08 guilders.

Legal tender are bank-notes, silver 10-guilder pieces, nickel 2½- and 1-guilder pieces, 25-cent, 10-cent pieces and bronze 5-cent pieces.

Banking. The Netherlands Bank, founded as a private institution, was nationalized on 1 Aug. 1948, the shareholders receiving, for a share of 1,000 guilders, a security of 2,000 guilders on the 2½% National Debt. Since 1863 the bank has the sole right of issuing bank-notes. The bank does the same business as other banks, but with more guarantees. The capital amounts to 20m. guilders.

Weights and Measures. The metric system of weights and measures was adopted in the Netherlands in 1820.

ENERGY AND NATURAL RESOURCES

Electricity. The total production of electrical energy (in 1m. kwh.) amounted in 1938 to 3,688; 1958, 13,854; 1970, 40,859; 1980, 64,806; 1981, 64,053; 1982, 60,313; 1983, 59,650.

Gas. Production of manufactured gas (milliard k joule): 1978, 181,033; 1979, 233,553; 1980, 210,011; 1981, 197,586. Production of natural gas in 1950, 8m. cu. metres; 1955, 139; 1960, 384; 1970, 31,688; 1980, 91,153; 1981, 84,617; 1982, 72,035; 1983, 76,536.

Minerals. On 1 Jan. 1975 all coalmines were closed.

The production of crude petroleum (in 1,000 tonnes) amounted in 1943 (first year) to 0·2; 1953, 820; 1970, 1,919; 1978, 1,402; 1979, 1,316; 1980, 1,280; 1981, 1,348; 1982, 1,637; 1983, 2,589.

There are saltmines at Hengelo and Delfzijl; production (in 1,000 tonnes), 1950, 412·6; 1960, 1,096; 1970, 2,871; 1978, 2,939; 1979, 3,951; 1980, 3,464; 1981, 3,578; 1982, 3,191; 1983, 3,124.

Agriculture. The net area of all holdings was divided as follows (in hectares):

	1980 [1]	*1981*	*1982* [1]	*1983* [1]	*1984* [1]
Field crops	704,710	702,510	702,287	706,120	715,887
Grass	1,197,592	1,187,719	1,178,098	1,181,297	1,178,534
Market gardening	87,121	89,600	94,210	89,371	91,031
Land for flower bulbs	14,307	14,390	14,189	14,165	14,558
Flower cultivation	5,180	5,267	5,472	5,615	5,824
Nurseries	6,228	6,413	6,386	6,431	6,498
Fallow land	5,099	4,769	4,577	5,713	3,763
Total	2,020,237	2,010,668	2,005,219	2,008,712	2,016,095

[1] Excluding holdings of less than 10 SFU (SFU = standard farm unit). 10 SFU is equal to a computed net value added at factor cost of about 4,000 guilders, in 1975.

The net areas [1] under special crops were as follows (in hectares):

Products	*1983*	*1984*	*Products*	*1983*	*1984*
Autumn wheat	141,724	140,584	Colza	13,211	13,163
Spring wheat	6,535	4,220	Flax	3,193	4,112
Rye	6,660	5,743	Agricultural seeds	18,149	18,056
Autumn barley	10,199	10,528	Potatoes, edible [2]	100,998	102,433
Spring barley	27,275	23,517	Potatoes, industrial [3]	62,458	58,230
Oats	13,527	12,495	Sugar-beet	116,739 [4]	129,304
Peas	7,636	11,051	Fodder-beet	2,119	2,169

[1] Excluding non-agrarian holdings of less than 10 SFU. [2] Including early and seed potatoes.
[3] Including seed potatoes. [4] Source, IRS.

The yield of the more important products, in tonnes, was as follows:

Crop	*Average 1940–49*	*Average 1950–58*	*1982* [1]	*1983* [1]	*1984* [1]
Wheat	322,003	348,464	967,263	1,042,914	1,046,855
Rye	439,055	454,992	26,492	25,674	24,503
Barley	145,892	258,049	247,116	176,920	193,009
Oats	315,642	464,041	136,122	61,110	67,133
Field beans	15,799	5,693	2,418	3,930	...
Peas	65,460	93,664	28,153	31,773	49,846
Colza	24,763	18,358	33,336	37,976	38,904
Flax, unrippled	82,906	138,165	25,062	20,848	35,970
Potatoes, edible [2]	2,861,793	2,745,505	4,145,765	3,338,196	4,262,987
Potatoes, industrial	1,242,326	1,003,994	2,072,857	1,974,243	...
Sugar-beet	1,667,711	2,935,881	7,945,554	5,445,498	...
Fodder-beet	...	...	213,457	164,600	...

[1] Excluding holdings of less than 10 SFU. 1984 figures provisional.
[2] Including early potatoes.

Livestock, May 1984: 5,516,243 cattle, 11,146,085 pigs; 64,318 horses and ponies; 765,529 sheep, 84·5m. poultry.

In 1983 the production of butter, under state control, amounted to 271,464 tonnes; that of cheese, under state control, to 477,664 tonnes. Export value (processed and unprocessed) of arable crops amounted to 16,420m. guilders; animal produce, 17,750m. guilders and horticultural produce, 8,661m. guilders.

Fisheries. The total produce of fish landed from the sea and inshore fisheries in 1981 was valued at 595m. guilders; the total weight amounted to 399,438 tonnes. In 1981 the herring fishery had a value of 26m. guilders and a weight of 16,710 tonnes. The quantity of oysters produced in 1981 amounted to 573 tonnes (10m. guilders).

INDUSTRY AND TRADE

Industry. Numbers employed (in 1,000) and turnover (in 1m. guilders) in manufacturing enterprises with 10 employees and more, excluding building:

Class in industry	*Numbers employed* 1981	1982	*Turnover* 1981	1982
Mining and quarrying	7·9	8·1	29,510	30,710
Manufacturing industry	860·1	816·2	223,440	226,030
Foodstuffs and tobacco products	142·6	138·0	60,460	63,990
Textile industry	28·7	25·6	4,230	4,270
Clothing	14·1	12·7	1,620	1,570
Leather and footwear	7·1	6·6	760	800
Wood and furniture industry	30·7	26·4	4,020	3,810
Paper industry	23·9	23·0	5,340	5,450
Graphic industry, publishers	62·5	60·1	9,660	9,810
Petroleum industry	10·8	10·0	32,560	31,170
Chemical industry, artificial yarns and fibre industry	85·5	83·7	33,710	33,260
Rubber and synthetic materials processing industry	24·1	23·6	4,230	4,440
Building materials, earthenware and glass	35·2	31·4	5,540	5,430
Basic metal industry	35·9	34·5	8,540	8,110
Metals products (excl. machinery and means of transport)	78·9	73·0	10,470	10,780
Machinery	81·5	78·1	11,380	11,600
Electrical industry	112·8	107·6	17,880	18,210
Means of transport	71·4	68·1	11,400	11,630
Instrument making and optical industry	9·0	8·6	1,080	1,130
Other industries	5·3	5·0	570	590
Public utilities	47·0	46·8	19,180	20,350

Commerce. On 5 Sept. 1944 and 14 March 1947 the Netherlands signed agreements with Belgium and Luxembourg for the establishment of a customs union. On 1 Jan. 1948 this union came into force and the existing customs tariffs of the Belgium–Luxembourg Economic Union and of the Netherlands were superseded by the joint Benelux Customs Union Tariff. It applies to imports into the 3 countries from outside sources, and exempts from customs duties all imports into each of the 3 countries from the other two. The Benelux tariff has 991 items and 2,400 separate specifications.

Returns of special imports and special exports (including parcel post and diamond trade, excluding unrefined and partly-worked gold, gold coins and coins in current circulation made of other metal) for calendar years (in 1,000 guilders):

	Imports	*Exports*		*Imports*	*Exports*
1949	5,331,569	3,851,126	1979 [1]	134,885,386	127,689,416
1959	14,968,454	13,702,927	1980 [1]	152,279,265	146,967,410
1969	39,955,406	36,205,110	1981 [1]	163,998,929	170,772,393
1978 [1]	114,371,926	108,205,427	1982 [1]	167,116,253	176,851,097

[1] Including unrefined and partly-worked gold and gold coins.

Value of the trade (including parcel post and diamond trade, excluding unrefined and partly-worked gold, gold coins and coins in current circulation made of other metal) with leading countries (in 1,000 guilders):

Country	Imports 1981	Imports 1982	Imports 1983	Exports 1981	Exports 1982	Exports 1983
Belgium–Luxembourg	18,627,846	18,312,904	18,804,391	24,486,748	25,092,899	25,832,167
France	10,535,248	10,865,041	11,684,553	17,860,028	18,404,759	19,303,857
Germany (Fed. Rep.)	35,202,710	37,022,529	38,617,811	50,272,569	52,188,052	57,053,530
Indonesia	582,710	419,327	696,904	678,251	601,520	769,393
Italy	4,892,484	5,087,217	5,491,599	9,543,802	9,766,040	10,186,070
Kuwait	2,506,535	1,131,699	1,868,200	344,519	318,363	269,894
Sweden	2,956,972	3,217,048	3,281,229	2,541,386	3,172,025	3,068,989
UK	14,003,953	15,723,378	15,329,336	14,112,136	16,359,875	16,884,880
USA	15,567,121	15,323,775	16,026,219	5,495,426	5,741,457	7,896,730
Venezuela	424,431	402,348	351,578	352,819	479,623	323,669

Total trade between the Netherlands and UK (British Department of Trade returns, in £1,000 sterling):

	1980	1981	1982	1983	1984
Imports to UK	3,406,928	3,895,486	4,474,663	5,097,673	6,147,298
Exports and re-exports from UK	3,845,412	4,019,435	4,653,416	5,440,701	6,127,991

Tourism. There were 2,991,300 foreign visitors in 1983 (hotels and boarding houses only). 601,100 came from the Federal Republic of Germany, 542,900 from UK and 475,600 from USA. Total income from tourism (1983) US$1,420m.

COMMUNICATIONS

Roads. In 1983 the length of the Netherlands network of surfaced inter-urban roads was 53,983 km, of which 1,749 km were motor highways. Number of private cars (1983), 4·7m.

Railways. All railways are run by the mixed company 'N.V. Nederlandsche Spoorwegen'. Length of line in 1983 was 2,852 km, of which 1,796 km were electrified. Passengers carried (1983), 202m.; goods transported, 10·0m. tonnes

Aviation. The Royal Dutch Airlines (KLM) was founded on 7 Oct. 1919. The company has a paid-up capital of 966m. guilders (1983–84). Revenue traffic, 1983–84: Passengers, 4·6m.; freight, 299m. kg; mail, 12m. kg.

Sea-going Shipping. Survey of the Netherlands mercantile marine as at 1 Jan. (capacity in 1,000 GRT):

Ships under Netherlands flag (including Netherlands Antilles)	*1982 Number*	*1982 Capacity*	*1983 Number*	*1983 Capacity*
Passenger ships [1]	9	144	9	122
Freighters (500 GRT and over)	457	2,524	474	2,641
Freighters (under 500 GRT)	64	27	62	26
Tankers	87	2,331	84	2,008
	617	5,026	629	4,796

[1] With accommodation for 13 or more cabin passengers.

In 1983, 43,391 sea-going ships of 323·6m. gross tons entered Netherlands ports (1982, 43,957 ships of 335·6m. gross tons).

Total goods traffic by sea-going ships in 1983 (with 1982 figures in brackets), in 1m. tonnes, amounted to 229 (241·7) unloaded, of which 110·9 (118·4) tankshipping, and 75·1 (75·7) loaded, of which 28·1 (31·7) tankshipping. The total seaborne freight traffic at Rotterdam was 233·4m. (246m.) and at Amsterdam 23·2m. (23·7m.) tonnes.

The number of containers at Rotterdam in 1983 was: unloaded from ships, 782,536, of which 199,777 from North America, and 836,011 loaded into ships, of which 139,225 to North America.

Inland Shipping. The total length of navigable rivers and canals is 4,387 km, of which about 1,974 km is for ships with a capacity of 1,000 and more tonnes. On 1

Jan. 1984 the Netherlands inland fleet actually used for transport (with carrying capacity in 1,000 tonnes) was composed as follows:

	Number	*Capacity*
Self-propelled barges	5,418	3,807
Dumb barges	433	431
Pushed barges	455	975
	6,306	5,213

In 1983, 247m. (1982: 238m.) tonnes of goods were transported on rivers and canals, of which 176m. (169m.) was international traffic. Goods transport on the Rhine across the Dutch–German frontier near Lobith amounted to 125m. (124m.) tonnes.

Post and Broadcasting. On 1 Jan. 1983 there were 5·5m. telephone connexions (38 per 100 inhabitants). Number of telex lines, 37,000; teleprinters, 38,000. *Nederlandse Omroep Stichting* (NOS) provides 5 programmes on medium-waves and FM in co-operation with broadcasting organizations. Regional programmes are also broadcast.

Advertisements are transmitted. NOS broadcasts 2 TV programmes. Advertisements, in the last quarter of 1980, were restricted to 4% of the transmission time in the evening. Television sets (1 Jan. 1984) totalled 4·5m.; holders of television licences may, in addition, have wireless receiving sets.

Cinemas (end 1982). There were 546 cinemas with a seating capacity of 146,000.

Newspapers (31 Dec. 1983). There were 79 daily newspapers with a total circulation of nearly 4·5m.

JUSTICE, RELIGION, EDUCATION AND WELFARE

Justice. Justice is administered by the High Court of the Netherlands (Court of Cassation), by 5 courts of justice (Courts of Appeal), by 19 district courts and by 62 cantonal courts; trial by jury is unknown. The Cantonal Court, which deals with minor offences, is formed by a single judge; the more serious cases are tried by the district courts, formed as a rule by 3 judges (in some cases one judge is sufficient); the courts of appeal are constituted of 3 and the High Court of 5 judges. All judges are appointed for life by the Sovereign (the judges of the High Court from a list prepared by the Second Chamber of the States-General). They can be removed only by a decision of the High Court.

At the district court the juvenile judge is specially appointed to try children's civil cases and at the same time charged with administration of justice for criminal actions committed by young persons between 12 and 18 years old, unless imprisonment of 6 months or more ought to be inflicted; such cases are tried by 3 judges.

Number of sentences, and cases in which prosecution was evaded by paying a fine to the public prosecutor (excluding violation of economic and tax laws):

Major offences		*Minor offences*	
1980	75,065	1980	1,528,772
1981	76,202	1981	1,491,879
1982	81,439	1982	1,317,213

In addition, prosecution was evaded by paying a fine to the police in 1,045,000 cases in 1981.

Police. There are both State and Municipal Police. The State Police, about 8,700 men strong, serves 630, and the Municipal Police, about 20,300 men strong, serves 140 municipalities. The State Police includes ordinary as well as water, mounted and motor police. The State Police Corps is under the jurisdiction of the Police Department of the Ministry of Justice, which also includes the Central Criminal Investigation Office, which deals with serious crimes throughout the country, and the International Criminal Investigation Office, which informs foreign countries of international crimes.

Religion. Entire liberty of conscience is granted to the members of all denominations. The royal family belong to the Dutch Reformed Church.

The number of adherents of the Churches according to survey estimates of 1983 was: Roman Catholics, 5,180,000; Dutch Reformed Church, 2,770,000; Reformed Churches, 1,134,000; other creeds, 631,000; no religion, 4,635,000.

The government of the Reformed Church is Presbyterian. On 1 July 1972 the Dutch Reformed Church had 1 synod, 11 provincial districts, 54 classes, 147 districts and 1,905 parishes.

Their clergy numbered 2,000. The Roman Catholic Church had, Jan. 1973, 1 archbishop (of Utrecht), 6 bishops and 1,815 parishes and rectorships. The Old Catholics had (1 July 1972) 1 archbishop (Utrecht), 2 bishops and 29 parishes. The Jews had, in 1970, 46 communities.

Education. Statistics for the scholastic year 1982–83:

	Full-time			*Part-time* [1]		
		Pupils			Pupils	
	Schools	*Total*	*Female*	*Schools*	*Total*	*Female*
Nursery schools	8,170	398,804	193,832	—	—	—
Primary Schools	8,745	1,201,512	593,650	—	—	—
Special schools	990	95,708	29,872	—	—	—
Secondary general schools	1,487	836,220	440,673	80	119,400	87,654
Secondary vocational schools:						
Junior—						
Technical, nautical	390	211,291	12,601	511	130,184	43,373
Agricultural	129	31,177	8,224	177	2,979	690
Domestic science	552	115,046	110,872	...	474	463
Other	228	47,588	28,228	14	943	13
Senior—						
Technical, nautical	125	68,233	4,812	55	6,063	228
Agricultural	49	15,045	2,458	29	2,553	170
Domestic science	184	42,883	41,017	16	2,928	2,878
Teachers' training (nursery schools)	49	8,069	7,961	49	2,630	2,614
Other	196	72,158	37,765	88	27,531	15,396
Third level non-university training:						
Technical, nautical	61	35,143	3,592	39	4,957	497
Agricultural	11	5,150	882	2	63	8
Arts	35	17,123	6,139	20	3,806	1,506
Teachers' training:						
Primary schools	91	11,532	7,611	126	22,641	20,028
Secondary general schools	32	22,535	11,412	101	29,201	16,070
Secondary vocational schools	—	—	—	23	5,458	224
Other	133	54,400	30,819	59	17,013	8,592

[1] Including apprenticeship schemes, young workers' educational institutes.

Academic Year 1983–84 [1]

		Full-time		*Part-time*	
		Students		*Students*	
	Schools	*Total*	*Female*	*Total*	*Female*
University education:					
Humanities	22	29,043	15,298	481	217
Social sciences		68,762	25,693	6,424	1,957
Natural sciences		15,003	3,231	56	5
Technical sciences		20,396	1,406		
Medical sciences		18,308	6,418		
Agricultural sciences		6,048	1,365		

[1] Provisional figures.

Health. On 1 Jan. 1984 there were 29,951 doctors and about 69,600 licensed hospital beds.

DIPLOMATIC REPRESENTATIVES

Of the Netherlands in Great Britain (38 Hyde Park Gate, London, SW7 5DP)
Ambassador: Jan Louis Reinier Huydecoper van Nigtevecht, GCVO (accredited 3 March 1982).

Of Great Britain in the Netherlands (Lange Voorhout, 10, The Hague)
Ambassador: J. W. D. Margetson, CMG.

Of the Netherlands in the USA (4200 Linnean Ave., NW, Washington, D.C., 20008)
Ambassador: Richard H. Fein.

Of the USA in the Netherlands (Lange Voorhout, 102, The Hague)
Ambassador: L. Paul Bremer, III.

Of the Netherlands to the United Nations
Ambassador: Max van der Stoel.

Books of Reference

Statistical Information: The 'Centraal Bureau voor de Statistiek' at Voorburg and Heerlen, is the official Netherlands statistical service. *Director-General of Statistics:* Prof. Dr W. Begeer.

The Bureau was founded in 1899. Prior to that year, statistical publications were compiled by the 'Centrale commissie voor de statistiek', the 'Vereniging voor staathuishoudkunde en statistiek' and various government departments. These activities have gradually been taken over and co-ordinated by the Central Bureau, which now compiles practically all government statistics.

Its current publications include:

Statistical Yearbook of the Netherlands. From 1923/24 (preceded by *Jaarcijfers voor het Koninkrijk der Nederlanden, 1898–1922);* latest issue, 1983
Statistisch zakboek (Pocket Year Book). From 1899/1924 (1 vol.); latest issue, 1984
CBS Select 1 (Statistical Essays), 1980.—*CBS Select 2 (Statistical Essays)*, 1983
Statistisch Bulletin (From 1945; weekly statistical bulletin)
Maandschrift (From 1944; monthly bulletin)
Denken en meten (Statistical Essays)
85 Jaren Statistiek In Tijdreeksen (historical series of the Netherlands 1899–1984)
Nationale Rekeningen (National Accounts). From 1948–50; latest issue, 1982
Statistisch Magazine. From 1981
Statistische onderzoekingen. From 1977
Statistical Studies. From 1953

Other Official Publications

Central Economic Plan. Centraal Plan bureau, The Hague (Dutch text), annually, from 1946
Netherlands. Organization for Economic Co-operation and Development. Paris, annual from 1964
Staatsalmanak voor het Koninkrijk der Nederlanden. Annual. The Hague, from 1814
Staatsblad van het Koninkrijk der Nederlanden. The Hague, from 1814
Staatscourant (State Gazette). The Hague, from 1813
Atlas van Nederland. Government Printing Office, The Hague, 1970 and supplements up to and including 1973
Memoranda on the Condition of the Netherlands State Finances. Ministry of Finance, The Hague, from 1906
Basic Guide to the Establishing of Industrial Operations in the Netherlands 1976. Ministry of Economic Affairs, The Hague, 1976
The Kingdom of the Netherlands. Ministry of Foreign Affairs, The Hague, Occasional
Huggett, F. E., *The Dutch Today.* Ministry of Foreign Affairs, The Hague, 1973.—*The Dutch Connection.* Ministry of Foreign Affairs, The Hague, 1982
Aspects of Dutch Agriculture. Ministry of Agriculture and Fisheries, The Hague, 1976

Non-Official Publications

Jansonius, H., *Nieuw Groot Nederlands—Engels Woordenboek Voor Studie en Praktijk.* 3 vols. Leiden, 1973 (Vols. 1–3)
Newton, G., *The Netherlands: An Historical and Cultural Survey, 1795–1977.* Boulder, 1978
Pinder, D., *The Netherlands.* Folkestone, 1976
Veldman, J., *Agriculture in the Netherlands.* Utrecht, 1974
Pyttersen's Nederlandse Almanak. Zaltbommel, annual, from 1899
Commerce and Industry in the Netherlands. Amsterdam–Rotterdam Bank. Amsterdam, 1977
Foreign Investment in the Netherlands. The Hague, 1975
The Information You Need When Planning a Business in the Netherlands. Algemene Bank Nederland. Amsterdam, 1975
A Compact Geography of the Netherlands. Utrecht, 1980

National Library: De Koninklijke Bibliotheek, Prinz Willem Alexanderhof 5, The Hague. *Director:* Dr C. Reedijk.

THE NETHERLANDS ANTILLES
De Nederlandse Antillen

AREA AND POPULATION. The Netherlands Antilles are an integral part of the Netherlands and comprise two groups of islands, viz., the Leeward Islands, Curaçao, Aruba and Bonaire, and the Windward Islands, St Maarten, St Eustatius and Saba. The Leeward Islands are situated 40–70 miles north of the Venezuelan coast between 12° and 13° N. lat. and 68° and 71° W. long. The Windward group lies east of Puerto Rico. For the constitutional position of the Netherlands Antilles *see* p. 883. The total area is 993 sq. km (383 sq. miles) and the population was 260,000 in 1983.

Leeward group	*Sq. km*	*Population*	*Windward group*	*Sq. km*	*Population*
Curaçao	444	165,011	St Maarten (St Martin)[1]	34	15,926
Aruba	193	67,014	St Eustatius	21	1,335
Bonaire	288	9,704	Saba	13	1,010

[1] The southern part belongs to the Netherlands Antilles, the northern to France.

The capital is Willemstad on Curaçao, population (1983) 50,000.

In 1975, 4,258 births, 1,193 deaths and 1,536 marriages were registered.

CLIMATE. All the islands have a tropical marine climate, with very little difference in temperatures over the year. There is a short rainy season from Oct. to Jan. Willemstad. Jan. 79°F (26·1°C), July 82°F (27·8°C). Annual rainfall 23″ (582 mm).

GOVERNMENT. Since Dec. 1954, the Netherlands Antilles have been fully autonomous in internal affairs, and constitutionally equal with the Netherlands and Suriname. The Sovereign of the Kingdom of the Netherlands is Head of the Government of the Netherlands Antilles and is represented by a Governor.

The executive power in internal affairs rests with the Governor and the Council of Ministers, who together form the Government. The Ministers are responsible to the unicameral legislature (*Staten*). This consists of 22 members (12 from Curaçao, 8 from Aruba, 1 from Bonaire, 1 from the Windward Islands) and is elected by general suffrage. It was agreed in 1977 that the 2 smallest islands, Saba and St Eustatius would each have a representative (non-voting) in the *Staten*.

The executive power in external affairs is vested in the Council of Ministers of the Kingdom, in which the Antilles is represented by a Minister Plenipotentiary with full voting powers.

In 1951 the Netherlands Antilles Islands Regulation provided for self-government of each of the 4 insular communities Aruba, Bonaire, Curaçao and the Windward Islands. The autonomous powers of the insular communities are divided between the Island Council (elected by general suffrage), the Executive Council and the Lieut.-Governor (*Gezaghebber*), who is responsible for maintaining public peace and order.

At the general election held on 25 June 1982, 6 of the 12 *Staten* seats in Curaçao were won by the *Movimiento Antijas Nobo,* 3 by the Democratic Party and 3 by the *Nationale Volkspartij-Unie;* of the 8 seats in Aruba, 5 were won by the *Movimiento Electoral di Puebla,* 2 by the *Arubaanse Volkspartij* and 1 by the *Partido Patriotico Arubano;* the 1 seat in Bonaire was won by the *Unión Patriotico Bonairiano* and the 1 seat in the Windward Islands by the Democratic Party. Following an earlier referendum, the government of the Netherlands announced on 28 Oct. 1981 that it had agreed that Aruba should at an early date proceed to independence separately from the other islands.

Governor: Dr B. M. Leito.

Prime Minister: Maria Liberia.

Flag: White, with a red vertical strip crossed by a blue horizontal strip bearing 6 white stars.

Dutch is the official language. In addition a 'lingua franca', *Papiamento* has evolved out of Spanish, Dutch and some other languages.

FINANCE. The central budget for 1979 envisaged 213m. guilders revenue and 256m. guilders expenditure.

The official rate of exchange was £1 = 1·92 *Antillian guilder*; US$1 = 1·80 *Antillian guilder* in March 1985.

ENERGY AND NATURAL RESOURCES

Electricity. Production (1981) totalled 2,275m. kwh.

Oil. The economy of the Netherlands Antilles is almost entirely based on the refining of oil imported from Venezuela to Curaçao and Aruba. About 25% (Curaçao) and 30% (Aruba) of the gainfully occupied are working at the refineries or their shipping establishments. On account of the activities of the oil companies (affiliated to the Royal Dutch/Shell and the Standard Oil of New Jersey), the prosperity on Curaçao and Aruba is good in comparison with the other islands. Refinery production (1981) 25m. tonnes.

Minerals. About 100,000 tons of calcium phosphate are annually mined in Curaçao.

Agriculture. Livestock (1983): Cattle, 9,000; goats, 23,000.

INDUSTRY AND TRADE

Industry. In Aruba there are some petrochemical factories; Curaçao has a paint factory, 2 cigarette factories, a textile factory, a brewery and some smaller industries. The Texas Instruments Co. and Electronic Fabriek have established electronic factories. Almost all products needed for consumption and production are imported, as the rocky soil permits little agriculture and local fishing is insufficient for home consumption. Bonaire has a textile factory and a modern-equipped salt plant. St Maarten has a rum factory and fishing is important. St Eustatius and Saba are of less economic importance.

Trade (1980). Total imports amounted to US$5,944m., total exports to US$6,054m.

Total trade between the Netherlands Antilles and UK (British Department of Trade returns, in £1,000 sterling):

	1980	*1981*	*1982*	*1983*	*1984*
Imports to UK	36,243	29,761	62,946	25,871	221,012
Exports and re-exports from UK	33,375	135,017	47,396	78,879	20,235

The Free-Zones Ordinance of 1956 has established free zones in the ports of Curaçao and Aruba.

Tourism. In 1981, 764,000 foreign tourists visited the Netherlands Antilles.

COMMUNICATIONS

Roads. In 1984, the Netherlands Antilles had 1,200 km of surfaced highway distributed as follows: Curaçao, 550; Aruba, 380; Bonaire, 210; St Maarten, 3. Number of motor vehicles (31 Dec. 1975): 41,955 in Curaçao, 15,393 in Aruba.

Shipping (1977). There entered the port of Curaçao, 11,432 vessels of 95m. gross tons; Aruba, 2,798 vessels of 52m. gross tons. Curaçao has a dry dock of 120,000 tons.

Post and Broadcasting. Number of telephones, 1 Jan. 1982, 72,168. Eight radio stations are operating on medium-waves from Curaçao, Aruba, Bonaire, and St Maarten. These stations broadcast in *Papiamento*, Dutch, English and Spanish and are mainly financed by income from advertisements. In addition, Radio Nederland and Trans World Radio have powerful relay stations operating on medium- and short-waves from Bonaire. There were (1980) 175,000 radio and 43,000 TV receivers.

Cinemas (1973). Curaçao and Aruba had 13 cinemas with a seating capacity of 11,000. There is a drive-in for 500 cars in Curaçao, for 200 cars in St Maarten and for 350 cars in Aruba.

JUSTICE, RELIGION, EDUCATION AND WELFARE

Justice. There is a Court of First Instance, which sits in each island, and a Court of Appeal in Willemstad.

Religion. In 1980, 82% of the population were Roman Catholics, 8% were Protestants (St Maartin and St Eustatius being chiefly Protestant).

Education (1977). There were 36,365 pupils and 1,458 teachers in primary schools, 10,685 pupils and 440 teachers in secondary schools, 7,825 students and 619 teachers in technical schools, and 358 students with 46 teachers in teacher-training colleges.

Health. In June 1973 there were 155 physicians, 55 specialists, 33 dentists and 18 pharmacists. In 1973, 11 hospitals had 2,037 beds.

DIPLOMATIC REPRESENTATIVE

USA Consul-General: Thomas M. Coony.

The British consulate closed on 1 Sept. 1976.

Books of Reference

Statistical Information: Statistical publications (on population, trade, cost of living, etc., are obtainable on request from the Statistical Office, Willemstad, Curaçao. *Statistical Jaarboek 1970* (text in Dutch, English and Spanish).

De West Indische Gids. The Hague. Monthly from 1919

Braam, H. L., *Hoe ons land geregeerd wordt.* Willemstad, 4th ed. 1972

Hartog, J., *Aruba.* Oranjestad, 1953.—*Bonairo.* Oranjestad, 1958.—*Curacao.* Oranjestad, 1961

Nordlohne, E., *De Economisch-geographische Structuur der Benedenwindse Eilanden.* Rotterdam, 1951

Poll, W. van de, *De Nederlandse Antillen.* The Hague, 1950

Walle, J. van de, *De Nederlandse Antillen.* Willemstad, 1954

Westerman, J. H., *Overzicht van de geologische en mijnbouwkundige kennis der Nederlandse Antillen.* Amsterdam, 1949

NEW ZEALAND

Capital: Wellington
Population: 3·2m. (1984)
GNP per capita: US$7,700 (1981)

HISTORY. The first European to discover New Zealand was Tasman in 1642. The coast was explored by Capt. Cook in 1769. From about 1800 onwards, New Zealand became a resort for whalers and traders, chiefly from Australia. By the Treaty of Waitangi, in 1840, between Governor William Hobson and the representatives of the Maori race, the Maori chiefs ceded the sovereignty to the British Crown and the islands became a British colony. Then followed a steady stream of British settlers.

The Maoris are a branch of the Polynesian race, having emigrated from the eastern Pacific before and during the 14th century. Between 1845 and 1848, and between 1860 and 1870, misunderstandings over land led to war, but peace was permanently established in 1871, and the development of New Zealand has been marked by racial harmony and integration.

AREA AND POPULATION. New Zealand lies south-east of Australia in the south Pacific, Wellington being 1,983 km from Sydney by sea. There are two principal islands, the North and South Islands, besides Stewart Island, Chatham Islands and small outlying islands, as well as the territories overseas (*see* pp. 911–13).

New Zealand (*i.e.*, North, South and Stewart Islands) extends over 1,750 km from north to south. Area, excluding territories overseas, 268,704 sq. km.; North Island, 11,469,000 hectares; South Island, 15,046,000 hectares; Stewart Island, 174,000 hectares; Chatham Islands, 96,000 hectares; minor islands, 82,900 hectares. Census population, exclusive of territories overseas:

	Total population	*Average annual increase %*		*Total population*	*Average annual increase %*
1858	115,462	—	1921	1,271,644	2·27
1874	344,984	—	1926	1,408,139	2·06
1878	458,007	7·33	1936	1,573,810	1·13
1881	534,030	5·10	1945[1]	1,702,298	0·83
1886	620,451	3·05	1951[1]	1,939,472	2·37
1891	668,632	1·50	1956[1]	2,174,062	2·31
1896	743,207	2·13	1961[1]	2,414,984	2·12
1901[1]	815,853	1·89	1966[1]	2,676,919	2·10
1906	936,304	2·75	1971[1]	2,862,631	1·34
1911	1,058,308	2·52	1976[1]	3,129,383	1·71
1916[1]	1,149,225	1·50	1981[1]	3,175,737	0·20

The census of New Zealand is quinquennial, but the census falling in 1931 was abandoned as an act of national economy, and owing to war conditions the census due in 1941 was not taken until 25 Sept. 1945.

[1] Excluding members of the Armed Forces overseas.

The areas and populations of statistical areas (with principal centres) as at 31 March 1983 were as follows [1]:

Statistical area [2]	*Sq. km*	*Total population*
Northland (Whangarei)	12,653	118,300
Central Auckland (Auckland)	5,581	863,900
South Auckland—Bay of Plenty (Hamilton)	36,882	506,500
East Coast (Gisborne)	10,885	48,900
Hawke's Bay (Napier, Hastings)	11,289	150,200
Taranaki (New Plymouth)	9,729	105,900
Wellington (Wellington)	27,766	585,800
Total, North Island	*114,785*	*2,379,500*

[1] For statistical purposes, the 9 provincial districts have now been replaced by 13 statistical areas.
[2] Listed from north to south.

Statistical area [1]	*Sq. km*	*Total population*
Marlborough (Blenheim)	10,210	36,500
Nelson (Nelson)	18,948	78,200
Westland (Greymouth)	15,477	23,200
Canterbury (Christchurch) [2]	43,346	422,500
Otago (Dunedin)	36,873	182,000
Southland (Invercargill) [3]	28,464	108,100
Total, South Island	*153,318*	*850,500*
Total, New Zealand	268,103	3,230,000

[1] Listed from north to south. [2] Includes Chatham Islands County.
[3] Includes Stewart Island County.

New Zealand-born residents made up 85·4% of the population at the 1981 census. Foreign-born (provisional): UK, 253,810; Australia, 44,500; Netherlands, 21,630; Samoa, 26,180; Cook Islands, 14,370; USA, 5,430; Ireland, 6,970; others, 97,070.

Maori population: 1896, 42,113; 1936, 82,326; 1945, 98,744; 1951, 115,676; 1961, 171,553; 1971, 227,414; 1976, 270,035; 1981, 279,255.

Populations of statistical divisions and main urban areas as at 31 March 1983 were as follows:

Auckland	863,900	Invercargill	54,000
Christchurch	322,200	Nelson	43,700
Dunedin	112,000	New Plymouth	45,000
Hamilton	164,600	Rotorua	50,000
Napier–Hastings	114,400	Tauranga	57,000
Palmerston North	93,700	Timaru	28,900
Wellington	342,500	Wanganui	39,600
Urban areas:		Whangarei	41,300
Gisborne	32,200		

Vital statistics for calendar years:

	Total live births	*Ex nuptial births*	*Deaths*	*Marriages*	*Divorces (decrees absolute)*
1981	50,794	11,441	25,150	23,660	8,590
1982	49,938	11,386	25,532	25,537	12,395
1983	50,474	11,979	25,991	24,678	9,750

Birth rate, 1983, 15·65 per 1,000; death rate, 8·06 per 1,000; marriage rate, 7·65 per 1,000; infant mortality, 12·54 per 1,000 live births.

External migration (exclusive of crews and through passengers) for years ended 31 March:

	Arrivals	*Departures*		*Arrivals*	*Departures*
1979	805,876	832,420	1982	946,287	951,030
1980	925,939	947,253	1983	915,463	900,021
1981	970,427	986,636	1984	922,868	912,311

Population and Migration: Part B—External Migration. Dept. of Statistics, Wellington, Annually

CLIMATE. Lying in the cool temperate zone, New Zealand enjoys very mild winters for its latitude owing to its oceanic situation, and only the extreme south has cold winters. The situation of the mountain chain produces much sharper climatic contrasts between east and west than in a north-south direction. Observations for 1983: Auckland. Jan. 65·5°F (18·6°C), July 50°F (10·2°C). Annual rainfall 41·5″ (1,053 mm). Christchurch. Jan. 61·3°F (16·3°C), July 42·4°F (5·8°C). Annual rainfall 29″ (737 mm). Dunedin. Jan. 57·4°F (14·1°C), July 43·2°F (6·2°C). Annual rainfall 38·1″ (968 mm). Hokitika. Jan. 56·1°F (13·4°C), July 43·5°F (6·4°C). Annual rainfall 132·2″ (3,357 mm). Rotorua. Jan. 61·2°F (16·2°C), July 43·7°F (6·5°C). Annual rainfall 49·9″ (1,268 mm). Wellington. Jan. 59·9°F (15·5°C), July 46·4°F (8·0°C). Annual rainfall 51·2″ (1,300 mm).

CONSTITUTION AND GOVERNMENT. Definition was given the status of New Zealand by the (Imperial) Statute of Westminster of Dec. 1931, which had received the antecedent approval of the New Zealand Parliament in July 1931. The Governor-General's assent was given to the Statute of Westminster Adoption Bill on 25 Nov. 1947.

The powers, duties and responsibilities of the Governor-General and the Executive Council under the present system of responsible government are set out in Royal Letters Patent and Instructions thereunder of 11 May 1917, published in the *New Zealand Gazette* of 24 April 1919. In the execution of the powers vested in him the Governor-General must be guided by the advice of the Executive Council.

The following is a list of Governors-General, the title prior to June 1917 being Governor:

Earl of Liverpool	1917–20	Lord Norrie	1952–57
Viscount Jellicoe	1920–24	Viscount Cobham	1957–62
Sir Charles Fergusson, Bt	1924–30	Sir Bernard Fergusson	1962–67
Lord Bledisloe	1930–35	Sir Arthur Porrit, Bt	1967–72
Viscount Galway	1935–41	Sir Denis Blundell	1972–77
Sir Cyril Newall	1941–46	Sir Keith Holyoake	1977–80
Lord Freyberg, VC	1946–52	Sir David Beattie	1980–

National flag: The British Blue Ensign with 4 stars of the Southern Cross in red, edged in white, in the fly.

National anthems: God Save the Queen; God Defend New Zealand (words by Thomas Bracken, music by John J. Woods).

Since Nov. 1977 both 'God Save the Queen' and 'God Defend New Zealand' have equal status as national anthems.

Parliament consists of the House of Representatives, the former Legislative Council having been abolished since 1 Jan. 1951.

The statute law on elections and the life of Parliament is contained in the Electoral Act, 1956. In 1974 the voting age was reduced from 20 to 18 years.

The House of Representatives from July 1984 consists of 95 members, including 4 members representing Maori electorates, elected by the people for 3 years. The 4 Maori electoral districts cover the whole country and adult Maoris of half or more Maori descent are the electors. From 1976 a descendant of a Maori is entitled to register either for a general or a Maori electoral district. Women's suffrage was instituted in 1893: women became eligible as members of the House of Representatives in 1919. The House in 1984 included 12 women members.

During Parliamentary sittings the proceedings of the House are broadcast regularly on sound radio.

House of Representatives as composed following the General Election in July 1984: Labour, 56; National Party, 37; Social Credit, 2.

The Executive Council was composed as follows in July 1984:

Governor-General and C.-in-C.: The Hon. Sir David Beattie, GCMG, GCVO, QC (from Oct. 1980).

Prime Minister, Foreign Affairs, Security Intelligence Service: David R. Lange.

Deputy Prime Minister, Attorney-General, Justice, the Legislative Department, the Government Printing Office: Geoffrey W. R. Palmer.

Minister of State, Defence, War Pensions, Rehabilitation: Francis D. O'Flynn.

Labour and State Services: Stanley J. Rodger.

Transport, Railways, Civil Aviation and Meteorological Services, Pacific Island Affairs: Richard W. Prebble.

Trade and Industry: David F. Caygill.

Education and Environment: Cedric R. Marshall.

Maori Affairs, Lands, Forests and the Valuation Department: Koro T. Wetere.

Health and Local Government: Michael E. R. Bassett.

Postmaster-General, Broadcasting: Jonathon L. Hunt.

Inland Revenue, Friendly Societies, Finance: Roger O. Douglas.

Overseas Trade and Marketing, Tourism, Publicity, Recreation and Sport: Michael K. Moore.

Social Welfare, Police, Women's Affairs: Margaret A. Hercus.

Energy, Statistics, Science and Technology, Audit Department: Robert J. Tizard.
Agriculture, Fisheries, Rural Banking and Finance Corporation: Colin J. Moyle.
Works and Development, Earthquake and War Damage Commission: Fraser M. Colman.
Regional Development, Employment, Immigration: Thomas K. Burke.
Customs, Consumer Affairs: M. K. Shields.
Internal Affairs, Civil Defence, Arts: Peter Tapsell.
Housing, Government Life Insurance Corporation, State Insurance Office, Public Trust Office: Philip B. Goff.

The Prime Minister (provided with residence) had in 1983 a salary of NZ$79,717 plus a tax-free expense allowance of $14,000 per annum; Ministers with portfolio, $55,115 plus a tax-free expense allowance of $5,750 (Minister of Foreign Affairs $10,750) per annum; Minister without portfolio, $44,572 plus a tax-free expense allowance of $4,500 per annum; Parliamentary Under-Secretaries, $42,814 plus an expense allowance of $4,500 per annum. In addition, Ministers and Parliamentary Under-Secretaries not provided with residence at the seat of Government receive $600 per annum house allowance. An allowance of $58 per day while travelling within New Zealand on public service is payable to Ministers.

The Speaker of the House of Representatives receives $51,161 plus an expense allowance of $7,100 per annum in addition to his electorate allowance, and residential quarters in Parliament House, and the Leader of the Opposition $55,115 plus expense allowance of $5,750 per annum, and allowances for travelling and housing.

Members were paid $32,271 per annum, plus an expense allowance varying from $4,500 to $9,250 according to the area of electorate represented.

There is a compulsory contributory superannuation scheme for members; retiring allowances are payable to a member after 9 years' service and the attainment of 50 years of age.

Dollimore, H. N., *The Parliament of New Zealand and Parliament House.* 3rd ed. Wellington, 1973
Scott, K. J., *The New Zealand Constitution.* OUP, 1962

Local Government. New Zealand is divided into 22 regions, excluding the Chatham Islands and various uninhabited minor islands. Of these, two (Auckland and Wellington Regions) are under directly-elected Regional Councils with direct rating powers, while the other twenty are under United Councils, appointed by constituent second-tier authorities upon which they precept. The regions are subdivided into (at 31 March 1983) 89 counties, 9 districts, 129 boroughs (and cities) and 3 town districts; further districts are being formed by the amalgamation of counties, boroughs and town districts, which they will eventually replace fully. The Chatham Islands form a 90th county outside the regional structure. There are also numerous other local authorities created for specific functions.

DEFENCE. The control and co-ordination of defence activities is obtained through the Ministry of Defence. This is a unitary department combining not only all joint-Service functions but also the former Departments of Army, Navy and Air.

Army. The Chief of the General Staff commands the Army, assisted by the General Staff and the staffs of Defence Headquarters. A regular force battalion is stationed in Singapore.

Regular personnel, at 31 March 1984, totalled 5,563 all ranks; territorial personnel totalled 6,299; the cadet corps totalled (1984) 1,170 Army School cadets.

Navy. The Royal New Zealand Navy is administered by the Chief of Naval Staff and the Deputy Chief of Naval Staff at Defence Headquarters.

The RNZN ships include 4 frigates (including *Wellington* (ex-*Bacchante*) and *Southland* (ex-*Dido*) transferred from the Royal Navy in 1982 and 1983 respectively), 1 surveying vessel, 4 patrol craft, 5 old harbour defence motor launches, 2 survey boats, 1 oceanographic research ship, 1 tug and 1 tender.

Personnel, in 1985, totalled 2,700 officers and ratings and 500 in the naval reserve.

Air Force. The Chief of Air Staff and Air Officer Commanding the RNZAF exercises command and administration of the RNZAF. Operational units of the RNZAF comprise a utility helicopter support unit (UH-1H Iroquois) based in Singapore as part of the NZ force, South-east Asia. A helicopter support unit is based in El Gorah, Sinai, with the Sinai Multinational Force and Observers. Two UH-1H Iroquois helicopters are leased from the US Army and 27 RNZAF and 2 NZ Army personnel are attached to the unit; maritime (P-3B Orion), long and medium-range transport (Boeing 727, C-130H Hercules, Andover, F.27 Friendship) and helicopter (Sioux, Iroquois, Wasp) squadrons based at RNZAF Base Auckland; and offensive support (A-4K Skyhawk) and medium-range transport/communications squadrons (Andover, F.27 Friendship, Cessna 421) at RNZAF Base Ohakea. Flying training units (Airtrainer, Strikemaster, TA-4K Skyhawks, Sioux) are located at RNZAF Bases Wigram and Ohakea; ground training is carried out at RNZAF Bases Auckland, Woodbourne and Wigram.

The strength as at 31 March 1984 was 4,296 regular personnel, 1,033 reserves.

INTERNATIONAL RELATIONS

Membership. New Zealand is a member of UN, the Commonwealth, OECD, ASEAN, South Pacific Forum and the Colombo Plan.

ECONOMY

Budget. The following tables of revenue and expenditure relate to the Consolidated Account, which covers the ordinary revenue and expenditure of the general government—*i.e.*, apart from capital items, commercial and special undertakings, advances, etc. Revenue in the Account (in NZ$1m.) was as follows:

Year ended 31 March	*Customs and excise*	*Sales tax*	*Income tax*	*Other taxes*	*Trading profits and departmental receipts*	*Interest*	*Total*
1981	413·6	775·6	5,298·9	373·4	493·1	597·8	7,952·4
1982	549·4	1,084·1	6,514·7	439·3	592·5	664·4	9,843·4
1983	660·9	1,211·7	7,455·5	536·3	709·7	719·5	11,293·6
1984	705·6	1,312·3	7,453·3	717·8	759·9	796·2	11,744·9

Expenditure from Consolidated Account, year ended 31 March, was as follows (in NZ$1m.):

	Debt services	*Social services* [1]	*Industrial development*	*Defence*	*Total (including other)*
1981	999·9	5,296·7	999·7	455·9	8,992·5
1982	1,327·2	6,205·9	1,337·4	593·6	11,123·8
1983	1,636·4	7,227·5	1,641·6	652·1	12,872·1
1984	2,229·2	7,618·5	2,134·8	673·0	14,221·5

[1] Includes education, health and social welfare.

Taxation receipts in 1983–84 for all purposes amounted to $10,431m., giving an average of $3,194 per head of mean population. Included in the total taxation is $242·3m. National Roads Fund taxation. The estimate for 1984–85 is $11,820m., the total being inclusive of an estimated $300m. of National Roads Fund taxation.

The gross public debt at 31 March 1984 was $21,789m., of which $13,652m. was held in New Zealand, $5,731m. in London, Europe and Asia, $2,433m. in USA and $63m. in Canada, Australia and other sources. The gross annual interest charge on the public debt at 31 March 1984 was $2,014,875,000.

New Zealand System of National Accounts. This replaces the National Income and Expenditure Accounts which have been produced since 1948. National Accounts aggregates for 4 years are given in the following table (in NZ$1m.):

Year ended 31 March	*Gross domestic product*	*Gross national product*	*National income*
1980	21,092	20,632	20,632
1981	24,461	23,950	23,950
1982	29,296	28,681	28,681
1983	32,240	31,380	31,380

Currency. The monetary unit is the New Zealand *dollar*, divided into 100 *cents*. In March 1985, £1 = 2·460NZ$; US$1 = 2·212NZ$.

Banking. The Reserve Bank is the sole note-issuing authority. Seven denominations of Reserve Bank notes are issued: NZ$1, 2, 5, 10, 20, 50, 100.

The New Zealand banking system comprises a central bank, the Reserve Bank of New Zealand, and 4 commercial or trading banks. There are also 12 trustee savings banks and the Post Office Savings Bank, while each trading bank has a private savings bank subsidiary. In addition, a number of trading companies, investment societies, etc., perform quasi-banking functions, accepting deposits and granting credits to clients.

The primary functions of the Reserve Bank are to act as the central bank, to advise the Government on matters relating to monetary policy, banking and overseas exchange, and to give effect to the monetary policy of the Government.

Of the 4 trading banks 2 are primarily Australian concerns, 1 until recently had its head office in London and the Bank of New Zealand has been state owned since 1 Nov. 1945.

At the end of March 1984 the amount on deposit at trading banks was NZ$8,727m., while advances amounted to NZ$6,630·2m. The weekly average of bank debits for 1983 was $5,797m. excluding government.

The number of accounts with the post office savings bank at 31 March 1984 was 3·32m.; amount deposited during year ended March 1984, $5,783m.; withdrawn, $5,600m., total amount to credit of depositors at end of year, $2,397m. At 31 March 1984, $3,016m. was on deposit in Trustee Savings Banks to the credit of 3·19m. depositors. The amount to the credit of depositors with savings accounts in the trading banks was $769·7m. at 31 March 1984.

Weights and Measures. Conversion to the metric system of weights and measures has been completed.

ENERGY AND NATURAL RESOURCES

Electricity. The general policy of the Government in regard to electric power is to supply power in bulk, leaving the reticulation and retail supply in the hands of local authorities; some of these are cities and boroughs but most are electric power boards. During the year ending 31 March 1983 hydro energy provided 74% of the national electricity supply, the balance coming from coal, oil, natural gas and geothermal energy. The last is obtained from Wairakei in the thermal region; natural steam is used to drive the turbines.

The transmission systems of the North and South Islands are linked by a high-voltage direct-current transmission and 40 km of submarine cable in Cook Strait.

Principal statistics for 4 years ended 31 March are:

	1980	*1981*	*1982*	*1983*
Number of establishments	79	81	82	82
Generators (capacity) AC (1,000 kw.)	5,860	6,018	5,827	5,820
Units generated (1m. kwh.)	21,607	22,111	22,963	24,301
Revenue ($1,000)	1,154,206	1,276,853	1,440,235	1,720,058
Expenditure:				
Operating ($1,000)	580,000	666,419	773,764	947,179
Management, etc. ($1,000)	96,933	118,898	142,714	163,403
Capital charges ($1,000)	266,611	299,756	329,162	359,989
Capital outlay:				
During year ($1,000)	350,500	370,700	459,200	491,286
To date ($1,000)	3,414,200	3,359,100	3,744,100	4,235,386

Natural Gas. Resources discovered in the Taranaki area of the North Island in 1961 are now supplying gas for household use to North Island cities including Auckland and Wellington. The much larger Maui offshore gasfield was discovered in 1969 and is at present being developed.

Minerals. New Zealand's production of minerals in 1983 included 301 kg of gold, 1,958 tonnes of bentonite, 97,944 tonnes of clay for bricks, tiles, etc., 23,917 tonnes of potters' clays, 2,700,400 tonnes of iron sand, 1,459,600 tonnes of limestone for agriculture and 206,500 tonnes of limestone for industry, 1,469,800 tonnes of limestone, marl, etc., for cement, 16,800 tonnes of pumice, 64,100 tonnes of serpentine, 148,400 tonnes of silica sand. Mineral fuel production amounted to 2,543,500 tonnes of coal, 845,000 cu. metres of petroleum condensate and 2,473m. cu. metres of natural gas. Salt produced by the solar evaporation of sea water amounted to 81,000 tonnes. Mineral production for the year was valued at $191·6m.

Agriculture. Two-thirds of the surface of New Zealand is suitable for agriculture and grazing. The total area under cultivation at 30 June 1983 was 11,155,000 hectares (including residential area and domestic orchards). There were 10,154,000 hectares of grassland, lucerne, and land in or prepared for fruit, grain, crops and vegetables, and 1,001,000 hectares of exotic timber plantations. The area of Crown lands (other than reserves) leased under various tenures at 31 March 1983 was 5,575,799 hectares.

The largest freehold estates are held in the South Island. The extent of occupied holdings as at 30 June 1983 (exclusive of holdings within borough boundaries) was as follows:

Size of holdings (hectares)	*Number*	*Aggregate area (hectares)*	*Size of holdings (hectares)*	*Number*	*Aggregate area (hectares)*
Under 5	8,670	26,231	400–799	4,417	2,407,526
5–19	13,345	133,459	800–999	816	726,468
20–39	7,409	210,325	1,000–1,199	470	515,775
40–79	12,922	740,061	1,200–1,999	951	1,454,506
80–99	4,350	384,299	2,000–3,999	568	1,551,961
100–149	6,912	846,908	4,000 and over	581	8,777,895
150–199	4,704	814,987			
200–299	6,370	1,551,997	Total	75,745	21,266,099
300–399	3,260	1,123,701			

The area and yield for each of the principal crops are given as follows (area and yield for threshing only, not including that grown for chaff, hay, silage, etc.):

	Wheat		*Maize*		*Barley*	
Crop years	*Area (1,000 hectares)*	*Yield (1,000 tonnes)*	*Area (1,000 hectares)*	*Yield (1,000 tonnes)*	*Area (1,000 hectares)*	*Yield (1,000 tonnes)*
1982	71·5	292·1	18·8	170·1	88·5	355·8
1983	70·9	300·8	17·2	142·8	81·7	346·4

Private air companies are carrying out such aerial work as top-dressing, spraying and crop-dusting, seed-sowing, rabbit poisoning, aerial photography and surveying, and dropping supplies to deer cullers and dropping fencing materials in remote areas. In 1983 a total area of 6,849,400 hectares was top-dressed with fertilizer and lime; 2,233,800 tonnes by ground spread and 909,600 by air.

Livestock at 30 June 1983: 7,631,000 cattle, 70·3m. sheep and 408,000 pigs. Total meat produced in the year ended 30 Sept. 1983 was estimated at 1·34m. tonnes (including 518,200 tonnes of beef and 510,200 tonnes of lamb). Total liquid milk produced in the year ended 31 May 1983 was 6,603m. litres.

Production of wool for 1982–83, 371,000 tonnes (greasy basis).

Agricultural Statistics. Dept. of Statistics, Wellington. Annual.
New Zealand Agriculture. Ministry of Agriculture and Fisheries, Wellington, 1974
Allsop, F., *The First Fifty Years of New Zealand's Forest Service.* Wellington, 1973
Evans, B. L., *A History of Agricultural Production and Marketing.* Palmerston North, 1969
Levy, E. B., *Grasslands of New Zealand.* Wellington, 1970

Forestry. Of the 6·2m. hectares of indigenous forest only about 1m. hectares are merchantable; they are being depleted at the rate of 5,000 hectares a year (although the rate of cutting is diminishing) and mainly for sawn timber. There are about 992,000 hectares of productive exotic forest, and this produces far more timber than the indigenous forests. Introduced conifer pines form the bulk of the large exotic forest estate and among these radiata pine is the best multi-purpose tree, reaching saw-log size in 25–30 years. Other major species are Douglas fir, Corsican pine and ponderosa pine. The table below shows production of rough sawn timber in cu. metres for years ending 31 March:

	Indigenous Rimu and Miro	Indigenous Beech	Indigenous Total	Exotic Exotic Pines	Exotic Douglas Fir	Exotic Total	All Species Total
1980–81	121,971	19,280	175,101	1,798,060	168,025	2,007,245	2,182,346
1981–82	111,614	18,208	164,442	1,885,761	173,377	2,105,991	2,270,433
1982–83	100,655	17,433	149,824	1,777,012	163,694	1,986,079	2,135,903

Forest industries consist of 394 saw-mills, 9 plywood and veneer plants, 3 particle board mills, 7 pulp and paper mills and 2 fibreboard mills.

The basic products of the pulp and paper mills are mechanical and chemical pulp which are converted into newsprint, kraft and other papers, paperboard and fibreboard. Production of woodpulp, 31 March 1983, amounted to 1·11m. tonnes and of paper (including newsprint paper and paperboard) to 725,700 tonnes.

Fisheries. The total value of New Zealand Fisheries exports during the year ended 30 June 1983 was $285·5m., an increase of $55·2m. (24·1%) over the previous year.

	Exports, 1982 Quantity kg (1,000)	*Exports, 1982* Value $ (1,000)	*Exports, 1983* Quantity kg (1,000)	*Exports, 1983* Value $ (1,000)
Finfish or wetfish	80,164	112,574	82,762	148,222
Rock lobster	2,375	41,386	2,585	48,054
Shellfish (squid, mussels, oysters, etc)	42,980	64,161	42,537	75,092
Total	125,519	218,121	127,884	271,368

INDUSTRY AND TRADE

Industry. Major industrial developments in recent years have included the establishment of an oil refinery, an iron and steel industry using New Zealand iron sands and an aluminium smelter using hydro-electric power.

Statistics of manufacturing industries:

Production year	*Persons engaged*	*Salaries and wages paid (NZ$1,000)*	*Cost of materials (NZ$1,000)*	*Sales and other income (NZ$1,000)*	*Net output (net value added) (NZ$1,000)*
1981–82	296,751	3,798,032	10,381,973	18,382,363	5,878,564

The following is a statement of the provisional value of the products (including repairs) of the principal industries for the year 1981–82 (in NZ$1,000):

Industry group	*Purchases & operating expenses*	*Sales and other income*	*Value added*	*Additions to fixed tangible assets*
		(NZ$1,000)		
Food, beverage and tobacco manufacturing	5,283,214	5,503,074	1,540,430	424,698
Textile, wearing apparel, leather industries	1,555,034	1,649,651	612,657	52,716
Wood and wood products (including furniture)	1,083,420	1,167,838	395,378	48,556
Paper and paper products, printing and publishing	1,771,428	1,958,810	684,629	106,890
Chemicals and chemical, petroleum, coal, rubber and plastic products	1,897,222	2,018,927	605,934	242,508
Non-metallic mineral products (excludes products of petroleum and coal)	563,227	631,980	226,723	57,075
Basic metal industries	688,896	717,817	214,338	121,591
Fabricated metal products, machinery and equipment	4,271,883	4,399,417	1,444,158	164,678
Other manufacturing industries	141,210	153,006	57,243	5,302
Total	17,575,722	18,382,363	5,878,564	1,248,108

Census of Manufacturing. Dept. of Statistics, Wellington. Annual

Labour. In Dec. 1982 there were 255 industrial unions of workers with a total of 527,797 members.

The industrial distribution of the labour force as estimated in Feb. 1982 was: Primary industries, 150,500; manufacturing, 312,700; construction, 85,800; commerce, 311,800; transport and communication, 106,400; services, 298,700; armed forces, 11,300; unemployed, 46,900; total labour force, 1,340,100.

By the Accident Compensation Act 1972 immediate compensation without proof of fault is provided for every injured person and wherever the accident occurred. Compensation is paid both for permanent physical disability and also—in the case of earners—for income losses on an income related basis. Regular adjustment in the level of payment is provided for in accordance with variations in the value of money. Non-earners such as tourists, housewives, children, students, retired people do not normally qualify for earnings related compensation but are eligible for all other benefits. These are not taxable. Housewives—including visiting women from overseas—who are non-earners are eligible for the benefits available to non-earners and home help can be paid for or the husband compensated for loss of earnings while he is looking after the home until the injured wife can resume her duties.

After the first week's incapacity and for the ensuing 4 weeks the earner can be paid 80% of his average earnings for the 28 days preceding the accident; after that the 80% is related to average earnings over the 12 preceding months. In addition—for earners—lump sums are payable for impairment, pain and disfigurement and for funeral expenses and weekly sums and lump payments to their widows and dependent children. All employees are covered by the Accident Compensation Act 1972.

Commerce. Trade (excluding specie and bullion) in NZ$1m. for 12 months ended 30 June:

	Total merchandise imported (v.f.d.)[1]	*Exports of domestic produce*	*Re-exports*	*Total merchandise exported (f.o.b.)*
1979–80	4,809·6	5,012·5	139·8	5,152·2
1980–81	5,587·3	5,830·0	235·2	6,065·3
1981–82	7,044·8	6,527·8	206·0	6,733·8
1982–83	6,928·2	7,427·7	266·6	7,694·3

[1] Value for duty.

The principal imports for the 12 months ended 30 June 1983 (provisional):

Commodity	*Value (NZ$1,000) (c.i.f.)*
Cereals and cereal preparations	32,851
Fruit and vegetables	105,758
Sugar and sugar preparations	66,953
Coffee, tea, cocoa, spices, etc.	67,960
Beverages	41,693
Tobacco and manufactures	24,626
Crude rubber	32,510
Textile fibres	20,924
Crude fertilizers and minerals other than coal	170,008
Petroleum and petroleum products	1,422,088
Organic chemicals	131,519
Inorganic chemicals	107,344
Dyeing, tanning, etc. materials	38,713
Medicinal and pharmaceutical products	136,273
Fertilizers, manufactured	74,713
Plastic materials, etc.	220,681
Miscellaneous chemical materials and products	82,836
Rubber manufactures [1]	61,139
Paper and paperboard manufactures	104,696
Textile yarn and fabrics, etc.	447,027
Non-metallic mineral manufactures [1]	94,995
Iron and steel	378,283
Non-ferrous metals	108,918
Manufactures of metals	198,953
General industrial machinery	551,039
Electric machinery	268,320
Road vehicles	497,501
Professional scientific instruments	139,017
Miscellaneous manufactured articles [1]	287,451
Total merchandise imported [2]	7,595,828

[1] Not elsewhere specified. [2] Including commodities not listed.

The principal exports of New Zealand produce for the 12 months ended 30 June 1983 (provisional) were:

Commodity	*Value (NZ$1,000)*	*Commodity*	*Value (NZ$1,000)*
Meat		Pulp and waste paper	161,479
Beef and veal	791,588	Wool	1,019,256
Lamb	904,322	Sausage casings (hanks)	50,183
Mutton	88,779	Tallow	55,476
Edible offals	70,809	Casein	199,224
Dairy products		Newsprint	60,855
Fresh milk and cream	13,500	Textile yarn	42,162
Butter	660,595	Carpets	58,688
Cheese	193,567	Aluminium	294,893
Fish	285,470	Metal manufactures	101,422
Cereals and cereal preparations	33,068	General industrial machinery	53,244
Apples	59,329	Electric machinery, etc.	74,380
Animal feeding stuff	103,623		
Wood and cork	100,252	Total produce exported	7,427,708

The following table shows the trade with different countries for the year ended 30 June (in NZ$1,000):

Countries	*Imports v.f.d. from* 1982	1983	*Exports and re-exports f.o.b. to* 1982	1983
Australia	1,400,519	1,367,934	1,031,743	953,207
Bahrain	92,781	23,787	9,755	14,296
Belgium	40,566	32,516	53,618	71,710
Canada	149,267	168,416	128,762	163,334
China	48,002	48,863	122,397	177,178
Fiji	22,493	29,687	91,715	103,863
France	72,725	96,397	107,327	143,036
Germany (Fed. Rep. of)	280,694	307,404	123,542	135,319
Greece	2,551	3,317	49,348	50,939
Hong Kong	89,974	97,097	95,600	92,322
India	[illegible]	79,367	60,912	15,611
Iran	166	213	103,709	355,999
Italy	86,871	105,761	112,995	119,762
Japan	1,199,913	1,165,997	876,067	1,062,423
Korea, Republic of	53,416	100,594	104,080	102,802
Kuwait	31,437	34,438	13,474	22,765
Malaysia	36,581	34,049	102,450	113,202
Netherlands	76,740	95,225	89,346	94,169
Philippines	8,346	9,676	98,886	90,318
Saudi Arabia	273,622	142,140	50,792	75,081
Singapore	278,813	395,062	97,319	138,522
Sweden	58,958	52,069	5,504	6,159
UK	636,056	637,759	962,540	990,143
USSR	34,618	9,023	361,772	344,763
USA	1,202,380	1,168,548	853,011	1,170,415

Total trade between New Zealand and UK was as follows (British Department of Trade returns, in £1,000 sterling):

	1980	*1981*	*1982*	*1983*	*1984*
Imports to UK	414,630	427,174	539,137	486,305	483,749
Exports and re-exports from UK	250,413	253,373	323,201	266,054	367,512

Tourism. The country has a growing tourist industry. In the year ended 31 March 1984, 518,441 travellers visited New Zealand (including 402,638 tourists), compared with 487,658 (including 372,669 tourists) in 1983.

COMMUNICATIONS

Roads. Total length of formed roads and streets in New Zealand at 31 March 1983 was 92,909 km. There were 14,532 bridges of over 3 metres in length with a total length of 328,365 metres at 31 March 1983. The network of state highways comprised, at 31 March 1983, 11,531 km, including the principal arterial traffic routes.

Total expenditure on roads, streets and bridges by the central government and local authorities combined for the financial year 1983–84 amounted to $336·7m.

In the main, roads are financed from the National Roads Fund which is administered by the National Roads Board. This fund which is derived largely from petrol tax is used for the maintenance and improvement of existing roads. The board's income is currently of the order of $343m. per annum. Funds are apportioned on the following basis: 43% or more of motor revenue to local authorities, 47% or more to state highways and the remaining 10% is allocated at the discretion of the board.

At 31 March 1984 motor vehicles licensed numbered 2,365,643, of which 1,447,298 were cars and 4,134 omnibuses and service vehicles. Included in the remaining numbers were 141,420 motor cycles, 1,379 power cycles, 294,033 trucks, 390,924 trailers and caravans, 713 contract vehicles and 74,318 farm tractors and other farm equipment.

Railways. On 31 March 1984 there were 4,273 km of 1,067 mm gauge railway open for traffic (200 km electrified). Operating earnings from government railways, 1983–84, $497,126,000; operating expenses, $478,331,000. In 1983–84 the tonnage of goods (including livestock) carried was 10·63m. tonnes, and passengers numbered 14,533,000. In addition, the railways road motor services carried 17·3m. passengers. Four rail/road ferries maintain a regular service between the North and South Islands.

The total revenue (including road motor and other subsidiary services) amounted to $626·6m., and total expenditure $583·4m. in 1983–84.

Aviation. International services are operated to and from New Zealand by a state-owned company, Air New Zealand Ltd, and by a number of overseas companies. Air New Zealand Ltd also operates most domestic scheduled passenger services. Non-scheduled services are run by the main companies and also by a number of small operators and aero clubs.

Domestic scheduled services during the 12 months ended Dec. 1983: Passengers carried, 2,361,000. International services: Passengers carried, 1,684,000; mail, 3,208 tonnes; freight, 76,794 tonnes.

Shipping. Container ships operate from Auckland, Wellington, Lyttelton and Port Chalmers to the UK, Europe, North America and Japan. The government-owned New Zealand Shipping Corporation has begun to increase its activity into New Zealand—UK and Pacific trades.

Entrances and clearances of vessels from overseas:

	Entrances		*Clearances*	
	No.	*Tons*	*No.*	*Tons*
1981	2,671	12,738,000	2,704	12,868,000
1982	2,855	13,083,000	2,846	13,071,000
1983	3,119	13,074,000	3,106	13,013,000

Post and Broadcasting. Receipts of the Post Office for year ended 31 March 1984 were $1,364·8m.; total expenditure was $1,075m. The average staff for 1983–84 was 37,957.

The telegraph and telephone systems are operated by the Post Office. At 31 March 1984 there were 2,010,684 telephones. The telecommunications receipts for the year 1983–84 were $867m.

An earth satellite station has been built north of Auckland to link with the Pacific satellite Intelsat III to augment the Compac and Seacon telecommunications systems which link New Zealand with overseas countries.

There are 2 TV channels both operated by the state-owned New Zealand Broadcasting Corporation, which also operates most of the broadcasting stations. Over 85% of New Zealand households have TV sets. There are 64 medium-wave broadcasting stations and 2 short-wave transmitters. Some commercial material is broadcast by both sound and TV services. Number of TV receiving licences at 31 March 1984 was 943,234.

Cinemas. There were in 1981, 154 cinemas with a seating capacity of 89,364.

Newspapers. There were (1984), 31 daily newspapers (8 morning and 23 evening) with a combined circulation of 1,058,805. Seven of these newspapers (2 each in

Auckland, Wellington and Christchurch and 1 in Dunedin) had a circulation of 715,760.

JUSTICE, RELIGION, EDUCATION AND WELFARE

Justice. The judiciary consists of the Court of Appeal, the High Court and District Courts. All exercise both civil and criminal jurisdiction. Other special courts include the Maori Land Court, Family Courts and Young Persons' Courts. At the end of Dec. 1983 the gaols and Borstal institutions contained 2,700 prisoners, 2,578 males and 122 females. The death penalty for murder was replaced by life imprisonment in 1961.

The Criminal Injuries Act, 1963, which came into force on 1 Jan. 1964, provided for compensation of persons injured by certain criminal acts and the dependants of persons killed by such acts. However, this has now been phased out in favour of the Accident Compensation Act, 1972, except in the residual area of property damage caused by escapers. Since 1970 legal aid in civil proceedings (except divorce) has been available for persons of small or moderate means. For the year ended 31 March 1984 expenditure amounted to $4,211,168 and 11,365 applications for aid were granted.

Police. The police in New Zealand are a national body maintained wholly by the central government. The total strength at 31 March 1984 was 5,088, the proportion of police to population being 1 to 642. The total cost of police services for the year 1983–84 was NZ$186m., equivalent to $57 per head of population. In New Zealand the police do not control traffic.

Ombudsmen. The office of Ombudsman was created in 1962. From 1975 additional Ombudsmen have been authorized. There are currently three. Ombudsmen's functions are to investigate complaints from members of the public relating to administrative decisions of government departments, local authorities and statutory organizations.

During the year ended 31 March 1984, 2,150 complaints were received, 138 of which were sustained.

Religion. No direct state aid is given to any form of religion. For the Church of England the country is divided into 7 dioceses, with a separate bishopric (Aotearoa) for the Maoris. The Presbyterian Church is divided into 23 presbyteries and the Maori Synod. The Moderator is elected annually. The Methodist Church is divided into 10 districts; the President is elected annually. The Roman Catholic Church is divided into 4 dioceses, with the Archbishop of Wellington as Metropolitan Archbishop.

Religious denomination	*Number of clergy (April 1977)*	*Number of adherents 1976 census*	*1981 census*
Church of England	780	915,202	814,740
Presbyterian	686	566,569	523,221
Roman Catholic (including 'Catholic' undefined)	931	478,530	456,858
Methodist	349	173,526	148,512
Baptist	254	49,442	50,043
Brethren	187	24,414	24,324
Ratana	142	35,082	35,781
Protestant (undefined)		33,309	16,986
Salvation Army	241	22,019	20,490
Latter-day Saints (Mormon)	162	36,130	37,686
Congregationalist	10	6,600	3,825
Seventh-day Adventist	55	11,958	11,523
Ringatu	88	6,230	6,114
Christian (undefined)	—	52,478	101,901
Jehovah's Witnesses	125	13,392	13,737
Hebrew	7	3,921	3,360
All other religious professions	—	194,271	279,768
Agnostic	—	14,136	24,201
Atheist	—	14,283	21,528
Not specified	—	39,380	108,015
Object to state	—	438,511	473,115
Total	4,712	3,129,383	3,175,737

Education. New Zealand has 6 universities, the University of Auckland, University of Waikato (at Hamilton), Victoria University of Wellington, Massey University (at Palmerston North), the University of Canterbury (at Christchurch) and the University of Otago (at Dunedin). There is, in addition, Lincoln College near Christchurch, a university college of agriculture, which is a constituent college of the University of Canterbury. The number of students in 1983 was 56,913. There were 7 teachers' training colleges with 4,503 students in 1983.

At 1 July 1983 there were 316 state secondary schools with 13,106 full-time teachers and 215,633 pupils. There were also 35 district high schools with 2,917 scholars in the secondary division. At 1 July 1983, 107,129 part-time pupils attended technical classes, and 29,899 received part-time instruction from the technical correspondence institute. At 1 July 1983, 885 pupils received tuition from the secondary department of the correspondence school. There were 15 registered private secondary schools with 759 teachers and 10,635 pupils.

At 1 July 1983, there were 2,432 state primary schools (including intermediate schools and departments), with 454,363 pupils; the number of teachers was 18,922. A correspondence school for children in remote areas and those otherwise unable to attend school had 1,383 primary pupils. There were 58 registered private primary schools with 553 teachers and 10,670 pupils.

Education is compulsory between the ages of 6 and 15. Children aged 3 and 4 years may enrol at the 539 free kindergartens maintained by Free Kindergarten Associations, which receive government assistance. There are also 681 play centres which also receive government subsidy. In July 1983 there were 40,895 and 16,170 children on the rolls respectively.

Total expenditure out of government funds in 1982–83 upon education was NZ$1,679m.

The universities and the affiliated agricultural colleges are autonomous bodies. Most secondary schools are controlled by their own boards. Virtually all state primary schools are controlled by the district education boards: there are 10 education districts. The Department of Education exercises certain defined functions in connexion with the general supervision of the education provided in state primary and secondary schools and disburses the government grants payable to controlling authorities for the running of those schools. Education in state schools is free for children under 19 years of age. Private schools are regularly visited by state school inspectors.

Report of the Minister of Education ('E.1. Report'). Annually. Wellington, Government Printer

NZ Committee on Secondary Education. *Towards Partnership.* Dept. of Education, 1976

Social Welfare. New Zealand's record for progressive legislation reaches back to 1898, when it was second only to Denmark in introducing non-contributory old-age pensions.

The present system came into operation from 1 April 1972. It provides for retirement, unemployment, widowhood, invalidity and sickness, as well as hospital and other medical care. Since 1 April 1969 the scheme has been financed from general taxation. Previously there was a special social security tax on virtually all income of individuals and companies in excess of $4 a week which met approximately three-quarters of the cost of the scheme, the balance being met from general taxation.

At 31 March 1984 the current weekly rates of widows', invalids', sickness, domestic purposes, unemployment and miners' benefits were $152·04 for a married couple, $91·22 for an unmarried person aged 20 years or over, and $69·41 for those under 20 years.

There are additional payments for dependent children.

All benefits except superannuation and family allowances are subject to an income test.

Family Benefit. A family benefit of $6 a week is payable for each dependent child.

Unemployment Benefit. The payment is subject to the condition that the applicant is capable and willing to undertake suitable employment.

Sickness Benefit. Payment is subject to medical evidence of incapacity of a person who has suffered a loss of weekly earnings as a result.

Other benefits include emergency benefits and additional benefits for those in need but who either do not qualify for one of the standard benefits or who have special needs or commitments for which a benefit at the standard rate is insufficient.

Medical, Hospital and Related Benefits. Medical, hospital and other related benefits are also provided under the Social Welfare scheme. These consist mainly of the payment of certain fees for medical attention by private practitioners, free treatment in public and mental hospitals, certain fees for treatment in private hospitals, maternity benefits (including ante-natal and post-natal treatment and services of doctors and nurses at confinements), pharmaceutical benefits (medicines, drugs, etc., prescribed by medical practitioners), etc. There are also benefits in connexion with dental services up to the age of 16, X-ray diagnosis, massage, home-nursing, artificial aids, etc.

Pensions. Provision is made for the payment of pensions and allowances to members or dependants of disabled, deceased or missing members, of the New Zealand Forces who served in the South African War, the two World Wars, the Korean War and the Vietnam War, to members of the New Zealand Mercantile Marine during the Second World War, or in connexion with any emergency whether arising out of the obligations undertaken by New Zealand in the Charter of the United Nations or otherwise. Principal rates are: War pensions are payable to widows at a rate of $49·05 a week, together with a mother's allowance of $54·82 a week, increased by $6 a week for each additional child, in addition to the normal child allowances of $6 per week for each child. These rates may be increased by an amount not exceeding $39·90 per week if the pensioner is suffering from total blindness, two or more serious disabilities or one extremely severe disability.

An 'economic pension' is defined as a supplementary pension granted on economic grounds and is additional to any pension payable as of right in respect of death or disablement. The maximum weekly rates are $76·02 to a married person (if unmarried, $91·22); to the widow or dependent widowed mother of a member, $91·22.

War veterans' allowances are $91·22 weekly for a single person and $76·02 for a married person, plus an equal amount to a wife, increased by $1.50 a week each at age 65, subject to income qualifications.

Domestic Purposes Benefit. A domestic purposes benefit is payable to unsupported male and female solo parents including divorced, separated and unmarried persons, prisoners' spouses and also to those who are required to give full-time care to a person (other than their spouse) who would otherwise have to be admitted to hospital.

Death Benefit. A death benefit of $1,000 is payable to a widow or widower if totally dependent on the deceased plus $500 for each dependent child but not exceeding $1,500.

Social Welfare Benefits and War Pensions:

Benefits	*Number in force at 31 March 1984*	*Total payments 1983–84 (NZ$1,000)*
SOCIAL WELFARE:		
Monetary—		
Superannuation	451,128	2,526,031
Widows	13,921	71,295
Orphans	384	1,186
Family	499,365	289,689
Invalids	20,187	87,410
Miners	13	70
Unemployment	50,136	315,849
Sickness	9,452	62,212
Domestic purposes	53,141	380,836
Total	1,097,730	3,734,586

Benefits	*Total payments 1982–83 (NZ$1,000)*
SOCIAL WELFARE (*contd.*):	
Health, etc.—	
Medical	41,072
Hospital	46,453
Maternity	11,052
Pharmaceutical	220,644
Supplementary	42,711
Total	377,361

WAR PENSIONS as at 31 March 1984:

Type of Person	*Number in Force*	*Dependent Wives Included*	*Annual Value NZ$ (1,000)*
War disablement	22,032	–	26,427
Dependants of disabled	93	–	365
Widows	4,445	–	11,435
Other dependants of deceased	57		
Economic	1,841	80	8,568
War service	2,705	1,736	18,327
War veteran's allowance	1,520	721	10,126
Police	34	–	44
Total	32,727	2,537	75,292

Reciprocity with Other Countries. There are reciprocal arrangements between New Zealand and Australia in respect of age, invalids', widows', family, unemployment and sickness benefits, and between New Zealand and the UK in respect of family, age, superannuation, widows', orphans', invalids', sickness and unemployment benefits.

Superannuation. Following the change of Government in Dec. 1975 the earnings-related superannuation scheme described in THE STATESMAN'S YEAR-BOOK, 1977–78, was abolished. Under the new system (operative from Feb. 1977) superannuation is payable to all New Zealanders on reaching the age of 60. It is taxable but not subject to an income test. The rates are based on the national average wage, of which married couples now receive 80% and single persons 60% of the married rate.

Health. At 30 June 1983 there were 7,597 doctors on the medical register. At 31 March 1983 there were 25,304 public hospital beds, of which 2,274 were for maternity cases.

MINOR ISLANDS

The minor islands (total area, 320 sq. miles, 829 sq. km) included within the geographical boundaries of New Zealand (but not within any local government area) are the following: Kermadec Islands (34 sq. km), Three Kings Islands (8 sq. km), Auckland Islands (114 sq. km), Campbell Island (62 sq. km), Antipodes Islands (606 sq. km), Bounty Islands (1 sq. km), Snares Islands (3 sq. km), Solander Island (1 sq. km). With the exception of Raoul Island in the Kermadec Group (population, 5, 1981 census) and Campbell Island (population, 10, 1981 census) both of which have staffed meteorological stations, none of these islands is inhabited.

The **Kermadec Islands** were annexed to New Zealand in 1887, have no separate administration and all New Zealand laws apply to them. Situation, 29° 10′ to 131° 30′ S. lat., 177° 45′ to 179° W. long., 600 miles NNE of New Zealand. The largest of the group is Raoul or Sunday Island, 20 miles in circuit, while Macaulay Island is 3 miles in circuit.

TERRITORIES OVERSEAS

Territories Overseas coming within the jurisdiction of New Zealand consist of Tokelau and the Ross Dependency.

Tokelau. Situated some 480 km to the north of Western Samoa between 8° and 10° S. lat., and between 171° and 173° W. long., are the 3 atoll islands of Atafu, Nukunonu and Fakaofo of the Tokelau (Union) group. Formerly part of the Gilbert and Ellice Islands Colony, the group was transferred to the jurisdiction of New Zealand on 11 Feb. 1926. By legislation enacted in 1948, the Tokelau Islands were declared part of New Zealand as from 1 Jan. 1949. The area of the group is 1,011 hectares; the population at census 25 Oct. 1976 was 1,575; estimate, 31 Dec. 1981, 1,572.

By the Tokelau Islands Act 1948 the Tokelau Group was included within the territorial boundaries of New Zealand; legislative powers are now invested in the Governor-General in Council. The inhabitants are British subjects and New Zealand citizens. In Dec. 1976 the territory was officially renamed 'Tokelau', the name by which it has customarily been known to its inhabitants.

From 8 Nov. 1974 the office of Administrator was invested in the Secretary of Foreign Affairs. Certain powers are delegated to the district officer in Apia, Western Samoa.

Because of the very restricted economic and social future in the atolls, the islanders agreed to a proposal put to them by the Minister of Island Territories in 1965 that over a period of years most of the population be resettled in New Zealand. Up to March 1975, 528 migrants entered New Zealand as permanent residents under Government sponsorship. At the request of the people the scheme has now been suspended.

New Zealand Government aid to Tokelau totalled $2·64m. for the year ended 31 March 1984.

Ross Dependency. By Imperial Order in Council, dated 30 July 1923, the territories between 160° E. long. and 150° W. long. and south of 60° S. lat. were brought within the jurisdiction of the New Zealand Government. The region was named the Ross Dependency. From time to time laws for the Dependency have been made by regulations promulgated by the Governor-General of New Zealand.

The mainland area is estimated at 400,000–450,000 sq. km and is mostly ice-covered. In Jan. 1957 a New Zealand expedition under Sir Edmund Hillary established a base in the Dependency. In Jan. 1958 Sir Edmund Hillary and 4 other New Zealanders reached the South Pole.

The main base—Scott Base—at Pram Point, Ross Island—is manned throughout the year, about 12 people being present during winter. Vanda Station in the dry ice-free Wright Valley is manned every summer.

Quartermain, L. B., *New Zealand and the Antarctic.* Wellington, 1971

SELF-GOVERNING TERRITORIES OVERSEAS

THE COOK ISLANDS

HISTORY. The Cook Islands, which lie between 8° and 23° S. lat., and 156° and 167° W. long., were proclaimed a British protectorate in 1888, and on 11 June 1901 were annexed and proclaimed part of New Zealand. In 1965 the Cook Islands became a self-governing territory in 'free association' with New Zealand.

AREA AND POPULATION. The islands within the territory fall roughly into two groups—the scattered islands towards the north (Northern group) and the islands towards the south known as the Lower group. The names of the islands with their populations as at the census of 1 Dec. 1981 were as follows:

Lower Group—	Area sq. km	Population	Northern Group—	Area sq. km	Population
Rarotonga	67·2	9,530	Nassau	1·2	134
Mangaia	51·8	1,364	Palmerston (Avarau)	2·0	51
Atiu	26·9	1,225	Penrhyn (Tongareva)	9·8	608
Aitutaki	18·0	2,335	Manihiki (Humphrey)	5·4	405
Mauke (Parry Is.)	18·4	681	Rakahanga (Reirson)	4·1	272
Mitiaro	22·3	256	Pukapuka (Danger)	5·1	796
Manuae and Te au-o-tu	6·2	12	Suwarrow (Anchorage)	0·4	—
Takutea	1·3	–			
			Total	293	17,754

In 1983, 414 live births and 129 deaths were registered. In 1983 there were 24,000 Cook Islanders living abroad, mainly in New Zealand.

CONSTITUTION AND GOVERNMENT. The Cook Islands Constitution Act 1964, which provides for the establishment of internal self-government in the Cook Islands, came into force on 4 Aug. 1965.

The Act establishes the Cook Islands as fully self-governing but linked to New Zealand by a common Head of State, the Queen, and a common citizenship, that of New Zealand. It provides for a ministerial system of government with a Cabinet consisting of a Premier and 6 other Ministers. The New Zealand Government is represented by a New Zealand Representative and the position of a Queen's Representative has recently been created by changes in the Constitution. New Zealand continues to be responsible for the external affairs and defence of the Cook Islands, subject to consultation between the New Zealand Prime Minister and the Prime Minister. The changed status of the Islands does not affect the consideration of subsidies or the right of free entry into New Zealand for exports from the group.

The capital is Rarotonga.

Prime Minister: Sir T. R. A. H. Davis.

ECONOMY AND TRADE

Budget. Revenue is derived chiefly from customs duties which follow the New Zealand customs tariff, income tax and stamp sales.

Grants from New Zealand, mainly for medical, educational and general administrative purposes totalled $7m. in 1982–83.

Currency. The Cook Island *dollar* is at par with the New Zealand *dollar*.

Agriculture. Livestock (1983): Pigs, 17,000; goats, 1,000.

Commerce. Exports, mainly to New Zealand, were valued at $4·9m. in 1983. Main items of export were fresh fruit and vegetables, fruit juice, copra and clothing. Imports totalled $27m. in 1982. The main items were foodstuffs, manufactured goods (including transport equipment), petrol and petroleum products.

COMMUNICATIONS

Aviation. New Zealand has financed the construction of an international airport at Rarotonga which became operational for jet services in Sept. 1973.

Shipping. A fortnightly cargo shipping service is provided between New Zealand, Niue and Rarotonga.

Telecommunications. Wireless stations are maintained at all the permanently inhabited islands. In 1982 there were 1,583 telephones.

EDUCATION AND HEALTH

Education. Twenty-eight primary schools are established in the various islands. Of these, two are Roman Catholic missionary schools and two are Seventh-Day Adventist missionary schools. Five primary schools have secondary school attachments, and there are also nine secondary schools. Two of these secondary schools are run by missions; one by the Roman Catholic Mission and the other by the Seventh-Day Adventist Mission. The number of students enrolled at school on 31 March 1983, was 8,276.

The instruction given at school is based on the New Zealand School syllabus and students can sit for the New Zealand School Certificate and University Entrance examinations. Most schools teach in both the English and Cook Island Maori languages, but the use of Cook Islands Maori is restricted to the primary school level.

There were 102 Government-funded students studying at overseas tertiary or technical institutes in 1983.

Health. All Cook Islanders receive free medical and surgical treatment in their villages, the hospital and the tuberculosis sanatorium. Cook Island Maori patients in the hospital and the sanatorium and all schoolchildren receive free dental treatment.

NIUE

History. Niue achieved internal self-government in Oct. 1974.

Area and Population. Distance from Auckland, New Zealand, 1,343 miles; from Rarotonga, 580 miles. Area, 100 sq. miles; circumference, 40 miles; height above sea-level, 220 ft. Population at 28 Sept. 1981 was 3,296; 1984, estimate, 3,019. During 1983 births registered numbered 94, deaths 25. Migration to New Zealand is the main factor in population change.

Constitution and Government. There is a Legislative Assembly of 20 members, and legislative measures apply as in the case of the Cook Islands.

Premier: Robert R. Rex, CMG, OBE.

Budget. Financial aid from New Zealand, 1983–84, totalled $7,138,000.

Agriculture. The most important products of the island are coconuts, passion fruit, honey, limes and root crops.

Trade. Exports, 1983, $632,976 (main export, canned coconut cream); imports, $3,158,778.

Communications. There is a wireless station at Alofi, the port of the island. Two weekly commercial air services link Niue with Western Samoa, Cook Islands, American Samoa and New Zealand. Telephones (1982) 205.

Education. There were 7 government schools with 832 pupils in 1984.

Health. There is a 30-bed hospital in Alofi and clinics in some villages.

DIPLOMATIC REPRESENTATIVES

Of New Zealand in Great Britain (New Zealand Hse, Haymarket, London, SW1Y 4TQ)
High Commissioner: J. A. Walding.

Of Great Britain in New Zealand (Reserve Bank of New Zealand Bldg., 2 The Terrace, Wellington, 1)
High Commissioner: T. D. O'Leary, CMG.

Of New Zealand in the USA (37 Observatory Cir., NW, Washington, D.C., 20008)
Ambassador: Rt. Hon. Sir Lancelot Adams-Schneider, KCMG.

Of the USA in New Zealand (29 Fitzherbert Terrace, Wellington)
Ambassador: H. Monroe Browne.

Of New Zealand to the United Nations
Ambassador: Bryce Harland.

Books of Reference

Statistical Information: The central statistical office for New Zealand is the Department of Statistics (Wellington, 1).

The beginning of a statistical service may be seen in the early 'Blue books' prepared annually from 1840 onwards under the direction of the Colonial Secretary, and designed primarily for the information of the Colonial Office in England. A permanent statistical authority was created in 1858. The Department of Statistics functions under the Statistics Act 1975 and reports to Parliament through the Minister of Statistics. A comprehensive statistical service has been developed to meet national requirements, and close contact is maintained with the United Nations Statistical Office and other international statistical organizations; through the Conference of Asian Statisticians assistance is being given with the development of statistics in the region.

The oldest publications consist of *(a)* census results from 1858 onwards and *(b)* annual volumes of statistics (first published 1858 but covering years back to 1853). Main current publications:

New Zealand Official Yearbook. Annual, from 1893
Catalogue of New Zealand Statistics. 1972
Statistical Reports of New Zealand. Annual
Monthly Abstract of Statistics. From 1914
Pocket Digest of Statistics. Annual, 1927–31, 1938 ff.

Parliamentary Reports of Government Departments. Annual
Pacific Islands Yearbook. Sydney, 1977
Dictionary of New Zealand Biography. 2 vols. Wellington, 1940
Encyclopaedia of New Zealand. 3 vols. Wellington, 1966
National Bibliography. Wellington, 1968
Alley, R., *New Zealand and the Pacific.* Boulder, 1983
Bedggood, D., *Rich and Poor in New Zealand.* Sydney, 1980
Bush, G., *Local Government and Politics in New Zealand.* Sydney, 1980
Easton, B., *Social Policy and the Welfare State in New Zealand.* Auckland, 1980
Grover, R. F., *New Zealand.* [Bibliography] Oxford and Santa Barbara, 1981
Holcroft, M. H., *The Shaping of New Zealand.* Auckland, 1975
Kennaway, R., Jackson, K., Henderson, J. (eds.) *Beyond New Zealand: The Foreign Policy of a Small State.* Auckland, 1980
Levine, S. (ed.), *Politics in New Zealand.* London, 1978.—*The New Zealand Political System.* London, 1979
Morrell, W. P., and Hall, D. O. W., *A History of New Zealand Life.* Christchurch and London, 1957
Oliver, W. H. (ed.), *The Oxford History of New Zealand.* OUP, 1981
Robson, J. L. (ed.), *New Zealand: The Development of its Laws and Constitution.* 2nd ed. London, 1967
Shadbolt, M. F. R., *The Shell Guide to New Zealand.* Christchurch, 1976
Sinclair, K., *A History of New Zealand.* Rev. ed. London, 1980
Traue, J. E., *Who's Who in New Zealand.* 11th ed. Wellington, 1978
Wards, I., *A Descriptive Atlas of New Zealand.* Wellington, Government Printer, 1976
Wise's New Zealand Guide. 7th ed. Auckland, 1979

NICARAGUA

Capital: Managua
Population: 2·9m. (1984)
GNP per capita: US$860 (1981)

República de Nicaragua

HISTORY. Active colonization of the Pacific coast was undertaken by Spaniards from Panama, beginning in 1523. After links with other Central American territories, and Mexico, Nicaragua became completely independent in 1838, but subject to a prolonged feud between the 'Liberals' of León and the 'Conservatives' of Granada. Mosquitia remained an autonomous kingdom on the Atlantic coast, under British protection until 1860.

On 5 Aug. 1914 the Bryan–Chamarro treaty between Nicaragua and the US was signed, under which the US in return for US$3m. acquired a permanent option for a canal route through Nicaragua and a 99-year option for a naval base in the Bay of Fonseca on the Pacific coast and Corn Islands on the Atlantic coast. It was ratified by Nicaragua on 7 April 1916 and by the US on 22 June 1916. US Marines finally left in 1933. The Bryan–Chamarro treaty was abrogated on 14 July 1970 and the Corn Islands handed back in 1971.

The 46-year political domination of Nicaragua by the Somoza family ended on 17 July 1979, after the 17 years long struggle by the Sandinista National Liberation Front flared into civil war. A Government Junta of National Reconstruction was established by the revolutionary government on 20 July 1979 and a 51-member Council of State later created; both were dissolved on 10 Jan. 1985 following new Presidential and legislative elections.

AREA AND POPULATION. Nicaragua is bounded north by Honduras, east by the Caribbean, south by Costa Rica and west by the Pacific. Area estimated at 148,000 sq. km (57,143 sq. miles) or 139,000 sq. km (54,296 sq. miles) if the lakes are excluded. The coastline runs 540 km on the Atlantic and 350 km on the Pacific. Population at the census of April 1971 was 1,877,972. Estimate (1984) 2,908,000.

Nicaragua is the largest in area and most thinly populated of the Central American republics, 23 inhabitants per sq. km in 1984. In 1981, births, 104,000; marriages, 16,000; deaths, 10,000.

The people of the western half of the republic are principally of mixed Spanish and Indian extraction, some of pure Spanish descent and many Indians. The population of the eastern half is composed mainly of Mosquito and other Indians and Zambos, and Negroes from Jamaica and other islands of the Caribbean. The main ethnic groups in 1974 were: Mestizo, 69%; white, 19%; Negro, 9%; Indio, 5%.

Nicaragua is administratively divided into the following 16 departments with population as in 1981:

Boaco	88,862	Jinotega	127,159	Matagalpa	220,548
Carazo	109,450	Léon	248,704	Nueva Segovia	97,765
Chinandega	228,573	Madriz	72,408	Río San Juan	29,001
Chontales	98,462	Managua	819,679	Rivas	108,913
Esteli	110,076	Masaya	149,015	Zelaya	202,462
Granada	113,102				

The capital is Managua, situated on the lake of the same name, 180 ft above sea level, with (1981) 615,000 inhabitants. Other cities: León, 158,577; Grenada, 72,640; Masaya, 78,308; Chinandega, 144,291.

CLIMATE. The climate is tropical, with a wet season from May to Jan. Temperatures vary with altitude. Managua. Jan. 79°F (26°C), July 86°F (30°C). Annual rainfall 45" (1,140 mm).

CONSTITUTION AND GOVERNMENT. Elections for a President and

Vice-President and for a 96-member National Assembly were held on 4 Nov. 1984. All elections were by direct vote, with that for the National Assembly being by proportional representation. The minimum voting age is 16 years.

President: Daniel Ortega Saavedra (elected 4 Nov. 1984, took office 10 Jan. 1985).

Vice-President: Sergio Ramírez Mercado.

In the legislative elections, 61 of the 96 National Assembly seats were won by the *Frente Sandinista de Liberación Nacional* (FSLN), 14 by the *Partido Conservador Demócrata,* 9 by the *Partido Liberal Independiente,* 6 by the *Partido Socialcristiano de Pueblo,* and 6 by 3 parties of the far left. The National Assembly is charged with drafting a new Constitution by 1987, replacing the 1974 Constitution which was abrogated on 20 July 1979.

National flag: Three horizontal stripes of blue, white, blue, with the national arms in the centre.

National anthem: Salve a ti Nicaragua (words by S. Ibarra Mayorga, 1937).

Local government. The republic is divided into a National District and 16 departments, each of which is under a political head (appointed by the President), who has supervision of finance, education and other matters. The departments have 134 *municipios*, headed by a mayor (*alcalde*). The Mosquito Reserve now forms part of the departments of Zelaya and Río San Juan.

DEFENCE. Conscription was introduced in 1983 for men between 17 and 22 years.

Army. The Army is organized into 3 armoured, 10 infantry, 3 artillery and 1 engineer battalions and 1 anti-aircraft artillery group. Equipment includes 45 T-54/-55 and 3 M-4A3 main battle tanks. Strength (1985) 22,000 with an additional 25,000 regular reservists. The Civilian Militia numbers about 30,000.

Navy. Includes 2 *ex*-Soviet fast gunboats, 2 *ex*-North Korean fast torpedo boats, 5 fast attack craft, 4 coastguard cutters, 11 coastal patrol craft and 2 minor landing craft operated by the marine section of the National Guard to picket the east and west coasts. Personnel in 1985 totalled 1,500 officers and men.

Air Force. Formed in June 1938 as the Nicaraguan Army Air Force, the Air Force has been semi-independent since 1947. Its combat units are reported to have more than 80 L-39 Albatross light jet attack/trainers, 4 Summit O2–337 Sentry counter-insurgency aircraft, 4 T-33 armed jet trainers, and 3 T-28 armed piston-engined trainers. Other equipment includes 4 C-47s, Spanish-built Arava STOL and 2 Israeli-built Arava STOL transports and smaller communications aircraft and helicopters, including 4 Mi-8s and a reported number of Mi-24 gunships.

INTERNATIONAL RELATIONS

Membership. Nicaragua is a member of the UN, OAS and the Central American Common Market.

ECONOMY

Budget. Revenue and expenditure for fiscal years, ending 31 Dec., in 1m. córdobas:

	1979	*1980*	*1981*	*1982*
Revenue	3,760·1	5,972·0	5,874·0	6,982·0
Expenditure	3,409·0	5,972·0	6,720·0	6,703·0

Currency. The monetary unit is the *córdoba* (C$), divided into 100 *centavos.* On 31 Dec. 1978 total money supply was 1,887·8m. córdobas. Bills form the greater part of the currency, in denominations from 1,000 córdobas to 1 córdoba. Silver coins struck, but now out of circulation, are 50, 25 and 10 centavos; copper–nickel and copper–zinc coins, 1 córdoba, 50, 25, 10 and 5 centavos. March 1985, US$1 = 10 *córdobas*; £1 = 29·95 *córdobas.*

Banking. The National Bank of Nicaragua at Managua founded in 1912, owned by the Government since 1924 was reorganized in July 1979, becoming the National Development Bank and including the National Development Institute (INFONAC) and Special Fund for Development (FED). This new law gave it increased responsibilities as a development bank. The Central Bank of Nicaragua came into operation on 1 Jan. 1961 as an autonomous bank of issue, absorbing the issue department of the National Bank.

In July 1979 private financial banking was nationalized and branches of foreign banks were prohibited from receiving deposits.

Weights and Measures. Since 1893 the metric system of weights and measures has been recommended.

ENERGY AND NATURAL RESOURCES

Electricity. Installed capacity for electric energy was 357,700 kw. in 1977 and 1,180·3 kwh. was produced.

Minerals. Production of gold in 1980 was 67,000 troy oz.; of silver, 167,000 troy oz.; of copper, 3,000 tonnes. There is no iron or coalmining. Large deposits of tungsten in Nueva Segovia were announced in 1961. Exploration for petroleum began off the Pacific and Atlantic coasts in 1965. A petroleum refinery of 650,000 tonnes capacity is functioning at Managua.

Agriculture. Agriculture is the principal source of national wealth, finding work for 65% of the labour force, and furnishing, 1975, 22% of the GNP.

Of the total land area (about 36·5m. acres), about 17·5m. acres are under timber 0·9m. acres are used for grazing and 2·1m. acres are arable. The unit of area used locally is the *manzana* (= 1·73 acres). Of the arable only 1·2m. acres are actively cultivated, 780,000 in annual crops such as cotton and rice and the remainder in perennial crops such as coffee and sugar-cane, or in two harvests a year in the cases of maize, sorghum and beans.

The products of the western half are varied, the most important being cotton, coffee, now under the aegis of the new *Instituto del Café*, sugar cane, cocoa, maize, sesame and beans. Production (1982): Coffee, 57,000 tonnes; sugar, 3m. tonnes; cotton, 190,000 tonnes.

There were about 2·2m. head of cattle in 1983. There were 520,000 pigs (1983).

Forestry. Timber production has been declining, though the forests, which cover 10m. acres, contain mahogany and cedar, which were formerly largely exported, three varieties of rosewoods, guayacán (*lignum vitae*) and dye-woods. Production of sawn wood in 1978, 270,000 tonnes.

Fishery. On the Atlantic coast fisheries are an important subsistence activity. Over 6·4m. lb. of shrimps were exported in 1978 and were processed in 3 plants at Schooner Cay and El Bluff. Catch (1981) 5,900 tonnes.

INDUSTRY AND TRADE

Industry. Chief local industries are cane sugar, cooking oil, cigarettes, beer, leather products, plastics, textiles, chemical products, metal products, cement (349,000 tonnes in 1980), strong and soft drinks, soluble coffee, dairy products, meat, plywood. Production of oil products, in 1978, was valued at 526m. córdobas; food products, 3,338·4m.; beverages, 565·8m.; textiles, 328·7m.; chemical substances and products, 1,054m.

Labour. In 1980 there were some 813,000 persons gainfully employed.

Commerce. The foreign trade of Nicaragua, in US$1m., was as follows in calendar years:

	1977	*1978*	*1979*	*1980*	*1981*
Imports	761·9	553·0	388·0	870·0	807·6
Exports	636·8	645·9	598·0	469·7	520·0

Total trade between Nicaragua and UK (British Department of Trade returns, in £1,000 sterling):

	1980	*1981*	*1982*	*1983*	*1984*
Imports to UK	1,510	1,030	3,282	1,810	2,176
Exports and re-exports from UK	2,478	4,269	4,940	2,367	4,755

COMMUNICATIONS

Roads. In 1984, 4,000 km were paved, out of a total of 25,000 km. The whole 368·5 km of the Nicaraguan section of the Pan-American Highway is now paved. The all-weather Roosevelt Highway linking Managua with the river port Rama was completed in 1968, to provide the first overland link with the Atlantic coast. There are paved roads to San Juan del Sur, Puerto Somoza and Corinto. In 1981 there were 66,000 vehicles in use including 23,000 cars.

Railways. The Pacific Railroad of Nicaragua, owned and operated by the Government, has a total length of 373 km, all single-track, and connects Corinto, Chinandega, León, Managua, Masaya and Granada. Passengers carried (1981) 640,000.

Aviation. LANICA, the Nicaraguan airline has daily flights to Miami and 6 flights a week to Guatemala and to the inner cities of Bluefields, Puerto Cabezas and the mining towns of Siuna and Bonanza. PANAM and TACA (Transportes Aéreos Centroamericanos), COPA (Compañía Panameña de Aviacíon), have daily services to Panama, Mexico, the other Central American countries and USA. SAM (Servicio Aéreo de Medellín) has 3 flights a week to Nicaragua and Colombia. In 1977, 223,420 passengers and 24·2m. tonnes of cargo were carried.

Shipping. The Pacific ports are Corinto (the largest), San Juan del Sur and Puerto Saudino through which pass most of the external trade. The chief eastern ports are El Bluff (for Bluefields) and Puerto Cabezas. The merchant marine consists solely of the Mamenic Line with 8 vessels. In 1980, 471,000 tonnes of goods were loaded and 1·14m. tonnes unloaded at Nicaraguan ports.

Post and Broadcasting. In 1982 there were 51,237 telephones.

The Tropical Radio Telegraph Company maintains a powerful station at Managua, and branch stations at Bluefields and Puerto Cabezas. The Government operates the National Radio with 47 broadcasting stations: there are 31 commercial stations and some 70 others. Number of wireless sets in 1981 was 140,000 and television sets 180,000. There are 2 television stations at Managua.

Cinemas. Cinemas numbered over 100 in 1977 and seated over 60,000.

Newspapers. In 1983 there were 3 daily newspapers (2 in Managua and 1 in León), with a total circulation of about 105,000.

JUSTICE, RELIGION, EDUCATION AND WELFARE

Justice. The judicial power is vested in a Supreme Court of Justice at Managua, 5 chambers of second instance (León, Masaya, Granada, Matagalpa and Bluefields) and 153 judges of inferior tribunals.

Religion. The prevailing form of religion is Roman Catholic, but religious liberty is guaranteed by the Constitution. The republic constitutes 1 archbishopric (seat at Managua) and 7 bishoprics (León, Granada, Estelí, Matagalpa, Juigalpa, Masaya and Puerto Cabezas). Protestants, established principally on the Atlantic coast, numbered 54,100 in 1966.

Education. There were, in 1981, 4,577 primary schools, with a total of 503,497 pupils and 14,113 teachers; and 377 secondary schools, with 139,743 pupils and 4,221 teachers. It was claimed that the illiteracy rate was 13% in 1980. In 1977 there were 6 universities and technical colleges with 1,204 professors and 23,171 students.

Social Welfare. In 1980 there were 1,600 physicians and 50 hospitals with 4,573 beds.

DIPLOMATIC REPRESENTATIVES

Of Nicaragua in Great Britain (8 Gloucester Rd., London, SW7 4PP)
Ambassador: Francisco d'Escoto.

Of Great Britain in Nicaragua
Ambassador and Consul-General: P. W. Summerscale (resides in San José).

Of Nicaragua in the USA (1627 New Hampshire Ave., NW, Washington, D.C., 20009)
Ambassador: Dr Carlos Tunnermann.

Of the USA in Nicaragua (Km. 4½ Carretera Sur., Managua)
Ambassador: Harry E. Bergold, Jr.

Of Nicaragua to the United Nations
Ambassador: Javier Chamorro Mora.

Books of Reference

Dirección General Estadística y Censos, *Boletín de Estadística* (irregular intervals); and *Indicadores Economicos.*
Black, G., *Triumph of the People: The Sandinista Revolution in Nicaragua.* London, 1981
Boletín de la Superintendencia de Bancos. Banco Central, Managua
Booth, J. A., *The End of the Beginning: The Nicaraguan Revolution.* Boulder, 1982
Rosset, P., and Vandermeer, J., (eds.) *The Nicaragua Reader: Documents of a Revolution under Fire.* New York, 1984
Walker, T. W., *Nicaragua: The Land of Sandino.* Boulder, 1982
Weber, H., *Nicaragua. The Sandinista Revolution.* London and New York, 1981
Woodward, R. L., *Nicaragua.* [Bibliography] Oxford and Santa Barbara, 1983

National Library: Biblioteca Nacional, Managua, D.N.

NIGER

Capital: Niamey
Population: 6·27m. (1984)
GNP per capita: US$330 (1981)

République du Niger

HISTORY. Niger was occupied by France between 1883 and 1899, and became a territory of French West Africa in 1904. It became an autonomous republic within the French Community on 18 Dec. 1958 and achieved full independence on 3 Aug. 1960.

On 15 April 1974 the first President, Hamani Diori, was overthrown in a military *coup* led by Lieut.-Col. Seyni Kountché, who suspended the constitution, dissolved the National Assembly and banned political groups.

AREA AND POPULATION. Niger is bounded north by Algeria and Libya, east by Chad, south by Nigeria, south-west by Benin and Burkina Faso, and west by Mali. Area, 1,186,408 sq. km (458,075 sq. miles), with a population at the 1977 census of 5,098,657. Estimate (1984) 6,265,000. The major towns (populations 1977) are: Niamey, the capital (225,314 inhabitants), Zinder (58,436), Maradi (45,852), Tahoua (31,265), Agadèz (20,475). Arlit (28,000), Akouta (26,000). The population is composed chiefly of Hausa (54%), Songhai and Djerma (23%), Fulani (10%), Beriberi-Manga (9%) and Tuareg (3%). The official language is French.

CLIMATE. Precipitation determines the geographical division into a southern zone of agriculture, a central zone of pasturage and a desert-like northern zone. The country lacks water, with the exception of the south-western districts, which are watered by the Niger and its tributaries, and the southern zone, where there are a number of wells. Niamey, 95°F (35°C). Annual rainfall varies from 22″ (560 mm) in the south to 7″ (180 mm) in the Sahara zone.

CONSTITUTION AND GOVERNMENT. The country is administered by a Supreme Military Council of 12 officers led by the President, who appoints a Council of Ministers to assist him. A system of elected Development Councils at all levels has been created, culminating in a 150-member National Development Council with limited legislative powers.

The Council of Ministers, in Sept. 1984, comprised:

Head of State, President of SMC, Defence and Interior: Maj.-Gen. Seyni Kountché.

Prime Minister: Hamid Algabid.

Ministers: Idé Oumarou *(Foreign Affairs and Co-operation)*, Boukari Adji *(Finance)*, Daouda Diallo *(Information)*, Issoufou Mayaki *(National Education)*, Annou Mahamane *(Planning)*, Amadou Nouhou *(Commerce and Transport)*, Salaou Barmou *(Posts and Telecommunications)*, Yahaya Tounkara *(Hydrology and Environment)*, Hadji Nadji *(Civil Service and Labour)* Sani Koutoubi *(Mines and Industry)*, Dr Ari Toubo Ibrahim *(Rural Development)*, Illa Maikassoua *(Higher Education and Research)*, Amadou Djibo *(Youth, Sports and Culture)*, Moumouni Yacouba *(Public Works and Town Planning)*, Dr Abdou Moudi *(Public Health and Social Affairs)*, al-Haji Allele Habibou *(Justice)*.

Minister-Delegate: Amadou Fity Maiga *(Interior)*.

Secretaries of State: Amadou Modieli *(National Education)*, al-Housseini Mouloul *(Planning)*, al-Moustapha Soumeila *(Commerce and Transport)*.

National flag: Three horizontal strips of orange, white and green, with an orange disc in the middle of the white strip.

Local government: Niger is divided into 7 *départements* (Agadez, Diffa, Dosso, Maradi, Niamey, Tahoua and Zinder), each under a prefect; they are sub-divided into 38 *arrondissements*, each under a sub-prefect and some 150 communes.

DEFENCE. Selective military service for 2 years operates.

Army. The Army consists of 2 armoured reconnaissance squadrons, 4 infantry, 1 engineer, 1 parachute and 1 support company. Equipment includes 10 M-8 and 30 ERC-60-20 armoured cars. Strength (1985) 2,150. There are additional paramilitary forces of some 2,500 men.

Air Force. The Air Force has 70 officers and men, 2 C-130H and 3 C-47 transports, 1 Boeing 737 VIP transport, 2 Cessna Skymasters, 3 Do 28D Skyservants and 1 Aero Commander 500 for communications duties.

INTERNATIONAL RELATIONS

Membership. Niger is a member of UN, OAU and is an ACP state of the EEC.

ECONOMY

Planning. The 5-year plan (1979–83) provided 116,400m. francs CFA for investment in the rural economy and francs CFA 70,000m. for mining, energy and industry.

Budget. The ordinary budget for 1983 balanced at 81,268m. francs CFA.

Currency. The unit of currency is the *franc CFA*, with a parity rate of 50 francs CFA to 1 French franc.

Banking. The *Banque Centrale des États de l'Afrique de l'Ouest* is the bank of issue, and there are 7 commercial banks in Niamey.

ENERGY AND NATURAL RESOURCES

Electricity. Production (1981) amounted to 60m. kwh.

Oil. Deposits in the Lake Chad area, located in 1978, are to be exploited.

Minerals. Large uranium deposits are mined at Arlit and Akouta, in the Aïr mountains of northern Niger, with French and Japanese assistance. Concentrate production (1981) 4,585 tonnes. Phosphates are mined in the Niger valley, and coal reserves are being exploited by open-cast mining. Salt and natron are produced at Manga and Agadez, tin ore in Aïr.

Agriculture. The chief agricultural products in 1982 (in 1,000 tonnes) were: Millet, 1,295; pulses, 305; sorghum, 357; cassava (1981), 225; sugar-cane, 130; in the river districts, cotton and rice (52,000 tonnes). Gum arabic is produced at Gouré, nearly all of which is exported to Nigeria.

Livestock (1983): Cattle, 3,521,000; horses, 283,000; asses, 501,000; sheep, 3,448,000; goats, 7,478,000; camels, 410,000; chickens, 11m.

INDUSTRY AND TRADE

Industry. Some small manufacturing industries, mainly in Niamey, produce textiles, food products, furniture and chemicals.

Trade Unions. The sole national body is the *Union Nationale des Travailleurs du Niger*, which has 15,000 members in 31 unions.

Commerce. Imports in 1982 were valued at 145,000m. francs CFA and exports at 109,000m. francs CFA. In 1981, France provided 36% of imports and took 36% of the exports. Main exports were uranium (79%) and livestock, 12%.

Total trade between Niger and UK (British Department of Trade returns, in £1,000 sterling):

	1980	*1981*	*1982*	*1983*	*1984*
Imports to UK	184	5,762	574	6,854	391
Exports and re-exports from UK	7,885	5,201	17,346	9,650	10,682

COMMUNICATIONS

Roads. In 1981 there were 8,547 km of roads. Niamey and Zinder are the termini of two trans-Sahara motor routes; the Hoggar–Aïr–Zinder road extends to Kano and the Tanezrouft-Gao-Niamey road to Benin. A 648-km 'uranium road' runs from Arlit to Niamey. There were (1980), 25,800 private cars and 4,400 commercial vehicles.

Shipping. Sea-going vessels can reach Niamey (300 km. inside the country) between Sept. and March.

Aviation. There are international airports at Niamey, Zinder and Maradi. Air Niger operates domestic services to over 20 other public airports.

Post and Broadcasting. There were (1978) 8,500 telephones. In Dec. 1982 there were 150,000 radio and 10,000 television receivers.

Cinemas. In 1970 there were 4 cinemas with a seating capacity of 3,800.

Newspapers. In 1984 there was 1 daily newspaper with a circulation of 3,000.

JUSTICE, RELIGION, EDUCATION AND WELFARE

Justice. There are Magistrates' and Assize Courts at Niamey, Zinder and Maradi, and justices of the peace in smaller centres. The Court of Appeal is at Niamey.

Religion. In 1979, 85% of the population was Moslem and the remainder mainly followed animist beliefs. There were about 20,000 Christians.

Education. There were, in 1979, 187,151 pupils and 4,762 teachers in primary schools, and, 45,846 (1981) and 866 teachers in secondary schools, 1,259 and 64 teachers in 4 teacher-training colleges, 354 students and 31 teachers in the technical school in Maradi. In 1982 there were 1,825 students and 273 teaching staff at the University of Niamey.

Health. In 1982 there were 2 hospitals, 36 medical centres and 116 dispensaries. In 1976 there were 110 doctors, 6 dentists, 8 pharmacists, 70 midwives and 575 nursing personnel.

DIPLOMATIC REPRESENTATIVES

Of Niger in Great Britain
Ambassador: Habou Saley (accredited 9 May 1984, resides in Paris).

Of Great Britain in Niger
Ambassador and Consul-General: J. M. Willson (resides in Abidjan).

Of Niger in the USA (2204 R. St., NW, Washington, D.C., 20008)
Ambassador: Joseph Diatta.

Of the USA in Niger (PO Box 11201, Niamey)
Ambassador: William R. Casey, Jr.

Of Niger to the United Nations
Ambassador: Arouna Mounkeila.

Books of Reference

Bonardi, P., *La République du Niger.* Paris, 1960
Fugelstad, F., *A History of Niger, 1850–1960.* OUP, 1984
Séré de Rivières, E., *Histoire du Niger.* Paris, 1965

NIGERIA

Capital: Lagos
Population: 82·39m. (1983)
GNP per capita: US$870 (1981)

Federal Republic of Nigeria

HISTORY. The Federal Republic comprises a number of areas formerly under separate administrations. Lagos, ceded in Aug. 1861 by King Dosunmu, was placed under the Governor of Sierra Leone in 1866. In 1874 it was detached, together with Gold Coast Colony, and formed part of the latter until Jan. 1886, when a separate 'colony and protectorate of Lagos' was constituted. Meanwhile the United African Company had established British interests in the Niger valley, and in July 1886 the company obtained a charter under the name of the Royal Niger Company. This company surrendered its charter to the Crown on 31 Dec. 1899, and on 1 Jan. 1900 the greater part of its territories was formed into the protectorate of Northern Nigeria. Along the coast the Oil Rivers protectorate had been declared in June 1885. This was enlarged and renamed the Niger Coast protectorate in 1893; and on 1 Jan. 1900, on its absorbing the remainder of the territories of the Royal Niger Company, it became the protectorate of Southern Nigeria. In Feb. 1906 Lagos and Southern Nigeria were united into the 'colony and protectorate of Southern Nigeria', and on 1 Jan. 1914 the latter was amalgamated with the protectorate of Northern Nigeria to form the 'colony and protectorate of Nigeria', under a Governor. On 1 Oct. 1954 Nigeria became a federation under a Governor-General.

On 1 Oct. 1960 Nigeria became sovereign and independent and a member of the Commonwealth and on 1 Oct. 1963 Nigeria became a republic.

For the history of Nigeria from 1961 to 1978, see THE STATESMAN'S YEAR BOOK, 1979–80, pp. 923-924.

AREA AND POPULATION. Nigeria is bounded north by Niger, east by Chad and Cameroon, south by the Gulf of Guinea and west by Benin. It has an area of 356,669 sq. miles (923,773 sq. km). Census population, Nov. 1963, 55,670,052. The results of the 1973 census have been officially repudiated. There is considerable uncertainty over the total population, but one estimate based on electoral registration in 1978 is 95m. Estimate (1983) 82·39m.

There are 19 states and a Federal Capital Territory:

States	*Area (in sq. km)*	*Population*	*States*	*Area (in sq. km)*	*Population*
Anambra	17,675	3,596,618	Kwara	66,869	1,714,485
Bauchi	64,605	2,431,296	Lagos	3,345	1,443,568
Bendel	35,500	2,460,962	Niger	65,037	1,194,508
Benue	45,174	2,427,017	Ogun	16,762	1,550,966
Borno	116,400	2,997,498	Ondo	20,959	2,729,690
Cross River	27,237	3,478,131	Oyo	37,705	5,208,884
Gongola	91,390	2,605,263	Plateau	58,030	2,026,657
Imo	11,850	3,672,654	Rivers	21,850	1,719,925
Kaduna	70,245	4,098,306	Sokoto	102,535	4,538,787
Kano	43,285	5,774,840			

See map in THE STATESMAN'S YEAR-BOOK, 1977–78.

The populations of the largest towns were (1975 estimate) as follows: Lagos, 1,060,848; and (in 1,000) Ibadan, 847; Ogbomosho, 432; Kano, 399; Oshogbo, 282; Ilorin, 282; Abeokuta, 253; Port Harcourt, 242; Zaria, 224; Ilesha, 224; Onitsha, 220; Iwo, 214, Ado Ekiti, 213; Kaduna, 202; Mushin, 197; Maiduguri, 189; Enugu, 187; Ede, 182; Aba, 177; Ife, 176; Ila, 155; Oyo, 152; Ikere Ekiti 145; Benin, 136; Iseyin, 129; Jos, 123; Katsina, 122; Ilobu, 122; Sokoto, 118; Offa, 117; Owo, 109; Shaki, 103; Calabar, 103, Ondo, 101.

It was announced in Feb. 1976 that the federal capital would be moved from Lagos to the Abuja area and, in Sept. 1982, Abuja was established as the future capital.

CLIMATE. Lying wholly within the tropics, temperatures everywhere are high. Rainfall varies very much, but decreases from the coast to the interior. The main rains occur from April to Oct. Lagos. Jan. 81°F (27·2°C), July 78°F (25·6°C). Annual rainfall 72″ (1,836 mm). Ibadan. Jan. 80°F (26·7°C), July 76°F (24·4°C). Annual rainfall 45″ (1,120 mm). Kano. Jan. 70°F (21·1°C), July 79°F (26·1°C). Annual rainfall 35″ (869 mm). Port Harcourt. Jan. 79°F (26·1°C), July 77°F (25°C). Annual rainfall 100″ (2,497 mm).

CONSTITUTION AND GOVERNMENT. Under the Constitution drafted and ratified in 1977–78, Nigeria is a sovereign, federal republic comprising 19 states and a federal capital district. Elections were held in Aug. 1983 and President Shagari was returned with 48% of the vote but in Dec. 1983 the military again took over control in a *coup* and on 3 Jan. 1984 a 18-member Supreme Military Council was sworn in.

The Supreme Military Council comprised in Jan. 1985:

Head of State and Government, Chairman of the SMC, and C.-in-C. of the Armed Forces: Maj.-Gen. Mohammed Buhari.

Chief of Staff: Brig. Tunde Idiagbon. *Minister of Defence:* Maj.-Gen. Domkat Yah Bali. *Chief of Army Staff:* Maj.-Gen. Ibrahim Babangida. *Chief of Naval Staff:* Cmdre. Augustine Aikomo. *Chief of Air Force Staff:* Air Vice-Marshal Ibrahim Alfa. *Minister for Federal Capital Territory:* Maj.-Gen. Mamman Vatsa. *Internal Affairs:* Brig. Mohammed Magoro. *Insp.-Gen. of Police:* Col. Salihu Ibrahim James Etim Nyang. *Director-Gen. of Nigeria Security Organisation:* Mohammed Rafindadi. *Attorney-General and Justice:* Chibe Offodile. *Other Members of the Council:* Brig. Sanni Abacha, Brig. Ola Oni, Brig. M. J. Nasco, Brig. Y. Y. Kure, Brig. Paul Omu, Capt. Ebelo Ukiwe, Air Cmdre. L. Koinyan.

The Federal Executive Council, appointed by the SMC, comprised in Jan. 1985 the four Ministers mentioned above and 14 other Ministers:

External Affairs: Dr I. A. Gambari. *Communications:* Lieut.-Col. A. Abdullahi. *Employment, Labour and Productivity:* Brig. S. A. Omojokun. *Information, Social Development, Youth, Sports and Culture:* Group-Capt. Samson Emeka Omeruah. *Health:* Dr Emmanuel Nyong Nsan. *Finance:* Dr Onaolapo Soleye. *Planning:* Chief M. S. Adigun. *Works and Housing:* Ibrahim Yarima Abdullahi. *Education, Science and Technology:* Abdullahi Ibrahim. *Agriculture, Water Resources and Rural Development:* Dr B. Shaib. *Transport and Aviation:* Cmdre. Patrick S. Koshoni. *Commerce and Industry:* Dr M. Tukur. *Mines, Power and Steel:* A. R. Lukman. *Petroleum and Energy:* T. David-West.

The official language is English but Hausa, Igbo and Yoruba languages are also used in the National Assembly, *i.e.* the Senate and the House of Representatives as well as in each of the State Houses of Assembly.

National flag: Three vertical strips of green, white, green.

Local Government: Each of the 19 states is administered by a military governor, who appoints and presides over a State Executive Council. The creation of further states by sub-division is under consideration.

DEFENCE

Army. The Army consists of 1 armoured division, 2 mechanized divisions and 1 airborne and amphibious forces division, each with supporting artillery, engineer and reconnaissance units, and 1 Guards brigade. Equipment includes 65 T-55 and Vickers Mk 3 main battle tanks. Strength (1985) 120,000 men.

Navy. The Nigerian Navy was established in 1958. It comprises the frigates *Aradu* (completed in the Federal Republic of Germany in 1982) and *Obuma* (*ex*-Nigeria) acting as training ship (completed in the Netherlands in 1965), 4 corvettes built in

Britain in 1970–72 (*Dorina* and *Otobo*), and 1975–80 (*Erinmi* and *Enyimiri*), 6 fast missile-armed attack vedettes (3 built in France and 3 in FR Germany), 9 patrol craft, 15 coastal patrol boats, 2 tank landing ships, 2 utility landing craft, 1 survey ship, 1 training ship, 60 launches and 5 tugs. There are also 80 small patrol launches operated by the Nigerian Police. Naval personnel in 1985 totalled 550 officers and 4,500 ratings.

Air Force. The Nigerian Air Force was established in Jan. 1964. Pilots were trained initially in Canada, India and Ethiopia. The Air Force was built up subsequently with the aid of a Federal Republic of Germany mission; much first-line equipment has since been received from the Soviet Union. It has 18 MiG-21 supersonic jet-fighters, 18 Jaguar attack aircraft and MiG-21U fighter-trainers, and 24 Alpha Jet light attack/trainers. Two F27 Maritime twin-turboprop aircraft are used for maritime patrol. About 20 BO 105 twin-turbine helicopters have been acquired from the Federal Republic of Germany for search and rescue. Transport units operate 9 C-130H-30 and C-130H Hercules 4-turboprop heavy transports, 5 twin-turboprop Aeritalia G222s and 5 F.27s, a Boeing 727, a Gulfstream II and a Fokker F.28 Fellowship twin-turbofan airliner for VIP use, 18 Dornier 128-6 twin-turboprop utility aircraft, 2 Navajos and a Navajo Chieftain. Training types include 30 Bulldog primary trainers and about 12 MB 339 jets for instrument training, transport and ambulance duties. Five heavy-lift CH-47C Chinooks, 13 medium-lift Aérospatiale Pumas and a few light helicopters are also in service. Personnel (1984) total about 8,000.

INTERNATIONAL RELATIONS

Membership. Nigeria is a member of UN, the Commonwealth, ECOWAS, OAU, OPEC and is an ACP state of EEC.

ECONOMY

Planning. The fourth plan (1981–85) was launched in 1981 but was rescheduled because of lower oil prices.

Budget. The 1984 budget provided for expenditure (capital and recurrent) of ₦10,100m. and revenue of ₦11,331m. (69% from oil revenues).

Currency. Since 1 Jan. 1973 a decimal currency has been issued by the Central Bank of Nigeria, consisting of *Naira* (₦) and divided into 100 *kobo* (k). Notes in circulation ₦20, ₦10, ₦5, ₦1, 50k. Coins, 25k, 10k, 5k, 1k, ½k.

In March 1985, £1 = ₦1·13; US$1 = ₦0·86.

Banking. There are 20 commercial banks including the First Bank of Nigeria (formerly Standard), Union Bank of Nigeria (formerly Barclays) and the United Bank of Africa. Eleven of the banks are indigenous. There are 3 merchant banks and 3 government-owned development banks in addition to the Post Office Savings Bank. In 1976 the Government took a 60% shareholding in all foreign banks.

Weights and Measures. The metric system is in force.

ENERGY AND NATURAL RESOURCES

Electricity. The National Electric Power Authority generated 7,260m. kwh. in 1981. The Niger dams at Kainji were completed in early 1969 (investment of £87m.) and provide cheap hydro-electricity for rapid industrialization.

Oil. There are refineries at Port Harcourt, Warri and at Kaduna. Oil represents 95% of exports. Production, 1983, 1·29m. bbls. per day.

Gas. Natural gas is being used at electric power stations at Afam and Ughelli. Reserves: 1,422,000m. cu.metres.

Minerals. Production: Tin, 1980, 2,527 tonnes; columbite, 1977 (the world's largest producer), 800 tonnes; coal (1981) 114,875 tonnes. There are large deposits of iron ore, coal (reserves estimate 245m. tonnes), lead and zinc. There are small quantities of gold and uranium.

Agriculture. Groundnuts, cotton and soybean come mainly or wholly from the north, palm produce, cocoa, timber and rubber from the south. Tobacco is grown in commercial quantities. Production (estimates) 1981 were (in tonnes): Groundnuts (unshelled), 580,000; cocoa, 160,000; cereals, 9·9m. In 1981, the National Rice Production Scheme was launched; production (1981), about 75,000 tons from 66,000 hectares.

Livestock (1983). There were 12·3m. cattle, 12·85m. sheep, 26·3m. goats, 1·3m. pigs and 150m. poultry.

Forestries. There are plywood factories at Epe, Sapele and Calabar, and numerous saw-mills. The most important timber species include mahogany, iroko, obeche, abwa, ebony and camwood.

Fisheries. The total catch (1981) was 496,200 tonnes.

INDUSTRY AND TRADE

Industry. There were more than 2,000 industrial establishments in 1982. Timber and hides and skins are major export commodities. Industrial products include soap, cigarettes, beer, margarine, groundnut oil, meat and cake, concentrated fruit juices, soft drinks, canned food, metal containers, ply-wood, textiles, ceramic products and cement (3m. tonnes, 1985). Of growing importance is the local assembly of motor vehicles, bicycles, radio equipment, electrical goods and sewing machines. In 1982, the Delta Steel Plant opened at Ovwian—Aladja.

Under a decree on indigenization Nigerians must have a minimum of 40% shareholding in all foreign enterprises.

Trade Unions. All trade unions were dissolved in 1976 and 42 new unions, each organized around a particular occupation, have since been created.

Commerce. There is a great deal of internal commerce in local foodstuffs and imported goods moving by rail, lorry and pack animals overland, and by launches, rafts and canoes along an extensive and complex network of inland waterways. Kano is still, as it has been for centuries, the focus of caravan routes linking a territory which stretches from the Sudan in the east to Senegal in the west, with branches northwards across the Sahara.

Total trade in ₦m. for 4 years:

	1981	*1982*	*1983*	*1984*
Imports (c.i.f.)	11,300	11,300	8,500	7,200
Exports and re-exports (f.o.b.)	10,900	8,700	7,500	8,700

Total trade between Nigeria and UK (according to British Department of Trade returns, in £1,000 sterling):

	1980	*1981*	*1982*	*1983*	*1984*
Imports to UK	151,563	95,069	356,802	387,975	375,796
Exports and re-exports from UK	1,204,358	1,428,018	1,225,164	798,276	768,449

Tourism. There were 114,000 foreign visitors in 1976.

COMMUNICATIONS

Roads (1980). There were 108,000 km of maintained roads.

In 1980, 633,268 vehicles were registered. Bus services, by private owners, operate in the larger towns and between the main towns in southern Nigeria, but the bulk of passenger and goods traffic by road is carried in lorries (mammy wagons).

Railways. There are 3,505 route-km of line 1,067 mm gauge, which in 1983 carried 1·7m. tonnes of freight and 12·9m. passengers.

Aviation. There is an extensive system of internal and international air routes, serving Europe, USA, Middle East and South and West Africa. Regular services are operated by Nigerian Airways (WAAC), British Caledonian, UTA, KLM, SABENA, Swissair, PANAM and other lines. In 1981, 2·3m. passengers were carried on domestic and international routes.

Shipping. The principal ports are Lagos, Port Harcourt, Warri and Calabar.

Post and Broadcasting. Postal facilities are provided at 1,667 offices and agencies; telegraph, money order and savings bank services are provided at 280 of these. Most internal letter mail is carried by air at normal postage rates. External telegraph services are owned and operated by Nigerian External Telecommunications, Ltd, at Lagos, from which telegraphic communication is maintained with all parts of the world. There were 708,390 telephones in use in 1982, of which 249,150 were in Lagos and 33,138 in Ibadan. There is also a telex service.

Federal and some state governments have established commercial corporations for sound and television broadcasting, which are widely used in schools. In 1983 there were 5·6m. radio and 455,000 television receivers.

Cinemas (1974). There were 120 cinemas, with a seating capacity of 60,000. Mobile cinemas are used by the Federal and States Information Services.

Newspapers. In 1983 there were 24 daily newspapers. The aggregate circulation is about 1m., of which the *Daily Times* (Lagos) has about 400,000. (Another 2 dailies were published in Lagos, 4 in Ikeja, 3 in Enugu, and 4 in Ibadan.)

JUSTICE, RELIGION, EDUCATION AND WELFARE

Justice. The highest court is the Federal Supreme Court, which consists of the Chief Justice of the Republic, and up to 15 Justices appointed by SMC. It has original jurisdiction in any dispute between the Federal Republic and any State or between States; and to hear and determine appeals from the Federal Court of Appeal, which acts as an intermediate appellate Court to consider appeals from the High Court.

High Courts, presided over by a Chief Justice, are established in each state. All judges are appointed by the SMC. Magistrates' courts are established throughout the Republic, and customary law courts in southern Nigeria. In each of the northern States of Nigeria there are the Sharia Court of Appeal and the Court of Resolution. Moslem Law has been codified in a Penal Code and is applied through Alkali courts.

Religion. Moslems, 48%; Christians, 34% (17% Protestants and 17% Roman Catholic); others, 18%. Northern Nigeria is mainly Moslem; Southern Nigeria is predominantly Christian and Western Nigeria is evenly divided between Christians, Moslems and animists.

Education. In 1976 primary education became free throughout the country. Literacy rate (1973) 25%.

In 1979 there were 12·6m. primary school pupils, and 1·9m. secondary school pupils.

Teacher-training institutions totalled 157 in 1973. There were also 67 trade centres and vocational training institutes for sub-professional technicians and tradesmen.

There are 24 universities in Nigeria, providing 3–5-year courses leading to the award of a first degree in various disciplines; these include 7 Federal Universities of Technology. There are also opportunities for taking higher degrees. Free tuition was provided from 1977. The total number of students (1982–83) was 88,636 in universities and 53,766 in polytechnics.

Health. Most tropical diseases are endemic to Nigeria. Blindness, yaws, leprosy, sleeping sickness, worm infections, malaria are major health problems which, however, are yielding to remedial and preventative measures. In co-operation with the World Health Organization river blindness and malaria are being tackled on a large scale, while annual campaigns are undertaken against the danger of smallpox epidemics. Dispensaries and travelling dispensaries are found in most parts of the country.

The teaching hospital at Lagos University has 350 beds; there is also a nursing school and a teaching hospital at Ibadan University. There are medical courses at Ahmadu Bello University, University of Ife, Benin University and at Nsukka.

DIPLOMATIC REPRESENTATIVES

Of Nigeria in Great Britain (9 Northumberland Ave., London, WC2N 5BX)
High Commissioner: Maj.-Gen. H. A. Hananiya (accredited 15 June 1984).

Of Great Britain in Nigeria (11 Eleke Cres., Victoria Island, Lagos)
High Commissioner: (Vacant).

Of Nigeria in the USA (2201 M. St., NW, Washington, D.C., 20037)
Ambassador: Ignatius C. Olisemeka.

Of the USA in Nigeria (2 Eleke Cres., Lagos)
Ambassador: Thomas W. M. Smith.

Of Nigeria to the United Nations
Ambassador: Maj.-Gen. Joseph N. Garba.

Books of Reference

Nigeria Digest of Statistics. Lagos, 1951 ff. (quarterly)
Annual Abstract of Statistics. Federal Office of Statistics. Lagos, 1960 ff.
Nigeria Trade Journal. Federal Ministry of Commerce and Industries (quarterly)
Barbour, K. M. (ed.), *Nigeria in Maps.* London, 1982
Blitz, F. (ed.), *The Politics and Administration of Nigerian Government.* Lagos and London, 1965
Comhaire, J., *Le Nigeria et ses populations.* Brussels, 1981.
Kirk-Greene, A., and Rimmer, D., *Nigeria since 1970.* London, 1981
Luckham, R., *The Nigerian Military: A Sociological Analysis of Authority and Revolt, 1960–67.* CUP, 1971
Nnoli, O., *Path to Nigerian Development.* Dakar, 1981
Nwabueze, B. O., *The Presidential Constitution of Nigeria.* Lagos and London, 1982
Olaloku, F. A., (ed.) *Structure of the Nigerian Economy.* London, 1980
Oyediran, O., *Nigerian Government and Politics under Military Rule, 1966–1979.* New York, 1980
Panter-Brick, S. K., *Nigerian Politics and Military Rule: Prelude to Civil War.* London, 1970.—*Soldiers and Oil.* London, 1978
Shaw, T. M., and Aluko, O., *Nigerian Foreign Policy: Alternative Perceptions and Projections.* London, 1984
Simmons, M., and Obe, O. A., *Nigerian Handbook 1982–83.* London, 1982
Tijjani, A. and Williams, D., (eds.) *Shehu Shagari: My Vision of Nigeria.* London, 1981
Van Apeldoorn, G. J., *Perspectives on Drought and Famine in Nigeria.* London, 1981
Williams, D., *President and Power in Nigeria.* London, 1982
Zartman, I. W., *The Political Economy of Nigeria.* New York, 1983

NORWAY

Capital: Oslo
Population: 4·1m. (1983)
GNP per capita: US$12,923 (1983)

Kongeriket Norge

HISTORY. By the Treaty of 14 Jan. 1814 Norway was ceded to the King of Sweden by the King of Denmark, but the Norwegian people declared themselves independent and elected Prince Christian Frederik of Denmark as their king. The foreign Powers refused to recognize this election, and on 14 Aug. a convention proclaimed the independence of Norway in a personal union with Sweden. This was followed on 4 Nov. by the election of Karl XIII (II) as King of Norway. Norway declared this union dissolved, 7 June 1905, and Sweden agreed to the repeal of the union on 26 Oct. 1905. The throne was offered to a prince of the reigning house of Sweden, who declined. After a plebiscite, Prince Carl of Denmark was formally elected King on 18 Nov. 1905, and took the name of Haakon VII.

Norwegian Sovereigns

Inge Baardssøn	1204	Erik of Pomerania	1389
Haakon Haakonssøn	1217	Kristofer af Bavaria	1442
Magnus Lagabøter	1263	Karl Knutssøn	1449
Eirik Magnussøn	1280	Same Sovereigns as in Denmark	1450–1814
Haakon V Magnussøn	1299	Christian Frederik	1814
Magnus Erikssøn	1319	Same Sovereigns as in Sweden	1814–1905
Haakon VI Magnussøn	1355	Haakon VII	1905
Olav Haakonssøn	1381	Olav V	1957
Margrete	1388		

AREA AND POPULATION. Norway is bounded north by the Arctic ocean, east by the USSR, Finland and Sweden, south by the Skagerrak Straits and west by the North Sea.

Fylker (counties)	*Area (sq. km)*	*Census population 1 Nov. 1980*	*Population 1 Jan. 1984*	*Pop. per sq km (total area) 1984*
Oslo (City)	471·0	452,023	447,257	985·1
Akershus	4,916·4	369,193	380,258	77·3
Østfold	4,183·4	233,301	234,938	56·2
Hedmark	27,388·3	187,223	187,475	6·8
Oppland	25,259·6	180,765	182,440	7·2
Buskerud	14,933·2	214,571	218,462	14·6
Vestfold	2,215·8	186,691	189,394	85·5
Telemark	15,315·3	162,050	162,153	10·6
Aust-Agder	9,211·8	90,629	93,603	10·2
Vest-Agder	7,280·3	136,718	139,141	19·1
Rogaland	9,140·6	305,490	316,534	34·6
Hordaland	15,633·7	391,463	396,222	25·3
Sogn og Fjordane	18,633·5	105,924	106,049	5·7
Møre og Romsdal	15,104·2	236,062	237,548	15·7
Sør Trøndelag	18,831·4	244,760	246,289	13·1
Nord-Trøndelag	22,463·3	125,835	127,051	5·7
Nordland	38,327·1	244,493	244,638	6·4
Troms	25,953·9	146,818	147,679	5·7
Finnmark	48,637·3	78,331	77,226	1·6
Mainland total	323,883·1 [1]	4,092,340	4,134,353	12·8

Svalbard and Jan Mayen have an area of 63,080 sq. km. Persons staying on Svalbard and Jan Mayen are registered as residents of their home Norwegian municipality.

[1] 125,051 sq. miles

On 1 Nov. 1980, 2,874,990 persons lived in densely populated areas and 1,197,939 in sparsely populated areas.

Population of the principal towns at 1 Jan. 1984:

Oslo	447,257	Sandnes	38,959	Halden	26,050
Bergen	207,332	Sandefjord	35,073	Gjøvik	25,990
Trondheim	134,143	Ålesund	35,095	Moss	24,881
Stavanger	92,883	Bodø	33,795	Lillehammer	22,092
Kristiansand	61,704	Porsgrunn	31,321	Harstad	21,851
Drammen	50,809	Fredrikstad	27,264	Molde	21,148
Tromsø	47,406	Haugesund	27,042	Steinkjer	20,654
Skien	46,693	Ringerike	26,797	Kongsberg	20,720

Vital statistics for calendar years:

	Marriages	*Divorces*	*Births*	*Still-born*	*Illegitimate* [1]	*Deaths*
1980	22,230	6,634	51,039	363	7,392	41,340
1981	22,271	7,136	50,708	299	8,169	41,893
1982	21,706	7,165	51,245	324	9,041	41,454
1983	20,803	7,668	49,937	303	9,616	42,177

[1] Excluding still-born.

CLIMATE. There is considerable variation in the climate because of the extent of latitude, the topography and the varying effectiveness of prevailing westerly winds and the Gulf Stream. Winters along the whole west coast are exceptionally mild but precipitation is considerable. Oslo. Jan. 25°F (–3·9°C), July 63°F (17°C). Annual rainfall 27″ (683 mm). Bergen. Jan. 35°F (1·5°C), July 61°F (16·1°C). Annual rainfall 78·3″ (1,958 mm). Trondheim. Jan. 26°F (–3·5°C), July 57°F (14°C). Annual rainfall 32·1″ (870 mm).

REIGNING KING. Olav V, born 2 July 1903, married on 21 March 1929 to Princess Märtha of Sweden (born 28 March 1901, died 5 April 1954), daughter of the late Prince Carl (son of King Oscar II). He succeeded on the death of his father, King Haakon VII, on 21 Sept. 1957. *Offspring:* Princess Ragnhild Alexandra, born 9 June 1930 (married, 1953, Hr. Erling Lorentzen); Princess Astrid Maud Ingeborg, born 12 Feb. 1932 (married, 12 Jan. 1961, Hr. Johan Martin Ferner); Crown Prince Harald, born 21 Feb. 1937, married, 29 Aug. 1968, Sonja Haraldsen. *Offspring:* Princess Märtha Louise, born 22 Sept. 1971; Prince Haakon Magnus, born 20 July 1973.

CONSTITUTION AND GOVERNMENT. Norway is a constitutional and hereditary monarchy. The royal succession is in direct male line in the order of primogeniture. In default of male heirs the King may propose a successor to the Storting, but this assembly has the right to nominate another, if it does not agree with the proposal.

The Constitution, voted by the constituent assembly at Eidsvoll on 17 May 1814 and modified at various times, vests the legislative power of the realm in the Storting (Parliament). The royal veto may be exercised; but if the same Bill passes two Stortings formed by separate and subsequent elections it becomes the law of the land without the assent of the sovereign. The King has the command of the land, sea and air forces, and makes all appointments.

Since June 1938 all branches of the Government service, including the state church, are open to women.

National flag: Red with a blue white-bordered Scandinavian cross.

National anthem: Ja, vi elsker dette landet (words by B. Bjørnson, 1865; tune by R. Nordraak, 1865).

The Storting assembles every year. The meetings take place *suo jure*, and not by any writ from the King or the executive. They begin on the first weekday in Oct. each year, until June the following year. Every Norwegian subject of 18 years of age is entitled to vote, unless he is disqualified for a special cause. Women are, since 1913, entitled to vote under the same conditions as men. The mode of election is direct and the method of election is proportional. The country is divided into 19 districts, each electing from 4 to 15 representatives.

At the elections for the Storting held in 1981 the following parties were elected: Labour, 66; Conservative, 53; Centre Party, 11; Christian Democratic Party, 15; Socialist Left Party, 4; Party of Progress, 4, and Liberal, 2.

The Storting, when assembled, divides itself by election into the *Lagting* and the *Odelsting*. The former is composed of one-fourth of the members of the Storting, and the other of the remaining three-fourths. Each Ting (the Storting, the Odelsting and the Lagting) nominates its own president. Most questions are decided by the Storting, but questions relating to legislation must be considered and decided by the Odelsting and the Lagting separately. Only when the Odelsting and the Lagting disagree, the Bill has to be considered by the Storting in plenary sitting, and a new law can then only be decided by a majority of two-thirds of the voters. The same majority is required for alterations of the Constitution, which can only be decided by the Storting in plenary sitting. The Storting elects 5 delegates, whose duty it is to revise the public accounts. The Lagting and the ordinary members of the Supreme Court of Justice (the *Høyesterett*) form a High Court of the Realm (the *Riksrett*) for the trial of ministers, members of the *Høyesterett* and members of the Storting. The impeachment before the *Riksrett* can only be decided by the Odelsting.

The executive is represented by the King, who exercises his authority through the Cabinet or Council of State *(Statsråd)*, composed of a Prime Minister (*Statsminster*) and (at present) 17 ministers *(Statsråder)*. The ministers are entitled to be present in the Storting and to take part in the discussions, but without a vote.

A Conservative Government was formed and took office on 14 Oct. 1981; after 16 Sept. 1983 the members of the Government were:

Prime Minister: Kåre Willoch.

Foreign Affairs: Svenn Stray. *Finance:* Rolf Presthus. *Defence:* Anders C. Sjaastad. *Agriculture:* Finn T. Isaksen. *Commerce and Shipping:* Asbjørn Haugstvedt. *Justice:* Mona Røkke. *Ecclesiastical Affairs and Education:* Kjell Magne Bondevik. *Culture:* Lars Roar Langslet. *Local Government and Labour:* Arne Rettedal. *Industry:* Jan P. Syse. *Communications:* Johan J. Jakobsen. *Environment:* Rakel S. Surlien. *Social Affairs:* Leif Arne Heløe. *Consumer Affairs and Government Administration:* Astrid Gjertsen. *Fisheries:* Thor Listau. *Oil and Energy:* Kåre Kristiansen. *Development Co-operation:* Reidun Brusletten.

The official languages are Bokmål (or Riksmål) and Nynorsk (or Landsmål).

Local Government. For the purposes of administration the country is divided into 19 counties *(fylker)*, in each of which the central government is represented by a county governor *(fylkesmannen)*. In addition, there are 47 urban districts *(bykommuner)* and 407 rural districts *(herredskommuner)*, each of which usually corresponds in size to a parish *(prestegjeld)*. The districts are administered by district councils *(kommunestyrer)*, whose membership may vary between 13 and 85 councillors, and by a committee *(formannskap)* which is elected by and from the members of the council. The council is four times the size of the committee. The council elects a chairman and a vice-chairman from among the committee members.

Each of the 18 counties forms a county district *(fylkeskommune)*, while the remaining one, Oslo, comprises an urban district. The supreme authority in a county district is the county council *(fylkesting)*. The members of the county council are elected directly by the electors of the county and the number of representatives varies between 25 and 85. In a county district the county committee *(fylkesutvalg)* occupies a position corresponding to that of the committee *(formannskap)* in the primary districts. The county committee is elected by and from among the members of the county council. The number of county committee members is one-fourth of the membership of the county council, but must be not more than 15. The county council elects from among the members of the county committee a county sheriff *(fylkesordfører)* and a deputy sheriff.

DEFENCE. Service is universal and compulsory, liability in peace-time commencing at the age of 19 and continuing till the age of 44. The training period in the Army is 12 months, in the Navy and Air Force, 15 months. The Norwegian Defence forces are organized into 2 integrated regional commands.

Army. In Northern Command the largest standing element is Brigade North. There are also 2 infantry battalions and 2 tank companies in the North. Southern Command comprises 1 infantry battalion, 1 tank company and 1 self-propelled field artillery battery. Equipment includes 78 Leopard I and 38 M-48A5 main battle tanks. Strength (1985) 24,200 (including 18,300 conscripts). Reserves number 122,000.

Navy. The Navy consists of the coastal batteries and other static defence systems and the following naval units: 14 coastal submarines, 5 small frigates, 2 minelayers, 1 submarine parent ship, 2 corvettes, 39 fast missile craft, 8 fast torpedo boats, 1 patrol vessel, 9 coastal minesweepers, 1 minehunter, 1 controlled minelayer, 2 coastal patrol boats, 1 research ship, 2 diving tenders, 7 coastal transports, 1 torpedo recovery vessel, 2 training craft, 7 landing craft, 2 tugs and the royal yacht.

Personnel in 1985 totalled 8,750 officers and ratings including 2,000 in the Coast Artillery. Reserves number 25,000.

Coastguard. The Coastguard was established in 1977 within the framework of the Armed Forces. Main tasks are Fishery Protection and Economic Zone Patrol. The Coastguard assists other government agencies in rescue service, environment, surveillance and police duties. It comprises 3 frigate-size monitors each equipped with a Lynx helicopter, 3 corvette type cutters, 7 armed trawlers (chartered until construction of patrol vessels), 12 survey and 8 inspection vessels.

Air Force. The Royal Norwegian Air Force consists of 3 squadrons of F-16 Fighting Falcons, 2 squadrons of F-5 fighter-bombers, 1 maritime patrol squadron of P-3B Orions, 1 squadron of C-130H Hercules transports and Jet Falcons equipped for EW duties, 1 squadron with Twin Otter light transports and UH-1B helicopters, 2 squadrons of UH-1B. Ground based air defence forces deploy 4 Nike surface-to-air missile batteries and several light anti-aircraft artillery units. Hawk missiles provide area and airfield defence. Ten Westland Sea King helicopters are used for search and rescue duties; 6 Lynx helicopters are operated for the Coast Guard.

Total strength (1985) is more than 10,000 personnel, including 4,700 conscripts.

Home Guard. The Home Guard is organized in small units equipped and trained for special tasks. Service after basic training is 1 week a year. The total strength is approximately 90,000.

INTERNATIONAL RELATIONS

Membership. Norway is a member of UN, NATO, EFTA, OECD, the Council of Europe and the Nordic Council.

ECONOMY

Budget. Current revenue and expenditure for years ending 31 Dec. (in 1,000 kroner):

	1979	*1980*	*1981*	*1982*	*1983*	*1984* [1]
Revenue	61,112,000	82,938,000	100,924,000	110,539,000	119,762,000	122,023,000
Expenditure	67,373,000	80,054,000	91,629,000	100,898,000	100,250,000	109,905,000

[1] Voted budget.

National debt [1] for years ending 31 Dec. (in 1,000 kroner):

1975	41,082,800	1978	86,556,000	1981	107,662,000
1976	50,290,300	1979	103,605,000	1982	103,799,400
1977	66,786,000	1980	106,908,000	1983	92,406,100

[1] At the rate of par on foreign loans: including treasury bills (in 1m. kroner) which amounted to 6,000 in 1978; 9,600 in 1979; 14,600 in 1980, 17,200 in 1981, 13,880 in 1982 and 13,400 in 1983.

Currency. The Norwegian *krone*, of 100 øre, is of the value of about 11 *kroner* to £1 sterling. National bank-notes of 10, 50, 100, 500 and 1,000 *kroner* are legal means of payment. March 1985, US$1 = 9·79 *kroner*; £1 = 10·31 *kroner*.

On 31 Aug. 1984 the nominal value of the coin in circulation was 1,016m. kroner; notes in circulation, 20,809m. kroner.

Banking. The Bank of Norway is a joint-stock bank; in 1949 the state acquired all the shares hitherto privately owned. The bank is governed by laws enacted by the State, and its directors are elected by the Storting, except the president and vice-president of the head office, who are nominated by the King. It is the only bank of issue.

At the end of 1983 there were 22 private joint-stock banks. Their total amount of capital and funds was 6,621m. kroner (capital 3,546m., funds 3,075m.). Deposits amounted to 127,184m. kroner, of which 29,976m. kroner were at call and notice, and 97,208m. kroner on time.

The number of savings banks at the end of 1983 was 235. The total amount of funds of the savings banks amounted to 6,345m. kroner, and total deposits 96,810m. kroner, of which 20,572m. kroner were at call and notice and 76,238m. kroner on time.

Weights and Measures. The metric system of weights and measures has been obligatory since 1875.

ENERGY AND NATURAL RESOURCES

Electricity. Norway is a large producer of hydro-electric energy. The potential total hydro-electric power, for a whole year at regulated minimum water flow and by 82% efficiency, is estimated at 15m. kw. or about 131,000m. kwh. annually. About 60% of the water power suitable for development consists of waterfalls with a height of at least 900 ft.

By the end of 1982 the capacity of the installations for production of thermo-electric energy amounted to only 247 mw. On 31 Dec. 1982, the total capacity of generators (of hydro-electric plants) was 26·03m. kva.

In 1982 the total production of electricity amounted to 93,156m. kwh. of which 99·7% was produced by hydro-electric plants.

Most of the electricity is used for industrial purposes, especially by the chemical and basic metal industries for production of nitrate of calcium and other nitrogen products, carbide, ferrosilicon and other ferro-alloys, aluminium and zinc. The paper and pulp industries are also big consumers of electricity.

Oil. In 1963 sovereignty was proclaimed over the Norwegian continental shelf and in 1966 the first exploration well was drilled. By 1982 production was 7 times the domestic consumption of petroleum and is valued at about 17% of the GNP. Production (1983) 30m. tonnes.

Minerals. Production and value of the chief concentrates, metals and alloys were:

	1981		*1982*	
Concentrates and minerals	*Tonnes*	*1,000 kroner*	*Tonnes*	*1,000 kroner*
Copper concentrates	110,550	180,490	107,448	185,257
Pyrites	435,493	36,684	425,251	41,254
Titanium ore	659,604	...	551,764	...
Zinc and lead concentrates	61,610	97,286	67,292	122,548
Metals and alloys				
Copper	31,951	...	24,358	...
Nickel	36,954	...	25,833	
Aluminium	633,585	4,749,804	638,091	4,826,972
Ferro-alloys	778,612	2,119,754	730,229	...
Pig-iron	586,584	...	456,490	...
Zinc	80,279	...	72,016	...
Lead and tin	189	...	88	...

Agriculture. Norway, including Svalbard and Jan Mayen, is a barren and mountainous country. The arable soil is found in comparatively narrow strips, gathered in deep and narrow valleys and around fiords and lakes. Large, continuous tracts fit for cultivation do not exist. Of the total area, 79·3% is unproductive, 18% productive forest and 2·6% under cultivation.

Principal crops	Area[1] (hectares) 1981	1982	1983	Produce[1] (tonnes) 1981	1982	1983
Wheat	12,850	16,690	23,270	57,600	75,500	96,800
Rye	880	700	1,000	2,900	2,200	3,400
Barley	176,130	169,530	181,160	607,400	623,300	569,400
Oats	126,060	133,550	119,260	464,000	495,100	400,700
Mixed corn	480	510	650	2,000	1,800	2,600
Potatoes	20,680	21,140	21,100	454,000	476,000	433,500
Hay	411,250	417,370	421,980	2,859,700	2,808,000	2,936,500

Livestock, 1983[1]: 14,900 horses, 975,100 cattle (380,600 milch cows), 2,272,100 sheep, 72,100 goats, 705,200 pigs, 3,582,800 hens.

Fur production in 1983–84 was as follows (1982–83 in brackets): Silver fox, 53,600 (32,000); silver-blue fox, 54,600 (17,000); blue fox, 321,000 (395,000); mink, 620,000 (737,000).

[1] Holdings with at least 5 decares agricultural area in use.

Forestry. The area covered with productive forests is 66,600 sq. km. About 81% of this consists of conifers and 19% of broadleaves. Forests in public ownership cover 8,470 sq. km of productive area. Between 1973–74 and 1983–84 an annual average of 8·3m. cu. metres was cut for sale: 8·1m. for industrial use, 0·2m. for fuel. Of industrial use, 4·5m. cu. metres in the lumber industry, 3m. as pulp, 200,000 as particle board. About 800,000 cu. metres are consumed annually on farms. The annual increment (estimate, 1982) is about 16m. cu. metres.

Fisheries. The total number of registered fishermen in 1983 was 28,305, of whom 5,916 had another chief occupation. In 1983, the number of fishing vessels (all with motor) was 26,045, and of these, 17,077 were open boats.

The value of sea fisheries in 1m. kroner in 1983 was: Cod, 1,304; capelin, 634; mackerel, 122; coal-fish (saithe), 551; deep-water prawn, 434; haddock, 148; herring, 82; dogfish, 12. The catch totalled in 1983, 2·6m. tons, valued at 3,982m. kroner.

From 1 Jan. 1977 Norway established an economic zone of 200 nautical miles, and from 3 June 1977 a fishery protection zone of 200 nautical miles around Svalbard.

INDUSTRY AND TRADE

Industry. Industry is chiefly based on raw materials produced within the country (wood, fish, etc.) and on water power, of which the country possesses a large amount. Crude petroleum and natural gas production, the manufacture of paper and paper products, industrial chemicals and basic metals are the most important export manufactures. In the following table are given figures for industrial establishments in 1982, excluding one-man units. Electrical plants, construction and building industry are not included. The values are given in 1m. kroner.

Industries	Establishments	Number of Salaried staff	Number of Wage earners	Gross value of production	Value added
Coalmining	1	149	675	206	60
Crude petroleum and natural gas	7	5,923	2,381	63,379	56,270
Metal-mining	13	783	2,878	1,264	409
Other-mining	445	483	2,571	1,391	675
Food manufacturing	2,390	9,245	40,299	37,161	3,585
Beverages	67	1,431	3,442	2,932	1,881
Tobacco	6	488	574	1,672	1,402
Textiles	437	1,867	8,222	2,757	960
Clothing, etc.	328	853	4,807	1,286	521
Footwear	43	135	911	228	93
Leather	70	153	900	260	90
Wood	1,520	4,827	17,333	10,288	3,095
Furniture and fixtures	529	1,662	7,045	2,986	1,155
Pulp and paper	159	3,737	11,691	10,143	2,471
Printing and publishing	1,603	12,784	21,731	10,201	4,201
Chemical, industrial	58	4,046	5,545	8,721	1,946
Chemical, other	165	3,229	3,972	3,949	1,390

Industries	*Establishments*	*Number of Salaried staff*	*Number of Wage earners*	*Gross value of production*	*Value added*
Petroleum, refined	3	349	548	12,374	280
Petroleum and coal	58	605	1,196	1,538	297
Rubber	78	380	1,431	589	247
Plastics	314	1,588	5,132	2,735	907
Ceramics	32	233	879	252	148
Glass	66	514	1,774	806	326
Other mineral products	493	1,860	6,027	4,588	1,642
Iron, steel and ferro-alloys	53	3,048	9,192	5,675	1,680
Non-ferrous metals	69	3,714	9,369	9,539	2,198
Metal products, except machinery	1,545	5,581	20,194	8,545	3,496
Machinery and equipment	1,120	11,434	23,097	19,531	6,347
Electrical apparatus and supplies	390	8,731	12,863	8,363	3,539
Transport equipment	1,008	8,183	33,933	16,826	5,720
Professional and scientific instruments, photographic and optical goods	50	322	881	383	188
Other manufacturing industries	301	612	2,183	789	324
Total (all included)	13,421	98,949	263,676	251,356	107,541

The following table sets forth the estimated value of net production, at factor cost by industries, in 1m. kroner:

	1978	*1979*	*1980*	*1981*	*1982*[1]	*1983*[1]
Agriculture	7,283	7,273	7,972	8,852	10,127	9,814
Forestry	1,410	1,535	1,716	2,260	2,146	1,941
Fishing	1,043	1,162	1,404	2,048	1,943	2,234
Mining and quarrying	767	809	836	1,179	1,198	1,219
Manufacturing	35,309	41,484	42,978	44,845	47,835	50,243
Crude petroleum and gas production	8,458	15,316	32,007	37,395	41,258	48,898
Electricity, gas and water	3,975	4,020	4,181	5,832	7,020	8,768
Construction [2]	13,476	13,326	14,753	17,274	19,110	19,747
Wholesale and retail trade	18,256	18,336	23,101	27,405	31,534	33,746
Restaurants and hotels	2,490	2,682	3,049	3,674	4,597	5,383
Water transport	3,235	4,708	6,747	6,263	3,835	4,131
Other transport [3]	8,386	9,192	10,461	12,912	15,380	17,114
Financial institutions	7,217	8,164	10,015	12,726	15,209	17,670
Real estate	6,731	7,407	8,321	7,600	9,018	10,616
Business services	4,278	5,665	6,380	9,710	11,046	12,513
Government services, social and personal services	40,825	43,596	49,423	57,074	65,220	72,358
Imputed bank service charge	-6,158	-7,278	-8,724	-11,349	-14,318	-17,139
Net production at factor cost	156,981	177,427	214,623	245,720	272,158	299,256
+ Indirect taxes	37,946	41,106	49,024	55,696	61,423	68,496
- Subsidies	16,446	16,743	19,960	21,795	23,680	24,652
Net domestic product (market price)	178,481	201,790	243,687	279,621	309,901	343,100

[1] Provisional figures.
[2] Including drilling of crude oil and natural gas wells.
[3] Including pipeline transport of oil and gas.

Labour. The distribution of the population according to professions in 1980, showed 142,025 (7%) economically active[1] in agriculture, forestry and gardening; 599,414 (29·6%) in mining, manufacturing, building, etc.; 308,408 (15·3%) in commerce; 176,853 (8·7%) in transport; 21,694 (1·1%) in fishery, sealing and whaling; 774,377 (38·3%) in public administration, liberal professions and services; 18,871 not reported; total, 2,041,642.

[1] Persons aged 16 or more with at least 100 hours paid work in one year.

Commerce. Total imports and exports in calendar years (in 1,000 kroner):

	1978	*1979*	*1980*	*1981*	*1982*	*1983*
Imports	60,168,613	69,338,924	83,601,605	89,687,802	99,747,271	98,407,773
Exports	57,083,799	68,527,167	91,672,433	104,265,370	113,236,296	131,396,960

Trading according to countries was as follows (in 1,000 kroner):

Countries	1982 Imports	1982 Exports	1983 Imports	1983 Exports
Argentina	103,205	53,139	99,219	44,237
Australia and New Zealand	495,595	258,667	754,662	344,581
Belgium and Luxembourg	2,320,466	1,207,635	2,519,246	1,338,509
Brazil	830,260	461,411	817,784	249,908
Canada	1,353,791	456,574	1,705,769	1,568,334
Czechoslovakia	231,509	120,708	208,616	147,697
Denmark	6,174,176	4,269,930	6,374,608	4,791,408
Fed. Republic of Germany	15,494,658	22,914,654	14,506,190	24,310,052
Finland	4,514,625	1,812,090	3,428,478	2,546,915
France	3,365,032	2,501,412	3,543,895	3,447,301
India	109,239	515,537	99,038	293,435
Italy	2,336,569	1,581,639	3,373,438	1,884,964
Netherlands	3,411,649	6,586,928	3,532,098	9,102,325
Poland	624,149	305,602	338,981	235,845
Portugal	533,508	324,805	637,128	405,140
Spain	706,612	550,927	719,096	510,135
Sweden	17,053,968	10,434,765	18,485,501	13,191,992
Switzerland	1,517,745	887,846	1,558,153	1,071,424
UK	11,822,301	41,291,127	10,264,385	46,091,803
USA	9,147,880	3,173,182	8,995,192	5,742,265
USSR	1,455,688	624,692	961,775	872,956

Principal items of import in 1983 (in 1,000 kroner): Machinery, transport equipment, etc., 36,170,483; fuel oil, etc., 10,270,603; base metals and manufactures thereof, 9,605,538; chemicals and related products, 6,882,069; textiles, 2,599,377.

Principal items of export in 1983 (in 1,000 kroner): Machinery and transport equipment, 17,440,506; base metals and manufactures thereof, 15,226,997; crude oil, 40,653,248; edible animal products, 6,523,733; pulp and paper, 5,035,890.

Total trade between Norway and UK (British Department of Trade returns, in £1,000 sterling):

	1980	1981	1982	1983	1984
Imports to UK	1,441,418	1,943,206	2,023,441	2,820,760	3,852,657
Exports and re-exports from UK	791,530	876,937	924,651	828,612	968,404

COMMUNICATIONS

Roads. On 31 Dec. 1983 the length of the public roads (including roads in towns) was 84,033 km. Of these, 57,235 km were main roads; 52,293 km had some kind of paving, mostly bituminous and oil-gravel treatment, the rest being gravel-surfaced.

Number of registered motor vehicles (31 Dec. 1983) was 1,912,725, including 1,383,367 passenger cars (including taxis), 179,434 lorries and vans, 15,199 buses, 167,614 motor cycles and mopeds. The scheduled bus and lorry services in 1983 drove 3,952m. passenger-km and 632m. net ton-km.

Railways. The length of state railways on 31 Dec. 1983 was 4,242 km; of private companies, 16 km. On 2,443 km of state and 16 km of private railways electric traction is installed. Total receipts of the state railways and road traffic in 1983 were 2,421m. kroner; total expenses (excluding depreciation and interest on capital), 3,314m. kroner. The state railways carried 19·4m. tonnes of freight (of which 9·8m. was iron ore on the Ofoten railway) and 35·9m. passengers.

Aviation. Det Norske Luftfartselskap (DNL) started its post-war activities on 1 April 1946. On 1 Aug. 1946 DNL, together with DDL (Danish Airlines) and ABA/SILA (Swedish Airlines), formed the 'Scandinavian Airlines System'—SAS. The 3 companies remained independent units, but all services were co-ordinated. In 1951 a new agreement was signed (retroactive from 1 Oct. 1950) according to which the 3 national companies became holding partners in a new organization which took over the entire operational system. Denmark and Norway hold each two-sevenths and Sweden three-sevenths of the capital, but they have joint responsibility towards third parties.

In the autumn of 1983 SAS had a fleet of 75 jet planes. Length of route network, about 252,000 km. Scheduled air services are run by SAS, Braathens South-American and Far East Air transport service (SAFE) and Wideroes Flyveselskap service. The Norwegian share of the scheduled air service run by SAS is two-sevenths of the SAS service on international routes and the total SAS service in Norway.

	1,000 km flown	*Passengers carried*	*1,000 passenger-km*	*Post, luggage, freight and passengers (1,000 ton-km) Total*	*Of which post*
1980	57,885	4,809,612	4,068,000	493,000	18,000
1981	55,091	4,967,880	4,062,000	498,000	19,000
1982	56,070	5,210,452	4,118,000	498,000	19,000
1983	59,638	5,610,866	4,345,000	514,000	19,000

Shipping. The total registered mercantile marine on 1 Jan. 1984 was 1,620 vessels, 18m. gross tons (steam and motor vessels above 100 gross tons). These figures do not include fishing and catching boats, tugs, salvage vessels, icebreakers and similar special types of vessels, totalling 772 vessels of 354,000 gross tons.

Vessels entering Norway from foreign countries 1980	*Total No.*	*Net tons*
Norwegian	7,720	13,635
Foreign	8,545	23,635
Total entered	16,265	37,270

Goods (in 1,000 tonnes) in 1983 discharged, 16,349; loaded, 39,575, of which 10,712 was Swedish iron ore shipped from Narvik.

Post and Broadcasting. Number of telephones on 31 Dec. 1983 was 2,394,712 (57·9 per 100 of population). Receipts, 7,880·4m. kroner; expenses, 6,716·01m. kroner (interest on capital included) for State Telecommunications. *Norsk Rikskringkasting* is a non-commercial enterprise operated by an independent state organization and broadcasts 1 programme (P1) on long-, medium-, and short-waves and on FM and 1 programme (P2) on FM. Local programmes are also broadcast. It broadcasts 1 TV programme from 1,644 transmitters. Colour programmes are broadcast by PAL system. Number of television licences, 1,316,272.

Cinemas. There were 446 cinemas with a seating capacity of 133,688 in 1982.

Newspapers. There were 65 daily newspapers with a combined circulation of 1,848,000 in 1983.

JUSTICE, RELIGION, EDUCATION AND WELFARE

Justice. The judicature is common to civil and criminal cases. The same professional judges, who are legally educated, preside over both kinds of cases. These judges are as such state officials. The participation of lay judges and jurors, both summoned for the individual case, varies according to the kind of court and kind of case.

The ordinary Court of First Instance *(Herredsrett* and *Byrett)* is in criminal cases composed of one professional judge and 2 lay judges, chosen by ballot from a panel elected by the district council. In civil cases 2 lay judges may participate. The ordinary Court of First Instance is in general competent in all kinds of cases with the exception of criminal cases where the maximum penalty prescribed in the Criminal Code for the offence in question exceeds five years imprisonment. Altogether there are 98 ordinary courts of first instance.

In every community there is a Conciliation Council *(Forliksråd)* composed of 3 lay persons elected by the district council. A civil lawsuit usually begins with mediation in the council which also has judicial authority in minor civil cases.

The ordinary Courts of Second Instance *(Lagmannsrett)*, of which there are 5, are composed of 3 professional judges. Additionally, in civil cases 2 or 4 lay judges may be summoned. In criminal cases a jury of 10 lay persons is summoned to determine whether the defendant is guilty according to the charge. In civil cases, the Court of Second Instance is an ordinary court of appeal. In criminal cases in which the lower court does not have judicial authority, it is itself the court of first instance. In other criminal cases it is an appeal court as far as the appeal is based on an attack against the lower court's assessment of the facts when determining the guilt of the defendant. An appeal based on any other alleged mistakes is brought directly before the Supreme Court.

The Supreme Court *(Høyesterett)* is the court of last resort. There are 18 Supreme Court judges. Each individual case is heard by 5 judges. Some major cases are determined in plenary session. The Supreme Court may in general examine every aspect of the case and the handling of it by the lower courts. However, in criminal cases the Court may not overrule the lower court's assessment of the facts as far as the guilt of the defendant is concerned.

The Court of Impeachment *(Riksretten)* is composed of 5 judges of the Supreme Court and 10 members of Parliament.

All serious offences are prosecuted by the State. The Public Prosecution Authority *(Påtalemyndigheten)* consists of the Attorney General *(Riksadvokaten)*, the district attorneys *(statsadvokater)* and legally qualified officers of the ordinary police force. Counsel for the defence is in general provided for by the State.

There are 3 central prisons in which were detained (11 Sept. 1984) 344 persons. There are also 35 local prisons in which were detained (11 Sept. 1984) 1,660 persons.

Religion. There is complete freedom of religion, the Evangelical Lutheran Church, however, being the national church, endowed by the State. Its clergy are nominated by the King. Ecclesiastically Norway is divided into 11 *Bispedømmer* (bishoprics), 89 *Prostier* (provostships or archdeaconries) and 618 *Prestegjeld* (clerical districts). There were 138,134 members of registered religious communities outside the Evangelical Lutheran Church, subsidized by central government and local authorities in 1983. The Roman Catholics are under a Bishop at Oslo, a Vicar Apostolic at Trondheim and a Vicar Apostolic at Tromsø.

Education. In Norway the children normally start their school attendance the year they complete 7 and finish compulsory school the year they complete 16.

On 1 Oct. 1983 the number of primary schools and pupils were as follows: 3,534 primary schools, 565,497 pupils; 89 special schools for the handicapped, 3,188 pupils.

On 1 Oct. 1982 the number of pupils in upper secondary schools, *i.e.*, folk high schools, secondary general schools and vocational schools, was 188,040.

There are in Norway 4 universities and 8 institutions equivalent to universities. In autumn 1982 the total number of students was 41,002. The University of Oslo, founded in 1811, had 19,078 students. The University of Bergen, founded in 1948, had 7,771 students. The University of Trondheim consists of the Norwegian Institute of Technology, founded in 1910, and the College of Arts and Science, founded in 1925. At each of them the number of students was in autumn 1982, 4,940 and 3,384 respectively. The University of Tromsø was established in 1968; 1,672 students were registered in autumn 1982. The other university institutions had 4,157 students.

In addition there were at other schools of higher education, 47,006 students. These included 13,546 at colleges for teachers, 6,654 at colleges for engineers and 6,651 at district colleges.

In 1983–84 there were 6,353 Norwegian students and pupils attending foreign universities and schools.

Health. In 1982 there were 9,722 doctors and 66,861 hospital beds.

Social Security. In 1983, about 63,000m. kroner were paid under different social insurance schemes, amounting to 18% of the net national income.

The National Insurance Act of 17 June 1966, which came into force on 1 Jan. 1967, replaced the schemes relating to old age pensions, disability benefits, widows' and mothers' pensions, benefits to unmarried women, 'survivors' benefit for children and rehabilitation aid. Schemes relating to health insurance, unemployment insurance and occupational injury insurance were revised and incorporated in National Insurance Scheme on 1 Jan. 1971. As from 1 Jan. 1981, benefits to divorced and separated supporters also are covered by the National Insurance Scheme.

The following conspectus gives a survey of schemes established by law. Many municipalities grant additional benefits to old-age, disablement and survivor's pensions.

Type of scheme	*Introduced*[1]	*Scope*	*Principal benefits as from 1 May 1984*
National insurance	1967 (1984)		
Sickness benefits[2]	1911	All residents	Medical benefits: all hospital expenses; cost share of expense of medical consultation, important medicines, travel expenses, etc. (such costs exceeding 800kr. a calendar year are paid in full by the National Insurance). Daily sickness allowances: kr. 38 to 745 per day cash (5 days a week). The new sickness allowance scheme (1 July 1978) entitles employees to a daily allowance equal to 100% of their gross earned income (within certain limits) from and including the first day of absence; self-employed persons, ordinarily 65% of gross earned income as from the 15th day. Supplementary insurance available. The allowances are taxable
Unemployment benefits[2]	1939	Nearly all wage-earners	Daily allowance during unemployment kr. 36 to 290 per day, excluding supplement for supported child(ren) (six days a week), taxable as from 1 Jan. 1980. Contributions to training and retraining, removal expenses, wage subsidies
Rehabilitation benefits[3]	1961	Persons unfit for work because of disablement and persons who have a substantially limited general functional capacity	Training; treatment; rehabilitation allowance grants and loans Full rehabilitation allowance equals old age pension (however, no special supplement is granted, see below.)
Disability benefits[3]	1961	All residents	*A basic grant* (ordinary rate kr. 3,348 per annum) and *an assistance grant* (ordinary rate kr. 5,580 per annum) to persons with special needs. In certain cases the benefits may be increased. The rates are fixed by the Storting, independent of the basic amount
		All residents between 16 and 67 years of age	*Disability pension* to persons between 16 and 67 years of age, occupationally disabled by at least 50%, unfit for rehabilitation Full disability pension equals old age pension
Occupational injury benefits[2] (industrial workers 1895; fishermen 1909; seamen 1913; military personnel 1953, combined in the act of occupational injury insurance *1960*)	1960	All employed persons, school children and students; self-employed on a voluntary basis	The ordinary benefits of the National Insurance, alternative calculation of pensions etc. which in almost all cases are more favourable for the insured person —or his survivors than the ordinary rules *An occupational injury compensation*, alone or in addition to a disability pension
Old age pensions[3]	1937	All persons above 67 years of age	Basic pensions: Single, kr. 24,200; couples, kr. 36,300 per annum; supplementary pensions based on previous pensionable income; *see below* under 'Special supplement' and 'Compensation supplement'
Death grants	1967	All residents	A certain amount fixed by the Storting, for the time being kr. 4,000

For notes *see* bottom of p. 940.

Type of scheme	*Introduced* [1]	*Scope*	*Principal benefits as from 1 May 1984*
Survivors' benefits [3]	1965	All residents	Full pension = kr. 24,200 per annum + 55% of the supplementary pension due to the deceased, *transitional benefits,* child care allowance and educational allowances (*see below* under 'Special supplement' and 'Compensation supplement')
Children's pension [3]	1958	Under 18 (20) years of age, after loss of one or both parents	40% of basic amount (kr. 9,680) for first child, 25% (kr. 6,050) for each additional child. If both parents are dead, full survivors' pension for first, 40% of basic amount for second, 25% third, etc., child
Benefits to unmarried supporters [3]	1965	Unmarried mothers or fathers	Maternity grant kr. 7,020, transitional benefit, full amount kr. 24,200 per annum, child care allowance and educational allowances (*see below* under 'Special supplement' and 'Family allowances')
Benefits to divorced and separated supporters [4]	1972	Divorced and separated supporters	Same kind of benefits as unmarried supporters above
Benefits to unmarried persons forced to live at home [3]	1965	Unmarried persons under 67 years of age having stayed at home for at least 5 years to give necessary care and attention to parents or other near relatives	Transitional benefit or a pension that equals the basic amount, educational allowances (*see below* under 'Special supplement')
Special supplement to National Insurance pensions or transitional benefits	1969 (1983)	Pensioners and persons with transitional allowance on basic rates	Full special supplement, 52·5% of basic amount, *i.e.* kr. 12,705. For a married pensioner full supplement is lower when spouse has her/his own pension (48·5%)
Compensation supplement to National Insurance pensions or transitional benefits	1970 (1972)	Pensioners, persons with transitional benefits (except unmarried, divorced and separated supporters) or rehabilitation allowances	Full compensation supplement kr. 500 for single persons and kr. 750 for married couples
Family allowances	1946 (1984)	All families with children under 16 years of age	Kr. 4,164 per annum for the first child, kr. 5,028 for the second, kr. 6,228 for the third, kr. 6,684 for the fourth and kr. 7,020 for the fifth and each additional child. Single supporters receive an additional benefit of kr. 5,028 per annum for the first, kr. 1,200 for the second, kr. 456 for the third and kr. 336 for the fourth child. (Limited to 4 children)
War pensions	1946 (1981)	War victims, 1939–45	Pensions up to kr. 98,244 per annum (excluding supplement for supported child(ren); widows' and children's pensions
Special pension schemes:		Persons with at least: [5]	Maximum old-age pension for couples:
Seamen	1948 (1983)	150 months service (360 ,, ,,)	Kr. 79,304 [6] per annum (officers) Kr. 56,646 [6] ,, ,, (others)

[1] Date of latest revision in brackets.
[2] Transferred to national insurance scheme and revised in 1971.
[3] Transferred to national insurance scheme and revised in 1967.
[4] Transferred to national insurance scheme and revised in 1981.
[5] Requirements for maximum pensions in brackets.
[6] Supplements for service during war not included.

Provisions have been laid down for the integration of more than one benefit, pension, etc., so as to limit the total amount.

Type of scheme	*Intro-duced*[1]	*Scope*	*Principal benefits as from 1 May 1984*
Forestry workers	1952 (1984)	750 premium weeks (1,500 ,, ,,)	Kr. 26,000 per annum (excluding supplement for supported child-(ren)
Fishermen	1958 (1983)	750 premium weeks (1,500 ,, ,,)	Kr. 31,500 ,, ,,

[1] Date of latest revision in brackets.

SVALBARD

An archipelago situated between 10° and 35° E. long. and between 74° and 81° N. lat. Total area, 62,000 sq. km (24,000 sq. miles).

The main islands of the archipelago are Spitsbergen (formerly called Vest-spitsbergen), Nordaustlandet, Edgeøya, Barentsøya, Prins Karls Forland, Bjørnøya, Hopen, Kong Karls Land, Kvitøya, and many small islands. The arctic climate is tempered by mild winds from the Atlantic.

The archipelago was probably discovered by Norsemen in 1194 and rediscovered by the Dutch navigator Barents in 1596. In the 17th century the very lucrative whale-hunting caused rival Dutch, British and Danish–Norwegian claims to sovereignty and quarrels about the hunting-places. But when in the 18th century the whale-hunting ended, the question of the sovereignty of Svalbard lost its significance; it was again raised in the 20th century, owing to the discovery and exploitation of coalfields. By a treaty, signed on 9 Feb. 1920 in Paris, Norway's sovereignty over the archipelago was recognized. On 14 Aug. 1925 the archipelago was officially incorporated in Norway.

Coal is the principal product. Of the 3 Norwegian and 3 Soviet mining camps, 2 Norwegian and 2 Soviet camps are operating. Total population on 31 Dec. 1983 was 3,457, of which 1,305 Norwegians, 2,143 Soviet citizens, and 9 Poles. In 1983, 448,000 tonnes of coal were exported from the Norwegian and 477,481 tonnes from the Soviet mines.

Norwegian and foreign companies have been prospecting for oil. So far 5 deep drillings have been made, but oil and gas finds have not been reported.

There are Norwegian meteorological and/or radio stations at the following places: Bjørnøya (since 1920), Hopen (1945), Isfjord Radio (1933), Longyearbyen (1930), Svalbard Lufthavn (1975) and Ny-Ålesund (1961). A research station, administered by Norsk Polarinstitutt, was erected at Ny-Ålesund in 1968 for various observations and investigations. An airport near Longyearbyen (Svalbard Lufthavn) opened in 1975.

Norsk Polarinstitutt, Skrifter, Oslo, from 1948 (under different titles from 1922)
Greve, T., *Svalbard: Norway in the Arctic.* Oslo, 1975
Hisdal, V., *Geography of Svalbard.* Norsk Polarinstitutt, Oslo, rev. ed., 1984
Orvin, A. K., 'Twenty-five Years of Norwegian Sovereignty in Svalbard 1925–1950' (in *The Polar Record,* 1951)

JAN MAYEN

This bleak, desolate and mountainous island of volcanic origin and partly covered by glaciers, is situated 71° N. lat. and 8° 30′ W. long., 300 miles NNE of Iceland. The total area is 380 sq. km (147 sq. miles). Beerenberg, its highest peak, reaches a height of 2,277 metres. Volcanic activity, which had been dormant, was reactivated in Sept. 1970.

The island was possibly discovered by Henry Hudson in 1608, and it was first named Hudson's Tutches (Touches). It was again and again rediscovered and renamed. Its present name derives from the Dutch whaling captain Jan Jacobsz May, who indisputably discovered the island in 1614. It was uninhabited, but occasionally visited by seal hunters and trappers, until 1921 when Norway established a radio and meteorological station. On 8 May 1929 Jan Mayen was officially proclaimed as incorporated in the Kingdom of Norway. Its relation to Norway was finally settled by law of 27 Feb. 1930. A LORAN station (1959) and a CONSOL station (1968) have been established.

BOUVET ISLAND
Bouvetøya

This uninhabited volcanic island, mostly covered by glaciers and situated 54° 25′ S. lat. and 3° 21′ E. long., was discovered in 1739 by a French naval officer, Jean Baptiste Loziert Bouvet, but no flag was hoisted till, in 1825, Capt. Norris raised the Union Jack. In 1928 Great Britain waived its claim to the island in favour of Norway, which in Dec. 1927 had occupied it. A law of 27 Feb. 1930 declared Bouvetøya a Norwegian dependency. The area is 50 sq. km (19 sq. miles). From 1977 Norway has had an automatic meteorological station on the island, and 5 men operated a meteorological station there during the 1978–79 season.

PETER I ISLAND
Peter I Øy

This uninhabited island, situated 68° 48′ S. lat. and 90° 35′ W. long., was sighted in 1821 by the Russian explorer, Admiral von Bellingshausen. The first landing was made in 1929 by a Norwegian expedition which hoisted the Norwegian flag. On 1 May 1931 Peter I Island was placed under Norwegian sovereignty, and on 24 March 1933 it was incorporated in Norway as a dependency. The area is 180 sq. km (69 sq. miles).

QUEEN MAUD LAND
Dronning Maud Land

On 14 Jan. 1939 the Norwegian Cabinet placed that part of the Antarctic Continent from the border of Falkland Islands dependencies in the west to the border of the Australian Antarctic Dependency in the east (between 20° W. and 45° E.) under Norwegian sovereignty. The territory had been explored only by Norwegians and hitherto been ownerless. Since 1949 expeditions from various countries have explored the area. In 1957 Dronning Maud Land was given the status of a Norwegian dependency.

DIPLOMATIC REPRESENTATIVES

Of Norway in Great Britain (25 Belgrave Sq., London, SW1X 8QD)
Ambassador: Rolf T. Busch.

Of Great Britain in Norway (Thomas Heftyesgate 8, 0264 Oslo, 2)
Ambassador: Sir William Bentley, KCMG.

Of Norway in the USA (2720 34th Street, NW, Washington, D.C., 20008)
Ambassador: Kjell Eliassen.

Of the USA in Norway (Drammensvien 18, 0255 Oslo, 2)
Ambassador: Robert D. Stuart, Jr.

Of Norway to the United Nations
Ambassador: Tom Eric Vraalsen.

Books of Reference

Statistical Information: The Central Bureau of Statistics, Statistisk Sentralbyrå (Skippergaten 15, P.B.8131 Dep.0033, Oslo 1), was founded in 1876 as an independent state institution. *Director general:* Arne Øien. The earliest census of population was taken in 1769. The Sentralbyrå publishes the series *Norges Offisielle Statistikk,* Norway's official statistics (from 1828), and *Social Economic Studies* (from 1954). The main publications are:

Statistisk Årbok for Norge (annual, from 1880; from 1952 bilingual Norwegian–English)
Økonomisk Utsyn (annual, from 1935; with English summary from 1952)
Historisk Statistikk 1978 (historical statistics; bilingual Norwegian–English)
Statistisk Månedshefte (monthly, from 1880; with English index)
Sosialt Utsyn 1983 (social survey). Irregular
Miljóstatistikk 1983 (environmental statistics). Irregular

Norges Statskalender. From 1816; annual from 1877
Facts about Norway. Ed. by Aftenposten. 17th ed. Oslo, 1982
Derry, T. K., *A History of Modern Norway, 1814–1972.* OUP, 1973.—*A History of Scandinavia.* London, 1979
Glässer, E., *Norwegen* [bibliography] Darmstadt, 1978
Gleditsch, Th., *Engelsk–norsk ordbok,* 2nd ed. Oslo, 1948
Greve, T., *Haakon VI of Norway, Founder of a New Monarchy.* London, 1983
Grønland, E., *Norway in English, Books on Norway . . . 1742–1959.* Oslo, 1961
Haugen, E., *Norwegian–English Dictionary,* Oslo, 1965
Helvig, M., *Norway: Land, People, Industries, a Brief Geography.* 3rd ed. Oslo, 1970
Holtedahl, O. (ed.), *Geology of Norway.* Oslo, 1960
Hornby, A. S., and Svenkerud, H., *Oxford engelsk-norsk ordbok.* Oslo, 1983
Hove, O., *The System of Education.* Oslo, 1968
Imber, W., *Norway.* Oslo, 1980
Knudsen, O., *Norway at Work.* Oslo, 1972
Larsen, K., *A History of Norway.* New York, 1948
Midgaard, J., *A Brief History of Norway.* Oslo, 1969
Nielsen, K., and Nesheim, A., *Lapp Dictionary: Lapp–English–Norwegian.* 5 vols., Oslo 1963
Orvik, N. (ed.), *Fears and Expectations: Norwegian Attitudes Toward European Integration.* Oslo, 1972
Paine, R., *Coast Lapp Society.* 2 vols. Tromsø, 1957–65
Popperwell, R. G., *Norway.* London, 1972
Udgaard, N. M., *Great Power Politics and Norwegian Foreign Policy.* Oslo, 1973
Vorren, Ø. (ed.), *Norway North of 65.* Oslo, 1960

National Library: The University Library, Drammensvein 42b, 0255 Oslo. *Director:* Ben Rugaas.

OMAN

Capital: Muscat
Population: 1·5m. (1982)
GNP per capita: US$5,920 (1981)

Sultanate of Oman

AREA AND POPULATION. The Sultanate of Oman, known as the Sultanate of Muscat and Oman until 1970, is an independent sovereign state, situated in south-east Arabia. Its coastline is over 1,000 miles long and extends from the Ras al Khaimah Shaikdom near Bukha on the west side of the Musandum Peninsula to Ras Dharbat Ali, which marks the boundary between Oman and the territory of the People's Democratic Republic of Yemen. The Sultanate extends inland to the borders of the Rub' al Khali ('Empty Quarter') across three geographical divisions—a coastal plain, a range of hills and a plateau. The coastal plain varies in width from 10 miles near Suwaiq to practically nothing in the vicinity of Mutrah and Muscat towns, where the hills descend abruptly into the sea. These hills are for the most part barren except at the highest part of the mountainous region of the Jebel Akhdar (summit 9,998 ft) where there is some cultivation. The plateau has an average height of 1,000 ft. With the exception of oases there is little or no cultivation. North-west of Muscat the coastal plain, known as the Batinah, is fertile and prosperous. The date gardens extend for over 150 miles. Whereas the coastline between the capital, Muscat, and the southern province of Dhofar is barren, Dhofar itself is highly fertile. Its principal town is Salalah on the coast which is served by the port of Raysut.

The area has been estimated at about 105,000 sq. miles and the population at 1·5m., chiefly Arabs; of these, some 40,000 live in Dhofar. The town of Muscat is the capital which, while formerly of some commercial importance, has now lost most of its trade to the adjacent port of Mutrah (combined populations, 80,000), the starting point for the trade routes into the interior. The population of both towns consists of pure Arabs, Indians, Pakistanis and Negroes; numerous merchants are Khojas (from Sind and Kutch) and Hindus (mostly from Gujarat and Bombay). Other ports are Sohar, Khaburah and Sur, Raysut in the south; none, however, affords shelter from bad weather.

The port of Gwadur and a small tract of country on the Balúchistán coast of the Gulf of Oman were handed over to Pakistan on 8 Sept. 1958.

The **Kuria Muria** islands were ceded to the UK in 1854 by the Sultan of Muscat and Oman for the purpose of a cable station. On 30 Nov. 1967 the islands were retroceded to the Sultan of Muscat and Oman, in accordance with the wishes of the population.

CLIMATE. Oman has a desert climate, with exceptionally hot and humid months from April to Oct., when temperatures may reach 117°F (47°C). From Dec. to the end of March, the climate is more pleasant. Light monsoon rains fall in the south from June to Sept., with highest amounts in the western highland region. Muscat. Jan. 72°F (22·2°C), July 91°F (33·3°C). Annual rainfall 4·0″ (99·1 mm). Salalah. Jan. 72°F (22·2°C), July 78°F (25·6°C). Annual rainfall 3·3″ (81·3 mm).

RULER. The present Sultan is Qaboos bin Said (born Nov. 1940). He took over from his father Said bin Taimur, on 23 July 1970 in a Palace *coup*.

In Oct. 1981 the Sultan issued three decrees establishing a 45-member State advisory council.

CONSTITUTION AND GOVERNMENT. Oman is an absolute monarchy and there is no formal constitution. The Sultan legislates by decree and appoints a Cabinet to assist him; he holds the posts of Prime Minister and Minister of Foreign Affairs, Defence and Finance. Besides 17 departmental Ministers, the Cabinet also includes:

Deputy Prime Minister for Security and Defence: Sayyid Fahar Bin-Taimur al-Said.

Deputy Prime Minister for Finance and Economy: Qais Abdel-Moneim al-Zawawi.

Deputy Prime Minister for Legal Affairs: Sayyid Fahad Bin-Mahmoud al-Said.

Special Advisor to Sultan, Governor of Muscat: Sayyid Thuwaini Bin-Shihab al-Said.

Special Advisor to Sultan on Religious and Historical Affairs: Mohammad Bin-Ahmad.

Minister of State for Foreign Affairs: Yusuf Alawi.

Minister of State, Governor of Dhofar: Hilal Bin-Saud Bin-Hareb al-Busaidi.

National flag: Red, with a white panel in the upper fly and a green one in the lower fly, and in the canton the national emblem in white.

Local government: Oman is divided into 10 provinces *(liwas)* and sub-divided into 41 governates *(wilayats)* each under a governor *(wali).*

DEFENCE

Army. The Army consists of 1 Royal Guard brigade; 1 armoured, 1 reconnaissance and 3 artillery regiments; 8 infantry battalions; 1 special force, 1 signals regiment, 1 engineer squadron and 1 parachute squadron. Equipment includes 6 M-60A1 and 12 Chieftain main battle tanks. Strength (1985) about 20,000.

Navy. The Navy comprises 3 new very fast missile-armed corvettes, 1 fast missile-armed patrol craft, 4 fast gunboats, 4 inshore patrol craft, 1 training ship/offshore patrol vessel, 2 logistic support ships, 1 supply ship, 5 landing craft, 1 survey craft, 1 supply ship and 1 training ship. All the warships are British-built. The marine police operate 10 coastal patrol boats, 2 logistics support craft, 2 inshore patrol boats and 7 launches. Naval personnel in 1985 totalled 2,000 officers and ratings.

Air Force. The Air Force, formed in 1959, had in 1984 two strike/interceptor squadrons of Jaguars, a ground attack/interceptor squadron of Hunters, a squadron of Strikemaster light jet training/attack aircraft, 1 DC-8, 3 BAC One-Eleven and 1 Falcon VIP transports, 3 C-130H Hercules, 2 twin-turboprop Buffalo, 7 Defender and 15 Skyvan light transports, 26 Agusta-Bell 205, 212, 214B and JetRanger helicopters for security duties, 2 Super Puma VIP helicopters and 2 Bravo piston-engined trainers. Air defence force has batteries of Rapier low-level surface-to-air missiles. Personnel (1984) about 2,200.

INTERNATIONAL RELATIONS

Membership. Oman is a member of UN, the Arab League, the Islamic Conference Organisation and the Gulf Co-operation Council.

Treaties. The Treaty of Friendship, Commerce and Navigation between Britain and the Sultan signed on 20 Dec. 1951, reaffirmed the close ties which have existed between the British Government and the Sultanate of Oman for over a century and a half. A Memorandum of Understanding signed in June 1982 provided for regular consultations on international and bilateral issues.

ECONOMY

Planning. The 5-year development plan (1976–80) had an expenditure of R.O. 2,556m. Expenditure for the second 5-year plan (1981–85) is (estimate) R.O. 7,368m. and a primary aim is to develop new sources of national income to augment and eventually to replace oil revenues.

Budget. Revenue (1984) R.O. 1,561m. (1,100m. from oil); expenditure, 1,765m.

Currency. The *Rial Omani* was introduced in Nov. 1972 replacing the *Rial Saidi*. It is divided into 1,000 *baiza*. There are notes of 100, 250 and 500 *baiza* and 1, 5 and 10 *Rial Omani* and coins of 2, 5, 10, 20, 50 and 100 *baiza*. The exchange rate in March 1985 was £1 = 373 *baiza*; US$1 = 346 *baiza*.

Banking. In 1983 there were 25 banks operating in Oman apart from the Central Bank of Oman.

Weights and Measures. The metric system of measurement is in operation. Transactions in the former measurements are now illegal.

ENERGY AND NATURAL RESOURCES

Oil. The economy of Oman is dominated by the oil industry, which provides nearly all Government revenue. In 1937 Petroleum Concessions (Oman) Ltd, a subsidiary of the Iraq Petroleum Co., was granted a 75-year oil concession extending over the whole of Oman, although it relinquished Dhofar in 1950. In 1951 the company's name was changed to Petroleum Development (Oman) Ltd. The company (PDO) regained the Dhofar concession area in 1969. When some of the IPC partners withdrew from Oman in 1960, Shell took over the management of PDO with an 85% interest (minority interests were held by Compagnie Française des Pétroles, 10% and Gulbenkian, 5%). At the beginning of 1974 the Oman Government bought a 25% share in PDO, increasing this retroactively to 60% in July. A Joint Management Committee was established. Other companies active in exploration activities in Oman, with mixed success, include Amoco, Elf-Acquitaine and a consortium of Deminex, Agip and Hispanoil with BP as operator.

Oil in commercial quantities was discovered in 1964 and production began at a rate of 200,000 bbls per day in 1967. Production has fluctuated from year to year, peaking in 1976 at 366,000 bbls per day. Due to conditions on the international oil market, production fell to a low of 282,000 bbls per day in 1980 but was restored to about 410,000 bbls per day in the first quarter of 1984. Production in 1983 was 141·6m. bbls. Total reserves were estimated in April 1984 to be 3,490m. bbls, or sufficient for 23 years at the current rate of production.

Oman is not a member of OPEC or OAPEC but tends to follow OPEC pricing policy.

Gas. Production (1982) 290m. cu. ft per day. In 1984 reserves were estimated at 7,600,000m. cu. ft.

Water Resources. Two water desalination units were being built in 1984 which will produce 12m. gallons of drinking water water a day. The project is due to be completed in 1986.

Minerals. Production of refined copper at the smelter at Sohar was about 6,700 tonnes in 1983. Copper mines produce about 11m. tonnes annually.

Agriculture. In the valleys of the interior, as well as on the Batinah, date cultivation has reached a high level, and there are possibilities of agricultural development subject to present water resources and soil surveys. The average annual crop of dates is estimated at 50,000 tons, most of which is exported to India. Camels (6,000 in 1983) are bred in large numbers by the inland tribes.

INDUSTRY AND TRADE

Industry. Apart from oil production, copper mining and smelting and cement production there are no industries of any importance. Fishing, water resources, soil and agricultural surveys are being undertaken.

Commerce. The total imports for 1983 were valued at R.O. 860·9m., including machinery and transport equipment (396·1m.), manufactured goods (166·8m.), food and live animals (107·1m.), petroleum products (14·1m.) and chemicals (31·7m.).

In 1983, 22% of imports came from Japan, 18·6% from UK, 17·5% from United Arab Emirates, 7·7% from USA and 7·3% from the Federal Republic of Germany; 50·2% of exports went to Japan, 11·1% to the Netherlands, 10·8% to the Federal Republic of Germany, 8·6% to Singapore and 7·7% to USA.

Total trade between Oman and UK (British Department of Trade returns, in £1,000 sterling):

	1980	*1981*	*1982*	*1983*	*1984*
Imports to UK	28,728	40,460	46,425	91,216	82,655
Exports and re-exports from UK	131,094	170,835	265,283	448,900	390,275

COMMUNICATIONS

Roads. A network of adequate graded roads links all the main sectors of population, and only a few mountain villages are not accessible by Land-Rover. A rapid road construction programme began in 1976, and by the end of 1981 there were 2,835 km of paved roads and 16,276 km of graded roads. There are good waterproof roads in the north of Oman, between Muscat and Sohar, Sohar and Buraimi, Nizwa and Buraimi and Nizwa and Seeb. In Dhofar tarmac roads have been completed from Raysut through Salalah to Taqa and also Bid Bid to Sur. A single arterial highway now links the interior, the Capital Area and the Batinah coast, and connects with the United Arab Emirates.

Aviation. Gulf Air run regional services in and out of Seeb international airport (20 miles from Muscat) to Bahrain, Doha, Abu Dhabi, Dubai, Karachi and Bombay. They and British Airways each operate daily flights to and from London. Other airlines serving Muscat are MEA, Kuwait Airlines, PIA, Air India, Iran Air, TMA (cargo) and Trade Winds (cargo).

Shipping. In Mutrah a deep-water port (named Mina Qaboos) was completed in 1974 at a cost of R.O. 18·2m. It provides 12 berths, 9 of which are deep-water berths, warehousing facilities and a harbour for dhows and coastal vessels. The annual handling capacity has been raised to 1·5m. tons. Mina Raysut, the port of Salalah, has a capacity of 1m. tons per year.

Post and Broadcasting. There are Sultanate post offices in Muscat and Mutrah, relying solely upon a Post Office Box system for delivery. Omantel maintain a telegraph office at Muscat and an automatic telephone exchange (23,000 lines, 1984) which includes Mutrah, Bait-al-Falaj and Mina al-Fahal, the oil company terminal. A high-frequency radio link with Bahrain was opened in Aug. 1972 providing communications with other parts of the world. Internally, there are radio telephone, telex and telegraph services direct between Salalah and Muscat, and a VHF radio link between Seeb international airport and Muscat. The airport is also served by a SITA telex system. Radio Oman broadcasts daily for 17 hours in Arabic and 2 hours in English.

A colour television service covering Muscat and the surrounding area started transmission in Nov. 1974. A television service for Dhofar opened in 1975.

Newspapers. There were (1984) 3 daily newspapers.

EDUCATION AND WELFARE

Education. In 1982–83, there were 455 schools with 140,582 pupils and 6,575 teachers. All Omanis desiring further education must obtain it abroad, but plans are being implemented for the development of technical and agricultural training and craft training at intermediate and secondary level. Oman's first university, in Nizwa, was under construction in 1984. There are also programmes to combat adult illiteracy.

Health. Health services in 1984 were widely spread with 14 hospitals in use and 2 more planned, 13 health centres, 62 clinics, 6 small health centres and 4 maternity clinics; total beds, 2,000. There are also Save the Children Fund Welfare Clinics at Sohar and Sur.

DIPLOMATIC REPRESENTATIVES

Of Oman in Great Britain (44A Montpelier Sq., London, SW7 1JJ)
Ambassador: Hussain bin Mohammed bin Ali (accredited 7 Dec. 1984).

Of Great Britain in Oman (PO Box 300, Muscat)
Ambassador: Duncan Slater, CMG.

Of Oman in the USA (2342 Massachusetts Ave., NW, Washington, DC., 20008)
Ambassador: Ali Salim Bader Al-Hinai.

Of the USA in Oman (PO Box 966, Muscat)
Ambassador: John R. Countryman.

Of Oman to the United Nations
Ambassador: Saoud Bin Salim Bin Hassan Al-Ansi.

Books of Reference

Achievements. Ministry of Health. Oman, 1975
Hints to Exporters: UAE and the Sultanate of Oman 1981–82. British Overseas Board
Oman in 10 years. Ministry of Information. Oman, 1980
Oman: A MEED Practical Guide. London, 1981
Clements, F. A., *Oman: The Reborn Land.* London and New York, 1980.—*Oman.* [Bibliography] Oxford and Santa Barbara, 1981
Graz, L., *The Omani's: Sentinals of the Gulf.* London, 1982
Hawley, D., *Oman and its Rennaissance.* London, 1977
Peterson, J. E., *Oman in the Twentieth Century.* London and New York, 1978
Shannon, M. O., *Oman and South-eastern Arabia: A Bibliographic Survey.* Boston, 1978
Thesiger, W., *Arabian Sands.* London, 1959
Townsend, J., *Oman.* London, 1977
Wikan, U., *Behind the Veil in Arabia: Women in Oman.* John Hopkins Univ. Press, 1982

PAKISTAN

Capital: Islamabad
Population: 88m. (1983)
GNP per capita: US$350 (1981)

Islamic Republic of Pakistan

HISTORY. Pakistan was constituted as a Dominion on 14 Aug. 1947, under the provisions of the Indian Independence Act, 1947, which received the royal assent on 18 July 1947. The Dominion consisted of the following former territories of British India: Balúchistán, East Bengal (including almost the whole of Sylhet, a former district of Assam), North-West Frontier, West Punjab and Sind; and those States which had acceded to Pakistan.

On 23 March 1956 an Islamic republic was proclaimed after the Constituent Assembly had adopted the draft constitution on 29 Feb.

On 7 Oct. 1958 President Mirza declared martial law in Pakistan, dismissed the central and provincial Governments, abolished all political parties and abrogated the constitution of 23 March 1956. Field Marshal Mohammad Ayub Khan, the Army Commander-in-Chief, was appointed as chief martial law administrator and assumed office on 28 Oct. 1958, after Maj.-Gen. Iskander Mirza had handed all powers to him. His authority was confirmed by a ballot in Feb. 1960. He proclaimed a new constitution on 1 March 1962.

On 25 March 1969 President Ayub Khan resigned and handed over power to the army under the leadership of Maj.-Gen. Agha Muhammad Yahya Khan who immediately proclaimed martial law throughout the country, appointing himself chief martial law administrator on the same day. On 29 March 1970 the Legal Framework Order was published, defining a new constitution: Pakistan to be a federal republic with a Moslem Head of State; the National Assembly and Provincial Assemblies to be elected in free and periodical elections, the first of which was held on 7 Dec. 1970.

At the general election the Awami League based in East Pakistan and led by Sheikh Mujibur Rahman gained 167 seats and the Peoples' Party 90. Martial law continued pending the settlement of differences between East and West, which developed into civil war in March 1971. The war ended in Dec. 1971 and the Eastern province declared itself an independent state, Bangladesh. On 20 Dec. 1971 President Yahya Khan resigned and Mr Z. A. Bhutto became President and chief martial law administrator. On 30 Jan. 1972, Pakistan withdrew from the Commonwealth.

A new Constitution was adopted by the National Assembly on 10 April 1973 and enforced on 14 Aug. 1973. It provided for a federal parliamentary system with the President as constitutional head and the Prime Minister as chief executive. President Bhutto stepped down to become Prime Minister and Fazal Elahi Chaudhry was elected President.

The Chief of the Army Staff, Gen. M. Zia-ul-Haq, proclaimed martial law on 5 July 1977 and the armed forces took control of the administration; scheduled elections were postponed. Mr Bhutto was hanged (for conspiracy to murder) on 4 April 1979. Gen. M. Zia-ul-Haq succeeded Fazal Elahi Chaudhry as President in Sept. 1978.

Governors-General of Pakistan: Quaid-I-Azam Mohummed Ali Jinnah (14 Aug. 1947–11 Sept. 1948); Khawaja Nazimuddin (14 Sept. 1948–18 Oct. 1951; took over the premiership after the assassination of Liaquat Ali Khan); Ghulam Mohammad (19 Oct. 1951–6 Aug. 1955); Maj.-Gen. Iskander Mirza (assumed office of President on 6 Oct. 1955, elected President on 5 March 1956).

Presidents of Pakistan: Maj.-Gen. Iskander Mirza (23 March 1956–28 Oct. 1958); Field Marshal Mohammad Ayub Khan (28 Oct. 1958–25 March 1969); Maj.-Gen. Agha Muhammad Yahya Khan (31 March 1969–20 Dec. 1971);

Zulfiqar Ali Bhutto (20 Dec.1971–14 Aug. 1973); Fazal Elahi Chaudhri (14 Aug. 1973–16 Sept. 1978); Gen. Mohammad Zia ul-Haq (16 Sept. 1978–).

AREA AND POPULATION. Pakistan is bounded north-west by Afghánistán, north by the USSR and China, east by India and south by the Arabian Sea. The total area of Pakistan is 307,293 sq. miles (796,095 sq. km); population (1981 census), 84·25m.; males, 44,232,000; females, 40,021,000. Density, 105·8 per sq. km. Estimate (1983) 88m. Urban population, 28·3%. Annual average growth rate, 1982–83, 2·8%. The crude birth rate was 41 (per 1,000 population); infant mortality 90 (per 1,000 live births); life expectancy, 55 years.

The population of the principal cities is:

Census of 1981

Islamabad	201,000	Multan	730,000
Karachi	5,103,000	Gujranwala	597,000
Lahore	2,922,000	Peshawar	555,000
Faisalabad	1,092,000	Sialkot	296,000
Rawalpindi	928,000	Sargodha	294,000
Hyderabad	795,000	Quetta	285,000

Population of the provinces (census of 1981) was (1,000):

	Area (sq. km)	*Total population*	*Male*	*Female*	*Urban*	*Density per sq. km (number)*
North-west Frontier Province	74,521	11,061	5,761	5,300	1,665	148
Federally administered Tribal Areas	27,219	2,199	1,143	1,056	–	81
Federal Capital Territory Islamabad	907	340	185	155	204	376
Punjab	205,344	47,292	24,860	22,432	13,051	230
Sind	140,914	19,029	9,999	9,030	8,243	135
Balúchistán	347,190	4,332	2,284	2,048	677	12

By June 1984 there were 2·3m. Afghan refugees in Pakistan, of whom some 78% were in the North-west Frontier Province, 17% in Baluchistan and 5% in the Punjab.

Language. The commonest languages are Urdu and Punjabi. Urdu is the national language while English is used in business and in central government. Provincial languages are Punjabi, Sindhi, Pushtu (North-West Frontier Province), Baluchi and Brahvi.

CLIMATE. A weak form of tropical monsoon climate occurs over much of the country, with arid conditions in the north and west, where the wet season is only from Dec. to March. Elsewhere, rain comes mainly in the summer. Summer temperatures are high everywhere, but winters can be cold in the mountainous north. Islamabad. Jan. 50°F (10°C), July 90°F (32·2°C). Annual rainfall 36″ (900 mm). Karachi. Jan. 61°F (16·1°C), July 86°F (30°C). Annual rainfall 8″ (196 mm). Lahore. Jan. 53°F (11·7°C), July 89°F (31·7°C). Annual rainfall 18″ (452 mm). Multan. Jan. 51°F (10·6°C), July 93°F (33·9°C). Annual rainfall 7″ (170 mm). Quetta. Jan. 38°F (3·3°C), July 80°F (26·7°C). Annual rainfall 10″ (239 mm).

CONSTITUTION AND GOVERNMENT. Under the Constitution of 1973 Parliament is bi-cameral, comprising the National Assembly and the Senate. The strength of the National Assembly is 210 including 10 women. The Senate consists of 63 members, 14 from each province, 5 from Federally Administered Tribal Areas and 2 from the federal capital area, elected by the members of the Provincial Assemblies. A constitutional amendment of 29 March 1976 provided 6 National Assembly seats reserved for non-Moslem minority representatives.

With the proclamation of martial law the Constitution kept in abeyance, but not abrogated: The Provisional Constitution Order, 1981, promulgated on 24 March 1981, retains 119 Articles in whole or in part.

The Constitution obliges the Government to use such ways and means as may enable the people to order their lives collectively and individually in accordance with the principles of Islam. The Council of Islamic Ideology was set up to this end under article 228 of the Constitution.

An Ombudsman was appointed in Jan. 1983.

In Jan. 1982 a Federal Council of 288 members was inaugurated, under the chairmanship of K. M. Safdar. The Council, of up to 350 members, was to act as an interim body until an elected Parliament could be set up.

In Jan. 1985 the President announced that national elections would be held 5 Feb. 1985 on the basis of the 1973 Constitution, amended to provide wider presidential powers. On 19 Dec. 1984 a referendum was held to determine whether the President should continue in office for a 5-year term, following the elections; results were announced as 98% in favour.

The Pakistan People's Party won 47 seats in the new Assembly, the Muslim League 17 and the Jamaat Islami Party, 9. In March 1985 the President set up a new National Security Council, led by himself; he assumed power to appoint and dismiss ministers. He retains the final decision on legislation.

President and Chief Martial Law Administrator, Chairman of the Planning Commission, Science and Technology, States and Frontier Regions, Establishment: Gen. M. Zia-ul-Haq.

Federal Cabinet in Jan. 1985:

Finance and Economic Affairs: G. Ishaq Khan. *Foreign Affairs:* S. Y. Khan. *Attorney-General:* S. Pirzada. *Interior:* Lieut.-Gen. S. F. S. Khan Lodhi. *Defence:* A. A. Talpur. *Planning and Development:* Mahboobul Haq. *Housing and Works:* Air Marshal I. Haq Khan. *Water and Power:* R. Sikandar Zaman. *Industry:* E. Bux Soomro. *Culture, Sports and Tourism:* A. Niaz Mohammad Arbab. *Local Government and Rural Development:* F. Imam. *Labour, Manpower and Overseas Pakistanis:* G. Dastegir Khan. *Kashmir and Northern Affairs:* Lieut.-Gen. J. Said Mian. *Education:* M. Afzal. *Food, Agriculture and Co-operatives:* Vice-Adm. M. F. Janjua. *Communications:* M. Baluch. *Railways:* N. A. Ghafoor Khan Hoti. *Information and Broadcasting:* Raja M. Zafarul Haq. *Without portfolio:* A. M. A. Khan Abbas.

National flag: Green, charged at the centre, with a white crescent and white 5-pointed star, a white vertical stripe at the mast to one-quarter of the flag.

Local Government. Pakistan comprises the provinces of the Punjab, the North-West Frontier, Sind and Balúchistán, the states of Bahawalpur and Khairpur, the Balúchistán States Union, the frontier states and the tribal areas of Balúchistán and the north-west. These were merged into a single unit on 14 Oct. 1955. In July 1970 the single unit was dissolved into the original 4 provinces. The provincial capitals are Peshawar (NW Frontier Province), Lahore (Punjab), Karachi (Sind) and Quetta (Balúchistán). Provincial governors are appointed by the President and are assisted by provincial councils.

Within the provinces there are divisions administered by Commissioners appointed by the President; the divisions are divided into districts and agencies administered by Deputy Commissioners or Political Agents who are responsible to the Provincial Governments. There are 4 provincial assemblies.

Kashmir. Between one-third and one-half of Kashmir is controlled by Pakistan. This area is the northern and western portion of the country. It has an area of 83,806 sq. km. and a population of about 1·3m. Under a United Nations resolution of 1949 its future was to be decided by plebiscite; it is still a disputed territory.

The people of Azad Kashmir have their own Assembly (42 members including 2 women), their own Council (of 14 members), High Court and Supreme Court. There is a Parliamentary form of Government with a Prime Minister as the executive head and the President as the Constitutional head. Elections to the Legislative's 40 general seats are to be held within 10 days of the general elections in Pakistan, according to a presidential proclamation of 8 Oct. 1977. The seat of government is Muzaffarabad.

The Pakistan Government is directly responsible for Gilgit and Baltistan.

DEFENCE

Army. The Army consists of 2 armoured and 16 infantry divisions; 4 independent armoured, 5 independent infantry, 7 artillery and 2 anti-aircraft brigades; 6 armoured reconnaissance regiments, 6 surface-to-air missile batteries and 1 Special Services Group. Equipment includes 370 M-47/-48, 51 T-54/-55 and 900 Type-59 main battle tanks. Strength (1985) 450,000, with a further 500,000 reservists. There are also 100,000 men in paramilitary units: National Guard, Frontier Corps, Pakistan Rangers, Coast Guard and Frontier Constabulary.

Navy. The fleet comprises 6 diesel-powered patrol submarines (completed in France in 1969–80), 3 midget submarines, 1 "County" class destroyer, *Babur* (*ex*-HMS *London*) transferred from the Royal Navy in 1982, the ex-British very old light cruiser (harbour training ship) *ex*-HMS *Diadem*, re-named *Jahangir*, 7 old destroyers (6 *ex*-US and 1 *ex*-British), 4 ex-Chinese corvette-type patrol vessels, 4 ex-Chinese fast missile craft, 12 *ex*-Chinese fast gunboats, 4 *ex*-Chinese fast (hydrofoil) torpedo boats, 1 seaward defence boat, 1 oceanographic survey ship, 6 coastal minesweepers, 1 fleet replenishment ship, 1 degaussing vessel, 1 rescue ship, 2 landing craft, 1 water carrier and 3 tugs.

The principal naval base and dockyard are at Karachi. Naval personnel in 1985 totalled 1,250 officers and 14,550 ratings.

The naval air arm comprises 4 fixed-wing aircraft and 10 helicopters.

Air Force. The Pakistan Air Force came into being on 14 Aug. 1947. It has its headquarters at Peshawar and is organized within 3 air defence sectors, in the northern, central and southern areas of the country. Tactical units include 5 squadrons of Mirage III-EP/5 supersonic fighters, 1 squadron equipped with Mirage III-RP reconnaissance aircraft, and C-130 Hercules turboprop transports. Delivery of 34 F-16A and 6 F-16B Fighting Falcons began in late 1982, for operational service with 3 interceptor squadrons from 1984. Flying training schools are equipped with Masshaq (Saab Supporter) armed piston-engined primary trainers, T-37B/C jet trainers supplied by the USA, Mirage III-DPs and Chinese-built FT-5s (two-seat MiG-17s). Three Breguet Atlantics, plus a small number of Alouette III helicopters, are available to perform maritime reconnaissance, search and rescue duties in co-operation with Sea King helicopters of the Pakistan Navy Air Arm. A VIP transport squadron operates the Presidential F27 turboprop aircraft, a twin-jet Falcon 20 and smaller types. There is a flying college at Risalpur and an aeronautical engineering college at Korangi Creek. Total strength in 1984 was about 260 combat aircraft and 18,000 all ranks.

INTERNATIONAL RELATIONS

External Debt (June 1983), about US$9,865m.

Membership. Pakistan is a member of the UN, the Colombo Plan, and Regional Co-operation for Development.

Treaties. A mutual defence assistance agreement between Pakistan and the USA was signed in Karachi on 19 May 1954.

ECONOMY

Planning. The sixth 5-year plan (1983–88) envisages a total fixed investment of Rs 495,000m. including Rs 77,000m. for industry, of which Rs 62,000m. would be spent in the private sector. Real growth in GDP is planned at 6·5% annually (agriculture 5%; industry 9%). Expenditure will be met mainly (75%) from internal resources. Allocations for energy (Rs 116,000m.), agriculture and irrigation (Rs 88,000m.), special development programmes (Rs 22,000m.) and family planning (Rs 1,800m.) have been made.

Budget. The following table shows the budget for the years 1982–83 and 1983–84 in Rs 1m.:

	1982–83 Revised	*1983–84 Budget*
Internal revenue	58,040·2	63,212·3
External revenue	14,973·9	16,775·3
Current expenditure	50,949·6	57,289·6
Development expenditure	28,255·0	31,000·0

Currency. The monetary unit is the Pakistan *rupee*. In March 1985 Rs 16·60 = £1; Rs 16·03 = US$1. Decimal coinage was introduced on 1 Jan. 1961. The rupee, which previously consisted of 64 *pice*, now consists of 100 *paisas*. The notes are of Rs 100, 50, 10 and 5 denominations issued by the State Bank in the name of the Government, and Rs 1 issued by the State Bank incurring no liability; the coinage in the decimal series is 0·5, 0·25, 0·1, 0·05 and 0·01 rupee.

Total monetary assets (including currency in circulation and deposits) in March 1980 amounted to Rs 93,087m. Currency in circulation, Oct. 1980, Rs 30,812·4m.

Banking. As from 1 Jan. 1985, banks and other financial institutions will abandon the payment of interest on new transactions. This does not apply to international business, but does apply to the domestic business of foreign banks operating in Pakistan. Investment partnerships, between bank and customer, are to replace straight loans at interest.

The State Bank of Pakistan is the central bank; it came into operation as the Central Bank on 1 July 1948 with an authorized capital of Rs 30m. and was nationalized in Jan. 1974. As on 27 Oct. 1983 total assets or liabilities of the issue department amounted to Rs 46,464m. and those of the banking department Rs 59,254m.; reserve fund, Rs 1,300m. and total deposits, Rs 36,745m. It is the sole bank of issue for Pakistan, custodian of foreign exchange reserves (US$1,670m. in Oct. 1983) and banker for the federal and provincial governments and for scheduled banks. It also manages the rupee public debt of federal and provincial governments. It provides short-term loans to the Government and commercial banks and short- and medium-term loans to specialized banks. The Bank's subsidiary Federal Bank for Co-operatives makes loans to provincial co-operative banks. Loans made 1979–80, Rs 601·2m.

There were 22 scheduled banks (banks with capital and reserves of an aggregate value of not less than Rs 500,000) in Pakistan on 30 June 1984. Of these 5 were Pakistani (National Bank of Pakistan, Habib Bank Ltd, United Bank Ltd, Muslim Commercial Bank Ltd and Allied Bank Ltd). Pakistani scheduled banks were nationalized in Jan. 1974. In addition, there were 17 foreign banks. Total deposits of all the scheduled banks stood at Rs 110,139m. on 27 Jan. 1983. The National Bank of Pakistan acts as an agent of the State Bank for transacting Government business and managing currency chests at places where the State Bank has no offices of its own.

Weights and Measures. The metric system is in general use.

ENERGY AND NATURAL RESOURCES

Electricity. Installed capacity (1981) by type of generation: Thermal 1,648,830 kw.; hydro-electric, 1,767,200 kw.; nuclear, 137,000 kw. Total generated electrical energy in 1982–83, 19,636m. kwh; 60% of this was hydro-electricity, the main source being the Tarbela Dam. By 1983 30% of the population had access to electric power.

Oil. Oil comes mainly from the Potowar Plain, from fields at Meyal, Tut, Balkassar, Joya Mair and Dhullian. Production in 1984 was 900,000 tonnes. Oil reserves were also found at Dhodak in Dec. 1976. Exploitation is mainly through government incentives and concessions to foreign private sector companies. The Pak Arab refinery pipeline runs 865 km. from Karachi to Multan; capacity, 4·5m. tonnes of oil annually.

Gas. Gas pipelines from Sui to Karachi (345 miles) and Multan (200) supply natural gas to industry and domestic consumers. A pipeline between Quetta and Shikarpur was constructed in 1982. There are 4 other productive fields. Reserves (1983), 500,000m. cu. metres; production in 1982–83 was 323,000m. cu. ft., or about 42% of energy needs.

Water. The Indus water treaty of 1960, concluded between India and Pakistan, has created the basis for a large-scale development programme. The Indus Basin Development Fund Agreement has been subscribed by Australia, Canada, Federal

Republic of Germany, New Zealand, UK and USA and is administered by the International Bank; the works to be constructed call for expenditure of US$1,000m. The main purpose of the treaty is the division of the water power of the Indus and its 5 tributaries between India and Pakistan. After the construction of some 460 miles of canals, the Indus and the 2 western tributaries will serve Pakistan and the entire flow of the 3 eastern tributaries will be released for use in India.

The largest project is the construction of the Tarbela Dam, an earth-and-rock filled dam on the river Indus, 485 ft high, which has a gross storage capacity of 11·1m. acre feet of water for irrigation.

The Lloyd Barrage and Canal Construction Scheme, consists of a barrage across the river Indus at Sukkur and 7 canals—4 on the left and 3 on the right bank. Another barrage across the Indus, 4½ miles north of Kotri, called the Ghulam Muhammad Barrage, was completed in 1955. The Taunsa barrage on the Indus, 80 miles downstream of Kalabagh, was completed in 1958. The Gudu barrage, 10 miles from Kashmore, was completed in 1962.

The province of the Punjab set up in 1949 the Thal Development Authority to colonize the Thal desert between the Indus and Jhelum rivers.

The Chashma canal will carry water 172 miles across Dera Ismail Khan from the Chashma barrage on the Indus. The Mangla Dam on the Jhelum was inaugurated in Nov. 1967.

Minerals. The main agencies are the Pakistan Mineral Development Corporation, the Resource Development Corporation and the Gemstone Corporation of Pakistan. Coal is mined at Sharigh and Harnai on the Sind–Pishin railway and in the Bolan pass, also in Sor Range and Degari in the Quetta–Pishin district and in the Punjab; total recoverable reserves, about 480m. tonnes, mainly low-grade. A further 55m. tonnes was found at Lakhra in 1980 and reserves of over 500m. tonnes were found in the 300 sq. mile Thatta Sadha field in 1981. Copper ore reserves at Saindak, in Baluchistan, 412m. tons, containing (1984 estimate) 1·69m. tons of copper; 2·24m. oz. of gold; 2·2m. oz. of silver. Chromite is extracted in and near Muslimbagh. Limestone is quarried generally. Gypsum is mined in the Sibi district and elsewhere; reserves (1983), about 370m. tonnes. Iron ore is being worked in Kalabagh and elsewhere; reserves, about 400m. tonnes, low-grade. A further 18m. tonnes, high-grade, has been found in Balúchistán. Uranium has been found in Dera Ghazi Khan. Production (tonnes, 1983): Coal, 1·54m.; chromite, 3,225; limestone, 4·2m.; gypsum, 215,000; rock salt, 526,000; china clay, 72,705. Other minerals of which useful deposits have been found are magnesite, sulphur, barites, marble, bauxite, antimony ore, bentonite, celestite, dolomite, fireclay, fluorite, fuller's earth, phosphate rock, silica sand and soapstone.

Agriculture. The entire area in the north and west is covered by great mountain ranges. The rest of the country consists of a fertile plain watered by 5 big rivers and their tributaries. Agriculture is dependent almost entirely on the irrigation system based on these rivers. It employs (1983) 55% of labour and provides about 30% of GNP and 35% of foreign exchange earnings. Growth rate, 1982–83, 4·8%. The main crops are wheat, cotton, maize, sugar-cane and rice, while the Quetta and Kalat divisions (Balúchistán) are known for their fruits and dates.

By 31 March 1977, 3·34m. acres of land had been taken away from landlords, and 1·48m. acres had been distributed to 137,005 tenants. An ordinance of Jan. 1977 reduced the upper limit of land holding to 100 irrigated or 200 non-irrigated acres; it also replaced the former land revenue system with a new agricultural income tax, from which holders of up to 25 irrigated or 50 unirrigated acres are exempt. Of about 4m. farms, 89% are of less than 25 acres. Of the surveyed area of 156m. acres, cultivated land accounts for 63m. acres, of which 11m. acres consist of fallow land, so that the net area sown is 52m. acres.

Pakistan is self-sufficient in wheat, rice and sugar.

Production, 1982–83 (in 1,000 tonnes): Rice (cleaned), 3,272; wheat, 12,300; sugar-cane (gur), 31,604; cotton (lint, 1,000 bales), 4,800.

Livestock (FAO estimate, 1983): Cattle, 16,157,000; buffaloes, 12,483,000; sheep, 23,531,000; goats, 27,716,000; poultry, 72m.

Forestry. There were (1976) 7·3m. acres of reserved and protected forests and 10·6m. acres managed as pasture ranges by the Forest Department. Of the forests 1·5m. acres are in Punjab, 1·66m. in Balúchistán, 1·46m. in Sind and 2·65m. in the North-West Frontier Province. Forests produce an annual average of over 20m. cu. ft of timber and 16m. cu. ft of fuel. Annual value of this and other produce, about Rs. 60m. Forest lands are also used as national parks, wildlife and game reserves.

Fisheries. Landings of inland water and marine fish, about 200,000 tonnes annually.

INDUSTRY AND TRADE

Industry. Industry employs about 10% of the population, contributing (1982–83) about 17·5% of GDP. The growth rate in manufacturing, 1982–83, was 8·3%. In 1972 public sector companies were re-organized under a Board of Industrial Management. Government policy since 1977 has been to encourage private industry, particularly small industry. The public sector, however, is still dominant in large industries; in 1981–82 its gross value added was Rs. 4,291·8m., number of employees 81,689, investment Rs. 45,886·98m., of which 60% was for Pakistan Steel. Pakistan is self-sufficient in cotton cloth and sugar. A public sector steel-mill (Pakistan Steel) has been built at Port Qasim near Karachi, capacity 1·1m. tonnes; production of coke and pig-iron began in autumn 1981 and of steel in 1983. Also recently completed are a heavy mechanical complex and a heavy forge and foundry plant at Taxila. There are plants processing barites and china clay. A private sector ferrous alloys plant has been approved near Peshawar, capacity 40 tonnes of ferrous silicon and manganese per day. There is an Export Processing Zone at Karachi, covering 500 acres; at 30 June 1981 investment here stood at US$58·8m. The largest project (approved Aug. 1981) is a Pakistan-Saudi aluminium extrusion plant. At Machi Goth there is a fertilizer plant, capacity 1,800 tonnes per day.

Production 1982–83 (tonnes): Refined sugar, 1·1m.; vegetable ghee, 522,000; jute textiles, 62,461; soda ash, 93,638; sulphuric acid, 61,659; caustic soda, 41,195; chip board and paper board, 58,690; cycle tyres and tubes, 9·2m. units; cotton cloth, 305m. sq. metres; cotton yarn, 399m. kg.; cement, 3·9m.

Labour. The Labour Force Survey of 1974–75 gave the total work force as 20·42m., of whom 54·8% (11·22m.) were engaged in agriculture, forestry and fishing, 13·6% (2·8m.) in manufacturing; the textile industry was the largest single manufacturing employer. Estimates (1979–80) gave a labour force of 22·97m., 5·6m. of them urban.

Commerce. Total value of exports during 1982–83 amounted to Rs 34,442m., and the total value of imports to Rs 68,151m. The value of the chief articles imported into and exported from Pakistan in 1982–83 was (in Rs 1m.):

Imports		*Exports*	
Minerals, fuels, lubricants etc.	20,909·5	Raw cotton	3,896·6
		Cotton cloth	3,579·0
Machinery and transport equipment	16,814·5	Cotton yarns	3,308·2
		Rice	3,682·6
Manufactured goods	8,896·3	Woollen carpets	1,885·5
Chemicals	7,508·2	Leather	1,195·0

Total trade between Pakistan and UK (British Department of Trade returns, in £1,000 sterling):

	1980	*1981*	*1982*	*1983*	*1984*
Imports to UK	58,289	63,249	81,531	80,277	93,136
Exports and re-exports from UK	139,692	149,370	199,178	191,647	282,356

Tourism. Earnings in 1980, US$154m. There were 292,000 tourists.

COMMUNICATIONS

Roads. At the end of financial year 1975–76 Pakistan had 31,029 miles of roads, of which 16,875 miles were all-weather roads. The Karakoram highway to the

Chinese border, through Kohistan and the Hunza valley, was opened in 1978. An all-weather road linking Skardu and the remote NE Indus valley to the highway was built in 1980.

In 1982 there were 1·3m. vehicles registered, including 635,196 motor-cycles and 304,449 cars, jeeps and station wagons.

Railways. Pakistan Railways had (1982) a route of 8,822 km (of which 290 km electrified) mainly on 1,676 mm. gauge, with some metre gauge and narrow gauge line. In 1981–82: ran 16,502 passenger-km and 7,067m. tonne-km..

Aviation. Karachi is served by British Airways, KLM, PANAM, Lufthansa, Swissair, SAS, Iran National Airlines, Air France, Garuda, Gulf Air and by Philippine, Japanese, Chinese, East African, Syrian, Iraqui, Kuwait, Jordanian, Saudi Arabian, Romanian, Egyptian and Russian airlines.

Pakistan International Airlines (founded 1955; the majority of shares is held by the Government) had 4 DC-10s, 7 Boeing 707Cs, 5 720Bs, 2 747Bs and 8 Fokker F27s in 1977; 2 other Boeing 720Bs were on lease to Air Malta. Services operate to 20 home airports, New York, Paris, Amsterdam, Copenhagen, İstanbul, Athens, Rome, Cairo, Tripoli, Nairobi, Dhahran, Damascus, Amman, Baghdad, Persian Gulf points, Tōkyō, Peking (Beijing), Zahedan, Singapore, Manila, Kuala Lumpur, Bangkok, Colombo, London, Frankfurt, Bombay, Delhi, Dacca, Kábul, Tehrán and Jeddah.

Shipping. There is a seaport at Karachi. A second port is being built at Phitti Creek on the Makram coast, 26 miles east of Karachi, to be called Port Muhammad Bin Qasim; this port will have iron and coal berths for Pakistan Steel Mills, multi-purpose berths, bulk-cargo handling, oil and container-traffic terminals; the first phase (handling bulk and bagged cargo) will be operational it is hoped in 1983. The Pakistan National Shipping Corporation had 51 vessels in 1982, of 700,000 DWT, carrying 38% of dry cargo handled. National flag carriers now operate between Pakistan and UK; USA and Canada; the Far East; the (Persian) Gulf, Arabian Gulf, Red Sea, Black Sea and Mekran Coast; Continental Europe and the Middle East. The Karachi Shipyard and Engineering Works Ltd construct all types of vessels up to 27,000 DWT and repairs all types; dry-dock and under-water repairs can be done on vessels up to 29,000 DWT, above-water repairs on vessels and drilling rigs of all sizes.

Post and Broadcasting. The telegraph and telephone system is government-owned. Telephones, on 1 Jan. 1982, numbered 393,010; a nationwide dialling system is in operation between 46 cities. In 1979 there were 10,488 post offices (8,193 rural) and 93 main telegraph offices; emphasis was laid on improving rural communications and 28 public call offices and 47 small exchanges were opened. Pakistan has international telephone connections by 102 satellite, 7 HF, 4 microwave and 10 carrier circuits. An international direct-dialling exchange with 25,000 connections was opened in July 1980. The Pakistan Broadcasting Corporation had 16 radio stations in Dec. 1983. Television stations operate in Lahore, Karachi, Peshawar, Quetta and Rawalpindi–Islamabad.

Cinemas (1983). There are about 600 cinemas.

Newspapers. Dailies and periodicals numbered 1,156 in 1983: 763 were in Urdu, 272 in English and 70 in Sindhi; 121 were dailies, 315 weeklies, 562 monthlies and 158 quarterlies. Top circulation 300,000 for an Urdu daily paper.

JUSTICE, RELIGION, EDUCATION AND WELFARE

Justice. The Central Judiciary consists of the Supreme Court of Pakistan, which is a court of record and has three-fold jurisdiction, namely, original, appellate and advisory. There are 4 High Courts in Lahore, Peshawar, Quetta and Karachi. Under the Constitution, each has power to issue directions of writs of *Habeas Corpus, Mandamus, Certiorari* and others. Under them are district and sessions courts of first instance in each division; they have also some appellate jurisdiction. Criminal cases not being sessions cases are tried by district magistrates and subordinate magistrates. There are subordinate civil courts also.

The Constitution provides for an independent judiciary, as the greatest safeguard of citizens' rights. The Laws (Continuance in Force) (Eleventh Amendment) Order, 1980, prescribed the date of 14 Aug. 1981 by which the judiciary shall be separated from the executive. There is an Attorney-General, appointed by the President, who has right of audience in all courts.

A Federal Shariat Court at the Supreme Court level has been established to decide whether any law is wholly or partially un-Islamic. Islamic law is to be enforced as the law of the state; penalties for offences involving intoxicating liquor, offences against property and sexual offences have been specified. Imprisonment remains as a penalty in general use, but some offences in all the above categories are liable to whipping and some property offences, to amputation.

Religion. Religious groups (1972 census): Moslems, 63·28m.; Christians, 907,861; Scheduled Castes, 603,369; Caste Hindus, 296,837; Parsees, 9,589; Buddhists, 4,318; others, 205,250. There is a Ministry to safeguard the constitutional rights of religious minorities.

Education. At the census of 1981, 23·3% of the population were able to read and write. Adult literacy programmes have been established.

The principle of free and compulsory primary education has been accepted as the responsibility of the state; duration has been fixed provisionally at 5 years. In 1982–83 there were 61,354 elementary schools with 7·1m. pupils; 5,686 middle schools with 1·6m.; 3,773 high schools with 600,000; 257 secondary vocational schools with 41,000. Present policy stresses vocational and technical education, disseminating a common culture based on Islamic ideology.

Sixth plan (1983–88) expenditure: Rs. 11,000m. on primary and secondary schools; Rs. 1,300m. on colleges and Rs. 2,100m. on universities.

There were 1983, 442 general colleges, 102 professional colleges. In 1983 there were 20 universities, including the open university at Islamabad and the privately-funded Aga Khan University. University and other college students, 1982–83, 379,000.

Health. In 1982 there were 613 hospitals and 3,457 dispensaries (50,335 beds) and about 29,930 doctors. Sixth plan (1983–88) expenditure: Rs. 15,750m.

Social Security. In 1981–82 expenditure on cash benefits under the employees' social security scheme was Rs15·3m., on medical care, Rs.93·2m.

DIPLOMATIC REPRESENTATIVES

Of Pakistan in Great Britain (35–36 Lowndes Sq., London, SW1X 9JN)
Ambassador: Ali Arshad (accredited 13 Feb. 1981).

Of Great Britain in Pakistan (Diplomatic Enclave, Ramna 5, Islamabad)
Ambassador: Richard Fyjis-Walker, CMG, CVO.

Of Pakistan in the USA (2315 Massachusetts Ave., NW, Washington, D.C., 20008)
Ambassador: Ejaz Azim.

Of the USA in Pakistan (AID/UN Bldg., Islamabad)
Ambassador: Deane R. Hinton.

Of Pakistan to the United Nations
Ambassador: S. Shah Nawaz.

Books of Reference

Pakistan Year-Book. Annual
Ahmed, A. S., *Religion and Politics in Muslim Society: Order and Conflict in Pakistan.* CUP, 1973
Ali, T., *Can Pakistan Survive? The Death of the State.* Harmondsworth, 1983
Burke, S. M., *Pakistan's Foreign Policy.* OUP, 1973
Burki, S. J., *Pakistan Under Bhutto.* London, 1980
Griffin, K., and Khan, A. R. (ed.), *Growth and Inequality in Pakistan.* London and New York 1972
Hasan, M., (ed.) *Pakistan in a Changing World.* Karachi, 1978
Jennings, Sir Ivor, *Constitutional Problems in Pakistan.* CUP, 1957
Siddiqui, K., *Conflict, Crisis and War in Pakistan.* London, 1972

PANAMA

Capital: Panama City
Population: 1·97m. (1983)
GNP per capita: US$1,910 (1981)

República de Panamá

HISTORY. A revolution, inspired by the USA, led to the separation of Panama from the United States of Colombia and the declaration of its independence on 3 Nov. 1903. The *de facto* Government was on 13 Nov. recognized by the USA, and soon afterwards by the other Powers. In 1914 Colombia agreed to recognize the independence of Panama. This treaty was ratified by the USA and Colombia in 1921, and on 8 May 1924 diplomatic relations between Colombia and Panama were established. On 10 Oct. 1979 Panama assumed sovereignty over what was previously known as the Panama Canal Zone and now called the Canal Area.

For the treaties regulating the relations between Panama and the USA *see* pp. 961–62.

AREA AND POPULATION. Panama is bounded north by the Caribbean, east by Colombia, south by the Pacific and west by Costa Rica. Extreme length is about 480 miles (772 km); breadth between 37 (60) and 110 miles (177 km); coastline, 426 miles (685 km) on the Atlantic and 767 (1,234 km) on the Pacific; total area (including the Canal Zone) is 30,134 sq. miles (78,046 sq. km); population according to the census of 11 May 1980 was 1,830,175. Over 75% are of mixed blood and the remainder Indians, negroid, white and Asiatic.

The capital is Panama City, on the Pacific coast; census population, 1980, 389,227. There are 9 provinces (with populations, 1980) as follows (the capitals in brackets): Bocas del Toro (Bocas del Toro), 53,579; Chiriquí (David), 287,801; Coclé (Penonomé), 140,320; Colón (Colón), 166,439; Los Santos (Las Tablas), 70,200; Herrera (Chitré), 81,866; Darién (La Palma), 26,497 ; Panama (Panama City), 830,278; Veraguas (Santiago), 173,195. The port of Colón on the Atlantic coast had 95,300 (78,000). Smaller ports on the Pacific are Aguadulce, Pedregal, Montijo, Puerto Mutis and Puerto Armuelles; in the Atlantic, Bocas del Toro, Almirante, Portobello, Mandinga and Permé. A new fishing port came into operation at Vacamonte in Aug. 1979.

Vital statistics (1980): Births, 52,626; marriages, 8,850; deaths, 7,959.

CLIMATE. A tropical climate, unvaryingly with high temperatures and only a short dry season from Jan. to April. Rainfall amounts are much higher on the north side of the isthmus. Panama City. Jan. 79°F (26·1°C), July 81°F (27·2°C). Annual rainfall 70″ (1,770 mm). Colón. Jan. 80°F (26·7°C), July 80°F (26·7°C). Annual rainfall 127″ (3,175 mm). Balboa Heights. Jan. 80°F (26·7°C), July 81°F (27·2°C). Annual rainfall 70″ (1,759 mm). Cristóbal. Jan. 80°F (26·7°C), July 81°F (27·2°C). Annual rainfall 130″ (3,255 mm).

CONSTITUTION AND GOVERNMENT. The 1972 Constitution, as amended in 1978 and 1983, provides for an Assembly of 505 representatives of municipal districts elected on a community rather than a party basis, a Legislative Council of 57 members and a directly-elected President and Vice-President. The formation of political parties is now permitted, subject to statutory regulations, and 5 such parties had achieved full legal recognition by Sept. 1981.

Elections, the first to be held in Panama for 12 years, for the National Legislative Council were held in Sept. 1980. The Democratic Revolutionary Party (PRD) gained 10 of the then 19 seats; Liberals, 5; Christian Democrats, 2; Independents, 2.

President: Nicolas Ardido Barletta (assumed office, 30 May 1984).

The Cabinet appointed in Sept. 1983 was composed as follows:

Foreign Affairs: Oyden Ortega. *Interior and Justice:* Dr Carlos Ozores Typaldos. *Treasury and Finance:* Dr Gabriel Castro. *Agriculutral Development:* Frank Pérez. *Public Works:* Carlos Clement. *Commerce and Industry:* Dr Carlos Hoffman. *Labour and Social Welfare:* Arturo Melo. *Health:* Dr Guillermo Gaspar García de Paredes. *Housing:* Raúl Rolando Rodríguez. *Education:* Sra. Susana Richa de Torrijos. *Planning and Economic Policy:* Menalco Solis. *Presidency:* Mario de Diago.

The official language is Spanish.

National flag: Quarterly: first a white panel with a blue star, second red, third blue, fourth white with a red star.

National anthem: Alcanzamos por fin la victoria (words by J. de la Ossa; tune by Santos Jorge, 1903).

Local government: The 9 provinces and a Special Territory (another is envisaged) are sub-divided into 64 municipal districts and 2 *comarcas* (special districts) and are further sub-divided into 505 *corregimientos* (electoral districts).

DEFENCE

Army. The Army numbered (1985) 1,500 men organized in 7 light infantry companies, equipped with 16 V-150 armoured cars. There is also a paramilitary force of about 7,500 men.

Navy. Divided between both coasts, the flotilla comprises 4 patrol craft, 2 coastguard cutters, 2 coastal launchers, 3 medium landing ships, 3 utility landing craft and 3 logistic support vessels. In 1985 personnel totalled 500 officers and men.

Air Force. The air force has 1 Lockheed Electra, 4 C-47, 3 CASA 212, 2 Islander and 3 Twin Otter transports, 3 Cessna and 2 DHC-3 Otter liaison aircraft, a Shorts Skyvan, a Falcon VIP jet transport, 21 UH-1B/D/H Iroquois, twin-engined UH-1N helicopters and 1 Boeing 727-100.

INTERNATIONAL RELATIONS

Membership. Panama is a member of UN and OAS.

ECONOMY

Budget. The 1982 budget provided for expenditure of 1,395m. balboas and revenue of 1,055m. balboas.

Public sector debt was 2,333m. balboas in Dec. 1981.

Currency. The monetary unit is the *balboa*, which is of the same size and fineness as the US silver dollar but is maintained equivalent to the gold dollar. Other coins whose metallic content is required by law to correspond exactly to that of similar US coins are the half-balboa (equal to 50 cents US); the quarter and tenth of a balboa piece; a cupro-nickel coin of 5 cents, and a copper coin of 1 cent. US coinage is also legal tender. Volume of the currency has not been disclosed since 31 Dec. 1950, when it stood at 1·5m. balboas. The only paper currency used is that of the USA. In March 1985, US$1 = 1 *balboa*, £1 = 1·07 *balboas*.

Banking. There is no statutory central bank. The Government accounts are handled through the *Banco Nacional de Panama*. The number of commercial banks rose from 9 in 1964 to 116 by Sept. 1981; 62 have a general licence, 42 an international licence and 12 a representational licence. Leading banks are the Citibank, Lloyds Bank International (Bahamas) Ltd., and the Chase Manhattan Bank of New York. Other foreign-owned banks include the Bank of America, as well as Canadian, Columbian, Swiss, Federal German, French, Spanish, Dutch, Taiwan, Japanese and Brazilian banks.

Weights and Measures. English weights and measures are in general use; those of the metric system are also used.

ENERGY AND NATURAL RESOURCES

Electricity. Production of electric energy, 1981, amounted to 1,792·38m. kwh.

Minerals. There are known to be copper deposits in the provinces of Chiriquí, Colón and Darien. The most important, containing possibly the largest undeveloped reserves in the world, is Cerro Colorado (Chiriquí) on which a feasibility study is being undertaken by the Rio Tinto Zinc Coporation Ltd. If it is eventually decided to develop the mine, it is expected that the annual production of copper will reach 260,000 to 280,000 tonnes within a few years. The cost of construction is estimated at about US$1,800m. The deposit has estimated reserves of 1,300m. tonnes, with an average grade of 0·76% copper.

Agriculture. Of the whole area (1975) 18·5% is cultivated, 57·1% is natural or artificial pasture land and 9·5% is fallow. Of the remainder only a small part is cultivated, though the land is rich in resources. About 60% of the country's food requirements are imported. The Ministry of Agricultural Development (MIDA) buys leading crops at field prices. Of the land under cultivation, 26·4% is owned and 44·7% is usufructuary. The most important export products are bananas, grown by an affiliate of the United Brands Company and sugar from 4 state-owned and 2 private mills. Production in 1982 totalled 1·1m. tonnes of bananas and in 1981 187,000 tonnes of raw sugar. Oranges (64,000 tonnes) and mangoes (27,000 tonnes) are also produced. Most important food crop, for home consumption, is rice, grown on 80% of the farms; Panama's *per capita* consumption is very high. Output of rough rice was 150,000 tonnes in 1982. Other products are maize (63,000 tonnes in 1982), cocoa (1,000 tonnes), coffee (8,000 tonnes) and coconuts (25,000 tonnes). Beer, whisky, rum, 'seco', anise and gin are produced. Coffee is mainly grown in the province of Chiriquí, near the Costa Rican frontier; total production in 1982 was 8,000 tonnes, and small amounts were exported. The country has great timber resources, notably mahogany. Livestock (1983): 1,459,000 cattle, 197,000 pigs and 6m. poultry.

Fisheries. The catch in 1981 was 132,000 tonnes.

INDUSTRY AND TRADE

Industry. Local industries include cigarettes, clothing, food processing, shoes, soap, cement factories; foreign firms are being encouraged to establish industries, and a petrol refinery is operating in Colón.

Commerce. The imports and exports (including re-exports) for the Republic of Panama, for 6 calendar years are as follows (in 1,000 balboas; 1 balboa = US$1):

	Imports	*Exports*		*Imports*	*Exports*
1975	789,700	262,000	1978	862,000	381,700
1976	783,500	378,200	1979	1,185,000	291,506
1977	777,761	243,051	1980	1,277,000	407,000

Chief exports (48·2% to the USA) in 1980 were: Petroleum products, bananas, sugar, shrimps.

Chief imports, 1979, were valued (in 1m. balboas f.o.b.): Machinery and transport material, 214·7; manufactured goods, 308·9; fuel, minerals and similar, 319·4; chemicals, 116·7; food, 77·1. USA provided 32% of imports in 1979.

Total trade between Panama (including Colón Free Zone) and UK (British Department of Trade returns, in £1,000 sterling):

	1980	*1981*	*1982*	*1983*	*1984*
Imports to UK	3,941	7,815	9,521	5,341	9,681
Exports and re-exports from UK [1]	24,032	35,855	83,250	42,276	74,322

[1] Including new ships built for foreign owners and registered in Panama.

Tourism. In 1980, 392,062 people visited Panama.

COMMUNICATIONS

Roads. Panama had on 1 Jan. 1980, 8,606 km of roads. The road from Panama

City westward to the cities of David and Concepción and to the Costa Rican frontier, with several branches, is part of the Pan-American Highway. A concrete highway connects Panama City and Colón.

On 1 Jan. 1980 registered motor vehicles, private and commercial, numbered 111,052, this excludes vehicles owned by government departments.

Railways. The *Ferrocarril de Panama* (Panama Railroad) (1,524 mm gauge) (through the Canal area), which connects Ancón on the Pacific with Cristóbal on the Atlantic, is the principal railway. It is 76 km long and runs along the banks of the Canal. As most vessels unload their cargo at Cristóbal (Colón), on the Atlantic side, the greater portion of the merchandise destined for Panama City is brought overland by the *Ferrocarril de Panama.* The United Brands Company runs 376 km of railway, and the Chiriqui National Railroad 126 km.

Aviation. Commercial aviation has developed rapidly. PANAM, Braniff Airways, British Airways, KLM, Iberia Airlines and other international companies operate at Tocumen Airport, 17 miles from Panama City. Air Panama provides services between Panama City and New York, Los Angeles, Miami, Central America and some countries in South America. The *Compañia Panameña de Aviación* (COPA) and *Aerolineas Las Perlas* provide a local service between Panama City and the provincial towns. COPA also provides an international service to Central America.

Shipping. Ships under Panamanian registry on 25 Sept. 1981 numbered 10,859 of 27·2m. gross tons; most of these ships elect Panamanian registry because fees are low and labour laws lenient. All the international maritime traffic for Colón and Panama runs through the Canal ports of Cristóbal, Balboa and Bahia Las Minas (Colón); Almirante is used for both the provincial and international trade. There is an oil transfer terminal at Puerto Armuelles on the Pacific coast.

Panama Canal. On 18 Nov. 1903 a treaty between the USA and the Republic of Panama was signed making it possible for the US to build and operate a canal connecting the Atlantic and Pacific oceans through the Isthmus of Panama. The treaty granted the US in perpetuity the use, occupation and control of a Canal Zone, approximately 10 miles wide, in which the US would possess full sovereign rights 'to the entire exclusion of the exercise by the Republic of Panama of any such sovereign rights, power or authority'. In return the US guaranteed the independence of the republic and agreed to pay the republic $10m. and an annuity of $250,000. The US purchased the French rights and properties—the French had been labouring from 1879 to 1899 in an effort to build the Canal—for $40m. and in addition, paid private landholders within what would be the Canal Zone a mutually agreeable price for their properites.

Two new treaties between Panama and USA were agreed on 10 Aug. and signed on 7 Sept. 1977. One deals with the operation and defence of the canal until the end of 1999 and the other guarantees permanent neutrality.

The USA maintains operational control over all lands, waters and installations, including military bases, necessary to manage, operate and defend the canal until 31 Dec. 1999. A new agency of the US Government, the Panama Canal Commission, operates the canal, replacing the Panama Canal Co. A policy-making board of 5 US citizens and 4 Panamanians serves on the Commission's board of directors. Until 1990 the canal administrator will be a US citizen and the deputy will be Panamanian. After that date the position will be reversed.

Six months after the exchange of instruments of ratification Panama assumed general territorial jurisdiction over the former Canal Zone and became able to use portions of the area not needed for the operation and defence of the canal. Panamanian penal and civil codes became applicable. At the same time Panama assumed responsibility for commercial ship repairs and supplies, railway and pier operations, passengers, police and courts, all of which were among other areas formerly administered by the Canal Co. and the Canal Zone Government.

66% of the electorate of Panama agreed to the ratification of the treaties when a referendum was held on 23 Oct. 1977 and on 18 April 1978 the treaty was ratified by the US Congress. The treaty went into effect on 1 Oct. 1979.

The treaty of 1936 increased the annuity to US$430,000 and, as desired by Panama, withdrew the guarantee of independence. In 1955 the annuity was increased to US$1·93m., and the Panama Canal Co. turned over to the Republic the Panama City railroad yards and other properties valued at US$22m. At the end of 1962 the US completed the construction of a high-level bridge over the Pacific entrance to the Canal, and the flags of Panama and the US were flown jointly over areas of the Canal Zone under civilian authority. Following the devaluation of the dollar in 1972 and 1973, the annuity was adjusted proportionally to US$2·1m. and US$2·33m. respectively.

The Panama Canal Commission, a US Government Agency, is concerned primarily with the actual operation of the Canal. On 8 July 1974, 18 Nov. 1976 and 10 Oct. 1979 tolls were increased. These were the first increases of toll rates in the history of the Canal. Tolls were raised again on 12 March 1983. The new rates are US$1.83 a Panama Canal ton for vessels carrying passengers or cargo and US$1·46 per ton for vessels in transit in ballast. A Panama Canal ton is equivalent to 100 cu. ft of actual earning capacity. The new toll rate for warships, hospital ships and supply ships, which pay on a displacement basis, is US$1·02 a ton.

The changes were designed to continue the approximately break-even financial operating results after paying its own expenses and paying interest on the net direct investment of the US in the Canal.

Administrator of the Panama Canal Commission: Dennis P. McAuliffe.
Deputy Administrator: Fernando Manfredo (Panama).

The total civilian and military population of the Canal area is 34,700 (estimate), of whom about 30,750 are US citizens. The total force employed by the Panama Canal Commission on 13 Oct. 1984 was 8,083, comprising 1,520 US citizens, 6,355 Panamanians and 208 others.

The Canal was opened to commerce on 15 Aug. 1914. It is 85 ft above sea-level. It is 51·2 statute miles in length from deep water in the Caribbean Sea to deep water in the Pacific ocean, and 36 statute miles from shore to shore. The channel ranges in bottom-width from 500 to 1,000 ft; the widening of Gaillard Cut to a minimum width of 500 ft was completed in 1969. Normally, the average time of a vessel in Canal waters is less than 30 hours, 8–12 of which are in transit through the Canal proper. A map showing the Panama, Suez and Kiel canals on the same scale will be found in THE STATESMAN'S YEAR-BOOK, 1959 and a new map in the 1978–79 edition.

Particulars of the ocean-going commercial traffic through the canal are given as follows (vessels of 300 tons Panama Canal net and 500 displacement tons and over; cargo in long tons):

Fiscal year ending 30 Sept.	*North-bound (Pacific to Atlantic)*		*South-bound (Atlantic to Pacific)*		*Total*		*Tolls levied (in US$)*
	Vessels	*Cargo*	*Vessels*	*Cargo*	*Vessels*	*Cargo*	
1981	6,623	81,902,966	7,261	89,318,796	13,884	171,221,762	301,762,600
1982	6,618	88,895,265	7,391	96,557,067	14,009	185,452,332	323,958,366
1983	5,540	57,762,250	6,167	87,828,509	11,707	145,590,759	285,985,719
1984	5,455	62,211,519	5,775	78,259,299	11,230	140,470,818	286,677,844

In the fiscal year ending 30 Sept. 1984, of the 11,230 ships which passed through the Canal, 1,770 were Panamanian; 1,379 Liberian; 1,191 Japanese; 788 Greek; 742 US; 454 British; 454 Ecuadorian; 435 Russian; 337 Norwegian; 250 Peruvian; 250 Danish; 232 Fed. German.

Statistical Information: The Panama Canal Commission Office of Public Affairs.

Annual Reports on the Panama Canal, by the Administrator of the Panama Canal Commission.
Rules and Regulations Governing Navigation of the Panama Canal. The Panama Canal Commission, Miami, Florida *or* Washington, DC
Cameron, I., *The Impossible Dream.* London, 1972
Le Feber, W., *The Panama Canal: The Crisis in Historical Perspective.* OUP, 1978
McCullough, D., *The Path Between the Seas.* New York and London, 1978

Post and Broadcasting. There are telegraph cables from Panama to North America and Central and South American ports, and from Colón to the USA and Europe. There is also inter-continental communication by satellite. There are 93 licensed commercial broadcasting stations, nearly all operated by private companies, one of which functions in the canal. There are 5 television stations, one of them run by the US Army at Fort Clayton. In 1980 there were 285,000 radio and 220,000 television sets. On 1 Jan. 1982 there were 212,992 telephones.

Cinemas. In 1977 there were 52 cinemas in the district of Panama. All films must have Spanish subtitles.

Newspapers. There are 1 English language and 4 Spanish language daily morning newspapers and 1 English/Spanish evening newspaper.

JUSTICE, RELIGION, EDUCATION AND WELFARE

Justice. The Supreme Court consists of 9 justices appointed by the executive. There is no death penalty.

Religion. 95% of the population is Roman Catholic and 5% Protestant. There is freedom of religious worship and separation of Church and State. Clergymen may teach in the schools but may not hold public office.

Education. Elementary education is compulsory for all children from 7 to 15 years of age, with an estimated 545,800 students in schools in 1977. The University of Panama at Panama City, inaugurated on 7 Oct. 1935, had a total enrolment (1978) of 32,868 students. The Catholic university Sta. Maria La Antigua, inaugurated on 27 May 1965, had 1,916 students in Sept. 1978.

DIPLOMATIC REPRESENTATIVES

Of Panama in Great Britain (109 Jermyn St., London, SW1)
Ambassador: Guillermo Vega (accredited 14 June 1984).

Of Great Britain in Panama (Apartado 889, Panama City 1)
Ambassador: T. H. Steggle.

Of Panama in the USA (2862 McGill Terr., NW, Washington, D.C., 20008)
Ambassador: Aquilino E. Boyd.

Of the USA in Panama (Ave. Balboa y Calle 38, Panama City)
Ambassador: Everett E. Briggs.

Of Panama to the United Nations
Ambassador: (Vacant)

Books of Reference

Statistical Information: The Comptroller-General of the Republic (Contraloria General de la República, Calle 35 y Avenida 6, Panama City) publishes an annual report and other statistical publications.

Jorden, W. J., *Panama Odyssey.* Univ. of Texas Press, 1984
Langstaff, E. DeS., *Panama.* [Bibliography] Oxford and Santa Barbara 1982
Ropp, S. C., *Panamanian Politics.* New York, 1982

National Library: Biblioteca Nacional, Departamento de Información. Calle 22, Panama.

PAPUA NEW GUINEA

Capital: Port Moresby
Population: 3·26m. (1984)
GNP per capita: US$706 (1983)

HISTORY. To prevent that portion of the island of New Guinea not claimed by the Netherlands or Germany from passing into the hands of a foreign power, the Government of Queensland annexed Papua in 1883. This step was not sanctioned by the Imperial Government, but on 6 Nov. 1884 a British Protectorate was proclaimed over the southern portion of the eastern half of New Guinea, and in 1887 Queensland, New South Wales and Victoria undertook to defray the cost of administration, and the territory was annexed to the Crown the following year. The federal government took over the control in 1901; the political transfer was completed by the Papua Act of the federal parliament in Nov. 1905, and on 1 Sept. 1906 a proclamation was issued by the Governor-General of Australia declaring that British New Guinea was to be known henceforth as the Territory of Papua. The northern portion of New Guinea was a German colony until the First World War. It became a League of Nations mandated territory in 1921, administered by Australia, and later a UN Trust Territory (of New Guinea).

The Papua New Guinea Act 1949–1972 provides for the administration of the UN Australian Trust Territory of New Guinea in an administrative union with the Territory of Papua, in accordance with Art. 5 of the New Guinea Trusteeship Agreement, under the title of Papua New Guinea.

Australia granted Papua New Guinea self-government on 1 Dec. 1973 and, on 16 Sept. 1975, Papua New Guinea became a fully independent state.

AREA AND POPULATION. Papua New Guinea extends from the equator to Cape Baganowa in the Louisiade Archipelago to 11° 40′ S. lat. and from the border of West Irian to 160° E. long. with a total area of 462,840 sq. km. According to the census the 1980 population was 3,010,727. Port Moresby, (1980) 123,624; Lae, 61,617; Rabaul, 14,954; Madang, 21,335; Mount Hagen, 13,441. Area and population of the provinces:

Provinces	*Sq.km*	*Census 1971*	*Census 1980*	*Capital*
Milne Bay	14,000	109,460	127,975	Alotau
Northern	22,800	66,514	77,442	Popondetta
Central	29,500	117,330	116,964	Port Moresby
National Capital District	240	76,507	123,624	—
Gulf	34,500	58,564	64,120	Kerema
Western	99,300	70,898	78,575	Daru
Southern Highlands	23,800	192,854	236,052	Mendi
Enga	12,800	346,032	164,534	Wabag
Western Highlands	8,500		265,656	Mount Hagen
Chimbu	6,100	160,245	178,290	Kundiawa
Eastern Highlands	11,200	239,640	276,726	Goroka
Morobe	34,500	249,032	310,622	Lae
Madang	29,000	170,953	211,069	Madang
East Sepik	42,800	181,893	221,890	Wewak
West Sepik	36,300	93,978	114,192	Vanimo
Manus	2,100	24,866	26,036	Lorengau
West New Britain	21,000	61,515	88,941	Kimbe
East New Britain	15,500	113,750	133,197	Rabaul
New Ireland	9,600	59,543	66,028	Kavieng
North Solomons	9,300	96,363	128,794	Arawa

Vital statistics (1983, estimate): Crude birth rate, 39 per 1,000; crude death rate, 17.

CLIMATE. There is a monsoon climate, with high temperatures and humidity the year round. Port Moresby which is in a rain shadow and is not typical of the rest of Papua New Guinea. Jan. 82°F (27·8°C), July 78°F (25·6°C). Annual rainfall 40″ (1,011 mm).

CONSTITUTION AND GOVERNMENT. Papua New Guinea has a Westminster type of government. A single legislative house, known as the National Parliament, is made up of 109 members from all parts of the country. The members are elected under universal suffrage and general elections are held every 5 years. All persons over the age of 18 who are Papua New Guinea citizens are eligible to vote and stand for election. Voting is by secret ballot and follows the preferential system.

The first Legislative Council was established in 1951. It was abolished in 1964 and replaced with the House of Assembly. In 1950 the first village council was formed which established the basis of the now extensive local government system. A system of provincial government was introduced in 1976.

In the national elections of 1982 a Pangu government, supported by the United Party, came to power with 67 members of Parliament.

The administrative centre and capital is located at Port Moresby. National administration is carried out by a public service under the direction of 28 ministries. The country is divided into the National Capital District and 19 provinces: Western, Gulf, Central, Milne Bay, Northern, Southern Highlands, Enga, Western Highlands, Chimbu, Eastern Highlands, Morobe, Madang, East Sepik, West Sepik, Manus, New Ireland, East New Britain, West New Britain, and North Solomons. Each of the provincial governments has a secretariat headed by an Administrative Secretary. In many provinces the system of local governments still operates, although the provinces may make changes to this if they wish.

Governor-General: Sir Kingsford Dibela, GCMG.

The Cabinet in Jan. 1985 was as follows:

Prime Minister: Michael Thomas Somare.

Deputy Prime Minister and Minister for National Planning: Paias Wingti. *Finance:* Philip Bouraga, OBE. *Foreign Affairs and Trade:* Rabbie Namaliu. *Public Service:* Anthony Siaguru. *Education:* Barry Holloway. *Defence:* Boyamo Sali. *Provincial Affairs:* John Nilkare. *Primary Industry:* Dennis Young. *Commerce and Industry:* Karl Stack. *Health:* Martin Tovadek. *Works and Supply:* Pato Kakarya. *Justice:* Anthony Bais. *Labour and Employment:* Caspar Anggua. *Lands:* Bebes Korowaro. *Planning and Physical Services:* Kala Swokim. *Environment and Conservation:* Halalu Mai. *Posts and Telecommunications:* Roy Evara. *Transport:* Mathew Bendumb. *Information and Broadcasting:* Epel Tito. *Minerals and Energy:* Francis Pusal. *Police:* John Giheno. *Civil Aviation:* Tom Pais. *Religion, Youth, Women and Recreation:* Tom Awasa. *Forestry:* Lukas Waka. *Administrative Services:* Sir Pita Lus. *Correctional Services and Liquor Licensing:* Pundia Kange. *Culture and Tourism:* McKenzie Javopa.

The seat of the Government is at Port Moresby.

National flag: Diagonally ochre-red over black, on the red a bird of paradise in gold, and on the black 5 stars of the Southern Cross in white.

DEFENCE. The Papua New Guinea Defence Force has a total strength of 3,800 (1985) consisting of land, maritime and air elements. The Army is organized in 2 infantry battalions, 1 engineer and 1 signals battalion with logistic units. The Navy has 4 large patrol craft and 2 landing craft. The nucleus of an Air Force was formed by 4 DC-3 piston-engined transports delivered from Australia in 1975; two more were delivered later. They have been followed by 7 Australian-built Missionmaster twin-turboprop support transports. A Gulfstream II and a Super King Air are available for VIP use. Personnel total 75.

INTERNATIONAL RELATIONS

Membership. Papua New Guinea is a member of UN, the Commonwealth, the Colombo Plan, the South Pacific Commission and is an ACP state of EEC.

ECONOMY

Budget. Revenue (in K1,000) for calendar years was:

Source	*1981*	*1982*	*1983*
Customs, excise and export tax	115,534	131,252	145,000
Other taxes	144,270	163,872	179,114
Foreign government grants [1]	184,348	186,684	212,238
Loans	57,178	81,736	93,563
Other revenue	127,545	84,867	82,724
Total	628,875	648,411	712,639

[1] Mainly from Australia.

Expenditure (in K1,000) for the same periods:

Source	*1981*	*1982*	*1983* [2]
Consumption	302,997	303,460	306,219
Capital	75,952	55,803	70,278
Other expenditure [1]	280,094	307,479	327,900
Total	659,043	666,760	704,397

[1] Includes transfers to provincial governments. [2] Preliminary.

Currency. The unit of currency is the *kina* divided into 100 *toea* and is the sole legal tender. In March 1985, £1 = K1·09; US$1 = K1·04.

Banking. The Bank of Papua New Guinea assumed the central banking functions formerly undertaken by the Reserve Bank of Australia on 1 Nov. 1973.

A national banking institution which has been named the Papua New Guinea Banking Corporation, has been established. This bank has assumed the Papua New Guinea business of the Commonwealth Trading Bank of Australia except where certain accounts give rise to special financial or contractual problems.

The subsidiaries of 3 Australian commercial banks also operate in Papua New Guinea. These are the Australia and New Zealand Banking Group (PNG) Ltd, the Bank of New South Wales (PNG) Ltd, and the Bank of South Pacific Ltd, all of which offer trading and savings facilities. As from 1 Nov. 1973 these banks operated under Papua New Guinea banking legislation.

In 1983, two additional commercial banks Indosuez Niugini Bank Ltd and Niugini Lloyds International Bank Ltd began operating, each with 51% national ownership, and the remaining 49% held by the affiliate of a major international bank.

In addition to these five commercial banks, the Papua New Guinea Development Bank has provided long-term development finance with a particular attention to the needs of small-scale enterprises since 1967. The country's first merchant bank, Resources and Investment Finance Ltd (RIFL), specializing in large-scale financial services began business in late 1979. Its shares are owned by the Hong Kong and Shanghai Banking Corporation, the Commonwealth Trading Bank of Australia and the Papua New Guinea Banking Corporation.

Weights and Measures. The metric system is in force.

ENERGY AND NATURAL RESOURCES

Electricity. In 1983 installed capacity was 402,900 mw, production 1,434·9m. kwh.

Minerals. Copper is the main mineral product. Oil companies have been searching for oil, but by 1983 no commercial deposits had been found. Gold, copper and silver are the only minerals produced in quantity. Major copper deposits in the Kieta district of Bougainville have proved reserves of about 800m. tonnes and are worked by Bougainville Copper Ltd and production of copper concentrates for export began in 1972 from this source. Copper and gold deposits which were found in the Star Mountains of the Western Province are being developed by Ok Tedi Mining Ltd at the Mt. Fubilan mine and production of gold commenced in 1984. In 1983, B.C.L. produced 636,932 tonnes of copper concentrate containing approximately 183,191 tonnes of copper, 18·00 tonnes of gold and 47·41 tonnes of silver.

Agriculture. At 31 Dec. 1982, the total area of larger holdings was 395,000 hectares, of which 242,000 hectares were for agricultural purposes, the principal crops being coffee, copra and cocoa. Production of palm oil is of growing importance. Minor commercial crops include pyrethrum, tea, peanuts and spices. Locally consumed food crops include sweet potatoes, taro, bananas, rice and sago. Tropical fruits grow abundantly. There is extensive grassland. A newly-established sugar industry has made the country self-sufficient in this commodity while a beef-cattle industry is being developed.

Livestock (1983): Cattle, 134,000; pigs, 1·45m.; goats, 16,000; poultry, 1m.

Forestry. Timber production is of growing importance for both local consumption and export. In 1983, about 2,004,500 cu. metres of logs were harvested; logs exported, 1,199,400 cu. metres.

Production of sawn timber, 1983, 297,000 cu. metres, exports, 21,200 cu. metres; exports of woodchips, 154,400 tonnes.

Fisheries. Tuna, both skipjack and yellowfin species, is the major fisheries resource; in 1980 the catch was 33,000 tonnes but has diminished sharply since then due to oversupply conditions on world markets. Exports of various crustacea, 1983, 1,171 tonnes, value K8·79m.

INDUSTRY AND TRADE

Industry. Secondary and service industries are expanding for the local market. Industries include the manufacture of paint, gases, concrete, twist tobacco and cigarettes, matches, soap, brewing, boat-building, furniture and the assembly of electrical appliances. In 1982 there were 720 factories employing 29,340 persons. Value of output K632m.

Labour. In 1980 about 733,000 were gainfully employed.

Trade. Imports (in K1,000) for calender years:

	1981	*1982*	*1983*
Food and live animals	136,339	138,692	134,813
Beverages and tobacco	8,362	8,388	8,769
Crude materials, inedible, except fuels	3,569	3,566	4,876
Mineral fuels, lubricants and related materials	158,369	146,093	167,380
Oils and fats (animal and vegetable)	1,877	2,212	2,525
Chemicals	45,033	39,319	64,050
Manufactured goods, chiefly by material	108,510	118,928	130,559
Machinery and transport equipment	224,595	230,393	232,770
Miscellaneous manufactured articles	54,593	53,873	60,339
Commodities and transactions of merchandise trade, not elsewhere specified	10,149	10,203	9,285
Total imports	751,419	751,667	814,866

Exports (in K1,000) for calendar years:

	1981	*1982*	*1983*
Coconut and copra products—			
Copra	19,476	12,878	23,891
Copra (coconut) oil	12,508	12,110	20,038
Copra cake and pellets	689	745	1,433
Total	32,673	25,733	45,452
Coffee beans	74,218	77,780	94,659
Cocoa beans	34,135	31,822	41,376
Crude rubber	3,403	1,406	2,153
Tea	7,131	6,682	10,391
Pyrethrum extract	890	498	397

	1981	1982	1983
Forest and timber products			
Logs	31,517	49,312	43,576
Sawn timber	3,897	3,508	2,495
Veneers	272	–	–
Plywood	3,000	2,151	1,394
Other	6,982	4,424	6,517
Total	45,667	59,395	53,982
Crocodile skins	1,320	2,341	936
Crayfish and prawns	6,851	6,463	8,788
Gold	7,132	6,242	8,058
Copper concentrate	...	298,034	364,862
Other domestic produce	332,170 [1]	28,412	31,878
Total domestic produce	545,589	545,396	662,932
Re-exports	19,334	24,351	19,236
Total exports	564,923	570,247	682,168

[1] Includes K292,336,000 for copper ore and concentrate.

Of exports in 1983, Japan took 35%, Federal Republic of Germany, 25% and Australia, 12%; of imports, Australia furnished about 40%, Singapore, 13% and Japan, 15%.

Total trade between Papua New Guinea and UK (British Department of Trade returns, in £1,000 sterling):

	1980	1981	1982	1983	1984
Imports to UK	22,861	18,506	28,031	28,142	68,245
Exports and re-exports from UK	10,978	11,316	15,911	18,236	14,643

Tourism. In 1983, there were 15,802 visitors.

COMMUNICATIONS

Roads. In Sept. 1976 there were approximately 19,538 km of roads including approximately 1,016 km of urban roads. Motor vehicles numbered (1980) 49,770 including 18,481 cars and station wagons.

Aviation. Frequent air services operate to and from Australia (Sydney, Brisbane and Cairns), and there are regular flights to Djayapura (Indonesia), Manila, Hong Kong, Singapore, Guam and Auckland. A service is also maintained to Honiara in the Solomon Islands. In addition to Air Niugini, the national flag carrier, Qantas, Philippine Airlines, Air New Zealand, Cathay Pacific and South Pacific Island Airways operate in and out of Papua New Guinea.

Shipping. There are regular shipping services between Australia and Papua New Guinea ports, and also services to New Zealand, Japan, Hong Kong, US west coast, Singapore, Solomon Islands, Vanuatu, Taiwan, Philippines and Europe. Small coastal vessels run between the various ports. In 1982 cargo discharged from overseas was 1·7m. tonnes; cargo loaded for overseas was 2·1m. tonnes.

Post and Broadcasting. Telephones numbered 51,483 on 31 Dec. 1983. The National Broadcasting Commission operates three networks. A national service is relayed throughout the country by a series of transmitters on medium- and short-wave bands. Local services operate in each of the 19 provinces, mainly on short-wave, while the larger urban centres are also covered by a commercial FM network relayed from Port Moresby.

JUSTICE, EDUCATION AND WELFARE

Justice. In 1983, over 1,500 criminal and civil cases were heard in the National Court and an estimated 120,000 cases in district and local courts.

Police. Total uniformed strength at 31 Dec. 1983, 4,497.

Education. At 30 June 1983 about 328,600 children attended 2,258 primary schools and 51,711 enrolled in 209 secondary, technical and vocational schools. The University of Papua New Guinea and the Papua New Guinea University of Technology had 3,245 students enrolled in full-time courses in 1983.

Health. In 1984, there were 19 hospitals, 459 health centres, 2,200 aid posts and 280 doctors.

DIPLOMATIC REPRESENTATIVES

Of Papua New Guinea in Great Britain (14 Waterloo Pl., London, SW1R 4AR)
High Commissioner: Ilinome Frank Tarua, OBE (accredited 25 Oct. 1983).

Of Great Britain in Papua New Guinea (Douglas St., Port Moresby)
High Commissioner: A. J. Collins, OBE.

Of Papua New Guinea in the USA (1140 19th St., NW, Washington D.C., 20036)
Ambassador: Renagi Renagi Lohia.

Of the USA in Papua New Guinea (Armit St., Port Moresby)
Chargé d'Affaires: Morton R. Dworken, Jr.

Of Papua New Guinea to the United Nations
Ambassador: Renagi Lohia.

Books of Reference

The Territory of Papua. Annual Report. Commonwealth of Australia. 1906–1940–41 and from 1945–46
The Territory of New Guinea. Annual Report. Commonwealth of Australia. 1914–1940–41 and from 1946–47
Papua New Guinea, Annual Report. From 1970–71
Hasluck, P., *A Time for Building.* Melbourne Univ. Press, 1976
Ross, A. C., and Langmore, J., *Alternative Strategies for Papua New Guinea.* OUP, 1974
Ryan, J., *The Hot Land.* London, 1970
Ryan, P. (ed.), *Encyclopaedia of Papua and New Guinea.* Melbourne Univ. Press, 1972
Skeldon, R., (ed.) *The Demography of Papua New Guinea.* Institute of Applied Social and Economic Research, 1979

PARAGUAY

Capital: Asunción
Population: 3·48m. (1983)
GNP per capita: US$1,630 (1981)

República del Paraguay

HISTORY. The Republic of Paraguay gained its independence from Spain on 14 May 1811. In 1814 Dr José Gaspar Rodríguez de Francia was elected dictator, and in 1816 perpetual dictator by the National Assembly. He died 20 Sept. 1840. In 1844 a new constitution was adopted, under which Carlos Antonio López (first elected in 1842, died 10 Sept. 1862) and his son, Francisco Solano López, ruled until 1870. During the devastating war against Brazil, Argentina and Uruguay (1865–70) Paraguay's population was reduced from about 600,000 to 232,000. Argentina, in Aug. 1942, and Brazil, in May 1943, voided the reparations which Paraguay had never paid. Further severe losses were incurred during the war with Bolivia (1932–35) over territorial claims in the Chaco. A peace treaty by which Paraguay obtained most of the area her troops had conquered was signed in July 1938.

AREA AND POPULATION. The area of the Oriental province is officially estimated at 159,827 sq. km (61,705 sq. miles) and the Occidental province at 246,925 sq. km (95,337 sq. miles), making the total area of the republic 406,752 sq. km (157,042 sq. miles).

The population according to the official census in 1983 was 3,477,000. The capital, Asunción (and metropolitan area), had 708,000 inhabitants; other principal cities: Presidente Stroessner (92,000), Pedro Juan Caballero (39,000), Encarnación (28,800), Pilar (25,600), Concepcíon (24,000).

The capital district and 19 departments had the following populations in 1982:

Asunción	455,517	Misiones	79,278
Central	494,575	Neembucu	70,689
Caaguazú	299,227	Amambay	68,422
Itapua	263,021	Canendiyú	65,807
Paraguari	202,152	*Oriente*	*2,959,568*
Cordillera	194,826	Presidente Hayes	43,787
San Pedro	189,751	Boquerón	14,685
Alto Paraná	188,351	Alto Paraguay	4,535
Guairá	143,374	Chaco	286
Concepción	135,068	Nueva Asunción	231
Caazapá	109,510	*Occidente*	*63,524*

Number of births, 1982, was 31,882; deaths, 10,201.

The population is overwhelmingly *mestizo* (mixed Spanish and Guaraní Indian) forming a homogeneous stock. There are some 46,700 unassimilated Indians of other tribal origin, in the Chaco and the forests of eastern Paraguay. There are some small traces of Negro descent. 40·1% of the population speak only Guaraní; 48·2% are bilingual (Spanish/Guaraní); and 6·4% speak only Spanish.

Mennonites who arrived in 3 groups (1927, 1930 and 1947) are settled in the Chaco and Oriental Paraguay and were estimated in 1969 to number 13,000, of whom 2,000 came from Canada and 11,000 from Germany. The Japanese colonists in the Oriental section, who first came in 1935, were reckoned to number 7,000 in 1983. Under an agreement signed with Japan in 1959 up to 85,000 Japanese were to be admitted over 30 years. An agreement with Korea was signed in 1966 and there were (1978) about 3,000 Korean families living in Paraguay.

CLIMATE. A tropical climate, with abundant rainfall and only a short dry season from July to Sept., when temperatures are lowest. Asunción. Jan. 81°F (27·2°C), July 64°F (17·8°C). Annual rainfall 53″ (1,316 mm).

CONSTITUTION AND GOVERNMENT. A new constitution replacing that of 1940 was drawn up by a Constituent Convention in which all legally recognized political parties were represented and was signed into law on 25 Aug. 1967. It provides for a two-chamber parliament consisting of a 30-seat Senate and a 60-seat Chamber of Deputies, each elected for a 5-year term. Two-thirds of the seats in each Chamber are allocated to the majority party and the remaining one-third shared among the minority parties in proportion to the votes cast. Voting is compulsory for all citizens over 18. The President is directly elected for a 5-year (renewable) term; he appoints the Cabinet and during parliamentary recess can govern by decree through the Council of State, the members of which are representatives of the Government, the armed forces and other bodies.

On 6 Feb. 1977 elections were held for a 60-member Constitutional Assembly to revise the 1967 Constitution.

President: Gen. Alfredo Stroessner, Commander-in-Chief, elected 11 July 1954 to complete the presidential period of his predecessor. He was re-elected as 'Colorado' candidate in 1958, 1963, 1968, 1973, 1978 and 1983.

The following is a list of past presidents since 1940, with the date on which each took office:

Gen. Higinio Morínigo, 7 Sept. 1940 (resigned).
Dr Juan Manuel Frutos, 3 June 1948.[1]
Dr J. Natalicio González, 15 Aug. 1948 (deposed).
Gen. Raimundo Rolón, 30 Jan. 1949.
Dr Felipe Molas López, 26 Feb. 1949[1] (resigned).
Dr Federico Chávez, 16 July 1950 (resigned).
Tomás Romero Pereira, 4 May 1954.

[1] Provisional, *i.e.*, following a *coup d'état.*

The President has a cabinet of 11 ministers which in March 1985 was composed as follows:

Interior: Dr Sabino A. Montanaro. *Foreign Affairs.* Dr Carlos A. Saldívar. *Finance:* César Barrientos. *Education and Worship:* Dr Carlos Ortiz Ramirez. *Public Works and Communications:* Juan A. Cáceres. *Agriculture and Livestock:* Hernando Bertoni. *National Defence:* Gen. Germán G. Martínez. *Public Health and Social Welfare:* Dr Adan Godoy Giménez. *Justice and Labour:* Dr Saúl González. *Industry and Commerce:* Dr Delfín Ugarte Centurión. *Without Portfolio:* (Vacant).

National flag: Red, white, blue (horizontal); the white stripe charged with the arms of the republic on the obverse, and, on the reverse, with a lion and the inscription *Paz y Justicia*—the only flag in the world with different obverse and reverse.

National anthem: ¡ Paraguayos, república o muerte! (words by F. Acuña de Figueroa; tune by F. Dupey).

The country is divided into 2 provinces: the 'Oriental', east of Paraguay River, and the 'Occidental', west of the same river. The Oriental section is divided into 14 departments and the capital. The more important departments are supervised by a *Delegado* appointed by and directly responsible to the central government. The Occidental province, or Chaco, is divided into 5 departments.

DEFENCE. The army, navy and air forces are separate services under a single command. The President of the Republic is the active Commander-in-Chief. The armed forces total about 15,500 officers and men

Army. The Army consists of 1 cavalry division, 8 infantry divisions, 1 independent infantry battalion, 1 Presidential Escort Regiment and supporting artillery, engineer and signals units. Equipment includes 6 M-4A3 main battle and 15 M-3A1 light tanks. Strength (1985) 12,500 (including 9,000 conscripts), and there are 25,000 reserves.

Navy. The flotilla comprises 6 armoured river defence gunboats (1 new Brazilian-built, 2 ancient monitors of 636 tons built in Italy and 3 old *ex*-Argentinian minesweepers of 620 tons), 1 helicopter carrying converted landing ship, 1 river patrol boat, 2 patrol launches, 6 coastal patrol craft, 2 landing craft, 1 survey craft, 1 transport training ship, 15 service craft and 2 tugs. There are 13 naval aircraft. Personnel in 1985 totalled 2,000 officers and men including coastguard and 500 marines.

Air Force. The Air Force came into being in the early thirties. After operating only transport and training aircraft for a number of years, it received 9 Xavante light jet strike/training aircraft from Brazil. Other types in service include 3 DC-6B and 2 C-54 four-engined transports more than 20 C-47 and 4 Bandeirante twin-engined transports, 1 Convair C-131A, a Twin Otter, an Otter, 8 Brazilian-built Uirapuru primary trainers, 12 T-6 Texan armed basic trainers and a number of light aircraft and helicopters. HQ and flying school are at Campo Grande, Asunción. Personnel total about 1,000.

INTERNATIONAL RELATIONS

Membership. Paraguay is a member of UN, OAS and LAIA (formerly LAFTA).

ECONOMY

Budget. In 1984 budget balanced at Gs. 306,143,627,637.

Currency. The *guaraní* was established on 5 Oct. 1943 equal to 100 old paper pesos. Total monetary circulation was Gs.81,531m. in Dec. 1983.

Rate of exchange, March 1985: 240 *guaraníes* = US$1; 256 *guaraníes* = £1.

Banking. The Banco Central del Paraguay opened 1 July 1952 to take over the central banking functions previously assigned to the National Bank of Paraguay, which had opened in March 1943 and been reorganized as the Banco del Paraguay in Sept. 1944 with a monetary, a banking and a mortgage department. The Banco del Paraguay closed in Nov. 1961 and has been replaced, with the aid of a US loan of US$3m., by the Banco Nacional de Fomento; the latter's assets in Jan. 1979 were Gs.47,621m.

The Banco Central in Dec. 1981 had gold and exchange reserves amounting to US$733·5m.; contribution to the IMF was Gs.47·7m.

The Banco Nacional de Fomento, Bank of London and South America, Ltd, Banco Exterior do Brasil, Citibank, Banco de Asunción, Banco Exterior SA, Banco Unión SA, Banco Paraguayo de Comercio, Banco Real del Paraguay SA, Banco Aleman Transatlantico, Banco Holandés Unido, Banco Nacional del Estado de São Paulo, Yegros y Azara, Bank of America, Chase Manhattan Bank, Bank of Boston, Interbanco, Banco Paraná and Banco de Inversiones all have agencies in Asunción and branches in some main towns.

Weights and Measures. The metric system was officially adopted on 1 Jan. 1901.

ENERGY AND NATURAL RESOURCES

Electricity. Electricity requirements are supplied by Acaray hydro-electric power plant. Production in 1983 was 847,748 kw.

Itaipú, the largest hydro-electric dam in the world, a joint effort of the governments of Brazil and Paraguay was inaugurated in 1982 and it is estimated that the whole project will be completed in 1990. Eventually it will have 18 turbogenerators, each with a capacity of 700,000 kw. In 1984 the first turbine started generating power. So far US$15,395,268,000 have been invested in this project which commenced in 1974.

The Yacyretá project is being carried out by the Binational Commission Yacyretá which was created by a treaty between the governments of Argentina and Paraguay. Work is being carried out on this project and it is hoped that the plant will be in full operation by the end of this decade. Initially 20 turbines each of 135,000 kw generating capacity will be installed giving the plant an initial output of 2·7m. kw.

Oil. The oil refinery at Villa Elisa, which has been in operation since 1966, has a production of about 3,500 bbls a day. Exploration for petroleum in the Chaco yielded negative results but prospecting was continuing in 1983–84.

Minerals. Iron, manganese and other minerals have been reported but have not been shown to be commercially exploitable. There are large deposits of limestone, and also salt, kaolin and apatite. National and international firms have acquired licences to prospect for oil and natural gas in the Chaco. A uranium survey was being carried out in 1978 in the Oriental region.

Agriculture. In 1981 it was estimated that agriculture absorbs some 51·4m. hectares. In 1982, the main agricultural products (in 1,000 tons) were: Mandioca, 1,826; soybeans, 750; maize, 521; cotton, 254; wheat, 70; rice, 65; tobacco, 18.

Wheat, soybean (750,000 tons, 1982), cotton, sugar, tobacco, coffee are increasing in importance, as are also essential oils and oilseeds. *Yerba maté*, or strongly flavoured Paraguayan tea, continues to be produced but is declining in importance; 80 tons were exported in 1983.

Livestock (1983). Paraguay had about 5·6m. cattle, 330,000 horses, 1·35m. pigs, 440,000 sheep.

Forestry. In the Oriental section there are reserves of hardwoods and cedars that have scarcely been exploited. Palms, tung and other trees are exploited for their oils. The Japanese are experimenting with mulberries for silk growing. Pines and firs have been introduced under a United Nations project. In the Chaco the accessible Quebracho forests have nearly been worked out but plans are being made to open up new areas. In 1983, 82,770 tons of timber were exported and 10,841 tons of quebracho.

INDUSTRY AND TRADE

Industry. Production, 1983 (tons): Hides, 11,036; frozen meat, 7,506; cotton fibre, 77,157 (1,000 metres); tannin, 12,678; petit grain, 86; tung oil, 17,033; cement, 152,953; sugar, 98,199; cigarettes (1m. packets), 46,598; matches (1,000 boxes), 8,979. There are 3 meat-packing plants and other factories producing vegetable oils. A textile industry in Pilar and Asunción meets a large part of local needs.

Labour. Trade unionists number about 30,000 (*Confederación Paraguaya de Trabajadores* and *Confederación Cristiana de Trabajadores*).

Commerce. Imports and exports (in US$1m.):

	1977	*1978*	*1979*	*1980*	*1981*	*1982*	*1983*
Imports	250·4	375	437·7	517·1	506·1	581·4	478·2
Exports	278·9	285	305·1	310·2	295·5	329·7	269·1

Chief exports in 1983 included (in US$1,000): Cotton, 85,126; soybeans, 84,445; sawn wood, 20,391; cakes and expellers, 13,839; tung oil, 11,604; tobacco, 10,171; hides, 9,285; sugar, 5,438; tannin, 5,373; processed beef, 5,272; coconut oil, 3,585; fruit and vegetables, 2,723.

Chief imports 1983 (in US$1,000): Fuels and lubricants, 120,024; machinery and motors, 107,802; iron and manufactures, 39,515; foodstuffs, 31,250; vehicles and accessories, 29,437; chemical and pharmaceutical products, 28,326; drinks and tobacco, 15,569.

Imports and exports (in US$), by country, 1983:

Country	*Imports*	*Exports*
Argentina	90,356	31,503
Belgium	1,778	6,313
Brazil	136,209	50,861
Federal Republic of Germany	32,320	28,809
France	16,948	4,885
Italy	4,894	3,130
Japan	20,168	3,653
Netherlands	1,712	35,354
Spain	16,082	2,815
Switzerland	4,932	18,842
UK	24,728	1,851
Uruguay	7,672	4,458
USA	30,795	22,856

Total trade between Paraguay and UK (British Department of Trade returns, in £1,000 sterling):

	1980	*1981*	*1982*	*1983*	*1984*
Imports to UK	1,279	2,241	2,790	3,129	2,961
Exports and re-exports from UK	13,384	13,105	16,915	15,263	16,884

Tourism. Visitors numbered 147,830 in 1983.

COMMUNICATIONS

Roads. In 1983 there were 20,000 km of roads, of which 2,000 were paved. The principal paved roads are Route No. 2/7 running from Asunción to the bridge over the Paraná at Puerto Presidente Stroessner, and thence down to the ocean at Paranaguá; and Route No. 1 to Encarnación in the south. The other main arteries are Coronel Oviedo-Pedro Juan Caballero road (unpaved from Coronel Oviedo) in the north and the Trans-Chaco road which starts from the bridge across the river Paraguay north of Asunción and ends at Nueva Asunción on the Bolivian border. Unpaved roads are closed when it rains. In the Argentine, a paved road starts from Pilcomayo, opposite Asunción, and provides good communication with Buenos Aires. Motor cars, 1976, numbered 17,600; commercial vehicles, 15,200, and passenger vehicles, 7,580.

Railways. The President Carlos Antonio López (formerly Paraguay Central) Railway runs from Asunción to Encarnación, on the Río Alto Paraná, with a length of 441 km (1,435 mm gauge). In 1982, traffic amounted to 244,400 tonnes and 280,459 passengers.

Aviation. International services are operated by 7 airlines (domestic and foreign) and internal routes by military airlines and some small private lines.

Shipping. In flood the Paraguay River, which divides the country into two distinct parts, is navigable for 12ft-draught vessels as far as Concepción, 180 miles north of Asunción, and for smaller vessels for a further distance of 600 miles northward. Drought conditions often restrict navigation to lighter traffic. The Paraná River is navigable by large boats from Corrientes up to Puerto Aguirre, at the mouth of the Yguazú River. Boats of a few hundred tons capacity navigate the tributary rivers.

Asunción, the chief port, is 950 miles from the sea. The cargo fleet includes 25 vessels of 300–1,000 tons, 3 tankers of 1,100–1,700 tons, 2 passenger river boats and 1 ocean-going freighter of 713 tons.

Post and Broadcasting. The national telegraph (137 offices) connects Asunción with Corrientes and Posadas in the Argentine Republic, and thus with the outside world; new direct links have been opened with the Federal Republic of Germany, USA, Bolivia and Chile. In addition, 34 stations are operated by the President Carlos Antonio López Railway; total, 2,070 miles. Three companies (12 stations) offer radio-telegraph and telex services to several countries. Telephones, 1982, 60,883, of which 45,797 were in Asunción and were automatic. There are 1 state and 9 commercial radio stations in Asunción, 22 in provincial towns, 2 commercial television stations in Asunción and 1 in Encarnación in the south.

Cinemas (1983). Cinemas numbered 9 in Asunción. The larger country towns usually have an outdoor cinema.

Newspapers (1983). There are 4 daily newspapers in Asunción.

JUSTICE, RELIGION AND EDUCATION

Justice. The highest court is the Supreme Court with 5 members. There are special Chambers of Appeal for civil and commercial cases, and criminal cases. Judges of first instance deal with civil, commercial and criminal cases in 6 departments. Minor cases are dealt with by Justices of the Peace.

The Attorney-General represents the State in all jurisdictions, with representatives in each judicial department and in every jurisdiction. In matters of revenue, taxes, etc., the State is represented by the *Abogado del Tesoro.*

Religion. Religious liberty is guaranteed by the 1967 constitution. Article 6 thereof recognizes Roman Catholicism as the official religion of the country. The same article disposes that relations between Paraguay and the Holy See shall be regulated by concordats or other bilateral agreements, but no such agreements have yet been negotiated.

The Roman Catholic Church is organized into the Archdiocese of Asunción, 3 other dioceses (San Juan Bautista de las Misiones, Concepción and Villarrica); 4 Prelatures (Coronel Oviedo, Encarnación, Alto Paraná and Caacupé); and 2 Vicariates Apostolic (Chaco and Pilcomayo). The bishops meet in a Conference of Paraguayan Bishops. Only civil marriages are legally valid. There are numerous non-catholic communities, the largest of whom are the Mennonites. There is a small Anglican church in Asunción, with missions in the Chaco, which comes under the jurisdiction of an Anglican Bishop resident in Asunción.

Education. Education is free and nominally compulsory, but schools are not everywhere available, and the system has been extensively revised to provide, *inter alia,* primary education for adults. Illiteracy is estimated at 22% (urban) and 30% (rural). In 1982 there were 3,071 government primary schools and 542 private schools, with 539,889 pupils and 20,746 teachers; 632 secondary schools had 135,829 students and 2,448 teachers. In 1978 there was an intensive school building programme in progress. The National University in Asunción had, in 1973, 7,919 students and 1,209 professors. In 1973 the Catholic University and associated colleges had 4,546 students and 355 professors.

DIPLOMATIC REPRESENTATIVES

Of Paraguay in Great Britain (51 Cornwall Gdns, London, SW7 4AQ)
Ambassador: Antonio R. Zuccolillo.

Of Great Britain in Paraguay (Calle Presidente Franco, 706, Asunción)
Ambassador and Consul-General: Bernard Coleman.

Of Paraguay in the USA (2400 Massachusetts Ave., NW, Washington, D.C., 20008)
Ambassador: Dr Marcos Martinez Mendieta.

Of the USA in Paraguay (1776 Mariscal López Ave., Asunción)
Ambassador: Arthur H. Davis, Jr.

Of Paraguay to the United Nations
Ambassador: Dr Alfredo Cañete.

Books of Reference

Gaceta Official, published by Imprenta Nacional, Estrella y Estero Bellaco, Asunción
Anuario Daumas. Asunción
Anuario Estadístico de la República del Paraguay. Asunción. Annual
Lewis, P. H., *Paraguay under Stroessner.* Univ. of North Carolina Press, 1980
Maybury-Lewis, D. and Howe, J., *The Indian Peoples of Paraguay: Their Plight and Their Prospects.* Cambridge, Mass., 1980

National Library: Biblioteca Nacional, De la Rosidenta, Asunción.

PERU

Capital: Lima
Population: 18·3m. (1982)
GNP per capita: US$1,170 (1981)

República del Perú

HISTORY. The Republic of Peru, formerly the most important of the Spanish vice-royalties in South America, declared its independence on 28 July 1821; but it was not till after a war, protracted till 1824, that the country gained its actual freedom.

AREA AND POPULATION. The total area of Peru is estimated to be 1,285,216 sq. km (496,093 sq. miles).

The long-standing dispute with Chile over the provinces of Tacna and Arica (*see* THE STATESMAN'S YEAR-BOOK, 1928, p. 1198) reached an amicable settlement on 3 June 1929 at Lima, Tacna going to Peru and Arica to Chile. In response to demands by Bolivia for permanent access to the Pacific Coast, proposals for a Bolivian corridor to the sea and a new Bolivian port to be built in the disputed area have been put forward by Chile and Peru. To date, little progress has been made. One result has been increased tension along the Chilean–Peruvian border, there is no sign of a settlement of the border dispute, and the armed forces of both countries remain on the alert in the disputed border area. Fighting broke out between Peruvian and Ecuadorean Forces, in early 1981, along part of the disputed border (the Cordillera del Condor) which has to date not been adequately mapped. A number of proposals for settling the issue permanently have been put forward but a final settlement is unlikely to be reached in the near future. For an account of the settlement of other boundary disputes, *see* THE STATESMAN'S YEAR-BOOK, 1948, p. 1173.

A map of the boundary with Ecuador is to be found in THE STATESMAN'S YEAR-BOOK, 1942.

The census taken in 1981 gave the population as 17,762,231. Children under 15 years, 7·2m. (41% of total population). Birth rate, 4·2%; death rate, 1·3%. Lima, the capital, had (1983) 5,258,600 population. Other major cities (with census population 1981), are Callao (478,500), Arequipa (447,431), Trujillo (354,557), Chiclayo (280,244), Chimbote (216,406), Piura (186,354), Cuzco (181,604), Huancayo (115,693, 1972), Iquitos (173,629), Ica (111,087). The language is Spanish, but the Indian population speak either Quechua (the second official language) or Aymará.

The area of the 24 departments and the constitutional province of Callao are given below with the population, according to the official census of 1981. The area of the department of Puno includes the Peruvian zone of Lake Titicaca, 4,996·28 sq. km. The chief towns are shown in brackets:

Departments	*Area (sq. km) 1959*	*Population 12 July 1981 (census)*	*Pop. per sq. km 1961*
Amazonas (Chachapoyas)	41,297·1	254,560	2·85
Ancash (Huaraz)	36,308·3	818,289	16·20
Apurímac (Abancay)	20,654·6	323,346	16·36
Arequipa (Arequipa)	63,527·6	706,580	6·47
Ayacucho (Ayacucho)[1]	45,503·1	430,289	9·85
Cajamarca (Cajamarca)	35,417·8	1,045,569	21·15
Callao (Callao)[2]	73·8	443,413	2,901·46
Cuzco (Cuzco)	84,140·9	832,504	7·30
Huancavelica (Huancavelica)	22,870·9	346,797	13·07
Huánuco (Huánuco)	35,314·6	484,780	10·24
Ica (Ica)	21,251·4	433,897	11·48
Junín (Huancayo)	32,354·4	852,238	15·64
La Libertad (Trujillo)	23,241·3	962,949	25·29
Lambayeque (Chiclayo)	16,585·9	674,442	20·93
Lima (Lima)	33,894·9	4,745,877	68·42
Loreto (Iquitos)	478,336·2	445,368	0·69

[1] 1961. [2] With province.

Departments	Area (sq. km.) 1959	Population 12 July 1981 (census)	Pop. per sq. km 1961
Madre de Dios (Maldonado)	78,402·7	33,007	0·19
Moquegua (Moquegua)	16,174·7	101,610	3·60
Pasco (Cerro de Pasco)	21,854·1	213,125	5·79
Piura (Piura)	33,067·1	1,125,865	21·68
Puno (Puno)	72,382·4	890,258	10·20
San Martín (Moyobamba)	53,063·6	319,751	3·06
Tacna (Tacna)	14,766·6	143,085	4·68
Tumbes (Tumbes)	4,731·5	103,839	21·10
Total	1,285,215·6	17,762,231	8·06

A new department of Ucayali is to be created in the central Amazon area, to include the provinces of Coronel Portillo and Ucayali, which were previously part of the department of Loreto. Pucallpa will be the capital of the new department.

CLIMATE. There is a very wide variety of climate, ranging from equatorial to desert, (or perpetual snow on the high mountains). In coastal areas, temperatures vary very little, either daily or annually, though humidity and cloudiness show considerable variation, with highest humidity from May to Sept. Little rain is experienced in that period. In the Sierra, temperatures remain fairly constant over the year, but the daily range is considerable. There the dry season is from April to Nov. Desert conditions occur in the extreme south, where the climate is uniformly dry, with a few heavy showers falling between Jan. and March. Lima. Jan. 74°F (23·3°C), July 62°F (16·7°C). Annual rainfall 2″ (48 mm). Cuzco. Jan. 56°F (13·3°C), July 50°F (10°C). Annual rainfall 32″ (804 mm).

CONSTITUTION AND GOVERNMENT. On 3 Oct. 1968 a military junta overthrew the government of President Fernando Belaúnde Terry and installed Gen. Juan Velasco Alvarado as President of a 'Revolutionary Government' with a cabinet composed entirely of officers of the armed services. Gen. Velasco was ousted in bloodless *coup* in Aug. 1975 and was replaced by Gen. Francisco Morales Bermudez. The new democratic government, under President Fernando Belaúnde Terry, took office on 28 July 1980.

The new Constitution, which became effective when a civilian government was installed in July 1980, provides for a Legislature consisting of a Senate (60 members) and a Chamber of Deputies (180 members) and an Executive formed of the President of the Republic and a Council of Ministers appointed by him. Elections were held in May 1980. They will be held every 5 years with the President and Congress elected, at the same time, by separate ballots. All Peruvians over the age of 18 are eligible to vote; in May 1980 the number of registered voters was over 6m., including 1m. in Lima province. Voting is compulsory; women were fully enfranchised in 1955.

Presidents since 1948 were:

Gen. Manuel A. Odría (Acting), 27 Oct. 1948–1 June 1950.[1]
Gen. Zenón Noriega, 1 June 1950–28 July 1950.
Gen. Manuel A. Odría, 28 July 1950–28 July 1956.
Dr Manuel Prado y Ugarteche, 28 July 1956–July 1962.
Gen. Ricardo Pérez Godoy, 18 July 1962–3 March 1963.[2]
Gen. Nicolás Lindley López, 3 March–28 July 1963.
Fernando Belaúnde Terry, 28 July 1963–3 Oct. 1968.[2]
Gen. Juan Velasco Alvarado, 3 Oct. 1968–29 Aug. 1975.[2]
Gen. Francisco Morales Bermudez, 29 Aug. 1975–28 July 1980.

[1] Resigned. [2] Deposed.

President: Fernando Belaúnde Terry.

The Cabinet was in Oct. 1984 composed as follows.

Prime Minister and Minister of Foreign Affairs: Luis Pércovich Roca.
Interior: Oscar Brush Noel. *War:* Julián Freyre. *Economy, Finance and Trade:*

José Benavides. *Agriculture:* Juan Hurtado Miller. *Labour:* Joaquin Leguia. *Health:* Juan Franco Ponce. *Education:* Andrés Cardó Franco. *Housing and Construction:* Carlos Pestana. *Transport and Communications:* Francisco Aramayo. *Energy and Mines:* Juan Incháustegui. *Fisheries:* Ismael Benavides Ferreyros. *Justice:* Max Arias Schreiber. *Industry, Integration and Tourism:* Alvaro Becerra Sotero. *National Development Institute:* Juan de Madalengoitia. *National Planning Institute:* Edgardo Quintanilla. *National Social Communication System:* Miguel Alva Orlandini. *Navy:* Jorge Du Bois. *Air Force:* José Zlatar Stambuk.

In 1984 the 24 departments were divided into 158 provinces (plus the constitutional province of Callao) and 1,690 districts; the province of Callao has some of the functions of a department.

National flag: Three vertical strips of red, white, red, with the national arms in the centre.

National anthem: Somos Libres, seámoslo siempre (words by J. de la Torre Ugarte; tune by J. B. Alcedo, 1821).

DEFENCE.

Army. While military service is compulsory youths are only conscripted to fill the annual quota. The term of service is 2 years and all males of 20–25 years of age are liable. The country is divided into 5 military regions.

The Army comprises (1985) approximately 75,000 men (including 51,000 conscripts). There are 8 infantry and mechanized brigades, 1 paracommando and 2 armoured brigades, 1 jungle brigade, 3 armoured reconaissance squadrons and 10 artillery and 4 engineer battalions. There is an air element of 4 Helio Courier 395 communications aircraft. Equipment consists of approximately 485 tanks (T-54/-55, M-4 and AMX-13), over 100 light armoured fighting vehicles and 105-mm./155-mm. field artillery.

The section of the national police force with a para-military role is known as the *Guardia Civil* and comprises approximately 25,000 personnel.

Navy. The principal surface ships of the Peruvian Navy are the cruisers:–

Completed	*Name*	*Standard Displacement (tons)*	*Main Guns*	*Aircraft*	*Shaft horsepower*	*Max. Speed (knots)*
1953	*Aguirre* (ex-*De Zeven Provincien*)	9,850	4 6in.	3	85,000	32
1953	*Almirante Grau*[1] (ex-*De Ruyter*)	9,530	8 6in.	–	85,000	32

[1] When the Dutch cruiser *De Ruyter* was purchased in 1973 she was re-named *Almirante Grau* after Peru's principal naval hero. In consequence the cruiser whose name had been changed from *Newfoundland* to *Almirante Grau* when she was purchased from Britain in 1959 was again re-named *Capitan Quinones*, after an air force hero; but this ship has since been retired (latterly used as harbour training ship); and her sister ship *Colonel Bolognesi* (*ex*- HMS *Ceylon*) was laid up in 1983. *Aquirre* was bought from the Netherlands in 1976.

There are also 12 submarines comprising 6 completed in Federal Republic of Germany in 1974–82, 4 completed in USA in 1954–57 and 2 old *ex*-USN; 2 reconstructed 'Daring' class destroyers delivered from Britain during 1973; 8 old destroyers purchased from the Netherlands in 1978–82, 2 Italian-built frigates and 1 Peruvian built to same design, 6 new French-built fast missile-armed corvettes, 2 landing ships; 2 medium landing ships; 5 river gunboats; 3 river patrol boats; 2 transports; 3 hospital craft; 1 research craft; 7 oilers; 3 survey vessels; 1 repair ship; 1 torpedo recovery vessel; 1 floating workshop, 4 floating docks; 4 water carriers, and 5 tugs.

The new construction programme includes 1 frigate being built in Peru (sister ship of *Montero* completed in Peru in 1984 and 2 completed in Italy in 1978–80).

All naval training takes place in the Callao area at various schools. The main naval base and dockyard are also in Callao. Smaller bases are at Iquitos on the Amazon, and at San Lorenzo.

Naval personnel in 1985 totalled 2,000 officers and 18,500 men including the Naval Air Arm which operates 44 aircraft.

The Coast Guard includes 6 modern patrol vessels built in Peru, 4 fast patrol craft built in Britain in 1964–65, 2 former US gunboats, 3 coastal patrol boats and 7 minor patrol craft.

Air Force. The Air Force is under the direction of the Air Minister, who is also C.-in-C.

The operational force consists of 3 combat groups. No. 13 Group has 2 squadrons of Mirage 5 jet fighters and 1 squadron of A-37B light attack aircraft; No. 21 Group has 2 squadrons of Canberra light jet bombers and 1 squadron of A-37Bs; No. 12 Group has about 40 Soviet-built Su-22 variable-geometry fighter bombers in 3 operational squadrons. Other aircraft in service include medium transports (1 F.28 Fellowship, 16 An-26, 6 L-100-20 Hercules), light transports (16 Twin Otter, 15 Buffalo, 1 twin-jet Falcon and 12 Turbo-Porter), helicopters (2 Mi-6 and a total of 54 Mi-8, Bell 212 and 214ST, BO 105, Alouette III and Bell 47G), 70 training aircraft (including Aermacchi MB 339, T-37 and T-41D) and a small number of miscellaneous types for photographic and communications duties. The T-37 trainers, and A-37B attack aircraft, will be replaced from 1985 by further MB 339s, built in Peru. Two DC-9s and some of the C-54 and C-130 aircraft are used by the Air Force to run a commercial airline network (SATCO). There are military airfields at Talara, Chiclayo, Piura, Pisco, Lima (2), Iquitos and La Joya, and a seaplane base at Iquitos. All officers and pilots are trained at the Air Academy at Lima (Las Palmas). The approximate strength of the Peruvian Air Force (1985) 10,000 personnel and 120 combat aircraft.

INTERNATIONAL RELATIONS

Membership. Peru is a member of UN, OAS, Andean Group and LAIA (formerly LAFTA).

ECONOMY

Planning. A Public Investment Programme for 1981–85 envisages expenditure of US$11,500m.

Budget. The authorized budget for 1984 envisaged expenditure of S/.10,729,000m.

The external debt was US$11,644m. in Dec. 1982.

Currency. The monetary unit is the *sol*. A new currency the *Sol Nuevo* is to be introduced in 1985. In March 1985, £1=7,958; US$1=7,521.

Coins include 50,000 soles (gold) and 10,000 soles (silver) coins as well as 10- and 5-sole pieces (copper 75%; nickel 25%), the sol and half sol (copper 30%; zinc 70%); the 20, 10 and 5 centavos (copper–zinc) and the 2- and 1-centavo pieces (zinc) have been discontinued. Peru has a paper currency issued by the Banco Central de la Reserva in denominations of 5,000, 1,000, 500, 200, 100 and 50. The 10 and 5 soles notes have been discontinued.

Banking. The government bank of issue is the Banco Central de la Reserva del Perú, which was established in 1922. A new charter for the bank was promulgated in Aug. 1968; this, *inter alia*, extended the bank's authority with regard to the organization of the commercial banking system.

The Government's fiscal agent is the Banco de la Nación which, since May 1970, has control of the 'giro' market through which most non-trade foreign currency transactions are channelled.

There were in 1983, 7 commercial banks (of which 3 state-owned), 4 foreign commercial banks, 9 development banks (5 state-owned), 6 regional commercial banks and a savings bank.

Weights and Measures. The metric system of weights and measures was established by law in 1869, and since 1916 has come into general use.

ENERGY AND NATURAL RESOURCES

Electricity. In 1972 control of electricity production and distribution passed to ELECTROPERU, a state company. In 1981 the production of electric energy was

3,200 mw (60% hydro-electric). An electrification programme to construct a series of large hydro-electric power stations, was started in 1980.

Oil. Proven oil reserves in the jungle region amount to about 900m. bbls. A further 75m. tonnes have been found in the north-west, some of it offshore. The new 850 km pipeline, linking the new jungle oilfields to coastal terminals, was opened in 1977. Output amounted to 9m. tonnes by 1984 and Peru became an oil exporter in that same year. The total value of exports in 1982 of petroleum and derivative was US$715m.

Minerals. Peru's mining industry produces 13 metals and 25 non-metallic minerals. Lead, copper, iron, silver, zinc and petroleum are the chief minerals exploited. In 1984 prospecting for uranium was in progress. Mineral exports in 1980: Copper, US$752m.; lead, US$383m.; zinc, US$210m.; silver, US$312m.; iron ore, US$95m.; gold, US$40m. Mineral production (in 1,000 tonnes, 1983) of iron, 2,800; zinc, 476; copper, 317; lead, 184; silver, 48m. oz.

Agriculture. There are 4 natural zones: the coast strip, with an average width of 80 km; the Sierra or Uplands, formed by the coast range of mountains and the Andes proper; the Montaña or high wooded region which lies on the eastern slopes of the Andes, and the jungle in the Amazon Basin, known as the Selva. In 1984 irrigation was increasing the amount of cultivable acreage in the arid coastal sections of the country, using the abundance of water flowing from the Andes mountains. US$3,000m. will be spent on irrigation-hydroelectric projects during 1981–85. A number of projects were underway or in the planning stages (1984) to irrigate or improve an area of approximately 900,000 hectares.

Nearly half of the population is dependent on agriculture, which accounted for 13·5% of the GDP in 1982–83. Peru's third land reform law, that of June 1969, is one of the most comprehensive. It provides for the large sugar estates in the north of Peru to be turned into co-operatives. Maximum permitted sizes for other types of land holding are stipulated for the various regions of the country. These range from 150 hectares for irrigated land on the coast to an area capable of supporting 5,000 sheep for pasture land in the Sierra. These sizes may be increased if certain efficiency criteria are met. Holdings too small to be economically viable are to be consolidated into co-operative units. The chief agricultural productions of Peru are, in the order named: Sugar, cotton, coffee and wool.

Production in 1981 (in 1,000 tonnes): Sugar-cane, 4,160; sugar, 493; cotton, 87; coffee, 95; wool, 13.

Output of cattle and buffalo hides (in tonnes), 1981, 13,220; sheepskins, 7,350; goatskins, 2,100. Output of sheep wool in 1976 was 9,000 tonnes. Exports, 1970, were sheep wool, unwashed, 606 tonnes; llama, alpaca and vicuña wool, 1,537 tonnes.

Livestock (1983): 653,000 horses, 3·2m. cattle, 1·9m. goats, 14·5m. sheep, 1·8m. swine, 40m. poultry.

Forestry. There are 209m. acres of forests containing valuable hardwoods; oak and cedar account for about 40%. In 1980, total lumber production was (estimate) 1,213,000 cu. metres; pulp production approximately 138,000 cu. metres.

Fisheries. Until the early 1970s Peru was the world's foremost fishing nation in terms of value of catch, due mainly to anchoveta which was converted into fishmeal for export as animal feed. Peru produced almost 45% of the world's fishmeal supplies, or nearly 2m. tonnes a year. However, abnormal marine conditions and over-fishing combined had, by 1983 considerably reduced the anchoveta catch.

Since then the industry has been partly denationalized and the number of fishing vessels reduced by approximately 50%, to some 700. Increased attention has been paid to fishing for human consumption.

Fish production 1980 (1,000 tonnes): Anchoveta, 720; other species, 1,006. Fresh, 155·7; frozen, 219·8; dried salted, 28·3; conserves, 567. Fish caught include (1980, tonnes): Anchoveta, 720,100; sardine, 1,480,400; hake, 159,400; black mackerel, 123,400; mackerel, 59,100; seafish, 6,800.

INDUSTRY AND TRADE

Industry. About 70% of Peru's manufacturing industries are located in or around the Lima/Callao metropolitan area.

Peru's first iron and steel mill came into production at Chimbote in April 1958. Products include pig-iron, blooms, billets, largets, round and round-deformed bars, wire rod, black and galvanized sheets and galvanized roofing sheets. Refractories are manufactured at Lima.

The Government has a monopoly of the import and/or local manufacture and sale of guano, salt, alcohol and explosives. The monopoly of matches was abandoned in 1954 and that of tobacco in June 1955.

Peru's manufacturing industry stagnated since 1972 but by 1980 had recovered substantially, mainly due to exports of non-traditional goods. In 1977 production in the following industries was (in tonnes):

Cement	1,964,000	Refined lead	169,000
Tyres (units)	700,000	TV receivers (units)	100,000
Refined zinc	389,000	Sulphuric acid	60,000
Refined copper	350,000	Vehicle assembly	11,300
Crude steel	347,000		

Labour. In 1983 the total labour was considered to number 6m. persons, of which 62·7% was either under-employed or unemployed. The population was distributed roughly as follows in 1981: Agriculture, stock-raising and fishing, 41%; manufacturing industry, 13%; commerce, 13%; construction, 4%; mining, 1%; services and others, 28%.

Trade Unions. Trade unions have about 2m. members (approximately 1·5m. in peasant organizations and 500,000 in industrial). The major trade union organization is the *Confederación de Trabajadores del Perú*, which was reconstituted in 1959 after being in abeyance for some years. The other labour organizations recognized by the Government are the *Confederación General de Trabajadores del Perú*, the *Confederación Nacional de Trabajadores* and the *Central de Trabajadores de la Revolución Peruana*.

Commerce. The value of trade has been as follows (in US$1m.):

	1976	*1977*	*1978*	*1979*	*1980*	*1981*	*1982*
Imports	1,360	1,726	1,601	2,090	3,062	3,803	3,502
Exports	2,100	2,095	1,941	3,474	3,898	3,255	3,212

In 1982 the principal imports were: Machinery and appliances, chemicals, foodstuffs; fuel, lubricants and other non-metallic minerals. Of exports, 32·7% went to USA, 15·4% to Japan; of imports, 31·5% came from USA and 9·1% from Japan.

Total trade between Peru and UK (British Department of Trade returns, in £1,000 sterling):

	1980	*1981*	*1982*	*1983*	*1984*
Imports to UK	77,487	66,726	92,120	118,414	119,423
Exports and re-exports from UK	46,541	50,280	39,370	32,947	33,841

Tourism. There were 336,000 visitors in 1981.

COMMUNICATIONS

Roads. In 1984 there were 65,000 km, of which 7,200 km were paved and (1980) 12,323 km gravel.

In 1981 there were 529,000 registered motor vehicles.

Railways. Since 1972 all public railways were nationalized and run by Peruvian National Railways (ENAFER). Total length (1984), 2,500 km on 1,435- and 914-mm gauges. In 1982 railways carried 2m. short tons and 2·9m. passengers.

Aviation. There are 3 international and 61 other airports.

Shipping. In 1966, 6,900 vessels of 26,602,270 tons entered, and 6,871 of 26,610,772 tons cleared the ports. Since 1928 the coasting trade has been largely reserved for Peruvian-owned vessels with Peruvian crews; in 1960 it handled 2,246,000 tonnes, valued at S/.1,665m.

Post and Broadcasting. An earth satellite ground communication station at Lurin connects Peru through Intelsat. III to the US and Europe. In 1981 there were 629,742 telephones, 371,673 in Lima. Radio-telephone circuits connect Lima with distant towns. Three submarine telegraph cables connect Peru and Chile, and one connects Peru and the republics to the north. There are 153 broadcasting stations, of which 29 are in Lima. Wireless receiving sets, about 2m. There are 4 television stations and 188 radio stations operating under government licenses.

Cinemas. In 1972 there were 276 cinemas.

Newspapers. The main Lima newspapers are *La Prensa, El Comercio, Expreso, Correo* and *La Crónica*.

JUSTICE, RELIGION, EDUCATION AND WELFARE

Justice. The Peruvian judicial system is a pyramid at the base of which are the justices of the peace who decide minor criminal cases and civil cases involving small sums of money. The apex is the Supreme Court with 17 members; in between are the judges of first instance, who usually sit in the provincial capitals, and the superior courts of which there are 18.

The Revolutionary Government decreed in Dec. 1969 that all judges, except justices of the peace, would in future be elected by the National Council of Justice, composed of representatives of the Executive, the Legislature, the Judiciary, the National Federation of the College of Lawyers and 2 of the university law faculties. Justices of the peace are appointed, by the superior courts.

Religion. Religious liberty exists, but the Roman Catholic religion is protected by the State, and since 1929 only Roman Catholic religious instruction is permitted in schools, state or private. In 1972 there were 1 Roman Catholic cardinal, 7 archbishops, 14 bishops, 3 vicars-general, 8 vicars apostolic, 2,672 priests, 506 cloistered monks and 4,558 members of religious orders.

Protestants numbered 128,000 in 1966.

All marriages must be civil, regardless of religion and preceded by medical examination; there are liberal divorce regulations, including divorce for 'absence without just cause for more than 2 years', and by mutual consent. Divorcees may remarry immediately. A law of 1936 emphasizes that the religious obligations of marriage are fully recognized.

Education. A new law for education was promulgated in March 1972. Elementary education is compulsory and free for both sexes between the ages of 7 and 16; secondary education is also free. But schools, despite substantial increases, are still too few. The system is highly centralized; all teaching appointments are made by the Minister of Education for the public schools; for the private schools he supervises plant and equipment and limits fees but does not appoint teachers.

In 1970 there were 20,034 public, private and primary schools, with 64,004 teachers and 2·75m. pupils; 1,452 secondary schools, with 21,863 teachers and 674,000 students. Training in 414 public technical schools is also free; in 1970 they had 6,333 teachers and 223,300 pupils. The 90 teacher-training schools had 1,075 teachers and 18,000 pupils. Total literacy (1975) was 68% of total population. Because of the increase in the number of pupils state schools have divided their teaching timetable into three divisions, morning, afternoon and evening. Those pupils in the last shift have to spend an extra year at school to make up for the difference in the length of the daily timetable.

In 1970 the total number of university students was 105,600.

Social Welfare. Contributory social security schemes exist for employees and workers. These are administered by the Ministry of Labour. There were in 1975, 182 hospitals (33,350 beds). In addition in 1969 there were 63 health centres, 307 medical posts and 842 sanitary posts, all administered by the authorities. In 1975 there were 9,445 doctors, 2,119 obstetricians, 115 chemists and 8,920 trained nurses.

DIPLOMATIC REPRESENTATIVES

Of Peru in Great Britain (52 Sloane St., London, SW1X 9SP)
Ambassador: Dr Andres A. Aramburú-Menchaca (accredited 10 May 1983).

Of Great Britain in Peru (Edificio El Pacifico Washington, Ave. Arequipa, Lima)
Ambassador: John W. R. Shakespeare, MVO.

Of Peru in the USA (1700 Massachusetts Ave., NW, Washington, D.C., 20036)
Ambassador: Luis Marchand.

Of the USA in Peru (PO Box 1995, Lima)
Ambassador: David C. Jordan.

Of Peru to the United Nations
Ambassador: Dr Javier Arias Stella.

Books of Reference

The official gazette is *El Peruano*, Lima.

Anario Estadistico del Perú. Annual.—*Boletin de Estadistica Peruana.* Quarterly.—*Demarcación Política del Perú.* (Dirección Nacional de Estadística), Lima
Estadística del Comercio Exterior (*Superintendencia de Aduanas*). Lima
Banco Central de Reserva. Monthly Bulletin.—*Renta Nacional del Perú.* Annual, Lima

Ministerio de Fomento Lima publishes separate annual statistics on the mining and petroleum industries and on general industry; the wool textile and cotton textile industries, the Peruvian Chamber of Commerce furnish annual studies.

Figueroa, A., *Capitalist Development and the Peasant Economy of Peru.* CUP, 1984
Fitzgerald, E. V. K., *The Political Economy of Peru 1958–78.* CUP, 1979
Hemming, J., *The Conquest of the Incas.* London, 1970
Lowenthal, A. F., *The Peruvian Experiment.* Princeton Univ. Press, 1975
McClintock, C., and Lowental, A. F., (eds.) *The Peruvian Experiment Reconsidered.* Princeton Univ. Press, 1983
Mejía Baca, J., and Tauro, A., *Diccionário Enciclopédico del Perú.* 3 vols. 1966
Philip, G. D. E., *The Rise and Fall of the Peruvian Military Radicals, 1968–1976.* London, 1978
Stepan, A., *The State and Society. Peru in Comparative Perspective.* Princeton Univ. Press, 1978
Thorp, R., and Bertram, G., *Peru 1890–1977.* London, 1978
Webb, R. C., *Government Policy and the Distribution of Income in Peru, 1963–1973.* Harvard Univ. Press, 1977

National Library: Avenida Abancay, Lima.

REPUBLIC OF THE PHILIPPINES

Capital: Manila
Population: 53·35m. (1984)
GNP per capita: US$790 (1981)

República de Filipinas— Republika ng Pilipinas

HISTORY. Before the Spanish discovery of the Philippines, the native Filipinos came in contact with India, China and Arabia. According to the early records of China, 'some Filipinos from the country of Ma-i arrived in Canton and sold their merchandise' as early as 982. The Philippine islands were discovered by Magellan in 1521 and conquered by Spain in 1565. Following the Spanish–American war, the islands were ceded to the USA on 10 Dec. 1898, after the Filipinos had tried in vain to establish an independent republic in 1896.

The Republic of the Philippines came into existence on 4 July 1946, by agreement with the US Government embodied in an Act of Congress signed by President Roosevelt on 24 March 1934, accepted by the Philippine Legislature on 1 May 1934 and ratified at a plebiscite on 14 May 1935. This Act established a 10-year transitional period, designated as that of the Philippine Commonwealth, at the end of which complete independence was automatically effective.

AREA AND POPULATION. The Philippines is situated between 21° 25′ and 4° 23′ N. lat. and between 116° and 127° E. long. It is composed of 7,100 islands and islets, 2,773 of which are named. Approximate land area, 115,830 sq. miles (300,000 sq. km). The 16 most important islands with their areas (in sq. miles) are: Luzon, 40,420; Mindanao, 36,537; Samar, 5,050; Negros, 4,906; Palawan, 4,550; Panay, 4,446; Mindoro, 3,759; Leyte, 2,786; Cebu, 1,707; Bohol, 1,492; Masbate, 1,262; Sulu group, 379; Tawi-tawi, 229; Romblon, 32; Marinduque, 347, and Siquijor, 129.

Census population 1980 was 48,098,460. Estimate (1984) 53·35m.

The population of Metropolitan Manila, in 1980 was 5,925,884, including the city of Manila, the present capital, Quezon City, the former capital (1,165,865), and Caloocan (467,816). Other large cities, with their population in May 1980 are: Iloilo on Panay, 244,827; Cebu on Cebu, 490,281; Zamboanga on Mindanao, 343,722; Davao on Mindanao, 610,375; Bacolod on Negros, 262,415; San Carlos on Negros Occidental, 91,627; San Carlos on Pangasinan, 101,243; Pasay on Rizal, 287,770.

On 7 June 1946 the President of the Philippines approved a law, effective 4 July 1946, making a new language (Pilipino) based on Tagalog (a Malayan dialect) the official national language of the republic. In 1970 about 16,409,133 people spoke English and about 1,335,945 Spanish; for government and commercial purposes these two languages are commonly used. Some 77 native languages are spoken in the Philippines, of which 9 are of major importance; they belong to the Malayo-Polynesian family.

CLIMATE. Some areas have an equatorial climate while others experience tropical monsoon conditions, with a wet season extending from May to Nov. Mean temperatures are high all year, with very little variation. Manila. Jan. 77°F (25°C), July 82°F (27·8°C). Annual rainfall 82″ (2,083 mm).

CONSTITUTION AND GOVERNMENT. The republic was governed by a constitution adopted on 14 May 1935 and amended in 1939, 1940 and 1947. On 17 Jan. 1973 a new constitution was ratified naming President Marcos President and Prime Minister without a fixed term of office. The President is assisted by 18 ministers in charge of Foreign Affairs, Finance, Justice, Agriculture, Public Works and Highways, Education, Culture and Sport, Labour and Employment, National Defence, Energy, Trade and Industry, Health, Social Services and Development, Agrarian Reform, Media Affairs, Local Government, Tourism, Natural Resources, Human Settlements, National Economic and Development Authority, Budget and Management, National Science and Technology Authority, the Presidential Executive Assistant, Muslim Affairs, Presidential Assistant on National Minorities and the Solicitor-General.

President: Ferdinand E. Marcos (re-elected for a third 6-year term in June 1981).
Prime Minister and Minister of Finance: Cesar Virata.

Martial law was introduced on 21 Sept. 1972. A referendum held in Dec. 1977 decreed that President Marcos should remain in power. On 12 June 1978 a limited experiment in parliamentary democracy began and the President also became Prime Minister. Limited power to legislate was given to the new Assembly but the right to legislate by decree was retained by the President and no date was given for lifting the martial law. On 17 Jan. 1981 martial law was lifted but the President retained wide powers under a National Security Code and Public Safety Act.

The 1973 Constitution provides that all male and female citizens 15 years of age or older who can read or write Spanish, English or a native dialect and who meet certain residential qualifications are entitled to vote.

The constitution vests in the republic all ownership of the country's natural resources, which, apart from public agricultural land, may not be alienated.

National flag: Horizontally blue over red, with a white triangle based on the hoist bearing a gold sun of 8 rays and 3 gold stars.

National hymn: 'Tierra Adorada', 'Land of the morning', lyric in English by M. A. Sane and C. Osias, in Spanish by José Palma (1899), tune by Julian Felipe (1898); 'Pambansang Awit ng Pilipinas', Tagalog lyric by the Institute of National Language, music by Julian Felipe.

Local Government. The country is administratively divided into 13 regions, 73 provinces, 60 cities, 1,493 municipalities, 21 municipal districts, 40,207 *barangays* with 241,242 councilmen. On 14 Nov. 1975 the name of provincial boards and city or municipal boards or councils was changed into *Sangguniang Bayan*. The latter assumes all the powers and responsibilities on matters of legislation of the defunct provincial, city or municipal boards.

The *Sangguniang Pambayan* is the direct successor of the old municipal council; *Sangguniang Panglunsod* for the old city council; *Sangguniang Panlalawigan* for the old provincial council and *Batasang Pambansa* for the defunct Congress.

DEFENCE. On 14 March 1947 the Philippine and US Governments signed a 99-year military-base arrangement since reduced to 25 years and will end in 1991. The USA was granted the use of a series of army, navy and air bases, with the right to use a number of others on mutual agreement. On 21 March a second agreement provided for a US Military Advisory Group as well as military assistance. A treaty of mutual assistance was signed in Washington on 30 Aug. 1951; the instruments of ratification were exchanged in Manila on 27 Aug. 1952. The Philippines is also a signatory of the S.E. Asia Collective Defence Treaty.

The Chief of Staff of the Armed Forces has overall command over the Army, Air Force, Navy and Constabulary.

Army. The Army comprises 5 infantry divisions, 1 special warfare brigade, 2 engineer brigades, 1 light armoured regiment and 4 artillery regiments. Equipment includes 28 Scorpion light tanks. Strength (1985) 60,000, with reserves totalling 90,000. There are also paramilitary forces; the Philippine Constabulary (44,000) and the Civil Home Defence Force (65,000).

Navy. The fleet includes 7 old frigates (3 former US destroyer escorts and 4 *ex*-USCG cutters, *ex*-USN seaplane tenders); 3 new fast missile craft; 10 corvettes (3 *ex*-US fleet minesweepers and 7 *ex*-US escorts), 2 *ex*-US PC-type patrol vessels, 8 other patrol craft, 5 gunboats, 72 coastal patrol craft, 1 training ship, 24 landing ships, 4 medium landing ships, 6 landing craft (3 LSSL and 3 LCU), 3 repair ships, 2 oilers, 3 water carriers, 1 supply ship, 4 survey ships, 5 tenders, 70 minor landing craft, 2 yachts (command ships), 6 tugs and 16 auxiliaries. There are some 30 patrol craft, cutters and tenders in the coast guard.

The Philippine Navy was considerably increased in 1976 by taking over many vessels (nearly all former US warships) from the Vietnamese Navy which escaped from Indo-China when the Saigon government collapsed in 1975. But some 60 of the larger ships are aged (40 years).

Naval personnel in 1985 totalled 1,600 officers and 13,070 men. There are also 330 officers and 6,500 enlisted men in the marine corps, and 300 officers and 1,700 men in the coast guard.

Air Force. The Air Force has a strength of 16,800 officers and men, with 390 aircraft, and was built up with US assistance. Its fighter-bomber wing is equipped with 1 squadron of F-5A and 1 squadron of F-8H Crusaders. There are transport, observation, air/sea rescue, helicopter and training units, for which recently acquired equipment has included 3 Fokker F27 Maritime patrol aircraft, a squadron of OV-1 Mohawk observation aircraft, 12 Australian-built Mission-master twin-turboprop STOL light transports, 4 HU-16 Albatross amphibians and a total of 44 Italian-built SF.260WP (armed) and SF.260MP piston-engined trainers. Many of the Air Force's other trainers are armed for counter-insurgency duties. No. 16 and 18 squadrons of the 15th Strike Wing each operate 16 T-28Ds. No. 17 has 16 SF.260WPs. Aircraft on order include 2 Sikorsky S-70A-5 assault helicopters and 17 S-76 utility helicopters.

Police. Public order is maintained partly through the Philippine constabulary and partly through the local police forces. The constabulary now forms part of the Armed Forces and has 27,000 personnel.

INTERNATIONAL RELATIONS

Membership. The Republic of the Philippines is a member of UN and the Colombo Plan.

External Debt. At 31 Dec. 1983 the external debt amounted to US$15,264·5m.

ECONOMY

Planning. A development plan, 1983–87, aims at an average growth rate of 6·5%.

Budget. The revenues and expenditures of the central government for calendar years were, in 1m. Philippine pesos, as follows:

	1981	*1982*	*1983*	*1984*[1]
Revenue	35,933	38,205	46,642	58,174
Expenditure	47,072	48,792	50,271	59,103

[1] Estimate.

Expenditure (1983) included (in 1m. pesos): National defence, 6,106; education, health and social services, 11,618; economic development, 11,618; public debt, 8,543.

At Feb. 1984 the total internal public debt outstanding of the national and local governments, including those of the government corporations, stood at P.62,514m.

Currency. Total money supply, Dec. 1984, was P.33,633·4m., of which P.21,797·9m. was currency in circulation and P.11,835·5m. were demand deposits. The coins used are: 5 *peso*, 1 *peso*, one-half *peso*, quarter *peso*, media *peseta* (10 *centavos*), all contain 70 grammes copper, 18 grammes zinc and 12 grammes nickel; 5 *centavo* in copper and zinc, and 1 *centavo* in aluminium and magnesium zinc. Central Bank notes are issued in 2, 5, 10, 20, 50, 100 *pesos* denominations.

In March 1985, £1 = 18·50 *pesos*; US$1 = 18·39 *pesos*.

Banking. In 1983 there were 1,905 branches of commercial banks operating under 34 head offices, with 4 overseas, 1 each in New York, Hong Kong, Taipei and London. Agencies exist in Honolulu, San Francisco and Los Angeles. Total deposits of the commercial banks in July 1983 were P.118,382·8m.

Under the law passed 15 June 1948 the Central Bank of the Philippines was created to have sole control of the credit and monetary supply, independent of the Treasury. It has a capital of P.10m. furnished solely by the Government. Its total assets, at 31 Dec. 1983 were P.130,371·7m.

Weights and Measures. The metric system of weights and measures was established by law in 1869, and since 1916 has come into general use but there are local units including the picul (63·25 kg) for sugar and fibres, and the cavan (16·5 gallons) for cereals.

ENERGY AND NATURAL RESOURCES

Electricity. Government and private electric systems furnish the Philippines with electric power, with total installed capacity of 5,634,100 mw (1983). The Manila Electric Co., was bought by the Government in July 1978. MECO plants sold 10,484m. kw in 1983 while the Government's National Power Corporation produced 18,688m. kw; others, 2,079m. kw.

Minerals. Mineral production in 1983 (in tonnes): Lead concentrate, 1,992; nickel metal, 13,900; nickel direct shipping ore, 345,310; zinc metal, 2,280; copper metal, 271,400; cobalt metal, 16,000; coal, 1·02m.; salt, 381,910; gold, 25,400 kg; silver, 56,700 kg. Other minerals include cement, rock asphalt, sand and gravel.

Agriculture. Of the total area of 30m. hectares, 7·04m. hectares are commercial forests; 5·4m. hectares non-commercial forests; 794,000 hectares open grassland; 115,000 hectares mangrove and marshes; 14,794,000 hectares cultivated.

About 98·4% of the total cultivated area is owned by Filipinos; the average size of the farm was 2·63 hectares in 1980. The principal products are unhusked rice (palay), Manila hemp (abaca), copra, sugar-cane, maize and tobacco. During the first quarter of 1984 9,187,000 persons were employed in agriculture (49·07% of the working population).

The products (in tonnes) are (1983, provisional): Rough rice, 7·7m.; copra, 2·5m.; coconut, 3·5m.; sugar (centrifugal muscovado and molasses), 3·4m.; shelled corn, 3·1m.; tobacco, 44,333; abaca fibre, 90,927.

Minor crops are fruits, nuts, root crops, vegetables, onions, beans, coffee, cacao, peanuts, ramie, rubber, maguey and kapok.

Livestock, estimated in 1983: 2·9m. carabaos (water buffaloes), 1·9m. cattle, 8m. pigs, 1·8m. goats and 67·7m. poultry.

Forestry. The forests covered some 11,204,000 hectares in 1983. Log production, 4,430,194 cu. metres, of which 786,037 cu. metres were exported in 1983.

Fisheries. Fish production from all sources was 1,896,983 tonnes and was valued at P.15,063,966 in 1983.

INDUSTRY AND TRADE

Industry. Manufacturing is a major source of economic development contributing 24·83% to GNP in 1984. Leading growth sectors were textile, footwear and wearing apparel, chemical and chemical products, beverage industries and food manufacture. In 1981 (annual survey), there were 84,931 manufacturing establishments, of which 29,199 were engaged in food; 28,148 wearing apparel, 1,370 footwear; 4,415 textile; 1,065 beverages; 4 petroleum refineries; 3,436 furniture and fixtures; 4,742 fabricated metal products and 874 transport equipment. The non-agricultural labour force during the first quarter of 1984 was 9,537,000 out of a total of 18,724,000 employed.

Commerce. The values of imports and exports (f.o.b.) for calendar years are stated as follows in US$1m.:

	1980	*1981*	*1982*	*1983*
Imports	7,727	7,946	7,667	7,487
Exports	5,788	5,722	5,021	5,005

The principal exports in 1984 were (in US$1m.): Electronics, 990; garments, 438; sugar, 205; coconut oil (crude), 436; copper concentrates, 91; gold, 80; fresh bananas, 96; petroleum products refined, 122; nickel, 85.

Main imports in 1982 (in US$1m.): Mineral fuels, lubricants and related materials, 2,105; machinery other than electric, 988; base metals, 528; transport equipment, 295; electric machinery apparatus and appliances, 289; chemical elements and components, 259; cereals and cereal preparations, 242; explosives and miscellaneous chemical materials and products, 216; metal manufactures, 172; unmanufactured textile fibres, 99.

For over a half-century the foreign trade has been chiefly with the USA.

Total trade between the Philippines and UK (British Department of Trade returns, in £1,000 sterling):

	1980	*1981*	*1982*	*1983*	*1984*
Imports to UK	99,018	105,535	127,061	160,701	199,659
Exports and re-exports from UK	88,998	85,650	97,908	102,949	91,751

Tourism. In 1983, 860,550 tourists visited the Philippines spending US$465m.

COMMUNICATIONS

Roads. In 1983 highways totalled 155,467·41 km; of this, 10,942·4 km were concrete; 17,849·22, asphalt; 54,922·61, earth; 71,753, macadam. In 1983 there were registered 1,200,803 motor vehicles of all types.

Railways. The National Railways totals 1,027 km of 1,067 mm gauge on Luzon, and Phividec Railways operates 116 km on Panay Island. In 1983, 4,307,588 passengers and 46,246 tonnes of freight were carried by rail.

Aviation. The Philippine Air Lines, Inc., with a working capital of P.3,061m., in 1983 carried 4,288,385 passengers, 43,171,880 kg of cargo and 459,171 kg of mail.

Shipping. In 1984 there were 622 public and 188 private ports, many serving coastal shipping. In 1981, 71,787 vessels of 24,608,624 net tons entered and 71,796 vessels of 23,834,150 net tons cleared all ports.

Post and Broadcasting. In 1983 there were in operation 2,108 post offices and 2,113 telegraph stations. The Philippine Long Distance Telephone Co. had 763,930 telephones in service in 1983 while other major operators had 62,429 connexions.

Licensed radio stations in 1983 numbered 44,672, including 3,546 ship stations and 790 aircraft stations.

Newspapers (1984). There were 472 registered publications (288 published in Manila), 26 of which were dailies.

JUSTICE, RELIGION, EDUCATION AND WELFARE

Justice. There is a Supreme Court which is composed of a chief justice and 14 associate justices; it can declare a law or treaty unconstitutional by the concurrent votes of the majority sitting. There is an intermediate appellate court, which consists of a presiding appellate justice and 49 associate appellate justices. There are 13 regional trial courts, one for each judicial region, with a presiding regional trial judge in its 720 branches. There is a metropolitan trial court in each metropolitan area established by law, a municipal trial court in each of the other cities or municipalities and a municipal circuit trial court in each area defined as a municipal circuit comprising one or more cities and/or one or more municipalities.

The Supreme Court may designate certain branches of the regional trial courts to handle exclusively criminal cases, juvenile and domestic relations cases, agrarian cases, urban land reform cases which do not fall under the jurisdiction of quasijudicial bodies and agencies and/or such other special cases as the Supreme Court may determine.

Religion. In 1970 there were 31,169,488 Roman Catholics, 1,434,688 Aglipayans, 1,584,963 Moslems, 1,122,999 Protestants, 475,407 members of the Iglesia ni Kristo, 33,639 Buddhists and 863,302 others.

The Roman Catholics are organized in 12 archbishoprics, 30 bishoprics, 12 prelatures nullius, 4 apostolic vicariates, 4 apostolic prefectures and some 1,633 parishes. The Philippine Independent Church, founded in 1902, and comprising about 3·9% of the population, denies the spiritual authority of the Roman Pontiff. It is divided into two groups, one of which has accepted ordinations by the Episcopalian Church.

Education. Formal education consists of 3 levels: elementary, secondary and further education. Public elementary education is free and public elementary schools are established in almost every *barangay* or *barrio*. The majority of the secondary and post-secondary schools are private, sectarian or non-sectarian. The number of years required to complete the elementary and secondary levels are 6 and 4 years respectively, while the tertiary level requires at least 4 years for an academic degree. Pre-school education is also offered mostly in private schools to children from ages 3–6.

Non-formal education consists of adult literacy classes, agricultural and farming training programmes, occupation skills training, youth clubs, and community programmes of instructions in health, nutrition, family planning and co-operatives.

Public and private schools in 1982–83 enrolled 8,591,267 pupils in primary schools, 3,074,219 in secondary schools and 1,411,515 students in further education. The University of the Philippines (founded in 1908) had 15,316 students in 1984.

Health. In 1982 there were 46,579 registered physicians and (1983) 76,653 hospital beds.

DIPLOMATIC REPRESENTATIVES

Of the Philippines in Great Britain (9A Palace Green, London, W8 4QE)
Ambassador: José V. Cruz (accredited 17 Dec. 1982).

Of Great Britain in the Philippines (115 Esteban St., Manila)
Ambassador: Robin J. T. McLaren.

Of the Philippines in the USA (1617 Massachusetts Ave., NW, Washington, D.C., 20036)
Ambassador: Benjamin T. Romualdez.

Of the USA in the Philippines (1201 Roxas Blvd., Manila)
Ambassador: Stephen W. Bosworth.

Of the Philippines to the United Nations
Ambassador: Luis Moreno-Salcedo.

Books of Reference

Philippine Yearbook 1985. National Census and Statistics Office, Manila, 1985
National Power Corporation. Annual Report '83
Foreign Trade Statistics of the Philippines, 1982. National Census and Statistics Office, Manila, 1982
Burley, T. M., *The Philippines. An Economic and Social Geography.* London, 1973
Golay, F. H., *The Philippines: Public Policy and National Economic Development.* Cornell Univ. Press, 1961
Lightfoot, K., *The Philippines.* London, 1973
Poole, F., and Vanzi, M., *Revolution in the Philippines.* New York, 1984

PITCAIRN ISLAND

HISTORY. It was discovered by Carteret in 1767, but remained uninhabited until 1790, when it was occupied by 9 mutineers of HMS *Bounty*, with 12 women and 6 men from Tahiti. Nothing was known of their existence until the island was visited in 1808. In 1856 the population having become too large for the island's resources, the inhabitants (194 in number) were, at their own request, removed to Norfolk Island; but 43 of them returned in 1859–64.

AREA AND POPULATION. Pitcairn Island (1·75 sq. miles; 4·6 sq. km) is situated in the Pacific Ocean, nearly equidistant from New Zealand and Panama (25° 04′S. lat., 130° 06′ W. long.). The population has been declining and on 30 June 1984 it was 57.

The uninhabited islands of Henderson (12 sq. miles), Ducie (1½ sq. miles) and Oeno (2 sq. miles) were annexed in 1902 and are included in the Pitcairn group.

CLIMATE. An equable climate, with average annual rainfall of 80″ (2,000 mm), spread evenly throughout the year. Mean monthly temperatures range from 75°F (24°C) in Jan. to 66°F (19°C) in July.

CONSTITUTION. Pitcairn was brought within the jurisdiction of the High Commissioner for the Western Pacific in 1898 and transferred to the Governor of Fiji in 1952. When Fiji became independent in Oct. 1970, the British High Commissioner in New Zealand was appointed Governor.

The Local Government Ordinance of 1964 constitutes a Council of 10 members, of whom 4 are elected, 5 are nominated (3 by the 4 elected members and 2 by the Governor) and the Island Secretary is an *ex-officio* member. The Island Magistrate, who is elected triennially, presides over the Council; other members hold office for only 1 year. Liaison between Governor and Council is through a Commissioner in the Auckland, New Zealand, office of the British Consulate-General.

Flag: British Blue Ensign with the whole arms of Pitcairn in the fly.

TRADE. Fruit, vegetables and curios are sold to passing ships; fuel oil, machinery, building materials, flour, sugar and other foodstuffs are imported.

Governor: T. D. O'Leary, CMG (resides in Wellington).
Island Magistrate: Ivan Christian (re-elected Dec. 1981).

Books of Reference

A Guide to Pitcairn. Pitcairn Island Administration, Auckland, revised ed. 1982
Ball, I., *Pitcairn: Children of the Bounty.* London, 1973
Ross, A. S. C., and Moverly, A. W., *The Pitcairnese Language.* London, 1964

POLAND

Capital: Warsaw
Population: 36·4m. (1983)
GNP per capita: US$3,900 (1980)

Polska Rzeczpospolita Ludowa

HISTORY. In 1966 Poland celebrated its millennium, but modern Polish history begins with the partitions of the once-powerful kingdom between Russia, Austria and Prussia in 1772, 1793 and 1795. For 19th century events *see* THE STATESMAN'S YEAR-BOOK 1980–81.

On 10 Nov. 1918 independence was proclaimed by Józef Piłsudski, the founder of the Polish Legions during the war. On 28 June 1919 the Treaty of Versailles recognized the independence of Poland.

On 1 Sept. 1939 Germany invaded Poland, on 17 Sept. 1939 Russian troops entered eastern Poland, and on 29 Sept. 1939 the fourth partition of Poland took place. After the German attack on Russia, the Germans occupied the whole of Poland. By March 1945 the country had been liberated by the Russians.

In July 1944 the USSR recognized the Polish Committee of National Liberation *(Polski Komitet Wyzwolenia Narodowego)* established in Lublin as an executive organ of the National Council of the Homeland *(Krajowa Rada Narodowa)*. The Committee was transformed into the Provisional Government in Dec. 1944, and on 28 June 1945, supplemented by members of the Polish Government in London (which had been recognized by the UK and USA), it was re-established in Moscow—as the Polish Provisional Government of National Unity and on 6 July recognized as such by the UK and USA.

Elections were held on 19 Jan. 1947. Of the 12·7m. votes cast, 11·24m. were recognized as valid and 9m. were given for the Communist-dominated 'Democratic Bloc'. After riots in Poznań in June 1956 nationalist anti-Stalinist elements gained control of the Communist Party, under the leadership of Wladyslaw Gomułka.

In 1970 the Federal Republic of Germany recognized Poland's western boundary as laid down by the Potsdam Conference of 1945 (the 'Oder–Neisse line').

In Dec. 1970 strikes and riots in Gdańsk, Szczecin and Gdynia led to the resignation of a number of leaders including Gomułka. He was replaced by Edward Gierek.

The introduction of price rises in June 1976 was again followed by strikes and riots. The rises were withdrawn and some demonstrators were imprisoned. In the campaign of protest which followed a Committee for the Defence of the Workers (KOR) was formed.

The raising of meat prices on 1 July 1980 resulted in a wave of strikes which broadened into generalized wage demands and eventually by mid-Aug. acquired a political character. Workers in Gdańsk, Gdynia and Sopot elected a joint strike committee, led by Lech Wałęsa demanding the right to strike and form independent Trade Unions, the abolition of censorship, access to the media and the release of political prisoners.

On 24 Aug. Gierek reshuffled the Party and Government leadership, and Józef Pińkowski replaced Edward Babiuch as Prime Minister. On 31 Aug. the Government and Wałęsa signed the 'Gdańsk Agreements' permitting the formation of independent Trade Unions.

On 5 Sept. Gierek suffered a heart attack and was replaced as First Secretary by Stanislaw Kania (Gierek was expelled from the Party in July 1981). On 17 Sept. various Trade Unions decided to form a national confederation ('Solidarity') and applied for legal status, which was granted on 24 Oct. after some Government resistance.

On 9 Feb. Pińkowski was replaced as Prime Minister by the Defence Minister, Gen. Wojciech Jaruzelski. At an extraordinary Communist Party congress in July a new leadership was elected. At Solidarity's first national congress (4–10 Sept. and 2–8 Oct. 1981) Wałęsa was re-elected chairman and a radical programme of action was adopted. On 18 Oct. Kania resigned from the Party leadership and was replaced by Jaruzelski. On 13 Dec. 1981 the Government imposed martial law (*stan wojenny*), banning a wide range of civil liberties, and establishing the rule of a 20-member Military Council of National Salvation (WRON). Solidarity was proscribed and its leaders detained. Government control was consolidated only after mass arrests and some bloodshed. Martial law was approved by the Sejm on 26 Jan. 1982 with one dissident vote and 5 abstentions. The Party Central Committee approved the measure on 25 Feb. Wałęsa was released in Nov. 1982. On 8 Oct. the Sejm voted (with 12 dissident votes and 9 abstentions) a law dissolving all registered trade unions including Solidarity. These have been replaced by workplace unions which are required to pledge support for the Communist Party and the Constitution. In Dec. 1982 martial law was suspended. Internment was ended and the Army withdrawn from many sectors of public life. Martial law was finally lifted in July 1983, although certain special legislation remains in force. An amnesty of 21 July 1984 freed 35,000 common and 652 political prisoners, including 7 Solidarity and 4 KOR leaders. The amnesty provides for rearrest should similar offences be committed.

AREA AND POPULATION. Poland is bounded north by the Baltic and the RSFSR, east by Lithuania, White Russia and the Ukraine, south by Czechoslovakia and west by the German Democratic Republic. Poland comprises an area of 312,683 sq. km (120,628 sq. miles). The country is divided into 49 voivodships (*wojewodztwo*) (including 3 urban: Warsaw, Kraków and Łódź) and these in turn are divided into 803 towns and 2,070 wards (*gmina*). The capital is Warsaw (Warszawa).

Area (in sq. km) and population (in 1,000, with urban in brackets) in 1981.

Voivodship	*Area*	*Population*	*Voivodship*	*Area*	*Population*
Biała Podlaska	5,348	288 (87)	Opole	8,535	979 (491)
Białystok	10,055	647 (358)	Ostrołęka	6,498	373 (109)
Bielsko–Biała	3,703	840 (408)	Piła	8,205	442 (234)
Bydgoszcz	10,349	1,043 (649)	Piotrków	6,266	613 (264)
Chełm	3,865	233 (89)	Płock	5,117	497 (215)
Ciechanów	6,362	407 (127)	Poznań	8,151	1,249 (866)
Częstochowa	6,182	751 (374)	Przemyśl	4,436	382 (132)
Elbląg	6,103	446 (257)	Radom	7,295	706 (296)
Gdańsk	7,394	1,345 (1,027)	Rzeszów	4,398	656 (236)
Gorzów	8,484	462 (276)	Siedlce	8,499	621 (166)
Jelenia Góra	4,378	495 (317)	Sieradz	4,869	392 (122)
Kalisz	6,512	673 (295)	Skierniewice	3,959	399 (162)
Katowice	6,650	3,806 (3,336)	Słupsk	7,453	374 (198)
Kielce	9,211	1,075 (461)	Suwałki	10,490	426 (202)
Konin	5,139	444 (165)	Szczecin	9,981	907 (670)
Koszalin	8,470	465 (282)	Tarnobrzeg	6,283	560 (185)
Kraków (Cracow)	3,255	1,177 (812)	Tarnów	4,151	613 (203)
Krosno	5,702	453 (143)	Toruń	5,348	616 (372)
Legnica	4,037	466 (298)	Wałbrzych	4,168	718 (522)
Leszno	4,154	361 (161)	Warsaw	3,788	2,342 (2,069)
Łódź	1,525	1,136 (1,038)	Włocławek	4,402	415 (181)
Łomża	6,684	328 (108)	Wrocław	6,287	1,083 (782)
Lublin	6,793	944 (508)	Zamość	6,980	476 (111)
Nowy Sącz	5,577	634 (224)	Zielona Góra	8,868	615 (385)
Olsztyn	12,320	690 (382)			

Population (in 1,000) of the largest towns (1982):

Warsaw	1,628	Bydgoszcz	356	Radom	198
Łódź	845	Lublin	314	Zabrze	196
Kraków (Cracow)	723	Sosnowiec	255	Kielce	192
Wrocław (Breslau)	627	Częstochowa	238	Toruń	183
Poznań	563	Bytom	238	Tychy	177
Gdańsk (Danzig)	462	Gdynia	237	Bielsko-Biala	170
Szczecin (Stettin)	390	Białystok	230	Ruda Słaska	162
Katowice	366	Gliwice	202	Chorzów	158

At the census of 7 Dec. 1978 the population was 35,032,000 (17m. males; 58% urban). Population on 1 Jan. 1983, 36,399,000 (18·7m. females; 21·7m. urban), density, 116 per sq. km. Vital statistics, 1982 (per 1,000): Marriages, 8·7; divorces, 1·3; live births, 19·4; deaths, 9·2; infant mortality (per 1,000 live births), 20·4.

The rate of natural growth, 1982, 10·2 per 1,000. Expectation of life in 1981 was 66·9 years for males, 75·4 years for females. In 1984, 55% of the population was under 30.

Ethnic minorities are not identified. There were estimated to be 1·2m. Germans in 1984. In 1982 there were 900 immigrants and 32,100 emigrants. In 1983 19,200 Germans emigrated. There is a large Polish diaspora, some 65% in USA.

CLIMATE. Climate is continental, marked by long and severe winters. Rainfall amounts are moderate, with a marked summer maximum. Warsaw. Jan. 25°F (–3·9°C), July 66°F (18·9°C). Annual rainfall 22·1" (553 mm). Gdańsk. Jan. 29°F (–1·7°C), July 63°F (17·2°C). Annual rainfall 22" (559 mm). Kraków. Jan. 27°F (–2·8°C), July 67°F (19·4°C). Annual rainfall 29" (729 mm). Poznań. Jan. 30°F (–1·1°C), July 67°F (19·4°C). Annual rainfall 21" (523 mm). Stettin. Jan. 30°F (–1·1°C), July 65°F (18·3°C). Annual rainfall 22" (550 mm). Wrocław. Jan. 30°F (–1·1°C), July 66°F (18·9°C). Annual rainfall 23" (574 mm).

CONSTITUTION AND GOVERNMENT. The present Constitution was adopted on 22 July 1952. Amendments were adopted in 1976 and 1983.

The titular head of state is the Chairman of the Council of State, Henryk Jabłoński. Deputy Chairmen: Tadeusz Mlynczak, Kazimierz Secomski, Bolesław Strużek, Jerzy Zietek.

Since 1983 the Constitution has defined the position of political parties as follows: 'The alliance and cooperation of the Polish United Workers' (*i.e.* Communist) Party with the United Peasant Party and the Democratic Party in the construction of socialism and their cooperation with those social organizations and associations that are grounded in the principles of the system of the Polish People's Republic form the basis of the Patriotic Movement of National Renaissance. (PRON). The latter was set up on 15 Oct. 1982. The National Unity Front was dissolved in July 1983.

At the 9th, extraordinary, congress of the Communist Party on 19 July 1981 a new Politburo was elected by democratic vote. Only four of the 16 former members were re-elected. Changes were made in the Party and Government leadership in July and Oct. 1982. In March 1985 the Politburo consisted of: Wojciech Jaruzelski *(First Secretary and Prime Minister)*; Kazimerz Barcikowski; Tadeusz Czechowicz; Józef Czyrek; Zofia Grzyb; Stanisław Kalkus; Hieronim Kubiak; Zbigniew Messner *(Deputy Prime Minister responsible for coordination)*; Mirosław Milewski; Stefan Olszowski *(Foreign Minister)*; Stanisław Opalko; Tadeusz Porebski; Jerzy Romanik; Albin Siwak; Marian Wozniak. Candidate members: Stanisław Bejger; Jan Główczyk; Czesław Kiszczak *(Minister of the Interior)*; Włodzimierz Mokrzyszczak; Marian Orzechowski; Gen. Florian Siwicki *(Defence)*. Ministers not in the Politburo include 8 *Deputy Prime Ministers:* Manfred Gorywoda *(Chairman, State Planning Commission)*; Zenon Komender *(Catholic representative),* Edward Kowalczyk; Roman Malinowski; Zbigniew Messner; Janusz Obodowski; Mieczysław Rakowski; Zbigniew Szalajda; Gen. Tadeusz Hupałowski *(Chairman, Supreme Chamber of Control)*; Zdzisław Krasiński *(Minister responsible for prices)*; Władysław Baka *(Plenipotentiary for the economic reform)*; Włodzimierz Oliwa *(Administration and Environment)*; Stanisław Zieba *(Agriculture and Food)*, Stanisław Nickarz *(Finance)*; Tadeusz Nesterowicz *(Foreign Trade)*; Anna Kedzierska *(Home Trade)*; Lech Domeracki *(Justice)*, Stefan Ciosek *(Trade Union affairs)*; Stanisław Gebala *(Labour)*.

In 1984 the Polish United Workers' Party had 2,186,000 (3,091,900 in 1980) members (39% workers, 89% over 30), the United Peasants' Party had 471,000, and the Democratic Party, 112,000 members. The Socialist Youth Union claimed nearly 2m. members in 1983.

The authority of the republic is vested in the Sejm, elected for 4 years by all citizens over 18. The Sejm elects a Council of State, composed of a Chairman, the Secretary and 16 members, including 4 vice-chairmen; and a Council of Ministers. Local government is carried out by People's Councils elected every 4 years at voivodship and community level. Alongside these are the offices of state administration. The chairman of the People's Council is the Secretary of the regional organization for the area.

The last elections for the Sejm were held on 23 March 1980. 646 candidates stood on the single list of the National Unity Front and obtained 99·52% of the vote. 98·87% of the electorate voted. The 460 seats are distributed as follows: 261 United Workers' Party, 113 United Peasants' Party, 37 Democratic Party, 49 independents, including 4 Catholics. There are 106 women deputies. The General Election due in March 1984 was postponed until 1985.

Local elections due in 1982 were postponed until 17 June 1984. Solidarity called for a boycott of the elections, but the Government announced that 74·95% of the 25·9m. electorate had voted (a figure claimed by Solidarity to be inflated by 12-15%). There were some 220,000 candidates, all selected by PRON.

National flag: Horizontally white over red.

National anthem: Jeszcze Polska nie zginęla (words by J. Wybicki, 1797; tune by M. Ogiński, 1796).

DEFENCE. A National Defence Committee was set up in Nov. 1983 with Gen. Jaruzelski at its head. Poland is divided into 3 military districts: Warsaw (the eastern part of Poland); Pomerania (Baltic coast, part of central Poland; headquarters at Bydgoszcz); Silesia (Silesia and southern Poland; headquarters at Wrocław).

Armed forces are on Soviet lines and divided into army and air force (2 years' conscription), navy (3 years), anti-aircraft, rocket and radio-technological units (3 years) and internal security forces (2 years). In 1965 the security forces were taken away from the Ministry of Internal Affairs and placed under the Defence Ministry. The military age extends from the 19th to the 50th year. The strength of the armed forces was (1985) 317,500, plus 85,000 security and frontier forces. Security forces include armoured brigades.

Army. The Army consists of 5 armoured, 8 mechanized, 1 airborne and 1 amphibious assault divisions; 3 artillery brigades and 1 regiment; 3 anti-tank regiments; 4 surface-to-surface missile brigades; 1 air defence brigade and 5 regiments. Equipment includes 3,400 T-54/-55 and 50 T-72 main battle tanks. Strength (1985) 230,000 (including 158,000 conscripts).

Navy. The fleet comprises 4 submarines, 1 destroyer, 24 fleet minesweepers, 13 missile craft, 23 patrol boats, 8 torpedo boats, 45 coastal patrol boats, 3 inshore minesweepers, 23 medium landing ships, 3 intelligence vessels, 8 training ships, 3 degaussing vessels, 2 salvage ships, 2 torpedo recovery vessels, 18 minor landing craft, 23 minesweeping boats, 6 surveying vessels, 7 oilers, 20 tugs and 40 auxiliaries and tenders. The Fleet Air Arm has 50 fixed-wing aircraft (including 40 MiG-17) and 25 helicopters. Personnel in 1985 totalled 22,500 comprising 7,500 afloat, 2,000 under training, 5,000 of coastal defence, 2,000 in naval aviation and 6,000 on shore support.

Air Force. The Air Force had a strength (1985) of some 75,000 officers and men and 700 first-line jet aircraft of Soviet design, forming 4 air divisions. There are 11 air defence regiments (33 squadrons) with about 400 MiG-21 supersonic interceptors, and 6 regiments (18 squadrons) operating variable-geometry MiG-23BM and Su-20, Su-7B and MiG-17 close-support fighters. Another fighter division supports the Navy. There are also reconnaissance, ECM, transport, helicopter (including Mi-24 gunship) and training units. Soviet 'Guideline' 'Goa', 'Ganef', 'Gainful' and 'Gaskin' surface-to-air missiles are operational.

Two Soviet armoured divisions are stationed on Polish territory.

INTERNATIONAL RELATIONS

Membership. Poland is a member of UN, Comecon and the Warsaw Pact.

ECONOMY

Planning. For planning history until 1980 *see* THE STATESMAN'S YEAR-BOOK 1981–82, p.1002. Industrialization without sufficient expenditure on infrastructure; neglect of agriculture and the inefficiency of the planning mechanism, exacerbated by higher prices and declining Western demand for exports, and the social unrest since 1980, brought the economy to a state of paralysis. Some foodstuffs are rationed, and price increases were introduced in 1982 and 1984. In Apr. 1982 a Consultative Economic Council was set up as an advisory body to the Government. A socio-economic plan for 1983–85 has the task of overcoming the economic crisis. The economy in 1983 showed some signs of recovery. Price rises announced for 1985 were modified in the face of official trade union opposition. Economic reforms involving a closer linking of credits, profits and wages with market forces and efficiency were introduced in 1982.

Budget. Budget in 1m. złotys, for calendar years:

	1977	*1978*	*1979*	*1980*	*1981*	*1982*
Revenue	993,948	1,103,457	1,154,800	1,215,200	1,334,600	2,346,100
Expenditure	887,599	994,158	1,107,700	1,246,200	1,465,600	2,433,600

Main items of 1982 revenue (in 1m. złotys): Sales tax and profits tax from state enterprises, 1,866,900; finance and insurance, 376,300; income tax, 20,900.

Main items of 1982 expenditure (in 1m. złotys): State enterprises, 1,095,900; welfare, 213,600; defence, 174,000; administration, 105,000; education, 192,900.

Currency. The currency unit is the *złoty*, divided into 100 *groszy*. The currency consists of notes of 10, 20, 50, 100, 500, 1,000, 2,000 and 5,000 złotys; and of coins of 10, 20 and 50 groszy and 1, 2, 5, 10, 20 and 50 złotys. In Jan. 1982 the złoty was substantially devalued against Western currencies. In March 1985, £1 sterling = 152 złotys, US$1 = 141 złotys.

Banking. The National Bank of Poland (established 1945) is the central bank, has exclusive authority to issue currency, is charged with control of money and credit, and has responsibility for financial implementation of the national economic plan. Since its merger with the former Investment Bank on 1 Jan. 1970 it exercises centralized control over investment financing. The Food Economics Bank (Bank Gospodarki Żywnościowej) has exclusive responsibility for direct financing of rural areas through both short-term and investment loans. It operates banks. The General Savings Bank (Powszechna Kasa Oszczedności) exercises central control over savings activities, transfers and checking transactions, including activities of workers' co-operative banks.

In addition to the National Bank of Poland other authorized foreign-exchange banks are, the Polish Welfare Bank (Bank Polska Kasa Opieki SA) and the Commercial Bank of Warsaw (Bank Handlowy w Warszawie SA).

Deposits in savings institutions amounted to 866,900m. złotys on 31 Dec. 1982.

Weights and Measures. The metric system is in general use.

ENERGY AND NATURAL RESOURCES

Energy. Power sources in 1979: Coal, 76%; lignite, 22%; hydroelectric, 2%. A nuclear power station is being built at Zarnowiec.

Minerals. Poland is a major producer of coal (reserves of some 71,000m. tonnes) and sulphur. Copper reserves are estimated at 10m. tonnes. There is also iron ore, lead and zinc. Production in 1982 (in 1,000 tonnes): Coal, 189,000; brown coal, 37,600; copper ore, 27,030; zinc-lead ores, 5,341; iron ore, 49.

Agriculture. In 1982 there were 18·9m. hectares of agricultural land, of which 14·3m. hectares were in private hands, 3·58m. in state farms, 0·74m. in co-operatives and 0·12m. in agricultural circles. There were 2·9m. private farms in 1982. Private holdings average 5·3 hectares, and may not exceed 100 hectares. 11m. hectares were arable, 233,000 orchards, 1·9m. meadows, 1m. pasture lands.

Collectivization has been largely abandoned but remains a long-term aim. There were 2,248 co-operatives in 1982. A new agricultural policy of 1981 gave more autonomy to co-operatives, linked wages to productivity and equalized resources between the state and private sectors. The peasants' trade union 'Rural Solidarity' won recognition in 1981 but was dissolved in Oct. 1982. A compulsory contributory pension scheme was introduced in 1978 for farmers who turn over their farms to their successors or the State. 250,000 such pensions had been paid by June 1980. 'Agricultural circles' numbered 26,000 with 2·2m. members in 1982. In 1981 there were 4,233 state agricultural holdings.

	Area (1,000 hectares)			*Yield (1,000 tonnes)*		
Crops	*1980*	*1981*	*1982*	*1980*	*1981*	*1982*
Wheat	1,609	1,418	1,456	4,175	4,203	4,476
Rye	3,039	3,002	3,273	6,566	6,731	7,792
Barley	1,322	1,294	1,236	3,420	3,540	3,647
Oats	997	1,156	1,086	2,245	2,730	2,608
Potatoes	2,344	2,258	2,178	26,391	42,562	31,951
Sugar-beet	460	470	493	10,139	15,867	15,085

Livestock (1983): 11·2m. cattle (5·7m. cows), 15·5m. pigs, 4·1m. sheep, 1·6m. horses, 61m. poultry. Milk production in 1982 was 14,749m. litres.

Tractors in use in 1982: 694,000 (in 15-h.p. units).

Forestry. In 1982, 8·4m. hectares were forests (predominantly coniferous). 61,000 hectares were afforested in 1982, and 23·3m. cu. metres of timber gained.

Fisheries. In 1981 the fishing fleet had 103 deep-sea vessels totalling 315,900 GRT. In 1982 the catch was 582,400 tonnes.

INDUSTRY AND TRADE

Industry. Production in 1981 (and 1982) (in 1,000 tonnes): Coke, 17,900 (17,300); pig-iron, 9,351 (8,524); crude steel, 15,719 (14,795); rolled steel, 11,064 (10,478); cement, 14,200 (16,035); sulphuric acid (100%), 2,776 (2,682); fertilizers, 2,242 (2,281); aluminium, 66 (43); electrolytic copper, 327 (348); lead, 69 (79); zinc, 167 (165); crude oil, 315 (240); salt, 4,271 (4,328); sugar, 1,685 (1,777); electricity, 115,000m. kwh. (118,000m.); natural gas, 6,172m. cu. metres (5,533m.). In 1982, 34 ships over 100 DWT were built (358,000 DWT), 229,000 cars, 37,800 lorries and 9,500 buses were built in 1982.

Output of light industry in 1981 (and 1982): Cotton fabrics, 738m. metres (693); woollen fabrics, 106m. metres (91); silk and synthetic fibres. 142m. metres (128); shoes, 145m. pairs (143); household glass, 71,500 tonnes (67,400); paper, 909,000 tonnes (966,000); washing machines 625,000 (712,000), refrigerators 553,000, and TV sets 764,400 (576,400).

Labour. In 1982 the total number in employment was 16·8m. (including 7·7m. women), of whom 12·2m. worked in the state-controlled sector and 4·6m. in the private sector, and including in agriculture 5m., industry 5m., building 1·2m., trade 1·3m. and transport and communications 1·1m. Founded in Aug. 1980 the 'independent self-governing union' organization Solidarity (Chairman Lech Wałęsa) was proscribed in Dec. 1981 and dissolved in Oct. 1982 along with all other trade unions. In 1983 some 2,500 new 'official' unions began operating at workplace level and in 115 national federations after Jan. 1984 with a membership of 3·8m. Membership of Solidarity had been 9,447,000 in Sept. 1981. Average wage in 1982, 11,138 złotys per month. A law of Oct. 1982 makes voluntary unemployment an offence; offenders are liable for compulsory labour for the state.

Commerce. Trade statistics for calendar years (in 1m. złotys):

	1977	*1978*	*1979*	*1980*	*1981* [1]	*1982*
Imports	48,600	50,938	54,015	58,299	963,447 (52,013)	862,040
Exports	40,800	44,685	50,141	51,908	846,209 (44,529)	947,384

[1] 'Official statistics for 1980 and before were expressed in exchange rate złotys, but thereafter in convertible złotys. The dramatic increase for 1981 is therefore only apparent. To facilitate comparison, the exchange rate złotys figure is also given (in brackets) for 1981.

Main imports in 1982 (in tonnes): Petroleum, 13·2m.; iron ore, 13·5m.; fertilizers, 5·7m.; wheat, 3·6m.; coal, 1m.; passenger cars, 46,759 units.

Main exports in 1982 (in tonnes): Coal, 28·5m.; coke, 1·7m.; sawn softwood, 616,000 cu. m.; ships, 334,000 DWT.

54% of Poland's trade is with Comecon countries.

Foreign trade deals should be made directly with the appropriate foreign trade enterprise. Information may be obtained from the Polish Chamber of Foreign Trade, Trebacka 4, 00–950 Warsaw. Joint ventures with Western firms are encouraged both at home and abroad. The Western partner may own up to 49% of the shares of ventures on Polish soil, and is guaranteed a share of profits and interest.

An over-ambitious programme of imports coinciding with the world recession and rise in oil prices was followed by a decline in output caused by the social and economic unrest of 1980–82. In 1982 Poland officially acknowledged debts to the West of 2,147,400m. złotys and to Comecon countries of 254,800m. złotys. Hard currency debt to the West in 1985 was US$22,500m. In Jan. 1985 a rescheduling agreement was signed with Western creditors. Poland does not accept liability for the £495,000 debts of pre-war Danzig (Gdańsk). 1982 saw a 27% drop in Western imports and a trade surplus of £250m.

Soviet exports include plant and equipment and raw materials; Polish exports, machinery, ships, coal, chemicals and consumer goods.

Total trade between Poland and UK for 5 years (British Department of Trade returns £1,000 sterling):

	1980	*1981*	*1982*	*1983*	*1984*
Imports to UK	194,523	133,605	151,737	177,057	266,961
Exports and re-exports from UK	296,254	175,728	133,340	151,721	169,962

An Anglo-Polish 10-year agreement on the development of economic, industrial, scientific and technical co-operation was signed on 20 March 1973, and a 10-year programme implementing this was signed on 4 Sept. 1975. Some Polish imports are subject to quota restrictions.

In Oct. 1982 the US suspended Poland's most-favoured-nation status and imposed some other economic sanctions as a response to the imposition of martial law. Some of these were lifted in Aug. and Dec. 1984.

Tourism. In 1982, 1,404,000 tourists visited Poland (388,000 from the West) and 995,000 Polish citizens made visits abroad (317,000 to the West).

COMMUNICATIONS

Roads. In 1982 Poland had 150,177 km of hard-surfaced roads. A road-improvement programme is bringing 75% of all roads up to suitability for heavy traffic. Number of motor vehicles: Passenger cars, 2,634,000 (of which, 2,587,000 private); lorries, 641,000 (180,000 private); motor cycles, 1,751,000.

In 1982 road transport carried 2,320m. passengers and 1,379m. tonnes of freight.

Railways. The length of the standard gauge railway system was (1983) 27,176 km (7,828 km electrified). In 1983 the railways carried 118,034 tonne-km of freight and 50,153m. passengers-km.

Aviation. In 1984 the state airline 'Lot' had 37 aircraft including 5 Il-62s, operated 10 internal routes and flew services to 30 countries. 907,000 passengers were flown and 9,000 tonnes of freight in 1982. There are British Airways, SABENA, KLM, PANAM, Alitalia, Swissair, Air France, Austrian Airlines and Lufthansa services to Okęcie (Warsaw) airport.

Shipping. The principal ports are Gdynia, Gdańsk (Danzig) and Szczecin (Stettin). The merchant marine is grouped into Polish Ocean Lines (179 vessels totalling 1·04m. DWT in 1975) based on Gdynia and operating regular liner services, and the Polish Shipping Company based on Szczecin and operating cargo services. Poland also has a share in the Gdynia America Line. There are 4,040 km of inland navigable waterways. 13·7m. tonnes of freight were carried in 1982.

In 1982 the merchant marine had 317 vessels totalling 3,005,000 GRT (including 19 vessels over 30,000 tons). There are regular lines to London, Hull, China, Indonesia, Australia, Vietnam and some African and Latin-American countries.

Total shipping entering Polish ports in 1982 was 7,242 vessels of 19·7m. NRT. Freight traffic in 1982 was 39·2m.

Pipeline. In 1982 there were 1,975 km of oil pipeline.

Post and Broadcasting. In 1982 there were 8,155 post offices and 3,648,000 telephones.

Polskie Radio i Telewizja broadcasts 3 programmes in Polish on long-, medium- and short-waves and on FM. There are 2 TV programmes. Colour programmes are transmitted by SECAM system. Wireless licences in 1982 numbered 8·87m.; television licences, 8·34m.

Cinemas and Theatres. In 1982 there were 2,089 cinemas, 96 theatres and 46 concert halls. Cinema attendance was 89·5m.; theatres, 7·4m.

Newspapers (1982). There were 90 papers with an overall circulation (in 1981) of 2,437m. 1,870 periodicals were published. The Party newspaper is *Trybuna Ludu* (People's Tribune), weekend circulation 1·1m.

JUSTICE, RELIGION, EDUCATION AND WELFARE

Justice. The penal code was adopted in 1969. Espionage and treason carry the severest penalties For minor crimes there is provision for probation sentences and fines.

There exist the following courts: The Supreme Court; voivodship, district and special courts. Judges and lay assessors are elected. The State Council elects the judges of the Supreme Court for a term of 5 years, and appoints the Prosecutor-General. The office of the Prosecutor-General is separate from the judiciary.

Family courts were established (1977) for cases involving divorce and domestic relations. Crimes reported in 1983 (and 1982) 466,000 (436,000) including 304 (250) murders and 1,055 (871) rapes. 35,000 criminals (40% of the prison population) were released under the amnesty of July 1984.

Religion. In 1978, 93% of the population was baptized into the Catholic Church, and 78% of the population attended church regularly. Church–State relations are regulated by agreements of 1950, 1956 and 1972. A joint government-episcopal commission was reactivated in Sept. 1980, and religious broadcasting began. The Church has a university (Lublin), an Academy of Catholic Theology and a seminary in every diocese. Religious education of children is conducted in 'catechism centres' of which there were 18,254 in 1973–74.

The archbishop of Warsaw and Gniezno is the primate of Poland (since 1981, Cardinal Józef Glemp). The Vatican considers the archbishoprics of Lwów and Vilnius (incorporated in the USSR in 1940) as still being under Polish jurisdiction. In 1977 there were 5 archbishoprics, 27 dioceses and 6,716 parishes, 75 bishops, 30,162 monks and nuns and 14,162 churches and chapels. In 1983 there were 2 cardinals and 21,643 priests. 100 churches were built. In Oct. 1978 Cardinal Karol Wojtyla, archbishop of Cracow, was elected Pope as John Paul II.

On 28 June 1972 the Vatican adjusted the Church boundaries, to coincide with the State's western frontier ('Oder–Neisse line') and the 4 apostolic administrators in the former German territories became bishops. In Oct. 1984, the radical priest, Jerzy Popiełuszko was murdered by secret policemen who were subsequently sentenced to long terms of imprisonment.

Figures for other churches in 1977: Polish Autocephalous Orthodox, 4 dioceses, 233 parishes, 301 churches, 221 priests, 2 monasteries (460,000 adherents in 1975). Lutheran, 6 dioceses, 122 parishes, 310 churches, 100 parsons (100,000 adherents in 1975). Uniate, 3 dioceses, 84 parishes, 89 churches, 90 priests (200,000 adherents in 1975). Old-Catholic Mariavite, 3 dioceses, 42 parishes, 56 churches, 33 priests (30,000 adherents in 1975). Methodist, 5 districts, 66 parishes, 65 chapels, 39 parsons (4,133 adherents in 1975). United Evangelical, 222 congregations, 68 chapels, 215 parsons. Seventh-day Adventist, 124 communities, 122 churches, 66 parsons. Baptist, 127 congregations, 53 chapels, 60 parsons (2,300 adherents in 1975). Jews, 16 congregations, 24 synagogues (12,000 adherents in

1978). Epiphany World Mission, 80 communities, 157 churches, 427 priests. In 1985 there were 2,500 Moslems with 3 mosques.

Education. Basic education from 7 to 15 is free and compulsory. Free secondary education is then optional in general or vocational schools. Primary schools are organized in complexes based on wards under one director ('gmina collective schools'). In 1982–83 there were: Kindergartens, 26,273 with 1·23m. pupils and 79,000 teachers; primary schools, 14,341 (of which 1,760 gmina collective schools) with 4,465,000 pupils and 245,000 teachers; secondary schools, 1,171 with 381,000 pupils and 23,000 teachers; vocational schools, 9,973 with 1,556,000 pupils and 85,000 teachers, and 91 institutions of higher education (including 10 universities, 18 polytechnics, 9 agricultural schools, 6 schools of economics, 11 teachers' training colleges and 10 medical schools) with 423,500 students and 55,450 teaching staff.

Beginning in 1978–79 the 8-year primary school is being progressively replaced by a 10-year general secondary school. In 1984 administration of schools was transferred from central to local government.

Health. In 1982 there were 686 hospitals (including 41 mental hospitals) with 240,000 beds, 5,893 dispensaries and 3,246 health centres. There were 66,848 doctors and 17,176 dentists.

Social Security. In 1982, 121,563m. złotys were paid out in 5·25m. retirement pensions, 32·51m. zlotys in family allowances and 49·82m. złotys in sick pay.

DIPLOMATIC REPRESENTATIVES

Of Poland in Great Britain (47 Portland Place, London, W1N 3AG)
Ambassador: Stefan Staniszewski (accredited 12 Feb. 1982).

Of Great Britain in Poland (Aleje Roz No. 1, Warsaw)
Ambassador: J. A. L. Morgan, CMG.

Of Poland in the USA (2640 16th St., NW, Washington, D.C., 20009)
Chargé d'Affaires: Zdzisław Ludwiczak.

Of the USA in Poland (Aleje Ujazdowskie 29/31, Warsaw)
Chargé d'Affaires: John R. Davis, Jr.

Of Poland to the United Nations
Ambassador: Włodzimierz Natorf.

Books of Reference

Statistical Information: The Central Statistical Office, Warsaw (Wawelska 1–3), publishes *Rocznik statystyczny* (annual, 1930–39; 1947–); *Concise Statistical Yearbook of Poland* (1959–); *Statystyka Polski* (irreg., 1947–); *Biuletyn statystyczny* (monthly, 1957–).

Constitution of the Polish People's Republic. Warsaw, 1964
Ascherson, N., *The Polish August: The Self-Limiting Revolution.* London, 1981
Ash, T. G., *The Polish Revolution: Solidarity 1980–82.* London, 1983
Beneš, V. L., and Pounds, N. G. J., *Poland.* London, 1970
Bromke, A., *Poland: the Protracted Crisis.* Oakville (Ontario), 1983
Brumberg, A., *Poland: Genesis of a Revolution.* New York, 1983
Bulas, K., and others, *English–Polish and Polish–English Dictionary.* 2 vols. The Hague, 1959
Burda, A., *Parliament of the Polish People's Republic.* Wrocław, 1978
Davies, N., *Poland, Past and Present: A Select Bibliography of Works in English.* Newtonville, 1977.—*God's Playground: A History of Poland.* 2 vols. OUP, 1981.—*Heart of Europe: a Short History of Poland.* OUP, 1984
De Weydenthal, J. B., et al. *The Polish Drama, 1980–1982.* Lexington, 1983
Dobbs, M., *Poland, Solidarity, Wałęsa.* New York, 1981
Dziewanowski, M. K., *Poland in the Twentieth Century.* Columbia Univ. Press, 1977
Eringer, R., *Strike for Freedom: The Story of Lech Wałesa and Polish Solidarity.* New York, 1982
Gieysztory, A., and others, *History of Poland. 2nd ed. Warsaw, 1979*
Halecki, O., *A History of Poland.* 4th ed. London, 1983
Karpiński, J., *Countdown: the Polish Upheavals of 1956, 1968, 1970, 1976, 1980.* NY, 1982

Kazimierz, B., *Warsaw Diary: 1978–1981.* New York, 1984
Kieniewicz, S. (ed.) *History of Poland.* 2nd ed. Warsaw, 1979
Lane, D., and Kolankiewicz, G. (ed.) *Social Groups in Polish Society.* London, 1973
Leslie, R. F., (ed.) *The History of Poland since 1863.* CUP, 1980
Lewanski, R. C., *Poland.* [Bibliography] Oxford and Santa Barbara, 1984
MacShane, D., *Solidarity: Poland's Independent Trade Union.* Nottingham, 1981
Polonsky, A. and Drukier, B., *The Beginnings of Communist Rule in Poland.* London, 1980
Pomian-Srzednicki, M. *Religious Change in Contemporary Poland: Secularization and Politics.* London, 1982
Potel, J.-I., *The Summer Before the Frost: Solidarity in Poland.* London, 1982
Preibisz, J. M., (ed.) *Polish Dissident Publications: an Annotated Bibliography.* New York, 1982
Rachman, A. R., *Poland between the Superpowers: Security vs. Economic Recovery.* Boulder, 1983
Raina P., *Political Opposition in Poland, 1954–1977.* London, 1978.—*Independent Social Movements in Poland.* London, 1981
Robinson, W.F. (ed.) *August 1980: the Strikes in Poland.* Munich, 1980
Roos, H., *A History of Modern Poland.* London, 1966
Ruane, K., *The Polish Challenge.* London, 1982
Sanford, G., *Polish Communism in Crisis.* London, 1983
Singer, D., *The Road to Gdańsk: Poland and the USSR.* New York and London, 1981
Staniszkis, J., *Poland's Self-Limiting Revolution.* Princeton, 1984
Steven, S., *The Poles.* London, 1982
Szczypiorski, A., *The Polish Ordeal: The View from Within.* London, 1982
Weschler, L., *Solidarity: Poland in the Season of its Passion.* NY, 1982
Who's Who in Poland. New York, 1983
Wielka Encyklopedia Powszechna. 13 vols. Warsaw, 1962–70
Woodall, J., (ed.) *Policy and Politics in Contemporary Poland: Reform, Failure and Crisis.* London, 1982

National Library: Biblioteka Narodowa, Rakowiecka 6, Warsaw.

PORTUGAL

República Portuguesa

Capital: Lisbon
Population: 9·93m. (1983)
GNP per capita: US$2,237 (1982)

HISTORY. Portugal has been an independent state since the 12th century, apart from one period of Spanish rule (1580–1640). The monarchy was deposed on 5 Oct. 1910 and a republic established.

A *coup* on 28 May 1926 established a military provisional government from 1 June. A corporatist constitution was adopted on 19 March 1933 under which a civil dictatorship governed until a fresh *coup* on 25 April 1974 established a Junta of National Salvation.

Following an attempted revolt on 11 March 1975, the Junta was dissolved and a Supreme Revolutionary Council formed which ruled until 25 April 1976 when constitutional government was resumed; the SRC was renamed the Council of the Revolution, becoming a consultative body until its abolition in 1982.

AREA AND POPULATION. Mainland Portugal is bounded north and east by Spain and south and west by the Atlantic ocean. The Atlantic archipelagoes of the Azores and of Madeira form autonomous but integral parts of the republic, which has a total area of 91,985 sq. km (35,516 sq. miles) and census populations:

1940	7,755,423	1960	8,889,392	1981	9,833,014
1950	8,510,240	1970	8,648,369		

The areas and populations of the districts and Autonomous Regions are:

Districts:	*sq. km*	*census 1981*		*sq. km*	*census 1981*
Aveiro	2,808	622,988	Portalegre	6,065	142,905
Beja	10,225	188,420	Porto	2,295	1,562,287
Braga	2,673	708,924	Santarém	6,747	454,123
Bragança	6,608	184,252	Setúbal	5,064	658,326
Castelo Branco	6,674	234,230	Viano de Castelo	2,225	256,814
Coimbra	3,947	436,324	Vila Real	4,328	264,381
Evora	7,393	180,277	Viseu	5,007	423,648
Faro	4,960	323,534	Total mainland	88,941	9,336,760
Guarda	5,518	205,631	*Autonomous Regions:*		
Leiria	3,515	420,229	Azores	2,247	243,410
Lisboa	2,761	2,069,467	Madeira	794	252,844

At the 1981 census, 29·7% of the population was urban (living in towns of 10,000 and more) and 48·2% were male. The chief cities (census, 1981) are Lisbon, the capital (817,627) and Porto (330,199); other towns are Amadora (93,663), Setúbal (76,812), Coimbra (71,782), Braga (63,771), Vila Nova de Gaia (60,962), Barreiro (50,745), Funchal (48,638), Almada (41,468), Queluz (41,112), Odivelas (38,546), Evora (34,072), Agualva-Cacem (34,041) and Oeiras (32,046).

The Azores islands lie in the mid-Atlantic ocean, between 1,200 and 1,600 km west of Lisbon. They are divided into 3 widely separated groups with clear channels between, São Miguel (747 sq. km) together with Santa Maria (97 sq. km) being the most easterly; about 100 miles north-west of them lies the central cluster of Terceira (397 sq. km), Graciosa (61 sq. km), São Jorge (238 sq. km), Pico (433 sq. km) and Faial (172 sq. km); still another 150 miles to the north-west are Flores (143 sq. km) and Corvo (17 sq. km), the latter being the most isolated and primitive of the islands. São Miguel contains over half the total population of the archipelago, including the regional capital, Ponta Delgada.

Madeira comprises the island of Madeira (740 sq. km), containing the capital, Funchal; the smaller island of Porto Santo (42 sq. km), lying 46 km. to the north-east of Madeira; and two groups of uninhabited islets, Ilhas Desertas being 20 km. south-east of Funchal and Ilhas Selvagens near the Canaries.

Vital statistics for calendar years:

	Births	*Still-births*	*Marriages*	*Divorces*	*Deaths*	*Emigrants*
1980	158,352	2,239	72,164	5,874	94,971	18,071
1981	152,102	1,977	76,283	6,827	95,892	16,513
1982	151,029	1,894	73,660	6,769	92,551	10,276
1983	144,327	1,791	74,417	7,837	96,150	7,096

In 1983 the births included 74,811 boys and 69,516 girls; deaths, 50,080 males and 46,100 females. In 1983, 4,373 emigrants went to France, 2,457 to USA, 1,376 to Venezuela and 825 to Canada.

CLIMATE. Because of westerly winds and the effect of the Gulf Stream, the climate ranges from the cool, damp Atlantic type in the north to a warmer and drier Mediterranean type in the south. July and Aug. are virtually rainless everywhere. Inland areas in the north have greater temperature variation, with continental winds blowing from the interior. Lisbon. Jan. 52°F (11°C), July 72°F (22°C). Annual rainfall 27·4″ (686 mm). Porto. Jan. 48°F (8·9°C), July 67°F (19·4°C). Annual rainfall 46″ (1,151 mm).

CONSTITUTION AND GOVERNMENT. A new Constitution, replacing that of 1976, was approved by the Assembly of the Republic (by 197 votes to 40) on 12 Aug. 1982 and promulgated in Sept. It abolished the (military) Council of the Revolution and reduced the role of the President of the Republic.

Portugal is a sovereign, unitary republic with all citizens possessing fundamental rights and duties before the law. Executive power is vested in the President of the Republic, directly elected for a 5-year term (for a maximum of 2 consecutive terms). Presidents since 1926:

Marshal António Oscar de Fragoso Carmona, 29 Nov. 1926–18 April 1951 (died).
Dr Antonio de Oliveira Salazar (acting), 18 April 1951–22 July 1951.
Marshal Francisco Higino Craveiro Lopez, 22 July 1951–9 Aug. 1958.
Rear-Adm. Américo de Deus Rodrigues Tomás, 9 Aug. 1958–25 April 1974. (deposed).
Gen. Antonio Sebastião Ribeiro de Spinola, 25 April 1974–30 Sept. 1974 (resigned).
Gen. Francisco da Costa Gomes, 30 Sept. 1974–14 July 1976.

President of the Republic: Gen. Antonio Ramalho Eanes, elected 27 June 1976 (took office 14 July 1976) and re-elected 7 Dec. 1980.

The President appoints a Prime Minister and, upon the latter's nomination, other members of the Council of Ministers, as well as Secretaries and Under-Secretaries of State, who are outside the Council.

The coalition government was composed as follows in March 1985:

Prime Minister: Dr Mário Alberto Nobre Lopes Soares (PS).

Deputy Prime Minister and Minister of Defence: Rui Machete (PSD). *Minister of State and Parliamentary Affairs:* Antonio de Almeida Santos (PS). *Interior:* Eduardo Ribeiro Pereira (PS). *Foreign Affairs:* Jaime Gama (PS). *Justice:* Mario Raposo (PSD). *Finance:* Ernani Lopes (Ind.). *Education:* Joao de Deus Pinheiro (PSD). *Labour and Social Security:* Amandio de Azevedo (PSD). *Health:* Antonio Maldonado Gonelha (PS). *Agriculture:* Alvaro Barreto (PSD). *Industry and Energy:* Jose Veiga Simao (PS). *Commerce and Tourism:* Joaquim Fereira do Amaral (PSD). *Culture:* Antonio Coimbra Martins (PS). *Public Works:* Joao Rosado Correia (PS). *Quality of Life:* Francisco Sousa Tavares (PSD). *Sea:* Carolos Melancia (PS).

There is a unicameral legislature, the Assembly of the Republic, comprising 250 deputies elected for 4 years by universal adult suffrage under a system of proportional representation. At the General Election of 25 April 1983, there were 101 seats won by the *Partido Socialista* (PS), 75 by the *Partido Social Democrata* (PSD), 44 by the *Partido Comunista Português* (PCP) and 30 by the *Partido do Centro Democrático Social* (CDS).

National flag: Vertical green and red, with the red of double width, and over all on the dividing line the national arms.

National anthem: A Portuguesa (words by Lopes de Mendonça, 1890; tune by Alfredo Keil).

Local government: Since 1976, the archipelagoes of the Azores and of Madeira are Autonomous Regions with their own legislatures and governments. Pending the formation of other regional governments, Continental Portugal is divided into 18 districts. Regions and districts are divided into 305 municipal authorities *(concelhos)* and sub-divided into 4,050 parishes. Each level is governed by an assembly elected by direct universal suffrage under a system of proportional representation, with an executive body responsible to the assembly.

DEFENCE. Military service is compulsory for 16 months in the Army, 24 months in the Navy and 21–24 months in the Air Force. Reserves for all services number about 90,000.

Army. The Army consists of 1 brigade, 2 cavalry regiments, 14 infantry regiments, 1 commando regiment, 3 field, 1 air-defence and 1 coast artillery regiments, 2 engineer regiments and 1 regiment of military police. Equipment includes 60 M-48A5 main battle tanks and 85 M113 armed personnel carriers. Strength (1985) 41,000 (including 32,000 conscripts). Security forces are National Republic Guard (15,700), and the Customs Guard (8,700).

Navy. The fleet comprises 3 small French-built diesel-powered patrol submarines, 17 frigates, 10 patrol vessels, 4 coastal minesweepers, 20 patrol launches, 1 sail training ship, 2 surveying vessels, 1 fleet oiler, 2 landing craft, 11 minor landing craft, 3 tugs, 2 training yachts and 1 harbour tanker. The navy personnel in 1985 totalled 14,000 officers and men including 2,000 marines.

Air Force. Formed in 1912, the Air Force has been independent since 1952, when it was combined with the naval air service and given equal status with the Army and Navy. In 1985, it had a strength of about 14,300 officers and men, including paratroops (3,776, operational force 2,905).

Equipment comprises a strike squadron of 40 A-7P Corsair IIs (10 more ordered); 2 squadrons of G.91Rs for ground attack; 1 squadron of 5 C-130H Hercules and 3 squadrons of CASA 212 Aviocars for transport and search and rescue operations, 32 Cessna 337 Skymasters and a force of Puma and Alouette III helicopters. Other aircraft in service include Chipmunk piston-engined trainers, T-37C jet basic trainers, T-33, T-38A Talon and G.91T jet advanced trainers.

INTERNATIONAL RELATIONS

Membership. Portugal is a member of UN, EFTA, OECD, NATO and the Council of Europe.

ECONOMY

Planning. The aim of the 1981–84 plan is to modernize existing industry and pave the way for entry into the European Community.

Budget. Revenue and expenditure (in 1m. escudos) have balanced as follows: 1979, 280,659; 1980, 374,780; 1981, 490,017.

Currency. The unit of currency is the *escudo* of 100 *centavos*, which contains 0·06651 gramme of fine gold. It was stabilized on 9 June 1931, and the paper currency re-linked to gold when the notes of the Bank of Portugal became payable in gold or its equivalent in foreign currency. 1,000 escudos is called a *conto*.

At present there are bank notes of 5,000, 1,000, 500, 100, 50 and 20 escudos; cupro-nickel coins of 25, 10, 5 and 2½ escudos; nickel-brass coins of 1 escudo; alpaca coins of 1 and ½ escudo (50 centavos), bronze coins of 1 and ½ escudo and 20 and 10 centavos and aluminium coins of 10 centavos. In March 1985, £1 = 198 *escudos*; US$1 = 188 *escudos*.

Banking. Since 1931, the central bank for Portugal and the only bank of issue for the country (including the Azores and Madeira) has been the Banco de Portugal, founded 19 Nov. 1846 and nationalized on 13 Sept. 1974. Its capital is fixed at 200m. escudos. All other Portuguese banks and insurance companies were nationalized on 14 March 1975.

The National Development Bank began operations on 4 Jan. 1960. Its total capital is 1,500m. escudos.

There are 12 commercial banks registered on the mainland and 1 in the Azores, with cash in hand on 31 Oct. 1984, 18,793m. escudos; bills, loans and other credits, 1,444,601m. escudos; deposits, 2,188,833m. escudos. The deposits in the savings banks including the general deposit bank (state) amounted to 891,119m. escudos.

There are also 4 foreign banks, the Bank of Brazil, Lloyds Bank International Ltd., Manufactures Hannover Trust and Crédit Franco-Portugais.

Weights and Measures. The metric system is the legal standard. The arroba (of 14·69 kg) is sometimes used locally.

ENERGY AND NATURAL RESOURCES

Electricity. Total production of electrical power in 1982 was 15,418m. kwh.; the installed capacity totalled 6,325,560 kva. of which 3,024,858 was hydro-electric.

Minerals. Portugal possesses considerable mineral wealth. Production in tonnes:

	1981	*1982*	*1983*		*1981*	*1982*	*1983*
Coal	183,760	178,540	185,228	Gold (refined)	0·244	0·211	0·199
Cupriferous pyrites	286,622	262,142	279,960	Uranium	119	134	122
Tin ores	506	585	525	Wolframite	2,365	2,300	2,010
Kaolin	107,978	63,021	73,273				

Uranium mining commenced in Aug. 1979. Annual production, 115 tonnes; reserves, 7,000 tonnes.

Agriculture. About 23% of the workforce is engaged in agriculture. The following figures show the area (in 1,000 hectares) and yield (in 1,000 tonnes) of the chief crops:

	1982		*1983*		*1984*	
Crop	*Area*	*Yield*	*Area*	*Yield*	*Area*	*Yield*
Wheat	353·0	424·5	330·8	326·8	289·9	469·0
Maize	351·8	421·2	311·1	424·4	319·4	483·2
Oats	169·7	85·8	191·4	99·3	181·4	194·8
Barley	76·8	51·3	87·8	54·1	96·7	135·3
Rye	194·0	119·4	131·5	92·4	131·0	115·3
Rice	33·7	143·4	26·5	109·1	29·9	134·0
Dried beans	245·0	35·3	228·0	39·3	231·5	41·4
Potatoes	114·4	982·8	120·8	905·3	125·6	1,021·6

Wine production (in hectolitres), 1984, 8m.; olive oil (hectolitres), 95,676. In 1978, 51,937 tonnes of port wine were exported.

Livestock (1983). 29,000 horses, 91,000 mules, 180,000 asses, 990,000 cattle, 750,000 goats, 5·22m. sheep and 3·48m. pigs.

Forestry. Forest area covers 3m. hectares, of which 1·38m. are pine, 680,390 cork oak, 534,370 other oak, 243,180 eucalyptus, 30,230 chestnut and 160,890 other species.

Portugal surpasses the rest of the world in the production of cork; 99,202 tonnes in 1982. Most of it is exported crude. Production of resin was 126,602 tonnes in 1982; more than two-thirds are exported.

Fisheries. The fishing industry for the continent and adjacent isles is of importance. At 31 July 1983 there were 37,637 men and boys employed, with 11,177 boats. The sardine catch, 1983, was 86,233 tonnes valued at 1,935,651 contos; The most important centres of the sardine industry are at Matosinhos, Peniche, Setúbal, Portimão and Olhão.

INDUSTRY AND TRADE

Industry. Industrial growth rate, 1983, 0·6%; manufacturing provided 30% of GDP and employed about 25% of the workforce. The main groups are textiles, shoes, leather goods, wood and cork products and ceramics; these are produced mainly by small companies. Nationalized steel, oil and engineering industries employed about 5% of the industrial workforce in 1983.

Commerce. Imports for consumption and exports (exclusive of coin and bullion and re-exports) for calendar years, in 1m. escudos:

	1979	*1980*	*1981*	*1982*	*1983*
Imports	331,927	475,486	609,014	753,981	899,340
Exports	176,051	231,623	256,913	331,743	508,568

The principal exports in 1981 were clothing (14% by value), textile yarns and fabrics (13%), machinery (9%), petroleum products (7%), chemicals (6%), cork and cork products (6%) and wine (5%).

The distribution of the imports and exports (in 1m. escudos):

	Imports (c.i.f.)			*Exports (f.o.b.)*		
From or to	*1981*	*1982*	*1983*	*1981*	*1982*	*1983*
Angola	941	1,812	1,506	13,839	6,743	11,058
Belgium	14,673	18,405	21,416	6,801	10,242	18,425
France	47,369	65,536	74,114	32,270	44,097	68,811
Germany, Fed. Rep. of	66,928	89,337	102,716	32,002	42,902	67,837
Italy	32,845	42,419	46,432	10,898	15,921	20,593
Mozambique	1,132	1,177	1,726	2,066	5,374	7,113
Netherlands	17,854	26,607	35,270	12,131	19,836	31,873
Spain	40,096	45,372	45,933	7,325	11,715	20,253
UK	49,182	58,626	68,728	37,104	49,082	75,278
USA	72,857	81,506	126,532	13,405	20,445	30,852

Total trade between Portugal (excluding the Azores and Madeira) and UK (British Department of Trade returns, in £1,000 sterling):

	1980	*1981*	*1982*	*1983*	*1984*
Imports to UK	335,112	333,355	379,949	475,902	644,520
Exports and re-exports from UK	389,849	368,080	430,684	396,988	385,799

Trade Unions. 331 unions had in 1976 a membership of 1,436,142.

Tourism. Tourism is of increasing importance for the invisible balance of payments. In 1983 there were 8,800,000 visitors and income from tourism represented 5·6% of GNP.

COMMUNICATIONS

Roads (1983). There were 18,832 km of road. There were registered in continental Portugal in 1983, 2,000,697 motor vehicles (excluding 100,058 motor cycles, 135,400 tractors and vehicles used by the armed forces).

Railways. In 1983 total railway length was 3,614 km (1,668 mm and metre gauges), of which 460 km of broad-gauge was electrified. In 1983, 5,195m. passenger-km were carried and 1,043m. tonne-km of merchandise transported.

Aviation. There are international airports at Portela (Lisbon), Pedras Rubras (Porto), Faro (Algarve), Santa Maria (Azores) and Funchal (Madeira). Regular services connect Lisbon with most major centres in North and South America, Western Europe and Africa. Airlines in 1983 carried 2m. passengers and 33,523 tonnes of freight. The national airline changed its name to Air Portugal in 1979.

Shipping. In 1983, 11,709 vessels of 54·1m. tons entered the ports (continental and islands), of which 4,050 (16·75m. tons) were Portuguese, 373 (2·1m. tons) British and 976 (3·0m. tons) Spanish. In 1982 the merchant marine consisted of 101 transport vessels of 1,259,573 gross tons.

Post and Broadcasting (1983). The number of telegraph offices was 1,574. The State owned 7,420,275 km of telephone line through the *Telefones de Lisboa e Porto* (nationalized in 1977). Number of telephones was 1,684,463 (1983)

Radio Difusão Portuguesa broadcasts 3 programmes on medium-waves and on FM as well as 3 regional services. *Radiotelevisão Portuguesa* broadcasts 2 commercial TV programmes. *Radio Renascença* is a commercial, nationwide network. In addition there are 6 local, commercial stations, operating on medium-waves. Radio Trans Europe is a high-powered short-wave station, retransmitting programmes of different broadcasting organizations, *e.g.*, IBRA, Radio Canada and Deutsche Welle. Radio Free Europe also has relay facilities on short-waves in Portugal. Number of receivers: Radio (1979), 1,575,000; TV (1981), 1,460,902.

Cinemas (1983). There were 415 cinemas with a seating capacity of 215,493.

Newspapers (1983). There were 28 daily newspapers with a combined circulation of 185,425m.; 14 of these, with a combined circulation of 129,548m., appeared in Lisbon.

JUSTICE, RELIGION, EDUCATION AND WELFARE

Justice. Portuguese law distinguishes civil (including commercial) and penal, labour, administrative and fiscal branches having higher and lower courts, courts of appeal and the Supreme Court.

The republic is divided for civil and penal cases into 214 *comarcas*; in every comarca there is a lower court. In the comarca of Lisbon there are 39 lower courts (22 for criminal procedure and 17 for civil or commercial cases); in the comarca of Oporto there are 21 lower courts (12 for criminal and 9 for civil or commercial cases); at Coimbra, Setúbal, Sintra and Vila Nova de Gaia there are 4 courts; at Almada, Braga, Cascais, Funchal, Guimarães, Leiria, Loures, Matosinhos, Oeiras, Santarém and Viseu there are 3 courts; 19 comarcas have 2 courts each. There are 4 courts of appeal *(Tribunal de Relação)* at Lisbon, Coimbra, Evora and Oporto, and a Supreme Court in Lisbon *(Supremo Tribunal de Justiça)*.

Capital punishment was abolished completely in the Constitution of 1976.

The prison population as at 31 Dec. 1982 was 5,127.

Religion. In 1976, 88% of the population were Roman Catholic, but there is freedom of worship, both in public and private, with the exception of creeds incompatible with morals and the life and physical integrity of the people.

Education. According to the latest statistics, 70% of the population over 7 years could read and write. Compulsory education has been in force since 1911. In 1981–82 there were 10,594 public primary schools with 844,773 pupils and 40,166 teachers. In 1981–82 private elementary schools numbered 617 with 64,233 pupils and 2,830 teachers. Basic preparatory schools numbered 1,885 with 354,503 pupils and 26,411 teachers. Secondary instruction is supplied in two types of schools: in the *liceus* and other grammar schools, and in schools of technical instruction. In 1981–82 there were 496 secondary schools, with 497,788 pupils and 42,781 teachers. There were also (1981–82) 27 schools which taught art activities (cinema, music and theatre) with 13,602 students. There are 11 universities, of which 5 are in Lisbon: the University of Lisbon (founded 1911), the Technical University (1930), the private Catholic University (1968), the New University (1973) and the Free University (1977); the other six are Coimbra (founded 1290), Porto (1911), Aveiro (1973), Minho, at Braga (1974), Evora (1979) and Azores, at Ponta Delgado (1980). Including other colleges, there were 73,070 students in higher education in 1981–82.

Health. In 1982 there were 491 hospitals, 22,009 doctors, 464 dentists, 5,061 pharmacists, 1,132 midwives and 23,714 nursing personnel.

DIPLOMATIC REPRESENTATIVES

Of Portugal in Great Britain (11 Belgrave Sq., London, SW1X 8PP)
Ambassador: João Hall Themido.

Of Great Britain in Portugal (35-37 Rua S. Domingos à Lapa, Lisbon)
Ambassador: H. C. Byatt, CMG.

Of Portugal in the USA (2125 Kalorama Rd., NW, Washington, D.C., 20008)
Ambassador: Leonardo Charles de Zaffiri Mathias.

Of the USA in Portugal (Ave. das Forcas Armadas, 1600 Lisbon)
Ambassador: H. Allen Holmes.

Of Portugal to the United Nations
Ambassador: Rui E. Barbosa de Medina.

Books of Reference

Statistical Information: The Instituto Nacional de Estatistica (Avenida Dr António José de Almeida, Lisbon) was set up in 1935 in succession to the Direcção-Geral de Estatistica. The Centro de Estudos Económicos and the Centro de Estudos Demográficos were affiliated to the Instituto in 1944. The main publications are:

Anuário Estatistico. Annuaire statistique. Annual, from 1875
Estatísticas do Comércio Externo. 2 vols. Annual from 1967 (replacing *Comércio Externo,* 1936–66, and *Estatística Comercial,* 1865–1935)
Censo da População de Portugal. 1864 ff. Decennial (latest ed. 1972)
Estatística da Organização Corporativa. 1938–49. Estatísticas da Organização Corporativa e Previdência Social. 1950 ff.
Estatísticas das Finanças, Publicas and *Estatísticas Nometárias.* 1969 ff. (replacing *Estatísticas Financeiras.* 1947–68 and *Situação Bancária,* 1919–46)
Estatísticas Agrícolas. Statistique Agricole. 1943–64; replaced by *Estatísticas Agrícolas e Alimentares.* From 1965. Annual
Estatísticas Industrials. 1967 ff. (replacing *Estatística Industrial. Statistique Industrielle.* 1943–66)
Estatísticas Demográficas. From 1967 (replacing *Anuário Demográfico,* 1929–66)
Boletim Mensal do Instituto Nacional de Estatística. Monthly since 1929
Centro de Estudos Económicos. Revista. 1945 ff.
Centro de Estudos Demográficos. Revista. 1945 ff.
Estatísticas das Contribuições e Impostos. Annual from 1967 (replacing *Anuário Estatístico das Contribuições e Impostos,* 1936–66)
Estatísticas da Educação. 1940 ff.
Estatísticas da Justica. 1968 ff. (replacing *Estatísticas Judiciária.* 1936–66)
Estatisticas das Sociedades. 1939 ff.
Estatísticas do Turismo. 1969 ff.
Estatísticas do Energia. 1969 ff.

Azevedo, Gonzaga de, *Historia de Portugal.* 6 vols. Lisbon, 1935–44
Ferreira, J. A., *Dictionario inglês-portugês.* 2 vols. Porto, 1948
Gallagher, T., *Portugal: A Twentieth Century Interpretation.* Manchester Univ. Press, 1983
Graham, L. S., and Wheeler, D. L., (eds.) *In Search of Modern Portugal: The Revolution and its Consequences.* Univ. of Wisconsin Press, 1983
Harvey R., *Portugal: Birth of a Democracy.* London, 1978
Robertson, I., *Blue Guide: Portugal.* London, 1982
Robinson, R., *Contemporary Portugal.* London, 1979
Rogers, F. M., *Atlantic Islanders of the Azores and Madeiras.* North Quincy, 1979
Soares, M., *Le Portugal Bâillonné: Une Témoignage.* Paris, 1972
Sobel, L. A. (ed.), *Portuguese Revolution 1974–76.* New York, 1976
Spinola, A. de, *Portugal e o Futoro.* Lisbon, 1974
Taylor, J. L., *Portuguese-English Dictionary.* London, 1959

National Library: Biblioteca Nacional, Campo Grande, Lisbon. *Director:* A. H. C. Marques.

MACAO

HISTORY. Macao was visited by Portuguese traders from 1513 and became a Portuguese colony in 1557; it remains a Portuguese-administered territory by virtue of a Sino-Portuguese treaty of 1 Dec. 1887. It was an Overseas Province of Portugal, 1961–74.

AREA AND POPULATION. The territory, which lies at the mouth of the Canton (Pearl) River, comprises a peninsula (5 sq. km) on which is built the city of Nome de Deus de Macao, and the islands of Taipa (4 sq. km), linked to Macao by a

2-km bridge, and Colôane (7 sq. km) linked to Taipa by a 2-km causeway (total area, 16 sq. km (6 sq. miles). The population (Census, 1981) is 261,680, of which 91·5% live in the city of Macao. The official language is Portuguese, but Cantonese is used by virtually the entire population.

Vital statistics (1983): Births, 6,168; marriages, 1,634; deaths, 1,514.

CONSTITUTION AND GOVERNMENT. By agreement with Beijing in 1974, Macao is a Chinese territory under Portuguese administration. An 'organic statute' was published on 17 Feb. 1976. It defined the territory as a collective entity, *pessoa colectiva,* with internal legislative authority which, while remaining subject to Portuguese constitutional laws, would otherwise enjoy administrative, economic and financial autonomy. The Governor is appointed by the Portuguese President, who also appoints up to 5 Secretaries-Adjunct on the Governor's nomination. The Legislative Assembly of 17 deputies, chosen for a 3-year term, comprises 6 members directly elected by universal suffrage, 6 indirectly elected by economic, cultural and social bodies and 5 appointed by the Governor.

Governor: Cdr Vasco Almeida e Costa.

ECONOMY

Budget. In 1983, revenue was 1,218,600,000 *patacas* (including receipts for the year, revenue carried over from previous years and autonomous funds) and expenditure 957,600,000 *patacas.*

Currency. The unit of currency is the *pataca,* of 100 *avos,* which is tied to the Hong Kong dollar at a rate of 103 *patacas*=HK$100.

Banking. The bank of issue is the Instituto Emissor de Macau. Commercial business is handled (1983) by 23 banks with 87 branches in Macao.

INDUSTRY AND TRADE

Industry. Textile manufacturing forms the basis of local industry. In 1982, it represented about 67% of industrial production.

Commerce. The trade, mostly transit, is handled by Chinese merchants. Imports, in 1983, were 5,402m. patacas and exports, 5,602m. patacas.

In 1983, 38·7% of imports came from Hong Kong, 28·3% from China and 9·4% from Japan; 26·6% of exports went to USA, 22% to Hong Kong, 11·8% to Federal Republic of Germany, 10·5% to France and 6·2% to UK; clothing and knitwear accounted for 73·3% of exports.

Total trade between Macao and UK (British Department of Trade returns, in £1,000 sterling):

	1982	*1983*	*1984*
Imports to UK	19,349	24,220	40,508
Exports and re-exports from UK	2,551	1,039	1,034

Tourism. There were 5,170,649 visitors in 1983.

COMMUNICATIONS.

Roads. In 1983 there were 90 km of roads, 16,882 passenger cars and 4,315 commercial vehicles.

Shipping. Macao is served by Portuguese, British and Dutch steamship lines. In 1981, 28,751 vessels of 9·77m. gross tons entered the port. Regular services connect Macao with Hong Kong, 65 km to the north-east.

Post and Broadcasting. The territory has 1,577 km of telephone line (17,712 instruments in 1983). One government and 1 private commercial radio station are in operation on medium-waves broadcasting in Portuguese and Chinese. Number of receivers (1977), 70,000. Macao receives television broadcasts from Hong Kong and had (1979) 50,000 receivers.

Newspapers. In 1979, there were 5 daily newspapers with a circulation of 59,000.

JUSTICE, RELIGION, EDUCATION AND WELFARE

Justice. There is a court of First Instance, from which there is appeal to the Court of Appeal and then the Supreme Court, both in Lisbon.

Religion. The majority of the Chinese population are Buddhists. About 6% are Roman Catholic.

Education. In 1982–83 education was provided at 25 grammar schools (10,876 pupils), 59 primary schools (29,699), 3 secondary-preparatory schools (435), 3 commercial schools (1,070), 1 industrial school (485), 2 teacher-training schools (80) and 4 art schools (338 pupils). The University of East Asia, established in 1981 on Taipa, had 1,165 students in 1983.

Health. In 1982 there were 2 hospitals with 1,350 beds; there were 120 doctors, 26 pharmacists, 10 midwives and 315 nursing personnel.

Books of Reference

Anuário Estatístico de Macau. Macao
Brazáo, E., *Macau.* Lisbon, 1957

QATAR

Dawlat Qatar

Capital: Doha
Population: over 260,000 (1982)
GNP per capita: US$27,720 (1981)

HISTORY. The State of Qatar declared its independence from Britain on 3 Sept. 1971, ending the Treaty of 3 Nov. 1916 which was replaced by a Treaty of friendship between the 2 countries.

AREA AND POPULATION. The State of Qatar, which includes the whole of the Qatar peninsula, extends on the landward side from Khor al Odeid to the boundaries of the Saudi Arabian province of Hasa. Area, 11,437 sq. km; population estimate in 1982 over 260,000, including a number of expatriate labourers from neighbouring states.

The capital is Doha (population, 190,000), which is the main port. Other towns are Dukhan, the centre of oil production, Umm Said, oil-terminal of Qatar and Ruwais, Wakra, Al-Khour and Umm-Bab.

CLIMATE. The climate is hot and arid. Doha. Jan. 62°F (16·7°C), July 98°F (36·7°C). Annual rainfall 2·5″ (62 mm).

RULER. *The Amir:* HH Shaikh Khalifa bin Hamad Al-Thani, assumed power on 22 Feb. 1972. On 31 May 1977, HH Shaikh Hamed bin Khalifa Al-Thani, was appointed Heir Apparent of the State of Qatar, the portfolio of Minister of Defence was added to his existing responsibility of Commander-in-Chief of the Armed Forces.

Foreign Minister: Shaikh Suhaim bin Hamad Al-Thani.

There is no Parliament, but the Ministers are assisted by a 30-member nominated Consultative Council.

Flag: Maroon, with white serrated border on hoist.

DEFENCE

Army. The Army consists of 1 Royal Guard regiment, 1 tank, 5 infantry battalions and 1 artillery battery. Equipment includes 24 AMX-30 tanks. Personnel (1985) 5,000.

Navy. The Navy has 3 new French-built fast gunboats, 6 British-built large patrol craft and 43 coastal patrol craft. Personnel (1985) exceeded 400.

Air Force. The Air Force has 2 Hunter jet fighter-bombers, 1 Hunter 2-seat trainer and 1 Islander transport aircraft, 4 Commando, 2 Whirlwind, 3 Lynx and some Puma helicopters, 6 Alpha Jet armed trainers and Tigercat surface-to-air missile systems. Personnel (1984) 300.

INTERNATIONAL RELATIONS

Membership. Qatar is a member of UN and the Arab League.

ECONOMY

Budget. Revenue (1984) 22,442m. riyals; expenditure 20,672m. riyals.

Currency. On 13 May 1973 the Qatar *Riyal* (of 100 *dirhams*) was introduced. In March 1985, £1 = 3·92 *riyals*, US$1 = 3·64 *riyals*.

Banking. Banks operating in Qatar include: Qatar National Bank, the Commercial Bank of Qatar (also Qatari-owned), the Arab Bank, Bank Al Mashrek, Bank Saderat Iran, Doha Bank, Banque de Paris et des Pays Bas, British Bank of the

Middle East, the Chartered Bank, the First National City Bank, Grindlays Bank, the Bank of Oman and United Bank.

ENERGY AND NATURAL RESOURCES

Electricity. Production (1980) 1,450m. kwh.

Oil. On 9 Feb. 1977 Qatar gained national control over its 2 natural resources, oil and gas, with the signing of an agreement with Shell Qatar over the procedure for the transfer to the State of the company's remaining 40% share. A similar agreement had been reached with the Qatar Petroleum Co. on 16 Sept. 1976.

The Qatar General Petroleum Corporation (QGPC) had been established by decree in July 1974 to assume overall responsibility for the State's domestic and foreign oil interests and operations. On 16 Oct. 1976 the Qatar Petroleum Producing Authority (QPPA) was established to serve as the executive arm of the QGPC—but in 1980 it was merged into the QGPC, which now directly oversees oil production through two operational divisions, Onshore and Offshore. A new 50,000 bbls a day refinery has been constructed at Umm Said to supplement the existing 10,000 bbls a day refinery.

Production, 1984, 18·8m. tonnes. Proven reserves (1982) 3,434,000m. bbls.

Gas. The North West Dome oilfield is being developed which contains 12% of the known world gas reserves. Production (1983) propane, 305,474 tonnes.

Agriculture. 10% of the working population is engaged in agriculture and between Jan.–May Qatar is self-sufficient in fruit and vegetables.

Livestock (1983): Cattle, 10,000; camels, 6,000; sheep, 53,000; goats, 57,000; poultry (1982), 380,000.

INDUSTRY AND TRADE

Industry. Several major projects have been established including the production of ammonia, urea and cement. The Qatar Iron and Steel Co. factory was opened in April 1978 and the Qatar Petro-chemical Company polyethylene plant in Feb. 1981, both in the Umm Said industrial zone.

Commerce. In 1983 exports totalled US$3,384m., and imports, US$1,402m. Japan provided 18% of imports, the UK 18% and the USA 11%, while 12% of exports went to the Netherlands, 11% to Japan and 11% to France; crude oil was 95% of exports.

Total trade between Qatar and UK (British Department of Trade returns, in £1,000 sterling):

	1980	*1981*	*1982*	*1983*	*1984*
Imports to UK	44,654	10,675	33,984	10,063	28,212
Exports and re-exports from UK	101,898	135,722	245,390	216,385	133,803

Tourism. Tourism was being developed in 1978.

COMMUNICATIONS

Roads. In 1981 there were about 800 miles of road.

Aviation. The Gulf Aviation Co., Ltd (owned equally by Qatar, Bahrain, Oman and the UAE), operates daily services from Bahrain; British Airways, Middle East and about 15 other airlines operate regular international flights from Doha airport.

Shipping. Ships of several lines used to call at Umm Said; with the completion in 1969 of the new Doha port, it has become the main port of Qatar.

Post and Telecommunications. Telephone and radio-telephone services connect Qatar with Europe and America; there were 67,500 telephones in Jan. 1982. An earth satellite station was inaugurated in March 1976.

Cinemas. In 1981 there were 5 cinemas with a seating capacity of 7,000.

Newspapers. In 1984 there were 4 daily and 4 weekly newspapers.

RELIGION, EDUCATION AND WELFARE

Religion. The population is almost entirely Moslem.

Education. There were, in 1983–84, 28,219 pupils (14,712 boys, 13,507 girls) at 85 elementary schools with 1,878 teachers in boys' and 2,346 teachers in girls' schools. In addition, 2,960 boys and 3,226 girls were attending 23 secondary schools. In 1983 the total number of pupils was 45,416. The University of Qatar had 3,815 students and 380 staff in 1982. Post-graduate students abroad numbered 1,305. In 1980, 7,458 men and 2,541 women attended evening classes.

Health. There are 5 hospitals (including 1 for women and 1 for gynaecology and obstetrics) with a total of 682 beds. The 660-bed hospital at Doha is nearing completion and clinics are being built throughout the State. In 1984 there were 891 doctors, and in 1983, 43 dentists, 9 pharmacists and 1,838 midwives and nursing personnel.

DIPLOMATIC REPRESENTATIVES

Of Qatar in Great Britain (27 Chesham Pl., London, SWIX 8HG)
Ambassador: Sharida Sa'ad Jubran Al Ka'abi (accredited 26 March 1981).

Of Great Britain in Qatar (Doha, Qatar)
Ambassador: Julian Walker, CMG, MBE.

Of Qatar in the USA (600 New Hampshire Ave., NW, Washington, D.C., 20037)
Ambassador: Abdelkader Braik Al-Ameri.

Of the USA in Qatar (Fariq Bin Omran, Doha)
Ambassador: Charles F. Dunbar.

Of Qatar to the United Nations
Ambassador: Hamad Abdel Aziz Al-Zuwari.

Books of Reference

Qatar into the Seventies. Information Ministry, Doha, 1973
El Mallakh, R., *Qatar: The Development of an Oil Economy.* New York, 1979
Unwin, P. T. H., *Qatar.* [Bibliography] Oxford and Santa Barbara, 1982

ROMANIA

Capital: Bucharest
Population: 22·6m. (1984)
GNP per capita: US$2,540 (1981)

Republica Socialistă România

HISTORY. 1918 is celebrated as the year of foundation of the 'unitary national Romanian state'. For the history and constitution of Romania from 1859 to 1947, *see* THE STATESMAN'S YEAR-BOOK, 1947, pp. 1187–89. On 30 Dec. 1947 King Michael abdicated under Communist pressure and parliament proclaimed the 'People's Republic'.

AREA AND POPULATION. The area of Romania is 237,500 sq. km (91,699 sq. miles). Pre-war Romania had an area of 113,918 sq. miles. Population at censuses: 1930, 18,057,208 (14,280,729 within present-day Romania); 1948, 15,872,624 (48·3% male); 1966, 19,103,163 (49% male, 38·2% urban); 1977, 21,559,910 (49·3% male, 47·5% urban).

On 1 Jan. 1984 the population was 22·6m., density per sq. km, 95. Vital statistics, 1982 (per 1,000 population): Live births, 14·3; deaths, 10·4; marriages, 7·3; divorces, 1·53; stillborn (per 1,000 live births), 8; infant mortality (per 1,000 live births), 23·9; population growth rate, 3·9 per 1,000. Expectation of life in 1982: men, 67·4 years; women, 72·4.

Administratively, Romania is divided into 40 counties (*judeţ*), 236 towns (*oraş*) (of which 56 are municipalities) and 2,705 local authorities (*comune*). The capital is Bucharest (Bucureşti) a municipality with county status.

District	*Area in sq. km*	*Population 1982*	*Capital*	*Population 1983*
Alba	6,231	410,080	Alba Iulia	56,625
Arad	7,652	509,168	Arad	171,198
Argeş	6,801	659,289	Piteşti	141,945
Bacău	6,606	695,693	Bacău	156,891
Bihor	7,535	649,009	Oradea	197,968
Bistriţa-Năsăud	5,305	306,936	Bistriţa	62,862
Botoşani	4,965	459,774	Botoşani	89,606
Braşov	5,351	668,415	Braşov	290,722
Brăila	4,724	393,467	Brăila	214,561
Buzău	6,072	517,434	Buzău	120,419
Caraş-Severin	8,503	400,761	Reşiţa	97,048
Călăraşi	5,075	339,942	Călăraşi	58,493
Cluj	6,650	741,580	Cluj-Napoca	270,820
Constanţa	7,055	680,472	Constanţa	284,801
Covasna	3,705	221,851	Sf. Gheorghe	59,262
Dîmboviţa	4,035	584,877	Tîrgovişte	80,044
Dolj	7,413	767,127	Craiova	243,117
Galaţi	4,425	619,587	Galaţi	254,636
Giurgiu	3,810	375,750	Giurgiu	59,070
Gorj	5,641	363,707	Tîrgu Jiu	78,730
Harghita	6,610	349,416	Miercurea-Ciuc	40,674
Hunedoara	7,016	543,643	Deva	73,420
Ialomiţa	4,449	299,717	Slobozia	41,175
Iaşi	5,469	765,791	Iaşi	265,176
Maramureş	6,215	526,556	Baia Mare	123,675
Mehedinţi	4,900	327,522	Drobeta-Turnu Severin	87,573
Mureş	6,696	612,618	Tîrgu Mureş	146,322
Neamţ	5,890	555,018	Piatra-Neamţ	100,549
Olt	5,507	528,661	Slatina	64,129
Prahova	4,694	852,785	Ploieşti	215,500
Satu Mare	4,405	405,739	Satu Mare	120,000
Sălaj	3,850	265,848	Zalău	47,085
Sibiu	5,422	502,851	Sibiu	159,599
Suceava	8,555	660,500	Suceava	80,725

District	Area in sq. km	Population 1982	Capital	Population 1983
Teleorman	5,760	510,523	Alexandria	46,850
Timiş	8,692	711,022	Timişoara	261,950
Tulcea	8,430	263,054	Tulcea	75,127
Vaslui	5,297	448,430	Vaslui	55,079
Vîlcea	5,705	419,398	Rîmnicu Vîlcea	81,179
Vrancea	4,863	379,232	Focşani	74,341
Bucharest [1]	1,521	2,211,460	Bucharest [2]	1,834,377

[1] Total conurbation. [2] Central area.

Ethnic groups: In 1978 there were 1·7m. Hungarians, mainly in Transylvania, and some 400,000 Germans. The official language is Romanian.

An 'education tax' was imposed on emigrants in Nov. 1982, but withdrawn in May 1983 after the USA had threatened to withdraw Romania's most-favoured-nation status.

CLIMATE. A continental climate with a large annual range of temperature and rainfall showing a slight summer maximum.

Bucharest. Jan. 27°F (–2·7°C), July 74°F (23·5°C). Annual rainfall 23·1″ (579 mm). Constanţa. Jan. 31°F (–0·6°C), July 71°F (21·7°C). Annual rainfall 15″ (371 mm).

CONSTITUTION AND GOVERNMENT. The present Constitution was adopted on 21 Aug. 1965 and supersedes those of 13 April 1948 and 24 Sept. 1952. Under it Romania becomes a 'Socialist' (as opposed to 'People's') Republic. The leading role of the Communist Party is reaffirmed. The Grand National Assembly of 369 is elected for 5 years (before 1972 for 4 years). It holds short sessions twice a year, and between sessions delegates its legislative rights to the State Council (the President, head of state; 3 Vice-presidents, 1 secretary and 20 members).

All citizens of 18 and over have the right to vote and electoral law provides for the nomination of 'one or more' candidates in each constituency.

Local government is carried out by 41 province, 236 municipal and 2,705 ward councils. 62,164 councillors were elected in Nov. 1982.

The National Council of the Socialist Democracy and Unity Front functions as a consultative body on home and foreign affairs. It has central and local councils in which workers, peasants, professional bodies, ethnic minorities and the Communist Party are represented. It replaced the Popular Democratic Front (*see* STATESMAN'S YEAR-BOOK, 1979–80).

Elections were held on 30 Nov. 1952, 3 Feb. 1957, 5 March 1961, 7 March 1965, 2 March 1969, 9 March 1975 and 9 March 1980.

At the 1980 elections 99·9% of the 15·6m. electorate voted, 98·52% of these for the Socialist Democracy and Unity Front. 2 candidates stood in 151, and 3 in 39, constituencies.

In 1965 the Romanian Workers' Party was renamed the Romanian Communist Party. The Party Congress elects the General Secretary, and its Central Committee elects the Executive Political Committee with its Permanent Bureau and the Secretariat (General Secretary and 7 secretaries). The Party had 3·37m. members in 1984 (of whom 23% were under 30, 10% ethnic minorities, 56% workers and 15% women). During 1982 extensive purges of Government and Party leaders took place, including the then Prime Minister, Ilie Verdeţ, and other members of President Ceauşescu's family.

President of the Republic and Chairman of the State Council: Nicolae Ceauşescu, succeeded Chivu Stoica in Dec. 1967. *Vice-Chairmen:* Stefan Voitec, Gheorghe Rădulescu, Iosif Kovacs, Maria Ciocan, Petru Enache, Mănea Mănescu.

In April 1985 the Permanent Bureau of the Party consisted of: Nicolae Ceauşescu (*General Secretary*); Emil Bobu; Elena Ceauşescu[1]; Nicu Ceauşescu[2]; Constantin Dăscălescu; Manea Mănescu; Gheorghe Oprea; Gheorghe Rădulescu; Ilie Verdeţ.

[1] Ceauşescu's wife. [2] Ceauşescu's son.

Council of Ministers (April 1985). *Chairman* (*Prime Minister*): Constantin Dăscălescu. *First Deputy Prime Ministers:* Elena Ceauşescu, Gheorghe Oprea, Ion Dinca; *Deputy Prime Ministers:* Alexandra Găinuşe; Gheorghe Petrescu; Ludovic Fazekaş; Marin Enache; Ion Totu; Nicolae Constantin; Ioan Avram. Other ministers include: Ştefan Bîrlea (*Chairman, State Planning Committee)* Ion Tesu (*Agriculture and Food*); Petre Gigea (*Finance*); Ştefan Andrei (*Foreign*); Maj.-Gen. Constantin Olteanu (*Defence*); Gheorghe Homoştean (*Interior*); Maxim Berghianu (*Labour*); Vasile Pungan (*Foreign Trade*); Gheorghe Chivulescu (*Justice*).

In July 1970 Romania signed a treaty of friendship, co-operation and mutual assistance with the USSR. A previous such treaty had expired in 1968. Since the mid-1960s Romania has been taking a relatively independent stand in foreign affairs generally, and within Comecon and the Warsaw Pact.

National flag: Three vertical strips of blue, yellow, red, with the national arms in the centre.

National anthem: Trei culori (Three colours). Introduced, 1977. Music by Ciprian Porumbescu.

DEFENCE. Defence is the responsibility of the Defence Council, which is controlled by the Council of State and headed by President Ceauşescu. Military service is compulsory for 16 months in the Army and Air Force and 30 months in the Navy.

Army. The 4 Army Areas consist of 2 tank and 8 motor rifle divisions; 3 mountain, 2 artillery, 2 anti-aircraft and 2 surface-to-surface missile brigades; and 3 artillery, 1 anti-aircraft, 5 anti-tank and 1 airborne regiments. Equipment includes 200 T-34, 1,000 T-54/-55, 30 T-72 and 150 M-77 main battle tanks. Strength (1985) 150,000 (including 95,500 conscripts), and 500,000 reservists. There are a further 37,000 men in paramilitary border guard and internal security forces.

Navy. The fleet comprises 2 new destroyers, 2 new frigates, 3 corvettes, 6 fast missile boats, 40 fast torpedo boats, 20 fast gunboats, 3 old patrol vessels, 4 old minesweepers (refitted recently), 32 inshore minesweepers, 2 logistic support ships, 1 oceanographic ship, 2 training ships, 8 minesweeping boats, 40 river patrol craft, 8 landing craft, 2 survey vessels and 4 tugs. Headquarters of the Navy is at Mangalia, and of the Danube flotilla at the main river port of Brăila. The naval school is in Constanţa. Personnel in 1985 totalled 9,700 officers and ratings including 900 in Coastal Defence, 500 under Training and 2,700 shore support.

Air Force. The Air Force numbers some 25,000 men, with 300 combat aircraft in 2 air divisions (4 regiments). These are organized into 12 interceptor squadrons with MiG-21 and MiG-23 fighters, 6 ground-attack and close-support squadrons with MiG-17 fighters, and 1 reconnaissance squadron of Il-28s. There are also more than 300 training aircraft, An-24/26/30 transports and helicopters. Under delivery are 185 IAR-93 close-support/interceptors, and Puma helicopters. 'Guideline' and 'Gainful' surface-to-air missiles are operational, and short-range surface-to-surface missiles have been displayed.

INTERNATIONAL RELATIONS

Membership. Romania is a member of UN, IMF, Comecon and the Warsaw Pact.

ECONOMY

Planning. In Oct. 1982 the Supreme Council of Economic and Social Development, presided over by Nicolae Ceauşescu, was raised to the level of an economic legislative chamber. Annual growth targets of the sixth 5-year plan (1981–85): GNP, 9%; national income, 10%; industrial production, 10%; agricultural production, 24·5–27·5%. Romania is committed to intensive industrialization and President Ceauşescu admitted in Feb. 1981 that agriculture had been neglected. Bread rationing was introduced in Oct. 1981 and food prices were raised by 35% in Feb. 1982. Virtual rationing was introduced in 1982 in the form of limitations of calorie intake. Industries scheduled for particular development: machine-building, iron and steel, non-ferrous metals, chemicals and electric power. A 10-year programme introduced in 1980 is designed to make Romania self-sufficient in energy. (For previous plans *see* THE STATESMAN'S YEAR-BOOK, 1976–77.)

There is no move towards any fundamental decentralization of planning authority but limited devolutions of responsibility in an attempt to improve efficiency were introduced in 1967, 1979 and 1983. There are 102 economic units intermediate between ministries and enterprises.

Budget. Revenue and expenditure (in 1m. lei) for calendar years:

	1979	*1980*	*1981*	*1982*	*1983*	*1984*	*1985*
Revenue	339,309	298,004	262,227	288,511	301,908	308,917	362,600
Expenditure	337,629	296,787	262,227	288,511	301,908	308,917	362,600

In 1984 sources of revenue (in 1m. lei) included: Profit payments of state enterprises and turnover tax, 190,736; personal taxes, 4,228; insurance contributions, 43,507; taxes on enterprise wage funds, 46,297. Expenditure: National economy, 153,962; social and cultural, 84,188; defence, 11,700.

Revenue and expenditure of local councils (included above) was 56,106m. lei in 1983.

In 1974 a Court of Preventive Financial control was set up to oversee most official transactions and combat waste and corruption.

By an agreement signed 12 Jan. 1976 Romania paid £3·5m. as 'full and final settlement' of defaulted Romanian bonds held by UK citizens in 4 annual instalments of £875,000 starting at the end of 1976. Payments of £1·25m. in settlement of UK claims arising out of the peace treaty were completed by 31 Jan. 1967.

Currency. The monetary unit is the *leu*, pl.*lei* (of 100 *bani*). On 1 Feb. 1954 the gold content of the leu was to 0·148112 gramme of fine gold. Exchange rates (March 1985): £1 = 5·13 lei; US$1 = 4·74 lei; 1 rouble = 6·67 lei. Tourist rates: £1 = 20·40 lei; US$1 = 11 lei; 1 rouble = 8·30 lei.

Bank-notes of 1, 5, 10, 25, 50 and 100 *lei* are issued by the National Bank, and there are coins of 5, 10, 15 and 25 *bani* and 1, 3 and 5 *lei*.

Banking. The National Bank of Romania (founded 1880, nationalized 1946) is the State Bank under the Minister of Finance. Half its profits are allotted to the State budget. There are also a Bank of Investments, a Foreign Trade Bank, an Agriculture and Food Industry Bank and a Savings Bank. In 1972 Romania joined IMF. The US Export-Import Bank has granted Romania borrowing rights. In 1974 the American bank Manufactures Hanover Trust Co. opened a branch in Bucharest, the first Western bank to do so in a Communist country.

Weights and measures. The Gregorian calendar was adopted in 1919. The metric system is in use. Tubes and pipes are measured in *tol* (= 1 inch).

ENERGY AND NATURAL RESOURCES

Electricity. Installed electric power 1980: 16,109,000 kw.; output (1983), 70,260m. kwh. There are two joint Romanian–Yugoslav hydro-electric power plants on the Danube at the 'Iron Gates' with a combined yearly output of 22,250m. kwh. A nuclear power programme has been subject to cut-backs and delays. A nuclear power station (capacity 660,000 kw.) was due to open in 1985.

Oil. The oilfields are in the Prahova, Băcau, Gorj, Crişana and Argeş districts. Petrol prices were raised by 60% and restrictions placed on official and private car use in 1979. Oil production in 1984 was 12m. tonnes. Oil reserves are expected to be exhausted by the mid-1990s.

Minerals. The principal minerals are oil and natural gas, salt, brown coal, lignite, iron and copper ores, bauxite, chromium, manganese and uranium. Salt is mined in the lower Carpathians and in Transylvania; production in 1983 was 4·6m. tonnes.

Output, 1983 (and 1982) (in 1,000 tonnes): Iron ore, 1,987 (2,146); crude oil,

11,593 (11,742); coal, 48,759 (41,433); methane gas (cu. metres), 27,719m. (28,620m.). The share of coal in the overall production of energy rose from 28% in 1975 to 47% in 1985 and is expected to reach 60% by 1990.

Agriculture. There were 14·98m. hectares of agricultural land in 1983, including (in 1,000 hectares): Arable, 9,904; meadows and pasture, 4,426; vineyards and fruit trees, 651.

Production in 1983 (in 1,000 tonnes): Wheat and rye, 5,250; barley, 2,193; maize, 11,982; potatoes, 6,209; sunflower seeds, 700; sugar-beet, 4,817.

Livestock (1983): 6m. cattle, 12m. pigs, 16·9m. sheep and 117m. poultry.

In 1980 there were 4,643 collective farms, with 9m. hectares of land (7·3m. arable; 921,200 in private plots). State farms numbered 407, with 2m. hectares of land, of which 1·64m. hectares were arable. A further 2·4m. hectares of land were in the hands of other state agricultural organizations. There were 714 agriculture mechanization stations with 140,074 tractors. Individual holdings totalled 1·41m. hectares. Since 1984 production quotas on private plots must be met on pain of confiscation. The National Union of Agricultural Co-operatives promotes self-management in collective farms, and gives guidance on planning and marketing. A minimum income is guaranteed to peasants. In 1984 there were 3·3m. hectares of irrigated land.

Forestry. Total forest area was 6·34m. hectares in 1982. In 1982, 52,183 hectares were afforested.

INDUSTRY AND TRADE

Industry. Output of main products in 1983 (and 1982) (in tonnes): Pig-iron, 8,190 (8,637); steel, 12,593 (13,055); steel tubes, 1,411 (1,422); blast furnace coke, 4,268 (3,513); rolled steel, 9,179 (9,346); chemical fertilizers, 2,913 (2,692); washing soda, 788 (870); caustic soda, 745 (760); paper, 798 (801); cement, 13,968 (14,995); sugar, 556 (596); edible oils, 371 (352); butter, 48 (20). Fabrics (in 1m. sq. metres): Cotton, 709 (707); woollens, 144 (142), man-made fibres, 235,520 (222,379). In 1,000 units: Radio sets, 542 (599); TV sets, 390 (412); bicycles, 248 (261); washing machines, 352 (372); refrigerators, 440 (431); motor cars, 90,200 (103,725).

Labour. The employed population in 1983 was 10·46m., of whom 3m. worked in agriculture and 4·63m. industry and building. Wage differentials (at a ratio of 5·25:1) are in accordance with the 'social evaluation' of the work and a range of incentives for productivity. The average monthly wage was 2,600 lei in 1984. Wages are cut if a firm's output falls below par. The working week is of 44 hours with alternate Saturdays free. Men retire at 62, women at 57.

Commerce. Some 53% of external trade is with Communist countries (20% with the USSR).

In 1983 exports totalled 173,324m. lei and imports 130,370m. lei.

Principal exports in 1983 were (in 1,000 tonnes): Petroleum products, 9,116; cement, 2,490; cereals, 530; oilfield equipment, 4,604m. lei; equipment for cement mills, 974m. lei; equipment for chemical factories, 1,477m. lei; shipbuilding, 1,979m. lei. Principal imports (in 1,000 tonnes): Iron ore, 14,477; industrial coke, 1,715; rolled ferrous metals, 733; electrical equipment, 2,563m. lei; motor cars, 517 units, and industrial and agricultural equipment.

In 1983 Romania's main trading partners (trade in 1m. lei) were: USSR (59,117), Poland (15,920), German Democratic Republic (15,824), Federal Republic of Germany (15,399), Iran (15,244), Italy (12,245), China (10,287).

Total trade between Romania and UK for calendar years (British Department of Trade returns, in £1,000 sterling):

	1980	*1981*	*1982*	*1983*	*1984*
Imports to UK	64,795	46,518	51,515	58,865	226,091
Exports and re-exports from UK	98,914	150,256	115,244	82,160	71,641

On 18 Sept. 1975 Romania and the UK signed a 10-year economic co-operation agreement. In Nov. 1976 Romania and the USA signed a 10-year

commercial agreement. Both the UK and the USA have joint economic commissions with Romania.

Romania owed some US$8,000m. to Western banks in 1985.

Joint companies with Western firms have been set up; at least 51% of the capital must be in Romanian hands. The 'Romconsult' and 'Publicom' agencies will carry out respectively market research and publicity campaigns on behalf of foreign firms.

Romania has a trade link with EEC under the generalized preference system.

Agreements with the EEC on industrial products and establishing a joint economic commission were reached in March 1980.

On 1 Jan. 1975 a 2-tier tariff system was introduced, graded according to the grant of most favoured nation status to Romania.

COMMUNICATIONS

Roads. There were in 1982, 14,675 km of national roads of which 11,673 km were modernized. Freight carried, 479m. tons; passengers, 1,000m.

Railways. Length of route (1,435 mm gauge) in 1983 was 10,589 km and (narrow-gauge), 472 km. A total of 2,868 km is electrified. Freight carried, 280m. tons; passengers, 414m.

Aviation. TAROM (*Transporturi Aeriene Române*), the state airline, operates all internal services, and also services to Amsterdam, Athens, Beirut, Belgrade, Berlin, Brussels, Budapest, Cairo, Cologne, Copenhagen, Düsseldorf, Frankfurt, Istanbul, London, Moscow, Paris, Prague, Rome, Sofia, Tel-Aviv, Vienna, Warsaw and Zürich. Bucharest is also served by British Airways, PANAM, SABENA, Aeroflot, Air France, Interflug, ČSA, MALEV, Austrian Air Lines, SAS, Lot, TABSO, El Al, Alitalia, Lufthansa and Swissair. An air agreement with China was signed in 1973.

Bucharest's airports are at Băneasa (internal flights) and Otopeni (international flights; 12 miles from Bucharest). Air transport in 1982 carried 1,304,000 passengers and 14,000 tons of freight.

Shipping. The main ports are Constanţa on the Black Sea and Galaţi and Brăila on the Danube. A new port has been constructed at Agigea on the Black Sea and the 64 km canal between the Danube and the Black Sea was opened in 1984. The largest shipyard is at Galaţi.

In 1985 the mercantile marine (NAVROM) some 200 sea-going ships. In 1982 sea-going transport carried 17·79m. tons of freight; river transport, 14·2m. tons.

Post and Broadcasting. *Radio-televiziunea Română* broadcasts 3 programmes on medium-waves and FM. There are also 6 regional programmes, including transmission in Hungarian, German and Serbo-Croat. Two TV programmes are broadcast. Number of telephone subscribers, in 1982, 1,748,000. Radio receiving sets, in 1982 3·2m.; TV sets, 3·86m.

Cinemas and Theatres. There were, in 1983, 5,643 cinemas and 149 theatres and concert halls. 32 full-length feature films were made in 1983.

Newspapers. There were, in 1982, 60 newspapers and 425 periodicals. These figures include 53 in minority languages. The party newspaper is *Scînteia* ('The Spark').

JUSTICE, RELIGION, EDUCATION AND WELFARE

Justice. Justice is administered by the Supreme Court, the 40 district courts, and lower courts. Lay assessors (elected for 4 years) participate in most court trials, collaborating with the judges. The Procurator-General exercises 'supreme supervisory power to ensure the observance of the law' by all authorities, central and local, and all citizens. The Procurator's Office and its organs are independent of any organs of justice or administration, and only responsible to the Grand National Assembly (which appoints the Procurator-General for 4 years) and between its sessions, to the State Council. The Ministry of the Interior is responsible for ordinary police work. State security is the responsibility of the State Security Council. A new penal code came into force on 1 Jan. 1969. It is based on 'the rule of law' and is aimed at preventing illegal trials. The death penalty is retained for 'specially serious offences' (treason, some classes of murder, theft of property having serious consequences).

Religion. Churches are organized and function in accordance with art. 30 of the Constitution. Churches administer their own affairs and run seminaries for the training of priests. Expenses and salaries are paid by the State. There are 14 Churches, all under the control of the 'Department of Cults'. The largest is the Romanian Orthodox Church, which claimed some 16m. members in 1985. It is autocephalous, but retains dogmatic unity with the Eastern Orthodox Church. It is administered by the consultative Holy Synod and National Ecclesiastical Assembly and the executive National Ecclesiastical Council and Patriarchal Administration. It is organized into 12 dioceses grouped into 5 metropolitan bishoprics (Hungaro-Wallachia; Moldavia-Suceava; Transylvania; Olt; Banat), and headed by Patriarch Justin Moisescu (since May 1948). There are some 11,800 churches, 2 theological colleges and 6 'schools of cantors', as well as seminaries.

The Uniate (Greek Catholic) Church (which severed its connexion with the Vatican in 1698) was suppressed in 1948. It had 1·6m. adherents and 1,818 priests. Estimates for 1973: 700,000 adherents and 600 priests.

Other churches: Serbs have a Serbian Orthodox Vicariate at Timişoara. In 1985 there were 1·5m. Roman Catholics, mainly among the Hungarian and German minorities. There are 8 dioceses. In 1985 6 were vacant. There is a bishop of Alba Iulia and an Apostolic Administrator was appointed to Bucharest in Oct. 1984. There were 734 priests in 1982. The Church has not secured approval for a Statute and has no hierarchical ties with the Vatican.

Calvinists (600,000; mainly Hungarian) have bishoprics at Cluj and Oradea; Lutherans (150,000, mainly Germans) a bishopric at Sibiu and Unitarians (60,000, Hungarians) a bishopric at Cluj. These sects share a seminary at Cluj. In 1985 there were about 200,000 Baptists and 100,000 other neo-Protestants.

In 1983 there were 32,000 Jews under a Chief Rabbi (Moses Rosen). There were 130 synagogues in 1973.

There were 40,000 moslems in 1983 and they have a Muftiate at Constanţa.

Education. Education is free and compulsory for 10 years (6 to 16), consisting of 8 years of primary school and 2 years of secondary (gymnasium). Further secondary education is available at *lycées*, professional schools or advanced technical schools.

In 1980–81[1] there were 13,467 kindergartens with 38,512 teachers and 935,711 children; 14,381 primary and secondary schools with 156,817 teachers and 3,308,462 pupils; 971 *lycées* with 46,500 teachers and 979,741 pupils; 603 professional schools with 1,954 teachers and 139,758 pupils; and 300 advanced technical schools with 257 teachers and 28,380 pupils. In 1983–84 there were 3,130 schools for 340,773 pupils of ethnic minorities with 15,922 teachers.

There are universities at Iaşi (founded 1860), Bucharest (1864), Cluj (1919), Timişoara (1962), Craiova (1965) and Braşov (1971). In 1983–84 there were in all 134 faculties of higher education, with a student population of 174,042. In 1983–84 there were 11,568 students at institutes of higher education for ethnic minorities with some 1,000 teachers.

The Academy, with seat at Bucharest, has 2 branches at Iaşi and Cluj. The National Council for Scientific Research co-ordinates research.

[1] Figures include evening classes.

Health. In 1983 there were 210,763 hospital beds and 44,484 doctors. Some hospitals began to charge fees in 1983.

DIPLOMATIC REPRESENTATIVES

Of Romania in Great Britain (4 Palace Green, London, W8 4QD)
Ambassador: Vasile Gliga

Of Great Britain in Romania (24 Strada Jules Michelet, Bucharest)
Ambassador: Philip McKearney, CMG.

Of Romania in the USA (1607 23rd St., NW, Washington, D.C., 20008)
Ambassador: Mircea Malitza.

Of the USA in Romania (7–9 Strada Tudor Arghezi, Bucharest)
Ambassador: David B. Funderburk.

Of Romania to the United Nations
Ambassador: Teodor Marinescu.

Books of Reference

Anuarul Statistic al R.S.R. Bucharest, annual
Atlas Geografic Republica Socialistă Romania. Bucharest, 1965
Dicţionar Enciclopedic Român. Bucharest, 1962–66
Economic and Commercial Guide to Romania. Bucharest, annual since 1969
Mic Dicţionar Enciclopedic. Bucharest, 1973
Revista de Statistică. Bucharest, monthly
Romania: An Encyclopaedic Survey. Bucharest, 1980
Romania Facts and Figures. Bucharest, 1980
Romania, the Industrialization of an Agrarian Economy under Socialist Planning: Report of a Mission sent to Romania by the World Bank. Washington, 1979
Academia Republicii Socialiste România. *Dicţionar Englez-Român.* Bucharest, 1974
Ceauçescu, N.,. *Romania on the Way of Completing Socialist Construction.* 3 vols. Bucharest, 1968–69.—*Romania on the Way of Completing the Many-sided Developed Socialist Society.* Bucharest, 1970 *ff.*
Fischer-Galati, S. A., *Rumania: A Bibliographical Guide.* Library of Congress, 1963.—*The New Rumania.* Mass. Inst. of Technology, 1968.—*The Socialist Republic of Rumania.* Baltimore, 1969.—*Twentieth Century Rumania.* New York, 1970
Gilberg, T., *Modernization in Romania Since World War II.* New York, 1975
Giurescu, C. C. (ed.), *Chronological History of Romania.* 2nd ed. Bucharest, 1974
Graham, L. S., *Romania, a Developing Socialist State.* Boulder, 1982
Hemy, G. W., *Romania: Business Opportunities.* London, 1977
Ionescu, A. (ed.), *The Grand National Assembly of the Socialist Republic of Romania: A Brief Outline.* Bucharest, 1974
King, R. R., *History of the Romanian Communist Party.* Stanford, 1980
Leviţchi, L., *Dicţionar Român-Englez.* 2nd ed. Bucharest, 1965
Morariu, T., and others, *The Geography of Rumania.* 2nd ed. Bucharest, 1969
Nelson, D. N. (ed.), *Romania in the 1980's.* Boulder, 1981
Turnock, D., *An Economic Geography of Romania.* London, 1974

RWANDA

Republika y'u Rwanda

Capital: Kigali
Population: 5·65m. (1984)
GNP per capita: US$250 (1981)

HISTORY. From the 16th century to 1959 the Tutsi kingdom of Rwanda shared the history of Burundi (*see* p. 256). In 1959 an uprising of the Hutu destroyed the Tutsi feudal hierarchy and led to the departure of the Mwami Kigeri V. Elections and a referendum under the auspices of the United Nations in Sept. 1961 resulted in an overwhelming majority for the republican party, the Parmehutu (*Parti du Mouvement de l'Emancipation du Bahutu*), and the rejection of the institution of the Mwami. The republic proclaimed by the Parmehutu on 28 Jan. 1961 was recognized by the Belgian administration (but not by the United Nations) in Oct. 1961. Internal self-government was granted on 1 Jan. 1962, and by decision of the General Assembly of the UN the Republic of Rwanda became independent on 1 July 1962. An agreement, signed with Burundi under United Nations auspices at Addis Ababa in April 1962, provided for a monetary and customs union. These and other common organizations came to an end by 1 Oct. 1964. The first President, Gregoire Kayibanda, was deposed in a *coup* on 5 July 1973.

AREA AND POPULATION. Rwanda is bounded south by Burundi, west by Zaïre, north by Uganda and east by Tanzania. A mountainous state of 26,338 sq. km (10,169 sq. miles), its western third drains to Lake Kivu on the border with Zaïre and thence to the Congo river, while the rest is drained by the Kagera river into the Nile system.

The population was 4,819,317 at the 1978 Census, of whom over 90% were Hutu, 9% Tutsi and 1% Twa (pygmy); latest estimate (1984) 5,650,000.

The areas and populations (1978 Census) of the 10 prefectures are:

Prefecture	*Sq. km*	*Census 1978*	*Prefecture*	*Sq. km*	*Census 1978*
Cyangugu	2,226	331,380	Kigali	3,251	698,063
Kibuye	1,320	337,729	Kibungo	4,134	360,934
Gisenyi	2,395	468,786	Gitarama	2,241	602,752
Ruhengeri	1,762	528,649	Gikongoro	2,192	369,891
Byumba	4,987	519,968	Butare	1,830	601,165

Kigali, the capital, had 156,650 inhabitants in 1981; other towns (1978) being Butare (21,691), Ruhengeri (16,025) and Gisenyi (12,436). Kinyarwanda, the language of the entire population, and French are official languages, and Kiswahili is spoken in the commercial centres, where most of the 1,200 Europeans and 750 Asians reside.

Vital statistics (1975): Live births, 113,154; deaths, 41,385; marriages, 13,899.

CLIMATE. Despite the equatorial situation, there is a highland tropical climate. The wet seasons are from Oct. to Dec. and March to May. Highest rainfall occurs in the west, at around 70" (1,770 mm), decreasing to 40–55" (1,020–1,400 mm) in the central uplands and to 30" (760 mm) in the north and east. Kigali. Jan. 67°F (19·4°C), July 70°F (21·1°C). Annual rainfall 40" (1,000 mm).

CONSTITUTION AND GOVERNMENT. A new Constitution was approved by referendum on 17 Dec. 1978; under it, the *Mouvement revolutionnaire national pour le développement* (MRND) founded 5 July 1975 becomes the sole political organisation. Executive power is vested in a President, elected by universal suffrage for a (renewable) 5-year term. He presides over a Council of Ministers, whom he appoints and dismisses.

President: Maj.-Gen. Junéval Habyarimana (took office July 1975; elected Dec. 1978 and re-elected Dec. 1983).

Foreign Affairs and Co-operation: François Ngarukiyintwari.

Legislative power rests with a National Development Council of 70 deputies, elected for a 5-year term; elections were held on 26 Dec. 1983.

National flag: Three equal vertical panels of red, yellow and green (left to right), the letter 'R' in black superimposed on the centre panel.

Local government: The 10 prefectures, each under an appointed Prefect, are divided into 144 communes, each with an appointed Burgomaster and an elected Council.

DEFENCE

Army. The Army consists of 1 commando battalion, 1 reconnaissance, 8 infantry and 1 engineer companies. Equipment includes 12 AML-60/-90 armoured cars. Strength (1985) about 5,000.

Air Force. Initial equipment ordered for the Air Force in 1972 comprised 3 Italian-built Aeritalia/Aermacchi AM.3C liaison aircraft, now supplemented by 2 Guerrier armed light aircraft, 3 armed Magister jet trainers, 1 twin-engined Defender, 2 C-47s, 1 Islander light transport, 6 Gazelle and 2 Alouette III helicopters. A Caravelle is operated on VIP duties. Personnel, about 150.

INTERNATIONAL RELATIONS

Membership. Rwanda is a member of UN, OAU and is an ACP state of EEC. With Burundi and Zaïre it forms part of the Economic Community of Countries of the Great Lakes.

ECONOMY

Planning. The 1981–90 Development Plan gave priority to rural development.

Budget. The budget for 1982 envisaged expenditure of 16,200m. Rwanda francs.

Currency. The currency is the *Rwanda franc.* The official rate of Rwanda francs 116·65 = £1; 108·18 = US$1 (March 1985).

Banking. On 5 April 1967 the Development Bank of Rwanda *(Banque Rwandaise de Développement—BRD)* was created with a capital of 50m. Rwanda francs, in 1983, 1,000m. Rwanda francs. Other banks are the Central Bank *(Banque Nationale du Rwanda)*; 2 commercial banks which are majority foreign owned—the *Banque Commerciale du Rwanda* and the *Banque de Kigali*; the People's Bank, the Savings Association and the *Caisse Hypothécaire.*

ENERGY AND NATURAL RESOURCES

Electricity. 4 hydro-electric installations and 1 thermal plant produced 69m. kwh in 1980, but over half of the country's needs come from Zaïre.

Minerals. Cassiterite and wolframite are mined east of Lake Kivu, from which (in 1979) 1,300 tons of tin and 505 tons of tungsten were respectively extracted. About 1m. cu. metres of natural gas are obtained from under the lake each year.

Agriculture. Subsistence agriculture accounts for most of the gross national product. Staple food crops (production 1981, in 1,000 tonnes) are sweet potatoes (938), cassava (494), beans (178), sorghum (175), potatoes (228), maize (85), peas and groundnuts. The main cash crops are *aravica* coffee (24), tea (7) and pyrethrum. There is a pilot rice-growing project.

Long-horned Ankole cattle, 639,000 head in 1980, play an important traditional role. Efforts are being made to improve their present negligible economic value. There were (1983) 652,000 cattle, 810,000 goats, 312,000 sheep and 150,000 pigs.

INDUSTRY AND TRADE

Industry. There are about 100 small-sized modern manufacturing enterprises in the country. Food manufacturing is the dominant industrial activity (64%)

followed by construction (15·3%) and mining (9%). There is a large modern brewery.

Commerce. In 1980 imports amounted to 22,568m. Rwanda francs and exports to 7,025m. of which coffee comprised 55%, tea 18% and tin 8%; Belgium provided 16% of imports, Japan 12% and Kenya 11%, while Tanzania took 63% of exports and Kenya 13%.

Total trade between Rwanda and UK (British Department of Trade returns, in £1,000 sterling):

	1980	*1981*	*1982*	*1983*	*1984*
Imports to UK	4,666	2,058	510	2,919	7,842
Exports and re-exports from UK	1,245	1,446	2,079	2,326	2,385

COMMUNICATIONS

Roads. There were (1982) 6,760 km of roads. There are road links with Burundi, Uganda, Tanzania and Zaïre. There were in 1976 3,352 cars and 4,456 trucks. Most imports and exports travel to and from Mombasa *via* Uganda.

Aviation. There are international airports at Kanombe, for Kigali, and at Kamembe, with services to Bujumbura, Bukavu, Entebbe, Goma, Lubumbashi, Athens and Brussels.

Post and Broadcasting. Telephones (1978) 4,543. In 1983 there were 2 radio stations and 155,000 receivers.

Cinemas. In 1975 there were 3 cinemas with a seating capacity of 1,000.

JUSTICE, RELIGION, EDUCATION AND WELFARE

Justice. A system of Courts of First Instance and provincial courts refer appeals to Courts of Appeal and a Court of Cassation situated in Kigali.

Religion. The population was (1983) predominantly Roman Catholic (56%); there is an archbishop (Kigali) and 3 bishops. 23% of the population follow traditional religions, 12% are Protestants and 9% Moslems.

Education. In 1981 there were 704,924 pupils attending 1,606 primary schools with 11,912 teachers. There were 118 secondary, technical and teacher-training schools with 10,667 students and 887 teachers. The National University, opened at Butare in 1963, had 1,266 students in 1981.

Health. In 1980 there were 248 hospitals and health centres with 7,889 beds; there were also 164 doctors, 1 dentist, 10 pharmacists, 464 midwives and 525 nursing personnel.

DIPLOMATIC REPRESENTATIVES

Of Rwanda in Great Britain
Chargé d'Affaires: Isidore Jean-Baptiste Rukira.

Of Great Britain in Rwanda
Ambassador: N. P. Bayre, CMG (resides in Kinshasa).

Of Rwanda in the USA (1714 New Hampshire Ave, NW, Washington, D.C., 20009)
Ambassador: Simon Insonere.

Of the USA in Rwanda (Blvd. de la Revolution, Kigali)
Ambassador: John Blane.

Of Rwanda to the United Nations
Ambassador: Jean-Marie Sibomana.

Books of Reference

Hance, W. A., *African Economic Development.* London, 1967
Lacroix, B., *Le Rwanda.* Montreal, 1966
Northumb, D., *Un Humanisme Africain.* Brussels, 1965

ST CHRISTOPHER (ST KITTS)—NEVIS

Capital: Basseterre
Population: 44,109 (1982)
GNP capita: US$1,040 (1981)

HISTORY. St Christopher (known to its Carib inhabitants as *Liamuiga*) and Nevis were discovered and named by Columbus in 1493. They were settled by Britain in 1623 and 1628 respectively, but ownership was disputed with France until 1713. Forming part of the Leeward Islands Federation from 1871 to 1956, and part of the Federation of the West Indies from 1958 to 1962. In Feb. 1967 the colonial status was replaced by an 'association' with Britain, giving the islands full internal self-government, while Britain remained responsible for defence and foreign affairs. St Christopher–Nevis became fully independent on 19 Sept. 1983.

AREA AND POPULATION. The islands form part of the Lesser Antilles in Eastern Caribbean. Population, estimate (1982) 44,109.

	sq. km	*Census 1980*	*Chief town*	*Census 1980*
St Christopher	168	35,104	Basseterre	14,725
Nevis	93	9,300	Charlestown	1,771
	261	44,404		

CLIMATE. A pleasantly healthy climate, with a cool breeze throughout the year, low humidity and no recognized rainy season. Average annual rainfall is about 55″ (1,375 mm).

CONSTITUTION AND GOVERNMENT. The 1983 Constitution described the country as 'a sovereign democratic federal state'. It allowed for a unicameral Parliament consisting of 11 elected Members (8 from St Kitts and 3 from Nevis) and 3 appointed Senators. Nevis was given its own Island Assembly and the right to secession from St Kitts. At the General Elections held on 21 June 1984, 6 seats from St Kitts were won by the People's Action Movement and 2 by the Labour Party, while the 3 Nevis seats were won by the Nevis Reformation Party.

Governor-General: Sir Clement Athelston Arrindell.

Prime Minister: Rt. Hon. Dr Kennedy Alphonse Simmonds.

Flag: Diagonally green, black, red, with the black fimbriated in yellow and charged with two white stars.

ECONOMY

Budget. The 1984 budget balanced at EC$75,409,791.

Banking. The National Bank operates 4 branches in St. Kitts and Nevis. The main office is located in Basseterre. Other banks include Barclay's Bank International, with a sub-branch in Nevis, Royal Bank of Canada, Bank of Commerce, and the Nevis Co-operative Bank in Charlestown. A branch of the Bank of Nova Scotia is located in Basseterre.

AGRICULTURE. The main crops are sugar and cotton. There are 30 sugar estates and 202 acres of cotton. Most of the farms are small-holdings and there are a number of coconut estates amounting to some 1,000 acres under private ownership. Sugar production (1984) 31,000 tons and 48 bales of cotton were produced in 1980.

Livestock (1983): Cattle, 8,000; pigs, 20,000; sheep, 24,000; goats, 15,000.

INDUSTRY AND TRADE

Industry. The main employer of labour is the sugar industry. Other industries are: Clothing, footwear and assembly of electronic equipment.

Commerce. Imports, (1983) EC$136·7m.; exports, EC$45·3m. Chief export (1983) was sugar (24,576 tons).

Total trade between St Christopher (St Kitts)–Nevis and UK (British Department of Trade returns, in £1,000 sterling):

	1982[1]	*1983*[1]	*1984*
Imports to UK	5,653	1,798	2,096
Exports and re-exports from UK	3,971	4,498	5,133

[1] Including Anguilla.

Tourism. In 1983, there were 34,274 tourists.

COMMUNICATIONS

Roads. There are about 200 km of roads.

Railways. There are 36 miles of railway operated by the sugar industry.

Aviation. There is an airport at Golden Rock (St Kitts). 35,296 passengers arrived by air in 1981. There is an airfield on Nevis (Newcastle).

Shipping. A deep water port was opened in 1981 at Bird Rock with accommodation for cargo, tourist, roll-on-roll-off ships and bulk sugar and molasses loading.

Post and Telecommunications. There is a general post office in Basseterre. Five branches are on the island. Charlestown has a general post office, and there are two branches in Nevis. There were 3,259 telephones at 30 June 1983.

JUSTICE, RELIGION, AND EDUCATION

Justice. Justice is administered by the Supreme Court and by Magistrates' Courts. They have both civil and criminal jurisdiction.

Religion. In 1970, 36% were Anglican, 32% Methodist, 8% other Protestant, and 8% Roman Catholic.

Education. There were (1983) 34 government, 14 private and 6 denominational schools in St Kitts and Nevis. Primary education is compulsory for all children between the ages of 5 and 14, but no pupil is required to leave school before the age of 16 years. There is an Extra-Mural Department of the University of the West Indies, a Technical College and a Teachers' Training College which prepares approximately 30 teachers annually in a two-year course.

Library: Public Library, Basseterre. *Librarian:* Miss V. Archibald.

DIPLOMATIC REPRESENTATIVES

Of St Christopher and Nevis in Great Britain (10 Kensington Ct., London W8)
High Commissioner: Dr Claudius C. Thomas, CMG.

Of Great Britain in St Christopher and Nevis
High Commissioner: G. L. Bullard, CMG.

Of St Christopher and Nevis in the USA (1730 Rhode Island Ave., NW, Washington, D.C., 20036)
Ambassador: Dr William Herbert.

Of St Christopher and Nevis to the United Nations
Ambassador: Dr William Herbert.

ST HELENA

Capital: Jamestown
Population: 5,499 (1982)

HISTORY. The island was administered by the East India Company from 1659 and became a British colony in 1834.

AREA AND POPULATION. St Helena, of volcanic origin, is 1,200 miles from the west coast of Africa. Area, 47 sq. miles (121·7 sq. km), with a cultivable area of about 600 acres (243 hectares). The port of the island is Jamestown, population (1976) 1,516.

Population (1982), 5,499. Births, 123; deaths, 52; marriages, 26.

CLIMATE. A mild climate, with little variation. Temperatures range from 75–85°F (24–29°C) in summer to 65–75°F (18–24°C) in winter. Rainfall varies between 13″ (325 mm) and 37″ (925 mm) according to altitude and situation.

GOVERNMENT. The Government of St Helena is administered by a Governor, with the aid of a Legislative Council consisting of the Governor, 2 *ex-officio* members (the Government Secretary and the Treasurer) and 12 elected members. Committees of the Legislative Council are responsible for the general oversight of the activities of government departments and have, in addition, statutory and administrative functions.

The Governor is also assisted by an Executive Council consisting of the 2 *ex-officio* members and the chairmen of the five Council committees.

Governor and C.-in-C.: F. E. Baker, CBE.

Government Secretary: P. Dale, OBE.

Flag: The British Blue Ensign with the shield of the colony in the fly.

FINANCE AND TRADE, for years from 1 April–31 March, in £ sterling:

	1977–78	*1978–79*	*1979–80*	*1980–81*	*1981–82*	*1982*[3]
Revenue[1]	2,244,550	2,683,681	4,226,899	4,488,257	5,656,518	4,126,548
Expenditure[1]	2,200,299	2,764,150	4,325,910	4,551,657	5,681,934	3,988,900
Imports[2]	1,758,337	1,164,437	1,835,000	2,117,126	2,485,819	2,381,632

[1] Including imperial grants (1977–78, £1,657,231; 1978–79, £1,771,618; 1979–80, £3,347,631; 1980–81, £3,232,093; 1981–82, £3,296,933; 1982, £2,819,256).
[2] Including government stores.
[3] April–Dec.

The revenue from customs was, in 1982, £305,635.

The colony's liabilities at 31 March 1982 exceeded the assets by £177,060; 31 Dec. 1982, £39,412.

Total trade between Ascension and St Helena and UK (British Department of Trade returns, in £1,000 sterling):

	1980	*1981*	*1982*	*1983*	*1984*
Imports to UK	476	224	754	457	979
Exports and re-exports from UK	3,016	3,471	7,049	10,343	6,294

BANKING. Savings-bank deposits on 31 Dec. 1982, £1,467,079, belonging to 3,800 depositors.

COMMUNICATIONS

Roads. There were 87 km of all-weather motor roads.

Shipping. The number of merchant vessels that called in 1982 (April–Dec.) was 30; total tonnage entered and cleared was 218,257.

Post and Broadcasting. The Cable & Wireless Ltd cable connects St Helena with Cape Town and Ascension Island. There is a telephone service with 85 miles of wire and (1982), 310 telephones.

St Helena Government Broadcasting Station broadcasts in English on medium-waves. Number of radio receivers (1982), 1,500.

JUSTICE, RELIGION, EDUCATION AND WELFARE

Justice. Police force, 32; cases dealt with by police magistrate, 205 in 1981.

Religion. There are 10 Anglican churches, 4 Baptist chapels, 3 Salvation Army halls, 1 Seventh Day Adventist church and 1 Roman Catholic church.

Education. Three pre-school playgroups, 8 primary, 3 senior and 1 secondary schools controlled by the Government had 980 pupils in Sept. 1982.

Health. There were 3 doctors, 1 dentist and 54 hospital beds in 1982.

Ascension is a small island of volcanic origin, of 34 sq. miles (88 sq. km), 700 miles north-west of St Helena. In Nov. 1922 the administration was transferred from the Admiralty to the Colonial Office and annexed to the colony of St Helena. There are 120 hectares providing fresh meat, vegetables and fruit. Population, 31 March 1982, was 1,625; St Helenians 759, others 866.

The island is the resort of sea turtles, which come to lay their eggs in the sand annually between Jan. and May. Rabbits, wild goats and partridges are more or less numerous on the island, which is, besides, the breeding ground of the sooty tern or 'wideawake', these birds coming in vast numbers to lay their eggs every eighth month.

Cable & Wireless Ltd own and operate a cable station, connecting the island with St Helena, Sierra Leone, St Vincent, Rio de Janeiro and Buenos Aires. There is an airstrip (Miracle Mile) near the settlement of Georgetown which was being extended in 1985.

Administrator: M. T. S. Blick.

Tristan da Cunha, a small group of islands in the Atlantic, halfway between the Cape and South America, in 37° 6′ S. lat., 12° 1′ W. long. Besides Tristan da Cunha and Gough Island, there are Inaccessible and Nightingale Islands, the former 2 and the latter 1 mile long, and a number of rocks. As from 12 Jan. 1938 the 4 islands have become dependencies of St Helena.

Tristan consists of a volcano rising to a height of 6,760 ft, with a circumference at its base of 21 miles. The volcano, believed to be extinct, erupted unexpectedly early in Oct. 1961. The whole population was evacuated without loss and settled temporarily in the UK. In 1963 they returned to Tristan where they all dwell in the settlement of Edinburgh.

Before the disaster occurred the habitable area was a small plateau on the north west side of about 12 sq. miles, 100 ft above sea-level. Only about 30 acres was under cultivation, three-quarters of it for potatoes. There were apple and peach trees. Potatoes remain the chief crop, cattle, sheep and pigs are now reared, and fish are plentiful.

The island is extremely lonely, but the community is growing. In 1880 it numbered 109, in 1982, 325. The original inhabitants were shipwrecked sailors and soldiers who remained behind when the garrison from St Helena was withdrawn in 1817.

At the end of April 1942 Tristan da Cunha was commissioned as HMS *Atlantic Isle*, and became an important meteorological and radio station. In Jan. 1949 a South African company commenced crawfishing operations. An Administrator was appointed at the end of 1948 and a body of basic law brought into operation. The Island Council, which was set up in 1932, in 1982 consisted of a Chief Islander, 3 nominated and 7 elected members under the chairmanship of the Administrator. Women's affairs are discussed by the Island Women's Council, which presents them for consideration to the general council.

Administrator: R. Perry.

Books of Reference

Booy, D. M., *Rock of Exile: A Narrative of Tristan da Cunha.* London, 1957
Crawford, A., *Tristan da Cunha and the Roaring Forties.* Edinburgh, 1982
Cross, A., *Saint Helena.* Newton Abbot, 1980
Munch, P. A., *Sociology of Tristan da Cunha.* Oslo, 1945.—*Crisis in Utopia.* New York, 1971
Stonehouse, B., *Wideawake Island* (Ascension). London, 1960

ST LUCIA

Capital: Castries
Population: 126,800 (1984)
GNP per capita: US$970 (1981)

HISTORY. St Lucia was discovered about 1500 A.D. Attempts to colonize the island by the English took place in 1605 and 1638. The French settled in 1650 and St Lucia was ceded to Britain in 1814. Self-government was achieved in 1967 and independence on 22 Feb. 1979.

AREA AND POPULATION. St Lucia is a small island of the Lesser Antilles situated in the Eastern Caribbean between Martinique and St Vincent, 240 sq. miles (622 sq. km); population (census, 1980) 120,300. Estimate (1984) 126,800. The capital is Castries (population, 1980, 45,000). Life expectancy (1983) was 65 (men) and 71 (women).

CLIMATE. The climate is tropical, with a dry season lasting from Jan. to April, a wet season from May to Aug., followed by an Indian summer for two months, but most rain falls in Nov. and Dec. Amounts vary over the year, according to altitude, from 60″ (1,500 mm) to 138″ (3,450 mm). Temperatures are uniform at about 80°F (26·7°C).

CONSTITUTION AND GOVERNMENT. There is a 17-seat House of Assembly elected for 5 years; an 11-seat Senate appointed by the Governor-General, 6 on the advice of the Prime Minister, 3 on the advice of the Leader of the Opposition, and 2 'after consultation with appropriate religious, economic or social bodies or associations'.

At the elections in May 1982, the United Workers' Party gained 14 seats, the St Lucia Labour Party, 2 and the Progressive Labour Party, 1.

Governor-General: Sir Allen Lewis.

Prime Minister: John George Melvin Compton.

Flag: Blue with a design of a black triangle edged in white, bearing a smaller yellow triangle, in the centre.

INTERNATIONAL RELATIONS

Membership. St Lucia is a member of UN, OAS, Caricom, the Commonwealth and is an ACP state of the EEC.

ECONOMY

Budget. The budget in 1983–84 amounted to EC$185·7m. expenditure.

Banking. There are Barclays Bank International with 2 branches and 4 agencies, the Royal Bank of Canada, the Bank of Nova Scotia and the Canadian Imperial Bank of Commerce (all of which have 1 branch each), the Chase Manhattan Bank, the St Lucia Co-operative bank, the National Development Bank with 1 branch and the Government Savings Bank. The Government Savings Bank (end of 1974), 8,400 depositors, $359,086 deposits.

INDUSTRY AND TRADE

Agriculture. Bananas, cocoa, copra and coconut oil are the chief products.

Livestock (1983): Cattle, 12,000; pigs, 11,000; sheep, 14,000; goats, 11,000.

Commerce. Value of imports (1980), EC$123·8m.; of exports, EC$40·4m., including coconut oil, cocoa beans, copra and bananas. Main items of imports were artificial silk and cotton piece-goods, cement, plastic goods, iron and steel products, hardware, motor vehicles, agricultural machinery, fertilizers, wheat flour, codfish and rice, meat and meat preparations.

Total trade between St Lucia and UK (British Department of Trade returns, in £1,000 sterling):

	1982	*1983*	*1984*
Imports to UK	15,530	21,950	28,563
Exports and re-exports from UK	6,273	6,276	8,236

Tourism. The total number of visitors during 1982 was 98,181.

COMMUNICATIONS

Roads. The island has 500 miles of main and secondary roads.

Aviation. The island is served on a scheduled basis by Leeward Islands Air Transport, British West Indian Airways and Eastern Airline. There are 2 air-fields—Hewanorra International Airport, with 9,000 ft runway, and Vigie.

Shipping. There are 2 ports, Castries and Vieux Fort.

Post and Broadcasting. There are 104 miles of telephone trunk lines, plus 300 miles of local lines. There were (1982) 9,500 telephone instruments coupled to some (1982) 4,881 exchange lines. There were 3,000 TV and 90,000 radio receivers in 1983.

Cinemas. There were 9 cinemas in 1970 with a seating capacity of 9,500.

JUSTICE, RELIGION, EDUCATION AND WELFARE

Justice. The island is divided into 2 judicial districts, and there are 9 magistrates' courts. Appeals lie with the Court of Appeal of the Windward and Leeward Islands, subject to exceptions and conditions as may be enacted by the St Lucia legislature.

Police establishment in 1974 was 11 officers, 11 inspectors and 267 others.

Religion. Over 90% of the population is Roman Catholic.

Education (1983–84). 81 primary schools (39 Roman Catholic, 3 Anglican, 3 Methodist, 35 government, 1 other), with 31,888 pupils on roll; government expenditure, 1982–83, $19,338,834. Primary education is free and compulsory by law, but the legislation is not enforced. There are 12 secondary schools (2 Roman Catholic, 1 Seventh-day Adventist, 9 government) with 4,984 pupils; government expenditure, 1982–83, $15,745,832. There is 1 technical college with (1982–83) 199 students and 1 teachers' college with (1982–83) 131 students.

Health. Victoria Hospital (in Castries) has 213 beds; there is also a 162-bed mental hospital, 3 other hospitals (150 beds) and 29 health centres. In 1983 there were 36 doctors, 5 dentists, 16 pharmacists and 246 nursing personnel.

Library: The Central Library, Castries. *Acting Librarian:* Frances Niles.

DIPLOMATIC REPRESENTATIVES

Of St Lucia in Great Britain (10 Kensington Ct., London, W8)
High Commissioner: Dr Claudius C. Thomas, CMG.

Of Great Britain in St Lucia (Colombus Sq., Castries)
High Commissioner: G. L. Bullard, CMG.

Of St Lucia in USA and to the United Nations
Ambassador: Dr Joseph Edsel Edmunds.

ST VINCENT AND THE GRENADINES

Capital: Kingstown
Population: 123,000 (1984)
GNP per capita: US$630 (1981)

HISTORY. The date of discovery of St Vincent is not known. In 1969 St Vincent became a self-governing Associated State of UK and acquired full independence on 27 Oct. 1979.

AREA AND POPULATION. The total area of 389 sq. km (150·3 sq. miles) comprises the island of St Vincent itself (345 sq. km) and the Northern Grenadines (44 sq. km) of which the largest are Bequia, Mustique, Canouan, Mayreau and Union. Population, estimate, 1984, 123,000. Capital, Kingstown, population (1980), 32,600. Vital statistics (1982): Live births, 3,352; still births, 0; deaths, 745; marriages, 380.

CLIMATE. The climate is tropical marine, with north-east Trades predominating and rainfall ranging from 150″ (3,750 mm) a year in the mountains to 60″ (1,500 mm) on the south-east coast. The rainy season is from June to Dec., and temperatures are equable throughout the year.

CONSTITUTION AND GOVERNMENT. The House of Assembly consists of 13 elected members, directly elected for a 5-year term from single-member constituencies, the Attorney-General (elected) and 6 Senators appointed by the Governor-General (4 on the advice of the Prime Minister and 2 on the advice of the Leader of the Opposition). At the General Elections held in July 1984, the New Democratic Party won 9 and the St Vincent Labour Party won 4 of the 13 elective seats in the House of Assembly.

Governor-General: Sir Sydney Gun-Munro, GCMG, MBE.
Prime Minister: James Fitz Allen Mitchell.

National Flag: Three vertical stripes of blue, yellow, green, with white fimbriations, charged in the centre with a green leaf of bread-fruit bearing the arms of St Vincent.

INTERNATIONAL RELATIONS

Membership. St Vincent and the Grenadines is a member of UN, OAS, Caricom, the Commonwealth and is an ACP state of the EEC.

ECONOMY

Budget. Revenue (estimate), 1984–85, $99,229,714; development aid, $6,378,506, and other sources, $45,205,788; expenditure, $97,443,992; $6,378,506 on British development projects and $45,205,788 on other projects. Public debt at the end of the financial year 1983–84 was $17,759,900.

Currency. The currency is the Eastern Caribbean *dollar.* In March 1985, £1 = EC$2·88; US$1 =EC$2·70.

Banking. There are branches of Barclays Bank International, the Royal Bank of Canada, the Canadian Imperial Bank of Commerce, the Bank of Nova Scotia. Locally-owned banks: the National Commercial Bank, St Vincent Co-operative Bank and the St Vincent Agricultural Credit and Loan Bank.

ENERGY AND NATURAL RESOURCES

Electricity. The electricity system is owned jointly by the Government (49%) and the Commonwealth Development Corporation (51%) and operated by the St Vincent Electricity Services (VINLEC). The system consists of 4 power stations: South Rivers Hydro (870 kw.); Cane Hall Diesel (3,640 kw.); Kingstown Diesel (2,075 kw.) and Richmond Hydro (1,100 kw.), which are linked by 11,000-volt transmission lines covering the island from Richmond through Kingstown to Georgetown. In Bequia there is one diesel station (800 kw.) with transmission at 11,000, 3,300 and 400 volts to Hamilton and Port Elizabeth. Current is supplied at 400 volts 3-phase, 50 cycles for industrial purposes and 230 volts single phase for domestic purposes. At 31 Dec. 1982 there were 11,384 consumers in St Vincent, 837 in Bequia and 266 in Union Island.

Agriculture. The estimated alienated area is about 47,000 of the total acreage of 85,120. 34,000 acres are under forest and woodland; of these about 5,000 acres are used for grazing; 3,000 are considered potentially productive for agriculture and 5,000 for forestry. About 14,000 acres are considered unsuitable for either agriculture or forestry. Of the total alienated area, 34,000 acres are considered arable land, of which 20,000 acres are under temporary crops, 4,000 acres under temporary meadows, 300 acres devoted to market-garden crops with temporary fallow and all other arable land making up a further 9,700 acres. About 11,000 acres are devoted to permanent crops, of which approximately 6,000 acres are under coconuts; the remainder produce cocoa, nutmegs, mangoes, avocado pears, guavas and miscellaneous crops. About 2,000 acres are under permanent meadow, of which 750 are cultivated.

Livestock (1983): Cattle, 8,000; pigs, 7,000; sheep, 13,000; goats, 4,000.

INDUSTRY AND TRADE

Industry. Manufactures include flour, furniture and concrete.

Trade (1982). Imports, EC$164,395,560; exports, EC$87,371,301.

Principal exports, 1982:

			EC$				*EC$*
Arrowroot starch	293,735	lb.	577,745	Coconut oil, crude	112,905	gals.	1,237,439
Eddoes	8,038,719	lb.	5,627,862	Coconut oil, refined	1,350	gals.	19,413
Bananas	58,865,459	lb.	23,503,964	Tannias	4,127,331	lb.	2,879,085
Sweet potatoes [1]	869,906	lb.	301,912				
Coconuts	1,022,051	nuts	423,361				

[1] July–Dec.

Total trade between St Vincent and the Grenadines and UK (British Department of Trade returns, in £1,000 sterling):

	1982	*1983*	*1984*
Imports to UK	10,891	12,496	14,167
Exports and re-exports from UK	3,265	4,357	5,811

Labour (1983). The Department of Labour serves both worker's and employers' organizations as a conciliatory body in case of dispute. Conciliatory meetings are held on dispute matters such as delay in the recognition of a union as collective bargaining agent for the workers, dismissals, overtime pay, delay in finalizing collective agreements and other conditions of work. There are 5 active trade unions: the St Vincent Union of Teachers, the Public Service Union, the Commercial, Technical and Allied Workers' Union, the National Workers' Movement and the National Farmers' Union.

Tourism. There were 86,350 visitors in 1983.

COMMUNICATIONS

Roads. There are 313 km of all-weather roads, 160 km of rough motorable roads and 161 km of tracks.

Aviation. Scheduled services are operated daily by LIAT, Air Martinique and WINLINK. Non-scheduled services are operated by Mustique Airways, Tropical Air Services, Aero-Services and St Lucia Airways. Passengers are able to travel daily through the chain of islands stretching as far north as San Juan, Puerto Rico and south to Trinidad. Connexions to the USA, Canada, South America and Europe are possible *via* Barbados, Antigua, Trinidad and St Lucia.

Shipping (1982): (*a*) 51 auxiliary sailing vessels of 1,597 NRT entered and cleared. (*b*) 19 steamships of 142,030 NRT entered and cleared. (*c*) 649 motor vessels of 226,826 NRT entered and cleared. (*d*) 60 tankers of 49,612 NRT bringing 16,169 tons of fuel entered. A deep-water harbour at Kingstown was completed in 1964.

Post and Broadcasting. There is a General Post Office at Kingstown and 47 district post offices. There is a telephone system with 2,000 miles of line and (1982), 6,047 subscribers; 5,745 stations and a radio telephone service to Bequia, Mustique, Union Island, Petit St Vincent and Palm Island. In 1983 there were 6,000 TV and 55,000 radio receivers.

Cinemas. There were 2 cinemas in 1983 with a seating capacity of 2,000.

JUSTICE, RELIGION, EDUCATION AND WELFARE

Justice (1981). There were 3,552 criminal matters disposed of in the 3 magisterial districts which comprise 11 courts. Strength of police force (1982), 525 (including 12 officers).

Religion. At the 1970 Census, 47% of the population was Anglican, 28% Methodist and 13% Roman Catholic.

Education (1983). Sixty-two primary schools; pupils on roll, 24,557, average attendance, 20,780. Expenditure on primary education, $16,867,048. There is also a secondary school for girls (658 pupils), a co-educational school (470 pupils), as well as 11 assisted secondary schools (2,706 pupils) and 6 junior secondary schools with 1,336 pupils. Expenditure on secondary education, $3,160,925.

Health. There is a General Hospital in Kingstown (216 beds), 3 rural hospitals at Chateaubelair, Georgetown and Bequia; 2 health centres at Union Island and Mesopotamia; 3 specialist hospitals and 34 medical clinics. In 1984 there were 24 doctors, 1 dentist, 19 technical staff, 290 nursing personnel and 34 community health aides.

Library: St Vincent Public Library, Kingstown. *Librarian:* Mrs Lorna Small.

DIPLOMATIC REPRESENTATIVES

Of St Vincent and the Grenadines in Great Britain (10 Kensington Ct, London, W8)
High Commissioner: Dr Claudius C. Thomas, CMG.

Of Great Britain in St Vincent and the Grenadines
High Commissioner: G. L. Bullard, CMG (resides in Bridgetown).

Of St Vincent and the Grenadines in the USA
Ambassador: Hudson Kemul Tannis.

Of St Vincent and the Grenadines to the United Nations
Ambassador: (Vacant).

SAN MARINO

Capital: San Marino
Population: 21,622 (1981)

Repubblica di San Marino

HISTORY. On 22 March 1862 San Marino concluded a treaty of friendship and co-operation, including a *de facto* customs union with the kingdom of Italy, preserving the independence of the ancient republic, although completely surrounded by Italian territory. The treaty was renewed on 27 March 1872, 28 June 1897 and 31 March 1939, with 7 amendments in 1942–71.

The republic has extradition treaties with Belgium, France, the Netherlands, UK and USA.

AREA AND POPULATION. San Marino is a land-locked state in central Italy, 20 km from the Adriatic. The frontier line is 38·6 km in length, area is 61·19 sq. km (24·1 sq. miles) and the population (30 June 1981), 21,622; some 20,000 citizens live abroad.

CONSTITUTION AND GOVERNMENT. The legislative power is vested in the Great and General Council of 60 members elected every 5 years by popular vote, 2 of whom are appointed every 6 months to act as regents *(Capitani reggenti).*

The elections held on 29 May 1983 gave 26 seats to the Christian Democrats, 15 to the Communists, 17 to Socialist parties, 2 to others.

The regents exercise executive power together with the Congress of State *(Congresso di Stato)*, which comprises 11 departments, and through Commissions on social welfare, public works, etc.

National flag: Horizontally white over light blue, with the national arms over all in the centre.

DEFENCE. The militia consists, in case of necessity, of all able-bodied citizens between the ages of 16 and 55, with certain exceptions (teachers and students, etc.).

ECONOMY. The budget (ordinary and extraordinary) for the financial year ending 31 Dec. 1981 balanced at 144,103,052,187 lire.

The chief exports are wood machinery, chemicals, wine, textiles, tiles, varnishes and ceramics.

Italian and Vatican City currency is in general use, but the republic issues its own postage stamps and coins.

In 1980, 3·5m. tourists visited San Marino.

COMMUNICATIONS

Roads. A bus service connects San Marino with Rimini.

Aviation. There is a helicopter service to Rimini in summer.

Post. In 1982 there were 8,712 telephones.

Cinemas. In 1974 there were 8 cinemas with a seating capacity of 2,300.

JUSTICE AND EDUCATION

Justice. Law is administered by a Commissioner for civil and commercial cases and a Commissioner for criminal cases (acting with a penal judge), from whom appeals can be made to a civil appeals judge and a criminal appeals judge respectively. The highest legal authority is, in certain cases, the *Consiglio dei XII.*

Education. There are 19 infant schools, 16 elementary schools, a secondary school and a grammar school, the diplomas of which are recognized by Italian universities. Civil marriage was instituted in Sept. 1953.

DIPLOMATIC REPRESENTATIVES

British Consul-General (resides at Florence): (Vacant).
Consul-General in London: Lord Forte.

Books of Reference

Information: Segreteria di Stato per gli Affari Esteri; Ente Governativo per il Turismo.

Garbeletto, A., *Evoluzione storica della costituzione di S. Marino.* Milan, 1956
Packett, C. N., *Guide to the Republic of San Marino.* Bradford, 1970
Rossi, G., *San Marino.* San Marino, 1954

SÃO TOMÉ E PRINCIPE

Capital: São Tomé
Population: 102,000 (1984)
GNP per capita: US$370 (1981)

HISTORY. The islands of São Tomé and Príncipe, were discovered in 1471 by Pedro Escobar and João Gomes, and from 1522 until independence had constituted a province of Portugal.

On 26 Nov. 1974 the Government of Portugal and the liberation movement of São Tomé e Príncipe signed an agreement granting independence to the archipelago on 12 July 1975 to become the Democratic Republic of São Tomé e Príncipe.

AREA AND POPULATION. The republic, which lies about 200 km off the west coast of Gabon, in the Gulf of Guinea, comprises the main islands of São Tomé (845 sq. km) and Príncipe and several smaller islets including Pedras Tinhosas and Rolas. It has a total area of 964 sq. km (372 sq. miles). Total population (census, 1970) 73,631 (São Tomé, 69,032; Príncipe, 4,599). Estimate (1984) 102,000. Capital, São Tomé (25,000).

Vital statistics (1982): Births, 3,236; deaths, 878.

CLIMATE. The tropical climate is modified by altitude and the effect of the cool Benguela current. The wet season is generally from Oct. to May, but rainfall varies very much, from 40″ (1,000 mm) in the hot and humid north-east to 150–200″ (3,800–5,000 mm) on the plateau. São Tomé. Jan. 79°F (26·1°C), July 75°F (23·9°C). Annual rainfall 38″ (951 mm).

CONSTITUTION AND GOVERNMENT. A new constitution was approved by the Constitutional Assembly (elected 6 July 1975) on 12 Dec. 1975. Under it, the sole legal party is the *Movimento de Libertação de São Tomé e Príncipe*, who nominate candidates for the Presidency and People's Assembly. The President is elected by the People's Assembly for a 4-year term; he is also head of government and appoints a Cabinet of Ministers to assist him. The 40-member People's Assembly is also elected for 4 years.

President, Prime Minister, National Security and Defence: Dr Manuel Pinto da Costa.

Foreign Affairs: Maria do Nascimento da Graça Amorim.

Flag: Three horizontal stripes of green, yellow, green, with the yellow of double width and bearing 2 black stars; in the hoist a red triangle over all.

INTERNATIONAL RELATIONS

Membership. São Tomé e Príncipe is a member of UN, OAU and is an ACP state of EEC.

DEFENCE. Initial equipment of the air force comprises a few L-39 jet trainers from Czechoslovakia and Soviet-built An-32 twin-turboprop transports. Police gendarmerie strength (estimate, 1984) 160.

ECONOMY

Budget. In 1977 the budget envisaged revenue of 179·6m. dobra and expenditure of 454·2m. dobra.

Currency. The currency is the *dobra*, introduced in 1977, divided into 100 *centavos*. In March 1985, £1 = 50·56 *dobra*; US$1 = 47·66 *dobra*.

Banking. *Banco Nacional de São Tomé e Príncipe* (established, 1975) is the central bank.

AGRICULTURE. The chief commercial products are cacao, copra, coconut, coffee, palm-oil and cinchona. In 1983 there were 4,000 goats, 2,000 sheep, 3,000 pigs and 3,000 cattle.

COMMERCE. Imports in 1975 amounted to 288,469,000 dobras and exports to 180,432,000 dobras, the main exports being cocoa (87%), copra (8%), coffee, bananas and palm-oil. In 1975 Portugal provided 61% of imports and Angola 13%, while the Netherlands took 52% of exports and Portugal 33%.

Total trade between São Tomé e Príncipe and UK (British Department of Trade returns, in £1,000 sterling):

	1981	*1982*	*1983*	*1984*
Imports to UK	207	494	218	450
Exports and re-exports from UK	625	1,510	597	962

COMMUNICATIONS

Roads. There were 288 km of roads in 1973.

Shipping. In 1975, 70 vessels entered the port of São Tomé to unload 26,693 tonnes and load 9,880 tonnes.

Aviation. São Tomé airport is linked by regular services to Douala, Lisbon, Luanda and Malabo, as well as to Príncipe. In 1975, 10,050 passengers arrived and 9,240 departed.

Post. There were, in 1973, 3 wireless stations with (1983) 25,000 radio receivers, 352 km of telephone lines and a telephone exchange (with 850 instruments in 1980).

Cinemas. In 1972 there was 1 cinema with a seating capacity of 1,000.

JUSTICE, RELIGION, EDUCATION AND WELFARE.

Justice. The members of the Supreme Court are appointed by the People's Assembly.

Religion. The vast majority of the population are Roman Catholic.

Education. In 1977 there were 14,162 pupils and 527 teachers in primary schools, 3,145 pupils and 81 teachers in 3 secondary schools, and 155 students and 30 teachers in technical schools.

Health. In 1976 there were 11 hospitals and dispensaries with 530 beds. In 1973 there were 12 doctors, 6 midwives and 63 nursing personnel.

DIPLOMATIC REPRESENTATIVES

Of Great Britain in São Tomé and Príncipe
Ambassador: M. I. Goulding, CMG (resides in Luanda).

Of São Tomé and Príncipe to the United Nations
Ambassador: Joaquim Rafael Branco.

Book of Reference

S. Tomé e Príncipe. Agência-Geral do Ultramar, 1964

SAUDI ARABIA

Capital: Riyadh
Population: 8·4m. (1984)
GNP per capita: US$12,600 (1981)

al-Mamlaka al-ʻArabiya as-Saʻudiya

HISTORY. Saudi Arabia was founded by Abdul Aziz ibn Abdur-Rahman al-Faisal Al Saʻud, GCB, GCIE (born about 1880; died 9 Nov. 1953), who had been proclaimed King of the Hejaz on 8 Jan. 1926 and had in 1927 changed his title of Sultan of Nejd and its dependencies to that of king, thus becoming 'King of the Hejaz and of Nejd and its Dependencies'. On 20 May 1927 a treaty was signed at Jiddah between Great Britain and Ibn Saʻud, by which the former recognized the complete independence of the dominions of the latter. The name of the State was changed to 'The Saudi Arabian Kingdom' by decree of 23 Sept. 1932.

AREA AND POPULATION. The total area of Saudi Arabia is estimated to be 927,000 sq. miles (2·4m. sq. km).

The principal cities of the Western Province (formerly *Hejaz*) are Jiddah (561,104 inhabitants at the 1974 Census), Mecca (366,801), Taif (204, 857) and Medina (198,196); of the Central Province (formerly *Nejd*) are Riyadh, the national capital (666,840), Buraidah (69,940), Ha'il (40,502), Anaiza and Al-Kharj; of the Northern Province are Tabouk (74,825), Al-Jawf and Sakaka; of the Eastern Province (formerly *Al-Hasa*) are Dammam (127,844), Hofuf (101,271), Haradh (100,000), Al-Mobarraz (54,325), Al-Khabar (48,817) and Qatif; and of the Southern Province (formerly *Asir*) are Khamis Mushait (49,581), Najran (47,501), Qizan (32,814) and Abha (30,150). New industrial cities are being built at Jubail (future pop. 300,000) and Yanbu (150,000).

Taif, about 3,800ft above sea-level and some 50 miles from Mecca,is a summer resort.

The total population was (1974 census) 7,012,642, of which 5,128,655 were categorized as settled and 1,883,987 as nomadic. Estimate (1984) 8·4m.

CLIMATE. A desert climate, with very little rain and none at all from June to Dec. The months May to Sept. are very hot and humid, but winter temperatures are quite pleasant. Riyadh. Jan. 58°F (14·4°C), July 92°F (33·3°C). Annual rainfall 4″ (100 mm). Jiddah. Jan. 73°F (22·8°C), July 87°F (30·6°C). Annual rainfall 3″ (81 mm).

KING. Fahd bin Abdul Aziz; succeeded in May 1982, after King Khalid's assassination. *Crown Prince:* Prince Abdullah ibn Abdul Aziz, First Deputy Prime Minister, Commander of the National Guard, brother of the King.

National flag: Green, with the text 'There is no God but Allah and Mohammed is his prophet' in white Arabic script, and beneath this a white sabre.

GOVERNMENT AND CONSTITUTION. The Kingdom has been welded together from Hejaz, Nejd, Asir and Al-Hasa. Riyadh is the political capital and Mecca the religious capital. There is no formal Constitution.

The King has the post of Prime Minister.

First Deputy Prime Minister and Commander of the National Guard: Prince Abdullah ibn Abdul Aziz.

Second Deputy Prime Minister and Defence and Aviation: Prince Sultan ibn Abdul Aziz.

Foreign Minister: Prince Saud al Faisal. *Interior:* Prince Nayef ibn Abdul Aziz. *Petroleum and Natural Resources:* Sheikh Ahmed Zaki Yamani. *Finance and*

Economy: Sheikh Muhammad Aba al Khail. *Health:* Faisal Hejailan. *Industry and Electricity:* Abdul Aziz Zamil.

There are provisions for the setting up of certain advisory councils, comprising a consultative Legislative Assembly in Mecca, municipal councils in each of the towns of Mecca, Medina and Jiddah, and village and tribal councils throughout the provinces. The country is divided for administrative purposes into 6 major and 12 minor provinces.

DEFENCE. In 1937 a Ministry of Defence and a training school for officers were established. British Military and Civil Air Missions helped in training the Army and civil aviation from 1947 to 1951. The US now maintains a Military Mission (with an Air Force element) as do France and Pakistan. UK provides small army and air force teams. Personnel are trained in Saudi Arabia, France, Pakistan, UK and the USA.

Army. The Army comprises 2 armoured brigades (1 manned by Pakistan troops), 3 mechanized brigades and 1 infantry brigade. Equipment is mainly US or French (M114, M101, M109 and M198 artillery, M113 APCs, M60 tanks; AMX10 APC, AMX30 tanks, CGT155mm Howitzer, HOT on AMX30 chassis. Ground-to-air defence provided by Shahine (with armoured brigades), 20mm Vulcan gun. There are two airborne battalions. Total strength of Army (1984) approximately 27,000. There are para-military forces with the Ministry of Interior; Frontier Force (approximately 9,000) and Special Security Force (1,800) of which the latter is equipped with anti-riot and internal security equipment (mostly West German).

National Guard. The National Guard comprises 1 mechanized brigade (trained by the US), 1 Special Security Unit. An additional mechanized brigade is planned. Additionally there are a number of regular and irregular units, the total strength of the National Guard amounting to approximately 30,000. The National Guard's primary role is the protection of the Royal Family and vital points in the Kingdom. It does not come under command of the Ministry of Defence and Aviation.

Navy. The Royal Saudi Naval Forces, with recent modernisation programme impetus under the aegis of USA and France, comprise 1 new French-built guided missile frigate of 2,600 tons, 4 new US-built missile-armed fast corvettes of 800 tons, 9 fast missile craft of 380 tons (all completed in 1980–82 in USA), 3 *ex*-German torpedo boats, 4 US-built MSC-type coastal minesweepers, 2 new French-built armed replenishment ships each with 2 helicopters, 1 *ex*-US coastguard cutter, 8 new French-built patrol craft, 35 coastal patrol boats, 24 hovercraft, 2 air-sea rescue launches, 1 training ship, 4 landing craft, 12 minor landing craft, 1 salvage vessel, 2 tugs, 16 customs craft and 2 royal yachts (with helicopter). New construction includes 3 more guided missile frigates in France. There are 24 helicopters. An intensive training programme continued in USA and Saudi Arabia. $70m. was spent on three naval bases. The main port facilities are at Jubail and Jedda.

Naval personnel in 1985 totalled 450 officers and 4,050 other ranks plus instructors and trainees. RSNF rely on considerable US and Pakistan support.

The Coast Guard operates 130 coastal patrol craft, 4 hovercraft, 300 inshore patrol cutters, 3 small oilers, 4 fire-fighting craft, 2 yachts and 12 service craft.

Air Force. Formed as a small army support unit in 1932, the Air Force has been built up considerably with British and US assistance since 1946. Complete re-equipment began in 1966 and delivery of 62 F-15 Eagles to equip 3 air superiority squadrons began in 1982; they will operate in conjunction with 5 E-3A Sentry AWACS aircraft and 6 KC-707 flight refuelling tankers. Current combat units include 1 squadron of Lightning F.53 supersonic interceptors, supported by 2-seat fighter-trainers. There are 3 squadrons of F-5E Tiger II supersonic fighter-bombers, supported by a conversion unit with F-5B/F combat trainers. Two squadrons of Strikemaster light jet attack/trainers are based at the King Faisal Air Academy, Riyadh, together with 12 Reims/Cessna FR172 piston-engined primary trainers. Other types in current service include 34 C-130E/H and 11 KC-130H Hercules transports and tankers, 2 C-130H hospital aircraft, 1 Boeing 747 SP, 1

Boeing 707, and 2 JetStar VIP jet transports, more than 70 Agusta-Bell 205, 212 and JetRanger helicopters, 2 Agusta AS-61A-4 VIP transport helicopters, 16 Kawasaki-Boeing Vertol KV-107 helicopters, and communications aircraft. On order are 10 RF-5E Tiger Eye reconnaissance-fighters and 40 Indonesian-built CASA Aviocar twin-turboprop transports. Personnel (1985), about 12,500.

Air Defence Command. This separate Command was formerly part of the Army, which retains a point air defence capability. It is heavily reliant on Pakistan assistance, particularly manpower. Equipment comprises approximately 18 Crotale missile systems, 15 batteries of Improved Hawk surface-to-air missiles, 30 mm Oerlikon and 20 mm Vulcan guns. Personnel strength about 3,000.

INTERNATIONAL RELATIONS

Membership. Saudi Arabia is a member of UN, the Arab League, the Gulf Co-operation Council and OPEC.

ECONOMY

Planning. The third development plan runs 1980–85, and emphasizes industrial development and the training of an indigenous work force. GDP is expected to grow at 6·2% in the non-oil economy: industrial growth will be much higher than this, but an anticipated decline in the construction sector depresses the figure. Government expenditure during the third plan is expected to total 783,000m. rials, of which 262,000m. for the development of economic resources, 130,000m. for education and training, 61,000m. for social welfare and 249,000m. for physical infrastructure.

Budget. The fiscal year runs from 1 Rajab to 30 Jumad II in the lunar calendar, and consequently starts approximately 10 days earlier each year. The 1983–84 budget envisaged expenditure of 260,000m. rials and revenue of 225,000m. rials.

Currency. The paper *rial* is divided into 100 *halalas*. In March 1985, £1 = 3·86 *rials*; US$1 = 3·60 *rials*.

Banking. There are 2 commercial banks of Saudi Arabian origin: the National Commercial Bank and the Riyadh Bank. It is government policy to encourage foreign banks operating in the kingdom to become Saudized. By 1982 there were 7 banks in which foreign capital represents only 40%: al Jazira Bank (National Bank of Pakistan), Saudi Dutch Bank (Algemene Bank Nederland), Saudi French Bank (Banque de l'Indochine et de Suez), Saudi British Bank (British Bank of the Middle East), Saudi Cairo Bank (Banque du Caire), the Saudi-American Bank (Citibank) and the Arab National Bank (Arab Bank of Jordan). All these banks are entitled to open branches nationwide.

In addition the Banque du Liban et d'Outremer and the Bank Melli in Jiddah and the United Bank (of Pakistan) in Dammam have invited subscription to an eighth bank that will operate by 1983.

ENERGY AND NATURAL RESOURCES

Electricity. 7,010m. kwh. was generated by the main electricity companies in 1977, 9,435m. kwh. in 1978 and 17,597m. kwh in 1980.

Oil. The first general geologic–geographical survey of Saudi Arabia was completed in 1961 under the joint sponsorship of the Saudi Arabian and US governments but surveying continues. Reserves (1984) 165,200m. bbls.

The original oil concession agreement was signed in 1933 with Standard Oil Co. of California. The name Aramco appeared in 1944, and by 1948 Exxon, Texaco and Mobil held shares in the company. In 1973 the Saudi Arabian Government acquired a 25% interest in Aramco. this became 60% in 1974, and in 1979 it was announced that the Government had taken full control of Aramco equity retroactively from Jan. 1976. By 1979 Aramco retained only 189,000 sq. km or 15·4% of the original concession areas.

Two other companies have concessions of Saudi Arabia's oil rights in the

Kuwait/Saudi Arabian Neutral Zone. Getty Oil's concession dates from 1953 and that of the Arabian Oil Co. (Japanese) from 1958.

Crude oil production in 1984 was 235m. tonnes. Crude oil exports in 1980 were 3,374m. bbls, of which Aramco provided 97·4%, Arabian Oil 1·94% and Getty Oil 0·6%. 1980 oil exports earned US$101,421m. (95m. for crude) and Aramco earned 98% of this total.

The agency responsible for co-ordination of national oil policy is Petromin (General Petroleum and Minerals Organization). Petromin manages exploration and concession agreements, oil refineries (except that of Aramco at Ras Tanura) and the distribution and marketing of oil and oil products.

In 1982, when Aramco produced 2,300m. bbls of crude oil, 55m. (2·38%) were sent by pipeline to Bahrain, and 1,500m. bbls (67·78%) were shipped out *via* Gulf terminals. The volume of crude exported will decline as the national refining capacity increases. In 1982 total refining capacity was 725,000 bbls per day including Ras Tanura (Aramco) 470,000 bbls per day, 120,000 bbls per day at Riyadh and 105,000 bbls per day at Jiddah (both Petromin). In 1982, 834,900 bbls per day of refined products were produced by Saudi Arabian refineries, of which fuel oil accounted for 382,700, gasoline, 194,000, Kerozene, 33,400.

About 3,000m. cu. ft per day of associated gas produced with crude oil is collected at gas-oil separator plants and piped to gas plants in the Eastern Province. There, impurities such as hydrogen sulfide are removed and a sweet, dry gas is extracted for use as an industrial fuel. From gas-processing centres at Shedgum and Uthmaniyah, the remaining natural gas liquids and ethane are piped to plants at Yanbu and Juaymah for fractionation. In 1981 Aramco produced 156m. bbls of natural gas liquids, obtained in association with crude production.

Water Resources. Intensive efforts are underway to provide adequate supplies of water for urban, industrial, rural and agricultural use. There is an important programme to tap non-renewable (3,450m. cu. metres per annum) and renewable (1,145m. cu. metres) water reserves by wells and small dams, and there are plans to reclaim urban waste water. Most investment however has gone into seawater desalination. By early 1982 14 plants in 10 towns had the capacity to produce 373,000 cu. metres per day and 5 more, totalling 1,143,000 cu. metres per day were under construction. Another 12, amounting to 554,000 cu. metres per day, were at various stages of planning.

Minerals. Surveys were launched during the second development plan to investigate potential mineral wealth other than oil. Deposits of several minerals including viable quantities of coal, iron and gold have been found. There are also reports of uranium deposits.

Agriculture. Since 1970 the Government has devoted huge resources to raise the Kingdom's agricultural potential, and spent substantially on desert reclamation, irrigation schemes, drainage and control of surface water and control of moving sands. Undeveloped land has been distributed to farmers and there are research and extension programmes. Large scale private investment has concentrated on meat, poultry and dairy production. Support finance from the Saudi Arabian Agricultural Bank in 1980 totalled 1,129m. rials, chiefly for equipment 223m., well drilling 196m. and purchases of poultry stock 121m.

Production, 1982 (in 1,000 tonnes) were: Alfalfa, 605; dates, 400; tomatoes, 19; sorghum, 110; water melons, 340; wheat, 400; dry onions, 60; grapes, 60. The use of greenhouses and hydroponics is increasing.

Livestock estimates for 1983 include 500,000 cattle, 110,000 asses, 160,000 camels, 3·5m. sheep and 2·3m. goats.

Fisheries. Total catch (1980) 24,000 tonnes.

INDUSTRY AND TRADE

Industry. The Government actively encourages the establishment of manufacturing industries in the country. The policy includes the provision of industrial estates and loans covering 50% of capital investment. The Government has also established two industrial poles at Jubail and Yanbu, to be the focus of heavy industrial development. Linked by gas and oil pipelines both are to have petrochemical complexes producing, initially, ethylene and methanol, for which agreements have been signed with American and Japanese companies. Six plants are under construction, to come on stream in 1985. In addition an integrated steel complex (German partners) and a urea fertilizer factory (Taiwanese), both in Jubail started production in 1983.

Commerce. Exports amounted to 261,000m. rials in 1982 and imports 139,355m. rials. In 1981 the USA was the main supplier, accounting for 21·4% of the total. Other major supplying countries were Japan (18·3%), Federal Republic of Germany (9·5%), Italy (6·2%) and the UK (6·2%). The main imports were machinery and electrical equipment (25·4%), metal articles (14·6%), transport equipment (14·4%) and foodstuffs (14·4%).

Total trade between Saudi Arabia and UK (British Department of Trade returns, in £1,000 sterling):

	1980	*1981*	*1982*	*1983*	*1984*
Imports to UK	1,927,583	1,892,605	1,447,775	897,702	545,149
Exports and re-exports from UK	1,050,145	1,133,921	1,361,665	1,478,587	1,387,163

Tourism. In 1984 there were nearly 2m. pilgrims to Mecca from abroad.

COMMUNICATIONS

Roads. All the main regions and population centres of the Kingdom are linked by asphalted roads, of which there were 22,501 km in 1981 and 28,586 km of graded, unpaved agricultural roads. An additional 12,492 km of roads were under construction including the Trans-Peninsula Expressway. There are road links with Yemen, Jordan, Kuwait and Qatar, and a causeway link to Bahrain is being built. In 1980 there were nearly 200,000 cars, over 142,000 commercial vehicles and about 4,500 buses.

Railways. A railway from Riyadh to Dammam on the Gulf (571 km, 1,435 mm gauge) *via* Dhahran and the oilfields Abqaiq, Ithmaniya (near Hofuf) and Haradh was completed in Oct. 1951. A 'dry port' at Riyadh station opened in 1981, and a new 465 km Dammam-Riyadh direct line was partially opened in 1984. There are plans to extend the line *via* Medina to Jiddah. That section of the Hejaz Railway which is in Saudi Arabian territory is not now in working order, but studies have been initiated to restore the whole line from Damascus to Medina. In 1981–82 railways carried 100m. passenger-km and 509m. tonne-km.

Aviation. Saudi Arabian Air Lines, a government-owned company operates regular internal air services, and international routes to Africa, the Middle East, Europe and the Far East, as well as special flights for pilgrims. There are 3 major international airports at Jiddah, Dhahran and Riyadh and 19 domestic airports. In 1981, 9·4m. passengers and 100,000 tonnes of cargo were carried.

Shipping. The ports of Dammam and Jubail on the Gulf and Jiddah, Yanbu and Jizan on the Red Sea had 101 deep-water piers at 31 Dec. 1981 and discharged 53·3m. freight tonnes.

Post and Broadcasting. Jiddah, Mecca, Taif, Riyadh and Dammam are linked by telephone, Jiddah and Cairo by radio-telephone. An international radio-telephone station at Riyadh was opened in 1956. Number of telephones (1982), 788,576. Number of post offices (1981) 437. In 1982 there were (estimate) 2·7m. radio receivers and 1·7m. television receivers.

Newspapers. In 1984 there were 8 daily newspapers in Arabic and 2 in English and 9 weekly or monthly magazines.

JUSTICE, RELIGION, EDUCATION AND WELFARE

Justice. The religious law of Islam is the common law of the land, and is administered by religious courts, at the head of which is a chief judge, who is responsible for the Department of Sharia (legal) Affairs.

Religion. About 85% are Sunni Moslems and 15% Shiites.

Education. Administration is in educational districts. Schooling is in three stages, primary, intermediate and secondary which is to prepare older pupils for university; pre-primary schools are being introduced. Education is free in all these stages; monthly scholarships are paid to students in higher education. Girls' education is separate. In 1981 there were 184 pre-primary schools with 27,843 pupils, 5,744 primary schools with 930,436 pupils and 50,010 teachers, and 2,181 intermediate/secondary schools with 377,681 students and 24,866 teachers. There were also adult literacy classes (136,103 students, 35% women), and special schools for 1,971 handicapped children. There were 107 teacher-training schools in 1980.

In 1981 there were 18 vocational centres, where 3,684 primary school graduates were instructed in basic trades. There were also 5 technical and 8 commercial secondary schools, taking 5,418 intermediate school graduates, and 4 industrial, one agricultural and 2 commercial higher institutes (1,466 students).

University courses concentrating on science, engineering, agriculture and medicine, but also covering education, commerce and arts, are available at the Riyadh University, King Abdul Aziz University, Jiddah, and King Faisal University, Dammam and Hofuf. New general universities are to be created in Abha and Mecca. Specialized engineering studies are available at the University of Petroleum and Minerals, Dhahran, and Arabic and Sharia law studies at the Islamic University, Medina and the Imam Muhammad bin Saud University, Riyadh. There were 54,397 university students (about 19% women) in 1981.

Welfare. The Ministry of Health is responsible for medical services, serving both Saudi citizens, foreign residents and pilgrims. In 1979 there were 65 hospitals with 10,978 beds, 824 clinics and health centres, 2,883 doctors, 5,159 nurses and midwives, 1,247 pharmacists and assistants and 1,161 X-ray and laboratory technicians. There were also 25 private hospitals (2,019 beds) and 22 private clinics employing 666 doctors. Five new hospitals with 2,275 beds opened in 1980 and a further five with 900 beds in 1981. In 1982 33 hospitals (7,112 beds) were under construction and another 11 (4,150 beds) were projected. The Jiddah Quarantine Centre, designed by WHO and primarily for pilgrims, can take 2,400 patients. In 1980 there were 7 schools for female nurses and 4 institutes for male trainees. There is a strict system of health controls for visiting pilgrims and strict supervision of sanitation and water supply.

DIPLOMATIC REPRESENTATIVES

Of Saudi Arabia in Great Britain (30 Belgrave Sq., London, SW1X 8QB)
Ambassador; Sheikh Nasser H. Almanaour, GCVO.

Of Great Britain in Saudi Arabia (PO Box 393, Jiddah)
Ambassador: Sir Patrick Wright, KCMG.

Of Saudi Arabia in the USA (601 New Hampshire Ave., NW, Washington, D.C., 20037)
Ambassador: HRH Prince Bandar bin Sultan.

Of the USA in Saudi Arabia (Palestine Rd., Ruwais, Jiddah)
Ambassador: Walter L. Cutler.

Of Saudi Arabia to the United Nations
Ambassador: Samir Shihabi.

Books of Reference

The Gulf Handbook. Bath (annual)
Anderson, N., *The Kingdom of Saudi Arabia.* (Rev. ed.). London, 1982
Clements, F. A., *Saudi Arabia.* [Bibliography] Oxford and Santa Barbara, 1979
Hajrah, H. H., *Land Distribution in Saudi Arabia.* London, 1982
Helms, C. M., *The Cohesion of Saudi Arabia.* Baltimore, 1981
Hobday, P., *Saudi Arabia Today: An Introduction to the Richest Oil Power.* London, 1978
Holden, D. and Johns, R., *The House of Saud.* London and New York, 1981
Looney, R. E., *Saudi Arabia's Development Potential.* Lexington, 1982
McMaster, B., *The Definitive Guide to Living in Saudi Arabia.* London, 1980
Niblock, T., *State, Society and Economy in Saudi Arabia.* New York, 1981
Presley, J. R., *A Guide to the Saudi Arabian Economy.* London, 1984
Quandt, W. B., *Saudi Arabia in the 1980's: Foreign Policy, Security and Oil.* Washington, 1981
Stacey International (ed.) *The Kingdom of Saudi Arabia.* (4th ed.) London, 1979

SENEGAL

Capital: Dakar
Population: 6·3m. (1984)
GNP per capita: US$430 (1981)

République du Sénégal

HISTORY. France established a fort at Saint-Louis in 1659 and later acquired other coastal settlements from the Dutch; the interior was occupied in 1854–65. Senegal became a territory of French West Africa in 1902 and an autonomous state within the French Community on 25 Nov. 1958. On 4 April 1959 Senegal joined with French Sudan to form the Federation of Mali, which achieved independence on 20 June 1960, but on 22 Aug. Senegal withdrew from the Federation and became a separate independent republic. Senegal was a one-Party state from 1966 until 1974, when a pluralist system was re-established. Léopold Sédar Senghor, President since independence, resigned on 31 Dec. 1980 and was succeeded by his Prime Minister, Abdou Diouf. From 1 Feb. 1982 Senegal joined with Gambia to form a Confederation of Senegambia.

AREA AND POPULATION. Senegal is bounded by Mauritania to the north and north-east, Mali to the east, Guinea and Guinea-Bissau to the south and the Atlantic to the west with The Gambia forming an enclave along that shore. The republic has a total area of 196,192 sq. km; the population (census, 1976) 5,085,388 (estimate, 1984) 6,274,000.

The areas (in sq. km), Census populations and capitals of the 8 regions are:

Region	*sq. km*	*1976 Census*	*Capital*	*1979 Estimate*
Cap-Vert	550	981,660	Dakar	978,553
Casamance	28,350	736,527	Ziguinchor	79,464
Diourbel	33,547	425,113	Diourbel	55,307
Louga		417,137	Louga	...
Fleuve	44,127	528,473	Saint-Louis	96,594
Sénégal-Oriental	57,602	286,148	Tambacounda	...
Sine-Saloum	23,945	1,007,736	Kaolack	115,679
Thiès	6,601	698,994	Thiès	126,886

In July 1984, 2 more regions were created.

Ethnic groups are the Wolof (29% of the population), Serer (17%), Fulani (17%), Tukulor (10%), Diola (8%), Malinke (6%), Bambara (6%) and Sarakole (2%).

CLIMATE. A tropical climate with wet and dry seasons. The rains fall almost exclusively in the hot season, from June to Oct., with high humidity. Dakar. Jan. 72°F (22·2°C), July 82°F (27·8°C). Annual rainfall 22″ (541 mm).

CONSTITUTION AND GOVERNMENT. Under the Constitution promulgated on 7 Mar. 1963 (as subsequently amended) there are simultaneous elections by universal adult suffrage for 5-year terms for both the Presidency and for the unicameral 120-member National Assembly; for the latter 60 members are elected in single-member constituencies and 60 by a form of proportional representation.

In the general election of Feb. 1983 the *Parti socialiste* gained 111 seats, the *Parti démocratique sénégalais* 8 seats and the *Rassemblement national democratique* 1.

On 14 Nov. 1981, President Diouf of Senegal and President Jawara of The Gambia issued a joint communiqué proposing the establishment of a confederation, to be known as Senegambia. Both parliaments ratified the agreement at the end of the year. The instruments of ratification were exchanged in Banjul on 11 Jan. 1982 and the Confederation formally came into existence on 1 Feb.

The agreement stated that each confederal state shall maintain its independence and sovereignty and calls for the integration of the armed security forces, economic and monetary union, co-operation in the fields of communications and external relations, and the establishment of joint institutions (*i.e.* President, Vice President, Council of Ministers, Confederal Parliament). The President of the Confederation would be President Diouf, and the Vice President President Jawara, The Confederal Parliament would have one third Gambian representation and two thirds Senegalese.

President Jawara said in Nov. 1981 that 'the Confederation would not compromise any of the agreements which link The Gambia direct to Britain and the rest of the Commonwealth'.

President of the Republic: Abdou Diouf (took office in Jan. 1981, re-elected Feb. 1983).

The Council of Ministers was composed as follows in Jan. 1985:

Foreign Affairs: Ibrahima Fall. *Defence:* Medoune Fall. *Interior:* Ibrahima Wone. *Finance and Economic Affairs:* Mamadou Touré. *Supply:* Robert Sagna. *Culture:* Abdel Kader Fall. *Education:* Iba der Thiam. *Rural Development:* Bator Diop. *Industrial Development and Handicrafts:* Serigne Lamine Diop. *Scientific and Technical Research:* Moussa Daffe. *Housing and Urban Affairs:* Hamidou Sakho. *Commerce:* Abdourahmane Touré. *Planning and Co-operation:* Cheikh Amidou Kané. *Information and Telecommunications:* Djibo Ka. *Justice and Keeper of the Seals:* Doudou Ndoye. *Civil Service, Employment and Labour:* André Sonko. *Public Health:* Mamadou Diop. *Social Affairs:* Mme. Maïmouna Kané. *Water Resources:* Samba Yella Diop. *Youth and Sports:* François Bob. *Environment:* Cheikh Cissokho. *Emmigration:* Mme. Fambaye Fall Diop. *Tourism:* Momar Talla Cisse. *Secretaries of State:* Landing Sané *(Decentralisation)*, Mme. Marie Sarr Mbodj *(Technical and Professional Training)*, Bocar Diallo *(Rural Development and Fisheries)*, Thierno Bâ *(Employment)*.

National flag: Three vertical strips of green, yellow, red, with a green star in the centre.

The official language is French.

Local Government. Senegal is divided into 10 *régions,* each with an appointed governor and an elected regional assembly. They are divided into 28 *départements,* each under an appointed *Préfet,* and thence into 99 *arrondissements.*

DEFENCE. There is selective conscription.

Army. The Army had a strength of 8,500 (1985), organized in 5 infantry battalions, 1 engineer battalion, 1 reconnaissance squadron and minor units. Equipment includes about 50 armoured cars. There is also a paramilitary force of some 7,000 men.

Navy. The flotilla includes 1 patrol vessel, 3 patrol craft, 3 fast gunboats, 19 small patrol craft, 1 fishery protection trawler, 4 coastal patrol launches, 1 landing craft, 2 minor amphibious craft, 12 service craft, 1 tug and 1 training tender. Personnel (1985) 350.

Air Force. The Senegal Air Force, formed with French assistance, has 1 Summit O2-337 Sentry counter-insurgency aircraft, 4 Rallye Guerrier armed trainers, 2 Magister jet trainers, 1 Boeing 727 and 1 Caravelle VIP transports, 5 DC-3/C-47 transports, 6 F.27 and 1 Twin Otter twin-turboprop transports, 2 Broussard liaison aircraft, 3 Puma, 1 Gazelle and 2 Alouette II helicopters. Personnel total about 500.

INTERNATIONAL RELATIONS

Membership. Senegal is a member of UN, OAU and is an ACP state of EEC.

ECONOMY

Planning. The sixth 4-year Development Plan (1981–85) provides 667,000m. francs CFA for investment in mineral exploration, tourism, cotton, fishing, livestock, seed selection, rice growing and fertilizers.

Budget. The budget for 1983–84 balanced at 273,984m. francs CFA.

Currency. The currency is the *franc* CFA, with a parity value of 50 *francs* CFA to 1 French *franc.*

Banking. The bank of issue is the *Banque Centrale des États de l'Afrique de l'Ouest.* The principal commercial bank is the *Union Sénégalaise de la Banque pour le Commerce et l'Industrie* (established 1961 with assistance from Crédit Lyonnais) in which the Senegalese government has the majority share-holding; also state controlled is the *Banque Nationale de Développement du Sénégal.* There are 3 private banks.

At 31 Dec. 1981 the savings banks had deposits of 85,120m. francs CFA.

ENERGY AND NATURAL RESOURCES

Electricity. Production (1979) was 636m. kwh.

Minerals. Extraction of phosphate rock in 1980 amounted to 1,756,100 tonnes. Titanium ores and zirconium are extracted from coastal (sand) deposits. Iron ore deposits amounting to an estimated 980m. tonnes have been located at La Faleme.

Agriculture. 80% of the labour force is engaged in agriculture. The main food crops (1981 production in 1,000 tonnes) are millet (750), sugar-cane (600), rice (120), maize (55), cassava and sorghum, while the primary cash crop is groundnuts (1,980).

Livestock (1983): 3·15m. sheep and goats, 2·25m. cattle, 150,000 pigs, 240,000 asses, 6,000 camels and 220,000 horses.

Forestry. Production (1981) amounted to 2·9m. cu. metres.

Fisheries. The 1982 catch totalled 226,481 tonnes; exports, 91,742 tonnes.

INDUSTRY AND TRADE

Industry. Dakar has numerous industrial works. A major ship-repairing complex has been constructed there for vessels of up to 28,000 tonnes. Cement production (1980) 371,300 tonnes; petroleum products, 726,400, groundnut oil, 125,200.

Trade Unions. There are two major unions, the *Union Nationale des Travailleurs Sénégalais* (government-controlled) and the *Conféderation Nationale des Travailleurs Sénégalais* (independent) which broke away from the former in 1969.

Commerce. In 1982 imports totalled 320,200m. francs CFA and exports 156,900m. francs CFA. In 1981 37% of imports came from France and 25% of exports went to France; petroleum products provided 24% of exports, fisheries 22%, phosphates 14% and peanut oil 5%.

Total trade between Senegal and UK (British Department of Trade returns, in £1,000 sterling):

	1980	*1981*	*1982*	*1983*	*1984*
Imports to UK	15,440	17,430	14,196	22,333	23,789
Exports and re-exports from UK	16,030	26,276	22,349	13,212	15,772

Tourism. In 1979, 198,433 tourists visited Senegal.

COMMUNICATIONS

Roads. The length of roads (1981) was 14,500 km of which 3,400 km was bitumenized. In 1978 there were 65,507 passenger cars and 9,558 commercial vehicles.

Railways. There are 5 railway lines: Dakar-Kidira (continuing in Mali), Thiès-Saint-Louis (193 km), Guinguinéo-Kaolack (22 km), Louga-Linguère (129 km), and Diourbel-Touba (46 km). Total length (1979), 1,186 km (metre gauge). In 1979–80 railways carried 732,000 passengers and 1·7m. tonnes of freight.

Aviation. In 1979 aircraft disembarked 297,170 and embarked 322,921 passengers and disembarked 7,676 tonnes and embarked 5,605 tonnes of freight at Yoff (Dakar).

Shipping. In 1978, 4,870 vessels entered the port of Dakar. There is a river service on the Senegal from Saint-Louis to Podor (363 km) open throughout the year, and to Kayes (924 km) open from July to Oct. The Senegal River is closed to foreign flags. The Saloum River is navigable as far as Kaolack, the Casamance River as far as Ziguinchor.

Post and Broadcasting. There were, in 1972, 74 post offices. Telephones in 1978 numbered 42,105, of which 33,863 were in Dakar. In 1981 there were 2 radio networks with 300,000 radio receivers and 2 television stations with 4,000 receivers.

Cinemas. In 1975 there were 77 with a seating capacity of 33,500.

Newspapers. The main daily is *Le Soleil,* circulation (1984) 30,000.

JUSTICE, RELIGION, EDUCATION AND WELFARE

Justice. There are *juges de paix* in each *département* and a court of first instance in each region. Assize courts are situated in Dakar, Kaolack, Saint-Louis and Ziguinchor, while the Court of Appeal resides in Dakar.

Religion. The population (1980) was 91% Moslem, 6% Christian (mainly Roman Catholic) and 3% animist.

Education. Secondary education is provided at 11 *lycées,* 66 *collèges d'enseignement secondaire, 2 lycées techniques,* 2 *écoles normales* and 3 *cours normaux.* Total pupils in the elementary schools in 1979 was 370,412, including 44,262 attending private schools; in the secondary schools, 82,631 (of whom 15,969 attend private colleges). The University in Dakar established on 24 Feb. 1957, had 9,549 students in 1982–83. A second university was being built (1985) at St Louis.

Health. In 1976 there were 43 hospitals with 6,025 beds; and in 1978, 391 doctors, 50 dentists, 116 pharmacists, 550 midwives and 3,193 nursing personnel.

DIPLOMATIC REPRESENTATIVES

Of Senegal in Great Britain (11 Phillimore Gdns., London, W8 7QG)
Ambassador: Gen. Idrissa Fall, MBE (accredited 1 Nov. 1984)

Of Great Britain in Senegal (20 Rue du Docteur Guillet, Dakar)
Ambassador: P. L. O'Keeffe, CMG, CVO.

Of Senegal in the USA (2112 Wyoming Ave., NW, Washington, D.C., 20008)
Ambassador: Falilou Kane.

Of the USA in Senegal (Ave. Jean XXIII, Dakar)
Ambassador: Charles W. Bray, III.

Of Senegal to the United Nations
Ambassador: Massamba Sarré

Books of Reference

Crowder, M., *Senegal: A Study in French Assimilation.* OUP, 1962
Gellar, S., *Senegal.* Boulder, 1982.—*Senegal: An African Nation between Islam and the West.* Aldershot, 1983
Samb, M. (ed.), *Spotlight on Senegal.* Dakar, 1972

SEYCHELLES

Capital: Victoria
Population: 64,718 (1984)
GNP per capita: US$1,800 (1981)

HISTORY. The islands were first colonized by the French in 1768, in order to establish plantations of spices to compete with the Dutch monopoly. They were captured by the English in 1794 and incorporated as a dependency of Mauritius in 1814. In Nov. 1903 the Seychelles archipelago became a separate colony. Internal self-government was achieved on 1 Oct. 1975 and independence as a republic within the Commonwealth on 29 June 1976. The first President, James Mancham, was deposed in a *coup* on 5 June 1977 and replaced by his Prime Minister.

AREA AND POPULATION. The Seychelles consists of 112 islands and islets in the Indian ocean, north of Madagascar, with a combined area of 156 sq. miles (444 sq. km) within two distinct groups. The Mahé or Granitic group of 40 islands cover 87 sq. miles (234 sq. km); the principal island is Mahé, with 56 sq. miles (144 sq. km) and 45,204 inhabitants at the 1971 census, the other inhabited islands of the group being Praslin, La Digue, Silhouette, Frigate and North, which together have 6,660 inhabitants.

The Outer or Coralline group comprises 60 islands spread over a wide area of ocean between the Mahé group and Madagascar, with a total land area of 69 sq. miles and a population of less than 1,000. The main islands are the Amirante Isles (including Desroches, Poivre, Daros and Alphonse), Coetivy Island and Platte Island, all lying south of the Mahé group; the Farquhar, St Pierre and Providence Islands, north of Madagascar; and Aldabra, Astove, Assumption and the Cosmoledo Islands, about 1,000 km south-west of the Mahé group. Aldabra (whose lagoon covers 55 sq. miles), Farquhar and Desroches were transferred to the new British Indian Ocean Territory in 1965, but were returned by Britain to the Seychelles on the latter's independence in 1976. Population (1984, estimate) 64,718.

Vital statistics (1983): Births, 1,662; deaths, 452.

CLIMATE. Though close to the equator, the climate is tropical. The hot, wet season is from Dec. to May, when conditions are humid, but south-east trades bring cooler conditions from June to Nov. Temperatures are high throughout the year, but the islands lie outside the cyclone belt. Victoria. Jan. 80°F (26·7°C), July 78°F (25·6°C). Annual rainfall 95″ (2,375 mm).

CONSTITUTION AND GOVERNMENT. A new Constitution came into force on 5 June 1979, under which the Seychelles People's Progressive Front is the sole legal Party and nominates all candidates for election. There is a unicameral People's Assembly comprising 23 members elected for 4 years with 2 further nominated members. There is an Executive President directly elected for a 5-year term, who nominates and leads a Council of Ministers.

The official languages are Creole, English and French but 95% of the population speak Creole.

President, Minister of Administration, Finance, Industry and Transport: Hon. France Albert René.

Foreign Affairs and Economic Planning: Dr Maxime Ferrari. *Development:* Jacques Hodoul. *Health:* Esmé Jumeau. *Labour and Social Security:* Joseph Belmont. *Education and Information:* Maj. James Michel. *Youth and Defence:* Ogilvy Berlouis.

National flag: Divided horizontally red over green by a wavy white stripe, with red of double width.

DEFENCE. A People's Liberation Army was created in 1977. Personnel (1985) 750 organized in 1 infantry battalion and 1 artillery troop.

INTERNATIONAL RELATIONS

Membership. Seychelles is a member of UN, the Commonwealth, OAU and is an ACP state of EEC.

ECONOMY

Budget, in 1m. rupees, for calender years:

	1980	*1981*	*1982*	*1983*[1]
Recurrent revenue	407·0	380·2	384·3	386·9
Recurrent expenditure	399·5	376·6	410·0	434·6

[1] Provisional.

Currency. The currency is the Seychelles *rupee.* In March 1985, £1 = 8 *rupees;* US$1 = 7·62 *rupees.*

Banking. Barclays Bank International, Standard Bank, Bank of Credit and Commerce, Banque Francaise Commerçiale, Habib Bank, Bank of Baroda and Seychelles Development Bank, have branches in Victoria, Mahé.

ENERGY AND NATURAL RESOURCES

Electricity. Production (1983) 56·7m. kwh.

Agriculture. Chief crops (production 1983, in tonnes) are copra (2,686), cinnamon bark (877) and tea (131). Food crop production is being increased for home consumption and fishing is actively pursued mainly for home consumption but also for export as frozen fish.

Livestock (1983): Cattle, 2,000; pigs, 13,000; goats, 4,000.

INDUSTRY AND TRADE

Industry. Local industry is expanding, the largest development in recent years being the brewery, (output, 1983, 3,872,000 litres), but steel fabricated goods, furniture, plastics, soap manufacturing form a growing element. In 1983, 3,370,000 litres of soft drinks and 51·6m. cigarettes were produced.

Commerce. Total trade, in rupees, for calendar years:

	1980	*1981*	*1982*	*1983*
Imports (less re-exports)	631,400,000	589,000,000	641,300,000	595,100,000
Domestic exports	32,900,000	27,500,000	20,400,000	25,200,000

Principal imports (1983): Manufactured goods, Rs 153·2m.; food, Rs 105·6m.; petroleum products, Rs 127·9m., machinery and transport equipment, Rs 135·8m. Principal exports (1983): Copra, Rs 11·3m.; frozen fish, Rs 9·9m.; cinnamon bark, Rs 3m.

Total trade between Seychelles and UK (British Department of Trade returns, in £1,000 sterling):

	1982	*1983*	*1984*
Imports to UK	696	615	586
Exports and re-exports from UK	10,086	7,502	7,540

Tourism. Tourism has now established itself as an important sector of the economy. The number of visitors has grown very rapidly since the opening of the international airport in 1978 and in 1979 there were 78,852, but the rapid growth has been reversed in 1983 (55,867) and 1982 (47,280).

COMMUNICATIONS

Roads. There is a good system of tarmac (154 km) and earth roads (105 km) in Mahé; extensive roadmaking is being undertaken.

Aviation. British Airways operates 1 service a week between London and Seychelles, and once a week from Johannesburg. Air France and Seychelles International Safari Airline operate 2 services a week. British Caledonian and Air Tanzania operate a weekly service. Kenya Airways operates a service 3 times a week. In 1982 aircraft movements were 1,722; passenger movements, 206,000 (including domestic flights); freight loaded, 195 tonnes, unloaded, 775 tonnes.

Shipping. Shipping (1983), goods unloaded, 163,500 tonnes, goods loaded, 5,000 tonnes. There are regular cargo vessels from Australia and the Far East, South Africa and Europe. The vessel *Cinq Juin* travels to and from Mauritius and visits the outlying islands.

Post and Broadcasting. Services operated by Cable & Wireless Ltd provide telegraphic communications with all parts of the world by satellite, the company's radio-telephone service also extends to all principal countries in the world. In 1978, an automatic dialling telex system was introduced. Telephones in Jan. 1983 numbered 4,512. There are 2 radio stations and (1983) 18,000 receivers.

Cinemas. In 1983 there were 3 cinemas with seating capacity of 1,038.

JUSTICE, RELIGION, EDUCATION AND WELFARE

Justice. The police force numbered 492 all ranks and 69 special constabulary.

Religion. 90% of the inhabitants are Roman Catholic and 8% Anglican.

Education. Equality of educational opportunity exists for all children for a minimum of 9 years. In Jan. 1983 there were 25 primary schools, 2 secondary schools and 1 Polytechnic school with 10 departments.

In Jan. 1983 there were 14,456 pupils in primary schools, 2,603 pupils in junior secondary and secondary grammar schools and 974 students in the Polytechnic. In 1983, a total of 239 students were undergoing training overseas, mainly in the UK; 153 were in university, 39 teacher-training and 6 nursing.

Health. In 1983 there were 43 doctors, 278 nurses and 352 hospital beds.

DIPLOMATIC REPRESENTATIVES

Of Seychelles in Great Britain (50 Conduit St., London, W1A 4PE)
High Commissioner: Danielle de St Jorre (accredited 27 July 1983).

Of Great Britain in Seychelles (Victoria Hse., Victoria)
High Commissioner: C. G. Mays.

Of Seychelles in the USA and to the United Nations
Ambassador: Giovinella Gonthier.

Of the USA in Seychelles (Victoria Hse., Victoria)
Ambassador: David J. Fischer.

Books of Reference

Statistical Information: Information Office, 52 Kingsgate House, Victoria, Mahé.
Report of Seychelles Constitutional Conference. HMSO, 1970
Agricultural Survey 1980. Government Printer
Benedict, M., and Benedict, B., *Men, Women and Money in Seychelles.* Univ. of California Press, 1983
Franda, M., *The Seychelles: Unquiet Islands.* Boulder, 1982
Lionnet, G., *The Seychelles.* Newton Abbot, 1972
Mancham, J. R., *Paradise Raped. Life, Love and Power in the Seychelles.* London, 1983

SIERRA LEONE

Capital: Freetown
Population: 3·35m. (1982)
GNP per capita: US$320 (1981)

HISTORY. The Colony of Sierra Leone originated in the sale and cession, in 1787, by native chiefs to English settlers, of a piece of land intended as a home for natives of Africa who were waifs in London, and later it was used as a settlement for Africans rescued from slave-ships. The hinterland was declared a British protectorate on 21 Aug. 1896. Sierra Leone became independent as a member state of the Commonwealth on 27 April 1961, and a republic on 19 April 1971.

AREA AND POPULATION. Sierra Leone is bounded on the north-west, north and north-east by the Republic of Guinea, on the south-east by Liberia and on the south-west by the Atlantic ocean. The coastline extends from the boundary of the Republic of Guinea to the north of the mouth of the Great Scarcies River to the boundary of Liberia at the mouth of the Mano River, a distance of about 212 miles (341 km). The area of Sierra Leone is 27,925 sq. miles (73,326 sq. km). Population (census 1982), 3,354,000, of whom about 2,000 are Europeans, 3,500 Asiatics and 30,000 non-native Africans. Estimate (1982) 3,354,000. The capital is Freetown, with 316,312 inhabitants.

Vital statistics (1983); Live births, 58,987; deaths, 22,894.

Sierra Leone is divided into 3 regions and the Western Area:

	Sq. km	*Estimate 1976*	*Capital*	*Census 1974*
Western Area	663	400,000	Freetown	314,350
Southern region	20,378	744,000	Bo	597,000
Eastern region	15,219	970,000	Kenema	773,500
Northern region	36,066	1,126,000	Makeni	1,046,000

The principal peoples are the Temnes, Limbas, Lokos and Korankos in the north, the Temnes in the centre, the Mendis in the south, and the Kissis and Konos in the east.

CLIMATE. A tropical climate, with marked wet and dry seasons and high temperatures throughout the year. The rainy season lasts from about April to Nov., when humidity can be very high. Thunderstorms are common from April to June and in Sept. and Oct. Rainfall is particularly heavy at Freetown because of the effect of neighbouring relief. Freetown. Jan. 80°F (26·7°C), July 78°F (25·6°C). Annual rainfall 135″ (3,434 mm).

CONSTITUTION AND GOVERNMENT. For earlier Constitutional history *see* THE STATESMAN'S YEAR-BOOK 1978–79, p. 1046. Following a referendum in June 1978, a new Constitution was instituted under which the ruling All People's Congress (APC) became the sole legal Party. The 104-member Parliament elected in May–June 1982 comprised 85 members all belonging to the APC, 12 Paramount Chiefs representing the 12 districts and 7 members appointed by the President.

President: Dr Siaka Probyn Stevens.
Vice-Presidents: Sorie Ibrahim Koroma, Francis M. Minah.
Finance: Dr Abdulai Conteh.
Foreign Affairs: Dr Sheka Kanu.

National flag: Three horizontal stripes of green, white, blue.

Local Government. The regions are administered through the Ministry of Internal Affairs and divided into 148 Chiefdoms, each under the control of a Paramount Chief and Council of Elders known as the Tribal Authorities, who are responsible for the maintenance of law and order and for the administration of justice (except for serious crimes). All of these Chiefdoms have been organized into local government units, empowered to raise and disburse funds for the development of the Chiefdom concerned.

DEFENCE

Army. The Army consists of 2 infantry battalions, 2 artillery batteries and 1 engineer squadron. Strength (1985), 3,000 officers and men.

Navy. There are 1 fast attack craft, 1 gunboat, 1 coastal patrol craft and 3 landing craft. Personnel did not exceed (1984), 150.

Air Force. The nucleus of an air arm for the defence forces came into existence in 1973. It operates currently a single MBB BO 105 helicopter. Personnel, about 30.

INTERNATIONAL RELATIONS

Membership. Sierra Leone is a member of UN, OAU, ECOWAS, the Commonwealth, the Mano River Union and is an ACP state of EEC.

ECONOMY

Planning. A 5-year plan (1974–79) was launched to develop industry and plantation agriculture but failed its main objectives.

Budget. Revenue and expenditure (in 1,000 leone) for years ending 30 June:

	1978–79	*1979–80*	*1980–81*	*1981–82*	*1982–83*	*1983–84*
Revenue	173,875	195,946	216,736	182,644	243,300	327,900
Expenditure	168,151	205,964	236,045	312,462	480,000	537,900

Currency. The Bank of Sierra Leone, which was established on 4 Aug. 1964, is responsible for providing the currency in the country. It introduced on 4 Aug. 1964 a decimal currency, the *leone* and the *cent*. The paper currency consists of 1, 2, 5, 10 and 20 *leone* and 50-*cent* notes; the coinage of 1, 5, 10, 20 and 50 *cents*.

At 30 June 1982 total Sierra Leone notes and coins in circulation was Le. 91·75m. In March 1985, £1 = 6·45 *leone*; US$1 = 6 *leone*.

Banking. The Standard Bank Sierra Leone, the National Commercial Bank, International Bank of Credit and Commerce, International Bank of Trade and Industry and Barclays Bank Sierra Leone have their headquarters at Freetown; the Standard Bank has 14, Barclays Bank 12 and the National Commercial Bank, 8 branches and agencies.

The Post Office Savings Bank had 94,910 depositors with total credit balance of nearly Le. 3,455,469 in 1983.

NATURAL RESOURCES

Electricity. Production (1981) 235m. kwh.

Minerals. The chief minerals mined are diamonds (303,000 carats, 1983), bauxite (701,400 tonnes, 1983–84), gold (12,200 oz., 1983–84 and rutile (35,000 tons, 1982). Molybdenite is being prospected. Rutile production started in 1979; potential production 100,000 tonnes per annum. Iron ore production was resumed in Feb. 1983 at Marampa by a new company, Austro Minerals, with a production of 417 tonnes.

Agriculture. In the western area farming is largely confined to the production of cassava and garden crops, such as maize, vegetables and mangoes, for local consumption. In the provincial areas the principal products include rice, which is the staple food of the country, cassava, groundnuts and export crops such as palm-kernels, cocoa beans, coffee, ginger and piassava. Cattle production is important in the northern part of the country, and most of the poultry, eggs and pork are produced in the Western Area. Production (1982, in 1,000 tonnes): Rice, 550; cassava, 95; palm oil, 48; palm kernels, 30; coffee, 11; cocoa, 10.

Livestock (1983): Cattle, 351,000; goats, 168,000; sheep, 320,000; chickens, 4m.

Fisheries. The estimated tonnage of catch of all species of fish during 1982 was 121,909 tonnes. The FAO has carried out a 5-year survey of pelagic fish resources along the coastline and continental shelf.

Total catch of fish is still below the demand of the country. In 1980, 247 tonnes of fish value Le. 483,488 were imported.

INDUSTRY AND TRADE

Industry. Four pioneer oil-mills for the expressing of palm-oil are operated by the Sierra Leone Produce Marketing Board. Government also operates 4 rice-mills, and there are a number of privately owned mills. At Kenema the Government Forest Industries Corporation produces sawn timber, joinery products (including prefabricated buildings) and high-class furniture. In addition, there is a smaller privately owned saw-mill at Panguma and several small furniture workshops are used internally. Village industries include fishing, fish curing and smoking, weaving and hand methods of expressing palm-oil and cracking palm kernels.

Labour. A large proportion of the population is engaged in agriculture and about 125,000 workers are in wage-earning employment. The number of workers in establishments employing 6 or more persons was 64,092 in 1982, distributed as follows: Services, 24,142; mining and quarrying, 6,170; transport, storage and communications, 4,814; construction, 9,721; commerce, 6,870; manufacturing, 9,407; agriculture, forestry and fishing, 5,834; electricity and water services, 24,142.

Commerce. Total trade (in 1,000 leone) for calendar years:

	1977	*1978*	*1979*	*1980*	*1981*	*1982*
Imports	206,228	290,844	333,920	447,476	360,440	368,473
Exports	156,734	194,000	201,251	220,797	168,576	133,245

Of the imports (1980) 22% came from the UK, 9% from Japan and 7% from Federal Republic of Germany. Of the exports (1980), 41% went to the UK, 11% to the USA, 8% to the Netherlands and 7% to Switzerland; diamonds formed 45%, coffee 13% and cocoa 13%.

Total trade between Sierra Leone and UK (British Department of Trade returns, in £1,000 sterling):

	1980	*1981*	*1982*	*1983*	*1984*
Imports to UK	65,697	43,303	14,438	17,710	25,971
Exports and re-exports from UK	36,785	24,591	19,110	13,735	19,532

Tourism. Tourism is being developed and was a major growth industry in 1983.

COMMUNICATIONS

Roads. There were (1977) about 4,406 miles of main roads, of which 665 miles are surfaced with bitumen.

Motor vehicles licensed in 1982 totalled 47,796; passenger cars, 27,925; buses and trucks, 3,801, and motor cycles, 9,018.

Railways (1983). The government railway closed in 1974, and an 84-km mineral line of 1,067-mm gauge connecting Marampa with the port of Pepel has been rehabilitated.

Aviation. Freetown Airport (Lungi), situated north of Freetown in the Port Loko District, is the only international airport in Sierra Leone.

The airport is served by Sierra Leone Airlines, Ghana/Nigeria Airways, British Caledonian, Union de Transport Aériens, KLM, Air Afrique and Aeroflot. A once weekly non-stop flight from London (Gatwick) to Freetown and *vice versa* is also provided.

Sierra Leone Airlines provide domestic flights daily (except Sundays) from Hastings (14 miles from Freetown) to Gbangbatoke, Bo, Kenema, Yengema, twice weekly to Bonthe and occasional flights to Marampa and Port Loko on charter basis.

Shipping. During 1982 the total imports handled by the port of Freetown amounted to 444,642 freight-tons and exports 61,078 freight-tons; a total of 576 vessels called at Freetown; 564 were cargo vessels and 12 were tourist ships with a total of 718 passengers. Freetown imports handled (1982), 444,642 freight-tons.

Bonthe-Sherbro, 80 miles south of Freetown, is used for the shipment of rutile and bauxite. Pepel lies some 12 miles from Freetown and exports iron ore.

Post and Broadcasting. The Posts and Telecommunications Department maintains a trunk network of radio and overhead telephone and telegraph routes of approximately 3,000 miles linking the Western Area with the other regions. Automatic telephone exchanges have been introduced at the regional centres of Bo, Kenema and Makeni; microwave radio relay link now replaces overhead open wire on main trunk routes. An extension programme to link important mining areas at Koidu, Mokanji and Pepel to the national network by microwave links has been established.

The wired broadcasting relay service was replaced in Jan. 1964 by a transistor radio service. Approximately 20,000 transistor radios purchased under this scheme are now in service.

Number of telephones (1981) 220,000. Telegraphic facilities are provided at 58 offices.

There were (1983) 37 post offices and 76 postal agencies.

The number of private wireless-licence holders (1981, estimate) was 500,000 and 20,000 television sets were in operation.

JUSTICE, RELIGION, EDUCATION AND WELFARE

Justice. The High Court has jurisdiction in civil and criminal matters. Subordinate courts are held by magistrates in the various districts. Native Courts, headed by court Chairmen, apply native law and custom under a criminal and civil jurisdiction. Appeals from the decisions of magistrates' courts are heard by the High Court. Appeals from the decisions of the High Court are heard by the Sierra Leone Court of Appeal. Appeal lies from the Sierra Leone Court of Appeal to the Supreme Court which is the highest court.

Police. The police force at 31 Dec. 1982 had an authorized strength of 136 superior police officers, 485 junior police officers and 4,934 other ranks including 415 women. In the provinces each Chiefdom keeps an additional force known as Chiefdom Police.

A non-pensionable force, known as the Auxiliary Force and consisting of 3 Junior police officers and 260 other ranks, are helping the regular force in maintaining law and order in the diamond protected area in the Eastern region.

Religion. The majority of the population follow traditional tribal religions. Islam was brought to the region by the nomadic cattle-rearing Fula people from the north around 1600. The Temne people in the north-west form the main part of the Moslem community who were estimated in 1977 to comprise about 20% of the population.

Christianity came to West Africa in the 16th century from Portugal and Spain. The Roman Catholics have 2 dioceses in Sierra Leone and number about 25,000 (1977).

The Evangelical group who led the anti-slavery movement in England founded the Sierra Leone Company in 1791 to settle freed slaves in and around Freetown. In 1966 there were 16 Protestant denominations with a total community of 77,000. Members of the Sierra Leone Church (Anglican) were 25,000 in 1977.

Education (1982). There were over 1,182 registered primary schools with a total enrolment of over 276,911. Primary education is partially free but not compulsory though parents and guardians are urged to send their children and wards to school. School attendance varies considerably in different parts of the country. There were 165 secondary schools with a total enrolment of 66,464 pupils; 71 of these schools are fully assisted by the Government. Technical education was provided in 4 technical institutes, 2 trade centres and in the technical training establishments of the mining companies. There is also a rural institute.

Fourah Bay College and Njala University College (1,863 students) are the 2 constituent colleges of the University of Sierra Leone. The Institute of Education, which is part of the University, is now responsible for teacher education, educational research and curriculum development in the country.

There is a paramedical school at Bo in the Southern region.

Health (1977). In the Western Area there are 12 government hospitals (1,108 beds and 217 cots), including a maternity hospital, a children's hospital and an infectious diseases hospital near Freetown. There are 6 government health centres in the Western Area. Three private hospitals are located in Freetown with 108 beds. A mental hospital at Kissy has accommodation for 224 patients. In the provinces there are 14 government hospitals, 4 hospitals associated with mining companies and 7 mission hospitals. There is a school of nursing in Freetown. There are 156 government dispensaries and health treatment centres and two military hospitals with 124 beds.

DIPLOMATIC REPRESENTATIVES

Of Sierra Leone in Great Britain (33 Portland Pl., London, W1N 3AG)
High Commissioner: Victor E. Sumner.

Of Great Britain in Sierra Leone (Standard Bank of Sierra Leone Ltd Bldg., Lightfoot Boston St., Freetown)
High Commissioner: Richard Clift, CMG.

Of Sierra Leone in the USA (1701 19th St., NW, Washington, D.C., 20009)
Ambassador: Dauda S. Kamara.

Of the USA in Sierra Leone (Corner Walpole and Siaka Stevens St., Freetown)
Ambassador: Arthur Winston Lewis.

Of Sierra Leone to the United Nations
Ambassador: Abdul G. Koroma.

Books of Reference

Atlas of Sierra Leone. Ed. Survey and Lands Dept. Freetown, 1953
Background to Sierra Leone. Freetown, 1980
Sierra Leone Studies. Ed. J. D. Hargreaves, Freetown, 1953 ff.
Fyfe, C., *A History of Sierra Leone*. OUP, 1962.—Fyfe, C., and Jones, E. (ed.), *Freetown*. Sierra Leone Univ. Press and OUP, 1968
Fyfe, C. N. and Jones, E. D., *A Krio–English Dictionary*. OUP and Sierra Leone Univ. Press, 1980
Kup, A. P., *Sierra Leone*. Newton Abbot, 1975
Porter, A. T., *Creoledom: A Study in the Development of Freetown Society*. OUP, 1963

REPUBLIC OF SINGAPORE

Population: 2·5m. (1984)
GNP per capita: US$6,521 (1983)

HISTORY. For the early history of the settlement (1819) and colony (1867) *see* THE STATESMAN'S YEAR-BOOK, 1959, pp. 246 f.

By an agreement entered into between the Governments of Malaysia and of the State of Singapore on 7 Aug. 1965, effective on 9 Aug. 1965, Singapore ceased to be one of the 14 states of the Federation of Malaysia and became an independent sovereign state. The separation was ratified by the Constitution and Malaysia (Singapore Amendment) Act of the Malaysian Parliament on 9 Aug. The 2 governments agreed to enter into a treaty on external defence and mutual assistance. The Singapore Government retains its executive authority and legislative powers under its State Constitution and took over the powers of the Malaysian Government under the Malaysian Constitution in Singapore. The sovereignty and jurisdiction of the head of the Malaysian State was transferred to the Singapore Government. Civil servants working in Singapore for the Federal Departments became Singapore civil servants. Singapore citizens ceased to be Malaysian citizens.

Singapore accepted responsibility for international agreements entered into by the Malaysian Government on its behalf.

AREA AND POPULATION. The Republic of Singapore consists of Singapore Island itself, and some 54 islets.

Singapore Island is situated off the southern extremity of the Malay peninsula, to which it is joined by a causeway carrying a road, railway and water pipeline. The Straits of Johore between the island and the mainland are about three-quarters of a mile wide. The island is some 26 miles (41·8 km) in length and 14 miles (22·9 km) in breadth, and about 238·6 sq. miles (618·1 sq. km) in area, including the adjacent islets.

Census of population (1980): 1,856,237 Chinese, 351,508 Malays, 154,632 Indians and 51,568 others; total 2,413,945. Estimate (mid-1984), 2,529,100.

Report on the Census of Population 1980. Dept. of Statistics, Singapore, 1980

CLIMATE. The climate is equatorial, with uniformly high temperatures and no defined wet or dry season, rain being copious throughout the year. Singapore. Jan. 80°F (26·7°C), July 81°F (27·2°C). Annual rainfall 95·1″ (2,413 mm).

CONSTITUTION AND GOVERNMENT. By a constitutional amendment the name of the state was changed to 'Republic of Singapore', the head of state was named 'President of Singapore' and the legislative assembly was renamed 'Parliament'.

Malay, Chinese, Tamil and English are the official languages; English is the language of administration.

Parliament consists of 75 members, elected by secret ballot from single-member constituencies, and is presided over by a Speaker, chosen by Parliament from its own members or from outside Parliament. In the latter case, the Speaker has no vote. With the customary exception of those serving criminal sentences, all citizens over 21 are eligible to vote irrespective of sex, race, education or property qualification. There is a common roll without communal electorates. Citizenship is automatic by birth; it can also be acquired by registration or by naturalization.

A Presidential Council was established under Part IVA of the Constitution enacted on 9 Jan. 1970. The general function of the Council is to consider and report on matters affecting persons of any racial or religious community in Singapore as referred to it by Parliament or the Government. The Council will draw attention to any bill or subsidiary legislation which in the opinion of the Council is a differentiating measure.

Parliament, as from Dec. 1984, is composed of 77 People's Action Party members, 1, Workers' Party and 1, Democratic Party.

President of Singapore: Devan Nair (sworn in 24 Oct. 1981).

The People's Action Party Cabinet at March 1985 was composed as follows: *Prime Minister:* Lee Kuan Yew.

Senior Minister (Prime Minister's Office): S. Rajaratnam. *First Deputy Prime Minister and Minister of Defence:* Goh Chok Tong. *Second Deputy Prime Minister:* Ong Teng Cheong. *Law:* E. W. Barker. *National Development:* Teh Cheang Wan. *Foreign Affairs and Community Development:* S. Dhanabalan. *Finance, Education and Health:* Dr Tony Tan. *Environment:* Dr Ahmad Mattar. *Communications and Information, Second Minister of Defence and National Development:* Dr Yeo Ning Hong. *Home Affairs and Second Minister for Law:* S. Jayakumar. *Trade and Industry:* Dr Richard Hu.

There are 7 Ministers of State.

National flag: Horizontally red over white, charged in the canton with a crescent and a circle of 5 stars, all in white.

DEFENCE. The Ministry of Defence exercises command and control over all armed forces in the republic. It comprises 5 major divisions, *i.e.*, the general staff, manpower, logistic, security and intelligence and finance divisions. Compulsory military service in peace-time was introduced in 1967. Periods of service are officers/n.c.o.s. 30 months, other ranks 24 months. Reserve liability is to 40 for men, 50 for officers.

The governments of Australia, Britain, Malaysia, New Zealand and Singapore continue to co-operate closely in defence arrangements and have agreed on a new 5-nation defence set-up in SE Asia designed to protect Malaysia and Singapore against outside attack. The new defence arrangement came into force on 1 Nov. 1971.

Army. The Army consists of 1 armoured and 3 infantry brigades, 6 artillery, 1 commando, 6 engineer and 3 signals battalions. Equipment includes 273 AMX-13 light tanks. Strength (1984) 45,000 (including 30,000 conscripts) and 150,000 reserves. Paramilitary forces number some 40,000.

Navy. The flotillas comprise 6 fast missile craft, all of German design but 4 built in Singapore, 6 fast patrol craft built by Vosper Thornycroft (2 at Portsmouth, Britain, and 4 in Singapore), 2 *ex*-US coastal minesweepers, 12 coastal patrol boats, 2 training vessels, 6 landing ships (*ex*-USN LST) and 6 small landing craft (2 *ex*-Australian). Personnel in 1985 numbered 3,500 officers and men. There are 50 coastal patrol craft deployed by the marine police and 4 small survey craft operated by the Singapore Port Authority.

Air Defence Command. The formation of an Air Defence Command began in 1968. The Republic of Singapore Air Force now has 1 squadron of F-5E supersonic fighters supported by 2-seat F-5Fs; 2 fighter-bomber squadrons equipped with A-4S Skyhawks, supported by TA-4S two-seat trainers; 2 squadrons of Hunter jet fighters and reconnaissance-fighters, supported by Hunter 2-seat trainers, a radar unit and Bloodhound, Rapier and Hawk surface-to-air missile squadrons; a transport squadron of C-130s (including 4 equipped as flight refuelling tankers) and Skyvans equipped for search and rescue; a squadron of Bell UH-1H Iroquois and Bell 212 helicopters; and training units equipped with SF.260MS piston-engined basic trainers, T-33A jets (to be replaced with SIAI-Marchetti S.211s), and AS 350 Ecureuil helicopters. Four E-2C Hawkeye AWACS aircraft are on order. Personnel strength (1985) about 6,000.

INTERNATIONAL RELATIONS

Membership. Singapore is a member of UN, the Commonwealth, the Colombo Plan and ASEAN.

ECONOMY

Planning. The GDP in 1983, at current factor cost was $32,252m., an increase of 9·5% over 1982.

Budget. Public revenue and expenditure for financial years (in S$1m.):

	1979	*1980*	*1981*	*1982*	*1983*[1]
Revenue	4,603	5,904	7,862	9,128	8,871
Expenditure	6,803	9,321	11,827	14,097	16,636

[1] Estimate.

Currency. The *Singapore dollar* (S$) is divided in 100 *cents*. Gross circulation on 31 Dec. 1983 was S$4,739·7m. In March 1985, £1 = 2·44 *dollars*; US$1 = 2·28 dollars.

Banking. The functions of the Commissioner of Banking have been assumed by the Monetary Authority of Singapore from 1 Jan. 1971.

The Development Bank of Singapore was established in 1968, primarily to provide long-term financing of manufacturing and other industries. In Dec. 1983 it had a paid up capital of S$230·7m. and shareholders' funds amounted to S$1,341·9m.

There were 122 commercial banks with 365 banking offices operating in Singapore as at 31 Dec. 1983. The total assets/liabilities amounted to S$60,024·9m. as at April 1984. Total deposits of non-bank customers amounted to S$26,679·9m. while loans and advances including bills financing, totalled S$35,857·8m.

In May 1984, the total balance of the Singapore Post Office Savings Bank was S$6,632m.

Weights and Measures. The metric system or the International System of Units (SI) was introduced in 1971 in Singapore.

ENERGY AND NATURAL RESOURCES

Electricity. The Public Utilities Board is responsible for the provision of electricity, gas and water. Electrical power is generated by 3 power stations, with a total generating capacity of 2,586 mw at the end of 1983.

Fisheries. As the prospect of increasing fish production from inshore waters is poor, in 1967 various projects were introduced, with the aim of making Singapore self-sufficient in fish as well as a major fishing base in the region.

The Jurong fishing port and fish market began operating 26 Feb. 1969. A Fishery Training Institute was established at Changi with the assistance of the United Nations Development Programme (Special Fund) to train youths and fishermen in modern fishing techniques. At Changi, too, a Marine Fisheries Research Department was set up under the sponsorship of the South-East Asian Fisheries Development Centre. Research on fish culture and ornamental fish was carried out at the Freshwater Fisheries Laboratory at Sembawang. The ornamental fish industry is fast becoming a valuable foreign exchange earner. Export of aquarium fish in 1983, S$32·3m. The local catch of fresh fish in 1983 was 19,099 tonnes.

INDUSTRY AND TRADE

Industry. The largest industrial area is the Jurong Industrial Estate with 1,451 factories employing 114,500 workers in March 1983.

Industries in Jurong include shipbuilding and those manufacturing steel rods, steel pipes, tyres, chemicals, pharmaceuticals, plywood and veneer, plastics, cement, bricks, cables, textiles and wiremesh. Smaller industrial estates have light industry factories producing food, paper and miscellaneous consumer goods

Labour. In June 1983, 1,169,598 persons were employed, of whom 986,157 were employees, 53,512 were employers, 103,731 were self-employed and 26,197 were unpaid family workers. The majority were working in manufacturing, 324,942; commerce, 266,003; transport and communications, 131,944.

There were 133 registered trade unions comprising 90 employee unions, 42 employer unions and 1 federation of trade unions in 1983. The total membership of employee unions numbered 205,155, of whom 197,701 of the unionized workers belonged to 68 employee unions affiliated to the National Trades Union Congress. Members of employer unions numbered 6,579.

The Employment Act and the Industrial Relations Act provide principal terms and conditions of employment such as hours of work, sick leave and other fringe benefits. A new labour legislation was introduced allowing youths of 14-16 years to work in industrial establishments, and also children from 12-14 years to be employed in approved apprenticeship schemes. A trade dispute may be referred to the Industrial Arbitration Court which was established in 1960.

The Ministry of Labour operates 3 employment exchanges to assist job seekers to obtain suitable employment and employers to recruit suitable workers. The Central Provident Fund was established in 1955 to make provision for employees in their old age. In 1983 there were about 1·8m. members with S$19,504·7m. standing to their credit in the fund. The total number of active employers registered with the board in 1982 was 80,253 comprising 63,391 business employers and 16,862 domestic employers.

Commerce. The major trading countries for 1983 were US (16·4%), Malaysia (15·9%), Japan (14·2%) and the EEC (9·8%). In 1983, imports (S$59,504m.) declined by 1·2%. Exports rose from S$44,473m. in 1982 to S$46,155m. in 1983.

In the following table (British Department of Trade returns, in £1,000 sterling) the imports include produce from Borneo, Sarawak and other eastern places, transhipped at Singapore, which is thus entered as the place of export:

	1980	*1981*	*1982*	*1983*	*1984*
Imports to UK	535,915	245,209	245,453	404,122	488,421
Exports and re-exports from UK	328,112	406,791	406,172	469,565	556,443

Tourism. There were 2,853,577 visitors in 1983.

COMMUNICATIONS

Roads. Singapore has 2,569 km of public roads, of which 2,468 km are asphalt-paved. In April 1984 motor vehicles registered in Singapore numbered 483,224, of which 208,188 were private cars, 8,108 buses, 140,246 motor cycles and scooters, 14,928 public cars including taxis, school taxis and private hire cars.

Railways. A 16-mile (25·8-km) main line runs through Singapore, connecting with the States of Malaysia and as far as Bangkok. Branch lines serve the port of Singapore and the industrial estate at Jurong. A metro was under construction in 1983.

Aviation. The new international airport at Changi was completed and operational from 1 July 1981. Thirty-six international airlines operated 997 scheduled services a week, totalling 61,000 aircraft movements at Singapore International Airport in Changi in 1983. Freight handled (1983) 258,000 tonnes and there were 8·6m. passengers.

Shipping. A total of 60,515 vessels of 562m. NRT entered into and cleared from Singapore during 1983.

Post. In Sept. 1982, 72 post offices and 63 postal agencies were in operation. Telephones numbered 795,737 in 1982.

Cinemas (1983). There were 57 cinemas with a total seating capacity of 63,000.

Newspapers (1984). There were 9 daily newspapers, in 4 languages, with a total daily circulation of 812,209.

JUSTICE, EDUCATION AND WELFARE

Justice. There is a Supreme Court in Singapore which consists of the High Court, the Court of Appeal and the Court of Criminal Appeal. The Supreme Court is composed of a Chief Justice and 6 Judges. An appeal from the High Court lies to the Court of Appeal in civil matters and to the Court of Criminal Appeal in criminal matters. Further appeal can in certain cases be made to the Judicial Committee of the Privy Council. The High Court has original civil and criminal jurisdiction as well as appellate civil and criminal jurisdiction in respect of appeals from the Subordinate Courts. There are 9 district courts, 11 magistrates' courts, 1 juvenile and 1 coroner's court.

Education. Statistics of schools in 1983:

	Schools	*Pupils*	*Teachers*
Primary			
Government schools	207	219,742	8,132
Government-aided schools	96	70,862	2,136
Private schools	2	196	6
Secondary			
Government schools	93	133,839 [1]	6,616
Government-aided schools	50	46,629 [1]	2,915
Private schools	4	1,875 [1]	73

[1] Includes pre-university classes.

The National University of Singapore was established on 8 Aug. 1980 following the merger of the University of Singapore and the Nanyang University. The National University of Singapore has 8 faculties: Arts and social sciences, law, science, medicine, dentistry, engineering, architecture and building, accountancy and business administration and 3 schools, post-graduate medical studies, post-graduate dental studies, and school of management.

The Department of Extramural Studies and the English Language Proficiency Unit are non-faculty departments. Total student enrolment for 1983 was 12,912. The Nanyang Technological Institute, situated in the former Nanyang University, was established on 8 Aug. 1981. The institute admitted about 650 second-year students of the University's Faculty of Engineering in July 1982. It will be developed into a University of Technology by 1992. The Singapore Polytechnic had 10,909 students and the Ngee Ann Polytechnic 4,825 students in 1983. The Institute of Education, established on 1 April 1973, is now the only institution responsible for teacher education in Singapore and for promoting research in education. There were 1,078 students in 1983.

The Adult Education Board and the Industrial Training Board were merged to form the Vocational and Industrial Training Board, on 1 April 1979. The VITB has taken over all the functions and responsibilities in vocational training and continuing education. The VITB runs 17 training institutes and centres offering full-time and part-time courses. The total student enrolment for 1983 was 15,610.

Health. There were 11 government hospitals with a total of 8,222 beds in 1983. There were 2,361 doctors registered.

DIPLOMATIC REPRESENTATIVES

Of Singapore in Great Britain (2 Wilton Cres., London, SW1X 8RW)
High Commissioner: Dr Ho Guan Lim (accredited 10 July 1984).

Of Great Britain in Singapore (Tanglin Rd, Singapore, 1024)
High Commissioner: W. E. Hamilton Whyte.

Of Singapore in the USA (1824 R St., NW, Washington, D.C., 20009)
Ambassador: T. T. B. Koh.

Of the USA in Singapore (30 Hill St., Singapore, 0617)
Ambassador: Harry E. T. Thayer.

Of Singapore to the United Nations
Ambassador: Kishore Mahbubani.

Books of Reference

Statistical Information: The Department of Statistics (PO Box 3010, Maxwell Road, Singapore 9050) was established 1 Jan. 1922. Its publications include: *Singapore Trade Statistics* (monthly), *Monthly Digest of Statistics, Yearbook of Statistics, Singapore Demographic*

Bulletin (monthly), *Census of Population 1980. Singapore Yearbook of Labour Statistics. Chief Statistician:* Khoo Chian Kim.

National Library. *Books About Singapore.* Singapore. Biennial
National Trades Union Congress, *Singapore. Towards Tomorrow.* Singapore, 1973
Singapore. Constitution. The Constitution of Singapore. Singapore, 1966
The Budget for the Financial Year 1984–85.
Singapore. Singapore, Publicity Division, Ministry of Culture (formerly *Annual Report*)
Singapore. Government Gazette (published weekly with supplement)
Economic Survey of Singapore, 1982. Ministry of Trade and Industry, Singapore, 1983
Singapore. Facts and Pictures. Singapore, Publicity Division, Ministry of Culture (annual)
Singapore Government Directory. Singapore, Publicity Division, Ministry of Culture
The Statutes of the Republic of Singapore. 8 vols., 1970 (with annual supplements). Singapore, Law Revision Commission, 1970—.
Practice of Economic Growth. Singapore, Federal Publications, 1977
Chen, P. S. J., *Singapore Development: Policies and Trends.* OUP, 1983
Josey, A., *Lee Kuan Yew, The Struggle for Singapore.* London, 1980.—*Singapore: Its Past, Present and Future.* Singapore, 1979
Saw, S.-H., *Population Control for Zero Growth in Singapore.* Singapore, 1980
Tan, C. H., *Financial Institutions in Singapore.* Singapore, 1984
Turnbull, C. M., *A History of Singapore, 1819–1975.* OUP, 1977
Wee, T.B. (ed.), *The Future of Singapore; The Global City.* Singapore, 1977
Yeo, K. W., *Political Development in Singapore, 1945–1955.* Singapore Univ. Press, 1973

National Library: National Library, Stamford Rd, Singapore. *Director:* Mrs Hedwig Anuar.

SOLOMON ISLANDS

Capital: Honiara
Population: 258,193 (1984)
GNP per capita: US$640 (1981)

HISTORY. The Solomon Islands were discovered in 1568 by Alvaro de Mendana, on a voyage of discovery from Peru; 200 years passed before European contact was again made with the Solomons. The Solomon Islands lie within the area 5° to 12° 30′ S. lat. and 155° 30′ to 169° 45′ E. long. The group includes the main islands of Guadalcanal, Malaita, San Cristobal, New Georgia, Santa Isabel and Choiseul; the smaller Florida and Russell groups; the Shortland, Mono (or Treasury), Vella La Vella, Kolombangara, Ranongga, Gizo and Rendova Islands; to the east, Santa Cruz, Tikopia, the Reef and Duff groups; Rennell and Bellona in the south; Ontong Java or Lord Howe to the north; and innumerable smaller islands. The 4 first-named were placed under British protection in 1893; the other islands were added in 1898 and 1899.

AREA AND POPULATION. The land area of the Solomons is estimated at 11,500 sq. miles (29,785 sq. km). The larger islands are mountainous and forest clad, with flood-prone rivers of considerable energy potential. Guadalcanal has the largest land area and the greatest amount of flat coastal plain.

Population of the Solomon Islands was (1984) 258,193. Census (1976) 196,823, over 50% being under 20 years (183,665 Melanesians, 7,821 Polynesians, 452 Chinese, 1,359 Europeans, 2,753 Gilbertese and 773 others).

The islands are administratively divided into 7 provinces. These provinces are (with 1984 population): Western Province (55,490), Guadalcanal, including Honiara (63,335), Central (18,462), Malaita (74,036), Makula (18,954), Temotu (13,928), Isabel (13,988).

The capital, Honiara, on Guadalcanal, is the largest urban area, with estimated population in 1984 of 23,500.

English is the official language but there are at least 87 vernacular languages.

CLIMATE. An equatorial climate with only small seasonal variations. South-east winds cause cooler conditions from April to Nov., but north-west winds for the rest of the year bring higher temperatures and greater rainfall, with annual totals ranging between 80″ (2,000 mm) and 120″ (3,000 mm).

CONSTITUTION AND GOVERNMENT. A Constitutional Conference was held in London during Sept. 1977, where it was agreed that there should be full independence for the Solomon Islands and this was granted on 7 July 1978.

The main provisions of the 1978 Constitution are that Solomon Islands is a constitutional monarchy with the British Sovereign (represented locally by a Governor-General, who must be a Solomon Island citizen) as Head of State, while legislative power is vested in the unicameral National Parliament composed of 38 members, elected by universal adult suffrage for four years (subject to dissolution), and executive authority is effectively held by the Cabinet, led by the Prime Minister.

The Governor-General is appointed for up to five years, on the advice of Parliament, and acts in almost all matters on the advice of the Cabinet. The Prime Minister is elected by and from members of Parliament. Other Ministers are appointed by the Governor-General on the Prime Minister's recommendation, from members of Parliament. The Cabinet is responsible to Parliament. Emphasis is laid on the devolution of power to provincial governments, and traditional chiefs and leaders have a special role within the arrangement.

The Constitution contains comprehensive guarantees of fundamental human rights and freedom, and provides for the introduction of a leadership code and the appointment of an Ombudsman and a Public Solicitor. It also provides for the establishment of the underlying law, based on customary law and concepts of the Solomon Islands people.

Solomon Islands citizenship was automatically conferred on the indigenous people of the islands and on other residents with close ties with the islands upon independence. The acquisition of land is reserved for indigenous inhabitants or their descendants.

Governor General: Sir Baddeley Devisi, GCMG, GCVO.
Prime Minister: Rt Hon. Sir Peter Kenilorea, KBE.
National flag: Divided blue over green by a diagonal yellow band, and in the canton 5 white stars.

INTERNATIONAL RELATIONS

Membership. The Solomon Islands is a member of UN and is an ACP state of EEC.

ECONOMY

Planning. The 1980–84 Development Plan envisages improvement in education and agricultural development.

Budget. The budget for 1981 envisaged revenue of SI$34·8m. and expenditure SI$61·3m.

Currency. The *Solomon Island dollar* (SI$) was introduced in 1977. In March 1985, US$1 = 1·44 *dollars*; £1 = 1·52 *dollars.*

NATURAL RESOURCES

Agriculture. Coconuts, cocoa, rice and other minor crops are grown. Oil-palm is being developed successfully with a total of 3,529 hectares having been planted by Dec. 1984. Production of copra (1980), 29,169 tonnes.

An oil-mill became operational in 1976. In 1983 19,238 tonnes of palm oil and 4,000 tonnes of palm kernel were exported.

Rice-cropping in 1983 yielded 4,608 tonnes of milled rice.

Livestock (1983): Cattle, 23,000; pigs, 48,000.

Forestry. Timber extraction is an important development in the Solomons. Timber (logs, sawn timber and veneer sheets) exports for 1980 were 258,000 cu. metres ($A149m.).

Fisheries. A total catch of 20,700 tonnes of skipjack was made in 1978. Exports of fish totalled 21,578 tonnes ($A19·8m.) in 1980.

INDUSTRY AND TRADE

Commerce. The main imports (1980) were food, fuels and capital goods and totalled $A61·5m. Exports comprised copra (316,821 tonnes, $A10·5m.), frozen fish (21,578 tonnes, $A19·8m.), rough timber (258,000 cu. metres, $A149m.), palm-oil (15,619 tonnes), marine shell, cocoa and manufactured tobacco; total exports, $A60·8m.

Total trade between Solomon Islands and UK (British Department of Trade returns, in £1,000 sterling):

	1982	*1983*	*1984*
Imports to UK	4,212	5,486	6,838
Exports and re-exports from UK	1,035	1,463	1,513

Tourism. In 1983, there were 11,113 tourists.

COMMUNICATIONS

Roads. There were 455 km of main roads in 1976.

Aviation. Regular flights from Fiji, Nauru, Australia (Papua New Guinea, New Zealand and Vanuatu) provide the main communication link. Solair, the internal airline, and innumerable small ships, provide inter-island transport.

Shipping. Shipping services are maintained with Australia, New Zealand, UK and the Far East.

Post and Broadcasting. In addition to the general post office, there are 3 post offices, 4 sub post offices and 96 Postal Agencies. In addition there are 125 licenced stamp dealers. Number of telephones (Jan. 1985), 3,827. A VHF radio telephone service operates internally as well as overseas. In 1982 there were about 25,000 radio receivers.

Newspapers. In 1984 there were 2 weekly newspapers and 1 monthly.

RELIGION, EDUCATION AND WELFARE

Religion. At the 1976 census, 34% of the population were Anglican, 19% Roman Catholic, 17% South Sea Evangelical and 25% other Protestant.

Education. In 1983 there were 34,906 primary school pupils. There were 4 aided national secondary schools, 2 private national secondary schools and 11 new secondary schools. Total enrolment secondary schools, 4,807 (1983).

Training of teachers is carried out at Solomon Islands Teachers' College and trade and vocational training is carried out at Honiara Technical Institute. There were 326 students on overseas scholarships in 1983.

Health. In 1985 there were 8 hospitals, 183 clinics and 2 health centres and 32 doctors.

DIPLOMATIC REPRESENTATIVES

Of the Solomon Islands in Great Britain
High Commissioner: (Vacant).

Of Great Britain in the Solomon Islands (Soltel House, Mendana Ave., Honiara)
High Commissioner: George Stansfield, OBE.

Of the Solomon Islands to the United Nations
Ambassador: Francis J. Saemala.

Books of Reference

B.S.I.P. Annual Report, 1969. Honiara, 1970
Solomon Islands Hand Book 1983. Government Information Service, Honiara, 1983
Amhurst, Lord, and Thompson, B., *The Discovery of the Solomon Islands in 1568.* London, 1967
Kent, J., *The Solomon Islands.* Newton Abbot, 1972
Miller, J., *Guadalcanal: The First Offensive.* Washington, 1949

SOMALIA

Capital: Mogadiscio
Population: 3·86m. (1982)
GNP per capita: US$280 (1981)

Jamhuriyadda Dimugradiga Somaliya

HISTORY. The Somali Republic came into being on 1 July 1960 as a result of the merger of the British Somaliland Protectorate, which became independent on 26 June 1960, and the Italian Trusteeship Territory of Somalia.

For the previous history of these territories *see* THE STATESMAN'S YEAR-BOOK, 1960, pp. 337 and 1367.

On 21 Oct. 1969 the Somali armed forces led by Maj.-Gen. Mohammed Siyad Barre took power in a *coup,* suspended the Constitution and formed a Supreme Revolutionary Council to administer the country, which was renamed the Somali Democratic Republic. Constitutional government was re-established on 23 Sept. 1979.

AREA AND POPULATION. Somalia is bounded north by the Gulf of Aden, east and south by the Indian ocean, and west by Kenya, Ethiopia and Djibouti. Total area of 637,657 sq. km (246,201 sq. miles). Census population (1975) 3,253,024 of whom 15% urban. Estimate (1982) 3,862,000 excluding an estimated 700,000 Somali-speaking refugees from the disputed Ogaden area of Ethiopia, were (1985) living in camps in Somalia.

The capital is Mogadiscio (600,000), other large towns being Hargeisa (150,000), Merca (100,000), Kisimayu (70,000) and Berbera (55,000).

There are long-standing territorial disputes with Kenya and Ethiopia.

CLIMATE. Much of the country is arid, though rainfall is more adequate towards the south. Temperatures are very high on the northern coasts. Mogadiscio. Jan. 79°F (26·1°C), July 78°F (25·6°C). Annual rainfall 17″ (429 mm). Berbera. Jan. 76°F (24·4°C), July 97°F (36·1°C). Annual rainfall 2″ (51 mm).

CONSTITUTION AND GOVERNMENT. A new Constitution was approved by referendum on 25 Aug. 1979 and came into force on 23 Sept. The sole legal Party (since 1 July 1976) is the Somali Revolutionary Socialist Party, administered by a 51-member Central Committee. There is an Executive President nominated by the Central Committee and elected for a 6-year term by the People's Assembly; the latter consists of 121 members elected by universal suffrage for a 5-year term and a further 6 members appointed by the President.

President: Maj.-Gen. Mohammed Siyad Barre.

Vice-President, Presidential Advisor on Government Affairs: Maj.-Gen. Hussein Kulmia Afrah. *Vice-President, Minister of Defence:* Lieut.-Gen. Mohammed Ali Samater. *Foreign Affairs:* Dr Abderrahman Jama Barre.

National flag: Light blue with a white star in the centre.

The national language is Somali. Arabic is also an official language and English and Italian are extensively spoken.

Local Government. There were (1982) 17 regions, sub-divided into 78 districts.

DEFENCE

Army. The Army consists of 3 tank, 20 infantry, 1 commando and 1 surface-to-air missile brigades. Equipment includes 100 T-34/-54/-55 and 40 Centurion main battle tanks. Strength (1985) 60,000. There are additional paramilitary forces: Police (8,000), Border Guards (1,500) and People's Militia (20,000).

Navy. The flotilla includes 4 submarine chasers (fast attack/torpedo/patrol craft), 2 fast missile craft, 7 fast torpedo boats, 6 patrol craft, 1 medium landing ship and 4 minor landing craft. All are former Soviet naval units which could deteriorate with the withdrawal of the Soviet element. Personnel increased to 700 officers and men by 1985.

Air Force. Formed with a nucleus of aircraft taken over from the former Italian Air Corps of Somalia, in 1960, the Air Corps was built up with Soviet aid. Current equipment includes a squadron of Hunter fighters and two-seat trainers, 7 MiG-21 and 30 J-6 (Chinese-built MiG-19) supersonic fighters, about 9 MiG-17 jet-fighters and 2 MiG-15UTI two-seat advanced trainers, and small transport, helicopter and training units. Latest equipment includes 2 Aeritalia G222 and 2 An-26 twin-turboprop transports, 16 SIAI-Marchetti SF.260W armed trainers and 4 Agusta-Bell 212 helicopters from Italy. Personnel total about 2,000.

INTERNATIONAL RELATIONS

Membership. Somalia is a member of UN, OAU, the Arab League and is an ACP state of EEC.

ECONOMY

Planning. The 1982–86 Development Plan envisages expenditure of Som.Sh. 16,000m. and a growth rate of 6%.

Budget. The budget for 1983 envisaged Som.Sh.4,664m. expenditure.

Currency. The currency is the *Somali shilling,* divided into 100 cents. The money is issued in notes of 5, 10, 20 and 100 shillings and coins of 1, 5, 10, 50 cents and 1 shilling. Currency in circulation (1979) Som.Sh.1,152·6m. In March 1985 £1 = 39·01 Som.Sh., US$1 = 36·60 Som.Sh.

Banking. The bank of issue is the Central Bank of Somalia (founded in 1960 as the Somali National Bank). All foreign banks were nationalised in May 1970, and the Commercial and Savings Bank of Somalia and the Somali Development Bank, both state-owned, are the only other banks.

Weights and Measures. The metric system is in use.

ENERGY AND NATURAL RESOURCES

Electricity. Electricity production (1981) was 69·1m. kwh.

Minerals. Deposits of iron ore in the south and gypsum in the north are known to exist. Beryl and columbite are also found in the north. None are commercially exploited. Several firms hold exploration and drilling licences for oil. Uranium is found in the Juba area.

Agriculture. Somalia is essentially a pastoral country, and about 80% of the inhabitants depend on livestock-rearing (cattle, sheep, goats and camels). In Southern Somalia, especially along the Shebeli and Juba rivers, there are banana and sugar-cane plantations with a cultivated area of some 90,000 hectares. Estimated production, 1982 (in 1,000 tons): Sugar, 460; bananas, 70; maize, 150, sorghum, 235; grapefruit, 6; cotton, 5. Fresh fruit and oil seeds are grown in increasing quantities.

Livestock (1983): 16·9m. goats; 10·4m. sheep; 5·65m. camels; 4m. cattle; 1,000 horses, 24,000 asses and 22,000 mules.

Fisheries. 21 co-operatives, including 4,000 full-time and 10,000 part-time fishermen, caught some 10,000 tonnes in 1981.

INDUSTRY AND TRADE

Industry. Production (1981): Textiles, 10·1m. yards; sugar, 26,800 tonnes; flour and pasta, 5,900 tonnes.

Trade. In 1982 imports were Som.Sh.2,377m. and exports Som.Sh.1,993m. The chief exports are fresh fruit, livestock, hides and skins.

In 1980, 35% of imports came from Italy, 9% from USA and 8% from the UK, while 66% of exports went to Saudi Arabia.

Total trade between the Somali Republic and UK (British Department of Trade returns, in £1,000 sterling):

	1980	*1981*	*1982*	*1983*	*1984*
Imports to UK	303	856	883	581	1,582
Exports and re-exports from UK	6,682	12,606	12,095	18,987	14,165

COMMUNICATIONS

Roads. Somalia has no developed transport system. Internal freight and passenger transport is almost entirely by means of road haulage. In 1978 there were 19,380 km of roads (2,153 km were paved). In 1977 there were 4,200 passenger cars and 5,700 commercial vehicles, including buses.

Aviation. There is a commercial national airline, Somali Airlines. Mogadiscio airport is used by Alitalia, Alyemda, Air Tanzania, PIA and Kenya Airways.

Shipping. There are 4 deep-water harbours at Kisimayu, Berbera, Marka and Mogadiscio. Because of the shape of the country, coastal shipping is an important form of internal transport. The merchant fleet (1982) amounted to 22 vessels of 17,525 gross tons.

Post and Broadcasting. There is a manual telephone system in several towns, but Mogadiscio has an automatic system; number of telephones (1980), about 7,000. The state radio stations transmit in Somali, Arabic, English and Italian from Mogadiscio, Hargeisa, Anhazic, Koti. Receivers (1982) 120,000. A television service was started in 1983.

Cinemas. In 1970 there were 26 cinemas with a seating capacity of 23,000.

JUSTICE, RELIGION, EDUCATION AND WELFARE

Justice. There are 84 district courts, each with a civil and a criminal section. There are 8 regional courts and 2 Courts of Appeal (at Mogadiscio and Hargeisa), each with a general section and an assize section. The Supreme Court is in Mogadiscio.

Religion. The population is almost entirely Sunni Moslems. There are very few Roman Catholics, mainly in the capital.

Education. The nomadic life of a large percentage of the population inhibits education progress. In 1981 there were 418,935 pupils and 12,007 teachers in primary schools, and 23,810 students and 2,380 pupils in technical schools; in 1979 there were 17,020 pupils and 925 students in secondary schools, and 2,156 students with 540 teachers at 2 teacher-training establishments.

The National University of Somalia in Mogadiscio (founded 1959) had 3,607 students in 1978.

Health. In 1976 there were 179 doctors, 21 pharmacists (1972), 586 medical assistants, 480 nurses (1972), 193 midwives (1972), 75 hospitals and 187 dispensaries (1972). There was a total of 5,691 beds.

DIPLOMATIC REPRESENTATIVES

Of Somalia in Great Britain (60 Portland Place, London, W1N 3DG)
Ambassador: Salah Mohamed Ali (accredited 15 Feb. 1985).

Of Great Britain in Somalia (Waddada Xasan Geeddi Abtoow 7/8, Mogadiscio)
Ambassador: Wiliam Fullerton.

Of Somalia in the USA (600 New Hampshire Ave., NW, Washington, D.C., 20037)
Ambassador: Mohamud Haji Nur.

Of USA in Somalia (Corso Primo Luglio, Mogadiscio)
Ambassador: Robert B. Oakley.

Of Somalia to the United Nations
Ambassador: Abdillahi Said Osman.

Books of Reference

Background to the Liberation Struggle of the Western Somalis. Ministry of Foreign Affairs, Mogadiscio, 1978

Legum, C. and Lee, B., *Conflict in the Horn of Africa.* London, 1977

Lewis, I. M., *A Pastoral Democracy.* London, 1962.—*The Modern History of Somaliland.* London, 1965

Touval, S., *Somali Nationalism.* Harvard Univ. Press and OUP, 1963

REPUBLIC OF SOUTH AFRICA

Capital: Pretoria
Population: 26·75m. (1984)
GNP per capita: US$2,770 (1981)

Republiek van Suid-Afrika

HISTORY. The Union of South Africa was formed in 1910 and comprised the former self-governing British colonies of the Cape of Good Hope, Natal, the Transvaal and the Orange Free State.

The Union remained a member of the British Commonwealth until it became a republic on 31 May 1961.

AREA AND POPULATION. South Africa is bounded north by South West Africa, Botswana and Zimbabwe, north-east by Mozambique and Swaziland, east by the Indian ocean, south and west by the South Atlantic. Lesotho forms an enclave between the Orange Free State and Natal. The total area of the republic was (1983) 433,678[1] sq. miles (1,123,226 sq. km), divided between the provinces as follows: Cape Province, 249,331 (645,767); Natal, 33,578 (86,967); Transvaal, 101,351 (262,499); Orange Free State, 49,418 (127,993).

On 25 Dec. 1947 the Union formally took possession of Prince Edward Island and, on 30 Dec., of Marion Island, about 1,200 miles south-east of Cape Town.

[1] Excludes Walvis Bay (434 sq. miles), which is an integral part of the Cape Province but is administered under Act No. 24 of 1922, South West Africa, Transkei, Ciskei, Bophuthatswana and Venda.

The census taken in 1904 in each of the 4 colonies was the first simultaneous census taken in South Africa. In 1911 the first Union census was taken.

	All races			*Whites*		*Non-whites*	
	Total	*Whites*	*Non-Whites*	*Males*	*Females*	*Males*	*Females*
1904	5,174,827	1,117,234	4,057,593	635,317	481,917	2,046,370	2,011,223
1911	5,972,757	1,276,319	4,696,438	685,206	591,113	2,383,879	2,312,559
1921	6,927,403	1,521,343	5,406,060	783,006	738,337	2,753,188	2,652,872
1936	9,587,863	2,003,334	7,584,529	1,017,557	985,777	3,818,211	3,766,318
1946	11,415,925	2,372,044	9,043,881	1,194,201	1,177,843	4,610,862	4,433,019
1951	12,671,452	2,641,689	10,029,763	1,322,754	1,318,935	5,109,331	4,920,432
1960	15,994,181	3,080,159	12,914,022	1,534,923	1,545,236	6,504,317	6,409,705
1970	21,402,470	3,726,540	17,675,930	1,856,180	1,870,360	8,689,920	8,986,010
1980[1]	24,885,960	4,528,100	20,357,860	2,265,400	2,262,700	10,393,780	9,964,080

[1] Excludes Transkei, Bophuthatswana and Venda, but includes Ciskei (677,820).

Of the non-White population in 1980, 16,923,760 were Black, 2,612,780 Coloured and 821,320 Asiatic. The numerically leading Black nations are the Zulu (5,682,520), Xhosa (2,987,340), Sepedi (North Sotho) (2,347,600), Seshoeshoe (South Sotho) (1,742,060), Tswana (1,357,360). Population, (1980) of the Black national areas: Kwa Zulu, 3,422,140 (of which 3,409,000 are Black); Gazankulu, 514,280 (512,000); Lebowa, 1,746,500 (1,739,000); Qwaqwa, 158,620 (156,000); Ka Ngwane, 161,160 (161,000); Kwa Ndebele, 156,380 (156,000). These places are included in the land area figures for the provinces where they lie, but their inhabitants are not included in the provincial population figures. Population of the Republic, 1984, 26,749,000 (18,238,000 Black, 4,807,000 White, 2,817,000 Coloured, 887,000 Asian). Growth rate 1970–80, 2·6% (Black, 2·7%; Coloured, 2%; Asian, 2·4%; White, 1·5%).

In 1980 (census) Afrikaans was the home language of 2,581,080 Whites, English of 1,763,220 Whites. Of the 15,970,019 Black about 50% could read and write, and 3·5m. (75%) of Black children of school-going age were attending school in 1981.

Vital statistics for calendar years:

	Whites					*Asians and Coloureds*		
	Births	*Deaths*	*Marriages*	*Immigrants*	*Emigrants*	*Births*	*Deaths*	*Marriages*
1979	73,090	35,814	41,813	18,680	15,694	91,360	28,618	26,746
1980	74,777	37,664	45,165	29,365	11,363	92,741	28,850	28,511
1981	79,061	39,376	46,653	41,542	8,791	98,163	30,707	29,502

Of the 41,542 immigrants in 1981, 41,429 were white; of the 8,791 emigrants 7,700 were white.

The registration of Black essential data was introduced on a compulsory basis many years ago. However, despite serious efforts on the part of the registering authorities, the Blacks are still largely reluctant to have their essential data registered. Consequently no complete vital statistics are available for this population group.

Principal cities (excluding suburbs) according to the latest statistics (1980) are:

Town	*Whites*	*Africans*	*Coloureds*	*Asians*	*Total*
Alberton (Trans.)	45,902	177,123	7,410	232	230,667
Benoni (Trans.)	56,508	135,752	997	13,553	206,810
Bloemfontein (O.F.S.)	90,625	124,768	15,295	...	230,688
Boksburg (Trans.)	61,337	73,385	15,408	157	150,287
Brakpan (Trans.)	31,902	46,135	1,674	21	79,732
Cape Town (C. Prov.)	124,876	5,608	80,748	2,598	213,830
Durban (Natal)	232,616	73,701	44,020	155,626	505,963
East London (C. Prov.)	62,735	77,372	18,150	2,325	160,582
Germiston (Trans.)	117,492	33,740	1,616	2,587	155,435
Johannesburg (Trans.)	435,586	947,290	101,769	51,812	1,536,457
Kempton Park (Trans.)	71,505	217,998	295	17	289,815
Kimberley (C. Prov.)	33,440	66,162	44,125	1,196	144,923
Krugersdorp (Trans.)	46,280	53,752	277	2,631	102,940
Pietermaritzburg (Natal)	53,780	62,330	11,424	51,438	178,972
Port Elizabeth (C. Prov.)	128,605	241,844	115,383	6,308	492,140
Pretoria (Trans.)	351,590	146,766	14,746	15,305	528,407
Roodepoort Maraisburg (Trans.)	83,217	77,511	3,620	967	165,315
Springs (Trans.)	49,752	101,691	1,254	1,277	153,974
Vereeniging (Trans.)	65,500	72,432	7,930	3,548	149,410
Welkom (O.F.S.)	38,027	133,679	4,902	...	176,608

CLIMATE. The climate is healthy and invigorating, with abundant sunshine and relatively low rainfall. The factors controlling this include the latitudinal position, the oceanic location of much of the country, and the existence of high plateaus. The south west has a Mediterranean climate, with rain mainly in winter, but most of the country has a summer maximum, though quantities show a clear decrease from east to west. Temperatures are remarkably uniform over the whole country. Pretoria. Jan. 70°F (21·1°C), July 52°F (11·1°C). Annual rainfall 31″ (785 mm). Bloemfontein. Jan. 73°F (22·8°C), July 47°F (8·3°C). Annual rainfall 23″ (564 mm). Cape Town. Jan. 69°F (20·6°C), July 54°F (12·2°C). Annual rainfall 20″ (508 mm). Durban. Jan. 75°F (23·9°C), July 62°F (16·7°C). Annual rainfall 40″ (1,008 mm). Johannesburg. Jan. 68°F (20°C), July 51°F (10·6°C). Annual rainfall 28″ (709 mm).

CONSTITUTION AND GOVERNMENT. The Republic of South Africa Constitution Act 1961 established with effect from 31 May 1961, the republic, consisting of the 4 provinces–the Cape of Good Hope, Natal, the Transvaal and the Orange Free State–which until then comprised the Union of South Africa.

On 5 Oct. 1960 a referendum was held among the white voters (1,800,426 on roll) to decide whether the Union should become a republic. Of the 1,634,240 votes polled, 850,458 were in favour of a republican constitution, 775,878 against it; 7,904 votes were invalid. The voting was as follows: Transvaal, 406,632 for, 325,041 against; Cape Province, 271,418 for, 269,784 against; Orange Free State,

110,171 for, 33,438 against; Natal, 42,299 for, 135,598 against; South West Africa, 19,938 for, 12,017 against.

The head of the republic was the State President; he was elected for a 7-year term (at a meeting specially convened for the purpose) by an electoral college consisting of members of the houses of Parliament and presided over by the Chief Justice or a judge of appeal designated by him.

On 29 May 1980 the Republic of South Africa Constitution Fifth Amendment Bill was passed and became operative on 1 Jan. 1981. The Senate was abolished from 1 Jan. 1981 and a 60-member President's Council was formed.

On 2 Nov. 1983 a referendum among white voters approved the South Africa Constitution Bill which had previously been passed in the House of Assembly by 119 votes to 35. Turnout for the referendum was 2,062,469 (76·02%), of whom 1,360,223 voted in favour.

The new constitution became effective on 4 Sept. 1984. It provides for a tricameral parliament: the House of Assembly with 178 members of whom 166 are directly elected and 8 indirectly elected by White voters; the House of Representatives with 85 members of whom 80 are directly elected by Coloured voters; the House of Deputies with 45 members of whom 40 are directly elected by Indian voters.

These houses choose respectively 50 White, 25 Coloured and 13 Indian members of an electoral college which elects an executive President. The President initiates legislation and resolves disputes between houses. He is helped by a 60-member President's Council, of which 35 members are elected by the houses, 15 are MPs nominated by himself and 10 are MPs nominated by Opposition parties.

The President appoints a Ministerial Council for each house, choosing members from the majority party; he appoints a central executive cabinet from the three Councils.

Each house discusses separately legislation on the affairs of its own community (education, housing, health and welfare, local government). Corporate discussion on national issues takes place through joint standing committee.

To hold an office of profit under the State (with certain exceptions) is a disqualification for membership of either House, as are also insolvency, crime and insanity. Pretoria is the seat of government, and Cape Town is the seat of legislature.

The state of the parties on 4 Sept. 1984: in the House of Assembly, National Party, 114; Progressive Federal Party, 26; Conservative Party, 17; New Republic Party, 8; South African Party, 3. In the House of Representatives, Labour Party, 76; others, 4. In the House of Delegates, National People's Party 18; Solidarity, 17; others, 5.

Indians voting in the elections to the new House of Delegates in Aug. 1984, 20·3% of registered voters; Coloured voters to the new House of Representatives, 30·9%.

President and Prime Minister: P. W. Botha (sworn in, 14 Sept. 1984).

The Cabinet sworn in on 17 Sept. 1984 was composed as follows:

Transport Services: H. Schoeman. *Constitutional Development and Planning:* J. C. Heunis. *Foreign Affairs:* R. F. Botha. *Home Affairs and National Education:* F. W. de Klerk. *Law and Order:* L. Le Grange. *Communications and Public Works:* Dr L. A. P. A. Munnik. *Health and Welfare and Chairman of the Ministers' Council for White Own Affairs:* Dr C. V. van der Merwe. *Co-operation and Development and (Black) Education:* Dr G. Viljoen. *Defence:* Gen. M. Malan. *Manpower:* P. T. du Plessis. *Industries and Commerce:* Dr D. J. de Villiers: *Justice:* H. J. Coetsee. *Agricultural Economics and Water Affairs:* J. J. G. Wentzel. *Mineral and Energy Affairs:* D. W. Steyn. *Finance:* B. J. du Plessis. *Environment and Tourism:* J. Wiley. *Chairman of the Ministers' Council for Coloured Own Affairs:* A. Hendrickse. *Chairman of the Ministers' Council for Indian Own Affairs:* A. Rajbansi.

The Prime Minister receives an annual salary of R43,000 and a reimbursive allowance of R20,000; a member of the Cabinet an annual salary of R23,500 and a reimbursive allowance of R6,500; and a Deputy Minister an annual salary of R19,000 and a reimbursive allowance of R6,500.

The English and Afrikaans languages are both official, subject to amendments carried by a two-thirds majority in joint session of both Houses of Parliament.

National flag: Three horizontal stripes of orange, white, blue, with the flags of the Orange Free State and the Transvaal, and the Union Jack side by side in the centre.

National anthem: The Call of South Africa/Die Stem van Suid-Afrika (words by C. J. Langenhoven, 1918; tune by M. L. de Villiers, 1921).

Provincial Administration. In each province there is an Administrator appointed by the State President-in-Council for 5 years, and a provincial council elected for 5 years, each council electing an executive committee of 4 (either members or not of the council), the Administrator acting as chairman. Members of the provincial council are elected on the same system as members of Parliament. The provincial committees and councils have authority to deal with local matters, of which provincial finance, education (primary and secondary, other than higher education and technical education), hospitals, roads and bridges, townships, horse and other racing, and game and fish preservation are the most important. In 1953 the administration and control of Black education was transferred from the provincial councils to the central government. All ordinances passed by a provincial council are subject to the veto of the State President-in-Council.

Black Administration. In 1951 the Bantu Authorities Act was enacted to provide a system of Black tribal, regional and territorial authorities. These were given limited administrative, executive and judicial functions and limited legislative powers. In 1959 the main ethnic groups received legislative recognition by the passing of the Promotion of Bantu Self-Government Act, which provided *inter alia* for the various ethnic groups to develop into self-governing national units, each with a Commissioner-General representing the Government of the Republic.

As the territorial authorities became experienced an executive body in the form of a government service was set up for each authority to increase their administrative power.

As the Act envisages eventual political autonomy for each of the various national units and as representation in the highest White governing bodies is regarded as a retarding factor, the representation of Blacks by Whites in Parliament and the Cape Provincial Administration was abolished with effect from 30 June 1960.

In 1968 the Ciskei (whose people are also Xhosa-speaking) and the Tswana Territorial Authorities were established, followed by the Lebowa (North Sotho), Machangana (Tsonga-Shangaan), Venda and South Sotho Territorial Authorities in 1969 and the Zulu Territorial Authority in 1970.

During 1971 these authorities, with the exception of the Zulu, were granted increased powers in terms of the Bantu Homelands Constitution Act 1971. In terms of the provisions of part I of this Act, 6 of the existing 7 territorial authorities in the Republic of South Africa (the Transkei became a self-governing territory in 1963 by virtue of the provisions of the Transkei Constitution Act of 1963) have been converted to Legislative Assemblies with extended legislative and administrative powers.

Part II of the Bantu Homelands Constitution Act makes provision for the areas of these legislative assemblies to be proclaimed self-governing territories with *inter alia* the power to repeal or amend, with minor exceptions, acts of the Republican Parliament. Executive power is vested in an Executive Council. These Councils, each headed by a Chief Councillor, consist of 6 members, except in the case of the South Sotho, where there are only 4. Each of these Councillors is responsible for the administration of a Department. A civil service has been established in each instance, staffed by citizens of the respective homelands. White officials will serve the homeland governments on secondment, until trained Black citizens are able to take over all duties.

In 1971 the Zulus established a Legislative Assembly. Their seat of government is Ulundi.

The Transkei, territory of the Xhosa nation, became independent on 25 Oct. 1976 (*see* p. 1093), Bophuthatswana on 6 Dec. 1977 (*see* p. 1091), Venda on 13 Sept. 1979 (*see* p. 1094) and Ciskei on 4 Dec. 1981 (*see* p. 1096).

There were (1984) 6 territories with a degree of self-government but still forming part of the Republic, Kwa Zulu, Gazankulu (Machangana-Tsonga people), Lebowa (North Soto), Qwaqwa (South Soto), Ka Ngwane (Swazi) and Kwa Ndebele (Southern Ndebele).

Rhoodie, N. J., and Venter, H. J., *Apartheid: A Socio-Historical Exposition of the Origin and Development of the Apartheid Idea.* Cape Town, 1959

DEFENCE. The South African Defence Force comprises a Permanent Force, a Citizen Force and a Commando organization. The Permanent Force consists of professional soldiers, airmen and seamen who are responsible for the administration and training of the whole Defence Force in peace-time, but who are gradually absorbed into the Citizen Force in time of war. The Permanent Force and the Citizen Force consist of Army, Air Force and Naval components; the Commando organization is an army and air organization.

Every white male citizen between 18 and 65 is liable to undergo training and to render personal service in time of war. Those between the ages of 16 and 25 are liable to undergo a compulsory course of peace training. Peace-time training in Commando organizations extends over a period of 16 years' intermittent training. Training in the Citizen Force takes the form of 2 years of continuous training, followed by 9 years during which training takes place at regular intervals.

Aliens have become liable for military service after 5 years' residence by Act of Parliament, 1967.

The S.A. Defence Force is administered by the Chief of the Defence Force, his advisers being the Chief of the Army, Chief of the Air Force and Chief of the Navy, Chief of Staff Operations, Chief of Staff Personnel, the Chief of Staff Management Services and the Surgeon-General.

Army. South Africa is divided into 9 territorial Commands: Western Province, Eastern Province, Natal, Orange Free State, North Western, Northern Transvaal, Witwatersrand, South West Africa and Southern Cape Commands. Within the various Commands are training units, of which members of the Permanent Force form the permanent staff. Courses of various types are held also at the S.A. Military College. The Army includes 1 armoured, 1 mechanized, 4 motorized and 1 parachute brigade; 1 special reconnaissance regiment and supporting artillery, engineer and signals units. Equipment includes some 250 Centurion/Olifant main battle tanks. Strength (1985) 67,400 (including 50,000 conscripts) with an Active Reserve of 130,000. Paramilitary forces are Commandos (90,000), South African Police (35,500) and Police Reserves (20,000).

Navy. The South African Navy has its headquarters at Pretoria.

A custom-built submarine complex incorporating an operations centre alongside a Syncholift marine elevator capable of docking all South African warships except the large tanker, was opened at Simonstown in July 1972. A new maritime headquarters was opened at Silvermine in March 1973.

The Navy includes 3 French-built diesel-powered patrol submarines, 1 British-built anti-submarine frigate, 9 fast missile armed patrol vessels (6 built in Durban and 3 in Israel), 10 coastal minesweepers (2 converted to minehunters and 2 employed for patrol), 5 seaward defence boats (1 used for surveying), 1 motor gunboat, 1 modern British-built survey ship, 1 fleet replenishment ship, 1 boom defence vessel, 1 small training vessel, 1 torpedo recovery vessel, 4 rescue launches, 30 harbour patrol boats and 7 tugs.

New construction includes 1 more missile-armed fast attack craft being built in South Africa.

Naval personnel in 1985 totalled 760 officers and 4,880 ratings, plus some 1,000 national service men.

Air Force. There is 1 light bomber squadron with 6 Canberra B.12 and 3 Canberra T.4; 1 light bomber squadron with 6 Buccaneer Mk.50; 1 coastal patrol squadron with 18 Piaggio P.166S; 1 fighter-bomber squadron with 32 Mirage F1-AZ ground attack aircraft; 1 general-purpose fighter squadron with Mirage IIICZ interceptors and Mirage IIIRZ reconnaissance fighters; and 1 squadron with Mirage F1-CZ interceptors. Transport squadrons have 9 Transall C-160s, 7 C-130B/E Hercules, more than 40 C-47s, 7 C-54s, 1 Viscount, 4 twin-jet HS.125s and 4 twin-turboprop Merlin IVA light transports. Four helicopter squadrons and No. 22 Flight have more than 80 Alouette IIIs, 60 Pumas and 14 Super Frelons. T-6Gs are used for primary training, followed by advanced training on Impalas and Mirage IIIEZ/DZ, weapons training on Impalas, and multi-engine/crew training on C-47s. Built under licence in the Republic of South Africa, about 150 two-seat Impala Mk. 1s have been followed by 75 single-seat Impala Mk. 2s, based on the Aermacchi MB.326M and 326K respectively. Three squadrons operate C4M Kudu and AM.3C Bosbok liaison aircraft.

The Citizen Force has 5 squadrons of Impalas for counter-insurgency duties and 1 squadron of C4M Kudu and AM.3C Bosbok liaison aircraft. CF personnel have additional functions in regular SAAF squadrons, notably those equipped with C-47 transports and P.166 light transport/coastal patrol aircraft. Total strength (1984) was about 10,000 regular officers and men and 4,000 Citizen Force.

INTERNATIONAL RELATIONS

Membership. The Republic of South Africa is a member of UN.

ECONOMY

Budget. A new basis of subsidy has, with effect from the 1971–72 financial year, been brought into operation by the Government following the investigation of the commission of enquiry into the financial relations between the central government and the provinces. The formula on which this subsidy is based is mainly derived from the calculation of: (1) The needs of the various provinces in respect of the services which they have to provide in the fields of education, health, roads and miscellaneous services; (2) the capacity to pay of the various provinces in respect of the different sources from which their 'own' revenue has to be derived; (3) the deficit which arises when the available revenue of each province, as reflected in its capacity to pay, is subtracted from its expenditure, as adjusted in accordance with its needs.

Total revenue and expenditure of the central government's State Revenue Account in R1m.:

	1980–81	*1981–82*	*1982–83*	*1983–84*[1]
Revenue	13,310·3	14,290·3	17,420·0	19,083·0
Expenditure	13,595·4	16,350·0	19,205·0	21,150·0

[1] Estimate.

Details of total revenue and expenditure (1983–84) of the State Revenue Account for year ended 31 March (in R1m.):

Revenue		*Expenditure*	
Direct taxes	11,272·0	Foreign affairs	779·8
Indirect taxes	6,922·2	Defence	3,534·6
Miscellaneous	1,416·0	Education	2,258·7
		Social welfare and pensions	1,112·3
		Public health	438·2
		Police	1,034·6
		Transfers and loans to provinces, national states and Development Trust Fund	5,417·0

Public debt on 31 March 1982, R25,729m., of which R1,456m. was foreign debt; internal debt, R24,273m.

Currency. Decimal coinage was introduced in 1959, the units being the *rand* (abbreviated as R) and the *cent* (abbreviated as c). The rand/cent coinage system came into operation on 14 Feb. 1961. The decimal coins are: *Gold coins*. 2 rand; 1 rand. *Silver coins*. 50 cents; 20 cents; 10 cents; 5 cents. *Bronze coins*. 2 cents; 1 cent. In March 1985, £1 = R2·22; US$1 = R2·06.

Banking. In Dec. 1920, under the South African Currency and Banking Act, 1920, a Central Reserve Bank was established at Pretoria. It commenced operations in June 1921, and began to issue notes in April 1922. The bank has branches in Pretoria (Head Office), Johannesburg, Cape Town, Durban, Port Elizabeth, East London, Bloemfontein, Pietermaritzburg and Windhoek. Total deposits, 31 Dec. 1982, R2,666m.; assets, R7,900m. The powers of the South African Reserve Bank to control banking and credit were extended by the Banks Act, 1965.

In Jan. 1983 there were 10 commercial banks and 24 general banks (total liabilities, 31 Dec. 1982, R26,092m.), 10 merchant banks (R1,452m.) and 3 discount houses. The Post Office Savings Bank had 2,447,197 current accounts on 31 March 1982; deposits, R236m.

Weights and Measures. Prior to 1969 the imperial system of weights and measures was generally used in the country. However, during 1969 the Weights and Measures Act was amended to provide for the gradual change-over to the metric system of weights and measures.

ENERGY AND NATURAL RESOURCES

Oil. Small amounts of oil and gas were found off-shore (south west of Mossel Bay) in Oct. 1982.

Electricity. The total capacity of the power plants controlled by the Electricity Supply Commission was 21,800 mw at the end of 1982. There were 20 coal-fired stations, 3 hydro-electric stations (1,540 mw) and 2 gas-turbine stations (342 mw).

Water. The government activities in respect of the control and utilization of water are governed by the Water Act, 1956 (as amended), which is administered by the Directorate of Water Affairs. A Water Research Commission was established in 1971 to co-ordinate and promote research; it is responsible for hydrological research, major water resource development, water pollution control. The combined average flow of South Africa's rivers is about 52,000m. cu. metres annually, most of it lost by evaporation and spillage. About 3,100m. cu. metres annually is available from storage dams, and 1,100m. cu. metres from ground water. Water demand (now mainly urban-industrial) grows at 7% annually.

The Orange River Project, launched in 1966, is near completion of its first phase. The estimated cost (at April 1984) was R490m. It is to embrace 3 major dams on the Orange River, 9 smaller dams or weirs, a 51½-mile tunnel, 20 hydro-electric power stations and a system of canals.

Minerals. Value of the main mineral production sales (in R1,000):

	1980	*1981*	*1982*	*1983*
Asbestos	102,148	117,335	107,420	113,279
Chrome ore	90,276	86,304	55,774	71,453
Coal	1,495,016	2,112,532	2,572,435	2,539,731
Copper	299,605	277,604	298,574	351,137
Diamonds	553,043	339,915	341,551	525,217
Fluorspar	36,673	48,042	29,467	30,744
Gold	10,369,611	8,556,613	8,779,328	10,180,209
Iron ore	296,141	361,162	366,320	309,919
Lime and limestone	119,052	142,222	154,092	162,493
Manganese	145,486	165,645	191,714	110,219
Nickel	65,295	...	49,680	53,287
Phosphate	69,135	64,153	75,513	74,271
Silver	81,693	70,143	51,712	79,342
Tin	38,424	30,575	38,048	34,785
Vermiculite	7,998	12,816	13,013	10,815
Zinc	17,304	...	38,925	46,237

Total value of all minerals sold (1983), R16,174·5m.

Mineral production 1983: Coal, 145·8m. tonnes; iron ore, 16·6m. tonnes; phosphates, 2·9m. tonnes; manganese ore, 2·9m. tonnes; chrome, 2·2m. tonnes; asbestos, 221,111 tonnes; copper, 204,984 tonnes; vermiculite, 153,034 tonnes; zinc concentrates, 109,981 tonnes; gold, 677,870 kg; silver, 172,916 kg; diamonds, 10,311,339 carats.

At 30 June 1983 the number of persons engaged in mining was 706,933. Of these, about 430,000 were engaged in goldmining.

The Mineral Resources of the Union of South Africa, With a Summary of the Mineral Resources of South West Africa. Geological Survey, Department of Mineral and Energy Affairs. 5th ed. Pretoria, 1976
Minerals. A Quarterly Report of Production and Sales. Department of Mineral and Energy Affairs. Pretoria, from 1936
Mining Statistics. Department of Mineral and Energy Affairs, Pretoria, from 1966

Agriculture. Much of the land suitable for mechanical farming has unreliable rainfall. Of the total area natural pasture occupies 58% (71·3m. hectares); about 14m. hectares are suitable for dry-land farming, of which 10·6m. are actually cultivated.

South African farmers produced mainly the following crops for the years indicated:

Product (1,000 tonnes)	*1979–80*	*1980–81*	*1981–82*
Maize	10,782	14,198	8,321
Sorghum	695	557	286
Wheat	2,086	1,470	2,339
Groundnuts	250	273	92
Sunflower seed	338	495	303
Sugar-cane	18,412	14,073	19,551
Citrus fruit	702	701	760
Deciduous fruit	897	821	706
Potatoes	686	814	982
Vegetables	1,445	1,561	1,726

Livestock, in 1,000 (1983): 13,086 cattle, 31,750 sheep, 5,950 goats, 1,450 pigs.

The 1982 production of red meat was 865,000 tonnes, poultry meat 411,000 tonnes, wool, 117,000 tonnes. Eggs produced, 260m. dozen; milk, 2,077m. litres.

Cotton-growing is now undertaken by many farmers, the plant being found a better drought resistant than either tobacco or maize. Gross value of production (1981–82), R64m.

Viticulture produced grapes and products valued at R166m. (1981–82).

In 1981–82 the gross value of agricultural production was R7,140m. (field crops, R3,011m.; livestock products, R3,067m.; horticultural products, R1,062m.).

Forestry. The commercial forests occupy about 1·62m. hectares, of which 148,000 hectares are indigenous trees and the rest exotic trees (pine, gum, wattle). The annual output of forest products is about 85m. cu. metres. Production now meets about 90% of domestic need. Capital invested is about R1,100m., and the number of employees about 100,000.

Fisheries. South Africa is no longer engaged in whaling.

About 90% of the catch is taken from the cold waters off the west coast. In 1982 sea fisheries caught 377,003 tonnes of pelagic shoal fish, mainly anchovy, and trawl fisheries (hake and sole) landed 135,000 tonnes. The fishing fleet consists (1983) of about 5,700 vessels, including 139 purse-seiners and 128 trawlers.

INDUSTRY AND TRADE

Industry. Net value of sales of the principal groups of industries (in R1m.) in 1981: Processed food, 7,146; beverages and tobacco, 3,115; motor vehicles, 4,208; basic metals, 5,250; chemicals and products, 9,952; non-electrical machinery, 3,147; non-metallic mineral products, 2,223; electrical machinery, 2,257; clothing, 1,379; paper and products, 1,777; textiles, 2,271; total net value including other groups, 56,047. Manufacturing industry contributed R17,328m. to gross domestic product of R72,777m. in 1982 (preliminary).

Industrial employment (except mining) in 1981: Manufacturing employed 1,468,400 workers (earning R8,348,978,000); construction, 440,600 (R1,868,346,000); transport, communications, 349,317 (R2,395,787,000); trade and accommodation services, 764,722 (R3,590,420,000); government and services, 976,135 (R5,283,077,000).

Of the above figures the following proportion of jobs and salaries were held by white South Africans: Total jobs in manufacturing, 322,500 (earning R4,386,540,000); construction, 57,800 (R758,721,000); transport, communications, 160,895 (R1,832,601,000); trade and accommodation services, 278,909 (R2,378,377,000); government and services, 342,725 (R3,373,738,000).

In 1981 in private manufacturing 174,600 workers were employed in the food industry (earning R696,092,000); textiles employed 118,400 (R437,742,000); clothing, 115,900 (R307,998,000); transport equipment, 115,800 (R831,572,000); non-metallic mineral products, 94,300 (R449,853,000).

Communications comprises the Department of Posts and Telegraphs. Transport comprises South African Railways and Harbours.

Trade Unions. At 1 Jan. 1983 there were 199 trade unions with an estimated total membership of 1,226,454. There were 71 White unions, 46 Coloured and Asian, and 26 Black. Thirty unions had members from all population groups.

The Industrial Conciliation Amendment Act (1979) provides for freedom of association to all workers irrespective of race; it is now possible for a Black trade union (as opposed to a union with some Black members) to register. Unions are barred from political activity.

Commerce. South Africa, Botswana, Lesotho, Swaziland and Transkei are members of a customs union and the foreign trade statistics shown below represent the combined imports and exports of these countries. The total value of the imports and exports, exclusive of specie and gold bullion, was as follows (in R1m.):

Imports		*Exports*	
1978	6,253	1978	7,333
1979	9,904	1979	14,811
1980	14,381	1980	19,915
1981	18,511	1981	18,014
1982	18,378	1982	19,129

The principal commodity groups of imports and exports (in R1m.) in 1982 (preliminary) were:

Imports		*Exports*	
Chemicals	1,347	Food, beverages and tobacco	505
Base metals and metal manufactures	803	Pearls, precious stones and precious metals	2,004
Machinery and parts	5,103	Base metals and metal manufactures	1,727
Textiles	788	Mineral products	2,150
Artificial resins, plastics and products	550	Vegetables and products	972
Vehicles, aircraft and other transport equipment	2,623		

The geographical origin of South Africa's imports and the direction of its export trade were mainly as follows (in R1m.) in 1982 (preliminary):

	Imports	*Exports*
Africa	329·3	925·5
Europe	7,858·4	5,222·0
America	3,083·0	1,692·9
Asia	2,640·2	2,546·4
Oceania	203·0	116·1

Total trade between South Africa and UK (British Department of Trade returns, in £1,000 sterling):

	1980	*1981*	*1982*	*1983*	*1984*
Imports to UK	756,397	649,166	745,803	764,909	725,631
Exports and re-exports from UK	1,002,073	1,219,949	1,192,891	1,109,039	1,205,143

Tourism. In 1981, 708,716 tourists visited the Republic of South Africa, spending approximately R550m.

COMMUNICATIONS

Roads. The railway administration operates the long-distance road motor services, together with private operators.

There were at 31 March 1981, 181,389 km of roads, of which some 1,742 km of national roads and 45,589 km of provincial roads were tarred.

South African Transport Services carried 17·9m. passengers and 3·7m. tonnes of goods by road in the year ended 31 March 1982; private operators carried 1m. passengers and 251·2m. tonnes of goods.

Motor vehicles in operation in 1981 included 2,448,968 passenger cars, 924,649 commercial vehicles, 104,183 buses and mini-buses and 258,288 motor cycles. Motor vehicles licensed in 1981, 4,056,710.

Railways. Railway history in South Africa begins in 1860 with the line Durban–Point. With the formation of the Union in 1910, the state-owned lines in the 4 provinces (12,194 km) were amalgamated into one state undertaking, which also took over the control of the harbours–the South African Railways and Harbours Administration.

Government-owned lines operated by the administration (1984) totalled 23,644 km (mostly 1,065 mm gauge), of which 7,275 km were electrified. Passenger journeys, 1982–83, 722m.; goods traffic, 158m. tonnes.

Aviation. Civil aviation in South Africa is controlled by the Department of Transport, which administers the following state-owned airports: Jan Smuts Airport, Johannesburg; D. F. Malan Airport, Cape Town; Louis Botha Airport, Durban; J. B. M. Hertzog Airport, Bloemfontein; Ben Schoeman Airport, East London; H. F. Verwoerd Airport, Port Elizabeth; B. J. Vorster Airport, Kimberley; P. W. Botha Airport, George; Upington Airport. At 13 other airports the Department provides air navigation services.

South African Airways, as the national air carrier, operate scheduled international air services within Africa and to Europe, South America, the USA, the Far East and Australia. Twenty-three other lines also operate scheduled international air services; they include British Airways, PANAM, KLM, SAS, TAP, Swissair, Olympic Air, El-Al, Alitalia, SABENA, Lufthansa, DETA, Air Zimbabwe, Iberia, DJA, UTA, LUXAIR, Lesotho Airways, Swazi Air, Air Malawi, Air Madagascar. Luxavia operate international non-scheduled flights.

Eighteen independent operators provide internal flights.

During 1982 South African Airways carried 3,937,217 passengers (3,142,956 on internal flights) and 77,548 tonnes of freight and mail (46,871).

Shipping. The main ports are Durban, Cape Town, Saldanha, Richards Bay, Port Elizabeth and East London. Smaller ports are Mossel Bay, Port Nolloth, Walvis Bay and Lüderitz. During 1981–82 these ports handled 78·0m. tons of cargo, of which Richards Bay handled 31·0m. tons and Durban handled 18·5m. tons.

Post and Broadcasting. On 31 March 1982 there were in South Africa 1,641 money-order post offices and 555 postal agencies.

On 30 Sept. 1982 the international telex switchboard served 26,323 telex subscribers in South Africa. Line capacity of automatic telephone exchanges, 2·1m.; there were 3,356,833 telephones.

The South African Broadcasting Corporation had, in Sept. 1980, 2·3m. listeners' licences.

On 5 Jan. 1976 the South African Television Service began official transmissions. There were 1·45m. licences in 1980.

Cinemas (1980). There were 620 including 140 drive-ins.

Newspapers (1981). There are 8 Afrikaans and 14 English daily newspapers.

JUSTICE, RELIGION, EDUCATION AND WELFARE

Justice. The common law of the republic is the Roman–Dutch law–that is, the uncodified law of Holland as it was at the date of the cession of the Cape in 1806. The law of England as such is not recognized as authoritative, though by statute the principles of English law relating to evidence and to mercantile matters, *e.g.*, companies, patents, trademarks, insolvency and the like, have been introduced. In shipping and insurance, English law is followed in the Cape Province, and it has also largely influenced civil and criminal procedure throughout the republic. In all other matters, family relations, property, succession, contract, etc., Roman–Dutch law rules, English decisions being valued only so far as they agree therewith.

The Supreme Court of South Africa is constituted as follows: (i) The Appellate Division, consisting of the Chief Justice and as many Judges of Appeal as the State President may stipulate, is the highest court and its decisions are binding on all courts. It has no original jurisdiction, but is purely a Court of Appeal. (ii) The Provincial Divisions: In each province there is a provincial division of the Supreme Court, while in the Cape there are three such divisions possessing both original and appellate jurisdiction. (iii) The Local Divisions: There is a local division each in the Transvaal and Natal exercising the same original jurisdiction within limited areas as the provincial divisions. The judges hold office till they attain the age of 70 years. No judge can be removed from office except by the State President upon an address from both Houses of Parliament on the ground of misbehaviour or incapacity. The circuit system is fully developed.

The Black appeal courts and 3 Black divorce courts have jurisdiction to some extent concurrent with and in certain respects exclusive of that of the Supreme Court in cases in which the parties are Black.

Each province is further divided into districts with a magistrate's court having a prescribed civil and criminal jurisdiction. From this court there is an appeal to the provincial divisions of the Supreme Court, and thence to the appellate division. Magistrates' convictions carrying sentences above a prescribed limit are subject to automatic review by a judge. In addition, several regional divisions consisting of a number of districts have been constituted. Convictions of such courts are not subject to automatic review by a judge.

Courts of Black affairs commissioners have been constituted in defined areas to hear all civil cases and matters between Black and Black only. An appeal lies to the Black appeal court, whose decision is final, unless the court consents to an appeal to the appellate division of the Supreme Court on a point stated by the court itself. Black affairs commissioners have concurrent criminal jurisdiction with magistrates' courts in respect of certain offences committed by Black, while a limited civil and criminal jurisdiction is conferred upon the Black chief or headman over his own tribe.

Police. In 1980 the staff of the Police department numbered 34,271 (18,370 White). There were 46 police stations manned exclusively by Blacks, 16 by Coloureds and 1 by Indians.

In 1983 there were 242 prisons with (Sept. 1983) a monthly average of 106,000 prisoners.

Religion. A sample tabulation of the 1980 census results as regards religious denominations shows the following: *Whites:* Nederduits Gereformeerd Kerk, 1,693,640; Anglicans, 456,020; Methodists, 414,080; Roman Catholics, 393,640; Nederduits Hervormde Kerk, 246,340; Presbyterians, 128,920; Gereformeerd Kerk, 128,360; Apostolics, 125,920; other Christians, 566,640; Jews, 119,220; others, 255,320. *Blacks:* Methodists, 11,554,280; Black independent churches, 4,954,000; Nederduits Gereformeerd kerk, 1,103,560; Roman Catholics, 1,676,680; Anglican, 797,040; Lutheran, 698,400; other Christian churches, 1,760,860; non-Christian churches, 101,700; others, 4,277,240. *Coloureds and Asians:* Nederduits Gereformeerd kerk, 678,380; Hindus, 512,360; Anglican, 360,380; Roman Catholic, 285,980; Islam 318,000; others, 1,279,020.

Education. *Higher Education.* There are 17 universities in the republic: (1) The University of Cape Town. (2) The University of Natal, Durban and Pietermaritzburg. (3) The University of the Orange Free State at Bloemfontein. (4) Potchefstroom University for Christian Higher Education, Potchefstroom. (5) The University of Pretoria. (6) Rhodes University, Grahamstown, C.P. (7) The University of Stellenbosch. (8) The University of the Witwatersrand, Johannesburg. (9) The University of South Africa, with its seat in Pretoria, which conducts a Division of External Studies by means of correspondence and vacation courses; it is also an examining body. (10) The University of Port Elizabeth. (11) Rand Afrikaans University, Johannesburg.

The University of Fort Hare (12), the University of the North (13) near Pietersburg and the University of Zululand (14) near Empangeni, Natal, are operated by the Department of Education and Training and provide education at university level for Blacks, the University of the Western Cape (15), Bellville (Cape), offers university facilities to the Coloured population and is administered by the Department of Internal Affairs as is the University for Indians (16), the University of Durban-Westville, at Durban. The Medical University of South Africa (17) is for Black students.

The following statistics refer to 1982:

University	*Students*	*University*	*Students*
Cape Town	10,834	Pretoria	15,976
Durban-Westville	4,950	Rand Afrikaans	5,523
Fort Hare	3,201	Rhodes	3,020
Medunsa	703	South Africa	52,200
Natal	8,722	Stellenbosch	11,534
North	4,095	West Cape	4,027
Orange Free State	8,052	Witwatersrand	14,045
Port Elizabeth	2,866	Zululand	3,011
Potchefstroom	6,644		

Technical and Vocational Education. Technical, vocational and special education for persons other than those for whom specific provision is made (*e.g.*, Black): The Department of National Education is responsible for the maintenance, management and control of or the payment of subsidies to colleges for advanced technical education, technical colleges, technical institutes, special schools, schools of industries and reform schools. Colleges for advanced technical education provide education on an advanced level for a variety of technical, commercial and general courses of study as well as secondary education on a part-time basis. Technical colleges and technical institutes are mainly responsible for the training of apprentices and the education, on a part-time basis, of persons not subject to compulsory school attendance. Special schools for handicapped children cater for the educational needs of those who are blind, partially sighted, deaf, hard of hearing, epileptic, cerebral palsied and physically handicapped. Children found to be in need of care by a children's court, are admitted to schools of industries and reform schools.

The Department of Internal Affairs has taken over all schools of this nature for Coloureds.

In 1982, 77 technical and training colleges for Whites had 95,184 students; 12 for Coloureds had about 9,160 students; 1 for Asians had 3,911 students. Provision is made for technical education for Black students at 4 institutions for advanced technical education and 33 industrial or trade schools; total enrolment at these institutions was 15,519 in 1982.

State and State-aided Education other than Higher Education. Primary and secondary public education, other than that specifically provided elsewhere, falls under the Provincial Administration. In terms of the National Education Policy Act, 1967, the Minister of Education, Arts and Science may, after consultation with the Provincial Administrators and the National Advisory Education Council, determine general educational policy within the framework of the Act. Black education is the responsibility of the Department of Black Education and Training, while education for Coloureds and Indians is controlled by the Department of Internal Affairs.

Public primary and secondary schools in 1984: For Whites there were 2,244 schools with 945,258 pupils and 49,273 teachers. Of these, 2,177 were provincial schools (927,531 and 47,907). For Coloureds, 2,030 schools with 781,339 pupils and 29,973 teachers. Of these, 931 were state schools (634,901 and 24,182) and the rest state-aided. For Indians there were 440 schools with 230,725 pupils and 10,011 teachers. Of these, 336 were state schools (206,003 and 9,014) and the rest state-aided. For Blacks there were 12,112 schools with 3,974,500 pupils and 97,560 teachers. Of these, the departments of education in the national states were responsible for 4,708 (2,279,428 and 52,631), and the Republic's Department of Education and Training for the others.

Private Schools. To a certain extent the activities of private schools are controlled by government regulations. Their pupils generally sit for the state schools' examinations. These schools make provision for kindergarten, elementary and preparatory, general primary, secondary and commercial education.

In 1984, 135 private schools for Whites had 3,130 teachers and 43,111 students; 12 schools for Coloureds had 115 teachers and 2,242 students; 84 for Blacks had 784 teachers and 25,434 students.

Teacher-training colleges in 1982: 20 for Whites had 1,248 teachers and 13,196 students;16 for Coloureds and Asians had 234 teachers and 2,909 students; 35 for Bantu had 12,900 students.

Health. At 1 Jan. 1983 there were 18,003 medical practitioners, 4,379 specialists, 3,140 hospital interns, 3,129 dental specialists and dentists; in 1980 there were 595 hospitals. In 1982 there were 21,727 beds in psychiatric hospitals; 484,701 mentally ill were treated as out-patients, and others treated in psychiatric wards in general hospitals.

All public health services rendered by government bodies are free, or charged according to the patient's means. The Department of Health and Welfare works according to the Health Act, 1977. The Department works with the Departments of Internal Affairs and of Co-operation and Development; it also co-operates with the health departments of Black national states.

In preventive medicine there are important programmes for controlling infectious diseases, genetic disorders and malnutrition. Notifiable diseases reported in recent years have been mainly tuberculosis, measles, typhoid, malaria, viral hepatitis, meningococcal infection and (1980–81) cholera.

Social Welfare. *Social Security.* Pensions paid in 1981:

	Beneficiaries	*Amount (R1,000)*
Old age	457,987	335,519
War veterans	22,389	25,868
Blind	7,232	3,907
Disability grants	185,209	117,025
Maintenance	95,271	114,320

Welfare Services. South Africa is not a welfare state, yet provides many services for the community. Welfare work on behalf of the Government is done by the Departments of Health and Welfare, Co-operation and Development, and Internal Affairs.

Voluntary organizations are numerous. The work of all these bodies is coordinated by the South African Welfare Council and regional welfare boards set up under the National Welfare Act, 1978.

The Children's Act, 1960, provides for the protection of children from neglect, ill-treatment and exploitation; the child is cared for within the family whenever possible, but there are also State subsidies to children's homes, crèches and foster families.

Welfare services for the aged are mainly provided by voluntary bodies with government subsidies; the same principle applies to the care of the handicapped, but there are State settlements for the permanently handicapped, and State sheltered-employment programmes for handicapped adults.

The National Advisory Board on Rehabilitation Matters advises and brings together the voluntary and government agencies working on drug abuse and alcoholism.

In all fields of welfare, State subsidies enable voluntary bodies to employ professional social workers.

DIPLOMATIC REPRESENTATIVES

Of South Africa in Great Britain (South Africa Hse., Trafalgar Sq., London, WC2N 5DP)
Ambassador: Dr Denis Worrall.

Of Great Britain in South Africa (6 Hill St., Arcadia, Pretoria, 0002)
Ambassador: P. H. Moberly, CMG.

Of South Africa in the USA (3051 Massachusetts Ave., NW, Washington, D.C., 20008)
Ambassador: Bernardus G. Fourie.

Of the USA in South Africa (225 Pretorius St., Pretoria)
Ambassador: Herman W. Nickel.

Of South Africa to The United Nations
Ambassador: Kurt Robert Samuel von Schirnding.

Books of Reference

Statistical Information: The Bureau (formerly Office) of Census and Statistics (Schoeman St., Pretoria), established on 1 April 1917 as a division of the Department of the Interior and now directly under the Minister of Economic Affairs, is based mainly on the Consolidated Census Act, No. 76, of 1957, and the Consolidated Statistics Act, No. 73, of 1957. Main publications:

Official Year Book of the Union of South Africa and of Basutoland, Bechuanaland Protectorate and Swaziland. From 1918 (preceded by the *Statistical Year Book, 1913–17)*
Union Statistics for 50 Years: Jubilee Issue, 1910–1960 (1960)
Statistical Year Book. From 1964
Statistics of Production: Industrial. Annual, from 1915/16 (but suspended from 1929/30 to 1931/32 and from 1938 to 1942)
Statistics of Production: Agricultural. Annual, from 1917/18 (but suspended from 1920/30 to 1931/32 and from 1939 to 1946)
Monthly Bulletin of Statistics (from 1922)
Population Census, 1970. (Various special reports in course of publication)
South African Reserve Bank, *Quarterly Bulletin of Statistics*
Homelands: The Role of the Corporations in the Republic of South Africa, Johannesburg, 1976

The Customs and Excise Office, Pretoria, publishes *Monthly Abstract of Trade Statistics* (from 1946) and *Trade and Shipping of the Union of South Africa* (annually, 1910–55); *Foreign Trade Statistics* (annually, from 1956)

Bissell, R. E., and Crocker, C. A., *South Africa in the 1980s.* Boulder, 1979
Böhning, W. R., *Black Migration to South Africa.* Geneva, 1981
Branford, J., *A Dictionary of South African English.* Rev. ed. OUP, 1980
de Villiers, L., *South Africa: A Skunk Among Nations.* London, 1975
Gann, L. H. and Duignan, P., *Why South Africa will Survive.* London, 1981
Hellmann, E. and Lever, H., *Race Relations in Africa, 1929–1979.* London, 1980
Lacour-Gayet, R., *A History of South Africa.* London, 1977
Metrowich, F. R., *Africa in the Sixties.* Pretoria, 1970
Muller, C. F. J., *500 Years of South African History.* Pretoria, 1969
Musiker, R., *South Africa,* [Bibliography] Oxford and Santa Barbara, 1980
Parker, F. J., *South Africa: Lost Opportunities.* Lexington, 1983
Talbot, A. M. and W. J., *Atlas of South African History.* Pretoria, 1969
Troup, F., *South Africa: An Historical Introduction.* London, 1972
Walker, E. A., *History of Southern Africa.* London, 1957
The Oxford History of South Africa. OUP, Vol. 1, 1969; Vol. 2, 1971

PROVINCE OF THE CAPE OF GOOD HOPE

Kaapprovinsie

HISTORY. The colony of the Cape of Good Hope was founded by the Dutch in the year 1652. Britain took possession of it from 1795 to 1803 and again in 1806, and it was formally ceded to Great Britain by the Convention of London, 13 Aug. 1814. Letters patent issued in 1850 declared that in the colony there should be a Parliament which should consist of the Governor, a Legislative

Council and a House of Assembly. On 31 May 1910 the colony was merged in the Union of South Africa, thereafter forming an original province of the Union.

AREA AND POPULATION. The following table gives the population of the Cape of Good Hope[1] (area (1980) 646,332 sq. km) at the last census:

		All races		*Whites*		*Non-Whites*	
	Total	*Males*	*Females*	*Males*	*Females*	*Males*	*Females*
1936	3,527,865	1,663,169	1,864,796	396,058	394,993	1,267,011	1,469,803
1946	4,051,424	1,924,334	2,127,090	433,849	436,300	1,490,485	1,690,790
1951	4,426,726	2,110,674	2,316,052	463,917	471,168	1,646,757	1,844,884
1960	5,360,234	2,553,245	2,806,989	493,370	507,398	2,059,875	2,299,591
1970[2]	4,293,726	2,151,629	2,142,097	546,761	567,448	1,604,868	1,579,649
1980[3]	5,091,360	2,575,460	2,515,900	624,680	639,360	1,950,780	1,876,540

[1] Including Walvis Bay (699 sq. km). [2] Excluding Transkei.
[3] Excluding Transkei, Ciskei and Bophuthatswana.

Present area (excluding Griqualand East, Mafikeng and the Republic of Bophuthatswana), 645,767 sq. km (249,331 sq. miles).

Of the non-White population in 1980, 32,120 were Asians, 1,569,040 were Blacks and 2,226,160 Coloureds.

Vital statistics for calendar years:

		Whites			*Asians and Coloureds*	
	Births	*Deaths*	*Marriages*	*Births*	*Deaths*	*Marriages*
1978	17,993	11,859	11,129	58,421	19,274	16,711
1979	17,755	11,594	11,081	63,145	20,591	16,488
1980	17,528	...	11,269	63,018	...	18,065

ADMINISTRATION. The division of parties in the Provincial Council (Sept. 1983) was: National Party, 45; Progressive Fed. Party, 10; New Republic Party, 1.

Cape Town is the seat of the provincial administration.

Administrator: Eugene Louw.

The province is divided into 128 magisterial districts and 38 divisional council divisions. Each division has a council of at least 6 members (15 in the Cape Division) elected quinquennially by the owners or occupiers of immovable property. The duties devolving upon divisional councils include the construction and maintenance of roads and bridges, local rating, vehicle taxation (except motor vehicle taxation) and preservation of public health. There are 219 municipalities, each governed by a mayor and councillors. Municipal elections are held biennially.

FINANCE. In 1984–85 revenue amounted to R1,773,570,000 and expenditure to R1,770,851,000.

MINING. For mineral production, *see* pp. 1074–75.

AGRICULTURE. Viticulture in the republic is almost exclusively confined to the Cape Province, but practically all other forms of agricultural and pastoral activity are pursued.

INDUSTRY. The province has brick, tile and pottery works, saw-mills, engineering works, foundries, grain-mills, distilleries and wineries, clothing factories, furniture, boot and shoe factories, etc.

RELIGION. Sample tabulation, 1980 census. *Whites:* Nederduits Gereformeerd Kerk, 585,400; Gereformeerd Kerk, 13,300; Nederduits Hervormde Kerk, 11,700; Anglicans, 155,460; Presbyterians, 36,120; Methodists, 113,760; Roman Catholics, 92,420; Apostolics, 19,940; other Christians, 141,500; Jews, 34,080; others, 6,280; object to state and no religion; 54,080. *Non-Whites:* Afrikaans Churches, 625,120; Anglicans, 298,520; Congregationalists, 153,880; Methodists, 117,360; Lutherans, 82,440; Roman Catholics, 186,080; Apostolics, 41,620; Black

Independent Churches, 93,840; other Christian Churches, 350,660; Islam, 157,960; Hindus, 6,940.

EDUCATION. *Training.* Higher education is under the control of the Department of National Education, Pretoria. Primary and secondary education (including vocational education and the training of primary teachers) are controlled by the Provincial Administration in respect of White pupils, by the Department of Education and Training in respect of Black pupils and by the Department of Internal Affairs in respect of Coloured pupils. Education is compulsory for all White children. Primary and secondary education is free to the end of the calendar year in which the age of 19 years is attained.

Whites (1984). There were 825 government and aided schools with 14,263 teachers and 239,547 pupils; 8 teacher-training colleges with 299 lecturers and 1,888 students; 53 private schools with 12,367 pupils.

Coloureds (1982). There were 1,810 state and aided schools with 24,499 teachers and 664,286 pupils; 12 teacher-training colleges with 3,748 students; 14 private schools with 2,687 pupils (1981).

Black (1981). There were 1,137 state schools with 5,703 teachers and 248,553 pupils and 17 private schools with 118 teachers and 5,063 pupils.

Asians (1982). There were 7 state schools with 191 teachers and 4,068 pupils.

PROVINCE OF NATAL

HISTORY. Natal was annexed to Cape Colony in 1844, placed under separate government in 1845, and on 15 July 1856 established as a separate colony. By this charter partially representative institutions were established, and in 1893 the colony obtained responsible government. The province of Zululand was annexed to Natal on 30 Dec. 1897. The districts of Vryheid, Utrecht and part of Wakkerstroom, formerly belonging to the Transvaal, were annexed in Jan. 1903. On 31 May 1910 the colony was merged in the Union of South Africa as an original province of the Union.

AREA AND POPULATION. The province (including Kwa Zulu, 10,375 sq. miles) has an area of 86,976 sq. km (33,578 sq. miles), with a seaboard of about 360 miles. The climate is sub-tropical on the coast and somewhat colder inland. The province is divided into 45 magisterial districts.

The census returns of population (excluding Kwa Zulu) for 1980 were:

	All races			*Whites*		*Non-Whites*	
	Total	*Males*	*Females*	*Males*	*Females*	*Males*	*Females*
1960	2,979,034	1,443,561	1,535,473	166,404	222,750	1,227,157	1,362,468
1970	4,236,770	2,009,410	2,227,360	171,005	214,960	1,794,430	2,004,610
1980	2,676,340	1,360,600	1,315,740	276,240	285,620	1,084,360	1,030,120

Of the non-White population in 1980, 665,340 were Asians, 91,020 Coloureds and 1,358,120 Blacks. Population of Kwa Zulu, *see* p. 1068.

ADMINISTRATION. State of parties Oct. 1984: New Republic Party, 14; National Party, 5; Progressive Federal Party, 1.

The seat of provincial government in Natal is Pietermaritzburg. In April 1978 the area of East Griqualand was transferred to Natal from Cape Province.

Administrator: The Hon. Radclyffe Macbeth Cadman.

FINANCE. In 1983–84 revenue amounted to R713·56m. and expenditure to R702·97m.

MINING. The province is rich in mineral wealth, particularly coal. For figures of mineral production, *see* pp. 1074–75.

AGRICULTURE. Sugar and citrus growing are of major importance. On the coast and in Zululand there are vast plantations of sugar-cane (about 800,000 acres), producing, in 1967, 15,547,000 tons. Cereals of all kinds (especially maize), fruits, vegetables, the *Acacia molissima* (the bark of which is much used for tanning purposes) and other crops are produced. Large areas are being afforested.

INDUSTRY. Natal is highly industrialized. There are metallurgical, chemical, paper, rayon and food-processing plants, iron and steel foundries, petrol refineries, pulp-mills, explosives and fertilizer plants, milk- and meat-canning factories.

EDUCATION. The Natal Provincial Administration controls primary and secondary education for Whites. Higher technical and vocational education for all races is provided by the central government. *See also* pp. 1078–80.

Whites (1984). There were 308 government and aided schools with 116,611 pupils; 3 residential teacher-training colleges with 1,203 students; 11 private schools with 786 pupils.

Coloureds (1983). There were 63 government and aided schools with 1,185 teachers and 29,072 pupils; 11 pre-primary schools with 30 teachers and 628 pupils (1982); 1 teacher-training college with 223 students and 25 lecturers; 1 technical college with 367 students and 36 lecturers (1982).

Blacks (1982). There were 1,000 schools with 4,584 teachers and 184,911 pupils. These schools are situated in the white area of Natal and the south-eastern Transvaal.

Asians (1984). There were 358 state and state-aided schools with 8,475 teachers and 195,969 pupils; 17 pre-primary schools with 1,207 children; 2 schools of industries with 275 pupils; 10 special schools and training centres with 995 pupils; 6 technical colleges with 4,452 full-time and part-time students and 1 College of Education with 1,246 students.

PROVINCE OF THE TRANSVAAL

HISTORY. The Transvaal was one of the territories colonized by the Boers who left the Cape Colony during the Great Trek in 1831 and following years. In 1852, by the Sand River Treaty, Great Britain recognized the independence of the Transvaal, which, in 1853, took the name of the South African Republic. In 1877 the republic was annexed by Great Britain, but the Boers took up arms towards the end of 1880. In 1881 peace was made and self-government, subject to British suzerainty and certain stipulated restrictions, was restored to the Boers. The London Convention of 1884 removed the suzerainty and a number of these restrictions but reserved to Great Britain the right of approval of the Transvaal's foreign relations, excepting with regard to the Orange Free State. In 1886 gold was discovered on the Witwatersrand, and this discovery, together with the great influx of foreigners which it occasioned, gave rise to many grave problems. Eventually, in 1899, war broke out between Great Britain and the Transvaal. Peace was concluded on 31 May 1902, the Transvaal and the Orange Free State both losing their independence. The Transvaal was governed as a crown colony until 12 Jan. 1907, when responsible government came into force. On 31 May 1910 the Transvaal became one of the four provinces of the Union.

AREA AND POPULATION. The area of the province is 262,499 sq. km or 101,351 sq. miles, including Gazankulu, Lebowa, Ka Ngwane and Kwa Ndebele. The province is divided into 53 districts. The following table shows the population, excluding Gazankulu, Lebowa, Ka Ngwane and Kwa Ndebele in 1980, at each of the last censuses:

		All races		Whites		Non-Whites	
	Total	Males	Females	Males	Females	Males	Females
1936	3,341,470	1,846,576	1,494,894	424,470	396,286	1,422,108	1,098,608
1946	4,283,038	2,374,323	1,908,715	541,053	522,068	1,833,270	1,386,647
1951	4,812,838	2,619,314	2,193,524	737,194	731,111	2,575,119	2,230,053
1960	6,270,711	3,310,948	2,959,763	735,845	729,730	2,575,103	2,230,034
1970	8,717,530	4,460,130	4,257,400	946,430	938,210	3,513,700	3,319,190
1980	8,350,500	4,567,500	3,783,000	1,190,740	1,171,320	3,376,760	2,611,680

Of the non-White population in 1980, 5,644,660 were Black, 115,560 Asians and 228,220 Coloureds. Population of Gazankulu, Lebowa, Ka Ngwane and Kwa Ndebele, *see* pp. 1068.

Important towns of the province are listed on p. 1069.

ADMINISTRATION. At the provincial council election in 1981 there were returned: National Party, 67; Progressive Federal Party, 9.

The seat of provincial government is at Pretoria, which is also the administrative capital of the Republic of South Africa.

Administrator: Willem A. Cruywagen.

FINANCE. In 1983–84 revenue amounted to R2,039,164,197 and expenditure to R1,972,487,646.

MINING. For mineral production, *see* p. 1074. Gold output in 1983 was 15,807,760 oz. worth R7,483,932,210.

AGRICULTURE. The province is in the main a stock-raising country, though there are considerable areas well adapted for agriculture, including the growing of tropical crops.

INDUSTRY. The province has iron and brass foundries and engineering works, grain-mills, breweries, brick, tile and pottery works, tobacco, soap, and candle factories, coach and wagon works, clothing factories, etc.

RELIGION. Sample tabulation, 1980 census. *Whites:* Nederduits Gereformeerde Kerk, 757,080; Gereformeerde Kerk, 96,020; Nederduits Hervormde Kerk, 212,860; Anglicans, 177,840; Presbyterians, 56,460; Methodists, 155,620, Roman Catholics, 214,240; other Christians, 314,360; Jews, 77,120; others, 13,280.

Non-Whites: Afrikaans Churches, 411,040; Anglicans, 341,800; Presbyterians, 78,080; Congregationalists, 53,080; Methodists, 444,060; Lutherans, 298,260; Roman Catholics, 532,720; Apostolics, 62,520; Black Churches, 1,857,460; other Christians, 484,700; Mohammedans, 68,180; Hindus, 33,580.

EDUCATION. All education for Whites except that of universities is under the provincial authority. The province has been divided for the purposes of local control and management into 21 school districts. Instruction in government schools, both primary and secondary, is free. The medium of instruction is the home language of the pupil. The teaching of the other language begins at the earliest stage at which it is appropriate on educational grounds. Both languages are taught as examination subjects to every pupil

Whites (1982). There were 1,153 public schools with 27,797 teachers and 547,452 pupils; 5 teacher-training colleges with 5,904 students; 84 private schools with 2,009 teachers and 31,597 pupils.

Coloureds (1982). There were 92 state and state-aided schools with 1,898 teachers and 59,547 pupils; 1 teacher-training college with 272 students.

Asians (1982). There were 71 public schools with 1,259 teachers and 28,958 pupils; 1 teacher-training college with 30 teachers and 377 students.

Blacks (1977). There were 2,170 public and private school sections with 15,450 teachers and 735,325 pupils (Homelands excluded).

PROVINCE OF THE ORANGE FREE STATE

Oranje-Vrystaat

HISTORY. The Orange River was first crossed by Europeans in the middle of the 18th century. Between 1810 and 1820, settlements were made in the southern parts of the Orange Free State, and the Great Trek greatly increased the number of settlers during and after 1836. In 1848, Sir Harry Smith proclaimed the whole territory between the Orange and Vaal rivers as a British possession called the 'Orange River Sovereignty'. However, in 1854, by the Convention of Bloemfontein, British sovereignty was withdrawn and the independence of the country was recognized.

During the first 5 years of its existence the Orange Free State was much harassed by incessant raids by the Basutos. These were at length conquered, but, owing to the intervention of the British Government, the treaty of Aliwal North incorporated only part of the territory of the Basutos in the Orange Free State.

On account of the treaty with the South African Republic, the Orange Free State took a prominent part in the South African War (1899–1902) and was annexed on 28 May 1900 as the Orange River Colony. Crown colony government continued until 1907, when responsible government was introduced. On 31 May 1910 the Orange River Colony was merged in the Union of South Africa as the province of the Orange Free State, and on 31 May 1961 became a province of the Republic of South Africa.

AREA AND POPULATION. The area of the province is 127,993 sq. km or 49,418 sq. miles, including Qwaqwa. The province is divided into 34 administrative and 57 magisterial districts. The census population (excluding Qwaqwa) in 1980 has varied as follows:

		All races		*Whites*		*Non-Whites*	
	Total	*Males*	*Females*	*Males*	*Females*	*Males*	*Females*
1936	772,060	381,903	390,157	101,872	99,106	280,031	291,051
1946	879,071	432,896	446,175	101,874	100,203	331,022	345,972
1951	1,016,570	519,166	497,404	115,637	112,015	403,529	385,389
1960	1,386,202	731,486	654,716	139,304	137,103	601,182	553,613
1970	1,716,350	899,140	817,210	148,110	148,030	751,030	669,180
1980	1,931,860	1,039,220	892,640	166,380	159,840	872,840	732,800

Of the non-White population in 1980, 1,549,600 were Black and 56,040 Coloureds. Population of Qwaqwa, *see* p. 1068.

ADMINISTRATION. At the provincial council election in 1981 there were returned 28 National Party.

The seat of provincial government is at Bloemfontein. There are 73 municipal councils, 2 local management boards and 1 village management board.

Administrator: L. J. Botha.

FINANCE. In 1983–84 revenue amounted to R475,355,956 and expenditure to R480,691,652.

MINING. For mineral statistics, *see* p. 1074. The production of the gold-fields in the province has increased tremendously since 1951, when the output was 18,545 oz. valued at R230,186. The output in 1983 was 5,978,046 oz. valued at R2,830,184,709.

AGRICULTURE. The province consists of undulating plains, affording excellent grazing and wide tracts for agricultural purposes. The rainfall is moderate. The country was mainly devoted to stock-farming, but now a rapidly increasing quantity of grain is being raised, especially in the eastern districts.

INDUSTRY. The more important manufacturing industries in the province are the oil-from-coal factory (as well as industries based on its by-products) at Sasolburg; fertilizer, agricultural implements, blanket and woollen products, clothing, hosiery, cement and pharmaceutical factories, grain-mills and brick, tile and pottery works.

EDUCATION. *Whites.* Primary, secondary and vocational education and the training of primary teachers are controlled and financed by the Provincial Administration. The province is divided into 11 regional office areas.

Education is free in all public schools up to the university matriculation standard. Attendance is compulsory between the ages of 7 and 16, but exemption may be granted in special cases. The home language of the pupil is the medium of instruction.

Whites (1984). There were 213 government and aided schools with 4,374 teachers and 76,644 pupils.

Coloureds (1982). There were 41 government and aided schools with 491 teachers and 14,000 pupils.

Blacks (1977). There were 2,406 school sections with 8,071 teachers and 344,064 pupils (Homelands excluded).

SOUTH WEST AFRICA

Suidwes-Afrika—Namibia

HISTORY. The territory (excluding Walvis Bay and certain islands) was proclaimed a German protectorate in 1884, but was surrendered to the Forces of the Union of South Africa on 9 July 1915 at Khorab. The administration was vested in the Government of the Union of South Africa by mandate of the League of Nations dated 17 Dec. 1920. In 1921 the Governor-General delegated certain of his functions to the Administrator of the Territory, who was assisted by an Advisory Council and, from 1925, by an Executive Committee and the Legislative Assembly. On 18 July 1966 the International Court of Justice decided, by the President's casting vote, that Ethiopia and Liberia had no legal right in applying for a decision on the international status of South West Africa. In 1971 the International Court of Justice ruled in an advisory opinion that the Republic of South Africa's presence in South West Africa was illegal. In Dec. 1973 the UN appointed Sean McBride as UN Commissioner for Namibia. The Republic of South Africa was given until May 1975 to declare its intentions on the future of Namibia, by the UN.

Independence was envisaged for 31 Dec. 1978. However in Dec. 1978 an election for a Constituent Assembly was held without UN supervision. The Democratic Turnhalle Alliance Party gained 41 of the 50 seats. The South West Africa People's Organisation (SWAPO) boycotted the election. The Constituent Assembly was not recognized by the UN, the Western Powers or SWAPO. UN plans for a ceasefire and UN-supervised elections were rejected by the Constituent Assembly on 20 April 1979. Discussions continued during 1980 aiming at solutions to the Namibia problem and in Jan. 1981 a UN Conference was held in Geneva but this also ended in failure as did various discussions held in 1982.

AREA AND POPULATION. The total area of the Territory, including the Caprivi-Zipfel, is 318,261 sq. miles (824,269 sq. km); this figure includes that of Walvis Bay, administered by South West Africa, 434 sq. miles (1,124 sq. km).

The country is bounded on the north by Angola and Zambia, on the west by the Atlantic ocean, on the south and southern portion of the eastern boundary by the Cape Province, and on the remainder of the eastern boundary by Botswana and Zambia. There are 3 main regions: the Namib, an extremely arid and desolate region stretching along the entire coastline to a width of between 80 to 130 km. The major portion of the Namib receives an annual rainfall of less than 50 mm. The

Central Plateau is the region lying to the east of the Namib. It varies in altitude between 1,000 and 2,000 metres and offers a diversified landscape of rugged mountains, rocky outcrops, sand-filled valleys and plains. It covers approximately 50% of the total area; the Kalahari covers the eastern, north-eastern and northern areas of South West Africa.

The rainfall increases steadily from less than 50 mm. in the west and south-west up to 600 mm. in the Caprivi Strip.

The Kunene River and the Okavango, which form portions of the northern border of the country, the Zambesi, which forms the eastern boundary of the Caprivi-Zipfel, the Kwando or Mashi, which flows through the Caprivi-Zipfel from the north between the Okavango and the Zambesi, and the Orange River in the south, are the only permanently running streams. But there is a system of great, sandy, dry river-beds throughout the country, in which water can generally be obtained by sinking shallow wells. In the Grootfontein area there are large supplies of underground water, but except for a few springs, mostly hot, there is no surface water in the country.

On 13 Oct. 1964 and 29 Jan. 1969 the Republic of South Africa and Portugal signed agreements on the common use of the Kunene River.

Owing to the difficulty of satisfactorily controlling that part of the Caprivi-Zipfel, east of the line running due south from Beacon 22, situated west of the Kwando (or Mashi) River, the control of this area was in Aug. 1939 transferred to the Union Department of Native Affairs.

The population at the census 1960 and 1970 and estimate 1982 was:

	1960	*1970*	*1982*
Ovambos	239,363	342,455	516,600
Whites	73,464	90,658	75,600
Damaras	44,353	64,973	76,800
Hereros	44,588	55,670	77,600
Namas	34,806	32,853	49,700
Kavangos	27,871	49,577	98,000
Caprivians	15,840	25,009	39,500
Coloureds	12,708	28,275	43,500
Basters	11,257	16,474	23,800
Bushmen	11,762	21,909	29,900
Tswana	...	4,407	6,800
	516,012	732,260	1,039,800

The population grew at a rate of 2·7% per annum between 1970 and 1981.

The Ovambos are a Bantu race and are both agriculturists and owners of stock. They still possess tribal organization to its full extent.

The Hereros are a pastoral people who formerly owned enormous herds of cattle. Wars with Namas and Germans destroyed their tribal organization. Under the Union and Republic administration, reserves have been set apart and they have considerably increased in numbers and in animal wealth.

The ethnic origin of the Bergdamaras or Damara is still not certain. They were alternatively the slaves of the Hereros and the Namas, whose language they now speak, in pre-European days.

The Namas consist of 2 distinct sections: one, the Hamitic, whose remnants are found in the central portions of the country, being of pure native extraction, is thought to have migrated from the region of the Central African lakes in prehistoric times; the other, the Khoisan, is composed of tribes whose members are descended from persons born in the Cape a couple of centuries ago with an admixture of European and Nama blood.

The Bushmen are among the oldest inhabitants of southern Africa.

In the centre of the country just south of the Windhoek district is the Rehoboth Gebiet, occupied by a race known as the Basters, who are of mixed Nama–European descent and whose ordinary language is Afrikaans.

ADMINISTRATION. The South West Africa Affairs Amendment Act, 1949, abolished the Advisory Council and the nominated members of the Legislative

Assembly. All 18 members of the Assembly are now elected by the registered voters of the Territory.

The election held on 24 April 1974 returned 18 Nationalists.

Until 1977 the Territory was represented in the South African House of Assembly by 6 members elected by the registered voters of the Territory, and in the Senate by 4 Senators, of which number 2 were elected by the members of the Legislative Assembly and the representatives of the Territory in the House of Assembly, and 2 nominated by the President of the Republic. Under the South West Africa Constitution Amendment Act 1977 this representation was abolished.

A commission of inquiry, appointed by the South African Government, in 1964 recommended the establishment of 'homeland areas' for the non-White groups. All these areas should be governed by legislative councils, headed by executive committees; franchise should be granted to males and females over 18 years who qualify for citizenship in their respective homelands.

On 17 Oct. 1968, 22 Oct. 1970 and 15 March 1973 respectively the first sessions of the Legislative Councils of Ovambo (77 members), Kavango (30 members) and Eastern Caprivi (28 members) were opened.

On 1 May 1973 and 9 May 1973 respectively Ovambo and Kavango obtained self-government.

On 13 Oct. 1966 the security and apartheid laws of the Republic of South Africa were extended to South West Africa, retrospective to 1950. The Legislative Assembly adopted a resolution on 22 Nov. 1974 inviting the representatives of the various population groups to deliberate with the representatives of the Whites on the manner in which they should exercise their right of self-determination in view of the South African government's desire that the inhabitants of South West Africa should themselves decide upon their future.

The seat of the administration is Windhoek. The country is divided into 22 districts controlled by magistrates and commissioners.

Administrator-General: Dr Willem van Niekerk.

ECONOMY

Budget. The revenue and expenditure (in R1,000) were:

	1978–79	*1979–80*	*1980–81*	*1982–83*	*1983–84*
Revenue	293,800	460,600	888,267	839,591	975,186
Expenditure	320,100	519,900	837,442	840,111	1,035,884

Banking. Barclays Bank International, Standard Bank, Bank Windhoek, Netherlands Bank, Trust Bank, South African Reserve Bank and Boland Bank have branches in the Territory. The only indigenous bank, The Bank of South West Africa, was established in 1973.

NATURAL RESOURCES

Minerals. Mineral export/sales amounted to R545·05m. in 1979. Diamonds, which constitute the principal production, are mainly recovered from alluvial terraces on a 60-mile stretch along the coastline from the Orange River mouth northward.

Agriculture. South West Africa is essentially a stock-raising country, the scarcity of water and poor rainfall rendering agriculture, except in the northern and north-eastern portions, almost impossible. Generally speaking, the southern half is suited for the raising of small stock, while the central and northern portions are better fitted for cattle.

Livestock (1983): 1·9m. cattle, 5·5m. sheep, 2·2m. goats. In 1981, 330,642 head of cattle and 48,889 beef carcasses and 583,182 head of small stock were exported.

In 1977–78, 188,402 kg of butter and 113,197 kg of factory cheese were manufactured. Other products produced are maize, 9,239 tons (1978); millet, 25,000 tons (1978); sunflower, 2,000 tons (1977); peanuts, 500 tons (1977).

The production of karakul pelts is of increasing importance. In 1983, 850,000 pelts, worth R9m. were produced.

Fisheries. The total catch in 1982 was 207,000 tonnes. The sales value of fish products (1977) was R67m.

COMMERCE. The statistics concerning the external trade of South West Africa are included in those of the Republic of South Africa (*see* p. 1076).

The bulk of the direct imports into the country is landed at Walvis Bay.

Total trade between South West Africa and UK (British Department of Trade returns, in £1,000 sterling):

	1980	*1981*	*1982*	*1983*	*1984*
Imports to UK	18,898	45,301	45,413	62,437	64,015
Exports and re-exports from UK	2,726	2,028	3,973	3,425	5,200

COMMUNICATIONS

Roads. In 1983 there were 4,361 km of trunk roads, 37,000 km of main and district roads, of which 4,133 km are bitumen surfaced. In 1983 there were 120,000 registered motor vehicles.

Railways. The South West Africa system connects with the main system of the South African Railways at De Aar. The total length of the line inside South West Africa is 2,340 km of 1,065 mm gauge.

Aviation. In 1981–82 the Territory's 4 major airports handled 194,170 passengers and 2,157,140 kg of freight.

Shipping. In 1979–80 Walvis Bay harbour handled 1,899 vessels, of which 570 were freighters, and Luderitz, 233 vessels.

Post and Broadcasting. At 31 March 1983 there were 82 post offices and postal agencies, and 656 private bag services distributed by rail or road transport.

There were 26,361 circuit km of trunk lines, 447,146 circuit km of microwave channels, 447,733 km of carrier circuits, 354,194 km of telegraph circuits and 50,100 km of farm telephone lines; 81 telegraph offices, 149 telephone exchanges, and 60,737 telephones. There were 9,297 licensed radio stations in operation.

In 1982–83, 45,296 wireless licences and 14,717 television licences were issued. There were 18,886 km of broadcast circuits.

A post office savings bank was established in 1916. The number of accounts opened in 1982–83 was 3,398. The balance due to holders as at 31 March 1983 amounted to R1,726,169.

EDUCATION AND WELFARE

Education (1983). There were 1,100 schools for all races, 272,615 pupils and 8,984 teachers. This included 36 academic high schools, 3 centres for handicapped children, 3 technical schools and 4 agricultural colleges.

Health (1983). There were 75 hospitals and 135 clinics. The ratio of beds per population was 7 per 1,000. There were 180 general practitioners, 19 specialists and 40 dentists. Nursing staff numbered 3,293.

Books of Reference

The Territory of South West Africa. (In *Official Year Book of the Republic of South Africa*)
Department of Mines: *Quarterly Information Circulars: Industrial Minerals*
Green, R. H., Kiljunen, K. and Kiljunen, M.-L. (eds.) *Namibia: The Last Colony.* London, 1982
Rotberg, R. I., *Namibia: Political and Economic Prospects.* Lexington, 1983
Schoeman, E. R., and H. S., *Namibia.* [Bibliography] Oxford and Santa Barbara, 1984
Thomas, W. H., *Economic Development in Namibia.* Munich, 1978
Tötemeyer, G. *Namibia Old and New.* New York, 1979
van der Merwe, J. H., *National Atlas of South West Africa.* Windhoek, 1983
Vigne, R., *A Dwelling Place of Our Own: The Story of the Namibian Nation.* London, 1973

BOPHUTHATSWANA

HISTORY. Bophuthatswana was first to obtain self-government under the Bantu Homelands Constitution Act of 1971 and was the second black homeland to ask the Republic of South Africa for full independence, which was granted on 6 Dec. 1977.

AREA AND POPULATION. The total area is 44,000 sq. km.

In 1980 there was a *de jure* population of 2·6m., of which 67% lived in the White areas. The remaining 35% (923,600) lived in the homeland. In addition, the homeland has a further population of about 405,000 non-Tswanas, giving the homeland a *de facto* population of about 1,328,637. Estimate (1984) 1·42m.

CONSTITUTION AND GOVERNMENT. The Bophuthatswana Government is a compromise between the traditional chief-in-council system and a democratic electoral system. There are 72 elected and 24 nominated members in the Legislative Assembly. Self-government was granted in 1972. Each regional authority (coinciding with the 12 districts of the homeland) nominates 2 members, and each district elects six members to the National Assembly and 12 designated by the President on account of their special knowledge, qualifications or experience.

Executive power vests in the President, who is directly elected by general suffrage of persons who are registered as voters, and he elects his Cabinet.

The first general election was held in Oct. 1972, 2 political parties taking part. Kgosi Lucas Mangope's Bophuthatswana National Party (BNP) won 20 of the 24 contested seats, but in 1974 he formed the Bophuthatswana Democratic Party which in 1979 held two-thirds of the seats in the Assembly and in the 1983 elections gained all the seats.

Members of regional authorities are elected from among the tribal and community authorities in their area.

The Cabinet in Sept. 1984 consisted of:

President, Minister of Economic Affairs and National Assembly: Kgosi L. M. Mangope.

Foreign Affairs: T. M. Molatlhwa. *Law and Order:* Kgosi B. L. M. Motsatsi. *Agriculture:* Kgosi F. M. Mokgoko. *Works and Water Affairs:* T. M. Tlhabane. *Lands and Rural Development:* D. C. Mokale. *Defence:* Brig. H. F. Riekert. *Health and Social Welfare:* Dr K. P. Mokhobo. *Transport:* G. J. Makodi. *Finance:* L. G. Young. *Post and Telecommunications:* C. M. A. V. Sehume. *Internal Affairs:* Rev. S. M. Seodi. *Manpower Utilization:* R. Cronje. *Local Government and Housing.* S. L. L. Rathebo. *Education.* G. L. Holele. *Speaker:* M. S. E. Motshumi.

There were 5 Deputy Ministers.

Flag: Blue, crossed by a diagonal orange stripe, and in the canton a white disc charged with a leopard's face in black and white.

INTERNATIONAL RELATIONS

Aid. The Republic of South Africa granted aid of R22m. in 1980–81.

ECONOMY

Budget. The 1984–85 budget balanced at R822m.

Currency. South African Rand.

NATURAL RESOURCES

Water. The Department of Agriculture inherited the following improvements from South Africa: 2,833 reservoirs; 6,845 boreholes, of which more than 4,000 have been equipped; 648 earth dams.

Minerals. The territory is particularly rich in minerals. In 1976 there were 34 mines employing 53,000 people. Minerals include platinum, asbestos, iron ore, manganese, chrome, vanadium, limestone, diamonds and fluorspar.

Exploration for more platinum, chrome and coal is currently being carried out both by the private sector and by the Mining and Geological Survey Division of the Department of Economic Affairs. The platinum mines around Rustenburg produce about 66% of the free world's total production. The major chrome mines are near Rustenburg and Marico, while vanadium is mined in the Odi district near Brits.

The Rustenburg, Western and Impala Platinum mines which Bophuthatswana shares with the Republic of South Africa produce about 1·9m. oz. a year.

AGRICULTURE. Bophuthatswana is a semi-arid area of bushveld and grass veld suitable for stock farming. The annual rainfall is 300 mm in the west and 700 mm in the east and there are 3 river catchment areas—those of the Molopo, Ngotwane, Limpopo and Vaal rivers.

Although the land tenure system militates against establishing large farms, some land which is unsuitable for building on is leased by the Government to successful farmers.

Livestock (1983): Cattle, 607,790; sheep, 201,893; goats, 429,769.

Only 6·6% of the territory is suited to dryland cropping, but crop yields have shown a steady improvement in recent years. In Ditsobotla district, 3,500 hectares of fertile land has been developed by 3 primary co-operatives comprising 190 Tswana farmers. Silkworm farming was being tried in 1983. By 1981 the country was self sufficient in maize and exported the surplus. Three rice projects are successfully expanding and vegetable production was increasing in 1984.

INDUSTRY. The first industries were started on an agency basis at Babelegi; the fastest growing industrial area in the homeland, in 1977 it covered 183 hectares and by March 1982 more than R234m. had been invested in the project. Other industries are situated at Garankuwa, Selosecha, Montshiwa and Mogwase. Border industries are also promoted by the central government, notably Rosslyn where 128 industries had been established by Dec. 1975.

COMMUNICATIONS

Roads. Total length (1977) 6,300 km, of which 63 km are tarred. 1976–77, 32 km were covered by bus, and 116m. passengers transported.

Post and Broadcasting. There were 18,232 telephones at 31 Aug. 1984.

EDUCATION AND WELFARE

Education. In 1982 the territory's total school attendance was 485,680 at 1,115 educational institutions which include special schools and technical schools. Primary school attendance in 1983 was 353,721; middle schools, 97,293; high schools, 44,599; teacher training college, 2,408; technical and vocational schools, 1,381; university (1984), 1,269. There were (1983) 13,708 teachers and lecturers.

Education is free apart from a nominal contribution to school funds, and hostel fees at post-primary schools.

Instruction from Grade I to Standard 2 is in Setswana, while Standard 3 to senior standards are taught in English. The education is controlled by the Department of Education with a budget of R144m.

Health. In 1982 there were 10 hospitals, 146 clinics, 4,806 hospital beds, 91 doctors and 3,342 nurses. The health budget in 1984–85 was R71m.

Book of Reference

Five Years of Independence: Republic of Bophuthatswana. Mafikeng, 1983

TRANSKEI

HISTORY. Transkei is the homeland of the Xhosa nation and was granted self-government by the Republic of South Africa in 1963. Over 1·5m. Transkeians live permanently in the Republic of South Africa but were deprived of their South African citizenship on independence.

AREA AND POPULATION. The total area is 16,910 sq. miles (43,798 sq. km). Population (1983 estimate) 2·5m., of which (1976) Coloured 7,650 and Whites 10,000. The capital is Umtata (population (1976) 24,805; 20,196 Blacks, 1,067 Coloured and 3,542 Whites). Other towns include Gcuwa, Kwabhaca, Umzimvubu and Lusikisiki.

CONSTITUTION AND GOVERNMENT. The Status of Transkei Bill passed its third reading in the South African House of Assembly on 11 June 1976 and received its second reading in the Senate on 17 June. The Bill gave Transkei a unicameral National Assembly instead of the then existing Legislative Assembly. Independence was achieved 25 Oct. 1976.

General elections were held on 29 Sept. 1976 and the Transkei National Independence Party gained 69 of the 75 elective seats in the National Assembly. Members were elected for a 5-year period. In addition there are 75 traditional (co-opted) members (70 chiefs and 5 paramount chiefs).

President: Paramount Chief Dr K. D. Matanzima.

Prime Minister: Chief George Matanzima.

Defence, Police, Foreign Affairs and Information: G. T. Vika. *Finance and Auditor-General:* R. Madikizela. *Local Government and Local Tenure:* G. S. Ndabankulu. *Interior:* S. N. Sigcau. *Education:* H. H. Bubu. *Works and Energy, Commerce and Industry:* W. S. Mbanga. *Posts, Telecommunications and Transport:* A. N. Jonas. *Health:* D. D. P. Ndamase. *Prisons and Justice:* T. T. Letlaka. *Agriculture and Forestry:* E. Z. Booi.

Flag: Three horizontal stripes of ochre, white, green.

FINANCE. The budget (1982–83) balanced at R627m.

AGRICULTURE. Notable examples of successful commercial enterprises in agriculture are the Magwa tea estate and various fibre plantations. 70,000 hectares of land are under indigenous forests and 61,000 hectares have been put under exotic plantations. There are 28 sawmills in the country.

Livestock (1976): Cattle, 1·3m.; sheep, 2·5m.; goats, 1·25m.

COMMUNICATIONS

Roads. There are above 8,800 km of roads.

Railways. There is a 209 km railway line linking Umtata with the port of East London in the Republic of South Africa.

Aviation. An international airport exists at Umtata.

Shipping. A start was made in 1978 on a 'free port' at Mnganzana. It will be completed in 5–6 years at a cost of R125m. by a French consortium.

Post. There were 11,498 telephones in 1978.

EDUCATION AND WELFARE

Education. In 1976 there were more than 500,000 pupils in nearly 2,000 schools with 10,000 teachers. The national university was inaugurated in Umtata in 1977.

Health. There are 31 hospitals with a total of 7,561 beds.

DIPLOMATIC REPRESENTATIVES

No country, other than the Republic of South Africa, has recognized Transkei as an independent state.

VENDA

HISTORY. Traditionally the territory of the Vhavenda, the country was granted self-government in 1973, and became the third black homeland to be granted independence by the Republic of South Africa on 13 Sept. 1979.

AREA AND POPULATION. The total area is 6,500 sq. km. Of the 381,000 Vhavenda living in the Republic of South Africa in 1970, nearly 70% lived in Venda. In 1980 the *de jure* population of Venda was estimated at 513,890, the *de facto* population at 343,480.

Vital statistics, 1981: Births, 13,568; deaths, 1,069; marriages, 228.

CONSTITUTION AND GOVERNMENT. Executive power is vested in the President, who is elected for the duration of each Parliament, which consists of the President and the National Assembly; legislative power is vested in Parliament. In addition to the National Assembly there is an Executive Council, or Cabinet, and a judiciary independent of the Executive. The National Assembly comprises the 28 chiefs, 15 members designated by 4 regional councils, 42 members elected by popular vote and 3 members nominated by the President. A new Assembly must be elected after every 5 years, but it may be dissolved at any time by the President. All existing tribal, community and regional councils were retained with their status and powers unchanged, like those of the tribal leaders.

The first general election was held in Aug. 1973; the sole political party, the Venda Independence People's Party (VIPP) won 10 of the 18 contested seats. Shortly after, the Chief Minister, Chief Mphephu, formed the Venda National Party (VNP); in the second general election of July 1978 the VIPP won 31 of the 42 contested seats, VNP the remaining 11. Chief Mphephu was re-elected Chief Minister.

President: Paramount Chief P. R. Mphephu.

Foreign Affairs: Chief A. M. Madzivhandila. *Economic Affairs:* Headman F. N. Ravele. *Education:* Headman E. R. B. Nesengani. *Urban Affairs and Land Tenure:* Chief C. A. Nelwamondo. *Justice:* Chief J. R. Rambuda. *Health and Welfare:* Chief C. N. Makuya. *Agriculture and Forestry:* G. M. Ramabulana. *Internal Affairs:* Chief M. M. Mphaphuli. *Transport, Works and Communications:* A. A. Tshivhase. *Deputy for Posts and Telecommunications:* Headman B. R. Nemulodi. *Deputy for Information and Broadcasting and of Public Service Commission:* W. R. Rabuma.

Flag: Three horizontal stripes of green, yellow, and brown, with a brown V on the yellow stripe, and a blue vertical strip in the hoist.

INTERNATIONAL RELATIONS

Aid. The Republic of South Africa granted aid of R45m. in 1981–82.

ECONOMY

Budget. The 1982–83 budget balanced at R115·07m.

Currency. South African Rand.

NATURAL RESOURCES

Water. In Oct. 1982 there were 118 hectares of canals, 250 dams and 520 boreholes.

Minerals. Venda is relatively poor in mineral resources, although there are large supplies of stone for construction. Coal is the most important mineral; there are large deposits in the west near Makhado and in the north-east, bordering on the Kruger National Park, which it is hoped will soon be exploited. In addition there are deposits of graphite, copper sulphides, phosphates and magnesite; in 1978 the 2 graphite and 2 magnesite mines provided employment for 233 people, and the value of their output was R963,900.

Agriculture. About 85% of Venda is suitable only for the raising of livestock because of insufficient rainfall and poor soils, while some 10% is suited to dry-land crop production. Over 10,965 hectares have been given over to forest, mainly pine and eucalyptus. Eighteen irrigation schemes are being developed and there is extensive reclamation and conservation of eroded or overgrazed land; nearly R2m. were spent on these projects in 1980–81. Only maize is grown on a comparatively large scale, but tea, sisal, groundnuts, coffee and sub-tropical fruits are increasing in importance. A fish-breeding project produced 3 tonnes in 1980–81.

Over 80% of the working population are engaged in agriculture. The Venda Agricultural Corporation (Agriven) was established on 1 April 1982 to promote agricultural development.

INDUSTRY. Industrial development is still in its early stages, and since Venda's location is unfavourable, the Government is concentrating on the promotion of agro-industries utilizing local produce, and small-scale industries. A chutney factory has recently been established, in addition to a tea processing plant, a furniture factory and several saw-mills. A copper-chrome arsenate preservation plant has been established at Phiphidi. At Shayandima a 20-hectare industrial area has been prepared. The construction industry is particularly important owing to the substantial increase in the demand for buildings caused by the recent expansion of government, educational and health services.

In Dec. 1982 total investment in industry was estimated at R18·9m. The Venda Development Corporation was established in 1975 to promote and finance economic developments.

COMMUNICATIONS

Roads. There were (1982) 1,226 km of roads, of which 50 km had a permanent surface.

Aviation. An airline, inaugurated in 1981, operates between Nwangundu in Thohoyandu and Johannesburg *via* Pietersburg and Pretoria.

Post and Broadcasting. In 1983 there were 30 post offices and postal agencies. Telephones (1982) numbered, 1,547. In 1984 the government-owned Radio Thohoyandu broadcast 17 hours daily.

EDUCATION AND WELFARE

Education. The Department of Education assumed responsibility for education on independence. Education is free up to Standard 2, and pupils are taught in the native tongue, Luvenda, for the first 4 years (up to Standard 2), after which English is gradually introduced. Secondary education comprises Standards 6 to 10.

The number of primary schools increased from 233 (1970) to 502 (1984), the number of pupils from 65,500 (1970) to 157,014 (1982) and the number of teachers from 956 (1970) to 4,586 (1982).

In 1970 there were 12 secondary schools, which had increased to 112 by 1982. Pupils numbered 2,465 in 1970, 33,432 in 1982, while the number of teachers increased from 100 (1970) to 1,062 (1982).

In addition there is a technical school at Sibasa with about 320 pupils, an agricultural school at Dimani with 476 pupils, and a school for the handicapped at Shayandima. There are 2 teacher-training colleges; enrolment was 704 in 1982. The University of Venda was established in 1981; 1,358 students (1984).

Health. In 1984 there were 5 hospitals/homes with 1,556 beds and 47 clinics. White doctors numbered 10 and coloured, 3; there were 712 nurses.

Welfare. In 1981–82 the Government spent R7·3m. on grants and pensions to 22,249 recipients. There is one welfare home.

CISKEI

HISTORY. On 4 Dec. 1981 the Republic of South Africa gave independence to Ciskei the fourth of the tribal homelands.

AREA AND POPULATION. Ciskei lies between latitudes 32° and 33°35′ and longitudes 26°20′ and 27°48′, and has a coastal boundary between East London and Port Alfred. The total area is about 8,300 sq. km. The population was (1981) 2·1m. but only 660,000 live in Ciskei. The remainder work in the Republic of South Africa and as a result can be deported as aliens.

Populations of towns (1984): Mdantsane, 300,000; Zwelitsha, 47,000; Sada, 30,000; Dimbaza, 17,800 and Litha, 5,326.

CONSTITUTION AND GOVERNMENT. In 1981 Ciskei became an independent democratic republic with an Executive Council consisting of the President, Vice-President and 11 ministers appointed by the President. The legislature is a National Assembly consisting of (1984) 41 Hereditary Chiefs, 22 elected and 5 nominated Members and the Paramount Chief's representatives of 37 are traditional leaders, the others being elected on the basis of adult suffrage every five years.

President: Dr Lennox Sebe.

Flag: Blue, a broad diagonal band from lower hoist to upper fly, charged with a black crane.

National Anthem: Nkosi Sikelel' i Afrika, composed by Enoch Sontonga.

ECONOMY

Budget. In 1984–85, revenue was R366,013,000 and expenditure R438,197,000.

Currency. South African Rand.

ENERGY AND NATURAL RESOURCES

Electricity. Ciskei is totally dependent on power supply lines maintained by the Republic of South Africa.

Minerals. Mineral resources are mainly undeveloped and in 1984 only one mine existed in Ciskei.

Agriculture. In 1977–78, total agricultural production was valued at R8·26m.

In 1983–84, the dryland products included (in tons): Maize, 1,075; wheat, 1,015; dry beans, 304; pumpkins, 14,500; potatoes, 21,750. The main crops produced under irrigation were (1979–80, in tons): Potatoes, 385; lucerne, 364; maize, 333; beans, 77; wheat, 64.

Livestock (1983): 75,000 cattle, 175,000 sheep, 226,000 goats, 15,000 pigs.

Forestry. In 1983–84, 5,500 hectares were planted mainly with conifers. The indigenous forest covered some 18,000 hectares. In 1984–85 (estimate), production of timber was valued at R600,000.

INDUSTRY AND TRADE

Industry. In 1983 total investment was R275·2m. The chief manufactures include textiles, wood and leather goods, metal products, crafts and light industrial articles.

Commerce. International trade is mainly with the Republic of South Africa and no separate figures are available. The main exports are pineapples, timber and manufactured goods.

Tourism. Tourism is an important and developing industry.

COMMUNICATIONS

Roads. In 1980 there were 407 km of tarred roads and 1,397 km of gravel roads.

Railways. There are two main railway lines serving the southern part of Ciskei only.

Aviation. Ciskei depends mainly on East London's airport though there is a small airfield at King William's Town and minor landing strips elsewhere.

Shipping. Ciskei has no harbour of its own but has full access to the facilities of East London in the Republic of South Africa.

Post and Broadcasting. All major centres have post offices and manual telephone exchanges; automatic exchanges and telex are gradually being provided. There were (1984) 10,924 telephones. Radio Xhosa broadcasts daily.

Newspapers (1981). There were two Ciskeian newspapers, one of which, *Imvo,* was first published in 1884.

JUSTICE, RELIGION, EDUCATION AND WELFARE

Justice. The Supreme Court acts as Court of Appeal for the eight Magistrates' Courts, which in turn act as Courts of Appeal for the chiefs' courts. Appeals from the Supreme Court are heard by the Appellate Division of Ciskei in Bisho.

Religion. In 1980 (estimate) the population was 24% Methodists, 21% Independent, 8% Presbyterian Congregationalists, 7% Anglicans, 6% Roman Catholics, 2% Dutch Reformed Church, 2% other Christians, 28% ancestor worship and 2% other religions.

Education. In 1981 there were 499 primary schools with 184,736 pupils and 4,240 teachers; 126 secondary and teacher-training schools with 48,838 pupils and 1,576 teachers; and 2 vocational schools with 304 pupils and 32 teachers. The University of Fort Hare had a total of 2,304 students in 1981.

Health. In 1983–84, there were 25 hospitals with 2,458 beds, and a total of 2,763 nursing staff.

Social Welfare. Pensions paid in 1984–85:

	Beneficiaries	*Amount (R1,000)*
Old age	42,573	20,435
Blind	564	270
Disability	5,421	2,602
War veterans	72	38
Leprosy	11	5

Books of Reference

Charlton, N., *Ciskei: Economics and Politics of Dependence in a South African Homeland.* London, 1980
Pauw, B. A., *Christianity and the Xhosa Tradition.* OUP, 1975
Van der Kooy, R. (ed.) *The Republic of Ciskei: A Nation in Transition.* Pretoria, 1981

SPAIN

Capital: Madrid
Population: 38·22m. (1983)
GNP per capita: US$4,173 (1983)

España

HISTORY. Although Spain has traditionally been a monarchy there have been two Republics, the first in 1873, which lasted for 11 months, and the second 1931–39; both were democratically and peacefully proclaimed. Part of the army rebelled against the republican government on 18 July 1936, thus beginning the Spanish Civil War, *see* THE STATESMAN'S YEAR-BOOK, 1939, pp. 1325–26. The new regime was led by Gen. Franco, who had been proclaimed Head of State and Government in 1936, and its institutions were based on single party rule, with the *Falange* as the only legal political organization.

In July 1969, Prince Don Juan Carlos de Borbón y Borbón, grandson of Alfonso XIII, was sworn in as successor to the Head of State and he had the title of HRH Prince of Spain until he became King.

Gen. Francisco Franco y Bahamonde died on 20 Nov. 1975 and on 22 Nov. Prince Juan Carlos de Borbón y Borbón took the oath as Juan Carlos I, King of Spain.

On 23 Feb. 1981 there was an attempted military *coup.* During 18 hours the deputies of the lower house of Parliament and the Cabinet were held hostage. The King, the only high authority who kept his liberty, obtained the surrender of the rebels without bloodshed.

AREA AND POPULATION. Spain is bounded north by the Bay of Biscay and the Pyrenees (which form the frontier with France and Andorra), east and south by the Mediterranean and the Straits of Gibraltar, south-west by the Atlantic and west by Portugal and the Atlantic. Continental Spain has an area of 492,592 sq. km, and including the Balearic and Canary Islands and the towns of Ceuta and Melilla 504,750 sq. km (194,884 sq. miles). Population (estimate, 1983), 38,219,534.

The growth of the population has been as follows:

Census year	*Population*	*Rate of annual increase*	*Census year*	*Population*	*Rate of annual increase*
1860	15,655,467	0·34	1950	27,976,755	0·81
1910	19,927,150	0·72	1960	30,903,137	0·88
1920	21,303,162	0·69	1970	33,823,918	0·94
1930	23,563,867	1·06	1981	37,746,260	1·15
1940	25,877,971	0·98			

Area and population of the autonomous communities and provinces, census of 1 March 1981:

Autonomous community Province	*Area (sq. km)*	*Population*	*Per sq. km*	*Autonomous community Province*	*Area (sq. km)*	*Population*	*Per sq. km*
Andalusia	*87,268*	*6,441,755*	*73*	Zaragoza	17,194	842,386	48
Almería	8,774	405,513	47	*Asturias*	*10,565*	*1,127,007*	*106*
Cádiz	7,385	1,001,716	135	*Baleares*	*5,014*	*685,088*	*136*
Córdoba	13,718	717,213	52	*Basque Country, The*	*7,261*	*2,134,967*	*296*
Granada	12,531	761,734	60	Álava	3,047	260,580	85
Huelva	10,085	414,492	41	Guipúzcoa	1,997	692,986	347
Jaén	13,498	627,598	46	Vizcaya	2,217	1,181,401	532
Málaga	7,276	1,036,261	142	*Canary Islands*	*7,273*	*1,444,626*	*200*
Sevilla	14,001	1,477,428	105	Palmas, Las	4,065	756,353	185
Aragón	*47,669*	*1,213,099*	*25*	Santa Cruz de Tenerife	3,208	688,273	217
Huesca	15,671	219,813	14				
Teruel	14,804	150,900	10				

Autonomous community Province	Area (sq. km)	Population	Per sq. km
Cantabria	*5,289*	*510,816*	*96*
Castilla-La Mancha	*79,226*	*1,628,005*	*20*
Albacete	14,858	334,468	22
Ciudad Real	19,749	468,327	23
Cuenca	17,061	210,280	12
Guadalajara	12,190	143,124	11
Toledo	15,368	471,806	30
Castilla-León	*94,147*	*2,577,105*	*27*
Ávila	8,048	178,997	22
Burgos	14,269	363,474	25
León	15,468	517,973	33
Palencia	8,029	186,512	23
Salamanca	12,336	368,055	29
Segovia	6,949	149,286	21
Soria	10,287	98,803	9
Valladolid	8,202	489,636	59
Zamora	10,559	224,369	21
Catalonia	*31,930*	*5,958,208*	*186*
Barcelona	7,773	4,618,734	598
Gerona	5,886	467,945	80
Lérida	12,028	355,451	29
Tarragona	6,283	516,078	82
Extremadura	*41,602*	*1,050,119*	*25*
Badajoz	21,657	635,375	29
Cáceres	19,945	414,744	20
Galicia	*29,434*	*2,753,836*	*93*
Coruña, La	7,876	1,083,415	137
Lugo	9,803	399,185	40
Orense	7,278	411,339	56
Pontevedra	4,477	859,897	192
Madrid	*7,995*	*4,726,986*	*591*
Murcia	*11,317*	*957,903*	*84*
Navarra	*10,421*	*507,367*	*48*
Rioja, La	*5,034*	*253,295*	*50*
Valencian Community	*23,305*	*3,646,765*	*156*
Alicante	5,863	1,148,597	195
Castellón	6,679	431,755	64
Valencia	10,763	2,066,413	192
Ceuta [1]	*18*	*70,864*	...
Melilla [1]	*14*	*58,449*	...
Total	*504,750*	*37,746,260*	*74*

[1] Ceuta and Melilla are municipalities located in the northern coast of Morocco.

The capitals of the autonomous communities are as follows: Andalusia, cap. Sevilla (Seville); Aragón, cap. Zaragoza (Saragossa); Asturias, cap. Oviedo; Baleares (Balearic Islands), cap. Palma de Mallorca; The Basque Country, cap. Vitoria; Canary Islands, dual and alternative capital, Las Palmas and Santa Cruz de Tenerife; Cantabria, cap. Santander; Catalonia, cap. Barcelona; Extremadura, cap. Mérida; Galicia, cap. Santiago de Compostela; Madrid, cap. Madrid; Murcia, cap. Murcia (but regional parliament in Cartagena); Navarra, cap. Pamplona; La Rioja, cap. Logroño; Valencian Community, cap. Valencia. Castilla-La Mancha and Castilla-León had not chosen (1984) a capital town; the actual seats of their legislative and executive institutions are at Toledo and Valladolid respectively.

The capitals of the provinces are in the towns from which they take the name, except in Álava (capital Vitoria), Asturias (Oviedo), Baleares (Palma de Mallorca), Cantabria (Santander), Guipúzcoa (San Sebastián), La Rioja (Logroño), Navarra (Pamplona) and Vizcaya (Bilbao).

In 1981 there were 19,216,496 females and 18,529,764 males.

By decree of 21 Sept. 1927 the islands which form the Canary Archipelago were divided into 2 provinces, under the name of their respective capitals, Santa Cruz de Tenerife and Las Palmas de Gran Canaria. The province of Santa Cruz de Tenerife is constituted by the islands of Tenerife, La Palma, Gomera and Hierro, and that of Las Palmas by Gran Canaria, Lanzarote and Fuerteventura, with the small barren islands of Alegranza, Roque del Este, Roque del Oeste, Graciosa, Montaña Clara and Lobos. The area of the islands is 7,273 sq. km; population (census 1981), 1,444,626. Places under Spanish sovereignty in Morocco are: Alhucemas, Ceuta, Chafarinas, Melilla and Peñón de Vélez.

The following were the registered populations of principal towns at census 1981:

Town	*Population*	*Town*	*Population*	*Town*	*Population*
Albacete	117,126	Burgos	156,449	Getafe	127,060
Alcalá de Henares	142,862	Cáceres	71,852	Gijón	255,969
Alcorcón	140,657	Cádiz	157,766	Granada	262,182
Algeciras	86,042	Cartagena	172,751	Hospitalet	294,033
Alicante	251,387	Castellón	126,464	Huelva	127,806
Almeria	140,946	Córdoba	284,737	Jerez de la Frontera	176,238
Ávila	86,584	Cornellá	90,956	Jaén	96,424
Badajoz	114,361	Coruña, La	232,356	Laguna, La	112,635
Badalona	227,744	Elche	162,873	Leganés	163,426
Baracaldo	117,422	Ferrol, El	91,764	León	131,134
Barcelona	1,754,900	Fuenlabrada	77,626	Lérida	109,573
Bilbao	433,030	Gerona	87,648	Logroño	110,980

Town	Population	Town	Population	Town	Population
Lugo	73,986	Reus	80,710	Santiago de Compostela	93,695
Madrid	3,188,297	Sabadell	184,943	Sevilla	653,833
Málaga	503,251	Salamanca	167,131	Tarragona	111,689
Mataró	96,467	San Baudilio del Llobregat	74,550	Tarrasa	155,360
Móstoles	149,649	San Fernando	71,846	Torrejón de Ardoz	75,398
Murcia	288,631	San Sebastián	175,576	Valencia	751,734
Orense	96,085	Santa Coloma de Gramanet	140,588	Valladolid	330,242
Oviedo	190,123	Santa Cruz de Tenerife	190,784	Vigo	258,724
Palencia	74,080	Santander	180,328	Vitoria	192,773
Palma de Mallorca	304,422			Zaragoza	590,750
Palmas, Las	366,454				
Pamplona	183,126				

Vital statistics for calendar years:

	Marriages	*Births*	*Deaths*
1977	262,015	656,357	294,324
1978	258,070	636,892	296,781
1979	246,349	601,992	291,213
1980[1]	213,363	565,401	287,621
1981[1]	199,057	532,255	286,400
1982[1]	188,597	509,685	282,266

[1] Provisional figures.

Languages. The Constitution states that 'Castilian is the Spanish official language of the State', but also that 'All other Spanish languages will also be official in the corresponding Autonomous Communities'.

Catalan is spoken by a majority of people in Catalonia and Baleares, and by a large minority in Valencian Community (where it is frequently called Valencian language); in Aragón, a narrow strip close to Catalonia and Valencian Community boundaries, speaks Catalan.

Galician, a language very close to Portuguese, is spoken by a majority of people in Galicia. Basque, by a significative minority in the Basque Country (33·3%, 1981 census); 54·3% in Guipúzcoa province, 25·7% in Vizcaya province and 11·7% in Álava province. Basque is also spoken by a small minority in north-west Navarra.

In bilingual communities, both Spanish and the regional language are taught in the schools.

CLIMATE. Most of Spain has a form of Mediterranean climate with mild, moist winters and hot, dry summers, but the northern coastal region has a moist, equable climate, with rainfall well-distributed throughout the year, mild winters and warm summers, though having less sunshine than the rest of Spain.

Madrid. Jan. 41°F (5°C), July 77°F (25°C). Annual rainfall 16·8″ (419 mm). Barcelona. Jan. 46°F (8°C), July 74°F (23·5°C). Annual rainfall 21″ (525 mm). Cartagena. Jan. 51°F (10·5°C), July 75°F (24°C). Annual rainfall 14·9″ (373 mm). La Coruña. Jan. 51°F (10·5°C), July 66°F (19°C). Annual rainfall 32″ (800 mm). Sevilla. Jan. 51°F (10·5°C), July 85°F (29·5°C). Annual rainfall 19·5″ (486 mm). Palma de Mallorca (Balearic Islands). Jan. 51°F (11°C), July 77°F (25°C). Annual rainfall 13·6″ (347 mm). Santa Cruz de Tenerife (Canary Islands). Jan. 64°F (17·9°C), July 76°F (24·4°C). Annual rainfall 7·72″ (196 mm).

KING. Juan Carlos I, born 5 Jan. 1938. The eldest son of Don Juan, Conde de Barcelona. Juan Carlos was given precedence over his father as pretender to the Spanish throne in an agreement in 1954 between Don Juan and Gen. Franco. Don Juan resigned his claims to the throne in May 1977. King (then Prince) Juan Carlos married, in 1962, Princess Sophia of Greece, daughter of the late King Paul of the Hellenes and Queen Frederika. *Offspring:* Elena, born 20 Dec. 1963; Cristina, 13 June 1965; Felipe, Prince of Asturias, Heir to the throne, 30 Jan. 1968.

CONSTITUTION AND GOVERNMENT. The *Cortes* (Parliament) was freely elected on 15 June 1977. The text of the new Constitution was approved by referendum on 6 Dec. 1978, and came into force 29 Dec. 1978. It established a parliamentary monarchy, with King Juan Carlos I as head of state. Legislative power is vested in the *Cortes,* a bicameral parliament composed of the Congress of Deputies (lower house) and the Senate (upper house). The Congress of Deputies has not less than 300 nor more than 400 members (350 in the general elections of 1977, 1979 and 1982), all elected in a proportional system regarding the population of every province. The members of the Senate are elected in a majority system: the 47 peninsular provinces elect 4 senators each, regardless of population; the insular provinces electing 5 (Baleares, Las Palmas) or 6 (Santa Cruz de Tenerife); and Ceuta and Melilla, 2 senators each. There are 208 senators, to whom are added some other members of the upper house elected by the parliaments of the autonomous communities. Deputies and senators are elected in universal (but not compulsory), direct, free, equal and secret suffrage, for a term of 4 years, liable to dissolution. Executive power is vested in the President of the Government (prime minister), with his Cabinet; he is elected by the Congress of Deputies.

A general election took place on 28 Oct. 1982.

Congress of Deputies (350 members): Spanish Workers Socialist Party (PSOE), 202; Popular Alliance (AP, conservative), 106; Centre Democratic Union (UCD), 12; Convergence and Union (CiU, Catalan nationalists), 12; Basque Nationalist Party (PNV), 8; Spanish Communist Party (PCE), 4; Social and Democratic Centre (CDS), 2; Herri Batasuna (Basque independentists), 2; Euskadido Eskerra (non-radical Basque independentists), 1; Esquerra Republicana de Catalunya (Catalan republican nationalists), 1.

Senate: 208 members, excluding those elected by regional parliaments (250 including them): PSOE, 134 (155); AP, 54 (64); CiU, 7 (9); PNV , 7 (9); UCD, 4; Asamblea Majorera (from Canary island of Fuerteventura). 1; independent from Soria province, 1.

The *Council of Ministers* appointed 2 Dec. 1982 was composed as follows in March 1985:

President of the Government (Prime Minister): Felipe González Márquez (Secretary-General of PSOE)

Vice-President of the Government (Deputy Premier): Alfonso Guerra González. *Foreign Affairs:* Fernando Morán López. *Economy, Finance and Commerce:* Miguel Boyer Salvador. *Industry and Energy:* Carlos Solchaga Catalán. *Interior:* José Barrionuevo. *Defence:* Narcís Serra i Serra. *Public Administration:* Javier Moscoso del Prado. *Education and Science:* José María Maravall. *Public Works:* Julián Campo. *Justice:* Fernando Ledesma Bartret. *Culture:* Javier Solana Madariaga. *Territorial Administration (relations with Autonomous Communities):* Tomás de la Quadra Salcedo. *Agriculture, Fisheries and Food.* Carlos Romero Herrero. *Health and Consumers Affairs:* Ernest Lluch i Martín. *Labour and Social Security:* Joaquín Almunia Amann. *Transport, Tourism and Communications:* Enrique Barón Crespo.

All ministers are members of PSOE, excepting the Minister of Justice, who is a non-party magistrate.

National flag: Three horizontal stripes of red, yellow, red, with the yellow of double width, and charged near the hoist with the national arms.

National anthem: Marcha real.

Regional and local government. The Constitution of 1978 establishes a semi-federal system of regional administration, with the autonomous community *(Comunidad Autónoma)* as its basic element. There are 17 autonomous communities, each of them having a Parliament, elected by universal vote, and a regional government; all possess exclusive legislative and executive power in many matters, as listed in the national Constitution and in their own fundamental law *(estatuto de autonomia).* The Basque Country and Catalonia elected their first parliaments in March 1980, Galicia in Oct. 1981 and Andalusia in May 1982. All others in May 1983. Basque and Catalan parliaments were renewed in their regional elections of Feb. 1984 and April 1984 respectively.

There are 7 autonomous communities composed of one only province, i.e., Asturias (*ex*-Oviedo province), Cantabria (*ex*-Santander province), La Rioja (*ex*-

Logroño province), Navarra, Baleares, Murcia and Madrid. The other 10 are formed by 2 or more provinces. In all, there are in Spain 50 provinces, since the administrative division established in 1833; Ceuta and Melilla, municipalities in the northern coast of Morocco, are not part of any province. The provincial council *(Diputación Provincial)* is the administrative organ of the province, except in the 7 autonomous communities composed of one only province, where there are only the regional legislative and executive powers. The provincial council is indirectly elected. Each of the 7 main islands of the Canaries (provinces of Las Palmas and Santa Cruz de Tenerife) has a directly elected corporation, the *Cabildo Insular,* to rule its special interests.

The provinces are constituted by the association of municipalities (8,022 in 1981 census). Municipalities are autonomous in their own sphere. At their head stands the municipal council *(Ayuntamiento),* members of which are elected in a universal ballot every 4 years, and they, in turn, elect one of them as Mayor *(Alcalde).*

DEFENCE. On 26 Sept. 1953 the US and Spain signed three agreements covering the construction and use of military facilities in Spain by the US, economic assistance, and military end-item assistance. These agreements were renewed several times, the last in July 1982. The American naval and air base at Rota (near Cádiz) is connected by pipelines with the American bomber bases at Morón de la Frontera (near Seville), Torrejón (near Madrid) and Zaragoza.

Length of service is 16 months in the army, 24 months in the navy and 18 months in the air force.

Army. The Army is divided into 2 principal parts: the Immediate Intervention Forces and Territorial Defence Forces. The former consist of 1 armoured, 1 mechanized and 1 motorized divisions; 1 armoured cavalry, 1 parachute and 1 airportable brigades; and supporting artillery, engineer and signals units. The Territorial Defence Forces are divided between 9 Military Regions, and include 3 mountain and 10 infantry brigades. There are also other reserve and independent units, and the Army Aviation forces. Equipment includes 300 AMX-30, 350 M-47E and 110 M-48 tanks. Strength (1985) 260,000 (including 190,000 conscripts). Of these 5,800 are stationed on the Balearic Islands, 16,000 on the Canary Islands and 19,000 in Ceuta/Melilla. The paramilitary National Police number 40,000 men and the Civil Guard 65,000.

Navy. Particulars of the principal ship:

Completed	*Name*	*Standard displacement Tons*	*Guns*	*Aircraft*	*Shaft horse-power*	*Speed Knots*
			Aircraft Carrier			
1943	Dédalo[1]	13,000	22 40-mm. A.A.	7 VSTOL aircraft and 20 helicopters	100,000	32 (original) now 24

[1] The former US fixed-wing aircraft carrier *Cabot*, converted in 1966 and transferred to Spain on loan in 1967 and purchased in 1973. Classed as a helicopter carrier until Harrier 'jump-jet' fixed wing aircraft were embarked.

There are also 10 diesel-powered patrol submarines (4 new French-built, 4 modern French-built and 2 old *ex*-US), 11 destroyers, 11 frigates, 4 old corvettes, 12 new fast attack craft, 10 new patrol vessels, 4 ocean minesweepers, 8 coastal minesweepers, 3 patrol ships (*ex*-coastal minesweepers), 38 coastal patrol craft, 33 inshore patrol launches, 1 dock landing ship, 6 survey ships, 3 landing ships, 8 landing craft, 140 minor landing craft, 1 replenishment ship, 15 oilers, 2 attack transports, 2 tenders, 2 training ships, 1 boom defence vessel, 1 fishery protection trawler, 30 tugs, 1 royal yacht, 10 water carriers, 40 auxiliary craft and 40 service barges.

The Spanish Navy is being renewed and modernized. Ships under construction include 1 small aircraft carrier scheduled to be completed in 1986 and 3 missile frigates. Ships projected include 2 more missile armed frigates and 6 corvettes, while a modified new construction programme is being considered including 2 large destroyers, 5 frigates and 4 minehunters.

Shipbuilding is mainly carried on at the dockyards at El Ferrol and Cartagena, Cádiz having a smaller share in it. Barcelona, Bilbao, Seville and Cádiz are the chief naval yards.

There are naval radio telegraphic stations at Cádiz, Barcelona, Mahón, Pontevedra, Cartagena and El Ferrol.

In 1985 naval personnel totalled 63,220, comprising 4,220 naval officers, 37,860 ratings, 8,940 civil branch, 700 marine officers and 11,500 marine other ranks.

The Naval Air Service operates 34 fixed-wing aircraft and 39 helicopters.

Air Force. The Air Force is organized as an independent service, dating from 1939. It is administered through 4 operational commands. These comprise Air Combat Command which controls interceptor squadrons (including USAF elements) and the control and warning radar network, Tactical and Transport Commands, and Air Command of the Canaries. Strength is about 33,000 and 215 combat aircraft.

The Tactical Air Command has 2 fighter-bomber squadrons of Spanish-built Northrop SF-5s, 1 squadron of HA-220 Super Saeta light attack jet aircraft of Spanish design and manufacture, 1 aero-naval co-operation squadron with 6 P-3A Orion anti-submarine aircraft, and a liaison flight at Tablada with CASA 127s and Bird Dogs. Air Combat Command has 2 squadrons of Mirage III-Es, 2 squadrons of F-4C/RF-4C Phantom IIs and 2 squadrons of Mirage F1-Cs, plus a flight of CASA/Dornier Do27 127 liaison aircraft. Five KC-130H tankers support the F-4C squadrons. Three wings of Air Transport Command operate C-130 Hercules, Caribou and Spanish-built CASA/Dornier Do27 Aviocars. Air Command of the Canaries has 3 squadrons, equipped with Aviocar transports; Mirage F1 fighter-bombers; F27 Maritime aircraft and Super Puma helicopters for search and rescue. Other equipment includes 2 DC-8s, 5 Falcons and helicopters for VIP transport; and aircraft for photographic, firefighting, target towing and research duties. Air-sea rescue units have Aviocars and Super Puma helicopters. Replacement of F-4s and SF-5s with a total of 72 F-18 Hornets will begin in 1986.

American-built F33 Bonanza, T-34A and T-6 piston-engined aircraft are used for basic training, after which pupil pilots progress to CASA C-101 and T-33A jet aircraft. Two-seat versions of operational types are used as advanced trainers. Other training types include Beechcraft King Air C90s for instrument flying and liaison duties.

INTERNATIONAL RELATIONS

Membership. Spain is a member of UN, the Council of Europe, NATO and OECD.

ECONOMY

Budget. Revenue and expenditure in 1m. pesetas:

	1979	*1980*	*1981*	*1982*	*1983*	*1984*
Revenue	1,747,500	2,284,456	2,823,000	3,533,820	4,513,305	5,399,997
Expenditure	1,747,500	2,284,456	2,823,000	3,533,820	4,513,305	5,399,997

The budget is made up as follows (in 1m. pesetas):

Revenue (1984)	
Direct taxes	1,806,840
Indirect taxes	1,651,100
Levies and various revenues	333,511
Current transactions	169,364
Real estate income	86,319
Miscellaneous income	21,375
Deficit (financed with public debt, treasury loans, etc)	1,331,488

Expenditure (1984)	
H.M. House	350
Cortes (Parliament)	7,179
Court of Accounts	1,439

Expenditure (1984) continued	
Constitutional Court	565
Council of State	319
Public Debt	517,380
Civil Service Pensions	328,676
General Council of the Judicial Power	727
Presidency of the Government	23,146
Ministry of Foreign Affairs	29,750
,, Justice	85,542
,, Defence	552,834
,, Finance	103,032
,, Interior	216,759
,, Public Works and Housing	263,450

Expenditure (1984) continued	
Ministry of Education and Science	524,073
,, Labour and Social Security	1,089,305
,, Industry and Energy	228,328
,, Agriculture and Food	234,355
,, Transport, Tourism and Communications	421,188

Expenditure (1984) continued	
Ministry of Culture	37,429
,, Territorial Administration	21,943
,, Health and Consumer Affairs	37,933
Regional governments	488,666
Regional Compensation Fund	127,674
Expenses in several ministries	77,948

Currency. The *peseta* is divided into 100 *céntimos*; but *céntimos* are no longer in legal use since 1 July 1984.

Bank-notes of 5,000, 2,000, 1,000, 500, 200 and 100 *pesetas* and coins of 1 *peseta* (copper and aluminium), 2, 5, 10, 25, 50, 100 *pesetas* (nickel and copper) are in circulation. In July 1984 the circulation of bank-notes was 1,953,518m. *pesetas* and of coins, 109,056m. *pesetas.*

In March 1985, £1 = 199 *pesetas*; US$1 = 190.

Banking. On 1 Jan. 1922 the Bank of Spain came under the Bank Ordinance Law, according to which the Government participate in its net profits.

The 10 largest banks are: Banco Central; Banco Español de Crédito; Banco Hispano Americano; Banco de Bilbao; Banco de Vizcaya; Banco de Santander; Banco Popular Español; Banco Exterior de España; Banco Pastor; Banco de Sabadell. All are privately owned except the Banco Exterior de España.

Private banks deposits and savings bank deposits (Popular Savings Banks) in Spain, 30 June 1983, amounted to 17,322,272m. pesetas. The Post office savings bank opened on 12 March 1916. Deposits, 30 June 1983, amounted to 316,919m. pesetas.

Weights and Measures. On 1 Jan. 1859 the metric system of weights and measures was introduced.

ENERGY AND NATURAL RESOURCES

Electricity. Electric power-stations in 1981 had a total installed capacity of 32·6m. kw., of which 13·4m. was hydro-electric. The total output 1983, amounted to 117,280m. kwh of which 28,990m. hydro-electric and 10,660m. nuclear.

Natural Gas. Production in 1981 was 317,821 tonnes.

Oil. Crude oil production (1984) 2,500,000 tonnes.

Minerals. Spain is relatively rich in minerals. The production of the more important minerals in 1981 were as follows (in 1,000 tonnes; net metal content):

Anthracite	4,876	Iron	3,816·0	Tin	0·6
Coal	9,938	Lead	83·9	Zinc	182·0
Lignite	20,886	Copper	50·9	Wolfram	0·5
Uranium	273	Mercury	1·7		

Agriculture. Spain is mainly an agricultural country. In 1982 the total value of agricultural produce was 959·1m. pesetas; of livestock, 770·3m.; of forestry, 53·6m. Land under cultivation in 1982 (in 1,000 hectares) included: Cereals, 7,308; vegetables, 385; potatoes, 332. In 1982, 580,053 tractors and 47,174 harvesters were in use.

Principal crops	*Area (in 1,000 hectares)*				*Yield (in 1,000 tonnes)*			
	1978[1]	*1979*[1]	*1980*	*1981*	*1979*[1]	*1980*	*1981*	*1982*
Wheat	2,752	2,551	2,698	2,635	4,082	6,039	3,408	4,410
Barley	3,519	3,477	3,575	3,506	6,251	8,705	4,758	5,270
Oats	442	436	458	464	456	680	445	443
Rye	228	220	217	220	221	283	212	169
Rice	68	69	68	69	427	433	444	402
Maize	443	467	454	429	2,212	2,313	2,157	2,330
Potatoes	371	355	355	343	5,637	5,737	5,470	5,222
Sugar-beet	235	166	183	218	5,124	6,908	7,941	9,085
Sunflower	...	...	...	...	...	...	...	654

[1]Provisional.

In 1981, 1,721,000 hectares were under vines; production of wine was (1982) 37·4m. hectolitres. The area of onions was 34,000 hectares, yielding (1982) 1,051,000 tonnes. Production of oranges and mandarines was 2,566,000 tonnes, lemons, 430,000. Other products are esparto, flax, hemp and pulse. Spain has important industries connected with the preparation of wine and fruits.

Industrial crops (1982 in 1,000 tonnes): Cotton, 159; olives, 269; olive oil, 666; tobacco, 42.

Livestock products (1982 in 1,000 tonnes): Pigmeat, 1,114; poultry meat, 852; cattle meat, 420; cows' milk, 5,947.

Livestock (1983): Horses, 250,000; mules, 169,000; cattle, 5,070,000; sheep, 17,000,000; goats, 2,500,000; pigs, 11,700,000; poultry, 54,000,000.

Forestry. Total forests (1981) 26m. hectares; production, 1981, 11,297,000 cu. metres of wood.

Fisheries. The most important catches are those of sardines, whiting, anchovy and hake. The total catch amounted in 1983 to 1·12m. tons. In the tinned fish industry there were, in 1978, 405 factories, producing 129,265 tons. The Spanish fishing fleet in 1982 consisted of 17,499 vessels of 738,468 tonnes, with a total crew of 106,584.

INDUSTRY AND TRADE

Industry. The manufacture of cotton and woollen goods is important, principally in Catalonia. In 1978 there were 3,756 textile factories in operation. Production, in 1,000 tonnes (1978): Wool yarn, 29; cotton (yarn, 61; fabrics, 62); rayon fabrics, 6. 245 paper-mills produced in 1977, 2m. tonnes of writing, printing, packing and other paper. The production of cement reached 29,488,000 tonnes in 1982. Steel production (1982) 13·1m. tonnes; the three great blast-furnaces concentrations are in Bilbao area, Avilés (Asturias) and Sagunto (Valencia). The chemical industry is located in the areas of Madrid, Barcelona and Bilbao; sulphuric acid production (1982) 2m. tonnes; nitrogenous fertilizers, 822,000 tonnes. The 9 oil refineries refined 47,583,000 tonnes of crude oil. In 1982 900,000 TV sets (550,000 colour sets), 1m. refrigerators, 918,000 washing machines and 880,000 bicycles were manufactured. Spain has important toys and shoe industries, toys especially in Alicante and Barcelona provinces and shoe in Alicante province and the Balearic islands.

Spanish shipyards launched 463,684 BRT in 1983. In 1983, 1,225,623 vehicles were built, including 910,000 passenger cars.

Labour. The daily minimum wage for workers is 1,239 pesetas (Jan. 1985).

The economically active population numbered 13,212,400 in Jan. 1983. Of these, 2,114,500 were occupied in agriculture and fishing, 3,176,400 in manufactures, 1,258,700 in construction industry, 5,746,700 in trade and other public and personal services and 916,300 in unspecified jobs. 18·42% of the active population was unemployed at the end of 1983 (2,433,700 persons).

Trade Unions. The Constitution guarantees the establishment and activities of trade unions provided they have a democratic structure. The two most important trade unions are *Unión General de Trabajadores* (UGT), founded in 1888 by Pablo Iglesias (who had founded in 1879 the Spanish Workers Socialist Party, PSOE), and *Comisiones Obreras*, which was gradually established 1958–63, then as a clandestine labour organization.

Commerce. Foreign trade of Spain (Peninsula, Baleares, Canaries, Ceuta, Melilla) (in 1m. pesetas).

	1978	*1979*	*1980*	*1981*	*1982*	*1983*
Imports	1,431,538	1,704,022	2,150,652	2,970,435	3,473,208	4,176,470
Exports	1,001,599	1,221,441	1,493,187	1,888,422	2,260,198	2,838,601

In 1983 the most important items of import were (in 1m. pesetas): Crude petroleum and other energetic sources, 1,671,335; boilers, machinery and mechanical hardware, 387,987; iron, steel and castings, 147,026; electric and electronic machinery and hardware, 157,373; vehicles, 155,081; organic chemical products, 134,342; cereals, 128,305; oleaginous seeds and fruits, 118,077; optical and photographic products, 95,011.

The most important exports in 1983 (in 1m. pesetas) were: Iron and steel castings, 308,905; vehicles, 349,537; boilers, machinery and mechanical hardware, 199,550; refined petroleum and related products, 252,093; citrus and other fruits, 122,532; electric and electronic machinery and hardware, 96,797; footwear, 90,848; cement, salt, sulphur, limestone, 70,092; organic chemical products, 70,714; vegetables and pulses, 54,812.

Distribution of Spanish foreign trade (in 1m. pesetas) according to origin and destination, for calendar years:

	Imports		*Exports*	
	1982	*1983*	*1982*	*1983*
Europe	1,366,122	1,703,259	1,260,853	1,657,251
EEC	1,087,705	1,348,860	1,036,930	1,370,571
France	277,516	344,334	370,217	448,737
Germany, Federal Republic	328,861	366,060	185,590	260,186
UK	171,112	256,671	161,022	219,886
Italy	155,634	180,853	127,284	150,801
EFTA	164,757	207,108	144,093	167,531
Comecon	98,867	132,060	52,320	80,269
USA	482,025	495,500	145,532	206,640
LAIA (ex LAFTA)	346,158	473,297	180,611	122,237
Mexico	206,584	270,097	56,970	36,291
Venezuela	40,779	29,030	38,515	23,163
Saudi Arabia	...	194,956	60,653	82,590
Iran	119,563	255,906	37,781	58,625
Japan	110,552	139,948	28,306	43,530
Libya	120,701	140,162	29,248	40,162
Oceania	19,109	20,581	8,862	11,871

Total trade between Spain and UK (British Department of Trade returns, in £1,000 sterling):

	1981	*1982*	*1983*	*1984*
Imports to UK	804,781	956,935	1,110,029	1,604,405
Exports and re-exports from UK	707,767	870,416	1,128,439	1,234,584

Total trade of the Spanish territories and UK (British Department of Trade returns, in £1,000 sterling):

	Imports to UK			*Exports from UK*		
	1982	*1983*	*1984*	*1982*	*1983*	*1984*
Canary Islands	44,574	55,305	83,456	83,508	93,600	78,850
North Africa	...	24	...	4,679	8,190	3,248

Tourism. In 1983, 41,263,646 tourists visited Spain (from France, 10·3m.; Portugal, 8·46m.; Federal Germany, 4·97m.; UK, 5·18m.). Receipts of foreign currency (1983) US$6·83m.

COMMUNICATIONS

Roads. In 1982 the total length of highways and roads in Spain was 149,337 km, of which 123,560 km were macadamized or had other good surface. Motorways, 1,963 km. Number of cars was 8,714,076, lorries, 1,529,081, buses, 43,759 and motorcycles, 1,310,037 in 1983.

Railways. The total length of the state railways in 1982 was 13,572 km, mostly 1,676-mm gauge. There are 6,162 km of lines electrified. On 1 Feb. 1941 the Spanish railways, of broad gauge only, passed into state ownership; they are under a board known as the *Red Nacional de Ferrocarriles Españoles* (RENFE). The gauge of the principal Spanish railways has, for strategic reasons, been kept different from that of France; passengers therefore must change trains at the French frontier stations except by certain trains having variable gauge axles. In 1982 freight carried was 10,504m. tonne-km and 14,705m. passenger-km.

Aviation. The most important Spanish airline is 'Iberia': it maintains a regular service with Europe, America, Africa and the Middle East. 'Aviaco' operates mainly internal flights. 'Spantax', based on Palma de Mallorca, operates charter flights only. There are 43 airports open to civil traffic; those of Madrid, Palma de Mallorca and Barcelona are the most active. A small airport in Seo de Urgel, in the Pyrenees, used especially for the air service of Andorra was opened in 1982.

Aircraft movements in 1983, 293,443 internal and 243,628 international, carrying 49·4m. passengers and 350,223 tonnes of merchandise.

Shipping. The merchant navy in 1982 contained 1,109 vessels of a gross tonnage of 7,299,000.

In 1983 (provisional), 89,788 ships entered Spanish ports, carrying 6,271,000 passengers and discharging 444·71m. tonnes of cargo.

Post and Broadcasting. The receipts of the post office in 1983 were 65,904m. pesetas; expenses, 75,542m. pesetas. There were in 1983, 11,723 post offices and 12,820,000 telephones, these all privately operated.

Radio Nacional de España broadcasts 4 programmes on medium-waves and FM, as well as many regional programmes; it does not broadcast advertising. There is another state broadcasting network, *Radio-Cadena Española,* this self-financing with advertising. The greatest radio audience is that of a private network, *Sociedad Española de Radiodifusión* (SER); *Cadena de Ondas Populares Españolas* (COPE) belongs to the Roman Catholic church. Two private broadcasting networks were established in 1982 covering the whole of Spain, *Antena 3* and *Radio 80. Televisión Española* broadcasts 2 programmes. Since 1983 *TV3* broadcasts entirely in Catalan and *Eusko Telebista* about 90% in Basque. Colour transmissions are carried by PAL system. Number of receivers (1979): radio, 9·6m.; television, 9·4m. (about 50% colour sets).

Cinemas (1981). There were 3,970 cinemas with an estimated seating capacity of 4m.

Newspapers (1984). There were about 100 daily newspapers with a total daily circulation of about 5m. copies. In 1983 the following dailies had a daily circulation of more than 100,000 copies: *El País* (Madrid, 296,176), *La Vanguardia* (Barcelona, 195,850), *As* (Madrid, [sports], 139,582), *ABC* (Madrid, 133,945), *Diario 16* (Madrid, 125,307), *El Periódico* (Barcelona, 122,893) and *Ya* (Madrid, 109,530).

JUSTICE, RELIGION, EDUCATION AND WELFARE

Justice. Justice is administered by *Tribunales* and *Juzgados* (Tribunals and Courts), which conjointly form the *Poder Judicial* (Judicial Power). Judges and magistrates cannot be removed, suspended or transferred except as set forth by law. The Constitution of 1978 has established a new organ, the *Consejo General del Poder Judicial* (General Council of the Judicial Power), formed by magistrates, judges, attorneys and lawyers, governing the Judicial Power in full independence from the other two powers of the State, the Legislative (Cortes) and the Executive (President of the Government and his Cabinet). The territorial organization of justice is being gradually changed, adapting it to the new map of the country in Autonomous Communities and when completed, in each of these it will be a *Tribunal Superior de Justicia* as the highest judicial organ, responsible only to the national *Tribunal Supremo.*

The Judicature is composed of the *Tribunal Supremo* (Supreme High Court); 16 *Audiencias Territoriales* (Division High Courts); 50 *Audiencias Provinciales* (Provincial High Courts); 518 *Juzgados de Primera Instancia* (Courts of First Instance), 742 *Juzgados de Distrito* (District Courts) and 7,532 *Juzgados Municipales y de paz* (Municipal and Peace Courts, Court of Lowest Jurisdiction held by Justices of the Peace).

The *Tribunal Supremo* consists of a President (appointed by the King, on proposal from the *Consejo General del Poder Judicial*) and various judges distributed among 6 chambers: 1 for trying civil matters, 3 for administrative purposes, 1 for criminal trials and 1 for social matters. The *Tribunal Supremo* has disciplinary faculties; is court of cassation in all criminal trials; for administrative purposes decides in first and second instance disputes arising between private individuals and the State, and in social matters resolves in the last instance all cases involving over 100,000 pesetas.

The *Audiencias Territoriales* have power to try in second instance sentences passed by judges in civil matters.

The *Audiencias Provinciales* try and pass sentence in first instance on all cases filed for delinquency. The jury system, re-established by the art. 125 of the Constitution, had not been applied by Jan. 1984, pending its parliamentary regulation.

The *Juzgados Municipales* try small civil cases and petty offences. The *Juzgados Comarcales* deal with the same charges, but their jurisdiction embraces larger districts.

Military cases are tried by the *Consejo Supremo de Justicia Militar* but its sentences can now pass to the (civil) *Tribunal Supremo,* as final cassation instance.

The *Tribunal Constitucional* (Constitutional Court) has power to solve conflicts between the State and the Autonomous Communities, to determine if legislation passed by the Cortes is contrary to the Constitution and to protect constitutional rights of the individuals violated by any authority. Its 12 members are appointed by the King in the following way: 4, on proposal of the Congress of Deputies; 4, on proposal of the Senate; 2 on proposal of the *Consejo General del Poder Judicial;* and 2 on proposal of the Cabinet.

The death penalty was abolished in 1978 by the Constitution (art. 15). Divorce is again in force since July 1981.

The prison population was, on 31 Dec. 1983, 14,050.

Religion. Roman Catholicism is the religion of the majority. There are 11 metropolitan sees and 52 suffragan sees, the chief being Toledo, where the Primate resides.

The archdioceses of Madrid-Alcalá and Barcelona depend directly from the Vatican.

The Constitution guarantees full religious freedom and states that no religion has an established legal condition (art. 16); so, since 29 Dec. 1978 there has been no official religion in Spain. A report issued in 1982 by the Episcopal Conference of the Roman Catholic Church claims that 82·76% of all children born in 1981 were baptized in that church.

There are about 150,000 other Christians, including several Protestant denominations, Jehovah Witnesses (about 60,000) and Mormons. The British and Foreign Bible Society was, on 10 March 1963, allowed to resume its activities.

The first synagogue since the expulsion of the Jews in 1492 was opened in Madrid on 2 Oct. 1959. The number of Jews is estimated at about 13,000.

Education. Primary education is compulsory and free between 6 and 14 years of age.

In 1982–83 pre-primary education (under 6 years) was conducted by 38,160 schools, with 37,343 teachers and 1,187,697 pupils. Primary or basic education (6 to 14 years): 180,618 schools, 190,926 teachers and 5,633,518 pupils. Secondary education (14-17 years) is conducted on two branches: 2,495 middle schools *(Institutos),* with 69,768 teachers and 1,117,600 pupils, and 2,366 vocational and technical centres *(Formación Profesional),* with 42,174 teachers and 650,929 pupils. For adult education there were (in 1982–83) 3,347 school units, with 3,085 teachers and 89,052 students. For the physically or mentally disabled there were 3,961 school units, with 3,904 teachers and 49,082 pupils.

In 1983 there were in all 33 universities: 22 State Universities, in Madrid, Barcelona, Valencia, Granada, Sevilla, Santiago de Compostela, Zaragoza, Bilbao (University of the Basque Country), Oviedo, Valladolid, Salamanca (founded in 1215), La Laguna (Canaries), Murcia, Málaga, Córdoba, Badajoz-Cáceres (University of Extremadura), Cádiz, León, Santander, Alicante, Palma de Mallorca and Alcalá de Henares; 4 Polytechnic Universities, in Madrid, Barcelona, Valencia and Las Palmas (Canaries); 2 Autonomous Universities, in Madrid and Barcelona; 4 private (catholic) universities, in Deusto (Bilbao), Pamplona, Salamanca and Madrid (University of Comillas); and the *Universidad Nacional de Educación a*

Distancia (National University for Education at Home), which teaches by mail, radio and TV, with its central seat at Madrid (32,854 students, 1981–82). The number of university students was 669,848 (1981–82).

DIPLOMATIC REPRESENTATIVES

Of Spain in Great Britain (24 Belgrave Sq., London SW1X 8QA)
Ambassador: José Joaquín Puig de la Bellacasa.

Of Great Britain in Spain (Calle de Fernando el Santo, 16, Madrid, 4)
Ambassador: Lord Nicholas Gordon Lennox, CMG, MVO.

Of Spain in the USA (2700 15th St., NW, Washington, D.C., 20009)
Ambassador: Gabriel Mañueco de Lecea.

Of the USA in Spain (Serrano 75, Madrid)
Ambassador: Thomas O. Enders.

Of Spain to the United Nations
Ambassador: Jaime de Piniés.

Books of Reference

Statistical Information: The Instituto Nacional de Estadistica (Paseo de la Castellana, 183, Madrid) combines the administrative work of a government department attached to the Presidency of the Government with a centre of statistical studies. *Director-General:* José Montes. Its publications include: *Anuario Estadístico de España.* Annual. *Edición manual* (latest vol., 1984).—*Reseñas estadísticas provinciales.*—*Nomenclátor de las ciudades, villas lugares, aldeas, y demás entidades de población de España.* 52 vols. Madrid, 1984.—*Poblaciones de Derecho y de Hecho de los Municipios Españoles: Censo de Poblacíon de 1981.* Madrid, 1982.—*Diccionario Corográfico de España.* 4 vols. Madrid, 1948.—*Boletín de Estadística.* Madrid. (No. 1, Jan.–March 1939: monthly from 1948).—*Estadística española. Revista trimestral* (from 1959).

Aguilar (ed.), *Nuevo Atlas de España.* Madrid, 1961
Altamira y Crevea, R., *A History of Spain.* New York and London, 1950
Anuario del Mercado Español. Madrid, 1965
Bell, D., (ed.), *Democratic Politics in Spain. Spanish Politics after Franco.* London, 1983
Carr, R., *Modern Spain, 1875–1980.* OUP, 1980
Enciclopedia Universal Ilustrada. 70 vols., 10 appendices, 10 supplements. Madrid
García Venero, M., *Historia del Nacionalismo Vasco, 1793–1936.* Madrid, 1945
Graham, R., *Spain: Change of a Nation.* London, 1984
Lafuente, M., and Valera, J., *Historia General de España.* New ed. 25 vols. Barcelona, 1925
Lieberman, S., *The Contemporary Spanish Economy: A Historical Perspective.* London, 1982
López Oliván, J., *Repertorio Diplomático Español. [Collection of treaties, 1125–1935.]* Madrid, 1944
Maravall, J., *The Transition to Democracy in Spain.* London, 1982
Morris, J., *Spain.* London, 1979
Reay-Smith, J., *Living in Spain in the '80's.* London, 1983
Russell, P. E. (ed.), *Spain: A Companion to Spanish Studies.* 6th ed. London, 1973
Vicens Vives, J., *Historia Económica de España.* 5 vols. Barcelona, 1959

National Library: Biblioteca Nacional, Madrid. *Director:* Guillermo Cuastavino Callent.

FORMER PROVINCE IN AFRICA (WESTERN SAHARA)

It was announced in Madrid on 14 Nov. 1975 that Spain, Morocco and Mauritania had reached agreement on the transfer of power over Western Sahara to Morocco and Mauritania on 28 Feb. 1976. Morocco occupied El Aiaún in late Nov. and on 12 Jan. 1976 the Spanish army withdrew from Western Sahara which had ceased to be a Spanish province on 31 Dec. 1975. The country was partitioned by Morocco and Mauritania. In Aug. 1979 Mauritania withdrew from the territory it took over in 1976. The area was taken over by Morocco and reorganized into provinces.

Algeria stated that the former province should be handed over to the people of the territory, objected to the partition and is (1982) backing the claims of *Frente Polisario* for an independent state. In spite of occupation of all western centres by Moroccan troops, Saharan guerrillas based in Algeria continue to attempt to liberate their country. They have renamed it the Democratic Saharan Arab Republic and hold most of the desert beyond a defensive line built by Moroccan troops encompassing Smara, Bu Craa and Laayoune.

In 1982 the Democratic Saharwi Arab Republic became a member of the Organization of African Unity (OAU).

The area was 266,769 sq. km (102,680 sq. miles). The population at the census (1970) was 76,425; Saharans, 59,777 and 16,648 Europeans. The capital was El Aaiún (Laayoune) (population, 24,048).

Rich phosphate deposits were discovered in 1963 at Bu Craa. Morocco holds 65% of the shares of the former Spanish state-controlled company. While production reached 5·6m. tonnes in 1975, exploitation has been severely reduced by guerrilla activity but in 1984 produced 1m. tonnes. After a nearly complete collapse, production and transportation of phosphate resumed in 1978, ceased again, and then resumed in 1982.

Books of Reference

Atlas Histórico y Geográfico de Africa Española. Madrid, 1955

Damis, J., *Conflict in Northwest Africa: The Western Sahara Dispute.* Stanford, 1983

Hernández-Pacheco, E., and others, *El Sahara español.* Madrid, 1949

Hodges, T., *Historical Dictionary of Western Sahara.* London, 1982.—*Western Sahara: The Roots of a Desert War.* London and Westport, 1984

Mercer, J., *Spanish Sahara.* London, 1976

Pélissier, R., *Les Territoires Espagnols d'Afrique.* Paris, 1963.—*Los Territorios Españoles de Africa.* Madrid, 1964

Rumeu de Armas, A., *España en el Africa Atlántica.* 2 vols. Madrid, 1956–57

Thompson, V. and Adloff, R., *The Western Saharans: Background to Conflict.* London, 1980

SRI LANKA

Ceylon

Capital: Colombo
Population: 14·9m. (1981)
GNP per capita: US$300 (1981)

HISTORY. According to the Mahawansa chronicle, an Indian prince from the valley of the Ganges, named Vijaya, arrived in the 6th century B.C. and became the first king of the Sinhalese. The monarchical form of government continued until the beginning of the 19th century when the British subjugated the Kandyan Kingdom in the central highlands.

In 1505 the Portuguese formed settlements on the west and south, which were taken from them about the middle of the next century by the Dutch. In 1796 the British Government annexed the foreign settlements to the presidency of Madras. In 1802 Ceylon was constituted a separate colony.

Ceylon reached fully responsible status within the British Commonwealth when the Ceylon Independence Act, 1947, came into force on 4 Feb. 1948. Sri Lanka became a republic in 1972.

EVENTS. Communal violence between Tamils and Sinhalese continued; there were frequent clashes between Tamil seperatists and the armed forces. On 19 Dec. 1984 a new Ministry of Manpower Mobilization was established, on 20 Dec. 1984 a new Ministry of Emergency Civil Administration. North Sri Lanka was under military restrictions in early 1985.

AREA AND POPULATION. Sri Lanka lies off the south-east coast of the Indian State of Tamil Nadu, separated from it by the Indian ocean but almost joined to it by the chain of islands called Adam's Bridge. On 28 June 1974 the frontier between India and Sri Lanka in the Palk Strait was re-defined, giving to Sri Lanka the island of Kachchativu. Area (in sq. km.) and census population on 17 March 1981.

Provinces	*Area*	*Population*	*Provinces*	*Area*	*Population*
Western	3,708·87	3,915,001	North-Central	10,723·21	850,575
Central	5,590·17	2,005,956	Uva	8,481·90	922,636
Southern	5,558·77	1,882,912	Sabaragamuwa	4,901·56	1,478,879
Northern	8,882·05	1,111,468			
Eastern	9,951·34	976,475	Total	65,609·63	14,850,001
North-Western	7,811·73	1,706,099			

Population (1981 census), 14,850,001, an increase of 17·1% since 1971. Population (in 1,000) according to race and nationality at the 1981 census: 10,986 Sinhalese, 1,872 Ceylon Tamils, 1,057 Ceylon Moors, 38 Burghers, 43 Malays, 825 Indian Tamils, 29 others. Non- nationals of Sri Lanka totalled 1,202,000. By agreement with the Government of India in 1964 and 1974, Indian nationals who have not been granted Sri Lanka citizenship were to be repatriated. The 1964 agreement covered 525,000 people; the 1974 agreement, 75,000.

Vital statistics, 1983: birth-rate (per 1,000 population), 26·2; death-rate, 6·1; infant death-rate (per 1,000 live births), 34·4 (provisional)

The urban population was 21·5% of the total in 1981. The principal towns and their population according to the census of 1981 are: Colombo, 585,776; Dehiwela-Mt. Lavinia, 174,385; Moratuwa, 135,610; Jaffna, 118,215; Kotte, 101,563; Kandy, 101,281; Galle, 77,183; Negombo, 61,376; Trincomalee, 44,913; Batticaloa, 42,934; Matara, 39,162; Ratnapura, 37,354; Anuradhapura, 36,248; Badulla, 32,954; Kalutara, 31,495. Population of the Greater Colombo area, 1980, about 1m.

The national languages are Sinhala, English and Tamil; Sinhala is the official language and Tamil is used in the northern and eastern provinces.

CLIMATE. Sri Lanka has an equatorial climate with low annual temperature variations, but it is affected by the north-east Monsoon (Dec. to Feb.) and the south-west Monsoon (May to Sept.). Rainfall is generally heavy but never lasts long; it is heaviest in the south-west and central highlands while the north and east are relatively dry. Thirty-year averages, 1951–80: Colombo. Jan. 79·7°F (26·5°C), July 81·1°F (27·3°C). Annual rainfall 99·5″ (2,527 mm). Trincomalee. Jan. 78·6°F (25·9°C), July 86°F (30°C). Annual rainfall 63·59″ (1,615 mm).

CONSTITUTION AND GOVERNMENT. A new constitution for the Democratic Socialist Republic of Sri Lanka was promulgated in Sept. 1978.

The Executive President is directly elected by the people and has to receive more than one-half of the valid votes cast. His term of office is six years and he shall not hold the office for more than two consecutive terms. He is the Head of the State, the Head of the Executive and of the Government and the Commander-in-chief of the Armed Forces. He does not have any veto power over legislation; even in a time of public emergency, he must act with Parliamentary control and approval.

Parliament consists of one chamber, composed of 168 members elected by universal suffrage. The Senate was abolished by constitutional amendment in Oct. 1971.

The term of Parliament is six years. In Nov. 1982 Parliament voted to extend its present term (expiring Aug. 1983) for a further six years. The vote was subject to national referendum on 20 Dec. 1982; 71% of the electorate voted and 55% approved the extension.

The Prime Minister and other Ministers, who must be members of Parliament, are appointed by the President. The President is head of the Cabinet.

The electorate consists of all who are 18 years of age and over.

National flag: A yellow field bearing 2 panels: in the hoist 2 vertical strips of green and orange; in the fly, dark red with a gold lion holding a sword and in each corner a gold 'bo' leaf.

The Cabinet was as follows in Sept. 1984:

President, Defence, Higher Education, Janata Estates Development, State Plantations, Power and Energy, and Plan Implementation: J. R. Jayawardene.

Prime Minister, Leader of the House, Local Government, Highways, Housing and Construction, Emergency Civil Administration: Ranasinghe Premadasa.

Land, Land Development and Mahaweli Development: Gamini Dissanayake. *Foreign Affairs:* A. C. S. Hameed. *Home Affairs:* K. W. Devanayagam. *National Security:* Lalith W. Athulathmudali. *Rural Development:* Wimala Kannangara. *Justice:* N. P. Wijeyeratne. *Finance and Planning:* Ronnie de Mel. *Labour:* C. P. J. Seneviratne. *Industries and Scientific Affairs:* Cyril Mathew. *Cultural Affairs:* E. L. B. Hurulle. *Fisheries:* M. F. W. Perera. *Health:* R. Atapattu. *Post and Telecommunications:* D. B. Wijetunge. *Parliamentary Affairs and Sports, Chief Government Whip:* M. Vincent Perera. *Transport:* M. H. Mohamed. *Agricultural Development and Research, Food Co-operatives:* G. Jayasuriya. *Public Administration and Plantation Industries:* M. Jayawickreme. *Textile Industry:* W. Mendis. *Social Services:* Asoka Karunaratne. *Rural Industrial Development:* S. Thondaman. *Youth Affairs, Education and Employment Manpower Mobilization:* R. Wickremasinghe. *State:* A. de Alwis. *Regional Development:* C. Rajadurai. *Women's Affairs and Teaching Hospitals:* S. Ranasinghe. *Trade and Shipping:* M. S. Amarasiri. *Without Portfolio:* M. A. Bakeer Markar.

For purposes of general administration, the island is divided into 25 districts, administered by government agents. There are 12 Municipal Councils and 24 District Councils.

The capital is Colombo.

DEFENCE

Army. The Army was constituted on 10 Oct. 1949. It consists of 5 infantry brigades, 1 reconnaissance, 1 field artillery, 1 anti-aircraft and 1 engineer regiments and 1 signals battalion. Equipment includes 18 Saladin armoured cars and 15 Ferret scout cars. Strength (1985) 11,000, with 14,000 reserves. There are also paramilitary forces: Police Force (14,500), Volunteer Force (5,000) and Home Guard.

Navy. The Navy was constituted on 9 Dec. 1950. It comprises 2 new Colombo-built patrol vessels, 5 (*ex*-Chinese) fast gunboats, 28 small patrol boats (17 built in Colombo, 5 in UK, 2 in Venice and 4 in Singapore by Thornycroft) and 1 service craft. Emphasis is now on indigenous building. *Gemunu* and *Rangalla* are commissioned as shore establishments. The naval base is at Trincomalee. Personnel in 1985 numbered 220 officers and 2,860 ratings. Naval personnel are sent to the UK for training. There is also a Volunteer Naval Reserve of 50 officers and 540 ratings, and a Naval Reserve of 35 officers and 300 men.

Air Force. The Air Force was formed on 10 Oct. 1950. Its flying bases are at Katunayake and China Bay, Trincomalee. Equipment of 4 squadrons comprises 7 Chipmunk and 4 Cessna 150/152 trainers, 4 Herons, 1 HS748, 2 DC-3s, 3 Cessna Skymasters, 1 Cessna 421 and a Cessna Cardinal for general transport and utility purposes; 3 Doves for navigation training; and 2 Dauphin and 9 JetRanger helicopters for internal security operations. In storage are 5 MiG-17F jet fighter-bombers. Total strength about 2,500 officers and airmen. There is also an Air Force Reserve.

INTERNATIONAL RELATIONS

Membership. Sri Lanka is a member of UN, the Commonwealth, the Non-Aligned Movement and the Colombo Plan.

External debt. External debt in Dec. 1983 was Rs46,025m. (provisional).

ECONOMY

Planning. The 1984–88 plan aims at 5·5% annual growth rate. Investment allocated is mainly for agriculture, including the Mahaweli energy and irrigation scheme. Total public investment, about Rs106,307m.

Budget. Revenue and expenditure of central government in Rs 1m. for financial years ending 31 Dec.:

		Expenditure		
Year	*Revenue*	*Recurrent*	*Capital*	*Total*
1982	17,809	19,231	16,056	35,287
1983	25,210	25,083	16,708	41,791
1984 [1]	30,770	28,950	19,492	48,442

[1] Estimate.

The principal sources of revenue in 1983 were (in Rs 1m.): Income tax, 3,367; import duties, 4,836; export duties, 2,459; other indirect taxes, 9,979.

The principal items of recurrent expenditure in 1983 (in Rs 1m.): Administration including defence, 4,273; food subsidies and food stamps, 1,508; education, social services and health, 3,756; interest on public debt, 6,624. Capital expenditure on agriculture, 1,526; communications, 1,502.

Currency. The Monetary Law Act provides that the standard monetary unit is the Ceylon *rupee*.

The Central Bank is the sole authority for the issue of currency and all currency notes and coins issued by the Central Bank are legal tender for the payment of any amount, except notes of Rs 50 and Rs 100 dated before 25 Oct. 1970. Currency notes are issued in the denominations of Rs 2, 5, 10, 20, 50, 100, 500 and 1,000. Coins are issued in the denominations of 1, 2, 5, 10, 25 and 50 cents; Rs 1, 2 and 5. The total circulation was Rs 8,641·5m. on 30 June 1984. In March 1985, £1 = Rs 28·35; US$1 = Rs 26·72.

Banking. The narrow money supply (M1) at 30 June 1984 stood at Rs 14,768·5m.

The main commercial banks in Sri Lanka are: The Bank of Ceylon and the People's Bank (state-managed), the State Bank of India, Grindlays Bank, the Hongkong and Shanghai Banking Corporation, the Chartered Bank, the Commercial Bank of Ceylon, the Hatton National Bank, the Habib Bank (Overseas) Ltd., Indo-Suez Bank, Bank of Credit and Commerce International, American Express and the Indian Overseas Bank Ltd. Total assets of 25 commercial banks at 30 June 1984, Rs 52,191·5m.

The state-owned Ceylon Insurance Corporation and the National Insurance Corporation have a monopoly of all insurance business.

Sri Lanka National Savings Bank at 30 June 1984 had a balance to depositors' credit of Rs 10,269·6m. Sri Lanka State Mortgage and Investment Bank, National Development Bank, Development Finance Corporation and the National Housing Department are the main long-term credit institutions.

Weights and Measures. The metric system has been established by the Weights and Measures (Amendment) Law No. 24 of 1974, and subsequent legislation.

ENERGY AND NATURAL RESOURCES

Electricity. Installed capacity of electric energy (1983), 592,000 kw. Energy produced, 2,114m. kwh; the main source is hydro-electricity. The Mahaweli power scheme (from 1984) has an installed capacity of 507mw.

Water. The Mahaweli Ganga irrigation scheme has entered phase 2 and will benefit 896,000 acres. Two major river diversions, at Polgolla near Kandy and at Bowatenna on the Amban Ganga River, will benefit 120,000 acres of land already cultivated and irrigate an extra 104,000 acres of new land. There is a Water Resources Board (set up in 1966) and a National Water Supply and Drainage Board (1974). Water supply to the city and area of Colombo comes from the Labugama and Kalatuwawa reservoirs. Consumption within Colombo city limits is estimated at 10,000m. gallons a year.

All domestic consumers receive a free water allowance; commercial consumers do not.

Minerals. Gems are among the chief minerals mined and exported. Precious and semi-precious stones are found among the layers of older alluvium and river gravels of quaternary age in the valleys of the Ratnapura district in the south-west. The most important are sapphire, ruby, crysoberyl, beryl, topaz, spinel, garnet, ziran and tourmaline. Value of gemstones exported in 1983, Rs 521m.

Graphite is also important. The State Graphite Corporation was set up in 1971. There were 3 large mines (Bogala, Kahatagaha and Kalangaha), and several smaller mines. Graphite produced (tonnes), 1982, 8,803; 1983 5,870.

The Ceylon Mineral Sands Corporation was established in 1957, mainly to extract ilmenite. Production of ilmenite, 1983, 76,462 tonnes. Some rutile is also produced (7,803 tonnes in 1983).

Salt extraction is the oldest industry in Sri Lanka and is now controlled by the National Salt Corporation. The method is solar evaporation of sea-water. Production, 1983, 128,471 tonnes.

Agriculture. The area of the island is approximately 6,560,963 hectares, of which 2,164,515 hectares are under cultivation. Agriculture engages about 45% of the labour force. The main crops in 1983 were as follows: Paddy (2·5m. tons from 778,038 hectares), rubber (139,997 tons, provisional), tea (179,287 tons) and coconuts (2,312m. nuts).

Livestock in 1983 (estimate): 1·7m. cattle, 910,000 buffaloes, 77,000 swine, 519,300 goats, 28,600 sheep, 6·5m. poultry.

Fisheries. The Government is implementing a programme (1979-83) for the development of fisheries. Production for 1983 was 220,866m. tons including 184,026m. tons of coastal water fish, 36,061m. tons of fresh water fish and 779m. tons from deep-sea fisheries. In 1983 (provisional) there were 27,407 fishing craft, of which 14,129 were not motorized.

INDUSTRY AND TRADE

Industry. The Business Undertakings (Acquisition) Act was passed in May 1971 empowering the Government to acquire any business for the state. The British Ceylon Corporation Ltd and its subsidiaries were nationalized in Feb. 1972. The nationalization of the oil industry was completed in Dec. 1971. The first objective was the development of heavy industry through state investment in small companies and the setting up of public corporations. Three such corporations have been established for the mining and processing of graphite; the importing, manufacture and distribution of pharmaceuticals; the importing and distribution of materials for textile manufacture. Other important manufactures are ceramics, vegetable oils, fertilizers, cement, wood and paper products, leather, rubber products and sugar. The government has set up Investment Promotion Zones; by Aug. 1980 these had 119 projects employing over 7,600; the main industry was clothing manufacture. Foreign investment is encouraged by a tax holiday of up to 10 years for approved industries. Export profits may have a 3-year tax holiday.

Trade unions. The registration and control of trade unions are regulated by the Trade Unions Ordinance (Ch. 138 of the Legislative Enactments). In 1983 there were 1,106 registered trade unions with a membership of 1,779,014.

Commerce. The values of total imports and exports (imports excluding bullion, specie and postal articles; exports, including re-exports and ship's stores) for calendar years (in Rs 1,000):

	1980	*1981*	*1982*	*1983*
Imports	33,637,000	35,530,235	36,875,519	42,020,529
Exports	17,273,000	19,657,851	20,728,491	24,843,439

Principal exports (domestic) in 1983 (in Rs 1m.): Tea, 8,296; rubber, 2,852; copra, coconut oil and desiccated coconut, 1,409; other crops, 1,486; textiles and garments, 4,738; precious and semi-precious stones, 941.

Principal imports (Rs 1m.) in 1983 were petroleum, 9,965m.; machinery and equipment, 7,879m.; vehicles and transport equipment, 3,176; food and beverages, 5,375.

In 1983 the principal sources of imports were (in Rs 1m.): Saudi Arabia, 1,859; Japan, 7,461; UK, 2,838; USA, 2,699; India, 2,709; Iran, 4,410; Singapore, 3,500; FRG, 1,766; South Korea, 844.

Principal export destinations 1983 were (in Rs 1m.): UK, 1,227; USA, 4,358; Japan, 1,130; Pakistan, 698; FRG, 1,537; Saudi Arabia, 805.

Total trade between Sri Lanka and UK (British Department of Trade returns, in £1,000 sterling):

	1980	*1981*	*1982*	*1983*	*1984*
Imports to UK	53,681	36,569	42,000	39,784	77,163
Exports and re-exports from UK	76,831	59,236	60,211	70,136	61,179

Tourism. About 337,340 tourists visited the country in 1983.

COMMUNICATIONS

Roads. There are about 25,466 km. of motorable roads, of which 75% are black-topped. Number of motor vehicles, 31 Dec. 1983, 439,661, including 136,853 private cars and cabs, 83,557 lorries, 66,973 tractors, 121,840 motor cycles, 30,438 buses.

Railways. In 1983 there were about 1,453 km of railway open, of which 1,394 km were broad gauge and 59 narrow gauge. In 1983 railways ran 2,447m. passenger-km and 223m. tonne-km.

Aviation. Air Lanka operates international services. Foreign airlines which operate scheduled services to Sri Lanka are British Airways, India Airlines Corporation, Swissair, Aeroflot, KLM, Singapore Airlines, Thai Airways International, Pakistan International Airlines, Korean Airlines, Gulf Air, Royal Nepal Airlines, Balkan Bulgarian Airlines, Kuwait Airlines and UTA French Airlines; various others operate charter services.

Shipping. In 1983, merchant vessels totalling 20·8m. GRT entered the ports of Sri Lanka. The Sri Lanka Shipping Corporation began functioning as ship-owners, charterers, brokers and shipping agents in 1979. The Sri Lanka Port Authority was also established in 1979.

Post and Broadcasting. In 1983 there were 446 post offices and 3,162 sub-post offices. In 1982 there were 1,900 telegraph offices and 109,900 telephones. Throughout the Greater Colombo Area inter-dialling facilities are now available between 52 stations.

The Overseas Telecommunication Service operates telegraph and telephone services to most parts of the world. Broadcasting is provided by the Sri Lanka Broadcasting Corporation, which assumed the functions of Radio Ceylon on 5 Jan. 1967.

Cinemas. In 1983 there were 350 cinemas with a seating capacity of 193,420. The National Film Corporation established in 1971 has exclusive rights to import films and arranges distribution of foreign and local films. Films released, 1983, 156.

Newspapers. There are 4 main newspaper groups: Associated Newspapers of Ceylon Ltd (5 daily and 3 weekly papers and other periodicals); Express Newspapers (Ceylon) Ltd (2 daily and 2 weekly papers); Independent Newspapers Ltd. (3 daily and 3 weekly papers and other periodicals); Upali Newspapers Ltd. (2 daily, 2 weekly papers and other periodicals).

There are 6 daily and 22 weekly papers in Sinhala; 6 daily and 6 weekly in Tamil; 7 daily and 9 weekly in English.

JUSTICE, RELIGION, EDUCATION AND WELFARE

Justice. The systems of law which obtain in Sri Lanka are the Roman-Dutch law, the English law, the Tesawalamai, the Moslem law and the Kandyan law.

The Kandyan law applies to the Kandyan Sinhalese in the Central, North-Central, Uva and Sabaragamuwa provinces in respect of all matters relating to inheritance, matrimonial rights and donations. The law of England is observed in most commercial matters. The law of Tesawalamai is applied to all Tamil inhabitants of Jaffna, in all matters relating to inheritance, marriages, gifts, donations, purchases and sales of land. The Moslem law is applied to all Moslems in respect of succession, donations not involving Fidei Commissa, marriage, divorce and maintenance. These customary and religious laws have been modified in many respects by local enactments.

The courts of original jurisdiction are the High Courts, District Courts, Magistrates' Courts and Primary Courts. The High Courts try major crimes and also exercise admiralty jurisdiction. The District Court has unlimited civil jurisdiction in civil, revenue, trust, insolvency and testamentary matters, over persons and estates of persons of unsound mind, and wards. Family Courts were estabished in 1978; District Courts act as Family Courts. The Magistrates' Courts exercise criminal jurisdiction carrying the power to impose terms of imprisonment not exceeding 2 years and fines not exceeding Rs 1,500. The Primary Courts which were established in 1978 exercise civil jurisdiction where the value of the subject matter does not exceed Rs 1,500 and also have jurisdiction in respect of by-laws of local authorities and matters relating to the recovery of revenue of such local authorities. Primary Courts exercise exclusive criminal jurisdiction in respect of offences which may be prescribed by regulation by the Minister. A Judge of a Primary Court has a duty to make every effort to settle matters whether civil or criminal, by conciliation. The Primary Courts have the power to impose sentences of imprisonment not exceeding three months and fines not exceeding Rs 250.

The Constitution of 1978 provided for the establishment of two superior courts, the Supreme Court and the Court of Appeal.

The Supreme Court is the highest and final superior court of record and exercises jurisdiction in respect of constitutional matters, jurisdiction for the protection of fundamental rights, final appellate jurisdiction, consultative jurisdiction, jurisdiction in election petitions and jurisdiction in respect of any breach of the privileges of Parliament. The Court of Appeal exercises appellate jurisdiction for the correction of all errors in fact or in law committed by any court, tribunal or institution, the power to grant and issue orders in the nature of writs of Certiorari, Prohibition, Procedendo, Mandamus, Quo Warrants and Habeas corpus, the power to grant injunctions and jurisdiction to try election petitions in respect of election of Members of Parliament.

Police. The strength of the police service in 1983 was 16,552.

Religion. Buddhism was introduced from India in the 3rd century B.C. and is the religion of 69·3% of the inhabitants. There were (1981) 10,292,586 Buddhists, 2,295,858 Hindus, 1,111,736 Christians, 1,134,556 Moslems and 15,265 others.

Education. Education is free from the kindergarten to the university and is imparted in the medium of the mother tongue. In 1981 about 86% of the population (10 years old and older) was literate.

In 1983 there were 9,947 schools including 9,575 government schools; the rest were private and estate schools, and Pirivenas. The government schools had 129,480 teachers and 3·5m. students from grades L.K.G. to XII. Department of Education expenditure (1983), Rs 2,447·8m. Education is now administered under 30 regional directors.

The overall control of the education regions is vested in the Ministry of Education.

There are 6 Universities: Peradeniya, Colombo, Jaffna, Sri Jayawardenepura, Moratuwa and Kelaniya, an Open University and two University Colleges: Ruhuna and Batticaloa. Dumbara Campus comes under Peradeniya University.

In 1983 there were 19,033 students and 2,168 teachers in the 6 Universities and 2 University Colleges. The Open University had 12,248 students. There were 22 institutions for technical education, 7 of which were polytechnics; total enrolment (1983), 21,730.

Health. In 1983 there were 497 hospitals, including 98 maternity homes, and 334 central dispensaries. Hospitals had 44,186 beds and there were 1,939 Department of Health doctors. Total state budget expenditure on health, 1983, Rs 1,735m.

Social Security. The activities of the Department of Social Services fall into five main divisions:

Public assistance (monthly allowances); casual relief; relief to leprosy and tuberculosis patients and their dependants.

Relief of widespread distress due to failure of crops, floods, storms, etc., including relief to individual cases of distress among fishermen due to acts of God such as fire, storms and accidents; rehabilitation and resettlement of flood victims.

State Homes for the aged, grants-in-aid to voluntary agencies and local authorities for charitable and welfare institutions, homes for the aged and creches.

Services for orthopaedically handicapped persons, services for the deaf and the blind, vagrancy and administration of the house of detention.

The education, vocational training, employment and rehabilitation of all categories of handicapped persons are functions of the Department of Social Services. The Department has established Vocational Training Centres for the handicapped and also helps the Voluntary Social Services Organizations with maintanence grants and ad-hoc grants to established homes. Grants are made to handicapped persons for higher education; orthopaedic appliances and hearing aids are supplied for handicapped persons in poor families.

The payment of compensation to workmen meeting with accidents in the course of their work has been administered by the Ministry of Justice since 1980.

DIPLOMATIC REPRESENTATIVES

Of Sri Lanka in Great Britain (13 Hyde Park Gdns., London, W2 2LX)
High Commissioner: L. B. C. Monerawela (accredited 15 May 1984).

Of Great Britain in Sri Lanka (190 Galle Rd., Kollupitiya, Colombo 3)
High Commissioner: J. A. B. Stewart, CMG, OBE.

Of Sri Lanka in the USA (2148 Wyoming Ave., NW, Washington, D.C., 20008)
Ambassador: Ernest Corea.

Of the USA in Sri Lanka (44 Galle Rd., Kollupitiya, Colombo 3)
Ambassador: John H. Reed.

Of Sri Lanka to the United Nations
Ambassador: Nissanka Wijewardane.

Books of Reference

The Sri Lanka Year Book. Department of Census and Statistics. Colombo, Annual
Census Publications from 1871
Economic Atlas. Department of Census and Statistics. Colombo, 1980
Performance 1983. Ministry of Plan Implementation, Colombo. 1983
Review of the Economy. Central Bank of Ceylon. Annual
Statistical Pocket-Book. Department of Census and Statistics. Colombo, 1984
Statistical Abstract. Department of Census and Statistics, Colombo, 1982

Coomaraswamy, R., *Sri Lanka: The Crisis of the Anglo-American Constitutional Traditions in a Developing Society.* Colombo, 1984
de Silva, K. M. (ed.), *Sri Lanka: A Survey.* London, 1977.—*A History of Sri Lanka.* London, 1980
Ferguson's *Ceylon Directory.* Annual (from 1858)
Johnson, B. L. C., and Scrivenor, M. le M., *Sri Lanka: Land, People and Economy.* London, 1981
Piyadasa, L., *Sri Lanka: The Holocaust and After.* London, 1984
Ponnambalam, S., *Dependent Capitalism in Crisis: The Sri Lankan Economy 1948–80.* London, 1980
Ratnasuriya, M. D., and Wijeratne, P. B. F., *Shorter Sinhalese-English Dictionary.* Colombo, 1949
Richards, P., and Gooneratne, W., *Basic Needs, Poverty and Government Policies in Sri Lanka.* Geneva, 1981
Robinson, M. S., *Political Structure in a Changing Sinhalese Village.* CUP, 1975
Schwarz, W., *The Tamils of Sri Lanka.* London, 1983
Wilson, A. J., *Politics in Sri Lanka 1947-73.* London, 1974.—*The Gaullist System in Asia: the Constitution of Sri Lanka.* London, 1980

THE DEMOCRATIC REPUBLIC OF SUDAN

Capital: Khartoum
Population: 20·56m. (1983)
GNP per capita: US$380 (1981)

Jamhuryat es-Sudan Al Democratia

HISTORY. Sudan was proclaimed a sovereign independent republic on 1 Jan. 1956. On 19 Dec. 1955 the Sudanese parliament passed unanimously a declaration that a fully independent state should be set up forthwith, and that a Council of State of 5 should temporarily assume the duties of Head of State. The Codomini, the UK and Egypt, gave their assent on 31 Dec. 1955.

For the history of the Condominium and the steps leading to independence, *see* THE STATESMAN'S YEAR-BOOK, 1955, pp. 340–341.

On 8 July 1965 the Constituent Assembly elected Ismail El-Azhari as President of the Supreme Council. Following a crisis in the coalition Cabinet the Prime Minister, Mohammed Ahmed Mahgoub resigned on 23 April 1969. For political history *see* THE STATESMAN'S YEAR-BOOK, 1973–74, p. 1333. The Government was taken over by a 10-man Revolutionary Council on 25 May 1969 under the Chairmanship of Col. Jaafar M. al Nemery. This Council was dissolved in 1972.

AREA AND POPULATION. Sudan is bounded north by Egypt, north-east by the Red Sea, east by Eritrea and Ethiopia, south by Kenya, Uganda and Zaïre, west by the Central African Republic and Chad, north-west by Libya. Sudan covers an area of 967,500 sq. miles (2,505,813 sq. km) and the population at the census of 14 Feb. 1983 was 20,564,364; latest estimate (1984) 21,440,000. The chief cities (census, 1983) are the capital, Khartoum (476,218), its suburbs Omdurman (526,287) and Khartoum North (341,146), Port Sudan (206,727), Wadi Medani (141,065), al-Obeid (140,024), Kassala (98,751 in 1973), Atbara (73,009), al-Qadarif (66,465 in 1973) and Kosti (65,257 in 1973).

The northern and central thirds of the country are populated by Arab and Nubian peoples, while the southern third is inhabited by Nilotic and Negro peoples; Arabic, the official language, is spoken by 51%, Darfurian by 6% and other northern languages by 12%, while Nilotic languages (chiefly Dinka and Nuer) are spoken by 18%, Nilo-Hamitic by 5%, Sudanic by 5% and others by 3%. In 1984 there were 700,000 refugees in Sudan (479,000 from Ethiopia).

The area and population (census, 1983) of the regions are as follows:

Region	*Sq km*	*1983*	*Region*	*Sq km*	*1983*
Northern	183,941	1,083,024	Dafur	196,555	3,093,699
Eastern	129,086	2,208,209	Equatoria	76,495	1,406,181
Central	53,716	4,012,543	Bahr al-Ghazal	77,625	2,265,510
Kurdufan	146,932	3,093,294	Upper Nile	92,269	1,599,605
Khartoum (province)	10,883	1,802,299			

Local government: Sudan is divided into Khartoum Province (centrally administered) and 8 Regions, each with an elected Regional Assembly and government, and sub-divided into 17 more Provinces.

CLIMATE. Lying wholly within the tropics, the country has a continental climate and only the Red Sea coast experiences maritime influences. Temperatures are generally high throughout the year, with May and June the hottest months. Winters are virtually cloudless and night temperatures are consequently cool. Summer is the rainy season inland, with amounts increasing from north to south, but the northern areas are virtually a desert region. On the Red Sea coast, most rain falls in winter. Khartoum. Jan. 74°F (23·3°C), July 89°F (31·7°C). Annual rainfall 6″ (157 mm). Juba. Jan. 83°F (28·3°C), July 78°F (25·6°C). Annual rainfall 39″ (968 mm). Port Sudan. Jan. 74°F (23·3°C), July 94°F (34·4°C). Annual rainfall 4″ (94 mm). Wadi Halfa. Jan. 60°F (15·6°C), July 90°F (32·2°C). Annual rainfall 0·1″ (2·5 mm).

CONSTITUTION AND GOVERNMENT. A new Constitution was introduced in 1973 (amended in 1975). Legislative power lies with a National Assembly of 151 members. The President is directly elected for 6 years.

A measure of autonomy has been given to southern Sudan and a People's Assembly of 60 was elected in May 1980. The Assembly is situated at Juba.

A State of Emergency was declared in May 1984.

The government in Dec. 1984 was composed as follows:

President and Prime Minister and Minister of Defence: Jaafar Mohammed Nemery (re-elected for a third term in April 1983).

First Vice-President, Director of State Security: Maj.-Gen. Umar Mohammed al Tayib.

Second Vice-President: Lieut.-Gen. Joseph Lagu. *Finance and Economic Planning:* Dr Abdul-Rahman Abdul-Wahab. *Industry:* Abdul-Kader Suliman. *Co-operation, Trade and Supply:* Fawzi Ibrahim Wasfi. *Health:* Gen. Abdebsalam Salam Isam. *Information and National Guidance:* Ali Muhammad Shummo. *Internal Affairs:* Kamal Hassan Ahmed. *Education:* Dr Osman Sidahmed Ismail. *Transport and Communications:* Khalid Hasan Abbas. *Foreign Affairs:* Hashim Osman. *Attorney-General:* Rashi al-Tahir Bakr.

On 9 Dec. 1965 the Constituent Assembly proscribed the Communist Party.

National flag: Three horizontal stripes of red, white, black, with a green triangle based on the hoist.

DEFENCE. Conscription had been legislated but not implemented in 1984.

Army. The Army is organized in 2 armoured, 1 parachute and 7 infantry brigades, with 3 artillery and 1 engineer regiments, and 3 Air Defence brigades. Equipment includes 70 T-54, 53 T-55, 17 T-34 and 20 M-60A3 main battle tanks. Strength (1985) 53,000 (including 3,000 in Air Defence brigades). Paramilitary forces are National Guard (500), Republican Guard (500) and Border Guard (2,500).

Navy. The Navy was established in 1962 to operate in the Red Sea and the River Nile, with 4 patrol boats built in Yugoslavia and a training mission from the Yugoslav Navy until 1972. There are also 1 larger *ex*-Yugoslav patrol craft, 3 *ex*-Iranian coastal patrol craft, 4 *ex*-Iranian very small coastguard cutters, 2 *ex*-Yugoslav landing craft, 1 small oiler, 1 small survey vessel and 1 water carrier. Personnel in 1985 totalled 2,000 officers and men.

Air Force. The Air Force was built up with Soviet and Chinese assistance, and is now receiving equipment from the USA. Three combat squadrons are equipped with 10 F-5E Tiger II and 2 F-5F fighters, about 10 MiG-21 fighters and 12 F-5 (Chinese-built MiG-17) and F-6 (MiG-19) fighter-bombers. There is 1 transport squadron, with 6 C-130H Hercules and 4 DHC-5D Buffalo turboprop transports; 2 Turbo-Porter light transports; 1 helicopter squadron with 10 BO 105s; 3 BAC Mk 55 jet armed trainers, and some Chinese-built FT-5 (MiG-17) advanced trainers. Personnel totalled (1985) about 2,500.

INTERNATIONAL RELATIONS

Membership. Sudan is a member of UN, OAU, the Arab League and is an ACP state of EEC.

ECONOMY

Planning. The 1978–83, 6-year development plan was published in 1977 and envisaged a total investment of £S2,670m.

Budget. The 1982–83 budget envisages revenue of £S1,300m. and expenditure of £S1,900m.

Currency. The monetary unit is the Sudanese *pound* (£S) divided into 100 *piastres* and 1,000 *milliemes.* Sudanese bank-notes of £S10, £S5, £S1, 50 and 25 *piastres* and Sudanese coins of P. 10, 5, 2; m/ms 10, 5, 2, 1 are in circulation. In March 1985, £1 = £S2·67; US$1 = £S2·50.

Banking. The Bank of Sudan opened in Feb. 1960 with an authorized capital of £S1·5m. as the central bank of the country; it has the sole right to issue currency. Its foreign reserves stood at £S12,631,000m. as at 31 Dec. 1978. All foreign banks were nationalized in 1970.

Weights and Measures. The metric system is in use.

ENERGY AND NATURAL RESOURCES

Electricity. Production (1981) 1,000m. kwh.

Oil. Two oil wells in the south-west produce 15,000 bbls per day of high quality oil. An oil refinery is being constructed and 2 oil companies are prospecting for oil and natural gas in the Red Sea area.

Minerals. The following minerals are known to exist in Sudan: gold, graphite, sulphur, chromium-ore (estimate, 9,400m. tonnes in 1979), iron-ore, manganese-ore, copper-ore, zinc-ore, fluorspar, natron, gypsum and anhydrite, magnesite, asbestos, talc, halite, kaolin, white mica, coal, diatomite (kieselguhr), limestone and dolomite, pumice, lead-ore, wollastonite, black sands, vermiculite pyrites.

Gold is being exploited on a small scale at Gabeit and at Abirkateib (in Kassala Province); alluvial gold is occasionally exploited in Southern Fung and Equatoria. Iron-ore was discovered in Red Sea area in 1976.

Manganese mining activities started in the 1950s but this industry did not develop well and in 1979 only 200 tonnes was produced. Processed and scrap white mica have been mined since the late fifties; it went out of production for almost a decade, but started again in 1970 when 170 tonnes were produced; 1979, 1,000 tonnes. A big deposit of vermiculite and a medium-sized deposit of pyrophyllite are known to occur in the Sinkat District. Reserves of metallurgical grade chromite occur in the Ingessana Hills, Blue Nile Province. Huge reserves of chrysotile asbestos are proved in this vicinity and also in Qala El Nahal area, Kassala Province. Deposits of magnesite, with or without talc, are known to occur in the Ingessana Hills and Qala El Nahal areas in addition to other occurrences in the Halaib area, Red Sea Province.

Agriculture. The Sudan is a predominantly agricultural country. Cotton is by far the most important cash crop on which the Sudan depends for earning foreign currency. The two types of cotton grown in the Sudan are: (*a*) long staple sakellaridis and sakel types (derivatives of sakellaridis), grown in Gezira, White Nile, Abdel Magid and private pump schemes; (*b*) short staple, mainly American types, in Equatoria and Nuba Mountains, generally by rain cultivation.

Production (1982) in 1,000 tonnes: Sorghum, 2,100; sugar-cane, 2,529; groundnuts, 800; cotton, 290; millet, 230; wheat, 150; sesame, 200; cotton seed, 300.

One of the largest sugar complexes in the world was opened at Kenana in March 1981. It is capable of processing 330,000 tonnes a year.

Livestock (1983): Cattle, 19·55m.; sheep, 19·5m.; goats, 12·9m.; poultry, 30m.

Forestry. Gum arabic, mainly hashab gum from *Acacia senegal*, is the sole forest produce exported from the Sudan on a major scale. Production (1981) 35·35m. cu. metres.

COMMERCE. Total trade for calendar years, in £S1,000:

	1980	*1981*	*1982*
Imports[1]	788,190	839,830	1,213,810
Exports	271,340	357,000	483,120

[1] Including government imports.

In 1981, the UK provided 13% of imports and Saudi Arabia 11%, while 21% of exports went to Saudi Arabia and 9% to Italy; cotton formed 24% by value of exports and groundnuts 19%, cereal 11%, sesame 10% and gum arabic 9%.

Total trade between Sudan and UK (British Department of Trade returns, in £1,000 sterling):

	1980	*1981*	*1982*	*1983*	*1984*
Imports to UK	13,362	10,889	9,929	18,693	16,858
Exports and re-exports from UK	124,697	118,647	136,636	133,432	95,627

Tourism. There were 27,000 visitors in 1977.

COMMUNICATIONS

Roads. In 1982 there were about 3,000 km of tarmac roads, including the new 1,190 km road from Khartoum to Port Sudan, and 45,000 km of tracks. There were 34,600 passenger cars and 38,000 commercial vehicles in 1980.

Railways. The main railway lines run from Khartoum to El Obeid *via* Wadi Medani, Sennar Junction, Kosti and El Rahad (701 km); El Rahad to Nyala *via* Abu Zabad, Babanousa and Ed-Daein (698 km); Sennar Junction to Kassala *via* Gedaref (455 km) and to Roseires *via* Singa (220 km); Kassala to Port Sudan *via* Haiya Junction and Sinkat (550 km); Khartoum to Wadi Halfa *via* Shendi, El Dammer, Atbara, Berber and Abu Hamad Junction (924 km); Abu Hamad to Karima (248 km); Atbara to Haiya Junction (271 km); Babanousa to Wau (444 km). The main flow of exports and imports is to and from Port Sudan *via* Atbara and Kassala. The total length of line open for traffic (1982) was 4,786 km. The gauge is 1,067 mm. Several new lines are planned, including a link from Wadi Halfa across the Egyptian border. In 1981–82, the railways carried 1,149m. passenger-km and 1·7m. tonne-km.

Aviation. Sudan Airways is a government-owned airline, with its headquarters in Khartoum, operating domestic and international services. The latter include services to Asmara, Addis Ababa, Aden, Jiddah, Cairo, Athens, Rome, London, Beirut, Nairobi, N'djamena, Tripoli and Entebbe. In 1980 Sudan Airways carried 519,000 passengers and 6·8m. ton-kg of mail and freight.

Shipping. Supplementing the railways are regular river steamer services of the Sudan Railways, between Karima and Dongola, 319 km; from Khartoum to Kosti, 319 km; from Kosti to Juba, 1,436 km, and from Kosti to Gambeila, 1,069 km. Port Sudan is the country's only seaport; it is equipped with 13 berths. A modernization programme began in Feb. 1980.

Post and Broadcasting (1975). There are 213 permanent post and telegraph offices, 24 travelling post and telegraph offices and 372 agencies. There are 27 wireless telegraph and 99 radio-telephone stations, 36 automatic telephone exchanges and 340 telephone call boxes; number of telephones in 1982 was 68,503 (43,923 in Greater Khartoum). Radio receivers (1982) 1·4m. The television service broadcasts for 35 hours per week. There were (1982) 107,000 TV receivers.

Cinemas. In 1975 there were 58, seating capacity 112,000 and also 43 mobile units.

JUSTICE, RELIGION, EDUCATION AND WELFARE

Justice. The judiciary is a separate and independent department of state directly and solely responsible to the President of the Republic. The general administrative supervision and control of the judiciary is vested in the High Judicial Council.

Civil Justice is administered by the courts constituted under the Civil Justice Ordinance, namely the High Court of Justice—consisting of the Court of Appeal and Judges of the High Court, sitting as courts of original jurisdiction—and Province Courts—consisting of the Courts of Province and District Judges. The law administered is 'justice, equity and good conscience' in all cases where there is no special enactment. Procedure is governed by the Civil Justice Ordinance.

Justice in personal matters for the Moslem population is administered by the Mohammedan law courts, which form the Sharia Divisions of the Court of Appeal, High Courts and Kadis Courts; President of the Sharia Division is the Grand Kadi. The religious law of Islam is administered by these courts in the matters of inheritance, marriage, divorce, family relationship and charitable trusts.

Criminal Justice is administered by the courts constituted under the Code of Criminal Procedure, namely major courts, minor courts and magistrates' courts. Serious crimes are tried by major courts, which are composed of a President and 2 members and have the power to pass the death sentence. Major Courts are, as a rule, presided over by a Judge of the High Court appointed to a Provincial Circuit or a Province Judge. There is a right of appeal to the Chief Justice against any decision or order of a Major Court, and all its findings and sentences are subject to confirmation by him.

Lesser crimes are tried by Minor Courts consisting of 3 Magistrates and presided over by a Second Class Magistrate, and by Magistrates' Courts consisting of a single Magistrate or a bench of lay magistrates.

Religion. In 1980 about 73% of the population was Moslem. The population of the 12 northern provinces is almost entirely Moslem (Sunni), while the majority of the 6 southern provinces are animist (18%) or Christian (9%).

Education (1980). 5,729 primary schools had 1·4m. pupils; there were 428,703 pupils in secondary schools and 28,985 in tertiary education. In 1979 Khartoum University with 10 faculties had 8,777 students. The Khartoum branch of Cairo University with 4 faculties had about 5,000 students and the Islamic University of Omdurman with 3 faculties had 1,472 students. Juba University, founded in 1975 with 5 faculties had 425 students.

Health. In 1976 the Ministry of Health maintained 151 hospitals, 1,500 dispensaries and dressing stations, 139 health centres and 620 clinics (with together 17,324 beds) and 1,652 doctors.

DIPLOMATIC REPRESENTATIVES

Of Sudan in Great Britain (3 Cleveland Row, London, SW1A 1DD)
Ambassador: Sayed Abdullah el Hassan (accredited 1 Dec. 1983).

Of Great Britain in Sudan (New Aboulela Bldg, Barlaman Ave., Khartoum)
Ambassador: Sir Alexander Stirling, KBE, CMG.

Of Sudan in the USA (2210 Massachusetts Ave., NW, Washington, D.C., 20008)
Ambassador: Omer Salih Eissa.

Of the USA in Sudan (Sharia Ali Abdul Latif, Khartoum)
Ambassador: Hume A. Horan.

Of Sudan to the United Nations
Ambassador: Omer Y. Birido.

Books of Reference

Sudan Almanac. Khartoum (annual)
al Rahim, M. Abd, *Changing Patterns of Civilian-Military Relations in the Sudan.* Uppsala, 1978
Barnett, T., *The Gezira Scheme: An Illusion of Development.* London, 1977
Daly, M. W., *Sudan.* [Bibliography] Oxford and Santa Barbara, 1983
Holt, P. M., *A Modern History of the Sudan.* New York, 3rd ed. 1979

Iten, O., *Le Soudan.* Zurich, 1983
Lees, F. A., *The Economic and Political Development of the Sudan.* London, 1977
Nimeiri, S., *Evaluation of the Six Year Development Plan 1977–78—1982–83.* Khartoum, 1978
Wai, D. M. (ed.), *The Southern Sudan: The Problem of National Integration.* London, 1973
Wickens, G. E., *The Flora of Jebel Marra.* London, 1977
Woodward, P., *Condominium and Sudanese Nationalism.* London, 1979

SURINAME

Capital: Paramaribo
Population: 370,000 (1984)
GNP per capita: US$3,030 (1981)

HISTORY. At the peace of Breda (1667) between Great Britain and the United Netherlands, Suriname was assigned to the Netherlands in exchange for the colony of New Netherland in North America, and this was confirmed by the treaty of Westminster of Feb. 1674. Since then Suriname has been twice in British possession, 1799–1802 (when it was restored to the Batavian Republic at the peace of Amiens) and 1804–16, when it was returned to the Kingdom of the Netherlands according to the convention of London of 13 Aug. 1814, confirmed at the peace of Paris of 20 Nov. 1815. On 25 Nov. 1975, Suriname gained full independence and was admitted to the UN on 4 Dec. 1975.

AREA AND POPULATION. Suriname is situated on the north coast of South America and bounded on the north by the Atlantic ocean, on the east by the Marowijne River, which separates it from French Guiana, on the west by the Corantijn River, which separates it from Guyana, and on the south by forests and savannas, which separate it from Brazil.

Area, 163,820 sq. km. Census population (1980), 354,860. Estimate (1984) 370,000. The capital, Paramaribo, had (1971 census) 103,738 inhabitants. Annual rate of growth decreased from 4·2% during 1950–64 to 2% during 1964–71, mainly through severe migration primarily to the Netherlands. It is estimated that Suriname lost a total of 150,000 persons by migration (1975–80).

Suriname is divided into 9 districts (populations census 1980): Paramaribo (urban district), 67,905; Commewijne, 14,351; Coronie, 2,777; Marowijne, 23,402; Nickerie, 34,480; Saramacca, 10,335; Suriname, 166,494; Brokopondo, 20,249 and Para, 14,867.

The official languages are Dutch and English. English is widely spoken next to Hindi, Javanese and Chinese as inter-group communication. A vernacular, called 'Sranan Tongo' or 'Surinamese', is used as a lingua franca. In 1976 the Government announced that Spanish would become the nation's principal working language.

CLIMATE. The climate is equatorial, with uniformly high temperatures and rainfall. There is no recognized dry season. Paramaribo. Jan. 80°F (26·7°C), July 81°F (27·2°C). Annual rainfall 89″ (2,225 mm).

CONSTITUTION AND GOVERNMENT. On 25 Feb. 1980 the Prime Minister, Henck Arron, was ousted in a *coup*. A National Military Council was established. In Feb. 1982 the civilian Prime Minister, Dr Henk Chin-a-Sen, was dismissed by the Military Council. In March there was an attempted *coup* by a right-wing military group but this failed. A 4-man military committee administered government departments from Feb. to April 1982 under the chairmanship of Lieut.-Col. Deysi Bouterse, the army commander and chairman of the National Military Council. In Jan. 1984 Errol Alibux was dismissed as Prime Minister by Lieut.-Col. Bouterse.

Before the 1982 *coup* there was a council of 13 ministers who were responsible to the Legislative Council (*Staten van Suriname*). The Legislative Council (39 members) was elected for a 4-year period by universal adult suffrage.

Flag: Horizontally green, red, green with the red of double width with yellow 5-pointed star in centre of red bar.

DEFENCE

Army. Armed forces of the Republic of Suriname consist of regular local officers and conscripted personnel with a strength of about 5,000 in 1983. At least 1 Defender twin-engined light transport has been delivered to the armed force of Suriname, from a total order for four. Other equipment includes a Cessna 206 liaison aircraft.

Navy. The flotilla comprises 3 patrol vessels, 3 coastal patrol craft, 3 river patrol launches and 1 coastal cutter. In 1985 personnel totalled 160 officers and men.

INTERNATIONAL RELATIONS

Membership. Suriname is a member of UN, OAS and is an ACP state of the EEC.

ECONOMY

Planning. For 15 years from independence approximately 3,500m. guilders is available from the Netherlands to carry out an extensive social and economic development programme devised by a joint Dutch and Surinamese team of experts. This programme envisaged, the creation of greater employment and the improvement of the living conditions of the people, but by 1980 only a third of the aid had been spent.

Budget. The expenditures and local revenues (derived from import, export and excise duties, taxes on houses and estates, personal imports and some indirect taxes) are as follows (in 1,000 Suriname guilders):

	1978	*1979*	*1980*	*1981*	*1982*	*1983*
Revenues	623,100	429,800	480,400	527,000	556,600	509,300
Expenditures	650,500	412,500	454,900	569,700	657,900	711,900

Outstanding loans in 1983: Local, 491·1m.; foreign, 37·3m. Suriname guilders. Public debt in 1980, 100·7m. Suriname guilders.

Currency. Notes ranging from 5 to 1,000 *Suriname guilders* are legal tender. Currency notes of 1·00 and 2·50 guilders are issued by the Government. In March 1985, US$1 = 1·78 Suriname guilders; £1 sterling = 1·90 Suriname guilders.

Banking. The Central Bank of Suriname is a bankers' bank and also a bank of issue; the Surinaamsche Bank, the Algemene Bank Nederland and the Handels-, Krediet- en Industriebank, are commercial banks; the Suriname People's Credit Bank operates under the auspices of the Government; Surinaamse Postspaarbank (postal savings bank); Surinaamse Hypotheekbank NV (mortgage bank); Surinaamse Investerings Mij. NV (investment bank); Agentschap van de Maatschappij tot financiering van het Nationaal Herstel NV (long-term investments); National Development Bank; The Agrarian Bank.

Weights and Measures. The metric system is in force.

NATURAL RESOURCES

Minerals. Bauxite is the most important mineral; it is being mined in the Suriname and Marowijne districts. Fresh deposits have been found in the western areas. The ore is exported mainly to USA, but partly processed locally into alumina and aluminium. Production (1983 in 1,000 tonnes): Bauxite, 2,641; alumina, 1,084; aluminium, 34·5.

Agriculture. Agriculture is restricted to the alluvial coastal zone; cultivated area in 1982, 87,442 hectares. The staple food crop is rice; 72,571 hectares of paddy were planted in 1982, chiefly in the Nickerie, Commewijne, Saramacca and Coronie districts. Principal products (in 1,000 units) in 1982:

Sugar (kg)	7,049	Maize on cob (kg)	211	Orange (pieces)	30,866
Cocoa (kg)	30	Bananas (kg)	42,399	Grapefruit (pieces)	2,394
Coffee (kg)	44	Rum 50% (litres)	1,047	Coconuts (pieces)	7,177
Paddy (kg)	301,130	Molasses (litres)	1,891	Palm oil (kg)	5,691

Livestock (1983): 53,000 head of cattle, 4,000 sheep, 10,000 goats, 18,000 pigs, 1m. poultry.

Forestry. Suriname has great timber resources. Production in 1983 included 204,251 cu. metres of logs, 18,420 cu. metres of sleepers (1982), 18,134 cu. metres of plywood and 3,155 cu. metres of particle board.

Fishery. The fish catch in 1980 amounted to 2,100 tonnes and the shrimp catch, 3,100 tonnes.

INDUSTRY AND TRADE

Industry. In 1981, there were 3 large bauxite plants, 1 alumina and 1 aluminium smelting plants, sugar- and rice-mills, 3 paint factories, 2 fruit-juice plants, 3 shrimp freezing plants, a plywood factory, timber-mills, a milk pasteurization plant, a butter and margarine factory and a number of various medium and small industries. Shortage of skilled personnel inhibits expansion.

Commerce. Imports and exports in calendar years (in 1m. Suriname guilders):

	1979	*1980*	*1981*	*1982*	*1983*[1]
Imports	733·5	900·3	1,013·7	921·2	762·5
Exports	792·7	918·2	845·7	765·1	605·4

[1] Estimate.

Principal exports in 1982 (in 1,000 Suriname guilders): Alumina, 411,500; bauxite, 52,400; aluminium, 124,000; rice, 72,100; shrimp, 53,300; wood and wood products, 20,600; bananas, 13,200.

Principal imports in 1982 (in 1,000 Suriname guilders): Raw and auxiliary materials, 356,700; fuels and lubricants, 209,900; investment goods, 117,800; foodstuffs, cars and motorcycles, 73,100; textile yarn and fabrics, 9,600.

Total trade between Suriname and UK (British Department of Trade returns, in £1,000 sterling):

	1980	*1981*	*1982*	*1983*	*1984*
Imports to UK	20,181	11,416	7,593	11,584	18,316
Exports and re-exports from UK	8,112	8,074	10,586	8,914	9,593

COMMUNICATIONS

Roads. There are 1,335 km of main roads. Two of them lead from Paramaribo to the bauxite centres of Smalkalden (29 km) and Paranam (30 km) and to the airport of Zanderij (49 km). Another main road runs across the districts of Saramacca (71 km) and Coronie (68 km), a fourth across the Commewijne district (41 km) and a fifth in the Marowijne district, from the bauxite centre Moengo to Albina (45 km). The 'East-West connexion' is almost completed, linking the Corantijn and the Marowijne rivers (375 km).

In 1983 there were 29,418 passenger cars, 9,452 trucks, 1,813 buses, 31,051 powered bicycles and 1,438 motor cycles.

Railway. There is a single-track railway, running from Onverwacht to Bronsweg (86 km); part of the track, from Paramaribo to Onverwacht (34 km) has been removed. Another single-track railway runs from Apoera to the Bakhuis Mountains.

Aviation. Regular air services are maintained by KLM, SLM, Aero Cubano and Cruzeiro do Sul. The international airfield at Zanderij is capable of handling all types of planes.

Suriname Airways Ltd provides daily services between all major districts and maintains also a charter service.

In 1975, 1,205 aircraft landed at Zanderij airport with 40,416 passengers and 1,225 tons of incoming mail and freight.

Shipping. The Royal Netherlands Steamship Co. plies between Amsterdam, Rotterdam, Antwerp, Hamburg and Paramaribo, and New York, Baltimore, New Orleans and Paramaribo. Regular sailings are made to Georgetown, Ciudad Bolivar and most Caribbean ports. The Suriname Navigation Co. maintains services from Paramaribo to Georgetown and Cayenne, and once a month to the Caribbean area. A French and an Italian company maintain passenger services to Europe. The Alcoa Steamship Co. has a fortnightly service to New York, Baltimore, Mobile and New Orleans; a Japanese line sails once a month from Hong Kong and Yokohama to Paramaribo; the Boomerang Line maintains a monthly freight and passenger service between Suriname and Australia. In 1981, 1,021 vessels totalling 4·93m. GRT entered Paramaribo.

Post and Broadcasting. Automatic telephone service links most of the districts in the interior. In 1982 there were 27,495 telephones. Wireless telephone connects Suriname with the Netherlands, USA, Curaçao, Guyana, French Guiana and Trinidad. There are 6 broadcasting and 1 television stations. In 1974 there were 170,000 radios and 36,000 TV sets. Automatic telex was established in 1972.

Cinemas. In 1981 there were 18 cinemas and 1 drive-in cinema.

Newspapers (1983). There is one daily newspaper, *De Ware Tijd*.

JUSTICE, RELIGION, EDUCATION AND WELFARE

Justice. There is a court of justice, whose members are nominated by the President. There are 3 cantonal courts.

Religion. There is entire religious liberty. At the end of 1983 the main religious bodies were: Hindus, 97,170; Roman Catholics, 80,922; Moslems, 69,638; Moravian Brethren, 55,625; Reformed, 6,265; Lutheran, 2,695; Jehovah's Witnesses, 1,626; Seventh Day Adventists, 1,061; others, 24,627.

Education. During school-year 1982–83 there were 703 schools with a total of 129,184 pupils and 6,051 teachers. There are also a University with faculties of medicine and law, social, technical and economic studies, 5 technical schools and 5 teachers' training colleges.

Schooling is compulsory from 6 to 12 years of age. Primary education is free and is undertaken by the Government in public schools and by the Roman Catholic and Protestant Missions in denominational schools.

Social Security. The Government subsidizes orphanages and other religious or philanthropical institutions, and maintains an almshouse and institutions for delinquent boys and girls. There are 13 modern hospitals in the country, 4 of which are operated by missions, 2 by a private company, 1 by the military forces and 6 by the Government.

DIPLOMATIC REPRESENTATIVES

Of Great Britain in Suriname
Ambassador: W. K. Slatcher, CMG, CVO (resides in Georgetown).

Of Suriname in the USA (2600 Virginia Ave., NW, Washington, D.C., 20037)
Ambassador: Donald A. McLeod.

Of the USA in Suriname (Dr Sophie Redmondstraat 129, Paramaribo)
Ambassador: Robert W. Duemling.

Of Suriname to the United Nations
Ambassador: H. A. M. Guda.

Books of Reference

Statistical Information: The General Bureau of Statistics in Paramaribo was established on 1 Jan. 1947. Its publications comprise trade statistics, *Suriname in Figures* (including, from 1953, the former *Handelsstatistiek*) and *Statistische Berichten*.

Economische Voorlichting Suriname. Ministry of Economic Affairs, Paramaribo
Annual Report of the Central Bank of Suriname

SWAZILAND

Capital: Mbabane
Population: 626,000 (1984)
GNP per capita: US$760 (1981)

HISTORY. The Swazi migrated into the country to which they have given their name, in the last half of the 18th century. They settled first in what is now southern Swaziland, but moved northwards under their chief, Sobhuza–known also to the Swazi as Somhlolo. Sobhuza died in 1838 and was succeeded by Mswati. The further order of succession has been Mbandzeni and Bhunu, whose son, Sobhuza II, was installed as King of the Swazi nation in 1921 after a long minority.

The independence of the Swazis was guaranteed in the conventions of 1881 and 1884 between the British Government and the Government of the South African Republic. In 1890, soon after the death of Mbandzeni, a provisional government was established representative of the Swazis, the British and the South African Republic Governments. In 1894 the South African Republic was given powers of protection and administration. In 1902, after the conclusion of the Boer War, a special commissioner took charge, and under an order-in-council in 1903 the Governor of the Transvaal administered the territory, through the Special Commissioner. Swaziland became independent on 6 Sept. 1968.

On 25 April 1967 the British Government gave the country internal self-government. It changed the country's status to that of a protected state with the Ngwenyama, Sobhuza II, recognized as King of Swaziland and head of state. King Sobhuza died on 21 Aug. 1982.

AREA AND POPULATION. Swaziland is bounded on the north, west and south by the Transvaal Province, and on the east by Mozambique and Zululand. The area is 6,705 sq. miles (17,400 sq. km).

The country is divided geographically into 4 longitudinal regions running from north to south; 3 of roughly equal width–Highveld (westernmost), Middleveld, Lowveld–and the Lubombo plateau in the east. The mountainous region on the west rises to an altitude of over 6,000 ft (1,800 metres). The Middleveld is mostly between 1,700 and 3,000 ft, while the Lowveld has an average height of not more than 1,000 ft (300 metres).

Population (census 1976), 527,791. Estimate (1984) 626,000. Mbabane, the administrative capital (23,109). The main urban areas with 1983 populations are: Manzini (18,818); Havelock Mine (4,838); Siteki (1,362); Big Bend (2,083); Mhlume (3,971); Nhlangano (2,097) and Pigg's Peak (2,192).

CLIMATE. A temperate climate with two seasons. Nov. to March is the wet season, when temperatures range from mild to hot, with frequent thunderstorms. The cool, dry season from May to Sept. is characterised by clear, bright sunny days. Mbabane. Jan. 68°F (20°C), July 54°F (12·2°C). Annual rainfall 56″ (1,402 mm).

CONSTITUTION AND GOVERNMENT. Britain's protection ended at independence, when a Constitution similar to the 1967 Constitution was brought into force. The general elections (by universal adult franchise) in April 1967 gave the royalist and traditional Imbokodvo National Movement all 24 seats. The Parliament consists of a House of Assembly, with 24 elected and 6 nominated members and the Attorney-General, who has no vote, and a Senate comprising 12 members, 6 of whom are elected by the House of Assembly and 6 appointed by the King. The executive authority is vested in the King and exercised through a Cabinet presided over by the Prime Minister, and consisting of the Prime Minister, the Deputy Prime Minister and up to 8 other ministers. In April 1973 the King assumed supreme power and the Constitution was suspended and in 1976 it was abolished. On 28 Oct. 1983 a general election took place to elect an electoral college of 80 members. This college elected 40 members for the National Assembly. The Queen Regent nominated 10 additional members.

Regent: Queen Ntombi.

In Oct. 1984, the Cabinet was composed as follows:

Prime Minister: Prince Bhekimpi Dlamini.

Foreign Affairs: M. M. P. Mnisi. *Labour and Public Service:* M. S. Matsebula. *Agriculture and Co-operatives:* H. S. Mamba. *Commerce, Industry, Mines and Tourism:* D. Von Wissel. *Works and Communications:* Chief Sipho Shongwe. *Education:* H. S. Dabulumjiva Nhlabatsi. *Finance:* B.S. Dlamini. *Health:* Prince Phiwokwakhe Dlamini. *Justice:* D. J. Mathse. *Interior:* K. Mtetwa. *Defence and Youth:* Brig. F. Dube. *Natural Resources, Land Utilization and Energy:* Prince Khuzulwandle Dlamini.

National flag. Horizontally 5 unequal stripes of blue, yellow, crimson, yellow, blue; in the centre of the crimson strip an African shield of black and white, behind which are 2 assegais and a staff, all laid horizontally.

Local Government. The country is divided into the 4 regions of Shiselweni, Lubombo, Manzini and Hhohho. They are administered by Regional Administrators.

DEFENCE

Army Air Wing. First military aircraft acquired by Swaziland, in mid-1979, were 2 Israeli-built Arava light twin-turboprop transports with underwing weapon attachments for light attack duties.

INTERNATIONAL RELATIONS

Membership. Swaziland is a member of UN, OAU, the Commonwealth and is an ACP state of EEC.

ECONOMY

Budget. Revenue and expenditure (in 1,000 emalangeni) for financial years ending 31 March:

	1981–82	*1982–83*	*1983–84*
Revenue	139,000	177,240	183,581
Expenditure	199,000	185,581	190,695

Currency. The currency in circulation in Swaziland is the *emalangeni,* but remains in the rand monetary area. In March 1985, £1=2·21 *emalangeni;* US$1=2·06 *emalangeni.*

Banking. Barclays Bank International and the Standard Bank Ltd maintain branches at Mbabane and Manzini; sub-branches and agencies are operated in 17 other places. Bank rates are those in force throughout South Africa and are prescribed by the main South African offices of the 2 banks. The Swaziland Credit and Savings Bank, now known as The Swazi Bank, a statutory body, was opened in 1965. It specializes in credit for agriculture and low-cost housing. Its head office is in Mbabane and it has branches or agencies at 3 other places. A fourth bank, The Bank of Credit and Commerce International opened in Sept. 1978; its head office is in Manzini and it has a branch in Mbabane.

ENERGY AND NATURAL RESOURCES

Minerals. Swaziland produced a large tonnage of iron ore from the Ngwenya mine near Mbabane (but mining has now ceased) and asbestos from the Havelock Mine (30,100 tons in 1982). Coal is mined at Mpaka (115,000 tons in 1982). Small quantities of quarry stone, kaolin, barytes and pyrophyllite are also mined.

A railway has been built from the Ngwenya hæmatite deposits to Goba, in Mozambique, chiefly for the transportation of iron ore. The extensive deposits of low-volatile bituminous coal in the Lowveld are being worked to provide coal for the railway, sugar-mills and export.

Agriculture. Some 60% of the country, which covers 4,290,944 acres, is reserved for occupation by the Swazi. The main crops are sugar (employing 13,000 people), citrus and rice, all of which are grown under irrigation, and cotton, maize (the staple product), sorghum, tobacco and pineapples. It is usually necessary to import maize from South Africa. Sugar, first produced in 1958, and woodpulp and other forest products are the two main agricultural exports.

Livestock (1983): Cattle, 700,000; goats, 335,000; sheep, 40,000; poultry, 1m.

COMMERCE. By agreement with the Republic of South Africa, Swaziland is united in a customs union with the republic and receives a *pro rata* share of the customs dues collected.

Total exports in 1983 amounted to E375m. The chief items were: Sugar, woodpulp and other forest products, asbestos, iron ore, citrus fruit, meat and meat products. Imports in 1983 were E580m.

Total trade between Swaziland and UK (British Department of Trade returns, in £1,000 sterling):

	1979	*1980*	*1981*	*1982*	*1983*	*1984*
Imports to UK	37,361	30,438	23,884	40,049	23,965	41,786
Exports and re-exports from UK	1,333	691	7,132	7,654	3,536	2,430

Tourism. There were 113,763 visitors in 1983.

COMMUNICATIONS

Roads. There is daily (except Sundays) communication by railway motor-buses between Manzini, Mbabane and Breyten; Manzini, Mankayana and Piet Retief. There are 241 km of tarred trunk roads. Total length of roads 2,750 km.

Railways. In 1982–83 the system comprised 312 km of route, and carried 1·3m. tonnes of freight.

Aviation. The country's chief airport is at Matsapa. It is served by Royal Swazi National Airways connecting with Johannesburg, Durban, Lusaka, Nairobi, Mauritius and Salisbury. South African Airways, connecting with Johannesburg and Durban. Lesotho National Airways flies from Matsapa to Maseru. El Al fly direct from Tel Aviv to Matsapa.

Post. There were (1980) 55 post offices, 2 telephone-telegraph agencies and 10 telephone agencies. There were, in Jan. 1982, 15,357 telephones in the country.

Cinemas. There were 5 cinemas in 1980 with a total seating capacity of 1,625.

Newspapers. There were in 1984 three dailies, two weeklies and one monthly newspaper.

JUSTICE, RELIGION, EDUCATION AND WELFARE

Justice. The judiciary is headed by the Chief Justice. A High Court having full jurisdiction and subordinate courts presided over by Magistrates and District Officers are in existence. During 1969 there were 6,624 convictions in subordinate courts and 36 convictions in the High Court.

There is a Court of Appeal with a President and 3 Judges. It deals with appeals from the High Court. There are 16 Swazi courts of first instance, 2 Swazi courts of appeal and a Higher Swazi Court of Appeal. The channel of appeal lies from Swazi Court of first instance to Swazi Court of Appeal, to Higher Swazi Court of Appeal, to the Judicial Commissioner and thence to the High Court of Swaziland.

Religion. In 1984 there were about 120,000 Christians and about 30,000 adults holding traditional beliefs. A large number of churches and missionary societies are established throughout the country and, in addition to evangelism, are doing important work in the fields of education and medicine. In the larger centres there are churches of several denominations—Protestant, Roman Catholics and others.

Education. In 1984 there were 554 schools with 125,303 pupils in primary classes and 26,469 in secondary classes. The Swaziland Agricultural College and University Centre at Luyengo was opened in Oct. 1966. Technical and vocational training classes are run at the Government's Industrial Training Institute and its Staff Training Institute. The Government also operates a police college. There are 2 teacher training colleges. In 1975 Botswana and Swaziland formed a joint university with campuses in each territory.

Health. In 1984 there were 80 doctors, 13 dentists and 1,608 hospital beds.

DIPLOMATIC REPRESENTATIVES

Of Swaziland in Great Britain (58 Pont St., London SW1X 0AE)
High Commissioner: George Mbikwakhe Mamba (accredited 16 Feb. 1978).

Of Great Britain in Swaziland (Allister Miller St., Mbabane)
High Commissioner: Martin Reith.

Of Swaziland in the USA (4301 Connecticut Ave., NW, Washington, D.C., 20008)
Ambassador: Peter H. Mtetwa.

Of the USA in Swaziland (PO Box 199, Mbabane)
Ambassador: Robert H. Phinny.

Of Swaziland to the United Nations
Ambassador: N. M. Malinga.

Books of Reference

Booth, A., *Swaziland: Tradition and Change in a Southern African Kingdom.* Aldershot and Boulder, 1984

Grotpeter, J. J., *Historical Dictionary of Swaziland.* Metuchen, 1975

Jones, D., *Aid and Development in Southern Africa.* London, 1977

Kuper, H., *An African Aristocracy.* New ed. London, 1961.—*The Uniform of Colour.* Johannesburg, 1947.—*The Swazi: An Ethnographical Survey.* London, 1952

Matsebula, J. S. M., *A History of Swaziland.* London, 1972

Nyeko, B., *Swaziland.* [Bibliography] Oxford and Santa Barbara, 1982

SWEDEN

Konungariket Sverige

Capital: Stockholm
Population: 8·3m. (1983)
GNP per capita: US$10,890 (1983)

HISTORY. Organized as an independent unified state in the 10th century, Sweden became a constitutional monarchy in 1809. In 1809 she also ceded Finland to Russia. In 1815 German possessions were ceded to Prussia and Sweden was united with Norway, which union lasted until 1905.

AREA AND POPULATION. The first census took place in 1749, and it was repeated at first every third year, and, after 1775, every fifth year. Since 1860 a general census has been taken every 10 years and, in addition, in 1935, 1945, 1965 and 1975.

Latest census figures: 1940, 6,371,432 (annual increase since 1935: 0·38%); 1950, 7,041,829 (1·1% since 1945); 1960, 7,495,316 (0·64% since 1950); 1965, 7,766,424 (1·04% since 1960); 1970, 8,076,903 (1·04% since 1965); 1975, 8,208,544 (1·02% since 1970); 1980, 8,320,438 (1·01% since 1975).

Counties (Län)	*Land area: sq. km*	*Census population 15 Sept. 1980*	*Estimated population 31 Dec. 1983*	*Pop. per sq. km 31 Dec. 1983*
Stockholm (city)[1] / Stockholm (county)[1]	6,488	1,527,330	1,551,165	239
Uppsala	6,989	243,273	248,103	35
Södermanland	6,061	252,515	251,000	41
Östergötland	10,569	393,141	392,310	37
Jönköping	9,944	303,354	301,036	30
Kronoberg	8,452	173,619	174,319	21
Kalmar	11,166	241,851	240,134	22
Gotland	3,140	55,362	55,987	18
Blekinge	2,941	153,880	151,884	52
Kristianstad	6,089	280,071	280,380	46
Malmöhus	4,939	743,746	745,434	151
Halland	5,454	230,679	236,319	43
Göteborg and Bohus	5,141	711,934	709,651	138
Älvsborg	11,395	425,189	425,544	37
Skaraborg	7,938	269,715	270,423	34
Värmland	17,582	284,477	281,205	16
Örebro	8,515	274,580	272,138	32
Västmanland	6,302	259,789	256,976	41
Kopparberg	28,264	287,250	285,610	10
Gävleborg	18,191	294,165	291,497	16
Västernorrland	21,711	268,385	264,803	12
Jämtland	49,916	135,084	134,946	3
Västerbotten	55,401	243,723	245,252	4
Norrbotten	98,919	267,321	264,457	3
Total	411,506[2]	8,320,438	8,330,577	20

[1] From Jan. 1968 Stockholm city and Stockholm county have been united in Stockholm county. [2] Total area of Sweden, 449,964 sq. km.

On 31 Dec. 1983 there were 4,116,133 males and 4,214,436 females.

On 31 Dec. 1983 aliens in Sweden numbered 397,140. Of these, 150,641 were Finns, 38,272 Yugoslavs, 26,195 Danes, 25,135 Norwegians, 14,852 Poles, 12,459 West Germans, 11,810 Greeks, 8,978 British, 8,910 Chileans, 6,027 Americans, 4,151 Italians and 3,541 Austrians.

Vital statistics for calendar years:

	Total living births	To mothers single, divorced or widowed	Stillborn	Marriages	Divorces	Deaths exclusive of still-born
1980	97,064	38,558	436	37,569	19,887	91,800
1981	94,065	38,742	380	37,793	20,198	92,034
1982	92,748	38,915	374	37,051	20,766	90,671
1983	91,780	40,059	340	36,210	20,618	90,791

Immigration: 1980, 39,426; 1981, 32,272; 1982, 30,381; 1983, 27,495. Emigration: 1980, 29,389; 1981, 29,440; 1982, 28,381; 1983, 25,269.

In 1860 the urban population numbered 435,000 (11% of the total population) and on 31 Dec. 1965, 4,177,212 (54%); including other densely populated areas, the urbanized population in 1965 was 77·4%.

On 15 Sept. 1980, population in densely populated areas was 6,910,431 (83·1%).

Population of largest communities, 31 Dec. 1983:

Stockholm	650,952	Halmstad	76,572	Falun	51,192
Göteborg	424,186	Skellefteå	74,247	Täby	50,787
Malmö	229,380	Karlstad	73,939	Solna	49,080
Uppsala	150,579	Kristianstad	69,354	Hässleholm	48,714
Norrköping	118,064	Huddinge	69,175	Trollhättan	48,592
Västerås	117,954	Luleå	66,512	Mölndal	48,327
Örebro	117,473	Växjö	65,859	Sollentuna	46,747
Linköping	114,681	Botkyrka	65,427	Kungsbacka	46,493
Jönköping	106,899	Nyköping	64,746	Borlänge	46,407
Helsingborg	103,870	Örnsköldsvik	60,105	Skövde	46,009
Borås	100,184	Haninge	59,837	Uddevalla	45,827
Sundsvall	93,947	Karlskrona	59,696	Varberg	45,367
Eskilstuna	88,987	Nacka	58,537	Norrtälje	41,833
Gävle	87,671	Östersund	56,305	Motala	41,432
Umeå	83,717	Gotland	55,987	Sandviken	41,319
Lund	80,458	Järfälla	55,419	Västervik	40,671
Södertälje	79,553	Kalmar	53,516		

Befolkningsförändringar (Population Changes). Annual. 3 vols. Statistics Sweden, Stockholm
Folkmängd 31 Dec. (Population). Annual. 3 vols. Statistics Sweden, Stockholm
Historisk statistik för Sverige. I: Befolkning (Population), 1720–1967. 2nd ed. Statistics Sweden, Stockholm, 1969

CLIMATE. North Sweden suffers from severe winters, with snow lying for 4–7 months. Summers are fine but cool, with long daylight hours. Further south, winters are less cold, summers are warm and rainfall generally well-distributed over the year, though with a slight summer maximum. Stockholm. Jan. 27°F (–2·7°C), July 62°F (16·5°C). Annual rainfall 21·5″ (536 mm).

REIGNING KING. Carl XVI Gustaf, born 30 April 1946, succeeded on the death of his grandfather Gustaf VI Adolf, 15 Sept. 1973, married 19 June 1976 to *Silvia* Renate Sommerlath, born 23 Dec. 1943 (Queen of Sweden). *Daughter* and *Heir Apparent:* Crown Princess Victoria Ingrid Alice Désirée, Duchess of Västergötland, born 14 July 1977; *son:* Prince Carl Philip Edmund Bertil, Duke of Värmland, born 13 May 1979; *daughter:* Princess Madeleine Thérèse Amelie Josephine, Duchess of Hälsingland and Gästrikland, born 10 June 1982.

Sisters of the King. Princess Margaretha, born 31 Oct. 1934, married 30 June 1964 to Mr John Ambler; Princess Birgitta (Princess of Sweden), born 19 Jan. 1937, married 25 May 1961 (civil marriage) and 30 May 1961 (religious ceremony) to Johann Georg, Prince of Hohenzollern; Princess Désirée, born 2 June 1938, married 5 June 1964 to Baron Niclas Silfverschiöld; Princess Christina, born 3 Aug. 1943, married 15 June 1974 to Tord Magnuson.

Uncles of the King. Sigvard, Count of Wisborg, born on 7 June 1907; Prince Bertil, Duke of Halland, born on 28 Feb. 1912, married 7 Dec. 1976 to Lilian May Davies, born 30 Aug. 1915 (Princess of Sweden, Duchess of Halland); Carl Johan, Count of Wisborg, born on 31 Oct. 1916.

Aunt of the King. Princess Ingrid (Princess of Sweden), born 28 March 1910, married 24 May 1935 to Frederik, Crown Prince of Denmark (King Frederik IX), died 14 Jan. 1972.

The following is a list of the kings and queens of Sweden, with the dates of their accession from the accession of the House of Vasa:

House of Vasa	
Gustaf I	1521
Eric XIV	1560
Johan III	1568
Sigismund	1592
Carl IX	1599
Gustaf II Adolf	1611
Christina	1632

House of Pfalz-Zweibrücken	
Carl X Gustaf	1654
Carl XI	1660

House of Pfalz-Zweibrücken (contd.)	
Carl XII	1697
Ulrica Eleonora	1719

House of Hesse	
Fredrik I	1720

House of Holstein-Gottorp	
Adolf Fredrik	1751
Gustaf III	1771
Gustaf IV Adolf	1792
Carl XIII	1809

House of Bernadotte	
Carl XIV Johan	1818
Oscar I	1844
Carl XV	1859
Oscar II	1872
Gustaf V	1907
Gustaf VI Adolf	1950
Carl XVI Gustaf	1973

The royal family of Sweden have a civil list of 11·2m. kronor; this does not include the maintenance of the royal palaces.

CONSTITUTION AND GOVERNMENT. Sweden's present Constitution came into force in 1975 and replaced the 1809 Constitution. Under the present Constitution Sweden is a representative and parliamentary democracy. Parliament (*Riksdag*) is declared to be the central organ of government. The executive power of the country is vested in the Government, which is responsible to Parliament. The King is Head of State, but he does not participate in the government of the country. Since 1971 Parliament has consisted of one chamber. It has 349 members, who are elected for a period of 3 years in direct, general elections.

Every man and woman who has reached the age of 18 years on election-day itself, and who is not under wardship has the right to vote and to stand for election.

The manner of election to the *Riksdag* is proportional. The country is divided into 28 constituencies. In these constituencies 310 members are elected. The remaining 39 seats constitute a nation-wide pool intended to give absolute proportionality to parties that receive at least 4% of the votes. A party receiving less than 4% of the votes in the country is, however, entitled to participate in the distribution of seats in a constituency, if it has obtained at least 12% of the votes cast there.

The *Riksdag*, elected 1982, has 166 Social Democrats, 86 Conservatives, 56 Centre Party, 21 Liberals and 20 Communists.

The Social Democratic Cabinet was composed as follows in Feb. 1984:

Prime Minister: Olof Palme.

Deputy Prime Minister and Minister with special responsibility for Research: Ingvar Carlsson. *Agriculture:* Svante Lundkvist. *Finance:* Kjell-Olof Feldt. *Health and Social Affairs, with special responsibility for the Social and Health Services:* Gertrud Sigurdsen. *Housing:* Hans Gustafsson. *Labour:* Anna-Greta Leijon. *Education and Cultural Affairs:* Lena Hjelm-Wallen. *Industry:* Thage Peterson. *Health and Social Affairs:* Sten Andersson. *Justice:* Sten Wickbom. *Transport and Communications:* Curt Boström. *Foreign Affairs:* Lennart Bodström. *Education, with special responsibility for cultural affairs, the mass media and comprehensive schools:* Bengt Göransson. *Labour, with special responsibility for immigrant and equality affairs:* Anita Gradin. *Industry, with special responsibility for energy questions:* Birgitta Dahl. *Industry, with special responsibility for state-owned enterprises:* Roine Carlsson. *Public Administration:* Bo Holmberg. *Foreign Affairs, with special responsibility for foreign trade:* Mats Hellström. *Defence:* Anders Thunborg.

Ministerial decisions are formally made by the Cabinet collectively and not (with some exceptions) by individual ministers.

Public administration in Sweden is characterized by a unique degree of functional decentralization. The Ministries are not really administrative agencies. Their main function is to prepare the decisions of the Cabinet; such decisions may concern bills for the *Riksdag,* general government directives and higher appointments. Only to a small extent does the Cabinet make individual administrative decisions. The routine administrative work is attended to by the central boards (*centrala ämbetsverk*). Each board is in principle subordinate to the government; its sphere of activity depends on the appropriations granted by the *Riksdag.* The Government often asks the boards' opinion on proposed measures.

National flag: Blue with a yellow Scandinavian cross.

National anthem: Du gamla, du fria, du fjällhöga nord (words by R. Dybeck, 1844; folk-tune).

The official language is Swedish. The capital is Stockholm.

Regional and Local Government. For national administrative purposes Sweden is divided into 24 counties (*län*), in each of which the central government is represented by a state county administrative board (*länsstyrelse*). The governor (*landshövding*), appointed by the government, is chairman of the board, which in addition to the governor has 14 members elected by the county council.

Local government and the levying of local taxes are based on the fundamental law and are regulated by the local government act and special acts. According to the local government act Sweden is divided into municipalities in which all men and women who have reached the age of 18 on election-day itself, and not under wardship, are entitled to elect the municipal council. These councils are named *kommunfullmäktige.* The number of municipalities has, since 1951, been reduced from about 2,500 to 284. The municipalities deal with a great variety of different tasks such as social welfare, education and culture, public health, town planning, housing etc. Each county, except Gotland, which consists of only one municipality, has a county council (*landsting*) elected by men and women who enjoy local suffrage. The county councils chiefly administer the health services and medical care. The municipalities of Gothenburg and Malmö do not belong to county councils. Ecclesiastical affairs in all parishes with more than 1,000 inhabitants are dealt with by church councils (*kyrkofullmäktige*); smaller parishes may make the same arrangement. All elections are conducted on a proportional basis.

Boalt, G., *The Political Process.* Stockholm, 1984
Gustafsson, A., *Local Government in Sweden.* Stockholm, 1983
Lewin, L., Jansson, B., and Sörbom, D., *The Swedish Electorate 1887–1968.* Stockholm, 1972
Vinde, P., *Swedish Government Administration.* 2nd rev. ed. Stockholm, 1978

DEFENCE. A Supreme Commander is, under the Government, in command of the three services. He is assisted by the Defence Staff under a chief of staff.

The military forces are recruited on the principle of national service, supplemented by voluntarily enlisted personnel who form the permanent cadres for training purposes, staff duties, etc.

Liability to service commences at the age of 18, and lasts till the end of the 47th year. The period of training for the Army and Navy is 7½-15 months and for the Airforce 8-15 months.

The territorial organization consists of 6 military commands each one under a general officer commanding.

Army. The C.-in-C. of the Royal Swedish Army has at his disposal the Army Staff under a chief of staff. The peace-time Army consists for training purposes of 16 infantry, 2 cavalry, 6 armour, 6 artillery, 5 AA, 3 engineer, 2 signal and 3 Army Service Corps units, most of which are called 'regiments' (*regementen*).

The Army is organized and equipped with regard to the varying geographical and climatic conditions of the country. The voluntary Home Guard (*Hemvärnet*) with a total strength of more than 100,000 men ready for action within 2 hours, raised during the War continues to be in force.

Sweden's ground forces, total 850,000 men (including the voluntary Home Guard), can be said to consist of an Army which for the most part is on indefinite leave, but which on short notice can be ready for action. One of the basic principles of the Swedish system of mobilization is the local recruitment of as many units as possible. The storage of equipment and supplies is decentralized on more than 3,000 places.

The active personnel of the Army comprises (1985) about 56,900, including 38,800 conscripts doing basic training.

Navy. The C.-in-C. of the Royal Swedish Navy is assisted by the Chief of Naval Staff, the Inspector of the Navy and the Inspector of the Coast Artillery. The Navy is divided into two branches, the Royal Navy and the Royal Coast Artillery. There are 3 Naval Base Areas: those of the southern, eastern and western coasts. The coast artillery defence areas are those of the Stockholm archipelago, Blekinge, Gothenburg, Gotland and Norrland. There are 5 coastal artillery regiments.

There are 12 diesel-powered patrol submarines, 2 old destroyers in reserve, 16 fast missile craft, 14 fast missile/torpedo boats, 6 fast torpedo boats, 2 patrol craft, 3 minelayers, 1 mine countermeasures support ship, 11 coastal minelayers, 2 new minehunters, 10 coastal minesweepers, 4 patrol vessels (*ex*-minesweepers), 23 inshore minesweepers, 25 coastal patrol craft, 2 mine transports, 22 minelaying boats, 1 surveillance ship, 3 torpedo recovery vessels, 17 tenders, 5 surveying vessels, 7 icebreakers, 3 oilers, 1 salvage vessel, 13 artillery landing craft, 81 utility landing craft, 54 minor landing craft, 2 sail training ships, 1 supply ship, 2 water carriers and 17 tugs.

Four submarines, 6 missile armed fast attack craft leaders (officially classed as corvettes), 2 coastal minelayers and 4 more minehunters are under construction or projected.

The Naval Air Arm comprises 10 Boeing Vertol 107 helicopters, 10 Jet Ranger helicopters and 5 Alouette II training helicopters. Four heavy helicopters are to be acquired for anti-submarine warfare.

The personnel of the navy and coast artillery in 1985 totalled 18,000 officers and men, comprising 3,500 regulars, 2,500 reservists and 12,000 national servicemen (refresher trainees). Additionally 6,250 conscripts train annually.

The Coast Guard operates 140 cutters, patrol boats and service craft and lists 5 aircraft. Personnel in 1985 numbered 600.

Air Force. The C-in C. of the Royal Swedish Air Force has at his disposal the Air Staff under a chief of staff.

The combat force consists of 3 fighter interceptor, 3 ground-attack and 3 mixed interceptor/reconnaissance wings (*flottiljer*), each with 2-3 squadrons of 12-15 aircraft, including 3 reconnaissance squadrons (*divisioner*). Total peace-time strength of the combat units is 20 squadrons with nearly 400 first-line aircraft.

Night and all-weather fighters are the Swedish-built Saab J35 Draken, equipping 7 squadrons, and JA37 Viggen, equipping 5 squadrons (3 more Draken squadrons are to convert to JA37s). The ground-attack wings have 5 squadrons of Saab AJ37 Viggens, and there is provision for 5 light ground-attack squadrons of twin-jet Saab-105s (Sk60s), most of which could be withdrawn in wartime from training units. One Sk60 squadron is designated as part of the primary ground attack force. The 3 reconnaissance squadrons have SF37 (photo) and SH37 (maritime, radar) Viggen reconnaissance aircraft; and there are transport, helicopter and other support units. The Sk60A is the Air Force's standard advanced trainer, to which pupils progress after initial training on piston-engined Bulldogs. Other trainers in service include the Sk61 Bulldog, Sk35C Draken and Sk37 Viggen.

Active strength consists of about 9,500 personnel, including 4,500 conscripts.

INTERNATIONAL RELATIONS

Membership. Sweden is a member of UN and EFTA.

ECONOMY

Budget. Revenue and expenditure of the total budget (Current and Capital) for financial years ending 30 June (in 1m. kr.):

	Revenue	*Expenditure*		*Revenue*	*Expenditure*
1980–81	155,287	215,238	1982–83	191,280	277,080
1981–82	167,131	235,104	1983–84[1]	221,165	298,266

[1] Preliminary.

The preliminary revenue and expenditure for the financial year 1 July 1983 to 30 June 1984 was as follows (in 1m. kr.):

Revenue		*Expenditure*	
Taxes:		Royal Household and residences	29
Taxes on income, capital gains and profits	48,903	Justice	9,093
Statutory social security fees	47,058	Foreign Affairs	7,592
Taxes on property	4,172	Defence	22,328
Value-added tax	48,520	Health and Social Affairs	70,441
Other taxes on goods and services	39,048	Transport and Communications	15,822
Total revenue from taxes	187,701	Ministry of Finance	13,744
Non-tax revenue	23,008	Education	35,490
Capital revenue	52	Agriculture	6,584
Loan repayment	4,357	Labour	18,695
Computed revenue	6,047	Housing and Physical Planning	21,501
Total revenue	221,165	Industry	12,049
		Civil Service Affairs	3,656
		Parliament and agencies	471
		Interest on National Debt, etc.	60,387
		Unforeseen expenditure	1
		Changed appropriation of short-term credits	383
		Total expenditure	298,266

On 31 Dec. 1983 the national debt amounted to 460,196m. kr.

Riksgäldskontoret (National Debt Office), *årsbok*. Annual. Stockholm, from 1920
Riksskatteverket (National Tax Board), *årsbok*. Annual. Stockholm, from 1971
The Swedish Budget. Ministry of Economic Affairs and Ministry of the Budget, from 1962/63

Currency. The monetary unit is the Swedish *krona,* of 100 *öre*. In March 1985, £1 = 10·20 *krona*; US$1 = 9·69 *krona.*

Gold coins do not exist as a currency. Central banknotes for 5, 10, 50, 100, 1,000 and 10,000 kr. are legal means of payment.

Banking. The Riksbank, or Central Bank of Sweden, belongs entirely to the State and is managed by directors elected for 3 years by the Parliament, except the chairman, who is designated by the Government. The bank is under the guarantee of the Parliament, its capital and reserve capital are fixed by its constitution. Since 1904, only the Riksbank has the right to issue notes. On 31 Dec. 1983 its note circulation amounted to 42,719m. kr.; its gold and foreign-exchange reserves totalled 32,153m. kr.

There are 15 commercial banks. On 31 Dec. 1983 their total deposits amounted to 225,214m. kr.; advances to the public amounted to 221,286m. kr.

On 31 Dec. 1983 there were 155 savings banks; their total deposits amounted to 108,516m. kr.; advances to the public were 77,712m. kr. Co-operative banks had total deposits of 26,565m. kr.; advances to the public were 17,986m. kr.

Sveriges Riksbank, årsbok. Annual. Stockholm, from 1908
Skandinaviska Enskilda Banken, Kvartalskrift. Quarterly Review (in English). Stockholm, from 1920

Weights and Measures. The metric system is obligatory.

ENERGY AND NATURAL RESOURCES

Electricity. Sweden is rich in hydro-power resources. The total electric energy production in 1982 was 100,050m. kwh. About 56% of this energy was produced in hydro-electric plants. Additional electric energy consumption will in the future mainly be covered by nuclear power and conventional thermal power.

Minerals. Sweden is one of the leading exporters of iron ore. The largest deposits are found north of the polar circle in the area of Kiruna and Gällivare-Malmberget. The ore is exported *via* the Norwegian port of Narvik and the Swedish port of Luleå. There are also important resources of iron ore in southern Sweden (Bergslagen). The most important fields are Grängesberg and Stråssa and the ores are shipped *via* the port of Oxelösund. Some of the southern deposits have, in contrast to the fields in North Sweden, a low phosphorus content.

There are also some deposits of copper, lead and zinc ores especially in the Boliden area in the north of Sweden. These ores are often found together with pyrites. Non-ferrous ores, except zinc ores, are used in the Swedish metal industry and barely satisfy domestic needs.

The total production of iron ores amounted to 14·7m. tons in 1982 and exports to 10m. tons. The production of copper ore was 234,644 tons, of lead ore 119,872 tons, of zinc ore 345,654 tons.

There are also deposits of raw materials for aluminium not worked at present. In southern Sweden there are big resources of alum shale, containing oil and uranium.

Agriculture. According to the farm register which is revised annually the following data was provided for 1983. The number of farms in cultivation of more than 2 hectares of arable land, was 113,888; of these there were 69,179 of 2-20 hectares; 41,321 of 20-100 hectares; 3,388 of above 100 hectares. Of the total land area of Sweden (41,161,500 hectares), 2,940,660[1] hectares were arable land, 348,767[1] hectares cultivated pastures and (1981) 22,742,235 hectares forests.

	Area (1,000 hectares)[1]			*Production (1,000 tonnes)*		
Chief crops	*1981*	*1982*	*1983*	*1981*	*1982*	*1983*
Wheat	230·8	293·1	346·7	1,066	1,490	1,721
Rye	52·4	56·8	64·9	180	211	237
Barley	729·3	677·4	659·9	2,452	2,378	2,026
Oats	507·8	509·4	432·1	1,816	1,663	1,268
Mixed grain	64·1	66·3	66·0	180	180	...
Peas and vetches	14·2	20·5	33·0	30	44	...
Potatoes	40·2	39·7	37·5	1,213	1,036	939
Sugarbeet	52·5	53·6	52·9	2,484	2,431	1,922
Tame hay	706·8	707·1	696·5	4,326	4,297	4,560
Oil seed	171·1	171·1	172·0	323	371	373

Area of rotation meadows for pasture was (in 1,000 hectares[1]): 1980, 191; 1981, 192; 1982, 193; 1983, 184.

Total production of milk (in 1,000 tonnes): 1980, 3,481; 1981, 3,514; 1982, 3,652; 1983, 3,715. Butter production in the same years was (in 1,000 tonnes): 66, 64, 69, 72; and cheese, 101, 108, 114, 115.

Livestock (1983): Cattle, 1·9m.; sheep, 437,000; pigs, 2·6m.; poultry, 7·3m.

Number of farm tractors in 1981, 189,654; combines in 1981, 48,990.

The number of pelts produced in 1982–83 was as follows: Fox, 38,639; mink, 1·4m.; others, 12,708.

[1] Figures refer to holdings of more than 2 hectares of arable land.

Forestry. In 1978–82 the forests covered an area of 23·5m. hectares, *i.e.* roughly 57% of the country's land area. Municipal and State ownership accounts for one fourth of the forests, companies own another fourth, and the remaining half is in private hands. In the felling seasons, 1981–82 and 1982–83 respectively, 49·4m. and 51·6m. cu. metres (solid volume excluding bark) of wood were removed from the forests in Sweden. The sawmill, wood pulp and paper industries are all of great importance. The number of sawmills in 1979 was about 2,600, 400 of which were commercial sawmills, with more than 90% of the total production of sawn hard- and soft-wood. In 1983 the total production was about 11·5m. cu. metres. The wood pulp factories total output amounted to 8·4m. tons (including dissolving pulp) (dry weight).

Fisheries. In 1983 the total catch of the sea fisheries was 247,300 tons, landed weight, value 662m. kr.

INDUSTRY AND TRADE

Manufacturing. The most important sector of Swedish manufacturing is the production of metals, metal products, machinery and transport equipment, covering almost half of the total value added by manufacturing. Production of high-quality steel is an old Swedish speciality. A large part of this production is exported. The production of ordinary steel is slightly decreasing and is still short of domestic demand. The total production of steel amounted to 3·9m. tons in 1982.

There is also a large production of other metals (aluminium, lead, copper) and rolled semi-manufactured goods of these metals.

These basic metal industries are an important basis for the production of more developed metal products, machinery and equipment, which are to a large extent sold on the world market, *i.e.*, hand tools, mining drills, ball-bearings, turbines, pneumatic machinery, refrigerating equipment, machinery for pulp and paper industries, etc., sewing machines, machine tools, office machinery, high-voltage electric machinery, telephone equipment, cars and trucks, ships and aeroplanes.

Another important manufacturing sector is based on Sweden's forest resources. This sector includes saw-mills, plywood factories, joinery industries, pulp- and paper-mills, wallboard and particle board factories, accounting for about 15% of the total value of manufacturing. A fast increasing sector is the chemical industry, especially the petro-chemical branch. Minerals industries include production of building materials, decorative arts products of glass and china.

Industry groups	*No. of establishments* 1981	1982	*Average no. of wage-earners* 1981	1982	*Sales value of production (gross) in 1m. kr.* 1981	1982
Mining and quarrying	*115*	*114*	*10,116*	*9,631*	*3,557*	*3,831*
Metal-ore mining	31	29	8,859	8,456	2,997	3,245
Other mining	84	85	1,257	1,175	560	586
Manufacturing	*9,821*	*9,423*	*579,003*	*547,915*	*329,047*	*364,987*
Manufacture of food, beverages and tobacco	918	886	53,015	51,191	46,052	53,178
Textile, wearing apparel and leather industries	791	726	29,338	27,200	7,823	8,173
Manufacture of wood products including furniture	1,624	1,525	51,666	47,520	23,564	24,628
Manufacture of paper and paper products, printing and publishing	1,080	1,070	70,635	67,128	45,820	48,879
Manufacture of chemicals and chemical, petroleum, coal, rubber and plastic products	700	688	42,401	40,809	50,066	56,754
Manufacture of non-metallic mineral products, except products of petroleum and coal	458	419	18,866	17,491	8,019	8,750
Basic metal industries	175	166	45,080	41,082	25,275	28,672
Manufacture of fabricated metal products, machinery and equipment	3,960	3,834	264,331	252,341	121,224	134,755
Other manufacturing industries	115	109	3,671	3,153	1,204	1,199
Electricity, gas and water	*850*	*831*	*11,464*	*11,733*	*44,546*	*49,460*
Electricity, gas and steam	720	705	10,827	11,121	43,373	48,150
Water works and supply	130	126	637	612	1,173	1,310

Arbetsmarknadsstatistik (Labour Market Statistics). Monthly. National Labour Market Board, Stockholm, from 1963

Arbetsmarknadsstatistisk Årsbok (Year Book of Labour Statistics). Statistics Sweden, Stockholm, from 1973

Historisk statistik för Sverige, II (Climate, land surveying, agriculture, forestry, fisheries). Statistics Sweden, Stockholm, 1959

Johansson, Ö., *The Gross Domestic Product of Sweden and its Composition 1861–1955.* Stockholm, 1967

Jörberg, L., *A History of Prices in Sweden 1732–1914.* 2 vols. Stockholm, 1972

Thalberg, B., and Marno, N., eds., *Economic Growth, Welfare and Industrial Relations: A Comparative Study of Japan and Sweden.* Tokyo, 1984

Jordbruksekonomiska meddelanden (Journal of Agricultural Economics, published monthly by the National Agricultural Market Board). Stockholm, from 1939

Jordbruksstatistisk årsbok (Yearbook of Agricultural Statistics). Statistics Sweden, Stockholm, from 1965

The Swedish Economy. Ministry of Economic Affairs and National Institute of Economic Research. Stockholm, from 1960

Trade Unions. The Swedish Confederation of Trade Unions (LO) had a total membership of 2,195,773 in 1983, including the Municipal Workers' Union with 594,078 members and the Metal Workers' Union with 440,469.

Commerce. The imports and exports of Sweden, unwrought gold and coin not included, have been as follows (in 1m. kr.):

	1977	*1978*	*1979*	*1980*	*1981*	*1982*	*1983*
Imports	90,246	92,717	122,952	141,641	146,040	173,932	200,225
Exports	85,678	98,205	118,147	131,002	144,876	168,134	210,311

Imports and exports by products (in 1m. kr.):

	Imports		*Exports*	
	1982	*1983*	*1982*	*1983*
Food and live animals chiefly for food	10,105	11,594	4,193	4,991
Cereals and cereal preparations	621	718	1,180	1,380
Vegetables and fruit	3,331	3,688	279	341
Coffee, tea, cocoa, spices and manufactures thereof	2,441	2,849	307	432
Feeding stuff for animals (not including unmilled cereals)	1,083	1,282	67	93
Beverages and tobacco	1,330	1,618	156	216
Crude materials, inedible, except fuels	6,918	7,907	17,695	23,172
Hides, skins and furskins, raw	300	366	454	544
Crude rubber (including synthetic and reclaimed)	374	496	91	125
Cork and wood	1,239	1,052	7,040	9,561
Pulp and waste paper	312	421	6,445	8,441
Textile fibres (other than wool tops) and their wastes (not manufactured into yarn or fabric)	271	331	299	357
Crude fertilizers and crude minerals (excluding coal, petroleum and precious stones)	1,025	1,162	294	372
Metalliferous ores and metal scrap	2,203	2,747	2,717	3,270
Mineral fuels, lubricants and related materials	42,528	46,077	9,001	13,411
Coal, coke and briquettes	1,518	1,570	176	122
Petroleum, petroleum products and related materials	40,155	43,576	8,353	12,648
Chemicals and related products, n.e.s.	15,369	19,076	9,673	12,887
Artificial resins and plastic materials, and cellulose esters and ethers	4,030	5,164	2,707	3,661
Manufactured goods classified chiefly by material	26,754	30,299	43,849	53,418
Paper, paperboard, and articles of paper pulp, of paper or of paperboard	1,733	2,130	16,148	19,459
Textile yarn, fabrics, made-up articles, n.e.s., and related products	4,507	5,182	2,177	2,622
Non-metallic mineral manufactures, n.e.s.	2,317	2,617	1,920	2,287
Iron and steel	6,676	6,877	10,870	12,512
Non-ferrous metals	3,896	4,801	3,475	5,116
Machinery and transport equipment	48,369	58,912	70,561	85,825
Power generating machinery and equipment	3,787	4,292	4,558	5,484
Machinery specialized for particular industries	5,071	6,037	8,245	9,299
Metal working machinery	1,489	1,614	1,751	1,800
General industrial machinery and equipment, n.e.s. and machine parts, n.e.s.	8,204	9,627	11,994	13,859
Office machines and automatic data processing equipment	5,028	7,699	3,529	5,926
Telecommunications and sound recording and reproducing apparatus and equipment	3,363	3,507	6,652	7,863
Electrical machinery apparatus and appliances, n.e.s., and electrical parts thereof (including non-electrical counterparts, n.e.s., of electrical household type equipment)	8,750	10,801	7,066	7,869

	Imports 1982	Imports 1983	Exports 1982	Exports 1983
Road vehicles (including air cushion vehicles)	11,374	13,088	22,262	26,370
Other transport equipment	1,301	2,247	4,504	7,352
Miscellaneous manufactured articles	20,786	22,980	11,056	14,045

Principal import and export countries (in 1m. kr.):

	Imports from 1982	Imports from 1983	Exports to 1982	Exports to 1983
Belgium-Luxembourg	5,284	5,666	6,076	8,705
Denmark	10,020	12,313	13,002	17,734
Federal Republic of Germany	30,076	34,235	17,605	23,918
Finland	9,904	11,803	10,916	12,258
France	6,996	9,271	9,530	10,479
Italy	5,407	6,083	5,252	6,743
Netherlands	7,848	8,268	8,365	10,051
Norway	12,470	14,959	17,763	21,250
Switzerland	3,276	3,973	3,160	3,433
USSR	5,022	7,313	2,221	2,228
UK	21,325	27,746	16,867	22,774
USA	14,678	16,686	11,957	18,483

Total trade between Sweden and UK (British Department of Trade returns, in £1,000 sterling):

	1980	1981	1982	1983	1984
Imports to UK	1,475,506	1,533,580	1,673,165	2,051,931	2,416,383
Exports and re-exports from UK	1,623,511	1,601,166	1,935,264	2,937,464	2,888,625

Historisk Statistik för Sverige, 3: Utrikeshandel [Foreign Trade], *1732–1970.* Statistics Sweden, Stockholm, 1972

Utrikeshandel, årsstatistik [Foreign Trade, Annual Bulletin]. Statistics Sweden, Stockholm. 5 vols. Statistical Reports, Series H

Utrikeshandel, månadsstatistik [Foreign Trade, Monthly Bulletin]. Statistics Sweden, Stockholm. Statistical Reports, Series H. Dec.

Utrikeshandel, kvartalsstatistik [Foreign Trade, Quarterly Bulletin]. Statistics Sweden, Stockholm. January – December. Exports respectively imports. Statistical Reports, Series H

Utrikeshandel, års statistik [Foreign Trade, Annual]. Official Statistics of Sweden, Statistics Sweden, Stockholm. Imports and exports. Distribution by country and commodity according to the SITC

Utrikeshandel, årsstatistik [Foreign Trade, Annual]. Official Statistics of Sweden, Statistics Sweden, Stockholm. Imports and exports. Commodities according to the CCCN.

COMMUNICATIONS

Roads. On 1 Jan. 1984 there were 200,000 km of public roads comprising State-administered roads, 98,100 km, municipal, 31,600 km, private roads with subsidies, 68,400 km, of which 87,136 km were surfaced. Motor vehicles on 31 Dec. 1983 included 3,006,760 passenger cars, 215,259 buses and lorries and 18,980 heavy motor cycles (all in use).

Railways. At the end of 1983 the total length of railways was 12,323 km, of which 11,706 km belonged to the State; 7,595 km were electrified. In 1983 the number of passengers on the railways was 96m.; weight of goods, 45m. tonnes.

Aviation. Commercial air traffic is maintained in (1) Sweden and other parts of the world by Scandinavian Airlines System (SAS), of which AB Aerotransport (ABA = Swedish Air Lines) is the Swedish partner (DDL = Danish Air Lines and DNL = Norwegian Air Lines being the other two); (2) only within Sweden by Linjeflyg AB. Scandinavian Airlines System have a joint paid-up capital of about Sw. kronor 733m. Capitalization of ABA, Sw. kronor 346m., of which 50% is owned by the Government and 50% by private enterprises. Capitalization of Linjeflyg, Sw. kronor 130m., of which 50% is owned by SAS and 50% by ABA.

In scheduled air traffic during 1981 the total number of km flown was 66·5m.; passenger-km, 5,450·6m.; goods, 180·2m. ton-km; mail, 21·6m. ton-km. These figures represent the Swedish share of the SAS traffic (Swedish domestic and three-sevenths of international traffic) and the Linjeflyg traffic.

Shipping. The Swedish mercantile marine consisted on 30 June 1984 of 476 vessels of 3·06m. gross tons (only vessels of at least 100 gross tons, and excluding fishing vessels and tugs). Stockholm and Göteborg, with together 226 vessels of 2·74m. gross tons in Dec. 1983, are the two major home ports for the Swedish mercantile marine.

Vessels entered from and cleared for foreign countries, exclusive of passenger liners and ferries, with cargoes and in ballast, in 1983, are as follows (only vessels of at least a gross tonnage of 75): With cargoes, 25,610 with a gross tonnage of 85·9m.; in ballast, 13,578 with a gross tonnage of 48·8m.

Post and Broadcasting. The length of telegraph circuits in Dec. 1979 was 1,591,000 km. The circuits of the telephone had a length of 28·2m. km at 31 Dec. 1980. On 1 Jan. 1983 there were 7·13m. instruments employed in the telephone service.

Number of combined radio and television reception fees paid at the end of 1983 was 3,245,000, of which 2·8m. included extra fees for colour television. As from 1 April 1978, special sound broadcasting licences were discontinued.

Sveriges Radio AB is a non-commercial semi-governmental corporation, transmitting 3 programmes on long-, medium-, and short-waves and on FM. There are also regional programmes. It also broadcasts 2 TV programmes. Colour programmes are broadcast by PAL system.

The overseas radio-telegraph and radio-telephone services are conducted by the Swedish Telecommunications Administration.

The number of post offices at the end of 1982 was 1,842. For receipts of the post and telecommunication services *see* the section on Economy.

Cinemas (1983). There were 1,252 cinemas.

Newspapers (1983). There were 171 daily newspapers with a total circulation of 4·8m.

JUSTICE, RELIGION, EDUCATION AND WELFARE

Justice. The administration of justice is entirely independent of the Government. The *Justitiekansler*, or Attorney General (a royal appointment) and the *Justitieombudsmän* (Parliamentary Commissioners appointed by the Diet), exercise a check on the administration. In 1968 a reform was carried through which meant that the offices of the former *Justiticombudsman* (Ombudsman for civil affairs) and the *Militieombudsman* (Ombudsman for military affairs) were turned into one sole institution with 3 Ombudsmen, each styled *Justitieombudsman.* They exert a general supervision over all courts of law, the civil service, military laws and the military services. In 1983–84 they received altogether 3,528 cases; of these, 101 were instituted on their own initiative and 3,397 on complaints.

The *Riksåklagaren* (a royal appointment) is the chief public prosecutor.

The kingdom has a Supreme Court of Judicature and is divided into 6 Courts of Appeal districts (*hovrätter*) and 97 district-court divisions (*tingsrätter*). There is also a Housing Appeal Court and 12 rent and tenancy tribunals.

Of the district courts 27 also serve as real estate courts and 6 as water rights courts.

These district courts (or courts of first instance) deal with both civil and criminal cases. Each member of the court has an individual vote and is legally responsible for the decision. In the voting, the majority rules. When the votes are evenly divided in a criminal case, the opinion implying the least severe sentence applies, and in cases where there is no opinion that could be considered the mildest, the Chair has the casting vote, as is also the case in family civil cases and matters; petty cases are tried by the judge alone. Civil cases are tried as a rule by 3 to 4 judges or in minor cases by 1 judge. Disputes of greater consequence relating to the Marriage Code or the Code relating to Parenthood and Guardianship are tried by a judge and a *nämnd* of 3-4 lay assessors. When cases concerning real estate are being tried the court consists of 2 qualified lawyers, 1 specialist on technical matters and 2 lay assessors.

Criminal cases are tried by a judge and a jury of 5 members (lay assessors) in felony cases, and of 3 members in misdemeanour cases. The cases in Courts of Appeal are generally tried by 4 or 5 judges, but the same cases, which are tried with a judge and a *nämnd* in the first instance, are tried by 3 or 4 judges and a *nämnd* of 2-3 members. In cases concerning real estate the court consists of a specialist on technical matters in place of one of the judges and in water-right cases of 3 or 4 judges and 1 or 2 specialists on technical water matters.

Those with low incomes can receive free legal aid out of public funds. In criminal cases a suspected person has the right to a defence counsel, paid out of public funds.

The Attorney-General (*Justitiekanslern*) and the Parliamentary Commissioner (*Justitieombudsmannen*) for the Judiciary and Civil Administration supervise the application in the public sector of acts of parliament and regulations. The Attorney-General is the Government's legal adviser and also the Public Prosecutor.

The holders of the office of Parliamentary Commissioner are 4 in number.

There were 76 penal and correctional institutions for offenders, with 4,549 male and 212 female inmates on 1 March 1984 (including offenders in remand prison). Besides, there were 19 institutions with 575 places for children and juveniles in need of care owing to viciousness, maladjustment or delinquency on 31 Dec. 1983; on 30 June 1983, 453 were committed to these institutions.

Anderman, S., ed., *Law and the Weaker Party: An Anglo-Swedish Comparative Study*. Abingdon, 1981–83

Bruzelius, A., and Ginsburg, R. B., *The Swedish Code of Judicial Procedure*. South Hackensack, Rev. ed., 1979

Strömholm, S., *An Introduction to Swedish Law*. Stockholm, 1981

al-Wahab, I., *The Swedish Institution of Ombudsmen*. Stockholm, 1979

Justitieombudsmännens ämbetsberättelse avgiven till Riksdagen. Annual. Stockholm

The Penal Code of Sweden: As Amended 1 Jan. 1972. South Hackensack, 1972

Rättsstatistisk årsbok (Year Book of Legal Statistics). Statistics Sweden, Stockholm, from 1975

Religion. The overwhelming majority of the population belong to the Evangelical Lutheran Church, which is the established national church. In 1983 there were 13 bishoprics (Uppsala being the metropolitan see) and 2,566 parishes. The clergy are chiefly supported from the parishes and the proceeds of the church lands. The nonconformists mostly still adhere to the national church. The largest denominations, on 1 Jan. 1983, were: Pentecost Movement, 99,717; The Mission Covenant Church of Sweden, 79,890; Salvation Army, 33,499; Swedish Evangelical Mission, 24,200; Swedish Baptist Church, 20,913 (1981); Orebro Missionary Society, 20,649; Swedish Alliance Missionary Society, 13,341; Holiness Mission, 6,110.

There were also 114,393 Roman Catholics (under a Bishop resident at Stockholm), about 35,000 Orthodox Catholics (1978) and about 15,000 Jews (1978).

Parliament and Convocation (*Kyrkomötet*) decided in 1958 to admit women to ordination as priests.

Murray, R., *L'église Suédoise. Son Histoire et Son Organisation*. Stockholm, 1970

Education. By the Swedish Higher Educational Act of 1977 a unified educational system was created by integrating institutions which had previously been administered separately. This new *högskola* includes not only traditional university studies but also those of various former professional colleges as well as a number of study programmes offered earlier by the secondary school system. One of the goals of the 1977 university reform was to introduce an increased element of vocational training into Swedish higher education and to widen admission. A Certificate of Education (B.Sc., M.Sc., U.C. etc.) is awarded on completion of a general study programme. This certificate states the number of courses taken as well as the points and grades obtained on each course in the study programme.

In autumn 1982 there were, in these new integrated institutions for higher education, *högskola*, about 168,000 enrolled for undergraduate studies of whom 105,100 were distributed by sector as follows: Education for technical professions, 26,000; education for social work, economic and administrative professions, 28,000;

education for medical and paramedical professions, 22,300; education for the teaching professions, 23,400; and education for information, communication and cultural professions, 5,400. The number of students enrolled for post-graduate studies was 12,800.

In autumn term in the school year 1982–83 there were 658,000 pupils in primary education (grades 1–6 in compulsory comprehensive schools). Secondary education at the lower stage (grades 7–9 in compulsory comprehensive schools) comprised 340,800 pupils. In secondary education at the higher stage (the integrated upper secondary school), there were 266,300 pupils (excluding about 37,400 pupils in the 4-year technical tier regarded as third-level education). The folk high schools, 'people's colleges', had 14,700 pupils in courses of more than 15 weeks.

In municipal adult education there were 154,500 pupils (corresponding to a gross number of 346,000 participants). Basic education for adults had 10,300 pupils.

There are also special schools for pupils with visual and hearing handicaps and those who are mentally retarded (about 13,500 pupils in 1982–83).

Education Policy for Planning: Goals for Educational Policy in Sweden. OECD, Paris, 1980
Educational Reforms in Sweden. OECD, Paris, 1981
Higher Education for Visiting Students.—Series Studying in Sweden.—National Board of Universities and Colleges. Stockholm, 1978
Boucher, L., *Tradition and Change in Swedish education.* OUP, 1982
Götberg, B., and Svärd, S., *The Swedish 'Folk High School': Its Background and its Present Situation.*
Kim, L., *Widened Admission to Higher Education in Sweden.* Stockholm, 1982
Marklund, S., *Educational Administration and Educational Development.* Univ. of Stockholm, 1979.—*The Democratization of Education in Sweden.* Univ. of Stockholm, 1980
Marklund, S. and Bergendal, G., *Trends in Swedish Educational Policy.* Stockholm, 1979
Paulston, C. B., *Swedish Research and Debate about Bilingualism.* Stockholm, 1983
Sundgvist, A., *New Rules for Swedish Study Circles.* Stockholm, 1983
Ueberschlag, G., *La Folkhögskola.* Paris, 1981

Social Welfare. The social security schemes are greatly expanding. Supported by a referendum, the Diet in 1958 and 1959 decided that the national pensions should be increased successively until 1968 and supplementary pensions paid from 1963. These pensions are of invariable value. In 1969 the Diet decided that as from 1 July 1969 an increment to the basic pension was to be paid to persons without supplementary pensions, and this amount is to be successively increased in a 10-year period. The basic and supplementary pensions consist of old-age and family pensions, as well as pensions paid to the disabled. The financing of the supplementary system is based on the current-cost method.

The most important social welfare schemes are described in the conspectus below.

Type of scheme	*Introduced*	*Scope*	*Principal benefits*
Sickness insurance (compulsory–current law, 1962)	1955	All residents	Hospital fees, most private doctors charge the insured person normally 50 kr., district physicians and doctors in hospitals charge the insured person only 40 kr. for full medical treatment, some reimbursement of cost of transportation as well as costs of physiotherapy, convalescent care, etc., medicines at reduced prices or free of charge. During sickness daily allowance 90% of the yearly income in between 6,000 and 152,200 kr. There is generally no maximum benefit period. Dental care is available to all residents from 17 years of age, the maximum payable by the patient being 60% up to 2,500 kr. and 25% thereafter.

Type of scheme	Introduced	Scope	Principal benefits
Employment injury insurance (compulsory–current law, 1976)	1901	All employed persons	Medical treatment, medicine and medical appliances, hospital care, sickness benefit 100% of the yearly income in between 6,000 and 152,200 kr. (first 90 days covered by sickness insurance), disability annuities, funeral benefit and survivor's pensions.
Unemployment insurance (current law, 1973)	1935	Members of recognized unemployment insurance societies (about 70% of all employees)	110-300 kr. per day subject to tax.
Basic pensions (current law, 1962)			
Old-age	1914	All citizens	Payable from the age of 65 or, at a reduced rate, from the age of 60. 51,360 kr. per annum for married couples, 29,232 kr. for others (including the special increment of 19,488 kr. and 9,744 kr. respectively for those without supplementary pension); about half of them receive municipal housing supplement.
Disability	1914	All citizens	Payable before the age of 65. Full pension 38,976 kr. per annum (including the special increment of 19,488 kr.).
Survivors	1948	All citizens	Widow's pension is payable before the age of 65. The pension is 29,232 kr. (including the special increment of 9,744 kr.) but less for those who have become widows before the age of 50 and have no child below 16. Many of them receive municipal housing supplements. Child pension is payable before the age of 18. The pension amounts to 8,323 kr. (fatherless or motherless) and 12,588 kr. (orphans).
Supplementary pensions (current law, 1962)			
Old-age	1960	All gainfully occupied persons	Payable from the same age as the basic pension (*see above*). The pension is in principle 60% of the insured person's average annual earnings during the best 15 years except an amount corresponding to the basic pension and subject to a ceiling.
Disability	1960	All gainfully occupied persons	Payable before the age of 65. Full pension corresponds in principle to supplementary old-age pension.

Type of scheme	Introduced	Scope	Principal benefits
Survivors	1960	All gainfully occupied persons	Payable to widow and children, before the age of 19, of a deceased person as a certain percentage of the deceased's supplementary pension.
Partial pensions (current law, 1979)	1976	All employees between 60–65 years of age	The pension is payable between 60-65 years of age. The insured must have reduced his working time by 5 hours on an average a week and the part-time work must thereafter comprise at least 17 hours per week. Furthermore the insured must have worked during at least 5 of the last 12 months and achieved a right to supplementary pension for 10 years after the age of 45. The partial pension is paid out by 50% of the loss of income in connection with the change-over to part-time work.
Parents benefit	1974	All resident parents in connection with confinement	Parents cash benefit of 37 kr. a day during 180 days. Employed parents entitled to daily parents cash benefit of 90% of the daily income (in between 6,000–152,200 kr. yearly) for 180 days. Maximum daily parents cash benefit 375 kr.
Special parents benefit	1978	All resident parents	Special parents cash benefit with the same amount as for parents cash benefit for care of each child during 180 days for the parents together until the child reaches 8 years of age or until the end of the child's first school year if that is later.
Children's allowances	1948	All children below 16	From 1 Jan. 1985 4,800 kr. per annum. An additional allowance is paid out for the third child with one-half of an allowance and a full allowance for each additional child.
		Children at school 16–18	275 kr. per month during school-courses.

Total social expenditure, including also hygiene, care of the sick and social assistance, amounted to 199,086m. kr. in 1982, representing 32% of the GDP.

The Cost and Financing of the Social Services in Sweden, 1981. Stockholm, 1983

Ministry of Health and Social Affairs, *The Evolution of the Swedish Health Insurance.* Stockholm, 1978

Socialnytt (Official Journal of the National Board of Health and Welfare). Stockholm, from 1968

Fry, John (ed.), *Limits of the Welfare State: Critical Views on Post war Sweden.* Farnborough, 1979

Heclo, H., *Modern Social Politics in Britain and Sweden: From Relief to Income Maintenance.* New Haven, 1974

Holgersson, L., *The Evolution of Swedish Social Welfare.* Stockholm, 1975

Lagerström, L., *Pension Systems in Sweden.* Stockholm, 1976.—*Social Security in Sweden.* Stockholm, 1976

Wilson, D., *The Welfare State in Sweden: A Study in Comparative Social Administration.* London, 1979

DIPLOMATIC REPRESENTATIVES

Of Sweden in Great Britain (11 Montagu Place, London, W1H 2AL)
Ambassador: Leif Leifland, GCVO (accredited on 10 Nov. 1982).

Of Great Britain in Sweden (Skarpögatan 6-8, 115 27 Stockholm)
Ambassador: Sir Richard Parsons, KCMG.

Of Sweden in the USA (600 New Hampshire Ave., NW, Washington, D.C., 20037)
Ambassador: Count Wilhelm H. F. Wachtmeister.

Of the USA in Sweden (Strandvägen 101, 115 27 Stockholm)
Ambassador: Franklin S. Forsberg.

Of Sweden to the United Nations
Ambassador: Anders Ferm.

Books of Reference

Statistical Information: The Statistics Sweden, (Statistiska, Centralbyrån, S-11581 Stockholm) was founded in 1858, in succession to the Kungl. Tabellkommissionen, which had been set up in 1756. *Director-General:* Sten Johansson. Its Publications include:

Levnadsförhållanden, årsbok (Living Conditions). Annual. From 1975.—*Rapport.* From 1976
Statistisk årsbok för Sverige (Statistical Abstract of Sweden). From 1914
Siffror om Sverige (Sweden). From 1971. Also in English as *Sweden*
Historisk statistik för Sverige (Historical Statistics of Sweden). 1955 ff. (4 vols. to date)
Allmän månadsstatistik (Monthly Digest of Swedish Statistics). From 1963
Statistiska meddelanden (Statistical Reports). From 1963

Andersson, L., *A History of Sweden.* Stockholm, 1962
Atlas över Sverige. Stockholm, 1953–71. [Publ. in separate parts dealing with population, economics, etc.]
Britten Austin, P., *The Swedes: How They Live and Work.* Newton Abbot, 1970.—*Days in Sweden.* Stockholm, 1979
Publications on Sweden. Stockholm, 1983
Documents on Swedish Foreign Policy, 1981. Stockholm, 1983
Fullerton, B., and Williams, A. F., *Scandinavia.* London, 1972
Furer, H. B. (ed.), *The Scandinavians in America 986–1970. A Chronology and Fact Book.* Dobbs Ferry, 1972
Gōranzon, B., *Job Design and Automation in Sweden.* Stockholm, 1982
Gullberg, I. E., *Swedish–English Dictionary of Technical Terms.—Svensk-Engelsk Fackordbok.* Stockholm, 2nd ed. 1977
Hancock, M. D., *Sweden. The Politics of Post-Industrial Change.* Hinsdale, Ill., 1972
Heilborn, A., *Travel, Study and Research in Sweden.* 6th ed. Stockholm, 1965
Mead, W. R., and Hall, W., *Scandinavia.* London, 1972
Nordic Council, *Yearbook of Nordic Statistics.* From 1962 (in English and one Nordic Language)
Paul, W. W., *The Story of Scandinavia.* Cincinnati, 1971
Scott, F. D., *Sweden: The Nation's History.* Univ. of Minnesota Press, 1977
Ståhle, N. K., *Alfred Nobel and the Nobel Prizes.* Stockholm, 1978
Stomberg, A. A., *A History of Sweden.* New York, 1970
Tomason, R. F., *Sweden: Prototype of Modern Society.* New York, 1970
Toyne, S. M., *The Scandinavians in History.* Freeport, 1970
Turner, B., *Sweden.* London, 1976
Sveriges statskalender. Published by Vetenskapsakademien. Annual, from 1813

National Library: Kungliga Biblioteket, Stockholm. *Director:* Lars Tynell.

SWITZERLAND

Schweiz—Suisse—Svizzera

Capital: Bern
Population: 6·4m. (1983)
GNP per capita: US$17,430 (1981)

HISTORY. On 1 Aug. 1291 the men of Uri, Schwyz and Unterwalden entered into a defensive league. In 1353 the league included 8 members and in 1513, 13. Various territories were acquired either by single cantons or by several in common, and in 1648 the league became formally independent of the Holy Roman Empire, but no addition was made to the number of cantons till 1798. In that year, under the influence of France, the unified Helvetic Republic was formed. This failed to satisfy the Swiss, and in 1803 Napoleon Bonaparte, in the Act of Mediation, gave a new Constitution, and out of the lands formerly allied or subject increased the number of cantons to 19. In 1815 the perpetual neutrality of Switzerland and the inviolability of her territory were guaranteed by Austria, France, Great Britain, Portugal, Prussia, Russia, Spain and Sweden, and the Federal Pact, which included 3 new cantons, was accepted by the Congress of Vienna. In 1848 a new Constitution was passed. The 22 cantons set up a Federal Government (consisting of a Federal Parliament and a Federal Council) and a Federal Tribunal. This Constitution, in turn, was on 29 May 1874 superseded by the present Constitution. In a national referendum held in Sept. 1978, 69·9% voted in favour of the establishment of a new canton, Jura, which was established on 1 Jan. 1979.

AREA AND POPULATION. Area and population, according to the census held on 1 Dec. 1980 and estimate 1 Jan. 1983.

Canton	*Area (sq. km)*	*Census 1 Dec. 1980*	*Estimate 1 Jan. 1983*	*Pop. per sq. km, 1980*
Zürich (Zurich) (1351)	1,729	1,122,839	1,128,000	650
Bern (Berne) (1553)	6,049	912,022	919,300	151
Luzern (Lucerne) (1332)	1,492	296,159	298,700	198
Uri (1291)	1,076	33,883	33,700	31
Schwyz (1291)	908	97,354	98,700	107
Obwalden (Obwald) (1291)	491	25,865	26,700	53
Nidwalden (Nidwald) (1291)	276	28,617	29,300	104
Glarus (Glaris) (1352)	685	36,718	36,200	54
Zug (Zoug) (1352)	239	75,930	77,200	318
Fribourg (Freiburg) (1481)	1,670	185,246	187,600	111
Solothurn (Soleure) (1481)	791	218,102	218,000	276
Basel-Stadt (Bâle-V.) (1501)	37	203,915	201,200	5,485
Basel-Land (Bâle-C.) (1501)	428	219,822	221,200	513
Schaffhausen (Schaffhouse) (1501)	298	69,413	69,800	233
Appenzell A.-Rh. (Rh.-Ext.) (1513)	243	47,611	48,400	196
Appenzell I.-Rh. (Rh.-Int.) (1513)	172	12,844	12,900	75
St Gallen (St Gall) (1803)	2,014	391,995	394,600	195
Graubünden (Grisons) (1803)	7,106	164,641	171,000	23
Aargau (Argovie) (1803)	1,405	453,442	459,100	323
Thurgau (Thurgovie) (1803)	1,013	183,795	186,600	181
Ticino (Tessin) (1803)	2,811	265,899	271,200	95
Vaud (Waadt) (1803)	3,218	528,747	532,600	164
Valais (Wallis) (1815)	5,226	218,707	224,500	42
Neuchâtel (Neuenburg) (1815)	797	158,368	156,100	199
Genève (Genf) (1815)	282	349,040	356,000	1,237
Jura (1979)	837	64,986	64,500	78
Total	41,293[1]	6,365,960	6,423,100	154

[1] 15,943 sq. miles.

Population (1983 estimate) 6·4m.

The German language is spoken by the majority of inhabitants in 19 of the 25 cantons above (French names given in brackets), the French in 6 (Fribourg, Vaud, Valais, Neuchâtel, Jura and Genève, for which the German names are given in brackets), the Italian in 1 (Ticino). In 1980, 65% spoke German, 18·4% French, 9·8% Italian, 0·8% Romansch and 6% other languages; counting only Swiss nationals, the percentages were 73·5, 20·1, 4·5, 0·9 and 1. On 8 July 1937 Romansch was made the fourth national language; it is spoken mostly in Graubünden.

At the end of 1983 the population figures of the principal towns (and their '*agglomérations*' or conurbations) were as follows: Zürich, 363,000 (840,000); Basel, 180,000 (365,000); Geneva, 159,000 (372,000); Bern, 144,000 (301,000); Lausanne, 127,000 (255,000); Winterthur, 86,000 (108,000); St Gallen, 74,000 (124,000); Luzern, 62,000 (158,000); Biel, 53,000 (84,000).

The number of foreigners resident in Switzerland in April 1983 was 926,000. Of these, 189,000 were in Zürich canton, 103,000 in Vaud and 102,000 in Geneva.

Vital statistics for calendar years:

	Live births					
	Total	*Illegitimate*	*Marriages*	*Divorces*	*Still births*	*Deaths*
1981	73,747	3,801	31,889	11,131	373	59,763
1982	74,800	4,100	37,000	11,600	360	59,000
1983	73,700	3,400	37,600	11,700	360	60,700

The excess of emigrants over remigrants was: 1974, 2,087; 1975, 2,967; 1976, 3,873; 1977, 3,510; 1978, 3,209; 1979, 3,129; 1980, 3,339.

CLIMATE. The climate is largely dictated by relief and altitude and includes continental and mountain types. Summers are generally warm, with quite considerable rainfall; winters are fine, with clear, cold air and cloudless skies. Bern. Jan. 32°F (0°C), July, 65°F (18·5°C). Annual rainfall 39·4" (986 mm).

CONSTITUTION AND GOVERNMENT. Switzerland is a republic. The highest authority is vested in the electorate, *i.e.*, all Swiss citizens of over 20. This electorate—besides electing its representatives to the Parliament—has the voting power on amendments to, or on the revision of, the Constitution. It also takes decisions on laws and international treaties if requested by 30,000 voters or 8 cantons (facultative referendum), and it has the right of initiating constitutional amendments, the support required for such demands being 50,000 voters (popular initiative).

The Federal Government is supreme in matters of peace, war and treaties; it regulates the army, the railway, telecommunication systems, the coining of money, the issue and repayment of bank-notes and the weights and measures of the republic. It also legislates on matters of copyright, bankruptcy, patents, sanitary policy in dangerous epidemics, and it may create and subsidize, besides the Polytechnic School at Zürich and at Lausanne, 2 federal universities and other educational institutions. There has also been entrusted to it the authority to decide concerning public works for the whole or great part of Switzerland, such as those relating to rivers, forests and the construction of national highways and railways. By referendum of 13 Nov. 1898 it is also the authority in the entire spheres of common law. In 1957 the Federation was empowered to legislate on atomic energy matters and in 1961 on the construction of pipelines of petroleum and gas.

National flag: Red with a white couped cross.

National anthem: Trittst im Morgenrot daher (words by Leonard Widmer, 1808–68; tune by Alberik Zwyssig, 1808–54); adopted by the Federal Council in 1962.

The legislative authority is vested in a parliament of 2 chambers, a *Ständerat*, or Council of States, and a *Nationalrat*, or National Council.

The *Ständerat* is composed of 46 members, chosen and paid by the 23 cantons of the Confederation, 2 for each canton. The mode of their election and the term of membership depend entirely on the canton. Three of the cantons are politically divided—Basel into Stadt and Land, Appenzell into Ausser-Rhoden and Inner-Rhoden, and Unterwalden into Obwalden and Nidwalden. Each of these 'half-cantons' sends 1 member to the State Council.

The *Nationalrat*—after the referendum taken on 4 Nov. 1962—consists of 200 National Councillors, directly elected for 4 years, in proportion to the population of the cantons, with the proviso that each canton or half-canton is represented by at least 1 member. The members are paid from federal funds at the rate of 150 francs for each day during the session and a nominal sum of 10,000 francs per annum.

In 1980 the 200 members were distributed among the cantons[1] as follows:

Zürich (Zurich)	35	Appenzell—Outer- and Inner-Rhoden	3
Bern (Berne)	29	St Gallen (St Gall)	12
Luzern (Lucerne)	9	Graubünden (Grisons)	5
Uri	1	Aargau (Argovie)	14
Schwyz	3	Thurgau (Thurgovie)	6
Unterwalden–Upper and Lower	2	Ticino (Tessin)	8
Glarus (Glaris)	1	Vaud (Waadt)	16
Zug (Zoug)	2	Valais (Wallis)	7
Fribourg (Freiburg)	6	Neuchâtel (Neuenburg)	5
Solothurn (Soleure)	7	Genève (Genf)	11
Basel (Bâle)—town and country	14	Jura	2
Schaffhausen (Schaffhouse)	2		

[1] The name of the canton is given in German, French or Italian, according to the language most spoken in it, and alternative names are given in brackets.

Composition of the National Council in 1983: Social Democrats, 47; Radicals, 54; Christian-Democratic People's Party, 42; Swiss People's Party, 23; Liberals, 8; Independents, 8; National Campaign/Vigilance, 5; Evangelical Party, 3; Progressive Organizations, 3; Environmentalists, 3; Others, 4.

Council of States (1983): Christian Democrats, 18; Radicals, 14; Social Democrats, 6; Swiss People's Party, 5.

A general election takes place by ballot every 4 years. Every citizen of the republic who has entered on his 20th year is entitled to a vote, and any voter, not a clergyman, may be elected a deputy. Laws passed by both chambers may be submitted to direct popular vote, when 50,000 citizens or 8 cantons demand it; the vote can be only 'Yes' or 'No'. This principle, called the *referendum*, is frequently acted on.

Women's suffrage, although advocated by the Federal Council and the Federal Assembly, was on 1 Feb. 1959 rejected, but in a subsequent referendum, held on 7 Feb. 1971, women's suffrage was carried.

The chief executive authority is deputed to the *Bundesrat*, or Federal Council, consisting of 7 members, elected from 7 different cantons for 4 years by the *Vereinigte Bundesversammlung*, *i.e.*, joint sessions of both chambers. The members of this council must not hold any other office in the Confederation or cantons, nor engage in any calling or business. In the Federal Parliament legislation may be introduced either by a member, or by either House, or by the Federal Council (but not by the people). Every citizen who has a vote for the National Council is eligible for becoming a member of the executive.

The President of the Federal Council (called President of the Confederation) and the Vice-President are the first magistrates of the Confederation. Both are elected by the Federal Assembly for 1 calendar year and are not immediately re-eligible to the same offices. The Vice-President, however, may be, and usually is, elected to succeed the outgoing President.

President of the Confederation for 1985: Kurt Furgler.

The 7 members of the Federal Council—each of whom has a salary of 203,000 francs per annum, while the President has 215,000 francs—act as ministers, or chiefs of the 7 administrative departments of the republic. The city of Berne is the seat of the Federal Council and the central administrative authorities.

The Federal Council was composed as follows in 1985.

Foreign Affairs: Pierre Aubert.
Interior: Alphons Egli.

Justice and Police: Elisabeth Kopp.
Military: Jean-Pascal Delamuraz.
Finance: Otto Stich.
Public Economy: Kurt Furgler.
Transport, Communications and Energy: Léon Schlumpf.

Local Government. Each of the cantons and demi-cantons is sovereign, so far as its independence and legislative powers are not restricted by the federal constitution; all cantonal governments, though different in organization (membership varies from 5 to 11, and terms of office from 1 to 5 years), are based on the principle of sovereignty of the people.

In all cantons a body chosen by universal suffrage, usually called *der Grosse Rat*, or *Kantonsrat*, exercises the functions of a parliament. In all the cantonal constitutions, however, except those of the cantons which have a *Landsgemeinde*, the referendum has a place. By this principle, where it is most fully developed, as in Zürich, all laws and concordats, or agreements with other cantons, and the chief matters of finance, as well as all revisions of the Constitution, must be submitted to the popular vote. In Appenzell, Glarus and Unterwalden the people exercise their powers direct in the *Landsgemeinde*, *i.e.*, the assembly in the open air of all male citizens of full age. In all the cantons the *popular initiative* for constitutional affairs, as well as for legislation, has been introduced, except in Lucerne, where the *initiative* exists only for constitutional affairs. In most cantons there are districts (*Amtsbezirke*) consisting of a number of communes grouped together, each district having a Prefect (*Regierungsstatthalter*) representing the cantonal government. In the larger communes, for local affairs, there is an Assembly (legislative) and a Council (executive) with a president, maire or syndic, and not less than 4 other members. In the smaller communes there is a council only, with its proper officials.

Basler Handelskammer, *La neutralité suisse*, 1962
Bonjour, E., *Swiss Neutrality*. London, 1946
Huber, H., *How Switzerland is Governed*. Zürich, 1947
Hughes, C., *The Federal Constitution of Switzerland. Translation and Commentary*. Oxford, 1954
Hughes, C. J., *The Parliament of Switzerland*. Hansard Society, 1962
Marx, Dr Paul, *Systematisches Register zu den geltenden Staatsverträgen der schweizerischen Eidgenossenschaft und der Kantone mit dem Auslande*. Zürich, 1918. *Appendix*, 1934
Rappard, W. E., *La Constitution fédérale de la Suisse*. Zürich, 1948.—*Collective Security in Swiss Experience*. London, 1948
Ruck, Erwin, *Schweizerisches Staatsrecht*. Zürich, 1933
Silbernagel-Caloyanni, Alfred, *Suisse: Organisation Politique, Administrative et Judiciaire de la Confédération Helvétique et de Chaque Canton*. Paris, 1936

DEFENCE. There are fortifications in all entrances to the Alps and on the important passes crossing the Alps and the Jura. Large-scale destructions of bridges, tunnels and defiles are prepared for an emergency.

Army. Switzerland depends for defence upon a *national militia*. Service in this force is compulsory and universal, with few exemptions except for physical disability. Those excused or rejected pay certain taxes in lieu. Liability extends from the 20th to the end of the 50th year for soldiers and of the 55th year for officers. The first 12 years are spent in the first line, called the *Auszug*, or *Élite*, the next 10 in the *Landwehr* and 8 in the *Landsturm*. The unarmed *Hilfsdienst* comprises all other males between 20 and 50 whose services can be made available for non-combatant duties of any description.

The initial training of the Swiss militia soldier is carried out in recruits' schools, and the periods are 118 days for infantry, engineers, artillery, etc. The subsequent trainings, called 'repetition courses', are 20 days annually; but after going through 8 courses further attendance is excused for all under the rank of sergeant. The *Landwehr* men are called up for training courses of 13 days every 2 years, and the *Landsturm* men have to undergo a refresher course of 13 days.

The Army is divided into 3 field corps each of 1 armoured and 2 infantry divisions, 11 independent frontier brigades, 3 mountain divisions, and independent redoubt-, fortress- and territorial-brigades, organized in 4 army corps. Strength on mobilization: 580,000, and 400,000 reserves.

The administration of the Swiss Army is partly in the hands of the Cantonal authorities, who can promote officers up to the rank of captain. But the Federal Government is concerned with all general questions and makes all the higher appointments.

In peace-time the Swiss Army has no general; only in time of war the Federal Assembly in joint session of both Houses appoints a general.

The Swiss infantry are armed with the Swiss automatic rifle and with machine-guns, bazookas and mortars. The field artillery is armed with a Q.F. shielded 10·5 Bofors and field howitzers of 10·5 cm calibre. The heavy artillery is armed with guns of 10·5 cm and howitzers of 15 cm calibre. The armoured troops are equipped with the light French AMX, the British Centurion and a modern Swiss tank.

Air Force. The Air Force has 3 flying regiments, with about 300 combat aircraft. The fighter squadrons are equipped with Swiss-built F-5E Tiger IIs (4 squadrons), Mirage IIIS supersonic interceptor/ground-attack (2 squadrons), Mirage IIIRS fighter/reconnaissance (1 squadron), and Hunter interceptor/ground-attack (9 squadrons) aircraft. Bloodhound surface-to-air missile batteries are operational.

Training aircraft are Pilatus P-2 and PC-7 Turbo-Trainer and Vampire; there are also communications and transport aircraft and helicopters. Personnel numbers, 45,000 on mobilization.

INTERNATIONAL RELATIONS

Membership. Switzerland is a member of OECD, EFTA and the Council of Europe.

ECONOMY

Budget. Revenue and expenditure of the Confederation, in 1m. francs, for calendar years:

	1978	*1979*	*1980*	*1981*	*1982*	*1983*
Revenue	15,106	15,050	16,460	17,400	18,900	19,400
Expenditure	15,824	16,764	17,332	17,570	19,300	20,300

The public debt, comprising consolidated debt and flowing debt, of the Confederation in 1980 amounted to 14,126m. francs. The floating debt in 1980 was 4,255m. francs.

Schweizerisches Finanz-Jahrbuch. Bern. Annual. From 1899
Staatstechnung der Schweizerischen Eidgenossenschaft. Bern, 1976

Currency. The *franc* of 100 *Rappen* or *centimes* is the monetary unit. On 10 May 1971 there was a revaluation to 0·21759 gramme of fine gold.

The legal gold coins are 20- and 10-franc pieces; cupro nickel coins are 5, 2, 1 and ½ franc, 20, 10 and 5 centimes; bronze, 2 and 1 centime. Notes are of 1,000, 500, 100, 50, 20, 10 and 5 francs.

On 10 July 1981 the notes in circulation (of francs of nominal value) was as follows: In 1,000 franc notes, 8,685·1m. francs; in 500, 4,201·9m. francs; in 100, 6,687·3m. francs; in 50, 1,058·3m. francs, and in lower denominations 1,195·8m.

In March 1985, £1 = 3·08 *francs*; US$1 = 2·93 *francs*.

Banking. The National Bank, with headquarters divided between Bern and Zürich, opened on 20 June 1907. It has the exclusive right to issue bank-notes. In 1983 the condition of the bank was as follows (in 1m. francs): Gold, 11,903·9, foreign exchange (currency), 25,495; currency in circulation, 24,759.

In 1976 there were 1,740 banking institutions with total assets of 347,710·5m. Swiss francs. They included 28 cantonal banks (79,376m. francs), 5 big banks (161,382m.), 225 regional banks (38,138m.), 185 other banks (43,267m.).

On 31 Dec. 1976 the total amount of savings deposits in Swiss banks was 73,903m. francs, with 11·2m. depositors.

National Bank: Bulletin mensuel—Das schweizerische Bankwesen. Yearly. From 1920

Weights and Measures. The metric system of weights and measures was made compulsory by the federal law on 3 July 1875 and since 1 Jan. 1887 only metric units have been legal. By the federal law of 24 June 1909 the international electric units were also adopted.

ENERGY AND NATURAL RESOURCES

Electricity. The total production of energy amounted to 51,819m. kwh. in 1983; 36,002m. kwh. were generated by hydro-electric plants.

Gas. The production of gas in 1983 was 44·36m. cu. metres.

Minerals. There are 2 salt-mining districts; that in Bex (Vaud) belongs to the canton, but is worked by a private company, and those at Schweizerhalle, Rheinfelden and Ryburg are worked by a joint-stock company formed by the cantons interested. The output of salt of all kinds in 1982 was 361,964 tonnes.

Agriculture. Of the total area of the country of 4,129,315 hectares, about 1,057,794 hectares (25·6%) are unproductive. Of the productive area of 3,071,521 hectares, 1,051,991 hectares are wooded. The agricultural area, in 1980, consisted of 287,283 hectares arable land (including vineyards), 106,406 hectares artificial meadows and 561,311 hectares permanent meadow. In 1980 there were 125,274 farms with a total area of 1,086,060 hectares. The gross value of agricultural products was estimated at 6,409·7m. francs in 1975 and 7,243·1m. francs in 1980.

In 1980, 176,942 hectares were planted with cereals, of which 85,301 hectares were wheat; barley, 46,111; rye, 8,058; potatoes, 23,664; sugar-beet, 13,075; vegetables, 8,196; tobacco, 769. Production, 1981 (in 1,000 tonnes): Potatoes, 1,048; sugar-beet, 900; wheat, 384; barley, 225; rye, 29; tobacco, 1·8. Milk production (in 1,000 tonnes): 1960, 3,112; 1970, 3,204; 1979, 3,671; 1980, 3,679; 1981, 3,680; 1982, 3,687.

The fruit production (in 1,000 tonnes) in 1981 was: Apples, 235; pears, 134; plums, 29; cherries, 28; nuts, 1.

Wine is produced in 18 of the cantons. In 1980 Swiss vineyards (13,736 hectares) yielded 854,804 hectolitres of wine, valued at 349,725 francs.

Livestock (1983): 47,000 horses, 349,000 sheep, 1,919,000 cattle (including about 835,000 milch cows), 2,166,000 pigs, 1m. poultry.

Forestry. Of the forest area of 999,795 hectares, 56,876 were owned by the Federation or the cantons, 636,069 by communes and 306,850 by private persons or companies in 1982. The utilization of timber, in 1981, was 4,385,931 cu. metres, of which 338,419 in state-owned, 2,747,112 in communal and 1,300,400 in private forests.

INDUSTRY AND TRADE

Industry. The chief food producing industries, based on Swiss agriculture, are the manufacture of cheese, butter, sugar and meat. The production in 1982 was (in tonnes): Cheese, 124,900; butter, 32,500; sugar (1981), 120,811. There are 46 breweries, producing in 1978, 4·05m. hectolitres of beer. Tobacco products in 1982: Cigars, 373·08m.; cigarettes, 26,497m.

Among the other industries, the manufacture of textiles, wearing apparel and footwear, chemicals and pharmaceutical products, bricks, glass and cement, the manufacture of basic iron and steel and of other metal products, the production of machinery (including electrical machinery and scientific and optical instruments) and watch and clock making are the most important. In 1981 there were 8,738 factories with 693,243 workers. In 1982, 41,200 were working in textile industries, 45,000 in the manufacture of clothing and footwear, 70,200 in chemical works, 194,700 in the construction industry, 168,600 in manufacture of metal products, 252,000 in the manufacture of machinery and 55,300 in watch and clock making and in the manufacture of jewellery.

Production in 1982 was: Woollen and blended yarn, 15,467 tonnes; woollen and blended cloth, 7,534 metres; footwear (1981), 5·87m. pairs; cement, 4,099,874 tonnes; raw aluminium, 75,256 tonnes; chocolate, 76,605 tonnes, 25·38m. watches and clocks were exported (1981).

Labour. In 1982, the total working population was 3,033,200, of which 213,600 were active in agriculture and forestry, 1,174,000 in manufacture and construction and 1,645,600 in services.

The foreign labour force with permit of temporary residence was 749,378 in Aug. 1982. Of the number recorded 295,699 were Italians, 90,899 Spaniards, 76,802 Frenchmen, 67,297 Germans and 27,918 Austrians.

The Swiss Federal Union of Administrative and Public Service Workers had, in 1981, a membership of 125,151. The Federation of Trade Unions had about 459,150 members.

Commerce. The special commerce, excluding gold (bullion and coins) and silver (coins), was (in 1m. Swiss francs) as follows:

	1977	*1978*	*1979*	*1980*	*1981*	*1982*	*1983*
Imports	43,026	42,299	48,730	60,859	60,094	58,059	61,064
Exports	42,159	41,779	44,024	49,607	52,821	52,658	53,723

The following table, in 1m. francs, shows the distribution of the special trade of Switzerland among the principal countries:

	Imports from				*Exports to*			
Countries	*1980*	*1981*	*1982*	*1983*	*1980*	*1981*	*1982*	*1983*
Federal Rep. of Germany	16,766·3	16,908·4	17,261·9	17,413·2	9,749·8	9,687·4	9,572·5	10,697·6
France	7,461·8	7,428·5	6,657·2	7,131·1	4,547·6	4,751·3	4,729·4	4,640·8
Italy	5,844·6	5,849·3	5,732·8	6,140·7	3,898·8	4,069·9	3,973·4	3,803·7
Netherlands	2,469·6	2,445·2	2,500·7	2,691·3	1,383·7	1,316·5	1,249·9	1,420·1
Belgium–Luxembourg	2,502·5	2,543·2	2,345·5	2,490·9	1,565·2	1,396·9	1,404·4	1,252·3
UK	5,072·6	3,457·6	3,180·6	3,303·2	3,134·4	3,428·6	3,268·1	3,481·5
Denmark	508·8	549·4	517·8	556·1	548·4	576·9	614·5	662·9
Ireland	150·9	176·1	197·0	240·9	91·1	134·7	154·0	162·6
Greece	...	90·9	75·1	79·1	...	370·4	422·9	302·2
EEC Total	40,777·2	39,448·6	38,469·4	40,046·5	24,919·0	25,732·6	25,389·1	26,424·2
Austria	2,184·4	2,262·7	2,153·6	2,166·8	2,271·0	2,263·0	2,141·6	2,211·1
Norway	229·1	186·3	168·0	222·2	428·9	444·7	439·2	419·1
Sweden	1,229·4	1,215·2	1,096·1	1,030·1	1,024·5	1,052·7	1,033·9	1,067·2
Portugal	179·4	190·0	168·5	183·3	400·7	476·5	444·6	390·8
Finland	343·5	338·3	319·9	350·0	397·2	454·4	441·8	453·9
Iceland	47·9	37·2	45·5	90·2	15·2	19·9	17·1	17·1
EFTA	4,213·7	4,229·7	3,951·6	4,042·7	4,537·5	4,711·2	4,518·2	4,559·2
Spain	578·8	617·2	655·0	883·1	903·1	1,020·4	1,263·8	1,264·7
Gibraltar, Malta	2·9	2·6	2·6	1·6	21·9	27·1	20·6	23·8
German Dem. Republic	68·5	79·9	81·6	91·6	220·3	232·9	221·6	145·6
Poland	240·1	103·5	82·4	75·1	287·5	181·4	179·8	191·2
Czechoslovakia	194·0	168·2	185·9	199·0	234·2	227·4	222·4	244·9
Hungary	166·5	236·3	191·5	229·0	285·5	339·5	335·0	305·9
Yugoslavia	173·5	145·8	141·9	199·6	552·7	567·5	437·2	421·7
Greece	66·3	...	...	...	300·4	...	...	...
Bulgaria	40·9	40·4	31·9	25·0	119·7	171·1	166·1	225·2
Romania	60·7	53·6	38·2	32·5	133·6	110·4	78·4	48·5
USSR	1,607·9	1,728·3	1,683·4	1,412·6	499·1	402·5	437·2	463·0
Turkey	113·4	141·4	119·2	118·3	265·5	423·5	368·9	408·0
Other European countries	8·4	8·0	10·6	18·3	45·0	25·0	31·1	33·1
Europe Total	48,312·8	47,003·5	45,645·2	47,374·9	33,325·0	34,172·5	33,669·4	34,759·0

Countries	Imports from 1980	1981	1982	1983	Exports to 1980	1981	1982	1983
Egypt	71·5	70·9	81·8	61·6	306·4	368·8	573·2	414·5
Sudan	4·4	2·2	1·0	4·2	42·2	53·7	48·9	67·2
Libya	516·5	368·2	526·9	868·2	143·6	195·2	175·6	209·1
Tunisia	11·9	13·3	44·2	159·6	46·8	57·7	50·4	52·1
Algeria	67·4	366·6	264·0	523·3	276·2	204·4	152·8	162·6
Morocco	46·1	21·2	23·6	18·4	66·4	78·6	69·7	82·6
Ivory Coast	35·8	48·1	40·9	33·6	41·4	31·0	33·6	39·8
Guinea	0·3	1·0	2·1	3·1	9·4	9·3	7·4	9·7
Ghana	48·9	33·5	27·4	32·6	23·1	31·5	11·3	20·6
Nigeria	356·5	195·3	454·4	155·8	530·5	683·2	517·2	340·3
Zaïre	20·9	6·7	15·6	5·9	25·2	29·9	31·3	28·7
Angola	11·6	10·8	14·1	13·3	52·6	46·1	40·4	15·1
S Africa, Rep. of	212·2	153·4	154·0	193·5	499·3	669·6	530·3	489·3
Zambia	21·9	43·5	26·0	13·9	14·3	14·7	24·3	12·3
Zimbabwe	8·7	29·6	35·7	43·5	17·4	40·4	36·5	24·8
Tanzania	3·8	6·4	5·3	5·0	29·8	16·5	21·4	26·5
Kenya	33·7	27·1	27·7	26·9	48·1	45·0	38·6	31·1
Other African countries	89·3	91·9	85·1	94·6	237·7	193·5	442·1	399·9
Africa Total	1,561·4	1,489·7	1,829·8	2,257·0	2,410·4	2,769·1	2,805·0	2,426·2
Syria	36·6	18·5	0·7	5·4	85·1	101·5	115·0	129·1
Lebanon	86·8	53·6	70·3	78·3	238·5	330·2	355·5	138·1
Israel	209·5	205·4	303·4	215·8	871·7	452·3	511·8	549·6
Iraq	0·4	0·8	0·2	5·2	354·9	527·2	680·4	419·9
Kuwait	44·6	2·7	6·3	6·3	128·3	200·8	255·8	202·9
Iran	136·8	81·6	148·8	89·2	463·7	464·4	391·1	642·8
Saudi Arabia	257·3	413·0	293·1	349·2	1,042·4	1,181·8	1,544·3	1,717·1
UAE	673·2	665·9	227·5	52·2	173·1	236·1	333·6	275·3
Pakistan	40·8	51·4	41·9	51·7	64·8	110·1	101·6	136·6
India	127·8	153·1	152·0	140·6	220·8	288·8	345·9	301·6
Thailand	191·9	104·8	102·2	118·8	103·6	144·0	125·7	175·2
Malaysia	52·1	51·1	44·6	47·2	58·1	67·0	95·9	186·1
Singapore	99·9	81·7	84·6	85·3	267·5	315·4	347·0	422·7
China	128·6	153·7	146·3	157·4	233·4	241·7	263·3	262·6
Hong Kong	572·4	610·0	644·6	688·6	934·6	999·0	867·2	875·2
Taiwan	164·1	170·0	173·2	181·9	184·2	200·6	172·5	240·9
Korea, Rep. of	113·7	143·5	155·1	165·4	122·9	110·7	134·5	174·7
Japan	1,989·8	2,297·8	2,147·5	2,342·4	1,273·5	1,435·8	1,365·4	1,508·2
Philippines	30·3	34·7	35·3	33·4	84·4	94·9	103·4	93·4
Indonesia	61·8	65·2	47·5	43·4	103·2	159·5	204·5	152·4
Other Asian countries	154·5	85·0	112·4	57·3	236·5	350·1	430·6	409·3
Asia Total	5,172·9	5,443·5	4,937·5	4,915·0	7,245·2	8,011·9	8,745·0	9,013·7
Canada	339·2	364·2	288·6	270·9	420·4	536·6	518·5	575·2
USA	4,104·9	4,475·5	4,153·2	4,993·3	3,552·0	4,129·1	4,095·2	4,594·1
Mexico	84·6	31·6	37·5	36·3	371·9	526·1	410·0	180·8
Guatemala	58·2	45·9	43·3	48·4	45·7	47·6	29·5	21·5
Honduras	42·4	43·9	40·6	34·1	11·2	10·6	16·8	26·7
Costa Rica	51·9	49·1	43·7	46·3	13·8	10·8	7·9	10·4
Panama	302·6	273·1	241·8	270·9	226·9	342·5	192·5	268·9
Cuba	21·1	12·4	14·2	11·7	45·9	61·6	35·6	56·0
Colombia	116·2	77·2	65·3	84·7	130·5	137·1	120·7	120·0
Venezuela	15·0	10·6	7·9	16·0	179·6	227·4	242·1	166·8
Brazil	263·6	287·6	282·0	271·7	497·6	451·9	414·3	383·1
Uruguay	20·6	30·9	27·6	28·2	29·1	33·0	28·2	27·5
Argentina	116·4	137·4	113·7	113·0	318·2	323·2	354·9	228·2
Chile	11·1	11·7	20·5	17·4	72·7	76·7	80·1	72·7
Bolivia	2·5	2·3	2·6	3·1	13·5	39·6	10·8	6·3
Peru	44·9	48·4	23·7	28·8	96·0	141·3	99·9	69·9
Ecuador	14·6	15·4	14·8	9·2	66·4	55·0	62·9	48·0

Countries	Imports from 1980	1981	1982	1983	Exports to 1980	1981	1982	1983
Other American countries	100·6	113·5	94·2	104·8	173·0	205·1	229·8	185·3
Australia and Oceania	110·7	126·7	132·0	128·5	362·6	513·2	489·6	483·1

Custom receipts (in 1,000 francs): 1977, 2,920,800; 1978, 2,989,707; 1979, 3,002,117; 1980, 3,170,700; 1981, 3,243,631.

Total trade between Switzerland (including Liechtenstein) and UK for calendar years (British Department of Trade, in £1,000 sterling):

	1980	1981	1982	1983	1984
Imports to UK	2,614,690	1,708,058	1,669,922	2,154,085	2,490,593
Exports and re-exports from UK	3,076,337	1,601,164	1,196,203	1,385,694	1,549,469

Federal Customs Office, *Statistique mensuelle du commerce extérieur de la Suisse.* From 1925.—*Statistique annuelle du commerce extérieur de la Suisse.* 2 vols. From 1840.—*Rapport annuel de la statistique du commerce Suisse.* From 1889

Tourism. Tourism is an important industry. In 1983, overnight stays in hotels and sanatoria were 35,233,000 (35,977,000 by foreign visitors) and in other accommodation 40,134,000.

COMMUNICATIONS

Roads. There are (1982) 66,544 km of main roads, including 1,170 km of 'national roads' for motor cars only. There is a postal autobus service, which, in 1976, carried 53·7m. passengers. Motor vehicles, as at 30 Sept. 1983, numbered 3,074,000, including 2,521,000 private cars, 190,000 trucks, 187,000 motor cycles, 11,000 buses and 165,000 commercial and agricultural vehicles.

Railways. Railway history in Switzerland begins in 1847. In 1983 the length of the general traffic railways was 4,997 km, and of special lines (funiculars etc.), 879 km. The operating receipts of general traffic lines amounted to (1980) 3,373,416,000 francs; operating expenses, 4,101,371,000 francs. Traffic (1981) was 45m. tonnes and 218m. passengers.

There are many privately-owned lines, the most important of which are the Bern–Lotschberg–Simplon (115 km) and Rhaetian (363 km) networks.

Aviation. In 1981 civil aviation on domestic and international routes carried 12,166,842 passengers, 331,391 tonnes of mail, freight and luggage.

The air transport organization Swissair (founded in 1931) in 1982 carried 189,139 tonnes of freight and 7,168,567 passengers. Swissair had a capital of 422m. francs on 15 May 1977. Its fleet consisted of 53 aircraft in Jan. 1983.

Shipping. A merchant marine was created by a decree of the Swiss Government dated 9 April 1941, the place of registry of its vessels being Basel. In 1981 it consisted of 33 vessels with a total of 319,631 GRT. In 1981, 8,277,359 tonnes of goods were handled in the port of Basel.

Post and Broadcasting. In 1981 there were 3,906 post offices. On 1 Jan. 1983 there were 5,113,000 telephones, all integrated in one dial system.

Wireless communication is furnished by 3 main medium-wave stations and 1 short-wave station. There are 3 television studios and more than 100 transmitters. TV programmes are financed by licence fees and advertisements. Advertisements are limited to 15 minutes each day. All stations are operated by the Federal Post, Telephone and Telegraph (PTT) services. Radio-telegraph circuits are operated by Radio Suisse SA, radio-telephone circuits by the PTT. Radio licences, 1982, 2,337,257; television licences, 2,057,062.

The total expenditure of the PTT in 1982 was 6,429 francs, the total gross receipts 6,562·2m. francs.

Cinemas (1982). There were 466 cinemas with a seating capacity of 149,975.

Newspapers (1984). The number of daily newspapers was estimated to be 126.

JUSTICE, RELIGION, EDUCATION AND WELFARE

Justice. The Federal Tribunal (*Bundes-Gericht*), which sits at Lausanne, consists of 26-28 members, with 11-13 supplementary judges, appointed by the Federal Assembly for 6 years and eligible for re-election; the President and Vice-President serve for 2 years and cannot be re-elected. The President has a salary of 170,000 francs a year, and the other members 158,000 francs. The Tribunal has original and final jurisdiction in suits between the Confederation and cantons; between cantons and cantons; between the Confederation or cantons and corporations or individuals, the value in dispute being not less than 8,000 francs; between parties who refer their case to it, the value in dispute being at least 20,000 francs; in such suits as the constitution or legislation of cantons places within its authority; and in many classes of railway suits. It is a court of appeal against decisions of other federal authorities, and of cantonal authorities applying federal laws. The Tribunal also tries persons accused of treason or other offences against the Confederation. For this purpose it is divided into 4 chambers: Chamber of Accusation, Criminal Chamber (*Cour d'Assises*), Federal Penal Court and Court of Cassation. The jurors who serve in the Assize Courts are elected by the people, and are paid 100 francs a day when serving.

On 3 July 1938 the Swiss electorate accepted a new federal penal code, to take the place of the separate cantonal penal codes. The new code, which abolished capital punishment, came into force on 1 Jan. 1942.

By federal law of 5 Oct. 1950 several articles of the penal code concerning crime against the independence of the state have been amended with a view to reinforcing the security of the State.

Thormann, P., and Overbeck, A. (ed.), *Das Schweizerische Strafgesetzbuch.* Zürich, 1939

Religion. There is complete and absolute liberty of conscience and of creed. No one is bound to pay taxes specially appropriated to defraying the expenses of a creed to which he does not belong. No bishoprics can be created on Swiss territory without the approbation of the Confederation.

According to the census of 1 Dec. 1980 Roman Catholics numbered 3,030,069 (47·6%) of the population; Protestants, 2,822,266 (44·3%) and others, 513,625 (8·1%). In 1960 Protestants were in a majority in 10 of the cantons and Catholics in 12. Of the more populous cantons, Zürich, Bern, Vaud, Neuchâtel and Basel (town and land) were mainly Protestant, while Luzern, Fribourg, Ticino, Valais and the Forest Cantons are mainly Catholic. The Roman Catholics are under 6 Bishops, viz., of Basel (resident at Solothurn), Chur, St Gallen, Lugano, Lausanne–Geneva–Fribourg (resident at Fribourg) and Sitten (Sion), all of them immediately subject to the Holy See. The Old Catholics have a theological faculty at the university of Bern.

Education. Education is administered by the cantons. Before the year 1848 most of the cantons had organized a system of primary schools, and since that year elementary education has steadily advanced. In 1874 it was made obligatory for the whole country (the school age varying in the different cantons) and placed under the civil authority. In some cantons the cost falls almost entirely on the communes, in others it is divided between the canton and communes. In all the cantons primary instruction is free.

In most cantons there are also secondary schools for youths of from 12 to 15, gymnasia, higher schools for girls, teachers' seminaries, commercial and administrative schools, trade schools, art schools, technical schools, schools for the instruction of girls in domestic economy and other subjects, agricultural schools, schools for horticulture, for viticulture, for arboriculture and for dairy management. There are also institutions for the blind, the deaf and dumb and feeble-minded.

There are 7 universities in Switzerland. These universities are organized on the model of those of Germany, governed by a rector and a senate, and divided into 4 faculties of theology, jurisprudence, philosophy and medicine. In 1980–81 the Federal Institute of Technology at Zürich (founded in 1855) had 658 teachers and (1981–82) 7,556 matriculated students; the Federal Institute of Technology at Lausanne, independent of the university since 1946, had 217 teachers and

(1981–82) 2,316 students; the St Gall School of Economics and Social Sciences, founded in 1899, had 148 teachers and (1981–82) 2,008 matriculated students.

University statistics in the winter of 1981–82:

	Theology	*Law*	*Economics*	*Medicine*	*Science*	*Others*	*Total*	*Teaching staff (1980–81)*
Basel (1460)	191	905	537	1,676	1,167	1,554	6,030	506
Zürich (1523 & 1833)	222	2,529	1,044	3,122	2,071	6,464	15,452	1,618
Bern (1528 & 1834)	224	1,556	488	1,823	1,405	2,312	7,808	810
Genève (1559[1] & 1873[1])	126	986	870	1,498	1,382	5,454	10,316	831
Lausanne (1537[1] & 1890[2])	93	818	717	1,491	780	1,809	5,708	433
Fribourg (1889)	432	635	593	375	471	2,012	4,518	465
Neuchâtel (1866 & 1909)	52	215	237	91	463	926	1,984	215

[1] Founded as an academy. [2] Reorganized as a university.

These numbers are exclusive of 'visitors', but inclusive of women students.

Social Security. The Federal Insurance Law against illness and accident, of 13 June 1911, entitles all Swiss citizens to insurance against illness; foreigners may be admitted to the benefits. Compulsory insurance against illness does not exist as yet, but cantons and communities are entitled to declare insurance obligatory for certain classes or to establish public benefit (sick fund) associations, and to make employers responsible for the payment of the premiums of their employees. In 1980 the 469 societies insuring against illness had 6,811,581 members.

Unemployment insurance is based since 13 June 1976 upon a Constitution amendment which stipulates unemployment insurance as compulsory for all wage-earners.

A federal law was in preparation in 1976. At 30 Sept. 1975 there existed 123 public and private unemployment insurance organizations with a total membership (31 March 1977) of 1,435,577 (53·5% of working population).

Insurance against accident is compulsory for all officials, employees and workmen of all the factories, trades, etc., which are under the federal liability law. The Swiss Accident Insurance Institution commenced operations on 1 April 1918.

On 6 July 1947 a federal law was accepted by a referendum, providing compulsory old age and widows and widowers insurance for the whole population, as from 1 Jan. 1948. In March 1981 the number of normal pensioners was 983,063, the number of interim pensioners, 34,379. On 1 Jan. 1960 the old-age insurance scheme was extended to cover invalidity. In March 1981, 184,174 invalids received a regular annuity and 20,731 invalids an interim annuity.

DIPLOMATIC REPRESENTATIVES

Of Switzerland in Great Britain (16–18 Montagu Place, London, W1H 2DQ)
Ambassador: François-Charles Pictet (accredited 9 Feb. 1984).

Of Great Britain in Switzerland (Thunstrasse 50, 30005 Bern)
Ambassador: John Powell-Jones, CMG.

Of Switzerland in the USA (2900 Cathedral Ave., NW, Washington, D.C., 20008)
Ambassador: Klaus Jacobi.

Of the USA in Switzerland (Jubilaeumstrasse 93, 3005, Bern)
Ambassador: John D. Lodge.

Books of Reference

Statistical Information: The Bureau fédéral de statistique (Hallwylstr. 15, 3003 Bern) was established in 1860. *Director:* J.-J. Senglet. Its principal publications are:

Annuaire statistique de la Suisse. Bâle. From 1891
Statistique de la Suisse. From 1930
Contributions à la Statistique Suisse. From 1930
Bibliographie Suisse de statistique et d'économie politique. Annual, from 1937

Swiss Confederation
Annuaire; Budget; Message du Budget; Compte d'Etat (annual) *Feuille Fédérale; Recueil des Lois fédérales* (weekly)

Recueil systématique des lois et ordonnances, 1848–1947 (in German, French and Italian). Bern, 1951
Sammlung der Bundes- und Kantonsverfassungen (in German, French and Italian). Bern, 1937

Federal Department of Economics
La vie économique (and supplements). Monthly. From 1928
Législation sociale de la Suisse. Annual, from 1928

Bonjour, E., Offler, H. S., and Potter, G. R., *A Short History of Switzerland.* Oxford, 1952
Dürrenmatt, P., *Schweizer Geschichte.* Zürich, 1963.—*Schweiz.* Zürich, 1962.—*Wir Schweizer und der totale Krieg.* Zürich, 1960
Imhof, E. (ed.), *Atlas der Schweiz.* Bern, 1965 ff.
McPhee, J., *The Swiss Army.* London, 1985
Riklin, A., *et al, Handbuch der schweizerischen Aussenpolitik.* Bern, 1975
Schwarz, U., *The Eye of the Hurricane: Switzerland in World War Two.* Boulder, 1980

National Library: Bibliothèque Nationale Suisse, Hallwylstr.15, 3003, Bern. *Director:* F. G. Maier.

SYRIA

Capital: Damascus
Population: 9·84m. (1983)
GNP per capita: US$1,570 (1981)

al-Jamhouriya al Arabia as-Souriya

HISTORY. For the history of Syria from 1920 to 1946 *see* THE STATESMAN'S YEAR-BOOK, 1957, pp. 1408 f. Complete independence was achieved on 12 Apr. 1946. Syria merged with Egypt to form the United Arab Republic from 2 Feb. 1958 until 29 Sept. 1961, when independence was resumed following a *coup* the previous day. Lieut.-Gen. Hafez al-Assad became Prime Minister following the fifth *coup* of that decade on 13 Nov. 1970, and assumed the Presidency on 22 Feb. 1971.

AREA AND POPULATION. Syria is bounded by the Mediterranean and the Lebanese Republic on the west, by Israel and Jordan on the south, by Iraq on the east and by Turkey on the north. The frontier between Syria and Turkey (Nisibim-Jeziret ibn Omar) was settled by the Franco-Turkish agreement of 22 June 1929.

The area of Syria is 185,180 sq. km (71,498 sq. miles), of which 35,000 sq. km have been surveyed. The census of 1981 gave a total population of 9,171,622, showing about 10% less than the estimates. Estimate (1983) 9·84m. The 14 *mohafaza* (administrative districts) with population, 1975, were: City of Damascus, 1,042,000; Damascus, excluding city, 732,000; Aleppo, 1,523,000; Homs, 629,000; Hama (1970), 514,748; Lattakia (1970), 389,552; Deir-el-Zor, 332,000; Idlib, 428,000; Hassakeh, 532,000; Raqqa, 281,000; Sweida, 162,000; Derá, 282,000; Tartous, 348,000; Kunaitra, 19,000.

Principal towns (census 1981), Damascus, 1,251,028; Aleppo, 976,727; Homs, 354,508; Lattakia, 196,791; Hama, 176,640.

Arabic is the official language.

CLIMATE. The climate is Mediterranean in type, with mild wet winters and dry, hot summers, though there are variations in temperatures and rainfall between the coastal regions and the interior, which even includes desert conditions. The more mountainous parts are subject to snowfall. Damascus. Jan. 45°F (7°C), July 81°F (27°C). Annual rainfall 9″ (225 mm).

CONSTITUTION AND GOVERNMENT. A new Constitution was approved by plebiscite on 12 March 1973 and promulgated on 14 March. It confirmed the Arab Socialist Renaissance *(Ba'ath)* Party, in power since 1963, as the 'leading party in the State and society'. Legislative power is held by a 195-member People's Council, elected for a 4-year term. At the latest elections on 10 Nov. 1981, all seats were won by the National Progressive Front, a coalition of the Ba'ath Party and 4 smaller ones.

President: Lieut.-Gen. Hafez al Assad (re-elected for further 7-year term in 1978).

First Vice-President: Abdul Halim Khaddam *(Political and Foreign Affairs). Second Vice-President:* Rifaat al Assad *(Defence and Security). Third Vice-President:* Mohammed Zuhair Mashrqa *(Party Affairs).*

Prime Minister: Dr Abdul Rauf al-Kasm.

National flag: Three horizontal stripes of red, white, black, with 2 green stars on the white stripe.

DEFENCE. Military service is compulsory for a period of 30 months.

Army. The Army is organized into 4 armoured and 2 mechanized infantry divisions, 2 armoured, 4 mechanized, 2 artillery brigades, 5 commando and 1 parachute regiment and 2 surface-to-surface missile regiments and 26 surface-to-air missile batteries. Strength (1985) about 170,000 (including 120,000 conscripts) and reserves 100,000. There are a further 10,000 men in paramilitary forces. Equipment includes 2,200 T-54/-55, 1,100 T-62 and 900 T-72 main battle tanks.

Navy. The Navy includes 2 small frigates, 20 missile boats, 8 torpedo boats, 2 minesweepers, 2 coastal minesweepers, 2 inshore minesweepers, 3 coastal patrol craft and 1 diving ship (all *ex*-Soviet) and the 3 patrol vessels (*ex*-French) transferred in 1962 to form the nucleus of the Syrian Navy. Personnel in 1985 totalled 2,500 officers and men.

Air Force. The Air Force, including Air Defence Command, was believed (1985) to have about 25,000 personnel and about 450 first-line jet combat aircraft, made up of about 200 MiG-21, 60 MiG-23 and 24 MiG-25 supersonic interceptors, 60 MiG-23, 40 Su-7, 60 Su-22 and 50 MiG-17 fighter-bombers, plus some MiG-25 reconnaissance aircraft. Additional aircraft are being purchased from the USSR with Saudi Arabian aid. Training units have Spanish-built Flamingo piston-engined primary trainers and Czechoslovakian L-29 Delfin jet basic trainers. There are also transport units with Il-76, An-12, An-24/26, C-47, Il-14 and other types, and helicopter units with Soviet-built Ka-25s, Mi-6s, Mi-8s and Mi-24 gunships, and French-built Gazelles. 'Guideline', 'Goa', 'Gainful' and 'Gaskin' surface-to-air missiles are widely deployed in Syria by Air Defence Command, and 'Gammon' long-range surface-to-air missiles in Lebanon.

INTERNATIONAL RELATIONS

Membership. Syria is a member of UN and the Arab League.

ECONOMY

Planning. The total investment envisaged in the fifth 5-year plan (1981–85) £Syr.101,493m.

Budget. The ordinary budget for the calendar year 1984 provides for expenditure of £Syr.41,289m.

Currency. The monetary unit is the Syrian *pound*, divided into 100 *piastres*. In March 1985, £1 = £Syr.4·91; US$1 = £Syr.3·92.

Banking. The Central Bank has the sole right of issuing currency. Other banks were nationalized in March 1963, namely, the Omaya Bank and its subsidiary, the Popular Mortgage Bank; the Orient Arab Bank; the Bank of Syria and Overseas; the Agricultural Bank; the Arab World Bank. Number of branches, 1973: Central Bank of Syria, 9; Commercial Bank of Syria, 22; Industrial Bank, 3; Agricultural Co-operative Bank, 50; Real Estate Bank, 3; Bank of Popular Discount, 27.

Weights and Measures. A decree dated 22 Aug. 1935 makes the use of the metric system legal and obligatory throughout the whole of the country. In outlying districts the former weights and measures may still be in use. They are: 1 *okiya* = 0·47 lb.; 6 *okiyas* = 1 *oke* = 2·82 lb.; 2 *okes* = 1 *rottol* = 5·64 lb.; 200 *okes* = 1 *kantar*.

ENERGY AND NATURAL RESOURCES

Oil. A branch of the Iraq Petroleum Co.'s oil pipeline from Kirkuk crosses Syria between Makaleb in the east and Nahr el Kebir valley in the west. The Iraq Petroleum Co. has constructed a new pipeline from Kirkuk to the small fishing port of Banias (south of Lattakia), which came into use in April 1952; the Trans-Arabian Pipeline Co.'s line to Sidon crosses southern Syria. Another pipeline is being constructed from the Karachouk oilfield *via* Homs to the port of Tartous. Crude oil production (1984) 9m. tonnes. Reserves (1983) 1,521m. bbls.

Gas. Gas reserves (1982) 700,000m. cubic ft.

Minerals. Phosphate deposits have been discovered at two places near al-Shargiya and at Khneifis. Production, 1981, 1·32m. tonnes; other minerals were salt,

110,800. There are indications of lead, copper, antimony, nickel, chrome and other minerals widely distributed. Manganese ore was mined before 1914. Sodium chloride and bitumen deposits are being worked. There is abundance of good calcareous building stone and basalt.

Agriculture. Syria is an agricultural country but is moving towards greater industrialization, the bulk of the population being engaged in the cultivation of the soil and in cattle breeding. In 1977 the irrigated area was 531,000 hectares; in 1980, 139,000 hectares under cotton and 1,449,000 hectares were under wheat, 1,587,000 hectares under barley. The total cultivable area was 14·47m. hectares, including 455,000 hectares of forest and 8,631,000 hectares of steppe and pasture.

Yield of principal crops, 1980 (in 1,000 tonnes): Wheat, 2,226; barley, 1,587; cotton (1982), 422; olives, 392; lentils, 83; millet, 19; sugar-beet, 505.

Livestock (1983): Cattle, 800,000; asses, 242,000; sheep, 11m.; goats, 1·1m.; poultry, 15m.

Fishing. The total catch in 1981 was 3,800 tonnes.

INDUSTRY AND TRADE

Industry. The most important industries are flour, oils, soap, cement, tanning, tobacco, textiles, knitwear, glassware, spinning, sugar, margarine, hosiery, footwear and brassware.

Industrial production in 1980 included (in 1,000 tonnes): Woollen fabrics, 1,200; cement, 2,310; sugar, 141; salt, 111; cotton yarn, 25·2; manufactured tobacco, 9·9.

Commerce. Trade in calendar years in £Syr.1m. was as follows:

	1979	*1980*	*1981*	*1982*
Imports	13,067	16,188	19,781	15,727
Exports	6,453	8,273	8,254	7,954

Cotton is one of the chief exports. Others include oil, cereals, live animals and phosphates. Imports include industrial raw materials, machinery, chemicals and electrical equipment.

Total trade between Syria and UK (British Department of Trade returns, in £1,000 sterling):

	1980	*1981*	*1982*	*1983*	*1984*
Imports to UK	12,241	4,555	25,644	18,859	59,245
Exports and re-exports from UK	81,584	85,244	89,535	72,320	91,909

Tourism. In 1981, 1,075,100 tourists visited Syria.

COMMUNICATIONS

Roads. In 1980 there were 13,000 km of asphalted roads, 1,300 km of macadam non-asphalted road and 6,000 km of earth roads. The first-class roads are capable of carrying all types of modern motor transport and are usable all the year round, while the second-class roads are usable during the dry season only, *i.e.*, for about 9 months. The Nairn Transport Company operate a trans-desert pullman motor coach service between Damascus and Baghdad. There are also two pullman transport companies (Elkarnak, Syrian, and Jett, Jordanian) operating a joint service between Damascus and Amman. The motor vehicles registered in 1981 were 93,000 motor cycles, 9,935 buses, 75,200 cars and 93,300 goods vehicles.

Railways. Network totals 1,686 km of 1,435 mm gauge (Syrian Railways) and 246 km of 1,050 mm gauge (Hedjaz-Syrian Railway). In 1983 the Syrian Railways network carried 1·8m. passengers and 3·1m. tonnes of freight.

Aviation. In 1980, 12,557 aircraft arrived at Damascus and Aleppo airports, disembarking 559,430 passengers.

Shipping. The amount of cargo discharged in 1980 was 2·6m. tons and the amount loaded 430,000 tons. Development of the port of Lattakia was in progress in 1983 and a new port was under construction at Tartous.

Post and Broadcasting. An automatic telephone system has been installed in Damascus, and most other towns. Number of telephones (1982), 471,127; of these, 154,615 were in Damascus and 72,981 in Aleppo. There were 1·8m. radio sets in 1983 and 405,000 television receivers.

Newspapers. There were (1984) 3 national daily newspapers in Damascus; other dailies and periodicals appear in Hama, Homs, Aleppo and Lattakia.

JUSTICE, RELIGION, EDUCATION AND WELFARE

Justice. Syrian law is based on both Islamic and French jurisprudence. There are 2 courts of first instance in each district, one for civil and 1 for criminal cases. There is also a Summary Court in each sub-district, under Justices of the Peace. There is a Court of Appeal in the capital of each governorate, with a Court of Cassation in Damascus.

Religion. The population is composed mainly of Sunni Moslems and there are also Shiites and Ismailis. There are also Druzes and Alawites. Christians include Greek Orthodox, Greek Catholics, Armenian Orthodox, Syrian Orthodox, Armenian Catholics, Protestants, Maronites, Syrian Catholics, Latins, Nestorians and Assyrians. There are also Jews and Yezides.

Education. The Syrian University was founded in 1924, although the faculties of law and of medicine had existed previously. In 1975 there were 3 universities with 94,794 students.

In 1980, state primary schools had 47,657 teachers and 1,407,388 pupils; secondary and intermediate schools, 28,847 teachers and 519,453 pupils; vocational schools, 3,161 teachers and 24,440 pupils; teacher-training colleges, 1,141 teachers and 10,612 students.

Health. In 1977 there were 7,479 hospital beds (1 per 983 persons) in 31 state hospitals, 69 private hospitals and 4 sanatoria.

DIPLOMATIC REPRESENTATIVES

Of Syria in Great Britain (8 Belgrave Sq., London, SW1X 8PH)
Ambassador: Dr Loutof Allah Haydar (accredited 9 Dec. 1982).

Of Great Britain in Syria (Quarter Malki, 11 Mohammed Kurd Ali St., Damascus)
Ambassador: W. R. Tomkys, CMG.

Of Syria in the USA (2215 Wyoming Ave., NW, Washington, D.C., 20008)
Ambassador: Dr Rafic Jouejati.

Of the USA in Syria (Abu Rumaneh, Al Mansur St., Damascus)
Ambassador: Robert P. Paganelli.

Of Syria to the United Nations
Ambassador: Dia-Allah El-Fattal.

Books of Reference

Statistical Information: There is a Central Statistics Bureau affiliated to the Council of Ministers, Damascus. It publishes a monthly summary and an annual Statistical Abstract (in Arabic and English).

Abd-Allah, U. F., *The Islamic Struggle in Syria.* Berkeley, 1983
Barthélemy, A., *Dictionnaire arabe-français. Dialectes de Syrie.* 4 vols. Paris, 1935–50
Devlin, J. F., *Syria: Modern State in an Ancient Land.* Boulder, 1983
Hourani, A. H., *Syria and Lebanon.* 2nd ed. R. Inst. of Int. Affairs, 1954
Petran, T., *Syria.* London, 1972

UNITED REPUBLIC OF TANZANIA

Capital: Dodoma
Population: 19·73m. (1983)
GNP per capita: US$280 (1981)

HISTORY. German East Africa was occupied by German colonialists from 1884 and placed under the protection of the German Empire in 1891. It was conquered in the First World War and subsequently divided between the British and Belgians. The latter received the territories of Ruanda and Urundi and the British the remainder, except for the Kionga triangle, which went to Portugal. The country was administered as a League of Nations mandate until 1946 and then as a UN trusteeship territory until 9 Dec. 1961.

Tanganyika achieved responsible government in Sept. 1960 and full self-government on 1 May 1961. On 9 Dec. 1961 Tanganyika became a sovereign independent member state of the Commonwealth of Nations. It adopted a republican form of government on 9 Dec. 1962. For history from the end of the 17th century until 1884 *see* THE STATESMAN'S YEAR-BOOK 1982–83, p. 1170.

On 24 June 1963 Zanzibar became an internal self-governing state and on 9 Dec. 1963 she became independent. On 24 June 1963 the Legislative Council was replaced by a National Assembly.

On 12 Jan. 1964 the sultanate was overthrown and the sultan sent into exile by a revolt of the Afro-Shirazi Party leaders who established the People's Republic of Zanzibar.

On 26 April 1964 Tanganyika, Zanzibar and Pemba combined to form the United Republic of Tanganyika and Zanzibar (named Tanzania on 29 Oct.).

AREA AND POPULATION. Tanzania is bounded north-east by Kenya, north by Lake Victoria and Uganda, north-west by Rwanda and Burundi, west by Lake Tanganyika, south-west by Zambia and Malawi and south by Mozambique. Total area 945,050 sq. km (364,886 sq. miles). The census of Aug. 1978 gave 17,551,925 for the United Republic, of which 17,076,270 were counted in mainland Tanzania and 475,655 in Zanzibar. Estimate (1983) 19·73m. There were also (1984) about 180,000 refugees living in Tanzania.

The chief towns (1978 census populations) are Dar es Salaam, the chief port and former capital (757,346), Zanzibar Town (110,669), Mwanza (110,611), Dodoma, the capital (45,703), Tanga (103,409), Arusha (55,281), Mbeya (76,606), Morogoro (61,890), Mtwara (48,510), Tabora (67,392), Iringa (57,182), and Kigoma (50,044).

The populations of the 22 regions were as follows at the 1978 Census:

Arusha	928,478	Mara	723,295	Rukwa	451,897
Dar es Salaam	851,522	Mbeya	1,080,241	Ruvuma	564,113
Dodoma	971,921	Morogoro	939,190	Shinyanga	1,323,482
Iringa	922,801	Mtwara	771,726	Singida	614,030
Kagera	1,009,379	Mwanza	1,443,418	Tabora	818,049
Kigoma	648,950	Pemba	205,850	Tanga	1,088,592
Kilimanjaro	902,394	Pwani	516,949	Zanzibar	273,365
Lindi	527,902				

Kiswahili is the national language.

CLIMATE. The climate is very varied and is controlled very largely by altitude and distance from the sea. There are three climatic zones: the hot and humid coast, the drier central plateau with seasonal variations of temperature, and the semi-temperate mountains. Dodoma. Jan. 75°F (23·9°C), July 67°F (19·4°C). Annual rainfall 23″ (572 mm). Dar es Salaam. Jan. 82°F (27·8°C), July 74°F (23·3°C). Annual rainfall 43″ (1,064 mm).

CONSTITUTION AND GOVERNMENT. A new Constitution was approved in April 1977. The country is a one-party state. The Tanganyika African National Union and the Afro-Shirazi Party in Zanzibar merged into one revolutionary party, *Chama cha Mapinduzi,* in Jan. 1977.

The President of the United Republic is head of state, chairman of the party and commander-in-chief of the armed forces. The vice-president is head of the executive in Zanzibar and vice-chairman of the party; the Prime Minister is also the leader of the National Assembly.

The National Assembly is composed of 111 elected members, 32 Parliament Members from the Zanzibar Revolutionary Council, 20 Nominated Members from Zanzibar, 25 National Members representing regions, 15 National Members representing mass organizations affiliated to the party, 10 Nominated Members from the mainland and 25 regional secretaries who are *ex-officio* members.

In Dec. 1979 a separate Constitution for Zanzibar was approved. Although at present (1981) under the same Constitution as Tanzania, Zanzibar has, in fact, been ruled by decree since 1964.

The Government was in March 1984 composed as follows:

President of the United Republic: Dr Julius K. Nyerere (re-elected for a further 5-year term in Oct. 1980). Presidential elections take place in April 1985.

Vice-President: Ali Hassan Mwinyi. *Prime Minister:* Salim Ahmed Salim. *Finance:* Cleopa Msuya. *Planning and Economic Affairs:* Kighoma Malima. *Foreign Affairs:* Salim Amour. *Defence and National Service:* Muhidin Kimaryo. *Agriculture and Livestock Development:* John Machunda. *Labour and Manpower Development:* Daudi Mwakawago. *Industry and Trade:* Basil Mramba. *Land, Natural Resources and Tourism:* Paul Bomani. *Water, Energy and Minerals:* Al Noor Kassum. *Communications and Works:* John Malecela. *National Education:* Jackson Makwetta. *Health:* Aaron Chiduo. *Justice:* Joseph Warioba.

National flag: Divided diagonally green, black, blue, with the black strip edged in yellow.

DEFENCE

Army. The Army consists of 8 infantry brigades; 1 tank, 2 artillery, 2 anti-aircraft, 2 mortar, 1 surface-to-air missile, 2 anti-tank and 2 signals battalions. Equipment includes 30 Chinese Type-59 main battle tanks. Strength (1985) 38,500. There is also a Citizen's Militia of 50,000 men.

Navy. There are 10 fast gunboats (7 *ex*-Chinese and 3 *ex*-GDR), 4 *ex*-Chinese fast torpedo hydrofoil boats, 4 *ex*-North Korean patrol craft, 4 *ex*-Chinese coastal patrol boats, 1 survey launch, 1 research vessel and 2 *ex*-Chinese minor landing craft. Personnel in 1985 totalled some 700.

Air Force. The Tanzanian People's Defence Force Air Wing was built up initially with the help of Canada, but combat equipment is now being acquired from China. Personnel totalled about 950 in 1983, with about 15 F-7 (MiG-21), 10 F-6 (MiG-19) and 3 F-5 (MiG-17) jet fighters; 1 F28 Fellowship VIP transport; 6 Buffalo twin-engined STOL transports; 3 HS 748 and some An-26 and An-32 turboprop transports; 2 Cessna 404 liaison aircraft; 2 Agusta-built Chinook helicopters; 6 Agusta-Bell JetRanger and 2 Bell 47G light helicopters; and Piper Cherokee, Cessna 310, L-39 Albatross and FT-5 (Chinese-built MiG-17) trainers.

INTERNATIONAL RELATIONS

Membership. Tanzania is a member of UN, OAU, the Commonwealth and is an ACP state of EEC.

ECONOMY

Planning. The fourth 5-year development (1981–86) plan envisages investment of Sh. 40,200m. and a growth rate of 6%.

Budget. Revenue and expenditure (in Tanzanian Sh. 1m.) for financial years ending 30 June:

	1979–80	*1980–81*	*1981–82*	*1982–83*[1]	*1983–84*[1]
Revenue	7,270·0	12,296·1	10,460	10,700	12,500
Expenditure	9,100·0	14,802·4	13,687	14,144	15,620

[1]Estimate.

Development expenditure, 1983–84 (estimate), was Sh. 5,830m.

Currency. The monetary unit is the *Tanzanian shilling* divided into 100 *cents*. The Tanzanian coinage has denominations of 5, 10, 20, 50 cents, 1 Sh., 5 Sh., 20 Sh. and 1,500 Sh.; notes, 10 Sh., 20 Sh. and 100 Sh. In March 1985, £1 = Sh. 19·86; US$ = Sh. 18·50.

Banking. On 14 June 1966 the central bank called the Bank of Tanzania, with a government-owned capital of Sh. 20m., began operations.

On 6 Feb. 1967 all commercial banks with the exception of National Co-operative Banks were nationalized and their interests vested in the National Bank of Commerce on the mainland and the Peoples' Bank in Zanzibar.

Weights. Tanzania has adopted the International System of Weights and Measures (SI), which has been introduced progressively since 1969. An important local unit of weight is the frasla (or frasila) = 35 lb. av.

ENERGY AND NATURAL RESOURCES

Electricity. A hydro-electric station on the Pangani River near Tanga has been built; £3m. of its estimated cost of £5·25m. is being provided by the Commonwealth Development Corporation. The second phase of the Kidatu power-station in Morogoro region is nearing completion; total power generated, 200 mw. Kiwira River power project, estimated to cost Sh.55m., has been completed, total capacity 24 mw. The Musoma power-station has also been completed with a capacity of 6 mw. The Mbeya-Iyunga power-station, capacity 12·5 mw, was completed in 1981.

Minerals. Production (1981): Diamonds, 237,000 carats; gold, ...; salt (1980) 33,000 tonnes; gemstones (1980) 3,052 kg. New discoveries of coal and iron ore were made in the south while copper, cobalt, nickel and tin deposits have been found in Western Tanganyika. Gas, at shallow depths, has been found off the coast.

Agriculture. Production of main agricultural crops in 1981 (in 1,000 tons) was: Maize, 750; sisal, 81; cotton, 167; sugar, 1,287; coffee, 68; wheat, 70; tobacco, 21. Production of sisal has been declining since 1967. The Tanganyika Sisal Corporation has embarked on a diversification programme by introducing various new crops. Crops already planned are cardamon, beans, cashew nuts, citrus, cocoa, coconuts, cotton, maize and timber. Cattle ranching, dairying and twine spinning have also been introduced.

Zanzibar provides the greater part of the world's supply of cloves. There are about 40,000 hectares under cloves with about 1·5m. trees; five-sixths of the clove output is produced on Pemba. Cloves and clove oil (distilled from the stems) form more than half Zanzibar's exports. In recent years cloves production has decreased from an average annual figure of 12,000 tons to 4,000 in 1974 but reached 10,000 tons in 1976.

The coconut industry ranks next in importance. There are about 5·5m. bearing trees in both islands. Chillies, cocoa, limes, other tropical fruits and coil tobacco are also cultivated. The chief food crops are rice, bananas, cassava, pulses, maize and sorghum.

Livestock (1983, including Zanzibar): 13,446,000 cattle, 4·02m. sheep, 6,031,000 goats, 19m. poultry.

Forestry. Total production (1981) 60,000 cu. metres.

Fisheries. A Fisheries Development Co. is catching sardines and tuna for export. Catch (1981) 226,000 tonnes of which, inland waters, 190,000 tonnes.

INDUSTRY AND TRADE

Industry. Industry is limited and is mainly textiles, petroleum and chemical products, food processing, tobacco and brewing.

Commerce. Total trade (in Sh. 1m.):

	1976	*1977*	*1978*	*1979*	*1980*	*1981*
Imports	5,350	6,200	8,582	8,941	10,047	10,065
Exports	4,108	4,537	3,514	4,296	4,165	5,248

In 1980, 17% of imports came from UK, 10% from Federal Republic of Germany, 9% from Japan, 6% Iraq, 6% Netherlands, and 6% USA; 18% of exports went to UK, 13% to Federal Republic of Germany, and 10% to Indonesia.

Major export items 1981 (in Sh. 1m.): Coffee, 1,456; cotton, 689; sisal, 291; cloves, 417; tea, 182; tobacco, 165.

Total trade between Tanzania and UK (British Department of Trade returns, in £1,000 sterling):

	1981	*1982*	*1983*	*1984*
Imports to UK	25,290	19,521	46,525	43,179
Exports and re-exports from UK	83,643	71,985	62,056	60,440

Tourism. In 1982 about 71,000 tourists visited Tanzania.

COMMUNICATIONS

Roads. In 1980 there were 45,631 km of roads and (1981) 43,248 cars and 27,000 commercial vehicles.

Railways. On 23 Sept. 1977 the independent Tanzanian Railway Corporation was formed following the break-up of the East African Railways administration. The network totals 2,600 km (metre-gauge), excluding the Tan-Zam Railway 969 km in Tanzania (1,067 mm gauge) operated by a separate administration. In 1980, the state railway carried 2.6m. passengers and 1.2m. tonnes of freight while in 1982–83 the Tan-Zam Railway carried 970,000 tonnes of freight and 564,000 passengers.

Aviation. There are 53 aerodromes and landing strips maintained or licensed by Government; of these, 2 are of international standards category (Dar es Salaam and Kilimanjaro) and 18 are suitable for Dakotas. Air Tanzania Corporation provide regular and frequent services to all the more important towns within the territory and to Mozambique, Zambia, Seychelles, Comoro, Rwanda, Burundi and Madagascar.

There is an all-weather landing-ground in Zanzibar and a smaller all-weather landing-ground in Pemba.

Shipping. In 1980 there were 1,296 ships of 3,176,000 NRT.

Post and Broadcasting. In 1982 there were 96,521 telephones. There are 2 broadcasting stations and colour television operates in Zanzibar. In 1984 there were 9,000 television receivers (on Zanzibar only) and 2m. radio receivers.

Newspapers (1985). There were 3 dailies, 2 weeklies and several monthly magazines.

JUSTICE, RELIGION, EDUCATION AND WELFARE

Justice. The Tanzanian Court of Appeal, which in Sept. 1979 replaced the former Court of Appeal for East Africa, comprises a Chief Justice and 4 Judges of Appeal. The High Court sits regularly in all Regions, but there is a District Court in each District (presided over by a Resident Magistrate) which hears appeals from the more than 800 Primary Courts with jurisdiction over customary and Islamic law.

Religion. In 1984 some 40% were Christian, including Roman Catholics under the Archbishops of Dar es Salaam and Tabora, Anglicans under the Archbishop of Tanzania, and Lutherans. Moslems amount to 33%, but reach 66% in the coastal towns; Zanzibar is 96% Moslem and 4% Hindu. Some 23% follow traditional religions.

Education. The educational system has been integrated on non-racial lines. Schools are maintained by the Government, private and agencies, including missions.

In 1981 there were 9,980 primary schools with 3,538,183 pupils.

Technical and vocational education is provided at several secondary and technical schools and at the Dar es Salaam Technical College.

There were, in 1981, 35 colleges of national education, including the college at Chang'ombe for secondary-school teachers, with 14,785 students and (1980) 170 secondary schools with 9,178 pupils. Five technical secondary schools had 3,129 students in 1981.

The University of Dar es Salaam, independent since 1970, has faculties of science, law, arts, social sciences, medicine, agriculture, engineering, commerce and management, veterinary science and forestry and had 3,780 students in 1982.

Health. In 1981 there were 599 doctors and 149 hospitals with 21,352 beds.

DIPLOMATIC REPRESENTATIVES

Of Tanzania in Great Britain (43 Hertford St., London, W1)
High Commissioner: Anthony Balthazar Nyakyi (accredited 15 Dec. 1982).

Of Great Britain in Tanzania (Hifadhi Hse., Samora Ave., Dar es Salaam)
High Commissioner: John Sankey, CMG.

Of Tanzania in the USA (2139 R St., NW, Washington, D.C., 20008)
Ambassador: Benjamin W. Mkapa.

Of the USA in Tanzania (36 Laibon Rd., Dar es Salaam)
Ambassador: David C. Miller, Jr.

Of Tanzania to the United Nations
Ambassador: Muhammad Ali Foum.

Books of Reference

Atlas of Tanganyika. 3rd ed. Dar es Salaam, 1956
Tanganyika Notes and Records. Tanganyika Society, Dar es Salaam. (Twice yearly, from 1936) *The Economic Development of Tanganyika. Report . . . by the International Bank.* Johns Hopkins Univ. Press and OUP, 1961
Ayany, S. G., *A History of Zanzibar.* Nairobi, 1970
Coulson, A., *Tanzania: A Political Economy.* OUP, 1982
Ingle, C. R., *From Village to State in Tanzania.* London, 1973
Mwansasu, B., *Towards Socialism in Tanzania.* Univ. of Toronto Press, 1979
Nellis, J. R., *A Theory of Ideology: The Tanzanian Example.* New York, OUP, 1972
Nyerere, J., *Freedom and Development.* New York, 1976
Resnick, I. N., *The Long Transition: Building Socialism in Tanzania.* New York and London, 1981
Samoff, J., *Tanzania: Local Politics and the Structure of Power.* Univ. of Wisconsin Press, 1975
Yeager, R., *Tanzania: An African Experiment.* Aldershot, 1982
Yu, G. T., *China's African Policy: A Study of Tanzania.* New York, 1975

THAILAND

Capital: Bangkok
Population: 50m. (1984)
GNP per capita: US$770 (1981)

Prathes Thai, or Muang-Thai

HISTORY. Until 24 June 1932 Siam was an absolute monarchy. On that date a *coup d'état* was effected and a Provisional Constitution Act was promulgated on 27 June. This was replaced by the constitution of 10 Dec. 1932, which in turn was superseded by new constitutions.

AREA AND POPULATION. The area of Thailand is 514,000 sq. km (198,250 sq. miles) and is bounded west by Burma and the Indian Ocean, east by the Gulf of Thailand, Cambodia and east and north by Laos.

At the census taken in 1979 the registration gave a population of 45,221,625 (22,775,852 males, 22,445,773 females), of whom 30·4% lived in the Central region, 35·2% in the North-East region, 12·5% in the South region, 21·9% in the North region. Estimate (1984) 50,060,477 (24,873,337 females).

Vital statistics, 1981: Births, 1,062,238 (518,836 females); deaths, 239,423 (98,494 females).

Thailand is divided into 72 provinces. Bangkok Metropolis is the capital (population 1982, 5,468,286). Other towns (1979 estimate) are Chiang Mai (105,230), Nakhon Ratchasima (87,371), Khon Kaen, (80,286), Udon Thani (76,173), Pitsanulok (73,175), Hat Yai (67,117), Songkhla (65,523), Nakhon Si Thammarat (61,049), Nakhon Sawan (55,741).

CLIMATE. The climate is tropical, with high temperatures and humidity. Over most of the country, 3 seasons may be recognized. The rainy season is June to Oct., the cool season from Nov. to Feb. and the hot season is March to May. Rainfall is generally heaviest in the south and lightest in the north east.

Bangkok. Jan. 78°F (25·6°C), July 83°F (28·3°C). Annual rainfall 56" (1,400 mm).

REIGNING KING. Bhumibol Adulyadej, born 5 Dec. 1927, younger brother of King Ananda Mahidol, who died on 9 June 1946. King Bhumibol married on 28 April 1950 Princess Sirikit, and was crowned 5 May 1950. Children: Princess Ubol Ratana (born 5 April 1951, married Aug. 1972 Peter Ladd Jensen), Crown-Prince Vajiralongkorn (born 28 July 1952, married 3 Jan. 1977 Soamsawali Kitiyakra), Princess Maha Chakri Sirindhorn (born 2 April 1955), Princess Chulabhorn (born 4 July 1957, married 27 Jan. 1982 Virayudth Didyasarin).

CONSTITUTION AND GOVERNMENT. The military government resigned on 14 Oct. 1973 and a new government was formed. New Constitutions were enacted on 7 Oct. 1974 and on 9 Nov. 1977. However on 20 Oct. 1977 a further military *coup* took place in order to return more swiftly to democracy. A new Constitution designed to restore democracy was promulgated in Dec. 1978 and elections took place on 22 April 1979. Elections were held in April 1983.

The cabinet in Aug. 1983 was composed as follows:

Prime Minister: Gen. Prem Tinsulanonda.

Deputy Prime Minister: Gen. Prachuab Soontarangkun; Boontheng Thongsawasdi; Bhichai Rattakul; Adm. Sonthi Boonyachai. *Defence:* Gen. Prem Tinsulanonda. *Finance:* Sommai Hoontrakul. *Foreign Affairs:* Air Chief Marshal Siddhi Savetsila. *Agriculture and Co-operatives:* Narong Wongwan. *Communications:* Samak Sundaravej. *Commerce:* Kosol Krairiksh. *Interior:* Gen. Sitthi

Chirarochana. *Justice:* Phipop Asitirat. *Education:* Chuan Leekpai. *Public Health:* Marut Bunnag. *Industry:* Ob Vasuratna. *Science, Technology and Energy:* Damrong Lathaphipat. *University Affairs:* Preeda Pathanathabutr.

National flag: Five horizontal stripes of red, white, blue, white, red, with the blue of double width.

Local Government. For purposes of administration Thailand is divided into 72 provinces *(changwads)*, each under the control of a *changwad* governor. The *changwads* are subdivided into 576 districts *(amphurs)* and 80 sub-districts *(king amphurs)*, 5,317 communes *(tambons)* and 49,841 villages *(moobans)*. Local legislative and executive bodies with limited powers are being established with functions, procedure and method of election modelled on those of central Assembly.

DEFENCE. Under the Ministry of Defence Organization Act of 1960 the Ministry of Defence has assumed the Supreme Command and the control of the Army, Navy and Air Force with the advice of the Defence Council headed by the Ministry of Defence. The National Defence College, the Armed Forces Staff College and the Military Preparatory School serve the education of officers. Each service has its own C.-in-C., service council, schools of arms and Command and General Staff College.

Under the Military Service Act of 1954 every able-bodied man between the ages of 21 and 30 is liable to serve 2 years with the colours; 7 years in the first reserve; 10 years in the second reserve; 6 years in the third reserve.

Army. The Army is organized in 4 Regions and consists of 1 cavalry, 1 armoured, 7 infantry, 1 special forces, 1 artillery and 1 anti-aircraft divisions; 11 engineer and 8 independent infantry battalions; and 4 reconnaissance companies. Equipment includes 55 M-48A5 main battle tanks. There is also an Army Aviation force. Strength (1985) 160,000, with 500,000 reserves.

Navy. The Fleet includes 4 frigates (1 modern built in Britain, 2 very old *ex*-US, and 1 very old *ex*-US destroyer escort), 2 corvettes (small frigates), 3 fast large attack gunboats, 6 fast missile craft, 4 coastal minesweepers, 10 patrol vessels, 1 mine counter-measures support ship, 20 gunboats, 24 coastal patrol boats, 8 landing ships, 13 landing craft, 42 minor landing craft, 5 minesweeping boats, 3 surveying ships, 3 surveying boats, 40 river patrol craft, 2 transports, 3 oilers, 3 training ships (old frigate, old corvette, old escort minesweeper), 2 transports, 2 water carriers and 4 tugs. There are 13 naval aircraft.

Two missile-armed corvettes are under construction by Tacoma and a third planned to be built in Thailand.

Naval personnel in 1985 totalled 30,000, including the Marine Corps. There is a Royal Naval Academy at Paknam.

At the mouth of the Chao Praya River are the Paknam forts. The naval dockyard was reconstructed.

The coast guard force operates 4 patrol vessels, 3 coastal patrol craft, 8 river patrol boats and a considerable number of service craft.

Air Force. The Royal Thai Air Force was reorganized with the assistance of a US Military Air Advisory Group. It has a strength of about 43,100 personnel, and is made up of a headquarters and Combat, Logistics Support, Training and Special Services Groups. The 3 squadrons of 1st Wing form the primary combat element, equipped with 40 F-5A/B/E/F supersonic fighter-bombers, some of the 45 OV-10C Bronco light reconnaissance/attack aircraft, and 18 T-33A/RT-33A and 4 RF-5A armed reconnaissance aircraft acquired from the USA. Six light attack squadrons in 2nd Wing operate the other OV-10Cs, about 20 T-28 armed piston-engined trainers, 12 A-37B light jet attack aircraft and 25 AU-23A Peacemakers, for security duties. There are transport units equipped with a total of about 70 C-130H/H-30 Hercules, DC-8-62F, HS 748, C-123B Provider, C-47 and smaller aircraft, including 20 Australian-built Missionmasters; training units with Airtrainer CT/4 primary trainers built in New Zealand, Italian-built SF.260MTs,

T-37 intermediate and T-33A advanced trainers; and large numbers of helicopters for assault and rescue duties. In 1984, delivery began of 31 Model 400 and 16 Model 600 Fantrainers, of which the first 6 will be built in the Federal Republic of Germany, the remainder partially manufactured and assembled in Thailand.

INTERNATIONAL RELATIONS

Planning. The Fifth National Development Plan, 1982–86 envisages a more equal distribution of income between the urban and rural population.

Membership. Thailand is a member of UN, ASEAN and the Colombo Plan.

ECONOMY

Budget. Ordinary expenditures in 1985 (in 1m. baht): Defence, 39,378; agriculture, 17,198; communications, 11,139; education, 34,294; public health, 9,508.

Revenue in 1980 derived from taxes and duties, sales and charges and government enterprises, 114,835m. baht.

In 1980 the national internal debt was 109,780·6m. baht and the external debt totalled 80,508·7m. baht.

Currency. The unit of currency is the *baht*, formerly called in English the *tical*, which is divided into 100 *satang*. Silver coins have gone out of circulation. Only nickel, copper, tin and bronze coins are now minted, in denominations of 1, 5 *baht*, 50, 25, 10 and 5 *satang*. Currency notes, first issued in 1902, now comprise, 5, 10, 20, 100, 500 *baht* notes.

On 31 March 1976 the total amount of notes and coins in circulation was 30,280m. baht.

In March 1985, £1 = 29·85 *baht*; US$1 = 28·25 *baht*.

Banking. In 1942 the Bank of Thailand was established under the Bank of Thailand Act, B.E. 2485 (1942) and began operations on 10 Dec. 1942, with the functions of a central bank. The Bank was organized on similar lines to the Bank of England, having its banking activities entirely separate from the management of the note issue. The Bank also took over the note issue previously performed by the Treasury Department of the Ministry of Finance. Although the entire capital is owned by the Government, the Bank is an independent body. Its gold and foreign-exchange reserves, at the end of Dec. 1973, amounted to US$1,082m.

In Jan. 1966 the Agricultural Bank and the Provincial Bank merged in the Krung Thai Bank (capital 105m. baht, of which 80% is owned by the Government).

Banks incorporated under Thai law include the Bangkok Bank Ltd, the Bangkok Bank of Commerce Ltd, the Bank of Asia for Industry & Commerce Ltd, the Bank of Ayudhya Ltd, Bangkok Metropolitan Bank Ltd, the Laem Thong Bank Ltd, the Siam City Bank Ltd, the Siam Commercial Bank Ltd, First Bangkok City Bank Ltd, Union Bank of Bangkok Ltd and the Wang Lee Chan Bank Ltd. Foreign banks include the Chartered Bank, the Hongkong and Shanghai Banking Corporation, the Mercantile Bank Ltd, Banque de l'Indochine, Bank of Canton Ltd, Bank of China Ltd, Bank of America, N.T. & S.A., the Mitsui Bank Ltd, The Asia Trust Bank Ltd, Bharat Overseas Bank Ltd, The Chase Manhattan Bank, United Malayan Banking Corporation and the Bank of Tokyo Ltd.

The commercial Thai banks had, in 1981, 1,484 branches in Thailand and 12 abroad; only Mae Hongson province has no commercial bank services. The deposits held by commercial banks in Nov. 1983 amounted to 407,597m. baht.

The Government Savings Bank, which was established as an independent organization in 1947, originated in 1913 when the Government Savings Office was established.

Weights and Measures. The metric system was made compulsory by a law promulgated on 17 Dec. 1923. The actual weights and measures prescribed by law are: Units of weight: 1 *standard picul* = 60 kg; 1 *standard catty* (1/100 picul) = 600 grammes; 1 *standard carat* = 20 centigrammes. Units of length: 1 *sen* = 40 metres; 1 *wah* (1/20 sen) = 2 metres; 1 *sauk* (1/2 wah) = 0·50 metre; 1 *keup* (1/2 sauk) = 0·25 metre. Units of square measure: 1 *rai* (1 sq. sen) = 1,600 sq. metres: 1 *ngan* (1/2 rai) = 400 sq. metres; 1 *sq. wah* (1/100 ngan) = 4 sq. metres. Units of capacity: 1 *standard kwien* = 2,000 litres; 1 *standard ban* (1/2 kwien) = 1,000 litres; 1 *standard sat* (1/50 ban) = 20 litres; 1 *standard tannan* (1/20 sat) = 1 litre.

Legislation passed in 1940 provided that the calendar year shall coincide with the Christian Year, and that the year of the Buddhist era 2484 shall begin on 1 Jan. 1941. (The New Year's Day was previously 1 April.) The years B.E. 2514–2518 therefore correspond to A.D. 1974 and 1975.

ENERGY AND NATURAL RESOURCES

Electricity. In 1981, steam power accounted for 52% of production (81% of the fuel being imported) and 34% hydro-electric. Only 20% of the population had access to electricity on 31 Dec. 1976.

Oil. Thailand is heavily dependent on oil. Extensive oil and gas exploration in the Gulf of Thailand were producing commercial quantities of 5,000 bbls a day in 1983.

Minerals. The mineral resources are extensive and varied, including cassiterite (tin ore), wolfram, scheelite, antimony, coal, copper, gold, iron, lead, manganese, molybdenum, rubies, sapphires, silver, zinc and zircons. By far the most important are tin and wolfram. Ore output in 1982 (in tonnes): Iron, 26,750; manganese, 7,746; tin, 35,644; lead, 43,718; antimony, 1,595; wolfram, 1,661; lignite, 1,963,764; gypsum, 753,433.

Agriculture. The chief produce of the country is rice, which forms the national food and the staple article of export. The area under paddy is about 18m. acres. With the completion of the Chao Phya dam located near Chainat in 1957 the irrigable area in the Central Plain had by 1962 been extended to about 8,409,000 rai (3,363,600 acres). Additional projects now under construction will bring the irrigable lands to the total of about 11,605,900 rai (4,642,360 acres). Tank irrigation projects which were designed to ensure water supply for upland crop cultivation, especially in the north-eastern part, irrigate 325,418 rai (130,167 acres).

Output of the major crops in 1982 was (in 1,000 tonnes): Paddy (1981), 19,000; maize, 4,200; sugar-cane, 27,000; kenaf, 270; tobacco, 50; tapioca-root, 16,000; soybeans, 150; coconut, 750; mung beans, 275; cotton, 250; groundnuts, 158.

Livestock, 1983 (in 1,000): horses, 19; buffaloes, 6,150; cattle, 4,600; pigs, 3,800; poultry, 65,000.

Forestry. About 60% of the land area of Thailand is under forest. In the north, mixed deciduous forests with teak *(Tectona grandis, Linn.)*, growing in mixture with several other species, predominate. In the north-eastern section hardwood of the *Dipterocarpus* species, especially *Shorea obtusa* and *Pentacme Siamensis, Kurz* exist in most parts. In all other regions of the country tropical evergreen forests are found, with the well-known timber of commerce, Yang (*Dipterocarpus alatus, Roxb* and *Dipterocarpus* spp.) as the outstanding crops. Most of the teak timber exploited in northern Thailand is floated down to Bangkok. Some, however, is exported through the Salween into Burma.

About one-third of the teak-forest area is being exploited by the Forest Industry Organization, and the remaining two-thirds is to be worked by timber company lessees and other private enterprises.

Output of main forestry products in 1981 was (in 1,000 tonnes): Teak, 60·9; yang and other woods, 1,807·7; firewood, 638·6; charcoal, 141·5.

Rubber production (in 1,000 tonnes), 1955, 133·3; 1960, 170·8; 1969, 281·8, 1973, 384; 1978, 467; 1979, 531; 1980, 501; 1981, 510; 1982, 540.

Fisheries. In 1981 the catch of sea fish was 1,415,600 tonnes; of freshwater fish, 161,200 tonnes, and (1979) of marine prawns, shrimps and crabs, 116,500 tonnes.

INDUSTRY AND TRADE

Industry. Production of manufactured goods in 1978 included 5,004,490 tonnes of cement, 46,818 tonnes of white cement, 1,584,453 tonnes of sugar, 149·8m. gunny bags, 39,721 tonnes of paper, 95,363 tonnes of sweetened condensed milk, 15,830 tonnes of evaporated milk, 108·3m. litres of beer, 875m. sq. yd of cotton textiles, 887·2m. sq. yd of man-made textiles, 4,673,432 sheets of plywood and 1,166,614 sq. metres of vinyl tiles.

Trade Unions. The Thai National Trade Union Congress is a member of the International Confederation of Free Trade Unions.

Commerce. The foreign trade (in 1m. baht) was as follows:

	1978	*1979*	*1980*	*1981*	*1982*	*1983*
Imports (c.i.f.)	108,899	146,161	188,686	216,746	193,332	217,475
Exports (f.o.b.)	83,065	108,179	133,197	153,001	157,203	146,438

In 1983 the main imports (in 1m. baht, provisional): Fuels and lubricants, 53,741; machinery, 26,379; base metals, 18,681; electrical machinery and parts, 17,940; vehicles and parts, 13,539; chemicals, 13,362.

In 1983 the main items of export (in 1m. baht, provisional): Rice, 20,135; crude materials, 16,270; tapioca products, 15,387; miscellaneous goods, 15,054; rubber, 11,822; maize, 8,485; machinery, 8,383; sugar, 6,331; tin, 5,263.

In 1981 imports from Japan (24%), Saudi Arabia (14%), USA (13%), Singapore (7%). Exports to Japan (14%), USA (13%), Netherlands (12%) and Singapore (8%).

Total trade between Thailand and UK (British Department of Trade returns, in £1,000 sterling):

	1980	*1981*	*1982*	*1983*	*1984*
Imports to UK	52,004	56,343	76,529	87,823	112,353
Exports and re-exports from UK	96,926	91,473	104,825	131,833	149,742

Tourism. In 1983 2,191,003 foreigners visited Thailand spending 24,600m. baht.

COMMUNICATIONS

Roads. In 1982 the length of highways and provincial roads open to traffic was approximately 44,200 km, of which about 13,226 km (1978) were concrete or asphalt-surfaced. Motor vehicles registered in 1981 included 432,312 passenger cars, 32,114 buses (1979), 419,143 lorries (1979) and 1,169,324 motor cycles.

Railways. In 1982 there were 3,735 km of state railways (metre gauge) open to traffic.

The northern line runs from Bangkok to Chiang Mai (741 km), the extreme northern terminus. The southern line (990 km) runs from Bangkok down the Peninsula to the frontier station of Padang Besar, where it connects with the Malayan railway from Penang, and to Singapore. Another line (214 km) branching off from Haad Yai on the southern line runs along the east coast of the peninsula to Su-gnai Kolok, where it connects with the Malayan railway line. There are branch lines (totalling 190 km) to Song Khla, Nakhon-Si Thammarat, Kan Tang and Tha-Kanon. The extensions of the north-eastern line (264 km) from Nakhon Ratsima (Korat) to Nong Khai (360 km) and from Kaeng Koi to Buayai (250 km) have been completed. The Nakhon Ratsima–Ubol line (311 km) has been completed as far as Ubol Rat Thani. The eastern line (255 km) runs from Makkasan to Aran Pradet on the Kampuchea frontier. The northern and southern railway systems are linked by a railway bridge over the Menam Chao Phya, and both systems terminate in Bangkok. All state railways are under one management and in 1983 carried 81·4m. passengers and 5·3m. tonnes of freight. A new line to the port of Sattahip opened in 1984.

Aviation. Thai Airways Co. Ltd (TAC), established in 1947, is the sole Thai air transport enterprise, with authorized capital of 300m. baht. The Company operates 11 domestic routes and 3 international routes. On 24 Aug. 1959 Thai Airways and the Scandinavian Airlines System set up a new company, Thai International Airways, to operate the international air services from Thailand. In 1981–82, more than 2m. passengers were carried.

Shipping. In 1981, 2,851 vessels of 12,135,183 NRT entered and 2,424 of 10,689,607 NRT cleared the port of Bangkok.

The port of Bangkok, about 30 km from the mouth of the Chao Phya River, is capable of berthing ocean-going vessels of 10,000 gross tons and 28 ft draught. Bangkok is now a port of entry for Laos, and goods arriving in transit are sent up by rail to Nong Khai and ferried across the river Mekhong to Vientiane.

Post and Broadcasting. In 1974 there were 555 post offices proper, 341 licensed and Amphur post offices and 545 railway-station post offices. In 1967, the length of telegraph lines was 21,203 km. In 1982 there were 529,106 telephones, of which 389,852 were in Bangkok.

In 1981, there were 265 radio stations and 9 television stations.

Cinemas (1983). There were 651 cinemas with a seating capacity of 438,787.

Newspapers (1984). There are 28 daily newspapers in Bangkok, including 3 in English and 6 in Chinese, with a combined circulation of more than 800,000.

JUSTICE, RELIGION, EDUCATION AND WELFARE

Justice. The judicial power is exercised in the name of the King, by *(a)* courts of first instance, *(b)* the court of appeal *(Uthorn)* and *(c)* the Supreme Court *(Dika)*. The King appoints, transfers and dismisses judges, who are independent in conducting trials and giving judgment in accordance with the law.

Courts of first instance are subdivided into 20 magistrates' courts *(Kwaeng)* with limited civil and minor criminal jurisdiction; 85 provincial courts *(Changwad)* with unlimited civil and criminal jurisdiction; the criminal and civil courts with exclusive jurisdiction in Bangkok; the central juvenile courts for persons under 18 years of age in Bangkok.

The court of appeal exercises appellate jurisdiction in civil and criminal cases from all courts of first instance. From it appeals lie to Dika Court on any point of law and, in certain cases, on questions of fact.

The Supreme Court is the supreme tribunal of the land. Besides its normal appellate jurisdiction in civil and criminal matters, it has semi-original jurisdiction over general election petitions. The decisions of Dika Court are final. Every person has the right to present a petition to the Government who will deal with all matters of grievance.

Religion. About 95% of the population are Buddhists, 4% Moslems, 1% Christians, Hindus and others.

Education. Primary education is compulsory for children between the ages of 7–14 and free in local municipal schools. In 1978 there were 7,612,534 students enrolled in 31,966 government schools and 1,119,528 in 2,327 private schools. In 1977 there were 45 teachers' training schools with 4,986 teachers and 115,117 students and 180 government vocational schools with 8,100 teachers and 147,997 students. In 1978 there were 12 universities: Chulalongkorn University (1917), Thammasat University (1934), Universities of Medical Science, Agriculture and Fine Arts; Ramkamhaeng University (1971)—all in Bangkok; Chiengmai University (1964), the Khon Kaen University (1966) in the north-east and Prince of Songkhla University (1968) in the south.

Health. In 1982 there were 434 hospitals and 6,496 health centres throughout the country. In 1982 there were 6,550 physicians, 1,122 dentists and (1977) 2,236 pharmacists.

DIPLOMATIC REPRESENTATIVES

Of Thailand in Great Britain (30 Queen's Gate, London, SW7 5JB)
Ambassador: Dr Owart Suthiwart-Narueput, CMG.

Of Great Britain in Thailand (Wireless Rd., Bangkok)
Ambassador: Justin Staples, CMG.

Of Thailand in the USA (2300 Kalorama Rd., NW, Washington, D.C., 20008)
Ambassador: M. R. Kasem S. Kasemsri.

Of the USA in Thailand (95 Wireless Rd., Bangkok)
Ambassador: John Gunther Dean.

Of Thailand to the United Nations
Ambassador: M. L. Birabhongse Kasemsri.

Books of Reference

Thailand into the 80's. Office of the Prime Minister, Bangkok, 1979
Thailand Statistical Yearbook. National Statistical Office, Bangkok
Thailand 1982: Plans, Problems and Prospects. Government's Public Relations Department, Bangkok, 1982
Thailand in Brief. Government's Public Relations Department, Bangkok, 1977
Bibliography of Materials About Thailand in Western Languages. Chulalongkorn University, Bangkok, 1960
Douner, W., *The Five Faces of Thailand.* Hamburg and London, 1978
Girling, J. I. S., *Thailand: Society and Politics.* Cornell Univ. Press, 1981
Haas, M. R., *Thai–English Student's Dictionary.* OUP, 1966
Morrell, D. and Samudavanija, C., *Political Conflict in Thailand.* Cambridge, Mass., 1981

TOGO

République Togolaise

Capital: Lomé
Population: 2·89m. (1984)
GNP per capita: US$380 (1981)

HISTORY. The Republic of Togo became independent on 27 April 1960, after having been a German protectorate (1894–1914, subsequently divided between the French and the British), a mandate of the League of Nations (20 July 1922) and a trusteeship territory of the United Nations (14 Dec. 1946).

On 28 Oct. 1956 a plebiscite was held to determine the status of the territory. Out of 438,175 registered voters, 313,458 voted for an autonomous republic within the French Union and the end of the trusteeship system. The trusteeship was abolished on the achievement of independence on 27 April 1960.

On 13 Jan. 1963 the President Sylvanus Olympio was murdered by n.c.o.s. of the army. Nicolas Grunitzky, a former prime minister and Olympio's brother-in-law, was appointed President of the Republic and head of government. On 13 Jan. 1967 in a bloodless *coup* the army under Col. Etienne Eyadéma made President Grunitzky 'voluntarily withdraw'. On 14 April 1967 Col. Eyadéma assumed the offices of President and Defence. There was a return to constitutional government in Jan. 1980.

AREA AND POPULATION. Togo is bounded west by Ghana, north by Burkina Faso, east by Benin and south by the Bight of Benin. Area, about 56,785 sq. km. The population of Togo in 1981 (census) was 2,703,000; 1984 (estimate) 2,890,000. The capital is Lomé (population, 1980, 283,000), other towns (1977, population) being Sokodé (33,500), Kpalimé (25,500), Atakpamé (21,800), Bassar (17,500), Tsévié (15,900) and Anécho (13,300).

The southern part of Togo is peopled by tribes using several different languages, of which the principal, Ewe and Mina, are languages of the Kwa group. The northern half contains, ethnologically, a totally different population descended largely from Hamitic tribes and speaking a fairly large number of different languages of the Voltaic (Gur) group, of which Dagomba, Tem and Kabre are the most important. French is the official language.

CLIMATE. The tropical climate produces wet seasons from March to July and from Oct. to Nov. in the south. The north has one wet season, from April to July. The heaviest rainfall occurs in the mountains of the west, south-west and centre. Lomé. Jan. 81°F (27·2°C), July 76°F (24·4°C). Annual rainfall 35″ (875 mm).

CONSTITUTION AND GOVERNMENT. Following approval in a referendum on 30 Dec. 1979, a new Constitution came into force on 13 Jan. 1980, when the Third Togolese Republic was proclaimed. It provides for an Executive President, directly elected for a 7-year term, and for a National Assembly of 67 deputies, elected on a regional list system for a 5-year term. Elections were held on 30 Dec. 1979.

All candidates are nominated by the *Rassemblement du peuple togolais*, the sole legal Party since 1969; it is administered by a 33-member Central Committee and a 9-member Political Bureau appointed by the President.

The government in Feb. 1985 was composed as follows:

President, Minister of Defence: Gen. Gnassingbe Eyadéma.

Foreign Affairs and Co-operation: Dr Anani Kuma Akakpo-Ahianyo. *Industry, Planning and Administrative Reform:* Koffi Walla. *Interior:* Kpotivi Têvi' Djidjogbé Laclé. *Economy and Finance:* Têtê Têvi Bénissan. *Public Works, Mines, Energy and Water Resources:* Barry Moussa Barque. *Health:* Hodabalo Bodjona. *Rural Development:* Anani Gassou. *Labour and Civil Service:* Nyandi Seibou

Napo. *Parliamentary Affairs:* Mme. Massa Dagadzi. *Rural Planning:* Samon Korto. *Information, Posts and Telecommunications:* Gbegnon Amegboh. *Youth, Sports and Culture:* Koffi Sama. *First and Second Cycle Education:* Komlan Agbetiafa. *Third and Fourth Cycle Education:* Ayssa Agbetra. *Justice:* Ayivi Mawuko Ajavon. *Commerce and Transport:* Phali Djalla. *Secretaries of State:* Sheffi Meatchi *(Social Affairs and Women's Promotion),* Bloua Yao Agbo *(Budget).*

National flag: Five horizontal stripes of green and yellow, a red quarter with a white star.

Local Government: There are 5 regions (Maritime, Des Plateaux, Du Centre, De La Kara and Des Savanes), each under an inspector appointed by the President; they are divided into 21 *prefectures,* each administered by a district chief assisted by an elected district council.

DEFENCE. Armed forces numbered (1985) about 5,080, all forming part of the Army.

Army. The Army consists of 2 infantry, 1 Presidential Guard commando and 1 para-commando regiments, with artillery and logistic support units. Equipment includes 7 T-34 and 2 T-54/-55 main battle tanks. Strength (1985) 4,000, with a further 750 men in a paramilitary force.

Navy. In 1985 there were 2 coastal patrol craft, 2 defence launches and a naval base at Lomé. Naval personnel, 105 officers and men.

Air Force. An Air Force, established with French assistance, has 6 Brazilian-built EMB-326 Xavante (Aermacchi MB.326) armed jet trainers; 5 Alpha Jet advanced trainers, with strike capability, 1 DC-8, 1 Boeing 720 and 1 twin-turbofan F28 Fellowship for VIP use, 2 turboprop Buffalo transports; 5 Magister jet trainers; 1 Puma and 1 Lama helicopter.

INTERNATIONAL RELATIONS

Membership. Togo is a member of UN, OAU and is an ACP state of EEC.

ECONOMY

Planning. The fourth 5-year development plan (1981–85) provides for investment of 368,490m. francs CFA, of which 116,397m. are for rural development, 98,625m. for industrial development and 100,690m. for infrastructure.

Budget. The ordinary budget for 1983 balanced at 75,800m. francs CFA.

Currency. The unit of currency is the *franc* CFA with a parity rate of 50 *francs* CFA to 1 French *franc.* The rate of exchange (March 1985) was 551·25 francs CFA to £1; US$1 = 523·75.

Banking. The bank of issue is the *Banque Centrale des Etats de l'Afrique de l'Ouest.* Seven commercial and 3 development banks are based in Lomé.

ENERGY AND NATURAL RESOURCES

Electricity. Production (1980) 75m. kwh.

Minerals. A Mines Department was set up in 1953 after the discovery of very rich deposits of phosphate and bauxite; mining began in 1961. Output of phosphate rock (1980) 2,895,000 tonnes. Other mineral deposits are limestone, estimated at 200m. tons; iron ore, estimated at 550m. tons with iron content varying between 40% and 55%, and marble estimated at 20m. tonnes.

Agriculture. Inland the country is hilly, rising to 3,600 ft, with streams and waterfalls. There are long stretches of forest and brushwood, while dry plains alternate with arable land. Maize, yams, cassava, plantains, groundnuts, etc., are cultivated; oil palms and dye-woods grow in the forests; but the main commerce is based on coffee, cocoa, palm-oil, palm-kernels, copra, groundnuts, cotton, manioc. There are considerable plantations of oil and cocoa palms, coffee, cacao, kola, cassava and cotton. Production, 1981 (in 1,000 tonnes): Cassava, 470; maize, 137; millet, 107; cottonseed (1980), 30; rice, 25; groundnuts, 20.

Livestock (1983): Cattle, 260,000; sheep, 840,000; swine, 380,000; horses, 3,000; asses, 1,000; goats, 760,000.

INDUSTRY AND TRADE

Industry. There is a cement works (production, 1978; 327,000 tonnes); a second is being built in co-operation with Ghana and Ivory Coast with a capacity of 1·2m. tonnes per annum. An oil refinery of 1m. tonne capacity opened in Lomé in 1978 and a steel mill (20,000 tonne capacity) in 1979. Industry, though small, is developing and there are about 40 medium sized enterprises in the public and private sectors, including textile and food processing plants.

Trade (in 1m. francs CFA):

	1976	*1977*	*1978*	*1979*	*1980*
Imports	44,420	69,834	85,887	110,208	116,357
Exports	24,914	39,115	53,035	46,432	71,285

In 1980, of the exports, phosphates amounted to 40%, cocoa beans 12% and coffee 8% by value; 20% of exports went to the Netherlands and 15% to France. Of the imports, France supplied 25% and Nigeria, 16%.

Total trade between Togo and UK (British Department of Trade returns, in £1,000 sterling):

	1980	*1981*	*1982*	*1983*	*1984*
Imports to UK	7,395	4,981	1,827	2,161	3,224
Exports and re-exports from UK	28,967	21,423	21,881	12,212	12,166

Tourism. There were about 131,000 tourists in 1982.

COMMUNICATIONS

Roads. There were, in 1981, 7,850 km of roads, of which 1,500 km were paved. In Dec. 1980 there were 26,067 passenger cars and 14,017 commercial vehicles.

Railways. There are 4 metre-gauge railways connecting Lomé with Anecho (continuing to Cotonou in Benin), Kpalimé, Tabligbo and (*via* Atakpamé) Blitta; total length 525 km. In 1982 the railways carried 16m. tonne-km and 105m. passenger-km.

Aviation: Air services connect Lomé with Paris, Dakar, Abidjan, Douala, Accra, Lagos, Cotonou and Niamey and by internal services with Sokodé, Mango, Dapaong, Atakpamé and Niamtougou.

Shipping. In 1979, 879 vessels landed 1,264,000 tonnes and cleared 323,000 tonnes at Lomé. The merchant marine comprises 7 vessels of 25,714 gross tons. In 1981 some 2·2m. tonnes of phosphate were loaded at the port of Kpémé.

Post and Broadcasting. There were (1972) 39 post offices and 16 postal agencies and (1981), 7,870 telephones. Togo is connected by telegraph and telephone with Ghana, Benin, Abidjan and Dakar, and by wireless telegraphy with Europe and America. There were 5,000 television receivers and 125,000 radio receivers in 1981.

Newspapers. There was (1984) 1 daily newspaper (circulation 10,000)

JUSTICE, RELIGION, EDUCATION AND WELFARE

Justice. The Supreme Court and two Appeal Courts are in Lomé, one for criminal cases and one for civil and commercial cases. Each receives appeal from a series of local tribunals.

Religion. In 1980, 28% of the population were Catholics, 17% Moslem (chiefly in the north) and 9% Protestant; while 46% follow animist religions.

Education. In 1981 there were 506,356 pupils and 9,193 teachers in primary schools, 128,175 pupils and (1980) 2,855 teachers in secondary schools, 7,793 (1980) students and (1978) 326 teachers in technical schools and 300 students and 22 teachers at the teacher-training college. The University of Benin at Lomé (founded in 1970) had 4,500 students in 1982.

Health. In 1977 there were 61 hospitals with 3,438 beds; and in 1979, 139 doctors, 7 dentists, 38 pharmacists, 586 midwives and 1,763 nursing staff.

DIPLOMATIC REPRESENTATIVES

Of Togo in Great Britain (116 Knightsbridge, London SW1)
Chargé d'Affaires: Kossi Fusuasu Metsoko.

Of Great Britain in Togo
Ambassador: K. F. X. Burns, CMG (resides in Accra).

Of Togo in the USA (2208 Massachusetts Ave., NW, Washington, D.C., 20008)
Ambassador: Ellom-Kodjo Schuppius.

Of the USA in Togo (Rue Pelletier Caventou, Lomé)
Ambassador: Howard K. Walker.

Of Togo to the United Nations
Ambassador: (Vacant).

Books of Reference

Cornevin, R., *Histoire du Togo.* 3rd ed., Paris, 1969
Feuillet, C., *Le Togo en general.* Paris, 1976
Piraux, M., *Le Togo aujourd'hui.* Paris, 1977

TONGA

Capital: Nuku'alofa
Population: 98,750 (1983)
GNP per capita: US$530 (1981)

Friendly Islands

HISTORY. The Kingdom of Tonga attained unity under Taufa'ahau Tupou (George I) who became ruler of his native Ha'apai in 1820, of Vava'u in 1833 and of Tongatapu in 1845. By 1860 the kingdom had become converted to Christianity (George himself having been baptized in 1831). In 1862 the king granted freedom to the people from arbitrary rule of minor chiefs and gave them the right to the allocation of land for their own needs. These institutional changes, together with the establishment of a parliament of chiefs, paved the way towards the democratic constitution under which the kingdom is now governed, and provided a background of stability against which Tonga was able to develop her agricultural economy.

The kingdom continued up to 1899 to be a neutral region in accordance with the Declaration of Berlin, 6 April 1886. By the Anglo-German Agreement of 14 Nov. 1899 subsequently accepted by the USA, the Tonga Islands were left under the Protectorate of Great Britain.

A protectorate was proclaimed on 18 May 1900, and a British Agent and Consul appointed. On 4 June 1970 the UK Government ceased to have any responsibility for the external relations of Tonga.

AREA AND POPULATION. The kingdom consists of some 169 islands and islets with a total area of 289 sq. miles (748 sq. km; including inland waters), and lies between 15° and 23° 30′ S. lat and 173° and 177° W. long., its western boundary being the eastern boundary of Fiji. The islands are split up into the following groups reading from north to south: The Niuas, Vava'u, Ha'apai, Kotu, Nomuka, Otu Tolu and Tongatapu. The 3 main groups, both from historical and administrative significance, are Tongatapu in the south, Ha'apai in the centre and Vava'u in the north. The Tongatapu group was discovered by Tasman in 1643.

The capital is Nuku'alofa on Tongatapu (18,312).

The islands to the east, being mostly of limestone formation, are low lying and with but a few exceptions seldom exceed 100 ft above sea-level. The islands to the west are of a volcanic nature, approximately 11, average between 350 and 3,433 ft in height. After a violent volcanic eruption in Sept. 1946 on the island of Niuafo'ou (Tin Can Island to philatelists, so named because of the method that was used of collecting and delivering mail) the 1,300 inhabitants were evacuated, most of them to Tongatapu and 'Eua, but more than 600 have returned since 1958. It was thought that a new island had been born when an eruption took place on the Metis Shoal on 12 Dec. 1967; during the volcanic activity a small rocky mass reached a maximum elevation of about 50 ft, but by Feb. 1968 the area was once more awash.

Census population (1976) 90,085 (males, 46,036); estimate, 1983, 98,750.

CLIMATE. Generally a healthy climate, though Jan. to March is hot and humid, with temperatures of 90°F (32·2°C). Rainfall amounts are comparatively high, being greatest from Dec. to March. Nuku'alofa. Jan. 78°F (25·6°C), July 70°F (21·1°C). Annual rainfall 63″ (1,576 mm). Vava'u. Jan. 80°F (26·7°C), July 73°F (22·8°C). Annual rainfall 110″ (2,750 mm).

CONSTITUTION AND GOVERNMENT. The present Constitution is almost identical with that granted in 1875 by King George Tupou I. There is a Privy Council, Cabinet, Legislative Assembly and Judiciary. The legislative assembly, which meets annually, is composed of 7 nobles elected by their peers, 7 elected representatives of the people and the Privy Councillors (numbering 8); the King appoints one of the 7 nobles to be the Speaker. The elections are held triennially. In 1960, women voted for the first time.

King: HM King Taufa'ahau Tupou IV, GCVO, GCMG, KBE, born 4 July 1918, succeeded on 16 Dec. 1965 on the death of his mother, Queen Salote Tupou III; his coronation took place on 4 July 1967.

Prime Minister: HRH Prince Tu'ipelehake, KCMG, KBE, younger brother of the King.

National flag: Red with a white quarter bearing a red couped cross.

INTERNATIONAL RELATIONS

Membership. Tonga is a member of the Commonwealth and is an ACP state of EEC.

ECONOMY

Planning. The Fourth Plan 1980–85 aims at increases in real income for the population and improved efficiency in both the public and private sectors. The Fifth Plan will run 1985–90.

Budget. Revenue and expenditure in T$1,000:

	1977–78	*1978–79*	*1979–80*	*1980–81*[1]	*1981–82*[1]
Revenue	8,628	8,722	10,596	12,147	14,744
Expenditure	8,515	8,932	10,538	11,899	14,736

[1] Estimate.

The principal sources of revenue are import dues, income tax, port and service tax, wharfage, philatelic revenue and telephone rentals.

The public debt at 30 June 1980 was T$16,428,909.

Currency. There is a government note issue of *pa'anga* (T$)10, 5, 2, 1 and ½ and coin issue of T$2, T$1 and *seniti* 50, 20, 10, 5, 2 and 1. In March 1985, £1 = 1·51 *pa'anga*; US$1 = 1·47 *pa'anga*.

AGRICULTURE. Tongan produce (exports 1977) consists of copra (T$3,931,390); packaged desiccated coconut (T$866,942); bananas (T$401,519); swamp taros (T$246,485).

Livestock (1983): Cattle, 11,000; horses, 15,000; pigs, 79,000; goats, 19,000; poultry (1982), 175,000.

COMMERCE. In 1982, imports were valued at T$41,204,705 while exports and re-exports were T$3,645,598 and T$642,308 respectively.

Main imports (in T$): Food 8,936,148, beverages and tobacco 2,316,709, crude materials 3,128,660, fuel and lubricants 5,714,938, oils and fats 38,575, chemicals 2,646,068, manufactured goods 9,417,568, machinery and transport equipment 6,028,881.

Principal destinations for Tongan exports/re-exports in 1982 were: Australia (T$1,814,386), New Zealand (T$1,643,274), USA (T$354,447), Fiji (T$174,440) and Hawaii (T$52,345). Of 1982 imports (in T$), New Zealand furnished 15,358,975; Australia, 9,675,775; USA, 3,914,705; Fiji, 2,938,194; Singapore, 2,700,893; Japan, 2,509,902; Taiwan, 740,680; China (Mainland), 679,135; UK, 594,797.

Total trade between Tonga and UK (British Department of Trade returns, in £1,000 sterling):

	1981	*1982*	*1983*	*1984*
Imports to UK	56	38	25	328
Exports and re-exports from UK	286	764	648	842

COMMUNICATIONS

Roads. In 1980 there were 2,849 registered motor vehicles.

Aviation. International air service connexions to Tongatapu are now provided by Air New Zealand, Polynesian Airlines, Air Pacific and SPIA with 5 flights per week to Auckland, 5 to Apia and 3 to Suva. SPIA provide a weekly B707 to Pangopango. Polynesian Airline and SPIA provide 2 local service flights a week from Apia and 4 from Pangopango to Vava'u in the Northern Group and through to Tongatapu. Internal air service flights are operated 5 days a week to 'Eua, Ha'apai, Vava'u and once to Niuatoputapu.

Shipping. Pacific Forum Line maintains a three weekly service New Zealand–Fiji–Samoas–Tonga from Sydney Australia–Noumea–Fiji–Samoas–Tonga. Warner Pacific Line maintains a monthly service New Zealand–Tonga–Samoas–Tonga–New Zealand and a monthly service Tonga–New Zealand–Australia–Funufuti–Tarawa–Samoas–Tonga.

Post. The kingdom has its own issue of postage stamps. Telephones numbered 2,608 in 1982.

JUSTICE, RELIGION AND EDUCATION

Justice. Since the lapse of British extra-territorial jurisdiction British and foreign nationals charged with an offence against the laws of Tonga (the enforcement of which is a responsibility of the Minister of Police) are fully subject to the jurisdiction of the Tongan courts to which they are already subject in all civil matters.

Religion. The Tongans are Christian, the vast majority being adherents of the Wesleyan Church.

Education. The Tongans enjoy free education, free medical attendance and dental treatment. In 1983 there were 99 government and 12 denominational primary schools, with a total of 16,329 pupils. There were 3 government and 47 non-government schools and 1 private school offering secondary education, with a total roll of 16,268. There was one government teacher-training college with 198 students; 4 government technical and vocational schools with 139 trainees and 8 non-government technical and vocational schools with 296 trainees. 193 students were undergoing training overseas.

DIPLOMATIC REPRESENTATIVES

Of Tonga in Great Britain (New Zealand Hse., Haymarket, London, SW1Y 4TE)
High Commissioner: Sonatane Tua Taumoepeau-Tupou (accredited 18 Feb. 1983). Also Ambassador to the USA.

Of Great Britain in Tonga (Nuku'alofa)
High Commissioner: G. F. Rance, MBE.

Of the USA in Tonga
Ambassador: F. Eckert, Jr (resides in Suva).

Books of Reference

Bain, K. R., *Royal Visit to Tonga: Tonga Government Official Record.* London, 1954.—*The Friendly Islanders.* London, 1967
Churchward, C. M., *Tongan Dictionary.* London, 1959
Luke, Sir Harry, *Queen Salote and Her Kingdom.* London, 1954

TRINIDAD AND TOBAGO

Capital: Port-of-Spain
Population: 1·16m. (1984)
GNP per capita: US$5,670 (1981)

HISTORY. Trinidad was discovered by Columbus in 1498 and colonized by the Spaniards in the 16th century. During the French Revolution a large number of French families settled in the island. In 1797, Great Britain being at war with Spain, Trinidad was occupied by the British and ceded to Great Britain by the Treaty of Amiens in 1802. Trinidad and Tobago were joined in 1889.

Under the Bases Agreement concluded between the governments of the UK and the USA on 27 March 1941, and the concomitant Trinidad–US Bases Lease of 22 April 1941, defence bases were leased to the US Government for 99 years. On 8 Dec. 1960 the US agreed to abandon 21,000 acres of leased land and the US has since given up the remaining territory, except for a small tracking station.

AREA AND POPULATION. Area: Trinidad, 1,864 sq. miles (4,828 sq. km); Tobago, 116 sq. miles (300 sq. km). Population (census 1980): 1,055,763 (526,234 males and 529,529 females) (Trinidad, 1,016,239; Tobago, 39,529). Capital, Port-of-Spain, 55,800; other important towns, San Fernando (38,395) and Arima (24,112). The majority are of African descent (40·8%), the balance being made up of Indians (40·7%), mixed races (16·3%), European, Chinese and others (2·2%). English is spoken generally.

Estimated population in 1984, 1·16m.

Vital statistics (rate per 1,000), 1980: Births, 26·4; deaths, 7; infant deaths, 19·7. Proportion of population under 15 years (1984) 39·2%.

Tobago is situated about 30·7 km north-east of Trinidad. Main town is Scarborough.

Principal goods shipped from Tobago to Trinidad are copra, cocoa, livestock and poultry, fresh vegetables, coconut oil and coconut fibre.

CLIMATE. A tropical climate whose dry season runs from Jan. to June, with a wet season for the rest of the year. Temperatures are uniformly high the year round. Port-of-Spain. Jan. 78°F (25·6°C), July 79°F (26·1°C). Annual rainfall 65″ (1,631 mm).

CONSTITUTION AND GOVERNMENT. On 31 Aug. 1962 Trinidad and Tobago became an independent member state of the British Commonwealth. A Republican Constitution was adopted on 24 Oct. 1976.

The Constitution provides for a bicameral legislature of a Senate and a House of Representatives. The Senate consists of 31 members, 16 being appointed by the President on the advice of the Prime Minister, 6 on the advice of the Leader of the Opposition and 9 at the discretion of the President.

The voting age in the 1976 election was reduced from 21 to 18 years and ballot boxes were re-introduced in place of the voting machines used in previous elections.

Tobago has a 15-man House of Assembly (with limited powers).

The House of Representatives consists of 36 (34 for Trinidad and 2 for Tobago) elected members and a Speaker elected from outside the House.

The Cabinet consists of the Prime Minister, appointed by the President, and other Ministers, including the Attorney-General.

In Nov. 1981 the People's National Movement held the 27 seats.

President: Ellis Clarke.

Prime Minister and Minister of Finance and Planning: George Chambers.

National flag: Red with a diagonal black strip edged in white.

DEFENCE. The Defence Force has a regular and a reserve infantry battalion and a support battalion equipped with 81mm mortars, and there is also a small air element, equipped with a Cessna 402 light transport, and 2 S-76 and 2 Gazelle helicopters for surveillance, liaison and casualty evacuation. Personnel in 1983 totalled 50.

In 1985 there are 2 Swedish (Karlskrona)-built patrol vessels, 4 British (Vosper, Portsmouth)-built patrol craft, 7 minor patrol boats, 2 launches and a training ketch. A Commodore is Chief of Defence Staff while a Commander directs the Coast Guard. Personnel strength (1985) 45 officers and 540 ratings.

INTERNATIONAL RELATIONS

Membership. Trinidad and Tobago is a member of UN, the Commonwealth, OAS, Caricom and is an ACP state of EEC.

ECONOMY

Budget. The 1984 budget envisaged revenue (in TT$) as 9,036·9m. and expenditure as 5,618·9m.

Total external debt at 31 Dec. 1983, US$1,774·4.

Currency. The currency is the *Trinidad and Tobago dollar* of 100 *cents.* £1 = TT$2·57; US$1 = TT$2·40 (March 1985).

Banking. Banks operating: Republic Bank of Trinidad and Tobago Ltd; Royal Bank of Trinidad and Tobago Ltd; Bank of Commerce, Trinidad and Tobago Ltd; Bank of Nova Scotia; United Bank of Trinidad and Tobago Ltd; National Commercial Bank of Trinidad and Tobago; Workers' Bank of Trinidad and Tobago; Trinidad Co-operative Bank Ltd. A Central Bank began operations in Dec. 1964.

Government savings banks are established in 69 offices, with a head office in Port-of-Spain.

ENERGY AND NATURAL RESOURCES

Electricity. In 1982, 25,735m. kwh was generated.

Oil. Oil production is one of Trinidad's leading industries and an important source of revenue. Commercial production began in 1909; production of crude oil in 1984 was 8m. tonnes. Trinidad also possesses 2 refineries, with rated distillation capacity of 305,000 bbls annually; crude oil is imported from Venezuela, Indonesia, Ecuador, Nigeria, Brazil, and Saudi Arabia and refined in Trinidad. The 'Pitch Lake' is an important source of asphalt; production, 1983, 38,200 tonnes.

Gas. In 1983 production was 631,817m. cu. feet, of which 119,417m. was flared and lost.

Agriculture. Hectares under cultivation and care include (1981): Forest, 229,000; cocoa, 20,000; sugar, 28,000. Sugar production in 1982 was 78,685 (1983: 77,400) tonnes. The territory is still largely dependent on imported food supplies, especially flour, dairy products, meat and rice. Areas have been irrigated for rice, and soil and forest conservation is practised.

Livestock (1983): Cattle, 76,000; sheep, 12,000; goats, 49,000; pigs, 62,000; poultry, 8m.

INDUSTRY AND TRADE

Industry. In 1983, 676,100 tonnes of iron and steel were produced at the first integrated steelworks to be constructed in the Caribbean which was opened in 1981. Other manufacturing include ammonia (production, 1983, 1,202,016 tonnes), fertilizers (1982 production, 939,700 tonnes), sugar, cement, paints, plastics and petrochemicals.

Labour. The working population in 1983 was 442,400 and unemployment was about 10·3%; about 30% of the labour force belong to unions.

Commerce. Exports in 1983 were TT$5,646·3m. of which TT$4,714·5m. was mineral fuels and products and chemicals, TT$456·8m. USA took 56·2% of exports. Imports totalled TT$6,196·7m. of which TT$2,291·5m. was for machinery and transport of which the USA supplied 42·3% and UK, 11·5%.

Total trade of Trinidad and Tobago with UK (British Department of Trade returns, in £1,000 sterling):

	1980	*1981*	*1982*	*1983*	*1984*
Imports to UK	35,088	37,153	65,154	52,748	164,715
Exports and re-exports from UK	120,270	121,465	158,436	148,811	113,312

Tourism. In 1981, 186,800 foreigners visited Trinidad and Tobago.

COMMUNICATIONS

Roads. There were (1984) about 6,435 km of main and local roads. Motor vehicles registered in 1982 totalled 365,010, including 110,910 private cars, 24,908 hired and rented cars, and 133,461 goods vehicles.

Aviation. The following airlines operate scheduled passenger, mail and freight services. British West Indian Airways, Ltd, Air Canada, PANAM, KLM, Linea Aeropostal Venezolana, Leeward Islands Air Transport, Air India, Caribair, British Airways, American Airlines, Guyana Airways, ALM Antillean Airline, Air Jamaica, Eastern Airlines, Cubana Airlines and Viasa.

Shipping. In 1977 48m. tons of cargo were handled.

Post and Broadcasting. International communications to all parts of the world are provided by Trinidad and Tobago External Telecommunications Co. Ltd (TEXTEL) by means of a satellite earth station and various high quality radio circuits. The marine radio service is also maintained by TEXTEL. Number of post offices (1984), 69; postal agencies, 166; number of telephones (1982), 81,949. Four wireless stations are maintained by the Trinidad Government and 3 by airline companies. There were 500,000 radio and 230,000 television receivers in 1981. A meteorological station is maintained at Piarco airport.

Cinemas (1984). There are 57 cinemas and 3 drive-in cinemas.

Newspapers (1984). There are 4 daily newspapers with a total daily circulation (1982) of 168,000, 2 Sunday newspapers with a total circulation (1982) of 167,000, and 3 weekly newspapers.

JUSTICE, RELIGION, EDUCATION AND WELFARE

Justice. The High Court consists of the Chief Justice and 11 puisne judges. In criminal cases a judge of the High Court sits with a jury of 12 in cases of treason and murder, and with 9 jurors in other cases. The Court of Appeal consists of the Chief Justice and 3 Justices of Appeal; there is a limited right of appeal from it to the Privy Council. There are 3 High Courts and 12 magistrates' courts.

Religion. In 1980, 15% of the population were Anglicans (under the Bishop of Trinidad and Tobago), 33·6% Roman Catholics (under the Archbishop of Port-of-Spain), 25% Hindus and 5·9% Moslems.

Education. In 1981–82 there were 464 primary and intermediate schools (government assisted) and 91 secondary schools and 12 vocational schools.

There were 167,452 pupils on roll in the primary and intermediate schools and 90,586 in the secondary schools (government and assisted). Education in government and assisted secondary schools was made free in 1960. There were also 5 training colleges. Technical and commercial education is provided by 4 government sponsored technical schools.

Literacy rate (1980) was 96·3%.

Health. State medical services are free and in 1972 a National Insurance Scheme was established.

DIPLOMATIC REPRESENTATIVES

Of Trinidad and Tobago in Great Britain (42 Belgrave Sq., London, SW1X 8NT)
High Commissioner: Frank O. Abdullah (accredited 9 March 1983).

Of Great Britain in Trinidad and Tobago (Furness Hse., 90 Independence Sq., Port-of-Spain)
High Commissioner: D. N. Lane, CMG.

Of Trinidad and Tobago in the USA (1708 Massachusetts Ave., NW, Washington, D.C., 20036)
Ambassador: Dr James O'Neil-Lewis.

Of the USA in Trinidad and Tobago (15 Queen's Park West, Port-of-Spain)
Ambassador: (Vacant).

Of Trinidad and Tobago to the United Nations
Ambassador: D. H. N. Alleyne.

Books of Reference

Statistical Information: The Central Statistical Office, Government of Trinidad and Tobago, 2 Edward St., Port-of-Spain. *Director:* J. Harewood. Publications include *Annual Statistical Digest, Quarterly Economic Report, Annual Overseas Trade Report, Population and Vital Statistics Annual Report, Report on Education Statistics.*

Report of the Trinidad and Tobago Independence Conference, 1962. (Cmnd. 1757.) HMSO, 1962
Facts on Trinidad and Tobago. Ministry of Information, Port-of-Spain, 1983
Immigration Guidelines. Government Printer, Port-of-Spain, 1980
Oil and Energy, Trinidad and Tobago. Government Printer, Port-of-Spain, 1980
Trinidad and Tobago Year Book. Port-of-Spain. Annual (from 1865)
Cooper, St G. C. and Bacon, P. R. (eds.), *The Natural Resources of Trinidad and Tobago.* London, 1981

Central Library: The Central Library of Trinidad and Tobago, Queen's Park East, Port-of-Spain. *Acting Librarian:* Mrs L. Hutchinson.

TUNISIA

Al-Djoumhouria Attunusia

Capital: Tunis
Population: 6·97m. (1984)
GNP per capita: US$1,420 (1981)

HISTORY. Tunisia was a French protectorate from 1883 and achieved independence on 20 March 1956. The Constituent Assembly, elected on 25 March 1956, abolished the monarchy (of the Bey of Tunis) on 25 July 1957 and proclaimed a republic.

AREA AND POPULATION. The boundaries are on the north and east the Mediterranean Sea, on the west Algeria and on the south Libya. The area is about 164,150 sq. km (63,362 sq. miles), including that portion of the Sahara which is to the east of the Djerid, extending towards Ghadamès.

At the census of 30 March 1984 there were 6,966,173 inhabitants (3,547,487 males and 3,419,026 females) of whom 49% were urban.

The census populations of the *gouvernorats* were as follows as at 30 March 1984:

Béja	274,706	Kassérine	297,959	Sfax	577,992
Bizerta	394,670	Le Kef	247,672	Sidi Bouzid	288,528
Gabès	245,016	Mahdia	270,435	Siliana	222,038
Gafsa	235,723	Médénine	295,889	Sousse	322,491
Jendouba	359,425	Monastir	278,478	Tunis Nord	944,130
Kairouan	421,607	Nabeul	461,405	Tunis Sud	205,907

Tunis, the capital, had (census, 1984) 556,654 inhabitants: Sfax, 231,911; Sousse, 83,509; Bizerta, 94,509; Djerba, 92,269; Kairouan, a holy city of the Moslems, 72,254; Gafsa, 60,870; Gabès, 92,259; Béja, 46,708.

Vital statistics (1976). Births, 208,728; deaths, 36,912; marriages, 47,940.

The official language is Arabic but the use of French is widespread.

CLIMATE. The climate ranges from warm temperate in the north, where winters are mild and wet and the summers hot and dry, to desert in the south. Tunis. Jan. 48°F (8·9°C), July 78°F (25·6°C). Annual rainfall 16″ (400 mm). Bizerta. Jan. 52°F (11·1°C), July 77°F (25°C). Annual rainfall 25″ (622 mm). Sfax. Jan. 52°F (11·1°C), July 78°F (25·6°C). Annual rainfall 8″ (196 mm).

CONSTITUTION AND GOVERNMENT. The Constitution of the republic was promulgated on 1 June 1959. The President and the National Assembly are elected simultaneously by direct universal suffrage for a period of 5 years. The President cannot be re-elected more than 3 times consecutively, however on 18 March 1975 the National Assembly proclaimed Bourguiba 'President for Life'. An amendment to the Constitution in 1969 gives the Prime Minister power to act as President in case of a sudden vacancy of the Presidency.

Elections were held on 1 Nov. 1981, when all 136 seats in the National Assembly were won by the *Front National*, an alliance of the ruling *Parti Socialiste Destourien* (109 seats) and the *Union générale des travailleurs tunisiens* (27 seats).

President of the Republic and Head of Government: Habib Ben Ali Bourguiba (elected 25 July 1957, re-elected 8 Nov. 1959, 8 Nov. 1964, 2 Nov. 1969, Nov. 1974). Declared President for life in 1975.

The Cabinet in Aug. 1984 was composed as follows:

Prime Minister and Interior: Mohammed M'Zali.

Special Adviser to the President: Habib Bourguiba, Jr. *Justice:* M'hamed Chaker. *Foreign Affairs:* Beji Caied Essebsi. *Defence:* Salaheddine Bali. *Planning:* Ismail

Khelil. *Finance:* Salah Ben M'Barkq. *National Economy:* Rashid Sfar. *Housing and Equipment:* Mohamed Sayah. *Information:* Abderrazak Kefi. *National Education:* Mohamed Frej Chedli. *Higher Education and Scientific Research:* Abdelaziz Ben Dhia. *Agriculture:* Lassaad Ben Osman. *Public Health:* Dr Souad Yacoubi. *Transport and Communications:* Brahim Ktlouaja. *Social Affairs:* Mohamed Ennaceur. *Youth and Sports:* Mohamed Kraiem. *Family and Women's Affairs:* Fathia M'zali. *Minister-Delegate responsible for Prime Minister's Office:* Mongi Kooli. *Minister-Delegate attached to Prime Minister responsible for Civil Service and Administrative Reform:* Mezri Chekir. *Secretary of State for International Co-operation:* Ahmed Ben Arfa. *Secretary of State for Foreign Affairs:* Mahmoud Mestiri.

Local Government. The country is divided into 18 *gouvernorats*, each subdivided into *délégations, communes and imadas.*

Flag: Red with a white circle in the middle, on which is a 5-pointed red star encircled by a red crescent.

DEFENCE. Selective military service is 1 year. Officer-cadets are being trained in France.

Army. The Army consists of 2 combined arms, 1 Sahara and 1 para-commando brigades; 1 armoured reconnaissance, 3 field, 2 anti-aircraft and 1 engineer regiments. Equipment includes 14 M-48 main battle, and 55 AMX-13 and 20 M-41 light tanks. Strength (1985) 23,000. There are also the paramilitary gendarmerie (5,000 men) and National Guard (3,500 men).

Navy. The flotilla consists of 1 frigate (*ex*-US 40-year-old destroyer-escort), 2 fast gunboats (*ex*-Chinese), 2 fast attack craft (British-built in 1977), 2 coastal minesweepers, 4 patrol vessels (French built), 10 coastal patrol boats, 4 protection launches and 1 large tug. In 1985 naval personnel totalled 2,600 officers and ratings.

Air Force. Equipment of the Air Force, acquired from various Western sources, includes 1 squadron of Aermacchi M.B.326K/L jet light attack aircraft (to be supplemented with 6 F-5E Tiger II fighters and 2 F-5Fs); 12 SF.260W piston-engined light trainer/attack aircraft; 3 Flamant light transports, 4 S.208 liaison aircraft, 6 SF.260M trainers, 12 T6 Texan advanced trainers, 7 M.B.326B and 4 F-5F jet trainers, 1 Puma, 4 UH-1H, 18 AB.205, 6 Ecureuil and about 12 Alouette II and III helicopters. Personnel (1985) about 2,000.

INTERNATIONAL RELATIONS

Membership. Tunisia is a member of UN, OAU and the Arab League.

ECONOMY

Planning. A sixth development plan (1982–86) envisaged investment of 8,000m. dinars.

Budget (in 1,000 dinars). Budget estimates, 1982, revenue, 1,042,000; expenditure, 954,000.

Currency. On 1 Nov. 1958 a new currency, the *dinar*, divided into 1,000 *millimes*, was established. Note circulation, Aug. 1980, was 910m. *dinars*.

Currency consists of coins of 1, 2, 5, 10, 20, 50, 100 and 500 *millimes*, and notes of 500 *millimes*, 1 *dinar*, 5 and 10 *dinars*. £1 = 0·97 *dinar*; US$1 = 0·93 *dinar* (March 1985).

Banking. The Central Bank of Tunisia is the bank of issue. In 1983 there were 39 banks operating in Tunisia, including 7 off-shore banks. Bank deposits amounted to 2,115m. dinars at 31 Dec. 1982.

Weights and Measures. The metric system of weights and measures has almost entirely taken the place of those of Tunisia, but corn is still sold in *kaffis* and *wibas*.

The *kfiz* (of 16 *wiba*, each of 12 *sa'*) = 16 bushels. The *ounce* = 31·487 grammes.
The principal measure of length is the metre.

ENERGY AND NATURAL RESOURCES

Electricity. The electricity, gas and water services, formerly run by a French company, were nationalized on 26 Nov. 1959 and are now run respectively by the Société Tunisienne d'Electricité et du Gaz (STEG) and the Société Nationale d'Exploitation et de Distribution du Eaux (SONEDE).

Electrical energy generated was 3,700m. kwh. in 1984, of which 85% was produced by STEG.

Oil. Crude oil production (1984) 5,400,000 tonnes.

Gas. Natural gas production (1983) 400m. cu. metres.

Minerals. Mineral production (in 1,000 tonnes) in 1983 (and 1981): Phosphate, 5,450 (4,978); iron ore, 230 (400); lead ore, 8·7 (14); zinc ore, 16 (15).

Processed minerals (in 1,000 tonnes) in 1982: Pig iron, 97; crude steel, 105.

Agriculture. Tunisia may be divided into 5 districts—the north, characterized by its mountainous formation, having large and fertile valleys (*e.g.*, the valley of the Medjerdah and the plains of Mornag, Mateur and Béja); the north-east, with the peninsula of Cap Bon, the soil being specially suited for the cultivation of oranges, lemons and tangerines; the Sahel, where olive trees abound; the centre, the region of high table lands and pastures, and the desert of the south, famous for its oases and gardens, where dates grow in profusion.

Agriculture is the chief industry, and large estates predominate. Of the total area of 15,583,000 hectares, about 9m. hectares are productive, including 2m. under cereals, 3·6m. used as pasturage, 900,000 forests and 1·3m. uncultivated.

Products		*1979–80*	*1980–81*	*1981–82*
Hard wheat	(in 1,000 tonnes)	740	800	963
Soft wheat		130	160	180
Barley		300	270	270
Olive oil		85	145	90
Oranges and lemons		160	220	170
Dates		47	46	53
Wine (in 1,000 hectolitres)		619	619	555

Other products are apricots, pears, apples, peaches, plums, figs, pomegranates, almonds, shaddocks, pistachios, esparto grass, henna and cork.

Livestock (1983): Horses, 53,000; asses, 208,000; mules, 73,000; cattle, 560,000; sheep, 5·1m.; goats, 920,000; camels, 175,000; pigs, 4,000.

Fisheries. In 1980, 6,209 boats with 22,555 men were engaged in fishing. In 1982 the catch amounted to 62,800 tonnes; 1981, 57,500.

INDUSTRY AND TRADE

Industry. Major modern plants include a sugar refinery in Béja (57,700 tonnes in 1975), a cellulose plant in Kassérine (22,000 tonnes in 1976), a petroleum refinery in Bizerta and a steel plant at Menzel Bourguiba. There is a marble work plant and a tyre factory at Mégrine.

In 1972 a phosphoric acid plant opened at Ghannouche with an annual capacity of 120,000 tonnes.

Production, 1982 (in 1,000 tonnes): Crude steel, 105; cement, 1,834; lime, 470·6.

Trade Unions. The Union Générale des Travailleurs Tunisiens won 27 seats in the parliamentary elections (1 Nov. 1981). There are also the Union Tunisienne de l'Industrie, du Commerce et de l'Artisanat (UTICA, the employers' union) and the Union National des Agriculteurs (UNA, farmers' union).

Commerce. The imports and exports for calendar years (in 1,000 dinars) were as follows:

	1976	*1977*	*1978*	*1979*	*1980*	*1981*	*1982*
Imports	656,700	735,000	834,000	1,156,800	1,483,170	1,649,000	1,937,900
Exports	338,300	390,000	440,000	726,700	891,410	1,042,200	1,153,900

Exports to France in 1982 totalled 219·2m. dinars, and imports from France, 520·9m. dinars and exports to USA were valued at 268·8m. dinars and imports from USA were valued at 149·9m. dinars.

Total trade between Tunisia and UK (British Department of Trade returns, in £1,000 sterling):

	1980	*1981*	*1982*	*1983*	*1984*
Imports to UK	17,566	22,070	12,628	18,125	21,086
Exports and re-exports from UK	29,872	35,157	38,632	44,559	47,077

Tourism. In 1981, 2·2m. tourists visited Tunisia, not counting ships' passengers in transit.

COMMUNICATIONS

Roads. In 1981 there were 23,700 km of roads, of which 10,800 km were main roads.

Number of motor vehicles, 1981, included 132,500 private cars, 126,785 commercial vehicles and 11,400 motor cycles.

Railways. In 1983 there were 2,136 km of railways (465 km of 1,435 mm gauge and 1,673 km of 1,000 mm gauge), of which 21 km electrified and ran 1,650m. tonne-km and 802m. passenger-km. A suburban railway links Tunis and La Marsa, and a light rail network opened in Tunis in 1985.

Aviation. The national airline is Tunis-Air. The main airport is at Tunis-Carthage. In 1981, 3,515,675 passengers were carried.

Shipping. The main port is Tunis, and its outer port is Tunis-Goulette. These two ports and Sfax, Sousse and Bizerta are directly accessible to ocean going vessels. The port of La Skhirra, in the south, is used for the shipping of Algerian and Tunisian oil.

In 1981, 5,055 ships of 20,422,000 tons entered Tunisian ports.

Post and Broadcasting. There were, in 1981, 188,476 telephones. There were, in 1978, 403 post offices, and 6 wireless transmitting stations. Wireless sets in use in 1983 were 1,124,000. Television began in 1966 and in 1983 there were 300,000 sets.

Cinemas (1976). There were 175 cinemas with a seating capacity of 44,000.

Newspapers. There were (1984) 2 Arabic and 3 French daily newspapers.

JUSTICE, RELIGION, EDUCATION AND WELFARE

Justice. There are 51 magistrates' courts, 13 courts of first instance, 3 courts of appeal (in Tunis, Sfax and Sousse) and the High Court in Tunis.

A Personal Status Code was promulgated on 13 Aug. 1956 and applied to Tunisians from 1 Jan. 1957. This raised the status of women, made divorce subject to a court decision, abolished polygamy and decreed a minimum marriage age.

Religion. The constitution recognizes Islam as the state religion. There are about 20,000 Roman Catholics, under the Prelate of Tunis. The Greek Church, the French Protestants and the English Church are also represented.

Education. All education was in 1956 made dependent on the Ministry of National Education. The 208 independent koranic schools have been nationalized and the distinction between religious and public schools has been abolished. All education is free from primary schools to university. A teachers' training college (*école normale supérieure*) was established in 1955. There are also a high school of law, 2 centres of economic studies, 2 schools of engineering, 2 medical schools, a faculty of agriculture and 2 institutes of business administration.

In 1980–81 there were 2,613 primary schools with 26,989 teachers and 1,045,011 pupils; 236 secondary schools with 12,629 teachers and 210,895 pupils; 60,137 students at technical and vocational schools and 4,101 students in teacher-training; higher education mainly at the University of Tunis had 31,887 students and 3,869 teaching staff.

Health. In 1976 there were 268 hospitals (13,145 beds). The registered medical personnel in Tunisia comprised 1,210 doctors (843 Tunisians and 367 foreigners), 313 pharmacists, 176 dentists and 60 veterinaries.

Social Security. A system of social security was set up in 1950 (amended 1963, 1964 and 1970).

DIPLOMATIC REPRESENTATIVES

Of Tunisia in Great Britain (29 Prince's Gate, London, SW7 1QG)
Ambassador: Sadok Bouzayen (accredited 26 Nov. 1981).

Of Great Britain in Tunisia (5 Place de la Victoire, Tunis)
Ambassador and Consul-General: W. J. Adams, CMG.

Of Tunisia in the USA (2408 Massachusetts Ave., NW, Washington, D.C., 20008)
Ambassador: Habib Ben Yahia.

Of the USA in Tunisia (144 Ave. de la Liberté, Tunis)
Ambassador: Walter L. Cutler.

Of Tunisia to the United Nations
Ambassador: Néjib Bouziri.

Books of Reference

Statistical Information: Institut National de la Statistique (27 Rue de Liban, Tunis) was set up in 1947. Its main publications are: *Annuaire statistique de la Tunisie* (latest issue, 1975).
Bannour, A. (ed.), *Economic Yearbook of Tunisia.* 2nd ed. Tunis, 1966
Findlay, Allan M., Findlay, Anne M., and Lawless, R. I., *Tunisia.* [Bibliography] Oxford and Santa Barbara, 1982
Knapp, W., *Tunisia.* London, 1970
Ling, D. L., *Tunisia: From Protectorate to Republic.* Indiana Univ. Press, 1967
Rudebeck, L., *The Tunisian Experience: Party and People.* London, 1970
Sylvester, A., *Tunisia.* London, 1969
Tomkinson, M., *Tunisia: A Holiday Guide.* London and Hammamet, 1984

TURKEY

Türkiye Cumhuriyeti

Capital: Ankara
Population: 48m. (1984)
GNP per capita: US$1,540 (1981)

HISTORY. The Turkish War of Independence (1919–22), following the disintegration of the Ottoman Empire, was led and won by Mustafa Kemal (Atatürk) on behalf of the Grand National Assembly which first met in Ankara on 23 April 1920. On 20 Jan. 1921 the Grand National Assembly voted a constitution which declared that all sovereignty belonged to the people and vested all power, both executive and legislative, in the Grand National Assembly. The name 'Ottoman Empire' was later replaced by 'Turkey'. On 1 Nov. 1922 the Grand National Assembly abolished the office of Sultan and Turkey became a republic on 29 Oct. 1923.

On 27 May 1960 the Turkish Army, directed by a National Unity Committee under the leadership of Gen. Cemal Gürsel, overthrew the government of the Democratic Party. The Grand National Assembly was dissolved and party activities were suspended. Party activities were legally resumed on 12 Jan. 1961. A new constitution was approved in a referendum held on 9 July 1961 and general elections were held the same year.

On 12 Sept. 1980, the Turkish armed forces overthrew the Demirel Government (Justice Party). Parliament was dissolved and all activities of political parties were suspended. The Constituent Assembly was convened in Oct. 1981, and prepared a new Constitution which was enforced after a national referendum on 7 Nov. 1982. New legislation regarding political parties and elections was being prepared in 1983.

AREA AND POPULATION. Turkey is bounded west by the Aegean Sea and by Greece, north by Bulgaria and the Black Sea, east by the USSR and Iran, and south by Iraq, Syria and the Mediterranean.

The area (including lakes) is 779,452 sq. km (300,947 sq. miles). Area in Europe (Trakya), 23,764 sq. km. Area in Asia (Anadolu), 755,855 sq. km; population estimate (1984), 48m.

The census population is given as follows:

	Total		*Total*		*Total*
1927	13,648,270	1950	20,947,188	1970	35,605,176
1935	16,158,018	1955	24,064,763	1975	40,347,719
1940	17,820,950	1960	27,754,820	1980	45,217,556
1945	18,790,174	1965	31,391,421		

The Treaty of Peace between the Allied Powers and Turkey, which was signed at Lausanne on 24 July 1923, defined the European frontier of the new Turkey and to some extent her Asiatic frontiers. This treaty was ratified by the Grand National Assembly in Ankara on 23 Aug. 1923 and entered into force 6 Aug. 1924.

The Treaty of Lausanne and the conventions attached to it provided for the demilitarization of zones adjoining the European frontier, the Dardanelles and the Bosphorus, subject to the right to maintain a garrison at Istanbul, for the demilitarization of Imroz, Bozcaada (Tenedos) and Tavşan Islands, as well as the islands in the Sea of Marmara with one exception and for a special administrative regime in İmroz and Bozcaada.

On 10 July 1936 a new Straits Convention was signed at Montreux (ratified on 9 Nov. 1936) to take the place of the 1923 Convention, whereby Turkey obtained the right of re-militarizing the zone of the Straits, and this area was re-occupied by Turkish troops on 21 July 1936. The International Commission of the Straits ceased to function on 30 Sept. 1936.

By an agreement between the Turkish and French Governments concluded at Ankara on 23 June 1939, the Sanjak of Alexandretta (the Hatay) was incorporated in the Turkish Republic.

The population of the provinces, at the census of Oct. 1980, was as follows:

Adana	1,485,743	Erzincan	282,022	Maraş	738,032
Adıyaman	367,595	Erzurum	801,809	Mardin	564,967
Afyonkarahisar	597,516	Eskişehir	543,802	Muğla	438,145
Ağrı	368,009	Gaziantep	808,697	Muş	302,406
Amasya	341,287	Gireşun	480,083	Nevşehir	256,933
Ankara	2,854,689	Gümüşane	275,191	Niğde	512,071
Antalya	748,706	Hakkari	155,463	Ordu	713,535
Artvin	228,997	Hatay	856,271	Rize	361,258
Aydin	652,488	İsparta	350,116	Sakarya	548,747
Balıkesir	853,177	İçel	843,931	Samsun	1,008,113
Bilecik	147,001	İstanbul	4,741,890	Siirt	445,483
Bingöl	228,702	İzmir	1,976,763	Sinop	276,242
Bitlis	257,908	Kars	700,238	Sivas	750,144
Bolu	471,751	Kastamonu	450,946	Tekirdağ	360,742
Burdur	235,009	Kayseri	778,383	Tokat	624,508
Bursa	1,148,492	Kırklareli	283,408	Trabzon	731,045
Çanakkale	391,568	Kırşehir	240,497	Tunceli	157,974
Çankırı	258,436	Kocaeli	596,899	Urfa	602,736
Çorum	571,831	Konya	1,562,139	Uşak	247,224
Denizli	603,338	Kütahya	497,089	Van	468,646
Diyarbakir	778,150	Malatya	606,996	Yozgat	504,433
Edirne	363,286	Manisa	941,941	Zonguldak	954,512
Elâziğ	440,808				

The population of towns of over 100,000 inhabitants, at the census of Oct. 1980, was as follows:

İstanbul	2,772,708	Samsun	198,749	Elaziğ	142,983
Ankara	1,877,755	İzmit	190,423	Denizli	135,373
İzmir	757,854	Erzurum	190,241	Adapazari	130,977
Adana	574,515	Malatya	179,074	İskenderun	124,824
Bursa	445,113	K. Maraş	178,557	Balikesir	124,051
Gaziantep	374,290	Kirikkale	178,401	Tarsus	121,074
Konya	329,139	Kağithane	175,540	Zonguldak	109,044
Eskişehir	309,431	Antalya	173,501	Trabzon	108,403
Kayseri	281,320	Sivas	172,864	Buca	103,105
Diyarbakir	235,617	Bayrampaşa	165,723	Küçükköy	100,406
Mersin	216,308	Urfa	147,488		

CLIMATE. Coastal regions have a Mediterranean climate, with mild, moist winters and hot, dry summers. The interior plateau has more extreme conditions, with low and irregular rainfall, cold and snowy winters and hot, almost rainless summers. Ankara. Jan. 32·5°F (0·3°C), July 73°F (23°C). Annual rainfall 14·7" (367 mm). Istanbul. Jan. 41°F (5°C), July 73°F (23°C). Annual rainfall 28·9" (723 mm). Izmir. Jan. 46°F (8°C), July 81°F (27°C). Annual rainfall 28" (700 mm).

CONSTITUTION AND GOVERNMENT. The Turkish Grand National Assembly was dissolved on 12 Sept. 1980. The National Security Council took over its functions and powers. On 23 Oct. 1981 a Consultative Assembly was inaugurated. In early 1983 the National Security Council was acting as the upper house and the Consultative Assembly as the lower house.

Religious courts were abolished in 1924, Islam ceased to be the official state religion in 1928, women were given the franchise and western-style surnames were adopted in 1934.

The task of the Consultative Assembly was to prepare a new Constitution to replace that of 1961. The Assembly began its work in Oct. 1981 under the presidency of Sadi Irmak and on 7 Nov. 1982 a national referendum established that 98% of the electorate were in favour of the new Constitution.

Turkish men and women are entitled to vote at the age of 21 and to become deputies at the age of 30 and second members of Senate at the age of 40. Secret ballot was introduced by law on 10 July 1948.

Elections were held on 6 Nov. 1983. Of the 399 seats in the Grand National Assembly the Motherland Party won 211; The Populist Party, 117; The National Democracy Party, 71.

Past Presidents of the Republic: Mustafa Kemal Atatürk (29 Oct. 1923–10 Nov. 1938), İsmet İnönü (11 Nov. 1938–21 May 1950), Celâl Bayar (22 May 1950–27 May 1960), Cemal Gürsel (26 Oct. 1961–27 March 1966), Cevdet Sunay (29 March 1966–28 March 1973), Fahri S. Korutürk (6 April 1973–6 April 1980).

President, Head of National Security Council: Kenan Evren.

The Cabinet, in Jan. 1985 was composed as follows:

Prime Minister: Turgut Özal.

Deputy Prime Minister and Minister of State: I. Kaya Erdem. *Justice:* Necat Eldem. *Defence:* Zeki Yavuztürk. *Interior:* Yildirim Akbulut. *Foreign Affairs:* Vahit Halefoğlu. *Finance and Customs:* Ahmet Alptemoçin. *Education, Youth and Sports:* Vehbi Dinçerler. *Public Works and Housing:* İ. Sefa Giray. *Health and Social Welfare:* Mehmet Aydin. *Transportation and Communication:* Veysel Atasoy. *Agriculture, Forestry and Rural Affairs:* H. Hüsnü Doğan. *Labour and Social Security:* Mustafa Kalemli. *Industry and Commerce:* Cahit Aral. *Energy and Natural Resources:* Sudi N. Türel. *Culture and Tourism:* M. Mükerrem Tascioğlu.

There are 6 Ministers of State.

National flag: A white crescent and star on red.

National anthem: Korkma! Sönmez bu şafaklarda yüzen al sancak (words by Mehmed Akif Ersoy; tune by Zeki Güngör; adopted 12 March 1921).

Local Government. The Constitution of 1921 provided for the administrative division of the country into *İl*, (province, now 67 in number), divided into *İlçe* (district), subdivided in their turn into *Bucak* (township or commune). At the head of each İl is a Vali representing the Government. Each İl has its own elective council.

The İlçe is regarded as a mere grouping of Bucaks for certain purposes of general administration. The Bucak or commune is an autonomous entity and possesses an elective council charged with the administration of such matters as are not reserved to the State.

According to the municipal law passed in 1930, Turkish women have the right to be electors and to be elected at local and national elections.

DEFENCE. Several bills for the reorganization of the armed forces were passed in June 1961 by the Grand National Assembly. One of these placed all organizations connected with national defence under the authority of the Minister of National Defence. Another created a Supreme Council of National Security, under the chairmanship of the Prime Minister, with the object of co-ordinating the resources of the country in case of war. Besides the Minister of National Defence and the Chief of the General Staff, the heads of economic Ministries are members of this council.

Military service in Army, Air Force and Navy is 18 months for officers and 20 months for other ranks. Men are called up when they reach the age of 20.

Army. The Army consists of 16 infantry divisions (2 mechanized), 6 armoured, 4 mechanized, 11 infantry, 1 parachute and 1 commando brigades; 4 surface-to-surface missile, 8 armoured reconnaissance, 32 artillery and 8 anti-aircraft battalions. Equipment includes 3,000 M-48, 500 M-47 and 77 Leopard main battle tanks. Strength (1985) 470,000 (including 420,000 conscripts), and reserves number 700,000. There is also a paramilitary gendarmerie of 125,000 men.

Navy. The fleet includes 16 diesel-powered submarines (6 new designed in Federal Republic of Germany and 10 old *ex*-US patrol submarines), 13 old *ex*-US destroyers, 5 frigates (2 modern Turkish-built and 3 *ex*-German Navy), 1 large minelayer, 6 coastal minelayers, 1 fast attack gunboat (light corvette type), 13 fast missile craft, 5 fast torpedo boats, 22 coastal minesweepers, 8 patrol vessels, 4 inshore minesweepers, 8 minehunting boats, 20 patrol craft, 3 repair ships, 2 submarine support ships, 1 large training ship, 1 training ship (*ex*-German support frigate), 6 landing ships, 43 landing craft, 20 minor landing craft, 3 submarine rescue ships, 9 oilers, 10 transports, 2 survey ships, 3 survey boats, 4 boom defence vessels, 3 depot ships, 4 training craft, 7 gate vessels, 25 auxiliary vessels, 14 tugs, 2 tenders, 9 water carriers, and 7 floating docks.

Future construction includes 6 diesel-electric patrol submarines designed in the Federal Republic of Germany, but to be built in Turkey; and 4 frigates, 2 in Germany and 2 of same design in Gölcük.

The naval bases are at Gölcük in the Gulf of İzmit, at İskenderun, at Taskizak (İstanbul) and at İzmir.

Personnel strength in 1985 totalled 45,000 officers and ratings.

The Coast Guard, formed in July 1982 from the naval wing of the Jandarma, with a rear-admiral as Commander-in-Chief, has 25 patrol vessels, 9 medium patrol craft and 10 coastal patrol cutters, and an establishment of 1,000 officers and men.

Air Force. The Air Force is under the control of the General Staff and, operationally, under 6 ATAF. It is organized as 2 tactical air forces, with headquarters at Eskisehir and Diyarbakir, each having a flight of C-47s, UH-1H helicopters, AT-11s and T-33s. Combat aircraft comprise F-104G and F-104S Starfighters in 8 squadrons; RF-104Gs in 1 squadron; RF-5As in 1 squadron; F-4E and RF-4E Phantoms in 8 squadrons; plus Nike-Hercules surface-to-air missile batteries. The 6 transport squadrons are equipped with Transall C-160, C-130 Hercules, Viscount and C-47 aircraft, and UH-IH helicopters. Training types include T-33A, T-37 and T-38 advanced trainers, T-34 basic and T-41 primary trainers and F-5A/Bs for weapons training. Personnel strength is about 53,000, with over 320 combat aircraft. Aircraft on order of a planned total of 126 F-16s.

INTERNATIONAL RELATIONS

Membership. Turkey is a member of UN, OECD, NATO and Council of Europe and an Associate of EEC.

ECONOMY

Planning. The first 5-year development plan, 1963–67, provided for investments of TL68,000m. (at 1965 prices); TL64,000m. were invested, the gross national product increasing at the rate of 6·7% per annum. The second 5-year plan (1968–72) aimed at achieving an annual growth of 7%; external financing amounting to US$1,716m. The third 5-year plan (1973–78) set out to achieve an annual growth of 7·4%. The fourth 5-year plan (1979–83) sets out to achieve an annual growth of 8%.

Budget. Estimates of revenue and expenditure (in TL1,000) for financial years 1 March–28/29 Feb.:

	1978–79	*1979–80*	*1980–81*	*1981–82*
Revenue	247,253,177	372,309,378	706,687,182	1,480,965,037
Expenditure	276,148,529	409,430,671	756,687,182	1,540,965,037

Currency. The Turkish *Lira* (TL) is divided into 100 *kuruş (piastres).* Coins in general circulation are of the following values: 25 and 50 *kurus,;* 1, 2½ and 5 *Lira.* Bank-notes in circulation are as follows: 5, 10, 20, 50, 100, 500, 1,000 and 5,000 *Lira.* In March 1985, US$1 = 493 *Lira*; £1 = 551.

Banking. The Turkish banking system is composed of the Central Bank of the Republic of Turkey (Merkez Bankası) and 44 other banks. Thirteen (including the Central Bank) are established by special laws.

The 13 banks established by special laws carry out specialized banking activities beside their general banking transactions. Five of them are state economic enterprises whose capital is owned wholly by the State. They include: Ziraat Bankası (rural credits, capital: TL1,500m.), Sümerbank (textiles, etc., capital: TL2,250m.), Etibank (mining, energy, capital: TL3,250m.), İller Bankası (urban works, capital: TL2,000m.), İstanbul Emniyet Sandığı (savings bank). Six of them are joint-stock companies; the majority of their share capital is owned by the public sector. They include: the Emlâk Kredi Bankası (housing, capital: TL1,000m.), Denizcilik Bankası (shipping, capital: TL2,000m.), Türkiye Vakıflar Bankası (investments of pious foundations, funds, capital: TL200m.), Türkiye Halk Bankası (small business, capital: TL1,000m.); Türkiye Öğretmenler Bankası (teachers' housing, capital: TL30m.), T. C. Turizm Bankası (tourism, capital: TL1,000m.).

The development banks are: Devlet Yatırım Bankası (investment credits to state economic enterprises, capital: TL1,000m.), Türkiye Sınaî Kalkınma Bankası (investment credit to the private sector, capital: TL328·66m.), Sınaî Yatırım ve Kredi Bankası (industrial medium-term credit, capital: TL40m.).

Of the 31 commercial banks, 5 are foreign banks established in Turkey, and one is a bank whose capital is shared by a foreign bank.

The total credit volume of banks at 31 Dec. 1982 amounted to TL2,703,102m.

Weights and Measures. The metric system came into force on 1 Jan. 1934. On 24 May 1928 the Grand National Assembly made European numerals obligatory as from 1 June 1929.

On 1 March 1917 the Gregorian calendar was introduced into Turkey, to be used side by side with the Hegira calendar, while as from 26 Dec. 1925 it was decided finally to adopt the Gregorian calendar alone.

ENERGY AND NATURAL RESOURCES

Electricity. The potential hydro-electric power in Turkey is estimated at 56,000m. kwh. In 1981 the electrical power plants (hydro-electric or thermal) produced 24,900m. kwh.

Oil. Oil is being produced in Garzan and Raman by the Turkish Petroleum Co. Under the oil law of 14 Oct. 1954 private companies can explore and produce oil. Crude oil production (1984) was 2m. tonnes. The 3 refineries refined 12m. tons of crude oil in 1975. With a fourth refinery, introduced in 1973, total refining capacity now reaches 24m. tons a year. The oil pipeline Batman–Iskenderun (494 km) was opened on 4 Jan. 1967. Imports (refined locally) in 1983 were 14·3m. tonnes.

Minerals. The Turkish provinces, especially those in Asia, are reported rich in minerals. Turkey is one of the four principal producers of chrome in the world.

Production of principal minerals (in 1,000 tonnes) was.

	1981	*1982*	*1983*
Coal	7,285	7,223	6,725
Lignite	18,951	20,542	23,847
Chrome	574	618	515
Copper concentrate	2,657	2,701	2,184
Sulphur	29	31	31
Wolfram concentrates (tonnes)	293	...	...
Phosphate	43	...	...
Alumina	131	...	...

Of the Government organizations producing these ores, Zonguldak coal mines operate under the Turkish State Coal Exploitation; while the copper mines at Murgul and Ergani, the Eastern chromite mines, Keçiborlu sulphur, Emet colemanite, Küre pyrite and cupriferous pyrite, Keban argentiferous lead mines operate under the Etibank.

Agriculture. The number of people aged 15 and over engaged in agriculture in 1980 was 10,482,856.

In 1982, 27,281,000 hectares were cultivated land, 20,667,000 hectares of its own and 6,614,000 hectares fallow; vineyards, fruit orchards and olive groves occupied 2,892,000 hectares; forest occupied 20,199,000 hectares.

The soil for the most part is very fertile; the principal products are cotton, tobacco, cereals (especially wheat), figs, silk, olives and olive oil, dried fruits, liquorice root, nuts, almonds, mohair, skins and hides, furs, wool, gums, canary seed, linseed and sesame. The principal tobacco districts are Samsun, Bafra, Çarşamba, İzmit and İzmir. Two-thirds of the exports of leaf tobacco goes to the USA. The principal centre for silk production is Bursa. The production of olive oil, mainly confined to the Ils of Aydın and Balıkesir, is very important (78,000 tonnes in 1983). Sugar production (refined) in 1982 was 1·05m. tonnes. Agricultural production (in tonnes) in 1983 included 3·5m. grapes, 730,000 oranges and lemons, 395,000 hazelnuts, 1·6m. apples, 1·75m. olives, 3m. potatoes. Tea production (fresh leaves, 1983) was 436,032 tonnes.

Turkey produced 385 tonnes of flax fibre and 9,800 tonnes of hemp fibre in 1982. Cotton production was 481,000 tonnes in 1982. Agricultural tractors numbered 513,516 in 1983.

Yield (in 1,000 tonnes) of principal crops:

	1979	*1980*	*1981*	*1982*	*1983*
Wheat	17,500	16,500	17,000	17,500	16,400
Barley	5,240	5,300	5,900	6,300	5,425
Maize	1,350	1,240	1,200	1,360	1,480
Rye	620	525	530	420	380
Tobacco	217	234	177	206	226
Oats	370	355	325	330	320
Rice	225	143	198	210	189

Livestock (1983): 49,636,000 sheep, 18,213,000 goats, 17·1m. cattle, 1·3m. asses, 770,000 horses, 808,000 buffaloes.

In 1981 Turkey produced 33·6m. tonnes of wool, 547,000 tonnes of cattle and sheep meat and 256,000 tonnes of poultry.

Forestry. On 8 Feb. 1937 a new forest law was voted, providing for state control of all forests, including those under private ownership. It contains measures for planting, protection against fire, marauders and insects, and lays down penalties for infringements of its clauses. The most wooded Ils are Kastamonu, Aydın, Bursa, Bolu, Trabzon, Konya and Balıkesir. Of the forest land, 10,417,560 hectares belonged to the State in 1951. In 1983 total forest land was 20,199,000 hectares.

Fisheries. On 25 Aug. 1964 Turkey extended her waters in which she has exclusive fishing rights to 12 nautical miles. In 1983, 557,278 tons of sea and fresh water food was produced; there were (1982) 7,263 fishing boats.

INDUSTRY AND TRADE

Industry. Production in 1983 included 13,595,000 tonnes of cement and 392,921 tonnes of paper. Industrial plants number about 30,000.

In 1981 Turkey produced (in tonnes) 4,203,000 of iron and steel, 10,449,000 of petroleum products, 2,364,000 of crude oil, 2,346,000 of iron ore (1978), 15,057,000 of lignite (clean), 3,973,000 of coal (clean), 208,000 of chrome, 27,300 of copper, 828,000 of boron (1978). There are steel works at Karabük, Ereğli and Iskenderun.

Trade Unions. The trade-union movement began in 1947. There are 4 national confederations (including Türk-İş and Disk) and 6 federations. There are 35 unions affiliated to Türk-İş and 17 employers' federations affiliated to Disk, whose activities were banned on 12 Sept. 1980. In 1983, labour unions totalled 109 and employers' unions, 69.

Employment, 1980: Manufacturing, 2,036,843; construction, 813,838; transport, communications and warehousing, 545,686; mining, 179,127; services, 41,923. There were 157,466 manufacturing firms, 236,995 trading establishments and 580,635 service establishments in 1975.

Commerce. Imports and exports (in US$1m.) for calendar years:

	1980	*1981*	*1982*	*1983*
Imports	7,909	8,933	8,735	9,179
Exports	2,910	4,703	5,746	5,728

Exports (1982) in US$1m.: Cotton, 308; hazelnuts, 240; tobacco, 349; textiles, 1,057; raisins, 101; cereals and pulses, 338.

Imports (1982) in US$1m.: Crude oil, 3,419; machinery, 1,690; chemicals, 843; transportation equipment, 604; iron and steel, 592; petroleum products, 221; non-ferrous metals, 122; rubber and plastics, 237.

In 1982 (provisional) imports (in US$1m.) from the Middle East and North Africa were 3,678; EEC, 2,466; Iraq, 1,310; Federal Republic of Germany, 1,009;

Libya, 920; US, 813. Exports to the Middle East and North Africa, 2,690; EEC, 1,755; Iran, 791; Federal Republic of Germany, 707; Iraq, 610.

Total trade between Turkey and UK (British Department of Trade returns, in £1,000 sterling):

	1980	*1981*	*1982*	*1983*	*1984*
Imports to UK	49,243	128,226	207,763	184,976	204,131
Exports and re-exports from UK	147,118	159,849	218,116	244,024	331,360

Tourism. A tourist industry is developing. The number of foreign tourists was about 1·6m. in 1983; earnings from tourism US$281·3m.

COMMUNICATIONS

Roads. Turkey had, in 1983, 59,297 km of national highways, of which 54,301 were hard surfaced. In 1982 there were registered 1,187,899 motor vehicles, including 746,506 passenger cars and 99,680 buses.

Railways. Total length of railway lines in 1983 was 8,373 km (1,435 mm gauge); 393 km electrified and carried 12·5m. passengers and 13·8m. tonnes of freight.

Aviation. The State Airways Administration, formed in 1938, has been converted into the mixed company Turkish Airlines (Türk Havayollari Anonim Ortaklıği); British Airways became a partner in July 1957. It conducts foreign services to Athens, Beirut, Brussels, Amsterdam, Munich, Rome, Frankfurt, Vienna, London, Paris, Belgrade, Nicosia, Tel-Aviv and Baghdad.

In 1983 Turkish Airlines flew a total of 21,112 flight km. İstanbul or Ankara are connected with all the principal countries by 27 national airlines.

Shipping. In 1982 Turkish Maritime Lines and private companies had a gross tonnage of 2,061,000, with a total of 3,083 ships. The main ports in order of tonnage capacity are: İstanbul, İzmir, Samsun, Mersin, İskenderun and Trabzon.

Ports built or extended since 1950 are İskenderun, Ereğli, Trabzon, Samsun, Mersin, Zonguldak, Giresun, Hopa, Antalya and Bandırma. New facilities have been provided at Haydarpaşa, Salıpazari, Hopa, Yarımca and İzmir.

Post and Broadcasting. Number of telephones in 1982 was 2,104,113; İstanbul, 656,908; Ankara, 385,819.

In 1983 there were 4,300,000 licensed wireless sets. There were 5,185,000 television receivers.

Newspapers. In 1984 there were over 2,000 daily newspapers and periodicals in the Turkish language, 2 in Greek, 1 in French, 1 in Armenian and 1 in English. In 1976, 27 dailies were published in Ankara, 40 dailies in İstanbul, 6 dailies in İzmir, 5 dailies in Bursa and 4 dailies in Konya.

JUSTICE, RELIGION, EDUCATION AND WELFARE

Justice. The unified legal system consists of: (1) justices of the peace (single judges with limited but summary penal and civil jurisdiction); (2) courts of first instance (single judges, dealing with cases outside the jurisdiction of (3) and (4)); (3) central criminal courts (a president and 2 judges, dealing with cases where the crime is punishable by imprisonment over 5 years); (4) commercial courts (3 judges); (5) state security courts, to prosecute offences against the integrity of the state (a president and 4 judges, 2 of the latter being military).

The civil and military Courts of Cassation sit at Ankara.

The Council of State is the highest administration tribunal; it consists of 5 chambers. Its 31 judges are nominated from among high-ranking personalities in politics, economy, law, the army, etc.

The Military Court of Cassation in Ankara is the highest military tribunal. The Military Administrative Court deals with the judicial control of administrative acts and deeds concerning military personnel.

The Constitutional Court, set up under the Constitution, can review and annul legislation and try the President of the Republic, Ministers and senior judges. It consists of 15 regular and 5 alternate members.

The Civil Code and the Code of Obligations have been adapted from the corresponding Swiss codes. The Penal Code is largely based upon the Italian Penal Code, and the Code of Civil Procedure closely resembles that of the Canton of Neuchâtel. The Commercial Code is based on the German.

Religion. Freedom of religion is guaranteed by the Constitution. Although Islam is not the official state religion of Turkey, Moslems form 98·2% of the population. The administration of the Moslem religious organizations is in charge of the Presidency of Religious Affairs, attached to the Prime Minister's office. The Turkish Republic is a secular state.

İstanbul is the seat of the Œcumenical Patriarch, who is the head of the Orthodox Church in Turkey. The Armenian Church (Gregorian) is ruled by a Patriarch in İstanbul who is subordinate to the Katholikos of Etchmiadzin, the spiritual head of all Armenians. The Armenian Apostolic Church is ruled by the Patriarch of Cilicia. The Chaldeans (Nestorian Uniats) have a Bishop at Mardin. The Syrian Uniats have a See of Mardin and Amida, but it is united with their Patriarchate of Antioch (residence, Damascus). Greek Uniats (Byzantine Rite) have as their Ordinary in İstanbul, the Titular Bishop of Gratianopolis. The Latins have an Apostolic Delegate in İstanbul and an Archbishop in İzmir, but their Patriarch of İstanbul is titular and non-resident. There is a Grand Rabbi (Hahambaşı) in İstanbul for the Jews, who are nearly all Sephardim.

A law passed in Dec. 1934 forbids the wearing of clerical garb for those other than religious leaders except in places of worship and during divine service. The constitution forbids the political exploitation of religion or any impairment of the secular character of the republic.

In lieu of religious formulae, all citizens take oaths on their honour.

Education. Elementary education is compulsory and co-educational and, in state schools, free. All children from 7 to 12 are to receive primary instruction, which may be given in state schools, schools maintained by communities, or private schools, or, subject to certain tests, at home. The state schools are under the direct control of the Ministry of Education. They include primary schools, secondary or middle schools, and *lycées* or secondary schools of a superior kind. There are also training schools for male and female teachers, and technical schools. In 1979 there were 18 universities and 102 other institutes of higher education; in 1982, a further 8 universities were founded. The important non-Moslem communities in İstanbul maintain their own schools, which, like all 'private' schools, are subject to the supervision of the Ministry of Education.

Literacy of the population of 6 years and over was 10·6% in 1927, 19·2% in 1935, 29% in 1945, 40·9% in 1955, 48·7% in 1965, 49% in 1970, 61·7% in 1975.

Religious instruction in schools, hitherto prohibited, was made optional in elementary and middle schools in May 1948. There are many training schools for Moslem clergy as well as a Faculty of Theology in Ankara.

Statistics for 1981–82	*Number*	*Teachers*	*Students*
Primary schools (state and private)	45,871	210,599	5,864,000
Secondary schools (state and private)	4,252	37,445	1,240,000
High schools (state and private)	1,169	43,173	541,000
Vocational and technical schools	1,900	36,327	531,000
Faculties (university and higher education)	334	22,223	241,000

On 1 Nov. 1928 the Grand National Assembly voted a law for the adoption of Latin characters as from 1 Dec. 1928. The publication of books in Arabic characters was forbidden after 1 Jan. 1929.

Health. Public health is the responsibility of the Ministry of Health and Social Welfare, established in 1920; social insurance for workers comes under the Workers' Insurance Institution attached to the Ministry of Labour. A law promulgated in 1961 and being implemented from 1963 provides for the nationalization of the health services within 15 years. In 1981, 2·2m. workers and employees were covered by social insurance, including free medical care.

In 1983 there were 32,265 doctors and 99,396 beds in some 646 hospitals.

DIPLOMATIC REPRESENTATIVES

Of Turkey in Great Britain (43 Belgrave Sq., London, SW1X 8PA)
Ambassador: Rahmi Gümrükçüoğlu (accredited 4 Aug. 1981).

Of Great Britain in Turkey (Sehit Ersan Caddesi 46/A, Cankaya, Ankara)
Ambassador: R. M. Russell, CMG.

Of Turkey in the USA (1606 23rd St., NW, Washington, D.C., 20008)
Ambassador: Dr Şükrü Elekdağ.

Of the USA in Turkey (110 Ataturk Blvd., Ankara)
Ambassador: Robert Strausz-Hupe.

Of Turkey to the United Nations
Ambassador: A. Coşkun Kirca.

Books of Reference

Statistical Information: The State Institute of Statistics in Ankara consists of a research bureau and 10 sections dealing with agriculture, education, foreign trade, etc. It published an *Annuaire Statistique/Istatistik Yılığı* (1928–53) and *Aylık Istatistik Bülteni*, Monthly Bulletin of Statistics.

Almanac: Turkey 1983. 1983
The Turkish Constitution, 1971. Ankara, 1972
Resmî Gazete, Official Gazette. Ankara
Konjonktür. Ministry of Commerce (three times a year, from 1940)
Banque Centrale de la République de Turquie. *Bulletin Mensuel* (from Jan. 1953)
Bulletins of the Chambers of Commerce of Istanbul and Izmir
Dodd, C. H., *The Crisis of Turkish Democracy.* Beverley, 1983
Goodwin, G., *A History of Ottoman Architecture.* London, 1971
Guclu, M., *Turkey.* [Bibliography] Oxford and Santa Barbara, 1981
Hale, W., *The Political and Economic Development of Modern Turkey.* London, 1981
Kazancigil, A. and Ozbudun, E., (eds.) *Atatürk: Founder of a Modern State.* London, 1981
Kinross, Lord, *Atatürk.* London, 1964
Landau, J. M., *Radical Politics in Modern Turkey.* Leiden, 1974
Mackenzie, K., *Turkey in Transition: The West's Neglected Ally.* London, 1984
Sezer, D. B., *Turkey's Security Policies.* London, 1981
Tamkoc, M., *The Warrior Diplomats.* Univ. of Utah Press, 1976
Weiker W., *The Modernization of Turkey.* New York, 1981

State Library: MilliKütüphane Müdürlüğü, Ankara.

THE TURKS AND CAICOS ISLANDS

Capital: Grand Turk
Population: 7,436 (1980)

HISTORY. After a long period of rival French and Spanish claims the islands were eventually secured to the British Crown by the appointment in 1766 of a Resident British Agent, and became a separate colony in 1973 after association at various times with the colonies of the Bahamas and Jamaica.

AREA AND POPULATION. The Turks and Caicos Islands are geographically part of the Bahamas extremity, of which they form the south-eastern archipelago. There are upwards of 30 small cays; area 192 sq. miles (430 sq. km). Only 6 are inhabited; the largest, Grand Caicos, is 30 miles long by 2 to 3 miles broad. The seat of government is at Grand Turk, 7 miles long by 1·25 broad; 3,146 inhabitants. Population, 1980 census, 7,436; South Caicos, 1,392; Middle Caicos, 371; North Caicos, 1,266; Providenciales, 979; Salt Cay, 282.

Vital statistics (1980): Births, 247; marriages, 32; deaths, 13.

CLIMATE. An equable and healthy climate as a result of regular trade winds, though hurricanes are sometimes experienced. Grand Turk. Jan. 76°F (24·4°C), July 83°F (28·3°C). Annual rainfall 29″ (725 mm).

CONSTITUTION AND GOVERNMENT. A new Constitution was introduced in Aug. 1976, providing for an Executive Council and a Legislative Council. The Governor retains responsibility for external affairs, internal security, defence and certain other matters. The Executive Council comprises 3 official members: the Chief Secretary, the Financial Secretary and the Attorney-General; a Chief Minister and 3 other ministers from among the elected members of the Legislative Council; and is presided over by the Governor. The Legislative Council consists of a Speaker, the 3 official members of the Executive Council, 11 elected members and 2 appointed members. At general elections held on 29 May 1984 for the 11 elective seats on the Legislative Council, 8 seats were won by the Progressive National Party and 3 seats by the People's Democratic Movement.

Governor: C. J. Turner, OBE.
Deputy Chief Minister: Nathaniel Francis.

Flag: British Blue Ensign with the shield of the Colony in the fly.

ECONOMY

Budget. 1982–83 revenue US$6,437,000; budgetary aid, US$2,149,000; expenditure, US$8,586,000.

Currency. The currency in circulation is US$.

Banking. In 1980 there were 6 commercial banks operating in the Islands. The Government Savings Bank has 3 branches. Barclays Bank International and the Oxford International Bank and Trust Co. Ltd have offices in Grand Turk with branches in South Caicos, North Caicos and Providenciales.

COMMERCE (1982–83). Exports, US$2,515,119, and imports, US$20,903,776. Principal imports, food, drink, tobacco and clothing. The main exports are crawfish, dried and fresh conch, and conch shells. The catch is processed in three plants operating in South Caicos.

Total trade between Turks and Caicos Islands and UK (British Department of Trade returns, in £1,000 sterling):

	1980	*1981*	*1982*	*1983*	*1984*
Imports to UK	8	5	5	18	12
Exports and re-exports from UK	295	973	405	902	1,533

TOURISM. Number of hotels and guest houses, 19 (beds 600). Number of visitors, 1983, 14,216.

COMMUNICATIONS

Aviation. There is a 6,335 ft paved airfield on Grand Turk. On South Caicos there is a 6,000 ft paved airstrip under construction and on Providenciales a 7,000 ft paved airstrip. There are small paved and unpaved airstrips on the other 3 inhabited islands. Air Florida Airlines operate a thrice weekly passenger service to Miami. Bahamas Air operate a twice weekly scheduled passenger service to the Bahamas. Air Turks and Caicos operate a twice daily service to the islands and 2 flights a week to Cap Haitien (Haiti). Turks Air Ltd operates a regular weekly cargo service to Miami.

Shipping. Registered shipping (1981), 165 sailing vessels of 2,366 tons and 34 motor vessels of 5,015 tons.

Post and Broadcasting. Air-mail is received and dispatched by Miami twice or thrice weekly. Surface mail from all parts of the world is routed *via* the US arriving at 3 weekly intervals from Miami, Florida. There is no regular outgoing surface mail. Cable & Wireless (West Indies) provide internal and international cable, telephone, telex and telegraph services. There were (1981) 932 telephones. North Caicos and Salt Cay are linked with the Providenciales and Grand Turk exchanges respectively. The Government operates a radio broadcasting service from the Islands to Grand Turk, call sign VSI radio Turks and Caicos, for a total of 106 hours a week on 1,460 KHZ medium wave. Number of receivers, approximately 6,000.

Newspapers. The *Turks and Caicos News* is published weekly.

EDUCATION AND WELFARE

Education. Education is free and compulsory up to 15 years of age in the 14 government primary and 3 government secondary schools. There are also 3 private primary schools. Pupils at Turks and Caicos High School, 372; South Caicos and Providenciales, 208; North Caicos Junior High, 91. Expenditure on education 1982–83 was US$1,086,936.

Health. In 1983 there were 4 doctors and 30 hospital beds.

TUVALU

Capital: Funafuti
Population: 7,349 (1979)
GNP per capita: US$680 (1981)

HISTORY. Formerly the Ellice Islands, a British Protectorate since 1892. On the recommendation of a Commissioner, appointed by the British Government, to consider requests that the island group be separated from the Gilbert Islands, a referendum was held in 1974. There was a large majority in favour of separation and this took place in Oct. 1975. Independence was achieved on 1 Oct. 1978.

AREA AND POPULATION. Tuvalu (formerly the Ellice Islands) lies between 5° 30′ and 11° S. lat. and 176° and 180° E. long. and comprise Nanumea, Nanumanga, Niutao, Nui, Vaitupu, Nukufetau, Funafuti (administrative centre), Nukulaelae and Niulakita. Population (census 1979) 7,349. Area approximately 9½ sq. miles (24 sq. km). The population is of a Polynesian race.

CLIMATE. A pleasant but monotonous climate with temperatures averaging 86°F (30°C), though trade winds from the east moderate conditions for much of the year. Rainfall ranges from 120″ (3,000 mm) to over 160″ (4,000 mm). Funafuti. Jan. 84°F (28·9°C), July 81°F (27·2°C). Annual rainfall 160″ (4,003 mm).

CONSTITUTION AND GOVERNMENT. The Constitution provides for a Prime Minister and 4 other Ministers to be elected from among the 12 elected members of the House of Parliament, for which general elections took place on 8 Sept. 1981. The Cabinet, chaired by the Prime Minister, consists of the 4 ministers and 2 *ex officio* members, the Attorney-General and the Secretary to Government, who are also *ex officio* members of the House of Assembly. Local Government services are provided by an elected Island Council on each of the 8 atolls.

Governor-General: Sir Fiatau Penitala Teo, GCMG, GCVO, MBE.
Prime Minister: Rt. Hon. Dr Tomasi Puapua.
Finance: Henry F. Naisali, CMG, MBE. *Social Services:* Falaile Pilitati. *Commerce and Natural Resources:* Lale Seluka. *Works and Communications:* Metia Tealofi.

National flag: Light blue with the Union Jack in the canton, and 9 gold stars in the fly arranged in the same pattern as the 9 islands.

Local Government. There is a town council on Funafuti and island councils on the 7 other main islands, each consisting of 6 elected members including a president. Since 1966 Members of Parliament and medical officers have been *ex-officio* members of Island Councils.

INTERNATIONAL RELATIONS

Membership. Tuvalu is a member of the Commonwealth and is an ACP state of EEC.

ECONOMY

Budget. In 1983 the budget envisaged expenditure of $A3·5m.

Currency. The unit of currency is the Australian *dollar* although Tuvaluan coins up to $A1 are in local circulation.

Banking. The Tuvalu National Bank was established at Funafuti in 1980 and is a joint venture between the Tuvalu Government and Barclay's Bank International.

NATURAL RESOURCES

Agriculture. Coconut palms are the main crop. Fruit and vegetables are grown for local consumption.

Fisheries. Sea fishing is excellent but is largely unexploited.

INDUSTRY AND TRADE

Industry. The main sources of income are from overseas remittances from Tuvaluans working abroad, philatelic and copra sales, and handicrafts.

Employment. A significant number of the population are employed in the phosphate industry on Nauru. The remainder are engaged in harvesting coconuts and fishing.

Commerce. Commerce is dominated by co-operative societies, the Tuvalu Co-operative Wholesale Society being the main importer. Imports (1982) $A2·89m.

Total trade between Tuvalu and UK (British Department of Trade returns, in £1,000 sterling):

	1980	*1981*	*1982*	*1983*	*1984*
Imports to UK	34	6	7	35	11
Exports and re-exports from UK	362	132	48	55	82

COMMUNICATIONS

Aviation. Tuvalu is linked to the outside world by Fiji Air which operates three a week, on Monday, Wednesday and Friday, and Air Marshal once a week on Sundays.

Shipping. Funafuti is the only port and a deep-water wharf was opened in 1980. Inter-island communication is by ship.

Post and Broadcasting. The Tuvalu Broadcasting Service transmits daily in Tuvaluan and English and all islands have daily radio communication with Funafuti. There were 120 telephones in 1984.

JUSTICE, RELIGION, EDUCATION AND WELFARE

Justice. There is a High Court presided over by the Chief Justice of Fiji. Appeals lie to the Fiji Court of Appeal.

Religion. The majority of the population are Christians mainly Protestant but with small groups of Roman Catholics, Seventh Day Adventists, Jehovah's Witnesses and Bahai's.

Education. In 1980 there was 1 secondary school jointly administered by the Government and the Church. In addition there were 8 primary schools with (1982, inclusive of 300 pupils in community training centres) 1,290 pupils run by Island Councils and subsidized by the central government. In 1979, a maritime school was opened on Amatuku islet. Tuvaluans requiring further education must seek it abroad.

Health. In 1984 there was 1 central hospital with 36 beds situated at Funafuti. There were 4 doctors.

DIPLOMATIC REPRESENTATIVES

Of Great Britain in Tuvalu
High Commissioner: R. A. R. Barltrop CVO. (resides in Suva).

Of Tuvalu in the USA
Ambassador: Ionatana Ionatana (resides in Tuvalu).

UGANDA

Capital: Kampala
Population: 13·99m. (1982)
GNP per capita: US$220 (1981)

HISTORY. Uganda became a British Protectorate in 1894, the province of Buganda being recognized as a native kingdom under its Kabaka. In 1961 Uganda was granted internal self-government with federal status for Buganda.

Uganda became a fully independent member of the Commonwealth on 9 Oct. 1962 after nearly 70 years of British rule. Full sovereign status was granted by the Uganda Independence Act, 1962, and the Constitution is embodied in the Uganda (Independence) Order in Council, 1962. The post of Governor-General was on 9 Oct. 1963 replaced by that of President as head of state, elected by the National Assembly for a 5-year term.

Uganda became a republic on 8 Sept. 1967. Under the 1967 Constitution, the executive authority is vested in the President.

In 1971, Dr A. Milton Obote was overthrown by troops led by Gen. Idi Amin.

In April 1979 a force of the Tanzanian Army and Ugandan exiles advanced into Uganda taking Kampala on 11 April. On 14 April Dr Yusuf Lule was sworn in as President and the country is to be administered, initially, by the Uganda National Liberation Front.

The former Attorney-General, Godfrey Lukongwa Binaisa, QC, was appointed President by the National Consultative Council on 20 June 1979. Dr Lule subsequently left the country. Dr Binaisa was subsequently overthrown in May 1980 by the Military Commission, the military arm of Uganda National Liberation Front.

AREA AND POPULATION. Uganda is bounded on the north by Sudan, on the east by Kenya, on the south by Tanzania and Rwanda, and the west by Zaïre. Total area 91,343 sq. miles (236,860 sq. km), including 15,217 sq. miles (39,459 sq. km) of swamp and water.

The population of Uganda was 13·99m. (1983 estimate). On 4 Aug. 1972 President Amin announced that he would ask the UK to take responsibility for Asians in Uganda holding British passports. Later that year 27,200 Asians had left Uganda for Britain. The majority of the Africans (1,044,000) are Baganda, the tribe from which the country takes its name.

About 3m. Africans speak Bantu languages; there are a few Congo pygmies living near the Semliki River; the rest of the Africans belong to the Hamitic, Nilotic and Sudanese groups. Ki-Swahili is generally understood in trading centres. The capital is Kampala; the population of greater Kampala (1975), 332,000.

The official language is English. Swahili is also widely spoken.

CLIMATE. Although in equatorial latitudes, the climate is more tropical, because of its elevation, and is characterized the year round by hot sunshine, cool breezes and showers of rain. The wettest months are March to June and there is no dry season. Temperatures vary little over the year. Kampala. Jan. 74°F (23·3°C), July 70°F (21·1°C). Annual rainfall 46″ (1,150 mm). Entebbe. Jan. 72°F (22·2°C), July 69°F (20·6°C). Annual rainfall 60″ (1,506 mm).

CONSTITUTION AND GOVERNMENT. At the elections held on 10–11 Dec. 1980, the Uganda People's Congress, led by Dr A. Milton Obote, was declared to have held 72 of the 124 elective seats in the new Parliament, the Democratic Party 51 seats, and the Uganda Patriotic Movement 1 seat. There are 17 specially elected members. Elections are due in 1985.

In Jan. 1985 the Cabinet was composed as follows:

President, Minister of Foreign Affairs and Finance: Dr A. Milton Obote.
Vice-President, Minister of Defence: Paulo Muwanga.

Prime Minister: Eric Otema Alimadi.

Public Service and Cabinet Affairs: Wilson Okwenje. *Health:* Dr Ezra Nkwasibwe. *Internal Affairs:* Dr J. Luwuliza Kirunda. *Education:* Isaac Ojok. *Lands, Minerals and Water Resources:* Max Choudry. *Information and Broadcasting:* Dr David Anyoti. *Agriculture and Forestry:* Samwiri Mugwisa. *Regional Co-operation:* Sam Tewungwa. *Local Government:* L. Kalule Settala. *Culture and Community Development:* Dr James Rwanyarare. *Animal Industry and Fisheries:* Dr John J. Otim. *Works:* Abner Nangwale. *Co-operatives and Marketing:* Yona Kanyomozi. *Planning and Economic Development:* Sam Odaka. *Rehabilitation:* Patrick Massettee Kuuya. *Tourism and Wildlife:* M. Ntege-Lubwama. *Commerce:* Joel M. Aliro Omara. *Industry:* Dr Adonia Tiberondwa. *Attorney-General and Minister of Justice:* Stephen O. Ariko. *Labour:* Anthony L. Butele. *Housing and Urban Development:* A. P. N. Waligo. *Supplies:* Dr Moses Apiliga. *Transport:* Yosamu Mugenyi. *Power, Posts and Telecommunications:* Akena P'Ojok. *Minister without Portfolio:* Shafiq Arain.

National flag: Six horizontal stripes of black, yellow, red, black, yellow, red, in the centre a small white disc bearing a representation of a Balearic Crested Crane.

For administrative purposes Uganda is divided into 33 districts. The provinces are: Busoga, Central, Eastern, Karamoja, Nile, North Buganda, Northern, South Buganda, Southern, Western.

DEFENCE

Army. The Army had a strength of 15,000 in 1985 and was organized in 3 brigades. Equipment includes 10 T-34/-54/-55 and 3 M-4 tanks.

Navy. A small lake patrol was initiated in 1977.

Air Force. The Air Force was formed in 1964 and later underwent rapid expansion with the assistance of Israeli and Czechoslovakian training missions. Prior to the events of 1979 equipment included about 10 MiG-21 and 12 MiG-17 jet fighter-bombers, 2 MiG-15 UTI two-seat trainers, about 5 L-29 Delfin and 8 Israeli-built Magister armed jet trainers, 11 Super Cub liaison aircraft, 5 Piaggio P 149 piston-engined trainers, 6 Swiss-built Bravo primary trainers, 6 Agusta-Bell 205, 2 Agusta-Bell 206 JetRanger and some Mi 8 helicopters. Personnel numbered about 1,000. In addition the Police Air Wing had 1 Twin Otter and 1 Caribou twin-engined STOL transports, 1 Turbo-Beaver and 1 Piper Aztec light transports, and about 7 Bell 205, JetRanger, Bell 212 and Scout helicopters. The status of these aircraft was unknown in early 1985.

INTERNATIONAL RELATIONS

Membership. Uganda is a member of UN, OAU, the Non-Aligned Movement, the Commonwealth and is an ACP state of EEC.

ECONOMY

Budget. The revenue and expenditure (exclusive of loan disbursements) for fiscal years (1 July–30 June) were (in Uganda Sh. 1m.):

	1978–79	*1979–80*	*1980–81*	*1981–82*
Revenue	3,197	3,810	2,835	25,292
Expenditure	5,441	4,224	7,568	21,422

Currency. The monetary unit is the *Uganda shilling* divided into 100 *cents.* In March 1985, £1 = 628 Uganda shillings; US$1 = 565 Uganda shillings.

Banking. The Bank of Uganda was set up on 16 May 1966; its external assets as at 31 Aug. 1967 were £9m. The Uganda Credit and Savings Bank, set up in 1950, was on 9 Oct. 1965 reconstituted as the Uganda Commercial Bank, with its capital fully owned by the Government.

Barclays Bank of Uganda Ltd. has 4 branches, Standard Bank Uganda Ltd. has 1 branch, Bank of Baroda Uganda Ltd. has 3 branches and the Libyan Arab Uganda

Bank for Foreign Trade and Development has 3 branches, the Uganda Commercial Bank has 56 branches, the Co-operative Bank which is owned by the Co-operative Movement. There are 2 Development Banks; the East African Development Bank and the Uganda Development Bank.

ENERGY AND NATURAL RESOURCES

Electricity. Industrial expansion is based on hydro-electric power provided by the Owen Falls scheme, which has a capacity of 150,000 kwh. Production (1978) 630m. kwh.

Minerals. The Kilembe Mines, which used to produce both copper for export and phosphate rock, ceased production in 1979. Preparations were under way (1985) to re-open fully the mine and other smaller mines and start exports.

Agriculture. In 1983, agriculture was still recovering from the administration of 1971–79. Cotton and coffee are the principal exports, the former being grown entirely and the latter very largely by African farmers. Production (1983) in 1,000 tonnes: Tobacco, 2·3; coffee, 172; cotton lint, 10·2; tea, 2·5; sugar, 2·5.

Livestock (1983): Cattle, 5m.; sheep, 1·3m.; goats, 2·4m.; pigs, 280,000; poultry, 8m.

Forestry. Exploitable forests consist almost entirely of hardwoods. Internal consumption is rising. About half of the timber exported goes to the UK and another quarter to Kenya and Tanganyika, from which the bulk of the softwood imports are obtained. Sawn wood production (1981) 5·97m. cu. metres.

Fishery. With its 13,600 sq. miles of lakes and many rivers, Uganda possesses one of the largest fresh-water fisheries in the world. In 1982 fish production was 170,800 tonnes. Fish farming (especially carp and tilapia) is a growing industry.

COMMERCE. Trade (in US$1m.):

	1981	*1982*	*1983*[1]
Imports	415	458	510
Exports	246	335	330

[1] Estimate.

Total trade between Uganda and UK (British Department of Trade returns, in £1,000 sterling):

	1980	*1981*	*1982*	*1983*	*1984*
Imports to UK	30,735	18,186	23,107	29,645	46,750
Exports and re-exports from UK	33,526	24,650	31,272	21,092	29,294

COMMUNICATIONS

Roads. There were (1985) 7,582 km of all-weather roads maintained by the Ministry of Works, of which 1,934 km are two-lane bitumenized highways, and some 19,640 km of other roads, maintained by district governments.

Railways. On 26 Aug. 1977 Uganda Railways was formed following break-up of the East African Railways administration. The network totals 1,286 km (metre gauge). In 1982 railways carried 3·3m. passengers and 313,000 tonnes of freight.

Aviation. Dr Obote International Airport, formerly Entebbe, has direct flights to Europe, Rhodesia, Sudan, Kenya, Burundi, Ghana, Ethiopia, Zaïre, Nigeria, USSR, and Rwanda by Sudan Airways, Air Congo, SABENA, Air France, Ethiopian Airlines, Air Zaïre and Aeroflot. Eleven other government airfields are used for internal communications.

Posts and Broadcasting. There were 48,884 telephones in use at 1 Jan. 1978. There were 275,000 radio receivers and about 75,000 television sets in 1982

Cinemas. In 1971 there were 16 cinemas with a seating capacity of 8,000.

JUSTICE, RELIGION, EDUCATION AND WELFARE

Justice. The High Court of Uganda, presided over by the Chief Justice and 15 puisne judges, exercises original and appellate jurisdiction throughout Uganda. Subordinate courts, presided over by Chief Magistrates and Magistrates of the first, second and third grade, are established in all areas: jurisdiction varies with the grade of Magistrate. Chief and first-grade Magistrates are professionally qualified; second-and third-grade Magistrates are trained to diploma level at the Law School, Entebbe. Chief Magistrates exercise supervision over and hear appeals from second- and third-grade courts.

The Court of Appeal of Uganda hears appeals from the High Court.

Religion. About 62% of the population are Christian and 6% Moslem.

Education. Education is a joint undertaking by the Government, local authorities and, to some extent, voluntary agencies. The education system is divided into 3 sectors, primary, secondary and post-secondary. The primary course covers 7 years. There were 1·4m. pupils in grant-aided primary schools in 1982. Education at secondary level falls into 4 categories, namely, secondary schools, which are the grammar type of schools with a course extending over 6 years to High School Certificate; technical schools; farm schools; and primary teacher-training colleges. Further education is provided at the Uganda Technical College, the National Teachers' College, the Uganda College of Commerce and Agricultural Colleges.

There are also several Departmental Training Schools for training staff for different departments.

The medical department has 8 such schools for training nurses, midwives, medical assistants, health inspectors, and other medical staff.

University level education is available at Makerere University College and the 2 other constituent Colleges of the University of East Africa; the University College, Nairobi, in Kenya, and the University College, Dar es Salaam, in Tanzania. Uganda students also go to universities and colleges outside East Africa for higher education.

Health. In 1983 there were 76 hospitals and 20,343 hospital beds.

DIPLOMATIC REPRESENTATIVES

Of Uganda in Great Britain (Uganda Hse., Trafalgar Sq., London, WC2N 5DX)
High Commissioner: Shafiq Arain.

Of Great Britain in Uganda (10/12 Obote Ave., Kampala)
High Commissioner: C. McLean, CMG, MBE.

Of Uganda in the USA (5909 16th St., NW, Washington, D.C., 20011)
Ambassador: John Wycliffe Lwamafa.

Of the USA in Uganda (British High Commission Bldg., Obote Ave., Kampala)
Ambassador: Allen C. Davis.

Of Uganda to the United Nations
Ambassador: Olara Otunnu.

Books of Reference

Atlas of Uganda. Dept. of Lands and Surveys. Kampala, 1962
Collison, R. L., *Uganda.* [Bibliography] Oxford and Santa Barbara, 1981
Hills, D., *The White Pumpkin.* New York, 1976
Jørgensen, J. J., *Uganda: A Modern History.* London, 1981
Kitching, A. L., and Blackledge, G. R., *A Luganda–English and English–Luganda Dictionary.* Kampala, 1925
Larimore, A. E., *The Alien Town: Patterns of Settlement in Uganda.* Chicago, 1959
Listowel, J., *Amin.* Irish Univ. Press, 1973
Mamdani, M., *Imperialism and Fascism in Uganda.* London, 1983

UNION OF SOVIET SOCIALIST REPUBLICS

Capital: Moscow
Population: 276·3m. (1985)

Soyuz Sovyetskikh Sotsialisticheskikh Respublik

POST-REVOLUTION HISTORY. Up to 12 March 1917 the territory now forming the USSR, together with that of Finland, Poland and certain tracts ceded in 1918 to Turkey, but less the territories then forming part of the German, Austro-Hungarian and Japanese empires–East Prussia, Eastern Galicia, Transcarpathia, Bukovina, South Sakhalin and Kurile Islands–which were acquired during and after the Second World War, was constituted as the Russian Empire. It was governed as an autocracy under the Tsar, with the aid of Ministers responsible to himself and a State Duma with limited legislative powers, elected by provincial assemblies chosen by indirect elections on a restricted franchise.

On 8 March 1917 a revolution broke out. The Duma parties, on 12 March, set up a Provisional Committee of the State Duma, while the factory workmen and the insurgent garrison of Petrograd elected a Council (Soviet) of Workers' and Soldiers' Deputies. Soviets were also elected by the workmen in other towns, in the Army and Navy and, as time went on, by the peasantry. On 15 March 1917 the Tsar abdicated, and the Provisional Committee, by agreement with the Petrograd Soviet, appointed a Provisional Government and, on 14 Sept., proclaimed a republic. However, a political struggle went on between the supporters of the Provisional Government–the Mensheviks and the Socialist-Revolutionaries–and the Bolsheviks, who advocated the assumption of power by the Soviets. When they had won majorities in the Soviets of the principal cities and of the armed forces on several fronts, the Bolsheviks organized an insurrection through a Military-Revolutionary Committee of the Petrograd Soviet. On 7 Nov. 1917 the Committee arrested the Provisional Government and transferred power to the second All-Russian Congress of Soviets. This elected a new government, the Council of People's Commissars, headed by Lenin.

On 25 Jan. 1918 the third All-Russian Congress of Soviets issued a Declaration of Rights of the Toiling and Exploited People, which proclaimed Russia a Republic of Soviets of Workers', Soldiers' and Peasants' Deputies; and on 10 July 1918 the fifth Congress adopted a Constitution for the Russian Soviet Federal Socialist Republic. In the course of the civil war other Soviet Republics were set up in the Ukraine, Belorussia and Transcaucasia. These first entered into treaty relations with the RSFSR and then, in 1922, joined with it in a closely integrated Union.

AREA AND POPULATION. The total area of the Soviet Union in April 1985 was 22·4m. sq. km (8·65m. sq. miles). The census population on 15 Jan. 1970 was 241·7m. (111·4m. males, 130·3m. females; 136m. urban, 105·7m. rural). The census population on 17 Jan. 1979 was 262·4m. (122·3m. males, 140·1m. females, 163·6m. urban, 98·9m. rural). The increase of 27·6m. in urban population between 1970 and 1979 was due to natural increase and 15·6m. rural dwellers becoming part of the urban population resulting from migration because of the development of industry and transport, and increased farm mechanization, and from the urbanization of large rural centres. Consequently, despite a natural increase of 8·7m. in rural areas, there was a net decrease of 6·9m. over this period. Population at 1 Jan. 1984, 273·8m. (128·3m. males, 145·5m. females; 177·5m. urban; 96·3m. rural).

Regions, towns, streets, factories, schools, etc., named after Stalin were renamed in Nov. 1961 when Stalin's body was removed from the Lenin-Stalin tomb in Red

Square in Moscow. Similarly, in Jan. 1962 towns bearing the names of Molotov, Kaganovich and Malenkov were renamed.

The areas (in 1,000 sq. km) and population (in 1m., in Jan. 1984) of the constituent republics are as follows (capitals in brackets):

Constituent Republics	*Area*	*Population*	*Constituent Republics*	*Area*	*Population*
RSFSR (Moscow)	17,075	142·1	Tadzhikistan (Dushanbe)	143	4·4
Ukraine (Kiev)	604	50·7	Kirgizia (Frunze)	199	3·9
Uzbekistan (Tashkent)	447	17·5	Lithuania (Vilnius)	65	3·5
Kazakhstan (Alma-Ata)	2,717	15·6	Armenia (Yerevan)	30	3·3
Belorussia (Minsk)	208	9·9	Turkmenistan (Ashkhabad)	488	3·1
Azerbaijan (Baku)	87	6·5	Latvia (Riga)	64	2·6
Georgia (Tbilisi)	70	5·2	Estonia (Tallinn)	45	1·5
Moldavia (Kishinev)	34	4·1			

Nationalities. The most numerous nationalities at the 1979 census were: 137·4m. Russians, 42·3m. Ukrainians, 12·5m. Uzbeks, 9·5m. Belorussians, 6·6m. Kazakhs, 6·3m. Tatars, 5·5m. Azerbaijanians, 4·1m. Armenians, 3·6m. Georgians, 3m. Moldavians, 2·9m. Tadzhiks, 2·9m. Lithuanians, 2m. Turkmenians, 1·9m. Germans, 1·9m. Kirgiz, 1·8m. Jews, 1·8m. Chuvashes, 1·4m. Latvians, 1·4m. Bashkirs, 1·2m. Mordovians, 1·2m. Poles, 1m. Estonians. The great majority (in each case 73-99%) indicated the language of their nationality as their native tongue; exceptions were the Bashkirs (67%), Germans (57%), Poles (29%) and Jews (14%).

Estimated losses of population in the Second World War, 20m., of which 7m. were military losses.

The following tables show the growth of the population in Russia:

1897 (Russian Empire)	126,900,000	1959 (census)	208,826,650
1913 (Russian Empire)	170,900,000	1970 (census)	241,720,134
1913 (present frontiers)	159,153,000	1979 (census)	262,436,227
1939 (census)	170,557,093		

The following was the population on 1 Jan. 1984 of the larger towns (in 1,000):

Aktyubinsk	224	Dushanbe	539	Komsomolsk-on-	
Alma-Ata	1,046	Dzerzhinsk (Gorky		Amur	291
Andizhan	267	region)	272	Kostroma	267
Andropov	249	Engels	175	Kramatorsk	189
Angarsk	254	Ferghana	191	Krasnodar	603
Arkhangelsk	403	Frunze	590	Krasnoyarsk	857
Armavir	168	Gomel	452	Kremenchug	222
Ashkhabad	346	Gorlovka	341	Krivoi Rog	680
Astrakhan	487	Gorky	1,392	Kuibyshev	1,250
Baku	1,661	Grodno	239	Kurgan	339
Barnaul	568	Grozny	389	Kursk	413
Belaya Tserkov	176	Irkutsk	589	Kustanai	191
Belgorod	274	Ivano-Frankovsk	200	Kutaisi	210
Berezniki	193	Ivanovo	476	Kzyl-Orda	180
Biisk	224	Kalinin	437	Leninakan	220
Blagoveshchensk	192	Kaliningrad	380	Leningrad	4,827
Bobruisk	218	Kaluga	291	Lipetsk	440
Bratsk	236	Kamensk-		Lvov	728
Brest	214	Uralski	198	Lyubertsy	166
Brezhnev	414	Karaganda	608	Magnitogorsk	421
Bryansk	424	Kaunas	400	Makeyevka	448
Bukhara	204	Kazan	1,039	Makhachkala	293
Cheboksary	378	Kemerovo	502	Melitopol	169
Chelyabinsk	1,086	Kerch	166	Minsk	1,442
Cherepovetz	295	Khabarovsk	568	Mogilev	334
Cherkassy	267	Kharkov	1,536	Moscow	8,537
Chernigov	270	Kherson	340	Murmansk	412
Chernovtsy	238	Kiev	2,409	Nalchik	227
Chimkent	360	Kirov	407	Namangan	265
Chita	331	Kirovabad		Nikolayev	480
Djambul	298	(Azerbaijan)	257	Nizhni Tagil	415
Dneprodzerzhinsk	268	Kirovograd	257	Norilsk	183
Dnepropetrovsk	1,140	Kishinev	605	Novgorod	215
Donetsk	1,064	Klaipeda	191	Novocherkassk	188

Novokuznetsk	572	Ryazan	488	Tselinograd	256
Novorossiisk	174	Samarkand	515	Tula	529
Novosibirsk	1,384	Saransk	301	Tyumen	411
Odessa	1,113	Saratov	893	Ufa	1,048
Omsk	1,094	Semipalatinsk	307	Ulan-Ude	329
Ordzhonikidze (Vladikavkaz)	300	Sevastopol	335	Ulyanovsk	524
Orel	325	Severodvinsk	224	Uralsk	188
Orenburg	513	Shakhty	219	Ustinov	603
Orsk	263	Simferopol	328	Ust-Kamenogorsk	302
Osh	194	Smolensk	326	Vilnius	535
Pavlodar	309	Sochi	307	Vinnitsa	360
Penza	522	Stavropol	287	Vitebsk	330
Perm	1,048	Sterlitamak	238	Vladimir	326
Petropavlovsk-Kamchatski	241	Sumgait	218	Vladivostok	590
Petropavlovsk (North Kazakhstan)	222	Sumy	252	Volgograd	969
Petrozavodsk	251	Sverdlovsk	1,286	Vologda	264
Podolsk	207	Syktyvkar	209	Volzhsky	238
Poltava	296	Syzran	173	Voronezh	840
Prokopyevsk	274	Taganrog	289	Voroshilovgrad	491
Pskov	189	Tallinn	458	Yaroslavl	623
Riga	875	Tambov	290	Yerevan	1,114
Rostov-on-Don	983	Tashkent	1,986	Yoshkar-Ola	227
Rovno	215	Tbilisi	1,140	Zaporozhye	844
Rubtsovsk	163	Temirtau	224	Zhdanov	520
		Togliatti	576	Zhitomir	270
		Tomsk	467	Zlatoust	204

Narodnoe khozyaistvo SSSR. Moscow, annual
Ezhegodnik Bol'shoi Sovetskoi Entsiklopedii. Moscow, annual
Itogi Vsesoyuznoi perepisi naseleniya 1959 goda. SSSR (svodnyi tom). Moscow, 1962
Itogi Vsesoyuznoi perepisi naseleniya 1970 goda, 7 vols. Moscow, 1972–74
Chislennost' i sostav naseleniya SSSR po dannym Vsesoyuznoi perepisi 1979 goda. Moscow, 1984
Sovetskii Soyuz. Geograficheskoe opisanie, 22 vols. Moscow, 1966–72
Cole, J. P., *Geography of the Soviet Union.* London, 1984.
Howe, G. Melvyn, *The Soviet Union: a Geographical Survey* (2nd ed.). London, 1983
Kish, G., (ed.), *An Economic Atlas of the Soviet Union.* (2nd ed.), Ann Arbor, 1971
Lorrimer, F., *The Population of the Soviet Union.* Geneva, 1946
Symons, L., (ed.), *The Soviet Union: a Systematic Geography.* London, 1983
Wixman, R., *The Peoples of Russia and the USSR.* London, 1984

CLIMATE. The USSR comprises several different climatic regions, ranging from polar conditions in the north, through sub-arctic and humid continental, to sub-tropical and semi-arid conditions in the south. Rainfall amounts are greatest in areas bordering the Baltic, Black Sea, Caspian Sea and eastern coasts of Asiatic Russia. In most cases, there is a summer maximum.

Moscow. Jan. 15°F (–9·4°C), July 65°F (18·3°C). Annual rainfall 25·2″ (630 mm). Arkhangelsk. Jan. 5°F (–15°C), July 57°F (13·9°C). Annual rainfall 20·1″ (503 mm). Kiev. Jan. 21°F (–6·1°C), July 68°F (20°C). Annual rainfall 22″ (554 mm). Leningrad. Jan. 17°F (–8·3°C), July 64°F (17·8°C). Annual rainfall 19·5″ (488 mm). Vladivostok. Jan. 6°F (–14·4°C), July 65°F (18·3°C). Annual rainfall 24″ (599 mm).

CONSTITUTION

Constituent Republics. The Union of Soviet Socialist Republics was formed by the union of the RSFSR, the Ukrainian Soviet Socialist Republic, the Belorussian Soviet Socialist Republic and the Transcaucasian Soviet Socialist Republic; the Treaty of Union was adopted by the first Soviet Congress of the USSR on 30 Dec. 1922. In Oct. 1924 the Uzbek and Turkmen Autonomous Soviet Socialist Republics and in Dec. 1929 the Tadzhik Autonomous Soviet Socialist Republic were declared constituent members of the USSR, becoming Union Republics.

At the 8th Congress of the Soviets, on 5 Dec. 1936, a new constitution of the USSR was adopted. The Transcaucasian Republic was split up into the Armenian Soviet Socialist Republic, the Azerbaijan Soviet Socialist Republic and the Georgian Soviet Socialist Republic, each of which became constituent republics of the Union. At the same time the Kazakh Soviet Socialist Republic and the Kirghiz Soviet Socialist Republic, previously autonomous republics within the RSFSR, were proclaimed constituent republics of the USSR.

In Sept. 1939 Soviet troops occupied eastern Poland as far as the 'Curzon line', which in 1919 had been drawn on ethnographical grounds as the eastern frontier of Poland, and incorporated it into the Ukrainian and Belorussian Soviet Socialist Republics. In Feb. 1951 some districts of the Drogobych Region of the Ukraine and the Lublin Voivodship of Poland were exchanged.

On 31 March 1940 territory ceded by Finland was joined to that of the Autonomous Soviet Socialist Republic of Karelia to form the Karelo-Finnish Soviet Socialist Republic, which was admitted into the Union as the 12th Union Republic. On 16 July 1956 the Supreme Soviet of the USSR adopted a law altering the status of the Karelo-Finnish Republic from that of a Union (constituent) Republic of the USSR to that of an Autonomous (Karelian) Republic within the RSFSR.

On 2 Aug. 1940 the Moldavian Soviet Socialist Republic was constituted as the 13th Union Republic. It comprised the former Moldavian Autonomous Soviet Socialist Republic and Bessarabia (44,290 sq. km, ceded by Romania on 28 June 1940), except for the districts of Khotin, Akerman and Ismail, which, together with Northern Bukovina (10,440 sq. km), were incorporated in the Ukrainian Soviet Republic. The Soviet-Romanian frontier thus constituted was confirmed by the peace treaty with Romania, signed on 10 Feb. 1947. On 29 June 1945 Ruthenia (Sub-Carpathian Russia, 12,742 sq. km) was by treaty with Czechoslovakia incorporated into the Ukrainian Soviet Socialist Republic.

On 3, 5 and 6 Aug. 1940 Lithuania, Latvia and Estonia were incorporated in the Soviet Union as the 14th, 15th and 16th Union Republics respectively. The change in the status of the Karelo-Finnish Republic reduced the number of Union Republics to 15.

After the defeat of Germany it was agreed by the governments of the UK, the USA and the USSR (by the Potsdam declaration) that part of East Prussia should be embodied in the USSR. The area (11,655 sq. km), which includes the towns of Konigsberg (renamed Kaliningrad), Tilsit (renamed Sovyetsk) and Insterburg (renamed Chernyakhovsk), was joined to the RSFSR by decree of 7 April 1946.

By the peace treaty with Finland, signed on 10 Feb. 1947, the province of Petsamo (Pechenga), ceded to Finland on 14 Oct. 1920 and 12 March 1940, was returned to the Soviet Union. On 19 Sept. 1955 the Soviet Union renounced its treaty rights to the naval base of Porkkala-Udd and on 26 Jan. 1956 completed the withdrawal of the forces from Finnish territory.

In 1945, after the defeat of Japan, the southern half of Sakhalin (36,000 sq. km) and the Kurile Islands (10,200 sq. km) were, by agreement with the Allies, incorporated in the USSR.[1]

[1] However, Japan asks for the return of the Etorofu and Kunashiri Islands as not belonging to the Kurile Islands proper. The Soviet Government informed Japan on 27 Jan. 1960 that the Habomai Islands and Shikotan would be handed back to Japan on the withdrawal of the American troops from Japan.

GOVERNMENT. The Soviet Union is a socialist state of the whole people (1977 constitution), the political units of which are the Soviets of People's Deputies. All central and local authority is vested in these Soviets.

The economic foundation of the USSR is the socialist system of economy and the socialist ownership of the means of production. There are two forms of socialist property: (1) state property (property of the whole people); (2) co-operative and collective farm (*kolkhoz*) property (property of individual collective farms and property of co-operative associations). The land, mineral deposits, waters, forests, mills, factories, mines, railways, water and air transport, banks, means of communication, state farms (*sovkhozy*), as well as municipal enterprises and the principal dwelling-house properties in the cities and industrial localities, are state property, but the land occupied by collective farmers is secured to them in perpetuity so long as they use it in accordance with the laws of the country. The members of the *kolkhozy* may have small plots of land attached to their dwellings for their own use. Peasants unwilling to enter a kolkhoz may retain their individual farms, but they are not allowed to employ hired labour. The right of personal property of citizens in their income from work and in their savings, in their dwelling houses and auxiliary household economy, their domestic furniture and utensils and objects of personal use and comfort, as well as the right of inheritance of personal property of citizens, are protected by law. The constitution recognizes the right of all citizens to work, rest, leisure, education, health protection, housing, maintenance in old age, sickness or incapacity, without distinction of sex, race or nationality, and lays down that any direct or indirect restriction of the rights of, or conversely, the establishment of direct or indirect privileges for, citizens on account of their race, or nationality, as well as the advocacy of racial or national exclusiveness, or hatred or contempt, is punishable by law. The franchise is enjoyed by all citizens of the USSR, including members of the Armed Forces, who have reached the age of 18, irrespective of sex, with the exception of the legally certified insane. Candidates for election to the Supreme Soviet of the USSR must be 21 years of age; for all other authorities the minimum age for candidates is 18. A member of any Soviet may be recalled by a decision of a majority of his or her electors if he or she fails to give satisfaction (law on procedure for this, 30 Oct. 1959).

The USSR consists of 15 Union Republics, each inhabited by a major nationality which gives its name to the republic. These are divided into 129 territories and regions, and these again into 3,213 districts and 2,138 towns and 3,937 urban settlements (1 Jan. 1984). Within the villages there are 41,963 rural districts (usually each including a number of villages). The territories and regions also include a number of smaller nationalities, forming their own self-governing units–20 Autonomous Soviet Socialist Republics, 8 Autonomous Regions and 10 Autonomous Areas.

The highest legislative organ is the Supreme Soviet of the USSR. It consists of two chambers with equal legislative rights, elected for a term of 5 years: the Council of the Union and the Council of Nationalities. Each has 750 members. The present Supreme Soviet, the 'Eleventh Convocation', was elected on 4 March 1984.

The Council of the Union is elected by the citizens of the USSR on the basis of constituencies with equal populations (approximately 1 deputy for every 360,000 population). Its Chairman (elected 1984) is L. N. Tolkunov. The Council of Nationalities is elected by the citizens of the USSR on the basis of national-territorial areas (32 deputies from each Union Republic, 11 from each Autonomous Republic, 5 from each Autonomous Region and 1 from each Autonomous Area). Its Chairman (elected 1984) is A. E. Voss. Plenary sessions of the Supreme Soviet are normally held twice a year for two or three days at a time.

Each chamber elects 17 standing commissions: mandates; legislative proposals; foreign affairs; planning and budget; industry; power engineering; transport and communications; construction and the building materials industry; agro-industrial complex; science and technology; consumer goods and services; housing and municipal services; health and social security; education and culture; women's work and social conditions and the protection of motherhood and childhood; youth affairs; and conservation and the rational use of natural resources. Membership of the commissions presently embraces 1,210 deputies (80·7% of the total).

Deputies are elected by the voters on the basis of universal, equal and direct suffrage by secret ballot. The only legal political party is the Communist Party of the Soviet Union; non-members are classed as non-party citizens. Candidates are selected at preliminary 'constituency electoral consultation' meetings (selection conferences), to which organizations which have put forward nominations send delegates, who discuss the various nominees. As a consequence, to date, a single candidate has been agreed upon in each constituency, whose name appears on the ballot paper to be endorsed (by non-deletion) or struck out as the voter desires. These procedures are governed by the Law on Elections to the Supreme Soviet of the USSR, adopted in April 1978. At the election on 4 March 1984, 184,006,373 electors voted (99·99% of the total); the vote in favour of the single list of candidates was 99·94% and 99·95% in each of the two chambers. The Supreme Soviet elected on that day consists of 1,071 Communist and 428 non-party deputies; 492 are women, 527 manual workers in industry and state farms, and 242 collective farmers.

The highest executive and administrative body of state authority in the USSR is the Council of Ministers of the USSR, which is appointed by the USSR Supreme Soviet at a joint sitting of the two chambers. It consists of a Chairman (in effect the Soviet Prime Minister), First Vice-Chairmen and Vice-Chairmen, Ministers of the USSR, and Chairmen of State Committees of the USSR. Chairmen of the Councils of Ministers of the Union Republics are *ex officio* members of the USSR Council of Ministers. The Council of Ministers of the USSR had more than 100 members in 1985, and day-to-day co-ordination of governmental matters is accordingly delegated to a smaller body, the Presidium of the Council of Ministers, which meets approximately every week. The Council of Ministers is responsible and accountable to the Supreme Soviet and is required to report regularly to the Supreme Soviet upon its work. Between sessions of the Supreme Soviet the Council of Ministers is responsible to the Presidium of the USSR Supreme Soviet.

The Presidium of the Supreme Soviet of the USSR is elected from among the deputies at a joint session of both chambers of the Supreme Soviet. It consists of a chairman (in effect the President of the USSR), a first vice-chairman, 15 vice-chairmen (1 from each Union Republic), 21 members and a secretary (39 members in all). The Presidium acts as the supreme state authority between sessions of the Supreme Soviet and is accountable to it for all its actions. The Presidium convenes sessions of the Supreme Soviet and co-ordinates the work of its standing commissions; it interprets the law of the USSR and ratifies and denounces international treaties; it confers medals, orders and other distinctions; it decides matters such as citizenship, amnesties, pardons, martial law and states of emergency; and it appoints the high command of the Soviet Armed forces and Soviet diplomatic representatives. It is empowered to adopt decrees *(ukazy)* and resolutions *(postanovleniya)*.

Soon after the adoption of the 1936 Constitution all the constituent republics of the Union held their Soviet congresses, at which they adopted their own constitutions based in all essentials upon the Constitution of the Union but adapted where necessary to local requirements. In April 1978 the Supreme Soviets of the Union Republics similarly adopted new republican constitutions based upon the new Constitution of the USSR approved by the Supreme Soviet in Oct. 1977. Article 73 of the 1977 Constitution of the USSR reserves to the central government the spheres of war and peace, diplomatic relations, defence, foreign trade, state security, economic planning, education, the basic principles of legislation, and other matters of 'all-Union significance'. The right of the constituent republics to withdraw from the Union is, however, formally recognized in Article 72. Union Republics have their own Supreme Soviets, Presidiums and Councils of Ministers, and exercise a wide range of devolved powers in local matters.

There are 20 Autonomous Republics in the USSR, which are similarly governed by their own Supreme Soviets, Presidiums and Councils of Ministers exercising devolved powers over local matters. Most (16) are in the RSFSR; 2 are in Georgia and 1 each in Azerbaijan and Uzbekistan. Five Autonomous Regions are in the RSFSR, 1 each in Azerbaijan, Georgia, and Tadzhikistan. All 10 Autonomous Areas are in the RSFSR. Elections are held every five years to the Supreme Soviets of Union and Autonomous Republics. At the most recent elections (Feb. 1985), 10,188 deputies were elected; 3,830 (37·6%) were women, 3,495 (34·3%) were non-Party, 3,605 (35·4%) were industrial workers and 1,557 (15·3%) were collective farmers.

Regions and territories, districts, towns and rural areas are similarly governed by their own Soviets, elected for a term of 2½ years. At the most recent elections (Feb. 1985), 2,340,703 deputies were elected to these Soviets; 1,159,597 (50·3%) were women, 1,317,220 (57·2%) were non-Party, 1,024,675 (44·5%) were industrial workers and 571,450 (24·8%) were collective farmers. On 1 Jan. 1984 there were 51,253 rural and urban Soviets in the USSR with 2·3m. deputies and over 30m. voluntary co-opted members participating in the work of their standing committees.

State flag: Red, with sickle and hammer in gold in the upper corner near the staff, and above them a 5-pointed star bordered in gold.

National anthem: Soyuz nerushimy respublik svobodnykh (words by S. Mikhalkov and G. El-Registan; music by A. V. Alexandrov; 1944, revised 1977).

Chairman of the Presidium of the Supreme Soviet of the USSR: (Vacant.)
First Vice-Chairman: Viktor Vasilievich Kuznetsov.
Secretary of the Presidium: Tengiz Menteshashvili.
Chairman of the Council of Ministers of the USSR: Nikolai Aleksandrovich Tikhonov.
First Vice-Chairmen: G. A. Aliev; A. A. Gromyko; I. V. Arkhipov.
Minister of Defence: Marshal S. L. Sokolov. *Minister of Foreign Trade:* N. S. Patolichev. *Minister for Foreign Affairs:* A. A. Gromyko. *Minister of Internal Affairs:* V. V. Fedorchuk. *Minister of Finance:* V. F. Garbuzov. *Chairman, State Security Committee (KGB):* V. M. Chebrikov. *Chairman, State Planning Committee (Gosplan):* N. K. Baibakov.

Constitution (Fundamental Law) of the USSR. Moscow, 1977
Konstitutsiya SSSR. Konstitutsii Soyuznykh Sovetskikh Respublik. Moscow, 1978
Unger, A. L., *Constitutional Development in the USSR.* London, 1981
F. J. M. Feldbrugge, (ed.), *The Constitution of the USSR and the Union Republics.* Alphen aan den Rijn, 1979

Communist Party of the Soviet Union. According to the rules adopted by the 22nd Congress of the Party on 31 Oct. 1961, the Communist Party of the Soviet Union 'unites, on a voluntary basis, the more advanced, politically more conscious section of the working class, collective-farm peasantry and intelligentsia of the USSR', whose principal objects are to build a Communist society by means of gradual transition from Socialism to Communism, to raise the material and cultural level of the people, to organize the defence of the country and to strengthen ties with the workers of other countries.

The Party is built on the territorial-industrial principle. The supreme organ is the Party Congress. Ordinary congresses are convened not less than every 5 years. The Congress elects a Central Committee which meets at least every 6 months, carries on the work of the Party between congresses, and guides the work of central Soviet and public organizations through Party groups within them.

The Central Committee forms a Political Bureau *(Politburo)* to direct the work of the Central Committee between plenary meetings, a Secretariat to direct current work and a Party Control Committee to deal with disciplinary matters; it also elects the General Secretary. Similar rules hold for the regional, territorial and republican levels of the party organization. The 'basis of the Party', the primary Party organization, exists in factories, state and collective farms, units of the Soviet Army and Navy, in villages, offices, educational establishments etc. where there are at least 3 Party members. There were over 425,000 primary Party organizations in 1983.

The Central Committee elected by the 26th Congress in March 1981 consisted of 319 members and 151 candidate (non-voting) members. Of these 39·6% were drawn from the central and regional party apparatus, and 5·7% were workers or peasants.

In March 1985 the Politburo of the Central Committee consisted of the following members: M. S. Gorbachev, G. A. Aliev, V. V. Grishin, A. A. Gromyko, D. A. Kunaev, G. V. Romanov, N. A. Tikhonov, V. V. Shcherbitsky, M. S. Solomentsev and V. I. Vorotnikov and the following candidate (non-voting) members: V. M. Chebrikov, P. N. Demichev, V. I. Dolgikh, V. V. Kuznetsov, B. N. Ponomarev, E. A. Shevardnadze.

Secretariat: M. S. Gorbachev *(General Secretary);* V. I. Dolgikh; I. V. Kapitonov; E. K. Ligachev; B. N. Ponomarev; G. V. Romanov; K. V. Rusakov; N. I. Ryzhkov and M. V. Zimyanin.

Chairman of the Party Control Committee: M. S. Solomentsev.
Chairman of the Central Auditing Commission: G. F. Sizov.

In Jan. 1984 the Communist Party had 18,443,521 members (about 9·3% of the adult population). Of these, 44·4% were classified as workers, 12·2% as collective farmers and 43·4% as office workers; 27·9% were women, and 59·7% were Russians. The party's youth wing, the Komsomol (All-Union Leninist Communist Union of Youth), had 42·0m. members in 1984. In Dec. 1982, V. M. Mishin was elected First Secretary of its Central Committee.

Istoriya Kommunisticheskoi partii Sovetskogo Soyuza, 6 vols. Moscow, 1964ff.
Istoriya Kommunisticheskoi partii Sovetskogo Soyuza, 7th ed. Moscow, 1984
Rules of the Communist Party of the Soviet Union. Moscow, 1977
KPSS v rezolyutsiyakh i resheniyakh s"ezdov, konferentsii i plenumov TsK, 8th ed., 14 vols. Moscow, 1970–1982
Resolutions and Decisions of the Communist Party of the Soviet Union, ed. R. H. McNeal, 5 vols. Toronto, 1974–82
Spravochnik partiinogo rabotnika. Moscow, annual
Hill, R. and Frank, P., *The Soviet Communist Party.* London, 1981
Schapiro, L. B., *The Communist Party of the Soviet Union.* 2nd ed., London, 1970

DEFENCE. On 25 Feb. 1946 the control of the Soviet Armed Forces was unified under a single Ministry of the Armed Forces. On 25 Feb. 1950 the Defence Ministry was divided into a War Ministry and a Navy Ministry; on 15 March 1953 a single Ministry of Defence was reconstituted.

In 1955 the Air Defence Command and in 1960 the Strategic Rocket Forces were established as the 4th and 5th 'branches' of the armed forces beside the army, navy and air force.

The direction of Party and political work in the Armed Forces is exercised by the Central Committee of the Communist Party of the Soviet Union through the chief political directorate of the Ministry of Defence. The chiefs of the political departments of military commands, fleets and armies must be Party members of 5 years' standing and the chiefs of political departments of divisions and regiments Party members of 3 years' standing. About 90% of the officers are members of the Communist Party or Young Communist League, and 50% have had an engineering and technical education.

Military service begins at the age of 19 (or 18 for graduates of secondary schools). Active service lasts 2 years for privates in the Army and M.V.D. troops, 3 years for n.c.o.s in the Army and M.V.D. troops and for privates and n.c.o.s in the Air Force, 4 years for privates and n.c.o.s in the Coastal Defence, 5 years for ratings in the Navy. Reserve service lasts up to the ages of 35, 45 or 50 years according to fitness, family status and other considerations. Conscientious objection is treated as a criminal offence. Students in places of higher education are freed from military service, but receive military instruction. About half the service personnel have had higher, or 10-year, education and over 80% are members of the Communist Party.

Total strength of the armed forces was over 5m. in 1984, with a probable 25m. reserves and a further 500,000 in paramilitary forces.

The estimated expenditure on defence (in 1m. rubles) for 1961 was 9,255; 1970, 17,900; 1980, 17,100; 1983, 17,050.

Army. The Army is thought to consist of 50 tank, 134 motor rifle, 7 airborne and 15 artillery divisions; 8 air assault brigades; and various independent tank, artillery, missile and engineer units. Equipment includes some 35,000 T-54/-55/-62, 7,500 T-64 and 7,500 T-72/-80 main battle tanks. Strength (1984) 1·8m. (including 1·4m. conscripts).

Navy. The Soviet Fleet is steadily expanding and progressively modernizing under a continuity of policy and technology given by the nearly three decades in office of Admiral of the Fleet of the Soviet Union Sergei Georgiyevich Gorshkov, C.-in-C. of the Soviet Navy and Deputy Minister of Defence. The overall picture is of an unprecedentedly powerful and well-balanced navy, the capacity of which is increasing annually by scientific application and numerical strength.

The principal surface ships of the Soviet Navy are as follows:

Completed	*Name*	*Standard displacement Tons*	*Aircraft*	*Principal armament*	*Shaft horse-power*	*Speed Knots*
			Aircraft Carriers [1]			
1985	Kharkov [2]	39,000	13 fixed wing aircraft 20 helicopters	4 twin SS missile launchers; 4 twin SA missile launchers; 1 twin AS missile launcher; 4 76-mm AA guns	140,000	32
1982	Novorossiisk					
1978	Minsk					
1976	Kiev					

[1] *See* Aircraft carriers under construction and projected, successors of *Kiev* class, next page.
[2] Scheduled for commissioning in late 1984.

			Battle Cruisers [1]			
1984	Frunze	22,000	3 helicopters	20 single SS missile launchers; 16 SA missile launchers; 2 AS missile launchers; 2 100-mm guns	160,000 (nuclear power)	35
1980	Kirov					

[1] The first battle cruisers, and the largest combatant warships, apart from aircraft carriers, to be built for any navy since the Second World War. Main engines comprise 2 nuclear reactors and oil-fired superheat boilers for steam turbines. Names proposed for sister ships reported to be Leoned Brezhnev and Baku.

			Helicopter Carriers			
1968	Leningrad	16,500	14 helicopters	2 twin SA missile launchers; 1 twin AS missile launcher; 2 twin 57-mm AA guns	100,000	31
1967	Moskva					

			Cruisers			
1984	Admiral Zakorov	8,500	2 helicopters	2 quadruple SS missile launchers; 8 SA missile launchers; 2 single 100-mm guns	100,000	33
1984	Marshal Vasilevsky					
1982	Vize Admiral Kulakov					
1982	Udaloy [1]					

[1] Four more light cruisers of the *Udaloy* class rated as large anti-submarine ships are being completed or under construction.

1984	Otlichnny	8,000	1 helicopter	8 SS missile launchers; 2 SA missile launchers; 4 130-mm guns	100,000	32
1983	Otchyanny					
1982	Sovremenny [1]					

[1] Four more light cruisers of the Sovremenny class are under construction.

1983	Slava	13,000	2 helicopters	16 SS missiles; SA vertical launchers; AS missile launchers; 100-mm guns	120,000	34

Two more heavy cruisers of this class are under construction.

1979	Tallin	8,200	1 helicopter	2 quadruple SS missile launchers; 8 twin SA missile launchers; 4 76-mm AA guns	124,000	34
1978	Tashkent					
1977	Petropavlovsk					
1976	Azov[3]					
1975	Kerch					
1974	Ochakov					
1973	Nikolaiev					

[3] *Azov*, nominally of this Kara class, is of a modified design, with a different guided missiles system, as trials ship for the armament of subsequent classes of cruisers.

Completed	Name	Standard displacement Tons	Aircraft	Principal armament	Shaft horse-power	Speed Knots
			Cruisers			
1958	Admiral Senyavin[1]	16,000		12 6-in.; 12 3·9-in.	110,000	32
1957	Mikhail Kutuzov					
1956	Dimitri Pojarski					
1956	Oktyabrskaya Revolutsiya [3]					
1956	Admiral Lazarev					
1955	Alexandr Suvorov					
1954	Admiral Ushakov					
1954	Dzerzhinski [2]					
1953	Alexandr Nevski					
1953	Murmansk					
1953	Zhdanov [1]					
1953	Sverdlov [4]					

[1] *Admiral Senyavin* now has a helicopter pad and hangar ('X' and 'Y' turrets removed), leaving her with only six 6-mm guns, while *Zhdanov* has high deckhouse ('X' turret removed). Each carries twin surface-air missile launchers. Both latterly employed as command and communications ships.

[2] *Dzerzhinski* has only nine 6-in. guns in 3 triple turrets, 'X' turret having been replaced by a twin surface-air missile launcher.

[3] This ship, first named *Molotovsk*, was renamed in 1957.

[4] Of the older cruisers, *Kirov* and *Slava* (ex-*Molotov*) were deleted from the effective list in 1976-77 and *Zheleznyakov* in 1978. *Komsomolets* was latterly used as a training ship.

Capital Support Ship

1977	Berezina [1]	40,000	2 helicopters	Twin SA missile launcher; 4 57-mm guns	54,000	22

[1] Very impressive militarised replenishment ship designed to support the new Soviet aircraft carriers.

Submarines

76(10)[3]	SSBN	Nuclear powered	Ballistic missile armed [1] *q.v.*
15	SSB	Diesel-electric powered	Ballistic missile armed
50	SSGN	Nuclear powered	Cruise (guided) missile armed
18	SSG	Diesel-electric powered	Cruise missile armed
76	SSN	Nuclear powered	Torpedo (only) armed
220[2]	SS	Conventionally (diesel) powered	Conventionally (torpedo) armed

[1] See table. All missile-carrying submarines are also armed with torpedoes.

[2] Including 73 patrol submarines in reserve or used for training only.

[3] Ten had missile tubes removed on conversion to fleet submarines, SSN (nuclear propelled).

Capital (Strategic) Submarines (SSBN)

Class	No.	Displacement Tons	Missile Tubes (vertical)	Nuclear Reactors	Shaft horse-power	Speed Knots
Typhoon [1]	2	30,000	20 SS–NX–20	2	120,000	24
D3	14	13,350	16 SS–N–18	1	60,000	24
D2	4	11,400	16 SS–N–8	1	60,000	25
D1	18	10,000	12 SS–N–8	1	60,000	25
Y	24 (10) [3]	9,300	16 SS–N–6	1	40,000	30
H3	1	5,750	3 SS–N–8	1	25,000	26
H2	3	5,600	3 SS–N–5	1	25,000	26

[1] These vessels, of battleship dimensions, are the largest submarines ever built. Launched in Sept. 1980 and Sept. 1982. The vertical missile cylinders are mounted forward of the fin.
Note: All these classes also carry six 21-inch torpedo tubes, except Typhoon, possibly

There are also 14 other missile-armed light-cruiser size leaders, 53 missile-armed destroyers, 37 gun-armed destroyers, (including 13 in reserve), 32 missile-armed frigates, 48 gun-armed frigates, 3 ocean minelayers, 87 missile-armed corvettes, 152 gun-armed corvettes, 32 patrol ships, 130 fleet minesweepers, 90 coastal minesweepers, 45 minehunters, 60 inshore minesweepers, 51 minesweeping boats, 130 fast missile craft, 10 fast torpedo boats, 95 fast anti-submarine boats, 55 patrol craft, 18 hydrofoil missile boats, 30 hydrofoil torpedo boats, 15 hydrofoil gunboats, 30 coastal patrol launches, 100 river patrol boats, 90 major amphibious and auxiliary roll-on roll-off ships, 2 dock landing ships, 30 tank landing ships, 60 medium landing ships, 35 utility landing craft, 70 minor landing craft, 65 intelligence collecting ships, 80 major support ships, 11 space associated ships, 147 survey ships, 75 oceanographic research ships, 7 missile range ships, 3 nuclear powered icebreakers, 63 icebreakers, 20 training ships, 190 fishery protection ships, 28 fleet replenishment ships, 55 oilers, 13 special tankers, 45 salvage vessels, 85 transports, 25 submarine rescue ships, 135 tenders, 10 lifting ships, 15 cable ships, 35 degaussing ships, 110 fleet tugs, 65 hovercraft and thousands of auxiliaries, para-military ships and service craft.

The new construction programme includes another aircraft carrier, considerably larger and nuclear-powered, 2 very large nuclear powered ballistic missile submarines, 2 nuclear powered cruise missile submarines, 6 nuclear powered torpedo-armed submarines, 3 diesel-electric propelled patrol submarines, a third nuclear powered guided missile armed battle cruiser, 10 guided missile cruisers and large anti-submarine leaders, 3 frigates and 4 corvettes.

In the progressive forward procurement programme more conventionally propelled aircraft carriers of improved 'follow-on' class are envisaged, together with nuclear powered surface ships, conventionally propelled submarines and specialized support ships, to fit into the Soviet global and strategic maritime pattern.

There are 5 shipyards in and near Leningrad; Black Sea yards are at Nikolaiev and Sevastopol, new shipyards are at Molotovsk in the White Sea region and at Komsomolsk on the Amur.

The completion of a through canal system between the Baltic and White Seas, allowing regular traffic *via* the North-East Passage (during the ice-free season), facilitates the navigation of suitable ships between the Baltic and Far East.

Estimated number of personnel in 1985 totalled 500,000, including naval aviation, naval infantry, coastal defence, cadets and apprentices (but excluding 75,000 civilians in administration and new construction). Some 25% of naval personnel are volunteers, *i.e.*, officers and petty officers, the remainder comprising national service men serving 3 years at sea and 2 if ashore.

Air Force. The Soviet Air Force (excluding the strategic bomber force and Voyska PVO air defence force) was believed to have a personnel strength, in 1983, of over 370,000 officers and men. To supplement long-range rocket missiles (estimated at 1,398 emplaced ICBM, 600 MRBM/IRBM), the strategic bomber force has still about 105 Tupolev Tu-95 ('Bear')[1] 4-turboprop bombers, 70 Myasishchev M-4 4-jet bombers and flight-refuelling tankers ('Bison'), 500 twin-jet Tupolev Tu-16 ('Badger'), and 135 supersonic Tupolev Tu-22 ('Blinder') bombers, ECM and reconnaissance aircraft, and at least 150 Tupolev ('Backfire') swing-wing bombers. All types are used also by the Naval Air Force for long-range maritime reconnaissance; the Tu-16, Tu-95, Tu-22 and 'Backfire' can carry air-to-surface guided self-propelled cruise missiles and all 5 types have provision for flight refuelling. A new swing-wing strategic bomber ('Blackjack'), larger and faster than the American B-1, is being flight tested.

The tactical air forces, under local army command in the field, have an estimated total of 6,000 ground attack, air combat, ECM and reconnaissance aircraft, including 2,400 MiG-23/27 ('Flogger') and 800 two-seat Sukhoi Su-24 ('Fencer') supersonic swing-wing aircraft, 200 twin-jet Yakovlev Yak-28 ('Brewer') reconnaissance aircraft, 100 single-jet Sukhoi Su-7B ('Fitter-A'), 800 swing-wing Su-17 ('Fitter-C/D/G/H/J'), and 600 MiG-21 ('Fishbed') fighter-bombers, 500 Su-15 ('Flagon'), 60 MiG-25 ('Foxbat') and some MiG-31 ('Foxhound') interceptors, and an increasing number of new Su-25 ('Frogfoot') twin-engined ground attack aircraft supported by 125 MiG-21 and 170 MiG-25 ('Foxbat') reconnaissance aircraft, and 3,500 helicopters, including very large Mi-26 ('Halo') transports and up to 1,000 heavily-

[1] For convenience Soviet aircraft and missiles are usually referred to by invented English names in non-Soviet military writings.

armed Mi-24 ('Hind') assault helicopters, in gunship/transport versions. Electronic warfare duties are performed by a variety of aircraft, including Yak-28s and Mi-8 and Mi-17 helicopters. The Voyska PVO defence forces, organized as a separate service, have an estimated total of 1,250 jet interceptors. A high proportion of the squadrons are equipped with MiG-23 ('Flogger'), Su-15 ('Flagon'), MiG-25 ('Foxbat') and improved MiG-31 ('Foxhound') all-weather interceptors, armed with air-to-air missiles. The twin-jet Yak-28P ('Firebar') and Tu-28P ('Fiddler') make up the balance of the force. Early warning and fighter-control duties are performed by about 10 radar-carrying adaptations of the Tu-114 turboprop transport, redesignated Tu-126 ('Moss'); these are being replaced by a more effective radar-equipped AWACS version ('Mainstay') of the Il-76 transport. Aircraft expected to enter service in 1984/85 include the Su-27 ('Flanker') and MiG-29 ('Fulcann') counter-air fighters, each with potential attack capability. Very large numbers of surface-to-air guided missiles are operational, on some 10,000 launchers, including the new high-performance SA-10 (low-altitude) and SA-12 (high-altitude) with capability against cruise and submarine-launched missiles respectively, the older 'Guild', 'Guideline', 'Goa', 'Gainful' and 'Ganef', the long-range 'Gammon' and the 'Galosh' which is deployed around Moscow on 32 launchers and has anti-missile capability.

Soviet Air Force transport squadrons have 400 An-12 ('Cub') 4-turboprop transports and 50 An-24s ('Coke') and An-26s ('Curl'), with 50 An-22s ('Cock'), and 250 Il-76 ('Candid') heavy four-jet freighters. The very large four-jet An-400 ('Condor') is under development to replace the An-22. Training aircraft include the piston-engined Yak-18 primary trainer, the Czech-built L-29 Delfin and L-39 jet basic trainers and versions of operational types such as MiG-21, MiG-23, MiG-25, MiG-15, Su-7, Su-15, Su-17, Yak-28 and Tu-22.

Naval Air Force. Operating 1,100 fixed-wing aircraft and helicopters, the Soviet Navy has the world's second largest naval air arm. Under the control of the various naval commands, *i.e.*, Baltic, Black Sea and Pacific, the Naval Air Arm has an estimated 220 Tu-16 ('Badger') twin-jet bombers, and 100 'Backfire' swing-wing bombers, able to carry air-to-surface missiles, 40 supersonic twin-jet Tu-22 ('Blinder') maritime reconnaissance aircraft, a small number of Su-17 ('Fitter') shore-based fighters, and 80 Beriev M-12 ('Mail') maritime patrol amphibians. For reconnaissance, anti-submarine and electronic warfare there are about 95 Tu-142 ('Bear') 4-engined bombers, 90 Tu-16s, and a few Tu-22s, plus a small number of Il-20s ('Coot-A') and 60 Il-38s ('May'). The Tu-142 also has an important targeting rôle for ships fitted with anti-shipping missile launchers. Over 250 anti-submarine and missile targeting/guidance helicopters, notably the Ka-27 ('Helix') and Ka-25 ('Hormone'), are carried in naval vessels, including 3 aircraft carriers (which also operate Yak-36 ('Forger') VTOL attack/reconnaissance aircraft) and 2 helicopter carriers. Several hundred transport, flight refuelling tanker ('Badger'), utility and training fixed-wing aircraft and Mi-14 ('Haze') shore-based ASW helicopters are also under Navy control.

Berman, H. J., and Kerner, M. (ed.), *Soviet Military Law and Administration.* 2 vols. Harvard Univ. Press, 1955
Scott, H. F., and Scott, W. F., *The Armed Forces of the USSR.* 2nd ed. Boulder, 1981
Smith, M. J., *The Soviet Navy, 1941–1978: A Guide to Sources in English.* Oxford and Santa Barbara, 1981
Suvorov, V., *The Liberators: The Soviet Army.* London, 1981
Watson, B. W., *Red Navy at Sea.* Boulder, 1982

INTERNATIONAL RELATIONS

Membership. USSR is a member of UN, Comecon and the Warsaw Pact.

ECONOMY

Planning. Planning is based on public ownership in industry and trade, and on mixed public and collective (co-operative) ownership in agriculture. The first plan drawn up by Gosplan (the State Planning Commission) was the 'Goelro' drawn up in 1920. This was to be the basis for the economic development of the country and for the construction of a system of electrical power plants with an aggregate capacity of 1·75m. kw., in the course of 15 years.

For details of Planning 1925–1942 *see* THE STATESMAN'S YEAR-BOOK, 1981–82 p. 1226.

For details of the fourth 5-year plan, 1946–50, *see* THE STATESMAN'S YEAR-BOOK, 1952, pp. 1424 f. The 1950 target of the gross output of industry was exceeded by 2%.

On 10 Oct. 1952 the 19th Congress of the Communist Party issued directives for the fifth 5-year plan, 1951–55; for details, *see* THE STATESMAN'S YEAR-BOOK, 1953, pp. 1435-36. During Sept. and Oct. 1953 the Government issued a number of decrees to stimulate the development of agriculture, the output of consumer goods and the expansion of the home trade. For details of these decrees, *see* THE STATESMAN'S YEAR-BOOK, 1955, pp. 1448-50.

The directives for the sixth 5-year plan, 1956-60, were adopted by the 20th Congress of the Communist Party on 25 Feb. 1956; for details *see* THE STATESMAN'S YEAR-BOOK, 1958, p. 1472.

In May 1955 Gosplan was reorganized to consist of 2 state commissions for long-term planning (Gosplan) and for current planning (Gosekonomkomissiya); at the same time a committee was set up to improve the application to industry of advanced science and technology (Gostekhnika).

Between 1954 and 1956 considerable changes were made in planning methods. In March 1954 collective farms were given greater authority over planning their own output, only the quantities required by the State in fixed deliveries being determined beforehand, and voluntary sales by contract. In 1955 they were authorized to make changes in their statutes, which had followed a fixed model since 1935. In 1955-57 over 15,000 industrial establishments in various basic industries, previously controlled by the Union Government, and later a number of entire light industries were turned over to the constituent (Union) Republics. By 1962 they controlled from 95 to 100% of all industrial output.

In 1957 a comprehensive plan for decentralization of management of industry was initiated. Industrial establishments responsible for about 71% of all Soviet industrial output were turned over to Economic Councils set up in 104 (in 1963: 47) economic administrative areas. These in 1962 controlled 73% of all industrial production. The Ministries previously responsible for the industries concerned were either abolished or transformed into purely planning and supervisory bodies. The State Committee for current planning was abolished, and Gosplan was given wider powers.

In consequence of this change a 7-year plan for 1959-65 was adopted by the 21st Congress of the Communist Party in Feb. 1959. Industrial output was to increase by 80%; it was in fact, in 1965, 84% above that of 1959. Capital investments would roughly equal the total for 1917-58: special attention was to be given to mechanization of agriculture and arduous industrial labour, automation and new technological processes, and housing. Diesel or electric traction of railway freight was to rise to 85%. Real incomes were to rise 40%, the 7-hour day (6 hours for miners) became general in 1960 and the 40-hour week in 1961, and introduction of the 35-hour week (30 hours for miners) began in 1964.

In Oct. 1965 the regional and Republic Economic Councils were abolished and also 28 Ministries for various branches of industry (17 Union-Republican, *i.e.*, corresponding to similar Ministries in the Union Republics, and 11 all-Union).

A 20-year plan was adopted by the 22nd Congress of the Communist Party on 31 Oct. 1961, which envisaged a ninefold growth in electricity output and big increases in production of steel, oil, coal, machinery and cement, and also in grain, milk and meat. Two new iron and steel centres were to be developed in Kazakhstan and in Kursk region. A single deepwater system was to link the main inland waterways in the European USSR. Some rivers in northern Asia were to be diverted south for irrigation purposes. A 6-hour day for a 6-day week or 35 hours for a 5-day week were to be achieved by 1970. Housing, water, gas, heating, public urban transport and school meals were to be free by 1980. These and cognate measures were to provide 'the material and technical basis of communism'.

The 23rd Congress of the Communist Party in April 1966 adopted directives for a 5-year plan for 1966-70. Under these, power output was to reach 830,000-850,000m. kwh.; oil, 345-355m. tons; coal, 665-675m. tons; steel, 124-129m. tons; mineral fertilizers, 62-65m. tons; machine-tools, 220,000-230,000; cars, 700,000-800,000; tractors, 600,000-625,000; paper, 5-5·3m. tons; cement, 100-105m. tons; fabrics, 9·5-9·8m. sq. metres; leather footwear, 610-630m. pairs; meat, 5·9-6·2m. tons; butter, 1·2m. tons; sugar, 9·8-10m. tons. The average annual output of grain was to increase by 30%; 7,000 km of new railway line, 63,000 km of new motor roads and 35-40 new airports were to be built; and marine tonnage was to be increased by 50%.

The 9th Five-Year Plan adopted in 1971 provided for an increase in electric power output to 1,065,000m. kwh.; oil to 496m. tons; gas, 320,000m. cu. metres; steel, 146m. tons; coal, 695m. tons; mineral fertilizers, 90m. tons; tractors, 575,000; passenger cars, 1·26m., and lorries, 750,000. Grain output was to rise to 195m. tons in 1975; meat, approximately 16m. tons; milk, 100m. tons; textiles, 11,000m. sq. metres; leather footwear, 830m. pairs. Average wages were to increase by 22%, incomes of collective farmers 30-35%, and the average of real incomes by 31%. 3,400 miles of new railway tracks were to be built and 3,700 miles electrified, with 17,000 miles of new oil pipelines, and 40% more cargo carried by sea. Over 16m. flats and houses were to be built.

By July 1972, 43,000 industrial plants had been transferred to the new system of decentralized cost-accounting; they produced 94% of total output of Soviet industry and 95% of its total profit. All public establishments in trade and catering and all the state farms have gone over to the new system.

On 29 Oct. 1976, the Supreme Soviet adopted the 10th Five-Year Plan (1976–80). This provided for an increase of industrial output from 104·3% of the 1975 level to 136%, an average annual increase of agricultural output by 16%, freight traffic (all forms) from 105·7% to 132%, state capital investments from 105·1% of the 1975 level in 1976 to 114·6% in 1980, real income per head from 103·7% to 121%, retail commodity turnover from 103·6% to 128·7%. 550m. sq. metres of new housing were to be built. Children in pre-school establishments would increase by 104·4% in 1976 and 125·5% in 1980, pupils in day schools from 108·9% to 148·8%, and students in higher education from 100·4% to 105·4%. Hospital beds were to increase from 102·2% in the first year to 109·7% in the final year.

In 1979 it was decided that from 1981 detailed plans would be drawn up at the outset for each year of a 5-year plan, so that enterprises could spread their potential more rationally over the whole period.

The 11th Five-Year Plan, adopted in 1981, aims to raise living standards. The focus is Siberia and the Soviet Far East, with their large resources of energy and raw materials, and also Central Asia, with its favourable combination of labour resources and raw materials. Virtually no industries will be developed in the European part of the USSR and the plan envisages speeding up the development of labour-intensive branches of agriculture, consumer goods and engineering industries in Central Asia. National income (in the Soviet definition) is to increase by 18% between 1981 and 1985; industrial production is to increase by 26%, capital investment by 5·4%, freight traffic by 19·4%, real incomes by 16·5%, agricultural production by 13%, and retail trade in the state and co-operative sectors by 23% over the same period. Pensions are to be raised and the minimum wage is to be increased to 80 rubles a month, and efforts are to be made to increase state assistance to families with young children and to improve the food and care given to them in schools and pre-school institutions.

In May 1982 the CPSU Central Committee adopted a series of resolutions intended to bring about an improvement in agricultural production more particularly. The resolutions, described as the party's 'food programme', are designed to achieve an expansion in all sectors of production and a reduction in imports from the West by means of a simplified and more decentralised system of management, increased procurement prices for many products, and enhanced bonuses and other incentives.

In July 1983 a limited devolution of authority to enterprise level was introduced in five ministries (heavy and transport machine-building, electro-technical industry, and three republican ministries), initially on an experimental basis, in order to raise the quality and effectiveness of their production. From 1985 these arrangements were extended nationally. Further measures have sought to reduce absenteeism and improve labour discipline.

Narodnoe khozyaistvo SSSR. Moscow, annual
Resheniya partii i pravitel'stva po khozyaistvennym voprosam. Vol. 1ff. Moscow, 1967ff
Istoriya sotsialisticheskoi ekonomiki SSSR. 7 vols. Moscow, 1976–80
Nove, A., *An Economic History of the USSR.* Rev. ed., Harmondsworth, 1982.—*The Soviet Economic System.* 2nd ed., London, 1980
US Congress, Joint Economic Committee, *The Soviet Economy in a Time of Change,* 2 vols. Washington D.C., 1979
Gregory, P. R. and Stuart, R. C., *Soviet Economic Structure and Performance.* 2nd ed., New York, 1981
Tikhonov, N. A., *Guidelines for the Economic and Social Development of the USSR for 1981–1985 and for the period ending in 1990.* Moscow, 1981

Budget. Revenue and expenditure in 1m. rubles for calendar years:

	1977	*1978*	*1979*	*1980*	*1983*	*1985* [1]
Revenue	247,800	265,800	275,600	302,700	354,106	391,687
Expenditure	242,800	260,200	275,100	294,600	353,905	391,479

[1] Estimate.

The 1985 budget allotted 222,427m. rubles to the national economy, 19,063m. to defence and 123,967m. to social and cultural services.

The social insurance budget, which is controlled by the Central Council for Trade Unions and its affiliated bodies, was 29,476m. rubles in 1977, 31,179m. in 1978, 33,089m. in 1979, 35,296 in 1980 and 37,417m. in 1981.

The national income was assessed (in 1,000m. rubles) at 152·9 in 1961, 289·9 in 1970, 305 in 1971, 313·6 in 1972, 337·8 in 1973, 354 in 1974, 440·6 in 1979, 462·2 in 1980, 523·4 in 1982 and 548·1 in 1983.

Income tax was abolished on 1 Oct. 1961 for earnings up to 60 rubles per month and reduced for earnings between 61 and 70 rubles; in Dec. 1967 further cuts of 25% were made for earnings from 61 to 80 rubles; in 1972 earnings up to 70 rubles were freed of income tax, and taxes on incomes up to 90 rubles were cut by about 33⅓%. Capital investment (1982) was 143,700m. rubles, including 129,600m. by State and co-operative enterprises, 12,400m. by collective farms and 1,700m. by individuals (on housing).

Currency. As from 1 Jan. 1961 the gold content of the *ruble* was raised from 0·222 168 to 0·987 412 gramme. The official exchange rates (March 1985) 0·968 *rubles* = £1; 0·92 *rubles* = US$1.

The gold holdings of the USSR were, in Dec. 1955, estimated at about 200m. fine oz. (US$7,000m.), or about 20% of the world total of monetary gold.

The currency in circulation is: (1) State Bank notes in denominations of 10, 25, 50 and 100 *rubles;* (2) Treasury notes in denominations of 1, 3 and 5 *rubles;* (3) cupro-nickel coins in denominations of 10, 15, 20 and 50 *kopeks* and 1 *ruble*; (4) cupro-zinc coins in denominations of 1, 2, 3 and 5 *kopeks.*

Banking. The State Bank began operations on 16 Nov. 1921. By an edict of 7 April 1959 a number of specialized banks for planned long-term investments, which had existed since 1932, were abolished. The State Bank, in addition to short-term credits, effects long-term investments in agriculture and in individual rural house building. The Bank for Financing Capital Investments (*Stroibank*) covers industry, transport, urban housing schemes and public utilities and individual house-building in towns.

Deposits in 79,000 savings banks were over 186·900m. rubles to the credit of 158·1m. depositors at 1 Jan. 1984.

Weights and Measures. The metric system has been in use since 1 Jan. 1927.

The Gregorian Calendar was adopted as from 14 Feb. 1918.

ENERGY AND NATURAL RESOURCES

Electricity. There were (1983) 57 fuel-burning power stations of over 1m. kw. capacity, and these account for over 80% of the country's electricity.

Hydro-electric stations have been constructed on major rivers. Among them are the Bratsk (4·5m. kw.), completed in 1967 — until recently the world's largest, Ust-Ilimsk, Central Siberia (3·6m. kw.), Krasnoyarsk (6m. kw.) and a 1·26m. kw. station on the River Pechora (Far North). The Sayano-Shushenskaya hydro-power station, part of the Yenisei chain, and already in part operation, will have a 6·4m. kw. capacity when completed in 1983. A 245m. high dam has to be built before completion, in a gorge in the Sayan Range. Another large hydro-electric station is under construction on the River Kureika, Siberia, to provide energy for the mining and metallurgical centre at Norilsk in the Arctic.

Total installed capacity of power stations in 1938 was 8·7m. kw. and 293·6m. kw. in 1983. Industry consumes about 70% of the total electricity. Over 35,000 small rural power stations have been closed in recent years owing to supply from State stations becoming available, but there are still many operating in the countryside. 800 towns and urban settlements were heated by central thermal plants.

The world's first commercial nuclear power station in Obninsk, built in 1954, was followed by the Beloyarsk, Novo-Voronezh, Leningrad, Kursk, Chernobyl, Armenian and Shevchenko nuclear stations. Soviet nuclear power plants so far have standard slow 1m. kw. reactors, but a 1·5m. kw. reactor has now been designed. A fast reactor is functioning at Shevchenko.

The general design for a nuclear thermal station has been developed, and practical experience in this field has been obtained at the Bilibino nuclear power station in the Arctic, which supplies electricity and heat to the inhabitants on the Chukchi Peninsula.

In 1979 a 500,000 kw. MHD pilot project was started in Ryazan. This first-generation MHD station will have an efficiency of 50% as against 40% in the best thermal power stations and will consume about 20% less fuel. An experimental tidal energy station is working at Kislaya Guba (Murman coast).

Total electricity output in 1983 was 1,418,000 kwh.

The country's integrated power grid is now in operation, covering over 900 power stations, which are handled by a central control panel in Moscow through (in 1983) 852,600 km. of cable of 35 kw. or greater capacity. A unified power grid ('Mir') with all the Socialist countries of eastern Europe was built up between 1962 and 1967.

Oil. In the 1930s practically all Soviet oil came from the Caucasian fields, of which the Baku fields yielded 75-80% and the Grozny and Maikop fields between them 15%. Since then, the distribution has considerably changed. The Ural-Volga area, the 'Second Baku', has 4 large centres in operation, at Samarska Luka (Kuibyshev), Tuimazy (Bashkiria), Ishimbaev (Bashkiria) and Perm, producing nearly 100m. tonnes annually.

A large new oilfield has been developed in the Trans-Volga area of the Saratov region. The Tyumen (West Siberian) complex now accounts for over 50% of the USSR's oil output. In 1983 the USSR extracted 616·3m. tonnes of oil.

The total length of pipeline on 1 Jan. 1939 was 4,212 km, divided as follows: Baku-Batumi, 1,717 km; Grozny-Makhachkala, 150 km; Grozny-Armavir-Tuapse, 618 km; Armavir-Trudovaya, 488 km; Guriev-Orsk, 845 km, and other, 394 km. One pipeline (1,700 km) was completed in 1955, connecting Tuimazy in Bashkiria with the refineries of Omsk. In 1957 the Almetyevsk-Gorky pipeline (580 km) and 479 km of the Stavropol-Moscow pipeline were completed. At the end of 1981 there were 70,800 km of pipeline, through which (in 1981) were conveyed 637·7m. tonnes of oil.

The construction of the 'Druzhba' pipeline of about 5,327 km from the oilfields near Kuibyshev to Poland and the German Democratic Republic (northern branch) and to Czechoslovakia and Hungary (southern branch)–separating in Belorussia–begun in 1960, was completed in 1965. Now a double line, it has an annual throughput of 50m. tonnes.

In 1976 the USSR exported 148·5m. tonnes of crude oil and oil products.

Meyerhoff, A. A., *The Oil and Gas Potential of the Soviet Far East.* Beaconsfield, 1981

Gas. A natural-gas pipeline from Gazli, near Khiva, to Voskresensk, near Moscow (2,750 km), with a planned capacity of 100m. cu. metres per day, began operating in Oct. 1967. Since then it has been extended to Czechoslovakia, where a 1,000 km extension, for transmission of Soviet gas to Austria, Italy and German Democratic Republic and Federal Republic of Germany, is under construction and another to Bulgaria. Another natural-gas pipeline, over 3,000 km from Medvezhye (Tyumen Region) to Moscow, began operating in Oct. 1974. A second pipeline from this region, linking the Urengoi deposit with Petrovsky in the Central European area of the USSR, became operational in 1980, and is to be continued to the southern Ukraine, to a total length of 3,000 km. A gas pipeline starting from Orenburg (Urals), passing across the Volga at Kamyshin, and continuing across the Ukraine *via* Kremenchug and Vinnitsa to Czechoslovakia (2,750 km), reached the Soviet frontier in Jan. 1979. When completed, it is to supply Czechoslovakia, Poland, Bulgaria and Hungary with 14,000m. cu. metres annually and Romania with 1,500m. A unified gas-grid exceeding 124,000 km now exists.

By Dec. 1981 construction work had begun on the 5,000 km Urengoi (West Siberia)-Uzhgorod-West Europe gas pipeline.

In 1983, 535,700m. cu. metres of gas were produced (in 1940, 3,200 m., in 1970, 197,900m.).

Minerals. Mining experts are trained in 6 mining, 3 oil and 1 peat institutes, the mining faculties of 17 higher educational establishments, oil faculties of 2 industrial institutes and a peat faculty at the Belorussian Polytechnical Institute.

The Soviet Union is rich in minerals. Soviet scientists claim that it contains 58% of the world's coal deposits, 58·7% of its oil, 41% of its iron ore, 76·7% of its apatite, 25% of all timber land, 88% of its manganese, 54% of its potassium salts and nearly one-third of its phosphates.

Estimated output (in tonnes) in 1962: Copper, 634,900; zinc, 399,000; lead, 363,000; tungsten, 10,500; antimony, 5,980; silver, 27m. fine oz. Output in 1963: Baryte, 199,500; magnesium, 31,745; aluminium, 961,400; manganese ore (1977), 8·6m.; graphite, 54,000; bauxite, 4·3m.; asbestos, 1·3m.; phosphate rock, 3·7m. (plus 7·4m. apatite); chromite, 1·23m.; gold, 12·5m. fine oz.; molybdenum, 12·5m. lb.; cadmium (1956), 160.

Output of iron and steel in the USSR (in 1m. tonnes):

	Pig-iron	*Ingot steel*	*Rolled steel*		*Pig-iron*	*Ingot steel*	*Rolled steel*
1913	4·2	4·2	3·5	1960	46·8	65·3	50·9
1928–29	4·0	4·8	3·9	1965	66·2	91·0	61·7
1932	6·2	5·9	4·4	1970	85·9	115·9	80·6
1940	14·9	18·3	13·1	1980	107·3	147·9	118·3
1946	10·0	13·4	9·6	1983	110·4	152·5	121·9
1950	19·2	27·3	20·9				

Coal production (in 1m. tonnes) was 29·1 in 1913, 64·4 in 1932, 165·9 in 1940, 261·1 in 1950, 509·6 in 1960, 624·1 in 1970, 701·3 in 1975, 716·4 in 1980, 704 in 1981, 716·1 in 1983.

The main centre of the atomic ore industry is at Ust-Kamenogorsk in the Altai Mountains. Uranium deposits are being worked near Taboshar (south-east of Tashkent), Andizhan (in the Tynya-Muyan Mountains), Slyudianka (near Lake Baikal), on the Kolyma River and in Southern Armenia.

Agriculture. The Soviet Union, up to about 1928 predominantly agricultural in character, has become an industrial-agricultural country. Of the gross social product, industry and transport accounted for 42·1% in 1913 and 66·5% in 1983; agriculture for 57·9% in 1913 and 15·9% in 1983. Of the total state land fund of 2,227·5m. hectares, agricultural land in use in 1983 amounted to 1,051·9m., state forests and state reserves to 1,109·7m. hectares. 20% of all gainfully employed in 1982 were engaged in agriculture and forestry (1913, 75%; 1940, 54%).

The total area under cultivation (including single-owner peasant farms, state farms and collective farms) was (in the same territory) 118·2m. hectares in 1913, 150·6m. in 1940, 146·3m. in 1950, 203m. in 1960, 206·7m. in 1970, 217·3 in 1980, and 226·8m. in 1983.

Collective farms in 1983 possessed 98·6m. hectares of cultivated land, of which 58·5m. were under crops of various kinds; state farms and other state agricultural undertakings possessed 114·3m. hectares, of which 69·1m. were under crops; manual and clerical workers held 4·2m. hectares as allotments.

In Nov. 1969 the Third Congress of collective farmers adopted a new model constitution, considerably enlarging the planning powers of collective farms and making payments to their members a priority.

Since 1969 conferences of collective farms have elected 2,417 district collective farm councils with 85,000 members, to study and co-ordinate local experience in methods and finance. Processing and other joint agricultural productive establishments in 1980 numbered 9,638.

State procurements (after consumption by farms) were, in 1m. tonnes, for the present area of the USSR:

	1950	*1960*	*1970*	*1983*		*1950*	*1960*	*1970*	*1983*
Grain	32·3	46·7	73·3	–	Meat[2] and fats	1·3	4·8	8·1	11·0
Raw Cotton[1]	3·5	4·3	6·9	9·2	Milk and milk products	11·4	29·1	48·0	63·4
Sugar-beet	19·7	52·2	71·4	74·5	Sunflower seed	1·1	2·3	4·6	4·0
Potatoes	14·0	13·7	18·1	18·3	Eggs (1,000m.)	3·5	10·5	22·1	48·2
Other vegetables	4·3	8·0	13·8	19·7					

[1] Seed-cotton unginned. [2] Slaughter weight.

Since 1954 grain crops have been measured in 'barn crop' (*i.e.*, net quantities delivered to barns) and not in 'gross harvest' or 'biological yield' (*i.e.*, calculated as growing crops) as previously. Average annual crops (in 1m. tonnes): 1909–13, 72·5; 1946–50, 64·8; 1951–55, 88·5; 1956–60, 121·5; 1961–65, 130·3; 1966–70, 167·5; 1971–75, 181·6; 1976–80, 205; 1980, 189·1; 1983 (Western estimate), 200.

Other produce (in 1m. tonnes) in 1982: Milk, 91; sugar-beet, 71·5; potatoes, 78·2; vegetables, 30; meat (slaughter weight), 15·4; raw cotton, 9·3; sunflower seed, 5·3; flax, 0·4; wool, 0·5; eggs, 72,400m.

In Dec. 1963 collective farms comprised 99·7% of all peasant holdings. In 1982 they produced 90% of all sugar-beet, cotton 65%, milk 38%, meat 30%, potatoes 20%, other vegetables 24%, eggs 6%, sunflower seed 74%, wool 30%.

Between 1953 and 1 Jan. 1983 the number of collective farms was reduced, mainly by amalgamation and partly by transformation into state farms, from 93,300 to 26,400, their cultivated area falling from 132m. hectares to 93·9m. The number of state farms rose in the same period from 4,857 to 22,000, their cultivated area from 15·2m. hectares to 114·3m.

By 1983 the main field work on state and collective farms and joint inter-farm enterprises (ploughing, sowing of grain, cotton and sugar-beet, and the harvesting of grain and silage crops) was fully mechanized; in 1982, 45% of potato harvesting was mechanized, 95% of sugar-beet pulling, and 50% of cotton-picking.

Rural power stations in 1940 had a capacity of 47·5 h.p.; in 1982, 663·8m. h.p. Energy consumption in 1982 was 28·3 h.p. per employee. In 1982 agriculture consumed 120,506m. kwh. of electric power.

Investments in agriculture in 1982 were 24,400m. rubles by the state and 10,800m. by collective farms. Total agricultural output in 1982 was valued at 127,400m. rubles.

In 1913 the total of irrigated land was 4m. hectares; in 1953, 11m.; in 1982, 18·6m. The total of land drained was 8·4m. hectares in 1956 and 17·5m. in 1982. In 1975 nearly 85m. hectares were treated from the air against weed, pest and disease.

In 1913, 188,000 tonnes of mineral fertilizers were used; in 1950, 5·3m. tonnes, and in 1981, 84m. On 1 Jan. 1983 there were 2·7m. tractors, 770,600 grain combine harvesters and 1·1m. motorized ploughs in the countryside.

An All-Union Academy of Agricultural Sciences, founded in 1929, has regional branches in Siberia and Central Asia and 310 research institutes.

Livestock (1 Jan. 1983), in 1m. head: Cattle, 117·2 (including 43·8 milch cows); pigs, 76·7; sheep, 148·5; horses, 5·6. Since 1957 the enumeration of livestock has been made on 1 Jan. instead of 1 Oct., *i.e.*, after the winter sales and slaughter for the market. Percentage of farm production in 1983:

	Cotton	*Sugar-beet*	*Pota-toes*	*Other vegetables*	*Meat*	*Milk*	*Eggs*	*Wool*
State	34	11	19	44	41	32	63	46
Collective	66	89	21	24	30	39	6	30
Private [1]	0	0	60	32	29	29	31	24

[1] *i.e.*, household plots of collective farmers.

Forestry. On the 791·6m. hectares of forest land of the USSR, 772·2m. hectares is administered and worked by the State; the remainder, 19·4m. hectares in extent, is granted for use to the peasantry free of charge.

The largest forest areas are 515m. hectares in the Asiatic part of USSR, 51·4m. along the northern seaboard, 25·4m. in the Urals and 17·95m. in the north-west.

On 24 Oct. 1948 a plan was published for planting crop-protecting forest belts, introducing crop rotation with grasses and building of ponds and water reservoirs in the steppe and forest-steppe areas of the European part of the USSR. By the middle of 1952 some 2·6m. hectares had been planted with shelter-belt trees and 13,500 ponds and reservoirs had been built. The planting of the shelter belts in the Kamyshin-Volgograd and Byelgorod-Don areas has in the main been completed. A Volga forest belt has been planted along 1,200 km of railway. Re-afforestation was carried out on 2·2m. hectares of land in 1982.

Fisheries. The fishing catch including whaling (in 1,000 tons): 1913, 1,051; 1940, 1,422; 1960, 3,541; 1980, 9,526.

Blandon, P., *Soviet Forest Industries.* Boulder, 1983
Johnson, D. G., and Brooks, K. M., *The Prospects for Soviet Agriculture in the 1980s.* Bloomington, 1983
Shaffer, H. G., *Soviet Agriculture.* New York, 1977
Symons, L., *Russian Agriculture: A Geographic Survey.* London, 1972
Vasiliev, P., and Kozlovsky, V., *Forest Wealth of the USSR* (in Russian). Moscow, 1959

INDUSTRY AND TRADE

Industry. The organization of industry in the USSR is based on state ownership and control, administered by a separate ministry for each large industry.

Under the successive 5-year plans, large-scale modern industrial works have been constructed, namely: 1st, over 1,500; 2nd, 4,500; 3rd (up to June 1941), 3,000; wartime, 3,500 (apart from reconstruction of destroyed plants); 4th, 6,200; 5th, 3,200; 6th, 2,700; 7th (1959–65), 5,470; 8th (1966–70), 1,870; 9th (1971–75), 2,000; 10th (1976–80), 1,200.

Output of some heavy industries was as follows:

Industry	*1913*	*1950*	*1960*	*1970*	*1980*	*1984*
Iron ore (1m. tonnes)	9·2	39·7	106·2	197·3	244·7	247·0
Oil (1m. tonnes)	9·2	37·9	148·0	353·0	603·2	613·0
Electric power (1,000m. kwh.)	1·9	91·2	292·0	740·9	1,295·0	1,493·0
Coal (1m. tonnes)	29·2	261·1	509·6	624·1	716·4	712·0
Steel (1m. tonnes)	4·2	27·3	65·3	115·9	147·9	154·0
Rolled steel (finished, 1m. tonnes)	3·3	18·0	43·7	80·6	102·9	107·0
Steam and gas turbines (1,000 kw.)	5·9	2,381·0	9,200·0	16,191·0	20,300·0	21,300·0
Steel pipe (1m. tonnes)	–	2·0	5·8	12·4	18·2	18·9
Chemical fibres (1m. tonnes)	–	0·0	0·2	0·6	1·2	1·4
Mineral fertiliser[2] (1m. tonnes)	0·0	1·3	3·3	13·1	24·8	30·8
Automobiles (1,000)	–	64·6	138·8	344·2	1,327·0	1,300·0
Tractors (1m. h.p.)	–	5·5	11·4	29·4	47·0	50·9
Sulphuric acid (1m. tonnes)	0·1	2·1	5·4	12·1	23·0	25·3
Excavators (no.)	–	3,540·0	12,290·0	30,800·0	42,000·0	41,800·0
Timber (commercial, 1m. cu. metres) [1]	27·2	161·0	261·5	298·5	277·7	280·0
Cement (1m. tonnes)	1·8	10·2	45·5	95·2	125·0	130·0

[1] Excluding collective farm production. [2] Recalculated base.

The process of industrial mechanization and the installation of automatic remote control is being pushed ahead. About 93% of Soviet pig-iron and 87% of the steel is produced in fully automatic furnaces. All hydro-electric plants (in terms of capacity) are fully automatic. Coal production in open-cast mines has been completely mechanized; hydraulic mining is coming into general use. Coal-cutting and underground haulage was over 99% mechanized by the end of 1962 (loading on inclined seams 56%); peat-cutting, 100%, and loading, nearly 80%; timber-cutting, 98%; haulage to loading centres, 93%, and despatch, 97%.

Output in some consumer industries was as follows:

Industry	*1913*	*1950*	*1960*	*1970*	*1980*	*1984*
Cotton fabrics (1m. linear metres)	2,672	3,899	6,387	7,482	8,063	
Woollen fabrics (1m. linear metres)	108	156	342	496	564	11,800
Silk fabrics (1m. linear metres)	43	130	810	1,241	1,632	
Leather footwear (1m. pairs)	60	203	419	679	744	764
Clocks and watches (1m.)	1	8	26	40	67	67
Radio receivers (1m.)	–	1	4	8	9	9
Television sets (1m.)	–	–	2	7	8	9
Refrigerators (1,000)	–	1	530	4,140	5,925	5,700
Paper (1,000 tonnes)	269	1,193	2,334	4,185	5,288	5,900
Meat (slaughter weight, 1m. tonnes)	5	5	9	12	15	17
Butter (1,000 tonnes)	104	336	737	963	1,278	1,500
Granulated sugar (1,000 tonnes)	1,363	2,523	6,360	10,221	10,127	12,500
Canned foods (1m. tins)	116	1,113	4,864	10,678	15,268	17,100

Since 1945 the cotton industry has expanded, especially in the Urals, Central Asia and Siberia. Large mills have been built at Kamyshin, Kherson, Barnaul, Engels, Alma-Ata, Chernigov and Frunze.

Trade Unions and Labour. Trade unions are organized on an industrial basis, all workers, whether manual or brain, in every branch of a given industry being eligible for membership of the same union. Collective farmers may join trade unions.

Since 1933 the trade unions have carried out the functions of the former Labour Commissariat; they control and supervise the application of labour laws, introduce new labour laws for approval by the Government and administer social insurance and factory inspection. Social insurance is non-contributory. The All-Union Congress has met at irregular intervals; the 14th Congress met in 1968, the 15th in 1972 and the 18th in 1982.

In 1944 there were 176 unions. This number was reduced by amalgamation of unions to 22 in 1958, but increased to 31 by 1980. Contributions range from 0·5 to 6% of wages. There are 173 regional and Republican Trades Councils. Membership (1984) 134·7m.

Chairman, Central Council of Trade Unions: S. A. Shalayev.

Industrial and clerical workers engaged (1983) in the whole national economy were 116·1m., 51% of them women; a further 13m. were engaged in collective-farm agriculture. The 7-hour day (6 hours for miners underground and other heavy trades) was generally in operation by the end of 1960. The average working week since 1970 has been 39·4 hours and the working day in industry 6·93 hours. The 5-day week (without reduction of total working hours) was introduced in 1967.

New 'Fundamentals of Labour Legislation', intended to codify and extend labour laws adopted in the last 40 years, were adopted by the Supreme Soviet in July 1970. They lay down, *inter alia*, the right to receive wages irrespective of the income of the enterprise concerned, the right to free vocational and advanced technical training; the right to form trade unions without state registration; the right of trade unions to participate in and supervise management and planning, labour legislation, safety regulation and housing, fixing of working conditions and wages, etc. Pensioners in Jan. 1984 numbered 53·6m., including 37m. old age. Average monthly wages in the state sector were 185 rubles in 1984.

Profsoyuzy SSSR. Dokumenty i materialy. 5 vols., Moscow, 1963–74
Sbornik postanovlenii VTsSPS. Moscow, 1960ff, quarterly
Ruble, B. A., *Soviet Trade Unions. Their Development in the 1970s.* CUP, 1981

Commerce. Retail home trade takes three forms–state, co-operative and the free market, *i.e.*, sales by individual collective-farm members and by the collective farms of their surplus products, after having fulfilled their statutory deliveries and made their regular allocations to their members.

In 1983 retail trade by the State, cooperatives and collective farms totalled 314,300m. rubles; of this state and cooperative trade amounted to 305,800m. rubles (in 1970, 159,400m. and 155,200m. rubles respectively). Employees in retail trade were 7·5m. in 1983 (annual average); there were 699,900 retail trade outlets with a total floor area of 49·8m. sq. metres. The state retail price index (1970 = 100) was 108 in 1983. Trade by collective farm markets amounted to 8,300m. rubles in 1983; this was 2·8% by value of all retail trade and 5·3% by value of all food sales.

Foreign trade is organized as a state monopoly. Importation and exportation of goods are effected under licences issued by the Ministry for Foreign Trade and its respective departments in pursuance of a plan annually sanctioned by the Government. The right of purchasing goods for importation, and that of selling Soviet exports abroad, is vested in trade delegations and representatives of the appropriate state corporations in foreign countries.

There are 29 state import and export organizations, including chartering and tourist corporations (one, Vostokintorg, dealing with Mongolia, Sinkiang and Afghánistán). The Central Union of Consumers' Societies (Tsentrosoyuz) is also authorized to conduct foreign trade operations.

For foreign trade up to 1938 *see* THE STATESMAN'S YEAR-BOOK, 1951, p. 1465. Foreign trade is in 1984 conducted with 143 foreign countries (in 1950, 45), and had by 1983 increased 15 times by value since 1950. Exports in 1983 were valued at 67,891m. rubles (37,714m. to the socialist countries), and imports at 59,585m. rubles (33,692m. from the socialist countries).

Russia's imports of machinery and equipment, between 1940 and 1983, rose from 32·4 to 38·2%, ores and concentrates fell from 26·6 to 8·8%, foodstuffs rose from 14·9 to 20·5% and manufactured consumer goods rose from 1·4 to 11·5% by value; exports of fuel and electricity increased from 13·2 to 53·7% and of machinery and equipment from 2 to 12·5% by value over the same period.

Main items of exports in 1983:

Oil and oil products (1m. rubles)	28,216·1	Gas (1m. rubles)	6,302·7
Iron ore (1m. tonnes)	33·2	Tractors (1m. rubles)	205·5
Iron and rolled metal (1m. rubles)	1,672·2	Motor cars (1,000)	237·9
Paper (1,000 tonnes)	668·9	Clocks and watches (1m.)	23·0
Cotton (1,000 tonnes)	773·9	Grain (1m. rubles)	241·8

Total trade between the USSR and UK for calendar years (British Department of Trade returns, in £1,000 sterling):

	1981	*1982*	*1983*	*1984*
Imports to UK	426,717	645,135	728,491	854,307
Exports and re-exports from UK	408,254	355,678	445,003	735,173

Tourism. Pre-revolutionary Russia was never a country for any but the most hardy and better-off tourists, as the introductory pages of Baedeker's guide made clear. For her subjects, too, touring was no more inviting. Acute shortage of hotels and boarding-houses, poor roads, lack of ordinary services for visitors were among the least of their difficulties. These have not by any means been fully overcome: but very great efforts to meet them have been made. The first tourist organizations came into existence in 1885–90 in St Petersburg, Tiflis and Odessa; and in 1901 the Russian Society of Tourists was formed (about 5,000 members in 1914). Organized tourism in the Soviet period began in the early 1920s; the Russian Society of Tourists was revived, and other tourist organizations, notably 'Intourist' (founded 1929), were established. The development of tourism on a massive scale is however a development of the post-Second World War period.

Tourist facilities for Soviet and foreign citizens are presently made available under state, trade union and other auspices, all of which come ultimately under the supervision of the State Committee on Tourism which is attached to the USSR Council of Ministers. The number of hotels available to such tourists increased from 222 in 1960 to 958 in 1983, with a total accommodation of 373,000 (in 1960, 36,000); the number of tourist bases, for the hire of equipment and shorter stays, increased to 6,959, with a total accommodation of 718,000. In 1983 these facilities were used by 26·5m. and 3·6m. tourists respectively (in 1970, 5m. and 1·7m.). A total of 45·4m. citizens in 1983 made use of all forms of tourist accommodation, including sanatoria and boarding houses (in 1960, 6·7m.; in 1970, 16·8m.). In 1983 a further 195m. citizens took part in tourist excursions.

Visitors to the USSR from foreign countries are catered for by 'Intourist' and its offices in foreign countries. In 1970, the USSR had 2,059,338 foreign visitors (43,490 from the UK, and 66,365 from the USA); in 1980 there were 5,590,000 foreign visitors. Intourist also arranges the visits of Soviet citizens to foreign countries, and in the 1970s assisted about 2m. annually.

COMMUNICATIONS

Roads. By 1940 there were over 1·5m. km of constructed roads, of which 143,000 km were suitable for motor traffic. The total length of motor roads in 1984 was 773,000 km. Road freights by lorry amounted to 859m. tonnes in 1940 and 26,406m. tonnes in 1983. Passengers carried were 590m. in 1940 and 44,548m. in 1983. In 1983, 22,200 inter-urban bus routes had a total length of 3,366,000 km.

Railways. The length of railways in Jan. 1984 was 143,630 km (1913: 58,500 km), of which 46,800 km was electrified. Diesel and electric traction now account for almost 100% of all movements, with the electrified network handling 56% of the traffic. In 1979 60% of all freight traffic and 40% of passengers went by rail (1913: 57% and 91% respectively), and railways ran 3,600,000m. tonne-km in 1983.

Operations are centred on 32 regions with headquarters at Baku, Alma-Ata, Tyndin, Minsk, Irkutsk, Gorki, Khabarovsk, Donetsk, Chita, Tbilisi, Aktyubinsk, Novosibirsk, Kemerovo, Krasnoyarsk, Kuibyshev, Lvov, Kishinev, Moscow, Odessa, Leningrad, Riga, Saratov, Dnepropetrovsk, Sverdlovsk, Yaroslavl, Rostov-on-Don, Tashkent, Tselinograd, Voronezh, Kharkov and Chelyabinsk.

Extensive railway construction is in progress, including routes northwards from Surgut to Urengoi and Nizhe-Vartovskoye, while the great Baikal-Amur Magistral (BAM) project was completed in 1985. This is a new main line to the east, sited well to the north of the existing Trans-Siberian route to the Pacific ports of Nakhodka and Vladivostok. It runs from Lena, on the Lena river, to Komsomolsk-on-Amur, 3,145 km distant. When open throughout in 1983–84, BAM will become the principal route for export traffic to the eastern ports, easing the very heavy pressure on the Trans-Siberian line, which is only partially electrified and not double-track throughout.

BAM was the most arduous railway building project ever tackled by Soviet engineers, and the greatest drawback to development of the region has been its severe geological and climatic conditions. There is permafrost throughout the area, and winter temperatures fall to –60°C. Construction work occupied nearly a decade, and has required over 3,200 bridges, tunnels and culverts.

Underground railways have been built in Moscow, Leningrad, Kiev, Tbilisi, Kharkov, Tashkent, Baku, Gorky, Minsk and Yerevan. Others are under construction at Novosibirsk, Omsk, Dnepropetrovsk, Kuibyshev and Sverdlovsk.

Aviation. In 1983 total length of internal airlines in the USSR was approximately 865,000 km; 110m. passengers were carried internally and externally. The Central Asian Airways in some instances provide the only means of communication across the desert and mountainous regions of the local republics. An 8,500-km air service was opened in Feb. 1941 between Moscow and Anadyr (Eastern Siberia), through Archangel, Igarka, Khatanga, Tiksi Bay and Cape Schmidt, *i.e.*, along the entire course of the Northern Sea Route. There are also other Arctic airlines, *e.g.*, Igarka-Gulf of Kozhevnikov, Igarka-Dickson Island; Yakutsk-Tiksi Bay; Yakutsk Viluisk; Yakutsk-Verkhoiansk.

Direct air services are maintained throughout the year between Moscow and the capitals of all Soviet republics as well as London, New York, Montreal, Tōkyō, Delhi, Rangoon, Belgrade, Peking, Pyongyang, Ulan Bator, Kábul, Tirana, Paris,

Warsaw, Prague, Budapest, Bucharest, Sofia, Vienna, Berlin, Helsinki, Stockholm, Copenhagen, Jakarta, Dakar and Gander. Soviet air services reached 87 countries in 1981, and 20 foreign lines have regular services to the USSR, including British Airways, KLM, SAS, Air France, SABENA, Air India, PANAM. The first Soviet airbus, the 350-seater IL-86, began flights on civil aviation routes in 1981. The 120-seater YAK-42 will gradually replace the TU-134 and AN-24 on major shorter routes.

MacDonald, H., *Aeroflot: Soviet Air Transport Since 1923.* London, 1975

Shipping. In 1977 the Soviet mercantile marine comprised 7,000 self-propelled vessels, of which 80% were built between 1957 and 1966. By May 1977 the gross cargo capacity was (including fishing vessels) 20·8m. registered tonnes (16m. tonnes dead-weight).

Freights carried were: In 1913 (present frontiers), 35·1m. tonnes; in 1940, 73·9m. tonnes; and in 1983, 607m. tonnes; 142m. passengers were carried. The Soviet share in world marine tonnage was 2% in 1960 and 6% in 1977. Deep-sea ports are under construction at Vostochny (Far East) and Grigorevsky (Black Sea) with new deep-sea wharves at Ventspils (Latvia), Murmansk and Archangel (for Arctic traffic). Archangel is kept open by icebreakers all the year round from 1979. Foreign freights in 1977 totalled 14% of all Soviet seaborne trade.

The North Sea route affords convenient communication between the European USSR and the Far East along the Soviet coast, for the produce of the basins of the Ob, Yenissei, Lena and Kolyma rivers.

The length of navigable rivers and canals in exploitation was (1983) 137,900 km, of which the length of floatable rivers is 86,200 km. There are several thousand miles of canals and other artificial waterways; among them the Baltic and White Sea Canal (235 km), the Moscow-Volga Canal (130 km). Goods turnover on inland waterways was 28,900m. tonne-km in 1913, 35,900m. in 1940, 45,900m. in 1950 and 273,200m. in 1983; freight carried rose from 35·1m. tonnes in 1913 to 606·7m. tonnes in 1983.

The Volga-Don Shipping Canal was opened for traffic in 1952. The Volga-Don waterway from Volgograd to Rostov is 540 km long, of which the Volga-Don canal comprises 101 km. The canal has transformed the section of the river from Kalach, where the Don is joined by the Volga-Don canal, to Rostov into a deep-water highway suitable for big Volga shipping. The canal links the White, Baltic, Caspian, Azov and Black Seas into a single water transport system. In Oct. 1964 the 2,430-km Baltic-Volga waterway, linking Klaipeda on the Baltic to Kakhovka at the mouth of the Dnieper and suitable for 5,000-tonne vessels, was begun. Reconstruction of the 18th-century Mariinsky canal system in north-west Russia was completed, providing a through waterway from Leningrad to Rybinsk (on the Upper Volga) and cutting the passage of freight from 18 to 2½ days.

At the end of 1977 the longest train ferry route in the world was opened between the Soviet Union and Bulgaria (Ilyichovsk-Varna).

The first section of Vostochny port, in Wrangel Bay on the Pacific coast, is completed. It will be the country's largest deep-sea port.

In 1962 a canal was completed across the Kara-Kum desert in southern Turkmenistan (replacing an earlier project for a more costly scheme across the north of the republic). The canal, from Bussag on the river Amu-Darya to Archnan, northwest of Ashkhabad, through the Murgab oasis, 900 km long, supplies water to an area exceeding 200,000 hectares, suitable for cotton, fruit, vineyards and livestock. An extension to the Caspian (500 km) is under construction: the complete system will irrigate 1m. hectares.

An irrigation canal system (250 miles), bringing water from Kakhovka on the Dnieper to the North Crimea, is nearing completion. Work to divert water from the Pechora and Vychegda rivers (flowing into the White Sea) south to the Volga is in progress. Work has begun on a 300-mile canal which will supply water from the Irtysh to Karaganda in Central Kazakhstan, irrigating over 150,000 acres; the first 37 miles were opened in 1965 and another 45 miles in Dec. 1967. Most of the 11 reservoirs required had been completed by 1 Jan. 1972. Other irrigation canals under construction are Kuibyshev (279 km long, to supply over 100,000 hectares) and Stavropol (481 km, irrigating 200,000 hectares); the second section of the latter went into commission in Nov. 1974, 14 months ahead of schedule. In Sept. 1972 the Saratov Canal (irrigating 1m. hectares) went into commission.

Post and Broadcasting. In Jan. 1984 the number of post, telegraph and telephone offices was 91,156 and of general telephones 27·8m.

The international radio-telecommunications services are operated by the Ministry of Communications of the USSR. The Great Northern Telegraph Co., Ltd, of Denmark, operates cables connecting Denmark with Leningrad, whence connexion is made by means of a trans-Siberian landline with Vladivostok. From the latter place the Great Northern Telegraph Co. owns cables connecting with Japan, China and Hong Kong. Direct radio and telephone communication with India is provided for in an agreement concluded in 1955.

The State Committee for Broadcasting and Television produces 3 programmes in Moscow, broadcasting throughout the Union. In addition the regional radio stations produce 1, 2 or 3 programmes for the republics as well as local programmes for a town or region. The foreign service from Moscow is beamed to all parts of the world, in 64 languages. Chinese has 28½ hours programme time a day. Several republics have their own foreign services. English is broadcast from Moscow, Kiev, Tashkent, Vilnius and Yerevan. There are 117 TV centres in the USSR, several of them producing more than 1 programme. In Moscow there are 4 programmes. Colour programmes are broadcast by the SECAM system. A nationwide system of space telecommunications, consisting of satellites and ground stations, takes TV broadcasts to distant parts of the country.

Number of receivers, Jan. 1983: radio, 145m. (1970, 94·6m); television, 85m. (1970, 34·8m.).

Cinemas and theatres (Jan. 1984). There were 141,700 permanent and 9,600 mobile cinemas. In Jan. 1984 there were 626 theatres, to which 124·9m. visits were made.

Newspapers. In 1983, 8,273 newspapers with a total daily circulation of 179m. copies were published in 57 languages of the USSR.

JUSTICE, RELIGION, EDUCATION AND WELFARE

Justice. The basis of the judicial system is the same throughout the Soviet Union, but the constituent republics have the right to introduce modifications and to make their own rules for the application of the codes of laws. The Supreme Court of the USSR is the chief court and supervising organ for all constituent republics and is elected by the Supreme Soviet of the USSR for 5 years. Chairman (1985) V. I. Terebilov. Supreme Courts of the Union and Autonomous Republics are elected by the Supreme Soviets of these republics, and Territorial, Regional and Area Courts by the respective Soviets, each for a term of 5 years. At the lowest level are the People's Courts, which are elected directly by the population.

Court proceedings are conducted in the local language with full interpreting facilities as required. All cases are heard in public, unless otherwise provided for by law, and the accused is guaranteed the right of defence.

Laws establishing common principles of legislation in various fields are adopted by the Supreme Soviet and are then enacted in more specific form and implemented by subordinate levels of state and judicial authority.

The Law Courts are divided into People's Courts and higher courts. The People's Courts consist of the People's Judge and 2 Assessors, and their function is to examine, as the first instance, most of the civil and criminal cases, except the more important ones, some of which are tried at the Regional Court, and those of the highest importance at the Supreme Court. The Regional Courts supervise the activities of the People's Courts and also act as Courts of Appeal from the decisions of the People's Court. Special chambers of the higher courts deal with offences committed in the Army and the public transport services.

People's Judges and Assessors, who serve on a rota basis, are elected directly by the citizens of each constituency: judges for 5 years, assessors for 2½. Should a judge be found not to perform his duties conscientiously and in accordance with the mandate of the people, he may be recalled by his electors.

The People's Assessors are called upon for duty for 2 weeks in a year. The People's Assessors for the Regional Court must have had at least 2 years' experience in public or trade-union work. The list of Assessors for the Supreme Court is drawn up by the Supreme Soviet of the republic.

The Labour Session of the People's Court supervises the regulations relating to the working conditions and the protection of labour and gives decisions on conflicts arising between managements and employees, or the violation of regulations.

Disputes between State institutions must be referred to an arbitration commission. Disputes between Soviet State institutions and foreign business firms may be referred by agreement to a Foreign Trade Arbitration Commission of the All-Union Chamber of Commerce.

The Procurator-General of the USSR (in 1985, A. M. Renkunov) is appointed for 5 years by the Supreme Soviet. All procurators of the republics, autonomous republics and autonomous regions are appointed by the Procurator-General of the USSR for a term of 5 years. The procurators supervise the correct application of the law by all state organs, and have special responsibility for the observance of the law in places of detention. The procurators of the Union republics are subordinate to the Procurator-General of the USSR, whose duty it is to see that acts of all institutions of the USSR are legal, that the law is correctly interpreted and uniformly applied; he has to participate in important cases in the capacity of State Prosecutor.

Capital punishment was abolished on 26 May 1947, but was restored on 12 Jan. 1950 for treason, espionage and sabotage, on 7 May 1954 for certain categories of murder, in Dec. 1958 for terrorism and banditry, on 7 May 1961 for embezzlement of public property, counterfeiting and attack on prison warders and, in particular circumstances, for attacks on the police and public order volunteers and for rape (15 Feb. 1962) and for accepting bribes (20 Feb. 1962).

In view of criminal abuses, extending over many years, discovered in the security system, the powers of administrative trial and exile previously vested in the security authorities (MVD) were abolished in 1953; accelerated procedures for trial on charges of high treason, espionage, wrecking, etc., by the Supreme Court were abolished in 1955; and extensive powers of protection of persons under arrest or serving prison terms were vested in the Procurator-General's Office (1955). Supervisory commissions, composed of representatives of trade unions, youth organizations and local authorities, were set up in 1956 to inspect places of detention.

Further reforms of the civil and criminal codes were decreed on 25 Dec. 1958. Thereby the age of criminal responsibility has been raised from 14 to 16 years; deportation and banishment have been abolished; a presumption of innocence is not accepted, but the burden of proof of guilt has been placed upon the prosecutor. Secret trials and the charge of 'enemy of the people' have been abolished. Articles 70 and 190 of the Criminal Code, which deal with 'anti-Soviet agitation and propaganda' and 'crimes against the system of administration' respectively, have however been widely used against political dissidents in more recent years.

Butler, W. E., *The Soviet Legal System. Selected Contemporary Legislation and Documents.* New York, 1978.—*Soviet Law.* London, 1983
Hazard, J., Butler, W. E. and Maggs, P., *The Soviet Legal System.* 3rd ed., New York, 1977
Simons, W. B., (ed.), *The Soviet Codes of Law.* Alphen aan den Rijn, 1980

Religion. With the Revolution the Orthodox Church lost its position as the dominant religion and all religions were placed on an equal footing. Article 52 of the 1977 Soviet Constitution reads as follows: 'Citizens of the USSR are guaranteed freedom of conscience, that is, the right to profess or not to profess any religion, and to conduct religious worship or atheistic propaganda. Incitement of hostility or hatred on religious grounds is prohibited. In the USSR the church is separated from the state, and school from the church.'

By decree of 2 Feb. 1918 the Orthodox Church was disestablished; its property, together with that of all other denominations, was nationalized. The congregations themselves have to maintain their churches and clergy, regardless of confession or denomination. A minimum of 20 persons may request and receive the use of a church building, free of charge, except for maintenance, insurance, land taxes, etc. About two-thirds of all the churches have been closed since 1917, but about 20,000 churches and 18 religious seminaries were reported to be in operation in 1984. Religious instruction may be given in private, but otherwise only in church classes. The income of religious communities is not subject to taxation. Religious instruction in classes for persons under 18 is forbidden. The state supplies paper and printing facilities to all denominations for producing the Bible, the Koran, prayer books, missals, etc.

Relations between the religious communities of all creeds and the Government are maintained through a Council for Religious Affairs which is attached to the Council of Ministers of the USSR. (*Chairman*, V. A. Kuroyedov).

The Russian Orthodox Church, represented by the Patriarchate of Moscow, had, in 1984, about 30m. regular worshippers. There are still many Old Believers, whose schism from the Orthodox Church dates from the 17th century. The Russian Church is headed by the Patriarch of Moscow and All Russia, assisted by the Holy Synod, which has 7 members–the Patriarch himself and the Metropolitans of Krutitsy and Kolomna (Moscow), Leningrad and Kiev *ex officio*, and 3 bishops alternating for 6 months in order of seniority from the 3 regions forming the Moscow Patriarchate. The Patriarchate of Moscow maintains jurisdiction over a few parishes of Russian Orthodox abroad, at Tehrán, Jerusalem, German Democratic Republic, France (1 archbishop), England, North and South America (2 bishops). There are 19 monasteries and nunneries, and 6 Orthodox academies and seminaries with 10 journals.

After the Russian Orthodox Church the next Christian community in importance are the Armenians; their Catholicos (Patriarch), whose seat is at Etchmiadzin, is head of all the Armenian (Gregorian) communities throughout the world. There is an Armenian Orthodox academy and a seminary.

The Georgian Orthodox Church has its own organization under a Catholicos (Patriarch) who is resident in Tbilisi and who directs the church's seminary in Mtskheta.

Protestantism is represented chiefly by the Evangelical Christian Baptists, with over 512,000 baptized adult members and some 5,000 churches; the Lutherans are concentrated mainly in the Baltic States (350,000 in Estonia, 600,000 in Latvia), the Reformed in the Transcarpathian Region of the Ukraine (70,000). Both Baptists and Lutherans conduct theological courses. The Methodist Church functions in Estonia.

The Roman Catholics are most numerous in Lithuania and the western Ukraine. There are 2 Roman Catholic arch-episcopates and 4 episcopates in Lithuania with 630 churches and a seminary at Kaunas providing a 5-year course. In 1946 some 3·5m. Uniates in the USSR were compelled to withdraw their allegiance to Rome and came under the jurisdiction of the Orthodox Patriarchate in Moscow. In Latvia there are an arch-episcopate and 1 episcopate (Riga and Liepaja) of the Roman Catholic Church.

The Moslems (estimate 30m. members, mainly Sunnis), are divided into 4 administrative regions, 3 of them (Central Asia and Kazakhstan, European Russia and Siberia, Northern Caucasus) headed by a Mufti; the largest (Transcaucasia, with its centre at Baku) by a Sheikh-ul-Islam.

There is a Moslem academy and a madrasah in Central Asia. Several editions of the Koran have appeared in recent years.

There are various Jewish communities, the chief being in Moscow and Kiev. Large synagogues maintain bakeries for producing unleavened bread. There is a Jewish Yeshiva in Moscow (established 1956) and 180 synagogues as well as several dozen minyans. The Central Buddhist Council of the USSR is headed by a Lama with communities in Buryatia, Tuva, Kalmykia and in the national (minority) areas of the Chita and Irkutsk regions.

O religii i tserkvi: sbornik vazhneishikh vyskazivanii klassikov Marksizma-Leninizma, dokumentov KPSS i sovetskogo gosudarstva. 2nd ed., Moscow, 1981

Bordeaux, M., *Opium of the People. The Christian Religion in the USSR.* London, 1965.—*Religious Ferment in Russia.* London, 1968

Curtiss, J. S., *The Russian Church and the Soviet State, 1917–50.* New York, 1953

Kochan, L., (ed.), *Jews in Soviet Russia since 1917.* 3rd ed., Oxford, 1977
Kolarz, W., *Religion in the Soviet Union.* London, 1961
Kuroedov, V. A., *Religiya i tserkov' v sovetskom gosudarstve.* Moscow, 1981
Lane, C., *Christian Religion in the Soviet Union.* London, 1978

Education. Education is free and compulsory from 7 to 16/17. There are 2 types of general schools, with an 8-year or a 10-year curriculum; the minimum school-leaving age is now 17. Pupils who leave an 8-year school continue their education at either a 10-year school or a vocational training school. A 10-year school pupil may also transfer to vocational school after the 8th year. Under directives adopted in 1984, there will be a gradual transition towards an 11-year school system, starting at 6, from 1986 onwards; efforts are also to be made to improve pupils' preparation for employment and the status and working conditions of teachers.

In 1983–84 there were 141,000 primary and secondary schools. Pupils in general educational schools numbered 44·5m. (8·7m. of them in the ninth and tenth forms) and the teachers 2·7m. Those at vocational and specialized technical secondary schools numbered 9·8m.

At the end of 1940 labour reserve schools (both vocational and industrial) were organized, admitting applicants from 14 to 17 years of age. From 1959 onwards these and other technical schools were reorganized as town and rural vocational and technical schools, at which pupils stay for a year longer than at general schools, combining completion of general secondary education with vocational training. From 1940 to 1977 inclusive they trained 35m. skilled workers. In 1978, 2·3m. graduated from such schools, including 628,000 for agriculture; 600,000 agricultural mechanics were trained in state and collective farms. Over 4,300 vocational training schools existed in 1981, training 2·17m. boys and girls, all of whom receive a full secondary education. In 1984, 15·5m. children of from 3 to 7 years of age attended kindergartens. Children in boarding schools numbered over 800,000 in 1972–73.

In 1983–84 there were 4,438 technical colleges with 4·5m. students, and 890 universities, institutes and other places of higher education, with 5·3m. students (including 1·7m. taking correspondence or evening courses). Among the 65 university towns are: Moscow, Leningrad, Kharkov, Odessa, Tartu, Kazan, Saratov, Tomsk, Kiev, Sverdlovsk, Tbilisi, Alma-Ata, Tashkent, Minsk, Gorky and Vladivostok.

On 1 Jan. 1984 there were 1·44m. scientific workers in places of higher education, research institutes and Academies of Sciences. There are 33,000 foreign students from 130 countries.

The Academy of Sciences of the USSR had 757 members and corresponding members. Total learned institutions under the USSR Academy of Sciences number 244, with 50,711 scientific staff. Each Union Republic (other than the RSFSR) has its own Academy of Sciences, with scientific staff numbering 49,079. There are also Siberian, Far Eastern and other branches of the USSR Academy. On 1 Jan. 1981 there were 96,820 post-graduate students in Academy and other higher educational institutions, 59% studying on a part-time basis.

The Academy of Pedagogical Sciences had 14 research institutes with 1,640 staff.

In 1984 over 106m. people were studying at schools, colleges and training or correspondence courses. 116 per 1,000 of the employed population had a higher education (1939, 13; 1959, 33).

Grant, N., *Soviet Education.* 4th ed., Harmondsworth, 1979
Matthews, M., *Education in the Soviet Union.* London, 1982

Health and Social Security. All health services are free of charge although payment is required for medicines; but private practice exists. The health service is administered by the Ministry of Health of the USSR, which supervises the work of the Health Ministries of the Union Republics and the Autonomous Republics.

In 1944 an Academy of Medical Sciences was formed; it has under its direct control 52 research institutes. In all, there were, in 1984, 393 medical research institutions with 70,000 research staff. Smallpox, trachoma and malaria have been virtually eliminated.

In 1981–82, 98 institutes and medical faculties had a total of 383,800 students taking a 6-year course.

In Jan. 1984 there were 23,100 civil hospitals with 3·5m. beds. There were 837,000 infants in day nurseries. 1,104,300 doctors (including dentists) were in the health service. All confinements in towns and 75% in the country were in hospital.

There were 37,000 outpatients' clinics, apart from the 25,800 women's consultation centres and children's clinics.

The death-rate in the USSR in 1983 was 10·3 per 1,000, and the birth rate 20·1 per 1,000. Infant death rate was 27·9 (per 1,000 live births) in 1974, compared with 273 in 1913, 184 in 1940 and 81 in 1950. Average expectation of life, 70 (1913, 32).

Social insurance is administered by the trade unions, through social insurance councils elected in places of work and social insurance sub-committees of factory committees: about 5m. volunteers are engaged in this work. 43·4m. people went to holiday sanatoria or rest homes in 1982. 52·4m. people, including 10·6m. collective farmers, were receiving state pensions in Jan. 1983; of these, 9·3m. were old-age pensioners.

Total number of holiday sanatoria providing toning-up treatment at resorts in 1982 was 2,352, with accommodation for 567,000; in addition, there were 2,766 overnight sanatoria at large plants for treatment of mild disorders without absence from work, accommodating 233,000. There were also 1,208 trade union-managed holiday hotels with a capacity of 380,000, holidays being partly or wholly at trade unions' expense.

State expenditure (in 1m. rubles) on health services and physical education: 1940, 0·9; 1970, 9,300; 1980, 14,800; 1983, 16,500.

Between 1950 and 1980 62,766,000 apartments (in towns) and houses (in rural areas) were built. In 1983, 2m. apartments and houses were built. Rents in the USSR have not been increased since 1928 and in 1983 account for about 3% of the expenditure of an average worker's family. By the end of 1983, 79% of all urban housing had a gas supply installed, 91% had running water, 88% had central heating and 80% of the urban population lived in individual rather than communal apartments. 57% of total housing space is publicly and 43% is privately owned.

DIPLOMATIC REPRESENTATIVES

Of the USSR in Great Britain (13 Kensington Palace Gdns., London, W8 4QX)
Ambassador: Viktor I. Popov.

Of Great Britain in the USSR (Naberezhnaya Morisa Toreza 14, Moscow 72)
Ambassador: Sir Iain Sutherland, KCMG.

Of the USSR in the USA (1125 16th St., NW, Washington, D.C., 20036)
Ambassador: Anatoly F. Dobrynin.

Of the USA in the USSR (Ulitsa Chaikovskogo 19, Moscow)
Ambassador: Arthur A. Hartman.

Of the USSR to the United Nations
Ambassador: Oleg Aleksandrovich Troyanovsky.

Books of Reference

Narodnoye Khozyaistvo SSSR 1922–1982 (National Economy of the USSR). Jubilee Statistical Yearbook. Moscow, 1982
Pravda (Truth). Daily organ of the Central Committee of the Communist Party
Izvestiya (News). Daily organ of the Presidium of the Supreme Soviet of the USSR
Vedomosti Verkhovnovo Soveta. Bulletin of the Supreme Soviet of the USSR in the languages of the 15 republics; published weekly
Sovetskaya Torgovlya. Twice-weekly publication of the Ministry of Trade of the USSR
Planovoye Khozyaistvo. Monthly. Moscow
Voprosy Torgovli. A monthly journal published by the Ministry of Trade of the USSR
Vneshnyaya Torgovlya. Published by the Ministry for Foreign Trade. Monthly. Moscow
Trud. The daily organ of the All-Union Central Council of Trade Unions
Professionalnye Soyuzy. A trade union fortnightly. Moscow
Kommunist. A fortnightly organ of the Communist Party of the Soviet Union
Finansy i Khozyaistvo. A weekly publication of the Ministry for Finance

Bolshaya Sovetskaya Entsiklopedia. 65 vols. Moscow, 1926–47; 2nd ed., 51 vols. Moscow, 1949–58; 3rd ed., Moscow, 1959–78; annual supplement (*Yezhegodnik*)
Soviet Union. A monthly pictorial. Moscow. (In English)
Soviet Import-Export Dictionary (in Russian, with English, etc., terms). Moscow, 1952
Soviet Studies; A Quarterly Review. Ed. R. A. Clarke. Glasgow, quarterly.
The Current Digest of the Soviet Press. Published by Joint Committee on Slavic Studies. Weekly. Washington, D.C.
Baylis, J., and Segal, G., (eds.) *Soviet Strategy.* London, 1981
Beloff, M., *The Foreign Policy of Soviet Russia, 1929–41.* 2 vols. 1947–49.—*Soviet Policy in the Far East.* Oxford, 1953.—*Soviet Policy in Asia, 1944–52.* Oxford, 1953
Brown, A., and Kaser, M., *The Soviet Union Since the Fall of Khrushchev.* London, 2nd ed. 1978.—*Soviet Policy for the 1980s.* London, 1982
Byrnes, J. F. (ed.), *After Brezhnev. Sources of Soviet Conduct in the 1980s.* London, 1983
Carr, E. H., *A History of Soviet Russia.* 14 vols. London, 1951–78
Clarke, R. A., and Matko, D. J. I., (eds.), *Soviet Economic Facts 1917–80.* London, 1983
Cracraft, J., *The Soviet Union Today.* Chicago, 1983
Degras, J. (compiler), *Soviet Documents on Foreign Policy, 1917–41.* 3 vols. London, 1948–52
Deutscher, I., *Trotsky.* 3 vols. OUP, 1954 ff.
Edmonds, R., *Soviet Foreign Policy: the Brezhnev Years.* Oxford, 1983
Falla, P. S., *The Oxford English-Russian Dictionary.* OUP, 1984
Fitzsimmons, T., and others, *USSR; Its People, Its Society, Its Culture.* New Haven, 1960
Galperin, I. R., *New English-Russian Dictionary.* 2 vols. Moscow, 1972
Gruzinov, V. F., *The USSR's Management of Foreign Trade.* London, 1980
Hammond, T. T. (ed.), *Soviet Foreign Relations and World Communism: A Selected Bibliography.* Princeton, 1965
Hough, J. F. and Fainsod, M., *How the Soviet Union is Governed.* Rev. ed. Harvard Univ. Press, 1979
Humphrey, C., *Karl Marx Collective: Economy, Society and Religion in a Siberian Collective Farm.* CUP, 1983
Hutchings, R., *The Soviet Budget.* London, 1983
Jones, D. L., *Books in English in the Soviet Union 1917–73: A Bibliography.* London and New York, 1975
Kaiser, R. G., *Russia: The People and the Power.* London, 1976
Kelley, D. R., (ed.), *Soviet Politics in the Brezhnev Era.* London, 1980
Lenin, V. I., *Collected Works.* 45 vols. London, 1960–70
McCauley, M., *The Soviet Union since 1917.* London, 1981
Nove, A., *The Soviet Economic System.* London, 1977
Pares, Sir B., *A History of Russia.* London, 1962
Paxton, J., *Companion to Russian History.* London and New York, 1984
Preobrazhensky, A. G., *Etymological Dictionary of the Russian Language.* Columbia Univ. Press, 1951
Riasanovsky, N. V., *A History of Russia.* 4th ed. OUP, 1984
Shabad, T., and Mote, V.L., *Gateway to Siberian Resources (The BAM).* New York and London, 1977
Schapiro, L., and Godson, J., *The Soviet Worker.* London, 1981
Slusser, R. M., and Triska, J. F., *A Calendar of Soviet Treaties, 1917–57.* Stanford Univ. Press, 1959—and Ginsburgs, G., *A Calendar of Soviet Treaties, 1958–1973,* Alphen aan den Rijn, 1981
Smirnitsky, A. I. (ed.), *Russko-angliiskii slovar.* 4th ed. Moscow 1959
Stalin, J. V., *Collected Works.* 13 vols. London, 1952–55
Thompson, A., *Russia/USSR: A Selective Annotated Bibliography of Books in English.* Oxford and Santa Barbara, 1979
Treadgold, D. W., *Twentieth Century Russia.* 5th ed. Boston, 1981
Utechin, S. V. (ed.), *Everyman's Concise Encyclopaedia of Russia.* London, 1961
Vernadsky, G., *A History of Russia.* 5th ed. Yale Univ. Press, 1961
Wheeler, M., *The Oxford Russian-English Dictionary.* OUP, 2nd ed., 1984

RUSSIAN SOVIET FEDERAL SOCIALIST REPUBLIC (RSFSR)

Rossiiskaya Sovyetskaya Federativnaya Sotsialisticheskaya Respublika

AREA AND POPULATION. The RSFSR occupies over 76% of the total area of the USSR stretching from the Far North to the Black Sea in the south and from the Far East to Kaliningrad in the west. 82·6% of its population in Jan. 1979 were Russians, the rest being 38 national minorities such as the Tatars, Ukrainians, Jews, Mordovians, Chuvashis, Bashkirs, Poles, Germans, Udmurts, Buryats, Mari, Yakuts and Ossetians. The 2 principal cities are Moscow, the capital, with a population (Jan. 1983) of 8·4m. (without suburbs, 8,202,000) and Leningrad, the second capital, 4,779,000 (without suburbs, 4,255,000). Among other important large towns are Gorky, Rostov-on-Don, Volgograd, Sverdlovsk, Novosibirsk, Chelyabinsk, Kazan, Omsk and Kuibyshev. Population, 1984, 142,117,000.

The RSFSR contains great mineral resources: iron ore in the Urals, the Kerch Peninsula and Siberia; coal in the Kuznets Basin, Eastern Siberia, Urals and the sub-Moscow Basin; oil in the Urals, Azov-Black Sea area, Bashkiria, and West Siberia. It also has abundant deposits of gold, platinum, copper, zinc, lead, tin and rare metals.

The RSFSR produces about 70% of the total industrial and agricultural output of the Soviet Union. Industrial and office workers averaged 66·2m. in 1981.

CONSTITUTION AND GOVERNMENT. The RSFSR adopted its present constitution at a meeting of the Supreme Soviet in April 1978, following 330,000 town and country meetings in which 25m. citizens took part.

Chairman, Presidium of the Supreme Soviet: M. A. Yasnov.
Chairman, Council of Ministers: V. I. Vorotnikov.
Foreign Minister: F. E. Titov.

The RSFSR consists of:

(1) *Territories:* Altai, Khabarovsk, Krasnodar, Krasnoyarsk, Primorye, Stavropol.

(2) *Regions:* Amur, Archangel, Astrakhan, Belgorod, Briansk, Chelyabinsk, Chita, Gorky, Irkutsk, Ivanovo, Kaluga, Kalinin, Kaliningrad, Kamchatka, Kemerovo, Kirov, Kostroma, Kuibyshev, Kurgan, Kursk, Leningrad, Lipetsk, Magadan, Moscow, Murmansk, Novgorod, Novosibirsk, Omsk, Orel, Orenburg, Penza, Perm, Pskov, Rostov, Ryazan, Sakhalin, Saratov, Smolensk, Sverdlovsk, Tambov, Tomsk, Tula, Tyumen, Ulyanovsk, Vladimir, Volgograd, Vologda, Voronezh, Yaroslavl.

(3) *Autonomous Soviet Republics:* Bashkir, Buryat, Checheno-Ingush, Chuvash, Daghestan, Kabardino-Balkar, Kalmyk, Karelian, Komi, Mari, Mordovian, North Ossetia, Karachayevo-Cherkess, Tartar, Tuva, Udmurt, Yakut.

(4) *Autonomous Regions:* Adygei, Karachai-Circassian, Gorno-Altai, Jewish, Khakass.

(5) *Autonomous Areas:* Aginsky-Buryat, Chukot, Evenki, Khanty-Mansi, Komi Permyak, Koryak, Nenets, Taimyr (Dolgano-Nenets), Ust-Ordynsky-Buryat, Yamalo-Nenets.

The Supreme Soviet, elected in Feb. 1985, consisted of 975 deputies (1 per 150,000 population); 649 were Communists, 344 women, 492 workers and collective farmers.

On 20 June 1982, 1,139,925 deputies were elected to local authorities; 578,461 (50·7%) were women, 658,241 (57·7%) non-Party and 773,073 (67·8%) industrial workers and collective farmers.

FINANCE. Revenue and expenditure balanced as follows (in 1m. rubles): 1985, 91,193; 1984 (estimate), 88,855. These figures, and those for the other 14 Union Republics, include grants from the Union Budget.

COMMUNICATIONS. Length of railways on 1 Jan. 1982 was 83,311 km, inland waterways, 126,000 km, hard-surface motor roads, 448,200 km

Newspapers. In 1982 there were 4,498 newspapers, 4,190 of them in Russian. Daily circulation of Russian-language newspapers, 117·8m., other languages, 3m.

EDUCATION. In 1981–82 there were 20·1m. pupils in primary and secondary schools; 3,067,200 students in 499 higher educational establishments (including correspondence students) and 2,587,200 students in 2,509 technical colleges of all kinds (including correspondence students). There were 8·4m. children attending pre-school institutions. There were, on 1 Jan. 1982, 963,400 scientific staff in over 3,000 learned and scientific institutions.

In 1957 a Siberian branch of the Academy of Sciences was organized, in charge of all scientific research institutions from the Urals to the Pacific.

There is an Academy of Municipal Economy (with 5 research institutions and a staff of 437).

HEALTH. Doctors at the end of 1981 numbered 579,900, and hospital beds 1·8m. (133,400 in 1913 and 482,000 in 1940).

BASHKIR AUTONOMOUS SOVIET SOCIALIST REPUBLIC

Area 143,600 sq. km (55,430 sq. miles), population (Jan. 1984) 3·85m. Capital, Ufa. Bashkiria was annexed to Russia in 1557. It was constituted as an Autonomous Soviet Republic on 23 March 1919. Population, census 1979, included 24·3% Bashkirians, 40·3% Russians, 24·5% Tatars, and 3·2% Chuvashes.

280 deputies were elected on 24 Feb. 1980, 109 of them women.

In 1982–83 there were 677,000 pupils in 3,400 secondary schools. There is a state university and a branch of the USSR Academy of Sciences with 8 learned institutions (511 research workers). There were 127,000 students in technical colleges and higher schools.

In Jan. 1982 there were 11,500 doctors and 48,400 hospital beds.

There are expanding chemical, coal, steel, electrical engineering, timber and paper industries. There were 629 collective farms and 159 state farms in 1980. Crop area was 4,587,000 hectares. Bashkiria is a major oil producer in USSR.

BURIAT AUTONOMOUS SOVIET SOCIALIST REPUBLIC

Area is 351,300 sq. km (135,650 sq. miles). The Buriat Republic, situated to the south of the Yakut Republic, adopted the Soviet system 1 March 1920. This area was penetrated by the Russians in the 17th century and finally annexed from China by the treaties of Nerchinsk (1689) and Kyakhta (1727). The population (Jan. 1981) was 929,000. Capital, Ulan-Udé. The name of the republic was changed from 'Buriat-Mongol' on 7 July 1958. The population (1979 census) includes 23% Buriats and 72% Russians. Population, 1984, 850,000.

170 deputies were elected on 24 Feb. 1980, 59 of them women.

The main industries are coal, timber, building materials, fisheries, sheep and cattle farming. In 1980 there were 105 state and 61 collective farms. Crop area was 827,100 hectares. Gold, molybdenum and wolfram are mined.

In 1983–84 there were 610 schools with 164,000 pupils, 22 technical colleges with 18,850 students and 4 higher educational institutions with 22,500 students. A branch of the Siberian Department of the Academy of Sciences had 4 learned institutions with 281 research workers.

In 1983 there were 3,000 doctors and 12,000 hospital beds.

CHECHENO-INGUSH AUTONOMOUS SOVIET SOCIALIST REPUBLIC

Area, 19,300 sq. km (7,350 sq. miles); population (Jan. 1984), 1·20m. Capital, Grozny. After 70 years of almost continuous fighting, the Chechens and Ingushes were conquered by Russia in the late 1850s. In 1918 each nationality separately established its 'National Soviet' within the Terek Autonomous Republic, and in 1920 (after the Civil War) were constituted areas within the Mountain Republic. The Chechens separated out as an Autonomous Region on 30 Nov. 1922 and the Ingushes on 7 July 1924. In Jan. 1934 the two regions were united, and on 5 Dec. 1936 constituted as an Autonomous Republic. This was dissolved in 1944, but reconstituted on 9 Jan. 1957: 232,000 Chechens and Ingushes returned to their homes in the next 2 years. The population (1979 census) includes 52·9% Chechens, 11·7% Ingushes, and 29·1% Russians.

175 deputies were elected on 24 Feb. 1980, 78 of them women.

The republic has one of the major Soviet oilfields: also a number of large engineering works, chemical factories, building materials works and food canneries. There is an expanding timber, woodworking and furniture industry. In 1983 there were 122 state and 39 collective farms. Crop area was 443,600 hectares.

There were, in 1982–83, 560 schools with 271,000 pupils, 12 technical colleges with 14,200 students and 2 places of higher education with 12,200 students.

In 1982 there were 3,800 doctors and 11,800 hospital beds.

CHUVASH AUTONOMOUS SOVIET SOCIALIST REPUBLIC

Area, 18,300 sq. km (7,064 sq. miles); population (Jan. 1984), 1,314,000. Capital, Cheboksary. The territory was annexed by Russia in the middle of the 16th century. On 24 June 1920 it was constituted as an Autonomous Region, and on 21 April 1925 as an Autonomous Republic. The population (1979 census) includes Chuvashes (68·4%), Russians (26%), Tatars (2·9%) and Mordovians (1·6%).

200 deputies were elected on 24 Feb. 1980, 79 of them women.

Like most of the Autonomous Republics, Chuvashia before 1914 was a region of primitive agriculture with a certain development of the timber industry. Today it has several big railway repair works, an expanding electrical and other engineering industries, building materials, chemicals, textiles and food industries; timber felling and haulage are largely mechanized. In 1983 there were 179 collective farms and 104 state farms. Grain crops account for nearly two-thirds of all sowings and fodder crops for nearly a quarter. Fruit and wine-growing are a developing branch of agriculture. Crop area was 798,800 hectares.

In 1982–83 there were 237,900 pupils at school, 25,000 students at technical colleges and 17,800 students undertaking higher education.

In 1982 there were 4,000 doctors and 15,600 hospital beds.

DAGESTAN AUTONOMOUS SOVIET SOCIALIST REPUBLIC

Area, 50,300 sq. km (19,416 sq. miles); population (Jan. 1984), 1·7m. Capital, Makhachkala. Over 30 nationalities inhabit this republic apart from Russians (11·6% at 1979 census); the most numerous are the Avartsy (25·7%), Dargintsy (15·2%), Lezginy (11·6%), Kumyki (12·4%), Laki (5·1%), Tabasarany (4·4%) and Azerbaidjanis (4%). Annexed from Persia in 1723, Dagestan was constituted an Autonomous Republic on 20 Jan. 1921.

210 deputies were elected on 24 Feb. 1980, 82 of them women.

There are large engineering, oil, chemical, woodworking, textile, food and other light industries. Agriculture is very varied, ranging from wheat to grapes, with sheep farming and cattle breeding; in 1983 there were 249 collective farms and 262 state farms. Crop area was 427,800 hectares. A chain of power stations is under construction in the Sulak River (total capacity 2·5m. kw.).

In 1982–83 there were 1,600 schools with 407,700 pupils, 33,900 technical students and 5 higher education establishments with 26,200 students; and a branch of the USSR Academy of Sciences with 4 learned institutions (373 research workers). In Jan. 1983 there were 6,300 doctors and 19,000 hospital beds.

KABARDINO-BALKAR AUTONOMOUS SOVIET SOCIALIST REPUBLIC

Area, 12,500 sq. km (4,825 sq. miles); population (Jan. 1984) 708,000. Capital, Nalchik. Kabarda was annexed to Russia in 1557. The republic was constituted on 5 Dec. 1936. Population (1979 census) includes Kabardinians (45·6%), Balkars (9%), Russians (35·1%).

160 deputies were elected on 24 Feb. 1980, 70 of them women.

Main industries are ore-mining, timber, engineering, coal, food processing, timber and light industries, building materials. Grain, livestock breeding, dairy farming and wine-growing are the principal branches of agriculture. There were, in 1983, 59 state and 66 collective farms.

In 1982–83 there were 266 schools with 127,700 pupils, 10,400 students in 11 technical colleges and 9,500 students receiving higher education; in Jan. 1983 there were 2,900 doctors and 8,100 hospital beds.

KALMYK AUTONOMOUS SOVIET SOCIALIST REPUBLIC

Area, 75,900 sq. km (29,300 sq. miles); population (Jan. 1984), 315,000. Capital, Elista (64,000). The population (1979 census) includes 41·5% Kalmyks, 42·6% Russians, 6·6% Kazakhs, Chechens and Dagestanis.

The Kalmyks migrated from western China to Russia (Nogai Steppe) in the early 17th century. The territory was constituted an Autonomous Region on 4 Nov. 1920, and an Autonomous Republic on 22 Oct. 1935; this was dissolved in 1943. On 9 Jan. 1957 it was reconstituted as an Autonomous Region and on 29 July 1958 as an Autonomous Republic once more.

130 deputies were elected on 24 Feb. 1980, 54 of them women.

Main industries are fishing, canning and building materials. Cattle breeding and irrigated farming (mainly fodder crops) are the principal branches of agriculture. In 1983 there were 79 state and 23 collective farms. Crop area was 859,000 hectares.

In 1982–83 there were 57,200 pupils in 266 schools, 10,400 students in technical colleges and 9,500 in higher education; 1,058 doctors and 4,605 hospital beds.

KARELIAN AUTONOMOUS SOVIET SOCIALIST REPUBLIC

HISTORY. Before 1917, Karelia (then known as the Olonets Province) was noted chiefly as a place of exile for political and other prisoners.

After the November Revolution of 1917, Karelia formed part of the RSFSR. In June 1920 a Karelian Labour Commune was formed and in July 1923 this was transformed into the Karelian Autonomous Soviet Socialist Republic (one of the autonomous republics of the RSFSR). On 31 March 1940, after the Soviet–Finnish war, practically all the territory (with the exception of a small section in the neighbourhood of the Leningrad area) which had been ceded by Finland to the USSR was added to Karelia and the Karelian Autonomous Republic was transformed into the Karelo-Finnish Soviet Socialist Republic as the 12th republic of the USSR. In 1946, however, the southern part of the republic, including its whole seaboard and the town of Viipuri (Vyborg) and Keksholm, was attached to the RSFSR and in 1956 the republic reverted to ASSR status with the RSFSR.

AREA AND POPULATION. The Karelian Autonomous Republic, capital Petrozavodsk, covers an area of 172,400 sq. km, with a population of 769,000 (Jan. 1984). Karelians represent 11·1% of the population, Russians, 71·3%, Belorussians 8·1%, Ukrainians 3·2%, Finns 2·7% (1979 census).

150 deputies were elected on 24 Feb. 1980, 53 of them women.

NATURAL RESOURCES. Karelia is chiefly noted for its wealth of timber, some 70% of its territory being forest land. It is also rich in other natural resources, having large deposits of diabase, spar, quartz, marble, granite, zinc, lead, silver, copper, molybdenum, tin, baryta, iron ore, etc. Karelia takes first place in the USSR for the production of mica. It has 43,643 lakes, which, as well as its rivers, are rich in fish.

Agriculture. There were 9 collective farms and 59 state farms in 1983. The crop area was 75,000 hectares (over 85% under fodder crops).

INDUSTRY. The republic has 25 large-scale enterprises, such as timber-mills, paper-cellulose works, mica, chemical plants, power stations and furniture factories. Output, 1982: Timber, 10·5m. cu. metres; paper, 1·2m. tonnes; cellulose, 755,000 tonnes; power, 3,677m. kwh.; confectionery, 5,600 tonnes.

The construction of the White Sea–Baltic Canal had a powerful influence on the economic development of Karelia. New refrigerating plants, cellulose factories and timber industry equipment began working in 1970.

COMMUNICATIONS. A railway between Petrozavodsk and Suoyarvi connects the capital and the Murmansk Railway with the main railway line Sortavala–Vyborg. A railway line was also laid between Kandalaksha and Kuolayarvi. Length of track, 1,600 km.

EDUCATION. In 1982–83 there were 115,200 pupils in 373 schools. There were 10,200 students in 3 places of higher education and 14,100 in 15 technical colleges.

There are in Petrozavodsk a university (4,028 full-time students, 2,036 taking correspondence courses and 622 evening students in 1971), 2 other higher institutes and a teachers' training college. A branch of the Academy of Sciences was set up in 1949 with 8 learned institutions (349 research workers).

HEALTH. In Jan. 1983 there were 3,400 doctors, and 11,600 hospital beds.

KOMI AUTONOMOUS SOVIET SOCIALIST REPUBLIC

Area, 415,900 sq. km (160,540 sq. miles); population (Jan. 1984), 1·2m. Capital, Syktyvkar (176,500). Annexed by the princes of Moscow in the 14th century and occupied by British and American forces in 1918–19, the territory was constituted as an Autonomous Region on 22 Aug. 1921 and as an Autonomous Republic on 5 Dec. 1936. The population (1979 census) includes Komi (25·3%), Russians (56·7%), Ukrainians and Belorussians (10·7%).

180 deputies were elected on 24 Feb. 1980, 59 of them women.

There are large coal, oil, timber, gas, asphalt and building materials industries; light industry is expanding. Livestock breeding (including dairy farming) is the main branch of agriculture. There were 56 state farms in 1983. Crop area, 92,000 hectares.

In 1982–83 there were 191,800 pupils in 620 schools, 12,400 students receiving higher education, 17,500 students in 18 technical colleges, and a branch of the Academy of Sciences with 4 learned institutions (297 research workers).

In Jan. 1983 there were 4,000 doctors and 16,200 hospital beds.

MARI AUTONOMOUS SOVIET SOCIALIST REPUBLIC

Area, 23,200 sq. km (8,955 sq. miles); population (Jan. 1984), 722,000. Capital, Yoshkar-Ola. The Mari people were annexed to Russia, with other peoples of the Kazan Tatar Khanate, when the latter was overthrown in 1552. On 4 Nov. 1920 the territory was constituted as an Autonomous Region, and on 5 Dec. 1936 as an Autonomous Republic. The population (1979 census) includes Mari (43·5%), Tatars (5·8%), Chuvashes (1·1%), Russians (47·5%).

150 deputies were elected on 24 Feb. 1980, 57 of them women.

There are over 300 modern factories. The main industries are metalworking, timber, paper, woodworking and food processing. In 1983 there were 89 collective farms and 82 state farms. Over 69% of cultivated land is grain, but flax, potatoes, fruit and vegetables are also expanding branches of agriculture, as is also livestock farming. 638,000 hectares were under crops.

Estimated reserves of the Pechora coalfield are 262,000m. tons.

In 1982–83 there were 467 schools with 112,900 pupils. Technical colleges and higher education establishments had a total of 28,000 students.

In Jan. 1983 there were 2,200 doctors and 8,500 hospital beds.

MORDOVIAN AUTONOMOUS SOVIET SOCIALIST REPUBLIC

Area, 26,200 sq. km (10,110 sq. miles); population (Jan. 1984), 971,000. Capital, Saransk. By the 13th century the Mordovian tribes had been subjugated by the Russian princes of Ryazan and Nizhni-Novgorod. In 1928 the territory was constituted as a Mordovian Area within the Middle-Volga Territory, on 10 Jan. 1930 as an Autonomous Region and on 20 Dec. 1934 as an Autonomous Republic. The population (1979 census) includes Mordovians (34·2%), Russians (59·7%), Tatars (4·6%)

175 deputies were elected on 24 Feb. 1980, 74 of them women.

The republic has a wide range of industries: electrical, timber, cable, building materials, furniture, textile, leather and other light industries. Agriculture is devoted chiefly to grain, sugar-beet, sheep and dairy farming. In 1983 there were 78 state and 273 collective farms.

There were 155,900 children at school, 36,200 students in technical colleges and at the state university and institutes, in 1982–83. In Jan. 1983 there were 3,096 doctors and 13,500 hospital beds.

NORTH OSSETIAN AUTONOMOUS SOVIET SOCIALIST REPUBLIC

Area, 8,000 sq. km (3,088 sq. miles); population (Jan. 1984), 610,000. Capital, Ordzhonikidze (formerly Vladikavkaz). The Ossetians, known to antiquity as Alani (who were also called by their immediate neighbours 'Ossi' or 'Yassi'), were annexed to Russia after the latter's treaty of Kuchuk-Kainardji with Turkey, and in 1784 the key fortress of Vladikavkaz was founded on their territory (given the name of Terek region in 1861). On 4 March 1918 the latter was proclaimed an Autonomous Soviet Republic, and after the Civil War this territory with others was set up as the Mountain Autonomous Republic (20 Jan. 1921), with North Ossetia as the Ossetian (Vladikavkaz) Area within it. On 7 July 1924 the latter was constituted as an Autonomous Region and on 5 Dec. 1936 as an Autonomous Republic. The population (1979 census) comprises chiefly Ossetians (50·5%), Russians (33·9%), Ingushi and other Caucasian nationalities (8·1%).

150 deputies were elected on 24 Feb. 1980, 68 of them women.

The main industries are non-ferrous metals (mining and metallurgy), maize-processing (at the Beslan Works, the largest in Europe), timber and woodworking, textiles, building materials, distilleries and food processing. There is also a prosperous and varied agriculture. In 1983 there were 38 state and 45 collective farms.

There were in 1982–83, 102,600 children in 238 schools, 14,100 students in technical colleges and 19,300 students in 4 higher educational establishments (pedagogical, agriculture, medical and mining-metallurgical institutes). In Jan. 1983 there were over 3,500 doctors and over 7,500 hospital beds.

TATAR AUTONOMOUS SOVIET SOCIALIST REPUBLIC

Area, 68,000 sq. km (26,250 sq. miles); population (Jan. 1984), 3,494,000. Capital, Kazan. From the 10th to the 13th centuries this was the territory of the flourishing Volga-Kama Bulgar State; conquered by the Mongols, it became the seat of the Kazan (Tatar) Khans when the Mongol Empire broke up in the 15th century, and in 1552 was conquered again by Russia. On 27 May 1920 it was constituted as an Autonomous Republic. The population (1979 census) includes Tatars (47·7%), Chuvashes, Mordovians and Udmurts (5·9%), Russians (44%).

250 deputies were elected on 24 Feb. 1980, 97 of them women.

The republic has highly developed engineering, oil and chemical industries, while timber, building materials, textiles, clothing and food industries are also expanding. The Kama works at Brezhnev plan to produce 400,000 vehicles annually. In 1983, 557 collective and 250 state farms served a total area under crops of 3·6m. hectares.

In 1982–83 there were 2,400 schools with 543,000 pupils, 59 technical colleges with 61,000 students and 13 higher educational establishments with 74,000 students (including a state university). There is a branch of the USSR Academy of Sciences with 5 learned institutions (512 research workers).

Doctors in Jan. 1983 numbered 12,000 and hospital beds 42,500.

TUVA AUTONOMOUS SOVIET SOCIALIST REPUBLIC

Area, 170,500 sq. km (65,810 sq. miles); population (Jan. 1984), 276,000. Capital, Kyzyl (71,000). Tuva was incorporated in the USSR as an autonomous region on 13 Oct. 1944 and elevated to an Autonomous Republic on 10 Oct. 1961. It is situated to the north-west of Mongolia, between 50° and 53°N. lat. and between 90° and 100°E. long. It is bounded to the east, west and north by Siberia, and to the south by Mongolia. The Tuvans are a Turkic people, formerly ruled by hereditary or elective tribal chiefs. (For the earlier history of the former Tannu-Tuva Republic, *see* THE STATESMAN'S YEAR BOOK, 1946, p. 798.) The population (1979 census) includes Tuvans (60·5%) and Russians (36·2%).

130 deputies were elected to its Supreme Soviet on 24 Feb. 1980, 53 of them women.

Tuva is well-watered and has much good pastoral land; 47 hydro-electric stations have been set into operation. The Tuvans are mainly herdsmen and cattle farmers, but, in 1983, 371,000 hectares were under crops. There are deposits of gold, cobalt and asbestos. The main exports are hair, hides and wool, and the imports manufactured goods and iron. There are 60 state farms. Mining, wood-working, garment, leather, food and other industries are rapidly developing.

In 1982–83 there were 173 schools with 65,100 pupils; 6 technical colleges with 4,100 students, and 2 higher education institutions with 2,800 students. In Jan. 1983 there were 881 doctors and 4,900 hospital beds.

A Soviet steamer-service along the river Yenisei maintains communication with Minussinsk, in Central Siberia. Internal transport is chiefly by lorry and motor coach. There is an air service from Kyzyl to Krasnoyarsk.

UDMURT AUTONOMOUS SOVIET SOCIALIST REPUBLIC

Area, 42,100 sq. km (16,250 sq. miles); population (Jan. 1984), 1,549,000. Capital, Izhevsk. The Udmurts (formerly known as 'Votyaks') were annexed by the Russians in the 15th and 16th centuries. On 4 Nov. 1920 the Votyak Autonomous Region was constituted (the name was changed to Udmurt—used by the people themselves—in 1932), and on 28 Dec. 1934 was raised to the status of an Autonomous Republic. The population (1979 census) includes Udmurts (32·2%), Tatars (6·6%), Russians (58·3%).

200 deputies were elected on 24 Feb. 1980, 78 of them women.

Heavy industry includes the manufacture of locomotives, machine tools and other engineering products, timber and building materials. There are also light industries—clothing, leather, furniture, food, etc.

There were 96 state and 244 collective farms in 1983; crop area 1·4m. hectares.

In 1982–83 there were 913 schools with 244,200 pupils; there were 22,900 students at technical colleges and 26,200 at 5 higher educational institutions.

In Jan. 1983 there were over 5,500 doctors and over 17,000 hospital beds.

YAKUT AUTONOMOUS SOVIET SOCIALIST REPUBLIC

The area is 3,103,200 sq. km (1,197,760 sq. miles); population (Jan. 1984); 963,000. Capital, Yakutsk (149,000). The Yakuts were subjugated by the Russians in the 17th century. The territory was constituted an Autonomous Republic on 27 April 1922. The population (1979 census) includes Yakuts (36·9%), other northern peoples (2·2%), Russians (50·4%).

205 deputies were elected on 24 Feb. 1980, 92 of them women.

The principal industries are mining (gold, tin, mica, coal) and livestock-breeding. The Soviet Soyuz-Zoloto Trust and a number of individual prospectors are working the fields. Silver- and lead-bearing ores and coal are worked; large diamond fields have been opened up. Timber and food industries are developing. There was 1 collective farm in 1983 with 88 state farms, with an area under crops of 103,400 hectares. Trapping and breeding of fur-bearing animals (sable, squirrel, silver fox, etc.) are an important source of income. A severe climate and lack of railways are serious obstacles to the economic development of the republic. There are, however, 10,000 km of roads and internal air lines totalling 10,000 km including an air service between Irkutsk and Yakutsk.

In 1982–83 there were 180,500 secondary school pupils, 9,700 technical college students and 7,500 at university and teacher training colleges.

In Jan. 1983 there were 3,400 doctors and 13,800 hospital beds.

ADYGEI AUTONOMOUS REGION

Part of Krasnodar Territory. Area, 7,600 sq. km (2,934 sq. miles); population (Jan. 1984), 417,000. Capital, Maikop (128,000). Established 27 July 1922.

Chief industries are timber, woodworking, food processing; but engineering is rapidly expanding. Cattle breeding predominates in agriculture. There were 38 collective and 33 state farms in 1983.

In 1982–83 there were 183 schools with 65,600 pupils, 6 technical colleges with 7,300 students and a pedagogical institute with 4,200 students. Regional newspapers are in Adygei and Russian. In Jan. 1983 there were 1,190 doctors and 5,400 hospital beds.

GORNO-ALTAI AUTONOMOUS REGION

Part of Altai Territory. Area, 92,600 sq. km (35,740 sq. miles); population (Jan. 1984), 178,000. Capital, Gorno-Altaisk (39,000). Established 1 June 1922 as Oirot Autonomous Region; renamed 7 Jan. 1948.

Chief industries are gold, mercury and brown-coal mining, timber, chemicals and dairying. Cattle breeding predominates; pasturages and hay meadows cover over 1m. hectares, but 142,000 hectares are under crops. There were 20 collective and 37 state farms in 1983.

In 1982–83 there were 30,800 school pupils; technical colleges had 4,251 students and 3,437 students were receiving higher education. There were 473 doctors and 2,700 hospital beds.

JEWISH AUTONOMOUS REGION

Part of Khabarovsk Territory. Area, 36,000 sq. km (13,895 sq. miles); population (Jan. 1984), 204,000 (1979 census, Russians, 84·1%; Ukrainians, 6·3%; Jews, 5·4%). Capital, Birobidjan (75,000). Established as Jewish National District in 1928, became an Autonomous Region 7 May 1934.

Chief industries are non-ferrous metallurgy, building materials, timber, engineering, textiles, paper and food processing. There were 161,000 hectares under cultivation in 1983; main crops are wheat, soya, oats, barley. There were 36 state farms and 2 collective farms in 1983.

In 1982–83 there were 33,500 schoolchildren; students in technical colleges numbered 5,300. There are a Yiddish national theatre, a Yiddish newspaper and a Yiddish broadcasting service. Doctors numbered 628 and hospital beds 3,000.

KARACHAYEVO-CHERKESS AUTONOMOUS REGION

Part of Stavropol Territory. Area, 14,100 sq. km (5,442 sq. miles); population (Jan. 1984), 384,000. Capital, Cherkessk (96,000). A Karachai Autonomous Region was established on 26 April 1926 (out of a previously united Karachayevo-Cherkess Autonomous Region created in 1922), and dissolved in 1943. A Cherkess Autonomous Region was established on 30 April 1928. The present Autonomous Region was re-established on 9 Jan. 1957.

Ore-mining, engineering, chemical and woodworking industries have been built up since 1917. There are 70 large factories, and a copper works and sugar factory are under construction. A large irrigation scheme, Kuban-Kalaussi, is being developed, to irrigate 200,000 hectares. Livestock breeding and grain growing predominate in agriculture; crop area in 1983 was 196,000 hectares. There were 15 collective farms and 37 state farms in 1983.

In 1982–83 there were 70,200 pupils in secondary schools, 6 technical colleges with 5,900 students and 2 institutes with 4,400 students. In Jan. 1983 there were over 900 doctors and over 7,300 hospital beds.

KHAKASS AUTONOMOUS REGION

Part of Krasnoyarsk Territory. Area, 61,900 sq. km (23,855 sq. miles); population (Jan. 1984), 533,000. Capital, Abakan (143,000). Established 20 Oct. 1930.

Coal- and ore-mining, timber and woodworking industries have been highly developed since 1917. The region is linked by rail with the Trans-Siberian line. Large textile and sugar factories are being built.

In 1983, 619,000 hectares were under crops. Livestock breeding, dairy and vegetable farming are developed. There are 56 state farms.

In 1982–83 there were 74,200 pupils in secondary schools, 8,900 students in technical colleges and 6,000 students in higher educational institutions. In Jan. 1983 there were 1,416 doctors and 7,600 hospital beds. A Khakass alphabet was created after the Revolution.

Books of Reference

Armstrong, T., *Russian Settlement in the North.* CUP, 1965
Conolly, V., *Beyond the Urals. Economic Developments in Soviet Asia.* London, 1967
Dallin, D. J., *The Rise of Russia in Asia.* New York, 1949.—*Soviet Russia and the Far East.* London, 1949
Kolarz, W., *The Peoples of the Soviet Far East.* London, 1954
Istoriya Sibiri s drevneishikh vremen do nashikh dnei. 5 vols., Leningrad, 1968–69

UKRAINE

Ukrainska Radyanska Sotsialistichna Respublika

HISTORY. The Ukrainian Soviet Socialist Republic was proclaimed on 25 Dec. 1917 and was finally established in Dec. 1919. In Dec. 1920 it concluded a military and economic alliance with the RSFSR and on 30 Dec. 1922 formed, together with the other Soviet Socialist Republics, the Union of Soviet Socialist Republics. On 1 Nov. 1939 Western Ukraine (about 88,000 sq. km) was incorporated in the Ukrainian SSR. On 2 Aug. 1940 Northern Bukovina (about 6,000 sq. km) ceded to the USSR by Romania 28 June 1940, and the Khotin, Akkerman and Izmail provinces of Bessarabia were included in the Ukrainian SSR, and on 29 June 1945 Ruthenia (Sub-Carpathian Russia), about 7,000 sq. km, was also incorporated. From the new territories 2 new regions (provinces) were formed, Chernovitz and Izmail.

AREA AND POPULATION. The Ukraine is in south-west USSR; it has a Black Sea coast and western frontiers with Romania, Hungary, Poland and Czechoslovakia. It is bounded north by Belorussia and otherwise by the RSFSR. In 1938 the Ukrainian SSR covered an area of 445,000 sq. km (171,770 sq. miles); it now covers 603,700 sq. km (231,990 sq. miles).

Population, Jan. 1984, 50,667,000 (in 1979, 73·6% Ukrainians, 21·1% Russians, 1·3% Jews, 0·8% Belorussians).

The principal towns are the capital Kiev, Kharkov, Donetsk, Odessa, Dnepropetrovsk, Lvov, Zaporozhye and Krivoi Rog.

The Ukrainian Soviet Socialist Republic consists of the following regions: Cherkassy, Chernigov, Chernovtzy, Crimea (transferred from the RSFSR on 19 Feb 1954), Dnepropetrovsk, Donetsk, Ivan Franko, Khmelnitsky (formerly Kamenets-Podolsk), Kharkov, Kherson, Kiev, Kirovograd, Lvov, Nikolayev, Odessa, Poltava, Rovno, Sumy, Ternopol, Vinnitsa, Volhynia, Voroshilovgrad, Zakarpatskaya (Transcarpathia), Zaporozhye, Zhitomir.

CONSTITUTION AND GOVERNMENT. The Supreme Soviet, elected on 24 Feb. 1985, consists of 650 deputies (1 per 90,000 population); 444 are Communists and 234 women. A new Constitution, based on that of the USSR, was adopted in April 1978.

At elections to regional district, urban and rural Soviets (19 June 1982), out of 525,500 deputies returned, 258,808 (49·2%) were women, 295,174 (56·2%) non-Party and 378,018 (72·4%) industrial workers and collective farmers.

Chairman, Presidium of the Supreme Soviet: (Vacant).
Chairman, Council of Ministers: A. P. Lyashko.
Foreign Minister: G. N. Martynenko.
First Secretary, Communist Party: V. V. Shcherbitsky.

FINANCE. Budget estimates (in 1m. rubles), 1985, 29,596; 1984, 27,787.

AGRICULTURE. The Ukraine contains some of the richest land in the USSR. It raises wheat, buckwheat, beet, sunflower, cotton, flax, tobacco, soya, hops, the rubber plant kok-sagyz, fruit and vegetables, and in 1982 produced over 23% by value of the USSR's crop production and over 21% by value of its livestock production. The area under cultivation was 27·9m. hectares in 1913, 27m. in 1939 before the new territories were added, and 33·3m. in 1983.

Output (in 1m. tonnes) in 1982 (1913 figures in tons in brackets): Sugar-beet, 42·3 (9·3); sunflower seed, 2·5 (0·07); potatoes, 20·1 (8·5); meat and fats, 3·5 (1·1); milk, 20·6 (4·7); wool, 0·027 (0·015); 15,561m. eggs (3,005m.); grain, 50·6m.

On 1 Jan. 1983 there were 25·5m. cattle, 20·8m. pigs, 8·9m. sheep and goats. In 1949 silver-fox breeding farms were started.

On 1 Jan. 1983 there were 2,162 state farms and 7,157 collective farms.

Irrigation networks supplied 1·82m. hectares of land; 2·2m. hectares were drained.

Tractors numbered 420,900 at 1 Jan. 1983 and combine harvesters, 98,100.

INDUSTRY. Coal in the Donets field (25,900 sq. km stretching from Donetsk to Rostov), estimated to contain 60% of the bituminous and anthracite-coal reserves of the USSR, yielded, in 1980, 197·1m. tonnes—about 28% of the USSR production. Large new seams have been found near Novo-Moskovsk (Dnepropetrovsk region), Kharkov, Lugansk (beyond the Don) and on the left bank of the Dnieper. Within the present frontiers of the Ukraine, coal output was 22·8m. tons in 1913, 83·8m. tons in 1940, 78m. tons in 1950 and 217m. tons in 1977.

Combining coal from the Donets field with the iron-ore from the mines in Krivoi Rog has made possible the development of a large ferrous metallurgical industry in the Ukraine. Output of iron ore was 6·9m. tons in 1913, 18·9m. tons in 1940 and 126m. tons in 1982.

Manganese is also available at Nikopol; output in 1976, 6·7m. tons.

Pig-iron output was 2·9m. tons in 1913, 9·6m. tons in 1940, 9·2m. tons in 1950 and 46·4m. tons in 1975. Steel output (within present frontiers) was 2·4m. tons in 1913, 8·9m. in 1940, 8·4m. in 1950 and 53·7m. in 1982.

The Ukraine also contains oil, rich deposits of salt and various important chemicals. Oil output was 1m. tons in 1913 (in present frontiers), 353,000 tons in 1940 and 10·5m. tons in 1977; with 68·7m. cu. metres of natural gas.

The Ukraine has highly developed chemical and machine-construction industries producing one-fifth of the total output of machinery and chemicals in the USSR. 142,000 tractors and 3,500 main-line diesel locomotives were produced in 1979.

In Northern Bukovina there are deposits of gypsum, oil, alabaster, brown coal and timber. Output of mineral fertilizers was 36,000 tons in 1913 and 21·1m. tons in 1981; cement output increased in the same years from 269,000 to 22·5m. tons (in present frontiers in both cases). Paper output in 1982 was 257,000 tons (1913: 26,900).

Consumer goods and food industries are important. Output of cotton fabrics was (in present frontiers) 4·7m. linear metres in 1913, 13·8m. in 1940, 20·6m. in 1950 and 429·4m. in 1975. Granulated sugar output was 1913, 1·1m. tons; 1940, 1·6m. tons; 1950, 1·8m. tons, and 1982, 6·6m. tons. Leather footwear manufactured in 1940 totalled 40·8m. pairs; 1982, 174m.

The number of industrial and office workers at the end of 1950 was 6·9m., and the average in 1982, 20·4m. There were 4·1m. collective farmers in 1982.

During the first 5-year plan (1929–32) the Dnieper power station was built; destroyed during the War, it was restored during the fourth plan (1946–50). Another large hydro-electric station at Kakhovka began operations during the fifth plan (1951–55). Power output (in 1,000m. kwh.) increased as follows: 1913, 0·5; 1940, 12·4; 1950, 14·7; 1982, 238.

COMMUNICATIONS. The total length of railways of the Ukrainian SSR in 1981 was 22,650 km, the navigable rivers, 3,900 km. Length of hard-surface motor roads was 171,900 km.

Airlines connect Kiev, Lvov, Chernovtsy and Odessa with Crimean and Caucasian spas, Kiev with Tbilisi, Odessa with Riga and Donetsk.

Newspapers (1982). Out of 1,778 newspapers, 1,305 were in Ukrainian. Daily circulation of Ukrainian-language newspapers, 15·0m., other languages, 7·7m.

RELIGION. Several Christian Churches have their adherents in the Ukraine, the chief being the Orthodox Greek Church and the Catholic Church. The Western Ukraine Uniate Church, which in 1596 had been forced by the Poles to establish unity with the Roman Church, severed this connexion in March 1946 and joined the Orthodox Church. There are also some Protestants as well as Jews and others.

EDUCATION. In 1982–83 the number of pupils in 22,500 primary and secondary schools was 7·4m.; 146 higher educational establishments had 885,000 students, and 728 technical colleges 795,400 students; 2·5m. children were attending 17,400 pre-school institutions.

The Ukrainian Academy of Sciences was established in 1919; in 1983 it had 77 institutions with 14,900 scientific staff. There is an academy of building and architecture. Total scientific staff in all institutions was 200,500 in 1981.

HEALTH. Doctors numbered 195,600 in 1982, and hospital beds, 644,200.

Books of Reference

Allen, W. E. D., *The Ukraine: A History.* London, 1940
Andrusyshen, C. H. (ed.), *Ukrainian-English Dictionary.* Toronto, 1955
Chamberlin, W. H., *The Ukraine.* New York, 1945
Chirovsky, N. L., *The Ukrainian Economy.* New York, Paris, Toronto, 1965
Hrushevsky, M., *A History of the Ukraine.* New Haven, 1941
Manning, C. A., *Twentieth-century Ukraine.* New York, 1951
Mirchuk, L. (ed.), *Ukraine and its People.* London, 1949
Istoriya Ukrainskoi SSR. 2 vols. Kiev, 1969
Soviet Ukraine. (English ed.) Ukrainian Soviet Encyclopaedia, 1970
Ukraine: A Concise Encyclopaedia. 2 vols. Toronto, 1963–71

BELORUSSIA

Belaruskaya Sovietskaya Sotsialistychnaya Respublika

HISTORY. The Belorussian Soviet Socialist Republic was set up on 1 Jan. 1919. It forms one of the constituent republics of the USSR.

AREA AND POPULATION. Belorussia is situated along the Western Dvina and Dnieper. It is bounded west by Poland, north by Latvia and Lithuania, east by the RSFSR and south by the Ukraine. The area is 207,600 sq. km (80,134 sq. miles). The capital is Minsk. Other important towns are Gomel, Vitebsk, Mogilev, Bobruisk, Grodno and Brest. On 2 Nov. 1939 western Belorussia was incorporated with an area of over 108,000 sq. km and a population of 4·8m. The population (Jan. 1984) was 9,878,000; 79·4% of this population in 1979 (census) were Belorussians, 4·2% Poles, 11·9% Russians, 2·4% Ukrainians and 1·4% Jews.

Belorussia now comprises the following regions: Brest, Gomel, Grodno, Mogilev, Minsk, Vitebsk.

CONSTITUTION AND GOVERNMENT. The Supreme Soviet, elected in 1980, consists of 485 deputies (1 per 20,000 population); 328 are Communists and 180 women. A new Constitution was adopted in April 1978.

At elections to regional, district, urban and rural Soviets (20 June 1982), of 85,394 deputies returned, 42,326 (49·6%) were women, 48,743 (57·1%) non-Party and 58,839 (68·9%) industrial workers and collective farmers.

Chairman, Presidium of the Supreme Soviet: I. E. Polyakov.
Chairman, Council of Ministers: V. I. Brovikov.
Foreign Minister: A. E. Gurinovich
First Secretary, Communist Party: N. Slyunkov.

FINANCE. Budget estimates (in 1m. rubles), 1985, 7,168; 1984, 6,697.

NATURAL RESOURCES. Belorussia is hilly, with a general slope towards the south. It contains large tracts of marsh land, particularly to the south-west, and valuable forest land wooded with oak, elm, maple and white beech: there are over 6,500 peat deposits.

AGRICULTURE. Agriculturally, Belorussia may be divided into three main sections—Northern: growing flax, fodder, grasses and breeding cattle for meat and dairy produce; Central: potato growing and pig breeding; Southern: good natural pasture land, hemp cultivation and cattle breeding for meat and dairy produce. The area under cultivation (in hectares) was 4·5m. in 1913, 5·2m. in 1940 and 6·3m. in 1983. There were 7·1m. cattle, 5·0m. pigs and 618,000 sheep and goats on 1 Jan. 1983.

Output of main agricultural products (in 1,000 tonnes) in 1982 (1913 figures in brackets): Flax, 117 (33); sugar-beet, 1,093 (0); potatoes, 8,829 (4,024); meat, 872 (219); milk, 6·0 (1·4); 3,220m. eggs (413m.); vegetables, 876 (000).

On 1 Jan. 1983 there were 1,753 collective farms and 907 state farms. About 2·5m. hectares of marsh land had been drained for agricultural use, 828,200 of these for crops. This land has been found to be as rich as the soil of the Black Earth Zone, and yields good harvests of grain, fodder, potatoes, kok-sagyz and other crops. In Jan. 1983 there were 122,400 tractors and 29,800 grain combine harvesters.

INDUSTRY. Industry in this republic was almost completely destroyed during the years 1941–45. By 1956, aggregate industrial output was three times what it had been in 1940. Plants producing tip-lorries, machine-tools and agricultural machinery are prominent.

The republic also contains timber works; a match factory in Borisov; building materials, machine, prefabricated house construction, glass-blowing and other factories; canneries, creameries and other food industries; chemical, textiles, artificial-silk, flax-spinning and leather works.

The automobile and tractor industry produced 90,900 tractors and 223,700 motor bikes in 1982. Cement output, 33,000 tons in 1913, was 2·17m. tons in 1975. Leather footwear output, 9·8m. pairs in 1940, was 42·0m. pairs in 1982. Linen fabrics, 13,000 linear metres in 1913, 70·4m. tonnes in 1982; paper, 51,000 tonnes in 1940, 192,800 tonnes in 1982.

Particular attention has been paid to the development of the peat industry with a view to making Belorussia as far as possible self-supporting in fuel, and in 1939 local peat provided 67·5% of her total requirements of fuel. The average annual output is about 18m. tonnes.

There are also rich deposits of rock salt. In 1951 the first sugar refinery in Belorussia was opened in Grodno; sugar output in 1982 was 305,600 tonnes.

Output of electricity in 1982, 34,000m. kwh. (508m. in 1940). New power-plants have been built in Baranovichi, Grodno, Molodechno and Lida.

The number of industrial and office workers in 1982 was 4,173,000.

COMMUNICATIONS. In 1983 there were 5,510 km of railways, 47,600 km of motor roads (38,900 km hard-surface) and 3,900 km of navigable waterways.

Newspapers (1982). Of 206 newspapers published 130 were in Belorussian. Daily circulation of Belorussian-language newspapers, 1·5m., other languages, 3·1m.

EDUCATION. In 1982–83 there were 182,200 students in 33 places of higher education and 162,100 students in 138 technical colleges. There were 39,400 scientific personnel in 178 institutions, and 340,000 specialists with a higher education employed in the national economy. The Belorussian Academy of Sciences controlled 32 learned institutions with 5,461 scientific staff. The number of children in primary and secondary schools was 489,000 in 1914–15, and 1·5m. in 1982–83. 532,000 children were attending pre-school institutions in Jan. 1983.

HEALTH. In 1982 there were 34,600 doctors and 124,200 hospital beds.

Books of Reference

Vakar, N. P., *Belorussia.* Harvard Univ. Press, 1956.—*A Bibliographical Guide to Belorussia.* Harvard Univ. Press, 1956

Istoriya Belorusskoi SSR. 2nd ed. 2 vols. Minsk, 1961

AZERBAIJAN

Azarbaijchan Soviet Sotsialistik Respublikasy

HISTORY. The 'Mussavat' (Nationalist) party, which dominated the National

Council or Constituent Assembly of the Tatars, declared the independence of Azerbaijan on 28 May 1918, with a capital, first at Ganja (Elizavetpol) and later at Baku. On 28 April 1920 Azerbaijan was proclaimed a Soviet Socialist Republic. From 1922, with Georgia and Armenia it formed the Transcaucasian Soviet Federal Socialist Republic. In 1936 it assumed the status of one of the Union Republics of the USSR.

AREA AND POPULATION. Azerbaijan covers an area of 86,600 sq. km (33,430 sq. miles) and has a population (Jan. 1984) of 6,506,000. Its capital is Baku. Other important towns are Kirovabad and Sumgait. Nakhichevan is the capital of the Autonomous Republic of the same name.

Azerbaijan includes the Nakhichevan Autonomous Republic and the Nagorno-Karabakh Autonomous Region. Situated in the eastern area of Transcaucasia, it is protected by mountains in the west and north, washed by the Caspian Sea in the east and bounded by Iran in the south. Its climate is inclined to drought.

In 1979 (census) 78·1% of the population were Azerbaijanis. Other nationalities were Russians (7·9%), Armenians (7·9%) and Daghestanis (3·4%).

CONSTITUTION AND GOVERNMENT. The Supreme Soviet, elected in 1985, consists of 450 deputies (1 per 10,000 population); 311 are Communists and 179 women. A new Constitution was adopted in April 1978.

At elections to the Nagorno-Karabakh regional Soviet and the district, urban and rural Soviets (20 June 1982), of 50,799 deputies returned, 24,432 (48·1%) were women, 28,775 (56·6%) non-Party and 34,059 (67%) industrial workers and collective farmers.

Chairman, Presidium of the Supreme Soviet: K. A. Khalilov.
Chairman, Council of Ministers: G. Seidov.
First Secretary, Communist Party: K. M. Bagirov.

FINANCE (in 1m. rubles). Budget estimates, 1985, 2,704; 1984, 2,551.

AGRICULTURE. The chief agricultural products are grain, cotton, rice, grapes, fruit, vegetables, tobacco and silk. The Mexican rubber plant *grayule* has been acclimatized. A new kind of high-yielding winter wheat has been produced for use in mountainous parts of the republic.

Livestock on 1 Jan. 1983: Cattle, 1·9m.; pigs, 184,900; sheep and goats, 5·3m.

Output of main agricultural products (in 1,000 tonnes) in 1982 (1913 figures in brackets): Cotton, 834 (4); potatoes, 184 (38); tea, 16 (0); meat, 151 (40); milk, 869 (203); wool, 11·3 (4·1); grapes, 1,816; fruit, 344; 830m. eggs (97m.).

Azerbaijan has become an important cotton-growing and sub-tropical base. About 70% of cultivated land is irrigated. On the irrigated land crops of Egyptian and Sea-Island cotton are obtained. Here, too, rice and lucerne are cultivated, and in the mountain valleys there are also orchards, vineyards and silk cultures.

In the south along the coast of the Caspian, where the climate is more moist, there are tea plantations, and citrus fruits and other sub-tropical plants are grown.

In 1941 a scientific research institute for sub-tropical research was opened to develop the culture of sub-tropical plants in Azerbaijan and other parts of Transcaucasia. A forestry research institute was opened in 1949.

There were on 1 Jan. 1983, 599 collective farms, 737 state farms, 37,800 tractors and 4,500 grain combine harvesters.

INDUSTRY. The republic is rich in natural resources: oil, iron, aluminium, copper, lead, zinc, precious metals, sulphur pyrites, limestone and salt. Iron and steel and aluminium works have been built at Sumgait.

The most important industry is the oil industry, especially in the Baku region. The output of oil was 7·7m. tonnes in 1913, 22·2m. tonnes in 1940 and 16·5m. tonnes in 1976. The largest producing area lies along the western shore of the Caspian Sea, north and south of Baku, where the largest refineries are located. Other wells lie west of Baku, and some have been drilled in the Caspian itself, off the Apsheron Peninsula. Baku is connected by a double pipeline with Batum on the Black Sea. All the oilfields have been electrified and are connected with Baku.

Azerbaijan has also copper, chemical, cement and building material, food, timber, salt, textiles and fishing industries. In 1982, 26·7m. tonnes of mineral fertilizers were produced, 298,800 tonnes of cotton fibre, 493 tonnes of raw silk, 19·4m. pairs leather footwear, and 257,000 tonnes of sawn timber.

In addition to Baku, other important industrial centres are Kirovabad, Nukha, Stepanakert, Nakhichevan, Lenkoran.

In 1982 electric power output was 16,900m. kwh. Output of gas, which began in 1928 with 176m. cu. metres, was 10,989m. in 1976. Pipelines from Karadag to Baku and Sumgait supply gas fuel for all oil-cracking factories and most engineering works.

Synthetic rubber works (Sumgait), tyre works and a worsted combine (Baku) and a large textile combine (Mingechaur) have been built.

The number of industrial and office workers in 1982 was 1,906,000.

COMMUNICATIONS. The first electrical railway (42 km) in the USSR was constructed in Azerbaijan in 1924; in 1949, 27 km was added, and the line now runs Baku-Surakhany-Sabunchi-Buzovny-Baku. The capital is also linked by rail with Tbilisi, Yerevan, Derbent, Julfa and Astara. Total length, Jan. 1983, 1,900 km. There were, in 1983, 27,400 km of motor roads (22,700 km hard-surface) and 500 km of inland waterways.

Newspapers (1982). There were 136 newspapers, 108 in the Azerbaijani language (circulation 2·1m.), other languages, 464,000.

EDUCATION. In 1982–83 there were 1·5m. pupils in 4,400 elementary and secondary schools and 153,000 children attending pre-school institutions. There were 75 technical colleges with 78,700 students, 18 higher educational institutions, including a state university at Baku, with 110,000 students (including correspondence students).

The Azerbaijan Academy of Sciences, founded in 1945, has 30 research institutions with 4,511 research workers. There are 142 learned and scientific institutions, with 22,700 research workers in all.

HEALTH. In 1982 there were 22,400 doctors and 62,200 hospital beds. There were also 619 maternity and infant welfare centres.

NAKHICHEVAN AUTONOMOUS SOVIET SOCIALIST REPUBLIC

Area, 5,500 sq. km (2,120 sq. miles), population (Jan. 1984), 262,000. Capital, Nakhichevan (37,000). This territory, on the borders of Turkey and Iran, forms part of the Azerbaijan SSR although separated from it by the territory of Soviet Armenia. Its population, mainly Azerbaijanis, had a chequered history for 1,500 years under the ancient Persians, Arabs, Seljuk Turks, Mongols, Ottoman Turks and modern Persians before being annexed by Russia in 1828. On 9 Feb. 1924 it was constituted as an Autonomous Republic within Azerbaijan. Its Supreme Soviet, elected 24 Feb. 1980, has 110 members including 52 women.

The republic has silk, clothing, cotton, canning, meat-packing and other factories. Nearly 70% of the people are engaged in agriculture, of which the main branches are cotton and tobacco growing. Fruit and grapes are also produced in increasing quantity. There are 35 collective and 37 state farms. Crop area 37,400 hectares.

In 1982–83 there were 219 primary and secondary schools with 70,800 pupils. There were 1,700 pupils in 4 technical colleges and a pedagogical institute with 2,400 students.

In Jan. 1983 there were 599 doctors and 2,500 hospital beds.

NAGORNO-KARABAKH AUTONOMOUS REGION

Area, 4,400 sq. km (1,700 sq. miles); population (Jan. 1984), 170,000. Capital, Stepanakert (33,000). Populated by Armenians (75·9%) and Azerbaijanis (23%), a separate khanate in the 18th century, it was established on 7 July 1923 as an Autonomous Region within Azerbaijan.

Main industries are silk, wine, dairying and building materials. Crop area is 67,200 hectares; cotton, grapes and winter wheat are grown. There are 33 collective and 38 state farms.

In 1982–83 there were 189 schools, 6 technical colleges, and a pedagogical institute; at all levels 41,600 were engaged in study. In Jan. 1983 there were 523 doctors and 1,800 hospital beds.

Books of Reference

Baddeley, J. F., *The Rugged Flanks of Caucasus.* 2 vols. Oxford, 1941
Tutaeff, D., *The Soviet Caucasus.* London, 1942

GEORGIA

Sakartvelos Sabchota Sotsialisturi Respublica

HISTORY. The independence of the Georgian Social Democratic Republic was declared at Tiflis on 26 May 1918 by the National Council, elected by the National Assembly of Georgia on 22 Nov. 1917. The independence of Georgia was recognized by the USSR on 7 May 1920. On 12 Feb. 1921 a rising broke out in Mingrelia, Abkhazia and Adjaria, and Soviet troops invaded the country, which, on 25 Feb. 1921, was proclaimed the Georgian Soviet Socialist Republic. At the first Transcaucasian Soviet Congress, 15 Dec. 1922, Georgia, together with Armenia and Azerbaijan, united to form the Transcaucasian Soviet Federal Socialist Republic, and a federal constitution was adopted and published 10 Jan. 1923. In 1936 the Georgian Soviet Socialist Republic became one of the constituent republics of the USSR and, like other republics of USSR, adopted a new Constitution.

AREA AND POPULATION. Georgia is bounded west by the Black Sea and south by Turkey, Armenia and Azerbaijan. It occupies the whole of the western part of Transcaucasia and covers an area of 69,700 sq. km (26,900 sq. miles). Its population on 1 Jan. 1984 was 5,167,000. The capital is Tbilisi (Tiflis). Other important towns are Kutaisi (207,000), Rustavi (139,000), Batumi (129,000), Sukhumi (122,000), Poti (54,000), Gori (59,000).

Protected from the north by the Caucasian mountains and receiving in the west the warm, moist winds from the Black Sea into which most of its rivers flow, Georgia is outstanding for its fine, warm climate and its natural wealth, variety and beauty. It has the highest snow-capped peaks of the Caucasian mountains. Georgia contains valuable sulphur and other medicinal springs. Georgians, an ancient people, were (1979 census) 68·8% of the population; Armenians 9%; Russians, 7·4%; Azerbaijanis, 5·1%; Ossetians, 3·2%; Abkhazians, 1·7%.

CONSTITUTION AND GOVERNMENT. The Georgian Soviet Socialist Republic includes the Abkhazian ASSR, the Adjarian ASSR and the South Ossetian Autonomous Region.

The Supreme Soviet, elected in 1985, consists of 440 deputies (1 per 10,000 population); 160 are women, 290 Communists. A new Constitution was adopted in April 1978.

At elections to the district, rural and urban Soviets, and that of the South Ossetian region (20 June 1982), of 50,643 deputies returned 25,403 (50·2%) were women, 29,083 (57·4%) non-Party and 34,780 (68·7%) industrial workers and collective farmers.

Chairman, Presidium of the Supreme Soviet: P. G. Gilashvili.
Chairman, Council of Ministers: D. L. Kartvelishvili.
First Secretary, Communist Party: E. A. Shevardnadze.

FINANCE (in 1m. rubles). Budget estimates, 1985, 2,899; 1984, 2,781.

AGRICULTURE. There are 3 main agricultural areas: (1) The moist subtropical area along the Black Sea Coast, where are cultivated tea, citrus fruits (lemons, oranges, mandarins, etc.), the tung tree (which yields special industrial oils), eucalyptus, bamboo, high-quality tobacco; (2) Imeretia (the Kutais region) where the chief cultures are grapes and silk, and (3) Kakhetia, along the Alazani (a tributary of the Kura river), famed for its orchards and wines. Land (in hectares) under cultivation was 748,000 in 1913, 896,000 in 1940, 778,000 in 1961, 732,800 in 1982.

Output of main agricultural products (in 1,000 tonnes) in 1982 (1913 figures in brackets): Sugar-beet, 122 (0); fruit, 592; grapes, 664; tea in leaf, 537; meat, 153 (49); wool, 5·5 (3·4); milk, 721 (222); vegetables, 587; 665m. eggs (119m.).

On 1 Jan. 1983 there were 697 collective farms working over 66% of all agricultural land, 532 state farms working nearly 34% of such land. In the Colchis area 115,000 hectares of extremely rich land have been reclaimed. There are 389,000 hectares of irrigated land. 151,400 hectares of marsh land have been drained. Tractors numbered 25,800 on 1 Jan. 1983; grain combines, 1,500.

Livestock on 1 Jan. 1983: Cattle, 1·6m.; pigs, 1m.; sheep and goats, 1·9m.

Georgia is rich in forest lands where fine varieties of timber are grown. Area covered by forests, 2·4m. hectares.

INDUSTRY. The most important mining industry of Georgia is the exploitation of the manganese deposits, the richest of which lie in the Chiatura region. Manganese deposits in Georgia are calculated at 250m. tonnes, distributed over an area of 140 sq. km. The most important coal seams are at Tkvarcheli (deposits estimated at 250m. tonnes) and Tkibuli (deposits of 80m. tonnes). Other important minerals are baryta, the best in the USSR, fire-resisting and other clays, diatomite shale, oil, agate, marble, cement, alabaster, iron and other ores, building stone, arsenic, molybdenum, tungsten and mercury. In 1941 a goldfield was discovered. Output of coal in 1976 was 1·9m. tonnes (625,000 in 1940).

Since the Second World War the Transcaucasian Metallurgical Plant has been built at Rustavi (near Tbilisi) and a motor works at Kutaisi. There are modern factories for processing green tea-leaves, creameries and breweries; Georgia has also textile and silk industries.

In 1982, 2·7m. tonnes of manganese ore were produced, 523,000 tonnes of steel pipe, 90,400 tonnes of mineral fertilizer, 21,800 lorries, 41,500 tonnes of paper, 15·2m. pairs leather footwear, 4,100 colour televisions and 36,900 tonnes of granulated sugar.

Georgia's fast flowing rivers form an abundant source of energy. One of the most powerful stations completed in recent years is Tbilisi (1m. kw.). Power output in 1982 was 15,200m. kwh. (742m. in 1940).

There were 2,056,000 industrial and office workers in 1982.

COMMUNICATIONS. Length of railways in 1983 was 1,450 km. The trunk line leading from Batumi through Tbilisi to Baku on the Caspian Sea has several narrow-gauge branches on Georgian territory to the coalmines of Tkibuli, to the port of Poti, to the manganese mines of Chiatura, to the mineral springs of Borjom and the health resort Bakuriani, to the towns Signakh and Telavi, in Kakhetia, and to the Armenian frontier, across the coalmine district of Alaverdi. The last branch divides in Armenia, going on the one side to Tabriz in Iran, and on the other to Erzerum in Anatolia. A railway line from Akhal-Senaki along the Black Sea coast, through Sukhumi to Tuapse, was completed in 1946. All lines are electrified or work on diesel traction. In 1983 there were 36,700 km of motor roads, 31,400 km of them hard-surfaced.

Newspapers (1982). Out of 143 newspapers, 124 were in Georgian. Daily circulation in Georgian language newspapers, 2·8m., other languages, 454,000.

EDUCATION. In 1982–83 there were 900,000 pupils in 3,800 primary and secondary schools, 52,800 in 90 technical colleges and 89,000 students in 19 higher educational institutions. Tbilisi University has 16,300 students. In towns, 11 years' education is usual. In Abastuman there is an astro-physical observatory. In 1936 a branch of the Academy of Sciences of the USSR was formed in Tbilisi, and in Feb. 1941 a Georgian Academy of Sciences was opened, which in 1983 had 42 institutions with scientific staff totalling 5,759. There were in all 194 research institutions with 26,500 scientific staff.

In Jan. 1983, 173,000 children were attending pre-school institutions.

HEALTH. There were 26,000 doctors and 55,000 hospital beds in 1982.

ABKHAZIAN AUTONOMOUS SOVIET SOCIALIST REPUBLIC

Area, 8,600 sq. km (3,320 sq. miles); population (Jan. 1984), 521,000. Capital Sukhumi. This area, the ancient Colchis, included Greek colonies from the 6th century B.C. onwards. From the 2nd century B.C. onwards, it was a prey to many invaders—Romans, Byzantines, Arabs, Ottoman Turks—before accepting a Russian protectorate in 1810. However, from the 4th century A.D. a West Georgian kingdom was established by the Lazi princes in the territory (known to the Romans as 'Lazica') and by the 8th century the prevailing language was Georgian and the name Abkhazia. In March 1921 a congress of local Soviets proclaimed it a Soviet Republic, and its status as an Autonomous Republic, within Georgia, was confirmed on 17 April 1930.

Population (1979 census) Abkhazians, 17·1%, Georgians, 43·9% and Russians, 16·4%.

140 deputies were elected on 24 Feb. 1980, 57 of them women.

The Abkhazian coast (along the Black Sea) possesses a famous chain of health resorts—Gagra, Sukhumi, Akhali-Antoni, Gulripsha and Gudauta—sheltered by thickly forested mountains.

The republic has coal, electric power, building materials and light industries. In 1983 there were 89 collective farms and 56 state farms; main crops are tobacco, tea, grapes, oranges, tangerines and lemons. Crop area 43,900 hectares.

Livestock, 1 Jan. 1984: 143,300 cattle, 110,700 pigs, 23,400 sheep and goats.

95,300 pupils were attending 351 schools in 1980–81. There were 6 technical colleges with 2,600 students; 6,200 students were receiving higher education (including correspondence courses). A university has been opened in Sukhumi.

In Jan. 1983 there were 2,000 doctors and 6,000 hospital beds; 956 scientific workers were employed in the republic.

ADJARIAN AUTONOMOUS SOVIET SOCIALIST REPUBLIC

Area, 3,000 sq. km (1,160 sq. miles); population (Jan. 1984), 375,000. Capital, Batumi. After a history similar to that of Abkhazia, it fell under Turkish rule in the 17th century, and was annexed to Russia (rejoining Georgia) after the Berlin Treaty of 1878. On 16 July 1921 the territory was constituted as an Autonomous Republic within the Georgian SSR.

Population (1979 census) Georgians, 80·1%, Russians, 9·8% and Armenians 4·6%.

110 deputies were elected on 24 Feb. 1980, 43 of them women.

The republic specializes in sub-tropical agricultural products. These include tea, mandarines and lemons, grapes, bamboo, eucalyptus, etc. Livestock (Jan. 1983): 128,600 cattle, 8,900 pigs, 10,300 sheep and goats. In 1980 there were 69 collective farms and 21 state farms.

There are shipyards at Batumi, modern oil-refining plant (the pipeline from the Baku oilfields ends at Batumi), food-processing and canning factories, clothing, building materials, drug factories, etc.

Health resorts are Kobuleti, Tsikhisdziri, Batumi on the coast and Beshumi in the hills. The sub-tropical climate and flora, and the combination of mountains and sea, make this republic (like Abkhazia) a favourite holiday area.

In 1982 there were 77,100 pupils at school, 8 technical colleges with 3,500 students, a pedagogical institute and several research institutions. 2,200 students were receiving a higher education.

In Jan. 1983 there were 1,300 doctors and 3,900 hospital beds; 396 scientific workers were employed in the republic.

SOUTH OSSETIAN AUTONOMOUS REGION

This area was populated by Ossetians from across the Caucasus (North Ossetia), driven out by the Mongols in the 13th century. The region was set up within the Georgian SSR on 20 April 1922. Area, 3,900 sq. km (1,505 sq. miles); population (Jan. 1984), 98,000 (1979 census, Ossetians, 66·4% and Georgians, 28·8%). Capital, Tskhinvali (34,000).

Main industries are mining, timber, electrical engineering and building materials. Crop area, chiefly grains, was 21,600 hectares in 1983; other pursuits are sheep-farming (154,000 sheep and goats) and vine-growing. There were 14 collective farms and 18 state farms.

There is a pedagogical institute (2,000 students) and 4 technical colleges (900 students). In 1982 there were 23,500 pupils in elementary and secondary schools.

In Jan. 1983 there were 500 doctors and 1,400 hospital beds.

Books of Reference

Lang, D. M., *A Modern History of Georgia.* London, 1962. — *The Georgians.* London, 1966
Tutaeff, D., *The Soviet Caucasus.* London, 1942
Istoriya Gruzii. 3 vols. Tbilisi, 1962–73

ARMENIA

Haikakan Sovetakan Sotsialistakan Respublika

HISTORY. On 29 Nov. 1920 Armenia was proclaimed a Soviet Socialist Republic. The Armenian Soviet Government, with the Russian Soviet Government, was a party to the Treaty of Kars (March 1921), which confirmed the Turkish possession of the former Government of Kars and of the Surmali District of the Government of Yerevan. From 1922 to 1936 it formed part of the Transcaucasian Soviet Federal Socialist Republic. In 1936 Armenia was proclaimed a constituent republic of the USSR.

AREA AND POPULATION. Armenia covers an area of 29,800 sq. km (11,490 sq. miles). It is bounded in the north by Georgia, in the east by Azerbaijan and in the south and west by Turkey and Iran. It is a very mountainous country with but little forest land, has many turbulent rivers and a highly fertile soil, but subject to drought. In Jan. 1984 the population was 3,267,000. Census (1979) 89·7% of the population were Armenians, the rest are Russians (2·3%), Kurds (1·7%), Azerbaijanians (5·3%). The capital is Yerevan. Other large towns are Leninakan (218,000) and Kirovakan (159,000).

CONSTITUTION AND GOVERNMENT. The Supreme Soviet, elected in 1985, consists of 338 deputies (1 per 5,000 population); 121 are women, 216 Communists. A new Constitution was adopted in April 1978.

At elections to the district, urban and rural Soviets (20 June 1982), of 27,165 deputies returned 13,513 (49·7%) were women, 15,376 (56·6%) non-Party and 18,975 (69·9%) industrial workers and collective farmers.

Chairman, Presidium of the Supreme Soviet: B. E. Sarkisov.
Chairman, Council of Ministers: F. T. Sarkisian.
First Secretary, Communist Party: K. S. Demirchian.

FINANCE. Budget estimates (in 1m. rubles), 1985, 1,848; 1984, 1,773.

AGRICULTURE. The chief agricultural area is the valley of the Arax and the area round Yerevan. Here there are considerable cotton plantations as well as orchards and vineyards. Sub-tropical plants, such as almonds and figs, are also grown. Olive groves and pomegranate plantations occupy large areas; experiments are being made to naturalize cork oak. In the mountainous areas the chief pursuit is livestock raising. In 1913 the total cultivated area of Armenia amounted to 346,000 hectares; in 1940, 434,000; in 1965, 400,000; in 1970, 409,000; in 1982, 444,000.

Output of main agricultural products (in 1,000 tonnes) in 1982 (1913 figures in brackets): Vegetables, 447; sugar-beet, 168 (0); potatoes, 309 (47); fruit, 189; grapes, 270; meat, 96·4 (19); milk, 542 (129); wool, 5 (2·3); and 502m. eggs (54m.).

Area of irrigated land in Armenia in 1982 was 284,000 hectares.

There were, on 1 Jan. 1983, 280 collective farms, and these together with the 447 state farms tilled 99·9% of the total cultivated area. Livestock included 265,000 pigs, 825,600 cattle and 2·2m. sheep and goats. All the state farms and collective farms had been electrified by the end of 1960. There were 13,000 tractors and 1,400 grain and cotton combines in Jan. 1983.

INDUSTRY. Armenia contains large deposits of copper, zinc, aluminium, molybdenum and other metals. It is also rich in marble, granite, cement and other building materials. The mining of these minerals is becoming more and more important. Among other industries are the chemical, producing chiefly synthetic rubber and fertilizers, and the extraction and processing of building materials such as cement, pumice-stone, tuffs, marble, volcanic basalt and fire-proof clay, ginning- and textile-mills, carpet weaving, food, including wine-making, fruit, meat-canning and creameries. Machine-tool and electrical engineering works have also been established. Among the industrial centres are Yerevan, Leninakan, Alaverdi, Kafan, Kirovakan, Daval, Megri and Oktemberyan. Output of electricity in 1982 was 13,500m. kwh. A chain ('cascade') of 8 hydro-electric stations on the river Razdan, as it falls about 3,300 ft from the mountain lake Sevan to its junction with the Arax, has been completed.

In 1982 there were produced 119,900 centrifugal pumps, 187m. electric light bulbs, 1·3m. cu. metres ferroconcrete, 3·3m. cu. metres carpet, 5·1m. watches and clocks, 15·3m. pairs leather footwear, 465·9m. cans of preserves, and 9·3m. decalitres of wine.

There were 1,260,000 industrial and office workers employed in the national economy in 1982.

COMMUNICATIONS. Length of railways in 1983, 760 km; motor roads, 10,800 km (hard surface, 9,300); airlines, 570 km.

Newspapers (1982). Out of 87 newspapers 77 appeared in Armenian. Daily circulation of Armenian-language newspapers, 1·4m., other languages, 116,000.

EDUCATION. In 1982–83 there were 600,000 pupils in 1,535 primary and secondary schools; 66 technical colleges with 48,100 students; 13 higher educational institutions with 59,200 students (including correspondence students). Yerevan houses the Armenian Academy of Sciences, 43 scientific institutes, a medical institute and other technical colleges, and a state university. In Jan. 1983, 31 learned institutions with 3,133 scientific staff are under the Academy of Sciences; scientific workers in 101 institutions totalled 21,000.

In Jan. 1983 there were 141,000 children in pre-school institutions.

HEALTH. In 1982 there were 11,600 doctors and 27,200 hospital beds.

Books of Reference

Kurkjian, V., *A History of Armenia.* New York, 1958

Lang, D.M., *Armenia: Cradle of Civilization.* London, 1978.—*The Armenians. A People in Exile.* London, 1981

Missakian, J., *A Searchlight on the Armenian Question, 1878–1950.* Boston, Mass., 1950

Shaginyan, M., *A Journey Through Soviet Armenia.* Moscow (English ed., 1954)

MOLDAVIAN SOVIET SOCIALIST REPUBLIC

Respublika Sovietike Sochialiste Moldovenyaske

HISTORY. The Moldavian Soviet Socialist Republic, capital Kishinev, was formed by the union of part of the former Moldavian Autonomous Soviet Socialist Republic (organized 12 Oct. 1924), formerly included in the Ukrainian Soviet Socialist Republic, and the areas of Bessarabia (ceded by Romania to the USSR, 28 June 1940) with a mainly Moldavian population. As from 2 Aug. 1940 the MSSR includes the following regions of the former Moldavian Autonomous Soviet Socialist Republic: Grigoriopol, Dubossarsk, Kamensk, Rybnits, Slobodzeisk and Tiraspol, and the following districts of Bessarabia: Beltsk, Bendery, Kagulsk, Kishinev, Orgeev and Sorok. The republic, however, is divided not into regions but into 36 rural districts, 21 towns and 15 urban settlements.

AREA AND POPULATION. Moldavia is bounded in the east and south by the Ukraine and on the west by Romania. The area is 33,700 sq. km (13,000 sq. miles). In Jan. 1984 the population was 4,080,000, of whom (1979 census) 63·9% are Moldavians. Others include Ukrainians (14·2%), Russians (12·8%), Gagauzi (3·5%), Jews (2%). Apart from Kishinev, larger towns are Tiraspol (154,000), Beltsy (139,000) and Bendery (114,000).

CONSTITUTION AND GOVERNMENT. The Supreme Soviet, elected in 1985, consists of 380 deputies (1 per 10,000 population); 138 are women, 253 Communists. A new Constitution was adopted in April 1978.

At elections to the district, urban and rural Soviets (20 June 1982), of 37,626 deputies returned, 18,865 (50·1%) were women, 21,286 (56·6%) non-Party and 26,519 (70·5%) industrial workers and collective farmers.

Chairman, Presidium of the Supreme Soviet: I. P. Kalin.
Chairman, Council of Ministers: I. G. Ustiyan.
First Secretary, Communist Party: S. K. Grossu.

FINANCE. Budget estimates (in 1m. rubles), 1985, 2,353; 1984, 2,265.

AGRICULTURE. On 1 Jan. 1983 there were 367 collective farms and 464 state farms. All ploughing and sowing is mechanized. Livestock included (1 Jan. 1983) 1·2m. cattle, 1·9m. pigs and 1·1m. sheep and goats. There were 53,500 tractors and 4,400 combine harvesters in Jan. 1983.

Output of main agricultural products (in 1,000 tonnes) in 1982 (1913 figures in tons in brackets): Sugar-beet, 2,321 (15); sunflower seeds, 233·2 (9); vegetables, 1,337; fruit, 736·1; grapes, 2,045; meat, 252 (53); milk, 1,072 (210); wool, 2·6 (3), 913m. eggs.

Bessarabia has an equable climate and very fertile soil. It contains nearly one quarter of the vineyards of the USSR. Bessarabia is also rich in fish in the south: sturgeon, mackerel, brill.

INDUSTRY. There are canning plants, wine-making plants, woodworking and metallurgical factories, a factory of ferro-concrete building materials, and footwear and textile plants. Moldavia takes third place in the USSR in the production of wine, tobacco and food-canning. Production in 1982 included 94,700 centrifugal pumps, 9,700 tractors, 15·5m. pairs leather footwear, 35,000 tons sausages, 427,100 tonnes granulated sugar, 1,620m. cans of preserves, 7,782m. cigarettes and 227,800 refrigerators. Meat and dairy produce are rapidly expanding food industries.

There are lignite, phosphorites, gypsum and valuable building materials.

In 1982 there were 1,579,000 industrial and office workers working in the national economy. Electricity generated (1982) 16,800m. kwh.

COMMUNICATIONS. Length of railways in Jan. 1983, 1,150 km. There is direct air communication with Leningrad, Moscow, Kiev, Lvov and across the Black Sea. There are 15,200 km of motor roads (10,600 hard surface), and 1,100 km of inland waterways.

Newspapers (1982). There were 185 newspapers, 79 in Moldavian. Daily circulation of Moldavian-language newspapers, 1,103,000, other languages, 899,000.

EDUCATION. In 1982–83 there were 700,000 pupils in 1,800 primary, secondary and special schools, 59,100 students in 51 technical colleges and 53,400 students in 8 higher educational institutions including the state university. A Moldavian Academy of Sciences was established in 1961: it had 17 research institutions and a scientific staff of 1,105 in Jan. 1983. In all, there are 68 learned institutions with 9,300 scientific staff. In Jan. 1983 there were 279,000 children attending pre-school institutions.

HEALTH. Moldavia has 800 medical centres, many district hospitals, a state medical institute and 9 medical schools with over 2,500 students. Doctors in 1982 numbered 13,800; hospital beds, 49,400.

Books of Reference

Zlatova, Y., and Kotelnikov, V., *Across Moldavia* (English ed.). Moscow, 1959
Istoriya Moldavskoi SSR. 2nd ed. 2 vols. Kishinev, 1965–68

ESTONIA

Eesti Nõukogude Sotsialistlik Vabariik

HISTORY. The workers' and soldiers' Soviets in Estonia took over power on 8 Nov. 1917, were overthrown by the German occupying forces in March 1918, and were restored to power as the Germans withdrew in Nov. 1918, establishing the 'Estland Labour Commune'. It was overthrown with the assistance of British naval forces in May 1919, and a democratic republic proclaimed. In March 1934 this regime was, in turn, overthrown by a fascist *coup*.

The secret protocol of the Soviet-German agreement of 23 Aug. 1939 assigned Estonia to the Soviet sphere of interest. An ultimatum (16 June 1940) led to the formation of a government acceptable to the USSR; on 21 July the State Duma proclaimed the establishment of an Estonian Soviet Socialist Republic and applied to join the USSR: on 6 Aug. the Supreme Soviet accepted the application. The incorporation has been accorded *de facto* recognition by the British Government, but not by the US Government, which continues to recognize an Estonian consul-general in New York.

AREA AND POPULATION. Estonia is bounded west and north by the

Baltic, east by the RSFSR and south by Latvia. Area, 45,100 sq. km (17,410 sq. miles); population, 1,518,000 (Jan. 1984). Census (1979) 64·7% were Estonians, 27·9% Russians, 2·5% Ukrainians and 1·6% Belorussians. The capital is Tallinn. Other large towns are Tartu (109,000), Pärnu, Narva (78,000). There are 15 districts, 33 towns and 26 urban settlements.

CONSTITUTION AND GOVERNMENT. The Supreme Soviet, elected in 1985, consists of 285 deputies (1 per 10,000 population); 102 are women, 192 Communists. A new Constitution was adopted in April 1978.

At elections to district, urban and rural Soviets (20 June 1982), out of 11,010 deputies returned 5,459 (49·6%) were women, 6,090 (55·3%) non-Party and 7,438 (67·6%) industrial workers and collective farmers.

Chairman, Presidium of the Supreme Soviet: A. F. Riutel.
Chairman, Council of Ministers: B. E. Saul.
First Secretary, Communist Party: K. G. Vaino.

FINANCE. Budget estimates (in 1m. rubles), 1985, 1,560; 1984, 1,447.

AGRICULTURE. Agriculture and dairy farming are the chief occupations. Area under cultivation was 697,000 hectares in 1913, 918,000 hectares in 1940 and 943,700 hectares in 1982. There were 142 agricultural and 8 fishery collectives and 154 state farms in 1983 using 19,600 tractors and 3,600 grain combines. 97% of state farms and 70% of collective farms were receiving electric power.

On 1 Jan. 1983 there were 835,500 head of cattle, 171,200 sheep and goats, and 1,080,100 pigs.

Output of main agricultural products (in 1,000 tonnes) in 1982 (1913 figures in brackets): Meat (slaughter weight), 173 (60); milk, 1,116 (415); eggs, 556m. (67m.); potatoes, 981 (689); vegetables, 125; fruit, 29.

INDUSTRY. Some 22% of the territory is covered by forests which provide good material for its sawmills, furniture, match and pulp industries, as well as wood fuel. Since the end of the war, 80,000 hectares have been afforested. 966,700 hectares of marsh land had been reclaimed by 1977.

Estonia has rich high-quality shale deposits (particularly in the north-east) which are estimated at 3,700m. tons. Shale output was 1·9m. tons in 1940 and 30m. in 1977. A factory for the production of gas from shale and a pipeline (208 km long) from Kohtla-Järve supplies shale gas to Leningrad and Tallinn. Estonian factories are now turning out agricultural and peat-digging machines, complex control and measuring instruments. The 'Volta' factory in Tallinn produces electric motors.

In the neighbourhood of Tallinn, phosphorites have been found, and in 1947 a plant for refining and for the production of super-phosphates was started. Estonia also contains valuable peat deposits, and some of her electrical stations work on peat. There are 350 rural electric stations. Electricity generated (1982) 18,500m. kwh. Output of paper in 1982 was 91,200 tonnes; leather footwear, 5·8m. pairs; cans of preserves, 316m.; felled timber, 2·5m. cubic metres; hosiery, 14·6m. pairs.

In 1982 there were 709,000 industrial and office workers engaged in the national economy.

COMMUNICATIONS. Length of railways in 1983, 1,010 km. Estonia has 20 ports, but Tallinn handles four-fifths of the total sea-going transport. Inland waterways total 500 km; motor roads, 27,700 km (hard surface, 25,500 km). Airlines link Tallinn with Moscow, Leningrad, Riga and the Estonian islands.

Newspapers (1982). There were 44 newspapers, 31 of them in Estonian. Daily circulation of Estonian-language newspapers, 1,022,000, other languages, 185,000.

EDUCATION. Estonia has retained an 11-year school curriculum, when it was reduced to 10 years elsewhere in the USSR. In 1982–83 pupils in 600 primary, secondary and special schools numbered 216,000. There were 25,400 students in 6 higher educational establishments, including Tartu (Dorpat) University, founded in 1632, and 23,400 students in 37 technical colleges.

The Estonian Academy of Sciences, founded in 1946, had 24 institutions with 1,095 scientific staff in Jan. 1983; in all, 6,700 scientists were working in 72 institutions.

In Jan. 1983 there were 86,000 children attending pre-school institutions.

HEALTH. In 1982 there were 6,600 doctors and 19,000 hospital beds.

Books of Reference

Istoriya Estonskoi SSR. 3 vols. Tallin, 1961–74
Küng, A., *A Dream of Freedom.* Cardiff, 1980
Misiuras, R-J., and Taagepera, R., *The Baltic States: Years of Dependence 1940–1980.* Farnborough, 1983
Parming, T., and Jarvesro, E., (eds.) *A Case Study of a Soviet Republic.* Boulder, 1978
Saagpakk, P. F., *Estonian-English Dictionary.* New Haven, 1982
Silvet, J., *Inglise—eestisõnaraamat.* Vadstena, 1949
Varetz, E. F., and Tarmisto, V. Y., *Estoniya.* Moscow, 1967 (in Russian)

LATVIA
Latvijas Padomju Socialistiska Republika

HISTORY. In the part of Latvia unoccupied by the Germans, the Bolsheviks won 72% of the votes in the Constituent Assembly elections (Nov. 1917). Soviet power was proclaimed in Dec. 1917, but was overthrown when the Germans occupied all Latvia (Feb. 1918). Restored when they withdrew (Dec. 1918), it was overthrown once more by combined British naval and German military forces (May–Dec. 1919), and a democratic government set up. This régime was in turn replaced when a fascist *coup* took place in May 1934.

The secret protocol of the Soviet–German agreement of 23 Aug. 1939 assigned Latvia to the Soviet sphere of interest. An ultimatum (16 June 1940) led to the formation of a government acceptable to the USSR. On 21 July a People's Diet proclaimed the establishment of the Latvian Soviet Socialist Republic and applied to join the USSR, whose Supreme Soviet accepted the application on 5 Aug. The incorporation has been accorded *de facto* recognition by the British Government, but not by the US Government, which continues to recognize the Chargé d'Affaires in Washington, D.C.

AREA AND POPULATION. Latvia is bounded north by Estonia and the Baltic Sea, west by the Baltic, south by Lithuania and Belorussia and east by the RSFSR. Latvia has a total area of 63,700 sq. km (25,590 sq. miles). Population, Jan. 1984, 2,587,000, of whom (1979 census) 53·7% are Latvians and 32·8% Russians. There are 26 districts, 56 towns and 37 urban settlements.

The chief town is Riga (the capital); other principal towns are Daugavpils (Dvinsk) (122,000), Liepāja (109,000), Jelgava (Mitau) (69,000) and Ventspils (Windau).

CONSTITUTION AND GOVERNMENT. The Supreme Soviet, elected in 1985, consists of 325 deputies (1 per 10,000 population); 115 are women, 219 Communists. A new Constitution was adopted in April 1978.

At elections to district, urban and rural Soviets (20 June 1982), of 23,369 deputies returned, 11,490 (49·2%) were women, 12,389 (53%) non-Party and 15,609 (66·8%) industrial workers and collective farmers.

Chairman, Presidium of the Supreme Soviet: P. Y. Strautmanis.
Chairman, Council of Ministers: Y. Y. Ruben.
First Secretary, Communist Party: B. K. Pugo.

FINANCE. Budget estimates (in 1m. rubles), 1985, 2,312; 1984, 2,154.

AGRICULTURE. Latvia is now no longer mainly an agricultural country. The urban population, 35% of the total in 1939, was 70% in Jan. 1984.

Latvian forest lands, state and private (2·4m. hectares), produced in 1937–38, 3·4m. cu. metres of timber; 1982 output, 3·9m. cu. metres.

Area under cultivation was 1·4m. hectares in 1913, 2m. in 1940, 1·7m. in 1982. 1·8m. hectares of marsh land have been drained (1983).

Cattle breeding and dairy farming are the chief agricultural occupations. Oats, barley, rye, potatoes and flax are the main crops.

After the establishment of the Soviet regime about 960,000 hectares were distributed among the landless peasants or those with very small holdings. On 1 Jan. 1983 there were 244 state farms and 330 collective farms. There were 34,600 tractors and 7,200 grain combine harvesters. By 1 Jan. 1964, all state farms and collective farms were using electric power.

Livestock (1 Jan. 1983): Cattle, 1·5m. (1939: 1·3m.); sheep, 208,000 (1939: 1·5m.); pigs, 1·7m. (1939: 891,500).

Output of main agricultural products (in 1,000 tonnes) in 1982 (1913 figures in brackets): Meat (slaughter weight), 275 (122); milk, 1,616 (673); eggs, 748m. (136m.); sugar-beet, 287 (0); potatoes, 1,484 (645); vegetables, 253; fruit, 65; wool, 0·5 (1·4); flax fibre, 4 (21).

INDUSTRY. Latvia is the main producer of electric railway passenger cars and long-distance telephone exchanges in the USSR, fourth in output of paper and woollen goods, fifth of sawn timber, sixth of mineral fertilizers.

Industrial output in 1982 (in 1,000 tons) included: Paper, 115; hosiery, 73m. pairs; knitwear, 44m. garments; leather footwear, 9·9m. pairs; radios, 2·2; washing machines, 597; mopeds, 293; granulated sugar, 270; cans of preserves, 420·4m. Electricity generated (1982) 4,700m. kwh.

Peat deposits extend over 645,000 hectares or about 10% of the total area, and it is estimated that total deposits are 3,000–4,000m. tons; output, 1971, 2·3m. tons. There are also gypsum deposits; amber is frequently found in the coastal districts.

In 1982 industrial and office workers numbered 1,209,000.

COMMUNICATIONS. In 1983 the length of railways was 2,380 km, and motor roads, 24,700 km (hard surface, 17,600 km). Riga is the largest port in the Baltic after Leningrad.

Newspapers (1982). There were 105 newspapers (63 in Lettish). Daily circulation of Lettish-language newspapers, 1·2m., other languages 471,000.

RELIGION. The Latvian Lutheran Church numbered 600,000 members in 1956.

EDUCATION. In 1982–83 there were 900 primary and secondary schools, with a total of 400,000 pupils: 119,000 children attended pre-school institutions. Ten places of higher education had 46,600 students, 55 technical colleges had 40,600 students; there were also 21 music and art schools, 3 teachers' training colleges and an agricultural academy. In 1946 an Academy of Sciences was opened which in Jan. 1983 had 16 research institutes with a staff of 1,703 scientific workers; there were over 13,300 scientific workers in 101 research institutions.

HEALTH. There were 11,700 doctors and 35,200 hospital beds in 1982.

Books of Reference

Latvian Academy of Sciences, *Istoriya Latviiskoi SSR.* Riga. 3 vols. 1952–58
Bilmanis, A., *A History of Latvia.* Princeton Univ. Press, 1951
Roze, B. and K., *Latviska–Angliska Vārdnīcā.* Göppingen, 1948
Spekke, A., *History of Latvia.* Stockholm, 1951
Turkina, E., *Angliski–Latviska Vārdnīca.* Riga, 1948.—*Latviešu-Anglu Vārdnīca.* Riga, 1962

LITHUANIA

Lietuvos Tarybu Socialistine Respublika

HISTORY. In 1914–15 the German army occupied the whole of Lithuania. On its withdrawal (Dec. 1918) Soviets were elected in all towns and a Soviet republic was proclaimed. In the summer of 1919 it was overthrown by Polish, German and nationalist Lithuanian forces, and a democratic republic established. In Dec. 1926 this regime was in turn overthrown by a fascist *coup*.

The secret protocol of the Soviet–German frontier treaty of 28 Sept. 1939 assigned the greater part of Lithuania to the Soviet sphere of influence. In Oct. 1939 the province and city of Vilnius (in Polish occupation 1920–39) were ceded by the USSR. An ultimatum (16 June 1940) led to the formation of a government acceptable to the USSR. A people's Diet, elected on 14–15 July, proclaimed the establishment of the Lithuanian Soviet Socialist Republic on 21 July and applied for admission to the USSR, which was effected by decree of the USSR Supreme Soviet on 3 Aug. and included also those parts of Lithuania which had been reserved for inclusion in Germany. This incorporation has been accorded *de facto* recognition by the British Government, but not by the US Government, which continues to recognize a Lithuanian Chargé d'Affaires in Washington, D.C.

AREA AND POPULATION. Lithuania is bounded north by Latvia, east and south by Belorussia, west by Poland, the Kaliningrad area of the RSFSR and the Baltic Sea. The total area of Lithuania is 65,200 sq. km (25,170 sq. miles) and the population (Jan. 1984) 3,539,000, of whom 80% were Lithuanians, 8·6% Russians and 7·7% Poles (1979 census).

The capital is Vilnius (Vilna). Other large towns are Kaunas (Kovno), Klaipeda (Memel), Šiauliai (130,000) and Panėvežys (112,000). There are 44 rural districts, 92 towns and 22 urban settlements.

CONSTITUTION AND GOVERNMENT. The Supreme Soviet, elected in 1985, consists of 350 deputies (1 per 15,000 population); 125 are women, 235 Communists. A new Constitution was adopted in April 1978.

At elections to district, urban and rural Soviets (20 June 1982), of 28,410 deputies returned, 14,140 (49·8%) were women, 16,139 (56·8%) non-Party and 19,291 (67·9%) industrial workers and collective farmers.

Chairman, Presidium of the Supreme Soviet: A. S. Barkauskas.
Chairman, Council of Ministers: R.-B. I. Songeila.
First Secretary, Communist Party: P. P. Griškevičius.

FINANCE. Budget estimates (in 1m. rubles), 1985, 3,495; 1984, 3,237.

AGRICULTURE. Lithuania before 1940 was a mainly agricultural country, but has since been considerably industrialized. The urban population was 23% of the total in 1937 and 64% in Jan. 1983. The resources of the country consist of timber and agricultural produce. Of the total area, 49·1% is arable land, 22·2% meadow and pasture land, 16·3% forests and 12·4% unproductive lands.

Area under cultivation in 1913 was 1·9m.; in 1938, 2·7m.; in 1983, 2·4m. hectares. By 1981 over 2·7m. hectares of swamps had been drained.

Output of main agricultural products (in 1,000 tonnes) in 1982 (1913 figures in brackets): Meat (slaughter weight), 414 (159); milk, 2,508 (832); eggs, 1,026m. (264m.); sugar-beet, 772 (0); flax, 18 (17); potatoes, 2,055 (1,375); vegetables, 349; fruit, 163; wool, 0·1 (1·5).

On 1 Jan. 1983 there were 2·4m. cattle, 2·6m. pigs, 94,000 sheep and goats.

Forests cover 1,554,000 hectares; 70% of the forests consist of conifers, mostly pines. Peat reserves total 4,000m. cu. metres.

Between 1940 and 1947 about 575,500 hectares (about 1·4m. acres) were distributed among the landless and poor peasant farmers. In 1983 there were 47,500 trators and 11,400 grain combines serving 741 collective farms and 311 state farms.

INDUSTRY. Heavy engineering, shipbuilding and building material industries are developing. Industrial output included, in 1982, 22,100 metal-cutting lathes; electric calculators, 3·3m.; sulphuric acid, 436,000 tonnes; paper, 111,000 tonnes; tape-recorders, 257,600; washing machines, 279,200; televisions, 496,700; leather footwear, 10m. pairs; granulated sugar, 225,300 tonnes; felled timber, 2·4m. cu. metres; hosiery, 94m. pairs; electric power, 12,400m. kwh.

In 1982 there were 1,504,000 industrial and office workers employed in the national economy.

COMMUNICATIONS. Length of railways in Jan. 1983, 2,040 km. Vilnius has one of the largest airports of the USSR. There are 33,900 km of motor roads (22,300 km hard surface) and 600 km of inland waterways. Klaipeda, as a non-freezing harbour and fishery base, is of national importance.

Newspapers (1982). Of 129 newspapers, 102 were in Lithuanian. Daily circulation of Lithuanian-language newspapers, 1·9m., other languages, 243,000.

RELIGION. In 1956, the Lithuanian Lutheran Church had 215,000 members; Roman Catholics, including those in Estonia and Latvia, numbered 2·5m.

EDUCATION. In 1982–83 there were 600,000 pupils in 2,300 primary and secondary schools. The University of Vytautas the Great, at Kaunas, was opened on 16 Feb. 1922. On 15 Jan. 1940 certain faculties were transferred to Vilnius to join the ancient University of Vilnius (founded 1570). In 1982–83 there were 12 higher educational institutions with 71,100 students: in 67 technical colleges of all kinds there were 64,600 students. The Lithuanian Academy of Sciences, founded in 1941, had 11 institutions with a total scientific staff of 1,807 in Jan. 1983; there were 88 scientific institutions with 14,600 research personnel. 168,000 children in Jan. 1983 were attending pre-school institutions.

HEALTH. In 1982 there were 14,200 doctors and 42,500 hospital beds.

Books of Reference

Griškevičius, P. P., *Land on the Nemunas.* Moscow, 1977

Jurgėla, C. R., *History of the Lithuanian Nation.* New York, 1948

Kantantas, F., *A Lithuanian Bibliography.* Univ. of Alberta Press, 1975

Peteraitis, V., *Lithuanian–English Dictionary.* 2 vols. Chicago, 1960

Vardys, S., (ed.) *Lithuania under the Soviets: Portrait of a Nation, 1940–45.* New York, 1965

SOVIET CENTRAL ASIA

Soviet Central Asia embraces the Kazakh Soviet Socialist Republic, the Uzbek Soviet Socialist Republic, the Turkmen Soviet Socialist Republic, the Tadzhik Soviet Socialist Republic and the Kirghiz Soviet Socialist Republic.

Turkestan (by which name part of this territory was then known) was conquered by the Russians in the 1860s. In 1866 Tashkent was occupied and in 1868 Samarkand, and subsequently further territory was conquered and united with Russian Turkestan. In the 1870s Bokhara was subjugated, the emir, by the agreement of 1873, recognizing the suzerainty of Russia. In the same year Khiva became a vassal state to Russia. Until 1917 Russian Central Asia was divided politically into the Khanate of Khiva, the Emirate of Bokhara and the Governor-Generalship of Turkestan.

In the summer of 1919 the authority of the Soviet Government became definitely established in these regions. The Khan of Khiva was deposed in Feb. 1920, and a People's Soviet Republic was set up, the medieval name of Khorezm being revived. In Aug. 1920 the Emir of Bokhara suffered the same fate, and a similar regime was set up in Bokhara. The former Governor-Generalship of Turkestan was constituted an Autonomous Soviet Socialist Republic within the RSFSR on 11 April 1921.

In the autumn of 1924 the Soviets of the Turkestan, Bokhara and Khiva Republics decided to redistribute the territories of these republics on a nationality basis; at the same time Bokhara and Khiva became Socialist Republics. The redistribution was completed in May 1925, when the new states of Uzbekistan, Turkmenistan and Tadzhikistan were accepted into the USSR as Union Republics. The remaining districts of Turkestan populated by Kazakhs were united with Kazakhstan which was established as an ASSR in 1925 and became a Union Republic in 1936. Kirghizia, until then part of the RSFSR, was established as a Union Republic in 1936.

Books of Reference

Akiner, S., *The Islamic Peoples of the Soviet Union.* London, 1983
Bennigsen, A., and Broxup, M., *The Islamic Threat to the Soviet State.* London, 1983
Nove, A. and Newth, J. A., *The Soviet Middle East.* London, 1967
Rwykin, M., *Moscow's Muslim Challenge.* New York, 1982
Wheeler, G., *The Modern History of Soviet Central Asia.* London, 1964.—*The Peoples of Soviet Central Asia.* London, 1966

KAZAKHSTAN

Kazak Soviettik Sotzialistik Respublikasy

HISTORY. On 26 Aug. 1920 Uralsk, Turgai, Akmolinsk and Semipalatinsk provinces formed the Kirgiz (in 1925 renamed Kazakh) Autonomous Soviet Socialist Republic within the RSFSR. It was made a constituent republic of the USSR on 5 Dec. 1936. To this republic were added the parts of the former Governorship of Turkestan inhabited by a majority of Kazakhs. It consists of the following regions: Aktyubinsk, Alma-Ata, Chimkent, Dzhambul, Dzhezkazgan, East Kazakhstan, Guryev, Karaganda, Kokchetav, Kustanai, Kzyl-Orda, Mangyshlak, North Kazakhstan, Pavlodar, Semipalatinsk, Taldy-Kurgan, Tselinograd, Turgai, Uralsk.

AREA AND POPULATION. Kazakhstan is bounded on the west by the Caspian Sea and the RSFSR, on the east by China, on the north by the RSFSR and on the south by Uzbekistan and Kirghizia. The area of the republic is 2,717,300 sq. km (1,049,155 sq. miles). It is the next in size to the RSFSR, is far larger than all the other Central Asian Soviet Republics combined and stretches nearly 3,000 km from west to east and over 1,500 km from north to south. Population (Jan. 1984) 15,648,000, of whom 55% live in urban areas. The Kazakhs form 36%, Russians 40·8% and Ukrainians 6·1% of the population (1979 census), as a result of the industrialization of the country since 1941 and the opening of virgin lands since 1945. The population includes over 100 nationalities.

The capital is Alma-Ata, formerly Verny; other large towns are Karaganda, Semipalatinsk, Chimkent and Petropavlovsk. In all there are 82 towns, 197 urban settlements and 221 rural districts.

CONSTITUTION AND GOVERNMENT. The Supreme Soviet, elected in 1985, consists of 510 deputies (1 per 20,000 population); 183 are women, 336 Communists. A new Constitution was adopted in April 1978.

At elections to the regional, district, urban and rural Soviets (20 June 1982), out of 128,365 deputies returned, 63,006 (49·1%) were women, 74,480 (58%) non-Party and 87,991 (68·6%) industrial workers and collective farmers.

President, Presidium of the Supreme Soviet: B. A. Ashimov.
Chairman, Council of Ministers: N. A. Nazarbaev.
First Secretary, Communist Party: D. A. Kunayev.

FINANCE. The budget (in 1m. rubles) balanced as follows: 1985, 10,982; 1984, 10,487.

AGRICULTURE. Kazakh agriculture has changed from primarily nomad cattle breeding to production of grain, cotton and other industrial crops. In 1983 the crop area was 35·3m. hectares—over 16% of the total cultivated area of the USSR (1913, 4·2m.; 1940, 6·8m.).

2,047,000 hectares of land have an irrigation network.

The 'Ukrainka' winter wheat has been transformed into a spring wheat suitable for cultivation in Kazakhstan. Tobacco, rubber plants and mustard are also cultivated. Kazakhstan has rich orchards and vineyards; 27,000 hectares were under vines and 95,000 under orchards in 1983. Between 1954 and 1959, over 23m. hectares of virgin and long fallow land were opened up, 544 new state grain farms being organized for the purpose. Grain deliveries to the state were 10·5m. tons in 1960; 2·4m. in 1965; 13·4m. in 1970; 5·1m. in 1975; 8·2m. in 1977; 16,784 in 1978.

Kazakhstan is noted for its livestock, particularly its sheep, from which excellent quality wool is obtained. The Akharomerino is a newly developed crossbreed of merino sheep and the wild Akhar mountain ram. Livestock on 1 Jan. 1983 included 9·02m. cattle, 35·6m. sheep and goats and 2·9m. pigs.

There were, on 1 Jan. 1983, 394 collective farms and 2,112 state farms with 240,000 tractors and 112,300 grain combine harvesters. There were 5,293 rural power stations of 307,800 kwh. capacity.

Output of main agricultural products (in 1m. tonnes) in 1982 (1913 figures in brackets): Meat (slaughter weight), 1·1 (0·44); milk, 4·5 (0·85); eggs, 3,478m. (233m.); wool, 0·1 (0·04); sugar-beet, 1·0 (0); cotton, 0·3 (0·015); potatoes, 1·9 (0·18); vegetables, 1·1; fruit, 0·3.

INDUSTRY. Kazakhstan is extremely rich in mineral resources. Coal and tungsten in Karaganda (in the centre), oil along the river Emba (in the west), copper, lead and zinc—Kazakhstan contains about one-half of the total deposits of these three metals contained in the USSR—Iceland spar (in the south), nickel and chromium in the Kustanai and Semipalatinsk regions, molybdenum and other minerals.

In 1943 big deposits of manganese were found in Eastern Kazakhstan; new coal seams were also discovered there. In South Kazakhstan new copper and bauxite deposits have been found.

Coal, oil, non-ferrous metallurgy, heavy engineering and chemical industries have brought Kazakhstan to the third place among the industrial republics of the USSR. Production (1m. tonnes) in 1982 included iron ore, 25·4; sulphuric acid, 1·8; ferroconcrete, 6m. cu. metres; leather footwear, 30·4m. pairs; granulated sugar, 0·3; cans of preserves, 403; felled timber, 2·3; cotton fibre, 0·1; hosiery, 72·6m. pairs. The Leninogorsk and Chimkent lead plants, the Balkhash, Irtysh and Karaskpai copper-smelting works and others supply the country with non-ferrous metals. A meat-packing plant has been built in Semipalatinsk, a fish cannery in Guryev, a chemical plant in Aktyubinsk, a tractor works at Pavlodar, and a superphosphate plant in Dzhambul. The oil industry in Emba and Aktyubinsk yields high-quality aviation oil.

Aviation plays an important part in agriculture. About 14m. hectares were in 1970 treated from the air (destruction of pests, surface feeding of sugar-beet plantations, pollination of orchards, etc.).

Among recent enterprises are a large textile combine at Kustanai, hosiery factories at Djezkazgan, Leninogorsk and Aktyubinsk, a sugar factory at Aksu, meat canneries at Djetygar and Kzyl-Orda.

Electric power output in 1982 was 62,800m. kwh.

There were, in 1982, 6,250,000 industrial and office workers in the national economy.

COMMUNICATIONS

Roads. In 1983 there were 106,000 km of motor roads (80,400 km hard surface).

Railways. A 430-km railway line between the settlements of Mointi and Chu in Kazakhstan to complete the Transkazakh trunk line, connecting Petropavlovsk,

Akmolinsk, Karaganda and Balkhash, was opened in 1953. The new line links the Transkazakh trunk line with the Turkestan–Siberian railway carrying Karaganda coal to South Kazakhstan. The Akmolinsk–Pavlodar railway (438 km), a section of the South Siberian line, was opened in Dec. 1953. Other lines in operation are Dzhambul–Chalaktan, Akmolinsk–Kartaly, Uralsk–Iletsk, Guriev–Kandagach. In 1983 the total length of railways in operation was 14,280 km. Over 600 km of narrow-gauge line and 700 km of broad-gauge line were built in the virgin lands area in 1951-57.

Inland waterways. Total length 5,500 km.

Newspapers (1982). Of 443 newspapers, 163 were in the Kazakh language. Daily circulation of Kazakh-language newspapers, 1·7m., other languages, 3·7m.

EDUCATION. Nearly the whole population is literate. In 1982–83 there were 3·3m. pupils at 8,700 elementary and secondary schools; 240 technical colleges with 270,000 students, 55 higher educational institutions with 275,600 students, and 207 research institutes with 34,700 scientific personnel. The Kazakh Academy of Sciences, founded in 1945, had, in 1983, 31 institutions, the scientific staff of which numbered 4,155. 926,000 children were attending pre-school institutions.

HEALTH. In 1982 there were 51,900 doctors and 203,100 hospital beds.

Books of Reference

Istoriya Kazakhskoi SSR. 2 vols. Alma-Ata, 1957–59
Alampiev, P., *Soviet Kazakhstan.* Moscow, 1958.—*Where Economic Inequality is No More.* Moscow, 1959

TURKMENISTAN
Tiurkmenostan Soviet Sotsialistik Respublikasy

HISTORY. The Turkmen Soviet Socialist Republic was formed on 27 Oct. 1924 and covers the territory of the former Trans-Caspian Region of Turkestan, the Charjiui vilayet of Bokhara and a part of Khiva situated on the right bank of the Oxus. In May 1925 the Turkmen Republic entered the Soviet Union as one of its constituent republics.

AREA AND POPULATION. Turkmenistan is bounded on the north by the Autonomous Kara-Kalpak Republic, a constituent of Uzbekistan, by Iran and Afghánistán on the south, by the Uzbek Republic on the east and the Caspian Sea on the west. The principal Turkmen tribes are the Tekkés of Merv and the Tekkés of the Attok, the Ersaris, Yomuds and Goklans. All speak closely related varieties of a Turkic language (of the south-western group); many are Sunni Mohammedans.

The country passed under Russian control in 1881, after the fall of the Turkoman stronghold of GökTépé. Census (1979) 68·4% of the population were Turkmenians, most of whom were nomads before the First World War. 12·6% are Russians living mostly in urban areas, and 8·5% Uzbeks. There are also Kazakhs (2·9%), Tatars, Ukrainians, Armenians and others.

The area of Turkmenistan is 488,100 sq. km (186,400 sq. miles), and its population in Jan. 1984 was 3,118,000.

There are 5 regions: Chardzhou, Mary, Ashkhabad, Tashauz and Krasnovodsk, comprising 42 rural districts, 15 towns and 74 urban settlements.

The capital is Ashkhabad (Poltoratsk); other large towns are Chardzhou (152,000), Mary (Merv) (81,000), Nebit-Dag (78,000) and Krasnovodsk (55,000).

CONSTITUTION AND GOVERNMENT. The Supreme Soviet, elected in 1985, consists of 330 deputies (1 per 5,000 population); 118 are women, 222 Communists. A new Constitution was adopted in April 1978.

At elections to regional, district, urban and rural Soviets (20 June 1982), of

23,478 deputies returned, 11,623 (49·5%) were women, 13,317 (56·7%) non-party and 16,312 (69·5%) industrial workers and collective farmers.

Chairman, Presidium of the Supreme Soviet: B. Yazkuliev.
Chairman, Council of Ministers: C. S. Karryev.
First Secretary, Communist Party: M. G. Gapurov.

FINANCE. Budget estimates (in 1m. rubles), 1985, 1,420; 1984, 1,346.

AGRICULTURE. The main occupation of the people is agriculture, based on irrigation. Turkmenistan produces cotton, wool, Astrakhan fur, etc. It is also famous for its carpets, and produces a special breed of Turkoman horses and the famous Karakul sheep.

There were 328 collective farms and 112 state farms in 1983, with 38,600 tractors and 1,200 grain combines. There were 608 rural power stations.

A considerable area is under Egyptian cotton, and from it has been evolved an original Soviet long-fibred cotton.

The main grain grown is maize. Sericulture, fruit and vegetable growing are also important; dates, olives, figs, sesame and other southern plants are grown. There is fishing in the Caspian. 950,000 hectares were under cultivation in 1982 (1913, 318,000; 1940, 411,000).

Between 1958 and 1970 the Kara-Kum Canal was extended to 860 km. In 1971 the fourth section, to reach the Caspian, was begun to reach 1,000 km. By 1982 over 1,011,000 hectares had been irrigated.

Livestock on 1 Jan. 1983: Cattle, 661,300; pigs, 193,700; sheep and goats, 4·5m.

Output of main agricultural products (in 1,000 tonnes) in 1982 (1913 figures in brackets): Meat (slaughter weight), 84·4 (58); milk, 324 (63); eggs, 274m. (18m.); cotton, 1,178 (69); vegetables, 288; fruit, 36; grapes, 62; wool, 13·4 (9·7).

INDUSTRY. Turkmenistan is rich in minerals, such as ozocerite, oil, coal, sulphur and salt. Industry is being developed, and there are now chemical, tailoring, textile, light, food, agricultural implements, cement and other factories, oil refineries, as well as ore-mining.

In the Kara-Kum Desert deposits of magnesium, minerals and coal have been discovered, as well as some 50 new saltmines. Here a new oil town, Nebit-Dag, has sprung up. On the Kara-Bogaz bay a sulphate industry has been developed. Industrial output in 1982 included 5·8m. sq. metres window glass, 358,000 tonnes cotton fibre, 5·2m. pairs hosiery, 3·5m. pairs leather footwear, 1·5m. Kanakul lambskins. Electric power output was 8,800m. kwh. (in 1982); 62,581m. cu. metres of natural gas were produced.

In 1982 there were 756,000 industrial and office workers in the national economy.

COMMUNICATIONS. Length of motor roads in 1983, 17,500 km (12,600 km hard surface). Motor communication exists between Ashkhabad and Meshed (Iran).

Length of railways, 2,120 km. The line Chardzhou–Kungrad crosses the Chardzhou and Tashauz regions of Turkmenia and runs across Uzbekistan. Another line connects Chardzhou and Urgench. Inland waterways, 1,300 km.

Airlines connect Leninsk and Tashauz, and Ashkhabad and remote areas in the west, north and east.

Newspapers (1982). Of 69 newspapers, 55 were in the Turkmen language. Daily circulation of Turkmenian-language newspapers, 771,000, other languages, 194,000.

EDUCATION. In 1982–83 there were 1,900 primary and secondary schools with 800,000 pupils, 8 higher educational institutions with 38,700 students, 35 technical colleges with 34,600 students, and 11 music and art schools. The Turkmen Academy of Sciences directs the work of 14 learned institutions with a staff of

1,047 scientists; there were 58 research institutions in all, with 5,300 research workers, in 1983. A Turkmenian State University was opened in 1951.

In Jan. 1983, 137,000 children were attending pre-school institutions.

HEALTH. In 1982 there were 8,900 doctors and 32,300 hospital beds.

Book of Reference

Istoriya Turkmenskoi SSR. 2 vols. Ashkhabad, 1957

UZBEKISTAN
Ozbekiston Soviet Sotsialistik Respublikasy

HISTORY. In Oct. 1917 the Tashkent Soviet assumed authority, and in the following years established its power throughout Turkestan. The semi-independent Khanates of Khiva and Bokhara were first (1920) transformed into People's Republics, then (1923–24) into Soviet Socialist Republics and finally merged in the Uzbek SSR and other republics.

The Uzbek Soviet Socialist Republic was formed on 27 Oct. 1924 from lands formerly included in Turkestan. It includes a large part of the Samarkand region, the southern part of the Syr Darya, Western Ferghana, the western plains of Bukhara, the Kara-Kalpak ASSR and the Uzbek regions of Khorezm. In May 1925 Uzbekistan, by the decision of the Congress of Soviets of the USSR, was accepted as one of the constituent republics of the Soviet Union.

AREA AND POPULATION. Uzbekistan is bordered on the north by the Kazakh Soviet Socialist Republic, on the east by the Kirghiz Soviet Socialist Republic and the Tadzhik Soviet Socialist Republic, on the south by Afghánistán and on the west by the Turkmen Soviet Socialist Republic. The Uzbeks, who form 68·7% (1979 census) of the population, were the ruling race in Central Asia until the arrival of the Russians during the third quarter of the 19th century. The several native states over which Uzbek dynasties formerly ruled were founded in the 15th century upon the ruins of Tamerlane's empire. The Uzbek speak Jagatai Turkish, which is related to Osmanli and Azerbaijan Turkish; many are Sunni Moslems. Russians numbered (census 1979) 10·8%, Tadzhiks, 3·9%, Tatars 4·2%.

The area of Uzbekistan is 447,400 sq. km (172,741 sq. miles). The population in Jan. 1984 was 17,498,000 (42% urban). The country comprises the following regions: Andizhan, Bukhara, Dzhizak, Ferghana, Kashkadar, Khorezm, Namangan, Navoi, Samarkand, Surkhan-Darya, Syr-Darya, Tashkent and the Autonomous Soviet Socialist Republic of Kara Kalpakia. The capital of the Republic is Tashkent; other large towns are Samarkand, Andizhan, Namangan. There are 109 towns, 93 urban settlements and 156 rural districts.

On 19 Sept. 1963 the Supreme Soviet of the USSR confirmed decisions of the Supreme Soviets of Kazakhstan and Uzbekistan, transferring over 40,000 sq. km from the former to the latter to ensure more efficient use of the 'Hungry Steppe'.

CONSTITUTION AND GOVERNMENT. The Supreme Soviet, elected in 1985, consists of 510 deputies (1 per 15,000 population); 183 are women, 346 Communists. A new Constitution was adopted in April 1978.

At elections to the regional, district, urban and rural Soviets (20 June 1982), of 102,699 deputies returned, 50,883 (49·5%) were women, 58,248 (56·7%) non-Party and 71,026 (69·2%) industrial workers and collective farmers.

President, Presidium of the Supreme Soviet: Au. Salimov.
Chairman, Council of Ministers: G. Kh. Kadyrov.
First Secretary, Communist Party: I. B. Usmankhodjayev.

FINANCE. Budget estimates (in 1m. rubles), 1985, 7,780; 1984, 7,256.

AGRICULTURE. Uzbekistan is a land of intensive farming, based on artificial irrigation. It is the chief cotton-growing area in the USSR and the third in the world. About 3·7m. hectares of collective and state farmland have irrigation networks, totalling over 150,000 km in length, and all are in full use.

In 1939 the Ferghana Canal (270 km) was built. During 1940, among the irrigation canals completed were: the North Ferghana Canal (165 km), and Andreyev South Ferghana Canal (108 km) and the first section of the Tashkent Canal (63 km). A canal from the Amu-Darya to Bokhara across the Kzyl-Kum and Ust-Urt deserts (180 km) was completed in 1965. A 200-km canal joining the river Zeravshan with the Kashka Darya at the village of Paruz was completed in Aug. 1955; it is part of the Iski–Angara Canal. The first section (93 km) of a canal irrigating the southern 'Hungry Steppe' was opened in 1960; 500,000 hectares of this desert were under cultivation in 1967.

Agriculture flourishes, particularly in the well-watered, warm, rich oases areas, such as the Ferghana valley, Zeravshan, Tashkent and Khorezm, where cotton, fruit, silk and rice are cultivated. In the higher-lying plains grain is grown; the wide desert and semi-desert area of Western Uzbekistan is mainly given to pasture land and the breeding of the Karakul sheep; there is a Karakul institute at Samarkand.

Orchards occupied 213,000 hectares and the vineyards 118,000 hectares in 1982. The Central Asian Branch of the Scientific Research Institute of Viticulture in Tashkent has produced new frost resistant grapes by crossing the wild Amur grape with Central Asian and European types. In 1983 there were 854 collective farms and 1,099 state farms, with 163,400 tractors and 10,400 cotton picking and grain combines. Ploughing, cotton-sowing and cultivation are completely mechanized; cotton picking over 46%.

Uzbekistan provides 65% of the total cotton, 50% of the total rice and 60% of the total lucerne grown in the USSR. The area under crops was 2,189,000 hectares in 1913, 3,036,000 hectares in 1940 and 4·1m. hectares in 1982.

Livestock on 1 Jan. 1983: 3·8m. cattle, 9·5m. sheep and goats and 694,400 pigs.

Output of main agricultural products (in 1,000 tonnes) in 1982 (1913 figures in tons in brackets). Meat (slaughter weight), 378 (89), milk, 2,448 (231), eggs, 1,717m. (87m.); wool, 23·5 (5·3); cotton, 6,003 (517); potatoes, 336 (46); vegetables, 2,537; fruit, 844; grapes, 548; wool, 24·5 (5·3).

Afforestation over an area of 50,000 hectares has been carried out to protect the Bokhara and Karakul oases from the advancing Kzyl-Kum sands and to stop the sand-drifts in a number of districts of Central Ferghana.

INDUSTRY. Of its mineral resources, in addition to oil and coal, copper and building materials and ozocerite deposits are now also exploited. New very rich coal deposits were discovered in 1944 and 1947 near Tashkent.

There are over 1,600 factories and mills. They include a factory of agricultural machinery (in Tashkent), a cement factory, a sulphur-mine, an oxygen factory, a paper-mill, a leather factory, textile-mills, clothing factories, iron and steel works, the Chirchik electro-chemical plant, a superphosphate plant in Kokand and oil refineries, coalmines, etc. Output in 1982 included 24,500 tractors, 102,000 refrigerators, 1·7m. tonnes cotton fibre, 127·7m. linear metres silk fabrics, 31·5m. pairs leather footwear, 751m. cans of preserves, 49·3m. pairs hosiery. Gold is being worked at Muruntau, Chadak and Kochbulak.

The Tashkent power station (2m. kw.) was completed in 1971. Power output in 1982 was 39,000m. kwh. (481m. kwh. in 1940). Two natural-gas pipelines (Djaikak–Tashkent, Ferghana–Kokand) and a third from Bokhara to the Urals are operating. Natural gas output (1976) was 36,100m. cu. metres.

In 1982 there were 4,556,000 industrial and office workers in the national economy.

COMMUNICATIONS. The total length of railway in 1983 was 3,480 km. Branches lead to Karshe-Kitab, Kerki-Termez, Jalal-Abad, Namangan, Andijan and other centres. In 1947–55 a new line was built from Chardzhou to Kungrad.

The Great Uzbek Highway was completed in April 1941. Total length of motor roads in 1983 was 69,500 km (hard surface, 58,200 km). Inland waterways, 1,100 km.

An airline, serving all of Central Asia, is most developed in Uzbekistan.

Newspapers (1982). There were 192 newspapers in the Uzbek language out of a total of 287. Daily circulation of Uzbek-language newspapers, 3·8m., other languages, 1·3m.

EDUCATION. In 1982–83 there were 9,400 elementary and secondary schools with 4·2m. pupils, 43 higher educational establishments with 288,800 students and 236 technical colleges with 251,500 students. Uzbekistan has an Academy of Sciences with 30 institutions and 3,950 academic staff; there were 188 research institutes with a scientific staff of 36,600 in Jan. 1983. There are universities and medical schools in Tashkent and Samarkand. In Jan. 1983, 1,026,000 children were attending pre-school institutions.

The Uzbek Arabic script was in 1929 replaced by the Latin alphabet which in 1940 was superseded by one based on the Cyrillic alphabet.

HEALTH. In 1982 there were 52,300 doctors and 199,900 hospital beds.

Book of Reference

Istoriya Uzbekskoi SSR. 4 vols. Tashkent, 1967–68

KARA-KALPAK AUTONOMOUS SOVIET SOCIALIST REPUBLIC

Area, 164,900 sq. km (63,920 sq. miles); population (Jan. 1984), 1,044,000. Capital, Nukus (127,000). The Karakalpaks are first mentioned in written records in the 16th century as tributary to Bokhara, and later to the Kazakh Khanate. In the second half of the 19th century, as a result of the Russian conquest of Central Asia, they came under Russian rule. On 11 May 1925 the territory was constituted within the then Kazakh Autonomous Republic (of the Russian Federation) as an Autonomous Region. On 20 March 1932 it became an Autonomous Republic within the Russian Federation, and on 5 Dec. 1936 it became part of the Uzbek SSR. Census (1979) Karakalpaks were 31·1% of population, Uzbeks, 31·5% and Kazakhs, 26·9%.

185 deputies were elected to its Supreme Soviet on 20 Feb. 1980, of whom 68 were women and 118 Communists.

Its manufactures are in the field of light industry—bricks, leather goods, furniture, canning, wine. Output of cotton fibre in 1982 was 118,900 tonnes; cattle numbered 315,000 and sheep and goats, 615,100, in Jan. 1983. There were 39 collective and 119 state farms. The total cultivated area in 1983 was 350,400 hectares.

In 1982–83 there were 278,800 pupils at schools, 32,283 at technical colleges, and 6,169 at university. There is a branch of the Uzbek Academy of Sciences with 190 scientific staff.

There were 2,200 doctors and 11,100 hospital beds.

TADZHIKISTAN

Respublikai Sovieth Sotsialistii Tojikiston

HISTORY. The Tadzhik Soviet Socialist Republic was formed from those regions of Bokhara and Turkestan where the population consisted mainly of Tadzhiks. It was admitted as a constituent republic of the Soviet Union on 5 Dec. 1929.

AREA AND POPULATION. Tadzhikistan is situated between 39° 40′ and

36° 40′ N. lat. and 67° 20′ and 75° E. long., north of the Oxus (Amu-Darya). On the west and north it is bordered by Uzbekistan and by the Kirghiz Soviet Socialist Republic; on the east by Chinese Turkestan and on the south by Afghánistán. It includes three regions (Leninabad, Kurgan-Tyube and Kulyab) and 43 rural districts, 18 towns and 49 urban settlements, together with the Gorno-Badakhshan Autonomous Region. Its highest mountains are Communism Peak (7,495 metres) and Lenin Peak (7,127 metres). Even the lowest valleys in the Pamirs are not below 3,500 metres above sea-level. The huge mountain glaciers are the source of many rapid rivers—the tributaries of the Amu-Darya, which flows from east to west along the southern border of Tadzhikistan. About 58·8% of the population are Tadzhiks. They speak an Iranian dialect, little different from Persian, and they are considered to be the descendants of the original Aryan population of Turkestan. Unlike the Persians, the Tadzhiks are mostly Sunnis. Of the rest, 22·9% are Uzbeks living in the north-west of the republic. Russians and Ukrainians number 10·4% (1979 census).

The area of the territory is 143,100 sq. km (55,240 sq. miles). Population (Jan. 1984), 4,365,000. The capital is Dushanbe. Other large towns are Leninabad (143,000), Kurgan-Tyube, Kulyab.

CONSTITUTION AND GOVERNMENT. The Supreme Soviet, elected in 1985, consists of 350 deputies (1 per 5,000 population); 126 are women and 238 Communists. A new Constitution was adopted in April 1978.

At elections to the district, urban and rural Soviets and the regional Soviet of Gorno-Badakhshan (20 June 1982), out of 26,627 deputies returned 13,216 (49·6%) were women, 15,227 (57·2%) non-Party and 18,677 (70·1%) industrial workers and collective farmers.

Chairman, Presidium of the Supreme Soviet: G. Pallaev.
Chairman, Council of Ministers: K. N. Makhkamov.
First Secretary, Communist Party: R. Nabiyev.

FINANCE. Budget estimates (in 1m. rubles), 1985, 1,626; 1984, 1,512.

AGRICULTURE. The occupations of the population are mainly farming, horticulture and cattle breeding. Area under crops in 1982 was 766,400 hectares (1913, 494,000; 1940, 807,000). Wine production in 1982 was 5·4m. decalitres.

There are 43,000 km of irrigation canals: the irrigation networks cover about 634,000 hectares of land.

Tadzhikistan grows many varieties of fruit, including apricots, figs, olives, pomegranates, a local variety of lemons and oranges, and in the south sugar-cane has been grown. Even on the highest mountain plateaux of the Pamirs, 'the roof of the world', the biological station of Tadzhikistan (3,860 metres above sea-level) has succeeded in raising crops of 60 varieties of barley, 10 varieties of oats, 4 of wheat, as well as vegetables. Eucalyptus and geranium are grown for the perfumery industry. Jute, rice and millet are also grown.

Tadzhikistan contains rich pasture lands, and cattle breeding is a very important branch of its agriculture. Livestock on 1 Jan. 1983: 1·3m. cattle, 3·1m. sheep and goats and 164,700 pigs.

The Gissar sheep is famous in the south for its meat and fat; the Karakul sheep is widely bred for its wool.

There were 159 collective farms (all with electric power) and 279 state farms in 1983, with 32,900 tractors and 1,200 cotton and grain combine harvesters.

Output of main agricultural products (in 1,000 tonnes) in 1982 (1913 figures in tons in brackets): Meat (slaughter weight), 101·3 (48); milk, 510·6 (102); eggs, 382·9m. (20m.); wool, 5 (2·1); cotton, 908 (32); potatoes, 160 (10); vegetables, 414; fruit, 238; grapes, 177.

INDUSTRY. The original small-scale handicraft industries have been replaced by big industrial enterprises, including mining, engineering, food, textile, clothing and silk factories.

There are rich deposits of brown coal, lead, zinc and oil (in the north of the republic), rare elements, such as uranium, radium, arsenic and bismuth. Asbestos, mica, corundum and emery, lapis lazuli, potassium salts, sulphur and other minerals have been found in other parts of the republic.

Industrial output in 1982 included 411,000 tonnes mineral fertilizer, 132,700 refrigerators, 999,000 cu. metres ferroconcrete, 309m. bricks, 294,600 tonnes cotton fibre, 10·9m. square metres carpet, 7·9m. pairs leather footwear.

There are 80 big electrical stations. The hydro-electric Varzob station began to operate in 1954, that at Kairak-Kum on the Syr Darya River was completed in 1957 and 2 more at Murgab in 1964. Output in 1982 was 12,000m. kwh. (in 1940, 62m. kwh.).

Construction of an electro-chemical combine, the largest in the USSR, has begun in the Yavan steppe in south Tadzhikistan, and the 3·2m. kw. power station in the upper reaches of the Vakhsh River was near completion in 1979.

In 1982 there were 1,003,000 industrial and office workers in the national economy.

COMMUNICATIONS

Roads. In Jan. 1983 there were 17,800 km of motor roads. Of these, 14,600 km are hard surface, including the Osh–Khorog (700 km), Yasui–Bazar–Charm (107 km) and Dushanbe–Khorog in the Pamirs (557 km) roads.

Railways. A railway line between Termez and Dushanbe (258 km) connects the republic with the railway system of the USSR. The mountainous nature of the republic makes ordinary railway construction difficult; accordingly 345 km of narrow gauge railways have been constructed (Kurgan–Tyube–Piandzh and Dushanbe–Kurgan–Tyube, connecting Dushanbe with the cotton-growing Vakhsh valley are particularly important). Length of railways, 1983, 470 km.

Aviation. Dushanbe is connected by air with Moscow, Tashkent, Baku and the regional and district centres of the republic.

Shipping. A steamship line on the Amu-Darya runs between Termez, Sarava and Jilikulam on the river Vakhsh (200 km).

Newspapers (1982). There were 67 newspapers, 58 in Tadzhik. Daily circulation of Tadzhik-language newspapers, 978,000; other languages, 346,000.

EDUCATION. In 1982–83 there were 3,100 primary and secondary schools with 1·1m. pupils, 10 higher educational institutions with 57,900 students and 38 technical colleges with 39,200 students; the Tadzhik state university had 12,467 students. In Jan. 1983, 116,000 children were attending pre-school institutions. In 1951 an Academy of Sciences was established; it has 17 institutions, the scientific staff of which numbers 1,324; there are 61 research institutions in all, with 8,000 scientific personnel in Jan. 1983. The Pamir research station is the highest altitude meteorological observatory in the world.

In 1940 a new alphabet based on Cyrillic was introduced.

HEALTH. There are 277 hospitals as well as maternity homes, clinics and special institutes to combat tropical diseases. There were 10,600 doctors in 1982 and 42,800 hospital beds.

GORNO-BADAKHSHAN AUTONOMOUS REGION

Comprising the Pamir massif along the borders of Afghánistán and China, the region was set up on 2 Jan. 1925. Area, 63,700 sq. km (24,590 sq. miles); population (Jan. 1984), 143,000 (83% Tadjiks, 11% Kirghiz). Capital, Khorog (14,800).

Mining industries are developed (gold, rock-crystal, mica, coal, salt). Wheat, fruit and fodder crops are grown and cattle and sheep are bred in the western parts.

In 1983 there were 71,300 cattle, 347,500 sheep and goats. Total area under cultivation, 18,400 hectares.

In 1981–82 42,900 pupils were attending 266 schools.

Books of Reference

Academy of Science of Tadzhikistan, *Istoriya Tadzhikskogo Naroda.* 3 vols. Moscow, 1963–65
Chumichev, D. A., *Tadzhikskaya SSR.* Moscow, 1954
Luknitsky, P., *Soviet Tajikistan* [In English]. Moscow, 1954

KIRGHIZIA

Kyrgyz Sovietik Sotsialistik Respublikasy

HISTORY. After the establishment of the Soviet regime in Russia, Kirghizia became part of Soviet Turkestan, which itself became an Autonomous Soviet Socialist Republic within the RSFSR in April 1921. In 1924, when Central Asia was reorganized territorially on a national basis, Kirghizia was separated from Turkestan and formed into an autonomous region within the RSFSR. On 1 Feb. 1926 the Government of the RSFSR transformed Kirghizia into an Autonomous Soviet Socialist Republic within the RSFSR, and finally in Dec. 1936 Kirghizia was proclaimed one of the constituent Soviet Socialist Republics of the USSR.

AREA AND POPULATION. The territory of Kirghizia covers 198,500 sq. km (76,460 sq. miles), and its population in Jan. 1984 was 3,886,000. The republic comprises 3 regions: Issyk-Kul, Naryn and Osh. There are 18 towns, 31 urban settlements and 40 rural districts. Its capital is Frunze (formerly Pishpek). Other large towns are Osh (188,000), Przhevalsk (56,000), Kyzyl-Kiya, Tokmak.

Kirghizia is situated on the Tien-Shan mountains and bordered on the east by China, on the west by Kazakhstan and Uzbekistan, on the north by Kazakhstan and in the south by Tadzhikistan. The Kirghizians are of Turkic origin and form 47·9% (1979 census) of the population; the rest are Russians (25·9%), Ukrainians (3·1%), Uzbeks (12·1%) and Tatars (2%).

CONSTITUTION AND GOVERNMENT. The Supreme Soviet, elected in 1985, consists of 350 deputies (1 per 5,000 population); 127 are women, 235 Communists. A new Constitution was adopted in April 1978.

At elections to the regional, district, urban and rural Soviets (20 June 1982), of the 27,875 deputies returned, 13,966 (50·1%) were women, 15,671 non-Party and 19,314 (69·3%) industrial workers and collective farmers.

Chairman, Presidium of the Supreme Soviet: T. Kh. Koshoev.
Chairman, Council of Ministers: A. Duisheev.
First Secretary, Communist Party: T. U. Usubaliev.

FINANCE. Budget estimates (in 1m. rubles), 1985, 1,944; 1984, 1,789.

AGRICULTURE. Kirghizia is famed for its livestock breeding. On 1 Jan. 1983 there were 1,013,600 cattle, 309,300 pigs, 10·2m. sheep and goats. Yaks are bred as meat and dairy cattle, and graze on high altitudes unsuitable for other cattle. Crossed with domestic cattle, hybrids are produced much heavier than ordinary Kirghiz cattle and giving twice the yield of milk. The Kirghizian horse is famed for its endurance, but it is of small stature; it has in recent years been crossed with Don, Arab and other breeds.

On 1 Jan. 1983 there were 180 collective and 252 state farms. Area under crops (1983), 1·2m. hectares (1913, 640,000; 1940, 1,056,000). There were 27,400 tractors and 4,900 grain combine harvesters in 1983; nearly all collective and state farms received electric power.

Kirghizia raises wheat sufficient for its own use and other grains and fodder, particularly lucerne; also sugar-beet, hemp, kenaf, kendyr, tobacco, medicinal plants and rice. Sericulture, fruit, grapes and vegetables and bee-keeping are major branches of Kirghiz agriculture. Agriculture is highly mechanized; nearly all the area under crops is worked by tractors. In 1983 irrigation networks in collective and state farms covered 974,000 hectares; practically all were in use. A canal in the western Tien-Shan ranges and a reservoir in the Urto-Tokoi mountains are being constructed.

The health resorts of Jety-Oguz (7,200 ft) and Jalal-Abad are famous for their mild alpine climate and mineral springs.

Output of main agricultural products (in 1,000 tonnes) in 1982 (1913 figures in tons in brackets): Meat (slaughter weight), 167 (39); milk, 693 (91); eggs, 428·1m. (19m.); wool, 35·3 (4·7); cotton, 78 (28); sugar-beet, 204 (0); potatoes, 336 (19); vegetables, 368; fruit, 196; grapes, 71.

INDUSTRY. Kirghizia contains over 500 large modern industrial enterprises including sugar refineries, tanneries, cotton and wool-cleansing works, flour-mills, a tobacco factory, food, timber, textile, engineering, metallurgical, oil and mining enterprises.

Production in 1982 included 360·3m. electric lamps, 22,300 lorries, 182,400 washing machines, 911,300 cu. metres ferroconcrete, 13·8m. pairs hosiery, 9·8m. pairs lether footwear, 41,300 tonnes cotton fibre.

Hydro-electric power stations are being built in the Central Tien-Shans and the cotton-growing districts in the Osh Region, the Chui valley and on the shore of Lake Issyk-Kul. Power output (1982) was 11,400m. kwh.

There were, in 1982, 1,161,000 industrial and office workers in the national economy.

COMMUNICATIONS. In the north a railway runs from Lugovaya through Frunze to Rybachi on Lake Issyk-Kul. Towns in the southern valleys are linked by short lines with the Ursatyevskaya–Andizhan railway in Uzbekistan. Total length of railway (Jan. 1983) is 370 km. Most of the traffic is by road; there were 27,600 km of motor roads (19,100 hard surface) in 1983. A road tunnel through the Tien-Shan mountains at an altitude of 9,600 ft, connecting Frunze and Osh, is being constructed. Inland waterways, 600 km. Airlines link Frunze with Moscow and Tashkent.

Newspapers (1982). Of 108 newspapers with a daily 1·2m. circulation, 61 with 757,000 circulation are in the Kirghiz language.

EDUCATION. Kirghizia had 1,700 primary and secondary schools with 900,000 pupils in 1982–83; 159,000 children were attending pre-school institutions. There were also 10 higher educational institutions with 58,900 students, 42 technical and teachers' training colleges with 50,600 students, as well as music and art schools. The Kirghizian Academy of Sciences was established in 1954. In 1983 there were 65 research institutes, 18 of them, with 1,517 scientific staff, operating under its auspices; the others have scientist staffs of 6,983. A university was opened in 1951. It has 13,370 students, 6,268 full-time, 1,054 evening and 6,048 correspondence students taking a full degree course. In Sept. 1940 a new alphabet, based on Cyrillic, was introduced.

HEALTH. In 1982 there were 11,700 doctors and 45,700 hospital beds.

Books of Reference

Istoriya Kirgizskoi SSR. 5 vols. Frunze, 1983ff.
Ryazantsev, S. N., *Kirghizia.* Moscow, 1951

UNITED ARAB EMIRATES

Federal Capital: Abu Dhabi
Population: 1·18m. (1983)
GNP per capita: US$24,660 (1981)

HISTORY. From Sha'am, 35 miles south-west of Ras Musam dam, for nearly 400 miles to Khor al Odeid at the south-eastern end of the peninsula of Qatar, the coast, formerly known as the Trucial Coast, of the Gulf (together with 50 miles of the coast of the Gulf of Oman) belongs to the rulers of the 7 Trucial States. In 1820 these rulers signed a treaty prescribing peace with the British Government. This treaty was followed by further agreements providing for the suppression of the slave trade and by a series of other engagements, of which the most important are the Perpetual Maritime Truce (May 1853) and the Exclusive Agreement (March 1892). Under the latter, the sheikhs, on behalf of themselves, their heirs and successors, undertook that they would on no account enter into any agreement or correspondence with any power other than the British Government, receive foreign agents, cede, sell or give for occupation any part of their territory save to the British Government.

British forces withdrew from the Gulf at the end of 1971 and the treaties whereby Britain had been responsible for the defence and foreign relations of the Trucial States were terminated, being replaced on 2 Dec. 1971 by a treaty of friendship between Britain and the United Arab Emirates. The United Arab Emirates (formed 2 Dec. 1971) consists of the former Trucial States: Abu Dhabi, Dubai, Sharjah, Ajman, Umm al Qawain, Ras al Khaimah (joined in Feb. 1972) and Fujairah. The small state of Kalba was merged with Sharjah in 1952.

AREA AND POPULATION. The Emirates are bounded north by the Persian Gulf, east by Oman, south and west by Saudi Arabia, north-west by Qatar. The area of these states is approximately 32,300 sq. miles (92,100 sq. km). The total population at census (1980), 1,040,275 (717,475 male). Estimate (1982) 1,175,000. About one tenth are nomads.

Population, 1980 census (1982, estimate): Abu Dhabi, 449,000 (516,000), Ajman, 36,100 (42,000); Dubai, 278,000 (296,000); Fujairah, 32,200 (38,000); Ras al Khaimah, 73,700 (83,000); Sharjah, 159,000 (184,000); Umm al Qawain, 12,300 (14,000).

The chief cities (1980 census) are Dubai (265,702), Abu Dhabi, the federal capital (242,975), Sharjah (125,149) and Al-Ain (101,663).

CLIMATE. The country experiences desert conditions, with rainfall both limited and erratic. The period May to Nov. is generally rainless, while the wettest months are Feb. and March. Temperatures are very high in the summer months. Dubai. Jan. 74°F (23·4°C), July 108°F (42·3°C). Annual rainfall 2·4" (60 mm). Sharjah. Jan. 64°F (17·8°C), July 91°F (32°C). Annual rainfall 4·2" (105 mm).

GOVERNMENT. The Emirates are a federation, headed by a Supreme Council which is composed of the 7 rulers and which in turn appoints a Council of Ministers. The Council of Ministers drafts legislation and a federal budget; its proposals are submitted to a federal National Council of 40 elected members which may propose amendments but has no executive power.

President: HH Sheikh Zayed bin Sultan al Nahyan, Ruler of Abu Dhabi.

Members of the Supreme Council of Rulers:

HH Sheikh Rashid bin Saeed al-Maktoum, Vice-President and Ruler of Dubai.
HH Sheikh Sultan bin Mohammed al-Qasimi, Ruler of Sharjah.
HH Sheikh Saqr bin Mohammed al-Qasimi, Ruler of Ras al Khaimah.
HH Sheikh Rashid bin Ahmed al-Mualla, Ruler of Umm al Qaiwain.
HH Sheikh Hamad bin Mohammed al Sharqi, Ruler of Fujairah.

HH Sheikh Humaid Rashid bin al-Nuaimi, Ruler of Ajman.

The Council of Ministers in Jan. 1985 was:

Prime Minister: H.H. Sheikh Rashid bin Said al-Maktoum.

Deputy Prime Ministers: Sheikh Maktoum bin Rashid al-Maktoum; Sheikh Hamdan bin Muhammad al-Nahayan.

Interior: Sheikh Mubarak bin Muhammad al-Nahayan. *Finance and Industry:* Sheikh Hamdan bin Rashid al-Maktoum. *Defence:* Sheikh Mohammed bin Rashid al-Maktoum. *Economy and Trade:* Saif al-Jarwan. *Information and Culture:* Sheikh Ahmed bin Hamed. *Communications:* Muhammad Saeed al-Mualla. *Public Works and Housing:* Muhammad Khalifa al-Kindi. *Education and Youth:* Faraj al-Mazroui. *Petroleum and Mineral Resources:* Dr Mana Said al-Oteiba. *Electricity and Water:* Hamaid Nasser al-Owais. *Justice:* Abdullah Hamid al-Mazroui. *Health:* Hamad Abdul Rahman al-Madfa. *Labour and Social Affairs:* Khalean Muhammad al-Roumi. *Planning:* Sheikh Humaid al-Mualla. *Agriculture and Fisheries:* Saeed al-Raghbani. *Minister of State for Internal Affairs:* Hamouda bin Ali Dhairi. *Minister of State for Foreign Affairs:* Rashid Abdulla Nuaimi. *Minister of State for Cabinet Affairs:* Said al-Ghaith. *Minister of State for Supreme Council Affairs:* Sheikh Abdel Aziz bin Humaid al-Qasimi. *Islamic Affairs and AWQAF:* Sheikh Muhammad bin Hassan al-Khazraji. *Minister of State for Finance and Industry:* Ahmad Hamid al-Tayer. *Without Portfolio:* Shaikh Ahmad bin Sultan al-Qasimi.

National flag: Three horizontal stripes of green, white, black, with a vertical red strip in the hoist.

DEFENCE

Army. The Army consists of 1 Royal Guard brigade, 5 armoured, 9 infantry, 3 artillery and 3 air defence battalions. Equipment includes 100 AMX-30 and 18 Lion OF-40 Mk 1 main battle tanks. The strength was (1985) 46,000.

Navy. The naval flotilla includes 6 new German-built missile armed fast attack craft, 9 British-built patrol craft, 1 maintenance craft and 2 tenders. Personnel in 1985 numbered 1,200 officers and ratings.

The Coast Guard flotilla comprises 13 armed coastal patrol craft, 16 armed small patrol cutters, 26 light launches, 1 amphibious craft, 2 diving tenders, 1 water carrier and 5 tugs.

Air Force. Formation of an air wing in Abu Dhabi, to support land forces, began in 1968 with the purchase of some light STOL transports and helicopters. Expansion has been rapid. Current equipment includes 25 Mirage 5 supersonic fighter-bombers, 3 Mirage 5R tactical reconnaissance aircraft and 2 Mirage 5D 2-seat trainers (to be replaced by Mirage 2000s, with delivery of first 18 to begin in 1986); 4 C-130 Hercules and 4 Buffalo turboprop transports; 4 CASA C-212 Aviocar ECM/elint aircraft; about 40 Gazelle, Alouette III, Puma, Super Puma and Agusta-Bell 205 helicopters; 14 PC-7 Turbo-Trainers and 6 Alpha Jets. On order are 16 Hawk light attack/trainers. Initial personnel were mostly British but considerable assistance is now being received from Arab countries and from Pakistan. The air wing became the Air Force of Abu Dhabi in 1972, in which year 3 JetRanger helicopters were transferred to the air wing of the Union Defence Force, since combined with the Dubai Police Air Wing to form a single component of the United Emirates Air Force. Current equipment of the Dubai Air Wing of the UEAF, bought mainly in Italy, comprises 6 Aermacchi MB 326K jet light attack aircraft, 1 Aeritalia G222 twin-turboprop transport, 1 piston-engined SF.260W armed basic trainer, 5 SF.260TP turboprop trainers, and 2 MB 326L jet trainers, 4 Bell 205A-1, 3 Bell 212 and 6 JetRanger helicopters and 1 Cessna 182 liaison aircraft, plus 2 L-100-30 Hercules transports and a Boeing 720B and a variety of other types for VIP use. Eight Hawks are on order.

INTERNATIONAL RELATIONS

Membership. The UAE is a member of UN and of the Arab League.

ECONOMY

Planning. The first 5-year plan (1981-85) envisages expenditure of UD 13,000m.

Budget. Revenue is principally derived from oil-concession payments. The federal budget (1984) was DH 17,239m.

Currency. The UAE issued its own currency in 1972 based on the *dirham*. 1 UAE *dirham* = 10 *dinar* = 1,000 *fils*. There are notes of 1, 5, 10, 50, 100 and 1,000 *dirham* and coins of 1, 5, 10, 25, 50 and 100 *fils*. Rate of exchange, March 1985: £1 = 3·94 *dirham*; US$1 = 3·68 *dirham*.

Banking. The British Bank of the Middle East has branches in Dubai, Abu Dhabi, Sharjah, Fujairah, Ajman and Ras al Khaimah; the Chartered Bank has branches in Dubai, Sharjah, Abu Dhabi and Al Ain; the National & Grindlays Bank (Ottoman Branch) has branches in Abu Dhabi and Sharjah. The Arab Bank has branches in Ajman, Ras al Khaimah, Sharjah, Abu Dhabi and Dubai; the Citibank has branches in Dubai, Sharjah and Abu Dhabi; the Habib Bank of Pakistan has branches in Abu Dhabi, Dubai and Sharjah and the United Bank Ltd of Pakistan branches in Dubai, Sharjah, Abu Dhabi and Al Ain. Barclays Bank International has branches in Abu Dhabi, Dubai, Ras Al Khaimah and Sharjah. There is also the National Bank of Dubai, formed in 1963 which has a branch in Abu Dhabi and Umm al Qaiwain, and the Bank of Oman Ltd, formed in 1967, which has branches in Ajman, Abu Dhabi and Dubai. The Commercial Bank opened in Dubai in 1969. The Bank Sadarat of Iran has branches in Abu Dhabi, Dubai and Sharjah. The National Bank of Fujeirah opened in 1984. The National Bank of Abu Dhabi, formed in 1967, has its head office in Abu Dhabi and a branch office in Dubai.

ENERGY AND NATURAL RESOURCES

Oil. Total production (1983) 75,011,263 bbls. Reserves (1984) 32,400m. bbls.

Abu Dhabi. Until the end of 1972 production was in the hands of 2 major companies, the Abu Dhabi Petroleum Co. and the Abu Dhabi Marine Area. The Government has acquired a 60% interest in both companies. Ownership in 1976 was as follows: *ADPC*, 60% Government; 9·5% BP; 9·5% Shell; 9·5% CFP; 4·75% Mobil; 2% Partex. *ADMA*, 60% Government; 26·7% BP/Japan Oil Development Co.; 13·3% CFP. A Japanese company, Abu Dhabi Oil Co. (ADOCO) began production from its Mubarraz field in 1973. There are other companies which have concessions in the State: Japan's Middle East Oil; a US consortium led by Pan Ocean Oil and Sunningdale Oils of Canada. A State Petroleum Co., the Abu Dhabi National Oil Co. (ADNOC), was formed in 1971 and began to set up its own tanker fleet known as the Abu Dhabi National Tankers Co. (ADNATCO). At the end of 1972 Abu Dhabi signed a participation agreement which would have given it an immediate 25% interest in the companies, rising to 51% by 1982. Oil production, 1983, 750,000 bbls.

Dubai. In July 1975 Dubai decided to take full control of all foreign oil and gas operations in the State. The companies were to remain however. A Dubai producing group was set up to comprise the foreign interests–US and continental companies. Dubai Petroleum Co. (DPC–a subsidiary of Continental Oil) has a 30% interest in this group; the other members are Dubai Marine Areas (*Compagnie Française des Pétroles*) with 50%; Deutsche Texaco with 10%; Dubai Sun Oil 5%; and Delfzee Dubai Petroleum (Wintershall) 5%. Oil production, 1983, 330,000 bbls.

Sharjah. In Sharjah the concession is given to Crescent Oil, its shareholders are: Ashland Oil, Skelly Oil, Kerr-McGee, Cities Services and Juniper. Other oil concessions have recently been given to the Crystal Oil Co. of USA and the Reserves Oil and Gas Co. Oil production, 1983, 10,000 bbls.

Ajman. An oil concession was awarded to United Refining in 1971.

Umm al Qawain. The concession here was given to US Occidental Petroleum; another was awarded to a consortium led by the US company United Refinery.

Ras al Khaimah. The Dutch oil firm Vitol took over Union's concession in 1973. Shell began prospecting in 1969 but pulled out in 1971. A concession in the same area was awarded to Peninsula Petroleum, a subsidiary of the US California Time Group, in 1973.

Gas. Abu Dhabi has reserves of natural gas, nationalized in 1976. The Abu Dhabi Gas Liquefaction Plant at Das Island (51% ADNOC) has a capacity of 2m. tons LNG, 1m. tons LPG, 220,000 tons of light distillate and 230,000 tons of pelletized sulphur. Gas exports (1983) DH5,000m.

Agriculture. The fertile Buraimi Oasis, known as Al Ain, is largely in Abu Dhabi territory, but owing to lack of water and good soil there is little agriculture in the rest of UAE. There are 15,000 hectares of cultivated land. However, since the establishment of an agricultural trials station and an agricultural school in Ras al Khaimah the number of gardens under cultivation has more than doubled and there have been remarkable increases in the variety of crops and the length of the agricultural season. An experimental agricultural farm exists in Al Ain which produces vegetables for Abu Dhabi.

Livestock (1983): Cattle, 30,000; camels, 70,000; sheep, 140,000; goats, 400,000.

Fisheries. The industry is still a major employer. Sharjah exports shrimps and prawns; a fishmeal plant is operating in Ras al Khaimah and plants are planned for Ajman and Sharjah.

INDUSTRY AND TRADE

Industry. Main industries in Abu Dhabi relate to the construction industry and to oil and gas extraction; there is also a steel rolling mill. Dubai has a cement factory of 500,000 tons annual capacity, and a dry dock. Twenty companies are now fully operational at the complex in Jebel Ali consisting of a liquefied petroleum gas plant. An aluminium smelter with power station and desalination plant was opened in Feb. 1979. Sharjah has a cement factory and various manufacturing estates. Ras al Khaimah also produces cement and crushed rock.

Commerce. Imports in 1983 for UAE were DH33,000m. Exports and re-exports (non-oil) totalled DH9,500m. Oil exports accounted for DH42,000m. and gas. DH5,000m.

Total trade between the UAE (excluding Abu Dhabi) and UK (British Department of Trade returns, in £1,000 sterling):

	1980	*1981*	*1982*	*1983*	*1984*
Imports to UK	239,519	118,697	82,706	107,574	60,550
Exports and re-exports from UK	287,615	245,388	286,079	254,862	296,948

Total trade between Abu Dhabi and UK (British Department of Trade returns, in £1,000 sterling):

	1980	*1981*	*1982*	*1983*	*1984*
Imports to UK	246,422	274,651	184,253	202,232	21,981
Exports and re-exports from UK	214,309	246,672	272,889	312,902	215,947

Tourism. In 1982 there were 9,836 rooms for tourists.

COMMUNICATIONS

Aviation. International airports at Dubai and Abu Dhabi are served by a large number of major airlines, as well as by Gulf Air partially owned by the Government of the UAE. Abu Dhabi's new airport opened and commenced operations in Jan. 1982. A new international airport was inaugurated at Sharjah in 1979. A Ras al Khaimah international airport was opened early in 1976 although it initially had only one scheduled service by Kuwait Airways. An airstrip exists at Al Ain, in the Buraimi Oasis, and in the oilfields, both onshore and offshore, on Das Island, while construction of a strip at Khor Fakkan is planned.

Abu Dhabi and Dubai are served by Alia, Air France, Air India, British Airways, Egyptair, Iran Air, Kuwait Airways, Middle East Airlines, PIA, KLM, Gulf Air,

Czechoslovak Airlines, Hungarian Airlines, Royal Nepal Airlines, Iberia, Turkish Airlines, Iraqi Airways, Olympic, SABENA, Saudia, Syrian Arab Airlines and TMA. Lufthansa and Singapore Airlines initiated scheduled flights to Dubai in mid-1976, while Sharjah is served by Gulf Air and TMA. A number of cargo airlines also fly regularly to the country's major airports. An air-taxi service, Emirates Air Services, flying between Abu Dhabi and Dubai, began in June 1976.

Shipping. In 1980 Port Rashid was enlarged to 37 berths. Abu Dhabi has dry docks and there are smaller ports at Sharjah and Ras al Khaimah. Jebel Ali is a port and industrial estate 35 km south-west of Dubai city and had (1982) 66 berths.

In 1976, the Government of the UAE joined with Qatar, Bahrain, Saudi Arabia, Kuwait and Iraq in forming the United Arab Shipping Co.

Post and Broadcasting. In 1982 there were 240,167 telephones, of which 71,344 were in Abu Dhabi and 82,158 in Dubai. In Sharjah a new telephone company has been formed and the other Northern States are now linked by telephone. The new Cable and Wireless Station at Jebel Ali in the State of Dubai links the system with the international communication network.

Television stations are at Abu Dhabi and Dubai, with extension of the service well advanced to the rest of the Emirates. Stations for The Voice of the United Arab Emirates began broadcasting in 1972 at Abu Dhabi, Dubai, Ras al Khaimah and Sharjah. Estimated radios (1976) 50,000 and television sets over 16,000.

Newspapers (1985). There are a number of daily and weekly publications mostly in Arabic, but some in English, notably *The Emirates News* of Abu Dhabi, *The Gulf News,* a daily, published in Dubai and the *Khaleej Times* (daily), also published in Dubai.

JUSTICE, RELIGION, EDUCATION AND WELFARE

Justice. UAE subjects and citizens of all Arab and Moslem states are subject to the jurisdiction of the local courts. In the local courts the rules of Islamic law prevail. A new code of law is being produced for Abu Dhabi. In Dubai there is a court run by a *qadi*, while in some of the other States all legal cases are referred immediately to the Ruler or a member of his family, who will refer to a *qadi* only if he cannot settle the matter himself. In Abu Dhabi a professional Jordanian judge presides over the Ruler's Court. The 95th article of the provisional Constitution of 1971 provided for the setting up of a Union Supreme Court and Union Primary Tribunals.

Religion. Nearly all the inhabitants are Moslem of the Sunni and Shi'ite sects.

Education (1982). Primary and secondary education for boys and girls is available in the UAE, and there are now 383 schools with over 113,000 pupils, with a further 379 planned. There are 4 junior colleges and 112 adult education centres, established to eliminate illiteracy. The education system is the same as that followed in Kuwait, and many of the teachers are supplied by the Kuwait, Qatar, Egypt, Jordan and Bahrain education departments. The oil companies in Abu Dhabi operate apprentice training schools and there is also a vocational training institute. A vocational training centre is under construction.

There are trade schools in Sharjah, Dubai and Ras al Khaimah. The UAE university had 3,500 students with 406 lecturers in 1981.

Health. A tuberculosis sanatorium is to be constructed by the State of Kuwait in Sharjah. In 1980 there were more than 20 hospitals (2,972 beds) and over 47 clinics. There were 1,202 doctors.

DIPLOMATIC REPRESENTATIVES

Of the UAE in Great Britain (30 Prince's Gate, London, SW7 1PT)
Ambassador: Mohamed Mahdi Al-Tajir (accredited 15 Nov. 1983).

Of Great Britain in the UAE
Ambassador: H. B. Walker, CMG (at the British Embassy, Abu Dhabi).

Of the UAE in the USA (600 New Hampshire Ave., NW, Washington, D.C., 20037)
Ambassador: Ahmed S. Al-Mokarrab.

Of the USA in the UAE (Al-Sudan St., Abu Dhabi)
Ambassador: George Quincy Lumsden, Jr.

Of the UAE to the United Nations
Ambassador: (Vacant).

Books of Reference

Middle East Annual Review. London
United Arab Emirates: A Record of Achievement, 1979–1981. Ministry of Information and Culture. Abu Dhabi, 1981
Abdullah, M.M. *The UAE: A Modern History.* London and New York, 1978
Bey, F.H., *From Trucial States to United Arab Emirates.* London, 1982
Fenelon, K. G., *The United Arab Emirates: An Economic and Social Survey.* 2nd ed. London, 1973
Hawley, D. F., *Courtesies in the Trucial States.* 1965.—*The Trucial States.* London, 1971
Heard-Bay, F., *From Trucial States to United Arab Emirates.* London, 1982
Hopwood, D., *The Arabian Peninsula.* London, 1972
Izzard, M., *The Gulf,* 1980
Khalifa, A. M., *The U.A.E.: Energy Development.* London, 1980
Mallakh, R.S., *The Economic Development of the United Arab Emirates,* London, 1981
Mostyn, T., *UAE-A MEED Practical Guide.* London, 1982
Soffan, L. U., *Women of the United Arab Emirates.* London, 1980
Tomkinson, M., *The United Arab Emirates: An Insight and a Guide.* London and Hammamet, 1975
Zahlan, R. S., *The Origins of the United Arab Emirates.* London, 1978

UNITED KINGDOM OF GREAT BRITAIN AND NORTHERN IRELAND

Capital: London
Population: 55·78m. (1981)
GNP per capita: US$9,110 (1981)

'Great Britain' is a geographical term describing the main island of the British Isles which comprises England, Scotland and Wales (so called to distinguish it from 'Little Britain' or Brittany). By the Act of Union, 1801, Great Britain and Ireland formed a legislative union as the United Kingdom of Great Britain and Ireland. Since the separation of Great Britain and Ireland in 1921 Northern Ireland remained within the Union which is now the United Kingdom of Great Britain and Northern Ireland. The United Kingdom does not include the Channel Islands or the Isle of Man which are direct dependencies of the Crown with their own legislative and taxation systems.

GREAT BRITAIN

AREA AND POPULATION. Area (in sq. km) and population (present on census night) at the census taken 5 April 1981:

Divisions	*Area*	*Total*
England	130,357	46,362,836
Wales (incl. Monmouthshire)	20,761	2,791,851
Scotland	78,762	5,130,735
	229,880	54,285,422

Population at the 4 previous decennial censuses:

Divisions	*1931*	*1951*	*1961*	*1971*
England	37,359,045	41,159,213	43,460,525	46,019,000
Wales	2,158,374	2,598,675	2,644,023	2,731,000
Scotland	4,842,980	5,096,415	5,178,490	5,228,963
Army, Navy and Merchant Seamen abroad	434,532	—	—	—
Total	44,794,931	48,854,303	51,283,038	53,978,963

Population (usually resident) at the census of 1981:

Divisions	*Males*	*Females*	*Total*
England	22,288,395	23,483,561	45,771,956
Wales (incl. Monmouthshire)	1,336,323	1,413,317	2,749,640
Scotland	2,428,472	2,606,843	5,035,315
Great Britain	26,053,190	27,503,721	53,556,911

In 1981 in Wales and Monmouthshire 21,283 persons 3 years of age and upwards were able to speak Welsh only, and 482,276 able to speak Welsh and English (preliminary figures): these totals represent 19% of the total population. In Scotland in 1981, 79,307 of the usually resident population could speak Gaelic (1·3%); 3,113 could read or write Gaelic, but could not speak it.

At the census of 1981, in England and Wales, there were 17,706,492 private households; in Great Britain, 19,500,113.

The age distribution in 1981 of the 'usually resident' population of England and Wales and Scotland was as follows (in 1,000):

Age-group	*England and Wales*	*Scotland*	*Great Britain*
Under 5	2,910	308	3,219
5 and under 10	3,207	344	3,551
10 ,, 15	3,846	425	4,271
15 ,, 20	4,020	447	4,467
20 ,, 25	3,564	394	3,959
25 ,, 35	6,931	701	7,632
35 ,, 45	5,885	588	6,473
45 ,, 55	5,474	575	6,049
55 ,, 65	5,410	541	5,951
65 ,, 70	2,426	241	2,667
70 ,, 75	2,062	204	2,265
75 ,, 85	2,280	221	2,501
85 and upwards	507	46	552
Total	48,522	5,035	53,557

At 30 June 1983 the estimated population of Great Britain was 54,804,100. Age and sex distribution: between 0 and 15, 5,572,400 males, 5,282,200 females; 15 and under 65, 17,863,000 males; 15 and under 60, 16,220,300 females; aged 65 and over, 3·23m. males; 60 and over, 7·5m. females.

England and Wales: The census population, (present on census night) of England and Wales 1801 to 1981:

Date of enumeration	*Population*	*Pop. per sq. mile*	*Date of enumeration*	*Population*	*Pop. per sq. mile*[1]
1801	8,892,536	152	1891	29,002,525	497
1811	10,164,256	174	1901	32,527,843	558
1821	12,000,236	206	1911	36,070,492	618
1831	13,896,797	238	1921	37,886,699	649
1841	15,914,148	273	1931	39,952,377	685
1851	17,927,609	307	1951	43,757,888	750
1861	20,066,224	344	1961	46,104,548	791
1871	22,712,266	389	1971	48,749,575	323
1881	25,974,439	445	1981	49,154,687	325

[1] Per sq. km from 1971

There is only one other major country in Europe, Netherlands (population density 421 persons per sq. km), more crowded than England and Wales.

The birth places of the 1981 'usually resident' population were: England, 41,552,500; Wales, 2,758,026; Scotland, 752,188; Northern Ireland, 209,042; Ireland, 579,833; Commonwealth, 1,429,407; foreign countries, 1,209,091.

Local authority areas in being from April 1974. Area in sq. km and population estimate 30 June 1983:

ENGLAND *Metropolitan counties*	*Area sq. km*	*Population*
Greater London	1,580	6,754,500
Greater Manchester	1,286	2,598,500
Merseyside	652	1,500,800
South Yorkshire	1,560	1,310,500
Tyne and Wear	540	1,145,300
West Midlands	899	2,657,600
West Yorkshire	2,039	2,059,300
Non-metropolitan counties		
Avon	1,338	935,900
Bedfordshire	1,235	512,900
Berkshire	1,256	706,900
Buckinghamshire	1,883	580,100
Cambridgeshire	3,409	601,400
Cheshire	2,322	933,200
Cleveland	583	564,800
Cornwall and Isles of Scilly	3,546	432,200
Cumbria	6,809	483,000

Non-Metropolitan counties—contd.	*Area sq. km*	*Population*
Derbyshire	2,631	911,100
Devon	6,715	973,000
Dorset	2,654	609,100
Durham	2,436	606,800
East Sussex	1,795	673,800
Essex	3,674	1,491,700
Gloucestershire	2,638	506,100
Hampshire	3,772	1,499,400
Hereford and Worcester	3,927	640,400
Hertfordshire	1,634	975,400
Humberside	3,512	854,000
Isle of Wight	381	119,800
Kent	3,732	1,486,300
Lancashire	3,043	1,377,600
Leicestershire	2,553	863,700
Lincolnshire	5,885	554,300
Norfolk	5,355	711,300
Northamptonshire	2,367	538,500
Northumberland	5,033	300,200
North Yorkshire	8,317	684,700

Non-Metropolitan counties—contd.	*Area sq. km*	*Population*
Nottinghamshire	2,164	992,200
Oxfordshire	2,611	550,300
Shropshire	3,490	382,500
Somerset	3,458	435,700
Staffordshire	2,716	1,018,000
Suffolk	3,800	612,500
Surrey	1,655	1,011,800
Warwickshire	1,981	477,800
West Sussex	2,016	678,900
Wiltshire	3,481	532,100
Total		46,794,800

WALES	*Area sq. km*	*Population*
Clwyd	2,425	395,300
Dyfed	5,765	335,300
Gwent	1,376	439,900
Gwynedd	3,868	232,000
Mid-Glamorgan	1,019	536,400
Powys	5,077	110,600
South Glamorgan	416	391,700
West Glamorgan	815	366,600
Total Wales		2,807,800
Total—England and Wales		49,653,700

County districts with populations of over 90,000 (estimate, 30 June 1983):

ENGLAND	
Allerdale	95,400
Amber Valley	109,100
Arun	122,700
Ashfield	105,800
Aylesbury Vale	134,700
Barnsley	224,800
Basildon	156,300
Basingstoke and Deane	134,000
Bassetlaw	103,300
Beverley	107,300
Birmingham	1,012,900
Blackburn	142,200
Blackpool	146,400
Bolton	261,800
Bournemouth	145,100
Bradford	463,900
Braintree	113,800
Breckland	99,100
Brighton	148,300
Bristol	399,300
Broadland	98,900
Broxtowe	104,200
Burnley	92,200
Bury	174,800
Calderdale	192,000
Cambridge	100,400
Canterbury	123,800
Carlisle	101,200
Charnwood	141,300
Chelmsford	143,300
Cherwell	113,000
Chester	115,000
Chesterfield	96,900
Chichester	99,800
Chiltern	91,400
Chorley	91,500
Colchester	140,000
Coventry	315,900
Crewe and Nantwich	97,500
Dacorum	132,300
Darlington	99,700
Derby	214,900
Doncaster	289,800
Dover	102,800
Dudley	300,000
Easington	98,800
East Devon	108,400
East Hampshire	93,600
East Hertfordshire	113,700
Eastleigh	96,000
East Lindsey	106,700
East Staffordshire	95,300
Elmbridge	111,100
Epping Forest	114,900
Erewash	103,500
Exeter	101,800
Fareham	90,800
Gateshead	210,200
Gedling	104,900
Gillingham	94,100
Gloucester	92,200
Gravesham	95,600
Grimsby	92,400
Guildford	124,700
Halton	122,600
Harrogate	141,100
Hartlepool	93,400
Havant	116,600
Hinckley and Bosworth	90,400
Horsham	103,200
Huntingdon	127,800
Ipswich	120,200
King's Lynn and West Norfolk	122,900
Kingston upon Hull	269,100
Kirklees	377,300
Knowsley	170,800
Lancaster	126,800
Langbaurgh	149,400
Leeds	714,000
Leicester	282,300
Liverpool	502,500
Luton	165,600
Macclesfield	148,500
Maidstone	131,300
Manchester	457,500
Mansfield	99,600
Mendip	91,800
Mid-Bedfordshire	105,800
Middlesbrough	148,600
Mid-Sussex	118,900
Milton Keynes	138,000
Newark	104,500
Newbury	122,500
Newcastle under Lyme	119,100
Newcastle upon Tyne	281,200
New Forest	149,000
Northampton	164,100
Northavon	121,600
North Bedfordshire	132,500
North East Derbyshire	97,300
North Hertfordshire	109,600
North Tyneside	195,000
North Wiltshire	106,700

ENGLAND—*contd.*	
Norwich	126,100
Nottingham	277,100
Nuneaton and Bedworth	113,600
Oldham	220,900
Oxford	116,400
Peterborough	138,900
Plymouth	255,200
Poole	121,500
Portsmouth	191,600
Preston	125,200
Reading	138,500
Reigate and Banstead	116,700
Rochdale	206,400
Rochester upon Medway	146,200
Rotherham	253,200
Rushcliffe	92,800
St Albans	126,600
St Helens	189,200
Salford	245,000
Salisbury	102,500
Sandwell	307,300
Scarborough	102,100
Sedgefield	91,200
Sedgemoor	90,900
Sefton	299,800
Sevenoaks	111,200
Sheffield	542,700
Slough	98,600
Solihull	199,900
Southampton	206,300
South Bedfordshire	109,000
South Cambridgeshire	112,000
Southend on Sea	157,700
South Kesteven	98,800
South Lakeland	96,400
South Norfolk	97,100
South Oxfordshire	131,900
South Ribble	98,000
South Staffordshire	99,900
South Tyneside	159,500
Spelthorne	91,100
Stafford	116,300
Staffordshire Moorlands	95,500
Stockport	288,900
Stockton on Tees	173,400
Stoke on Trent	250,400
Stratford on Avon	101,900
Stroud	102,700
Suffolk Coastal	99,900
Sunderland	299,400

ENGLAND—*contd.*	
Swale	110,200
Tameside	216,300
Teignbridge	96,800
Tendring	116,600
Test Valley	95,500
Thamesdown	154,700
Thanet	121,400
Thurrock	125,300
Tonbridge and Malling	99,300
Torbay	113,100
Trafford	218,700
Tunbridge Wells	98,600
Vale of White Horse	105,100
Vale Royal	112,100
Wakefield	312,100
Walsall	265,300
Warrington	174,200
Warwick	115,600
Waveney	101,500
Waverley	112,700
Wealden	121,800
Welwyn Hatfield	94,200
West Lancashire	107,600
West Wiltshire	102,100
Wigan	308,200
Winchester	92,300
Windsor and Maidenhead	134,700
Wirral	338,500
Wokingham	124,400
Wolverhampton	255,400
Woodspring	166,600
Worthing	93,400
Wrekin	127,600
Wychavon	95,900
Wycombe	155,600
Wyre	98,400
Wyre Forest	91,900
Yeovil	135,200
York	102,700
WALES	
Cardiff	279,800
Newport	130,200
Ogwr	130,400
Rhymney Valley	104,700
Swansea	187,900
Taff Ely	94,300
Torfaen	90,200
Vale of Glamorgan	111,900
Wrexham Maelor	113,900

The following table shows the distribution of the urban and rural population of England and Wales in 1951, 1961, 1971, and 1981.

		Population		*Percentage*	
	England and Wales	*Urban districts* [1]	*Rural districts* [1]	*Urban* [1]	*Rural*
1951	43,757,888	35,335,721	8,422,167	80·8	19·2
1961	46,071,604	36,838,442	9,233,162	80·0	20·0
1971	48,755,000	38,151,000	10,598,000	78·2	21·5
1981	49,011,417	37,686,863	11,324,554	76·9	23·1

[1] As existing at each census.

Conurbations. These are aggregates of local-authority areas with high population densities. In April 1981 there were 6 in England and Wales, with a population of 14·7m. (30% of total population). Their populations were: Greater London, 6·7m.; Tyneside, 0·7m.; W. Yorks., 1·67m.; S.E. Lancs., 2·24m.; Merseyside, 1·13m.; W. Midlands, 2·24m.

Greater London Boroughs. Estimated population on 30 June 1983.

Barking and Dagenham	150,100	Hammersmith and Fulham	150,300	Lambeth	245,000
Barnet	294,400	Haringey	204,700	Lewisham	231,900
Bexley	217,900	Harrow	199,400	Merton	165,400
Brent	254,000	Havering	240,300	Newham	210,300
Bromley	299,200	Hillingdon	234,200	Redbridge	227,000
Camden	175,500	Hounslow	200,900	Richmond-on-Thames	160,900
Croydon	320,600	Islington	162,700	Southwark	215,400
Ealing	283,900	Kensington and Chelsea	134,100	Sutton	169,700
Enfield	263,100	Kingston upon Thames	133,600	Tower Hamlets	144,000
Greenwich	216,100			Waltham Forest	215,200
Hackney	186,700			Wandsworth	258,400
				Westminster	184,100

The City of London (677 acres) is part of the County of Greater London but retains some independent powers. Resident population (1983 estimate) 5,500.

Census of England and Wales, 1961. HMSO. 1961–65
Royal Commission on Local Government in Greater London, Report. HMSO, 1960 (Cmnd. 1164)
Census 1971, England and Wales. HMSO, 1971–75
Census 1971, Great Britain; Advance Analysis. HMSO, 1972
Census 1981, Great Britain. HMSO, 1981–83
Census 1981, England and Wales. HMSO, 1981–83

Scotland: Area 78,762 sq. km, including its islands, 186 in number, and inland water 1,580 sq. km.

Population (including military in the barracks and seamen on board vessels in the harbours) at the dates of each census:

Date of enumeration	*Population*	*Pop. per sq. mile*	*Date of enumeration*	*Population*	*Pop. per sq. mile* [1]
1811	1,805,864	60	1901	4,472,103	150
1821	2,091,521	70	1911	4,760,904	160
1831	2,364,386	79	1921	4,882,497	164
1841	2,620,184	88	1931	4,842,980	163
1851	2,888,742	97	1951	5,096,415	171
1861	3,062,294	100	1961	5,179,344	174
1871	3,360,018	113	1971	5,229,963	68
1881	3,735,573	125	1981	5,130,735	66
1891	4,025,647	135			

[1] per sq. km from 1971.

The 1981 population present on census night included 2,466,000 males, 2,664,000 females.

Population of the local authority areas:

Regions	*Districts*	*Area sq.km*	*Estimated population 1983*
Borders		4,662	101,202
	Berwickshire		18,370
	Ettrick and Lauderdale		33,249
	Roxburgh		35,210
	Tweeddale		14,373
Central		2,590	272,662
	Clackmannan		47,875
	Falkirk		143,921
	Stirling		80,866
Dumfries and Galloway		6,475	146,159
	Annandale and Eskdale		35,758
	Nithsdale		57,076
	Stewartry		23,033
	Wigtown		30,292
Fife		1,308	342,826
	Dunfermline		127,484
	Kirkcaldy		149,491
	N.E. Fife		65,851

Regions	*Districts*	*Area sq. km*	*Estimated population 1983*
Grampian		8,550	494,491
	Aberdeen City		214,100
	Banff and Buchan		83,086
	Gordon		67,344
	Kincardine and Deeside		44,314
	Moray		85,647
Highland		26,136	196,079
	Badenoch and Strathspey		10,003
	Caithness		27,494
	Inverness		57,526
	Lochaber		19,561
	Nairn		10,039
	Ross and Cromarty		47,351
	Skye and Lochalsh		10,963
	Sutherland		13,142
Lothian		1,756	744,802
	E. Lothian		80,838
	Edinburgh City		440,902
	Midlothian		82,362
	W. Lothian		140,700
Strathclyde		13,856	2,383,077
	Argyll and Bute		65,031
	Bearsden and Milngavie		39,697
	Clydebank		51,498
	Clydesdale		57,599
	Cumbernauld and Kilsyth		62,794
	Cumnock and Doon Valley		44,166
	Cunninghame		137,683
	Dumbarton		78,780
	E. Kilbride		82,524
	Eastwood		54,371
	Glasgow City		751,014
	Hamilton		108,440
	Inverclyde		99,684
	Kilmarnock and Loudoun		81,459
	Kyle and Carrick		112,934
	Monklands		109,984
	Motherwell		149,914
	Renfrew		206,971
	Strathkelvin		88,534
Tayside		7,668	394,895
	Angus		93,163
	Dundee		180,748
	Perth and Kinross		120,984
Island Authority Areas			
Orkney Islands		974	19,239
Shetland Islands		1,427	23,454
Western Isles		2,901	31,519

Population of cities and large towns:

	Census population 1961	*1971*	*1981*		*Census population 1961*	*1971*	*1981*
Glasgow	1,055,017	893,790	762,288	Kilmarnock	47,509	48,992	52,080
Edinburgh	468,361	453,025	419,187	Dunfermline	47,151	51,738	52,057
Dundee	182,978	182,930	174,746	Clydebank	49,651	48,170	51,656
Aberdeen	185,390	181,785	190,200	Hamilton	41,928	46,376	51,529
Paisley	95,750	95,067	84,789	Coatbridge	53,825	51,985	50,866
Greenock	74,560	69,171	57,324				

Larger New Towns: East Kilbride, 71,316; Irvine, 55,278.

The birthplaces of the 1981 "usually resident" population were: Scotland, 4,548,708; England, 297,784; Wales, 12,733; Northern Ireland, 33,927; Ireland 27,018; Commonwealth, 48,515; foreign countries, 65,384.

The population of the Central Clydeside conurbation in 1981 was 1,713,287.

At 30 June 1983 the estimated sex distribution of the population in Scotland was: between 0 and 15, 580,800 males, 552,000 females; 15 and 65, 1,627,200 males, 15 and 60, 1,510,700 females; 65 and over, 277,000 males, 60 and over, 602,800 females.

Isle of Man and Channel Islands:

Islands	*Area in sq. km*	*Census population 1961*	*1971*	*1981*
Isle of Man	572	48,151	56,289	64,679
Jersey	116	57,200	69,329	77,000
Guernsey, Herm and Jethou	64			
Alderney	8	47,178	53,734	56,000
Sark, Brechou and Lihou	6			

Vital statistics for England and Wales:

	Estimated home population at 30 June [1]	*Total live births*	*Illegitimate live births*	*Deaths*	*Marriages*	*Divorces, annulments and dis-solutions*
1977	49,440,400	569,259	55,379	575,928	356,954	129,053
1978	49,442,500	596,418	60,637	585,901	368,258	143,667
1979	49,508,200	638,028	69,467	593,019	368,853	138,706
1980	49,603,000	656,234	77,372	581,385	370,022	148,301
1981	49,634,300	634,492	80,983	577,890	351,973	145,713
1982	49,601,400	625,931	89,857	581,861	342,166	146,698
1983	49,653,700	629,134	99,211	579,608	344,334	147,479

[1] The population actually in England and Wales.

In 1983 the proportion of male to female births was 1,056 male to 1,000 female; the live birth rate was 12·7 and the death rate 11·7 per 1,000 of the population; infant mortality rate 10·8 per 1,000 of live births. The average age at marriage in 1983 was 30 years for males and 27·2 years for females.

Vital statistics for Scotland:

	Estimated home population at 30 June [1]	*Total births*	*Illegitimate births*	*Deaths*	*Marriages*	*Divorces, annulments and dis-solutions*
1976	5,205,100	64,895	6,025	65,253	37,543	8,692
1977	5,195,000	62,342	5,968	62,294	37,288	8,823
1978	5,179,400	64,295	6,304	65,123	37,814	8,458
1979	5,167,000	68,366	6,960	65,747	37,860	8,837
1980	5,153,000	68,892	7,678	63,299	38,501	10,530
1981	5,149,500	69,054	8,447	63,828	36,237	9,895
1982	5,166,557	66,196	9,395	65,022	34,942	11,288
1983	5,150,405	65,078	9,581	63,454	34,962	13,238

[1] Includes merchant navy at home and forces stationed in Scotland.

In 1982 the proportion of male to female births was 1,071 male to 1,000 female; the live birth rate was 12·6 and the death rate 12·3 per 1,000 of the population; infant mortality rate, 10 per 1,000 live births. The average age of marriage was 28 years for males and 26 years for females.

Emigration and Immigration. During the last hundred years the UK has most often been a net exporter of population. Throughout the period 1881–1931 there was a consistent net loss from migration, though the fifteen years 1931–46 brought a reversal of the trend as a result of immigration from Europe. Since the Second World War the loss has largely continued. However, during the five years 1956–1961, increased immigration particularly from the new Commonwealth and Pakistan, resulted in a net gain. Decreased emigration in 1979 and 1983 also produced net gains.

Since 1964 migration figures have been available from the International Passenger Survey. This is a sample survey conducted by the Office of Population Censuses and Surveys, covering all the principal air and sea routes between the UK and overseas, except those to and from the Republic of Ireland. For the years 1964–73 the survey shows an average annual net loss for the UK of 63,000. During the decade 1974–1983 the annual net outflow has been an average of 37,000. Since 1964 levels of both immigration and emigration have decreased.

The table below, derived from the International Passenger survey, summarizes migration statistics for 1983 (in 1,000):

By country of last or future intended residence	*Into UK*	*Out from UK*	*Balance*
All Countries	201·9	184·9	+17·0
Australia, Canada, New Zealand	31·7	40·9	−9·1
India, Bangladesh, Sri Lanka	13·5	4·5	+9·0
Other Commonwealth	40·0	27·9	+12·1
EEC	30·8	29·3	+1·5
USA	25·5	31·7	−6·2
South Africa	6·5	8·6	−2·1
Rest of World	53·8	42·1	+11·7
By sex/age			
Males 0–14	25·5	20·3	+5·2
15–24	26·9	17·2	+9·6
25–44	45·0	40·3	+4·8
45 and over	9·7	12·2	− 2·5
All ages	107·2	90·1	+17·1
Females 0–14	18·2	20·3	−2·1
15–24	28·0	26·2	+ 1·9
25–44	39·7	38·8	+0·9
45 and over	8·8	9·5	− 0·8
All ages	94·7	94·8	−0·1

Walvin, J., *Passage to Britain: Immigration in British History and Politics.* London, 1984

CLIMATE. The climate is cool temperate oceanic, with mild conditions and rainfall evenly distributed over the year, though the weather is very changeable because of cyclonic influences. In general, temperatures are higher in the west and lower in the east in winter and rather the reverse in summer. Rainfall amounts are greatest in the west, where most of the high ground occurs.

London. Jan. 40°F (4·5°C), July 64°F (18°C). Annual rainfall 24″ (600 mm). Aberdeen. Jan. 39°F (4°C), July 57°F (14°C). Annual rainfall 33″ (823 mm). Belfast. Jan. 40°F (4·5°C), July 61°F (16°C). Annual rainfall 34·6″ (865 mm). Birmingham. Jan. 38°F (3·3°C), July 61°F (16·1°C). Annual rainfall 30″ (749 mm). Cardiff. Jan. 40°F (4·4°C), July 61°F (16·3°C). Annual rainfall 42·6″ (1,065 mm). Edinburgh. Jan. 38°F (3·5°C), July 58°F (14·5°C). Annual rainfall 28″ (708 mm). Glasgow. Jan. 39°F (4°C), July 60°F (15·5°C). Annual rainfall 37·2″ (930 mm). Manchester. Jan. 41°F (5°C), July 62°F (16·5°C). Annual rainfall 34·1″ (853 mm).

QUEEN, HEAD OF THE COMMONWEALTH. Elizabeth II Alexandra Mary, born 21 April 1926 daughter of King George VI and Queen Elizabeth; married on 20 Nov. 1947 Lieut. Philip Mountbatten (formerly Prince Philip of Greece), created Duke of Edinburgh, Earl of Merioneth and Baron Greenwich on the same day and created Prince Philip, Duke of Edinburgh, 22 Feb. 1957; succeeded to the crown on the death of her father, on 6 Feb. 1952. Offspring: *Charles* Philip Arthur George, Prince of Wales (Heir Apparent), born 14 Nov. 1948, married Lady Diana Spencer on 29 July 1981. Offspring: *William* Arthur Philip Louis, born 21 June 1982; *Henry* Charles Albert David, born 15 Sept. 1984. Princess *Anne* Elizabeth Alice Louise, born 15 Aug. 1950, married Mark Anthony Peter Phillips on 14 Nov. 1973. Offspring: *Peter* Mark Andrew, born 15 Nov. 1977; *Zara* Anne Elizabeth, born 15 May 1981. Prince *Andrew* Albert Christian Edward, born 19 Feb. 1960; Prince *Edward* Antony Richard Louis, born 10 March 1964.

The Queen Mother: Queen Elizabeth, born 4 Aug. 1900, daughter of the 14th Earl of Strathmore and Kinghorne; married the Duke of York, afterwards King George VI, on 26 April 1923.

Sister of the Queen: Princess Margaret Rose, born 12 Aug. 1930; married Antony Armstrong-Jones (created Earl of Snowdon, 3 Oct. 1961) on 6 May 1960; divorced, 1978. Offspring: *David* Albert Charles (Viscount Linley), born 3 Nov. 1961; Lady *Sarah* Frances Elizabeth Armstrong-Jones, born 1964.

Children of the late Duke of Gloucester (died 10 June 1974): William Henry Andrew Frederick, born 18 Dec. 1941, died 28 Aug. 1972; Richard Alexander Walter George, Duke of Gloucester, born 26 Aug. 1944, married Birgitte van Deurs on 8 July 1972 (offspring: Alexander Patrick Gregers Richard Windsor, Earl of Ulster, born 24 Oct. 1974; Davina Elizabeth Alice Benedikte Windsor, born 19 Nov. 1977; Rose Victoria Birgitte Louise Windsor, born 1 March 1980).

Children of the late Duke of Kent (died 25 Aug. 1942): Edward George Nicholas Patrick, Duke of Kent, born 9 Oct. 1935; married Katharine Worsley on 8 June 1961 (offspring: George Philip Nicholas, Earl of St Andrews, born 26 June 1962; Lady Helen Windsor, born 28 April 1964; Lord Nicholas Charles Edward Jonathan Windsor, born 25 July 1970). Alexandra Helen Elizabeth Olga Christabel, born 25 Dec. 1936; married 24 April 1963, Angus Ogilvy (offspring: James Robert Bruce, born 29 Feb. 1964; Marina Victoria Alexandra, born 31 July 1966). Michael George Charles Franklin, born 4 July 1942; married Marie-Christine von Reibnitz on 30 June 1978 (offspring: Lord *Frederick* Michael George David Louis Windsor, born 6 April 1979; Lady *Gabriela* Marina Alexander Ophelia Windsor, born 23 April 1981).

The Queen's legal title rests on the statute of 12 and 13 Will. III, ch. 3, by which the succession to the Crown of Great Britain and Ireland was settled on the Princess Sophia of Hanover and the 'heirs of her body being Protestants'. By proclamation of 17 July 1917 the royal family became known as the House and Family of Windsor. On 8 Feb. 1960 the Queen issued a declaration varying her confirmatory declaration of 9 April 1952 to the effect that while the Queen and her children should continue to be known as the House of Windsor, her descendants, other than descendants entitled to the style of Royal Highness and the title of Prince or Princess, and female descendants who marry and their descendants should bear the name of Mountbatten-Windsor. For the Royal Style and Titles of Queen Elizabeth *see* Commonwealth section.

By letters patent of 30 Nov. 1917 the titles of Royal Highness and Prince or Princess are restricted to the Sovereign's children, the children of the Sovereign's sons and the eldest living son of the eldest son of the Prince of Wales.

Provision is made for the support of the royal household by the settlement of the Civil List soon after the beginning of each reign. (For historical details, *see* THE STATESMAN'S YEAR-BOOK, 1908, p. 5, and 1935, p. 4). According to the Civil List Act of 1 Jan. 1972 and the Civil List (Increase of Financial Provision) Order 1975, the Civil List of the Queen, after the usual surrender of hereditary revenues, was (1985) £3,976,000.

The Civil List Acts of 1985 provide for an annuity of £120,000 to the Princess Anne; £192,600 to Prince Philip; £345,300 to Queen Elizabeth (the Queen Mother); £116,800 to the Princess Margaret; £20,000 to Prince Andrew; £20,000 to Prince Edward.

Sovereigns of Great Britain, from the Restoration (with dates of accession):

House of Stewart	
Charles II	29 May 1660
James II	6 Feb. 1685
House of Stewart-Orange	
William and Mary	13 Feb. 1689
William III	28 Dec. 1694
House of Stewart	
Anne	19 March 1702
House of Hanover	
George I	1 Aug. 1714
George II	11 June 1727
George III	25 Oct. 1760
George IV	29 Jan. 1820
William IV	26 June 1830
Victoria	20 June 1837
House of Saxe-Coburg and Gotha	
Edward VII	22 Jan. 1901
House of Windsor	
George V	6 May 1910
Edward VIII	20 Jan. 1936
George VI	11 Dec. 1936
Elizabeth II	6 Feb. 1952

CONSTITUTION AND GOVERNMENT. The supreme legislative power is vested in Parliament, which in its present form, as divided into two Houses of

Legislature, the Lords and the Commons, dates from the middle of the 14th century.

Parliament is summoned by the writ of the sovereign issued out of Chancery, by advice of the Privy Council, at least 20 days previous to its assembling. A Parliament may last up to 5 years, normally divided into annual sessions. A session is ended by prorogation, and all Bills which have not been passed then lapse. A Parliament ends by dissolution, either by will of the sovereign (that is, on the advice of the Prime Minister) or by lapse of the 5-year period. A dissolution is followed by a general election.

Under the Parliament Acts 1911 (1 and 2 Geo. V, ch. 13) and 1949 (12, 13 and 14 Geo. VI, ch. 103), all Money Bills (so certified by the Speaker of the House of Commons), if not passed by the House of Lords without amendment, may become law without their concurrence on the royal assent being signified within 1 month. Public Bills, other than Money Bills or a Bill extending the maximum duration of Parliament, if passed by the House of Commons in 2 successive sessions, whether of the same Parliament or not, and rejected each time, or not passed, by the House of Lords, may become law without their concurrence on the royal assent being signified, provided that 1 year has elapsed between the second reading in the first session of the House of Commons and the third reading in the second session. All Bills coming under this Act must reach the House of Lords at least 1 month before the end of the session.

The House of Lords consists of: (1) 794 hereditary peers and peeresses sitting by virtue of creation or descent, other than those who have disclaimed their titles for life under the provisions of the Peerage Act, 1963; (2) life peers being *(a)* 19 Lords of Appeal (active and retired), under the Appellate Jurisdiction Act, 1876, as amended; *(b)* (26 Jan. 1985) 338 life peers (including 45 women peers) under the Life Peerages Act, 1958: (3) 2 archbishops and 24 bishops of the Church of England (as long as they hold their sees).

The full House thus consists of 1,177, and the average attendance is about 300; at the end of Jan. 1985 149 peers were on leave of absence and 100 peers (including 5 minors) were without writs of summons.

The House of Commons consists of members (of both sexes) representing constituencies determined by the Parliamentary Boundary Commissions. Persons under 21 years of age, Clergy of the Church of England and of the Scottish Episcopal Church, Ministers of the Church of Scotland, Roman Catholic clergymen, civil servants, members of the regular armed forces, policemen, most judicial officers and other office-holders named in the House of Commons (Disqualification) Act are disqualified from sitting in the House of Commons. No English or Scottish peer can be elected to the House of Commons unless he has disclaimed his title for life under the Peerage Act, 1963, but Irish peers and holders of courtesy titles, who are not members of the House of Lords, are eligible.

In Aug. 1911 provision was first made for the payment of a salary of £400 per annum to members, other than those already in receipt of salaries as officers of the House, as Ministers or as officers of Her Majesty's household. As from 1 Jan. 1985 the salaries of members are £16,904 per annum, with income-tax relief on expenses incurred in the course of parliamentary duties. There is a secretarial allowance of up to £12,437 per annum and a living allowance, for an additional home, of up to £6,518 per annum. Members of the House of Lords are unsalaried but may recover expenses incurred in attending sittings of the House within maxima for each day's attendance of £16 for day subsistence, £40 for night subsistence and £17 for secretarial and research assistance or general office expenses. Additionally, Members of the House who are disabled may recover the extra cost of attending the House incurred by reason of their disablement. In connection with their attendance at the House and for parliamentary duties within the UK Lords may also recover the cost of travelling to and from their main place of residence.

Select Committees consisting of 10–15 Members of all parties exist in order to investigate most areas of public policy.

The Representation of the People Act 1948, abolished the business premises and

University franchises, and the only persons entitled to vote at Parliamentary elections are those registered as residents or as service voters. No person may vote in more than one constituency at a general election. Persons may apply on certain grounds to vote by post or by proxy.

All persons over 18 years old and not subject to any legal incapacity to vote and who are either British subjects or citizens of Ireland are entitled to be included in the register of electors for the constituency containing the address at which they were residing on the qualifying date for the register and are entitled to vote at elections held during the period for which the register remains in force. The current register was published in Feb. 1984.

Members of the armed forces, Crown servants employed abroad, and the wives accompanying their husbands, are entitled, if otherwise qualified, to be registered as 'service voters' provided they make a 'service declaration'. To be effective for a particular register, the declaration must be made on or before the qualifying date for that register.

The Representation of the People Act 1969, abolished the occupier's qualification for voting in Local Government elections.

The House of Commons (Redistribution of Seats) Acts 1944, 1949 and 1958, provided for the setting up of Boundary Commissions for England, Wales, Scotland and Northern Ireland. The Commissions are required to make general reports at intervals of not less than 10 and not more than 15 years and to submit reports from time to time with respect to the area comprised in any particular constituency or constituencies where some change appears necessary. Any changes giving effect to reports of the Commissions are to be made by Orders in Council laid before Parliament for approval by resolution of each House. The electorate of the United Kingdom and Northern Ireland in the register in 1984 numbered 42,983,727, of whom 35,800,362 were in England, 2,148,484 in Wales, 3,957,276 in Scotland and 1,077,605 in Northern Ireland.

At the general election held in June 1983, 650 members were returned, 523 from England, 72 from Scotland, 38 from Wales and 17 from Northern Ireland. Every constituency returns a single member.

The following is a table of the duration of Parliaments called since Nov. 1935.

Reign	*When met*	*When dissolved*	*Duration (years*	*and days)*
George V, Edward VIII and George VI	26 Nov. 1935	15 June 1945	9	205
George VI	1 Aug. 1945	3 Feb. 1950	4	188
,,	1 Mar. 1950	5 Oct. 1951	1	219
George VI and Elizabeth II	31 Oct. 1951	6 May 1955	3	188
Elizabeth II	7 June 1955	18 Sept. 1959	4	105
,,	20 Oct. 1959	25 Sept. 1964	4	341
,,	27 Oct. 1964	10 Mar. 1966	1	134
,,	18 Apr. 1966	29 May 1970	4	81
,,	29 June 1970	8 Feb. 1974	3	225
,,	12 Mar. 1974	20 Sept. 1974	0	224
,,	22 Oct. 1974	7 April 1979	4	167
,,	9 May 1979	13 May 1983	4	4
,,	15 June 1983	—	—	—

The executive government is vested nominally in the Crown, but practically in a committee of Ministers, called the Cabinet, which is dependent on the support of a majority in the House of Commons.

The head of the Ministry is the Prime Minister, a position first constitutionally recognized, and special precedence accorded to the holder, in 1905. His colleagues in the Ministry are appointed on his recommendation, and he dispenses the greater portion of the patronage of the Crown.

Heads of the Administrations since 1935 (C. = Conservative, L. = Liberal, Lab. = Labour, Nat. = National, Coal. = Coalition, Care. = Caretaker):

S. Baldwin (Nat.)	7 June 1935	H. Macmillan (C.)	10 Jan. 1957
N. Chamberlain (Nat.)	28 May 1937	Sir Alec Douglas-Home (C.)	18 Oct. 1963
W. S. Churchill (Coal.)	10 May 1940	H. Wilson (Lab.)	16 Oct. 1964
W. S. Churchill (Care.)	23 May 1945	E. Heath (C.)	19 June 1970
C. R. Attlee (Lab.)	26 July 1945	H. Wilson (Lab.)	12 Mar. 1974
W. S. Churchill (C.)	26 Oct. 1951	J. Callaghan (Lab.)	5 Apr. 1976
Sir Anthony Eden (C.)	6 Apr. 1955	M. Thatcher (C.)	4 May 1979

In March 1985 the Government consisted of the following members:

(a) MEMBERS OF THE CABINET

1. *Prime Minister and First Lord of the Treasury and Minister for Civil Service:* Rt Hon. Margaret Thatcher, MP, born 1925. (Salary £31,271 per annum.)

2. *Lord President of the Council and Leader of the House of Lords:* Rt Hon. Viscount Whitelaw, CH, MC, born 1918. (£33,260.)

3. *Lord Chancellor:* Rt Hon. The Lord Hailsham, CH, born 1907. (£31,680.)

4. *Secretary of State for Foreign and Commonwealth Affairs:* Rt Hon. Sir Geoffrey Howe, QC, MP, born 1926. (£31,271.)

5. *Secretary of State for the Home Department:* Rt Hon. Leon Brittan, QC, MP, born 1939. (£31,271.)

6. *Chancellor of the Exchequer:* Rt Hon. Nigel Lawson, MP, born 1932. (£31,271.)

7. *Secretary of State for Education and Science:* Rt Hon. Sir Keith Joseph, Bt, MP, born 1918. (£31,271.)

8. *Secretary of State for Northern Ireland:* Rt Hon. Douglas Hurd, CBE, MP, born 1930. (£31,271.)

9. *Secretary of State for Energy:* Rt Hon. Peter Walker, MBE, MP, born 1932. (£31,271.)

10. *Secretary of State for Defence:* Rt Hon. Michael Heseltine, MP, born 1933. (£31,271.)

11. *Secretary of State for Scotland:* Rt Hon. George Younger, TD, MP, born 1931. (£31,271.)

12. *Secretary of State for Wales:* Rt Hon. Nicholas Edwards, MP, born 1934. (£31,271.)

13. *Secretary of State for the Environment:* Rt Hon. Patrick Jenkin, MP, born 1926. (£31,271.)

14. *Lord Privy Seal and Leader of the House of Commons:* Rt Hon. John Biffen, MP, born 1930. (£31,271.)

15. *Secretary of State for Social Services:* Rt Hon. Norman Fowler, MP, born 1938. (£31,271.)

16. *Secretary of State for Trade and Industry:* Rt Hon. Norman Tebbit, MP, born 1931. (£31,271.)

17. *Chancellor of the Duchy of Lancaster and Minister for the Arts:* Rt Hon. Earl of Gowrie, born 1939. (£33,260.)

18. *Secretary of State for Employment:* Rt Hon. Tom King, MP, born 1933. (£31,271.)

19. *Minister of Agriculture, Fisheries and Food:* Rt Hon. Michael Jopling, MP, born 1930. (£31,271.)

20. *Chief Secretary to the Treasury:* Rt Hon. Peter Rees, QC, MP, born 1926. (£31,271.)

21. *Secretary of State for Transport:* Rt Hon. Nicholas Ridley, MP, born 1929. (£31,271.)

22. *Minister without Portfolio:* Lord Young of Graffham, born 1932.

(b) LAW OFFICERS

23. *Attorney-General:* Rt Hon. Sir Michael Havers, QC, MP, born 1923. (£33,281.)

24. *Lord Advocate:* Rt Hon. Lord Cameron of Lochbroom, QC, born 1931. (£33,320.)

25. *Solicitor-General:* Sir Patrick Mayhew, QC, MP, born 1929. (£27,131.)

26. *Solicitor-General for Scotland:* Peter Fraser, QC, MP, born 1945. (£22,991.)

(c) MINISTERS NOT IN THE CABINET

27. *Parliamentary Secretary, Treasury (Chief Whip):* Rt Hon. John Wakeham, MP, born 1932. (£25,881.)

28. *Paymaster-General:* John Selwyn Gummer, MP, born 1939.

29. *Minister of State, Foreign and Commonwealth Office:* Rt Hon. The Baroness Young, born 1926. (£28,000.)

30. *Minister of State, Foreign and Commonwealth Office, Minister for Overseas Development:* Rt Hon. Timothy Raison, MP, born 1929. (£21,881.)

31. *Minister of State, Foreign and Commonwealth Office:* Malcolm Rifkind, MP, born 1946. (£21,881.)

32. *Minister of State, Foreign and Commonwealth Office:* Richard Luce, MP, born 1936. (£21,881.)

33. *Minister of State, Home Office:* Giles Shaw, MP, born 1931. (£21,881.)

34. *Minister of State, Home Office:* David Waddington, QC, MP, born 1929. (£21,881.)

35. *Financial Secretary, Treasury:* John Moore, MP, born 1937. (£21,881.)

36. *Minister of State, Treasury:* Barney Hayhoe, MP, born 1925. (£21,881.)

37. *Minister of State, Treasury:* Ian Stewart, MP, born 1935. (£21,881.)

38. *Minister of State, Northern Ireland Office:* Dr Rhodes Boyson, MP, born 1925. (£21,881.)

39. *Minister of State, Department of Energy:* Rt Hon. Alick Buchanan-Smith, MP, born 1932. (£21,881.)

40. *Minister of State, Ministry of Defence, Armed Forces:* Rt Hon. John Stanley, MP, born 1942. (£21,881.)

41. *Minister of State, Ministry of Defence, Defence Procurement:* Rt Hon. Adam Butler, MP, born 1931. (£21,881.)

42. *Minister of State, Scottish Office:* Rt Hon. The Lord Gray, born 1927. (£28,000.)

43. *Minister of State, Welsh Office:* John Stradling Thomas, MP, born 1925. (£21,881.)

44. *Minister of State, Department of the Environment, Minister for Local Government and Environmental Services:* Rt Hon. Kenneth Baker, MP, born 1934. (£21,881.)

45. *Minister of State, Department of the Environment, Minister for Housing and Construction:* Ian Gow, TD, MP, born 1937. (£21,881.)

46. *Minister of State, Department of Health and Social Security, Minister for Health:* Rt Hon. Kenneth Clarke, QC, MP, born 1940. (£21,881.)

47. *Minister of State, Department of Health and Social Security, Minister for Social Security:* Anthony Newton, OBE, MP, born 1937. (£21,881.)

48. *Minister of State, Department of Trade and Industry, Minister for Trade:* Rt Hon. Paul Channon, MP, born 1935. (£21,881.)

49. *Minister of State, Department of Trade and Industry, Minister for Information Technology:* Geoffrey Pattie, MP, born 1936. (£21,881.)

50. *Minister of State, Department of Trade and Industry:* Norman Lamont, MP, born 1942. (£21,881.)

51. *Minister of State, Department of Employment:* Hon. Peter Morrison, MP, born 1944. (£21,881.)

52. *Minister of State, Ministry of Agriculture, Fisheries and Food:* Rt Hon. The Lord Belstead, born 1932. (£28,000.)

53. *Minister of State, Ministry of Agriculture, Fisheries and Food:* John MacGregor, OBE, MP, born 1937. (£28,881.)

54. *Minister of State, Department of Transport:* Lynda Chalker, MP, born 1942. (£21,881.)

Leader of the Opposition in the House of Commons: Rt Hon. Neil Kinnock, MP, born 1942. (£28,601.)

Leader of the Opposition in the House of Lords: The Lord Cledwyn of Penrhos, born 1916. (£22,520.)

The Constitution of the House of Commons after the general election held on 9 June 1983 was as follows: Conservative, 397; Labour, 209; Alliance 23 (Liberals, 17, SDP, 6); Others, 21.

Herman, V., and Att, J. E., *Cabinet Studies.* London, 1976
Jennings, Sir I., *Cabinet Government.* 3rd. ed. CUP, 1959.—*The British Constitution.* 5th ed. CUP, 1966.—*Parliament.* 2nd ed. CUP, 1957.—*Party Politics.* 3 vols. CUP, 1960–62
Jones, J. M., *British Nationality Law.* Rev. ed. London, 1955
King, A. (ed.), *The British Prime Minister.* Rev. ed. London, 1985.—*British Members of Parliament.* London, 1974
Laundy, P., *The Office of Speaker.* London, 1964
Mackintosh, J. P., *The British Cabinet.* 3rd ed. London, 1977.—*The Government and Politics of Britain.* 4th ed. London, 1977
May, Sir T. E., *Treatise on the Law, Privileges, Proceedings and Usage of Parliament.* 19th ed., London, 1976
Mellors, C., *The British MP.* London, 1982
Pelling, H., *A Short History of the Labour Party.* London, 1976
Rush, M., and Shaw, M., *House of Commons.* London, 1974
Taylor, E., *The House of Commons at Work.* 7th ed. London, 1967
The Times Guide to the House of Commons, June 1983. London, 1983
Wilding, N., and Laundy, P., *An Encyclopaedia of Parliament.* 4th ed. London, 1972
Young, R., *The British Parliament.* London, 1962

European Parliament: On 14 June 1984 Great Britain elected 81 representatives to the European Parliament, of which 66 came from England, 8 from Scotland and 4 from Wales, each constituency returning a single member by a first past the post system. Northern Ireland returned 3 members by single transferable vote. The seats were won as follows: Conservative 45, Labour 32, Scottish Nationalists 1, Ulster Unionists 1, Democratic Unionists 1, Social, Democratic and Labour Party 1.

Local Government. Local Administration is carried out by four different types of bodies, namely: (i) local branches of some central ministries, such as the Department of Health and Social Security; (ii) local sub-managements of nationalized industries (coal, electricity, gas, public transport and the post office); (iii) specialist authorities such as water authorities; and (iv) the system of *local government* described below. The phrase 'local government' has come to mean that part of the local administration conducted by elected councils.

There are two separate systems: one for England and Wales and one for Scotland, but both systems are financed by a species of tax on property, levied locally, supplemented by government grants. This local tax is called 'the rate'. The system of financing local government was the subject of a major review in 1975.

Local Government: England and Wales—*Outside London.* England and Wales have slightly differing systems. Each country has three types of councils namely, county, district and English parish or Welsh Community Councils. In addition, England has some metropolitan county and district councils.

Councillors are elected by their local electors for 4 years. The chairman of the council is one of the councillors elected by the rest. In a district with the status of city or borough his title is mayor, or in a few famous places Lord Mayor. Any parish or community council can by simple resolution adopt the style 'town council' and the status of town for the parish or community. The chairman of the council will be known as the town mayor.

Counties and Districts: There are 47 non-metropolitan counties (of which 8 are in Wales) and 6 metropolitan counties (Greater Manchester, Merseyside, South Yorkshire, Tyne and Wear, West Yorkshire and West Midlands). Within the counties there are 369 districts (36 metropolitan and 333 non-metropolitan, of which 37 are in Wales).

Parishes and Communities: There are some 10,000 parishes within the English districts, of which 7,000 or so have councils. About 300 are former small boroughs or urban districts which became successor parishes. Parishes generally, however, remain comparatively unaffected by reorganization.

In Wales, parishes have been replaced by communities. Unlike England, where many areas are not in any parish, communities have been established for the whole of Wales. There is one for each former parish, county borough, borough or urban district (or part thereof where the former area is divided by a new boundary). There are about 1,000 communities altogether, of which 800 or so have councils.

The Local Government Act 1972 laid down the boundaries for all the counties and districts in England and Wales except the English non-metropolitan districts.

Permanent Local Government Boundary Commissions for England and for Wales advise the Secretaries of State on boundaries and electoral arrangements.

A council has only those powers which have been conferred upon it expressly by Act of Parliament, and no more. The relationship between the different types of council is one of specialization, not of hierarchy. The larger do not supervise the smaller; each being, within its own sphere, entitled to make its own decisions. Government sanction, however, is required to borrow money and to sell land below its market value, and certain types of land use are subject to planning control.

Councils are kept within the law by a system of publicly regulated audit, and in the last resort they can be restrained from exceeding their powers by the courts.

Local government functions may be classified into county, district and parish or community functions, but whereas county and district functions are distinct, the parish and community functions are mostly concurrent with those of the districts. Arrangements may, however, be made so that any council may discharge functions of any other as its agent.

The following is the classification of powers given above: *Parish and Community Functions.* Allotments, burial and cremation, halls, meeting places and entertainments, facilities for exercise and recreation, public lavatories, street lighting, off-street vehicle parking, footpaths, the support of local arts and crafts, the encouragement of tourism and the right to be consulted by the district council on planning applications and certain byelaws. *District Functions.* In addition to the Parish and Community functions, aerodromes, civic restaurants, housing, markets, refuse collection, the administration of planning control, the formulation of local plans, sewerage, on behalf of the water authority, museums, the licensing of places of entertainment and refreshment, and the constitutional oversight of parishes and communities. *County Functions.* The formulation of structure plans, traffic, transportation and roads, education, public libraries and museums, youth employment and social services.

There are, in addition, a number of special arrangements. Four district councils in Wales are designated as library authorities and Welsh district councils have powers in relation to allotments currently with community councils. The county councils in England and Wales separately or jointly appoint the fire and police authorities, and the bodies responsible for national parks. In Metropolitan counties the district not the county councils are responsible for education, social services and libraries.

The total number of local government electors in England and Wales was 37,950,002 in 1984.

Greater London. Since 1965 London has been governed by the Greater London Council covering the whole metropolitan area, and by 32 London Boroughs and the City of London, each with responsibilities in its own area. In the City and the 12 boroughs covering the inner part of Greater London education is the responsibility of the Inner London Education Authority, a special Committee of the GLC but independent of it, while in the 20 outer boroughs the London Borough Council is the education authority. Other functions are divided between the GLC and the boroughs. The main responsibilities of the GLC are strategic planning, major roads, housing, major parks and open spaces, the fire service, refuse disposal and Thames flood prevention. The boroughs are the primary housing authorities in their own areas, while the GLC is concerned with matters affecting the whole of London. The City has preserved a large measure of independence and has its own powers regarding police, justice, bridges, sanitation, etc. Except in the City the police authority covering the whole of Greater London is the Metropolitan Police, which is responsible direct to the Central Government.

Estimated population of Greater London in June 1984 was 6,744,210, and rateable value at 1 April 1984 was £2,025,338,254. Estimated gross revenue expenditure of the GLC in 1984–85 was £3,062·8m. (including £1,065·8m. for the ILEA). Estimated gross capital expenditure, 1984–85 was £507m., including ILEA £20m. and £19·5m. for housing loans. The GLC outstanding debt at 1 April 1984 was £1,879,158; ILEA, £195,664m.

Scotland. Under the system, which came into effect in 1975, the Scots mainland is divided into 9 regions, and in addition there are the 3 islands areas of Orkney, Shetland and the Western Isles. There is no equivalent to the English metropolitan county. The regions are divided into districts which total 53. All these units have a council consisting of councillors elected for 4 years and a chairman elected by the councillors for 4 years. Community councils have been established under schemes submitted by district and islands councils. These community councils cannot claim public funds as of right, nor do they have powers directly conferred by Statute: consequently they are not local authorities in the sense that Welsh Community Councils are.

As in England and Wales a permanent Local Government Boundary Commission advises the Secretary of State on Local Authority Boundaries and electoral arrangements.

On the mainland, functions are allocated between regional and district authorities, in the same way (with minor exceptions) as they are allocated between English counties on the one hand and English districts and parishes on the other, but the councils of the islands areas, which have no districts, perform both sets of functions.

Despite differences of nomenclature the effect of the reforms of 1972 (England) and 1973 (Scotland) is to assimilate the systems of mainland Scotland and of England and Wales more closely than has been the case in the past.

The total number of local government electors in Scotland was 3,957,276 in 1982.

Complaints. Under both systems, complaints, by members of the public, of maladministration may be investigated by a Commissioner for Local Administration. Initially a complaint must be referred to him through a councillor, but a direct approach to him is possible if this fails. He can deal only with matters for which there is no other remedy; he reports to the council concerned and may publish his report.

For map of regions *see* THE STATESMAN'S YEAR-BOOK, 1974–75.

Our Changing Democracy: Devolution to Scotland and Wales. HMSO, 1975
Arnold-Baker, C., *The Local Government Act 1972.* London, 1973

DEFENCE. The Defence Council was established on 1 April 1964 under the chairmanship of the Secretary of State for Defence, who is responsible to the Sovereign and Parliament for the defence of the realm. Vested in the Defence Council are the functions of commanding and administering the Armed Forces. The Secretary of State heads the Ministry of Defence as a Department of State. There are 4 subordinate Ministers; 2 Ministers of State and 2 Parliamentary Under Secretaries of State.

Defence Council membership comprises the Secretary of State, 2 Ministers of State, the 2 Parliamentary Under-Secretaries, the Chief of the Defence Staff, the 3 single Service Chiefs of Staff, the Vice-Chief of Defence Staff, the Chief of Defence Procurement, the Chief Scientific Adviser, the Permanent Under-Secretary of State and the Second Permanent Under Secretary of State.

There are 3 Service Boards, each of which enjoys delegated powers for the administration of matters relating to the naval, military and air forces respectively.

Defence policy decision making is a collective Governmental responsibility. Important matters of policy are considered by the full Cabinet or, more frequently, by the Defence and Oversea Policy Committee under the chairmanship of the Prime Minister. Other members of this Committee include the Secretary of State for Defence, the Foreign and Commonwealth Secretary and the Home Secretary.

Logistics Services. Since the inception of a unified Ministry of Defence in 1964, progress has been made in the rationalization of the logistics services of the Royal Navy, the Army and the Royal Air Force. The Air Force Department is responsible for accommodation stores for maintenance and for the initial furnishing of new buildings; the Army Department is the single management authority for the design, development, procurement and inspection of clothing other than certain specialized clothing; the Navy Department has for some time been responsible for ration policy provisioning, procurement, storing and distribution of food to main depots and to Army forward supply depots in BAOR and is responsible for water transport to its tri-service responsibilities. The supply of Naval air stores has been integrated with those of the RAF.

The Procurement Executive. An important development in 1971 was the creation of a Procurement Executive to combine the Defence Procurement responsibilities of the Ministry of Defence and the former Ministry of Aviation Supply.

Service Strengths at 31 Dec. 1984, all ranks, males and females, UK personnel only: Royal Navy and Royal Marines, 63,104; Army, 163,003; Royal Air Force, 93,230; Total, 326,849. The Ministry of Defence employed 178,056 civilians in Dec. 1984.

Defence Budget Estimates: 1985–86, £18,050m.; 1986–87, £18,560m.

Army. Control of the British Army is vested in the Defence Council and is exercised through the Army Board. The Secretary of State for Defence is Chairman of the Army Board. The other civilian members are the Ministers of State for the

Armed Forces and Defence Procurement and the Parliamentary Under Secretaries of State for the Armed Forces and Defence Procurement; the Chief of Establishments and Research Nuclear and the Second Permanent Under Secretary of State.

The Military members of the Army Board are the Chief of the General Staff, the Adjutant-General, the Quartermaster-General and the Master-General of the Ordnance. The Chief of the General Staff is the professional head of his Service and the professional adviser to Ministers on the Army aspects of military problems. He is responsible for the fighting efficiency of his Service; for Army advice on the conduct of operations; and for the issuing of such single Service operational orders as may be appropriate resulting from defence policy decisions. He is also responsible for the Territorial Army. The Chief of the General Staff is a member of the Chiefs of Staff Committee which is collectively responsible to HM Government for professional advice on strategy and military operations and on the military implication of defence policy. This advice is tendered to the Secretary of State for Defence by the Chief of the Defence Staff. The Adjutant-General is responsible for Army manpower within the policy set up by the General Staff; for recruiting and selection; for the administration and individual training of military personnel; for the discipline of the Army; for pay and allowances and pensions; for legal services; for the veterinary and remount services; for the Army Cadet Forces; for questions of Army welfare and education including school children overseas; and for resettlement and sports. The Quartermaster-General is responsible for logistic planning for the Army; for the storage, distribution, maintenance, repair and inspection of equipment, stores and ammunition; for development of stores; for supply, transport and accommodation; for the development, production and inspection of clothing; for military movements and transportation; for the Army postal, catering, salvage and fire services; and for questions connected with canteens, institutes and military labour. The Master General of the Ordnance is a member of both the Army Board and of the Procurement Executive Management Board. He is responsible to the Chief of Defence Procurement for the financial and technical management of the approved programme for the procurement of land service equipment for the Armed Services, and to the Army Board for the co-ordination of the Army's total equipment programme.

Headquarters United Kingdom Land Forces at Wilton commands all Army units in UK except Ministry of Defence controlled units. The Ministry of Defence retains direct operational control of units in Northern Ireland. Command by HQ United Kingdom Land Forces is exercised through 9 district headquarters. There are 3 major overseas Commands: Land Forces Cyprus, Hong Kong and the British Army of the Rhine. There are also garrisons in Berlin, Gibraltar, Falkland Islands and Belize.

The strength of the Regular Army (less the Brigade of Gurkhas and locally enlisted personnel) on 1 Jan. 1984 was 154,600 men and 6,400 women. Strength of reserve forces were: Regular reserves, 141,000; territorial army, 70,600.

The Territorial Army role is to provide a national reserve for employment on specific tasks at home and overseas and to meet the unexpected when required; and, in particular, to complete the Army Order of Battle of NATO committed forces and to provide certain units for the support of NATO Headquarters, to assist in maintaining a secure UK base in support of forces deployed on the Continent of Europe and to provide a framework for any future expansion of the Reserves. In addition, men who have completed service in the Regular Army normally have some liability to serve in the Regular Reserve. All members of the TA and Regular Reserve may be called out by a Queen's Order in time of emergency of imminent national danger and most of the TA and a large proportion of the Regular Reserve may be called out by a Queen's Order when warlike operations are in preparation or in progress. There is a special reserve force in Northern Ireland, the Ulster Defence Regiment, 7,000 strong, which gives support to the regular army.

Men, women and juniors enlist in the Army for 22 years' active and reserve service. However, under a scheme introduced in May 1981 they are entitled to give 12 months' notice (18 months' for women) to leave active service provided they serve for a minimum of 3 years. Alternatively, they can agree to serve for 6 or 9 years to receive the benefit of higher rates of pay. Those enlisting in certain technical trades must agree to serve for a minimum of 6 years. Recruits under the age of 17½ on reaching the age of 18 are entitled either to confirm their original engagement or to reduce their period of service to 3 years.

Women serve in both the Regular Army and the TA in the Queen Alexandra's Royal Army Nursing Corps, the Ulster Defence Regiment and the Women's Royal Army Corps, the latter's employments including communications, motor transport, clerical and catering duties. Some officers of the Women's Royal Army Corps are employed on the staffs of military headquarters.

Barnett, C., *Britain and her Army 1509–1970.* London, 1970
Blaxford, G., *The Regiments Depart: A History of the British Army 1945–70.* London, 1971
Haswell, J., *The British Army.* London, 1975
Johnson, F. A., *Defence by Ministry: The British Ministry of Defence 1944–1974.* London, 1980
Stanhope, H., *The Soldiers: An Anatomy of the British Army.* London, 1979

Navy. Control of the Royal Navy is vested in the Defence Council and is exercised through the Admiralty Board, which consists of 8 civilian and 5 service members. The Secretary of State for Defence is chairman of the Army Board. The other civilian members are the Ministers and Under Secretaries of State for the Armed Forces and for Defence Procurement; the Second Permanent Under Secretary of State; the Controller, Research and Development Establishments, Research and Nuclear; and the Deputy Under Secretary of State (Navy).

The duties of the civilian members of the Admiralty Board are as described in the section on the Army. The Service Board members are as follows: the Chief of the Naval Staff and First Sea Lord (with broadly parallel responsibilities to the Chief of the General Staff); the Chief of Naval Personnel and Second Sea Lord (with broadly parallel duties to the Adjutant-General); the Controller of the Navy (with broadly parallel duties to the Master-General of the Ordnance); the Chief of Fleet Support (with broadly parallel duties to the Quartermaster-General); and the Vice-Chief of the Naval Staff (with broadly parallel duties to the Vice Chief of the General Staff). These parallels are, however, purely indicative: Chief of Fleet Support, for example, is head of the naval dockyard organization and of the Royal Fleet Auxiliary.

The Commander in Chief Fleet at Northwood exercises Command of the Fleet. Naval Air Stations and units at non-naval Air Stations and establishments in the United Kingdom are commanded by the Flag Officer Naval Air Command. Command of all other naval establishments in the UK, except Ministry of Defence-controlled units including Royal dockyards and the Naval Air Repair Organization, and those under the full command of the Commandant General Royal Marines, is exercised by the C.-in-C. Naval Home Command at Portsmouth through Area Flag Officers.

The Royal Naval Reserve (RNR) and the Royal Marines Reserve (RMR) currently have provision for 5,500 and 1,500 personnel respectively. The role of the RNR is to provide a reserve of trained personnel who will be available in times of war to undertake such duties as Naval Control of Shipping, Mine Counter Measures, HQ Command and Communications, and Rotary Wing Aircrew. The main roles of the RMR are to provide reinforcements and to carry out other specialist tasks with the UK-Netherlands Amphibious Force. In addition, men who have completed service in the Royal Navy and the Royal Marines have a liability to serve in the Royal Fleet Reserve. All members of the RNR, the RMR and the Royal Fleet Reserve have a liability to be called out under the provisions of the Reserve Forces Act 1980. Officers of the Retired and Emergency Lists and Pensioners also have a Reserve liability.

Royal Navy ratings enlist to complete 22 years' active service with the option to leave at 18 months notice on completion of a minimum of 2½ years' productive service. Those who leave before completing 22 years have a liability for up to 3 years' service in the Royal Fleet Reserve. Royal Marine ranks, WRNS ratings and QARNNS ratings enlist to complete an initial 9 year engagement but they may apply to re-engage to complete 14 years and 22 years. Servicewomen have no reserve liability.

Women serve in both the WRNS and the QARNNS, and their reserves. In the former, they are employed on a wide range of duties including communications, stores accounting, catering, education, training support and motor transport.

The following is a summary of the more important units:

Category	*1977*	*1978*	*1979*	*1980*	*1981*	*1982*	*1983*	*1984*	*1985*
Aircraft carriers	3	3	3	3	3	3	3	3	3
Submarines	31	30	31	31	32	33	31	32	32
Destroyers	10	11	14	14	15	13	14	15	14
Frigates	56	54	56	55	47	47	46	48	42

There are also 2 helicopter support ships, 2 assault ships, 1 repair ship, 2 maintenance ships, 4 ice patrol ships, 17 patrol vessels of corvette size, 12 surveying vessels, 23 minehunters, 14 coastal minesweepers, 4 trawler minesweepers, 1 mine countermeasures support ship, 1 large seabed operations vessel, 4 trials ships, 1 submarine tender, 10 patrol boats, 10 mooring, salvage and boom vessels, 10 fleet support and supply ships, 14 fleet oilers, 50 other auxiliaries, 7 logistic landing ships, 50 minor landing craft, 9 fleet tugs, 55 other tugs, and 70 tenders.

In the following table the principal surface warships are grouped in classes, in descending order of modernity.

Completed	*Name*	*Standard displacement Tons*	*Aircraft*	*Armament*	*Shaft horse-power*	*Speed knots*
			Aircraft Carriers			
1985 1982 1980	Ark Royal Illustrious [1] Invincible [2]	16,000	5 Sea Harriers; 9 Sea King helicopters	Twin 'Sea Dart' surface-to-air missile launchers; 2 Phalanx guns; 2 20 mm guns	112,000 (gas)	28·0
1959	Hermes [3] (reserve)	24,000	Latterly carried; 5 Sea Harriers; 9 Sea King helicopters	2 quadruple 'Seacat' missile launchers	78,000 (steam)	28·0

[1] Two AEW (airborne early warning) Sea Kings added to complement – to be increased to three in each ship.

[2] Originally designed as 'Command Cruiser', subsequently re-rated as 'Through-deck Cruiser' (meaning long underdeck hangar with flat-top or near full-length flight deck) and later designated 'Anti-Submarine Cruiser'. Officially listed as anti-submarine warfare carrier in 1980. Slightly angled deck and 7 degree ski-jump ramp, like *Illustrious*, but *Ark Royal* has 15 degree ski-jump for Harriers. During the Falklands campaign *Invincible* embarked ten Harriers and nine Sea Kings.

[3] Refitted 1980 with 7·5 degree 'ski-jump' ramp for launching Harrier aircraft. She carried 37 aircraft during the Falklands campaign. Rehabilitated early 1984 as harbour training ship and standby for operational contingency. She is being kept in a high state of reserve until the new *Ark Royal* is fully operational.

Note: For disposals of the large fixed-wing aircraft carriers *Ark Royal* and *Eagle*, the original sister ships of *Hermes* (*Bulwark*, *Albion* and *Centaur*) and the rebuilt *Victorious*; the helicopter cruisers *Blake* and *Tiger*, original sister ship *Lion*, and the other orthodox cruisers *Belfast* (museum ship on the *Thames*), *Ceylon*, *Newfoundland*, *Birmingham*, *Jamaica*, *Superb*, *Kenya*, *Swiftsure*, *Bermuda*, *Mauritius*, *Sheffield* and *Gambia*, *see* 1983–84 and earlier editions.

Capital (Strategic) Submarines

Class	*No.*	*Displacement (submerged) tons*	*Missile Tubes (vertical)*	*Nuclear Reactors*	*Shaft horse-power*	*Speed Knots*
"R"	4 [1]	8,400	16 Polaris A3	1	15,000	25 dived 20 surface

[1] *Renown, Repulse, Resolution* and *Revenge* (former battleship names) completed in 1967–69. All also have six 21-in. torpedo tubes.

Other submarines are of the following classes: 'Trafalgar' (nuclear propelled), 2; 'Swiftsure' (nuclear propelled), 6; 'Churchill' (nuclear propelled), 3; 'Valiant' (nuclear propelled), 2; 'Oberon', 13; 'Porpoise', 2.

The destroyers of the Royal Navy are of the following classes: 'Sheffield' (Type 42), 11; 'Bristol' (Type 82), 1; 'County', 2.

Frigates are of the following classes; 'Broadsword' (Type 22), 6; 'Amazon' (Type 21), 6; 'Leander', 24; 'Rothesay', 6.

Ships under construction or on order include 4 nuclear propelled submarines, 1 diesel driven patrol submarine, 1 destroyer, 8 frigates, and 12 mine countermeasures vessels.

The total number of male and female personnel (including Royal Marines) was (in 1,000) 1981–82, 74·3; 1982–83, 70·4; 1983–84, 71·7; 1984–85, 71·1.

Blackman, R. V. B., *The World's Warships.* London, annual
Blackman, R. V. B., *Ships of the Royal Navy.* London, annual
Moore, J. E. (ed.), *Jane's Fighting Ships.* London, annual

Air Force. In May 1912 the Royal Flying Corps first came into existence with military and naval wings, of which the latter became the independent Royal Naval Air Service in July 1914. On 2 Jan. 1918 an Air Ministry was formed, and on 1 April 1918 the Royal Flying Corps and the Royal Naval Air Service were amalgamated, under the Air Ministry, as the Royal Air Force.

In 1937 the units based on aircraft carriers and naval shore stations again passed to the operational and administrative control of the Admiralty, as the Fleet Air Arm. In 1964 control of the RAF became a responsibility of the Ministry of Defence.

The Royal Air Force is administered by the Air Force Board, of which the Secretary of State for Defence is Chairman. The Minister of State for the Armed Forces is Vice-Chairman, and normally acts as Chairman on behalf of the Secretary of State. Other members of the Board are the Under-Secretary of State for the Armed Forces, the Under-Secretary of State for Defence Procurement, the Chief of the Air Staff, Vice-Chief of the Air Staff, Air Member for Personnel, Air Member for Supply and Organization, Controller of Aircraft, Chief Scientist (Royal Air Force), Deputy Under-Secretary of State (Air) and Second Permanent Under-Secretary of State for Administration. The RAF is organized into commands:

Home Commands. Strike and Support Commands. The Air Training Corps and the Air Sections of the Combined Cadet Force are under the administrative control of Support Command and functionally controlled by the Ministry of Defence.

The RAF College, which trains general-duties, engineering, and supply and secretarial graduates for permanent commissions, is at Cranwell. The RAF Staff College is at Bracknell. The Department of Air Warfare is at Cranwell. The RAF Central Flying School is at Scampton. Estimated strength in Sept. 1984, including WRAF and boys, was 93,002.

Strike Command is made up of 3 Groups. Nos 1 and 38 Groups merged in late 1983 to form a new No 1 Group, responsible for the strike/attack, reconnaissance, tanker, battlefield support and transport forces. The Tornado GR1 and Jaguar provide the strike/attack and reconnaissance. Victor and Hercules tanker aircraft are being supplemented by ex-civil VC10s and TriStars converted to air refuelling. Battlefield support forces comprise Harrier GR3s, and Chinook, Puma and Wessex support helicopters. The strategic and tactical transport force comprises VC10s and Hercules, and communications aircraft. No 11 Group controls the air defence forces: Lightning and Phantom supersonic all-weather intercepters, Bloodhound surface-to-air missiles, and ground environment radars, the associated communication systems, and the Ballistic Missile Early Warning System at Fylingdales. No 11 Group also controls the Hawks of the Tactical Weapons Units which, in war, would supplement air defence fighters at bases throughout the UK. UK air defence is undergoing major improvements. The Tornado F2 entered service in Nov. 1984 and will gradually replace the Lightning and some Phantoms. Nimrod AEW3 will shortly enter service, replacing the Shackleton, and in the ground environment, there are new radars and communications systems entering service. No 18 Group is responsible for maritime air operations. ASW is the duty of the Nimrod Mk 2, which also has a capability against surface ships, although Buccaneers provide the main offensive force against a maritime surface threat. No 18 Group also operates Canberras in a multitude of roles, including photo-reconnaissance, target towing and ECM training, as well as Nimrod special-purpose aircraft. Search and rescue units are equipped with Sea King and Wessex helicopters. RAF Regiment short-range air defence squadrons, armed with Rapier, and the field squadrons form part of 1 Group, as does The Queen's Flight, which is due to receive 2 BAe 146s but is presently equipped with 3 Andovers and 2 Wessex helicopters. The Military Air Traffic Operations organization also has the status of a Group. Strike Command has NATO commitments, but is available for overseas reinforcement. The training element of RAF Support Command utilizes Bulldog and Chipmunk primary trainers, Jet Provost basic trainers, Hawk advanced trainers, Jetstreams for multi-engine pilot training, twin-jet Dominies for training navigators and other non-pilot aircrew, and Gazelle and Wessex helicopters.

Overseas Commands. Royal Air Force Germany. Small units in Gibraltar, the Falkland Islands, Belize, Cyprus and Hong Kong.

Squadrons of RAF Germany, which form part of NATO's 2nd Allied Tactical Air Force under SACEUR, have Tornado GR1, Harrier and Jaguar attack and reconnaissance aircraft, Phantom fighters, Chinook and Puma Helicopters, Pembroke communications aircraft, and Rapier surface-to-air missile squadrons of the RAF Regiment.

A squadron of Phantom aircraft and a flight of Harriers and Chinooks, together with detachments of Hercules tankers and search and rescue Sea Kings, are based in the Falkland Islands; a squadron of Wessex helicopters is based in Hong Kong.

The Royal Air Force, 1939–45. Vols. I, II, III. HMSO, 1953–54
Taylor J. W. R. (ed.), *Jane's All the World's Aircraft.* London. Annual from 1909

INTERNATIONAL RELATIONS

Membership. The UK is a member of UN, Commonwealth, EEC, OECD, the Council of Europe, NATO and the Colombo Plan.

ECONOMY

Budget. Revenue and expenditure for years ending 31 March, in £ sterling:

Revenue	*Estimated in the Budgets*	*Actual receipts into the Exchequer*	*More than estimates*
1981	65,415,000,000	66,814,000,000	1,399,000,000
1982	75,524,000,000	76,288,000,000	764,000,000
1983	82,895,000,000	83,350,000,000	455,000,000
1984	87,800,000,000	88,700,000,000	900,000,000
1985	98,000,000,000	98,400,000,000	400,000,000

The Budget estimate of ordinary revenue for 1985–86 is £106,500m.

Expenditure	*Budget and supplementary estimates*	*Actual payments out of the Exchequer*	*More than estimates*
1981	73,175,000,000	76,728,000,000	3,553,000,000
1982	83,697,000,000	85,425,000,000	1,728,000,000
1983	90,891,000,000	89,041,000,000	−850,000,000
1984	95,600,000,000	97,400,000,000	1,800,000,000
1985	103,400,000,000	105,800,000,000	2,400,000,000

The Budget estimate of ordinary expenditure for 1985–86 is £159,500m.

The imperial revenue in detail for 1984–85 and the expenditure, are given below, as is the budget estimate for 1985–86 (in £1m.):

Sources of revenue	*Net receipts 1984–85*	*Budget estimate 1985–86*
Inland Revenue:		
Income	32,700	35,200
Corporation tax	8,200	10,100
Petroleum revenue tax	7,200	8,200
Capital Gains tax	720	790
Development land tax	80	55
Capital transfer tax	680	760
Stamp duties	910	1,100
Total Inland Revenue	50,500	56,200
Customs and Excise:		
Value Added Tax	18,400	18,300
Oil	6,100	6,500
Tobacco	4,100	4,300
Spirits, beer, wine, cider and perry	3,800	4,200
Betting and gaming	670	700
Car tax	750	760
Other excise duties	20	20
Customs duties	1,300	1,400
Agricultural levies	120	100
Total Customs and Excise	*35,300*	*36,300*
Vehicle Excise duties	2,200	2,500
National insurance surcharge	920	30
Total taxation	88,900	95,100
Miscellaneous receipts:		
Broadcasting receiving licences	790	790
Interest and dividends	500	870
Gas levy	500	520
Oil royalties	2,400	2,500
Other	5,300	6,700
Total	98,400	106,500

The following are the branches of expenditure for year ended 31 March 1985 and the estimates for the year 1985–86 (in £1m.):

	Estimates 1984–85	*Estimates 1985–86*
Central Government:		
Social Security	35,200	37,200
Defence	17,100	18,100
Health and Personal Social Services	13,400	14,100
Other	26,500	27,100
Local Authorities:		
Educational and Science	11,500	11,200
Other	23,200	21,900
National Industries' External Finance	4,100	1,300
	129,700	134,200
Interest Payments	16,500	18,000
Other Adjustments	3,300	7,300
Total	149,500	159,500

A single graduated income tax came into operation on 6 April 1973, replacing the existing income tax and surtax.

Rates of Personal Tax from 6 April 1985	%
Income between	
£0–£16,200	30
£16,201–£19,200	40
£19,201–£24,400	45
£24,401–£32,300	50
£32,301–£40,200	55
Over £40,200	60

Surcharge on investment income was abolished. Life assurance premium relief for contracts made after 13 March 1984 was abolished.

Under the tax system, the amounts of the personal allowances are adjusted so that they retain their equivalent in relation to earned income.

Personal Allowances	*1985–86* £
Single person / Wife's earned income	2,205
Married man	3,455
Additional allowance	1,250
Dependent relative:	
Single woman claimant	145
Others	100
Housekeeper	100
Relative taking charge of younger brother or sister	100
Daughter's services	55
Blind person	360

Deductions of tax under PAYE extend over the full range of unified tax rates and not merely the basic rate. Similarly, assessment on business profits and on other income which was directly assessed to tax, such as rents and interest on bank deposits, are made by reference to the full scale of rates, including where appropriate the investment income surcharge.

The standard rate of 30% is the rate at which tax is deducted from payments of interest, etc., and corresponds under the new corporation tax system, to the tax credit on dividends. Where an individual's total income is such that he is liable on this taxed investment income at rates exceeding 30%, or if his investment income is high enough to make him liable to the surcharge, the higher rate or surcharge liability on this taxed investment income will in general be assessed separately after the end of the tax year.

Corporation Tax. Corporation Tax applies, with certain exceptions, to trades or businesses carried on by bodies corporate or by unincorporated societies or other bodies and this tax came into force from April 1966 replacing Profits Tax. There are reduced rates of Corporation Tax for small companies and for 1984–85 the rate is 45% reducing to 35% by 1986–87. Small companies rates until 1986–87, 30%.

Capital Gains Tax. Gains resulting from the disposal of capital assets (other than British Government and Government guaranteed securities and certain exempted forms of property such as a private car and personal residences) are taxed under the Finance Act 1965. In 1985–86 exemption was granted for all gains made in a financial year which in total did not exceed £5,900 and most trusts on the first £2,950.

Value Added Tax. Value Added Tax was introduced from 1 April 1973 at the rate of 10% on the supply of goods (with certain exceptions) and services. From 18 June 1979 the rate of tax was fixed at 15%.

Kay, J. A. and King, M. A., *The British Tax System.* OUP, 1980

Local Taxation. The rateable value on which rates were leviable in England and

Wales on 1 April 1984 was £7,731m. In England and Wales, the average amount of the rates collected per £ of rateable value was £0·34 in 1913–14; and estimated to be 179·5p for 1984–85. In Scotland the rateable value on which rates are leviable on 1 April 1983 was £1,169m. and the average amount per £ of rateable value of the rates was 124·9p. The average domestic water rate was 9p in the £.

Under the Local Government Planning and Land Act 1980, the Government gives general financial assistance to local authorities by means of rate support grants. The Rate Support Grant Supplementary Report (England) 1983–84 deals with the distribution of these grants to local authorities in England only. The grants for 1984–85 contain (i) Block Grant £8,179m., the object of which is to give authorities sufficient grant to put them in a position where they can provide similar standards of service for a similar rate in the £, and (ii) Domestic Grant £692m., which will provide a relief of 18½p for domestic ratepayers except for those in the Cities of London and Westminster where the relief provided is 36·5p and 26·5p respectively. There is also provision in the 1980 Act for payment of National Parks Supplementary Grant (£5·5m.) to county councils with all or part of a national park in their area, and Transport Supplementary Grant (£400m.) payable to county councils and the Greater London Council. Grants are also payable on revenue expenditure for specific services, including police and housing, and capital expenditure on certain services also attracts grant.

In Scotland, rate support grants are paid under the Local Government (Scotland) Act 1966 as amended. The total rate support grant and the amounts of the component parts for the local authority financial year 1985–86, as prescribed in the Rate Support Grant (Scotland) Order 1985 are as follows: total £1,691·8m. comprising needs element £1,424·5m.; resources element £203·5m.; domestic element £63·8m. The domestic element is paid to rating authorities to offset the cost of reducing by 5p in the £ rates payable on domestic properties. A small part of the needs element, £1·1m. in 1985–86, is apportioned among those local authorities which incurred extraordinary expenses in connection with developments relating to exploration for or exploitation of offshore petroleum in 1981–82. As in England and Wales capital and revenue grants are also payable on expenditure for certain specified services.

Rates and Rateable Values, 1974–75. HMSO
Rates and Rateable Values in Scotland, 1977–78. HMSO
Estimates, 1982–83. GLC
Analysis of Rateable Values List. GLC, 1977
Report on Rate Support Grant Order 1979. HMSO

Gross National Product:	*1946*	*1960*	*1970*	*1980*	*1983*
Expenditure (£1m.)					
Consumers' expenditure	7,273	16,939	31,773	135,738	182,427
Central government final consumption	2,282	4,206	8,961	48,424	65,859
Gross domestic fixed capital formation	925	4,190	9,462	39,411	49,559
Value of physical increase in stocks and work in progress	–126	562	425	–2,706	267
Total domestic expenditure at market prices	10,354	25,897	50,581	220,867	298,112
Exports of goods and services	1,775	5,153	11,533	63,158	79,768
Less Imports of goods and services	–2,083	–5,549	–11,122	–57,913	–76,582
Less Taxes on expenditure	–1,573	–3,378	–8,416	36,882	49,865
Subsidies	384	493	884	5,308	6,056
Gross domestic product at factor cost	8,855	22,616	43,460	194,538	257,489

Factor incomes (£1m.)	*1946*	*1960*	*1970*	*1980*	*1983*
Income from employment	5,758	15,174	30,404	136,050	170,072
Income from self-employment[1]	1,126	2,008	3,735	17,581	23,123
Gross trading profits of companies[1]	1,476	3,730	5,935	27,708	41,530
Gross trading surplus of public corporations[1]	20	534	1,447	6,222	9,661
Gross trading surplus of other public enterprises[1]	86	189	151	242	–109
Rent[2]	429	1,086	2,833	13,390	17,424
Total domestic income before providing for depreciation and stock appreciation	8,895	22,863	44,837	203,304	264,157
Less Stock appreciation	–125	–122	–1,090	–6,456	–4,326
Residual error	...	–125	–287	–2,310	–2,342
Gross domestic product at factor cost	8,770	22,616	43,460	194,538	257,489
Net property income from abroad	85	233	559	273	1,948
Gross national product	8,855	22,849	44,019	194,265	259,437
Less Capital consumption	...	–2,047	–4,420	–27,223	–36,490
National income	...	20,802	39,599	167,042	222,947

[1] Before providing for depreciation and stock appreciation.
[2] Before providing for depreciation.

National Economic Development Council. The NEDC (Neddy), which first met in 1962, is the national forum for economic consultation between government, management and unions. It includes leading representatives of the Government, CBI and TUC and also chairmen of nationalized industries and independent members. It meets usually under the chairmanship of the Chancellor of the Exchequer although the Prime Minister takes the chair from time to time. Discussions at the monthly council meetings are normally based on papers, presented by the participating parties, which deal primarily with questions of medium-term national economic performance and prospects, besides seeking to agree on ways of improving industrial efficiency. Council meetings are held in private to encourage the frank exchange of views between members, and discussions are summarized at a press conference taken by the Director-General of the National Economic Development Office (NEDO) following each meeting. The Economic Development Committees (Little Neddies), like the NEDC, bring together representatives of management and unions and officials from Government, who use this neutral meeting place to study the efficiency and prospects of individual industries and sectors and to suggest ways in which these could be improved. The National Economic Development Office (NEDO) provides the professional staff for the NEDC and the EDCs.

Currency. The monetary unit of Great Britain is the *pound sterling*. A gold standard was adopted in 1816, the sovereign or twenty-shilling piece weighing 7·98805 grammes 0·916⅔ fine. Currency notes for £1 and 10*s.* were first issued by the Treasury in 1914, replacing the circulation of sovereigns. The issue of £1 and 10*s.* notes was taken over by the Bank of England in 1928. The issue of 10*s.* notes ceased on the issue of the 50p coin in 1969.

Following the post-war fluctuations in the value of the pound, Great Britain returned to the Gold Standard in 1925 with the pound fixed at the pre-war parity of US$4.8665. But the world financial crisis of 1931 forced the country off the Gold Standard again, and in the following year the Exchange Equalization Account was set up for the purpose of checking undue fluctuations in the exchange value of the pound. With the relative stability of the pound which followed, a 'Sterling Bloc' emerged consisting of most Empire countries and those others who voluntarily pegged their currencies to the pound.

The Bloc was superseded at the outbreak of the Second World War by the 'Sterling Area'. The pound was then fixed at $4.03 and remained at that rate until Sept. 1949, when it was devalued to $2.80. On 18 Nov. 1967 it was further devalued to $2.40. Following the general international currency re-alignment of Dec. 1971, the rate for the pound, in terms of the US$, was fixed at £1 = $2.6057 but in June 1972 the pound was allowed to float. March 1985, £1 = US$ 1·07.

When the pound was floated in June 1972 measures were also introduced to control payments between the 'Scheduled Territories' (*i.e.*, the UK including the Channel Islands, the Isle of Man and Ireland), and the rest of the Sterling Area as well as the rest of the world. Exchange control restrictions were lifted in Oct. 1979 except for Rhodesia (Zimbabwe) and these were lifted in Dec. 1979.

Coinage. The sovereign (£1) weighs 123·27447 grains, or 7·98805 grammes, 0·916⅔ (or eleven-twelfths) fine, and consequently it contains 113·00159 grains or 7·32238 grammes of fine gold. On 15 Feb. 1971 (Decimalization Day) a decimal currency system was introduced retaining the *pound sterling* as the major unit but now divided into 100 *new pence* instead of 240 old pence. The decimal coins are the £1 (22·5 mm diameter, 9·5 grammes weight); 50p (equilateral curve heptagon, 30 mm diameter, 13·5 grammes); 20p (equilateral curved heptagon 21·4 mm diameter, 5 grammes); 10p (28·5 mm, 11·31 grammes); 5p (23·6 mm, 5·65 grammes); 2p (25·9 mm, 7·12 grammes) and 1p (20·3 mm, 3·56 grammes). The ½p was demonetized on 31 Dec. 1984. The Decimal Currency Act, 1967 and the Proclamation of 27 Dec. 1968 required that the 50p, 10p and 5p be made of cupro-nickel and the 2p, 1p and ½p of mixed metal; copper, tin and zinc (bronze). The Decimal Currency Act, 1969, provided that the coins of the Queen's Maundy Money should continue to be made in silver to a millesimal fineness of 925.

By Proclamation dated 28 July 1971, which came into force on 30 Aug. 1971, the crown, double-florin, the florin, the shilling and the sixpence are to be treated as coins of the new currency and as being of the denominations respectively of 25, 20, 10, 5 and 2½ new pence. The sixpence was demonetised on 30 June 1980.

The Coinage Act, 1971, specified that the legal tender limits for coins were: Gold coins, for payment of any amount; coins of cupro-nickel and silver of denominations of more than 10p, for payment of any amount not exceeding £10; coins of cupro-nickel and silver of not more than 10p, for payment of any amount not exceeding £5; coins of bronze, for payment of any amount not exceeding 20p. The £1 coin is legal tender to any amount.

UK coins issued in the 12 months up to March 1984 totalled £744m.

It is estimated that the following coins were in circulation in the UK at 31 March 1984, in millions: £1 166, 50p 966, 20p 860, 10p 1,750, 5p 1,920, 2p 2,450, 1p 3,700, ½p 2,400.

Bank-notes. The Bank of England issues notes in denominations of £1, £5, £10, £20 and £50 for the amount of the fiduciary note issue. Under the provisions of the Currency and Bank Notes Act, 1954, which came into force on 22 Feb. 1954, the amount of the fiduciary note issue was fixed at £1,575m., but this figure might be altered by direction of HM Treasury after representations made by the Bank of England.

All Bank of England notes are legal tender in England and Wales, and notes of denominations less than £5 are legal tender in Scotland and Northern Ireland. The banks in Scotland and Northern Ireland have certain note-issuing powers.

The total amount of notes issued at 30 Dec. 1983 was £12,950m., of which £12,949m. were in the hands of other banks and the public and £900,000 in the Banking Department of the Bank of England.

Banking. The Bank of England, Threadneedle Street, London, is the Government's banker and the 'banker's bank'. It has the sole right of note issue in England and Wales and manages the National Debt. The Bank operates under royal charters of 1694 and 1946 and the Bank of England Act, 1946. The capital stock has, since 1 March 1946, been held by the Treasury.

The statutory return is published weekly. End-Dec. figures for the past 5 years are as follows (in £1m.):

	Notes in circulation	*Notes and coin in Banking Department*	*Public deposits (government)*	*Other deposits*[1]
1980	10,819	6	36	1,292
1981	11,577	23	45	2,260
1982	12,014	11	109	2,668
1983	12,623	7	51	2,152
1984	13,477	13	106	2,082

[1] Including Special Deposits.

The fiduciary note issue was £12,950m. at 31 Dec. 1984. All the profits of the note issue are passed on to the National Loans Fund.

Official reserves of gold and convertible currencies, SDR and reserve position in the IMF at the end of Dec. 1984 were US$15,694m.

The value of paper debit bank clearings for 1984, £7,545m. Paper credit clearings for 1984, £69m. Automatic direct debits, 1984, £59m.; automatic credit transfers, 1984, £131m.

The following statistics relate to the London clearing banks' groups at mid-Dec. 1984. Total deposits (sterling and currency), £171,226m.; sterling market loans £24,416m.; advances (sterling and currency), £87,009m.; sterling investments £6,838m.

Total net profits from the operations of the main 4 London clearing bank groups in 1984 amounted to £862m., of which £296m. in gross dividends, £566m. transferred to reserves.

The clearing banks cover all aspects of banking business in UK including corporate business, and are also actively involved in international banking.

Trustee Savings Banks. Trustee Savings Banks started in Scotland in 1810. They operate under the terms of the Trustee Savings Bank Act 1981. There are 4 banks with a network of 1,624 branches throughout the UK and the Channel Islands. The banks are supervised by the TSB Central Board, a statutory body established by the TSB Act 1976.

On 20 Nov. 1984 the funds of all Trustee Savings Banks totalled £9,001m., the total number of accounts exceeded 13m.

National Savings Bank. Statistics for 1982 and 1983:

	Ordinary accounts		*Investment accounts*	
	1982	*1983*	*1982*	*1983*
Accounts open at 31 Dec.	19,907,123[1]	19,743,370[1]	2,186,267	2,463,815
Amounts—	*£1,000*	*£1,000*	*£1,000*	*£1,000*
Received	588,815	694,397	1,234,774	1,195,200
Interest credited	78,913	77,880[2]	382,388	414,510
Paid	684,216	700,885	718,224	967,905
Due to depositors at 31 Dec.	1,675,977	1,747,369	3,770,287	4,412,092
Average amount due to each depositor in active accounts	£84·18	£88·50	£1,724·53	£1,790·75

[1] Excluding accounts with balances of less than £1 which have been inactive for 3 years or more.

[2] From 1 Jan. 1983, a two-tier interest structure was introduced, 6% per annum was payable on accounts with a minimum balance of £500; accounts with a minimum balance of less than £500 received 3% per annum.

The amount due to depositors in Ordinary Accounts on 1 Jan. 1985 was approximately £1,766,192,263 and in Investment Accounts £4,951,604,987.

The National Girobank (founded 1968) had (1984) 1·6m. customers with balances of £810m.

Bank of England Quarterly Bulletin. Bank of England
Bank of England Annual Report. Bank of England
British Banking and other Financial Institutions. HMSO, 1977
Central Statistical Office, Financial Statistics. HMSO (monthly)
Report of the Committee on the Working of the Monetary System. HMSO, 1959

Report of the Select Committee on Nationalised Industries—The Bank of England. HMSO, 1970
The Royal Mint. 6th ed. HMSO, 1977
Clapham, Sir J. H., *The Bank of England: A History.* 2 vols. CUP, 1944
Sayers, R. H., *The Bank of England 1891–1944.* CUP, 1976

Weights and Measures. Conversion to the metric system was in progress (1985) which will replace the imperial system at present in force.

ENERGY AND NATURAL RESOURCES

Electricity. The electricity industry was vested in the British Electricity Authority on 1 April 1948. Following the re-organization of the electricity supply industry after the passing of the Electricity Act, 1957, the statutory bodies comprising the electricity service in England and Wales are the Electricity Council, the Central Electricity Generating Board and the 12 Area Electricity Boards.

The Electricity Council has functioned from Jan. 1958 as the central council for the supply industry in England and Wales for consultation on, and formulation of, general policy; its main functions are to advise the Secretary of State for Energy on all matters affecting the supply industry, and to promote and assist the maintenance and development by the Central Electricity Generating Board and the Area Boards (known collectively as Electricity Boards) of an efficient, co-ordinated and economical system of electricity supply. The Council can also perform services for the Boards, and, in addition, has certain specific functions, particularly in matters of finance, research and industrial relations.

The Central Electricity Generating Board is responsible for the generation and bulk supply of electricity to the 12 Area Boards in England and Wales. It therefore plans the provision of new generating and transmission capacity, including the siting and construction of new generating stations, both conventional and nuclear, and is responsible for the operation and maintenance of generating stations and the main transmission system.

Area Electricity Boards. Each of the 12 Area Electricity Boards acquires bulk supplies of electricity from the Generating Board and is responsible for distribution networks and sales of electricity to its Area consumers. Thus distribution and utilization of electricity, and also the contracting and sale of appliances side of the industry, are their responsibilities.

The number of power stations owned by the Generating Board in England and Wales on 31 March 1984 was 90 with a total output capacity, of 51,028 mw. Total number of customers in England and Wales on 31 March 1984 was 21,047,102 (on 31 March 1983, 20,828,334).

Electricity sold in England and Wales in 1983–84 amounted to 199,690m. units. Revenue from sales of electricity in 1983–84 was £901m. Coal used for electricity generation in 1983–84 amounted to 77·2m. tonnes (75·3m. tonnes in 1982–83). Total fuel (coal equivalent) used in 1982–83 amounted to 93·1m. tonnes and in 1983–84 to 95·5m. tonnes. Nine nuclear stations of total output capacity 4,485 mw provided 14·7% of total units supplied in 1983–84. Eight of these are gas cooled graphite-moderated stations using natural uranium fuel canned in magnesium alloy (Magnox) and 1 is an advanced gas-cooled station (AGR). With 4 AGR stations under construction, output capacity will reach 10,350 mw by Dec. 1988.

The number of persons employed by the Generating Board, the Electricity Council and Area Boards at the end of March 1984 was 137,210.

The North of Scotland Hydro-Electric Board, established under the Hydro-Electric Development (Scotland) Act 1943, is the nationalized authority responsible not only for generating and transmitting electricity but also for distributing and selling it to over 562,000 consumers.

The Board's district covers a quarter of the land mass of Great Britain and lies generally north and west of a line joining the firths of Clyde and Tay as well as all the island groups extending to the Outer Hebrides, Orkney and Shetland. Over 99% of potential consumers have now been provided with supply. On the mainland the Board operates generating stations with a total installed generating capacity of 3,179 mw consisting of 1,758 mw of hydro power and pumped storage, together with 1,260 mw of steam. Diesel stations with a total installed capacity of 126 mw supply the principal island groups together with 35 mw gas turbine. A 1,320 mw of oil/gas fired thermal plant is now operating at Peterhead.

The main transmission system consists of 5,097 circuit km of 275 kv and 132 kv lines linking the power stations and the bulk supply points serving the distribution networks. The system control centre at Pitlochry co-ordinates the operation of the transmission system and power stations together with the continuous interchange of power with the South of Scotland Electricity Board. The number of staff at the end of the year was 3,840.

The South of Scotland Electricity Board was established in April 1955 by the Electricity Reorganisation (Scotland) Act 1954, replacing in South Scotland 2 Electricity Boards and 2 Divisions of the British Electricity Authority. The area of Scotland served by the Board lies south of a line from the Firth of Clyde to the Firth of Tay and extends to about 8,000 sq. miles (21,000 sq. km), including the industrial belt of Scotland, with a population of 4m. By special arrangement a small part of North-East England is also supplied. The remainder of Scotland is served by the North of Scotland Hydro-Electric Board.

The Board differs from those established in England and Wales in that its responsibilities cover not only the distribution of electricity and retail sale of electrical appliances but also the generation and transmission of bulk power within South Scotland.

At 31 March 1984 the Board operated 16 generating stations (including 2 nuclear and 7 hydro-electric stations) with a total output capacity of 6,188 mw (total effective capacity however, has been reduced by placing 1,284 mw of plant at 1 station in storage for an indefinite period). In 1983–84 the Board sold 17,770m. units to more than 1·6m. consumers and had a total revenue of £782m. The number of staff employed at the end of the year was 12,304.

Oil. Production 1983, in 1,000 tonnes (1982 in brackets): Throughput of crude and process oils, 76,876 (77,130); refinery use, 5,297 (5,549); gases, 1,538 (1,475); naphtha, 3,550 (3,492); motor spirit, 21,053 (19,134); kerosene, 6,493 (6,308); diesel oil, 21,029 (20,581); fuel oil, 13,483 (15,808); lubricating oils, 936 (990); bitumen, 1,798 (1,862). Total output of refined products, 70,927 (70,747).

Gas. The British gas industry, nationalized in 1949, was reorganized as the British Gas Corporation on 1 Jan. 1973. Under the terms of the Gas Act 1972, the Corporation has the general duty 'to develop and maintain an efficient, co-ordinated and economical system of gas supply'. The chairman and members of the Corporation are appointed by the Secretary of State for Energy. British Gas explores for and produces natural gas, manufactures substitute natural gas, transmits, distributes and sells gas, and sells, installs and maintains gas appliances.

Gas Council (Exploration) Ltd and Hydrocarbons Great Britain Ltd, wholly owned subsidiaries of British Gas, have been involved in exploration for oil and gas in the Irish Sea, the English Channel and Celtic Sea and, in partnership with oil companies, in the North Sea and onshore. British Gas is a partner in gasfields in the southern North Sea and discovered the Morecambe gasfield in the Irish Sea.

In 1983–84, British Gas sold 17,281m. therms of gas. Conversion to natural gas was completed in 1977. There were 15·64m. domestic customers, who used 9,128m. therms; 82,000 industrial customers, who used 5,753m. therms; and 494,000 commercial customers, who used 2,400m. therms.

The turnover of British Gas in 1983–84 was £6,422m. and the average net assets employed at current cost was £12,631m. The surplus for the year was £668m. before tax. In March 1984, there were 97,200 employees.

Minerals. Coal. The number of National Coal Board producing collieries on 31 March 1984 was 170. Statistics of the coalmining industry (including licensed mines) for recent years are as follows:

	1980–81	*1981–82*	*1982–83*	*1983–84* [1]
Saleable output of coal:				
Total deep-mined (1m. tonnes)	111·4	110·0	106·2	92·0
Opencast (1m. tonnes)	15·3	14·3	14·7	14·1
Average weekly number of wage-earners on colliery books:				
All workers (NCB only)	229,808	218,519	207,640	191,305
Underground workers (NCB only)	183,631	176,036	167,876	155,638
Coal exports:				
Total (1m. tonnes)	4·84	9·37	7·13	6·92

[1] 53 week year.

Total stocks of coal on 31 March 1984 amounted to 46·2m. tonnes (24·5m. tonnes distributed, 21·7m. tonnes undistributed). Trading profit made by the NCB for the year ended 31 March 1984 amounted to £410m. Interest payable was £467m., of which to the Secretary of State for Energy, £402m. There was a Deficit grant of £875m. from the Government for the year ended 31 March 1984.

Production of coke (including coke breeze) amounted in 1983–84 to 3·2m. tonnes.

In 1983–84 inland consumption (in 1,000 tonnes) of coal is estimated to have been 113,685, some of the principal users being: Power stations, 83,987; coke ovens, 10,576; domestic, 7,792; other conversion industries, 2,204; collieries, 437; industry, 7,006.

The UK is among the 10 largest steel producing countries in the world. Output in recent years was as follows (in 1,000 tonnes):

	Pig-iron	*Crude steel*	*Home consumption* [1]
1980[2]	6,316	11,277	15,990
1981	9,554	15,573	15,650
1982	8,389	13,704	15,120
1983	9,560	14,986	14,760
1984	9,562	15,120	...

[1] Finished steel (crude steel equivalent).
[2] 1980 figures affected by 3-month industrial dispute.

Exports of finished steel products were 3·9m. tonnes in 1983 and 4m. tonnes in 1984. Imports were 3·9m. tonnes in 1983 and 3·6m. tonnes in 1984.

The industry is divided between the 'public sector' and the 'private sector'.

The British Steel Corporation, which was established by the Iron and Steel Act 1967, took over the 14 largest UK iron and steel making concerns (and their subsidiaries) in July 1967 and merged them into a single publicly owned business. With a turnover of more than £3,358m. and a liquid steel output of 13·4m. tonnes in 1983–84, the British Steel Corporation ranks as one of Britain's major manufacturing industries and is one of the world's largest steel makers. The number of employees at the end of 1984 was 69,000. A substantial part of the British steel industry remains in private ownership and there were in 1984 a number of significant producers in mixed public/private ownership. Although responsible for only 15% of UK crude steel production, companies other than the British Steel Corporation produce much higher proportions of steel in finished form. For some products such as wire rod, reinforcement steel, bright bars, wire, open-die forgings and high speed and tool steels, they cover nearly all UK production and hold approximately 25% of the total UK demand for finished steel products.

Iron Castings. Production of iron castings was 1·5m. tonnes in 1983 (1·5m. tonnes in 1982).

Production of non-ferrous metals in 1983 (in 1,000 tonnes): Refined copper, 144·3 (134·2 in 1982); refined lead, 322·2 (306·2); tin metal, 13·6 in 1982; virgin aluminium, 252·5 (240·8); slab zinc, 87·7 (79·3).

Agriculture. The total land area of the UK is 24m. hectares, of which 18·74m. (1983) is agricultural.

Distribution of the cultivated area in the UK (in 1,000 hectares):

	1982	*1983*
Corn crops[1]	4,030	3,961
Green crops[2]	975	1,003
Hops	6	6
Fruit	61	58
Bare fallow	55	97
Rotation grasses including lucerne	1,859	1,846
Permanent pasture	5,097	5,107

[1] Includes wheat, barley, rye and oats.
[2] Green crops include beans, potatoes, turnips and swedes, mangolds, sugar-beet, cabbage, etc., for fodder, vegetables, and all other crops.

The number of workers employed in agriculture, forestry and fishing in the UK was, in June 1983, 349,000; 328,000 were solely engaged in agriculture; there were also (Dec. 1982) 186,400 farmers, partners and directors.

Principal crops in the UK as at June in each year:

	Wheat	*Barley*	*Oats*	*Beans*	*Potatoes*	*Fodder crops*	*Sugar-beet*	*Rape for oilseed*
				Area (1,000 hectares)				
1979	1,371	2,343	136	60	204	204	214	74
1980	1,441	2,330	148	61	206	200	213	92
1981	1,491	2,327	144	58	191	222	210	125
1982	1,663	2,222	129	52	192	166	204	174
1983	1,695	2,143	108	45	195	180	199	222
				Total product (1,000 tonnes)				
1979	7,140	9,550	535	286	6,485	9,049	7,660	198
1980	8,470	10,320	600	251	7,105	8,335	7,380	300
1981	8,710	10,230	620	209	6,215	7,945	7,395	325
1982	10,310	10,960	575	229	6,875	7,565	10,005	581
1983	10,880	10,080	465	188	4,780	6,160	7,494	563

Livestock in the UK as at June in each year (in 1,000):

	1979	*1980*	*1981*	*1982*	*1983*
Cattle	13,543	13,426	13,137	13,242	13,290
Sheep	29,860	31,446	32,091	33,053	34,069
Pigs	7,844	7,815	7,828	8,023	8,174
Poultry	134,700	135,105	132,286	135,363	128,260

Forestry. On 31 March 1984 the area of productive woodland in Britain was 2,018,000 hectares of which the Forestry Commission managed 902,000 hectares and the private sector 1,116,000 hectares.

The Forestry Commission employed 6,745 staff in 1984. In addition a further 11,350 were employed in private forestry with an estimated 8,100 engaged in the wood processing industry.

In 1983–84 a total of 4·61m. cu. metres of timber was thinned and felled (3·71m. conifer; 2·77m. by the Forestry Commission).

New Planting (1983–84) 25,300 hectares (8,400, Forestry Commission; 16,900, private woodlands).

James, N. D. G., *A History of English Forestry*. London, 1981

Fisheries. Quantity (in 1,000 tonnes) and value (in £1,000) of fish of British taking landed in Great Britain (excluding salmon and sea-trout):

Quantity	*1979*	*1980*	*1981*	*1982*	*1983*
Wet fish	764·1	679·0	664·6	689·4	659·2
Shell fish	62·5	68·6	62·9	60·0	66·9
	826·6	747·6	727·5	749·4	726·1
Value					
Wet fish	211,892	184,847	188,152	213,108	224,625
Shell fish	35,545	32,245	34,405	38,685	47,243
	247,437	217,092	222,557	251,793	271,868

The fishing fleet of England and Wales comprised (1983) 4,662 vessels including

1,750 trawlers and 678 line fishing vessels; the Scottish fleet (1983) 2,214 vessels including 740 trawlers and 878 creel fishing vessels.

INDUSTRY AND TRADE

Industry. Statistics of a cross-section of industrial production are as follows (in 1,000 tonnes):

	1981	*1982*	*1983*
Sulphuric acid	2,889	2,587	2,631
Synthetic resins	1,973	1,662	1,415
Cotton single yarn	43	42	41
Wool tops	39	37	39
Woollen yarn	72	53	56
Man-made fibres (rayon, nylon, etc.)	395	334	389
Newsprint	113	86	80
Other paper and board	3,265	3,140	3,132
Cement	12,729	12,962	13,396
Fabricated aluminium (to consumers)	444	455	461

Engineering. Manufacturers' sales (in £1m.) for 1983 (1982 in brackets): Motor vehicles and engines, 4,778 (4,843); motor vehicle bodies and parts, 3,424 (3,111); boilers and process plant, 1,557 (1,530); constructional steelwork, 1,151 (1,234); mechanical lifting and handling equipment, 1,177 (1,111); refrigerating, space-heating, ventilating and air conditioning equipment, 1,094 (986); construction and earth-moving equipment, 821 (936), wheeled tractors, 903 (881); industrial (including marine) engines, 750 (872).

Electrical Goods. Manufacturers' sales (in £1m.) for 1983 (1982 in brackets): Radio and electronic capital goods, 2,127 (1,933); basic electrical equipment, 2,124 (2,174); electronic data processing equipment, 1,464 (1,097); telephone and telegraph apparatus and equipment, 1,434 (1,284); domestic electrical appliances, 1,055 (902).

Textile Manufacturers. Production of woven cloth for 1983 (1982 in brackets): cotton (1m. metres), 255 (261); man-made fibres (1m. metres), 176 (205); woven woollen and worsted fabrics (1m. sq. metres), deliveries, 94 (100).

Construction. Total value (in £1m.) of constructional work by all agencies in 1983 was 24,343 (22,540 in 1982), including new work, 13,396 (12,629) of which new housing, 4,849 (3,920). Houses for private developers, 3,729 (2,899). New work (other than housing) for private developers, 4,817 (5,038), for public authorities, 3,729 (3,671).

Annual Abstract of Statistics. HMSO
Chester, Sir N., *The Nationalisation of British Industry, 1945–51.* HMSO, 1976
Kelf-Cohen, R., *British Nationalization: 1945–1973.* New York, 1973
Statistical Summary of the Mineral Industry. HMSO, annual

Labour. The distribution of total manpower in Great Britain was in June 1983 (in 1,000): Total working population, 26,136 (15,775 males, 10,361 females). Total employed in armed forces and women's services, 322. Total in civil employment, 20,744, including agriculture, 320; energy and water supply, 653 (of which coal-mining, 256); manufacture, 5,539; public administration and defence, 1,547; transport and communications, 1,313; construction, 991; distributive trades, 2,930; insurance, banking, business services, 2,706; education, 1,543; medicine, 1,292.

The average monthly numbers (based on claimants in 1,000) of registered unemployed in Great Britain were: 1978, 1,321 (males, 966; females, 355), 1979, 1,234 (887; 347); 1980, 1,591 (1,129; 461); 1981, 2,422 (1,773; 649); 1982, 2,809 (2,056; 753); 1983, 2,988 (2,134; 854).

Trade Unions. In Dec. 1983 there were 102 unions affiliated to the Trades Union Congress with a total membership of 10,510,157 (including about 3·5m. women). The unions affiliated to the TUC in 1983 ranged in size from the Transport and General Workers' Union, with 1,632,957 members, to the Cloth Pressers' Society with 16 members. Non-manual workers accounted for nearly a third of the total TUC membership.

The TUC's executive body, the General Council, is elected at the annual Congress. It is composed of 51 members made up of 34 members nominated by unions with a membership of over 100,000, entitled to automatic representation in proportion to their size, 11 members elected by and from unions smaller than 100,000 and 6 members elected by Congress as a whole to represent women workers.

The General Secretary is elected by the Congress but is not subject to annual re-election.

The TUC General Council appoints committees, which draw upon the services of specialist departments in preparing policies on economic, education, international, employment, industrial organization, and social questions.

The TUC is affiliated to the International Confederation of Free Trade Unions, the Trade Union Advisory Committee of OECD, the Commonwealth Trade Union Council and the European Trade Union Confederation. The TUC provides a service of trade union education. It provides members to serve, with representatives of employers, on joint committees advising the Government on issues of national importance (e.g., National Economic Development Council and various Royal Commissions) and on the managing boards of such bodies as the Health and Safety Commission; Advisory, Conciliation and Arbitration Service; and Manpower Services Commission.

The following table is a statistical summary relating to trade disputes for recent years:

	No. of workers involved	*Working days lost through stoppages*
1981	1,499,000	4,266,000
1982	2,101,000	5,313,000
1983	538,000	3,593,000

Lovell, J., and Robert, B. C., *A Short History of the T.U.C.* London, 1968
Pelling, H., *A History of British Trade Unionism.* 2nd ed. London, 1972

Commerce. Value of the imports and exports of merchandise (excluding bullion and specie and foreign merchandise transhipped under bond) of the UK for 6 recent years (in £1,000):

	Total imports	*Total exports*		*Total imports*	*Total exports*
1979	48,467,400	42,803,609	1982	56,940,267	55,538,408
1980	51,650,267	49,510,791	1983	65,993,096	60,533,692
1981	51,163,579	50,995,080	1984	78,705,170	70,511,345

The value of goods imported is generally taken to be that at the port and time of entry, including all incidental expenses (cost, insurance and freight) up to the landing on the quay. For goods consigned for sale, the market value in this country is required and recorded in the returns. For exports, the value at the port of shipment (including the charges of delivering the goods on board) is taken. Imports are entered as from the country whence the goods were consigned to the UK, which may, or may not, be the country whence they were last shipped. Exports are credited to the country of ultimate destination as declared by the exporters.

For details of imports and exports for 1983 and 1984, *see* pp. 1317–21.

Trade according to countries for 1983 and 1984 (in £1,000):

Countries	*Imports of merchandise from* 1983[1]	1984[1]	*Exports of merchandise to* 1983[1]	1984[1]
Foreign countries				
Europe and Overseas Possessions—				
Albania	240	1,097	2,983	4,481
Austria	438,446	529,620	273,702	320,901
Belgium and Luxembourg	3,133,905	3,691,794	2,572,673	3,051,722
Bulgaria	12,355	17,345	44,577	55,917
Czechoslovakia	101,302	117,188	69,456	78,075
Denmark and Faroe Islands	1,528,552	1,678,096	1,161,516	1,202,521
Finland	995,017	1,248,561	539,721	684,477
France	5,043,118	5,885,715	5,651,521	7,082,389
German Dem. Rep.	167,625	198,130	60,997	92,270
Germany (Fed. Rep. of)	9,667,444	11,090,227	6,063,989	7,458,042
Greece	164,917	279,367	280,204	354,332
Hungary	53,834	75,905	91,845	100,502
Iceland	66,505	86,104	65,176	64,242
Italy	3,188,219	3,814,163	2,292,788	2,902,666
Netherlands	5,097,763	6,147,298	5,440,701	6,127,991
Netherlands Antilles	97,486	221,012	84,289	20,235
Norway	2,820,760	3,852,657	828,612	968,404
Poland	177,067	266,961	151,721	169,962
Portugal, Azores and Madeira	475,902	644,520	396,988	385,799
Romania	58,865	226,091	82,160	71,641
Spain	1,110,029	1,604,405	1,128,439	1,234,584
Canary Islands	56,305	63,456	98,603	84,550
Sweden	2,051,931	2,416,383	2,397,464	2,888,625
Switzerland and Liechtenstein	2,154,085	2,490,593	1,385,894	1,549,469
Turkey	184,976	204,131	244,024	331,360
USSR	728,491	854,307	445,008	735,173
Yugoslavia	83,951	108,479	148,645	163,871
EEC	30,098,053	35,204,049	26,516,335	31,568,022
EFTA	9,003,645	11,268,439	5,887,557	6,861,917
Africa—				
Algeria	157,645	274,155	233,426	272,438
Angola	45,732	158,636	22,847	35,581
Burundi	3,485	1,924	3,155	1,710
Cameroon	52,481	132,539	26,445	23,254
Egypt	79,826	164,946	370,489	427,688
Ethiopia	12,071	13,733	34,092	63,434
Ivory Coast	79,255	93,875	25,591	25,347
Liberia	7,181	6,975	13,877	30,980
Libya	224,050	155,276	274,169	246,467
Mali	3,833	5,646	15,856	5,471
Mauritania	6,044	10,343	1,719	2,656
Morocco	75,602	79,738	99,727	79,850
Mozambique	9,175	8,589	28,618	15,671
Rwanda	2,919	7,842	2,326	2,385
Senegal	22,333	23,789	13,212	15,772
South Africa, Republic of	764,909	725,631	1,109,039	205,143
S.W. Africa/Namibia	62,437	64,015	3,425	5,200
Sudan	18,693	16,858	133,432	95,627
Tunisia	18,126	21,086	44,659	47,077
Zaïre	11,192	7,720	21,129	36,254
Asia—				
Afghánistán	19,837	20,776	10,310	11,892
Bahrain	37,488	28,240	150,264	138,614
Burma	4,726	6,420	21,927	16,488
China	231,417	278,474	159,722	317,256
Indonesia	169,454	181,490	193,642	186,732
Iran	100,545	368,572	629,980	703,097
Iraq	30,334	69,047	400,259	343,120
Israel	311,110	392,757	334,860	393,025
Japan	3,355,450	3,768,019	797,848	925,311
Jordan	28,680	18,114	262,503	192,508
Korea (South)	440,354	443,819	168,942	219,406
Kuwait	67,281	141,606	333,273	301,520

[1] Provisional figures.

Countries	Imports of merchandise from 1983[1]	1984[1]	Exports of merchandise to 1983[1]	1984[1]
Asia—(contd.)				
Lebanon	11,521	5,869	81,435	76,223
Pakistan	80,277	93,136	191,647	282,536
Philippines	160,701	199,659	102,949	91,751
Qatar	10,063	28,212	216,385	133,803
Saudi Arabia	897,702	545,149	1,478,587	387,163
Syria	18,859	59,245	72,320	91,909
Thailand	87,823	112,353	131,833	149,742
America—				
Argentina	194	65	4,472	5,232
Bolivia	14,834	20,052	4,711	17,170
Brazil	560,277	637,702	157,758	238,717
Chile	107,644	108,420	43,520	74,997
Colombia	56,458	80,387	51,023	43,485
Costa Rica	22,299	21,248	11,041	9,138
Cuba	14,010	13,020	45,737	64,377
Dominican Republic	6,662	5,620	11,594	12,535
Ecuador	11,022	12,951	35,008	34,323
El Salvador	425	2,551	7,653	7,589
Guatemala	9,764	9,565	7,440	10,660
Haiti	1,646	1,402	4,171	3,736
Honduras	7,082	12,360	9,539	7,382
Mexico	160,978	175,487	95,674	150,126
Nicaragua	1,810	2,176	2,367	4,755
Panama	5,341	9,681	42,276	74,322
Paraguay	3,129	2,961	15,263	16,884
Peru	118,414	119,423	32,947	33,841
Puerto Rico	58,804	76,854	35,936	72,695
Uruguay	33,361	33,292	10,763	13,980
USA	7,442,671	9,356,029	8,336,979	10,149,479
Venezuela	183,731	253,770	87,937	102,400
Total (including those not specified above)	57,352,440	68,638,338	50,833,257	59,426,563
Commonwealth countries:				
In Europe—				
Cyprus	87,436	94,381	127,837	146,773
Gibraltar	4,266	5,333	26,495	31,978
Malta	40,852	45,076	71,895	89,468
In Africa				
West Africa:				
Gambia	3,781	3,407	13,261	10,233
Ghana	58,192	61,561	82,234	82,897
Nigeria, Federation of	387,975	375,976	798,276	768,479
Sierra Leone	17,710	25,971	13,735	19,532
South Africa:				
Botswana	21,713	14,913	3,250	9,015
Lesotho	216	78	2,080	1,633
Malawi	42,050	65,327	18,183	22,995
Swaziland	23,966	41,786	3,536	2,430
Zambia	50,242	48,069	55,501	66,746
Zimbabwe	68,446	74,090	64,734	68,636
East Africa:				
Kenya	128,454	203,243	111,249	176,061
Mauritius	128,437	160,042	22,499	24,358
Tanzania	46,525	43,179	62,055	60,449
Uganda	29,645	46,750	21,092	29,294
Seychelles	615	586	7,502	7,540
St Helena	457	979	10,343	6,294
In Asia—				
Bangladesh	4,726	46,506	50,979	51,591
Hong Kong	1,178,343	1,266,964	726,711	897,419
India	366,928	571,470	804,779	780,997
Malaysia	222,673	320,325	248,239	283,269
Singapore	404,122	488,421	469,155	556,443
Sri Lanka	25,189	77,163	70,136	61,179

[1] Provisional figures.

Countries	Imports of merchandise from 1983[1]	1984[1]	Exports of merchandise to 1983[1]	1984[1]
In Oceania—				
Australia	552,642	612,087	940,279	186,521
Fiji Islands	46,943	70,209	12,184	11,281
Nauru	1,421	916	1,715	1,332
New Zealand	486,305	483,747	286,054	367,512
Papua New Guinea	28,142	68,245	18,236	14,643
Western Samoa	156	421	468	1,183
In America—				
Bahamas	24,013	38,478	17,815	220,356
Barbados	11,899	22,509	31,938	30,654
Belize	11,565	15,911	8,726	11,501
Bermuda	4,019	3,037	24,924	22,843
Canada	1,522,187	1,617,476	968,269	1,183,231
Falkland Islands	4,022	5,202	7,269	9,516
Guyana	42,810	57,884	13,685	14,845
Jamaica	94,036	77,895	116,188	48,088
Leeward Islands	3,852	3,045	20,577	30,698
Trinidad and Tobago	52,748	164,715	148,811	113,312
Windward Islands	39,843	63,394	17,926	30,725
Total, Commonwealth countries (including those not specified above)	6,350,589	7,431,793	6,645,160	7,691,283
Ireland	2,290,067	2,635,039	3,055,277	3,393,499
Grand Total	65,993,096	78,705,170	60,533,692	70,511,345

[1] Provisional figures.

Imports and exports for 1983 and 1984 (Great Britain and Northern Ireland) (in £1,000):

Import values c.i.f. *Export values f.o.b.*	Total imports 1983[1]	1984[1]	Domestic exports 1983[1]	1984[1]
0. *Food and Live Animals*				
Live animals (excluding zoo animals, dogs and cats)	170,334	196,896	187,356	190,990
Meat and meat preparations	1,313,480	1,342,391	496,238	491,051
Dairy products and eggs	629,191	605,612	305,866	246,589
Fish and fish preparations	505,590	537,896	203,617	224,435
Cereals and cereal preparations	595,340	628,983	736,712	992,742
Fruit and vegetables	1,718,946	1,931,057	163,162	190,761
Sugar, sugar preparations, honey	424,436	524,300	144,917	165,669
Coffee, tea, cocoa, spices	800,004	1,291,896	291,318	363,470
Feeding stuff for animals	523,629	501,522	78,735	96,782
Miscellaneous food preparations	210,385	262,624	140,691	152,314
Total of Section 0	6,891,336	7,823,177	2,748,612	3,114,803
1. *Beverages and Tobacco*				
Beverages	617,339	705,466	1,051,195	1,156,994
Tobacco and tobacco manufactures	344,743	407,053	434,976	420,896
Total of Section 1	962,083	1,112,519	1,486,172	1,577,890
2. *Crude Materials, Inedible, except Fuels*				
Hides, skins and furskins, undressed	184,878	235,278	200,179	280,261
Oil seeds, oil nuts and oil kernels	216,929	235,416	37,841	53,963
Crude rubber (including synthetic and reclaimed)	197,445	223,535	141,667	166,678
Wood and cork	937,988	1,009,197	24,148	25,503
Pulp and waste paper	428,033	611,687	15,784	27,214
Textile fibres and their waste	475,571	596,818	374,695	427,921
Crude fertilizers and crude minerals (excluding fuels)	285,695	312,945	223,857	249,065

[1] Provisional figures.

Import values c.i.f. *Export values f.o.b.*	*Total imports* *1983*[1]	*1984*[1]	*Domestic exports* *1983*[1]	*1984*[1]
2. *Crude Materials, Inedible, except Fuels*—Contd.				
Metalliferous ores and metal scrap	1,358,103	1,344,217	444,200	591,439
Crude animal and vegetable materials, not elsewhere specified	279,852	317,389	64,914	75,644
Total of Section 2	4,364,493	4,886,482	1,527,285	1,697,688
3. *Mineral Fuels, Lubricants and Related Materials*				
Coal, coke and briquettes	276,081	674,255	239,437	88,957
Petroleum and petroleum products	5,738,044	8,078,417	12,524,959	14,909,767
Gas, natural and manufactured	1,052,938	1,439,915	362,115	367,860
Total of Section 3	7,067,063	10,192,587	13,126,511	15,366,584
4. *Animal and Vegetable Oils and Fats*	358,811	533,460	59,106	90,966
5. *Chemicals*				
Chemical elements and compounds	2,017,606	2,573,564	2,627,096	3,192,870
Dyeing, tanning and colouring materials	235,064	269,668	568,714	633,269
Medicinal and pharmaceutical products	470,122	542,280	1,074,213	1,222,449
Essential oils and perfume; toilet and cleansing preparations	305,258	377,080	574,323	690,489
Fertilizers, manufactured	172,546	219,420	69,682	64,383
Plastic materials	1,323,445	1,609,679	980,133	1,179,944
Total[2] of Section 5	5,119,501	6,311,527	6,929,252	8,214,762
6. *Manufactured Goods Classified Chiefly by Material*				
Leather and dressed furs	183,981	245,085	232,944	312,487
Rubber	419,604	457,185	451,844	481,903
Wood and cork (excluding furniture)	578,767	622,423	85,189	104,578
Paper, paperboard	1,906,348	2,281,465	543,136	678,514
Textile yarn, fabrics	2,320,056	2,706,248	1,284,638	1,484,821
Non-metallic mineral manufactures	2,085,501	2,269,201	1,994,994	2,298,698
Iron and steel	1,260,654	1,487,190	1,330,851	1,529,079
Non-ferrous metals	1,975,277	1,996,637	1,614,520	1,656,622
Manufactures of metal, not elsewhere specified	1,108,937	1,385,187	1,324,047	1,464,579
Total of Section 6	11,840,125	13,450,620	8,862,164	10,011,281
7. *Machinery and Transport Equipment*				
Boilers, engines, motors and power-units	1,569,162	1,782,626	2,472,470	2,686,353
Agricultural and Industrial machinery	3,919,818	4,754,764	5,085,687	5,754,539
Office machinery	3,019,923	4,112,261	2,049,184	3,046,240
Electrical machinery, apparatus, not elsewhere specified	4,723,665	5,696,995	3,281,166	3,921,945
Transport equipment	6,998,124	7,321,035	5,425,152	6,075,811
Total of Section 7	20,230,691	23,667,681	18,313,659	21,484,888

[1] Provisional figures.
[2] Includes items not specified here.

Import values c.i.f. *Export values f.o.b.*	*Total imports* *1983*[1]	*1984*[1]	*Domestic exports* *1983*[1]	*1984*[1]
8. *Miscellaneous Manufactured Articles*				
Sanitary, plumbing, heating and lighting fixtures	126,737	151,254	108,340	119,041
Furniture	490,473	591,791	257,784	282,112
Travel goods, handbags and similar articles	131,104	161,948	19,266	22,437
Clothing	1,601,480	2,013,149	865,394	996,392
Footwear	541,985	642,195	123,428	142,680
Scientific instruments; cameras, watches and clocks	1,303,670	2,660,702	1,472,374	2,473,128
Miscellaneous manufactured articles, not elsewhere specified	3,522,243	3,235,089	2,967,477	2,921,438
Total of Section 8	7,714,693	9,456,128	5,814,062	6,957,228
9. *Commodities and Transactions not Classified According to Kind*				
Total of Section 9	1,444,299	1,270,989	1,666,870	1,795,254
Total[2] of all classes	65,993,096	78,705,170	60,533,692	70,511,345

[1] Provisional figures. [2] Includes items not specified here.

Tourism. There were an estimated 13·5m. overseas visitors in 1984. Foreign exchange from tourism was more than £5,000m. including fares paid to British air and shipping lines.

COMMUNICATIONS

Roads. Central government responsibility for highways in England rests with the Secretary of State for Transport. His responsibilities are administered by the Department of Transport through a number of Directorates at Headquarters together with 9 Regional Offices. For Welsh and Scottish roads central government responsibility rests with the Secretaries of State for Wales and Scotland respectively.

The Secretary of State is the highway authority responsible for all trunk roads. Under the local government system introduced in 1974, the highway authority for local roads are the County Councils. In London responsibility is shared between the Greater London Council, the London Boroughs and the Common Council of the City of London.

The Secretary of State has powers to provide roads designed for limited classes of motor traffic, and to confirm schemes for the provision of such special roads by local authorities. The former have the status of trunk roads; the latter principal roads. They are generally referred to as motorways. 2,353 km of motorways in England were open to traffic in 1983 and some 122 km of trunk motorway are under construction.

The design and supervision of the construction of major trunk road schemes is carried out by firms of consulting engineers and by local authorities which act as the Secretary of State's agents. The Regional Offices ensure that schemes progress in accordance with the Secretary of State's statutory and financial responsibilities. Directors (Transport) are responsible for smaller trunk road schemes and for the maintenance of all trunk roads, including motorways. Local authorities can act as the Secretary of State's agents for construction and maintenance. The work is carried out by them or by contractors on their behalf and the cost borne by Central Government.

Aid to local authorities' transport expenditure is now given through Rate Support Grant and through Transport Supplementary Grant; the latter is paid to County Councils on capital expenditure on roads and traffic regulation accepted by the Secretary of State as being of more than local importance.

Public highways in Great Britain in 1983, excluding lengths of unsurfaced roads (green lanes), totalled 343,978 km (England, 262,293 km; Wales, 32,382 km; Scotland, 50,343 km). There were 12,653 km of all-purpose trunk roads, 2,709 km of trunk and principal motorways, 34,587 km of principal roads (excluding motorways) and 295,361 km of other roads.

Motor vehicles for which licences were current under the Vehicles (Excise) Act, 1971, at 31 Dec. 1983, numbered 20·22m., including 17·16m. private cars and private vans, 1·29m. mopeds, scooters and motor cycles, 113,000 public transport vehicles and 2·2m. goods vehicles.

New vehicle registrations in 1983 numbered 2·3m.

Road casualties in Great Britain numbered in 1983, 309,000 including 5,445 killed; in 1982, 334,000 including 5,934 killed.

Railways. The British Railways Board as a public authority owns and manages British Rail, the national rail network, British Rail Engineering Ltd., British Rail Property Board, Freightliners Ltd., Transportation Systems and Market Research Ltd. (Transmark) and Travellers-Fare. The role of the Board is to determine policies and objectives, establish the organisation to carry them out, monitor performance and take major decisions.

The Group turnover in 1983 was nearly £2,260m. and just under 200,000 staff were employed, of which 155,000 were involved in the railway business.

The management of the railways is the responsibility of the Chief Executive (Railways). He establishes plans and budgets for the achievement of objectives set by the Board, monitors and achieves results against the plans and budgets, and directs the organisation and deployment of manpower resources. He is assisted by other Board members with responsibility for functions such as Engineering, Research, Finance and Planning, Marketing, Operating, Productivity and Personnel.

In 1983, British Rail carried 145m. tonnes of freight and parcels and 695m. passenger journeys were made.

The rail business is split into 5 sectors and directors act on behalf of the Chief Executive (Railways) to control policy. The sectors are InterCity, London and South East Services, Provincial Services, Freight and Parcels. A director is responsible for efficient operation and budgeting within his sector, each of which bears its fair share of the fixed costs of operation, such as signalling and track maintenance. The day-to-day running of the rail network is the responsibility of 5 regional managers to whom local area and station managers report.

		1982	*1983*
Passenger Receipts and Traffic			
1 Receipts	£m.	924·1	1,149·5
Passenger journeys	m.	630·1	695·2
Passenger miles (estimated)	m.	17,100·0	18,700·0
Freight Train Traffic			
Receipts	£m.	478·2	582·6
Traffic	m. tonnes	141·9	145·1
Net tonne miles (trainload and wagonload)	m.	9,867·0	10,653·0
Locomotives			
Diesel		2,750	2,603
Electric		266	247
High Speed Tains			
Power cars		197	197
Passenger carriages		709	709
Coaching vehicles		16,889	16,224
Freight vehicles (excluding brake vans)		71,452	54,510
Stations		2,711	2,619
Route open for traffic	miles	10,706	10,541

The London Regional Transport (formerly London Transport Executive) is the authority responsible for the operation of the capital's Underground and bus services. Overall policy and financial control is exercised by the Secretary of State for Transport. In Jan. 1984, London Transport had 241 route miles of railway open for traffic and also operated over 13 route miles owned by British Rail. Rolling stock owned: Underground, 3,875 (2,457 motor cars, 1,418 trailer cars); buses, 5,638. Number of train miles run in passenger service (1983) was 29m.; number of bus miles run in passenger service (1983) was 163m. The number of passengers carried in 1983 was: Underground 563m.; buses 1,088m. Average fare per passenger journey (1983): Underground 50·7p; buses 24·4p.

Gross receipts in 1980 for these Boards were: British Railways Board, from 1975 the Railways Act 1974 introduced, *inter alia*, new arrangements for the financial support of the railway passenger system and provided for the reconstruction of the finances of the Board (1981) £1,664·8m.[1]; London Transport, (1983), £578m.[1]; British Transport Docks Board, £131·2m.; National Bus Company, £4,603m.[1]; National Freight Corporation, £417m., and British Waterways Board, £13·1m.[1].

[1] Excludes support grants.

Railway Finances. [Serpell Report] HMSO, London, 1983

Aviation. British Airways plc took over the business and undertaking of British Airways Board from 1 April 1984. March 1985 the company was government owned but there are plans for 'privatisation'. Initially it acted as a holding corporation for the two state airlines British Overseas Airways Corporation (BOAC) and British European Airways Corporation (BEA), but as from 1 April 1974 the business of BOAC and BEA were transferred to and vested in British Airways Board and BOAC and BEA were dissolved.

British Airways is engaged in the provision of air transport services for passengers, cargo and mail worldwide, both on scheduled and charter services. It operates long and short haul international services, as well as an extensive domestic network. In 1983–84, it carried 14·2m. passengers, and at 31 March 1984 it had a fleet of 183 aircraft (including 33 helicopters) and it employed 36,933 personnel.

In addition to British Airways, there were 1983 about 41 independent air transport operators, the principal ones being British Caledonian Airways, Britannia Airway and British Midland Airways. In recent years there has been a significant expansion of the independent operators.

Pursuant to the Civil Aviation Act 1980, the business and undertaking of British Airways Board was transferred to and vested in a limited liability company, British Airways Plc, with effect from 1 April 1984. Although HM Government will initially hold all the shares in the new company, it is the Government's intention, pursuant to its 'privatization' polices, to introduce private capital into the company at the earliest suitable opportunity.

Following the Civil Aviation Act 1971, the Civil Aviation Authority was established as an independent public body responsible for the economic and safety regulation of British civil aviation. It took over the responsibilities of the former Air Transport Licensing Board and Air Registration Board, and also runs the National Air Traffic Services in conjunction with the Ministry of Defence.

In addition to the public transport operators there are a number of companies engaged in miscellaneous aviation activities such as crop-spraying, aerial survey and photography, and flying instruction.

The operating and traffic statistics of the UK airlines on scheduled services during the calendar year 1982 (and 1983) are as follows: Aircraft km flown, 332m. (325m.); revenue passengers carried, 20·6m. (20·4m.); cargo (freight and mail) carried 263,798 (294,247) tonnes.

Traffic between the UK airports and places abroad in 1982 (and 1983) on all services included 511,375 (526,509) air transport aircraft movements.

There were 7,283 civil aircraft registered in the UK at 31 Dec. 1984.

Shipping. The UK flag merchant fleet in July 1984 totalled 23·2m. DWT (dry cargo, 9·6m. DWT; tankers 13·6m. DWT) representing 3·5% of the world fleet. The total number of UK flag ships was 1,151. The number of UK nationality seafarers was about 36,000 as at 31 Dec. 1984.

Capital investment in new tonnage and facilities by British shipping companies 1977–83 (inclusive) was over £2,400m. In 1983 capital expenditure was an estimated £253m. The average age of UK owned and registered tonnage in mid-1983 was 9·4 years.

Total gross earnings by UK owned and registered ships in 1983 amounted to £2,199m. The net contribution to UK balance of payments was £548m. and, in addition, there were gross import savings of £589m.

On 30 Nov. 1984, 64 UK flag ships (3·6m. DWT) were laid up out of a world total of 1,368 ships (65·7m. DWT).

GCBS Facts and Figures 1980. 1980
Committee of Inquiry into Shipping. Cmnd 4337. HMSO, 1970

Inland Waterways. There are approximately 2,500 miles of navigable canals and locked river navigations in Great Britain. Of these, the British Waterways Board is responsible for some 300 miles of commercial waterways (maintained for freight traffic) and some 1,100 miles of cruising waterways (maintained for pleasure cruising, fishing and amenity). The Board is also responsible for a further 600 miles of canals, some of which are no longer navigable and whose future is being considered in conjunction with local authorities; a number of these lengths have been restored for cruising or as local amenities. The Board's gross receipts for the year 1983 were £18·5m. The total traffic on their waterways was 4.9m. tonnes.

The most important of the river navigations and canals under other authorities include the rivers Thames, Great Ouse, Nene and Yorkshire Ouse, the Norfolk Broads and the Manchester Ship Canal.

The Port of Manchester was opened to maritime traffic in 1894 by the construction of the Manchester Ship Canal, which is 35¼ miles in length and owned and operated by the Manchester Ship Canal Company. The entrance lock is 80 ft (24·38 metres) wide and the maximum width of other locks within the canal is 65 ft (19·81 metres). Ships up to 28 ft 10 in. (8·78 metres) freshwater draught can navigate to Ince Oil Berth; ships up to 24 ft (7·31 metres) draught can navigate to Manchester docks but within these docks draught is limited to 22 ft (6·70 metres).

The Port of Manchester includes the Queen Elizabeth II Oil Dock at Eastham (separate entrance lock 100 ft wide), the oil docks at Stanlow and a considerable number of public and private wharves and installations along the canal, as well as the container terminal at Ellesmere Port. Total sea-borne and barge traffic in 1984 amounted to 11m. tonnes; operating revenue, £23·1m.; profit after tax, £1·13m. The total issued capital at 31 Dec. 1983 was £17·2m.

Edwards, L. A., *Inland Waterways of Great Britain and Northern Ireland.* 5th ed. St. Ives, 1972
Farnie, D. A., *The Manchester Ship Canal and the Rise of the Port of Manchester.* Manchester Univ. Press, 1980
Hadfield, C., *British Canals.* 6th ed. Newton Abbot, 1979
McKnight, H., *The Shell Book of Inland Waterways.* Newton Abbot, 1975
Paget-Tomlinson, E. W., *Complete Book of Canal and River Navigations.* Albrighton, 1978

Posts and Telecommunications. In Oct. 1981 the Post Office ceased to control telecommunications services, which became the responsibility of a separate corporation, British Telecom. The Post Office provides: Royal Mail general collection and delivery services, handling 42m. letters and parcels a day; Royal Mail Special Services including guaranteed delivery to UK addresses on the same day and overnight (Datapost), and by facsimile transmission to many UK and overseas centres; International Datapost offering guaranteed swift delivery to 155 countries; postal, National Girobank and many agency services on behalf of government departments at 22,000 post office counters; full banking facilities through National Girobank, a separately managed business within the Corporation. Number of post offices at 31 March 1984 was 22,058; number of posting boxes including those at post offices, over 100,000; staff employed, 175,000 (including 20,500 sub-postmasters employed on an agency basis).

	1980–81 (1m.)	*1981–82 (1m.)*	*1982–83 (1m.)*	*1983–84 (1m.)*
Correspondence (incl. registered items) posted	9,969	9,883	10,500	10,700
Parcels handled	172	183	193	195

Income (1983–84) £2,844m. Profit, £117m.

In July 1984 there were 6,096 local exchanges, 266 automanual centres, 365 main network switching centres, 76,500 call offices, 23·6m. exchange connections and 29m. telephone stations. During the year 18,750m. local telephone calls, 3,931m. trunk calls and 369m. international calls were made.

There were 94,000 telex exchange connexions, 110·3m. inland telex calls were made and 494m. international telex minutes recorded.

Broadcasting. Radio and television services are provided by the BBC and by the Independent Broadcasting Authority and its programme contractors. The BBC, constituted by Royal Charter until 31 Dec. 1996, has responsibility for providing domestic and external broadcast services, the former financed from the television licence revenue, the latter by Government grant. The domestic services include 2 national television services, 4 national radio network services and an expanding local radio service.

The IBA constituted until 31 Dec. 1996 by the Broadcasting Act 1981 provides an independent television service on a regional basis, with programmes provided by its programme contractors. The 1981 Act provided for the establishment of the fourth television channel and of the Welsh Fourth Channel Authority (WFCA) which provides a Welsh service on that channel in Wales; they started broadcasting in Nov. 1982. The IBA also provides independent local radio services. All these services are financed by the sale of broadcast advertising time.

The BBC's domestic radio services are available on LF, MF and VHF; those of the IBA on MF and VHF. The television services of the 2 authorities BBC1, BBC2, ITV, and Channel 4 are broadcast at UHF in 625-line definition and in colour.

The broadcasting authorities, whose governing bodies are appointed (by HM the Queen in the case of the BBC and by the Home Secretary in the case of the IBA and WFCA) as trustees for the public interest in broadcasting, are independent of government in matters of programme content and are publicly accountable to Parliament for the discharge of their responsibilities.

In 1981 the Broadcasting Complaints Commission was set up to consider and adjudicate upon complaints of unfair or unjust treatment in broadcast programmes or of unwarranted infringement of privacy in or in the making of programmes. The number of broadcast receiving licences in force on 30 Nov. 1982 was 18·41m., including 14·41m. for colour.

Cinemas. In 1983 there were 1,500 screens in 803 cinemas and there were 60m. admissions.

Newspapers. In 1983 there were 11 national dailies.

Benn's Press Directory. Tunbridge Wells, Annual

JUSTICE, RELIGION, EDUCATION AND WELFARE

Justice. *England and Wales.* The legal system of England and Wales, divided into civil and criminal courts has at the head of the superior courts, as the ultimate court of appeal, the House of Lords, which hears each year a number of appeals in civil matters, including a certain number from Scotland and Northern Ireland, as well as some appeals in criminal cases. In order that civil cases may go from the Court of Appeal to the House of Lords, it is necessary to obtain the leave of either the Court of Appeal or the House itself, although in certain cases an appeal may lie direct to the House of Lords from the decision of the High Court. An appeal can be brought from a decision of the Court of Appeal or the Divisional Court of the Queen's Bench Division of the High Court in a criminal case provided that the Court is satisfied that a point of law 'of general public importance' is involved, and either the Court or the House of Lords is of the opinion that it is desirable in the public interest that a further appeal should be brought. As a judicial body, the House of Lords consists of the Lord Chancellor, the Lords of Appeal in Ordinary, commonly called Law Lords, and such other members of the House as hold or have held high judicial office. The final court of appeal for certain of the Commonwealth countries is the Judicial Committee of the Privy Council which, in addition to Privy Counsellors who are or have held high judicial office in the UK, includes others who are or have been Chief Justices or Judges of the Superior Courts of Commonwealth countries.

Civil Law. The main courts of original civil jurisdiction are the county courts for less important cases, and the High Court for the more important ones.

There are about 300 county courts located throughout the country, grouped in districts, and each presided over by a circuit judge. They have a general jurisdiction to determine all actions founded on contract or tort involving sums of not more than £5,000 and can also deal with other classes of case, such as landlord and tenant, probate, equity and admiralty, up to certain limits. Certain matters, such as actions of libel and slander, are entirely reserved for the High Court. In addition, certain designated county courts have jurisdiction in matrimonial proceedings. Divorce proceedings must now commence in these courts and, subject to being transferred to the High Court upon becoming defended, are determined in the county court.

The High Court has both appellate and original jurisdiction, covering virtually all civil causes not determined in the county court. The judges of the High Court are attached to one of its 3 divisions: Chancery; Queen's Bench; and Family; each with its separate field of jurisdiction. There are 77 such judges, called puisne judges. For the hearing of cases at first instance, the High Court judges sit singly. Appellate jurisdiction is usually exercised by Divisional Courts consisting of 2 (sometimes 3) judges, though in certain circumstances a judge sitting alone may hear the appeal.

The Restrictive Practices Court was set up in 1956 under the Restrictive Trade Practices Act, and is responsible for deciding whether a restrictive trade agreement is in the public interest. It is presided over by a High Court judge, but laymen sit on the bench also. Another specialist court is the Employment Appeal Tribunal, with similar composition, which hears appeals in employment cases from lower tribunals.

The Court of Appeal (Civil Division) hears appeals in civil actions from the High Court and county courts and certain special courts such as the Restrictive Practices Court and the Employment Appeal Tribunal. Its President is the Master of the Rolls, aided by 18 Lords Justices of Appeal sitting in 6 or 7 divisions of 2 or 3 judges each.

Civil proceedings are instituted by the aggrieved person, but, as they are a private matter, they are frequently settled by the parties to a dispute through their lawyers before the matter actually comes to court. In some cases, at the instance of either party, a jury may sit to decide questions of fact and award of damages.

Criminal Law. At the base of the system of criminal courts in England and Wales are the magistrates' courts which try over 97% of criminal cases. In general, in exercising their summary jurisdiction, they have power to pass a sentence of up to six months imprisonment and to impose a fine of up to £2,000. They also deal with the preliminary hearing of cases triable only at the Crown Court. In addition to dealing summarily with over 2m. cases, which include thefts, assaults, road traffic infringements, drug abuse, etc, they also have a limited civil jurisdiction.

Magistrates' courts normally comprise three lay justices. Although unpaid they are entitled to loss of earnings and travel and subsistence allowance. They undergo training after appointment and they are advised by a professional justices' clerk. In central London and in some provincial areas full-time stipendiary magistrates have been appointed. They possess the same powers as the lay bench, but they sit alone.

At 1st January 1985 the total strength of the lay magistracy was 27,244 including 11,264 women. Justices are appointed on behalf of the Queen by the Lord Chancellor, except in Greater Manchester, Merseyside and Lancashire where they are appointed by the Chancellor of the Duchy of Lancaster.

Specially qualified justices sit in juvenile courts to deal with cases involving persons under 17 years of age charged with criminal offences (other than homicide and other grave offences) or brought before the court as being in need of care or control. These courts normally sit with three justices, including at least one man or one woman, and are accommodated separately from other courts.

Justices also sit in Domestic Proceedings courts which deal with matrimonial applications, custody, guardianship and maintenance of children, affiliation and adoption. These courts normally sit with three justices including at least one man or one woman.

The Employment Appeal Tribunal. The Employment Appeal Tribunal which is a superior Court of Record with the like powers, rights, privileges and authority of the High Court, was set up in 1976 to hear appeals on questions of fact and law against decisions of industrial tribunals and of the Certification Officer. The appeals are heard by a High Court Judge sitting with 2 members (in exceptional cases 4) appointed for their special knowledge or experience of industrial relations either on the employer or the trade union side; with always an equal number on each side. Industrial tribunals are responsible for deciding questions under Employment Protection (Consolidation) Act, 1978, Equal Pay Act, 1970, Sex Discrimination Act 1975, Employment Protection Act 1975, Employment Act 1980, Race Relations Act, 1976, and Employment Acts 1980 and 1982. The great bulk of their work is concerned with the problems which can arise between employees and their employers. The Certification Officer is responsible for deciding questions under the Trade Union Act 1913, the Trade Union (Amalgamations, etc.) Act 1964, the Trade Union and Labour Relations Act 1974 and the Employment Protection Act 1975.

Military Courts. Offences by persons subject to service law against the system of military law created under the powers of the Army Act, Air Force Act or Naval Discipline Act are dealt with either summarily or by courts-martial. Petitions may be made to the Defence Council. Subsequent appeals lie to a Courts-Martial Appeals Court, and from that court an appeal may lie to the House of Lords.

The Personnel of the Law. All judicial officers except the Lord Chancellor (who is a member of the Cabinet) are independent of Parliament and the Executive. They are all appointed by the Crown on the advice of the Prime Minister or the Lord Chancellor and hold office until retiring age. The legal profession is divided; barristers, who advise on legal problems and conduct cases in court, usually act for the public only through solicitors, who deal directly with the legal business brought to them by the public. Most judicial appointments are made from barristers of long standing, though solicitors are eligible for appointment as Recorders, who may, after 3 years, be appointed Circuit Judges.

Legal Aid. Broadly there are 3 kinds of legal aid. Firstly there is legal advice and assistance, otherwise known as the 'Green Form' scheme. This includes advice and help on any question of English law, both civil and criminal, but does not normally cover any form of representation before a court or tribunal. As an extension of the scheme, however, assistance by way of representation has been available for certain proceedings, chiefly civil, in magistrates' courts. Secondly, under Part I of the Legal Aid Act 1974, there is legal aid for civil court proceedings. Under the provisions of the Act, aid is available to those of low or moderate means either free or subject to a contribution, depending on means. In 1983–84 there were over 831,000 applications for advice and assistance under the Legal Advice and Assistance Scheme and over 205,000 civil legal aid certificates were issued. The cost of legal aid in civil cases is met from (*a*) contributions from assisted persons; (*b*) the operation of the statutory charge which gives the Law Society a first charge on money or property recovered or preserved for an assisted person to the extent of that person's liability for his own costs; (*c*) costs recovered from opposing parties and (*d*) a grant from the

Exchequer. The net cost of civil legal aid to the state in the year 1983–84 amounted to £86·7m. and the cost of the legal advice and assistance scheme was £45·4m. of which £9·6m. was accounted for by assistance by way of representation.

Under Part II of the Legal Aid Act 1974 a court dealing with criminal proceedings may order legal aid to be given if it considers it is desirable in the interests of justice and if it also considers that the defendant (or appellant) requires financial assistance in meeting the costs he may incur. The interests of justice are not statutorily defined but may include, for example, situations where the defendant is in real danger of going to prison or losing his job, where substantial questions of law are to be argued or where the defendant is unable to follow the proceedings and explain his case due to inadequate knowledge of English, mental illness or other mental or physical disability. Legal aid must be granted, subject to means, in the following circumstances: where a person is committed for trial on a charge of murder, where the prosecutor appeals or applies for leave to appeal from the criminal division of the Court of Appeal or the Courts-Martial Appeal Court to the House of Lords, and in certain circumstances where the court is considering depriving a defendant of his liberty.

The costs of legal aid in criminal proceedings are paid by the central government, but courts have power to require legally aided persons to contribute towards the cost of legal aid given to them. The net cost of legal aid in criminal proceedings in the year 1983–84 was £119·1m., £58·3m. of this was for legal aid in the higher courts which is paid for out of the Lord Chancellor's vote and £60·8m. for legal aid in the magistrates' courts which is paid from the legal aid fund.

Under the Parliamentary Commissioner Act, passed 22 March 1967, M.P.s may refer to the Parliamentary Commissioner complaints received from the public regarding improper or inequitable administration in most spheres of central government affairs. Generally, other available remedies (such as legal action) must be exhausted before a complaint can be investigated. If a complaint is found to require a remedy the Parliamentary Commissioner makes a report to Parliament.

Commissions for Local Administration in England and Wales were set up under the Local Government Act 1974. The Commissioners carry out similar functions in relation to local government bodies to those the Parliamentary Commissioner discharges with regard to maladministration in central government.

Police. The authorized establishment of the police force in England and Wales in Dec. 1984 was 122,233: the actual strength was 109,490 men and 11,083 women. In addition there were 16,056 special constables (including 4,307 women). Total police net expenditure (estimated) in England and Wales for 1982–83 was £2,569·9m.

SCOTLAND. The High Court of Justiciary is the supreme criminal court in Scotland and has jurisdiction in all cases of crime committed in any part of Scotland, unless expressly excluded by statute. It consists of the Lord Justice-General, the Lord Justice-Clerk and 22 other judges, who are the same judges as of the Court of Session, the Scottish supreme civil court. One judge is seconded to the Scottish Law Commission. The Court, which is presided over by the Lord Justice-General, whom failing, the Lord Justice-Clerk, exercises an appellate jurisdiction as well as one of first instance, sits as business requires in Edinburgh both as a Court of Appeal (the *quorum* being 3 judges) and as a court of first instance and on circuit as a court of first instance. The decisions of the Court in either case are not subject to review by the House of Lords. One judge sitting with a jury of 15 persons can, and usually does, try cases, but 2 or more (with a jury) may do so in important or complex cases. It has a privative jurisdiction over cases of treason, murder, rape, deforcement of messengers and breach of duty by magistrates. It also, in practice, is the only court which tries cases of incest, sodomy and other serious or aggravated crimes against person or property and generally those cases in which a sentence greater than imprisonment for 2 years may be imposed either under statute or common law. Moreover, the Court has inherent power to try and to punish all acts which are plainly criminal though previously unknown and not dealt with by any statute.

The appellate jurisdiction of the High Court of Justiciary extends to all cases tried on indictment, whether in the High Court or the Sheriff Court, and persons so convicted may appeal to the Court against conviction or sentence or both except that there is no appeal against any sentence fixed by law. By such an appeal, a person may bring under review of the High Court of Justiciary any alleged miscarriage of justice including any alleged miscarriage of justice on the basis of the existence and significance of additional evidence which was not heard at the trial and which was not available and could not reasonably have been made available at the trial. It is also a court of review from courts of summary criminal jurisdiction, and on the final determination of any summary prosecution either party may appeal to the Court by way of stated case on questions of law, procedure, etc., but not on questions of fact, except in relation to a miscarriage of justice alleged by the person accused on the basis of the existence and significance of additional evidence which was not heard at the trial and which was not available and could not reasonably have been made available at the trial. A further or complementary form of process of review which can be resorted to by convicted persons in these courts is by Bill of Suspension (and Liberation), but it is of strictly limited application. A prosecutor in cases tried on indictment or under summary criminal procedure may also bring under review a decision in law, prior to final judgment of the case, by way of Bill of Advocation. The Court also hears appeals under the Courts-Martial (Appeals) Act 1951.

The Sheriff Court has an inherent universal criminal jurisdiction (as well as an extensive civil one) limited in general to crimes and offences committed within a sheriffdom (a specifically defined region), which has, however, been curtailed by statute or practice under which the High Court of Justiciary has exclusive jurisdiction in relation to the crimes above-mentioned. This Court is presided over by a Sheriff-Principal or Sheriff, and when trying cases on indictment sits with a jury of 15 persons. His power of awarding punishment involving imprisonment is restricted to 2 years in the maximum, but he may under certain statutory powers remit the prisoner to the High Court for sentence. The Sheriff also exercises a wide summary criminal jurisdiction and when doing so sits without a jury; and he has concurrent jurisdiction with every other court within his sheriffdom in regard to all offences competent for trial in summary courts. The great majority of offences which come before the courts are of a minor nature and, as such, are disposed of in the Sheriff Courts. In cases to be tried on indictment either in the High Court of Justiciary or in the Sheriff Court, the judge may, and in some cases must, before the trial, hold a Preliminary Diet to decide questions of a preliminary nature, whether to the competency or relevancy or otherwise. Any decision at a preliminary diet can be the subject of an appeal to the High Court of Justiciary prior to the trial.

District Courts in each local authority district have jurisdiction in minor offences occurring within the district. These courts are presided over by lay magistrates, known as justices, and have limited powers of fine and imprisonment.

The Court of Session, presided over by the Lord President (the Lord Justice-General in criminal cases), is divided into an Inner House comprising 2 divisions of 4 judges each with mainly appellate function, and an Outer House comprising 13 single judges, sitting individually at first instance; it exercises the highest civil jurisdiction in Scotland, with the House of Lords as a court of appeal.

Police. The police forces in Scotland at the end of 1983 had an authorized establishment of 13,321; the strength was 12,494 men and 714 women. There were 2,643 part-time special constables. The total police net expenditure in Scotland was £230·2m. for 1982–83.

Civil Judicial Statistics

England and Wales	1981	1982	1983
Appellate Courts			
Judicial Committee of the Privy Council	54	62	58
House of Lords	65	71	86
Court of Appeal	. . .	1,627	1,452
High Court of Justice (appeals and special cases from inferior courts)	1,306	1,495	1,619
Courts of First Instance (excluding Magistrates' Courts and Tribunals)			
High Court of Justice:			
Chancery Division[1]	15,650	17,119	18,340
Queen's Bench Division[2]	183,574	165,491	180,178
Family Division: Principal Registry matters[3]	972	1,014	990
District Registry wardships	1,081	1,426	1,338
Official Referee's	909	827	990
County courts: Matrimonial suits[4]	176,162	181,853	176,745
Other[5]	1,888,125	2,120,207	2,177,427
Restrictive Practices Court	. . .	. . .	10
Scotland			
House of Lords (Appeals from Court of Session)	12	11	11
Court of Session—General Department	30,043	31,471	32,673
Sheriff's Ordinary Cause	37,364	35,949	39,862
Sheriff's Summary Cause	131,855	166,127	149,500

[1] Including Companies Court, Bankruptcy petitions and Patents Court.
[2] Including Admiralty Court.
[3] Adoption, guardianship and wardship.
[4] Including petitions filed at Principal Registry.
[5] Plaint, Admiralty, Bankruptcy and Companies, Adoption, Guardship and miscellaneous.

Criminal Statistics

England and Wales	Total number of offenders 1982	Total number of offenders 1983	Indictable offences[1] 1982	Indictable offences[1] 1983
Aged 10 and over				
Proceeded against in magistrates' courts[2]	2,221,326	2,302,811	538,806	530,110
Found guilty at magistrates' courts	1,963,600	2,022,646	407,694	388,140
Found guilty at the Crown Court	67,443	72,883	67,437	72,883
Cautioned[3]	160,482	165,517	111,315	114,905
Aged 10 and under 17				
Proceeded against in magistrates' courts[2]	121,468	112,234	90,169	81,820
Found guilty at magistrates' courts	108,709	99,194	80,447	72,055
Found guilty at the Crown Court	1,309	1,251	1,309	1,251
Cautioned[3]	112,684	115,437	92,907	94,623

[1] Includes offences which can be tried either at the Crown Court or at magistrates' courts.
[2] Almost all defendants are initially proceeded against in magistrates' courts.
[3] Offenders who, on admission of guilt, are given an oral caution by or on the instruction of a senior police officer as an alternative to court proceedings. Such cautions are not given for motoring offences.

CRIMINAL STATISTICS

SCOTLAND

	All Crimes and Offences 1982	All Crimes and Offences 1983	Crimes[1] 1982	Crimes[1] 1983
All persons and companies				
Proceeded against in all courts	235,452	246,127	68,622	71,053
Charge proved	215,718	225,498	59,903	62,165
Children (aged 8–15)				
Proceeded against in all courts	796	816	514	556
Given formal police warning/ referred to reporter	21,325	23,097	16,938	17,609

[1] Crimes are generally the more serious criminal acts and offences the less serious. 'Crimes' are not equivalent in coverage to 'indictable/triable either way offences'.

Average population in prisons, borstals, youth custody centres and detention centres (1983) in England and Wales was 43,462 (convicted 37,136; untried 6,003, and 323 non-criminal prisoners); in Scotland (1983), 5,052 (sentenced, 4,189; remanded, 863 and 6 others).

Criminal statistics, England and Wales. 1984
Prison statistics, England and Wales, 1983. HMSO, 1984
Paterson, A., *The Law Lords.* London, 1982

Religion. The Anglican Communion has originated from the Church of England and parallels in its fellowship of autonomous churches the evolution of British influence beyond the seas from colonies to dominions and independent nations. There is no terrestrial head of the Anglican Communion; the Archbishop of Canterbury presides as *primus inter pares* at the decennial meetings of the bishops of the Anglican Communion at the Lambeth Conference.

The Anglican churches, in addition to the Church of England, comprise the churches, councils, and provinces in communion with the see of Canterbury; which are situated in Wales; Ireland; Scotland; United States of America; Canada; Australia; New Zealand; West Indies; Brazil; South Africa; Central Africa; West and East Africa; Jerusalem and the Middle East; South East Asia, Burma; Sri Lanka; Japan; South America; China; Indian Ocean; South Pacific.

In addition to the dioceses included within the Provinces of Canterbury and York, there are several dioceses overseas over which the Archbishop of Canterbury exercises metropolitical jurisdiction, while Church of England chaplaincies in North and Central Europe formerly under the jurisdiction of the Bishop of London now form the diocese of Europe. There are also two small Iberian churches which have been accepted into membership.

England and Wales. The established Church of England, which baptizes about 35% of the children born in England (*i.e.* excluding Wales but including the Isle of Man and the Channel Islands), is Protestant Episcopal. Civil disabilities on account of religion do not attach to any class of British subject. Under the Welsh Church Acts, 1914 and 1919, the Church in Wales and Monmouthshire was disestablished as from 1 April 1920, and Wales was formed into a separate Province.

The Queen is, under God, the supreme governor of the Church of England, with the right, regulated by statute, to nominate to the vacant archbishoprics and bishoprics. The Queen, on the advice of the First Lord of the Treasury, also appoints to such deaneries, prebendaries and canonries as are in the gift of the Crown, while a large number of livings and also some canonries are in the gift of the Lord Chancellor.

There are 2 archbishops (at the head of the 2 Provinces of Canterbury and York), and 42 diocesan bishops including the bishop of the diocese of Europe, which is part of the Province of Canterbury. Each archbishop has also his own particular diocese, wherein he exercises episcopal, as in his Province he exercises metropolitan, jurisdiction. In Dec. 1984 there were 70 suffragan and assistant bishops, 41 deans and provosts of cathedrals and 105 archdeacons. The General Synod, in England, consists of a House of Bishops, a House of Clergy and a House of Laity, and has power to frame legislation regarding Church matters. The first two Houses consist of the members of the Convocations of Canterbury and York, each of which consists of the diocesan bishops and elected representatives of the suffragan bishops, 6 for Canterbury province and 3 for York (forming an Upper House), deans, provosts, and archdeacons, and a certain number of proctors elected as the representatives of the inferior clergy, together with, in the case of Canterbury Convocation, representatives of the Universities of Oxford, Cambridge and London and in the case of York a representative for the Universities of Durham and Newcastle; the chaplains in the Forces (forming the Lower House). They are elected by their fellow suffragans. The House of Laity is elected by the lay members of the Deanery Synods. Parochial affairs are managed by annual parochial church meetings and parochial church councils. Every Measure passed by the General Synod must be submitted to the Ecclesiastical Committee, consisting of 15 members of the House of Lords nominated by the Lord Chancellor and 15 members of the House of Commons nominated by the Speaker. This committee reports on each Measure to Parliament, and the Measure receives the Royal Assent and becomes law if each House of Parliament resolves that the Measure be presented to the Queen.

At 31 Dec. 1984 there were 13,420 ecclesiastical parishes, inclusive of the Isle of Man and the Channel Islands. These parishes do not, in many cases, coincide with civil parishes. Owing to the pastoral re-organization, although most parishes have their own churches, not every parish nowadays can have its own incumbent or minister; so that in some areas one or more parishes may be served by a clergyman, who must be in priest's orders, and in these cases he holds the parishes in plurality or as part of a united benefice. In Dec. 1984 there were 7,020 beneficed clergymen excluding dignitaries, 1,320 other clergymen of incumbent status and 1,734 assistant curates working in the parishes.

Private persons possess the right of presentation to over 2,000 benefices; the patronage of the others belongs mainly to the Queen, the bishops and cathedrals, the Lord Chancellor, and the universities of Oxford and Cambridge. In addition to the 10,074 parochial incumbents and assistant curates, there were (1984) 378 dignitaries, 297 non-parochial clergymen working within the diocesan framework and approximately 2,000 non-parochial clergymen outside the framework.

In 1982 there were estimated to be 1·7m. Easter and 1·7m. Christmas Communicants.

Of the 40,446 churches and chapels registered for the solemnization of marriages at 30 June 1983, 16,640 belonged to the Established Church and the Church in Wales and 23,806 to other religious denominations. Of the 344,334 marriages celebrated in 1983 (342,166 in 1982), 34% were in the Established Church and the Church in Wales, 17% in churches or chapels of other denominations and 49% were civil marriages in a Register Office.

Roman Catholics in England and Wales were 4,240,262 in 1984. There were 5 archdioceses and 16 dioceses, 6,816 clergy and 2,679 parish churches and 1,220 other churches open to the public. Convents, 1,273.

The Unitarians have about 250 places of worship, the Catholic Apostolic Church over 80, the New Jerusalem Church about 75. The Salvation Army, a religious body with a quasi-military organization, carries on both spiritual and social work at home and abroad, and had, in British Territory, 1982, 2,135 officers, 1,042 corps. There were also 38 eventide homes, 13 maternity homes, 2 maternity hospitals, 46 hostels for men, 14 hostels for women and girls, and 9 approved and training schools.

The following is a summary of statistics of certain churches in England and Wales, Channel Islands and Isle of Man:

Denomination	*Full members*	*Ministers in charge*	*Local and lay preachers*
Methodist	487,972	3,506	14,847
Independent Methodist	4,515	151	—
Wesleyan Reform Union	3,455	24	171
United Reform	150,000	1,800	—
Baptist	221,766	1,714	—
Calvinistic Methodist Church of Wales	85,041	230	—
Moravian	4,000	40	—
Society of Friends	18,303	—	—

There are about 354,000 Jews in the UK with about 240 synagogues.

Scotland. The Church of Scotland (established in 1560 at the Reformation and re-established in 1688 as part of the Revolution Settlement) is Presbyterian, the ministers all being of equal rank. There is in each parish a kirk session consisting of the minister and a number of laymen called elders. There are presbyteries (formed by groups of parishes), meeting frequently throughout the year, and these are again grouped in synods, which meet half-yearly and can be appealed to against the decisions of the presbyteries.

The supreme court is the General Assembly, which now consists of some 1,250 members, half clerical and half lay, chosen by the different presbyteries. It meets annually in May (under the presidency of a Moderator appointed by the Assembly, the Sovereign being present or represented by a Lord High Commissioner, appointed by the Queen on the nomination of the Government of the day), and sits for 7 days. Any matters not decided during this period may be left to a Commission which will sit if required.

On 2 Oct. 1929 the Church of Scotland and the United Free Church of Scotland were reunited under the name of The Church of Scotland, and the two bodies met in General Assembly in Edinburgh as one. The united Church had, in Scotland, on 31 Dec. 1983, 1,780 congregations, 902,714 members; 18,633 teachers and 104,552 scholars in attendance in Sunday schools. The Church courts are the General Assembly, 12 synods, 46 presbyteries in Scotland, 1 in England and 2 on the Continent. Income in 1981 was £41,740,070. There are divinity faculties in 4 Scottish universities of Edinburgh, Glasgow, Aberdeen and St Andrews, with 60 professors and lecturers who are mostly ministers of the Church of Scotland.

The Episcopal Church of Scotland is a province of the Anglican Church and is one of the historic Scottish churches. It consists of 7 dioceses. As at 31 Dec. 1984 it had 275 churches and missions, 241 clergy and 65,951 members, of whom 38,420 were communicants.

There are in Scotland some small outstanding Presbyterian bodies and also Baptists, Congregationalists, Methodists and Unitarians.

The Roman Catholic Church which celebrated the centenary of the restoration of the hierarchy in 1978, had in Scotland (1984) 1 cardinal, 1 archbishop and 9 bishops, 1,103 clergy, 478 parishes, and 807,900 adherents.

The proportion of marriages in Scotland according to the rites of the various Churches in 1982 was: Church of Scotland, 39·5%; Roman Catholic, 13·6%; Episcopal, 1·4%; United Free, 0·4%; others, 4·6%; civil, 40·9%.

Education. *The Publicly Maintained System of Education England and Wales:* Compulsory schooling begins at the age of 5 and the minimum leaving age for all pupils is 16. No tuition fees are payable in any publicly maintained school (but it is open to parents, if they choose, to pay for their children to attend other schools). The post-school stage, which is voluntary, includes universities, polytechnics and other further education establishments (including those which provide courses for the training of teachers), as well as adult education and the youth service. Financial assistance is generally available to students on higher education courses in the university and non-university sectors and to some students on other courses in further education.

Nursery Education. Children under 5 may be provided for in nursery schools and nursery classes in primary schools. In the public sector no fees are payable. There were (1984) 565 nursery schools accommodating 49,487 children while some 3,921 primary schools contained nursery classes accommodating 209,987 children. Over 80% of all these children attend on a part-time basis. There are also 236,417 children under 5 attending maintained primary schools.

Primary Schools. Children normally begin primary school when they are 5. Nearly half of the 20,020 primary schools take the complete age-range from 5 upwards. About 3,200 take infants only, up to about 7 years; the rest take juniors only, from 7 or 8 on. The great majority of primary schools take both boys and girls. Just over 13,000 of these schools had between 100 and 300 pupils each; of the remainder, over half had 100 pupils or less.

There are 1,822 primary schools in Wales. In those primary schools (and some secondary schools) which are in the predominantly Welsh-speaking areas, the main language of instruction is Welsh. There are also 'Welsh', or, more accurately, bilingual schools in mainly English-speaking parts of Wales. Generally children transfer from primary to secondary schools at 11.

[1] As a result of the Education (School Leaving Dates) Act 1976, one of the two former leaving dates was amended. This means that pupils whose dates of birth fall between 1 Feb. and 31 Aug. (inclusive) cease to be of compulsory school age on the Friday before the last Monday in May. Some of these pupils will leave school before their 16th birthdays. Pupils whose dates of birth fall between 1 Sept. and 31 Jan. (inclusive) remain of compulsory school age until the end of the Easter term following their 16th birthdays.

Middle Schools. In some areas middle schools have been developed. These cover the age-ranges 8 to 12, 9 to 12, 9 to 13, 10 to 13 or 10 to 14. In Jan. 1984 there were 1,333 middle schools, 72 fewer than in 1983; this stabilizing of numbers comes after a decade of rapid growth (there were only 15 middle schools in 1969).

Secondary Education. In some areas, pupils are still selected at 11 for grammar schools on the basis of ability. The grammar schools, of which there were 175 at Jan. 1984, provide a mainly academic course from age 11 to 18. There were also a small number of technical schools which are the academic equals of grammar schools but can specialize to a greater or lesser extent in technical studies. Modern schools provide a general education up to the minimum school leaving age, though some pupils can, and increasingly do, stay on beyond that age. At Jan. 1984 there were 285 of these schools. There are also a small number of other schools which are various combinations of grammar, technical and modern schools.

All authorities now operate some comprehensive schools to which pupils are admitted without reference to ability or aptitude. In Jan. 1984 there were 3,291 fully comprehensive schools with over 3·08m. pupils, in comparison with 221 such schools with about 210,000 pupils in 1965. With the development of comprehensive education various patterns of secondary school organization have come into operation, of which the main ones are: all through schools with an age-range of 11–18 or 11–16 (with possible transfer to an 11–18 school or to a sixth form college (*i.e.*, 16–19) for further studies); 3-tier systems, which incorporate middle schools with a transfer age of 12, 13 or 14, and corresponding 12–18, 13–18 or 14–18 schools; or a system of junior and senior comprehensive schools, catering for the 11–18 age group with a transfer age of 13 or 14.

Direct Grant Grammar Schools. These schools receive grants direct from the Department of Education and Science for their secondary departments (or 'upper schools') and are independent of local education authorities. With the phasing out of the direct grant system now in its final stages, however, there were (1985) only 5 schools receiving grant in respect of pupils attending them. It is expected that direct grant payments will cease in 1987.

Assisted Places Scheme. In order to give able children a wider range of educational opportunity the government set up, in 1981, the assisted places scheme to give help with tuition fees at independent schools to parents who could not otherwise afford them. In the school year 1984–85, the 226 participating schools offered a total of 5,857 assisted places, 4,825 for entry at age 11, 12 or 13, and 1,032 for entry at sixth form level.

Special Education. Since 1971, when the education of severely mentally handicapped children became the responsibility of the education service, the right to education of all handicapped children has been recognised.

The Education Act 1981, which came into force in April 1983, switched the focus of attention from a child's disability to his special educational needs. The Act restated the Government's policy that no child should be placed in a special school if his needs can be met in an ordinary school.

The majority of handicapped children attend special schools of which there are at present around 1,550 catering for approximately 120,000 pupils. Some 3,000 pupils are educated in hospital schools and around 7,000 in independent schools under arrangements made by local education authorities.

Increasingly, however, handicapped children are being integrated into ordinary schools either in designated classes or on an individual basis. At present around 18,500 pupils with special educational needs are in designated special classes at maintained ordinary schools. Of maintained special schools, 1,144 are day schools and a further 306 have boarding facilities. Attendance is compulsory from 5–16. In addition, local authorities can make special educational provision below the age of 5 for those ascertained as being in need of it and until the age of 18 for those who want it (education from 16–18 may be provided either in a school or in a college of further education). In addition to the provision in ordinary and special schools, authorities make special arrangements for educating children at home, in small groups or in hospitals. There are also some establishments which provide further education, P.E. vocational training and for assessment for employment purely for handicapped school leavers. The statistics in this and the preceding paragraph are for England only and are valid at Jan. 1984.

Ancillary Services. Local education authorities may provide registered pupils at any school maintained by them with milk, meals and refreshment and they may make such charges as they think fit for anything they provide. For pupils whose parents are in receipt of supplementary benefit or family income supplement, however, authorities are required to ensure that such provision is made for the pupil at mid-day as appears to them to be requisite and anything which is provided must be free of charge. Authorities are also required to remit the charge for anything they provide for other pupils if having regard to their circumstances, they consider it appropriate to do so. Facilities must also be provided, free of charge, for consuming any meals or other refreshments which pupils bring to school themselves.

Local education authorities also have power to provide milk, meals and refreshment for pupils in non-maintained schools, if they wish to do so, under such terms as may be agreed with the proprietors as long as the cost does not exceed what it would have been if the pupils had been at a school maintained by an authority.

Further and Higher Education (Non-University). In Nov. 1983 there were about 566 institutions in England and Wales providing courses of further education, ranging from shorthand instruction to degree-level, postgraduate work and courses of teacher-training. Course enrolments numbered 605,724 full-time (including 78,282 sandwich students) and 1·32m. part-time and evening; students released by their employers numbered 479,723. There were in addition 4,513 adult education centres (formerly known as evening institutes), and youth clubs which provided mainly part-time courses of non-advanced general education and were attended by 1,734,000 students. At the top end of this range, outside the university sector, are the 30 polytechnics. These are engaged mainly in higher education, offering degrees of a standard comparable to those of universities, professional qualifications and courses in a wide range of disciplines leading to awards of the Business and Technician Education Council. Many other colleges of further education are however involved to a greater or lesser extent in the higher education sector of further education. Most polytechnics and further education colleges cater for a mixture of full and part-time students, and also sandwich students whose periods of study at college alternate with periods of practical training in industry or other employment. The Secretary of State receives advice on the funding and management of advanced further education from the National Advisory Body for Local Authority Higher Education (NAB) whose remit covers almost all non-university provision at this level, most of which is maintained by local education authorities.

Courses were also provided by the Workers' Educational Association (8,188), the University extramural departments (8,684) and the Welsh National Council of YMCAs (65). The total number of students registered at these courses was 306,004.

Education at institutions of further education is not free, but fees are generally low, and are remitted for most students under the age of 18 by the local authority.

The Youth Service. A wide range of facilities for the leisure-time recreation and informal social education of young people primarily of post-school age is provided by local education authorities and voluntary youth organizations. A duty is laid upon local education authorities by the provisions of the 1944 Education Act to secure the adequacy of such facilities for young people in their area; to this end they either provide, maintain and staff youth clubs, centres and other facilities themselves or assist voluntary agencies to do so.

Grants to voluntary agencies to help meet the cost of regional and national capital projects and to national voluntary bodies towards their headquarters and training expenses are made by the Government.

Awards to Students. Local education authorities are responsible for making mandatory awards to suitably qualified students taking first-degree and comparable courses, courses of initial teacher-training and certain other advanced level courses. These awards cover fees and maintenance but the maintenance grants are subject to the income of the student and his parents or spouse. In addition scholarships may be available both from universities and other sources. The authorities may also give discretionary awards to students who do not qualify for mandatory awards including those taking non-degree level courses.

In 1982–83 there were 415,967 full value awards current in all, 48% at university and 31,732 were for teacher-training courses. Lesser value awards, for which the maximum rate of grant payable is below the full cost of the student's fees and maintenance, were also made by the authorities. There were 85,862 such awards taken up in the academic year 1982–83.

The Research Council gave 7,200 new awards in 1984–85 and there were 14,090 current awards in that academic year. The Department gave 1,497 new awards (state studentships and state bursaries) in 1983–84 and in 1984–85 awards totalled 1,497.

Teachers. In order to qualify for work in maintained schools, most teachers take a course of professional training. Graduates and holders of some specialist qualifications obtained before 1 Jan. 1970 are regarded as qualified to teach without training, but anyone obtaining these qualifications after that date is obliged to take a training course before being appointed for the first time to a primary school, and since 1 Jan. 1974 before first appointment to a secondary school.

In 1984 there were some 64 non-university institutions (including 23 polytechnics) and 31 university departments of education providing courses of initial teaching in England and Wales.

In Nov. 1983 there were about 25,000 students on initial teacher-training courses.

On 30 Sept. 1984, 414,000 full-time teachers were employed by local education authorities in maintained nursery, primary and secondary schools in England and Wales.

Finance. Total current and capital expenditure on education in England from public funds (excluding university education) is estimated at £11,031m. for 1984–85 as compared with £10,727m. for 1983–84.

Scotland. The statistics on schools relate to education authority and grant-aided schools. From 1974–75 all teachers employed in these schools require to be qualified; figures given are full-time equivalents.

Nursery Education. In Sept. 1982 there were 541 nursery schools and departments, with a total enrolment of 34,862 pupils.

Primary Education. In Sept. 1982 there were 2,509 primary schools and departments and the number on the registers was 474,234.

In Sept. 1982, 23,289 teachers were employed in primary schools and departments.

Secondary Education. In Sept. 1982 there were 463 secondary schools with

410,048 pupils. Of these schools, 382 were all-through comprehensive establishments providing the full range of Scottish Certificate of Education courses and also non-certificate courses. A further 59 schools were comprehensive in intake and provided both non-certificate and certificate courses, the latter however only up to Ordinary grade. Of the remaining 22 schools, these were selective in intake, 19 provided certificate courses only (Ordinary grade and Higher grade) and 3 non-certificate and certificate courses, the latter again not extending beyond Ordinary grade. Pupils who start their secondary education in schools which do not cater for courses beyond Ordinary grade may in the light of their performance, or for other reasons, be transferred at the end of their second or fourth year to schools providing Higher grade courses.

There were 28,765 teachers in secondary schools at Sept. 1982.

Special Schools. In Sept. 1982 there were 330 special schools and departments. The total number of handicapped children under instruction was 10,871, of which 8,011 were mentally handicapped, 859 were physically handicapped, 302 were blind or partially blind and 582 were deaf or partially deaf, and 1,117 were otherwise handicapped.

At Sept. 1982 there were 24 'List D' schools (these establishments correspond to Community Homes in England and Wales) with a total enrolment of 1,077.

Further Education. Centres and colleges for formal further education numbered 196 in 1982–83.

The student population was 221,130, of whom 54,596 attended full-time (advanced courses, 26,178; non-advanced, 28,418) and 166,534 part-time (advanced courses, 29,044; non-advanced, 137,490).

Teacher-Training. In Nov. 1982 there were 3,782 students in 7 colleges of education on pre-service courses of teacher-training.

Finance. Total expenditure on education met from revenue in 1982–83 was £1,247m. (excluding university education and loan charges).

Independent Schools. Outside the state system of education there were in England nearly 2,343 independent schools in Jan. 1984, ranging from large 'public' schools to small local ones. There were (Jan. 1983) 510,074 full-time and 13,191 part-time pupils in these schools. In Wales 11,331 full-time pupils attended 70 independent schools. Fees are charged by all these schools, which receive no grant from central government sources. All independent schools in England are required to be registered by the Department and are liable to the inspection by HM Inspector. The term 'public schools' refers to independent schools in membership of the Headmasters' Conference, Governing Bodies Association or the Governing Bodies of Girls' Schools Association. Qualifications under which a school may be represented at the Headmasters' Conference include the measure of independence enjoyed by the governing body and the amount of advanced courses undertaken. Some of these schools are for boarders only, but the majority include non-resident 'day-pupils'. In Scotland there were 86 independent schools, with a total of 14,996 pupils in Sept. 1983. A small number of the Scottish independent schools are of the 'public school' type but they are not known as 'public schools' since in Scotland this term is used to denote education authority (*i.e.*, state) schools.

The earliest of the schools were founded by, and attached to, the medieval churches. Many were founded as 'grammar' (classical) schools in the 16th century, receiving charters from the reigning sovereign. Reformed mainly in the middle of the 19th century, these schools now provide the highest form of English pre-university education. Among the most well-known independent schools are Eton College, founded in 1440 by Henry VI, with 1,250 boys; Winchester College, 1394, founded by William of Wykeham, Bishop of Winchester, 600 boys; Harrow School, founded in 1560 as a grammar school by John Lyon, a yeoman, 740 boys; Charterhouse, 1611, 670 boys. Among the earliest foundations are King's School, Canterbury, founded 600; King's School, Rochester, 604; St Peter's, York, 627.

Universities. In *England* there are 33 traditional degree-giving universities. In addition there are the University of Manchester Institute of Science and Technology; the London and Manchester Business Schools and the Open University. Eight new universities have been established since 1961 and 8 former Colleges of Advanced Technology gained university status in the 1960's.

In *Wales* there is 1 university, the University of Wales, with colleges at Aberystwyth, Bangor, Cardiff, Lampeter and Swansea. The Welsh National School of Medicine is a school of the University, and the University of Wales Institute of Science and Technology became a constituent college in Nov. 1967.

In *Scotland* there are 8 universities, Aberdeen, Dundee, Edinburgh, Stirling, Strathclyde, Heriot-Watt, Glasgow and St Andrews. The Carnegie Trust for Scottish Universities (founded, 1901) has a capital (1984) of £8m. and an annual income of £650,000; 50% of the income is devoted to the improvement and expansion of Scottish Universities and 50% to assist students with their fees.

All these universities and colleges are independent, self-governing institutions, although they receive substantial aid from the State (in the case of the Open University by direct grant from the Department of Education and Science, and the traditional universities through the University Grants Committee). The UGC is a committee appointed by the Secretary of State for Education and Science designed to advise the Government on the needs of the universities, and to prepare plans for future development. The members are drawn from education and industry. The Government receives advice on the universities' requirements for central computing facilities from the Computer Board for the Universities and Research Councils whose members are also drawn from the universities and industry.

The Royal College of Art and the Cranfield Institute of Technology are primarily postgraduate institutions which award higher degrees under charters granted in 1967 and 1969 respectively. They receive grants direct from the Department of Education and Science.

The local education authorities have no responsibility for universities.

The Open University received its Royal Charter on 1 June 1969 and is an independent, self-governing institution, awarding its own degrees. It is financed by the Government through the Department of Education and Science and by the receipt of students' fees.

Tuition is by means of correspondence textbooks, radio and television broadcasts and summer schools. Students can also attend one of 250 local study centres. No formal qualifications are required for entry to undergraduate or associate student courses.

Anyone resident in the UK aged 18 or over may apply. There are 134 undergraduate courses; many are available on a one-off basis to associate students.

In 1984 it had 66,763 undergraduates, about 26,500 continuing education students and some 850 postgraduate students. The university has 2,900 full-time staff working at its Milton Keynes headquarters and in 13 regional offices throughout the country. There are 5,000 part-time tutors and counsellors.

The University of Buckingham, formerly the University College at Buckingham offers two-year degree courses. The academic year commencing in Jan. and consisting of four ten-week terms. There are four Schools of Studies: Accounting, Business, and Economics; Humanities; Law; and Sciences. A number of postgraduate courses are also offered. In 1984, there were 528 full-time students. Opened in 1976, the University of Buckingham received its Royal Charter in March 1983.

All universities charge fees, but financial help is available to students from several sources.

The universities themselves provide scholarships of various kinds and all local education authorities have a system of awards to help suitable students to attend university.

The amount of aid given generally depends upon the parents' means. The majority of the students at the English and Welsh universities are in receipt of some form of financial assistance.

Awards known as state studentships are offered on a competitive basis by the

Department from among candidates considered by the universities and other higher education institutions to be qualified for post-graduate studies in the humanities; similar awards, tenable at universities or other higher education institutions, are offered by the Research Councils to students studying topics within the broad spectrum of agriculture and food; the biological sciences; man's natural environment; science and engineering and the social sciences at post-graduate level.

The following table gives the number of professors, lecturers, etc., and students (full-time and sandwich courses) for 1983–84:

University or college	*Students*	*Staff*
Aston	4,054	468
Bath	3,730	462
Birmingham	8,736	1,396
Bradford	4,574	513
Bristol	6,907	1,101
Brunel	2,654	344
Cambridge	11,598	1,656
City	2,798	340
Durham	4,704	588
East Anglia	4,031	531
Essex	3,188	333
Exeter	4,758	524
Hull	5,025	525
Keele	2,729	300
Kent	4,159	476
Lancaster	4,438	534
Leeds	10,569	1,331
Leicester	4,668	608
Liverpool	7,519	1,069
London Business School	252	60
London	40,512	7,816
Loughborough	5,232	654
Manchester Business School	206	42
Manchester	10,931	1,391
Univ. of Manchester Inst. of Science and Technology	4,301	648
Newcastle	7,538	1,136
Nottingham	6,829	951
Oxford	11,708	2,050
Reading	5,576	738
Salford	3,835	373
Sheffield	7,648	1,025
Southampton	6,416	996
Surrey	3,240	508
Sussex	4,360	608
Warwick	5,377	623
York	3,338	431
Wales—		
Aberystwyth U.C.	2,981	388
Bangor U.C.	2,673	338
Cardiff U.C.	5,103	691
St David's, Lampeter	739	70
Swansea U.C.	3,695	486
Welsh Nat. School of Medicine	743	289
Univ. of Wales Institute of Science and Technology	2,801	358
Scotland—		
Aberdeen	5,470	762
Dundee	3,198	479
Edinburgh	9,866	1,512
Glasgow	10,043	1,350
Heriot-Watt	3,185	396
St Andrews	3,454	383
Stirling	2,470	308
Strathclyde	7,163	899

Women students are admitted on equal terms with men. Number of women students: England, 88,206; Wales, 7,819; Scotland, 18,934. There are, however, colleges exclusively for female students at Oxford and Cambridge. Total number of full-time or sandwich students at universities listed above: England, 228,138; Wales, 18,735; Scotland, 44,849; total, 291,722.

McIntosh, N. E., Calder, J.A. and Swift, B., *A Degree of Difference.* London, 1976
Perry, W., *Open University: A Personal Account.* Open Univ. Press, 1976
Tunstall, J., *The Open University.* London, 1974

The British Council. The British Council was established in Nov. 1934 and incorporated by Royal Charter in 1940. Its aims are the promotion of an enduring understanding and appreciation of Britain in other countries through cultural, educational and technical co-operation.

The Council's expenditure in 1981–82 amounted to £147·1m. Funds were provided by a grant-in-aid of £34·1m. from the Overseas Information (Foreign and Commonwealth Office) Vote and a contribution of £19·4m. from the Overseas Aid Vote. A further £57·4m. was provided by the Overseas Development Administration to cover the cost of administration of, and the reimbursement of sums expended on technical co-operation schemes. The balance of £36·2m. was derived from Council earnings and from international agencies, overseas governments, etc. for educational services.

The Council is governed by a board consisting of up to 30 members, 2 of whom are nominated by Ministers. There are advisory committees for Scotland and Wales and also advisory committees for the main branches of the Council's work. In Jan. 1983 the Council had staff in 81 countries.

The Council is designated by the British Government to carry out over 30 bilateral cultural agreements, including that with the Soviet Union. The Council's work broadly divides into English language teaching; education and training; the development of university links and interchange; the promotion of wider use and availability of British books and periodicals; the development of personal contacts and the provision of information abroad on British experience and resources in the fields of education, medicine, science, technology and the arts.

The general policy in the field of English language teaching is to advise and assist education authorities overseas, particularly in curriculum and materials development and the training of local teachers of English; courses are provided in Britain and abroad for the further training of English language teaching experts from overseas. In many countries the Council runs its own English teaching centres. The Council acts as a centre for the dissemination of information about British educational thought and practice at all levels and, through its complement of education specialists working overseas, it has become closely involved with the administration of aid on behalf of the Overseas Development Administration. It assists in producing English teaching and other educational television and radio programmes overseas and arranges overseas consultancies and training in TV, radio and the application of media to development both in Britain and overseas. A prominent aspect of its education work is the assistance given in developing countries to the adoption of modern and locally relevant methods of science and mathematics teaching in schools. Following the merger with TETOC in 1982, the Council is responsible for advising ODA on its policies in the fields of technical education, industrial training, agricultural education, public administration and management development. Over 850 lecturers etc., mainly in the field of English language, are working overseas, having been recruited by the British Council on behalf of universities, schools, etc. in over 100 different countries. The Council is concerned to promote closer international academic collaboration through a variety of interchange and linking schemes, and through the provision of information and advice on educational institutions; it also administers the British Government's Technical Co-operation Training Programme and scholarship programmes on behalf of a large number of international organizations, notably UN and EEC. It administers examinations on behalf of a number of British examining boards.

During recent years the Council has collaborated with British educational institutions and firms in designing and implementing a wide range of education projects, for which overseas authorities or multilateral agencies pay the full cost.

The sciences, including medicine, technology and agriculture, form an increasingly important part of Council work. Contacts are built up and information collected and distributed through the specialist departments in London and the qualified scientists serving overseas, who also advise on training in Britain and the provision of experts abroad.

The importance of the arts as a medium for fostering cultural relations is reflected in the Council's encouragement of the appreciation of British achievements in the performing and the visual arts, both by supporting local activity and by sending theatre and ballet companies, orchestras and chamber groups, and exhibitions both of fine arts, crafts and photographs, from Britain on tours overseas. The Council also produces booklets, records and tapes on a wide range of literary and artistic subjects and in addition makes extensive use of films and video cassettes in support of its arts and educational work.

The Council runs, or is associated with, over 100 libraries in the countries in which it is represented. It arranges touring exhibitions of new British books and periodicals (some 80,000 books were exhibited in 272 exhibitions 1983–84). Additional publicity for British books is provided by the publication *British Book News*, and the distribution of specialized book lists. The Council also administers ODA funds (approximately £2·6m. in 1982–83) for the presentation of books to educational institutions in developing countries and the subsidized publication of low-priced books for students under the imprint of the English Language Book Society.

The Council arranges short advisory tours overseas by British experts. In a number of countries it is also the overseas administrative arm of the British Volunteer Programme. It awards scholarships and bursaries and arranges study programmes for some 30,000 visitors a year in Britain. It administers central government funds for youth exchanges with other countries.

In Britain the Council administers the programmes of award schemes for overseas students, meets many students on arrival from overseas, and provides an accommodation service for students from overseas for whom it has a special responsibility. The Council runs offices in Britain, mainly in university cities, for these purposes.

The Council is increasingly called on to administer training schemes and educational services financed by overseas authorities, or by multilateral agencies, on a contractual basis. The Council's specialist courses and summer schools provide advanced study in a number of fields, notably medicine, science, literature and the arts, English language and education. Payment is made by the student, or his parent organization, or by some other sponsor.

The Council produces the following periodicals: *Studying in Britain, Media in Education and Development* and *British Book News*. Other publications include the series *Writers and their Work, Notes on Literature, British Education, British Books and Libraries* and a number of booklets including *Scholarships Abroad, Introducing Wales, How to Live in Britain* and *Statistics of Overseas Students in the United Kingdom*. The Council has sponsored two major series of literature recordings, *The Complete Works of Shakespeare* and *The English Poets from Chaucer to Yeats*.

Chairman: Sir David Orr, MC.
Director-General: Sir John Burgh, KCMG, CB.
Headquarters: 10 Spring Gdns., London, SW1A 2BN.

Arts Council of Great Britain. The Arts Council is an independent organization established by Royal Charter in 1946, and is the principal channel for British Government aid to the arts. The Council's objects are to develop and improve the knowledge, understanding and practice of the arts, to increase their accessibility to the public, and to advise and co-operate with government departments, local authorities and other organizations.

The Council consists of a Chairman and not more than 19 other members who are appointed by the Minister for the Arts, after consultation with the Secretaries of State for Scotland and Wales. The Council is advised by panels and committees concerned with different aspects of the arts. With the approval of the appropriate Minister, the Council appoints committees for Scotland and Wales known respectively as the Scottish Arts Council and the Welsh Arts Council.

The Council receives a grant-in-aid from the Government voted annually by Parliament. The grant-in-aid for 1985–86 is £105m.

As well as giving financial help and advice to several hundred artistic organizations from the major opera, dance, drama companies, orchestras and festivals, to the smallest touring theatre and experimental group, the Council encourages such diverse interests as contemporary dance, photography, art films, and helps professional creative writers, dramatists, poets, musicians, composers, artists and photographers by means of bursary and award schemes. The Council provides funds for specialist training courses in the arts, and gives advice on projects for the construction of new buildings, or improvements to existing ones under its 'Housing the Arts' scheme.

A growing proportion of the Council's funds is channelled to the network of regional arts associations which practically covers the whole of England and Wales. The regional arts associations are not branches of the Arts Council, but are autonomous bodies, financed by a combination of Arts Council, local authority and private funds.

The Council mounts art exhibitions at the Hayward and Serpentine and other galleries in London and also in the regions. Other direct promotions include tours of opera and drama companies, of the Council's own films on the arts and of music groups under the Contemporary Music Network scheme. The Council has a library of contemporary British poetry at its headquarters and library and information service covering cultural policy, also administration and funding.

Chairman: Sir William Rees-Mogg.
Secretary-General: Luke Rittner.
Headquarters: 105 Piccadilly, London W1V 0AU. *The Scottish Arts Council:* 19–20 Charlotte Sq., Edinburgh, EH2 4DF. *The Welsh Arts Council:* 9 Museum Place, Cardiff, CF1 3NX.

National Insurance. The National Insurance Act, 1946, came into operation on 5 July 1948, repealing the existing schemes of health, pensions and unemployment insurance. This Act, along with later legislation, was consolidated as the National Insurance Act, 1965.

The Social Security Act 1975 introduced, from 6 April 1975, a new system of national insurance contributions to replace the previous system of flat-rate and graduated contributions. Since 6 April 1975, Class 1 contributions have been related to the employee's earnings and are collected with PAYE income tax, instead of by affixing stamps to a card. Class 2 and Class 3 contributions remain flat-rate, but, in addition to Class 2 contributions, those who are self-employed may be liable to pay Class 4 contributions, which for the year 1985–86 will be at the rate of 6·3% on profits or gains between £4,150 and £13,780, which are assessable for income tax under Schedule D. The non-employed and others whose contribution record is not sufficient to give entitlement to benefits are able to pay a Class 3 contribution voluntarily to qualify for a limited range of benefits. Class 2 contributions for 1984–85 are £4·75 a week for men and women. Class 3 contributions are £4·65 a week.

From 6 April 1978 the Social Security Pensions Act 1975 introduced earnings-related retirement, invalidity and widows' pensions. Employee's national insurance contribution liability depends on whether he is in contracted out or not contracted out employment. The not-contracted out employee pays 9% on all earnings up to £265 a week. The employer's rate is 10·45%. An employee's contracted-out contribution is 9% of the first £35.50 a week of earnings and 6·85% of earnings between £35.50 and £265 a week. The employer's contribution is 10·45% of the first £35.50 of weekly earnings and 6·35% of earnings between £35.50 and £265 a week.

The State supplements the contributions paid by contributors and employers, from general taxation. Contributions and supplement together with interest on investments form the income of the National Insurance Fund from which benefits are paid.

Statutory Sick Pay (SSP). The Social Security and Housing Benefits Act 1982 provides that, since 6 April 1983, employers are responsible for paying statutory sick pay (SSP) to their employees for up to 8 weeks of sickness absence in a tax year. SSP replaces the employee's entitlement to State sickness benefit which will not be payable as long as any employer's responsibility for SSP remains.

Benefits. Qualification for any benefit depends upon fulfilment of the appropriate contribution conditions. Persons who are incapable of work as the result of an industrial accident may get sickness benefit followed by invalidity benefit without having to satisfy the contributions conditions. Employed persons may qualify for all the benefits; self-employed may not qualify for unemployment benefit.

Sickness Benefit. From 29 Nov. 1984 the rate is £27·25 a week plus £16·80 a week for an adult dependant.

Unemployment Benefit is paid through the local unemployment benefit offices of the Department of Employment. The rate is £28·45 a week plus £17·55 a week for an adult dependant.

Invalidity Benefit replaces sickness benefit after 168 days of entitlement. It comprises a basic invalidity pension of £34·25 weekly and an invalidity allowance of £7·50 if incapacity began before age 40: £4·80 if incapacity began between 40 and 50 or £2·40 if it began between 50 and 60 (55 for women). Increases are: £20·55 for an adult dependant plus £7·65 for each child for whom child benefit is payable.

Maternity Benefit. For a confinement a woman may receive a maternity grant of £25 and, where 2 or more children are born at the confinement, a further grant of £25 for each additional child who is alive 12 hours after its birth. There are no contribution conditions. The grant is paid on the satisfaction of a simple 'presence in Great Britain' test by the mother. If the woman has been gainfully employed or self-employed, and has paid sufficient full-rate national insurance contributions in the relevant income tax year, she may receive a maternity allowance of £27·25 a week normally payable for 18 weeks commencing 11 weeks before the expected week of confinement, but not for any part of that period she does any paid work. Maternity allowance may be increased in certain circumstances in respect of dependants in the same way as sickness and unemployment benefits.

Widow's Benefit. On her husband's death a widow normally qualifies for 26 weeks for an allowance of £50·10 a week for herself plus an increase of £7·65 a week for each child for whom child benefit is payable. At the end of the 26 weeks she may qualify for a widowed mother's allowance of £35·80 for herself, and the increases for the children for whom child benefit is payable continue at the same rate as for the first 26 weeks of widowhood. She may also receive her allowance at the personal rate of £35·80 a week if she has living with her a son or daughter who is under 19. The child increase for widow's allowance and widowed mother's allowance is, generally speaking, payable only in respect of a child for whom child benefit is payable.

A widow's pension may be paid to: (i) A widow after the termination of her widow's allowance, if she does not qualify for widowed mother's allowance and was aged 40 or more when her husband died; (ii) A widow after she ceases to be entitled to a widowed mother's allowance if she is then aged 40 or more. The standard rate of this pension is £35·80 a week if the widow was 50 or more when her husband died or when her entitlement to widowed mother's allowance ended. If she was between 40 and 50, however, the standard rates of total pension range in 7% steps from 93% of the full age-50 rate (*i.e.*, £33·29 a week) for the widow who was 49 at that time to 30% (*i.e.*, £10·74 a week) for the widow who was then 40.

Child's Special Allowance. An allowance may be payable for the children of divorced parents where the father has died. It is payable to the mother if she has not remarried and her former husband was contributing, or legally liable to contribute, at least 25p a week towards the children's support in cash or kind or if she took reasonable steps to enforce maintenance and she was entitled to child benefit for the child(ren) when her former husband died or it is her child by her former husband and he was entitled to child benefit for the child(ren) when he died. It is similar to the increases for widow's children and is payable at the same rates.

Guardian's Allowance. A person who is responsible for an orphan child may be entitled to a guardian's allowance of £7·65 a week in addition to the amount of child benefit payable in respect of that child. Normally both the child's parents must be dead but when the child is illegitimate, or the parents were divorced, or one parent is missing, or serving a long sentence of imprisonment, the allowance may, in certain circumstances, be paid on the death of one parent only.

Retirement Pension. In order to receive a retirement pension, men between 65 and 70, and women between 60 and 65 must have retired from regular employment. From 6 April 1979 a woman divorced over the age of 60 must satisfy the retired conditions before a pension is payable. The standard rates of basic pensions are £35·08 a week for a man or woman on his or her own contributions and £21·50 for a married woman through her husband's contributions. Proportionately reduced pensions are payable where contribution records are deficient. For a person who reaches pension age on or after 6 April 1979, additional pension may also be payable. This is based on the earnings on which he or she has paid Class 1 contributions in each complete tax year between April 1978 and pension age. If the person has been a member of a contracted-out occupational pension scheme, that scheme will be responsible for paying the whole or part of the additional pension. An increase of £21·50 a week may be payable for a dependent wife. If she resides with the beneficiary the increase is gradually reduced for earnings over £45 a week. If she does not reside with the beneficiary an increase is not payable if she earns more than £21·50 a week. In addition £7·65 a week may be payable for each child for whom child benefit is payable. In certain circumstances an increase of £21·50 a week may be payable for a woman having care of the pensioner's children. In addition, a man who had paid graduated contributions receives 4·67p per week for every £7·50 of graduated contributions paid, and a woman 4·67p per week for every £9 paid. Although no further graduated contributions have been paid after April 1975, pension already earned will be paid along with the basic pension in the normal way. If, after being awarded a retirement pension, a man under 70 or a woman under 65 earns more than £70 in a calendar week the pension for the next pension week, including any increase for dependants, will be reduced by 5p for every 10p earned between £70 and £74 and by 5p for every 5p earned over £74. If retirement is postponed after minimum pension age increments of basic pension can be earned for periods of deferred retirement. From 6 April 1979 increments are earned at the rate of one-seventh penny per £1 of basic pension for every 6 days (excluding Sundays) for which pension has been foregone. Any days for which another benefit has been paid will not count. These increments must be at least 1% of the pension rate unless the minimum was earned under the arrangements which applied before 6 April 1979. For periods between 6 April 1975 and that date, the rate was one-eighth penny per £1 of the basic pension rate for every 6 days and for periods of deferred retirement before 6 April 1975 increments were based on the number of contributions paid as an employed or self-employed person. At age 70 for a man (65 for a woman) the pension for which a person has qualified may be paid in full whether a person continues in work or not irrespective of the amount of earnings. At the age of 80 an age addition of £0·25 a week is payable. In addition non-contributory pensions are now payable, subject to residence conditions, to persons aged 80 and over who do not qualify for a retirement pension or qualify for one at a low rate. The rates of these pensions, which are financed by Exchequer funds, are £21·50 a week for a single person and £12·85 for a married woman. These amounts do not include the £0·25 age addition.

Death Grant. This is a lump sum paid on the death of an insured person or his close relative. The normal amount of the payment is: For an adult, £30; for a child aged 6 but under 18, £22·50; for a child aged 3 but under 6, £15; for a child under 3, £9. For the death of a person who was within 10 years of pensionable age on 5 July 1948 (*i.e.*, a man over 55 and a woman over 50 on that date) only half the standard amount is payable. No grant is payable for the death of a person who was over the pensionable age on 5 July 1948.

The Industrial Injuries Provisions of the Social Security Act, 1975. The Industrial Injuries Act, which also came into operation on 5 July 1948, with its later amending Acts, was consolidated as the National Insurance (Industrial Injuries) Act, 1965. This legislation was incorporated in the Social Security Act, 1975. The scheme provides a system of insurance against 'personal injury by accident arising out of and in the course of employment' and against certain prescribed diseases and injuries due to the nature of the employment. It takes the place of the Workmen's Compensation Acts and covers persons who are employed earners under the Social Security Act. There are no contribution conditions for the payment of benefit. Three types of benefit are provided:

(1) Disablement benefit. This is payable where, as the result of an industrial accident or prescribed disease, there is a loss of faculty. The loss of faculty will be assessed as a percentage by comparison with a person of the same age and sex whose condition is normal. If the assessment is 20%, or more, benefit will be a pension varying according to the assessment, from £11·68 a week to £58·40 a week. If the assessment is under 20% benefit will normally be a gratuity of an amount not exceeding £3,880. Unemployability supplement plus age additions

similar to invalidity allowance, may be payable to a disablement pensioner who, as a result of the relevant loss of faculty is incapable of work and likely to remain permanently so incapable. Increases for dependants at the same rates as for invalidity pension are also payable to a disablement pensioner who is entitled to unemployability supplement. The supplement cannot be paid at the same time as certain other benefits payable under the Social Security Act or out of public funds. Other increases of disablement benefit may be payable *(i)* where the loss of faculty causes special hardship, *i.e.*, it prevents the beneficiary from undertaking his regular job or one of an equivalent standard of earnings; *(ii)* there is a need for constant attendance; *(iii)* there is exceptionally severe disablement and the need for constant attendance is likely to be permanent; or *(iv)* disablement is assessed at less than 100% and the beneficiary is in hospital for treatment for his injury or prescribed disease. Pensions for persons under 18 are at a reduced rate. When injury benefit was abolished for industrial accidents occurring and prescribed diseases commencing on or after 6 April 1983, a common start date was introduced for the payment of disablement benefit 90 days (excluding Sundays) after the date of the relevant accident or onset of the disease.

(2) *Death Benefit.* On the death of a person as the result of an industrial accident or a prescribed disease, certain dependants may qualify for benefit. Benefit for a widow is a pension normally of £50·10 weekly for the first 26 weeks and thereafter £36·35, depending on such factors as age, entitlement to a child's allowance and permanent incapacity for self-support. If the conditions for pension at the higher rate are not satisfied the widow may receive a pension of £10·74 a week. Child allowances may be payable to the widow, or other person, entitled to child benefit for children of the deceased. For widows, these allowances are usually at the rate of £7·65 a week for each child; other persons do not normally qualify for these allowances. An allowance of £1 is payable to a woman having care of a child of the deceased. Benefit for widowers, parents and certain other relatives takes the form of pensions, allowances or gratuities according to the relationship to, and degree of maintenance by, the deceased.

War Pensions. The number of beneficiaries in receipt of war (1914–18) pensions or allowances as at 28 Sept. 1984 was 19,600. The number of beneficiaries in receipt of war (1939–45 and later) pensions or allowances in payment as at 28 Sept. 1984 was 285,000. The expenditure for both wars for 1983–84 was £524m. The expenditure is exclusive of administrative expenses.

National Insurance Fund. At 1 April 1983 the balance of the National Insurance Fund amounted to £4,023,461,000. Income during the period 1 April 1983 to 31 March 1984, consisting of contributions from insured persons and employers, payments from the Exchequer and interest on investments, etc., was £21,089m. Payments of benefit in respect of unemployment were £1,496,518,000; sickness, £254,363,000; invalidity, £1,871,952,000; maternity, £141m.; widows, £771m.; guardian's allowance and child's special allowance, £2m.; retirement pension, £14,613,112,000; death grants, £16,749,000; injury benefit, £7,322,000; disablement benefits, £369,107,000; death benefit, £54m. Included in these figures are the following estimated amounts of graduated retirement benefit, £289m.; additional component, £142m.; earning related supplement having ceased. Administrative and other payments cost approximately £912,010,000. The balance at 31 March 1984 was £4,603,840,000.

From 1 April 1975 the National Insurance Reserve Fund and the Industrial Injuries Fund were merged with the National Insurance Fund. All basic scheme contributions payable under the 1975 Social Security Act are paid into the single fund out of which the existing range of benefits will continue to be financed. The new national insurance fund will continue to receive a Treasury Supplement set at a level of 13% of total contribution income.

Child Benefit. Child benefit is a tax-free cash allowance for all children. The weekly rate for each child is £6·85 from Nov. 1984. Child benefit is payable for all children under age 16 and for those under age 19 receiving full-time non-advanced education at a college or school. One Parent Benefit. This is a tax-free cash allowance for certain people bringing up children alone. It is payable for the first or only child in the family in addition to child benefit. The weekly rate from Nov. 1984 is £4·25.

Family Income Supplement. Family income supplement is payable to families with at least 1 dependent child where the man or woman is in remunerative work for at least 30 hours a week (24 hours for lone parents), and where the family's normal gross weekly income (but excluding child benefits) is below a prescribed amount. The prescribed amount for a 1-child family is £90, this amount being increased by £10 for each additional child in the family. The weekly rate of benefit payable is one-half of the difference between the prescribed amount and the family's normal income, subject to a maximum weekly payment of £23 for families with 1 child, increasing by £2 for each additional child. Benefit is usually payable for 52 weeks and is not affected by changes in circumstances. The prescribed amounts are the same for both 1- and 2-parent families.

Attendance allowance. This is a tax-free allowance for severely disabled people, including children aged 2 or over, who require a lot of help from another person. There are 2 rates, the higher rate of £28·60 a week for those who require attention or supervision by day and night, and the lower rate of £19·10 a week for those who need the attendance either by day or night. In addition to the medical requirements a simple test of residence and presence in Great Britain must also be satisfied.

Invalid Care Allowance. May be paid to those under pensionable age who stay at home to care for a person who is receiving attendance allowance or constant attendance allowance. In general married women do not qualify for this benefit. Current rate £21·50 a week, with increases for dependants.

Supplementary Benefit. Under the Supplementary Benefits Act, 1976, as amended by the Social Security Act 1980, benefit is payable to any persons in Great Britain aged 16 years or over (excluding persons at school or college or anyone directly involved in a trade dispute) who are not in full-time remunerative work and who are without resources, or whose resources (including national insurance benefits) need to be supplemented in order to meet their requirements. A person who is excluded from benefit under the normal rules may, nevertheless, receive payments to meet urgent need. The general standards by reference to which supplementary benefit is granted are determined by statutory regulations approved by Parliament. Persons who are dissatisfied with the amount of benefit granted to them may appeal to an independent Appeal Tribunal established under the Act.

During the financial year 1983–84 net payments on supplementary benefit amounted to £5,591m.

Newman, T. S., *Digest of British Social Insurance.* London, 1947 (and supplements, to date)

National Health. The National Health Service in England and Wales started on 5 July 1948 under the National Health Service Act, 1946. There is a separate Act for Scotland and also one for Northern Ireland, where the Health Services are run on similar lines to those in England and Wales.

The National Health Service, which is available to every man, woman and child, is a charge on the national income in the same way as the armed forces and other facilities.

Every person normally resident in this country is entitled to use any complete part of the services, and no insurance qualification is necessary. Most of the cost of running the service is met from the national exchequer, *i.e.*, from taxes.

Since Sept. 1957 a small weekly National Health Service contribution has been payable by contributors and where applicable by their employers. For convenience this contribution is collected with the National Insurance contribution and for 1982–83 is estimated to be £1,618m. for Great Britain.

Organization. Under the provisions of the NHS Act 1977 and the Health Service Act 1980, the administration of the National Health Service in England and Wales is organized under a system of regional and district health authorities accountable to the Secretary of State for the Social Services and the Secretary of State for Wales. In Scotland the National Health Service is administered under the National Health Service (Scotland) Act 1978, by 15 Health Boards and a Common Services Agency all accountable to the Secretary of State for Scotland.

There are 192 district health authorities in England responsible for the administration and development of health services in their district. Fourteen regional health authorities, each consisting of a number of health districts, are responsible for allocating resources between the district health authorities in their regions and for monitoring their performance. The regional authorities are responsible for developing strategic plans and priorities and for carrying out certain executive functions.

Services. The National Health Service broadly consists of hospital and specialist services, general medical, dental and ophthalmic services, pharmaceutical services, community health services and school health services. All these services are free of charge except for such things as prescriptions, spectacles, dentures and dental treatment, amenity beds in hospitals and for some of the community services, for which charges are made with certain exemptions.

The total cost of the Health and Personal Social Services (Great Britain) is estimated at £17,483m. for 1982–83 and the estimated net expenditure by the Exchequer (except for the Local Authority Personal Social Services, where the rates and the Exchequer grants are estimated at about £2,341m.) in 1982–83 is £12,651m.

The provisional number of abortions performed in 1982 under the provisions of the Abortion Act, 1967, was 162,797, of which 128,328 related to England and Wales residents. Of these 128,328 abortions, 71,717 (55·9%) were to single women, 40,427 (31·5%) were to married women, and 16,184 (12·6%) were to widowed, divorced or separated women and to women who did not state their marital status.

The number of abortion notifications received in Scotland in 1983 under the provisions of the Abortion Act 1967, was 8,419, of which 8,407 related to Scottish residents. Of these 8,419 notifications, 4,933 (58·6%) were to single women, 2,447 (29·4%) were to married women, and 1,009 (12%) were to widowed, divorced or separated women and to women who did not state their marital status.

In 1977 there were 26,810 general medical practitioners, 13,564 general dental practitioners and 219,900 qualified nurses and midwives. There were (1977) 469,849 allocated hospital beds.

Personal Social Services. Under the Local Authority Social Services Act 1970 and in Scotland the Social Work (Scotland) Act 1968 the welfare and social work services provided by local authorities were made the responsibility of a new local authority department—the Social Services Department in England and Wales, and Social Work Departments in Scotland headed by a Director of Social Work. The social services thus administered include: the fostering, care and adoption of children, welfare services and social workers for the mentally disordered, the disabled and the aged, and accommodation for those needing residential care services. In Scotland the social work departments' functions also include the supervision of persons on probation, of adult offenders and of persons released from penal institutions or subject to fine supervision orders.

The number of supported residents in residential accommodation for the elderly and younger disabled was as follows:

England and Wales (31 March)	*Residential accommodation Adults and Children*	*Scotland (31 March)*	*Residential accommodation Adults and Children*
1982	134,152	1982	15,823
1983	132,749	1983	15,685
1984	129,093	1984	...

England and Wales. Expenditure and income relating to the personal social services administered by local authorities (in £1,000 sterling):

Year ended 31 March	*Gross current expenditure*	*Income from sales, fees and charges*	*Net current expenditure*
1979	1,335,252	214,757	1,120,495
1980	1,623,758	247,611	1,376,147
1981	1,997,761	294,710	1,703,051
1982	2,214,296	326,915	1,887,381
1983[1]	2,430,706	359,321	2,071,385

[1] Provisional.

Scotland. The total local authority expenditure for 1982–83 in respect of residential accommodation and welfare services under the Social Work (Scotland) Act, 1968, was £294·1m. Central Government expenditure on social work totalled £12·1m.

Klein, R., *The Politics of the National Health Service.* London, 1983
Watkin, B., *The National Health Service.* London, 1978

DIPLOMATIC REPRESENTATIVES

Of the USA in Great Britain (Grosvenor Sq., London, W1A 1AE)
Ambassador: John J. Louis, Jr.

Of Great Britain in the USA (3100 Massachusetts Ave., NW, Washington, D.C., 20008)
Ambassador: Sir Oliver Wright, GCMG, GCVO, DSC.

Of Great Britain to the United Nations
Ambassador: Sir John Thomson, KCMG.

Books of Reference

The annual and other publications of the various Public Departments, and the Reports, etc. of Royal Commissions and Parliamentary Committees. (These may be obtained from HM Stationery Office.)
Bickmore, D. P., and Shaw, M. A. (ed.), *The Atlas of Great Britain and Northern Ireland.* OUP, 1963
Central Statistical Office. *Annual Abstract of Statistics.* HMSO.—*Monthly Digest of Statistics.* HMSO
Central Office of Information. *Britain: An Official Handbook.* HMSO, annual.
Demangeon, A., *The British Isles.* 3rd ed. London, 1952
Directory of British Associations. Beckenham, annual
Government Statistical Service. *Social Trends.* HMSO.—*Regional Statistics.* HMSO
Government Statistics: A Brief Guide to Sources. HMSO, 1984
Halsey, A. H., *Trends in British Society Since 1900.* London, 1972
History of the Second World War. HMSO, 1949 ff.
Jenkin, M., *British Industry and the North Sea.* London, 1981
Kendall, M. G. (ed.), *The Source and Nature of the Statistics of the United Kingdom.* 2 vols. London, 1952–1957
Mitchell, B. R., *Abstract of British Historical Statistics.* OUP, 1962
Oxford History of England. 15 vols. OUP, 1936–75
Woodward, Sir E. L., and Butler, R., *Documents on British Foreign Policy, 1919–39.* HMSO, 1957 ff.

Scotland

Scottish Council (Development and Industry). *Inquiry into the Scottish Economy, 1900–61.* Edinburgh, 1961
Scottish Office. *Scottish Economic Bulletin.* HMSO (quarterly).—*Scottish Abstract of Statistics.* HMSO (annual)
The New Scottish Local Authorities: Organisation and Management Structures. HMSO, 1973
Brand, J., *The National Movement in Scotland.* London, 1978
Campbell, R. H., *The Rise and Fall of Scottish Industry, 1707–1939.* Edinburgh, 1981
Donaldson, G. (ed.) *The Edinburgh History of Scotland.* 4 vols. Edinburgh, 1965–75
Drucker, N. and H. M., *The Scottish Government Year Book.* London, 1980

Grant, E., *Scotland.* [Bibliography] Oxford and Santa Barbara, 1982
Hogg, A., and Hutcheson, A. MacG., *Scotland and Oil.* 2nd ed. Edinburgh, 1975
Johnston, T. L., *Structure and Growth in the Scottish Economy.* London, 1971
Kellas, J. G., *The Scottish Political System.* 2nd ed. CUP, 1975
Meikle, H. W. (ed.), *Scotland: A Description of Scotland and Scottish Life.* London, 1947
Turnock, D., *Patterns of Highland Development.* London, 1970

Wales

Wales: The Way Ahead (Cmnd 3334.) HMSO, 1971
Wales: Employment and the Economy. Cardiff, 1972
Digest of Welsh Statistics. HMSO (annual)
Thomas, B. (ed.), *The Welsh Economy.* Cardiff, 1962
Williams, D., *A History of Modern Wales.* New ed. London, 1977
Williams, G., (ed.) *Social and Cultural Change in Contemporary Wales.* London, 1978

NORTHERN IRELAND

AREA AND POPULATION. Area (revised by the Ordnance Survey Department) and population (estimate) of 30 June 1983 were as follows:

District	*Population 1983*	*Area (Hectares)*
Antrim	45,500	40,527
Ards	59,700	36,779
Armagh	49,900	66,733
Ballymena	55,400	63,384
Ballymoney	23,400	41,687
Banbridge	30,600	44,131
Belfast	322,600	13,017
Carrickfergus	28,400	8,484
Castlereagh	59,800	8,441
Coleraine	47,400	47,763
Cookstown	29,300	51,207
Craigavon	73,400	27,989
Down	54,000	63,835
Dungannon	45,700	76,266
Fermanagh	51,600	169,952
Larne	29,300	33,744
Limavady	28,000	58,523
Lisburn	87,900	43,595
Londonderry [1]	96,100	37,258
Magherafelt	34,200	56,186
Moyle	14,500	49,378
Newry and Mourne	83,400	88,589
Newtownabbey	71,900	15,108
North Down	66,800	7,241
Omagh	46,900	112,354
Strabane	37,000	86,090
Northern Ireland	1,572,700	1,348,261

[1] Name changed to Derry in 1984.

Vital statistics for calendar years:

	Marriages	*Divorces*	*Births*	*Deaths*
1979	10,214	757	28,178	16,811
1980	9,923	896	28,582	16,835
1981	9,636	775	27,302	16,256
1982	9,913	1,383	27,028	15,918
1983 [1]	9,990	1,502	27,255	16,039

[1] Provisional.

CONSTITUTION AND GOVERNMENT. Northern Ireland is part of the United Kingdom. As such it is subjected to the fundamental constitutional provisions which apply to the rest of the United Kingdom. However, in the Northern Ireland Constitution Act 1973 and the Northern Ireland Act 1982, Parliament provides for a measure of devolved government in Northern Ireland. This can only be introduced if both Houses of Parliament agree that the arrangements for devolution are likely to command widespread acceptance throughout the community in Northern Ireland.

Such matters as the Crown, Parliament, international relations, the armed forces and the raising of taxes cannot be devolved in any circumstances and remain the responsibility of the UK Parliament and Government. In the event of agreement on widely-acceptable arrangements for devolution, powers over a range of social and economic matters would be devolved first. The Northern Ireland Assembly would have power to make laws on these subjects and Members of the Assembly would be appointed as heads of the relevant Northern Ireland government departments. Such powers were devolved on 1 Jan. 1974, following an agreement among the Northern Ireland political parties to form a power-sharing Executive. This collapsed on 28 May 1974 and there had been no devolution by March 1985.

In the interim and in the absence of devolved arrangements which command widespread acceptance, Northern Ireland is governed by 'direct rule' under the provisions of the Northern Ireland Act 1974. This provides for Parliament to approve all laws for Northern Ireland and places the Northern Ireland departments under the direction and control of a UK Cabinet Minister, the Secretary of State for Northern Ireland.

The 78-member Assembly was elected by proportional representation in 1982. The present party balance is: Ulster Unionist Party (UUP), 27 seats; Democratic Unionist Party (DUP), 20 seats; Social Democratic and Labour Party (SDLP), 13 seats; Alliance Party, 10 seats; Sinn Fein, 5 seats; others (Independent Unionists), 3 seats. Since 1982 the SDLP Members have declined to take their seats in the Assembly as presently constituted. Sinn Fein have said that it will not take part in Assembly proceedings under any circumstances.

The Assembly has, pending agreement on the devolution of powers, important consultative and scrutinising functions. By May 1984 it had produced 66 reports, considered 18 proposals for draft Orders in Council, and in addition some 380 pieces of subordinate legislation had been referred to it. As a result of the Assembly's work, direct rule has been made more responsive to local needs. In May 1984 the Assembly set up a Committee on Devolution to consider and report on how the Assembly might be strengthened and progress made towards legislative and selective devolution.

What began ostensibly as a Civil Rights campaign in 1968 escalated into a full-scale offensive designed to overthrow the State. This offensive was originally mounted by an illegal organization, the Irish Republican Army (not to be confused with the legitimate Army of the Republic of Ireland). At times counter-measures have required the services of over 20,000 regular troops, in addition to the Royal Ulster Constabulary, the RUC Reserve and the part-time Ulster Defence Regiment.

Secretary of State for Northern Ireland: Right Hon. Douglas Hurd, MP.

Local Government. Northern Ireland has a single-tier system of 26 district councils based on main centres of population.

The district councils are responsible for the provision of a wide range of local services including refuse collection and disposal, street cleansing, litter prevention, consumer protection, environmental health, miscellaneous licensing including dog control, the provision and management of recreational and cultural facilities, the promotion of tourist development schemes, the enforcement of building regulations and gas supply. They have in addition both a representative role in which they send forward representatives to sit as members of statutory bodies including the Northern Ireland Housing Council, the Fire Authority and the Area Boards for health and personal social services and education and libraries; and a consultative role under which the Department of Environment (NI) and the Northern Ireland Housing Executive, among others, have an obligation to consult them regarding the provision of the regional services for which these bodies are responsible.

The Government's policy for the future development of the Province is contained in the *Regional Physical Development Strategy 1975–95* which was published in May 1977. Basically the policy advocates that the main town in each District Council area should be developed to fulfil its function as the prime centre in the district and for any other specialized rôles it may have such as an industrial centre, port or tourist resort. The Strategy also recognizes that the smaller towns and villages have an important rôle to play, depending on the availability of services, as locations for smaller scale industries service centres and as dormitory centres for people not wishing to live in the towns where they find employment.

The Regional Strategy provides a framework within which development plans can be prepared for all the districts. Since its adoption of the Strategy the Department has been engaged in formulating the detailed policies and proposals for future communications, the location of industry, housing and major services in the light of anticipated population growth and distribution.

A development plan sets down the broad policies and proposals for the development or other use of land in the area covered by the plan over a period of up to 20 years ahead. Development plans have been published for the Belfast Urban Area, North Down, Derry, West Tyrone, East Tyrone, Newry, Limavady, Armagh, East Antrim, Magherafelt, Fermanagh, the North East of the Province which incorporates the Coleraine-Portrush-Portstewart area and Lisburn. A review of the Derry area plan has also been published.

FINANCE. There exists a separate Northern Ireland Consolidated Fund from which is met the expenditure of Northern Ireland Departments. Its main sources of revenue are: *(i)* The Northern Ireland attributed share of UK taxes; *(ii)* A non-specific grant in aid of Northern Ireland's revenue, payable by the Secretary of State for Northern Ireland; *(iii)* Rates and other receipts of Northern Ireland Departments.

The general principle underlying the financial arrangements is that Northern Ireland should have parity of taxation and services with Great Britain.

Since the financial year 1982–83 the income of the Northern Ireland Consolidated Fund has been as follows (in £ sterling):

	1982–83	*1983–84*	*1984–85*
Attributed share of UK taxes	1,607,112,320[1]	1,603,034,464[2]	1,757,400,000[3]
Payments by UK Government:			
Grant in Aid	630,000,000	775,000,000	732,916,000
Refund of value added tax	18,119,788	27,278,536	25,000,000
Regional and district rates	166,150,000	170,650,000	201,000,000
Other receipts	260,262,632	302,246,314	305,403,000
Total	2,681,644,740	2,878,209,314	3,021,719,000

[1] Including final adjustment for 1980–81.
[2] Including final adjustment for 1981–82.
[3] Provisional.

The public debt at 31 March 1984 was as follows: Northern Ireland 7% Exchequer Stock 1982–84, £20m.; Ulster Savings Certificates, £163,681,000;

Ulster Development Bonds, £864,700; borrowing from UK Government, £798,473,762; borrowing from Northern Ireland Government Funds, £345,328,700; short term borrowing from external sources, £31·2m.; borrowing from building societies, £10m.; European Investment Bank Loan, £18,804,738; total, £1,388,352,900.

The above amount of public debt is offset by equal assets in the form of loans from Government to public and local bodies and of cash balances.

ENERGY AND NATURAL RESOURCES

Electricity. The planning, generation and distribution of electricity supplies are the responsibility of the Northern Ireland Electricity Service.

The installed capacity of the system is 2,400 mw largely provided from 4 thermal power-stations.

The total sales of electricity in Northern Ireland in the year ended 31 March 1984 amounted to 4,663m. units supplied to a total of 543,546 consumers.

Water Supplies and Sewerage. The Water Service Division of the Department of the Environment (NI) is responsible for water supply and sewerage. Some 151m. gallons of water a day are supplied throughout the Province. More than 96% of the population have a mains supply of water and live in property connected to a public sewerage system.

The Department is also responsible for the conservation and planned development of water resources in Northern Ireland.

Minerals. The output of minerals (in 1,000 tonnes) during 1983 was approximately: Basalt and igneous rock (other than granite), 6,140; grit and conglomerate, 2,532; limestone, 3,249; sand and gravel, 3,207; and other minerals (rocksalt, flint, sandstone, diatomite, granite, chalk, clay and shale), 557. Lignite has been discovered near Crumlin in County Antrim and in some other areas.

Agriculture. Estimated gross output in 1983:

	Unit	*Quantity (1,000)*	*Value (£m.)*
Fat cattle	head	479	240·1
Calves	head	8	1·4
Store cattle	head	4	1·3
Exports of breeding livestock	head	6	1·3
Fat sheep and lambs	head	715	23·1
Fat pigs	head	1,151	72·7
Poultry (tonnes)		57	41·3
Eggs: for human consumption (dozen)		85,671	27·4
Wool (tonnes)		1,851	1·6
Milk (litres)		1,415,632	199·1
Potatoes	tonnes	300	25·7
Oats	tonnes	5	0·6
Barley	tonnes	92	11·0
Wheat	tonnes	5	0·6

	Unit	*Quantity (1,000)*	*Value (£m.)*
Grass seed	tonnes	—	—
Hay and straw	tonnes	9	0·4
Fruit	tonnes	24	3·4
Vegetables	tonnes	33	4·3
Mushrooms	tonnes	5	5·9
Flowers		—	1·9
Other items		—	54·7
Total receipts			714·8
Value of changes in stocks due to volume			+4·2
Gross output			722·0

Area (in 1,000 hectares) of crops at June census (1983 and 1984):

	1983	*1984*
Oats	2·9	2·7
Barley	45·4	45·1
Other cereals and pulses	2·0	3·5
Potatoes	12·9	14·1
Turnips, swedes, kale and cabbage[1]	0·6	6·7
Vegetables	1·2	1·2
Other crops	6·8	6·2
Fruit	2·3	2·2
Grass for mowing	256·3	257·6
Grass for grazing	509·5	508·7
Rough grazing (excluding common land)	190·3	188·4

[1] Stock feeding only.

Livestock (1,000) at June census (1983 and 1984):

	1983	*1984*		*1983*	*1984*
Dairy cows	294	299	Total sheep	1,324	1,450
Beef cows	194	196	Breeding sows	70	63
Total cattle	1,472	1,507	Total pigs	651	615
Breeding ewes	670	709	Total poultry	10,513	10,775

INDUSTRY AND TRADE

Industry. In 1984 (Sept.) employment in manufacturing and construction amounted to 126,130, some 27% of the total workforce. Of this number, 30,770 (24%) were engaged in the engineering and allied industries, which include shipbuilding and aircraft manufacture. The former predominance of shipbuilding has diminished, and the engineering sector now produces an impressive variety of goods; from textile machinery, air-conditioning plant and oilfield equipment to automobile and aero-engine components, data-processing equipment, and electronic components. The textile industry, with a workforce of 12,350 includes longer established sectors such as spinning and weaving as well as more recently established activities such as the production of carpets, man-made fibres and hosiery. The related clothing and footwear sector employs 16,070 people. Taken together, food, drink and tobacco account for 19,660 jobs, the remainder of the manufacturing sector comprising a multiplicity of activities, such as chemicals, rubber and plastic goods, and furniture accounting for 23,310. The construction industry employs 22,970 people.

In 1984 the average number of unemployed was 121,418, this represents an average of 21% of all employees. The Department of Economic Development provides an all-age guidance and placement service through a network of jobmarkets situated in the principal towns of Northern Ireland. They maintain registers of persons voluntarily seeking employment (either full- or part-time) and those already in employment who wish to change their job. In 1984 the number of vacancies filled in Northern Ireland by the Employment Service was 25,124 (adults and young persons), and 16,912 were placed in centres of training.

The Government offers a comprehensive range of incentives to encourage the establishment of new and the expansion of existing industry. At 30 June 1984 there were 201 new projects and 175 expansions of existing projects giving employment to 67,035 workers.

Through the Department of Economic Development, there are various employment and training grants available to assist employers with recruitment and training of workers. These grants cover a wide spectrum of industry, age groups, and types of training.

Assistance is available to employers who transfer key workers temporarily or permanently to Northern Ireland from other countries or within Northern Ireland in connection with the establishment or expansion of an industrial undertaking.

The Department of Economic Development maintains a register of disabled persons who are in the employment field and under the provisions of the Disabled Persons (Employment) Acts (NI) 1945 and 1960, makes efforts to find suitable work for those who are unemployed. Employment rehabilitation courses are provided at the Employment Rehabilitation Unit at Felden House, Newtownabbey and training courses at various locations are available to assist unemployed disabled persons to readjust themselves to working conditions and to enhance their prospects of obtaining suitable employment. Allowances are paid to persons attending these courses.

The Department of Economic Development and the Department of Education co-ordinate jointly a Youth Training Programme to assist all 16 and 17 year olds to make the transition from school to adult life and acquire a range of basic skills and knowledge. The programme provides:

(a) a guaranteed year of training with work experience in further education for young people aged 16 who do not wish to continue their education full-time;

(b) a combination of training and work for 17 year olds either as private sector employees or as unemployed trainees with voluntary bodies; and

(c) additional vocational preparation for young people remaining in full-time education.

In 1985–86 the Programme is providing some 10,500 training places for the unemployed and assisting with the training of some 5,000 employees.

Enterprise Ulster is an independent statutory body whose objective as a direct labour organization is to recruit workers from the unemployed register. Work is carried out mainly for public bodies and projects are of a community and amenity nature such as play areas, parks, playing fields, etc. In Dec. 1984, 125 projects were in operation providing employment for 1,100 employees.

The Action for Community Employment Scheme, which came into operation in April 1981, provides temporary employment for long-term unemployed adults by funding projects which are of benefit to the community. In Dec. 1984 some 1,050 such projects were operational, providing employment for 3,150 people.

There are 12 Government Training Centres in Northern Ireland which provide over 3,000 training places and an annual output of over 5,000 trainees.

Government Training Centres contribute to the Youth Training Programme having up to 2,400 places available for 16–17 year olds who have been unable to find employment. A special six-month broad-based modular course provides basic training in a wide variety of skills and the six-month craft skill courses provide initial apprentice training. Advanced vocational training is available to young people who have completed the basic training course and have been unable to obtain a place in an apprentice course. The remaining places are for adult trainees.

To supplement the Government Training Centres facilities, arrangements have been made for the use of spare training capacity in industry and commerce to attach people to firms for training courses. By this means a wide variety of training is made available and this has been further supplemented by use of spare capacity in other training agencies and in Colleges of Further Education.

The Department of Economic Development administers an Entry to Management Programme for unemployed trainees and a Management Development Programme for private sector firms. The former Programme contains training opportunities schemes for those wishing to enter or re-enter management or to set up new businesses – at the peak time of the training year almost 200 men and women can be in training at any one time. The latter Programme is designed to encourage private sector firms to develop management structures and to train individual managers in a planned way to a high level of competence. Since the Management Development Programme was introduced in Oct. 1982, 2,900 have been trained in this way. 2,000 places are available in the period Aug. 1983 to March 1985 under the Enterprise Allowance Scheme to encourage unemployed people to forego receipt of unemployment benefit and set up in business, by paying them £40 a week for up to 52 weeks as a business receipt.

Labour. The main source of statistics in Northern Ireland is the census of employment which was last conducted in 1981. In June 1984 there were 461,550 jobs for employees in Northern Ireland; of which 245,000 were taken up by males.

TOURISM. Tourism earns a substantial amount of revenue for Northern Ireland and total spending by some 865,000 visitors in 1983 was 72m.; day excursions provided an additional £120m. Altogether tourism provides over 9,000 permanent jobs and some 3,000 temporary or seasonal jobs. The Northern Ireland Tourist Board plays a major role in promoting the development of tourist traffic in Northern Ireland.

The protection of scenic beauty, scientific and nature interest, and wildlife is fostered under the Amenity Lands Act (NI) 1965 and the Wild Birds Protection Acts (NI) 1931 to 1968 by the Department of the Environment for Northern Ireland, which is advised by the Ulster Countryside Committee, the Nature Reserves Committee and the Wild Birds Advisory Committee. Eight Areas of Outstanding Natural Beauty and 47 Areas of Scientific Interest have been designated, and in these areas special attention is given respectively to the amenity and scientific aspects of planning applications. Country Parks have been established at Crawfordsburn, Redburn and Scrabo, Co. Down, at the Roe Valley and Ness Wood, Co. Derry, at Castle Archdale, Co. Fermanagh and at The Birches

('Peatlands') in N. Armagh. The Lagan Valley between Belfast and Lisburn is being administered as Northern Ireland's first Regional Park. Forty-one National Nature Reserves have been declared, and steady progress is being made with the acquisition of further reserves. Ten areas have been designated as Bird Sanctuaries.

The Department is advised by the Historic Monuments Council on the exercise of its powers under the Historic Monuments Act (NI) 1971 in respect of the conservation of historic monuments and the preservation of objects of archaeological or historic interest. At present there are some 153 monuments in State care and approximately 470 are scheduled. The Department, advised by the Historic Buildings Council, is also responsible for listing buildings of special architectural or historic interest and for designating areas of similar interest the character or appearance of which it is desirable to preserve or enhance. To date some 6,400 buildings have been listed and 19 conservation areas have been designated. Grants are payable by the Department to assist in the repair or maintenance of listed buildings and for schemes of enhancement in conservation areas.

COMMUNICATIONS

Road and Rail. All train services are operated by the Northern Ireland Railways Co. Ltd which is a subsidiary of the Northern Ireland Transport Holding Co. The number of track miles operated is 357; passenger route miles, 210. In 1983–84 railways carried 5·5m. passengers. Most bus services are operated by two other subsidiaries, Ulsterbus Ltd and Citybus Ltd. Ulsterbus runs services outside the Belfast area (except for a few services provided by privately owned bus undertakings) while all the services within the Belfast area are run by Citybus.

The Department of the Environment (NI) administers a licensing system for professional hauliers with the objective of maintaining standards and conditions necessary for the safe operation of vehicles and fair competition between hauliers. The level of services provided and the rates charged by the industry are determined by the normal economic forces of supply and demand. At 31 March 1984 there were 1,475 professional hauliers and 2,481 vehicles licensed to engage in road haulage.

The number of motor vehicles licensed at 31 Dec. 1983 was 481,854, comprising private cars, 422,310; motor cycles, 14,790; hackney vehicles, 2,200; goods vehicles, 18,870; agricultural tractors, 9,870. In addition, there were 13,764 vehicles which were not subject to licence duty.

The Department of the Environment (NI) is responsible for the provision and maintenance of all public roads, bridges and street lighting in the Province, the provision and operation of car parks, and for the operation of the Strangford Ferry. In addition to Headquarters Division the Roads Service of the Department operates through Divisional Offices in Ballymena, Belfast, Coleraine, Craigavon, Downpatrick and Omagh and smaller offices in other centres.

At 1 April 1984 the total mileage of roads was 14,802, graded for administrative purposes as follows: Motorway 70 miles; all purpose trunk, 343 miles; Class I, 1,025 miles; Class II, 1,765 miles; Class III, 2,954 miles; unclassified, 8,645 miles.

Aviation. Northern Ireland Airports Ltd is responsible for the operation of Belfast International Airport. A major 4-stage development programme was started in 1977 and the first 2 stages have now been completed, while the design of Stage 3 works is under way. The completion of the programme will leave the airport better equipped to handle traffic growth in the foreseeable future. Passenger and freight services operate between Belfast International Airport and airports throughout the UK. In 1983–4, 1·4m. passengers and 24,000 tonnes of freight and mail were handled.

Scheduled air services are available from Belfast (Harbour) Airport to 5 destinations in the UK.

There are 3 other licensed airfields in Northern Ireland and apart from some scheduled services during the summer months, these airfields are used principally by flying clubs, by private owners and by expanding air taxi businesses flying to destinations in Ireland, the UK and continental Europe.

Shipping. Passenger services operate between Belfast and Liverpool and between Larne and (i) Cairnryan and (ii) Stranraer. Conventional cargo services have given way in many cases to container, unit load and drive on/drive off services. The latter type of service now operates between Belfast and Larne to various ports in UK.

JUSTICE, RELIGION, EDUCATION AND WELFARE

Justice. The Lord Chancellor has responsibility for the administration of all courts in Northern Ireland through the Northern Ireland Court Service, and is responsible for the appointment of judges and resident magistrates.

The court structure in Northern Ireland has 3 tiers–the Supreme Court of Judicature of Northern Ireland (comprising the Court of Appeal, the High Court and the Crown Court), the County Courts and the Magistrates' Courts. There are 25 Petty Sessions districts which when grouped together for administration purposes form 7 County Court Divisions and 4 Circuits.

The County Court has general civil jurisdiction subject to an upper monetary limit of £5,000. Appeals from the Magistrates' Courts lie to the County Court, while appeals from the County Court lie to the High Court or, on a point of law, to the Court of Appeal by way of case stated. Circuit Registrars have jurisdiction to deal with most defended actions up to £500 and most undefended actions up to £5,000. They also deal, by an informal arbitration procedure, with small claims whose value does not exceed £300. An appeal from the decision of a Circuit Registrar lies to the High Court other than in small claims cases.

Police. The police force consists of the Royal Ulster Constabulary, supported by the Royal Ulster Constabulary Reserve, a mainly part-time force.

Religion. The religious professions at the census of 1981 were: Roman Catholics, 414,532; Presbyterians, 339,818; Church of Ireland, 284,253 (including Church of England, 2,503 and Episcopal Church of Scotland, 278); Methodists, 58,731; others, 110,041 and not stated, 274,584.

Education. Education in Northern Ireland is administered centrally by the Department of Education and locally by 5 education and library boards. The Department is concerned with the whole range of education from nursery education through to higher education and continuing education; for sport and recreation; for youth services; for the arts and culture (including libraries) and for community relations and community development. District councils are the main providers of sport, recreation and community facilities and the education and library boards have a responsibility where the facilities are intended primarily for education and youth service activities. The Department assists with grants as far as the district councils are concerned and meets the full cost in relation to education and library boards.

The 5 education and library boards which took over responsibility for the local administration of the education and library services on 1 Oct. 1973 are required to ensure that there are sufficient schools of all kinds to meet the needs of their area. They provide primary and secondary schools, special schools for handicapped pupils and institutions of further education. The boards also make contributions towards the cost of maintaining voluntary schools; award university and other scholarships; meet the tuition fees of the great majority of pupils attending grammar schools; provide milk and meals; free books and transport for pupils; enforce school attendance; regulate the employment of children and young people and secure the provision of recreational and youth service facilities. They are also required to develop a comprehensive and efficient library service for their areas. The following are the statistics for the 1982–83 academic year:

Universities. The Queen's University of Belfast (founded in 1849 as a college of the Queen's University of Ireland and reconstituted as a separate university in 1908) had 111 professors, 238 readers and senior lecturers, 491 lecturers and tutors and 6,645 full-time students. In Oct. 1984, the New University of Ulster and the Ulster Polytechnic merged to form a new institution, the University of Ulster, with campuses in Belfast, Coleraine, Jordanstown and Derry.

The New University of Ulster at Coleraine, of which Magee University College, Derry, is an integral part, had 21 professors, 53 readers and senior lecturers, 169 lecturers and demonstrators and 2,264 full-time students.

The Ulster Polytechnic, a central institution providing higher non-university education for the whole of Northern Ireland, had a full-time academic staff of 562, and 5,169 full-time and sandwich, and 2,471 part-time students.

Secondary Education. 78 grammar schools with 58,754 pupils and 3,627 full-time teachers; 183 secondary (intermediate) schools with 103,166 pupils and 6,872 full-time teachers.

Primary Education. 1,017 primary schools with 181,395 pupils and 7,739 teachers; 84 nursery schools with 4,499 pupils and 154 teachers.

Further Education. 26 institutions of further education with 2,138 full-time and 1,875 part-time teachers and an enrolment of 13,464 full-time, 13,314 part-time day and 17,245 evening students on vocational courses; and 43,828 students on non-vocational (mostly evening) courses.

Special Educational Treatment. 34 special schools, including hospital schools with 2,830 pupils and 352 teachers.

Teachers. There were 20,882 full-time teachers (8,630 men and 12,252 women) in grant-aided schools and institutions of further education. The minimum general teacher-training course is of 3 years' duration and there were 1,498 students (448 men and 1,050 women) in training; these included students following teacher-training courses at university establishments and at Ulster Polytechnic and North West College of Technology, and the 3 Colleges of Education.

Expenditure. Expenditure by the Department of Education in 1983–84 was £556·5m.

Health and Personal Social Services. Under the provisions of the Health and Personal Social Services (NI) Order 1972, the Department of Health and Social Services is responsible for the provision of integrated health and personal social services in Northern Ireland, designed to promote the physical and mental health of the people of Northern Ireland through the prevention, diagnosis and treatment of illness, and also to promote their social welfare. Four Health and Social Services Boards, Eastern, Northern, Southern and Western, established under the above Order, administer health and personal social services, as the Department directs, within their designated areas.

Social Security. The social security schemes in Northern Ireland are similar to those in force in Great Britain.

National Insurance. During the year ended 31 March 1984, £13·9m. sickness benefit was paid to an average of 9,100 persons and £48·1m. unemployment benefit was paid to an average of 33,500 persons. Widows' benefits amounting to £27·9m. were paid to 14,700 persons and retirement pensions totalling £319·5m. were paid to an average of 201,300 persons. Invalidity pensions and allowances totalling £87·3m. were paid to approximately 34,900 persons. Industrial disablement benefit amounting to £10·6m. was paid to an average of 5,100 persons. Maternity benefit totalling £4·4m. was paid to approximately 11,600 persons. Receipts, of the Northern Ireland Insurance Fund in the year ended 31 March 1984 were £544·1m. and payments were £546·8m.

Child Benefit. During the year ended 31 March 1984, £152m. was paid to an average of 215,600 families.

Supplementary Benefits. In 1983–84, £280·3m. was paid to an average of 175,000 persons.

Family Income Supplement. In 1983–84, £10·4m. was paid to an average of 12,800 persons.

Books of Reference

The annual and other publications of the various Departments and the Reports, etc., of Parliamentary Committees may be obtained from HM Stationery Office, Belfast.

Northern Ireland Social Security Statistics
Ulster Year Book, 1985. (Bi-annual). Belfast, HMSO, 1985
Census of Population Reports, Northern Ireland. Belfast, HMSO, 1981
Annual Abstract of Statistics. Belfast, HMSO
Northern Ireland Development 1970–75. Belfast, HMSO, 1970
Northern Ireland: A Trade Directory. Belfast, HMSO, 1st ed. 1985
Reports on the Census of Production of Northern Ireland. Belfast, HMSO
Re-organization of Secondary Education in Northern Ireland. Belfast, HMSO, 1976
The Statutes Revised: Northern Ireland. HMSO, 1982
Bell, G., *The Protestants of Ulster.* London, 1976
Bew, P., Gibbon, P. and Patterson, H., *The State in Northern Ireland, 1921–1972.* New York, 1980
Biggs-Davison, J., *The Hand is Red.* London, 1974
Boal, F. W. and Douglas, J. N. H., *Integration and Division.* London, 1982
Farrell, M., *Northern Ireland: The Orange State.* London, 1976
Flackes, W. D., *Northern Ireland: Political Directory 1968–83.* London, 1983
Heskin, K., *Northern Ireland: A Psychological Analysis.* Dublin, 1980
Hull, R. H., *The Irish Triangle.* Princeton Univ. Press, 1976
Kelly, K., *The Longest War: Northern Ireland and the IRA.* Dingle, Westport and London, 1982
Quekett, Sir A. S., *The Constitution of Northern Ireland.* 3 pts. Belfast, 1928–47
Rose, R., *Northern Ireland: A Time of Choice.* London, 1976
Wallace, M., *British Government in Northern Ireland: From Devolution to Direct Rule.* Newton Abbot, 1982
Watt, D. (ed.), *The Constitution of Northern Ireland.* London, 1981
Winchester, S., *Northern Ireland in Crisis: Reporting the Ulster Troubles.* New York, 1975

ISLE OF MAN

AREA AND POPULATION. Area, 221 sq. miles (572 sq. km); resident population census April 1981, 64,679. The principal towns are Douglas (population, 19,944), Ramsey (5,818), Peel (3,688), Castletown (3,141). Vital statistics, 1983: Births, 680; deaths, 943; marriages, . The number of Manx-speaking people was 284 in 1971 (165 in 1961 and 4,657 in 1901), all of whom were bilingual.

CONSTITUTION AND GOVERNMENT. The Isle of Man is administered in accordance with its own laws by the Court of Tynwald, consisting of the Governor, appointed by the Crown; the Legislative Council, composed of the Lord Bishop of Sodor and Man, the Attorney-General (who does not vote) and 8 members selected by the House of Keys, total 10 members; and the House of Keys, a representative assembly of 24 members chosen on adult suffrage with 12 months' residence for 5 years by the 6 'sheadings' or local sub-divisions, and the 4 municipalities. The Island is not bound by Acts of the Imperial Parliament unless specially mentioned in them.

A special relationship exists between the Isle of Man and the European Economic Community providing for free trade and adoption by the Isle of Man of the EEC's external trade policies with third countries. The Island remains free to levy its own system of rates and taxes.

The elections to the House of Keys, Nov. 1981, resulted in the return of 21 Independents and 3 Labour. Number of voters, 47,449.

An Executive Council to advise the Governor on all matters of government was set up under the Isle of Man Constitution Act, 1961. It consists at present of 5 members of the House of Keys and 3 of the Legislative Council.

Lieut.-Governor: Sir Nigel Cecil, KBE, CB (term of office began Sept. 1980).
Government Secretary: P. J. Hulme.
Government Treasurer: W. Dawson.

Flag: Red, with 3 steel-coloured legs armoured and spurred (knees and spurs, yellow) in the centre.

ECONOMY

Budget. Revenue is derived from customs duties, value added tax and from income tax. In 1984–85 the budget allowed for gross revenue and capital expenditure of £145,722,290. Income tax was 20p in the £. No death duties or surtaxes are levied. Company registration tax is levied at a flat rate of £250 on every company incorporated in the Isle of Man which trades and is controlled outside the island. A Land Speculation Tax applies at the same rate as income tax.

The Island currently makes an annual contribution to the UK Government of 2·5% of net 'common purse' receipts (share of customs and excise duties and VAT received by Treasury) towards the cost of defence and other common services provided by the UK Government. That contribution currently amounts to about £1,030,000.

Currency. Notes to the value of £50, £20, £10, £5, £1 and 50p are issued by the Isle of Man Government. Annual minting of decimal coinage takes place, and in 1973, 1974, 1977 and 1979 and thereafter legal tender gold coins in half sovereign, sovereign, £2 and £5 pieces were issued. Commemorative crowns have also been issued since 1970, and silver and platinum decimal sets have been minted more recently. From 1978 onwards £5, £1, and 20p coins were minted for general circulation. Plastic £1 notes and a platinum bullion coin were introduced in 1983.

AGRICULTURE. The principal agricultural produce of the Island consists of oats, wheat, barley, potatoes, grasses, fatstock dairy products. The total area under grass and crops in 1983 was 80,363 acres and of rough grazings, 36,737 acres. The total area under cereals was 11,084 acres, including 1,423 under oats, 916 under wheat and 8,552 under barley or bere. There were also 1,040 acres under turnips and swedes, 795 under potatoes and 65,940 acres of grassland.

Livestock in 1983: 951 horses, 34,762 cattle, 131,588 sheep, 5,031 pigs and 73,537 poultry.

TOURISM. In 1982–83 tourism contributed 11% of national income and about 5,000 were employed in the industry during the summer season.

COMMUNICATIONS

Roads. There are 500 miles of good roads. The International TT Motor Cycle Races and cycle races take place annually. Omnibus services operate to all parts of the island.

Number of vehicles (1983–84): 28,098 cars, 3,748 goods vehicles and engineering plant, 1,052 agricultural vehicles, 2,897 motor cycles and scooters and 627 taxis and public service vehicles.

Railways. Several novel transport systems operate on the Island during the summer season, including 100-year-old horse-drawn trams, and the Manx Electric Railway, linking Douglas, Ramsey and Snaefell Mountain (2,036 ft). The Isle of Man Steam Railway also operates between Douglas and Port Erin.

Aviation. Ronaldsway Airport handles scheduled services operated by Manx Airlines, Dan-Air, Avair, Genair, Spacegrand, Air Ecosse, and Loganair to and from London, Manchester, Belfast, Dublin, Glasgow, Liverpool, Blackpool, etc. Air taxi services also operate.

Shipping. Car ferries of the Isle of Man Steam Packet Co. link the Island with Liverpool throughout the year and similar services operate to Fleetwood, Ardrossan, Dublin and Belfast during the summer season.

Manx Line provides a roll-on roll-off service between Douglas and Heysham. A roll-on roll-off service for commercial vehicles is also operated to Liverpool by the Isle of Man Steam Packet Co.

Broadcasting. The first constitutionally licensed commercial radio station in the British Isles, Manx Radio, is operated by Government on medium and VHF wavelengths from Douglas.

Newspapers. In 1983 there were 5 weekly newspapers.

JUSTICE AND EDUCATION

Police. The police force numbered 175 all ranks and 14 cadets in 1983.

Education. Education is compulsory between the ages of 5 and 15. In Jan. 1984 there were 36 primary schools with 5,188 pupils in attendance. The net expenditure on education for 1984–85 amounted to £17·1m.; in addition, capital expenditure of £1·5m. was made for school buildings. There are 7 secondary schools, 5 provided by the Board of Education (4,587 registered pupils), 1 direct grant school for girls (283 registered pupils), 1 independent public school for boys (340 registered pupils), 1 college of further education (3,790 full-, part-time and evening pupils).

Books of Reference

Isle of Man Digest of Economic and Social Statistics, 1983–84. Isle of Man Government, 1984
Isle of Man Family Expenditure Survey 1981–82. Isle of Man Government, 1983
Isle of Man Tourist Survey 1981 and Passenger Survey 1982–83. Isle of Man Government, 1984
A Businessman's Briefing 1982–83. Isle of Man Government 1982
Tynwald Companion 1983. Isle of Man Government, 1983
Policy Planning Programme. Isle of Man Government, 1982
A Guide to Industrial and Financial Opportunities. Isle of Man Government, 1983
Kinvig, R. H., *History of the Isle of Man.* Oxford, 1945.—*The Isle of Man: A Social, Cultural and Political History.* Liverpool Univ. Press, 1975
Mais, S. P. B., *Isle of Man.* London, 1954
Solly, M., *The Isle of Man: A Low Tax Area.* London, 1984
Stenning, E. H., *Portrait of the Isle of Man.* London, 1958

CHANNEL ISLANDS

AREA. The Channel Islands are situated off the north-west coast of France and are the only portions of the 'Duchy of Normandy' now belonging to the Crown of England, to which they have been attached since the Conquest. They consist of Jersey (28,717 acres), Guernsey (15,654 acres) and the following dependencies of Guernsey–Alderney (1,962), Brechou (74), Great Sark (1,035), Little Sark (239), Herm (320), Jethou (44) and Lihou (38), a total of 48,083 acres, or 75 sq. miles (194 sq. km).

The climate is mild. Total rainfall (1983), Jersey, 729·7 mm; Guernsey, 658·3 mm. Temperature registered (1983): highest, Jersey, 32·2°C.; Guernsey, 30·3°C.; lowest, Jersey, –1·5°C.; Guernsey, –1·3°C.

CONSTITUTION. The Lieut.-Governors and Cs.-in-C. of Jersey and Guernsey are the personal representatives of the Sovereign, the Commanders of the Armed Forces of the Crown and the channel of communication between the Crown and the insular governments. They are appointed by the Crown and have a voice but no vote in the Assemblies of the States (the insular legislatures). The Secretaries to the Lieut.-Governors are their staff officers.

The Bailiffs are appointed by the Crown and are Presidents both of the Assembly of the States and of the Royal Courts of Jersey and Guernsey. They have in the States a casting vote.

LANGUAGE. The official languages are French and English, but English is gradually supplanting French. The language commonly used is English, but in the country districts of Jersey and Guernsey and throughout Sark some people also speak a Norman-French dialect; that of Alderney has died out.

TRADE. From 1958 the trade of the Channel Islands with the UK has been regarded as internal trade.

COMMUNICATIONS

Road. Omnibus services operate in all parts of Jersey and Guernsey.

Aviation. Scheduled air services are maintained by British Airways, British Caledonian, Aer Lingus, Air UK, Jersey European, British Midland, Aurigny Air Services, Dan-Air, Brymon Airways, Guernsey Airlines, NLM City Hopper and other companies between the islands and airports in the UK, Ireland, the Netherlands and France. During the summer months these services are greatly increased, both in the number of airports served and in the frequency of flights.

Shipping. Passenger and cargo steam services between Jersey, Guernsey and England are maintained by Sealink, British Ferries and Channel Island Ferries; between Guernsey, Jersey and England and St Malo by the Commodore Shipping Co.; between Guernsey, Jersey, Alderney and France by Condor Ltd (hydrofoil), and between Guernsey and Alderney and England and Guernsey and Sark by local companies.

Post and Broadcasting. Postal and overseas telephone and telegraph services are maintained by the respective Postal Administrations of each bailiwick. The local telephone services are maintained by the insular authorities. There were, in 1983, 55,461 subscribers in Jersey and 38,634 in Guernsey.

There is an independent television station in Jersey and local radio stations, BBC Radio Jersey and Guernsey, opened in 1982.

JUSTICE AND RELIGION

Justice. Justice is administered by the Royal Courts of Jersey and Guernsey, each of which consists of the Bailiff and 12 Jurats, the latter being elected by an electoral college. There is an appeal from the Royal Courts to the Courts of Appeal of Jersey and of Guernsey. A final appeal lies to the Privy Council in certain cases. A stipendiary magistrate in each, Jersey and Guernsey, deals with minor civil and criminal cases.

Church. Jersey and Guernsey each constitutes a deanery within the diocese of Winchester. The rectories (12 in Jersey; 10 in Guernsey) are in the gift of the Crown. The Roman Catholic and various Nonconformist Churches are represented.

Books of Reference

Ambrière, F., *Les Iles Anglo-Normandes.* Paris, 1971

Coysh, V., *The Channel Islands: A New Study.* Newton Abbot, 1977

Cruickshank, C., *The German Occupation of the Channel Islands.* London, 1975

Jee, N., *The Landscape of the Channel Islands.* Chichester, 1982

Lempière, R., *Portrait of the Channel Islands.* London, 1970.—*History of the Channel Islands.* London, 1974

Myhill, H., *Introducing the Channel Islands.* London, 1964

Uttley, J., *The Story of the Channel Islands.* London, 1966

JERSEY

POPULATION (census 1981), 76,050. In the year ended 31 Dec. 1983 there were 920 births and 944 deaths. The town is St Helier on the south coast.

CONSTITUTION. The States consist of 12 senators (elected for 6 years, 6 retiring every third year), 12 Constables (triennial) and 29 Deputies (triennial), all elected on universal suffrage by the people.

The island legislature is 'The States of Jersey'. The States comprises the Bailiff, the Lieut.-Governor, 12 Senators, the Constables of the 12 parishes of the island, 29 Deputies, the Dean of Jersey, the Attorney-General and the Solicitor-General. They all have the right to speak in the Assembly, but only the 53 elected members (the Senators, Constables and Deputies) have the right to vote; the Bailiff has a casting vote. General elections for Senators and Deputies are held every third year. Except in specific instances, enactments passed by the States require the sanction of The Queen-in-Council. The Lieut.-Governor has the power of veto on certain forms of legislation.

Flag: White with a red diagonal cross. In the top centre of the flag a shield of the arms of Jersey ensigned with the Plantagenet Crown.

Lieut.-Governor and C.-in-C. of Jersey: Adm. Sir William Pillar, GBE, KCB.
Secretary and ADC to the Lieut.-Governor: Cdr D. M. L. Braybrooke, LVO, RN (Retd).

Bailiff of Jersey and President of the States: Sir Frank Ereaut.
Deputy Bailiff: P. L. Crill, CBE.

ECONOMY

Budget (year ending 31 Dec. 1982). Revenue, £130,074,676; expenditure, £112,535,570; public debt, £349,543. The standard rate of income tax is 20p in the pound. No super-tax or death duties are levied. Parochial rates of moderate amount are payable by owners and occupiers.

Currency. The States issue bank-notes in denominations of £10, £5 and £1.

INDUSTRY AND TRADE

Industry. Principal activities: Tourism; total number of hotel and guesthouse bedrooms (1983), 24,949; expenditure of tourists (1983), £160m. Agriculture, total output (1983), £28·8m.; total exports (1983), £19·8m. Light industry, mainly electrical goods, textiles and clothing. Total exports (1980), £29m. Banking and finance, total bank deposits and balances due to parent companies by deposit-taking institutions (1983), £17,500m.

Commerce (1980). Principal imports: Machinery and transport equipment, £57·3m.; manufactured goods, £43·4m.; food, £40m.; mineral fuels, £21·5m.; chemicals, £15·1m., and miscellaneous, £53·6m. Principal exports (1980): Machinery and transport equipment, £28m.; food, £22·2m; manufactured goods, £15·6m., and miscellaneous, £24·1m.

COMMUNICATIONS

Aviation. The Jersey airport is situated at St Peter. It covers approximately 375 acres. Number of aircraft movements (1983) 27,112; number of passenger arrivals, 690,688.

Shipping (1983). All vessels arriving in Jersey from outside Jersey waters report at St Helier or Gorey on first arrival. There is a harbour of minor importance at St Aubin. Number of commercial vessels entering St Helier, 3,693; number of registered craft (of 15 ft and over), 1,553. Passengers arrived in 1983, 530,639.

EDUCATION (1983). There were 7 States secondary schools and 24 States primary schools; 4,212 pupils attended the primary schools, 4,143 the secondary schools. There were 9 private primary schools with 1,260 pupils and 5 private secondary schools with 932 pupils. Highlands College offers full- and part-time courses to Ordinary and National Certificate and Diploma levels or similar standards and, together with Les Quennevais Adult Community Centre, evening classes in technical and recreational subjects.

Books of Reference

Balleine, G. R., *Biographical Dictionary of Jersey.* London, 1948.—*A History of the Island of Jersey.* London, 1950.—*The Bailiwick of Jersey.* 3rd ed. London, 1970
Bois, F. de L., *The Constitutional History of Jersey.* Jersey, 1970
Carre, A. L., *English–Jersey Language Vocabulary.* Jersey, 1972
Le Maistre, F., *Dictionnaire Jersiais-Français.* Jersey, 1966
Powell, G. C., *Economic Survey of Jersey.* Jersey, 1971

States of Jersey Library: Royal Square, St Helier. *Librarian:* J. K. Antill, FLA.

GUERNSEY

POPULATION. Census population (1981) 53,313. Births during 1983 were 659; deaths, 639. The town is St Peter Port.

CONSTITUTION. The government of the island is conducted by committees appointed by the States.

The States of Deliberation, the Parliament of Guernsey, is composed of the following members: The Bailiff, who is President *ex officio;* 12 Conseillers; H.M. Procureur and H.M. Comptroller (Law Officers of the Crown), who have a voice but no vote; 33 People's Deputies elected by popular franchise; 10 Douzaine Representatives elected by their Parochial Douzaines; 2 representatives of the States of Alderney.

The States of Election, an electoral college, elects the Jurats and Conseillers. It is composed of the following members: The Bailiff (President *ex officio*); the 12 Jurats or 'Jurés-Justiciers'; the 12 Conseillers; H.M. Procureur and H.M. Comptroller; the 33 People's Deputies; 34 Douzaine Representatives; and (for the election of Conseillers) 4 representatives of the States of Alderney.

Since Jan. 1949 all legislative powers and functions (with minor exceptions) formerly exercised by the Royal Court have been vested in the States of Deliberation. Projets de Loi (Bills) require the sanction of The Queen-in-Council.

Flag: White with a red cross.

Lieut.-Governor and C.-in-C. of Guernsey and its Dependencies: Lieut.-Gen. Sir Alexander Boswell, KCB, CBE.
Secretary and ADC to the Lieut.-Governor: Capt. D. P. L. Hodgetts.

Bailiff of Guernsey and President of the States: Sir Charles Frossard.
Deputy Bailiff of Guernsey: G. M. Dorey.

FINANCE (year ending 31 Dec. 1983). Revenue, £63,835,841 (including £1,924,358 for Alderney); expenditure, £65,707,734 (including £2,010,059 for Alderney). States' funded debt less sinking fund provisions, £686,111; note and coin issue, £25,485,208. The standard rate of income tax is 20p in the pound. States and parochial rates are very moderate. No super-tax or death duties are levied.

COMMERCE (1983). Principal imports: Coal, 28,751 tonnes; petrol and oils, 133,378,549 litres. Principal exports: Tomatoes (1983), £15,376,273; flowers and fern, £14,939,043; sweet peppers, £418,467; aubergines, £227,812, other vegetables, £590,355; plants, £670,448.

COMMUNICATIONS

Aviation. The airport in Guernsey, situated at La Villiaze, has a landing area of approximately 124 acres and a tarmac runway of 4,800 ft. In 1983, 188,396 passengers arrived from places outside the Channel Islands.

Shipping. The principal harbour is that of St Peter Port, and there is a harbour at St Sampson's (used mainly for commercial shipping). In 1983 the number of ship tonnes gross entering and leaving Guernsey was 10,717,168. 152,455 passengers arrived from places outside the Channel Islands. Ships registered in Guernsey at 31 Dec. 1983 numbered 882 and 449 fishing vessels. Small craft registered, 3,755. In 1983, 10,485 yachts visited Guernsey.

EDUCATION. There are 2 public schools in the island: Elizabeth College, founded by Queen Elizabeth in 1563, for boys, and the Ladies' College, for girls. The States grammar schools provide for education up to University entrance requirements, and there are numerous modern secondary and primary schools and a College of Further Education. The total number of school children is 8,883. Facilities are available for the study of art, domestic science and many other subjects of a technical nature. There is also a convent school with boarding facilities for girls.

ALDERNEY. Population (census, 1971), 1,686 (1981 estimate, 2,086). The island has an airport. The constitution of the island (reformed 1949) provides for its own popularly elected President and States (12 members), and its own Court. The town is St Anne's.

Flag: White with a red cross with the island badge in the centre.

President of the States: J. Kay-Mouat.
Clerk of the States: W. R. Jones, MA.
Clerk of the Court: P. J. Beer.

SARK. Population (census, 1971), 584 (1978 estimate, 600). The Constitution is a mixture of feudal and popular government with its Chief Pleas (parliament), consisting of 40 tenants and 12 popularly elected deputies, presided over by the Seneschal. The head of the island is the Seigneur. Sark has no income tax. Motor vehicles, except tractors, are not allowed.

Flag: White with a red cross and a red first quarter bearing two gold lions.

The Seigneur: J. M. Beaumont.
Seneschal: L. P. de Carteret.

Books of Reference

Carteret, A. R. de, *The Story of Sark.* London, 1956
Clark, L., *Sark Discovered.* London, 1956
Coysh, V., *Alderney.* Newton Abbot, 1974
Durand, R., *Guernsey, Present and Past.* Guernsey, 1933.—*Guernsey under German Rule.* London, 1946
Hathaway, Sybil, *Dame of Sark: An Autobiography.* London, 1961
Le Huray, C. P., *The Bailiwick of Guernsey.* London, 1952
Marr, L. J., *A History of Guernsey.* Guernsey, 1982
Robinson, G. W. S., *Guernsey.* Newton Abbot, 1977
Wood, A. and M. S., *Islands in Danger.* 2nd ed. London, 1957
Wood, J., *Herm, Our Island Home.* London, 1973

UNITED STATES OF AMERICA

Capital: Washington, D.C.
Population: 234m. (1983)
GNP per capita: US$12,820 (1981)

HISTORY. The Declaration of Independence of the 13 states of which the American Union then consisted was adopted by Congress on 4 July 1776. On 30 Nov. 1782 Great Britain acknowledged the independence of the USA, and on 3 Sept. 1783 the treaty of peace was concluded and was ratified by the USA on 14 Jan. 1784.

AREA AND POPULATION. Population of conterminous USA at each census from 1790 to 1950, and for USA including Alaska and Hawaii, from 1960. Residents of Puerto Rico, the Philippine Islands, Guam, American Samoa and the Virgin Islands of the USA, and persons in the military and naval service stationed abroad are not included in the figures of this table. Residents of Indian reservations are excluded prior to 1890.

	White	*Negroes* [1]	*Other races* [2]	*Total*	*Decennial increase %*
1790	3,172,464 [3]	757,208	—	3,929,672	—
1800	4,306,446	1,002,037	—	5,308,483	35·1
1810	5,862,073	1,377,808	—	7,239,881	36·4
1820	7,866,797	1,771,562	—	9,638,359	33·1
1830	10,537,378	2,328,642	—	12,866,020	33·5
1840	14,195,805	2,873,648	—	17,069,453	32·7
1850	19,553,068	3,638,808	—	23,191,876	35·9
1860	26,922,537	4,441,830	78,954 [4]	31,443,321	35·6
1870 [5]	33,589,377	4,880,009	88,985	38,558,371	22·6
1870 [5]	*34,337,292*	*5,392,172*	*88,985*	*39,818,449*	*26·6*
1880	43,402,970	6,580,793	172,020	50,155,783	30·1
1890	55,101,258	7,488,676	357,780	62,947,714	25·5
1900	66,809,196	8,833,994	351,385	75,994,575	21·0
1910	81,731,957	9,827,763	412,546	91,972,266	21·0
1920	94,820,915	10,463,131	426,574	105,710,620	14·9 [6]
1930	110,286,740 [7]	11,891,143	597,163	122,775,046	16·1 [6]
1940	118,214,870	12,865,518	588,887	131,669,275	7·3
1950	134,942,028	15,042,286	713,047	150,697,361	14·5
1960 [8]	158,831,732	18,871,831	1,619,612	179,323,175	18·5
1970	177,748,975	22,580,289	2,882,662	203,211,926	13·3
1980	188,371,622	26,495,025	11,679,158	226,545,805	11·4

[1] Seventeen southern states (including D.C.) in 1900 had 7,922,969 Negroes (89·7% of the total Negro population); in 1920, 8,912,231 (85·2%); in 1940, 9,904,619 (77%); in 1950, 10,225,407 (68%); in 1960, 11,311,607 (59·9%); in 1970, 11,969,961 (53%); in 1980, 14,048,000 (53%).

[2] 1870: 63,199 Chinese, 55 Japanese and 25,731 Indians; 1880, 105,465 Chinese, 148 Japanese and 66,407 Indians; 1890, 107,488 Chinese, 2,039 Japanese and 248,253 Indians; 1900, 89,863 Chinese, 24,326 Japanese and 237,196 Indians; 1910, 71,531 Chinese, 72,157 Japanese, 265,683 Indians and 3,175 other races; 1920, 61,639 Chinese, 111,010 Japanese, 244,437 Indians and 9,488 other races; 1930, 332,397 Indians, 74,954 Chinese, 138,834 Japanese and 50,978 other races; 1940, 333,969 Indians, 77,504 Chinese, 126,947 Japanese and 50,467 other races; 1950, 343,410 Indians, 141,768 Japanese, 117,629 Chinese, 110,240 other races; 1960, 523,591 Indians, 464,332 Japanese, 237,292 Chinese, 176,310 Filipino, 218,087 other races; 1970, 792,730 Indians, 591,290 Japanese, 435,062 Chinese, 343,060 Filipino, 720,520 other races; 1980, 1,420,400 Indians, 701,000 Japanese, 806,000 Chinese, 774,700 Filipino, 7,977,000 other races.

[3] Made up of Anglo-Scottish, 89·1%; German, 5·6%; Dutch, 2·5%; Irish, 1·9%; French, 0·6%.

[4] 34,933 Chinese and 44,021 Indians.

[5] Enumeration in 1870 incomplete. Figures in italics represent estimated corrected population.

[*Footnotes continued on p. 1366.*]

Total population in 1980 at 226,545,805 comprised 110,053,161 males and 116,492,644 females; 167,050,992 were urban and 59,494,813 were rural. Negroes, 12,519,189 males and 13,975,836 females.

Estimated population, including Alaska and Hawaii, and armed forces overseas, on 1 July 1950, 152,271,000; 1955, 165,931,000; 1960, 180,671,000; 1965, 194,303,000; 1970, 204,878,000; 1975, 215,973,000; 1980, 227,658,000; 1981, 229,807,000; 1982, 232,100,000; 1983, 234,200,000.

The age distribution by sex of the total population of the US (excluding armed forces overseas, US population abroad and outlying areas) at the 1980 census was as follows:

Age-group	*Male*	*Female*	*Total*
Under 5	8,362,009	7,986,245	16,348,254
5–9	8,539,080	8,160,876	16,699,956
10–14	9,316,221	8,925,908	18,242,129
15–19	10,755,409	10,412,715	21,168,124
20–24	10,663,231	10,655,473	21,318,704
25–34	18,381,903	18,699,936	37,081,839
35–44	12,569,719	13,064,991	25,634,710
45–54	11,008,919	11,790,868	22,799,787
55–59	5,481,863	6,133,391	11,615,254
60–64	4,669,892	5,417,729	10,087,621
65–74	6,756,502	8,824,103	15,580,605
75 and over	3,548,413	6,402,409	9,968,822
Total	110,053,161	116,492,644	226,545,805

The following table includes population statistics, the year in which each of the original 13 states ratified the constitution, and the year when each of the other states was admitted into the Union. Postal abbreviations for the names of the states are shown in brackets. Land area includes land temporarily or partially covered by water, and lakes, etc., of less than 40 acres. (For census population by states and regions in 1940 and 1950 *see* THE STATESMAN'S YEAR-BOOK, 1952, pp. 552 and 553.)

Geographic divisions and states		*Land area: sq. miles 1980*	*Census population 1 April 1970*	*Census population 1 April 1980*	*Pop. per sq. mile, 1980*
United States		3,539,289	203,235,298	226,545,805	64·0
New England		63,012	11,847,186	12,348,493	196·0
Maine (1820)	*(Me.)*	30,995	993,663	1,124,660	36·3
New Hampshire (1788)	*(N.H.)*	8,993	737,681	920,610	102·4
Vermont (1791)	*(Vt.)*	9,273	444,732	511,456	55·2
Massachusetts (1788)	*(Mass.)*	7,824	5,689,170	5,737,037	733·3
Rhode Island (1790)	*(R.I.)*	1,055	949,723	947,154	897·8
Connecticut (1788)	*(Conn.)*	4,872	3,032,217	3,107,576	637·8
Middle Atlantic		99,733	37,283,339	36,786,790	368·9
New York (1788)	*(N.Y.)*	47,377	18,241,266	17,558,072	370·6
New Jersey (1787)	*(N.J.)*	7,468	7,168,164	7,364,823	986·2
Pennsylvania (1787)	*(Pa.)*	44,888	11,793,909	11,863,895	264·3

[6] Between the 1910 census (15 April 1910) and the 1920 census (1 Jan. 1920), the period covered was 116 months (less than a full decade). Adjusting for this, the exact rate of increase for the decade was 15·4%. Similarly correcting for the 123 months between the 1920 and 1930 censuses, the true rate of increase was 15·7%.

[7] Figures for 1930 have been revised to include Mexicans (1,422,533), who were classified with 'Other Races' in the 1930 census reports.

[8] Figures for 1960 strictly comparable with those given for other years (*i.e.*, excluding Alaska and Hawaii) are: White, 158,454,956; Negroes, 18,860,117; other races, 1,149,163; total, 178,464,236; decennial increase, 18·4%.

Geographic divisions and states		Land area: sq. miles 1980	Census population 1 April 1970	Census population 1 April 1980	Pop. per sq. mile, 1980
East North Central		243,961	40,252,678	41,682,217	170·9
Ohio (1803)	*(Oh.)*	41,004	10,652,017	10,797,630	263·3
Indiana (1816)	*(Ind.)*	35,932	5,193,669	5,490,224	152·8
Illinois (1818)	*(Ill.)*	55,645	11,113,976	11,426,518	205·3
Michigan (1837)	*(Mich.)*	56,954	8,875,083	9,262,078	162·6
Wisconsin (1848)	*(Wis.)*	54,426	4,417,933	4,705,767	86·5
West North Central		508,132	16,344,389	17,183,453	33·8
Minnesota (1858)	*(Minn.)*	79,548	3,805,069	4,075,970	51·2
Iowa (1846)	*(Ia.)*	55,965	2,825,041	2,913,808	52·1
Missouri (1821)	*(Mo.)*	68,945	4,677,399	4,916,686	71·3
North Dakota (1889)	*(N.D.)*	69,300	617,761	652,717	9·4
South Dakota (1889)	*(S.D.)*	75,952	666,257	690,768	9·1
Nebraska (1867)	*(Nebr.)*	76,644	1,483,791	1,569,825	20·5
Kansas (1861)	*(Kans.)*	81,778	2,249,071	2,363,679	28·9
South Atlantic		266,910	30,671,337	36,959,123	138·5
Delaware (1787)	*(Del.)*	1,932	548,104	594,338	307·6
Maryland (1788)	*(Md.)*	9,837	3,922,399	4,216,975	428·7
Dist. of Columbia (1791)	*(D.C.)*	63	756,510	638,333	10,132·3
Virginia (1788)	*(Va.)*	39,704	4,648,494	5,346,818	134·7
West Virginia (1863)	*(W. Va.)*	24,119	1,744,237	1,949,644	80·8
North Carolina (1789)	*(N.C.)*	48,843	5,082,059	5,881,766	120·4
South Carolina (1788)	*(S.C.)*	30,203	2,590,516	3,121,820	103·4
Georgia (1788)	*(Ga.)*	58,056	4,589,575	5,463,105	94·1
Florida (1845)	*(Fla.)*	54,153	6,789,443	9,746,324	180·0
East South Central		178,824	12,804,552	14,666,423	82·0
Kentucky (1792)	*(Ky.)*	39,669	3,219,311	3,660,777	92·3
Tennessee (1796)	*(Tenn.)*	41,155	3,924,164	4,591,120	111·6
Alabama (1819)	*(Al.)*	50,767	3,444,165	3,893,888	76·7
Mississippi (1817)	*(Miss.)*	47,233	2,216,912	2,520,638	53·4
West South Central		427,271	19,322,458	23,746,816	55·6
Arkansas (1836)	*(Ark.)*	52,078	1,923,295	2,286,435	43·9
Louisiana (1812)	*(La.)*	44,521	3,643,180	4,205,900	94·5
Oklahoma (1907)	*(Okla.)*	68,655	2,559,253	3,025,290	44·1
Texas (1845)	*(Tex.)*	262,017	11,196,730	14,229,191	54·3
Mountain		855,193	8,283,585	11,372,785	13·3
Montana (1889)	*(Mont.)*	145,388	694,409	786,690	5·4
Idaho (1890)	*(Id.)*	82,412	713,008	943,935	11·5
Wyoming (1890)	*(Wyo.)*	96,989	332,416	469,557	4·8
Colorado (1876)	*(Colo.)*	103,595	2,207,259	2,889,964	27·9
New Mexico (1912)	*(N. Mex.)*	121,335	1,016,000	1,302,894	10·7
Arizona (1912)	*(Ariz.)*	113,508	1,772,482	2,718,215	23·9
Utah (1896)	*(Ut.)*	82,073	1,059,273	1,461,037	17·8
Nevada (1864)	*(Nev.)*	109,894	488,738	800,493	7·3
Pacific		896,253	26,525,774	31,799,705	35·5
Washington (1889)	*(Wash.)*	66,511	3,409,169	4,132,156	62·1
Oregon (1859)	*(Oreg.)*	96,184	2,091,385	2,633,105	27·4
California (1850)	*(Calif.)*	156,299	19,953,134	23,667,902	151·4
Alaska (1959)	*(Ak.)*	570,833	302,173	401,851	0·7
Hawaii (1960)	*(Hi.)*	6,425	769,913	964,691	150·1

Geographic divisions and states	Land area: sq. miles 1980	Census population 1 April 1970	Census population 1 April 1980	Pop. per sq. mile, 1980
Outlying Territories, total	4,691	4,720,306	3,565,376	760
Puerto Rico (1898)	3,515	2,712,033	3,196,520	909
Virgin Islands (1917)	132	62,438	96,569	731
American Samoa (1900)	77	27,159	32,297	419
Guam (1898)	209	84,996	105,979	507
Northern Marianas (1947)	184	9,640	16,780	91
Trust Territory of the Pacific (1947)	533	81,300	116,149	217
Midway Islands (1867)	2	2,220	453	226
Wake Island (1898)	3	1,647	302	100
Johnston and Sand Islands (1858)	...	1,007	327	...

The 1980 census showed 9,323,946 foreign-born Whites. The 9 countries contributing the largest numbers who were foreign-born were Mexico, 2,199,221; Germany, 849,384; Canada, 842,859; Italy, 831,922; UK, 669,149; Cuba, 607,814; Philippines, 501,440; Poland, 418,128; USSR, 406,022.

Increase or decrease of native White, and foreign-born White, population from 1860 to 1980, by decades:

	Native White			Foreign-born White		
	Total	Increase	Per cent increase	Total	Increase or decrease (–)	Per cent. change
1860	22,825,784	5,513,251	31·8	4,096,753	1,856,218	82·8
1870	28,095,665	5,269,881	23·1	5,493,712	1,396,959	34·1
1880	36,843,291	8,747,626	31·1	6,559,679	1,065,967	19·4
1890	45,979,391	9,018,732 [1]	24·5	9,121,867	2,562,188	39·1
1900	56,595,379	10,615,988	23·1	10,213,817	1,091,950	12·0
1910	68,386,412	11,791,033	20·8	13,345,545	3,131,728	30·7
1920	81,108,161	12,721,749	18·6	13,712,754	367,209	2·8
1930	96,303,335	15,195,174	18·7	13,983,405	270,651	2·0
1940	106,795,732	10,492,397	10·9	11,419,138	–2,564,267	–18·3
1950	124,780,860	17,985,128	16·8	10,161,168	–1,257,970	–11·0
1960	149,543,638	24,762,778	19·8	9,293,992	– 867,176	– 8·5
1970	169,385,451	19,841,813	13·3	8,733,770	– 560,222	– 6·0
1980	179,711,066	10,325,615	6·0	9,323,946	590,176	6·7

[1] Exclusive of population specially enumerated in 1890 in Indian Territory and on Indian reservations.

The population of leading cities (with over 100,000 inhabitants) at the censuses of 1970 and 1980 were as follows:

Cities	1 April 1970	1 April 1980	Cities	1 April 1970	1 April 1980
New York, N.Y.	7,895,563	7,071,639	Boston, Mass.	641,071	562,994
Chicago, Ill.	3,369,357	3,005,072	New Orleans, La.	593,471	557,927
Los Angeles, Calif.	2,811,801	2,968,579	Jacksonville, Fla.	504,265	540,920
Philadelphia, Pa.	1,949,996	1,688,210	Seattle, Wash.	530,831	493,846
Houston, Tex.	1,233,535	1,595,138	Denver, Colo.	514,678	492,365
Detroit, Mich.	1,514,063	1,203,339	Nashville-Davidson,		
Dallas, Tex.	844,401	904,078	Tenn.	426,029	455,651
San Diego, Calif.	697,471	875,538	St Louis, Mo.	622,236	453,085
Phoenix, Ariz.	584,303	789,704	Kansas City, Mo.	507,330	448,033
Baltimore, Md.	905,787	786,741	El Paso, Tex.	322,261	425,259
San Antonio, Tex.	645,153	786,023	Atlanta, Ga.	495,039	425,022
Indianapolis, Ind.	736,856	700,807	Pittsburgh, Pa.	520,089	423,959
San Francisco, Calif.	715,674	678,974	Oklahoma City, Okla.	368,164	403,484
Memphis, Tenn.	623,988	646,174	Cincinnati, Ohio	453,514	385,457
Washington, D.C.	756,668	638,333	Fort Worth, Tex.	393,455	385,164
Milwaukee, Wisc.	717,372	636,297	Minneapolis, Minn.	434,400	370,951
San José, Calif.	459,913	629,531	Portland, Oregon	379,967	366,383
Cleveland, Ohio	750,879	573,822	Honolulu, Hawaii	630,528	365,048
Columbus, Ohio	540,025	565,032	Long Beach, Calif.	358,879	361,355

Cities	*1 April 1970*	*1 April 1980*
Tulsa, Okla.	330,350	360,919
Buffalo, N.Y.	462,768	357,870
Toledo, Ohio	383,062	354,635
Miami, Fla.	334,859	346,865
Austin, Tex.	253,539	345,890
Oakland, Calif.	361,561	339,337
Albuquerque, N. Mex.	244,501	332,239
Tucson, Ariz.	262,933	330,537
Newark, N.J.	381,930	329,248
Charlotte, N.C.	241,420	314,447
Omaha, Nebr.	346,929	313,939
Louisville, Ky.	361,706	298,694
Birmingham, Ala.	300,910	284,413
Wichita, Kans.	276,554	279,835
Sacramento, Calif.	257,105	275,741
Tampa, Fla.	277,714	271,523
St Paul, Minn.	309,866	270,230
Norfolk, Va.	307,951	266,979
Virginia Beach, Va.	172,106	262,199
Rochester, N.Y.	295,011	241,741
St Petersburg, Fla.	216,159	238,647
Akron, Ohio	275,425	237,177
Corpus Christi, Tex.	204,525	232,134
Jersey City, N.J.	260,350	223,532
Baton Rouge, La.	165,921	219,844
Anaheim, Calif.	166,408	219,494
Richmond, Va.	249,332	219,214
Fresno, Calif.	165,655	217,129
Colorado Springs, Colo.	135,517	214,821
Shreveport, La.	182,064	205,820
Lexington-Fayette, Ky.	108,137	204,165
Santa Ana, Calif.	155,710	204,023
Jackson, Miss.	153,968	202,895
Mobile, Ala.	190,026	200,452
Yonkers, N.Y.	204,297	195,351
Dayton, Ohio	243,023	193,536
Des Moines, Iowa	201,404	191,003
Grand Rapids, Mich.	197,649	181,843
Montgomery, Ala.	133,386	177,857
Knoxville, Tenn.	174,587	175,045
Anchorage, Alaska	48,081	174,431
Lubbock, Tex.	149,101	173,979
Fort Wayne, Ind.	178,269	172,349
Lincoln, Nebr.	149,518	171,932
Spokane, Wash.	170,516	171,300
Madison, Wisc.	140,089	170,591
Riverside, Calif.	171,809	170,616
Huntington Beach, Calif.	115,960	170,505
Syracuse, N.Y.	197,297	170,105
Chattanooga, Tenn.	119,923	169,728
Columbus, Ga.	155,028	169,441
Las Vegas, Nev.	125,787	164,674
Salt Lake City, Utah	175,885	163,034
Worcester, Mass.	176,572	161,799
Kansas City, Kans.	168,213	161,148
Warren, Mich.	179,260	161,134
Arlington, Tex.	90,229	160,113
Flint, Mich.	193,317	159,611
Little Rock, Ark.	132,483	158,915
Aurora, Colo.	74,974	158,588
Tacoma, Wash.	154,407	158,501
Providence, R.I.	179,116	156,804
Greensboro, N.C.	144,076	155,642
Fort Lauderdale, Fla.	139,590	153,279
Mesa, Ariz.	63,049	152,453

Cities	*1 April 1970*	*1 April 1980*
Springfield, Mass.	163,905	152,319
Gary, Ind.	175,415	151,953
Raleigh, N.C.	122,830	150,255
Stockton, Calif.	109,963	149,779
Amarillo, Tex.	127,010	149,230
Hialeah, Fla.	102,452	145,254
Newport News, Va.	138,177	144,903
Bridgeport, Conn.	156,542	142,546
Huntsville, Ala.	139,282	142,513
Savannah, Ga.	118,349	141,651
Rockford, Ill.	147,370	139,712
Glendale, Calif.	132,664	139,060
Garland, Tex.	81,437	138,857
Paterson, N.J.	144,824	137,970
Hartford, Conn.	158,017	136,392
Springfield, Mo.	120,096	133,116
Fremont, Calif.	100,869	131,945
Winston-Salem, N.C.	133,683	131,885
Evansville, Ind.	138,764	130,496
Lansing, Mich.	131,403	130,414
Torrance, Calif.	134,968	129,881
Orlando, Fla.	99,006	128,291
New Haven, Conn.	137,707	126,101
Peoria, Ill.	126,963	124,160
Garden Grove, Calif.	121,155	123,307
Hampton, Va.	120,779	122,617
Hollywood, Fla.	106,873	121,323
Erie, Pa.	129,265	119,123
San Bernadino, Calif.	106,869	118,794
Beaumont, Tex.	117,548	118,102
Pasadena, Calif.	112,951	118,072
Macon, Ga.	122,423	116,896
Youngstown, Ohio	140,909	115,436
Topeka, Kans.	125,011	115,266
Chesapeake, Va.	89,580	114,486
Lakewood, Colo.	92,743	113,808
Pasadena, Tex.	89,957	112,560
Independence, Mo.	111,630	111,806
Cedar Rapids, Iowa	110,642	110,243
Irving, Tex.	97,260	109,943
South Bend, Ind.	125,580	109,727
Sterling Heights, Mich.	61,365	108,999
Oxnard, Calif.	71,225	108,195
Ann Arbor, Mich.	100,035	107,969
Tempe, Ariz.	63,550	106,920
Sunnyvale, Calif.	95,976	106,618
Modesto, Calif.	61,712	106,602
Elizabeth, N.J.	112,654	106,201
Eugene, Oregon	79,028	105,624
Bakersfield, Calif.	69,515	105,611
Livonia, Mich.	110,109	104,814
Portsmouth, Va.	110,963	104,577
Concord, Calif.	85,164	103,763
Allentown, Pa.	109,871	103,758
Berkeley, Calif.	114,091	103,328
Waterbury, Conn.	108,033	103,266
Davenport, Iowa.	98,469	103,264
Alexandria, Va.	110,927	103,217
Stamford, Conn.	108,798	102,466
Boise City, Idaho	74,990	102,160
Fullerton, Calif.	85,987	102,034
Albany, N.Y.	115,781	101,727
Pueblo, Colo.	97,774	101,686
Waco, Tex.	95,326	101,261
Columbia, S.C.	113,542	101,229
Reno, Nev.	72,863	100,756
Durham, N.C.	95,438	100,538
Roanoke, Va.	92,115	100,220

Vital Statistics: Vital statistics are based on records of births, deaths, fœtal deaths, marriages and divorces filed with registration officials of states and cities. Figures for the US include Alaska beginning with 1959 and Hawaii beginning with 1960.

Annual collection of mortality records from a national death-registration area was inaugurated in 1900. A national birth-registration area was established in 1915. These areas, which at their inception comprised 10 states and the District of Columbia, expanded gradually until 1933, when both the birth- and death-registration areas covered the entire continental US. Marriage and divorce statistics are compiled from reports furnished by state and local officials. Data on annulments are included in the divorce statistics. The marriage-registration area was established in 1957 with 30 states and 3 other areas. The divorce-registration area was established in 1958 with 14 states and 2 other areas. In Jan. 1980 the marriage-registration area included 42 states and D.C., and the divorce-registration area included 30 states.

	Live births [1]	*Deaths* [2]	*Marriages* [3]	*Divorces* [4]	*Maternal deaths* [5]	*Deaths under 1 year* [6]
1900	—	343,217	709,000	56,000	—	—
1910	2,777,000	696,856	948,000	83,000	—	—
1920	2,950,000	1,118,070	1,274,476	170,505	16,320	170,911
1930	2,618,000	1,327,240	1,126,856	195,961	14,915	143,201
1940	2,559,000	1,417,269	1,595,874	264,000	8,876	110,984
1950	3,632,000	1,452,454	1,667,231	385,144	2,960	103,825
1960	4,257,850 [7]	1,711,982	1,523,000	393,000	1,579	110,873
1970	3,731,386 [7]	1,921,031	2,158,802	708,000	803	74,667
1980	3,612,258	1,989,841	2,390,252	1,189,000	334	45,526
1982	3,704,000	1,986,000	2,495,000	1,180,000	330	41,700
1983 [8]	3,614,000	2,010,000	2,444,000	1,179,000	290	39,400

[1] Figures through 1959 include adjustment for under-registration (the 1959 registered count was 4,244,796); beginning 1960 figures represent number registered.

[2] Excluding fœtal deaths and deaths among the armed forces overseas.

[3] Estimates for all years except 1970.

[4] Includes reported annulments. Estimated for all years.

[5] Deaths for 1979–81 (Ninth Revision, International Classification of Diseases, 1975). Deaths from complications of pregnancy, childbirth and the puerperium. Deaths for 1968–78 were classified according to the Eighth Revision, International Classification of Diseases, adopted, 1965. Deaths for 1958–67 were classified according to the Seventh Revision of the International Lists of Diseases and Causes of Death, those for 1949–57 according to the Sixth Revision and those for 1939–48, according to the Fifth Revision.

[6] Excluding fœtal deaths. [7] Based on a 50% sample. [8] Provisional.

The crude birth rate, based on total live-birth estimates per 1,000 total population, fell from 29·5 in 1915 to 18·4 in 1933; it rose to a peak of 26·6 in 1947—its highest for 25 years. This peak reflects demobilization (1945–46), the record marriage rate that followed, and the high levels of employment and income. The decrease in the following 3 years was moderate. In 1951 the rate moved upward and levelled off in 1957 at about 25 per 1,000 population. Since 1957 the crude birth rate has declined every year to 18·4 live births per 1,000 population in 1966. The crude birth rate for 1983 was 15·5. Estimated number of illegitimate births in 1980 was 665,747, a ratio of 184·2 illegitimate births per 1,000 registered live births.

Deaths, excluding fœtal deaths (per 1,000 population), declined from 17·2 in 1900 to 10 in 1946. The death rate has been below 10 per 1,000 since 1947, fluctuating slightly from year to year, mainly under the impact of occurrences of outbreaks of severe respiratory diseases. Since the record low of 9·2 in 1954 the rate has changed only between 9·3 and 9·7. The rate for 1970, 9·5; for 1976, 8·8; 1977, 8·6; 1978, 8·7; 1979, 8·5; 1980, 8·8; 1981, 8·6; 1982, 8·6; 1983, 8·6.

Leading causes of death, 1983, per 100,000 population: Diseases of heart, 327·6; malignant neoplasms, 188·3; cerebrovascular diseases, 66·8; accidents, 39. Suicides in 1983 were 12·4 per 100,000 population; homicides, 8·2.

The marriage rate per 1,000 population for selected years are: 1920, 12; 1932, 7·9; 1946, 16·4; 1951, 10·4; 1961, 8·5; 1970, 10·6; 1975, 10; 1977, 9·9; 1978, 10·3; 1979, 10·4; 1980, 10·6; 1981, 10·6; 1982, 10·8; 1983, 10·5. The divorce rates per 1,000 population for selected years are: 1920, 1·6; 1946, 4·3; 1951, 2·5; 1961, 2·3; 1971, 3·7; 1979, 5·3; 1980, 5·2; 1981, 5·3; 1982, 5·1; 1983, 5.

Maternal mortality rates (deaths of mothers from conditions associated with deliveries and complications of pregnancy, childbirth and the puerperium) per 100,000 live births, were 1915–19, 727·9 and thereafter declined: 493·9 for 1935–39; 376 for 1940; 207·2 for 1945; 83·3 for 1950; 47 for 1955; 37·1 for 1960; 31·6 for 1965; 21·5 for 1970; 12·8 for 1975; 9·2 for 1980; 8·5 for 1981; 8·9 for 1982; 8 for 1983. The 1980 rate for white women was 6·7 and for all other women 19·8. By state, the average maternal mortality rate for 1976–78 was highest for Wyoming (32·9) and lowest for Connecticut (3·7).

The infant mortality rates, per 1,000 live births were: 1915–19, 95·7; 1920–24, 76·7; 1925–29, 69; 1930–34, 60·4; 38·3 in 1945; 29·2 in 1950; 26·4 in 1955; 26 in 1960; 20 in 1970; 16·1 in 1975; 12·6 in 1980; 11·9 in 1981; 11·2 in 1982; 10·9 in 1983. In 1979 the rate for whites was 11·4; for all other, 19·8. In 1980, white, 11, all other, 19·1.

Immigration: The Immigration and Nationality Act, as amended, provides for the numerical limitation of most immigration. Public Law 96–212, the Refugee Act of 1980, reduced the worldwide numerical limitation to 280,000 for 1980 and 270,000 thereafter, with a maximum of 20,000 visas available for one country. The colonies and dependencies of a foreign state are limited to 600 per year, chargeable to the country limitation of the mother country. Visas are allocated under a system of 6 preference categories, 4 of which are designed to reunite close relatives of US citizens and resident aliens of the US, and 2 for skilled and professional workers. Visa numbers not used in the preference categories are made available to qualified non-preference immigrants. The non-preference category has not been available since 1978 due to high demand in other categories. Immigrants not subject to any numerical limitation are spouses, children, and parents of US citizens, who are 21 years of age or older; certain former US citizens; ministers of religion; certain long-term US government employees; and refugees adjusting to immigrant status.

Immigrant aliens admitted to US for permanent residence, by country or region of birth.

	Immigrants admitted			
Country or region of birth	*1978*	*1979*	*1980*	*1981*
All countries	601,442	460,348	530,639	596,600
Europe	73,198	60,845	72,121	66,695
Germany (GDR and FRG)	6,739	6,314	6,595	6,552
Greece	7,035	5,090	4,699	4,361
Italy	7,415	6,174	5,467	4,662
Poland	5,050	4,413	4,725	5,014
Portugal	10,445	7,085	8,408	7,049
Spain	2,297	1,933	1,879	1,711
UK	14,245	13,907	15,485	14,997
Yugoslavia	2,621	2,171	2,099	2,048
Other Europe	17,351	13,758	22,764	20,301
Asia	249,776[1]	189,293	236,097	264,343
China and Taiwan	21,315	24,264	27,651	25,803
Hong Kong	5,158	4,119	3,860	4,055
India	20,753	19,708	22,607	21,522
Japan	4,010	4,048	4,225	3,896
Korea (North and South)	29,288	29,248	32,320	32,663
Philippines	37,216	41,300	42,316	43,772
Thailand	3,574	3,194	4,115	4,799
Other Asia	128,462	63,412	99,003	127,833
North America	220,778	157,579	164,772	210,427
Canada	16,863	13,772	13,609	11,191
Mexico	92,367	52,096	56,680	101,268
Cuba	29,754	15,585	15,054	10,858
Dominican Republic	19,458	17,519	17,245	18,220
Haiti	6,470	6,433	6,540	6,683
Jamaica	19,265	19,714	18,970	23,569
Trinidad and Tobago	5,973	5,225	5,154	4,599
Other Caribbean	10,441	9,598	10,333	9,372
Central America	20,153	17,547	20,968	24,509
Other North America	34	90	219	158

[1] Year ending 30 Sept.

Country or region of birth	Immigrants admitted 1978	1979	1980	1981
South America	41,764	35,344	39,717	35,913
Colombia	11,032	10,637	11,289	10,335
Ecuador	5,732	4,383	6,133	5,129
Other South America	25,000	20,324	22,295	20,449
Africa	11,524	12,838	13,981	15,029
Australia and New Zealand	2,184	1,999	2,209	1,947
Other countries	2,218	2,450	1,742	2,246

The total number of immigrants admitted from 1820 up to 30 Sept. 1981 was 50,252,552; this included 6,998,056 from Germany (GDR and FRG), and from Italy 5,310,516.

Aliens coming to the US for temporary periods of time are classified as non-immigrants. During fiscal year 1981, a total of 11,756,903 non-immigrants were admitted. This is inclusive of multiple entry documents and excludes border crossers, crewmen and insular travellers. Tourists, primarily from Mexico, Japan, the UK, the Caribbean, Germany (GDR and FRG) and Canada numbered 5,395,648 (total tourists, 9,515,170). There were 1,196,517 aliens expelled during fiscal year 1981. Of this number, 16,595 were deported and 1,179,922 were required to depart without formal orders of deportation.

In accordance with the Immigration and Nationality Act, 5,381,106 aliens reported their address in Jan. 1980. Of this total, 4,532,647 were permanent residents and 848,459 were aliens here temporarily. Of the permanent resident aliens who reported the best represented nationalities were the following: Mexico, 992,765; Canada, 301,085; Cuba, 279,100; UK, 273,521; Philippines, 223,743; Italy, 163,700; Germany (GDR and FRG), 147,647. Over 76% of the permanent resident aliens reported their states of residence as: California, 1,261,069; New York, 690,383; Texas, 411,163; Florida, 335,457; Illinois, 256,091; New Jersey, 238,883; Massachusetts, 152,916, and Michigan, 118,588.

In the year ended 30 Sept. 1981, 166,317 persons became US citizens through naturalization; this includes, 139,909 naturalized under the general provisions of 5-year residence in the US, 22,230 spouses and children of US citizens, 4,090 military and 88 who were naturalized under other provisions. Of the total, there were 11,329 former nationals of Cuba, 16,976 of the Philippines, 12,048 of China and Taiwan, 13,258 of Korea, 8,120 of UK, 4,287 of Italy, 9,545 of Mexico and 5,791 of Jamaica.

CLIMATE. For temperature and rainfall figures, see entries on individual states as indicated by regions, below, of mainland USA.

Pacific Coast. The climate varies with latitude, distance from the sea and the effect of relief, ranging from polar conditions in North Alaska through cool to warm temperate climates further south. The extreme south is temperate desert. Rainfall everywhere is moderate. *See* Alaska, California, Oregon, Washington.

Mountain States. Very varied, with relief exerting the main control; very cold in the north in winter, with considerable snowfall. In the south, much higher temperatures and aridity produce desert conditions. Rainfall everywhere is very variable as a result of rain-shadow influences. *See* Arizona, Colorado, Idaho, Montana, Nevada, New Mexico, Utah, Wyoming.

High Plains. A continental climate with a large annual range of temperature and moderate rainfall, mainly in summer, although unreliable. Dust storms are common in summer and blizzards in winter. *See* Nebraska, North Dakota, South Dakota.

Central Plains. A temperate continental climate, with hot summers and cold winters, except in the extreme south. Rainfall is plentiful and comes at all seasons, but there is a summer maximum in western parts. *See* Mississippi, Missouri, Oklahoma, Texas.

Mid-West. Continental, with hot summers and cold winters. Rainfall is moderate, with a summer maximum in most parts. *See* Indiana, Iowa, Kansas.

Great Lakes. Continental, resembling that of the Central Plains, with hot summers but very cold winters because of the freezing of the lakes. Rainfall is moderate with a slight summer maximum. *See* Illinois, Michigan, Minnesota, Ohio, Wisconsin.

Appalachian Mountains. The north is cool temperate with cold winters, the south warm temperate with milder winters. Precipitation is heavy, increasing to the south but evenly distributed over the year. *See* Kentucky, Pennsylvania, Tennessee, West Virginia.

Gulf Coast. Conditions vary from warm temperate to sub-tropical, with plentiful rainfall, decreasing towards the west but evenly distributed over the year. *See* Alabama, Arkansas, Florida, Louisiana.

Atlantic Coast. Temperate maritime climate but with great differences in temperature according to latitude. Rainfall is ample at all seasons; snowfall in the north can be heavy. *See* Delaware, District of Columbia, Georgia, Maryland, New Jersey, New York, North Carolina, South Carolina, Virginia.

New England. Cool temperate, with severe winters and warm summers. Precipitation is well distributed with a slight winter maximum. Snowfall is heavy in winter. *See* Connecticut, Maine, Massachusetts, New Hampshire, Rhode Island, Vermont. *See* also Hawaii and Outlying Territories.

CONSTITUTION AND GOVERNMENT. The form of government of the USA is based on the constitution of 17 Sept. 1787.

By the constitution the government of the nation is composed of three co-ordinate branches, the executive, the legislative and the judicial.

The National Government has authority in matters of general taxation, treaties and other dealings with foreign Powers, foreign and inter-state commerce, bankruptcy, postal service, coinage, weights and measures, patents and copyright, the armed forces (including, to a certain extent, the militia), and crimes against the USA; it has sole legislative authority over the District of Columbia and the possessions of the US.

The 5th article of the constitution provides that Congress may, on a two-thirds vote of both houses, propose amendments to the constitution, or, on the application of the legislatures of two-thirds of all the states, call a convention for proposing amendments, which in either case shall be valid as part of the constitution when ratified by the legislatures of three-fourths of the several states, or by conventions in three-fourths thereof, whichever mode of ratification may be proposed by Congress. Ten amendments (called collectively 'the Bill of Rights') to the constitution were added 15 Dec. 1791; two in 1795 and 1804; a 13th amendment, 6 Dec. 1865, abolishing slavery; a 14th in 1868, including the important 'due process' clause; a 15th, 3 Feb. 1870, establishing equal voting rights for white and coloured; a 16th, 3 Feb. 1913, authorizing the income tax; a 17th, 8 April 1913, providing for popular election of senators; an 18th, 16 Jan. 1919, prohibiting alcoholic liquors; a 19th, 18 Aug. 1920, establishing woman suffrage; a 20th, 23 Jan. 1933, advancing the date of the President's and Vice-President's inauguration and abolishing the 'lame-duck' sessions of Congress; a 21st, 5 Dec. 1933, repealing the 18th amendment; a 22nd, 26 Feb. 1951, limiting a President's tenure of office to 2 terms, or to 2 terms plus 2 years in the case of a Vice-President who has succeeded to the office of a President; a 23rd, 30 March 1961, granting citizens of the District of Columbia the right to vote in national elections; a 24th, 4 Feb. 1964, banning the use of the poll-tax in federal elections; a 25th, 10 Feb. 1967, dealing with Presidential disability and succession; a 26th, 22 June 1970, establishing the right of citizens who are 18 years of age and older to vote.

National flag: Seven red and 6 white alternating stripes, horizontal; with a blue canton, extending down to the lower edge of the 4th red stripe from the top, and displaying 50 white 5-pointed stars, one for each state. The stars have one point directed vertically upward, and they are arranged in 6 rows of 5 each, alternating with 5 rows of 4 each. On the admission of additional states, stars are added, effective on 4 July following the date of admission. Congress, by law of 22 Dec. 1942, has codified 'existing rules and customs' pertaining to the display of the flag, for civilians.

National anthem: The Star-spangled Banner, 'Oh say, can you see by the dawn's early light' (words by F. S. Key, 1814; tune by J. S. Smith; formally adopted by Congress 3 March 1931).

National motto: 'In God we trust'; formally adopted by Congress 30 July 1956.

Presidency. The executive power is vested in a president, who holds office for 4 years, and is elected, together with a vice-president chosen for the same term, by electors from each state, equal to the whole number of senators and representatives to which the state may be entitled in the Congress. The President must be a natural-born citizen, resident in the country for 14 years, and at least 35 years old.

The presidential election is held every fourth (leap) year on the Tuesday after the first Monday in November. Technically, this is an election of presidential electors, not of a president directly; the electors thus chosen meet and give their votes (for the candidate to whom they are pledged, in some states by law, but in most states by custom and prudent politics) at their respective state capitals on the first Monday after the second Wednesday in December next following their election; and the votes of the electors of all the states are opened and counted in the presence of both Houses of Congress on the sixth day of January. The total electorate vote is one for each senator and representative.

If the successful candidate for President dies before taking office the Vice-President-elect becomes President; if no candidate has a majority or if the successful candidate fails to qualify, then, by the 20th amendment, the Vice-President acts as President until a president qualifies. The duties of the Presidency, in absence of the President and Vice-President by reason of death, resignation, removal, inability or failure to qualify, devolve upon the Speaker of the House under legislation enacted 18 July 1947. And in case of absence of a Speaker for like reason, the presidential duties devolve upon the President *pro tem.* of the Senate and successively upon those members of the Cabinet in order of precedence, who have the constitutional qualifications for President.

The presidential term, by the 20th amendment to the constitution, begins at noon on 20 Jan. of the inaugural year. This amendment also installs the newly elected Congress in office on 3 Jan. instead of—as formerly—in the following December. The President's salary is $200,000 per year, plus $50,000 to assist in defraying expenses resulting from official duties. Also he may spend up to $100,000 non-taxable for travel and $20,000 for official entertainment. The office of Vice-President carries a salary of $91,000, plus $10,000 allowance for travel, all taxable.

The President is C.-in-C. of the Army, Navy and Air Force, and of the militia when in the service of the Union. The Vice-President is *ex-officio* President of the Senate, and in the case of 'the removal of the President, or of his death, resignation, or inability to discharge the powers and duties of his office', he becomes the President for the remainder of the term.

President of the United States: Ronald Reagan, of California, born at Tampico, Illinois, in 1911; Governor of California, 1967–75.

At the Presidential election on 6 Nov. 1984 total vote cast, including men and women in the armed services, was 89,296,029 (preliminary), of which Ronald Reagan (R.) received 52,609,797 (59%), Walter Mondale (D.) 36,450,613 (41%) and David Bergland (Libertarian Party) 235,619. Electoral college votes: Reagan 525; Mondale 13; Bergland 0.

PRESIDENTS OF THE USA

Name	*From state*	*Term of service*	*Born*	*Died*
George Washington	Virginia	1789–97	1732	1799
John Adams	Massachusetts	1797–1801	1735	1826
Thomas Jefferson	Virginia	1801–09	1743	1826
James Madison	Virginia	1809–17	1751	1836
James Monroe	Virginia	1817–25	1759	1831
John Quincy Adams	Massachusetts	1825–29	1767	1848

Name	*From state*	*Term of service*	*Born*	*Died*
Andrew Jackson	Tennessee	1829–37	1767	1845
Martin Van Buren	New York	1837–41	1782	1862
William H. Harrison	Ohio	Mar.–Apr. 1841	1773	1841
John Tyler	Virginia	1841–45	1790	1862
James K. Polk	Tennessee	1845–49	1795	1849
Zachary Taylor	Louisiana	1849–July 1850	1784	1850
Millard Fillmore	New York	1850–53	1800	1874
Franklin Pierce	New Hampshire	1853–57	1804	1869
James Buchanan	Pennsylvania	1857–61	1791	1868
Abraham Lincoln	Illinois	1861–Apr. 1865	1809	1865
Andrew Johnson	Tennessee	1865–69	1808	1875
Ulysses S. Grant	Illinois	1869–77	1822	1885
Rutherford B. Hayes	Ohio	1877–81	1822	1893
James A. Garfield	Ohio	Mar.–Sept. 1881	1831	1881
Chester A. Arthur	New York	1881–85	1830	1886
Grover Cleveland	New York	1885–89	1837	1908
Benjamin Harrison	Indiana	1889–93	1833	1901
Grover Cleveland	New York	1893–97	1837	1908
William McKinley	Ohio	1897–Sept. 1901	1843	1901
Theodore Roosevelt	New York	1901–09	1858	1919
William H. Taft	Ohio	1909–13	1857	1930
Woodrow Wilson	New Jersey	1913–21	1856	1924
Warren Gamaliel Harding	Ohio	1921–Aug. 1923	1865	1923
Calvin Coolidge	Massachusetts	1923–29	1872	1933
Herbert C. Hoover	California	1929–33	1874	1964
Franklin D. Roosevelt	New York	1933–Apr. 1945	1882	1945
Harry S. Truman	Missouri	1945–53	1884	1972
Dwight D. Eisenhower	New York	1953–61	1890	1969
John F. Kennedy	Massachusetts	1961–Nov. 1963	1917	1963
Lyndon B. Johnson	Texas	1963–69	1908	1973
Richard M. Nixon	California	1969–74	1913	—
Gerald R. Ford	Michigan	1974–77	1913	—
James Earl Carter	Georgia	1977–81	1924	—
Ronald Reagan	California	1981–	1911	—

VICE-PRESIDENTS OF THE USA

John Adams	Massachusetts	1789–97	1735	1826
Thomas Jefferson	Virginia	1797–1801	1743	1826
Aaron Burr	New York	1801–05	1756	1836
George Clinton	New York	1805–12 [1]	1739	1812
Elbridge Gerry	Massachusetts	1813–14 [1]	1744	1814
Daniel D. Tompkins	New York	1817–25	1774	1825
John C. Calhoun	South Carolina	1825–32 [1]	1782	1850
Martin Van Buren	New York	1833–37	1782	1862
Richard M. Johnson	Kentucky	1837–41	1780	1850
John Tyler	Virginia	Mar.–Apr. 1841 [1]	1790	1862
George M. Dallas	Pennsylvania	1845–49	1792	1864
Millard Fillmore	New York	1849–50 [1]	1800	1874
William R. King	Alabama	Mar.–Apr. 1853 [1]	1786	1853
John C. Breckinridge	Kentucky	1857–61	1821	1875
Hannibal Hamlin	Maine	1861–65	1809	1891
Andrew Johnson	Tennessee	Mar.–Apr. 1865 [1]	1808	1875
Schuyler Colfax	Indiana	1869–73	1823	1885
Henry Wilson	Massachusetts	1873–75 [1]	1812	1875
William A. Wheeler	New York	1877–81	1819	1887
Chester A. Arthur	New York	Mar.–Sept. 1881 [1]	1830	1886
Thomas A. Hendricks	Indiana	Mar.–Nov. 1885 [1]	1819	1885
Levi P. Morton	New York	1889–93	1824	1920

[1] Position vacant thereafter until commencement of the next presidential term.

Name	*From state*	*Term of service*	*Born*	*Died*
Adlai Stevenson	Illinois	1893–97	1835	1914
Garret A. Hobart	New Jersey	1897–99 [1]	1844	1899
Theodore Roosevelt	New York	Mar.–Sept. 1901 [1]	1858	1919
Charles W. Fairbanks	Indiana	1905–09	1855	1920
James S. Sherman	New York	1909–12 [1]	1855	1912
Thomas R. Marshall	Indiana	1913–21	1854	1925
Calvin Coolidge	Massachusetts	1921–Aug. 1923 [1]	1872	1933
Charles G. Dawes	Illinois	1925–29	1865	1951
Charles Curtis	Kansas	1929–33	1860	1935
John N. Garner	Texas	1933–41	1868	1967
Henry A. Wallace	Iowa	1941–45	1888	1965
Harry S. Truman	Missouri	1945–Apr. 1945 [1]	1884	1972
Alben W. Barkley	Kentucky	1949–53	1877	1956
Richard M. Nixon	California	1953–61	1913	—
Lyndon B. Johnson	Texas	1961–Nov. 1963 [1]	1908	1973
Hubert H. Humphrey	Minnesota	1965–69	1911	1978
Spiro T. Agnew	Maryland	1969–73	1918	—
Gerald R. Ford	Michigan	1973–74	1913	—
Nelson Rockefeller	New York	1974–77	1908	1979
Walter Mondale	Minnesota	1977–81	1928	—
George Bush	Texas	1981–	1924	—

[1] Position vacant thereafter until commencement of the next presidential term.

Cabinet. The administrative business of the nation has been traditionally vested in several executive departments, the heads of which, unofficially and *ex officio*, formed the President's Cabinet. Beginning with the Interstate Commerce Commission in 1887, however, an increasing amount of executive business has been entrusted to some 60 so-called independent agencies, such as the Veterans Administration, Housing and Home Finance Agency, Tariff Commission, etc.

All heads of departments and of the 60 or more administrative agencies are appointed by the President, but must be confirmed by the Senate.

The Cabinet consisted of the following (March 1985):

1. *Secretary of State* (created 1789). George P. Shultz; businessman, Secretary of Labor, 1969–70, Secretary of the Treasury, 1972–74; born 1920.

2. *Secretary of the Treasury* (1789). James Addison Baker III, of Texas, lawyer; Presidential Chief of Staff 1981–85; born 1930.

3. *Secretary of Defense* (1947). Caspar Weinberger, Vice-President of the Bechtel Power Corporation; lawyer, former Secretary of Health, Education and Welfare; born 1918.

4. *Attorney-General* (Department of Justice, 1870). Edwin Meese, of California; lawyer and special counsellor to the President; born 1931.

5. *Secretary of the Interior* (1849). Donald P. Hodel, of Oregon, lawyer; former Secretary of Energy; born 1935.

6. *Secretary of Agriculture* (1889). John R. Block, of Illinois; farmer; director of the Illinois Farm Bureau; born 1935.

7. *Secretary of Commerce* (1903). Malcolm Baldridge, of Connecticut; manufacturer; born 1922.

8. *Secretary of Labor* (1913). William Emerson Brock; Chairman, Republican National Committee 1977–80, Special Trade Representative 1981–85; born 1930.

9. *Secretary of Health and Human Services* (1953). Margaret M. Heckler, of Massachusetts; lawyer and congresswoman; born 1931.

10. *Secretary of Housing and Urban Development* (1966). Samuel J. Pierce, of New York; lawyer; born 1922.

11. *Secretary of Transportation* (1967). Elizabeth H. Dole, of North Carolina; lawyer, Federal Trade Commissioner 1973–79, President's public liaison assistant, 1981; born 1936.

12. *Secretary of Energy* (1977). John Herrington, of California, lawyer; formerly special assistant to the President; born 1939.

13. *Secretary of Education* (1979). William Bennett; chairman of National Endowment of the Humanities 1981–85; born 1943.

Each of the above Cabinet officers receives an annual salary of $80,100 and holds office during the pleasure of the President.

Congress: The legislative power is vested by the Constitution in a Congress, consisting of a Senate and House of Representatives.

Electorate: By amendments of the constitution, disqualification of voters on the ground of race, colour or sex is forbidden. Accordingly, the electorate consists theoretically of all citizens of both sexes over 18 years of age, but the franchise is not universal. There are requirements of residence varying in the several states as to length from 6 months to 2 years and differing requirements as to registration. In 20 states the ability to read (usually an extract from the constitution) is required—in Alaska the ability to read English; in Hawaii, English or Hawaiian; in Louisiana, English or one's native tongue. In Alabama the voter must take an 'anti-Communist oath' and fill out a questionnaire to the satisfaction of the registrars. In some southern states voters are required to give a reasonable explanation of what they read. In most states convicts are excluded from the franchise, in some states duellists and fraudulent voters.

Legislation designed to discourage the rise of third parties has been adopted in a few states. In Illinois a new party must present a petition signed by at least 25,000 voters, including at least 200 in each of 50 of the 102 counties.

The method of balloting varies greatly. Seventeen states use different ballots for federal, state and local elections. In Delaware and South Carolina the various political parties furnish their own ballot-papers to the voters as he or she enters the polling-booth.

Senate: The Senate consists of 2 members from each state, chosen by popular vote for 6 years, one-third retiring or seeking re-election every 2 years. Senators must be no less than 30 years of age; must have been citizens of the USA for 9 years, and be residents in the states for which they are chosen. The Senate has complete freedom to initiate legislation, except revenue bills (which must originate in the House of Representatives); it may, however, amend or reject any legislation originating in the lower house. The Senate is also entrusted with the power of giving or withholding its 'advice and consent' to the ratification of all treaties initiated by the President with foreign Powers, a two-thirds majority of senators present being required for approval. (However, it has no control over 'international executive agreements' made by the President with foreign governments; such 'agreements', representing an important but very recent development, cover a wide range and are actually more numerous than formal treaties.) It also has the power of confirming or rejecting major appointments to office made by the President, but it has no direct control over the appointment by the President of 'personal representatives' or 'personal envoys' on missions abroad. Members of the Senate constitute a High Court of Impeachment, with power, by a two-thirds vote, to remove from office and disqualify any civil officer of the USA impeached by the House of Representatives, which has the sole power of impeachment.

The Senate has 16 Standing Committees to which all bills are referred for study, revision or rejection. The House of Representatives has 24 such committees. In both Houses each Standing Committee has a chairman and a majority representing the majority party of the whole House; each has numerous sub-committees. The jurisdictions of these Committees correspond largely to those of the appropriate executive departments and agencies. Both Houses also have a few special Committees with limited duration; there were (1984) 4 Joint Committees.

House of Representatives: The House of Representatives consists of 435 members elected every second year. The number of each state's representatives is determined by the decennial census, in the absence of specific Congressional legislation affecting the basis. The states, in 1984, had the following representatives:

Alabama	7	Indiana	10	Nebraska	3	South Carolina	6
Alaska	1	Iowa	6	Nevada	2	South Dakota	1
Arizona	5	Kansas	5	New Hampshire	2	Tennessee	9
Arkansas	4	Kentucky	7	New Jersey	14	Texas	27
California	45	Louisiana	8	New Mexico	3	Utah	3
Colorado	6	Maine	2	New York	34	Vermont	1
Connecticut	6	Maryland	8	North Carolina	11	Virginia	10
Delaware	1	Massachusetts	11	North Dakota	1	Washington	8
Florida	19	Michigan	18	Ohio	21	West Virginia	4
Georgia	10	Minnesota	8	Oklahoma	6	Wisconsin	9
Hawaii	2	Mississippi	5	Oregon	5	Wyoming	1
Idaho	2	Missouri	9	Pennsylvania	23		
Illinois	22	Montana	2	Rhode Island	2		

The Supreme Court decided on 17 Feb. 1964, that the federal constitution requires congressional districts within each state to be substantially equal in population. By almost invariable custom the representative lives in the district from which he is elected.

Representatives must be not less than 25 years of age, citizens of the USA for 7 years and residents in the state from which they are chosen. The District of Columbia, Guam, American Samoa and the Virgin Islands have one non-voting delegate each. The House also admits a 'resident commissioner' from Puerto Rico, who has the right to speak on any subject and to make motions, but not to vote; he is elected in the same manner as the representatives but for a 4-year term. Each of the two Houses of Congress is sole 'judge of the elections, returns and qualifications of its own members'; and each of the Houses may, with the concurrence of two-thirds, expel a member. The period usually termed 'a Congress' in legislative language continues for 2-years, terminating at noon on 3 Jan.

The salary of a senator is $60,662 per annum, with tax-free expense allowance and allowances for travelling expenses and for clerical hire. The salary of the Speaker of the House of Representatives is $90,100 per annum, with a taxable allowance. The salary of a Member of the House is $69,800.

No senator or representative can, during the time for which he is elected, be appointed to any *civil* office under authority of the USA which shall have been created or the emoluments of which shall have been increased during such time; and no person holding *any* office under the USA can be a member of either House during his continuance in office. No religious text may be required as a qualification to any office or public trust under the USA or in any state.

The 99th Congress (1984–85) was constituted (Jan 1985) as follows: Senate, 53 Republicans, 47 Democrats; House of Representatives, 253 Democrats, 182 Republicans and 6 seats subject to re-election.

Indians: By an Act passed on 2 June 1924 full citizenship was granted to all Indians born in the USA, though those remaining in tribal units were still under special federal jurisdiction. Those remaining in tribal units constitute from one-half to three-fourths of the Indian population. The Indian Reorganization Act of 1934 gave the tribal Indians, at their own option, substantial opportunities to self-government and of self-controlled corporate enterprises empowered to borrow money, buy land, machinery and equipment; these corporations are controlled by democratically elected tribal councils; by 1945 roughly a third of the Indians had taken advantage of this Act. Recently a trend towards releasing Indians from federal supervision has resulted in legislation terminating supervision over specific tribes. Indian lands (1979) amounted to 52,468,000 acres, of which 42,008,000 was tribally owned and 10·01m. in trust allotments. Indian lands are held free of taxes. Total Indian population at the 1980 census was 1,418,195, of which Oklahoma, Arizona, California and New Mexico accounted for 628,400.

State and Local Government: The Union comprises 13 original states, 7 states which were admitted without having been previously organized as territories, and

30 states which had been territories—50 states in all. Each state has its own constitution (which the USA guarantees shall be republican in form), deriving its authority, not from Congress, but from the people of the state. Admission of states into the Union has been granted by special Acts of Congress, either (1) in the form of 'enabling Acts' providing for the drafting and ratification of a state constitution by the people, in which case the territory becomes a state as soon as the conditions are fulfilled, or (2) accepting a constitution already framed, and at once granting admission.

Each state is provided with a legislature of two Houses (except Nebraska, which since 1937 has had a single-chamber legislature), a governor and other executive officials, and a judicial system. Both Houses of the legislature are elective, but the senators (having larger electoral districts usually covering 2 or 3 counties compared with the single county or, in some states, the town, which sends 1 representative to the Lower House) are less numerous than the representatives, while in 38 states their terms are 4 years; in 12 states the term is 2 years. Of the 4-year senates, Illinois, Montana and New Jersey provide for two 4-year terms and one 2-year term in each decade. Terms of the lower houses are usually shorter; in 45 states, 2 years.

Members of both Houses are paid at the same rate, which varies from $200 per biennium (New Hampshire) to $46,800 per year (Alaska). The trend is towards annual sessions of state legislatures; in 1984, 36 were constitutionally required to meet annually (in 1939, only 4), the other 14 holding biennial sessions, 12 in the odd-numbered and 2 in the even-numbered years. Of these 14, 6 met annually in practice by invoking flexible constitutional powers to reconvene at intervals during the biennium.

The Governor has power to summon an extraordinary session, but not to dissolve or adjourn. The duties of the two Houses are similar, but in many states money bills must be introduced first in the Lower House. The Senate sits as a court for the trial of officials impeached by the other House, and often has power to confirm or reject appointments made by the Governor.

State legislatures are competent to deal with all matters not reserved for the federal government by the federal constitution nor specifically prohibited by the federal or state constitutions. Among their powers are the determination of the qualifications for the right of suffrage, and the control of all elections to public office, including elections of members of Congress and electors of President and Vice-President; the criminal law, both in its enactment and in its execution, with unimportant exceptions, and the administration of prisons; the civil law, including all matters pertaining to the possession and transfer of, and succession to, property; marriage and divorce, and all other civil relations; the chartering and control of all manufacturing, trading, transportation and other corporations, subject only to the right of Congress to regulate commerce passing from one state to another; labour; education; charities; licensing; fisheries within state waters, and game laws (apart from the hunting of migratory birds, which is a federal concern under treaties with Canada and Mexico). Taxes on income were left to the states until 1913, when the 16th amendment authorized the imposition of federal taxes on income without regard to apportionment.

The Governor is chosen by direct vote of the people over the whole state. His term of office varies in the several states from 2 to 4 years, and his salary from $35,000 (Arkansas, Maine) to $100,000 (New York). His duty is to see to the faithful administration of the law, and he has command of the military forces of the state. He may recommend measures but does not present bills to the legislature. In some states he presents estimates. In all but one of the states (North Carolina) the Governor has a veto upon legislation, which may, however, be overridden by the two Houses, in some states by a simple majority, in others by a three-fifths or two-thirds majority. In some states the Governor, on his death or resignation, is succeeded by a Lieut.-Governor who was elected at the same time and has been presiding over the state Senate. In several states the Speaker of the Lower House succeeds the Governor.

The chief officials by whom the administration of state affairs is carried on (secretaries, treasurers, members of boards of commissioners, etc.) are usually chosen by the people at the general state elections for terms similar to those for which governors hold office.

Local Government. The chief unit of local government is the county, of which there were (1982) 2,992 with definite functions; in addition, Rhode Island has 5 'counties' which have no functions; Alaska does not have 'counties' as such and, since Oct. 1960, there has been no active county government in Connecticut. Louisiana has 64 'parishes'. The counties maintain public order through the sheriff and his deputies, who may, in a crisis, be drawn temporarily from willing citizens; in many states the counties maintain the smaller local highways; other functions are the granting of licences and the apportionment and collection of taxes. In a few states they also manage the schools.

The unit of local government in New England is the rural township, governed directly by the voters, who assemble annually or oftener if necessary, and legislate in local affairs, levy taxes, make appropriations and appoint and instruct the local officials (selectmen, clerk, school-committee, etc.). Townships are grouped to form counties. Where cities exist, the township government is superseded by the city government.

The **District of Columbia,** ceded by the State of Maryland for the purposes of government in 1791, is the seat of the US Government. It includes the city of Washington, and embraces a land area of 61 sq. miles. The Reorganization Plan No. 3 of 1967 instituted a Mayor Council form of government with appointed officers. In 1973 an elected Mayor and elected councillors were introduced; in 1974 they received power to legislate in local matters. Congress retains power to enact legislation and to veto or supersede the Council's acts. Since 1961 citizens have had the right to vote in national elections. On 23 Aug. 1978 the Senate approved a constitutional amendment giving the District full voting representation in Congress. This has still to be ratified.

The **Commonwealth of Puerto Rico, American Samoa, Guam and the Virgin Islands** each have a local legislature, whose acts may be modified or annulled by Congress, though in practice this has seldom been done. Puerto Rico since its attainment of commonwealth status on 25 July 1952, enjoys practically complete self-government, including the election of its governor and other officials. The conduct of foreign relations, however, is still a federal function and federal bureaux and agencies still operate in the island.

General supervision of territorial administration is exercised by the Office of Territories in the Department of Interior.

Congress and the Nation, 4 vols., Congressional Quarterly, Washington, from 1965.—*Congressional Ethics,* Rev. ed., 1980.—*Congressional Quarterly Almanac,* annual
Constitution of the US, National and State. 2 vols. [with subsequent amendments]. Dobbs Ferry, 1962
Political profiles. 5 vols. New York, from 1978
Adrian, C. R., *State and Local Government.* 4th ed. New York, 1977
Barone, M. (ed.), *The Almanac of American Politics.* New York and London, Annual
Bone, H. A., *American Politics and the Party System.* 4th ed. New York, 1971
Brenner, P., *The Limits and Possibilities of Congress.* New York, 1983
Corwin, E. S., *Presidential Power and the Constitution.* Cornell Univ. Press, 1976
Egger, R. A., *The President of the United States.* 2nd ed. New York, 1972
Ferguson, J. H., and McHenry, D. E., *Elements of American Government.* 6th ed. New York, 1963.—*The American Federal Government.* 12th ed. New York, 1973.—*The American System of Government.* 12th ed. New York, 1973
Fisher, L., *Presidential Spending Power.* Princeton Univ. Press, 1975
Hardin, C. M., *Presidential Power and Accountability: Towards a New Constitution.* Univ. of Chicago Press, 1974
Kelly, A. H., and Harbison, W. A., *The American Constitution, Its Origin and Development.* 4th ed. New York, 1970
Koenig, L. W., *The Chief Executive.* 3rd ed. New York, 1975
Levine, E. L., *An Introduction to American Government.* 2nd ed. New York, 1974
Maddox, R. W., and Fuquay, R. F., *State and Local Government.* 3rd ed. New York, 1975
Ogg, F. A., and Ray, P. O., *Introduction to American Government.* 12th ed. New York, 1962.—*Essentials of American National Government.* 10th ed. New York, 1969.—*Essentials of American State and Local Government.* 10th ed. New York, 1969

Pritchett, C. H., *The American Constitution*. 2nd ed. New York, 1968.—*The American Constitutional System*. New York, 1977
Ripley, R. B., *American National Government and Public Policy*. New York, 1974
Robinson, J. A., *State Legislative Innovation*. New York, 1973
Scheer, R., *America after Nixon: The Politics of the New World Order*. New York, 1975
Seymour-Ure, C., *The American President: Power and Communication*. London, 1982
Tugwell, R. G., *The Enlargement of the Presidency*. Garden City, N.Y., 1960.—*The Emerging Constitution*. New York, 1974
White, T. H., *The Making of the President*. New York, 1960.—*The Making of the President, 1964*. New York, 1965.—*The Making of the President, 1968*. New York, 1969

DEFENCE. The President is C.-in-C. of the Army, Navy and Air Force.

The National Security Act of 1947 provides for the unification of the Army, Navy and Air Forces under a single Secretary of Defense with cabinet rank. The President is also advised by a National Security Council and the Office of Civil and Defense Mobilization.

The major components of the Department of Defense are the Office of the Secretary of Defense and the Joint Chiefs of Staff, who provide immediate staff assistance and advice to the Secretary; the departments of the Army, Navy and Air Force, each separately organized under a civilian head (not of cabinet rank); and the unified and specified commands.

Army. *Secretary of the Army:* John O. Marsh Jr.

Central Administration. The Secretary of the Army is the head of the Department of the Army. Subject to the authority of the President as C.-in-C. and of the Secretary of Defense, he is responsible for all affairs of the Department.

The Secretary of the Army is assisted by the Under Secretary of the Army, 5 Assistant Secretaries of the Army (Installations, Logistics and Financial Management; Research and Development; Manpower and Reserve Affairs, and Civil Works), the General Counsel, an Administrative Assistant, Chief of Legislative Liaison, Chief of Public Affairs and the Army Staff headed by the Chief of Staff, US Army. The office of the Under Secretary of the Army includes a Deputy Under Secretary (Operations Research).

The Chief of Staff is the principal military adviser of the Secretary of the Army, and performs his duties under the direction of the Secretary of the Army, except as otherwise prescribed by law, by the President or by the Secretary of Defense. He has supervision of all members and organizations of the Army. The Vice Chief of Staff assists and advises the Chief of Staff.

The Army General Staff is the principal element of the Army Staff and includes the offices of the Chief of Staff, Vice Chief of Staff, Director of Staff, the 4 Deputy Chiefs of Staff (Military Operations, Personnel, Logistics, and Research, Development and Acquisition), the Comptroller of the Army, the Assistant Chief of Staff for Intelligence, the Ballistic Missile Defense Program Manager and the Army Reserve Forces Policy Committee. Other elements of the Army Staff are the offices of the Judge Advocate General, Surgeon General, Adjutant General, Inspector General and Auditor General, Chief of Chaplains, Chief, Army Reserve, Chief, National Guard Bureau, and Chief of Engineers.

The Army consists of the Regular Army, the Army National Guard of the US, the Army Reserve and civilian workforce; and all persons appointed to or enlisted into the Army without component; and all persons serving under call or conscription, including members of the National Guard of the States, etc., when in the service of the US.

The strength of the Army was (1984) 780,800 (including some 84,000 women).

The US Army Forces Command, with headquarters at Fort McPherson, Georgia, commands the continental US Armies and all assigned Active Army and US Army Reserve troop units in the continental US, Alaska, Hawaii, Panama, Guam, Johnston Island, the Commonwealth of Puerto Rico, and the Virgin Islands of the USA. The headquarters of the continental US Armies are: First US Army, Fort George G. Meade, Maryland; Fifth US Army, Fort Sam Houston, Texas; Sixth US Army, Presidio of San Francisco, California. The US Army Training and Doctrine Command, with headquarters at Fort Monroe, Virginia, co-ordinates and integrates the total combat development effort of the Army as well as developing, managing and supervising the training of individuals of the US Army and authorized foreign nationals. The US Army Health Services Command, with headquarters at Fort Sam Houston, Texas, provides health services in the continental US for the US Army and provides professional education and training for medical personnel of the US Army and authorized foreign national personnel. The US Army Materiel Development and Readiness Command, with headquarters in Alexandria, Virginia, is responsible for all US Army operations dealing with equipment development, procurement, delivery, supply and maintenance. The US Army Communications Command, with headquarters at Fort Huachuca, Arizona, provides worldwide communication to the Department of the Army and supports the Defense Communications Systems. The US Army Military District of Washington, with headquarters at Fort McNair, Washington, D.C. provides support to the Department of the Army and the Department of Defense at the seat of Government.

Some 43% of the Army is deployed overseas. Two divisions two-thirds of which are located in the USA keep equipment in the Federal Republic of Germany and can be flown there in 48–72 hours. Headquarters of US Seventh and Eighth Armies are in Europe and Korea respectively.

Operational Commands and Weapons. The larger commands are the theater army and the corps. The typical theater army may consist of a variable number of corps; combat forces of armour and infantry; air defense artillery (*Nike-Hercules* and *Hawk* and short-range missile battalions); field artillery and Pershing missile battalions; combat support forces of aviation, engineer and signal elements; and combat service support forces. A typical corps consists of a variable number and mixture of infantry, mechanized infantry, armoured, airmobile, and airborne divisions; one or more separate infantry brigades; one or more armoured cavalry regiments; corps artillery (155-mm howitzer, 8-in. howitzer, 175-mm gun, *Lance* missile battalions); an air defense element of a size commensurate with the hostile air threat (*Nike-Hercules, Hawk* and *Chaparral/Vulcan* battalions), and a target acquisition unit; combat support and combat service support forces.

US Army Divisions have a common base (containing command, aviation divisional artillery, combat, combat support units and combat service support units) and a varying mixture of 'combat manoeuvre battalions' (usually 10 in number in 3 brigades) to make up airborne, infantry, armoured, mechanized infantry and airmobile divisions. Divisions can in this way be 'tailored' to fit a variety of strategic or tactical situations. An infantry division, with about 18,200 men, may have 8 infantry battalions, an armoured battalion and a mechanized infantry battalion; a mechanized infantry division, with about 16,500 men, may have 5 mechanized infantry battalions and 5 armoured battalions; an armoured division, with about 16,500 men, may have 4 mechanized infantry battalions and 6 armoured battalions; an airborne division, with 16,700 men, may have 9 infantry (airborne) battalions.

The newly created 10,000-man light divisions consist of infantry, airborne or air assault forces. All offer rapid strategic force projection, especially the airborne division. Infantry divisions can operate in all environments and are general purpose forces. The air assault division is a highly specialized force capable of battlefield helicopter operations for infantry, artillery and necessary support forces.

Small arms include the M-16, which fires a 5·56-mm cartridge. The standard general-purpose machine-gun is the M-60 (23 lb.; 550 rounds of 7·63-mm per minute). Infantry weapons also include M-203 grenade launcher attachment for the M16A1 rifle, which fire a 40-mm grenade up to 400 metres, the *Tow* and *Dragon* anti-tank missile system, and the M-72 rocket, a light anti-tank weapon.

Combat vehicles of the US Army are the tank, armoured personnel carrier (infantry fighting vehicle), armoured reconnaissance airborne assault vehicle and the armoured command and reconnaissance vehicle. The first-line tanks are the M1 Abrams tank, and the M-60A3 with 105-mm main armament. The standard armoured infantry personnel carrier is the Bradley Fighting Vehicle (BFU); it carries a mechanized infantry squad, a 25-mm Bushmaster gun and *Tow* missile launchers. The BFU is also being utilized as the ground scout vehicle in armoured cavalry regiments, squadrons and in scout platoons of armoured and mechanized infantry battalions.

The approved calibres of artillery are: light, 105-mm howitzer, medium 155-mm howitzer; the heavy, 8-in. howitzer. The 4·2-in. mortars and the 81-mm mortar are used by combat manoeuvre elements. The *Tow* is the primary anti-tank weapons. *Chaparral* and *Vulcan*, forward-area air-defence weapons, provide the capability of low-altitude defence against high-performance aircraft.

The Army has two categories of missiles—surface-to-surface (field artillery) and surface-to-air (air defence artillery). Surface-to-surface missiles are: *Pershing II*, ballistic, nuclear warhead, range about 400 miles operational; *Lance*, guided, nuclear warhead, storable, liquid propellant, operational. Surface-to-air missiles, for air defence, are: *Nike-Hercules*, guided, field or fixed installation, nuclear warhead, operational; *Hawk*, homing type, low-to-mid-altitude, field, operational (an improved system has replaced the basic *Hawk*); *Chaparral*, infra-red homing, low-altitude, forward area, operational (improvements to the basic system are under development); *Redeye*, hand-held, infra-red homing, low-altitude, forward area, operational; *Patriot*, mid-to-high-altitude, replacement for *Hawk* and *Nike-Hercules*, under limited production; *Stinger*, hand-held infra-red homing, low-altitude, forward area, replacement for *Redeye* is under development. Anti-tank missiles are: *Tow*, tube launched, optically tracked, wire guided, anti-armour, forward area, operational; *Hellfire*, terminal homing under development.

The Army employs rotary- and fixed-wing aircraft as organic elements of its ground formations where their use is required on a full-time basis and their immediate and constant availability is essential. The front line commander exploits the benefits of aviation technology to perform traditional land battle tasks in the third dimension. This concept of airmobility for ground formation utilizes aerial vehicles as a highly integrated team to perform all five functions of land combat: reconnaissance, command and control, logistics and that inseparable combination, firepower and manoeuvre.

Enlistment, Terms of Service. Since 1974 the Army has operated a 'zero draft' system making it, in effect, an all-regular force. Terms of service may be 2, 3, 4, 5 or 6 years. Men who enlist incur a 6-year obligation and must serve in the reserve any part of the period not served on active duty.

The Army National Guard is a reserve military component with a dual status and rôle. Enlistment is voluntary. The members are recruited by each state, but are equipped and paid by the federal government. Training is supervised by the active Army (FORSOM), and unit organization parallels that for the active army; training facilities are made available by the USA and each state. As the organized militia of the several states, the District of Columbia, Puerto Rico and the Territory of the Virgin Islands, the Guard may be called into service for local emergencies by the sovereigns in those jurisdictions; and may be called into federal service by the President to thwart invasion or rebellion or to enforce federal law. In its role as a reserve component of the Army, the Guard is subject to the order of the President in the event of national emergency.

The Army Reserve is designed to supply qualified and experienced units and individuals in an emergency. US Army Forces Command is charged with the command, support and training supervision of US Army Reserve units. Members are assigned to one category, the Ready. The Ready Reservists is subject to call by the President in case of national emergency without declaration of war by Congress. The Standby Reserve and the Retired Reserve may be called only after declaration of war or national emergency by Congress.

The Army Almanac. Dept. of the Army, Washington, D.C.
Coker, C., *US Military Power in the 1980s.* London, 1984

Navy. *Secretary of the Navy:* Hon. John H. Lehman, Jr.

The Department of the Navy is administered under the Secretary of Defense by the Secretary of the Navy, assisted by the Under Secretary; 4 Assistant Secretaries, for Financial Management; for Shipbuilding and Logistics; for Manpower and Reserve Affairs; and for Research, Engineering and Systems, as well as by the Chief of Naval Operations and the Commandant of the Marine Corps. The 3 divisions of the Department of the Navy are:

Navy Department, comprised of staff offices of the Secretary for Legislative Affairs, Information, the Judge Advocate General, Auditor General, Program Appraisal, General Counsel, Naval Research and Comptroller; offices of the Chief of Naval Operations which include the Vice Chief, the Assistant Vice Chief/ Director of Naval Administration, 6 Deputy Chiefs and 8 Directors; Naval Inspector General; the Surgeon General; and headquarters of the Chief of Naval Material, Bureau of Medicine and Surgery, and Bureau of Naval Personnel.

The Shore Establishment comprises commands dealing with air, electronic, facilities engineering, sea (including ordnance) and supply systems; and other commands: Space, Medical, Education and Training, Data Automation, Telecommunications, Intelligence, Oceanography, Legal Service, Security Group, and Investigative Service; as well as supporting establishment of the Marine Corps and Marine Corps Reserve.

The Operating Forces are the Military Sealift Command, U. S. Naval Forces Europe, the Atlantic and Pacific Fleet including Fleet Marine Forces; operating forces of the Marine Corps, the Mine Warfare Command, Operational Test and Evaluation Force, Naval Forces Southern and Central Commands.

Major shore activities include 8 shipyards, 32 air stations and facilities, 2 amphibious bases, 3 submarine bases and 12 naval stations and bases. By agreement dated 2 Sept. 1940, Britain granted leases for naval and air bases in Newfoundland, Bermuda, Bahamas, Jamaica, St Lucia, Trinidad, Antigua and Guyana; but these are not all now active.

Naval appropriations in recent fiscal years: 1980, $47,084m.; 1981, $57,834m.; 1982, $68,792m.; 1983, $81,936m.; 1984, $81,999m.; 1985 (planned) $101,299m.

The active personnel on duty on 30 Sept. 1984 was 572,006 Navy officers and enlisted men, plus 205,439 Marine Corp officers and men.

The following is a tabulated statement of US vessels listed on 31 Dec.:

Category	*1977*	*1978*	*1979*	*1980*	*1981*	*1982*	*1983*	*1984*
Multi-purpose aircraft carriers	15	15	15	15	15	15	14	14
ASW and other carriers	5[1]	5[1]	5[1]	5[1]	4[1]	5[1]	5[1]	5[1]
Helicopter carriers	9	10	11	12	12	25[2]	25[2]	25[2]
Command ships	3[3]	3[3]	3[3]	3[3]	3[3]	3[3]	3[3]	3[3]
Nuclear powered submarines	109	113	115	118	124	129	135[7]	139[7]
Submarines (conventional)	15	13	10	10	8	6	6	5
Battleships	4	4	4	4	4	4	4	4
Cruisers	35[4]	36[4]	32[4]	29[4]	31[4]	32[4]	33[4]	32[4]
Destroyers	97[5]	93[5]	96[5]	98[5]	93[5]	88[5]	86[5]	84[5]
Frigates	65[6]	65[6]	69[6]	67[6]	77[6]	82[6]	102[6]	105[6]

[1] Comprises 1 training carrier and 2 anti-submarine carriers and 2 other Essex class carriers in reserve.

[2] Comprises 5 flat-top hangar/dock heavy amphibious assault ships and 7 lighter flat-top hangar ships and 13 lighter semi-flat-top amphibious transports dock.

[3] Includes 1 Middle East Flagship (converted amphibious transport dock).

[4] Includes 24 frigates (destroyer leaders, DLG) reclassified as cruisers in 1975.

[5] Includes 10 frigates (destroyer leaders, DLG) reclassified as destroyers in 1975. Of the 84 destroyers 41 are classified as DDG.

[6] Includes 65 escort ships reclassified as frigates on 1 July 1975.

[7] Includes 5 Trident (Ohio class) ballistic missile armed very large (see Table) vessels, 31 other ballistic missile submarines and 103 attack submarines.

The table below shows principal surface ships, guns under 3-in. calibre not given:

Completed	Name	Standard displacement Tons	Aircraft	Principal armament	Shaft horse-power	Speed Knots
			Multi-Purpose (Former Attack) Aircraft Carriers			
1982	Carl Vinson	81,600	90	3 BPDMS[3] launchers with Sea Sparrow missiles	260,000 (nuclear power)	33
1977	Eisenhower	81,600				
1975	Nimitz	81,600				
1968	John F. Kennedy	61,000	85	3 BPDMS launchers with NATO Sea Sparrow missiles	280,000	34
1965	America	60,300				
1962	Enterprise	75,700	84	3 NATO Sea Sparrow missile launchers	300,000 (nuclear power)	35
1962	Constellation	61,000	85	2 twin Terrier missile launchers	280,000	34
1961	Kitty Hawk	61,000	85	3 BPDMS launchers with NATO Sea Sparrow missiles	280,000	34
1959	Independence	60,000	80 to 75	3 BPDMS launchers with Sea Sparrow missiles	280,000	34
1957	Ranger	60,000				
1956	Saratoga	59,100	80 to 75	3 BPDMS launchers with Sea Sparrow missiles	260,000	33
1955	Forrestal	59,100	70			
1950	*Oriskany[1]	33,250	70	2 5-in. guns	150,000	33
1947	Coral Sea[2]	52,500	75	Guided missiles	212,000	33
1945	Midway[2]	51,000	75	Guided missiles 2 BPDMS launchers with Sea Sparrow to be fitted	212,000	33
1944	*Bon Homme Richard[1]	33,100	70	4 5-in. guns	150,000	33

[1] In reserve, *Bon Homme Richard* CVA, *Oriskany* CV.
[2] Sister ship *Franklin D. Roosevelt* was stricken in 1977.
[3] Basic Point Defence Missile System.

Anti-Submarine Support Aircraft Carriers

Completed	Name	Standard displacement Tons	Aircraft	Principal armament	Shaft horse-power	Speed Knots
1944	*Bennington	33,000	45	4 5-in. guns	150,000	33
1943	*Hornet[1]					

[1] Sister ship *Intrepid* was stricken in 1982 to become a memorial ship at New York City. *Shangri La* was scrapped in 1983.

Training Carrier

Completed	Name	Standard displacement Tons	Aircraft	Principal armament	Shaft horse-power	Speed Knots
1943	Lexington	32,800	—	Removed	150,000	33

The 'Essex' class originally comprised 24 ships, the *Essex, Yorktown, Intrepid, Hornet, Franklin, Lexington, Bunker Hill, Wasp, Ticonderoga, Hancock, Randolph, Bennington, Bon Homme Richard, Shangri-La, Tarawa, Antietam, Boxer, Kearsarge, Lake Champlain, Leyte, Philippine Sea, Princeton, Valley Forge, Oriskany*. Only the above 4* now remain in reserve. For dates and other details of the 18 stricken during 1964–81, and of the 'Bogue' class, 'Commencement Bay' class, and other former aircraft carriers, see 1981–82 and earlier editions.

Helicopter Carriers[1] (Amphibious Assault Ships)

Completed	Name	Standard displacement Tons	Aircraft	Principal armament	Shaft horse-power	Speed Knots
1981	Pelileu	39,300 (full load)	26 to 42 helicopters (or V/STOL aircraft)	2 Sea Sparrow missile launchers (BPDMS); 3 5-in. guns	140,000	24
1980	Nassau					
1978	Belleau Wood					
1977	Saipan					
1976	Tarawa[2]					

[1] According to official statistics eleven of the 12 amphibious transports dock (the other is a command ship) of the Austin class; of 12,000 tons, and the two of the Raleigh class, each with a capacity of six helicopters, are now listed under the generic heading of helicopter carriers.
[2] In many ways these five heavy through deck Hangar ships are equivalent to orthodox large aircraft carriers in other principal navies.

Completed	Name	Standard displacement Tons	Aircraft	Principal armament	Shaft horse-power	Speed Knots
		Helicopter Carriers [1] *(Amphibious Assault Ships)*				
1970	Inchon	18,800 (full load)	20 to 26 helicopters (or 4 V/STOL aircraft instead of helos)	2 Sea Sparrow missile launchers (BPDMS); 4 3-in. guns	23,000	23
1968	New Orleans					
1966	Tripoli					
1965	Guam [1]					
1963	Guadalcanal					
1962	Okinawa					
1961	Iwojima					

[1] *Guam* was modified in 1971–72 as 'interim' sea control ship and operated Harrier aircraft but reverted to the amphibious role in 1974.

Command Ships [1]

Completed	Name	Standard displacement Tons	Aircraft	Principal armament	Shaft horse-power	Speed Knots
1971	Mount Whitney	19,100 (full load)	1 helicopter	2 Sea Sparrow missile launchers; 4 3-in. guns (twin)	22,000	23
1970	Blue Ridge					

[1] *Northampton*, originally heavy cruiser; and: *Wright*, originally light fleet aircraft carrier, converted into Command Ships were stricken from the Navy List in 1977–78.

The amphibious transport dock *Coronado* has been converted to a command ship to relieve *La Salle* as flagship of the Middle East Force.

Battleships

Completed	Name	Standard displacement Tons	Aircraft	Principal armament	Shaft horse-power	Speed Knots
1944	Missouri [1] Wisconsin [1]	45,000		9 16-in.; 20 5-in.	212,000	33
1943	Iowa [1] New Jersey [2]			9 16-in.; 12 5m.; Tomahawk cruise missile launchers; 4 quadruple launch cannisters		

[1] All laid up in reserve since 1955–58 but reactivation scheduled for recommissioning and modernisation and conversion to cruise missile carrier in 1984 (*Iowa*) followed by *Missouri* and *Wisconsin* in 1986 and 1988 if approved.

[2] Reactivated in 1967 and commissioned 1968–69, reserve 1969 to July 1981. Reactivated Oct. 1981 and recommissioned Dec. 1982 on modernisation and conversion to cruise missile carrier. Began first operational deployment in March 1983.

Cruisers

Completed	Name	Standard displacement Tons	Aircraft	Principal armament	Shaft horse-power	Speed Knots
1984	Yorktown	9,000	2 helicopters	2 octuple 'Harpoon' and 2 twin Standard/ASROC launchers; 2 5-in.	80,000 (gas)	30
1983	Ticonderoga [1]					
1961	Long Beach	14,200	deck for helicopter	2 quadruple Harpoon and 2 twin Terrier/Standard; guided missile launchers; 2 5-in.	80,000 (nuclear power)	30
1949	Salem*	17,000	—	9 8-in.; 12 5-in; 20 3-in.	120,000	32
1948	Des Moines					
1946	Albany	13,700	deck for utility helicopters	2 twin 'Tartar' launchers 2 5-in.	120,000	32

[1] Originally rated as guided missile destroyers. *Ticonderoga*, DDG 47, was redesignated CG47 in 1980 when the new type were reclassified as guided cruisers.

* Sister ship *Newport News* was stricken from the Navy List on 31 July 1978.

Albany and *Chicago* were to have been disposed of in 1980 but in 1981 it was planned to retain these ships in reserve for a minimum of three years and *Oklahoma City* retained for logistic support but she was again listed for disposal in 1983. *Chicago* was again listed for disposal in 1984.

For conversions and disposals of other cruisers of the 'Oregon City', 'Baltimore', 'Cleveland' and 'Juneau' classes see 1981–82 and earlier editions.

Completed	Name	Standard displacement Tons	Aircraft	Principal armament	Shaft horse-power	Speed Knots
Cruisers, Former Frigates (Destroyer Leaders)						
1980 1978 1977 1976	Arkansas Mississippi Texas Virginia	9,000	2 helicopters	2 quadruple Harpoon; 2 twin Standard/ ASROC'; 2 5-in.	80,000 (nuclear power)	30
1974 1973	South Carolina California	9,560	—	2 quadruple Harpoon; 2 single Standard; 2 5-in.	70,000 (nuclear power)	30
1967	Truxtun	8,200	1 helicopter	2 quadruple Harpoon; 1 twin 'Standard'; 1 5-in.; 2 3-in.	60,000 (nuclear power)	30
1962	Bainbridge	7,600	—	2 quadruple Harpoon; 2 twin 'Standard'		
1964–67	9 Belknap Class [1]	6,570	—	2 quadruple Harpoon; 1 twin Standard; 1 5-in.	85,000	34
1962–64	9 Leahy Class [2]	5,670	—	2 quadruple Harpoon; 2 twin Standard	85,000	34

[1] The 'Belknap' class comprises *Belknap, Biddle, Fox, Horne, Josephus Daniels, Jouett, Sterett, Wainwright* and *William H. Standley.*

[2] The 'Leahy' class comprises *Dale, England, Gridley, Halsey, Harry E. Yarnell, Leahy, Reeves, Richmond K. Turner* and *Worden.*

The 10 'Coontz' class comprises *Coontz, Dahlgren, Dewey, Farragut, King, Luce, Macdonough, Mahan, Preble* and *William V. Pratt.* They were reclassified from frigates (DLG) to destroyers (DDG) on 1 July 1975 when the later frigates above were reclassified as cruisers. See 1981–82 edition for earlier destroyer leader/frigates.

Capital (Strategic) Submarines

Class	No.	Displacement (submerged) Tons	Missile Tubes (Vertical)	Nuclear Reactors	Shaft Horse-power	Speed Knots
'726'	5	18,700	24 Trident	1	60,000	30 dived 20 surface
'640'	12	8,500	16 Poseidon	1	15,000	30 dived 20 surface
'616'	19	8,250	16 Poseidon	1	15,000	30 dived 21 surface
'608'	4 [1]	7,880	16 Polaris	1	15,000	30 dived 20 surface
'598'	3 [2]	6,888	16 Polaris	1	15,000	31 dived 20 surface

Completion:- '726' or 'Ohio' class in 1981–85 (five more to follow in 1985–89); '640' or 'Benjamin Franklin' class 1965–67; '616' or 'Lafayette' class in 1963–64; '608' or 'Ethan Allen' class in 1961–63; '598' or 'George Washington' class in 1959–61. All these ballistic missile armed submarines also have four 21-inch torpedo tubes.

[1] This class reclassified as fleet submarines. *Ethan Allen* (608) stricken in 1983 (target).

[2] Three of this class converted to fleet submarines and two scrapped, *Theodore Roosevelt* (600) and *Abraham Lincoln* (602) both targets.

In addition to the above named principal surface ships there are 139 nuclear-powered submarines (including the ballistic missile armed vessels in the table), 5 conventionally propelled submarines, 84 destroyers, 105 frigates, 21 ocean minesweepers, 4 patrol vessels, 6 hydrofoil missile patrol craft, 1 fast patrol boat, 70 amphibious warfare ships, 95 landing craft, 37 replenishment ships, 100 sealift ships, 125 fleet support ships and auxiliaries, 60 oilers, 100 minor landing craft and 1,010 service craft.

Ships under construction include 8 submarines of 18,700 tons submerged with nuclear propulsion and ballistic missiles, 17 nuclear propelled attack (fleet) submarines of 6,900 tons submerged; the giant nuclear propelled aircraft carrier *Theodore Roosevelt* and 2 sister ships each of 93,400 tons war load; 3 destroyers and 16 guided missile frigates.

Projected new construction includes 11 more 'Ohio' class nuclear propelled deterrent or 'strategic' submarines; 18 more nuclear propelled fleet or 'attack' submarines; 2 more large aircraft carriers; 60 guided missile destroyers and 10 frigates.

Naval Aviation. The official figures given in the total aircraft inventory are: 6,222 in the Navy and the Marine Corps of which 5,670 are active and 5,073 are operating. There are 597 naval aircraft in the pipeline.

The US Coast Guard operates under the Department of Transportation in time of peace and as a part of the Navy in time of war or when directed by the President. The act of establishment stated the Coast Guard 'shall be a military service and branch of the armed forces of the United States at all times'. The Coast Guard did operate as part of the Navy during the First and Second World Wars. It also had some units serving in Vietnam. It comprises 250 ships including cutters of destroyer, frigate, corvette and patrol vessel types, powerful icebreakers, and paramilitary auxiliaries and tenders, plus some 2,000 small rescue and utility craft. It also maintains 50 fixed-wing aircraft and 110 helicopters. The Coast Guard missions include maintenance of aids to navigation, enforcement of maritime laws, enforcement of international treaties, environmental protection (especially waterway pollution), commercial vessel safety programmes, recreational boating safety, and search and rescue efforts. In the new construction programme are 11 cutters of frigate size and utility each capable of carrying a helicopter. The strength of personnel on 1 Jan. 1985 was 4,500 officers, 1,350 warrant officers and 26,220 enlisted personnel. A few ships had several women assigned as permanent members of the crew.

Air Force. *Secretary of the Air Force:* Verne Orr.

The Department of the Air Force was activated within the Department of Defense on 18 Sept. 1947, under the terms of the National Security Act of 1947. It is administered by a Secretary of the Air Force, assisted by an Under Secretary and 3 Assistant Secretaries (Research, Development and Logistics; Financial Management; and Manpower, Reserve Affairs and Installations). The USAF, under the administration of the Department of the Air Force, is supervised by a Chief of Staff, who is a member of the Joint Chiefs of Staff. He is assisted by a Vice Chief of Staff, Assistant Vice Chief of Staff, and 5 Deputy Chiefs of Staff (Manpower and Personnel; Programs and Resources; Research, Development and Acquisition; Plans and Operations; and Logistics and Engineering).

The USAF consists of active duty Air Force officers and enlisted personnel, civilian employees, the Air National Guard and the Air Force Reserve. For operational purposes the service is organized into 13 major commands, 15 separate operating agencies and 4 direct reporting units. The Strategic Air Command, equipped with long-range bombers based both in the USA and overseas, and with intercontinental ballistic missiles, is maintained primarily for strategic air operations anywhere on the globe. Tactical Air Command is the Air Force's mobile strike force, able to deploy US general-purpose air forces anywhere in the world for tactical air combat operations. The Military Airlift Command provides air transportation of personnel and cargo for all military services on a worldwide basis; and is also responsible for Air Force audio-visual products, weather service, and aerospace rescue and recovery operations.

The other major commands are the Air Force Systems Command, Air Force Logistics Command, Air Force Communications Command, Electronic Security Command, Air Training Command, Alaskan Air Command, Pacific Air Forces, Space Command, United States Air Forces in Europe, and Air University. The Alaskan, Pacific and European commands conduct, control and co-ordinate offensive and defensive air operations according to tasks assigned by their respective theatre commanders.

The separate operating agencies are the Air Force Accounting and Finance Center, Air Force Audit Agency, Air Force Commissary Service, Air Force Engineering and Services Center, Air Force Inspection and Safety Center, Air Force Intelligence Service, Air Force Office of Security Police, Air Force Manpower and Personnel Center, Air Force Medical Service Center, Air Force Service Information and News Center, Air Force Legal Services Center, Air Force Office of Special Investigations, Air Force Operational Test and Evaluation Center, Air Force Reserve, and Air Reserve Personnel Center. Air Force direct reporting units are the Air Force Academy, Air National Guard, Air Force Technical Applications Center and USAF Historical Research Center.

Of the fighter and interceptor aircraft in service, the F-15 Eagle, F-5 Tiger II, F-16 Fighting Falcon, F-106 Delta Dart, F-111 and F-4 Phantom II fly faster than the speed of sound in level flight and can carry a variety of armament. The E-3 Sentry (AWACS) is a large long-range airborne warning and control aircraft; the EF-111A Raven is a tactical electronics jamming aircraft produced by conversion of the F-111A fighter. The subsonic A-7 Corsair II and the A-10 Thunderbolt II are close-support aircraft. Strategic bombers are the B-52 Stratofortress heavy bomber (to be supplemented by B-1B from mid-80s) and the 'swing-wing' FB-111A. The Strategic Air Command also operates the KC-10A Extender and KC-135 Stratotanker for aerial refuelling, and the SR-71 Blackbird, U-2, and TR-1 for reconnaissance. Primary transport types include the C-141 StarLifter, C-5 Galaxy, KC-10A Extender and the turboprop-powered C-130 Hercules. Intercontinental ballistic missiles in USAF service are Titan II (to be retired) and Minuteman II and III.

In June 1984, the Air Force had about 594,000 personnel. The service operates, or has on order, 6,912 frontline and 4,927 support aircraft.

INTERNATIONAL RELATIONS

Membership. USA is a member of UN, OAS, NATO, OECD and the Colombo Plan.

ECONOMY

Budget. The budget covers virtually all the programmes of federal government, including those financed through trust funds, such as for social security, Medicare and highway construction. Receipts of the Government include all income from its sovereign or compulsory powers; income from business-type or market-orientated activities of the Government is offset against outlays. Budget receipts and outlays (in $1m.):

Year ending 30 June	*Receipts*[2]	*Outlays*[2]	*Surplus* (+) *or deficit* (–)
1945	45,216	92,690	47,474
1950	39,485	42,597	– 3,112
1955	65,469	68,509	– 3,041
1960	92,492	92,223	+ 269
1970	192,807	195,652	– 2,845
1981[1]	599,272	657,204	–57,932
1982	617,766	728,424	–110,658
1983	600,563	795,917	–195,354

[1] From 1977 the fiscal year changed from a 1 July–30 June basis to a 1 Oct.–30 Sept. basis.
[2] From 1970, revised to include Medicare premiums and collections.

Budget receipts, by source, for fiscal years (in $1m.):

Source	*1981*[1]	*1982*[1]	*1983*[1]
Individual income taxes	285,917	298,111	288,938
Corporation income taxes	61,137	49,207	37,022
Social insurance taxes and contributions	182,720	201,132	209,001
Excise taxes	40,839	36,311	35,300
Estate and gift taxes	6,787	7,991	6,053
Customs	8,083	8,854	8,655
Miscellaneous	13,790	16,161	15,594
Total	599,272	617,766	600,563

[1] From 1977, the fiscal year changed from a 1 July–30 June basis to a 1 Oct.–30 Sept. basis.

Budget outlays, by function, for fiscal years (in $1m.):

Source	*1981* [1]	*1982* [1]	*1983* [1 4]
National defence [2]	159,765	187,397	221,502
International affairs	11,130	9,983	12,091
General science, space, and technology	6,359	7,096	7,636
Energy	10,277	4,844	4,151
Natural resources and environment	13,525	13,086	10,438
Agriculture	5,572	14,808	10,411
Commerce and housing credit	3,946	3,843	431
Transportation	23,381	20,589	19,886
Community and regional development	9,394	7,410	7,347
Education, training, employment and social services	31,402	25,411	23,783
Health	65,982	74,018	78,493
Income security	225,099	248,807	259,286
Veterans benefits and services	22,988	23,973	24,220
Administration of justice	4,698	4,648	4,646
General government	4,614	4,833	5,007
General purpose fiscal assistance	6,856	6,161	6,535
Interest	82,537	100,777	111,117
Allowances [3]	...	...	−4,687
Undistributed offsetting receipts	−30,320	−29,261	−40,777
Total budget outlays	657,204	728,424	761,516

[1] From 1977, the fiscal year changed from a 1 July–30 June basis to a 1 Oct.–30 Sept. basis.
[2] Includes allowances for civilian and military pay raises for the Department of Defense.
[3] Includes allowances for civilian agency pay raises and contingencies.
[4] Estimate.

Budget outlays, by agency, for fiscal years (in $1m.):

Agency	*1981* [1]	*1982* [1]	*1983* [1]
Legislative branch	1,209	1,362	2,215 (Legislative branch and The judiciary)
The judiciary	637	705	
Executive Office of the President	96	95	94
Funds appropriated to the President	7,010	6,073	5,417
Agriculture	26,030	36,213	46,372
Commerce	2,226	2,045	1,913
Defence—Military [2]	156,035	182,850	205,012
Defence—Civil	3,148	2,971	2,927
Education [3]	15,089	14,081	14,555
Energy [3]	11,797	7,577	8,348
Health and Human Services	226,987	251,259	274,131
Housing and Urban Development	14,033	14,491	15,312
Interior	4,262	3,922	4,485
Justice	2,682	2,584	2,832
Labour	30,084	30,736	38,176
State	1,897	2,193	2,263
Transportation	22,554	19,917	20,591
Treasury	92,633	110,521	116,787
Environmental Protection Agency	5,232	5,004	4,301
National Aeronautics and Space Administration	5,421	6,026	6,657
Veterans Administration	22,903	23,937	24,805
Other independent agencies:			
Foundation for Education Assistance	...	...	...
Office of Personnel Management	18,089	19,973	21,275
Postal Service	1,343	707	789
Railroad Retirement Board	5,308	5,733	6,236
All other	10,803	6,697	5,991
Allowances [4]	...	...	...
Undistributed offsetting receipts	−30,306	−29,261	−35,566
Total budget outlays	657,204	728,424	795,917

[1] From 1977, the fiscal year changed from a 1 July–30 June basis to a 1 Oct.–30 Sept. basis.
[2] Includes allowances for civilian and military pay raises for the Department of Defense.
[3] The Administration proposed in the 1983 Budget that the Departments of Education and Energy be eliminated and that their programmes be transferred to other agencies. Many of the Education programmes went to the proposed Foundation for Education Assistance.
[4] Includes allowances for civilian agency pay raises and contingencies.

National Debt: Gross federal debt outstanding (in $1m.), and *per capita* debt (in $1) on 30 June to 1970 and then on 30 Sept.:

	Public debt	*Per capita*[2]		*Public debt*	*Per capita*[2]
1919[1]	25,485	243	1970	382,603	1,867
1920	24,299	228	1980	914,317	4,021
1930[1]	16,185	132	1981	1,003,941	4,365
1940	50,696	382	1982[3]	1,137,131	4,900
1950	256,853	1,687	1983[3]	1,273,505	5,420
1960	290,862	1,610			

[1] On 31 Aug. 1919 gross debt reached its First World War (1914–18) peak of $26,596,702,000, which was the highest ever reached up to 1934; on 31 Dec. 1930 it had declined to $16,026m., the lowest it has been since the First World War. On the 30 Nov. 1941, just preceding Pearl Harbor, debt stood at $61,363,867,932. The highest Second World War debt was $279,764,369,348 on 28 Feb. 1946.

[2] *Per capita* figures, beginning with 1960, have been revised; they are based on the Census Bureau's estimates of the total population of the US, including Alaska and Hawaii.

[3] Estimate.

State and Local Finance: Revenue of the 50 states and all local governments (82,688 in 1982) from their own sources amounted to $416,433m. in fiscal year 1980–81; in addition they received $80,294m. in revenue from fiscal aid, shared revenues and reimbursements from the federal government, bringing total revenue from all sources to $506,728m. Of the revenue from state and local sources, taxes provided $244,514m., of which property taxes (mainly imposed by local governments) yielded $74,969m. or 31% of all tax revenue; and sales taxes, both general sales taxes and selective excises, provided $85,971m. (35%).

State tax revenue totalled $149,738m. in fiscal year 1981. Largest sources of state tax revenue are general sales taxes (imposed during 1980 by 45 states), motor fuel sales taxes (all states), individual income (44 states), motor vehicle and operators' licences (49 states), corporation income (46 states), tobacco products (all states) and alcoholic beverage sales taxes (all states).

General revenue of local units from own sources in fiscal year 1980–81 totalled $145,736m. In addition they received $111,443m. from state and federal aids. Property taxes provided 28% of total general revenue.

Total expenditures of state and local governments were $487,048m. in 1980–81, of which approximately 71% was for current operation. Education took $145,784m. in current and capital expenditure; highways, $34,603m.; welfare (chiefly public assistance), $54,121m., and health and hospitals, $36,101m. Capital outlays (construction, equipment and land purchases) totalled $67,596m.

Gross debt of state and local governments totalled $363,892m. or $1,606 *per capita* at the close of their 1980–81 fiscal year. Total cash and investment assets of state and local governments were $454,393m., about 23% being in cash and deposits, and the remainder in investments, mainly non-governmental securities.

US Bureau of the Census, *Governmental Finances in 1980–81.* Washington, 1982
American Economic Association, *Readings in Fiscal Policy.* Homewood, Ill., 1955
Brookings Institute and National Bureau of Economic Research, *Role of Direct and Indirect Taxes in the Federal Revenue System.* Washington, D.C., 1964

National Income. The Bureau of Economic Analysis of the Department of Commerce prepares detailed estimates on the national income and product of the United States. The principal tables are published monthly in *Survey of Current Business;* the complete set of national income and product tables are published in the *Survey* regularly each July, showing data for recent years. *The National Income and Product Accounts of the United States, 1929–1976: Statistical Tables* (1981) and the July 1982, July 1983 and July 1984 *Survey* contain complete sets of tables from 1929 through 1983. The conceptual framework and statistical methods underlying the US accounts were described in *National Income, 1954.* Subsequent limited changes were described in *US Income and Output* (1958), and in *Survey of Current Business* (Aug. 1965, Jan. 1976 and Dec. 1980).

These latest figures[1] in $1,000m. for various years are as follows:

	1929[2]	*1933*[3]	*1950*	*1960*	*1970*	*1980*	*1983*
I. Gross National Product	103·4	55·8	286·5	506·5	992·7	2,631·7	3,304·8
(a) Personal consumption expenditures	77·3	45·8	192·0	324·9	612·7	1,668·1	2,155·9
(b) Gross private domestic investment	16·2	1·4	53·8	75·9	144·2	401·9	471·7
(c) Net exports of goods and services	1·1	0·4	2·2	5·5	6·7	23·9	–8·3
(d) Government purchases of goods and services	8·8	8·2	38·5	100·3	220·1	537·8	685·5
1. GNP *less* capital consumption allowances with capital consumption adjustment, indirect business tax and non-tax liability, business transfer payments, statistical discrepancy, *plus* subsidies less current surplus of government enterprises, equals:							
2. National Income	84·8	39·9	237·6	415·7	810·7	2,116·6	2,646·7
which, *less* corporate profits with inventory valuation and capital consumption adjustments, contributions for social insurance, wage accruals less disbursements, *plus* government transfer payments to persons, interest paid by government to persons and business less interest received by government, interest paid by consumers, personal dividend income, business transfer payments, equals:							
3. Personal income whereof	85·0	47·0	227·2	402·3	811·1	2,165·3	2,744·2
4. Personal tax and non-tax payments take leaving	2·6	1·4	20·6	50·4	115·8	336·1	404·2
5. Disposal personal income divided into	82·4	45·6	206·6	352·0	695·3	1,828·9	2,340·1
(e) Personal outlays[4]	79·1	46·5	194·7	332·3	639·5	1,718·7	2,222·0
(f) Personal saving	3·3	–0·9	11·9	19·7	55·8	110·2	118·1
IA. GNP in constant (1972) $s	315·7	222·1	534·8	737·2	1,085·6	1,475·0	1,534·7
(a) Personal consumption expenditures	215·1	170·5	337·3	452·0	672·1	931·8	1,009·2
(b) Gross private domestic investment	55·8	8·4	93·5	104·7	158·5	208·5	221·0
(c) Net exports of goods and services	3·7	0·4	5·9	7·7	3·9	50·3	12·6
(d) Government purchases of goods and services	41·0	42·9	98·1	172·8	251·1	284·3	291·9
II. National Income composed of	84·8	39·9	237·6	415·7	810·7	2,116·4	2,646·7
Compensation of employees	*51·1*	*29·5*	*154·8*	*294·9*	*612·0*	*1,599·6*	*1,984·9*
(g) Salaries and wages	50·5	29·0	147·0	271·9	548·7	1,356·6	1,658·8
(h) Supplements to wages and salaries	0·6	0·5	7·8	23·0	63·2	243·0	326·2
Proprietors' income[5]	*15·0*	*5·9*	*38·7*	*47·2*	*66·2*	*117·4*	*121·7*
(i) Farm[5]	6·1	2·5	13·7	11·7	14·3	21·8	13·8
(j) Business and professional[5]	8·9	3·3	25·0	35·5	51·9	95·6	107·9
Personal income from rents[6]	*4·9*	*2·2*	*7·1*	*14·5*	*19·7*	*31·5*	*58·3*
Net interest	*4·7*	*4·1*	*3·0*	*11·4*	*41·4*	*192·6*	*256·6*
Corporate profits with inventory valuation and capital consumption adjustments	*9·0*	*–1·7*	*33·9*	*47·6*	*71·4*	*191·7*	*192·0*
(k) Tax liabilities	1·4	0·5	17·9	22·7	34·2	84·8	75·8
(l) Inventory valuation adjustment	0·5	–2·1	–5·0	–0·2	–6·6	–42·9	–11·2
(m) Capital consumption adjustment	–1·4	0·6	–4·0	–2·0	2·5	–16·3	33·2
(n) Dividends	5·8	2·0	8·8	12·9	22·5	58·6	72·9
(o) Undistributed profits	2·8	–1·6	16·2	14·3	18·8	32·0	76·5

[1] The inclusion of statistics for Alaska and Hawaii beginning in 1960 does not significantly affect the comparability of the data.

[2] Peak year between First and Second World Wars. [3] Low point of the depression.

[4] Includes personal consumption expenditures, interest paid by consumers and personal transfer payments to foreigners (net).

[5] With inventory valuation and capital consumption adjustment.

[6] With capital consumption adjustment.

Currency. Prior to the banking crisis that occurred early in 1933, the monetary system had been on the gold standard for more than 50 years. An Act of 14 March 1900 required the Secretary of the Treasury to maintain at a parity with gold all forms of money issued by the USA. For a description of these, *see* THE STATESMAN'S YEAR-BOOK, 1934, p. 491.

The old gold dollar had a par value of 49·32*d*., or \$4·8666 to the £ sterling; it contained 25·8 grains (or 1·6718 grammes) of gold 0·900 fine. By the act of 12 May 1933 the President of the USA was given authority to reduce the gold content of the dollar by not more than 50% and by the Gold Reserve Act of 30 Jan. 1934 the minimum reduction which he could make was fixed at 40%; on 31 Jan. 1934 he fixed its value at 59·06%, or 15⁵⁄₂₁ grains of gold 0·900 fine. This was equal to a price for gold of \$35 a fine oz. (old price, \$20·67183). The President's power to alter the gold content of the dollar to 50% of its value, which was extended by Congress in 1937, 1939 and 1941, was not yet again extended in 1943.

The Par Value Modification Act (Public Law 92–268), enacted on 31 March 1972, authorized and directed the Secretary of the Treasury to take the steps necessary to establish a new par value of the dollar of \$1 = 0·818513 gramme of fine gold or \$38 per fine troy oz. of gold. The Secretary of the Treasury, pursuant to the statutory directive, proposed the new par value for the US dollar to the International Monetary Fund, which par value became effective on 8 May 1972.

In Public Law 93–110, enacted on 21 Sept. 1973, Congress amended the Par Value Modification Act of 1972, and authorized and directed the Secretary of the Treasury to take the steps necessary to establish a new par value of \$1 equals 0·828948 Special Drawing Right or 1/42²⁄₉ of a fine troy ounce of gold. Pursuant to the statutory directive, the Secretary of the Treasury notified the International Monetary Fund that, effective 18 Oct. 1973, the par value of the dollar would be changed from 1/38 to 1/42²⁄₉ a fine troy ounce of gold. Expressed in terms of gold, the new par value of the dollar was 0·736662 gramme of gold per dollar, or \$42.2222 per fine troy ounce of gold. Expressed in percentage, the change in the par value of the dollar amounted to a reduction of 10% in the former gold content of the dollar. This is the equivalent to an 11·1% increase in the former dollar price of gold.

The USA, on 1 April 1978, accepted the second amendment to the Articles of Agreement of the International Monetary Fund. The par value of the dollar is no longer defined in terms of the Special Drawing Right and gold, and the USA is not obliged to establish and maintain a par value for the dollar.

At the time of the banking crisis in March 1933 gold payments by banks and the Treasury were suspended by the Government, and an embargo was placed on gold exports. Steps were taken to withdraw from circulation all gold coin and gold certificates and to prohibit the private ownership of all gold certificates, gold bullion and gold coin except for numismatic purposes. Public Law 93–373, 14 Aug. 1974, amended the Par Value Modification Act so as to provide for the termination of all governmental restrictions on private ownership of gold, including gold coins, no later than 31 Dec. 1974.

Currency in the USA for many years has comprised several varieties. Prior to May 1933 the legal tender qualities of the classes varied, but in that month all types of currency were made equally legal tender. Under the Coinage Act of 1965, all coins and currencies of the USA, regardless of when coined or issued, are legal tender for all debts, public and private.

Only one of the eight kinds of notes outstanding is now significant: Federal Reserve notes in denominations of \$1, \$2, \$5, \$10, \$20, \$50 and \$100. The issue of *(a)* \$500, \$1,000, \$5,000 and \$10,000 Federal Reserve notes; of *(b)* silver certificates, and of *(c)* \$100, \$5 and \$2 US notes have been discontinued, although they are still outstanding. The following issues were stopped many years ago and have been in process of retirement: (1) Federal Reserve Bank notes; (2) National Bank notes; (3) Treasury notes of 1890; (4) fractional currency.

Federal Reserve notes are obligations of the USA and a first lien on the assets of the Federal Reserve Banks, through which they are issued. Each of the 12 banks issues them against the security of an equal volume of collateral.

Gold coins (of the old weight and fineness) were $20, $10, $5 and $2½ pieces called *double eagles, eagles, half-eagles* and *quarter-eagles*. The old eagle weighed 258 grains or 16·7181 grammes 0·900 fine, and therefore contained 232·2 grains or 15·0463 grammes of fine gold. Except for collector's holdings, these are no longer in circulation. The stock of gold bullion held by the Treasury on 31 Aug. 1982 was 264m. fine oz., valued at $11,100m.; stock of silver bullion was 38·7m. fine oz. (excluding 137·5m. fine oz. held for defence stockpile). Estimated stock of domestic coin in circulation on 30 June 1983 was $13,909m., including standard silver dollars and silver and other subsidiary coin.

The silver dollar weighs 412·5 grains or 26·7296 grammes 0·900 fine, and contains 371·25 grains or 24·0566 grammes of fine silver. Subsidiary, 0·900 fine, silver coins contain 347·22 grains of fine silver per dollar. These are the half-dollar, quarter-dollar and dime (one-tenth). Minor coins currently issued are the cupro-nickel 5-cent piece and the bronze 1-cent piece. Pursuant to the Coinage Act of 1965, Congress authorized the minting and issuance of new silver clad half-dollars containing 40% silver and cupro-nickel quarter-dollars and dimes containing no silver. In an amendment to the Coinage Act enacted on 31 Dec. 1970, Congress provided that all coins minted thereafter, including dollar and half-dollar coins, be made of cupro-nickel composition. However, a provision in the 1970 law permitted the coining of 1·500 inch dollar coins containing 40% silver. These dollar coins, which bear the likeness of the late President Eisenhower, are sold at premium price to coin collectors. In Oct. 1978 there was authorization of a new dollar bearing the likeness of suffragette Susan B. Anthony. The new dollars, which are 1·043 inches in diameter and weigh 8·1 grammes, replace the cupro-nickel Eisenhower dollars. In 1981 the Mint began producing 1-cent coins made of 97·6% zinc and 2·4% copper (zinc and copper alloy blanks, barrel electro-plated with copper), pursuant to its authority under 31 USC 317(b) to alter the composition of the alloy of the 1-cent coin. In 1983 it was in the process of phasing out production of bronze cents and will shortly only be producing zinc cents.

On 22 July 1982, the Olympic Commemorative Coin Act authorized the limited issue of not more than 50m. one dollar silver coins and 2m. ten dollar gold coins to commemorate the 1984 Olympics. The coins are to be minted in proof and uncirculated condition. The 1·500 inch dollar coins containing 90% silver will be issued in 1983 and 1984. The 1983 Olympic silver dollar will feature the classic Greek discus thrower, while the 1984 Olympic silver dollar will depict the gateway for the entrance to the Los Angeles Memorial Coliseum. The 1·06 inch 1984 ten dollar gold coin weighs 16·718 grammes of an alloy of 90% gold, 10% copper. It features two Olympic Torch bearers and will be the first US coin to carry the 'W' mint mark of the US. Bullion Depository, West Point, N.Y. The coins are being sold at a premium price with the surcharge above the cost of manufacturing and marketing going to support equally the efforts of the US. Olympic Committee and the Los Angeles Olympic Organizing Committee.

Banking. On 31 Aug. 1983 there were 14,795 domestic banks doing a general deposit business with the public and having aggregate deposits of $1,420,200m.

The Federal Reserve System, established under an Act of 1913, comprises the Board of 7 Governors, the 12 regional Federal Reserve Banks with their 25 branches, the Federal Open Market Committee and the Federal Advisory Council. The 7 members of the Board of Governors are appointed by the President with the consent of the Senate. Each Governor is appointed to a full term of 14 years or an unexpired portion of a term, one term expiring every 2 years. No two may come from the same Federal Reserve District. The Board supervises the Reserve Banks and the issue and retirement of Federal Reserve notes; it designates 3 of the 9 directors of each Reserve Bank and designates the Chairman and Deputy Chairman; it passes on the admission of state banks to the System and has power to correct unsound conditions in State member banks or violations of banking law by them, including, if necessary, disciplinary action to remove officers and directors for unsafe or unsound banking practices or for continuous violations of banking laws; it also authorizes State member bank branches and approves mergers and consolidations if the acquiring, assuming or resulting bank is to be a State member; and it has power to control the expansion of bank holding companies and to require divestment of certain non-banking interests. The 12 members of the Federal Open Market Committee include the 7 members of the Board of Governors and 5 of the 12 Federal Reserve Bank presidents. The latter serve 1-year terms on the Committee in rotation except for the President of the Federal Reserve Bank of New York, who is a permanent member. The Federal Open Market Committee influences credit market conditions, money and bank credit, by buying or selling US Government securities; and it also supervises System operations in foreign currencies for the purpose of helping to safeguard the value of the dollar in international exchange markets and facilitating co-operation and efficiency in the international monetary system. The Board also influences credit conditions through powers to set reserve requirements, to approve discount rates at Federal Reserve Banks, and to fix margin requirements on stock-market credit.

The Reserve Banks hold bank reserves, advance funds to depository institutions, issue Federal Reserve notes, which are the principal form of currency in the US, act as fiscal agent for the Government and afford nation-wide cheque-clearing and fund transfer arrangements. They may issue notes, fully secured; discount paper for depository institutions; increase or reduce the country's supply of reserve funds by buying or selling Government securities and other obligations at the direction of the Federal Open Market Committee. Their capital stock is held by the member banks, but it carries no voting rights except in the election of directors.

Every member bank is required to subscribe to stock in the Reserve Bank of its district in an amount equal to 6% of its paid-up capital and surplus. Only one-half of the par value of the stock is paid in, the other half remaining subject to call by the Board of Governors. However, no call has been made for the second half of the subscription. All depository institutions with certain transaction accounts and time deposits are required to hold reserves with the Federal Reserve.

Beginning in 1968, the Congress passed a number of consumer credit protection acts, the first of which was the Truth in Lending Act (and including the Equal Credit Opportunity Act), Home Mortgage Disclosure Act, Consumer Leasing Act and the Fair Credit Billing Act, for which it has directed the Board to write implementing regulations and assume partial enforcement responsibility. To manage these responsibilities the Board has established a Division of Consumer and Community Affairs. To assist it, the Board consults with a Consumer Advisory Council, established by the Congress as a statutory part of the Federal Reserve System.

The Consumer Advisory Council was established by Congress in 1976 at the suggestion of the Board of Governors. Representing both consumers and creditors, the Council meets several times a year to advise the Board on its implementation of consumer regulations and other consumer related matters.

Another statutory body, the Federal Advisory Council, consists of 12 members (one from each district); it meets in Washington at least four times a year to advise the Board of Governors on general business and financial conditions.

Following the passage of the Monetary Control Act of 1980, the Board of Governors established the Thrift Institutions Advisory Council to provide information and views on the special needs and problems of thrift institutions. The group is comprised of representatives of mutual savings banks, savings and loan associations, and credit unions.

Banks which participate in the federal deposit insurance fund have their deposits insured against loss up to $100,000 for each depositor. The fund is administered by the Federal Deposit Insurance Corporation established in 1933; it obtains resources through annual assessments on participating banks.

All members of the Federal Reserve System are required to insure their deposits through the Corporation, and non-member banks may apply and qualify for insurance. On 31 Dec. 1982, 14,487 commercial banks and 315 mutual savings banks with insured deposits of $1,100,000m. were members of the insurance fund. There were 647 uninsured banks comprising 644 commercial banks and trust companies and 103 mutual savings banks.

There are also banks which operate solely in the field of agricultural credits under the Farm Credit Administration; Federal Home Loan Banks makes advances to financial associations and institutions upon the security of home mortgages.

US Board of Governors of the Federal Reserve System. *The Federal Reserve System Purposes and Functions.* 6th ed., 1974.—*Federal Reserve Bulletin.* Monthly.—*Annual Report.—Annual Statistical Digest.—The Federal Reserve Act, As Amended Through 1978*
Beckhart, B. H., *Federal Reserve System.* New York, 1972
Chandler, L. V., *Economics of Money and Banking.* 7th ed. New York, 1977
Clifford, A. J., *The Independence of the Federal Reserve System.* Philadelphia, 1965
Horovitz, P. M., *Monetary Policy and the Financial System.* 4th ed. Englewood Cliffs, 1979
Maisel, S. J., *Managing the Dollar.* New York, 1973
Timberlake, R. H., *The Origins of Central Banking in the United States.* Cambridge, Massachusetts, 1978
Young, R. A., *Instruments of Monetary Policy in the United States; the Role of the Federal Reserve System.* Washington, 1973

Weights and Measures. British weights and measures are usually employed, but the old Winchester bushel and wine gallon are used instead of the new or Imperial standards: *Wine gallon* = 0·83268 Imperial gallon; *Bushel* = 0·9690 Imperial bushel. Instead of the British cwt of 112 lb., one of 100 lb. is used; the *short* or *net ton* contains 2,000 lb.; the *long* or *gross ton*, 2,240 lb.

ENERGY AND NATURAL RESOURCES

Minerals. Total value of non-fuel minerals produced in US (including Alaska and Hawaii) in 1983 was estimated at $21,134m. ($19,675m. in 1982). Details are given in the following tables.

Production of metallic minerals (long tons, 2,240 lb.; short tons, 2,000 lb.):

	1982		*1983*	
Metallic minerals	*Quantity*	*Value ($1,000)*	*Quantity*	*Value ($1,000)*
Bauxite (dried equiv.) tonnes	732	12,334	679	11,309
Copper (recoverable content), tonnes	1,146,975	1,840,856	1,038,098	1,751,476
Gold (recoverable content), troy oz.	1,465,686	550,968	1,957,379	829,929
Iron ore (usable)[1], 1,000 long tons, gross	35,751	1,491,705	44,295	1,938,496
Lead (recoverable content), tonnes	512,516	288,579	449,038	214,623
Molybdenum (content of concentrate), 1,000 lb.	76,135	504,089	49,163	167,164
Silver (recoverable content), 1,000 troy oz.	40,248	319,975	43,415	496,671
Zinc (recoverable content), tonnes	303,160	257,116	275,294	251,204
Other metals	—	251,378	—	205,128
Total metals	—	5,517,000	—	5,866,000

[1] Excluding by-product iron sinter.

The two world wars and record levels of industrial production have hastened the depletion of once abundant supplies of metal and US is increasingly an importer. US is wholly or almost wholly dependent upon imports for industrial diamonds, bauxite, tin, chromite, nickel, strategic-grade mica and long-fibre asbestos; it imports the bulk of its tantalum, platinum, manganese, mercury, tungsten, cobalt and flake graphite, and substantial quantities of antimony, cadmium, arsenic, fluorspar, zinc and bismuth.

In 1983 precious metals were mined mainly in Idaho, Nevada, Montana, Utah and Arizona (in order of combined output of gold and silver). US output of gold (troy oz.), 1930–39, 31,453,370; 1940–49, 24,171,646; 1950–59, 18,817,241; total 1792–1970, 316,620,436. Output of silver (troy oz.), 1930–39, 466,412,499; 1940–49, 434,656,631; 1950–59, 374,055,521; total 1792–1970, 4,701,429,507.

Statistics of important non-metallic minerals and mineral fuels are:

	1982		*1983*	
Non-metallic minerals	*Quantity*	*Value ($1,000)*	*Quantity*	*Value ($1,000)*
Boron minerals, short tons	1,234,000	384,597	1,303,000	439,181
Cement:				
Portland, 1,000 short tons	61,080	3,084,439	67,183	3,315,690
Masonry, 1,000 short tons	2,364	145,172	2,921	186,240
Clays, 1,000 short tons	35,345	825,064	40,858	931,091
Gypsum, 1,000 short tons	10,538	89,131	12,884	101,361

	1982		*1983*	
Non-metallic minerals	*Quantity*	*Value ($1,000)*	*Quantity*	*Value ($1,000)*
Lime, 1,000 short tons	14,075	696,207	14,867	757,611
Phosphate rock, 1,000 tonnes	37,414	950,326	42,573	1,020,901
Potassium salts, 1,000 tonnes (K_2O equivalent)	1,784	265,600	1,513	220,800
Salt (common), 1,000 short tons	37,894	671,424	34,573	597,081
Sand and gravel, 1,000 short tons	621,400	1,997,800	681,720	2,270,200
Stone, 1,000 short tons	791,360	3,063,413	863,886	3,486,483
Sulphur (Frasch-process), 1,000 tonnes	3,598	434,660	4,111	445,131
Other non-metallic minerals	—	1,550,167	—	1,496,230
Total non-metallic minerals	—	14,158,000	—	15,268,000
Mineral fuels	*1981*		*1982*	
Coal: Bitum. and lignite, 1,000 short tons	823,800	21,510,000	824,000	22,380,000
Pennsylv. anthracite,[1] 1,000 short tons	5,400	240,000	4,200	200,000
Gas: Natural gas,[2] 1m. cu. ft	19,690,000	39,950,009	8,090,000	44,580,000
Petroleum (crude), 1,000 bbls of 42 gallons	3,129,000	99,400,000	3,165,000	90,330,000

[1] Includes a small quantity of anthracite mined in states other than Pennsylvania.
[2] Value at wells.

Minerals Yearbook. Bureau of Mines. Washington, D.C. Annual from 1932–33; continuing the *Mineral Resources of the United States* series (1866–1931); from 1963 in 3 vols. *(Metals, Minerals, Fuels; Area Reports, Domestic; and Area Reports, International)*

Agriculture. Agriculture in the USA is characterized by its ability to adapt to widely varying conditions, and still produce an abundance and variety of agricultural products. From colonial times to about 1920 the major increases in farm production were brought about by adding to the number of farms and the amount of land under cultivation. During this period nearly 320m. acres of virgin forest were converted to crop land or pasture, and extensive areas of grass lands were ploughed. Improvident use of soil and water resources was evident in many areas.

During the next 20 years the number of farms reached a plateau of about 6·5m., and the acreage planted to crops held relatively stable around 330m. acres. The major source of increase in farm output arose from the substitution of power-driven machines for horses and mules. Greater emphasis was placed on development and improvement of land, and the need for conservation of basic agricultural resources was recognized. A successful conservation programme, highly co-ordinated and on a national scale—to prevent further erosion, to restore the native fertility of damaged land and to adjust land uses to production capabilities and needs—has been in operation since early in the 1930s.

Following the Second World War the uptrend in farm output has been greatly accelerated by increased production per acre and per farm animal. These increases are associated with a higher degree of mechanization; greater use of lime and fertilizer; improved varieties, including hybrid maize and grain sorghums; more effective control of insects and disease; improved strains of livestock and poultry; and wider use of good husbandry practices, such as nutritionally balanced feeds, use of superior sites and better housing. During this period land included in farms decreased slowly, crop land harvested declined somewhat more rapidly, but the number of farms declined sharply.

Some significant changes during these transitions are:

All land in farms totalled less than 500m. acres in 1870, rose to a peak of over 1,200m. acres in the 1950s and declined to 1,039m. acres in 1982, even with the addition of the new States of Alaska and Hawaii in 1960. The number of farms declined from 6·35m. in 1940 to 2·4m. in 1982, as the average size of farms doubled. The average size of farms in 1982 was 433 acres, but ranged from a few acres to many thousand acres. In 1978, 215,088 farms (128,254 in 1974) were less than 10 acres; 475,241 (379,543), 10–49 acres; 814,689 (827,884), 50–179 acres; 596,356 (616,098), 180–499 acres; 215,112 (207,297), 500–999 acres; 98,521 (92,712), 1,000–1,999 acres; 63,635 (62,225) 2,000 acres or more.

Farms operated by owners or part-owners, 1978, were 2,165,000 (87% of all farms), by all tenants, 314,000 (13%). The average size of farms in 1978 was 235 acres for full-owners, 792 acres for part-owners and 396 acres for tenants. Farms with white operators numbered 2,398,726, and those with operators who were black or of other races were 79,916. A higher proportion of blacks and operators of other races were tenants and operated a significantly smaller acreage than white operators.

In 1982 (with 1960 figures in parentheses) large-scale, highly mechanized farms with sales of agricultural products totalling $20,000 and over per farm made up 40% (8·6%) of all farms and accounted for 90% (48·3%) of the value of farm products sold. Farms selling between $19,999 and $2,500 worth of products per farm were 39% (44·8%) of all farms and sold 8·2% (43·3%) of all sales. The remaining 21% (46·6%) of all farms sold less than $2,500 worth of products per farm, 1·8% (8·4%) of total sales. Operators in every sales category received off-farm income, but operators selling less than $2,500 per year received 91·7% of their average income of $22,063 from non-farm sources in 1980.

A century ago three-quarters of the total US population was rural, and practically all rural people lived on farms. In April 1980 26% of the population was rural, and 6m. farm residents accounted for 3% of the total population.

Hired farm workers in 1982 averaged about 2·5m., and farm family workers, including operators, about 2·6m. In 1950 there were nearly 10m. farm workers. At that time each farm worker supplied farm products for 15 people; in 1974, 55 people, in 1977, 60 people and in 1982, 76 people.

Cash receipts from farm marketings and government payments (in $1m.):

	Crops	*Livestock and livestock products*	*Government payments*	*Total*
1932	1,996	2,752	—	4,748
1945	9,655	12,008	742	22,405
1950	12,356	16,105	283	28,744
1960	15,259	18,989	702	34,950
1970	20,976	29,563	3,717	54,256
1979	63,394	68,522	1,375	133,291
1980	69,026	67,405	1,286	137,717
1981	74,920	68,478	1,930	145,328
1982	74,353	70,199	3,492	148,043
1983	69,516	69,203	9,294	148,014

Realized gross farm income (including government payments), in $1m., was 144,205 in 1981, compared with 148,043 in 1982; net income of farm operators (only from farm sources), 22,051 (25,100). Farm real estate debt, in 1982, was $105,539m.; 1983, $109,507m.

US agricultural exports, fiscal year, totalled: 1974–75, $21,854m.; 1975–76, $22,760m.; 1976–77, $23,974m.; 1977–78, $27,290m.; 1978–79, $31,975m.; 1979–80, $40,481m.; 1980–81, $43,780m.; 1982, 39,094m.

Total area of farm land under irrigation in 1978 was 50,837,940 acres (302,674 farms).

Federal income taxes paid by farm people was $15m. in 1941, $1,365m. in 1948, $1,182m. in 1967, $3,434m. in 1971, $5,309m. in 1972, $8,364m. in 1973 and $8,277m. in 1974. Total taxes levied on farm real estate were $3,039m. in 1977, $3,021m. in 1978, $3,215m. in 1979, $3,450·9m. in 1980, $3,695·5m. in 1981; $3,907·1m. in 1982.

According to census returns and estimates of the Economic Research Service, the acreage and specified values of farms has been as follows (area in 1,000 acres; value in $1,000):

	Farm area [1]	*Crop land available for crops*	*Value, land, bldgs, machinery, livestock*	*Value of products sold in preceding year*
1910	878,798	432,000	41,089,000	...
1930	986,771	480,000	57,815,000	9,609,924
1940	1,060,852	467,000	41,829,000	6,681,581
1950	1,158,566	478,000	99,366,000	22,051,129
1959	1,125,508	448,100	164,200,000	30,492,721
1969	1,063,346	459,048	206,751,000	44,519,658
1978	1,029,695	461,341	5,653,400,000	108,113,519

[1] Acreages are for the preceding year except for 1959.

The areas and production of the principal crops for 3 years were:

	1980			*1981*			*1982*		
	Harvested 1,000 acres	*Production 1,000 bu.*	*Yield per acre bu.*	*Harvested 1,000 acres*	*Production 1,000 bu.*	*Yield per acre bu.*	*Harvested 1,000 acres*	*Production 1,000 bu.*	*Yield per acre bu.*
Corn for grain	73,030	6,644,841	91·0	74,700	8,201,598	109·8	73,152	8,397,334	114·8
Oats	8,652	458,263	53·0	9,415	509,167	54·1	10,561	616,981	58·4
Barley	7,275	360,956	49·6	9,158	479,333	52·3	9,113	522,387	57·3
All wheat	70,984	2,374,306	33·4	81,013	2,798,738	34·5	78,841	2,808,737	35·6
Rice (cwt)	3,312	146,150	4,413	3,792	182,742	4,819	3,252	154,216	4,742
Soybeans for beans	67,856	1,792,062	26·4	66,368	2,000,145	30·1	70,783	2,276,976	32·2
Flaxseed	683	7,928	11·6	617	7,799	12·6	815	11,635	14·3
Cotton lint (bale)	13,215	11,122	404	13,841	15,646	543	9,728	11,963	590
Potatoes (cwt)	1,155	302,857	262	1,237	338,591	274	1,273	349,268	274
Tobacco (lb.)	920	1,786,192	1,940	976	2,063,611	2,114	907	1,982,245	2,183

Wheat. The chief wheat-growing states (1982) were (estimated yield in 1,000 bu.): Kansas, 462,000; N. Dakota, 330,785; Oklahoma, 227,700; Montana, 183,560; Texas, 144,000; Washington, 138,880; Minnesota, 126,809; Nebraska, 101,500; Idaho, 94,200; Colorado, 87,504; California, 81,625; Missouri, 75,820.

Cotton. Leading production, 1982, by state (in 1,000 bales, 480 lb. net weight) was: California, 3,073; Texas, 2,700; Mississippi, 1,760; Arizona, 1,095; Louisiana, 870; Arkansas, 534; Alabama, 460; Tennessee, 339; Oklahoma, 238; Missouri, 204.

Tobacco. Output (1,000 lb.) of the chief tobacco-growing states (92% of the crop) was, in 1982: N. Carolina, 700,689; Kentucky, 577,100; Tennessee, 178,117; Virginia, 125,384; S. Carolina, 124,195; Georgia, 105,500.

Fruit. A wide variety of fruits are grown; the chief products are as follows:

	1980		*1981*		*1982*	
	Production 1,000 tons	*Value $1,000*	*Production 1,000 tons*	*Value $1,000*	*Production 1,000 tons*	*Value $1,000*
Apples	4,414	762,509	3,877	852,981	4,055	803,723
Citrus Fruit	16,484	1,905,648	15,105	1,866,685	12,113	1,712,712
Grapes	5,595	1,341,052	4,458	1,322,431	6,616	1,349,808

Dairy produce. In 1982, production of milk was 135,795m. lb.; milkfat, 4,961m. lb.; cheese (not including cottage cheese), 4,540m. lb.; butter, 1,257m. lb.; eggs, 69,680m.

Livestock (1983). Cattle, 115·2m.; pigs, 53·2m.; sheep, 11·9m.; goats, 1·33m.; poultry, 544m.

The value (in $1,000) was:

	1981	*1982*	*1983* [2]
Cattle of all kinds	54,292,044	47,966,517	46,749,210
Sheep and lambs	903,332	737,777	615,691
Swine (hogs and pigs) [1]	4,113,725	4,783,560	...

[1] At 1 Dec. of previous year. [2] Preliminary.

Total value of livestock, excluding poultry and goats and, from 1961, horses and mules (in $1m.) on farms in the USA on 1 Jan. was: 1930, 6,061; 1933 (low point of the agricultural depression), 2,733; 1970, 22,886; 1978, 31,952; 1979, 50,612; 1980, 60,598; 1981, 60,016; 1982, 53,601; 1983 (preliminary), 52,148.

In 1982 the production of shorn wool was 105m. lb. from 13·1m. sheep (average 1970–74, 320m. lb. from 18·2m. sheep); of pulled wool 1·15m. lb. (1970–74, 10·1m. lb.).

Forestry. In 1977 the US forest lands, including Alaska and Hawaii, capable of producing timber for commercial use, covered 482,485,900 acres (more than one-fifth of the land area), classified as follows: Saw-timber stands, 215,435,700 acres; pole timber stands, 135,609,900 acres, seedling and sapling stands, 115,032,100 acres; non-stocked and other areas, 16,408,200 acres. Ownership of commercial forest land is distributed as follows: Federal government, 99,410,400 acres; state, county, municipal and Indian, 36,311,200 acres; privately owned, 346,764,300 acres, including 115,777,100 acres on farms. Of the saw-timber stand (2,578,940m. bd ft) Douglas fir constitutes 514,317; Southern yellow pine, 321,563; Western yellow (ponderosa and jeffrey) pine, 192,070; other softwoods, 947,458; hardwoods, 593,532. In 1976 growing stock timber removals amounted to 14,229,023,000 cu. ft compared to net annual growth of about 21,664,316,000 cu. ft. Saw-timber removals amounted to 65,176,618,000 bd ft against an annual growth of 74,620,832,000 bd ft. The net area of the 155 national forests and other areas in USA and Puerto Rico administered by the US Department of Agriculture's Forest Service, including commercial and non-commercial forest land, was in May 1983, 191m. acres.

Fire takes a heavy annual toll in the forest; total area burned over in 1982 was 2,382,037 acres; 1,500m. acres of land are now under organized fire-protection service. The area planted or seeded in forest and wind barrier nursery stock in the year ending 30 Sept. 1983 was 425,561 acres.

Land Areas of National Forest System. Forest Service, US Dept. of Agriculture, 1982
Report of the Forest Service, 1982

Fisheries. The main fishing industries are in California (anchovy, tuna and sole); Alaska (notably salmon); Washington (salmon and halibut); Florida (the main source of turtles and sponges); Massachusetts, Maine, North Carolina and Oregon. Total catch, 1981 (preliminary), 5,977m. lb. valued at $2,388m.

Tennessee Valley Authority. Established by Act of Congress, 1933, the TVA is a multiple-purpose federal agency which carries out its duties in an area embracing some 41,000 sq. miles, in 125 counties (aggregate population, about 7·9m.) in the 7 Tennessee River Valley states: Tennessee, Kentucky, Mississippi, Alabama, North Carolina, Georgia and Virginia. In addition, 76 counties outside the Valley are served by TVA power distributors. Its 3 directors are appointed by the President, with the consent of the Senate; headquarters are in Knoxville, Tenn. There were 33,352 employees in May 1984.

In the 1930s and 1940s, the Tennessee Valley offered the world a model of the first effort to develop all resources of a major river valley under one comprehensive programme, the Tennessee Valley Authority. The multipurpose development of the Tennessee River for flood control, navigation, and electric power production was the first big task for TVA. But there were other needs; controlling erosion on the land, introducing better fertilizers and new farming practices, eradicating malaria, demonstrating ways electricity could lighten the burdens in the home and increase production on the farm, and a multitude of potential job-producing enterprises.

In the depression year, 1933, the average *per capita* income in the Valley was $168, compared with the national average of $375. Through the years, TVA has placed a strong emphasis on the economic development of the Valley. An abundant supply of reasonably priced power, combined with a reliable navigation system, has provided a strong incentive for industry to locate in the Valley. By 1981, the region's *per capita* income had multiplied over 48 times to $8,078, while the national average had increased 28 times.

Taming the Tennessee River has had two positive effects on the Valley: flood damages averted by river control now total nearly $2,250m., and a navigable channel system 650 miles long, connecting with the American system of inland waterways, provides a readily accessible transportation system for industry. In 1982, 27m. (estimate) tons of barge-traffic travelled the TVA river system.

Another activity is experimentation in the development and manufacture of chemical fertilizers, accompanied by programmes designed to encourage proper fertilizer use in all parts of the United States and the world. TVA's National Fertilizer Development Center is recognized world-wide for its expertise in fertilizer technology. TVA also works closely with other federal agencies, and with state and local authorities in combating soil erosion, improving forest resources, improving agriculture, and in the development of local industries based on natural resources.

In recent years, attention has focused mainly on TVA's power programme. TVA supplies electric power to 160 local distribution systems serving 2·9m. customers. The power system originated with the water-power development of the Tennessee River, but has become predominantly a coal-fired system as power requirements have outgrown the region's hydro-electric potential. In fiscal year 1983, the TVA system generated 114,331m. kwh. Installed capacity in 1983 was 32·1m. kw, with another 5·2m. kw under construction at TVA's nuclear plants.

Because of the ever-increasing cost of energy in today's world, TVA has focused a good deal of its attention and resources on the research and demonstration of new and alternative energy sources. TVA is playing a lead rôle in the development of atmospheric fluidized bed combustion (AFBC) technology, an innovative process of burning high-sulphur coal cleanly and cheaply. TVA is continuing its research and demonstrations into solar energy, both for residential and commercial uses; energy from wood and waste products, and electric vehicle development. Other TVA activities include demonstration of effective ways of reclaiming strip-mined areas and development of new and improved methods of controlling air and water pollution.

Power operations are financially self-supporting from revenues. In fiscal year 1983 power revenues were $4,114m., and net income $332m. Power facilities are financed from revenues and the sale of revenue bonds and notes, and TVA is repaying appropriations previously invested in power facilities. Other TVA resource development programmes continue to be financed from congressional appropriations, which amount to $125·5m. in 1983–84.

Annual Report of the TVA. Knoxville, 1934 to date

Clapp, G.R., *The TVA; An Approach to the Development of a Region*. Univ. of Chicago Press, 1955

Lilienthal, D. E., *TVA; Democracy on the March*. 20th Anniversary ed. New York and London, 1953

Owen, M., *The Tennessee Valley Authority*. New York, 1973

Tennessee Valley Authority. *A History of the Tennessee Valley Authority*. Knoxville, Tennessee, 1982.—*TVA. The First Twenty Years* (ed. R. C. Martin), Univ. of Tennessee Press, 1956

INDUSTRY AND TRADE

Industry. The following table presents industry statistics of manufactures as reported at various censuses from 1909 to 1977 and from the Annual Survey of Manufactures for years in which no census was taken. The figures for 1958 to 1977 include data for some establishments previously classified as non-manufacturing. The figures for 1939, but not for earlier years, have been revised to exclude data for establishments classified as non-manufacturing in 1954. The figures for 1909–33 were previously revised by the deduction of data for industries excluded from manufacturing during that period.

The statistics for 1958, 1963, 1967, 1972 and 1977 relate to all establishments employing 1 or more persons anytime during the year; for 1950, 1956–57, 1959–62, 1966 and 1968–74 on a representative sample of manufacturing establishments of 1 or more employees; for 1929 through 1939, those reporting products valued at $5,000 or more; and for 1909 and 1919, those reporting products valued at $500 or more. These differences in the minimum size of establishments included in the census affect only very slightly the year-to-year comparability of the figures.

The annual Surveys of Manufactures carry forward the key measures of manufacturing activity which are covered in detail by the Census of Manufactures. The estimate for 1950 is based on reports for approximately 45,000 plants out of a total of more than 260,000 operating manufacturing establishments; those for 1956–57 on about 50,000, and those for 1959–62, 1966 and 1968–74 on about 60,000 out of about 300,000. Included are all large plants and representative samples of the much more numerous small plants. The large plants in the surveys account for approximately two-thirds of the total employment in operating manufacturing establishments in the US.

	Number of establishments	Production workers (average for year)	Production workers' wages total ($1,000)	Value added by manufacture[1] ($1,000)
1909	264,810	6,261,736	3,205,213	8,160,075
1919	270,231	8,464,916	9,664,009	23,841,624
1929	206,663	8,369,705	10,884,919	30,591,435
1933	139,325	5,787,611	4,940,146	14,007,540
1939	173,802	7,808,205	8,997,515	24,487,304
1950	260,000	11,778,803	34,600,025	89,749,765
1960	...	12,209,514	55,555,452	163,998,531
1963	306,317	12,232,041	62,093,601	192,082,900
1966	...	13,826,500	78,256,400	250,880,100
1967	305,680	13,955,300	81,393,600	261,983,800
1968	...	14,041,200	87,480,400	285,058,900
1969	...	14,357,800	93,459,600	304,440,700
1970	...	13,528,000	91,609,000	300,227,600
1971	...	12,874,900	93,231,700	314,138,400
1972	312,662	13,526,500	105,494,700	353,974,200
1973	...	14,233,100	118,332,300	405,623,500
1974	...	13,970,900	124,983,200	452,468,400
1975	...	12,567,900	121,427,200	442,485,800
1976	...	13,051,200	137,564,000	511,470,900
1977	350,757	13,691,000	157,163,700	585,165,600
1978	...	14,228,700	176,416,800	657,412,000
1979	...	14,537,800	192,881,500	747,480,500
1980	...	13,900,100	198,164,000	773,831,300
1982	...	12,389,700	204,523,100	...

[1] For the period 1954–67 value added represents adjusted value added and for earlier years unadjusted value added. Unadjusted is obtained by subtracting cost of materials, supplies and containers, fuel, electricity and contract work from the value of shipments for products manufactured plus receipts for services rendered. Adjusted value added also takes into account value added by merchandizing operations plus net change in finished goods and work-in-process inventories between the beginning and end of the year.

For comparison of broad types of manufacturing, the industries covered by the Census of Manufactures have been divided into 20 general groups according to the *Standard Industrial Classification.*

Code No.	Industry group	Census year	Production workers (average for year)	Production workers' wages, total ($1,000)	Value added by manufacture[1] ($1,000)
20.	Food and kindred products	1980	1,091,200	14,814,400	75,490,900
		1981	1,068,700	15,707,100	80,794,700
		1982	1,048,200	16,409,800	...
21.	Tobacco manufactures	1980	46,600	767,400	6,147,600
		1981	49,100	891,400	6,429,600
		1982	45,400	957,100	...
22.	Textile mill products	1980	706,200	7,212,400	18,983,300
		1981	678,500	7,439,000	19,463,200
		1982	617,700	6,976,200	...
23.	Apparel and related products	1980	1,129,500	8,503,400	23,425,500
		1981	1,078,600	8,734,400	25,639,900
		1982	1,007,700	8,826,300	...
24.	Lumber and wood products	1980	581,700	6,719,900	18,029,900
		1981	543,800	6,752,900	17,321,000
		1982	480,400	6,439,700	...
25.	Furniture and fixtures	1980	383,800	3,926,000	11,631,100
		1981	374,100	4,189,100	12,668,700
		1982	349,500	4,179,200	...
26.	Paper and allied products	1980	493,900	8,203,500	29,760,500
		1981	486,600	8,820,400	32,366,700
		1982	459,100	9,018,000	...
27.	Printing and publishing	1980	716,000	9,599,100	44,374,700
		1981	719,700	10,454,000	49,351,600
		1982	712,600	11,287,200	...

[1] Figures represent adjusted value added. For definitions see footnote to previous table.

Code No.	Industry group	Census year	Production workers (average for year)	Production workers' wages, total ($1,000)	Value added by manufacture [1] ($1,000)
28.	Chemical and allied products	1980	544,700	9,482,600	74,384,100
		1981	532,600	10,230,100	80,032,300
		1982	504,100	10,463,900	...
29.	Petroleum and coal products	1980	99,800	2,135,000	24,815,600
		1981	101,000	2,522,100	26,740,300
		1982	99,200	2,612,800	...
30.	Rubber and plastics products, not elsewhere classified [2]	1980	544,400	6,777,300	22,568,700
		1981	541,900	7,392,700	26,005,900
		1982	521,700	7,684,500	...
31.	Leather and leather products	1980	200,500	1,635,300	4,851,200
		1981	196,800	1,766,000	5,230,300
		1982	172,300	1,625,200	...
32.	Stone, clay and glass products	1980	479,700	7,190,300	24,051,000
		1981	462,500	7,568,600	24,853,900
		1982	407,500	7,153,900	...
33.	Primary and metal industries	1980	854,200	17,306,200	47,619,200
		1981	825,900	18,564,100	49,550,600
		1982	638,500	14,460,100	...
34.	Fabricated metal products [2]	1980	1,224,000	17,908,500	57,917,100
		1981	1,182,800	19,134,000	61,558,200
		1982	1,065,800	18,339,300	...
35.	Machinery (except electrical)	1980	1,595,700	25,771,300	99,435,400
		1981	1,561,000	27,762,200	111,393,700
		1982	1,346,900	24,903,900	...
36.	Electrical machinery [2]	1980	1,303,000	17,762,600	73,149,500
		1981	1,278,100	19,192,400	79,720,400
		1982	1,200,900	19,369,900	...
37.	Transportation equipment [2]	1980	1,213,000	24,109,000	76,591,800
		1981	1,185,300	26,096,600	82,938,200
		1982	1,069,500	24,513,800	...
38.	Instruments and related products [2]	1980	370,700	5,021,400	27,913,100
		1981	368,300	5,536,700	31,493,800
		1982	362,300	5,896,000	...
39.	Miscellaneous manufacturing	1980	321,500	3,318,400	12,691,100
		1981	307,500	3,447,100	13,953,500
		1982	280,400	3,406,300	...

[1] Figures represent adjusted value added. For definitions see footnote to previous table, p. 1402.

[2] Figures for 1967 are not comparable to 1972 due to revisions in the Standard Industrial Classification System.

Iron and Steel: Output of the iron and steel industries (in net tons of 2,000 lb.), according to figures supplied by the American Iron and Steel Institute, was:

	Furnaces in blast 31 Dec.	Pig-iron (including ferro-alloys)	Raw steel	Steel by method of production [1] Open hearth	Bessemer	Electric [2]	Basic Oxygen
1932 [3]	44	9,835,227	15,322,901	13,336,210	1,715,925	270,044	...
1939	195	35,677,097	52,798,714	48,409,800	3,358,916	1,029,067	
1944 [4]	218	62,866,198	89,641,600	80,363,953	5,039,923	4,237,699	
1950	234	66,400,311	96,336,075	86,262,509	4,534,558	6,039,008	...
1960	114	68,566,384	99,281,601	86,367,506	1,189,196	8,378,743	3,346,156
1970	152	87,933,000	131,514,000	48,022,000	—	20,162,000	63,330,000
1980	...	70,329,000	111,835,000	13,054,000	—	31,166,000	67,617,000
1982		43,309,000	74,577,000	6,110,000		23,150,000	45,309,000
1983	...	48,706,000	84,615,000	5,951,000	—	26,615,000	52,050,000

[1] The sum of these 4 items should equal the total in the preceding column; any difference appearing is due to the very small production of crucible steel, omitted prior to 1950.

[2] Includes crucible production beginning 1950.

[3] Low point of the depression.

[4] Peak year of war production.

Wholesale price index of iron and steel mill products (1967 = 100) was: 1950, 59·4; 1960, 96·4; 1970, 114·3; 1978, 254·4; 1979, 280·4; 1980, 302·7; 1982, 349·7; 1983, 352·5.

Consumption of ore, 1983, was 68·3m. net tons, of which blast-furnaces took 56·9m. net tons; agglomerating plants, 11·2m. net tons; and steel producing furnaces, 248,000 net tons.

The iron and steel industry in 1983 employed 168,852 wage-earners (compared with 449,888 in 1960), who worked an average of 36·9 hours per week and earned an average of $15·09 per hour: total wages were $4,900m. and total salaries for 73,893 employees were $2,477m.

Annual Statistics Report. American Iron and Steel Institute

Labour. The American labour movement comprises about 190 national and international labour organizations plus a large number of small independent local or single-firm labour organizations. In 1980 total membership was approximately 23·9m., including 1·7m. Canadian workers affiliated with American labour organizations and under 120,000 others outside the USA. The American Federation of Labor (founded 1881 and taking its name in 1886) and the Congress of Industrial Organizations merged into one organization, named the AFL–CIO, in Dec. 1955, representing 16·8m. workers in 1980.

Unaffiliated or independent labour organizations, inter-state in scope, including those organizing coalminers, teamsters and government employees and railroad workers, had an estimated total membership excluding all foreign members (1980) of about 6·8m. Labour organizations represented approximately 20% of the labour force in 1980.

The Labor–Management Relations (Taft–Hartley) Act, 1947, applicable to industries affecting inter-state commerce, prohibits the closed shop, but permits union shop arrangements except where forbidden by state laws. Statutes regulating, restricting or prohibiting union shop or other types of union security agreements are in effect in 20 states (Alabama, Arizona, Arkansas, Florida, Georgia, Iowa, Kansas, Louisiana, Mississippi, Nebraska, Nevada, North Carolina, North Dakota, South Carolina, South Dakota, Tennessee, Texas, Utah, Virginia and Wyoming). Colorado and Wisconsin ban all-union agreements unless a certain percentage of employees have voted for them; in Hawaii an all-union agreement may be entered into unless a majority of employees votes against it. Thirteen states have acts to prevent industrial disputes between public utilities and their employees by means of compulsory arbitration or seizure; however, a number of these laws have been declared unconstitutional in so far as industries in inter-state commerce are concerned. Laws to restrict or regulate picketing or other strike activities have been enacted in over half the states. About one-half of the states also prohibit certain types of strikes, as 'sit down', jurisdictional or sympathy strikes.

The Employee Retirement Income Security Act of 1974 protects the interests of workers and their beneficiaries who are entitled to benefits from employee pension and welfare plans. The law requires disclosure of plan provisions and financial information and establishes standards of conduct for trustees and administrators of welfare and pension plans. It provides funding, participation and vesting requirements for pension plans and makes termination insurance available for most pension plans. The law does not require a company to establish a welfare or pension plan.

Minimum wage laws governing private employers are in operation in 45 jurisdictions: 41 states, the District of Columbia, Guam, Puerto Rico and the Virgin Islands have minimum wage laws and minimum wage rates. As of 1 Aug. 1978, all but one of the laws cover men, women and, usually, minors. The exception covers only women and minors. The minimum wage rate under federal law is $3.35 per hour for employees who are engaged in commerce, in the production of goods for commerce or in certain enterprises which are engaged in commerce as well as federal employees.

A total of 81 strikes and lockouts of 1,000 workers or more occurred in 1983, involving 909,000 workers and 17·5m. idle days; the number of idle days was 0·08% of the year's total working time of all workers.

There are 3 federal agencies which provide formal machinery for the adjustment of labour disputes: (1) The Federal Mediation and Conciliation Service, now an independent agency, whose mediation services are available 'in any labor dispute in any industry affecting commerce'; under Executive Order 11491, as amended, to federal agencies and organizations of federal employees involved in negotiation disputes; and in state and local government collective bargaining disputes when adequate dispute resolution machinery is not available to the parties. Its aim is to prevent and minimize work stoppages. (2) The National Mediation Board (1934) provides much the same facilities for the railroad and air-transport industries pursuant to the Railway Labor Act. (3) The National Railroad Adjustment Board (1934) acts as a board of final appeal for grievances arising over the interpretation of existing collective agreements under the Railway Labor Act; its decisions are binding upon both sides and enforceable by the courts.

The National Labor Relations Act, as amended by the Labor–Management Relations (Taft–Hartley) Act, 1947 (*see* THE STATESMAN'S YEAR-BOOK, 1955, p. 617), was amended by the Labor–Management Reporting and Disclosure Act, 1959, and again amended in 1974. The 1959 Act requires extensive reporting and disclosure of certain financial and administrative practices of labour organizations, employers and labour relations consultants. In addition, certain powers are vested in the Secretary of Labor to prevent abuses in the administration of trusteeships by labour organizations, to provide minimum standards and procedures for the election of union officers and to establish rules prescribing minimum standards for determining the adequacy of union procedures for the removal of officers. Other provisions impose a fiduciary responsibility upon union officers and provide for the exclusion of those convicted of certain named felonies from office for specified periods; more stringently regulate secondary boycotts and banning of 'hot' cargo agreements; put limitations upon organizational and recognition picketing and permit States to assert jurisdiction over labour disputes where the National Labor Relations Board declines to act. The Act also contains a 'Bill of Rights' for union members (enforceable directly by them) dealing with such things as equal rights in the nomination and election of union officers, freedom of speech and assembly subject to reasonable union rules, and safeguards against improper disciplinary action.

The Bureau of Labor Statistics estimated that in 1983 the labour force was 113,226,000 (64·4% of those 16 years and over); the resident armed forces accounted for 1,676,000 and the civilian labour force for 111·55m., of whom 100,834,000 were employed and 10,717,000—or 9·6%—were unemployed. The following table shows civilian employment by industry and sex and percentage distribution of the total:

Industry Group	*Male*	*Female*	*Total*	*Percentage distribution*
Employed (1,000 persons):	56,787	44,047	100,834	100·0
Agriculture, forestry and fisheries	2,838	705	3,542	3·5
Mining	761	161	921	0·9
Construction	5,640	509	6,149	6·1
Manufacturing:				
Durable goods	8,629	3,079	11,708	11·6
Non-durable (including not specified)	4,825	3,412	8,238	8·2
Transportation, communication and other public utilities	5,204	1,784	6,988	6·9
Wholesale and retail trade	11,197	9,948	21,145	21·0
Finance, insurance and real estate	2,752	3,758	6,510	6·5
Business and repair services	3,204	1,711	4,916	4·9
Personal services (including private household)	1,161	2,916	4,077	4·0
Entertainment and recreation services	739	476	1,215	1·2
Professional and related services	7,009	13,707	20,716	20·5
Public administration	2,829	1,880	4,709	4·7

Bureau of Labor Statistics, US Dept. of Labor. *Directory of National Unions and Employee Associations in the US.* 1979. *Brief History of the American Labor Movement.* 1976.—*Analysis of Work Stoppages.* 1979.—*Employment and Earnings.* Monthly

A Guide to Basic Law and Procedures under the National Labor Relations Act, National Labor Relations Board, Washington, D.C., 1976

Brody, D., *Workers in Industrial America: Essays on the Twentieth-century Struggle.* New York, 1980

Commerce. The subjoined table gives the total value of the imports and exports of merchandise by yearly average or by year (in $1m.):

	Exports		General		Exports [2]		General
	Total	US mdse.[1]	imports		Total	US mdse.[1]	imports [2]
1946–50	11,829	11,673	6,659	1979	181,816	178,578	210,285
1951–55	15,333	15,196	10,832	1980	220,783	216,668	245,262
1956–60	19,204	19,029	13,650	1981	233,739	228,961	260,982
1961–65	24,006	24,707	17,659	1982	212,275	207,158	243,952
1970	43,224	42,590	39,952	1983	200,538	195,969	258,048

[1] Excludes re-exports. [2] Includes US Virgin Islands trade with foreign countries.

For a description of how imports and exports are valued, see *Explanation of Statistics of Report FT990, Highlights of US Export and Import Trade,* Bureau of the Census, US Department of Commerce, Washington, D.C., 1946.

The 'most favoured nation' treatment in commerce between Great Britain and US was agreed to for 4 years by the treaty of 1815, was extended for 10 years by the treaty of 1818, and indefinitely (subject to 12 months' notice) by that of 1827.

Imports and exports of gold and silver bullion and specie in calendar years (in $1,000):

	Gold		Silver	
	Exports	Imports	Exports	Imports
1932	809,528	363,315	13,850	19,650
1940	4,995	4,749,467	3,674	58,434
1944	959,228	113,836	126,915	23,373
1955	7,257	104,592	8,331	72,932
1960	1,647	335,032	25,789	57,438
1965	1,285,097	101,669	54,061	64,769
1970	36,887	227,472	53,003	58,838
1975	429,278	406,583	104,086	274,106
1980	2,787,431	2,508,520	1,326,878	1,336,009
1982	590,947	1,650,719	105,977	786,154
1983	825,418	1,575,570	169,383	1,926,102

The domestic exports of US produce, including military, and the imports for consumption by economic classes for 3 calendar years were (in $m.):

	Exports (US merchandise)			Imports for consumption		
	1981	1982	1983	1981	1982	1983
Food and live animals	30,291	23,950	24,166	15,233	14,453	15,412
Crude materials	20,993	19,248	18,596	11,193	8,585	9,590
Machinery and transport equipment	95,736	87,148	82,578	69,627	73,320	86,131
Chemicals	21,187	19,890	19,751	9,448	9,493	10,779
Total	168,207	150,236	145,091	105,501	105,851	121,912

Leading exports of US merchandise are listed below for the calendar year 1983: Special category merchandise is included. Data for major subdivisions of certain classes are also given:

Commodity	$1m.	Commodity	$1m.
Machinery, total	54,309	Chemicals	19,751
Power generating machinery	8,718	Chemical elements and compounds	8,378
Metalworking machinery	1,121	Plastic materials and resins	3,732
Agricultural machines and tractors	2,346	Soybeans	5,925
Office machines	11,669	Cotton	1,817
Telecommunications apparatus	3,804	Textiles and apparel	2,368
Electrical apparatus	11,936	Tobacco and manufactures	2,587
Electrical power machinery and switchgear	2,379	Iron and steel-mill products	1,415
		Non-ferrous base metals and alloys	1,606
Automobiles (and parts)	14,463	Pulp, paper and products	4,469
Aircraft (and parts)	12,189	Coal	4,115
Grains and preparations	15,152	Fruits, nuts and vegetables	2,444
Wheat (and flour)	6,509	Petroleum and products	4,557
Coarse grains	7,408	Firearms of war and ammunition	3,092

Chief imports for 28 commodity classes for consumption for the calendar year 1983:

Commodity	*$1m.*	*Commodity*	*$1m.*
Petroleum and products	52,325	Rubber	655
Petroleum	36,809	Textiles and apparel	12,808
Petroleum products	15,516	Clothing	9,583
Non-ferrous base metals	7,422	Cotton fabrics, woven	560
Copper	1,341	Machinery, total	46,975
Aluminium	1,629	Electrical machinery and parts	12,499
Nickel	524	Agricultural machines and tractors	1,196
Bauxite, crude	...	Office machines	6,759
Tin	453	Coffee	2,590
Pulp, paper and products	5,723	Chemicals	10,779
Newsprint	2,759	Chemical elements and compounds	6,044
Wood pulp	1,470	Uranium oxide	199
Fertilizers	997	Plywood	754
Sugar	1,047	Oils and fats	495
Iron and steel-mill products	6,338	Cocoa (and cacao beans)	349
Cattle, meat and preparations	2,335	Glass and pottery	1,602
Automobiles and parts	35,034	Footwear	4,010
Fish (and shellfish)	3,594	Toys and sports goods	2,506
Fruit, nuts and vegetables	2,920	Furs, undressed	126
Alcoholic beverages	2,626	Telecommunications apparatus	11,278
Wool and other hair	176	Artworks and antiques	2,017
Metal manufactures	4,504	Grains and animal feeds	483
Diamonds (excl. industrial)	2,275		

Total trade beween the USA and the UK for 5 years (British Department of Trade returns, in £1,000 sterling):

	1980	*1981*	*1982*	*1983*	*1984*
Imports to UK	6,043,774	6,048,305	6,638,250	7,442,671	9,356,029
Exports and re-exports from UK	6,668,342	6,258,157	7,457,114	8,336,979	10,149,479

Imports and exports by continents, areas and selected countries for calendar years (in $1m.):

	General imports		*Exports incl. re-exports* [1]	
Area and country	*1982*	*1983*	*1982*	*1983*
Canada	46,477	52,130	33,720	38,244
20 American Republics	32,513	35,683	30,086	22,618
Western Europe	52,346	53,884	60,054	55,980
Western Hemisphere	84,467	93,873	67,312	63,970
Canada	46,477	52,130	33,720	38,244
20 American Republics	32,513	35,683	30,086	22,618
Central American Common Market	1,467	1,585	1,405	1,494
Costa Rica	358	387	330	382
El Salvador	319	348	292	365
Guatemala	336	371	390	316
Honduras	365	381	275	299
Nicaragua	90	97	119	132
Panama	255	337	839	748
Latin American FTA	29,850	32,611	26,879	19,378
Argentina	1,128	853	1,294	965
Brazil	4,285	4,946	3,423	2,557
Chile	666	969	925	729
Colombia	801	970	1,903	1,514
Ecuador	1,131	1,429	828	597
Mexico	15,566	16,776	11,817	9,082
Paraguay	39	32	78	37
Peru	1,099	1,151	1,117	900
Uruguay	258	381	190	86
Dominican Republic	629	814	664	632
Haiti	310	336	299	366
Bolivia	109	166	99	102
Venezuela	4,768	4,938	5,206	2,811
Bahamas	1,050	1,687	590	452
Netherlands Antilles	2,117	2,291	660	553
Jamaica	294	273	468	452
Trinidad and Tobago	1,627	1,318	894	728

[1] 'Special category' exports are included in these totals.

Area and country	General imports 1982	General imports 1983	Exports incl. re-exports[1] 1982	Exports incl. re-exports[1] 1983
Europe				
Western Europe	52,346	53,884	60,054	55,980
OECD Countries	51,966	53,468	59,378	55,261
European Economic Community[2]	42,509	43,892	47,932	44,311
Belgium and Luxembourg	2,396	2,412	5,229	5,049
Denmark	904	1,067	732	649
France	5,545	6,025	7,110	5,961
Germany (Fed. Rep.)	11,975	12,695	9,291	8,737
Ireland	556	560	983	1,115
Italy	5,301	5,455	4,616	3,908
Netherlands	2,494	2,970	8,604	7,767
UK	13,095	12,470	10,645	10,621
Greece	242	238	721	503
Turkey	274	320	868	783
EFTA countries	...	...	...	...
Austria	491	447	371	371
Norway	1,973	1,358	950	813
Portugal	283	280	838	1,212
Sweden	1,993	2,429	1,689	1,581
Switzerland	2,340	2,494	2,707	2,960
Finland	414	496	489	413
Iceland	184	219	77	53
Spain	1,505	1,533	3,456	2,763
Yugoslavia	360	386	494	572
Soviet bloc.	1,067	1,359	3,610	2,891
Poland	212	189	295	324
USSR	228	347	2,587	2,003
Asia[3] [4]	85,686	91,743	67,409	66,483
Near East	11,812	7,135	15,950	13,796
Egypt	547	303	2,875	2,813
Iran	585	1,130	122	190
Iraq	39	59	846	512
Israel	1,164	1,255	2,271	2,017
Kuwait	40	130	941	741
Lebanon	19	17	294	484
Saudi Arabia	7,443	3,627	9,026	7,903
Japan	37,744	41,183	20,966	21,894
Other Asia	45,139	48,035	40,912	39,725
Bangladesh	70	88	227	190
Hong Kong	5,540	6,394	2,453	2,564
India	1,404	2,191	1,599	1,828
Indonesia	4,224	5,285	2,025	1,466
Korea, Republic of	5,637	7,148	5,529	5,925
Malaysia	1,885	2,124	1,736	1,684
Singapore	2,195	2,868	3,214	3,759
Pakistan	165	167	700	812
Philippines	1,806	2,001	1,854	1,807
Sri Lanka	175	185	198	75
Thailand	884	967	915	1,063
Taiwan (Formosa)	8,893	11,204	4,367	4,667
Vietnam	–	–	32	21
China	2,284	2,244	2,912	2,173
Oceania	3,131	3,044	5,700	4,827
Australia	2,287	2,222	4,535	3,954
New Zealand and W. Samoa	777	737	900	625

[1] See note on previous page.
[2] 1982 and 1983 figures include Greece.
[3] Includes Egypt.
[4] Excludes Yemen (Aden) (formerly Southern Yemen), and Bahrain.

Area and country	General imports 1982	1983	Exports incl. re-exports[1] 1982	1983
Africa[2]	17,223	14,122	7,396	5,955
Algeria	2,673	3,551	909	594
Ethiopia	102	87	43	43
Libya	512	–	301	191
Morocco	45	31	397	440
Ghana	362	120	116	119
Liberia	91	91	113	110
Nigeria	7,045	3,736	1,295	864
Kenya	71	65	98	69
Zaïre	407	366	91	83
South Africa, Republic of[3]	1,973	2,028	2,376	2,133

[1] See note on p. 1407.
[2] Excludes Egypt.
[3] Includes also South-West Africa (Namibia).

US Department of Commerce, Bureau of Census. Report FT 990, Highlights of US Export and Import Trade

Tourism. In 1983, 21·7m. tourists visited the USA and spent over US$11,400m. They came mainly from Canada (12m.), Europe (3m.), Mexico (1·9m.) and Asia (2·1m.). Approximately 24·9m. US tourists travelled abroad, mainly to Canada (11·2m.), Europe (4·7m.), Mexico (3·9m.) and the Caribbean and Central America (2·9m.).

COMMUNICATIONS

Roads. On 31 Dec. 1983 the total US public road[1] mileage, including rural and urban roads, amounted to 3,879,638 miles, of which 3,424,530 miles were surfaced roads. The total mileage cited includes 817,206 miles of rural roads under control of the states, 2,137,960 miles of local rural roads, 263,015 miles of federal park and forest roads, and 662,350 miles of urban roads and streets. Expenditures for construction and maintenance amounted to $34,541m. in 1983.

By the end of 1983, toll roads, financed by private capital through bond issues and administered by state toll authorities, totalled 4,679 miles (including some under construction) compared with 344 miles in 1940.

Motor vehicles registered in the calendar year 1983 were (Federal Highways Administration) 163,861,169, including 126,727,870 automobiles, 585,515 buses and 36,547,781 trucks.

Inter-city trucks (private and for hire) averaged 502,000m. revenue net ton-miles in 1982. Of the 585,515 buses in service in 1983, 470,727 were school buses. Inter-city service operated a total of 1,140m. bus-miles and carried a total of 390m. revenue passengers in 1982.

There were 42,595 deaths in road accidents in 1983.

[1] Public road mileage excludes that mileage not open to public travel, not maintained by public authority, or not passable by standard four-wheel vehicles. This excluded mileage was reported to the US Federal Highway Administration prior to 1981.

Railways. Railway history in the USA commences in 1828, but the first railway to convey both freight and passengers in regular service (between Baltimore and Ellicott's Mills, Md., 13 miles) dates from 24 May 1830. Mileage rose to 52,922 miles in 1870; to 167,191 miles in 1890, and to a peak of 266,381 miles in 1916, falling thereafter to 261,871 in 1925; 246,739 in 1940 and 222,164 in 1969 (these include some duplication under trackage rights and some mileage operated in Canada by US companies). The ordinary gauge is 4 ft 8½ in. (about 99·6% of total mileage). The USA has about 29% of the world's railway mileage.

In addition to the independent railroad companies, railway service is provided by two federally-assisted organizations, the National Railroad Passenger Corporation (Amtrak), and the Consolidated Rail Corporation (Conrail).

Amtrak was set up on 1 May 1971 to maintain a basic network of inter-city passenger trains with government assistance, and is responsible for almost all non-commuter services with 27,000 miles of route. From 1 Jan. 1983, an Amtrak commuter division took over from Conrail all commuter services not acquired by State or regional agencies.

Conrail was established on 1 April 1976 to run freight services in the industrial north-east formerly operated by the bankrupt Penn Central, Reading, Lehigh Valley, Central of New Jersey, Erie Lackawanna, Lehigh & Hudson railroads, and Pennyslvania-Reading Seashore Lines which is being returned to the private sector in 1985.

The following table, based on the figures of the Interstate Commerce Commission, shows some railway statistics for 4 calendar years:

	1960	*1970*	*1980*[2]	*1983*[1 2]
Classes I and II Railroads				
Mileage owned (first main tracks)	223,779	204,621	157,078	144,506
Revenue freight originated (1m. short tons)	1,421	1,572	1,537	1,279
Freight ton-mileage (1m. ton-miles)	591,550	771,012	932,748	825,250
Passengers carried (1,000)	488,019	289,469	281,503	[3]
Passenger-miles (1m.)	31,790	10,786	6,557	[3]
Operating revenues ($1m.)	9,587	12,209	28,708	26,559
Operating expenses ($1m.)	7,135	9,806	26,761	23,980
Net railway operating income ($1m.)	1,055	506	1,364	1,817
Net income after fixed charges ($1m.)	855	126	2,029	2,642
Class I Railroads:				
Locomotives in service	40,949	27,086	28,240	25,495
Steam locomotives	25,640	—	—	—
Freight-train cars (excluding caboose cars)	1,721,269	1,423,921	1,101,343	943,799
Passenger-train cars	57,146	11,177	2,219	714
Average number of employees	1,220,784	566,282	458,996	322,050
Average wage per week ($1)	72.59	188.71	474.21	617.79

[1] Class I railroads only. From 1981, Class II railroads were no longer required to file annual reports.
[2] Data for National Railroad Passenger Corporation excluded.
[3] This data has been discontinued.

Aviation. In civil aviation there were, on 31 Dec. 1983, 718,004 certified pilots (including 147,197 student pilots) and 264,866 registered civil aircraft.

Airports on 31 Dec. 1983: Air carrier, 677; general aviation, 15,352. Of these airports, 12,653 were conventional land-based, while 392 were seaplane bases, 2,918 were heliports and 66 stolports (STOL—Short Take-Off and Landing).

Statistics from the Civil Aeronautics Board indicate that for 12 months ended June 1984 on US flag carriers in scheduled international service there were 23·04m. enplanements with 313·9m. aircraft miles (excluding all-cargo) for a total of 64,710m. revenue passenger-miles. The non-scheduled airlines had a total of 13,104m. revenue passenger-miles internationally and domestically. Domestically US scheduled airlines in 1984 had 304·3m. enplanements with a total of 2,615m. aircraft miles for 230,647m. revenue passenger-miles. (A revenue passenger-mile is one paying passenger carried per mile.) The Civil Aeronautics Board ceased to exist as an independent agency on 31 Dec. 1984 and its functions were transferred to the Department of Transportation.

Shipping. On 1 Sept. 1984 the US merchant marine included 752 sea-going vessels of 1,000 gross tons or over, with aggregate dead-weight tonnage of 24m. This included 274 tankers of 16·1m. DWT.

On 1 Sept. 1984 US merchant ocean-going vessels were employed as follows: Active, 399 of 15·6m. DWT, of which 147 of 5m. tons were foreign trade, 188 of 9·4m. tons in domestic trade and 64 of 1·4m. tons in other US agency operations. Inactive vessels totalled 8m. DWT; 112 of 5·6m. DWT privately owned were laid up and 241 of 2·8m. tons were Government-owned National Defense reserve fleet. Of the total vessels in the US fleet, 501 of 21m. DWT were privately owned.

US exports and imports carried on dry cargo and tanker vessels in the year 1983 totalled 630m. long tons, of which 36·7m. long tons or 5·8% were carried in US flag vessels.

Post and Broadcasting. Until the beginning of 1984 the telephone business was largely in the hands of the American Telephone and Telegraph Company (AT & T) and its telephone operating subsidiaries, which together were known as the Bell System. Pursuant to a government anti-trust suit, the Bell System was broken up, with the telephone operating companies being divested from AT & T to create seven regional companies for providing local service. There are also many hundreds of smaller telephone companies having no common ownership affiliation with the Bell companies, but which connect with them for universal service, countrywide and worldwide. In addition, several new entrants have begun to compete with AT & T in the long-distance telephone market. The message telegraph and telex services are in the hands of The Western Union Telegraph Company, and the international record carriers, which compete with the telephone industry in providing leased private lines. Western Union also provides an inter-city telephone service.

The number of telephones in service in the USA has increased in the period since 1945 at a much faster rate than has the population. Among principal reasons are the significant increase in the percentage of households with telephone service and the enormous growth in the number of extension telephones.

In marked contrast, the number of public telegrams has decreased by a substantial amount. Telegrams have lost favour due to shifts in user preference to the air-mail and to the telephone. The telex services of the telegraph company have also found broad acceptance in place of telegrams for business purposes. The following table contains key data items on a comparative basis for the domestic telephone and message telegraph services:

	1960	*1970*	*1980*	*1983*[1]
All telephone systems:				
Total telephones	74,342,000	120,218,000	180,425,000	181,891,000[2]
Bell System:				
Total telephones	60,735,100	96,561,000	141,674,000	142,386,000[2]
Average daily telephone calls	219,093,000	368,363,000	580,230,000	601,200,000[2]
Local	209,373,000	346,505,000	527,543,000	544,886,000[2]
Long distance	9,720,000	21,858,000	52,687,000	56,314,000[2]
Total plant in service ($1,000)	24,072,499	54,813,202	132,831,794	163,052,567
Total operating revenues ($1,000)	7,958,125	17,094,846	51,203,404	69,229,482
Employees, number	580,405	772,980	847,768	...
Western Union Telegraph Co.:				
Public telegrams for year	102,931,000	46,084,000	40,801,398	29,805,460
Total plant ($1,000)	398,023	1,029,149	2,101,007	2,285,678
Revenue from public telegrams ($1,000)	160,746	126,739	115,612	116,143
Total operating revenues ($1,000)	262,365	402,456	696,972	722,096
Employees, number	32,655	24,293	12,649	...

[1] Preliminary. [2] 1981.

International communication services, providing overseas connexions with all parts of the world, are furnished principally by the American Telephone and Telegraph Company and three telegraph companies. The old submarine cable telegraph systems have all been abandoned in favour of using telegraph circuits derived from voice channels in the newer telephone ocean cables, which have also made inroads on the use of high-frequency radio. More recently, satellite communications facilities have been utilized not only for telephone and telegraph services but for television and data transmission as well.

International overseas telegrams, inbound to and outbound from the continental US, numbered 9·2m. in 1982 (11·7m. in 1980). This service has tended to decline in volume in recent years. It first lost ground to the air-mail and then to the telex and telephone services. For the US and its possessions the volume of international overseas telephone calls has grown enormously with the availability of the excellent voice-transmission qualities provided in the telephone ocean cables and in the satellite radio relays. Whereas international telephone calls were 990,000 in 1955, the last year in which there was no cable service available, there were 149·6m. such calls in 1980.

Postal business for the years ended 30 Sept. included the following items:

	1980	*1981*	*1982*	*1983*
Number of post offices, on 30 June [1]	39,486	39,457	39,447	39,445
Postal operating revenue ($1,000) [2]	17,142,760	19,133,041	22,599,937	23,581,667
Postal expenses ($1,000) [3]	19,412,587	21,369,139	22,826,217	24,083,100

[1] The US Postal Service was established 1 July 1971. Financial statements prior to that date are those of the Post Office Department. Such statements for 1968–71 have been restated to be in a format and on an accounting principle basis generally consistent with 1972.

[2] Operating revenue excludes government appropriations, operating reimbursements and other income.

[3] Operating expenses are stated net of operating reimbursements and exclude certain costs financed by revenue.

On 1 Jan. 1975 there were in the USA and Territories, 7,068 authorized commercial radio stations, 711 commercial television stations: of non-commercial stations 717 were for radio, 241 for television.

Cinemas. Cinemas increased from 17,003 in 1940 to 20,239 in 1950 and decreased to 42,187 in 1967.

Newspapers. Of the daily newspapers being published in the USA in 1971, 339 were morning papers with a circulation of 26,116,000, and 1,425 were evening papers with a circulation of 36,115,000. The 590 Sunday papers had a total circulation of 49·7m.

JUSTICE, RELIGION, EDUCATION AND WELFARE

Justice. Legal controversies may be decided in two systems of courts: the federal courts, with jurisdiction confined to certain matters enumerated in Article III of the Constitution, and the state courts, with jurisdiction in all other proceedings. The federal courts have jurisdiction exclusive of the state courts in criminal prosecutions for the violation of federal statutes, in civil cases involving the government, in bankruptcy cases and in admiralty proceedings, and have jurisdiction concurrent with the state courts over suits between parties from different states, and certain suits involving questions of federal law.

The highest court is the Supreme Court of the US, which reviews cases from the lower federal courts and certain cases originating in state courts involving questions of federal law. It is the final arbiter of all questions involving federal statutes and the Constitution; and it has the power to invalidate any federal or state law or executive action which it finds repugnant to the Constitution. This court, consisting of 9 justices who receive salaries of $94,700 a year (the Chief Justice, $100,700), meets from Oct. until June every year and disposes of about 4,450 cases, deciding about 380 on their merits. In the remainder of cases it either summarily affirms lower court decisions or declines to review. A few suits, usually brought by state governments, originate in the Supreme Court, but issues of fact are mostly referred to a master.

The US courts of appeals number 12 (in 11 circuits composed of 3 or more states and 1 circuit for the District of Columbia); the 132 circuit judges receive salaries of $77,300 a year. Any party to a suit in a lower federal court usually has a right of appeal to one of these courts. In addition, there are direct appeals to these courts from many federal administrative agencies. In the year ending 30 June 1983, 29,630 appeals were filed in the courts of appeals.

The trial courts in the federal system are the US district courts, of which there are 89 in the 50 states, 1 in the District of Columbia and 1 each in the territories of Puerto Rico, Virgin Islands, Guam and the Northern Marianas. Each state has at least 1 US district court, and 3 states have 4 apiece. Each district court has from 1 to 27 judgeships. There are 515 US district judges ($73,100 a year), who handle about 241,850 civil cases and 48,450 criminal defendants every year.

In addition to these courts of general jurisdiction, there are special federal courts of limited jurisdiction. US Claims Court (6 judges at $77,300 a year) decides claims for money damages against the federal government in a wide variety of matters; the Court of International Trade determines controversies concerning the classification and valuation of imported merchandise.

The judges of all these courts are appointed by the President with the approval of the Senate; to assure their independence, they hold office during good behaviour and cannot have their salaries reduced. This does not apply to the territorial judges, who hold their offices for a term of years. The judges may retire with full pay at the age of 70 years if they have served a period of 10 years, or at 65 if they have 15 years of service, but they are subject to call for such judicial duties as they are willing to undertake. Only 9 US judges up to 1984 have been involved in impeachment proceedings, of whom 3 district judges and 1 commerce judge were convicted and removed from office.

Of the 241,842 civil cases filed in the district courts in the year ending 30 June 1983, about 95,295 arose under various federal statutes (such as labour, social security, tax, patent, securities, antitrust and civil rights laws); 34,210 involved personal injury or property damage claims; 67,276 dealt with contracts; and 8,812 were actions concerning real property.

Of the 35,872 criminal cases filed in the district courts in the year ending 30 June 1983, about 1,900 were charged with alleged infractions of the immigration laws; 3,400, the transport of stolen motor vehicles; about 3,400 larceny and theft; 7,650, embezzlement and fraud; and 7,650 narcotics laws.

Persons convicted of federal crimes are either fined, released on probation under the supervision of the probation officers of the federal courts, confined in prison for a period of up to 6 months and then put on probation (known as split sentencing) or confined in one of the following institutions: 3 for juvenile and youths; 7 for young adults; 7 for intermediate term adults; 7 for short-term adults; 2 for females; 1 hospital and 15 community service centres. In addition, prisoners are confined in centres operated by the National Institutes of Mental Health. In addition, prisoner drug addicts may be committed to US Public Health Service hospitals for treatment. Prisoners confined in institutions operated by the US Bureau of Prisons for the year ending 30 Sept. 1982, numbered 28,133.

The state courts have jurisdiction over all civil and criminal cases arising under state laws, but decisions of the state courts of last resort as to the validity of treaties or of laws of the US, or on other questions arising under the Constitution, are subject to review by the Supreme Court of the US. The state court systems are generally similar to the federal system, to the extent that they generally have a number of trial courts and intermediate appellate courts, and a single court of last resort. The highest court in each state is usually called the Supreme Court or Court of Appeals with a Chief Justice and Associate Justices, usually elected but sometimes appointed by the Governor with the advice and consent of the State Senate or other advisory body; they usually hold office for a term of years, but in some instances for life or during good behaviour. Their salaries range from $24,000 to $84,584 a year. The lowest tribunals are usually those of Justices of the Peace; many towns and cities have municipal and police courts, with power to commit for trial in criminal matters and to determine misdemeanours for violation of the municipal ordinances; they frequently try civil cases involving limited amounts.

The death penalty is illegal in Alaska, Hawaii, Iowa, Maine, Minnesota, Oregon, West Virginia, Wisconsin and Michigan; in North Dakota it is legal only for treason and first-degree murder committed by a prisoner serving a life sentence for first-degree murder, in Rhode Island only for murder committed by a prisoner serving a life sentence and in Vermont and New York for the murder of a peace officer in the line of duty and for first-degree murder by those who kill while serving a life sentence for murder. The death penalty is legal in 37 states. Until 1982 it had fallen into disuse and had been abolished *de facto* in many states. The US Supreme Court had held the death penalty, as applied in general criminal statutes, to contravene the eighth and fourteenth amendments of the US constitution, as a cruel and unusual punishment when used so irregularly and rarely as to destroy its deterrent value.

In 1967 only 2 persons were executed under civil authority; both for murder. There were no executions 1968–76. In 1977 a convicted murderer requested that he should be executed and after a lengthy legal dispute the sentence was carried out at Utah state prison. Six persons were executed between 1977 and 1982. In Jan. 1983, 1,050 prisoners in 31 states were reported under sentence of death.

The total number of civilian executions carried out in the US from 1930 to 1982 was 3,866.

Federal 'Political' Crimes. Prosecutions for what may be loosely described as 'political' offences, or crimes directed towards the overthrow by violence of the federal government, which were somewhat numerous in the early 1950s, have declined sharply over the last 20 years and are now exceedingly rare.

A Guide to Court Systems. Institute of Judicial Administration. New York, 1960
The United States Courts. Administrative Office of the US Courts, Washington, D.C., 20544
Blumberg, A. S., *Criminal Justice: Issues and Ironies.* 2nd ed. New York, 1973
Huston, L. A., *The Department of Justice.* New York, 1967
Huston, L. A., and others, *Roles of the Attorney General of the United States.* New York, 1968
McCloskey, R. G., *The Modern Supreme Court.* Harvard Univ. Press, 1972
McLauchlan, W. P., *American Legal Processes.* New York, 1977
Walker, S. E., *Popular Justice.* New York, 1980

Religion. *The Yearbook of American and Canadian Churches for 1984,* published by the National Council of the Churches of Christ in the USA, New York, presents the latest figures available from official statisticians of church bodies. The large majority of reports are for the calendar year 1982, or a fiscal year ending 1982. The 1982 reports indicated that there were 139,603,059 members with 341,111 local churches. There were 329,802 clergymen serving in local congregations. The principal religious bodies (numerically or historically) or groups of religious bodies are shown below:

Denominations	*Local churches*	*Total membership*
Summary:		
Protestant bodies	310,284	76,754,009
Roman Catholic Church	24,071	52,088,774
Jews [1]	3,500	5,725,000
Eastern Churches	1,632	3,859,668
Old Catholic, Polish National Catholic and Armenian	427	924,861
Buddhists	62	100,000
Miscellaneous [2]	1,135	150,747
1982 totals	341,111	139,603,059 [3]

Protestant Church Membership	*Total membership*
Baptist bodies	
Southern Baptist Convention	13,991,709
National Baptist Convention, USA	5,500,000
National Baptist Convention of America, Inc.	2,668,799
National Primitive Baptist Convention	250,000
American Baptist Churches in the USA	1,621,795
American Baptist Association	225,000
Progressive National Baptist Convention	521,692
Conservative Baptist Association of America	225,000
Regular Baptist Churches	300,839
Free Will Baptists	243,658
Baptist Missionary Association of America	226,953
Christian Church (Disciples of Christ)	1,156,458
Christian Churches and Churches of Christ	1,063,254
Church of the Nazarene	498,491
Churches of Christ	1,605,000
The Episcopal Church	2,794,139
Latter-Day Saints:	
Church of Jesus Christ of Latter-Day Saints	3,521,000
Reorganized Church of Jesus Christ of Latter-Day Saints	201,460
Lutheran Bodies:	
Lutheran Church in America	2,925,655
The Lutheran Church-Missouri Synod	2,630,823

[1] Includes Orthodox, Conservative and Reformed bodies.
[2] Includes non-Christian bodies such as Spiritualists, Ethical Culture, Unitarian-Universalists.
[3] Care should be taken in interpreting membership statistics for the US Churches. Some statistics are accurately compiled and others are estimates. Also statistics are not always comparable.

Protestant Church Membership	*Total membership*
Lutheran Bodies *(contd.)*:	
The American Lutheran Church	2,346,710
Wisconsin Evangelical Lutheran Synod	412,529
Methodist Bodies:	
United Methodist Church	9,457,012
African Methodist Episcopal Church	2,210,000
African Methodist Episcopal Zion Church	1,134,179
Christian Methodist Episcopal Church	786,707
Pentecostal Bodies:	
Assemblies of God	1,879,182
Church of God in Christ, International	200,000
Church of God in Christ	3,709,661
Church of God (Cleveland, Tenn.)	463,992
United Pentecostal Church, International, Inc.	465,000
Presbyterian Bodies: [1]	
United Presbyterian Church in the USA	2,342,441
Presbyterian Church in the US	814,931
Reformed Churches:	
Reformed Church in America	346,293
Christian Reformed Church	223,976
The Salvation Army	419,475
Seventh-day Adventists	606,310
United Church of Christ	1,716,723

[1] In June 1983, these two Presbyterian Bodies merged to form Presbyterian Church (USA).

Yearbook of American and Canadian Churches. Annual, from 1951. New York
Clarke, E. T., *The Small Sects in America.* Rev. ed. New York, 1949
Johnson, A. W., and Yost, F. H., *Separation of Church and State in the United States.* Minneapolis and London, 1949
Mead, F. S., *Handbook of Denominations in the US.* 6th ed. Nashville, 1975

Education. Under the system of government in the USA, elementary and secondary education is committed in the main to the several states. Each of the 50 states and the District of Columbia has a system of free public schools, established by law, with courses covering 12 years plus kindergarten. There are 3 structural patterns in common use; the K8–4 plan, meaning kindergarten plus 8 elementary grades followed by 4 high school grades; the K6–3–3 plan, or kindergarten plus 6 elementary grades followed by a 3-year junior high school and a 3-year senior high school; and the K6–6 plan, kindergarten plus 6 elementary grades followed by a 6-year high school. All plans lead to high-school graduation, usually at age 17 or 18. Vocational education is an integral part of secondary education. In addition, some states have, as part of the free public school system, 2-year colleges in which education is provided at a nominal cost. Each state has delegated a large degree of control of the educational programme to local school districts (numbering 15,840 in autumn 1982), each with a board of education (usually 3 to 9 members) selected locally and serving mostly without pay. The school policies of the local school districts must be in accord with the laws and the regulations of their state Departments of Education. While regulations differ from one jurisdiction to another, in general it may be said that school attendance is compulsory between the ages of 7 to 16.

The Census Bureau estimates that in Nov. 1979 only 1m. or 0·6% of the 170m. persons who were 14 years of age or older were unable to read and write; in 1930 the percentage was 4·8. In 1940 a new category was established—the 'functionally illiterate', meaning those who had completed fewer than 5 years of elementary schooling; for persons 25 years of age or over this percentage was 3 in March 1982 (for the non-white population alone it was 7·4%); it was 0·8% for white and 0·7% for non-whites in the 25–29-year-old group. The Bureau reported that in March 1982 the median years of school completed by all persons 25 years old and over was 12·6, and that 17·7% had completed 4 or more years of college. For the 25–29-year-old group, the median school years completed was 12·8 and 21·7% had completed 4 or more years of college.

In the autumn of 1983, 12,465,000 students (6,024,000 men and 6,441,000 women) were enrolled in 3,284 colleges and universities; 2,444,000 were first-time students. About 26% of the population between the ages of 18 and 24 were enrolled in colleges and universities.

Public elementary and secondary school revenue is supplied from the county and other local sources (44·6% in 1982–83), state sources (48·3%) and federal sources (7·1%). In 1982–83 expenditure for public elementary and secondary education totalled about $119·1m., including $108·1m. for regular day school programmes, $2·1m. for other programmes, $6,500m. for capital outlay and $2·4m. for interest on school debt. The current expenditure per pupil in average daily attendance was about $2,948. The total cost per pupil, also including capital outlay and interest, amounted to about $3,190. Estimated total expenditures, for private elementary and secondary schools in 1982–83 were about $9,000m. In 1981–82 the 3,280 universities and colleges expended $70,339m. from current funds, of which $46,219m. was spent by institutions under public control. The federal government contributed 11·5% of total current-fund revenue; state governments, 30·3%; student tuition and fees, 21·9%; and all other sources, 36·3%.

Vocational education below college grade, including the training of teachers to conduct such education, has been federally aided since 1918. During the school year 1979–80 enrolments in the vocational classes were: Agriculture, 879,000; distributive occupations, 961,000; health occupations, 834,000; home economics, 3,938,000; trade and industry, 3,216,000; technical education, 499,000; office occupations, 3·4m.; other programmes, 2,726,000. Federal support funds were $745,481,000.

Summary of statistics of regular schools (public and private), teachers and pupils in autumn 1983 (compiled by the US National Center for Education Statistics):

Schools by level	*Number of schools 1980–81*	*Teachers autumn 1983*	*Enrolment autumn 1983*
Elementary schools:			
Public	61,069	1,175,000	23,655,000
Private	16,792	230,000	4,200,000
Secondary schools:			
Public	24,362	950,000	15,673,000
Private	5,678	100,000	1,500,000
Higher education:			
Public	1,497	515,000	9,683,000
Private	1,734	200,000	2,782,000
Total	111,132	3,170,000	57,493,000

Most of the private elementary and secondary schools are affiliated with religious denominations. Of the children attending private elementary and secondary schools in 1983, nearly 3,200,000 or 55·7% were enrolled in Roman Catholic schools.

During the school year 1982–83 high-school graduates numbered about 2,910,000 (about 49% boys and 51% girls). Institutions of higher education conferred 952,998 bachelor's degrees for the academic year 1981–82, 473,364 to men and 479,634 to women; 295,546 master's degrees, 145,532 to men and 150,014 to women; 32,707 doctorates, 22,224 to men and 10,483 to women; and 72,032 first professional degrees, 52,223 to men and 19,809 to women.

During the academic year, 1983–84, 338,900 foreign students were enrolled in American colleges and universities. The percentages of students coming from various areas in 1983–84 were: South and East Asia, 39; Middle East, 17·9; Latin America, 15·5; Africa, 12·3; Europe, 9·4; North America, 4·6; Oceania, 1·2.

School enrolment, Oct. 1983, embraced 95% of the children who were 5 and 6 years old; 99% of the children aged 7–13 years; 95% of those aged 14–17, 50% of those aged 18 and 19, 32% of those aged 20 and 21, and 17% of those aged 22–24 years.

The US National Center for Education Statistics estimates the total enrolment in the autumn of 1984 at all of the country's elementary, secondary and higher educational institutions (public and private) at 56,970,000 (57,493,000 in the autumn of 1983); this was 24·1% of the total population of the USA as of 1 Sept. 1984.

Enrolment at the elementary and secondary school level was expected to be down by 0·9% in autumn 1984 and total enrolment in the colleges and universities to decline by about 1%.

The number of teachers in regular public and private elementary and secondary schools in the autumn of 1984 was expected to decrease slightly to 2,450,000. The average annual salary of the public school teachers was about $22,000 in 1983–84.

Digest of Education Statistics. Annual. Dept. of Education, Washington 20202, D.C. (from 1962)
American Community, Technical and Junior Colleges. 9th ed. American Council on Education. Washington, 1984
American Universities and Colleges. 12th ed. American Council on Education. Washington, 1983
Ayer's Directory of Newspapers and Periodicals. Annual, from 1880. Philadelphia

Health and Welfare. Admission to the practice of medicine (for both doctors of medicine and doctors of osteopathic medicine) is controlled in each state by examining boards directly representing the profession and acting with authority conferred by state law. Although there are a number of variations, the usual time now required to complete basic training is 8 years beyond the secondary school with up to 3 years of additional graduate training. Certification as a specialist may require between 3 and 5 more years of graduate training plus experience in practice. In academic year 1981–82 the 141 US schools (15 osteopathic and 126 allopathic) graduated 16,669 physicians. About 30·2% of first-year students were women. In Dec. 1981 the estimated number of active physicians (MD and DO—in all forms of practice) in the US, Puerto Rico and outlying US areas was 467,700 (1 active physician to 504 population). The distribution of physicians throughout the country is uneven, both by state and by urban–rural areas.

In 1981–82 the 60 dental schools graduated 5,371 dentists. Active dentists in Dec. 1982 numbered 132,000 (1 active dentist to 1,766 population).

In academic year 1981–82, there were 1,422 registered nursing programmes in the US and 74,975 graduates. In Dec. 1981 registered nurses employed full- or part-time were 1 to 188 population.

Number of hospitals listed by the American Hospital Association in 1980 was 6,965, with 1,365,000 beds and 38,892,000 admissions during the year; average daily census was 1·06m. Of the total, 359 hospitals with 117,000 beds were operated by the federal government; 1,835 with 212,000 beds by state and local government; 3,339 with 693,000 beds by non-profit organizations (including church groups); 730 with 87,000 beds are proprietary. The categories of non-federal hospitals are 5,904 short-term general and special hospitals with 992,000 beds; 157 non-federal long-term general and special hospitals with 39,000 beds; 534 psychiatric hospitals with 215,000 beds; 11 tuberculosis hospitals with 2,000 beds.

Social welfare legislation was chiefly the province of the various states until the adoption of the Social Security Act of 14 Aug. 1935. This as amended provides for a federal system of old-age, survivors and disability insurance; health insurance for the aged and disabled; supplemental security income for the aged, blind and disabled; federal state unemployment insurance; and federal grants to states for public assistance (medical assistance for the aged and aid to families with dependent children generally) and for maternal and child-health and child-welfare services. The Social Security Administration of the Department of Health and Human Services has responsibility for the programmes—old-age, survivors and disability insurance, supplemental security income and aid to families with dependent children. The Health Care Financing Administration, an agency of the same Department, has federal responsibility for health insurance for the aged and disabled (Medicare) and medical assistance (Medicaid). The Department's Office of Human Development administers human service programmes for such groups as the elderly, children, youth, native Americans and persons with developmental disabilities, and its Public Health Service supports maternal and child-health services. Unemployment insurance is the responsibility of the Department of Labor.

The Social Security Act provides for protection against the cost of medical care through the two-part programme of health insurance for people 65 and over and for certain disabled people under 65, who receive disability insurance payments or who have permanent kidney failure (Medicare). During fiscal year 1982, payments totalling $34,343m. were made under the hospital insurance part of Medicare on behalf of 29·1m. people. During the same period, $14,806m. was paid under the voluntary medical insurance part of Medicare on behalf of 28·4m. people.

In 1982 about 116m. persons worked in employment covered by old-age, survivors and disability insurance.

In Dec. 1982 over 35·8m. beneficiaries were on the rolls, and the average benefit paid to a retired worker (not counting any paid to his dependants) was about $419 per month.

Benefits paid during calendar year 1982 totalled $156,173m., including $17,339m. paid to disabled workers and their dependants.

In Dec. 1982, 10·5m. persons (adults and children) were receiving payments under aid to families with dependent children (average monthly payment, $310 per family). Total payments under aid to families with dependent children were $12,941m. for the calendar year 1982.

In Dec. 1982, about 3·8m. persons were receiving supplementary security income payments, including over 1·5m. persons aged 65 or over; 77,000 blind persons, and over 2·2m. disabled persons. Payments, including supplemental amounts from various states, totalled $9,200m. in 1982.

In 1981, block grants supplanted some categorical grants to states for services. In 1982, federal appropriations for the social services block grant amounted to $2,400m. In addition, 1982 federal appropriations for human services to selected target groups totalled $2,296m. Included in this amount were $1,416m. for children and youth; $729m. for the elderly; $58m. for persons with developmental disabilities; and $28m. for native Americans. During 1982, the public Health Services awarded a total of $373·8m. for maternal and child health services, $316·2m. as block grants to the states and the remaining $57·6m. for special projects of regional and national significance. In addition, approximately $2·6m. was spent for research and $28·3m. for training in the fields of maternal and child health.

Burns, E. M., *Social Security and Public Policy.* New York, 1956 (Repr. 1976).—*Health Services for Tomorrow.* New York, 1973
Friedlander, W. A., *Introduction to Social Welfare.* 4th ed. New York, 1974
Grob, G. N., (ed.), *Social Problems and Social Policy Series.* 51 vols. New York, 1975
Grob, G. N., *et al.*, (eds.), *Mental Illness and Social Policy: The American Experience.* 41 books. New York, 1973

DIPLOMATIC REPRESENTATIVES

Of the United States in Great Britain (Grosvenor Sq., London, W1A 1AE)
Ambassador: Charles H. Price II (accredited 20 Dec. 1983).

Of Great Britain in the USA (3100 Massachusetts Ave., Washington, D.C., 20008)
Ambassador: Sir Oliver Wright, GCMG, GCVO, DSC.

Of the United States to the United Nations
Ambassador: (Vacant).

Books of Reference

I. Statistical Information

Within the federal government of the USA, responsibilities for the collection, compilation, analysis and publication of statistics are decentralized among a number of agencies, with specified responsibilities for general-purpose statistics in particular areas. In addition, most agencies of the Government collect statistical data as a by-product of their administrative or operating responsibilities in specific fields. Responsibility for co-ordinating the decentralized statistical activities rests in the Office of Statistical Standards Bureau of the Budget, Washington 25, D.C., as a part of the Executive Office of the President. This Office reviews all proposed collections of statistical data to avoid duplication or overlapping; promotes the use of improved statistical techniques; develops standard definitions and classifications so that the data collected by different agencies are comparable; serves as liaison between federal agencies and international organizations and as an information centre on government statistical programmes. The Division does not itself collect or publish statistics.

The major general-purpose statistical agencies and their principal areas of responsibility are:

(1) Bureau of the Census in the Department of Commerce (A. Ross Eckler, Director). Decennial censuses of population and housing and quinquennial censuses of agriculture, manufactures and business; current statistics on population and the labour force, manufacturing activity and commodity production, retail and wholesale trade and services, foreign trade, and state and local government finances and operations.

(2) Bureau of Labor Statistics in the Department of Labor (Geoffrey H. Moore, Commissioner). Current statistics on employment, earnings, man-hours, labour turnover, industrial accidents, work stoppages, wage rates; collective bargaining agreements; construction; industrial productivity; wholesale prices, retail prices and urban consumers' price indexes; income and expenditures of urban families.

(3) Statistical Reporting Service and Economic Research Service in the Department of Agriculture. Statistics on crop and livestock production and inventories; crop forecasts; food processing and food consumption; farm population, labour and wages; farm management; farm ownership values, transfers; taxation and finance; prices farmers pay and receive; farm income; accidents; studies of land and water uses.

(4) National Center for Health Statistics in the Public Health Service, Department of Health, Education and Welfare (Theodore D. Woolsey, Chief). Current statistics on births, deaths, marriages and divorce.

(5) Bureau of Mines in the Department of the Interior (John F. O'Leary, Director). Statistics on production, consumption and stocks of metals and minerals, and on injuries in mineral industries.

Other agencies in which statistics are an important by-product of regulatory or other administrative functions include: Social Security Administration in the Department of Health, Education and Welfare; Internal Revenue Service in the Treasury Department; Federal Power Commission; Federal Trade Commission; Interstate Commerce Commission, and the Securities and Exchange Commission.

Among the more important statistical publications of a fairly general nature are:

Statistical Abstract of the United States, published by the Bureau of the Census, Department of Commerce. Annual. Important summary statistics on the industrial, social, political and economic organization of the USA, with a representative selection from most of the important statistical publications. *Survey of Current Business*, published by the Office of Business Economics, Department of Commerce. Monthly. Interpretative text and charts reviewing business trends, etc.; official estimates of national income. *Economic Indicators*, prepared by the Council of Economic Advisers and published by the Congressional Joint Committee on the Economic Report. Monthly. Tables and charts presenting current data on the total output of the economy; prices; employment and wages; production and business activity; purchasing power; money, banking and federal finance. *Monthly Labor Review*, published by the Bureau of Labor Statistics, Department of Labor. *Federal Reserve Bulletin*, published by the Board of Governors of the Federal Reserve System. Monthly. Current data on money and banking and selected other economic series. Federal Reserve indexes of industrial production, etc.; international financial statistics. *Treasury Bulletin*, published by the Office of the Secretary, Department of the Treasury. Monthly. Current coverage of federal fiscal statistics; international capital movements. *Minerals Yearbook*, published by the Bureau of Mines, Department of the Interior. Annual. *Agricultural Statistics*, published by the Department of Agriculture. Annual. *Crops and Markets*, published by the Bureau of Agricultural Economics in the Department of Agriculture. Monthly. Crop report and market statistics. *Foreign Agriculture*, published by the Office of Foreign Agriculture Service, Department of Agriculture. Monthly. Foreign agricultural production, foreign government policies relating to agriculture and international trade in agricultural products. *Vital Statistics of the United States*, published by the Public Health Service, US Department of Health, Education and Welfare. Monthly and Annual. Natality and mortality data tabulated by place of occurrence, with supplemental tables for Puerto Rico and the Virgin Islands; and tabulated by place of residence.

An annotated bibliography of about 100 periodical statistical publications is included in *Statistical Services of the United States Government*, a pamphlet issued by the Division of Statistical Standards, Bureau of the Budget, describing the general organization of the statistical system of the USA and the principal types of economic statistics.

II. Other Official Publications

Guide to the Study of the United States of America. General Reference and Bibliography Division, Library of Congress. 1960.

Historical Statistics of the United States, Colonial Times to 1957: A Statistical Abstract Supplement. Washington, 1960.—*Continuation to 1962 and Revisions*, 1965.

United States Government Manual. Washington. Annual.

The official publications of the USA are issued by the US Government Printing Office and are distributed by the Superintendent of Documents, who issued in 1940 a cumulative *Catalog of the Public Documents of the ... Congress and of All the Departments of the Government of the United States.* This *Catalog* is kept up to date by *United States Government Publications, Monthly Catalog* with annual index and supplemented by *Price Lists.* Each *Price List* is devoted to a special subject or type of material, *e.g., American History* or *Census.* Useful guides are Schmeckebier, L. F., and Eastin, R. B. (eds.), *Government Publications and Their Use.* 2nd ed., Washington, D.C., 1961; Boyd, A. M., *United States Government Publications.* 3rd ed. New York, 1949, and Leidy, W. P., *Popular Guide to Government Publications.* 2nd ed. New York and London, 1963.

Treaties and other International Acts of the United States of America (Edited by Hunter Miller), 8 vols. Washington, 1929–48. This edition stops in 1863. It may be supplemented by *Treaties, Conventions ... Between the US and Other Powers, 1776–1937* (Edited by William M. Malloy and others). 4 vols. 1909–38. A new Treaty Series, *US Treaties and Other International Agreements* was started in 1950.

Writings on American History. Washington, annual from 1902 (except 1904–5 and 1941–47).

III. Non-Official Publications

A. Handbooks

National Historical Publications Commission. *Guide to Archives and Manuscripts in the United States,* ed. P. M. Hamer. Yale Univ. Press, 1961
Adams, J. T. (ed.), *Dictionary of American History.* 2nd ed. 7 vols. New York, 1942
Dictionary of American Biography, ed. A. Johnson and D. Malone. 23 vols. New York, 1929–64.—*Concise Dictionary of American Biography.* New York, 1964
Current Biography. New York, annual from 1940; monthly supplements
Handlin, O., and others. *Harvard Guide to American History.* Cambridge, Mass., 1954
Herstein, S. R. and Robbins, N., *United States of America.* [Bibliography] Oxford and Santa Barbara, 1982
Lord, C. L. and E. H., *Historical Atlas of the US.* Rev. ed. New York, 1969
Who's Who in America. Chicago, 1899–1900 to date; monthly Supplement. 1940 to date

B. General History

Barck, Jr, O. T., and Blake, N. M., *Since 1900: A History of the United States.* 5th ed. New York, 1974
Bellot, H. H., *American History and American Historians.* London, 1952, repr. 1974
Billington, R. A., *Westward Expansion.* 4th ed. New York, 1974
Carman, H. J., and others, *A History of the American People.* 3rd ed. 2 vols. New York, 1967
Commager, H. S. (ed.), *Documents of American History.* 8th ed. New York, 1966
Divine, R. A., *Since 1945: Politics and Diplomacy in Recent American History.* New York, 1975
Hicks, J. D., *The American Nation, A History of the United States from 1865.* 5th ed. Boston, 1971
Link, A. S., and Catton, W. B., *American Epoch: A History of the United States Since the 1890s.* 4th ed. New York, 1967
Morison, S. E., *The Oxford History of the American People.* OUP, 1968
Morison, S. E., with Commager, H. S., *The Growth of the American Republic.* 2 vols. 5th ed. OUP, 1962–63
Nicholas, H. G., *The Nature of American Politics.* OUP, 1980
Parkes, H. B., *The United States of America, A History.* 3rd ed. New York, 1968
Scammon, R. N. (ed.), *American Votes: A Handbook of Contemporary American Election Statistics.* Washington, D.C., 1956 to date (biennial)
Schlesinger, A. M., *The Rise of Modern America, 1865–1951.* 4th ed. New York, 1951.—*The Age of Roosevelt.* 4 vols. New York and London, 1957–62.—*A Thousand Days: John F. Kennedy in the White House.* New York and London, 1965
Snowman, D., *America Since 1920.* London, 1978
Watson, R. A., *The Promise and Performance of American Democracy.* 2nd ed. New York, 1975

C. Minorities

Bennett, M. T., *American Immigration Policies: A History.* Washington, D.C., 1963
Burma, J. J., *Spanish-speaking Groups in the US.* Duke University Press, 1954, repr. 1974
Frazier, E. F., *The Negro Family in the United States.* Chicago Univ. Press, 1966
McNickle, D., *The Indian Tribes of the United States.* OUP, 1962.—*Native American Tribalism.* OUP, 1973
Sklare, M., *The Jew in American Society.* New York, 1974
Wissler, Clark, *Indians of the United States.* Rev. ed. New York, 1966

D. Economic History
The Economic History of the United States. 9 vols. New York, 1946 ff.
Bining, A. C., and Cochran, T. C., *The Rise of American Economic Life.* 4th ed. New York, 1963
Dorfman, J., *The Economic Mind in American Civilization.* 5 vols. New York, 1946–59
Faulkner, H. U., *American Economic History.* 8th ed. New York, 1960
Friedman, M., and Schwartz, A. J., *A Monetary History of the United States, 1867–1960.* New York, 1963
Mund, V. A., *Government and Business.* 4th ed. New York, 1965

E. Foreign Relations
Documents on American Foreign Relations. Princeton, from 1948. Annual
The United States in World Affairs. 1931 ff. Council on Foreign Relations. New York, from 1932. Annual
Allison, G., and Szanton, P., *Remaking Foreign Policy: The Organizations Connection.* New York, 1976
Bartlett, R. (ed.), *The Record of American Diplomacy; Documents and Readings in the History of American Foreign Relations.* 4th ed. New York, 1964
Beloff, M., *The United States and the Unity of Europe.* London, 1963, repr. 1976
Connell-Smith, G., *The United States and Latin America.* London, 1975
DeConde, A., *The American Secretary of State.* London, 1963, repr. 1976
Morgan, R., *The United States and West Germany, 1945–73.* OUP, 1975
Schwab, G., (ed.), *United States Foreign Policy at the Crossroads.* Westport, 1982
Smith, R. F., *The United States and Cuba: Business and Diplomacy, 1917–1960.* New York, 1962
Stebbins, R. P., and Adam, E. A., *Documents of American Foreign Relations, 1968–69.* New York, 1972
Vance, C., *Hard Choices: Critical Years in America's Foreign Policy.* New York, 1983
Wilcox, F. O., and Frank, R. A., *The Constitution and the Conduct of Foreign Policy.* New York, 1976

F. National Character
Coan, O. W., *America in Fiction, An Annotated List of Novels.* 5th ed. Stanford Univ. Press, 1967
Curti, M. B., *The Growth of American Thought.* 3rd ed. New York, 1964
Degler, C. N., *Out of Our Past: The Forces That Shaped Modern America.* Rev. ed. New York, 1970
Duignan, P., and Rabushka, A., (eds.), *The United States in the 1980s.* Stanford, 1980
Fawcett, E., and Thomas, T., *America and the Americans.* London, 1983

National Library: The Library of Congress. Washington 25, D.C. *Librarian:* Lawrence Quincy Mumford, AB, MA, BS.

STATES AND TERRITORIES

For information as to State and Local Government, see under UNITED STATES, *pp.* 1378–80.

Against the names of the Governors and the Secretaries of State, (D.) stands for Democrat and (R.) for Republican.

Figures for the revenues and expenditures of the various states are those of the Federal Bureau of the Census unless otherwise stated, which takes the original state figures and arranges them on a common pattern so that those of one state can be compared with those of any other.

Official publications of the various states and insular possessions are listed in the *Monthly Check-List of State Publications*, issued by the Library of Congress since 1910. Their character and contents are discussed in J. K. Wilcox's *Manual on the Use of State Publications* (1940). Of great importance bibliographically are the publications of the Historical Records Survey and the American Imprints Inventory, which record local archives, official publications and state imprints. These publications supplement those of state historical societies which usually publish journals and monographs on state and local history. An outstanding source of statistical data is the material issued by the various state planning boards and commissions, to which should be added the annual *Governmental Finances* issued by the US Bureau of the Census.

The Book of the States. Biennial. Council of State Governments, Lexington, 1953 ff.
State Government Finances. Annual. Dept. of Commerce, 1966 ff.

Regionalism
Odum, H. W., *American Regionalism, A Cultural–Historical Approach to National Integration.* New York, 1938
Visher, S. X., *Climatic Atlas of the USA.* Harvard Univ. Press, 1954

A. North-East
Gottman, J., *Megalopolis, the Urbanized North-eastern Seaboard of the US.* New York, 1964

B. The South
Clement, E., *A History of the Old South.* New York, 1949
Ezell, J. S., *The South Since 1865.* New York and London, 1963
Heseltine, W. B., and Smiley, D. L., *The South in American History.* 2nd ed. Englewood Cliffs, 1960
Stephenson, W. H., and Coulter, E. M. (ed.), *A History of the South.* 10 vols. Louisiana State Univ. Press, 1947–67

C. The Middle West
Lynd, R. S. and H. M., *Middletown: A Study in Contemporary American Culture.* New York and London, 1929.—*Middletown in Transition: A Study in Cultural Conflicts.* New York and London, 1937
Nye, R. B., *Midwestern Progressive Politics, 1870–1938.* Michigan State Univ. Press, 1959

D. The West
Fogelson, R. U., *The Fragmented Metropolis: Los Angeles, 1850–1930.* Harvard Univ. Press, 1967
Fuller, G. W., *History of the Pacific Northwest.* 2nd ed. New York, 1938
Johansen, D. O., and Gates, C. M., *Empire of the Columbia: A History of the Pacific North-West,* New York, 1957
Parrish, P. H., *Before the Covered Wagon.* Portland, Oreg., 1931
Quiett, G. C., *They Built the West: An Epic of Rails and Cities.* New York and London, 1934
Scott, H. W., *History of the Oregon Country.* 6 vols. Cambridge, Mass., 1924
Winther, O. O., *The Great Northwest: A History.* 2nd ed., rev. New York, 1950

ALABAMA

HISTORY. Alabama, settled in 1702 as part of the French Province of Louisiana, and ceded to the British in 1763, was organized as a Territory, 1817, and admitted into the Union on 14 Dec. 1819.

AREA AND POPULATION. Alabama is bounded north by Tennessee, east by Georgia, south by Florida and the Gulf of Mexico and west by Mississippi. Area, 51,998 sq. miles, including 1,535 sq. miles of inland water. Census population, 1 April 1980, 3,893,888, an increase of 13·06% over that of 1970. Estimate (1981) 3,917,000. Births, 1983, 59,057 (14·4 per 1,000 population); deaths, 35,471 (8·7); infant deaths (under 28 days), 486 (8·2 per 1,000 live births); marriages, 47,469 (11·6); divorces, 25,190 (6·2).

Population in 5 census years was:

	White	*Negro*	*Indian*	*Asiatic*	*Total*	*Per sq. mile*
1910	1,228,832	908,282	909	70	2,138,093	41·4
1930	1,700,844	944,834	465	105	2,646,248	51·3
1960	2,283,609	980,271	1,726	915	3,266,521	64·0
			All others			
1970	2,533,831	903,467	6,867		3,444,165	66·7
1980	2,872,621	996,335	24,932		3,893,888	74·9

Of the total population in 1980, 49% were male, 61% were urban and 65% were 21 years or older.

The large cities (1980 census) were: Birmingham, 284,413 (metropolitan area, 847,487); Mobile, 200,452 (443,536); Huntsville, 142,513 (308,593); Montgomery (capital), 177,857 (272,687); Tuscaloosa, 75,211 (137,541).

CLIMATE. Birmingham. Jan. 46°F (7·8°C), July 80°F (26·7°C). Annual rainfall 54″ (1,346 mm). Mobile. Jan. 52°F (11·1°C), July 82°F (27·8°C). Annual rainfall 63″ (1,577 mm). Montgomery. Jan. 49°F (9·4°C), July 81°F (27·2°C). Annual rainfall 53″ (1,321 mm). *See* Gulf Coast, p. 1373. The growing season ranges from 190 days (north) to 298 days (south).

CONSTITUTION AND GOVERNMENT. The present constitution dates from 1901; it has had 447 amendments (at 2 Oct. 1984). The legislature consists of a Senate of 35 members and a House of Representatives of 105 members, all elected for 4 years. The Governor and Lieut.-Governor are elected for 4 years.

The state is represented in Congress by 2 senators and 7 representatives. Applicants for registration must take an oath of allegiance to the United States and fill out a questionnaire to the satisfaction of the registrars. In the 1984 presidential election Reagan polled 844,299 votes, Mondale, 540,445.

Montgomery is the capital.

Governor: George C. Wallace (D.), 1983–86 ($68,838).
Lieut.-Governor: Bill Baxley (D.) ($1,900 a month plus daily allowances).
Secretary of State: Don Siegelman (D.) ($32,940).

BUDGET. The total receipts for the fiscal year ending 30 Sept. 1981 were $13,845·5m.; total expenditure was $6,896·3m.

The net long-term debt on 30 Sept. 1981 amounted to $13,366·7m.

Per capita income (1980) was $7,434.

ENERGY AND NATURAL RESOURCES

Minerals. Production of principal minerals (financial year 1982): Coal, about 27·5m. short tons; limestone, 15·2m. short tons. Total (non-fuel) mineral output was valued at $300m.

Agriculture. The number of farms in 1984 was 54,000, covering 11·5m. acres; average farm had 213 acres and was valued at about $183,000.

Cash receipts from farm marketings, 1983: Crops, $759m.; livestock and poultry products, $1,259m.; and total, $2,018m. Principal crops: soybeans, cotton, wheat, corn and peanuts; potatoes, hay, sorghum, pecans and tomatoes are also important. In 1983, poultry accounted for the largest percentage of cash receipts from farm marketings; cattle and calves were second, soybeans third, peanuts fourth.

Forestry. Area of national forest lands, Oct. 1983, 644,432 acres; state forest, 147,400; industrial forest, 4,458,000; private non-industrial forest, 16m.; other government-owned forest, 321,200.

INDUSTRY. Alabama is predominantly industrial. In 1981, 6,448 manufacturing establishments employed 364,130 production workers, earning over $5,725m. Pig-iron, 1981, amounted to 2·5m. net tons.

TOURISM. In 1983 about 28m. travelled to or through Alabama from other states. Total income from tourism (including receipts from Alabama holiday-makers) was about $2,900m.

COMMUNICATIONS

Roads. Paved roads of all classes at 1 Jan. 1984 totalled 59,173 miles; total highways, 87,598 miles.

Railways. At 1 Jan. 1984 the railways had a length of 4,576 miles.

Aviation. In 1982–83 the state had 88 publicly owned and 29 privately owned licensed airfields.

Shipping. The only deep water port is Mobile, with a large ocean-going trade; total tonnage (1983), 34·9m. tons. The docks can handle 33 ocean-going vessels at once. The 9-ft channel of the Tennessee River traverses North Alabama for 200 miles; the Tennessee-Tombigbee waterway (232 miles), open Feb. 1985, connects the Tennessee River with the Tombigbee River for access to the Gulf of Mexico. The Warrier–Tombigbee system (476 miles) connects the Birmingham industrial area to the Gulf. The Coosa-Alabama River system reaches central Alabama as far north as Montgomery from Mobile and the Gulf Intracoastal Waterway. The

Alabama State Docks also operates a system of 11 inland docks; there are several privately-run inland docks.

JUSTICE, RELIGION, EDUCATION AND WELFARE

Justice. The prison population on 30 Sept. 1984 was 10,301.

From 1 Jan. 1927 to 1 June 1983 there were 154 executions (electrocution): 122 for murder, 25 for rape, 5 for armed robbery, 1 for burglary and 1 for carnal knowledge. Before 1 Jan. 1927, persons executed in Alabama were hanged locally by the sheriffs in the counties of their conviction.

In 41 counties the sale of alcoholic beverage is permitted, and in 26 counties it is prohibited.

Religion. Chief religious bodies (in 1980) are: Southern Baptist Convention (about 1,182,018), Churches of Christ (113,919), United Methodist (about 344,790), Roman Catholic (106,123), African Methodist Episcopal Zion (139,714), Christian Methodist Episcopal (about 53,493) and Assemblies of God (48,610).

Education. In 1983 the 1,400 public elementary and high schools required 31,550 teachers to teach 721,900 pupils enrolled in grades K-12. In 1983 there were 15 senior public institutions with 102,769 students and 4,160 faculty members. In 1982 the 21 junior colleges had 38,858 students and 1,250 teachers, 22 technical schools had 24,743 students and 822 teachers.

Health. In Sept. 1984 there were 137 hospitals (21,102 beds) licensed by the State Board of Health. In 1982–83 hospitals for mental diseases had 2,545 beds. Facilities for the mentally retarded (1 Sept. 1983) had 1,455 cases.

Pensions and Security. In Aug. 1984 Alabama paid supplements (to federal welfare payments) to 13,992 recipients of old-age assistance, receiving an average of $59.76 each; 5,244 permanently and totally disabled, $63.78; 131 blind, $60.54. Combined state–federal aid to dependent children was paid to 54,752 families, average $111.40 per family.

Books of Reference

Alabama Official and Statistical Register. Montgomery. Quadrennial
Alabama Encyclopædia. Vol. I. Northport, 1965
Economic Abstract of Alabama. Center for Business and Economic Research, Univ. of Alabama, 1975
The Deep South in Transformation: A Symposium. Univ. of Alabama Press, 1964
Farmer, H., *The Legislative Process in Alabama.* Univ. of Alabama, 1949

ALASKA

HISTORY. Discovered in 1741 by Vitus Bering, its first settlement, on Kodiak Island, was in 1784. The area known as Russian America with its capital (1806) at Sitka was ruled by a Russo-American fur company and vaguely claimed as a Russian colony. Alaska was purchased by the United States from Russia under the treaty of 30 March 1867 for $7·2m. It was not organized until 1884, when it became a 'district' governed by the code of the state of Oregon. By Act of Congress approved 24 Aug. 1912 Alaska became an incorporated Territory; its first legislature in 1913 granted votes to women, 7 years in advance of the Constitutional Amendment.

Alaska officially became the 49th state of the Union on 3 Jan. 1959.

AREA AND POPULATION. Alaska is bounded north by the Beaufort Sea, west and south by the Pacific and east by Canada. It has the largest area of any state, being more than twice the size of Texas. The gross area (land and water) is 591,004 sq. miles; the land area is 586,412 sq. miles of which 85% was in federal ownership in 1984. Census population, 1 April 1980, was 401,851, including military personnel, an increase of 33·5% over 1970. Estimate (1983), 510,600. Births,

1983, were 11,834 (23·2 per 1,000 population); deaths, 1,897 (3·7); infant deaths (1982), 117 (12·3 per 1,000 live births); marriages (1982), 5,361 (13·4); divorces (1982), 3,517 (8·7).

Population in 5 census years was:

	White	*Negro*	*All Others*	*Total*	*Per sq. mile*
1940	39,170	...	33,354	72,524	0·13
1950	92,808	...	35,835	128,643	0·23
1960	174,649	...	51,518	226,167	0·40
1970	236,767	8,911	54,704	300,382	0·53
1980	309,728	13,643	78,480	401,851	0·70

Of the total population in 1980, 53·01% were male, 64·34% were urban and 68·57% were aged 21 years or over.

The largest city is Anchorage, which had a 1980 census area population of 174,430 (1983 estimate, 227,100). Other census area populations, 1980 (and 1983 estimate), Fairbanks North Star, 53,983 (64,800); Juneau, 19,528 (26,000); Kenai Peninsula, 25,282 (34,900); Ketchikan Gateway, 11,316 (12,700); Kodiak Island, 9,939 (12,900); Matanuska-Susitna 17,816 (29,800). There are 11 boroughs and 142 incorporated cities.

CLIMATE. Anchorage. Jan. 12°F (–11·1°C), July 57°F (13·9°C). Annual rainfall 15″ (371 mm). Fairbanks. Jan. –11°F (–23·9°C), July 60°F (15·6°C). Annual rainfall 12″ (300 mm). Sitka. Jan. 33°F (0·6°C), July 55°F (12·8°C). Annual rainfall 87″ (2,175 mm). *See* Pacific Coast, p. 1372.

CONSTITUTION AND GOVERNMENT. An important provision of the Enabling Act is that the state has the right to select 103·55m. acres of vacant and unappropriated public lands in order to establish 'a tax basis'; it can open these lands to prospectors for minerals, and the state is to derive the principal advantage in all gains resulting from the discovery of minerals. In addition, certain federally administered lands reserved for conservation of fisheries and wild life have been transferred to the state. Special provision is made for federal control of land for defence in areas of high strategic importance.

The constitution of Alaska was adopted by public vote, 24 April 1956. The state legislature consists of a Senate of 20 members (elected for 4 years) and a House of Representatives of 40 members (elected for 2 years). The state sends 2 senators and 1 representative to Congress. The franchise may be exercised by all citizens over 18.

The capital is Juneau. A new capital site near Anchorage was chosen in 1976.

In the 1984 presidential election Reagan polled 138,392 votes, Mondale, 62,018.

Governor: William Sheffield (D.), 1983–86 ($81,648).
Lieut.-Governor: Steve McAlpine (D.) 1983–86 ($76,188).

ECONOMY

Budget. Total state government revenue for the year ended 30 June 1984 (Annual Financial Report figures) was $3,935·8m. ($2,914m. from petroleum revenue, $109·4m. from taxation). Total expenditure was $3,931·3m.

In 1976 a Permanent Fund was set up for the deposit of at least 25% of all mineral-related revenue; total assets at 30 June, 1984, $5,530·8m.

General obligation bonds at 30 June 1984, $169·5m.

Per capita income (1983) was $16,820.

Banking. Total bank assets 1981, $2,782m., total deposits $2,216m.

ENERGY AND NATURAL RESOURCES

Oil and Gas. Commercial production of crude petroleum began in 1959 and by 1961 had become the most important mineral by value. Production: 1961, 6·3m. bbls (of 42 gallons); 1976, 67m. bbls; 1977, 169m. bbls; 1981, 587m. bbls; 1984, 630m. bbls. Oil comes mainly from Prudhoe Bay, the Kuparuk River field and several Cook Inlet fields. Natural gas marketed production, 1984,

200,296,680m. cu. ft. Value of crude oil and gas (1981), $12,479m. Alaska receives 84% of its total revenue from petroleum. Revenue to the state from oil production in 1984 was $2,861·6m. from corporate petroleum tax $265·1m. and from royalties $1,047·5m., severance tax, $1,393·1m., property tax, $131m., bonus sale, $10·1m., rents, $3·8m., intergovernmental receipts, $11·1m.

Oil from the Prudhoe Bay arctic field is now carried by the Trans-Alaska pipeline to Prince William Sound on the south coast, where a tanker terminal has been built at Valdez.

Minerals. Value of production, 1983: gold (169,000 troy oz.) $67·6m.; antimony (22,400 lb.) $25,000; platinum $100,000; silver (33,200 troy oz.) $332,000; tin (215,000 lb.) $1·1m.; jade and soapstone (2·3 tons) $42,000; sand and gravel (50m. short tons) $120m.; building stone (5·27m. short tons) $25m.; coal (803,000m. short tons) $18m. Total value, $232,399,000.

Agriculture. In some parts of the state the climate during the brief spring and summer (about 100 days in major areas and 152 days in the south-eastern coastal area) is suitable for agricultural operations, thanks to the long hours of sunlight, but Alaska is a food-importing area. In 1982 about 2m. acres was farmland; 90% of this was unimproved pasture primarily government leases for grazing of sheep and beef cattle in south-west Alaska. In 1980 (preliminary) there were 8,400 cattle, 1,100 milch cows, 1,800 hogs and 4,300 sheep stock.

Farm income in 1981: $13m. of which $8m. was from crops (mainly hay and potatoes) and $5m. from livestock and dairy products.

There were about 25,000 reindeer in western Alaska in 1980, owned by individual Eskimo herders except for 750 at Nome owned by the Government.

Forestry. In south-eastern Alaska timber fringes the shore of the mainland and all the islands extending inland to a depth of 5 miles. The state's enormous forests could produce an estimated annual sustained yield of 1,500m. bd ft of lumber, nearly twice Alaska's record 1973 cut. Alaska has 2 national forests: the Tongass of 16·9m. acres and the Chugach of 5·9m. acres. An estimated total of 446m. bd ft was cut in 1981, of which 387·5m. came from national forests and 53,687,000 from state forests, 4,275,000 from land held by the Bureau of Indian Affairs and 362,000 from the Bureau of Land Management. Alaska has 2 large pulp-mills at Ketchikan and Sitka.

Fisheries. The catch for 1982 was 1,300m. lb. of fish and shellfish having a value to fishermen of $600m. and a wholesale value of over $1,000m. King crab, 39m. lb., snow (tanner) crab, 69m. lb., herring, 52m. lb., shrimp, 17m. lb. Salmon accounts for more than half of the US catch.

INDUSTRY. Main industries with employment, 1984: Government, 66,400; trade, 44,700; services, 42,300; contract construction, 22,200; manufacturing, 9,600; mining including oil and gas, 7,900; transport, communication and utilities, 19,600; finance, insurance and property, 11,400; agriculture, forestry and fishing, 1,360 in 1982.

The major manufacturing industry was food processing, followed by timber industries. Total non-agricultural employment, 1984, 224,100. Total wages and salaries, 1983, $6,075·7m.

TOURISM. About 691,200 tourists visited the state in 1984.

COMMUNICATIONS

Roads. Alaska's highway and road system, 1984, totalled 15,315 miles, including marine highway systems, local service roads, borough and city streets, national park, forest and reservation roads and military roads. Registered motor vehicles, 1983, 475,378.

The Alaska Highway extends 1,523 miles from Dawson Creek, British Columbia, to Fairbanks, Alaska. It was built by the US Army in 1942, at a cost of $138m. The greater portion of it, because it lies in Canada, is maintained by Canada.

Railways. There is a railway of 111 miles from Skagway to the town of Whitehorse, the White Pass and Yukon route, in the Canadian Yukon region (this service was suspended in 1982 but may reopen). The government-owned Alaska Railroad runs from Seward to Fairbanks, a distance of 471 miles. This is a freight service with only occasional passenger use. A passenger service operates from Anchorage to Fairbanks via Denali National Park in the tourist season.

Aviation. In 1982 the state had about 1,070 airports, of which about half were publicly owned. Commercial passengers by air from Alaska's largest international airports Anchorage and Fairbanks numbered 1·1m. at Anchorage and 273,512 at Fairbanks. General aviation aircraft in the state per 1,000 population was about ten times the US average.

Shipping. Regular shipping services to and from the US are furnished by 2 steamship and several barge lines operating out of Seattle and other Pacific coast ports. A Canadian company also furnishes a regular service from Vancouver, B.C. Freight handled at the Port of Anchorage, 1981 (short tons): Bulk petroleum, 365,999; vans, flats and containers, 1,154,060; cement and drilling mud, 32,497; vehicles, 39,822; total 1·65m.

A 1,435 nautical-mile ferry system for motor cars and passengers (the 'Alaska Marine Highway') operates from Seattle, Washington and Prince Rupert (British Columbia) to Juneau, Haines (for access to the Alaska Highway) and Skagway. A second system extends throughout the south-central region of Alaska linking the Cook Inlet area with Kodiak Island and Prince William Sound.

JUSTICE, RELIGION, EDUCATION AND WELFARE

Justice. There is no death penalty in Alaska.

Religion. Many religions are represented, including the Russian Orthodox, Roman Catholic, Episcopalian, Presbyterian, Methodist and other denominations.

Education. During 1984 there were 100,000 pupils at public schools, 3,868 at private schools. The Bureau of Indian Affairs schools had 1,005 pupils attending schools in the state. The University of Alaska (founded in 1922) had (Spring 1984) 11,808 students in Fairbanks, Anchorage and Juneau and 19,296 in community colleges. Other colleges had 1,775 students in 1984.

Health. In 1982 there were 28 acute care hospitals with 1,397 beds, of which 7 were federal public health hospitals; there was 1 mental hospital; there were 24 mental health clinics.

Welfare. Old-age assistance was established under the Federal Social Security Act; in 1982 aid to dependent children covered a monthly average of 6,617 households; payments, an average of $409 per month; aid to the blind and to the disabled was given to a monthly average of 2,170 persons receiving on average $185 per month. An average of 5,492 people per month received Medicaid.

Books of Reference

Statistical Information: Department of Commerce and Economic Development, Economic Analysis Section, Juneau.

Alaska Blue Book, Department of Education, Juneau. Biennial
Alaska Economic Outlook, Department of Labor, Juneau.
Alaska Economy, The. Division of Economic Enterprise, Juneau. Annual
Alaska Statistical Review. Office of the Governor, Juneau. Biennial
Annual Financial Report, Department of Administration, Juneau.
Gardey, J., *Alaska: The Sophisticated Wilderness.* London, 1976
Hulley, Clarence C., *Alaska Past and Present.* Portland, Oregon, 1970
Hunt, W. R., *Alaska, a Bicentennial History.* New York, 1976
Pearson, R. W., and Lynch, D. F., *Alaska, a Geography.* Boulder, 1984
Thomas, L., Jr., *Alaska and the Yukon.* New York, 1983
Tourville, M., *Alaska, a Bibliography, 1570–1970.* 1971

State Library: Pouch G, Juneau. *Librarian:* Richard Engen.—Alaska Historical Library, Pouch G, Juneau. *Librarian:* Phyllis de Muth.

ARIZONA

HISTORY. Arizona was settled in 1752, organized as a Territory in 1863 and became a state on 14 Feb. 1912.

AREA AND POPULATION. Arizona is bounded north by Utah, east by New Mexico, south by Mexico, west by California and Nevada. Area, 113,909 sq. miles, including 492 sq. miles of inland water. Of the total area (72,586,880 acres) 42,826,259 were owned by the federal government in 1980, including 20,324,326 acres held by the Office of Indian Affairs. Census population on 1 April 1980 was 2,718,215, an increase of 53·4% over 1970. Estimate (1984) 2,794,000. Births, 1983, 52,919; deaths, 22,482; infant deaths (1983), 509; marriages, 30,819; divorces, 19,875.

Population in 5 census years:

	White	*Negro*	*Indian*	*Chinese*	*Japanese*	*Total*	*Per sq. mile*
1910	171,468	2,009	29,201	1,305	371	204,354	1·8
1930	378,551	10,749	43,726	1,110	879	435,573	3·8
1960	1,169,517	43,403	83,387	2,937	1,501	1,302,161	11·3
				All others			
1970	1,604,498	53,344		117,557		1,775,399	15·6
1980	2,260,288	74,159		383,768		2,718,215	23·9

Of the population in 1980, 1,338,943 were male, 2,278,728 were urban and 1,822,127 were aged 20 and over.

The 1980 census population of Phoenix was 789,704; Tucson, 330,537; Scottsdale, 88,412; Tempe, 106,743; Mesa, 152,453; Glendale, 97,172.

CLIMATE. Phoenix. Jan. 52°F (11·1°C), July 90°F (32·2°C). Annual rainfall 8″ (191 mm). Yuma. Jan. 55°F (12·8°C), July 91°F (32·8°C). Annual rainfall 3″ (75 mm). *See* Mountain States, p. 1372.

CONSTITUTION AND GOVERNMENT. The state constitution (1910, with 103 amendments) placed the government under direct control of the people through the Initiative, Referendum and the Recall. The state Senate consists of 30 members, and the House of Representatives of 60, all elected for 2 years. Arizona sends to Congress 2 senators and 5 representatives. In the 1984 presidential election Reagan polled 669,353 votes, Mondale, 325,924.

The state capital is Phoenix. The state is divided into 15 counties.

Governor: Bruce Babbitt (D.), 1978– ($62,500).
Secretary of State: Rose Mofford (D.) ($35,000).

BUDGET. General revenues, year ending 30 June 1983 (US Census Bureau figures), were $1,692·9m. (taxation, $1,440·3m.); general expenditures, $1,762·4m. (education, $1,034·1m.; transport $2·4m., and public welfare, $240·2m.).

Per capita income (1982) was $10,173.

NATURAL RESOURCES

Minerals. The mining industries of the state are important, but less so than agriculture and manufacturing. By value the most important mineral produced is copper. Production (1982): Copper (769,974 tonnes); gold (61,050 troy oz.) and silver (6·3m. troy oz.) are both largely recovered from copper ore. Other minerals include sand and gravel (19,231,000 short tons) and lead (359 tonnes). Total value of minerals mined in 1982 was $1,619·3m.

Agriculture. Arizona, despite its dry climate, is well suited for agriculture along the water-courses and where irrigation is practised on a large scale from great reservoirs constructed by the US as well as by the state government and private interests.

Irrigated area, 1982, 1·1m. acres. The wide pasture lands are favourable for the rearing of cattle and sheep, but numbers are either stationary or declining compared with 1920.

In 1983 Arizona contained 7,334 farms and ranches with 1·05m. acres of crop land, out of a total farm and pastoral area of 37·7m. acres. The average farm was estimated at 5,148 acres. Farming is highly commercialized and mechanized and concentrated largely on cotton picked by machines and by Indian, Mexican and migratory workers.

Area under cotton (1983), 313,390 acres; 771,900m. bales (of 480 lb.) of cotton were harvested.

Cash income, 1982, from crops, $974·9m.; from livestock, $682·4m. Most important cereals are wheat, corn and barley; other crops include oranges, grapefruit and lettuce. On 1 Jan. 1984 there were 980,000 all cattle, 82,000 milch cows, 306,000 sheep and (1983) 150,000 swine.

Forestry. The national forests in the state had an area (1983) of 11·22m. acres.

INDUSTRY. In 1982 there were 3,041 manufacturing establishments with 154,278 production workers, earning $3,076m.

TOURISM. In 1982 15·7m. tourists visited Arizona; direct employment, 71,700; indirect, 114,600; state tax revenue, $204m.

COMMUNICATIONS

Roads. In 1982 there were 76,290 miles of public roads and streets; 2,215,549 motor vehicles were registered in the state.

Aviation. Airports, 1984, numbered 251, of which 82 were for public use; 6,079 aircraft were registered.

JUSTICE, RELIGION, EDUCATION AND WELFARE

Justice. A 'right-to-work' amendment to the constitution, adopted 5 Nov. 1946, makes illegal any concessions to trade-union demands for a 'closed shop'.

The Arizona prisons 30 June 1981 held 5,199. There have been no executions since 1963; from 1930 to 1963 there were 38 executions (lethal gas) all for murder, and all men (28 whites, 10 Negro).

Religion. The leading religious bodies are Roman Catholics and Mormons (Latter Day Saints); others include Methodists, Presbyterians, Baptists and Episcopalians. No recent statistics of membership are available.

Education. School attendance is compulsory to grade 9 (from 1985–86) and to grade 10 (from 1986–87). In autumn 1983 there were 597,537 pupils enrolled in grades K-12. The state maintains 3 universities: the University of Arizona (Tucson) with an enrollment of 30,292 in autumn 1983; Arizona State University (Tempe) with 39,319; Northern Arizona University (Flagstaff) with 11,665.

Health. In 1983 there were 80 hospitals reported by the State Department of Health; capacity 12,125 beds; the hospitals had 582 physicians and dentists, 9,015 registered nurses and 2,508 licensed practical nurses.

Social Security. Old-age assistance (maximum depending on the programme) is given, with federal aid, to needy citizens 65 years of age or older. In June 1984, federal Social Security Insurance payments of $6,802,000 went to 10,448 aged, 598 blind, 19,643 disabled; 2,412 persons receive state administered supplementation. Average weekly benefit for total unemployment was $102.41 in 1983; average weekly number of beneficiaries 16,762.

Books of Reference

Arizona Statistical Review. 39th ed. Valley National Bank, Phoenix, 1983
Federal Writers' Project. *Arizona: The Grand Canyon State.* 4th ed. New York, 1966
Comeaux, M. L., *Arizona: a Geography.* Boulder, 1981
Goff, J. S., *Arizona Civilization.* 2nd ed. Cave Creek, 1970
Mason, B. B., and Hink, H., *Constitutional Government of Arizona.* 7th ed. Tempe, 1982

State Library: Department of Library, Archives and Public Records, Capitol, Phoenix 85007. *Director:* Sharon G. Turgeon.

ARKANSAS

HISTORY. Arkansas was settled in 1686, made a territory in 1819 and admitted into the Union on 15 June 1836. The name originated with the Quapaw Indian tribe. The constitution, which dates from 1874, has been amended 61 times.

AREA AND POPULATION. Arkansas is bounded north by Missouri, east by Tennessee and Mississippi, south by Louisiana, south-west by Texas and west by Oklahoma. Area, 53,187 sq. miles (1,109 sq. miles being inland water). Census population on 1 April 1980 was 2,286,435, an increase of 18·9% from that of 1970. Estimate (1983) 2,328,000. Births, 1982, were 35,295 (15·3 per 1,000 population); deaths, 22,327 (9·7); infant deaths, 355 (10·1 per 1,000 live births); marriages, 28,041 (12·2); divorces 15,739 (6·8).

Population in 5 census years was:

	White	*Negro*	*Indian*	*Asiatic*	*Total*	*Per sq. mile*
1910	1,131,026	442,891	460	72	1,574,449	30·0
1930	1,375,315	478,463	408	296	1,854,482	35·2
1960	1,395,703	388,787	580	1,202	1,786,272	34·0
			All others			
1970	1,565,915	352,445	4,935		1,923,295	37·0
1980	1,890,332	373,768	22,335		2,286,435	43·9

Of the total population in 1980, 48·3% were male, 51·6% were urban, 60·2% were 21 years of age or older.

Little Rock (capital) had a population of 158,461 in 1980; Fort Smith, 71,626; North Little Rock, 64,288; Pine Bluff, 56,636; Fayetteville, 36,608; Hot Springs, 35,781; Jonesboro, 31,530; West Memphis, 28,138. The population of the largest standard metropolitan statistical areas: Little Rock–North Little Rock, 393,774; Fayetteville–Springdale, 178,609; Fort Smith (Arkansas portion), 132,064; Pine Bluff, 90,718; Memphis (Arkansas portion), 49,499; Texarkana (Arkansas portion), 37,766.

CLIMATE. Little Rock. Jan. 42°F (5·6°C), July 81°F (27·2°C). Annual rainfall 49″ (1,222 mm). *See* Gulf Coast, p. 1373.

GOVERNMENT. The General Assembly consists of a Senate of 35 members elected for 4 years, partially renewed every 2 years, and a House of Representatives of 100 members elected for 2 years. The sessions are biennial and usually limited to 60 days. The Governor and Lieut.-Governor are elected for 2 years. The state is represented in Congress by 2 senators and 4 representatives.

In the 1984 presidential election Reagan polled 533,624 votes, Mondale, 338,829.

The state is divided into 75 counties; the capital is Little Rock.

Governor: Bill Clinton (D.), 1985–86 ($35,000).
Lieut.-Governor: Winston Bryant (D.) ($14,000).
Secretary of State: W. J. McCuen (D.) ($22,500).

FINANCE

Budget. The state's general revenue for the fiscal year 1982 was $2,238·4m., of which taxation furnished $1,263·7m. and federal aid, $691·1m. General expenditure was $2,159·1m., of which education took $934·4m.; highways, $289·2m., and public welfare, $358·6m.

Net long-term debt for the financial year 1982 was $127·6m.

Per capita income (1983) was $9,242.

Banking. In 1983 total bank deposits were $12,016·8m.

ENERGY AND NATURAL RESOURCES

Minerals. In 1982 crude petroleum amounted to 18·4m. bbls; natural gas, 150·7m. cu. ft; the state is an important source of bauxite, bromine, silica stone and barite, and also produces gallium, tripoli and vanadium. Value of mineral production, 1981, $1,099m.

Agriculture. In 1982 (Federal Census Report), 50,525 farms had a total area of 14·7m. acres; average farm was of 291 acres; 7·5m. acres were harvested cropland; 2,022,695 acres were irrigated.

The largest sources of income in 1982 were chickens including broilers ($681·4m.); soybeans ($588·3m.); cattle and calves ($316·3m.); rice ($658·2m.); wheat ($223·6m.). Cash farm income (1982) was $3,416·5m.; from crops, $1,790·8m., and from livestock, $1,625·8m.

Livestock on 1 Jan. 1984 included 2m. all cattle, 84,000 milch cows and 395,000 swine.

INDUSTRY.

In Aug. 1984 total employment averaged 973,600 (74,600 agricultural, 213,300 manufacturing, 175,000 wholesale and retail trade, 128,800 government). The Arkansas Department of Labor estimated that 173,900 factory production workers earned an average $298.56 per week (40·4 hours). The most important manufacturing group was food and kindred products employing 37,900, followed by electric and electronic equipment (26,200) and lumber and wood products (20,300). Construction employed 34,100.

COMMUNICATIONS

Roads. Total road mileage, 82,647 miles. State-maintained highways (1 Jan. 1984) total 16,105 miles; local county highways, 49,682 miles; city streets, 9,628 miles; federal roads, 1,639 miles; roads not publicly maintained, 5,593 miles. In 1983 there were 1,451,356 registered motor vehicles.

Railways. In 1984 there were in the state 5,308·4 miles of commercial railway.

Aviation. Seven air carrier and 4 commuter airlines serve the state; there were, in 1984, 140 airports (86 public use and 54 private).

Waterways. There are about 1,000 miles of navigable streams: the Mississippi, Arkansas, Red, White and Ouachita Rivers and the Kerr-McClellan Channel which flows eastward across the state and gives access to the sea *via* the Mississippi River.

RELIGION, EDUCATION AND WELFARE

Religion. The most numerous religious bodies in 1980 were Baptist (603,884), Methodist (214,925), Church of Christ (90,671), Roman Catholic (56,911) and Assembly of God (53,555).

Education. In the school year 1982–83 public elementary and secondary schools had 420,262 enrolled pupils and 24,874 classroom teachers. Average salaries of teachers in elementary schools was $14,579, secondary $15,459. Expenditure on elementary and secondary education was $894·8m.

An educational TV network began operating in 1966 with a full 12-hour-day telecasting, it had 5 stations in 1984.

Higher education is provided at 32 institutions: 10 state universities, 1 medical college, 12 private or church colleges, 10 community or junior colleges. Total enrolment in institutions of higher education, 1983–84, was 73,905.

There were (1983–84) 23 vocational-technical schools with 26,500 students, including extension class students. Total expenditure, $23·2m.

Health. There were 98 licensed hospitals (11,702 beds) in 1984, and 231 licensed nursing homes (20,958 beds).

Social Welfare. In Oct. 1983, 409,000 persons were drawing old-age assistance at an average amount of $317.85 per month; 22,085 families (43,618 children),

$130.43 per family; 44,000 persons were receiving disability benefits at an average of $409.09 per month.

State prisons in Sept. 1984 had 4,269 inmates (187 per 100,000 population).

Books of Reference

Current Employment Developments. Arkansas Employment Security Division, Little Rock
Arkansas State and County Economic Data. Industrial Research and Extension Center, Little Rock
State Government Finances. U.S. Dept. of Commerce, Bureau of the Census.
Agricultural Statistics for Arkansas. U.S. Dept. of Agriculture, Crop Reporting Service, Little Rock, 1982
Ferguson and Atkinson, *Historic Arkansas.* Little Rock, 1966

CALIFORNIA

HISTORY. California, first settled in July 1769, was from its discovery down to 1846 politically associated with Mexico. On 7 July 1846 the American flag was hoisted at Monterey, and a proclamation was issued declaring California to be a portion of the US. On 2 Feb. 1848, by the treaty of Guadalupe–Hidalgo, the territory was formally ceded by Mexico to the US, and was admitted to the Union 9 Sept. 1850 as the thirty-first state, with boundaries as at present.

AREA AND POPULATION. Area, 158,706 sq. miles (2,407 sq. miles being inland water). In 1983 the federal government owned 45m. acres (45·03% of the land area); in 1975, 546,000 acres were under jurisdiction of the Bureau of Indian Affairs, of which 472,000 acres were tribal. Public lands, vacant in 1975, totalled 15,607,125 acres, practically all either mountains or deserts.

Census population, 1 April 1980, 23,667,902, an increase of 18·5% over 1970, making California the most populous state of the USA (New York: 17,557,288). Estimate (1983) 25,174,000. Births in 1982, 429,902 (17·3 per 1,000 population); deaths, 189,075 in 1981; infant deaths, 4,218 (9·8 per 1,000 live births); marriages, 217,348 in 1981 (9); divorces, dissolutions and nullities, 140,473 in 1981 (5·8).

Population in 5 census years was:

	White	*Negro*	*Japanese*	*Chinese*	*Total (incl. all others)*	*Per sq. mile*
1910	2,259,672	21,645	41,356	36,248	2,377,549	15·0
1930	5,408,260	81,048	97,456	37,361	5,677,251	35·8
1960	14,455,230	883,861	157,317	95,600	15,717,204	99·0
1970	17,761,032	1,400,143	213,280	170,131	19,953,134	125·7
			All other			
1980	18,030,893	1,819,281	3,817,728		23,667,902	149·1

Of the 1980 population 49·3% were male, 91·3% were urban and 67·2% were 21 years old or older.

The largest cities with 1980 census population are:

Los Angeles	2,966,850	Anaheim	219,494	Fremont	131,945
San Diego	875,538	Fresno	217,289	Torrance	129,881
San Francisco	678,974	Santa Ana	204,023	Garden Grove	123,307
San José	629,546	Riverside	170,591	San Bernardino	118,794
Long Beach	361,334	Huntington Beach	170,505	Pasadena	118,550
Oakland	339,337	Stockton	149,779	Oxnard	108,195
Sacramento	275,741	Glendale	139,060		

Urbanized areas (1980 census): Los Angeles–Long Beach, 9,477,926; San Francisco–Oakland, 3,191,913; San Diego, 1,704,352; San José, 1,243,900; Sacramento, 796,266; San Bernardino–Riverside, 703,316; Oxnard–Ventura–Thousand Oaks, 378,420; Fresno, 331,551.

CLIMATE. Los Angeles. Jan. 55°F (12·8°C), July 70°F (21·1°C). Annual rainfall 15″ (381 mm). Sacramento. Jan. 45°F (7·2°C), July 74°F (23·3°C). Annual rainfall 19″ (472 mm). San Diego. Jan. 55°F (12·8°C), July 69°F (20·6°C). Annual rainfall

10″ (259 mm). San Francisco. Jan. 50°F (10°C), July 59°F (15°C). Annual rainfall 22″ (561 mm). Death Valley. Jan. 52°F (11°C), July 100°F (38°C). Annual rainfall 1·6″ (40 mm). *See* Pacific Coast, p. 1372.

CONSTITUTION AND GOVERNMENT. The present constitution became effective from 4 July 1879; it has had numerous amendments since 1962. The Senate is composed of 40 members elected for 4 years—half being elected each 2 years—and the Assembly, of 80 members, elected for 2 years. Two-year regular sessions convene in Dec. of each even-numbered year. The Governor and Lieut.-Governor are elected for 4 years.

California is represented in Congress by 2 senators and 45 representatives.

In the 1984 presidential election Reagan polled 5,291,747 votes, Mondale, 3,803,913.

The capital is Sacramento. The state is divided into 58 counties.

Governor: George Deukmejian (R.), 1983–86 ($49,100).
Lieut.-Governor: Leo McCarthy (D.), 1983–86 ($42,500).
Secretary of State: March Fong Eu (D.) ($42,500).

BUDGET. For the year ending 30 June 1984 total General Fund revenues were $23,195m.; total General Fund expenditures were $22,282m. ($11,682m. for education, $7,171m. for health and welfare).

The long-term state debt (general obligation bonds outstanding) was $6,903m. on 30 June 1984.

Per capita personal income (1983) was $13,257.

ENERGY AND NATURAL RESOURCES

Minerals. California is one of the three most important petroleum-producing states of the US (Texas and Louisiana being the other two); crude oil output was estimated at 375m. bbls in 1983. Output of natural gas was 400,872m. cu. ft; of natural gas liquids, (1983) 259m. bbls. Gold output was 6,300 troy oz. (1981); asbestos, boron minerals, diatomite, tungsten, sand and gravel, salt, magnesium compounds, lead, zinc, copper and iron ore are also produced. The estimated value of all the minerals produced (other than fuels) was $1,831m. in 1983.

Agriculture. Extending 700 miles from north to south, and intersected by several ranges of mountains, California has almost every variety of climate, from the very wet to the very dry, and from the temperate to the semi-tropical.

In 1982 there were 82,000 farms, comprising 32m. acres; average farm, 390 acres. Cotton, fruit, poultry and vegetables are important. Cash receipts, 1983, from crops, $8,054m.; from livestock and poultry, $4,160m. Dairy produce, cattle, grapes, cotton, hay, nursery products (in that order) are the main sources of farm income.

Production of cotton lint, 1983, was 473,000 short tons; other field crops included sugar-beet (4·0m. short tons). Cereal crops include maize, 1m. short tons; wheat, 1·4m. short tons, and rice, 1·2m. short tons. Principal crops include wine, table and raisin grapes (4·9m. short tons); peaches (527,000 short tons); pears (267,700 short tons); apricots (91,000 short tons); prunes (145,000 short tons); plums, nectarines, avocados, olives and cherries. Citrus fruit crops were: oranges, 2·9m. short tons; lemons, 756,000 short tons; grapefruit, 238,000 short tons.

On 1 Jan. 1984 the farm animals were: 962,000 milch cows, 5m. all cattle, 900,000 sheep and 155,000 swine.

Forestry. Total forest area in 1979 was 32,558,000 acres, of which 15,795,000 acres were commercial forest. California ranks third to Oregon and Washington in volume of standing timber; total annual cut is about 3,358m. bd ft (1983). National forest service land in 1982 was 19·6m. acres.

Fishery. California ranks fourth as a fishing state (by value of fishery products). The catch in 1983 was 641m. lb.; leading species were anchovy, tuna and mackerel.

INDUSTRY. In 1983, manufacturing employed about 2m. The fastest-growing industries were instruments and related products, non-electrical machinery, electric and electronic equipment, transport equipment and fabricated metal products. The aerospace industry is important, as is also food-processing.

COMMUNICATIONS

Roads. In 1983 California had 53,891 miles of roads inside cities and 120,142 miles outside. In 1983 there were about 13·8m. registered cars and over 3·7m. commercial vehicles, leading all states in all items by a wide margin.

Railways. Total mileage of railways, 1 Jan. 1977, was 7,600 miles. There are 2 systems: Amtrak and Southern Pacific Railroad commuter trains. Amtrak carries about 900,000 passengers per year, Southern Pacific about 5m. Amtrak services run from Oakland (San Francisco) to Seattle, Chicago, Bakersfield and Los Angeles, and also from Los Angeles to San Diego. Southern Pacific runs the Caltrains commuter route from San Francisco to San José. There is a metro (BART) and light rail (Muni) system in San Francisco, and a light rail line in San Diego.

Aviation. In 1980 there were 311 public airports and 950 private airstrips.

Shipping. The chief ports are San Francisco and Los Angeles.

JUSTICE, RELIGION, EDUCATION AND WELFARE

Justice. State prisons, 1 Jan. 1983, had 32,439 male and 1,512 female inmates. From 1893 to 1942, 307 inmates were executed by hanging. From 1938 to 1976, 194 inmates were executed by lethal gas. No further death sentences were passed until 1980.

Religion. The Roman Catholic Church is much stronger than any other single church; next are the Jewish congregations, then Methodists, Presbyterians, Baptists and Episcopalians.

Education. Full-time attendance at school is compulsory for children from 6 to 16 years of age for a minimum of 175 days per annum, and part-time attendance is required from 16 to 18 years. In autumn 1983 there were 4m. pupils enrolled in elementary and secondary schools. Estimated expenditure on public schools, 1982–83, was $11,838m.

Community Colleges had 1,199,269 students in autumn 1983.

California has two publicly supported higher education systems: the University of California (1868) and the California State University and Colleges. In autumn 1983, the University of California with campuses for resident instruction and research at Berkeley, Los Angeles, San Francisco and 6 other centres, had 130,913 full-time students. California State University and Colleges with campuses at Sacramento, Long Beach, Los Angeles, San Francisco and 15 other cities had 199,800 full-time students. In addition to the 28 publicly supported institutions for higher education there are 117 private colleges and universities which had a total estimated enrolment of 171,084 in the autumn of 1983.

Health. In 1984 there were 587 general hospitals; capacity, 112,225 beds. On 30 June 1984 state hospitals for the mentally disabled had 5,142 patients and state hospitals for the developmentally disabled had 7,451 patients.

Social Security. On 1 Jan. 1974 the federal government (Social Security Administration) assumed responsibility for the Supplemental Security Income/State Supplemental Program which replaced the State Old-Age Security. The SSI/SSP provides financial assistance for needy aged (65 years or older), blind or disabled persons. An individual recipient may own assets up to $1,500; a couple up to $2,250, subject to specific exclusions. There are federal, state and county programmes assisting the aged, the blind, the disabled and needy children. In July 1984, 462,000 families with one or more children were receiving an average of $439 per month per family.

Books of Reference

California Almanac, 1984–85. Fay, J. S., (ed.) Oxford, 1984
California Government and Politics. Hoeber, T. R., et al, (eds.) Sacramento, Annual
California Handbook. California Institute, 1981
California Statistical Abstract. 25th ed. Dept. of Finance, Sacramento, 1984
Economic Report of the Governor. Governor's Office, Sacramento, Annual
Lavender, D. S., *California.* New York, 1976

State Library: The California State Library, Library-Courts Bldg, Sacramento 95814.

COLORADO

HISTORY. Colorado was first settled in 1858, made a Territory in 1861 and admitted into the Union on 1 Aug. 1876.

AREA AND POPULATION. Colorado is bounded north by Wyoming, north-east by Nebraska, east by Kansas, south-east by Oklahoma, south by New Mexico and west by Utah. Area, 104,090 sq. miles (496 sq. miles being inland water). Federal lands, 1974, 23,974,000 acres (36% of the land area).

Census population, 1 April 1980, was 2,889,964, an increase of 680,368 or 30·8% since 1970. Estimated (1982), 3,045,000. Births, 1982, were 54,786 (18 per 1,000 population); deaths, 19,638 (6·4); infant deaths, 497 (9 per 1,000 live births); marriages (1981), 37,210 (12·5); dissolutions (1981), 19,515 (6·6).

Population in 5 census years was:

	White	*Negro*	*Indian*	*Asiatic*	*Total*	*Per sq. mile*
1910	783,415	11,453	1,482	2,674	799,024	7·7
1930	1,018,793	11,828	1,395	3,775	1,035,791	10·0
1950	1,296,653	20,177	1,567	5,870	1,325,089	12·7
1970	2,112,352	66,411	8,836	10,388	2,207,259	21·3
			All others			
1980	2,570,615	101,702	216,517		2,888,834 [1]	27·7

[1] Preliminary.

Of the total population in 1980, 49·6% were male, 80·6% were urban; 68% were aged 20 years or older. Large cities with 1980 census population (and 1983 estimate): Denver, 492,365 (500,600); Colorado Springs, 215,150 (230,553); Aurora, 158,588 (178,665); Lakewood, 112,860 (117,436); Pueblo, 101,686 (99,619); Arvada, 84,576 (91,262); Boulder, 76,685 (80,651); Fort Collins, 65,092 (68,307); Wheat Ridge, 30,293 (54,995); Greeley, 53,006 (54,063); Westminster, 50,211.

CLIMATE. Denver. Jan. 31°F (–0·6°C), July 73°F (22·8°C). Annual rainfall 14″ (358 mm). Pueblo. Jan. 30°F (–1·1°C), July 83°F (28·3°C). Annual rainfall 12″ (312 mm). *See* Mountain States, p. 1372.

CONSTITUTION AND GOVERNMENT. The constitution adopted in 1876 is still in effect with (1983) 78 amendments. The General Assembly consists of a Senate of 35 members elected for 4 years, one-half retiring every 2 years, and of a House of Representatives of 65 members elected for 2 years. Sessions are annual, beginning 1951. The Governor, Lieut.-Governor, Attorney-General and Secretary of State are elected for 4 years. Qualified as electors are all citizens, male and female (except convicted, incarcerated criminals), 18 years of age, who have resided in the state and the precinct for 32 days immediately preceding the election. The state is divided into 63 counties. The state sends to Congress 2 senators and 6 representatives.

In the 1984 presidential election Reagan polled 768,711 votes, Mondale, 434,560.

The capital is Denver.

Governor: Richard D. Lamm (D.), 1983–86 ($60,000).
Lieut.-Governor: Nancy Dick (D.), 1983–86 ($32,500).
Secretary of State: Natalie Meyer (R.), 1983–86 ($32,500).

BUDGET. The state's total budget, 1983–84, is $3,889m., of which taxation and other revenue furnish $2,904m. and federal grants $985m. Education takes $1,708m.; health, welfare and rehabilitation, $1,136m., and highways, $672m. Total state and local taxes *per capita* (1983–84) were $860.

The state has no general debt. The net long-term debt (in revenue bond) on 30 June 1984 was $154m.

Per capita personal income (1982) was $12,302.

ENERGY AND NATURAL RESOURCES

Minerals. Colorado has a variety of mineral resources. Among the most important are crude oil, metals and coal. Mineral production in 1983 (estimate) $2,050m. in value. An estimated 29,000 people were employed in extracting petroleum and natural gas in 1984; 9,800 in metals and 4,500 in coal and non-metals.

Agriculture. In May 1984 farms numbered 27,000, with a total area of 33·5m. acres. (66·7% of the land area); 6,625,600 acres (1982) were harvested crop land; average farm (1984), 1,400 acres. Cash income, 1984, from crops $2,200m.; from livestock, $2,020m. In 1984 there were 3,200,000 acres under irrigation.

Production of principal crops in 1982: Maize for grain, 110·4m. bu. (from 830,000 acres); wheat, 87·5m. bu. (3·0m.); hay, 3·7m. tons (1·4m.); dry beans, 2·1m. cwt (170,000); potatoes, 14·2m. cwt (51,400); sugar-beet, 920,000 tons (46,000); oats, barley and sorghums are grown, as well as fruit.

On 1 Jan. 1984 the number of farm animals was: 75,000 milch cows, 3·1m. all cattle, 690,000 sheep, 260,000 swine. The wool clip in 1984 yielded 7m. lb. of wool.

INDUSTRY. In 1983 1,456,000 were employed in non-agricultural sectors, of which 328,000 were in trade; 288,200 in services; 238,800 in government; 185,100 in manufacturing; 80,000 in construction; 82,700 in transport and public utilities; 39,700 in mining; 84,400 in finance, insurance and property. In manufacturing the biggest employers were non-electrical machinery, foods and kindred products, and printing. Value added by manufacturing was $7,748m. (1984 estimate).

TOURISM. In 1984 about 13·5m. people spent holidays in Colorado, of whom about 3% were Colorado residents. Overall expenditure, $2,500m.; $45m. of this was from ski-ing holidays.

COMMUNICATIONS

Roads. The state highway system (1983) included 9,232 miles of highway. County roads totalled 56,898, and city streets, 9,352 miles. Total road mileage, 80,483, of which 5,001 miles are unmaintained county and city roads.

Railways. In 1982 there were in the state 4,500 miles of main-track and branch railway.

Aviation. There were (1984) 233 airports in the state. Of these, 68 are publicly owned and open to the public; 16 are privately owned and open to the public; 149 are private and not open to the public.

JUSTICE, RELIGION, EDUCATION AND WELFARE

Justice. At 30 Sept. 1984 there were 3,050 people committed to the State Department of Corrections, inmates of the State Penitentiary, the State Reformatory and other institutions. In 1967 there was 1 execution; since 1930 executions (by lethal gas) numbered 47, including 41 whites, 5 Negroes and 1 other; all were for murder.

Colorado has a Civil Rights Act (1935) forbidding places of public accommodation to discriminate against any persons on the grounds of race, religion, sex, colour or nationality. No religious test may be applied to teachers or students in the public schools, 'nor shall any distinction or classification of pupils be made on account of race or colour'. In 1957 the General Assembly prohibited discrimination in employment of persons in private industry and in 1959 adopted the Fair Housing

Act to discourage discrimination in housing. A 1957 Act permits marriages between white persons and Negroes or mulattoes.

Religion. In 1984 the Roman Catholic Church had 550,300 members; the ten main Protestant denominations had 350,900 members; the Jewish community had 45,000 members. Buddhism is among other religions represented.

Education. In autumn 1983 the public elementary and secondary schools had 545,174 pupils and 34,500 teachers and administrators; total instructional salaries averaged $20,600. Enrolments in universities and larger colleges, autumn 1983, were: US Air Force Academy (Colorado Springs), 6,000 students; University of Colorado (Boulder), 25,500; University of Colorado (Denver), 10,560; University of Colorado (Colorado Springs), 5,500; University of Colorado (Medical Center), 1,585; Colorado State University (Fort Collins), 17,500; University of Denver (Denver), 9,300; Colorado School of Mines (Golden), 3,200; University of Northern Colorado (Greeley), 10,700; University of Southern Colorado (Pueblo), 5,000; Western State College (Gunnison), 1,700; Adams State College (Alamosa), 2,000; Metropolitan State College (Denver), 17,690; Colorado College (Colorado Springs), 1,950; Fort Lewis College (Durango), 3,650; Mesa College (Grand Junction), 3,400.

Health. Approved hospitals, 1983, numbered 98. In 1983, there were 25 public mental health centres and clinics.

Social Security. A constitutional amendment, adopted 1956, provides for minimum old age pensions of $100 per month, which may be raised on a cost-of-living basis; for a $5m. stabilization fund and for a $10m. medical and health fund for pensioners. In 1984 the maximum monthly retirement pension (for citizens of 65 and older) was $703; maximum monthly benefit for a disabled worker, $854.

Books of Reference

Directory of Colorado Manufacturers, 1982. Business Research Division, School of Business, Univ. of Colorado, Boulder, 1982

Economic Outlook Forum, 1982. Colorado Division of Commerce and Development, and the College of Business, Univ. of Colorado, Denver, 1981

Griffiths, M., and Rubright, L., *Colorado: a Geography.* Boulder, 1983

Sprague, M., *Colorado: A History.* New York, 1976

State Library: Colorado State Library, State Capitol, Denver, 80203.

CONNECTICUT

HISTORY. Connecticut was first settled in 1634 and has been an organized commonwealth since 1637. In 1629 a written constitution was adopted which, it is claimed, was the first in the history of the world formed under the concept of a social compact. This constitution was confirmed by a charter from Charles II in 1662, and replaced in 1818 by a state constitution, framed that year by a constitutional convention.

AREA AND POPULATION. Connecticut is bounded north by Massachusetts, east by Rhode Island, south by the Atlantic and west by New York. Area, 5,018 sq. miles (147 sq. miles being inland water).

Census population, 1 April 1980, 3,107,576, an increase of 2·5% since 1970. Estimate (1982) 3,153,000. Births (1980) were 34,069 (11 per 1,000 population), deaths, 26,597 (8·5); infant deaths, 343 (10 per 1,000 live births); marriages, 25,761 (8·3); divorces, 11,448.

Population in 5 census years was:

	White	*Negro*	*Indian*	*Asiatic*	*Total*	*Per sq. mile*
1910	1,098,897	15,174	152	533	1,114,756	231·3
1930	1,576,700	29,354	162	687	1,606,903	328·0
1960	2,423,816	107,449	923	3,046	2,535,234	517·5
			All others			
1970	2,835,458	181,177	15,074		3,031,709	629·0
1980	2,799,420	217,433	4,533	18,970	3,107,576	634·3

Of the total population in 1980, 1,498,005 persons were male, 2,449,774 persons were urban. Those 19 years old or older numbered 2,228,805.

The chief cities and towns, with census population 1 April 1980, are:

Bridgeport	142,546	New Britain	73,840
Hartford	136,392	Danbury	69,470
New Haven	126,109	Bristol	57,370
Waterbury	103,266	Meriden	57,118
Stamford	102,453	West Haven	53,184
Norwalk	77,767	Milford	50,898

Larger urbanized areas, 1980 census: Hartford, 726,114; Bridgeport, 395,455; New Haven, 417,592; Waterbury, 228,178; Stamford, 198,854.

CLIMATE. New Haven: Jan. 28°F (–2·2°C), July 72°F (22·2°C). Annual rainfall 46″ (1,151 mm). *See* New England, p. 1373.

CONSTITUTION AND GOVERNMENT. The 1818 Constitution was revised in June 1953 effective 1 Jan. 1955. On 30 Dec. 1965 a new constitution went into effect, having been framed by a constitutional convention in the summer of 1965 and approved by the voters in Dec. 1965.

The 1965 Constitution provides for 30 to 50 members of the Senate (instead of 24 to 36) and for 125 to 225 members of the House of Representatives, to be elected from assembly districts, rather than 2 or 1 from each town, as in the former constitution. The convention has added a new provision for a 3-day session following each regular or special session, solely to reconsider bills vetoed by the Governor.

The General Assembly consists of a Senate of 36 members and a House of Representatives of 151 members. Members of each House are elected for the term of 2 years (annual salary $9,500 first year, $7,500 second year; expenses $2,000 and mileage allowance). Legislative sessions are annual. The Governor and Lieut.-Governor are elected for 4 years. All citizens (with necessary exceptions and the usual residential requirements) have the right of suffrage.

Connecticut is one of the original 13 states of the Union. The state is represented in Congress by 2 senators and 6 representatives.

In the 1984 presidential election Reagan polled 883,486 votes, Mondale, 560,712. The state capital is Hartford.

Governor: William A. O'Neill (D.), 1983–86 ($65,000).
Lieut.-Governor: Joseph J. Fauliso (D.), ($40,000).
Secretary of State: Julia Tashjian (D.) ($35,000).

BUDGET. For the year ending 30 June 1982 (state government figures) general revenues were $5,588m. (taxation, $3,723m., and federal aid, $998m.); general expenditures were $5,330m. (education, $1,843m., highways, $376m., and public welfare, $737m.).

The total long-term debt on 30 June 1982 was $4,452m.

Per capita income, 1982, was $13,748.

NATURAL RESOURCES

Minerals. The state has some mineral resources: sheet mica, sand, gravel, clays and stone; total production in 1981 was valued at $63m.

Agriculture. In 1983 the state had 5,000 farms with a total area of about 500,000 acres; average farm was of 111 acres, valued at $2,687 per acre. Total cash income, 1982, was $309m., including $117m. from crops and $192m. from livestock and products (mainly from dairy products and poultry). Principal crops are hay, silage, forest, greenhouse and nursery products, tobacco, potatoes, sweet corn, tomatoes, apples, peaches, pears, vegetables and small fruit.

Livestock (1 Jan. 1980): 108,000 all cattle (value $70·7m.), 5,200 sheep ($387,000), 11,000 swine ($699,000) and 5·8m. poultry ($12m.).

Forestry. The state had (1980) 137,782 acres of state forest land, which is about 4·2% of the total land area.

INDUSTRY. Manufacturing establishments employed 417,560 production workers in Aug. 1980 who earned average weekly wages of $294.47; value added by manufacture (1980), $15,973m. Total non-agricultural employment in 1982 was 1,426,000. The main employers are manufacturers (transport equipment, non-electrical machinery and fabricated metals); trade (303,000 workers); services (301,000) and government (180,000).

COMMUNICATIONS

Roads. The state (1 Jan. 1981) maintains 4,035 miles of highways, all surfaced. Motor vehicles registered in 1979 numbered 2,229,000 (licences issued 1980, 1,688,373).

Railways. In 1981 there were 950 miles of railway track.

Aviation. In 1981 there were 61 airports (27 commercial including 5 state-owned, and 34 heliports).

JUSTICE, RELIGION, EDUCATION AND WELFARE

Justice. In 1981 there were no executions; since 1930 there have been 22 executions (19 by electrocution, 3 by hanging), including 19 whites and 3 Negroes, all for murder. In 1982 there were 3,809 inmates of the state prisons.

The Civil Rights Act makes it a punishable offence to discriminate against any person or persons 'on account of alienage, colour or race' and to hold up to ridicule any persons 'on account of creed, religion, colour, denomination, nationality or race'. Places of public resort are forbidden to discriminate. Insurance companies are forbidden to charge higher premiums to persons 'wholly or partially of African descent'. Schools must be open to all 'without discrimination on account of race or colour'.

Religion. The leading religious denominations (1980) in the state are the Roman Catholic (1·4m. members), United Churches of Christ, Protestant Episcopal, Jewish, Greek Orthodox, Methodist, Baptist, Presbyterian.

Education. Elementary instruction is free for all children between the ages of 4 and 16 years, and compulsory for all children between the ages of 7 and 16 years. In 1981 there were 783 public elementary schools, 236 secondary schools and 5 combined. In 1982 there were 486,470 pupils and 83,301 classroom teachers. The 17 state vocational technical schools had 527,152 students. Expenditure of the state on public schools, 1981, $1,383m. Average salary of teachers in public schools, 1983, $20,800.

Connecticut has 47 colleges, of which one state university, 4 state colleges, 5 state technical colleges and 12 regional community colleges are state funded. The University of Connecticut at Storrs, founded 1881, had 1,253 faculty and 22,407 students in 1980–81. Yale University, New Haven, founded in 1701, had 2,088 faculty and 9,626 students. Wesleyan University, Middletown, founded 1831, had 297 faculty and 2,775 students. Trinity College, Hartford, founded 1823, had 145 faculty and 2,007 students. Connecticut College, New London, founded 1915, had 203 faculty and 1,974 students. The University of Hartford, founded 1877, had 305 faculty and 9,836 students. The regional community colleges (2-year course) had 514 faculty and 34,082 students.

Health. Hospitals listed by the American Hospital Association, 1981, numbered 65, with 17,935 beds. The state operated one general hospital, one veterans' hospital, 8 hospitals for the mentally ill (2,450 patients in Jan. 1981), 2 training schools for the mentally retarded (and 12 regional centres), one chronic disease hospital (56 in-patients in Jan. 1981) and a state-aided institution for the blind.

Social Security. Disbursements during the year ending 30 June 1981 amounted to $10,751,924 for old-age assistance, and medical aid to the aged, $5,413,444. The average monthly number of cases, 1980–81, was 4,782. In other areas of welfare, there was an average of 47,096 cases for aid to families with dependent children; 889 cases for such aid where the parent is unemployed; 84 cases for aid to the blind; 6,357 for aid to the disabled; 1,411 for Connecticut Assistance and Medical Aid to the disabled.

Books of Reference

The Register and Manual of Connecticut. Secretary of State. Hartford. Annual
The Structure of Connecticut's State Government. Connecticut Public Expenditure Council. Hartford, 1973
Adams, V. Q., *Connecticut: The Story of Your State Government.* Chester, 1973
Smith, Allen R., *Connecticut, a Thematic Atlas.* Newington, 1974

State Library: Connecticut State Library, Capitol Avenue, Hartford, 06015. *State Librarian:* Clarence R. Walters.

DELAWARE

HISTORY. Delaware, permanently settled in 1638, is one of the original 13 states of the Union, and the first one to ratify the Federal Constitution.

AREA AND POPULATION. Delaware is bounded north by Pennsylvania, north-east by New Jersey, east by Delaware Bay, south and west by Maryland. Area 2,044 sq. miles (112 sq. miles being inland water). Census population, 1 April 1980 was 594,338, an increase of 46,234 or 8·4% since 1970. Estimate (1983), 606,000. Births in 1983, 9,546; deaths, 5,085; infant deaths, 102; marriages, 5,572; divorces, 3,060.

Population in 5 census years was:

	White	*Negro*	*Indian*	*Asiatic*	*Total*	*Per sq. mile*
1910	171,102	31,181	5	34	202,322	103·0
1930	205,718	32,602	5	55	238,380	120·5
1960	384,327	60,688	597	410	446,292	224·0
			All others			
1970	466,459	78,276	3,369		548,104	276·5
1980	488,002	96,157	10,179		594,338	290·8

Of the total population in 1980, 48·4% were male, 70·7% were urban and 65·7% were 21 years old or older.

The 1980 census figures show Wilmington with population of 70,195; Newark, 25,241; Dover, 23,512; Elsmere Town, 6,493; Milford City, 5,356; Seaford City, 5,256.

CLIMATE. Wilmington. Jan. 32°F (0°C), July 75°F (23·9°C). Annual rainfall 43″ (1,076 mm). *See* Atlantic Coast, p. 1373.

CONSTITUTION AND GOVERNMENT. The present constitution (the fourth) dates from 1897, and has had 51 amendments; it was not ratified by the electorate but promulgated by the Constitutional Convention. The General Assembly consists of a Senate of 21 members elected for 4 years and a House of Representatives of 41 members elected for 2 years. The Governor and Lieut.-Governor are elected for 4 years.

With necessary exceptions, all adult citizens, registered as voters, who are *bona fide* residents, and have complied with local residential requirements, have the right to vote.

Delaware is represented in Congress by 2 senators and 1 representative, elected by the voters of the whole state.

In the 1984 presidential election Reagan polled 151,494 votes, Mondale, 100,632.

The state capital is Dover. Delaware is divided into 3 counties.

Governor: Michael N. Castle (R.), 1984–88 ($70,000).

Lieut.-Governor: S. B. Woo (D.), ($19,200).
Secretary of State: Glenn C. Kenton (R.) ($49,300) (appointed by the Governor).

FINANCE. For the year ending 30 June 1984 general receipts were $1,040·6m., of which federal grants were $271·8m. Total expenditure was $992·5m.
On 30 June 1984 the total debt was $563·5m.
Per capita income (1983) was $12,665.

ENERGY AND NATURAL RESOURCES

Minerals. The mineral resources of Delaware are not extensive, consisting chiefly of clay products, stone, sand and gravel and magnesium compounds. Value of mineral production in 1980 was $2m.

Agriculture. Delaware is mainly an industrial state, but 685,465 acres is in farms, which in 1982 numbered 3,338; average farm was of 196 acres and the average farm was valued (land and buildings) at $364,448.
Cash income, 1983, from crops and livestock, $455m., of which $316m. was from livestock and products. The chief crops are corn and soybeans.

INDUSTRY. In 1981 manufacturing establishments employed 70,512 people; value added by manufacture (1980), $2,466m., mainly from chemicals, transport equipment and food.

COMMUNICATIONS

Roads. The state in 1982 maintained 4,671 miles of roads and streets and 1,369 miles of federally-aided highways. There were also 598 miles of municipal maintained streets. Vehicles registered in year ended 30 June 1984, 468,019.

Railways. In 1984 the state had 285 miles of railway.

Aviation. Delaware had 12 airports, all of which were for general use in 1984.

JUSTICE, RELIGION, EDUCATION AND WELFARE

Justice. State prisons, 1 July 1983–30 June 1984, had daily average of 1,921 inmates. The death penalty was illegal from 2 April 1958 to 18 Dec. 1961. Executions since 1930 (by hanging) have totalled 12 (none since 1946).

Religion. Membership, 1979–80: Methodists, 60,489, Roman Catholics, 103,060; Episcopalians, 18,696; Lutherans, 10,000.

Education. The state has free public schools and compulsory school attendance. In Sept. 1983 the elementary and secondary public schools had 91,406 enrolled pupils and 5,429 classroom teachers. Appropriation for public schools (financial year 1984–85) was about $245·7m. Average salary of classroom teachers (financial year 1983–84), $20,934. The state supports the University of Delaware at Newark (1834) which had 626 full-time faculty members and 17,859 students in Sept. 1983, Delaware State College, Dover (1892), with 74 full-time faculty members and 2,113 students, and the 4 campuses of Delaware Technical and Community College (Wilmington, Stanton, Dover and Georgetown) with 124 full-time faculty members and 7,177 students.

Health. In 1983 there were 7 short-term general hospitals. During financial year 1982 patients in mental hospitals numbered 1,963.

Social Security. In 1974 the federal Supplemental Security Income (SSI) programme lessened state responsibility for the aged, blind and disabled. SSI payments in Delaware (1983), $13m. Provisions are also made for the care of dependent children; in 1983 there were 26,000 recipients in 9,500 families (average monthly payment per family, $233). The total state programme for the year ending 30 June 1983 was $27·02m. for the care of dependent children.

Books of Reference

Information: Division of Historical and Cultural Affairs, Hall of Records, Dover.
State Manual, Containing Official List of Officers, Commissions and County Officers. Secretary of State, Dover. Annual

Hoffecker, C. E., *Delaware: a Bicentennial History.* New York, 1977
Smeal, L., *Delaware Historical and Biographical Index.* New York, 1984
Weslager, C. A., *Delaware Indians, a History.* Rutgers Univ. Press, 1972
Topical History of Delaware. Division of Historical and Cultural Affairs. Dover, 1977

DISTRICT OF COLUMBIA

HISTORY. The District of Columbia, organized in 1790, is the seat of the Government of the US, for which the land was ceded by the states of Maryland and Virginia to the US as a site for the national capital. It was established under Acts of Congress in 1790 and 1791. Congress first met in it in 1800 and federal authority over it became vested in 1801. In 1846 the land ceded by Virginia (about 33 sq. miles) was given back.

AREA AND POPULATION. The District forms an enclave on the Potomac River, where the river forms the south-west boundary of Maryland. The area of the District of Columbia is 68·68 sq. miles, 6 sq. miles being inland water.

Census population, 1 April 1980, was 638,333, a decrease of 16% from that of 1970. Estimate (1982) 631,000. Metropolitan statistical area of Washington, D.C.–Md–Va. (1980), 3m. Density of population in the District, 1980, 10,453 per sq. mile. Births, 1980, in the District were 9,257 (14·5 per 1,000 population); resident deaths, 6,982 (10·9); infant deaths, 228 (24·6 per 1,000 live births); marriages, 5,182 (8·1); divorces, 3,473 (5·4).

Population in 5 census years was:

	White	*Negro*	*Indian*	*Chinese and Japanese*	*Total*	*Per sq. mile*
1910	236,128	94,446	68	427	331,069	5,517·8
1930	353,981	132,068	40	780	486,869	7,981·5
1960	345,263	411,737	587	3,532	763,956	12,523·9
			All others			
1970	209,272	537,712	9,526		756,510	12,321·0
1980	171,768	448,906	17,659		638,333	10,184·0

CLIMATE. Washington. Jan. 34°F (1·1°C), July 77°F (25°C). Annual rainfall 43″ (1,064 mm). *See* Atlantic Coast, p. 1373.

GOVERNMENT. Local government, from 1 July 1878 until Aug. 1967, was that of a municipal corporation administered by a board of 3 commissioners, of whom 2 were appointed from civil life by the President, and confirmed by the Senate, for a term of 3 years each. The other commissioner was detailed by the President from the Engineer Corps of the Army. Reorganization Plan No. 3 of 1967 submitted by the President to Congress on 1 June 1967 abolished the Commission form of government and instituted a new Mayor Council form of government with officers appointed by the President with the advice and consent of the Senate. On 24 Dec. 1973 the appointed officers were replaced by an elected Mayor and councillors, with full legislative powers in local matters as from 1974. Congress retains the right to legislate, to veto or supersede the Council's acts. The 23rd amendment to the federal constitution (1961) conferred the right to vote in national elections; in the 1984 presidential election Mondale polled 172,459 votes, Reagan, 26,805. On 23 Aug. 1978 the Senate approved a constitutional amendment giving the District full voting representation in Congress. In order to become part of the constitution the amendment must be ratified by 38 state legislatures within 7 years. It would give the District 2 senators and a number of representatives according to population.

BUDGET. The District's revenues are derived from a tax on real and personal property, sales taxes, taxes on corporations and companies, licences for conducting various businesses and from federal payments. In financial year 1982 the Council authorized a budget of $1,513,255,700.

The District of Columbia has no bonded debt not covered by its accumulated sinking fund. *Per capita* personal income, 1982, $14,550.

INDUSTRY. The District's main industries (1982) are government service (37%); services (31%); wholesale and retail trade (10%); finance, real estate, insurance, communications, transport and utilities (12%); total employed, 1982, 282,000 (residents).

TOURISM. About 17m. visitors stay in the District every year and spend about $1,000m.

COMMUNICATIONS

Roads. Within the District are 340 miles of bus routes. There are 1,101 miles of streets maintained by the District; of these, 673 miles are local streets, 262 miles are major arterial roads.

Railways. There is a rapid rail transit system including a town subway system. This coordinates with the bus system and connects with Union railway station and the National Airport. Nine rail lines serve the District.

Aviation. The District is served by 3 general airports; across the Potomac River in Arlington, Va., is National Airport, in Chantilly, Va., is Dulles International Airport and in Maryland is Baltimore—Washington International Airport.

JUSTICE, RELIGION, EDUCATION AND WELFARE

Justice. Since 1958 there have been no executions; from 1930 to 1957 there were 40 executions (electrocution) including 3 whites for murder and 35 Negroes for murder and 2 for rape. The death penalty was declared unconstitutional in the District of Columbia on November 16, 1973

The District's Court system is the Judicial Branch of the District of Columbia. It is the only completely unified court system in the United States, possibly because of the District's unique city-state jurisdiction. Until the District of Columbia Court Reform and Criminal Procedure Act of 1970, the judicial system was almost entirely in the hands of Federal Government. Since that time, the system has been similar in most respects to the autonomous systems of the states.

Religion. The largest churches are the Protestant and Roman Catholic Christian churches; there are also Jewish, Eastern Orthodox and Islamic congregations.

Education. In 1981–82 there were about 90,000 pupils in secondary and elementary schools. Expenditure on public schools, 1982–83, averages $3,530 per pupil. There are also 17,560 pupils in private elementary and secondary schools. Higher education is given through the Consortium of Universities of the Metropolitan Washington Area, which consists of six universities and three colleges: Georgetown University, founded in 1795 by the Jesuit Order (12,000 students in 1982); George Washington University, non-sectarian founded in 1821 (17,000); Howard University, founded in 1867 (11,000); Catholic University of America, founded in 1887 (7,700; American University (Methodist) founded in 1893 (12,500); University of D.C., founded 1976 (13,500); Gallandet College, founded 1864 (1,000); Mount Vernon College, founded 1875 (500); Trinity College, founded 1897 (1,000). There are four other schools of higher education.

All benefit from such facilities as the 12 museums of the Smithsonian Institution, the Library of Congress, National Archives, and the Legal Libraries of the US Supreme Court and Department of Justice.

Social Security The District government provides primary health care for residents, mainly through its Department of Human Services, (about 6,280 employees). Departmental budget, 1981, $470m. of District, Federal and other funds.

Books of Reference

Statistical Information: The Metropolitan Washington Board of Trade publications.
Reports of the Commissioners of the District of Columbia. Annual. Washington
Federal Writers' Project. *Washington, D.C.: A Guide to the Nation's Capital.* New York

FLORIDA

HISTORY. White men, probably Spaniards but possibly English, saw Florida for the first time in the period 1497–1512. Juan Ponce de Leon sighted Florida on 27 March 1513. Going ashore between 2 and 8 April in the vicinity of what is now St Augustine, he named the land 'Pasqua de Flores' because his landing was 'in the time of the Feast of Flowers'. The first permanent settlement in the entire US was made at St Augustine, 8 Sept. 1565. It was claimed by Spain until 1763, then ceded to England; back to Spain in 1783, and to the US in 1821. Florida became a Territory in 1821 and was admitted into the Union on 3 March 1845.

AREA AND POPULATION. Florida is a peninsula bounded west by the Gulf of Mexico, south by the Straits of Florida, east by the Atlantic, north by Georgia and north-west by Alabama. Area, 58,664 sq. miles, including 4,510 sq. miles of inland water. Census population, 1 April 1980, was 9,746,324, an increase of 43·4% since 1970. Estimate (1984) 10,925,000. Births in 1980 were 131,923; deaths, 106,815; infant deaths, 1,904; marriages, 110,575; divorces, 71,409.

Population in 5 federal census years was:

	White	*Negro*	*All Others*	*Total*	*Per Sq. Mile*
1940	1,381,986	514,198	1,230	1,897,414	35·0
1950	2,166,051	603,101	2,153	2,771,305	51·1
1960	4,063,881	880,168	7,493	4,952,788	91·5
1970	5,719,343	1,041,651	28,449	6,789,443	125·6
1980	8,319,448	1,342,478	84,398	9,746,324	180·1

Of the population in 1980, 48% of the total were male; 84·3% were urban and 72·4% were 20 years of age or over.

The largest cities in the state (1980 census) are: Jacksonville, 540,898; Miami, 346,931; Tampa, 271,523; St Petersburg, 236,893; Fort Lauderdale, 153,256; Hialeah, 145,254; Orlando, 128,394; Hollywood, 117,188; Miami Beach, 96,298; Clearwater, 85,450; Tallahassee, 81,548; Gainesville, 81,371; West Palm Beach, 62,530; Largo, 58,977; Pensacola, 57,619.

CLIMATE. Jacksonville. Jan. 55°F (12·8°C), July 81°F (27·2°C). Annual rainfall 54″ (1,353 mm). Key West. Jan. 70°F (21·1°C), July 83°F (28·3°C). Annual rainfall 39″ (968 mm). Miami. Jan. 67°F (19·4°C), July 82°F (27·8°C). Annual rainfall 60″ (1,516 mm). Tampa. Jan. 61°F (16·1°C), July 81°F (27·2°C). Annual rainfall 51″ (1,285 mm). *See* Gulf Coast, p. 1373.

CONSTITUTION AND GOVERNMENT. The 1968 Legislature revised the constitution of 1885. The state legislature consists of a Senate of 40 members, elected for 4 years, and House of Representatives with 120 members elected for 2 years. Sessions are held annually, and are limited to 60 days. The Governor is elected for 4 years, and can hold two terms in office. Two senators and 19 representatives are elected to Congress.

In the 1984 presidential election Reagan polled 2,512,318 votes and Mondale, 1,373,137.

The state capital is Tallahassee. The state is divided into 67 counties.

Governor: Robert Graham (D.), 1983–86 ($69,550).
Lieut.-Governor: Wayne Mixson (D.), 1983–86 ($60,455).
Secretary of State: George Firestone (D.), 1983–86 ($59,385).

FINANCE. There is no state income tax on individuals. For the year ending 30 June 1983 the state had a total revenue of $20,858m. and total expenditure of $20,681m. General revenue fund expenditure was $5,159m., of which education took $2,997m.; public welfare, $392m.; and highways, $98m.

Net long-term debt, 30 June 1981, amounted to $1,940·8m.

Per capita personal income (1983) was $11,592 (preliminary).

NATURAL RESOURCES

Minerals. Chief mineral is phosphate rock, of which marketable production in 1981 was 41·7m. tonnes, leading all states (national production 53·6m. tons). Total value of mineral production, 1981, $1,725·5m.

Agriculture. In 1981, there were 40,000 farms; net income per farm was $21,817. Total value of all farm land and buildings, 1981, $19,600m. There were 847,056 acres in citrus groves and 12·2m. acres of other farms and ranches. Total cash receipts from crops and livestock (1981), $4,144m., of which crops provided $3,114·6m. Oranges, grapefruit, melons and vegetables are important. Other crops are soybeans ($68m.), sugar-cane, tobacco and peanuts. On 1 Jan. 1981 the state had 2·1m. cattle, including 189,000 milch cows, and 257,000 swine.

The national forests area in Sept. 1980 was 1,097,930 acres. There were (1983) 16m. acres of commercial forest.

Fisheries. Florida has extensive fisheries for oysters, shrimp, red snapper, crabs, mackerel and mullet. Catch (1980), 187·4m. lb. valued at $132·8m.

INDUSTRY. In 1982 there were 13,610 manufacturers. They employed 469,745 persons. The metal-working, lumber, chemical, woodpulp, food-processing and instruments industries are important.

TOURISM. During 1983 38·9m. tourists visited Florida. They spent $22,800m. making tourism one of the biggest industries in the state. There are 121 state parks, 4 state forests, 1 national park and 4 national forests. The state parks were visited by 15m. people in 1982, 1·3m. of them campers.

COMMUNICATIONS

Roads. The state (1981) had 97,186 miles of road and streets including 8,854 miles of primary federally-aided highways.

In 1980–81, 10·3m. vehicle licence plates were issued.

Railways. In 1980 there were 3,681 miles of railway.

Aviation. In 1984 Florida had 591 airports, including 137 public use airports of which 16 are international, 20 have air carrier service and 10 have scheduled commuter service. There are 3 public and 9 private seaplane bases.

JUSTICE, RELIGION, EDUCATION AND WELFARE

Justice. Since 1968 there have been 3 executions, by electrocution, for murder; from 1930 to 1968 there were 168 executions (electrocution), including 130 for murder, 37 for rape and 1 for kidnapping. State prisons, 30 June 1982, had 26,036 in-mates.

Religion. The main Christian churches are Roman Catholic, Baptist, Methodist, Presbyterian and Episcopalian.

Education. Attendance at school is compulsory between 7 and 16.

In 1981–82 the public elementary and secondary schools had 1,488,073 enrolled pupils. State expenditure on public schools (1981–82) was $4,133·5m. The state maintains 28 community colleges with 357,993 enrolments in 1982.

There are 9 universities in the state system, namely the University of Florida at Gainesville (founded 1853) with 34,061 students in 1982; the Florida State University (founded at Tallahassee in 1857) with 22,116 students; the University of

South Florida at Tampa (founded 1960) with 24,978 students; Florida A. & M. University at Tallahassee (founded 1887) with 4,728 students; Florida Atlantic University (founded 1964) at Boca Raton with 8,296 students; the University of West Florida at Pensacola with 5,279 students; the University of Central Florida at Orlando with 13,093 students; the University of North Florida at Jacksonville with 4,998 students; Florida International University at Miami with 11,892 students.

Health. Hospitals, 1983, numbered 263 with 59,048 beds; there were 225 general, 38 special and 1 tuberculosis hospitals.

Social Security. From 1974 aid to the aged, blind and disabled became a federal responsibility. The state continued to give aid to families with dependent children and general assistance. Monthly payments 1981–82: aid to 4,800 blind averaged $188.44; aid to 174,089 dependent children averaged $63.46; aid to 145,000 disabled averaged $181.91; aid to 123,000 aged averaged $149.49.

Books of Reference

Florida Population: Summary of the 1980 Census. Univ. of Florida Press, 1981
Florida Statistical Abstract. Univ. of Florida Press, 1983
Florida Tourist Study. Florida Department of Commerce, Tallahassee. Annual
Historical Florida Economic Data 1970–83. Florida Dept. of Commerce, 1983
Report. Florida Secretary of State. Tallahassee. Biennial
Report of the Comptroller. Tallahassee. Biennial
Dimensions. Bureau of Business and Economic Research, Univ. of Florida, Gainesville. Monthly
Morris, Allen. *The Florida Handbook.* Tallahassee. Biennial
Fernald, E. A., (ed.) *Atlas of Florida.* Florida State Univ., 1981

State Library: Gray Building, Tallahassee. *Librarian:* Barratt Wilkins.

GEORGIA

HISTORY. Georgia (so named from George II) was founded in 1733 as the 13th original colony; she became the 4th original state.

AREA AND POPULATION. Georgia is bounded north by Tennessee and North Carolina, north-east by South Carolina, east by the Atlantic, south by Florida and west by Alabama. Area, 58,910 sq. miles, of which 854 sq. miles are inland water. Census population, 1 April 1980, was 5,464,265. Estimate (1981), 5,639,000. Births, 1980, were 95,980 (17·5 per 1,000 population); deaths, 43,519 (7·9); infant deaths, 1,208 (12·6 per 1,000 live births); marriages, 69,416 (12·7); divorces and annulments, 33,636 (6·2).

Population in 5 census years was:

	White	*Negro*	*Indian*	*Asiatic*	*Total*	*Per sq. mile*
1910	1,431,802	1,176,987	95	237	2,609,121	44·4
1930	1,837,021	1,071,125	43	317	2,908,506	49·7
1960	2,817,223	1,122,596	749	2,004	3,943,116	67·7
			All others			
1970	3,391,242	1,187,149	11,184		4,589,575	79·0
1980	3,948,007	1,465,457	50,801		5,464,265	92·7

Of the 1980 population, 2,641,030 were male, 3,406,171 were urban and those 20 years of age and over numbered 3,601,895.

The largest cities are: Atlanta (capital), with population, 1980 census, of 422,293 (urbanized area, 2,010,368); Columbus, 168,598 (238,593); Savannah, 133,672 (225,581); Macon, 116,044 (251,736); Albany, 74,471 (112,257).

CLIMATE. Atlanta. Jan. 43°F (6·1°C), July 78°F (25·6°C). Annual rainfall 49″ (1,234 mm). *See* Atlantic Coast, p. 1373.

CONSTITUTION AND GOVERNMENT. A new constitution was ratified in the general election of 2 Nov. 1976, proclaimed on 22 Dec. 1976 and became effective 1 Jan. 1977. The General Assembly consists of a Senate of 56 members and a House of Representatives of 180 members, both elected for 2 years. The Governor and Lieut.-Governor are elected for 4 years. Legislative sessions are annual, beginning the 2nd Monday in Jan. and lasting for 40 days.

Georgia was the first state to extend the franchise to all citizens 18 years old and above. The state is represented in Congress by 2 senators and 10 representatives.

Registered voters, 1976, numbered 2,178,623. At the 1984 presidential election Reagan polled 1,050,852 votes, Mondale, 696,181.

The state capital is Atlanta. Georgia is divided into 159 counties.

Governor: Joe F. Harris (D.), 1982–86 ($71,314).
Lieut.-Governor: Zell Miller (D.), ($41,496).
Secretary of State: Max Cleland (D.), ($51,896).

BUDGET. For the fiscal year ending 30 June 1982 general revenue was $9,009m. (taxes, $4,666m.; federal aid, $2,158m.); general expenditure was $8,401m. (education, $2,900m.; public welfare, $895m.; hospitals, $1,384m.).

On 30 June 1982 total liability was $6,877m.

Estimated *per capita* personal income (1982), was $9,583.

NATURAL RESOURCES

Minerals. Georgia is the leading producer of kaolin. The state ranks first in production of crushed and dimensional granite, second in production of fuller's earth and marble (crushed and dimensional).

Mineral products, 1981, had a value of $804m.

Agriculture. In 1983, 55,000 farms covered 15m. acres; average farm was of 273 acres; average value per acre, $817. For 1982 cotton output was 235,000 bales (of 480 lb.). Other crops, 1982, included tobacco, 106m. lb; corn, 69m. bu.; soybeans, peanuts and pecans. Cash income, 1982, $3,210m: from crops, $1,550m.; from livestock, $1,660m.

On 1 Jan. 1983 farm animals included 1·9m. all cattle, including 130,000 milch cows, and 1·4m. swine.

Forestry. The forested area in 1980 was 25m. acres.

INDUSTRY. In 1982 the state's manufacturing establishments had 501,000 workers; the main groups were textiles, transport equipment, food, wood products and paper, chemicals. Trade employed 520,000, services 372,000.

TOURISM. In 1982 tourists spent $6,380m.

COMMUNICATIONS

Roads. Total road mileage (Dec. 1980) was 134,500 including 88,900 rural and 11,850 primary federal-aided. Motor vehicles registered, 1981, numbered 3,850,000.

Railways. In 1976 there were 5,417 miles of railways. A metro opened in Atlanta in 1979.

Aviation. In 1981 there were 125 public and 168 private airports.

Shipping. The principal port is Savannah.

JUSTICE, RELIGION, EDUCATION AND WELFARE

Justice. State prisons, 31 Dec. 1982, had 14,049 inmates. Since 1964 there have been two executions (for murder). From 1924 to 1964 there were 415 executions (electrocution), including 75 whites and 268 Negroes for murder, 3 whites and 63 Negroes for rape and 6 Negroes for armed robbery.

Under a Local Option Act, the sale of alcoholic beverages (not including malt beverages and light wines) is prohibited in more than half the counties.

Religion. An estimated 78% of the population are church members. Of the total population, 74·3% are Protestant, 3·2% are Roman Catholic and 1·5% Jewish.

Education. Since 1945 education has been compulsory; tuition is free for pupils between the ages of 6 and 18 years. In 1981 there were 1,305 public elementary schools and 451 public secondary schools; in autumn 1982 they had 1m. pupils and 56,510 teachers. Teachers' salaries averaged $17,400 in 1983. Integration in public schools is now an accepted practice.

The University of Georgia (Athens) was founded in 1785 and was the first chartered State University in the US. Other institutions of higher learning include Georgia Institute of Technology (Atlanta), Emory University (Atlanta), Agnes Scott College (Decatur), Georgia College (Milledgeville), Georgia State University (Atlanta) and Mercer University (Macon). The Atlanta University Center, devoted primarily to Negro education, includes Clark College and Morris Brown College, co-educational, Morehouse, a liberal arts college for men, Interdenominational Theological Center, a co-educational theological school, and Spelman College, the first liberal arts college for Negro women in the US. Atlanta University serves as the graduate school centre for the complex. Wesleyan College near Macon is the oldest chartered women's college in the US. Total enrolment, 1982, was 198,000 in 80 institutions of higher education.

Health. Hospitals licensed by the Department of Human Resources, 1980, numbered 191 with 31,100 beds. State facilities for the mentally retarded had 1,363 resident patients in 1980; there were 4,527 in mental care hospitals.

Social Security. In Dec. 1980, 71,100 persons were receiving SSI old-age assistance of an average $104 per month; 89,900 families were receiving as aid to dependent children an average of $133 per family; aid to 80,500 disabled persons was $163 monthly.

Books of Reference

Georgia History in Outline. Univ. of Georgia Press, Athens, 1978

Bonner, J. C., and Roberts, L. E., eds., *Studies in Georgia History and Government.* Reprint Company, Spartanburg, 1940 Repr.

Pound, M. B., and Saye, A. B., *Handbook on the Constitution of the U.S. and Georgia.* Univ. of Georgia Press, Athens, 1978

Rowland, A. R., *A Bibliography of the Writings on Georgia History.* Hamden, Conn., 1978

Saye, A. B., *A Constitutional History of Georgia, 1732–1968.* Univ. of Georgia, Athens, Rev. ed., 1970

State Library: Judicial Building, Capital Sq., Atlanta. *State Librarian:* John D. M. Folger.

HAWAII

HISTORY. The Hawaiian Islands, formerly known as the Sandwich Islands, were discovered by Capt. James Cook in Jan. 1778. During the greater part of the 19th century the islands formed an independent kingdom, but in 1893 the reigning Queen, Liliuokalani (died 11 Nov. 1917), was deposed and a provisional government formed; in 1894 a Republic was proclaimed, and in accordance with the request of the people of Hawaii expressed through the Legislature of the Republic, and a resolution of the US Congress of 6 July 1898 (signed 7 July by President McKinley), the islands were on 12 Aug. 1898 formally annexed to the US. On 14 June 1900 the islands were constituted as a Territory of Hawaii.

Statehood was granted to Hawaii on 18 March 1959.

AREA AND POPULATION. The Hawaiian Islands lie in the North Pacific Ocean, between 18° 50′ and 28° 15′ N. lat. and 154° 40′ and 178° 15′ W. long., about 2,090 nautical miles south-west of San Francisco. There are more than 20 islands in the group, of which 7 are inhabited. The land and inland water area of the state is 6,471 sq. miles, with census population, 1 April 1980, of 964,691, an increase of 194,778 or 25·4% since 1970; density was 150 per sq. mile.

The principal islands are Hawaii, 4,035 sq. miles (population, 1980, 92,053); Maui, 735 (62,823); Oahu, 618 (762,534); Kauai, 558 (38,856); Molokai, 264 (6,049); Lanai, 141 (2,119); Niihau, 71 (226); Kahoolawe, 46 (0). The capital Honolulu, on the island of Oahu, had a population in 1980 of 365,017 and Hilo on the island of Hawaii, 35,269.

Figures for racial groups, 1980, are: 331,925 White, 239,734 Japanese, 132,075 Filipinos, 118,251 Hawaiian, 55,916 Chinese, 17,453 Korean, 17,687 Negroes, 51,650 all others. Of the total, approximately 92% were citizens of the US.

Inter-marriage between the races is popular. Of the 11,856 persons married in the calendar year 1980, 37·6% married a wife or husband of a different race. Births, 1982, were 18,675; deaths, 5,123; infant deaths, 158; marriages, 13,483; divorces and annulments, 4,233.

CLIMATE. All the islands have a tropical climate, with an abrupt change in conditions between windward and leeward sides, most marked in rainfall. Temperatures vary little. Honolulu. Jan. 71°F (21·7°C), July 78°F (25·6°C). Annual rainfall 31″ (775 mm).

CONSTITUTION AND GOVERNMENT. The constitution took effect on 21 Aug. 1959.

The Legislature consists of a Senate of 25 members elected for 4 years, and a House of Representatives of 51 members elected for 2 years. The constitution provides for annual meetings of the legislature with 60-day regular sessions. The Governor and Lieut.-Governor are elected for 4 years. The registered voters, 1982, numbered 405,005.

The state sends to Congress 2 senators and 2 representatives.

In the 1984 presidential election Reagan polled 183,998 votes, Mondale, 145,975.

Governor: George R. Ariyoshi (D.), 1983–86 ($59,400).
Lieut.-Governor: John Waihee (D.), 1983–86 ($53,460).

BUDGET. Revenue is derived mainly from taxation of sales and gross receipts, real property, corporate and personal income, and inheritance taxes, licences, public land sales and leases. For the year ending 30 June 1982 state general fund receipts amounted to $1,148·3m.; special fund receipts, $841·1m., and federal grants, $370·65m. State expenditures were $1,958·5m. (education, $632·6m.; highways, $48·9m.; public welfare, $317·2m.; figures include both special and general funds).

Net long-term debt, 31 Dec. 1982, amounted to $2,359·5m.

Estimated *per capita* personal income (1982) was $11,652.

NATURAL RESOURCES

Minerals. Total value of mineral production, 1981, amounted to $58·7m. Cement shipped from plants amounted to 312,000 short tons; stone, 6·04m. short tons.

Agriculture. Farming is highly commercialized, aiming at export to the American market, and highly mechanized. In 1981 there were 4,400 farms with an acreage of 1·97m.

Sugar and pineapples are the staple crops. Income from crop sales, 1982, was $434·3m., and from livestock, $78·3m. The sugar crop was valued at $230·8m.; pineapples, $99·5m.; other crops, $104m.

Forestry. Commercial forests totalled 948,000 acres (1977 census); state lands in 1983, 1·2m. acres. Land held by the federal government in 1983 totalled 328,414 acres.

INDUSTRY AND TRADE

Industry. In 1978 manufacturing establishments employed 23,700 production workers who earned an estimated $285·2m.; value added by manufacture was estimated at $782·9m.

Commerce. In 1981 imports of newsprint, fertilizer, lumber, feed, crude oil and other products from foreign countries such as Saudi Arabia, Indonesia and Japan were $1,982·2m.; exports, primarily food and manufactures, amounted to $237·7m.

Tourism. Tourism is an outstanding factor in Hawaii's economy. Tourist arrivals numbered 109,798 in 1955, and reached 4·24m. in 1982. Tourist expenditures, totalling $55m. in 1955, contributed $3,700m. to the state's economy in 1982.

COMMUNICATIONS

Roads. In 1982 there were 671,513 motor vehicles, and a total of 4,060 miles of highways (including 36 miles of federally assisted highways).

Aviation. There were 8 commercial airports in 1982; passengers arriving from overseas numbered 4·6m., and there were 7·3m. passengers between the islands.

Shipping. Several lines of steamers connect the islands with the mainland USA, Canada, Australia, the Philippines, China and Japan. In 1980, 10,096 inbound vessels entered Hawaiian ports.

Post. There were 728,352 telephones at 31 Dec. 1981.

JUSTICE, RELIGION, EDUCATION AND WELFARE

Justice. There is no capital punishment in Hawaii.

Religion. The residents of Hawaii are mainly Christians, though there are many Buddhists. A sample survey in 1979 showed that 31% were Roman Catholic, 34% Protestant, 12% Buddhist, 2·5% Latter Day Saints.

Education. Education is free, and compulsory for children between the ages of 6 and 18. The language in the schools is English. In 1982–83 there were 233 public schools (162,024 pupils with 8,083 teachers) and 140 private schools (38,105 pupils and 2,219 teachers) ranging from kindergarten through the 12th grade. The University of Hawaii, founded in 1907, had 20,629 day students in 1981; total university and college attendance 1982–83, 67,778 at the University and Community colleges, 6,619 at private colleges (1981–82).

Social Security. During 1981 the state spent $286·7m., the federal government provided $137·7m. of this. In 1981 there were 25 non-military hospitals (2,925 beds) listed by the Department of Health. During 1982 the average number of persons served by major welfare programmes was 68,835.

Books of Reference

Government in Hawaii. Tax Foundation of Hawaii. Honolulu, 1984
Guide to Government in Hawaii. 8th ed. Legislative Reference Bureau. State of Hawaii, Honolulu, 1984
All About Hawaii: Thrum's Hawaiian Annual and Standard Guide. Honolulu, 1875 to 1974
Current Hawaiiana (quarterly bibliography). Hawaii Library Association, Honolulu
Allen, G. E., *Hawaii's War Years.* 2 vols. Hawaii Univ. Press, 1950–52
Bell, R. J., *Last Among Equals: Hawaiian Statehood and American Politics.* Honolulu, 1984
Kuykendall, R. S., and Day, A. G., *Hawaii, A History.* Rev. ed. New Jersey, 1961
Morgan, J. R., *Hawaii.* Boulder, 1982
Pukui, M. K., and Elbert, S. H., *Hawaiian–English Dictionary.* Honolulu, 1957

IDAHO

HISTORY. Idaho was first permanently settled in 1860, although there was a mission for Indians in 1836 and a Mormon settlement in 1855. It was organized as a Territory in 1863 and admitted into the Union as a state on 3 July 1890.

AREA AND POPULATION. Idaho is bounded north by Canada, east by the Rocky Mountains of Montana and Wyoming, south by Nevada and Utah, west by Oregon and Washington. Area, 83,564 sq. miles, of which 1,153 sq. miles are inland water. In 1970 the federal government owned 33,979,389 acres (64% of the state area). Census population, 1 April 1980, 943,935, an increase of 32·4% since 1970. Estimate (1983) 989,000.

Births, 1983, 18,742 (19·2 per 1,000 population); deaths, 7,204 (7·4); infant deaths, 195 (10 per 1,000 live births); marriages, 13,421 (13·8); divorces, 6,228 (6·4).

Population in 5 census years was:

	White	*Negro*	*Indian*	*Asiatic*	*Total*	*Per sq. mile*
1910	319,221	651	3,488	2,234	325,594	3·9
1930	438,840	668	3,638	1,886	445,032	5·4
1960	657,383	1,502	5,231	2,958	667,191	8·1
1970	693,375	3,655	5,413	2,526	713,008	8·5
			All others			
1980	901,641	2,716	39,578		943,935	11·3

Of the total 1980 population, 471,155 were male, 509,702 were urban and those 20 years of age or older 600,242.

The largest cities are Boise (capital) with 1980 census population of 102,160 (1982 estimate, 104,586); Pocatello, 46,340 (46,494); Idaho Falls, 39,734 (40,700); Lewiston, 27,986 (27,762); Twin Falls, 26,209 (26,947); Nampa, 25,112 (26,242).

CLIMATE. Boise. Jan. 29°F (−1·7°C), July 74°F (23·3°C). Annual rainfall 12" (303 mm). *See* Mountain States, p. 1372.

CONSTITUTION AND GOVERNMENT. The constitution adopted in 1890 is still in force; it has had 104 amendments. The Legislature consists of a Senate of 42 members and a House of Representatives of 84 members, all the legislators being elected for 2 years. The Governor, Lieut.-Governor and Secretary of State are elected for 4 years. Voters are citizens, over the age of 18 years. The state is represented in Congress by 2 senators and 2 representatives.

In the 1984 presidential election Reagan polled 296,687 votes, Mondale, 108,447.

The state is divided into 44 counties. The capital is Boise.

Governor: John V. Evans (D.), 1983–86 ($50,000).
Lieut. Governor: David Leroy (R.), 1983–86 ($14,000).
Secretary of State: Pete Cenarrusa (R.), 1983–86 ($37,500).

BUDGET. For the year ending 30 June 1984 (State Auditor's Office) general revenues were $504·5m. and general expenditures included education, $506·8m. (which includes $7·7m. outstanding obligations), transport, $183·5m., and health and welfare, $195·8m. (which includes $66·6m. General Account money).

Per capita personal income (1982) was $9,210.

NATURAL RESOURCES

Minerals. Production of the most important minerals (1983): Lead, 25,726 tonnes; silver, 17·7m. troy oz.; copper, 3,556 tonnes; antimony, 585 short tons. There is some gold, zinc and vanadium. Non-metallic minerals include phosphate rock, barite, clay, garnet, gypsum, perlite, lime, cement, pumice, sand and gravel and dimension stone. Value of total mineral output was $415m. in 1983.

Agriculture. Agriculture is the leading industry, although a great part of the state is naturally arid. Extensive irrigation works have been carried out, bringing an estimated 4m. acres under irrigation; 83 reservoirs have a total capacity of 10·4m. acre-ft, 7·3m. acre-ft of which is primarily used for irrigation.

In 1984 there were 24,000 farms with a total area of 14·7m. acres (27% of the land area); average farm had 598 acres with land and buildings valued at approximately $700 per acre.

In 1984 there were 51 soil conservation districts, managed by local farmers and ranchers, covering most of the state.

Cash receipts from marketings, 1983, was $2,082m. ($1,134m. from crops and $894m. from livestock). The most important crops are potatoes and wheat—potatoes leading all states; in 1983 the production amounted to 83·6m. cwt, cash receipts $288m. Other crops are sugar-beet, alfalfa, barley, field peas and beans, onions and apples. On 1 Jan. 1984 the number of sheep was 383,000; milch cows, 174,000; all cattle, 1·89m.; swine, 120,000.

Forestry. In 1983 a total of 20,635,700 acres (37·6% of the state's area) was in forests; 13,540,600 acres of this was commercial (non-reserved) forest. The volume of sawtimber in commercial forests was 139,600m. bd ft. The stumpage value of forest products was about $124m., and about $531m. was added by processing. Ownership of commercial forests is 70% federal, 6·5% state and local government, 0·5% Indian, 22·3% private. Some 16,100 workers are involved in forestry.

INDUSTRY. In 1980 there were about 1,500 manufacturing establishments and they employed about 48,000 workers; value added by manufacture was $1,931m.

TOURISM. Money spent by travellers in 1983 was about $1,100m. Estimated state and local tax receipts from tourism, $48m. Jobs generated, 25,000 (pay-roll over $300m.).

COMMUNICATIONS

Roads. The state maintained in 1983, 4,951 miles of the total of 67,254 miles of public roads; 722,401 passenger vehicles were registered in 1983.

Railways. The state had (1984) 1,910 miles of railways (including 2 AMTRAK routes) operated by 3 companies and serving all but 3 counties.

Aviation. There were 71 municipally owned airports in 1983.

Shipping. Water transport is provided from the Pacific to the Port of Lewiston, by way of the Columbia and Snake rivers, a distance of 464 miles.

JUSTICE, RELIGION, EDUCATION AND WELFARE

Justice. The death penalty may be imposed for first degree murder, but the judge must consider mitigating circumstances before imposing a sentence of death. Since 1926 only 3 men (white) have been executed, by hanging (2 in 1951 and 1 in 1957). At 1 Oct. 1984 12 prison inmates (11 men and 1 woman) were under sentence of death. Execution is now by lethal injection. The state prison system, 1 Oct. 1984, had 1,137 inmates.

Religion. The leading religious denominations are the Church of Jesus Christ of Latter Day Saints (Mormon Church), Roman Catholics, Methodists, Presbyterians, Episcopalians and Lutherans.

Education. In 1983–84 public elementary schools (grades K to 6) had 116,474 pupils and 5,285 classroom teachers; secondary schools had 91,891 pupils and 4,844 classroom teachers.

Average salary, 1983–84, of elementary and secondary classroom teachers, $18,012. The University of Idaho, founded at Moscow in 1889, had 451 professors and 9,239 students in 1983–84. There are 9 other institutions of higher education; 5 of them are public institutions with a total enrolment (1983–84) of 23,880 (excluding vocational-technical colleges).

Social Welfare. Old-age assistance is granted to persons 65 years of age. In Aug. 1984, 1,020 persons were drawing an average of $104.85 per month; 6,337 families with 11,551 children were drawing an average of $244.05 per case (or $88.74 per eligible person); 23 blind persons, $88.08; 508 children were receiving $207.37 per child for foster care.

Health. In Sept. 1984 skilled nursing covered 4,535 beds; intermediate care,

119; intermediate care for the mentally retarded 568. Hospitals had 3,524 beds and home health agencies totalled 29.

Books of Reference

Idaho Blue Book. Secretary of State. Boise, 1981–82
Idaho. Idaho First National Bank
Idaho Almanac. Division of Economic and Community Affairs, 1977
Idaho's Yesterdays. State Historical Society. Quarterly

ILLINOIS

HISTORY. Illinois was first discovered by Joliet and Marquette, two French explorers, in 1673. In 1763 the country was ceded by the French to the British. In 1783 Great Britain recognized the United States' title to the land that became Illinois; it was organized as a Territory in 1809 and admitted into the Union on 3 Dec. 1818.

AREA AND POPULATION. Illinois is bounded north by Wisconsin, north-east by Lake Michigan, east by Indiana, south-east by the Ohio River (forming the boundary with Kentucky), west by the Mississippi River (forming the boundary with Missouri and Iowa). Area, 56,400 sq. miles, of which 652 sq. miles are inland water. Census population, 1980, 11,426,518, an increase of 2·71% since 1970. Estimate (1982), 11,448,000. Births in 1980 were 186,578; deaths, 100,356; infant deaths, 2,693; marriages 110,667; divorces, 50,405.

Population in 5 census years was:

	White	*Negro*	*Indian*	*All others*	*Total*	*Per sq. mile*
1910	5,526,962	109,049	188	2,392	5,638,591	100·6
1930	7,295,267	328,972	469	5,946	7,630,654	136·4
1960	9,010,252	1,037,470	4,704	28,732	10,081,158	180·3
			All others			
1970	9,600,381	1,425,674	87,921		11,113,976	199·4
1980	9,233,327	1,675,398	517,793		11,426,518	203·0

Of the total population in 1980, 5,537,737 were male, 9,518,039 persons were urban and 5,597,360 were 18 years of age or older.

The most populous cities with population (1980 census), are:

Chicago	3,005,072
Rockford	139,712
Peoria	124,160
Springfield (cap.)	99,637
Decatur	94,081
Joliet	77,956
Aurora	81,293
Evanston	73,706
Waukegan	67,653
Elgin	63,798

Standard Metropolitan Statistical Area population, 1980 census (and 1982 estimate). Chicago, 7,102,378 (7,215,200); East St Louis, 565,874 (300,300); Peoria, 365,864 (363,500); Rockford, 279,514 (279,200); Springfield, 176,089 (187,700); Decatur, 131,375 (129,900).

CLIMATE. Chicago. Jan. 25°F (–3·9°C), July 73°F (22·8°C). Annual rainfall 33" (836 mm). *See* Great Lakes, p. 1373.

CONSTITUTION AND GOVERNMENT. The present constitution became effective 1 July 1971. The General Assembly consists of a House of Representatives of 118 members, elected for 2 years and a Senate of 59 members who are divided into three groups; in one, they are elected for terms of four years, four years, and two years; in the next, for terms of four years, two years, and four years; and in the last, for terms of two years, four years, and four years. Sessions are annual. The Governor and Lieut.-Governor are elected as a team for 4 years; the Comptroller and Secretary of State are elected for 4 years. Electors are citizens 18 years of age, having the usual residential qualifications.

The state is divided into legislative districts, in each of which 1 senator is chosen; each district is divided into 2 representative districts, in each of which 1 representative is chosen.

Illinois is represented in Congress by 2 senators and 22 representatives.

In the 1984 presidential election Reagan polled 2,667,721 votes, Mondale, 2,036,337.

The capital is Springfield. The state has 102 counties.

Governor: James R. Thompson (R.), 1983–86 ($58,000).
Lieut.-Governor: George Ryan (R.), 1983–86 ($45,500).
Secretary of State: Jim Edgar, 1983–86 ($50,500).

BUDGET. For the year ending 30 June 1983 general revenues were $14,595m. and general expenditures were $14,671m.

Total net long-term debt, 30 June 1981, was $6,919·6m.

Per capita personal income (1983) was $12,626.

ENERGY AND NATURAL RESOURCES

Minerals. Chief mineral product is coal; 61 operative mines had an output (1982) of 61·43m. tons. Mineral production also included: Crude petroleum and fluorspar. Total value of mineral products, 1980, was $2,770m.

Agriculture. In 1982, 98,467 farms had an area of 28·7m. acres; the average farm was 292 acres.

Cash receipts, 1982, from crops, $5,890·9m.; from livestock and livestock products, $2,221m. Illinois is a large producer of maize and soybeans, the state's leading cash commodities. Output, 1981: maize, 1,453m. bu.; soybeans, 355m. bu; wheat, 92·5m. bu. In Jan. 1982 there were 234,000 milch cows, 2·8m. all cattle, 195,000 sheep and 5·4m. swine. The wool clip in 1981 was 1·3m. lb.

Forestry. National forest area under the US Forest Service administration, 1981, was 262,000 acres. Total forest land, 3·8m. acres.

INDUSTRY AND TRADE

Industry. In 1982, manufacturing establishments employed 1,117,477 workers; annual payroll, $23,314·14m. Largest industry was machinery (excluding electrical).

Labour. In 1983 there were 4·5m. employees, of whom 951,000 were in manufacturing, 1·1m. in trade, 1·01m. in services, 700,000 in government.

COMMUNICATIONS

Roads. In 1983 there were 5·9m. passenger cars, 1·1m. trucks and buses, 12,912 taxis, liveries and ambulances, 562,068 trailers, 325,969 motor cycles and 234,067 other vehicles registered in the state. In 1983 there were 17,307 miles of state administered roads. There were 4,291 miles of interstate or freeway roads.

Railways. There were 1981, 10,143 miles of Class I railway. Chicago is served by Amtrak long-distance trains on several routes, and by a metro (CTA) system, and by 7 groups of commuter railways controlled by the Northeast Illinois Railroad Corporation.

Shipping. In 1981 the seaport of Chicago handled 31,599,167 short tons of cargo.

Aviation. There were (1984) 125 public airports and 780 restricted landing areas.

JUSTICE, RELIGION, EDUCATION AND WELFARE

Justice. In 1980 there were no executions; since 1930 there have been 90 executions (electrocution), including 58 white men, 1 white woman and 31 Negro men, all for murder. In Dec. 1984 the total average daily prison population was 18,010.

A Civil Rights Act (1941), as amended, bans all forms of discrimination by places of public accommodation, including inns, restaurants, retail stores, railroads, aeroplanes, buses, etc., against persons on account of 'race, religion, colour, national ancestry or physical or mental handicap'; another section similarly mentions 'race or colour.'

The Fair Employment Practices Act of 1961, as amended, prohibits discrimination in employment based on race, colour, sex, religion, national origin or ancestry, by employers, employment agencies, labour organizations and others. These principles are embodied in the 1971 constitution.

Religion. Among the larger religious denominations are: Roman Catholic, Jewish, United Presbyterian Church, USA, Lutheran Church in America, Lutheran Church Missouri Synod, American Baptist, Disciples of Christ, and Methodist.

Education. Education is free and compulsory for children between 7 and 16 years of age. In autumn 1983 public school elementary enrolments were 1,271,525 pupils and 40,025 teachers; secondary enrolments, 581,791 pupils and 24,096 teachers. Enrolment (1982–83) in non-public schools was 263,146 elementary and 89,041 secondary. Teachers' salaries, 1980–81, averaged $19,519. Total enrolment in 179 institutions of higher education (autumn 1982) was 744,636.

Colleges and universities with over 3,000 students:

Founded	*Name*	*Place*	*Control*	*Autumn 1982 Enrolment*
1851	Northwestern University	Evanston	Methodist	15,703
1857	Illinois State University	Normal	Public	20,565
1867	University of Illinois	Urbana	Public	65,483
1867	Chicago State University [1]	Chicago	Public	7,389
1869	Southern Illinois University	Carbondale	Public	34,831
1870	Loyola University	Chicago	Roman Catholic	11,860
1890	University of Chicago	Chicago	Non-Sect.	9,013
1895	Eastern Illinois University	Charleston	Public	10,354
1895	Northern Illinois University	DeKalb	Public	25,676
1897	Bradley University	Peoria	Non-Sect.	5,637
1898	DePaul University	Chicago	Roman Catholic	12,867
1899	Western Illinois University	Macomb	Public	12,411
1940	Illinois Institute of Technology [2]	Chicago	Non-Sect.	6,926
1945	Roosevelt University	Chicago	Non-Sect.	6,685
1961	Northeastern Illinois University [3]	Chicago	Public	10,349

[1] Formerly Illinois Teachers College (South).
[2] Illinois Institute of Technology formed in 1940 by merger of two older technical schools.
[3] Formerly Illinois Teachers' College (North).

Health. In 1983 hospitals listed by the American Hospital Association numbered 281, with 71,211 beds. In 1980 state institutions for the mentally retarded had 3,791 residents and state hospitals for the mentally ill, 4,368.

Social Security. State-administered Supplemental Security Income (SSI) was paid to 31,834 recipients in financial year 1984; payments totalled $31m.; medical payments, $79·3m. Aid to families with dependent children was paid to 245,767 families, average monthly payment per family, $293·07; total payments, $864·3m.; medical payments, $442·5m.

Books of Reference

Blue Book of the State of Illinois. Edited by Secretary of State. Springfield. Biennial

Angle, P. M., and Beyer, R. L., *A Handbook of Illinois History.* Illinois State Historical Society, Springfield, 1943

Clayton, J., *The Illinois Fact Book and Historical Almanac 1673–1968.* Southern Illinois Univ., 1970

Howard, R. P., *Illinois: A History of the Prairie State.* Grand Rapids, 1972

Pease, T. C., *The Story of Illinois.* 3rd ed. Chicago, 1965

The Illinois State Library: Springfield, Il.62756. *State Librarian:* Jim Edgar.

INDIANA

HISTORY. Indiana, first settled in 1732–33, was made a Territory in 1800 and admitted into the Union on 11 Dec. 1816.

AREA AND POPULATION. Indiana is bounded west by Illinois, north by Michigan and Lake Michigan, east by Ohio and south by Kentucky across the Ohio River. Area, 36,185 sq. miles, of which 253 sq. miles are inland water. Census population, 1 April 1980, was 5,490,224, an increase of 294,832 or 5·7% since 1970. Estimate (1983) 5,479,000. In 1983 births were 80,777 (14·7 per 1,000 population); deaths 47,698 (8·7); infant deaths, 923 (11·4 per 1,000 live births); marriages 53,982 (9·9).

Population in 5 census years was:

	White	*Negro*	*Indian*	*Asiatic*	*Total*	*Per sq. mile*
1910	2,639,961	60,320	279	316	2,700,876	74·9
1930	3,125,778	111,982	285	458	3,238,503	89·4
1960	4,388,554	269,275	948	2,447	4,662,498	128·9
			All others			
1970	4,820,324	357,464	15,881		5,193,669	143·9
1980	5,004,394	414,785	71,045		5,490,224	152·8

Of the total in 1980, 2,665,805 were male, 3,525,298 were urban and 3,545,431 were 21 years of age or older.

The largest cities with population (census 1980) are: Indianapolis (capital), 711,539; Fort Wayne, 172,196; Gary, 151,953; Evansville, 130,496; South Bend, 109,727; Hammond, 93,714; Muncie, 77,216; Anderson, 64,695; Terre Haute, 61,125.

CLIMATE. Indianapolis. Jan. 29°F (–1·7°C), July 76°F (24·4°C). Annual rainfall 41″ (1,034 mm). *See* The Mid-West, p. 1372.

CONSTITUTION AND GOVERNMENT. The present constitution (the second) dates from 1851; it has had (as of Nov. 1983) 34 amendments. The General Assembly consists of a Senate of 50 members elected for 4 years, and a House of Representatives of 100 members elected for 2 years.

A constitutional amendment of 1970 allows the legislators to set the length and frequency of sessions, which are currently held annually. The Governor and Lieut.-Governor are elected for 4 years. The state is represented in Congress by 2 senators and 10 representatives.

In the 1984 presidential election Reagan polled 1,332,679 votes, Mondale, 814,659.

The state capital is Indianapolis. The state is divided into 92 counties and 1,008 townships.

Governor: Robert D. Orr (R.), 1984–88 ($66,000 plus expenses).
Lieut.-Governor: John Mutz (R.), 1984–88 ($51,000 plus expenses).
Secretary of State: Edwin Simcox (R.), 1982–86 ($46,000).

BUDGET. In the fiscal year 1982–83 (US Census Bureau figures) total revenues were $6,166·4m. ($1,271·5m. from federal government, $3,195·7m. from taxes), total expenditures were $5,843·3m. ($2,385m. for education, $837m. for public welfare and $546m. for highways).

Total long-term debt, on 30 June 1983, was $1,061m.

Per capita personal income (1981) was $9,720.

ENERGY AND NATURAL RESOURCES

Minerals. The state produced 30·9m. short tons of crushed limestone and 161,000 short tons of dimension limestone in 1980; the output of coal was 30·9m. short tons; petroleum, 5m. bbls (of 42 gallons).

Agriculture. Indiana is largely agricultural, about 75% of its total area being in farms. In 1982, 77,200 farms had 16m. acres (average, 211 acres). Cash income, 1982, from crops, $2,439m.; from livestock and products, $1,792m.

The chief crops (1982) were maize (815m. bu.), winter wheat (46·4m. bu.), oats (6·1m. bu.), soybeans (183·2m. bu.), popcorn, rye, barley, hay (alfalfa, clover, timothy), lespedeza seed, mint, clover seed, apples, strawberries, tomatoes, watermelons and tobacco.

The livestock on 1 Jan. 1982 included 1·75m. all cattle, 207,000 milch cows, 138,000 sheep and lambs, 4·1m. swine, 21·9m. chickens. In 1982 the wool clip yielded 852,000 lb. of wool from 124,000 sheep.

Forestry. The national forests area, 9 Sep. 1983, was 188,252 acres; 13 state forests and 2 state nurseries totalled 142,336 acres in July 1983.

INDUSTRY. Manufacturing establishments employed, in 1981, 649,032 workers, earning $13,541·8m. The steel industry is the largest in the country.

COMMUNICATIONS

Roads. In 1981 there were 91,469 miles of highways, roads and streets, of which 66,412 miles were county highways and 11,148 miles state highways. Motor vehicles registered, 1982, 4,342,071.

Railways. In 1980 there were 5,252 miles of mainline railway, 921 miles of secondary track and 3,295 miles of side and yard track.

Aviation. Of airports, 1981, 125 were for public use, 401 were private and 3 were military.

JUSTICE, RELIGION, EDUCATION AND WELFARE

Justice. In 1963–80 there were no executions; in 1981 there was one (electrocution), for murder; since 1930 there have been 2 others (electrocution), both for murder. State correctional institutions, 1 Oct. 1983, had 9,971 inmates.

The Civil Rights Act of 1885 forbids places of public accommodation to bar any persons on grounds not applicable to all citizens alike; no citizen may be disqualified for jury service 'on account of race or colour'. An Act of 1947 makes it an offence to spread religious or racial hatred.

A 1961 Act provided 'all . . . citizens equal opportunity for education, employment and access to public conveniences and accommodations' and created a Civil Rights Commission.

Religion. Religious denominations include Methodists, Roman Catholic, Disciples of Christ, Baptists, Lutheran, Presbyterian churches, Society of Friends.

Education. School attendance is compulsory from 7 to 16 years. In 1981–82 public and parochial schools, had 1,123,812 pupils and 49,019 teachers. Teachers' salaries, grades 1–12, averaged $18,645. Total expenditure for public schools, $2,455·9m.

The principal institutions for higher education are (1981–82):

Founded	*Institution*	*Control*	*Students (full-time)*
1801	Vincennes University	State	3,724
1824	Indiana University, Bloomington	State	38,930
1837	De Pauw University, Greencastle	Methodist	2,034
1842	University of Notre Dame	R.C.	5,851
1850	Butler University, Indianapolis	Independent	2,067
1859	Valparaiso University, Valparaiso	Evangelical Lutheran Church	3,555
1870	Indiana State University, Terre Haute	State	10,118
1874	Purdue University, Lafayette	State	33,095
1898	Ball State University, Muncie	State	13,917
1963	Indiana Vocational Technical College, Indianapolis	State	45,000[1]

[1] 1982–83.

Health. Hospitals listed by the Indiana State Board of Health (1981) numbered 120 (23,929 beds). On 30 June 1982, 11 state mental hospitals had 6,512 patients enrolled (4,519 present).

Social Security. Old-age assistance, assistance to the blind and to the disabled were transferred from state to federal programmes in June 1974. In Jan.–June 1983, state supplemental assistance and/or Federal Supplemental Security assistance was paid to an average of 12,164 elderly persons per month (total $7·6m.), 1,175 blind ($1·3m.) and 25,798 disabled ($26·89m.).

Books of Reference

Indiana State Chamber of Commerce. *Here is Your Indiana Government.* 21st ed. Indianapolis, 1983

State Library: Indiana State Library, 140 North Senate, Indianapolis 46204. *Director:* C. Ray Ewick.

IOWA

HISTORY. Iowa, first settled in 1788, was made a Territory in 1838 and admitted into the Union on 28 Dec. 1846.

AREA AND POPULATION. Iowa is bounded east by the Mississippi River (forming the boundary with Wisconsin and Illinois), south by Missouri, west by the Missouri River (forming the boundary with Nebraska), north-west by the Big Sioux River (forming the boundary with South Dakota) and north by Minnesota. Area, 56,275 sq. miles, including 310 sq. miles of inland water. Census population, 1 April 1980, 2,913,387, an increase of 3·17% since 1970. Estimate, 1984, 2,836,890. Births, 1983, were 43,247; deaths, 27,509; infant deaths, 385; marriages, 26,769; dissolutions of marriages, 10,588.

Population in 5 census years was:

	White	*Negro*	*Indian*	*Asiatic*	*Total*	*Per sq. mile*
1870	1,188,207	5,762	48	3	1,194,020	21·5
1930	2,452,677	17,380	660	222	2,470,939	44·1
1960	2,729,286	25,354	1,708	1,022	2,757,537	49·2
			All others			
1970	2,782,762	32,596	10,010		2,825,368	50·5
1980	2,838,805	41,700	32,882		2,913,387	51·7

At the census of 1980, 1,416,195 were male, 1,624,547 were urban and 1,971,502 were 20 years of age or older.

The largest cities in the state, with their census population in 1980 are: Des Moines (capital), 191,003; Cedar Rapids, 110,243; Davenport, 103,243; Sioux City, 82,003; Waterloo, 75,985; Dubuque, 62,321; Council Bluffs, 56,449; Iowa City, 50,508; Ames, 45,775; Cedar Falls, 36,322; Clinton, 32,828; Mason City, 30,144; Burlington, 29,529; Fort Dodge, 29,423; Ottumwa, 27,381.

CLIMATE. Cedar Rapids. Jan. 18·5°F (−7·5°C), July 74·3°F (23·5°C). Annual rainfall 36″ (903 mm). Des Moines. Jan. 18·6°F (−7·5°C), July 76·3°F (29·6°C). Annual rainfall 31″ (773 mm). *See* The Mid-West, p. 1372.

CONSTITUTION AND GOVERNMENT. The constitution of 1857 still exists; it has had 37 amendments. The General Assembly comprises a Senate of 50 and a House of Representatives of 100 members, meeting annually for an unlimited session. Senators are elected for 4 years, half retiring every second year: representatives for 2 years. The Governor and Lieut.-Governor are elected for 4 years. The state is represented in Congress by 2 senators and 6 representatives. Iowa is divided into 99 counties; the capital is Des Moines.

In the 1984 presidential election Reagan polled 698,239 votes, Mondale, 601,946.

Governor: Terry Branstad (R.), 1983–86 ($64,000).
Lieut.-Governor: Robert Anderson (D.), 1983–86 ($21,900).
Secretary of State: Mary Jane Odell (R.) ($41,000).

BUDGET. For fiscal year 1983 state tax revenue was $1,732·0m. General expenditures were $1,526m. for education, $586·3m. for public welfare, and $971·5m. for transport.

On 30 June 1982 the net long-term debt was $857·3m.

Per capita personal income (1983) was $10,791.

ENERGY AND NATURAL RESOURCES

Minerals. The leading products by value are crushed stone (28·4m. tons in 1983) and cement (1·68m. short tons in 1983). Coalfields produced 526,929 tons in 1982. The value of mineral products, 1983, was $247·4m.

Agriculture. Iowa is the wealthiest of the agriculture states, partly because nearly the whole area (95·5%) is arable and included in farms. It has escaped large-scale commercial farming. The average farm (in 1983) was 293 acres.

Cash farm income (1983 estimate) was $9,986·9m.; from livestock, $5,960·9m., and from crops, $4,026m. Production of corn in 1983 was 744m. bu. Red meat production in 1983 totalled 5,955m. lb. On 1 Dec. 1983 livestock included swine, 14·8m. (leading all states); milch cows, 385,000; all cattle, 6·0m., and sheep and lambs, 425,000. The wool clip (1983) yielded 3·9m. lb. of wool.

INDUSTRY. In 1981 manufacturing establishments employed 235,800 people with annual payroll at $4,520·4m., value added by manufacture was $11,570m.

COMMUNICATIONS

Roads. On 1 Jan. 1983 number of miles of streets and highways was 112,362; there were 2·6m. licensed drivers and 2·9m. registered vehicles.

Railways. The state, 1983, had 5,027 miles of track, and 6 Class I railways.

Aviation. Airports (1983), numbered 350, including 138 lighted airports and 93 all-weather runways. There were almost 3,100 private aircraft.

JUSTICE, RELIGION, EDUCATION AND WELFARE

Justice. There is now no capital punishment in Iowa. State prisons, 14 Oct. 1984, had 2,703 inmates.

Religion. Chief religious bodies in 1980 were: Roman Catholic (542,698 members); United Methodists, 258,252; American Lutheran, 200,712 baptised members; United Presbyterians, 85,000; United Church of Christ, 50,679.

Education. School attendance is compulsory for 24 consecutive weeks annually during school age (7–16). In 1983–84 553,851 were attending primary and secondary schools; 50,735 pupils attending non-public schools. Classroom teachers numbered 20,140 with average salary of $19,257. Total expenditure on public schools in 1983–84 was $1,323,969,054. Leading institutions for higher education (1983–84) were:

Founded	*Institution*	*Control*	*Full-time Professors*	*Students*
1843	Clarke College, Dubuque	Independent	50	906
1847	University of Iowa, Iowa City	State	1,601	29,599
1847	Grinnell College, Grinnell	Independent	102	1,131
1852	Wartburg College, Waverly	American Lutheran	65	1,140
1853	Cornell College, Mount Vernon	Independent	63	962
1858	Iowa State University, Ames	State	1,554	26,020
1876	Univ. of Northern Iowa, Cedar Falls	State	570	11,204
1881	Drake University, Des Moines	Independent	273	6,008
1881	Coe College, Cedar Rapids	Independent	75	1,371
1894	Morningside College, Sioux City	Methodist	66	1,233

Health. In 1984, the state had 137 hospitals (about 20,019 beds). In Oct. 1983 hospitals for mental diseases had 2,022 resident patients.

Social Security. Iowa has a Civil Rights Act (1939) which makes it a misdemeanour for any place of public accommodation to deprive any person of 'full and equal enjoyment' of the facilities it offers the public.

Supplemental security income (SSI) assistance is available for the aged (65 or older), the blind and the disabled. In May 1984, 9,093 elderly persons were drawing an average of $105 per month, 1,052 blind persons $206 per month, and 15,871 disabled persons $206 per month. Aid to dependent children, established in 1974, was received by 39,700 families representing 113,100 persons at a monthly average of $334 per family.

Books of Reference

Statistical Information: State Departments of Health, Public Instruction and Social Services; State Aeronautics, Commerce and Development Commissions; Crop and Livestock Reporting Services, Des Moines; Iowa Dept. of Transportation, Ames; Geological Survey, Iowa City; Iowa College Aid Commission.

Annual Survey of Manufactures. US Department of Commerce
Government Finance. US Department of Commerce
Official Register. Secretary of State. Des Moines. Biennial
Petersen, W. J., *Iowa History Reference Guide.* Iowa City, 1952
Smeal, L., *Iowa Historical and Biographical Index.* New York, 1984
Vexler, R. I., *Iowa Chronology and Factbook.* Oceana, 1978

Iowa State Library: Des Moines 50319.

KANSAS

HISTORY. Kansas, settled in 1727, was made a Territory (along with part of Colorado) in 1854, and was admitted into the Union with its present area on 29 Jan. 1861.

AREA AND POPULATION. Kansas is bounded north by Nebraska, east by Missouri, with the Missouri River as boundary in the north-east, south by Oklahoma and west by Colorado. Area, 82,277 sq. miles, including 499 sq. miles of inland water. Census population, 1 April 1980, 2,364,236, an increase of 5·1% since 1970. Estimate (1982) 2,408,000. Vital statistics, 1981: Births, 41,202 (17·2 per 1,000 population); deaths, 21,579 (9); infant deaths, 452 (11 per 1,000 live births); marriages, 26,137 (10·9); divorces 13,484 (5·6).

Population in 5 federal census years was:

	White	*Negro*	*Indian*	*Asiatic*	*Total*	*Per sq. mile*
1870	346,377	17,108	914	—	364,399	4·5
1930	1,811,997	66,344	2,454	204	1,880,999	22·9
1960	2,078,666	91,445	5,069	2,271	2,178,611	26·3
			All others			
1970	2,122,068	106,977	17,533		2,249,071	27·5
1980	2,168,221	126,127	69,888		2,364,236	28·8

Of the total population in 1980, 1,156,941 were male, 1,575,899 were urban and those 20 years of age or older numbered 1,620,368.

Cities, with 1980 census population, are Wichita, 279,835; Kansas City, 161,148; Topeka (capital), 115,266; Overland Park, 81,784; Lawrence, 52,738.

CLIMATE. Dodge City. Jan. 29°F (–1·7°C), July 78°F (25·6°C). Annual rainfall 21″ (518 mm). Kansas City. Jan. 30°F (–1·1°C), July 79°F (26·1°C). Annual rainfall 38″ (947 mm). Topeka. Jan. 28°F (–2·2°C), July 78°F (25·6°C). Annual rainfall 35″ (875 mm). Wichita. Jan. 31°F (–0·6°C), July 81°F (27·2°C). Annual rainfall 31″ (777 mm). *See* Mid-West, p. 1372.

CONSTITUTION AND GOVERNMENT. The year 1861 saw the adoption of the present constitution; it has had 78 amendments. The Legislature includes a Senate of 40 members, elected for 4 years, and a House of Representatives of 125 members, elected for 2 years. Sessions are annual. The Governor and Lieut.-Governor are elected for 4 years. The right to vote (with the usual exceptions) is possessed by all citizens. The state is represented in Congress by 2 senators and 5 representatives.

The state was the first (of 42 states) to establish in 1933 a Legislative Council; this is now called the Legislative Coordinating Council and has 7 members.

In the 1984 presidential election Reagan polled 649,423 votes, Mondale, 321,010.

The capital is Topeka. The state is divided into 105 counties.

Governor: John Carlin (D.), 1983–86 ($54,784).
Lieut.-Governor: Thomas Docking (D.), 1983–86 ($16,436).
Secretary of State: Jack H. Brier (R.) ($33,480).

BUDGET. For the year ending 30 June 1982 (Governor's Budget Report) general revenue fund was $2,641,221,484. General expenditures were $1,333,496,424.

Bonded debt outstanding for 1982 amounted to $316·9m.

Per capita personal income (1981) was $10,824.

ENERGY AND NATURAL RESOURCES

Minerals. Important minerals are coal, petroleum, natural gas, lead and zinc. Value of production (1980), $2,478m.

Agriculture. Kansas is pre-eminently agricultural, but sometimes suffers from lack of rainfall in the west. In 1982, 76,000 farms covered 48·5m. acres; average farm, 638 acres.

Cash income, 1982, from crops was $2,470m.; from livestock and products, $3,305·3m.

Kansas is a great wheat-producing state. Its output in 1982 was 462m. bu. Other crops in 1982 (in bushels) were maize, 140·2m.; sorghum, 207·7m.; soybeans, 47m.; oats, 7·5m.; barley, 2·3m. The state has an extensive livestock industry, comprising, on 1 Jan. 1983, 127,000 milch cows, 5 75m. all cattle, 190,000 sheep and lambs 1·67m. swine. Wool clip (1981), 1,684,000 lb. from 230,000 sheep.

INDUSTRY. Employment distribution (1982): 24·7% in trade; 20·3% in government; 18·8% in services; 18·1% in manufacturing; 6·7% in transport and utilities; 4.3% in finance, insurance and real estate; 4·1% in construction; 2% in mining. Value added by manufacture in 1980 was $7,498m. The slaughtering industry, other food processing, aircraft, the manufacture of transport equipment and petroleum refining are important.

COMMUNICATIONS

Roads. The state in Dec. 1982 had 135,087 miles of roads and streets including 8,916 miles of interstate and other primary and federally-aided highways.

Railways. There were 7,273 miles of railway in Jan. 1982.

Aviation. There were 384 airports and landing strips in 1983, of which 168 were public.

JUSTICE, RELIGION, EDUCATION AND WELFARE

Justice. There were 3,390 prisoners in state institutions, 30 June 1983. The death penalty (by hanging) for murder was abolished in 1907 and restored in 1935; there have been no executions since 1968; executions 1934 to 1968 have been 15 (all for murder).

For the various Civil Rights Acts forbidding racial or political discrimination, *see* THE STATESMAN'S YEAR-BOOK, 1955, p. 666. The 1965 Kansas Act against

Discrimination declared that it is the policy of the state to eliminate and prevent discrimination in all employment relations, and to eliminate and prevent discrimination, segregation or separation in all places of public accommodations covered by the Act.

Religion. The most numerous religious bodies are Roman Catholic, Methodists and Disciples of Christ.

Education. In 1982–83 organized school districts had 1,519 elementary and secondary schools which had 407,074 pupils and 26,053 teachers. Average salary of public school teachers, $18,231 (elementary and secondary). There were 20 independent colleges, 20 community colleges, 2 Bible colleges, 1 municipal university.

Kansas has 6 state-supported institutions of higher education: the University of Kansas, Lawrence, founded in 1865; Kansas State University, Manhattan (1863); Emporia State University, Emporia; Pittsburg State University, Pittsburg; Fort Hays State University, Hays and Wichita State University, Wichita. The state also supports a two-year technical school, Kansas Technical Institute, at Salina.

Health. In 1982 the state had 166 hospitals (188,512 beds) listed by the American Hospital Association; hospitals had an average daily occupancy rate of 70·3%.

Social Security. In Dec. 1980, 92,100 persons received state and federal aid under programmes of aid to the aged or disabled and aid to dependent children. Total payments amounted to $114·9m. in 1980.

Books of Reference

Annual Economic Report of the Governor. Topeka

Directory of State Officers, Boards and Commissioners and Interesting Facts Concerning Kansas. Topeka, Biennial

Drury, J. W., *The Government of Kansas.* Lawrence, Univ. of Kansas, 1970

Zornow, W. F., *Kansas: A History of the Jayhawk State.* Norman, Okla., 1957

State Library: Kansas State Library, Topeka.

KENTUCKY

HISTORY. Kentucky, first settled in 1765, was originally part of Virginia; it was admitted into the Union on 1 June 1792 and its first legislature met on 4 June.

AREA AND POPULATION. Kentucky is bounded north by the Ohio River (forming the boundary with Illinois, Indiana and Ohio), north-east by the Big Sandy River (forming the boundary with West Virginia), east by Virginia, south by Tennessee and west by the Mississippi River (forming the boundary with Missouri). Area, 40,409 sq. miles, of which 740 sq. miles are water. Census population, 1980 3,660,777, an increase of 13·6% since 1970. Estimate (1982) 3,668,000. Births in 1981, 57,212 (15·6 per 1,000 population); deaths, 33,260 (9·1); infant deaths, 563 (9·8 per 1,000 live births); marriages, 32,217 (8·8); divorces, 16,671 (4·6).

Population in 5 census years was:

	White	*Negro*	*All others*	*Total*	*Per sq. mile*
1930	2,388,364	226,040	185	2,614,589	65·1
1950	2,742,090	201,921	795	2,944,806	73·9
1960	2,820,083	215,949	2,124	3,038,156	76·2
1970	2,981,766	230,793	6,147	3,218,706	81·2
1980	3,379,006	259,477	22,294	3,660,777	92·3

Of the total population in 1980, an estimated 1,789,000 were male, 1,862,183 were urban and 2,359,614 were 21 years old or older.

The principal cities with census population in 1980 are: Louisville, 298,451 (urbanized area, 654,938); Lexington-Fayette, 204,165; Owensboro, 54,450; Covington, 49,563; Bowling Green, 40,450; Paducah, 29,315; Hopkinsville, 27,318; Ashland, 27,064; Frankfort (capital), 25,973.

CLIMATE. Kentucky has a temperate climate. Temperatures are moderate during both winter and summer, precipitation is ample without a pronounced dry season, and there is little snow during the winter. Lexington. Jan. 33°F (0·6°C), July 76°F (24·4°C). Annual rainfall 45″ (1,126 mm). Louisville. Jan. 33°F (0·6°C), July 77°F (25°C). Annual rainfall 43″ (1,077 mm). *See* Appalachian Mountains, p. 1373.

CONSTITUTION AND GOVERNMENT. The constitution dates from 1891; there had been 3 preceding it. The 1891 constitution was promulgated by convention and provides that amendments be submitted to the electorate for ratification. The General Assembly consists of a Senate of 38 members elected for 4 years, one half retiring every 2 years, and a House of Representatives of 100 members elected for 2 years. A constitutional amendment approved by the voters in Nov. 1979, changes the year in which legislators are elected from odd to even numbered years and establishes an organizational session of the legislature, limited to ten legislative days, in odd-numbered years. The amendment provides for regular sessions limited to 60 legislative days between the first Tuesday after the first Monday of Jan. and 15 April of even numbered years. The Governor and Lieut.-Governor are elected for 4 years. All citizens are (with necessary exceptions) qualified as electors; the voting age was in 1955 reduced from 21 to 18 years. Registered votes, Aug. 1981: 1,819,075. In the 1980 presidential election Reagan polled 816,444 votes, Mondale, 535,704.

The state is represented in Congress by 2 senators and 7 representatives.

The capital is Frankfort. The state is divided into 120 counties.

Governor: Martha Layne Collins (D.), 1983–86 ($60,000).
Lieut.-Governor: Stephen L. Beshear (D.) ($51,008).
Secretary of State: Drexell R. Davis (D.) ($51,008).

BUDGET. For the fiscal year ending 30 June 1983 revenues received within the five major operating funds amounted to $4,296·4m. Included in this figure are $2,211·9m. General Fund revenues and $844m. Federal Fund revenues. Total expenditures amounted to $4,424·8m. including education and humanities, $1,286·9m.; human resources benefits payments, $590·9m.; and transport, $723·3m.

The general obligation bonded indebtedness on 30 June 1983 was $226m.

Per capita personal income (1983) was $9,397.

ENERGY AND NATURAL RESOURCES

Minerals. The principal mineral product of Kentucky is coal, 131·2m. short tons mined in 1983, value $3,801m. Output of petroleum, 7·9m. bbls (of 42 gallons); natural gas, 46,720m. cu. ft; stone, 36·5m. short tons, value $135m.; clay 597,000 short tons, value $2·2m.; sand and gravel, 6m. short tons, value $13m. Total value of non-fuel mineral products in 1983 was $241,520,000. Other minerals include fluorspar, ball clay, lead, zinc, silver, cement, lime, industrial sand and gravel, oil shale and tar sands.

Agriculture. In 1983, 103,000 farms had an area of 14·5m. acres. The average farm was 141 acres.

Cash income, 1983, from crops, $1,300m., and from livestock, $1,500m. The chief crop is tobacco: production, in 1983, 324m. lb., ranking second to N. Carolina in US. Other principal crops include corn, soybeans, wheat, barley, sorghum grain, hay, oats and rye.

Stock-raising is important in Kentucky, which has long been famous for its horses. The livestock in 1983 included 243,000 milch cows, 2·7m. cattle and calves, 23,000 sheep, 960,000 swine.

Forestry. Total forests area, 1978, 12,160,800 acres. Total commercial forest land, 1978, 11,901,900 acres; 92% is privately owned.

INDUSTRY. In 1983 the state's 3,406 manufacturing plants had 185,622 production workers; value added by manufacture in 1981 was $12,000m. The leading manufacturing industries (by employment) are non-electrical machinery, electrical equipment, apparel and other fabric products and foods. Direct foreign investment in manufacturing by foreign investors was $910m. in 1984.

TOURISM. In 1983 tourist expenditure was $2,280m., producing over $157m. in tax revenues and generating 101,708 jobs. The state had (1984) 751 hotels and motels, 211 campgrounds and 43 state parks.

COMMUNICATIONS

Roads. In 1983 the state had over 69,000 miles of federal, state and local roads. There were over 2·7m. motor vehicle registrations in 1983.

Railways. In 1983 there were about 3,300 miles of railway.

Aviation. There are (1983) 117 aircraft landing areas and 2,000 registered aircraft in Kentucky. Seven airports served 5–6m. passengers with scheduled services in 1982.

Shipping. There is an increasing amount of barge traffic on 1,090 miles of navigable rivers. There are 5 river ports, 1 under construction and 3 planned.

JUSTICE, RELIGION, EDUCATION AND WELFARE

Justice. There are 10 prisons within the Department of Adult Institutions; average daily population (1983–84), 4,636.

There has been no execution since 1962. A session of Congress in 1976 limited the death penalty to cases of kidnap and murder.

Total executions, 1911–62, were 162, including 76 whites and 86 Negroes; 144 were for murder, 7 for rape, 6 for criminal offences, 5 for armed robbery.

Religion. The chief religious denominations in 1980 were: Southern Baptists, with 883,096 members, Roman Catholic (365,277), United Methodists (234,536), Christian Churches and Church of Christ (81,222) and Christian (Disciples of Christ) (78,275).

Education. Attendance at school between the ages of 6 and 15 years (inclusive) is compulsory, the normal term being 175 days. In 1983–84, 21,064 teachers were employed in public elementary and 11,396 in secondary schools, in which 431,243 and 216,171 pupils enrolled respectively. Expenditure on elementary and secondary day schools in 1983–84 was $1,618·3m.; public school classroom teachers' salaries (1983–84) averaged $19,663.

There were also 4,260 teachers working in private elementary and secondary schools with 72,668 students.

The state has 24 universities and senior colleges, 5 junior colleges and 13 community colleges, with a total (autumn 1982) of 134,841 students. Of these universities and colleges, 22 are state-supported, and the remainder are supported privately. The largest of the institutions of higher learning are (autumn 1982): University of Kentucky, with 22,829 students; University of Louisville, 19,744 students; Western Kentucky University, 12,855 students; Eastern Kentucky University, 13,041 students; Murray State University, 7,587 students; Morehead State University, 6,370 students; Northern Kentucky University, 9,339 students. Five of the several privately endowed colleges of standing are Berea College, Berea; Centre College, Danville; Transylvania University, Lexington; Georgetown College, Georgetown; and Bellarmine College, Louisville.

Health. In 1984 the state had 109 licensed acute care hospitals (15,507 beds), 11 psychiatric hospitals (2,488 beds) and 4 children's hospitals (211 beds). There were 3 drug-dependency treatment centres (141 beds) and 2 acute rehabilitation hospitals (164 beds).

Welfare. In July 1984 there were 262,435 persons receiving financial assistance;

96,813 of these persons received the Federal Supplemental Security Income (SSI); 37,723 of them were aged, 2,120 blind, 56,970 disabled. Also, in the all state funded Supplementation programme payments were made in July 1984 to 7,539 persons, of which 4,042 were aged, 107 blind and 3,390 disabled. The average State Supplementation payment was $109.60 to aged, $62.81 to blind and $112.77 to disabled.

In the Aid to Families with Dependent Children Programme as of June 1984, aid was given to 158,083 persons in 60,170 families. The average payment per person was $72.71, per family $191.02.

In addition to money payments, medical assistance, food stamps and social services are available.

Books of Reference

Kentucky 1985 Economic Statistics. 21st ed. Department of Economic Development, Frankfort, 1984

LOUISIANA

HISTORY. Louisiana was first settled in 1699. That part lying east of the Mississippi River was organized in 1804 as the Territory of New Orleans, and admitted into the Union on 30 April 1812. The section west of the river was added very shortly thereafter.

AREA AND POPULATION. Louisiana is bounded north by Arkansas, east by Mississippi, with the Mississippi River forming the boundary in the north-east, south by the Gulf of Mexico and west by Texas, with the Sabine River forming most of the boundary. Area, 52,453 sq. miles, including lakes, rivers and coastal waters inside 3-mile limit; land area, 44,873 sq. miles. Census population, 1 April 1980, 4,205,900, an increase of 15·5% since 1970. Estimate (1982) 4,362,000. Births, 1981, 81,105 (18·8 per 1,000 population); deaths, 35,747 (8·3); infant deaths, 1,112 (13·7 per 1,000 live births); marriages, 44,929; divorces, 17,377.

Population in 5 census years was:

	White	*Negro*	*Indian*	*Asiatic*	*Total*	*Per sq. mile*
1910	941,086	713,874	780	648	1,656,388	36·5
1930	1,322,712	776,326	1,536	1,019	2,101,593	46·5
1960	2,211,715	1,039,207	3,587	2,004	3,257,022	72·2
			All others			
1970	2,541,498	1,086,832	12,976		3,641,306	81·1
1980	2,911,243	1,237,263	55,466		4,203,972 [1]	93·5

[1] Preliminary.

Of the 1980 total, 2,039,894 were male, 2,885,535 were urban; those 20 years of age or older numbered 2,699,100.

The largest cities with their 1980 census population are: New Orleans, 557,482; Baton Rouge (capital), 219,486; Shreveport, 205,815; Lafayette, 81,961; Kenner, 66,382.

CLIMATE. New Orleans. Jan. 54°F (12·2°C), July 83°F (28·3°C). Annual rainfall 58″ (1,458 mm). *See* Gulf Coast, p. 1373.

CONSTITUTION AND GOVERNMENT. The present constitution dates from 1974.

The Legislature consists of a Senate of 39 members and a House of Representatives of 105 members, both chosen for 4 years. Sessions are annual; a fiscal session is held in odd years. The Governor and Lieut.-Governor are elected for 4 years.

A Governor may serve a second consecutive term. Qualified electors are (with the usual exceptions) all registered citizens with the usual residential qualifications.

In the 1984 presidential election Reagan polled 1,030,091 votes, Mondale, 648,040.

The state sends to Congress 2 senators and 8 representatives. Louisiana is divided into 64 parishes (corresponding with the counties of other states).

Governor: Edwin W. Edwards (D.), 1984–88 ($73,440).
Lieut.-Governor: Robert Freeman (D.), 1980–84 ($63,367).
Secretary of State: James Brown (D.), 1984–88 ($60,169).

BUDGET. For the fiscal year ending 30 June 1982 (Louisiana State Budget Office figures) general revenues were $6,091,714,373, of which $1,236,983,444 were federal funds; total expenditures were $6,067,203,315 (education, $2,077,432,518; transport and development, $416,170,800; health, hospitals and public welfare, $1,578,334,592).

Per capita personal income (1982) was $10,231.

ENERGY AND NATURAL RESOURCES

Minerals. The yield in 1982 of crude petroleum was 458m. bbls; marketed production of natural gas, 6,131,000m. cu. ft. Rich sulphur mines are found in the state, and wells for the extraction of sulphur by means of hot water and compressed air are in operation; output, 1980, 2·6m. tonnes.

Louisiana is the USA's main salt producer. Output of salt (1980) was 12·6m. short tons valued at $132·2m. Total output of raw, non-fuel minerals in 1981 was valued at $574m.

Agriculture. The state is divided into two parts, the uplands and the alluvial and swamp regions of the coast. A delta occupies about one-third of the total area. Manufacturing is the leading industry, but agriculture is important. In 1983 there were about 37,000 farms with annual average sales of at least $1,000; average farm, 277 acres; average value per acre $1,481.

Cash income, 1983, from crops $1,370m.; from livestock, $483m. Production of crops: corn for grain, 5m. bu.; cotton lint, 540,000 bales; hay, 735,000 tons; soybeans, 67m. bu.; wheat, 7·5m.bu. Rice and sugar are also important.

In 1983 the state contained 102,000 milch cows, 1·4m. all cattle, 9,000 sheep and 135,000 swine.

Forestry. Forests, 14·5m. acres, represent 47% of the state's area. Income from manufactured products exceeds $2,500m. annually. In 1982 pulpwood cut, 3,867,994·3 cords; sawtimber cut, 927·4m. bd ft.

INDUSTRY. The manufacturing industries are chiefly those associated with petroleum, chemicals, lumber, food, paper. Investment in manufacturing, 1980–81, about $9,000m. In 1982 206,000 were employed in manufacturing, 368,000 in trade and 302,000 in service industries.

TOURISM. Travellers spent an estimated $3,300m. in 1982. State tax revenue, $99·3m. (3% of state tax revenue). New Orleans is the site of the Louisiana World Exposition in 1984.

COMMUNICATIONS

Roads. The state has more than 16,326 miles of public roads. In June 1982, over 4·6m. vehicles were registered in the state.

Railways. In 1980 the railways in the state had a length of about 3,700 miles.

Aviation. There were, 1981, about 240 commercial and private airports.

Shipping. In 1981 New Orleans handled 188·9m. tons of cargo. The Mississippi and other waterways provide 7,500 miles of navigable water.

JUSTICE, RELIGION, EDUCATION AND WELFARE

Justice. Prisons, Oct. 1982, had 9,257 inmates.

Execution is by electrocution; there were 135 between 1930 and 1961; between 1977 and 1985 there were 6.

Religion. The Roman Catholic Church is the largest denomination in Louisiana, with 1,316,441 members in 1979. The leading Protestant Churches are Southern Baptist, with (1979) 524,566 members; Methodist, (1979) 136,972.

Education. School attendance is compulsory between the ages of 7 and 15, both inclusive. In 1981–82 there were 1,493 public elementary and high schools which had 808,322 pupils with a current expenditure of $2,297 per pupil. Private schools had 157,330. In 1981–82, instructional staff had an average salary of $18,500. There are 16 four-year public colleges and universities and 12 non-public four-year institutions of higher learning. There are 53 state trade and vocational-technical schools. Superior instruction is given in the Louisiana State University system with 56,520 students (1982). Tulane University in New Orleans had 10,400; The Roman Catholic Loyola University in New Orleans had 4,550; Dillard University in New Orleans had 12,000; and the Southern University system, 11,800.

Health. In 1982 the state had 156 licensed hospitals (25,410 beds); 3 mental hospitals cared for 12,381 patients.

Social Security. In Dec. 1982, assistance was being given to 94,264 elderly persons; 64,709 families with dependent children; 4,120 general assistance cases and 635 Vietnamese and Cambodian refugees. Supplemental Security assistance was given to 68,915 blind and physically disabled people. Aid was from state and federal sources.

Books of Reference

Louisiana Almanac. New Orleans, 1979–80

The History and Government of Louisiana. Legislative Council, Baton Rouge, 1975

Louisiana State Agencies Handbook. Public Affairs Research Council of Louisiana. Baton Rouge, 1979

The State of the State: an Economic and Social Report to the Governor. Louisiana State Planning Office, New Orleans, 1978

Statistical Abstract of Louisiana. Division of Business and Economic Research, Univ. of New Orleans, 1977

Davis, E. A., *Louisiana, the Pelican State.* Louisiana State Univ. Press, Baton Rouge, 1975

Hansen, H., (ed.), *Louisiana, a Guide to the State.* Rev. ed. New York, 1971

Kniffen, F. B., *Louisiana, its Land and People.* Louisiana State Univ. Press, Baton Rouge, 1968

State Library: The Louisiana State Library, Baton Rouge, Louisiana. *State Librarian:* Thomas F. Jaques.

MAINE

HISTORY. After a first attempt in 1607, Maine was settled in 1623. From 1652 to 1820 it was part of Massachusetts and was admitted into the Union on 15 March 1820.

AREA AND POPULATION. Maine is bounded west, north and east by Canada, south-east by the Atlantic, south and south-west by New Hampshire. Area, 33,265 sq. miles, of which 2,269 are inland water. Of the state's total area, about 17·2m. acres (87%) are in timber and wood lots. Census population, 1 April 1980 1,125,027, an increase of 13·29% since 1970. Estimate (1982) 1,133,000. In 1981 live births numbered 16,695; deaths, 10,451; infant deaths, 146; marriages, 12,388; divorces 5,804.

Population for 5 census years was:

	White	Negro	Indian	Asiatic	Total	Per sq. mile
1910	739,995	1,363	892	121	742,371	24·8
1930	795,185	1,096	1,012	130	797,423	25·7
1950	910,846	1,221	1,522	185	913,774	29·4
			All others			
1970	985,276	2,800	3,972		992,048	31·0
1980	1,109,850	3,128	12,049		1,125,027	36·3

Of the total population in 1980, 48·5% were male, 40·7% were urban and 60·5% were 21 years or older.

The largest city in the state is Portland with a census population of 61,572 in 1980. Other cities (with population in 1980) are: Lewiston, 40,481; Bangor, 31,643; Auburn, 23,128; South Portland, 22,712; Augusta (capital), 21,819; Biddeford, 19,638; Waterville, 17,779.

CLIMATE. Average maximum temperatures range from 56·3°F in Waterville to 48·3°F in Caribou, but record high (since *c.* 1950) is 103°F. Average minimum ranges from 36·9°F in Rockland to 28·3°F in Greenville, but record low (also in Greenville) is –42°F. Average annual rainfall ranges from 48·85″ in Machias to 36·09″ in Houlton. Average annual snowfall ranges from 118·7″ in Greenville to 59·7″ in Rockland. *See* New England, p. 1373.

CONSTITUTION AND GOVERNMENT. The constitution of 1820 is still in force, but it has been amended 143 times. In 1951, 1965 and 1973 the Legislature approved recodifications of the constitution as arranged by the Chief Justice under special authority.

The Legislature consists of the Senate with 33 members and the House of Representatives with 151 members, both Houses being elected simultaneously for 2 years. Apart from these legislators and the Governor (elected for 4 years), no other state officers are elected. The Justices of the Supreme Judicial Court give their opinion upon important questions of law and upon solemn occasions when required by the Governor, Senate or House of Representatives. The suffrage is possessed by all citizens, 18 years of age; persons under guardianship for reasons of mental illness have no vote. Indians residing on tribal reservations and otherwise qualified have the vote in all county, state and national elections but retain the right to elect their own tribal representative to the legislature.

In the 1984 presidential election Reagan polled 336,500 votes, Mondale, 214,515.

The state sends to Congress 2 senators and 2 representatives.

The capital is Augusta. The state is divided into 16 counties.

Governor: Joseph E. Brennan (D.), 1983–86 ($35,000).
Secretary of State: Rodney S. Quinn (D.), 1983–86 ($30,000).

BUDGET. For the financial year ending 30 June 1984 total general revenue was $1,459,560,121 and expenditure was $1,440,274,458.

Total net long-term debt on 30 June 1984 was $294·5m.

Per capita personal income (Dec. 1983) was $9,487.

NATURAL RESOURCES

Minerals. Minerals include sand and gravel, stone, lead, clay, copper, peat, silver and zinc. Non-fuel mineral output, 1982, was valued at over $35·4m.

Agriculture. In 1983, 8,100 farms occupied 1·56m. acres; the average farm was 193 acres.

Cash receipts, 1983, $413·1m., of which $91·7 came from potatoes; Maine is the third largest producer of potatoes (about 7% of the country's total of 325·7m. cwt). Other important items include eggs ($94m.), dairy products ($107·5m.) and poultry ($29·7m.); these with potatoes provide 78% of receipts. Sweet corn, peas and beans, oats, hay, apples and blueberries are also grown. On 1 Jan. 1983 the farm animals included 57,000 milch cows, 146,000 all other cattle, and 14,000 sheep.

Forestry. Lumber, wood turnings and pulp are important. In 1982 the cut of softwood was 769,195m. bd ft; hardwood, 150,878m. bd ft, and pulpwood, 3,417,586 cords. Spruce and fir, white pine, hemlock, white and yellow birch, sugar maple, northern white cedar, beech and red oak are the most important species cut. There were (1982) 17,600,000 acres of commercial forest (98% in private ownership). National forests comprise 37,500 acres; other federal, 35,800; state forests, 163,000 acres; municipal, 75,200 acres. Wood products industries are of great economic importance; in 1982 the lumber, wood and paper industries' production was valued at $3,355,731. There were (1982) 342 primary manufacturers and over 1,400 secondary.

Fisheries. In 1983, 202,657,000 lb. of fish and shellfish (valued at $107,889,000 were landed; the catch included 21,976,000 lb. of lobsters (valued at $51,234,000). 1·97m. lb. of scallops ($10·8m.); 4·14m. lb. of soft clams ($7·24m.); 12·31m. lb of dabs ($6·0m.); 42·4m. lb. of menhaden ($846,000); 40m. lb. of herring ($2·14m.).

INDUSTRY. In 1982, 2,289 manufacturing establishments reported 108,330 workers, earning $1,769·5m.; gross value of production, $7,948·9m. (increase of 1·2% from 1981). Leading industry is paper with 47 plants, 17,957 workers and output valued at $2,714·2m. (34% of the state's total manufactures).

LABOUR. The four largest employers are government, education, health and tourism.

TOURISM. In 1983 there were about 4m. tourists (including state residents on holiday), generating about $655·5m. in business. Eating, drinking and accommodation produce 12·4% of sales tax.

COMMUNICATIONS

Roads. In 1983 there were 22,098 miles of roads, of which 3,973 miles were state highways and 4,359 miles were state-aided; town streets and miscellaneous, 13,766 miles. In July 1984, 847,922 motor vehicles were registered, including 669,240 passenger vehicles, 87,267 commercial vehicles and 40,361 motorcycles.

Railways. In 1984 there were 1,516 miles of mainline railway tracks.

Aviation. Licensed airports, 1984, numbered 76, including 37 commercial public airports, 12 non-commercial and 4 commuter airports, 15 commercial and 4 non-commercial seaplane bases, and 4 air-carrier airports. There were also 2 military airports and 23 private landing strips.

JUSTICE, RELIGION, EDUCATION AND WELFARE

Justice. The state's penal system in Sept. 1984 held 435 adults in the State Prison, 237 in the Correctional Center and 332 juveniles in the Youth Center. There is no capital punishment. Inmates serving life sentences are eligible for parole consideration after 15 years, less remission for good conduct, provided they were imprisoned before the passage of a new Criminal Code by the 107th Maine Legislature, which abolished the parole system.

Religion. The largest religious bodies are: Roman Catholic (270,283 members), Baptists (36,808 members) and Congregationalists (40,750 members), and other Christian Churches (34,066 members).

Education. Education is free for pupils from 5 to 21 years of age, and compulsory from 7 to 17. In 1983–84 the 756 public schools (610 elementary, 105 secondary and 41 combined elementary and secondary) had 12,283 staff and 209,753 enrolled pupils. In 1983–84 there were 126 private schools with 1,035 teachers and 15,461 pupils. Public school teachers' salaries, 1983–84, averaged $17,328. Total public expenditure on public elementary and secondary education in 1982–83, $461,252,847.

The state University of Maine, founded in 1865, had (1983–84) 1,003 teaching staff and 28,591 students at 7 locations; Bowdoin College, founded in 1794 at Brunswick, (107 and 1,371); Bates College at Lewiston, (104 and 1,424); Colby College at Waterville, (125 and 1,733); Husson College, Bangor, (31 and 1,465); Westbrook College at Westbrook, (56 and 1,120); Unity College at Unity, (23 and 325), and the University of New England (formerly St Francis College) at Biddeford, (55 and 848).

Health. In 1984 the state had 42 general hospitals (4,571 beds for acute care); 3 hospitals for mental diseases, acute and psychiatric care (541 beds); 144 nursing homes (10,220 beds).

Social Security. Supplemental Security Income (SSI) (maximum payment for single person, $324·30 per month) is administered by the Social Security Administration. It became effective on 1 Jan. 1974 and replaces former aid to the aged, blind and disabled, administered by the state with state and federal funds. SSI is supplemented by Medicaid for nursing home patients or hospital patients. State payments for SSI recipients for Jan. 1983 totalled $381,000, covering 21,000 cases. Aid to families with dependent children is granted where one or both parents are disabled or absent and income is insufficient; aid was being granted in Aug. 1984 to 17,209 families (32,592 children) with an average payment per family of $292·95 per month. Total aid under the programme, Aug. 1984, $5·4m. Payments under Maine Medicaid Assistance programme totalled $217m. for the financial year 1983–84. There is a programme of assistance for catastrophic illness. Child welfare services include basic child protective services, enforcing child support, establishing paternity and finding missing parents, foster home placements, adoptions; services in divorce cases and licensing of foster homes, day care and residential treatment services, and public guardianship. There are also protective services for adults.

Books of Reference

Maine Register, State Year-Book and Legislative Manual. Tower Publishing, Portland. Annual
Banks, R., *Maine Becomes A State.* Wesleyan U.P., 1970
Caldwell, B., *Rivers of Fortune.* Gannett, 1983
Calvert, M. R., *Dawn over the Kennebec.* Private Pr., 1983
Clark, C., *Maine.* New York, 1977

MARYLAND

HISTORY. Maryland, first settled in 1634, was one of the 13 original states.

AREA AND POPULATION. Maryland is bounded north by Pennsylvania, east by Delaware and the Atlantic, south by Virginia and West Virginia, with the Potomac River forming most of the boundary, and west by West Virginia. Chesapeake Bay almost cuts off the eastern end of the state from the rest. Area, 10,460 sq. miles, of which 623 sq. miles are inland water; in addition, water area under Maryland jurisdiction in Chesapeake Bay amounts to 1,726 sq. miles. Census population, 1 April 1980, 4,216,975, an increase since 1970 of 293,078 or 7·5%. Estimate (1983) 4,304,000. In 1982 births were 63,759 (14·9 per 1,000 population); deaths, 34,094 (7·8); infant deaths, 767 (12 per 1,000 live births); marriages, 47,867 (11·2); divorces, 16,083 (3·8).

Population for 5 federal censuses was:

	White	*Negro*	*Indian*	*Asiatic*	*Total*	*Per sq. mile*
1920	1,204,737	244,479	32	413	1,449,661	145·8
1930	1,354,226	276,379	50	871	1,631,526	165·0
1960	2,573,919	518,410	1,538	5,700	3,100,689	314·0
			All others			
1970	3,194,888	499,479	28,032		3,922,399	396·6
1980	3,158,838	958,150	99,987		4,216,975	428·7

Of the total population in 1980, 2,042,810 were male, 3,386,555 persons were urban and those 20 years old or older numbered 2,890,196.

The largest city in the state (containing 18·7% of the population of the state) is Baltimore, with 786,775 in 1980; population of metropolitan area, 3,273,015. Maryland residents in the Washington, D.C., metropolitan area total more than 1·3m.; other cities (1980) are Dundalk (71,293); Towson (51,083); Silver Spring (72,893); Bethesda (62,736), Bowie (33,695), Hagerstown (34,132), Annapolis (capital), 31,740. Incorporated places: Cumberland, 25,933; Cambridge, 11,703; Frederick, 28,086; Gaithersburg, 26,424; Rockville, 43,811.

CLIMATE. Baltimore. Jan. 36°F (2·2°C), July 79°F (26·1°C). Annual rainfall 41″ (1,026 mm). *See* Atlantic Coast, p. 1373.

CONSTITUTION AND GOVERNMENT. The present constitution dates from 1867; it has had 125 amendments. The General Assembly consists of a Senate of 47, and a House of Delegates of 141 members, both elected for 4 years, as are the Governor and Lieut.-Governor. Voters are citizens who have the usual residential qualifications. At the 1984 presidential election Reagan polled 836,295 votes, Mondale, 757,635.

Maryland sends to Congress 2 senators and 8 representatives.

The state capital is Annapolis. The state is divided into 23 counties and Baltimore City.

Governor: Harry R. Hughes (D.), 1983–86 ($75,000).
Lieut.-Governor: J. Joseph Curran (D.), 1983–86 ($62,500).
Secretary of State: Patricia Holtz ($45,000).

BUDGET. For the fiscal year ending 30 June 1983 general revenues were $5,017,775,000 ($3,492,540,000 from taxation). General expenditures, $5,341,502,000, including $956,799,000 for education and $1,546,808,000 for public welfare and health; $775,800,000 for highways.

Total authorized long-term state debt, 30 June 1983 was $2,998,191,000. (Issued and outstanding, $2,409,890,000; authorized but not issued, $588,301,000.)

Per capita personal income (1983) was $12,994.

ENERGY AND NATURAL RESOURCES

Minerals. Value of non-fuel mineral production, 1983, was $201·9m. Sand and gravel (10m. short tons) and stone (16·9m. short tons) account for over 54% of the total value. Coal is the leading mineral commodity by value followed by Portland cement, stone, sand and gravel. Output of coal was 3·1m. short tons, valued at about $87m. Natural gas is produced from 1 field in Garrett County; 30·8m. cu. ft in 1983. A second gas field in the same county is used for natural gas storage.

Agriculture. Agriculture is an important industry in the state. In 1983 there were approximately 18,000 farms with an area of 2·7m. acres (43% of the land area).

Farm animals, 1 Jan. 1984, were: Milch cows, 125,000; all cattle, 420,000; swine, 200,000 (1983); sheep and lambs, 20,000; chickens (not broilers), 4·7m. (1983). The most important crops, 1983, were: corn for grain, 37·7m. bu.; soybeans, 9·3m. bu.; tobacco, 30m. lb., and hay, 627,000 tons.

Cash receipts from farm marketings, 1983, were $1,032·5m.; from livestock and livestock products, $702m., and crops, $330·5m. Dairy products and broilers are important.

INDUSTRY. In 1978 manufactories had 169,700 production workers earning $2,218·8m.; value added by manufacture, $7,739·2m. Chief industries are food and kindred products, primary metal products, electrical and electronic equipment, chemicals and products, transport equipment.

TOURISM. Tourism is one of the state's leading industries. In 1983 tourists spent over $3,362m.

COMMUNICATIONS

Roads. The state highway department maintained, 1 Jan. 1982, 5,241 miles of highways, of which 80 miles were toll roads. The 23 counties maintained 17,245 miles of highways, and the 159 municipalities (including the city of Baltimore) maintained 3,916 miles of streets and alleys. Total mileage, 1 Jan. 1982, of public highways, streets and alleys, 26,402 miles. In 1983, about 3·2m. automobiles were registered.

Railways. Railways, in 1983, had 1,100 miles of line.

Aviation. There were, 1983, 41 commercially licensed airports.

Shipping. In 1983 Baltimore was the sixth largest US seaport in value of trade, sixth in tonnage handled.

JUSTICE, RELIGION, EDUCATION AND WELFARE

Justice. Prisons on 21 Sept. 1984 had about 12,700 men and 450 women; the total equalled 277 per 100,000 population, a high rate, which may be explained by the fact that Maryland incarcerates domestic relations law violators in state prisons; state prisons also receive a considerable number of persons committed for misdemeanours by magistrates' courts of the counties as well as from Baltimore's court system.

Since 1930 there have been 68 executions (by lethal gas since 1957; earlier by hanging)—7 whites and 37 Negroes for murder, and 6 whites and 18 Negroes for rape. Last execution was June 1961.

Maryland's prison system has conducted a work-release programme for selected prisoners since 1963. All institutions have academic and vocational training programmes.

In accordance with the 1950 Supreme Court decisions declaring segregation unconstitutional, the University of Maryland and other public and private colleges admitted Negro students in Sept. 1956. Elementary and secondary schools accept the ruling, and gradual integration is under way in all counties under different methods.

Religion. Maryland was the first US state to give religious freedom to all who came within its borders. Present religious affiliations of the population are approximately: Protestant, 32%; Roman Catholic, 24%; Jewish, 10%; remaining 34% is non-related and other faiths.

Education. Education is compulsory from 6 to 16 years of age. In Sept. 1983 the public elementary schools (including kindergartens and secondary schools) had 683,491 pupils. Teachers and principals in the elementary and secondary schools numbered 40,089. Average salary of instructional staff (1982–83) was $22,786. Current expenditure by local school boards on education, 1983–84, was $2,260m., of which the state's contribution was $900m.

In 1983 there were 35 degree-granting 4-year institutions and 21 2-year colleges. The largest two were the University of Maryland system, with 62,851 students (Sept. 1983) and Towson State College with 15,157 students (Sept. 1983).

Health. In Jan. 1984, 83 hospitals (21,561 beds) were licensed by the State Department of Health and Mental Hygiene.

The Maryland State Department of Health, organized in 1874, was in 1969 made part of the Department of Health and Mental Hygiene which performs its functions through its central office, 23 county health departments and the Baltimore City Health Department. For the financial year 1983 the department's budget was $1,021m., of which $721·6m. were general funds and $17m. special funds appropriated by the General Assembly. The balance of the budget, $282·4m., derives from federal funds.

During financial year 1983 Maryland's programme of medical care for indigent and medically indigent patients covered an average of 351,109 persons. The programme, which covers in-patient and out-patient hospital services, laboratory services, skilled nursing home care, physician services, pharmacy services, dental services and home health services, cost approximately $535·7m.

Social Security. Under the supervision of the Department of Human Resources, local social service departments administer public assistance for needy persons. In June 1984 families with dependent children received $16,704,311 (187,409 recipients, average actual monthly payment $89.13); general public assistance payments were $2,390,304 (19,909 recipients, average actual monthly payments $120.06).

Books of Reference

Statistical Information: Maryland Department of Economic and Community Development, Annapolis, 21401.

Maryland Manual: A Compendium of Legal, Historical and Statistical Information Relating to the State of Maryland. Annapolis. Biennial

DiLisio, J. E., *Maryland.* Boulder, 1982

Papenfuse, E. C., et al., *Maryland, a New Guide to the Old Line State.* Johns Hopkins Univ. Press, 1976

Rollo, V. F., *Maryland's Constitution and Government.* Maryland Hist. Press, Rev. ed., 1982

State Library: Maryland State Library, Annapolis. *Director:* Michael S. Miller.

MASSACHUSETTS

HISTORY. The first permanent settlement within the borders of the present state was made at Plymouth in Dec. 1620, by the Pilgrims from Holland, who were separatists from the English Church, and formed the nucleus of the Plymouth Colony. In 1628 another company of Puritans settled at Salem, forming eventually the Massachusetts Bay Colony. In 1630 Boston was settled. In the struggle which ended in the separation of the American colonies from the mother country, Massachusetts took the foremost part, and on 6 Feb. 1788 became the sixth state to ratify the US constitution.

AREA AND POPULATION. Massachusetts is bounded north by Vermont and New Hampshire, east by the Atlantic, south by Connecticut and Rhode Island and west by New York. Area, 8,284 sq. miles, 460 sq. miles being inland water. The census population 1 April 1980, was 5,737,037, an increase of 47,867 or 0·8% since 1970. Estimate (1984) 5,741,000. Births, 1982 were 75,749 (13·1 per 1,000 population); deaths, 52,868 (9·2 per 1,000); infant deaths, 764 (10·1 per 1,000 live births); marriages, 48,654 (8·5); divorces, 19,531 (3·4).

Population at 4 federal census years was:

	White	*Negro*	*Other*	*Total*	*Per sq. mile*
1950	4,611,503	73,171	5,840	4,690,514	598·4
1960	5,023,144	111,842	13,592	5,148,578	656·8
1970	5,477,624	175,817	35,729	5,689,170	725·8
1980	5,362,836	221,279	152,922	5,737,037	732·0

Of the total population in 1980, 47·6% were male, 83·8% were urban and 32% were 21 years old or older.

In 1980 the population of the principal towns and cities was:

Boston	562,994	Fall River	92,574	Framingham	65,113
Worcester	161,799	Lowell	92,418	Lawrence	63,175
Springfield	152,319	Quincy	84,743	Waltham	58,200
New Bedford	98,478	Newton	83,622	Medford	58,076
Cambridge	95,322	Lynn	78,471	Weymouth	55,601
Brockton	95,172	Somerville	77,372	Chicopee	55,112

The largest of 10 standard metropolitan statistical areas, 1980 census were: Boston, 2,763,357; Springfield–Chicopee–Holyoke, 530,668; Worcester, 372,940.

CLIMATE. Boston. Jan. 28°F (–2·2°C), July 71°F (21·7°C). Annual rainfall 41″ (1,036 mm). *See* New England, p. 1373.

CONSTITUTION AND GOVERNMENT. The constitution dates from 1780 and has had 116 amendments. The legislative body, styled the General Court of the Commonwealth of Massachusetts, meets annually, and consists of the Senate with 40 members, elected biennially, and the House of Representatives of 160 members, elected for 2 years. The Governor and Lieut.-Governor are elected for 4 years. The state sends 2 senators and 11 representatives to Congress.

At the 1984 presidential election Reagan polled 1,293,367 votes, Mondale, 1,219,513.

Electors are all citizens 18 years of age or older.

The capital is Boston. The state has 14 counties, 39 cities and 312 towns.

Governor: Michael S. Dukakis (D.), 1983–86 ($75,000).
Lieut.-Governor: (Vacant).
Secretary of the Commonwealth: Michael J. Connolly (D.) ($60,000).

BUDGET. For the fiscal year ending 30 June 1984 the total revenue of the state was $8,763,776,497 ($5,659·5m. from taxes and $1,800·3m. from federal aid); general expenditures, $8,649,394,825 ($603·4m. for education, $330·5m. for highway and transport construction and $2,097m. for public welfare).

The net long-term debt on 30 June 1984 amounted to $3,346m.

Per capita personal income (1983) was $13,244.

NATURAL RESOURCES

Minerals. There is little mining within the state. Total mineral output in 1983 was valued at $95·7m., of which most came from sand, gravel and stone.

Agriculture. On 1 Jan. 1984 there were 5,300 farms (11,179 in 1959) with an area of 598,900 acres.

Cash income, 1983, totalled $366·9m.; dairy, $91·3m.; greenhouse and nursery, $100m.; poultry, $26·8m.; vegetables, $32m.; tobacco, $4·5m.; cranberries, $65m.; other fruit, $18·1m.; potatoes, $2·3m.; all other, $27·1m.

Principal 1983 crops include cranberries, 1,460,000 bbls; apples, 2·3m. (42-lb. units); potatoes, 646,000 cwt, and tobacco, 0·8m. lb. On 1 Jan. 1982 farms in the state had 48,000 milch cows, 98,000 all cattle, 49,000 swine. In 1982 farms produced 145,000 turkeys and 0·8m. chickens.

Forestry. About 68% of the state is forest. State forests cover about 256,000 acres. Total forest land covers about 3m. acres. Commercially important hardwoods are sugar maple, northern red oak and white ash; softwoods are white pine and hemlock. About 240m. bd ft of timber are cut annually.

Fisheries. The 1983 catch amounted to 324·7m. lb. of finfish valued at $117m.; 27·8m. lb. of shellfish ($74m.); including 12·6m. lb. of lobster ($29·6m.).

INDUSTRY. In 1983, 10,503 manufacturing establishments employed an average of 632,375 workers, who earned $13,321. The 3 most important manufacturing groups, based on employment, were electric and electronic equipment, machinery (except electrical), instruments and related products.

LABOUR. In May 1984 the work force was 3,019,000. Changes in the industrial pattern have caused the loss of jobs in the shoe and textile industries. In 1981 there were 102 work stoppages involving 28,700 workers which resulted in 696,000 man-days idle.

COMMUNICATIONS

Roads. In Oct. 1984 the state had 33,800 miles of roads and streets and in 1984 registered 4m. motor vehicles.

Railways. In 1984 there were 1,310 miles of mainline railway.

Aviation. There were, in 1983, 52 aircraft landing areas for commercial operation, of which 27 were publicly owned.

Shipping. The state has 3 deep-water harbours, the largest of which is Boston (port trade (1983), 16,767,585 short tons). Other ports are Fall River and New Bedford.

JUSTICE, RELIGION, EDUCATION AND WELFARE

Justice. On 12 Sept. 1984 state penal institutions held 4,970 inmates. There have been no executions since 1947.

Religion. The principal religious bodies are the Roman Catholics, Jewish Congregations, Methodists, Episcopalians and Unitarians.

Education. A regulation effective from 1 Sept. 1972 makes school attendance compulsory for ages 6–16. In 1982–83 expenditure by cities and towns on public schools was $3,249m., including $199m. debt retirement and service payments. In 1983–84 there were 49,754 classroom teachers and 882,283 pupils.

Within the state there were (1982) 126 degree-granting institutions of higher learning (including 89 colleges and universities) with (1982–83) 14,274 full-time teaching staff and about 415,320 students. Some leading institutions are:

Year opened	*Name and location of universities and colleges*	*Students 1982*
1636	Harvard University, Cambridge [1]	21,252
1793	Williams College, Williamstown [1]	2,006
1821	Amherst College, Amherst [1]	1,561
1837	Mount Holyoke College, South Hadley [2]	1,979
1843	College of the Holy Cross, Worcester [1]	2,511
1852	Tufts University, Medford [1,3]	6,778
1861	Mass. Institute of Technology, Cambridge [1]	9,510
1863	University of Massachusetts, Amherst [1]	26,638
1863	Boston College (RC), Chestnut Hill [1]	14,171
1865	Worcester Polytechnic Institute, Worcester [1]	3,552
1869	Boston University, Boston [1]	28,042
1870	Wellesley College, Wellesley [2]	2,220
1875	Smith College, Northampton [1]	2,971
1879	Radcliffe College, Cambridge [1]	2,435
1885	Springfield College, Springfield [1]	2,511
1887	Clark University, Worcester [1]	3,169
1894	University of Lowell [1]	14,562
1898	Northeastern University, Boston [1,4]	42,406
1899	Simmons College, Boston [2]	2,773
1948	Brandeis University, Waltham [1]	3,580

[1] Co educational. [3] Includes Jackson College for women.
[2] For women only. [4] Includes Forsyth Dental Center School.

Health. In 1982 the state had 182 hospitals (with 40,270 beds); average daily census, 32,736, including patients in public and private mental hospitals and institutions for the mentally retarded.

Social Security. The Department of Public Welfare had an appropriation of $1,828m. in financial year 1984 and paid $388m. in aid to families with dependent children (average 95,798 families per month); other main items were general relief (average 27,242 cases), Supplemental Security Income (average 105,402 cases) and Medical Assistance only (average 65,841 cases).

Books of Reference

Annual Reports. Massachusetts and US Boards, Commissions, Departments and Divisions, Boston, annual

Business Climate Studies (1983). Alexander Grant, Boston 1983

Manual for the General Court. By Clerk of the Senate and Clerk of the House of Representatives, Boston, Mass. Biennial

Levitan, D., with Mariner, E. C., *Your Massachusetts Government.* Newton, Mass., 1984
Higher Education Publications, Washington, D.C., 1983

MICHIGAN

HISTORY. Michigan, first settled by Marquette at Sault Ste Marie in 1668, became the Territory of Michigan in 1805, with its boundaries greatly enlarged in 1818 and 1834; it was admitted into the Union with its present boundaries on 26 Jan. 1837.

AREA AND POPULATION. Michigan is divided into two by Lake Michigan. The northern part is bounded south by the lake and by Wisconsin, west and north by Lake Superior, east by the North Channel of Lake Huron; between the two latter lakes the Canadian border runs through straits at Sault Ste Marie. The southern part is bounded west and north by Lake Michigan, east by Lake Huron, Ontario and Lake Erie, south by Ohio and Indiana. Area, 58,527 sq. miles, of which 56,954 sq. miles are land area, 1,573 sq. miles are inland water. Census population, 1 April 1980, 9,262,078, an increase of 380,252 or 4·3% since 1970. Estimate (1983) 9,069,000. In 1983 births were 131,873; deaths, 74,302; infant deaths, 1,474; marriages, 70,735; divorces, 39,733.

Population of 5 federal census years was:

	White	*Negro*	*Indian*	*Asiatic*	*Total*	*Per sq. mile*
1910	2,785,247	17,115	7,519	292	2,810,173	48·9
1930	4,663,507	169,453	7,080	2,285	4,842,325	84·9
1960	7,085,865	717,581	9,701	10,047	7,823,194	137·2
			All others			
1970	7,833,474	991,066	50,543		8,875,083	156·2
1980	7,872,241	1,199,023	190,814		9,262,078	162·6

Of the total population in 1980, 4,513,951 were male, 6,547,842 persons were urban and those 20 years old or older numbered 6,144,925. 162,440 were of Spanish origin.

Population of the chief cities (census of 1 April 1980) was:

Detroit	1,203,339	Dearborn	90,660	Royal Oak	70,893
Grand Rapids	181,843	Westland	84,603	Dearborn Heights	67,706
Warren	161,134	Kalamazoo	79,722	Troy	67,102
Flint	159,611	Taylor	77,568	Wyoming	59,616
Lansing (capital)	130,414	Saginaw	77,508	Farmington Hills	58,056
Sterling Heights	108,999	Pontiac	76,715	Roseville	54,311
Ann Arbor	107,316	St Clair Shores	76,210		
Livonia	104,814	Southfield	75,568		

Larger standard metropolitan areas, 1980 census: Detroit, 4,344,139; Grand Rapids, 601,106; Flint, 521,541; Lansing, 467,584.

CLIMATE. Detroit. Jan. 25°F (–3·9°C), July 72°F (22·2°C). Annual rainfall 32″ (813 mm). Grand Rapids. Jan. 23°F (–5°C), July 72°F (22·2°C). Annual rainfall 32″ (803 mm). Lansing. Jan. 23°F (–5°C), July 71°F (21·7°C). Annual rainfall 30″ (754 mm). *See* Great Lakes, p. 1373.

CONSTITUTION AND GOVERNMENT. The present constitution was adopted in April 1963 and became effective on 1 Jan. 1964. The Senate consists of 38 members, elected for 4 years, and the House of Representatives of 110 members, elected for 2 years. The Governor and Lieut.-Governor are elected for 4 years. Electors are all citizens over 18 years of age meeting the usual residential requirements. The state sends to Congress 2 senators and 18 representatives.

At the 1984 presidential election Reagan polled 2,147,147 votes, Mondale, 1,468,512.

The capital is Lansing. The state is organized in 83 counties.

Governor: James J. Blanchard (D.), 1983–86 ($78,000).
Lieut.-Governor: Martha Griffiths (D.), 1983–86 ($53,500).
Secretary of State: Richard H. Austin (D.), 1983–86 ($75,000).

BUDGET. For the financial year ending 30 Sept. 1983, the general fund revenue was $8,267,328,000 (taxation, $7,333,434,000, and federal aid, $2,768,773,000); total revenue, $11,158,538,000; special revenue funds, $2,891,210,000; general expenditures, $10,804,575,000.

Per capita personal income (1983 estimate) was $11,466.

ENERGY AND NATURAL RESOURCES

Minerals. Most important minerals by value of production are iron ore, petroleum and cement. Output (1982): Iron ore, 6·7m. long tons ($313m.); Portland cement, 3·1m. short tons ($147·3m.); petroleum, 31·6m. bbls ($1,036·3m.); copper, 32,000 short tons ($35·9m.); sand and gravel, 24m. short tons ($72·4m.); stone, 21·7m. short tons ($70·9m.); lime, 680,000 short tons ($32·6m.); natural gas, 143,319m. cu. ft ($460·6m.). Total value of natural salines, $182m. Mineral output in 1982 was valued at $2,475·1m.

Agriculture. The state, formerly agricultural, is now chiefly industrial. In 1982 it contained 65,000 farms with a total area of 11·5m. acres; the average farm was 177 acres. Cash income, 1982, from crops, $1,687·6m.; from livestock and products, $1,175m. Principal crops are maize (production, 1983, 166m. bu. for grain), oats (15·6m. bu.), wheat (35·7m. bu.), sugar-beet (1·97m. tons); soybeans (32·3m. bu.), hay (4·5m. tons). On 1 Jan. 1984 there were in the state 110,000 sheep, 402,000 milch cows, 1·47m. all cattle; on 31 Dec. 1983, 1,250,000 swine, 7·5m. chickens and 38,000 turkey breeder hens. In 1983 the wool clip yielded 902,000 lb. of wool.

Forestry. The forests of Michigan consist of 18·3m. acres, about 50% of total state land area. About 17·5m. acres of this total is commercial forest, 64% of which is privately owned, 20% state forest, 14% federal forest and 1·5% in various public ownerships. Three-fourths of the timber volume is hardwoods, principally hard and soft maples, aspen, oak and birch. Christmas trees are another important forest crop.

Michigan leads in the number of state parks and public campsites. There are 79 state parks and recreation areas, 33 state forests, 3 national forests and 3 national parks. There are 171 state forest campgrounds and 64 state game areas.

INDUSTRY. Transport equipment and non-electrical machinery are the most important manufactures. The state ranks first in 19 manufacturing categories; among principal products are motor vehicles and trucks, cement, chemicals, furniture, paper, cereal, baby food and pharmaceuticals. Total labour force, 1983, 4,216,000, of which 932,800 are in manufacturing.

COMMUNICATIONS

Roads. State trunk-line mileage (31 July 1980) totalled, 9,500, all hard surfaced. Passenger car registrations, 18 Sept. 1983, 5,101,748.

Railways. On 1 Jan. 1980 there were 6,153 miles of railway and 383 miles of active car-ferry routes.

Aviation. Airports (1980) numbered 205 licensed airports, 88 certified but not licensed and 23 air carrier airports.

JUSTICE, RELIGION, EDUCATION AND WELFARE

Justice. The 1963 Constitution provides that no person shall be denied the equal protection of the law; nor shall any person be denied the enjoyment of his civil or political rights or be discriminated against in the exercise thereof because of religion, colour or national origin. A Civil Rights Commission was established, and its powers and duties were implemented by legislation in the extra session of 1963. Earlier statutory enactments guaranteeing civil rights in specific areas are as follows. An Act of 1885, last amended in 1956, orders all places of public accommodation and resort, etc., to furnish equal accommodations without discrimination. An Act of 1941, as last amended, forbids the Civil Service in counties with population exceeding 1m. to discriminate against employees or applicants on the ground of political, racial or religious opinions or affiliations. An Act of 1881 incorporated into the school code of 1955 forbids any discrimination in school facilities. An Act of 1893 incorporated in the insurance code of 1956 prohibits insurance companies from discriminating between white and coloured persons.

In 1951 the legislature restored the unique one-man grand jury system abandoned in 1949.

Religion. There were 2,004,288 Roman Catholics in 1979; largest Protestant denominations, Lutherans, 500,000; United Methodists, 278,245; United Presbyterians, 155,864; Episcopalians, 63,873.

Education. Education is compulsory for children from 6 to 16 years of age. The operating expenditure for graded and ungraded public schools for the fiscal year ending 30 June 1982, was $4,479,187,725; total, including capital and debt expenditures, $5,102,796,831. In 1982–83 there were 573 school districts (elementary and secondary schools) with 1,742,831 pupils and 78,814 teachers. Teachers' salaries in 1983 averaged $25,712.

In the autumn of 1981 the public 4-year institutions reported 235,027 students and the non-public institutions reported 67,509 students. The community colleges had an autumn enrolment (1981) of 211,871 students.

Universities and students (1983):

Founded	*Name*	*Students*
1817	University of Michigan	34,593
1849	Eastern Michigan University	18,880
1855	Michigan State University	41,765
1884	Ferris State College	10,767
1885	Michigan Technological University	7,414
1868	Wayne State University	29,639
1892	Central Michigan University	17,259
1889	Northern Michigan University	8,054
1903	Western Michigan University	20,296
1946	Lake Superior State College	2,820
1959	Oakland University	12,084
1960	Grand Valley State College	6,710
1965	Saginaw Valley College	4,612

Social Welfare. Old-age assistance is provided for persons 65 years of age or older who have resided in Michigan for one year before application; assets must not exceed various limits. In 1974 federal Supplementary Security Income (SSI) replaced the adults' programme. In 1982–83 aid was supplied to a monthly average of 1,186,943 dependent children in 239,848 families at $424.85 per family.

Health. In 1981 the state had 236 hospitals (41,000 beds) licensed by the state and 11 psychiatric hospitals, 11 centres for developmental disabilities, 5 centres for emotionally disturbed children.

In 1957 a programme came into force which provided for free medical care and hospital treatment for certain categories of persons. On 1 Oct. 1966 this programme was superseded by a more comprehensive programme called 'Medicaid' which, with federal support, disbursed in 1981, $1,297·8m. to 480,299 persons.

Books of Reference

Michigan Department of Economic Development. *Publications.* Lansing
Michigan Manual. Dept of State. Lansing. Biennial
Bureau of Business Research, Wayne State University. *Michigan Statistical Abstract.* Detroit, 1983
Bald, F. C., *Michigan in Four Centuries.* 2nd ed. New York, 1961
Blanchard, J. J., *Economic Report of the Governor 1983.* Lansing, 1983
Catton. B., *Michigan—a Bicentennial History.* Norton, New York, 1976
Lewis, F. E., *State and Local Government in Michigan.* Lansing, 1979
Dunbar, W. F., and May, G. S., *Michigan: A History of the Wolverine State.* Grand Rapids, 1980
Sommers, L. (ed.), *Atlas of Michigan.* East Lansing, 1977

State Library Services: Library of Michigan, Lansing 48909. *State Librarian:* James W. Fry.

MINNESOTA

HISTORY. Minnesota, first explored in the 17th century and first settled in the 20 years following the establishment of Fort Snelling (1819), was made a Territory in 1849 (with parts of North and South Dakota), and was admitted into the Union, with its present boundaries, on 11 May 1858.

AREA AND POPULATION. Minnesota is bounded north by Canada, east by Lake Superior and Wisconsin, with the Mississippi River forming the boundary in the south-east, south by Iowa, west by South and North Dakota, with the Red River forming the boundary in the north-west. Area, 84,402 sq. miles, of which 4,854 sq. miles are inland water. Census population, 1 April 1980, 4,075,970, an increase of 7·1% since 1970. Estimate (1983), 4,145,667. Births in 1981, 68,652 (16·7 per 1,000 population); deaths, 32,815 (8·0); infant deaths, 701 (10·2 per 1,000 live births); marriages, 37,638 (9·2); divorces, 16,505 (4).

Population in 5 census years was:

	White	*Negro*	*Indian*	*Asiatic*	*Total*	*Per sq. mile*
1910	2,059,227	7,084	9,053	344	2,075,708	25·7
1930	2,542,599	9,445	11,077	832	2,563,953	32·0
1960	3,371,603	22,263	15,496	3,642	3,413,864	42·7
			All others			
1970	3,736,038	34,868	34,163		3,805,069	47·6
1980	3,935,770	53,344	86,856		4,075,970	51·4

Of the 1980 population, 1,997,826 were male; 2,725,270 were urban; those 21 years of age or older numbered 2,656,947.

The largest cities are Minneapolis, 370,951; St Paul (capital), 270,230 (Minneapolis–St Paul standard metropolitan statistical area, 2,113,533 in 1980); Duluth, 92,811; Bloomington, 81,831; Rochester, 57,890.

CLIMATE. Duluth. Jan. 8°F (–13·3°C), July 63°F (17·2°C). Annual rainfall 29" (719 mm). Minneapolis-St. Paul. Jan. 12°F (–11·1°C), July 71°F (21·7°C). Annual rainfall 26" (656 mm). *See* Great Lakes, p. 1373.

CONSTITUTION AND GOVERNMENT. The present constitution dates from 1858; it has had 94 amendments. The Legislature consists of a Senate of 67 members, elected for 4 years, and a House of Representatives of 134 members, elected for 2 years. The Governor and Lieut.-Governor are elected for 4 years. The state sends to Congress 2 senators and 8 representatives.

In the 1984 presidential election Mondale polled 971,648 votes, Reagan 941,609.

The capital is St Paul. There are 87 counties, four containing less than 400 sq. miles, the largest being 6,092 sq. miles.

Governor: Rudy Perpich (D.), 1983–86 ($84,560).
Lieut.-Governor: Marlene Johnson (D.), 1983–86 ($46,510).
Secretary of State: Joan Anderson Growe (DFL.), 1983–86 ($46,510).

BUDGET. The general fund budget for the 1983–85 2-year period was $9,407m.; tax relief $1,674m., education $3,456m., public welfare $1,986m., transport $48m.

Net long-term debt, 30 June 1980, was $881m.

Per capita personal income (1983) was $11,913.

NATURAL RESOURCES

Minerals. The iron ore and taconite industry is the most important in the USA. Production of usable iron ore in 1981 was 50m. tons, value $2,062m. Other important minerals are sand and gravel, crushed and dimension stone, lime and manganiferous ore. Total value of mineral production, 1981, $2,151·9m.

Agriculture. Agriculture, including processing, is the leading industry. In 1983 there were 103,000 farms with a total area of 30·4m. acres (60% of the land area); the average farm was of 295 acres. Average value of land and buildings (1982) $348,800. Commercial farms in 1982 numbered 94,385; 12% of the farms were operated by tenant-farmers. Cash income, 1982, from crops, $3,132m.; from livestock, $3,541m. In 1983 Minnesota ranked first in sugarbeet and wild rice, and second in spring wheat, oats, hay, rye, non-fat dry milk, processing sweet corn and turkeys. Other important products are butter, eggs, sheep, flaxseed, milch cows, milk, corn, barley, swine, cattle for market, soybeans, honey, potatoes, chickens, sunflower seed, dry edible beans, and green peas for processing. Of livestock, cattle represents 15·1% of total farm income, swine 12·6% and milk 20%. Of crops, corn represents 15·3% and soybeans 17%. On 1 Jan. 1984 the farm animals included 3·69m. all cattle, 910,000 milch cows, 255,000 sheep and lambs, 4·27m. swine, 13·9m. chickens and 443,000 breeder hen turkeys. Turkey production, 1981, 27m. In 1983 the wool clip amounted to 2·11m. lb. of wool from 305,000 sheep.

Honey production (1981), 8·2m. lb; beeswax, 188,000 lb. About 95% of US commercial wild rice paddies are in Minnesota. Production from 20,000 acres (1983), 3·2m. lb. of processed wild rice.

Forestry. Forests of commercial timber cover 13·69m. acres, of which 53·5% is government-owned. The value of forest products in 1982 was $2,544m.; $674·3m. of this was from pulpwood and $1,595m. from secondary manufacturing. Logging, pulping, saw-mills and associated industries employed 46,800 in 1982.

INDUSTRY. In 1982 manufacturing establishments employed 359,600 workers; value added by manufacture was $14,305m.

TOURISM. In 1982, tourists spent about $2,500m.

COMMUNICATIONS

Roads. The state highway system (interstate and state trunk highways) covered 12,100 miles in 1981; total highway, road and street mileage, 130,800. In 1981, 2,092,170 passenger automobiles were registered.

Railways. There are 6 Class I and 9 Class II railroads operating, with total mileage of 5,318.

Aviation. Airports in 1980 numbered 593 (139 municipal, 27 privately owned for public use, 387 personal use, 11 public seaplane bases, 14 private, 74 for personal use).

JUSTICE, RELIGION, EDUCATION AND WELFARE

Justice. A Civil Rights Act (1927) forbids places of public resort to exclude persons 'on account of race or colour' and another section forbids insurance companies to discriminate 'between persons of the same class on account of race'. Contractors on public works may have their contracts cancelled if 'in the hiring of common or skilled labour' they are found to have discriminated on the grounds of 'race, creed or colour'. The state's penal reformatory system on 1 Jan. 1984 held 2,228 men and women. There is no death penalty in Minnesota.

Religion. The chief religious bodies are: Lutheran with 1,112,495 members in 1970; Roman Catholic, 1,061,614; Methodist, 213,084. Total membership of all denominations, 3,044,055.

Education. In 1983, there were 52,528 kindergarten students, 297,102 elementary students, and 362,084 secondary students enrolled in 1,504 public schools. There were 7,925 kindergarten students, 51,395 elementary students and 32,982 secondary students enrolled in 603 private schools. There were 39,704 public school classroom teachers and 5,382 private. The average salary for a public classroom teacher was $22,367. Total public school expenditures for 1983 were $2,333m. and total revenues were $2,322m. Of the total revenues, $1,923m. came from State funds and $113m. came from Federal funds. The University of Minnesota, chartered in 1851 and opened in 1869, had a total enrolment in 1982 of 59,290 students. The 14 public community colleges (2-year) had a total enrolment of 37,445. Seven state universities (4-year) had 1982 enrolment of 43,270, State universities are at Bemidji, Mankato, Marshall, Moorhead, St Cloud, Winona, Minneapolis and St Paul.

Health. In 1983 the state had 172 general acute hospitals with 20,752 beds. Patients resident in institutions under the Department of Public Welfare on 30 June 1982 included 1,303 mentally ill, 2,368 mentally retarded and 581 chemically dependent. There are 2 state nursing homes with 774 residents in 1983.

Social Security. On 1 Jan. 1974 the state administered programmes of old age assistance, aid to the disabled, and aid to the blind were given over to federal administration under the Supplemental Security Income (SSI) Programme. For some states, the new maintenance grants were less than under the state administered programmes. These states could establish a supplemental programme to correct the deficiency. The Minnesota Supplemental Aid (MSA) programme was later expanded to cover individuals who were not receiving SSI and to provide one-time payment for certain special needs such as major home repair, replacement of essential basic furniture or appliances, moving expenses and fuel and utility adjustments.

Books of Reference

Statistical Information: Current information is obtainable from the State Planning Agency (101 Capitol Square Building, 550 Cedar Street, St Paul 55101); non-current material from the Reference Library, Minnesota Historical Society, St Paul 55101.

Legislative Manual. Secretary of State. St Paul. Biennial
Manufacturers' Directory. Nelson Name Service, Minneapolis, Biennial
Minnesota Agriculture Statistics. Dept. of Agric., St Paul. Annual
Minnesota Pocket Data Book, Minneapolis, 1983

MISSISSIPPI

HISTORY. Mississippi, settled in 1716, was organized as a Territory in 1798 and admitted into the Union on 10 Dec. 1817. In 1804 and in 1812 its boundaries were extended, but in March 1817 a part was taken to form the new Territory of Alabama, leaving the boundaries substantially as at present.

AREA AND POPULATION. Mississippi is bounded north by Tennessee, east by Alabama, south by the Gulf of Mexico and Louisiana, west by the Mississippi River forming the boundary with Louisiana and Arkansas. Area, 47,689 sq. miles, 457 sq. miles being inland water. Census population, 1 April 1980, 2,520,638, an increase of 13·6% since 1970. Estimate (1983), 2,587,000. Births, occurring in the state, 1983, were 43,689; deaths, 23,314; infant deaths, 629; marriages, 26,921; divorces, 13,436.

Population of 6 federal census years was:

	White	*Negro*	*Indian*	*Asiatic*	*Total*	*Per sq. mile*
1910	786,111	1,009,487	1,253	263	1,797,114	38·8
1930	998,077	1,009,718	1,158	568	2,009,821	42·4
1950	1,188,632	986,494	2,502	1,286	2,178,914	46·1
1960	1,257,546	915,743	3,119	1,481	2,178,141	46·1
			All others			
1970	1,393,283	815,770	7,859		2,216,912	46·9
1980	1,615,190	887,206	18,242		2,520,638	53·0

Of the population in 1980, 1,213,878 were male, 1,192,805 were urban and 1,601,157 were 20 years old or older.

The largest city (1980) is Jackson, 202,895. Others are: Biloxi, 49,311; Meridian, 46,577; Hattiesburg, 40,829; Greenville, 40,613; Gulfport, 39,676; Pascagoula, 29,318; Columbus, 27,383; Vicksburg, 25,434; Tupelo, 23,905.

CLIMATE. Jackson.Jan. 47°F (8·3°C), July 82°F (27·8°C). Annual rainfall 49″ (1,221 mm). Vicksburg. Jan. 48°F (8·9°C), July 81°F (27·2°C). Annual rainfall 52″ (1,311 mm). *See* Central Plains, p. 1372.

CONSTITUTION AND GOVERNMENT. The present constitution was adopted in 1890 without ratification by the electorate; it has since had 48 amendments.

The Legislature consists of a Senate (52 members) and a House of Representatives (122 members), both elected for 4 years, as are also the Governor and Lieut.-Governor. Electors are all citizens who have resided in the state 1 year, in the county 1 year, in the election district 6 months next before the election and have been registered according to law. In the 1984 presidential election Reagan polled 577,378 votes, Mondale, 351,195.

The state is represented in Congress by 2 senators and 5 representatives.

The capital is Jackson; there are 82 counties.

Governor: William A. Allain (D.), 1984–88 ($53,000).
Lieut.-Governor: Bradford Johnson Dye (D.) ($34,000).
Secretary of State: Dick Molpus (D.) ($34,000).

BUDGET. For the fiscal year ending 30 June 1984 the general revenues were $2,912,094,406 (taxation, $1,809,145,191; federal aid, $875,137,182; other state resources, $227,812,033), and general expenditures were $2,867,245,829 ($989,800,154 for education, $322,241,426 for highways and $174,967,870 for public welfare).

On 30 June 1984 the total net long-term debt was $1,070·9m.

Per capita personal income (1982) was $7,778 (lowest in US).

ENERGY AND NATURAL RESOURCES

Minerals. Petroleum and natural gas account for about 90% (by value) of mineral production. Output of petroleum, 1981, was 34,381,093 bbls and of natural gas 229,404,669m. cu. ft. There are 6 oil refineries. Value of oil and gas products sold 1981 was $1,807,679,550.

Agriculture. Agriculture is the leading industry of the state because of the semi-tropical climate and a rich productive soil. In 1984 there were 82 soil conservation districts covering 26,342,406 acres. In 1983 farms with annual sales of $1,000 or more numbered 51,000 with an area of 14·3m. acres. Average size of farm was 280 acres. This compares with an average farm size of 138 acres in 1960.

Cash income from all crops and livestock during 1982, including government payments, was $2,535·2m. Cash income from crops was $1,488·1m. and from livestock and products, $943·2m. The chief product is cotton, cash income $651·9m. from 1m. acres producing 1·76m. bales of 480 lb. Soybeans (92·3m. bu. from 3·5m. acres), rice, corn, hay, wheat, oats, sorghum, peanuts, pecans, sweet potatoes, peaches, other vegetables, nursery and forest products continue to contribute.

On 1 Jan. 1983 there were 1·8m. head of cattle and calves on Mississippi farms. Milch cows and heifers which had calved totalled 96,000, beef cows and heifers that had calved, 874,000; hogs and pigs, 280,000. Of cash income from livestock and products, 1982, $267·4m. was credited to cattle and calves. Cash income from poultry and eggs totalled $427·7m.; dairy products, $127·3m.; swine, $56·9m.

In 1983 there were 82 soil-conservation districts covering 26,342,406 acres.

Forestry. In 1983 income from forestry amounted to $484m.; output of logs, lumber, etc., was 1,153·4m. bd ft; pulpwood, 4,764,132 cords; distillate wood, 16,862 tons; turpentine gum, 4,355 bbls. There are about 16·2m. acres of forest (53% of the state's area). National forests area, 1983, 1·1m. acres.

INDUSTRY. In 1983 the 2,968 manufacturing establishments employed 204,821 workers, earning $3,118,208,376.

TOURISM. Total receipts, 1984, $1,400m. from about 9m. tourists.

COMMUNICATIONS

Roads. The state in July 1984 maintained 10,240 miles of highways, of which 10,199 miles were paved. In 1984, 1,643,997 cars were registered.

Railways. The state in 1984 had 2,970·36 miles of railway.

Aviation. There were 77 public airports in 1984, 67 of them general. There were also 5 privately owned airports open to the public.

JUSTICE, RELIGION, EDUCATION AND WELFARE

Justice. In 1983 there was 1 execution; from 1955 to 1983 executions (by gas-chamber) totalled 32 (8 whites and 14 Negroes for murder, 9 Negroes for rape and 1 Negro for armed robbery). On 20 Oct. 1983 the state prisons had 5,552 inmates.

Religion. Southern Baptists in Mississippi (1983), 638,235 members; United Methodists (1984) 200,336; Roman Catholics (1984), 98,420 in Biloxi and Jackson dioceses; Negro Baptists about 475,000.

The number of churches relative to the population is the highest in the US (one church per 289 persons; national average, 814).

Education. Attendance at school is compulsory as laid down in the Education Reform Act of 1982. The public elementary and secondary schools in 1982–83 had 471,663 pupils and 25,256 classroom teachers.

In 1982–83, teachers' average salary was $14,135. The expenditure per pupil in average daily attendance, 1981–82, was $1,863.

There are 22 universities and senior colleges, of which 8 are state-supported. The University of Mississippi, at Oxford (1844), had, 1983–84, 575 instructors and 8,715 students; Mississippi State University, Starkville, 842 instructors and 11,720 students; Mississippi University for Women, at Columbus, 143 instructors and 2,198 students; University of Southern Mississippi, Hattiesburg, 634 instructors and 11,169 students; Jackson State University, Jackson, 353 instructors and 6,088 students; Delta State University, Cleveland, 202 instructors and 3,445 students; Alcorn State University, Lorman, 159 instructors and 2,400 students; Mississippi Valley State University, Itta Bena, 144 instructors and 2,396 students. State support for the 8 universities (1984–85) was $153·2m.

Junior colleges had (1983–84) 58,075 students and 2,279 instructors. The state appropriation for junior colleges, 1983–84, was $47·7m.

Health. In 1984 the state had 125 acute general hospitals (13,007 beds) listed by the Mississippi Health Care Commission. In 1984, 11 hospitals with facilities for care of the mentally ill had 2,428 beds.

Social Security. Department of Public Welfare figures show (June 1984) 20 persons receiving State Mandatory Supplementation payments amounting to $198 or an average of $9.90 per case. The state Medicaid commission paid (1983–84) $324·8m. for medical services, including $40m. for drugs, $45·96m. for skilled nursing home care, $82m. for hospital services. There were 70,689 persons eligible for Aged Medicaid, 1,981 persons eligible for Blind Medicaid and 62,989 persons eligible for Disabled Medicaid benefits at 30 June 1984. In June 1984 52,899 families with 111,923 dependent children received $4,821,906 in the Aid to Dependent Children programme. The average payment was $91.15 per family or $43.08 per child.

Books of Reference

1980 Census of Population and Housing: Mississippi.
Mississippi Official and Statistical Register. Secretary of State. Jackson. Biennial
Bettersworth, J. K., *Mississippi: A History.* Rev. ed. Austin, Tex., 1964

Mississippi Library Commission: PO Box 10700 Jackson, MS. 39209–0700. *Manager of Information Services:* Sharman B. Smith.

MISSOURI

HISTORY. Missouri, first settled in 1735 at Ste Genevieve, was made a Territory on 1 Oct. 1812, and admitted to the Union on 10 Aug. 1821. In 1837 its boundaries were extended to their present limits.

AREA AND POPULATION. Missouri is bounded north by Iowa, east by the Mississippi River forming the boundary with Illinois and Kentucky, south by Arkansas, south-west by Oklahoma, west by Kansas and Nebraska, with the Missouri River forming the boundary in the north-west. Area, 68,945 sq. miles, 752 sq. miles being water.

Census population, 1 April 1980, 4,916,686, an increase since 1970 of 5·1%. Estimate (1982), 4,951,000. Births, 1981, were 76,758 (15·9 per 1,000 population); deaths, 49,780 (10·1); infant deaths, 971 (12·7 per 1,000 live births); marriages, 54,124 (11·0); divorces, 27,975 (5·7).

Population of 5 federal census years was:

	White	*Negro*	*Indian*	*Asiatic*	*Total*	*Per sq. mile*
1910	3,134,932	157,452	313	638	3,293,335	47·9
1930	3,403,876	223,840	578	1,073	3,629,367	52·4
1960	3,922,967	390,853	1,723	3,146	4,319,813	62·5
			All others			
1970	4,177,495	480,172	19,732		4,677,399	67·0
1980	4,345,521	514,276	56,889		4,916,686	71·3

Of the total population in 1980, 2,365,487 were male, 3,350,746 persons were urban and those 18 years of age or older numbered 3,554,203.

The principal cities at the 1980 census (and estimates, 1982) are:

St Louis	453,085 (419,004)	Columbia	62,061 (64,004)
Kansas City	448,159 (436,002)	Florissant	55,372 (56,006)
Springfield	133,116 (137,006)	University City	42,738 (41,007)
Independence	111,806 (111,009)	Joplin	38,893 (39,002)
St Joseph	76,691 (76,008)	St Charles	37,379 (41,004)

Metropolitan areas, 1980: St Louis, 2,356,000; Kansas City, 1,327,000.

CLIMATE. Kansas City. Jan. 30°F (–1·1°C), July 79°F (26·1°C). Annual rainfall 38″ (947 mm). St. Louis. Jan. 32°F (0°C), July 79°F (26·1°C). Annual rainfall 40″ (1,004 mm). *See* Central Plains, p. 1372.

CONSTITUTION AND GOVERNMENT. A new constitution, the fourth, was adopted on 27 Feb. 1945; it has been amended 26 times. The General Assembly consists of a Senate of 34 members elected for 4 years (half for re-election every 2 years), and a House of Representatives of 163 members elected for 2 years. The Governor and Lieut.-Governor are elected for 4 years. Missouri sends to Congress 2 senators and 9 representatives.

Voters (with the usual exceptions) are all citizens and those adult aliens who, within a prescribed period, have applied for citizenship. In the 1984 presidential election Reagan polled 1,242,678, Mondale, 808,601.

Jefferson City is the state capital. The state is divided into 114 counties and the city of St Louis.

Governor: John D. Ashcroft (R.), 1985–88 ($75,000).
Lieut.-Governor: Harriett Woods (D.), 1985–88 ($45,000).
Secretary of State: Roy D. Blunt (R.), 1985–88 ($60,000).

BUDGET. For the year 1981–82 the total revenues from all funds were $4,951·5m. (federal revenue, $1,543·3m., general revenue, $2,833·3m.).

Total outstanding debt, 1981–82, was $3,181·4m.
Per capita personal income (1982) was $10,188.

NATURAL RESOURCES

Minerals. Principal minerals are lead (ranks first in USA), zinc (ranks second), clays, coal, iron ore, and stone for cement and lime manufacture. Value of production (1982) $733·8m., a 16·2% decrease from that of 1981.

Agriculture. In 1983 there were (preliminary) 117,000 farms in Missouri covering 31·4m. acres. The average size of farms is 268 acres. Production of principal crops, 1983: Corn, 74·36m. bu.; soybeans, 101·4m. bu.; wheat, 70·3m. bu.; sorghum grain, 40·8m. bu.; oats, 2·48m. bu.; cotton, 73,000 bales (of 480 lb.). Cash receipts from farming, 1983, $3,906·5m. (preliminary). Export value of farm produce, $1,018m., to which soybeans contributed $629m.

Forestry. Forest land area, 1982, 32·4m. acres.

INDUSTRY. The largest employer in 1982 (preliminary) was manufacturing, in which the transport equipment industry employed 56,009 workers. Other large industries are food and kindred products, electrical equipment and supplies, apparel and related products and non-electrical machinery, leather products, chemicals, paper, metal industries, stone, clay and glass. Retail trade employed 326,375 in 1981, 103,233 of them in eating and drinking places; wholesale trade employed 135,282.

LABOUR. The State Board of Mediation has jurisdiction in labour disputes involving only public utilities. The Prevailing Wage Law (1959) provides that no less than the local hourly rate of wages for work of a similar character shall be paid to any workmen engaged in public works. The Industrial Commission has authority to inspect records and to institute actions for penalties described in the Act. There is a state programme for industrial safety in hand, under the Federal Occupational and Health Act. In June 1984 the estimated number of employed was 2,428,500, and 172,700 were unemployed. The unemployment rate was 7·1% (estimate).

COMMUNICATIONS

Roads. Federal and state highways, Dec. 1981, totalled 118,403 miles. In 1981 there were 3·3m. vehicles licensed in the state, of which 3,741 were private and commercial buses.

Railways. The state has 10 Class I railways; approximate total mileage, 8,081. There are 7 other railways (switching, terminal or short-line), total mileage 229.

Aviation. In 1984 there were 116 public airports and 277 private airports.

Shipping. Ten carrier barge lines (1984) operated on about 1,000 miles of navigable waterways including the Missouri and Mississippi Rivers. Boat shipping seasons: Missouri River, April–end Nov.; Mississippi River, all seasons.

Post and Broadcasting. There were 243 commercial radio stations and 30 TV stations in 1983 (preliminary). The number of telephones in 1980 was 3·87m.

Newspapers. There were (1984) 44 daily and 226 weekly newspapers.

JUSTICE, RELIGION, EDUCATION AND WELFARE

Justice. State prisons in 1984 had an average of 8,167 inmates. Of those committed, 70% are aged 17–29. There have been no executions since 1965 although the death penalty was reinstated in 1978, since 1930 executions (by lethal gas) have totalled 40, including 31 for murder, 6 for rape and 3 for kidnapping. The Missouri Law Enforcement Assistance Council was created in 1969 for law reform.

Religion. Chief religious bodies (1980) are Catholic, with 800,228 members, Southern Baptists (700,053), United Methodists (270,469), Christian Churches

(175,101), Lutheran (157,928), Presbyterian (38,254). Total membership, all denominations, about 2·6m. in 1980.

Education. School attendance is compulsory for children from 7 to 16 years for the full term. In the 1983–84 school year, public schools (kindergarten through grade 12) had 795,453 pupils. Total expenditure for public schools in 1983, $2,065·2m. Salaries for teachers (kindergarten through grade 12), 1982–83, averaged $18,000. Institutions for higher education include the University of Missouri, founded in 1839 with campuses at Columbia, Rolla, St Louis and Kansas City, with 6,052 accredited teachers and 54,662 students in 1982. Washington University at St Louis, founded in 1857, and St Louis University (1818), are both private universities. Fifteen state colleges had 114,232 students in 1982. Private colleges had (1982) 43,171 students. Church-affiliated colleges (1982) had 28,689 students. Public junior colleges had 52,423 students. There are about 89 secondary and post-secondary institutions offering vocational courses, and about 201 private career schools. There were 244,238 students in higher education in autumn 1982.

Health. There were 9 state mental health hospitals and centres and 2 children's psychiatric hospitals in 1983, admitting 23,692 patients.

Social Security. In 1981 the number of recipients of medicaid was 361,000. The number of recipients of Aid to Dependent Children was 177,000 with an average monthly payment per family of $219.

Books of Reference

Missouri Final Production Count, Office of Comptroller and Budget Director, Jefferson City
Missouri Corporate Planner, Division of Commerce and Industrial Development, Jefferson City
Statistical Abstract for Missouri. State and Regional Fiscal Studies Unit, College of Business and Public Administration, Columbia 1983

MONTANA

HISTORY. Montana, first settled in 1809, was made a Territory (out of portions of Idaho and Dakota Territories) in 1864 and was admitted into the Union on 8 Nov. 1889.

AREA AND POPULATION. Montana is bounded north by Canada, east by North and South Dakota, south by Wyoming and west by Idaho and the Bitterroot Range of the Rocky Mountains. Area, 147,138 sq. miles, including 1,551 sq. miles of water, of which the federal government, 1979, owned 27,741,000 acres or 29·7%. US Bureau of Indian Affairs administered 5·26m. acres, of which 2,204,000 were allotted to tribes. Census population, 1 April 1980, 786,690, an increase of 13·3% since 1970. Estimate (1982), 801,000. Births, 1981, were 13,999 (18 per 1,000 population); deaths, 6,709 (8·5); infant deaths, 153 (10·7 per 1,000 live births); marriages, 8,209 (10·4); divorces 5,004 (6·3).

Population in 5 census years was:

	White	*Negro*	*Indian*	*Asiatic*	*Total*	*Per sq. mile*
1910	360,580	1,834	10,745	2,870	376,053	2·6
1930	519,898	1,256	14,798	1,239	537,606	3·7
1950	572,038	1,232	16,606	—	591,024	4·1
1970	663,043	1,995	27,130	1,099	694,409	4·7
1980	740,148	1,786	37,270	2,503	786,690	5·3

Of the total population in 1980, 392,625 were male, 416,402 persons (52·9%) were urban. Persons 20 years of age or older numbered 524,836. Median age, 29 years. Households, 283,742.

The largest cities (1980) are Billings, 66,798; Great Falls, 56,725. Others, 1980: Butte-Silver Bow, 37,205; Missoula, 33,388; Helena (capital), 23,938; Bozeman, 21,645; Anaconda-Deer Lodge County, 12,518; Havre, 10,891; Kalispell, 10,648.

CLIMATE. Helena. Jan. 18°F (−7·8°C), July 69°F (20·6°C). Annual rainfall 13″ (325 mm). *See* Mountain States, p. 1372.

CONSTITUTION AND GOVERNMENT. A new constitution was ratified by the voters on 6 June 1972, and fully implemented on 1 July 1973; the Senate to consist of 50 senators, elected for 4 years, one half at each biennial election. The 100 members of the House of Representatives are elected for 2 years.

The Governor and Lieut.-Governor are elected for 4 years. Montana sends to Congress 2 senators and 2 representatives.

In the 1984 presidential election Reagan polled 207,163 votes, Mondale, 131,975.

The capital is Helena. The state is divided into 56 counties.

Governor: Ted Schwinden (D.), 1985–89 ($47,963).
Lieut.-Governor: George Turman (D.), 1985–89 ($34,344).
Secretary of State: Jim Waltermire (R.), 1985–89 ($31,692).

BUDGET. Total state revenues for the year ending 30 June 1981 were $1,269,327,000 ($465m. taxes); total expenditures were $1,096,301,000 ($307·8m. for education, $193m. for highways and $116·8m. for public welfare).

Total net long-term debt on 30 June 1981 was $82,034,000.

Per capita personal income (1981) was $9,412.

ENERGY AND NATURAL RESOURCES

Electricity. Electric power generated in June 1983 was 1,027 gwh., of which 902 gwh. was hydro-electric and 123 gwh. from coal-fired plants; minimal amounts were from oil and gas-fired plants and 1 gwh. from other sources.

Minerals (1981). Output of crude petroleum, 31m. bbls; copper, 62,485 tonnes; sand and gravel, 6·1m. short tons; phosphate rock, undisclosed; silver, 2·9m. troy oz.; gold, 54,267 troy oz.; zinc, 25 tonnes; natural gas, 56,565m. cu. ft; coal, 33·5m short tons. Value of total mineral production (1981), $1,894·3m., with petroleum ($1,073·9m.) the first, coal ($407·2m.) the second, copper ($117·3m.) the third and natural gas ($108m.) the fourth most important commodity.

Agriculture. In 1982 there were 24,000 farms and ranches (50,564 in 1935) with an area of 62·1m. acres (47,511,868 acres in 1935). Large-scale farming predominates; in 1982 the average size per farm was 2,588 acres. Income from all farm marketings was $1,483·3m. in 1981 (crops, $854·2m.; livestock, $629m.). Irrigated area harvested in 1981 was 1·73m. acres; non-irrigated, 7·98m. acres.

The chief crops are wheat, amounting in 1981 to 172·8m. bu., ranking sixth in US; barley, 56·7m. bu., oats, 4·8m. bu.; sugar-beet, hay, potatoes, alfalfa, dry beans, flax and cherries. In 1981 there were 29,000 milch cows, 2·9m. all cattle; 200,000 swine.

The wool clip in 1981 was 5·56m. lb. from 616,000 head of sheep.

Forestry. Total forest area (1977), 22·5m. acres. In 1981 there were 16·8m. acres within 11 national forests.

INDUSTRY. In 1981 manufacturing establishments numbering 612 had 17,264 production workers; value added by manufacture was (1978) $850·6m.

LABOUR (Aug. 1983). Work force, 393,200; total employed, 362,600; total non-agricultural workers, 320,900; agricultural workers, 41,700. Workers employed by major industry group: Mining, 7,000 (average net weekly earnings, $492.78), contract construction, 12,900 ($569.65); manufacturing, 21,000 ($422.75); transport and public utilities, 18,900 ($465.37; wholesale/retail trade, 73,700 ($206.38); finance/insurance/real estate, 13,100 ($207.27); services, 55,300 ($200.63); government, 64,200 (no income figures available). Average weekly earnings for all workers in private non-agricultural industries $281.60. Total unemployed 30,600 (7·8% of the work force in Aug. 1983 as compared to 9·2% nationally for that month).

There were 16 work stoppages in 1980 involving 4,900 workers, with a total of 96,900 man days idle during the year.

COMMUNICATIONS

Roads. In Dec. 1982 the state had 63,151 miles of maintained public roads and streets including 11,733 miles of the federal-aid system. At 26 Oct. 1983 there were 506,080 passenger vehicles, 319,515 trucks and 50,688 motor cycles registered.

Railways. In Dec. 1983 there were 4,314 route miles of railway in the state.

Aviation. There were 126 airports open for public use in Dec. 1983, of which 120 were publicly owned.

JUSTICE, RELIGION, EDUCATION AND WELFARE

Justice. On 1 Nov. 1983 the Montana state prison held 777 inmates and the Women's Correctional Center, 17. Since 1943 there have been no executions; total since 1930 (all by hanging) was 6; 4 whites and 2 Negroes, for murder.

Religion. The leading religious bodies are (1982): Roman Catholic with 131,000 active members; Lutheran, 68,000; Methodist, 25,000 (church estimates).

Education. In Oct. 1982 public elementary and secondary schools had 152,335 pupils. Public elementary and secondary school teachers (9,517 full-time) had an average salary of $19,488. Expenditure on public school education (1982–83) (excluding special education programmes) was $360·9m.; expenditure per pupil was $2,373. The Montana University system consists of the Montana State University, at Bozeman (autumn 1983 enrolment: 11,447 students), the University of Montana, at Missoula, founded in 1895 (9,371), the Montana College of Mineral Science and Technology, at Butte (2,306), Northern Montana College, at Havre (1,859), Eastern Montana College, at Billings (4,424) and Western Montana College, at Dillon (941).

Social Security. In Sept. 1983, 3,569 persons over age 65 were receiving in medical assistance an average of $772.21 per month; 52 blind persons, $579.42; 2,983 totally disabled, $599.85; 6,823 families (12,369 dependent children) receiving in aid-to-dependent children assistance an average of $307.03 per month. Aid was from state and federal sources.

Health. In Aug. 1983 the state had 61 hospitals (3,426 beds) listed by the Montana Board of Health. Four centres for mental disease and development disorders had 962 beds and 841 patients.

Books of Reference

Montana Agricultural Statistics. U.S. Dept. of Agriculture, Montana Crop and Livestock Reporting Service. Biennial from 1946

Montana Employment and Labor Force. Montana Dept. of Labor and Industry. Monthly from 1971

Montana Federal-Aid Road Log. Montana Dept. of Highways and US Dept. of Transportation, Federal Highway Administration. Annual from 1938

Montana Vital Statistics. Montana Dept. of Health and Environmental Sciences. Annually from 1954

Statistical Report. Montana Dept. of Social and Rehabilitation Services. Monthly from 1947

Lang, W, L., and Myers, R. C., *Montana, Our Land and People.* Pruett, 1979

Malone, M. P., and Roeder, R. B., *Montana, A History of Two Centuries.* Univ. of Washington Press, 1976

Spence, C. C., *Montana, a History.* New York, 1978

NEBRASKA

HISTORY. The Nebraska region was first reached by white men from Mexico under the Spanish general Coronado in 1541. It was ceded by France to Spain in

1763, retroceded to France in 1801, and sold by Napoleon to the US as part of the Louisiana Purchase in 1803. Its first settlement was in 1847, and on 30 May 1854 it became a Territory and on 1 March 1867 a state. In 1882 it annexed a small part of Dakota Territory, and in 1908 it received another small tract from South Dakota.

AREA AND POPULATION. Nebraska is bounded north by South Dakota, with the Missouri River forming the boundary in the north-east and the boundary with Iowa and Missouri to the east; south by Kansas, south-west by Colorado and west by Wyoming. Area, 77,355 sq. miles, of which 711 sq. miles are water. Census population, 1980: 1,569,825, an increase of 5·7% since 1970. Estimate (1982), 1,586,000. Births, 1982, were 26,954 (17·0 per 1,000 population); deaths, 14,567 (9·2); infant deaths, 269 (10 per 1,000 live births); marriages, 14,350 (9): divorces, 6,357 (4).

Population in 5 census years was:

	White	*Negro*	*Indian*	*Asiatic*	*Total*	*Per sq. mile*
1910	1,180,293	7,689	3,502	730	1,192,214	15·5
1920	1,279,219	13,242	2,888	1,023	1,296,372	16·9
1960	1,374,764	29,262	5,545	1,195	1,411,330	18·3
			All others			
1970	1,432,867	39,911	10,715		1,483,791	19·4
1980	1,490,381	48,390	31,054		1,569,825	20·5

Of the total population in 1980, 48·8% were male,62·9% were urban 65·6% were 21 years of age or older. The largest cities in the state are: Omaha, with a census population, 1980, of 313,911; Lincoln (capital), 171,932; Grand Island, 33,180; North Platte, 24,509; Fremont, 23,979; Hastings, 23,045; Bellevue, 21,813; Kearney, 21,158; Norfolk, 19,449.

The Bureau of Indian Affairs, as of 30 June 1981, administered 65,000 acres, of which 23,000 acres were allotted to tribal control.

CLIMATE. Omaha. Jan. 22°F (–5·6°C), July 77°F (25°C). Annual rainfall 29" (721 mm). *See* High Plains, p. 1372.

CONSTITUTION AND GOVERNMENT. The present constitution was adopted in 1875; it has been amended 176 times. By an amendment adopted in Nov. 1934 Nebraska has a single-chambered legislature (elected for 4 years) of 49 members—the only state in the Union to have one. The Governor and Lieut.-Governor are elected for 4 years. Amendments adopted in 1912 and 1920 provide for legislation through the initiative and referendum and permit cities of more than 5,000 inhabitants to frame their own charters. A 'right-to-work' amendment adopted 5 Nov. 1946 makes illegal the 'closed shop' demands of trade unions. Nebraska is represented in Congress by 2 senators and 3 representatives.

In the 1984 presidential election Reagan polled 446,938 votes, Mondale, 183,838.

The capital is Lincoln. The state has 93 counties.

Governor: Robert Kerrey (D.), 1983–86 ($40,000).
Lieut.-Governor: Donald F. McGinley (D.) ($32,000).
Secretary of State: Allen Beerman (R.) ($32,000).

BUDGET. For the fiscal year ending 30 June 1980 (US Census Bureau figures) the state's revenues were $1,506m. (taxation, $817m. and federal aid, $361m.); general expenditures were $1,341m. ($416m. for education, $265m. for highways and $191m. for public welfare).

The state has a bonded indebtedness limit of $100,000.

Per capita personal income (1981) was $10,641.

ENERGY AND NATURAL RESOURCES

Minerals. The total output of minerals, 1983, was valued at $282·2m., petroleum (6m. bbls) and sand and gravel (12m. tons) being the most important.

Agriculture. Nebraska is one of the most important agricultural states. In 1983 it contained approximately 63,000 farms, with a total area of 45m. acres. The average farm was 746 acres.

In 1982, 7·7m. acres were irrigated and 70,233 irrigation wells were registered.

Cash income from crops (1982), $2,855·4m., and from livestock, $4,231·4m. Principal crops, with estimated 1983 yield: Maize, 475·2m. bu. (ranking third in US); wheat, 98·9m. bu.; sorghums for grain, 60m. bu.; oats, 13·6m. bu.; soybeans, 59·5m. bu. About 753 farms grow sugar-beet for 5 factories; output, 1983, 1·2m. short tons. On 1 Jan. 1984 the state contained 6·9m. all cattle (ranking third in US), 121,000 milch cows, 195,000 sheep and 3·5m. swine.

Forestry. The area of national forest, 1982, was 352,000 acres.

INDUSTRY. In 1978 there were 1,969 manufacturing establishments; 66,900 production workers earned $786·5m. and value added by manufacturing was $3,249·7m. The chief industry is meat-packing, employing (1978), 8,200 (7,100 production workers) and value added was $258·3m.

COMMUNICATIONS

Roads. The state-maintained highway system embraced 9,888 miles in 1982; local roads, 96,072 miles. In 1983, 821,002 automobiles were registered.

Railways. In 1981 there were 7,394 miles of railway.

Aviation. Airports (1982) numbered 323, of which 112 were publicly owned.

JUSTICE, RELIGION, EDUCATION AND WELFARE

Justice. A 'Civil Rights Act' revised in 1969 provides that all people are entitled to a 'full and equal enjoyment of the accommodations, advantages, facilities and privileges' of hotels, restaurants, public conveyances, amusement places and other places. The state university is forbidden to discriminate between students 'because of age, sex, color or nationality'. An Act of 1941 declares it to be 'the policy of this state' that no trade union should discriminate, in collective bargaining, 'against any person because of his race or color'.

The state's prisons had, 23 Oct, 1984, 1,700 inmates (93 per 100,000 population). From 1930 to 1962 there were 4 executions (electrocution), 3 white men and 1 American Indian, all for murder, and none since.

Religion. The Roman Catholics had 334,352 members in 1983; Protestant Churches, 671,000; Jews, 7,900 members. Total, all denominations, 1,013,252 (unofficial figures).

Education. School attendance is compulsory for children from 7 to 16 years of age. Public elementary schools, autumn 1982, had 144,425 enrolled pupils. Teachers' salaries, 1983–84, averaged $18,785. Estimated public school expenditure for year ending 30 Aug. 1983 was $690·4m. Total enrolment in 30 institutions of higher education, autumn 1983, was 95,162 students. The largest institutions were (1983):

Opened	*Institution*	*Students*
1867	Peru State College, Peru (State)	1,130
1869	Univ. of Nebraska, Lincoln (State)	27,372
1878	Creighton Univ., Omaha (RC)	6,301
1883	Midland Lutheran College, Fremont (Lutheran)	881
1887	Nebraska Wesleyan Univ. (Methodist)	1,222
1891	Union College, Lincoln (Seventh Day Adventist)	1,040
1894	Concordia Teachers' College, Seward (Lutheran)	960
1905	Kearney State College, Kearney (State)	7,664
1908	Univ. of Nebraska, Omaha (State)	14,531
1910	Wayne State College, Wayne (State)	2,405
1911	Chadron State College, Chadron (State)	1,916
1923	College of St. Mary	1,207
1966	Bellevue College, Bellevue (Private)	2,717

The state holds 1·52m. acres of land as a permanent endowment of her schools; permanent public school endowment fund in Sept. 1984 was $79·2m.

Health. In 1984 the state had 113 hospitals and 570 patients in mental hospitals.

Social Security. The administration of public welfare is the responsibility of the County Divisions of Welfare with policy-forming, regulatory, advisory and supervisory functions performed by the State Department of Public Welfare. In 1983 public welfare provided financial aid and/or services as follows: for 6,588 individuals who were aged, blind or disabled, with an average state supplement of $55.82; for 14,639 families with dependent children, with an average payment of $318.60 per family; for 82,874 individuals who had medical needs, $1,753.97, per individual; for 1,842 children in need of child welfare services; for 3,516 children who were in need of crippled children's services and medical care. The amount of aid is based on need in accordance with State assistance standards; the programme of aid to families with dependent children is limited to a maximum maintenance payment of $293 for 1 child plus $71 for each additional child.

Books of Reference

Agricultural Atlas of Nebraska. Univ. of Nebraska Press, 1977
Climatic Atlas of Nebraska. Univ. of Nebraska Press, 1977
Economic Atlas of Nebraska. Univ. of Nebraska Press, 1977
Nebraska. A Guide to the Cornhusker State. Univ. of Nebraska Press, 1979
Nebraska Statistical Handbook, 1984–85. Nebraska Dept. of Econ. Development, Lincoln
Nebraska Blue-Book. Legislative Council. Lincoln. Biennial
Olson, J. C., *History of Nebraska.* Univ. of Nebraska Press, 1955

State Library: State Law Library, State House, Lincoln. *Librarian:* Larry D. Donelson.

NEVADA

HISTORY. Nevada, first settled in 1851, when it was a part of the Territory of Utah (created 1850), was made a Territory in 1861, enlarged in 1862 by an addition from Utah Territory and admitted into the Union on 31 Oct. 1864 as the 36th state. In 1866 and 1867 the area of the state was significantly enlarged at the expense of the Territories of Utah and Arizona.

AREA AND POPULATION. Nevada is bounded north by Oregon and Idaho, east by Utah, south-east by Arizona, with the Colorado River forming most of the boundary, south and west by California. Area 110,561 sq. miles, 667 sq. miles being water. The federal government in 1973 owned 60,908,872 acres, or 86·5% of the land area. Vacant public lands, 48,340,876 acres. The Bureau of Indian Affairs controlled 1·35m. acres in 1975, of which 1,062,047 acres have been assigned to Indian tribes.

Census population on 1 April 1980, 799,184, an increase of 310,446 or 63·5% since 1970. Estimate (1981) 845,000. Births, 1980, were 13,156 (16·5 per 1,000 population); deaths, 6,408 (8); infant deaths, 157 (12 per 1,000 live births); marriages, 115,411 (144·5 per 1,000 population, largest of any state); divorces, 13,659 (17·1).

Population in 5 census years was:

	White	*Negro*	*Indian*	*Asiatic and all others*	*Total*	*Per sq. mile*
1910	74,276	513	5,240	1,846	81,875	0·7
1930	84,515	516	4,871	1,156	91,058	0·8
1960	263,443	13,484	6,681	1,670	285,278	2·6
1970	449.850	27,579	7,329	3,980	488,738	4·4
			All others			
1980	699,377	50,791	49,016		799,184	7·2

Of the total population in 1980, 404,372 were male, 681,682 were urban and 556,021 were 20 years of age or older.

The largest cities are Las Vegas, with population at the 1980 census of 164,674 (1982 estimate, 183,184); Reno, 100,756 (107,607); North Las Vegas, 39,196 (47,543); Sparks, 38,114 (42,604); Carson City, 30,807 (33,929); and Henderson,

20,905 (28,680). Clark County (Las Vegas, North Las Vegas and Henderson) and Washoe County (Reno and Sparks) together had 81% of the total state population in 1980 (82% in 1982).

CLIMATE. Las Vegas. Jan. 44°F (6·7°C), July 85°F (29·4°C). Annual rainfall 4" (112 mm). Reno. Jan. 32°F (0°C), July 69°F (20·6°C). Annual rainfall 7" (178 mm). *See* Mountain States, p. 1372.

CONSTITUTION AND GOVERNMENT. The constitution adopted in 1864 is still in force, with over 60 amendments. The Legislature meets biennially (and in special sessions) and consists of a Senate of 20 members elected for 4 years, half their number retiring every 2 years, and an Assembly of 40 members elected for 2 years. The Governor, Lieut.-Governor and Attorney-General are elected for 4 years. Qualified electors are all citizens with the usual residential qualification. Nevada is represented in Congress by 2 senators and 2 representatives. A Supreme Court of 5 members is elected for 4 years on a non-partisan ballot.

In the 1984 presidential election Reagan polled 188,794 votes, Mondale, 91,654.

The state capital is Carson City. There are 16 counties, 17 incorporated cities and towns, 44 unincorporated towns and 1 city-county (Carson City).

Governor: Richard Bryan (D.), 1983–86 ($65,000).
Lieut.-Governor: Bob Cashell (D.) ($10,500).
Secretary of State: William D. Swackhammer (D.) ($42,500).

BUDGET. For the fiscal year ending 30 June 1985 budget state general fund revenues were $433m., including federal receipts; budget expenditures were $415·5m. Education followed by human resources and public safety received the largest appropriations.

State bonded indebtedness on 30 June 1984, was $45·9m. The state has no franchise tax, capital stock tax, special intangibles tax, chain stores tax, stock transfer tax, admissions tax, estate tax, gift tax, income taxes or inheritance tax. The sales and use tax and gaming taxes are the largest revenue producers.

Per capita personal income (1982) was $11,981.

ENERGY AND NATURAL RESOURCES

Electricity. Electricity power stations supplied 8,463m. mwh. in 1978. There were about 316,484 private and commercial customers in 1979. There are 8 suppliers of natural gas producing 51,696,121m.cu. ft in 1978.

Minerals. Production, 1981, in order of value was gold, barite, silver, and sand and gravel. Other minerals are gypsum, iron ore, mercury, lime, lithium, petroleum, gemstones, lead, molybdenum, fluorspar, perlite, pumice, clays, talc, salt, tungsten, magnesite, diatonite and zinc. Value of mineral output for 1981, $504m.

Agriculture. In 1982, an estimated 2,900 farms had a farm area of 8·9m. acres (9·2m. in 1960). Farms averaged (1981) 2,871 acres. Area under irrigation (1979) was 1·3m. acres compared with 542,976 acres in 1959.

Gross income, 1981, from crops, livestock and government payments, $249·1m. Cattle, dairy products, hay, potatoes and sheep are the principal commodities in order of cash receipts. Total value of crops produced, $13·2m., of which hay accounted for 17·1%. On 1 Jan. 1982 there were 16,000 milch cows, 359,000 beef cattle, 129,000 sheep and 129 lambs.

Forestry. The area of national forests (1983) under US Forest Service administration was 5,150,088 acres. National forests: Toiyabe (2,561,441 acres); Humboldt (2,527,938), Inyo (60,656); Eldorado (53).

INDUSTRY. The main industries are the service industry, especially tourism and legalized gambling, mining and smelting, livestock and irrigated agriculture, chemical manufacturing, and lumber processing. In 1981 there were 843 manufacturing establishments with 20,094 employees, earning $362m.

Gaming industry gross revenue for financial year 1983, $2,847m. There were at the same time 1,637 licences in force.

LABOUR. The annual average unemployment for 1983 was 9·8% of the work force. All industries employed 404,900 workers. Main industries and employees, 1983: Mining, 5,900; contract construction, 19,700; manufacturing, 19,000; transport (except railways), public works and utilities, 24,500; service industries, 178,800; retail trade, 66,700; government, 58,000; finance, insurance and real estate, 18,600.

COMMUNICATIONS

Roads. Highway mileage (federal, state and local) totalled 51,118 in 1984, of which 16,798 miles were surfaced; motor vehicle registrations at 31 Dec. 1983 numbered 812,281.

Railways. In 1973 there were 1,553 miles of main-line railway. Nevada is served by Southern Pacific, Union Pacific and Western Pacific railways, and Amtrac passenger service for Carlin, Elko, Reno and Sparks.

Aviation. There were (1974) 114 civil airports and heliports (1,307 civil aircraft registered); 16 scheduled airlines operated. During 1983 McCarren International Airport handled 10·3m. passengers and Cannon International Airport handled 2·5m. passengers.

Post. In 1976 there were 11 telephone exchanges with (1980), 787,232 telephones in service.

JUSTICE, RELIGION, EDUCATION AND WELFARE

Justice. Prohibition of marriage between persons of different race was repealed by statute in 1959.

A 1965 Civil Rights Act makes it illegal for persons operating public accommodations, employers of 15 or more employees, labour unions, and employment agencies to discriminate on the basis of race, colour, religion or national origin; a 1971 law makes racial discrimination in the sale or renting of houses illegal. A Commission on Equal Rights of Citizens is charged with enforcing these laws.

Between 1924 and 1967 executions (by lethal gas—the first state to adopt this method, in 1921), numbered 31. Capital punishment was abolished in 1972 and later re-introduced; there was 1 execution (by lethal gas) in 1979.

Religion. Roman Catholics are the most numerous religious group, followed by members of the Church of Jesus Christ of Latter-day Saints (Mormons) and various Protestant churches.

Education. School attendance is compulsory for children from 7 to 17 years of age. In Oct. 1982 the 184 public elementary schools, including kindergartens, had 73,315 pupils; there were 95 secondary public schools, including junior and high schools, with 66,794. Special schools for handicapped pupils had 10,995. There were 3,411 elementary teachers (average salary $21,822), 2,827 secondary teachers with an average salary of $22,740. There were 36 parochial and private schools. The University of Nevada, Reno, had, in 1983–84, 351 full-time instructors and 9,875 students (regular, non-degree and correspondent), and University of Nevada, Las Vegas, 339 instructors and 11,401 students. Two-year community colleges operate as part of the University of Nevada system in Carson City, Elko and Las Vegas. There were (1983) 20,833 students.

Health. In 1984 the state had 31 hospitals (3,730 beds) and 25 skilled nursing units (2,169 beds).

Social Security. Old-age assistance is granted to all 65 years of age or older who are in need, and have assets not over $750 ($1,500 for married couples); end of fiscal year 1974–75, total expenditure was $6,179,040 at an average of $140 each person per month, for 3,678 people. Families with dependent children received

$7,613,458 at $45.52 monthly average per person. The blind received $328,440 at $170 for 161 people. Nevada is the only state without aid to the permanently and totally disabled.

Books of Reference

Information: Bureau of Business and Economic Research (Univ. of Nevada).

Handbook of the Nevada Legislature, 55th Session, 1969. Legislative Counsel Bureau. Carson City

Legislative Manual, State of Nevada, 55th Session, 1969. Legislative Counsel Bureau. Carson City

Political History of Nevada. Secretary of State. Carson City, 1965

Bushnell, E., and Driggs, D. W., *The Nevada Constitution: Origin and Growth.* Univ. of Nevada Press, 5th ed., 1980

Hulse, James W., *The Nevada Adventure, A History.* Univ. of Nevada Press, 2nd ed., 1969

Laxalt, R., *Nevada: A History.* New York, 1977

Mack, E. M., and Sawyer, B. W., *Here is Nevada: A History of the State.* Sparks, Nevada, 1965

Paher, S. W., *Nevada, an Annotated Bibliography.* Nevada, 1980

State Library: Nevada State Library, Carson City. *State Librarian:* Mildred J. Heyer.

NEW HAMPSHIRE

HISTORY. New Hampshire, first settled in 1623, is one of the 13 original states of the Union.

AREA AND POPULATION. New Hampshire is bounded north by Canada, east by Maine and the Atlantic, south by Massachusetts and west by Vermont. Area, 9,279 sq. miles, of which 286 sq. miles are inland water. Census population, 1 April 1980, 920,610, an increase of 24·8% since 1970. Estimate (1982), 951,000. Births, 1980, were 12,330; deaths, 7,190; infant deaths, 101; marriages, 9,049; divorces, 4,471.

Population at 5 federal censuses was:

	White	*Negro*	*Indian*	*Asiatic*	*Total*	*Per sq. mile*
1910	429,906	564	34	68	430,572	47·7
1930	464,351	790	64	88	465,293	51·6
1960	604,334	1,903	135	549	606,921	65·2
			All others			
1970	733,106	2,505	2,070		737,681	81·7
1980	910,099	3,990	6,521		920,610	101·9

Of the total population in 1980, 448,462 were male, 480,325 were urban; those 20 years of age or older numbered 625,562.

The largest city of the state is Manchester, with a 1980 census population of 90,757. Other cities are: Nashua, 67,817; Concord (capital), 30,; Portsmouth, 26,214; Dover, 22,265; Keene, 21,385; Rochester, 21,579; Berlin, 13,090; Laconia, 15,579; Claremont, 14,575; Lebanon, 11,052; Somersworth, 10,313.

CLIMATE. Manchester. Jan. 22°F (–5·6°C), July 70°F (21·1°C). Annual rainfall 40″ (1,003 mm). *See* New England, p. 1373.

CONSTITUTION AND GOVERNMENT. While the present constitution dates from 1784, it was extensively revised in 1792 when the state joined the Union. Since 1775 there have been 16 state conventions with 49 amendments adopted to amend the constitution.

The Legislature consists of a Senate of 30 members, elected for 2 years, and a House of Representatives, restricted to between 375 and 400 members, elected for 2 years. The Governor and 5 administrative officers called 'Councillors' are also elected for 2 years.

Electors must be adult citizens, able to read and write, duly registered and not paupers or under sentence for crime. New Hampshire sends to the Federal Congress 2 senators and 2 representatives.

In the 1984 presidential election Reagan polled 244,790 votes, Mondale, 110,268.

The capital is Concord. The state is divided into 10 counties.

Governor: John Sununu (R.), 1985–88 ($44,520).
Secretary of State: William M. Gardner (D.) ($31,270).

BUDGET. The state government's general revenue for the fiscal year ending 30 June 1982 (US Census Bureau figures) was $1,306m. ($732m. from taxes, $320m. from federal aid); general expenditures, $1,392m. ($504m. on education, $188m. on public welfare, $174m. on highways).

Net long-term debt, 30 June 1982, was $1,480m.

Per capita personal income (1982) was $10,729.

NATURAL RESOURCES

Minerals. Minerals are little worked; they consist mainly of sand and gravel, stone, and clay for building and highway construction. Value of mineral production, 1981, $26m.

Agriculture. In 1983, there were 3,000 farms occupying 1m. acres; average farm was 169 acres. Average value per acre, $1,109. The US Soil Survey estimates that the state has 164,167 acres of excellent soil, 486,615 acres of fair soil, 530,630 of poor soil and 3,843,798 of non-arable soil. Only 636,195 acres (11% of the total area) show moderate erosion.

Cash income, 1983, from crops, $39·9m., and livestock, $78m. The chief field crops are hay and vegetables; the chief fruit crop is apples. On 1 Jan. 1975 animals on farms were 40,000 milch cows, 69,000 all cattle, 4,800 sheep, 8,700 swine, 1·8m. poultry, 28,000 turkeys and about 36,225 horses.

Forestry. In 1979 forest land totalled 5m. acres; national forest, 705,000 acres.

INDUSTRY. In 1982, manufacturing establishments employed 112,000 workers; value added by manufacture (1980) was $3,606m.; 54% of manufacturing employment is accounted for in durable goods. Total non-agricultural employment, 393,000.

Principal industries are, electrical machinery, non-electrical machinery, metal products, textiles and shoes.

COMMUNICATIONS

Roads. On 1 Jan. 1982 the state's highway mileage was 12,400 miles of rural roads, 2,100 miles of urban roads; there were 1,352 miles of federal-aid highways (primary), of which 202 miles were interstate. Motor vehicles registered, 1982, numbered 773,000.

Railways. In 1975 the length of railway in the state was 826 miles.

Aviation. In 1981 there were 15 public and 37 private airports.

JUSTICE, RELIGION, EDUCATION AND WELFARE

Justice. The state prison held 445 persons on 31 Dec. 1982. Since 1930 there has been only one execution (by hanging)—a white man, for murder, in 1939.

Religion. The Roman Catholic Church is the largest single body. The largest Protestant churches are Congregational, Episcopal, Methodist and United Baptist Convention of N.H.

Education. School attendance is compulsory for children from 6 to 14 years of age during the whole school term, or to 16 if their district provides a high school.

Employed illiterate minors between 16 and 21 years of age must attend evening or special classes, if provided by the district.

In autumn 1982 the public elementary and secondary schools had 160,197 pupils and 9,758 classroom teachers. Public school salaries, 1983, averaged $15,400. Total expenditure on public schools in 1981 was estimated at $365m.

Total enrolment, 1982, in 27 institutions of higher education was 52,000 students. Dartmouth College, at Hanover was founded in 1769, the University of New Hampshire, at Durham was founded in 1866.

Health. In 1980 the state had 33 hospitals (4,680 beds). On 1 Jan. 1980 mental hospitals had 608 patients, and there were 679 persons in state institutions for the mentally retarded.

Social Security. The Division of Welfare handles public assistance for (1) aged citizens 65 years or over, (2) needy aged aliens, (3) needy blind persons, (4) needy citizens between 18 and 64 years inclusive, who are permanently and totally disabled, (5) needy children under 21 years, (6) Medicaid and the medically needy not eligible for a monthly grant.

In Dec. 1980, 2,100 persons were receiving SSI old-age assistance of an average $87 per month; 3,200 permanently and totally disabled, $166 per month; 8,600 families with dependent children, $271 per month.

Books of Reference

N.H. Register. State Year Book and Legislative Manual. Portland, Maine, 1965
Delorme, D. (ed.), *New Hampshire Atlas and Gazetteer.* Freeport, 1983
Morison, E. E., and E. F., *New Hampshire.* New York, 1976

NEW JERSEY

HISTORY. New Jersey, first settled in the early 1600s, is one of the 13 original states in the Union.

AREA AND POPULATION. New Jersey is bounded north by New York, east by the Atlantic with Long Island and New York City to the north-east, south by Delaware Bay and west by Pennsylvania. Area (US Bureau of Census), 7,787 sq. miles (319 sq. miles being inland water). Census population, 1 April 1980, 7,364,823, an increase of 2·7% since 1970. Estimate (1982) 7,438,000. Births, 1982, were 98,225 (13·3 per 1,000 population); deaths, 67,470 (9·1); infant deaths, 1,153 (11·7 per 1,000 live births); marriages (1982), 59,900 (8·1); divorces (1982), 30,322 (4·1).

Population at 5 federal censuses was:

	White	*Negro*	*Indian*	*Asiatic*	*All others*	*Total*	*Per sq. mile*
1910	2,445,894	89,760	168	1,345	—	2,537,167	337·7
1930	3,829,663	208,828	213	2,630	122	4,041,334	537·3
1960	5,539,003	514,875	1,699	8,778	2,427	6,066,782	739·5
1970	6,349,908	770,292	4,706	20,537	22,721	7,168,164	953·1
1980	6,127,467	925,066	8,394	103,847	200,048	7,364,823	986·2

Of the population in 1980, 3,533,012 were male, 6,557,377 persons were urban, 5,116,581 were 20 years of age or older.

Census population of the larger cities and towns in 1980 was:

Newark	329,248	Irvington	61,493	Parsippany-Troy Hills	49,868
Jersey City	223,532	Union City	55,593	Middletown	62,574
Paterson	137,970	Vineland	53,753	Union Township	50,184
Elizabeth	106,201	Passaic	52,463	Bloomfield	47,792
Trenton (capital)	92,124	Woodbridge	90,074	Atlantic City	40,199
Camden	84,910	Hamilton	82,801	Plainfield	45,555
Clifton	74,388	Edison	70,193	Hoboken	42,460
East Orange	77,025	Cherry Hill	68,785	Montclair	38,321
Bayonne	65,047				

Largest urbanized areas (1980) were: Newark, 1,963,000; Jersey City, 555,483; Paterson-Clifton-Passaic, 447,785; Trenton (NJ–Pa.), 305,678.

CLIMATE. Jersey City. Jan. 31°F (–0·6°C), July 75°F (23·9°C). Annual rainfall 41" (1,025 mm). Trenton. Jan. 32°F (0°C), July 76°F (24·4°C). Annual rainfall 40" (1,003 mm). *See* Atlantic Coast, p. 1373.

CONSTITUTION AND GOVERNMENT. The legislative power is vested in a Senate and a General Assembly, the members of which are chosen by the people, all citizens (with necessary exceptions) 18 years of age, with the usual residential qualifications, having the right of suffrage. The present constitution, ratified by the registered voters on 4 Nov. 1947, has been amended 27 times. In 1966 the Constitutional Convention proposed, and the people adopted, a new plan providing for a 40-member Senate and an 80-member General Assembly. This plan, as certified by the Apportionment Commission and modified by the courts, provides for 40 legislative districts, with 1 senator and 2 assemblymen elected for each. Assemblymen serve 2 years, senators 4 years, except those elected at the election following each census, who serve for 2 years. The Governor is elected for 4 years.

The state sends to Congress 2 senators and 14 representatives.

In the 1984 presidential election Reagan polled 1,861,774 votes, Mondale, 1,229,206.

The capital is Trenton. The state is divided into 21 counties, which are subdivided into 567 municipalities—cities, towns, boroughs, villages and townships.

Governor: Thomas H. Kean (R.), 1982–85 ($85,000).
Secretary of State: Jane Burgio ($66,000).

BUDGET. For the year ending 30 June 1985 (budget figures) general revenues were $7,670·7m. (taxation $4,439m. and federal aid, $2,438·8m.), general expenditures were $7,574·6m. (education, $2,404m.; highways, $438·7m., and public welfare, $1,465·5m.).

Total net long-term debt, 30 June 1984, was $2,307·5m.

Per capita personal income (1982) was $13,169.

NATURAL RESOURCES

Minerals. The chief minerals are stone ($15m., 1984) and sand and gravel ($34·3m.), others are zinc ($3m.), clay products ($986,000), peat and gemstones. New Jersey is a leading producer of greensand marl, magnesium compounds and peat. Total value of mineral products, 1984, was $149m.

Agriculture. Livestock raising, market-gardening, fruit-growing, horticulture and forestry are pursued. In 1982–83, 9,500 farms had a total area of 1·03m. acres; average farm in 1982 had 108 acres valued at $3,118 per acre.

Cash income, 1983, from crops and livestock, $532m.

Leading crops are tomatoes (value, $20·5m., 1982), all corn ($32·2m.), peaches ($21·5m.), hay ($27·3m.), blueberries ($18·2m.), soybeans ($29·7m.).

Farm animals on 1 Jan. 1982 included 41,000 milch cows, 100,000 all cattle, 9,700 sheep and lambs and 45,000 swine.

INDUSTRY. In 1984 manufacturing establishments employed 731,200 workers, receiving (preliminary) $19,700m. in wages. The principal industries by value are: Chemicals and allied products, construction, electrical and electronic equipment, machinery (except electrical).

COMMUNICATIONS

Roads. In 1982 there were 33,692 miles of roads (municipal, 23,890 miles; state, 2,237 miles; county, 6,655 miles; others, 910 miles).

Railways. In Jan. 1984, the state had 1,411·3 route miles of railway.

Aviation. There were (1984) 90 airports, of which 14 were publicly owned and 60 allowed public use.

JUSTICE, RELIGION, EDUCATION AND WELFARE

Justice. State prisons in 1984 had 12,645 inmates. The last execution (by electrocution) was in 1963; it was the 160th, all for murder. Future executions would be by lethal injection.

The constitution of New Jersey forbids discrimination against any person on account of 'religious principles, race, color, ancestry or national origin'. The state has had, since 1945, a 'fair employment act', *i.e.*, a Civil Rights statute forbidding any employer, public or private (with 6 or more employees), to discriminate against any applicant for work (or to discharge any employee) on the grounds of 'race, creed, color, national origin or ancestry'. Trade unions may not bar Negroes from membership.

Religion. The Roman Catholic population of New Jersey in 1984 was 3·1m. The five largest Protestant sects were United Methodists, 150,000; United Presbyterians, 174,000; Episcopalians, 147,000; Lutherans, 89,000; American Baptists, 74,000. There were 40,000 African Methodists and 4,000 Christian Methodist Episcopalians. The main Jewish sects were Reform (38,000) and Conservative (27,000).

Education. Elementary instruction is compulsory for all from 6 to 16 years of age and free to all from 5 to 20 years of age. In autumn 1984 public elementary schools had 725,700 and secondary schools had 422,138 enrolled pupils; public colleges in autumn 1984 had 313,985 students, including 117,212 in community colleges, and independent colleges had 63,607. The total cost of public schools, 1983–84, $6,799·6m. Average salary of all elementary and secondary classroom teachers in public schools 1982–83 was $21,751.

Rutgers, the State University (founded as Queen's College in 1766) had, in 1984, an opening autumn enrolment of 47,200 full- and part-time students. Princeton (founded in 1746) had 4,500 undergraduate and 1,500 graduate students. Fairleigh Dickinson (1941), had 9,770 undergraduate and 5,658 graduate students; Kean College, 12,930 students in 1983; Montclair State College, 14,949 in 1983; Glassboro State College, 8,960 in 1983; Trenton State College, 9,268 in 1983.

Health. In 1983 the state had 131 hospitals (42,362 beds), listed by the American Hospital Association.

Social Security. In the financial year 1982 gross expenditure for all public assistance programmes was $563,000,000. Average monthly total of cases was $358,000 with an average grant per case of $350.

Books of Reference

Legislative District Data Book. Bureau of Government Research. Annual
Manual of the Legislature of New Jersey. Trenton. Annual
Boyd, J. P. (ed.), *Fundamentals and Constitutions of New Jersey, 1664–1954.* Princeton, 1964
Cunningham, J. T., *New Jersey: America's Main Road.* Rev. ed. New York, 1976
League of Women Voters of New Jersey. *New Jersey: Spotlight on Government.* Rutgers Univ. Press, 3rd ed., 1978
Lehne, R., and Rosenthal, A. (eds.), *Politics in New Jersey.* Rev. ed., Rutgers Univ. Press, 1979

State Library: 185 W. State Street, Trenton, N.J. 08625. *State Librarian:* Barbara F. Weaver.

NEW MEXICO

HISTORY. The first European settlement was established in 1598. Until 1771 New Mexico was the Spanish kings' 'Kingdom of New Mexico'. In 1771 it was annexed to the northern province of New Spain. When New Spain won its independence in 1821, it took the name of Republic of Mexico and established New

Mexico as its northernmost department. When the war between the US and Mexico was concluded on 2 Feb. 1848 New Mexico was recognized as belonging to the US, and on 9 Sept. 1850 it was made a Territory. Part of the Territory was assigned to Texas; later Utah was formed into a separate Territory; in 1861 another part was transferred to Colorado, and in 1863 Arizona was disjoined, leaving to New Mexico its present area. New Mexico became a state in Jan. 1912.

AREA AND POPULATION. New Mexico is bounded north by Colorado, north-east by Oklahoma, east by Texas, south by Texas and Mexico and west by Arizona. Land area 121,335 sq. miles (258 sq. miles water). Public lands, administered by federal agencies (1975) amounted to 26·7m. acres or 34% of the total area. The Bureau of Indian Affairs held 7·3m. acres; the State of New Mexico held 9·4m. acres; 34·4m. acres were privately owned.

Census population, 1 April 1980, 1,302,894, an increase of 285,839 or 28% since 1970. Estimate (1983) 1,399,000. Vital statistics, 1983: Births, 27,508 (19·7 per 1,000 population); deaths, 9,138 (6·5); infant deaths, 274 (10 per 1,000 live births); marriages, 16,728 (12); divorces, 9,063 (6·5).

The population in 5 census years was:

	White	*Negro*	*Indian*	*Asian and Pacific Islander*	*Other*	*Total*	*Per sq. mile*
1910	304,594	1,628	20,573	506		327,301	2·7
1940	492,312	4,672	34,510	324		531,818	4·4
1960	875,763	17,063	56,255	1,942		951,023	7·8
1970	915,815	19,555	72,788	7,842 [1]		1,016,000	8·4
1980	1,164,053	24,406	106,119	6,825	1,491	1,302,894	10·7

[1] Includes unspecified races, 1970.

Of the 1980 total, 642,157 were male. 939,963 persons were urban; 884,987 were 18 years of age or older.

Before 1930 New Mexico was largely a Spanish-speaking state, but since 1945 an influx of population from other states has reduced the percentage of persons of Spanish origin or descent to 36·6%.

The largest cities are Albuquerque, with census population, 1980, 332,336 (and 1982 estimate, 341,978); Santa Fé (capital), 48,953 (50,957); Las Cruces, 45,086 (46,476); Roswell, 39,676 (42,296); Farmington, 31,222 (35,659).

CLIMATE. Santa Fé. Jan. 29°F (−1·7°C), July 68°F (20°C). Annual rainfall 15″ (366 mm). *See* Mountain States, p. 1372.

CONSTITUTION AND GOVERNMENT. The constitution of 1912 is still in force with 104 amendments. The state Legislature, which meets annually, consists of 42 members of the Senate, elected for 4 years, and 70 members of the House of Representatives, elected for 2 years. The Governor and Lieut.-Governor are elected for 4 years. The state sends to Congress 2 senators and 3 representatives.

In the 1984 presidential election Reagan polled 304,950 votes, Mondale 200,953.

The state capital is Santa Fé. For local government the state is divided into 33 counties.

Governor: Toney Anaya (D.), 1983–86 ($60,000).
Lieut.-Governor: Mike Runnells (D.), 1983–86 ($38,500).
Secretary of State: Clara Jones (D.), 1983–86 ($38,500).

BUDGET. For the year ending 30 June 1982 (US Census Bureau figures) general revenues were $2,773m. ($1,227m. from taxation and $454·9m. from federal government); general expenditures, $2,272·4m. (education, $1,010m.; highways, $287·9m., and public welfare, $215·1m.).

Long-term debt on 30 June 1982 was $820·8m.

Per capita personal income (1983) was $9,640.

ENERGY AND NATURAL RESOURCES

Minerals. New Mexico is the country's largest domestic source of uranium, perlite and potassium salts. Production of recoverable U_3O_8 was 7·8m. lb. in 1982; perlite (1982), 408,000 short tons; potassium salts, 1·5m. tonnes; petroleum, 71m. bbls (of 42 gallons); natural gas, 992,000m. cu. ft; natural gas liquids, 42·9m. bbls (of 42 gallons); copper, 59,693 tonnes; coal, 19·1m. short tons marketed. The value of the total mineral output (1982) was $5,932m. An average of 26,300 persons were employed monthly in the mining industry in 1982.

Agriculture. New Mexico produces cereals, vegetables, fruit, livestock and cotton. Dry farming and irrigation have proved profitable in periods of high prices. There were 13,500 farms and ranches covering 47·0m. acres in 1983, average farm (or ranch) was valued (land and buildings) at $618,708 in the 1982 US Census of Agriculture; 3,732 farms and ranches were of 1,000 acres and over.

Cash income, 1983 (preliminary), from crops, $329·3m., and from livestock products, $634·7m. Principal crops are wheat (13·6m. bu. from 470,000 acres), hay (1·4m. tons from 320,000 acres) and grain sorghums (6·3m. bu. from 150,000 acres). Farm animals on 1 Jan. 1984 included 62,000 milch cows, 1·4m. all cattle, 589,000 sheep and 30,000 swine. National forest area (1982) covered 9·3m. acres.

INDUSTRY. Average monthly non-agricultural employment during 1983 was 478,000: 34,400 were employed in manufacturing, 127,200 in government. Value of manufactures shipments, 1981, $3,229·6m.; leading commodities, petroleum, food, electrical and electronic equipment.

COMMUNICATIONS

Roads. On 1 Jan. 1984 the state had 79,082 miles of road, of which the state maintained 12,905 miles. Motor vehicle registrations, 1983, 1,391,770.

Railways. In 1983 there were 2,061 miles of railway.

Aviation. There were 78 public-use airports in Dec. 1983.

JUSTICE, RELIGION, EDUCATION AND WELFARE

Justice. The number of state prison inmates on 18 Nov. 1984 was 2,511, including 417 in juvenile centres; there were also 95 New Mexico prisoners held outside the state. The death penalty (by electrocution formerly, and now by lethal injection) has been imposed on 8 persons since 1933, 6 whites and 2 Negroes, all for murder. The last execution was in 1961.

Since 1949 the denial of employment by reason of race, colour, religion, national origin or ancestry has been forbidden. A law of 1955 prohibits discrimination in public places because of race or colour. An 'equal rights' amendment was added to the constitution in 1972.

Religion. There were (1975) approximately 356,530 Protestant Church members and 315,470 Roman Catholics.

Education. Elementary education is free, and compulsory between 6 and 17 years or high-school graduation age. In 1982–83 the 89 school districts had an estimated enrolment of 258,862 students in public elementary and secondary schools. Private and parochial schools had 22,953 pupils. There were 14,012 teachers receiving an average salary of $20,380. Public education expenditure was $871m.

The state-supported 4-year institutes of higher education are (1983–84):

	Full-time Faculty	*Students*
University of New Mexico, Albuquerque	784	27,144
New Mexico State University, Las Cruces	582	16,463
Eastern New Mexico University, Portales	177	6,950
New Mexico Highlands University, Las Vegas	119	2,326
Western New Mexico University, Silver City	62	1,750
New Mexico Institute of Mining and Technology, Socorro	93	1,345

Health. In 1982 the state had 53 short-term hospitals (4,599 beds).

Social Security. In Dec. 1983, 14,874 persons were receiving federal supplemental security income for the disabled (average $223.93 per month); 9,234 persons were receiving old-age assistance (average $137.73 per month); 483 persons were receiving aid to the blind (average $227.68 per month). In 1982 a monthly average of 49,252 people received aid to families with dependent children (average $73.90 per month).

Books of Reference

New Mexico Business (monthly; annual review in Jan.–Feb. issue). Bureau of Business and Economic Research, Univ. of N.M., Albuquerque
New Mexico Statistical Abstract: 1984. Bureau of Business and Economic Research, Univ. of N.M., Albuquerque, 1984
Beck, W., *New Mexico: a History of Four Centuries.* Univ. of Oklahoma, 1979
Garcia, C., Haine, P., and Rhodes, H., *State and Local Government in New Mexico.* Albuquerque, 1979
Jenkins, M., and Schroeder, A., *A Brief History of New Mexico.* Univ. of New Mexico, 1974
Muench, D., and Hillerman, T., *New Mexico.* Belding, Portland, Oregon, 1974

NEW YORK STATE

HISTORY. From 1609 to 1664 the region now called New York was claimed by the Dutch; then it came under the rule of the English, who governed the country until the outbreak of the War of Independence. On 20 April 1777 New York adopted a constitution which transformed the colony into an independent state; on 26 July 1788 it ratified the constitution of the US, becoming one of the 13 original states. New York dropped its claim to Vermont after the latter was admitted to the Union in 1791. With the annexation of a small area from Massachusetts in 1853, New York assumed its present boundaries.

AREA AND POPULATION. New York is bounded west and north by Canada with Lake Erie, Lake Ontario and the St Lawrence River forming the boundary; east by Vermont, Massachusetts and Connecticut, south-east by the Atlantic, south by New Jersey and Pennsylvania. Area, 49,108 sq. miles (1,731 sq. miles being water). Census population, 1 April 1980, 17,557,288, a decrease of 3·7% since 1970. Estimate (1982) 17,659,000. Births in 1983 (provisional) were 219,618; deaths, 170,464; infant deaths (1979), 3,177; marriages, 156,440; divorces, 64,480 (includes all dissolutions).

Population in 5 census years was:

	White	*Negro*	*Indian*	*Asiatic*	*Total*	*Per sq. mile*
1910	8,966,845	134,191	6,046	6,532	9,113,614	191·2
1930	12,143,191	412,814	6,973	15,088	12,588,066	262·6
1960	15,287,071	1,417,511	16,491	51,678	16,782,304	350·2
			All others			
1970	15,834,090	2,168,949	233,828		18,236,967	380·3
1980	13,961,106	2,401,842	1,194,340		17,557,288	367·0

Of the 1980 population, 8,338,961 were male, 14,857,202 were urban; those 20 years of age or older numbered 12,232,284. Aliens registered in Jan. 1980 numbered 801,411.

The population of New York City, by boroughs, census of 1 April 1980 was: Manhattan, 1,427,533; Bronx, 1,169,115; Brooklyn, 2,230,936; Queens, 1,891,325; Staten Island, 352,121; total, 7,071,030. The New York metropolitan statistical area had, in 1980, 9,080,777.

Population of other large cities and incorporated places census, April 1980, was:

Buffalo	357,002	Albany (capital)	101,767	Schenectady	67,877
Rochester	241,509	Utica	75,435	Mount Vernon	66,023
Yonkers	194,557	Niagara Falls	71,344	Troy	56,614
Syracuse	170,292	New Rochelle	70,345	Binghamton	55,745

White Plains	46,999	N. Tonawanda	35,760	Lindenhurst	26,919
Rome	43,826	Elmira	35,327	Rockville Center	25,405
Hempstead	40,404	Auburn	32,548	Newburgh	23,438
Freeport	38,272	Poughkeepsie	29,757	Garden City	22,927
Jamestown	35,775	Watertown	27,861	Massapequa Park	19,779
Valley Stream	35,769				

Other large urbanized areas, census 1980; Buffalo, 1·2m.; Rochester, 970,313; Albany–Schenectady–Troy, 794,298.

CLIMATE. Albany. Jan. 24°F (–4·4°C), July 73°F (22·8°C). Annual rainfall 34″ (855 mm). Buffalo. Jan. 24°F (–4·4°C), July 70°F (21·1°C). Annual rainfall 36″ (905 mm). New York. Jan. 30°F (–1·1°C), July 74°F (23·3°C). Annual rainfall 43″ (1,087 mm). *See* Atlantic Coast, p. 1373.

CONSTITUTION AND GOVERNMENT. The present constitution dates from 1894; a later constitutional convention, 1938, is now legally considered merely to have amended the 1894 constitution, which has now had 93 amendments. The Constitutional Convention of 1967 (4 April through 26 Sept.) was composed of 186 delegates who proposed a new state constitution; however this was rejected by the registered voters on 7 Nov. 1967. The Senate consists of 60 members, and the Assembly of 150 members, both elected every 2 years. The Governor and Lieut.-Governor are elected for 4 years. The right of suffrage resides in every adult who has been a citizen for 90 days, and has the residential qualifications; new voters must establish, by certificates or test, that they have had at least an elementary education.

The state is represented in Congress by 2 senators and 34 representatives.

In the 1984 presidential election Reagan polled 3,525,266 votes, Mondale, 3,013,521.

The state capital is Albany. For local government the state is divided into 62 counties, 5 of which constitute the city of New York. New York leads in state parks and recreation areas, covering 252,984 acres in 1979.

Cities are in 3 classes, the first class having each 175,000 or more inhabitants and the third under 50,000. Each is incorporated by charter, under special legislation. The government of New York City is vested in the mayor (Edward Koch), elected for 4 years, and a city council, whose president and members are elected for 4 years. The council has a President and 37 members, each elected from a state senatorial district wholly within the city. The mayor appoints all the heads of departments, except the comptroller, who is elected. Each of the 5 city boroughs (Manhattan, Bronx, Brooklyn, Queens and Richmond) has a president, elected for 4 years. Each borough is also a county bearing the same name except Manhattan borough, which, as a county, is called New York, and Brooklyn, which is Kings County.

Governor: Mario Cuomo (D.), 1983–86 ($100,000).
Lieut.-Governor: Alfred del Bello (D.), 1983–86 ($85,000).
Secretary of State: Gail Schaefer (D.), 1983–86 ($65,700).

BUDGET. The state's general revenues for the financial year ending 31 March 1982 were $16,142m. ($14,959m. from taxes); general expenditures were $16,126m. ($5,298m. for education, $8,049m. for social services, $1,893m. for transport).

Per capita personal income was $12,314 in 1982.

The assessed valuation in 1980 of taxable real property in New York City was $38,056m. The assessed valuation of the state was $86,741m.

ENERGY AND NATURAL RESOURCES

Minerals. Production of principal minerals in 1980: Sand and gravel (22,000 short tons), salt (5,500 short tons), zinc (33,629 tonnes), petroleum (824,296 bbls), natural gas (15,680m. cu. ft). The state is a leading producer of titanium concentrate, talc, abrasive garnet, wollastonite and emery. Quarry products include trap rock, slate, marble, limestone and sandstone. Value of mineral output in 1980 $497·9m.

Agriculture. New York has large agricultural interests. In 1983 it had 50,000 farms, with a total area of 10m. acres; average farm was 190 acres; average value per acre, $770.

Cash income, 1982, from crops $721m. and livestock, $1,867m. Dairying, with 18,500 farms, 1981, is an important type of farming with produce at a market value of $1,520m. Field crops comprise maize, winter wheat, oats and hay. New York (1981) ranks second in US in the production of apples, and maple syrup. Other products are grapes, tart cherries, peaches, pears, plums, strawberries, raspberries, cabbages, onions, potatoes, maple sugar. Estimated farm animals, 1983, included 2m. all cattle, 935,000 milch cows, 63,000 sheep, 100,000 swine and (1981) 10·6m. chickens.

INDUSTRY. In 1981 manufacturing establishments numbering 31,849 employed 1,439,872 workers whose average weekly earnings were $385. Leading industries were clothing, non-electrical machinery, printing and publishing, electrical equipment, instruments, food and allied products and fabricated metals.

COMMUNICATIONS

Roads. There were (1981) 109,485 miles of municipal and rural roads. The New York State Thruway extends 559 miles from New York City to Buffalo; in 1981 receipts from tolls amounted to $183,289,532. The Northway, a 176-mile toll-free highway, is a connecting road from the Thruway at Albany to the Canadian border at Champlain, Quebec.

Motor vehicle registrations in 1981 were 8·7m., most of which (7m.) were private passenger vehicles.

Railways. There were in 1981, 3,891 miles of Class I railways. New York City has NYCTA and PATH metro systems, and commuter railways run by Metro-North, New Jersey Rail and Long Island Rail Road.

Aviation. There were 471 airports and landing areas in 1981.

Shipping. The canals of the state, combined in 1918 in what is called the Improved Canal System, have a length of 524 miles, of which the Erie or Barge canal has 340 miles. In 1981 the canals carried 807,925 tons of freight.

JUSTICE, RELIGION, EDUCATION AND WELFARE

Justice. The State Human Rights Law was approved 12 March 1945, effective 1 July, 1945. The State Division of Human Rights is charged with the responsibility of enforcing this law. The division may request and utilize the services of all governmental departments and agencies; adopt and promulgate suitable rules and regulations; test, investigate and pass judgment upon complaints alleging discrimination in employment, in places of public accommodation, resort or amusement, education, and in housing, land and commercial space; hold hearings, subpoena witnesses and require the production for examination of papers relating to matters under investigation; grant compensatory damages and require repayment of profits in certain housing cases among other provisions; apply for court injunctions to prevent frustration of orders of the Commissioner.

On 30 Dec. 1982, 27,951 persons were in state prisons.

In 1963–81 there were no executions. Total executions (by electrocution) from 1930 to 1962 were 329 (234 whites, 90 Negroes, 5 other races; all for murder except 2 for kidnapping).

In 1980 murders reported in New York were 2,225; total violent crimes, 179,981. Police strength (sworn officers) in 1980 was 55,222 (27,394 New York City).

Religion. The churches are Roman Catholic, with 6,367,576 members in 1981, Jewish congregations (about 2m. in 1981) and Protestant Episcopal (299,929 in 1980).

Education. Education is compulsory between the ages of 7 and 16. In autumn 1982 the public elementary and secondary schools had 2,718,678 pupils; classroom teachers numbered 144,591 in public schools. Total expenditure on public schools in 1980–81 was $9,069,092,216. Teachers' salaries, 1983, averaged $25,100.

The state's educational system, including public and private schools and secondary institutions, universities, colleges, libraries, museums, etc., constitutes (by legislative act) the 'University of the State of New York', which is governed by a Board of Regents consisting of 15 members appointed by the Legislature. Within the framework of this 'University' was established in 1948 a 'State University' which controls 64 colleges and educational centres, 30 of which are locally operated community colleges. The 'State University' is governed by a board of 16 Trustees, appointed by the Governor with the consent and advice of the Senate.

Higher education in the state is conducted in 296 institutions (642,000 full-time and 371,000 part-time students in autumn 1982); 573,000 students are in public-control colleges and 439,000 in private.

In autumn 1980 the institutions of higher education in the state included:

Founded	*Name and place*	*Teachers*	*Students*
1754	Columbia University, New York	3,965	17,410
1795	Union University, Schenectady and Albany	178	2,071
1824	Rensselaer Polytechnic Institute, Troy	442	6,145
1831	New York University, New York	2,615	45,000
1846	Colgate University, New York	205	2,550
1846	Fordham University, New York	958	14,653
1847	University of the City of New York, New York	12,426	172,683
1848	University of Rochester, Rochester	1,549	11,159
1854	Polytechnic Institute of New York	242	4,583
1856	St Lawrence University, Canton	173	2,375
1857	Cooper Union Institute of Technology, New York	161	872
1861	Vassar College, Poughkeepsie	230	2,364
1863	Manhattan College, New York	291	3,498
1865	Cornell University, Ithaca	1,863	17,866
1870	Syracuse University, Syracuse	1,100	11,819
1948	State University of New York	13,228	372,415

The Saratoga Performing Arts Centre (5,100 seats), a non-profit, tax-exempt organization, which opened in 1966, is the summer residence of the New York City Ballet and the Philadelphia Orchestra—two groups which present special educational programmes for students and teachers.

Health. In 1981 the state had 278 hospitals (67,798 beds), 585 skilled nursing homes (62,435 beds) and 241 other institutions (24,302 beds). In 1980 mental health facilities had 27,309 patients and institutions for the mentally retarded had 18,577 patients.

Social Security. The federal Supplemental Security Income programme covered aid to the needy aged, blind and disabled from 1 Jan. 1975. In the state programme for 1980, $4,543m. was paid in Medicaid to 2,288,000 people; aid to dependent children in 1980 went to 1,248,900 recipients, average benefits $371 per family per month.

Books of Reference

New York Red Book. Albany, 1979–80
Legislative Manual. Department of State, 1980–81
New York State Statistical Yearbook, 1979–80. Albany
Connery, R. and G. B., *Governing New York State: The Rockefeller Years.* Academy of Political Science, New York, 1974
Ellis, D. M., *History of New York State.* Cornell Univ. Press, 1967
Flick, A. (ed.), *History of the State of New York.* Columbia Univ. Press, 1933–37
Lincoln, C., *Constitutional History of New York 1809–1877.* Rochester, 1906
Rosenwhike, I., *Population History of New York City.* Syracuse Univ. Press, 1972
Wolfe, G. R., *New York: A Guide to the Metropolis.* New York Univ. Press, 1975

State Library: The New York State Library, Albany 12230. *State Librarian and Assistant Commissioner for Libraries:* Joseph Shubert.

NORTH CAROLINA

HISTORY. North Carolina, first settled in 1585 by Sir Walter Raleigh and permanently settled in 1663, was one of the 13 original states of the Union.

AREA AND POPULATION. North Carolina is bounded north by Virginia, east by the Atlantic, south by South Carolina, south-west by Georgia and west by Tennessee. Area, 52,669 sq. miles, of which 3,826 sq. miles are inland water. Census population, 1 April 1980, 5,874,429, an increase of 15·5% since 1970. Estimated population (1982), 6,058,154.

Births, 1979, were 83,782 (14·9 per 1,000 population); marriages, 45,064 (8); deaths, 46,640 (8·3); infant deaths, 1,270 (15·2 per 1,000 live births); divorces and annulments, 27,445 (4·9).

Population in 6 census years was:

	White	*Negro*	*Indian*	*Asiatic*	*Total*	*Per sq. mile*
1910	1,500,511	697,843	7,851	82	2,206,287	45·3
1930	2,234,958	918,647	16,579	92	3,170,276	64·5
1950	2,983,121	1,047,353	3,742	—	4,061,929	82·7
1960	3,399,285	1,116,021	38,129	2,012	4,556,155	92·2
			All others			
1970	3,901,767	1,126,478	53,814		5,082,059	104·1
1980	4,453,010	1,316,050	105,369		5,874,429	111·5

Of the total population in 1980, 2,852,012 were male, 2,818,794 were urban and 3,976,359 were 20 years old or older; 14·8% were non-white.

Cities (with census population in 1980) are: Charlotte, 310,799; Greensboro, 154,763; Winston-Salem, 131,211; Raleigh (capital), 148,299; Durham (1970), 95,438; High Point, 63,169; Asheville, 57,708; Fayetteville, 59,476.

CLIMATE. Climate varies sharply with altitude; the warmest area is in the south east near Southport and Wilmington; the coldest is Mount Mitchell (6,684 ft). Raleigh. Jan. 42°F (5·6°C), July 79°F (26·1°C). Annual rainfall 46″ (1,158 mm). *See* Atlantic Coast, p. 1373.

CONSTITUTION AND GOVERNMENT. The present constitution dates from 1971 (previous constitution, 1776 and 1868/76); it has had 12 amendments. The General Assembly consists of a Senate of 50 members and a House of Representatives of 120 members; all are elected by districts for 2 years. The Governor and Lieut.-Governor are elected for 4 years. The Governor may succeed himself but has no veto. There are 17 other executive heads of department, 8 elected by the people and 7 appointed by the Governor. All registered citizens with the usual residential qualifications have a vote.

The state is represented in Congress by 2 senators and 11 representatives.

In the presidential election of 1984 Reagan polled 1,314,802 votes, Mondale, 809,876.

The capital is Raleigh, established in 1792.

Governor: James G. Martin, (R.), 1985–89 ($60,768).
Lieut.-Governor: Robert B. Jordan, III (D.) ($50,328).
Secretary of State: Thad Eure (D.) ($50,328).

BUDGET. General revenue for the year ending 30 June 1983 was $2,403·8m. General expenditure was $3,440·7m.

On 30 June 1981 the net total long-term debt amounted to $853·2m.

Per capita personal income (1982) was $9,032.

NATURAL RESOURCES

Minerals. Mining production in 1982 was valued at $275·1m. Principal minerals were stone, sand and gravel, phosphate rock, feldspar, clay, mica, lithium minerals, olivine, kaolin and talc. North Carolina ranked first in the production of mica, feldspar, olivine spodumene and phrophyllite. It is also the leading producer of bricks, making about 13% of the total US production.

Agriculture. In 1981 there were 93,000 farms in North Carolina covering 11·7m. acres; average size of farms was 126 acres and average value $167,400.

The state leads in producing tobacco, sweet potatoes, turkeys and farm forest products. Cash receipts from farming (1981), $4,200m., of which $2,600m. was from crops and $1,600m. from livestock, dairy and poultry products. Value of crop production: flue-cured tobacco, $1,300m.; maize, $380m.; soybeans, $289m.; peanuts, $157m.; sweet potatoes, $64m.; wheat, $54m.; hay, $41m. On 1 Jan. 1981 farms had 1·16m. all cattle, 1·98m. swine and 18·5m. chickens.

Forestry. Commercial forest covered 19·5m. acres (62·6% of land area), in 1983. Main products are hardwood veneer and hardwood plywood.

Fisheries. Commercial fish catch, 1980, amounted to 356m. lb.; value approximately $68·8m. The catch is mainly of menhaden, crabmeat, bay scallops, flounder, croaker, shrimps, sea trout, spots and clams.

INDUSTRY. North Carolina's 9,668 industrial establishments in 1980 had 824,200 production workers. The leading industries are textile goods, manufacture of cigarettes, chemicals, electronics and electrical machinery, processing of food crops and the manufacture of furniture and bricks. In 1982 investment in new and expanded industry was $1,290m.

TOURISM. Total receipts of the travel industry, $3,400m. in 1983.

COMMUNICATIONS

Roads. The state maintained, 1981, 76,032 miles of highways, comprising all rural roads and 4,388 miles of urban streets which are major thoroughfares. In Sept. 1981, 2,989,776 automobiles, 904,708 trucks and 572,550 other vehicles were registered.

Railways. The state in 1983 contained 4,117 miles of railway operating in 91 of the 100 counties. There are 23 Class I, II and III rail companies.

Aviation. In 1981 there were 71 public airports of which 9 are served by major airlines and 5 by commuter airlines.

Shipping. There are 2 ocean ports, Wilmington and Morehead City.

JUSTICE, RELIGION, EDUCATION AND WELFARE

Justice. Total executions 1910–62, 362. There was one execution (by lethal injection) in 1984. Prison population at 8 Oct. 1983, 15,995.

Religion. Leading denominations are the Baptists (48·9% of church membership), Methodists (20·7%), Presbyterians (7·7%), Lutherans (3%) and Roman Catholics (2·7%). Total estimate of all denominations in 1983 was 2·6m.

Education. School attendance is compulsory between 6 and 16.

Public school enrolment, 1982–83, was 1,107,490; elementary and secondary schools numbered 2,005. Instructional staff (1980) consisted of 67,586 classroom teachers and administrators. Expenditure for public schools is 63·3% from state, 23·6% from local and 13·1% from federal sources.

In autumn 1982–83 state-supported colleges and universities included 23 community colleges with 60,730 students; 35 technical institutes with 55,897 students. The 16 senior universities are all part of the University of North Carolina system, the largest campus being at Chapel Hill, where the university was founded in 1789 and first opened in 1792. Its 1982 enrolment was 100,912 undergraduates. The total enrolment of public institutions of higher learning in 1982 was 218,606.

In addition to the state-supported institutions there were 8 private junior colleges with an enrolment of 4,760 and 30 private senior institutions with a total enrolment of 41,904. The total enrolment in private institutions for 1982 was 52,538.

Health. In Oct. 1983 the state had 157 hospitals (32,345 beds).

Social Security. In June 1982 there were 900,070 persons receiving $300·4m. in social security benefits. Of that number 496,020 were retired, receiving $186·67m.; 85,640 were disabled ($34·7m.); 318,410 others received $79m.

Books of Reference

North Carolina Manual. Secretary of State. Raleigh. Biennial
Clay, J. W., *et al*, (eds.), *North Carolina Atlas: Portrait of a Changing Southern State.* Univ. of North Carolina Press, 1975
Corbitt, D. L., *The Formation of the North Carolina Counties.* Raleigh, 1969
Lefler, H. T., and Newsome, A. R., *North Carolina: The History of a Southern State.* Univ. of N.C., Chapel Hill, 1963

NORTH DAKOTA

HISTORY. North Dakota was admitted into the Union, with boundaries as at present, on 2 Nov. 1889; previously it had formed part of the Dakota Territory, established 2 March 1861.

AREA AND POPULATION. North Dakota is bounded north by Canada, east by the Red River (forming a boundary with Minnesota), south by South Dakota and west by Montana. Land area, 69,262 sq. miles, and 1,403 sq. miles of water. The Federal Bureau of Indian Affairs administered (1971) 850,000 acres, of which 153,000 acres were assigned to tribes. Census population, 1 April 1980, 652,717, an increase of 34,956 or 5·7% since 1970. Estimate (1983), 680,000. Births in 1983 were 12,380 (18 per 1,000 population); deaths, 5,569 (8·2); infant deaths, 110; marriages, 5,976; divorces, 2,321.

Population at 5 census years was:

	White	*Negro*	*Indian*	*Asiatic*	*Total*	*Per sq. mile*
1910	569,855	617	6,486	98	577,056	8·2
1930	671,851	377	8,617	194	680,845	9·7
1960	619,538	777	11,736	274	632,446	9·1
			All others			
1970	599,485	2,494	15,782		617,761	8·9
1980	625,557	2,568	24,692		652,717	9·4

Of the total population in 1980, 328,126 were male, 317,821 were urban and 419,234 were 21 years old or older. Estimated outward migration, 1970–80, 16,983.

The largest cities are Fargo with population (census), 1980, of 61,383; Grand Forks, 43,765; Bismarck (capital), 44,485, and Minot, 32,843.

CLIMATE. Bismarck. Jan. 8°F (−13·3°C), July 71°F (21·1°C). Annual rainfall 16″ (402 mm). Fargo. Jan. 6°F (−14·4°C), July 71°F (21·1°C). Annual rainfall 20″ (503 mm). *See* High Plains, p. 1372.

CONSTITUTION AND GOVERNMENT. The present constitution dates from 1889; it has had 95 amendments. The Legislative Assembly consists of a Senate of 53 members elected for 4 years, and a House of Representatives of 106 members elected for 2 years. The Governor and Lieut.-Governor are elected for 4 years. Qualified electors are (with necessary exceptions) all citizens and civilized Indians. The state sends to Congress 2 senators elected by the voters of the entire state and 1 representative.

In the 1984 presidential election Reagan polled 155,856 votes, Mondale, 80,839.

The capital is Bismarck. The state has 53 organized counties.

Governor: George A. Sinner (D.), 1985–89 ($60,812 plus expenses).
Lieut.-Governor: Ruth Meiers (D.), 1985–89 ($12,500 plus expenses).
Secretary of State: Ben Meier (R.), 1985–89 ($43,380 plus expenses).

FINANCE. General revenue of state and local government year ending 30 June 1981, was $1,457m.; general expenditures, $1,271m., taxation provided $643m. and federal aid, $289m.; education took $479m.; highways, $179m., and public welfare, $115m.

Total net long-term debt (local government) on 30 June 1981, $818m.

Per capita personal income (1983) was $11,666.

ENERGY AND NATURAL RESOURCES

Minerals. The mineral resources of North Dakota consist chiefly of oil which was discovered in 1951. Production of crude petroleum in 1983 was 50·7m. bbls; of natural gas, 73,000m. cu. ft. Output (1983) of lignite coal was 20·1m. short tons. Total value of mineral output, 1983, $1,870m.

Agriculture. Agriculture is the chief pursuit of the North Dakota population. In 1983 there were 37,500 farms (61,963 in 1954) with an area of 42m. acres (41,876,924 in 1954); the average farm was of 1,112 acres. The greater number of farms are cash-grain or livestock farms with annual sales of $20,000–$39,999.

Cash income, 1983, from crops, $2,086·1m., and from livestock, $628·9m. North Dakota leads in the production of barley, sunflowers, flaxseed and durum. Other important products are wheat, pinto beans, sugar-beet, potatoes, hay, oats, rye and maize.

The state has also an active livestock industry, chiefly cattle raising. On 1 Jan. 1984 the farm animals were: 99,000 milch cows, 2m. all cattle, 224,000 sheep and 260,000 swine. The wool clip yielded (1983), 1·6m. lb. of wool from 180,000 sheep.

Forestry. National forest area, 1977, 422,000 acres, of which 115,000 acres are federally owned or managed.

INDUSTRY. From 1970 to 1983 agricultural employment fell from 51,920 to 51,480; non-agricultural jobs rose from 148,910 to 267,180. Between 1970 and 1982, employment in manufacturing rose from 9,910 to 16,100, in trade from 43,890 to 65,530 and in government from 49,240 to 61,130.

COMMUNICATIONS

Roads. The state highway department maintained, in 1982, 7,224 miles of highway; local authorities, 95,900 miles, and municipal, 3,234 miles.

Car and truck registrations in 1983 numbered 705,056.

Railways. In 1984 there were 5,262 miles of railway.

Aviation. Airports in 1984 numbered 262, of which 107 were publicly owned.

JUSTICE, RELIGION, EDUCATION AND WELFARE

Justice. The state penitentiary, on 24 Jan. 1984, held 424 inmates. Of these, 55 were incarcerated at the North Dakota State Farm. There is no death penalty.

Religion. The leading religious denominations are the Roman Catholics, with 171,185 members in 1975; Combined Lutherans, 216,579; Methodists, 28,880; Presbyterians, 18,636.

Education. School attendance is compulsory between the ages of 7 and 16, or until the 17th birthday if the eighth grade has not been completed. In Oct. 1983 the public elementary schools had 81,797 pupils; secondary schools, 34,892 pupils. State expenditure on public schools, 1980, $427m. Private schools had 9,569 elementary pupils and 3,149 secondary pupils in 1983.

The university at Grand Forks, founded in 1883, had 9,440 students in 1982; the state university of agriculture and applied science, at Fargo, 8,079 students. Total enrolment in the 8 public institutions of higher education, 1982, 35,011.

Health. In 1982 the state had 60 hospitals (5,880 beds), and 79 nursing homes (5,100).

Social Security. In 1980 grants were made to 107,000 people, including 78,000 retired workers, 22,000 survivors of workers and 7,000 disabled workers.

Books of Reference

North Dakota Growth Indicators, 1984. 20th ed. Economic Development Commission, Bismarck, 1984
North Dakota Blue Book. Secretary of State, Bismarck, 1981
Statistical Abstract of North Dakota, 1983. Bureau of Business and Economic Research, Univ. of North Dakota, 1983
Glaab, C. L., et al, *The North Dakota Political Tradition.* Iowa State Univ. Press, 1981
Jelliff, T. B., *North Dakota: A Living Legacy.* Fargo, 1983
Robinson, E. B., *History of North Dakota.* Univ. of Nebraska Press, 1966

OHIO

HISTORY. Ohio, first settled in 1788, unofficially entered the Union on 19 Feb. 1803; entrance was made official, retroactive to 1 March 1803, on 8 Aug. 1953.

AREA AND POPULATION. Ohio is bounded north by Michigan and Lake Erie, east by Pennsylvania, south-east and south by the Ohio River (forming a boundary with West Virginia and Kentucky) and west by Indiana. Area, 41,330 sq. miles, of which 325 sq. miles are inland water. Census population, 1 April 1980 (preliminary), 10,797,419, an increase of 145,402 or 1·4% since 1970. Estimate (1982) 10,791,000. In 1980 births numbered 169,359 (15·7 per 1,000 population); deaths, 97,779 (9); infant deaths, 2,020 (12 per 1,000 live births); marriages, 99,522 (9·2); divorces and annulments, 58,225 (5·4).

Population at 5 census years was:

	White	*Negro*	*Indian*	*Asiatic*	*Total*	*Per sq. mile*
1910	4,654,897	111,452	127	645	4,767,121	117·0
1930	6,335,173	309,304	435	1,785	6,646,697	161·6
1960	8,909,698	786,097	1,910	8,692	9,706,397	236·9
			All others			
1970	9,646,997	970,477	34,543		10,652,017	260·0
1980	9,597,266	1,076,734	123,419		10,797,419	263·5

Of the total population in 1980, 5,217,027 were male, 7,914,500 persons were urban. Those 20 years old or older numbered 7,294,471.

Census population of chief cities on 1 April 1980 was:

Cleveland	572,532	Hamilton	62,845	Cuyahoga Falls	43,710
Columbus	561,943	Lakewood	61,921	Mentor	42,065
Cincinnati	383,058	Kettering	61,223	Newark	41,200
Toledo	354,265	Euclid	59,896	Marion	37,040
Akron	236,820	Elyria	57,039	East Cleveland	36,957
Dayton	193,319	Cleveland Heights	55,563	North Olmsted	36,486
Youngstown	115,429	Warren	55,456	Upper Arlington	35,648
Canton	94,632	Mansfield	53,907	Lancaster	34,953
Parma	92,378	Lima	47,381	Garfield Heights	33,380
Lorain	75,339	Middletown	43,719	Zanesville	28,655
Springfield	72,098				

Urbanized areas, 1980 census: Cleveland, 1,895,997; Cincinnati, 1,392,394; Columbus (the capital), 1,088,973; Dayton, 826,891; Akron, 660,233; Toledo, 791,137; Youngstown-Warren, 529,887; Canton, 403,847.

CLIMATE. Cincinnati. Jan. 33°F (0·6°C), July 78°F (25·6°C). Annual rainfall 39″ (978 mm). Cleveland. Jan. 27°F (–2·8°C), July 71°F (21·1°C). Annual rainfall 35″ (879 mm). Columbus. Jan. 29°F (–1·7°C), July 75°F (23·9°C). Annual rainfall 34″ (850 mm). *See* Great Lakes, p. 1373.

CONSTITUTION AND GOVERNMENT. The question of a general revision of the constitution drafted by an elected convention is submitted to the people every 20 years. The constitution of 1851 had 105 amendments by 1978.

In the 112th General Assembly the Senate consisted of 33 members and the House of Representatives of 99 members. The Senate is elected for 4 years, half each 2 years; the House is elected for 2 years; the Governor, Lieut.-Governor and Secretary of State for 4 years. Qualified as electors are (with necessary exceptions) all citizens 18 years of age who have the usual residential qualifications. Ohio sends 2 senators and 21 representatives to Congress.

In the 1984 presidential election Reagan polled 2,653,691 votes, Mondale, 1,804,870.

The capital (since 1816) is Columbus. Ohio is divided into 88 counties.

Governor: Richard Celeste (D.), 1983–86 ($50,000).
Lieut.-Governor: Myrl H. Shoemaker (D.), 1983–86 ($50,000).
Secretary of State: Sherrod Brown (D.), 1983–86 ($50,000).

BUDGET. For the year ending 30 June 1982 (Budget of the State of Ohio) total general revenue was $16,461m. and general expenditure was $16,972m.

The total debt outstanding on 30 June 1982 was $11,268m.

Per capita personal income (1982) was $10,677.

ENERGY AND NATURAL RESOURCES

Minerals. Ohio has extensive mineral resources, of which coal is the most important by value: output (1981) 37·4m. short tons. Production of crude petroleum, 1982, 15m. bbls; natural gas, 123,000m. cu. ft. Other minerals include stone, clay, sand and gravel. Value of fuel minerals, 1981, $1,887m.; non-fuel, $554m.

Agriculture. Ohio is extensively devoted to agriculture. In 1983, 92,000 farms covered 16m. acres; average farm value per acre, $1,297.

Cash income 1982, from crop and livestock and products, $3,674m. The most important crops in 1983 were: Maize (232m. bu.), wheat (58·6m. bu.), oats (15·4m. bu.), soybeans (101·7m. bu.). On 1 Jan. 1983 there were 1·8m. swine 1·9m. all cattle and 275,000 sheep.

Forestry. State forest area, 1978, 170,000 acres including reclamation area.

INDUSTRY. In 1981, manufacturing employed 1,219,000 workers. The value of shipments was $122,287m. The largest industry was manufacturing of non-electrical machinery, then transport equipment and fabricated metals.

COMMUNICATIONS

Roads. In 1981 the state had 29,000 miles of urban and 81,900 miles of rural highway. The federal-aid highway system included 7,872 miles of primary roads, of which 1,535 miles were interstate. In 1982 there were (estimate) 7·7m. cars, trucks and buses, and 274,000 motorcycles.

Railways. The railroads had 7,400 route miles of track in 1978.

Aviation. Ohio had (1978) 719 airports and airfields, of which 212 are commercial and 527 private, 130 heliports and 2 seaplane bases. There were 6,600 licensed aeroplanes.

JUSTICE, RELIGION, EDUCATION AND WELFARE

Justice. A Civil Rights Act (1933) forbids inns, restaurants, theatres, retail stores and all other places of public resort to discriminate against citizens on grounds of 'colour or race'; none may be denied the right to serve on juries on the grounds of 'colour or race'; insurance companies are forbidden to discriminate between 'white persons and coloured, wholly or partially of African descent'.

A state Civil Rights Commission (created 1959) has general administrative powers to prevent discrimination because of race, colour, religion, national origin or ancestry in employment, labour organization membership, use of public accommodations and in obtaining 'commercial housing' or 'personal residence'. Ohio has no *de jure* segregation in the public schools.

The state's adult correctional institutions, 30 Oct. 1978, held 8,285 inmates (average daily count). Total executions (by electrocution) since 1930 were 170, all for murder. There have been no executions since 1963. The Department of Rehabilitation and Correction was created in July 1972, and has established probation services in 51 counties where services would otherwise be inadequate or non-existent.

Religion. Many religious faiths are represented, including (but not limited to) the Baptist, Jewish, Lutheran, Methodist, Presbyterian and Roman Catholic.

Education. School attendance during full term is compulsory for children from 6 to 18 years of age. In autumn 1982 public schools had 1,860,245 enrolled pupils and 94,126 classroom teachers. Teachers' salaries (1983) averaged $21,000 (secondary) and $19,900 (elementary). Operating expenditure on elementary and secondary schools for 1981 was $4,182m. The state's universities and colleges had a total enrolment (1982) of 532,000 students; the following had 7,000 or more students, autumn 1977:

Founded	*Institutions*	*Enrolments*
1804	Ohio University, Athens (State)	13,021
1809	Miami University, Oxford (State)	14,759
1826	Case Western Reserve University, Cleveland	8,108
1850	University of Dayton (R.C.)	9,620
1870	University of Akron (State)	23,121
1872	Ohio State University, Columbus (State)	51,003
1872	University of Toledo (State)	16,933
1874	University of Cincinnati (State-affiliated)	32,952
1887	Sinclair Community College, Dayton	13,752
1908	Youngstown University (State)	15,696
1910	Bowling Green State University (State)	16,439
1912	Kent State University (State)	19,396
1962	Cuyahoga Community College (Municipal)	27,250
1964	Cleveland State University (State)	17,627
1964	Wright State University (State)	13,067

Health. In 1981 the state had 239 hospitals (63,600 beds) listed by the American Hospital Association. State and county mental care hospitals had 5,915 resident patients on 31 Dec. 1980. State facilities for the mentally retarded, 3,710 in 1982.

Social Security. Public assistance is administered through 4 basic programmes: aid to dependent children, emergency assistance, Medicaid and general relief. Total public assistance expenditures during the year ending 30 June 1978 were $1,322·4m. In 1976–77 the number of persons receiving public assistance averaged 626,100 per month. Under the aid to dependent children programme $429·9m. provided assistance to an average of 526,434 recipients per month. Payments for Medicaid were $603·5m.; for social services, $189m.; for general relief, $78·4m., and emergency assistance, $21·6m. Recipients of general relief averaged 47,923 per month, emergency assistance, 30,585. Recipients of Medicaid during the year, 799,915.

Books of Reference

Official Roster: Federal State, County Officers and Department Information. Secretary of State, Columbus. Biennial

Rosebloom, E. H., and Weisenburger, F. P., *A History of Ohio.* State Arch. and Hist. Soc., Columbus, 1953

OKLAHOMA

HISTORY. An unorganized area in the centre of the present state was thrown open to white settlers on 22 April 1889. The Territory of Oklahoma, organized in 1890 to include this area and other sections, was opened to white settlements by runs or lotteries during the next decade. In 1893 the Territory was enlarged by the addition of the Cherokee Outlet, which fixed part of the present northern boundary. On 16 Nov. 1907 Oklahoma was combined with the remaining part of the Indian Territory and admitted as a state with boundaries substantially as now.

AREA AND POPULATION. Oklahoma is bounded north by Kansas, north-east by Missouri, east by Arkansas, south by Texas (the Red River forming part of the boundary) and, at the western extremity of the 'panhandle', by New Mexico and Colorado. Area 69,919 sq. miles, of which 1,137 sq. miles are water. Census population, 1 April 1980, 3,025,266, an increase of 465,803 or 18% since 1970. Estimate (1983), 3,298,000. Births, 1980, were 52,065; deaths, 28,908; infant deaths 660; marriages, 46,509; divorces, including annulments, 24,226.

The population at 5 federal censuses was:

	White	*Negro*	*Indian*	*Asiatic*	*Total*	*Per sq. mile*
1910	1,444,531	137,612	74,825	187	1,657,155	23·9
1930	2,130,778	172,198	92,725	339	2,396,040	34·6
1960	2,107,900	153,084	68,689	1,414	2,328,284	33·8
			All others			
1970	2,280,362	171,892	106,999		2,559,253	37·2
1980	2,597,783	204,658	222,825		3,025,266	43·2

In 1980, 1,476,719 were male, 2,035,082 were urban and those 20 years of age or older numbered 2,052,729. The US Bureau of Indian Affairs is responsible for 37 Indian tribes, 201,456 Indians on 1,229,341 acres (1984).

The most important cities with population, 1980 are Oklahoma City (capital), 403,213, Tulsa, 360,919; Lawton, 80,054; Norman, 68,020; Enid, 50,363; Midwest City, 49,559.

CLIMATE. Oklahoma City. Jan. 37°F (2·8°C), July 81°F (27·2°C). Annual rainfall 32" (803 mm). Tulsa. Jan. 37°F (2·8°C), July 82°F (27·8°C). Annual rainfall 37" (925 mm). *See* Central Plains, p. 1372.

CONSTITUTION AND GOVERNMENT. The present constitution, dating from 1907, provides for amendment by initiative petition and legislative referendum; it has had 106 amendments.

The Legislature consists of a Senate of 48 members, who are elected for 4 years, and a House of Representatives elected for 2 years and consisting of 101 members. The Governor and Lieut.-Governor are elected for 4-year terms; the Governor can only be elected for two terms in succession. Electors are (with necessary exceptions) all citizens 18 years or older, with the usual qualifications.

The state is represented in Congress by 2 senators and 6 representatives.

In the 1984 presidential election Reagan polled 793,258 votes, Mondale, 362,771.

The capital is Oklahoma City. The state has 77 counties.

Governor: George Nigh (D.), 1983–86 ($70,000).
Lieut.-Governor: Spencer Bernard (D.), 1983–86 ($40,000).
Secretary of State: Jeanette B. Edmondson (D.), 1983–86 ($37,500).

BUDGET. Total revenue for the year ending 30 June 1983 (State Budget Office figures) was $1,763·4m. Total expenditure, $4,790·5m.

Bonded indebtedness for the year ending 30 June 1984, $135·96m.

Per capita personal income (1984) was $11,187.

ENERGY AND NATURAL RESOURCES

Minerals. Resources include petroleum, helium, natural gas, coal (bituminous), cement, granite, gypsum, olivestone, sand, gravel and some copper and silver. Production for 1982 (preliminary) was: Petroleum, 159m. bbls; natural gas, 1,934,000m. cu. ft. In March 1981 there were 82,639 oilwells and 16,994 natural gaswells in production. Total value of mineral production, 1981, $8,677,798.

Agriculture. In 1980 the state had 73,000 farms with a total area of 35m. acres; average farm was 479 acres with an average gross income of $49,569. In 1980, there were 43,792 full-time farmers or ranchers, 25,719 part-owners and 10,019 tenants. Large-scale commercial farming is predominant.

The conservation and development of the renewable natural resources of the state has received close attention by local, county and state governments during the past 40 years. All of the land in the state is within the boundaries of one of the 88 conservation districts. Of the total surface (44m. acres), 92% is under a basic conservation plan prepared by the conservation district with assistance from the Soil Conservation Service. The Oklahoma Conservation Commission reported that good conservation measures by farmers, such as minimum tillage and crop residue management, are helping to conserve moisture and protect crops from erosion. Through Jan. 1980, 125 work plans had been approved for watersheds established in 1946 to aid flood control. In addition, 2,540 flood-prevention dams and 62 multi-purpose dams have been built or approved under this project. In 1981 there were 4 active Resource Conservation and Development Areas covering 16·8m. acres in 31 counties. Plans for 5 other areas covering another 32 counties have been submitted.

A trend of the last 40 years has been the conversion of arable land to grass; cattle and calves rank first in agricultural products, valued, 1981, at $1,460m.; winter wheat is second, at $845m.

Cash income from crops and livestock products 1981, $2,855m. The most valuable crop is winter wheat (production, 1981, 172m. bu.). Other crops (production, 1981) included hay (3·3m. tons), cotton (440,000 bales of 480 lb.), grain sorghums (22m. bu.) and peanuts (189m. lb.). On 1 Jan. 1982 the stock included 111,000 milch cows, 5·8m. all cattle, 105,000 sheep and lambs, 4·2m. farm chickens and 245,000 swine.

Forestry. There are 8·5m. acres of forest, one half considered commercial. The forest products industry, concentrated in the southeastern counties, employs approximately 7,000 in over 100 manufacturing plants with an estimated combined annual payroll of $75m. Value of shipments of lumber and forest products in 1980 was over $50m.

INDUSTRY. The retail trade and service industries each employed 15% of the working population in 1981. Among other industries the most important by payroll employment (1982) were: mining (103,700); construction (49,300); transport and utilities (67,700); manufacturing (193,700); government (245,000); finance, insurance and property (58,800). In 1982 the civilian non-agricultural labour force averaged 1·2m.

COMMUNICATIONS

Roads. In 1982 there were 12,178 miles of inter-state, federal and state highway open, 81,304 miles of county roads, 15,458 miles of city streets, 487 miles of turnpike and 344 miles of park and forest roads. Motor vehicle registrations, 1980, 2,731,628.

Railways. In 1983 Oklahoma had 5,005 miles of railway operated by 12 companies.

Aviation. Airports, 1982, numbered 288, of which 131 were municipally owned. Seven cities were served by CAB-certificated airlines.

Shipping. The McClellan-Kerr Arkansas Navigation System provides access from east central Oklahoma to New Orleans through the Verdigris, Arkansas and Mississippi rivers. The main ports are Catoosa and Muskogee.

JUSTICE, RELIGION, EDUCATION AND WELFARE

Justice. Penal institutions, 30 Sept. 1984, held 7,500 inmates. There are 12 correction centres and 8 community treatment centres.

The death penalty was suspended in 1966 and re-imposed in 1974. Since 1915 there have been 83 (52 whites, 27 Negroes, 4 other races) executions. Electrocution was replaced (1977) by lethal injection.

Religion. The chief religious bodies in 1980 were Baptists, 674,766; United Methodists, 248,635; Roman Catholics, 122,820; Churches of Christ, about 80,000; Assembly of God, 63,992; Disciples of Christ, 45,070; Presbyterian, 38,605; Lutheran, 33,664; Nazarene, 22,090; Episcopal, 21,500.

Education. In 1982–83 there were 622,630 pupils enrolled in elementary and secondary schools, 39,901 teachers at elementary schools and secondary schools had average salaries of $19,163. Total expenditure on public schools, $19,973·7m.

In 1980–81, there were 3,415 special education units with 65,598 students in class.

The University of Oklahoma (founded at Norman in 1890) had 753 full-time faculty and 20,333 enrolled students in spring 1981; Oklahoma State University of Agriculture and Applied Science (founded in 1890 at Stillwater) had 718 full-time faculty and 20,739 students; Central State University (founded at Edmond in 1890) had 320 full-time faculty and 10,820 students. There are 10 other institutions of higher learning in the state system at the senior level and 14 junior colleges. Total enrolment in institutions of higher education, spring 1981, 154,266.

Health. In 1981 there were 134 hospitals (15,642 beds). In 1981 institutions for the mentally retarded had 1,828 inmates; the schools for deaf and blind had 234 children, 3 schools for delinquents, 862 children, 2 children's homes, 679 children.

Social Security. Public assistance, financial year 1981 was being drawn by 148,435 persons, receiving an average monthly payment of $930. This includes old age assistance, aid to families with dependent children, AFDC emergency, AFDC foster home care, aid to the blind and aid to the disabled. Medical payments were made for 234,393 persons, totalled $317·9m. and averaged $1,356.50 per person. Intermediate care was provided for 26,664 persons at an average of $5,914.05 per person. Non-technical medical care was provided for 10,129 persons at an average of $2,127.96 per person. A total of $29,954,310 was spent for vocational rehabilitation.

Books of Reference

Directory of Oklahoma. Dept. of Libraries, Oklahoma City
Chronicles of Oklahoma. State Historical Society, Oklahoma City (from 1921, quarterly)
Statistical Abstract of Oklahoma, 1982. Centers for Economic and Management Research, Univ. of Oklahoma, Norman, 1982
Dale, E. E., and Aldrich, G., *History of Oklahoma.* New York, 1969
Gibson, A. M., *The History of Oklahoma.* Rev. ed., Univ. of Oklahoma, Norman, 1984
McReynolds, Edwin C., *Oklahoma: A History of the Sooner State.* Rev. ed. Univ. of Oklahoma, Norman, 1964
Ruth, K., *et al.*, (eds.), *Oklahoma: A Guide to the Sooner State.* Rev. ed. Univ. of Oklahoma, Norman, 1957
Strain, J. W., *Outline of Oklahoma Government.* Rev. ed., Central State Univ., Edmond, 1983

State Library: Oklahoma Dept. of Libraries, 200 N.E. 18th Street, Oklahoma City 73105. *State Librarian and State Archivist:* Robert L. Clark, Jr.

OREGON

HISTORY. Oregon was first settled in 1811 by the Pacific Fur Co. at Astoria, a provisional government was formed on 5 July 1834; a Territorial government was organized, 14 Aug. 1848, and on 14 Feb. 1859 Oregon was admitted to the Union.

AREA AND POPULATION. Oregon is bounded north by Washington, with the Columbia River forming most of the boundary, east by Idaho, with the Snake River forming most of the boundary, south by Nevada and California and west by the Pacific. Area, 97,073 sq. miles, 889 sq. miles being inland water. The federal government owned (1976) 32,370,216 acres (52·55% of the state area). Census population, 1 April 1980, 2,633,105, an increase of 541,720 or 26% since 1970. Estimated population (1982), 2,656,185. In 1980 births numbered 43,998 (16·7 per 1,000 population); deaths, 21,793 (8·2); infant deaths 556 (12 per 1,000 live births); marriages, 23,115 (8·8), and divorces, 17,925 (6·8).

Population at 5 federal censuses was:

	White	*Negro*	*Indian*	*Asiatic*	*Total*	*Per sq. mile*
1910	655,090	1,492	5,090	11,093	672,765	7·0
1930	938,598	2,234	4,776	8,179	953,786	9·9
1960	1,732,037	18,133	8,026	9,120	1,768,687	18·4
1970	2,032,079	26,308	13,510	13,290	2,091,385	21·7
1980	2,490,610	37,060	27,314	34,775	2,633,105	27·3

Of the total population in 1980, 1,296,566 were male, 1,788,354 persons were urban. Those 18 years and older numbered 1,910,048.

The US Bureau of Indian Affairs (area headquarters in Portland) administers (1976) 742,151·74 acres, of which 597,222·94 acres are held by the US in trust for Indian tribes, and 144,928·8 acres for individual Indians.

The largest towns, according to 1980 census figures, are: Portland, 366,383; Eugene, 105,664; Salem (the capital), 89,233; Corvallis, 40,960; Medford, 39,603; Springfield, 41,621; Beaverton, 31,926; Albany, 26,678. Metropolitan areas (1980): Portland, 1,236,294; Eugene-Springfield, 273,114; Salem, 249,655.

CLIMATE. Portland. Jan. 39°F (3·9°C), July 67°F (19·4°C). Annual rainfall 44″ (1,100 mm). *See* Pacific Coast, p. 1372.

CONSTITUTION AND GOVERNMENT. The present constitution dates from 1859; some 80 items in it have been amended. The Legislative Assembly consists of a Senate of 30 members, elected for 4 years (half their number retiring every 2 years), and a House of 60 representatives, elected for 2 years. The Governor is elected for 4 years. The constitution reserves to the voters the rights of initiative and referendum and recall. In Nov. 1912 suffrage was extended to women.

The state sends to Congress 2 senators and 5 representatives.

In the 1984 presidential election Reagan polled 618,824 votes, Mondale, 496,237.

The capital is Salem. There are 36 counties in the state.

Governor: Victor Atiyeh (R.), 1983–86 ($53,394 plus $1,000 monthly for expenses).

Secretary of State: Barbara Roberts (D.) ($45,619).

BUDGET. Oregon has 2-year financial periods. Total resources for the biennium 1981–83 were $13,957,634,165 (federal funds, $1,003m.; individual taxes, $2,123·7m.; business taxes, $1,587·4m.); total expenditures, $10,052,272,033 (education, $2,451·9m.; economic development and consumer services, $2,983·5m.; human resources, $2,398·6m.).

In Feb. 1983 the outstanding bonded debt was $6,000m.

Per capita personal income (1982) was $10,335.

ENERGY AND NATURAL RESOURCES

Electricity. On 1 Jan. 1982 four privately owned utilities, 11 municipally owned utilities, 18 co-operatives and 4 utility districts provided electricity in the state. The privately owned companies provided 73% of the electricity. Hydroelectricity plants (67 in 1983) have an installed capacity of 5m. kw., of which multi-purpose federal projects like the Bonneville Power Administration accounted for 3·5m. kw. The Trojan Nuclear plant has a capacity of 1,080mw., and Boardman coal-fired plant, 530mw.

Minerals. Oregon's mineral resources include gold, silver, nickel copper, lead, mercury, chromite, sand and gravel, stone, clays, lime, silica, diatomite, expansible shale, scoria, pumice and uranium. There is geothermal potential. Value of mineral products, 1981, was $163m.

Agriculture. Oregon, which has an area of 61,557,184 acres, is divided by the Cascade Range into two distinct zones as to climate. West of the Cascade Range there is a good rainfall and almost every variety of crop common to the temperate zone is grown; east of the Range stock-raising and wheat-growing are the principal industries and irrigation is needed for row crops and fruits.

There were, in 1983, 37,000 farms with an acreage of 18·3m. (29·7% of the land area); average farm size was 492 acres; most are family-owned corporate farms. Average value per acre, $580.

Cash receipts from crops in 1983 amounted to $1,145m., and from livestock and livestock products, $555m., of which cattle and calves made most. Principal crops are hay (1·3m. tons), wheat (65·6m. bu.), potatoes, peppermint, ryegrass seed, pears, onions, snap beans, sweet corn and barley.

Livestock, 1 Jan. 1983: Milch cows, 100,000; cattle and calves, 1·7m.; sheep and lambs, 500,000; swine, 90,000.

Forestry. About 29·8m. acres is forested, almost half of the state. Of this amount, 24·2m. is commercial forest land suitable for timber production; ownership is as follows (acres): US Forestry service, 11·6m. (48%); Forest Industry, 5·5m. (22·8%); Small non-industrial landowners, 3·6m. (14·7%); US Bureau of Land Management, 2·2m. (9%); State of Oregon, 820,000 acres (3·4%) and other owners (city, county, Indian), 496,000 acres (2·1%). Oregon's commercial forest lands provided an estimated 1982 harvest of 5,200m. bd ft of logs, as well as the benefits of recreation, water, grazing, wildlife and fish. Trees vary from the coastal forest of hemlock and spruce to the state's primary species, Douglas-fir, throughout much of western Oregon. In eastern Oregon, ponderosa pine, lodgepole pine and true firs are found. Here, forestry is often combined with livestock grazing to provide an economic operation. Along the Cascade summit and in the mountains of northeast Oregon, alpine species are found.

Production, 1981: plywood, 5,561m. sq. ft (value $991·5m.); Douglas Fir lumber, 3,842m. bd. ft ($948·3m.); Ponderosa Pine lumber, 1,273m. bd. ft ($386m.); pulp and paper, 4·8m. tons ($8·5m.).

Fisheries. All food and shellfish landings in the calendar year 1981 amounted to a value of $58m. The most important are: tuna, crabs, bottom fish, shrimp.

INDUSTRY. Forest products manufacturing is Oregon's leading industry, and provides for 20% of the country's softwood lumber needs, 40% of its plywood and more than 25% of the hardboard. More than one-third of the economy depends directly or indirectly on timber industries; about 78,130 (1981) people are employed. The payroll was $1,600m. and value of production, $3,490m. During 1981, manufacturing employed 203,300, of which 148,500 made durable goods; trade, 253,700, construction, 37,600.

TOURISM. In 1982, 14,391,400 out-of-state tourists visited Oregon; the total income from tourism was estimated to be $1,300m.

COMMUNICATIONS

Roads. The state maintains (1982) 7,555 miles of primary and secondary highways, almost all surfaced; counties maintain 27,697 miles, and cities 6,913 miles; there were 79,167 miles in national parks and federal reservations. Registered motor vehicles, 31 Dec. 1981, totalled 2·3m.

Railways. The state had (1980) 19 common carrier railways with a total mileage of 4,428.

Aviation. In Oct. 1982 there were 4 public-use and 85 personal-use heliports; 5 public-use seaplane bases; 206 personal-use airports; 110 public-use airports including 37 state-owned airports.

Shipping. Portland is a major seaport for large ocean-going vessels and is 101 miles inland from the mouth of the Columbia River. In 1982 the port handled 6·6m. short tons of cargo; main commodities for this and other Columbia River ports are grain and petroleum.

Post and Broadcasting. In Dec. 1982 there were 137 commercial radio stations and 13 educational radio stations. There were 14 commercial television stations and 6 educational television stations. There were also 5 campus limited radio stations and 1 subscription radio station.

Newspapers. In 1982 there were 21 daily newspapers with a circulation of 653,392 and 89 non-daily newspapers.

JUSTICE, RELIGION, EDUCATION AND WELFARE

Justice. There are 3 correctional institutions in Oregon, all in Salem. The Oregon State Penitentiary, on 30 June 1982, held 1,779 males; the Women's Correctional Center had a resident population of 73; and the Oregon Correctional Institution, which is for first offenders, had a population of 926. The Oregon Correctional Division's Release Center in Salem held 323 inmates, 110 inmates were held in Oregon State Hospital wards and 16,174 offenders were on parole or probation.

The sterilization law, originally passed in 1917, was amended in 1967. The amendments changed the number of persons on the Board of Social Protection from 15 to 7 and provided that the Public Defender would automatically represent all persons examined. The basis on which a person would be subject to examination by the Board are: *(a)* if such person would be likely to procreate children having an inherited tendency to mental retardation or mental illness, or *(b)* if such person would be likely to procreate children who would become neglected or dependent because of the person's inability by reason of mental illness or mental retardation to provide adequate care.

Religion. The chief religious bodies are Catholic, Baptist, Lutheran, Methodists, Presbyterian and Mormon.

Education. School attendance is compulsory from 7 to 18 years of age if the twelfth year of school has not been completed; those between the ages of 16 and 18 years, if legally employed, may attend part-time or evening schools. Others may be excused under certain circumstances. In 1981–82 the public elementary schools had 330,810 students and the secondary schools, 148,458. Total expenditure on elementary and secondary education (1980–81) was $1,726·7m.

Leading state-supported institutions of higher education (autumn 1982) included:

	Students
University of Oregon, Eugene	15,467
Oregon Health Sciences University:	1,431
Oregon State University, Corvallis	16,759
Portland State University, Portland	14,541
Western Oregon State College, Monmouth	2,473
Southern Oregon State College, Ashland	4,161
Eastern Oregon State College, La Grande	1,764
Oregon Institute of Technology, Klamath Falls	2,653

Largest of the privately endowed universities are Lewis and Clark College, Portland, with (1982) 3,054 students; University of Portland, 2,872 students; Willamette University, Salem, 1,859 students; Reed College, Portland, 1,122 students, and Linfield College, McMinnville, 1,496 students. There are 13 community colleges and 1 area education district with an estimated enrolment of 293,886 students in 1981–82.

Health. In Oct. 1982 there were 91 licensed hospitals. In Oct. 1979 there were 4 state hospitals for mentally ill and mentally retarded (2 for mentally ill, 1 for mentally retarded and 1 with both programmes). On 30 June 1982 there were 931 mentally ill patients and 1,629 mentally retarded.

Social Security. Old-age assistance is provided for all needy persons 65 years or older who meet certain eligibility requirements. In financial year 1979–80, 3,598 cases per month received average payments of $5.36 cash and $87.54 services. For the same period 98,278 persons in 36,166 families with dependent children received an average $279.74 per month; 552 blind recipients $38.56 cash and $62.52 services; 7,009 disabled $15.94 cash and $41.86 services; 4,501 general assistance cases $134.73 cash and $5.45 services.

Medical assistance and mental health costs averaged $14,494,000 per month.

A system of unemployment benefit payments, financed by employers, with administrative allotments made through a federal agency, started 2 Jan. 1938, and covers about 66,500 employers with average employment in 1979 of 1,024,535. By June 1980, $1,717m. in taxes had been paid into the trust fund plus $297·3m. in interest and reimbursed benefits. About $1,691m. has been paid in benefits which from July 1980 range from $38 to $138 weekly and up to $3,588 per year. About 38,406 state employees, 48,060 school employees, 5,507 community college employees and 18,879 political subdivision employees are participants in the public employees retirement programme. The same employees are covered under the federal old-age, survivors and disability insurance programme. Approximately 31,016 retired employees are receiving monthly benefit cheques.

Books of Reference

Oregon Blue Book. Issued by the Secretary of State. Salem. Biennial

Federal Writers' Project. *Oregon: End of the Trail.* Rev. ed. Portland, 1972

Baldwin, E. M., *Geology of Oregon.* Rev. ed. Dubuque, Iowa, 1976

Carey, C. H., *General History of Oregon, prior to 1861.* 2 vol. (1 vol. reprint, 1971) Portland, 1935

Corning, H. M. (ed.), *Dictionary of Oregon History.* New York, 1956

Dicken, S. N., *Oregon Geography.* 5th ed. Eugene, 1973.—with Dicken, E. F., *Making of Oregon: a Study in Historical Geography.* Portland, 1979.—with Dicken, E. F., *Oregon Divided: A Regional Geography.* Portland, 1982

Dodds, G. B., *Oregon: A Bicentennial History.* New York, 1977

Friedman, R., *Oregon for the Curious.* 3rd ed. Portland, 1972

Highsmith, R. M. Jr. (ed.), *Atlas of the Pacific Northwest.* Corvallis, 1973

McArthur, L. A., *Oregon Geographic Names.* 4th ed., rev. and enlarged. Portland, 1974

Patton, Clyde P., *Atlas of Oregon.* Univ. Oregon Press, Eugene, 1976

State Library: The Oregon State Library, Salem. *Librarian:* Marcia Lowell.

PENNSYLVANIA

HISTORY. Pennsylvania, first settled in 1682, is one of the 13 original states in the Union.

AREA AND POPULATION. Pennsylvania is bounded north by New York, east by New Jersey, south by Delaware and Maryland, south-west by West Virginia, west by Ohio and north-west by Lake Erie. Area, 45,308 sq. miles, of which 420 sq. miles are inland water. Census population, 1 April 1980, 11,863,895, an increase of 63,129 or 0·5% since 1970. Estimate (1982) 11,885,330. Births, 1982, 161,561; deaths, 118,450; infant deaths, 1,853; marriages, 93,350; reported divorces, 38,545.

Population at 5 census years was:

	White	*Negro*	*Indian*	*All others*	*Total*	*Per sq. mile*
1910	7,467,713	193,919	1,503	1,976	7,665,111	171·0
1930	9,196,007	431,257	523	3,563	9,631,350	213·8
1960	10,454,004	852,750	2,122	10,490	11,319,366	251·5
			All others			
1970	10,745,219	1,015,884	39,663		11,800,766	262·9
1980	10,652,320	1,046,810	164,765		11,863,895	264·3

Of the total population in 1980, 47·9% were male, 69·3% were urban and 68·1% were 21 years of age or older.

The population of the larger cities and townships, 1980 census, was:

Philadelphia	1,688,210	Scranton	88,117	Lancaster	54,725
Pittsburgh	423,938	Reading	78,686	Harrisburg	53,264
Erie	119,123	Bethlehem	70,419	Wilkes-Barre	51,551
Allentown	103,758	Altoona	57,078	York	44,619

Larger urbanized areas, 1980 census: Philadelphia (in Pennsylvania), 3,682,709; Pittsburgh, 2,263,894; Northeast, 640,396, Allentown–Bethlehem–Easton (in Pennsylvania), 551,052; Harrisburg, 446,576.

CLIMATE. Philadelphia. Jan. 32°F (0°C), July 77°F (25°C). Annual rainfall 40″ (1,006 mm). Pittsburgh. Jan. 31°F (–0·6°C), July 74°F (23·3°C). Annual rainfall 37″ (914 mm). *See* Appalachian Mountains, p. 1373.

CONSTITUTION AND GOVERNMENT. The present constitution dates from 1968. The General Assembly consists of a Senate of 50 members chosen for 4 years, one-half being elected biennially, and a House of Representatives of 203 members chosen for 2 years. The Governor and Lieut.-Governor are elected for 4 years. Every citizen 18 years of age, with the usual residential qualifications, may vote. The state sends to Congress 2 senators and 23 representatives. Registered voters in 1983, 5,707,163.

In the 1984 presidential election Reagan polled 2,564,273 votes, Mondale, 2,209,137.

The state capital is Harrisburg. The state is organized in counties (numbering 67), cities, boroughs, townships and school districts.

Governor: Richard Thornburgh (R.), 1979–86 ($75,000).
Lieut.-Governor: William W. Scranton (R.) ($54,500).

BUDGET. Total revenues for the year ending 30 June 1983 were $7,320·7m.; general fund expenditure, $7,604·4m. (education, $3,508·9m.; transport, $155·6m.; public welfare, $2,716·6m.; environment, $112·7m.)

On 30 June 1984 outstanding long-term debt (excluding highway bonds) amounted to $3,340·9m.

Per capita personal income (1983) was $11,448.

ENERGY AND NATURAL RESOURCES

Minerals. Pennsylvania is almost the sole producer of anthracite coal; its output reached a peak of 100,445,299 short tons in 1917 with a labour-force of 156,148 men. Production in 1983: Anthracite, 4·02m. tons, with about 1,700 men; bituminous coal, 62·21m. tons, with about 16,400 men; crude petroleum (1982), 4·28m. bbls; natural gas (1982), 121,111m. cu. ft. Total value of minerals produced (1981), $3,880m., of which $3,247m. was for fuel minerals.

Agriculture. Agriculture, market-gardening, fruit-growing, horticulture and forestry are pursued within the state. In 1983 there were 59,000 farms with a total farm area of 8·3m. acres (4·4m. acres in crops); the average farm was 149 acres with average value per acre of $1,520. Cash income, 1982, from crops, $825·4m., and from livestock, $2,166m.

Pennsylvania ranks first in the production of mushrooms (246·6m. lb., value $172·6m. in 1983). Other crops are (1983) tobacco (22m. lb., $20·72m.), winter wheat (7·6m. bu.), oats (16·2m. bu.), maize (72·5m. bu.), barley (3·71m. bu.) and potatoes (4·30m. cwt). On 1 Jan. 1984 there were on farms: 1·97m. cattle and calves, including 735,000 milch cows, 104,000 sheep, 950,000 swine. Milk production, 1983, was 9,510m. lb. valued at $1,351m., and eggs numbered 4,716m. valued at $232m. Pennsylvania is also a major fruit producing state; in 1983 apples totalled 500m. lb.; peaches, 94m. lb.; tart cherries, 8·5m. lb.; sweet cherries, 800 tons; and grapes, 62,500 tons. Other important items are soybeans (3·48m. bu.), vegetables for processing (102,000 tons), fresh vegetables (1·2m. cwt) and broiler-chickens (102·6m.).

Forestry. In 1982 national forest lands totalled 510,517 acres; state forests, 2,064,533 acres; state parks, 278,930 acres; state game land, 1,250,980 acres; game land leased but not owned by the state, 3,957,438 acres (co-operative and safety-zone programmes).

INDUSTRY. Pennsylvania is third in national production of iron and steel. Output of steel, 1982, 10·9m. net tons.

In 1981, 16,388 manufacturing establishments employed 1,321,109 workers (wages, $25,069m.).

COMMUNICATIONS

Roads. Highways and roads in the state (federal, local and state combined) totalled (1984) 114,797 miles. Registered motor vehicles for 1983 numbered 7,562,726 (including 5,659,975 passenger cars, 1,582,096 trucks, truck-tractors and trailers).

Railways. In 1983, 41 railways operated within the state with a line mileage of about 6,300.

Aviation. There were (1982) 161 commercial airports, 3 public landing strips, 242 heliports, 391 airports for personal use and 16 seaplane bases.

Shipping. Trade at the Ports of Philadelphia (1983), imports 48·3m. short tons, exports 5·7m.

Post and Broadcasting. Broadcasting stations comprised (1982) 41 television stations and 378 radio stations.

Newspapers. There were (1983) 111 daily and 219 weekly newspapers.

JUSTICE, RELIGION, EDUCATION AND WELFARE

Justice. No executions took place in 1963–84; since 1930 there have been 149 executions (electrocution), all for murder.

State prison population, on 31 Dec. 1983, was 11,798.

Religion. The chief religious bodies in 1977 were the Roman Catholic, with 3,717,667 members; Protestant, 3,150,920 (1971); and Jewish, 469,078. The 5 largest Protestant denominations (by communicants) were: Lutheran Church in America, 766,276; United Methodist, 728,915 (1971), United Presbyterian Church in the USA, 573,905 (1971); United Church of Christ, 257,138; Episcopal, 193,399 (1971).

Education. School attendance is compulsory for children 8–17 years of age. In 1983–84 the public kindergartens and elementary schools had 846,145 pupils; public secondary schools had 891,807 pupils. Non-public schools had 285,372 elementary pupils and 110,861 secondary pupils. Average salary, public school professional personnel, men $25,218; women $22,283; for classroom teachers, men $23,678, women $21,997.

Leading senior academic institutions included:

Founded	*Institutions*	*Faculty (Autumn 1983)*	*Students (Autumn 1983)*
1740	University of Pennsylvania (non-sect.)	1,005	22,277
1787	University of Pittsburgh	1,486	35,613
1832	Lafayette College, Easton (Presbyterian)	159	2,383
1842	Villanova University (R.C.)	473	11,728
1846	Bucknell University (Baptist)	212	3,264
1851	St Joseph's College, Philadelphia (R.C.)	139	6,061
1852	California University of Pennsylvania	269	4,959
1855	Pennsylvania State University	2,425	63,989
1855	Millersville University of Pennsylvania	302	6,768
1863	LaSalle College, Philadelphia (R.C.)	200	6,725
1866	Lehigh University, Bethlehem (non-sect.)	349	6,355

Founded	Institutions	Faculty (Autumn 1983)	Students (Autumn 1983)
1871	West Chester University of Pennsylvania	457	9,586
1875	Indiana University of Pennsylvania	639	12,526
1878	Duquesne University, Pittsburgh (R.C.)	274	6,362
1884	Temple University, Philadelphia	1,140	28,900
1885	Bryn Mawr College	131	1,832
1888	University of Scranton (R.C.)	174	4,801
1891	Drexel University, Philadelphia	341	12,682
1900	Carnegie-Mellon University, Philadelphia	440	5,998

Health. In 1983 the state had 226 hospitals (54,617 beds) listed by the State Health Department, excluding federal hospitals and mental institutions.

Social Security. During the year ending 30 June 1983 the monthly average number of cases receiving public assistance was: aid to families with dependent children, 577,740; blind pension, 4,455; general assistance, 186,771.

Payments for medical assistance for the year ending 30 June 1983 totalled $2,067m. Under the medical assistance programme payments are made for inpatient hospital care ($683·6m.); care in public institutions (nursing homes, mental institutions and geriatric centres) ($697m.); private nursing home care ($345m.); other medical care ($356·7m.).

Books of Reference

Encyclopaedia of Pennsylvania, New York, 1984
Pennsylvania Manual. General Services, Bureau of Publications, Harrisburg. Biennial
Pennsylvania's Regions, A Survey of the Commonwealth. State Planning Board. Harrisburg, 1967
Pennsylvania Statistical Abstract. Dept. of Commerce, Harrisburg. Annual
Pennsylvania State Industrial Directory. New York. Annual
Cochran, T. C., *Pennsylvania,* New York, 1978
Klein, P. S., and Hoogenboom, A., *A History of Pennsylvania.* New York, 1973
League of Women Voters of Pennsylvania, *Key to the Keystone State.* Philadelphia, 1972
Majumdar, S. K., and Miller, E. W., *Pennsylvania Coal: Resources, Technology and Utilisation.* Pennsylvania Science, 1983
Pennsylvania Chamber of Commerce, *Pennsylvania Government Today.* State College, Pa., 1973
Weigley, R. F., (ed.) *Philadelphia: A 300-year History.* New York, 1984
Wilkinson, N. B., *Bibliography of Pennsylvania History.* Pa. Historical & Museum Commission. Harrisburg, 1957

RHODE ISLAND

HISTORY The earliest settlers in the region which now forms the state of Rhode Island were colonists from Massachusetts who had been driven forth on account of their non-acceptance of the prevailing religious beliefs. The first of the settlements was made in 1636, settlers of every creed being welcomed. In 1647 a patent was executed for the government of the settlements, and on 8 July 1663 a charter was executed recognizing the settlers as forming a body corporate and politic by the name of the 'English Colony of Rhode Island and Providence Plantations, in New England, in America'. On 29 May 1790 the state accepted the federal constitution and entered the Union as the last of the 13 original states.

AREA AND POPULATION. Rhode Island is bounded north and east by Massachusetts, south by the Atlantic and west by Connecticut. Area, 1,214 sq. miles, of which 165 sq. miles are inland water. Census population, 1 April 1980, 947,154 a decrease of 0·3% since 1970. Estimate (1983), 950,000.

Births, 1983, were 13,060; deaths (excluding foetal deaths), 9,486; infant deaths, 157; marriages, 8,043; divorces, 3,521.

Population of 5 census years was:

	White	Negro	Indian	Asiatic	Total	Per sq. mile
1910	532,492	9,529	284	305	542,610	508·5
1930	677,026	9,913	318	240	687,497	649·3
1960	838,712	18,332	932	1,190	859,488	812·4
1970	914,757	25,338	1,390	5,240	949,723 [1]	905·0
			All other			
1980	896,692	27,584	22,878		947,154	903·0

[1] Through tabulation errors there were 2,998 people unaccounted for, as to race and sex, in 1970.

Of the total population in 1980, 451,251 were male, 824,004 were urban and 665,054 were 20 years of age or older.

The chief cities and their population (census, 1980) are Providence, 156,304; Warwick, 87,127; Cranston, 71,992; Pawtucket, 71,204; East Providence, 59,980; Woonsocket, 45,914; Newport, 29,259; North Providence (town), 29,188; Cumberland (town), 27,069. The Providence–Pawtucket–Warwick Standard Metropolitan Statistical Area had a population of 919,216 in 1980.

CLIMATE. Providence. Jan. 28°F (−2·2°C), July 72°F (22·2°C). Annual rainfall 43″ (1,079 mm). *See* New England, p. 1373.

CONSTITUTION AND GOVERNMENT. The present constitution dates from 1843; it has had 36 amendments. The General Assembly consists of a Senate of 50 members and a House of Representatives of 100 members, both elected for 2 years, as are also the Governor and Lieut.-Governor. Every citizen, 18 years of age, who has resided in the state for 30 days, and is duly registered, is qualified to vote.

Rhode Island sends to Congress 2 senators and 2 representatives.

At the 1984 presidential election Reagan polled 212,080 votes, Mondale, 197,106.

The capital is Providence. The state has 5 counties (unique in having no political functions) and 39 cities and towns.

Governor: Edward DiPrete (R.), 1985–87 ($49,500).
Lieut.-Governor: Richard Licht (D.), 1985–87 ($35,500).
Secretary of State: Susan Farmer (R.), 1985–87 ($35,500).

BUDGET. For the fiscal year ending 30 June 1984 (Office of the State Controller) total revenues were $1,272·4m. (taxation, $791·5m., and federal aid, $310·5m.); general expenditures were $1,241·8m. (education, $347·6m.; highways, $65·8m.; and public welfare, $378m.).

Total net long-term debt on 30 June 1984 was $245·3m.

Per capita personal income (1983) was $11,670.

NATURAL RESOURCES

Minerals. The small mineral output, mostly stone, sand and gravel, was valued (1984) at $9·1m.

Agriculture. While Rhode Island is predominantly a manufacturing state, agriculture contributed $33·1m. to the general cash income in 1983. In 1982 it had 728 farms with an area of 80,000 acres (12% of the total land area), of which 31,000 acres were crop land; the average farm was 86 acres.

Fisheries. In 1983 the catch was 113m. lb (live weight) valued at $66m.

INDUSTRY. Total non-agricultural employment in 1984 was 403,600, of which 119,600 were manufacturing, 284,000 non-manufacturing. Manufacturing firms totalled 3,039; average weekly earnings for production workers in manufacturing, $283.50; value added by manufacture (1980), $3,545m. Principal industries are metals and machinery, textiles and jewellery–silverware.

COMMUNICATIONS

Roads. The state had (1 Jan. 1983) 6,396 miles of road, of which 1,366 were state-owned. In 1983, 630,000 motor vehicles were registered.

Railways. In 1984, 5 railways operated 135 line-miles.

Aviation. In 1984 there were 6 state-owned airports. Theodore Francis Green airport at Warwick, near Providence, is served by 10 airlines, and handled 989,000 passengers and 13m. lb. of freight in 1984.

Shipping. Waterborne freight through the Port of Providence (1983) totalled 2m. tons.

Broadcasting. There are 24 radio stations and 5 television stations in the state.

JUSTICE, RELIGION, EDUCATION AND WELFARE

Justice. The state's penal institutions, Dec. 1982, had 781 inmates (81 per 100,000 population).

The death penalty is illegal, except that it is mandatory in the case of murder committed by a prisoner serving a life sentence.

Religion. Chief religious bodies are (estimated figures Sept. 1984): Roman Catholic with 550,000 members; Protestant Episcopal (baptized persons), 50,000; Baptist, 22,500; Congregational, 12,000; Methodist, 10,000; Jewish, 24,000.

Education. In 1982–83 the 223 public elementary schools had 3,756 teachers and total enrolment of 64,563 pupils; about 22,000 pupils were enrolled in private and parochial schools. The 60 senior and vocational high schools had 3,834 teachers and 67,833 pupils. Teachers' salaries (1983) averaged $23,200. Local expenditure, for schools (including evening schools) in 1982–83 totalled $419·1m.

There are 12 institutions of higher learning in the state, including 1 junior college. The state maintains Rhode Island College, at Providence, with 800 faculty members, and 8,500 full-time students (1984), and the University of Rhode Island, at South Kingstown, with over 900 faculty members and over 14,000 students (including graduate students). Brown University, at Providence, founded in 1764, is now non-sectarian; in 1984 it had over 500 full-time faculty members and 6,000 full-time students. Providence College, at Providence, founded in 1917 by the Order of Preachers (Dominican), had (1984) 250 professors and 4,000 students. The largest of the other colleges are Bryant College, at Smithfield, with 125 faculty and over 4,600 students, and the Rhode Island School of Design, in Providence, with about 100 faculty and 1,400 students.

Health. In 1984 the state had 22 hospitals (over 7,000 beds), including 4 mental hospitals.

Social Security. In 1982 aid to dependent children was granted to 44,900 children in 15,800 families at an average payment per family of $345 per month, and the state also had a general assistance programme. (All other aid programmes were taken over by the federal government.)

Books of Reference

Rhode Island Manual. Prepared by the Secretary of State. Providence
Providence Journal Almanac: A Reference Book for Rhode Islanders. Providence. Annual
Rhode Island Basic Economic Statistics. Rhode Island Dept. of Economic Development. Providence, 1982–83
McLoughlin, W. G., *Rhode Island: a History.* Norton, 1978
Wright, M. I., and Sullivan, R. J., *Rhode Island Atlas.* Rhode Island Pubs., 1983

State Library: Rhode Island State Library, State House, Providence 02908. State Librarian: Elliott E. Andrews.

SOUTH CAROLINA

HISTORY. South Carolina, first settled permanently in 1670, was one of the 13 original states of the Union.

AREA AND POPULATION. South Carolina is bounded in the north by North Carolina, east and south-east by the Atlantic, south-west and west by Georgia. Area, 31,113 sq. miles, of which 909 sq. miles are inland water. Census population, 1 April 1980, 3,121,833, an increase of 20·5 since 1970. Estimate (1983) 3,204,094. Births, 1983, were 50,731 (15·3 per 1,000 population); deaths, 26,130 (7·9); infant deaths, 730 (15 per 1,000 live births); marriages, 53,691 (16·2); divorces and annulments, 13,601 (4·1).

The population in 5 census years was:

	White	*Negro*	*Indian*	*Asiatic*	*Total*	*Per sq. mile*
1910	679,161	835,843	331	65	1,515,400	49·7
1930	944,049	793,681	959	76	1,738,765	56·8
1960	1,551,022	829,291	1,098	946	2,382,594	78·7
			All others			
1970	1,794,432	789,040	3,588		2,587,060	83·2
1980	2,150,507	948,623	22,703		3,121,833	100·3

Of the total population in 1980, 49% were male, 54·1% were urban and 55% were 25 years old or older.

Populations of large towns at the 1980 census (with those of associated metropolitan areas): Columbia (capital), 101,457 (422,900); Charleston, 70,776 (455,300); Greenville, 57,490; Spartanburg, 43,522 (Greenville–Spartanburg, 581,053).

CLIMATE. Columbia. Jan. 47°F (8·3°C), July 81°F (27·2°C). Annual rainfall 45″ (1,125 mm). *See* Atlantic Coast, p. 1373.

CONSTITUTION AND GOVERNMENT. The present constitution dates from 1895, when it went into force without ratification by the electorate. The General Assembly consists of a Senate of 46 members, elected for 4 years, and a House of Representatives of 124 members, elected for 2 years. The Governor and Lieut.-Governor are elected for 4 years. Only registered citizens have the right to vote. South Carolina sends to Congress 2 senators and 6 representatives.

At the 1984 presidential election Reagan polled 615,539 votes, Mondale 344,459 and Bergland 4,359.

The capital is Columbia.

Governor: Richard W. Riley (D.), 1983–87 ($60,000).
Secretary of State: John Tucker Campbell (D.), 1983–87 ($55,000).

BUDGET. For the fiscal year ending 30 June 1984 general revenues were $2,210m.; general expenditures were $2,110·7m.

On 30 June 1984 the total bonded debt was $611·6m.

Per capita personal income (1982) was $8,475.

NATURAL RESOURCES

Minerals. Non-metallic minerals are of chief importance: value of mineral output in 1983 was $230·6m., chiefly from limestone for cement, clay, stone, sand and gravel. Production of kaolin, vermiculite, scrap mica and fuller's earth is also important.

Agriculture. In 1984 there were 28,000 farms covering a farm area of 6m. acres. The average farm was of 190 acres. Of the 24,931 farms of the 1982 Census of Agriculture, there were 1,030 of 1,000 acres or more, average farm 224 acres; owners operated 14,761 farms; tenants 2,160. There were 2,334 farms with $100,000 or more in value of sales.

Cash receipts from farm marketing in 1982 amounted to $601·8m. for crops and $366·6m. for livestock, including poultry. Chief crops are tobacco ($205m.), soybeans ($200m.), and corn ($62m.). Production, 1982: Cotton 147,822 bales; peaches, 144m. lb.; soybeans, 29m. bu.; tobacco, 119·78m. lb.; eggs, 1,656m. bu. Livestock on farms, 1982: 660,000 all cattle, 440,000 swine.

Forestry. The forest industry is important; state and private forest land (1983), 12·5m. acres. National forests amounted to 610,294 acres.

INDUSTRY. A monthly average of 363,364 workers were employed in manufacturing in 1983, earning $6,096·3m. Major sectors are textiles (31·3%), apparel (13%) and chemicals (8·9%).

Tourism is important; tourists spent an estimated $2,600m. in 1983.

COMMUNICATIONS

Roads. Total highway mileage in the combined highway system in 1983 was 39,824 miles. Motor vehicle registrations numbered 2m. in 1982.

Railways. In 1984 the length of railway in the state was about 3,000 miles.

Aviation. In 1984 there were 73 public airports, 58 private airports and 11 private heliports, and 1,120 registered aircraft.

Shipping. The state has 3 deep-water ports.

JUSTICE, RELIGION, EDUCATION AND WELFARE

Justice. In Sept. 1984 penal institutions held 8,367 inmates.

Education. In 1983–84 the total public-school enrolment (K-12) was 618,590; there were 358,227 white pupils and 260,363 non-white pupils. The total number of teachers was 31,859; average salary was $17,384.

For higher education the state operates the University of South Carolina, founded at Columbia in 1801, with, 1983–84, 24,296 enrolled students; Clemson University, founded in 1889, with 12,459 students; The Citadel, at Charleston, with 3,040 students; Winthrop College, Rock Hill, with 4,999 students; Medical University of S. Carolina, at Charleston 2,254 students; S. Carolina State College, at Orangeburg, with 4,123 students, and Francis Marion College, at Florence, with 3,131 students; the College of Charleston has 5,323 students and Lander College, Greenwood, 2,136. There are 16 technical institutions (34,965).

There are also 472 private kindergartens, elementary and high schools with total enrolment (1983–84) of 51,219 pupils, and 31 private and denominational colleges and junior colleges with (1983–84) enrolment of 27,503 students.

Health. In 1984 the state had 181 hospitals and nursing homes and 108 intermediate care institutions licensed by the South Carolina Department of Health and Environmental Control

Social Security. In 1983 (preliminary) there were 462,000 recipients of social security benefits. The average monthly expenditure in benefits was $163m.

Books of Reference

Reports of the South Carolina State Development Board. Columbia. Annual
South Carolina Legislative Manual. Columbia. Annual
South Carolina Statistical Abstract, 1983. South Carolina Budget and Control Board, Columbia, 1983

Jones, L., *South Carolina: A Synoptic History for Laymen.* Lexington, 1978
League of Women Voters of South Carolina, *Know Your State.* Columbia, 2nd ed., 1977
State Library. South Carolina State Library, Columbia.

SOUTH DAKOTA

HISTORY. South Dakota was first visited by Europeans in 1743 when Verendrye planted a lead plate (discovered in 1913) on the site of Fort Pierre, claiming the region for the French crown. Beginning with a trading post in 1794, it was settled from 1857 to 1861 when Dakota Territory was organized. It was admitted into the Union on 2 Nov. 1889.

AREA AND POPULATION. South Dakota is bounded north by North Dakota, east by Minnesota, south-east by the Big Sioux River (forming the boundary with Iowa), south by Nebraska (with the Missouri River forming part of the boundary) and west by Wyoming and Montana. Area, 77,116 sq. miles, of which 1,164 sq. miles are water. Area administered by the Bureau of Indian Affairs, 1980, covered 5m. acres (10% of the state), of which 2·6m. acres were held by tribes. The federal government, 1979, owned 3,492,000 acres or 7·1% of the total.

Census population, 1 April 1980, 690,178, an increase of 3·5% since 1970. Estimate (1981) 686,000. Births, 1982, were 12,839 (18·6 per 1,000 population); deaths, 6,588 (9·5); infant deaths, 131 (10·2 per 1,000 live births); marriages, 8,353 (12·1); divorces, 2,564 (3·7).

Population in 5 federal censuses was:

	White	*Negro*	*Indian*	*Asiatic*	*Total*	*Per sq. mile*
1910	563,771	817	19,137	163	583,888	7·6
1930	669,453	646	21,833	101	692,849	9·0
1960	653,098	1,114	25,794	336	680,514	8·9
			All others			
1970	630,333	1,627	34,297		666,257	8·8
1980	638,955	2,144	49,079		690,178	9·0

Of the total population in 1980, 340,370 were male, 320,223 were urban and 441,851 were 21 years of age or older.

Population of the chief cities (census of 1980) was: Sioux Falls, 81,071; Rapid City, 46,340; Aberdeen, 25,973; Watertown, 15,632, Mitchell, 13,917; Brookings, 14,915; Huron, 13,000.

CLIMATE. Rapid City. Jan. 25°F (–3·9°C), July 73°F (22·8°C). Annual rainfall 19″ (474 mm). Sioux Falls. Jan. 14°F (–10°C), July 73°F (22·8°C). Annual rainfall 25″ (625 mm). *See* High Plains, p. 1372.

CONSTITUTION AND GOVERNMENT. Voters are all citizens 18 years of age or older who have complied with certain residential qualifications. The people reserve the right of the initiative and referendum. The Senate has 35 members, and the House of Representatives 70 members, all elected for 2 years; the Governor and Lieut.-Governor are elected for 4 years. The state sends 2 senators and 1 representative to Congress.

In the 1984 presidential election Reagan polled 198,119 votes, Mondale, 114,967.

The capital is Pierre (population, 1980, 11,973). The state is divided into 66 organized counties.

Governor: William Janklow (R.), 1983–86 ($50,975).
Lieut.-Governor: Lowell Hansen, 1983–86 ($7,075 plus expense allowance).
Secretary of State: Alice Kundert, 1983–86 ($34,600).

BUDGET. For the fiscal year ending 30 June 1983 general revenues were $627·8m. and expenditures, $544·7m. Taxes and fees from state sources furnished $273·7m. and federal receipts $268·3m.

Per capita personal income (1981) was $8,833.

NATURAL RESOURCES

Minerals. The mineral products include gold (185,038 troy oz. in 1982, second largest yield of all states), silver (26,000 troy oz.). Mineral products, 1982, were valued at $135·6m., of which gold accounts for $69·5m.

Agriculture. In 1982, 37,148 farms had an acreage of 45m.; the average farm had 1,179 acres. Farm units are large; in 1982 there were only 4,024 farms of 50 acres or less, compared with 10,165 exceeding 1,000 acres. 17,371 farms sold produce valued at $40,000 or over.

South Dakota ranks first in the US as producer of oats (133·8m. bu. in 1982) and rye (4·68m. bu.) and second in flaxseed (3·33m. bu.) and hay (8·63m. tons). The other important crops (1982) are sorghum (17·25m. bu.), and sunflower seeds (659·98m. bu.) The farm livestock on 1 Jan. 1983 included 4·06m. cattle, 680,000 sheep, 1·51m. swine.

Forestry. National forest area, 1981, 1,998,000 acres.

INDUSTRY. In 1982, manufacturing establishments had 24,881 workers who earned $398·2m. Food processing is by far the largest industry with 96 plants employing 7,678 workers. There are 168 printing and publishing plants employing 2,423 workers. Also significant are dairy, lumber and wood products, machinery, transport equipment, electronics, stone, glass and clay products.

COMMUNICATIONS

Roads. Total highway mileage was 17,056 in 1981. Registered passenger cars numbered 637,000 in 1981.

Railways. In 1983 there were 1,927 miles of railway in operation. The state owns 837·8 miles of track of which 435 miles is operating.

Aviation. In 1981 there were 69 general aviation airports and 9 air carrier airports.

JUSTICE, RELIGION, EDUCATION AND WELFARE

Justice. The State prisons had, in 1982, 693 inmates. The death penalty was illegal from 1915 to 1938; since 1938, one person has been executed, in 1949 (by electrocution), for murder.

Religion. The chief religious bodies are: Lutherans, Roman Catholics, Methodist, Disciples of Christ, Presbyterian, Baptist and Episcopal.

Education. Elementary and secondary education are free from 6 to 21 years of age. Between the ages of 8 and 16, attendance is compulsory. In 1982–83 128,625 pupils were attending elementary and high (including parochial) schools (8,124 full-time equivalent classroom teachers)

Teachers' salaries (1981–82) averaged an estimated $14,717. Total expenditure on public schools (1982–83), $362·7m.

The School of Mines at Rapid City, established 1885, had, spring 1984, 2,694 students; the State University at Brookings, 6,554 students; the University of South Dakota, founded at Vermillion in 1882, 5,753 students; Northern State College, 2,571 students; Black Hills State College, 2,072 students; Dakota State College, 1,081 students. The 9 private colleges had 6,041 students. The federal Government maintains Indian schools on its reservations and 2 outside at Flandreau and Pierre.

Health. In Aug. 1983 the state Health Department listed 57 licensed hospitals (3,572 licensed beds).

Social Security. In financial year 1982–83, 37,259 aged persons received $3,829,956; 1,623 blind persons received $339,744; 49,910 disabled persons received $8,627,820. Aid to dependent children was $17,542,976, to 11,554 children.

Books of Reference

Governor's Budget Report. South Dakota Bureau of Finance and Management. Annual
South Dakota Historical Collections. 1902–80
South Dakota Legislative Manual. Secretary of State, Pierre, S.D. Biennial
Berg, F. M., *South Dakota: Land of Shining Gold.* Hettinger, 1982
Karolevitz, Robert F., *Challenge: the South Dakota Story.* Sioux Falls, 1975
Milton, John R., *South Dakota; a Bicentennial History.* New York, W. W. Norton, 1977
Schell, H. S., *History of South Dakota.* 3rd ed. Lincoln, Neb., 1975
Vexler, R. I., *South Dakota Chronology and Factbook.* New York, 1978

State Library: South Dakota State Library, State Library Building, Pierre, S.D., 57501. *State Librarian:* Clarence L. Coffindaffer.

TENNESSEE

HISTORY. Tennessee, first settled in 1757, was admitted into the Union on 1 June 1796.

AREA AND POPULATION. Tennessee is bounded north by Kentucky and Virginia, east by North Carolina, south by Georgia, Alabama and Mississippi and west by the Mississippi River (forming the boundary with Arkansas and Missouri). Area, 42,144 sq. miles (989 sq. miles water). Census population, 1 April 1980, 4,591,120, an increase of 665,102 or 16·9% since 1970. Estimate (1984), 4,716,752. Vital statistics, 1983 (provisional): Births, 65,724 (13·9 per 1,000 population); deaths, 41,461 (8·8); infant deaths 880 (13·4 per 1,000 live births); marriages, 55,840 (23·6); divorces, 28,199 (11·9).

Population in 6 census years was:

	White	*Negro*	*Indian*	*Asiatic*	*Total*	*Per sq. mile*
1910	1,711,432	473,088	216	53	2,184,789	52·4
1930	2,138,644	477,646	161	105	2,616,556	62·4
1950	2,760,257	530,603	339	334	3,291,718	78·8
1960	2,977,753	586,876	638	1,243	3,567,089	85·4
			All others			
1970	3,293,930	621,261	8,496		3,923,687	95·3
1980	3,835,452	725,942	29,726		4,591,120	111·6

Of the population in 1980, 2,216,600 were male, 2,773,573 were urban and those 21 years of age or older numbered 3,026,398.

The cities, with population, 1980, are Memphis, 646,356; Nashville (capital), 455,651; Knoxville, 175,030; Chattanooga, 169,565; Clarksville, 54,777; Jackson, 49,131; Johnson City, 39,753; Murfreesboro, 32,845; Kingsport, 32,027; Oak Ridge, 27,662. Standard metropolitan areas (1980): Memphis, 810,043; Nashville, 850,505; Knoxville, 476,517; Chattanooga, 320,761; Johnson City–Bristol–Kingsport, 343,041; Clarksville, 83,342.

CLIMATE. Memphis. Jan. 41°F (5°C), July 82°F (27·8°C). Annual rainfall 49" (1,221 mm). Nashville. Jan. 39°F (3·9°C), July 79°F (26·1°C). Annual rainfall 48" (1,196 mm). *See* Appalachian Mountains, p. 1373.

CONSTITUTION AND GOVERNMENT. The state has operated under 3 constitutions, the last of which was adopted in 1870 and has been since amended 22 times (first in 1953). Voters at an election may authorize the calling of a convention limited to altering or abolishing one or more specified sections of the constitution. The General Assembly consists of a Senate of 33 members and a House of Representatives of 99 members, senators elected for 4 years and representatives for 2 years. Qualified as electors are all citizens (with the usual residential and age (18) qualifications). Tennessee sends to Congress 2 senators and 9 representatives.

In the 1984 presidential election Reagan polled 990,212 votes, Mondale, 711,714.

For the Tennessee Valley Authority *see* pp. 1400–01.

The capital is Nashville. The state is divided into 95 counties.

Governor: Andrew Lamar Alexander (R.), 1983–86 ($68,226).
Lieut.-Governor: John S. Wilder (D.), 1983–86 ($8,308).
Secretary of State: Gentry Crowell (D.), ($51,510).

BUDGET. For 1981–82 total revenue was $4,521·3m.; general expenditure, $4,298·4m.

Total net long-term debt on 30 June 1982 amounted to $1,350m.

Per capita personal income (1983) was $9,362.

ENERGY AND NATURAL RESOURCES

Minerals. Total value of mineral production 1980: fuel minerals (mainly coal), $280m.; non-fuel (mainly stone and zinc), $408m.

Agriculture. In 1982, 90,564 farms covered 12·47m. acres. The average farm was of 138 acres (only a few states had a smaller average) valued, land and buildings, at $1,014 per acre.

Cash income (1982) from crops was $848·8m.; from livestock, $835m. Main crops were cotton, tobacco and soybeans.

On 1 Jan. 1982 the domestic animals included 217,234 milch cows, 2·2m. all cattle, 11,385 sheep, 866,226m. swine.

Forestry. Forests occupy 13·16m. acres (50% of total land area). The forest industry and industries dependent on it employ about 40,000 workers, earning $150m. per year. Wood products are valued at over $500m. per year. National forest system land (1981) 623,000 acres.

INDUSTRY. The manufacturing industries include iron and steel working, but the most important products are chemicals, including synthetic fibres and allied products, electrical equipment and food. In 1980, manufacturing establishments employed 491,000 workers; value added by manufactures was $16,138m.

TOURISM. 22·2m. out-of-state tourists spent $3,000m. in 1983.

COMMUNICATIONS

Roads. In 1982 there were 83,757 miles of municipal and rural roads. The state is served by 115 intrastate bus companies and 31 privately owned internal bus services.

Motor-vehicle registrations, 1983, totalled 3,849,449, of which 3,232,032 were cars.

Railways. The state had (1982) 5,696 miles of track on 10 railways.

Aviation. The state is served by 11 major airlines. In 1981 there were 74 public airports and 78 private; there were 71 heliports and 2 military air bases.

JUSTICE, RELIGION, EDUCATION AND WELFARE

Justice. There has been no execution since 1960; since 1930 there have been 22 whites and 44 Negroes executed (by electrocution) for murder and 5 whites and 22 Negroes for rape. A US Supreme Court ruling prohibits the use of capital punishment under present Tennessee law, except for first degree murder.

Prison population, 31 July 1984, 7,488.

The law prohibiting the inter-marriage of white and Negro was declared unconstitutional by the US Supreme Court in June 1967.

Religion. The leading religious bodies are the Southern Baptists, Methodists and Negro Baptists.

Education. School attendance has been compulsory since 1925 and the employment of children under 16 years of age in workshops, factories or mines is illegal.

In 1982–83 there were 1,691 public schools with a net enrolment of 860,708 pupils. In 1982–3 46,691 teachers earned an average salary of $17,697·58. Total expenditure for operating county and city public schools (kindergarten to Grade 12) in 1982–83, $1,658·5m. Tennessee has 49 accredited colleges and universities, 18 2-year colleges and 28 vocational schools. The universities include the University of Tennessee, Knoxville (founded 1794), with 26,752 students in 1982–83; Vanderbilt University, Nashville (1873) with 8,782, Tennessee State University (1912) with 8,011, the University of Tennessee at Chattanooga (1886) with 7,543 and Fisk University (1866) with 743.

Health. In 1983 the state had 150 hospitals with 27,806 beds. State facilities for the mentally retarded had 2,174 resident patients; mental hospitals had 3,200 (1 Jan. 1980).

Social Security. In 1980 Tennessee paid $2,233m. to retired workers and their survivors and to disabled workers. Total beneficiaries: 448,000 retired; 169,000 survivors and 122,000 disabled. 354,000 people received $380m. in Medicaid. 56,000 families received aid to dependent children ($85m.). Supplemental Security Income ($198·7m.) was paid to 130,600.

Books of Reference

Tennessee Dept. of Finance and Administration, Annual Report, Annual
Dept. of Education Annual Report for Tennessee, Annual
Tennessee Blue Book. Secretary of State, Nashville
Tennessee Statistical Abstract, Center for Business and Economic Research, Univ. of Tennessee. Annual

Corlew, R. E., *Tennessee: A Short History.* Univ. Tennessee, 2nd ed., 1981
Davidson, D., *Tennessee: Vol. I, The Old River Frontier to Secession,* Univ. Tennessee, 1979
Dykeman, W., *Tennessee,* Rev. Ed., New York, 1984
State Library: State Library and Archives, Nashville. *Librarian:* Miss O. Young. *State Historian:* Wilma Dykeman.

TEXAS

HISTORY. In 1836 Texas declared its independence of Mexico, and after maintaining an independent existence, as the Republic of Texas, for 10 years, it was on 29 Dec. 1845 received as a state into the American Union. The state's first settlement dates from 1686.

AREA AND POPULATION. Texas is bounded north by Oklahoma, north-east by Arkansas, east by Louisiana, south-east by the Gulf of Mexico, south by Mexico and west by New Mexico. Area, 266,807 sq. miles (including 4,790 sq. miles of inland water). Census population, 1 April 1980 (provisional), 14,228,383, an increase of 27% since 1970. Estimate (1982), 15,280,000. Vital statistics for 1980: Births, 268,717 (18·9 per 1,000 population); deaths, 108,586 (7·6); infant deaths, 3,226 (12 per 1,000 live births); marriages, 187,118 (13·2); divorces, 97,161 (6·8).

Population for 5 census years was:

	White	*Negro*	*Indian*	*Asiatic*	*Total*	*Per sq. mile*
1910	3,204,848	690,049	702	943	3,896,542	14·8
1930	4,967,172	854,964	1,001	1,578	5,824,715	22·1
1960	8,374,831	1,187,125	5,750	9,848	9,579,677	36·5
			All others			
1970	9,717,128	1,399,005	80,597		11,196,730	42·7
1980	11,197,663	1,710,250	1,320,470		14,228,383	54·2

Of the population in 1980, 6,998,301 were male, 11,327,159 persons were urban. Those 20 years old and older numbered 9,357,309. A census report, 1980, showed, 2,985,643 persons of Spanish origin.

The largest cities, with census population in 1980, are:

Houston	1,554,992	Amarillo	149,167	Odessa	89,797
Dallas	901,450	Beaumont	118,031	Garland	138,749
San Antonio	783,296	Wichita Falls	93,543	Laredo	91,229
Fort Worth	382,349	Irving	109,575	San Angelo	72,655
El Paso	424,522	Waco	101,267	Galveston	61,601
Austin (capital)	343,390	Arlington	159,117	Midland	70,291
Corpus Christi	230,715	Abilene	98,231	Tyler	70,720
Lubbock	174,157	Pasadena	111,884	Port Arthur	61,106

Larger urbanized areas, 1980: Houston, 2,891,146; Dallas-Fort Worth, 2,964,342; San Antonio, 1,070,245.

CLIMATE. Dallas. Jan. 45°F (7·2°C), July 84°F (28·9°C). Annual rainfall 38″ (945 mm). El Paso. Jan. 44°F (6·7°C), July 81°F (27·2°C). Annual rainfall 9″ (221 mm). Galveston. Jan. 54°F (12·2°C), July 84°F (28·9°C). Annual rainfall 46″ (1,159 mm). Houston. Jan. 52°F (11·1°C), July 83°F (28·3°C). Annual rainfall 48″ (1,200 mm). *See* Central Plains, p. 1372.

CONSTITUTION AND GOVERNMENT. The present constitution dates from 1876; it has been amended 233 times. The Legislature consists of a Senate of 31 members elected for 4 years (half their number retire every 2 years), and a House of Representatives of 150 members elected for 2 years.

The Governor and Lieut.-Governor are elected for 4 years. Qualified electors are all citizens with the usual residential qualifications. Texas sends to Congress 2 senators and 27 representatives.

In the 1984 presidential election Reagan polled 3,301,024 votes, Mondale, 1,873,499.

The capital is Austin. The state has 254 counties.

Governor: Mark White (D.), 1983–86 ($88,900).
Lieut.-Governor: William P. Hobby (D.), 1983–86 ($7,200).
Secretary of State: John W. Fainter, Jr. (D.), ($61,200).

BUDGET. In the fiscal year ending 31 Aug. 1982 general revenues were $23,617m. ($13,671m. from taxes, $4,154m. federal aid); general expenditures, $21,334m. ($8,743m. on education, $2,506m. on highways, $2,067m. on hospitals, $1,741m. on public welfare). Texas has a large revenue derived from the severance tax (*i.e.*, tax on the removal of oil, natural gas and sulphur from the soil or waters of the state).

Net long-term debt, 31 Aug. 1982, was $22,516m.

Per capita personal income (1982) was $11,419.

ENERGY AND NATURAL RESOURCES

Minerals. In 1975 Texas had 31% of proved US crude oil reserves. Production, 1981: Crude petroleum, 945m. bbls. Other mineral products include natural gas (7,010,000 m.c.f.), natural gasoline, butane and propane gases, helium, crude gypsum, granite and sandstone, salt and cement. Total value of mineral products in 1981, $48,708m., of which $47,050 was for fuels.

Agriculture. Texas is one of the most important agricultural states of the Union. In 1983 it had 184,000 farms covering 138m. acres; average farm was of 752 acres valued, land and buildings, at $593 per acre. Large-scale commercial farms, highly mechanized, dominate in Texas; farms of 1,000 acres or more in number far exceed that of any other state. But small-scale farming persists.

Soil erosion is serious in some parts. For some 97,297,000 acres drastic curative treatment has been indicated and for 51,164,000 acres, preventive treatment.

Production, 1983: Cotton, 2,391,500 bales (of 480 lb); maize (104·7m. bu.), wheat (161m. bu.), oats (24m. bu.) and barley (2·5m. bu.), soybeans (9·6m. bu.), peanuts, oranges, grapefruit, peaches, potatoes, sweet potatoes.

Cash income, 1983, from crops was $3,448·2m.; from livestock, $5,522·2m.

The state has a very great livestock industry, leading in the number of all cattle, 15m. on 1 Jan. 1983, and sheep, 2·2m.; it also had 335,000 milch cows, and 550,000 swine.

Forestry. There were (1980) 23·3m. acres of forested land.

INDUSTRY. In 1980 manufacturing establishments employed 1m. workers; value added by manufacturing, $47,145m. Chemical industries along the Gulf Coast, such as the production of synthetic rubber and of primary magnesium (from sea-water), are increasingly important.

COMMUNICATIONS

Roads. In 1979 there were 264,900 miles of roads including 199,500 miles of rural roads. Motor registration in 1980, 10·2m.

Railways. The railways (1974) had a total mileage of 19,134 miles, of which 13,303 miles were main lines.

Aviation. In 1981 there were 322 public and 1,109 private airports.

Shipping. The port of Houston, connected by the Houston Ship Channel (50 miles long) with the Gulf of Mexico, is the largest inland cotton market in the world. Cargo handled 1981, 100·9m. tonnes.

JUSTICE, RELIGION, EDUCATION AND WELFARE

Justice. On 31 Dec. 1982 the state prison held 36,149 men and women. Execution is by lethal injection; there were 300 between 1930 and 1968; between 1977 and 1984 there were 2.

Texas has adopted 11 laws governing the activities of trade unions. An Act of 1955 forbids the state's payment of unemployment compensation to workers engaged in certain types of strikes.

Religion. The largest religious bodies are Roman Catholics, Baptists, Methodists, Churches of Christ, Lutherans, Presbyterians and Episcopalians.

Education. School attendance is compulsory from 7 to 17 years of age.

In autumn 1982 public elementary and secondary schools had 2,985,659 enrolled pupils and there were 166,961 classroom teachers. Teachers' salaries, 1983, averaged $19,500. Total public school expenditure, 1981, $6,403m.

The state has 157 institutions of higher learning with an estimated enrolment, Sept. 1982, of 759,000 students. The largest institutions, with faculty numbers and student enrolment, spring 1983, were:

Founded	*Institutions*	*Control*	*Faculty*	*Students*
1845	Baylor University, Waco	Baptist	587	10,473
1852	St Mary's University, San Antonio	R.C.	187	3,311
1869	Trinity University, San Antonio	Presb.	316	3,103
1873	Texas Christian University, Fort Worth	Christian	422	6,283
1876	Texas A. and M. Univ., College Station	State	2,093	36,127
1876	Prairie View Agr. and Mech. Coll., Prairie View	State	288	4,495
1879	Sam Houston State University	State	486	9,856
1883	University of Texas System (every campus)	State	10,270	114,800
1890	North Texas State University, Denton	State	1,173	18,782
1891	Hardin-Simmons University, Abilene	Baptist	123	1,948
1889	East Texas State University, Commerce	State	401	7,768
1899	South West Texas State University, San Marcos	State	668	16,038
1903	Texas Woman's University, Denton	State	622	7,827
1906	Abilene Christian College, Abilene	Church of Christ	286	4,546
1911	Southern Methodist University, Dallas	Methodist	622	9,150
1923	Stephen F. Austin State University	State	585	11,881
1923	Texas Technical University, Lubbock	State	1,539	23,000
1925	Texas Arts and Industries University, Kingsville	State	202	5,245
1934	University of Houston, Houston	State	3,236 [1]	49,241 [1]
1947	Texas Southern University, Houston	State	453	9,147
1951	Lamar University, Beaumont	State	650	14,600

[1] 1982.

Health. In 1980, the state had 561 hospitals (81,800 beds) listed by the American Hospital Association; on 1 Jan. 1980 mental hospitals had 6,559 resident patients and state institutions for the mentally retarded, 11,178 resident patients (1980).

Social Security. Aid is from state and federal sources. Old-age assistance (SSI) was being granted in Dec. 1980 to 146,800 persons, who received an average of $101 per month; aid was given to 320,000 dependent children (average payment per family, $109 per month).

Books of Reference

Texas Almanac. Dallas. Biennial
Texas Factbook. Univ. of Texas, 1983
Benton, W. E., *Texas, its Government and Politics.* 4th ed., Englewood Cliffs, 1977
Cruz, G. R. and Irby, J. A. (eds.), *Texas Bibliography.* Austin, 1982
Jordan, T. G., and Bean, J. L., Jr., *Texas.* Boulder, 1983
MacCorkle, S. A., and Smith, D., *Texas Government.* 7th ed. New York, 1974
Richardson, R. N., *Texas, the Lone Star State.* 3rd ed. New York, 1970

Legislative Reference Library: Box 12488, Capitol Station, Austin, Texas 78811. *Director:* James R. Sanders.

UTAH

HISTORY. Utah, which had been acquired by the US during the Mexican war, was settled by Mormons in 1847, and organized as a Territory on 9 Sept. 1850. It was admitted as a state into the Union on 4 Jan. 1896 with boundaries as at present.

AREA AND POPULATION. Utah is bounded north by Idaho and Wyoming, east by Colorado, south by Arizona and west by Nevada. Area, 84,899 sq. miles, of which 2,826 sq. miles are water. The federal government (1967) owned 35,397,274 acres or 67·1% of the area of the state. The area of unappropriated and unreserved lands was 23,268,250 acres in 1974. The Bureau of Indian Affairs in 1974 administered 3,035,190 acres, all of which were allotted to Indian tribes.

Census population, 1 April 1980, 1,461,037, an increase of 38% since 1970. Estimate (1982), 1,554,000. Births in 1980 were 43,708 (29·9 per 1,000 population); deaths, 8,556 (5·9); infant deaths, 505 (11·5 per 1,000 live births); marriages, 17,074 (11·7); divorces, 7,957 (5·4).

Population at 5 federal censuses was:

	White	*Negro*	*Indian*	*Asiatic*	*Total*	*Per sq. mile*
1910	366,583	1,144	3,123	2,501	373,851	4·5
1930	499,967	1,108	2,869	3,903	507,847	6·2
1960	873,828	4,148	6,961	5,207	890,627	10·8
1970	1,031,926	6,617	11,273	6,230	1,059,273	12·9
1980	1,382,550	9,225	19,256	15,076	1,461,037	17·7

Of the total in 1980, 724,501 were male, 1,232,908 persons were urban; 860,304 were 20 years of age or older.

The largest cities are Salt Lake City (capital), with a population (census, 1980) of 162,960; Provo, 74,007; Ogden, 64,444; Bountiful, 32,877; Orem, 52,399; and Logan, 26,844.

CLIMATE. Salt Lake City. Jan. 29°F (−1·7°C), July 77°F (25°C). Annual rainfall 16″ (401 mm). *See* Mountain States, p. 1372.

CONSTITUTION AND GOVERNMENT. Utah adopted its present constitution in 1896 (now with 61 amendments). It sends to Congress 2 senators and 3 representatives.

The Legislature consists of a Senate (in part renewed every 2 years) of 30 members, elected for 4 years, and of a House of Representatives of 75 members elected for 2 years. The Governor is elected for 4 years. The constitution provides for the initiative and referendum. Electors are all citizens, who, not being insane or criminal, have the usual residential qualifications.

The capital is Salt Lake City. There are 29 counties in the state.

In the 1984 presidential election Reagan polled 461,535 votes, Mondale, 154,239.

Governor: Norman Bangerter (R.), 1985–88 ($52,000).
Lieut.-Governor: W. Val Oveson (R.), 1985–88 ($35,500).

BUDGET. For the year ending 30 June 1982 general revenue was $2,490m. ($1,332m. from taxes, $612m. from federal aid) while general expenditures were $2,490m. ($1,104m. on education, $279m. on highways, $234m. on public welfare).

The net long-term debt on 30 June 1982 was about $2,171m.

Per capita personal income (1982) was $8,875.

ENERGY AND NATURAL RESOURCES

Minerals The principal minerals are: copper, gold, petroleum, lead, silver and zinc. The state also has natural gas, clays, tungsten, molybdenum, uranium and phosphate rock. Total value of mineral production, 1981, $2,067m.

Agriculture. In 1983 Utah had 13,000 farms covering 12m. acres, of which about 2m. acres were crop land and about 300,000 acres pasture. About 1m. acres had irrigation; the average farm was of 953 acres.

Of the total surface area, 9% is severely eroded and only 9·4% is free from erosion; the balance is moderately eroded.

Cash income, 1982, from crops, $130m. and from livestock, $412m. The principal crops (1983) are: Barley, 11m. bu.; wheat (spring and winter), 8m. bu.; oats, 884,000 bu.; potatoes, 1·2m. cwt; hay (alfalfa, sweet clover and lespedeza), 270,000 tons; maize, 1·5m. bu. In 1983 there were 565,000 sheep; 84,000 milch cows; 950,000 all cattle; 32,000 swine.

Forestry. Area of national forests, 1981, was 9,129,000 acres, of which 8·05m. acres were under forest service administration.

INDUSTRY. In 1980 manufacturing establishments had 93,000 workers; value added by manufacture was $3,415m. Leading manufactures by value added are primary metals, ordinances and transport, food, fabricated metals and machinery, petroleum products.

COMMUNICATIONS

Roads. The state has about 50,000 miles of highway. In 1980 there were 1,009,000 motor vehicles registered.

Railways. On 1 July 1974 the state had 1,734 miles of railways.

Aviation. In 1981 there were 57 public and 45 private airports.

JUSTICE, RELIGION, EDUCATION AND WELFARE

Justice. The number of inmates of the state prison on 31 Dec. 1982 was 1,199. Since 1930 total executions have been 14 (13 by shooting, 1 by hanging—the condemned man has choice), all whites, and all for murder.

Religion. Latter-day Saints (Mormons) form about 73% of the church membership of the state, with approximately 829,990 members in 1974; their church is a substantial property-owner. There were (1970) about 50,483 Catholics. Most Protestant denominations are represented.

Education. School attendance is compulsory for children from 6 to 18 years of age. There are 40 school districts. Teachers' salaries, 1983, averaged $19,700. There were (autumn 1982) 370,183 pupils in public elementary and secondary schools, and 15,227 classroom teachers. In 1981 estimated public school expenditure was $752m.

The University of Utah (1850) (24,364 students in 1983) is in Salt Lake City; the Utah State University (1890) (11,112 students) is in Logan. The Mormon Church maintains the Brigham Young University at Provo (1875) with 2,700 students. Other colleges include: Westminster College, Salt Lake City, 1,120 students in 1982; Weber State College, Ogden, 10,000; Southern Utah State College, Cedar City, 2,400; College of Eastern Utah, Price, 1,250 in 1982; Snow College, Ephraim, 1,404 in 1982; Dixie College, St George, 2,010; L.D.S. Business College, Salt Lake

City, 895. Total higher education students in 14 institutions, 1981, 97,000. A state bond of $70m. was approved in July 1975 for the University of Utah medical centre.

Health. In 1980, the state had 42 hospitals (5,300 beds) listed by the Utah Department of Social Services. Mental hospitals had 317 resident patients on 1 Jan. 1980; state facilities for the mentally retarded had 763.

Social Security. The state department of public welfare provided assistance during Dec. 1980 to 43,700 persons receiving aid to dependent children at an average $314 per family per month; aid to the aged, the blind and disabled is provided from federal funds.

Books of Reference

Compiled Digest of Administrative Reports. Secretary of State, Salt Lake City. Annual
Statistical Abstract of Government in Utah. Utah Foundation, Salt Lake City. Annual
Utah Agricultural Statistics. Dept. of Agriculture, Salt Lake City. Annual
Utah: Facts. Bureau of Economic and Business Research, Univ. of Utah, 1975
Arrington, L., *Great Basin Kingdom: An Economic History of the Latter-Day Saints, 1830–1900.* Cambridge, Mass., 1958
Petersen, C. S., *Utah, a History.* New York, 1977

VERMONT

HISTORY. Vermont, first settled in 1724, was admitted into the Union as the fourteenth state on 4 March 1791. The first constitution was adopted by convention at Windsor, 2 July 1777, and established an independent state government.

AREA AND POPULATION. Vermont is bounded north by Canada, east by New Hampshire, south by Massachusetts and west by New York. Area, 9,614 sq. miles, of which 341 sq. miles are inland water. Census population, 1 April 1980, 511,456, an increase of 15% since 1970. Estimate (1984) 515,700. Births, 1982, were 8,028 (15·5 per 1,000 population); deaths, 4,479 (8·6); infant deaths, 75 (9·3 per 1,000 live births); marriages, 5,570 (10·7); divorces, 2,620 (5).

Population at 5 census years was:

	White	*Negro*	*Indian*	*Asiatic*	*Total*	*Per sq. mile*
1910	354,298	1,621	26	11	355,956	39·0
1930	358,966	568	36	41	359,611	38·8
1960	389,092	519	57	172	389,881	42·0
1970	442,553	761	229	787	444,732	48·0
1980	506,736	1,135	984	1,355	511,456	55·1

Of the population in 1980, 249,080 were male, 172,735 persons were urban; those 20 years of age or older numbered 343,666. The largest cities are Burlington, with a population in 1980 of 37,712; Rutland, 18,436; Barre, 9,824.

CLIMATE. Burlington. Jan. 17°F (–8·3°C), July 70°F (21·1°C). Annual rainfall 33″ (820 mm). *See* New England, p. 1373.

CONSTITUTION AND GOVERNMENT. The constitution was adopted in 1793 and has since been amended. Amendments are proposed by two-thirds vote of the Senate every 4 years, and must be accepted by two sessions of the legislature; they are then submitted to popular vote. The state Legislature, consisting of a Senate of 30 members and a House of Representatives of 150 members (both elected for 2 years), meets in Jan. in odd-numbered years. The Governor and Lieut.-Governor are elected for 2 years. Electors are all citizens who possess certain residential qualifications and have taken the freeman's oath set forth in the constitution.

The state is divided into 14 counties; there are 251 towns and cities and other minor civil divisions. The state sends to Congress 2 senators and 1 representative, who are elected by the voters of the entire state.

In the 1984 presidential election Reagan polled 134,252 votes, Mondale, 94,518.

The capital is Montpelier (8,241, census of 1980).

Governor: Madeleine Kunin (D.), 1985–87 ($50,003).
Lieut.-Governor: Peter Smith (R.) ($22,006).
Secretary of State: James Douglas (R.) ($29,993).

BUDGET. The total revenue for the year ending 30 June 1984 was $763·9m.; total disbursements, $786·9m.

Total net long-term debt, 1 July 1984, was $273,900,000.

Per capita personal income (1983) was $9,979.

NATURAL RESOURCES

Minerals. Stone, chiefly granite, marble and slate, is the leading mineral produced in Vermont, contributing about 60% of the total value of mineral products. Other products include asbestos, talc, peat, sand and gravel. Total value of mineral products, 1981, $51m.

Agriculture. Agriculture is the most important industry. In 1978 the state had 7,273 farms covering 29·6% of the land area; the average farm was of 241 acres. Cash income, 1981, from livestock and products, $365·4m.; from crops, $30·2m. The dairy farms produce about 2,300m. lb. of milk annually. The chief agricultural crops are hay, apples and maple syrup. In 1981 Vermont had 355,000 cattle, 11,000 sheep, 9,000 swine, 425,000 poultry.

Forestry. In 1982 the harvest was 82m. bd ft hardwood and 93m. bd ft softwood saw-logs, and 267,000 cords of pulpwood and boltwood. About 600,000 cords was cut for firewood.

The state is nearly 80% forest, with 12% in public ownership. National forests area (1983), 285,000 acres. State-owned forests, parks, fish and game areas, 250,000 acres; municipally-owned, 38,500 acres.

INDUSTRY. In 1983, manufacturing establishments employed an average 47,785 workers who earned $926·5m.; main manufactures include machine tools and electronic components.

COMMUNICATIONS

Roads. The state had 14,000 miles of roads in 1984, including 12,900 miles of rural roads. Motor vehicle registrations, 1984, 510,267.

Railways. There were, in 1983, 756 miles of main line railway, 300 of which was leased by the state to private operators.

Aviation. There were 22 airports in 1983, of which 10 were state operated, 2 municipally owned and 10 privately owned but open to public use.

JUSTICE, RELIGION, EDUCATION AND WELFARE

Justice. In financial year 1984 6 prisons and centres had an average of 524 inmates; average total inmates, 576; there were an average of 4,350 people on probation and 313 on parole.

Religion. The principal denominations are Roman Catholic, United Church of Christ, United Methodist, Protestant Episcopal, Baptist and Unitarian–Universalist.

Education. School attendance during the full school term is compulsory for children from 7 to 16 years of age, unless they have completed the 10th grade or undergo approved home instruction. In 1982–83 the public elementary schools had 48,166 enrolled pupils; the public secondary schools had 43,344 pupils; the 82 private schools had 8,580 pupils. Full-time teachers for public elementary schools numbered 2,941, secondary schools 3,310. Teachers' salaries for 1983 averaged $15,794 (elementary) and $16,747 (secondary).

The University of Vermont (1791) had 9,218 full-time students in 1981–82, of whom 7,833 were undergraduates; Middlebury College (1800), 1,932 students; Norwich University (1834 but founded as an academy 1819), 2,308 students (including Vermont College); St Michael's College, 1,721 students; the 5 state colleges, 3,796 students; all other colleges, 3,120.

Health. In Sept. 1983 the state had 16 general hospitals (898 beds), 2 mental hospitals and 1 T.B. hospital. There was 1 federal general hospital with 224 beds.

Social Security. Old-age assistance (SSI) was being granted in 1980 to 2,400 persons, drawing an average of $108 per month; aid to dependent children was being granted to 24,300 persons, drawing an average of $340 per family per month; and aid to the permanently and totally disabled was being granted to 5,200 persons, drawing an average of $192.

Books of Reference

Legislative Directory. Secretary of State, Montpelier. Biennial
Vermont Facts and Figures. Office of Statistical Co-ordination, Montpelier
Vermont Year-Book, formerly *Walton's Register.* Chester. Annual
Bassett T., and Seymour D. (eds.), *Vermont: A Bibliography of its History,* Boston, 1981
Delorme, D. (ed.), *Vermont Atlas and Gazetteer,* Rev. ed., Freeport, 1983
Morrissey, C. T., *Vermont,* New York, 1981

State Library: Vermont Dept. of Libraries, Montpelier. *State Librarian:* Patricia Klinck.

VIRGINIA

HISTORY. The first English Charter for settlements in America was that granted by James I in 1606 for the planting of colonies in Virginia. The state was one of the 13 original states in the Union. Virginia lost just over one-third of its area when West Virginia was admitted into the Union (1863).

AREA AND POPULATION. Virginia is bounded north-west by West Virginia, north-east by Maryland, east by the Atlantic, south by North Carolina and Tennessee and west by Kentucky. Area, 40,767 sq. miles including 1,063 sq. miles of inland water. Census population, 1 April 1980, 5,346,818, an increase of 695,370 or 14·9% since 1970. Estimate (1982) 5,479,000. In 1983 there were 80,779 births (14·6 per 1,000 population); 43,734 deaths (7·9); 984 infant deaths (12·2 per 1,000 live births); 61,858 marriages and 25,482 divorces.

Population for 5 federal census years was:

	White	*Negro*	*Indian*	*Asiatic*	*Total*	*Per sq. mile*
1910	1,389,809	671,096	539	168	2,061,612	51·2
1930	1,770,441	650,165	779	466	2,421,851	60·7
1960	3,142,443	816,258	2,155	4,725	3,966,949	99·3
			All others			
1970	3,761,514	861,368	25,612		4,648,494	116·9
1980	4,230,000	1,008,311	108,517		5,346,818	134·7

Of the total population in 1980, 49% were male, 66% were urban and 59% were 21 years of age or older.

The population (census of 1980) of the principal cities was: Norfolk, 266,979; Virginia Beach, 262,199; Richmond, 219,214; Newport News, 144,903; Hampton, 122,617; Chesapeake, 114,226; Portsmouth, 104,577; Alexandria, 103,219; Roanoke, 100,427; Lynchburg, 66,743.

CLIMATE. Average temperatures in Jan. are 41°F in the Tidewater coastal area and 32°F in the Blue Ridge mountains; July averages, 78°F and 68°F respectively. Precipitation averages 36″ in the Shenandoah valley and 44″ in the south. Snowfall is 5-10″ in the Tidewater and 25-30″ in the western mountains. Norfolk. Jan. 41°F (5°C), July 79°F (26·1°C). Annual rainfall 46″ (1,145 mm). *See* Atlantic Coast, p. 1373.

CONSTITUTION AND GOVERNMENT. The present constitution dates from 1971.

The General Assembly consists of a Senate of 40 members, elected for 4 years, and a House of Delegates of 100 members, elected for 2 years. The Governor and Lieut.-Governor are elected for 4 years. Qualified as electors are (with few exceptions) all citizens 18 years of age, fulfilling certain residential qualifications, who have registered. The state sends to Congress 2 senators and 10 representatives.

In the 1984 presidential election Reagan polled 1,325,516 votes, Mondale, 793,711.

The state capital is Richmond; the state contains 95 counties and 41 independent cities.

Governor: Charles S. Robb (D.), 1983–86 ($60,000).
Lieut.-Governor: Richard J. Davis (D.) $16,000.
Secretary of the Commonwealth: Laurie Naismith (D.) ($21,400).

BUDGET. General revenue for the year ending 30 June 1983 was $5,064m. (taxation, $3,336m., and federal aid, $1,157m.); general expenditures, $4,705·5m. ($1,335m. for education, $985·6m. for transport and $1,510m. for public welfare).

Total net long-term debt, 30 June 1983, amounted to $348,770,279.

Per capita personal income (1982) was $11,095.

ENERGY AND NATURAL RESOURCES

Minerals (1981). Coal is the most important mineral, with output of 41,977,807 short tons. Lead and zinc ores, stone, sand and gravel, lime and titanium ore are also produced. Total mineral output was 53m. tons.

Agriculture. In 1978 there were 57,000 farms with an area of 10m. acres; average farm had 175 acres and was valued at $163,918.

Income, 1982, from crops, $674m., and from livestock and livestock products, $1,005m. The chief crops (1982) are corn, hay and peanuts (330·8m. lb.), tobacco (158m. lb.).

Animals on farms on 1 Jan. 1982 included 170,000 milch cows, 1·85m. all cattle, 170,000 sheep and 640,000 swine (Dec. 1981).

Forestry. National forests, 1982, covered 1,628,000 acres.

INDUSTRY. The manufacture of cigars and cigarettes and of rayon and allied products and the building of ships lead in value of products.

TOURISM. Tourists spend about $3,700m. a year in Virginia, attracted mainly by the state's outstanding scenery, coastline and historical interest.

COMMUNICATIONS

Roads. The state highways system, 31 Dec. 1982, had 61,801 miles of highways, of which 8,958 miles were primary roads. Motor registrations, 1982, 3·9m.

Railways. In 1983 there were 3,693 miles of railways.

Aviation. There were, in 1981, 260 airports, of which 58 were publicly owned.

JUSTICE, RELIGION, EDUCATION AND WELFARE

Justice. Executions (by electrocution) since 1930 totalled 97. Prison population, 31 Dec. 1982, 9,715 in federal and state prisons.

Religion. The principal churches are the Baptist, Methodist, Protestant-Episcopal, Roman Catholic and Presbyterian.

Education. Elementary and secondary instruction is free, and for ages 6–17 attendance is compulsory. No child under 12 may be employed in any mining or manufacturing work.

In 1983 the 139 school districts had, in primary schools, 653,495 pupils and 22,783·8 teachers and in public high schools, 280,991 pupils and 17,124 teachers.

Teachers' salaries (1982–83) averaged $18,467. Total expenditure on education, 1982–83, was $2,773·5m. The more important institutions for higher education (1982) were:

Founded	*Name and place of college*	*Staff*	*Students*
1693	William and Mary College, Williamsburg (State)	557	6,520
1749	Washington and Lee University, Lexington	178	1,714
1776	Hampden-Sydney College, Hampden-Sydney (Pres.)	64	770
1819	University of Virginia, Charlottesville (State)	1,681	17,118
1832	Randolph-Macon College, Ashland (Methodist)	92	884
1832	University of Richmond, Richmond (Baptist)	295	4,469
1838	Virginia Commonwealth University, Richmond	2,520	20,211
1839	Virginia Military Institute Lexington (State)	133	1,309
1865	Virginia Union University, Richmond	90	1,300
1868	Hampton Institute	260	3,824
1872	Virginia Polytechnic Institute and State University	2,594	21,510
1882	Virginia State University, Petersburg	228	4,564
1908	James Madison University, Harrisonburg	521	9,048
1910	Radford University (State)	315	5,903
1930	Old Dominion University, Norfolk	830	14,712
1956	George Mason University (State)	750	14,273

Health. In 1981 the state had 136 hospitals (31,400 beds) listed by the American Hospital Association.

Social Security. In 1938 Virginia established a system of old-age assistance under the Federal Security Act; in March 1983 persons in 2,034 cases were drawing an average grant of $202.79; aid to permanently and totally disabled, 1,766 cases, average grant $218.96; aid to dependent children, 164,383 persons, average grant $85.77; general relief, 6,642 persons, average grant $146.62.

Books of Reference

Virginia Facts and Figures. Annual Division of Industrial Development, Richmond. Annual
Dabney, V., *Virginia, the New Dominion.* 1971
Friddell, G., *The Virginia Way.* Burda, 1973
Gottmann, J., *Virginia in our Century.* Charlottesville, 1969
Morton, R. L., *Colonial Virginia.* 2 vols. Univ. Press of Virginia, 1960
Rouse, P. *Virginia: a Pictorial History.* Scribner, 1975
Rubin, L. D., Jr., *Virginia: a Bicentennial History.* Norris, 1977

State Library: Virginia State Library, Richmond 23219. *State Librarian:* Donald Haynes.

WASHINGTON

HISTORY. Washington, formerly part of Oregon, was created a Territory in 1853, and was admitted into the Union as a state on 11 Nov. 1889. Its settlement dates from 1811.

AREA AND POPULATION. Washington is bounded north by Canada, east by Idaho, south by Oregon with the Columbia River forming most of the boundary, and west by the Pacific. Area, 68,139 sq. miles, of which 1,627 sq. miles are inland water. Lands owned by the federal government, 1977, were 12·4m. acres or 29·1% of the total area. Census population, 1 April 1980 (preliminary), 4,130,163, an increase of 730,994 or 21·4% since 1970. Estimated population (1982), 4,265,400. Births, 1980 were 67,518; deaths, 32,304; infant deaths, 143; marriages, 47,836; divorces and annulments, 28,733.

Population in 5 federal census years was:

	White	*Negro*	*Indian*	*Asiatic and others*	*Total*	*Per sq. mile*
1910	1,109,111	6,058	10,997	15,824	1,141,990	17·1
1930	1,521,661	6,840	11,253	23,642	1,563,396	23·3
1960	2,751,675	48,738	21,076	31,725	2,853,214	42·8
1970	2,351,055	71,308	33,386	53,420	3,409,169	51·2
1980	3,777,296	105,544	60,771	186,552	4,130,163	62·0

Of the total population in 1980, 2,051,369 were male, 3,037,765 persons were urban; 2,837,607 were 20 years of age or older.

There are 24 Indian reservations, the largest being held by the Yakima tribe. Indian reservations in Sept. 1979 covered 2,496,423 acres, of which 1,996,018 acres were tribal lands and 497,218 acres were held by individuals. Total Indian population, 1980, 60,771.

Leading cities are Seattle, with a population (1980 census) of 491,897; Spokane, 170,993; Tacoma, 158,101; Bellevue, 73,711. Others : Yakima, 49,826; Everett, 54,413; Vancouver, 42,834; Bellingham, 45,794; Bremerton, 36,208; Richland, 33,578; Longview, 31,052; Renton, 30,612; Edmonds, 27,526; Walla Walla, 25,618. Urbanized areas (1980 census): Seattle–Everett, 1,600,944; Tacoma, 482,692; Spokane, 341,058.

CLIMATE. Seattle. Jan. 40°F (4·4°C), July 63°F (17·2°C). Annual rainfall 34″ (848 mm). Spokane. Jan. 27°F (–2·8°C), July 70°F (21·1°C). Annual rainfall 14″ (350 mm). *See* Pacific Coast, p. 1372.

CONSTITUTION AND GOVERNMENT. The constitution, adopted in 1889, has had 63 amendments. The Legislature consists of a Senate of 49 members elected for 4 years, half their number retiring every 2 years, and a House of Representatives of 98 members, elected for 2 years. The Governor and Lieut.-Governor are elected for 4 years. The state sends 2 senators and 7 representatives to Congress.

Qualified as voters are (with some exceptions) all citizens 18 years of age, having the usual residential qualifications.

In the 1984 presidential election Reagan polled 939,124 votes, Mondale, 731,440.

The capital is Olympia (population, 1980 census, 27,447). The state contains 39 counties.

Governor: Booth Gardner (D.), 1985–89 ($63,000).
Lieut.-Governor: John A. Cherberg (D.), 1985–89 ($28,600).
Secretary of State: Ralph Munro (R.), 1985–89 ($31,000).

BUDGET. For the 2-year budget period 1981–83 the state's total revenue is (projected) $13,545·2m.; general expenditure is (projected) $13,873·5m. (education, $6,150·7m.; transportation, $706·6m., and human resources, $3,636m.). State revenue in the period 1979–81 was $10,623·7m. and expenditure $10,857·8m.

Total net long-term debt on 30 June 1980 was $627,784,980.

Per capita personal income (1982) was $11,635.

ENERGY AND NATURAL RESOURCES

Electricity. With about 20% of potential water-power resources of US, the state is first in developed and potential hydro-electricity. Electric energy produced in 1982, 99,684m. kw.

Minerals. Mining and quarrying employed about 3,000 in 1981, and the sector is not as important as forestry, agriculture or manufacturing. Uranium is mined but figures are not disclosed; other minerals include sand and gravel, stone, coal and clays.

Agriculture. Agriculture is constantly growing in value because of more intensive and diversified farming and because of the 1m.-acre Columbia Basin Irrigation Project. Irrigated land in farms (1974) amounted to 1,286,412 acres.

In 1983 there were 38,000 farms with an acreage of 16m.; average farm was of 429 acres. Average value per acre, $888.

Value of farm production, 1982, was $3,057m. (from field crops, $1,359m.; from speciality products, including flowers, bulbs, Christmas trees, $170m., fruit and vegetables, $621·4m., and from livestock and dairy products, $906·5m.). Wheat, the leading farm commodity, was valued at $555·5m. Cattle and calves were valued at $348m. Other major commodities are milk ($440m.), apples ($297m.).

On 1 Jan. 1983 animals on farms included 213,000 milch cows, 1·57m. all cattle, 65,000 sheep and 51,000 swine.

Forestry. Forests cover about 23m. acres, of which 9m. acres are national forest. In 1982, lumber production was 3,014m. bd ft; plywood, 1,200m. bd ft, and pulp wood (1981) 3,494,000 short tons.

Fisheries. Washington ranks second only to Alaska in the catch of salmon and halibut, and in the production of canned salmon.

INDUSTRY. In 1981 manufacturing employed 301,900 workers, of whom 79,100 were in aerospace and 61,200 in the forest products industry. Gross manufacturing income (1 Oct. 1980–30 Sept. 1981): aerospace, $8,380·6m.; forest products, $6,415·6m., of which paper and pulp made $2,571·4m.; food products, $4,801·4m.; primary metals, $2,728·9m.; refining petroleum, $2,227·2m.

Abundance of electric power has made Washington the leading producer of primary aluminium.

COMMUNICATIONS

Roads. The state (1979) maintained 6,920 miles of highway; the counties, 40,767 miles; municipalities, 9,888 miles. Motor vehicle registrations (1980), 3,566,639.

Railways. The railways had, in 1980, 6,057 miles.

Aviation. There were in 1979, 365 airports, 120 publicly owned. In 1978 Seattle–Tacoma Airport traffic was 8·3m. passengers, 48,000 tons of mail and 185,000 tons of freight and express.

JUSTICE, RELIGION, EDUCATION AND WELFARE

Justice. The average daily adult population in state prisons in Jan. 1982 was 4,674. Since 1963 there have been no executions; total 1930–63 (by hanging) was 47, including 40 whites, 5 Negroes and 2 other races, all for murder, except 1 white for kidnapping.

Religion. Chief religious bodies are the Roman Catholic, United Methodist, Lutheran, Presbyterian, Latter-day Saints and Episcopalian.

Education. Education is given free to all children between the ages of 5 and 21 years, and is compulsory for children from 8 to 15 years of age. In autumn 1982 there were 739,215 pupils in public elementary and secondary schools, with 34,056 classroom teachers. In 1983 the average salary of teaching staff was $23,400. The total expenditure on public elementary and secondary schools for the school year 1980–81 was $1,791·6m.

The University of Washington, founded 1861, at Seattle, had, autumn 1982, 34,769 students, and Washington University at Pullman, founded 1890, for science and agriculture, had 16,829 students. Twenty-seven community colleges had (1981) a total enrolment of 161,244 students (89,263 full-time equivalent).

Health. In 1981 the 2 state hospitals for mental illness had a daily average of 1,204 patients; schools for handicapped children, 1,999 residents in Sept. 1981.

In 1981 the state had 109 licensed general hospitals (13,201 beds), 3 licensed psychiatric hospitals (181 beds) and 3 alcoholism hospitals (174 beds).

Social Security. Old-age assistance is provided for persons 65 years of age or older without adequate resources (and not in need of continuing home care) who are residents of the state. In July 1981, 14,287 people were drawing an average of $130·93 per month; aid to 139,514 children in 52,781 families averaged $333·86 per family monthly; to 500 blind persons, $218·03 per person monthly; to 25,557 totally disabled, $216·59 monthly. 5,057 persons, under foster care, received payments of $366·11 per person. Total unemployment in 1981 averaged 176,000 (9·1% of the population). In June 1980 the unemployment insurance system covered 90·5% of employers (103,391). Benefits ranged from $41 to $150 per week and averaged $117·75 per week.

Books of Reference

Washington State Research Council. *Handbook: A Compendium of Statistical and Explanatory Information about State and Local Government in Washington.* 4th ed. Olympia, 1973.—*The Book of Numbers: A Statistical Handbook on Washington State Government.* Olympia, 1977

Washington (State) Office of Financial Management. *Pocket Data Book 1978*

Avery, M. W., *Washington, a History of the Evergreen State.* Univ. of Wash. Press, 1965.—*Government of Washington State.* Univ. of Wash. Press, revised ed. 1973

State Library: Washington State Library, Olympia. *State Librarian:* Roderick Swartz.

WEST VIRGINIA

HISTORY. In 1862, after the state of Virginia had seceded from the Union, the electors of the western portion ratified an ordinance providing for the formation of a new state, which was admitted into the Union by presidential proclamation on 20 June 1863, under the name of West Virginia. Its constitution was adopted by the voters almost unanimously on 26 March 1863.

AREA AND POPULATION. West Virginia is bounded north by Pennsylvania and Maryland, east and south by Virginia, south-west by the Sandy River (forming the boundary with Kentucky) and west by the Ohio River (forming the boundary with Ohio). Area, 24,282 sq. miles, of which 102 sq. miles are water. Census population, 1 April 1980, 1,949,644, an increase of 11·8% since 1970. Estimate (1982), 1,948,000. Births, 1980, 29,438; deaths, 19,178; infant deaths, 347; marriages, 17,391; divorces, 10,275.

Population in 5 federal census years was:

	White	*Negro*	*Indian*	*Asiatic*	*Total*	*Per sq. mile*
1910	1,156,817	64,173	36	93	1,221,119	50·8
1940	1,614,191	114,893	18	103	1,729,205	71·8
1960	1,770,133	89,378	181	419	1,860,421	77·3
1970	1,673,480	67,342	751	1,463	1,744,237	71·8
1980	1,874,751	65,051	1,610	5,194	1,949,644	80·3

Of the total population in 1980, 945,408 were male, 705,319 were urban; those 20 years of age or older numbered 1,319,566.

The 1980 census population of the principal cities was: Huntington, 63,684; Charleston, 63,968. Others: Wheeling, 43,070; Parkersburg, 39,967; Morgantown, 27,605; Weirton, 24,736; Fairmont, 23,863; Clarksburg, 22,371.

CLIMATE. Charleston. Jan. 34°F (1·1°C), July 76°F (24·4°C). Annual rainfall 40″ (1,010 mm). *See* Appalachian Mountains, p. 1373.

CONSTITUTION AND GOVERNMENT. The present constitution was adopted in 1872; it has had 51 amendments.

The Legislature consists of the Senate of 34 members elected for a term of 4 years, one-half being elected biennially, and the House of Delegates of 100 members, elected biennially. The Governor is elected for 4 years and may succeed himself once. Voters are all citizens (with the usual exceptions) 18 years of age and meeting certain residential requirements. The state sends to Congress 2 senators and 4 representatives.

In the 1984 presidential election Reagan polled 396,332 votes, Mondale, 322,142.

The state capital is Charleston. There are 55 counties.

Governor: Arch Moore Jr. (R.), 1985–89 ($60,000).
Secretary of State: Ken Hechler (D.), ($36,000).

FINANCE. General revenues for the year ending 30 June 1982 were $3,169m. ($1,632m. from taxes, $898m. from federal funds); general expenditures were $3,170m. (education, $1,138m.; highways, $535m.; public welfare, $267m.).

Debts outstanding were $3,700m. on 30 June 1982.
Estimated *per capita* personal income (1982) was $8,769.

ENERGY AND NATURAL RESOURCES

Minerals. 55% of the state is underlain with mineable coal; 128·8m. short tons of coal were produced in 1982. Petroleum output, 3m. bbls; natural gas production was 152,000m. cu. ft. Salt, sand and gravel, sandstone and limestone are also produced. The total value of mineral output in 1981 was $5,000m.

Agriculture. In 1983 the state had 21,000 farms with an area of 4·2m. acres; average size of farm was 203 acres and valued at $829 per acre. Livestock farming predominates.

Cash income, 1983, from crops was $54·7m.; from government payments, $3·9m., and from livestock and products, $172·87m. Major crops harvested, 1983: hay (594,000 tons); all corn (4·3m. bu.); tobacco (3·3m. lb.). Apples and peaches are important fruit crops. Livestock on farms, 1 Jan. 1980, included 545,000 cattle, of which 37,000 were milch cows; sheep, 113,000; hogs, 56,000; chickens, 940,000 excluding broilers. Production, 1980, included 21·8m. broilers, 149m. eggs; 2·3m. turkeys.

Forestry. State forests, 1980, covered 79,307 acres; national forests, 1,647,146 gross acres; 75% of the state is woodland.

INDUSTRY. In 1980, 1,730 manufactories had 116,552 production workers who earned $2,167·9m. Value added by manufacture (estimate) was $3,660m. Leading industries are primary and fabricated metals, glass, chemicals, wood products, textiles and apparel, and machinery.

In 1982 non-agricultural employment was 609,000 of whom 128,000 were in trade, 126,000 in government and 103,000 in service industries.

The first commercial coal liquefaction plant in the USA is being built near Morgantown with the co-operation of the governments of Federal Republic of Germany and Japan and the Gulf Oil Co.

COMMUNICATIONS

Roads. Total highways in 1980, 37,527 miles (state maintained, 33,436 miles; inter-state, 390 miles; national parks and other roads, 4,091 miles; West Virginia Turnpike, 87 miles). Registered motor vehicles, financial year ending 30 June 1980, numbered 1,140,673.

Railways. In 1980 the state had 3,941 miles of railway, all operated by diesel or electric trains.

Aviation. There were 42 licensed airports in 1980.

Post and Broadcasting. There are 65 AM radio stations, 41 FM radio stations. Television stations number 9 VHF and 3 UHF.

Newspapers. Daily newspapers number 25; weekly newspapers 78.

JUSTICE, RELIGION, EDUCATION AND WELFARE

Justice. The state court system consists of a Supreme Court and 31 circuit courts. The Supreme Court of Appeals, exercising original and appellate jurisdiction, has 5 members elected by the people for 12-year terms. Each circuit court has from 1 to 7 judges (as determined by the Legislature on the basis of population and case-load) chosen by the voters within each circuit for 8-year terms.

Effective on 1 July 1967, the West Virginia Human Rights Act prohibits discrimination in employment and places of public accommodations based on race, religion, colour, national origin or ancestry.

There are 8 penal and correctional institutions which had, on 30 June 1980, 1,590 inmates. In 1965 the State Legislature abolished capital punishment.

Religion. Chief denominations in 1980 were United Methodist (175,000 members, estimate), Baptists (141,000) and Roman Catholics (102,600).

Education. Public school education is free for all from 5 to 21 years of age, and school attendance is compulsory for all between the ages of 7 and 16 (school term, 200 days—180–185 days of actual teaching). The public schools are non-sectarian. In autumn 1982 public elementary and secondary schools had 375,115 pupils and 22,159 classroom teachers. Average salary of teachers in 1983, $17,400. Total 1981 expenditures for public schools, $849m.

Leading institutions of higher education in 1981:

Founded		*Full-time students*
1837	Marshall University, Huntington	11,482
	School of Medicine	401
1837	West Liberty State College, West Liberty	2,668
1867	Fairmont State College, Fairmont	5,262
1868	West Virginia University, Morgantown	19,874
	School of Medicine	1,437
1872	Concord College, Athens	2,174
1872	Glenville State College, Glenville	1,920
1872	Shepherd College, Shepherdstown	3,001
1891	West Virginia State College	4,368
1895	West Virginia Institute of Technology, Montgomery	3,343
1895	Bluefield State College, Bluefield	2,340
1901	Potomac State College of West Virginia Univ., Keyser	1,104
1972	West Virginia College of Graduate Studies	3,323
1976	School of Osteopathic Medicine, Lewisburg	231

In addition to the universities and state-supported schools, there are 3 community colleges (8,326 students in 1981), 10 denominational and private institutions of higher education (11,221 students in 1981) and 14 business colleges.

Health. In 1980–81 the state had 66 hospitals and 34 licensed personal care homes, 71 skilled-nursing homes and 6 mental hospitals.

Social Security. The Department of Welfare, originating in the 1930s as the Department of Public Assistance, is both state and federally financed. In the year ending 30 June 1981 day care for 5,288 children per month was provided; aid was given to 24,158 families with dependent children (average award, $173·05 per month); handicapped children's services conducted 134,640 examinations; 65,526 families per month received food stamps.

On 1 Jan. 1974 all blind, aged and disabled services were converted to the Federal Supplemental Security Income programme.

Books of Reference

West Virginia Blue Book. Legislature, Charleston. Annual, since 1916
West Virginia Statistical Handbook, 1974. Bureau of Business Research, W. Va. Univ., Morgantown, 1974
Bibliography of West Virginia. 2 parts. Dept. of Archives and History, Charleston, 1939
West Virginia History. Dept. of Archives and History. Charleston. Quarterly, from 1939
Conley, P., and Doherty, W. T., *West Virginia History.* Charleston, 1974
Davis, C. J., and others, *West Virginia State and Local Government.* West Virginia Univ. Bureau for Government Research, 1963
Williams, J. A., *West Virginia: A Bicentennial History.* New York, 1976

State Library: Division of Archives and History, Dept. of Culture and History, Charleston.

WISCONSIN

HISTORY. Wisconsin was settled in 1670 by French traders and missionaries. Originally a part of New France, it was surrendered to the British in 1763 and in 1783, when ceded to the US, became part of the North-west Territory. It was then contained successively in the Territories of Indiana, Illinois and Michigan. In 1836 it became part of the Territory of Wisconsin, which also included the present states of Iowa, Minnesota and parts of the Dakotas. It was admitted into the Union with its present boundaries on 29 May 1848.

AREA AND POPULATION. Wisconsin is bounded north by Lake Superior and the Upper Peninsula of Michigan, east by Lake Michigan, south by Illinois, west by Iowa and Minnesota, with the Mississippi River forming most of the boundary. Area, 56,153 sq. miles, including 1,727 sq. miles of inland water, but excluding any part of the Great Lakes. Census population, 1 April 1980 4,705,335, an increase of 6·5% since 1970. Estimated population (1984), 4,774,383. Births in 1983 were 72,499 (15·3 per 1,000 population); deaths, 40,985 (8·6); infant deaths, 688 (9·2 per 1,000 live births); marriages, 40,754 (8·6); divorces and annulments, 16,503.

Population in 5 census years was:

	White	*Negro*	*All others*	*Total*	*Per sq. mile*
1910	2,320,555	2,900	10,405	2,333,860	42·2
1930	2,916,255	10,739	12,012	2,939,006	53·7
1960	3,858,903	74,546	18,328	3,951,777	72·2
1970	4,258,959	128,224	30,750	4,417,933	80·8
1980	4,442,598	182,593	80,144	4,705,335	86·4

Of the total population in 1980, 49% were male, 64·2% were urban and 67% were 20 years old or older.

Population of the larger cities, 1980 census, was as follows:

Milwaukee	636,212	Appleton	59,032	Beloit	35,207
Madison	170,616	Oshkosh	49,678	Fond du Lac	35,863
Racine	85,725	La Crosse	48,347	Manitowoc	32,547
Green Bay	87,889	Sheboygan	48,085	Wausau	32,426
Kenosha	77,685	Janesville	51,071	Superior	29,571
West Allis	63,982	Eau Claire	51,509	Brookfield	34,035
Wauwatosa	51,308	Waukesha	50,319		

Population of larger urbanized areas, 1980 census: Milwaukee, 1,207,008; Madison, 213,678, Duluth–Superior (Minn.–Wis.), 132,585; Racine, 118,987; Green Bay, 142,747.

CLIMATE. Milwaukee. Jan. 19°F (–7·2°C), July 70°F (21·1°C). Annual rainfall 29″ (727 mm). *See* Great Lakes, p. 1373.

CONSTITUTION AND GOVERNMENT. The constitution, which dates from 1848, has 118 amendments. The legislative power is vested in a Senate of 33 members (1985 term: 19 Democrats, 14 Republicans) elected for 4 years, one-half elected alternately, and an Assembly of 99 members (1985 term: 52 Democrats, 47 Republicans) all elected simultaneously for 2 years. The Governor and Lieut.-Governor are elected for 4 years. All 6 constitutional officers serve 4-year terms.

Wisconsin has universal suffrage for all citizens 18 years of age or over; but, as there is no official list of voters, the size of the electorate is unknown; 2,211,689 voted for President in 1984.

Wisconsin is represented in Congress by 2 senators and 9 representatives.

In the 1984 presidential election Reagan polled 1,198,584 votes, Mondale, 995,740.

The capital is Madison. The state has 72 counties.

Governor: Anthony S. Earl (D.), 1983–87 ($75,337).
Lieut.-Governor: James T. Flynn (D.), 1983–87 ($41,390).
Secretary of State: Douglas La Follette (D.), 1983–87 ($37,334).

BUDGET. For the year ending 30 June 1984 (Wisconsin Bureau of Financial Operations figures) total revenue for all funds was $10,581,177,270 ($4,909,439,067 from taxation and $1,813,137,493 from federal aid). General expenditure from all funds was $8,888,929,927 ($2,549,387,301 for education, $2,631,115,550 for human resources).

Per capita personal income (1982) was $10,774.

ENERGY AND NATURAL RESOURCES

Electricity. There were, Dec. 1983, 89 hydro-electric power plants (15 of them municipal, 59 private in Wisconsin; 15 private outside the state) operated by public utilities with a total installed capacity of 452,930 kw.; output, 1983, was 2,510,704m. kwh. The 15 outside plants are in Michigan; installed capacity 99,990 kw., output 561,189m. kwh.

Fossil fuel and nuclear plants numbered 24 (4 municipal); the former had a total installed capacity of 6,235,266 kw.; total output, (1983), 23,772,507m. kwh; the 2 nuclear plants had an installed capacity of 1,540,682 kw. and a total output (1983) of 9,099,277m. kwh.

There were also 31 internal combustion reciprocating plants (one in Michigan), with a total installed capacity of 105,498 kw. and a total output of (1983) 2,568m. kwh., and 17 internal combustion turbine plants with a total installed capacity of 1,285,950 kw.; total output was (1983) 69,688m. kwh.

There was a total of 161 plants, with a total installed capacity of 9,620,326 kw. and a total output of (1983) 35,454,744m. kwh.

Minerals. Sand and gravel, crushed stone and lime are the chief mineral products. Mineral production in 1983 was valued at $111·5m. This value included $38m. for sand and gravel, $48m. for crushed stone and about $18m. for lime. Value of all other minerals including natural abrasives, peat, cement and gemstones, $7m.

The large Forest County sulphide deposit (5,000 ft long, about 200 ft wide and over 1,500 ft deep and almost vertical) south of Crandon is estimated at over 77m. tons, averaging 5% zinc, 1% copper and lesser amounts of lead, silver and gold. The company owning the Crandon zinc-copper deposit initiated the process to acquire mine permits in 1982. In 1981, northern Wisconsin was explored for base metal deposits in Price, Forest, Lincoln, Rusk, and Marathon counties.

Agriculture. The total number of farms has declined in the last 48 years, but farms have become larger and more productive. On 1 Jan. 1983 there were 90,000 farms with a total acreage of 18·2m. acres and an average size of 202 acres, compared with 142,000 farms with a total acreage of 22·4m. acres and an average of 158 acres in 1959.

Cash income from products sold by Wisconsin farms in 1983, $4,984m.; $3,911m. from livestock and livestock products and $1,072m. from crops.

Wisconsin ranked first among the states in 1983 in the number of milch cows, milk and butter production, output of American, both Brick and Munster, Italian and Blue Mold Cheese. Production of all cheese accounted for 35·9% of the nation's total. The state also ranked first in bulk whole condensed milk and bulk sweetened skim condensed milk and dry whey. In crops the state ranked first for snap beans for processing, green peas for processing, all hay, beets for canning, corn for silage and sweet corn for processing. Production of the principal field crops in 1983 included: Corn for grain, 223m. bu.; corn for silage, 10·38m. tons; oats, 45·1m. bu.; all hay, 12·2m. tons. Other crops of importance 18·9m. cwt of potatoes, 16·1m. lb. of tobacco, 1·1m. bbls of cranberries, 1·5m. cwt of carrots and the processing crops of 568,280 tons of sweet corn, 110,160 tons of green peas and 210,680 tons of snap beans.

Forestry. In June 1984 national forests comprised 1·5m. acres; state forests, 426,312 acres; the county forests, 2·28m. acres. Wisconsin has an estimated 14·4m. acres of forest land (about 41·5% of land area) which consists of private (about 58%) and industrial forest. The production and remanufacture of wood and wood-products is one of the state's most important industries.

INDUSTRY. Wisconsin has much heavy industry, particularly in the Milwaukee area. In 1982 the state ranked thirteenth in manufactured exports; non-electrical machinery was the major industrial group (20% of all manufacturing employment), followed by food processing, fabricated metals, electrical machinery, paper and products, transport equipment, primary metals and printing. Manufacturing establishments in 1983 provided 26·9% of all employment, 32·4% of all earnings; exports (1981) $4,030m. The total number of establishments was 9,197 in 1983; the biggest concentration is in the south-east.

TOURISM. The tourist-vacation industry ranks among the first three in economic importance. The decline of lumbering and mining in the northern section of the state has increased dependency on the recreation industry. The Division of Tourism of the Department of Development spent $914,000 to promote tourism in financial year 1982–83.

COMMUNICATIONS

Roads. The state had on 1 Jan. 1984, 108,093 miles of highway. 74% of all roads in the state have a bituminous (or similar) surface. There are 11,920 miles of state trunk roads and 19,534 miles of county trunk roads.

In the year ending 1 Jan. 1984 Wisconsin registered, 3,580,684 motor vehicles.

Railways. On 1 July 1983 the state had 4,534 road-miles of railway.

Aviation. There were, in 1984, 96 publicly operated airports. Fifteen scheduled air carrier airports were served by 9 national air carriers and 7 by regional air carriers.

Shipping. With the opening of the St Lawrence Seaway in 1959, 14 Wisconsin ports became accessible to ocean-going vessels. Green Bay, Kenosha, Manitowoc, Marinette, Milwaukee, Sheboygan and Superior (one of the world's largest iron ore and grain ports) have developed foreign waterborne commerce. Cargo is also carried by barge on the river Mississippi. Other ports handle mainly Great Lakes traffic.

JUSTICE, RELIGION, EDUCATION AND WELFARE

Justice. The state's penal, reformatory and correctional system on 30 June 1984 held 4,591 men and 212 women in 13 state-owned and other institutions for adult and juvenile offenders; the probation and parole system was supervising 19,998 men and 3,910 women. Wisconsin does not impose the death penalty.

Religion. Wisconsin church affiliation, as a percentage of the 1980 population, was estimated at 32·2% Catholic, 20·06% Lutheran, 3·74% Methodist, 10·41% other churches and 32·6% un-affiliated.

Education. All children between the ages of 7 and 16 are required to attend school full-time to the end of the school term in which they become 16 years of age. Children living in a district with a vocational school must attend until 18. In 1983–84 the public school grades kindergarten–8 had 501,319 pupils and 28,828 (full-time equivalent) teachers; school grades 9–12 had 273,327 pupils and 16,582 teachers. Grade kindergarten–8 teachers' salaries, 1983–84, averaged $21,062; grade 9–12 teachers, $22,024.

In 1983–84 vocational, technical and adult schools had an enrolment of 460,158, and there were 6,840 faculty members in 1982–83. There is a school for the visually handicapped and a school for the deaf.

The University of Wisconsin, established in 1848, was joined by law in 1971 with the Wisconsin State Universities System to become the University of Wisconsin System with 13 degree granting campuses, 13 two-year campuses in the Center System, and the University Extension. The 26 campuses had, in 1983–84, 6,835 full-time professors and instructors and 2,104 (full-time equivalent) teaching assistants. In autumn 1983, 161,693 students enrolled (11,072 at Eau Claire, 4,880 at Green Bay, 8,958 at La Crosse, 42,921 at Madison, 26,468 at Milwaukee, 11,053 at Oshkosh, 6,008 at Parkside, 5,488 at Platteville, 5,368 at River Falls, 8,871 at Stevens Point, 7,470 at Stout, 2,219 at Superior, 10,493 at Whitewater and 10,454 in the Center System freshman-sophomore centres). There are also several independent institutions of higher education. These (with 1983–84 enrolment) include 2 universities (12,696), 21 liberal arts colleges (16,337), 5 technical and professional schools (3,916), and 4 theological seminaries (509).

The total expenditure, 1983–84, for all public education (except capital outlay and debt service) was $3,964m.

The state maintains an educational broadcasting and television service.

Health. In Oct. 1984 the state had 145 general and allied special hospitals (21,967 beds), 19 mental hospitals (1,803 beds), 11 treatment centres for alcoholism and 1 rehabilitation centre. Patients in state and county mental hospitals and institutions for the mentally retarded in June 1982 averaged 2,699.

Social Security. On 1 Jan. 1974 the US Social Security administration assumed responsibility for financial aid (Supplemental Security Income) to persons 65 years old and over, blind persons and totally disabled persons, who satisfy requirements as to need. Recipients receive a federal payment plus a federally administered state supplementary payment, except for those who reside in a medical institution. In Oct. 1984, there were 65,069 SSI recipients in the state. In Jan. 1984 payment levels increased to $413 for a single individual, $463 for an eligible individual with an ineligible spouse, and $633 for an eligible couple. A special payment level of $511 for an individual and $975 for a couple may be paid with special approval for SSI recipients who are developmentally disabled or chronically mentally ill, living in a non-medical living arrangement not his or her own home. All SSI recipients receive state medical assistance coverage.

Under the Aid to Families with Dependent Children programme, 92,699 families constituting 279,847 persons received an average of $482.38 per family in Aug. 1984. Medicaid in financial year 1982 cost $932·6m.

Books of Reference

Wisconsin Statistical Abstract. Wis. Dept. of Administration, State Bureau of Planning and Budget, Madison, 1979
Dictionary of Wisconsin Biography. Wis. Historical Society, Madison, 1960
Wisconsin Blue Book. Wis. Legislative Reference Bureau, Madison. Biennial
Current, R. N., *The History of Wisconsin,* Vol. II. State Historical Society of Wisconsin, Madison, 1976.—*Wisconsin, a History.* New York, 1977
Nesbit, R. C., *Wisconsin, A History.* State Historical Society of Wisconsin, Madison, 1973
Smith, Alice E., *The History of Wisconsin,* Vol. 1. State Historical Society of Wisconsin, Madison, 1973
Vexler, R. I., *Wisconsin Chronology and Factbook.* New York, 1978

State Information Agency: Legislative Reference Bureau, State Capitol, Madison, Wis. 53702. *Chief:* Dr H. Rupert Theobald.

WYOMING

HISTORY. Wyoming, first settled in 1834, was admitted into the Union on 10 July 1890. The name originated with the Delaware Indians.

AREA AND POPULATION. Wyoming is bounded north by Montana, east by South Dakota and Nebraska, south by Colorado, south-west by Utah and west by Idaho. Area 97,809 sq. miles, of which 820 sq. miles are water. The Yellowstone National Park occupies about 2,221,733 acres; the Grand Teton National Park has 310,350 acres. The federal government in 1979 owned 28,888,546 acres (46·1% of the total area of the state). The Federal Bureau of Land Management administers 17,546,188 acres.

Census population, 1 April 1980, 469,557, an increase of 41·25% since 1970. Estimate (1984) 487,243. Births in 1980 were 10,546 (22 per 1,000 population); deaths, 3,215 (7); infant deaths, 104 (10 per 1,000 live births); marriages, 6,868; divorces, 4,003.

Population in 5 census years was:

	White	Negro	Indian	Asiatic	Total	Per sq. mile
1910	140,318	2,235	1,486	1,926	145,965	1·5
1930	221,241	1,250	1,845	1,229	225,565	2·3
1960	322,922	2,183	4,020	805	330,066	3·4
			All others			
1970	323,619	2,568	6,229		332,416	3·4
1980	446,488	3,364	19,705		469,557	4·8

Of the total population in 1980, 240,560 were male, 295,898 were urban and those over 21 years of age numbered 295,908.

The largest towns are Cheyenne (capital), with census population in 1980 of 47,283; Casper, 51,016; Laramie, 24,410; Rock Springs, 19,458.

CLIMATE. Cheyenne. Jan. 25°F (–3·9°C), July 66°F (18·9°C). Annual rainfall 15″ (376 mm). Yellowstone Park. Jan. 18°F (–7·8°C), July 61°F (16·1°C). Annual rainfall 18″ (444 mm). *See* Mountain States, p. 1372.

CONSTITUTION AND GOVERNMENT. The constitution, drafted in 1890, has since had 43 amendments. The Legislature consists of a Senate of 30 members elected for 4 years, and a House of Representatives of 64 members elected for 2 years. The Governor is elected for 4 years.

The state sends to Congress 2 senators and 1 representative, elected by the voters of the entire state. The suffrage extends to all citizens, male and female, who have the usual residential qualifications.

In the 1984 presidential election Reagan polled 131,998 votes, Mondale, 53,154.

The capital is Cheyenne. The state contains 23 counties.

Governor: Ed Herschler (D.), 1983–86 ($70,000).
Secretary of State: Mrs Thyra Thomson (R.), 1983–86 ($52,500).

BUDGET. In the fiscal year ending 1 July 1984 (State Treasurer's figures) general revenues were $1,913,858,323; general expenditures were $1,454,378,833.

Per capita personal income (1983) was $11,969.

ENERGY AND NATURAL RESOURCES

Minerals. Wyoming is largely an oil-producing state. In 1983 the output of petroleum was valued at $3,182·4m.; natural gas, $978·5m. Other mining: Coal, $989·7m.; trona, $121·6m.; uranium, $45·5m.; other minerals mined include iron ore, feldspar, gypsum, limestone, phosphate, sand, gravel and marble, taconite, bentonite and hematite.

Agriculture. Wyoming is semi-arid, and agriculture is carried on by irrigation and by dry farming. In 1983 there were 9,200 farms and ranches; total land area 35·3m. acres.

Cash receipts, 1982, from crops, $115·7m.; from livestock and products, $414·5m. Principal commodities are wheat, cattle and calves, lambs and sheep, sugar-beet, barley, hay and wool. Animals on farms on 1 Jan. 1983 included 12,000 milch cows, 1·5m. all cattle, 1m. sheep and lambs and 33,000 swine.

INDUSTRY AND TRADE

Industry. In 1981–82 there were 570 manufacturing establishments. There were 458 mining establishments. A large portion of the manufacturing in the state is based on natural resources, mainly oil and farm products. Leading industries are food, wood products (except furniture) and machinery (except electrical). Casper is the most industrialized city, with 64 manufacturers and 145 mining companies. There were 1,541 new business incorporations in 1983. The Wyoming Industrial Development Corporation assists in the development of small industries by providing credit. Available capital, $3m.

Labour. Mining is the largest employer in the state with 26,900 workers in 1984. The total civilian labour force for June 1984 was 266,931; non-agricultural, 209,200. The average unemployment rate was 5·4% and average weekly earnings were $362.50 for manufacturing production workers.

Tourism. There are over 5m. tourists annually, mainly sportsmen. The state has the largest elk and pronghorn antelope herds in the world, 11 fish hatcheries and numerous wild game. Receipts from hunters and fishermen in 1983, $14,529,948.

COMMUNICATIONS

Roads. The roads in 1983 comprised 5,670 miles of federal highways, 353 miles of state highways and 917 miles of inter-state highway. There were (1981) 554,264 registered motor vehicles and 11 bus companies.

Railways. The railways, 1983, had a length of 2,070 mainline miles.

Aviation. There were 9 towns with regular scheduled services and 5 towns on jet routes in 1979.

JUSTICE, RELIGION, EDUCATION AND WELFARE

Justice. The state penitentiary in July 1982 held 657 inmates, the Womens' Center, 32. There are 2 other state correctional institutions. There have been 14 executions in Wyoming, 8 by hanging and 6 by lethal gas.

Religion. Chief religious bodies are the Roman Catholic (with 45,917 members in 1974), Mormon (28,954 in 1971) and Protestant churches (83,327 in 1974). There were 5,000 members of the Eastern Orthodox Church in 1972.

Education. In 1984–85 public elementary and secondary schools had 101,261 pupils. Enrolment in the parochial elementary and secondary schools was about 4,000. Approximately 7,791 public school teachers earned an average of $25,439. The average total expenditure per pupil for 1982–83 was $4,085.

The University of Wyoming, founded at Laramie in 1887, had in autumn 1984, 9,866 students. There are 2-year colleges at Casper, Riverton, Torrington, Cheyenne, Powell, Rock Springs and Sheridan with 38,187 students in 1982–83.

Social Welfare. In Jan. 1974 the federal government assumed many of the previous state programmes including old age assistance, aid to the blind and disabled. In 1983 financial year, $10,895,373 was distributed in food stamps; $10,331, 324 in aid to families with dependent children; $651,587 in emergency aid and $599,577 in general assistance. Total state expenditure on public assistance and social services programmes, financial year 1983, $47·8m.

Health. In 1983 the state had 28 hospitals. There are 33 registered nursing homes.

Books of Reference

News of Big Wyoming. Cheyenne, 1975
Official Directory. Secretary of State. Cheyenne. Biennial
1983 Wyoming Data Handbook. Dept. of Administration and Fiscal Control. Division of Research and Statistics, Cheyenne, 1983
Brown, R. H., *Wyoming: A Geography.* Boulder, 1980
Larsen, T. A., *History of Wyoming.* Rev. ed. Univ. of Nebraska, 1979
Treadway, T., *Wyoming.* New York, 1982
Vexler, R. I., *Wyoming Chronology and Factbook.* New York, 1978

OUTLYING TERRITORIES

Non-Self-Governing Territories: Summaries of Information Transmitted to the Secretary-General of the United Nations. Annual
Coulter, J. W., *The Pacific Dependencies of the United States.* New York, 1957
Perkins, W. T., *The United States and its Dependencies.* Leiden, 1962
Wiens, H. J., *Pacific Island Bastions of the US.* New York and London, 1962

GUAM

HISTORY. Magellan is said to have discovered the island in 1521; it was ceded by Spain to the US by the Treaty of Paris (10 Dec. 1898). The island was captured by the Japanese on 10 Dec. 1941, and retaken by American forces from 21 July 1944. Guam is of great strategic importance; substantial numbers of naval and air force personnel occupy about one-third of the usable land.

AREA AND POPULATION. Guam is the largest and most southern island of the Marianas Archipelago, in 13° 26′ N. lat., 144° 43′ E. long. The length is 30 miles, the breadth from 4 to 10 miles, and there are about 209 sq. miles (541 sq. km). Agaña, the seat of government is about 8 miles from the anchorage in Apra Harbour. The census on 1 April 1980 showed a population of 105,979, an increase of 20,983 or 24·7% since 1970; those of Guamanian ancestry numbered about 50,794; foreign-born, 28,572; density was 507 per sq. mile. Estimated population (1984), 115,756. On 1 July 1980 transient residents connected with the military were estimated at 20,000. The Malay strain is predominant. The native language is Chamorro; English is the official language and is taught in all schools.

CLIMATE. Tropical maritime, with little difference in temperatures over the year. Rainfall is copious at all seasons, but is greatest from July to Oct. Agaña. Jan. 81°F (27·2°C), July 81°F (27·2°C). Annual rainfall 93″ (2,325 mm).

CONSTITUTION AND GOVERNMENT. Guam's constitutional status is that of an 'unincorporated territory' of the US. Entry of US citizens is unrestricted; foreign nationals are subject to normal regulations. In 1949 the President transferred the administration of the island from the Navy Department (who held it from 1899) to the Interior Department. The transfer was completed by 1 Aug. 1950, on the passage of the Organic Act, which conferred full citizenship on the Guamanians, who had previously been 'nationals' of the US.

The Governor and his staff constitute the executive arm of the government. The Legislature is unicameral; its powers are similar to those of an American state legislature. At the general election of Nov. 1982, the Democratic Party won 14 seats and the Republicans 7. All adults 18 years of age or over are enfranchised. Guam returns one non-voting delegate to the House of Representatives.

Governor: Ricardo Bordallo (D.), 1982–85. ($50,000).
Lieut.-Governor: Edward D. Reyes (D.), 1982–85.

ECONOMY

Budget. At 30 Sept. 1983 total assets were $65·1m.; federal grants $35·2m., taxes, $26·7m.: total liabilities were $149·3m.

Banking. Recent changes in banking law make it possible for foreign banks to operate in Guam; the first to obtain a licence was the First Commercial Bank of Taiwan.

ENERGY AND NATURAL RESOURCES

Water. Supplies are from springs, reservoirs and groundwater; 65% comes from water-bearing limestone in the north. The Navy and Air Force conserve water in reservoirs. The Water Resources Research Centre is at Guam University.

Agriculture. The major products of the island are sweet potatoes, cucumbers, water melons and beans. In 1982 there were 140 full-time and 1,904 part-time farmers. Livestock (1983) included 790 cattle, 2,932 hogs, and 36,430 poultry. Commercial productions (1983) amounted to 6·6m. lb. of fruit and vegetables ($3·4m.), 667,000 doz. eggs ($811,093). There is an agricultural experimental station at Inarajan.

Fisheries. Fresh fish caught in 1982, 319,300 lb. Offshore fishing produced 100,687 lb., including 6,080 lb. of shrimps.

INDUSTRY AND TRADE

Industry. Guam Economic Development Authority controls three industrial estates: Cabras Island (32 acres); Calvo estate at Tamuning (26 acres); Harmon estate (16 acres). Industries include textile manufacture, cement and petroleum distribution, warehousing, printing, plastics and ship-repair. Other main sources of income are construction and tourism.

Labour. In 1983 51% of employment was in government, 18% in trade, 5% in construction, 13% in services, 4% in manufacturing, 5% in transport and 4% in finance.

Trade. Guam is the only American territory which has complete 'free trade'; excise duties are levied only upon imports of tobacco, liquid fuel and liquor. In the year ending 31 Dec. 1980 imports were valued at \$544·1m. and accounted for 90% of trade.

Tourism. Tourism is developing; there were 1,900 visitors in 1964 and 345,805 in 1983, 294,429 of them from Japan.

COMMUNICATIONS

Roads. There are 419 miles of all-weather roads.

Aviation. Seven commercial airlines serve Guam.

Post and Broadcasting. Overseas telephone and radio dispatch facilities are available. In 1983 there were 23,442 telephones.

There are 4 commercial stations, a commercial television station, a public broadcasting station and a cable television station with 24 channels.

Newspapers. There is 1 daily newspaper, a twice-weekly paper, and 4 weekly publications (all of which are of military or religious interest only).

JUSTICE, RELIGION, EDUCATION AND WELFARE

Justice. The Organic Act established a District Court with jurisdiction in matters arising under both federal and territorial law; the judge is appointed by the President subject to Senate approval. There is also a Supreme Court and a Superior Court; all judges are locally appointed except the Federal District judge. Misdemeanours are under the jurisdiction of the police court. The Spanish law was superseded in 1933 by 5 civil codes based upon California law.

Religion. About 98% of the Guamanians are Roman Catholics; others are Baptists, Episcopalians, Bahais, Lutherans, Mormons, Presbyterians, Jehovah's Witnesses and members of the Church of Christ and Seventh Day Adventists.

Education. Elementary education is compulsory. There are Chamorro Studies courses and bi-lingual teaching programmes to integrate the Chamorro language and culture into elementary and secondary school courses. There were, Dec. 1983, 24 elementary schools, 6 junior high schools, 5 senior high schools, one vocational-technical school for high school students and adults and 1 school for handicapped children. There were 17,725 elementary school pupils, 7,418 junior high and 5,776 senior high school pupils. Department of Education staff included 1,258 teachers. The Catholic schools system also operates 3 senior high schools, 3 junior high and 5 elementary schools. The Seventh Day Adventist Guam Mission Academy operates a school from grades 1 through 12, serving over 100 students. St John's Episcopal Preparatory School provides education for 530 students between kindergarten and the 9th grade. The University of Guam (an accredited institution) had 2,774 students, 1983–84.

Health. There is a hospital, 8 nutrition centres, a school health programme and an extensive immunization programme. Emphasis is on disease prevention, health education and nutrition.

Books of Reference

Report (Annual) of the Governor of Guam to the US Department of Interior
Carano, P., and Sanchez, P. C., *Complete History of Guam.* Rutland, Vt, 1964
Guam Annual Economic Review. Economic Research Center, Agana

COMMONWEALTH OF PUERTO RICO

HISTORY. Puerto Rico, by the treaty of 10 Dec. 1898 (ratified 11 April 1899), was ceded by Spain to the US. The name was changed from Porto Rico to Puerto Rico by an Act of Congress approved 17 May 1932. Its territorial constitution was determined by the 'Organic Act' of Congress (2 March 1917) known as the 'Jones Act', which ruled until 25 July 1952, when the present constitution of the Commonwealth of Puerto Rico was proclaimed.

AREA AND POPULATION. Puerto Rico is the most easterly of the Greater Antilles and lies between the Dominican Republic and the US Virgin Islands. The island has a land area of 3,459 sq. miles and a population, according to the census of 1980, of 3,196,520, an increase of 484,487 or 17·9% over 1970. Of the population in 1970 about 529,000 were bilingual, Spanish being the mother tongue and (with English) one of the two official languages. Urban population (1980) 2,134,365 (66·8%).

Vital statistics (1981–82): Births, 69,336 (21·2 per 1,000 population); deaths, 21,522 (6·5); deaths under 1 year, 1,193 (17·6 per 1,000 live births).

Chief towns (1980) are: San Juan, 434,849; Bayamón, 196,207; Ponce, 189,046; Carolina, 165,954; Caguas, 117,959; Mayaguez, 96,193; Arecibo, 86,766.

The Puerto Rican island of Vieques, 10 miles to the east, has an area of 51·7 sq. miles and 7,662 inhabitants. The island of Culebra, with 1,265 inhabitants, between Puerto Rico and St Thomas, has a good harbour.

CONSTITUTION AND GOVERNMENT. Puerto Rico has representative government, the franchise being restricted to citizens 18 years of age or over, residence (1 year) and such additional qualifications as may be prescribed by the Legislature of Puerto Rico, but no property qualification may be imposed. Women were enfranchised in 1932 (with a literacy test) and fully in 1936. Puerto Ricans do not vote in the US presidential elections, though individuals living on the mainland are free to do so subject to the local electoral laws. The executive power resides in a Governor, elected directly by the people every 4 years. Fourteen heads of departments form the Governor's advisory council, also designated as his Council of Secretaries. The legislative functions are vested in a Senate, composed of 27 members (2 from each of the 8 senatorial districts and 11 senators at large), and the House of Representatives, composed of 51 members (1 from each of the 40 representative districts and 11 elected at large). Puerto Rico sends to Congress a Resident Commissioner to the US, elected by the people for a term of 4 years, but he has no vote in Congress. Puerto Rican men are subject to conscription in US services.

On 27 Nov. 1953 President Eisenhower sent a message to the General Assembly of the UN stating 'if at any time the Legislative Assembly of Puerto Rico adopts a resolution in favour of more complete or even absolute independence' he 'will immediately thereafter recommend to Congress that such independence be granted'.

For an account of the constitutional developments prior to 1952, *see* THE STATESMAN'S YEAR-BOOK, 1952, p. 742. The new constitution was drafted by a Puerto Rican Constituent Assembly and approved by the electorate at a referendum on 3 March 1952. It was then submitted to Congress, which struck out Section 20 of Article 11 covering the 'right to work' and the 'right to an adequate standard of living'; the remainder was passed and proclaimed by the Governor on 25 July 1952.

At the election on 4 Nov. 1984 the Popular Democratic Party, headed by Rafael

Hernández Colon, polled 822,783 votes (47·8% of the total); the New Progressive Party, headed by Carlos Romero Barceló, polled 768,742 votes (44·6% of the total); the Independence Party (full independence by constitutional means), 61,316 (3·6% of the total); Renewal Puerto Rican Party, 69,865 votes (3·6% of the total).

Governor: Rafael Hernández Colon (Popular Democratic Party), 1985–89 ($35,000).

ECONOMY

Budget. Receipts and disbursements (US$) in central government fund for the year ending 30 June 1982 were:

Balance, 1 July 1981	16,632,000	Disbursements	3,818,678,000
Receipts	3,878,806,000	Balance, 1 July 1979	76,760,000
Total	3,895,438,000		

Assessed value of property, 30 June 1984, was $9,341·9m., and bonded indebtedness (30 June 1984), $1,917·5m.

The US administers and finances the postal service and maintains air and naval bases. US payments in Puerto Rico, including direct expenditures (mainly military), grants-in-aid and other payments to individuals and to business totalled: 1977–78, $2,563·4m.; 1978–79, $2,814·4m.; 1979–80, $3,176m.; 1980–81, $3,426·5m.; 1981–82, $3,553·6m.; 1982–83, $3,626·3m.

Banking. Banks on 30 June 1984 had total deposits of $15,149·1m. Bank loans were $8,422·7m. This includes 18 commercial banks, 2 government banks and 4 trust companies.

NATURAL RESOURCES

Minerals. Production: Cement (1983–84), 1m. short tons; stone (1981), 20·5m. short tons, value $96·2m. Total value of mineral production in 1981 was $208m.

Agriculture. In 1974 there were 47 'proportional profit' farms of 22,051 cords (about 22,704 acres) (mostly sugar-cane). The land had been bought from the big corporations by the Land Authority.

Production of raw sugar, 96 degrees basis, 1984 crop year, was 95,751 tons.

Livestock (1984): Cattle, 591,972; pigs, 202,764; goats, 15,531; and poultry, 6·4m.

COMMERCE. In 1983–84 imports amounted to $9,529m., of which $5,456·5m. came from US; exports were valued at $9,145·9m., of which $7,559·7m. went to US.

In financial year 1984 the US took: Sugar, 11,585 short tons; tobacco and products, 2,298,062 lb.; rum, 21,975,086 proof gallons.

Puerto Rico is not permitted to levy taxes on imports.

Total trade between Puerto Rico and UK (British Department of Trade returns, in £1,000 sterling):

	1980	*1981*	*1982*	*1983*	*1984*
Imports to UK	33,002	29,085	33,445	58,804	76,854
Exports and re-exports from UK	16,970	19,819	25,735	35,936	72,695

COMMUNICATIONS

Roads. The Department of Public Works had under maintenance in June 1983, 6,562 miles of paved road. Motor vehicles registered 30 June 1984, 1,227,000.

Shipping. In financial year 1983–84, 7,965 American and foreign vessels of 47,244,352 gross tons entered and cleared Puerto Rico.

Post and Broadcasting. In 1984 there were 99 broadcasting stations and 11 television companies. There were (1984) 730,949 telephones.

Cinemas (1981–82). Cinemas had an annual attendance of 7·3m.

Newspapers. In Sept. 1984 there were 5 main newspapers, *El Nuevo Día* had a circulation of about 194,679; *El Vocero*, 206,247; *San Juan Star*, 38,000; *El Mundo*, 107,000 and *El Reportero*, 50,000.

JUSTICE AND EDUCATION

Justice. The Commonwealth judiciary system is headed by a Supreme Court of 7 members, appointed by the Governor, and consists of a Superior Tribunal with 11 sections and 92 superior judges, a District Tribunal with 38 sections and 99 district judges, and 60 municipal judges all appointed by the Governor. The police force (1982) consisted of 10,051 men and women.

Education. Education was made compulsory in 1899, but in 1981, 3·6% of the children still had no access to schooling. The percentage of illiteracy in 1976 was 8·7% of those 10 years of age or older. Total enrolment in public schools, 1983–84, was 709,135. Accredited private schools had 87,055 pupils (1983–84). All instruction below senior high school standard is given in Spanish only.

The University of Puerto Rico, in Río Piedras, 7 miles from San Juan, had 53,816 students in 1983–84 of which 19,756 were in 8 Regional Colleges. Higher education is also available in the Inter-American University of Puerto Rico (39,123 students in 1983–84), the Catholic University of Puerto Rico (13,808), the Sacred Heart College (7,985) and the Fundacion Educativa Ana G. Méndez (16,226). These and other private colleges and universities had 106,387 students.

Books of Reference

Statistical Information: The area of Economic Research and Evaluation of the Puerto Rico Planning Board publishes: *(a)* annual *Economic Report to the Governor; (b) Statistical Yearbook* (since 1940–41); *(c) External Trade Statistics* (annual report); *(d) Economic Bulletin* (monthly); *(e) Reports on national income and balance of payments; (f) Socio-Economic Statistics* (since 1940); *(g) Puerto Rico Monthly Economic Indicators.* In addition there are annual reports by various Departments.

Annual Reports. Governor of Puerto Rico. Washington
Bird, A., *Bibliografia Puertorriqueña, 1930–45.* Social Science Research Centre, Univ. of Puerto Rico, 2 vols. 1946–47
Carr, R., *Puerto Rico: A Colonial Experiment.* New York Univ. Press, 1984
Cevallos, E., *Puerto Rico.* [Bibliography], Oxford and Santa Barbara, 1985
Crampsey, R. A., *Puerto Rico.* Newton Abbot, 1973
Jones, C. F., and Pico, R. (eds.), *Symposium on the Geography of Puerto Rico.* Univ. of P.R. Press, 1955

Commonwealth Library: Univ. of Puerto Rico Library, Rio Piedras. *Librarian:* José Lázaro.

AMERICAN SAMOA

HISTORY. The Samoan Islands were first visited by Europeans in the 18th century; the first recorded visit was in 1722. On 14 July 1889 a treaty between the USA, Germany and Great Britain proclaimed the Samoan islands neutral territory, under a 4-power government consisting of the 3 treaty powers and the local native government. By the Tripartite Treaty of 7 Nov. 1899, ratified 19 Feb. 1900, Great Britain and Germany renounced in favour of the US all rights over the islands of the Samoan group east of 171° long. west of Greenwich, the islands to the west of that meridian being assigned to Germany (now the Independent State of Western Samoa, *see* p. 1591). The islands of Tutuila and Aunu'u were ceded to the US by their High Chiefs on 17 April 1900, and the islands of the Manu'a group on 16 July 1904. Congress accepted the islands under a Joint Resolution approved 20 Feb. 1929. Swain's Island, 210 miles north of the Samoan Islands, was annexed in 1925 and is administered as an integral part of American Samoa.

AREA AND POPULATION. The islands (Tutuila, Aunu'u, Ta'u, Olosega, Ofu and Rose) are approximately 650 miles east-north-east of Fiji. The total area of

American Samoa is 76·1 sq. miles (197 sq. km); population, 1980, 32,297, nearly all Polynesians or part-Polynesians. The island's 3 Districts are Eastern (population, 1980, 17,311), Western (13,227) and Manu'a (1,732). There is also Swain's Island, with an area of 1·9 sq. miles and 29 inhabitants (1980), which lies 210 miles to the north west. Rose Island (uninhabited) is 0·4 sq. mile in area. In 1981 there were 1,158 births and 153 deaths.

CLIMATE. A tropical maritime climate with a small annual range of temperature and plentiful rainfall. Pago-Pago. Jan. 83°F (28·3°C), July 80°F (26·7°C). Annual rainfall 194" (4,850 mm).

CONSTITUTION AND GOVERNMENT. American Samoa is constitutionally an unorganized unincorporated territory of the US administered under the Department of the Interior. Its indigenous inhabitants are US nationals and are classified locally as citizens of American Samoa with certain privileges under local laws not granted to non-indigenous persons. Polynesian customs (not inconsistent with US laws) are respected.

Fagatogo is the seat of the Government.

The islands are organized in 15 counties grouped in 3 districts; these counties and districts correspond to the traditional political units. On 25 Feb. 1948 a bicameral legislature was established, at the request of the Samoans, to have advisory legislative functions. With the adoption of the Constitution of 22 April 1960, and the revised Constitution of 1967, the legislature was vested with limited law-making authority. The lower house, or House of Representatives, is composed of 20 members elected by universal adult suffrage and 1 non-voting member for Swain's Island. The upper house, or Senate, is comprised of 18 members elected, in the traditional Samoan manner, in meetings of the chiefs.

Governor: A. P. Lutali.
Lieut.-Governor: High Chief Tufele Lia.

ECONOMY

Planning. The first formal Economic Development and Planning Office completed its first year in 1971. Much has been done to promote economic expansion within the Territory and a large amount of outside investment interest has been stimulated.

The Office initiated the first Territorial Comprehensive Plan. This plan when completed will, with periodic updating, provide a guideline to territorial development for the next 20 years. The planning programme was made possible under a Housing and Urban Development '701' grant programme, and Economic Development Administration '302' planning programmes.

The focus will be on physical development and the problems of a rapidly increasing population with severely limited labour resources.

Budget. The chief sources of revenue are annual federal grants from the US, and local revenues from taxes, and duties, and receipts from commercial operations (enterprise and special revenue funds), utilities, rents and leases and liquor sales. During the financial year 1983–84 the Government had a revenue of $76·6m. including local appropriations of $9·5m., federal appropriations of $39·6m. and enterprise funds of $17·5m.

Banking. The American Samoa branch of the Bank of Hawaii and the American Samoa Bank offer all commercial banking services. The Development Bank of American Samoa, government owned, is concerned primarily through loans and guarantees with the economic advancement of the Territory.

ENERGY AND NATURAL RESOURCES

Electricity. Net power generated (financial year 1981) was 72·2m. kwh., of which 23·1m. kwh. was supplied to large power users and 20·2m. kwh. to householders. All the Manu'a islands have electricity.

Agriculture. Of the 48,640 acres of land area, 11,000 acres are suitable for tropical crops; most commercial farms are in the Tafuna plains and west Tutuila. Principal crops are taro, bread-fruit, yams, bananas and coconuts. Local sales (1982): taro, 770,315 lb.; bananas, 1m. lb.; vegetables, 584,143 lb.

Livestock (1981): Pigs, 8,000; goats, 8,000; poultry, 45,000.

INDUSTRY AND TRADE

Industry. Fish canning is important, employing the second largest number of people (after government). Attempts are being made to provide a variety of light industries. Tuna fishing and local inshore fishing are both expanding.

Commerce. In 1982 American Samoa exported goods valued at $186,782,060 and imported goods valued at $119,416,918. Chief exports are canned tuna, watches, pet foods and handicrafts. Chief imports are building materials, fuel oil, food, jewellery, machines and parts, alcoholic beverages and cigarettes.

COMMUNICATIONS

Roads. There are (1983) about 76 miles of paved roads and 16 miles of unpaved within the Federal Aid highway system. There are 21 miles of other unpaved roads. Motor vehicles registered, 1983, 3,657.

Aviation. South Pacific Island Airways and Polynesian Airlines operate daily services between American Samoa and Western Samoa. South Pacific Island Airways also operates between Pago Pago and Honolulu, and between Pago Pago and Tonga. The islands are also served by Air Nauru which operates between Pago Pago, Tahiti and Auckland, and Air Pacific (Fiji and westward). South Pacific and Manu'a Air Transport run local services.

Shipping. The harbour at Pago Pago, which nearly bisects the island of Tutuila, is the only good harbour for large vessels in Samoa. By sea, there is a twice-monthly service between Fiji, New Zealand and Australia and regular service between US, South Pacific ports, Honolulu and Japan.

Post and Broadcasting. A commercial radiogram service is available to all parts of the world through 2 principal trunks, United States and Western Samoa. Commercial phone and telex services are operated to all parts of the world on a 24-hour service. Number of telephones (Sept. 1983), 6,029; telex subscribers, 78.

JUSTICE, EDUCATION AND WELFARE

Justice. Judicial power is vested firstly in a High Court. The trial division has original jurisdiction of all criminal and civil cases. The probate division has jurisdiction of estates, guardianships, trusts and other matters. The land and title division decides cases relating to disputes involving communal land and Matai title court rules on questions and controversy over family titles. The appellate division hears appeals from trial, land and title and probate divisions as well as having original jurisdiction in selected matters. The appellate court is the court of last resort. Two American judges sit with 5 Samoan judges permanently. In addition there are temporary judges or assessors who sit occasionally on cases involving Samoan customs. There is also a District Court with limited jurisdiction and there are 69 village courts.

Education. Education is compulsory between the ages of 6 and 18. The Government (1983) maintains 24 consolidated elementary schools, 5 senior high schools with technical departments, 1 community college, special education classes for the handicapped and 92 Early Childhood Education Centres for pre-school children. Total elementary and secondary enrolment (1983), 8,300; in ECE schools, 1,611; classes for the handicapped, 68; total elementary and secondary classroom teachers, 480. Ten private schools had 2,108 students. Learning is by a variety of media including television.

Health. The Department of Health provides the only curative and preventive medical and dental care in American Samoa. It operates a general hospital (173 beds including 49 bassinets), 3 dispensaries on Tutuila, 4 dispensaries in the Manu'a group, 1 on Aunu'u and 1 on Swain's Island. A $3·5m. tropical medical centre was completed and placed in service in 1968. This now embraces the general hospital as well as preventive health services and out-patient clinics for surgery, obstetrics, gynaecology, emergencies, family practice, internal medicine, paediatrics; there are clinics for treatment of the eye, ear, nose and throat, dental and public health departments.

In 1983 there were 27 doctors, 7 dentists, 2 optometrists, 3 nurse anaesthetists, and 3 physician assistants. Total number of health service employees, 397.

VIRGIN ISLANDS OF THE UNITED STATES

HISTORY. The Virgin Islands of the United States, formerly known as the Danish West Indies, were named and claimed for Spain by Columbus in 1493. They were later settled by Dutch and English planters, invaded by France in the mid-17th century and abandoned by the French *c.* 1700, by which time Danish influence had been established. St Croix was held by the Knights of Malta between two periods of French rule.

They were purchased by the United States from Denmark for $25m. in a treaty ratified by both nations and proclaimed 31 March 1917. Their value was wholly strategic, inasmuch as they commanded the Anegada Passage from the Atlantic Ocean to the Caribbean Sea and the approach to the Panama Canal. Although the inhabitants were made US citizens in 1927, the islands are, constitutionally, an 'unincorporated territory'.

AREA AND POPULATION. The Virgin Islands group, lying about 40 miles due east of Puerto Rico, comprises the islands of St Thomas (32 sq. miles), St Croix (84 sq. miles), St John (20 sq. miles) and about 50 small islets or cays, mostly uninhabited. The total area of the 3 principal islands is 132 sq. miles, of which the US Government owns 9,599 acres as National Park.

The population, according to the census of 1 April 1980, was 95,591, an increase of 33,123 or 53% since 1970. Estimate (1984) 100,000. Population had slowly declined since 1835, when it stood at 43,000, but began to recover in the 1940s. Population of St Croix, 49,013; St Thomas, 44,218; St John, 2,360. About 20–25% are native-born, 35–40% from other Caribbean islands, 10% from mainland USA and 5% from Europe. St Croix has over 40% of Puerto Rican origin or extraction, Spanish speaking. In financial year 1983, live births were 2,593 and deaths, 510.

The capital and only city, Charlotte Amalie, on St Thomas, had a population (1980) of 11,756; there are two towns on St Croix. Christiansted with 2,856 and Frederiksted with 1,054.

CONSTITUTION AND GOVERNMENT. The Organic Act of 22 July 1954 gives the US Department of the Interior full jurisdiction; some limited legislative powers are given to a single- chambered legislature, composed of 15 senators elected for 2 years representing the two legislative districts of St Croix and St Thomas-St John.

The Governor is elected by the residents. A new Constitution was under consideration in March 1979, but was rejected by the electorate; a further constitutional convention was held in 1980. A new document was submitted to the President of the United States and to Congress; it was approved and submitted to the Virgin Islands electorate and was defeated in a referendum in Nov. 1981.

For administration, there are 13 executive departments, 12 of which are under commissioners and the other, the Department of Law, under an Attorney-General. The US Department of the Interior appoints a Federal Comptroller of government revenue and expenditure.

The franchise is vested in residents who are citizens of the United States, 18 years of age or over. In 1984 there were 30,430 voters, of whom 22,274 (or 73·2%) participated in the local elections that year.

They do not participate in the US presidential election but they have a non-voting representative in Congress.

The capital is Charlotte Amalie, on St Thomas Island.

Governor: Juan Luis ($51,000).
Lieut.-Governor: Julio A. Brady ($47,000).

ECONOMY

Budget. Under the 1954 Organic Act finances are provided partly from local revenues—customs, federal income tax, real and personal property tax, trade tax, excise tax, pilotage fees, etc.—and partly from Federal Matching Funds, being the excise taxes collected by the federal government on such Virgin Islands products transported to the mainland as are liable.

Budget for financial year 1984, $259·8m.

Currency and Banking. United States currency became legal tender on 1 July 1934. Banks are the Chase Manhattan Bank; the Bank of Nova Scotia; the First Federal Savings and Loan Association of Puerto Rico; Barclays Bank International; Bank of America; Citibank; First Pennsylvania Bank, Banco Popular de Puerto Rico, and the Royal Bank of Canada.

ENERGY AND NATURAL RESOURCES

Electricity. The Virgin Islands Water and Power Authority provides electric power from generating plants on St Croix and St Thomas; St John is served by power cable and emergency generator.

Water. Large de-salinization plants have been established, but rain-water remains the most reliable source. Every building must have a cistern to provide rain-water for drinking, even in areas served by mains (10 gallons capacity per sq. ft of roof for a single-storey house).

Agriculture. With the phasing out of the sugar-cane industry in St Croix, and the accelerated construction activities carried on in all three islands, the number of farms decreased, but there has recently been a revival of interest in food crops. The government has bought 2,000 acres on St Croix, partly for farming.

Land for fruit, vegetables and animal feed is available on St Croix, and there are tax incentives for development. Sugar has been terminated as a commercial crop and over 4,000 acres of prime land could be utilized for food crops.

Livestock (1983): Cattle, 7,188; goats, 6,724; pigs, 2,469; sheep, 3,018.

Fisheries. There is a fishermen's co-operative with a market at Christiansted. There is a shellfish-farming project at Rust-op-Twist, St Croix.

INDUSTRY AND TRADE

Industry. The main occupations on St Thomas are tourism and government service; on St Croix manufacturing is more important. Manufactures include textiles, pharmaceuticals, rum and fragrances. The Martin Marietta Alumina plant processes bauxite from Africa for refining in mainland USA. The Amerada Hess oil refinery has a capacity of 700,000 bbls per day.

The Virgin Islands offer liberal tax exemptions to persons, firms or companies prepared to invest $50,000 in new industries or in the promotion of tourism.

Commerce. Exports, calendar year 1984, totalled $3,600m. and imports $4,700m.

Total trade between the US Virgin Islands and UK (financial years, British Department of Trade returns, in £1,000 sterling):

	1981	*1982*	*1983*	*1984*
Imports to UK	13	137	9,706	56,871
Exports and re-exports from UK	2,882	27,450	4,981	3,657

Tourism. Tourism is the most important business. There were about 1·3m. visitors in 1984 spending $360m.

About 657,460 tourists came on cruise ships which made 789 calls, mainly at St Thomas which has a good, natural deepwater harbour.

COMMUNICATIONS

Roads. The Virgin Islands have (1984) 660 miles of roads, and 42,669 motor vehicles registered.

Aviation. There is a daily cargo and passenger service between St Thomas and St Croix. Alexander Hamilton Airport on St Croix can take all aircraft except Concorde. Harry S. Truman Airport on St Thomas takes 727-class aircraft; it is being enlarged (1983) to take larger aircraft. There are air connexions to mainland USA, other Caribbean islands, Latin America and Europe.

Shipping. The whole territory has free port status; there is a container port in St. Croix. There is an hourly boat service between St Thomas and St John.

Post and Broadcasting. All three Virgin Islands have a dial telephone system. In Jan. 1985 there were 53,306 telephones. Direct dialling to Puerto Rico and the mainland is now possible. Worldwide radio telegraph service is also available.

The islands are served by 7 radio stations, 3 television stations and cable TV, 2 daily newspapers and several monthlies.

RELIGION AND EDUCATION

Religion. There are churches of the Protestant, Roman Catholic and Jewish faiths in St Thomas and St Croix and Protestant and Roman Catholic churches in St John.

Education. Education is compulsory between the ages of 5½ and 16 years, inclusive. In 1984–85 there were 37 public schools (ranging from kindergarten to high schools); enrolment was 25,568; 27 private schools had 7,030 pupils; the public school budget was $66·2m. In 1984 the College of the Virgin Islands had 2,862 registered students; 777 full-time undergraduates, 1,906 part-time undergraduates and 179 graduate students. The College is part of the United States land-grant network of higher education; it has campuses on St. Thomas and St. Croix.

Books of Reference

Boyer, W. W., *America's Virgin Islands.* Durham, N.C., 1983

Dookhan, I., *A History of the Virgin Islands of the United States.* Caribbean Univ. Press, 1974

McGuire, J. W., *Geographic Dictionary of the Virgin Islands of the United States.* US Coast and Geodetic Survey. Special Publication No. 103. Washington, 1925

Reid, C. F., *Bibliography of the Virgin Islands of the United States.* New York, 1941

TRUST TERRITORY OF THE PACIFIC ISLANDS

HISTORY. Under the Treaty of Versailles (1919) Japan was appointed mandatory to the former German possessions north of the Equator. In 1946 the US agreed to administer the former Japanese-mandated islands of the Caroline, Marshall and Mariana groups (except Guam) as a Trusteeship for the United Nations; the trusteeship agreement was approved by the Security Council 27 April 1947 and came into effect on 18 July 1947. The Trust Territory was administered by the US Navy until 1951, when all the islands except Tinian and Saipan in the Marianas were transferred to the Secretary of the Interior. In 1962 the Interior Department assumed responsibility for them also. On 17 June 1975 the voters of the Northern Mariana Islands, in a plebiscite observed by the UN, adopted the covenant to establish a Commonwealth of the Northern Mariana Islands in Union with the USA. In April 1976 the US government approved the convenant and separated the administration of the Northern Marianas from that of the rest of the Trust Territory; the group has a constitution and a constitutional government, installed 9 Jan. 1978; population, 1 April 1980, 16,800. The rest of the Trust Territory is divided into 3 entities, each with its own constitution. The Marshall Islands and the Federated States of Micronesia (Yap, Kosrae, Truk and Ponape) had negotiated compacts of free association with the US in 1984; the Republic of Palau was still negotiating. Free association gives the USA the authority to control military and defence activities in return for federal government assistance and budget supports to the autonomous constitutional governments. Termination of the UN Trusteeship Agreement is contingent upon establishing a political status, either free association or independence, for the islands.

AREA AND POPULATION. The Trust Territory extends from 1° to 22° N. lat. and from 142° to 172° E. long. The area is generally known as Micronesia, or 'land of the small islands' (Guam, Kiribati and Nauru not part of the Trust Territory, are also ethnically and geographically Micronesian); total land area 708 sq. miles; population (1980 census), 116,974. This excludes the Northern Marianas, which had (1980 census) an area of 471 sq. km (182 sq. miles) and a population of 16,800.

The census population of the 6 administrative districts as of Sept. 1980 was: Truk, 37,742; Ponape, 22,319; Marshall Islands, 31,042; Palau, 12,177; Yap, 8,172; Kosrae, 5,522. Nine different languages are spoken, each with variations; English is used in the schools and is the official language.

CLIMATE. Marked by high temperatures throughout the year and high rainfall. Marshall Islands, Jaluit. Jan. 81°F (27·2°C), July 82°F (27·8°C). Annual rainfall 161″ (4,034 mm). Caroline Islands, Ponape. Jan. 80°F (26·7°C), July 79°F (26·1°C). Annual rainfall 194″ (4,859 mm).

CONSTITUTION AND GOVERNMENT. Constitutional governments are functioning in the Mariana Islands (1978), the Marshall Islands (1979), the Federated States of Micronesia (1979) and the Republic of Palau (1981). Each of the 4 entities is autonomous from the other 3 but all are still legally under the Trust Territory system. The citizens are Trust Territory citizens until the termination of the Trusteeship. Majuro is the capital of the Marshall Islands. Kolonia, Ponape, is the capital of the Federated States, Koror is the headquarters of Palau and Saipan is the capital of the Commonwealth of the Northern Marianas, as well as the US administrative headquarters.

High Commissioner: Janet J. McCoy.

INDUSTRY. Tourism is the main source of income from overseas; industrial development is limited. There is some commercial fishing and agriculture, a coconut-processing plant and a tuna-freezing plant.

COMMUNICATIONS

Aviation. The island groups are served by Continental Air Micronesia *via* Honolulu. Internal commuter airlines operate in Ponape, Yap, Marshalls, Belau and the Marianas. There are connexions to international routes in Guam, Hawaii, Taiwan, Papua-New Guinea, the Philippines and Japan.

JUSTICE, RELIGION, EDUCATION AND WELFARE

Justice. Local constitutions and government statutes are the basis for law; the Trust Territory Code operates if a local constitution or statute fails to cover a particular area which the Code covers. The Trust Territory High Court is confined to specific areas of responsibility, most areas are covered by the constitutional courts. Local customs are recognized and protected in legal practice, when not in conflict with higher law.

Religion. Freedom of religion is guaranteed in the Trust Territory Code and all constitutions.

Education. Education is free and compulsory through elementary school (grades 1–8). There are public and private elementary and secondary schools and government post-secondary education.

Health. The public health system, which includes 6 district hospitals as well as other hospitals and clinics in outlying areas, is carried on by a staff consisting chiefly of trained Micronesian medical and dental officers and assistants, and senior US doctors.

Books of Reference

Report to the United Nations Trusteeship Council, 1979. Dept. of State, Washington, D.C., 1980

Basic Information. High Commissioner's Office, Saipan; Office of the Governor, Commonwealth of the Northern Mariana Islands, Saipan; Office of the President, Republic of the Marshall Islands, Majuro; Office of the President, Federated States of Micronesia, Ponape, Caroline Islands; Office of the President, Republic of Palau, Palau, Caroline Islands.

UNINCORPORATED TERRITORIES

Johnston Atoll. Two small islands 1,150 km south-west of Hawaii, administered by the US Air Force. Area, under 1 sq. mile; population (1980 census) 327, with Sand Island.

Midway Islands. Two small islands at the western end of the Hawaiian chain, administered by the US Navy. Area, 2 sq. miles; population (1980 census) 453.

Wake Island. Three small islands 3,700 km west of Hawaii, administered by the US Air Force. Area, 3 sq. miles; population (1980 census) 302.

URUGUAY

Capital: Montevideo
Population: 2·99m. (1983)
GNP per capita: US$2,820 (1981)

República Oriental del Uruguay

HISTORY. The Republic of Uruguay, formerly a part of the Spanish Viceroyalty of Río de la Plata and subsequently a province of Brazil, declared its independence 25 Aug. 1825 which was recognized by the treaty between Argentina and Brazil signed at Rio de Janeiro 27 Aug. 1828. The first constitution was adopted 18 July 1830.

AREA AND POPULATION. Uruguay is bounded on the north-east by Brazil, on the south-east by the Atlantic, on the south by the Río de la Plata and on the west by Argentina. The area is 186,926 sq. km (72,172 sq. miles). The following table shows the area and the population of the 19 departments (capitals in brackets) as estimated in May 1975:

Departments	*Area sq. km*	*Population*	*Pop. per sq. km*
Artigas (Artigas)	11,378	57,528	4·6
Canelones (Canelones)	4,752	313,858	54·3
Cerro-Largo (Melo)	14,929	73,204	4·8
Colonia (Colonia)	5,682	110,820	18·5
Durazno (Durazno)	14,315	54,990	3·7
Flores (Trinidad)	4,519	24,684	5·2
Florida (Florida)	12,107	66,092	5·3
Lavalleja (Minas)	12,485	65,240	5·3
Maldonado (Maldonado)	4,111	75,607	14·9
Montevideo (Montevideo City)	664	1,345,858	2,102·4
Paysandú (Paysandú)	13,252	98,735	6·6
Río Negro (Fray Bentos)	8,471	49,816	5·5
Rivera (Rivera)	9,829	79,330	7·8
Rocha (Rocha)	11,089	59,952	5·0
Salto (Salto)	12,603	100,407	7·3
San José (San José)	6,963	88,281	11·1
Soriano (Mercedes)	9,223	80,114	8·4
Tacuarembó (Tacuarembó)	21,015	84,829	3·7
Treinta y Tres (Treinta y Tres)	9,539	45,680	4·5
Total	186,926	2,843,296	15·2

Estimated population in 1983 was 2,991,341. In 1980 Montevideo (the capital) had an estimated population of 1,362,000. Other cities (1975): Salto, 80,000; Paysandú, 80,000; Mercedes, 53,000.

CLIMATE. A warm temperate climate, with mild winters and warm summers The wettest months are March to June, but there is really no dry season. Montevideo. Jan. 72°F (22·2°C), July 50°F (10°C). Annual rainfall 38'' (950 mm).

CONSTITUTION AND GOVERNMENT. Since 1900 Uruguay has been unique in her constitutional innovations, all designed to protect her from the emergence of a dictatorship. The favourite device of the group known as the 'Batllistas' (a *Colorado* faction) which, until defeated at the 1958 elections, held the majority for over 90 years, has been the collegiate system of government, in which the two largest political parties were represented.

One such pattern lasted from 1917 to 1933, when it was abolished by a dictator who re-established the system of an individual President. Until 1951 Presidents were elected every 4 years and they selected their own Cabinet Ministers (*see* list of Presidents in THE STATESMAN'S YEAR-BOOK, 1956, p. 1493). In 1951, on the initiative of the 'Batllistas', the Constitution was amended. Parliament was dissolved in June 1973, and a military government installed.

Presidential elections were held on 25 Nov. 1984 and Julio Maria Sanguinetta of the Colorado Party was elected. The first-choice candidates of the National (Blanco) Party and the Broad Front Party were vetoed by the military government. Gen. Gregorio Alvarez resigned on 12 Feb. 1985 and a return to civilian rule took place on 1 March 1985.

President: Julio Maria Sanguinetta (sworn in on 1 March 1985).

The Cabinet in March 1985 was as follows:

Defence: Juan Vicente Chiarino. *Foreign Affairs:* Enrique Iglesias. *Interior:* Carlos Manini Rios. *Economy:* Ricardo Zerbino. *Public Health:* Raul Ugarte. *Industry and Energy:* Carlos Piran. *Transport and Public Works:* Jorge Sanguinetti. *Labour:* Hugo Fernandez. *Agriculture:* Roberto Vasquez Platero. *Justice, Education and Culture:* Adela Reta.

National flag: Nine horizontal stripes of white and blue, a white canton with the 'Sun of May' in gold.

National anthem: Orientales, la patria ó la tumba (words by Francisco Acuña de Figueroa; music by Francisco José Deballi).

DEFENCE

Army. The Army consists of volunteers who enlist for 1-2 years service. There are 3 cavalry, 5 infantry, 1 artillery and 1 engineer brigades, 1 air defence and 1 parachute battalion. Equipment includes 17 M-24, 29 M-3A1 and 22 M-41 light tanks. Strength was (1985) 22,300, with about 120,000 former regulars as reserve.

Navy. The Navy consists of 3 frigates (*ex*-US old destroyer escorts), 1 corvette (*ex*-US fleet minesweeper), 1 patrol vessel (*ex*-coastal minesweeper), 3 coastal patrol craft, 1 transport, 1 training ship, 1 salvage vessel, 7 minor amphibious craft, 2 oilers and 1 tender. Personnel in 1985: totalled 5,500 officers and ratings including naval infantry (marines) and Coastguard, and the small US-equipped naval air service of 30 aircraft and 4 helicopters.

Air Force. Organized with US aid, the Air Force has about 3,500 personnel and 110 aircraft, including 1 counter-insurgency squadron with 4 IA 58 Pucara, 4 AT-33 armed jet trainers and 8 A-37B light strike aircraft, a reconnaissance and training squadron with 10 T-6Gs, 3 transport squadrons with 4 turboprop FH-227/F.27 Friendships, 5 Brazilian-built EMB-110 Bandeirantes (1 equipped for photographic duties), 5 CASA C-212 Aviocars and 6 Queen Airs, a search and rescue squadron with Cessna U-17A aircraft and light helicopters, and a number of Cessna 182 light aircraft for liaison duties. Basic training types are the T-41 and T-34.

INTERNATIONAL RELATIONS

Membership. Uruguay is a member of UN, OAS and LAIA (formerly LAFTA).

ECONOMY

Budget. The receipts and expenditure of the national accounts as approved by the National Council of Government (UR$1m.):

	1980	*1981*	*1982*	*1983*
Revenue	14,954,800	21,260,000	19,551,900	29,486,400
Expenditure	14,879,900	21,368,600	30,761,400	36,897,300

Now covering a 5-year period the budget is presented during the year following election of each new government; differences in actual annual income and expenditure and amendments to the budget (including new taxes) must be approved by Parliament each year-end; these usually come forward in July each year.

Expenditures in 1983 included: Salaries and social security payments, 66·5%; other current expenditure, 11·1%; subsidies and transfer payments, 5·8%; interests of public debts, 6·1%; and investments, 10·5%. Expenditure on public works is separately financed from specific revenues (*e.g.,* fuel tax). A law inaugurating income tax came into operation on 1 July 1961, but was repealed on 1 March 1974.

Foreign debt outstanding in Dec. 1983 was US$4,589m. Total reserves of the Banco Central in Dec. 1983 were US$258·4m.

Currency. The unit of currency is the *Nuevo Peso* (1,000 old pesos) of 100 *centésimos.* The actual circulating medium consists of paper notes issued by the Central Bank in *Nuevo Peso* denominations of 50, 100, 500 and 1,000 *Nuevo Peso*, and 1, 2, 5 and 10 coins.

In March 1985, US$1 = 90·05 *pesos*; £1 = 96·08 *pesos.*

Banking. The Bank of the Republic (founded 1896), whose president and directors are appointed by the Government has a paid-up capital of N$1,852m. The Banco Central was inaugurated on 16 May 1967. Note circulation in Dec. 1983 was N$10,538·7m.

A state-owned National Insurance Bank *(Banco de Seguros del Estado)* has a monopoly of new insurance business of all kinds. The Bank re-insures much of its business in London.

Of the 25 banks in Uruguay the Bank of London and South America (British) has a main office and 16 branch agencies.

Weights and Measures. The metric system was adopted in 1862.

ENERGY AND NATURAL RESOURCES

Electricity. The supply of electricity for light, power and traction has been a State monopoly since 1897. In Jan. 1949 the first hydro-electric plant at the site of the dam of Rincón del Bonete was completed with an installed capacity of 128 megawatts. Another plant at Rincón de Baygorria on the Río Negro came into operation in 1960, with a capacity of 108 megawatts. Palmar hydro-electric dam came into operation in early 1982 with an installed capacity of 330 mw. Salto Grande came into full operation in Dec. 1982 with an installed capacity of 1,890 mw, of which Uruguay is getting one-sixth at present. Power output in Dec. 1983 was 3,653,000 mwh.

Oil. An extension of the ANCAP refining plant, opened at Montevideo on 6 Dec. 1961, gives a capacity of 7,500 cu. metres daily of high-octane petrol and high-grade gas for domestic and industrial use.

Agriculture. Uruguay is primarily a pastoral country. Of the total land area of 46m. acres some 41m. are devoted to farming, of which 90% to livestock and 10% to crops. Some large *estancias* have been divided up into family farms; rural landlordism is much less than elsewhere. Uruguay is said to be the only Latin American country in which agricultural workers have the protection of a minimum-wage law. Animals and animal products constituted 34·9% of the exports in 1983.

There were (1983) 10m. cattle, 21·2m. sheep, 530,000 horses, 450,000 pigs, 12,000 goats and 8m. poultry.

The wool clip in 1981–82 was 81,300 tonnes.

Agricultural products are raised chiefly in the departments of Paysandú, Río Negro, Colonia, San José, Soriano and Florida. The average farm is about 250 acres. The principal crops and their estimated yield (in tonnes) in 2 crop years were as follows:

	1982	*1983*		*1982*	*1983*
Wheat	387,800	363,100	Barley	85,300	45,000
Linseed	11,000	4,700	Maize	97,300	103,700
Oats	20,600	26,600	Rice	418,900	323,100

Uruguay is self-sufficient in rice, with a surplus for export. Three sugar refineries handle cane and (mainly) beet, their total production being approximately 92,000 tonnes, and approaching self-sufficiency.

Wine is produced chiefly in the departments of Montevideo, Canelones and Colonia, about enough for domestic consumption. The country has some 6m. fruit trees, principally peaches, oranges, tangerines and pears.

Forestry. In 1980 roundwood removals were 1,729,000 cu. metres, of which 100,000 cu. metres was softwood.

Fisheries. In 1983, the total catch was 142,300 tonnes. Exports were valued at US$43m.

INDUSTRY AND TRADE

Industry. In 1978 there were nearly 77,000 registered enterprises with 405,000 employees. These cover activities such as meat packing, oil refining, cement manufacture, foodstuffs, beverages, leather and textile maufacture, chemicals, light engineering and transport equipment. There are about 100 textile mills, but with the exception of half a dozen large plants, these are on the whole small.

The development of industry is an important economic policy objective and there is a liberal attitude to foreign investment for industrial promotion.

There are a number of public works programmes including airport modernization, port of Montevideo modernization, highways improvements, Montevideo sewage disposal, power production and transmission and telecommunications.

Trade Unions. Trade unions number about 150,000 members. About 1·05m. (35%) population are classed as gainfully occupied. Unemployment rate (average for the country) was 15·5% in Dec. 1983.

Commerce. The foreign trade (officially stated in US$, with the figure for imports based on the clearance permits granted and that for exports on export licences utilized) was as follows (in US$1,000):

	1980	*1981*	*1982*	*1983*
Imports	1,602·5	1,598·9	1,057·9	705·0
Exports	1,209·3	1,215·4	975·8	1,044·5

Of the imports in 1983 (in US$1m.) USA, 53·6; Nigeria, 116·9; Brazil, 94·1; Venezuela, 19·6; Middle East, 78·5; Iran, 78; Argentina, 73·2; Federal Republic of Germany, 40·2; UK, 17·8. Of the exports in 1983 Brazil took 121·4; Argentina, 91; Federal Republic of Germany, 82·4; USSR, 61·9; USA, 102·2; Iran, 121·6; Egypt, 83·5; UK, 41·9.

Principal imports and exports (in US$1,000):

Imports	*1982*	*1983*	*Exports*	*1982*	*1983*
Chemicals	112,100	96,900	Meat and meat products	170,300	222·5
Transport materials	109,800	26,300	Hides, furs and leather manufactures	135,600	139·2
Fuel and lubricants	416,000	286,200	Wool and manufactures	262,600	266·6
Machinery and accessories	141,500	87,000	Vegetable products	147,300	139·3

Total trade between Uruguay and UK (British Department of Trade returns, in £1,000 sterling):

	1980	*1981*	*1982*	*1983*	*1984*
Imports to UK	16,884	26,330	23,107	33,361	33,292
Exports and re-exports from UK	26,619	20,103	13,926	10,763	13,980

Tourism. There were 480,900 tourists in 1981 spending an estimated US$283m.

COMMUNICATIONS

Roads. The main highways, linking Montevideo with the interior, have a total length of 9,899 km, of which about 5,000 km are paved. Other roads, unpaved, are about 4,726 km. Considerable improvements, financed both internally and by international loans, have been carried out in the last few years.

Registered motor vehicles, 31 Dec. 1978, are estimated at 220,000 passenger cars and 92,150 trucks and buses.

Railways. The 4 principal railway systems, embracing 2,987 km, were all built by British capital amounting to £14,513,000. The Uruguayan Government in 1948 bought these railways for £7·15m., assuming control that year. The East Coast Railway (125·5 km) and 3 minor lines were already controlled by the State under a separate administration. In Oct. 1952 the railways were brought under a single administration and a major programme of track upgrading and rolling stock rehabilitation is being carried out. The total railway system open for traffic was (1980) 3,004 km of 1,435 mm gauge. In 1981 it carried 3·3m. passengers and 1·2m. tonnes of freight. In 1979 the 27 km line between Mercedes and Ombucito was opened, providing a direct route from Montevideo to Fray Bentos, while a link with Argentina across the Salto Grande dam was completed in 1982.

Aviation. Carrasco, 22·5 km from Montevideo, is the most important airport. US, Argentine, Brazilian, Chilean, Dutch, French, Fed. German, Scandinavian and Paraguayan airlines fly to and from Uruguay. The state-operated civil airline PLUNA runs services in the interior of the country and to Brazil, Paraguay and Argentina, and Spain.

Shipping. In 1983 there were 13 merchant vessels and 3 tankers. In 1982, 1,115 vessels cleared Montevideo, 17 being British. River transport (1,270 km) is extensive, its main importance being to link Montevideo with Paysandú and Salto.

Post and Broadcasting. The telegraph lines in operation have a total length of 12,083 km. The telephone system in Montevideo is controlled by the State; small companies operate in the interior. Telephone instruments, 1982, numbered 294,350. There are 1,277 post offices. Uruguay has 85 long-wave and 17 short-wave broadcasting stations. There are about 1m. wireless sets and 440,000 television receivers. There are 4 television stations in Montevideo and 11 in the interior. The State itself operates one of the most powerful sound broadcasting stations in South America. Colour television was inaugurated 1981.

Cinemas (1980). Cinemas numbered 85 with seating capacity of 47,000.

Newspapers (1984). There were 5 daily newspapers in Montevideo with aggregate daily circulation of about 210,000; most of the 25–30 provincial newspapers appear bi-weekly.

JUSTICE, RELIGION, EDUCATION AND WELFARE

Justice. The Ministry of Justice was created in 1977 to be responsible for relations between the Executive Power and the Judiciary and other jurisdictional entities. The Court of Justice is made up by 5 members appointed by the Council of the Nation at the suggestion of the Executive Power, for a period of 5 years. This court has original jurisdiction in constitutional, international and admiralty cases and hears appeals from the appellate courts, of which there are 4, each with 3 judges.

In Montevideo there are also 8 courts for ordinary civil cases, 3 for government *(Juzgado de Hacienda)*, as well as criminal and correctional courts. Each departmental capital has a departmental court; each of the 224 judicial divisions has a justice of peace court. In Sept. 1907 the death penalty was abolished, replaced by penal servitude for a period of 30–40 years.

Religion. State and Church are separated, and there is complete religious liberty. The faith professed by the majority of the inhabitants is Roman Catholic. The archbishop of Montevideo has 10 suffragan bishops in Salto, Melo, Florida, Minas, San José, Canelones, Tacuarembó, Mercedes, Maldonado and Montevideo (Auxiliary Bishop).

Protestants numbered about 10,500 in 1957.

Education. Primary education is obligatory; both primary and superior education are free.

In 1979 there were 1,050 primary public schools with 364,910 pupils and approximately 10,300 teachers; in 1979, 249 secondary schools had 196,462 pupils. There are also evening courses for adults. Illiteracy is now confined largely to the older age groups.

The University of the Republic at Montevideo, inaugurated in 1849, has about 16,200 students; tuition is free to both native-born and foreign students; there are 10 faculties. There are 43 normal schools for males and females, and a college of arts and trades with about 33,000 students. There are also many religious seminaries throughout the Republic with a considerable number of pupils, a school for the blind, 2 for deaf and dumb and a school of domestic science.

Health. Hospital beds, 1981, numbered (estimate) 23,000; physicians numbered 5,600.

DIPLOMATIC REPRESENTATIVES

Of Uruguay in Great Britain (48 Lennox Gdns., London, SW1X 0DL)
Ambassador: Dr Luis M. de Posadas Montero (accredited 6 May 1983).

Of Great Britain in Uruguay (Calle Marco Bruto 1073, Montevideo)
Ambassador: Charles William Wallace, CMG, CVO.

Of Uruguay in the USA (1918 F St., NW, Washington, D.C., 20006)
Ambassador: Walter Ra Venna.

Of the USA in Uruguay (Calle Lauro Muller 1776, Montevideo)
Ambassador: Thomas Aranda, Jr.

Of Uruguay to the United Nations
Ambassador: Dr Juan Carlos Blanco.

Books of Reference

The official gazette is the *Diario Oficial*
Statistical Reports of the Government. Montevideo. Annual and biennial
Anales de Instruccion Primaria. Montevideo. Quarterly

Arcas, J. A., *Historia del siglo XX uruguayo, 1897–1943.* Montevideo, 1950
Fernández Saldaña, J. M., *Diccionario Uruguayo de Biografias.* Montevideo, 1945
Finch, M.H.J., *A Political Economy of Uruguay Since 1870.* London, 1981
Montañés, M. T., *Desarrollo de la agricultura en el Uruguay.* Montevideo, 1948
Porzecanski, A. C., *Uruguay's Tupamaros.* London and New York, 1973
Salgado, José, *Historia de la Republica O. del Uruguay.* 8 vols. Montevideo, 1943

National Library: Biblioteca Nacional del Uruguay, Guayabo 1793, Montevideo. It publishes *Anuario Bibliográfico Uruguayo.*

VANUATU

Capital: Vila
Population: 117,000 (1980)
GNP per capita: US$350 (1981)

Republic of Vanuatu

HISTORY. The group was administered for some purposes jointly, for others unilaterally, as provided for by Anglo-French Convention of 27 Feb. 1906, ratified 20 Oct. 1906, and a protocol signed at London on 6 Aug. 1911 and ratified on 18 March 1922. On 30 July 1980 the Condominium of the New Hebrides achieved independence and became the Republic of Vanuatu.

AREA AND POPULATION. The Vanuatu group lies roughly 500 miles west of Fiji and 250 miles north-east of New Caledonia. The estimated land area is 5,700 sq. miles (14,760 sq. km). The larger islands of the group are: Espiritu Santo, Malekula, Epi, Pentecost, Aoba, Maewo, Paama, Ambrym, Efate, Erromanga, Tanna and Aneityum. They also claim Matthew and Hunter islands. Population at the census (1979) 112,596. Estimate (1980) 117,000. Vila (the capital) 14,000.

There are 3 active volcanoes, on Tanna, Ambrym and Lopevi, respectively. Earth tremors are of common occurrence.

CLIMATE. The climate is tropical, but moderated by oceanic influences and by trade winds from May to Oct. High humidity occasionally occurs and cyclones are possible. Rainfall ranges from 90″ (2,250 mm) in the south to 155″ (3,875 mm) in the north. Vila. Jan. 80°F (26·7°C), July 72°F (22·2°C). Annual rainfall 84″ (2,103 mm).

CONSTITUTION AND GOVERNMENT. General elections took place in Nov. 1975 to elect a 42-member Representative Assembly, replacing the former advisory council. Further general elections took place in Nov. 1979. A committee system was instituted and the Assembly chose its own President from its own members in 1977. The President replaced the Co-Presidents, who were the Resident Commissioners.

President: (Vacant).

The cabinet in Jan. 1984 was composed as follows:

Prime Minister: Walter Hadye Lini, CBE.

Home Affairs and Deputy Prime Minister: S. Regenvanu. *Foreign Affairs:* D Kalpokas. *Education:* O. Tahi. *Finance:* K. Kalsakau. *Health:* W. Korisa. *Transport, Communications and Public Works:* A. Sande. *Agriculture, Forestry, Fisheries:* J. Hopa. *Lands:* S. Molisa.

Flag: Red over green, with a black triangle in the hoist, the three parts being divided by fimbriations of black and yellow, and in the centre of the black triangle a boar's tusk overlaid by two crossed fern leaves.

Language: The national language is Bislama; English and French are also official languages.

ECONOMY

Planning. A National Development Plan (1982-86) envisages expenditure of US$12m.

Budget. The budget for 1982-83 envisages expenditure of 2,472m. Vatu. The main sources of revenue were import and export duties.

Currency. In 1982 a new currency, the *Vatu* was introduced.

Banking. A Central Bank was established in 1980. Because of the absence of direct taxation, with the exception of an added value tax on sales of sub-divided land, there has been growing interest in Vanuatu as a finance centre and 500 overseas companies are using Vila and have contributed 450m. Vatu in invisible export earnings. There were 8 banks in Vila in 1980. There is a National Development Bank and a Central Bank operated by the government and branches of the Bank of Indochine et de Suez at Vila and Santo. Barclays Bank International has a branch in Vila and Santo. Other overseas banks are: ANZ Bank, Westpac Banking Corporation and Hongkong and Shanghai Bank.

NATURAL RESOURCES

Minerals. The manganese mine, established at Forari on Efate by the Compagnie Française de Phosphates de l'Océanie, closed in 1968 but was reopened in 1970 by Southland Mining of Australia. Manganese exports, all to Japan, 1979, 25m. Vatu.

Agriculture. The main commercial crops are copra, cocoa and coffee. Yams, taro, manioc and bananas are grown for local consumption. A large number of cattle are reared on plantations, and an up-grading programme using pure-bred Charolais, Limousins and Illawarras has begun. A beef industry is developing.

Livestock (1983): Cattle, 100,000; goats, 8,000; pigs, 70,000.

Forestry. An active forestry development programme is in progress and more than 26 plantations of South American hardwoods have been established.

Fisheries. The principal catch is tuna (1980, 10,000 tonnes) mainly exported to USA.

INDUSTRY AND TRADE

Industry. Industries include a saw-mill, a soft drinks factory, meat canneries and a modern abattoir, and a fish-freezing plant. A few indigenous crafts, such as basketry, canoe-building and pottery, are practised. Subsistence fishing is done by the Vanuatuan, and a plant for freezing of tuna and bonito commenced operation in 1957. This plant, which is sited on Santo, freezes and packages for export to Japan and elsewhere, fish caught by Taiwanese and other vessels under contract to the British company running the plant. There are over 300 co-operative societies handling 85% of the distribution of goods in the islands.

Commerce. Imports and exports were (in 1m. Vatu):

	1979	*1980*	*1981*	*1982*
Imports	4,276	4,220	5,123	5,794
Exports	2,851	1,759	2,832	2,199

In 1979 the main exports were: Copra, 39,821 tonnes, 1,505m. NH francs; fish, 7,623 tonnes, 831m. NH francs; beef, 750 tonnes, 135m. NH francs. Australia, France and Japan were the major sources of imports and principal imports were food and drink, manufactured goods and petroleum products.

Total trade between Vanuatu and UK (British Department of Trade returns, in £1,000 sterling):

	1982	*1983*	*1984*
Imports to UK	21	28	80
Exports and re-exports from UK	294	811	479

Tourism. Tourism is a growing industry and in 1980 there were 22,000 visitors to Vanuatu.

COMMUNICATIONS

Roads. There are approximately 1,000 km of roads in Vanuatu, of these about 35 km are sealed, mostly on Efate Island. There were 7,000 registered motor vehicles in Vanuatu (1980).

Aviation. External air services are provided by Air Pacific, Solair and Air Vanuatu. Solair has a weekly service Honiara–Santo–Vila and return. Air Vanuatu has 3 services a week Sydney–Vila–Sydney, UTA (Unions de Transports Aériens) and Air Nauru. Air Pacific has two services a week Nandi–Vila–Honiara–Brisbane, and one Nandi–Vila–Noumea–Brisbane. UTA has daily flights from Noumea, and a weekly flight to Wallis. Air Nauru gives a weekly service Vila–Nauru. Inter-island flights are provided by Air Melanesiae. The principal airports are Bauer Field (for Vila) and Pekoa (for Santo). Seventeen smaller airfields provide an internal network. In 1977 there were 1,001 overseas aircraft arrivals in Vila, carrying 59,141 passengers.

Shipping. Several international shipping lines serve Vanuatu, linking the country with Australia, New Zealand, other Pacific territories notably Hong Kong, Japan, North America and Europe. The chief ports are Vila and Santo. In 1977, 394 vessels arrived including 48 cruise ships carrying 40,412 visitors. 92,340 tons of cargo were exported and 102,867 tons discharged. Small vessels provide frequent inter-island services.

Telecommunications. Internal telephone and telegram services are provided by the Posts and Telecommunications and Radio Departments. There are automatic telephone exchanges at Vila and Santo; rural areas are served by a network of tele-radio stations. In 1981 there were 3,000 telephones.

External telephone, telegram and telex services are provided by VANITEL, through their satellite earth station at Vila. There are direct circuits to Noumea, Sydney, Hong Kong and Paris and high quality communications are available on a 24-hour basis to most countries in the world. Air radio facilities are provided. Marine coast station facilities are available at Vila and Santo. Radio New Hebrides operates a service 7 days a week in 3 languages, French, English and Pidgin.

JUSTICE, RELIGION, EDUCATION AND WELFARE

Justice. A study was being made in 1980 which could lead to unification of the judicial system.

Religion. The Presbyterian, Anglican, Roman Catholic, Seven Day Adventists, Church of Christ, Apostolic and Assemblies of God have churches and chapels in Vanuatu.

Education. Primary and secondary education facilities are provided in both English and French. There is one technical training facility in Vila and students undergo higher (university) education either at the University of the South Pacific in Fiji, or University of Papua New Guinea or in France. Teacher training for both English and French language teachers is conducted in Vanuatu.

There were (1980) 115 French language primary and 3 secondary schools and 161 English language primary and 5 secondary schools.

Health. Medical care is provided through a network of 106 hospitals, health centres, clinics and dispensaries administered by the Government with the help of a number of voluntary agencies, and WHO. Public health measures and the control of communicable diseases are the responsibility of the public health administration. Local training schemes are devoted to basic community nurse training at hospitals in Vila, to rural health training and refresher courses at a special training health centre in North Efate, or by attachment to other suitable clinics and health centres, and to training of village sanitarians or health orderlies.

DIPLOMATIC REPRESENTATIVES

Of Vanuatu in Great Britain
High Commissioner: Barak Teme Sope (accredited 4 June 1981).

Of Great Britain in Vanuatu (Melitco Hse., Rue Pasteur, Vila)
High Commissioner: R. B. Dorman, CBE.

VATICAN CITY STATE

Stato della Città del Vaticano

HISTORY. For many centuries the Popes bore temporal sway over a territory stretching across mid-Italy from sea to sea and comprising some 17,000 sq. miles, with a population finally of over 3m. In 1859–60 and 1870 the Papal States were incorporated with the Italian Kingdom. The consequent dispute between Italy and successive Popes was only settled on 11 Feb. 1929 by three treaties between the Italian Government and the Vatican: (1) A Political Treaty, which recognized the full and independent sovereignty of the Holy See in the city of the Vatican; (2) a Concordat, to regulate the condition of religion and of the Church in Italy; and (3) a Financial Convention, in accordance with which the Holy See received 750m. lire in cash and 1,000m. lire in Italian 5% state bonds. This sum was to be a definitive settlement of all the financial claims of the Holy See against Italy in consequence of the loss of its temporal power in 1870. The treaty and concordat were ratified on 7 June 1929. The treaty has been embodied in the Constitution of the Italian Republic of 1947. A revised Concordat between the Italian Republic and the Holy See was signed on 18 Feb. 1984 and on its ratification, the 1929 Concordat will lapse.

The Vatican City State is governed by a Commission appointed by the Pope. The reason for its existence is to provide an extra-territorial, independent base for the Holy See, the government of the Roman Catholic Church.

In 1930 the issue of Papal coinage was resumed, after a lapse of 60 years. In virtue of a special convention between the Vatican City and the Italian Government (last renewed in 1962), each state allows the currency of the other to circulate in its territory. The Vatican City has, however, given an undertaking that the total value of its coins issued in ordinary years will not exceed 100m. lire, 200m. lire in years of 'Sede vacante' or holy years, or 300m. in the year of the opening of a Council.

AREA AND POPULATION. The area of the Vatican City is 44 hectares (108·7 acres). It includes the Piazza di San Pietro (St Peter's Square), which is to remain normally open to the public and subject to the powers of the Italian police. It has its own railway station (opened Nov. 1932), postal facilities, coins and radio. Twelve buildings in and outside Rome enjoy extra-territorial rights, including the Basilicas of St John Lateran, St Mary Major, St Paul without the Walls and the Pope's summer villa at Castel Gandolfo. On 8 Oct. 1951 extra-territorial rights were also granted to a new Vatican radio station on Italian soil. *Radio Vaticana* is broadcasting an extensive service in 34 languages from transmitters in the Vatican City and in Italy.

The Vatican City has about 1,000 inhabitants.

CONSTITUTION. The Pope exercises the sovereignty and has absolute legislative, executive and judicial powers. The judicial power is delegated to a tribunal in the first instance, to the Sacred Roman Rota in appeal and to the Supreme Tribunal of the Signature in final appeal.

The Pope is elected by the College of Cardinals, meeting in secret conclave. The election is by scrutiny and requires a two-thirds majority.

Name and family	*Election*	*Name and family*	*Election*
Benedict XIV *(Lambertini)*	1740	Pius VI *(Braschi)*	1775
Clement XIII *(Rezzonico)*	1758	Pius VII *(Chiaramonti)*	1800
Clement XIV *(Ganganelli)*	1769	Leo XII *(della Genga)*	1823

Name and family	Election	Name and family	Election
Pius VIII *(Castiglioni)*	1829	Pius XI *(Ratti)*	1922
Gregory XVI *(Cappellari)*	1831	Pius XII *(Pacelli)*	1939
Pius IX *(Mastai-Ferretti)*	1846	John XXIII *(Roncalli)*	1958
Leo XIII *(Pecci)*	1878	Paul VI *(Montini)*	1963
Pius X *(Sarto)*	1903	John Paul I *(Luciani)*	1978
Benedict XV *(della Chiesa)*	1914	John Paul II *(Wojtyla)*	1978

Supreme Pontiff: **John Paul II** (Karol Wojtyla), born at Wadowice near Cracow, Poland, 18 May 1920. Archbishop of Cracow 1964–78, created Cardinal in 1967, elected Pope 16 Oct. 1978, inaugurated 22 Oct. 1978.

Pope John Paul II was the first non-Italian to be elected since Pope Adrian VI (a Dutchman) in 1522.

Secretary of State: Cardinal Agostino Casaroli (appointed May 1979).

Flag: Vertically yellow and white, with on the white the crossed keys and tiara of the Papacy.

ROMAN CATHOLIC CHURCH. The Roman Pontiff (in orders a Bishop, but in jurisdiction held to be by divine right the centre of all Catholic unity, and consequently Pastor and Teacher of all Christians) has for advisers and coadjutors the Sacred College of Cardinals, consisting in Oct. 1984 of 124 Cardinals appointed by him from senior ecclesiastics who are either the bishops of important Sees or the heads of departments at the Holy See. In addition to the College of Cardinals, the Pope has created a 'Synod of Bishops'. This consists of the Patriarchs and certain Metropolitans of the Catholic Church of Oriental Rite, of elected representatives of the national episcopal conferences and religious orders of the world, of the Cardinals in charge of the Roman Congregations and of other persons nominated by the Pope. The Synod meets as and when decided by the Pope; its first session was held in the autumn of 1967 and its sixth General Assembly in Sept.–Oct. 1983.

The central administration of the Roman Catholic Church is carried on by a number of permanent committees called Sacred Congregations, each composed of a number of Cardinals and diocesan bishops (both appointed for 5-year periods), with Consultors and Officials. Besides the Secretariat of State and the Council for Public Affairs of the Church (which deals with external relations) there are now 9 Sacred Congregations, viz: Doctrine, Oriental Churches, Bishops, the Sacraments and Divine Worship, Clergy, Religious, Catholic Education, Evangelization of the Peoples and Causes of the Saints. There are also 3 Secretariats: for Christian Unity, Non-Christians and Non-Believers; a Prefecture of Economic Affairs, a Prefecture of the Pontifical Household and a Statistical Office. Furthermore, the Roman Curia contains 3 tribunals, the Apostolic Penitentiary, the Supreme Tribunal of the Apostolic Signature and the Sacred Roman Rota; and, lastly, various other councils and commissions dealing with the Laity, Justice and Peace, Women, the Family, the Information and Revision of Canon Law, Social Communications, Migration and Tourism and Culture. The Pontifical Academy of Sciences was revived by Pius XI in 1936 with 70 members.

More than 2,500 Roman Catholic prelates and 99 observer-delegates from 27 other Christian Churches attended the Second Vatican Council which met 11 Oct. 1962 and 8 Dec. 1965. Sixteen Constitutions and Decrees were approved at the Council, and 7 commissions were set up to implement these decisions.

DIPLOMATIC REPRESENTATIVES

In its diplomatic relations with foreign countries the Holy See is represented by the Council for Public Affairs of the Church. It maintains permanent observers to the UN in New York and Geneva and to UNESCO and FAO. The Holy See is a member of IAEA and the Vatican City State is a member of UPU and ITU. It therefore attends as a member those international conferences open to State members of the UN and specialized agencies.

Of the Holy See in Great Britain
Apostolic Pro-Nuncio in Great Britain: Mgr Bruno Heim, Titular Archbishop of Xanto.

Of Great Britain at the Holy See
Ambassador: David Lane. *First Secretary:* R. J. Griffiths.

Of the Holy See in the USA
Apostolic Pro Nuncio: Most Rev. Pio Laghi.

Of the USA at the Holy See
Ambassador: William A. Wilson.

Books of Reference

Acta Apostolicæ Sedis Romanæ. Rome
Annuario Pontificio. Rome. Annual
L'Attivià della Santa Sede. Rome. Annual
The Catholic Directory. London. Annual
Code of Canon Law. London, 1983
The Catholic Directory for Scotland. Glasgow. Annual
Bilan du Monde: Encyclopédie catholique du monde chrétien. Tournai, 1964
Cardinale, Mgr. Igino, *Le Saint-Siège et la diplomatie.* Paris and Rome, 1962.—*The Holy See and the International Order.* Gerrards Cross, 1976
Hales, E. E., *The Catholic Church and the Modern World.* London, 1958
Mayer, F. *et al, The Vatican: Portrait of a State and a Community.* Dublin, 1980
Nichols, P., *The Politics of the Vatican.* London, 1968
Pallenborg, C., *Vatican Finances.* Harmondsworth, 1971
Walsh, M. J., *Vatican City State.* [Bibliography] Oxford and Santa Barbara, 1983

VENEZUELA

Capital: Caracas
Population: 15·26m. (1984)
GNP per capita: US$4,644 (1982)

República de Venezuela

HISTORY. Venezuela formed part of the Spanish colony of New Granada until 1821 when it became independent in union with Colombia. A separate, independent republic was formed in 1830.

AREA AND POPULATION. Venezuela is bounded north by the Caribbean, east by Guyana, south by Brazil, south-west and west by Colombia. The official estimate of the area is 912,050 sq. km (352,143 sq. miles); the frontiers with Colombia, Brazil and Guyana extend for 2,972 miles and its Atlantic coastline stretches for some 2,000 miles. Over half the population live in the valleys of Caracas and Valencia (once the capital). There are 20 states, 2 territories, the federal district and the federal dependencies (*i.e.* 72 islands in the Antilles); further states may be created from the territories. Bolívar, the largest state, has an area of 91,868 sq. miles; the other states are far smaller. The federal district embraces 745 sq. miles.

The language of the country is Spanish.

Population according to the 1971 census (estimate (1984) 15·26m.):

State	*Capital*	*Population*	*State*	*Capital*	*Population*
Anzoátegui	Barcelona	506,297	Portuguesa	Guanare	297,044
Apure	San Fernando	164,705	Sucre	Cumaná	469,006
Aragua	Maracay	543,170	Táchira	San Cristóbal	511,344
Barinas	Barinas	231,046	Trujillo	Trujillo	381,335
Bolívar	Ciudad Bolivar	391,665	Yaracuy	San Felipe	223,540
Carabobo	Valencia	659,339	Zulia	Maracaibo	1,229,037
Cojedes	San Carlos	94,351	Ter. Amazonas	Puerto Ayacucho	21,696
Falcón	Coro	407,957	Ter. Delta Amacuro	Tucupita	48,139
Guárico	San Juan	318,905	Federal District	Caracas	1,860,637
Lara	Barquisimeto	671,410	Federal Dependencies	—	463
Mérida	Mérida	347,095			
Miranda	Los Teques	856,272			
Monagas	Maturin	298,239			
Nueva Esparta	La Asunción	118,830		Total	10,721,522

The 1971 census excluded tribal Indians estimated at 31,800, of whom 20,000 are in Ter. Amazonas and 4,000 in Zulia. Excluding illegal immigrants, estimated (1979) at about 3m.

The 1971 population of Caracas was 1,035,499; Maracaibo 651,574; Barquisimeto, 330,815; Valencia, 367,154; Maracay, 255,134; San Cristóbal, 152,239; Ciudad Guyana, 143,540; Cabimas, 122,239; Maturín, 121,662; Baruta, 121,066; Cumaná, 119,751; Ciudad Bolívar, 103,728.

Vital statistics, 1979 (estimate): 484,700 births, 74,950 deaths. Life expectancy (1978) 66 years with 53% of population under 18 years.

CLIMATE. The climate ranges from warm temperate to tropical. Temperatures vary little throughout the year and rainfall is plentiful. The dry season is from Dec. to April. Caracas. Jan. 65°F (18·3°C), July 69°F (20·6°C). Annual rainfall 32″ (833 mm). Ciudad Bolivar. Jan. 79°F (26·1°C), July 81°F (27·2°C). Annual rainfall 41″ (1,016 mm). Maracaibo. Jan. 81°F (27·2°C), July 85°F (29·4°C). Annual rainfall 23″ (577 mm).

CONSTITUTION AND GOVERNMENT. The constitution of 1961 provides for popular election for a term of 5 years of a President, a National Congress, and State and Municipal legislative assemblies, and guarantees the freedom of labour, industry and commerce. Aliens are assured of treatment equal to that extended to nationals.

Congress consists of a Senate and a Chamber of Deputies. At least 2 Senators are elected for each State and for the Federal District. Senators must be Venezuelans by birth and over 30 years of age. Deputies must be native Venezuelans over 21 years of age; there is 1 for every 50,000 inhabitants. The territories, on reaching the population fixed by law, also elect deputies. Voting (by proportional representation) is compulsory for men and women over 18. Owing to the high rate of illiteracy, voting is by coloured ballot cards.

The President must be a Venezuelan by birth and over 30 years of age; he has a qualified power of veto.

The following is a list of presidents since 1941:

	Took Office		*Took Office*
Gen. Isaias Medina Angarita	6 May 1941	Dr Edgard Sanabria	14 Nov. 1958[3]
Rómulo Betancourt	20 Oct. 1945	Rómulo Betancourt	13 Feb. 1959
Rómulo Gallegos	15 Feb. 1948	Raul Leoni	11 March 1964
Lieut.-Col. Carlos Delgado Chalbaud	24 Nov. 1948[4]	Rafael Caldera	11 March 1969
Dr G. Suárez Flamerich	27 Nov. 1950[2]	Carlos Andrés Pérez Rodríguez	12 March 1974
Col. Marcos Pérez Jiménez.	3 Dec. 1952[1]	Dr Luis Herrera Campíns	12 March 1979
Rear-Adm. Wolfgang Larrazábal Ugueto	23 Jan. 1958[2] [3]	Dr Jaime Lusinchi	2 Feb. 1984

[1] Deposed. [2] Resigned. [3] Provisional. [4] Assassinated 13 Nov. 1950.

President: Dr Jaime Lusinchi, elected 4 Dec. 1983 with 57% of the votes, assumed office on 2 Feb. 1984.

Foreign Minister: Isidro Morales Paul. *Finance Minister:* Manuel Azpurua.

At the Congressional elections held 4 Dec. 1983, 112 of the 200 seats in the Chamber of Deputies were won by Acción Democrática, 61 by COPEI (the Social Christians) and 27 by other parties.

The city of Caracas is the capital. The 20 states, autonomous and politically equal, have each a legislative assembly and an elected governor. The states are divided into 156 districts and 613 municipalities. There are also 2 federal territories with 7 departments, and a federal district with 2 departments and 2 parishes. Each district has a municipal council, and each municipio a communal junta. The federal district and the 2 territories are administered by the President of the Republic.

National flag: Three horizontal stripes of yellow, blue, red, with an arc of 7 white stars in the centre, and the national arms in the canton.

National anthem: Gloria al bravo pueblo (1811; words by Vicente Salias, tune by Juan Landaeta).

DEFENCE. All Venezuelans on reaching 18 years of age are liable for 2 years in the Armed Forces.

Army. The Army consists of 1 armoured and 1 Ranger brigades; 1 horsed cavalry, 26 infantry and 5 engineer battalions; and 5 artillery groups. Equipment includes 75 AMX-30 main battle and 40 AMX-13 light tanks. Army aviation comprises 30 helicopters and 2 STOL transports. Strength (1985) 27,500.

Navy. Strength includes 3 diesel-powered patrol submarines (2 modern built in Federal Republic of Germany and 1 very old *ex*-US submarine), 8 frigates built in Italy (6 new and 2 old), 6 fast missile-armed patrol craft built in Britain in 1974–75, 5 tank landing ships, 1 medium landing ship, 1 transport landing ship (*ex*-repair ship), 2 new utility landing craft, 12 minor landing craft, 1 survey ship, 2 survey launches, 2 transports, 1 training ship and 8 tugs. Coastal patrol boats operated by the National Guard *(Fuezzas Armadas de Cooperacion)* now number 46, and there are some 30 service craft.

New construction planned includes 4 corvettes, 2 more submarines from the Federal Republic of Germany, 6 fast attack craft, 6 mine countermeasures vessels, 2 landing ships and 1 survey ship.

There is a naval academy and sail training ship for the training of officer cadets and a school of staff studies and various technical training schools. Personnel in 1985 totalled: 13,500 officers and men including 5,500 of the Marine Corps and pilots and crew of the Naval Air Arm comprising 8 S2E Trackers, 6 Agusta AB-212 shipborne helicopters, 6 Bell 47s helicopters and 10 other light aircraft for various and coastguard duties.

Air Force. Formed in 1920, the Air Force of some 4,500 officers and men is a small, but well-equipped service with a total of about 200 aircraft. There are 6 combat squadrons. One is equipped with 18 F-16A and 6 F-16B Fighting Falcons. Two others have 14 Canadair CF-5A fighter-bombers and 6 two-seat CF-5Ds, and 16 Mirage III/5s respectively. Two bomber squadrons are equipped with 19 modernized Canberra jet-bombers and a single reconnaissance Canberra. Another operational squadron has 15 OV-10E Bronco twin-turboprop counter-insurgency aircraft. A helicopter force consists of more than 40 Bell JetRangers, 212s, 214STs and 412s, UH-1B/D/H Iroquois, Agusta A 109s and Alouette IIIs. Transport units are equipped with 12 C-123 Providers, 5 C-130H Hercules and 6 Aeritalia G222s. Communications aircraft are Queen Airs and other types. T-34 Mentors are used for training, together with 20 T-2D Buckeye advanced jet trainers, which have a secondary attack role. A battalion of paratroops comes within Air Force responsibility. There is a staff college and a cadet academy.

National Guard, a volunteer force of some 15,000 under the Ministry of Defence, is broadly responsible for internal security. It includes customs and forestry duties among its tasks.

INTERNATIONAL RELATIONS

Membership. Venezuela is a member of UN, OAS, LAIA (formerly LAFTA), OPEC and the Andean Group.

ECONOMY

Planning. The sixth 5-year plan (1981–85) aims to achieve economic growth but with a reorientation of priorities towards social programmes: Education, housing and public services. There are 5 major projects: Caracas metro, Guri hydro-electric scheme, INOS water supply, major housing schemes and the Corpozulia coal and steel complex. These will cost Bs. 67,000m. over 5 years.

Budget. The revenue and expenditure for calendar years were, in Bs.1m., as follows:

	1979	*1980*	*1981*	*1982*	*1983*
Revenue	50,588	71,508	94,865	82,101	87,978
Expenditure	51,236	72,868	94,544	86,884	86,110

Currency. The *bolívar* (Bs.) is divided into 100 *céntimos*. Gold coins, 100 (*pachanos*), 20 and 10 *bolívars* have been minted but are no longer in circulation; silver coins are 5 (*fuerte*), 2, 1 *bolívars*; nickel, 50 (*real*), 25 (*medio*) and 12·5 *céntimos* (*locha*), coppernickel, 5 *céntimos* (*puya*).

The bank-notes in circulation are 500, 100, 50, 20 and 10 bolívars. The circulation of foreign bank-notes is forbidden.

In March 1985, £1 = Bs.14·11; US$1 = 13·40.

Banking. The major banks include: Banco Industrial de Venezuela, Banco de Venezuela, Banco nacional de Descuento, Banco Unión, Banco Mercantil y Agrícola, Banco de los Trabajadores de Venezuela, Banco Provincial SAICA, Banco Latino, Banco de Maracaibo, Banco Unido.

ENERGY AND NATURAL RESOURCES

Oil. The oil-producing region around Maracaibo, covering some 30,000 sq. miles, produces about three-quarters of Venezuelan petroleum. Deposits in the Orinoco region are likely to prove one of the largest heavy oil reserves in the world. Nationalization of the privately owned oil sector in 1976 has proved successful. New distribution channels have been established, with the result that the major transnational companies which took 80% of Venezuela's oil in 1976 handled only 50% in 1980. Crude oil production (1984) 95m. tonnes.

Proven reserves in mid-1979 stood at 18,500m. bbls, probable reserves at 15,000m. and possible at 102,000m. However, these are considered conservative estimates and new fields off-shore have estimated reserves of 6,000–40,000m. bbls. The Orinoco tar sands belt has reserves variously estimated at between 700,000m. bbls. and 3,000,000m. bbls.

Gas. Production (1978) 34,842m cu. metres.

Minerals. Bauxite is being exploited in the Guayana region by Bauxien, a state agency. There are important goldmines in the region south-east of Bolívar State, and new deposits have been discovered near El Callao (1959) and Sosa Méndez (1961) in the Guayana region. Output, 1982, amounted to 902 kg. Diamond output, from Amazonas territory, was 687,000 carats in 1977. Manganese deposits, estimated at several million tons, were discovered in 1954. Phosphate-rock deposits (yielding from 64 to 82% tricalcium phosphate) are found in the state of Falcón; reserves of 15m. tons of high-quality rock have been established. The state of Sucre has large sulphur deposits. Coal is worked in the states of Táchira, Aragua and Anzoátegui. Coal proven reserves in Zulia (160m. tons) are to be developed to service a new thermal power station in the Maracaibo area. An important nickel deposit (at Loma de Hierro near Tejerías) is estimated to equal 600,000 tons of pure nickel. Saltmines are now worked by the Government on the Araya peninsula. Asbestos and copper pyrite are being exploited. There were proven reserves (1984) of bauxite totalling 200m. tonnes and production of about 3m. per annum are scheduled from 1986.

Iron ore is exploited in Bolívar State by the Orinoco Mining Co. and Iron Mines of Venezuela, subsidiaries respectively of the US Steel Corp. and the Bethlehem Steel Co. Proven reserves at the end of 1980 were 1,800m. tonnes. National output of iron ore, 1983, 9·3m. tonnes of which 7·4m. was exported.

Agriculture. Venezuela is divided into 3 distinct zones—the agricultural, the pastoral and the forest zone. In the first are grown coffee, cocoa, sugar-cane, maize, rice, wheat (grown in the Andes), tobacco, cotton, beans, sisal, etc.; the second affords grazing for more than 6m. cattle and numerous horses; and in the third, which covers a very large portion of the country, tropical products, such as caoutchouc, balatá (a gum resembling rubber), tonka beans, dividivi, copaiba, vanilla, growing wild, are worked by the inhabitants. The 1983 livestock estimate showed cattle, 12,092,000; pigs, 3·2m.; goats, 1,322,000; sheep, 412,000; poultry, 42m. Area under cultivation is 5,530,898 acres. Over 50% of all farmers are engaged in subsistence agriculture and growth rates in agricultural production have not kept pace with the high population increase. Government has introduced a programme of price support, tax incentives and price increases but cattle farming is at present the only profit opportunity.

Production (1982, in 1,000 tonnes) rice, 670; maize, 501; cassava, 360; raw sugar, 367 (sugar-cane, 5,000); sorghum, 337; bananas, 926; oranges, 370; potatoes, 216; tomatoes, 135; coffee, 59; sesame seed, 53; tobacco, 17; cocoa, 15.

The coffee plantations number 62,673, covering 543,400 acres with 135m. bushes. The Venezuelan cocoa, from 13,000 plantations, is considered to be of high quality; it is grown chiefly in the states of Sucre and Miranda. The sugar industry has 6 government and 20 privately owned mills.

Forestry. Resources have been barely tapped; 600 species of wood have been identified. Output of roundwood timber, 1977, broadleaved, 8m. cu. metres.

Fisheries. Total catch (1981) was 181,000 tonnes.

INDUSTRY AND TRADE

Industry. Production (1982): Steel, 1·99m. tonnes; aluminium, 273,000; ammonia, 535,000; fertilizers, 630,000; cement, 5·43m.; paper, 481,000; vehicles (units) 155,000.

Industrial development is concentrated in capital intensive areas where it can have a competitive advantage within the Andean Group, whereas in more labour intensive industries, the low labour costs of other member countries gives them an advantage. However, Venezuela currently produces 90% of its requirements of processed food, beverages, tobacco, clothing and textiles.

Labour. The labour force in 1983 was 6m., 19·5% were in agriculture, 18·8% in manufacturing and 9·6% in construction.

Wages are the highest in Latin America, there is a high turnover of labour and a corresponding rate of absenteeism.

45% of the labour force is unionized. The most powerful confederation is the CTV (*Confederacion de Trabajadores de Venezuela*, formed 1947), which is dominated by the Accion Democratica party. Estimated membership, 1·1m., claims 2m. Comprises 68 regional and industrial federations with over 6,000 unions, including: FCV (peasants), 700,000; FETRACONS (construction workers), 1m.; FETRASALUD (health workers), 45,000; FETRAMETAL (metal workers and miners), 32,000; the very important FEDEPETROL (oil workers), 6,000; Federacion Venezolana de Maestros (teachers).

Other confederations are CUTV (*Confederacion Unitaria de Trabajadores Venezolanos*, formed 1963). Estimated membership, 40,000, claims 100,000. Comprises 8 regional and 5 industrial federations in 185 local unions; and, CODESA (*Confederacion de Sindicatos Autonomos de Venezuela*, formed 1964). Estimated membership, 10,000, claims 35,000. Dominated by COPEI party. Comprises 120 local unions, including textile, petrol distribution, public health and education workers' federations.

Commerce. Venezuela's exports and imports (in US$1m.):

	1980	*1981*	*1982*	*1983*
Exports	19,281	20,100	16,549	16,180
Imports	11,318	12,400	13,200	6,115

Main export markets in 1982 were USA, Netherlands Antilles because of its oil refining and transhipment facilities, Canada, Puerto Rico, Italy and Spain.

Principal imports are machinery and equipment, manufactured goods, chemical products, foodstuffs.

The USA supplied 47% of all imports in 1982, followed by Federal Republic of Germany, Japan, Italy and the UK.

Total trade between UK and Venezuela (British Department of Trade returns, in £1,000 sterling):

	1980	*1981*	*1982*	*1983*	*1984*
Imports to UK	117,614	124,020	141,892	183,731	253,770
Exports and re-exports from UK	131,684	125,315	148,666	87,937	102,400

Tourism. 652,000 tourists visited Venezuela in 1977.

COMMUNICATIONS

Roads. There were, 1983, 61,059 km of road fit for traffic the year round; of these 20,000 km are paved. There are 10,097 km of high-speed 4-lane motorway type. The motorway system runs from Caracas to Puerto Cabello *via* Valencia and will shortly be linked direct with one from La Guaira to Caracas.

Railways. Plans have existed since 1950 for large-scale railway construction but only the Puerto Cabello to Barquisimeto line (175 km–1,435 mm gauge) has been completed. A metro is under construction in Caracas the first section of which was opened in March 1983.

Aviation. In 1984 there were 7 international airports, 51 national and over 200 private airports. The chief Venezuelan airlines are LAV (Líneas Aéreas Venezolanas), a government-owned concern, and AVENSA (Aerovías Venezolanas). Both operate numerous internal services. VIASA operates international routes in conjunction with KLM. There are also 3 specialist air freight companies. In all there are over 100 commercial aircraft in operation. In addition to Venezuelan international services, a number of US and Latin American and European lines operate services to Venezuela. British Caledonian operates twice-weekly flights between London and Caracas.

Shipping. Foreign vessels are not permitted to engage in the coasting trade, except by special concessions or by contract with the Government. La Guaira, Maracaibo, Puerto Cabello, Puerto Ordaz and Guanta are the chief ports. In Dec. 1978 the merchant fleet had an aggregate gross tonnage of 824,000; this included tankers of 368,000 gross tons.

The principal navigable rivers are the Orinoco and its tributaries Apure and Arauca, from San Fernando to Tucupita through Ciudad Bolívar, Puerto Ordaz and San Félix; San Juan from Carípito to the Gulf of Paria; and Esculante in Lake Maracaibo.

Post and Broadcasting. There were 1,377,630 telephones in 1982; 511,336 were in Caracas. An international telex service operates in the Caracas metropolitan zone. There is a submarine telephone link with USA.

In 1983 there were 5m. radio receivers and there were 77 radio stations at Caracas, Maracaibo, Maracay and other towns. There were 3 television stations in Caracas (two privately owned), of which 2 cover, with relays, most of the country. In 1983 there were about 2m. homes with TV receivers.

Cinemas (1977). There were 563 cinemas and 25 drive-ins.

Newspapers (1983). There were 25 leading daily newspapers with a circulation of over 1·7m.

JUSTICE, RELIGION, EDUCATION AND HEALTH

Justice. The Supreme Court, which operates in Divisions, each with 5 members, is elected by Congress for 5 years. The country is divided into 20 legal districts. They select their own President and Vice-President. The Federal Procurator-General is appointed for 5 years. There are lower federal courts.

Each state has a Supreme Court with 3 members, a superior court, or superior tribunal, courts of first instance, district courts and municipal courts. In the territories there are civil and military judges of first instance, and also judges in the municipios. Finally, there is an income-tax claims tribunal.

Religion. The Roman Catholic is the prevailing religion, but there is toleration of all others. There are 4 archbishops, 1 at Caracas, who is Primate of Venezuela, 2 at Mérida and 1 at Ciudad Bolívar. There are 19 bishops. In the state primary schools instruction is given only to those children whose parents expressly request it. Protestants number about 20,000.

Education. In 1979–80 there were 12,753 primary schools with 88,493 teachers and 2,456,815 pupils; there were 751,356 pupils in secondary schools, 40,264 in technical schools and 29,040 in teacher-training establishments, with a total of 45,888 teachers in the 1,447 establishments in this sector; the number of students in higher education was 299,773 with 27,025 teaching staff in the 68 establishments, including 17 universities.

Health. In 1976 there were 14,211 doctors and 386 hospitals and dispensaries with 36,126 beds.

DIPLOMATIC REPRESENTATIVES

Of Venezuela in Great Britain (1 Cromwell Rd., London SW7)
Ambassador: Dr José Luis Salcedo-Bastardo (accredited 25 Oct. 1984).

Of Great Britain in Venezuela (Torre Las Mercedes, Avenida La Estancia, Chuao, Caracas 1060)
Ambassador: M. J. Newington.

Of Venezuela in the USA (2445 Massachusetts Ave., NW, Washington, D.C., 20008)
Ambassador: Valentin Hernandez.

Of the USA in Venezuela (Avenida Francisco de Miranda and Avenida Principal de la Floresta, Caracas)
Ambassador: George W. Landau.

Of Venezuela to the United Nations
Ambassador: José Francisco Sucre-Figarella.

Books of Reference

Statistical Information: The following are some of the principal publications:
Dirección General de Estadística, Ministerio de Fomento, *Boletín Mensual de Estadística.—Anuario Estadístico de Venezuela, 1978.* Caracas, 1979
Banco Central, *Memoria Annual* and *Boletin Mensual*
Ministerio de Sanidad y Asistencia Social, Dirección de Salud Pública, *Anuario de Epidemiología y Asistencia Social*

Betancourt, R., *Venezuela's Oil.* London, 1978
Bigler, G. E., *Politics and State Capitalism in Venezuela.* Madrid, 1981
Buitrón, A., *Causas y Efectos del Exodo Rural en Venezuela.—Efectos Económicos y Sociales de las Inmigraciones en Venezuela.—Las Inmigraciones en Venezuela.* Pan American Union, Washington, D.C., 1956
Ewell, J., *Venezuela: A Century of Change.* London, 1984
Gil Yepes, J. A., *The Challenge of Venezuelan Democracy.* London, 1981
Lombard, J., *Venezuelan History: A Comprehensive Working Bibliography.* Boston, 1977.—*Venezuela: The Search for Order, the Dream of Progress.* OUP, 1982
Salazar-Carrillo, J., *Oil in the Economic Development of Venezuela.* New York, 1976

VIETNAM

Capital: Hanoi
Population: 60m. (1985)
GNP per capita: US$100 (1984)

Công Hòa Xã Hôi Chu Nghĩa Viêt Nam—The Socialist Republic of Vietnam

HISTORY. The recorded history of Vietnam can be traced to Tonkin (now known as the northern part of Vietnam) at the beginning of the Christian era. Conquered by the Chinese in B.C. 111, the kingdom of Nam-Viet, as it was then called, broke free of Chinese domination in 939, though at many subsequent periods it became a nominal vassal of the Chinese emperors.

By the end of the 15th century the Vietnamese had conquered most of the kingdom of Champa (in Annam, now known as the central part of Vietnam) and by the end of the 18th had acquired Cochin-China (now known as the southern part of Vietnam), formerly Cambodian territory.

French interest in Vietnam started in the late 16th century with the arrival of French and Portuguese missionaries. The most notable of these was Alexander of Rhodes, who, in the following century, romanized Vietnamese writing. At the end of the 18th century France helped to establish the Emperor Gia-Long (with whom Louis XVI had signed a treaty in 1787) as ruler of a unified Vietnam, known then as the Empire of Annam.

An expedition sent by Napoleon III in 1858 to avenge the death of some French missionaries led in 1862 to the cession to France of part of Cochin-China, and thence, by a series of treaties between 1874 and 1884, to the establishment of French protectorates over Tonkin and Annam, and to the formation of the French colony of Cochin-China. By a Sino-French treaty of 1885 the Empire of Annam (including Tonkin) ceased to be tributary to China. Cambodia had become a French protectorate in 1863, and in 1899, after extension of French protection to Laos in 1893, the Indo-Chinese Union was proclaimed.

In 1940 Vietnam was occupied by the Japanese. During the occupation there was considerable underground activity among nationalist, revolutionary and Communist organizations. In 1941 a nominally nationalist coalition of such organizations, known as the Vietminh League, was founded by the Communists.

On 9 March 1945 the Japanese interned the French authorities and proclaimed the 'independence' of Indo-China. In Aug. 1945 they allowed the Vietminh movement to seize power, dethrone Bao Dai, the Emperor of Annam, and establish a republic known as Vietnam, including Tonkin, Annam and Cochin-China, with Hanoi as capital. In Sept. 1945 the French re-established themselves in Cochin-China and on 6 March 1946, after a cease-fire in the sporadic fighting between the French forces and the Vietminh had been arranged, a preliminary convention was signed in Hanoi between the French High Commissioner and President Ho Chi Minh by which France recognized 'the Democratic Republic of Vietnam' as a 'Free State within the Indo-Chinese Federation'. Two conferences in 1946 broke down chiefly over the question of whether Cochin-China should be included in the new republic. On 19 Dec. Vietminh forces made a surprise attack on Hanoi, the signal for hostilities which were to last for nearly 8 years.

An agreement signed by Emperor Bao Dai on 8 March 1949 recognized the independence of Vietnam within the French Union, and certain sovereign powers were transferred to Vietnam. The Paris agreements of 29 Dec. 1954 completed the transfer of sovereignty. Treaties of independence and association were initialled by the French and Vietnamese governments on 4 June 1954.

An agreement on the cessation of hostilities in Vietnam was reached on 20 July 1954 at the Geneva conference. The agreement was signed on behalf of the C.-in-C.

of the French Forces in Indo-China and on behalf of the C.-in-C. of the People's Army of Vietnam. The Government of Vietnam did not sign the agreement.

The final declaration of the Geneva conference (21 July 1954) declared that general elections should take place in July 1956. With the departure of the French Ngo Dinh Diem became Prime Minister of South Vietnam (Republic of Vietnam) in 1954 and President in 1955. Elections were never held. In 1963 Diem was overthrown. In 1965 Nguyen Van Thieu took power as chairman of a National Leadership Committee, becoming President in 1967. From 1959 the North promoted insurgency in the South; US involvement began in 1961.

In Paris on 27 Jan. 1973 an agreement was signed ending the war in Vietnam. After the US withdrawal, however, hostilities continued between the North and the South until the latter's defeat in 1975. President Thieu resigned on 21 April. Gen. Duong Van Minh surrendered to the Communist forces on 30 April. 150,000–200,000 South Vietnamese fled the country, including the former President Thieu.

For details of the former Republic of Vietnam (South Vietnam), see THE STATESMAN'S YEAR-BOOK, 1975–76. After the collapse of President Thieu's regime the Provisional Revolutionary Government established an administration in Saigon on 6 June 1975 under the presidency of Huynh Tan Phat. A North–South conference on reunification of Nov. 1975 announced that agreement on 'the basic problems' had been reached. A general election was held on 25 April 1976 for a National Assembly representing the whole country. Voting was by universal suffrage of all citizens of 18 or over, except former functionaries of South Vietnam undergoing 're-education'. The unification of North and South Vietnam into the Socialist Republic of Vietnam took place formally on 2 July 1976. After previous US vetoes the new administration of President Carter indicated that it was not opposed to Vietnam's application to join the UN, and Vietnam was admitted unanimously and without a vote on 20 Sept. 1977. In June 1978 Vietnam was admitted to Comecon and in Nov. 1978 signed a 25-year treaty of friendship and co-operation with the USSR. Relations with China correspondingly deteriorated, an especially exacerbating factor being the successful Vietnamese military intervention in Kampuchea. On 17 Feb. 1979 China invaded North Vietnam, but claimed that its troops had all withdrawn by 19 March. Peace negotiations were commenced on 18 April 1979 but broken off by the Chinese on 6 March 1980. Skirmishing continues along the frontier.

AREA AND POPULATION. The country has a total area of 329,566 sq. km and is divided administratively into 36 provinces and 1 special area. Areas and populations (in 1,000) at the census of Oct. 1979 were as follows:

Province	*Sq. km*	*1979*
Lai Chau	17,408	322,077
Son La	14,656	487,793
Hoang Lien Son	14,125	778,217
Ha Tuyen	13,519	782,453
Cao Bang	13,731 (Cao Bang and Lang Son)	479,823
Lang Son		484,657
Bac Thai	8,615	815,105
Quang Ninh	7,076	750,055
Vinh Phu	5,187	1,488,348
Ha Bac	4,708	1,662,671
Ha Son Binh	6,860	1,537,190
Hanoi (city) [1]	597	2,570,905
Hai Hung	2,526	2,145,662
Thai Binh	1,344	1,506,235
Hai Phong (city) [1]	1,515	1,279,067
Ha Nam Ninh	3,522	2,781,409
Thanh Hoa	11,138	2,532,261
Nghe Tinh	22,380	3,111,989
Binh Tri Thien	19,048	1,901,713
Quang Nam – Da Nang	11,376	1,529,520
Nghia Binh	14,700	2,095,354
Gia Lai – Kon Tum	18,480	595,906
Dac Lac	18,300	490,198
Phu Khanh	9,620	1,188,637
Lam Dong	10,000	396,657
Thuan Hai	11,000	938,255
Dong Nai	12,130	1,304,799
Song Be	9,500	659,093
Tay Ninh	4,100	684,006
Long An	5,100	957,264
Dong Thap	3,120	1,182,787
Thanh Pho – Ho Chi Minh [1]	1,845	3,419,978
Tien Giang	2,350	1,264,498
Ben Tre	2,400	1,041,838
Cuu Long	4,200	1,504,215
An Giang	4,140	1,532,362
Hau Giang	5,100	2,232,891
Kien Giang	6,000	994,673
Minh Hai	8,000	1,219,595
Vung Tau – Con Dao [2]	—	91,160
	329,466	52,741,766

[1] Autonomous city. [2] Special area.

At the census of Oct. 1979 the population was 52,741,766 (25,580,582 male; 19·7% urban).

Population (1985), 60m. (Ho Chi Minh 3·5m. (1981); Hanoi, 2m. (1979); growth rate (1983) 2·3% per annum. Contraception is encouraged, and women urged to confine their families to two children, one not before 22 and one 5 years later.

84% of the population are Vietnamese (Kinh). There are also over 60 minority groups thinly spread in the extensive mountainous regions. The largest minorities are (1976 figures in 1,000): Tay (742); Khmer (651); Thai (631); Muong (618); Nung (472); Meo (349); Dao (294). In 1981 0·5m. Vietnamese were living abroad, mainly in USA.

From 1979 to July 1984 59,730 persons emigrated legally. Between Apr. 1975 and Aug. 1984 a further 554,000 'boat people' succeeded in finding refuge abroad. By 1983 more 'boat people' were arriving in countries of first asylum than were leaving under the UN's orderly departure scheme. (For previous details *see* THE STATESMAN'S YEAR-BOOK, 1981–82). In Sept. 1984 the USA announced a plan to offer asylum to Vietnamese political prisoners and to accept all Asian-American children in Vietnam as refugees.

CLIMATE. The humid monsoon climate gives tropical conditions in the south and sub-tropical conditions in the north, though real winter conditions can affect the north when polar air blows south over Asia. In general, there is little variation in temperatures over the year. Hanoi. Jan. 62°F (16·7°C), July 84°F (28·9°C). Annual rainfall 72" (1,830 mm).

CONSTITUTION AND GOVERNMENT. A new Constitution was adopted in Dec. 1980. It states that Vietnam is a state of proletarian dictatorship and is developing according to Marxism–Leninism.

At the elections for the new National Assembly held on 26 April 1981, 613 candidates stood and 496 were elected. 70% of the candidates were standing for the first time.

Local government authorities are the people's councils, which appoint executive committees. Local elections were held in Ho Chi Minh City and the 38 provinces of the former South Vietnam on 5 May 1977.

The 1980 Constitution replaced the Presidency with the State Council, 'the standing organ of the National Assembly and presidium of the Republic'.

Chairman: Truong Chinh. *Vice-Chairmen:* Nguyen Huu Tho, Le Thanh Nghi, Chu Huy Man, Huynh Tan Phat. The *Prime Minister* is the Chairman of the Council of Ministers, Pham Van Dong.

Chairman of the National Assembly: Nguyen Huu Tho.

All political power stems from the Communist Party of Vietnam (until Dec. 1976 known as the Workers' Party of Vietnam), founded in 1930; it had 1m. members in Dec. 1979 (8·8% workers; 17% women). In April 1984 the Politburo consisted of Le Duan *(First Secretary)*; Truong Chinh; Pham Van Dong; Pham Hung *(Deputy Prime Minister and Minister of the Interior)*; Le Duc Tho; Gen. Van Tien Dung *(Minister of Defence)*; Vo Chi Cong; Gen. Chu Huy Man; To Huu *(First Deputy Prime Minister)*; Vo Van Kiet *(Deputy Prime Minister and Chairman, State Planning Commission)*; Do Muoi *(Deputy Prime Minister)* Le Duc Anh; Nguyen Duc Tam. Candidate members: Nguyen Co Thach *(Foreign Minister)*; Dong Si Nguyen *(Deputy Prime Minister)*. Ministers not in the Politburo include: Vo Nguyen Giap; Tran Quynh; Vu Dinh Lieu; Tran Phuong *(Deputy Prime Ministers)*; Chu Tham Phuc *(Finance)*; Le Khac *(Foreign Trade)*; Le Duc Thinh *(Home Trade)*; Dong Si Nguyen *(Transport)*; Mme. Nguyen Thi Binh *(Education)*; Nguyen Ngoc Triu *(Agriculture)*; Phan Hien *(Justice)*.

There are 2 puppet parties, the Democratic (founded 1944) and the Socialist (1946), which are unified with the trade and youth unions in the Fatherland Front.

National flag: Red, with a yellow 5-pointed star in the centre.

National anthem: 'Tien quan ca' ('The troops are advancing').

DEFENCE. Men between the ages of 18 and 35 and women between 18 and 25 are liable for conscription.

Army. The Army consists of 1 armoured division, 58 infantry divisions (of varying strengths), 7 engineer and 15 economic construction divisions, 10 marine brigades, 5 field and 4 anti-aircraft artillery brigades, 4 engineer brigades, and 6 independent armoured regiments. Equipment includes some 2,000 main battle and 600 light tanks. Strength was (1985) about 1·2m. Paramilitary forces are Border Defence (60,000) and Militia (1·5m.). In 1985 some 45,000 troops were stationed in Laos and 150,000 in Cambodia.

Navy. Before the North Vietnamese victory in 1975 the Navy comprised 3 old coastal escorts, 2 fast missile boats, 28 fast torpedo boats, 22 fast motor gunboats, 34 small patrol boats, 24 landing craft, 4 minesweeping boats, 10 tenders, 100 auxiliaries and 200 armed junks. It also had 10 Mi-4 SAR helicopters.

At least 1 frigate, several other major warships and a considerable number of auxiliaries were captured after the South Vietnamese surrender.

The fleet reportedly includes 4 *ex*-Soviet escorts, 2 old frigates, 2 old corvettes, 1 minesweeper, 6 old submarine chasers, 8 fast missile boats, 16 fast torpedo boats, 18 fast gunboats, 16 fast patrol craft, 5 seaward defence boats, 9 landing ships, 12 landing craft, 1 torpedo recovery vessel, 15 riverine craft, 24 minesweeping launches, 1 survey ship, 15 auxiliaries and 100 armed junks; but due to the lack of maintenance, spares and trials it is difficult to accurately assess the operational availability, fitness for sea or steaming capacity of this heterogeneous collection or the availability of trained personnel.

It is estimated that 4 missile craft, 12 torpedo boats, 22 gunboats, 3 minesweepers, 24 patrol craft, 25 coastguard cutters and 100 motor launches are non-operational together with 550 riverine craft, 100 landing craft, 30 monitors, 100 converted amphibious craft, 26 vedettes, 36 auxiliaries and 75 service craft.

In 1985 there were an estimated 4,000 naval personnel regulars, with additional conscripts on three to four year terms.

Air Force. The Air Force, built up with Soviet and Chinese assistance, has about 12,000 personal and 275 combat aircraft (plus many stored), including modern US types captured in war. There are reported to be 2 squadrons of variable-geometry MiG-23s, 3 squadrons of MiG-17s, Su-7s and Su-20s, about 180 MiG-21 interceptors; An-2, Li-2, An-24, An-26 and Il-14 transports; and a strong helicopter force with UH-1 Iroquois, Mi-6 and Mi-8 helicopters. 'Guideline', 'Goa' and 'Gainful' missiles are operational in large numbers.

INTERNATIONAL RELATIONS

Membership. Vietnam is a member of UN, Comecon and IMF.

ECONOMY

Planning. Long-term forward planning gives priority to creating self-sufficiency in agriculture before progressing to further industrialization. Targets for the second 5-year plan 1976–80) were not met. Growth in agriculture, 18·7%, industry, 17·3%. The third 5-year plan covered 1981–85. An agreement co-ordinating this plan with the current Soviet plan was signed with the USSR in July 1981. (For previous plans *see* THE STATESMAN'S YEAR-BOOK, 1976–77, p. 1473).

Curtailment of Western imports, and the effect of floods and resistance to the Government's economic measures have contributed to a serious shortage of consumer goods and widespread malnutrition, which it is hoped to correct by stimulating regional industry and utilizing the expertise of former businessmen.

Currency. The monetary unit is the *dong* = 10 *hao*, the *hao* = 10 *xu*. There are coins of 1, 2 and 5 *xu*, 1, 2 and 5 *hao*, 1 *dong*, and notes of 1, 2, 5, 10, 20, 30, 50 and 100 *dong*. In March 1985, £1 = 11·59 *dong*; US$1 = 10·93 *dong*.

Banking. The bank of issue is the National Bank of Vietnam (founded in 1951). There is also a Bank for Foreign Trade (Vietcombank). In 1980 this bank ceased all transactions with US banks.

ENERGY AND NATURAL RESOURCES

Electricity. In 1982, 4,045m. kwh. of electricity were produced. A hydro-electric power station with a capacity of 2m. kw. is being built at Hoa-Binh with Soviet assistance.

Minerals. North Vietnam is rich in anthracite, lignite and hard coal: total reserves are estimated at 20,000m. tonnes. Anthracite production in 1975 was 5m. tonnes. Coal production was 5·3m. tonnes in 1980. There are deposits of iron ore, manganese, titanium, chromite, bauxite and a little gold. Chromite production in 1962 was 35,000 tons. Reserves of apatite are some of the biggest in the world. Estimated production of phosphates in 1971, 1·1m. tonnes; salt, 150,000 tonnes. Western companies have pulled out of exploration for oil as uneconomic, but a Soviet-Vietnamese enterprise claims to have struck oil in May 1984. There are large limestone deposits in Kien Giang, Chau Doc and Thua Thien provinces. A recent geological survey reported on the prospects of valuable bauxite deposits. There is a small coal-bearing region at Nong-Son.

Agriculture. In 1980, 71% of the population was engaged in agriculture. In 1977 there were 15,200 co-operatives in the North averaging 300–500 hectares (less than 100 hectares in mountain regions) and a workforce of 1,000–2,000. The intemperate collectivization of agriculture in the South after 1977 had disastrous effects which the Government is now trying to rectify by a system of incentives to peasants which allows them small private plots and the right to market some of their own produce. There were 105 state farms employing in all 70,000 workers and with 55,000 hectares arable and 50,000 hectares of pasture. Other crops include maize, sugar-cane, sweet potatoes and cotton. The cultivated area in 1980 was 6·97m. hectares (5·54m. hectares for rice).

In 1984 there were some 23,000 production collectives and 268 agricultural cooperatives in the South accounting for 47% of the cultivated area. There were about 300 state farms.

Production in 1,000 tonnes in 1980: Soybeans (32), tea (21), rubber (45), maize (475), oil seed plants (595), tobacco (15·6), potatoes (684). (1979) sweet potatoes (from 380,000 hectares), sorghum (35) from 30,000 hectares), beans (45) from 93,000 hectares), coffee (15). The main crop is rice. Cereals production was 14m. tonnes in 1982, 17m. tonnes in 1983.

Livestock (1983): Cattle 2m.; pigs, 10,785,000; goats, 200,000; poultry, 50m.

Animal products, 1980: Eggs, 1,129m., meat, 427,000 tonnes.

Forestry. 1,626,000 cu. metres of timber were produced in 1980.

Fisheries. Fishing is important, especially in Halong Bay. In 1976, 6m. tonnes of sea fish and 180,000 tonnes of freshwater fish were caught (representing only 83% of the planned target).

INDUSTRY AND TRADE

Industry. Next to mining, food processing and textiles are the most important industries; there is also some machine building. Older industries include cement, cotton and silk manufacture. Local industries and handicrafts account for 50% of production.

Private businesses were taken over in 1978. Foreign firms, principally French, are continuing to function, but all US property has been nationalized. There is little heavy industry. Most industry is concentrated in the Ho-Chi-Minh area.

Production (1980, in 1,000 tonnes) iron, 125; steel, 106; sulphuric acid, 6,700; caustic soda, 4,500; mineral fertilizer, 260; pesticides, 18,400; paper, 54,000; sugar, 94,000, cement, 705. 1,500 tractors were built in 1980, and 621 railway coaches. Footwear production, 200,000 pairs. Beer, 942,000 hectolitres. Kenaf yarn production was 1,615 tons in 1972.

Labour. Average wage (1984) 200 dong per month. Non-agricultural workforce (1980) 3,587,000, of whom 2,238,000 in industry.

Commerce. USSR and Japan are Vietnam's main trading partners; others are

Singapore and Hong Kong. Main exports are coal, farm produce, sea produce and livestock. Imports: technical equipment, industrial raw materials, foodstuffs and medical supplies. The Vietnamese Government recognizes a need for foreign aid and credit for the development of an industrial base. An aid agreement was reached with the USSR in Sept. 1981 for 5 years under which the USSR will participate in 40 construction projects and oil exploration in exchange for foodstuffs. Western aid has been significantly curtailed since the Vietnamese occupation of Cambodia. In 1982 Vietnam's total indebtedness was estimated at US$3,000m. In 1978 the IMF approved a virtually interest-free loan of US$90m. repayable over 50 years, but in July 1982 refused Vietnam's request for US$150m. in Special Drawing Rights until there are reforms in the economy. Foreign investments are encouraged and guaranteed for 15 years. Profits may be transferred and indemnities paid in the event of nationalization. In the case of foreign firms installed in Vietnam all capital may remain in foreign hands if goods are produced for export only; otherwise the Vietnamese Government will retain 51% of shares.

Trade between Vietnam and UK (British Department of Trade returns, in £1,000 sterling):

	1981	*1982*	*1983*	*1984*
Imports to UK	130	133	603	1,154
Exports and re-exports from UK	1,180	876	951	1,787

COMMUNICATIONS

Roads. In 1973 there were about 9,500 km of roads in the North. In 1970 there were 20,905 km of roads in the South. Of these, 5,908 km were asphalted.

Railways. 'Project Reunification', the rebuilding of the Hanoi–Ho Chi Minh City railway, is a major part of the new authorities' programme to repair and extend all communications systems and link them with the North. The Da Nang–Hue railway was reopened in 1975. Important sections of railway have been reconstructed rapidly since the cessation of hostilities in 1975. The systems total 2,600 km.

Aviation. Civil Aviation of Vietnam operates internal services from Hanoi to Ho Chi Minh City, Cao Bang, Na Son and Dien Bien, Vinh and Hue, and from Ho Chi Minh City to Ban Me Thuot and Da Nang, Can Tho, Con Son Island and Quan Long. Aeroflot (USSR) operate regular services from Ho Chi Min City to Moscow and from Hanoi to Moscow, Rangoon and Vientiane, Interflug (German Dem. Rep.) to Berlin, Moscow and Dacca and Air France to Paris.

Shipping. The major ports are Haiphong, which can handle ships of 10,000 tons, Ho Chi Minh City and Da Nang, and there are ports at Hong Gai and Haiphong Ben Thuy. There are regular services to Hong Kong, Singapore, Kampuchea and Japan. In 1953 there were 830 km of navigable waterways in the North and, in 1971, 4,783 km in the South.

Cargo is handled by the Vietnam Ocean Shipping Agency; other matters by the Vietnam Foreign Trade Transport Corporation.

Post and Broadcasting. In 1966 there were 1·4m. radios. There were 46,509 telephones in the South in 1974. There were 2m. TV sets in 1980.

Cinemas and theatres. 116 films were produced in 1980 (including 10 full-length). There were 145 theatres.

Newspapers and books. The Party daily is *Nhan Dan* ('The People') circulation, 1984: 300,000. The official daily in the South is *Giai Phong.* Two unofficial dailies, *Cong Giao Va Dan Toc* (Catholic) and *Tin Sang* (independent) are also published. 2,564 books were published in 1980 totalling 90·9m. copies.

JUSTICE, RELIGION, EDUCATION AND WELFARE

Justice. There are the Supreme People's Court, local people's courts and military courts. The president of the Supreme Court is responsible to the National Assembly, as is the Procurator-General, who heads the Supreme People's Office of Supervision and Control.

Religion. Taoism is the traditional religion but Buddhism is widespread. At a Conference for Buddhist Reunification in Nov. 1981, 9 sects adopted a charter for a new Buddhist church under the Council of Sangha. The Hoa Hao sect, associated with Buddhism, claimed 1·5m. adherents in 1976. Caodaism, a synthesis of Christianity, Buddhism and Confucianism founded in 1926, has some 2m. followers. There are some 3m. Roman Catholics headed by Cardinal Trinh Van Can, Archbishop of Hanoi and 13 bishops. In 1983 the Government set up a Solidarity Committee of Catholic Patriots.

Education. Primary education consists of a 10-year course divided into 3 levels of 4, 3 and 3 years respectively. Numbers of pupils and students in 1980–81: nurseries, 2·66m.; primary schools, 12·1m.; complementary education, 2·19m.; vocational secondary education, 130,000. In 1980–81 there were 92,913 nurseries. There were 11,400 schools and 280 vocational secondary schools, with 357,000 and 13,000 teachers respectively.

In 1980–81 there were 83 institutions of higher education (including 3 universities: (Hanoi, Ho Chi Minh City, Central Highlands University at Ban Me Thuot), 13 industrial colleges, 7 agricultural colleges, 5 economics colleges, 9 teacher-training colleges, 7 medical schools and 3 art schools, in all with 16,000 teachers and 159,000 students. In 1981 there were 5,000 Vietnamese studying in the USSR.

Health. In 1975 there were 1,996 hospitals and dispensaries and 93 sanatoria. There were some 13,300 doctors and dentists in 1980 and 197,000 hospital beds.

DIPLOMATIC REPRESENTATIVES

Of Vietnam in Great Britain (12–14 Victoria Rd, London, W8)
Ambassador: Dang Nghiem Bai (accredited 5 Nov. 1982).

Of Great Britain in Vietnam (16 Pho Ly Thuong Kiet, Hanoi)
Ambassador: M. E. Pike, CMG.

Of Vietnam to the United Nations
Ambassador: Hoang Bich Son.

Books of Reference

Chen, J. H.-M., *Vietnam: A Comprehensive Bibliography.* London, 1973
Duiker, W. J., *The Communist Road to Power in Vietnam.* Boulder, 1981.—*Vietnam: Nation in Revolution,* Boulder, 1983
Goodman, A. E., *The Lost Peace: America's Search for a Negotiated Settlement of the Vietnam War.* Stanford Univ. Press, 1978
Harrison, J. P., *The Endless War: Fifty Years of Struggle in Vietnam.* New York, 1982
Higgins, H., *Vietnam.* 2nd ed. London, 1982
Ho Chi Minh, *Selected Writings, 1920–1969.* Hanoi, 1977
Hodgkin, T., *Vietnam: The Revolutionary Path:* London, 1981
Karnow, S., *Vietnam: A History.* New York, 1983
Le Thanh Khoi, *Socialisme et Développement au Vietnam.* Paris, 1978
Le Van Hung, *Vietnamese–English Dictionary.* Paris, 1955
Lewy, G., *America in Vietnam.* OUP, 1979
Leitenberg, M., and Burns, R. D., *War in Vietnam.* 2nd ed. Oxford and Santa Barbara, 1982
Nguyen Tien Hung, C., *Economic Developments of Socialist Vietnam, 1955–80.* New York, 1977
Nguyen Van Canh, *Vietnam under Communism, 1975–1982.* Stanford Univ. Press, 1983
Popkin, S. L., *The Rational Peasant: The Political Economy of Rural Society in Vietnam.* Berkeley, 1979
Smith, R. B., *An International History of the Vietnam War.* London, 1983–
Viet Tran, *J'ai Choisi l'Exil.* Paris, 1979
Voronin, A. S. and Ognetov, I. A. *Sotsialisticheskaia Respublika V'etnam: Spravochnik.* (2nd ed). Moscow, 1981

BRITISH VIRGIN ISLANDS

Capital: Road Town
Population: 12,034 (1980)

HISTORY. The Virgin Islands were discovered by Colombus on his second voyage in 1493. The British Virgin Islands were first settled by the Dutch in 1648 and taken over in 1666 by a group of English planters. In 1774 constitutional government was granted and in 1834 slavery was abolished.

AREA AND POPULATION. The British Virgin Islands form the eastern extremity of the Greater Antilles and, exclusive of small rocks and reefs, number 36, of which 16 are inhabited. The largest are Tortola (1980 population, 9,322), Virgin Gorda (1,443), Anegada (169) and Jost Van Dyke (136). Other islands in the group have a total population of 82; Marine population, 220; Institutional population, 662. Total area about 59 sq. miles (130 sq. km); population (1980), 12,034. Road Town, on the south-east of Tortola, is a port of entry; population, approximately 3,976.

CLIMATE. A pleasantly healthy sub-tropical climate with summer temperatures lowered by sea breezes. Nights are cool and rainfall averages 50″ (1,250 mm).

CONSTITUTION AND GOVERNMENT. In 1950 representative government was introduced and in 1967 a new Constitution was granted (amended 1977). The Governor is responsible for defence and internal security, external affairs, the public service, and the courts. The Executive Council consists of the Governor, 1 *ex-officio* member who is the Attorney-General and 4 ministers in the Legislature. The Legislative Council consists of 1 *ex-officio* member who is the Attorney-General and 9 elected members, one of whom is the Chief Minister and Minister of Finance; the Speaker is elected from outside the Council.

Governor: David Robert Barwick, CBE, QC.
Chief Minister: Cyril B. Romney.
Flag: The British Blue Ensign with the arms of the Territory in the fly.

ECONOMY

Planning. In 1984, there was an increase of about 35% in the government's expenditure provision to facilitate the construction of the new extensions of piped water supplies to the West End and the East End areas of Tortola.

Budget. In 1984 revenue (estimate) was US$19,788,000 Capital expenditure (estimate) was US$19,048,315.

Currency. The unit of currency is the US dollar.

Banking. Barclays Bank International, the First Pennsylvania Bank, the Bank of Nova Scotia and the Chase Manhattan Bank have branches in the islands. There are also a large number of Trust Companies.

INDUSTRY AND TRADE

Industry. Agricultural production is now very limited with the chief products being livestock (including poultry), fish, fruit and vegetables. The export trade is carried on almost entirely with the Virgin Islands of the USA. The main industry is tourism and related activities, notably construction.

Livestock (1983): Cattle, 2,000; pigs, 3,000; sheep, 8,000; goats, 12,000.

Trade. In 1980 imports were US$36m. and exports US$1,087,000.

Total trade between the British Virgin Islands and UK (British Department of Trade returns, in £1,000 sterling):

	1982	*1983*	*1984*
Imports to UK	460	172	1,427
Exports and re-exports from UK	2,348	3,455	2,543

Tourism. There were 155,715 visitors in 1982.

COMMUNICATIONS

Roads. There were (1983) over 66 miles of roads and 3,000 licensed vehicles.

Aviation. Beef Island Airport, about 16 km from Road Town, is capable of receiving 48-seat turbo-prop aircraft. Air BVI operates internal services and external flights to the USVI, St Kitts, Antigua and Puerto Rico. Also, operating services to the BVI are Coral Air, Crown Air, LIAT, Prinair, Davair and British Caribbean Airways.

Shipping. There are services to Europe, the USA and other Caribbean islands, and daily services by motor launches to the US Virgin Islands.

Post and Broadcasting. There were (1983) over 2,000 telephones, and an external telephone service links Tortola with Bermuda and the rest of the world, and cable communications also exist to all parts of the world. Radio ZBVI transmits 10,000 watts and has stand-by transmitting facilities of 1,000 watts. Cable and Wireless, also, operates reception of approximately 7 television channels plus a number of FM stereo broadcasting stations.

RELIGION, EDUCATION AND WELFARE

Religion. There are Anglican, Methodist, Seventh-Day Adventist, Roman Catholic and Baptist Churches in the Territory. The Church of God is also represented.

Education. Primary education is provided in 16 government schools, two with secondary divisions, and 9 private schools. Total number of pupils (Dec. 1980) 2,748.

Secondary education to the GCE level and Caribbean Examination Council level is provided at the B.V.I. High School. Total pupils in Dec. 1980, 791.

Government expenditure, 1984 (estimate), US$3,426,897. In 1983 the total number of teachers in all the schools was 198.

Health. In 1983 there were 10 doctors and more than 50 hospital beds. Expenditure, 1984 (estimate) was US$2,577,744.

Books of Reference

Dookhan, I., *A History of the British Virgin Islands.* Epping, 1975
Elkan, W., and Morley, R., *Employment in a Tourist Economy, British Virgin Islands*
Harrigan, N., and Varlack, P., *British Virgin Islands: A Chronology*
Pickering, V. W., *Early History of the British Virgin Islands.*

Library: Public Library, Road Town. *Librarian:* Mrs Verna Penn-Mall, MLS, ALA.

WESTERN SAMOA

Capital: Apia
Population: 156,349 (1981)
GNP per capita: US$350 (1976)

Samoa i Sisifo

HISTORY. Western Samoa, a former German protectorate (1900 to the First World War), was administered by New Zealand from 1920 to 1961, at first under a League of Nations Mandate and since 1946 under a United Nations Trusteeship Agreement. In May 1961 a plebiscite held under the supervision of the United Nations on the basis of universal adult suffrage voted overwhelmingly in favour of independence as from 1 Jan. 1962, on the basis of the Constitution, which a Constitutional Convention had adopted in Aug. 1960. In Oct. 1961 the General Assembly of the United Nations passed a resolution to terminate the trusteeship agreement as from 1 Jan. 1962, on which date Western Samoa became an independent sovereign state.

Under a treaty of friendship signed on 1 Aug. 1962 New Zealand acts, at the request of Western Samoa, as the official channel of communication between the Samoan Government and other governments and international organizations outside the Pacific islands area. Liaison is maintained by the New Zealand High Commissioner in Apia.

AREA AND POPULATION. Western Samoa lies between 13° and 15° S. lat. and 171° and 173° W. long. It comprises the two large islands of Savai'i and Upolu, the small islands of Manono and Apolima, and several uninhabited islets lying off the coast. The total land area is 1,093 sq. miles (2,830·8 sq. km), of which 659·4 sq. miles (1,707·8 sq. km) are in Savai'i, and 431·5 sq. miles (1,117·6 sq. km) in Upolu; other islands, 2·1 sq. miles (5·4 sq. km). The islands are of volcanic origin, and the coasts are surrounded by coral reefs. Rugged mountain ranges form the core of both main islands and rise to 3,608 ft in Upolu and 6,094 ft in Savai'i. The large area laid waste by lava-flows in Savai'i is a primary cause of that island supporting less than one-third of the population of the islands despite its greater size than Upolu.

The population at the 1981 census was 156,349, of whom 113,000 were in Upolu (including Manono and Apolima) and 42,218 in Savai'i. The capital and chief port is Apia in Upolu (population 33,170 in 1981).

CLIMATE. A tropical marine climate, with cooler conditions from May to Nov. and a rainy season from Dec. to April. The rainfall is unevenly distributed, with south and east coasts having the greater quantities. Average annual rainfall is about 100″ (2,500 mm) in the drier areas. Apia. Jan. 80°F (26·7°C), July 78°F (25·6°C). Annual rainfall 112″ (2,800 mm).

CONSTITUTION AND GOVERNMENT. The Constitution provides for a Head of State known as 'Ao o le Malo', which position from 1 Jan. 1962 was held jointly by the representatives of the two royal lines of Tuiaana/Tuiatua and Malietoa. On the death of HH Tupua Tamasese Mea'ole, CBE, on 5 April 1963, HH Malietoa Tanumafili II, CBE, became, as provided by the constitution, the sole Head of State for life. Future Heads of State will be elected by the Legislative Assembly and hold office for 5-year terms.

The executive power is vested in the Head of State, who appoints the Prime Minister and, on the Prime Minister's advice, the 8 Ministers to form the Cabinet which has general direction and control of the executive Government.

The Legislative Assembly has 45 members elected from territorial constituencies on a franchise confined to matais or chiefs (of whom there are about 11,000) and 2 members elected on universal adult suffrage from the individual voters roll, which has replaced the old European roll (approximately 1,350 in 1971). One Member is elected as Speaker. The Constitution also provides for a Council of Deputies of 3 members.

Elections, Feb. 1985, the Human Rights Protection Party won 31 seats.

The official languages are English and Samoan.

Head of State: HH Malietoa Tanumafili II, CBE.
Prime Minister: Tofilau Eti Alesana.
National flag: Red with a blue quarter bearing 5 white stars of the Southern Cross.

INTERNATIONAL RELATIONS

Membership. Western Samoa is a member of UN, the Commonwealth and is an ACP state of EEC.

ECONOMY

Budget. In 1983 budgeted revenue was $WS41·3m.; expenditure, $WS69·2m.

Currency. The Western Samoa currency is the *talà* (dollar). In March 1985, £1 = 2·48; US$1 = 2·21.

Banking. A Central Bank was established in 1984. In 1959 the Bank of Western Samoa was established with a capital of $WS500,000, of which $WS275,000 was subscribed by the Bank of New Zealand and $WS225,000 by the Government of Western Samoa. In 1977 the Pacific Commercial Bank was established jointly by Australia's Bank of New South Wales and the Bank of Hawaii.

NATURAL RESOURCES

Agriculture. The main products are coconut oil, cocoa, taro, copra and bananas.

Fisheries. The total catch (1983) was 3,150 tonnes, valued at $WS5·1m.

INDUSTRY AND TRADE

Industry. Some industrial activity is being developed associated with agricultural products and forestry.

Commerce. In 1980, imports were valued at $WS57,438,000 and exports at $WS15,828,000. Principal exports were copra (25,317 tons; $WS8,404,700), cocoa (1,503 tons; $WS3,012,600), taro (86,085 cases, $WS1,048,300), timber (1,287,900 sq. ft; $WS324,400), and bananas (70,427 cases; $WS439,700). Chief imports in 1980 included food and live animals ($WS12,352,100), manufactured goods ($WS13,066,700) and machinery and transport equipment ($WS11,708,500) and mineral fuels, lubricants and other materials ($WS9,561,000).

Total trade between Western Samoa and UK (British Department of Trade returns, in £1,000 sterling):

	1980	*1981*	*1982*	*1983*	*1984*
Imports to UK	572	90	107	156	421
Exports and re-exports from UK	710	431	285	468	1,183

Tourism. There were 32,000 visitors in 1982.

COMMUNICATIONS

Roads (1980). Western Samoa has over 396 km of main roads, 403 km of town and secondary roads and 1,243 km of plantation roads fit for light traffic.

In 1980 there were 1,583 passenger cars and 2,503 commercial vehicles.

Aviation. Western Samoa is linked by daily air service with American Samoa, which is on the route of the weekly New Zealand–Tahiti and New Zealand–Honolulu air services, with connexions to Fiji, Australia, USA and Europe. There are also services throughout the week to and from Tonga, Fiji, Nauru, the Cook Islands and New Zealand. Internal services link Upolu and Savai'i.

Shipping. Western Samoa is linked to Japan, USA, Europe, Fiji, Australia and New Zealand by regular shipping services.

Post and Broadcasting. There is a radio communication station at Apia. Radio telephone service connects Western Samoa with American Samoa, Fiji, New Zealand, Australia, Canada, USA and UK. Telephone subscribers numbered 5,942 in 1982. In 1982 there were 70,000 radio receivers and about 2,500 television sets.

Cinemas. In 1977 there were 10 cinemas with a seating capacity of 7,168.

Newspapers. In 1985, there were 4 weeklies, circulation 12,000 and 2 monthlies (8,000); all were in Samoan and English.

EDUCATION AND WELFARE

Education. In 1980 there were 158 primary, (including intermediate), 38 secondary, 3 secondary vocational and 5 higher education vocational schools, and 2 teacher-training colleges with a total of 55,025 students.

Health. In 1980 there were 30 hospitals (674 beds) and 34 Samoan doctors.

DIPLOMATIC REPRESENTATIVES

Of Great Britain in Western Samoa
High Commissioner: T. D. O'Leary, CMG (resides in Wellington, New Zealand).

Of Western Samoa in the USA and to the United Nations
Ambassador: Maiava Iulai Toma.

Books of Reference

Statistical Year-Book. Annual
Economic Prospects. 1978
The Economy of Western Samoa. 1968
Clare, B. L., *A Review of Social, Labour and Economic Conditions in Western Samoa.* Apia, 1962, reprinted 1963.—*The Parliament of Western Samoa.* Rev. ed. Apia, 1964
Fox, J. W. (ed.), *Western Samoa.* Univ. of Auckland, 1963
Milner, G. B., *Samoan–English, English–Samoan Dictionary.* OUP, 1965

YEMEN ARAB REPUBLIC

Capital: San'a
Population: 7·7m. (1980)
GNP per capita: US$460 (1981)

al Jamhuriya al Arabiya al Yamaniya

HISTORY. On the death of the Iman Ahmad on 18 Sept. 1962, army officers seized power on 26–27 Sept., declared his son, Saif Al-Islam Al-Badr (Iman Mansur Billah Muhammad), deposed and proclaimed a republic. The republican régime was supported by Egyptian troops, whereas the royalist tribes received aid from Saudi Arabia. On 24 Aug. 1965 President Nasser and King Faisal signed an agreement according to which the two powers are to support a plebiscite to determine the future of the Yemen; a conference of republican and royalist delegates met at Haradh on 23 Nov. 1965, but no plebiscite was agreed upon. At a meeting of the Arab heads of state in Aug. 1967 the President and the King agreed upon disengaging themselves from the civil war in Yemen. At the time there were still about 50,000 Egyptian troops in the country, holding San'a, Ta'iz, Hodeida and the plains, whereas the mountains were in the hands of the royalist tribes. By the end of 1967 the Egyptians had withdrawn.

AREA AND POPULATION. In the north the boundary between the Yemen and Saudi Arabia has been defined by the Treaty of Taif concluded in June 1934. This frontier starts from the sea at a point some 5 or 10 miles north of Maidi and runs due east inland until it reaches the hills some 30 miles from the coast, whence it runs northwards for approximately 50 miles so as to leave the Sa'da Basin within the Yemen. Thence it runs in an easterly and south-easterly direction until it reaches the desert area near Nejran. The area is about 73,300 sq. miles (195,000 sq. km) with a population of 7,160,851, census 1981. There were 1,395,123 citizens working abroad mainly in Saudi Arabia and the United Arab Emirates not included in the census total. The capital is San'a with a population of (1981) 277,817. Other important towns are the port of Hodeida (population, 126,386), and Ta'iz (119,572); other towns are Ibb, Yerim, Dhamar and the ports of Mokha and Loheiya.

CLIMATE. A desert climate, modified by relief. San'a. Jan. 57°F (13·9°C), July 71°F (21·7°C). Annual rainfall 20″ (508 mm).

CONSTITUTION AND GOVERNMENT. A provisional Constitution was promulgated on 19 June 1974 by the Command Council, which later established a 99-member People's Constituent Assembly on 6 Feb. 1978 (membership raised to 159 on 8 May 1979) before dissolving itself on 22 April 1978. The Assembly elects the President of the Republic, who appoints a Prime Minister and other members of the Cabinet. A General People's Congress met in 1982 composed of 1,000 members (700 elected).

President of the Republic: Col. Ali Abdullah Saleh (elected 17 July 1978; re-elected 22 May 1983).

The Council of Ministers on 12 Nov. 1983 was composed of:

Chairman (Prime Minister), Vice-President of the Republic: Maj. Abdel Aziz Abdel Ghani.

Deputy Prime Minister for Internal Affairs: Lieut.-Col. Mujahid Abu Shawrib.

Foreign Affairs: Dr Ahmad Abd al-Malik al-Asfahi. *Interior:* Lieut.-Col. Muhsin Mohammad al-Ulufi. *Economy and Industry:* Ahmad Qa'id Barakat. *Public Works:* Abdullah Husayn al-Kurshumi. *Electricity, Water and Drainage:* Mohammad Hasan Sabra. *Waqfs and Guidance:* Qadi Ali bin Ali as-Samman. *Local Government:* Mohammad Abdullah al-Jayfi. *Labour, Youth and Social Affairs:* Ahmad Salih ar-Ra'ini. *Agriculture and Fisheries:* Dr Ahmad al-Hamadani. *Civil Service and Administrative Reform:* Ismail Ahmad al-Wazir. *Education:* Dr Abd al-Wahid Aziz az-Zindani. *Communications and Transport:* Ahmad Mohammad al-Unsi. *Justice:* Qadi Ahmad al-Jubi. *Information and Culture:* Hasan Ahmad al-Lawzi. *Municipalities and Housing:* Ahmad Mohammad Luqman. *Finance:* Ahmad Khadin al-Wajih. *Supply and Trade:* Dr Mohammad Yahya al-Adhi. *Development and Planning:* Mohammad Ahmad Junaid. *Health:* Dr Mohammad Ahmad al-Kabab. There are also 3 Ministers of State.

National flag: Three horizontal stripes of red, white, black, with a green star in the centre.

Local government: There are 8 provinces *(Liwa'):* Sa'dah, al-Bayda, San'a, al-Hudaydah (Hodeida), Hajjah, Rida, Ibb and Ta'iz.

DEFENCE. Military service for 3 years is compulsory.

Army. The Army consists of 5 armoured, 1 mechanized, 9 infantry, 1 parachute and 3 artillery brigades, 1 central guard force and 3 anti-aircraft artillery and 2 air defence battalions. Equipment includes 150 T-34, 500 T-54/-55 and 64 M-60 main battle tanks. Strength (1985) 20,000.

Navy. The flotilla consists of 2 fast missile craft, 3 fast torpedo boats, 3 patrol craft, 2 inshore minehunters, 12 small coastal patrol boats and 4 landing craft (all 26 *ex*-Soviet). Personnel in 1985 numbered 600 officers and men.

Air Force. Built up with aid from both the USA and USSR, as well as Saudi Arabia, the Air Force is believed to be receiving many new Soviet aircraft. Current equipment includes 15 Su-22 fighter-bombers, 25 MiG-21 fighters, a total of 11 Il-14, C-47, An-24/26, C-130 Hercules and Skyvan transports, Mi-8 and Agusta-Bell JetRanger and 212 helicopters. Personnel (1983) about 1,500.

INTERNATIONAL RELATIONS

Membership. The Yemen Arab Republic is a member of UN and the Arab League.

ECONOMY

Planning. A development plan (1982–86) envisages expenditure of 27,400m. riyals.

Budget. The budget for 1984 provided for expenditure of 8,123,738,000 riyal and revenue of 5,455,738,000 riyal.

Currency. The currency is the paper *riyal* of 100 rial. In March 1985, 6·31 *riyal* = £1 and 6·45 *riyal* = US$1.

NATURAL RESOURCES

Minerals. The only commercial mineral being exploited is salt and (1981) production was 64,000 tons. Reserves (estimate) 25m. tonnes.

Agriculture. Wherever water-supply allows, and in general throughout the south-western part of the country, millet (*dhurra*) is grown as a subsistence crop. The traditional cultivation of coffee (no longer exported through Mokha) continues but is giving place to that of *qat* (*cathula edulis*), a narcotic shrub. Cotton (production, 1982, 5,000 tonnes) is grown in the Tihama, the coastal belt, round Bait al Faqih and Zabid (seat of a medieval university). Fruit is plentiful, especially fine grapes from the San'a district. Production (1982, in 1,000 tonnes): Sorghum, 583; potatoes, 138 (1981); grapes, 64 (1981); dates, 90; wheat, 70 (1981); barley, 53; maize, 50.

Livestock (1983): Cattle, 950,000; camels, 108,000; sheep, 3·15m.; goats, 7·5m.; poultry, 4m.

Fisheries. Total catch (1980) 17,000 tonnes.

INDUSTRY AND TRADE

Industry. There is very little industry. In 1970 there were over 60 industrial enterprises employing 4,750. The largest is a textile factory at San'a. A cement factory with a capacity of 100,000 tonnes a year exists.

Commerce. Imports totalled 8,022m. riyals in 1981, the largest items being food and live animals. Exports totalled 217m. in 1981.

Total trade between Yemen Arab Republic and UK (British Department of Trade returns, in £1,000 sterling):

	1980	*1981*	*1982*	*1983*	*1984*
Imports to UK	469	966	1,340	1,857	2,536
Exports and re-exports from UK	36,428	31,599	52,593	56,315	58,761

COMMUNICATIONS

Roads. There were (1983) 19,223 km of roads of which 1,924 are asphalted.

Aviation. There are 3 international airports: San'a, Ta'iz and Hodeida.

Shipping. Hodeida, Mokha, Salif and Loheiya are the 4 main ports.

Post and Broadcasting. There were about 90,350 telephones in 1981. In 1983 there were 25,000 television and 110,000 radio receivers.

RELIGION, EDUCATION AND WELFARE

Religion. The population is almost entirely Moslem, comprising both Sunni (Shafi'i) and Shi'a (Zaidi).

Education. There were (1980–81) 418,263 pupils at primary schools, 25,037 at intermediate, and 9,895 at higher secondary schools, and 2,450 at teacher-training establishments. In 1982 the University of San'a (founded in 1974) had 6,719 students.

Health. In 1983 there were 60 hospitals and health centres with 4,000 beds.

DIPLOMATIC REPRESENTATIVES

Of Yemen Arab Republic in Great Britain (41 South St., London, W1Y 5PD)
Ambassador: Ahmed Daifellah Al-Azeib (accredited 16 Oct. 1982).

Of Great Britain in Yemen Arab Republic (23/25 Qasr al Jumhuri St., San'a)
Ambassador: D. E. Tatham.

Of Yemen Arab Republic in the USA (600 New Hampshire Ave., NW, Washington, D.C., 20037)
Chargé d'Affaires: Muhammad A. M. Basalamah.

Of the USA in Yemen Arab Republic (P.O. Box 1088, San'a)
Ambassador: David E. Zweifel.

Of Yemen Arab Republic to the United Nations
Ambassador: Muhammad Abdul Aziz Sallam.

Books of Reference

Bidwell, R., *The Two Yemens.* Boulder and London, 1983
Heyworth-Dunne, G. E., *Al-Yemen. Social, Political and Economic Survey.* Cairo, 1952
Ingrams, H., *The Yemen.* London, 1963
Peterson, J. E., *Yemen: The Search for a Modern State.* London, 1982
Smith, G. R., *The Yemens.* [Bibliography] Oxford and Santa Barbara, 1984
Stookey, R. W., *Yemen: The Politics of the Yemen Arab Republic.* Boulder, 1978

THE PEOPLE'S DEMOCRATIC REPUBLIC OF YEMEN

Capital: Aden
Population: 2m. (1981)
GNP per capita: US$460 (1981)

Jumhurijah al-Yemen al Dimuqratiyah al Sha'abijah— Southern Yemen

HISTORY. Between Aug. and Oct. 1967 the 17 sultanates of the Federation of South Arabia (*see* map in the STATESMAN'S YEAR-BOOK, 1965–66) were overrun by the forces of the National Liberation Front (NLF). The rulers were deposed, resigned or fled. At the same time the rival organization of FLOSY (Front for the Liberation of Occupied South Yemen) fought a civil war against NLF and harassed the British forces and civilians in Aden. In Nov. the UAR withdrew its support from FLOSY, and with the backing of the Army the NLF took over throughout the country.

The last British troops left Aden on 29 Nov., and on 30 Nov. the Southern Yemen People's Republic was proclaimed and the name subsequently changed to the People's Democratic Republic of Yemen.

AREA AND POPULATION. The People's Democratic Republic of Yemen is bounded north by Yemen Arab Republic and Saudi Arabia, east by Oman, south by the Gulf of Aden and west by the Yemen Arab Republic. The Republic covers an area of approximately 111,074 sq. miles (287,682 sq. km) The population was (estimate, 1981) 2,030,000. The main towns are Aden (capital) (population, 264,326), including Shaikh Othman (30,000), Mukalla, (100,000) and Maalla (44,626).

The island of **Kamaran** in the Red Sea (area 70 sq miles) was in British occupation from 1915 to 1967, when the inhabitants opted in favour of remaining with the Republic but Yemen Arab Republic occupied it in 1972.

The island of **Perim** was first occupied by the French in 1738. In 1799 the British took formal possession but evacuated the island the same year. It was re-occupied by the British in Jan. 1851 and was later used as a coaling station. In Nov. 1967 the inhabitants opted in favour of remaining with the Republic.

The island of **Socotra** lying to the east of the Horn of Africa in the Arabian sea (area 1,400 sq. miles) was formerly part of the Sultanate of Qishn and Socotra and became part of the Republic in 1967.

CLIMATE. A desert climate prevails, modified in parts by altitude, which affects temperatures by up to 12°C, as well as rainfall, which is very low in coastal areas. Aden. Jan. 75°F (24°C), July 90°F (32°C). Annual rainfall 1·8″ (46 mm).

CONSTITUTION AND GOVERNMENT

An amended Constitution was approved by the Supreme People's Council on 31 Oct. 1978.

Meetings took place during 1981–83 between President Mohammed and the President Saleh of the Yemen Arabic Republic, to discuss further steps towards unification.

Cabinet at Oct. 1984 was composed as follows:

Secretary General of the Yemen Socialist Party, Chairman of the Presidium of the Supreme People's Council and Prime Minister: Ali Nasser Mohammed.

Deputy Chairman of the Presidium and First Deputy Prime Minister: Ali Ahmed Nasser Antar. *Deputy Prime Minister and Chairman of Government Information Committee:* Ali Abdul Ar-razzaq Ba Dhib. *Chairman of the State Security Committee:* Saleh Minassar Al-Siyayli. *Foreign Affairs:* Dr Abdul Aziz Al-Dali. *Defence:* Saleh Musleh Qassam. *The Interior:* Mohammed Abdullah Al-Butani. *Finance:* Mahmood Said Madhi. *Health:* Dr Abdulla Ahmed Bakair. *Constructions:* Haidar Abubaker Al Attas. *Labour and Civil Service:* Nasr Nasser Ali. *Culture and Tourism:* Rashid Mohammed Thabit. *Education:* Hassan Ahmed Asalami. *Communications:* Abdulla Mohammed Aziz. *Agriculture:* Mohammed Suleiman Nasser. *Industry:* Abdul Kader Bagamal. *Justice:* Khaled Fadhal Mansour. *Trade and Supply:* Ahmed Obeid Al Fadhli. *Planning:* Dr Farag Bin Ghamen. *Housing:* Ahmed Mohammed Alqaatbi. *Fisheries:* Dr Yassin Saeed Nouman. *Minister of State for the Council of Ministers:* Abdulla Ahmed Ghanim. *Local Government:* Ali Salem Al-Biedh.

National flag. Three horizontal stripes of red, white, black, with a blue triangle based on the hoist bearing a red star.

Local Government. There are 6 governorates, sub-divided into 27 provinces.

DEFENCE. Military service for 2 years is compulsory.

Army. The Army comprises 1 armoured, 2 mechanized, 9 infantry, 1 artillery, 1 rocket and 1 surface-to-surface missile brigades and 10 artillery battalions. Equipment includes 450 T-54/-55/-62 main battle tanks. Strength (1985) about 22,000.

Navy. The Navy comprises 8 fast missile craft, 4 fast torpedo-boats, 2 fast attack craft, 6 coastal patrol boats, 1 fleet minesweeper, 1 tank landing ship, 3 medium landing ships and 3 minor landing craft, all transferred from the Soviet Navy and 3 *ex*-British inshore minesweepers and 6 very small British-built launches. Personnel in 1985 totalled 1,000 officers and men.

Air Force. Formed in 1967, the Air Force is now equipped mainly with aircraft of Soviet design. It has received about 50 MiG-21 fighters, 35 MiG-17 fighter-bombers, 30 Su-20 attack aircraft, 15 Mi-24 gunship helicopters, 4 An-24 twin-turboprop transports and about 16 Mi-8 and 6 Mi-4 helicopters. Personnel (1985) about 1,500.

INTERNATIONAL RELATIONS

Membership. The People's Democratic Republic of Yemen is a member of UN and the Arab League.

ECONOMY

Planning. The revised 5-year plan (1980–85) envisaged expenditure of 425m. dinars.

Budget. The budget of the Republic (in 1m. Yemeni dinars) for 1980–81 envisaged revenue at 86 and expenditure at 96.

Currency. The currency is the South Yemen *dinar* and is divided into 1,000 *fils*. Coins: 50, 25, 5 *fils*; notes: 10, 5 and 1 *dinar,* 500 and 250 *fils*. In March 1985, £1 = 0·366 *dinars*; US$1 = 0·343 *dinars*.

Banking. The only commercial bank is the National Bank of Yemen with the Bank of Yemen carrying on the functions of the Central Bank. All foreign banks have been nationalized.

ENERGY AND NATURAL RESOURCES

Electricity. Production (1981) 260m. kwh.

Agriculture. Agriculture is the main occupation of the people. This is largely of a subsistence nature, sorghum, sesame and millet being the chief crops, and wheat and barley widely grown at the higher elevations. Of increasing importance, however, are the cash crops which have been developed since the Second World War, by far the most important of which is the Abyan long-staple cotton, now the country's major export.

Owing to paucity of rainfall, cultivation is largely confined to fertile valleys and flood plains on silt, built up and irrigated in the traditional manner. These traditional methods are being augmented and replaced by the use of modern earth moving machinery and pumps. Irrigation schemes with permanent installations are in progress. Production (1982 in 1,000 tonnes): Millet, 60; wheat, 15; cotton lint, 4; cotton seed, 8; sesame, 4; barley, 2.

Livestock (1983): Cattle, 120,000; sheep, 1m.; goats, 1·35m.; poultry, 2m.

Fisheries. There is a thriving fisheries industry, fish being the Republic's major export after cotton. Catch (1981) 75,000 tonnes.

INDUSTRY AND TRADE

Industry. Light industry is being established and paint, match and textile factories are in production.

Commerce. Trade is mainly transhipment and entrepôt, Aden serving as a centre of distribution to and from neighbouring territories. Transit trade is mainly in cotton piece-goods, grains, coffee, hides and skins, and cheap consumer goods.

In 1980 imports totalled 527m. dinar; exports and re-exports, 269m. dinar.

Total trade between Republic of Yemen and UK (British Department of Trade returns, in £1,000 sterling):

	1980	*1981*	*1982*	*1983*	*1984*
Imports to UK	5,685	7,272	26,631	10,627	18,238
Exports and re-exports from UK	25,425	31,480	35,577	36,673	45,221

COMMUNICATIONS

Roads. There are 1,150 miles of roads. Registered motor vehicles in 1980 numbered 33,000.

Aviation. Nine airlines operate scheduled services: Alyemda, Air-India, Ethiopian Airlines, Middle East Airlines, Yemen Airlines, Aeroflot, Saudi Airlines, Kuwait Airways, and Air Djibouti.

Shipping. Because of its favourable geographical position and its efficient service to ships, Aden used to be one of the busiest oil-bunkering ports in the world, handling some 550 ships a month.

Post and Broadcasting. The automatic telephone system provided service to about 9,876 subscribers in 1973.

In 1983 there were 150,000 radio and 26,000 television receivers.

Cinemas (1971). There were 19 cinemas with a seating capacity of about 20,000.

JUSTICE, RELIGION, EDUCATION AND WELFARE

Justice. There is a Supreme Court and Magistrates' Courts. In some areas Moslem and local Common Law are administered.

Religion. The majority of the population is Moslem. There are small numbers of Christians and Hindus.

Education. There were (1982, estimate) 229,000 primary school pupils and 28,000 secondary school pupils. A state university was founded in 1975.

Welfare. There were (1979) 44 hospitals with 2,700 beds and about 250 doctors.

DIPLOMATIC REPRESENTATIVES

Of the People's Democratic Republic of Yemen in Great Britain (57 Cromwell Rd., London, SW7 2ED)
Ambassador: Salah Abdulla Muthana (accredited 22 Nov. 1983).

Of Great Britain in the People's Democratic Republic of Yemen (28 Shara Ho Chi Minh, Khormaksar, Aden)
Ambassador: Peter K. Williams.

Of the People's Democratic Republic of Yemen to the United Nations
Ambassador: Abdalla Saleh Al-Ashtal.

The US Embassy in Aden was closed on 26 Oct. 1969 and UK acts as the protective power.

Books of Reference

Hickinbotham, Sir T., *Aden.* London, 1959
Ingrams, H., *Arabia and the Isles.* London
Kostiner, J., *The Struggle for South Yemen.* London and New York, 1984
Smith, G. R., *The Yemens.* [Bibliography] Oxford and Santa Barbara, 1984
Stookey, R. W., *South Yemen: A Marxist Republic in Arabia.* Boulder and London, 1982
Thesiger, W., *Arabian Sands.* London, 1959

YUGOSLAVIA

Capital: Belgrade
Population: 22·85m. (1983)
GNP per capita: US$2,790 (1981)

Socijalistička Federativna Republika Jugoslavija—Socialist Federal Republic of Yugoslavia

HISTORY. In 1917 the Yugoslav Committee in London drew up the Pact of Corfu, which proclaimed that all Yugoslavs would unite after the first world war to form a kingdom under the Serbian royal house. The Kingdom of Serbs, Croats and Slovenes was proclaimed on 1 Dec. 1918. In 1929 the name was changed to Yugoslavia. During the Second World War Tito's partisans set up a provisional government (AVNOJ) which was the basis of a Constituent Assembly after the war. On 29 Nov. 1945 Yugoslavia was proclaimed a republic.

The peace treaty with Italy, signed in Paris on 10 Feb. 1947, stipulated the cession to Yugoslavia of the greater part of the Italian province of Venezia Giulia, the commune of Zara and the island of Pelagosa and the adjacent islets.

By an agreement of 10 Nov. 1975 the city of Trieste ('Zone A') was recognized as Italian and the Adriatic coastal portion of the former Free Territory of Trieste ('Zone B') as Yugoslav. A free industrial zone was set up in the Fernetici–Sezana region on both sides of the frontier.

AREA AND POPULATION. Yugoslavia is bounded in the north by Austria and Hungary, north-east by Romania, east by Bulgaria, south by Greece and west by Albania, the Adriatic Sea and Italy. The area is 225,804 sq. km. Population at the 1981 census: 22,427,585. Population by sex at the 1971 census: males, 10,077,282; females, 10,445,690. Estimate (1983) 22·85m.

The federal capital is Belgrade (Beograd). Population (1981) 1,407,073 and of other principal towns (B = Bosnia and Herzegovina; C = Croatia; K = Kosovo; Ma = Macedonia; Mo = Montenegro; Se = Serbia; Sl = Slovenia; V = Vojvodina):

Banja Luka (B)	183,618	Priština (K)	216,040
Bitolj (Ma)	137,835	Prizren (K)	134,526
Čačak (Se)	110,676	Rijeka (C)	193,044
Čakovec (C)	116,825	Šabac (Se)	119,669
Gostivar (Ma)	101,188	Sarajevo (B)	448,500
Kragujevac (Se)	164,823	Skopje (Ma)	506,547
Kraljevo (Se)	121,622	Slavonski Brod (C)	106,400
Kruševac (Se)	132,972	Smederevo (Se)	107,366
Kumanovo (Ma)	126,368	Split (C)	235,922
Leskovac (Se)	159,001	Subotica (V)	154,611
Ljubljana (Sl)	305,211	Tetovo (Ma)	162,414
Maribor (Sl)	185,699	Titograd (Mo)	132,290
Mostar (B)	110,377	Titova Mitrovica (K)	105,323
Niš (Se)	230,711	Tuzla (B)	121,717
Novi Sad (V)	257,685	Uroševac (K)	113,680
Osijek (C)	158,790	Zadar (C)	116,174
Pančevo (V)	123,791	Zagreb (C)	1,174,512
Peć (K)	111,071	Zenica (B)	132,733
Prijedor (B)	108,868	Zrenjanin (V)	139,300

Population (1981 census) by ethnic group was *(i)* the 6 'leading nations': Serbs, 8,140,507; Croats, 4,428,043; Moslems, 1,999,890; Slovenes, 1,753,571; Macedonians, 1,341,598; Montenegrins, 579,043; *(ii)* of the 18 other 'nationalities': Albanians, 1,730,878; Hungarians, 426,867. 1,219,024 persons declared themselves 'Yugoslavs' (i.e. not wanting to be listed with any minority). In 1984 about 600,000 nationals worked abroad.

Vital statistics for calendar years:

	Live births	*Still-born*	*Deaths*	*Infantile deaths*	*Marriages*	*Divorces*
1980	382,120	2,675	197,361	12,012	171,439	22,583
1981	369,047	2,534	201,196	11,354	173,036	22,557

Vital statistics, 1983 (per 1,000 population: Live births, 16·7; deaths, 9·5; marriages, 7·5; infant mortality, 31·7; natural increase, 7·2. Divorces per 1,000 marriages: 161·8. Expectation of life in 1981: males, 67·2; females, 73·6.

The Yugoslav (*i.e.*, South Slav) languages proper are Slovene, Macedonian and Serbo-Croat, the latter having 2 variants (Serbian and Croatian) which are regarded as constituting one language. There are claims, largely politically-motivated, that Croatian is a separate language and Macedonian a dialect of Bulgarian. Macedonian is and Serbian may be written in the Cyrillic alphabet. There are also substantial Albanian and Hungarian-speaking minorities. Art. 246 of the Constitution lays down that 'The languages of the nations and nationalities and their alphabets shall be equal throughout the territory of Yugoslavia'. In practice Serbo-Croat serves as a *lingua franca* throughout the country.

CLIMATE. Most parts have a central European type of climate, with cold winters and hot summers, but the whole coast experiences a Mediterranean climate with mild, moist winters and hot, brilliantly sunny summers with less than average rainfall. Belgrade. Jan. 32°F (0°C), July 72°F (22°C). Annual rainfall 24·4" (610 mm). Sarajevo. Jan. 31°F (–0·5°C), July 67°F (19·6°C). Annual rainfall 34" (856 mm). Šibenik. Jan. 45°F (7°C), July 78°F (25·5°C). Annual rainfall 32·5" (813 mm). Split. Jan. 47°F (8·5°C), July 78°F (25·6°C). Annual rainfall 35" (870 mm). Zagreb. Jan. 32°F (0°C), July 72°F (22°C). Annual rainfall 34·6" (865 mm).

CONSTITUTION AND GOVERNMENT. The Constitution passed on 31 Jan. 1946 declared the Federal Republic to be composed of 6 republics: Serbia, Croatia, Slovenia, Bosnia and Herzegovina, Macedonia and Montenegro.

On 13 Jan. 1953 a new Constitution (Fundamental Law) confirmed the management of all public affairs by the workers and their representatives (which was introduced in 1950) as the basis of the entire social, economic and political system of Yugoslavia.

The Constitution promulgated 7 April 1963 changed the name of the country into the Socialist Federal Republic of Yugoslavia, composed of the socialist republics of Bosnia and Herzegovina, Croatia, Macedonia, Montenegro, Serbia and Slovenia, and the 2 socialist autonomous provinces of Kosovo and Vojvodina within the framework of Serbia.

Under this Constitution, social self-government was exercised by the representative bodies of communes, districts, autonomous provinces, republics and the Federation and the rights to self-government and distribution of income proclaimed in 1953 were extended to those employed in public services. The former Council of Producers, in which only workers and employees engaged in economic production were represented, was replaced by Councils of Working Communities representing the working people employed in every field of social activity.

All the means of production and all natural resources are social property. Exceptions are peasants' holdings (up to 10 hectares of arable land) and handicrafts. Citizens may be owners of houses and dwellings for personal and family needs.

A new Constitution was proclaimed on 21 Feb. 1974. The political principle of this Constitution is the direct transfer of economic and political decision making power to the working people through the 'assembly system'. An assembly is defined (Art. 132) as 'a body of social self-management and the supreme organ of power within the framework of the rights and duties of its socio-political community'. Assemblies are based upon the work-place or community and take various forms depending upon the nature of employment. Art. 133 states, 'Working people in basic self-managing organizations and communities and in socio-political organizations shall form delegations for the purpose of the direct exercise of their rights, duties and responsibilities and of organized participation in the performance of the functions of the assemblies of the socio-political communities', and Art. 135, 'Candidates for members of delegations of basic self-managing organizations and communities shall be proposed and determined by the working people in these organizations and communities in the Socialist Alliance of the Working People ... or in trade union organizations'. At the apex of the assembly system is the federal legislature, the Assembly of the Socialist Federal Republic of Yugoslavia which has 2 Chambers: the Federal Chamber and the Chamber of Republics and Provinces.

The Federal Chamber consists of 30 delegates of self-managing organizations, communities and socio-political organizations from each Republic, and 20 delegates from each Autonomous Province. The Chamber of Republics and Provinces consists of 12 delegates from each Republican Assembly and of 8 delegates from each Provincial Assembly.

Every citizen over the age of 18 has the suffrage (16 if employed). The last elections were held from Jan. to April 1982.

The State Presidency is elected every 5 years. It has 9 members: 8 representatives of the Republics and Autonomous Provinces, and the President of the Presidium of the League of Communists *ex officio*. The annual President is head of state.

Membership of the state Presidency:

Bosnia and Herzegovina: Branko Mikulić; *Croatia:* Josip Vrhovec; *Macedonia:* Lazar Mojsov; *Montenegro:* Veselin Djuranović *(President until May 1985); Serbia:* Gen. Nikola Ljubičić; *Slovenia:* Stane Dolanc; *Kosovo:* Sinan Hasani; *Vojvodina:* Radovan Vlajković *(Vice-President).*

The League of Communists had 2·2m. members in 1984. It is headed by a Presidium of its Central Committee led by Ali Šukrija (till June 1985). *Secretary:* Dimce Belovski (until June 1985). Other members of the Presidium: Jure Bilić, Dušan Dragosavac, Kiro Hadži-Vasilev, Franjo Herljević, Milan Kučan, Dragoslav Marković, Petar Matić, Veljko Milatović, Miljan Radović, Mitja Ribičić, Nikola Stojanović, Dobrivoje Vidić. There are also 9 *ex-officio* members.

President of the Assembly of the SFRY: Vojo Srzentić (elected May 1983).

The Federal Executive Council consists of 29 ministers. Members of the Council are elected in conformity with the principle of equal representation of the Republics with corresponding representation of Autonomous Provinces.

The President of the Council is elected by the Chambers of the Assembly of the SFRY at the proposal of the Presidency; Members, at the proposal of the candidate Chairman.

President of the Federal Executive Council (Prime Minister): Milka Planinc. *Vice-Presidents:* Borislav Srebrić; Mijat Suković; Janez Zemljarič.

Federal Secretary Defence: Adm. Branko Mamula; *Finance:* Vlado Klemenčič; *Foreign Affairs:* Raif Dizdarević; *Foreign Trade:* Milenko Bojanić; *Information:* Mitko Calovski; *Internal Affairs:* Dobrosav Ćulafić; *Justice:* Borislav Krajina; *Market and Economic Affairs:* Siniša Korića.

National flag: Three horizontal stripes of blue, white, red, with a large red, yellow-bordered star in the centre.

National anthem: Hej, Slaveni, jošte živi reč naših dedova—O Slavs, our ancestors' words still live.

DEFENCE. Military service for 15 months is compulsory. The General People's Defence Law of 1969 bases Yugoslavia's defence on the principle of a nation in arms ready to wage partisan war against any invader. The partisan Territorial Defence Force number about 3m.

Army. The Army is divided into 7 Military Regions and comprises 8 infantry divisions; 8 independent tank, 17 independent infantry, 1 mountain and 1 airborne brigades; 12 field artillery, 12 anti-aircraft, 6 anti-tank and 3 surface-to-air missile regiments. Equipment includes 1,240 T-34/-54/-55 and 60 M-47 main battle tanks. Strength (1985) 191,000 (including 140,000 conscripts), with a reserve of 500,000.

Navy. The Navy comprises 7 diesel powered patrol submarines, 2 midget (2-man) submarines, 2 new *ex*-Soviet frigates, 16 fast missile boats, 15 fast torpedo boats, 3 patrol vessels, 6 fast attack craft, 4 minehunters, 13 patrol boats, 10 inshore minesweepers, 23 river minesweepers, 1 tank landing ship, 13 minelaying landing craft, 1 survey ship, 1 salvage vessel, 2 headquarters ships, 9 transports, 2 training ships, 22 minor landing craft, 4 ammunition carriers, 6 oilers, 6 water carriers and 12 tugs. Personnel in 1985 totalled: 1,500 officers and 12,500 ratings.

Air Force. The Air Force has about 250 combat aircraft and is organized in 2 Air Corps, with HQ at Zagreb and Zemun. There are 2 fighter divisions equipped primarily with about 125 Russian-built MiG-21s, 2 ground-attack divisions of locally-built Jastreb light jet attack aircraft (being replaced with Super Galeb), and 2 squadrons of Jastreb jet reconnaissance aircraft. Transport units fly Il-14 and An-26 twin-engined aircraft, 4-turboprop An-12s, and a few other types in small numbers, notably Turbo-Porters and Yak-40s, Mystère 50s and Learjets for VIP duties. Training types are the nationally-designed UTVA-75 armed primary trainer, Galeb jet basic trainer and the T-33A jet advanced trainer (being replaced with Super Galeb). A large number of Gazelle, Agusta-Bell 205, Mi-4 and Mi-8 helicopters are in service. 'Guideline' and 'Goa' surface-to-air missiles have been supplied by the USSR. Personnel number 37,000.

INTERNATIONAL RELATIONS

Membership. Yugoslavia is a member of UN and has special relationships with Comecon and OECD.

ECONOMY

Planning. A 5-year plan of economic development for 1981–85 envisaged that industrial production should increase by 4·5–5%, and that of agriculture by 4·5%. A long-term Economic Stabilisation Programme was introduced in 1983 to deal with the economic crisis, and laws were passed to ensure the prompt repayment of foreign debts. Foreign indebtedness was US$21,000m. in 1984. Control of some prices and increases in others were introduced in Dec. 1983 in an attempt to control inflation, which had nevertheless reached 62% by July 1984. As a condition of IMF aid, price freezes were ended in Sept. 1984 on 55% of industrial products. Balance of payments (in US$1m.) in 1982: receipts, 19,671; expenditure, 20,135.

Budget. Revenue and expenditure for 1984, 374,000m. dinars. 231,600m. dinars were allotted to defence.

Currency. On 26 July 1965 the value of 1 *dinar*, divided into 100 *para*, was fixed at 0·710937 milligrammes of fine gold instead of 2·96224 milligrammes. A new *dinar*, equivalent of 100 old dinars, was introduced on 1 Jan. 1966. There are coins of 5, 10, 20, 25 and 50 *paras* and 1, 2, 5 and 10 *dinars*, and notes of 5, 10, 20, 50, 100, 500 and 1,000 *dinars*. Currency in circulation in 1983 was 1,438,100m. *dinars*. The *dinar* was devalued by 30% in June 1980 and again by 20% in Oct. 1982. In March 1985, £1 = 270 *dinars*; US$1 = 255 *dinars*.

Banking. The National Bank is the bank of issue. There are also republican National Banks, 115 (in 1980) 'internal banks', 160 'basic banks' and 9 'associated banks'. At 30 June 1982 total credits amounted to 2,108,300m. dinars. Savings deposits totalled 271,300m. dinars in 1983.

Weights and Measures. The metric weights and measures have been in use since 1883. The *wagon* of 10 tonnes is used as a unit of measure for coal, roots and corn. The Gregorian calendar was adopted in 1919.

ENERGY AND NATURAL RESOURCES

Electricity. Generation of electricity in 1983 (and 1982) was 64,600m. kwh. (62,324m.), of which 21,691m. was hydro-electric.

Minerals. Yugoslavia has considerable mineral resources, including coal (chiefly brown coal), iron, copper ore, gold, lead, chrome, antimony and cement. The most important iron mines are at Vareš and Ljubija in Bosnia, and there are also considerable siderite and limonite iron ores between Prijedor, Sanski Most and Topusko. Copper ore is exploited chiefly at Bor (Serbia). The principal lead mines are at Trepča and Mežice. Chrome mines are in southern Serbia (Kosovo) and Macedonia (Skopje, Kumanovo). There are 2 antimony mines in western Serbia (Podrinje).

Mining output, in 1,000 tonnes, in 1983 (and 1982): Coal, 392 (389); lignite, 47,697 (43,454); bauxite, 3,500 (3,668); salt, 425 (428); manganese ore, 32 (27); iron ore, 5,018 (5,106); copper ore, 23,443 (19,733); lead and zinc ore, 4,063 (4,252); antimony ore, 51 (63); crude petroleum, 4,125 (4,340); pyrite concentrates, 694 (810); magnesite, 300 (328). In 1982, gold output was 4,211 kg; silver (1981), 138,000 kg.

Agriculture. The economically active agricultural population was 2,488,000 in 1981 (47·5% female). The cultivated area was 9·89m. hectares in 1983 of which 8·23m. were in private farms and 1·67m. in agricultural organizations, of which there were 4,853 in 1982. In 1984 only 6·5% of the 2·6m. private farms were more than 10 hectares of land.

Area (in hectares) and yield (in 1,000 tonnes) in 1983: Maize, 2·3m. (10,688); wheat, 1·6m. (5,525); sugar beet, 141,000 (5,650); rye, 51,000 (83); tobacco, 60,000 (65); sunflower, 76,000 (139); potatoes, 274,000 (2,587).

Livestock, Jan. 1983: cattle, 5·35m.; pigs, 8·37m.; sheep, 7·45m.; poultry, 69·68m.

1983 yield of fruit (in 1,000 tonnes): Apples, 589; grapes, 1,625; plums, 987. 7·6m. hectolitres of wine were produced in 1982.

There were 622,385 tractors in 1983, of which 594,000 were in private hands.

Forestry. The forest areas consist largely of beech, oak and fir. Forest area in 1982: 9,278,000 hectares (2,354,000 in private hands). Gross timber cut: 21,108,000 cu. metres.

Fisheries. In 1982 the landings of fish were (in tonnes): salt-water, 40,489; freshwater, 26,235. The number of fishing craft was 220 motor vessels (9,430 GRT) and 1,117 sailing and rowing vessels.

INDUSTRY AND TRADE

Employment. In 1982 there were 9,763 large industrial enterprises and 1,500 small businesses in the social sector, and 141,128 small businesses in the private sector. In Dec. 1983 (women in brackets) there were 126,000 (47,000) employed in the private sector and 6·1m. in the social sector (excluding armed forces) of whom 2·37m. (0·84m.) were in manufacturing and mining, and 1·05m. (0·63m.) in the social services. There were 912,000 unemployed in 1983, of whom 694,000 were under 30 and 520,000 were women. Average income per worker in 1983: 15,540 dinars. In 1982 60% of workers received less than the average income. There were (1982) 5,485,000 trade union members.

Industry. The majority of industries are situated in the north-west part of the country.

Industrial output (in 1,000 tonnes) in 1982 (and 1983): Pig-iron, 2,703 (2,870); steel, 3,850 (4,165); cement, 9,718 (9,880), sulphuric acid, 1,183 (1,320); fertilizers, 2,314 (2,350); plastics, 409 (505). Fabrics (in 1m. sq. metres): Cotton, 372 (377); woollen, 94 (95). Sugar (1,000 tonnes), 683 (695). Motor cars (in 1,000s), 219 (215).

Commerce. Foreign trade, in 1m. dinars, for calendar years:

	1979	*1980*	*1981*	*1982*	*1983*
Imports	382,709	411,257	430,166	557,353	789,330
Exports	185,470	245,086	298,360	428,071	637,170

Structure of exports (and imports) in 1983 (%): investment goods, 17·2 (15); intermediate goods, 52·3 (79·4); consumer goods, 30·5 (5·6). Largest suppliers in

1983 (goods in 1m. dinars): USSR, 165,328; Federal Republic of Germany, 102,549; Italy, 62,357; USA, 52,966; Iraq, 43,832; Czechoslovakia, 43,776. Largest export markets: USSR, 170,263; Federal Republic of Germany, 52,572; Italy, 52,465; Czechoslovakia, 40,656; Iraq, 30,352; USA, 22,353.

The main imports (by value) in 1982 were (in 1m. dinars): Machinery, electrical goods, transport means and parts, 154,984; fuel and lubricants, 143,487; manufactured goods, 83,875; chemical products, 62,232; crude articles, 59,449; food, 28,063. The main exports: Machinery, electrical goods, transport means and parts, 133,178; fuel and lubricants, 7,902; manufactured goods, 94,106; chemical products, 44,848; crude articles, 20,764; foods, 38,519.

In April 1983 a five-year trade and co-operation agreement with the EEC was signed. A trade pact was signed with the USSR in March 1983.

Total trade between Yugoslavia and UK (British Department of Trade returns, in £1,000 sterling):

	1980	*1981*	*1982*	*1983*	*1984*
Imports to UK	56,802	42,405	52,115	83,951	108,479
Exports and re-exports from UK	190,503	194,846	158,881	148,645	163,871

Tourism. In 1983, 5,947,000 (1982: 5,925,000) tourists visited Yugoslavia.

COMMUNICATIONS

Roads (1983). There were 62,111 km of asphalted roads and 34,924 km of macadamized roads. There were 2,770,739 passenger motor cars and 244,770 trucks and buses in 1983. In 1983, 1,051m. passengers and 180m. tonnes of freight were carried by public road transport. The north–south highway is being converted to 6-lane motorway.

Railways. In 1983 Yugoslavia had 9,399 km of railway, of which 3,451 km are electrified, and ran 11,643m. passenger-km and 27,860m. tonne-km of freight.

Aviation. The national airline, Jugoslovenski Aero Transport (Inex Adria-aviopromet, Panadria and Aviogenex) in 1983 flew on its home and international services, 49·3m. km and carried 4·7m. passengers and 85m. ton-km of freight; international services (without Panadria), 5·1m. passengers and 42·9m. ton-km of freight. The chief airfields are Belgrade, Zagreb, Ljubljana, Sarajevo, Skopje, Dubrovnik, Split, Titograd, Tivat, Pula and Zadar.

Shipping. In 1982 Yugoslavia possessed a total of 460 vessels of 2·5m. gross tons.

In 1982 vessels of 46·4m. net tons entered the ports of Yugoslavia.

In 1982 Yugoslavia had 1,248 river craft with 2,426 passenger capacity. The length of the navigable rivers amounted to 1,673 km, that of canals to 664 km. There are 2 navigable lakes: Skadar (391 sq. km, of which 243 in Yugoslavia) and Ohrid (348 sq. km, of which 230 in Yugoslavia). A Tisza-Danube canal system is under construction.

Pipeline. An oil pipeline runs from Krk to Pančevo.

Post and Broadcasting. There were 3,871 post offices and 2,796,000 telephone subscribers in 1983. *Jugoslovenska Radiotelevizija* consists of almost 250 main, relay and local stations operating on medium-waves and FM. *Radio Koper* also broadcasts commercial programmes in Italian for northern parts of Italy. National and regional TV programmes are broadcast. Advertisements are broadcast for maximum 170 minutes each week. Number of receivers in 1983: radio, 4·7m.; television, 4m.

Cinemas (1982). 1,278, seating 424,000. 27 full-length films were made in 1983.

Theatres (1982–83). 68, seating 27,691.

Newspapers and Books (1982). There were 27 dailies and 4,532 other newspapers and periodicals. There are no party newspapers but *Borba* and *Politika* (circulation in 1983: 44,000 and 278,000) enjoy semi-official status. 10,535 book titles (1,006 by foreign authors) were published in 1982.

JUSTICE, RELIGION, EDUCATION AND WELFARE

Justice. There are county tribunals, district courts, supreme courts of the constituent republics and a Supreme Court. There are also self-management courts, including courts of associated labour. In county tribunals and district courts the judicial functions are exercised by professional judges and by lay assessors constituted into collegia. There are no assessors at the supreme courts.

All judges are elected by the socio-political communities in their jurisdiction. The judges exercise their functions in accordance with the legal provisions enacted since the liberation of the country.

The constituent republics enact their own criminal legislation, but offences concerning state security and the administration are dealt with at federal level.

Religion. Religious communities are separate from the State and are free to perform religious affairs. All religious communities recognized by law enjoy the same rights.

Serbia has been traditionally Orthodox and Croatia Roman Catholic. Moslems are found in the south as a result of the Turkish occupation. The 1953 percentage of the denominations was: Orthodox, 41·2%; Roman Catholic, 31·7%; Moslems, 12·3%; Protestants, 0·9%; without religion, 12·6%. 1984 estimates of believers: Orthodox, 9m.; Roman Catholic, 7m.; Moslems, 4m.

The Serbian Orthodox Church with its seat in Belgrade has 20 bishoprics within the country and 4 abroad, 3 in US and Canada and 1 in Hungary. The Serbian Orthodox Church numbers about 2,000 priests.

The Macedonian Orthodox Church with the Archbishop of Ohrid and Macedonia as its head in Skopje, has 4 bishoprics in the country and 1 abroad (American–Canadian–Australian). The Macedonian Orthodox Church numbers about 300 priests.

The Roman Catholic Church is divided into two provinces: Zagreb with 4 suffragan sees, and Sarajevo with 2 suffragan sees. In addition, the Roman Catholic Church has 4 archbishoprics, 10 independent bishoprics directly connected with the Vatican and 3 Apostolic Administrators. There is a National Conference of Bishops with the Archbishop of Zagreb, Cardinal Franjo Kuharič, at its head. The Roman Catholic Church has about 4,000 priests, 2 theological faculties and 15 seminaries. Relations with the Vatican are regulated by a 'Protocol' of 1966.

The Moslem Religious Union has 4 republic Superiorates in Sarajevo, Skopje, Titograd and Priština. The highest authority is the supreme synod of the Islamic Religious Community, which elects the Reis-ul-Ulema and the Supreme Islamic Superiorate. The Moslem religious community has about 2,000 priests.

The Protestant churches covering 4 independent Lutheran Churches, numbering about 150,000 believers, the Reformed Christian Church, numbering about 60,000 believers, include also several much smaller churches of Baptists, Methodists, Adventists, Nazarenes, etc., numbering together about 100,000 believers. The Protestant churches have about 450 priests.

Also there are independent Old Catholic Churches with Synodal Council at Zagreb.

The Jewish religion has about 35 communities making up a common league of Jewish Communities with its seat in Belgrade.

Education. Compulsory general education lasts 8 years, secondary 3–4 years. In 1982–83 there were 12,402 primary schools with 134,208 teachers and 2,819,788 pupils, secondary schools (440 in 1981–82, currently in course of reform) with 63,868 teachers and 1,025,139 pupils, 178 primary schools for adults with 16,662 pupils, and secondary schools for adults (585 in 1981–82) with 35,186 pupils. 86·6% of primary school leavers entered secondary school.

Primary (and secondary schools) of ethnic minorities: Albanian, 1,342 (278), Hungarian, 167 (64); Bulgarian, 49; Czech, 13; Slovak, 19 (10); Italian, 28 (17); Romanian, 29 (7); Turkish, 64 (11); Ukrainian, 3 (3).

In 1982–83 there were 357 institutes of higher education with 386,356 students and 24,905 teachers. 9·5% of the population over ten years old was illiterate in 1981.

Health. In 1982 there were 42,852 doctors and dentists, and 138,340 hospital beds (11,062 psychiatric).

Health insurance benefits totalled 105,251m. dinars and pensions 204,379m. dinars in 1982.

DIPLOMATIC REPRESENTATIVES

Of Yugoslavia in Great Britain (5 Lexham Gdns., London, W8 5JJ)
Ambassador: Dragi Stamenković.

Of Great Britain in Yugoslavia (46 Generala Ždanova, Belgrade)
Ambassador: K. B. A. Scott, CMG.

Of Yugoslavia in the USA (2410 California St., NW, Washington, D.C., 20008)
Ambassador: Mico Rakic.

Of the USA in Yugoslavia (50 Kneza Miloša, Belgrade)
Ambassador: David Anderson.

Of Yugoslavia to the United Nations
Ambassador: Ignac Golob.

Books of Reference

Statistical Information: The Federal Statistical Office (Savezni Zavod za Statistiku; Kneza Miloša 20, Belgrade) was founded in Dec. 1944. *Director:* Franta Kornel. It publishes: *Indeks* (from April 1952, with English and French translations); *Statistički bilten* (1950 ff., with English or French translations); *Statistical Yearbook* (from 1954, with English, Russian and French translations); *Statistics of Foreign Trade of the SFR Yugoslavia* (annual, from 1946; half-yearly, from 1951); *Statistical Pocket-book* (from 1955; in 5 eds.: Yugoslav, English, French, Russian, German).

The Assembly of the SFR of Yugoslavia. Belgrade, 1974
The Constitution of the Socialist Federal Republic of Yugoslavia. Belgrade, 1974
Alexander, S., *Church and State in Yugoslavia since 1945.* CUP, 1979
Auty, P., *Yugoslavia.* New York, 1965.—*Tito: A Biography.* London, 1970
Burg, S. L., *Conflict and Cohesion in Socialist Yugoslavia: Political Decision-Making since 1966.* Princeton Univ. Press, 1983
Carter, A., *Democratic Reform in Yugoslavia: The Changing Role of the Party.* Princeton Univ. Press and London, 1982
Cohen, L. J., *Political Cohesion in a Fragile Mosaic: The Yugoslav Experience.* Boulder, 1983
Dedijer, V., *et al., History of Yugoslavia.* New York, 1974
Denitch, B. D., *The Legitimation of a Revolution: The Yugoslav Case.* Yale Univ. Press, 1976
Djilas, M., *Memoir of a Revolutionary.* New York, 1973
Doder, D. *The Yugoslavs.* New York, 1978
Drvodelić, M., *Croatian or Serbian-English Dictionary.* 4th ed. Zagreb, 1978
Filipović, R., *English-Croatian or Serbian Dictionary.* Zagreb, 1980
Horton, J. J., *Yugoslavia.* [Bibliography] Oxford and Santa Barbara, 1978
Horvat, B., *The Yugoslav Economic System.* White Plains, 1976
Kotnik, J., *Slovensko–angleski slovar.* 4th ed. Ljubljana, 1959
Minić, M., *The Foreign Policy of Yugoslavia, 1973–1980.* Belgrade, 1982
Rusinow, D. I., *The Yugoslav Experiment, 1948–1974.* London, 1977
Ristić, Simić, Popović: *An English–Serbocroatian Dictionary.* 2 vols. Belgrade, 1956
Singleton, F., *Twentieth Century Yugoslavia.* London, 1976.—(with B. Carter) *The Economy of Yugoslavia.* London, 1982
Sirc, L., *The Yugoslav Economy under Self-Management.* London, 1979
Stojanović, R., (ed.) *The Functioning of the Yugoslav Economy.* New York, 1982
Tito, J. B., *The Essential Tito.* New York, 1970

REPUBLICS AND AUTONOMOUS PROVINCES

The Federal Republic of Yugoslavia comprises the 6 republics of Bosnia and Herzegovina, Croatia, Macedonia, Montenegro, Serbia and Slovenia, and the 2 autonomous provinces of Kosovo and Vojvodina within the Republic of Serbia.

Each has its own Constitution, Assembly of 3 Chambers (of Associated Labour; of Communes; Socio-Political) and League of Communists within the League of

Communists of Yugoslavia, though the latter is not formally a federal institution. League of Communist Presidents and Secretaries in 1985: *Bosnia and Herzegovina:* Mato Andrić, Živko Grubor; *Croatia:* Mika Špiljak, Stanko Stojčević; *Kosovo:* Svetislav Dolašević, Bajram Seljani; *Macedonia:* Milan Pančevski, Jakov Lazarovski; *Montenegro:* Vidoje Žarković, Velisav Vuksanović; *Serbia:* Ivan Stambolić, Radiša Gačić; *Slovenia:* Andrej Marinc, Miha Ravnik; *Vojvodina:* Boško Krunić, Katalin Hajnal.

Indicators (in %) for 1982:

	Population	*Workers*	*Social product*	*Investments*
Yugoslavia	*100*	*100*	*100*	*100*
Bosnia and Herzegovina	18·5	14·8	13·6	16·7
Croatia	20·4	24·2	25·8	24·4
Macedonia	8·6	7·5	5·7	5·7
Montenegro	2·6	2·3	2	4·4
Serbia	41·5	37·9	37·9	36·2
Slovenia	8·4	13·3	15	12·6

BOSNIA AND HERZEGOVINA

HISTORY. The country was settled by Slavs in the 7th century, the original clan system evolving between the 12th and 14th centuries into a principality under a *Ban,* during which time the Bogomil Christian heresy became entrenched. Bosnia was conquered by the Turks in 1463, and the majority of the Bogomils were converted to Islam. At the Congress of Berlin (1878) the territory was assigned to Austro-Hungarian administration under nominal Turkish suzerainty. Austria-Hungary's outright annexation in 1908 generated tensions which contributed to the outbreak of the first world war.

AREA AND POPULATION. The republic is bounded in the north and west by Croatia, in the east by Serbia and in the south-east by Montenegro. It is virtually land-locked, having a coastline of only 20 km with no harbours. Its area is 51,129 sq km. The capital is Sarajevo.

Population at the 1981 census: 4,124,008 (2,073,343 females), of whom the predominating ethnic groups were Moslems (1,629,924), Serbs (1,320,644) and Croats (758,136). Population density per sq. km: 80·7.

Vital statistics:

	Live births	*Marriages*	*Deaths*	*Growth rate per 1,000*
1982	71,763	36,533	25,131	10·9
1983	72,355	36,729	28,428	10·4

ECONOMY

Agriculture. In 1983 the agricultural area was 2·56m. hectares. Yields (in 1,000 tonnes) and areas sown (in 1,000 hectares) of principal crops were: wheat, 439 (151); barley, 66 (37); maize, 821 (251); soya, 8,881 (4,549); potatoes, 351 (50). Livestock in 1984 (1,000 head): horses, 134; cattle, 996; sheep, 1,471; pigs, 820. Timber cut in 1982: 6·9m. cu. metres.

Industry. Production (1983): Electricity, 11,447m. kwh; lignite, 7·43m. tonnes; iron ore, 4·23m. tonnes; pig iron, 1·69m. tonnes; bauxite, 2·28m. tonnes; cement, 725m. tonnes; cotton fabrics, 44m. sq. metres; cars, 26,000.

Employment. Population of working age, 1983, 2·75m.; non-agricultural workforce, 0·94m., of whom 0·72m. worked in production.

CROATIA

HISTORY. The Croats migrated to their present territory in the 6th century and were converted to Roman Catholicism. Croatia was conquered by Hungary in

1091 and remained under Hungarian domination until after the first world war. During the second world war an independent fascist state was set up.

AREA AND POPULATION. Croatia is bounded in the north by Slovenia and Hungary and in the east by Serbia. It has an extensive Adriatic coastline well provided with ports, and includes the historical areas of Dalmatia, Istria and Slavonia, which no longer have administrative status. The capital is Zagreb. Its area is 56,538 sq. km. Population at the 1981 census was 4,601,469 (2,374,579 females), of whom the predominating ethnic groups were Croats (3,454,661), Serbs (531,502), and Hungarians (25,439). Population density per sq. km: 81·4.

Vital statistics:

	Live births	*Marriages*	*Deaths*	*Growth rate per 1,000*
1982	66,289	33,828	51,275	3·3
1983	66,325	33,623	54,377	2·6

ECONOMY

Agriculture. In 1983 the agricultural area was 3·24m. hectares. Yields (in 1,000 tonnes) and areas sown (in 1,000 hectares) of principal crops were: wheat, 1,303 (323); barley, 161 (55); maize, 2,481 (511); sugar beet, 1,172 (28); soya, 23,790 (10,918); potatoes, 716 (81). Livestock in 1984 (1,000 head): horses, 69; cattle, 970; sheep, 723; pigs, 2,095. Timber cut in 1982: 5·11m. cu. metres.

Industry. Production (1983): Electricity, 7,582m. kwh; coal, 260,000 tonnes; bauxite, 448; crude petroleum, 2·86m. tonnes; steel, 383,000 tonnes; plastics, 169,000 tonnes; cement, 3·4m. tonnes; cotton fabrics, 65m. sq. metres; sugar, 151,000 tonnes.

Employment. Population of working age, 1983: 3·03m.; non-agricultural workforce, 1·5m., of whom 1·25m. worked in production.

MACEDONIA

HISTORY. The Slavs settled in Macedonia since the 6th century, who had been Christianized by Byzantium, were conquered by the non-Slav Bulgars in the 7th century and in the 9th century formed a Macedo-Bulgarian empire, the western part of which survived until Byzantine conquest in 1014. In the 14th century it fell to Serbia, and in 1355 to the Turks. After the Balkan Wars of 1912-13 Turkey was ousted, and Serbia received the greater part of the territory, the rest going to Bulgaria and Greece. In 1918 Yugoslav Macedonia was incorporated into Serbia as 'South Serbia'. Possession of this territory has long been a source of contention between Bulgaria and Yugoslavia.

AREA AND POPULATION. Macedonia is land-locked, and is bounded in the north by Serbia and Kosovo, in the east by Bulgaria, in the south by Greece and in the west by Albania. The capital is Skopje. Its area is 25,713 sq. km. Population at the 1981 census was 1,912,257 (940,993 females), of whom the predominating ethnic groups were Macedonians (1,281,195), Albanians (377,726) and Turks (86,691). Population density per sq. km, 74·4.

Vital statistics:

	Live births	*Marriages*	*Deaths*	*Growth rate per 1,000*
1982	39,845	16,648	14,558	13·4
1983	39,806	16,436	14,558	12·8

ECONOMY

Agriculture. In 1983 the agricultural area was 1·34m. hectares. Yields (in 1,000 tonnes) and areas sown (in 1,000 hectares) of principal crops were: wheat, 246 (115); barley, 97 (54); maize, 99 (40); cotton, 719 (1,113); tobacco, 27 (25); Livestock in 1984 (1,000 head): horses, 81; cattle, 302; sheep, 2,131; pigs, 197. Timber cut in 1982: 976,000 cu. metres.

Industry. Production (1983): Electricity, 3,040m. kwh; lignite, 2·26m. tonnes; iron ore, 642,000 tonnes; pig-iron, 212,000 tonnes; steel, 350,000 tonnes; copper ore, 3·84m. tonnes; sulphuric acid, 76,000 tonnes; cement, 699,000 tonnes; cotton fabrics, 51m. sq. metres.

Employment. Population of working age, 1983: 1·24m.; non-agricultural work-force, 0·48m., of whom 0·4m. worked in production.

MONTENEGRO

HISTORY. Montenegro emerged as a separate entity on the break-up of the Serbian Empire in 1355. It was never effectively subdued by Turkey. It was ruled by Bishop Princes until 1851, when a royal house was founded.

AREA AND POPULATION. Montenegro is a mountainous region which opens to the Adriatic in the south-west. It is bounded in the north-west by Bosnia and Herzegovina, in the north-east by Serbia and in the south-east by Albania. The capital is Titograd. Its area is 13,812, sq. km. Population at the 1981 census was 584,310 (294,571 females), of whom the predominating ethnic groups were Montenegrins (400,488), Moslems (78,080) and Albanians (37,735). Population density per sq. km: 42·3.

Vital statistics:

	Live births	*Marriages*	*Deaths*	*Growth rate per 1,000*
1982	11,012	4,593	3,483	12·7
1983	10,972	4,211	3,954	11·7

ECONOMY

Agriculture. In 1983 the agricultural area was 517,000 hectares. Yields (in 1,000 tonnes) and areas sown (in 1,000 hectares) of principal crops were: wheat, 10 (4); barley, 9 (6); maize, 16 (8), potatoes, 42 (6). Livestock in 1984 (1,000 head): horses, 24; cattle, 184; sheep, 488; pigs, 28. Timber cut in 1982: 808,000 cu. metres.

Industry. Production (1983): Electricity, 2,264m. kwh; lignite, 2·15m. tonnes; bauxite, 670,000 tonnes; cement, 164,000 tonnes.

Employment. Population of working age, 1983: 0·38m.; non-agricultural work-force, 0·14m., of whom 0·12m. worked in production.

SERBIA

HISTORY. The Serbs received Orthodox Christianity from the Byzantines. They threw off the latter's suzerainty to become a large prosperous medieval state, which was destroyed by the Turks at the Battle of Kosovo in 1389. After revolutions in 1804 and 1815 Serbia won increasing degrees of autonomy from Turkey; complete independence came with the Treaty of Berlin in 1878. Its prince took the title of king in 1881.

AREA AND POPULATION. Serbia is land-locked and is bounded in the north-west by Croatia, in the north by Hungary, in the north-east by Romania, in the east by Bulgaria, in the south by Macedonia and in the west by Albania, Montenegro and Bosnia and Herzegovina. It includes the Autonomous Provinces of Kosovo in the south and Vojvodina in the north, which have substantial Albanian and Hungarian populations respectively. Without these its area is 55,968 sq. km. The capital is Belgrade. Population at the 1981 census was 5,694,464

(2,876,909 females), of whom the predominating ethnic group was Serbs (4,865,283). Population density per sq. km: 101·7.

Vital statistics:

	Live births	Marriages	Deaths	Growth rate per 1,000
1982	80,222	42,062	55,539	4·3
1983	81,630	41,005	59,314	3·9

ECONOMY

Agriculture. In 1983 the agricultural area was 3·38m. hectares. Yields (in 1,000 tonnes) and areas sown (in 1,000 hectares) of principal crops were: Wheat, 1,332 (474); barley, 80 (45); maize, 2,637 (623); sugar-beet, 532 (14); soya, 16,932 (8,912); potatoes, 572 (61). Livestock in 1984: (in 1,000 head): horses, 64; cattle, 1,611; sheep, 1,926; pigs, 3,072. Timber cut in 1982: 2·74m. cu. metres.

Industry. (1983): Electricity, 24,803m. kwh; coal, 132,000 tonnes; lignite, 23·67m. tonnes; pig-iron, 567,000 tonnes; steel, 649,000 tonnes; copper ore, 19·6m. tonnes; lorries, 11,110; cars, 42,797; sulphuric acid, 911,000 tonnes; plastics, 64,000 tonnes; cement, 1·23m. tonnes; sugar, 46,000 tonnes; cotton fabrics, 53m. sq. metres; woollens, 32m. sq. metres.

Employment. Population of working age, 1983: 3·87m.; non-agricultural workforce, 1·56m., of whom 1·28m. were in production.

KOSOVO

AREA AND POPULATION. Area: 10,887 sq. km. The capital is Priština. Population at the 1981 census, 1,584,441 (766,048 females), of whom the predominating ethnic groups were Albanians (1,226,736), and Serbs (209,498). Population density per sq. km: 145·5.

Vital statistics:

	Live births	Marriages	Deaths	Growth rate per 1,000
1982	51,870	11,994	9,792	25·8
1983	53,322	12,113	10,850	25·3

ECONOMY

Agriculture. The agricultural area in 1983 was 584,000 hectares. Yields (in 1,000 tonnes) and sown areas (in 1,000 hectares) of principal crops were: Wheat, 229 (99); maize, 274 (93); sugar-beet, 25 (1); potatoes, 73 (8). Livestock in 1984 (1,000 head): horses, 35; cattle, 392; sheep, 374; pigs, 69. Timber cut in 1982, 378,000 cu. metres.

Industry. Production (1983): Electricity, 3,539m. kwh; lignite, 7·15m. tonnes; sulphuric acid, 77,000 tonnes; cement, 295,000 tonnes.

Employment. Population of working age, 1983: 0·89m.; non-agricultural workforce, 200,000, of whom 150,000 worked in production.

VOJVODINA

AREA AND POPULATION. Area: 10,887 sq. km. The capital is Novi Sad. Population at the 1981 census, 2,034,772 (1,041,392 females), of whom the predominating ethnic groups were Serbs (1,107,378) and Hungarians (385,356). Population density per sq. km: 94·6.

Vital statistics:

	Live births	Marriages	Deaths	Growth rate per 1,000
1982	26,397	15,435	23,112	1·6
1983	26,673	15,417	23,890	1·4

ECONOMY

Agriculture. The agricultural area in 1983 was 1·79m. hectares. Yields (in 1,000 tonnes) and sown areas (in 1,000 hectares) of principal crops were: Wheat, 1,805 (396); barley, 198 (59); maize, 4,132 (678); sugar-beet, 3,595 (87); soya, 160,307 (82,574); potatoes, 287 (23). Livestock in 1984 (1,000 head): horses, 39; cattle, 329; sheep, 320; pigs, 2,420. Timber cut in 1982: 629,000 cu. metres.

Industry. Production (1983): Electricity, 1,290m. kwh; crude petroleum, 1·26m. tonnes; sulphuric acid, 33,000 tonnes; plastics, 144,000 tonnes; cement, 1·64m. tonnes.

Employment. Population of working age, 1983: 1·36m.; non-agricultural work-force, 0·59m., of whom 0·5m. worked in production.

SLOVENIA

HISTORY. The lands originally settled by Slovenes in the 6th century were steadily encroached upon by Germans. Slovenia developed as part of Austria-Hungary and only gained independence in 1918.

AREA AND POPULATION. Slovenia is bounded in the north by Austria, in the north-east by Hungary, in the south-east by Croatia and in the west by Italy. There is a small strip of coast south of Trieste. Its area is 20,251 sq. km. The capital is Ljubljana. Population at the 1981 census: 1,891,864 (973,098 females), of whom the predominating ethnic group were Slovene (1,712,445). Population density per sq. km: 93·4.

Vital statistics:

	Live births	*Marriages*	*Deaths*	*Growth rate per 1,000*
1982	30,667	11,562	19,830	5·7
1983	29,130	12,076	21,125	4·2

ECONOMY

Agriculture. In 1983 the agricultural area was 880,000 hectares. Yields (in 1,000 tonnes) and sown areas (in 1,000 hectares) of principal crops were: Wheat, 160 (47); maize, 259 (61); sugar-beet, 142 (4); potatoes, 463 (33). Livestock in 1984 (1,000 head): horses, 17; cattle, 575; sheep, 25; pigs, 635. Timber cut in 1982: 3·52m. cu. metres.

Industry. Production (1983): Electricity, 12,429m. kwh; lignite, 5m. tonnes; steel, 818,000 tonnes; lorries, 5,292; cars, 45,000; sulphuric acid, 203,000 tonnes; sugar, 21,000 tonnes; cement, 1·39m. tonnes; cotton fabrics, 143m. sq. metres; woollens, 27m. sq. metres.

Employment. Population of working age, 1983: 1·23m.; non-agricultural work-force, 0·82m., of whom 0·69m. worked in production.

ZAÏRE

Capital: Kinshasa
Population: 31·94m. (1983)
GNP per capita: US$210 (1981)

République du Zaïre

HISTORY. Until the middle of the 19th century the territory drained by the Congo River was practically unknown. When Stanley reached the mouth of the Congo in 1877, King Leopold II of the Belgians recognized the immense possibilities of the Congo Basin and took the lead in exploring and exploiting it. The Berlin Conference of 1884–85 recognized King Leopold II as the sovereign head of the Congo Free State.

The annexation of the state to Belgium was provided for by treaty of 28 Nov. 1907, which was approved by the chambers of the Belgian Legislature in Aug. and Sept. and by the King on 18 Oct. 1908. The law of 18 Oct. 1908, called the Colonial Charter (last amended in 1959), provided for the government of the Belgian Congo, until the country became independent on 30 June 1960. The country's name was changed from Congo to Zaïre in Oct. 1971. For subsequent history to 1977 *see* THE STATESMAN'S YEAR-BOOK, 1980–81, p. 1613.

AREA AND POPULATION. Zaïre is bounded north by the Central African Republic, north-east by Sudan, east by Uganda, Rwanda, Burundi and Lake Tanganyika, south by Zambia, south-west by Angola, north-west by Congo. There is a 40-km Atlantic coastline separating Angola's province of Cabinda from the rest of that country.

The area of the republic is estimated at 2,344,885 sq. km (905,365 sq. miles). The population is composed almost entirely of Bantu groups, with minorities of Sudanese (in the north), Nilotes (northeast), Pygmies and Hamites (in the east). In the census (1976) the population was 25,568,640. Estimate (1983) 31,944,000; annual growth rate, 2·9%. In 1983 there were about 283,500 refugees in Zaïre including 215,000 from Angola.

The area (in sq. km) and populations (estimate) 1981 of the regions were as follows, together with their capitals:

Region	*Sq. km*	*Population 1981*	*Chief town*	*Population 1976*
Bandundu	295,658	4,119,524	Bandundu (Banningville)	74,467 [1]
Bas-Zaïre	53,920	1,921,524	Matadi	162,396
Equateur	403,293	3,418,296	Mbandaka (Coquilhatville)	149,118
Haut-Zaïre	503,239	4,541,655	Kisangani (Stanleyville)	339,210
Kasai Occidental	156,967	2,935,036	Kananga (Luluabourg)	704,211
Kasai Oriental	168,216	2,336,951	Mbuji-Mayi (Bakwanga)	382,632
Kinshasa City	9,965	2,338,246	Kinshasa (Leopoldville)	2,443,876
Kivu	256,662	4,713,761	Bukavu (Costermansville)	209,051
Shaba	496,965	3,823,172	Lubumbashi (Elizabethville)	451,332

[1] 1970.

Other large towns: Kikwit, 172,450 in 1976; Likasi (Jadotville), 185,328 in 1975.

French is the only official language, but of more than 200 languages spoken, 4 are recognized as national languages. Of these, Kiswahili is used in the east, Tshiluba in the south, Kikongo in the area between Kinshasa and the coast, while Lingala is spoken widely in and around Kinshasa and along the river; Lingala has become the *lingua franca* after French.

CLIMATE. Because of the size and the relief of the country, the climate is very varied, the central region having an equatorial climate, with year-long high temperatures and rain at all seasons. Elsewhere, depending on position north or south of the Equator, there are well-marked wet and dry seasons. The mountains of the east and south have a temperate mountain climate, with the highest summits having considerable snowfall. Kinshasa. Jan. 79°F (26·1°C), July 73°F (22·8°C). Annual rainfall 45″ (1,125 mm). Kananga. Jan. 76°F (24·4°C), July 74°F (23·3°C). Annual rainfall 62″ (1,584 mm). Kisangani. Jan. 78°F (25·6°C), July 75°F (23·9°C). Annual rainfall 68″ (1,704 mm). Lubumbashi. Jan. 72°F (22·2°C), July 61°F (16·1°C). Annual rainfall 50″ (1,237 mm).

CONSTITUTION AND GOVERNMENT. A new Constitution was promulgated on 15 Feb. 1978 and amended in Nov. 1980. The supreme institution is the sole political party, the *Mouvement Populaire de la Révolution* (MPR), whose leader and President is automatically Head of State, of the National Executive Council and of the National Legislative Council. His nomination by the Political Bureau of the MPR (whose 38 members are all nominated by him) is confirmed for a 7-year term (renewable once) by election by universal adult suffrage (all Zaïreans acquire automatic membership of the MPR at birth).

Former President: Joseph Kasavubu, 1 July 1960–25 Nov. 1965 (deposed in coup).

President: Marshal Mobutu Sésé Séko Kuku Ngbendu wa Zabanga (took office 25 Nov. 1965, elected 1 Nov. 1970 and re-elected Dec. 1977 and July 1984).

The National Executive Council is composed of State Commissioners appointed by the President. In June 1984 it was composed as follows:

First State Commissioner (Prime Minister): Kengo wa Dondo.

Territorial Administration: Mozagba Ngbuka. *Foreign Affairs and International Co-operation:* Umba-Di-Lutete. *Justice:* Bayona Ba Meya. *Information, Propaganda, Mobilization and Political Animation:* Sakombi Inongo. *Planning:* Mulumba Lukoji. *Agriculture and Rural Development:* Nyembo Shabani. *Economy, Industry and Foreign Trade:* Pay Pay wa Syakasighe. *Finance, Budget and State Investment Holdings:* Kiakwama Kiakiziki. *Mines and Energy:* Umba Kyamitala. *Public Works and Territorial Development:* Bokana W'Ondangela. *Transport and Communications:* Mwamba Nduba. *Land Affairs:* Unen Kam. *Higher Education, Universities and Scientific Research:* Takizala Luyan Muis Mbingin. *Primary and Secondary Education:* Nzenge. *Public Health:* Dr Tshibasu Mubiay. *Environment and Tourism:* Njoli Balanga. *Women's and Social Affairs:* Ekila Liyonda. *Civil Service:* Kilolo Musamba Lubemba. *Labour and Social Security:* Kande Buloba Kasumpata. *Posts and Telecommunications:* Mukuku W'Etonda. *Culture and the Arts:* Masengabio. *Sports, Leisure and Youth:* Sampasa Kaweta Milombe.

Parliament consists of a unicameral National Legislative Council comprising People's Commissioners (one per 100,000 inhabitants) elected by universal suffrage for a 5-year term. At the latest elections (Sept. 1982) 310 People's Commissioners were elected from a list of 1,409 candidates presented by the MPR.

National flag: Green, with a yellow disc bearing an arm holding a flaming torch.

Local government: Zaïre is composed of the *ville neutre* of Kinshasa (administered by a Governor) and 8 regions, each under a Regional Commissioner and 6 Councillors; all are appointed by the President.

DEFENCE

Army. The Army is divided into 3 Military Regions and comprises 1 division; 1 armoured, 2 infantry, 1 parachute, 1 commando and 1 Presidential Guard brigades. Equipment includes 60 Chinese Type-62 light tanks, and 95 AML-60 and 60 AML 90 armoured cars. Strength (1985) 22,000. There is a paramilitary gendarmerie which is responsible for security and also numbered (1985) about 22,000, organized in 40 battalions.

Navy. The Navy consists of 3 flotillas, 1 coastal, 1 river and 1 lake, comprising 4 fast gunboats (*ex*-Chinese), 7 fast torpedo boats (4 *ex*-Chinese and 3 *ex*-North Korean), and 42 coastal patrol boats including 12 US-built and 29 French-built. Personnel in 1985 numbered 1,500 officers and men including 600 marines.

Air Force. The Air Force has been built up with training assistance from Italy. In 1984 it operated 5 Mirage 5 supersonic fighters, 12 Aermacchi MB.326GB and 3 MB.326K armed jet trainers, 5 C-130 Hercules and 3 DHC-5 Buffalo turboprop transports, 8 C-47, 12 Super Frelon, Alouette and Puma helicopters, 20 SIAI-Marchetti SF.260MC basic trainers and a variety of other transport and training aircraft. Personnel, approximately 2,500.

INTERNATIONAL RELATIONS

Membership. Zaïre is a member of UN, OAU and is an ACP state of EEC.

ECONOMY

Budget. Revenue was envisaged at 6,773m. zaïres in 1983, and expenditure, 9,173m.

Currency. The currency unit, is the *zaïre*, divided into 100 *makuta*. Each *likuta* (plural *makuta*) is divided into 100 *sengi*. Bank-notes are issued in the following denominations: 10, 5 and 1 *zaïre*, 50, 20, 10 *makuta*; there are coins of 5 *makuta*, 1 *likuta* and 10 *sengi*. In March 1985, £1 sterling = 49·23 *zaïre*; US$1 = 44·86 *zaïre*.

Banking. The central bank is Banque du Zaïre. A development bank with state backing is the Société Financière de Développement (SOFIDE). Commercial banks operating in Zaïre are Banque de Paris et des Pays-Bas, Banque de Kinshasa, National & Grindlays Bank, Barclays Bank SZPRL, First National City Bank, Union Zaïroise de Banques, Banque Commerciale Zaïroise, Bank du Peuple, Caisse Nationale d'Epargne et de Crédit Immobilier and Banque Internationale pour L'Afrique au Zaïre.

Weights and Measures. The metric system was introduced by law on 17 Aug. 1910.

ENERGY AND NATURAL RESOURCES

Electricity. The installed generating capacity (1978) was 1,692 mw, of which 98% was hydroelectric. Production (1981) 4,560m. kwh. A huge new dam at Inga, on the Zaïre River near Matadi, has a potential capacity of 39,600 mw.

Oil. Offshore oil production began in Nov. 1975; crude production (1984) was 1·2m. tonnes.

Minerals. In 1982 most of Zaïre's foreign exchange was derived from mining of copper (505,385 tonnes), zinc concentrates (64,425 tonnes), cobalt (5,573), as well as manganese, gold and silver. The most important mining area is in the region of Shaba (formerly Katanga). The principal mining companies are the State-owned Gécamines; the Zaïre-Japanese Sodimiza; the international Société Minière du Tenke-Fungurume which started production in 1976; and 2 diamond companies, MIBA and British Zaïre Diamond Distributors. Production (1982) 5·7m. metric carats.

Agriculture. In 1979, 75% of the 11·7m. workforce were engaged in agriculture. There were 5·65m. hectares of arable land and 24·8m. hectares of pastures and meadows. The main food crops (1981 production in 1,000 tonnes) are: Cassava, 13,000; plantains, 1,450; sugar-cane, 700; maize, 520; groundnuts, 320; bananas, 317; yams, 309; rice, 250. Cash crops (1982) include palm oil, 160; coffee, 85; palm kernels, 65; rubber, 23; cotton 10. There are also (1982) pineapples, 153; mangoes, 137; oranges, 141.

Livestock (1983): Cattle, 1·3m.; sheep, 760,000; goats, 2·9m.; pigs, 750,000; poultry, 16m.

Forestry. Equatorial rain forests cover 55% of Zaïre's land surface, and 10·57m. cu. metres of timber were produced in 1981.

Fisheries. The catch for 1981 was 102,000 tonnes, almost entirely from inland waters.

INDUSTRY AND TRADE

Industry. In 1981 about 341,000 tonnes of petroleum products were refined, and about 400,000 tonnes of cement produced.

Commerce. Imports in 1982 totalled 2,759·7m. zaïres, exports totalled 9,924·9m. zaïres. In 1982, 40% of the exports (by value) consisted of copper, 19% of coffee, 12% of diamonds and 7% of cobalt. 36% of all exports went to USA, 31% to Belgium and 6% to France, while 22% of imports came from Belgium, 13% from France, 10% from USA and 10% from Federal Republic of Germany.

Total trade between Zaïre and UK (British Department of Trade returns, in £1,000 sterling):

	1980	*1981*	*1982*	*1983*	*1984*
Imports to UK	52,585	17,986	15,801	11,192	7,720
Exports and re-exports from UK	27,629	22,452	20,557	21,129	36,254

Tourism. There were 18,942 visitors in 1976 spending US$11m.

COMMUNICATIONS

Roads. In 1984 of 160,000 km of roads only 20,600 km are of national importance and all roads are earth-surfaced. There were 177,931 motor vehicles registered in Dec. 1975. Of these, 95,978 were cars, 33,505 trucks, 2,989 buses, 9,153 motor cycles, and other types, 36,306.

Railways. There are two railway operators, the Zaïre National Railways (SNCZ) and the National Office of Transport and Communications (Onatra), which leases two lines from SNCZ. Length in 1983 was 4,104 km on four gauges, of which 858 km is electrified. In 1983 SNCZ carried 372m. passenger-km and 1,860m. tonne-km.

Aviation. There are 4 international airports at Kinshasa (Ndjili), Lubumbashi (Luano), Kisangani and Bukavu. There are another 40 airports with regular scheduled internal services, and over 150 other landing strips.

More than twelve international airlines, including British Caledonian Airways, operate in and out of Kinshasa from Europe, Africa and the USA. The national airline Air Zaïre, operates on all the main internal routes as well as on international routes to Europe and other African cities.

Shipping. The Zaïre River and its tributaries are navigable for about 13,700 km. Regular traffic has been established between Kinshasa and Kisangani as well as Ilebo, on the Lualaba (*i.e.*, the river above Kisangani), on some tributaries and on the lakes. Zaïre has only 40 km of sea coast. The merchant marine in 1981 comprised 34 vessels with a total tonnage of 92,044 GRT. Kinshasa, Matadi and Boma are the main seaports; in 1978, 629,422 tonnes of freight were unloaded and 498,380 loaded.

Post and Broadcasting. In 1970 there were 351 post offices. Length of telegraph lines, 2,459 km. There were 15 broadcasting stations, 161 stations of wireless telegraphy and 206 telegraph offices; telephones numbered 30,284 in 1980. There is a ground satellite communications station outside Kinshasa. In 1979 there were 245,000 radio and 7,700 television receivers.

Cinemas (1974): 91 cinemas had a seating capacity of 23,300.

Newspapers. There were (1984) 4 dailies: *Salongo* (mornings) and *Elima* (evenings) in Kinshasa; *Njumbe* in Lubumbashi and *Boyoma* in Kisangani.

JUSTICE, RELIGION, EDUCATION AND WELFARE

Justice. A Justice Department was established in Jan. 1980 to replace the Judicial Council. There is a Supreme Court at Kinshasa, 9 Courts of Appeal and 32 courts of first instance.

Religion. In 1980 there were about 10m. Roman Catholics, 7m. Protestants and

4m. Kimbanguistes, as well as some 200,000 Moslems and 2,000 Jews. The remaining inhabitants adhere to animist beliefs.

Education. In 1978–79 there were 3,919,395 pupils in 5,924 primary schools, 611,349 in secondary schools, 84,995 (1977–78) in technical schools and 138,170 in teacher-training colleges. In 1971 all Institutes of Higher Education combined to form the National University of Zaïre, but in 1981 this was divided to form 3 Universities at Kinshasa, Kisangani and Lubumbashi; in 1978–79 in all there were 28,430 students and 2,782 teaching staff at 36 higher education establishments.

Health. In 1979 there were 1,900 doctors, 58 dentists, 414 pharmacists, 3,043 midwives, 14,661 nursing personnel and 942 hospitals and medical centres with 79,244 beds.

DIPLOMATIC REPRESENTATIVES

Of Zaïre in Great Britain (26 Chesham Place, London, SW1X 8HH)
Ambassador: Mukamba Kadiata Nzemba (accredited 14 Nov. 1984).

Of Great Britain in Zaïre (Ave. de l'Equateur, Kinshasa)
Ambassador: Nicholas P. Bayne, CMG.

Of Zaïre in the USA (1800 New Hampshire Ave., NW, Washington, D.C., 20009)
Ambassador: Kasongo Mutuale.

Of the USA in Zaïre (310 Ave. des Aviateurs, Kinshasa)
Ambassador: Peter D. Constable.

Of Zaïre to the United Nations
Ambassador: Inonga Lokongo L'Ome.

Books of Reference

Area Handbook for the Democratic Republic of the Congo (Kinshasa). US Government Printing Office, Washington, 1971
Atlas Général du Congo. Académie Royale, Brussels
Cornevin, R., *Histoire de Congo.* Paris, 1963
Gran, G., *Zaire: The Political Economy of Underdevelopment.* New York, 1979
Slade, R. M., *King Leopold's Congo: Aspects of the Development of Race Relations in the Congo's Independent State.* OUP, 1962

ZAMBIA

Capital: Lusaka
Population: 6·24m. (1982)
GNP per capita: US$600 (1981)

HISTORY. The independent Republic of Zambia (formerly Northern Rhodesia) came into being on 24 Oct. 1964 after 9 months of internal self-government following the dissolution of the Federation of Rhodesia and Nyasaland on 31 Dec. 1963.

By an Order in Council dated 4 May 1911 the two provinces of North-eastern and North-western Rhodesia were amalgamated under the name of Northern Rhodesia, with effect from 17 Aug. 1911.

By an Order in Council dated 20 Feb. 1924, the office of Governor was created, an executive council constituted and provision made for the institution of a legislative council which, since 1945, had an unofficial majority. On 1 April 1924 the British South Africa Company was relieved of the administration of the territory by the Crown.

AREA AND POPULATION. Zambia is bounded by Tanzania in the north, Malawi in the east, Mozambique in the south-east and by Zimbabwe and South West Africa (Namibia) in the south. The area is 290,586 sq. miles (752,620 sq. km). Population (1982 estimate) 6,242,000 of which 40% urban.

The republic is divided into 9 provinces. Their names, headquarters, area (in sq. km) and estimated population in 1980 were as follows:

Province	*Headquarters*	*Area*	*Population*	*Province*	*Headquarters*	*Area*	*Population*
Copperbelt	Ndola	31,328	1,248,888	Eastern	Chipata	69,106	656,381
Luapula	Mansa	50,567	412,789	Southern	Livingstone	85,283	686,469
Northern	Kasama	147,826	677,894	N.-Western	Solwezi	125,827	301,677
Central (including Lusaka)	Kabwe	116,290	1,207,713	Western	Mongu	126,386	487,988

The seat of Government is at Lusaka (population, 1980, 538,469). The other important centres are Livingstone, the old capital (71,987), Ndola (282,439), Luanshya (132,164), Mufulira (149,778), Kitwe (314,794), Chililabombwe (61,928), Kalulushi (59,213) and Chingola on the Copperbelt (145,869); Kabwe, the oldest mining township (143,635); Chipata, centre of a tobacco farming area.

CLIMATE. The climate is tropical, but has three seasons. The cool, dry one is from May to Aug., a hot dry one follows until Nov., when the wet season commences. Frosts may occur in some areas in the cool season. Lusaka. Jan. 70°F (21·1°C), July 61°F (16·1°C). Annual rainfall 33″ (836 mm). Livingstone. Jan. 75°F (23·9°C), July 61°F (16·1°C). Annual rainfall 27″ (673 mm). Ndola. Jan. 70°F (21·1°C), July 59°F (15°C). Annual rainfall 52″ (1,293 mm).

CONSTITUTION AND GOVERNMENT. The Constitution provides for a President, elected in the first instance by the General Conference of the ruling party, the United National Independence Party, and thereafter he is elected by the electorate. On 13 Dec. 1972 President Kaunda signed a new Constitution based on one-party rule.

The single political party is the United National Independence Party. Its full-time executive organ (headed by a Secretary-General) is the Central Committee, whose 24 members are elected by the General Conference of the Party. The Central Committee has precedence over the legislative body, the National Assembly, which is led by the Prime Minister and consists of 125 elected members and up to 10 nominated members, including a cabinet of 18 ministers.

Presidential elections were held in Oct. 1983 and on 30 Oct. President Kaunda was sworn in for a fifth 5-year term.

The Cabinet, as in Sept. 1984, was composed as follows:

President and Commander-in-Chief: Kenneth David Kaunda.
Prime Minister: Nalumino Mundia.
Secretary of Defence and Security: A. G. Zulu. *Higher Education:* R. Kunda. *Defence:* C. M. Mwananshiku. *Foreign Affairs:* L. K. H. Goma. *Works and Supply:* H. Y. Mwale. *Agriculture and Water Development:* Gen. G. K. Chinkuli. *Tourism:* R. C. Sakuhuka. *General Education and Culture:* K. S. K. Musokotawne. *Health:* Mark Tambatamba. *Home Affairs:* F. M. Chomba. *National Guidance:* A. K. Simuchimba. *Youth and Sport:* B. C. Kakoma. *Legal Affairs and Attorney-General:* G. G. Chigaga. *National Commission for Development Planning:* Dr H. S. Meebelo. *Mines:* B. R. Kabwe. *Labour and Social Services:* F. S. Hapunda. *Power, Transport and Communications:* F. Chuula. *Information and Broadcasting Services:* C. Chibanda. *Co-operatives:* J. J. Mukando. *Finance:* L. J. Mwananshiku. *Commerce and Industry:* L. S. Subulwa. *Lands and Natural Resources:* F. Chela.

Flag: Green, with in the fly a panel of 3 vertical strips of dark red, black and orange, and above these a soaring eagle in gold.

The provinces are administered by Central Committee Members for the provinces who are responsible for the overall government and Party administration of their respective areas.

DEFENCE

Army. The Army consists of 1 armoured regiment and 6 infantry battalions, with supporting artillery, engineer and signals units. Equipment includes some 34 main battle tanks and 130 armoured cars. Strength (1985) 12,500. There are also para-military police units numbering 1,200 men.

Air Force. Creation of the Zambian Air Force was assisted initially by an RAF mission. Training and expansion of the Air Force was next taken over by Italy, with the purchase of 23 Aermacchi M.B.326G armed jet basic trainers (of which 18 remain in service), 6 SIAI-Marchetti SF.260M piston-engined trainers and the 10 surviving Agusta-Bell 47G/205/212/JetRanger helicopters. Twelve F-6 (MiG-19) jet fighter-bombers and some CF-6 primary trainers have since been acquired from China, a squadron of 17 MiG-21 fighters, 3 Yak-40 light jet transports, some An-26 twin-turboprop transports and 6 Mi-8 helicopters from the Soviet Union, 6 SOKO Jastreb jet light attack aircraft and 6 Galeb jet trainers from Yugoslavia, 5 DHC-5 Buffalo twin-turboprop transports from Canada, 6 C-47s built in the USA, 10 Do 28D Skyservant light transports from Germany, 20 Supporter armed light trainers from Sweden.

INTERNATIONAL RELATIONS

Membership. Zambia is a member of UN, the Commonwealth, SADCC, OAU and is an ACP state of EEC.

ECONOMY

Budget. Revenue and expenditure for 1984 (in K1m.): envisaged expenditure of 1,508 and revenue of 1,240.

Currency. Decimal currency was introduced on 16 Jan. 1968. The *Kwacha* (K) is divided into 100 *ngwee* (n). Notes of K20, K10, K5, K2 and K1 are in use. In March 1985, £1 = 2·50 *Kwacha*; US$1 = 2·45 *Kwacha*.

Banking. Barclays Bank International has 25 branches, 6 sub-branches and 17 agencies; Standard Bank has 18 branches and 17 agencies; National & Grindlays, 10 branches and 1 sub-branch; Zambia National Commercial Bank, 10 branches and 1 in London; the post office saving bank has branches throughout the republic.

The Finance Development Corporation (FINDECO) controls the building societies, all insurance companies, one commercial bank and has shares in a second one. The Agricultural Finance Corporation provides loans to farmers, co-operatives, farmers' associations and agricultural societies.

ENERGY AND NATURAL RESOURCES

Electricity. The total installed capacity of hydro and thermal power stations, excluding Zambia's share of Kariba South, amounts to 855 mw and the energy consumption during 1978 amounted to some 5,626·3m. kwh. Zambia exports electricity to Zaïre, Zimbabwe and Angola.

The hydro stations are located at Mbala, Mansa, Kasama, Mulungushi, Lunsemfwa and Victoria Falls, Lusiwasi and Kafue Gorge. Work has started on the Kariba North Project. The thermal stations are located on the Copperbelt. A number of diesel power stations have been installed, mostly in the North-Western and Northern Provinces.

Minerals. The total value of minerals produced in 1982 was:

	Output (1,000 tonnes)	*Value (K1,000)*		*Output (1,000 tonnes)*	*Value (K1,000)*
Copper	584·2	710,636	Coal	603·9	22,346
Zinc	38·9	27,648	Cobalt	2·4	45,257
Lead	14·5	6,050	Other	–	43,227

Agriculture. Although 70% of the population is dependent on agriculture only 10% of GDP is provided by the industry. Principal agricultural products (1983) were maize, 630,622 tonnes; sugar, 132,000 tonnes; cotton, 32,019 tonnes; tobacco, 2,290 tonnes; groundnuts, 97,987 tonnes.

Livestock (1983): 2·38m. cattle; 250,000 pigs; 40,000 sheep; 350,000 goats, and 18m. poultry.

Fishing. Total catch (1980) 51,000 tonnes.

INDUSTRY AND TRADE

Industry. In Dec. 1982 there were 34,020 persons employed in agriculture, forestry and fisheries; 60,270 in mining and quarrying; 48,070 in manufacturing; 8,060 in electricity and water; 42,150 in construction and 25,350 in transport and communications.

Commerce. In 1982 imports totalled K773m., exports 985m. Copper exports (1981) totalled 552,000 tons valued at K874m.

Total trade between Zambia and UK (British Department of Trade returns, in £1,000 sterling):

	1981	*1982*	*1983*	*1984*
Imports to UK	41,398	39,957	50,242	48,069
Exports and re-exports from UK	68,223	61,248	55,501	66,746

Tourism. There were 117,000 tourists in 1982.

COMMUNICATIONS

Roads. There were (1982) over 5,583 km of tarred roads.

Railways. Zambia Railways are that part of the old Rhodesia Railways north of the Victoria Falls. In 1983 the total route-km was 1,204 km (1,067 mm gauge). In 1983 the Zambian railways (excluding Tan-Zam) carried 1·9m. passengers and 5·3m. tonnes of freight. The Tan–Zam railway, giving Zambia access to Dar es Salaam, was opened in 1975, comprising 892 km of route in Zambia.

Aviation. There were (1982) 130 airports in Zambia (46 government owned). Lusaka is the principal international airport. Seven foreign airlines use Lusaka.

Post. There were (1982) 13 head post offices and 236 other post offices. On 1 Jan. 1982 there were 32,659 telephones.

Cinemas. In 1971 there were 28 cinemas with a seating capacity of 13,400.

Newspapers. There were (1984) 2 national daily papers: *The Times of Zambia* (circulation, 65,000) and *Zambia Daily Mail* (45,000).

JUSTICE, RELIGION, EDUCATION AND WELFARE

Justice. The Judiciary consists of the Supreme Court, the High Court and 4 classes of magistrates' courts; all have civil and criminal jurisdiction.

The Supreme Court hears and determines appeals from the High Court. Its seat is at Lusaka.

The High Court exercises the powers vested in the High Court in England, subject to the High Court ordinance of Zambia. Its sessions are held where occasion requires, mostly at Lusaka and Ndola.

All criminal cases tried by subordinate courts are subject to revision by the High Court.

Religion. Freedom of worship is one of the constitutional rights of Zambian citizens. The Christian faith has largely replaced traditional African religion, and the Christian Churches number about 500,000 members and adherents.

Education. In 1981 the primary school enrolments were 1·07m., secondary school enrolments were 99,000 and 4,485 students were enrolled for teacher-training. In 1981 the University of Zambia had 3,603 full-time students.

Health. In 1978 there were 82 hospitals and over 1,000 children's clinics served by 423 doctors.

DIPLOMATIC REPRESENTATIVES

Of Zambia in Great Britain (2 Palace Gate, London, W8 5LS)
High Commissioner: Lieut.-Gen. Peter D. Zuze (accredited 24 June 1982).

Of Great Britain in Zambia (Independence Ave., Lusaka)
High Commissioner: W. K. K. White, CMG.

Of Zambia in the USA (2419 Massachusetts Ave., NW, Washington, D.C., 20008)
Ambassador: Putteho M. Ngonda.

Of the USA in Zambia (PO Box 31617, Lusaka)
Ambassador: Nicholas Platt.

Of Zambia to the United Nations
Ambassador: Paul John Firmino Lusaka.

Books of Reference

General Information: The Director, Zambia Information Services, PO Box RW20, Lusaka.

Laws of Zambia. 13 vols. Govt. Printer, Lusaka

Beveridge, A. A., and Oberschall, A. R., *African Businessmen and Development in Zambia.* Princeton Univ. Press, 1980

Bliss, A. M. and Riggs, J. A., *Zambia.* [Bibliography] Oxford and Santa Barbara, 1984

Bond, G. C., *The Politics of Change in a Zambian Community.* Univ. of Chicago Press, 1976

Gertzel, C. (ed.), *The Dynamics of a One-Party State in Zambia.* Manchester Univ. Press, 1984

Kaunda, Kenneth D., *Zambia Shall be Free.* London, 1962.—*Humanism in Zambia.* Lusaka. 2 vols. 1967 and 1974.—*Zambia's Economic Revolution.* Lusaka, 1968.—*Zambia's Guidelines for the Next Decade.* Lusaka, 1968.—*Letter to my Children.* Lusaka, 1973

Roberts, A., *A History of Zambia.* London, 1977

ZIMBABWE

Capital: Harare
Population: 7·5m. (1982)
GNP per capita: US$780 (1984)

HISTORY. Prior to Oct. 1923 Southern Rhodesia, like Northern Rhodesia, was under the administration of the British South Africa Co. In Oct. 1922 Southern Rhodesia voted in favour of responsible government. On 12 Sept. 1923 the country was formally annexed to His Majesty's Dominions, and on 1 Oct. 1923 government was established under a governor, assisted by an executive council, and a legislature, with the status of a self-governing colony. For the history of the period 1961–1979 including the period of unilateral declaration of independence *see* THE STATESMAN'S YEAR-BOOK, 1980–81, pp. 1623–25. Rhodesia (Southern Rhodesia) became the Republic of Zimbabwe on 18 April 1980.

AREA AND POPULATION. Zimbabwe is situated between the northern border of the Transvaal and the Zambezi River and is bordered on the east by Mozambique and on the west by the republic of Botswana. The area is 150,699 sq. miles (390,308 sq. km). The capital is Harare (Salisbury). The total population was (1982 census) 7,532,000.

Population of main urban areas (1982 census): Bindura, 18,000; Bulawayo, 414,000; Masvingo (Fort Victoria) 31,000; Kadoma (Gatooma) 45,000; Gweru (Gwelo) 79,000; Chegutu (Hartley) 20,000; Marondera (Marandellas) 20,000; Kwekwe (Que Que) 48,000; Redcliffe, 22,000; Harare (Salisbury) 656,000; Zvishavane (Shabani) 27,000; Chinhoyi (Sinoia) 24,000; Mutare (Umtali) 70,000; Hwange (Wankie) 39,000; Chitungwiza, 175,000.

Vital statistics (1980): Deaths, 22,431. Many living in remote areas do not register births.

CLIMATE. Though situated in the tropics, conditions are remarkably temperate throughout the year because of altitude, and an inland position keeps humidity low. The warmest weather occurs in the three months before the main rainy season, which starts in Nov. and lasts till March. The cool season is from mid-May to mid-Aug. and, though days are mild and sunny, nights are chilly. Harare. Jan. 69°F (20·6°C), July 57°F (13·9°C). Annual rainfall 33″ (828 mm). Bulawayo. Jan. 71°F (21·7°C), July 57°F (13·9°C). Annual rainfall 24″ (594 mm). Victoria Falls. Jan. 78°F (25·6°C), July 61°F (16·1°C). Annual rainfall 28″ (710 mm).

CONSTITUTION AND GOVERNMENT. At the Commonwealth Conference held in Lusaka in Aug. 1979 agreement was reached for a new Constitutional Conference to be held in London and this took place between 10 Sept. and 15 Dec. 1979 at Lancaster House. It was attended by the various factions in Zimbabwe-Rhodesia, including Abel Muzorewa, Robert Mugabe and Joshua Nkomo, and was chaired by Lord Carrington. It achieved 3 objectives: (*i*) the terms of the Constitution for an independent Zimbabwe; (*ii*) terms for a return to legality: and (*iii*) a ceasefire. Lord Soames became Governor-General of Southern Rhodesia in Dec. 1979 and elections took place in March 1980.

Zimbabwe African National Union (ZANU, PF) won 57 of the 80 black seats, Zimbabwe African People's Party (ZAPU), 20 and United National Council (UANC), 3. Elections are due in 1985.

President: Canaan Banana.

The Cabinet in March 1985 was composed as follows:

Prime Minister and Minister of Defence and Industry and Technology: R. G. Mugabe.

Deputy Prime Minister and Minister of Energy and Water Resources and Development: S. V. Muzenda. *National Supplies:* E. M. Nkala. *Finance, Economic Plan-*

ning and Development: B. T. G. Chidzero. *Trade and Commerce:* R. C. Hove. *Home Affairs:* S. V. Mubako. *Education:* D. B. Mutumbuka. *Community Development and Women's Affairs:* T. R. Nhongo. *Agriculture:* D. R. Norman. *Health:* S. T. Sekeramayi. *Information, Posts and Telecommunications:* N. M. Shamuyarira. *Justice, Legal and Parliamentary Affairs:* E. J. M. Zvobgo. *Youth, Sport and Culture:* E. R. Kadungure *(Acting)*. *Foreign Affairs:* W. M. Mangwende. *Labour, Manpower Planning and Social Welfare:* F. M. M. Shava. *Local Government and Town Planning:* E. C. Chikowore. *Natural Resources and Tourism:* V. F. Chitepo. *Lands, Resettlement and Rural Development:* M. E. Mahachi. *Construction and National Housing:* S. S. Mumbengegwi. *Energy and Water Resources and Development:* O. M. Munyaradzi. *Transport:* H. S. M. Ushewokunze. *Ministers of State in the Prime Minister's Office:* T. M. Nyagumbo *(Political Affairs and Provincial Development Co-ordination)*, E. R. Kadungure *(Defence)*, K. M. Kangai *(Industry and Technology)*, E. D. Mnangagwa.

National flag: Seven horizontal stripes of green, yellow, red, black, red, yellow and green; on a white black-edged triangle in the hoist a red star surmounted by the Zimbabwe Bird in yellow.

The first municipal elections were held in Nov. 1980.

DEFENCE

Army. The Army consists of 1 armoured and 1 artillery regiments; 18 infantry, 1 commando and 3 parachute battalions; and 8 engineer and 7 signals squadrons. Equipment includes 10 T-34 and 18 T-54 main battle tanks. Strength was (1985) 40,000, and there are a further 10,000 paramilitary police.

Air Force. The Zimbabwe Air Force (regular) has a strength of about 1,300 personnel and 130 aircraft in 8 squadrons, of which 2 are intended primarily for a training role. Headquarters ZAF and New Sarum ZAF station are in Harare; the second main base is at Thornhill, Gweru, with many secondary airfields throughout the country. Equipment includes 1 squadron of Canberra bombers with added underfuselage rocket racks; 1 squadron of Hunter FGA.9 fighter-bombers, supported by Hawk training and light attack aircraft, a transport squadron with 6 turboprop CASA Aviocars, 4 twin-engined Islanders and 12 C-47s; a squadron with 9 Reims/Cessna 337 Lynx attack aircraft; a squadron with 14 SIAI-Marchetti SF.260W Genet and 5 turboprop SF.260TP light attack aircraft and 17 SF.260C Genet trainers; a helicopter liaison/transport squadron with 40 Alouette II/IIIs, a helicopter casualty evacuation/transport squadron with 10 Bell 205s and 2 Bell 412s. One fighter squadron is expected to equip with Chinese-built F-6 (MiG-19) aircraft and another with J-7s (MiG-21s).

INTERNATIONAL RELATIONS

Membership. Zimbabwe is a member of UN, OAU, the Non-Aligned Movement and is an ACP state of EEC.

ECONOMY

Budget. Revenue and expenditure (in Z$1,000) for years ending 30 June:

	1980–81	*1981–82*	*1982–83*	*1983–84*	*1984–85*
Revenue	949,109	1,359,115	1,764,503	1,940,158	2,100,000
Ordinary expenditure:					
From revenue and loan funds	1,411,904	1,897,383	2,558,894	2,866,133	3,389,163

Receipts during the year ended 30 June 1984 were (in Z$1,000): Income and profits tax, 801,569; taxes on goods and services, 923,184; miscellaneous taxes and other income, 215,405.

The gross amount of the public debt outstanding in June 1984 was Z$3,175,953,984.

Currency. On 17 Feb. 1970 decimal currency was adopted. The unit of currency is the Zimbabwe *dollar* divided into 100 *cents*. In March 1985, £1 = Z$1·77; US$1 = Z$1·65.

Banking. The Reserve Bank of Zimbabwe is the country's central bank; it became operative when the Bank of Rhodesia and Nyasaland ceased operations on 1 June 1965. It acts as banker to the Government and to the commercial banks and as agent of the Government for important financial operations. It is also the central note-issuing authority and co-ordinates the application of the Government's monetary policy.

The post office savings bank had Z$534·8m. deposits at 31 Aug. 1984.

The 5 commercial banks are Barclays Bank of Zimbabwe Ltd, Grindlays Bank Ltd, Zimbabwe Banking Corporation Ltd, Standard Chartered Bank Zimbabwe Ltd, Bank of Credit and Commerce Zimbabwe (Pvt) Ltd.

Weights and Measures. The metric system is in use but the US short ton is also used.

ENERGY AND NATURAL RESOURCES

Minerals. The total value of all minerals produced in 1982 was Z$383,044,000. Output (in 1,000 tonnes) and value (in Z$1,000):

	Output			*Value*		
	1981	*1982*	*1983*	*1981*	*1982*	*1983*
Asbestos	247·6	194·4	153·2	91,276	76,634	69,335
Gold (1,000 oz.)	371·0	426·0	453·2	117,380	122,773	193,914
Chrome ore	536·0	431·6	420·3	20,406	19,873	25,629
Coal	2,867·0	2,800·0	2,536·9	29,469	35,834	42,174
Copper	24·6	24·8	21·6	27,900	26,839	32,953
Nickel	13·1	13·3	10·1	51,734	49,753	42,100
Iron Ore	1,097·7	837·0	926·5	14,841	13,949	14,628
Silver (1,000 oz.)	857·0	918·0	938·4	5,997	5,271	10,552

Agriculture. The most important single food crop in Zimbabwe is maize, the staple food of a large proportion of the population; deliveries to the Grain Marketing Board in 1983 were 616,900 tonnes. Drought reduced crop by 50%. The export potential for the livestock industry has increased with the possibility of new markets in EEC countries. Milk production by the Dairy Marketing Board in 1984 was 181·1m. litres.

The country is suitable for the production of both citrus and deciduous fruits and fruit production is now well established. In 1982–83 seed cotton production was 168,465 tonnes and irrigated wheat production (1983) was 124,250 tonnes. Tea is grown in the Inyanga and Chipinge districts and production in 1982 was 9,920 tonnes. Coffee growing is of increasing importance (production, 1982–83, 9,729 tonnes) as is sugar; sugar exports (1982) were valued at about Z$41m. Other crops grown in substantial quantities include small grains (sorghums and millet), soya beans and groundnuts. A wide variety of vegetable crops are also produced.

Tobacco is the most important single product, accounting for over 40% of the value of earnings from agricultural exports. In 1982 tobacco exports accounted for 17% of all Zimbabwean foreign exchange earnings.

Livestock (1983): Cattle, 5·35m.; pigs, 192,000; sheep, 455,000; goats, 1m.

INDUSTRY AND TRADE

Industry. The manufacturing industry has developed from the service and maintenance operations that initially provided the back-up needed by the mining and agricultural sectors, and it now supplies a comprehensive range of consumer goods and a growing number of capital goods to the local market. A high reputation for quality has been won by many manufacturers, including producers of clothing, footwear, furniture, radio equipment, steel sections, agricultural implements and pharmaceutical products.

The Customs Agreement with the Republic of South Africa was extended in March, 1982 pending further discussion. Zimbabwe has also entered into Trade

Agreements with Zambia, Mozambique, Tanzania, Angola and Swaziland. There is a Customs Union with Botswana. In 1981 agriculture and forestry formed 18% and manufacturing (1983) 25% of the GDP.

Labour. The labour force (1983) was 2·5m.; 1,991,000 (40%) are employed in the formal sector; 750,000 (30%) are peasant cultivators. The remaining 750,000 are either self-employed in the informal sector or unemployed. Nearly 108,500 new job-seekers entered the employment market this year.

Commerce. Imports and exports (in Z$1,000):

	1978	*1979*	*1980*	*1981*	*1982*
Imports	404,239	550,908	809,400	1,017,700	999,000
Exports	612,364	702,302	784,000	959,300	1,118,000

Principal imports in 1981 (in Z$1,000): Machinery and transport equipment, 372,400; petroleum products, 189,056; textiles, 67,394; chemicals, 48,424; steel products, 41,224; insecticides and disinfectants, 18,486; medicines and drugs, 16,216.

Principal exports in 1981 (in Z$1,000): Unmanufactured tobacco, 218,280; gold, 117,380; ferrochrome, 79,517; asbestos, 75,947; cotton lint, 60,299; nickel and nickel alloys, 46,787; raw sugar, 45,908; iron and steel, 42,638; maize, 34,738; copper, 18,317; clothing, 12,308; meat, 4,526.

Total trade between Zimbabwe and UK (British Department of Trade returns, in £1,000 sterling):

	1980	*1981*	*1982*	*1983*	*1984*
Imports to UK	28,632	38,331	62,584	68,445	74,090
Exports and re-exports from UK	16,209	45,314	95,019	64,734	66,636

Tourism. In 1983, 298,041 tourists visited Zimbabwe.

COMMUNICATIONS. The Ministry of Transport is responsible for the Government's relations with the National Railways of Zimbabwe and with Air Zimbabwe.

Roads. The Ministry of Transport is responsible for the construction and maintenance of all State roads and bridges, and all bridges outside municipal areas. The Ministry assists and supervises junior road authorities who look after the secondary and tertiary roads. State roads are those connecting all the main centres of population, international routes, major links in the system and main roads serving rural communities. The total length of roads is approximately 85,000 km including surfaced, 12,000; gravel, 46,000; earth, 27,000.

Number of motor vehicles, 1982: Passenger cars, 219,000; commercial vehicles, 17,000; motor cycles, 20,000; trailers, 29,000; tractors, 5,000.

Railways. Zimbabwe is served by the National Railways of Zimbabwe, which connect with the South African Railways to give access to the South African ports; with the Mozambique Railways to give access to the ports of Beira and Maputo; and with the Zambia railway system. In Sept. 1974 the National Railways of Zimbabwe opened another line from Rutenga to connect with South African Railways at Beitbridge. In 1983 there were 3,394 km (1,067 mm gauge) of railways including 480 km electrified. In 1982–83 National Railways of Zimbabwe carried 13·9m. tons of freight and 2m. passengers.

Aviation. Air Zimbabwe operates domestic services and also regular flights to Zambia, Kenya, Malawi, Botswana and South Africa, and to London, Frankfurt and Athens in Europe and also to Perth and Sydney in Australia in association with Qantas. The country is also served by British Airways, Kenya Airways, Ethiopian Airlines, Air Tanzania, Air Malawi, Zambian Airways, Mozambique Airlines, South African Airways, Air India, Air Botswana, the Royal Swazi Airlines, UTA French Airlines, Air Portugal, Swissair and Qantas. In 1982–83, 554,510,000 passenger-km were flown.

Shipping. Zimbabwe outlets to the sea are Maputo and Beira in Mozambique and the South African ports.

Post and Broadcasting. At Aug. 1984 there were 166 full post offices, 38 postal telegraph agencies and 65 postal agencies. In June 1984 there were 246,384 telephones in Zimbabwe served by 97 exchanges; 1,749 telex connexions, served by 1 telex exchange. Zimbabwe Broadcasting Corporation is an independent statutory body broadcasting general service in English and African service in English, Shona, N'debele and Nyanja and 3 regional commercial services in English on medium- and short-waves. Zimbabwe Television Ltd broadcasts one programme 45 hours a week *via* 8 transmitters. In June 1984 there were 90,500 television and 180,500 radio licences.

JUSTICE, RELIGION, EDUCATION AND WELFARE

Justice. The Supreme Court consists of the Chief Justice, the Judge President and at least one other judge of appeal. The High Court consists of a number of puisne judges. The Supreme Court considers appeals from the High Court and lower courts; the High Court has full jurisdiction, civil and criminal, over all persons and matters within Zimbabwe. The Judge President presides over the Supreme Court in the absence of the Chief Justice. The Courts sit at Harare and Bulawayo, and sittings of the High Court are held at three other principal towns three times a year.

Regional Courts, established in Harare and Bulawayo, are intermediate in jurisdiction between the magistrates' courts and the High Court, and have civil jurisdiction.

The tribal courts and District Commissioners' Courts of colonial days have now been replaced by a system of Primary Courts, comprising village courts and community courts. By 1982, 1,100 village and 50 Community Courts had been established. Village courts are presided over by officers selected for that purpose from the local population. They sit with two assessors, and apply customary law. They are not yet able to exercise criminal jurisdiction, but it is anticipated that this will soon come about.

Community Courts are presided over by a Presiding Officer, who is a Government Officer. They have a limited amount of criminal jurisdiction.

Religion. The largest religious groups are the Anglicans and Roman Catholics. Other denominations include Presbyterians, the Methodist Church in Zimbabwe and the United Methodist Church.

Education. Education is non racial at all levels and not compulsory.

All primary schools offer free tuition; government secondary schools charge from Z$8–Z$25 per term. All instruction is given in English. There are also over 3,800 private primary schools and over 950 private secondary schools, all of which must be registered by the Ministry of Education.

There are 10 teachers' training colleges, 8 of which are in association with the University of Zimbabwe. In addition, there are 4 special training centres for teacher trainees in the Zimbabwe Integrated National Teacher Education Course.

The University of Zimbabwe provides facilities for higher education. In 1982 the total enrolment of full- and part-time students in the 9 Faculties of Agriculture, Arts, Commerce and Law, Education, Engineering, Medicine, Science, Social Studies and Veterinary Science, was 4,124 (1984), 3,136 full-time.

Health. In 1983 there were 161 hospitals, and 1985, 622 static rural clinics and health centres and 24 mobile rural clinics operated by the Ministry of Health. All mission health institutions get 100% government grants-in-aid for recurrent expenditure. There was one medical practitioner for every 7,020 inhabitants in Zimbabwe. There is a medical school attached to the University of Zimbabwe in Harare, four government training schools attached to the 4 central hospitals for training state registered nurses, 14 training schools for medical assistants out of which 11 are administered by missions, and two for training maternity assistants, health assistants/health inspectors.

Social Services. It is a statutory responsibility of the government in many areas to provide: Processing and administration of war pensions and old age pensions; protection of children; administration of remand, probation and correctional institutions; registration and supervision of welfare organisations.

DIPLOMATIC REPRESENTATIVES

Of Zimbabwe in Great Britain (Zimbabwe Hse., 429 Strand, London, WC2R 0SA)
High Commissioner: Dr Herbert M. Murerwa (accredited 1 March 1984).

Of Great Britain in Zimbabwe (Stanley Hse., Stanley Ave., Harare)
High Commissioner: Michael Ramsay Melhuish.

Of Zimbabwe in the USA (2852 McGill Terr., NW, Washington, D.C., 20008)
Ambassador: Edmund O. Z. Chipamaunga.

Of the USA in Zimbabwe (78 Enterprise Rd., Highlands, Harare)
Ambassador: David C. Miller, Jr.

Of Zimbabwe to the United Nations
Ambassador: Dr Stanley Mudenge.

Books of Reference

Statistical Information: The Central Statistical Office, PO Box 8063, Causeway, Harare, Zimbabwe, originated in 1927 as the Southern Rhodesian Government Statistical Bureau. Ten years later its name was changed to Department of Statistics, and in 1948 it assumed its present title when it took over responsibility for certain Northern Rhodesian and Nyasaland statistics (which it relinquished in Dec. 1963 on the dissolution of the Federation). It publishes *Monthly Digest of Statistics.*

Akers, M., *Encyclopaedia Rhodesia.* Harare, 1973
Caute, D., *Under the Skin: The Death of White Rhodesia.* London, 1983
Davies, D. K., *Race Relations in Rhodesia.* London, 1975
Keppel-Jones, A., *Rhodes and Rhodesia: The White Conquest of Zimbabwe, 1884–1902.* Univ. of Natal Press, 1983
Linden, I., *The Catholic Church and the Struggle for Zimbabwe.* London, 1980
Martin, D., and Johnson, P., *The Struggle for Zimbabwe.* London, 1981
Meredith, M., *The Past is Another Century: Rhodesia 1890–1979.* London, 1979
Morris-Jones, W. H., (ed.) *From Rhodesia to Zimbabwe.* London, 1980
Murphee, M. W. (ed.), *Education, Race and Employment.* Lichfield, 1975
Nkomo, J., *Nkomo: The Story of My Life.* London, 1984
O'Meara, P., *Rhodesia: Racial Conflict or Co-Existence.* Cornell Univ. Press, 1975
Palley, C., *The Constitutional History and Law of Southern Rhodesia, 1888–1965.* OUP, 1966
Pollak, K. and Pollak, O. B., *Rhodesia/Zimbabwe* [Bibliography] Oxford and Santa Barbara, 1979
Stoneham, C., *Zimbabwe's Inheritance.* London, 1982
Wiseman, H. and Taylor, A. M., *From Rhodesia to Zimbabwe: The Politics of Transition.* Elmsford, N.Y., 1981

Reference Library: National Archives of Zimbabwe, PO Box 8043, Causeway, Harare.

PLACE AND INTERNATIONAL ORGANIZATIONS INDEX

Desroches (Seychelles), 1047
Dessau (GDR), 511

PRODUCT INDEX